Contemporary Business and Online Commerce Law

Legal, Internet, Ethical, and Global Environments

Sixth Edition

HENRY R. CHEESEMAN

Clinical Professor of Business Law

Director of the Legal Studies Program

Marshall School of Business

University of Southern California

D0146050

PEARSON

Prentice Hall

Upper Saddle River, New Jersey 07458

Library of Congress Cataloging-in-Publication Data

Cheeseman, Henry R.
    Contemporary business and online commerce law / Henry R. Cheeseman.— 6th ed.
        p. cm.
    Includes bibliographical references and index.
    ISBN-13: 978-0-13-601500-0
    ISBN-10: 0-13-601500-X
        1. Business law—United States. 2. Electronic commerce—Law and legislation—United
States. I. Title.
    KF889.C4332 2008
    346.7307—dc22

                                                                2007044211

AVP/Editor-in-Chief: Eric Svendsen
Product Development Manager: Ashley Santora
Editorial Project Manager: Kierra Kashickey
Editorial Assistant: Mauricio Escoto
Senior Marketing Manager: Jodi Bassett
Associate Director, Production Editorial: Judy Leale
Production Project Manager: Kerri Tomasso
Permissions Coordinator: Charles Morris
Senior Operations Supervisor: Arnold Vila
Operations Specialist: Michelle Klein
Cover photo: Stanley Rowin Photography
Cover Design: Wee Design Group
Interior design: Wee Design Group
Art Director: Steven Frim
Manager, Cover Visual Research & Permissions: Karen Sanatar
Composition/Full-Service Project Management: Heidi Allgair, GGS Book Services
Printer/Binder: Quebecor Printing/Dubuque
Typeface: 10/12 Times Roman

Credits and acknowledgments borrowed from other sources and reproduced, with permission,
in this textbook appear on appropriate page within text.

Microsoft® and Windows® are registered trademarks of the Microsoft Corporation in the
U.S.A. and other countries. Screen shots and icons reprinted with permission from the
Microsoft Corporation. This book is not sponsored or endorsed by or affiliated with
the Microsoft Corporation.

**Copyright © 2009, 2006, 2003, 2000, 1997 by Pearson Education, Inc., Upper Saddle
River, New Jersey, 07458.** Pearson Prentice Hall. All rights reserved. Printed in the United
States of America. This publication is protected by Copyright and permission should be
obtained from the publisher prior to any prohibited reproduction, storage in a retrieval
system, or transmission in any form or by any means, electronic, mechanical, photocopying,
recording, or likewise. For information regarding permission(s), write to: Rights and
Permissions Department.

Pearson Prentice Hall™ is a trademark of Pearson Education, Inc.
Pearson® is a registered trademark of Pearson plc
Prentice Hall® is a registered trademark of Pearson Education, Inc.

Pearson Education LTD., London   Pearson Education Australia PTY, Limited
Pearson Education Singapore, Pte. Ltd   Pearson Education North Asia Ltd
Pearson Education, Canada, Ltd   Pearson Educación de Mexico, S.A. de C.V.
Pearson Education–Japan   Pearson Education Malaysia, Pte. Ltd.

10 9 8 7 6 5 4 3 2 1
ISBN-13: 978-0-13-601500-0
ISBN-10: 0-13-601500-X

Dedication

Jin Du

杜劲

"十分钟"

About the Author

Henry R. Cheeseman is Clinical Professor of Business Law and Director of the Legal Studies Program at the Marshall School of Business of the University of Southern California (USC), Los Angeles, California.

Professor Cheeseman earned a bachelor's degree in Finance from Marquette University, both a master's in business administration and a master's in business taxation from USC, a juris doctor degree from the University of California at Los Angeles School of Law, a master's of business administration with emphasis on Law and Economics from the University of Chicago, and a master's in law degree in Financial Institutions Law from Boston University.

Professor Cheeseman has earned the "Golden Apple" Teaching Award on many occasions by having been voted by the students as the best professor at the Marshall School of Business of USC. He was named a Faculty Fellow of the Center for Excellence in Teaching at USC by the dean of the Marshall School of Business. The USC's Torch and Tassel Chapter of the Mortar Board has named Professor Cheeseman Faculty of the Month of USC.

Professor Cheeseman writes leading business law and legal environment textbooks that are published by Prentice Hall. These include *Business Law: Legal Environment, Online Commerce, Business Ethics, and International Issues*; *Contemporary Business and Online Commerce Law*; *The Legal Environment of Business and Online Commerce*; *Essentials of Contemporary Business Law*; and *Introduction to Law: Its Dynamic Nature*.

Professor Cheeseman is an avid traveler and amateur photographer. All interior photos for this book were taken by Professor Cheeseman.

Brief Contents

Contents

Preface

To The Students

Each semester, as I stand up in front of a new group of business majors in my business law and legal environment classes, I am struck by the thought that, cases and statutes aside, I know two very important things that they have yet to learn. The first is that I draw as much from them as they do from me. Their youth, enthusiasm, questions, and even the doubts a few of them hold about the relevance of law to their futures fuel my teaching. They don't know that every time they open their minds to look at an issue from a new perspective or critically question something they have previously taken for granted, I get a wonderful reward for the work that I do.

The other thing I know is that both teaching and learning the legal environment are all about stories. These stories come from the legal cases in this book, as well as the important cases and stories that each professor personally brings to the classroom. These stories provide the framework on which students will hang everything they learn about the law in class. It is my hope that long after the specific language of cases or statutes have faded, students will retain that framework. Several years from now, "unintentional torts" may draw only a glimmer of recognition with business managers who learn about them as students in my class this year. However, they will likely recall the story of the woman who sued McDonald's for damages for serving her coffee that was too hot and caused her injuries. The story sticks and gives students the hook on which to hang the concepts.

I remind myself of these two facts every time I sit down to work on writing and revising *Contemporary Business and Online Commerce Law*, as well. My goal is to present business law and ethics in a way that will spur students to ask questions, to go beyond rote memorization.

Business law is an evolving outgrowth of its environment, and the legal environment keeps changing. This new sixth edition of *Contemporary Business and Online Commerce Law* emphasizes coverage of Internet law and electronic commerce as key parts of the legal environment. In addition, this book covers social, ethical, and international issues important to the study of business law.

It is my wish that my commitment to these goals shines through in this labor of love, and I hope you have as much pleasure in using it as I have had in creating it for you.

Henry Cheeseman

New to the Sixth Edition

Cases

More than 120 new cases in this book bring modern business law to life. These exciting new cases apply legal concepts in today's business environment. There are more than 210 cases in total in the sixth edition of *Contemporary Business and Online Commerce Law*, including more than 60 U.S. Supreme Court cases. The edited language of the reasoning in each case is in the words of the U.S. Supreme Court justices. The text also retains "Landmark Cases," such as *Brown v. Board of Education*, *Heart of Atlanta Motel v. United States*, and others. Full versions of the cases featured in *Contemporary Business and Online Commerce Law* are available at www.prenhall.com/cheesemancases.

Text and Examples

The text of this sixth edition of *Contemporary Business and Online Commerce Law* has been time tested, reviewed by contemporary business law and legal environment professors, and praised for its clarity and understandability by students. More than 700 examples are integrated throughout to help students understand and apply the legal theories and concepts covered in the text. More than 90 "Contemporary Environment" special feature boxes cover modern cases, statutes, and laws that affect managers and businesses today.

Web-Based Learning

More than 1,100 relevant websites and web exercises engage students to explore business law further by using the Internet as a resource. Websites and web exercises appear after each case in the book. They also appear after special feature boxes and within the text of the sixth edition.

Cyber Law

Chapter 15, "E-Contracts, Internet Law, and Cyber Crimes," is a newly written chapter that covers important digital laws related to e-contracts, e-commerce, software licensing, domain names, computer law, and cyber crimes. There are 44 "Internet & Technology" special feature boxes that cover Internet law, cyber law, and e-commerce are presented throughout the text. This sixth edition also identifies the changes to the Uniform Commercial Code (UCC) that recognizes digital documents, signatures, and filings that promote e-commerce.

Business Ethics

Chapter 8, "Ethics of Managers and Social Responsibility of Business," examines the moral theories of business ethics and applies these theories to actual ethical issues confronted by today's managers and businesses. More than 70 "Ethics Spotlight" special feature boxes that address business ethics issues are presented throughout the chapters. The cases and special feature boxes in this sixth edition of *Contemporary Business and Online Commerce Law* are followed by more than 430 ethics questions that relate to the cases and issues. There are more than 100 end-of-chapter "Ethics Issue" cases.

Special Coverage

The Sarbanes-Oxley Act is covered extensively in Chapter 28, "Corporate Governance and the Sarbanes-Oxley Act," and other chapters of the sixth edition. Chapter 24, "Bankruptcy and Reorganization," has been completely rewritten to incorporate the major changes made by the Bankruptcy Abuse Prevention and Consumer Protection Act of 2005. Chapter 41, "International and World Trade Law," covers public and private laws that apply to the global business environment. This sixth edition of *Contemporary Business and Online Commerce Law* contains more than 40 "International Law" special feature boxes that discuss international law.

New Custom Database Option

Do you want to use a book tailored to your course? This new edition of Cheeseman is designed to do so. Now part of the Pearson Custom Database solution, we are making it easier for users and new adopters to make Cheeseman fit their course perfectly. Pick the material that you want, include other material as needed, and order and cover to your choice. All will come produced from our custom database ready for your course. Use the order form in the front of sample copies to learn more about this option, preview, and order. Please contact your local Pearson sales rep for more information or if the form is missing.

Supplements that Accompany the Sixth Edition

To ensure consistency of style, approach, and coverage among the key print and online supplements, these critical pieces were created by an author team working in conjunction with Henry Cheeseman. Supplements are provided for both instructors and students.

For Instructors

We offer a variety of both print and electronic supplements to meet the unique teaching needs of each instructor. Electronic versions of the supplements that accompany this text are available for download by instructors only at our Instructor Resource Center, at www.prenhall.com.

COMPANION WEBSITE This edition's companion website, accessible at www.prenhall.com/cheeseman, contains an online study guide, including true/false and multiple-choice questions, as well as PowerPoint presentations for each chapter. Also available online at www.prenhall.com/cheesemancases are the full-length versions of the cases featured in this sixth edition of *Contemporary Business and Online Commerce Law*.

INSTRUCTOR'S MANUAL The Instructor's Manual (978-0-13-601502-4) provides a comprehensive outline of each text chapter. Also included are "teacher-to-teacher dialogues" that offer teaching suggestions for each chapter, as well as key chapter objectives.

TEST ITEM FILE The Test Item File (978-0-13-601504-8) is a bank of questions specifically designed to aid in the preparation of tests. Each question includes a corresponding difficulty level, allowing for the creation of tailor-made testing material.

TESTGEN TestGen is test management software that contains all the material from the Test Item File. This user-friendly software allows instructors to view, edit, and add test questions with just a few clicks of the mouse.

POWERPOINT PRESENTATION A ready-to-use PowerPoint slideshow, designed for classroom presentation, is available. Instructors can use it as-is or edit content to fit particular classroom needs.

INSTRUCTOR'S RESOURCE CENTER ON CD-ROM The Instructor's Resource Center (978-0-13-601471-3) is a compilation of instructor's tools, including the Instructor's Manual, PowerPoint presentation, Test Item File, and TestGen.

VIDEOS Available in DVD format, 10 videos (978-0-13-601474-4) demonstrate how law works in everyday situations. Scenarios include contracts, product liability, employment discrimination, torts, third-party rights, and more.

For Students

STUDY GUIDE The Study Guide is a student aid designed to facilitate learning by enforcing key concepts. Each chapter contains a chapter overview, a list of objectives, and an explanation of the practical applications of the chapter. Also included are a "helpful hints" section, a sample quiz, and several exercises.

Acknowledgments

When I first began writing this book, I was a solitary figure, researching cases in the law library and writing text at my desk. As time passed, others entered the scene—editors, research assistants, reviewers, production personnel—and touched the project and made it better. Although my name appears on the cover of this book, the project is no longer mine alone. I humbly thank the following persons for their contributions to this project:

The Exceptional Supplements Team and Prentice Hall Professionals

Many thanks to Kerri Tomasso, who held the positions of both the project manager and production manager for this book, for shepherding this sixth edition of *Contemporary Business and Online Commerce Law* through the many phases of editing and production at Prentice Hall. I'd also like to thank Heidi Allgair of GGS Book Services, as the editor who skillfully and cheerfully navigated this complex project to publication. Kerri and Heidi have worked on several of my previous books, and I hope that they will each work on my future books.

The supplements package was authored by a remarkable team, with exceptional contributions from Gregory Cermignano of Widener University, Melinda Hickman of Fort Hays State University, and Michael Katz of Delaware State University.

I also appreciate the support of the management at Prentice Hall, including Kierra Kashickey, project manager; Steve Sartori, acquisitions editor; Eric Svendsen, editor-in-chief; Sally Yagan, editorial director; and Jerome Grant, president of Prentice Hall Business Publishing, for their support in the publication of this book.

I would especially like to thank the professionals of the sales staff of Prentice Hall Publishing, including Jodi Bassett, marketing manager, and all the knowledgeable sales representatives without whom the success of this textbook book would be impossible.

Personal Acknowledgments

My family

Your family counts the most, no matter how far away they are geographically. My parents—Henry B. and Florence, deceased—who have had a profound effect on me and my ability to be a professor and writer; my brother Gregory and the special bond that exists between us as twins; and to the rest of my family, Gregory's wife Lana, my sister Marcia, my nephew Gregory and niece Nikki, and my great-nieces Lauren and Addison. My entire family lives in Saint Ignace, Michigan, which I will always call "home."

Students

The students at the Marshall School of Business at the University of Southern California (USC). Their spirit, energy, and joy are contagious, and I love teaching them (and, as importantly, they teaching me). At the end of each semester, I am sad that the students I have come to know are moving on. But each new semester brings another group of students, who it will be a joy to teach. And the cycle continues.

Research Assistant Ashley Anderson

Ashley is an undergraduate and pre-law student at the Marshall School of Business at USC who has been my research assistant for the past three years. Ashley has done an absolutely excellent job in finding new cases to be used in the sixth edition of *Contemporary Business and Online Commerce Law*. Ashley has also done a superb job working with the editors of

Prentice Hall in the proofreading and production of my business law books. She is president of the pre-law society and a member of USC's moot court team. Next year, she will move on to law school, and I will miss her.

Research Assistant Jason Towne

Jason is an undergraduate and pre-law student at the Marshall School of Business at USC. Jason has been my research assistant for two years, and in that capacity has researched cases, statutes, and current events. Jason has also used his excellent writing ability to create special feature boxes on contemporary law, ethics, and international law for this book. Next year, Jason will also be on to law school, and I will miss him.

Colleagues at USC

There are certain people and colleagues who are enjoyable to work with and who have made my life easier as I have endeavored to write this revision of *Contemporary Business and Online Commerce Law*. I would like to thank Kerry Fields, my colleague professor who teaches other business law courses at USC, who is an excellent professor and wonderful friend. I would also like to thank Helen Pitts, Marilyn Johnson, Terry Lichvar, Debra Jacobs, and Jean Collins at the Marshall School of Business, who are always a joy to work with.

While writing this Preface and Acknowledgment, I have thought about the many hours I have spent researching, writing, and preparing this manuscript. I have loved every minute, and the knowledge gained has been sufficient reward for the endeavor.

I hope this book and its supplementary materials will serve you as well as they have served me.

With joy and sadness,
emptiness and fullness,
honor and humility,
I surrender the fruits of this labor.

Henry R. Cheeseman

UNIT 1
Legal, Ethical, and Digital Environment

CHAPTER 1

Legal Heritage and the Information Age

> **"**Where there is no law, there is no freedom. **"**

—JOHN LOCKE
Second Treatise of Government, Sec. 57

CHAPTER OBJECTIVES

After studying this chapter, you should be able to:

1. Define *law* and describe the functions of law.
2. Explain the development of the U.S. legal system.
3. List and describe the sources of law in the United States.
4. Describe the international civil law legal system used in some other countries.
5. Apply critical legal thinking in analyzing judicial decisions.

CHAPTER CONTENTS

- Introduction to Legal Heritage and the Information Age
- What Is Law?
- Schools of Jurisprudential Thought
- History of American Law
- Sources of Law in the United States
- Briefing a Case: The IRAC Method
- Chapter Summary
- Test Review Terms and Concepts
- Case Problems
- Ethics Issues
- IRAC Writing Assignment

  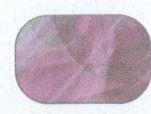 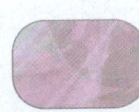 

Introduction to Legal Heritage and the Information Age

Every society makes and enforces laws that govern the conduct of the individuals, businesses, and other organizations that function within it. In the words of Judge Learned Hand, "Without law we cannot live; only with it can we insure the future which by right is ours. The best of men's hopes are enmeshed in its success."[1]

Although the law of the United States is primarily based on English common law, other legal systems, such as Spanish and French civil law, also influenced it. The sources of law in this country are the U.S. Constitution, state constitutions, federal and state statutes, ordinances, administrative agency rules and regulations, executive orders, and judicial decisions by federal and state courts.

Businesses that are organized in the United States are subject to its laws. They are also subject to the laws of other countries in which they operate. Businesses organized in other countries must obey the laws of the United States when doing business here. In addition, businesspeople owe a duty to act ethically in the conduct of their affairs, and businesses owe a responsibility not to harm society.

This chapter discusses the nature and definition of law, the history and sources of law, and critical legal thinking, as applied by the U.S. Supreme Court in deciding actual cases.

Statue of Liberty, New York Harbor

The United States of America is a country of laws. For centuries it has attracted people from around the world because of its democratic principles and constitutional protections.

What is Law?

The law consists of rules that regulate the conduct of individuals, businesses, and other organizations within society. It is intended to protect persons and their property against unwanted interference from others. In other words, the law forbids persons from engaging in certain undesirable activities. Consider the following passage:

> Hardly anyone living in a civilized society has not at some time been told to do something or to refrain from doing something, because there is a law requiring it, or because it is against the law. What do we mean when we say such things? Most generally, how are we to understand statements of the form "x is law"? This is an ancient question. In his Memorabilia (I, ii), Xenophon reports a statement of the young Alcibiades, companion of Socrates, who in conversation with the great Pericles remarked that "no one can really deserve praise unless he knows what a law is."
>
> At the end of the 18th century, Immanuel Kant wrote of the question "What is law?" that it "may be said to be about as embarrassing to the jurist as the well-known question 'What is truth?' is to the logician."[2]

A lawyer without history or literature is a mechanic, a mere working mason: if he possesses some knowledge of these, he may venture to call himself an architect.

Sir Walter Scott
Guy Mannering, Chapter 37
(1815)

INTERNET AND TECHNOLOGY
Students Plug In to the Internet

Every year millions of students arrive on college campuses and unpack an array of items—clothes, books, furniture, decorations, and their computers. College students used to be judged by the size of their stereo speakers; today it is their computers and their Internet savvy. Almost all college students now own personal computers.

The Internet has revolutionized campus life. Computer kiosks abound around college campuses, occupying space in libraries, dorm rooms, and hallways of athletic departments. Traditional libraries have become obsolete for many students as they conduct almost all their research online. More than 80 percent of college students check out the Web daily, and most students communicate through e-mail, pick up course assignments, download course notes, and socialize online. Current university and college students use modern technology and are leading their parents, employers, and sometimes even their professors into the new world of high technology. Today's college students are the leaders of the technology generation.

Universities and colleges are now rated on not only how well they are connected with alumni but also on how well they are connected to computer technology. Some universities have installed software that allows their students to sit anywhere on campus with their laptops and "plug" in to the school's computers. The computer is no longer just a study tool; it has become totally integrated into the lives of college students. Students of the new generation study online, shop online, and even date online.

To help students understand their legal rights and duties, this business law book fully integrates online commerce and Internet law. Through this total integration of online commerce and Internet law, students will learn traditional business law topics and will also become well versed in their legal rights while using the Internet.

Definition of Law

The concept of **law** is broad. Although it is difficult to state a precise definition, *Black's Law Dictionary* gives one that is sufficient for this text:

> Law, in its generic sense, is a body of rules of action or conduct prescribed by controlling authority, and having binding legal force. That which must be obeyed and followed by citizens subject to sanctions or legal consequences is a law.[3]

Functions of the Law

The law is often described by the function it serves within a society. The primary *functions* served by the law in this country are:

> Commercial law lies within a narrow compass, and is far purer and freer from defects than any other part of the system.
>
> Henry Peter Brougham
> *House of Commons,*
> *February 7, 1828*

1. Keeping the peace, which includes making certain activities crimes
2. Shaping moral standards (e.g., enacting laws that discourage drug and alcohol abuse)
3. Promoting social justice (e.g., enacting statutes that prohibit discrimination in employment)
4. Maintaining the status quo (e.g., passing laws preventing the forceful overthrow of the government)
5. Facilitating orderly change (e.g., passing statutes only after considerable study, debate, and public input)
6. Facilitating planning (e.g., well-designed commercial laws allow businesses to plan their activities, allocate their productive resources, and assess the risks they take)
7. Providing a basis for compromise (e.g., approximately 90 percent of all lawsuits are settled prior to trial)
8. Maximizing individual freedom (e.g., the rights of freedom of speech, religion, and association granted by the First Amendment to the U.S. Constitution)

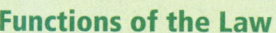 **CONCEPT SUMMARY**

Functions of the Law

1. Keep the peace
2. Shape moral standards
3. Promote social justice
4. Maintain the status quo

5. Facilitate orderly change
6. Facilitate planning
7. Provide a basis for compromise
8. Maximize individual freedom

Fairness of the Law

On the whole, the U.S. legal system is one of the most comprehensive, fair, and democratic systems of law ever developed and enforced. Nevertheless, some misuses and oversights of our legal system—including abuses of discretion and mistakes by judges and juries, unequal applications of the law, and procedural mishaps—allow some guilty parties to go unpunished.

In *Standefer v. United States*,[4] the Supreme Court of the United States *affirmed* (let stand) the criminal conviction of a Gulf Oil Corporation executive for aiding and abetting the bribery of an Internal Revenue Service agent. The agent had been acquitted in a separate trial. In writing the opinion of the Court, Chief Justice Warren Burger stated, "This case does no more than manifest the simple, if discomforting, reality that different juries may reach different results under any criminal statute. That is one of the consequences we accept under our jury system."

> The law, in its majestic equality, forbids the rich as well as the poor to sleep under bridges.
>
> Anatole France

Flexibility of the Law

U.S. law evolves and changes along with the norms of society, technology, and the growth and expansion of commerce in the United States and the world. The following quote by Judge Jerome Frank discusses the value of the adaptability of law:

The law always has been, is now, and will ever continue to be, largely vague and variable. And how could this be otherwise? The law deals with human relations in their most complicated aspects. The whole confused, shifting helter-skelter of life parades before it—more confused than ever, in our kaleidoscopic age.

Men have never been able to construct a comprehensive, eternalized set of rules anticipating all possible legal disputes and formulating in advance the rules which would apply to them. Situations are bound to occur which were never contemplated when the original rules were made. How much less is such a frozen legal system possible in modern times?

The constant development of unprecedented problems requires a legal system capable of fluidity and pliancy. Our society would be straightjacketed were not the courts, with the able assistance of the lawyers, constantly overhauling the law and adapting it to the realities of ever-changing social, industrial, and political conditions; although changes cannot be made lightly, yet rules of law must be more or less impermanent, experimental and therefore not nicely calculable.

Much of the uncertainty of law is not an unfortunate accident; it is of immense social value.[5]

LANDMARK CASE

Brown v. Board of Education

❝*We conclude that in the field of public education the doctrine of "separate but equal" has no place.*❞

—Justice Warren

When the original 13 states ratified the Constitution of the United States of America in 1788, that document created a democratic form of government and granted certain rights to its people. But all persons were not treated equally, as many people, including drafters of the Constitution such as Thomas Jefferson, owned African American slaves. It was more than 75 years before the Civil War was fought between the northern states and the southern Confederate states over the preservation of the Union and slavery. Slavery was abolished by the Thirteenth Amendment to the Constitution in 1865. In addition, the Fourteenth Amendment of 1868 provided that no state shall "deny to any person within its jurisdiction the equal protection of the laws." The original intent of this amendment was to guarantee equality to freed African Americans.

But equality was denied to African Americans for years to come. This included discrimination in housing, transportation, education, jobs, service at restaurants, and other activities. In 1896, the U.S. Supreme Court decided the case **Plessy v. Ferguson**.[6] In that case, the state of Louisiana had a law that provided for separate but equal accommodations for African American and white railway passengers. An African American passenger challenged the state law. The Supreme Court held that the "separate but equal" state law did not violate the Equal Protection Clause of the Fourteenth Amendment. The "separate but equal" doctrine was then applied to other areas of life, including public education. Thus, African American and white children attended separate schools, often with unequal facilities.

It was not until 1954 that the U.S. Supreme Court decided a case that challenged the separate but equal doctrine as it applied to public elementary and high schools. In **Brown v. Board of Education**,[7] a consolidated case that challenged the separate school systems of four states—Kansas, South Carolina, Virginia, and Delaware—the Supreme Court decided to revisit the separate but equal doctrine announced by its forbearers in another century. This time a unanimous Supreme Court, in an opinion written by Chief Justice Earl Warren, reversed prior precedent and held that the separate but equal doctrine violated the Equal Protection Clause of the Fourteenth Amendment to the Constitution. In its opinion, the Court stated:

We cannot turn the clock back to 1868 when the Amendment was adopted, or even to 1896 when Plessy v. Ferguson was written. Today, education is perhaps the most important function of state and local governments.

We conclude that in the field of public education the doctrine of "separate but equal" has no place. Separate educational facilities are inherently unequal. Therefore, we hold that the plaintiffs and others similarly situated for whom actions have been brought are, by reason of the segregation complained of, deprived of the equal protection of the laws guaranteed by the Fourteenth Amendment.

After *Brown v. Board of Education* was decided, it took court orders as well as federal army enforcement to integrate many of the public schools in this country. The *Brown v. Board of Education* case demonstrates that one Supreme Court case can overrule prior Supreme Court cases to promote justice.

Law & Ethics Questions

1. It has been said that the U.S. Constitution is a "living document"—that is, one that can adapt to changing times. Do you think this is a good policy? Or should the U.S. Constitution be interpreted more narrowly and literally?

2. **ETHICS** Do you think it was ethical for the justices to adopt the "separate but equal" rule in *Plessy v. Ferguson*?

3. **ETHICS** Was it ethical for the U.S. Supreme Court to wait until 1954 to overturn the separate but equal rule adopted in 1868?

Web Exercises

1. **WEB** For the complete opinion of *Plessy v. Ferguson*, go to *www.prenhall.com/cheesemancases*.

2. **WEB** For the complete opinion of *Brown v. Board of Education of Topeka*, go to *www.prenhall.com/cheesemancases*.

3. **WEB** Visit the website of the Supreme Court of the United States, at *www.supremecourtus.gov*. Can you find any documents that relate to the *Brown v. Board of Education* case?

4. **WEB** Use *www.google.com* to find an article that discusses the significance of the *Brown v. Board of Education* case. Read it.

The decision of the U.S. Supreme Court is set forth in Exhibit 1.1

Supreme Court of the United States

No. 1 ———— , *October Term, 19* 54

Oliver Brown, Mrs. Richard Lawton, Mrs. Sadie Emmanuel et al.,

Appellants,

vs.

Board of Education of Topeka, Shawnee County, Kansas, et al.

Appeal from *the United States District Court for the* ——————————— *District of* Kansas.

This cause *came on to be heard on the transcript of the record from the United States District Court for the* ———————— *District of* Kansas, ——————————— *and was argued by counsel.*

On consideration whereof, *It is ordered and adjudged by this Court that the judgment of the said* District ——————————— *Court in this cause be, and the same is hereby,* reversed with costs; and that this cause be, and the same is hereby, remanded to the said District Court to take such proceedings and enter such orders and decrees consistent with the opinions of this Court as are necessary and proper to admit to public schools on a racially nondiscriminatory basis with all deliberate speed the parties to this case.

Per Mr. Chief Justice Warren,

May 31, 1955.

Schools of Jurisprudential Thought

The philosophy or science of the law is referred to as **jurisprudence**. There are several different philosophies about how the law developed, ranging from the classical natural theory to modern theories of law and economics and critical legal studies. Classical legal philosophies are discussed in the following paragraphs.

Natural Law School

The **Natural Law School** of jurisprudence postulates that the law is based on what is "correct." Natural law philosophers emphasize a **moral theory of law**—that is, law should be based on morality and ethics. Natural law is "discovered" by humans through the use of reason and choosing between good and evil. Documents such as the U.S. Constitution, the Magna Carta, and the United Nations Charter reflect this theory.

Historical School

The **Historical School** of jurisprudence believes that the law is an aggregate of social traditions and customs that have developed over the centuries. It believes that changes in the norms of society will gradually be reflected in the law. To these legal philosophers, the law is an evolutionary process. Thus, historical legal scholars look to past legal decisions (precedent) to solve contemporary problems.

Analytical School

> Law must be stable and yet it cannot stand still.
>
> Roscoe Pound
> *Interpretations of Legal History*
> *(1923)*

The **Analytical School** of jurisprudence maintains that the law is shaped by logic. Analytical philosophers believe that results are reached by applying principles of logic to the specific facts of the case. The emphasis is on the logic of the result rather than on how the result is reached.

Sociological School

The **Sociological School** of jurisprudence asserts that the law is a means of achieving and advancing certain sociological goals. The followers of this philosophy, known as *realists*, believe that the purpose of law is to shape social behavior. Sociological philosophers are unlikely to adhere to past law as precedent.

Command School

The philosophers of the **Command School** of jurisprudence believe that the law is a set of rules developed, communicated, and enforced by the ruling party rather than a reflection of the society's morality, history, logic, or sociology. This school maintains that the law changes when the ruling class changes.

Critical Legal Studies School

> The law is not a series of calculating machines where definitions and answers come tumbling out when the right levers are pushed.
>
> William O. Douglas
> *The Dissent, A Safeguard of Democracy (1948)*

The **Critical Legal Studies School** proposes that legal rules are unnecessary and are used as an obstacle by the powerful to maintain the status quo. Critical legal theorists (the *Crits*) argue that legal disputes should be solved by applying arbitrary rules that are based on broad notions of what is "fair" in each circumstance. Under this theory, subjective decision making by judges would be permitted.

Law and Economics School

The **Law and Economics School** (or the "Chicago School," named after the University of Chicago, where it was first developed) believes that promoting market efficiency should be the central goal of legal decision making.

Example Proponents of law and economics theory suggest that the practice of appointing counsel, free of charge, to prisoners who bring civil rights cases should be abolished. If a prisoner cannot find a lawyer who will take the case on a contingency-fee basis or *pro bono* (free of charge), it probably means the case is not worth bringing.

CONCEPT SUMMARY

Schools of Jurisprudential Thought

SCHOOL	PHILOSOPHY
Natural Law	Postulates that law is based on what is "correct." It emphasizes a moral theory of law—that is, law should be based on morality and ethics.
Historical	Believes that law is an aggregate of social traditions and customs.
Analytical	Maintains that law is shaped by logic.
Sociological	Asserts that the law is a means of achieving and advancing certain sociological goals.
Command	Believes that the law is a set of rules developed, communicated, and enforced by the ruling party.
Critical Legal Studies	Maintains that legal rules are unnecessary and that legal disputes should be solved by applying arbitrary rules based on fairness.
Law and Economics	Believes that promoting market efficiency should be the central concern of legal decision making.

INTERNATIONAL LAW

Immigration to the United States of America

❝ *. . . that I will support and defend the Constitution and laws of the United States of America against all enemies, . . .* **❞**

—Oath of Citizenship
—United States of America

The United States of America was originally founded by immigrants, primarily those from western Europe. Many sought wealth and prosperity; some sought religious freedom, while others were running from their debts. But no matter the reason, during the sixteenth, seventeenth, and eighteenth centuries, the immigrants kept coming, and they moved farther inland from the Atlantic Ocean. Many immigrants also came from the continent of Africa; most of them were forcibly brought to become slaves.

After this country won its bloody revolution and gained freedom from Great Britain, immigrants continued to pour into the United States during the nineteenth and twentieth centuries, and they continue to do so in the twenty-first century. Immigrants to the United States come from all over the world.

In 1921, the first immigration quota law was enacted by the United States. This law set a quota on the number of immigrants that could be admitted to the United States from each foreign country each year. During different times, the quotas for each foreign country have been raised or lowered, depending on the world situation. For example, after World War II, the United States increased the quotas dramatically to accept many persons who had been displaced by the war. This quota system is still in effect today.

Currently, the immigration laws of this country are administered by the **United States Citizenship and Immigration Services (USCIS)**, which is part of the U.S. Department of Homeland Security.

Foreign nationals who qualify and have met the requirements may become citizens of the United States. During their swearing-in ceremony, they must take the following Oath of Citizenship:

The Oath of Citizenship

I hereby declare, on oath, that I absolutely and entirely renounce and adjure all allegiance and fidelity to any foreign prince, potentate, state, or sovereignty of whom or which I have heretofore been a subject or citizen; that I will support and defend the Constitution and laws of the United States of America against all enemies, foreign and domestic; that I will bear true faith and allegiance to the same; that I will bear arms on behalf of the United States when required by law; that I will perform noncombatant service in the Armed Forces of the United States when required by the law; that I will perform work of national importance under civilian direction when required by the law; and that I take this obligation freely without any mental reservation or purpose of evasion; so help me God. In acknowledgement whereof I have hereunto affixed my signature.

Web Exercises

1. **WEB** Go to *www.uscis.gov*. Use this website to find information that shows how to become a citizen of the United States of America.

2. **WEB** Visit the website *www.umass.edu/complit/aclanet/USMigrat.html* for a history of migration and immigration laws of the United States of America.

3. **WEB** Use *www.google.com* to find an article that discusses immigration to this country. Read it.

History of American Law

> Two things most people should never see made: sausages and laws.
>
> An old saying

When the American colonies were first settled, the English system of law was generally adopted as the system of jurisprudence. This was the foundation from which American judges developed a common law in America.

English Common Law

English common law was law developed by judges who issued their opinions when deciding cases. The principles announced in these cases became *precedent* for later judges deciding similar cases. The English common law can be divided into cases decided by the *law courts*, *equity courts*, and *merchant courts*.

LAW COURTS Prior to the Norman Conquest of England in 1066, each locality in England was subject to local laws as established by the lord or chieftain in control of the local area. There was no countrywide system of law. After 1066, William the Conqueror and his successors to the throne of England began to replace the various local laws with one uniform system of law. To accomplish this, the king or queen appointed loyal followers as judges in all local areas. These judges were charged with administering the law in a uniform manner in courts that were called **law courts**. Law at that time tended to emphasize the form (legal procedure) over the substance (merit) of a case. The only relief available in law courts was a monetary award for damages.

CHANCERY (EQUITY) COURTS Because of the unfair results and the limited remedy available in the law courts, a second set of courts—the **Court of Chancery** (or **equity court**)—was established. These courts were under the authority of the Lord Chancellor. Persons who believed that the decision of the law court was unfair or believed that the law court could not grant an appropriate remedy could seek relief in the Court of Chancery. Rather than emphasize legal procedure, the Chancery Court inquired into the merits of the case. The Chancellor's remedies were called *equitable remedies* because they were shaped to fit each situation. Equitable order and remedies of the Court of Chancery took precedence over the legal decisions and remedies of the law courts.

MERCHANT COURTS As trade developed in the Middle Ages, the merchants who traveled about England and Europe developed certain rules to solve their commercial disputes. These rules, known as the "law of merchants," or the **Law Merchant**, were based on common trade practices and usage. Eventually, a separate set of courts was established to administer these rules. This court was called the **Merchant Court**. In the early 1900s, the Merchant Court was absorbed into the regular law court system of England.

INTERNATIONAL LAW
Adoption of English Common Law in America

All the states of the United States of America (except Louisiana) base their legal systems primarily on the English *common law*. In the United States, the law, equity, and merchant courts have been merged. Thus, most U.S. courts permit the aggrieved party to seek both law and equitable orders and remedies.

The importance of common law to the U.S. legal system is described in the following excerpt from Justice Douglas's opinion in the 1841 case *Penny v. Little*:

The common law is a beautiful system, containing the wisdom and experiences of ages. Like the people it ruled and protected, it was simple and crude in its infancy and became enlarged, improved, and polished as the nation advanced in civilization, virtue, and intelligence. Adapting itself to the conditions and circumstances of the people and relying upon them for its administration, it necessarily improved as the condition of the people was elevated. The inhabitants of this country always claimed the common law as their birthright, and at an early period established it as the basis of their jurisprudence.[8]

INTERNATIONAL LAW
The Civil Law System

One of the major legal systems that has developed in the world in addition to the Anglo-American common law system is the **Romano-Germanic civil law system**. This legal system, which is commonly called **civil law**, dates to 450 B.C., when Rome adopted the Twelve

Tables, a code of law applicable to the Romans. A compilation of Roman law, called the *Corpus Juris Civilis* ("Body of Civil Law"), was completed in A.D. 534. Later, two national codes—the French Civil Code of 1804 (the Napoleonic Code) and the German Civil Code of 1896—became models for countries that adopted civil codes.

In contrast to the Anglo-American common law, where laws are created by the judicial system as well as by congressional legislation, the civil code and parliamentary statutes that expand and interpret it are the sole sources of the law in most civil law countries. Thus, the adjudication of a case is simply the application of the code or the statutes to a particular set of facts. In some civil law countries, court decisions do not have the force of law.

Many countries in Europe still follow the civil law system.

Eiffel Tower, Paris, France

The French legal system is based on the civil law system.

Sources of Law in the United States

In the more than 200 years since the founding of the United States and adoption of the English common law, the lawmakers in this country have developed a substantial body of law. The *sources of modern law* in the United States are discussed in the paragraphs that follow.

Constitutions

The **Constitution of the United States of America** is the *supreme law of the land*. This means that any law—whether federal, state, or local—that conflicts with the U.S. Constitution is unconstitutional and, therefore, unenforceable.

The principles enumerated in the Constitution are extremely broad because the founding fathers intended them to be applied to evolving social, technological, and economic conditions. The U.S. Constitution is often referred to as a "living document" because it is so adaptable.

The U.S. Constitution established the structure of the federal government. It created the following three branches of government and gave them each particular powers:

- *Legislative (Congress).* Power to make (enact) the law.
- *Executive (president).* Power to enforce the law.
- *Judicial (courts).* Power to interpret and determine the validity of the law.

Powers not given to the federal government by the Constitution are reserved for the states. States also have their own constitutions. These are often patterned after the U.S. Constitution, although many are more detailed. State constitutions establish the legislative, executive, and judicial branches of state government and establish the powers of each branch. Provisions of state constitutions are valid unless they conflict with the U.S. Constitution or any valid federal law.

> The Constitution of the United States is not a mere lawyers' document: it is a vehicle of life, and its spirit is always the spirit of age.
>
> Woodrow Wilson
> *Constitutional Government in the United States (1927)*

Treaties

The U.S. Constitution provides that the president, with the advice and consent of two-thirds of the Senate, may enter into **treaties** with foreign governments. Treaties become part of the supreme law of the land. With increasing international economic relations among nations, treaties will become an even more important source of law that will affect business in the future.

Codified Law

Statutes are written laws that establish certain courses of conduct that must be adhered to by covered parties. The U.S. Congress is empowered by the Commerce Clause and other provisions of the U.S. Constitution to enact *federal statutes* to regulate foreign and inter-state commerce. Federal statutes include antitrust laws, securities laws, bankruptcy laws, labor laws, equal employment opportunity laws, environmental protection laws, consumer protection laws, and such. State legislatures enact *state statutes*. State statutes include corporation laws, partnership laws, workers' compensation laws, the Uniform Commercial Code, and the like. The statutes enacted by the legislative branches of the federal and state governments are organized by topic into code books. This is often called **codified law**.

State legislatures often delegate lawmaking authority to local government bodies, including cities and municipalities, counties, school districts, water districts, and such. These governmental units are empowered to adopt **ordinances**. Examples of ordinances are traffic laws, local building codes, and zoning laws. Ordinances are also codified.

Web Exercises

1. **WEB** Visit the website *www.senate.gov*. What does the U.S. Senate do?
2. **WEB** Visit the website *www.house.gov*. What does the U.S. House of Representatives do?
3. **WEB** Use *www.google.com*. Find the website of the legislative branch(es) of your state.

U.S. Congress, Washington, DC

The U.S. Congress, which is a bicameral system made up of the U.S. Senate and the U.S. House of Representatives, creates federal law by enacting statutes. Each state has two senators and is allocated a certain number of representatives, based on population.

Executive Orders

The executive branch of government, which includes the president of the United States and state governors, is empowered to issue **executive orders**. This power is derived from express delegation from the legislative branch and is implied from the U.S. Constitution and state constitutions.

Example When the United States is at war with another country, the president of the United States usually issues executive orders prohibiting U.S. companies from selling goods or services to that country.

Web Exercises

1. **WEB** Visit the website *www.whitehouse.gov/president*. Who is the current president of the United States of America?

2. **WEB** Visit the website *www.whitehouse.gov*. What information do you find?

Regulations and Order of Administrative Agencies

The legislative and executive branches of federal and state governments are empowered to establish **administrative agencies** to enforce and interpret statutes enacted by Congress and state legislatures. Many of these agencies regulate business. Congress has created the Securities and Exchange Commission (SEC) and the Federal Trade Commission (FTC), among others.

Congress or the state legislatures usually empower administrative agencies to adopt **administrative rules and regulations** to interpret the statutes that the agency is authorized to enforce. These rules and regulations have the force of law. Administrative agencies usually have the power to hear and decide disputes. Their decisions are called *orders*. Because of their power, administrative agencies are often informally referred to as the "fourth branch of government."

Web Exercises

1. **WEB** Visit the website of the Securities and Exchange Commission (SEC), at *www.sec.gov*. What is the mission of the SEC?

2. **WEB** Visit the website of the Federal Trade Commission (FTC), at *www.ftc.gov*. What is the mission of the FTC?

CONTEMPORARY ENVIRONMENT
Department of Homeland Security

On September 11, 2001, the World Trade Center buildings in New York City were destroyed and the Pentagon in Washington, DC, was damaged by terrorist attacks. After the attacks, President George W. Bush issued an executive order creating the Office of Homeland Security. The president called for the office to be made into a Cabinet-level agency. Congress responded by enacting the **Homeland Security Act of 2002**, which created the Cabinet-level **Department of Homeland Security (DHS)**. The creation of the DHS was the largest government reorganization in over 50 years.

The act placed 22 existing federal agencies with more than 180,000 employees under the umbrella of the DHS. The DHS is the second-largest government agency, after the Department of Defense. The DHS contains the Bureau of Customs and Border Protection, the Bureau of Citizenship and Immigration Services, the U.S. Secret Service, the Federal Emergency Management Agency, the Federal Computer Incident Response Center, the National Domestic Preparedness Office, the U.S. Coast Guard, and portions of the Federal Bureau of Investigation, Treasury Department, Commerce Department, Justice Department, and other federal government agencies.

The mission of the DHS is to prevent domestic terrorist attacks, reduce vulnerability to terrorist attacks, minimize the harm caused by such attacks, and assist in the recovery if a terrorist attack occurs. The DHS provides services in the following critical areas: (1) border and transportation security, including protecting airports, seaports, and borders and providing immigration and visa processing; (2) chemical, biological, radiological, and nuclear countermeasures, including metering the air for biological agents and developing vaccines and treatments for biological agents; (3) information analysis and infrastructure protection, including protection of communications systems, power grids, transportation networks, telecommunications, and cyber systems; and (4) emergency preparedness and response to terrorist incidents, including training first responders and coordinating government disaster relief.

Web Exercise

1. **WEB** Visit the website of the Department of Homeland Security, at *www.dhs.gov*.

Judicial Decisions

When deciding individual lawsuits, federal and state courts issue **judicial decisions**. In these written opinions, the judge or justice usually explains the legal reasoning used to decide the case. These opinions often include interpretations of statutes, ordinances, and administrative regulations and the announcement of legal principles used to decide the case. Many court decisions are printed (reported) in books that are available in law libraries and in some cases online legal databases.

DOCTRINE OF *STARE DECISIS* Based on the common law tradition, past court decisions become **precedent** for deciding future cases. Lower courts must follow the precedent established by higher courts. That is why all federal and state courts in the United States must follow the precedents established by U.S. Supreme Court decisions.

The courts of one jurisdiction are not bound by the precedent established by the courts of another jurisdiction, although they may look to each other for guidance. For example, state courts of one state are not required to follow the legal precedent established by the courts of another state.

Adherence to precedent is called ***stare decisis*** ("to stand by the decision"). The **doctrine of *stare decisis*** promotes uniformity of law within a jurisdiction, makes the court system more efficient, and makes the law more predictable for individuals and businesses. A court may later change or reverse its legal reasoning if a new case is presented to it and change is warranted. The doctrine of *stare decisis* is discussed in the following excerpt from Justice Musmanno's decision in *Flagiello v. Pennsylvania*:

> *Without* stare decisis, *there would be no stability in our system of jurisprudence.* Stare decisis *channels the law. It erects lighthouses and flies the signal of safety. The ships of jurisprudence must follow that well-defined channel which, over the years, has been proved to be secure and worthy.*[9]

Web Exercises

1. **WEB** Visit the website of the U.S. Supreme Court, at *www.supremecourtus.gov*. Where is the Supreme Court located?

2. **WEB** Use *www.google.com* to find the website of the highest court in your state.

PRIORITY OF LAW IN THE UNITED STATES   As mentioned previously, the U.S. Constitution and treaties take precedence over all other laws in the United States. Federal statutes take precedence over federal regulations. Valid federal law takes precedence over any conflicting state or local law. State constitutions rank as the highest state law. State statutes take precedence over state regulations. Valid state law takes precedence over local laws.

CONCEPT SUMMARY

Sources of Law in the United States

SOURCE OF LAW	DESCRIPTION
Constitutions	The U.S. Constitution establishes the federal government and enumerates its powers. Powers not given to the federal government are reserved to the states. State constitutions establish state governments and enumerate their powers.
Treaties	The president, with the advice and consent of the Senate, may enter into treaties with foreign countries.
Codified law: statutes and ordinances	Statutes are enacted by Congress and state legislatures. Ordinances are enacted by municipalities and local government agencies. They establish courses of conduct that covered parties must follow.
Executive orders	Issued by the president and governors of states, executive orders regulate the conduct of covered parties.
Regulations and orders of administrative agencies	Administrative agencies are created by the legislative and executive branches of government. They may adopt rules and regulations that regulate the conduct of covered parties as well as issue orders.
Judicial decisions	Courts decide controversies. In doing so, a court issues a decision that states the holding of the case and the rationale the court used in reaching that decision.

U.S. SUPREME COURT DECISIONS The U.S. Supreme Court is often called upon to decide cases that have immense social implications. One of these issues is affirmative action in school admissions based on an applicant's race. For years, blacks and other minorities were discriminated against in many facets of society. To remedy this discrimination, Congress enacted the federal **Civil Rights Act of 1964**. This monumental act outlawed discrimination in housing, education, employment, and other areas of life.

Because of the Civil Rights Act of 1964, university admissions became open to applicants of all races. Many educational institutions adopted affirmative action programs that gave preference in admission to racial minority candidates. Proponents of affirmative action argue that anti-discrimination laws should be interpreted by the U.S. Supreme Court very broadly and that under such an interpretation, affirmative action programs in college and university admission is justified to make up for centuries of discrimination. Opponents to affirmative action counter that the Civil Rights Act of 1964 does not provide for affirmative action and that the law should be interpreted literally—that is, it should ban discrimination in admissions, not create reverse discrimination.

In the following two cases, the Supreme Court applied the Equal Protection Clause in determining the lawfulness of affirmative action programs in college and law school admissions.

CASE **1.1**

Affirmative Action

U.S. SUPREME COURT

Gratz v. Bollinger and the Regents of the University of Michigan

529 U.S. 244, 123 S.Ct. 2411, 156 L.Ed.2d 257,
Web 2003 U.S. Lexis 4801 (2003)
Supreme Court of the United States

> 66 *To withstand our strict scrutiny analysis, respondents must demonstrate that the University's use of race in its current admission program employs narrowly tailored measures that further compelling governmental interests.* 99

—Justice Rehnquist

Facts

Jennifer Gratz, a Caucasian resident of the state of Michigan, applied for admission to the College of Literature, Science, and the Arts at the University of Michigan, a state government–supported university. In its review of applicants, the University of Michigan considered high school grade point average, standardized test scores (SAT or ACT), high school quality, curriculum strength, geography, alumni relationships, and leadership. Each item was assigned a certain number of points for each applicant. If an applicant received 100 points, he or she would be guaranteed admission to the university. Minority applicants, defined as African Americans, Hispanics, and Native Americans, were automatically given 20 points, or one-fifth of the points needed to guarantee admission. Gratz was originally placed in a postponed decision category but was ultimately rejected for admission. A minority applicant with Gratz's score, who would receive an extra 20 points, would have been admitted.

Gratz brought a class action lawsuit against the University of Michigan, alleging that the university violated the Equal Protection Clause of the Fourteenth Amendment to the U.S. Constitution. Plaintiff Gratz sought damages for past violations and an injunction prohibiting the university from continuing to discriminate on the basis of race in violation of the Fourteenth Amendment. The District Court granted the university's motion for summary judgment and upheld the university's policy of adding 20 points to minority applicants' applications for admission. The U.S. Supreme Court granted certiorari to hear the appeal of this issue.

Issue

Does the University of Michigan's automatic award of 20 points to minority applicants for admission to the university's undergraduate College of Literature, Sciences, and the Arts violate the Equal Protection Clause of the Fourteenth Amendment to the U.S. Constitution?

Language of the U.S. Supreme Court

Each applicant received points based on high school grade point average, standardized test scores, academic quality of an applicant's high school, strength or weakness of high school curriculum, in-state residency, alumni relationships, personal essay, and personal achievement or leadership. Of particular significance here, under a "miscellaneous" category, an applicant was entitled to 20 points based upon his or her membership in an underrepresented racial or ethnic minority group. During all periods relevant to this litigation, the University has considered African-Americans, Hispanics, and Native Americans to be underrepresented minorities, and it is undisputed that the University admits virtually every qualified applicant from these groups.

We granted certiorari in this case to decide whether the University of Michigan's use of racial preferences in undergraduate admissions violates the Equal Protection Clause. All racial classifications reviewable under the Equal Protection Clause must be strictly scrutinized. To withstand our strict scrutiny analysis, respondents must demonstrate that the University's use of race in its current admission program employs narrowly tailored measures that further compelling governmental interests. We find that the University's policy, which automatically distributes 20 points, or one-fifth of the points needed to guarantee admission, to every single underrepresented minority applicant solely because of race, is not narrowly tailored to achieve the interest in educational diversity that respondents claim justify their program.

Decision

The U.S. Supreme Court held that the University of Michigan's undergraduate admission policy that automatically assigned 20 points, or one-fifth of the points needed to guarantee admission, to minority applicants did not pass the strict scrutiny test and was not narrowly tailored to accomplish the compelling state interest of obtaining a diverse student population. The Supreme Court held that the University of Michigan had violated the Equal Protection Clause of the Fourteenth Amendment. The Supreme Court reversed and remanded the case for further proceedings.

C A S E **1.2**

Affirmative Action

U.S. SUPREME COURT

Grutter v. Bollinger and the University of Michigan Law School

539 U.S. 306, 123 S.Ct. 2325, 156 L.Ed.2d 304,
Web 2003 U.S. Lexis 4800 (2003)
Supreme Court of the United States

> ❝ *Universities occupy a special niche in our constitutional tradition. In order to cultivate a set of leaders with legitimacy in the eyes of the citizenry, it is necessary that the path to leadership be visibly open to talented and qualified individuals of every race and ethnicity.* ❞
>
> —Justice O'Conner

Facts

Barbara Grutter, a Caucasian resident of the state of Michigan, applied to the Law School of the University of Michigan, a state government–supported institution, in 1996 with a 3.8 undergraduate grade point average and a 161 LSAT score. The Law School rejected her application. The Law School received 3,500 applications for a class of 350 students. The Law School used race as one of the factors in considering applicants for admission to law school. The race of minority applicants, defined as African-Americans, Hispanics, and Native Americans, was considered as a "plus factor" in considering their applications to law school. Caucasians and Asians were not given such a plus factor. The Law School stated that it used race as a plus factor to obtain a critical mass of underrepresented minority students in order to create diversity at the school.

Grutter brought a class action lawsuit against the Law School of the University of Michigan, alleging that its use of a minority's race as a plus factor in admissions violated the Equal Protection Clause of the Fourteenth Amendment to the U.S. Constitution. The District Court held that the Law School's use of race as a factor in admissions violated the Equal Protection Clause. The Court of Appeals reversed. The U.S. Supreme Court granted certiorari to hear the appeal.

Issue

Does the University of Michigan Law School's use of race as a plus factor in accepting minority applicants for admission to the Law School violate the Equal Protection Clause of the Fourteenth Amendment to the U.S. Constitution?

Language of the U.S. Supreme Court

The Equal Protection Clause provides that no State shall "deny to any person within its jurisdiction the equal protection of the laws." Racial classifications imposed by government must be analyzed by a reviewing court under strict scrutiny. When race-based action is necessary to further a compelling governmental interest, such action does not violate the constitutional guarantee of equal protection so long as the narrow-tailoring requirement is also satisfied. Universities occupy a special niche in our constitutional tradition. In order to cultivate a set of leaders with legitimacy in the eyes of the citizenry, it is necessary that the path to leadership be visibly open to talented and qualified individuals of every race and ethnicity.

To be narrowly tailored, a race-conscious admissions program cannot use a quota system. Instead, a university may consider race or ethnicity only as a "plus" in a particular applicant's file. We find that the Law School's admissions program bears the hallmarks of a narrowly tailored plan. Universities cannot establish quotas for members of certain racial groups or put members of those groups on separate admissions tracks. Nor can universities insulate applicants who belong to certain racial or ethnic groups from the competition for admission. Universities can, however, consider race or ethnicity more flexibly as a "plus" factor in the context of individualized consideration of each and every applicant.

The Law School's goal of attaining a critical mass of underrepresented minority students does not transform its program into a quota. Here, the Law School engages in a highly individualized, holistic review of each applicant's file, giving serious consideration to all the ways an applicant might contribute to a diverse educational environment. The Law School affords this individualized consideration to applicants of all races. We agree that, in the context of its individualized inquiry into the possible diversity contributions of all applicants, the Law School's race conscious admissions program does not unduly harm nonminority applicants.

We take the Law School at its word that it would like nothing better than to find a race-neutral admissions formula and will terminate its race-conscious admissions program as soon as practicable. We expect that 25 years from now, the use of racial preferences will no longer be necessary to further the interest approved today.

Decision

The U.S. Supreme Court held that the University of Michigan Law School's policy of using race as a plus factor in admitting minority applicants furthers a compelling state interest and is narrowly tailored to accomplish that interest. The Supreme Court held that the Law School's race-conscious admission policy does not violate the Equal Protection Clause of the Fourteenth Amendment to the U.S. Constitution.

Law & Ethics Questions

1. What does the Equal Protection Clause provide? Should the government ever be allowed to treat persons differently because of their race? Explain.

2. **ETHICS** Is it socially responsible for the University of Michigan or the University of Michigan Law School to consider a minority applicant's race as a plus factor in its admissions decisions?

3. Is anyone hurt by the University of Michigan Law School's race-conscious admissions policy? Explain.

4. What is the difference between the Supreme Court's decisions in these two cases? Explain.

Web Exercises

1. **WEB** For the complete opinion of the *Gratz v. Bollinger and the Regents of the University of Michigan* decision, go to *www.prenhall.com/cheesemancases*.

2. **WEB** For the complete opinion of the *Grutter v. Bollinger and the University of Michigan Law School*, go to *www.prenhall.com/cheesemancases*.

3. **WEB** Visit the website of the University of Michigan, at *www.umich.edu*. Does the application procedure for undergraduate admissions mention anything about affirmative action?

4. **WEB** Visit the website of the University of Michigan Law School, at *www.law.umich.edu*. Does the law school application procedure mention anything about affirmative action?

5. **WEB** Use *www.google.com* to find a recent article that discusses affirmative action in college and university admissions. Read it.

Moscow, Russia

The legal heritages of countries differ considerably. After the fall of communism, Russia adopted capitalism. New laws have been enacted to allow for the private ownership of property, to provide for the enforcement of contracts, and to otherwise support trade and commerce.

Briefing a Case: The IRAC Method

Judges apply *legal reasoning* in reaching a decision in a case. That is, a judge must specify the issue presented by the case, identify the key facts in the case and the applicable law, and then apply the law to the facts to come to a conclusion that answers the issue presented. This process is called **critical legal thinking**. Skills of analysis and interpretation are important in deciding legal cases.

Key Legal Terms

Before you embark on the study of law, you should know the following key legal terms:

- *Plaintiff.* The **plaintiff** is the party who originally brought the lawsuit.
- *Defendant.* The **defendant** is the party against whom the lawsuit has been brought.
- *Petitioner,* or *appellant.* The **petitioner** (or **appellant**) is the party who has appealed the decision of the trial court or lower court. The petitioner may be either the plaintiff or the defendant, depending on who lost the case at the trial court or lower court level.
- *Respondent,* or *appellee.* The **respondent** (or **appellee**) is the party who must answer the petitioner's appeal. The respondent may be either the plaintiff or the defendant, depending on which party is the petitioner. In some cases, both the plaintiff *and* the defendant may disagree with the trial court's or lower court's decision, and both parties may appeal the decision.

Briefing a Case Using the IRAC Method

It is often helpful for a student to "brief" a case to clarify the legal issues involved and to gain a better understanding of the case. One procedure for briefing a case is to use the IRAC method. After reading the facts of a case, the student then uses the following approach in analyzing the case:

I = What is the legal *issue* in the case?

R = What is the *rule* (law) of the case?

A = What is the court's *analysis* and rationale?

C = What was the *conclusion* or outcome of the case?

The procedure for briefing a case using the IRAC method is as follows: The student must summarize, or brief, the court's decision in no more than 600 words (some professors may shorten or lengthen this limit). The brief's format is highly structured, consisting of five parts, each of which is numbered and labeled (see Exhibit 1.2).

EXHIBIT 1.2

Briefing a Case Using the IRAC Method

Part	Maximum Words
1. The case name, citation, and court	50
2. A summary of the key facts in the case	150
3. I = The *issue* presented by the case, stated as a one-sentence question answerable only by *yes* or *no*	50
4. R = The *rule of law* of the case, stated in one sentence	50
5. A = A summary of the court's *analysis* and reasoning justifying the holding	250
6. C = The court's *conclusion* of the issue (the "holding")	50
Total words	600

Elements of a Case Brief

Briefing a case consists of making a summary of each of the following items of the case:

1. *Case name, citation, and court.* The name of the case should be placed at the beginning of each briefed case. The case name usually contains the names of the parties

to the lawsuit (for example, *PGA Tour, Inc. v. Martin*). Where there are multiple plaintiffs or defendants, however, some of the names of the parties may be omitted from the case name. Abbreviations are often used in case names as well

The case citation, which consists of a number plus the year in which the case was decided, such as "532 U.S. 661, 121 S.Ct. 1879, 149 L.Ed.2d 904, **Web** 2001 U.S. Lexis 4115," is set forth below the case name. The case citation identifies the book in the law library or the Internet site where the case may be found. For example, the case in the above citation may be found on page 661 in volume 532 of the *United States Reports*, on page 1879 in volume 121 of the *Supreme Court Reporter*, on page 904 in volume 149 of the *Lawyer's Edition* second edition, and on the **Lexis Nexis website**, at 2001 U.S. Lexis 4115. The name of the court that decided the case should be set forth below the case name for the case.

2. *Key facts.* The important facts of a case should be stated briefly. Extraneous facts and facts of minor importance should be omitted from the brief. The facts of the case can usually be found at the beginning of the case, but not necessarily. Important facts may be found throughout the case.

3. *I = Issue.* In the briefing of a case, it is crucial to identify the issue presented to the court to decide. The issue on appeal is most often a legal question, although questions of fact are sometimes the subject of an appeal. The issue presented in each case is usually quite specific and should be asked in a one-sentence question that is answerable only by *yes* or *no*. For example, the issue statement "Is the PGA Tour, Inc., liable?" is too broad. A proper statement of the issue would be "Does the Americans with Disabilities Act require the PGA to accommodate Martin by permitting him to use a golf cart while playing in PGA tournaments?"

4. *R = Rule of law.* In setting forth the brief of the case, you should state the rule of law at issue in the case. This could be a provision in the federal or state constitutions, a federal or state statute, or other law that is presented in the case.

5. *A = Analysis.* When an appellate court or a supreme court issues a decision, which is often called an *opinion*, the court will normally state the reasoning it used in reaching its decision. The rationale for the decision may be based on the specific facts of the case, public policy, prior law, or other matters. In stating the reasoning of the court, the student should reword the court's language into his or her own language. This summary of the court's reasoning should pick out the meat of the opinions and weed out the nonessentials.

6. *C = Conclusion.* The conclusion is the decision reached by the present court. It should be *yes* or *no*. The holding should also state which party won. The conclusion is sometimes called the *holding*.

The following is an excerpted decision by the Supreme Court of the United States. The case is presented in the language of the Supreme Court.

Case Name, Citation, and Court	**PGA TOUR, Inc. v. Martin, 532 U.S. 661, 121 S.Ct. 1879, 149 L.Ed.3d 904, Web 2001 U.S. Lexis 4115 (2001) Supreme Court of the United States**
Opinion of the Court	*OPINION, STEVEN, JUSTICE This case raises two questions concerning the application of the Americans with Disabilities Act of 1990 [42 U.S.C. § 12101 et seq.] to a gifted athlete: first, whether*
Issue	*the Act protects access to professional golf tournaments by a qualified entrant with a disability, and second, whether a disabled contestant may be denied the use of a golf cart because it would "fundamentally alter the nature" of the tournaments to allow him to ride when all other contestants must walk.*
Facts	*Petitioner PGA TOUR, Inc., a nonprofit entity formed in 1968, sponsors and cosponsors professional golf tournaments conducted on three annual tours. About 200 golfers participate in the PGA TOUR; about 170 in the NIKE TOUR; and about 100 in the SENIOR PGA TOUR. PGA TOUR and*
Petitioner: **PGA TOUR, Inc.**	*NIKE TOUR tournaments typically are four-day events, played on courses leased and operated by petitioner. The revenues generated by television, admissions, concessions, and contributions from cosponsors amount to about $300 million a year, much of which is distributed in prize money. The "Conditions of Competition and Local Rules," often described as the "hard card," apply specifically to petitioner's professional tours. The hard cards for the PGA TOUR and NIKE TOUR*

required players to walk the golf course during tournaments, but not during open qualifying rounds. On the SENIOR PGA TOUR, which is limited to golfers age 50 and older, the contestants may use golf carts. Most seniors, however, prefer to walk.

Casey Martin is a talented golfer. As an amateur, be won 17 Oregon Golf Association junior events before he was 15, and he won the state championship as a high school senior. He played on the Stanford University golf team that won the 1994 National Collegiate Athletic Association (NCAA) championship. As a professional, Martin qualified for the NIKE TOUR in 1998 and 1999, and based on his 1999 performance, qualified for the PGA TOUR in 2000. In the 1999 season, be entered 24 events, made the cut 13 times, and had six top-10 finishes, coming in second twice and third once.

Respondent: Casey Martin

Martin is also an individual with a disability, as defined in the Americans with Disabilities Act of 1990 (ADA or Act). Since birth he has been afflicted with Klippel-Trenaunay-Weber Syndrome, a degenerative circulatory disorder that obstructs the flow of blood from his right leg back to his heart. The disease is progressive; it causes severe pain and has atrophied his right leg. During the latter part of his college career, because of the progress of the disease, Martin could no longer walk an 18-hole golf course. Walking not only caused him pain, fatigue, and anxiety, but also created a significant risk of hemorrhaging, developing blood clots, and fracturing his tibia so badly that an amputation might be required.

When Martin turned pro and entered petitioner's Qualifying-School, the hard card permitted him to use a cart during his successful progress through the first two stages. He made a request, supported by detailed medical records, for permission to use a golf cart during the third stage. Petitioner refused to review those records or to waive its walking rule for the third stage. Martin therefore filed this action.

At trial, petitioner PGA TOUR did not contest the conclusion that Martin has a disability covered by the ADA, or the fact that his disability prevents him from walking the course during a round of golf. Rather, petitioner asserted that the condition of walking is a substantive rule of competition and that waiving it as to any individual for any reason would fundamentally alter the nature of the competition. Petitioner's evidence included the testimony of a number of experts, among them some of the greatest golfers in history. Arnold Palmer, Jack Nicklaus, and Ken Venturi explained that fatigue can be a critical factor in a tournament, particularly on the last day, when psychological pressure is at a maximum. Their testimony makes it clear that, in their view, permission to use a cart might well give some players a competitive advantage over other players who must walk.

District Court's Decision: 994 F. Supp. 1242, Web 1998 U.S. Dist. Lexis 1980 [U.S. District Court, Oregon (1998)]

The judge found that the purpose of the rule was to inject fatigue into the skill of shot-making, but that the fatigue injected "by walking the course cannot be deemed significant under normal circumstances." Furthermore, Martin presented evidence, and the judge found, that even with the use of a cart, Martin must walk over a mile during an 18-hole round, and that the fatigue he suffers from coping with his disability is "undeniably greater" than the fatigue his able-bodied competitors endure from walking the course. As a result, the judge concluded that it would "not fundamentally alter the nature of the PGA Tour's game to accommodate him with a cart." The judge accordingly entered a permanent injunction requiring petitioner to permit Martin to use a cart in tour and qualifying events.

The Court of Appeals concluded that golf courses remain places of public accommodation during PGA tournaments. On the merits, because there was no serious dispute about the fact that permitting Martin to use a golf cart was both a reasonable and a necessary solution to the problem of providing him access to the tournaments, the Court of Appeals regarded the central dispute as whether such permission would "fundamentally alter" the nature of the PGA TOUR or NIKE TOUR. Like the District Court, the Court of Appeals viewed the issue not as "whether use of carts generally would fundamentally alter the competition, but whether the use of a cart by Martin would do so." That issue turned on "an intensively fact-based inquiry," and, the court concluded, had been correctly resolved by the trial judge. In its words, "all that the cart does is permit Martin access to a type of competition in which he otherwise could not engage because of his disability."

Court of Appeals Decision: 204 F.3d 994, Web 2000 U.S. App. Lexis 3376 [U.S. Court of Appeals (2000)]

Congress enacted the ADA in 1990 to remedy widespread discrimination against disabled individuals. To effectuate its sweeping purpose, the ADA forbids discrimination against disabled individuals in major areas of public life, among them employment (Title I of the Act), public services (Title II), and public accommodations (Title III). At issue now is the applicability of Title III to petitioner's golf tours and qualifying rounds, in particular to petitioner's treatment of a qualified disabled golfer wishing to compete in those events.

Federal Statute Being Interpreted

It seems apparent, from both the general rule and the comprehensive definition of "public accommodation," that petitioner's golf tours and their qualifying rounds fit comfortably within the coverage of Title III, and Martin within its protection. The events occur on "golf courses," a type of place specifically identified by the Act as a public accommodation [Section 12181(7)(L)]. In this case, the narrow dispute is whether allowing Martin to use a golf cart, despite the walking requirement that applies to the PGA TOUR, the NIKE TOUR, and the third stage of the Qualifying-School, is a modification that would "fundamentally alter the nature" of those events.

U.S. Supreme Court's Reasoning

As an initial matter, we observe that the use of carts is not itself inconsistent with the fundamental character of the game of golf. From early on, the essence of the game has been shotmaking—using clubs to cause a ball to progress from the teeing ground to a hole some distance away with as few strokes as possible. Golf carts started appearing with increasing regularity on American golf courses in the 1950s. Today they are everywhere. And they are encouraged. For one thing, they often speed up play, and for another, they are great revenue producers. There is nothing in the rules of golf that either forbids the use of carts or penalizes a player for using a cart.

Petitioner, however, distinguishes the game of golf as it is generally played from the game that it sponsors in the PGA TOUR, NIKE TOUR, and the last stage of the Qualifying-School—golf at the "highest level." According to petitioner, "the goal of the highest-level competitive athletics is to assess and compare the performance of different competitors, a task that is meaningful only if the competitors are subject to identical substantive rules." The waiver of any possibly "outcome-affecting" rule for a contestant would violate this principle and therefore, in petitioner's view, fundamentally alter the nature of the highest-level athletic event. The walking rule is one such rule, petitioner submits, because its purpose is "to inject the element of fatigue into the skill of shot-making," and thus its effect may be the critical loss of a stroke. As a consequence, the reasonable modification Martin seeks would fundamentally alter the nature of petitioner's highest-level tournaments.

The force of petitioner's argument is, first of all, mitigated by the fact that golf is a game in which it is impossible to guarantee that all competitors will play under exactly the same conditions or that an individual's ability will be the sole determinant of the outcome. For example, changes in the weather may produce harder greens and more head winds for the tournament leader than for his closest pursuers. A lucky bounce may save a shot or two. Whether such happenstance events are more or less probable than the likelihood that a golfer afflicted with Klippel-Trenaunay-Weber Syndrome would one day qualify for the NIKE TOUR and PGA TOUR, they at least demonstrate that pure chance may have a greater impact on the outcome of elite golf tournaments than the fatigue resulting from the enforcement of the walking rule.

Further, the factual basis of petitioner's argument is undermined by the District Court's finding that the fatigue from walking during one of petitioner's 4-day tournaments cannot be deemed significant. The District Court credited the testimony of a professor in physiology and expert on fatigue, who calculated the calories expended in walking a golf course (about five miles) to be approximately 500 calories—"nutritionally less than a Big Mac." What is more, that energy is expended over a 5-hour period, during which golfers have numerous intervals for rest and refreshment. In fact, the expert concluded, because golf is a low-intensity activity, fatigue from the game is primarily a psychological phenomenon in which stress and motivation are the key ingredients. And even under conditions of severe heat and humidity, the critical factor in fatigue is fluid loss rather than exercise from walking. Moreover, when given the option of using a cart, the majority of golfers in petitioner's tournaments have chosen to walk, often to relieve stress or for other strategic reasons. As NIKE TOUR member Eric Johnson testified, walking allows him to keep in rhythm, stay warmer when it is chilly, and develop a better sense of the elements and the course than riding a cart. As we have demonstrated, the walking rule is at best peripheral to the nature of petitioner's athletic events, and thus it might be waived in individual cases without working a fundamental alteration.

Holding and Remedy

Under the ADA's basic requirement that the need of a disabled person be evaluated on an individual basis, we have no doubt that allowing Martin to use a golf cart would not fundamentally alter the nature of petitioner's tournaments. As we have discussed, the purpose of the walking rule is to subject players to fatigue, which in turn may influence the outcome of tournaments. Even if the rule does serve that purpose, it is an uncontested finding of the District Court that Martin "easily endures greater fatigue even with a cart than his able-bodied competitors do by walking." The purpose of the walking rule is therefore not compromised in the slightest by allowing Martin to use a cart. A modification that provides an exception to a peripheral tournament rule without impairing its purpose cannot be said to "fundamentally alter" the tournament. What it can be said to do, on the other hand, is to allow Martin the chance to qualify for and compete in the athletic events petitioner offers to those members of the public who have the skill and desire to enter. That is exactly what the ADA requires. As a result, Martin's request for a waiver of the walking rule should have been granted.

The judgment of the Court of Appeals is affirmed. It is so ordered.

Dissenting Opinion

DISSENTING OPINION, SCALIA, JUSTICE *In my view today's opinion exercises a benevolent compassion that the law does not place it within our power to impose. The judgment distorts the text of Title III, the structure of the ADA, and common sense. I respectfully dissent.*

Agility, strength, speed, balance, quickness of mind, steadiness of nerves, intensity of concentration—these talents are not evenly distributed. No wild-eyed dreamer has ever suggested that the managing bodies of the competitive sports that test precisely these qualities should try to take account of the uneven distribution of God-given gifts when writing and enforcing the rules of competition. And I have no doubt Congress did not authorize misty-eyed judicial supervision of such a revolution.

Web Exercises

1. **WEB** For the complete opinion of this case, go to *www.prenhall.com/cheesemancases*.
2. **WEB** Visit the website of the U.S. Supreme Court, at *www.supremecourtus.gov* and try to find documents that relate to this case.

EXHIBIT 1.3

IRAC Brief of the Case

1. **Case Name, Citation, and Court**

   PGA TOUR, Inc. v Martin

   532 U.S. 661, 121 S.Ct. 1879, 149 L.Ed.3d 904, **Web** 2001 Lexis 4115 (2001)

   Supreme Court of the United States

2. **Key Facts**
   A. PGA TOUR, Inc., is a nonprofit organization that sponsors professional golf tournaments.
   B. The PGA establishes rules for its golf tournaments. A PGA rule requires golfers to walk the golf course and not use golf carts.
   C. Casey Martin is a professional golfer who suffers from Klippel-Trenaunay-Weber Syndrome, a degenerative circulatory disorder that atrophied Martin's right leg and causes him pain, fatigue, and anxiety when walking.
   D. When Martin petitioned the PGA to use a golf cart during golf tournaments, the PGA refused.
   E. Martin sued the PGA, alleging discrimination against a disabled individual in violation of the Americans with Disabilities Act of 1990, a federal statute.

3. **I = Issue**

   Does the Americans with Disabilities Act require the PGA to accommodate Martin by permitting him to use a golf cart while playing in PGA tournaments?

4. **R = Rule**

   The Americans with Disabilities Act requires employers to make reasonable accommodations to persons with disabilities where such rule does not cause an undue burden on the employer.

5. **A = Analysis**

   The Supreme Court held that:
   A. Martin was disabled and covered by the act.
   B. Golf courses are "public accommodations" covered by the act.
   C. The use of golf carts is not a fundamental character of the game of golf.
   D. Other than the PGA rule, there is no rule of golf that forbids the use of golf carts.
   E. It is impossible to guarantee that all players in golf will play under exactly the same conditions, so allowing Martin to use a golf cart gives him no advantage over other golfers.
   F. Martin, because of his disease, will probably suffer more fatigue playing golf using a golf cart than other golfers will suffer without using a cart.
   G. The PGA's "walking rule" is only peripheral to the game of golf and not a fundamental part of golf.
   H. Allowing Martin to use a golf cart will not fundamentally alter the PGA's highest-level professional golf tournaments.

6. **C = Conclusion**

   The Supreme Court held that the PGA must allow Martin to use a golf cart when competing in PGA golf tournaments. Affirmed.

Chapter Summary

What is Law? p. 3
Definition of Law

Law is a body of rules of action or conduct that has binding legal force. Laws must be obeyed by citizens, subject to sanction or legal consequences.

Functions of the Law

1. Keep the peace
2. Shape moral standards
3. Promote social justice
4. Maintain the status quo
5. Facilitate orderly change
6. Facilitate planning
7. Provide a basis for compromise
8. Maximize individual freedom

Fairness of the Law

Although the U.S. legal system is one of the fairest and most democratic systems of law, abuses of process and mistakes in the application of the law do occur.

Flexibility of the Law

The law must be flexible to meet social, technological, and economic changes in the United States and the world.

Schools of Jurisprudential Thought, p. 8
Natural Law School

The Natural Law School postulates that law is based on what is "correct." It emphasizes a moral theory of law—that is, law should be based on morality and ethics.

Historical School

The Historical School believes that law is an aggregate of social traditions and customs.

Analytical School

The Analytical School maintains that law is shaped by logic.

Sociological School

The Sociological School asserts that law is a means of achieving and advancing certain sociological goals.

Command School

The Command School believes that law is a set of rules developed, communicated, and enforced by the ruling party.

Critical Legal Studies School

The Critical Legal Studies School maintains that legal rules are unnecessary and that legal disputes should be solved by applying arbitrary rules based on fairness.

Law and Economics School

The Law and Economics School believes that promoting market efficiency should be the central concern of legal decision making.

History of American Law, p. 10
English Common Law

The English common law (judge-made law) forms the basis of the legal systems of most states in the United States. Louisiana, however, bases its law on the French civil code.

Sources of Law in the United States, p. 12
Constitutions

The U.S. Constitution establishes the federal government and enumerates its powers. Powers not given to the federal government are reserved to the states. State constitutions establish state governments and enumerate their powers.

Treaties

The president, with the advice and consent of the Senate, may enter into treaties with foreign countries.

Codified Law

Statutes are enacted by the federal Congress and state legislatures. Ordinances are passed by municipalities and local government bodies. They establish courses of conduct that must be followed by covered parties.

Executive Orders

Issued by the president and governors of states, executive orders regulate the conduct of covered parties.

Regulations and Order of Administrative Agencies

Administrative agencies are created by the legislative and executive branches of government. They may adopt administrative regulations and issue orders.

Judicial Decisions

Federal and state courts decide controversies. In doing so, they issue decisions that state the holding of each case and the reasoning used by the court in reaching its decision.

Doctrine of *Stare Decisis*. This doctrine provides for the adherence to precedent. *Stare decisis* means "to stand by the decision."

Briefing a Case: the IRAC Method, p. 18
Briefing a Case Using the IRAC Method

1. Case name, citation, and court.
2. Summary of the key facts in the case.
3. *I* = Issue presented by the case.
4. *R* = Rule of law that applies to the case.
5. *A* = Summary of the court's analysis.
6. *C* = Conclusion reached by the court.

Test Review Terms and Concepts

Administrative agencies   13
Administrative rules and
    regulations   14
Analytical School   8
Civil law System   11
Codified law   12
Command School   8

Constitution of the United States of
    America   12
Court of Chancery (equity
    court)   10
Critical Legal Studies
    School   8
Critical legal thinking   19

Defendant   19
Department of Homeland Security
    (DHS)   14
Doctrine of *stare decisis*   15
English common law   10
Executive branch (president)   12
Executive orders   13

Case Problems

1.1 Fairness of the Law: In 1909, the state legislature of Illinois enacted a statute called the "Woman's 10-Hour Law." The law prohibited women who were employed in factories and other manufacturing facilities from working more than 10 hours per day. The law did not apply to men. W. C. Ritchie & Co., an employer, brought a lawsuit that challenged the statute as being unconstitutional in violation of the Equal Protection Clause of the Illinois constitution. In upholding the statute, the Supreme Court of Illinois stated:

It is known to all men (and what we know as men we cannot profess to be ignorant of as judges) that woman's physical structure and the performance of maternal functions place her at a great disadvantage in the battle of life; that while a man can work for more than 10 hours a day without injury to himself, a woman, especially when the burdens of motherhood are upon her, cannot; that while a man can work standing upon his feet for more than 10 hours a day, day after day, without injury to himself, a woman cannot; and that to require a woman to stand upon her feet for more than 10 hours in any one day and perform severe manual labor while thus standing, day

after day, has the effect to impair her health, and that as weakly and sickly women cannot be mothers of vigorous children.

We think the general consensus of opinion, not only in this country but in the civilized countries of Europe, is, that a working day of not more than 10 hours for women is justified for the following reasons: (1) the physical organization of women, (2) her maternal function, (3) the rearing and education of children, (4) the maintenance of the home; and these conditions are, so far, matters of general knowledge that the courts will take judicial cognizance of their existence.

Surrounded as women are by changing conditions of society, and the evolution of employment which environs them, we agree fully with what is said by the Supreme Court of Washington in the Buchanan case; "law is, or ought to be, a progressive science."

Is the statute fair? Would the statute be lawful today? Should the law be a "progressive science"? *W. C. Ritchie & Co. v. Wayman, Attorney for Cook Country, Illinois,* 244 Ill. 509, 91 N.E. 695, **Web** 1910 Ill. Lexis 1958 (Supreme Court of Illinois)

Ethics Issues

1.2 Ethics: In 1975, after the war in Vietnam, the U.S. government discontinued draft registration for men in this country. In 1980, after the Soviet Union invaded Afghanistan, President Jimmy Carter asked Congress for funds to reactivate draft registration. President Carter suggested that both males and females be required to register. Congress allocated funds only for the registration of males. Several men who were subject to draft registration brought a lawsuit that challenged the law as being unconstitutional in violation of the Equal Protection Clause of the U.S. Constitution. The U.S. Supreme Court upheld the constitutionality of the draft registration law, reasoning as follows:

The question of registering women for the draft not only received considerable national attention and was the subject of wide-ranging public debate, but also was extensively considered by Congress in hearings, floor debate, and in committee. The foregoing clearly establishes that the decision to exempt women from registration was not the "accidental by-product of a traditional way of thinking about women."

This is not a case of Congress arbitrarily choosing to burden one of two similarly situated groups, such as would be the case with an all-black or all-white, or an all-Catholic or all-Lutheran, or an all-Republican or all-Democratic registration. Men and women are simply not similarly situated for purposes of a draft or registration for a draft.

Justice Marshall dissented, stating that "The Court today places its imprimatur on one of the most potent remaining public expressions of 'ancient canards about the proper role of women.' It upholds a statute that requires males but not females to register for the draft, and which thereby categorically excludes women from a fundamental civil obligation. I dissent."

Is the decision fair? Is the law a "progressive science" in this case? Is it ethical for males, but not females, to have to register for the draft? *Rostker, Director of Selective Service v. Goldberg*, 453 U.S. 57, 101 S. Ct. 2646, 69 L. Ed. 2d 478, **Web** 1981 U.S. Lexis 126 (Supreme Court of the United States)

IRAC Writing Assignment

Read Case A-1 in Appendix A [*Anheuser-Busch Incorporated v Schmoke, Mayor of Baltimore City*]. Read the case and use the IRAC method to prepare a written analysis of the case.

Endnotes

1. *The Spirit of Liberty*, 3rd ed. (New York: Alfred A. Knopf, 1960).
2. "Introduction," *The Nature of Law: Readings in Legal Philosophy*, ed. M. P. Golding (New York: Random House, 1966).
3. *Black's Law Dictionary*, 5th ed. (St. Paul, MN: West, 1979).
4. 447 U.S. 10, 100 S.Ct. 1999, 64 L.Ed.2d 689, **Web** 1980 U.S. Lexis 127 (Supreme Court of the United States).
5. Jerome Frank, *Law and the Modern Mind* (New York: Brentano's, 1930).
6. 163 U.S. 537, 16 S.C. 1138, 141 L.Ed 256, **Web** 1896 U.S. Lexis 3390 (Supreme Court of the United States, 1896).
7. 347 U.S. 483, 74 S.Ct. 686, 98 L.Ed. 873, **Web** 1954 U.S. Lexis 2094 (Supreme Court of the United States, 1954).
8. 4 Ill. 301, 1841 Ill. Lexis 98 (Ill.).
9. 417 Pa. 486, 208 A.2d 193, **Web** 1965 Pa. Lexis 442 (Supreme Court of Pennsylvania).

CHAPTER 2

Constitutional Law for Business and E-Commerce

> **"** *We the People of the United States, in Order to form a more perfect Union, establish Justice, insure domestic Tranquility, provide for the common defense, promote the general Welfare, and secure the Blessings of Liberty to ourselves and our Posterity, do ordain and establish this Constitution for the United States of America.* **"**
>
> —PREAMBLE TO THE CONSTITUTION OF THE UNITED STATES OF AMERICA

CHAPTER OBJECTIVES

After studying this chapter, you should be able to:

1. Describe the concept of federalism and the doctrine of separation of powers.
2. Define and apply the Supremacy Clause of the U.S. Constitution.
3. Explain the federal government's authority to regulate foreign commerce and interstate commerce.
4. Explain how speech is protected by the First Amendment.
5. Explain the doctrines of equal protection and due process.

CHAPTER CONTENTS

- Introduction to Constitutional Law for Business and Online Commerce
- Constitution of the United States of America
- Supremacy Clause
- Commerce Clause
- Bill of Rights
- Freedom of Speech
- Freedom of Religion
- Equal Protection Clause
- Due Process Clause
- Privileges and Immunities Clause
- Chapter Summary
- Test Review Terms and Concepts
- Case Problems
- Ethics Issues
- IRAC Writing Assignment

Introduction to Constitutional Law for Business and E-Commerce

Prior to the American Revolution, each of the 13 original colonies operated as a separate sovereignty under the rule of England. In September 1774, representatives of the colonies met as a Continental Congress. In 1776, the colonies declared independence from England, and the American Revolution ensued. The Declaration of Independence was the document that declared independence from England.

This chapter examines the major provisions of the U.S. Constitution and the amendments that have been added to the Constitution. Of particular importance, this chapter discusses how these provisions affect the operations of business in this country. The Constitution, with amendments, is set forth as Appendix B to this book.

> The nation's armour of defence against the passions of men is the Constitution. Take that away, and the nation goes down into the field of its conflicts like a warrior without armour.
>
> Henry Ward Beecher
> *Proverbs from Plymouth Pulpit (1887)*

Web Exercises

1. **WEB** Use *www.google.com* to find an article about the American Revolution. Read it.

2. **WEB** Use *www.ushistory.org* to find a copy of the Declaration of Independence. Read it.

3. **WEB** Use *www.google.com* to find an article about the drafting of the Declaration of Independence. Read it.

New York City, New York

The Constitution of the United States of America establishes the structure of the federal government, delegates powers to the federal government, and guarantees certain fundamental rights.

Constitution of the United States of America

In 1778, the Continental Congress formed a *federal government* and adopted the **Articles of Confederation**. The Articles of Confederation created a federal Congress composed of representatives from each of the 13 new states. The Articles of Confederation was a

particularly weak document that gave limited power to the newly created federal government. For example, it did not provide Congress with the power to levy and collect taxes, to regulate commerce with foreign countries, or to regulate interstate commerce among the states.

The **Constitutional Convention** was convened in Philadelphia in May 1787. The primary purpose of the convention was to strengthen the federal government. After substantial debate, the delegates agreed to a new **Constitution of the United States of America**. The constitution was reported to Congress in September 1787. State ratification of the Constitution was completed in 1788. Many amendments, including the Bill of Rights, have been added to the Constitution since that time.

The U.S. Constitution serves two major functions:

1. It creates the three branches of the federal government (i.e., the executive, legislative, and judicial branches) and allocates powers to these branches.
2. It protects individual rights by limiting the government's ability to restrict those rights.

The Constitution itself provides that it may be amended to address social and economic changes. Some important constitutional concepts are discussed in the following paragraphs. Exhibit 2.1 shows the U.S. Constitution.

Web Exercises

1. **WEB** To view a map of the original 13 colonies, go to *http://en.wikipedia.org/wiki/Thirteen_colonies*.
2. **WEB** Use *www.google.com* to find an article about the Continental Congress. Read it.

Federalism and Delegated Powers

Our country's form of government is referred to as **federalism**, which means the federal government and the 50 state governments share powers.

When the states ratified the Constitution, they *delegated* certain powers, called **enumerated powers**, to the federal government. The federal government is authorized to deal with national and international affairs. Any powers that are not specifically delegated to the federal government by the Constitution are reserved to the state governments. State governments are empowered to deal with local affairs.

Doctrine of Separation of Powers

As mentioned previously, the federal government is divided into three branches:

1. *Legislative branch.* Article I of the Constitution establishes the **legislative branch** of government. This branch is bicameral; that is, it consists of the Senate and the House of Representatives. Collectively, they are referred to as *Congress.*[1] Each state has two senators. The number of representatives to the House of Representatives is determined according to the population of each state. The current number of representatives is determined from the 2000 census.
2. *Executive branch.* Article II of the Constitution establishes the **executive branch** of government by providing for the election of the president and vice president. The president is not elected by popular vote but instead is selected by the *electoral college*, whose representatives are appointed by state delegations.[2]
3. *Judicial branch.* Article III establishes the **judicial branch** of the government by establishing the Supreme Court and providing for the creation of other federal courts by Congress.[3]

Web Exercises

1. **WEB** Visit the website of the U.S. Senate, at *www.senate.gov*.

2. **WEB** Visit the website of the U.S. House of Representatives, at *www.house.gov*.

3. **WEB** Visit the website of the president of the United States, at *www.whitehouse.gov/president*.

4. **WEB** Visit the website of the Supreme Court of the United States, at *www.supremecourtus.gov*.

EXHIBIT 2.1

The Constitution of the United States of America

Checks and Balances

Certain **checks and balances** are built into the Constitution to ensure that no one branch of the federal government becomes too powerful. Some of the checks and balances in our system of government are as follows:

1. The judicial branch has authority to examine the acts of the other two branches of government and determine whether those acts are constitutional.[4]
2. The executive branch can enter into treaties with foreign governments only with the advice and consent of the Senate.
3. The legislative branch is authorized to create federal courts and determine their jurisdiction and to enact statutes that change judicially made law.

CONCEPT SUMMARY

Basic Constitutional Concepts

CONCEPT	DESCRIPTION
Federalism	The Constitution created the federal government. The federal government and the 50 state governments and Washington, DC, share powers in this country.
Delegated powers	When the states ratified the Constitution, they delegated certain powers to the federal government. These are called *enumerated powers*.
Reserved powers	Those powers not granted to the federal government by the Constitution are reserved to the states.
Separation of powers	Each branch of the federal government has separate powers. These powers are: a. Legislative branch—power to make the law. b. Executive branch—power to enforce the law. c. Judicial branch—power to interpret the law.
Checks and balances	Certain checks and balances are built into the Constitution to ensure that no one branch of the federal government becomes too powerful.

Supremacy Clause

The **Supremacy Clause** establishes that the federal Constitution, treaties, federal laws, and federal regulations are the supreme law of the land.[5] State and local laws that conflict with valid federal law are unconstitutional. The concept of federal law taking precedence over state or local law is commonly called the **preemption doctrine**.

Congress may expressly provide that a particular federal statute *exclusively* regulates a specific area or activity. No state or local law regulating the area or activity is valid if there is such a statute. More often, though, federal statutes do not expressly provide for exclusive jurisdiction. In these instances, state and local governments have *concurrent jurisdiction* to regulate the area or activity. However, any state or local law that "directly and substantially" conflicts with valid federal law is preempted under the Supremacy Clause.

In the following case, the U.S. Supreme Court applied the Supremacy Clause.

C A S E **2.1**

Supremacy Clause

U.S. SUPREME COURT

Engine Manufacturers Association v. South Coast Air Quality Management District

541 U.S. 246, 124 S.Ct. 1756, 158 L.Ed. 529,
Web 2004 U.S. Lexis 3232 (2004)
Supreme Court of the United States

> " *But if one state or political subdivision may enact such rules, then so may any other, and the end result would undo Congress's carefully calibrated regulatory scheme.* "
>
> —Justice Scalia

Facts

The Clean Air Act, a federal statute, establishes national air pollution standards for fleet vehicles such as buses, taxicabs, and trucks. The South Coast Air Quality Management District (South Coast) is a political entity of the state of California. South Coast establishes air pollution standards for the Los Angeles, California, metropolitan area. South Coast enacted fleet rules that prohibited the purchase or lease by public and private fleet operators of vehicles that do not meet stringent air pollution standards set by South Coast. South Coast's fleet emission standards are more stringent than those set by the federal Clean Air Act.

The Engine Manufacturers Association (Association), a trade association that represents manufacturers and sellers of vehicles, sued South Coast, claiming that South Coast's fleet rules are preempted by the federal Clean Air Act. The U.S. District Court and the U.S. Court of Appeals upheld South Coast's fleet rules. The Association appealed to the U.S. Supreme Court.

Issue

Are South Coast's fleet rules preempted by the federal Clean Air Act?

Language of the U.S. Supreme Court

Clearly, Congress contemplated the enforcement of emission standards. But if one state or political subdivision may enact such rules, then so may any other, and the end result would undo Congress's carefully calibrated regulatory scheme. The fleet purchase standards must comply strictly with federal specifications, being neither more lenient nor more demanding. What is the use of imposing such a limitation if the states are entirely free to impose their own fleet purchase standards with entirely different specifications?

Decision

The U.S. Supreme Court held that the federal Clean Air Act fleet emission standards preempted South Coast's more stringent fleet emission standards. The Supreme Court vacated the judgment of the Court of Appeals and remanded the case for further proceedings.

Law & Ethics Questions

1. What does the preemption doctrine provide? Do businesses sometimes favor uniform national laws over state laws? Explain.
2. **ETHICS** Did the Engine Manufacturers Association act ethically in trying to avoid South Coast's more stringent emission standards?
3. What would have been the consequences if the Supreme Court had upheld South Coast's more stringent fleet rules? Explain.

Web Exercises

1. **WEB** For the complete opinion of this case, go to *www.prenhall.com/cheesemancases*.
2. **WEB** Visit the website of Engine Manufactures Association, at *www.enginemanufacturers.org*.
3. **WEB** Visit the website of South Coast Air Quality Management District, at **www.aqmd.gov**.
4. **WEB** Visit the website of the U.S. Supreme Court, at *www.supremecourtus.gov* and try to find documents that relate to this case.
5. **WEB** Use *www.google.com* to find the current law or an article that discusses the Environmental Law in your state. Read it.

Commerce Clause

The **Commerce Clause** of the U.S. Constitution grants Congress the power "to regulate commerce with foreign nations, and among the several states, and with Indian tribes."[6] Because this clause authorizes the federal government to regulate commerce, it has a greater impact on business than any other provision in the Constitution. Among other things, this clause is intended to foster the development of a national market and free trade among the states.

Commerce Regulation with Native American Tribes

When the United States was first founded over 200 years ago, it consisted of the original 13 colonies, all located in the east, primarily on the Atlantic Ocean. At that time, these colonies (states) delegated to the federal government the authority to regulate commerce with the Native American tribes. In the original states, as well as the territory that was to eventually become the United States of America, there existed many Native American nations. The federal government entered into treaties with many of the Native American nations, exchanging money and goods for property. The government obtained many of these treaties through unscrupulous means, and it violated some of the treaties over the years. Many Native Americans lived on reservations set aside for various tribes. Today, many Native Americans live and work in modern society.

The following case is an example of the enforcement of Native American treaty rights.

C A S E   2.2
Native Americans

U.S. SUPREME COURT
Minnesota v. Mille Lacs Band of Chippewa Indians

526 U.S. 172, 119 S.CT. 1187, 143 L.Ed.2d 270,
Web 1999 U.S. LEXIS 2190 (1999)
Supreme Court of the United States

> **❝***There is no clear evidence of congressional intent to abrogate the Chippewa Treaty rights here.* **❞**

—Justice O'Connor

Facts

When the Constitution was ratified by the original colonies in 1788, it delegated to the federal government the exclusive power to regulate commerce with Native American tribes. During the next 100 years, as the colonists migrated westward, the federal government entered into many treaties with Native American nations. One such treaty was with the Ojibwe Indians in 1837, whereby the Ojibwe sold land located in the Minnesota territory to the United States. The treaty provided: "The privilege of hunting, fishing, and gathering wild rice, upon the lands, the rivers and the lakes included in the territory ceded, is guaranteed to the Indians." The state of Minnesota was admitted into the Union in 1858.

In 1990, the Mille Lacs Band of the Ojibwe tribe sued the state of Minnesota, seeking declaratory judgment that they retained the hunting, fishing, and gathering rights provided in the 1837 treaty and an injunction to prevent Minnesota from interfering with those rights. The state of Minnesota argued that when Minnesota entered the Union in 1858, those rights were extinguished. The U.S. District Court and the U.S. Court of Appeals held in favor of the Ojibwe. Minnesota appealed to the U.S. Supreme Court.

Issue

Are the hunting, fishing, and gathering rights guaranteed to the Ojibwe in the 1837 treaty still valid and enforceable?

Language of the U.S. Supreme Court

The State of Minnesota argues that the Chippewa's rights under the 1837 treaty were extinguished when Minnesota was admitted to the Union in 1858. In making this argument, the state faces an uphill battle. There is no clear evidence of congressional intent to abrogate the Chippewa [Ojibwe] Treaty rights here. The relevant statute—Minnesota's enabling act—provides in relevant part: "The State of Minnesota shall be one, and is hereby declared to be one, of the United States of America, and admitted into the Union on an equal footing with the original

states in all respects whatever." This language, like the rest of the act, makes no mention of Indian treaty rights.

Decision

The U.S. Supreme Court held that the hunting, fishing, and gathering rights provided to the Ojibwe in the 1837 treaty with the United States of America were valid and enforceable and had not been extinguished when Minnesota was admitted to the Union.

Law & Ethics Questions

1. **ETHICS** Did the state of Minnesota act ethically in arguing that the hunting, fishing, and gathering rights of the Chippewa had been extinguished? Why do you think that the state of Minnesota took this position?

2. **ETHICS** Do the Native Americans have any legal claim to the lands that now comprise the United States of America? Explain.

3. **ETHICS** The federal government enacted federal legislation that permits gambling on Native American reservation land (with the permission of state governments). Do these gambling statutes make up for past wrongs caused to Native Americans by the federal government?

Web Exercises

1. **WEB** For the complete opinion of this case, go to *www.prenhall.com/cheesemancases*.

2. **WEB** Visit the website of state of Minnesota, at *www.state.mn.us*.

3. **WEB** Visit the website of the U.S. Supreme Court, at *www.supremecourtus.gov* and try to find documents related to this case.

4. **WEB** Visit the website of the Mille Lacs Band of Ojibwe Native Americans, at *www.millelacsojibwe.org*.

5. **WEB** Use *www.google.com* to find the current law or an article that discusses the current law regarding the enforcement of treaties made with Native Americans. Read it.

CONTEMPORARY ENVIRONMENT
Native American Law

Before Europeans arrived in the "New World," the land had been occupied for thousands of years by the people we now refer to as Native Americans or American Indians. There were many different Native American tribes, each with its own independent and self-governing system of laws. However, when Native Americans came under U.S. authority, they lost much of their political power. Many of the larger tribes were able to enter into treaties with the U.S. that allowed them to keep their own governments, but they were placed under the "protection" of the U.S. government.

The U.S. federal government was given the power to regulate commerce with the Native American tribes through the Commerce Clause in the Constitution. Appropriately, Native American legal matters that cannot be dealt with within the tribe are generally taken to federal courts. State courts do not have jurisdiction over laws that are broken on Native American land. The two federal agencies generally responsible for making sure Native Americans are treated fairly under the law are the **Bureau of Indian Affairs (BIA)** and the **Indian Health Service (IHS)**. In general, the United States treats Native Americans as a separate nation, just as Spain or France; however, they are still considered a "domestic dependent" nation with limited sovereignty. The U.S. government has an obligation to protect Native Americans' land, resources, and rights of self-government.

On Native American reservations, tribal governments act as the governing authority. The tribes can choose what form of government to take and how to operate it. These governing bodies, called **tribal councils**, are able to collect taxes, regulate property, and maintain their own law and order. The fact that the states cannot regulate or tax Native Americans within their borders has caused many legal battles and ill will between some tribes and the states where they live.

One of the main reasons states frown upon Native Americans not having to pay taxes is due to the success of Native American gambling casinos. In 1987, the Supreme Court ruled that federally recognized Native American tribes can operate gaming facilities without state regulation. A year later, Congress passed the **Indian Gaming Regulatory Act**, which sets the terms of casino gambling and other gaming activities on tribal land. This act allows Native Americans to negotiate with the states for gaming compacts and ensures that the states do so in good faith. If a state fails to do so, a tribe can bring suit in federal court, forcing the state to comply. However, Native American casinos are typically only allowed in states where gambling is already legal.

Web Exercises

1. **WEB** To learn more about Native American law, visit *www.megalaw.com/top/native.php*.

2. **WEB** Visit the website of the Bureau of Indian Affairs, at *www.doi.gov/bureau-indian-affairs.html*.

St. Ignace, Michigan

The U.S. Constitution gives the federal government the authority to regulate commerce with Native American tribes. The Sault Ste. Marie Chippewa Tribe owns and operates casinos in St. Ignace, Michigan, and several other locations in northern Michigan, pursuant to federal law.

Foreign Commerce Clause

The Commerce Clause of the U.S. Constitution gives the federal government the *exclusive power* to regulate commerce with foreign nations. For example, the federal government could enact a law that prohibits U.S. companies from doing business with a foreign country that engages in terrorist activities.

Direct and indirect regulation of foreign commerce by state or local governments that unduly burdens foreign commerce violates the Commerce Clause and is therefore unconstitutional.

Examples The state of Michigan is the home of General Motors Corporation, Ford Motor Company, and Chrysler Corporation, the three largest automobile manufacturers in the United States. Suppose the Michigan state legislature enacted a law that imposed a 100 percent tax on any automobile imported from a foreign country sold in Michigan but did not impose the same tax on domestic automobiles sold in Michigan. The Michigan tax would violate the Foreign Commerce Clause and would therefore be unconstitutional and void. If, on the other hand, Michigan enacted a law that imposed a 100 percent tax on all automobiles sold in Michigan, domestic and foreign, the law would not discriminate against foreign commerce and therefore would not violate the Foreign Commerce Clause. The federal government could enact a 100 percent tax on all foreign automobiles but not domestic automobiles sold in the United States, and that law would be valid.

In the following case, the U.S. Supreme Court struck down a state law as violating the Foreign Commerce Clause within the Constitution.

C A S E **2.3**

Foreign Commerce Clause

U.S. SUPREME COURT

Crosby, Secretary of Administration and Finance of Massachusetts v. National Foreign Trade Council

530 U.S. 363, 120 S.Ct. 2288, 147 L.Ed.2d 352,
Web 2000 U.S. Lexis 4153 (2000)
Supreme Court of the United States

❝ *Within the sphere defined by Congress, then, the federal statute has placed the president in a position with as much discretion to exercise economic leverage against Burma, with an eye toward national security, as our law will admit.* ❞

—Justice Souter

Facts

The military regime of the country of Myanmar (called Burma prior to 1989) has been accused of major civil rights violations, including using forced and child labor, imprisoning and torturing political opponents, and harshly repressing ethnic minorities. These inhumane actions have been condemned by human rights organizations around the world. The state legislators in the state of Massachusetts were so appalled at these actions that in June 1996, they enacted a state statute banning the state government from purchasing goods and services from any company that did business with Myanmar.

In the meantime, the U.S. Congress enacted a federal statute that delegated power to the president of the United States to regulate U.S. dealings with Myanmar. The federal statute (1) banned all aid to the government of Myanmar except for humanitarian assistance, (2) authorized the president to impose economic sanctions against Myanmar, and (3) authorized the president to develop a comprehensive multilateral strategy to bring democracy to Myanmar.

The National Foreign Trade Council—a powerful Washington, DC–based trade association with more than 500 member companies—filed a lawsuit against Massachusetts to have the state law declared unconstitutional. The council argued that the Massachusetts "anti-Myanmar" statute was preempted by the Supremacy Clause of the U.S. Constitution, which makes federal law the "supreme law of the land" and gives the federal government the power to regulate foreign affairs. The U.S. District Court and U.S. Court of Appeals ruled in favor of the council. Massachusetts appealed to the U.S. Supreme Court.

Issue

Did the Massachusetts anti-Myanmar state statute violate the Supremacy Clause of the U.S. Constitution?

Language of the U.S. Supreme Court

Within the sphere defined by Congress, then, the federal statute has placed the president in a position with as much discretion to exercise economic leverage against Burma, with an eye toward national security, as our law will admit. And it is just this plenitude of executive authority that we think controls the issue of preemption here. The president has been given this authority not merely to make a political statement but to achieve a political result, and the fullness of his authority shows the importance in the congressional mind of reaching that result. It is simply implausible that Congress would have gone to such lengths to empower the president if it had been willing to compromise his effectiveness by deference to every provision of state statute or local ordinance that might, if enforced, blunt the consequences of discretionary presidential action.

We find it unlikely that Congress intended both to enable the president to protect national security by giving him the flexibility to suspend or terminate federal sanctions and simultaneously to allow Massachusetts to act at odds with the president's judgment of what national security requires. And that is just what the Massachusetts Burma law would do in imposing a different, state system of economic pressure against the Burmese political regime.

Decision

The U.S. Supreme Court held that the Massachusetts anti-Myanmar law conflicted with federal law and was therefore preempted by the Supremacy Clause of the Constitution. The Supreme Court affirmed the decisions of the U.S. District Court and U.S. Court of Appeals in favor of the council.

Law & Ethics Questions

1. What does the Foreign Commerce Clause provide? Explain.
2. Should the federal government have sole power to regulate the foreign affairs of the United States? Or should the states share in this power?
3. **ETHICS** Do you think companies that have goods manufactured in Myanmar violate any ethical principles? Explain.
4. **ETHICS** Was it ethical for the National Foreign Trade Council to argue against the Massachusetts anti-Myanmar law? Why or why not?
5. Did the Massachusetts anti-Myanmar law have any economic implications for business? What would have been the economic consequences if the U.S. Supreme Court had held that the Massachusetts anti-Myanmar statute was lawful?

Web Exercises

1. **WEB** For the complete opinion of this case, go to *www.prenhall.com/cheesemancases*.
2. **WEB** Visit the website of the U.S. Supreme Court, at *www.supremecourtus.gov* and try to find documents that relate to this case.
3. **WEB** Visit the website of the National Foreign Trade Council, at *www.nftc.org*. What is the mission of this organization?
4. **WEB** Visit the website *www.unicef.org/myanmar* for information on Myanmar.
5. **WEB** Use *www.google.com* to find an article that discusses the labor practices used in Myanmar. Read it.

Golden Pavilion, Kyoto, Japan

Each country has developed its own laws. A company conducting business in a foreign country is subject to that country's laws.

LANDMARK CASE

Heart of Atlanta Motel v. United States

> ❝*One need only examine the evidence which we have discussed . . . to see that Congress may . . . prohibit racial discrimination by motels serving travelers, however "local" their operations may appear.* ❞
>
> —Justice Clark

The Heart of Atlanta Motel, which was located in the state of Georgia, had 216 rooms available to guests. The motel was readily accessible to motorists using U.S. interstate highways 75 and 85 and to Georgia state highways 23 and 41. The motel solicited patronage from outside the state of Georgia through various national advertising media, including magazines of national circulation. The motel maintained more than 50 billboards and highway signs within the state of Georgia. Approximately 75 percent of the motel's registered guests were from out of state. The Heart of Atlanta Motel refused to rent rooms to blacks.

Congress enacted the **Civil Rights Act of 1964**, which made it illegal for motels, hotels, and other public accommodations to discriminate against guests based on their race. After the act was passed, the motel continued not to rent rooms to Blacks. The owner-operator of the motel brought a declaratory relief action in U.S. District Court, **Heart of Atlanta Motel v. United States**,[7] to have the Civil Rights Act of 1964 declared unconstitutional. The plaintiff argued that Congress, in passing the act, had exceeded its powers to regulate interstate commerce under the Commerce Clause of the U.S. Constitution. The U.S. District Court upheld the Civil Rights Act and enjoined the owner-operator of the Heart of Atlanta Motel from discriminating against blacks. The owner-operator of the motel appealed to the U.S. Supreme Court.

The U.S. Supreme Court held that the provisions of the Civil Rights Act of 1964 that prohibited discrimination in accommodations properly regulated interstate commerce. In reaching its decision, the U.S. Supreme Court stated:

The power of Congress over interstate commerce is not confined to the regulation of commerce among the states. It extends to those activities intrastate which so affect interstate commerce or the exercise of the power of Congress over it as to make regulation of them appropriate means to the attainment of a legitimate end, the exercise of the granted power of Congress to regulate interstate commerce.

Thus the power of Congress to promote interstate commerce also includes the power to regulate the local incidents thereof, including local activities in both the States of origin and destination, which might have a substantial and harmful effect upon that commerce. One need only examine the evidence which we have discussed above to see that Congress may—as it has—prohibit racial discrimination by motels serving travelers, however "local" their operations may appear.

The U.S. Supreme Court held that the challenged provisions of the Civil Rights Act of 1964 were constitutional as a proper exercise of the commerce power of the federal government.

Web Exercises

1. **WEB** For the complete opinion of this case, go to *www.prenhall.com/cheesemancases*.

2. **WEB** Use *www.google.com* to find an article that discusses the significance of this case.

Interstate Commerce

The Commerce Clause gives the federal government the authority to regulate **interstate commerce**. Originally, the courts interpreted this clause to mean that the federal government could only regulate commerce that moved *in* interstate commerce. The modern rule, however, allows the federal government to regulate activities that *affect* interstate commerce.

Under the **effects on interstate commerce test**, the regulated activity does not itself have to be in interstate commerce. Thus, any local (*intrastate*) activity that has an effect on interstate commerce is subject to federal regulation. Theoretically, this test subjects a substantial amount of business activity in the United States to federal regulation.

Example In the famous case **Wickard, Secretary of Agriculture v. Filburn**,[8] a federal statute limited the amount of wheat a farmer could plant and harvest for home consumption. Congress had enacted this federal statute during the Great Depression, a time of substantial economic disruption and unemployment in the United States. Filburn, a farmer,

> The American Constitution is, so far as I can see, the most wonderful work ever struck off at a given time by the brain and purpose of man.
>
> W. E. Gladstone
> *Kin Beyond Sea (1878)*

violated the law. The case went to the U.S. Supreme Court, where Filburn, the accused farmer argued that the federal statute did not involve interstate commerce and that the statute was therefore unconstitutional. The U.S. Supreme Court sided with the government and upheld the federal statute on the grounds that it involved interstate commerce because the statute was designed to prevent nationwide surpluses and shortages of wheat during the Depression. The Court reasoned that wheat grown for home consumption would affect the supply of wheat available in interstate commerce.

The federal government's authority to enact federal statutes pursuant to the Commerce Clause was at issue in the following two cases.

CASE 2.4
Interstate Commerce

U.S. SUPREME COURT
Reno, Attorney General of the United States v. Condon, Attorney General of South Carolina

528 U.S. 141, 120 S.Ct. 666, 145 L.Ed.2d 587,
Web 2000 U.S. Lexis 503 (2000)
Supreme Court of the United States

> "*Because drivers' information is, in this context, an article of commerce, its sale or release into the interstate stream of business is sufficient to support congressional regulation.*"

—Justice Rehnquist

Facts

State departments of motor vehicles (DMVs) register automobiles and issue driver's licenses. State DMVs require automobile owners and drivers to provide personal information—including a person's name, address, telephone number, vehicle description, Social Security number, medical information, and a photograph—as a condition for registering an automobile or obtaining a driver's license. Many states' DMVs sold this personal information to individuals, advertisers, and businesses. These sales generated significant revenues for the states.

After receiving thousands of complaints from individuals whose personal information had been sold, the U.S. Congress enacted the Driver's Privacy Protection Act of 1994 (DPPA).[9] This federal statute prohibits a state from selling the personal information of a person unless the state obtains that person's affirmative consent to do so. South Carolina sued the United States, alleging that the federal government violated the Commerce Clause by adopting the DPPA. The District Court and the Court of Appeals held for South Carolina. The U.S. Supreme Court granted review.

Issue

Was the Driver's Privacy Protection Act properly enacted pursuant to the Commerce Clause power granted to the federal government by the U.S. Constitution?

Language of the U.S. Supreme Court

The United States asserts that the DPPA is a proper exercise of Congress's authority to regulate interstate commerce under the Commerce Clause. The United States bases its Commerce Clause argument on the fact that the personal, identifying information that the DPPA regulates is a thing in interstate commerce, and that the sale or release of that information in interstate commerce is therefore a proper subject of congressional regulation. We agree with the United States' contention.

The motor vehicle information which the States have historically sold is used by insurers, manufacturers, direct marketers, and others engaged in interstate commerce to contact drivers with customized solicitations. The information is also used in the stream of interstate commerce by various public and private entities for matters related to interstate motoring. Because drivers' information is, in this context, an article of commerce, its sale or release into the interstate stream of business is sufficient to support congressional regulation.

Decision

The U.S. Supreme Court held that Congress had the authority under the Commerce Clause to enact the federal Driver's Privacy Protection Act. The Supreme Court reversed the decisions of the District Court and Court of Appeals that held in favor of South Carolina.

Law & Ethics Questions

1. How often do you think one government (the federal government) saves people from the intrusiveness of another government (state or local government)?
2. **ETHICS** Was it ethical for the states to sell the personal information of automobile owners and drivers?
3. Who benefited from this decision? Who was hurt by this decision?

Web Exercises

1. **WEB** For the complete opinion of this case, go to *www.prenhall.com/cheesemancases*.
2. **WEB** Visit the website of the U.S. Supreme Court, at *www.supremecourtus.gov* and try to find documents that relate to this case.
3. **WEB** Use *www.google.com* to find an article that discusses the Driver's Privacy Protection Act. Read it.

C A S E 2.5

Interstate Commerce

U.S. SUPREME COURT
Gonzales, Attorney General of the United States v. Raich

545 U.S. 1, 125 S.Ct. 2195, 162 L.Ed.2d 1,
Web 2005 U.S. Lexis 4656 (2005)
Supreme Court of the United States

> **"***Indeed, . . . the California exemptions will have a significant impact on both the supply and demand sides of the market for marijuana.* **"**
>
> —Justice Stevens

Facts

Congress enacted the federal Controlled Substances Act (CSA) in 1970.[10] This act gives the federal government the authority to regulate legitimate and illegitimate manufacture, cultivation, distribution, and use of controlled substances. Marijuana is a controlled substance pursuant to the CSA, and its cultivation, distribution, and use is prohibited by the CSA.

California voters passed Proposition 215, now codified as the California Compassionate Use Act of 1996. This state law allows seriously ill residents of California to use marijuana for medical purposes. The act creates an exemption from criminal prosecution for physicians, patients, and primary caregivers who possess or cultivate marijuana for medicinal purposes with the recommendation or approval of a physician.

Angel Raich and Diane Monson (collectively Raich) are California residents who suffer from a variety of serious medical conditions and use marijuana medicinally pursuant to California's Compassionate Use Act. Raich sued the federal government, seeking an injunction and declaratory relief prohibiting the enforcement of the federal CSA as it pertains to medical marijuana. The U.S. District Court denied Raich's motion. The U.S. Court of Appeals, however, reversed and entered the injunction. The United States appealed to the U.S. Supreme Court.

Issue

Does the Commerce Clause of the U.S. Constitution grant the power to the federal government to enact the Controlled Substances Act, which prohibits local cultivation and use of marijuana as permitted under the California Compassionate Use Act?

Language of the U.S. Supreme Court

Indeed, . . . the California exemptions will have a significant impact on both the supply and demand sides of the market for marijuana. The exemption for physicians provides them with an economic incentive to grant their patients permission to use the drug. In contrast to most prescriptions for legal drugs, which limit the dosage and duration of the usage, under California law the doctor's permission to recommend marijuana use is open-ended. The authority to grant permission whenever the doctor determines that a patient is afflicted with "any other illness for which marijuana provides relief," is broad enough to allow even the most scrupulous doctor to conclude that some recreational uses would be therapeutic. And our cases have taught us that there are some unscrupulous physicians who overprescribe when it is sufficiently profitable to do so.

The exemption for cultivation by patients and caregivers can only increase the supply of marijuana in the California market. The likelihood that all such production will promptly terminate when patients recover or will precisely match the patients' medical needs during their convalescence seems remote; whereas the danger that excesses will satisfy some of the admittedly enormous demand for recreational use seems obvious. Moreover, that the national and international narcotics trade has thrived in the face of vigorous criminal enforcement efforts suggests that no small number of unscrupulous people will make use of the California exemptions to serve their commercial ends whenever it is feasible to do so. Taking into account the fact that California is only one of at least nine States to have authorized the medical use of marijuana, Congress could have rationally concluded that the aggregate impact on the national market of all the transactions exempted from federal supervision is unquestionably substantial.

Decision

The U.S. Supreme Court held that the passage of the federal Controlled Substances Act by Congress was a constitutional exercise of its Commerce Clause powers. The Supreme Court found that the intrastate, noncommercial cultivation and possession of marijuana for personal medical purposes under California's Compassionate Use Act is subject to and is prohibited by the CSA. The Supreme Court vacated the judgment of the Court of Appeals and remanded the case for further proceedings consistent with the Supreme Court's opinion.

Law & Ethics Questions

1. What does the Commerce Clause provide regarding the ability of the federal government to regulate intrastate commerce? Explain.
2. Was the federal Controlled Substances Act enacted pursuant to the federal government's Commerce Clause powers?
3. **ETHICS** What was the public policy that was to be served by the California Compassionate Use Act?

Web Exercises

1. **WEB** For the complete opinion of this case, go to *www.prenhall.com/cheesemancases*.
2. **WEB** Visit the website of the U.S. Supreme Court, at *www.supremecourtus.gov* and try to find documents that relate to this case.
3. **WEB** Use *www.google.com* to find an article that discusses the use of marijuana for medical purposes.

No Undue Burden on Intrastate Commerce

The states did not delegate all power to regulate business to the federal government. They retained the power to regulate *intrastate* and much interstate business activity that occurs within their borders. This is commonly referred to as states' **police power**.

Police power permits states (and, by delegation, local governments) to enact laws to protect or promote the *public health, safety, morals, and general welfare*. This includes the authority to enact laws that regulate the conduct of business. Zoning ordinances, state environmental laws, corporation and partnership laws, and property laws are enacted under this power.

State and local laws cannot **unduly burden interstate commerce**. If they do, they are unconstitutional because they violate the Commerce Clause.

Example Each state has enacted a corporations code that regulates the establishment and operations of corporations in that state. Assume that one state's corporations code permits only corporations from that state, but from no other state, to conduct business in that state. That state law would unduly burden interstate commerce and would be unconstitutional.

In the following case, the U.S. Supreme Court had to decide whether a state law unduly burdened interstate commerce.

CASE 2.6
Undue Burden on Interstate Commerce

U.S. SUPREME COURT
Granholm, Governor of Michigan v. Heald
544 U.S. 460, 125 S.Ct. 1885, 161 L.Ed.2d 796,
Web 2005 U.S. Lexis 4174 (2005)
Supreme Court of the United States

> "*State bans on interstate direct shipping represent the single largest regulatory barrier to expanded e-commerce in wine.*"
>
> —Justice Kennedy

Facts

The state of Michigan regulates the sale of wine within its boundaries. Michigan law permits in-state wineries to sell wine directly to consumers, including by mail, Internet, and other means of sale. Michigan law prohibits out-of-state wineries from selling wine directly to Michigan consumers and instead requires out-of-state wineries to sell their wine to Michigan wholesalers, who then sell the wine to Michigan retailers, who then sell the wine to Michigan consumers. Many small wineries across the country rely on mail order and the Internet to sell wine to residents in other states. Out-of-state wineries that are required by law to sell wine to Michigan wholesalers would incur a cost that in-state wineries would not incur, thus making it more costly and often unprofitable for out-of-state wineries to sell to Michigan consumers.

Domaine Alfred, a small winery located in San Luis Obispo, California, and several other out-of-state wineries that were prohibited from selling wine directly to Michigan consumers sued Michigan. The plaintiff wineries alleged that the Michigan law caused an undue burden on interstate commerce in violation of the Commerce Clause of the U.S. Constitution. The U.S. District Court ruled in favor of Michigan. The wineries appealed to the U.S. Court of Appeals for the Sixth Circuit, which reversed in favor of the out-of-state wineries. The state of Michigan appealed to the Supreme Court of the United States, which agreed to hear the case.

Issue

Does the state of Michigan law that permits in-state wineries to sell wine directly to Michigan consumers but that restricts the ability of out-of-state wineries to do so violate the Commerce Clause of the U.S. Constitution?

Language of the U.S. Supreme Court

Technological improvements, in particular the ability of wineries to sell wine over the internet, have helped make direct shipments an attractive sales channel. State bans on interstate direct shipping represent the single largest regulatory barrier to expanded e-commerce in wine.

Time and again this court has held that, in all but the narrowest circumstances, state laws violate the Commerce Clause if they mandate differential treatment of in-state and out-of-state economic interests that benefits the former and burdens the latter. This rule is essential to the foundations of the Union. The mere fact of non-residence should not foreclose a producer in one state from access to markets in other states. States may not enact laws that burden out-of-state producers or shippers simply to give a competitive advantage to in-state businesses. Rivalries among the states are thus kept to a minimum, and a proliferation of trade zones is prevented.

Laws of the type at issue in the instant case contradict these principles. They deprive citizens of their right to have access to the markets of other states on equal terms. Allowing states to discriminate against out-of-state wine invites a multiplication of preferential trade areas destructive of the very purpose of the Commerce Clause. State laws that discriminate against interstate commerce face a virtually per se rule of invalidity. The Michigan law by its terms violates this proscription.

Decision

Yes. The United States Supreme Court held that the Michigan state law that discriminated against out-of-state wineries in favor of in-state wineries violated the Commerce Clause of the U.S. Constitution. The Supreme Court affirmed the decision of the U.S. Court of Appeals in favor of the out-of-state wineries.

Law & Ethics Questions

1. **ETHICS** Why did the state of Michigan adopt this discriminatory wine sales law? Who do you think lobbied the legislators of Michigan to enact such a law?

2. What would have been the consequences if the Michigan law had been allowed? Explain.
3. How important are the Internet and e-commerce to small businesses that sell goods?

Web Exercises

1. **WEB** For the compete opinion of this case, go to *www.prenhall.com/cheesemancases*.
2. **WEB** Visit the website of the U.S. Supreme Court, at *www.supremecourtus.gov* and try to find documents that relate to this case.
3. **WEB** Visit the website of the Domaine Alfred winery, at *www.domainealfred.com*. Does the winery sell wines via the Internet?
4. **WEB** Use *www.google.com* to find other sources of wine sold over the Internet.

Bill of Rights

The U.S. Constitution provides that it may be amended. In 1791, the 10 amendments that are commonly referred to as the **Bill of Rights** were approved by the states and became part of the U.S. Constitution. The Bill of Rights guarantees certain fundamental rights to natural persons and protects these rights from intrusive government action. Most of these rights have also been found applicable to so-called artificial persons (i.e., corporations).

In addition to the Bill of Rights, 17 other **amendments** have been added to the Constitution. These amendments cover a variety of subjects.

Example Amendments have abolished slavery, prohibited discrimination, authorized the federal income tax, given women the right to vote, and specifically recognized that persons 18 years of age and older have the right to vote.

Originally, the Bill of Rights limited intrusive actions by the *federal government* only. Intrusive actions by state and local governments were not limited until the **Due Process Clause** of the Fourteenth Amendment was added to the Constitution in 1868. The Supreme

Protest, Los Angeles, California

The Freedom of Speech Clause of the First Amendment to the U.S. Constitution protects the right to engage in political speech.

Court has applied the **incorporation doctrine** and held that most of the fundamental guarantees contained in the Bill of Rights are applicable to state and local government action. The amendments to the Constitution that are most applicable to business are discussed in the paragraphs that follow.

Web Exercises

1. **WEB** Use *www.google.com* to find a copy of the Bill of Rights.
2. **WEB** Use *www.google.com* to find an article about the adoption of the Bill of Rights. Read it.

Freedom of Speech

One of the most honored freedoms guaranteed by the Bill of Rights is the **freedom of speech** of the First Amendment. Many other constitutional freedoms would be meaningless without it. The First Amendment's Freedom of Speech Clause protects speech only, not conduct. The U.S. Supreme Court places speech into three categories: (1) *fully protected*, (2) *limited protected*, and (3) *unprotected speech*. These types of speech are discussed in the following paragraphs.

Fully Protected Speech

Fully protected speech is speech that the government cannot prohibit or regulate. Political speech is an example of such speech.

Example The government could not enact a law that forbids citizens from criticizing the current administration. The First Amendment protects oral, written, and symbolic speech.

> I disapprove of what you say, but I will defend to the death your right to say it.
>
> Voltaire

The following case demonstrates the application of the Freedom of Speech Clause.

CASE **2.7**

Freedom of Speech

U.S. SUPREME COURT

United States v. Playboy Entertainment Group, Inc.

529 U.S. 803, 120 S.Ct. 1878, 146 L.Ed.2d 803,
Web 2000 U.S. Lexis 3427 (2000)
Supreme Court of the United States

❝Section 505 . . . silences the protected speech for two-thirds of the day in every home in a cable service area, regardless of the presence or likely presence of children or of the wishes of the viewers.❞

—Justice Kennedy

Facts

Many entertainment companies, including Playboy Entertainment Group, Inc., produce and distribute sexually explicit adult entertainment features for transmission over cable television stations. These shows are usually offered on a pay-per-view subscription service basis. Cable operators provide viewers with a converter box that attaches to the television set and scrambles these sexually explicit materials so they can only be viewed by subscribers who pay the subscription fee. However, with analog television sets, there often occurs "signal bleed" of either a blurred visual image or muted audio transmission of these materials. Digital television eliminates the signal bleed problem.

To address the signal bleed problem, Congress enacted Section 505 of the Telecommunications Act of 1996, which requires cable operators not to transmit sexually explicit materials during the hours from 6:00 A.M. to 10:00 P.M. if the signal bleed problem can occur.

Playboy Entertainment Group, Inc., a cable operator of Playboy Television and Spice, two adult entertainment cable television networks, sued the federal government, alleging that Section 505 violated its free speech rights guaranteed by the U.S. Constitution. The District Court declared Section 505 unconstitutional. The Court found it feasible to allow cable operators to block individual cable boxes in the home and therefore found Section 505 to be an overly broad restriction on content-based speech. The U.S. Supreme Court agreed to hear the case on direct appeal.

Issue

Is Section 505 an overly broad restriction on content-based speech that violates the free speech rights of Playboy Entertainment Group, Inc.?

Language of the U.S. Supreme Court

As this case has been litigated, the programming is not alleged to be obscene; adults have a constitutional right to view it.

The effect of the federal statute on the protected speech is now apparent. It is evident that the only reasonable way for a substantial number of cable operators to comply with the letter of Section 505 is to "time channel", which silences the protected speech for two-thirds of the day in every home in a cable service area, regardless of the presence or likely presence of children or of the wishes of the viewers. According to the District Court, 30 to 50 percent of all adult programming is viewed by households prior to 10 P.M., when the safe harbor period begins. To prohibit this much speech is a significant restriction of communication between speakers and willing adult listeners, communication which enjoys First Amendment protection.

Cable systems have the capacity to block unwanted channels on a household-by-household basis. Simply put, targeted blocking is less restrictive than banning, and the Government cannot ban speech if targeted blocking is a feasible and effective means of furthering its compelling interests. If a less restrictive means is available for the Government to achieve its goals, the Government must use it.

Decision

The U.S. Supreme Court held that Section 505 was an overly broad restriction on legal content-based speech and was therefore an unconstitutional violation of free speech rights. The Supreme Court affirmed the judgment of the District Court.

Law & Ethics Questions

1. Do you think that Section 505 was an overly broad restriction on free speech rights? Why or why not?
2. **ETHICS** Why do you think Congress enacted Section 505 rather than require each home to choose to individually block the challenged programming?
3. What economic consequences did the Supreme Court's ruling have for Playboy Entertainment and other adult entertainment cable companies?

Web Exercises

1. **WEB** For the complete opinion of this case, go to *www.prenhall.com/cheesemancases*.
2. **WEB** Visit the website of the U.S. Supreme Court, at *www.supremecourtus.gov* and try to find documents that relate to this case.
3. **WEB** Use *www.google.com* to find an article about free speech rights. Read it.

Limited Protected Speech

The Supreme Court has held that certain types of speech have only *limited protection* under the First Amendment. The government cannot forbid **limited protected speech**, but it can subject this speech to *time, place, and manner restrictions*. Two types of speech are accorded limited protection: *offensive speech* and *commercial speech*.

OFFENSIVE SPEECH **Offensive speech** is speech that offends many members of society. (It is not the same as obscene speech, however.) The Supreme Court has held that the government may restrict offensive speech under time, place, and manner restrictions.

Example The Federal Communications Commission (FCC) can regulate the use of offensive language on television by limiting such language to time periods when children would be unlikely to be watching (e.g., late at night).

COMMERCIAL SPEECH **Commercial speech**, such as advertising, was once considered unprotected by the First Amendment. The Supreme Court's landmark decision in *Virginia State Board of Pharmacy v. Virginia Citizens Consumer Council, Inc.*[11] changed this rule. In that case, the Supreme Court held that a state statute prohibiting a pharmacist from advertising the price of prescription drugs was unconstitutional because it violated the Freedom of Speech Clause. However, the Supreme Court held that commercial speech is subject to time, place, and manner restrictions. For example, a city can prohibit billboards along its highways for safety and aesthetic reasons as long as other forms of advertising (e.g., print media) are available.

In the following case, the court had to decide whether the government had properly regulated commercial speech.

CASE **2.8**
Commercial Speech

U.S. SUPREME COURT

Mainstream Marketing Services, Inc. v. Federal Trade Commission and Federal Communications Commission

358 F.3d 1228, **Web** 2004 U.S. App. Lexis 2564 (2004)

> ❝*The national do-not-call registry offers consumers a tool with which they can protect their homes against intrusions that Congress has determined to be particularly invasive.* ❞

—Judge Ebel

Facts

Pursuant to enabling statutes, two federal administrative agencies—the Federal Trade Commission (FTC) and the Federal Communications Commission (FCC)—created the national do-not-call registry. The national do-not-call registry is a list that contains the personal telephone numbers of telephone users who have voluntarily placed themselves on this list to indicate that they do not want to receive unsolicited calls from commercial telemarketers. Commercial telemarketers are prohibited from calling phone numbers that have been placed on the do-not-call registry. Telemarketers must pay an annual fee to access the phone numbers on the registry so that they can delete those numbers from their solicitation lists. The national do-not-call registry restrictions apply only to telemarketers' calls made by or on behalf of sellers of goods or services. Charitable and fundraising calls are exempt from the do-not-call registry's restrictions. Persons who do not voluntarily place their phone numbers on the do-not-call registry may still receive unsolicited telemarketers' calls.

Mainstream Marketing Services, Inc., and other telemarketers sued the FTC and the FCC in several lawsuits, alleging that their free speech rights were violated and that the do-not-call registry was unconstitutional. The FTC and FCC defended, arguing that unsolicited telemarketing calls was commercial speech that could be regulated by the government's do-not-call registry's restrictions. The separate lawsuits were consolidated for appeal.

Issue

Do unsolicited telemarketing calls constitute commercial speech that can be constitutionally regulated by the do-not-call registry restrictions?

Language of the U.S. Supreme Court

Four key aspects of the do-not-call registry convince us that it is consistent with **First Amendment** requirements. First, the list restricts only core commercial speech—i.e., commercial sales calls. Second, the do-not-call registry targets speech that invades the privacy of the home, a personal sanctuary that enjoys a unique status in our constitutional jurisprudence. Third, the do-not-call registry is an opt-in program that puts the choice of whether or not to restrict commercial calls entirely in the hands of consumers. Fourth, the do-not-call registry materially furthers the government's interests in combating the danger of abusive telemarketing and preventing the invasion of consumer privacy, blocking a significant number of the calls that cause these problems.

A number of additional features of the national do-not-call registry, although not dispositive, further demonstrate that the list is consistent with the First Amendment rights of commercial speakers. The challenged regulations do not hinder any business' ability to contact consumers by other means, such as through direct mailings or other forms of advertising. Moreover, they give consumers a number of different options to avoid calls they do not want to receive. Namely, consumers who wish to restrict some but not all commercial sales calls can do so by using company-specific do-not-call lists or by granting some businesses express permission to call. In addition, the government chose to offer consumers broader options to restrict commercial sales calls than charitable and political calls after finding that commercial calls were more intrusive and posed a greater danger of consumer abuse.

The national do-not-call registry offers consumers a tool with which they can protect their homes against intrusions that Congress has determined to be particularly invasive. Just as a consumer can avoid door-to-door peddlers by placing a "No Solicitation" sign in his or her front yard, the do-not-call registry lets consumers avoid unwanted sales pitches that invade the home via telephone, if they choose to do so. We are convinced that the **First Amendment** does not prevent the government from giving consumers this option.

For the reasons discussed above, the government has asserted substantial interests to be served by the do-not-call registry (privacy and consumer protection), the do-not-call registry will directly advance those interests by banning a substantial amount of unwanted telemarketing calls, and the regulation is narrowly tailored because its opt-in feature ensures that it does not restrict any speech directed at a willing listener. In other words, the do-not-call registry bears a reasonable fit with the purposes the government sought to advance. Therefore, it is consistent with the limits the **First Amendment** imposes on laws restricting commercial speech.

Decision

The U.S. Supreme Court held that unsolicited telemarketing calls constituted commercial speech that was subject to government regulation and that the do-not-call registry restrictions did not violate the free speech rights of the plaintiff telemarketers.

Law & Ethics Questions

1. What is the do-not-call registry? How does it work?
2. **ETHICS** Is it ethical for telemarketers to make unsolicited phone calls to persons' houses? What time of day are many of these calls made?

3. **ETHICS** Do you think telemarketers commit fraud? Explain.
4. What is the economic effect on telemarketers of the do-not-call registry?

Web Exercises

1. **WEB** For the complete opinion of this case, go to *www.prenhall.com/cheesemancases*.

2. **WEB** Visit the website of the U.S. Court of Appeals for the Tenth Circuit, at *www.ck10.uscourts.gov*.
3. **WEB** Visit the website of the Federal Trade Commission (FTC), at *www.ftc.gov*. What are the goals of the FTC?
4. **WEB** Go to *www.donotcall.gov*. How easy is it to place your telephone number on the national do-not-call registry?
5. **WEB** Use *www.google.com* to find an article that discusses telemarketing fraud. Read it.

INTERNET AND TECHNOLOGY
Commercial Speech: Junk Faxes

The use of fax machines has made the conduct of business and individuals' transactions more efficient. However, faxes have also spurned a growth industry that sends unsolicited advertising "junk faxes" to fax machines all over the country. The recipients of junk faxes complained to the government that these faxes tied up their fax machines and cost them money to receive and process. In order to regulate this practice, Congress enacted a provision in the **Telephone Consumer Protection Act of 1991** (TCPA) that outlaws junk faxes.[12]

Fax.com. Inc., which provides promotional services to clients, continued to transmit unsolicited advertisements to fax machines of potential customers after the TCPA was enacted. In response to numerous consumer complaints, the U.S. government sued Fax.com for violating the TCPA. Fax.com argued in defense that the TCPA's regulation of unsolicited faxes violated its free speech rights under the First Amendment to the U.S. Constitution. The U.S. government argued that junk faxes were commercial speech that it could regulate in this manner. The U.S. District Court held that the TCPA violated Fax.com's free speech rights and dismissed the government's lawsuit. The U.S. government appealed.

The Court of Appeals held that unsolicited advertising faxes—junk faxes—constituted commercial speech. The court cited legislative history of the passage of the TCPA as well as evidence from the District

Court which proved that unsolicited junk faxes caused recipients of these faxes substantial costs and time loss. The Court of Appeals held that the federal government's enactment of the TCPA, which prohibits junk faxes, was a constitutional "time, place, and manner" regulation of commercial speech and did not violate Fax.com's free speech rights. The court stated, "There is a substantial governmental interest in protecting the public from the cost shifting and interference caused by unwanted fax advertisements." The Court of Appeals held that the TCPA's prohibition against unsolicited advertising faxes was a lawful constitutional regulation of commercial speech. *Fax.com, Inc. v. United States of America*, 323 F.3d 649, **Web** 2003 U.S. App. Lexis 5469 (United States Court of Appeals for the Eighth Circuit, 2003)

Law & Ethics Questions

1. **ETHICS** Was Fax.com making profits from its endeavors? Did it shift costs to the recipients of its junk faxes?
2. **ETHICS** Did Fax.com act ethically in sending unsolicited junk faxes to unsuspecting parties?

Web Exercise

1. **WEB** Use *www.google.com* to find an article that discusses the Telephone Consumer Protection Act of 1991 (TCPA). Read it.

Unprotected Speech

The Supreme Court has held that the following types of speech are **unprotected speech**; they are not protected by the First Amendment and may be totally forbidden by the government:

> The Constitution of the United States is not a mere lawyers' document: It is a vehicle of life, and its spirit is always the spirit of the age.
>
> Woodrow Wilson
> *Constitutional Government in the United States 69 (1927)*

1. Dangerous speech (including such things as yelling "fire" in a crowded theater when there is no fire)
2. Fighting words that are likely to provoke a hostile or violent response from an average person[13]
3. Speech that incites the violent or revolutionary overthrow of the government (However, the mere abstract teaching of the morality and consequences of such action is protected.)[14]
4. Defamatory language[15]
5. Child pornography[16]
6. Obscene speech[17]

The definition of **obscene speech** is quite subjective. One Supreme Court justice stated, "I know it when I see it."[18] In ***Miller v. California***, the Supreme Court determined that speech is obscene when:

1. The average person, applying contemporary community standards, would find that the work, taken as a whole, appeals to the prurient interest.
2. The work depicts or describes, in a patently offensive way, sexual conduct specifically defined by the applicable state law.
3. The work, taken as a whole, lacks serious literary, artistic, political, or scientific value.[19]

States are free to define what constitutes obscene speech. Movie theaters, magazine publishers, and so on are often subject to challenges that the materials they display or sell are obscene and therefore not protected by the First Amendment.

INTERNET AND TECHNOLOGY
Broad Free Speech Rights Granted in Cyberspace

❝ *As the most participatory form of mass speech yet developed, the internet deserves the highest protection from government intrusion.* **❞**

—Justice Stevens

Once or twice a century, a new medium comes along that presents new problems for applying freedom of speech rights. The most recent problem was the Internet. In 1996, Congress enacted the **Computer Decency Act**, which made it a felony to knowingly make "indecent" or "patently offensive" materials available on computer systems, including the Internet, to persons under 18 years of age. Immediately, more than 50 cyberspace providers and users filed a lawsuit, challenging the act as a violation of their free speech rights granted under the First Amendment to the Constitution. The U.S. District Court agreed with the plaintiffs and declared the act an unconstitutional violation of the Freedom of Speech Clause.

On appeal, the U.S. Supreme Court agreed and held that the act was an unconstitutional violation of free speech rights. The Supreme Court concluded that the Internet allows an individual to reach an audience of millions at almost no cost, setting it apart from TV, radio, and print media, which are prohibitively expensive to use. The Court stated, "As the most participatory form of mass speech yet developed, the internet deserves the highest protection from government intrusion." The Court declared emphatically that the Internet must be given the highest possible level of First Amendment free speech protection.

Proponents of the act argued that it was necessary to protect children from indecent materials. The Supreme Court reasoned that limiting the content on the Internet to what is suitable for a child would result in unconstitutionally limiting adult speech. The Court noted that children are far less likely to trip over indecent material on the Internet than on TV or radio because the information must be actively sought out on the Internet. The Court noted that less obtrusive means for protecting children are available, such as requiring parents to regulate their children's access to materials on the Internet and placing filtering and blocking software on computers to control what their children see on the Internet. It still remains a crime under existing laws to transmit *obscene* materials over the Internet. *Reno v. American Civil Liberties Union*, 521 U.S. 844, 117 S.Ct. 2329, 138 L.Ed.2d 874, **Web** 1997 U.S. Lexis 4037 (Supreme Court of the United States)

Web Exercises

1. **WEB** For the complete opinion of this case, go to *www.prenhall.com/cheesemancases*.
2. **WEB** Visit the website of the American Civil Liberties Union (ACLU), at *www.aclu.org*. What is one of the issues that the ACLU has taken a position on?

Freedom of Religion

The U.S. Constitution requires federal, state, and local governments to be neutral toward religion. The First Amendment contains two separate **freedom of religion** clauses: the *Establishment Clause* and the *Free Exercise Clause*. These two clauses are discussed in the following paragraphs.

Establishment Clause

The **Establishment Clause** prohibits the government from either establishing a state religion or promoting one religion over another. Thus, it guarantees that there will be no state-sponsored religion. The Supreme Court used this clause as its reason for ruling that an Alabama statute that authorized a one-minute period of silence in school for "meditation or voluntary prayer" was invalid.[20] The Court held that the statute endorsed religion.

In the following two cases, the U.S. Supreme Court had to decide whether the Establishment Clause had been violated.

C A S E **2.9**

Establishment Clause

U.S. SUPREME COURT

McCreary County, Kentucky v. American Civil Liberties Union of Kentucky

545 U.S. 844, 125 S.Ct. 2722, 162 L.Ed.2d 729,
Web 2005 U.S. Lexis 5211 (2005)
Supreme Court of the United States

❝*The touchstone for our analysis is the principle that the First Amendment mandates governmental neutrality between religion and religion, and between religion and nonreligion. Government action must have a secular purpose, . . .*❞

—Justice Souter

Facts

McCreary County and Pulaski County (the Counties), Kentucky, placed in their courthouses large, gold-framed copies of the Ten Commandments. In both courthouses, the Ten Commandments were prominently displayed so that visitors could see them. The Ten Commandments hung alone, not with other paintings and such. The American Civil Liberties Union of Kentucky (ACLU) sued the Counties in U.S. District Court, alleging that the placement of the Ten Commandments in the courthouses violated the Establishment Clause of the U.S. Constitution.

The U.S. District Court granted a preliminary injunction ordering the removal of the Ten Commandments from both courthouses. The Counties added copies of the Magna Carta, the Declaration of Independence, the Bill of Rights, and other nonreligious items to the display of the Ten Commandments. The U.S. District Court reissued the injunction against this display, and the U.S. Court of Appeals affirmed. The Counties appealed to the U.S. Supreme Court.

Issue

Does the display of the Ten Commandments in the Counties' courthouses violate the Establishment Clause?

Language of the U.S. Supreme Court

The touchstone for our analysis is the principle that the First Amendment mandates governmental neutrality between religion and religion, and between religion and nonreligion. Government action must have a secular purpose, and after a host of cases it is fair to add that although a legislature's stated reasons will generally get deference, the secular purpose required has to be genuine, not a sham, and not merely secondary to a religious objective. But it is nonetheless the duty of the courts to distinguish a sham secular purpose from a sincere one.

Hence, we look to the record of evidence showing the progression leading up to the third display of the Commandments.

The first one in the sequence set out a text of the Commandments as distinct from any traditionally symbolic representation and not part of an arguably secular display. This is not to deny that the Commandments have had influence on civil or secular law; a major text of a majority religion is bound to be felt. The point is simply that the original text viewed in its entirety is an unmistakably religious statement dealing with religious obligations and with morality subject to religious sanction. When the government initiates an effort to place this statement alone in public view, a religious object is unmistakable.

In this second display, unlike the first, the Commandments were not hung in isolation, merely leaving the Counties' purpose to emerge from the pervasively religious text of the Commandments themselves. The display's unstinting focus was on religious passages, showing that the Counties were posting the Commandments precisely because of their sectarian content. That demonstration of the government's objective was enhanced by serial religious references and the accompanying resolution's claim about the embodiment of ethics in Christ. Together, the display and resolution presented an indisputable, and undisputed, showing of an impermissible purpose.

After the Counties changed lawyers, they mounted a third display, without a new resolution or repeal of the old one. The result was the "Foundations of American Law and Government" exhibit, which placed the Commandments in the company of other documents the Counties thought especially significant in the historical foundation of American government. These new statements of purpose were presented only as a litigating position. No reasonable observer could swallow the claim that the Counties had cast off the objective so unmistakable in the earlier displays.

Decision

The U.S. Supreme Court held that the Counties' display of the Ten Commandments violated the Establishment Clause.

Law & Ethics Questions

1. What does the Establishment Clause provide? Explain.
2. What is the difference between religious and secular purposes? Explain.
3. **ETHICS** Do you think that the Counties acted ethically in changing their display of the Ten Commandments? What was the purpose of adding documents such as the Declaration of Independence to the display?
4. **ETHICS** Is it ethical for the U.S. Supreme Court to strike down the display of the Ten Commandments in the Kentucky courthouses when the U.S. Supreme Court has displays of the Ten Commandments in the U.S. Supreme Court building in Washington, DC?

Web Exercises

1. **WEB** For the complete opinion of this case, go to *www.prenhall.com/cheesemancases*.
2. **WEB** Visit the website of the U.S. Supreme Court, at *www.supremecourtus.gov* and try to find documents that relate to this case.
3. **WEB** Visit the website of the American Civil Liberties Union of Kentucky, at *www.aclu-ky.org*. Find a case that the ACLU of Kentucky is currently involved in.
4. **WEB** Use *www.google.com* to find a photo of the Ten Commandment displays in either the McCreary County courthouse or the Pulaski County courthouse.

C A S E **2.10**

Establishment Clause

U.S. SUPREME COURT

Van Orden v. Perry, Governor of Texas

545 U.S. 677, 125 S.Ct. 2854, 162 L.Ed.2d 607,
Web 2005 U.S. Lexis 5215 (2005)
Supreme Court of the United States

> ❝*Such acknowledgments of the role played by the Ten Commandments in our Nation's heritage are common throughout America. We need only look within our own Courtroom.*❞
>
> —Justice Rehnquist

Facts

The 22 acres surrounding the Texas State capital contain 17 monuments and 21 historical markers commemorating the people, ideals, and events that compose Texas identity. The monuments include the Heroes of the Alamo, Confederate Soldiers, Texas Cowboys, the Spanish-American War, Texas Pioneer Women, Pearl Harbor Veterans, Soldiers of World War II, and the monolith challenged in this case, a 6-foot-high and 3½-foot-wide monument containing an eagle grasping the American flag, the eye inside a pyramid, two Stars of David, the two Greek letters chi and rho, which represent Christ, and the Ten Commandments. The monument was erected in 1961, and its construction and erection were paid for by the Eagles fraternal organization.

The plaintiff, Thomas Van Orden, is a native Texan and former lawyer who uses the law library in the Texas Supreme Court building, which is just to the northwest of the Capitol building. After six years of walking by the monument containing the Ten Commandments, Van Orden sued the state of Texas, alleging that the monument violated the Establishment Clause of the U.S. Constitution. The U.S. District Court held that the monument did not violate the Establishment Clause, and the U.S. Court of Appeals agreed. Van Orden appealed to the U.S. Supreme Court.

Issue

Does the monument on the grounds of the Texas Capitol building that contains the Ten Commandments violate the Establishment Clause?

Language of the U.S. Supreme Court

In this case we are faced with a display of the Ten Commandments on government property outside the Texas State Capitol. Such acknowledgments of the role played by the Ten Commandments in our Nation's heritage are common throughout America. We need only look within our own Courtroom. Since 1935, Moses has stood, holding two tablets that reveal portions of the Ten Commandments written in Hebrew, among other lawgivers in the south frieze. Representations of the Ten Commandments adorn the metal gates lining the north and south sides of the Courtroom as well as the doors leading into the Courtroom. Moses also sits on the exterior east facade of the building holding the Ten Commandments tablets.

Similar acknowledgments can be seen throughout a visitor's tour of our Nation's Capital. For example, a large statue of Moses holding the Ten Commandments, alongside a statue of the Apostle Paul, has overlooked the rotunda of the Library of Congress' Jefferson Building since 1897. And the Jefferson Building's Great Reading Room contains a sculpture of a woman beside the Ten Commandments with a quote above her from the Old Testament (Micah 6:8). A medallion with two tablets depicting the Ten Commandments decorates the floor of the National Archives. Inside the Department of Justice, a statue entitled "The Spirit of Law" has two tablets representing the Ten Commandments lying at its feet. So too a 24-foot-tall sculpture, depicting, among other things, the Ten Commandments and a cross, stands outside the federal courthouse that houses both the Court of Appeals and the District Court for the District of Columbia. Moses is also prominently featured in the Chamber of the United States House of Representatives.

Of course, the Ten Commandments are religious—they were so viewed at their inception and so remain. The monument, therefore, has religious significance. According to Judeo-Christian belief, the Ten Commandments were given to Moses by God on Mt. Sinai. But Moses was a lawgiver as well as a religious leader. And the Ten Commandments have an undeniable historical meaning, as the foregoing examples demonstrate. Simply having religious content or promoting a message consistent with a religious doctrine does not run afoul of the Establishment Clause. Texas has treated its Capitol grounds monuments as representing the several strands in the State's political and legal history. The inclusion of the Ten Commandments monument in this group has a dual significance, partaking of both religion and government. We cannot say that Texas' display of this monument violates the Establishment Clause of the First Amendment.

Decision

The U.S. Supreme Court held that the monument on the grounds of the Texas Capitol building served a secular purpose and therefore did not violate the Establishment Clause.

Law & Ethics Questions

1. Define the difference between *religious* and *secular* purpose. Is this an easy differentiation to make?
2. How did the U.S. Supreme Court distinguish this case from the case *McCreary County, Kentucky v. American Civil Liberties Union of Kentucky*?
3. **ETHICS** Did the U.S. Supreme Court act unethically by allowing the Ten Commandments in its own building? Explain.

Web Exercises

1. **WEB** For the complete opinion of this case, go to *www.prenhall.com/cheesemancases*.
2. **WEB** Visit the website of the U.S. Supreme Court, at *www.supremecourtus.gov* and try to find documents that relate to this case.
3. **WEB** Use *www.google.com* to find a photo of the Ten Commandments displayed on the grounds of the Texas Capitol building.

Free Exercise Clause

The **Free Exercise Clause** prohibits the government from interfering with the free exercise of religion in the United States. Generally, this clause prevents the government from enacting laws that either prohibit or inhibit individuals from participating in or practicing their chosen religions. For example, in *Church of Lukumi Babalu Aye, Inc. v. City of Hialeah, Florida*,[21] the U.S. Supreme Court held that a city ordinance that prohibited ritual sacrifices of animals (chickens) during church services violated the Free Exercise Clause and that such sacrifices should be allowed. Of course, this right to be free from government intervention in the practice of religion is not absolute. For example, human sacrifices are unlawful and are not protected by the First Amendment.

CONCEPT SUMMARY

Freedom of Religion

CLAUSE	DESCRIPTION
Establishment Clause	Prohibits the government from establishing a government-sponsored religion and from promoting one religion over other religions.
Free Exercise Clause	Prohibits the government from enacting laws that either prohibit or inhibit individuals from participating in or practicing their chosen religions.

Equal Protection Clause

The Fourteenth Amendment was added to the U.S. Constitution in 1868. Its original purpose was to guarantee equal rights to all persons after the Civil War. The provisions of the Fourteenth Amendment prohibit discriminatory and unfair action by the government. Several of these provisions—namely, the *Equal Protection Clause*, the *Due Process Clause*, and the *Privileges and Immunities Clause*—have important implications for business. The Equal Protection Clause is discussed in this section. The Due Process Clause and the Privileges and Immunities Clause are discussed in following sections.

Federal, State, and Local Government Action

The **Equal Protection Clause** provides that a state cannot "deny to any person within its jurisdiction the equal protection of the laws." Although this clause expressly applies to state and local government action, the Supreme Court has held that it also applies to federal government action.

This clause prohibits state, local, and federal governments from enacting laws that classify and treat "similarly situated" persons differently. It also protects artificial persons, such as corporations. Note that this clause is designed to prohibit invidious discrimination: It does not make the classification of individuals unlawful per se.

Standards of Review

The Supreme Court has adopted three different standards for reviewing equal protection cases:

1. *Strict scrutiny test.* Any government activity or regulation that classifies persons based on a *suspect class* (i.e., race) is reviewed for lawfulness using a **strict scrutiny test**. Under this standard, most government classifications of persons based on race are found to be unconstitutional.

   Example A government rule that permitted persons of one race but not of another race to receive government benefits such as Medicaid, would violate this test. However, affirmative action programs that give racial minorities a "plus factor" when considered for public university admission is lawful, as long as it does not constitute a quota system.

2. *Intermediate scrutiny test.* The lawfulness of government classifications based on *protected classes* other than race (e.g., sex, age) is examined using an **intermediate scrutiny test**. Under this standard, the courts determine whether the government classification is "reasonably related" to a legitimate government purpose.

   Example A rule prohibiting persons over a certain age from military combat would be lawful, but a rule prohibiting persons over a certain age from acting as government engineers would not be. With regard to a person's sex, the U.S. Supreme Court has held that the federal government can require males, but not females, to register with the military for a possible draft.

3. *Rational basis test.* The lawfulness of all government classifications that do not involve suspect or protected classes is examined using a **rational basis test**. Under this test, the courts will uphold government regulation as long as there is a justifiable reason for the law. This standard permits much of the government regulation of business.

   Example Providing government subsidies to farmers but not to those in other occupations is permissible.

Due Process Clause

The Fifth and Fourteenth Amendments to the U.S. Constitution both contain **Due Process Clauses**. These clauses provide that no person shall be deprived of "life, liberty, or property" without due process of the law. The Due Process Clause of the Fifth Amendment applies to federal government action; that of the Fourteenth Amendment applies to state and local government action. It is important to understand that the government is not prohibited from taking a person's life, liberty, or property. However, the government must follow due process to do so. There are two categories of due process: *substantive* and *procedural*.

Substantive Due Process

The **substantive due process** category of due process requires that government statutes, ordinances, regulations, or other laws be clear on their face and not overly broad in scope.

The test of whether substantive due process is met is whether a "reasonable person" could understand the law to be able to comply with it. Laws that do not meet this test are declared *void for vagueness*.

Example   A city ordinance that made it illegal for persons to wear "clothes of the opposite sex" would be held unconstitutional as void for vagueness because a reasonable person could not clearly determine whether his or her conduct violated the law.

Procedural Due Process

The **procedural due process** form of due process requires that the government give a person proper *notice* and *hearing* of legal action before that person is deprived of his or her life, liberty, or property.

Example   If the federal government or a state government brings a criminal lawsuit against a defendant, the government must notify the person of its intent (by charging the defendant with a crime) and provide the defendant with a proper hearing (a trial).

Example   If the government wants to take a person's home by eminent domain to build a highway, the government must (1) give the homeowner sufficient notice of its intention and (2) provide a hearing. Under the Just Compensation Clause of the Fifth Amendment, the government must pay the owner just compensation for taking the property. Oftentimes, a lawsuit is brought for a court to determine just compensation.

Privileges and Immunities Clause

The purpose of the U.S. Constitution is to promote nationalism. If the states were permitted to enact laws that favored their residents over out-of-state residents, the concept of nationalism would be defeated. Both Article IV of the Constitution and the Fourteenth Amendment contain **Privileges and Immunities Clauses** that prohibit states from enacting laws that unduly discriminate in favor of their residents.

Example   A state cannot enact a law that prevents residents of other states from owning property or businesses in that state. Only invidious discrimination is prohibited. Thus, state universities are permitted to charge out-of-state residents higher tuition than in-state residents. Note that this clause applies only to citizens; it does not protect corporations.

United States Post Office, Alhambra, California

The United States is the world's leading democracy. The country, however, has had many blemishes on its citizens' constitutional rights. For example, during World War II, Japanese Americans were involuntarily placed in camps. During the McCarthy hearings of the 1950s, citizens who were communists or associated with communists were "blackballed" from their occupations, most notably in the film industry. It was not until the mid-1960s that equal opportunity laws outlawed discrimination in the workplace based on race and sex.

Chapter Summary

Constitution of the United States of America, p. 31

The U.S. Constitution

The Constitution consists of 7 articles and 26 amendments. It establishes the three branches of the federal government, enumerates their powers, and provides important guarantees of individual freedom. The Constitution was ratified by the states in 1788.

Federalism

The Constitution created the federal government. The federal government and the 50 state governments and Washington, DC, share powers in this country.

Delegated Powers

When the states ratified the Constitution, they delegated certain powers to the federal government. These are called enumerated powers.

Reserved Powers

Those powers not granted to the federal government by the Constitution are reserved to the states.

Separation of Powers

Each branch of the federal government has separate powers:
1. **Legislative branch.** Power to make the law.
2. **Executive branch.** Power to enforce the law.
3. **Judicial branch.** Power to interpret the law.

Checks and Balances

Certain checks and balances are built into the Constitution to ensure that no one branch of the federal government becomes too powerful.

Supremacy Clause, p. 32

The Supremacy Clause stipulates that the U.S. Constitution, treaties, and federal law (statutes and regulations) are the *supreme law of the land*. State or local laws that conflict with valid federal law are unconstitutional. This is called the *preemption doctrine*.

Commerce Clause, p. 33

The Commerce Clause authorizes the federal government to regulate commerce with foreign nations, among the states, and with Native American tribes.

Native Americans

The Commerce Clause along with various treaties regulates commerce on Native American lands. Generally, Native American tribes are self-governing and considered "domestic dependants" of the Federal Government.

Foreign Commerce Clause

The Commerce Clause gives the federal government the exclusive power to regulate commerce with foreign nations.

Interstate Commerce

Under the broad effects test, the federal government may regulate any activity (even intrastate commerce) that affects interstate commerce.

No Undue Burden on Intrastate Commerce

Any state or local law that causes an undue burden on intrastate commerce is unconstitutional as a violation of the Commerce Clause.

Bill of Rights, p. 42

The Bill of Rights consists of the first 10 amendments to the Constitution, which establish basic individual rights. The Bill of Rights was ratified in 1791.

Freedom of Speech, p. 43

The *Freedom of Speech Clause* is a clause of the First Amendment which guarantees that the government shall not infringe on a person's right to speak. It protects oral, written, and symbolic speech. This right is not absolute—that is, some speech is not protected, and some speech is granted only limited protection.

Fully Protected Speech

Fully protected speech is speech that cannot be prohibited or regulated by the government.

Limited Protected Speech

Some types of speech are granted only limited protection under the Freedom of Speech Clause—that is, they are subject to governmental *time, place,* and *manner restrictions*:
1. Offensive speech
2. Commercial speech

Unprotected Speech

Some speech is not protected by the Freedom of Speech Clause:
1. Dangerous speech
2. Fighting words
3. Speech that advocates the violent overthrow of the government
4. Defamatory language
5. Child pornography
6. Obscene speech

Freedom of Religion, p. 47

There are two religion clauses in the First Amendment: the Establishment Clause and the Free Exercise Clause.

Establishment Clause

The Establishment Clause prohibits the government from establishing a state religion or promoting religion.

Free Exercise Clause

The Free Exercise Clause prohibits the government from interfering with the free exercise of religion. This right is not absolute; for example, human sacrifices are forbidden.

Equal Protection Clause, p. 50
Federal, State, and Local Government Action

The Equal Protection Clause prohibits the government from enacting laws that classify and treat "similarly situated" persons differently. This standard is not absolute, and the government can treat persons differently in certain situations.

Standards of Review

The U.S. Supreme Court has applied the following tests to determine whether the Equal Protection Clause has been violated:
1. **Strict scrutiny test.** Applies to suspect classes (e.g., race, national origin).
2. **Intermediate scrutiny test.** Applies to protected classes other than race (e.g., sex, age).
3. **Rational basis test.** Applies to government classifications that do not involve a suspect or protected class.

Due Process Clause, p. 51

The Due Process Clause provides that no person shall be deprived of "life, liberty, or property" without due process. There are two categories of due process: substantive and procedural.

Substantive Due Process

Substantive due process requires that laws be clear on their face and not overly broad in scope. Laws that do not meet this test are *void for vagueness*.

Procedural Due Process

Procedural due process requires that the government give a person proper *notice* and *hearing* before that person is deprived of his or her life, liberty, or property. An owner must be paid *just compensation* if the government takes his or her property.

Privileges and Immunities Clause, p. 52

The Privileges and Immunities Clause prohibits states from enacting laws that unduly discriminate in favor of their residents over residents of other states.

Test Review Terms and Concepts

amendments   42
Articles of Confederation   29
Bill of Rights   42
Bureau of Indian Affairs (BIA)   35
Checks and balances   32
Church of Lukumi Babalu Aye, Inc.
   v. City of Hialeah, Florida   50
Civil Rights Act of 1964   38
Commerce Clause   33
Commercial speech   44
Computer Decency Act   47
Constitutional Convention   30
Constitution of the United States
   of America   30
Due Process Clause   42
Effects on interstate commerce
   test   38
Enumerated powers   30
Equal Protection Clause   51

Establishment clause   48
Executive branch   30
Federalism   30
Free Exercise Clause   50
Freedom of religion   47
Freedom of speech   43
Fully protected speech   43
Heart of Atlanta Motel v.
   United States   38
incorporation doctrine   43
Indian Gaming Regulatory Act   35
Indian Health Service (IHS)   35
Intermediate scrutiny test   51
Interstate commerce   38
Judicial branch   30
Legislative branch   30
Limited protected speech   44
Miller v. California   47
Obscene speech   47

Offensive speech   44
Police power   41
Preemption doctrine   32
Privileges and Immunities
   Clause   52
Procedural due process   52
Rational basis test   51
Strict scrutiny test   51
Substantive due process   51
Supremacy clause   32
Telephone Consumer Protection
   Act of 1991   46
Tribal councils   35
unduly burden interstate
   commerce   41
Unprotected speech   46
Wickard, Secretary of Agriculture
   v. Filburn   38

Case Problems

2.1. Separation of Powers: In 1951, a dispute arose between steel companies and their employees about the terms and conditions that should be included in a new labor contract. At the time, the United States was engaged in a military conflict in Korea that required substantial steel resources from which to make weapons and other military goods. On April 4, 1952, the steelworkers' union gave notice of a nationwide strike called to begin at 12:01 A.M. on April 9. The indispensability of steel as a component in weapons and other war materials led President Dwight D. Eisenhower to believe that the proposed strike would jeopardize the national defense and that governmental seizure of the steel mills was necessary in order to ensure the continued availability of steel. Therefore, a few hours before the strike was to begin, the president issued Executive Order 10340, which directed the secretary of commerce to take possession of most of the steel mills and keep them running. The steel companies obeyed the order under protest and brought proceedings against the president. Was the seizure of the steel mills constitutional? *Youngstown Co. v. Sawyer, Secretary of Commerce*, 343 U.S. 579, 72 S.Ct. 863, 96 L.Ed.2d 1153, **Web** 1952 U.S. Lexis 2625 (Supreme Court of the United States)

2.2. Commerce and Supremacy Clauses: Congress enacted a federal statute called the Ports and Waterways Safety Act that established uniform standards for the operation of boats on inland waterways in the United States. The act coordinated its provisions with those of foreign countries so that there was a uniform body of international rules that applied to vessels that traveled between countries. Pursuant to the act, a federal rule was adopted that regulated the design, length, and size of oil tankers, some of which traveled the waters of the Puget Sound area in the state of Washington. Oil tankers from various places entered Puget Sound to bring crude oil to refineries located in Washington. The state of Washington enacted a statute that established different designs, smaller lengths, and smaller sizes for oil tankers serving Puget Sound than allowed by the federal law. Oil tankers used by the Atlantic Richfield Company (ARCO) to bring oil into Puget Sound met the federal standards but not the state standards. ARCO sued to have the state statute declared unconstitutional. Who wins? *Ray, Governor of Washington v. Atlantic Richfield Co.*, 435 U.S. 151, 98 S.Ct. 988, 55 L.Ed.2d 179, **Web** 1978 U.S. Lexis 18 (Supreme Court of the United States)

2.3. Undue Burden on Interstate Commerce: Most trucking firms, including Consolidated Freightways Corporation, use 65-foot-long "double" trailer trucks to ship commodities on the highway system across the United States. Almost all states permit these vehicles on their highways. The federal government does not regulate the length of trucks that can use the nation's highways. The state of Iowa enacted a statute that restricted the length of trucks that could use highways in the state to 55 feet. This meant that if Consolidated wanted to move goods through Iowa, it needed to either use smaller trucks or detach the double trailers and shuttle them through the state separately. Its only other alternative was to divert its 65-foot doubles around Iowa. Consolidated filed suit against Iowa, alleging that the state statute was unconstitutional. Is it? *Kassel v. Consolidated Freightways Corporation*, 450 U.S. 662, 101 S.Ct. 1309, 67 L.Ed.2d 580, **Web** 1981 U.S. Lexis 17 (Supreme Court of the United States)

2.4. Privileges and Immunities Clause: During a period of a booming economy in Alaska, many residents of other states moved there in search of work. Construction work on the Trans-Alaska Pipeline was a major source of employment. The Alaska legislature enacted an act titled the Local Hire Statute. This act required employers to hire Alaska residents in preference to nonresidents. Is this statute constitutional? *Hicklin v. Orbeck, Commissioner of the Department of Labor of Alaska*, 437 U.S. 518, 98 S.Ct. 2482, 57 L.Ed.2d 397, **Web** 1978 U.S. Lexis 36 (Supreme Court of the United States)

2.5. Commercial Speech: The city of San Diego, California, enacted a city zoning ordinance that prohibited outdoor advertising display signs—including billboards. On-site signs at a business location were exempted from this rule. The city based the restriction on traffic safety and aesthetics. Metromedia, Inc., a company in the business of leasing commercial billboards to advertisers, sued the city of San Diego, alleging that the zoning ordinance was unconstitutional. Is it? *Metromedia, Inc. v. City of San Diego*, 453 U.S. 490, 101 S.Ct. 2882, 69 L.Ed.2d 800, **Web** 1981 U.S. Lexis 50 (Supreme Court of the United States)

2.6. Substantive Due Process: The village of Hoffman Estates, Illinois, enacted an ordinance regulating drug paraphernalia. The ordinance made it unlawful for any person "to sell any items, effect, paraphernalia, accessory or thing which is designed or marketed for use with illegal cannabis or drugs as defined by Illinois Revised Statutes, without obtaining a license therefore." The license fee was $150. A violation was subject to a fine of not more than $500. The Flipside, a retail store located in the village, sold a variety of merchandise, including smoking accessories, clamps, roach clips, scales, water pipes, vials, cigarette rolling papers, and other items. Instead of applying for a license, Flipside filed a lawsuit against the village, alleging that the ordinance was unconstitutional as a violation of substantive due process because it was overly broad and vague. Who wins? *Village of Hoffman Estates v. Flipside, Hoffman Estates, Inc.*, 455 U.S. 489, 102 S.Ct. 1186, 71 L.Ed.2d 362, **Web** 1982 U.S. Lexis 78 (Supreme Court of the United States)

2.7. Equal Protection Clause: The state of Alabama enacted a statute that imposed a tax on premiums earned by insurance companies. The statute imposed a 1 percent tax on domestic insurance companies (i.e., insurance companies that were incorporated in Alabama and had their principal office in the state). The statute imposed a 4 percent tax on the premiums earned by out-of-state insurance companies that sold insurance in Alabama. Out-of-state insurance companies could reduce the premium tax by 1 percent by investing at least 10 percent of their assets in Alabama. Domestic insurance companies did not have to invest any of their assets in Alabama. Metropolitan Life Insurance Company, an out-of-state insurance company, sued the state of Alabama, alleging that the Alabama statute violated the Equal Protection Clause of the U.S. Constitution. Who wins? *Metropolitan Life Insurance Co. v. Ward, Commissioner of Insurance of Alabama*, 470 U.S. 869, 105 S.Ct. 1676, 84 L.Ed.2d 751, **Web** 1985 U.S. Lexis 80 (Supreme Court of the United States)

Ethics Issues

2.8. Ethics: The Raiders are a professional football team and a National Football League (NFL) franchise. Each NFL franchise is independently owned. Al Davis was an owner and the managing general partner of the Raiders. The NFL establishes schedules, negotiates television contracts, and otherwise promotes NFL football, including conducting the Super Bowl each year. The Raiders play home and away games against other NFL teams.

For years, the Raiders played their home games in Oakland, California. The owners of the Raiders decided to move the team from Oakland to Los Angeles, California, to take advantage of the greater seating capacity of the Los Angeles Coliseum, the larger television market of Los Angeles, and other economic factors. The renamed team was to be known as the Los Angeles Raiders. The city of Oakland brought an eminent domain proceeding in court to acquire the Raiders as a city-owned team. Can the city of Oakland acquire the Raiders through eminent domain? Is it socially responsible for a professional sports team to move to another location? *City of Oakland, California v. Oakland*

Raiders, 174 Cal.App.3d 414, 220 Cal.Rptr. 153, **Web** 1985 Cal. App. Lexis 2751 (Court of Appeal of California)

2.9. Ethics: Congress enacted the Flag Protection Act, which made it a crime to knowingly mutilate, deface, physically defile, burn, or trample the U.S. flag. The law provided for fines and up to one year in prison upon conviction [18 U.S.C. Section 700]. Certain individuals set fire to several U.S. flags on the steps of the U.S. Capitol in Washington, DC, to protest various aspects of the federal government's foreign and domestic policy. In a separate incident, other individuals set fire to a U.S. flag to protest the act's passage. All these individuals were prosecuted for violating the act. The District Courts held that the Flag Protection Act was unconstitutional, in violation of the defendants' First Amendment free speech rights, and dismissed the charges. The government appealed to the U.S. Supreme Court, which consolidated the two cases. Who wins? Does a flag burner exhibit any morals? *United States v. Eichman*, 496 U.S. 310, 110 S.Ct. 2404, 110 L.Ed.2d 287, **Web** 1990 U.S. Lexis 3087 (Supreme Court of the United States)

IRAC Writing Assignment

Read Case A-2 in Appendix A [*Lee v. Weisman*]. Read the case and use the IRAC method to prepare a written analysis of the case.

Endnotes

1. To be elected to Congress, an individual must be a U.S. citizen, either naturally born or granted citizenship. To serve in the Senate, a person must be 30 years of age or older. To serve in the House of Representatives, a person must be 25 years of age or older.
2. To be president, a person must be 35 years of age or older and a natural citizen of the United States. By amendment to the Constitution (Amendment XXII), a person can serve only two full terms as president.
3. Federal court judges and justices are appointed by the president with the consent of the Senate.
4. The principle that the U.S. Supreme Court is the final arbiter of the U.S. Constitution evolved from *Marbury v. Madison*, 1 Cranch 137, 5 U.S. 137, 2 L.Ed. 60, **Web** 1803 U.S. Lexis 352 (Supreme Court of the United States, 1803). In that case, the Supreme Court held that a judiciary statute enacted by Congress was unconstitutional.
5. Article VI, Section 2.
6. Article I, Section 8, clause 3.
7. 379 U.S. 241, 85 S.Ct. 348, 13 L.Ed.2d 258, **Web** 1964 U.S. Lexis 2187 (Supreme Court of the United States, 1964).
8. 317 U.S. 111, 63 S.Ct. 82, 87 L.Ed. 122, **Web** 1942 U.S. Lexis 1046 (Supreme Court of the United States, 1942).
9. 18 U.S.C. Sections 2721–2775.
10. 21 U.S.C.S. Section 801.
11. 425 U.S. 748, 96 S.Ct. 1817, 48 L.Ed.2d 346, **Web** 1976 U.S. Lexis 55 (Supreme Court of the United States, 1976).
12. 47 U.S.C. Section 227.
13. *Chaplinsky v. New Hampshire*, 315 U.S. 568, 62 S.Ct. 766, 86 L.Ed. 1031, **Web** 1942 U.S. Lexis 851 (Supreme Court of the United States, 1942).
14. *Brandenburg v. Ohio*, 395 U.S. 444, 89 S.Ct. 1827, 23 L.Ed.2d 430, **Web** 1969 U.S. Lexis 1367 (Supreme Court of the United States, 1969).
15. *Beauharnais v. Illinois*, 343 U.S. 250, 72 S.Ct. 725, 96 L.Ed. 919, **Web** 1952 U.S. Lexis 2799 (Supreme Court of the United States, 1952).
16. *New York v. Ferber*, 458 U.S. 747, 102 S.Ct. 334, 73 L.Ed.2d 1113, **Web** 1982 U.S. Lexis 12 (Supreme Court of the United States, 1982).
17. *Roth v. United States*, 354 U.S. 476, 77 S.Ct. 1304, 1 L.Ed.2d 1498, **Web** 1957 U.S. Lexis 587 (Supreme Court of the United States, 1957).
18. Justice Stewart in *Jacobellis v. Ohio*, 378 U.S. 184, 84 S.Ct. 1676, 12 L.Ed.2d 793, **Web** 1964 U.S. Lexis 822 (Supreme Court of the United States, 1964).
19. 413 U.S. 15, 93 S.Ct. 2607, 37 L.Ed.2d 419, **Web** 1973 U.S. Lexis 149 (Supreme Court of the United States, 1973).
20. *Wallace v. Jaffree*, 472 U.S. 38, 105 S.Ct. 2479, 86 L.Ed.2d 29, **Web** 1985 U.S. Lexis 91 (Supreme Court of the United States, 1985).
21. 508 U.S. 520, 113 S.Ct. 2217, 124 L.Ed.2d 472, **Web** 1993 U.S. Lexis 4022 (Supreme Court of the United States, 1993).

CHAPTER **3**

Court Systems and Jurisdiction

> **❝***I was never ruined but twice; once when I lost a lawsuit, and once when I won one.* **❞**
>
> —VOLTAIRE

CHAPTER OBJECTIVES

After studying this chapter, you should be able to:

1. Describe state court systems.
2. Describe the federal court system.
3. Compare the jurisdiction of state courts with that of federal courts.
4. List and describe the types of decisions that are issued by the U.S. Supreme Court.
5. Define *standing to sue* and *venue*.

CHAPTER CONTENTS

- Introduction to Court Systems and Jurisdiction
- State Court Systems
- Federal Court System
- United States Supreme Court
- Personal Jurisdiction of Courts
- Jurisdiction of Federal and State Courts
- Chapter Summary
- Test Review Terms and Concepts
- Case Problems
- Ethics Issues
- IRAC Writing Assignment

    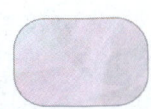

Introduction to Court Systems and Jurisdiction

There are two major court systems in the United States: (1) the federal court system and (2) the court systems of the 50 states and the District of Columbia. Each of these systems has jurisdiction to hear different types of lawsuits.

This chapter discusses the various court systems and the jurisdiction of courts to hear and decide cases.

Supreme Court of the United States, Washington, DC

The highest court in the land is the Supreme Court of the United States, located in Washington, DC. The Supreme Court's unanimous and majority decisions are precedent for all the other courts in the country.

State Court Systems

Each state and the District of Columbia has a separate court system. Most state court systems include the following: *limited-jurisdiction trial courts, general-jurisdiction trial courts, intermediate appellate courts,* and a *supreme court.*

Limited-Jurisdiction Trial Courts

State **limited-jurisdiction trial courts**, which are sometimes referred to as **inferior trial courts**, hear matters of a specialized or limited nature. In many states, traffic courts, juvenile courts, justice-of-the-peace courts, probate courts, family law courts, and courts that hear misdemeanor criminal law cases and civil cases involving lawsuits under a certain dollar amount are examples of such courts. Because these courts are trial courts, evidence can be introduced and testimony can be given. Most limited-jurisdiction courts keep records of their proceedings. Their decisions can usually be appealed to a general-jurisdiction court or an appellate court.

Many states have also created **small claims courts** to hear civil cases involving small dollar amounts (e.g., $5,000 or less). Generally, the parties must appear individually and cannot have lawyers represent them. The decisions of small claims courts are often appealable to general-jurisdiction trial courts or appellate courts.

General-Jurisdiction Trial Courts

Every state has a **general-jurisdiction trial court**. These courts are often referred to as **courts of record** because the testimony and evidence at trial are recorded and stored for future reference. These courts hear cases that are not within the jurisdiction of limited-jurisdiction trial courts, such as felonies, civil cases over a certain dollar amount, and so on. Some states divide their general-jurisdiction courts into two divisions, one for criminal cases and another for civil cases. Evidence and testimony are given at general-jurisdiction trial courts. The decisions handed down by these courts are appealable to an intermediate appellate court or the state supreme court, depending on the circumstances.

Intermediate Appellate Courts

In many states, **intermediate appellate courts** (also called *appellate courts* or *courts of appeal*) hear appeals from trial courts. They review the trial court record to determine whether there have been any errors at trial that would require reversal or modification of the trial court's decision. Thus, an appellate court reviews either pertinent parts or the whole trial court record from the lower court. No new evidence or testimony is permitted. The parties usually file legal *briefs* with the appellate court, stating the law and facts that support their positions. Appellate courts usually grant a brief oral hearing to the parties. Appellate court decisions are appealable to the state's highest court. In sparsely populated states that do not have intermediate appellate courts, trial court decisions can be appealed directly to the state's highest court.

Highest State Court

Each state has a highest court in its court system. Most states call this highest court the **state supreme court**. Some states use other names for their highest courts. The function of a state's highest court is to hear appeals from intermediate state courts and certain trial courts. It hears no new evidence or testimony. The parties usually submit pertinent parts of or the entire lower court record for review. The parties also submit legal briefs to the court and are usually granted a brief oral hearing. Decisions of highest state courts are final unless a question of law is involved that is appealable to the U.S. Supreme Court.

Exhibit 3.1 portrays a typical state court system.

EXHIBIT 3.1

Typical State Court System

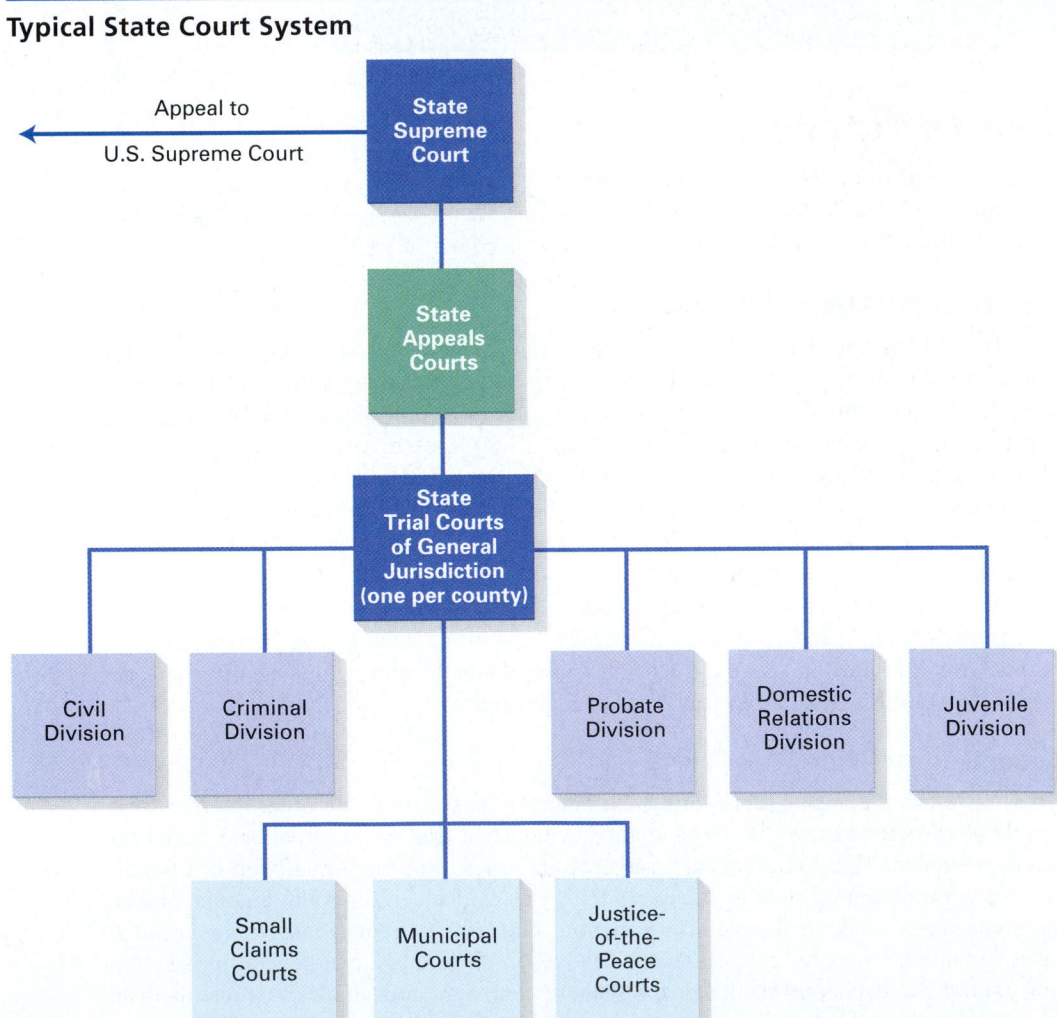

CONTEMPORARY ENVIRONMENT
Specialized Courts Hear Commercial Disputes

In most states, business and commercial disputes are heard by the same courts that hear and decide criminal, landlord–tenant, matrimonial, medical malpractice, and other non-business-related cases. The one major exception to this standard has been the state of Delaware, where a special Chancery Court hears and decides business litigation. The court, which deals mainly with cases involving corporate government disputes, has earned a reputation for its expertise in handling and deciding corporate matters. Perhaps the existence of this special court and a corporation code that tends to favor corporate management are the primary reasons that more than 60 percent of the corporations listed on the New York Stock Exchange are incorporated in Delaware.

Businesses tend to favor special commercial courts because the judges presiding over them are expected to have the expertise to handle complex commercial lawsuits. The courts are also expected to be more efficient in deciding business-related cases, thus saving time and money for the parties. Other states are also establishing courts that specialize in commercial matters.

Web Exercises

1. **WEB:** Visit the website of the Delaware court system, at *www.courts.state.de.us.*
2. **WEB:** Use *www.google.com* to find an article on why the state of Delaware is considered "business friendly." Read it.

Courthouse, St. Louis, Missouri

State courts hear and decide the majority of cases in the United States.

Exhibit 3.2 lists the websites for the court systems of the 50 states and jurisdictions associated with the United States.

EXHIBIT 3.2

State Court Systems

State	Website
Alabama	www.judicial.state.al.us
Alaska	www.state.ak.us/courts
Arizona	www.supreme.state.az.us
Arkansas	www.courts.state.ar.us
California	www.courtinfo.ca.gov/courts
Colorado	www.courts.state.co.us
Connecticut	www.jud.state.ct.us
Delaware	www.courts.state.de.us
District of Columbia	www.dccourts.gov
Florida	www.flcourts.org
Georgia	georgiacourts.org
Guam	www.guamsupremecourt.com
Hawaii	www.courts.state.hi.us
Idaho	www.isc.idaho.gov
Illinois	www.state.il.us/court
Indiana	www.in.gov/judiciary
Iowa	www.judicial.state.ia.us
Kansas	www.kscourts.org
Kentucky	www.courts.ky.gov
Louisiana	www.lasc.org
Maine	www.courts.state.me.us
Maryland	www.courts.state.md.us
Massachusetts	www.mass.gov/courts
Michigan	www.courts.michigan.gov
Minnesota	www.courts.state.mn.us
Mississippi	www.mssc.state.ms.us
Missouri	www.courts.mo.gov
Montana	www.montanacourts.org
Nebraska	http://court.nol.org
Nevada	www.nvsupremecourt.us
New Hampshire	www.courts.state.nh.us
New Jersey	www.judiciary.state.nj.us
New Mexico	www.nmcourts.com
New York	www.courts.state.ny.us
North Carolina	www.nccourts.org
North Dakota	www.ndcourts.com
Ohio	www.sconet.state.oh.us
Oklahoma	www.oscn.net/oscn/schome
Oregon	www.ojd.state.or.us
Pennsylvania	www.courts.state.pa.us
Puerto Rico	www.tribunalpr.org

State	Website
Rhode Island	*www.courts.state.ri.us*
South Carolina	*www.judicial.state.sc.us*
South Dakota	*www.sdjudicial.com*
Tennessee	*www.tsc.state.tn.us*
Texas	*www.courts.state.tx.us*
Utah	*www.utcourts.gov*
Vermont	*www.vermontjudiciary.org*
Virginia	*www.courts.state.va.us*
Virgin Islands	*www.visuperiorcourt.org*
Washington	*www.courts.wa.gov*
West Virginia	*www.wv.gov*
Wisconsin	*www.wicourts.gov*
Wyoming	*www.courts.state.wy.us*

Web Exercises

1. **WEB** Find the court system that serves your state or territory and visit the website of that court.
2. **WEB** What is the name of the highest court of your state?
3. **WEB** How many judges does the highest court of your state have?

Federal Court System

Article III of the U.S. Constitution provides that the federal government's judicial power is vested in one "Supreme Court." This court is the U.S. Supreme Court. The Constitution also authorizes Congress to establish "inferior" federal courts. Pursuant to this power, Congress has established special federal courts, the U.S. District Courts, and the U.S. Courts of Appeals. Federal judges are appointed for life by the president, with the advice and consent of the Senate (except bankruptcy court judges, who are appointed for 14-year terms).

Special Federal Courts

The **special federal courts** established by Congress have limited jurisdiction. They include the following:

- *U.S. Tax Court.* The **U.S. Tax Court** hears cases that involve federal tax laws. Its website is *www.ustaxcourt.gov*.
- *U.S. Court of Federal Claims.* The **U.S. Court of Federal Claims** Hears cases brought against the United States. Its website is *www.uscfc.uscourts.gov*.
- *U.S. Court of International Trade.* The **U.S. Court of International Trade** hears appeals of rulings of the U.S. Customs offices that involve tariffs and international commercial disputes. Its website is *www.cit.uscourts.gov*.
- *U.S. Bankruptcy Court.* The **U.S. Bankruptcy Court** hears cases that involve federal bankruptcy laws. Its website is *www. uscourts.gov/bankruptcycourts.html*.
- *U.S. Court of Appeals for the Armed Services.* The **U.S. Court of Appeals for the Armed Services** exercises appellate jurisdiction over members of the armed services. Its website is *www.armfor.uscourts.gov*.
- *U.S. Court of Appeals for Veterans Claims.* The **U.S. Court of Appeals for Veterans Claims** exercises jurisdiction over decisions by the Department of Veterans Affairs. Its website is *www.vetapp.uscourts.gov*.

U.S. District Courts

The **U.S. District Courts** are the federal court system's trial courts of general jurisdiction. There are 94 U.S. District Courts. There is at least one federal District Court in each state and the District of Columbia, and heavily populated states have more than one District Court. The geographic area served by each court is referred to as a *district*. The federal District Courts are empowered to impanel juries, receive evidence, hear testimony, and decide cases. Most federal cases originate in federal District Courts.

U.S. Courts of Appeals

The **U.S. Courts of Appeals** are the federal court system's intermediate appellate courts. There are 13 circuits in the federal court system. The first 12 are geographic. Eleven are designated by numbers, such as the "First Circuit," "Second Circuit," and so on. The geographic area served by each court is referred to as a *circuit*. The 12th Circuit Court is located in Washington, DC, and is called the **District of Columbia Circuit**.

Congress created the 13th Court of Appeals in 1982. It is called the **Court of Appeals for the Federal Circuit** and is located in Washington, DC.[1] This court has special appellate jurisdiction to review the decision of the Court of Federal Claims, the Patent and Trademark Office, and the Court of International Trade. This court was created to provide uniformity in the application of federal law in certain areas, particularly patent law.

As an appellate court, each Court of Appeals hears appeals from the District Courts located in its circuit as well as from certain special courts and federal administrative agencies. The Court reviews the record of the lower court or administrative agency proceedings to determine whether there has been any error that would warrant reversal or modification of the lower court decision. It hears no new evidence or testimony. The parties file legal briefs with the Court and are given a short oral hearing. Appeals are usually heard by a three-judge panel. After a decision is rendered by the three-judge panel, a petitioner can request a review *en banc* by the full court.

Exhibit 3.3 shows a map of the 13 U.S. Courts of Appeals. Exhibit 3.4 lists the websites for the 13 U.S. Courts of Appeals.

Web Exercises

1. **WEB** From the map in Exhibit 3.3, find the circuit that serves your geographic area and visit the website of that court.

2. **WEB** What states are represented by your circuit court?

3. **WEB** How many judges does your circuit court have?

EXHIBIT 3.3

Map of the Federal Circuit Courts

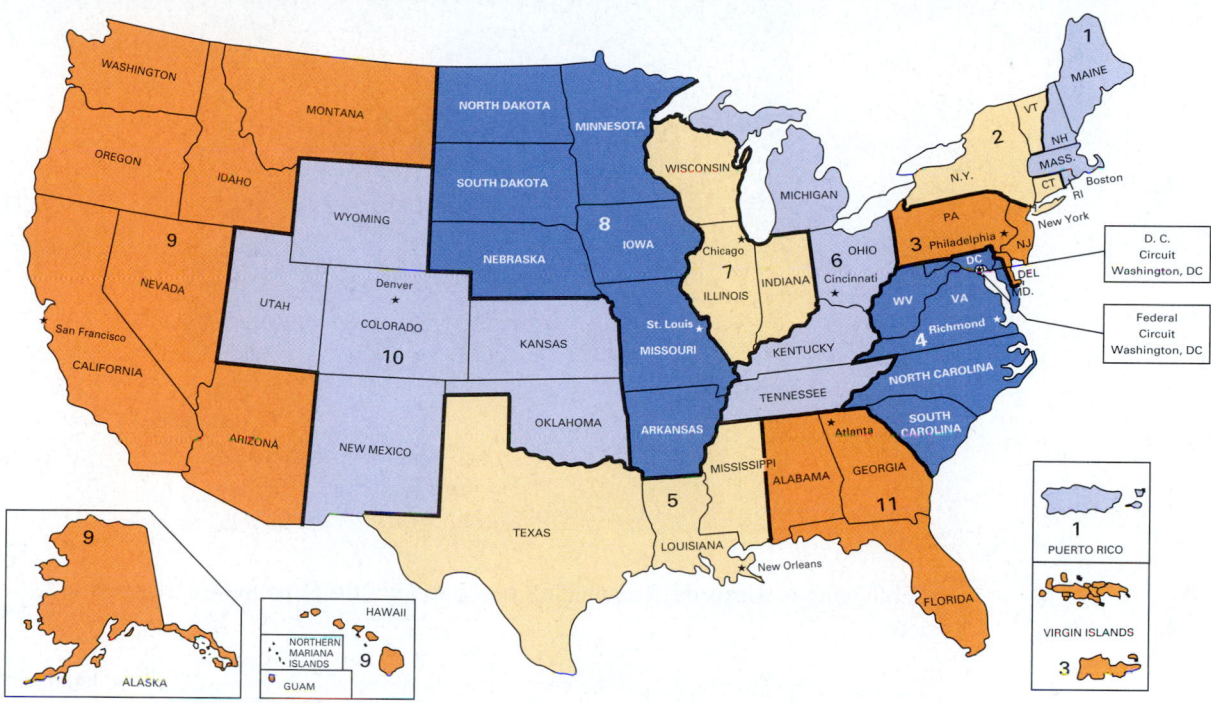

EXHIBIT 3.4

Federal Courts of Appeals

United States Court of Appeals	Main Office	Website
First Circuit	Boston, Massachusetts	www.ca1.uscourts.gov
Second Circuit	New York, New York	www.ca2.uscourts.gov
Third Circuit	Philadelphia, Pennsylvania	www.ca3.uscourts.gov
Fourth Circuit	Richmond, Virginia	www.ca4.uscourts.gov
Fifth Circuit	Houston, Texas	www.ca5.uscourts.gov
Sixth Circuit	Cincinnati, Ohio	www.ca6.uscourts.gov
Seventh Circuit	Chicago, Illinois	www.ca7.uscourts.gov
Eighth	St. Paul, Minnesota	www.ca8.uscourts.gov
Ninth	San Francisco, California	www.ca9.uscourts.gov
Tenth	Denver, Colorado	www.ca10.uscourts.gov
Eleventh	Atlanta, Georgia	www.ca11.uscourts.gov
District of Columbia	Washington, DC	www.dcd.uscourts.gov
Court of Appeals for the Federal Circuit	Washington, DC	www.fedcir.gov

United States Supreme Court

The highest court in the land is the **U.S. Supreme Court**, located in Washington, DC. The Court is composed of nine justices who are nominated by the president and confirmed by the Senate. The president appoints one justice as **chief justice**, who is responsible for the administration of the Supreme Court. The other eight justices are **associate justices**.

Following is Alexis de Tocqueville's description of the Supreme Court's role in U.S. society:

> The peace, the prosperity, and the very existence of the Union are vested in the hands of the [justices] of the Supreme Court. Without them, the Constitution would be a dead letter: the executive appeals to them for assistance against the encroachments of the legislative power; the legislature demands their protection against the assaults of the executive; they defend the Union from the disobedience of the states, the states from the exaggerated claims of the Union; the public interest against private interests, and the conservative spirit of stability against the fickleness of the democracy.

LANDMARK LAW
The Process of Choosing a Supreme Court Justice

In an effort to strike a balance of power between the executive and legislative branches of government, Article II, Section 2 of the U.S. Constitution gives the president the power to appoint Supreme Court justices "with the advice and consent of the Senate."

President George Bush, a Republican, was given the chance to cast a conservative shadow over the Court's decisions when Justice Thurgood Marshall retired in 1991. Marshall, who had served 24 years, was one of the most liberal members of the Court. President Bush nominated Clarence Thomas, an African American conservative, whom the U.S. Senate confirmed with a 52–48 vote.

The election of Bill Clinton as President swung the pendulum back to the Democrats. President Clinton, with the consent of the Senate, replaced Justice Byron White, a Democrat-appointed liberal, with Ruth Bader Ginsburg, a moderate liberal.

President George W. Bush, a Republican, became president of the United States in January 2001 and served two terms. In 2005, then presiding Chief Justice Rehnquist died. President Bush nominated John G. Roberts, Jr., to be the next chief justice of the Supreme Court.

Justice Roberts, a conservative, was easily confirmed by the Senate. In the same year, Justice Sandra Day O'Conner, the centrist vote on the Court, resigned from the Supreme Court. President Bush nominated Samuel A. Alito, Jr., a conservative, to fill the vacancy. Justice Alito was confirmed by a 58–42 vote of the Senate.

Future presidents, with their nominations and with the help of the Senate, will be able to cast their ideologies on the U.S. Supreme Court.

Web Exercises

1. **WEB:** Visit the website of the U.S. Supreme Court, at *www.supremecourtus.gov*. Who are the nine justice of the U.S. Supreme Court? Who is the Chief Justice?

2. **WEB:** Visit the website of the U.S. Supreme Court, at *www.supremecourtus.gov*. What president appointed each of the nine justices, and what political party (e.g., Democrat, Republican) did that president belong to? What is the ratio of Democrat-appointed justices to Republican-appointed justices?

Jurisdiction of the U.S. Supreme Court

The Supreme Court, which is an appellate court, hears appeals from U.S. Courts of Appeals and, under certain circumstances, from U.S. District Courts, special federal courts, and the highest state courts. It hears no new evidence or testimony. As with other appellate courts, the Supreme Court reviews the lower court record to determine whether there has been an error that warrants a reversal or modification of the decision. Legal briefs are filed, and the parties are granted a brief oral hearing. The Supreme Court's decision is final.

The federal court system is illustrated in Exhibit 3.5.

Decisions by the U.S. Supreme Court

The U.S. Constitution gives Congress the authority to establish rules for the appellate review of cases by the Supreme Court, except in the rare case in which mandatory review is required. Congress has given the Supreme Court discretion to decide what cases it will hear.[2]

A petitioner must file a **petition for certiorari** asking the Supreme Court to hear the case. If the Court decides to review a case, it issues a **writ of certiorari**. Because the Court issues only about 100 opinions each year, writs are granted only in cases involving constitutional and other important issues.

Each justice of the Supreme Court, including the chief justice, has an equal vote. The Supreme Court can issue several types of decisions, as described in the following paragraphs.

UNANIMOUS OPINION If all the justices voting agree as to the outcome and reasoning used to decide a case, it is a **unanimous opinion**. Unanimous opinion are precedent for later cases.

EXHIBIT 3.5

Federal Court System

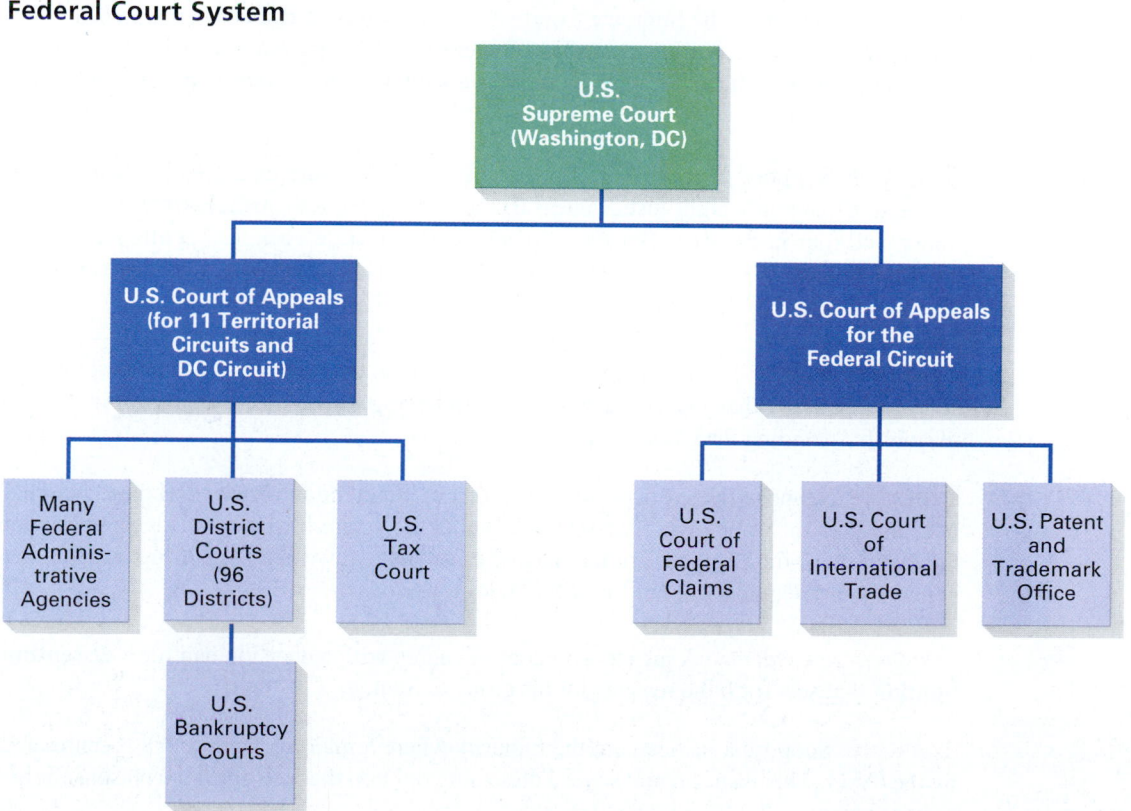

Example Suppose all nine justices hear a case, and all nine agree to the outcome (e.g., the petitioner wins) and the reason (e.g., the Equal Protection Clause of the U.S. Constitution had been violated); this is a unanimous decision. This unanimous decision becomes precedent for later cases.

MAJORITY OPINION If a majority of the justices agree as to the outcome and reasoning used to decide a case, it is a **majority opinion**. Majority opinion are precedent for later cases. A majority decision occurs if five, six, seven, or eight justices vote for the same outcome for the same reason.

Example If all nine justices hear a case, and five of them agree as to the outcome (e.g., the petitioner wins) and all of these five justices agree to the same reason (e.g., the Equal Protection Clause of the U.S. Constitution has been violated), it is a majority opinion. The majority opinion becomes precedent for later cases and has the same force of law as a unanimous decision. The remaining four justices' vote for the respondent has no legal effect whatsoever.

PLURALITY OPINION If a majority of the justices agree as to the outcome of a case but not as to the reasoning for reaching the outcome, it is a **plurality opinion**. A plurality opinion settles the case but is not precedent for later cases.

Example If all nine justices hear a case, and five of them agree as to the outcome (e.g., the petitioner wins), but not all of these five agree to the reason (e.g., three base their vote on a violation of the Equal Protection Clause and two base their vote on a violation of the Freedom of Speech Clause of the U.S. Constitution), this is a plurality decision. Five justices have agreed to the same outcome, but those five have not agreed to the same reason. The petitioner wins his or her case, but the decision is not precedent for later cases. The remaining four justices' votes for the respondent have no legal effect whatsoever.

TIE VOTE Sometimes the Supreme Court sits without all nine justices being present. This could happen because of illness, conflict of interest, or a justice not having been confirmed to fill a vacant seat on the Court. If there is a **tie vote**, the lower court decision is affirmed. Such votes are not precedent for later cases.

Example Suppose a petitioner won her case at the Court of Appeals. At the U.S. Supreme Court, only eight justices hear the case. Suppose four justices vote for the petitioner, and four justices vote for the respondent. This is a tie vote. The petitioner remains the winner because she won at the Court of Appeals. This decision of the Supreme Court sets no precedent for later cases.

CONCURRING OPINION A justice who agrees with the outcome of a case but not the reason proffered by other justices can issue a **concurring opinion** that sets forth his or her reasons for deciding the case.

Example Suppose five justices vote for a certain outcome in a case, and these five justices agree to the same legal theory to justify their decision. If another justice agrees with the outcome of the case, but not the reason, he or she can write a concurring opinion that concurs with the judgment but for different legal reasons.

DISSENTING OPINION A justice who does not agree with a decision can file a **dissenting opinion** that sets forth the reasons for his or her dissent.

Example Suppose a justice is in the minority where a majority opinion has been issued by the Court. This justice could write a dissenting opinion that sets forth the reasons for his or her vote.

> Sancho: But if this is hell, why do we see no lawyers?
> Clarindo: They won't receive them, lest they bring lawsuits here.
> Sancho: If there are no lawsuits here, hell's not so bad.
>
> Lope de Vega
> *The Star of Seville, Act 3, Scene 2*

CONTEMPORARY ENVIRONMENT

"I'll Take You to the U.S. Supreme Court!"

In reality, the chance of ever having your case heard by the highest court is slim to none. Each year, more than 7,000 petitioners ask the Supreme Court to hear their cases. These petitioners usually pay big law firms from $30,000 to $100,000 or more to write the appeal petition. In recent years, the Supreme Court has accepted only fewer than 100 of these cases for full review each term.

Each of the nine Supreme Court justices has three law clerks—recent law school graduates usually chosen from elite law schools across the country—who assist them. The justices rarely read the appellate petitions but instead delegate this task to their law clerks. A clerk writes a short memorandum, discussing the key issues raised by the appeal, and recommends to the justices whether they should grant or deny a review. The justices meet once a week to discuss what cases merit review. The votes of four justices are necessary to grant an appeal and schedule an oral argument before the Court (this is called the **"rule of four"**). Written opinions by the justices are usually issued many months later.

So what does it take to win a review by the Supreme Court? The U.S. Supreme Court usually decides to hear cases involving major constitutional questions such as freedom of speech, freedom of religion, equal protection, and due process. The Supreme Court also hears many cases involving the interpretation of statutes enacted by Congress. The Court rarely decides day-to-day legal issues such as breach of contract, tort liability, or corporations law unless they involve more important constitutional or federal law questions.

So the next time you hear someone say, "I'll take you to the U.S. Supreme Court!" just say, "Not!"

Jurisdiction of Federal and State Courts

Federal courts and state courts each have jurisdiction to hear and decide certain types of cases. Article III, Section 2 of the U.S. Constitution sets forth the jurisdiction of federal courts. Federal courts have *limited jurisdiction* to hear cases involving federal questions and cases based on diversity of citizenship.

Federal Questions

The federal courts have jurisdiction to hear cases involving *federal questions*. **Federal question** cases are cases arising under the U.S. Constitution, treaties, and federal statutes and regulations. There is no dollar-amount limit on federal question cases that can be brought in federal court.[3]

Example Larry has been sued by the United States for engaging in insider trading in violation of the Securities Exchange Act of 1934 and regulations adopted by the federal Securities and Exchange Commission (SEC). This lawsuit involves federal questions—a federal statute and a federal regulation—and therefore qualifies to be brought in the appropriate U.S. District Court.

Diversity of Citizenship

A case may be brought in federal court if there is **diversity of citizenship**. Diversity of citizenship occurs if the lawsuit involves either citizens of different states or a citizen of a state and a citizen or subject of a foreign country. Diversity of citizenship is used to bring or maintain a lawsuit in federal court when the subject matter of the lawsuit involves a nonfederal question. A corporation is considered to be a citizen of the state in which it is incorporated and in which it has its principal place of business.

The reason for providing diversity of citizenship jurisdiction was to prevent state court bias against nonresidents. The federal court must apply the appropriate state's law in deciding the case. The dollar amount of the controversy must exceed $75,000.[4] If this requirement is not met, action must be brought in the appropriate state court.

Example Henry, a resident of Idaho, is driving his automobile when he negligently hits Mary, a pedestrian. Mary is from New York. There is no federal question involved in this case. It is an automobile accident that involves state negligence law. However, there is diversity of citizenship in this case: Henry is from the state of Idaho, while Mary is from another state, the state of New York. In this case Mary, the plaintiff, may bring her lawsuit in federal court, and if she does so, the case will remain in federal court. If Mary brings the case in state court (usually the state in which the automobile accident occurred), it will remain in state court if Henry agrees; however, Henry can move the case to federal court.

Exclusive Jurisdiction

Federal courts have **exclusive jurisdiction** to hear cases involving federal crimes, antitrust, and bankruptcy; patent and copyright cases; suits against the United States; and most admiralty cases. State courts may not hear these matters.

CONCEPT SUMMARY

Jurisdiction of Federal Courts

TYPE OF JURISDICTION	DESCRIPTION
Federal question	Cases arising under the U.S. Constitution, treaties, and federal statutes and regulations. There is no dollar-amount limit in federal question cases.
Diversity of citizenship	Cases between citizens of different states or between a citizen of a state and a citizen or subject of a foreign country. Federal courts must apply the appropriate state law in such cases. The controversy must exceed $75,000 for the federal court to hear the case.

Jurisdiction of State Courts

State courts have jurisdiction to hear cases that federal courts do not have jurisdiction to hear. These usually involve state law, such as real estate law, corporation law, partnership law, limited liability company law, contract law, sales and lease contracts law, negotiable instruments law, and other state law (nonfederal question) subject matters that do not involve diversity of citizenship.

State courts have **concurrent jurisdiction** with federal courts to hear cases involving diversity of citizenship and federal questions over which federal courts do not have exclusive jurisdiction (e.g., cases involving federal securities laws). If a case involving concurrent jurisdiction is brought by a plaintiff in federal court, the case remains in federal court. If the plaintiff brings a case involving concurrent jurisdiction in state court, the defendant can either let the case be decided by the state court or remove the case to federal court.

If a case does not qualify to be brought in federal court, it must be brought in the appropriate state court.

Exhibit 3.6 illustrates the jurisdiction of federal and state courts.

Personal Jurisdiction of Courts

Not every court has the authority to hear all types of cases. First, to bring a lawsuit in a court, the plaintiff must have *standing to sue*. In addition, the court must have *personal jurisdiction* to hear the case, and the case must be brought in the proper *venue*. These topics are discussed in the following paragraphs.

Standing to Sue

To bring a lawsuit, a plaintiff must have **standing to sue**. This means the plaintiff must have some stake in the outcome of the lawsuit.

Example Suppose Linda's friend Jon is injured in an accident caused by Emily. Jon refuses to sue. Linda cannot sue Emily on Jon's behalf because she does not have an interest in the result of the case.

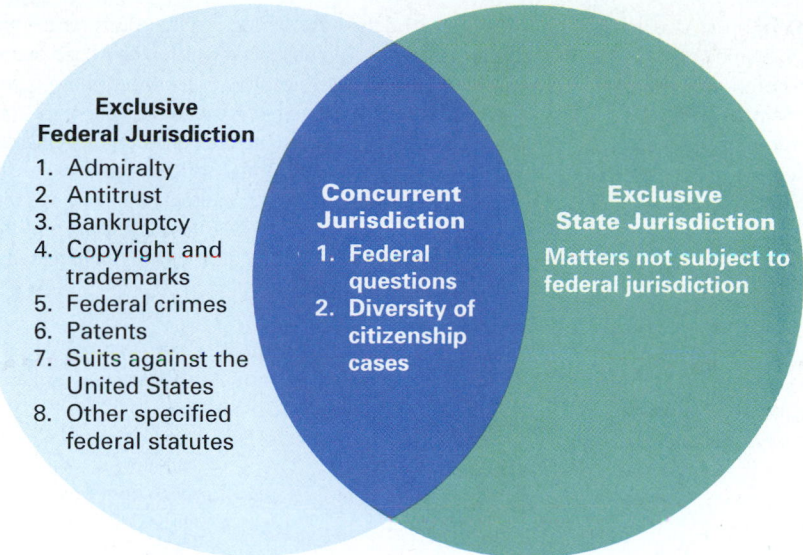

EXHIBIT 3.6

Jurisdiction of Federal and State Courts

A few states now permit investors to invest money in a lawsuit for a percentage return of any award of judgment. Courts hear and decide actual disputes involving specific controversies. Hypothetical questions will not be heard, and trivial lawsuits will be dismissed.

In Personam Jurisdiction

Jurisdiction over a person is called *in personam* **jurisdiction**, or **personal jurisdiction**. A *plaintiff*, by filing a lawsuit with a court, gives the court *in personam* jurisdiction over himself or herself. The court must also have *in personam* jurisdiction over the *defendant*, which is usually obtained by having a summons served to that person within the territorial boundaries of the state (i.e., **service of process**).

Service of process is usually accomplished by personal service of the summons and complaint on the defendant. If this is not possible, alternative forms of notice, such as mailing of the summons or publication of a notice in a newspaper, may be permitted. A corporation is subject to personal jurisdiction in the state in which it is incorporated, has its principal office, and is doing business.

A party who disputes the jurisdiction of a court can make a *special appearance* in that court to argue against imposition of jurisdiction. Service of process is not permitted during such an appearance.

L A N D M A R K   C A S E

International Shoe Company v. State of Washington

How far can a state go to require a person or business to defend himself or itself in a court of law in that state? That question was presented to the U.S. Supreme Court in the landmark case ***International Shoe Company v. State of Washington***.[5]

The International Shoe Company was a Delaware corporation that had its principal place of business in St. Louis, Missouri. The company manufactured and distributed shoes throughout the United States. The company maintained a sales force throughout the United States. In the state of Washington, its sales representatives did not have a specific office but sold shoes door-to-door and sometimes at temporary locations. The

sales representatives were paid commissions based on the number of shoes they sold.

The state of Washington assessed an unemployment tax on International Shoe for the sales representative it had in the state. When International Shoe failed to pay, Washington served personal service on a sales representative of the company in Washington and mailed the service of process to the company's headquarters in St. Louis. International Shoe appeared specially to argue that it did not do sufficient business in Washington to warrant having to pay unemployment taxes in that state. The unemployment office ruled against International Shoe, and the appeals tribunal, the superior court, and supreme court of Washington agreed. International Shoe appealed to the U.S. Supreme Court.

In its decision, the U.S. Supreme Court noted, "Due process requires only that in order to subject a defendant to a judgment *in personam*, if he be not present within the territory of the forum, he have certain minimum contacts with it such that the maintenance of that suit does not offend 'traditional notions of fair play and substantial justice.'"

The Supreme Court stated:

Applying these standards, the activities carried on in behalf of International Shoe in the State of Washington were neither irregular nor causal. They were systematic and continuous throughout the years in question. They resulted in a large volume of interstate business, in the course of which International Shoe received the benefits and protection of the laws of the state, including the right to resort to the courts for the enforcement of its rights. The obligation which is here sued upon arose out of those very activities. It is evident that these operations establish sufficient contacts or ties with the state of the forum to make it reasonable and just, according to our traditional conception of fair play and substantial justice, to permit the state to enforce the obligations which International Shoe has incurred there. Hence, we cannot say that the maintenance of the present suit in the State of Washington involves an unreasonable or undue procedure.

Thus, the "minimum contacts" test and "traditional notions of fair play and substantial justice" establish when a state may subject a person or business to the walls of its courtrooms. Obviously, this is not a bright-line test, so battles of *in personam* jurisdiction abound to this day.

In Rem Jurisdiction

A court may have jurisdiction to hear and decide a case because it has jurisdiction over the property of the lawsuit. This is called ***in rem* jurisdiction** ("jurisdiction over the thing").

Example   Suppose John, a resident of the state of Massachusetts, owns a piece of vacant real estate in the state of New Hampshire. Sarah, a resident of the state of Florida owns the property adjacent to John's property. John and Sarah dispute the boundary line between the two parcels of property. John claims that an old fence line sets the boundary between the two parcels of property; Sarah claims that the lot line determined by a legal survey sets the boundary line between the two parcels of property. In this case, the court of New Hampshire will hear and decide the lot line dispute because it has *in rem* jurisdiction—that is, the property in dispute is located in New Hampshire.

CONCEPT SUMMARY

In Personam and *in Rem* Jurisdiction

TYPE OF JURISDICTION	DESCRIPTION
In personam jurisdiction	With *in personam* jurisdiction, a court has jurisdiction over the parties to the lawsuit. The plaintiff submits to the jurisdiction of the court by filing the lawsuit there. Personal jurisdiction is obtained over the defendant through *service of process* to that person.
In rem jurisdiction	With *in rem* jurisdiction, a court has jurisdiction to hear and decide a case because it has jurisdiction over the property at issue in the lawsuit (e.g., real property located in the state).

Long-Arm Statutes

In most states, a state court can obtain jurisdiction over persons and businesses located in another state or country through the state's **long-arm statute**. Such a statute extends a state's jurisdiction to nonresidents who were not served a summons within the state.

The nonresident must have had some *minimum contact* with the state.[6] In addition, the maintenance of the suit must uphold the traditional notions of fair play and substantial justice.

The exercise of long-arm jurisdiction is generally permitted over nonresidents who have (1) committed torts within the state (e.g., caused an automobile accident in the state), (2) entered into a contract either in the state or that affects the state (and allegedly breached the contract), or (3) transacted other business in the state that allegedly caused injury to another person.

Parties to a contract may include a forum-selection clause that designates a certain court to hear any dispute concerning nonperformance of the contract.

Venue

Venue requires lawsuits to be heard by the court with jurisdiction nearest the location in which the incident occurred or where the parties reside.

Example Harry, a Georgia resident, commits a felony crime in Los Angeles County, California. The California superior court located in Los Angeles is the proper venue because the crime was committed there, the witnesses are probably from the area, and so on.

Occasionally, pretrial publicity may prejudice jurors located in the proper venue. In such cases, a **change of venue** may be requested so that a more impartial jury can be found. The courts generally frown upon *forum shopping* (i.e., looking for a favorable court without a valid reason).

Forum-Selection and Choice-of-Law Clauses

One issue that often comes up when parties from different states have a legal dispute is which state's court will be used, or which federal courts in either of the states will hear the case. When the parties have not agreed in advance, courts must make the decision about which court has jurisdiction. This determination costs time and money. Therefore, parties sometimes agree in their contract as to what state's courts, federal courts, or country's court will have jurisdiction to hear a legal dispute should one arise. Such clauses in contracts are called **forum-selection clauses**.

In addition to agreeing to a forum, the parties to a contract also often agree as to what state's law or country's law will apply in resolving a dispute. These clauses are called **choice-of-law clauses**.

Example Retail Outlet Store is located in the state of Maine. Southeast Clothing Company, which designs and manufactures women's clothing, is located in the state of Illinois. Retail Outlet contracts to purchase $100,000 of merchandise from Southeast Clothing. The parties place a clause in the contract that states that if any dispute arises concerning the contract, the lawsuit will be brought in the state court of Maine. This is a forum-selection clause. The contract also provides that the laws of Maine will apply in deciding the dispute. This is a choice-of-law clause.

Example American Import Company is a company located in the United States, with its headquarters in Los Angeles, California. Tata Motors is a truck and automobile manufacturer located in the country of India. American Import enters into a contract to purchase 1,000 designated vehicles from Tata to be imported into the United States. This international contract specifies that any dispute regarding the contract will be heard and decided by the courts of India. This is a forum-selection clause. The contract also specifies that the law of India will apply. This is a choice-of-law clause.

The following case illustrates the application of a forum-selection clause.

CASE 3.1
Forum-Selection Clause

U.S. SUPREME COURT
Carnival Cruise Lines, Inc. v. Shute

499 U.S. 585, 111 S.Ct. 1522, 113 L.Ed.2d 622,
Web 1991 U.S. Lexis 2221(1991)
Supreme Court of the United States

> ❝ *A clause establishing the forum for dispute resolution has the salutary effect of dispelling any confusion where suits arising from the contract must be brought and defended, sparing litigants the time and expense of pretrial motions to determine the correct forum, . . .* ❞
>
> —Justice Blackmun

Facts

Mr. and Mrs. Shute, residents of the state of Washington, purchased passage for a seven-day cruise on the *Tropicale*, a cruise ship operated by Carnival Cruise Lines, Inc. (Carnival). They paid the fare to the travel agent, who forwarded the payment to Carnival's headquarters in Miami, Florida. Carnival prepared the tickets and sent them to the Shutes. Each ticket consisted of five pages, including contract terms. The ticket contained a forum-selection clause that designated the state of Florida as the forum for any lawsuits arising under or in connection with the ticket and cruise. The Shutes boarded the *Tropicale* in Los Angeles, which set sail for Puerto Vallarta, Mexico. While the ship was on its return voyage and in international waters off the coast of Mexico, Mrs. Shute was injured when she slipped on a deck mat during a guided tour of the ship's galley. Upon return to Washington, she filed a negligence lawsuit against Carnival in U.S. District Court in Washington, seeking damages. Carnival filed a motion for summary judgment, contending that the lawsuit could be brought only in a court located in the state of Florida. The District Court granted Carnival's motion. The Court of Appeals reversed, holding that Mrs. Shute could sue Carnival in Washington. Carnival appealed to the U.S. Supreme Court.

Issue

Is the forum-selection clause in the Carnival Cruise Lines ticket enforceable?

Language of the U.S. Supreme Court

As an initial matter, we do not adopt the court of appeals' determination that a non-negotiated forum-selection clause in a form ticket contract is never enforceable simply because it is not the subject of bargaining. Including a reasonable forum clause in a form contract of this kind may well be permissible for several reasons: First, a cruise line has a special interest in limiting the fora in which it potentially could be subject to suit. Because a cruise ship typically carries passengers from many locales, it is not unlikely that a mishap on a cruise could subject the cruise line to litigation in several different fora.

Additionally, a clause establishing the forum for dispute resolution has the salutary effect of dispelling any confusion where suits arising from the contract must be brought and defended, sparing litigants the time and expense of pretrial motions to determine the correct forum, and conserving judicial resources that otherwise would be devoted to deciding those motions. Finally, it stands to reason that passengers who purchase tickets containing a forum clause like that at issue in this case benefit in the form of reduced fares reflecting the savings that the cruise line enjoys by limiting the fora in which it may be sued.

Decision

The U.S. Supreme Court held that the forum-selection clause in Carnival's ticket is fair and reasonable and therefore enforceable against Mrs. Shute. If she wishes to sue Carnival, she must do so in a court in the state of Florida, not in a court in the state of Washington. The U.S. Supreme Court reversed the decision of the Court of Appeals.

Law & Ethics Questions

1. Should forum-selection clauses be enforced? Why or why not?
2. **ETHICS** Did Carnival Cruise Lines act ethically by placing the forum-selection clause in its tickets?
3. Do forum-selection clauses serve any legitimate business purpose? Explain.

Web Exercises

1. **WEB** For a complete opinion of this case, go to *www.prenhall.com/cheesemancases*.
2. **WEB** Visit the website of the U.S. Supreme Court, at *www.supremecourtus.gov* and try to find documents that relate to this case.
3. **WEB** Visit the website of Carnival Cruise Lines, Inc., at *www.carnival.com*. Does the company disclose its current passenger contract?
4. **WEB** Use *www.google.com* to find an advertisement for a Carnival Cruise Lines cruise. Is there any information in this advertisement about a forum-selection clause?

INTERNET AND TECHNOLOGY
Obtaining Personal Jurisdiction in Cyberspace

Obtaining personal jurisdiction over a defendant in another state has always been difficult for the courts. Today, thanks to the ability the Internet gives persons and businesses to reach millions of people in other states electronically, modern issues arise as to whether courts have jurisdiction in cyberspace.

In one case, Zippo Manufacturing Company (Zippo) sued Zippo Dot Com, Inc., in federal District Court in Pennsylvania. Zippo manufacturers its well-known line of tobacco lighters in Bradford, Pennsylvania, and sells them worldwide. Zippo Dot Com, a California corporation with its principal place of business and its servers located in Sunnyvale, California, operates an Internet website that transmits information and sexually explicit material to its subscribers.

Three thousand of Zippo Dot Com's 140,000 paying subscribers worldwide are located in Pennsylvania. Zippo sued Zippo Dot Com in federal District Court in Pennsylvania for trademark infringement. Zippo Dot Com alleged that it was not subject to personal jurisdiction in Pennsylvania. The U.S. District Court applied the *International Shoe* "minimum contacts" and "traditional notions of fair play and substantial justice" standard and held that Zippo Dot Com was subject to personal jurisdiction under the Pennsylvania long-arm statute and ordered Zippo Dot Com to defend itself in Pennsylvania. *Zippo Manufacturing Company v. Zippo Dot Com, Inc.*, 952 Fed.Supp. 1119, **Web** 1997 U.S. Dist. Lexis 1701 (United States District Court for the Western District of Pennsylvania, 1997)

Samarkan, Uzbekistan

Each country has its own national courts that hear and decide legal disputes in that country. This photo is of an Islamic mosque in the country of Uzbekistan.

Chapter Summary

State Court Systems, p. 59

Limited-Jurisdiction Trial Court

Limited-jurisdiction trial courts are state courts that hear matters of a specialized or limited nature (e.g., misdemeanor criminal matters, traffic tickets, civil matters under a certain dollar amount). Many states have created small claims courts that hear small-dollar-amount civil cases (e.g., under $5,000) where the parties cannot be represented by lawyers.

General-Jurisdiction Trial Court

General-jurisdiction trial courts are state courts that hear cases of a general nature that are not within the jurisdiction of limited-jurisdiction trial courts.

Intermediate Appellate Court

Intermediate appellate courts are state courts that hear appeals from state trial courts. The appellate court reviews the trial court record in making its decision. No new evidence is introduced at this level.

Highest State Court

Each state has a highest court in its court system. This court hears appeals from appellate courts and, where appropriate, trial courts. This court reviews the record in making its decision. No new evidence is introduced at this level. Most states call this court the supreme court.

Federal Court System, p. 63

Special Federal Courts

Special federal courts have specialized or limited jurisdiction. They include:
1. *U.S. Tax Court.* This court hears cases involving federal tax laws.
2. *U.S. Court of Federal Claims.* This court hears cases brought against the United States.
3. *U.S. Court of International Trade.* This court hears cases involving tariffs and international commercial disputes.
4. *U.S. Bankruptcy Court.* This court hears cases involving federal bankruptcy law.
5. *U.S. Court of Appeals for the Armed Forces.* This court hears cases involving members of the armed forces.
6. *U.S. Court of Appeals for Veterans Claims.* This court hears cases involving veterans of the armed forces.

U.S. Districts Courts

U.S. District Courts are federal trial courts of general jurisdiction that hear cases not within the jurisdiction of specialized courts. There is at least one U.S. District Court per state: More populated states have several District Courts. The area serviced by one of these courts is called a *district*.

U.S. Courts of Appeals

U.S. Courts of Appeals are intermediate federal appellate courts that hear appeals from District Courts located in their circuits and, in certain instances, from special federal courts and federal administrative agencies. There are 12 geographic circuits in this country. Eleven serve areas that comprise several states, and another is located in Washington, DC. A 13th circuit court—the Court of Appeals for the Federal Circuit—is located in Washington, DC, and it reviews patent, trademark, and international trade cases.

United States Supreme Court, p. 65

Jurisdiction of the U.S. Supreme Court

The U.S. Supreme Court is the highest court of the federal court system. It hears appeals from the circuit courts and, in some instances, from special courts and U.S. District Courts. The Supreme Court, which is located in Washington, DC, is composed of nine justices, one of whom is named chief justice.

Decisions by the U.S. Supreme Court

To have a case heard by the U.S. Supreme Court, a petitioner must file a *petition for certiorari* with the Court. If the Court decides to hear the case, it issues a *writ of certiorari*. The Court may issue the following decisions:
1. *Unanimous opinion.* In this type of decision, all the justices agree as to the outcome and reasoning used to decide the case. The decision becomes precedent.
2. *Majority opinion.* In this type of decision, a majority of the justices agree as to the outcome and reasoning used to decide the case. The decision becomes precedent.
3. *Plurality opinion.* In this type of decision, a majority of the justices agrees as to the outcome but not as to the reasoning. The decision is not precedent.

4. *Tie opinion.* If there is a tie vote, the lower court's decision stands. The decision is not precedent.

5. *Concurring opinion.* A justice who agrees as to the outcome of the case but not the reasoning used by other justices may write a concurring opinion, setting forth his or her reasoning.

6. *Dissenting opinion.* A justice who disagrees with the outcome of a case may write a dissenting opinion, setting forth his or her reasoning for dissenting.

Jurisdiction Of Federal And State Courts, p. 69

Federal courts may hear cases involving federal questions and cases involving diversity of citizenship.

Federal Questions

Federal questions are cases arising under the U.S. Constitution, treaties, and federal statutes and regulations. There is no dollar-amount limit in federal question cases.

Diversity of Citizenship

Cases involving diversity of citizenship are cases between either citizens of different states or a citizen of a state and a citizen or subject of a foreign country. Federal courts must apply the appropriate state law in such cases. The controversy must exceed $75,000 for the federal court to hear the case.

Exclusive Jurisdiction

Federal courts have exclusive jurisdiction to hear cases involving federal crimes, antitrust, and bankruptcy; patent and copyright cases; suits against the United States; and most admiralty cases. State courts may not hear these matters.

Jurisdiction of State Courts

State courts hear some cases that may be heard by federal courts. State courts have *concurrent jurisdiction* to hear cases involving diversity of citizenship and federal questions over which the federal courts do not have exclusive jurisdiction. The defendant may have the case removed to federal court.

PERSONAL JURISDICTION OF COURTS, p. 70
Standing to Sue

To bring a lawsuit, the plaintiff must standing to sue, which is some stake in the outcome of the lawsuit.

In personam *Jurisdiction*

The court must have jurisdiction over the parties to a lawsuit. This is called *in personam* (or personal) jurisdiction. The plaintiff submits to the jurisdiction of the court by filing the lawsuit there. Personal jurisdiction is obtained over the defendant through service of process to that person.

In rem *Jurisdiction*

A court may have jurisdiction to hear and decide a case because it has jurisdiction over the property at issue in the lawsuit (e.g., real property located in the state). This is called *in rem* jurisdiction.

Long-Arm Statutes

Long-arm statutes permit a state to obtain personal jurisdiction over an out-of state defendant as long as the defendant had the requisite minimum contact with the state. The out-of-state defendant may be served process outside the state in which the lawsuit has been brought.

Venue

A case must be heard by the court that has jurisdiction nearest to where the incident at issue occurred or where the parties reside. A *change of venue* is granted if prejudice would occur because of pretrial publicity of another reason.

Forum-Selection and Choice-of-Law Clauses

A *forum-selection clause* in a contract designates the court that will hear any disputes that arise out of the contract. A choice-of-law clause in a contract designates the law that will apply to any dispute that arises out of the contract.

Test Review Terms and Concepts

Case Problems

3.1 Federal Question: Nutrilab, Inc., manufactured and marketed a product known as "Starch Blockers." The purpose of the product is to block the human body's digestion of starch as an aid in controlling weight. The U.S. FDA classified Starch Blockers as a drug and requested that it be removed from the market until the FDA approved of its use. The FDA claimed that it had the right to classify new products as drugs and prevent their distribution until their safety could be determined. Nutrilab disputed the FDA's decision and wanted to bring suit to halt the FDA's actions. Do the federal courts have jurisdiction to hear this case? *Nutrilab, Inc. v. Schweiker*, 713 F.2d 335, **Web** 1983 U.S. App. Lexis 25121 (United States Court of Appeals for the Seventh Circuit)

3.2 Jurisdiction: James Clayton Allison, a resident of the state of Mississippi, was employed by the Tru-Amp Corporation as a circuit breaker tester. As part of his employment, Allison was sent to inspect, clean, and test a switch gear located at the South Central Bell Telephone Facility in Brentwood, Tennessee. One day when he attempted to remove a circuit breaker manufactured by ITE Corporation (ITE) from a bank of breakers, a portion of the breaker fell off. The broken piece fell behind a switching bank and, according to Allison, caused an electrical fire and explosion. Allison was severely burned in the accident. Allison brought suit against ITE in a Mississippi state court,

claiming more than $50,000 in damages. Can this suit be removed to federal court? *Allison v. ITE Imperial Corp.*, 729 F. Supp. 45, **Web** 1990 U.S. Dist. Lexis 607 (United States District Court for the Southern District of Mississippi)

3.3 Long-Arm Statute: Sean O'Grady, a professional boxer, was managed by his father, Pat. Sean was a contender for the world featherweight title. Pat entered into a contract with Magna Verde Corporation, a Los Angeles–based business, to co-promote a fight between Sean and the then-current featherweight champion. The fight was scheduled to take place in Oklahoma City, Oklahoma. To promote the fight, Pat O'Grady scheduled a press conference. At the conference, Pat was involved in a confrontation with a sportswriter named Brooks. He allegedly struck Brooks in the face. Brooks brought suit against Pat O'Grady and Magna Verde Corporation in an Oklahoma state court. Court records showed that the only contact Magna Verde had with Oklahoma was that a few of its employees had taken several trips to Oklahoma to plan the title fight. The fight was never held. Oklahoma has a long-arm statute. Magna Verde was served by mail and made a special appearance in Oklahoma state court to argue that Oklahoma does not have personal jurisdiction over it. Does Oklahoma have jurisdiction over Magna Verde Corporation? *Brooks v. Magna Verde Corp.*, 1980 OK. CIV. APP. 40, 619 P.2d 1271, **Web** 1980 Okla. Civ. App. Lexis 118 (Court of Appeals of Oklahoma)

3.4 Minimum Contacts: The National Enquirer, Inc., is a Florida corporation with its principal place of business in Florida. It publishes the *National Enquirer*, a national weekly newspaper with a total circulation of more than 5 million copies. About 600,000 copies, almost twice the level in the next highest state, are sold in California. The *Enquirer* published an article about Shirley Jones, an entertainer. Jones, a California resident, filed a lawsuit in California state court against the *Enquirer* and its president, who was a resident of Florida. The suit sought damages for alleged defamation, invasion of privacy, and intentional infliction of emotional distress. Are the defendants subject to suit in California? *Calder v. Jones*, 465 U.S. 783, 104 S.Ct. 1482, 79 L.Ed.2d 804, **Web** 1984 U.S. Lexis 4 (Supreme Court of the United States)

Ethics Issues

3.5 Ethics One day Joshua Gnaizda, a three-year-old, received what he (or his mother) thought was a tantalizing offer in the mail from Time, Inc. The front of the envelope contained a see-through window that revealed the following statement: "Joshua Gnaizda, I'll give you this versatile new calculator watch free just for opening this envelope." Beneath the offer was a picture of the calculator watch itself. When Joshua's mother opened the envelope, she realized that the see-through window had not revealed the full text of Time's offer. Not viewable through the see-through window were the following words: "And mailing this certificate today." The certificate required Joshua to purchase a subscription to *Fortune* magazine in order to receive the free calculator watch. Joshua (through his father, a lawyer) sued Time in a class action suit, seeking compensatory damages in an amount equal to the value of the calculator watch and $15 million in punitive damages. The trial court dismissed the lawsuit as being too trivial for the court to hear. Joshua appealed. Should Joshua be permitted to maintain his lawsuit against Time, Inc.? Did Time act ethically? Should Joshua's father have sued for $15 million? *Harris v. Time, Inc.*, 191 Cal. App.3d 449, 237 Cal. Rptr. 584, **Web** 1987 Cal. App. Lexis 1619 (Court of Appeal of California)

IRAC Writing Assignment

Read Case A-3 in Appendix A [***Peoples Trust Company v. Kozuck***]. Read the case and use the IRAC method to prepare a written analysis of the case.

Endnotes

1. Federal Courts Improvement Act of 1982. Public Law 97-164, 96 Stat. 25, 28 U.S.C. Section 1292 and Section 1295.
2. Effective September 25, 1988, mandatory appeals were all but eliminated, except in reapportionment cases and cases brought under the Civil Rights Act and Voting Rights Act, antitrust laws, and the Presidential Election Campaign Fund Act.
3. Prior to 1980, there was a minimum dollar-amount controversy requirement of $10,000 to bring a federal question action in federal court. This minimum amount was eliminated by the Federal Question Jurisdictional Amendment Act of 1980, Public Law 96-486.
4. The 1996 Federal Courts Improvement Act raised the amount from $50,000 to $75,000.
5. 326 U.S. 310, 66 S.Ct. 154, 90 L.Ed 95, Web 1945 U.S. Lexis 1447 (Supreme Court of the United States).
6. International Shoe Co. v. Washington, 326 U.S. 310, 66 S.Ct. 154, 90 L.Ed. 95, Web 1945 U.S. Lexis 1447 (Supreme Court of the United States).

CHAPTER 4

Judicial, Administrative, Alternative, and Online Dispute Resolution

> **❝***We're the jury, dread our fury!***❞**

—WILLIAM S. GILBERT
Trial by Jury

CHAPTER OBJECTIVES

After studying this chapter, you should be able to:

1. Describe the pretrial litigation process.
2. Describe how a case proceeds through trial.
3. Describe how a trial court decision is appealed.
4. Explain the use of arbitration and other nonjudicial methods of alternative dispute resolution.
5. Define *administrative law* and explain the functions of administrative agencies.

CHAPTER CONTENTS

- Introduction to Judicial, Administrative, Alternative, and Online Dispute Resolution
- Pretrial Litigation Process
- Dismissals and Pretrial Judgments
- Settlement Conference
- Trial
- Appeal
- Alternative Dispute Resolution
- Administrative Law
- Chapter Summary
- Test Review Terms and Concepts
- Case Problems
- Ethics Issues
- IRAC Writing Assignment

Introduction to Judicial, Administrative, Alternative, and Online Dispute Resolution

The process of bringing, maintaining, and defending a lawsuit is called *litigation*. Litigation is a difficult, time-consuming, and costly process that must comply with complex procedural rules. Although it is not required, most parties employ a lawyer to represent them when they are involved in a lawsuit.

Several forms of *nonjudicial* dispute resolution have developed in response to the expense and difficulty of bringing a lawsuit. These methods, collectively called *alternative dispute resolution*, are being used more and more often to resolve commercial and e-commerce disputes.

Federal and state governments enact laws that regulate business. The legislative and executive branches of government have created numerous administrative agencies to assist in implementing and enforcing these laws. The operation of these administrative agencies is governed by a body of *administrative law*. Because of their importance, administrative agencies are informally referred to as the "fourth branch of government."

This chapter discusses the judicial litigation process and alternative dispute resolution, and it examines administrative agencies and administrative law.

Federal Courthouse, Santa Ana, California

Parties to a dispute can use the court system to have their dispute decided.

Pretrial Litigation Process

The bringing, maintaining, and defense of a lawsuit are generally referred to as the *litigation process*, or **litigation**. The pretrial litigation process can be divided into the following major phases: *pleadings, discovery, dismissals and pretrial judgments*, and *settlement conference*. Each of these phases is discussed in the paragraphs that follow.

Pleadings

The paperwork that is filed with the court to initiate and respond to a lawsuit is referred to as the **pleadings**. The major pleadings are the *complaint*, the *answer*, the *cross-complaint*, and the *reply*.

COMPLAINT AND SUMMON To initiate a lawsuit, the party who is suing (the **plaintiff**) must file a **complaint** with the proper court. The complaint must name the parties to the lawsuit, allege the ultimate facts and law violated, and contain a "prayer for relief" for a remedy to be awarded by the court. The complaint can be as long as necessary, depending on the complexity of the case. A sample complaint appears in Exhibit 4.1.

Once a complaint has been filed with the court, the court issues a **summons**. A summons is a court order directing the defendant to appear in court and answer the complaint. The complaint and summons are served on the defendant by a sheriff, another government official, or a private process server.

Web Exercises

1. **WEB** Go to *www.eff.org/IP/digitalradio/XM_complaint.pdf* to view a copy of a complaint filed in U.S. District Court.

2. **WEB** Use *www.google.com* to find a copy of a complaint filed in a lawsuit in a state court in your state.

EXHIBIT 4.1

Sample Complaint

In the United States District Court for the District of Idaho

John Doe   Civil No. 2-1001
         Plaintiff

         v.   COMPLAINT

Jane Roe

         Defendant

The plaintiff, by and through his attorney, alleges:

1. The plaintiff is a resident of the State of Idaho, the defendant is a resident of the State of Washington, and there is diversity of citizenship between the parties.
2. The amount in controversy exceeds the sum of $75,000, exclusive of interest and costs.
3. On January 10, 2008, plaintiff was exercising reasonable care while walking across the intersection of Sun Valley Road and Main Street, Ketchum, Idaho when defendant negligently drove her car through a red light at the intersection and struck plaintiff.
4. As a result of the defendant's negligence, plaintiff has incurred medical expenses of $104,000 and suffered severe physical injury and mental distress.

WHEREFORE, plaintiff claims judgment in the amount of $1,000,000 interest at the maximum legal rate, and costs of this action.

By _____
Edward Lawson
Attorney for Plaintiff
100 Main Street
Ketchum, Idaho

ANSWER The defendant must file an **answer** to the plaintiff's complaint. The defendant's answer is filed with the court and served on the plaintiff. In the answer, the defendant admits or denies the allegations contained in the plaintiff's complaint. A judgment is entered against a defendant who admits all the allegations in the complaint. The case proceeds if the defendant denies all or some of the allegations. If the defendant does not answer the complaint, a *default judgment* is entered against him or her. A default judgment establishes the defendant's liability. The plaintiff then has only to prove damages.

In addition to answering the complaint, a defendant's answer can assert *affirmative defenses*. For example, if a complaint alleges that the plaintiff was personally injured by the defendant, the defendant's answer could state that he or she acted in self-defense. Another affirmative defense would be an assertion that the plaintiff's lawsuit is barred because the *statute of limitations* (time within which to bring the lawsuit) has expired.

> Pieces of evidence, each by itself insufficient, may together constitute a significant whole and justify by their combined effect a conclusion.
>
> Lord Wright
> *Grant V. Australian Knitting Mills, Ltd. (1936)*

Web Exercise

1. **WEB** Use *www.google.com* to find a copy of an answer filed in a lawsuit.

In the following case, the U.S. Supreme Court held that a complaint successfully pleaded the elements of the case.

C A S E   **4.1**
Complaint

U.S. SUPREME COURT
Swierkiewicz v. Sorema N.A.

534 U.S. 506, 122 S.Ct. 992, 152 L.Ed.2d 1,
Web 2002 U.S. Lexis 1374 (2002)
Supreme Court of the United States

"*A complaint must include only a short and plain statement of the claim showing that the pleader is entitled to relief.***"**

—Justice Thomas

Facts

Akos Swierkiewicz, a native of Hungary, worked for Sorema N.A., a reinsurance company headquartered in New York. Swierkiewicz was initially employed as senior vice president and chief underwriting officer. Nearly six years later, the chief executive officer of the company demoted Swierkiewicz to a marketing position and removed him from his underwriting responsibilities. Swierkiewicz's underwriting responsibilities were transferred to a 32-year-old employee with les than 1 year of underwriting experience. Sorema dismissed Swierkiewicz, who was 53 years old at the time and had 26 years of experience in the insurance industry. Swierkiewicz sued Sorema to recover monetary damages for alleged age and national origin discrimination in violation of federal anti-discrimination laws. Sorema moved to have Swierkiewicz's complaint dismissed. The U.S. District Court dismissed Swierkiewicz's complaint for not being specific enough. The U.S. Court of Appeals affirmed. Swierkiewicz appealed to the U.S. Supreme Court.

Issue

Under the federal notice pleading system, was Swierkiewicz's complaint sufficiently pleaded to permit the case to go to trial?

Language of the U.S. Supreme Court

When a federal court reviews the sufficiency of a complaint, its task is necessarily a limited one. The issue is not whether a plaintiff will ultimately prevail but whether the claimant is entitled to offer evidence to support the claims. Under a notice pleading system, it is not appropriate to require a plaintiff to plead facts establishing a **prima facie** case.

Imposing the court of appeals' heightened pleading standard in employment discrimination cases conflicts with Federal Rule of Civil Procedure 8(a)(2), which provides that a complaint must include only "a short and plain statement of the claim showing that the pleader is entitled to relief." Such a statement must simply give the defendant fair notice of what the plaintiff's claim is and the grounds upon which it rests. For example, Form 9 sets forth a complaint for negligence in which plaintiff simply states in relevant part: "On June 1, 1936, in a public highway called Boylston Street in Boston, Massachusetts, defendant negligently drove a motor vehicle against plaintiff who was then crossing said highway." Applying the relevant standard, petitioner Swierkiewicz's complaint easily satisfies the requirements of Rule 8(a) because it gives respondent Sorema N.A. fair notice of the basis for petitioner's claims.

Decision

The U.S. Supreme Court held that Swierkiewicz's complaint met the requirements of notice pleading and was sufficient to withstand Sorema's motion to dismiss. The Supreme Court reversed the judgment of the Court of Appeals and remanded the case for further proceedings.

Law & Ethics Questions

1. Describe "notice pleading." What is the public policy supporting notice pleading?
2. **ETHICS** Did Sorema N.A. act ethically in trying to have Swierkiewicz's complaint dismissed? Did Sorema know why it was being sued?
3. What are the benefits of notice pleading? Are there any detriments?

Web Exercises

1. **WEB** For the complete opinion of this case, go to *www.prenhall.com/cheesemancases*.
2. **WEB** Visit the website of the U.S. Supreme Court, at *www.supremecourtus.gov*, and try to find documents that relate to this case.
3. **WEB** Use *www.google.com* to find an article concerning age discrimination against an employee. Read it.

CROSS-COMPLAINT AND REPLY A defendant who believes that he or she has been injured by the plaintiff can file a **cross-complaint** against the plaintiff in addition to an answer. In the cross-complaint, the defendant (now the **cross-complainant**) sues the plaintiff (now the **cross-defendant** for damages or some other remedy. The original plaintiff must file a **reply** (answer) to the cross-complaint. The reply, which can include affirmative defenses, must be filed with the court and served on the original defendant.

CONCEPT SUMMARY

Pleadings

TYPE OF PLEADING	DESCRIPTION
Complaint	A document filed by a plaintiff with a court and served with a *summons* on the defendant. It sets forth the basis of the lawsuit.
Answer	A document filed by a defendant with a court and served on the plaintiff. It usually denies most allegations of the complaint.
Cross-complaint and reply	A document filed and served by a defendant if he or she countersues the plaintiff. The defendant is the *cross-complainant*, and the plaintiff is the *cross-defendant*. The cross-defendant must file and serve a *reply* (answer).

INTERVENTION AND CONSOLIDATION If other persons have an interest in a lawsuit, they may **intervene** and become parties to the lawsuit. For instance, a bank that has made a secured loan on a piece of real estate can intervene in a lawsuit between parties who are litigating ownership of the property.

If several plaintiffs have filed separate lawsuits stemming from the same fact situation against the same defendant, the court can **consolidate** the cases into one case if doing so would not cause undue prejudice to the parties.

Example: Suppose, for example, that a commercial airplane crashes, killing and injuring many people. The court could consolidate all the lawsuits against the defendant airplane company.

In the following case, the court had to decide which state's law applied to a case.

CASE 4.2
State Law

Bertram v. Norden, et al.

159 Ohio App.3d 171, 823 N.E.2d 478,
Web 2004 Ohio App. Lexis 5500 (2004)
Court of Appeals of Ohio

> *We note that Michigan is a known snowmobiling destination, and, as such, Michigan lawmakers have taken steps to deal with the liability issues that go along with the dangers of snowmobiling.*
>
> —Judge Rogers

Facts

Four friends, John Bertram, Matt Norden, Scott Olson, and Tony Harvey, all residents of Ohio, traveled to the Upper Peninsula of Michigan to go snowmobiling. On their first day of snowmobiling, after going about 135 miles, the lead snowmobiler, Olson, came to a stop sign on the snowmobile trail where it intersected a private driveway. As Olson approached the sign, he gave the customary hand signal and stopped his snowmobile. Harvey, second in line, was going too fast to stop, so Olson pulled his snowmobile to the right side of the private driveway. Harvey, to avoid hitting Olson, pulled his snowmobile to the left and went over a 5- to 6-foot snow embankment. Bertram, third in line, going about 30 miles per hour, slammed on his break, turned 45 degrees, and slammed into Olson's snowmobile. Bertram was thrown from his snowmobile. Norden, fourth in line, could not stop, and his snowmobile hit Bertram's leg. Bertram's tibia and fibula were both fractured and protruded through his skin. Bertram underwent surgery to repair the broken bones.

Bertram filed a lawsuit against Olson, Harvey, and Norden in a trial court in Ohio, claiming that each of his friends were liable to him for their negligent snowmobile operation. The Ohio court held that Michigan law applied and that a Michigan statute specifically stated that snowmobilers assumed the risks associated with snowmobiling. The court therefore held that the three friends were not liable to Bertram and granted their motions for summary judgment. Ohio law did not contain an assumption of the risk rule regarding snowmobiling. Bertram appealed, alleging that Ohio law applied to the case because all the parties were from Ohio.

Issue

Does Michigan or Ohio law apply to this case?

Language of the Court

Because the accident took place in Michigan, we must presume that Michigan law applies absent any other jurisdiction having more substantial contacts. Bertram, however, contends that Ohio law should apply, because all of the parties were residents of Ohio at the time of the accident and all consequences flowing from his injury occurred in Ohio. We disagree.

We again note that the accident itself took place in Michigan. Additionally, the place where the conduct causing injury occurred was Michigan. Bertram, Norden, and the others all traveled to Michigan specifically to go snowmobiling. It was while they were in Michigan that the conduct causing the accident, as well as the accident itself, occurred. Additionally, we note that Michigan is a known snowmobiling destination, and, as such, Michigan lawmakers have taken steps to deal with the liability issues that go along with the dangers of snowmobiling.

Because the snowmobiling accident took place in Michigan, the place where the conduct causing Bertram's injury occurred in Michigan and Michigan has enacted specific legislation involving the risks of snowmobiling, we find that Michigan law clearly controls in this case. While all parties are residents of and have their relationships in the State of Ohio, we are not persuaded by Bertram's argument that this issue should control.

Decision

The court of appeals of Ohio held that the law of the state of Michigan, where the accident occurred, and not the law of the state of Ohio, the state of the residence of the parties, should apply. The court upheld the trial court's application of Michigan's assumption of the risk statute to this case and affirmed the trial court's grant of summary judgment to the three defendant friends of plaintiff Bertram.

Law & Ethics Questions

1. What does the doctrine of assumption of the risk provide? Explain.

2. **ETHICS** Was it ethical for Bertram to sue his three friends for negligence? Why or why not?

3. **ETHICS** Why did Bertram want Ohio law, and not Michigan law, to apply to the case?

Web Exercises

1. **WEB** For the complete opinion of this case, go to *www.prenhall.com/cheesemancases*.

2. **WEB** Visit the website of the court of appeals of Ohio, Third Appellate District, Defiance County, at *www.third.courts.state.oh.us*.

3. **WEB** Visit the snowmobiling website of the Upper Peninsula of Michigan, at *www.upsnowmobiling.com* to see the type of equipment that is used in snowmobiling.

INTERNET AND TECHNOLOGY
E-Filings

When litigation ensues, the clients, lawyers, and judges involved in the case are usually buried in papers. These papers include pleadings, interrogatories, documents, motions to the court, briefs, and memorandums; the list goes on and on. By the time a case is over, reams of paper are stored in dozens, if not hundreds, of boxes. In addition, court appearances, for no matter how small the matter, must be made in person. For example, lawyers often wait hours for a 10-minute scheduling or other conference with the judge. The time it takes to drive to and from court can also be considerable, in some areas amounting to hours.

Today, because of the Internet and other technologies, a virtual courthouse is being developed. Technology allows for the electronic filing—**e-filing**—of pleadings, briefs, and other documents related to a lawsuit.

E-filing includes using CD-ROMs for briefs, scanning evidence and documents into a computer for storage and retrieval, and e-mailing correspondence and documents to the court and the opposing counsel. Scheduling and other conferences with the judge or opposing counsel are held via telephone conferences and e-mail.

Many courts have instituted e-filing. In some courts, e-filing is now mandatory. Companies such as Microsoft and LexisNexis have developed systems to manage e-filings of court documents.

Web Exercises

1. **WEB** Use *www.google.com* to find out if your state court system allows for the electronic filing of complaints, answers, and other documents filed with the court.

Statute of Limitations

A **statute of limitations** establishes the period during which a plaintiff must bring a lawsuit against a defendant. If a lawsuit is not filed within this time period, the plaintiff loses his or her right to sue. A statute of limitations begins to "run" at the time the plaintiff first has the right to sue the defendant (e.g., when the accident happens, when the breach of contract occurs).

Federal and state governments have established statutes of limitations for each type of lawsuit. Most are from one to four years, depending on the type of lawsuit.

Example   A one-year statute of limitations is common for ordinary negligence actions. Thus, if on July 1, 2008, Otis negligently causes an automobile accident in which Cha-Yen is injured, Cha-Yen has until July 1, 2009, to bring a negligence lawsuit against Otis. If she waits longer than that, she loses her right to sue him.

In the following case, the court applied a statute of limitations.

CASE 4.3
Statute of Limitations

Norgart v. The Upjohn Company

21 Cal.4th 383, 87 Cal.Rpt.2nd 453,
Web 1999 Cal. Lexis 5308
Supreme Court of California

> " *Pursuant to this rule, the Norgarts were too late, exactly five years too late.* "
>
> —Justice Mosk

Facts

Kristi Norgart McBride lived with her husband in Santa Rosa, California. Kristi suffered from manic-depressive mental illness (now called bipolar disorder). In this disease, the person cycles between manic (ultrahappy, expansive, extroverted) episodes to depressive episodes. The disease is often treated with prescription drugs. In April 1984,

Kristi attempted suicide. A psychiatrist prescribed an antianxiety drug. In May 1985, Kristi attempted suicide again by overdosing on drugs. The doctor prescribed Halcion, a hypnotic drug, and added Darvocet-N, a mild narcotic analgesic. On October 16, 1985, after descending into a severe depression. Kristi committed suicide by overdosing on Halcion and Darvocet-N. On October 16, 1991, exactly six years after

Kristi's death, Leo and Phyllis Norgart, Kristi's parents, filed a lawsuit against the Upjohn Company, the maker of Halcion, for wrongful death based on Upjohn's alleged failure to warn of the unreasonable dangers of taking Halcion. The trial court granted Upjohn's motion for summary judgment based on the fact that the one-year statute of limitations for wrongful death actions had run. The court of appeals reversed, and Upjohn appealed to the supreme court of California.

Issue

Is the plaintiff's action for wrongful death barred by the one-year statute of limitations?

Language of the Court

The court noted that the statute of limitations has a purpose to protect defendants from the stale claims of dilatory plaintiffs. It has as a related purpose to stimulate plaintiffs to assert fresh claims against defendants in a diligent fashion. The court stated that under the statute of limitations, a plaintiff must bring a cause of action from wrongful death within one year of accrual—that means that the date of accrual of a cause of action for wrongful death is the date of death. The Norgarts had to bring the cause of action for wrongful death within one year of accrual. The court stated, "They did not do so. Pursuant to this rule, the Norgarts were too late, exactly five years too late."

Decision

The supreme court of California held that the defendant, the Upjohn Company, was entitled to judgment as a matter of law, based on the fact that the one-year statute of limitations for wrongful death actions had run out, thus barring the plaintiff's lawsuit. The state supreme court reversed the decision of the court of appeals.

Law & Ethics Questions

1. What is a statute of limitations? What is the public policy behind having statutes of limitations?

2. **ETHICS** Was it ethical for the Upjohn Company to avoid facing the merits of the lawsuit by asserting the one-year statute of limitations?

3. What are the business implications for having statutes of limitations?

Web Exercises

1. **WEB** For the complete opinion of this case, go to *www.prenhall.com/cheesemancases*.

2. **WEB** Visit the website of the Supreme Court of California, at *www.courtinfo.ca.gov/courts/supreme*.

3. **WEB** Visit the website of the Upjohn Company, at *www.upjohn.com*.

4. **WEB** Use *www.google.com* to find an article that describes bipolar disorder. Read it.

Discovery

The legal process provides for a detailed pretrial procedure called **discovery**. During discovery, each party engages in various activities to discover facts of the case from the other party and witnesses prior to trial. Discovery serves several functions, including preventing surprise, allowing parties to thoroughly prepare for trial, preserving evidence, saving court time, and promoting the settlement of cases. The major forms of discovery are discussed in the following paragraphs.

DEPOSITION A **deposition** is the oral testimony given by a party or witness prior to trial. The person giving the deposition is called the **deponent**. A *party* to the lawsuit must give a deposition, if called upon by the other party to do so. The deposition of a *witness* can be given voluntarily or pursuant to a subpoena (court order). The deponent can be required to bring documents to the deposition. Most depositions are taken at the office of one of the attorneys. The deponent is placed under oath and then asked oral questions by one or both of the attorneys. The questions and answers are recorded in written form by a court reporter. Depositions can also be videotaped. The deponent is given an opportunity to correct his or her answers prior to signing the deposition. Depositions are used to preserve evidence (e.g., if the deponent is deceased, ill, or not otherwise available at trial) and impeach testimony given by witnesses at trial.

INTERROGATORIES **Interrogatories** are written questions submitted by one party to a lawsuit to another party. The questions can be very detailed. In addition, certain documents might be attached to the answers. A party is required to answer the interrogatories in writing within a specified time period (e.g., 60 to 90 days). An attorney usually helps with the preparation of the answers. The answers are signed under oath.

PRODUCTION OF DOCUMENTS   Often, particularly in complex business cases, a substantial portion of a lawsuit may be based on information contained in documents (e.g., memorandums, correspondence, company records). One party to a lawsuit may request that the other party produce all documents that are relevant to the case prior to trial. This is called **production of documents**. If the documents sought are too voluminous to be moved or are in permanent storage, or if their movement would disrupt the ongoing business of the party who is to produce them, the requesting party may be required to examine the documents at the other party's premises.

PHYSICAL AND MENTAL EXAMINATION   In cases that concern the physical or mental condition of a party, a court can order the party to submit to certain **physical or mental examinations** to determine the extent of the alleged injuries. This would occur, for example, if the plaintiff has been injured in an accident and is seeking damages for physical injury and mental distress.

CONCEPT SUMMARY

Discovery

TYPE	DESCRIPTION
Deposition	Oral testimony given by a *deponent*, either a party or witness. Depositions are transcribed.
Interrogatories	Written questions submitted by one party to the other party. They must be answered within a specified period of time.
Production of documents	Copies of all relevant documents obtained by a party to a lawsuit from another party upon order of the court.
Physical and mental examination	Court-ordered examination of a party where injuries are alleged that could be verified or disputed by such examination.

Dismissals and Pretrial Judgments

There are several **pretrial motions** that parties to a lawsuit can make to try to dispose of all or part of a lawsuit prior to trial. The two major pretrial motions are motion for judgment on the pleadings and motion for summary judgment.

Motion for Judgment on the Pleadings

A **motion for judgment on the pleadings** can be made by either party once the pleadings are complete. This motion alleges that if all the facts presented in the pleadings are true, the party making the motion would win the lawsuit when the proper law is applied to these facts. In deciding this motion, the judge cannot consider any facts outside the pleadings.

Motion for Summary Judgment

The trier of fact (i.e., the jury or, if there is no jury, the judge) determines factual issues. A **motion for summary judgment** asserts that there are no factual disputes to be decided by the jury and that the judge should apply the relevant law to the undisputed facts and decide the case. Motions for summary judgment, which can be made by either party, are supported by evidence outside the pleadings. Affidavits from the parties and witnesses, documents (e.g., a written contract between the parties), depositions, and such are common forms of evidence.

If, after examining the evidence, the court finds no factual dispute, it can decide the issue or issues raised in the summary judgment motion. This may dispense with the entire case or with part of the case. If the judge finds that a factual dispute exists, the motion is denied, and the case goes to trial.

In the following case, the court had to decide whether to grant a motion for summary judgment.

CASE 4.4
Summary Judgment

Toote v. Canada Dry Bottling Company of New York, Inc. and Pathmark Stores, Inc.

7 A.D.3d 251, 776 N.Y.S.2d 42,
Web 2004 N.Y. App. Div Lexis 6470 (2004)
Supreme Court of New York, Appellate Division

> **"** *Plaintiff alleges that she tripped over cases of soda that were stacked on the floor of defendant's supermarket.* **"**

—Judge Lerner

Facts

Plaintiff Phyllis Toote filed a lawsuit against Pathmark Stores, Inc., a grocery store, and Canada Dry Bottling Company of New York, a bottler and distributor of soda. In her complaint, plaintiff alleged that the defendants were liable for negligence for injuries she suffered when she fell over cases of soda that were stacked on the floor of the supermarket when she was shopping at the supermarket.

Defendant Pathmark took plaintiff Toote's deposition in which she stated that she had entered the supermarket, and upon entering the store, she immediately walked to the soda aisle. Toote stated that she did not see the soda stacked on the floor before she fell over the soda. In the deposition, Toote stated that she did not know how long the soda had been on the floor before she tripped and fell. Pathmark made a motion for summary judgment, alleging that plaintiff Toote could not establish how long the soda had been on the floor before she fell. The motion court denied Pathmark's motion for summary judgment, finding that there were questions of fact to be decided by the jury. Pathmark appealed.

Issue

Should the motion court have granted Pathmark's motion for summary judgment?

Language of the Court

Plaintiff alleges that she tripped over cases of soda that were stacked on the floor of defendant's supermarket. It appears that at the time of the accident, the supermarket's shelves, in accordance with usual practice, were being "packed out" with soda by an employee of either defendant bottling company or defendant soda distributor. The supermarket moved for summary judgment, contending that it did not create the alleged dangerous condition and that plaintiff's deposition testimony, to the effect that she walked to the soda aisle immediately after entering the store and did not see any soda on the floor before falling, shows that she cannot establish how long the soda had been on the floor before she fell. The motion court correctly held that such

testimony does not establish, *prima facie*, the supermarket's lack of prior actual or constructive notice of the soda on the floor, or that it may not be held liable for an independent contractor's negligence on the basis of the supermarket's non-delegable duty to keep the public areas of its premises reasonably safe.

Decision

The appellate court decided that there were issues of fact to be decided by a jury and affirmed the motion court's denial of Pathmark's motion for summary judgment

Law & Ethics Questions

1. What is a motion for summary judgment? When will a motion for summary judgment be granted?

2. When will a motion for summary judgment be denied?

3. **ETHICS** Was it ethical for Pathmark, the supermarket, to make a motion for summary judgment based on the facts of this case? Explain.

4. **ETHICS** Do you think supermarkets face a significant number of "faked" slip-and-fall cases?

Web Exercises

1. **WEB** For the complete opinion of this case, go to *www.prenhall.com/cheesemancases*.

2. **WEB** Visit the website of the supreme court of New York, Appellate Division, First Department, at *www.courts.state.ny.us/courts/ad1*.

3. **WEB** Visit the website of defendant Pathmark Stores, Inc., at *www.pathmark.com*.

4. **WEB** Use *www.google.com* to find an article about a slip-and-fall negligence case. Read it.

Settlement Conference

Federal court rules and most state court rules permit the court to direct the attorneys or parties to appear before the court for a **settlement conference**, or *pretrial hearing*. One of the major purposes of such hearings is to facilitate the settlement of the case. Settlement conferences are often held informally in the judge's chambers. If no settlement is reached, the pretrial hearing is used to identify the major trial issues and other relevant factors. More than 90 percent of all cases are settled before they go to trial.

CONTEMPORARY ENVIRONMENT
Cost–Benefit Analysis of a Lawsuit

In most civil lawsuits, each party is responsible for paying its own attorneys' fees, whether the party wins or loses. This is called the "American rule." The court can award lawyers' fees to the winning party if a statute so provides, the parties have so agreed (e.g., in a contract), or the losing party has acted maliciously or pursued a frivolous case.

An attorney in a civil or criminal lawsuit can represent his or her client on an hourly or project-fee basis. Hourly fees usually range from $100 to $500 per hour, depending on the type of case, the expertise of the lawyer, and the locality of the lawsuit. In a civil lawsuit, plaintiffs' lawyers often work under a *contingency fee arrangement*, where the lawyer receives a percentage of the amount recovered for the plaintiff upon winning or settling the case. Contingency fees normally range from 20 to 50 percent of the award or settlement, with the average being about 35 percent. Lawyers for defendants in civil lawsuits are normally paid on an hourly basis.

The choice of whether to bring or defend a lawsuit should be analyzed like any other business decision. This includes performing a **cost-benefit analysis** of the lawsuit. For the plaintiff, it may be wise not to sue. For the defendant, it may be wise to settle. The following factors should be considered in deciding whether to bring or settle a lawsuit:

- The probability of winning or losing
- The amount of money to be won or lost
- Lawyers' fees and other costs of litigation
- Loss of time by managers and other personnel
- The long-term effects on the relationship and reputation of the parties
- The amount of prejudgment interest provided by law
- The aggravation and psychological costs associated with a lawsuit
- The unpredictability of the legal system and the possibility of error
- Other factors peculiar to the parties and lawsuit

CONTEMPORARY ENVIRONMENT
Ford Settles Lawsuit

Approximately 90 percent of civil lawsuits are settled prior to trial. Settlements are reached when both parties believe that a trial provides too much risk of loss and the amount of the settlement is reasonable in light of that risk. Consider the settlement in the following case. Nabil Boury was driving a Ford Explorer SUV on the Eisenhower Expressway in Chicago, with five passengers in the vehicle. When another car clipped the Explorer on the driver's-side rear wheel well, the Explorer immediately rolled over. By the time it came to rest, the Explorer had rolled over three times and ejected several of the passengers. Boury's sister and another teenager were killed, Boury's cousin lost vision in one eye, and another passenger was rendered a quadriplegic; Boury and his mother suffered minor injuries.

After the accident, the injured persons and the estates of the two deceased teenagers sued Ford Motor Company in a product liability lawsuit, alleging that there was a defect in the design of the Explorer SUV that caused it to roll over. The plaintiffs sued Michelin Tire Corporation, alleging that the Michelin tires on the SUV were inappropriate for the vehicle and that Michelin had not warned of this fact. The plaintiffs sued Packey Webb Ford, the car dealer that sold the Explorer, for putting Michelin tires on the SUV in a size and type specifically contrary to the warnings in the Ford owner's manual. The plaintiffs also sued Cassidy Tire Company, the distributor of the Michelin tires.

Several months before the case was to proceed to trial, the parties reached settlement. Ford agreed to pay $8 million, Packey Webb $10.5 million, Cassidy Tire $3 million, and Michelin Tire $500,000. The plaintiffs reached a separate agreement as to how to divide the settlement proceeds. This is just one example of the hundreds of thousands of civil lawsuits that are settled each year. *Boury v. Ford Motor Company*, Cook County Circuit Court, Illinois (2001)

Law & Ethics Questions

1. What is a settlement of a lawsuit? Explain.

2. Why are so many lawsuits settled instead of going to trial?

3. **ETHICS** Does entering into a settlement admit to any wrongdoing?

Web Exercise

1. **WEB** Use *www.google.com* to find an article about a recent settlement of a lawsuit. Read it.

Trial

Pursuant to the Seventh Amendment to the U.S. Constitution, a party to an action at law is guaranteed the right to a *jury trial* in a case in federal court.[1] Most state constitutions contain a similar guarantee for state court actions. If either party requests a jury, the **trial** is by jury. If both parties waive their right to a jury, the trial occurs without a jury. The judge sits as the **trier of fact** in nonjury trials. At the time of trial, each party usually submits to the judge a *trial brief* that contains legal support for its side of the case.

Phases of a Trial

A trial can last less than one day to many months, depending on the type and complexity of the case. A typical trial is divided into stages. The stages of a trial are discussed in the following paragraphs.

JURY SELECTION The pool of potential jurors is usually selected from voter or automobile registration lists. Individuals are selected to hear specific cases through a process called **voir dire** ("to speak the truth"). Lawyers for each party and the judge can ask prospective jurors questions to determine whether they would be biased in their decisions. Biased jurors can be prevented from sitting on a particular case. Once the appropriate number of jurors is selected (usually 6 to 12 jurors), they are *impaneled* to hear the case and are sworn in. The trial is ready to begin. A jury can be *sequestered* (i.e., separated from family) in important cases. Jurors are paid minimum fees for the service.

OPENING STATEMENTS Each party's attorney is allowed to make an **opening statement** to the jury. In an opening statement, an attorney usually summarizes the main factual and legal issues of the case and describes why he or she believes the client's position is valid. The information given in an opening statement is not considered as evidence.

THE PLAINTIFF'S CASE A plaintiff bears the **burden of proof** to persuade the trier of fact of the merits of his or her case. This is called the **plaintiff's case**. The plaintiff's attorney calls witnesses to give testimony. After a witness has been sworn in, the plaintiff's attorney examines (i.e., questions) the witness. This is called *direct examination*. Documents and other evidence can be introduced through each witness. After the plaintiff's attorney has completed his or her questions, the defendant's attorney can question the witness. This is called *cross-examination*. The defendant's attorney can ask questions only about the subjects that were brought up during the direct examination. After the defendant's attorney completes his or her questions, the plaintiff's attorney can ask questions of the witness. This is called *re-direct examination*.

THE DEFENDANT'S CASE The **defendant's case** proceeds after the plaintiff has concluded his or her case. The defendant's case must (1) rebut the plaintiff's evidence, (2) prove any affirmative defenses asserted by the defendant, and (3) prove any allegations contained in the defendant's cross-complaint. The defendant's witnesses are examined in much the same way that the plaintiff's attorney cross-examines each witness. This is followed by re-direct and re-cross-examination.

REBUTTAL AND REJOINDER After the defendant's attorney has finished calling witnesses, the plaintiff's attorney can call witnesses and put forth evidence to rebut the defendant's case.

This is called a **rebuttal**. The defendant's attorney can call additional witnesses and introduce other evidence to counter the rebuttal. This is called the **rejoinder**.

CLOSING ARGUMENTS At the conclusion of the presentation of the evidence, each party's attorney is allowed to make a **closing argument** to the jury. Both attorneys try to convince the jury to render a verdict for their clients by pointing out the strengths in the client's case and the weaknesses in the other side's case. Information given by the attorneys in their closing statements is not evidence.

JURY INSTRUCTIONS Once the closing arguments are completed, the judge reads **jury instructions** (or *charges*) to the jury. These instructions inform the jury about what law to apply when they decide the case. For example, in a criminal trial, the judge reads the jury the statutory definition of the crime charged. In an accident case, the judge reads the jury the legal definition of *negligence*.

JURY DELIBERATION AND VERDICT The jury then retires to the jury room to deliberate its findings. This can take from a few minutes to many weeks. After the **jury deliberation**, the jury reaches a **verdict**. In civil cases, the jury assesses damages against the defendant if it has held in favor of the plaintiff. The jury often assesses penalties in criminal cases.

ENTRY OF JUDGMENT After the jury has returned its verdict, in most cases the judge enters **judgment** to the successful party based on the verdict. This is the official decision of the court.

The court may, however, overturn the verdict if it finds bias or jury misconduct. This is called a **judgment notwithstanding the verdict** (or **judgment n.o.v. or j.n.o.v.**).

In a civil case, the judge may reduce the amount of monetary damages awarded by the jury if he or she finds the jury to have been biased, emotional, or inflamed. This is called *remittitur*.

The trial court usually issues a *written memorandum* setting forth the reasons for the judgment. This memorandum, together with the trial transcript and evidence introduced at trial, constitutes the permanent *record* of the trial court proceeding.

In the following case, the court was asked to grant a judgment notwithstanding the verdict.

C A S E 4.5

Judgment n.o.v.

Ferlito v. Johnson & Johnson Products, Inc.

771 F.Supp. 196,
Web 1991 U.S. Dist. Lexis 11747
United States District Court for the Eastern District of Michigan

❝*Plaintiffs' showing that the product may be used for decorative purposes failed to demonstrate the foreseeability of an adult male encapsulating himself from head to toe in cotton batting and then lighting up a cigarette.*❞

—Judge Paul V. Gadola

Facts

Susan and Frank Ferlito were invited to a Halloween party. They decided to attend as "Little Bo Peep" (Mrs. Ferlito) and her little sheep (Mr. Ferlito). Mrs. Ferlito constructed a lamb costume for her husband by gluing cotton batting manufactured by Johnson & Johnson Products, Inc., to a suit of long underwear. She used the same cotton batting to fashion a headpiece, complete with ears. The costume covered Mr. Ferlito from his head to his ankles, except for his face and hands, which were blackened with paint. At the party, Mr. Ferlito attempted to light a cigarette with a butane lighter. The flame passed close to his left arm, and the cotton batting ignited. He suffered burns over one-third of his body. The Ferlitos sued Johnson & Johnson to recover damages, alleging that Johnson & Johnson failed to warn them of the ignitability of cotton batting. The jury returned a verdict for Mr. Ferlito in the amount of $555,000 and for Mrs. Ferlito in the amount of $70,000. Johnson & Johnson filed a motion for judgment notwithstanding the verdict (j.n.o.v.).

Issue

Should defendant Johnson & Johnson's motion for j.n.o.v. be granted?

Language of the Court

Both plaintiffs testified that they knew that cotton batting burns when it is exposed to flame. Susan Ferlito testified that the idea for the costume was hers alone. As described on the product's package, its intended uses are for cleansing, applying medications, and infant care. Plaintiffs' showing that the product may be used for decorative purposes failed to demonstrate the foreseeability of an adult male encapsulating himself from head to toe in cotton batting and then lighting up a cigarette.

If after reviewing the evidence the trial court is of the opinion that reasonable minds could not come to the result reached by the jury, then the motion for j.n.o.v. should be granted. In the instant action no reasonable jury could find that JJP's failure to warn of the flammability of cotton batting was a proximate cause of plaintiffs' injuries.

Decision

The trial court granted defendant Johnson & Johnson's motion for j.n.o.v. By doing so, the court vacated the verdict entered by the jury in favor of Mr. and Mrs. Ferlito. The Court of Appeals affirmed the grant of j.n.o.v.

Law & Ethics Questions

1. Should trial courts have the authority to enter a j.n.o.v., or should jury verdicts always be allowed to stand? Explain your answer.

2. **ETHICS** Did the Ferlitos act ethically in suing Johnson & Johnson in this case? Were they responsible for their own injuries?

3. What would have been the business implications had Johnson & Johnson been found liable?

Web Exercises

1. **WEB** For the complete opinion of this case, go to *www.prenhall.com/cheesemancases*.

2. **WEB** Visit the website of the U.S. District Court for the Eastern District of Michigan at *www.mied.uscourts.gov*.

3. **WEB** Visit the website of Johnson & Johnson, at *www.jnj.com*.

4. **WEB** Use *www.google.com* to find an article about j.n.o.v. Read it.

Appeal

In a civil case, either party can **appeal** the trial court's decision once a *final judgment* is entered. Only the defendant can appeal in a criminal case. The appeal is made to the appropriate appellate court. A *notice of appeal* must be filed within a prescribed time after judgment is entered (usually within 60 or 90 days).

The appealing party is called the **appellant**, or *petitioner*. The responding party is called the **appellee**, or the *respondent*. The appellant is often required to post a bond (e.g., one-and-one-half times the judgment) on appeal.

The parties may designate all or relevant portions of the trial record to be submitted to the appellate court for review. The appellant's attorney may file an *opening brief* with the court that sets forth legal research and other information to support his or her contentions on appeal. The appellee can file a *responding brief*, answering the appellant's contentions. Appellate courts usually permit a brief oral argument at which each party's attorney is heard.

An appellate court reverses a lower court's decision if it finds an *error of law* in the record. An error of law occurs if the jury was improperly instructed by the trial court judge, prejudicial evidence was admitted at trial when it should have been excluded, prejudicial evidence was obtained through an unconstitutional search and seizure, and the like. An appellate court does not reverse a *finding of fact* unless such finding is unsupported by the evidence or is contradicted by the evidence.

In the following case, the U.S. Supreme Court reviewed the legality of an appeals court decision.

C A S E 4.6
Appeal

U.S. SUPREME COURT
Weisgram v. Marley Company
528 U.S. 440, 120 S.Ct. 1011, 145 L.Ed.2d 958,
Web 2000 U.S. Lexis 1011 (2000)
Supreme Court of the United States

> ❝*Courts of appeals should be constantly alert to the trial judge's firsthand knowledge of witnesses, testimony, and issues; in other words, appellate courts should give due consideration to the first-instance decision maker's "feel" for the overall case.*❞
>
> —Justice Ginsburg

Facts

Bonnie Weisgram died from carbon monoxide poisoning from a fire at her home. Her son, Chad Weisgram, brought a wrongful death tort action against Marley Company to recover damages, alleging that a defect in the electric baseboard heater manufactured by Marley had caused the fire and his mother's death. At trial, over Marley's objections, Weisgram introduced the evidence from three expert (i.e., paid-for) witnesses. The jury returned a verdict against Marley. Marley requested judgment as a matter of law, asserting that the expert testimony was unreliable and therefore inadmissible. The U.S. Court of Appeals agreed with Marley, finding that the expert witnesses' testimony was speculative and not scientifically sound. The U.S. Court of Appeals granted judgment as a matter of law for Marley and refused to grant Weisgram's motion for a new trial. Weisgram appealed to the U.S. Supreme Court.

Issue

Can an appellate court enter judgment as a matter of law against a jury-verdict winner if it determines on appeal that evidence was erroneously admitted at trial and concludes that the other properly admitted evidence is not sufficient to constitute a submissible case?

Language of the U.S. Supreme Court

Our decision is guided by Federal Rule of Civil Procedure 50, which governs the entry of judgment as a matter of law. Courts of appeals should be constantly alert to the trial judge's first-hand knowledge of witnesses, testimony, and issues; in other words, appellate courts should give due consideration to the first-instance decision maker's "feel" for the overall case. But the court of appeals has authority to render the final decision. If, in the particular case, the appellate tribunal determines that the district court is better positioned to decide whether a new

trial, rather than judgment for defendant, should be ordered, the court of appeals should return the case to the trial court for such an assessment. But if, as in the instant case, the court of appeals concludes that further proceedings are unwarranted because the loser on appeal has had a full and fair opportunity to present the case, including arguments for a new trial, the appellate court may appropriately instruct the district court to enter judgment against the jury-verdict winner.

Decision

The U.S. Supreme Court held that an appellate court may enter judgment as a matter of law against a jury-verdict winner if it determines that evidence was erroneously admitted at trial and that other properly admitted evidence is not sufficient to remand the case for a new trial.

Law & Ethics Questions

1. Define *expert witness*. Is the testimony of expert witnesses important at many types of trials? Explain.
2. **ETHICS** Do you think an expert witness is totally objective? Why or why not?
3. What implications does the Supreme Court's opinion have for business? Explain.

Web Exercises

1. **WEB** For the complete opinion of this case, go to *www.prenhall.com/cheesemancases*.
2. **WEB** Visit the website of the U.S. Supreme Court, at *www.supremecourtus.gov*, and try to find documents that relate to this case.
3. **WEB** Use *www.google.com* to find an article that discusses the recent appeal of a case to the U.S. Supreme Court. Read it.

INTERNATIONAL LAW
Japan's Legal System

Japan nurtures the attitude that confrontation should be avoided. In Japan, a country with about half the population of the United States, there are only one-fiftieth the number of lawyers as in the United States. In Japan, no class actions or contingency fee arrangements are allowed. Plaintiffs must pay their lawyers a front fee of up to 8 percent of the damages sought, plus a nonrefundable filing fee to the court of one-half of 1 percent of the damages sought. No discovery is permitted. Even if the plaintiff wins the lawsuit, damage awards are low. Most legal disputes in Japan are settled or decided by private arbitrators.

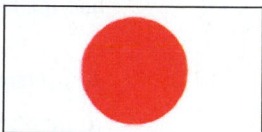

Kyoto, Japan
Many other countries are not as litigious as the United States.

Alternative Dispute Resolution

The use of the court system to resolve business and other disputes can take years and cost thousands or even millions of dollars in legal fees and expenses. In commercial litigation, the normal business operations of the parties are often disrupted. To avoid or lessen these problems, businesses are increasingly turning to methods of **alternative dispute resolution (ADR)** and other aids to resolving disputes. The most common form of ADR is *arbitration*. Other forms of ADR are *negotiation, arbitration, mediation, conciliation, minitrial, fact-finding*, and using a *judicial referee*.

Negotiation

The simplest form of alternative dispute resolution is engaging in negotiations between the parties to try to settle a dispute. Negotiation is a procedure whereby the parties to a dispute engage in negotiations to try to reach a voluntary settlement of their dispute. Negotiation may take place either before a lawsuit is filed, after a lawsuit is filed, or before other forms of alternative dispute resolution are used.

In a negotiation, the parties, who often are represented by attorneys, negotiate with each other to try to reach an agreeable solution to their dispute. During negotiation proceedings, the parties usually make offers and counteroffers to one another. The parties or their attorneys also may provide information to the other side to assist the other side in reaching an amicable settlement.

Many courts require that the parties to a lawsuit engage in settlement discussions prior to trial to try to negotiate a settlement of the case. The judge must be assured that a settlement of the case is not possible before he or she permits the case to go to trial. Judges often convince the parties to engage in further negotiations if the judge determines that the parties are not too far apart in the negotiation of a settlement.

If a settlement of a dispute is reached through negotiation, a settlement agreement is drafted that contains the terms of the agreement. The parties to a dispute voluntarily enter into a **settlement agreement** to settle the dispute. Each side must sign the settlement agreement for it to be effective. The settlement agreement is usually submitted to the court, and the case is dismissed based on the execution of the settlement agreement.

Arbitration

In **arbitration**, the parties choose an impartial third party to hear and decide the dispute. This neutral party is called the **arbitrator**. Arbitrators are usually members of the American Arbitration Association (AAA) or another arbitration association. Labor union agreements, franchise agreements, leases, and other commercial contracts often contain **arbitration clauses** that require disputes arising out of the contract to be submitted to arbitration. If there is no arbitration clause, the parties can enter into a **submission agreement** whereby they agree to submit a dispute to arbitration after the dispute arises.

Congress enacted the **Federal Arbitration Act (FAA)** to promote the arbitration of disputes.[2] About half of the states have adopted the **Uniform Arbitration Act**. This act promotes the arbitration of disputes at the state level. Many federal and state courts have instituted programs to refer legal disputes to arbitration or another form of ADR.

LANDMARK LAW
Federal Arbitration Act

> ❝ *By agreeing to arbitrate a statutory claim, a party does not forgo the substantive rights afforded by the statute, it only submits to their resolution in an arbitral, rather than a judicial, forum.* ❞
>
> —Justice White

The Federal Arbitration Act (FAA) was originally enacted in 1925 to reverse the long-standing judicial hostility to arbitration agreements that had existed at English common law and had been adopted by American courts. The act provides that arbitration agreements involving commerce are valid, irrevocable, and enforceable contracts, unless some grounds exist at law or equity (e.g., fraud, duress) to revoke them. The FAA permits one party to obtain a court order to compel arbitration if the other party has failed, neglected, or refused to comply with an arbitration agreement.

Since the FAA's enactment, the courts have wrestled with the problem of which types of disputes should be arbitrated. Breach of contract cases, tort claims, and such are clearly candidates for arbitration if there is a valid arbitration agreement. In addition, the U.S. Supreme Court has enforced arbitration agreements that call for the resolution of disputes arising under federal statutes. The Supreme Court has stated, "By agreeing to arbitrate a statutory claim, a party does not forgo the substantive rights afforded by the statute, it only submits to their resolution in an arbitral, rather than a judicial, forum."[3]

ARBITRATION PROVIDERS ADR services are usually provided by private organizations or individuals who qualify to hear and decide certain disputes.

Example The American Arbitration Association (AAA) is the largest private provider of ADR services. The AAA employs persons who are qualified in special areas of the law to provide mediation and arbitration services in those areas. These persons are called *neutrals*. For example, the AAA has a special group of neutrals that can hear and decide contract disputes involving employment contracts, construction contracts, and other commercial contract or business disputes. Other arbitration and mediation associations are located throughout the United States and the world.

Web Exercises

1. **WEB** Visit the website of the American Arbitration Association (AAA), at *www.adr.org*.
2. **WEB** Use *www.google.com* to find an arbitration and mediation service in your area.

ARBITRATION PROCEDURE An arbitration agreement often describes the specific procedures that must be followed for a case to proceed to and through arbitration. If one party seeks to enforce an arbitration clause, that party must give notice to the other party. The parties then select an arbitration association or arbitrator, as provided in the agreement. The parties usually agree on the date, time, and place of the arbitration. This can be at the arbitrator's office, at a law office, or at any other agreed-upon location.

At the arbitration, the parties can call witnesses to give testimony and introduce evidence to support their case and refute the other side's case. Rules similar to those followed by federal courts are usually adhered to at the arbitration. Often, each party pays a filing fee and other fees for the arbitration. Sometimes the agreement provides that one party pays all the costs of the arbitration. Arbitrators are paid by the hour or day or using another agreed-upon method of compensation.

DECISION AND AWARD After the hearing is complete, the arbitrator reaches a decision and issues an award. The parties often agree in advance to be bound by an arbitrator's decision and remedy. This is called *binding arbitration*. In this situation, the decision and award of the arbitrator cannot be appealed to the courts. If the arbitration is not binding, the decision and award of the arbitrator can be appealed to the courts. This is called *nonbinding arbitration*. Courts usually give great deference to an arbitrator's decision and award.

If an arbitrator has rendered a decision and an award but a party refuses to abide by the arbitrator's decision, the other party may file an action in court to have the arbitrator's decision enforced.

Example Assume that there has been a contract dispute between NorthWest Corporation and SouthEast Corporation that goes to binding arbitration. The arbitrator issues a decision that awards SouthEast Corporation $5 million against NorthWest Corporation. If NorthWest Corporation fails to pay the award, SouthEast Corporation can file an action in court to have the award enforced by the court.

Mediation

Mediation is a form of negotiation in which a neutral third party assists the disputing parties in reaching a settlement of their dispute. The neutral third party is called a **mediator**. The mediator is usually a person who is an expert in the area of the dispute or a lawyer or retired judge. The mediator is selected by the parties as provided in their agreement, or as otherwise selected by the parties.

Unlike an arbitrator, a mediator does not make a decision or an award. A mediator's role is to assist the parties in reaching a settlement. The mediator usually acts as an intermediary between the parties. In many cases, the mediator meets with the two parties at an agreed-upon location, often the mediator's office or the office of one of the parties. The mediator then meets with each party, usually separately, to discuss its side of the case.

After discussing the facts of the case with both sides, the mediator encourages settlement of the dispute and transmits settlement offers from one side to the other. In doing so, the mediator points out the strengths and weaknesses of each party's case and gives his or her opinion to each side about why they should decrease or increase their settlement offers. The mediator's job is to facilitate settlement of the case.

The mediator gives his or her opinion to the parties as to what he or she believes to be a reasonable settlement of the case and usually proposes settlement of the dispute. The parties are free to accept or reject such proposal. If the parties agree to a settlement, a settlement agreement is drafted that expresses their agreement. Execution of the settlement agreement ends the dispute. The parties, of course, must perform their duties under the settlement agreement. If an agreement is not reached, the parties may proceed to a judicial resolution of their case.

Conciliation

Conciliation is another form of alternative dispute resolution. In conciliation, a **conciliator** helps the parties try to reach a resolution of their dispute. Conciliation is often used when the parties refuse to face each other in an adversarial setting. The conciliator schedules meetings and appointments during which information can be transferred to the parties. A conciliator usually carries offers and counteroffers for a settlement back and forth between the disputing parties. A conciliator cannot make a decision or an award.

Although the role of a conciliator is not to propose a settlement of the case, many often do. In many cases, conciliators are neutral third parties, although in some circumstances, the parties may select an interested third party to act as the conciliator. If the parties reach a settlement of their dispute through the use of conciliation, a settlement agreement is drafted and executed by the parties.

Minitrial

A **minitrial** is a voluntary private proceeding in which lawyers for each side present a shortened version of their case to the representatives of both sides. The representatives of each side who attend the minitrial have the authority to settle the dispute. In many cases, the parties also hire a neutral third party, often someone who is an expert in the field concerning the disputed matter or a legal expert, who presides over the minitrial. After hearing the case, the neutral third party often is called upon to render an opinion as to how the court would most likely decide the case.

During a minitrial, the parties get to see the strengths and weaknesses of their own position and that of the opposing side. Once the strengths and weaknesses of both sides are exposed, the parties to a minitrial often settle the case. The parties also often settle a minitrial based on the opinion rendered by the neutral third party. If the parties settle their dispute after a minitrial, they enter into a settlement agreement setting forth their agreement.

Minitrials serve a useful purpose in that they act as a substitute for a real trial, but they are much briefer and not as complex and expensive to prepare for. Because a minitrial exposes the strengths and weaknesses of both sides' cases, the parties usually are more realistic regarding their own positions and the merits of settling the case prior to an expensive, and often risky, trial.

Fact-Finding

In some situations, called **fact-finding**, the parties to a dispute employ a neutral third party to act as a fact-finder to investigate the dispute. The fact-finder is authorized to investigate the dispute, gather evidence, prepare demonstrative evidence, and prepare reports of his or her findings.

A fact-finder is not authorized to make a decision or an award. In some cases, a fact-finder recommends settlement of the case. The fact-finder presents the evidence and findings to the parties, who then may use the information in negotiating a settlement if they wish.

Judicial Referee

If the parties agree, the court may appoint a **judicial referee** to conduct a private trial and render a judgment. Referees, who are often retired judges, have most of the powers of trial judges, and their decisions stand as judgments of the court. The parties usually reserve their right to appeal.

In the following case, the U.S. Supreme Court applied alternative dispute resolution.

C A S E **4.7**
Arbitration

U.S. SUPREME COURT

Circuit City Stores, Inc. v. Adams

532 U.S. 105, 121 S.Ct. 1302, 149 L.Ed.2d 234,
Web 2001 U.S. Lexis 2459 (2001)
Supreme Court of the United States

> ❝*Congress enacted the Federal Arbitration Act (FAA) in 1925. The FAA was a response to hostility of American courts to the enforcement of arbitration agreements.*❞

—Justice Kennedy

Facts

Saint Clair Adams was hired as a sales counselor by Circuit City Stores, Inc., a national retailer of consumer electronics. Adams signed an employment contract that included the following arbitration clause:

I agree that I will settle any and all previously unasserted claims, disputes or controversies arising out of or relating to my application or candidacy for employment, employment and/or cessation of employment with Circuit City, exclusively by final and binding arbitration before a neutral Arbitrator. By way of example only, such claims include claims under federal, state, and local statutory or common law, such as the Age Discrimination in Employment Act, Title VII of the Civil Rights Act of 1964, the Americans with Disabilities Act, the law of contract and the law of tort.

Two years later, Adams filed an employment discrimination lawsuit against Circuit City in court. Circuit City sought to enjoin the court proceeding and to compel arbitration, pursuant to the FAA. The U.S. District Court granted Circuit City's request. The U.S. Court of Appeals reversed, holding that employment contracts are not subject to arbitration. Adams appealed to the U.S. Supreme Court.

Issue

Are employment contracts subject to arbitration if the parties have entered into a valid arbitration agreement?

Language of the U.S. Supreme Court

Congress enacted the Federal Arbitration Act (FAA) in 1925. The FAA was a response to hostility of American courts to the enforcement of arbitration agreements. To give effect to this purpose, the FAA compels judicial enforcement of a wide range of written arbitration agreements. The FAA's coverage provision, Section 2, provides that "a written provision in any contract evidencing a transaction involving commerce to settle by arbitration a controversy thereafter arising out of such contract or transaction, or the refusal to perform the whole or any part thereof, shall be valid, irrevocable, and enforceable, save upon such grounds as exist at law or in equity for the revocation of any contract."

Decision

The U.S. Supreme Court held that employment contracts, including the one in this case between Circuit City and Adams, are subject to arbitration if a valid arbitration agreement has been executed. The Supreme Court reversed the decision of the Court of Appeals and remanded the case for further proceedings.

Law & Ethics Questions

1. What is arbitration? What does the Federal Arbitration Act provide?
2. **ETHICS** Is it ethical for employers to include arbitration clauses in employment contracts? Or should employers face judicial litigation? Explain.
3. **ETHICS** Who do you think benefits most from arbitration clauses in employment contracts: employers or employees? Why?

Web Exercises

1. **WEB** For the complete opinion of this case, go to *www.prenhall.com/cheesemancases*.
2. **WEB** Visit the website of the U.S. Supreme Court, at *www.supremecourtus.gov*, and try to find documents that relate to this case.
3. **WEB** Visit the website of Circuit City Stores, Inc., at *www.circuitcity.com*.
4. **WEB** Use *www.google.com* to find an article that discusses the use of arbitration clauses in contracts. Read it.

INTERNET AND TECHNOLOGY
Online Dispute Resolution

Online arbitration services are now offered. Most of these services allow a party to a dispute to register the dispute with the service and then notify the other party by e-mail of the registration of the dispute. Most online arbitration requires the registering party to submit an amount that the party is willing to accept or pay to the other party in the online arbitration. The other party is afforded the opportunity to accept the offer. If that party accepts the offer, a settlement is reached. The other party, however, may return a counteroffer. The process continues until a settlement is reached or one or both of the parties remove themselves from the online ADR process.

Also, several websites offer **online meditation** services. In an online mediation, the parties sit before their computers and sign onto the website. Two chat rooms are assigned to each party. One chat room is used for private conversations with the online mediator, and the other chat room is for conversations with both parties and the mediator.

Online arbitration and mediation services charge fees for their services. The fees are reasonable. In an online arbitration or mediation, a settlement can be reached rather quickly, without lawyers' fees and court costs. The parties act through an objective online process rather than meeting face-to-face or negotiating over the telephone, either of which could conclude in verbal arguments.

Web Exercises

1. **WEB** Use *www.google.com* to find a website that offers online arbitration and mediation services.

2. **WEB** Visit the website of the American Arbitration Association (AAA), at *www.adr.org*. Does the AAA provide online dispute resolution?

Administrative Law

Administrative agencies are created by federal, state, and local governments. They range from large, complex federal agencies, such as the federal Department of Health and Human Services, to local zoning boards. At the federal government level, the legislative branch (Congress) and the executive branch (the president) have created more than 100 administrative agencies. Thousands of other administrative agencies have been created by state and local governments.

When Congress enacts a statute, it often creates an administrative agency to administer and enforce the statute (see Exhibit 4.2). When Congress enacts some statutes, it authorizes an existing administrative agency to administer and enforce the new statute. For example, when Congress enacted the Securities Act of 1933 and the Securities Exchange Act of 1934,

EXHIBIT 4.2

Administrative Agency

Legislature
(Enacts a
statue)

Legislature enacts a
statute and creates an
administrative agency to
administer and enforce
the statute.

ADMINISTRATIVE
AGENCY
(Administer
the statute)

it created the Securities and Exchange Commission (SEC), a federal administrative agency, to administer and enforce those statutes.

Federal Administrative Agencies

Federal administrative agencies can be created by either the legislative or the executive branch of the federal government.

Congress has established many federal administrative agencies. These agencies have broad regulatory powers over key areas of the national economy. Examples are the Securities and Exchange Commission (SEC), which regulates the issuance and trading in securities, and the Commodity Futures Trading Commission (CFTC), which regulates trading in commodities futures contracts.

Other federal administrative agencies are created by the president of the United States to operate the federal government. These include the U.S. Department of Justice, the Labor Department, and the Commerce Department.

State Administrative Agencies

All states have created administrative agencies to enforce and interpret state law. For example, most states have a corporations department to enforce state corporations law, a banking department to regulate the operation of banks, fish and game departments, and workers' compensation boards. **State administrative agencies** have a profound effect on business. Local governments and municipalities create administrative agencies, such as zoning commissions, to administer local law.

Baldy Mountain, Sun Valley, Idaho

Federal and state governments regulate the logging, mineral extraction, and recreational uses of government-owned land.

Government Regulation

Many administrative agencies, and the laws they enforce, regulate businesses and industries collectively.

Example The National Labor Relations Board (NLRB) is empowered to regulate the formation and operation of labor unions in most industries, the Occupational Health and Safety Administration (OSHA) is authorized to formulate and enact safety and health standards for the workplace, and the Consumer Product Safety Commission (CPSC) is empowered to establish mandatory safety standards for products sold in this country.

Some administrative agencies, and the laws they enforce, are created to regulate specific industries.

Example The Federal Communications Commission (FCC) regulates the operation of television and radio stations, the Federal Aviation Administration (FAA) regulates

> The great can protect themselves, but the poor and humble require the arm and shield of the law.
>
> Andrew Jackson

commercial airlines, and the Office of the Comptroller of the Currency (OCC) regulates national banks.

Administrative Law

Administrative law is a combination of substantive and procedural law. Substantive law is the law that has been created that the administrative agency enforces.

Example   The federal Environmental Protection Agency (EPA) enforces laws that protect the environment. The EPA must follow certain procedural laws (e.g., notice, hearing) in enforcing these laws.

Administrative Procedure Act

In 1946, Congress enacted the **Administrative Procedure Act (APA)**.[4] This act establishes certain administrative procedures that federal administrative agencies must follow in conducting their affairs. The APA establishes notice and hearing requirements, rules for conducting agency adjudicative actions, and procedures for rule making. Most states have enacted administrative procedural acts that govern state administrative agencies.

Administrative Law Judge

Administrative law judges (ALJs) preside over administrative proceedings. They decide questions of law and fact concerning a case. There is no jury. An ALJ is an employee of the administrative agency. Both the administrative agency and the respondent may be represented by counsel. Witnesses may be examined and cross-examined, evidence may be introduced, objections may be made, and such.

An ALJ's decision is issued in the form of an **order**. The order must state the reasons for the ALJ's decision. The order becomes final if it is not appealed. An appeal consists of a review by the agency. Further appeal can be made to the appropriate federal court (in federal agency actions) or state court (in state agency actions).

Delegation of Powers

When an administrative agency is created, it is delegated certain powers. The agency has only the legislative, judicial, and executive powers that are delegated to it. This is called the **delegation doctrine**. Thus, an agency can adopt a rule or regulation (a legislative function), prosecute a violation of the statute or rule (an executive function), and adjudicate the dispute (a judicial function). The courts have upheld this combined power of administrative agencies as being constitutional. If an administrative agency acts outside the scope of its delegated powers, it is an unconstitutional act.

Administrative agencies have been delegated legislative powers that consist of substantive rule making, interpretative rule making, issue of statements of policy, and granting of licenses. Administrative agencies have also been delegated certain executive powers and judicial powers. These powers are discussed in the following paragraphs.

RULE MAKING   Many federal statutes expressly authorize an administrative agency to issue **substantive rules**. A substantive regulation is much like a statute: It has the force of law and must be adhered to by covered persons and businesses. Violators may be held civilly or criminally liable, depending on the rule. All substantive rules are subject to judicial review.

Administrative agencies can issue **interpretive rules** that interpret existing statutory language. Such rules do not establish new laws. Neither public notice nor public participation is required. Administrative agencies may issue **statements of policy**. Such a statement announces a proposed course of action that an agency intends to follow in the future. Statements of policy do not have the force of law. Again, public notice and participation are not required.

LICENSING POWER   Statutes often require the issuance of a government **license** before a person can enter certain types of industries (e.g., the operation of banks, television and radio stations, and commercial airlines) or professions (e.g., doctors, lawyers, dentists, certified public accountants, and contractors). Most administrative agencies are granted the power to determine whether to grant licenses to applicants.

Applicants must usually submit detailed applications to the appropriate administrative agency. In addition, the agency usually accepts written comments from interested parties and holds hearings on the matter. Courts generally defer to the expertise of administrative agencies in licensing matters.

JUDICIAL POWER Many administrative agencies have the judicial authority to adjudicate cases through an administrative proceeding. Such a proceeding is initiated when an agency serves a complaint on a party the agency believes has violated a statute or an administrative rule or order.

In adjudicating cases, an administrative agency must comply with the Due Process Clause of the U.S. Constitution (and state constitution, where applicable). **Procedural due process** requires the respondent to be given (1) proper and timely notice of the allegations or charges against him or her and (2) an opportunity to present evidence on the matter.

EXECUTIVE POWER Administrative agencies are usually granted **executive powers**, such as the power to investigate and prosecute possible violations of statutes, administrative rules, and administrative orders. To perform these functions successfully, an agency must often obtain information from the persons and businesses under investigation as well as from other sources. If the required information is not supplied voluntarily, the agency may issue an administrative subpoena to search the business premises; this is called an **administrative search**.

An administrative agency can issue an **administrative subpoena** to a business or person subject to its jurisdiction. The subpoena directs the party to disclose the requested information to the administrative agency. The administrative agency can seek judicial enforcement of the subpoena if the party does not comply with the subpoena.

CONCEPT SUMMARY

Powers of Administrative Agencies

POWER	DESCRIPTION OF POWER
1. Legislative Power	
A. Substantive rule making	To adopt rules that advance the purpose of the statutes that the agency is empowered to enforce. These rules have the force of law. Public notice and participation are required.
B. Interpretive rule making	To adopt rules that interpret statutory language. These rules do not establish new laws. Neither public notice nor participation is required.
C. Statements of policy	To announce a proposed course of action the agency plans to take in the future. These statements do not have the force of law. Public participation and notice are not required.
D. Licensing	To grant licenses to applicants (e.g., television station licenses, bank charters) and to suspend or revoke licenses.
2. Judicial Power	The power to adjudicate cases through an administrative proceeding. This includes the power to issue a complaint, hold a hearing by an administrative law judge (ALJ), and issue an order deciding the case and assessing remedies.
3. Executive Power	The power to prosecute violations of statutes and administrative rules and orders. This includes the power to investigate suspected violations, issue administrative subpoenas, and conduct administrative searches.

CONTEMPORARY ENVIRONMENT
Federal Administrative Agencies

With so many different federal agencies operating within the United States, it can sometimes be confusing who's who and who oversees what. It's important to be familiar with the following federal agencies that operate in the business sector:

- **Federal Trade Commission (FTC).** The FTC focuses on consumer protection and deals with anticompetitive business practices. Things such as consumer fraud, false advertising, and monopolistic practices all fall under the authority of the FTC.

Web Exercise

1. **WEB** Visit the FTC's website, at *www.ftc.gov*.

- **Securities and Exchange Commission (SEC).** The SEC regulates federal securities laws and the stock market. All public companies as well as their investors are subject to SEC rules and regulations. Things such as accounting fraud and insider trading fall under the authority of the SEC.

Web Exercise

1. **WEB** Visit the SEC's website, at *www.sec.gov*.

- **Equal Employment Opportunity Commission (EEOC).** The EEOC is responsible for preventing and ending employment discrimination. The EEOC is the agency charged with making sure businesses and organizations follow federal mandates such as the Civil Rights Act, the Age Discrimination in Employment Act, and the Americans with Disabilities Act.

Web Exercise

1. **WEB** Visit the EEOC's website, at *www.eeoc.gov*.

- **Consumer Product Safety Commission (CPSC).** The CPSC is responsible for protecting people against unreasonable risk of injuries associated with consumer products. The CPSC has the authority to regulate the manufacture and sale of tens of thousands of different consumer products, from toys to swimming pools.

Web Exercise

1. **WEB** Visit the CPSC's website, at *www.cpsc.gov*.

- **Occupational Safety and Health Administration (OSHA).** OSHA is a federal agency operating under the U.S. Department of Labor that is charged with preventing work-related injuries, illnesses, and deaths by issuing and enforcing standards for workplace health and safety.

Web Exercise

1. **WEB** Visit OSHA's website, at *www.osha.gov*.

- **Federal Communications Commission (FCC).** The FCC is charged with regulating all interstate and international communications by radio, television, wire, satellite, and cable. Its main powers are issuing fines and revoking licenses. Some violations include censorship and acts deemed indecent.

Web Exercise

1. **WEB** Visit the FCC's website, at *www.fcc.gov*.

- **Small Business Administration (SBA).** The SBA is an independent federal agency that provides a wide variety of support to small businesses, including small business loans and grants, business and legal counseling services, and help with issues such as marketing, networking, and creation of business plans.

Web Exercise

1. **WEB** Visit the SBA's website, at *www.sba.gov*.

- **Internal Revenue Service (IRS).** The IRS is a bureau of the Department of the Treasury that is charged with collecting taxes and enforcing the internal revenue laws. The IRS oversees the taxes for individuals, businesses, and nonprofit organizations.

Web Exercise

1. **WEB** Visit the IRS's website, at *www.irs.gov*.

- **U.S. Department of Justice, Antitrust Division (DOJ).** The Antitrust Division of the DOJ is in charge of enforcing business antitrust laws, similar to the job of the FTC. The difference is that the FTC is responsible only for the civil enforcement of antitrust laws, whereas the Antitrust Division of the DOJ has the power to bring both civil and criminal actions against a business.

Web Exercise

1. **WEB** Visit the Antitrust Division's website, at *www.usdoj.gov/atr*.

- **Office of Special Counsel (OSC).** The OSC is an independent federal investigative prosecutorial agency. Its basic authority comes from three federal statutes: the Civil Service Reform Act, the Whistleblower Protection Act, and the Hatch Act. The primary mission of the OSC is to protect government and business whistleblowers from revenge or retaliation tactics.

Web Exercise

1. **WEB** Visit the OSC's website, at *www.osc.gov*.

Judicial Review of Administrative Actions

Many federal statutes expressly provide for judicial review of administrative agency actions. Where an enabling statute does not provide for review, the Administrative Procedure Act (APA) authorizes judicial review of federal administrative agency actions.[5] The party appealing the decision of an administrative agency is called the **petitioner**.

Decisions of federal administrative agencies are appealed to the appropriate federal court. Decisions of state administrative agencies may be appealed to the proper state court.

Kathmandu, Nepal

Many other countries do not have administrative law systems as extensive as that of the United States.

Chapter Summary

Pretrial Litigation Process, p. 81

Pleadings

Pleadings are paperwork that initiates and responds to a lawsuit. Pleadings include:

1. *Complaint.* The complaint is filed by the plaintiff with the court and served with a *summons* on the defendant. It sets forth the basis of the lawsuit.
2. *Answer.* The answer is filed by the defendant with the court and served on the plaintiff. It usually denies most allegations of the complaint.
3. *Cross-complaint.* The cross-complaint is filed and served by the defendant if he or she countersues the plaintiff. The defendant is the *cross-complainant*, and the plaintiff is the *cross-defendant*. The cross-defendant must file and serve a *reply* (answer).
4. *Intervention.* A person who has an interest in a lawsuit may intervene and become a party to the lawsuit.
5. *Consolidation.* A court may consolidate separate cases against the same defendant arising from the same incident into one case if doing so would not cause prejudice to the parties.

Statute of Limitations

Statute of limitations establishes the period during which a plaintiff must bring a lawsuit against a defendant.

Discovery

Discovery is the pretrial litigation process for discovering facts of the case from the other parties and witnesses. Discovery consists of:

1. *Depositions.* Depositions are oral testimony given by a *deponent*, either a party or witness. Depositions are transcribed.

2. *Interrogatories.* These written questions are submitted by one party to the other party. They must be answered within a specified period of time.

3. *Production of documents.* A party to a lawsuit may obtain copies of all relevant documents from the other party.

4. *Physical and mental examination.* These examinations of a party are permitted upon order of the court where injuries are alleged that could be verified or disputed by such examination.

Dismissals and Pretrial Judgments, p. 88
Motion for Judgment on the Pleadings

A motion for judgment on the pleadings alleges that if all facts as pleaded are true, the moving party would win the lawsuit. No facts outside the pleadings may be considered.

Motion for Summary Judgment

A motion for summary judgment alleges that there are no factual disputes, so the judge may apply the law and decide the case without a jury. Evidence outside the pleadings may be considered (e.g., affidavits, documents, depositions).

Settlement Conference, p. 90

The settlement conference (also called the pretrial hearing) occurs prior to trial between the parties in front of the judge to facilitate the settlement of the case. If a settlement is not reached, the case proceeds to trial.

Trial, p. 91
Phases of a Trial

1. *Jury selection.* Jury selection occurs through a process called *voir dire.* Biased jurors are dismissed and replaced.

2. *Opening statements.* The parties' lawyers make opening statements, which are not evidence.

3. *The plaintiff 's case.* The plaintiff bears the burden of proof. The plaintiff calls witnesses and introduces evidence to try to prove his or her case.

4. *The defendant's case.* The defendant calls witnesses and introduces evidence to rebut the plaintiff's case and to prove affirmative defenses and cross-complaints.

5. *Rebuttal and rejoinder.* The plaintiff and defendant may call additional witnesses and introduce additional evidence.

6. *Closing arguments.* The parties' lawyers make closing arguments, which are not evidence.

7. *Jury instructions.* The judge reads instructions to the jury as to what law they are to apply to the case.

8. *Jury deliberation and verdict.* The jury retires to the jury room and deliberates until it reaches a *verdict.*

9. *Entry of judgment.* The judge may:
   a. Enter the verdict reached by the jury as the court's *judgment.*
   b. Grant a motion for *judgment n.o.v.* if the judge finds that the jury was biased. This means that the jury's verdict does not stand.
   c. Order *remittitur* (reduction) of any damages awarded if the judge finds the jury to have been biased or emotional.

Appeal, p. 93

Both parties in a civil suit and the defendant in a criminal trial may appeal the decision of the trial court. *Notice of appeal* must be filed within a specified period of time. The appeal must be made to the appropriate appellate court.

Alternative Dispute Resolution, p. 95

Alternative dispute resolution (ADR) is a *nonjudicial* means of solving legal disputes. ADR usually saves time and money compared to litigation.

Arbitration

In arbitration, an impartial third party, called an arbitrator, hears and decides a dispute. The arbitrator makes an award. The award is appealable to a court if the parties have not given up this right. Arbitration is designated by the parties pursuant to:

1. *Arbitration clause.* An agreement contained in a contract which stipulates that any dispute arising out of the contract will be arbitrated.
2. *Submission agreement.* An agreement to submit a dispute to arbitration after the dispute arises.

Mediation

In mediation, a neutral third party, called a *mediator*, assists the parties in trying to reach a settlement of their dispute. The mediator does not make an award.

Conciliation

In conciliation, an interested third party, called a *conciliator*, assists the parties in trying to reach a settlement of their dispute. The conciliator does not make an award.

Minitrial

A minitrial is a short session in which the lawyers for each side present their cases to representatives of each party who have the authority to settle the dispute.

Fact-finding

The parties may hire a neutral third person, called a *fact-finder*, to investigate a dispute and report his or her findings to the adversaries.

Judicial Referee

With consent of the parties, the court may appoint a judicial referee (usually a retired judge or lawyer) to conduct a private trial and render a judgment. The judgment stands as the judgment of the court and may be appealed to the appropriate appellate court.

Administrative Law, p. 100

Administrative Agencies

1. *Administrative agencies.* Administrative agencies are created by federal and state legislative and executive branches. They consist of professionals having an area of expertise in a certain area of commerce, who interpret and apply designated statutes.
2. *Administrative rules and regulations.* Administrative agencies are empowered to adopt rules and regulations that interpret and advance the laws they enforce.
3. *Administrative Procedure Act.* This act establishes procedures (i.e., notice, hearing) to be followed by federal agencies in conducting their affairs. States have enacted their own procedural acts to govern state agencies.

Test Review Terms and Concepts

Administrative agency   100
Administrative law   102
Administrative law judge
  (ALJs)   102
Administrative Procedure Act
  (APA)   102
Administrative search   103

Administrative subpoena   103
Alternative dispute resolution
  (ADR)   95
Answer   82
Appeal   93
Appellant   93
Appellee   93

Arbitration   96
Arbitration clause   96
Arbitrator   96
Burden of proof   91
Closing arguments   92
Complaint   82
Conciliation   98

Case Problems

4.1 Physical Examination: Robert Schlagenhauf worked as a bus driver for the Greyhound Corporation. One night, the bus he was driving rear-ended a tractor-trailer. Seven passengers on the bus who were injured sued Schlagenhauf and Greyhound for damages. The complaint alleged that Greyhound was negligent for allowing Schlagenhauf to drive a bus when it knew that his eyes and vision "were impaired and deficient." The plaintiffs petitioned the court to order Schlagenhauf to be medically examined concerning these allegations. Schlagenhauf objected to the examination. Who wins? *Schlagenhauf v. Holder*, 379 U.S. 104, 85 S.Ct. 234, 13 L.Ed.2d 152, **Web** 1964 U.S. Lexis 152 (Supreme Court of the United States)

4.2 Interrogatories: Cine Forty-Second Street Theatre Corporation operates a movie theater in New York City's Times Square area. Cine filed a lawsuit against Allied Artists Pictures Corporation, alleging that Allied Artists and local theater owners illegally attempted to prevent Cine from opening its theater, in violation of federal antitrust law. The suit also alleged that once Cine opened the theater, the defendants conspired with motion picture distributors to prevent Cine from exhibiting first-run, quality films. Attorneys for Allied Artists served a set of written questions concerning the lawsuit on Cine. Does Cine have to answer these questions? *Cine Forty-Second Street Theatre Corp. v. Allied Artists Pictures Corp.*, 602 F.2d 1062, **Web** 1979 U.S. App. Lexis 13586 (United States Court of Appeals for the Second Circuit)

4.3 Judgment n.o.v.: Mr. Simblest was driving a car that collided with a fire engine at an intersection in Burlington, Vermont. The accident occurred on a night on which a power blackout had left most of the state without lights. Mr. Simblest, who was injured in the accident, sued the driver of the fire truck for damages. During the trial, Simblest testified that when he entered the intersection, the traffic light was green in his favor. All the other witnesses testified that the traffic light had gone dark at least 10 minutes before the accident. Simblest testified that the accident was caused by the fire truck's failure to use any warning lights or sirens. Simblest's testimony was contradicted by four witnesses, who testified that the fire truck had used both its lights and sirens. The jury found that the driver of the fire truck had been negligent and rendered a verdict for Simblest. The defense made a motion for judgment n.o.v. Who wins? *Simblest v. Maynard*, 427 F.2d 1, **Web** 1970 U.S. App. Lexis 9265 (United States Court of Appeals for the Second Circuit)

4.4 Arbitration: AMF Incorporated and Brunswick Corporation both manufacture electric and automatic bowling center equipment. In 1983, the two companies became involved in a dispute over whether Brunswick had advertised certain automatic scoring devices in a false and deceptive manner. The two parties settled the dispute and signed an agreement that any future problems between them involving advertising claims would be submitted to the National Advertising Council for arbitration. Brunswick advertised a new product, Armor Plate 3000, a synthetic laminated material used to make bowling lanes. Armor Plate 3000 competed with wooden lanes produced by AMF. Brunswick's advertisements claimed that bowling centers could save up to $500 per lane per year in maintenance and repair costs if they switched to Armor Plate 3000 from wooden lanes. AMF disputed this claim and requested arbitration. Is the arbitration agreement enforceable? *AMF Incorporated v. Brunswick Corp.*, 621 F.Supp. 456, **Web** 1985 U.S. Dist. Lexis 14205 (United States District Court for the Eastern District of New York)

4.5 Administrative Procedure: The Federal Deposit Insurance Corporation (FDIC) insures the deposit accounts of banks up to $100,000. Federal law [12 U.S.C. Section 1818(g)] permits the FDIC to suspend from office any officer of a federally insured bank who is criminally indicted if that person's continued service poses a threat to the interest of the bank's depositors or threatens to impair public confidence in the bank. The statute entitles suspended bank officers to a hearing before the FDIC within 30 days of a written request and to a final decision within 60 days of the hearing. At the administrative hearing, the officer may submit written material or, at the discretion of the FDIC, oral testimony.

The FDIC suspended James E. Mallen, the president and director of Farmers State Bank in Kanawha, Iowa, upon his indictment for conspiracy to commit mail fraud and for making false statements in violation of federal law. The FDIC issued an order suspending Mallen as president and director. A hearing was scheduled to occur within 19 days after his written request. The FDIC did not permit oral testimony in this case. Mallen sued, alleging that the FDIC's refusal to allow oral testimony at the administrative hearing violated the Due Process Clause of the U.S. Constitution. Is Section 1818(g) constitutional? *Federal Deposit Insurance Corporation v. Mallen*, 486 U.S. 230, 108 S.Ct. 1780, 100 L.Ed.2d 265, **Web** 1988 U.S. Lexis 2477 (Supreme Court of the United States)

4.6 Rule Making: The Food and Drug Administration (FDA), a federal administrative agency, is charged with enforcing the Food, Drug, and Cosmetic Act. This statute mandates that the FDA limit the amount of "poisonous or deleterious substances" in food. Pursuant to this authority, the FDA established certain "action levels" of unavoidable contaminants, such as aflatoxins, in food. Food producers that sell products that are contaminated above the set action level are subject to enforcement proceedings initiated by the FDA. In announcing these action levels, the FDA did not comply with the notice and comment procedure required for the adoption of a substantive or legislative rule. The FDA argued that the "action levels" are merely interpretive rules or statements of policy that do not require notice and comment. The Community Nutrition Institute, a consortium of consumer

public interest groups, sued to require the FDA to follow the notice and comment procedure. Who wins? *Community Nutrition Institute v. Young*, 260 U.S. App. D.C. 294, 818 F.2d 943, **Web** 1987 U.S. App. Lexis 6385 (United States Court of Appeals for the District of Columbia Circuit)

4.7 Rule Making: The Federal Communications Commission (FCC) is a federal administrative agency that is empowered to enforce the Communications Act of 1934. This act, as amended, gives the FCC power to regulate broadcasting of radio and television. The act provides that "broadcasting shall not be deemed to common carrier." In *United States v. Midwest Video Corporation*, 406 U.S. 649, 92 S.Ct. 1860, 32 L.Ed.2d 390, **Web** 1972 U.S. Lexis 166 (1972), the U.S. Supreme Court held that the FCC also has the power to regulate cable television.

The FCC promulgated rules requiring cable television operators that have 3,500 or more subscribers to (1) develop a 20-channel capacity, (2) make 4 channels available for use by public, educational, local, governmental, and leased-access users (with 1 channel assigned to each), (3) make equipment available for those utilizing these public-access channels, and (4) limit the fees cable operators charge for their services. Do these rules exceed the statutory authority of the FCC? *Federal Communications Commission v. Midwest Video Corporation*, 440 U.S. 689, 99 S.Ct. 1435, 59 L.Ed.2d 692, **Web** 1979 U.S. Lexis 82 (Supreme Court of the United States)

4.8 Administrative Regulation: George Carlin, a satiric humorist, recorded a 12-minute monologue called "Filthy Words." He began by referring to his thoughts about "the words you couldn't say on the public airwaves" and then proceeded to list those words, repeating them over and over again in a variety of colloquialisms. At about 2 o'clock in the afternoon, a New York radio station owned by Pacifica Foundation (Pacifica) broadcast Carlin's "Filthy Words" monologue. A father who heard the broadcast while driving with his young son filed a complaint with the Federal Communications Commission (FCC), a federal administrative agency charged with regulating broadcasting. The Federal Communications Act forbids the use of "any obscene, indecent, or profane language by means of radio communications." Therefore, the FCC issued an order granting the complaint and informing Pacifica that the order would be considered in future licensing decisions involving Pacifica. Is the FCC regulation legal? *Federal Communications Commission v. Pacifica Foundation*, 438 U.S. 726, 98 S.Ct. 3026, 57 L.Ed.2d 1073, **Web** 1978 U.S. Lexis 135 (Supreme Court of the United States)

4.9 License: The Interstate Commerce Commission (ICC) is a federal administrative agency empowered to regulate motor carriers involved in interstate commerce. Trucking companies must apply to the ICC to obtain a license before they can offer trucking services on a route.

The Interstate Commerce Act empowers the ICC to grant an application for a license if it finds that (1) the applicant is fit, willing, and able to properly perform the service proposed and (2) the service proposed is or will be required by the present or future "public convenience or necessity."

Thirteen motor carriers applied to offer trucking services between points in the Southwest and Southeast. After reviewing the applications and extensive written evidence (including the testimony of more than 900 witnesses), the ICC granted licenses to three of the applicants. Arkansas-Best Freight System, Inc., a rejected applicant, brought an action seeking to annul the ICC's order. Should the ICC's grant of the license be overturned on appeal? *Browman Transportation, Inc. v. Arkansas-Best Freight System, Inc.*, 419 U.S. 281, 95 S.Ct. 438, 42 L.Ed.2d 447, **Web** 1974 U.S. Lexis 51 (Supreme Court of the United States)

Ethics Issues

4.10 Ethics: Dennis and Francis Burnham were married in 1976 in West Virginia. In 1977, the couple moved to New Jersey, where their two children were born. In July 1987, the Burnhams decided to separate. Mrs. Burnham, who intended to move to California, was to have custody of the children. Mr. Burnham agreed to file for divorce on grounds of irreconcilable differences. Mr. Burnham threatened to file for divorce in New Jersey on grounds of desertion. After unsuccessfully demanding that Mr. Burnham adhere to the prior agreement, Mrs. Burnham brought suit for divorce in California state court in early January 1988. In late January, Mr. Burnham visited California on a business trip. He then visited his children in the San Francisco Bay area, where his wife resided. He took the older child to San Francisco for the weekend. Upon returning the child to Mrs. Burnham's home, he was served with a California court summons and a copy of Mrs. Burnham's divorce petition. He then returned to New Jersey. Mr. Burnham made a special appearance in the California court and moved to quash the service of process. Did Mr. Burnham act ethically in trying to quash the service of process? Did Mrs. Burnham act ethically in having Mr. Burnham served on his visit to California? Is the service of process good? *Burnham v. Superior Court of California*, 495 U.S. 604, 110 S.Ct. 2105, 109 L.Ed.2d 631, **Web** 1990 U.S. Lexis 2700 (Supreme Court of the United States)

4.11 Ethics: The Federal Mine Safety and Health Act requires the Secretary of Labor to develop detailed mandatory health and safety standards to govern the operation of the nation's mines. The act provides that federal mine inspectors are to inspect underground mines at least four times a year and surface mines at least twice a year to ensure compliance with these standards and to make inspections to determine whether previously discovered violations have been corrected. The act also grants mine inspectors "a right of entry to, upon or through any coal or other mine" and states that "no advance notice of an inspection shall be provided to any person."

A federal mine inspector attempted to inspect quarries owned by Waukesha Lime and Stone Company (Waukesha) to determine whether all 25 safety and health violations uncovered during a prior inspection had been corrected. Douglas Dewey, Waukesha's president, refused to allow the inspector to inspect the premises without first obtaining a search warrant. Are the warrantless searches of stone quarries authorized by the Mine Safety and Health Act constitutional? Did Dewey act ethically in refusing to allow the inspections? *Donovan, Secretary of Labor v. Dewey*, 452 U.S. 594, 101 S.Ct. 2534, 69 L.Ed.2d 262, **Web** 1980 U.S. Lexis 58 (Supreme Court of the United States)

4.12 Ethics: A statute of the state of Wisconsin forbids the practice of medicine without a license granted by the Examining Board (Board), a state administrative agency composed of practicing physicians. The statute specifically prohibits certain acts of professional misconduct. Board may investigate alleged violations, issue charges against a licensee, hold hearings, and rule on the matter. Board also has the authority to warn and reprimand violators, suspend or revoke their licenses, and institute criminal actions.

Dr. Larkin was a physician licensed to practice medicine in the state of Wisconsin. Board sent a notice to Larkin that it would hold a hearing to determine whether he had engaged in prohibited acts. Larkin was represented by counsel at the hearing. Evidence was introduced, and witnesses gave testimony at the hearing. Board found Larkin guilty and temporarily suspended his license to practice medicine. Larkin then filed suit, alleging that it was an unconstitutional violation of due process to permit an administrative agency to adjudicate a charge that it had investigated and brought. Is there a violation of due process? Did Larkin act ethically in challenging the authority of the administrative agency? *Withrow v. Larkin*, 421 U.S. 35, 95 S.Ct. 1456, 43 L.Ed.2d 712, **Web** 1975 U.S. Lexis 56 (Supreme Court of the United States)

IRAC Writing Assignment

Read Case A-4 in Appendix A [**_Gnazzo v. G.D. Searle & Co._**]. Read the case and use the IRAC method to prepare a written analysis of the case.

Endnotes

1. There is no right to a jury trial for actions in equity (e.g., injunction-specific performance).
2. 9 U.S.C. Section 1 et seq.
3. _Gilmer v. Interstate/Johnson Lane Corporation_, 500 U.S. 20, 111 S.Ct. 1647, 114 L.Ed.2d 26, **Web** 1991 U.S. Lexis 2529 (Supreme Court of the United States).
4. 5 U.S.C. Section 551–706.
5. 5 U.S.C. Section 702.

CHAPTER 5

Torts and Strict Liability

> **"**Negligence is not actionable unless it involves the invasion of a legally protected interest, the violation of a right. Proof of negligence in the air, so to speak, will not do. **"**
>
> —JUSTICE CARDOZO
>
> Palsgraf v. Long Island Railroad Co., 248 N.Y. 339, 162 N.E. 99, 1928 N.Y. Lexis 1269 (1928)

CHAPTER OBJECTIVES

After studying this chapter, you should be able to:

1. List and describe intentional torts against persons and against property.
2. List and explain the elements necessary to prove negligence.
3. Describe the business torts of disparagement and fraud.
4. Describe and apply the doctrine of strict liability.
5. Describe negligent and intentional infliction of emotional distress.

CHAPTER CONTENTS

- Introduction to Torts and Cyber Torts
- Intentional Torts Against Persons
- Intentional Torts Against Property
- Unintentional Torts (Negligence)
- Special Negligence Doctrines
- Defenses Against Negligence
- Strict Liability
- Chapter Summary
- Test Review Terms and Concepts
- Case Problems
- Ethics Issues
- IRAC Writing Assignment

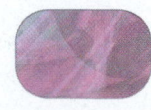

Introduction to Torts and Cyber Torts

Tort is the French word for a "wrong." Tort law protects a variety of injuries and provides remedies for them. Under tort law, an injured party can bring a *civil lawsuit* to seek compensation for a wrong done to the party or to the party's property. Many torts have their origin in common law. The courts and legislatures have extended tort law to reflect changes in modern society.

Tort damages are monetary damages that are sought from the offending party. They are intended to compensate the injured party for the injury suffered. Such injury may consist of past and future medical expenses, loss of wages, pain and suffering, mental distress, and other damages caused by the defendant's tortious conduct. If the victim of a tort dies, his or her beneficiaries can bring a *wrongful death action* to recover damages from the defendant. *Punitive damages*, which are awarded to punish the defendant, may be recovered in intentional tort and strict liability cases. Other remedies, such as injunctions, may be available, too.

This chapter discusses various tort laws, including intentional torts, negligence, strict liability, and cyber torts.

Exposition Boulevard, Los Angeles, California.

Automobile accidents cause thousands of deaths each year. Few of us can pass one of these familiar roadside memorials without thinking about the pain and suffering of the occupants of the vehicle and their surviving loved ones.

Intentional Torts Against Persons

The law protects a person from unauthorized touching, restraint, or other contact. In addition, the law protects a person's reputation and privacy. Violations of these rights are actionable as torts. **Intentional torts** against persons are discussed in the paragraphs that follow.

Assault

Assault is (1) the threat of immediate harm or offensive contact or (2) any action that arouses reasonable apprehension of imminent harm. Actual physical contact is unnecessary. Threats of future harm are not actionable.

Example Suppose a 6-foot-5-inch, 250-pound male makes a fist and threatens to punch a 5-foot, 100-pound woman. If the woman is afraid that the man will physically harm her, she can sue him for assault. If she is a black-belt karate champion and laughs at the threat, there is no assault because the threat does not cause any apprehension.

Battery

Battery is unauthorized and harmful or offensive physical contact with another person. Basically, the interest protected here is each person's reasonable sense of dignity and safety.

Example Intentionally hitting someone is considered battery because it is harmful. Note that there does not have to be direct physical contact between the victim and the perpetrator. If an injury results, throwing a rock, shooting an arrow or a bullet, knocking off a hat, pulling a chair out from under someone, and poisoning a drink are all instances of actionable battery. The victim need not be aware of the harmful or offensive contact (e.g., it may take place while the victim is asleep). Assault and battery often occur together, although they do not have to (e.g., the perpetrator hits the victim on the back of the head without any warning).

TRANSFERRED INTENT DOCTRINE Sometimes a person acts with the intent to injure one person but actually injures another. The **transferred intent doctrine** applies to such situations. Under this doctrine, the law transfers the perpetrator's intent from the target to the actual victim of the act. The victim can then sue the defendant.

False Imprisonment

The intentional confinement or restraint of another person without authority or justification and without that person's consent constitutes **false imprisonment**. The victim may be restrained or confined by physical force, barriers, threats of physical harm, or the perpetrator's false assertion of legal authority (i.e., *false arrest*). A threat of future harm or moral pressure is not considered false imprisonment. The false imprisonment must be complete.

Example Merely locking one door to a building when other exits are not locked is not false imprisonment. In such a case, a person is not obliged to risk danger or an affront to his or her dignity by attempting to escape.

MERCHANT PROTECTION STATUTES Shoplifting causes substantial losses to merchants each year. Almost all states have enacted **merchant protection statutes**, also known as the **shopkeeper's privilege**. These statutes allow merchants to stop, detain, and investigate suspected shoplifters without being held liable for false imprisonment if:

1. There are *reasonable grounds* for the suspicion.
2. Suspects are detained for only a *reasonable time*.
3. Investigations are conducted in a *reasonable manner*.

Proving these elements is sometimes difficult. The following case demonstrates the application of these elements to a case of alleged shoplifting and false imprisonment.

ETHICS SPOTLIGHT

Wal-Mart Liable for False Imprisonment

LaShawna Goodman went to a local Wal-Mart store in Opelika, Alabama, to do some last-minute holiday shopping. She brought along her two young daughters and a telephone she had purchased earlier at Wal-Mart to exchange. She presented the telephone and receipt to a Wal-Mart employee, who took the telephone. Unable to find another telephone she wanted, Goodman retrieved the previously purchased telephone from the employee, bought another item, and left. Outside, Ms. Goodman was stopped by Wal-Mart security personnel and was accused of stealing the phone. Goodman offered to show the Wal-Mart employees the original receipt, but the Wal-Mart employees detained her and called the police. Ms. Goodman was handcuffed in front of her children. Wal-Mart filed criminal charges against Ms. Goodman.

At the criminal trial, Ms. Goodman was acquitted of all charges. Now it was Ms. Goodman's turn: She filed a civil lawsuit against Wal-Mart Stores, Inc., to recover damages for falsely accusing her of stealing the telephone. Ms. Goodman presented her evidence. Wal-Mart asserted the defense that it was within its rights to have detained Ms. Goodman as it did and to have prosecuted Ms. Goodman based on its investigation. Wal-Mart asserted that the merchant protection statute protected its actions in this case.

The jury did not accept Wal-Mart's plea that it had acted reasonably. The jury rejected Wal-Mart's defenses, including the shopkeeper's privilege and its allegations that it had not maliciously prosecuted her. The jury determined that Ms. Goodman should be awarded $200,000 in compensatory damages for her suffering. The jury then decided that Wal-Mart had acted so badly in this case that it tacked on punitive damages to its award to Ms. Goodman just to teach Wal-Mart a lesson.

The supreme court of Alabama upheld liability, the award of $200,000 in compensatory damages, and an award of $600,000 in punitive damages *Wal-Mart Stores, Inc. v. Goodman*, 789 So.2d 166, **Web** 2000 Ala. Lexis 548 (Supreme Court of Alabama, 2000)

Law & Ethics Questions

1. Define *false imprisonment*.
2. What does a merchant sued for false imprisonment have to prove to avoid liability under the merchant protection statute?
3. **ETHICS** Did Wal-Mart act responsibly by filing criminal charges against Ms. Goodman in this case? Explain.
4. **ETHICS** Do you think Wal-Mart presented sufficient evidence to be protected by the merchant protection statute?

Web Exercises

1. **WEB** For a complete opinion of this case, go to *www.prenhall.com/cheesemancases*.
2. **WEB** Visit Wal-Mart's website, at *www.walmartstores.com*. Find Wal-Mart's code of ethics and read it.
3. **WEB** Visit the website of the supreme court of Alabama, at *www.judicial.state.al.us/supreme.cfm*.
4. **WEB** Use *www.google.com* to find other cases where Wal-Mart has been sued.

Misappropriation of the Right to Publicity

Each person has the exclusive legal right to control and profit from the commercial use of his or her name and personality during his or her lifetime. This is a valuable right, particularly to well-known persons such as sports figures and movie stars. Any attempt by another person to appropriate a living person's name or identity for commercial purposes is actionable. The wrongdoer is liable for the **tort of misappropriation of the right to publicity** (also called the **tort of appropriation**). In such cases, the plaintiff can (1) recover the unauthorized profits made by the offending party and (2) obtain an injunction against further unauthorized use of his or her name or identity. Many states provide that the right to publicity survives a person's death and may be enforced by the deceased's heirs.

Example Brad Pitt is a famous movie star. If an advertising agency places Brad Pitt's likeness (e.g., photo) on a billboard advertising a product without Brad Pitt's permission, it has engaged in the tort of misappropriation of the right to publicity. Brad Pitt could sue and recover the profits made by the offending party as well as obtain an injunction to prevent unauthorized use of his likeness by the offending party.

Invasion of the Right to Privacy

The law recognizes each person's right to live his or her life without being subjected to unwarranted and undesired publicity. A violation of this right constitutes the tort of **invasion of the right to privacy**. If a fact is public information, there is no claim to privacy. However, a fact that was once public (e.g., commission of a crime) may become private after the passage of time.

Example Secretly taking photos of another person with a cell phone camera in a men's or women's locker room would constitute invasion of the right to privacy. Reading someone else's mail, wiretapping someone's telephone, and reading someone else's e-mail without authorization to do so are also examples of invasion of the right to privacy.

Placing someone in a "false light" constitutes an invasion of privacy. For example, sending an objectionable telegram to a third party and signing another's name would place the purported sender in a false light in the eyes of the receiver. Falsely attributing beliefs or acts to another can also form the basis of a lawsuit.

Defamation of Character

A person's reputation is a valuable asset. Therefore, every person is protected from false statements made by others during his or her lifetime. This protection ends upon a person's death. The tort of **defamation of character** requires a plaintiff to prove that (1) the defendant made an *untrue statement of fact* about the plaintiff and (2) the statement was intentionally or accidentally *published* to a third party. In this context, *publication* simply means that a third person heard or saw the untrue statement. It does not just mean appearance in newspapers, magazines, or books.

The name for an oral defamatory statement is **slander**. A false statement that appears in a letter, newspaper, magazine, book, photograph, movie, video, and the like is called **libel**. Most courts hold that defamatory statements in radio and television broadcasts are considered libel because of the permanency of the media.

The publication of an untrue statement of fact is not the same as the publication of an opinion. The publication of opinions is usually not actionable. Because defamation is defined as an untrue statement of fact, truth is an absolute defense to a charge of defamation.

Example The statement "My lawyer is lousy" is an opinion. The statement "My lawyer has been disbarred from the practice of law," when she has not been disbarred, is an untrue statement of fact and is actionable as defamation.

PUBLIC FIGURES AS PLAINTIFFS In ***New York Times Co. v. Sullivan***,[1] the U.S. Supreme Court held that *public officials* cannot recover for defamation unless they can prove that the defendant acted with "actual malice." Actual malice means that the defendant made the false statement knowingly or with reckless disregard of its falsity. This requirement has since been extended to *public figure* plaintiffs such as movie stars, sports personalities, and other celebrities.

CONTEMPORARY ENVIRONMENT
Eminem's Rap Song Is Not Slander

Eminem is a famous white rapper who won a Grammy award for his music in the movie *8 Mile* in which he starred. Eminem's lyrics often contain references to his personal experiences. In "Brain Damage," a song from his 1999 CD *The Slim Shady LP*, Eminem sang lyrics he had written, which read in part:

> *I was harassed daily by this fat kid named DeAngelo Bailey.*
>
> *He banged my head against the urinal till he broke my nose.*
>
> *Soaked my clothes in blood.*
>
> *Grabbed me and choked my throat.*

DeAngelo Bailey sued Eminem for $1 million, alleging that the lyrics were untrue and slanderous. Eminem's mother publicly defended her son's account of the bullying by Bailey. After hearing all the evidence, Judge Deborah Servitto wrote:

> *Mr. Bailey complains that his rap is trash*
>
> *So he's seeking compensation in the form of cash.*
>
> *Bailey thinks he's entitled to some money gain*
>
> *Because Eminem used his name in vain.*

> *The lyrics are stories no one would take as fact*
>
> *They're an exaggeration of a childish act.*
>
> *It is therefore this court's ultimate position*
>
> *That Eminem is entitled to summary disposition.*

Judge Servitto ruled in favor of Eminem. *Bailey v. Eminem* (2005 Mich. App. LEXIS 930 [Trial Court of Michigan, 2000])

Law & Ethics Questions

1. Define *defamation*. What elements must be proved to find defamation?

2. **ETHICS** What are parody and satire? Should parody be granted First Amendment free speech protection? Why or why not?

Web Exercises

1. **WEB** Visit Eminem's website, at *www.eminem.com.*

2. **WEB** Visit the website of Michigan courts, at *www.courts.michigan.gov.*

DISPARAGEMENT OR TRADE LIBEL Business firms rely on their reputation and the quality of their products and services to attract and keep customers. That is why state unfair-competition laws protect businesses from disparaging statements made by competitors or others. A disparaging statement is an untrue statement made by one person or business about the products, services, property, or reputation of another business.

To prove **disparagement**, which is also called *trade libel*, *product disparagement*, and *slander of title*, the plaintiff must show that the defendant (1) made an untrue statement about the plaintiff's products, services, property, or business reputation; (2) published that untrue statement to a third party; (3) knew the statement was not true; and (4) made the statement maliciously (i.e., with intent to injure the plaintiff).

In the following case, the court had to decide whether trade libel had occurred.

CASE 5.1
Trade Libel

Themed Restaurants, Inc., Doing Business as Lucky Cheng's v. Zagat Survey, LLC

801 N.Y.S.2d 38,
Web 2005 N.Y. App. Div. Lexis 9275 (2005)
Supreme Court of New York, Appellate Division

> ❝*Indeed, restaurant ratings and reviews almost invariably constitute expressions of opinion.*❞
>
> —Judge Sullivan

Facts

Zagat Survey, LLC, publishes the famous Zagat series of dining, travel, and leisure guides for different cities and locations. The Zagat restaurant guides lists and ranks each reviewed restaurant from 0 to 30 for categories such as food, décor, and service. These ratings are calculated from surveys of customers of the restaurants, and the Zagat guide often quotes anonymous consumer comments.

Lucky Cheng's is a restaurant owned by Themed Restaurants, Inc., that is located in Manhattan, New York City. Lucky Cheng's is a theme restaurant with a drag queen cabaret where female impersonators are both waiters and performers, and customer participation contributes to the entertainment. The "Zagat Survey of New York City Restaurants" rated the food at Lucky Cheng's as 9 and rated the décor and service as 15. The Zagat guide then stated:

> God knows "you don't go for the food" at this East Village Asian-Eclectic—rather you go to "gawk" at the "hilarious" "cross-dressing" staff who "tell dirty jokes", perform "impromptu floor shows" and offer "lap dances for dessert"; obviously, it "can be exhausting", and weary well-wishers suggest they "freshen up the menu—and their makeup."

Themed Restaurants sued Zagat for defamation and trade libel. Zagat defended, arguing that the ratings and comments about Lucky Cheng's restaurant that appeared in the Zagat guide were opinions and not statements of fact, and were therefore not actionable as defamation and trade libel. The trial court agreed with Zagat and dismissed the case. Themed Restaurants appealed.

Issue

Were the statements made in Zagat's restaurant guide statements of fact or statements of opinion?

Language of the Court

The allegedly libelous statements can only be construed as statements of opinion and thus are constitutionally protected. Indeed, restaurant ratings and reviews almost invariably constitute expressions of opinion.

Decision

The appellate court held that the ratings and comments about Lucky Cheng's restaurant in Zagat's restaurant guide were statements of opinion and not statements of fact. Therefore, defamation or trade libel did not occur. The appellate court affirmed the trial court's judgment in favor of Zagat.

Law & Ethics Questions

1. Define *trade libel*. What is the difference between a statement of fact and a statement of opinion? Explain.

2. Do you think that the statements in question were statements of fact or statements of opinion?

3. **ETHICS** Do you think that restaurant ratings in Zagat guides impact the earnings of reviewed restaurants? Does Zagat's violate any ethical standards by publishing its guides? Explain.

4. Do you think Lucky Cheng's had much of a chance to win this case? Explain.

Web Exercises

1. **WEB** For the complete opinion of this case, see *www.prenhall.com/cheesemancases*.

2. **WEB** Visit the Zagat website, at *www.zagat.com*. Locate one of your favorite restaurants.

3. **WEB** Visit the website of the court that decided this case, the supreme court of New York, Appellate Division, First Department, at *www.courts.state.ny.us/courts/ad1*.

4. **WEB** Use *www.google.com* to find another restaurant rating service other than Zagat.

Intentional Misrepresentation (Fraud)

One of the most pervasive business torts is **intentional misrepresentation**. This tort is also known as **fraud** or *deceit*. It occurs when a wrongdoer deceives another person out of money, property, or something else of value. A person who has been injured by an intentional misrepresentation can recover damages from the wrongdoer. Four elements are required to find fraud:

1. The wrongdoer made a false representation of material fact.
2. The wrongdoer had knowledge that the representation was false and intended to deceive the innocent party.
3. The innocent party justifiably relied on the misrepresentation.
4. The innocent party was injured.

> He that's cheated twice by the same man, is an accomplice with the Cheater.
>
> Thomas Fuller
> *Gnomologia (1732)*

Item 2, which is called **scienter**, includes situations in which the wrongdoer recklessly disregards the truth in making a representation that is false. Intent or recklessness can be inferred from the circumstances.

Intentional Infliction of Emotional Distress

In some situations, a victim may suffer mental or emotional distress without first being physically harmed. The *Restatement (Second) of Torts* provides that a person whose *extreme and outrageous* conduct intentionally or recklessly causes severe emotional distress to another is liable for that emotional distress.[2] This is called the **tort of intentional infliction of emotional distress**, or the **tort of outrage**. The plaintiff must prove that the defendant's conduct was "so outrageous in character and so extreme in degree as to go beyond all possible bounds of decency, and to be regarded as atrocious and utterly intolerable in a civilized society."[3] An indignity, an annoyance, rough language, or an occasional inconsiderate or unkind act does not constitute outrageous behavior. However, repeated annoyances or harassment coupled with threats are considered outrageous.

The tort does not require any publication to a third party or physical contact between the plaintiff and defendant.

Example A credit collection agency making harassing telephone calls to a debtor every morning between 1:00 and 5:00 A.M. is outrageous conduct.

The mental distress suffered by the plaintiff must be severe. Many states require that this mental distress be manifested by some form of physical injury, discomfort, or illness, such as nausea, ulcers, headaches, or miscarriage. This requirement is intended to prevent false claims. Some states have abandoned this requirement.

Example Shame, humiliation, embarrassment, anger, fear, and worry constitute severe mental distress.

The tort of intentional infliction of emotional distress was asserted in the following case.

CASE 5.2
Intentional Infliction of Emotional Distress

Roach v. Stern

252 A.D.2d 488, 675 N.Y.S.2d 133,
Web 1998 N.Y. App. Div. Lexis 799
Supreme Court of New York, Appellate Division

> **"** *In light of Stern's reputation for vulgar humor . . . , a jury might reasonably conclude that the manner in which Tay's remains were handled, for entertainment purposes . . . , went beyond the bounds of decent behavior.* **"**
>
> —Judge O'Brien

Facts

Howard Stern is a famous television talk-show host who emcees an irreverent daily show on the radio. The show was syndicated by Infinity Broadcasting, Inc. (Infinity), and was listened to by millions of people across the country. Deborah Roach, a self-described topless dancer and cable-access television host, was a perennial guest on the Howard Stern radio show. She was famous for her stories about encounters with aliens. Roach died of a drug overdose at the age of 27. Roach's sister, Melissa Driscoll, had Roach's body cremated and gave a portion of the remains to Roach's close friend Chaunce Hayden. Driscoll said she did so with the understanding that Hayden would "preserve and honor said remains in an appropriate and private manner."

On July 18, 1995, Hayden brought a box containing Roach's cremated remains to Stern's radio show. Hayden said she did so as a memorial to Roach because "the only happiness Debbie had was the Howard Stern show." Thereafter, Stern, Hayden, and other participants in the broadcast played with Roach's ashes and made crude comments about the remains. The radio show was videotaped and later broadcast on a national cable television station. Roach's sister and brother sued Stern, Infinity, and Hayden to recover damages for intentional infliction of emotional distress. The trial court dismissed the complaint. The plaintiffs appealed.

Issue

Did the plaintiffs sufficiently plead a cause of action to recover damages for the intentional infliction of emotional distress?

Language of the Court

Upon our review of the allegations in the case at bar, we conclude that the Supreme Court erred in determining that the element of outrageous conduct was not satisfied as a matter of law. Although the defendants contend that the conduct at issue was not particularly shocking, in light of Stern's reputation for vulgar humor and Tay's actions during her guest appearances on his program, a jury might reasonably conclude that the manner in which Tay's remains were handled, for entertainment purposes and against the express wishes of her family, went beyond the bounds of decent behavior.

In light of Stern's reputation for vulgar humor . . . , a jury might reasonably conclude that the manner in which Tay's remains were handled, for entertainment purposes . . . , went beyond the bounds of decent behavior.

Decision

The court held that the complaint and the facts of the case as pleaded sufficiently stated a cause of action to recover damages for intentional infliction of emotional distress. The supreme court reversed the judgment of the trial court and reinstated the case against Stern and Infinity.

Law & Ethics Questions

1. Should the tort of intentional infliction of emotional distress be recognized by the law? What difficulties arise in trying to apply this tort?

2. **ETHICS** Was the conduct of Stern and the other participants on the radio show tasteless? Did it amount to "outrageous conduct" for which legal damages should be awarded?

3. If Stern and Infinity were found liable, would a chilling effect on future broadcasts result?

Web Exercises

1. **WEB** For the complete opinion of this case, go to *www.prenhall.com/cheesemancases*.

2. **WEB** Visit the website of Howard Stern, at *www.howardstern.com*.

3. **WEB** Visit the website of the New York Supreme Court, Appellate Division, at *www.courts.state.ny.us/courts/ad2*.

4. **WEB** Use *www.google.com* to find an article that discusses the tort of outrage.

Malicious Prosecution

Businesses and individuals often believe they have a reason to sue someone to recover damages or other remedies. If the plaintiff has a legitimate reason to bring a lawsuit and does so, but the plaintiff does not win the lawsuit, he or she does not have to worry about being sued by the person whom he or she sued. But a losing plaintiff does have to worry about being sued by the defendant in a second lawsuit for **malicious prosecution** if certain elements are met. In a lawsuit for malicious prosecution, the original defendant sues the original plaintiff. In this second lawsuit, which is a *civil* action for damages, the original defendant is the plaintiff, and the original plaintiff is the defendant. To succeed in a malicious prosecution lawsuit, the courts require the plaintiff to prove all of the following:

1. The plaintiff in the original lawsuit (now the defendant) instituted or was responsible for instituting the original lawsuit.
2. There was no *probable cause* for the first lawsuit (that is, it was a frivolous lawsuit).
3. The plaintiff in the original action brought it with *malice*. (Caution: This is a very difficult element to prove.)
4. The original lawsuit was terminated in favor of the original defendant (now the plaintiff).
5. The current plaintiff suffered injury as a result of the original lawsuit.

The courts do not look favorably on malicious prosecution lawsuits because they feel such lawsuits inhibit the original plaintiff's incentive to sue.

Intentional Torts against Property

There are two general categories of property: real property and personal property. *Real property* consists of land and anything permanently attached to that land. *Personal property* consists of things that are movable, such as automobiles, books, clothes, pets, and such. The law recognizes certain torts against real and personal property. These torts are discussed in the paragraphs that follow.

> Thoughts much too deep for tears subdue the court when I assumpsit bring, and godlike waive a tort.
>
> J. L. Adolphus
> *The Circuiteers (1885)*

Trespass to Land

Interference with an owner's right to exclusive possession of land constitutes the tort of **trespass to land**. There does not have to be any interference with the owner's use or enjoyment of the land; the ownership itself is what counts. Thus, unauthorized use of another person's land is trespass even if the owner is not using it. Actual harm to the property is not necessary.

Example Entering another person's land without permission, remaining on the land of another after permission to do so has expired (e.g., a guest refuses to leave), and causing something or someone to enter another's land (e.g., one person builds a dam that causes another person's land to flood) are examples of trespass to land.

A person who is pushed onto another's land or enters that land with good reason is not liable for trespass.

Example A person may enter onto another person's land to save a child or a pet from harm.

Trespass to and Conversion of Personal Property

The tort of **trespass to personal property** occurs when one person injures another person's personal property or interferes with that person's enjoyment of his or her personal property. The injured party can sue for damages. For example, breaking another's car window is trespass to personal property.

Depriving a true owner of the use and enjoyment of his or her personal property by taking over such property and exercising ownership rights over it constitutes the tort of **conversion of personal property**. Conversion also occurs when someone who originally is given possession of personal property fails to return it (e.g., fails to return a borrowed car). The rightful owner can sue to recover the property. If the property was lost or destroyed, the owner can sue to recover its value.

Santa Monica Pier, California
Who would be liable if the roller coaster broke, causing injury to a rider?

Unintentional Torts (Negligence)

Under the doctrine of **unintentional tort**, commonly referred to as **negligence**, a person is liable for harm that is the *foreseeable consequence* of his or her actions. *Negligence* is defined as "the omission to do something which a reasonable man would do, or doing something which a prudent and reasonable man would not do."[4]

To be successful in a negligence lawsuit, the plaintiff must prove that (1) the defendant owed a *duty of care* to the plaintiff, (2) the defendant *breached* this duty of care, (3) the plaintiff suffered *injury*, and (4) the defendant's negligent act *caused* the plaintiff's injury. Each of these elements is discussed in the paragraphs that follow.

> Negligence is the omission to do something which a reasonable man would do, or doing something which a prudent and reasonable man would not do.
>
> B. Alderson Blyth v. Brimingham Waterworks Co. (1856)

CONCEPT SUMMARY

Elements of Negligence

1. The defendant owed a *duty of care* to the plaintiff.
2. The defendant *breached this duty*.
3. The plaintiff suffered *injury*.
4. The defendant's negligent act was the *actual cause* (or *causation in fact*) of the plaintiff's injuries.
5. The defendant's negligent act was the *proximate cause* (or *legal cause*) of the plaintiff's injuries. The defendant is liable only for the *foreseeable* consequences of his or her negligent act.

Duty of Care

To determine whether a defendant is liable for negligence, it must first be ascertained whether the defendant owed a **duty of care** to the plaintiff. Duty of care refers to the obligation people owe each other—that is, the duty not to cause any unreasonable harm or risk of harm.

Example Each person owes a duty to drive his or her car carefully, not to push or shove on escalators, not to leave skateboards on the sidewalk, and the like. Businesses owe a duty to make safe products, not to cause accidents, and so on.

The courts decide whether a duty of care is owed in specific cases by applying a *reasonable person standard*. Under this test, the courts attempt to determine how an *objective, careful, and conscientious person would have acted in the same circumstances* and then measure the defendant's conduct against that standard. The defendant's subjective intent ("I did not mean to do it") is immaterial in assessing liability. Certain impairments do not affect the reasonable person standard. For example, there is no reasonable alcoholic standard.

> No court has ever given, nor do we think ever can give, a definition of what constitutes a reasonable or an average man.
>
> Lord Goddard C.J.R. v. McCarthy (1954)

Defendants with a particular expertise or competence are measured against a *reasonable professional standard*. This standard is applied in much the same way as the reasonable person standard.

Example A brain surgeon is measured against a reasonable brain surgeon standard rather than a less specialized reasonable doctor standard. Children are generally required to act as a *reasonable child* of similar age and experience would act.

McDonald's found itself embroiled in one of the most famous negligence cases of modern times. This case follows.

CONTEMPORARY ENVIRONMENT
Ouch! McDonald's Coffee's Is Too Hot!

Many studies have shown that people care less about how good their coffee tastes than whether it is hot. So restaurants, coffee shops, and other sellers make their coffee hot. McDonald's, however, discovered that it was in hot water for making its coffee too hot. Consider this case.

Stella Liebeck, an 81-year-old resident of Albuquerque, New Mexico, visited a drive-through window of a McDonald's restaurant with her grandson. Her grandson, the driver of the vehicle, placed the order. When it came, he handed a hot cup of coffee to Liebeck. As her grandson drove away from the drive-through window, Liebeck took the lid off the coffee cup she held in her lap. The coffee spilled all over Liebeck, who suffered third-degree burns on her legs, groin, and buttocks. She required medical treatment, was hospitalized, and suffered permanent scars from the incident.

Liebeck sued McDonald's for selling coffee that was too hot and for failing to warn her of the danger of the hot coffee it served. McDonald's rejected Liebeck's pretrial offer to settle the case for $300,000 and went to trial.

At trial, McDonald's denied that it had been negligent and asserted that Liebeck's own negligence—opening a hot coffee cup on her lap—had caused her injuries. The jury heard evidence that McDonald's enforces a quality-control rule requiring its restaurants and franchises to serve coffee at 180 to 190 degrees Fahrenheit. Evidence showed that this was 10 to 30 degrees hotter than coffee served by competing restaurant chains and approximately 40 to 50 degrees hotter than normal house-brewed coffee.

Based on this evidence, the jury concluded that McDonald's acted recklessly and awarded Liebeck $200,000 compensatory damages (reduced by $40,000 for her own negligence) and $2.7 million punitive damages. After the trial court judge reduced the amount of punitive damages to $480,000, the parties reached an out-of-court settlement for an undisclosed amount. Because of this case, McDonald's and other purveyors of coffee have reduced the temperature at which they sell coffee and have placed warnings on their coffee cups.

Law & Ethics Questions

1. If you were Ms. Liebeck's lawyer, what evidence would you try to introduce at trial to help win your client's case against McDonald's?

2. Do you think McDonald's owed a duty to Ms. Liebeck and that McDonald's breached this duty?

3. **ETHICS** Do you think McDonald's acted recklessly?

4. **ETHICS** Was an award of punitive damages warranted? If so, do you think that the award of punitive damages in this case was warranted? What amount of punitive damages would you have awarded in this case?

Web Exercises

1. **WEB** Visit the McDonald's website, at *www.mcdonalds.com*. Find the McDonald's code of ethics.

2. **WEB** Use *www.google.com* to find an article about this case and read the article.

3. **WEB** Use *www.google.com* to find an article about copycat lawsuits against McDonald's. Read it.

Breach of Duty

Once a court finds that a defendant actually owed the plaintiff a duty of care, it must determine whether the defendant breached that duty. A **breach of the duty of care** is a failure to exercise care. In other words, it is the failure to act as a reasonable person would act. A breach of this duty may consist of either an action (e.g., throwing a lit match on the ground in the forest and causing a fire) or a failure to act when there is a duty to act (e.g., a firefighter refusing to put out a fire). Generally, passersby are not expected to rescue others gratuitously to save them from harm.

In the following two cases, the courts had to determine whether the defendants were liable for negligence.

C A S E **5.3**
Negligence

Wilhelm v. Flores
133 S.W.3d 726, **Web** 2003 Tex. App. Lexis 9335 (2003)
Court of Appeals of Texas

> **"** *We examine whether the plaintiffs established a duty to warn of the dangerousness of bees.* **"**

—Judge Valdez

Facts

Curtis R. Wilhelm owned beehives and kept the hives on property he owned. John Black, who operated a honeybee business, contracted to purchase some beehives from Wilhelm. Black employed Santos Flores, Sr. to help him pick up the beehives from Wilhelm. Black provided Flores with a protective suit to wear while picking up the beehives. Neither Wilhelm nor Black informed Flores of the danger of working with bees. After picking up beehives from Wilhelm's home, Black and Flores drove to remote property owned by Wilhelm to pick up other beehives. Flores opened the veil on his protective suit. After loading one beehive onto the truck, Flores started staggering and yelling for help. Flores sustained several bee stings, suffered anaphylactic shock reaction, and died before an ambulance could reach him. Flores's wife and children sued Wilhelm and Black for negligence for failing to warn Flores of the dangers of working with beehives and the possibility of dying of anaphylactic shock if stung by a bee. The jury found Wilhelm and Black each 50 percent liable and awarded $1,591,000 to the plaintiffs. Wilhelm appealed.

Issue

Did Wilhelm act negligently by failing to warn Flores of the dangers of working with beehives?

Language of the Court

Whether a legal duty exists is a threshold question of law for the court to decide from the facts surrounding the occurrence in question. The plaintiffs' allegations of negligence included failure to provide proper instructions. We examine whether the plaintiffs established a duty to warn of the dangerousness of bees. Foreseeability is the foremost and dominant consideration. There must be sufficient evidence indicating that the defendant knew or should have known that harm would eventually befall the victim. An expert witness testified that bees are probably the number one cause of insect deaths. Appellant Wilhelm himself testified that he was an expert concerning insects, with a degree in entomology. At the time of this incident, Wilhelm had owned beehives for about five years. Accordingly, we hold that there is sufficient evidence to support the jury's verdict and that such verdict is not manifestly unreasonable or unjust.

Decision

The court of appeals held that Wilhelm owed a duty of care to warn Flores of the dangers of working with beehives and was negligent in not doing so. The court of appeals affirmed the award of damages to Flores's estate.

Law & Ethics Questions

1. Should failure to warn be a basis for a negligence lawsuit? Explain.

2. Do you think most businesses carry liability insurance to protect against lawsuit judgments? What type of businesses most likely carry such insurance? What businesses are least likely to carry such insurance?

3. **ETHICS** Do you think Wilhelm should have been held liable in this case? Why or why not?

4. **ETHICS** Do you think Wilhelm acted ethically in this case?

Web Exercises

1. **WEB** For the complete opinion of this case, go to *www.prenhall.com/cheesemancases*.

2. **WEB** Visit the website of the Texas court of appeals, at *www.13thcoa.courts.state.tx.us*.

3. **WEB** Use *www.google.com* to find a website that shows the proper use of equipment that should be worn when handling bees.

CASE 5.4
Negligence

James v. Meow Media, Inc.

300 F.3d 683,
Web 2002 U.S. App. Lexis 16185 (2002)
United States Court of Appeals for the Sixth Circuit

> **“** *Our inquiry is whether the deaths of James, Steger, and Hadley were the reasonably foreseeable result of the defendants' creation and distribution of their games, movie, and Internet sites.* **”**
>
> —Judge Boggs

Facts

Michael Carneal was a 14-year-old freshman student at Heath High School in Paducah, Kentucky. Carneal regularly played the violent interactive video and computer games "Doom," "Quake," "Castle Wolfenstein," "Rampage," "Nightmare Creatures," "Mech Warrior," "Resident Evil," and "Final Fantasy." These games involved the player shooting virtual opponents with computer guns and other weapons. Carneal also watched videotaped movies, including one called *The Basketball Diaries*, in which a high-school-student protagonist dreams of killing his teacher and several of his fellow classmates. On December 1, 1997, Carneal took a .22-caliber pistol and five shotguns into the lobby of Heath High School and shot several of his fellow students, killing three and wounding many others. The three students killed were Jessica James, Kayce Steger, and Nicole Hadley.

The parents of the three dead children (collectively "James") sued the producers and distributors of the violent video games and movies that Carneal had watched previous to the shooting. The parents sued to recover damages for wrongful death, alleging that the defendants were negligent in producing and distributing such games and movies to Carneal. The U.S. District Court applied Kentucky law and held that the defendants did not owe or breach a duty to the plaintiffs and therefore were not liable for negligence. The plaintiffs appealed.

Issue

Did the defendant video and movie producers and distributors owe a duty of care to the plaintiffs by selling and licensing violent video games and movies to Carneal, who killed the three children?

Language of the Court

Kentucky courts have held that the determination of whether a duty of care exists is whether the harm to the plaintiff resulting from the defendant's negligence was "foreseeable." Kentucky courts have struggled with the formless nature of this inquiry. Our inquiry is whether the deaths of James, Steger, and Hadley were the reasonably foreseeable result of the defendants' creation and distribution of their games, movie, and Internet sites.

It appears simply impossible to predict that these games, movie, and Internet sites would incite a young person to violence. We find that it is simply too far a leap from shooting characters on a video screen (an activity undertaken by millions) to shooting people in a classroom (an activity undertaken by a handful, at most) for Carneal's actions to have been reasonably foreseeable to the manufacturers of the media that Carneal played and viewed. Carneal's reaction was not a normal reaction. Indeed, Carneal is not a normal person. Individuals are generally entitled to assume that third parties will not commit intentional criminal acts.

Decision

The Court of Appeals held that the defendant video game and movie producers and distributors did not owe a duty of care to the plaintiffs by selling and licensing violent video games and movies to Carneal, who murdered the three children.

Law & Ethics Questions

1. How does the Court define *foreseeability*? Did the court use a narrow, middle, or broad interpretation of foreseeability in deciding this case? Explain.

2. What would have been the consequences for the video game and movie industries if the Court had held in favor of the plaintiffs? Explain.

3. **ETHICS** Do producers and distributors of video games and movies owe a duty of care to society not to produce and distribute violent games and movies?

4. Are any free speech rights involved in this case? Explain.

Web Exercises

1. **WEB** For the complete opinion of this case, go to *www.prenhall.com/cheesemancases*.

2. **WEB** Use *www.google.com* to see if you can find a video game that contains violence. Do you think this game contains violent activities that expose the producer to liability?

3. **WEB** Visit the website of U.S. Court of Appeals for the Sixth Circuit, at *www.ca6.uscourts.gov*.

Injury to Plaintiff

Even though a defendant's act may have breached a duty of care owed to the plaintiff, this breach is not actionable unless the plaintiff suffers **injury**.

Example A business's negligence causes an explosion and fire to occur at its factory at night. No one is injured, and there is no damage to the neighbors' property. The negligence is not actionable.

The damages recoverable depend on the effect of the injury on the plaintiff's life or profession. Suppose two men injure their hands when a train door malfunctions. The first man is a professional basketball player. The second is a college professor. The first man can recover greater damages than the second.

In the following case, the jury had to determine damages.

C A S E **5.5**
Damages

Clancy v. Goad

858 N.E.2d 653,
Web 2006 Ind. App. Lexis 2576 (2006)
Court of Appeals of Indiana

> ❝*Although the amount of the award in this case is sizeable, we cannot conclude that it is unreasonable given the evidence.*❞

—Judge Vaidik

Facts

One morning, after being awake part of the night at work, Tim Clancy was driving a Chevrolet S-10 pickup truck on State Road 231. Clancy fell asleep at the wheel of the truck. Robert and Dianna Goad, husband and wife, were riding separate motorcycles on the other side of the road. Clancy's truck crossed the center line of the road, and, after narrowly missing two other vehicles and Robert's motorcycle, collided with Dianna's motorcycle. The collision immediately severed Dianna's leg above the knee, and she was thrown from her motorcycle into a water-filled ditch at the side of the road. Clancy was awakened by the sound of the impact, and the truck veered into the ditch as well. Robert stopped his motorcycle, ran back to the scene of the accident, and held Dianna's head out of the water-filled ditch. Clancy called 911, and when the paramedics arrived, she was taken to the hospital. Dianna remained in a coma for two weeks. Her leg had to be amputated. In addition, Dianna suffered from a fractured pelvic bone, a fractured left elbow, and a lacerated spleen, which had to be removed.

Dianna sued Clancy to recover damages based on his negligence. The jury returned a verdict finding Clancy 100 percent at fault for the accident and awarded Dianna $10 million in compensatory damages. Clancy appealed, arguing that the damages were excessive.

Issue

Were the damages awarded to Dianna Goad excessive?

Language of the Court

The record indicates that before the accident, Dianna was an active and athletic person. She was an avid runner, often jogging three-and-a-half miles a day. She belonged to a health club where she regularly trained with free weights. Dianna enjoyed rollerblading, hiking, and cross country skiing. Dianna also worked full-time in a managerial accounting position where she earned approximately $45,000 per year and where she planned to work until she retired.

The injuries Dianna received in the accident as a result of Clancy's accident were catastrophic. She spent two weeks in a coma. Surgeries were performed to medically amputate her leg above the knee and to set her broken pelvic bones and her broken elbow. Dianna's spleen could not be repaired and was inevitably removed, resulting in an increased lifetime risk of infection. Dianna has endured multiple skin graft procedures. At the time of the trial, Dianna had undergone seven surgeries, taken more than 6,800 pills, and her medical expenses totaled more than $368,000. Furthermore, Dianna's medical expenses and challenges continue and are expected to continue indefinitely. In addition, Dianna has been fitted with a "C-leg," a computerized prosthetic leg. A C-leg needs to be replaced every three to five years at full cost. The trial court took judicial notice that Dianna's life expectancy is 35.4 years.

We see no tangible indication that the jury acted out of prejudice, passion, or partiality to punish Clancy. Although the amount of the award in this case is sizeable, we cannot conclude that it is unreasonable given the evidence.

Decision

The court of appeals affirmed the judgment of the trial court finding Clancy liable for negligence and upheld the jury verdict awarding Dianna $10 million in damages.

Law & Ethics Questions

1. Was Clancy liable for negligence in this case? What is negligence?

2. **ETHICS** Was the award of $10 million to plaintiff Dianna Goad reasonable? Would you have awarded these damages? Or would you have awarded more or less?

3. **ETHICS** Was it ethical for defendant Clancy to appeal this case? Why or why not?

Web Exercises

1. **WEB** For the complete opinion of this case, go to *www.prenhall.com/cheesemancases*.

2. **WEB** Visit the website of the court of appeals of Indiana, at *www.state.in.us/judiciary/appeals*.

3. **WEB** Use *www.google.com* to find an article that discusses statistics of the accident rate of motorcycles.

Actual Cause

A defendant's negligent act must be the **actual cause**, or the **causation in fact**, of the plaintiff's injuries.

Example Suppose a corporation negligently pollutes the plaintiff's drinking water. The plaintiff dies of a heart attack unrelated to the polluted water. Although the corporation has acted negligently, it is not liable for the plaintiff's death. There were a negligent act and an injury, but there was no cause-and-effect relationship between them. If, instead, the plaintiff had died from the pollution, there would have been causation in fact, and the polluting corporation would have been liable.

If two (or more) persons are liable for negligently causing the plaintiff's injuries, both (or all) can be held liable to the plaintiff if each of their acts is a substantial factor in causing the plaintiff's injuries.

LANDMARK CASE

Palsgraf v. The Long Island Railroad Company

> ❝Negligence is not actionable unless it involves the invasion of a legally protected interest, the violation of a right. Proof of negligence in the air, so to speak, will not do.❞
>
> —Justice Cardozo

The landmark case establishing the doctrine of proximate cause is *Palsgraf v. The Long Island Railroad Company*,[5] a New York case decided in 1928. Helen Palsgraf was standing on a platform, waiting for a passenger train. The Long Island Railroad Company owned and operated the trains and employed the station guards. As a man carrying a package wrapped in a newspaper tried to board the moving train, railroad guards tried to help him. In doing so, the package was dislodged from the man's arm, fell to the railroad tracks, and exploded. The package contained hidden fireworks. The explosion shook the railroad platform, causing a scale located on the platform to fall on Helen Palsgraf, injuring her. She sued the railroad for negligence. Justice Cardozo eloquently addressed the issue of proximate cause:

The conduct of the defendant's guard, if a wrong in its relation to the holder of the package, was not a wrong in its relation to the plaintiff, standing far away. Relatively to her it was not negligence at all. Nothing in the situation gave notice that the falling package had in it the potency of peril to persons thus removed. Negligence is not actionable unless it involves the invasion of a legally protected interest, the violation of a right. Proof of negligence in the air, so to speak, will not do. In every instance, before negligence can be predicated of a given act, back of the act must be sought and found a duty to the individual complaining, the observance of which would have averted or avoided the injury.

The argument for the plaintiff is built upon the shifting meanings of such words as "wrong" and "wrongful," and shares their instability. What the plaintiff must show is "a wrong" to herself, *i.e.*, a violation of her own right, and not merely a wrong to some one else, nor conduct "wrongful" because unsocial. The risk reasonably to be perceived defines the duty to be obeyed, and risk imports relation; it is risk to another or to others within the range of apprehension. Here, by concession, there was nothing in the situation to suggest to the most cautious mind that the parcel wrapped in newspaper would spread wreckage through the station. If the guard had thrown it down knowingly and willfully, he would not have threatened the plaintiff's safety, so far as appearances could warn him. His conduct would not have involved, even then, an unreasonable probability of invasion of her bodily security. Liability can be no greater where the act is inadvertent.

Negligence, like risk, is thus a term of relation. Negligence in the abstract, apart from things related, is surely not a tort, if indeed it is understandable at all. One who seeks redress at law does not make out a cause of action by showing without more that there has been damage to his person. If the harm was not willful, he must show that the act as to him had possibilities of danger so many and apparent as to entitle him to be protected against the doing of it though the harm was unintended.

Justice Cardozo denied Palsgraf's recovery, finding that the railroad was not the proximate cause of her injuries.

Law & Ethics Questions

1. Define *proximate cause*.

2. **ETHICS** Do you think that the railroad should have been held liable in this case? Why or why not?

Web Exercises

1. **WEB** For the complete opinion of this case, go to *www.prenhall.com/cheesemancases*.

2. **WEB** Visit the website of the court that decided this case, at *www.courts.state.ny.us/ctapps*.

3. **WEB** Use *www.google.com* to find an article about Justice Cardozo's decision in *Palsgraf*.

Proximate Cause

Under the law, a negligent party is not necessarily liable for all damages set in motion by his or her negligent act. Based on public policy, the law establishes a point along the damage chain after which the negligent party is no longer responsible for the consequences of his or her actions. This limitation on liability is referred to as **proximate cause**, or **legal cause**. The general test of proximate cause is *forseeability*. A negligent party who is found to be the actual cause—but not the proximate cause—of the plaintiff's injuries is not liable to the plaintiff. Situations are examined on a case-by-case basis.

The following case examines whether the defendant proximately caused the plaintiff's injuries.

CASE 5.6
Duty of Care and Proximate Cause

Carter v. Indianapolis Power & Light Company and Indiana Bell Telephone Company, Inc.

837 N.E.2d 509,
Web 2005 Ind. App. Lexis 2129 (2005)
Court of Appeals of Indiana

> “*The utility poles did not cause Mitchell to drive 80 m.p.h. on a road with a 40 m.p.h. speed limit, or to deliberately surrender control of her car by becoming airborne, . . .*”
>
> —Judge Crone

Facts

Seventeen-year-olds Adam C. Jacobs and David Messer made the acquaintance of 17-year-old waitress Sarah Mitchell at a pizza restaurant in Indianapolis, Indiana. Jacobs and Messer returned to the restaurant when Mitchell's shift ended at midnight, and the trio went to Messer's home. At approximately 2:30 A.M., Mitchell drove her Honda Accord with Jacobs in the front seat and Messer in the back seat. Jacobs suggested that they "jump the hills" on Edgewood Avenue, which he had done at least 20 times before. The speed limit for Edgewood Avenue, a two-lane road, was 40 miles per hour. Mitchell accelerated to approximately 80 miles per hour to jump the "big hill" on Edgewood Avenue near its crossroad at Emerson Avenue. The car crested the hill at 80 mills per hour, went airborne for a considerable distance, and landed in the middle of the road. Mitchell lost control of the car and over-steered to the right. The car sideswiped an Indiana Bell Telephone Company, Inc., utility pole (pole 65), and spun clockwise several times. The car then slammed broadside into an Indianapolis Power & Light Company utility pole (pole 66) and caught on fire. The two utility poles were located approximately 25 feet from Edgewood Avenue at the edge of the utility companies' right of way. Messer escaped from the burning wreckage but was unable to rescue the unconscious Mitchell and Jacobs, both of whom died.

Susan J. Carter, the personal representative of the estate of Adam C. Jacobs, sued Indiana Bell and Indianapolis Power, alleging that the companies were negligent in the placement of their utility poles along Edgewood Avenue. The trial court held that the defendants had not breached their duty of care to Jacobs and were therefore not liable to Jacobs. The trial court granted summary judgment to the utility companies. Carter appealed.

Issue

Did Indiana Bell or Indianapolis Power breach their duty of care to Jacobs and proximately cause his death?

Language of the Court

To recover in negligence, the plaintiff must establish: (1) a duty on the part of the defendant to conform his conduct to a standard of care arising from his relationship with the plaintiff; (2) a failure on the part of the defendant to conform his conduct to the requisite standard of care; and (3) an injury to the plaintiff proximately caused by the breach. The duty, when found to exist, is the duty to exercise reasonable care under the circumstances. The duty never changes. However, the standard of conduct required to measure up to that duty varies depending upon the particular circumstances. Carter contends that the Utilities owe a duty to the motoring public to exercise reasonable care when placing utility poles along the roadway. We believe that the utility companies owe a duty to the motoring public to exercise reasonable care in placing utility poles along Indiana's public roads and highways.

The Utilities argue that only one conclusion can be drawn from the undisputed facts of this case: Jacobs' death was the direct result of the superseding, intentional act of Mitchell's reckless driving. The causal chain between any alleged negligence of the Utilities and the Plaintiff's harm was broken by Mitchell's willful, criminal actions. The utility poles did not cause Mitchell to drive 80 m.p.h. on a road with a 40 m.p.h. speed limit, or to deliberately surrender control of her car by becoming airborne, or to over-steer when she landed, or to leave the roadway. It strains reason to suggest that Utilities should foresee the sort of willful disregard for the law and personal safety that indisputably led to this accident.

We agree. The undisputed evidence indicates that Edgewood Avenue is a straight two-lane thoroughfare with a speed limit of forty miles per hour. The utility poles are located on or near the edge of the right-of-way, approximately three feet from the edge of the roadway. There is nothing to suggest that the poles' location is inherently dangerous to those who engage in the ordinary and normal public use of Edgewood Avenue. In sum, we conclude as a matter of law that the Utilities could not reasonably have foreseen that Mitchell would intentionally jump the hills on Edgewood Avenue at high speed and that her negligence therefore relieves the Utilities from any and all liability to Carter for their placement of poles 65 and 66.

Decision

The court of appeals held that the defendant utilities were not liable for the death of Jacobs. The court of appeals affirmed the trial court's summary judgment in favor of the two utility companies.

Law & Ethics Questions

1. Define *duty of care*. Does this duty change, depending on the facts of the case? Explain.

2. Define *proximate cause*. Is this an easy standard to apply?

3. **ETHICS** Should the utility companies have anticipated such conduct as occurred in this case and designed the location of their utility poles accordingly?

4. **ETHICS** Was it ethical for the plaintiff to pursue the claim in this case? Why or why not?

Web Exercises

1. **WEB** For the complete opinion of this case, go to *www.prenhall.com/cheesemancases*.

2. **WEB** Visit the website of the court of appeals of Indiana, at *www.state.in.us/judiciary/appeals*.

3. **WEB** Use *www.google.com* to locate the intersection of Edgewood Avenue and Emerson Avenue in Indianapolis, Indiana.

Special Negligence Doctrines

The courts have developed many *special negligence doctrines*. The most important of these are discussed in the paragraphs that follow.

Professional Malpractice

Professionals, such as doctors, lawyers, architects, accountants, and others, owe a duty of ordinary care in providing their services. This duty is known as the *reasonable professional standard*. A professional who breaches this duty of care is liable for the injury his or her negligence causes. This liability is commonly referred to as **professional malpractice**.

Example A doctor who amputates a wrong leg is liable for *medical malpractice*. A lawyer who fails to file a document with the court on time, causing the client's case to be dismissed, is liable for *legal malpractice*. An accountant who fails to use reasonable care, knowledge, skill, and judgment in providing auditing and other accounting services to a client is liable for *accounting malpractice*.

Negligent Infliction of Emotional Distress

Some jurisdictions have extended the tort of emotional distress to include the **negligent infliction of emotional distress**. The most common examples of this involve bystanders who witness the injury or death of a loved one that is caused by another's negligent conduct. The bystander, even though not personally physically injured, can sue the negligent party for his or her own mental suffering under this tort.

Generally, to be successful in this type of case, the plaintiff must prove that (1) a relative was killed or injured by the defendant, (2) the plaintiff suffered severe emotional distress, and (3) the plaintiff's mental distress resulted from a sensory and contemporaneous observance of the accident. Some states require that the plaintiff's mental distress be manifested by some physical injury; other states have eliminated this requirement.

Example A father is driving his young daughter to school in his automobile when another driver negligently runs a red light and hits their automobile. Suppose that the young daughter dies from her injuries, and the father is uninjured. The father suffers severe emotional distress because of the loss of his daughter and manifests this distress by suffering physically. In this case, the father can sue the driver for negligence (1) to recover for his daughter's death and (2) for negligent infliction of emotional distress to recover damages for the severe distress he suffers.

In the following case, the court had to decide whether the elements for liability for negligent infliction of emotional distress existed.

CASE 5.7
Negligent Infliction of Emotional Distress

Colbert v. Moomba Sports, Inc. and Skier's Choice, Inc.

135 P.3d 485,
Web 2006 Wash. App. Lexis 975 (2006)
Court of Appeals of Washington

> **"***The tort of negligent infliction of emotional distress is a limited, judicially-created cause of action that allows bystander family members to obtain damages for "foreseeable" intangible injuries caused by viewing a physically-injured loved one shortly after a traumatic accident.***"**
>
> —Judge Hunt

Facts

Shortly after 2:00 A.M. one summer night, 12-year-old Denise Colbert and several friends took a motor boat out on Lake Tapps. Denise had been drinking. Skier's Choice, Inc., had manufactured the Moomba brand boat they were using. Denise and several of her friends jumped off the boat into the water and held onto the boat's rear platform as the boat drove slowly toward shore. When the boat neared 200 yards from shore, Denise and Lindsay Lynam began swimming to shore. Sometime between 3:00 and 3:30 A.M. Lindsay noticed that Denise had disappeared beneath the water's surface. The friends called 911 and began searching for Denise. One of the friends called Denise's father, Jay Colbert, and told him that Denise had fallen off the boat and they could not find her.

Police and other rescuers arrived around 3:45 A.M., and Mr. Colbert arrived sometimes thereafter. Mr. Colbert went to a friend's dock, where they could watch the rescuers search for Denise. The rescuers search with boats, spotlights, and divers. Some time after 6:00 A.M., rescuers found Denise's body. About 10 minutes later Mr. Colbert saw rescuers, about 100 yards away, pull a body out of the water and onto a boat. The rescuers wrapped the body in a blanket and placed the body in an ambulance while Mr. Colbert looked on. The medical examiner reported the cause of Denise's death as drowning. The examiner noted two other significant conditions: high levels of carbon monoxide and ethanol toxicity that would come from a boat's engine.

Thereafter, Mr. Colbert saw a psychologist, who later testified that Mr. Colbert was suffering from severe emotional distress caused by the death of his daughter. Mr. Colbert sued Skier's Choice, Inc., the manufacturer of the boat, to recover damages under the doctrine of negligent infliction of emotional distress. The trial court dismissed Mr. Colbert's claim. Mr. Colbert appealed.

Issue

Is the defendant liable to Mr. Colbert under the legal theory of negligence infliction of emotional distress?

Language of the Court

The tort of negligent infliction of emotional distress is a limited, judicially-created cause of action that allows bystander family members to obtain damages for "foreseeable" intangible injuries caused by viewing a physically-injured loved one shortly after a traumatic accident.

We agree with the trial court and hold that the following undisputed facts here do not, as a matter of law, meet the "shortly thereafter" requirement for establishing a bystander relative's cause of action for negligent infliction of emotional distress. Unlike the usual negligent infliction of emotional distress case, where a family member either witnesses a loved one in an accident or comes upon the scene minutes later and observes the loved one's agonized state, Colbert was not at the scene either to witness Denise's drowning or soon enough thereafter to witness the final seconds of her disappearance under the lake's surface. Instead, he arrived at least 10 to 15 minutes after learning that his daughter has fallen off a boat and disappeared in the lake.

Not only was Denise not visible anywhere when Colbert arrived at the lake, but also he arrived only after many rescuers were already present and searching for his missing daughter. Before ever laying eyes on his daughter, or her body, Colbert primarily witnessed these rescue workers' futile attempts off shore for several hours. When the rescuers pulled her body from the lake onto the boat, she was a football field away, or about 100 yards, from Colbert's vantage point on the dock, her features were not visible, and the rescuers immediately covered her body in a blanket.

Decision

The court of appeals held that the elements for finding negligent infliction of emotional distress were not met in this case. The court of appeals affirmed the trial court's dismissal of Mr. Colbert's cause of action alleging negligent infliction of emotional distress.

Law & Ethics Questions

1. Define the legal doctrine of *negligent infliction of emotional distress*.

2. Do you think that Mr. Colbert suffered emotional distress sufficient to award damages for negligent infliction of emotional distress?

3. Why did the court not find negligent infliction of emotional distress in this case?

4. **ETHICS** Was it ethical for the defendant to argue against liability for negligent infliction of emotional distress in this case? Why or why not?

Web Exercises

1. **WEB** For the complete opinion of this case, go to www.prenhall.com/cheesemancases.

2. **WEB** Visit the website of Skier's Choice, Inc., at www.skierschoice.com. Find the Moomba line of boats.

3. **WEB** Visit the website of the Court of Appeals of Washington, at www.courts.wa.gov.

4. **WEB** Use www.google.com to find an article that discusses negligent infliction of emotional distress. Read it.

Negligence Per Se

Statutes often establish duties owed by one person to another. The violation of a statute that proximately causes an injury is **negligence per se**. The plaintiff in such an action must prove that (1) a statute existed, (2) the statute was enacted to prevent the type of injury suffered, and (3) the plaintiff was within a class of persons meant to be protected by the statute.

Example Most cities have an ordinance that places the responsibility for fixing public sidewalks in residential areas on the homeowners whose homes front the sidewalks. A homeowner is liable if he or she fails to repair a damaged sidewalk in front of his or her home and a pedestrian trips and is injured because of the damage. The injured party does not have to prove that the homeowner owed the duty because the statute establishes that.

Res Ipsa Loquitur

If a defendant is in control of a situation in which a plaintiff has been injured and has superior knowledge of the circumstances surrounding the injury, the plaintiff might have difficulty proving the defendant's negligence. In such a situation, the law applies the doctrine of *res ipsa loquitur* (Latin for "the thing speaks for itself"). This doctrine raises a presumption of negligence and switches the burden to the defendant to prove that he or she was not negligent. *Res ipsa loquitur* applies in cases where the following elements are met:

1. The defendant had exclusive control of the instrumentality or situation that caused the plaintiff's injury.
2. The injury would not have ordinarily occurred but for someone's negligence.

Example Haeran goes in for major surgery and is given anesthesia to put her to sleep during the operation. Sometime after the operation, it is discovered that a surgical instrument was left in Haeran during the operation. She suffers severe injury because of the left-in instrument. Haeran would be hard-pressed to identify which doctor or nurse had been careless and left the instrument in her body. In this case, the court can apply the doctrine of *res ipsa loquitur* and place the presumption of negligence on the defendants. Any defendant who can prove that he or she did not leave the instrument in Haeran escapes liability; any defendant who does not disprove his or her negligence is liable. Other typical *res ipsa loquitur* cases involve commercial airplane crashes, falling elevators, and the like.

Good Samaritan Laws

In the past, liability exposure made many doctors, nurses, and other medical professionals reluctant to stop and render aid to victims in emergency situations, such as highway accidents. Almost all states have enacted **Good Samaritan laws** that relieve medical professionals from liability for injury caused by their ordinary negligence in such circumstances. Good Samaritan laws protect medical professionals only from liability for their *ordinary negligence*, not for injuries caused by their gross negligence or reckless or intentional conduct. Most Good Samaritan laws protect licensed doctors, nurses, and laypersons who have been certified in CPR. Laypersons not trained in CPR are not generally protected by Good Samaritan statutes—that is, they are liable for injuries caused by their ordinary negligence in rendering aid.

Example Sam is injured in an automobile accident and is unconscious in his automobile alongside the road. Doctor Pamela Heathcoat, who is driving by the scene of the accident, stops, pulls Sam from the burning wreckage, and administers first aid. In doing so, Pamela negligently breaks Sam's shoulder. If Pamela's negligence is ordinary negligence, she is not liable to Sam because the Good Samaritan law protects her from liability; if Pamela was grossly negligent or reckless in administering aid to Sam, she is liable to him for the injuries she caused. It is a question of fact for the jury to decide whether a doctor's conduct was ordinary negligence or gross negligence or recklessness.

Example If Cathy, a layperson not trained in CPR, had rendered aid to accident-injured Sam and caused Sam injury because of her ordinary negligence, the Good Samaritan law would not protect her, and she would be liable to Sam.

Dram Shop Acts

Many states have enacted **dram shop acts** that make taverns and bartenders civilly liable for injuries caused to or by patrons who are served too much alcohol. The alcohol must be either served in sufficient quantity to make the patron intoxicated or served to an already intoxicated person. Both the tavern and the bartender are liable to third persons injured by the patron and for injuries suffered by the patron. They are also liable for injuries caused by or to minors served by the tavern, regardless of whether the minors are intoxicated.

Guest Statutes

Many states have enacted **guest statutes** which provide that if a driver voluntarily and without compensation give a ride in a vehicle to another person (e.g., a hitchhiker), the driver is not liable to the passenger for injuries caused by the driver's ordinary negligence. However, if the passenger pays compensation to the driver, the driver owes a duty of ordinary care to the passenger and will be held liable. The driver is always liable to the passenger for wanton and gross negligence—for example, injuries caused because of excessive speed.

Fireman's Rule

Under the **fireman's rule**, a firefighter who is injured while putting out a fire may not sue the party whose negligence caused the fire. This rule has been extended to police officers and other government workers. The bases for this rule are (1) people might not call for help if they could be held liable; (2) firefighters, police officers, and other such workers receive special training for their jobs; and (3) these workers have special medical and retirement programs that are paid for by the public.

"Danger Invites Rescue" Doctrine

The law recognizes a **"danger invites rescue" doctrine**. Under this doctrine, a rescuer who is injured while going to someone's rescue can sue the person who caused the dangerous situation.

Example A passerby who is injured while trying to rescue children from a fire set by an arsonist can bring a civil suit against the arsonist.

Social Host Liability

Several states have adopted the **social host liability** rule. This rule provides that a social host is liable for injuries caused by guests who are served alcohol at a social function (e.g., birthday party, wedding reception) and later cause injury because they are intoxicated. The injury may be to a third person or to the guest himself or herself. The alcohol served at the social function must be the cause of the injury. A few states have adopted statutes that relieve social hosts from such liability.[6]

> Every unjust decision is a reproach to the law or the judge who administers it. If the law should be in danger of doing injustice, then equity should be called in to remedy it. Equity was introduced to mitigate the rigour of the law.
>
> Lord Denning
> *M.R. Re Vandervell's Trusts (1974)*

Liability of Landowners

Owners and renters of real property owe certain duties to protect visitors from injury while on the property. A landowner's or tenant's liability generally depends on the status of the visitor. Visitors fall into the following categories:

1. *Invitees and licensees.* An **invitee** is a person who has been expressly or impliedly invited onto the owner's premises for the *mutual benefit* of both parties (e.g., guests invited for dinner, the mail carrier, customers of a business). A **licensee** is a person who, *for his or her own benefit*, enters onto the premises with the express or implied consent of the owner (e.g., an Avon representative, salespersons, Jehovah's Witnesses). An owner owes a **duty of ordinary care** to invitees and licensees. An owner is liable if he or she negligently causes injury to an invitee or a licensee.

   Example A homeowner is liable if she leaves a garden hose across the walkway on which an invitee or a licensee trips and is injured.

2. *Trespassers.* A **trespasser** is a person who has no invitation, permission, or right to be on another's property. Burglars are a common type of trespasser. Generally, an owner does not owe a duty of ordinary care to a trespasser.

   Example If a trespasser trips and injures himself on a bicycle the owner negligently left out, the owner is not liable. An owner does owe a **duty not to willfully or wantonly injure a trespasser**. Thus, an owner cannot set traps to injure trespassers.

A few states have eliminated the invitee/licensee/trespasser distinction. These states hold that owners and renters owe a duty of ordinary care to all persons who enter upon the property.

Liability of Common Carriers and Innkeepers

The common law holds common carriers and innkeepers to a higher standard of care than it does most other businesses. Common carriers and innkeepers owe a **duty of utmost care**—rather than a duty of ordinary care—to their passengers and guests. For example, innkeepers must provide security for their guests. The concept of utmost care is applied on a case-by-case basis. Obviously, a large hotel must provide greater security to guests than a "mom-and-pop" motel. Some states and cities have adopted specific statutes and ordinances relating to this duty.

In the following case, the court found that a landowner had engaged in *willful and wanton conduct*, and it awarded punitive damages.

C A S E 5.8
Liability of Landowners

Matthias v. Accor Economy Lodging, Inc. and Motel 6 Operating L.P.

347 F.3d 672,
Web 2003 U.S. App. Lexis 21299
United States Court of Appeals for the Seventh Circuit

“ *Motel 6 could not have rented any rooms at the prices it charged had it informed guests that the risk of being bitten by bedbugs was appreciable.* ”

—Judge Posner

Facts

The defendants, Accor Economy Lodging, Inc., and Motel 6 Operating L.P. (hereinafter referred to as Motel 6) operate the Motel 6 nationwide chain of motels and hotels. One of these hotels is in downtown Chicago. In 1998, EcoLab, an extermination service that the motel used, discovered bedbugs in several rooms in the motel and recommended that it be hired to spray every room, for which EcoLab would charge the motel $500 total, but the motel refused. The next year, bedbugs were again discovered in a room, but EcoLab was hired to spray just that room. By the spring of 2000, the motel had given refunds to several guests bitten by bedbugs in their rooms. The motel manager looked at several rooms and found bedbugs. Further incidents of guests being bitten by bedbugs led the motel's manager to recommend that the motel be closed while every room was sprayed, but Motel 6 refused. The infestation continued, and several of the rooms were placed on "Do not rent, bugs in room" status.

In November 2000, Burl Matthias and Desiree Matthias, brother and sister, checked in to the Motel 6 in downtown Chicago. They were given Room 514, even though it was on the "Do not rent, bugs in room" list. That night, 190 of the motel's 191 rooms were rented. That night the Matthiases were severely bitten by bedbugs. The Matthiases sued Motel 6 to recover damages, alleging that it had engaged in willful and wanton conduct. The jury agreed and awarded each plaintiff $5,000 in compensatory damages and $186,000 in punitive damages. Motel 6 appealed.

Issue

Was Motel 6 liable for willful and wanton conduct that supported the award of punitive damages of $186,000 to each plaintiff?

Language of the Court

Although bedbug bites are not as serious as the bites of some other insects, they are painful and unsightly. Motel 6 could not have rented any rooms at the prices it charged had it informed guests that the risk of being bitten by bedbugs was appreciable. Its failure to warn guests or to take effective measures to eliminate the bedbugs amounted to fraud and probably to battery as well. There was, in short, sufficient evidence of "willful and wanton conduct" to permit an award of punitive damages in this case.

But what amount? The term "punitive damages" implies punishment, and a standard principle of penal theory is that "the punishment should fit the crime." All things considered, we cannot say that the award of punitive damages was excessive, albeit the precise number chosen by the jury was arbitrary. It is probably not a coincidence that $5,000 + $186,000 = $191,000/191 = $1,000: i.e., $1,000 per room in the motel.

Decision

The Court of Appeals held that Motel 6's willful and wanton conduct warranted the trial court's award of $186,000 in punitive damages to each defendant. The Court of Appeals affirmed the judgment of the District Court.

Law & Ethics Questions

1. What standard of care is owed by innkeepers to their guests?
2. Define *punitive damages*. Why are punitive damages awarded? Explain.
3. **ETHICS** Did Motel 6 act ethically in this case? Explain.
4. **ETHICS** Does the possibility of an award of punitive damages make businesses act more responsibly?

Web Exercises

1. **WEB** For the complete opinion of this case, go to *www.prenhall.com/cheesemancases*.
2. **WEB** Visit the website of the U.S. Court of Appeal for the Sixth Circuit, at *www.ca6.uscourts.gov*.
3. **WEB** Visit the website of Motel 6, at *www.motel6.com*.

CONTEMPORARY ENVIRONMENT
Federal Tort Claims Act

The **doctrine of sovereign immunity** provides that a government is not liable to anyone hurt by the government and its employees. A government can, however, make itself liable. The federal government has enacted the **Federal Tort Claims Act (FTCA)**,[7] which is a federal statute that provides that the federal government is liable for its actions in most cases. Thus, the federal government is generally liable for the ordinary negligence of its employees.

Example Cynthia works for the federal government. One day while she is on business for the federal government and driving a federal government vehicle, she accidentally causes an automobile accident in which Jason, a pedestrian, is severely injured. The federal government is liable to Jason for any damages he has suffered.

The FTCA lists several exceptions where it has declared that it will not be liable for these listed activities. One of the express exceptions is that the federal government is not liable for "discretionary function." This would include making decisions about applications to the government for licenses, approvals, and such.

Example Wei files for a patent at the U.S. Patent and Trademark Office (PTO). After a review of the evidence, the PTO makes a decision that Wei's invention does not qualify for a patent and denies Wei's application. The PTO has made a discretionary decision. Wei cannot sue the decision makers at the PTO for negligence. Wei can challenge the decision regarding whether her invention qualified for a patent in court, however.

The following U.S. Supreme Court case examines the issue of whether the federal government could be held liable.

CASE 5.9
Federal Tort Claims Act

U.S. SUPREME COURT

Dolan v. United States Postal Service

546 U.S. 481, 126 S.Ct. 1252, 163 L.Ed.2d 1079,
Web 2006 U.S. Lexis 1820 (2006)
Supreme Court of the United States

> *"The question is whether, when mail left by the Postal Service causes the slip and fall, the exception for "loss, miscarriage, or negligent transmission of letters or postal matter" preserves sovereign immunity"*

—Justice Kennedy

Facts

Barbara Dolan fell over letters, packages, and periodicals placed by a United States Postal Service (USPS) employee on her porch. As a result of the fall, Dolan suffered serious injury. Dolan filed a claim with the Postal Service, and when her claim was denied, she filed a lawsuit against the USPS in U.S. District Court. At trial, the USPS argued that since it was a government unit, and that although the Federal Tort Claims Act (FTCA) generally assessed liability against the government for torts, it was protected by one of the exceptions in the FTCA that provides for non-liability. The exception that USPS relied on stated that the federal government shall not be liable for "any claim arising out of the loss, miscarriage, or negligent transmission of letters or postal matters." Dolan countered that the USPS was liable because the language of the exemption did not apply to the tort of the USPS employee in this case. The U.S. District Court agreed with the USPS and dismissed Dolan's lawsuit. The U.S. Court of Appeals agreed. Dolan appealed to the U.S. Supreme Court.

Issue

Does the exception in the FTCA that protects the USPS from any claim arising out of loss, miscarriage, or negligent transmission of letters or postal matters prevent plaintiff Dolan's lawsuit?

Language of the U.S. Supreme Court

The FTCA waives sovereign immunity in two different sections of the United States Code. The first confers federal-court jurisdiction in a defined category of cases involving negligence committed by federal employees in the course of their employment. This jurisdictional grant covers: "claims against the United States, for money damages, for injury or loss of property, or personal injury or death caused by the negligent or wrongful act or omission of any employee of the Government while acting within the scope of his office or employment, under circumstances where the United States, if a private person, would be liable to the claimant in accordance with the law of the place where the act or omission occurred." As to claims falling within this jurisdictional grant, the FTCA, in a second provision, makes the United States liable "in the same manner and to the same extent as a private individual under like circumstances, though not for interest prior to judgment or for punitive damages."

The FTCA qualifies its waiver of sovereign immunity for certain categories of claims (13 in all). If one of the exceptions applies, the bar of sovereign immunity remains. The relevant subsection for our purposes, pertaining to postal operations, states: "The provisions of this chapter of this title shall not apply to any claim arising out of the loss, miscarriage, or negligent transmission of letters or postal matter."

We assume, that under the applicable state law a person injured by tripping over a package or bundle of papers negligently left on the porch of a residence by a private party would have a cause of action for damages. The question is whether, when mail left by the Postal Service causes the slip and fall, the exception for "loss, miscarriage, or negligent transmission of letters or postal matter" preserves sovereign immunity despite the FTCA's more general statements of waiver.

Here, as both parties acknowledge, mail is "lost" if it is destroyed or misplaced and "miscarried" if it goes to the wrong address. Since both those terms refer to failings in the postal obligation to deliver mail in a timely manner to the right address it would be odd if "negligent transmission" swept far more broadly to include injuries like those alleged here—injuries that happen to be caused by postal employees but involve neither failure to transmit mail nor damage to its contents.

We think it more likely that Congress intended to retain immunity, as a general rule, only for injuries arising, directly or consequentially, because mail either fails to arrive at all or arrives late, in damaged condition, or at the wrong address. The Government raises the specter of frivolous slip-and-fall claims inundating the Postal Service. Slip-and-fall liability, however, to the extent state tort law imposes it, is a risk shared by any business that makes home deliveries. The postal exception is inapplicable and Dolan's claim falls within the FTCA's general waiver of federal sovereign immunity.

Decision

The U.S. Supreme Court held that the Federal Tort Claims Act allowed plaintiff Dolan to pursue her case against the Postal Service. The Supreme Court reversed the judgment of the U.S. Court of Appeals and remanded the case for further proceedings consistent with this opinion.

Law & Ethics Questions

1. What does the doctrine of sovereign immunity provide? Explain.
2. What does the Federal Tort Claims Act do? Explain.
3. What does the postal exception in the FTCA provide? Explain.
4. **ETHICS** Do you think that there will be many frivolous lawsuits, as the Postal Service alleges?

Web Exercises

1. **WEB** For the complete opinion of this case, go to *www.prenhall.com/cheesemancases*.
2. **WEB** Visit the website of the United States Postal Service, at *www.usps.com*.
3. **WEB** Visit the website of the U.S. Supreme Court, at *www.supremecourtus.gov*, and try to find documents that relate to this case.
4. **WEB** Use *www.google.com* to find an article that discusses the Federal Tort Claims Act. Read it.

Defenses against Negligence

A defendant in a negligence lawsuit may raise several defenses to the imposition of liability. These defenses are discussed in the following paragraphs.

Superseding, or Intervening, Event

Under negligence, a person is liable only for foreseeable events. Therefore, an original negligent party can raise a **superseding**, or **intervening, event** as a defense to liability.

Example Assume that an avid golfer negligently hits a spectator with a golf ball, knocking the spectator unconscious. While lying on the ground waiting for an ambulance to come, the spectator is struck by a bolt of lightning and killed. The golfer is liable for the injuries caused by the golf ball. He is not liable for the death of the spectator, however, because the lightning bolt was an unforeseen intervening event.

Assumption of the Risk

If a plaintiff knows of and voluntarily enters into or participates in a risky activity that results in injury, the law recognizes that the plaintiff assumed, or took on, the risk involved. Thus, the defendant can raise the defense of **assumption of the risk** against the plaintiff. This defense assumes that the plaintiff (1) had knowledge of the specific risk and (2) voluntarily assumed that risk. For example, under this theory, a race car driver assumes the risk of being injured or killed in a crash.

In the following two cases, the court had to decide whether the plaintiff had assumed the risk.

C A S E **5.10**
Assumption of the Risk

Lilya v. The Greater Gulf State Fair, Inc.

855 So.2d 1049,
Web 2003 Ala. Lexis 57 (2003)
Supreme Court of Alabama

> 66 *Here, the only evidence of danger stemming from the mechanical bull ride is the most open and obvious characteristic of the ride: the possibility of falling off the mechanical bull.* 99
>
> —Judge Houston

Facts

The Greater Gulf State Fair, Inc., operated the Gulf State Fair in Mobile County, Alabama. One of the events at the fair was a mechanical bull ride for which participants paid money to ride the mechanical bull. A mechanical bull is a ride where the rider sits on a motorized device shaped like a real bull, and the ride simulates a real bull ride as the mechanical bull turns, twists, and bucks. The challenge is to stay on the bull and not be thrown off the bull. A large banner above the ride read "Rolling Thunder."

John Lilya and a friend watched as a rider was thrown from the mechanical bull. Lilya also watched as his friend paid and rode the bull but also was thrown off. Lilya then paid the $5 admission charge and signed a release agreement that stated: "I acknowledge that riding a mechanical bull entails known and unanticipated risks which could result in physical or emotional injury, paralysis, death, or damage to myself, to property, or to third parties. I expressly agree and promise to accept and assume all of the risks existing in this activity. My participation in this activity is purely voluntary, and I elect to participate in spite of the risks."

Lilya boarded the mechanical bull and was immediately thrown off onto a soft pad underneath the bull. Lilya reboarded the bull for a second ride. The bull ride began again and became progressively faster, spinning and bucking to the left and right until Lilya fell off the bull. On the fall, Lilya landed on his head and shoulders, and he suffered a fractured neck. Lilya sued Gulf State Fair to recover damages for his severe injuries. The trial court granted summary judgment to Gulf State Fair, finding that Lilya had voluntarily assumed an open and obvious danger. Lilya appealed.

Issue

Was riding a mechanical bull an open and obvious danger for which Lilya had voluntarily assumed the risk when he rode the mechanical bull?

Language of the Court

As the landowner, Gulf State Fair would owe Lilya, its invitee, the duty to use reasonable care. The owner of premises has no duty to warn an invitee of open and obvious defects in the premises which the invitee is aware of or should be aware of in the exercise of reasonable care. Here, the only evidence of danger stemming from the mechanical bull ride is the most open and obvious characteristic of the ride: the possibility of falling off the mechanical bull. Lilya was aware that the two riders who had ridden the mechanical bull immediately before he rode it had fallen off. He noticed the thick floor mat, and he knew that the mat was there to protect riders when they fell. Also, he signed a release that explicitly stated that riding

the mechanical bull involved inherent risks and that the risks included falling off or being thrown from the bull which could result in head, neck, and back injuries. Additionally, the very name of the ride—"Rolling Thunder"—hanging on a banner above the ride, gives a somewhat graphic indication of what is the very nature of bull riding: an extremely turbulent ride the challenge of which is to hang on and not fall off. The entertainment value—and, indeed, the concept—of bull riding becomes meaningless without the inherent possibility of falling off. *"Volenti non fit injuria"* (a person who knowingly and voluntarily risks danger cannot recover for any resulting injury).

Decision

The supreme court of Alabama held that riding a mechanical bull and being thrown and injured by the bull is an open and obvious danger and that Lilya had voluntarily assumed the risk when he rode the bull and was thrown and injured. The supreme court affirmed the trial court's grant of summary judgment in favor of Gulf State Fair.

Law & Ethics Questions

1. Do you think the doctrine of assumption of the risk should be recognized by the law? Explain.

2. **ETHICS** Did Gulf State Fair act ethically by making money from such a dangerous activity as mechanical bull riding?

3. Give several examples of sports or activities that rely on the doctrine of assumption of the risk.

Web Exercises

1. **WEB** For a complete opinion of this case, go to *www.prenhall.com/cheesemancases*.

2. **WEB** Use *www.google.com* to find the website of the Greater Gulf State Fair in Alabama.

3. **WEB** Visit the website of the Alabama supreme court, at *www.judicial.state.al.us/supreme*.

4. **WEB** Use *www.google.com* to find a video clip of a mechanical bull.

CASE **5.11**

Assumption of the Risk

Hurst v. East Coast Hockey League, Inc. and Knoxville Cherokees Hockey, Inc.

637 S.E.2d 560,
Web 2002 S.C. Lexis 366 (2006)
Supreme Court of South Carolina

❝*After a hearing on the matter, the circuit court determined the risk of pucks leaving the ice rink and entering the spectator area is well-known, obvious, and inherent to the game of hockey.***❞**

—Justice Burnett

Facts

Knoxville Cherokees Hockey, Inc., is a member of the East Coast Hockey League, a professional hockey league. During a pregame warmup, Craig A. Hurst entered the spectator area at the Florence City and County Civic Center. As he was standing in the spectator area, he was hit in the face by a hockey puck. The ice rink at the civic center was encircled by wooden dasher boards and protective Plexiglas up to a certain height. Hurst sued Knoxville Cherokees Hockey, Inc., the East Coast Hockey League, and the City and County of Florence (collectively "Respondents"). The circuit court held that Hurst had assumed the risk of flying hockey pucks when he attended the game. The court granted summary judgment to the Respondents. Hurst appealed.

Issue

Does the doctrine of implied assumption of risk protect the Respondents from liability to Hurst?

Language of the Court

After a hearing on the matter, the circuit court determined the risk of pucks leaving the ice rink and entering the spectator area is well-known, obvious, and inherent to the game of hockey. Under the doctrine of implied primary assumption of risk, Respondents' duty of care did not encompass the risk involved. The risk of a hockey spectator being struck by a flying puck is inherent to the game of hockey and is also a common, expected, and frequent risk of hockey. Respondents did not have a duty to protect Appellant Hurst, a spectator, from inherent risks of the game of hockey. Based on the foregoing analysis, we conclude Appellant's action fails as a matter of law under primary implied assumption of risk.

Decision

The Supreme Court held that the doctrine of implied assumption of the risk protected the Respondents from liability to Hurst. The Supreme Court affirmed the judgment of the circuit court in favor of the Respondents.

Law & Ethics Questions

1. Define *doctrine of assumption of the risk*.

2. Do you think hockey rinks should increase the height of the Plexiglas that encircles the rinks? Why or why not?

3. **ETHICS** Did any of the parties in this case act unethically? Explain.

Web Exercises

1. **WEB** For a complete opinion of this case, go to *www.prenhall.com/cheesemancases*.

2. **WEB** Visit the website of the East Coast Hockey League, at *www.echl.com*.

3. **WEB** Use *www.google.com* to locate a history of the Knoxville Cherokees hockey team.

4. **WEB** Visit the website of the supreme court of South Carolina, at *www.sccourts.org/supreme*.

5. **WEB** Use *www.google.com* to find a video stream of a hockey game. How high is the Plexiglas that encircles the hockey rink?

Contributory Negligence

Sometimes a plaintiff is partially liable for causing his or her own injuries. Under the common law doctrine of **contributory negligence**, a plaintiff who is partially at fault for his or her own injury cannot recover against the negligent defendant. Many states follow this rule.

Example Suppose a driver who is driving over the speed limit negligently hits and injures a pedestrian who is jaywalking. Suppose the jury finds that the driver is 80 percent responsible for the accident, and the jaywalker is 20 percent responsible. The pedestrian suffered $100,000 in injuries. Under the doctrine of contributory negligence, the pedestrian cannot recover any damages from the driver.

LAST CLEAR CHANCE RULE There is one major exception to the doctrine of contributory negligence: The defendant has a duty under the law to avoid the accident if at all possible. This rule is known as the *last clear chance rule*.

Example A driver who sees a pedestrian walking across the street against a "Don't Walk" sign must avoid hitting him or her if possible. When deciding cases involving this rule, the courts consider the attentiveness of the parties and the amount of time each had to respond to the situation.

Comparative Negligence

The application of the doctrine of contributory negligence could reach an unfair result where a party only slightly at fault for his or her injuries could not recover from an otherwise negligent defendant. Many states have replaced the doctrine of contributory negligence with the doctrine of **comparative negligence**. Under this doctrine, damages are apportioned according to fault.

Example When the comparative negligence rule is applied to the previous example, the result is much fairer. The plaintiff-pedestrian, who was 20 percent at fault for causing his own injuries, can recover 80 percent of his damages (or $80,000) from the defendant-driver. This is an example of *pure comparative negligence*. Several states have adopted *partial comparative negligence*, which provides that a plaintiff must be less than 50 percent responsible for causing his or her own injuries to recover under comparative negligence; otherwise, contributory negligence applies.

Nepal

Each country has developed its own liability laws. Individuals conducting business in foreign countries must be aware of the liability laws of those countries.

Strict Liability

Strict liability is a unique category of torts. Strict liability is *liability without fault*. That is, a participant in a covered activity will be held liable for any injuries caused by the activity, even if he or she was not negligent. This doctrine holds that (1) there are certain activities that can place the public at risk of injury even if reasonable care is taken and (2) the public should have some means of compensation if such injury occurs.

Strict liability was first imposed for *abnormally dangerous activities*, such as crop dusting, blasting, fumigation, burning of fields, storage of explosives, and the keeping of wild animals as pets.

In the following case, the court imposed strict liability.

CASE **5.12**
Strict Liability

Cook v. Whitsell-Sherman

796 N.E.2d 271,
Web 2003 Ind. Lexis 793 (2003)
Supreme Court of Indiana

❝ *The statute reflects a policy choice that the dog's owner and keeper should bear the loss rather than the injured public employee.* **❞**

—Judge Boehm

Facts

Tamara Cook owned a 100-pound Rottweiler dog named Maggie. Maggie had never demonstrated any aggressive or violent tendencies. Cook went out of town and left Maggie in the care of Marva and Joseph Hart. When Kenneth Whitsell-Sherman was delivering mail as a letter carrier for the U.S. Postal Service to the Harts' home, the Harts were on the sidewalk outside their yard, and their eight-year-old daughter was several feet away, holding Maggie on a lease. Maggie broke free and bit Whitsell-Sherman on the left hand, causing injuries. Whitsell-Sherman sued Cook to recover damages based on an Indiana statute that made dog owners strictly liable for pets who injured postal carriers. The trial court found Cook strictly liable and awarded Whitsell-Sherman $87,000 in damages. The court of appeals reversed, and Whitsell-Sherman appealed.

Issue

Is the owner of a dog strictly liable for injuries caused by the dog biting a postal carrier?

Language of the Court

At the time Maggie bit Whitsell-Sherman, Cook was Maggie's owner but not her custodian. Cook argues that the statute does not apply to her in this situation because at the time of the incident she was not in possession of the dog. Indiana law was intended to alter the common law negligence framework if the victim is a letter carrier. In this case, the statute reflects a policy choice that the dog's owner and keeper should bear the loss rather than the injured public employee. Accordingly, Cook is subject to strict liability for Maggie's biting Whitsell-Sherman.

Decision

The Indiana supreme court held that Indiana law made a dog owner strictly liable to mail carriers for injuries caused by his or her dog biting a mail carrier and upheld the liability of Maggie's owner. The supreme court held that the damages were incorrectly calculated by the trial court and remanded the case for a proper determination of damages.

Law & Ethics Questions

1. Describe the doctrine of strict liability. How does it differ from the doctrine of negligence? Explain.
2. **ETHICS** Did Cook act ethically by trying to avoid liability in this case?
3. Does household liability insurance cover injuries caused by the homeowner's pets?

Web Exercises

1. **WEB** For the complete opinion of this case, go to www.prenhall.com/cheesemancases.
2. **WEB** Visit the website of the supreme court of Indiana, at www.state.in.us/judiciary/supreme.
3. **WEB** Visit the website for the U.S. Postal Service, at www.usps.com.
4. **WEB** Use www.google.com to find a photograph of a Rottweiler dog.

Chapter Summary

Intentional Torts against Persons, p. 113

Assault

Assault is threat of immediate harm or offensive contact, or any action that arouses reasonable apprehension of imminent harm.

Battery

Battery is unauthorized and harmful or offensive physical contact with another person.

Transferred intent doctrine. If a person intends to injure one person but actually harms another person, the law transfers the perpetrator's intent from the target to the actual victim.

False Imprisonment

False imprisonment is intentional confinement or restraint of another person without authority or justification and without that person's consent.

Merchant protection statutes. These statutes permit businesses to stop, detain, and investigate suspected shoplifters (and not be held liable for false imprisonment) if the following requirements are met:

1. There are reasonable grounds for the suspicion.
2. Suspects are detained for only a reasonable time.
3. Investigations are conducted in a reasonable manner.

Misappropriation of the Right to Publicity

Misappropriation of the right to publicity refers to appropriating another person's name or identity for commercial purposes without that person's consent. Also called the tort of appropriation.

Invasion of the Right to Privacy

Invasion of the right to privacy is the unwarranted and undesired publicity of a private fact about a person. The fact does not have to be untrue. Truth is not a defense.

Defamation of Character

With defamation of character, the defendant makes an untrue statement of fact about the plaintiff that is published to a third party. Truth is an absolute defense. There are two types of defamation:

1. *Slander.* Oral defamation is called slander.
2. *Libel.* Written defamation is called libel.

Public figures as plaintiffs. These plaintiffs must prove the additional element of *malice*.

Intentional Misrepresentation (Fraud)

It occurs when a wrongdoer deceives another person out of money, property, or something else of value. A person who has been injured by an intentional misrepresentation can recover damages from the wrongdoer. Four elements are required to find fraud:

1. The wrongdoer made a false representation of material fact.
2. The wrongdoer had knowledge that the representation was false and intended to deceive the innocent party.
3. The innocent party justifiably relied on the misrepresentation.
4. The innocent party was injured.

Intentional Infliction of Emotional Distress

The tort of intentional infliction of emotional distress involves extreme and outrageous conduct intentionally or recklessly done that causes severe emotional distress. Some states require that the mental distress be manifested by physical injury. Also known as the *tort of outrage*.

Malicious Prosecution

A successful defendant in a prior lawsuit can sue the plaintiff if the first lawsuit was frivolous.

Intentional Torts against Property, p. 120

Trespass to Land

Trespass to land involves interference with a landowner's right to exclusive possession of his or her land.

Trespass to and Conversion of Personal Property

Trespass to personal property occurs when a person injures another person's personal property or interferes with that person's enjoyment of his or her property. *Conversion of personal property* involves taking over another person's personal property and depriving him or her of the use and enjoyment of the property.

Unintentional Torts (Negligence), p. 121

Negligence is "the omission to do something which a reasonable man would do, or doing something which a prudent and reasonable man would not do." To establish negligence, the plaintiff must prove the following elements of negligence:

1. The defendant owed a *duty of care* to the plaintiff.
2. The defendant *breached this duty*.

3. The plaintiff suffered *injury*.
4. The defendant's negligent act was the *actual cause* (or *causation in fact*) of the plaintiff's injuries.
5. The defendant's negligent act was the *proximate cause* (or *legal cause*) of the plaintiff's injuries. The defendant is liable only for the *foreseeable* consequences of his or her negligent act.

Duty of Care

To determine whether a defendant is liable for negligence, it must first be ascertained whether the defendant owed a *duty of care* to the plaintiff. Duty of care refers to the obligation people owe each other—that is, the duty not to cause any unreasonable harm or risk of harm.

Breach of Duty

Once a court finds that a defendant actually owed the plaintiff a duty of care, it must determine whether the defendant breached that duty. A *breach of the duty of care* is a failure to exercise care. In other words, it is the failure to act as a reasonable person would act. A breach of this duty may consist of either an action or a failure to act when there is a duty to act.

Injury to Plaintiff

Even though a defendant's act may have breached a duty of care owed to the plaintiff, this breach is not actionable unless the plaintiff suffers *injury*.

Actual Cause

A defendant's negligent act must be the *actual cause*, or the *causation in fact*, of the plaintiff's injuries.

Proximate Cause

Under the law, a negligent party is not necessarily liable for all damages set in motion by his or her negligent act. Based on public policy, the law establishes a point along the damage chain after which the negligent party is no longer responsible for the consequences of his or her actions. This limitation on liability is referred to as *proximate cause*, or *legal cause*. The general test of proximate cause is *forseeability*.

Special Negligence Doctrines, p. 128
Professional Malpractice

Doctors, lawyers, architects, accountants, and other professionals owe a duty of ordinary care in providing their services. They are judged by a *reasonable professional standard*. Professionals who breach this duty are liable to clients and some third parties for *professional malpractice*.

Negligent Infliction of Emotional Distress

A person who witnesses a close relative's injury or death may sue the negligent party who caused the accident to recover damages for any emotional distress suffered by the bystander. To recover for *negligent infliction of emotional distress*, the plaintiff must prove:

1. A relative was killed or injured by the defendant.
2. The plaintiff suffered severe emotional distress.
3. The plaintiff's mental distress resulted from a sensory and contemporaneous observance of the accident. Some states require that the mental distress be manifested by physical injury.

Negligence Per Se

With negligence per se, a statute or an ordinance establishes the duty of care. A violation of the statute or ordinance constitutes a breach of this duty of care.

Res Ipsa Loquitur

With *res ipsa loquitur*, a presumption of negligence is established if the defendant had exclusive control of the instrumentality or situation that caused the plaintiff's injury and the injury would not have ordinarily occurred but for someone's negligence. The defendant may rebut this presumption.

Good Samaritan Laws

Good Samaritan laws relieve doctors and other medical professionals from liability for ordinary negligence when rendering medical aid in emergency situations.

Dram Shop Acts

Dram shop acts are state statutes that make taverns and bartenders liable for injuries caused to or by patrons who are served too much alcohol and cause injury to themselves or others.

Guest Statutes

Guest statutes provide that a driver of a vehicle is not liable for ordinary negligence to passengers he or she gratuitously transports. The driver is liable for gross negligence.

Fireman's Rule

Based on the fireman's rule, firefighters, police officers, and other government employees who are injured in the performance of their duties cannot sue the person who negligently caused the dangerous situation that caused the injury.

"Danger Invites Rescue" Doctrine

Based on the "danger invites rescue" doctrine, a person who is injured while going to someone's rescue may sue the person who caused the dangerous situation.

Social Host Liability

Some states make social hosts liable for injuries caused by guests who are served alcohol at a social function and later cause injury because they are intoxicated.

Liability of Landowners

Landowners (and tenants) owe the following duties to persons who come upon their property:
1. *Invitees.* Invitees are owed a duty of ordinary care
2. *Licensees.* Licensees are owed a duty of ordinary care
3. *Trespassers.* Trespassers are owed a duty not to willfully and wantonly injure trespassers.

Liability of Common Carriers and Innkeepers

Common carriers and innkeepers have a *duty of utmost care*, rather than the duty of ordinary care, to protect their passengers and patrons from injury.

Defenses against Negligence, p. 135

Superseding, or Intervening, Event

A superseding event is an intervening event caused by another person that caused the plaintiff's injuries and relieves the defendant from liability.

Assumption of the Risk

A defendant is not liable for the plaintiff's injuries if the plaintiff had knowledge of a specific risk and voluntarily assumed that risk.

Contributory Negligence

Sometimes a plaintiff is partially liable for causing his on her own injuries. Under the common law doctrine of *contributory negligence*, a plaintiff who is partially at fault for his or her own injury cannot recover against the negligent defendant. Many states follow this rule.

Comparative Negligence

The application of the doctrine of contributory negligence could reach an unfair result where a party only slightly at fault for his or her injuries could not recover from an otherwise negligent defendant. Many states have replaced the doctrine of contributory negligence with the doctrine of *comparative negligence*. Under this doctrine, damages are apportioned according to fault.

Strict Liability, p. 138

Strict liability is *liability without fault*. Strict liability is applied to dangerous activities. A defendant can be held liable for any injury caused by his or her participation in such activity, even if he or she was not negligent.

Test Review Terms and Concepts

Actual cause (causation in fact)   126
Assault   113
Assumption of the risk   135
Battery   114
Breach of the duty of care   122
Comparative negligence   137
Contributory negligence   137
Conversion of personal property   120
"Danger invites rescue" doctrine   131
Defamation of character   116
Disparagement   117
Doctrine of sovereign immunity   133
Dram shop act   131
Duty of care   121
Duty of ordinary care   132
Duty of utmost care   132
Duty not to willfully or wantonly
   injure a trespasser   132
False imprisonment   114
Federal Tort Claims Act
   (FTCA)   133

Fireman's rule   131
Good Samaritan law   130
Guest statute   131
Injury   124
Intentional misrepresentation
   (fraud)   118
Intentional tort   113
Invasion of the right to privacy   115
Invitee   132
Libel   116
Licensee   132
Malicious prosecution   120
Merchant protection statute
   (shopkeeper's privilege)   114
Negligence (unintentional tort)   121
Negligence per se   130
Negligent infliction of emotional
   distress   128
New York Times Co. v. Sullivan   116
*Palsgraf v. The Long Island Railroad
   Company*   126

Professional malpractice   128
Proximate cause (legal cause)   127
Res ipsa loquitur   130
Scienter   118
Slander   116
Social host liability   131
Strict liability   138
Superseding (intervening)
   event   135
Tort   113
Tort of intentional infliction of
   emotional distress (tort of
   outrage)   118
Tort of misappropriation of the
   right to publicity (tort of
   appropriation)   115
Transferred intent doctrine   114
Trespass to land   120
Trespass to personal property   120
Trespasser   132

Case Problems

5.1 Intentional Tort: The Baltimore Orioles, a professional baseball team, visited Boston's Fenway Park to play the Boston Red Sox, another professional baseball team. Ross Grimsley was a pitcher for the visiting Baltimore club. During one period of the game, Grimsley was warming up in the bullpen, throwing pitches to a catcher. During this warmup, Boston spectators in the stands heckled Grimsley. After Grimsley had completed warming up, Grimsley wound up as if he were going to throw the ball in his hand at the plate but then turned and threw the ball at one of the hecklers in the stand. The ball traveled at about 80 miles an hour, passed through a wire fence protecting the spectators, missed the heckler that Grimsley was aiming at, and hit another spectator, David Manning, Jr., causing injury.

Manning sued Grimsley and the Baltimore Orioles. Are the defendants liable? *Manning v. Grimsley*, 643 F.2d 20, **Web** 1981 U.S. App. Lexis 19782 (United States Court of Appeals for the First Circuit)

5.2 Merchant Protection Statute: At about 7:30 P.M., Deborah A. Johnson entered a Kmart store located in Madison, Wisconsin, to purchase some diapers and several cans of motor oil. She took her small child along to enable her to purchase the correct size diapers, carrying the child in an infant seat that she had purchased at Kmart two or three weeks previously. A large Kmart price tag was still attached to the infant seat. Johnson purchased the diapers and oil and some children's clothes. She was in a hurry to leave because it was 8:00 P.M., her child's feeding time, and she hurried through the checkout lane. She paid for the diapers, the oil, and the clothing. Just after leaving the store, she heard someone ask her to stop. She turned around and saw a Kmart security officer. He showed her a badge and asked her to come back into the store, which she did. The man stated, "I have reason to believe that you have stolen this car seat." Johnson explained that she had purchased the seat previously. She demanded to see the manager, who was called to the scene. When Johnson pointed out that the seat had cat hairs, food crumbs, and milk stains on it, the man said, "I'm really sorry, there's been a terrible mistake. You can go." Johnson looked at the clock, which read 8:20 P.M., when she left. Johnson sued Kmart for false imprisonment. Is Kmart liable? *Johnson v. K-Mart Enterprises, Inc.*, 98 Wis.2d 533, 297 N.W.2d 74, **Web** 1980 Wisc. App. Lexis 3197 (Court of Appeals of Wisconsin)

5.3 Trespass: A. C. Wade operated a liquor store in Cordele, Georgia. Because the store had been burglarized on several occasions and money had been stolen from a cigarette vending machine, Wade booby-trapped the machine with dynamite, with the intent to scare away thieves when they tried to steal money from the vending machine. Robert McKinsey, a 16-year-old, was killed when the dynamite attached to the vending machine exploded while McKinsey was burglarizing the liquor store. Mrs. Ella McKinsey, Robert's mother, although admitting her son was committing a crime at the time he was killed, brought action for damages against Wade for the wrongful death of her son. Who wins? *McKinsey v. Wade*, 136 Ga.App. 109, 220 S.E.2d 30, **Web** 1975 Ga.App. Lexis 1264 (Court of Appeals of Georgia)

5.4 Negligence: George Yanase was a paying guest at the Royal Lodge-Downtown Motel in San Diego, California. Yanase was a member of the Automobile Club of Southern California. The Auto Club publishes a "Tourbook" in which it lists hotels and motels and rates the quality of their services, including the cleanliness of rooms, quality of the restaurant, level of personal service, and the like. Yanase had selected the Royal from the Tourbook. On the night of his stay at the Royal, Yanase was shot in the parking lot adjacent to the motel and died as a result of his injuries. Yanase's widow sued the Auto Club for negligence. Is the Auto Club liable? *Yanase v. Automobile Club of Southern California*, 212 Cal.App.3d 468, 260 Cal.Rptr. 513, **Web** 1989 Cal.App. Lexis 746 (Court of Appeal of California)

5.5 Causation: W. L. Brown purchased a new large Chevrolet truck from Days Chevrolet. The truck had been manufactured by General Motors Corporation. One month later, an employee of Brown's was operating the truck when it ceased to function in rush-hour traffic on Interstate Highway 75 in the Atlanta suburbs. A defect within the alternator had caused a complete failure of the truck's elec-

trical system. The defect was caused by General Motors's negligence in manufacturing the truck. When the alternator failed to operate, the truck came to rest in the right-hand lane of two north-bound lanes of freeway traffic. Because of the electrical failure, no blinking lights could be used to warn traffic of the danger. The driver, however, tried to motion traffic around the truck. Some time later, when the freeway traffic had returned to normal, the large Chevrolet truck was still motionless on the freeway. At approximately 6:00 P.M., a panel truck approached the stalled truck in the right-hand lane of traffic at freeway speed. Immediately behind the panel truck, Mr. Davis, driving a Volkswagen fastback, was unable to see the stalled truck. At the last moment, the driver of the panel truck saw the stalled truck and swerved into another lane to avoid it. Mr. Davis drove his Volkswagen into the stalled truck at freeway speed, causing his death. Mr. Davis's wife brought a wrongful death action based on negligence against General Motors. Is there causation linking the negligence of the defendant to the fatal accident? *General Motors Corporation v. Davis*, 141 Ga.App. 495, 233 S.E.2d 825, **Web** 1977 Ga.App. Lexis 1961 (Court of Appeals of Georgia)

5.6 Negligence Per Se: Julius Ebanks set out from his home in East Elmhurst, Queens, New York, en route to his employment in the downtown district of Manhattan. When Ebanks reached the Bowling Green subway station, he boarded an escalator owned and operated by the New York City Transit Authority. While the escalator was ascending, Ebanks's left foot became caught in a two-inch gap between the escalator step on which he was standing and the side wall of the escalator. Ebanks was unable to free himself. When he reached the top of the escalator he was thrown to the ground, fracturing his hip and causing other serious injuries. The two-inch gap exceeded the three-eighths-inch standard required by the city's building code. Ebanks sued the Transit Authority to recover damages for his injuries. Who wins? *Ebanks v. New York City Transit Authority*, 70 N.Y.2d 621, 518 N.Y.S.2d 776, **Web** 1987 N.Y. Lexis 17294 (Court of Appeals of New York)

5.7 Liability of Landowners: George and Beverly Wagner owned a 1.6-acre parcel of land on which they operated "Bowag Kennels," which catered to training, boarding, and caring for show dogs. The property was entirely surrounded by land owned by Reuben Shiling and W. Dale Hess. In August 1964, Shiling and Hess granted the Wagners an easement right-of-way over their land that connected the kennel to Singer Road, a public road. Singer Road was a rural, unlit two-lane road running through a wooded area. The right-of-way was an unpaved, unlit, narrow road that crossed an uninhabited wooded area leading to Bowag Kennels. On numerous occasions, unauthorized motorcyclists drove on the right-of-way. On several occasions, the bikers had loud parties along the right-of-way. In September 1982, the Wagners stretched a large metal chain between two poles at the entrance of the right-of-way. The Wagners testified that they marked the chain with reflectors and signs. Just before midnight on October 2, 1982, William E. Doehring, Jr., and his passenger, Kelvin Henderson, drove their motorcycle off Singer Road and turned on to the right-of-way. The motorcycle they were riding was not equipped with a headlight, and the riders were not wearing helmets. Doehring and Henderson had not been granted permission by the Wagners or Shiling or Hess to use the right-of-way. The motorcycle struck the chain, and the riders were thrown off. Doehring died several hours later at a hospital. Doehring's father filed a wrongful death and survival action against the Wagners. Who wins? *Wagner v. Doehring*, 315 Md. 97, 553 A.2d 684, **Web** 1989 Md. Lexis 29 (Court of Appeals of Maryland)

5.8 Liability of Common Carrier: The Southern California Rapid Transit District (RTD) is a public common carrier that operates public buses throughout the Los Angeles area. Carmen and Carla Lopez were fare-paying passengers on an RTD bus when a group of juveniles began harassing them and other passengers. When the bus driver was notified of this problem, he failed to take any precautionary measures and continued to operate the bus. The juveniles eventually physically assaulted Carmen and Carla, who were injured. The RTD was aware of a history of violent attacks on its bus line. Carmen and Carla sued the RTD to recover damages for their injuries. Who wins? *Lopez v. Southern California Rapid Transit District*, 40 Cal.3d 780, 710 P.2d 907, 221 Cal.Rptr. 840, **Web** 1985 Cal. Lexis 434 (Supreme Court of California)

5.9 Emotional Distress: Gregory and Demetria James, brother and sister, were riding their bicycles north on 50th Street in Omaha, Nebraska. Spaulding Street intersects 50th Street. A garbage truck owned by Watts Trucking Service, Inc., and driven by its employee, John Milton Lieb, was backing up into the intersection of 50th and Spaulding streets. The truck backed into the intersection, through a stop sign, and hit and ran over Demetria, killing her. Gregory helplessly watched the entire accident but was not in danger himself. As a result of watching his sister's peril, Gregory suffered severe emotional distress. Gregory sued Watts and Lieb to recover damages for his emotional distress. Who wins? *James v. Watts Trucking Service, Inc.*, 221 Neb. 47, 375 N.W.2d 109, **Web** 1985 Neb. Lexis 1209 (Supreme Court of Nebraska)

5.10 Defense: The New York Yankees professional baseball team played the Chicago White Sox at Shea Stadium, New York. Elliot Maddox played center field for the Yankees that night. It had rained the day before, and the previous night's game had been canceled because of bad weather. On the evening of the game, the playing field was still wet, and Maddox commented on this fact several times to the club's manager but continued to play. In the ninth inning, when Maddox was attempting to field a ball in center field, he slipped on a wet spot, fell, and injured his right knee. Maddox sued the City of New York, which owned Shea Stadium; the Metropolitan Baseball Club, Inc., as lessee; the architect; the consulting engineer; and the American League. Maddox alleged that the parties were negligent in causing the field to be wet and that the injury ended his professional career. Who wins? *Maddox v. City of New York*, 66 N.Y.2d 270, 487 N.E.2d 553, 496 N.Y.S.2d 726, **Web** 1985 N.Y. Lexis 17254 (Court of Appeals of New York)

Ethics Issues

5.11 Ethics: Radio station KHJ was a successful Los Angeles broadcaster of rock music that commanded a 48 percent market share of the teenage audience in the Los Angeles area. KHJ was owned and operated by RKO General, Inc. KHJ inaugurated a promotion titled "The Super Summer Spectacular." As part of this promotion, KHJ had a disc jockey known as "The Real Don Steele" ride around the Los Angeles area in a conspicuous red automobile. Periodically KHJ would announce to its radio audience Steele's location. The first listener to thereafter locate Steele and answer a question received a cash prize and participated in a brief interview on the air with Steele. One KHJ broadcast identified Steele's next destination as Canoga Park. Robert Sentner, 17 years old, heard the broadcast and immediately drove to Canoga Park. Marsha Baime, 19 years old, also heard the broadcast and drove to Canoga Park. By the time Sentner and Baime located Steele, someone else had already claimed the prize. Without the knowledge of the other, Sentner and Baime each decided to follow Steele to the next destination and to be first to "find" him.

Steele proceeded onto the freeway. For the next few miles, Sentner and Baime tried to jockey for position closest to the Steele vehicle, reaching speeds of up to 80 miles per hour. There is no evidence that the Steele vehicle exceeded the speed limit. When Steele left the freeway at the Westlake off ramp, Sentner and Baime tried to follow. In their attempts to do so, they knocked another vehicle, driven by Mr. Weirum, into the center divider of the freeway, where it overturned. Mr. Weirum died in the accident. Baime stopped to report the accident. Sentner, after pausing momentarily to relate the tragedy to a passing police officer, got back into his car, pursued and successfully located Steele, and collected the cash prize. The wife and children of Mr. Weirum brought a wrongful death negligence action against Sentner,

Baime, and RKO General. Who wins? Did RKO General, Inc., act responsibly in this case? *Weirum v. RKO General, Inc.*, 15 Cal.3d 40, 539 P.2d 36, 123 Cal.Rptr. 468, **Web** 1975 Cal. Lexis 220 (Supreme Court of California)

5.12 Ethics: Guy Portee, a seven-year-old, resided with his mother in an apartment building in Newark, New Jersey. Edith and Nathan Jaffee owned and operated the building. One day, Guy became trapped in the building's elevator, between its outer door and the wall of the elevator shaft. When someone activated the elevator, the boy was dragged up to the third floor. Another child who saw the accident ran to seek help. Soon afterward, Renee Portee, the boy's mother, and officers at the Newark Police Department arrived. The officers worked for hours, trying to release the boy, during which time the mother watched as her son moaned, cried out, and flailed his arms. The police contacted the Atlantic Elevator Company, which was responsible for the installation and maintenance of the elevator, and requested that the company send a mechanic to assist in the effort to free the boy. Apparently no one came. The boy suffered multiple bone fractures and massive internal hemorrhaging. He died while still trapped, his mother a helpless observer.

After her son's death, Renee became severely distressed and seriously self-destructive. On March 24, 1979, she attempted to take her own life. She survived, and the wound was repaired by surgery, but thereafter she required considerable physical therapy. She had received extensive counseling and psychotherapy to help overcome the mental and emotional problems associated with her son's death. Renee sued the Jaffees and Atlantic to recover damages for her emotional distress. Who wins? Did either of the defendants act unethically in this case? *Portee v. Jaffee*, 84 N.J. 88, 417 A.2d 521, **Web** 1980 N.J. Lexis 1387 (Supreme Court of New Jersey)

IRAC Writing Assignment

Read Case A-5 in Appendix A [*Braun v. Soldier of Fortune Magazine, Inc.*]. Read the case and use the IRAC method to prepare a written analysis of the case.

Endnotes

1. **376** U.S. 254, 84 S.Ct. 710, 11 L.Ed.2d 686, **Web** 1964 U.S. Lexis 1655 (Supreme Court of the United States, 1964).
2. Restatement (Second) of Torts, Section 46.
3. Restatement (Second) of Torts, Section 46, comment d.
4. Justice B. Anderson, *Blyth a Birmingham Waterworks Co.,* 11 Exch. 781, 784 (1856).
5. 248 N.Y. 339, 162 N.E. 99, **Web** 1928 N.Y. Lexis 1269 (Court of Appeals of New York, 1928).
6. For example, see California Civil Code, Section 1714(c).
7. 28 U.S.C. Section 1346(b) and 28 U.S.C. Sections 2671-2680.

CHAPTER **6**

Criminal Law and White-Collar Crime

> ❝ *In our complex society the accountant's certificate and the lawyer's opinion can be instruments for inflicting pecuniary loss more potent than the chisel or the crowbar.* ❞
>
> —JUSTICE BLACKMUN, DISSENTING OPINION
> Ernest & Ernst v. Hochfelder, 425 U.S. 185 (1976)

CHAPTER OBJECTIVES

After studying this chapter, you should be able to:

1. Define and list the essential elements of a crime.
2. Describe criminal procedure, including arrest, indictment, arraignment, and the criminal trial.
3. Define major white-collar crimes, such as embezzlement, bribery, and criminal fraud.
4. Explain the constitutional safeguards provided by the Fourth, Fifth, Sixth, and Eighth Amendments to the U.S. Constitution.
5. Describe corporate criminal liability.

CHAPTER CONTENTS

    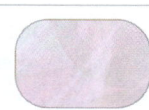

Introduction to Criminal Law and Internet Crimes

For members of society to peacefully coexist and commerce to flourish, people and their property must be protected from injury by other members of society. Federal, state, and local governments' *criminal laws* are intended to accomplish this by providing an incentive for persons to act reasonably in society and imposing penalties on persons who violate them.

The United States has one of the most advanced and humane criminal law systems in the world. It differs from other criminal law systems in several respects. A person charged with a crime in the United States is *presumed innocent until proven guilty*. The *burden of proof* is on the government to prove that the accused is guilty of the crime charged. Further, the accused must be found guilty **beyond a reasonable doubt**. Conviction requires unanimous jury vote. Under many other legal systems, a person accused of a crime is presumed guilty unless the person can prove he or she is not. A person charged with a crime in the United States is also provided with substantial constitutional safeguards during the criminal justice process.

Many crimes are referred to as "white-collar" crimes. These crimes are most often committed by managers and businesses. These crimes include fraud, bribery, and other business-related crimes. The Internet and computer technology has brought on a new wave of criminal activity. Many preexisting crimes are committed using the Internet, while many new crimes have been invented using computer technology. These are commonly called **cyber crimes**.

This chapter discusses crimes, criminal procedure, crimes affecting business, white-collar crime, Internet and digital crimes, international crime, criminal penalties, and the constitutional safeguards afforded criminal defendants.

Homeless Persons' Wall Postings, Los Angeles, California

Should the death penalty be permitted in the United States?

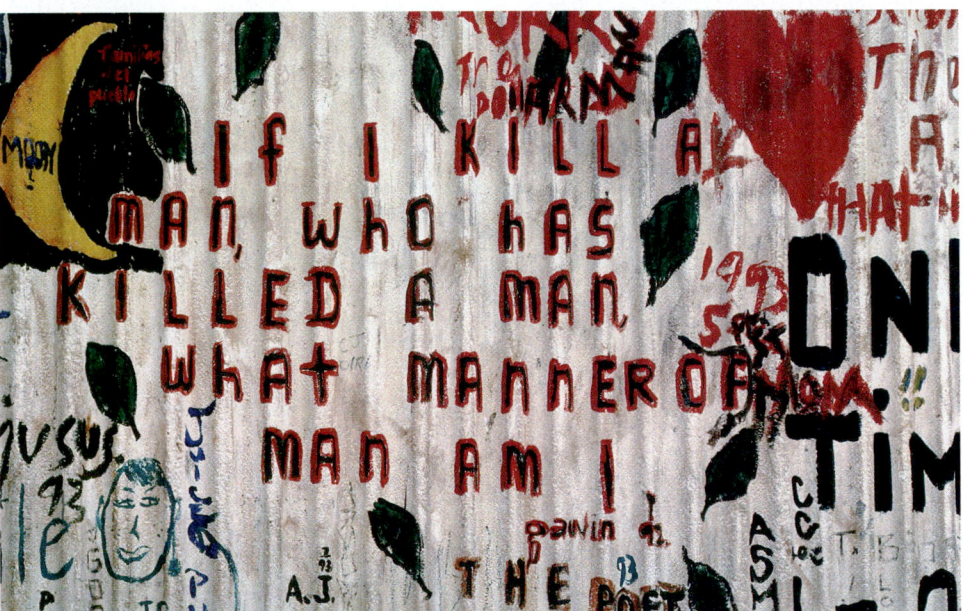

Definition of *Crime*

A **crime** is defined as any act done by an individual in violation of the duties that he or she owes to society and for the breach of which the law provides that the wrongdoer shall make amends to the public. Many activities have been considered crimes through the ages, whereas other crimes are of recent origin.

Penal Codes and Regulatory Statutes

Statutes are the primary source of criminal law. Most states have adopted comprehensive **penal codes** that define in detail the activities considered to be crimes within their jurisdictions and the penalties that will be imposed for their commission. A comprehensive federal criminal code defines federal crimes.[1] In addition, state and federal **regulatory statutes** often provide for criminal violations and penalties. The state and federal legislatures are continually adding to the list of crimes.

The penalty for committing a crime may consist of the imposition of a fine, imprisonment, both, or some other form of punishment (e.g., probation). Generally, imprisonment is imposed to (1) incapacitate the criminal so he or she will not harm others in society, (2) provide a means to rehabilitate the criminal, (3) deter others from similar conduct, and (4) inhibit personal retribution by the victim.

Parties to a Criminal Action

In a criminal lawsuit, the government (not a private party) is the *plaintiff*. The government is represented by a lawyer called the **prosecutor**. The accused, which is usually an individual or a business, is the *defendant*. The accused is represented by a **defense attorney**. If the accused cannot afford a defense lawyer, the government will provide one free of charge.

> Law cannot persuade, where it cannot punish.
>
> Thomas Fuller
> *Gnomologia (1732)*

Classification of Crimes

A crime is generally classified as a *felony*, *misdemeanor*, or *violation*.

FELONY **Felonies** are the most serious kinds of crimes. Felonies include crimes that are *mala in se*—that is, inherently evil. Most crimes against persons (e.g., murder, rape) and certain business-related crimes (e.g., embezzlement, bribery) are felonies in most jurisdictions. Felonies are usually punishable by imprisonment. In some jurisdictions, certain felonies (e.g., first-degree murder) are punishable by death. Federal law[2] and some state laws require mandatory sentencing for specified crimes. Many statutes define different degrees of crimes (e.g., first-, second-, and third-degree murder), with each degree earning different penalties. Serious violations of regulatory statutes are also felonies.

MISDEMEANOR **Misdemeanors** are less serious than felonies. They are crimes *mala prohibita*; that is, they are not inherently evil but are prohibited by society. Many crimes against property, such as robbery, burglary, and less serious violations of regulatory statutes, are included in this category. Misdemeanors carry lesser penalties than felonies. They are usually punishable by fines and/or imprisonment for one year or less.

VIOLATION Crimes such as traffic violations, jaywalking, and such are neither felonies nor misdemeanors. These crimes, which are called **violations**, are generally punishable by fines. Occasionally, a few days of imprisonment are imposed.

CONCEPT SUMMARY

Classification of Crimes

CLASSIFICATION	DESCRIPTION
Felony	The most serious kinds of crimes. They are *mala in se* (inherently evil), and they are usually punishable by imprisonment.
Misdemeanor	Crimes that are less serious than felonies. They are *mala prohibita* (prohibited by society), and they are usually punishable by fine and/or imprisonment for less than one year.
Violation	Crimes that are neither felonies not misdemeanors. Violations are generally punishable by a fine.

Elements of a Crime

The following two elements must be proven for a person to be found guilty of most crimes: (1) criminal act and (2) criminal intent. These elements are discussed in the following paragraphs.

CRIMINAL ACT (*ACTUS REUS*) The defendant must have actually performed the prohibited act. The actual performance of the criminal act is called the ***actus reus*** (guilty act).

Example Killing someone without legal jurisdiction is an example of *actus reus*.

Sometimes, the omission of an act constitutes the requisite *actus reus*.

Example A crime has been committed if a taxpayer who is under a legal duty to file a tax return fails to do so.

Merely thinking about committing a crime is not a crime because no action has been taken.

CRIMINAL INTENT (*MENS REA*) To be found guilty of a crime, the accused must be found to have possessed the requisite state of mind (i.e., specific or general intent) when the act was performed. This is called the ***mens rea*** (evil intent). **Specific intent** is found where the accused purposefully, intentionally, or with knowledge commits a prohibited act. **General intent** is found where there is a showing of recklessness or a lesser degree of mental culpability. The individual criminal statutes state whether the crime requires a showing of specific or general intent. Juries may infer an accused's intent from the facts and circumstances of the case. There is no crime if the requisite *mens rea* cannot be proven. Thus, no crime is committed if one person accidentally injures another person.

CONCEPT SUMMARY

Elements of an Intent Crime

ELEMENT	DESCRIPTION
Actus reus	Guilty act.
Mens rea	Evil intent.

Non-Intent Crimes

Most states provide for certain **non-intent crimes**. The crime of *involuntary manslaughter* is often imposed for reckless conduct.

Example If a driver of an automobile drives too fast (e.g., 20 miles over the speed limit) on a city street and hits and kills a pedestrian, the driver most likely would be found guilty of the crime of involuntary manslaughter and be sentenced to jail.

Criminal Acts as the Basis for Tort Actions

> The magnitude of a crime is proportionate to the magnitude of the injustice which prompts it. Hence, the smallest crimes may be actually the greatest.
>
> Aristotle
> *The Rhetoric, Book 1, Chapter XIV*

An injured party may bring a *civil tort action* against a wrongdoer who has caused the party injury during the commission of a criminal act. Civil lawsuits are separate from the government's criminal action against the wrongdoer. In many cases, a person injured by a criminal act will not sue the criminal to recover civil damages. This is because the criminal is often *judgment proof*—that is, the criminal does not have the money to pay a civil judgment.

CONCEPT SUMMARY

Civil and Criminal Law Compared

ISSUE	CIVIL LAW	CRIMINAL LAW
Party who brings the action	The plaintiff	The government
Trial by jury	Yes, except actions for equity	Yes
Burden of proof	Preponderance of the evidence	Beyond a reasonable doubt
Jury vote	Judgment for plaintiff requires specific jury vote (e.g., 9 of 12 jurors)	Conviction requires unanimous jury vote
Sanctions and penalties	Monetary damages and equitable remedies (e.g., injunction, specific performance)	Imprisonment, capital punishment, fine, probation

ETHICS SPOTLIGHT

Martha Stewart Guilty of a Crime

Martha Stewart is an icon of fine living. Through her company Maratha Stewart Living Omnimedia, Inc. (Omnimedia), Stewart built a business conglomerate involved in publishing magazines and cookbooks, selling clothing and home-based merchandise, and producing a syndicated television program. She and her business became so successful that when the company went public in 1999, Stewart became an instant billionaire.

In 2003, Stewart's friend Sam Waksal, the primary owner of ImClone Systems Inc. (ImClone), received news that the U.S. Food and Drug Administration (FDA) had not given approval for ImClone to market a cancer-fighting drug. Waksal received this information one day before the news would be made public. Waksal and a number of his family members tried to sell their ImClone stock through a securities broker named Peter E. Bacanovic. Bacanovic was also Martha Stewart's stockbroker, and Stewart was a shareholder of ImClone. Bacanovic had his assistant, Douglas Faneuil, notify Stewart of Waksal's activities. Stewart sold her ImClone stock at $58 per share. When the FDA's negative decision regarding the anticancer drug was released, ImClone stock fell in value. Stewart saved $45,000 by selling her ImClone stock early.

When the U.S. government investigated the substantial selling activity in ImClone stock prior to the public announcement of the FDA's adverse ruling, they netted the Waksal family *and* Martha Stewart. Sam Waksal pleaded guilty to insider trading and was sent to jail. When the federal government questioned Stewart about her sale of ImClone stock, she said that she had a prior $60 "sell order" (to sell the stock if it ever dropped to $60). Although both Bacanovic and Faneuil first collaborated this story, eventually Faneuil reached a plea bargain with the government and became a witness: He then told the government that the $60 sell order story was a lie and cover-up.

The U.S. government brought criminal charges against Stewart for criminal conspiracy, lying to the federal government, and obstruction of justice. Stewart pleaded the Fifth Amendment and did not testify at trial. The government called many witnesses, including Faneuil and several of Stewart's friends to whom she had talked to about the ImClone stock sale. One witness testified that Stewart told her that Stewart knew of Waksal's trading before she sold her ImClone stock and then stated, "Isn't it nice to have brokers who tell you these things?" The jury returned a verdict of guilty on all charges. On the day the judgment was announced, Stewart's Omnimedia stock plummeted, and Stewart lost about $100 million in one day. Stewart served four and a half months in jail. *United States v. Stewart* (2004)

Law & Ethics Questions

1. **ETHICS** Did Stewart act ethically in this case?

2. **ETHICS** Why do you think Stewart sold her ImClone stock to save only $45,000?

Web Exercises

1. **WEB** Visit Martha Stewart's website, at *www.marthastewart.com.*

2. **WEB** Use *www.google.com* to find an article that discusses the Martha Stewart case. Read it.

Criminal Procedure

The procedure for initiating and maintaining a criminal action is quite detailed. It includes both pretrial procedures and the actual trial.

Arrest

Before the police can **arrest** a person for the commission of a crime, they usually must obtain an **arrest warrant** based on a showing of probable cause. *Probable cause* is defined as the substantial likelihood that the person either committed or is about to commit a crime. If there is no time for the police to obtain a warrant (e.g., if the police arrive during the commission of a crime, when a person is fleeing from the scene of a crime, or when it is likely that evidence will be destroyed), the police may still arrest the suspect. *Warrantless arrests* are also judged by the probable cause standard.

After a person is arrested, he or she is taken to the police station to be booked. **Booking** is the administrative procedure for recording the arrest, fingerprinting, and so on.

In the following case, the U.S. Supreme Court held that a police officer may make a warrantless arrest pursuant to a minor criminal offense.

C A S E 6.1
Arrest

U.S. SUPREME COURT
Atwater v. Lago Vista, Texas

532 U.S. 318, 121 S.Ct. 1536, 149 L.Ed.2d 549,
Web 2001 U.S. Lexis 3366 (2001)
Supreme Court of the United States

> ❝ *If an officer has probable cause to believe that an individual has committed even a very minor criminal offense in his presence, he may, without violating the Fourth Amendment, arrest the offender.* ❞

—Justice Souter

Facts

Texas law requires that front-seat drivers and passengers wear seat belts and that a driver secure any small child riding in front. In March 1997, Gail Atwater was driving her pickup truck in Lago Vista, Texas, with her three-year-old son and five-year-old daughter in the front seat. None of them were wearing seat belts. Bart Turek, a Lago Vista police officer, observed the seat belt violation and pulled Atwater over. A friend of Atwater's arrived at the scene and took charge of the children. Turek handcuffed Atwater, placed her in his squad car, and drove her to the police station. Atwater was booked, her mug shot was taken, and she was placed in a jail cell for about one hour until she was released on $310 bond. Atwater ultimately pleaded no contest to the misdemeanor seat belt offenses and paid a $50 fine. Atwater sued the City of Lago Vista and the police officer for compensatory and punitive damages for allegedly violating her Fourth Amendment right to be free from unreasonable seizure. The U.S. District Court ruled against Atwater, and the U.S. Court of Appeals affirmed. Atwater appealed to the U.S. Supreme Court.

Issue

Does the Fourth Amendment permit police to make a warrantless arrest pursuant to a minor criminal offense?

Language of the U.S. Supreme Court

There is no support for Atwater's position in this Court's cases. Both the legislative tradition of granting warrantees misdemeanor arrest authority and the judicial tradition of sustaining such statutes against constitutional attack are buttressed by legal commentary that for more than a century now has almost uniformly recognized the constitutionality of extending warrantless arrest power to misdemeanors without limitation to breaches of the peace. If an officer has probable cause to believe that an individual has committed even a very minor criminal offense in his presence, he may, without violating the Fourth Amendment, arrest the offender.

Decision

The U.S. Supreme Court held that the Fourth Amendment permits police officers to make a warrantless arrest pursuant to a minor criminal offense. The Supreme Court affirmed the decisions of the U.S. District Court and the U.S. Court of Appeals.

Law & Ethics Questions

1. Do you agree with the U.S. Supreme Court's decision in this case? Why or why not?

2. **ETHICS** Did the police officer act ethically in this case? Should he have used more discretion?
3. What would be the consequences if the Supreme Court had held in favor of Atwater? Explain.

Web Exercises

1. **WEB** For the complete opinion of this case, go to *www.prenhall.com/cheesemancases*.

2. **WEB** Visit the website of the U.S. Supreme Court, at *www.supremecourtsu.gov*, and try to find documents that relate to this case.
3. **WEB** Visit the website of the Chamber of Commerce of Lago Vista, Texas, at *www.lagovista.org*.

Indictment or Information

Accused persons must be formally charged with a crime before they can be brought to trial. This is usually done through the issuance of a *grand jury indictment* or a *magistrate's information statement*.

Evidence of serious crimes, such as murder, is usually presented to a **grand jury**. Most grand juries comprise between 6 and 24 citizens who are charged with evaluating the evidence presented by the government. Grand jurors sit for a fixed period of time, such as one year. If the grand jury determines that there is sufficient evidence to hold the accused for trial, it issues an **indictment**. Note that the grand jury does not determine guilt. If an indictment is issued, the accused will be held for later trial.

For lesser crimes (e.g., burglary, shoplifting), the accused will be brought before a **magistrate** (judge). A magistrate who finds that there is enough evidence to hold the accused for trial will issue **information**.

The case against the accused is dismissed if neither an indictment nor an information is issued.

Web Exercise

1. **WEB** Use *www.google.com* to find out about the grand jury in your area, such as how many members are on it, is the length of their term, and other relevant information.

Arraignment

If an indictment or information is issued, the accused is brought before a court for an **arraignment** proceeding, during which the accused is (1) informed of the charges against him or her and (2) asked to enter a **plea**. The accused may plead *guilty*, *not guilty*, or *nolo contendere*. A plea of **nolo contendere** means that the accused agrees to the imposition of a penalty but does not admit guilt. A *nolo contendere* plea cannot be used as evidence of liability against the accused at a subsequent civil trial. Corporate defendants often enter this plea. The government has the option of accepting a *nolo contendere* plea or requiring the defendant to plead guilty or not guilty.

Plea Bargaining

Sometimes the accused and the government enter into a **plea bargaining agreement**. The government engages in plea bargaining to save costs, avoid the risks of a trial, and prevent further overcrowding of the prisons. This type of arrangement allows the accused to admit to a lesser crime than charged. In return, the government agrees to impose a lesser penalty or sentence than might have been obtained had the case gone to trial.

The Criminal Trial

At a criminal trial, all jurors must *unanimously* agree before the accused is found *guilty* of the crime charged. If even one juror disagrees (i.e., has reasonable doubt) about the guilt of the accused, the accused cannot be found guilty of the crime charged. If all the jurors agree

> There can be no equal justice where the kind of trial a man gets depends on the amount of money he has.
>
> J. Black
> *Griffin v. Illinois (1956)*

that the accused did not commit the crime, the accused is found *not guilty* of the crime charged. After trial, the following rules apply:

- If the defendant is found guilty, he or she may appeal.
- If the defendant is found not guilty, the government cannot appeal.
- If the jury cannot come to a **unanimous decision** about the defendant's guilt one way or the other, the jury is considered a **hung jury**. The government may choose to retry the case before a new judge and jury.

Common Crimes

Many crimes are committed against business property. These crimes often involve the theft, misappropriation, or fraudulent taking of property. Many of the most important crimes against business property are discussed in the following paragraphs.

Murder

Murder is defined as the unlawful killing of a human being by another with malice aforethought. There are several degrees of murder—such as first degree, second degree, and third degree—depending on the circumstances of the case. Each degree carries different penalties. The statutory definition of murder from the Florida Penal Code is set forth in Exhibit 6.1.

EXHIBIT 6.1

Definition of Murder

FLORIDA PENAL CODE (Highlights)

782.04 Murder.—
(1)(a) The unlawful killing of a human being:

First Degree Murder
(1) When perpetrated from a premeditated design to effect the death of the person killed or any human being;

(2) When committed by a person engaged in the perpetration of, or in the attempt to perpetrate, any: trafficking offense prohibited by s. 893.135(1), arson, sexual battery, robbery, burglary, kidnapping, escape, aggravated child abuse, aggravated abuse of an elderly person or disabled adult, aircraft piracy, unlawful throwing, placing, or discharging of a destructive device or bomb, carjacking, home-invasion robbery, aggravated stalking, murder of another human being, resisting an officer with violence to his or her person, felony that is an act of terrorism or is in furtherance of an act of terrorism; or . . .

(3) Which resulted from the unlawful distribution of any substance controlled under s. 893.03(1), cocaine as described in s. 893.03(2)(a)4., or opium or any synthetic or natural salt, compound, derivative, or preparation of opium by a person 18 years of age or older, when such drug is proven to be the proximate cause of the death of the user, is murder in the first degree and constitutes a capital felony, punishable as provided in s. 775.082.

(b) In all cases under this section, the procedure set forth in s. 921.141 shall be followed in order to determine sentence of death or life imprisonment.

Second Degree Murder
(2) The unlawful killing of a human being, when perpetrated by any act imminently dangerous to another and evincing a depraved mind regardless of human life, although without any premeditated design to effect the death of any particular individual, is murder in the second degree and constitutes a

felony of the first degree, punishable by imprisonment for a term of years not exceeding life or as provided in s. 775.082, s. 775.083, or s. 775.084.

(3) When a person is killed in the perpetration of, or in the attempt to perpetrate, any: trafficking offense prohibited by s. 893.135(1), arson, sexual battery, robbery, burglary, kidnapping, escape, aggravated child abuse, aggravated abuse of an elderly person or disabled adult, aircraft piracy, unlawful throwing, placing, or discharging of a destructive device or bomb, carjacking, home-invasion robbery, aggravated stalking, murder of another human being, resisting an officer with violence to his or her person, or a felony that is an act of terrorism or is in furtherance of an act of terrorism, by a person other than the person engaged in the perpetration of or in the attempt to perpetrate such felony, the person perpetrating or attempting to perpetrate such felony is guilty of murder in the second degree, which constitutes a felony of the first degree, punishable by imprisonment for a term of years not exceeding life or as provided in s. 775.082, s. 775.083, or s. 775.084.

Third Degree Murder

(3) The unlawful killing of a human being, when perpetrated without any design to effect death, by a person engaged in the perpetration of, or in the attempt to perpetrate, any felony other than any: trafficking offense prohibited by s. 893.135(1), arson, sexual battery, robbery, burglary, kidnapping, escape, aggravated child abuse, aggravated abuse of an elderly person or disabled adult, aircraft piracy, unlawful throwing, placing, or discharging of a destructive device or bomb, carjacking, home-invasion robbery, aggravated stalking, murder of another human being, resisting an officer with violence to his or her person, a felony that is an act of terrorism or is in furtherance of an act of terrorism, or . . .

The unlawful distribution of any substance controlled under s. 893.03(1), cocaine as described in s. 893.03(2)(a)4., or opium or any synthetic or natural salt, compound, derivative, or preparation of opium by a person 18 years of age or older, when such drug is proven to be the proximate cause of the death of the user; is murder in the third degree and constitutes a felony of the second degree, punishable as provided in s. 775.082, s. 775.083, or s. 775.084.

(4) The unlawful killing of a human being, when perpetrated without any design to effect death, by a person engaged in the perpetration of, or in the attempt to perpetrate, any felony other than any: trafficking offense prohibited by s. 893.135(1), arson, sexual battery, robbery, burglary, kidnapping, escape, aggravated child abuse, aggravated abuse of an elderly person or disabled adult, aircraft piracy, unlawful throwing, placing, or discharging of a destructive device or bomb, unlawful distribution of any substance controlled under s. 893.03(1), cocaine as described in s. 893.03(2)(a)4., or opium or any synthetic or natural salt, compound, derivative, or preparation of opium by a person 18 years of age or older, when such drug is proven to be the proximate cause of the death of the user, carjacking, home-invasion robbery, aggravated stalking, murder of another human being, resisting an officer with violence to his or her person, or a felony that is an act of terrorism or is in furtherance of an act of terrorism, is murder in the third degree and constitutes a felony of the second degree, punishable as provided in s. 775.082, s. 775.083, or s. 775.084.

(5) As used in this section, the term "terrorism" means an activity that:

    (a) 1. Involves a violent act or an act dangerous to human life which is a violation of the criminal laws of this state or of the United States; or

       2. Involves a violation of s. 815.06; and

    (b) Is intended to:

       1. Intimidate, injure, or coerce a civilian population;

       2. Influence the policy of a government by intimidation or coercion; or

       3. Affect the conduct of government through destruction of property, assassination, murder, kidnapping, or aircraft piracy.

Manslaughter

782.07 Manslaughter; aggravated manslaughter of an elderly person or disabled adult; aggravated manslaughter of a child; aggravated manslaughter of an officer, a firefighter, an emergency medical technician, or a paramedic.—

(1) The killing of a human being by the act, procurement, or culpable negligence of another, without lawful justification according to the provisions of chapter 776 and in cases in which such killing shall not be excusable homicide or murder, according to the provisions of this chapter, is manslaughter, a felony of the second degree, punishable as provided in s. 775.082, s. 775.083, or s. 775.084.

(2) A person who causes the death of any elderly person or disabled adult by culpable negligence under s. 825.102(3) commits aggravated manslaughter of an elderly person or disabled adult, a felony of the first degree, punishable as provided in s. 775.082, s. 775.083, or s. 775.084.

(3) A person who causes the death of any person under the age of 18 by culpable negligence under s. 827.03(3) commits aggravated manslaughter of a child, a felony of the first degree, punishable as provided in s. 775.082, s. 775.083, or s. 775.084.

(4) A person who causes the death, through culpable negligence, of an officer as defined in s. 943.10(14), a firefighter as defined in s. 112.191, an emergency medical technician as defined in s. 401.23, or a paramedic as defined in s. 401.23, while the officer, firefighter, emergency medical technician, or paramedic is performing duties that are within the course of his or her employment, commits aggravated manslaughter of an officer, a firefighter, an emergency medical technician, or a paramedic, a felony of the first degree, punishable as provided in s. 775.082, s. 775.083, or s. 775.084.

Felony Murder Rule

782.051 Attempted felony murder.—

(1) Any person who perpetrates or attempts to perpetrate any felony enumerated in s. 782.04(3) and who commits, aids, or abets an intentional act that is not an essential element of the felony and that could, but does not, cause the death of another commits a felony of the first degree, punishable by imprisonment for a term of years not exceeding life, or as provided in s. 775.082, s. 775.083, or s. 775.084, which is an offense ranked in level 9 of the Criminal Punishment Code. Victim injury points shall be scored under this subsection.

(2) Any person who perpetrates or attempts to perpetrate any felony other than a felony enumerated in s. 782.04(3) and who commits, aids, or abets an intentional act that is not an essential element of the felony and that could, but does not, cause the death of another commits a felony of the first degree,

punishable as provided in s. 775.082, s. 775.083, or s. 775.084, which is an offense ranked in level 8 of the Criminal Punishment Code. Victim injury points shall be scored under this subsection.

(3) When a person is injured during the perpetration of or the attempt to perpetrate any felony enumerated in s. 782.04(3) by a person other than the person engaged in the perpetration of or the attempt to perpetrate such felony, the person perpetrating or attempting to perpetrate such felony commits a felony of the second degree, punishable as provided in s. 775.082, s. 775.083, or s. 775.084, which is an offense ranked in level 7 of the Criminal Punishment Code. Victim injury points shall be scored under this subsection.

FELONY MURDER RULE Sometimes a murder is committed during the commission of another crime even though the perpetrator did not originally intend to commit murder. Most states hold the perpetrator liable for the crime of murder in addition to the other crime. This is called the **felony murder rule**. The intent to commit the murder is inferred from the intent to commit the other crime. Many states also hold accomplices liable under this doctrine.

In the following case, the court found that the accused had committed murder.

Web Exercises

1. **WEB** To see the Florida penal code in its entirety, visit *www.leg.state.fl.us/statutes*.
2. **WEB** Use *www.google.com* to find the definition of *murder* in your state's penal code.

CASE 6.2
Murder

State of Ohio v. Wilson

2004 Ohio 2838,
Web 2004 Ohio App. Lexis 2503 (2004)
Court of Appeals of Ohio

> "In determining whether a verdict is against the manifest weight of the evidence, the appellate court acts as a "thirteenth juror.""
>
> —Judge Sadler

Facts

Gregory O. Wilson, who had been arguing earlier in the day with his girlfriend, Melissa Spear, approached a parked car within which Ms. Spear was seated, and poured gasoline from a beer bottle over her head. When Ms. Spear exited the car, Wilson ignited her with his cigarette lighter, setting her body on fire. As Ms. Spear became engulfed in flames, and while bystanders tried to assist her, Wilson walked away and down the street as if nothing had happened.

Paramedics arrived at the scene. One paramedic described Ms. Spear's burns as the worst he had ever seen. A witness described her after the fire as "totally black, no hair, laying there with her skin melted off of her, the flesh looked like it was melted. She was black, look up at me saying 'help me.'"

Ms. Spear was transported from the scene to the hospital. When she arrived, she had third-degree burns on her face, neck, trunk, arms, hands, and thighs. She was put in a medically induced coma and

placed on a respirator. She remained in a coma for 45 days, during which time she underwent 10 surgeries that excised her burn wounds and placed synthetic skin dressing or skin grafts onto her wound sites. Ms. Spear was transferred to a rehabilitation facility. Upon her release from the rehabilitation facility, she received continual treatment and medicine for pain, infection, and depression. Nine months after the incident occurred, and five days before her 30th birthday, Ms. Spear's 7-year-old son found her lying dead in her bed.

The State of Ohio brought criminal charges against Wilson. He was convicted by a jury of aggravated murder and was sentenced to 30 years to life in prison. Mr. Wilson appealed his conviction.

Issue

Was there sufficient causation between Wilson's act of setting Ms. Spear on fire and Ms. Spear's death nine months later to warrant a conviction for murder?

Language of the Court

Wilson argues that the evidence was insufficient to support his conviction for aggravated murder, and that the verdict on this charge was against the manifest weight of the evidence. He contends that the state failed to prove the element of causation beyond a reasonable doubt. Specifically, appellant argues that the nine-month lapse of time between his act of setting Ms. Spear on fire and her eventual death render the verdict of guilty beyond a reasonable doubt on the aggravated murder charge unsupported by the manifest weight and sufficiency of the evidence.

An appellate court's function when reviewing the sufficiency of the evidence to support a criminal conviction is to examine the evidence admitted at trial to determine whether such evidence, if believed, would convince the average mind of the defendant's guilt beyond a reasonable doubt. In determining whether a verdict is against the manifest weight of the evidence, the appellate court acts as a "thirteenth juror." Under this standard of review, the appellate court weighs the evidence in order to determine whether the trier of fact clearly lost its way and created such a manifest miscarriage of justice that the conviction must be reversed and a new trial ordered.

A causal connection between the criminal agency and the cause of death is an essential element in a conviction for murder. Thus, the state must produce evidence to support each link in the chain of causation between the defendant's criminal act and the eventual death of the victim. Proximate causation is the strongest if the victim dies immediately or shortly after being injured by the defendant. However, a defendant is not relieved of culpability for the natural consequences of inflicting serious wounds on another merely because the victim later died of complications brought on by the injury. The passing of nine months between appellant's act of setting Ms. Spear on fire and her eventual death does not, alone, render appellant's conviction for aggravated murder reversible. The evidence sufficiently demonstrates that the physical maladies that brought about the death of Ms. Spear were the natural, probable and foreseeable results of appellant's conduct. In short, there was sufficient evidence presented upon which the jury could have rationally concluded that appellant's act of setting Melissa Spear ablaze was the direct and proximate cause of both of the physical conditions that the coroner determined precipitated her death.

Decision

The court of appeals affirmed the trial court's conviction of Wilson of the crime of the murder of Ms. Spear. The court of appeals remanded the case to the trial court to permit Wilson to make a statement on his behalf prior to sentencing.

Law & Ethics Questions

1. What is murder? Is it easy to define?

2. If you were a juror in this case, would you have voted for the death penalty? Why or why not?

3. **ETHICS** Do you think Wilson's argument on appeal was justified?

Web Exercises

1. **WEB** For the complete version of this case, go to *www.prenhall.com/cheesemancases*.

2. **WEB** Visit the website of the court of appeals of Ohio, Tenth Appellate District, Franklin County, at *www.franklincountyohio.gov/appeals*.

3. **WEB** Use *www.google.com* to find an article that discusses the death penalty. Read it.

CONTEMPORARY ENVIRONMENT
The Crime of Manslaughter

> *"He never once expressed in court any remorse for his actions."*
>
> —Judge Michael Johnson

In the summer of 2003, an elderly man plowed 50 miles per hour through a crowded outdoor shopping district in Santa Monica, California, killing 10 people and injuring more than 60 more. The driver was 86-year-old George Weller, who had driven for 2½ blocks through the farmer's market at Santa Monica's Third Street Promenade, swerved to avoid hitting parked cars, and finally came to a stop about 100 yards later. Witnesses reported that Weller then got out of his car, glanced around, and casually inquired to onlookers about how many people he had hit.

Weller was arrested and charged with 10 counts of vehicular manslaughter with gross negligence but was released on his on recognizance. His attorney, Mark Overland, argued that there was no crime but rather the incident was simply an unfortunate accident attributed to "pedal error," claiming that Weller mistakenly stepped on the gas instead of the brake.

Prosecutors said Weller was careless to the point of criminal negligence. Several witnesses testified that Weller got out of the car asking the injured, "Why didn't you get out of my way?" and "How do you think I felt?" Santa Monica Police Chief James Butts, Jr., commented, "Mr. Weller was conscious throughout the collision sequence; no evidence exists that he attempted to take the car out of gear; there is no indication of braking throughout the entire collision sequence."

After arguments concluded, the jury came back with a unanimous guilty verdict on all 10 counts of vehicular manslaughter with gross negligence. According to many experts, the now 89-year-old Weller faced up to 18 years in prison but would not likely be sentenced to the max. A month before his 90th birthday, Weller remained in his sick bed when Los Angeles County Superior Court Judge Michael Johnson blasted the elderly man, saying that, "He never once expressed in court any remorse for his actions." Judge Johnson then turned around and gave Weller a total of 5 years probation, saying that although he deserved prison, it would most likely kill him due to his poor health and that it would be a burden on taxpayers. Weller was also ordered to pay $57,500 in restitution to the victims' families and $44,200 in fines. He never spent a day in jail.

Web Exercises

1. **WEB** Use *www.google.com* to find your state's definition of *manslaughter*.

2. **WEB** Visit the website of Santa Monica's Third Street Promenade, where the event happened, at *www.downtownsm.com*.

Robbery

In common law, **robbery** is defined as the taking of personal property from another person or business by the use of fear or force.

Example If a robber threatens to physically harm a storekeeper unless that victim surrenders the contents of the cash register, it is robbery. If a criminal pickpockets somebody's wallet, it is not robbery because there has been no use of force or fear. Robbery with a deadly weapon is generally considered aggravated robbery (or armed robbery) and carries a harsher penalty.

Burglary

In common law, **burglary** is defined as "breaking and entering a dwelling at night" with the intent to commit a felony. Modern penal codes have broadened this definition to include daytime thefts from offices and commercial and other buildings. In addition, the "breaking in" element has been abandoned by most modern definitions of burglary. Thus, unauthorized entering of a building through an unlocked door is sufficient. Aggravated burglary (or armed burglary) carries stiffer penalties.

Larceny

In common law, **larceny** is defined as the wrongful and fraudulent taking of another person's personal property. Most personal property—including tangible property, trade secrets, computer programs, and other business property—is subject to larceny.

Example Stealing of automobiles and car stereos, pickpocketing, and such are larceny. Neither the use of force nor the entry of a building is required. Some states distinguish between grand larceny and petit larceny. This distinction depends on the value of the property taken.

Theft

Some states have dropped the distinction among the crimes of robbery, burglary, and larceny. Instead, these states group these crimes under the general crime of **theft**. Most of these states distinguish between grand theft and petit theft. The distinction depends on the value of the property taken.

Receiving Stolen Property

It is a crime for a person to (1) knowingly **receive stolen property** and (2) intend to deprive the rightful owner of that property. Knowledge and intent can be inferred from the circumstances. The stolen property can be any tangible property (e.g., personal property, money, negotiable instruments, stock certificates).

Arson

In common law, **arson** is defined as the malicious or willful burning of the dwelling of another person. Modern penal codes have expanded this definition to include the burning of all types of private, commercial, and public buildings. Thus, in most states, an owner who burns his or her own building to collect insurance proceeds can be found liable for arson. If the owner is determined to have perpetrated arson on his or her own property, the insurance company does not have to pay proceeds of any insurance policy on the burned property.

The Bahamas

Certain countries have enacted bank secrecy laws that protect the identity of depositors from disclosure. The Bahamas has such laws, and many of its chartered "banks" are no more than lawyers' offices in office buildings. Who do you think uses these bank accounts?

White-Collar Crime

Certain types of crime are prone to being committed by businesspersons. These crimes are often referred to as **white-collar crimes**. These crimes usually involve cunning and deceit rather than physical force. Many of the most important white-collar crimes are discussed in the paragraphs that follow.

Forgery

The crime of **forgery** occurs if a written document is fraudulently made or altered and that change affects the legal liability of another person. Counterfeiting, falsifying public records, and materially altering legal documents are examples of forgery.

Example Signing another person's signature to a check and changing the amount of a check without the owner's permission are examples of forgery.

Note that signing another person's signature without the intent to defraud is not forgery.

Example Forgery has not been committed if one spouse signs the other spouse's payroll check for deposit in a joint checking or savings account at the bank.

Embezzlement

Unknown in common law, the crime of **embezzlement** is a statutory crime. Embezzlement is the fraudulent conversion of property by a person to whom that property was entrusted. Typically, embezzlement is committed by an employer's employees, agents, or representatives (e.g., accountants, lawyers, trust officers, treasurers). Embezzlers often try to cover their tracks by preparing false books, records, or entries.

The key element here is that the stolen property was *entrusted* to the embezzler. This differs from robbery, burglary, and larceny, where property is taken by someone not entrusted with the property.

Example Embezzlement has been committed if a bank teller absconds with money that was deposited by depositors. The employer (the bank) entrusted the teller to take deposits from its customers.

Bribery

Bribery is one of the most prevalent forms of white-collar crime. A bribe can be money, property, favors, or anything else of value. The crime of commercial bribery entails the payment of bribes to private persons and businesses. This type of bribe is often referred to as a *kickback* or *payoff*. Intent is a necessary element of this crime. The offeror of a bribe commits the crime of bribery when the bribe is tendered. The offeree is guilty of the crime of bribery when he or she accepts the bribe. The offeror can be found liable for the crime of bribery even if the person to whom the bribe is offered rejects the bribe.

Example Harriet Landers is the purchasing agent for the ABC Corporation and is in charge of purchasing equipment to be used by the corporation. Neal Brown, the sales representative of a company that makes equipment that can be used by the ABC Corporation, offers to pay her a 10 percent kickback if she buys equipment from him. She accepts the bribe and orders the equipment. Both parties are guilty of bribery.

In common law, the crime of bribery is defined as the giving or receiving of anything of value in corrupt payment for an "official act" by a public official. Public officials include legislators, judges, jurors, witnesses at trial, administrative agency personnel, and other government officials. Modern penal codes also make it a crime to bribe public officials.

Example If a developer who is constructing an apartment building offers to pay the building inspector to overlook a building code violation, this is bribery.

INTERNATIONAL LAW
Foreign Corrupt Practices Act

It is well known that the payment of bribes is pervasive in conducting international business. To prevent U.S. companies from engaging in this type of conduct, the U.S. Congress enacted the **Foreign Corrupt Practices Act (FCPA)**.[3] The FCPA makes it illegal for U.S. companies, or their officers, directors, agents, or employees, to bribe a foreign official, a foreign political party official, or a candidate for foreign political office. A bribe is illegal only where it is meant to influence the awarding of new business or the retention of a continuing business activity.

The FCPA imposes criminal liability where a person pays the illegal bribe himself or herself or supplies a payment to a third party or an agent, knowing that it will be used as a bribe. A firm can be fined up to $2 million, and an individual can be fined up to $100,000 and imprisoned for up to five years for violations of the FCPA.

The 1988 amendments to the FCPA created two defenses. One excuses a firm or person charged with bribery under the FCPA if the firm or person can show that the payment was lawful under the written laws of that country. The other allows a defendant to show that a payment was a reasonable and bona fide expenditure related to the furtherance or execution of a contract. This latter exemption is difficult to interpret.

Some people argue that U.S. companies are placed at a disadvantage in international markets where commercial bribery is commonplace and firms from other countries are not hindered by laws similar to the FCPA.

Law & Ethics Questions

1. What does the Foreign Corrupt Practices Act (FCPA) make illegal?

2. Do you think bribery in international business transactions occurs very often?

3. **ETHICS** Will the FCPA have much of an impact in reducing bribery? Why or why not?

St. Petersburg, Russia
Criminal laws and the enforcement of these laws vary by country.

Extortion

The crime of **extortion** involves the obtaining of property from another, with his or her consent, induced by wrongful use of actual or threatened force, violence, or fear.

Example Extortion occurs when a person threatens to expose something about another person unless that other person gives money or property. The truth or falsity of the information is immaterial. Extortion of private persons is commonly referred to as **blackmail**. Extortion of public officials is called *extortion "under color of official right."*

Criminal Fraud

Obtaining title to property through deception or trickery constitutes the crime of **false pretenses**. This crime is commonly referred to as **criminal fraud**, or *deceit*.

Example Bob Anderson, a stockbroker, promises Mary Greenberg, a prospective investor, that he will use any money she invests to purchase interests in oil wells. Based on this promise, Ms. Greenberg decides to make the investment. Mr. Anderson never intended to invest the money. Instead, he used the money for his personal needs. This is criminal fraud.

> There are some frauds so well conducted that it would be stupidity not to be deceived by them.
>
> C. C. Colton
> *Lacon, Volume 1 (1820)*

MAIL FRAUD AND WIRE FRAUD Federal law prohibits the use of mails or wires (e.g., telegraphs, telephone, the Internet) to defraud another person. These crimes are called **mail fraud**[4] and **wire fraud**[5], respectively. The government often prosecutes a suspect under these statutes if there is insufficient evidence to prove the real crime that the criminal was attempting to commit or did commit. The maximum penalty for mail, wire, and Internet fraud is 20 years in prison.

LANDMARK STATUTE
Racketeer Influenced and Corrupt Organizations Act (RICO)

Organized crime has a pervasive influence on many parts of the American economy. In 1980, Congress enacted the Organized Crime Control Act, of which the **Racketeer Influenced and Corrupt Organizations Act (RICO)** is part.[6] Originally, RICO was intended to apply only to organized crime. However, the broad language of the RICO statute has been used against non–organized crime defendants as well. RICO, which provides for both criminal and civil penalties, is one of the most important laws affecting business today.

Criminal RICO

RICO makes it a federal crime to acquire or maintain an interest in, use income from, or conduct or participate in the affairs of an enterprise through a pattern of racketeering activity. An *enterprise* is defined as a corporation, a partnership, a sole proprietorship, another business or organization, or the government.

Racketeering activity consists of a number of specifically enumerated federal and state crimes, including such activities as gambling, arson, robbery, counterfeiting, and dealing in narcotics. Business-related crimes, such as bribery, embezzlement, mail fraud, and wire

fraud, are also considered racketeering. To prove a *pattern of racketeering*, at least two of these acts must be committed by the defendant within a 10-year period. For example, committing two different frauds would be considered a pattern.

Individual defendants found criminally liable for RICO violations can be fined up to $25,000 per violation, imprisoned for up to 20 years, or both. In addition, RICO provides for the *forfeiture* of any property or business interests (even interests in a legitimate business) that were gained because of RICO violations. This provision allows the government to recover investments made with monies derived from racketeering activities. The government may also seek civil penalties for RICO violations. These include injunctions, orders of dissolution, reorganization of business, and the divestiture of the defendant's interest in an enterprise.

Civil RICO

Persons injured by a RICO violation can bring a private *civil* action against the violator to recover injury to business or property. A successful plaintiff may recover *treble damages* (three times actual loss) plus attorneys' fees.

Law & Ethics Questions

1. Define *racketeering* under RICO.
2. What does criminal RICO provide? Explain.
3. What does civil RICO provide? Explain.
4. **ETHICS** Do you think that professional criminals will be deterred from engaging in crime because the RICO statute has been enacted? Why or why not?
5. Why did the federal government enact RICO? Explain.

CRIMINAL CONSPIRACY A **criminal conspiracy** occurs when two or more persons enter into an *agreement* to commit a crime. To be liable for a criminal conspiracy, an *overt act* must be taken to further the crime. The crime itself does not have to be committed, however.

Example Two securities brokers agree over the telephone to commit a securities fraud. They obtain a list of potential victims and prepare false financial statements necessary for the fraud. Because they entered into an agreement to commit a crime and took overt action, the brokers are guilty of the crime of criminal conspiracy even if they never carry out the securities fraud. The government usually brings criminal conspiracy charges if (1) the defendants have been thwarted in their efforts to commit the substantive crime or (2) there is insufficient evidence to prove the substantive crime.

ETHICS SPOTLIGHT
Money Laundering

When criminals make money from illegal activities, they are often faced with the problem of having large sums of money and no record of how this money was earned. This could easily tip the government off to their illegal activities. In order to "wash" the money and make it look as though it was earned legitimately, many criminals purchase legitimate businesses and run the money through that business to clean it before the criminal receives the money. The legitimate business has "cooked" books showing faked expenditures and receipts, in which the illegal money is buried. Restaurants, motels, and other cash businesses make excellent money laundries.

To address this problem, the federal government enacted the **Money Laundering Control Act**.[7] This act makes it a crime to:

- Knowingly engage in a *monetary transaction* through a financial institution involving property, obtained illegally, worth more than $10,000. For example, this would include making deposits, making withdrawals, conducting transactions between accounts, or obtaining monetary instruments such as cashiers' checks, money orders, and travelers' checks from a bank or other financial institution.

- Knowingly engage in a *financial transaction* involving the proceeds of an illegal activity. For example, this would include

buying real estate, automobiles, personal property, intangible assets, or anything else of value with money obtained from illegal activities.

Thus, **money laundering** itself is now a federal crime. The money that is washed could have been made from illegal gambling operations, drug dealing, fraud, and other crimes, including white-collar crimes. Persons convicted of money laundering can be fined up to $500,000 or twice the value of the property involved, whichever is greater, and sentenced to up to 20 years in federal prison. In addition, violation of the act subjects any property involved in or traceable to the offense to forfeiture to the government.

Law & Ethics Questions

1. Define *money laundering*.

2. **ETHICS** Will the money laundering statute deter much crime? Why or why not?

3. Why did the federal government enact the Money Laundering Control Act? Explain.

ETHICS SPOTLIGHT
Corporate Criminal Liability

A *corporation* is a fictitious legal person that is granted legal existence by the state when certain requirements are met. A corporation cannot act on its own behalf. Instead, it must act through *agents*, such as managers, representatives, and employees.

The question of whether a corporation can be held criminally liable has intrigued legal scholars for some time. Originally, under the common law, it was generally held that corporations lacked the criminal mind (*mens rea*) to be held criminally liable. Modern courts, however, impose **corporate criminal liability**. These courts have held that corporations are criminally liable for the acts of their managers, agents, and employees. In any event, because corporations cannot be put in prison, they are usually sanctioned with fines, loss of a license or franchise, and the like.

Corporate directors, officers, and employees are individually liable for crimes that they personally commit, whether for personal benefit or on behalf of the corporation. In addition, under certain circumstances, a corporate manager can be held criminally liable for the criminal activities of his or her subordinates. To be held criminally liable, the manager must have failed to supervise the subordinate appropriately. This is an evolving area of the law.

Law & Ethics Questions

1. Explain corporate criminal liability.

2. **ETHICS** Who gets hurt when a corporation is required to pay a criminal fine because of criminal activity by a member of the board of directors, an officer, or other employee?

Protection against Unreasonable Search and Seizure

In many criminal cases, the government relies on information obtained from searches of individuals and businesses. The *Fourth Amendment* to the U.S. Constitution protects persons and corporations from overzealous investigative activities by the government. It protects the rights of the people from **unreasonable search and seizure** by the government. It permits people to be secure in their persons, houses, papers, and effects.

"**Reasonable**" **search and seizure** by the government is lawful. **Search warrants** based on probable cause are necessary in most cases. Such a warrant specifically states the place and scope of the authorized search. General searches beyond the specified area are forbidden. *Warrantless searches* are permitted only (1) incident to arrest, (2) where evidence is in "plain view," or (3) where it is likely that evidence will be destroyed. Warrantless searches are also judged by the probable cause standard.

Exclusionary Rule

Evidence obtained from an unreasonable search and seizure is considered tainted evidence ("fruit of a tainted tree"). Under the **exclusionary rule**, such evidence can generally be prohibited from introduction at a trial or an administrative proceeding against the person searched. However, this evidence is freely admissible against other persons. The U.S. Supreme Court created a *good faith exception* to the exclusionary rule.[8] This exception allows evidence otherwise obtained illegally to be introduced as evidence against the accused if the police officers who conducted the unreasonable search reasonably believed that they were acting pursuant to a lawful search warrant.

The following cases examine the reach of the Fourth Amendment's protection against unreasonable search and seizure.

CASE 6.3
Search

U.S. SUPREME COURT
Kyllo v. United States
533 U.S. 27, 121 S.Ct. 2038, 150 L.Ed.2d 94,
Web 2001 U.S. Lexis 4487 (2001)
Supreme Court of the United States

> " *At the very core of the Fourth Amendment stands the right of a man to retreat into his own home and there be free from unreasonable government intrusion.* "

—Justice Scalia

Facts

Government agents suspected that marijuana was being grown in the home of Danny Kyllo, which was part of a triplex building in Florence, Oregon. Indoor marijuana growth typically requires high-intensity lamps. In order to determine whether an amount of heat was emanating from Kyllo's home consistent with the use of such lamps, federal agents used a thermal imager to scan the triplex. Thermal imagers detect infrared radiation and produce images of the radiation. The scan of Kyllo's home, which was performed from an automobile on the street, showed that the roof over the garage and a side wall of Kyllo's home were "hot." The agents used this scanning evidence to obtain a search warrant authorizing a search of Kyllo's home. During the search, the agents found an indoor growing operation involving more than 100 marijuana plants.

Kyllo was indicted for manufacturing marijuana, a violation of federal criminal law. Kyllo moved to suppress the imaging evidence and the evidence it led to, arguing that it was an unreasonable search that violated the Fourth Amendment to the U.S. Constitution. The U.S. District Court disagreed with Kyllo and let the evidence be introduced and considered at trial. Kyllo then entered a conditional guilty plea and appealed the trial court's failure to suppress the challenged evidence to the U.S. Court

of Appeals. The U.S. Court of Appeals affirmed the trial court's decision admitting the evidence. Kyllo appealed to the U.S. Supreme Court.

Issue

Is the use of a thermal-imaging device aimed at a private home from a public street to detect relative amounts of heat within the home a "search" within the meaning of the Fourth Amendment?

Language of the U.S. Supreme Court

At the very core of the Fourth Amendment stands the right of a man to retreat into his own home and there be free from unreasonable government intrusion. With few exceptions, the question whether a warrantless search of a home is reasonable and hence constitutional must be answered no. The present case involves officers on a public street engaged in more than naked-eye surveillance of a home. The question we confront today is what limits there are upon this power of technology to shrink the realm of guaranteed privacy. We think that obtaining by sense-enhancing technology any information regarding the interior of the home that could not otherwise have been obtained without physical intrusion into a constitutionally protected area. This assures preservation of that degree of privacy against government that existed when the Fourth Amendment was adopted. On the basis of this criterion, the information obtained by the thermal imager in this case was the product of a search.

Decision

The U.S. Supreme Court held that the use of a thermal-imaging device aimed at a private home from a public street to detect relative amounts of heat within the home is a "search" within the meaning of the Fourth Amendment. The Supreme Court reversed the decision of the U.S. Court of Appeals and remanded the case for further proceedings.

Law & Ethics Questions

1. Is the Fourth Amendment's prohibition against unreasonable search and seizure an easy standard to apply? Explain.

2. **ETHICS** Did the police act ethically in obtaining the evidence in this case? Did Kyllo act ethically in trying to suppress the evidence?

3. How can the government catch entrepreneurs such as Kyllo? Explain.

Web Exercises

1. **WEB** For the complete opinion of this case, go to *www.prenhall.com/cheesemancases*.

2. **WEB** Visit the website of the U.S. Supreme Court, at *www.supremecourtus.gov*, and try to find documents that relate to this case.

3. **WEB** Use *www.google.com* to find a recent case in which the Fourth Amendment prohibition against unreasonable search and seizures was violated.

CASE 6.4
Search

United States of America v. Garcia

474 F.3d 994, **Web** 2007 U.S. App. Lexis 2272 (2007)
United States Court of Appeals for the Seventh Circuit

> **"** *The Supreme Court has insisted that the meaning of a Fourth Amendment search must change to keep pace with the march of science.* **"**
>
> —Judge Posner

Facts

Bernardo Garcia had served time in jail for methamphetamine (meth) offenses. Upon release from prison, a person reported to the police that Garcia had brought meth to her and used it with her. Another person told police that Garcia bragged that he could manufacture meth in front of a police station without being caught. A store's security video system recorded Garcia buying ingredients used in making meth. From someone else, the police learned that Garcia was driving a Ford Tempo.

The police found the car parked on the street near where Garcia was staying. The police placed a global positioning system (GPS) tracking device underneath the rear bumper of the car so the device could receive and store satellite signals that indicate the device's location. Using the device, the police learned that Garcia had been visiting a large tract of land. With permission of the owner of the land, the police conducted a search and discovered equipment and materials to manufacture meth. While the police were there, Garcia arrived in his car.

The police had not obtained a search warrant authorizing them to place the GPS tracker on Garcia's car. At Garcia's criminal trial in U.S. District Court, the evidence the police obtained using the GPS system was introduced. Based upon this evidence, Garcia was found guilty of crimes related to the manufacture of meth. Garcia appealed to the U.S. Court of Appeals, arguing that the use of the GPS tracking system by the police was an unreasonable search in violation of the Fourth Amendment to the Constitution.

Issue

Did the police officers' use of the GPS system without first obtaining a search warrant constitute an unreasonable search in violation of the Fourth Amendment?

Language of the Court

The Fourth Amendment forbids unreasonable searches and seizures. There is nothing in the amendment's text to suggest that a warrant is required in order to make a search or seizure unreasonable. The Supreme Court, however, has created a presumption that a warrant is required, unless infeasible for a search to be reasonable. But was there a search? The Supreme Court has held that the mere tracking of a vehicle on public streets by means of a similar though less sophisticated device (a beeper) is not a search. The Supreme Court has insisted that the meaning of a Fourth Amendment search must change to keep pace with the march of science. So far as appears, the police of Polk County (a rural county in northwestern Wisconsin), where the events of this case unfolded, are not engaged in mass surveillance. They do GPS tracking only when they have a suspect in their sights. They had, of course, abundant grounds for suspecting the defendant.

Decision

The U.S. Court of Appeals held that the warrantless use of a GPS tracking system was not a search and therefore did not violate the Fourth Amendment. The U.S. Court of Appeals upheld the U.S. District Court's judgment that convicted Garcia of crimes involving the manufacture of meth.

Law & Ethics Questions

1. What is a warrantless search?

2. When are warrantless searches permitted?

3. **ETHICS** Is it ethical for a defendant to try to keep incriminating evidence out of a trial when he or she is aware of having committed the crime? Explain.

Web Exercises

1. **WEB** For the full opinion of this case, go to *www.prenhall.com/cheesemancases*.

2. **WEB** Use *www.google.com* to see if you can find an article describing how to manufacture meth.

3. **WEB** Use *www.google.com* to see if you can find a GPS system for sale like the one used in this case. How much does such a device cost?

4. **WEB** Visit the website of the U.S. Court of Appeals for the Seventh Circuit, at *www.ca7.uscourts.gov*.

C A S E   **6.5**
Search and Seizure

U.S. SUPREME COURT
City of Indianapolis v. Edmond

531 U.S. 32, 121 S.Ct. 447, 148 L.Ed.2d 333,
Web 2000 U.S. Lexis 8084 (2000)
Supreme Court of the United States

> "*Because the primary purpose of the Indianapolis narcotics checkpoint program is to uncover evidence of ordinary criminal wrongdoing, the program contravenes the Fourth Amendment.*"
>
> —Justice O'Connor

Facts

The police of the city of Indianapolis, Indiana, began to operate vehicle roadblock checkpoints on Indianapolis roads in an effort to interdict unlawful drugs. Once a car had been stopped, police questioned the driver and passengers and conducted an open-view examination of the vehicle from the outside. A narcotics-detection dog walked around outside each vehicle. The police conducted a search and seizure of the occupants and vehicle only if particular suspicion developed from the initial investigation. The overall "hit rate" of the program was approximately 9 percent.

James Edmond and Joel Palmer, attorneys who had both been stopped at one of the Indianapolis checkpoints, filed a lawsuit on behalf of themselves and the class of all motorists who had been stopped or were subject to being stopped at such checkpoints. They claimed that the roadblocks violated the Fourth Amendment to the Constitution. The District Court found for Indianapolis, but the Court of Appeals reversed. The U.S. Supreme Court granted certiorari to hear the appeal.

Issue

Does the Indianapolis highway checkpoint program, whereby police, without individualized suspicion, stop vehicles for the primary purpose of discovering and interdicting illegal narcotics, violate the Fourth Amendment to the U.S. Constitution?

Language of the U.S. Supreme Court

The Fourth Amendment requires that searches and seizures be reasonable. A search or seizure is ordinarily unreasonable in the absence of individualized suspicion of wrongdoing. We have recognized only limited circumstances in which the usual rule does not apply. We have upheld brief, suspicionless seizures of motorists at a fixed border patrol checkpoint designed to intercept illegal aliens, and at a sobriety checkpoint aimed at removing drunk drivers from the road. We have never approved a checkpoint program whose primary purpose was to detect evidence of ordinary criminal wrongdoing. Because the primary purpose of the Indianapolis narcotics checkpoint program is to uncover evidence of ordinary criminal wrongdoing, the program contravenes the Fourth Amendment. Of course, there are circumstances that may justify a law enforcement checkpoint where the primary purpose would otherwise, but for some emergency, relate to ordinary crime control. For example, the Fourth Amendment would almost certainly permit an appropriately tailored roadblock set up to thwart an imminent terrorist attack or to catch a dangerous criminal who is likely to flee by way of a particular route.

Decision

The U.S. Supreme Court held that the Indianapolis general highway checkpoint, whereby police, without individualized suspicion, stopped vehicles for the primary purpose of discovering and interdicting narcotics, was an unreasonable search and seizure in violation of the Fourth Amendment. The Supreme Court affirmed the decision of the Court of Appeals.

Law & Ethics Questions

1. How did the Supreme Court reconcile its decision in this case with its prior decisions that permitted warrantless checkpoint road checks to intercept illegal aliens and drunk drivers?
2. Do you think that the "terrorist" exception that the Supreme Court announced is reasonable? Explain.

3. **ETHICS** Should the 9 percent of criminals who were caught in the Indianapolis roadblock program get off because of the Fourth Amendment?

Web Exercises

1. **WEB** For the complete opinion of this case, go to *www.prenhall.com/cheesemancases*.
2. **WEB** Visit the website of the U.S. Supreme Court, at *www.supremecourtus.gov*, and try to find documents that relate to this case.
3. **WEB** Use *www.google.com* to find a recent article that discusses the police's use of road checkpoint stops in your state and whether it violated the Fourth Amendment prohibition against unreasonable search and seizures.

> The criminal is to go free because the constable has blundered.
>
> Justice Cardozo
> *People v. Defore (1926)*

Searches of Business Premises

Generally, the government does not have the right to search business premises without a search warrant.[9] Certain hazardous and regulated industries—such as sellers of firearms and liquor, coal mines, and the like—are subject to warrantless searches if proper statutory procedures are met.

In the following case, the U.S. Supreme Court had to decide whether a warrantless search of business premises was lawful.

C A S E 6.6
Search of Business Premises

U.S. SUPREME COURT
New York v. Burger

482 U.S. 691, 107 S.Ct. 2636, 96 L.Ed.2d 601,
Web 1987 U.S. Lexis 2725
Supreme Court of the United States

> ❝ *An expectation of privacy in commercial premises, however, is different from, and indeed less than, a similar expectation in an individual's home.* ❞
>
> —Justice Blackmun

Facts

Joseph Burger was the owner of a junkyard in Brooklyn, New York. His business consisted, in part, of dismantling automobiles and selling their parts. The state of New York enacted a statute that requires automobile junkyards to keep certain records. The statute authorizes warrantless searches of vehicle dismantlers and automobile junkyards without prior notice. One day, five plain-clothes officers of the Auto Crimes Division of the New York City Police Department entered Burger's junkyard to conduct a surprise inspection. Burger did not have either a license to conduct the business or records of the automobiles and vehicle parts on his premises, as required by state law. After conducting an inspection of the premises, the officers determined that Burger was in possession of stolen vehicles and parts. He was arrested and charged with criminal possession of stolen property. Burger moved to suppress the evidence. The New York supreme court and appellate division held the search to be constitutional. The New York court of appeals reversed. New York appealed.

Issue

Does the warrantless search of an automobile junkyard pursuant to a state statute that authorizes such search constitute an unreasonable search and seizure in violation of the Fourth Amendment to the U.S. Constitution?

Language of the Supreme Court

The court has long recognized that the Fourth Amendment's prohibition on unreasonable searches and seizures is applicable to commercial premises, as well as to private homes. An expectation of privacy in commercial premises, however, is different from, and indeed less than, a similar expectation in an individual's home. This expectation is particularly attenuated in commercial property employed in "closely regulated" industries.

Because the owner or operator of commercial premises in a closely regulated industry has a reduced expectation of privacy, the warrant and probable cause requirements—which fulfill the traditional Fourth Amendment standard of reasonableness for a government search—have a lessened application in this context. The nature of the regulatory statute reveals that the operation of a junkyard, part of which is devoted to vehicle dismantling, is a closely regulated business in the state of New York. A warrantless inspection of commercial premises may well be reasonable within the meaning of the Fourth Amendment.

The New York regulatory scheme satisfies the criteria necessary to make reasonable warrantless inspections. The state has substantial interest in regulating the vehicle dismantling and automobile junkyard industry because motor vehicle theft has increased in the state of New York and because the problem of theft is associated with this industry. Regulation of the vehicle dismantling industry reasonably serves the state's substantial interest in eradicating automobile theft. It is well established that the theft problem can be addressed effectively by controlling the receiver of, or market in, stolen property. Automobile junkyards and vehicle dismantlers provide the major market for stolen vehicles and vehicle parts. The New York law provides a constitutionally adequate substitute for a warrant. The statute informs the operator of a vehicle dismantling business that inspections will be made on a regular basis.

Decision

The U.S. Supreme Court held that the New York statute that authorizes warrantless searches of vehicle dismantling businesses and automobile junkyards does not constitute an unreasonable search in violation of the Fourth Amendment to the U.S. Constitution. The Supreme Court reversed the judgment of the New York court of appeals and remanded the case for further proceedings consistent with its decision.

Law & Ethics Questions

1. Should the Fourth Amendment's protection against unreasonable searches and seizures apply to businesses? Why or why not?
2. **ETHICS** Was it ethical for the defendant to assert the Fourth Amendment's prohibition against unreasonable searches and seizures? Why did he raise this defense?
3. Is auto theft a big business? Will the New York law that regulates vehicle dismantling businesses and junkyards help to alleviate this crime?

Web Exercises

1. **WEB** For the complete opinion of this case, go to *www.prenhall.com/cheesemancases*.
2. **WEB** Visit the website of the U.S. Supreme Court, at *www.supremecourtus.gov*, and try to find documents that relate to this case.
3. **WEB** Use *www.google.com* to find a recent article that discusses the search of business premises.
4. **WEB** Visit the website of the New York City Police Department, at *www.nyc.gov/html/nypd/home.html*.

CONTEMPORARY ENVIRONMENT
Federal Antiterrorism Act

The devastating terrorist attacks on the World Trade Center in New York and the Pentagon in Washington, DC, on September 11, 2001, shocked the nation. The attacks were organized and orchestrated by terrorists who crossed nations' borders easily, secretly planned and prepared for the attacks undetected, and financed the attacks using money located in banks in the United States, Great Britain, and other countries. In response, Congress enacted the federal **Antiterrorism Act**, which assists the government in detecting, investigating, and prosecuting terrorists. The bill was signed into law on October 26, 2001. The act contains the following main features:

- **Special Intelligence Court.** The act authorizes the Special Intelligence Court to issue expanded wiretap orders and subpoenas to obtain evidence of suspected terrorism.
- **Nationwide search warrant.** The act creates a nationwide search warrant to obtain evidence of terrorist activities.

- **Roving wiretaps.** The act permits "roving wiretaps" on a person suspected of involvement in terrorism so that any telephone or electronic device used by the person may be monitored.
- **Detention of noncitizens.** The act gives the federal government authority to detain a nonresident in the United States for up to seven days without filing charges against that person. Nonresidents who are certified by a court as a threat to national security may be held for up to six months without a trial.

Law & Ethics Questions

1. Do you think that the provisions of the federal Antiterrorism Act will help prevent terrorist attacks? Why or why not?
2. **ETHICS** Do you think that any of the provisions of the federal Antiterrorism Act violate the U.S. Constitution?

Web Exercises

1. **WEB** Use *www.google.com* to find a video that shows the September 11, 2001, terrorist attack on the World Trade Center in New York City.

2. **WEB** Use *www.google.com* to find a video that shows the September 11, 2001, terrorist attack on the U.S. Pentagon building in Washington, DC.

3. **WEB** Use *www.google.com* to find an article about the fourth plane taken over by terrorists on September 11, 2001.

Fifth Amendment Privilege against Self-Incrimination

The *Fifth Amendment* to the U.S. Constitution provides that no person "shall be compelled in any criminal case to be a witness against himself." Thus, a person cannot be compelled to give testimony against himself or herself, although nontestimonial evidence (e.g., fingerprints, body fluids) may be required. A person who asserts this right is described as having "taken the Fifth." This protection applies to federal cases and is extended to state and local criminal cases through the Due Process Clause of the Fourteenth Amendment.

The **protection against self-incrimination** applies only to natural persons who are accused of crimes. Therefore, artificial persons (such as corporations and partnerships) cannot raise this protection against incriminating testimony.[10] Thus, business records of corporations and partnerships are not generally protected from disclosure, even if they incriminate individuals who work for the business. However, certain "private papers" of businesspersons (such as personal diaries) are protected from disclosure.

Miranda Rights

Most people have not read and memorized the provisions of the U.S. Constitution. The U.S. Supreme Court recognized this fact when it decided the landmark case *Miranda v. Arizona* in 1966.[11] In that case, the Supreme Court held that the Fifth Amendment privilege against self-incrimination is not useful unless a criminal suspect has knowledge of this right. Therefore, the Supreme Court required that the following warning—colloquially called the *Miranda* **rights**—be read to a criminal suspect before he or she is interrogated by the police or other government officials:

- You have the right to remain silent.
- Anything you say can and will be used against you.
- You have the right to consult a lawyer and to have a lawyer present with you during interrogation.
- If you cannot afford a lawyer, a lawyer will be appointed free of charge to represent you.

> At the present time in this country there is more danger that criminals will escape justice than that they will be subjected to tyranny.
>
> J. Holmes Dissenting
> *Kepner v. United States (1904)*

Any statements or confessions obtained from a suspect prior to being read his or her *Miranda rights* can be excluded from evidence at trial. In 2000, the U.S. Supreme Court upheld *Miranda* in *Dickerson v. United States*. Chief Justice Rehnquist said: "We do not think there is justification for overruling *Miranda*. *Miranda* has become embedded in routine police practice to the point where the warnings have become part of our national culture."[12]

Attorney–Client Privilege and Other Privileges

To obtain a proper defense, the accused person must be able to tell his or her attorney facts about the case without fear that the attorney will be called as a witness against the accused. The **attorney–client privilege** is protected by the Fifth Amendment. Either the client or the attorney can raise this privilege. For the privilege to apply, the information must be told to the attorney in his or her capacity as an attorney, and not as a friend or neighbor or such.

The following privileges have also been recognized under the Fifth Amendment: (1) **psychiatrist/psychologist–patient privilege**, (2) **priest/rabbi/minister/imam–penitent privilege**, (3) **spouse–spouse privilege**, and (4) **parent–child privilege**. There are some exceptions.

Example A spouse or child who is beaten by a spouse or parent may testify against the accused.

The U.S. Supreme Court has held that there is no accountant–client privilege under federal law.[13] Thus, an accountant could be called as a witness in cases involving federal securities laws, federal mail or wire fraud, or other federal crimes. Nevertheless, approximately 20 states have enacted special statutes that create an **accountant–client privilege**. An accountant cannot be called as a witness against a client in a court action in a state where these statutes are in effect. Federal courts do not recognize these laws, however.

> It is better that ten guilty persons escape, than that one innocent suffer.
>
> Sir William Blackstone
> *Commentaries on the Laws of England (1809)*

Immunity from Prosecution

On occasion, the government may want to obtain information from a suspect who has asserted his or her Fifth Amendment privilege against self-incrimination. The government can often achieve this by offering the suspect **immunity from prosecution**. Immunity from prosecution means that the government agrees not to use against a person granted immunity any evidence given by that person. Once immunity is granted, the suspect loses the right to assert his or her Fifth Amendment privilege.

Grants of immunity are often given when the government wants the suspect to give information that will lead to the prosecution of other, more important, criminal suspects. Partial grants of immunity are also available.

Example A suspect may be granted immunity from prosecution for a serious crime, but not a lesser crime, in exchange for information. The suspect must agree to a partial grant of immunity.

Other Constitutional Protections

There are many other provisions in the U.S. Constitution and its amendments that guarantee and protect certain other rights in the criminal process. Several of these additional rights are described in the paragraphs that follow.

Fifth Amendment Protection Against Double Jeopardy

The **Double Jeopardy Clause** of the Fifth Amendment protects persons from being tried twice for the same crime.

Example If a state tries a suspect for the crime of murder and the suspect is found not guilty, the state cannot bring another trial against the accused for the same crime.

If the same criminal act involves several different crimes, the accused may be tried for each of the crimes without violating the Double Jeopardy Clause.

Example Suppose the accused kills two people during a robbery. The accused may be tried for two murders and robbery.

If the same act violates the laws of two or more jurisdictions, each jurisdiction may try the accused.

Example If an accused kidnaps a person in one state and brings the victim across a state border into another state, the act violates the laws of two states and the federal government. Thus, three jurisdictions can prosecute the accused without violating the Double Jeopardy Clause.

Sixth Amendment Right to a Public Jury Trial

The *Sixth Amendment* guarantees certain rights to criminal defendants. These rights are (1) to be tried by an impartial jury of the state or district in which the alleged crime was committed, (2) to confront (cross-examine) the witnesses against the accused, (3) to have the assistance of a lawyer, and (4) to have a speedy trial.[14]

Eighth Amendment Protection Against Cruel and Unusual Punishment

The *Eighth Amendment* protects criminal defendants from **cruel and unusual punishment**. For example, it prohibits the torture of criminals. However, this clause does not prohibit capital punishment.[15]

INTERNATIONAL LAW
International Extortion and Bribery

> **❝** *The payments made by the company were always motivated by our good faith concern for the safety of our employees.* **❞**
>
> —Fernando Aguirre
> Chief Executive Officer, Chiquita Brands International

The Cincinnati, Ohio–based banana company Chiquita Brands International admitted to the U.S. Justice Department that it had been paying protection money to Columbian terrorists for over seven years. The company voluntarily confessed that it had paid in excess of $1.7 million of extortion money to at least three groups, the United Self-Defense Forces of Columbia (AUC), the National Liberation Army (ELN), and the Revolutionary Armed Forces of Columbia (FARC), in order to protect its Columbian plant employees. The Justice Department labeled all three groups as known "foreign terrorist organizations" and federal law prohibits U.S. companies from doing business with them.

Although Chiquita claimed it didn't realize that it was dealing with a group that had been officially designated a terrorist organization, its financial records showed that the company had switched its payments to the AUC to cash and continued to pay them off even after outside counsel warned the company of the illegality. The payments were disguised in the company's financial statements as payments made to "security companies."

The payments were made through a subsidiary of Chiquita known as Banadex, which insisted that the payments were made due to terrorist extortion. According to federal documents, Banadex executives said that the AUC sent an "unspoken, but clear message that failure to make the payments could result in physical harm to Banadex personnel and property." Chiquita CEO Fernando Aguirre insisted that the payments were made for protection, saying "The payments made by the company were always motivated by our good faith concern for the safety of our employees."

After Chiquita had learned that the Justice Department had been investigating the company's financial dealings with the organizations, the banana producers decided to come forward on their own. Soon thereafter, Chiquita agreed to a settlement deal that forced a guilty plea, a full disclosure, and a $25 million fine. Soon after, the company sold off its Columbian banana plant.

Law & Ethics Questions

1. What is extortion? Explain.

2. **ETHICS** Did Chiquita do the "right thing" by paying the extortionists?

3. **ETHICS** Did Chiquita act ethically by selling off the troublesome Columbian banana plant?

4. **ETHICS** Do you think that the payment of extortion money or bribes is a usual cost of doing business? Explain.

Web Exercises

1. **WEB** Visit the website of Chiquita Brands International, at *www.chiquita.com*.

2. **WEB** View the list of the groups designated as "foreign terrorist organizations" at the website of the U.S. Department of State, at *www.state.gov/s/ct/rls/rpt/fto/2001/5258.htm*.

3. **WEB** Use *www.google.com* to find an article that discusses a recent case of bribery or extortion in conducting business. Read it.

The Forbidden City, Beijing, China
Multinational corporations have to obey the criminal laws of all the countries in which they conduct business.

Chapter Summary

Definition of Crime, p. 148

A *crime* is any act done by a person in violation of the duties that he or she owes to society and for the breach of which the law provides a penalty. In the United States:

1. The accused is *presumed innocent until proven guilty*.
2. The plaintiff (the government) bears the *burden of proof*.
3. The government must prove *beyond a reasonable doubt* that the accused is guilty of the crime charged.
4. The accused does not have to testify against him- or herself.
   A conviction requires a unanimous jury.

Penal Codes and Regulatory Statutes

State and federal statutes define many crimes. Criminal conduct is also defined in many *regulatory statutes*.

Parties to a Criminal Action

Parties to a criminal lawsuit are:

1. *Plaintiff.* The government, which is represented by the *prosecuting attorney* (or *prosecutor*).
2. *Defendant.* The person or business accused of the crime, who is represented by a *defense attorney*.

Classification of Crimes

1. *Felony.* The most serious kinds of crimes are felonies. They are *mala in se* (inherently evil), and they are usually punishable by imprisonment.
2. *Misdemeanor.* Misdemeanors are less serious crimes than felonies. They are *mala prohibita* (prohibited by society), and they are usually punishable by fine and/or imprisonment for less than one year.
3. *Violation.* A violation is neither a felony nor a misdemeanor. Violations are generally punishable by a fine.

Elements of a Crime

Most crimes require that the following two elements be proven:

1. *Actus reus.* Guilty act.
2. *Mens rea.* Evil intent.

Non-Intent Crimes

Most states provide for certain non-intent crimes, such as the crime of involuntary manslaughter.

Criminal Procedure, p. 152

Arrest

An arrest is made pursuant to an *arrest warrant*, based on a showing of "probable cause," or, where permitted, by a *warrantless* arrest.

Indictment or Information

Grand juries issue *indictments*, magistrates (judges) issue *information*. These formally charge the accused with specific crimes.

Arraignment

The accused is informed of the charges against him or her and enters a *plea* in court. The plea may be *not guilty, guilty*, or *nolo contendere*.

Plea Bargaining

In a plea bargain, the government and the accused may negotiate a settlement agreement wherein the accused agrees to admit to a lesser crime than charged.

   A criminal trial may result in the following verdicts:
1. *Guilty.* Requires unanimous vote of the jury.
2. *Not guilty.* Requires unanimous vote of the jury.
3. *Hung jury.* Nonunanimous vote of the jury. The government may prosecute the case again.

   An appeal involves the following:
1. *Defendant.* May appeal his or her conviction.
2. *Plaintiff (government).* May not appeal a verdict of innocent.

Common Crimes, p. 154

Murder

Murder is the unlawful killing of a human being by another with malice aforethought.

Robbery

Robbery is the taking of personal property from another by fear or force.

Burglary

Burglary is the unauthorized entering of a building to commit a felony.

Larceny

Larceny is the wrongful taking of another's property other than from his person or building.

Theft

Theft is the wrongful taking of another's property, whether by robbery, burglary, or larceny.

Receiving Stolen Property

A person may knowingly receive stolen property with the intent to deprive the rightful owner of that property.

Arson

Arson is the malicious and willful burning into a building.

White-Collar Crime, p. 160

White-collar crimes are generally committed by businesspersons, and they involve cunning and trickery rather than physical force.

Forgery

Forgery involves fraudulently making or altering a written document that affects the legal liability of another person.

Embezzlement

Embezzlement is the fraudulent conversion of property by a person to whom the property was *entrusted*.

Bribery

Bribery is the offer of payment of money or property or something else of value in return for an unwarranted favor. The party who pays the bribe and the recipient are both guilty of the crime of bribery.

1. *Commercial bribery* is the offer of a payment of a bribe to private persons and business. This is often referred to as a *kickback* or *payoff*.
2. Bribery of public officials for an "official act" is a crime.

Foreign Corrupt Practice Act

The FCPA is a federal statute that makes it a crime for U.S. companies, or their officers, directors, agents, or employees, to bribe a foreign official, a foreign political party official, or a candidate for foreign political office, where the bribe is paid to influence the awarding of new business or the retention of a continuing business activity.

Extortion

Extortion involves a threat to expose something about another person unless that person gives up money or property.

Criminal Fraud

Criminal fraud involves obtaining title to another's property through deception or trickery. Also called *false pretenses* or *deceit*.

Mail Fraud and Wire Fraud

Mail fraud is the use of mail to defraud another person. *Wire fraud* is the use of wire (telephone or telegraph) to defraud another person.

Racketeer Influenced and Corrupt Organizations Act (RICO)

This federal statute makes it a federal crime to acquire or maintain an interest in, use income from, or conduct or participate in the affairs of an enterprise through a pattern of racketeering activity. Criminal penalties include the *forfeiture* of any property or business interests gained through a RICO violation.

Criminal Conspiracy

A crime that occurs when two or more persons enter into an agreement to commit a crime and takes some overt act in furtherance of the crime.

Money Laundering Control Act

This federal statute makes it a crime to:

1. Knowingly engage in a *money transaction* through a financial institution involving property worth more than $10,000.
2. Knowingly engage in a *financial transaction* involving the proceeds of an illegal activity.

Corporate Criminal Liability

1. Corporate directors, officers, and employees are criminally liable for crimes they commit for personal benefit or on behalf of the corporation.
2. A corporation is criminally liable for crimes committed by directors, officers, and employees while acting on behalf of the corporation.

Protection against Unreasonable Search and Seizure, p. 164

This amendment protects persons and corporations from *unreasonable search and seizures*. *Reasonable search and seizure* based on *probable cause* is lawful. A search warrant stipulates the place and scope of the search.

A *warrantless search* is permitted only:

1. Incident to an arrest.
2. Where evidence is in plain view.
3. Where it is likely that evidence will be destroyed.

Exclusionary Rule

Evidence obtained from an unreasonable search and seizure is *tainted evidence* that may not be introduced at a government proceeding against the person searched.

Searches of Business Premises

Business premises are protected by the Fourth Amendment, except that certain *regulated industries* may be subject to warrantless searches authorized by statute.

Fifth Amendment Privilege against Self-Incrimination, p. 170

This amendment provides that no person "shall be compelled in any criminal case to be a witness against himself." A person asserting this privilege is said to have "taken the Fifth." Nontestimonial evidence (e.g., fingerprints, body fluids) is not protected. In addition, the privilege applies only to natural persons; businesses cannot assert the privilege.

Miranda Rights

A criminal suspect must be informed of his or her Fifth Amendment rights before the suspect can be interrogated by the police or government officials.

Attorney-Client Privilege and Other Privileges

An accused's lawyer cannot be called as a witness against the accused. The following privileges have been recognized, with some limitations:

1. Psychiatrist/psychologist–patient
2. Priest/rabbi/minister/imam–penitent
3. Spouse–spouse
4. Parent–child

Accountant–client privilege is not recognized at the federal level. Some states recognize this privilege in state law actions.

Immunity from Prosecution

Immunity is granted by the government to obtain otherwise privileged evidence. The government agrees not to use the evidence given against the person who gave it.

Other Constitutional Protections, p. 171

The Constitution provides several other important protections in criminal cases.

Fifth Amendment Protection Against Double Jeopardy

The Fifth Amendment protects persons from being tried twice by the same jurisdiction for the same crime. If the act violates the law of two or more jurisdictions, each jurisdiction may try the accused. The Fifth Amendment guarantees criminal defendants the following rights:

1. To be tried by an impartial jury.
2. To confront the witness.
3. To have the assistance of a lawyer.
4. To have a speedy trial.

Sixth Amendment Right to a Public Jury Trial

The Sixth Amendment permits the accused to be tried by an impartial jury, to confront witnesses, have the assistance of a lawyer, and to have a speedy trial.

Eighth Amendment Protection Against Cruel and Unusual Punishment

The Eighth Amendment protects criminal defendants from cruel and unusual punishment. Capital punishment is permitted by this amendment.

Test Review Terms and Concepts

Accountant–client privilege 171
Actus reus 150
Antiterrorism Act 169
Arraignment 153
Arrest 152
Arrest warrant 152
Arson 159
Attorney–client privilege 170
Beyond a reasonable doubt 148
Blackmail 162
Booking 152
Bribery 161
Burglary 159
Civil RICO 163
Corporate criminal liability 164
Crime 148
Criminal conspiracy 163
Criminal fraud (false pretenses) 162
Criminal RICO 163
Cruel and unusual punishment 172
Cyber crimes 148
Defense attorney 149
Double Jeopardy Clause 171
Embezzlement 160
Exclusionary rule 165

Extortion 162
Felony 149
Felony murder rule 157
Foreign Corrupt Practice Act (FCPA) 161
Forgery 160
General intent 150
Grand jury 153
Hung jury 154
Immunity from prosecution 171
Indictment 153
Information 153
Larceny 159
Magistrate 153
Mail fraud 162
Mala in se 149
Mala prohibita 149
Mens rea 150
Miranda rights 170
Misdemeanor 149
Money laundering 164
Money Laundering Control Act 164
Nolo contendere 153
Non-intent crime 150
Parent–child privilege 171
Penal code 148

Plea 153
Plea bargaining agreement 153
Priest/rabbi/minister/imam–penitent privilege 171
Prosecutor 149
Protection against self-incrimination 170
Psychiatrist/psychologist–patient privilege 171
Racketeer Influenced and Corrupt Organizations Act (RICO) 163
Reasonable search and seizure 165
Receiving stolen property 159
Regulatory statute 149
Robbery 159
Search warrant 165
Specific intent 150
Spouse–spouse privilege 171
Theft 159
Unanimous decision 154
Unreasonable search and seizure 165
Violation 149
White-collar crime 160
Wire fraud 162

Case Problems

6.1 Criminal Liability of Corporations: Representatives of hotels, restaurants, hotel and restaurant supply companies, and other businesses located in Portland, Oregon, organized an association to attract conventions to their city. Members were asked to make contributions equal to 1 percent of their sales to finance the association. To aid collections, hotel members, including Hilton Hotels Corporation, agreed to give preferential treatment to suppliers who paid their assessments and to curtail purchases from those who did not. This agreement violated federal antitrust laws. The United States sued the members of the association, including Hilton Hotels, for the crime of violating federal antitrust laws. Can a corporation be held criminally liable for the acts of its representatives? If so, what criminal penalties can be assessed against the corporation? *United States v. Hilton Hotels Corp.*, 467 F.2d 1000, **Web** 1972 U.S. App. Lexis 7414 (United States Court of Appeals for the Ninth Circuit)

6.2 Forgery: Evidence showed that there was a burglary in which a checkbook belonging to Mary J. Harris, doing business as The Report Department, and a check encoder machine were stolen. Two of the checks from that checkbook were cashed at the Citizens & Southern National Bank branch office in Riverdale, Georgia, by Joseph Leon Foster, who was accompanied by a woman identified as Angela Foxworth. The bank teller who cashed the checks testified that the same man and woman cashed the checks on two different occasions at her drive-up window at the bank and that on both occasions they were in the same car. Each time the teller wrote the license tag number of the car on the back of the check. The teller testified that both times the checks and the driver's license used to identify the woman were passed to her by the man driving and that the man received the money from her. What crime has been committed? *Foster v. State of Georgia*, 193 Ga. App. 368, 387 S.E.2d 637, **Web** 1989 Ga. App. Lexis 1456 (Court of Appeals of Georgia)

6.3 Extortion: The victim (Mr. X) went to the premises at 42 Taylor Terrace in New Milford, Connecticut, where his daughter and her husband lived. Lisa Percoco, who was

Gregory Erhardt's girlfriend, was at the residence. Mr. X and Percoco were in the bedroom, partially dressed, engaging in sexual activity, when Erhardt entered the room and photographed them. He then informed Mr. X that unless he procured $5,000 and placed it in a mailbox at a designated address by 8 P.M. that night, Erhardt would show the photographs to Mr. X's wife. Mr. X proceeded to make telephone arrangements for the procurement and placement of the money according to Erhardt's instructions. If the money were paid, what crime would have been committed? *State of Connecticut v. Erhardt*, 17 Conn. App. 359, 553 A.2d 188, **Web** 1989 Conn. App. Lexis 21 (Appellate Court of Connecticut)

6.4 Criminal Fraud: Miriam Marlowe's husband purchased a life insurance policy on his own life, naming his wife as the beneficiary. Three years later, after Marlowe's husband died in a swimming accident, Marlowe received payment on the life insurance policy. Marlowe later met John Walton, a friend of a friend. He convinced her and her representative that he had a friend who worked for the State Department and had access to gold in Brazil and that the gold could be purchased in Brazil for $100 an ounce and sold in the United States for $300 an ounce. Walton convinced Miriam to invest $25,000. Instead of investing the money in gold in Brazil, Walton opened an account at Tracy Collins Bank in the name of Jeffrey McIntyre Roberts and deposited Miriam's money in the account. He later withdrew the money in cash. What crime is Walton guilty of? *State of Utah v. Roberts*, 711 P.2d 235, **Web** 1985 Utah Lexis 872 (Supreme Court of Utah)

6.5 Bribery: The city of Peoria, Illinois, received federal funds from the Department of Housing and Urban Development (HUD) to be used for housing rehabilitation assistance. The city of Peoria designated United Neighborhoods, Inc. (UNI), a corporation, to administer the funds. Arthur Dixon was UNI's executive director, and James Lee Hinton was its housing rehabilitation coordinator. In these capacities, they were responsible for contracting with suppliers and tradespeople to provide the necessary goods and services to rehabilitate the houses. Evidence showed that Dixon and Hinton used their positions to extract 10 percent payments back on all contracts they awarded. What crime have they committed? *Dixon and Hinton v. United States*, 465 U.S. 482, 104 S.Ct. 1172, 79 L.Ed.2d 458, **Web** 1984 U.S. Lexis 35 (Supreme Court of the United States)

6.6 Administrative Search: Lee Stuart Paulson owned the liquor license for My House, a bar in San Francisco. The California Department of Alcoholic Beverage Control is the administrative agency that regulates bars in that state. The California Business and Professions Code, which the department administers, prohibits "any kind of illegal activity on licensed premises." An anonymous informer tipped the department that narcotics sales were occurring on the premises of My House and that the narcotics were kept in a safe behind the bar on the premises. A special department investigator entered the bar during its hours of operation, identified himself, and informed Paulson that he was conducting an inspection. The investigator, who did not have a search warrant, opened the safe without seeking Paulson's consent. Twenty-two bundles of cocaine, totaling 5.5 grams, were found in the safe. Paulson was arrested. At his criminal trial, Paulson challenged the lawfulness of the search. Was the warrantless search of the safe a lawful search? *People v. Paulson*, 216 Cal.App.3d 1480, 265 Cal.Rptr. 579, **Web** 1990 Cal.App. Lexis 10 (Court of Appeal of California)

6.7 Search Warrant: The Center Art Galleries–Hawaii sells artwork. Approximately 20 percent of its business involves art by Salvador Dalí. The federal government, which suspected the center of fraudulently selling forged Dalí artwork, obtained identical search warrants for six locations controlled by the center. The warrants commanded the executing officer to seize items that were "evidence of violations of federal criminal law." The warrants did not describe the specific crimes suspected and did not stipulate that only items pertaining to the sale of Dalí's work could be seized. There was no evidence of any criminal activity unrelated to that artist. Are these search warrants valid? *Center Art Galleries–Hawaii, Inc. v. United States*, 875 F.2d 747, **Web** 1989 U.S. App. Lexis 6983 (United States Court of Appeals for the Ninth Circuit)

6.8 Privilege Against Self-Incrimination: John Doe is the owner of several sole-proprietorship businesses. During the course of an investigation of corruption in awarding county and municipal contracts, a federal grand jury served several subpoenas on John Doe, demanding the production of certain business records. The subpoenas demanded the production of the following records: (1) general ledgers and journals, (2) invoices, (3) bank statements and canceled checks, (4) financial statements, (5) telephone-company records, (6) safe-deposit box records, and (7) copies of tax returns. John Doe filed a motion in federal court, seeking to quash the subpoenas, alleging that producing these business records would violate his Fifth Amendment privilege of not testifying against himself. Do the records have to be disclosed? *United States v. John Doe*, 465 U.S. 605, 104 S.Ct. 1237, 79 L.Ed.2d 552, **Web** 1984 U.S. Lexis 169 (Supreme Court of the United States)

Ethics Issues

6.9 Ethics: Leo Shaw, an attorney, entered into a partnership agreement with three other persons to build and operate an office building. From the outset, it was agreed that Shaw's role was to manage the operation of the building. Management of the property was Shaw's contribution to the partnership; the other three partners contributed the necessary capital. Ten years later, the other partners discovered that the loan on the building was in default and that foreclosure proceedings were imminent. Upon investigation, they discovered that Shaw had taken approximately $80,000 from the partnership's checking account. After heated discussions, Shaw repaid $13,000. When no further payment was forthcoming, a partner filed a civil suit against Shaw and notified the police. The state filed a criminal complaint against Shaw. Subsequently, Shaw repaid the remaining funds as part of a civil settlement. At his criminal trial, Shaw argued that the repayment of the money was a defense to the crime of embezzlement. Did Shaw act ethically in this case? Would your answer be different if he had really only "borrowed" the money and had intended to return it? *People v. Shaw*, 10 Cal.App. 4th 969, 12 Cal.Rptr.2d 665, **Web** 1992 Cal.App. Lexis 1256 (Court of Appeal of California)

6.10 Ethics: Ronald V. Cloud purchased the Cal-Neva Lodge, a hotel and casino complex located in the Lake Tahoe area near the California–Nevada border, for $10 million. Cloud was a sophisticated 68-year-old entrepreneur who was experienced in buying and selling real estate and had real estate holdings valued at more than $65 million. He also had experience in banking and finance, having been the founder and chairman of Continental National Bank of Fresno. After two years of mounting operation losses, Cloud closed the Cal-Neva Lodge and actively began seeking a new buyer. Cloud met with Jon Perroton and orally agreed to transfer the lodge to Perroton for approximately $17 million. Perroton met with an executive of Hibernia Bank (Hibernia) to discuss a possible loan to finance the purchase of the lodge. Perroton made multiple false representations and presented false documents to obtain a $20 million loan from Hibernia. In particular, Perroton misrepresented the sale price for the lodge ($27.5 million) and stated that $7.5 million had already been paid to Cloud. An escrow account was opened with Transamerica Title Company (Transamerica).

Cloud and his attorney and Perroton met at Transamerica to sign mutual escrow instructions. Cloud reviewed the instructions and noticed that the sale price and down payment figures were incorrectly stated at $27.5 million and $7.5 million, respectively, and that the Hibernia loan was for $20 million, almost $3 million above what he knew to be the true sale price. Cloud signed the escrow instructions. Later, Cloud signed a settlement statement containing the same false figures and signed a grant deed to the property. The sale closed on January 23, 1985, with Hibernia making the $20 million loan to Perroton. Subsequently, when the loan went into default, Continental Insurance Company (Continental) paid Hibernia its loss of $7.5 million on the bank's blanket bond insurance policy. The United States sued Cloud for aiding and abetting a bank fraud in violation of federal law (18 U.S.C. Sections 2 and 1344). The jury convicted Cloud of the crime and ordered him to make restitution of $7.5 million to Continental. Cloud appealed. Did cloud act ethically in this case? Explain. Is Cloud guilty of aiding and abetting a bank fraud? *United States v. Cloud*, 872 F.2d 846, **Web** 1989 U.S. App. Lexis 4534 (United States Court of Appeals for the Ninth Circuit)

IRAC Writing Assignment

Read Case A.6 in Appendix A [*Schalk v. Texas*]. Read the case and use the IRAC method to prepare a written analysis of the case.

Endnotes

1. Title 18 of the U.S. Code contains the federal criminal code.
2. Sentencing Reform Act of 1984, 18 U.S.C. Section 3551 et. seq.
3. 15 U.S.C. Section 78m.
4. 18 U.S.C. Section 1341.
5. 18 U.S.C. Section 1343.
6. 18 U.S.C. Sections 1961–1968.
7. 18 U.S.C. Section 1957.
8. *United States v. Leon*, 468 U.S. 897, 104 S.Ct. 3405, 82 L.Ed.2d 677, **Web** 1984 U.S. Lexis 153 (Supreme Court of the United States).

9. *Marshall v. Barlow's Inc.*, 436 U.S. 307, 98 S.Ct. 1816, 56 L.Ed.2d 305, Web 1978 U.S. Lexis 26 (Supreme Court of the United States).

10. *Bellis v. United States*, 417 U.S. 85, 94 S.Ct. 2179, 40 L.Ed.2d 678, **Web** 1974 U.S. Lexis 58 (Supreme Court of the United States).

11. 384 U.S. 436, 86 S.Ct. 1602, 16 L.Ed.2d 694, **Web** 1966 U.S. Lexis 2817 (Supreme Court of the United States).

12. *Dickerson v. United States*, 530 U.S. 428, 120 S.Ct. 2326, 147 L.Ed.2d 405, **Web** 2000 U.S. Lexis 4305 (Supreme Court of the United States).

13. 409 U.S. 322, 93 S.Ct. 611, 34 L.Ed.2d 548, **Web** 1973 U.S. Lexis 23 (Supreme Court of the United States).

14. The Speedy Trial Act requires that a criminal defendant be brought to trial within 70 days after indictment [18 U.S.C. Section 316(c) (1)]. Continuances may be granted by the court to serve the "ends of justice."

15. *Baldwin v. Alabama*, 472 U.S. 372, 105 S.Ct. 2727, 86 L.Ed.2d 300, **Web** 1985 U.S. Lexis 106 (Supreme Court of the United States).

CHAPTER **7**

Intellectual Property and Piracy

"The Congress shall have the power ... to promote the Progress of Science and useful Arts, by securing for limited Times to Authors and Inventors the exclusive Right to their respective Writings and Discoveries."

—U.S. CONSTITUTION, ARTICLE 1, SECTION 8, CLAUSE 8

CHAPTER OBJECTIVES

After studying this chapter, you should be able to:

1. Describe the business tort of misappropriating a trade secret.
2. Describe how an invention can be patented under federal patent laws and the penalties for patent infringement.
3. List the items that can be copyrighted and describe the penalties of copyright infringement.
4. Define *trademarks* and *service marks* and describe the penalties for trademark infringement.
5. Describe the international protection of patents, copyrights, and trademarks.

CHAPTER CONTENTS

- Introduction to Intellectual Property and Internet Law
- Trade Secrets
- Patents
- Copyrights
- Trademarks
- Chapter Summary
- Test Review Terms and Concepts
- Case Problems
- Ethics Issues
- IRAC Writing Assignment

    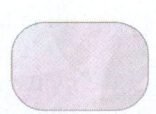

Introduction to Intellectual Property and Internet Law

The U.S. economy is based on the freedom of ownership of property. In addition to real estate and personal property, **intellectual property rights** have value to both businesses and individuals. This is particularly the case in the modern era of the Information Age, computers, and the Internet.

Trade secrets form the basis of many successful businesses, and they are protected from misappropriation. State law imposes civil damages and criminal penalties against persons who misappropriate trade secrets. Federal law provides protections for intellectual property rights, such as patents, copyrights, and trademarks. Certain federal statutes provide for either civil damages or criminal penalties, or both, to be assessed against infringers of patents, copyrights, and trademarks.

This chapter discusses the protection of trade secrets, patents, copyrights, and trademarks.

Reflecting Pool, Los Angeles County Museum of Art

Photographs such as this one, titled "Colorful Dream," are copyrighted.

Trade Secrets

Many businesses are successful because their **trade secrets** set them apart from their competitors. Trade secrets may be product formulas, patterns, designs, compilations of data, customer lists, or other business secrets. Many trade secrets do not qualify to be—or simply are not—patented, copyrighted, or trademarked. Many states have adopted the **Uniform Trade Secrets Act** to give statutory protection to trade secrets.

State unfair competition laws allow the owner of a trade secret to bring a lawsuit for **misappropriation of a trade secret** against anyone who steals a trade secret. For the lawsuit to be actionable, the defendant (often an employee of the owner or a competitor) must have obtained the trade secret through unlawful means, such as theft, bribery, or industrial espionage. No tort has occurred if there is no misappropriation. For example, a competitor can lawfully discover a trade secret by performing reverse engineering (i.e., taking apart and examining a rival's product).

The owner of a trade secret is obliged to take all reasonable precautions to prevent that secret from being discovered by others. Such precautions include fencing in buildings, placing locks on doors, hiring security guards, and the like. If the owner fails to take such actions, the secret is no longer subject to protection under state unfair competition laws.

Generally, a successful plaintiff in a trade secret action can (1) recover the profits made by the offender from the use of the trade secret, (2) recover for damages, and (3) obtain an injunction prohibiting the offender from divulging or using the trade secret.

INTERNET AND TECHNOLOGY
The Economic Espionage Act

Stealing of trade secrets exposes the offender to a civil lawsuit by the injured party to recover economic damages. In addition, the enactment by Congress of the federal **Economic Espionage Act** of 1996[1] makes it a federal crime to steal another's trade secrets. Under the Espionage Act, it is a federal crime for any person to convert a trade secret to his or her benefit or for the benefit of others, knowing or intending that the act would cause injury to the owner of the trade secret. The definition of *trade secret* under the Espionage Act is very broad and parallels the definition used under the civil laws of misappropriating a trade secret.

One of the major reasons for the passage of the Espionage Act was to address the ease of stealing trade secrets through computer espionage and using the Internet. For example, hundreds of pages of confidential information can be downloaded onto a small computer disc or jump drive, placed in a pocket, and taken from the legal owner. In addition, computer hackers can crack into a company's computers and steal customer lists, databases, formulas, and other trade secrets. The Espionage Act is a very important weapon in addressing and penalizing computer and internet espionage.

The Espionage Act provides for severe criminal penalties. An organization can be fined up to $5 million per criminal act and $10 million if the criminal act was committed to benefit a foreign government. The act imposes prison terms on individuals of up to 15 years per criminal violation, which can be increased to 25 years per violation if the criminal act was done with the intent to benefit a foreign government.

ETHICS SPOTLIGHT
Coca-Cola Worker Convicted of Trying to Sell a Trade Secret to Pepsi-Cola

> *" What if you knew the markets [Coca-Cola was] going to move into and out of . . . and beat them to the punch. "*

—Letter to PepsiCo

In February 2007, former Coca-Cola secretary Joya Williams was convicted by a federal jury of conspiring to steal trade secrets and attempting to sell them to arch rival Pepsi for $1.5 million. Along with Williams, two other co-conspirators were arrested and pled guilty.

Federal prosecutors asserted that Williams was in deep debt, unhappy with her job, and was seeking a big payday. She was fired as a secretary in Coca-Cola's global branding department when the initial allegations came to light. Two of the more damaging pieces of evidence the jury considered was a letter written by a co-conspirator to PepsiCo, trying to sell the stolen items and FBI surveillance videotape of Williams smuggling out secret documents.

The conspiracy was initially foiled when rival Pepsi produced a letter sent to them by one of the co-conspirators that offered Coca-Cola trade secrets to the highest bidder. "What if you knew the markets [Coca-Cola was] going to move into and out of . . . and beat them to the punch," the letter stated. PepsiCo notified Coca-Cola officials and federal authorities, who initiated an FBI investigation into the matter.

During trial, prosecutors produced videotape of Williams putting confidential documents into her bag, along with samples of Coke products that were still in development. According to court records, the stolen materials included details of an upcoming Coke product code-named Project Lancelot. Coke's 120-year-old "secret formula" recipe was not involved.

After the jury members initially instructed the court that they were deadlocked, U.S. District Judge J. Owen Forrester ordered them to try again, and they returned with a guilty verdict. Referring to several witnesses that testified on Williams' behalf that she did not pose a risk to society, Judge Forrester said, "We never really know people." The judge ordered Williams to jail.

Law & Ethics Questions

1. What is a trade secret? Explain.
2. Did the Coca-Cola information that Williams was trying to sell qualify as a trade secret?
3. **ETHICS** Did Williams act ethically in this case?
4. **ETHICS** Did PepsiCo act ethically in this case?

Web Exercises

1. **WEB** Visit the website of Coca-Cola, at *www.coca-cola.com*.
2. **WEB** Visit the website of PepsiCo, at *www.pepsico.com*.
3. **WEB** Use *www.google.com* to find an article about a recent case of misappropriation of a trade secret.

Patents

When drafting the Constitution of the United States of America, the founders of the United States provided for protection of the work of inventors and writers. Article I, Section 8 of the Constitution provides, "The Congress shall have Power ... to promote the Progress of Science and useful Arts, by securing for limited Times to Authors and Inventors the exclusive Right to their respective Writings and Discoveries."

Federal Patent Statute

Pursuant to the express authority granted in the U.S. Constitution, Congress enacted the **Federal Patent Statute** of 1952.[2] This law is intended to provide an incentive for inventors to invent and make their inventions public and to protect patented inventions from infringement. Federal patent law is exclusive; there are no state patent laws. Applications for **patents** must be filed with the **U.S. Patent and Trademark Office (PTO)** in Washington, DC.

Web Exercise

1. **WEB** Visit the website of the U.S. Patent and Trademark Office (PTO), at *www.uspto.gov*. Read the basic facts about patents.

U.S. Court of Appeals for the Federal Circuit in Washington, DC

The **U.S. Court of Appeals for the Federal Circuit** in Washington, DC, was created in 1982 to hear patent appeals and to promote uniformity in patent law.

Web Exercise

1. **WEB** Visit the website of the U.S. Court of Appeals for the Federal Circuit in Washington, DC, at *www.fedcir.gov*. Click on "About the Court." Read about the authority of this court.

Patent Period

In 1995, in order to bring the U.S. patent system into harmony with the systems of the majority of other developed nations, Congress made the following important changes in U.S. patent law:

1. Patents for inventions are valid for *20 years* (instead of the previous term of 17 years). Design patents are valid for 14 years.
2. The patent term begins to run from the date the patent application is *filed* (instead of when the patent is issued, as was previously the case).

After the patent period runs out, the invention or design enters the *public domain*, which means that anyone can produce and sell the invention without paying the prior patent holder.

The United States still follows the *first-to-invent rule* rather than the *first-to-file rule* followed by some other countries. Thus, in the United States, the first person to invent an item or a process is given patent protection over another party who was first to file a patent application.

Example On January 3, 2008, Nerdette, a straight-A student in college, invents "smork," a chemical formula that can be released into the air and eliminate air pollution. Smork causes no harmful effects to humans, any other living being, or the environment. She keeps her discovery secret, however. Two years later, Nerd, who is a straight-C student in college, invents "dork," which is exactly the same chemical formula as previously invented by Nerdette. The next day, Nerd rushes out and files a patent application with the U.S. Patent and Trademark Office (PTO). Subsequently, Nerd is issued a patent for Dork. Nerdette later discovers this fact, challenges Nerd's patent, and wishes to patent Smork. Nerdette will win her patent challenge against Nerd because she was the first to invent the invention. Nerd, although he was the first to file for a patent, loses his patent.

Exhibit 7.1 shows Thomas Edison's patent for the electric light bulb.

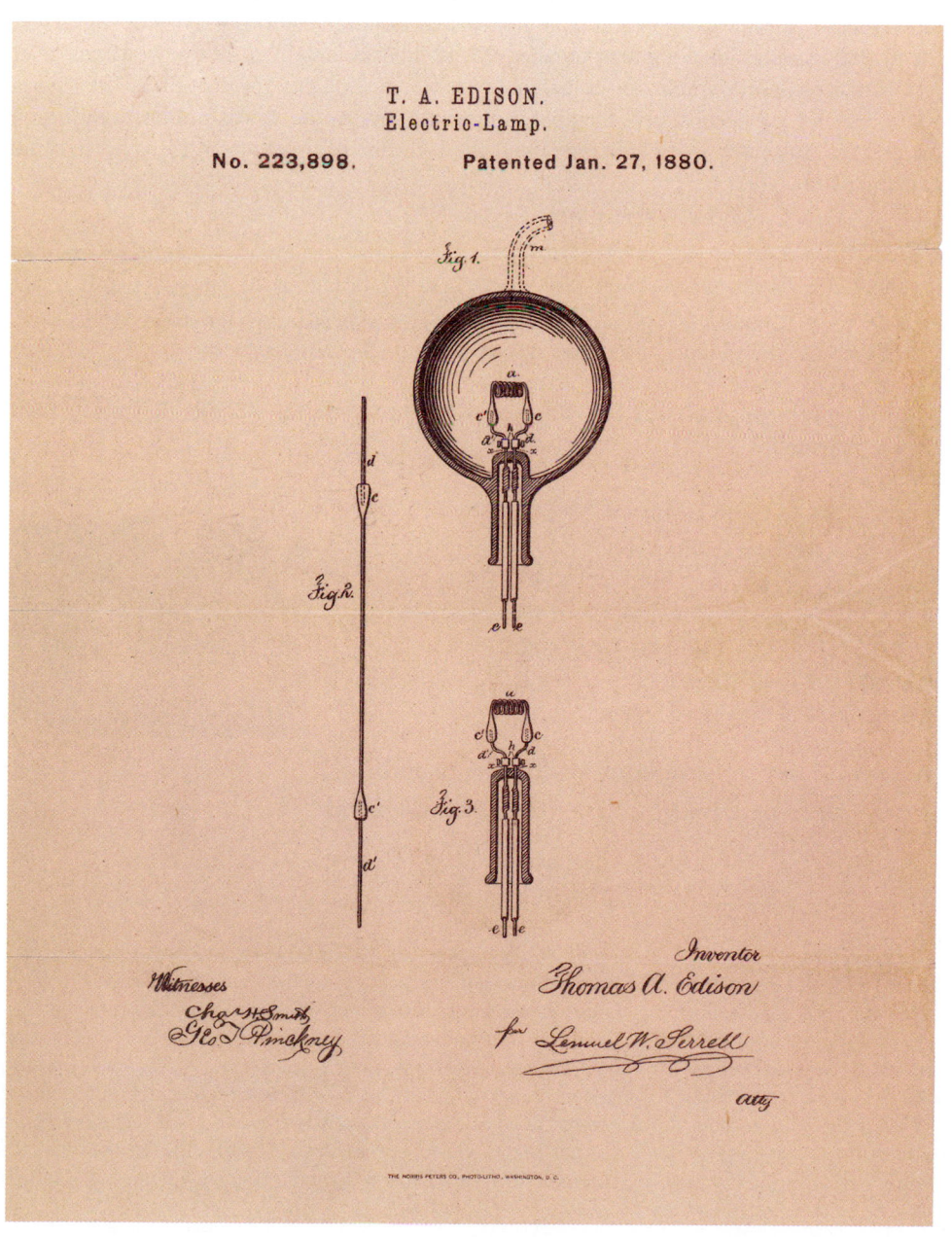

EXHIBIT 7.1

Thomas Edison's Patent for the Electric Light Bulb

Web Exercise

1. **WEB** Use *www.google.com* to find and read a short bibliography of Thomas Edison. Did he make any other inventions and have any other patents?

Patenting an Invention

To be patented, an invention must be **novel**, **useful**, and **nonobvious**. In addition, only certain subject matters can be patented. Patentable subject matters include (1) machines; (2) processes; (3) compositions of matter; (4) improvements to existing machines, processes, or compositions of matter; (5) designs for an article of manufacture; (6) asexually reproduced plants; and (7) living material invented by a person. Abstractions and scientific principles cannot be patented unless they are part of the tangible environment.

Example Einstein's Theory of Relativity ($E = mc^2$) cannot be patented.

> The patent system added the fuel of interest to the fire of genius.
>
> Abraham Lincoln
> *Lectures on Discoveries, Inventions, and Improvements (1859)*

A **patent application** must contain a written description of the invention and be filed with the PTO in Washington, DC. Patent applications are complicated. An inventor should hire a patent attorney to assist in obtaining a patent for an invention. If a patent is granted, the invention is assigned a patent number. Patent holders usually affix the word *patent* or *pat*, and the patent number to the patented article. If a patent application is filed but a patent has not yet been issued, the applicant usually places the words **patent pending** on the article. Any party can challenge either the issuance of a patent or the validity of an existing patent.

Web Exercises

1. **WEB** Go to *www.uspto.gov/patft*. Search to find a patent for an item you are interested in.
2. **WEB** The PTO provides for the online submission of patent applications and documents through its EFS-Web system. Read about this system at *www.uspto.gov/ebc/efs_help.html*.

In the following case, the U.S. Supreme Court had to decide whether the subject matter was patentable.

CASE 7.1
Patent

U.S. SUPREME COURT
J.E.M. Ag Supply, Inc., d.b.a. Farm Advantage, Inc. v. Pioneer Hi-Bred International, Inc.

534 U.S. 124, 122 S.Ct. 593, 151 L.Ed.2d 508,
Web 2001 U.S. Lexis 10949 (2001)
Supreme Court of the United States

"*Congress employed broad general language in drafting Section 101 precisely because new types of inventions are often unforeseeable.*"

—Justice Thomas

Facts

Pioneer Hi-Bred International, Inc. (Pioneer), holds patents that cover the company's inbred and hybrid corn and corn seed products. A hybrid plant patent protects the plant, its seeds, variants, mutants, and modifications of the hybrid. Pioneer sells its patented hybrid seeds under a limited label license that provides: "License is granted solely to produce grain and/or forage." The license states that it "does not extend to the use of seed from such crop or the progeny thereof for propagation or seed multiplication."

J.E.M. Ag Supply, Inc., doing business as Farm Advantage, Inc. (Farm Advantage), purchased patented hybrid seeds from Pioneer in bags bearing this license agreement. Farm Advantage created seed from the hybrid corn products it grew from Pioneer's patented hybrid seed. Pioneer sued Farm Advantage, alleging that Farm Advantage had infringed its patent. Farm Advantage filed a counterclaim of patent invalidity, arguing that Pioneer hybrid plant seed patents are not patentable subject matter. The U.S. District Court held that the seed patents were valid and granted summary judgment to Pioneer.

The U.S. Court of Appeals affirmed. Farm Advantage appealed to the U.S. Supreme Court.

Issue

Are sexually reproducing hybrid plants patentable subject matter?

Language of the U.S. Supreme Court

"Whoever invents or discovers any new and useful process, machine manufacture, or composition of matter, or any new and useful improvement thereof, may obtain a patent therefor, subject to the conditions and requirements of this title." As this Court recognized over 20 years ago in *Diamond v. Chakrabarty*, 447 U.S. at 308 (1980), the language of Section 101 is extremely broad. "Congress plainly contemplated that the patent laws would be given wide scope." This Court thus concluded in *Chakrabarty* that living things were patentable under Section 101, and held that a manmade microorganism fell within the scope of the statute.

It has been the unbroken practice of the PTO since to confer patents for plants. To obtain patent protection, a plant breeder must show that the plant he has developed is new, useful, and non-obvious. Petitioner Farm Advantage essentially asks us to deny utility patent protection for sexually reproduced plants because it was unforeseen in 1930 that each plant could receive protection under Section 101. Denying patent protection under Section 101 simply because such coverage was thought technologically infeasible in 1930, however, would be inconsistent with the forward-looking perspective of the utility patent statute. As we noted in *Chakrabarty*, "Congress employed broad general language in drafting Section 101 precisely because new types of inventions are often unforeseeable."

Decision

The U.S. Supreme Court held that sexually reproducing hybrid plants are patentable subject matter. The Supreme Court affirmed the judgment of the U.S. Court of Appeals in favor of the patent holder, Pioneer.

Law & Ethics Questions

1. Do you think sexually reproducing hybrid plants should be patentable subject matter? Why or why not?
2. **ETHICS** Did Farm Advantage act ethically in this case? Explain.
3. What are the economic implications of the U.S. Supreme Court's decision in this case?

Web Exercises

1. **WEB** For the complete opinion of this case, go to *www.prenhall.com/cheesemancases*.
2. **WEB** Visit the website of the U.S. Supreme Court, at *www.supremecourtus.gov*, and try to find documents that relate to this case.
3. **WEB** Visit the website of the U.S. Patent and Trademark Office (PTO), at *www.uspto.gov*. Find information about obtaining plant patents.

CONTEMPORARY ENVIRONMENT

The Cost of Protecting a Patent

An inventor spends years dreaming up new products and inventions and then files an application with the Patent and Trademark Office and waits to see if the patent is granted. The day the patent is issued is a cause for celebration—or is it? Ask Donald BonAsia. The young entrepreneur invented "forkchops"—two eating utensils with chopsticks on one end and a knife and fork on the other end. He spent two years and $7,500 to receive a patent on his invention.

But his worst fear happened. Other manufacturers began copying his invention and selling knockoff forkchops without seeking BonAsia's permission or paying him a royalty fee. BonAsia contacted a patent lawyer and found out the following: The normal cost to pursue a patent infringement case through trial is $1.5 million and $1 million if it settles near trial. Attorneys typically want over $100,000 in retainer fees before filing a patent infringement case.

BonAsia discovered that he had a patent but not enough money to protect it.

BonAsia's plight is typical for small-time inventors who are under the misconception that a patent gives the holder an exclusive right to make the item. Wrong. What a patent gives the holder is the right to defend the patent and try to stop others from making the patented article. BonAsia learned a valuable lesson: Justice can be obtained only at a price. Thus, an inventor needs to determine how valuable the patent is before making a decision to defend it.

Web Exercise

1. **WEB** Go to *www.forkchops.com/products.html* to view pictures of forkchops.

CONTEMPORARY ENVIRONMENT
Amazon.com Denied Patent

❝Barnesandnoble.com has raised substantial questions as to the validity of the '411 patent.❞

—Judge Clevenger

Amazon.com has become one of the biggest online retailers. Amazon.com, Inc., enables customers to find and purchase books, music, videos, consumer electronics, games, toys, gifts, and other items over the Internet by using its website, *www.amazon.com*. As an early entrant into this market, Amazon.com became a leader in electronic commerce. Other e-commerce retailers began offering goods and services for sale over the web.

One problem that Amazon.com and other e-commerce retailers faced was that more than 50 percent of potential customers who went shopping online and selected items for purchase abandoned their transactions before checkout. To address this problem, Amazon.com devised and implemented a method that enabled online customers to purchase selected items with a single click of a computer mouse button. A customer who had previously registered his or her name, address, and credit card number with Amazon.com could complete purchases by clicking an instant "buy" button. Amazon.com applied for a software patent for its one-click ordering system, and the U.S. Patent and Trademark Office (PTO) granted patent no. 5,960,411 ('411 patent) to Amazon.com. Amazon.com designated this as the "1-click®" ordering system.

While Amazon.com's patent application was pending, other online retailers began offering similar one-click ordering systems. One was Barnesandnoble.com, which operates a website through which it sells books, software, music, videos, and other items. Amazon.com sued Barnesandnoble.com, alleging patent infringement, and sought an injunction against Barnesandnoble.com from using its one-click ordering system. Barnesandnoble.com defended, asserting that a one-click ordering system was clearly obvious and, therefore, did not meet the required "nonobvious" test of federal patent law for an invention to qualify for a patent.

After examining the evidence, the U.S. District Court decided that Amazon.com's 1-click system was nonobvious and therefore qualified for a patent. The District Court issued a temporary injunction against Barnesandnoble.com's use of its one-click ordering system. Barnesandnoble.com appealed to the U.S. Court of Appeals for the Federal Circuit, the appellate court for patent appeals.

Barnesandnoble.com argued that Amazon.com's 1-click ordering system was not novel or nonobvious, as required by patent law. Barnesandnoble.com cited the following evidence that one-click ordering systems existed in the prior art before Amazon.com filed for its patent: (1) Since the 1990s, the CompuServe Trend System provided for single-click ordering of stock charts over the Internet; (2) another Internet vendor's "WebBasket" allowed one-click ordering; (3) the "Oliver's Market" ordering system of another online vender permitted one-click ordering; and (4) the book *Creating the Virtual Store*, published before Amazon.com filed for its '411 patent, suggested modifying software to provide for one-click ordering online.

The U.S. Court of Appeals relied on these prior art references and held that the one-click ordering system was obvious and therefore not patentable. The Court of Appeals stated that Barnesandnoble.com "has raised substantial questions as to the validity of the '411 patent." The Court of Appeals reversed the U.S. District Court's grant of an injunction against Barnesandnoble.com. The Court of Appeals allowed Barnesandnoble.com to use its one-click ordering system. *Amazon.com, Inc. v. Barnesandnoble.com, Inc.*, 239 F.3d 1343, **Web** 2001 U.S. App. Lexis 2163 (United States Circuit Court of Appeals for the Federal Circuit, 2001)

Law & Ethics Questions

1. If the U.S. Patent and Trademark Office grants an applicant a patent, can this later be challenged in court?

2. **ETHICS** Was there any unethical conduct in this case? Was this a legitimate legal dispute?

Web Exercises

1. **WEB** For the complete opinion of this case, go to *www.prenhall.com/cheesemancases*.

2. **WEB** Visit the website of the United States Court of Appeals for the Federal Circuit, at *www.fedcir.gov*.

3. **WEB** Visit the website of Amazon.com, at *www.amazon.com*.

4. **WEB** Visit the website of Barnesandnoble.com, at *www.barnesandnoble.com*.

5. **WEB** Go to the website of the U.S. Patent and Trademark Office, at *www.uspto.gov*. Can you find patent number 5,960,411?

One-Year On-Sale Doctrine

Under the **one-year on-sale doctrine**, also called the **public use doctrine**, a patent may not be granted if the invention was used by the public for more than one year prior to the filing of the patent application. This doctrine forces inventors to file their patent applications in a timely manner.

Example Suppose Cindy Parsons invents a new invention on January 1. She allows the public to use this invention and does not file a patent application until February of the following year. Cindy has lost the right to patent her invention.

In the following case, the U.S. Supreme Court was called on to examine whether the one-year on-sale doctrine had been violated.

C A S E 7.2
On-Sale Doctrine

U.S. SUPREME COURT
Pfaff v. Wells Electronics, Inc.
525 U.S. 55, 119 S.Ct. 304, 142 L.Ed.2d 261,
Web 1998 U.S. Lexis 7268
Supreme Court of the United States

> *"The primary meaning of the word invention in the Patent Act unquestionably refers to the inventor's conception rather than to a physical embodiment of that idea."*
>
> —Justice Stevens

Facts

Wayne K. Pfaff commenced work on designing a computer chip socket in November 1980. Pfaff prepared detailed engineering drawings that described the design, dimensions, and materials to be used in making the socket. Prior to March 17, Pfaff showed a sketch of his design to representatives of Texas Instruments, a large company. On April 8, Texas Instruments and Pfaff signed a written contract confirming a previously placed verbal purchase order for 30,100 of his new sockets, for a total price of $91,000. Pfaff did not make a prototype of the new socket device before offering it for sale to Texas Instruments.

Pfaff filled the order in July. The socket achieved substantial commercial success, as other companies placed orders. On April 19 of the following year, Pfaff filed an application for a patent on his computer chip socket, and a patent was issued. When a competitor made a similar socket, Pfaff sued for patent infringement. The competitor countered that Pfaff did not have a valid patent because the one-year on-sale doctrine of Section 102(b) of the federal patent statute had been violated. The U.S. District Court held that the Pfaff's patent was valid. The U.S. Court of Appeals held that Pfaff violated the one-year on-sale doctrine and reversed the judgment of the U.S. District Court. Pfaff appealed to the U.S. Supreme Court.

Issue

Was the one-year on-sale doctrine violated, thus invalidating Pfaff's patent on the computer chip socket?

Language of the U.S. Supreme Court

The primary meaning of the word *invention* in the Patent Act unquestionably refers to the inventor's conception rather than to a physical embodiment of that idea. The statute does not contain any express requirement that an invention must be reduced to practice before it can be patented.

It is well settled that an invention may be patented before it is reduced to practice. In 1888, this Court upheld a patent issued to Alexander Graham Bell even though he had filed his application before constructing a working telephone. [*The Telephone Cases*, 126 U.S. 1, 8 S.Ct. 778, 31 L.Ed. 863,

Web 1888 U.S. Lexis 2509 (1888).] When we apply the reasoning of *The Telephone Cases* to the facts of the case before us today, it is evident that Pfaff could have obtained a patent on his novel socket when he accepted the purchase order from Texas Instruments for 30,100 units.

Decision

The U.S. Supreme Court held that the one-year on-sale doctrine started to run on or before April 8, the date when Pfaff contracted in writing to sell sockets to Texas Instruments. Because the filing of his patent application on April 19 of the following year was more than one year later, his patent was invalidated pursuant to the one-year on-sale doctrine. The Supreme Court affirmed the judgment of the U.S. Court of Appeals that invalidated Pfaff's patent.

Law & Ethics Questions

1. What does the one-year on-sale doctrine provide? What is the public policy behind this rule?
2. **ETHICS** Was it ethical for the competitor to copy and produce Pfaff's computer chip socket?
3. How valuable is a patent? What were the economic consequences to Pfaff of the Supreme Court's decision? What were the economic consequences to others?

Web Exercises

1. **WEB** For the complete opinion of this case, go to *www.prenhall.com/cheesemancases*.
2. **WEB** Visit the website of the U.S. Supreme Court, at *www.supremecourtus.gov*, and try to find documents that relate to this case.
3. **WEB** Visit the website of the U.S. Patent and Trademark Office (PTO), at *www.uspto.gov*. Click on "Patents." Click on "Search Aids." Click on "How to Search." Click on "Search Patents now." Type in the patent numbers 174,465 and 186,787. Who owned these patents?
4. **WEB** Use *www.google.com* to find a short bibliography of Alexander Graham Bell. Besides the telephone, did he make any other inventions or have any other patents?

The American Inventors Protection Act

In 1999, Congress enacted the **American Inventors Protection Act**. This statute does the following:

- Permits an inventor to file a **provisional application** with the PTO, pending the preparation and filing of a final and complete patent application. This part of the law grants "provisional rights" to an inventor for three months, pending the filing of the final application.
- Requires the PTO to issue a patent within three years after the filing of a patent application unless the applicant engages in dilatory activities.
- Provides that non–patent holders may challenge a patent as being overly broad by requesting a contested reexamination of the patent application by the PTO. The reexamination will be within the confines of the PTO; the decision of the PTO can be appealed to the U.S. Court of Appeals for the Federal Circuit in Washington, DC.

INTERNET AND TECHNOLOGY
Cyber Business Plans Are Patentable

Federal patent law recognizes four categories of innovation: (1) machines, (2) articles of manufacture, (3) compositions, and (4) processes. For centuries, most patents involved tangible inventions, such as the telephone and the light bulb. Next, chemical, polymer, and biotechnology patents were granted. Now, the computer and the Internet have added to what can be patented.

Signature Financial Group, Inc. (Signature), filed for and was granted a patent for a computerized accounting system that determines share prices through a series of mathematical calculations and is then used to manage mutual funds [U.S. patent no. 5,193,056]. State Street Bank, another financial institution that wanted to offer a similar mutual fund investment program to clients, sued to have Signature's patent declared invalid. Signature defended, arguing that its intangible financial business model was a "process" that was protected under

federal patent law. The U.S. Court of Appeals for the Federal Circuit upheld the patent as a "practical application of a mathematical algorithm, formula, or calculation, because it produces a useful, concrete and tangible result."

Taking the lead from the *State Street* case, many persons and businesses have filed for and received patents for business and financial models that are used over the Internet. Critics contend that Congress did not intend to grant patents for intangible processes when it enacted federal patent law. Business plan patent holders counter that the trend reflects a necessary evolution in patent law and claim that business plan patterns are to the Internet Age what machine patents were to the Industrial Age. *State Street Bank & Trust Co. v. Signature Financial Group, Inc.*, 149 F.3d 1368, **Web** 1998 U.S. App. Lexis 16869 (United States Court of Appeals for the Federal Circuit)

Patent Infringement

Patent holders own exclusive rights to use and exploit their patents. **Patent infringement** occurs when someone makes unauthorized use of another's patent. In a suit for patent infringement, a successful plaintiff can recover (1) money damages equal to a reasonable royalty rate on the sale of the infringed articles, (2) other damages caused by the infringement (such as loss of customers), (3) an order requiring the destruction of the infringing article, and (4) an injunction preventing the infringer from such action in the future. The court has the discretion to award up to treble damages if the infringement was intentional.

ETHICS SPOTLIGHT
Inventor Wipes Ford's and Chrysler's Windshields Clean

Robert Kearns, a professor at Wayne State University in Detroit, Michigan, patented his design for the electronic intermittent-speed windshield wiper for automobiles and other vehicles. He peddled his invention around to many automobile manufacturers but never

reached a licensing deal with any of them. Two years later, automobile manufacturers began producing cars using Kearns's intermittent-speed windshield wiper invention. Virtually all cars sold in the United States today now have these wipers as standard equipment. Kearns filed patent infringement lawsuits against virtually all automobile manufacturers.

The Ford case went to trial first. Ford alleged that Kearns's patents were not valid because of obviousness and prior art. The jury disagreed with Ford, decided that Kearns's patents were valid, and ordered Ford to pay $5.2 million, plus interest, for patent infringement. Ford settled by paying Kearns $10.2 million and agreeing to drop all appeals. This represented 50¢ per Ford vehicle that used the wiper system.

In the Chrysler case, Kearns fired his lawyers and represented himself. Kearns won a second victory: The jury found that Chrysler had infringed Kearns's patents and awarded him $11.3 million. Kearns received over $21 million from Chrysler, which amounted to 90¢ for every vehicle sold by Chrysler with the wiper system.

Over the next two years, the court dismissed Kearns's lawsuits against 23 other automobile manufacturers, including General Motors, Porsche, Nissan, Toyota, and Honda, because Kearns failed to comply with court orders to disclose documents. This ended Kearns's legal battle with the automobile industry.

Law & Ethics Questions

1. Do you think that intermittent-speed windshield wipers were obvious when Kearns invented them?

2. **ETHICS** Did the automobile manufacturers that used Kearns's invention without paying him act ethically? Explain.

ETHICS SPOTLIGHT

Microsoft Slapped with $1.52 Billion MP3 Verdict

In one of the leading patent cases of all time, the giant software company Microsoft Corporation tussled with Alcatel-Lucent, a large French networking equipment company, over who owned the patent rights to the basic technology behind the MP3 format. Microsoft used the MP3 technology in its industry-leading software Microsoft Windows Media. Alcatel-Lucent argued that it owned the patent rights to the MP3 technology and that it had not been compensated by Microsoft for the licensing rights. Microsoft contended that it did not know of Alcatel's patent claim and, in fact, had paid $16 million to another firm that it thought owned the MP3 patent rights.

The case came as part of a maze of lawsuits filed by technology companies in what amounts to MP3 legal warfare. Alcatel-Lucent had previously sued PC makers Dell and Gateway for permitting the preinstalled Windows Media Player software to play MP3s. Microsoft inserted itself into the mix by suing Alcatel-Lucent for a declaration that it had not violated Alcatel-Lucent's patent rights. Alcatel-Lucent promptly turned around and countersued Microsoft, leading to the 2007 trial.

After three weeks of highly technical testimony, the jury announced its verdict. The jury found Microsoft liable for patent infringement over its use of the MP3 music technology and awarded $1.52 billion in damages to Alcatel-Lucent. The jury was unable to agree on whether the

infringement was willful, thus allowing Microsoft to barely escape liability for triple damages. This could go down as the largest patent award in history.

The result of this case will have an enormous effect on other tech companies because nearly all music-based desktop software and digital media players use the MP3 format, including Apple iPod and iTunes, RealNetworks's RealPlayer, and Nullsoft's Winamp. These could now all be future targets of Alcatel-Lucent lawsuits.

Law & Ethics Questions

1. How complex was this patent lawsuit?

2. **ETHICS** Do you think any party in this lawsuit acted unethically? Or was this just a major legal dispute?

Web Exercises

1. **WEB** Visit the website of Microsoft Corporation, at *www.microsoft.com*.

2. **WEB** Visit the website of Alcatel-Lucent, at *www.alcatel-lucent.com*.

3. **WEB** Use *www.google.com* to find information that describes Microsoft Windows Media.

Copyrights

Article I, Section 8 of the Constitution of the United States of America authorizes Congress to enact statutes to protect the works of writers for limited times.

Pursuant to this authority, Congress has enacted **copyright** laws. The **Copyright Revision Act** of 1976 currently governs copyright law.[3] The act establishes the requirements for obtaining a copyright and protects copyrighted works from infringement. Federal copyright law is exclusive; there are no state copyright laws. Federal copyright law protects the work of authors and other creative persons from the unauthorized use of their copyrighted materials and provides a financial incentive for authors to write, thereby increasing the number of creative works available in society.

Only *tangible writings*—writings that can be physically seen—are subject to **copyright registration** and protection. The term *writing* has been broadly defined.

Example Books, periodicals, and newspapers; lectures, sermons, addresses, and poems; musical compositions; plays, motion pictures, and radio and television productions; maps; works of art, including paintings, drawings, sculpture, jewelry, glassware, tapestry, and lithographs; architectural drawings and models, photographs, including prints, slides, and filmstrips, greeting cards and picture postcards; photoplays, including feature films, cartoons, newsreels, travelogues, and training films; and sound recordings published in the form of tapes, cassettes, and compact discs and MP3s qualify for copyright protection.

Exhibit 7.2 shows a copyrighted poem.

EXHIBIT 7.2

Copyrighted Poem

Like oceans, we have spent
this time together before.
In galley slave pits you fed me
water and removed my slivers.
Riding Ch'u dynasty chariots
we perished on Mongol swords.
We toiled rocks in chains
and built Stonehenge,
drank with King Arthur
and danced with Black Elk.
We fled, hand-in-hand, dodging
Hitler's bullets, and
I carried you over the border
to have our baby in freedom.
During past full moons, the sun set
the seas in orbit
and as driftwood we tumbled
onto the shores of Los Angeles.
Another life together, my love?

Henry Cheeseman

Registration of Copyrights

To be protected under federal copyright law, a work must be the original work of the author. A copyright is created when an author produces his or her work. For example, when a student writes a term paper for her class, she owns a copyright to her work.

Published and unpublished works may be registered with the **U.S. Copyright Office** in Washington, DC. Registration is permissive and voluntary and can be affected at any time during the term of the copyright.

In 1989, the United States signed the **Berne Convention**, an international copyright treaty. This law eliminated the need to place the symbol © or the word "copyright" or "copr." on a copyrighted work.

The **Sonny Bono Copyright Term Extension Act** of 1998 grants individuals copyright protection for their life plus 70 years. Copyrights owned by businesses are protected for 95 years from the year of first publication or for 120 years from the year of creation, whichever is shorter. After the copyright period runs out, the work enters the *public domain*, which means that anyone can publish the work without paying the prior copyright holder.

Example At age 30, Ernst Hummingbird writes the great novel *To Save a Hummingbird*. Ernst lives until he is 70. The copyright period of Ernst's great novel is 110 years, which includes the 40 remaining years of his life and 70 years after he is deceased. Thus, Ernst's heirs will receive any royalties or other payments due for the publication of the novel after Ernst's death.

Web Exercises

1. **WEB** Visit the website of the U.S. Copyright Office, at *www.copyright.gov*.

2. **WEB** When visiting the U.S. Copyright Office website, at *www.copyright.gov*, click on "Frequently Asked Questions (FAQ)" and then click on "Do I have to register with your office to be protected?" Click on "Copyright Registration." What are the advantages of registering a copyright with the U.S. Copyright Office?

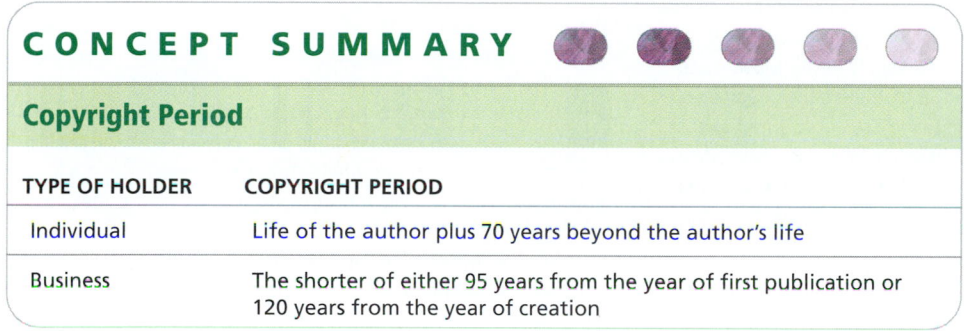

CONCEPT SUMMARY

Copyright Period

TYPE OF HOLDER	COPYRIGHT PERIOD
Individual	Life of the author plus 70 years beyond the author's life
Business	The shorter of either 95 years from the year of first publication or 120 years from the year of creation

> The law in respect to literature ought to remain upon the same footing as that which regards the profits of mechanical inventions and chemical discoveries.
>
> William Wordsworth
> *Letter (1838)*

INTERNET AND TECHNOLOGY
Computer Software Copyright Act

In 1980, Congress enacted the **Computer Software Copyright Act**,[4] which amended the Copyright Act of 1976. The 1980 amendments include computer programs in the list of tangible items protected by copyright law. The creator of a copyrightable software program obtains automatic copyright protection. The Registrar of Copyright is authorized to accept and record any document pertaining to computer software and to issue a **certificate of recordation** to the recorder.

Congress passed the **Semiconductor Chip Protection Act** of 1984[5] to provide greater protection of the hardware components of a computer. This law protects masks that are used to create computer chips. A *mask* is an original layout of software programs that is used to create a semiconductor chip. This act is sometimes referred to as the "Mask Work Act." Notice on the work is optional, but when used, it must contain the words *mask work* or the symbol *M* or (M) and the name of the owner.

Copyright Infringement

Copyright infringement occurs when a party copies a substantial and material part of the plaintiff's copyrighted work without permission. The copying does not have to be either word for word or the entire work. A successful plaintiff can recover (1) the profit made by the infringer from the copyright infringement, (2) damages suffered by the plaintiff, (3) an order requiring the impoundment and destruction of the infringing works, and (4) an injunction preventing the infringer from doing so in the future. The court, in its discretion, can award statutory damages up to $150,000 for willful infringement in lieu of actual damages.

The following two cases involve peer-to-peer software file sharing of music.

CASE 7.3
Copyright Infringement

BMG Music v. Gonzalez

430 F.3d 888, **Web** 2005 U.S. App. Lexis 26903 (2005)
United States Court of Appeals for the Seventh Circuit

> *"Nor can she defend by observing that other persons were greater offenders; Gonzalez's theme that she obtained "only 30" (or "only 1,300") copyrighted songs is no more relevant than a thief's contention that he shoplifted "only 30" compact discs, planning to listen to them at home and pay later for any he liked."*
>
> —Judge Easterbrook

Facts

Cecilia Gonzalez downloaded 1,370 copyrighted songs on her computer using the Kazaa file-sharing network during a few weeks and kept them on her computer until she was caught. BMG Music sued Gonzalez for copyright infringement of 30 of these songs. Gonzalez defended, arguing that her downloading of these copyrighted songs was lawful. The U.S. District Court granted summary judgment in favor of BMG Music, assessed $22,500 in damages against Gonzalez, and issued an injunction against Gonzalez, enjoining her from further copyright infringement. Gonzalez appealed.

Issue

Did Gonzalez engage in copyright infringement?

Language of the Court

Gonzalez's position is that she was just sampling music to determine what she liked enough to buy at retail. Instead of erasing songs that she decided not to buy, she retained them. A copy downloaded, played, and retained on one's hard drive for future use is a direct substitute for a purchased copy. Gonzalez was not engaged in a nonprofit use; she downloaded (and kept) whole copyrighted songs and she did this despite the fact that these works often are sold per song as well as per album.

As she tells the tale, downloading on a try-before-you-buy basis is good advertising for copyright proprietors, expanding the value of their inventory. As file sharing has increased, the sales of recorded music have dropped. The events likely are related. Music downloaded for free from the Internet is a close substitute for purchased music; many people are bound to keep the downloaded files without buying originals. That is exactly what Gonzalez did for at least 30 songs.

Think of radio. Authors and publishers collect royalties on the broadcast of recorded music. Downloads from peer-to-peer networks such as Kazaa compete with licensed broadcasts and hence undermine the income available to authors. Many radio stations stream their content over the Internet, paying a fee for the right to do so. Gonzalez could have listened to this streaming music to sample songs for purchase; had she done so, the authors would have received royalties from the broadcasters.

Licensed Internet sellers, such as the iTunes Music Store, offer samples—but again they pay authors a fee for the right to do so, and the teasers are just a portion of the original. Other intermediaries (Yahoo! Music Unlimited and Real Rhapsody but also the revived Napster) offer licensed access to large collections of music; customers may rent the whole library by the month or year, sample them all, and purchase any songs they want to keep. New technologies, such as SNOCAP, enable authorized trials over peer-to-peer systems. Authorized previews share the feature of evanescence: if a listener decides not to buy (or stops paying the rental fee), no copy remains behind.

With all of these means available to consumers who want to choose where to spend their money, downloading full copies of copyrighted material without compensation to authors cannot be deemed "fair use." Nor can she defend by observing that other persons were greater offenders; Gonzalez's theme that she obtained "only 30" (or "only 1,300") copyrighted songs is no more relevant than a thief's contention that he shoplifted "only 30" compact discs, planning to listen to them at home and pay later for any he liked.

BMG Music elected to seek statutory damages under 17 U.S.C. Section 504(c)(1) instead of proving actual injury. This section provides that the author's entitlement, per infringed work, is "a sum of not less than $ 750 or more than $ 30,000 as the court considers just." Gonzalez asked the district court to reduce the award, but the judge concluded that Section 402(d) bars any reduction in the minimum award. But BMG was content with $750 per song, which the district judge awarded on summary judgment.

As for the injunction: Gonzalez contends that this should be vacated because she has learned her lesson, has dropped her broadband access to the Internet, and is unlikely to download copyrighted material again. A private party's discontinuation of unlawful conduct does not make the dispute moot, however. An injunction remains appropriate to ensure that the misconduct does not recur as soon as the case ends. The district court did not abuse its discretion in awarding prospective relief.

Decision

The U.S. Court of Appeals held that Gonzalez had engaged in copyright infringement. The Court of Appeals affirmed the judgment of the U.S. District Court in favor of BMG Music and the award of $22,500 in damages and injunction against Gonzalez.

Law & Ethics Questions

1. Is music copyrighted?

2. What is copyright infringement? Did Gonzalez engage in copyright infringement in this case?

3. **ETHICS** Do you think that Gonzalez knew that she was engaging in copyright infringement when she copied the music onto her computer?

4. **ETHICS** Have you ever downloaded music using a peer-to-peer file-sharing network without paying the musician or the music company?

Web Exercises

1. **WEB** For the complete opinion of this case, go to *www.prenhall.com/cheesemancases*.

2. **WEB** Visit the website of the United States Court of Appeals for the Seventh Circuit, at *www.ca7.uscourts.gov*.

3. **WEB** Visit the website of BMG Music, at *www.bmg.com*.

4. **WEB** Use *www.google.com* to find an article that discusses the lawfulness of downloading music for free using file-sharing programs. Read it.

CASE 7.4
Contributory Copyright Infringement

U.S. SUPREME COURT
Metro-Goldwyn-Mayer Studios v. Grokster, Ltd. and StreamCast Networks, Inc.

545 U.S. 913, 125 S.Ct. 2764, 162 L.Ed.2d 781,
Web 2005 U.S. Lexis 5212 (2005)
Supreme Court of the United States

> ❝*The ease of copying songs or movies using software like Grokster's or StreamCast's is fostering distain for copyright protection.*❞
>
> —Justice Souter

Facts

Grokster, Ltd., and StreamCast Networks, Inc., distribute free software that allows computer users to share electronic files through peer-to-peer networks where users' computers communicate directly with each other. These peer-to-peer networks are primarily used to share copyrighted music and video files without authorization of the copyright holder. Thus, music and video filers stored on one computer can be downloaded onto another computer using Grokster's and StreamCast's software. Statistical evidence shows that nearly 90 percent of the files available for download are copyrighted works. The parties downloading copyrighted music and videos are liable for copyright infringement.

Metro-Goldwyn-Mayer Studios, Inc., and other owners of copyrighted music and movies (collectively "MGM") sued Grokster and StreamCast, alleging that they are secondarily liable for the resulting acts of infringement by third parties using their peer-to-peer software. The U.S. District Court granted the defendants' motion for summary judgment. The U.S. Court of Appeals affirmed. MGM appealed to the U.S. Supreme Court.

Issue

Is a party who distributes a device with the object of promoting its use to infringe copyrighted works liable for the resulting acts of infringement by third parties using such device?

Language of the U.S. Supreme Court

MGM's evidence gives reason to think that the vast majority of users' downloads are acts of infringement, and because well over 100 million copies of the software in question are known to have been downloaded, and billions of files shared across the networks each month, the probable scope of copyright infringement is staggering.

Grokster and StreamCast are not merely passive recipients of information about infringing use. The record is replete with evidence that from the moment Grokster and StreamCast began to distribute their free software, each one clearly voiced the objective that recipients use it to download copyrighted works, and each took active steps to encourage infringement. The business models employed by Grokster and StreamCast confirm that their principal object was use of their software to download copyrighted works. Grokster and StreamCast receive no revenue from users, who obtain the software itself for nothing. Instead, both companies generate income by selling advertising space, and they stream advertising to users while they are employing the programs. As the number of users of each program increases, advertising opportunities become worth more. The ease of copying songs or movies using software like Grokster's and StreamCast's is fostering distain for copyright protection.

The argument of imposing indirect liability in this case is a powerful one, given the number of infringing downloads that occurs everyday using Grokster's and StreamCast's software. When a widely shared service or product is used to commit infringement, it may be impossible to enforce rights in the protected work effectively against all direct infringers, the only practical alternative being to go against the distributor of the copying device for secondary liability on a theory of contributory or vicarious infringement. One infringes contributory by intentionally inducing or encouraging direct infringement.

Decision

The U.S. Supreme Court held that a party who distributes a device with the object of promoting its use to infringe copyright is liable for the resulting acts of infringement by third parties. The Supreme Court held that the summary judgment in favor of Grokster and StreamCast was in error. The Supreme Court vacated the judgment of the U.S. Court of Appeals and remanded the case for further proceedings.

Law & Ethics Questions

1. **ETHICS** Do you think Grokster and StreamCast knew that their software was being used to facilitate copyright infringement?
2. Who suffers financial loss from the illegal downloading of music and videos? How big do you think this loss is?
3. **ETHICS** Do you think downloading copyrighted music, videos, or movies without paying the copyright holder is illegal? Is it unethical?

Web Exercises

1. **WEB** For the complete opinion of this case, go to *www.prenhall.com/cheesemancases*.
2. **WEB** Visit the website of the U.S. Supreme Court, at *www.supremecourtus.gov*, and try to find documents that relate to this case.
3. **WEB** Use *www.google.com* to find a recent of peer-to-peer file-sharing program that accomplishes the same result as Grokster and StreamCast.

The Fair Use Doctrine

The copyright holder's rights in a work are not absolute. The law permits certain limited unauthorized use of copyrighted materials under the **fair use doctrine**. The following uses are protected under this doctrine: (1) quotation of the copyrighted work for review or criticism or in a scholarly or technical work, (2) use in a parody or satire, (3) brief quotation in a news report, (4) reproduction by a teacher or student of a small part of the work to illustrate a lesson, (5) incidental reproduction of a work in a newsreel or broadcast of an event being reported, and (6) reproduction of a work in a legislative or judicial proceeding. The copyright holder cannot recover for copyright infringement where fair use is found.

In the following case, the court had to decide whether there was copyright infringement or fair use.

CASE 7.5
Fair Use

Newton v. Beastie Boys

349 F.3d 591, **Web** 2003 U.S. App. Lexis 22635 (2003)
United States Court of Appeals for the Ninth Circuit

> 66 *The dispute between Newton and Beastie Boys centers around the copyright implications of the practice of "sampling," a practice now common to many types of popular music.* 99

—Judge Schroeder

Facts

James W. Newton, Jr., is an accomplished avant-garde jazz composer and flutist. In 1978, Newton wrote a composition for the song "Choir," a piece for flute and voice that incorporated elements of African American gospel music. Newton owns the copyright to the composition "Choir." In 1992, the Beastie Boys, a rap and hip-hop group, used six seconds of Newton's "Choir" composition in their song "Pass the Mic" without obtaining a license from Newton to do so. Newton sued the Beastie Boys for copyright infringement. The Beastie Boys defended, arguing that their use of six seconds of Newton's song was fair use. The District Court found that the Beastie Boys's use of Newton's composition was *de minimis* and therefore fair use. The U.S. District Court granted summary judgment in favor of the Beastie Boys. Newton appealed.

Issue

Does the incorporation of a short segment of a copyrighted musical composition into a new musical recording constitute fair use, or is it copyright infringement?

Language of the Court

The dispute between Newton and Beastie Boys centers around the copyright implications of the practice of "sampling," a practice now common to many types of popular music. Sampling entails the incorporation of short segments of prior sound recordings into new recordings. For an unauthorized use of a copyrighted work to be actionable, there must be substantial similarity between the plaintiff's and defendant's works. This means that even where the fact of copying is conceded, no legal consequences will follow from that fact unless the copying is substantial. The focus on the sample's relation to the plaintiff's work as a whole embodies the fundamental question in any infringement action: whether so much is taken that the value of the original is sensibly diminished. When viewed in relation to Newton's composition as a whole, the sampled portion is neither quantitatively nor qualitatively significant. Quantitatively, the three-note sequence appears only once in Newton's composition. When played, the segment lasts six seconds and is roughly two percent of the four-and-a-half-minute "Choir." Beastie Boys' use of the "Choir" composition was de minimis. We hold today that Beastie Boys' use of a brief segment of the "Choir" composition is not sufficient to sustain a claim for copyright infringement.

Decision

The U.S. Court of Appeals held that the Beastie Boys's *de minimis* sampling of Newton's "Choir" composition constituted fair use and not copyright infringement. The U.S. Court of Appeals affirmed the U.S. District Court's grant of summary judgment in favor of the Beastie Boys.

Law & Ethics Questions

1. Describe sampling. Should sampling be allowed as fair use? Why or why not?

2. **ETHICS** Did the Beastie Boys act ethically when they used part of Newton's "Choir" composition in their song?

3. Has the use of sampling become a big part of today's music recordings? Why do you think recording artists engage in sampling?

Web Exercises

1. **WEB** For the complete opinion of this case, go to *www.prenhall.com/cheesemancases*.

2. **WEB** Visit the website of the United States Court of Appeals for the Ninth Circuit, at *www.ca9.uscourts.gov*.

3. **WEB** Visit the website of the Beastie Boys, at *www.beastieboys.com*.

ETHICS SPOTLIGHT

Elvis Presley's Videos Copied

> **"***The King is dead. His legacy, and those who wish to profit from it, remain very much alive.***"**
>
> —Judge Tallman

Elvis Presley became a musical icon during a career that spanned more than 20 years, until he died August 16, 1977. Many companies and individuals own copyrights to Presley's songs, lyrics, photographs, movies, and appearances on TV shows. Millions of dollars of these copyrighted materials are sold or licensed annually.

Passport Video produced a video documentary titled *The Definitive Elvis*, comprising 16 one-hour episodes. The producers interviewed more than 200 people regarding virtually all aspects of Elvis's life. Passport sold the videos commercially for a profit. Approximately 5 to 10 percent of the videos were composed of copyrighted music and appearances of Presley on TV and in movies owned by copyright holders other than Passport. Passport did not obtain permission to use those copyrighted works. Elvis Presley Enterprises, Inc., and other companies and individuals that owned copyrights to the Presley works used by Passport sued Passport for copyright infringement. Passport defended, arguing that its use of the copyrighted materials was fair use. The U.S. District Court held in favor of the plaintiff copyright holders and enjoined Passport from further distribution of its documentary videos. Passport appealed.

The U.S. Court of Appeals held that Passport's use of the copyrighted Elvis Presley materials was not fair use but instead constituted copyright infringement. The Court of Appeals stated, "The King is dead. His legacy, and those who wish to profit from it, remain very much alive." The Court of Appeals held that Passport's use of others' copyrighted materials was for commercial use rather than for a nonprofit purpose. The Court rejected Passport's claim that the videos consisted of scholarly research that would be protected as fair use. The court found that Passport's use of the copyrighted material caused market harm to the copyright holders because it would act as a substitute for the original copyrights and thus deny the copyright holders of the value of their copyrights. The Court of Appeals denied Passport's claim of fair use and affirmed the District Court's judgment that enjoined Passport from distributing its videos containing these copyrighted materials. *Elvis Presley Enterprises, Inc. v. Passport Video*, 349 F.3d 622, **Web** 2003 U.S. App. Lexis 22775 (United States Court of Appeals for the Ninth Circuit).

Law & Ethics Questions

1. How valuable do you think the copyrights to Elvis Presley songs, movies, and TV appearances are?

2. **ETHICS** Did Passport Video act ethically in this case? Do you think Passport Video knew it was engaging in copyright infringement?

Web Exercises

1. **WEB** Use *www.google.com* to find a video clip of Elvis Presley singing one of his songs.

2. **WEB** Use *www.google.com* to find a short bibliography of Elvis Presley.

INTERNET AND TECHNOLOGY
The NET Act: Criminal Copyright Infringement

In 1997, Congress enacted the **No Electronic Theft Act (NET Act)**, which criminalizes certain copyright infringement. The NET Act prohibits any person from willfully infringing a copyright for the purpose of either commercial advantage or financial gain, or by reproduction or distribution, even without commercial advantage or financial gain, including by electronic means, where the retail value of the copyrighted work exceeds $1,000. Criminal penalties for violating the act include imprisonment for up to one year and fines of up to $100,000.

The NET Act adds a new law for the federal government to criminally attack copyright infringement and curb digital piracy.

Law & Ethics Questions

1. What does the NET Act provide?
2. **ETHICS** Will criminalizing copyright infringement reduce the amount of copyright infringement?

INTERNET AND TECHNOLOGY
Digital Millennium Copyright Act

The Internet makes it easier than ever before for people to illegally copy and distribute copyrighted works. To combat this, software and entertainment companies have developed "wrappers" and encryption technology to protect their copyrighted works from unauthorized access. Not to be outdone, software pirates and other Internet users have devised ways to crack these wrappers and protection devices. Software and entertainment companies lobbied Congress to enact legislation to make the cracking of their wrappers and selling of technology to do so illegal. In response, Congress enacted the **Digital Millennium Copyright Act (DMCA)** [17 U.S.C. 1201], which does the following:

- Prohibits unauthorized access to copyrighted *digital* works by circumventing the wrapper or encryption technology that protects the intellectual property. This "black box" protection prohibits simply accessing the protected information and does not require that the accessed information be misused.
- Prohibits the manufacture and distribution of technologies, products, or services primarily designed for the purpose of circumventing wrappers or encryption technology protecting digital works. However, multipurpose devices that can be used in ways other than for cracking wrappers or encryption technology can be manufactured and sold without violating the DMCA.

Thus, for digital protected works, the DMCA makes it illegal to merely access copyrighted material by breaking through the digital wrapper or encryption technology that protects the work.

Congress granted exceptions to DMCA liability to (1) software developers to achieve compatibility of their software with the protected work; (2) federal, state, and local law enforcement agencies conducting criminal investigations; (3) parents who are protecting children from pornography or other harmful materials available on the Internet: (4) Internet users who are identifying and disabling cookies and other identification devices that invade their personal privacy rights; and (5) nonprofit libraries, educational institutions, and archives that access a protected work to determine whether to acquire the work.

The DMCA imposes civil and criminal penalties. A successful plaintiff in a civil action can recover actual damages from first-time offenders and treble damages from repeat offenders, costs and attorneys' fees, an order for the destruction of illegal products and devices, and an injunction against future violations by the offender. As an alternative to actual damages, a plaintiff can recover statutory damages of not less than $2,500 and up to $25,000 per act of circumvention. The following criminal penalties can be assessed for willful violations committed for "commercial advantage" or "private financial gain": First-time violators can be fined up to $500,000 and imprisoned for up to 5 years; subsequent violators can be fined up to $1 million and imprisoned for up to 10 years.

The following case involves the application of the DMCA.

CASE 7.6
Digital Millennium Copyright Act

Sony Computer Entertainment America, Inc. v. Filipiak

406 F.Supp.2d 1068, **Web** 2005 U.S. Dist. Lexis 35850 (2005)
United States District Court for the Northern District of California

> **"** *The evidence clearly shows that Filipiak was aware at all times that he was violating the DMCA when he sold mod chips and HDLoader. Therefore, the Court concludes that Filipiak willfully violated the DCMA.* **"**
>
> —Judge Spero

Facts

Sony Computer Entertainment America, Inc. (Sony), owns and distributes PlayStation and PlayStation2 (PlayStation) video game consoles that play video games. Sony also distributes video games played on PlayStation consoles. Sony incorporates technological protection in these devices to prevent copied games from being play on PlayStations.

Steven Filipiak began selling modification chips (mod chips) that circumvent the technological copyright protection measures in PlayStation consoles that allow users to play unauthorized and illegal copies of PlayStation video games. Filipiak sold the mod chips on two websites, http://the-console-corner.com and http://systems-modz.com. Filipiak also began selling "HDLoader," software that permits a user to make unauthorized copies of Sony's PlayStation video games and that allows users to play unlawful copies of Sony's video games on Sony's PlayStation consoles. This software also circumvents the technological copyright protection measures in PlayStation consoles.

Sony's lawyers sent a cease-and-desist letter to Filipiak's lawyer, demanding that Filipiak and his websites agree to an injunction prohibiting the marketing, sale, and distribution of mod chips and HDLoader. Filipiak signed the letter. After Filipiak removed the devices from his websites, he continued to sell them to existing and new customers through e-mail correspondence. Sony sued Filipiak and proposed, and Filipiak signed, a consent judgment that stipulated that he had sold mod chips and HDLoader in violation of the Digital Millennium Copyright Act (DMCA). Under the terms of the injunction in the judgment, Filipiak was prohibited from marketing or selling mod chips or HDLoader software. Sony subsequently discovered that Filipiak continued to ship HDLoader software to his customers. Filipiak signed a consent judgment agreeing not to sell mod chips or HDLoader as well as prohibiting Filipiak from destroying or deleting any documents or computer files reflecting sales of mod chips and HDLoader software.

The U.S. District Court entered the consent judgment in which Filipiak stipulated to liability under the DMCA. The judgment contained a provision ordering discovery proceedings. Pursuant to a discovery request, Filipiak delivered to Sony a hard drive that he said he used in his business. A computer forensics expert, however, determined that thousands of files had been deleted from the hard drive within a three-day period prior to production of the hard drive to Sony. In response to Sony's interrogatories, Filipiak did not disclose the total number of mod chips or HDLoader software copies he had sold.

Sony pursued its lawsuit against Filipiak. After hearing the evidence, the U.S. District Court awarded damages against Filipiak in the amount of $6,018,700. Filipiak filed a motion with the Court, challenging the award of damages.

Issue

Was the award of $6,018,700 against Filipiak for violating the DMCA supported by the evidence?

Language of the Court

The Court finds that Filipiak knew at the time he was selling them that the sale of mod chips and HDLoader was illegal under the DMCA. The evidence shows that Filipiak experienced difficulties with suppliers who were either shut down or who temporarily stopped supplying these devices to him and that he knew these shut-downs and stoppages were caused by legal problems experienced by these suppliers because their circumvention devices were alleged or found to violate the DMCA. The Court finds that Filipiak, at the time he signed the letter agreement, did not intend to abide by it and willfully violated the agreement after he signed it.

The DMCA makes it illegal to "manufacture, import, offer to the public, provide, or otherwise traffic in any technology, product, service, device, component, or part thereof, that . . . is primarily designed or produced for the purpose of circumventing a technological measure that effectively controls access to a work protected" by copyright [17 U.S.C. Section 1201(a)(2)]. Filipiak has stipulated to liability under this provision and on that basis the Court concludes that Filipiak has violated the DMCA.

Under the DMCA, a plaintiff may elect to recover statutory damages. The DMCA provides for an award of statutory damages in the sum of not less than $200 or more than $2,500 per act of circumvention, device, product, component, offer, or performance of service, as the court considers just. The Court concludes that the DMCA authorizes a separate award of statutory damages for each device sold.

The evidence clearly shows that Filipiak was aware at all times that he was violating the DMCA when he sold mod chips and HDLoader. Therefore, the Court concludes that Filipiak willfully violated the DCMA. Accordingly, the Court finds that SCEA is entitled to statutory damages in the amount of $5,631,200 (that is, 7,039 × 800) for the pre-June 12, 2004 sales and

$387,500.00 (that is, 155 × 2,500) for the sales after June 12, 2004, giving rise to a total of $6,018,700 in damages. While this award of damages is substantial, the Court concludes that it is both consistent with Congressional intent and necessary to discourage wrongful conduct by other potential retailers who might be tempted to engage in what might otherwise appear to be a lucrative business selling illegal contravention devices.

Decision

The U.S. District Court held that the award of $6,018,700 against Filipiak for violating the DMCA was supported by the evidence.

Law & Ethics Questions

1. What does the Digital Millennium Copyright Act (DMCA) provide? Explain.

2. **ETHICS** Did Filipiak act ethically in this case? Do you think he had intended to violate the DMCA, as the U.S. District Court found?

3. **ETHICS** Do you think that the award of damages in this case will deter others from violating the DMCA?

Web Exercises

1. **WEB** For the complete opinion of this case, go to *www.prenhall.com/cheesemancases*.

2. **WEB** Visit the website of the United States District Court for the Northern District of California, at *www.cand.uscourts. gov*.

3. **WEB** Visit the website of Sony Computer Entertainment America, Inc., at *www.scea.com*.

Trademarks

Businesses often develop company names, as well as advertising slogans and commercial logos, to promote the sale of their goods and services. Companies such as Nike, Microsoft, Louis Vuitton, and McDonald's spend millions of dollars annually to gain market recognition from consumers. The U.S. Congress has enacted trademark laws to provide legal protection for these names, slogans, and logos.

Federal Lanham Trademark Act

In 1946, Congress enacted the **Lanham Act**[6] to provide federal protection to trademarks, service marks, and other marks. This act, as amended, is intended to (1) protect the owner's investment and goodwill in a **mark** and (2) prevent consumers from being confused as to the origin of goods and services.

Trademarks are registered with the U.S. PTO in Washington, DC. The original registration of a mark is valid for 10 years and can be renewed for an unlimited number of 10-year periods. The registration of a trademark, which is given nationwide effect, serves as constructive notice that the mark is the registrant's personal property. The registrant is entitled to use the registered trademark symbol ® in connection with a registered trademark or service mark. Use of the symbol is not mandatory. Note that the frequently used notations "TM" and "SM" have no legal significance.

An applicant can register a mark if it has been used in commerce (e.g., actually used in the sale of goods or services). An applicant can also register a mark six months prior to its proposed use in commerce, but if the mark is not used within this period, the applicant loses the mark. A party other than the registrant can submit an opposition to a proposed registration of a mark or the cancellation of a previously registered mark.

Marks That Can Be Trademarked

The word *mark* collectively refers to *trademarks, service marks, certification marks*, and *collective marks*:

- *Trademarks.* A **trademark** is a distinctive mark, symbol, name, word, motto, or device that identifies the *goods* of a particular business. For example, *Chevrolet, Coca-Cola*, and *IBM* are trademarks.
- *Service marks.* A **service mark** is used to distinguish the *services* of the holder from those of its competitors. For example, *United Air Lines, Marriott International*, and *Weight Watchers* are service marks.
- *Certification marks.* A **certification mark** is a mark that is used to certify that goods and services are of a certain quality or originate from particular geographical areas. Example of certification marks are wines from the *Napa Valley* of California

and *Florida* oranges. The owner of the mark is usually a nonprofit corporation that licenses producers that meet certain standards or conditions to use the mark.

■ *Collective marks.* A **collective mark** is a mark used by cooperatives, associations, and fraternal organizations. *Boy Scouts of America* is an example of a collective mark.

Certain marks cannot be registered. They include (1) the flag or coat of arms of the United States, any state, municipality, or foreign nation; (2) marks that are immoral or scandalous; (3) geographical names standing alone (e.g., "South"); (4) surnames standing alone (note that a surname can be registered if it is accompanied by a picture or fanciful name, such as *Smith Brothers cough drops*); and (5) any mark that resembles a mark already registered with the federal PTO.

Napa Valley, California

This certification mark designates California cheese manufacturers.

Distinctiveness of a Mark

To qualify for federal protection, a mark must be **distinctive** or have acquired a **secondary meaning**.

Example Marks such as *Xerox* and *Acura* are *distinctive*. Nike, Inc., has trademarked its *Just Do It* slogan which has taken on a secondary meaning. Words that are *descriptive* but have no secondary meaning cannot be trademarked. The word *cola* alone could not be trademarked.

Web Exercises

1. **WEB** Visit the website of Nike, at *www.nike.com*. Can you find any trademarks or service marks?
2. **WEB** Visit the website of McDonald's Corporation, at *www.mcdonalds.com*. Can you find any trademarks or service marks?
3. **WEB** Visit the website of Microsoft Corporation, at *www.microsoft.com*. Can you find any trademarks or service marks?
4. **WEB** Visit the website of Louis Vuitton, at *www.louisvuitton.com*. Can you find any trademarks or service marks?
5. **WEB** Visit the website of Harley-Davidson, at *www.harley-davidson.com*. Can you find any trademarks or service marks?

In the following case, the court had to decide whether there was a trademark.

C A S E **7.7**
Trademark

Menashe v. Victoria's Secret Stores, Inc.

409 F.Supp.2d 412, **Web** 2006 U.S. Dist. Lexis 7763 (2006)
United States District Court for the Southern District of New York

> **66** *I find that because Victoria's Secret made bona fide trademark use of "SEXY LITTLE THINGS" in commerce before Plaintiffs … Victoria's Secret has acquired priority in the Mark.* **99**

—Judge Baer

Facts

As early as Fall 2002, Victoria's Secret, a woman's lingerie manufacturer and retailer, began to develop the concept and making of a line of lingerie named "SEXY LITTLE THINGS." Victoria's Secret rolled out its "SEXY LITTLE THINGS" collection at its stores. The collection was also available to consumers through catalogues and online.

On or about June 1, 2004, Ronit Menashe and Audrey Quock (collectively "Menashe") embarked on a joint venture to produce and launch a line of women's underwear. In late July or early August 2004, Menashe came up with the phrase "SEXY LITTLE THING" and "SEXY LITTLE THINGS" for a line of lingerie. On September 13, 2004, Menashe filed an intent-to-use (ITU) application with the U.S. Patent and Trademark Office (PTO) for these two names for lingerie. A the subsequent trial, both Menashe and Quock denied knowing that Victoria's Secret had been using the term "SEXY LITTLE THINGS" when they filed their ITU application with the PTO.

On November 11, 2004, Victoria's Secret applied to register "SEXY LITTLE THINGS" for lingerie on the PTO's Principal Register, based on its first use in commerce dating from July 28, 2004. At about the same time, Victoria's Secret learned of Menashe's ITU application for "SEXY LITTLE THING" and "SEXY LITTLE THINGS."

On November 16, 2004, Menashe received a cease-and-desist letter from Victoria's Secret, informing her that Victoria's Secret had been using "SEXY LITTLE THINGS" as a trademark for lingerie since prior to the filing date of Menache's ITU application. The letter demanded that Menashe cease and desist from using "SEXY LITTLE THING" and "SEXY LITTLE THINGS" and abandon the ITU application.

Menashe halted the production of the underwear project. Menashe filed a lawsuit against Victoria's Secret, seeking a declaratory judgment that asked the court to order that she had not infringed Victoria's Secret's claimed trademark in "SEXY LITTLE THINGS" in violation of the Lanham Act. Menashe sought damages from Victoria's Secret. On March 28, 2005, the PTO suspended further action on Victoria's Secret's trademark application, pending the disposition of Menashe's ITU application.

Issue

Should Menashe be granted a declaratory judgment of trademark non-infringement for using the terms "SEXY LITTLE THING" and "SEXY LITTLE THINGS" for their lingerie?

Language of the Court

At trial—while it stretches credulity—Menashe testified that since the time she received the cease and desist letter, she has not been in a Victoria's Secret store or looked at a Victoria's Secret catalogue to see whether Victoria's Secret was selling merchandise under the name "SEXY LITTLE THINGS." Quock testified that she did not visit a Victoria's Secret store nor look at a Victoria's Secret catalogue until some time after receipt of the cease and desist letter, when she walked into a Victoria's Secret store and saw a display for "SEXY LITTLE THINGS."

Plaintiffs' determination to ignore the model for the underwear fails to overcome the overwhelming evidence that Victoria's Secret used "SEXY LITTLE THINGS" as a trademark in commerce beginning on July 28, 2004. I find that because Victoria's Secret made bona fide trademark use of "SEXY LITTLE THINGS" in commerce before Plaintiffs filed their ITU application, and has continued to use that Mark in commerce, Victoria's Secret has acquired priority in the Mark. Consequently, Plaintiffs are not entitled to a declaratory judgment of non-infringement under the Lanham Act or at common law.

Decision

The U.S. District Court held that Victoria's Secret had obtained priority in the mark "SEXY LITTLE THINGS." The District Court dismissed Menashe's petition for declaratory judgment and dismissed the case against Victoria's Secret.

Law & Ethics Questions

1. What is the value of having a trademark?

2. Did Victoria's Secret use the term "SEXY LITTLE THINGS" in commerce before Menashe and Quock decided to use the same term? What was the significance of this fact?

3. **ETHICS** Do you think Menashe and Quock had knowledge of Victoria's Secret's use of the term "SEXY LITTLE THINGS" before they filed their application with the PTO?

Web Exercises

1. **WEB** For the complete opinion of this case, go to *www.prenhall.com/cheesemancases.*

2. **WEB** Visit the website of the United States District Court for the Southern District of New York, at *www.nysd.uscourts.gov*.

3. **WEB** Visit the website of Victoria's Secret, at *www.victoriassecret.com*. Can you find the "SEXY LITTLE THINGS" line of lingerie?

4. **WEB** Visit the website of the U.S. Patent and Trademark Office, at *www.uspto.gov*. Can you find the trademark for "SEXY LITTLE THINGS"?

Knockoff Goods

These counterfeit knockoff goods are an example of how companies' trademarks and copyrights are being infringed around the world. Knockoff goods cause a huge monetary loss to the owners' intellectual property rights.

Trademark Infringement

The owner of a mark can sue a third party for the unauthorized use of a mark. To succeed in a **trademark infringement** case, the owner must prove that (1) the defendant infringed the plaintiff's mark by using it in an unauthorized manner and (2) such use is likely to cause confusion, mistake, or deception of the public as to the origin of the goods or services. A successful plaintiff can recover (1) the profits made by the infringer through the unauthorized use of the mark, (2) damages caused to the plaintiff's business and reputation, (3) an order requiring the defendant to destroy all goods containing the unauthorized mark, and (4) an injunction preventing the defendant from such infringement in the future. The court has discretion to award up to treble damages where intentional infringement is found.

ETHICS SPOTLIGHT

Apple Computer Sued for Infringing the "iPhone" Trademark

Computer networking giant Cisco Systems didn't take to kindly to Apple Computer using the name "iPhone" on its handheld digital device. In fact, shortly after Apple released the much-hyped phone/music/video player "iPhone," Cisco leveled Apple with a civil suit claiming trademark infringement.

Several years before this battle of Fortune 500 companies, Cisco had acquired a small startup company named InfoGear, which had obtained the iPhone trademark and used it in its popular Linksys brand of Voice over IP phones. Shortly thereafter, Apple began contacting Cisco in hopes of purchasing the iPhone name to use on its much-anticipated upcoming cell phone. Cisco rejected the multiple offers. Apple created a front company called Ocean Telecom Services in hopes of obtaining the trademark through it. When that didn't work, Apple resorted to blunt force.

At the 2007 Macworld Expo in San Francisco, Apple CEO Steve Jobs went before a huge crowd and the world media to unveil Apple's hottest new item—the "iPhone." Cisco execs were stunned at the audacity of Apple, calling the move "a blatant disrespect for trademark law." Cisco immediately filed a federal lawsuit, seeking an injunction to prevent Apple from using the name, as well as damages. In public, Apple seemed to brush off the suit, saying, "We think Cisco's trademark suit is silly." However, legal experts insisted that behind closed doors, Apple had to be concerned. Cisco was indeed the clear trademark holder of record and had already released products using the iPhone name.

A trial would have been high risk for Apple as not only do courts tend to side with the original trademark holder when products are similar, but if Apple were to lose, it could be forced to pay Cisco all the profits from the sale of the iPhone. Apparently Apple didn't like their odds, and after a few weeks, the two companies announced a settlement for an undisclosed amount. According to the agreement, Apple and Cisco will both continue to use the iPhone name, and they will explore opportunities to work together in the future.

Law & Ethics Questions

1. What is trademark infringement?
2. **ETHICS** Did Apple act ethically in this case?

Web Exercises

1. **WEB** To see the iPhone, visit the website of Apple Computer, at *www.apple.com*.
2. **WEB** Visit the website of Cisco Systems, at *www.cisco.com*.
3. **WEB** Go to *www.google.com* and find an article relating to this case.

Trade Dress

Section 43(a) of the Lanham Act protects certain forms of **trade dress**. This consists of the "look and feel" of a product, a product's packaging, or a service establishment. The area of trade dress protection is an evolving area of the law.

The following case involves the issue of trade dress.

C A S E **7.8**
Trade Dress

U.S. SUPREME COURT
Two Pesos, Inc. v. Taco Cabana, Inc.
505 U.S. 763, 112 S.Ct. 2753, 120 L.Ed.2d 615,
Web 1992 U.S. Lexis 4533
Supreme Court of the United States

❝*Trade dress is the total image of the business.*❞

—Justice White

Facts

Taco Cabana, Inc. (Taco Cabana), had operated a chain of fast-food Mexican restaurants in Texas. Its restaurants provided a festive eating atmosphere of interior dining and patio areas decorated with artifacts, bright colors, paintings, and murals. The exterior of its buildings had a vivid color scheme, using top border paint and neon stripes. Bright awnings and umbrellas continued the theme. Ten years later, Two Pesos, Inc. (Two Pesos), opened a chain of competing Mexican fast-food restaurants in Texas. When Two Pesos adopted a motif similar to Taco Cabana's, Taco Cabana sued Two Pesos, alleging trade dress infringement in violation of Section 43(a) of the Lanham Act. Two Pesos argued that Taco Cabana's trade dress should not be protected because it had not yet acquired a secondary meaning. The U.S. District Court found that Taco Cabana's trade dress was protected. The U.S. Court of Appeals affirmed. Two Pesos appealed to the U.S. Supreme Court.

Issue

Does a restaurant's design have to have acquired a secondary meaning before it is protected as trade dress under Section 43(a) of the Lanham Act?

Language of the U.S. Supreme Court

Trade dress is the total image of the business. Taco Cabana's trade dress may include the shape and general appearance of the exterior restaurant, the identifying sign, the interior kitchen floor plan, the decor, the menu, the equipment used to serve food, the servers' uniforms and other features reflecting on the total image of the restaurant. The trade dress of a product is essentially its total image and overall appearance. The user of a trade dress should be able to maintain what competitive position it has and continue to seek wider identification among potential customers.

We see no basis for requiring secondary meaning for inherently distinctive trade dress protection. Adding a secondary meaning requirement could have anticompetitive effects, creating particular burdens on the start-up of small companies. It would present special difficulties for a business, such as Taco Cabana, that seeks to start a new product in a limited area and then expand into new markets. Denying protection for inherently distinctive trade dress until after secondary meaning has been established would allow a competitor, which has not adopted a distinctive trade dress of its own, to appropriate the originator's dress in other markets and to deter the originator from expanding into and competing in these areas.

Decision

The U.S. Supreme Court held that distinctive trade dress is protectable under the Lanham Act without proof that it has acquired a secondary meaning. The Supreme Court affirmed the decision of the U.S. Court of Appeals, which held that Taco Cabana's trade dress was protected from copying by Two Pesos.

Law & Ethics Questions

1. Should trade dress be protected under the Lanham Act? Why or why not?
2. **ETHICS** Did Two Pesos act ethically in copying Taco Cabana's trade dress?
3. Does the Supreme Court decision in this case have a pro- or anti-competitive effect on business? Explain.

Web Exercises

1. **WEB** For the complete opinion of this case, go to *www.prenhall.com/cheesemancases*.
2. **WEB** Visit the website of the U.S. Supreme Court, at *www.supremecourtus.gov*, and try to find documents that relate to this case.
3. **WEB** Use *www.google.com* to find an article that discusses a recent case of trade dress infringement.

INTERNATIONAL LAW
Chinese Courts Uphold Intellectual Property Rights

Ever since China entered the World Trade Organization (WTO), the protection of intellectual property rights from infringement has been a major concern among foreign companies doing business in China. The sale of counterfeit consumer goods carrying illegal trademarks have been an especially big problem in China. Dozens of international companies, however, are now suing in Chinese courts to stop the sale of imitation items.

In one case, luxury French fashion and leather goods maker Louis Vuitton sued Chaowai Men's Department Store in Beijing for failing to stop the sale of fake handbags. The case was brought before the Beijing No. 2 Intermediate People's Court. The Chinese court ruled in favor of Louis Vuitton and ordered Chaowai to pay 150,000 yuan in damages. The ruling found that Chaowai had been selling the fake handbags in over 20 stalls at the store at a price 50 times cheaper than the genuine item.

In another lawsuit, Louis Vuitton teamed up with fellow luxury brand companies Chanel, Prada, Burberry, and Gucci in an effort to stop Silk Alley, another Beijing indoor market, from selling counterfeit goods. The Chinese court in that case ruled in favor of the companies and ordered Silk Alley to pay each of them 20,000 yuan for violating their intellectual property rights.

Law & Ethics Questions

1. What is a knockoff good?
2. How hard is it for trademark holders to police the sale of knockoff items around the world? Explain.

Web Exercises

1. **WEB** Visit the website of Louis Vuitton, at *www.louisvuitton.com*.
2. **WEB** Read about the WTO's attempts to stop trademark infringement at *www.wto.org*.

Generic Names

If a word, name, or slogan is too generic, it cannot be registered as a trademark.

Example The words *water* and *watermark* are generic names that do not, alone, qualify as a trademark. The name *WaterColor Computer* would not be generic and could be registered as a trademark, however.

Most companies promote their trademarks and service marks to increase the public's awareness of the availability and quality of their products and services. At some point in time, however, the public may begin to treat the mark as a common name to denote the type of product or service being sold, rather than as the trademark or trade name of an individual seller. A trademark that becomes a common term for a product line or type of service is called a **generic name**. When a trademark becomes a generic name, the term loses its protection under federal trademark law (see Exhibit 7.3).

In the following case, the court had to decide whether a registered trademark was generic.

EXHIBIT 7.3

Generic Names

Reprinted with permission of Xerox Corporation

CASE **7.9**	**Retail Services Inc. v. Freebies Publishing**
Generic Name	364 F.3d 535, **Web** 2004 U.S. App. Lexis 7130 (2004)
	United States Court of Appeals for the Fourth Circuit

> ❝*The district court concluded that the evidence of genericness was so one-sided that no genuine issue of fact existed as to whether, in the public's mind, "freebies" indicates free or almost free products and is not identified with defendants....*❞
>
> —Judge Traxler

Facts

Eugene F. Zannon and Gail Zannon filed an application on behalf of Freebies Publishing with the U.S. Patent and Trademark Office (PTO) to register the word "Freebies" as a trademark. After first denying the application, the PTO subsequently granted the applicant Freebies Publishing the registration of the word "Freebies." Thereafter, Freebies Publishing registered the Internet domain name *www.freebies.com*. Freebies Publishing shifted its focus from traditional print media to cyberspace and operated the business from the website *www.freebies.com*.

Two years after Freebies Publishing was granted the trademark to "Freebies," Retail Services Inc. (RSI) registered the Internet domain name *www.freebie.com* and began operating a website offering an Internet service that promoted free offerings of goods and services for clients. RSI filed an action in U.S. District Court, seeking an order that RSI's use of the domain and website name *www.freebie.com* did not infringe Freebies Publishing's trademark "Freebies" and that this mark was generic and should be cancelled.

The U.S. District Court concluded that the word *freebies* was generic and could not be registered as a federal trademark. Thus, without a valid trademark before it, the District Court granted declaratory judgment to RSI, permitting it to use the domain name *www.freebie.com*. Freebies Publishing appealed, alleging that the word *freebies* was not generic and that RSI possessed the trademark "Freebies."

Issue

Is the word *freebies* a generic word that does not qualify as a trademark?

Language of the Court

The issuance of a certificate of registration arms the registrant with prima facie evidence of the validity of the registered mark and of the registration of the mark. The certificate of registration supplies the registrant with prima facie evidence that its mark is not generic in the eyes of the relevant public. This is a significant procedural advantage for the registrant. The effect of the presumption is to satisfy that burden in the absence of rebutting evidence. The presumption of validity flowing from trademark registration, therefore, has a burden-shifting effect, requiring the party challenging a registered mark to produce sufficient evidence to establish that the mark is generic by a preponderance of evidence.

The district court considered various dictionary definitions that were roughly uniform in defining "freebie" as a slang term meaning "Something given or received without charge" (*Webster's Collegiate Dictionary*); "An article or service given free" (*The American Heritage College Dictionary*); and "Something given or received gratis" (*Webster's II New Riverside University Dictionary*). The district court noted that, according to the *Oxford English Dictionary*, "freebie" has been understood to mean "something that is provided free" since its 1942 inclusion in *The American Thesaurus of Slang*.

Freebie Publishing's use of the term "freebies" is consistent with the use of that term by scores of other websites on the Internet. Freebie Publishing's website is but one of the 1,600-plus websites (or more) that incorporate the word "freebie" or "freebies" into their domain names. These websites are now so common that the term "freebie site" is often used by these sites to refer to other sites that, like Freebie Publishing's, offer information about free products or services. Finally, RSI offered a list of fifty-one newspaper or news media reports using the phrase "freebie site" to refer to websites similar to Freebie Publishing's freebie.com.

The district court concluded that the evidence of genericness was so one-sided that no genuine issue of fact existed as to whether, in the public's mind, "freebies" indicates free or almost free products and is not identified with defendants or their website in particular. Such one-sided evidence necessarily rebuts the presumption of non-genericness. A registration is subject to cancellation at any time if the registered mark becomes the generic name for the goods or services for which it is registered. A generic word can never function as a trademark.

Decision

The U.S. Court of Appeals held that the word *freebies* was a generic word that could not be registered as a federal trademark. The U.S. Court of Appeals affirmed the declaratory judgment issued by the U.S. District Court in favor of RSI, allowing it to use the domain name *www.freebie.com*.

Law & Ethics Questions

1. What is a generic name? Can a generic name be registered as a trademark?

2. Once a word has been granted a valid trademark, can this trademark be lost in the future? Explain.

3. **ETHICS** Did RSI act ethically in registering the domain name *www.freebie.com*?

Web Exercises

1. **WEB** For the complete opinion of this case, go to *www.prenhall.com/cheesemancases*.

2. **WEB** Visit the website of the United States Court of Appeals for the Fourth Circuit, at *www.ca4.uscourts.gov*.

3. **WEB** Use *www.google.com* to find another name that was either denied registration as a trademark or that was cancelled as a trademark because it was a generic word.

CONCEPT SUMMARY

Types of Intellectual Property Protected by Federal Law

TYPE	SUBJECT MATTER	TERM
Patent	Inventions (e.g., machines; processes; compositions of matter; designs for articles of manufacture; and improvements to existing machines and processes). Invention must be novel, useful, and nonobvious. *Public use doctrine:* Patent will not be granted if the invention was used in public for more than one year prior to the filing of the patent application.	Patents on articles of manufacture and processes: 20 years; design patents: 14 years.
Copyright	Tangible writing (e.g., books, magazines, newspapers, lectures, operas, plays, screenplays, musical compositions, maps, works of art, lithographs, photographs, postcards, greeting cards, motion pictures, newsreels, sound recordings, computer programs, and mask works fixed to semiconductor chips). Writing must be the original work of the author. The *fair use doctrine* permits the use of copyrighted material without consent for limited uses (e.g., scholarly work, parody or satire, and brief quotation in news reports).	Individual holder: life of author plus 70 years. Corporate holder: the shorter of either 120 years from the date of creation or 95 years from the date of first publication
Trademark	Marks (e.g., name, symbol, word, logo, or device). Marks include trademarks, service marks, certification marks, and collective marks. Mark must be distinctive or have acquired a secondary meaning. *Generic name:* A mark that becomes a common term for a product line or type of service loses its protection under federal trademark law.	Original registration: 10 years. Renewal registration: unlimited number of renewals for 10-year terms.

Federal Dilution Act

Companies owning trademarks often spend millions of dollars each year advertising and promoting the quality of the goods and services sold under their names. Many of these become household names that are recognized by millions of consumers, such as Coca-Cola, McDonald's, Microsoft, and Nike.

Traditional trademark law protected these marks where an infringer used the mark and confused consumers as to the source of the goods or services.

Example If a knockoff company sold athletic shoes and apparel under the name "Nike," there would be trademark infringement.

Often, however, a party would use a name similar to, but not exactly identical to, a holder's trademark. Congress enacted the **Federal Dilution Act** of 1995 to protect *famous marks* from *dilution*. The Federal Dilution Act provides that owners of marks have a valuable property right in their marks that should not be *eroded, blurred, tarnished*, or *diluted* in any way by another. The Federal Dilution Act has three fundamental requirements:

1. The mark must be famous.
2. The use by the other party must be commercial.
3. The use must cause dilution of the distinctive quality of the mark. *Dilution* is broadly defined as the lessening of the capacity of a famous mark to identify and distinguish its holder's goods and services, regardless of the presence or absence of competition between the owner of the mark and the other party.

Example If someone other than Nike had the website *www.nikeathletesrun.com*, it would be unlawful dilution.

Congress enacted the **Trademark Dilution Revision Act**, which became law in 2006. This act provides that a dilution plaintiff does not need to show that it has suffered actual harm to prevail in its dilution lawsuit. The act also lists factors that help in defining dilution, blurring, and tarnishment. The act permits truthful comparative advertising and provides a "fair use" defense for parodying someone else's famous mark.

INTERNATIONAL LAW
International Protection of Intellectual Property Rights

For centuries, national patent, copyright, and trademark laws defined the rights of inventors, authors, and businesses. These laws offered protection within a country's borders but not in other countries. Beginning in the late 1800s, countries began entering into treaties and conventions with other countries that provided international protection of intellectual property rights. For example, the **Paris Convention** is an international treaty that protects patents and trademarks, and the Berne Convention is an international treaty that protects copyrights.

The **World Intellectual Property Organization (WIPO)** is an international organization that was founded to promote and protect intellectual property rights worldwide. The WIPO is a specialized agency of the United Nations that has more than 180 member countries. The WIPO can propose intellectual property rights treaties that its members may choose to join. Two of the recent WIPO treaties are:

1. *WIPO Copyright Treaty.* The **WIPO Copyright Treaty** is an international treaty that protects copyrights to computer programs and data compilations.

2. *WIPO Phonogram Treaty.* The **WIPO Phonogram Treaty** is an international treaty that gives performers and producers the exclusive right to broadcast, reproduce, and distribute copies of their performances.

Web Exercise

1. **WEB** Visit the website of the WIPO, at *www.wipo.int*.

Arc de Triomphe, Paris, France

International treaties and conventions protect intellectual property rights in most countries of the world.

Chapter Summary

Trade Secrets, p. 182

A *trade secret* is a product formula, pattern, design, compilation of data, customer list, or other business secret that makes a business successful. The owner of a trade secret must take reasonable precautions to prevent its trade secret from being discovered by others.

Misappropriation of a Trade Secret

Obtaining another's trade secret through unlawful means such as theft, bribery, or espionage is a tort. A successful plaintiff can recover profits, damages, and an injunction against the offender.

The Economic Espionage Act

The Economic Espionage Act is a federal statute that makes it a crime for any person to convert a trade secret for his or her own or another's benefit, knowing or intending to cause injury to the owners of the trade secret.

Patents, p. 184

Patent law is exclusively federal law; there are no state patent laws. Patentable subject matter includes inventions such as machines; processes; compositions of matter; improvements to existing machines, processes, or compositions of matter; designs for articles of manufacture; asexually reproduced plants; and living matter invented by a person. To be patented, an invention must be novel, useful, and nonobvious.

Federal Patent Statute

This law is intended to provide an incentive for inventors to invent and make their inventions public and to protect patented inventions from infringement.

Patent Period

Patents are valid for 20 years. The patent term begins to run from the date the patent application is filed.

Patenting an Invention

An invention must be novel, useful, and nonobvious. Patentable subject matters include (1) machines; (2) processes; (3) compositions of matter; (4) improvements to existing machines, processes, or compositions of matter; (5) designs for an article of manufacture; (6) asexually reproduced plants; and (7) living material invented by a person.

Business Plans

In *State Street Bank & Trust Co. v. Signature Financial Group, Inc.*, the U.S. Court of Appeals held that business plans are patentable.

Patent Application

An application containing a written description of the invention must be filed with the *U.S. Patent and Trademark Office* in Washington, DC.

Patent Appeals

Patent appeals are heard by the *U.S. Court of Appeals for the Federal Circuit* in Washington, DC.

One-Year On-Sale Doctrine, p. 188

Public Use Doctrine

A patent may not be granted if the invention was used by the public for more than one year prior to the filing of the patent application.

The American Inventors Protection Act

The American Inventors Protection Act is a federal statute that does the following:
1. Permits an inventor to file a *provisional application* with the U.S. Patent and Trademark Office (PTO) three months before the filing of a final patent application.
2. Requires the PTO to issue a patent within three years after the filing of a patent application.
3. Provides that non-patent holders may challenge a patent as being overly broad by requesting a contested reexamination of the patent application by the PTO.

Patent Infringement

The unauthorized use of an author's patent constitutes patent infringement. The patent holder may recover damages and other remedies against the infringer.

Copyrights, p. 191

Copyright law is exclusively federal law; there are no state copyright laws. Only tangible writings can be copyrighted. These include books, newspapers, addresses, musical compositions, motion pictures, works of art, architectural plans, greeting cards, photographs, sound recordings, computer programs, and mask works fixed in semiconductor chips. The writing must be the original work of the author.

Registration of Copyrights

Copyright registration is permissive and voluntary. Published and unpublished works may be registered with the *U.S. Copyright Office* in Washington, DC. Registration itself does not create the copyright. Copyrights are for the following terms:
1. *Individual holder.* Life of the author plus 70 years.
2. *Corporate holder.* Either 120 years from the date of creation or 95 years from the date of publication, whichever is shorter.

Copyright Infringement

Copyright infringement is the copying of a substantial and material part of a copyrighted work without the holder's permission. The copyright holder may recover damages and other remedies against the infringer.

The Fair Use Doctrine, p. 196

The fair use doctrine permits use of copyrighted material without the consent of the copyright holder for limited uses (e.g., scholarly work, parody or satire, and brief quotation in news reports).

No Electronic Theft Act (NET Act)

The No Electronic Theft Act (NET Act) is a federal statute that makes it a crime for a person to willfully infringe a copyright work exceeding $1,000 in retail value.

Digital Millennium Copyright Act (DMCA)

The Digital Millennium Copyright Act (DMCA) is a federal statute, enacted in 1998, that provides civil and criminal penalties that:
1. Prohibit the manufacture and distribution of technologies, products, or services primarily designed for the purpose of circumventing wrappers or encryption protection.

2. Prohibit unauthorized *access* to copyrighted digital works by circumventing the wrapper or encryption technology that protects the intellectual property.

Trademarks, p. 200

Federal Lanham Trademark Act

The *Lanham Act* provides federal protection to trademarks, service marks, and other marks. A *mark* is a trade name, symbol, word, logo, design, or device that distinguishes the owner's goods or services. Marks are registered with the *U.S. Patent and Trademark Office* in Washington, DC. The original registration of a mark is valid for 10 years and can be renewed for an unlimited number of 10-year periods. Marks are often referred to collectively as trademarks.

Marks That Can Be Trademarked

The following types of marks can be trademarked:
1. *Trademark.* Identifies goods of a particular business.
2. *Service mark.* Identifies services of a particular business.
3. *Certification mark.* Certifies that goods or services are of a certain quality or origin.
4. *Collective mark.* Used by cooperatives, associations, and fraternal organizations.

Distinctiveness of a Mark

A mark must either (a) be *distinctive* or (b) have acquired a *secondary meaning*. The mark must have been used in commerce or the holder must intend to use the mark in commerce and actually do so within six months after registering the mark.

Trademark Infringement

The unauthorized use of another's registered mark is called trademark infringement. The mark holder may recover damages and other remedies from the infringer.

Trade Dress

Trade dress involves the protection of the "look and feel" of a product, a product's packaging, or a service establishment.

Generic Name

A mark that becomes a common term for a product line or type of service loses its protection under federal trademark law.

Federal Dilution Act

The Federal Dilution Act is a federal statute that protects famous marks from dilution. A violation of the act requires that the mark be famous, the use by the other party be commercial, and the use cause dilution of the distinctive quality of the mark.

International Protection of Intellectual Property Rights

1. *Paris Convention.* An international treaty that protects patents and trademarks.
2. *Berne Convention.* An international treaty that protects copyrights.
3. *WIPO Copyright Treaty.* An international treaty that protects copyrights to computer programs and data compilations.
4. *WIPO Phonogram Treaty.* An international treaty that gives performers and producers the exclusive right to broadcast, reproduce, and distribute copies of their performances.

Test Review Terms and Concepts

American Inventors Protection Act   190
Berne Convention   192
certificate of recordation   193
Certification mark   200
Collective mark   201

Computer Software Copyright Act   193
Copyright   191
Copyright infringement   193
Copyright registration   192
Copyright Revision Act   191

Digital Millennium Copyright Act (DMCA)   198
Distinctive   201
Economic Espionage Act   183
Fair use doctrine   196

Case Problems

7.1. Trade Secret: CRA-MAR Video Center, Inc., sells electronic equipment and videocassettes, as does its competitor, Koach's Sales Corporation. Both CRA-MAR and Koach's purchased computers from Radio Shack. CRA-MAR used the computer to store customer lists, movie lists, personnel files, and financial records. Because the computer was new to CRA-MAR, Randall Youts, Radio Shack's salesman and programmer, agreed to modify CRA-MAR's programs when needed, including the customer list program. At one point, CRA-MAR decided to send a mailing to everyone on its customer list. The computer was unable to perform the function, so Youts took the disks containing the customer lists to the Radio Shack store to work on the program. Somehow Koach's came into possession of CRA-MAR's customer lists and sent advertising mailings to the parties on the lists. When CRA-MAR discovered this fact, it sued Koach's, seeking an injunction against any further use of its customer lists. Is a customer list a trade secret that can be protected from misappropriation? *Koachs Sales Corp. v. CRA-MAR Video Center, Inc.*, 478 N.E.2d 110, **Web** 1985 Ind. App. Lexis 2432 (Court of Appeals of Indiana)

7.2. Patent: Patent no. 3,397,928 (928) was issued to Edward M. Galle, an executive of Hughes Tool Company. Galle assigned the patent, and other related patents, to Hughes. The patent was for an O-ring rubber seal that was used to seal bearings in the cone of a rock bit that rotated to drill holes in rocks. Rock bits were used to drill oil wells. Hughes did not license its 928 patent, which was a substantial commercial success. Smith International, Inc., was Hughes's major competitor in this industry. For 13 years, Smith made more than 460,000 rock bits (reaping sales of about $1.3 billion) that contained rubber seals that infringed on Hughes's patents. Hughes sued Smith for patent infringement and requested $1.2 billion in lost royalties and interest. Smith offered $20 million to $60 million in settlement. The case went to trial, and the court found Smith liable for patent infringement. How much should Hughes be awarded in damages? *Smith Internat'l, Inc. v. Hughes Tool Co.*, 759

F.2d 1572, **Web** 1985 U.S. App. Lexis 14777 (United States Court of Appeals for the Federal Circuit)

7.3. Copyright: When Spiro Agnew resigned as vice president of the United States, President Richard M. Nixon appointed Gerald R. Ford as vice president. Amid growing controversy surrounding the Watergate scandal, President Nixon resigned, and Vice President Ford acceded to the presidency. As president, Ford pardoned Nixon for any wrongdoing regarding the Watergate affair and related matters. Ford served as president until he was defeated by Jimmy Carter in the presidential election. Ford entered into a contract with Harper & Row, Publishers, Inc., to publish his memoirs in book form. The memoirs were to contain significant unpublished materials concerning the Watergate affair and Ford's personal reflections on that time in history. The publisher instituted security measures to protect the confidentiality of the manuscript. Several weeks before the book was to be released, an unidentified person secretly brought a copy of the manuscript to Victor Navasky, editor of *The Nation*, a weekly political commentary magazine. Navasky, knowing that his possession of the purloined manuscript was not authorized, produced a 2,250-word piece titled "The Ford Memoirs" and published it in an issue of *The Nation*. Verbatim quotes of between 300 and 400 words from Ford's manuscript, including some of the most important parts, appeared in the article. Harper & Row sued the publishers of *The Nation* for copyright infringement. Who wins? *Harper & Row, Publishers, Inc. v. Nation Enterprises*, 471 U.S. 539, 105 S.Ct. 2218, 85 L.Ed.2d 588, **Web** 1985 U.S. Lexis 17 (Supreme Court of the United States)

7.4. Fair Use Doctrine: Once in the past, when the City of New York teetered on the brink of bankruptcy, on the television screens of America there appeared an image of a top-hatted Broadway showgirl, backed by an advancing phalanx of dancers, chanting: "I-I-I-I-I Love New Yo-o-o-o-o-o-rk." As an ad campaign for an ailing city, it was an unparalleled success. Crucial to the campaign was a brief but exhilarating musical theme written by Steve Karmin called "I Love New York." Elsmere Music, Inc., owned the copyright to the music. The success of the campaign did not go unnoticed. The popular weekly variety program *Saturday Night Live (SNL)* performed a comedy sketch over National Broadcasting Company's network (NBC). In the sketch, the cast of *SNL*, portraying the mayor and members of the chamber of commerce of the biblical city of Sodom, were seen discussing Sodom's poor public image with out-of-towners and its effect on the tourist trade. In an attempt to recast Sodom's image in a more positive light, a new advertising campaign was revealed, with the highlight of the campaign being a song "I Love Sodom" sung a cappella by a chorus line of *SNL* regulars to the tune of "I Love New York." Elsmere Music did not see the humor of the sketch and sued NBC for copyright infringement. Who wins? *Elsmere Music, Inc. v. National Broadcasting Co., Inc.*, 623 F.2d 252, **Web** 1980 U.S. App. Lexis 16820 (United States Court of Appeals for the Second Circuit)

7.5. Trademark: Clairol Incorporated manufactures and distributes hair tinting, dyeing, and coloring preparations. Clairol embarked on an extensive advertising campaign to promote the sale of its "Miss Clairol" hair-color preparations that included advertisements in national magazines, on outdoor billboards, on radio and television, in mailing pieces, and on point-of-sale display materials to be used by retailers and beauty salons. The advertisements prominently displayed the slogans "Hair Color So Natural Only Her Hairdresser Knows for Sure" and "Does She or Doesn't She?" Clairol registered these slogans as trademarks. During the next decade, Clairol spent more than $22 million for advertising materials, resulting in more than a billion separate audio and visual impressions using the slogans. Roux Laboratories, Inc., a manufacturer of hair-coloring products and a competitor of Clairol's, filed an opposition to Clairol's registration of the slogans as trademarks. Do the slogans qualify for trademark protection? *Roux Laboratories, Inc. v. Clairol Inc.*, 427 F.2d 823, **Web** 1970 CCPA Lexis 344 (United States Court of Customs and Patent Appeals)

7.6. Trademark: Mead Data Central, Inc., has provided computer-assisted legal research services to lawyers and others under the trademark "Lexis." Lexis is based on *lex*, the Latin word for law, and *IS*, for information systems. Through extensive sales and advertising, Mead has made Lexis a strong mark in the computerized legal research field, particularly among lawyers. However, Lexis is recognized by only 1 percent of the general population, with almost half of this 1 percent being attorneys. Toyota Motor Corporation has for many years manufactured automobiles, which it markets in the United States through its subsidiary Toyota Motor Sales, U.S.A., Inc. Toyota announced a new line of luxury automobiles to be called Lexus. Toyota planned on spending almost $20 million for marketing and advertising Lexus during the first nine months of 1989. Mead filed suit against Toyota, alleging that Toyota's use of the name Lexus violated New York's anti-dilution statute and would cause injury to the business reputation of Mead and a dilution of the distinctive quality of the Lexis mark. Who wins? *Mead Data Central, Inc. v. Toyota Motor Sales, U.S.A., Inc.*, 875 F.2d 1026, **Web** 1989 U.S. App. Lexis 6644 (United States Court of Appeals for the Second Circuit)

7.7. Generic Name: The Miller Brewing Company, a national brewer, produces a reduced-calorie beer called Miller Lite. Miller began selling beer under this name and spent millions of dollars promoting the Miller Lite brand name on television, in print, and via other forms of advertising. Falstaff Brewing Corporation has brewed and distributed a reduced-calorie beer called "Falstaff Lite." Miller brought suit under the Lanham Act, seeking an injunction to prevent Falstaff from using the term *Lite*. Is the term *Lite* a generic name that does not qualify for trademark protection? *Miller Brewing Co. v. Falstaff Brewing Corp.*, 655 F.2d 5, **Web** 1981 U.S. App. Lexis 11345 (United States Court of Appeals for the First Circuit)

Ethics Issues

7.8. Ethics: Integrated Cash Management Services, Inc. (ICM), designs and develops computer software programs and systems for banks and corporate financial departments. ICM's computer programs and systems are not copyrighted, but they are secret. After Alfred Sims Newlin and Behrouz Vafa completed graduate school, they were employed by ICM as computer programmers. They worked at ICM for several years, writing computer programs. They left ICM to work for Digital Transactions, Inc. (DTI). Before leaving ICM, however, they copied certain ICM files onto computer disks. Within two weeks of starting to work at DTI, they created prototype computer programs that operated in substantially the same manner as comparable ICM programs and were designed to compete directly with ICM's programs. ICM sued Newlin, Vafa, and DTI for misappropriation of trade secrets. Are the defendants liable? Did the defendants act ethically in this case? *Integrated Cash Management Services, Inc. v. Digital Transactions, Inc.*, 920 F.2d 171, **Web** 1990 U.S. App. Lexis 20985 (United States Court of Appeals for the Second Circuit)

7.9. Ethics: John W. Carson was the host and star of *The Tonight Show*, a well-known nightly television talk show broadcast by the National Broadcasting Company (NBC) until he retired. Carson also appeared as an entertainer in theaters and night clubs around the country. For the

30 years, he hosted *The Tonight Show*, he had been introduced on the show each night with the phrase "Here's Johnny." The phrase "Here's Johnny" was generally associated with Carson by a substantial segment of the television viewing public. Carson had licensed the use of the phrase to a chain of restaurants, a line of toiletries, and other business ventures. Johnny Carson Apparel, Inc., founded in 1970, manufactured and marketed men's clothing to retail stores. Carson, president of Apparel and owner of 20 percent of its stock, had licensed Apparel to use the phrase "Here's Johnny" on labels for clothing and in advertising campaigns. The phrase had never been registered by Carson or Apparel as a trademark or service mark.

Earl Broxton was the owner and president of Here's Johnny Portable Toilets, Inc., a Michigan corporation that engages in the business of renting and selling "Here's Johnny" portable toilets. Broxton was aware when he formed the corporation that the phrase "Here's Johnny" was the introductory slogan for Carson on *The Tonight Show*. Broxton indicated that he coupled the phrase "Here's Johnny" with a second one, "The World's Foremost Commodian," to make a good play on the phrase. Shortly after Toilets went into business in 1976, Carson and Apparel sued Toilets, seeking an injunction prohibiting the further use of the phrase "Here's Johnny" as a corporate name for or in connection with the sale or rental of its portable toilets. Who wins? Did Broxton act ethically by appropriating the phrase "Here's Johnny" to promote the sale and rental of portable toilets? *Carson v. Here's Johnny Portable Toilets, Inc.*, 698 F.2d 831, **Web** 1983 U.S. App. Lexis 30866 (United States Court of Appeals for the Sixth Circuit)

IRAC Writing Assignment

Read Case A-7 in Appendix A [*Feist Publications, Inc. v. Rural Telephone Service Company, Inc.*]. Read the case and use the IRAC method to prepare a written analysis of the case.

Endnotes

1. 18 U.S.C. Sections 1831–1839.
2. 35 U.S.C. Section 10 et seq.
3. 17 U.S.C. Section 101 et seq.
4. 17 U.S.C. Section 101.
5. 17 U.S.C. Section 901–914.
6. 15 U.S.C. Section 1114 et seq.

CHAPTER 8

Ethics of Managers and Social Responsibility of Business

> **"** *Ethical considerations can no more be excluded from the administration of justice, which is the end and purpose of all civil laws, than one can exclude the vital air from his room and live.* **"**
>
> —JOHN F. DILLON
> Laws and Jurisprudence of England and America Lecture I (1894)

CHAPTER OBJECTIVES

After studying this chapter, you should be able to:

1. Describe how law and ethics intertwine.
2. Describe the moral theories of business ethics.
3. Describe the theories of the social responsibility of business.
4. Describe corporate social audits.
5. Examine how international ethical standards differ from country to country.

CHAPTER CONTENTS

- Introduction to Ethics of Managers and Social Responsibility of Business
- Ethics and the Law
- Business Ethics
- Social Responsibility of Business
- Chapter Summary
- Test Review Terms and Concepts
- Case Problems
- Ethics Issues
- IRAC Writing Assignment

Introduction to Ethics of Managers and Social Responsibility of Business

Businesses organized in the United States are subject to its laws. They are also subject to the laws of other countries in which they operate. In addition, businesspersons owe a duty to act ethically in the conduct of their affairs, and businesses owe a social responsibility not to harm society.

Although much of the law is based on ethical standards, not all ethical standards have been enacted as law. The law establishes a minimum degree of conduct expected by persons and businesses in society. Ethics demands more. This chapter discusses business ethics and the social responsibility of business.

Myanmar
Some companies refuse to do business with Myanmar because of allegations that its military-led government engages in humanitarian violations.

Ethics and the Law

Sometimes the rule of law and the golden rule of **ethics** demand the same response by a person confronted with a problem. For example, federal and state laws make bribery unlawful. A person violates the law if he or she bribes a judge for a favorable decision in a case. Ethics would also prohibit this conduct. However, the law may permit something that would be ethically wrong.

Example Occupational safety laws set standards for emissions of dust from toxic chemicals in the workplace. Suppose a company can reduce the emission below the legal standard by spending additional money. The only benefit from the expenditure would be better employee health. Ethics would require the extra expenditure; the law would not.

Another alternative occurs where the law demands certain conduct but a person's ethical standards are contrary.

Example Federal law prohibits employees from hiring certain illegal alien workers. Suppose an employer advertises the availability of a job and receives no response except from a person who cannot prove he or she is a citizen of this country or does not posses a required visa. The worker and his or her family are destitute. Should the employer hire him or her? The law says no, but ethics says yes (see Exhibit 8.1).

> Ethics precede laws as man precedes society.
>
> Jason Alexander
> *Philosophy for Investors (1979)*

Law   Ethics

EXHIBIT 8.1

Law and Ethics

He who seeks equality must do equity.

Joseph Story
Equity Jurisprudence (1836)

Business Ethics

How can ethics be measured? The answer is very personal: What is considered ethical by one person may be considered unethical by another. However, there do seem to be some universal rules about what conduct is ethical and what conduct is not. The following discussion highlights five major theories of ethics.

ETHICS SPOTLIGHT

Wal-Mart Pays Big for Meal Break Violations

❝*At Wal-Mart, not only is there no such thing as a free lunch for employees but, in this sad case, there is no lunch at all.*❞

—Wal-Mart Watch

In recent years, the retail giant Wal-Mart has been the target of hundreds of lawsuits by employees in dozens of states, claiming the company violated wage-and-hour laws. In Colorado, Wal-Mart settled with a group of employees for $50 million because of denied meal break violations. In Oregon, workers were rewarded with nearly $2,000 each for similar violations.

A group of California Wal-Mart employees became the first in a series of class-action lawsuits involving the denied meal breaks. In *Wal-Mart Stores v. S.C. (Savaglio),* **Web** 2004 Cal. Lexis 3284 (Supreme Court of California, 2004), both current and former employees argued that Wal-Mart had violated California's meal period law. Wal-Mart fought back, saying that it didn't break any law.

The Oakland, California, jury watched four months of testimony and deliberated for three days before coming back with its verdict: 116,000 current and former Wal-Mart employees were to receive $172 million in general and punitive damages. Wal-Mart employees and community activists felt vindicated and insisted that the company fix the broken system. Wal-Mart Watch, a union-backed group that keeps a very close eye on everything the company does, commented, "At Wal-Mart, not only is there no such thing as a free lunch for employees but, in this sad case, there is no lunch at all."

Less than a year after the meal break case, Wal-Mart was in court in Pennsylvania. This time the jury hit the company with over $78 million in damages for forcing employees to work "off the clock" and during rest breaks.

Law & Ethics Questions

1. **ETHICS** Did Wal-Mart act ethically in this case?
2. **ETHICS** Why does Wal-Mart engage in such practices?

Web Exercises

1. **WEB** Visit the website of Wal-Mart, at *www.walmart.com.*
2. **WEB** Use *www.google.com* to find a recent case in which Wal-Mart has been found to engage in an illegal activity.
3. **WEB** Use *www.google.com* to find Wal-Mart's code of ethics.
4. **WEB** Visit the website of the Wal-Mart watchdog group, at *www.walmartwatch.com.* What is one of the current issues discussed?

Ethical Fundamentalism

Under **ethical fundamentalism**, a person looks to an *outside source* for ethical rules or commands. This may be a book (e.g., the Bible, the Koran) or a person (e.g., Karl Marx). Critics argue that ethical fundamentalism does not permit people to determine right and wrong for themselves. Taken to an extreme, the result could be considered unethical under most other moral theories. For example, a literal interpretation of the maxim "an eye for an eye" would permit retaliation.

ETHICS SPOTLIGHT
Qui Tam Lawsuit

The Bayer Corporation (Bayer) is a U.S. subsidiary corporation of giant German-based Bayer A.G. Bayer is a large pharmaceutical company that produces prescription drugs, including its patented antibiotic Cipro. Bayer sold Cipro to private health providers and hospitals, including Kaiser Permanente Medical Care Program, the largest health maintenance organization in the United States. Bayer also sold Cipro to the federal government's Medicaid program, which provides medical insurance to the poor. Federal law contains a "best price" rule that prohibits a company that sells a drug to Medicaid to charge Medicaid a price higher than the lowest price for which it sells the drug to private purchasers.

Kaiser told Bayer that it would not purchase Cipro from Bayer—and would switch to a competitor's antibiotics—unless Bayer reduced the price of Cipro. Bayer's executives came up with a plan whereby Bayer would put a private label on its Cipro and not call it Cipro and sell the antibiotic to Kaiser at a 40 percent discount. Thus, Bayer continued to charge Medicaid the full price for Cipro while giving Kaiser a 40 percent discount through the private labeling program. One of Bayer's executives who negotiated this deal with Kaiser was corporate account manager George Couto.

Everything went well for Bayer until Couto attended a mandatory ethics training class at Bayer at which a video of Heige Wehmeier, then company chief executive, was shown. When the video stated that Bayer employees were to obey not only "the letter of the law but the spirit of the law as well," some of the Bayer executives laughed. Later that day, Couto attended a staff meeting at which it was disclosed that Bayer kept $97 million from Medicaid by using the discounted private labeling program for Kaiser and other health care companies. Two days later, Couto wrote a memorandum to his boss, questioning the legality of the private labeling program in light of Medicaid's "best price" law.

When he received no response to his memo, Couto contacted a lawyer. Couto filed a *qui tam* lawsuit under the federal **False Claims Act**—also known as the **Whistleblower Statute**—which permits private parties to sue companies for fraud on behalf of the government. The riches: The whistleblower can be awarded up to 25 percent of the amount recovered on behalf of the federal government, even if the informer has been a co-conspirator in perpetrating the fraud.

Once the case was filed, the U.S. Department of Justice took over the case, as allowed by law, and filed criminal as well as civil charges against Bayer. After discovery was taken, Bayer pleaded guilty to one criminal felony and agreed to pay federal and state governments $257 million to settle the civil and criminal cases. Couto, age 39, died of pancreatic cancer three months prior to the settlement. Couto was awarded $34 million, which will go to his three children. *United States v. Bayer Corporation.*

Law & Ethics Questions

1. **ETHICS** Was it very difficult for the Bayer executives to devise the private labeling plan to cheat the federal government?

2. **ETHICS** Did Couto act ethically in this case? Should a fraudulent co-conspirator be allowed to recover an award under the Whistleblower Statute? Explain.

Web Exercises

1. **WEB** Visit the website of the Bayer Corporation, at *www.bayer.com*. Can you find the corporation's code of ethics?

2. **WEB** Use *www.google.com* to find an article that discusses a recent application of the Whistleblower Statute.

Utilitarianism

Utilitarianism is a moral theory with origins in the works of Jeremy Bentham (1748–1832) and John Stuart (1806–1873). This moral theory dictates that people must choose the actions or follow the rule that provides the *greatest good to society*. This does not mean the greatest good for the greatest number of people. For instance, if an action would increase the good of 25 people 1 unit each and an alternative action would increase the good of 1 person 26 units, the latter action should be taken.

Utilitarianism has been criticized because it is difficult to estimate the "good" that will result from different actions, it is hard to apply in an imperfect world, and it treats morality as if it were an impersonal mathematical calculation.

Example A company is trying to determine whether it should close an unprofitable plant located in a small community. Utilitarianism would require that the benefits to shareholders from closing the plant be compared to the benefits to employees, their families, and others in the community in keeping it open.

The following case examined the ethics of a fast-food restaurant chain.

Bradley v. McDonald's Corporation

Web 2003 U.S. Dist. Lexis 15202 (2003)
United States District Court for the Southern District of New York

> **"***Advertising campaigns run by McDonald's claimed that it sold "Good basic nutritious food. Food that's been the foundation of well-balanced diets for generations. And will be for generations to come."***"**
>
> —Judge Sweet

Facts

McDonald's Corporation operates the largest fast-food restaurant chain in the United States and the world. It produces such famous foods as the "Big Mac" hamburger, chicken McNuggets, the egg McMuffin, French fries, shakes, and other foods. A McDonald's survey showed that 22% of its customers are "Super Heavy Users," meaning that they eat at McDonald's 10 times or more a month. Super Heavy Users make up approximately 75% of McDonald's sales. The survey also found that 72% of McDonald's customers were "Heavy Users," meaning they ate at McDonald's at least once a week.

Jazlyn Bradley consumed McDonald's foods her entire life during school lunch breaks and before and after school, approximately five times per week, ordering two meals per day. When Bradley was 19 years old, she sued McDonald's Corporation for causing her obesity and health problems associated with obesity.

Plaintiff Bradley sued McDonald's in U.S. District Court for violating the New York Consumer Protection Act, which prohibits deceptive and unfair acts and practices. She alleged that McDonald's misled her, through its advertising campaigns and other publicity, that its food products were nutritious, of a beneficial nutritional nature, and easily part of a healthy lifestyle if consumed on a daily basis. The plaintiff sued on behalf of herself and a class of minors residing in New York State who purchased and consumed McDonald's products. McDonald's filed a motion with the U.S. District Court to dismiss the plaintiff's complaint.

Issue

Did the plaintiff state a valid case against McDonald's for deceptive and unfair acts and practices in violation of the New York Consumer Protection Act?

Language of the Court

It is well-known that fast food in general, and McDonald's products in particular, contain high levels of cholesterol, fat, salt and sugar, and that such attributes are bad for one. The plaintiff therefore either knew or should have known enough of the critical facts of her injury that her claims accrued upon being injured. The complaint does specify how often the plaintiff ate at McDonald's. Jazlyn Bradley is alleged to have "consumed McDonald's foods her entire life during school lunch breaks and before and after school, approximately five times per week, ordering two meals per day."

What the plaintiff has not done, however, is to address the role that a number of other factors other than diet may come to play in obesity and the health problems of which the plaintiff complains. In order to allege that McDonald's products were a significant factor in the plaintiff's obesity and health problems, the complaint must address these other variables and, if possible, eliminate them or show that a McDiet is a substantial factor despite these other variables. Similarly, with regards to plaintiff's health problems that she claims resulted from her obesity, it would be necessary to allege that such diseases were not merely hereditary or caused by environmental or other factors. Without this additional information, McDonald's does not have sufficient information to determine if its foods are the cause of the plaintiff's obesity, or if instead McDonald's foods are only a contributing factor.

Decision

The U.S. District Court granted the motion of defendant McDonald's to dismiss the plaintiff's complaint. *Note:* Because of this case and other threatened obesity-related litigation, fast-food franchisors introduced salads, low-fat fare, and low-carb offerings to their menus.

Law & Ethics Questions

1. What is the purpose of consumer protection laws?

2. **ETHICS** Do you think McDonald's has a duty to warn consumers of the dangers of eating its fast food? Do parents owe a duty to their children not to let them eat fast food too often?

3. What would have been the effect on McDonald's and other fast-food companies if the plaintiff had won her lawsuit against McDonald's? Explain.

Web Exercises

1. **WEB** For the complete opinion of this case, go to *www.prenhall.com/cheesemancases*.

2. **WEB** Visit the website of the United States District Court for the Southern District of New York, at *www.nysd.uscourts.gov*.

3. **WEB** Visit the website of McDonald's Corporation, at *www.mcdonalds.com*. Can you find the corporation's code of ethics?

4. **WEB** Use *www.google.com* to find the nutrition facts about BigMacs, French fries, and chocolate shakes.

Amid the controversy around how to handle the country's increasing weight problem, New York City's Board of Health voted unanimously to ban nearly all the artificial trans fats from the city's 24,000 restaurants. This is believed to be the first law of its kind in the nation and could possibly lead to other cities creating similar laws.

Trans fats are the artery-clogging cooking oils that are used in foods such as French fries, donuts, pies, chips, cookies, and even bread. Trans fats are known to dramatically increase the risk of heart disease and stroke, even more than the better-known saturated fats. They do so by raising bad cholesterol while simultaneously lowering good cholesterol. Restaurants were given 18 months to phase out the oils and find safer alternatives.

While health officials and consumers around the country praised the new law, not everyone was happy. Restaurant owners argued that getting rid of trans fats should be on a voluntary basis only and that the government should not force the issue. The National Restaurant Association threatened to sue the city because it feared the law would quickly spread across the nation, putting some restaurants out of business due to the high cost. But New York City's health commissioner, Thomas Frieden, called the matter a public health issue and applauded

the Board of Health decision, saying that the new law could, "save between 200 and 500 lives per year."

Law & Ethics Questions

1. **ETHICS** Do food manufacturers, restaurants, and other food-service businesses owe a duty of social responsibility to warn consumers of dangerous propensities of the food they sell and serve?

2. **ETHICS** Why do food companies use trans fats in their products? Should food companies voluntarily remove all trans fats from their products?

3. **ETHICS** Should New York City have enacted this law? Why or why not?

Web Exercises

1. **WEB USE** *www.google.com* to find an article that discusses the health risks of trans fats.

2. **WEB** To read more about New York City's new law, visit *www.nyc.gov/html/doh/html/cardio/cardio-transfat.shtml.*

Kantian Ethics

Immanuel Kant (1724–1804) is the best-known proponent of **duty ethics**, also called **Kantian ethics**. Kant believed that people owe moral duties that are based on *universal* rules. For example, keeping a promise to abide by a contract is a moral duty even if that contract turns out to be detrimental to the obligated party. Kant's philosophy is based on the premise that people can use reasoning to reach ethical decisions. His ethical theory would have people behave according to the *categorical imperative* "Do unto others as you would have them do unto you."

The universal rules of Kantian ethics are based on two important principles: (1) consistency—that is, all cases are treated alike, with no exceptions—and (2) reversibility—that is, the actor must abide by the rule he or she uses to judge the morality of someone else's conduct. Thus, if you are going to make an exception for yourself, that exception becomes a universal rule that applies to all others. For example, if you rationalize that it is all right for you to engage in deceptive practices, it is all right for competitors to do so also. A criticism of Kantian ethics is that it is hard to reach a consensus as to what the universal rules should be.

In the following case, a company alleged that a competitor had engaged in false advertising.

CASE 8.2	Pizza Hut, Inc. v. Papa John's International, Inc.
Ethics	227 F.3d 489, **Web** 2000 U.S. App. Lexis 23444 (2000) United States Court of Appeals for the Fifth Circuit

"This simple statement, "Better Pizza.," epitomizes the exaggerated advertising, blustering and boasting by a manufacturer upon which no consumer would reasonably rely."

—Judge Jolly

Facts

Papa John's International, Inc., is the third-largest pizza chain in the United States, with more than 2,050 locations. Papa John's adopted a new slogan—"Better Ingredients. Better Pizza."—and applied for and received a federal trademark for this slogan. Papa John's spent over $300 million building customer recognition and goodwill for this slogan. This slogan has appeared on millions of signs, shirts, menus, pizza boxes, napkins, and other items, and it has regularly appeared as the tag line at the end of Papa John's radio and television advertisements.

Pizza Hut, Inc., is the largest pizza chain in the United States, with more than 7,000 restaurants. Two years after Papa John's advertisements began, Pizza Hut launched a new advertising campaign in which it declared "war" on poor-quality pizza. The advertisements touted the "better taste" of Pizza Hut's pizza and "dared" anyone to find a better pizza.

A few weeks later, Papa John's countered with a comparative advertising campaign that touted the superiority of Papa John's pizza over Pizza Hut's pizza. Papa John's claimed it had superior sauce and dough to Pizza Hut. Many of these advertisements were accompanied by the Papa John's slogan "Better Ingredients. Better Pizza."

Pizza Hut filed a civil action in U.S. District Court, charging Papa John's with false advertising in violation of Section 43(a) of the federal Lanham Act. The U.S. District Court found that the Papa John's slogan "Better Ingredients. Better Pizza." standing alone was mere puffery and did not constitute false advertising. The District Court found, however, that Papa John's claims of superior sauce and dough were misleading and that Papa John's slogan "Better Ingredients. Better Pizza." became tainted because it was associated with these misleading statements. The U.S. District Court enjoined Papa John's from using the slogan "Better Ingredients. Better Pizza." Papa John's appealed.

Issue

Is the Papa John's slogan "Better Ingredients. Better Pizza." false advertising?

Language of the Court

Essential to any claim under Section 43(a) of the Lanham Act is a determination whether the challenged statement is one of fact—actionable under Section 43(a)—or one of general opinion—not actionable under Section 43(a). One form of non-actionable statements of general opinion under Section 43(a) of the Lanham Act has been referred to as "puffery." We think that non-actionable "puffery" comes in at least two possible forms: (1) an exaggerated, blustering, and boasting statement upon which no reasonable buyer would be justified in relying; or (2) a general claim of superiority over comparable products that is so vague that it can be understood as nothing more than a mere expression of opinion. Prosser and Keeton on the Law of Torts (5th edition) define "puffing" as "a seller's privilege to lie his head off, so long as he says nothing specific, on the theory that no reasonable man would believe him, or that no reasonable man would be influenced by such talk."

We turn now to consider the case before us. Reduced to its essence, the question is whether the evidence established that Papa John's slogan "Better Ingredients. Better Pizza." is misleading and violative of Section 43(a) of the Lanham Act. Bisecting the slogan "Better Ingredients. Better Pizza.," it is clear that the assertion by Papa John's that it makes a "Better Pizza." is a general statement of opinion regarding the superiority of its product over all others. This simple statement, "Better Pizza.," epitomizes the exaggerated advertising, blustering and boasting by a manufacturer upon which no consumer would reasonably rely. Consequently, it appears indisputable that Papa John's assertion "Better Pizza." is non-actionable puffery.

Moving next to consider the phrase "Better Ingredients," the same conclusion holds true. Like "Better Pizza." it is typical puffery. The word "better," when used in this context, is unquantifiable. What makes one food ingredient "better" than another comparable ingredient, without further description, is wholly a matter of individual taste or preference not subject to scientific quantification. Indeed, it is difficult to think of any product, or any component of any product, to which the term "better," without more quantifiable measurements. Thus, it is equally clear that Papa John's assertion that it uses "Better Ingredients." is one of opinion not actionable under the Lanham Act.

Consequently, the slogan as a whole is a statement of non-actionable opinion. Thus, there is no legally sufficient basis to support the jury's finding that the slogan is a "false or misleading" statement of fact.

Decision

The U.S. Court of Appeals held that the Papa John's trademarked slogan "Better Ingredients. Better Pizza." was mere puffery and a statement of opinion that was not false advertising and did not violate Section 43(a) of the Lanham Act. The U.S. Court of Appeals reversed the judgment of the U.S. District Court and remanded the case to the District Court for entry of judgment for Papa John's.

Law & Ethics Questions

1. What is false advertising? What is puffery? How do they differ from one another?

2. **ETHICS** Do businesses sometimes make exaggerated claims about their products? Are consumers smart enough to see through companies' puffery?

3. If the Court of Appeals had found in favor of Pizza Hut, what would have been the effect on advertising in this country? Explain.

Web Exercises

1. **WEB** For the complete opinion of this case, go to *www.prenhall.com/cheesemancases*.

2. **WEB** Visit the website of the United States Court of Appeals for the Fifth Circuit, at *www.ca5.uscourts.gov*.

3. **WEB** Visit the website of Papa John's International, Inc., at *www.papajohns.com*. Can you find the corporation's code of ethics?

4. **WEB** Visit the website of Pizza Hut, Inc., at *www.pizzahut.com*. Can you find the corporation's code of ethics?

5. **WEB** Use *www.google.com* to find a comparative advertising campaign. How exaggerated are the company's claims in this campaign?

ETHICS SPOTLIGHT

Procter & Gamble Wins "Satanism" Lawsuit

> **"** *The ram's horn will form the number 666, which is known as Satan's number.* **"**
>
> —Amway distributor flier

A U.S. District Court jury found that the Devil is not in cahoots with Procter & Gamble (P&G), the world's largest consumer products company, and rewarded the company $19.25 million in unfair competition and false advertising damages. The verdict concluded a 12-year lawsuit in which P&G had accused four distributors of its rival, Amway Corporation, of propagating rumors that P&G was involved in Satanism and that the president of P&G had gone on national television to announce that a large portion of P&G profits would go to support the Church of Satan.

Procter & Gamble, the maker of such household names as Tide and Pampers, claimed in court documents that four Amway distributors had told customers that P&G's logo—which featured a bearded man looking over a field of 13 stars—was a symbol of Satan. P&G lawyers also produced a transcript of a voice mail message in which an Amway distributor could be heard alleging that the P&G president had avowed his personal allegiance to Satan on the *Phil Donahue* show, a nationally televised talk show. Other damaging evidence in trial was a written flier that spread like wildfire through mail, fax, and later e-mail that listed all of P&G's products and gave supposed details on the company's undying love for the Prince of Darkness. According to an Amway distributor flier:

> If you are not sure about the product, look for Procter & Gamble written on the products, or the symbol of a ram's horn, which will appear on each product beginning in April. The ram's horn will form the number 666, which is known as Satan's number.

The case was originally dismissed by a three-judge panel of the U.S. Circuit Court of Appeals, who proclaimed that the rumors were not defamatory and that P&G had not made a case for specific damages. However, P&G successfully got the case reinstated through further appeals. "This is about protecting our reputation," said Jim Johnson, P&G's chief legal officer. Amway, which focuses on direct selling through independent business owners, claimed that it acted quickly and thoroughly to stop the rumors, and the company was subsequently dismissed from the case, leaving only the four ex-distributors. "We are stunned. All of us," replied one of the distributors after the trial.

Law & Ethics Questions

1. **ETHICS** What is false advertising?

2. **ETHICS** Why did the Amway distributors make the claims about P&G that they did?

Web Exercises

1. **WEB** Visit the website of Proctor & Gamble, at *www.pg.com*. Locate P&G's logo.

2. **WEB** Visit the website of Amway Corporation, at *www.amway.com*. Can you find this corporation's code of ethics?

3. **WEB** Use *www.google.com* to find a recent article or website that criticizes P&G for Satanism.

Rawls's Social Justice Theory

John Locke (1632–1704) and Jean-Jacques Rousseau (1712–1778) proposed a **social contract** theory of morality. Under this theory, each person is presumed to have entered into a social contract with all others in society to obey moral rules that are necessary for people to live in peace and harmony. This implied contract states, "I will keep the rules if everyone else does." These moral rules are then used to solve conflicting interests in society.

The leading proponent of the modern justice theory is John Rawls, a contemporary philosopher at Harvard University. Under **Rawls's social justice theory**, fairness is considered the essence of justice. The principles of justice should be chosen by persons who do not yet know their station in society—thus, their "veil of ignorance" would permit the fairest possible principles to be selected. For example, the principle of equal opportunity would be promulgated by people who would not yet know if they were in a favored class. As a caveat, Rawls also propose that the least advantaged in society must receive special assistance to allow them to realize their potential.

Rawls's theory of social justice is criticized for two reasons. First, establishing the blind "original position" for choosing moral principles is impossible in the real world.

> The notion that a business is clothed with a public interest and has been devoted to the public use is little more than a fiction intended to beautify what is disagreeable to the sufferers.
>
> Justice Holmes
> *Tyson & Bro-United Theatre Ticket Officers v. Banton (1927)*

Second, many persons in society would choose not to maximize the benefit to the least advantaged persons in society.

In the following case, the U.S. Supreme Court examined the legality of giving gifts to politicians.

CASE 8.3
Ethics

U.S. SUPREME COURT
United States v. Sun-Diamond Growers of California
526 U.S. 398, 119 S.Ct. 1402, 143 L.Ed.2d 576,
Web 1999 U.S. Lexis 3001
Supreme Court of the United States

> "*The Solicitor General of the United States contends that the statute requires only a showing that a gift was motivated, at least in part, by the recipient's capacity to exercise governmental power or influence in the donor's favor without necessarily showing that it was connected to a particular official act.*"
>
> —Justice Scalia

Facts

The Sun-Diamond Growers of California is a trade association that engages in marketing and lobbying activities on behalf of its 5,000 member-growers of raisins, figs, walnuts, prunes, and hazelnuts. Sun-Diamond gave Michael Epsy, U.S. secretary of agriculture, tickets to sporting events (worth $2,295), luggage ($2,427), meals ($665), and a crystal bowl ($524) while several matters in which Sun-Diamond members had an interest in were pending before the secretary. The two matters were decided in Sun-Diamond's favor. The United States sued Sun-Diamond for making illegal gifts to a public official in violation of the federal antibribery and gratuity statute [18 U.S.C. Sections 201(b) and 201(c)]. The jury convicted Sun-Diamond, and the U.S. District Court ordered it to pay a fine of $400,000. The U.S. Court of Appeals reversed, finding that Sun-Diamond had not violated the federal antibribery and gratuity statute. The United States appealed to the U.S. Supreme Court.

Issue

Does a conviction under the federal antibribery and gratuity statute require a showing of a direct nexus between the value conferred on the public official and the official act performed by the public official in favor of the giver?

Language of the U.S. Supreme Court

The Solicitor General of the United States contends that the statute requires only a showing that a gift was motivated, at least in part, by the recipient's capacity to exercise governmental power or influence in the donor's favor without necessarily showing that it was connected to a particular official act. We are inclined to believe this meaning incorrect because of the peculiar results that the government's reading would produce. It would criminalize, for example, token gifts to the President based on his official position and not linked to any identifiable act—such as the replica jerseys given by championship sports teams each year during ceremonial White House visits. Similarly, it would criminalize a high school principal's gift of a school baseball cap to the secretary of education, by reason of his office, on the occasion of the latter's visit to the school.

Decision

The U.S. Supreme Court held that there must be proof of a direct nexus between the gratuity given and the public official's act before the federal antibribery and gratuity statute is violated. Because no such direct nexus was proven in this case, there is no violation of the federal antibribery and gratuity statute. The U.S. Supreme Court affirmed the judgment of the U.S. Court of Appeals that found that Sun-Diamond had not violated the federal antibribery and gratuity statute.

Law & Ethics Questions

1. What does the federal antibribery and gratuity statute prohibit? Explain.
2. Do you think the Supreme Court should have read the statute so narrowly? Why or why not?
3. **ETHICS** Is it ethical for a government official to accept gifts and gratuities from parties who have actions or matters pending before the official? Do you think such gifts and gratuities are given with any return favor in mind?
4. **ETHICS** What is lobbying? Are there any winners and losers of successful lobbying? Explain.

Web Exercises

1. **WEB** For the complete opinion of this case, go to *www.prenhall.com/cheesemancases*.
2. **WEB** Visit the website of the U.S. Supreme Court, at *www.supremecourtus.gov*, and try to find documents that relate to this case.

3. **WEB** Use *www.google.com* to find an article that discusses a lobbying effort to get a new law enacted or one deleted. Who was the group lobbying for the law? Did it get the result it wanted?

Ethical Relativism

Ethical relativism holds that individuals must decide what is ethical based on their own feelings as to what is right or wrong. Under this moral theory, if a person meets his or her own moral standard in making a decision, no one can criticize him or her for it. Thus, there are no universal ethical rules to guide a person's conduct. This theory has been criticized because action that is usually thought to be unethical (e.g., committing fraud) would not be unethical if the perpetrator thought it was in fact ethical. Few philosophers advocate ethical relativism as an acceptable moral theory.

ETHICS SPOTLIGHT

Disney Losses "Pooh Bear" Lawsuit

For years, the Walt Disney Company had battled a Beverly Hills family over millions of dollars in Winnie the Pooh royalties. In early 2007, a federal judge dismissed Disney's lawsuit, essentially clearing the way for the family to seek its own lawsuit for lost profits and damages. The ruling was a major turning point in the legal copyright drama that has spanned decades.

In 1930, Stephen Slesinger, a cartoon character marketer, had acquired the rights to "Winnie the Pooh" merchandise from the author A.A. Milne. When Slesinger died in 1953, Shirley Slesinger, his widow, continued to market Pooh by herself. In 1961, the Slesingers dealt the Pooh rights to Disney in exchange for continuous royalty payments. Disney used its marketing might to turn the bear into its most profitable cartoon character, pulling in over $1 billion a year. In 1983, Mrs. Slesinger renegotiated the deal with Disney, agreeing that Disney would keep 98% of gross worldwide royalties and that the Slesingers would get the other 2%. Today, Disney makes over $6 billion annually from Winnie the Pooh sales and licensing.

One decade after granting Disney the Pooh rights, the Slesingers slapped Disney with a fraud and breach-of-contract lawsuit, alleging that the media giant had been cheating them out of hundreds of millions in profits from Pooh products. Specifically, the family accused Disney of failing to report Winnie the Pooh computer software and video sales of $3 billion, which would have brought the family tens of millions in royalties. The court appointed a task force of so-called forensic accountants to examine Disney's books, but before the court could rule, Disney produced evidence that the Slesingers had stolen confidential documents from the company's trash, lied about it, and altered court filings to cover it up. The judge dismissed the lawsuit with prejudice.

Disney wasn't finished, however. In 2002, the families of Pooh author A.A. Milne and illustrator E.H. Shepard filed a copyright lawsuit against the Slesingers which was funded by Walt Disney Co. The lawsuit sought to get all of the Pooh rights removed from the Slesingers and given to the other families, which in turn would revert them to Disney permanently. Disney hoped this would stop all royalty payments to the Slesingers and end the family's pending appeal for lost profits and damages. Unfortunately for Disney, that didn't happen.

In February 2007, U.S. District Court Judge Florence-Marie Cooper dismissed the Disney-sponsored lawsuit against the Slesingers. The Slesinger family immediately launched a $2 billion lawsuit against the company for damages, trademark and copyright infringement, breach of contract, and fraudulent underpayment of royalties. The long legal battle over Pooh is not yet over.

Law & Ethics Questions

1. What are royalty payments?
2. **ETHICS** How could the Slesinger family determine if Disney had been cheating them out of royalties over the years?

Web Exercises

1. **WEB** Visit the website of the Walt Disney Company, at *www.disney.com*.
2. **WEB** Find out all about Winnie the Pooh at *http://disney.go.com/characters/pooh/index.html*.

CONCEPT SUMMARY

Theories of Ethics

THEORY	DESCRIPTION
Ethical fundamentalism	Persons look to an outside source (e.g., the Bible, the Koran) or a central figure for ethical guidelines.
Utilitarianism	Persons choose the alternative that would provide the greatest good to society.
Kantian ethics	A set of universal rules establishes ethical duties. The rules are based on reasoning and require (1) consistency in application and (2) reversibility.
Rawls's social justice theory	Moral duties are based on an implied social contract. Fairness is justice. The rules are established from an original position of a "veil of ignorance."
Ethical relativism	Individuals decide what is ethical based on their own feelings as to what is right or wrong.

Vietnam

Many U.S. multinational corporations "outsource" the manufacture of goods to workers in foreign countries. The goods are then imported into the United States and sold to consumers. Are there any ethical problems with this practice?

The ultimate justification of the law is to be found, and can only be found, in moral considerations.

Lord Macmillan
Law and Other Things (1937)

Social Responsibility of Business

Businesses do not operate in a vacuum. Decisions made by businesses have far-reaching effects on society. In the past, many business decisions were based solely on a cost–benefit analysis and how they affected the "bottom line." Such decisions, however, may cause negative externalities for others. For example, the dumping of hazardous wastes from a manufacturing plant into a river affects the homeowners, farmers, and others who use the river's waters. Thus, corporations are considered to owe some degree of **social responsibility** for their actions. Four theories of the social responsibility of business are discussed in the following paragraphs.

Maximizing Profits

The traditional view of the social responsibility of business is that business should **maximize profits** for shareholders. This view, which dominated business and the law during the nineteenth century, holds that the interests of other constituencies (e.g., employees, suppliers, residents of the communities in which businesses are located) are not important in and of themselves.

In the famous case *Dodge v. Ford Motor Company*,[1] a shareholder sued the car company when Henry Ford introduced a plan to reduce the prices of cars so that more people would be put to work and more people could own cars. The shareholders alleged that such a plan would not increase dividends. Mr. Ford testified, "My ambition is to employ still more men, to spread the benefits of this industrial system to the greatest number, to help them build up their lives and their homes." The court sided with the shareholders and stated that:

> [Mr. Ford's] testimony creates the impression that he thinks the Ford Motor company has made too much money, has had too large profits and that, although large profits might still be earned, a sharing of them with the public, by reducing the price of the output of the company, ought to be undertaken.

> There should be no confusion of the duties which Mr. Ford conceives that he and the stockholders owe to the general public and the duties which in law he and his codirectors owe to protesting, minority stockholders. A business corporation is organized and carried on primarily for the profit of the stockholders. The powers of the directors are to be employed for that end. The discretion of directors is to be exercised in the choice of means to attain that end and does not extend to a change in the end itself, to the reduction of profits, or to the nondistribution of profits among stockholders in order to devote them to other purposes.

> Public policy: That principle of the law which holds that no subject can lawfully do that which has a tendency to be injurious to the public or against the public good.
>
> Lord Truro
> *Egerton v. Brownlow (1853)*

Milton Friedman, who won the Nobel Prize in economics when he taught at the University of Chicago, advocated this theory. Friedman asserted that in a free society, "there is one and only one social responsibility of business—to use its resources and engage in activities designed to increase its profits as long as it stays within the rules of the game, which is to say, engages in open and free competition without deception and fraud."[2]

In the following case, one company was accused of knocking off another company's product design.

CASE 8.4
Business Ethics

U.S. SUPREME COURT
Wal-Mart Stores, Inc. v. Samara Brothers, Inc.
529 U.S. 205, 120 S.Ct. 1339, 146 L.Ed.2d 182,
Web 2000 U.S. Lexis 2197 (2000)
Supreme Court of the United States

> "*Their suspicions aroused, however, Samara officials launched an investigation, which disclosed that Wal-Mart [was] selling the knockoffs of Samara's outfits.*"
>
> —Justice Scalia

Facts

Samara Brothers, Inc. (Samara), is a designer and manufacturer of children's clothing. The core of Samara's business is its annual new line of spring and summer children's garments. Samara sold its clothing to retailers, who in turn sold the clothes to consumers. Wal-Mart Stores, Inc. (Wal-Mart), operates a large chain of budget warehouse stores that sell thousands of items at very low prices. Wal-Mart contacted one of its suppliers, Judy-Philippine, Inc. (JPI), about the possibility of making a line of children's clothes just like Samara's successful line. Wal-Mart sent photographs of Samara's children's clothes to JPI (the name "Samara" was readily discernible on the labels of the garments) and directed JPI to produce children's clothes exactly like those in the photographs. JPI produced a line of children's clothes for Wal-Mart that copied the designs,

colors, and patterns of Samara's clothing. Wal-Mart then sold this line of children's clothing in its stores, making a gross profit of over $1.15 million on these clothes sales during the 1996 selling season.

Samara discovered that Wal-Mart was selling the knockoff clothes at a price that was lower than Samara's retailers were paying Samara for its clothes. After sending unsuccessful cease-and-desist letters to Wal-Mart, Samara sued Wal-Mart, alleging that Wal-Mart stole Samara's trade dress (i.e., look and feel) in violation of Section 43(a) of the Lanham Act. Although not finding that Samara's clothes had acquired a *secondary meaning* in the minds of the public, the U.S. District Court held in favor of Samara and awarded damages. The U.S. Court of Appeals affirmed the award to Samara. Wal-Mart appealed to the U.S. Supreme Court.

Issue

Must a product's design have acquired a secondary meaning before it is protected as trade dress?

Language of the U.S. Supreme Court

The Lanham Act, in Section 43(a), gives a producer a cause of action for the use by any person of "any word, term, name, symbol, or device, or any combination thereof which is likely to cause confusion as to the origin, sponsorship, or approval of his or her goods." The text of Section 43(a) provides little guidance as to the circumstances under which unregistered trade dress may be protected. It does require that a producer show that the allegedly infringing feature is likely to cause confusion with the product for which protection is sought. In an action for infringement of unregistered trade dress a product's design is protectable only upon a showing of secondary meaning.

Decision

The U.S. Supreme Court held that a product's design has to have acquired a secondary meaning in the public's eye before it is protected as trade dress under Section 43(a) of the Lanham Act. The Supreme Court reversed the decision of the U.S. Court of Appeals and remanded the case for further proceedings consistent with its opinion.

Law & Ethics Questions

1. What is trade dress? Should it have been protected in this case?
2. **ETHICS** Even though Wal-Mart's conduct was ruled legal, was it ethical?
3. Before reading this case, had you heard or read about Samara's children's clothing?

Web Exercises

1. **WEB** For the complete opinion of this case, go to *www.prenhall.com/cheesemancases*.
2. **WEB** Visit the website of the Supreme Court of the United States, at *www.supremecourtus.gov*, and try to find documents that relate to this case.
3. **WEB** Visit the website of Wal-Mart, at *www.walmart.com*. Can you find the corporation's code of ethics?
4. **WEB** Use *www.google.com* to find a recent article about another legal dispute that Wal-Mart is currently engaged in.

ETHICS SPOTLIGHT

Student Loan Scandal Comes to Light

> **❝** *Loan decisions should be made in the best interest of the students and not the best interest of the school.* **❞**
>
> —Andrew Cuomo, New York Attorney General

Sallie Mae, the largest U.S. student-loan provider, has agreed to pay $2 million and alter its business practices after being caught up in an ever-widening scandal. New York Attorney General Andrew Cuomo, who is spearheading the investigation into the $85 billion student loan industry, said he has found numerous deceptive practices that benefit lenders and colleges at the expense of students.

Some of the arrangements Cuomo's office have investigated include revenue sharing between school employees and lenders, kickbacks to school officials who steer students toward certain lenders, and paid trips to exotic locations for school financial aid officers who direct students to "preferred lenders." Some college officials were fired after Cuomo's office accused them of receiving stock or consulting fees from student loan lenders.

Sallie Mae has also agreed to stop offering perks to college employees and to adopt a code of conduct created by Cuomo. The new code is aimed at making the loan process more transparent. It prohibits revenue sharing between schools and lenders, sets restrictions on how lenders are chosen to be preferred lenders, insists on full disclosure of the relationship between lenders and schools, and bans gifts and trips from lenders to college employees.

"The $2 million," Cuomo said, "will be paid into a fund to help educate college-bound students and their parents on financial aid issues."

Sallie Mae is not alone. So far, six colleges in the New York area, including New York University and Syracuse University, have agreed to reimburse students millions of dollars' worth of inflated loan prices, due to the revenue-sharing agreements with lenders. The probe is just beginning, as Sallie Mae alone has relationships with more than 5,600 colleges throughout the nation and serves nearly 10 million borrowers.

Law & Ethics Questions

1. **ETHICS** Did Sallie Mae act ethically in giving bribes to college loan officers for steering student loan business its way? Why do you think Sallie Mae did this?
2. **ETHICS** Did the college administrators act ethically in accepting "perks" from student lenders? Should these college administrators be fired?
3. Do you have a student loan? Are you concerned that you may not have gotten the best loan terms you could have?

Web Exercises

1. **WEB** Visit the website of Sallie Mae, at *www.salliemae.com*.
2. **WEB** Visit the website of the New York Attorney General's Office, at *www.oag.state.ny.us*.

Moral Minimum

Some proponents of corporate social responsibility argue that a corporation's duty is to *make a profit while avoiding causing harm to others*. This theory of social responsibility is called the **moral minimum**. Under this theory, as long as business avoids or corrects the social injury it causes, it has met its duty of social responsibility.

Example A corporation that pollutes the waters and then compensates those whom it injures has met its moral minimum duty of social responsibility.

The legislative and judicial branches of government have established laws that enforce the moral minimum of social responsibility on corporations. For example, occupational safety laws establish minimum safety standards for protecting employees from injuries in the workplace. Consumer protection laws establish safety requirements for products and make manufacturers and sellers liable for injuries caused by defective products. Other laws establish similar minimum standards for conduct for business in other areas.

ETHICS SPOTLIGHT

Media Giant Pays for Bomb Scare

❝ *It's all about corporate greed.* **❞**

—Thomas Menino, Mayor of Boston, Massachusetts

On January 31, 2006, Boston, Massachusetts went in panic mode as multiple 911 calls were made, reporting suspicious blinking bomb-like structures attached to a subway station, a hospital, Fenway Park baseball stadium, and other high-profile spots. Local, state, and federal authorities shut down a university, bridges, and highways. The Department of Homeland Security and the U.S. Northern Command began monitoring the situation.

What authorities found was 38 blinking electronic signs with duct-tape wrapped around a package and black wires protruding from the back, but these weren't bombs. Instead, they were box-like cartoon characters giving an obscene gesture, paid for by one of the country's biggest media giants—Time Warner.

The entire debacle was part of a marketing campaign by Time Warner subsidiaries Turner Broadcasting Systems (TBS), the Cartoon Network, and Adult Swim. The campaign was part of a nationwide guerrilla marketing effort to promote the network's cartoon "Aqua Teen Hunger Force."

Not long after the devices were found, authorities arrested two men for installing the boxes and charged them with the placing of a hoax device and disorderly conduct. The men were traced back to Interference, Inc., a New York City marketing firm that Time Warner had hired to conduct the campaign. Boston's proximity to the terrorist attacks of 9/11 made it particularly sensitive to perceived threats.

After learning that the devices were part of a publicity stunt, local politicians blasted those involved. Massachusetts Attorney General Martha Coakley, Mayor Thomas Menino, and others threatened criminal charges and a civil suit. Menino told reporters, "I just think this is outrageous, what they've done. It's all about corporate greed."

Within days, all corporate parties issued public apologies, with TBS and Interference agreeing to pay $2 million in compensation for the emergency response. Officials said $1 million will be used to reimburse the agencies that dealt with the incident and the other half will go toward homeland security. The agreement also resolved any potential civil or criminal claims against the companies.

Law & Ethics Questions

1. Was this a very smart advertising campaign?
2. **ETHICS** Should TBS have been punished more harshly for its actions?

Web Exercises

1. **WEB** Visit the website of Time Warner, at *www.timewarner.com*.
2. **WEB** Visit *www.interferenceinc.com*, the website of the marketing firm that developed this hoax.
3. **WEB** Go to *www.adultswim.com/shows/athf* to view the "Aqua Teen Hunger Force" characters.

Stakeholder Interest

Businesses have relationships with all sorts of people besides their stockholders, including employees, suppliers, customers, creditors, and the local community. Under the **stakeholder interest** theory of social responsibility, a corporation must consider the effects its actions have on these *other stakeholders*. For example, a corporation would violate the stakeholder interest theory if it viewed employees solely as a means of maximizing stockholder wealth.

The stakeholder interest theory is criticized because it is difficult to harmonize the conflicting interests of stakeholders. For example, in closing a plant, certain stakeholders may benefit (e.g., stockholders and creditors) while other stakeholders may not (e.g., current employees and the local community).

BUSINESS ETHICS
State Farm: Not Such a Good Neighbor

> **❝** *The punitive award of $ 145 million, therefore, was neither reasonable nor proportionate to the wrong committed, and it was an irrational and arbitrary deprivation of the property of the defendant.* **❞**

—Justice Kennedy

Curtis Campbell was driving with his wife in Utah when he decided to pass six vans traveling ahead of him on a two-lane highway. Todd Ospital, who was driving on the opposite side of the road toward Campbell, swerved to avoid a collision with Campbell and collided with an automobile driven by Robert Slusher. Ospital was killed; Slusher was rendered permanently disabled; the Campbells escaped unscathed. Early investigations determined that Campbell made an unsafe pass and had caused the crash. Ospital's heirs and Slusher sued Campbell for wrongful death and injuries, respectively. Campbell's insurance company, State Farm Mutual Automobile Insurance Company (State Farm) declined offers by Ospital's estate and Slusher to settle their claims for the insurance policy limit of $50,000 and took the case to trial. The jury determined that Campbell was 100 percent at fault and returned a judgment for $185,000.

Campbell reached a settlement with Ospital's and Slusher's attorneys whereby Campbell agreed to pursue a bad faith tort action against State Farm, and Ospital's estate and Slusher would receive 90 percent of any verdict against State Farm. One and one-half years after the initial judgment, State Farm paid all of the $185,000 judgment against Campbell, even though it exceeded the $50,000 policy limit.

State Farm has consistently used the advertising slogan "Like a good neighbor, State Farm is there." The plaintiffs did not think so, and their bad faith tort case went to trial against State Farm in a Utah trial court. At trial, evidence was introduced that State Farm had a policy to take many cases to trial even though they could be settled within the insurance policy limits. The jury held against State Farm and awarded Campbell $2.6 million in compensatory damages and $145 million in punitive damages. The trial court judge reduced the compensatory damages to $1 million and punitive damages to $25 million. The Utah supreme court reinstated the $145 million punitive damages award. State Farm appealed to the U.S. Supreme Court.

The issue on appeal was whether an award of $145 million in punitive damages, where compensatory damages were $1 million, was excessive and a violation of the Due Process Clause of the Fourteenth Amendment to the Constitution of the United States.

The U.S. Supreme Court noted that while states possess discretion over the imposition of punitive damages, it is well established that there are procedural and substantive constitutional limitations on these awards. The Due Process Clause of the Fourteenth Amendment prohibits the imposition of grossly excessive or arbitrary punishments on a tortfeasor. The U.S. Supreme Court held that this case was neither close nor difficult: It was an error to reinstate the jury's $145 million punitive damages award.

The U.S. Supreme Court stated that this case was used as a platform to expose and punish the perceived deficiencies of State Farm's operations throughout the country. The Utah supreme court's opinion makes explicit that State Farm was being condemned for its nationwide policies rather than for the conduct directed toward the Campbells. The Utah court awarded punitive damages to punish and deter conduct that bore no relation to the Campbells' harm. The U.S. Supreme Court held that a defendant's dissimilar acts, independent from the acts on which liability was premised, may not serve as the basis for punitive damages. A defendant should be punished for the conduct that harmed the plaintiff, not for being an unsavory individual or business. The Court concluded that due process does not permit courts, in the calculation of punitive damages, to adjudicate the merits of other parties' hypothetical claims against a defendant, under the guise of the reprehensibility analysis.

The U.S. Supreme Court stated that few awards exceeding a single-digit ratio between punitive and compensatory damages, to a significant degree, will satisfy due process. The Supreme Court noted that single-digit multiples are more likely to comport with due process, while still achieving the state's goals of deterrence and retribution, than awards with ratios in the range of 500 to 1, or, in this case, 145 to 1. The Supreme Court concluded that there may be a few cases in which particularly egregious conduct could justify a larger ratio of punitive damages to economic damage.

The U.S. Supreme Court held that an award of $145 million in punitive damages where compensatory damages were $1 million was excessive and violated the Due Process Clause of the Fourteenth Amendment to the U.S. Constitution. The Supreme Court stated, "The punitive award of $145 million, therefore, was neither reasonable nor proportionate to the wrong committed, and it was an irrational and arbitrary deprivation of the property of the defendant." The U.S.

Supreme Court reversed the decision of the Utah supreme court and remanded the case for proceedings consistent with the U.S. Supreme Court's opinion. *State Farm Mutual Automobile Insurance Company v. Campbell*, 538 U.S. 408, 123 S.Ct. 1513, 155 L.Ed.2d 585, **Web** 2003 U.S. Lexis 2714 (Supreme Court of the United States, 2003)

Law & Ethics Questions

1. **ETHICS** What is the purpose of punitive damages? Why are they awarded?

2. What is the protection afforded by the Due Process Clause? Explain.

3. **ETHICS** Did Campbell act ethically in this case?

4. **ETHICS** Did State Farm act ethically in this case?

Web Exercises

1. **WEB** For the complete opinion of this case, go to *www.prenhall.com/cheesemancases*.

2. **WEB** Visit the website of the Supreme Court of the United States, at *www.supremecourtus.gov*, and try to find documents that relate to this case.

3. **WEB** Visit the website of State Farm Insurance, at *www.statefarm.com*. Can you find the corporation's code of ethics?

Corporate Citizenship

The **corporate citizenship** theory of social responsibility argues that business has a responsibility to do well. That is, business is responsible for helping to solve social problems that it did little, if anything, to cause. For example, under this theory, corporations owe a duty to subsidize schools and help educate children.

This theory contends that corporations owe a duty to promote the same social goals as do individual members of society. Proponents of this "do good" theory argue that corporations owe a debt to society to make it a better place and that this duty arises because of the social power bestowed on them. That is, this social power is a gift from society and should be used to good ends.

A major criticism of this theory is that the duty of a corporation to do good cannot be expanded beyond certain limits. There is always some social problem that needs to be addressed, and corporate funds are limited. Further, if this theory were taken to its maximum limit, potential shareholders might be reluctant to invest in corporations.

CONCEPT SUMMARY

Theories of Social Responsibility

THEORY	SOCIAL RESPONSIBILITY
Maximizing profits	To maximize profits for stockholders.
Moral minimum	To avoid causing harm and to compensate for harm caused.
Stakeholder interest	To consider the interests of all stakeholders, including stockholders, employees, customers, suppliers, creditors, and the local community.
Corporate citizenship	To do well and solve social problems.

ETHICS SPOTLIGHT

Sarbanes-Oxley Act Prompts Public Companies to Adopt Codes of Ethics

In the late 1990s and early 2000s, many large corporations in the United States were found to have engaged in massive financial frauds. Many of these frauds were perpetrated by the chief executive officers and other senior officers of the companies. Financial officers, such as chief financial officers and controllers, were also found to have been instrumental in committing these frauds. In response, Congress enacted the **Sarbanes-Oxley Act** of 2002, which makes certain conduct illegal and establishes criminal penalties for violations. In addition, the Sarbanes-Oxley Act prompts companies to encourage senior officers of public companies to act ethically in their dealings with shareholders, employees, and other constituents.

Section 406 of the Sarbanes-Oxley Act requires a public company to disclose whether it has adopted a **code of ethics** for senior financial officers, including its principal financial officer and principal accounting officer. In response, public companies have adopted codes of ethics for their senior financial officers. Many public companies have included all officers and employees in the coverage of their codes of ethics.

A typical code of ethics is illustrated in Exhibit 8.2.

Law & Ethics Questions

1. Do you think the Sarbanes-Oxley Act will be effective in promoting ethical conduct by officers and directors? Explain.

2. **ETHICS** Can ethics be mandated? In other words, will crooks still be crooks?

EXHIBIT 8.2

Code of Ethics

Big Cheese Corporation
Code of Ethics

Big Cheese Corporation's mission includes the promotion of professional conduct in the practice of general management worldwide. Big Cheese's Chief Executive Officer (CEO), Chief Financial Officer (CFO), corporate Controller, and other employees of the finance organization and other employees of the corporation hold an important and elevated role in the corporate governance of the corporation. They are empowered and uniquely capable to ensure that all constituents' interests are appropriately balanced, protected, and preserved.

This Code of Ethics embodies principles to which we are expected to adhere and advocate. The CEO, CFO, finance organization employees, and other employees of the corporation are expected to abide by this Code of Ethics and all business conduct standards of the corporation relating to areas covered by this Code of Ethics. Any violation of the Code of Ethics may result in disciplinary action, up to and including termination of employment. All employees will:

- Act with honesty and integrity, avoiding actual or apparent conflicts of interest in their personal and professional relations.
- Provide stakeholders with information that is accurate, fair, complete, timely, objective, relevant, and understandable, including in our filings with and other submissions to the U.S. Securities and Exchange Commission.
- Comply with rules and regulations of federal, state, provincial, and local governments and other appropriate private and public regulatory agencies.
- Act in good faith, responsibly, with due care, competence, and diligence, without misrepresenting materials facts or allowing one's independent judgment to be subordinated.
- Respect the confidentiality of information acquired in the course of one's work, except when authorized or otherwise legally obligated to disclose. Confidential information acquired in the course of one's work will not be used for personal advantage.
- Share knowledge and maintain professional skills important and relevant to stakeholders' needs.
- Proactively promote and be an example of ethical behavior as a responsible partner among peers, in the work environment and the community.
- Achieve responsible use, control, and stewardship over all Big Cheese's assets and resources that are employed or entrusted to us.
- Not unduly or fraudulently influence, coerce, manipulate, or mislead any authorized audit or interfere with any auditor engaged in the performance of an internal or independent audit of Big Cheese's financial statements or accounting books and records.

If you are aware of any suspected or known violations of this Code of Ethics or other Big Cheese policies or guidelines, you have a duty to promptly report such concerns either to your manager, another responsible member of management, a Human Resources representative, or the Director of Compliance or the 24-hour Business Conduct Line.

If you have a concern about a questionable accounting or auditing matter and wish to submit the concern confidentially or anonymously, you may do so by sending an e-mail to (bc.codeofethics@bigcheese.cc) or calling the Business Conduct Line 24-hour number at 1-888-666-BIGC (2442).

Big Cheese will handle all inquiries discretely and make every effort to maintain, within the limits allowed by law, the confidentiality of anyone requesting guidance or reporting questionable behavior and/or a compliance concern.

It is Big Cheese's intention that this Code of Ethics to be its written code of ethics under Section 406 of the Sarbanes-Oxley Act of 2002 complying with the standards set forth in Securities and Exchange Commission Regulation S-K Item 406.

ETHICS SPOTLIGHT

The Corporate Social Audit

It has been suggested that corporate audits should be extended to include not only audits of the financial health of a corporation but also of its moral health. It is expected that corporations that conduct **corporate social audits** would be more apt to prevent unethical and illegal conduct by managers, employees, and agents. The audit would examine how well employees have adhered to the company's code of ethics and how well the corporation has met its duty of social responsibility.

Such audits would focus on the corporation's efforts to promote employment opportunities for members of protected classes, worker safety, environmental protection, consumer protection, and the like. Social audits are not easy. First, it may be difficult to conceptualize just what is being audited. Second, it may be difficult to measure results. Despite these factors, a growing number of companies are expected to undertake social audits.

Companies should institute the following procedures when conducting a social audit:

- An independent outside firm should be hired to conduct the audit. This ensures autonomy and objectivity in conducting the audit.

- The company's personnel should cooperate fully with the auditing firm while the audit is being conducted.

- The auditing firm should report its findings directly to the company's board of directors.

- The results of the audit should be reviewed by the board of directors.

- The board of directors should determine how the company can better meet its duty of social responsibility and can use the audit to implement a program to correct any deficiencies it finds.

Law & Ethics Questions

1. What is a corporate social audit? What purpose would such an audit serve?

2. **ETHICS** Would a corporate social audit encourage more ethical behavior by corporate officers and employees?

Web Exercises

1. **WEB** Go to *www.thecoca-colacompany.com/citizenship/ index.html*. Pick out several categories that interest you and read how the Coca-Cola Company is helping in that area.

2. **WEB** Pick out a company that interests you. Use *www.google.com* to find the code of ethics of that company.

The actions of transnational corporations impact everything from local and global economies to human rights and labor laws. In the 1970s the United Nations recognized this important and increasing role of transnational corporations in the world and as a result began a committee to draft the **United Nations Code of Conduct for Transnational Corporations**.

INTERNATIONAL LAW

United Nations Code of Conduct for Transnational Corporations

Respect for National Sovereignty

Transnational corporations shall respect the national sovereignty of the countries in which they operate and the right of each state to exercise its permanent sovereignty over its natural wealth and resources.

Transnational corporations should carry out their activities in conformity with the development policies, objectives, and priorities set out by the governments of the countries in which they operate and work seriously toward making a positive contribution to the achievement of such goals at the national and, as appropriate, the regional level, with the framework of regional integration programs. Transnational corporations should cooperate with the governments of the countries in which they operate, with a view to contributing to the development process and should be responsible to requests for consultation in this respect, thereby establishing mutually beneficial relations with these countries.

Adherence to Sociocultural Objectives and Values

Transnational corporations should respect the social and cultural objectives, values, and traditions of the countries in which they operate. While economic and technological development is normally accompanied by social change, transnational corporations should avoid practices, products, or services that cause detrimental effects on cultural patterns and sociocultural objectives, as determined by governments. For this purpose, transnational corporations should respond positively to requests for consultations from governments concerned.

Respect for Human Rights and Fundamental Freedoms

Transnational corporations shall respect human rights and fundamental freedoms in the countries in which they operate. In their social and industrial relations, transnational corporations shall not discriminate on the basis of race, color, sex, religion, language, social, national and ethnic origin, or political or other opinion. Transnational corporations shall conform to government policies designed to extend quality of opportunity and treatment.

Abstention from Corrupt Practices

Transnational corporations shall refrain, in their transactions, from the offering, promising, or giving of any payment, gift, or other advantage to or for the benefit of a public official as consideration for performing or refraining from the performance of his duties in connection with those transactions.

Law & Ethics Questions

1. Do the rules of ethics vary from country to country? Explain.

2. **ETHICS** Should a multinational corporation refuse to engage in bribery or other corrupt practices even if such behavior is common in its industry or the country in which it is operating?

Louang-Phrabang, Laos

The local customs of a country should be honored when conducting business in that country.

Chapter Summary

Ethics and the Law, p. 217

Ethics is a set of moral principles on values that governs the conduct of an individual or a group.

Business Ethics, p. 218

A number of moral theories have been applied to business ethics.

Ethical Fundamentalism

Under the moral theory of ethical fundamentalism, persons look to an outside source (e.g., Bible, Koran) or a central figure to set ethical guidelines.

Utilitarianism

Under the moral theory of utilitarianism, persons choose the alternative that would provide the greatest good to society.

Kantian Ethics

Under the moral theory of Kantian ethics, also called duty ethics, a set of universal rules establishes ethical duties. The rules are based on reasoning and require (1) consistency in application and (2) reversibility.

Rawls's Social Justice Theory

Under Rawls's social justice theory, moral duties are based on an implied social contract. Fairness is justice, and the rules are established from an original position of a "veil of ignorance."

Ethical Relativism

Under the moral theory of ethical relativism, individuals decide what is ethical based on their own feelings of what is right or wrong.

Social Responsibility of Business, p. 226

A number of theories of social responsibility have been posited.

Maximizing Profits

The goal of the maximizing profits theory is to maximize profits for shareholders.

Moral Minimum

The goal of the moral minimum theory is to make a profit and avoid harm and to compensate for harm caused.

Stakeholder Interest

The goal of the stakeholder interest theory is to consider the interests of stakeholders other than shareholders, such as employees, suppliers, customers, creditors, and the local community.

Corporate Citizenship

The goal of the corporate citizenship theory is to do good and help solve social problems.

Corporate Social Audit

A social audit is an audit of a corporation by independent auditors that examines how well employees have adhered to the company's code of ethics and how well the company has met its duty of social responsibility.

Test Review Terms and Concepts

Business ethics 218	False Claims Act 219	Social contract 223
Code of ethics 232	Kantian ethics (duty ethics) 221	Social responsibility of business 226
Corporate citizenship 231	Maximizing profits 226	Stakeholder interest 229
Corporate social audit 233	Moral minimum 229	United Nations Code of Conduct for
Ethical fundamentalism 218	*Qui tam* lawsuit 219	Transnational Corporations 233
Ethical relativism 225	Rawls's social justice theory 223	Utilitarianism 219
Ethics 217	Sarbanes-Oxley Act 231	Whistleblower Statute 219

Case Problems

8.1 Fraud: The Warner-Lambert Company has manufactured and distributed Listerine antiseptic mouthwash since 1879. Its formula has never changed. Ever since Listerine's introduction, the company has represented the product as being beneficial in preventing and curing colds and sore throats. Direct advertising of these claims to consumers began in 1921. Warner-Lambert spent millions of dollars annually advertising these claims in print media and in television commercials.

After 100 years of Warner-Lambert's making such claims, the Federal Trade Commission (FTC) filed a complaint against the company, alleging that it had engaged in false advertising in violation of federal law. Four months of hearings were held before an administrative law judge that produced an evidentiary record of more than 4,000 pages of documents from 46 witnesses. After examining the evidence,

the FTC issued an opinion which held that the company's representations that Listerine prevented and cured colds and sore throats were false. The U.S. Court of Appeals affirmed.

Is Warner-Lambert guilty of fraud? If so, what remedies should the court impose on the company? Did Warner-Lambert act ethically in making its claims for Listerine? *Warner-Lambert Company v. Federal Trade Commission*, 183 U.S. App. D.C. 230, 562 F.2d 749, **Web** 1977 U.S. App. Lexis 11599 (United States Court of Appeals for the District of Columbia Circuit)

8.2 Liability: The Johns-Manville Corporation was a profitable company that made a variety of building and other products. It was a major producer of asbestos, which was used for insulation in buildings and for a variety of other uses. It has been medically proven that excessive exposure to asbestos causes asbestosis, a fatal lung disease. Thousands of employees of the company and consumers who were exposed to asbestos and contracted this fatal disease sued the company for damages. Eventually, the lawsuits were being filed at a rate of more than 400 per week.

In response to the claims, Johns-Manville Corporation filed for reorganization bankruptcy. It argued that if it did not, an otherwise viable company that provided thousands of jobs and served a useful purpose in this country would be destroyed and that without the declaration of bankruptcy, a few of the plaintiffs who first filed their lawsuits would win awards of hundreds of million of dollars, leaving nothing for

the remainder of the plaintiffs. Under the bankruptcy court's protection, the company was restructured to survive. As part of the release from bankruptcy, the company contributed money to a fund to pay current and future claimants. The fund is not large enough to pay all injured persons the full amounts of their claims.

Was Johns-Manville liable for negligence? Was it ethical for Johns-Manville to declare bankruptcy? Did it meet its duty of social responsibility in this case? *In re Johns-Manville Corporation*, 36 B.R. 727, **Web** 1984 Bankr. Lexis 6384 (United States Bankruptcy Court for the Southern District of New York)

Ethics Issues

8.3 Ethics: The Reverend Leon H. Sullivan, a Baptist minister from Philadelphia who was also a member of the board of directors of General Motors Corporation, proposed a set of rules to guide American-owned companies doing business in the Republic of South Africa. The *Sullivan Principles*, as they became known, call for the nonsegregation of races in South Africa. They call for employers to (a) provide equal and fair employment practices for all employees and (b) improve the quality of employees' lives outside the work environment in such areas as housing, schooling, transportation, recreation, and health facilities. The principles also require signatory companies to report regularly and to be graded on their conduct in South Africa.

Eventually, the Sullivan Principles were subscribed to by several hundred U.S. corporations with affiliates doing business in South Africa. Which of the following theories of social responsibility are the companies that subscribed to the Sullivan Principles following?

1. Maximizing profits
2. Moral minimum
3. Stakeholder interest
4. Corporate citizenship

To put additional pressure on the government of the Republic of South Africa to end apartheid, Reverend Sullivan called for the complete withdrawal of all U.S. companies from doing business in or with South Africa. Very few companies agreed to do so. Do companies owe a social duty to withdraw from South Africa? Should universities divest themselves of investments in companies that do not withdraw from South Africa?

8.4 Ethics: Kaiser Aluminum & Chemical Corporation entered into a collective bargaining agreement with the United Steelworkers of America, a union that represented employees at Kaiser's plants. The agreement contained an affirmative-action program to increase the representation of minorities in craft jobs. To enable plants to meet these goals, on-the-job training programs were established to teach unskilled production workers the skills necessary to become

craft workers. Assignment to the training program was based on seniority, except that the plan reserved 50 percent of the openings for black employees.

Thirteen craft trainees were selected from Kaiser's Gramercy plant for the training program. Of these, 7 were black and 6 white. The most senior black selected had less seniority than several white production workers who had applied for the positions but were rejected. Brian Weber, one of the white rejected employees, instituted a class action lawsuit alleging that the affirmative action plan violated Title VII of the Civil Rights Act of 1964, which made it "unlawful to discriminate because of race" in hiring and selecting apprentices for training programs. The U.S. Supreme Court upheld the affirmative-action plan in this case. The decision stated:

> We therefore hold that Title VII's prohibition against racial discrimination does not condemn all private, voluntary, race-conscious affirmative action plans. At the same time, the plant does not unnecessarily trammel the interests of the white employees. Moreover, the plan is a temporary measure; it is not intended to maintain racial balance, but simply to eliminate a manifest racial imbalance.

Do companies owe a duty of social responsibility to provide affirmative-action programs? *Steelworkers v. Weber*, 443 U.S. 193, 99 S.Ct. 2721, 61 L.Ed.2d 480, **Web** 1979 U.S. Lexis 40 (Supreme Court of the United States)

8.5 Ethics: Iroquois Brands, Ltd., a Delaware corporation, had $78 million in assets, $141 million in sales, and $6 million in profits. As part of its business, Iroquois imported pâté de foie gras (goose pâté) from France and sold it in the United States. Iroquois derived only $79,000 in revenues from sales of such pâté. The French product force-fed the geese from which the pâté was made. Peter C. Lovenheim, who owned 200 shares of Iroquois common stock, proposed to include a shareholder proposal in Iroquois's annual proxy materials to be sent to shareholders. His proposal criticized the company because the force-feeding caused "undue stress, pain and suffering" to the geese and requested that shareholders vote to have Iroquois discontinue importing and selling pâté produced by this method.

Iroquois refused to allow the information to be included in its proxy materials. Iroquois asserted that its refusal was based on the fact that Lovenheim's proposal was "not economically significant" and had only "ethical and social" significance. The company reasoned that because corporations are economic entities, only an economic test applied to its activities, and it was not subject to an ethical or a social responsibility test. Is the company correct? That is, should only an economic test be applied in judging the activities of a corporation? Or should a corporation also be subject to an ethical or a social responsibility test? *Lovenheim v. Iroquois Brands, Ltd.*, 618 F.Supp. 554, **Web** 1985 U.S. Dist. Lexis 21259 (United States District Court for the District of Columbia)

IRAC Writing Assignment

Read Case A-8 in Appendix A [***Ramirez v. Plough, Inc.***]. Read the case and use the IRAC method to prepare a written analysis of the case.

Endnotes

1. 204 Mich. 459, 170 N.W. 668, **Web** 1919 Mich. Lexis 720 (Supreme Court of Michigan).
2. Milton Friedman, "The Social Responsibility of Business Is to Increase Its Profits," *New York Times Magazine*, September 13, 1970.

UNIT 2

Contracts and E-Commerce

CHAPTER 9

Nature of Traditional and Online Contracts

> *"The movement of the progressive societies has hitherto been a movement from status to contract."*
>
> —SIR HENRY MAINE
> Ancient Law, Chapter 5

CHAPTER OBJECTIVES

After studying this chapter, you should be able to:

1. Define *contract*.
2. List the elements necessary to form a valid contract.
3. Distinguish between bilateral and unilateral contracts.
4. Describe and distinguish between express and implied-in-fact contracts.
5. Describe and distinguish among valid, void, voidable, and unenforceable contracts.

CHAPTER CONTENTS

- Introduction to Nature of Traditional and Online Contracts
- Definition of a *Contract*
- Sources of Contract Law
- Classifications of Contracts
- Equity
- Chapter Summary
- Test Review Terms and Concepts
- Case Problems
- Ethics Issues
- IRAC Writing Assignment

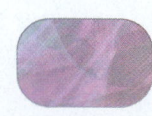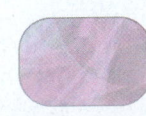

Introduction to Nature of Traditional and Online Contracts

Contracts are the basis of many of our daily activities. They provide the means for individuals and businesses to sell and otherwise transfer property, services, and other rights. The purchase of goods, such as books and automobiles, is based on sales contracts; the hiring of employees is based on service contracts; the lease of an apartment is based on a rental contract; the sale of goods and services over the Internet is based on electronic contracts. The list is almost endless. Without enforceable contracts, commerce would collapse.

Parties voluntarily enter into contracts. The terms of a contract become *private law* between the parties. One court has stated, "The contract between parties is the law between them and the courts are obliged to give legal effect to such contracts according to the true interests of the parties."[1]

Nevertheless, most contracts are performed without the aid of the court system. This is usually because the parties feel a moral duty to perform as promised. Although some contracts, such as illegal contracts, are not enforceable, most are **legally enforceable**.[2] This means that if a party fails to perform a contract, the other party may call upon the courts to enforce the contract.

This chapter introduces the study of traditional and Internet contract law. Such topics as the definition of *contract*, requirements for forming a contract, sources of contract law, and the various classifications of contracts are discussed.

Finland

Contracts support the conduct of trade, business, and e-commerce worldwide.

Definition of a *Contract*

A **contract** is an agreement that is enforceable by a court of law or equity. A simple and widely recognized definition of *contract* is provided by the *Restatement (Second) of Contracts*: "A contract is a promise or a set of promises for the breach of which the law gives a remedy or the performance of which the law in some way recognizes a duty."[3]

Parties to a Contract

Every contract involves at least two parties. The **offeror** is the party who makes an offer to enter into a contract. The **offeree** is the party to whom the offer is made (see Exhibit 9.1). In making an offer, the offeror promises to do—or to refrain from doing—something.

EXHIBIT 9.1

Parties to a Contract

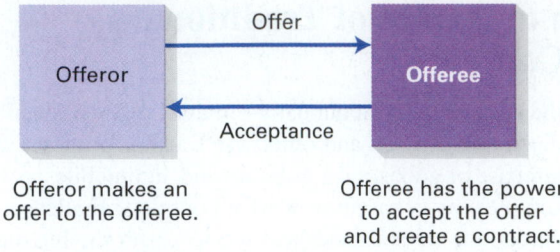

Offeror makes an
offer to the offeree.

Offeree has the power
to accept the offer
and create a contract.

The offeree then has the power to create a contract by accepting the offeror's offer. A contract is created if the offer is accepted. No contract is created if the offer is not accepted.

Elements of a Contract

For a contract to be enforceable, the following four basic requirements must be met:

1. *Agreement.* To have an enforceable contract, there must be an **agreement** between the parties. This requires an *offer* by the offeror and an *acceptance* of the offer by the offeree. There must be mutual assent by the parties.
2. *Consideration.* The promise must be supported by a bargained-for **consideration** that is legally sufficient.

> Contracts must not be the sports of an idle hour, mere matters of pleasantry and badinage, never intended by the parties to have any serious effect whatever.
>
> Lord Stowell
> *Dalrymple v. Dalrymple (1811)*

Example Gift promises and moral obligations are not considered supported by valid consideration.

3. *Contractual capacity.* The parties to a contract must have **contractual capacity**.

Example Certain parties, such as persons adjudged insane, do not have contractual capacity.

4. *Lawful object.* The object of a contract must be **lawful**.

Example Contracts to accomplish illegal objects or contracts that are against public policy are void.

CONCEPT SUMMARY

Elements of a Contract

1. Agreement
2. Consideration
3. Contractual capacity
4. Lawful object

Defenses to the Enforcement of a Contract

Two *defenses* may be raised to the enforcement of contracts:

1. *Genuineness of assent.* The consent of the parties to create a contract must be **genuine**. If the consent is obtained by duress, undue influence, or fraud, there is no real consent.
2. *Writing and form.* The law requires that certain contracts be in **writing** or in a certain **form**. Failure of such a contract to be in writing or to be in proper form may be raised against the enforcement of the contract.

CONTEMPORARY ENVIRONMENT
The Evolution of the Modern Law of Contracts

The use of contracts originally developed in ancient times. The common law of contracts developed in England around the fifteenth century. American contract law evolved from the English common law.

At first, the United States adopted a *laissez-faire* approach to the law of contracts. The central theme of this theory was *freedom of contract*. The parties (such as consumers, shopkeepers, farmers, and traders) generally dealt with one another face-to-face, had equal knowledge and bargaining power, and had the opportunity to inspect the goods prior to sale. Contract terms were openly negotiated. There was little, if any, government regulation of the right to contract. This "pure," or classical law of contracts, produced objective rules, which, in turn, produced certainty and predictability in the enforcement of contracts. It made sense until the Industrial Revolution.

The Industrial Revolution changed many of the underlying assumptions of pure contract law. For example, as large corporations developed and gained control of crucial resources, the traditional balance of parties' bargaining power shifted: Large corporations now had the most power. The chain of distribution for goods also changed because (1) buyers did not have to deal face-to-face with sellers and (2) there was not always an opportunity to inspect the goods prior to sale.

Form Contracts

Eventually, sellers began using *form contracts* that offered their goods to buyers on a take-it-or-leave-it basis. The majority of contracts in this country today are form contracts.

Example Automobile contracts, mortgage contracts, sales contracts for consumer goods, and such are examples of form contracts.

Both federal and state governments have enacted statutes intended to protect consumers, debtors, and others from unfair contracts. In addition, the courts have developed certain common law legal theories that allow some oppressive or otherwise unjust contracts to be avoided. Today, under this **modern law of contracts**, there is substantial government regulation of the right to contract.

Sources of Contract Law

There are several sources of contract law in the United States, including the *common law of contracts*, the *Uniform Commercial Code*, and the *Restatement (Second) of Contracts*. The following paragraphs explain these sources in more detail.

The Common Law of Contracts

A major source of contract law is the **common law of contracts**. The common law of contracts developed from early court decisions that became precedent for later decisions. There is a limited federal common law of contracts that applies to contracts made by the federal government. The larger and more prevalent body of common law has been developed from state court decisions. Thus, although the general principles remain the same throughout the country, there is some variation from state to state.

The Uniform Commercial Code (UCC)

Another major source of contract law is the **Uniform Commercial Code (UCC)**. The UCC, which was first drafted by the National Conference of Commissioners on Uniform State Laws in 1952, has been amended several times. Its goal is to create a uniform system of commercial law among the 50 states. The provisions of the UCC normally take precedence over the common law of contracts. (The provisions of the UCC are discussed in other chapters in this book.)

The UCC is divided into nine main articles. Every state has adopted at least part of the UCC. In the area of contract law, two of the major provisions of the UCC are:

■ *Article 2 (Sales).* **Article 2** prescribes a set of uniform rules for the creation and enforcement of contracts for the sale of goods. These contracts are often referred to as *sales contracts*.

Example The sale of equipment is a sales contract subject to Article 2 of the UCC.

■ ***Article 2A (Leases).* Article 2A** prescribes a set of uniform rules for the creation and enforcement of contracts for the lease of goods. These contracts are referred to as *lease contracts*.

Example The lease of an automobile is a lease subject to Article 2A of the UCC.

The *Restatement of the Law of Contracts*

In 1932, the American Law Institute completed the ***Restatement of the Law of Contracts***. The *Restatement* is a compilation of contract law principles as agreed upon by the drafters. The *Restatement*, which is currently in its second edition, is cited in this book as ***Restatement (Second) of Contracts***. Note that the *Restatement* is not law. However, lawyers and judges often refer to it for guidance in contract disputes because of its stature.

INTERNET AND TECHNOLOGY

Uniform Computer Information Transactions Act (UCITA)

The National Conference of Commissioners on Uniform State Laws (a group of lawyers, judges, and legal scholars) drafted the **Uniform Computer Information Transactions Act (UCITA)**. The UCITA establishes uniform legal rules for the formation and enforcement of electronic contracts and licenses. The UCITA addresses most of the legal issues that are encountered while conducting e-commerce over the Internet.

The UCITA is a model act that does not become law until a state legislature adopts it as a statute for the state. Although most states have not adopted the UCITA, the UCITA has served as a model for states that have enacted their own statutes that govern e-commerce. Because of the need for uniformity of e-commerce rules, states are attempting to adopt uniform laws to govern the creation and enforcement of cyberspace contracts and licenses.

Objective Theory of Contracts

The **objective theory of contracts** holds that the intent to enter into an express or implied-in-fact contract is judged by the **reasonable person standard**. Would a hypothetical reasonable person conclude that the parties intended to create a contract after considering (1) the words and conduct of the parties and (2) the surrounding circumstances? For example, no valid contract results from offers that are made in jest, anger, or undue excitement.

Under the objective theory of contracts, the subjective intent of a party to enter into a contract is irrelevant. The following two cases illustrate the application of the objective theory of contracts.

CASE **9.1**

Objective Theory of Contracts

City of Everett, Washington v. Mitchell

631 P.2d 366, **Web** 1981 Wash. Lexis 1139
Supreme Court of Washington

> "The objective manifestation theory of contracts lays stress on the outward manifestation of assent made by each party to the other. The subjective intention of the parties is irrelevant. "
>
> —Judge Dolliver

Facts

Al and Rosemary Mitchell owned a small secondhand store. The Mitchells attended Alexander's Auction, where they frequently shopped to obtain merchandise for their business. While at the auction, they purchased a used safe for $50. They were told by the auctioneer that the inside compartment of the safe was locked and that no key could be found to unlock it. The safe was part of the Sumstad Estate. Several days after the auction, the Mitchells took the safe to a locksmith to have the locked compartment opened. When the locksmith opened the compartment, he found $32,207 in cash. The locksmith called the City of Everett Police, who impounded the money. The City of Everett commenced an interpleader action against the Sumstad Estate and the Mitchells. The trial court entered summary judgment in favor of Sumstad Estate. The court of appeals affirmed. The Mitchells appealed.

Issue

Was a contract formed between the seller and the buyer of the safe?

Language of the Court

The objective manifestation theory of contracts lays stress on the outward manifestation of assent made by each party to the other. The subjective intention of the parties is irrelevant. A contract is an obligation attached by the mere force of law to certain acts of the parties, usually words, which ordinarily accompany and represent a known intent. If, however, it were proved by twenty bishops that either party, when he used the words, intended something else than the usual meaning that the law imposes, he would still be held.

The Mitchells were aware of the rule of the auction that all sales were final. Furthermore, the auctioneer made no statement reserving rights to any contents of the safe to the Estate. Under these circumstances, we hold reasonable persons would conclude that the auctioneer manifested an objective intent to sell the safe and its contents and that the parties mutually assented to enter into that sale of the safe and the contents of the locked compartment.

Decision

The state supreme court held that under the objective theory of contracts, a contract was formed between the seller and the buyer of the safe. The court reversed the appellate court's grant of summary judgment to the Sumstad Estate and remanded the case to the trial court for entry of judgment in favor of the Mitchells.

Law & Ethics Questions

1. Does the objective theory of contracts work? Is it easy to define a "reasonable person"?

2. **ETHICS** Did the seller of the safe act ethically in alleging that no contract had been made with the Mitchells?

3. What do you think would be the economic consequences to business if the courts recognized a subjective theory of contracts?

Web Exercises

1. **WEB** For the complete opinion of this case, go to *www.prenhall.com/cheesemancases*.

2. **WEB** Visit the website of the Supreme Court of Washington, at *www.courts.wa.gov*.

3. **WEB** Use *www.google.com* to find an article about the objective theory of contracts. Read it.

CASE 9.2

Objective Theory of Contracts

Welles v. Academy of Motion Picture Arts and Sciences

Web 2004 U.S. Dist. Lexis 5756 (2004)
United States District Court for the Central District of California

> 66 *Courts presume that a contract, deliberately entered into, expresses the true intent and meaning of the parties. A court will not set aside contractual obligations because one party misunderstood, or failed to read, the contract.* 99
>
> —Judge Pregerson

Facts

Orson Welles won an Academy Award (Oscar) from the Academy of Motion Picture Arts and Sciences for the Best Original Screenplay for the 1941 film *Citizen Kane*. After Orson Welles died, the right of ownership to the original Oscar passed to his wife, and when she died, it passed to her daughter, Beatrice Welles (Welles). In 1988, Welles requested a duplicate Oscar from the Academy, stating that her father had lost the original Oscar many years before. The Academy provided her with a duplicate Oscar, and she signed the following Receipt and Addendum:

Receipt

I hereby acknowledge receipt from you of replica No. 2527 [duplicate Oscar] of your copyrighted statuette, commonly known as the "Oscar", as an award for Orson Welles, Original Screenplay—"Citizen Kane". I acknowledge that my receipt of said replica does not entitle me to any right whatsoever in your copyright, trade-mark and service mark of said statuette and that only the physical replica itself shall belong to me. In consideration of your delivering said replica to me, I agree to comply with your rules and regulations respecting its use and not to sell or otherwise dispose of it, not permit it to be sold or disposed of by operation of law, without first offering to sell it to you for the sum of $1.00. You shall have thirty days after any such offer is made to you within which to accept it. This agreement shall be binding not only on me, but also on my heirs, legatees, executors, administrators, estate, successors and assigns. My legatees and heirs shall have the right to acquire said replica, if it becomes part of my estate, subject to this agreement.

Addendum

Any member of the Academy who has heretofore received any Academy trophy shall be bound by the forgoing receipt and agreement with the same force and effect as though he or she had executed and delivered the same in consideration of receiving such trophy.

In 1994, Welles discovered and obtained possession of the original Oscar. Welles decided that she wanted to sell the original Oscar through public auction at Christie, Manson & Woods International (Christie's). The Academy objected, and Christie's withdrew the original Oscar from auction, pending the resolution of the dispute between Welles and the Academy. Welles sued the Academy for a judicial declaration that she was the rightful owner of the original Oscar and had the right to sell it. The Academy defended that the Receipt and Addendum prevented her from selling the original Oscar. Welles argued that the language of the Addendum "Any member of the Academy . . . " did not apply to her because she was not a member of the Academy. The Academy responded that it intended that the language should apply to Welles and asked the court to reform the Receipt and Addendum to apply to Welles and to order that the Academy had a right of first refusal to purchase the original Oscar for $1.00.

Issue

Does the Receipt and Addendum prohibit Welles from selling the original Oscar?

Language of the Court

A written contract, once executed, carries with it a legal presumption that it correctly expresses the intention of the parties. Where one party claims that a contract was entered into pursuant to a unilateral mistake, in order to be granted reformation, that party must prove that the other party knew of or suspected the mistake at the time the contract was executed. The Academy asserts that it committed a unilateral mistake by using the form Receipt that contained the Addendum concerning "members" in its agreement with Welles, a nonmember. The burden is on the Academy to show that Welles knew or suspected the Academy's mistake—namely, that the Academy intended that the Addendum apply to her.

In order for a court to reform a contract, there must be a mutual intention of the parties for the reformed contract to express. Welles states in her declaration that she "did not and

would not under any circumstances agree to give the Academy a right of first refusal for $1.00 on the original statuette awarded to my father." The Academy asserts that it intended to preclude Welles from selling any Oscar. Thus, the court finds that there was no meeting of the minds, and no mutual intention of the parties on which a reformed contract would be based. The intention of the parties must be derived from the language of the contract if possible. The Academy does not dispute that the plain language of the Addendum does not apply to Welles. Instead, the Academy argues that because Welles was unique—the replacement Oscar given to her was the first one given to a nonmember who was not the original recipient of the award—the Academy erred and sent Welles a form that did not apply to her. Courts presume that a contract, deliberately entered into, expresses the true intent and meaning of the parties. A court will not set aside contractual obligations because one party misunderstood, or failed to read, the contract. Here, the Academy failed to ensure that the Addendum applied to Welles. The Academy drafted the document, and the court will not set aside the contract because the Academy failed to review its own form. Per the Receipt's terms, the Addendum does not apply to Welles's original Oscar which she received from her father's estate.

Decision

The U.S. District Court applied the objective theory of contracts and decided that the Academy's subjective belief that the Addendum applied to Welles did not change the express language of the contract. The District Court granted Welles's motion for summary judgment, holding that the Academy did not have a right of first refusal in Welles's original Oscar. The District Court held that Welles had unrestricted property rights in the original Oscar, which she could dispose of as she saw fit.

Law & Ethics Questions

1. What does the objective theory of contracts provide? Explain.

2. Do you think that the Academy had the subjective intent to provide in the contract that it had the right of first refusal if Welles tried to sell the original Oscar? Does this matter in contract interpretation?

3. **ETHICS** Was it ethical for the Academy to try to get out from under the terms of a contract that it drafted?

Web Exercises

1. **WEB** For the complete opinion of this case, go to *www.prenhall.com/cheesemancases*.

2. **WEB** Visit the website of the U.S. District Court for the Central District of California, at *www.cacd.uscourts.gov*.

3. **WEB** Use *www.google.com* to find a short bibliography of Orson Welles. Read it.

4. **WEB** Visit the website of the Academy of Motion Picture Arts and Sciences at *www.oscars.org*.

5. **WEB** Use *www.google.com* to find a movie clip from the movie *Citizen Kane*.

INTERNET AND TECHNOLOGY
E-Commerce

As we entered the twenty-first century, a new economic shift brought the United States and the rest of the world into the Information Age. Computer technology and the use of the Internet increased dramatically. A new form of commerce—**electronic commerce**, or **e-commerce**—is flourishing. All sorts of goods and services are now sold over the Internet. You can purchase automobiles and children's toys, participate in auctions, purchase airline tickets, make hotel reservations, and purchase other goods and services over the Internet.

Much of the new cyberspace economy is based on electronic contracts and the licensing of computer information. E-commerce has created problems for forming contracts over the Internet, enforcing e-commerce contracts, and providing consumer protection. In many situations, traditional contract rules apply to e-contracts. Many states have adopted rules that specifically regulate e-commerce transactions. The federal government has also enacted several laws that regulate e-contracts. Contract rules that apply to e-commerce are discussed in this chapter and in the following chapters.

Classifications of Contracts

There are several types of contracts. They differ somewhat in formation, enforcement, performance, and discharge. The different types of contracts are discussed in the following paragraphs.

Bilateral and Unilateral Contracts

Contracts are either *bilateral* or *unilateral*, depending on what the offeree must do to accept the offeror's offer. A contract is a **bilateral contract** if the offeror's promise is answered with the offeree's promise of acceptance. In other words, a bilateral contract is a "promise for a promise." This exchange of promises creates an enforceable contract. No act of performance is necessary to create a bilateral contract.

A contract is a **unilateral contract** if the offeror's offer can be accepted only by the performance of an act by the offeree. There is no contract until the offeree performs the requested act. An offer to create a unilateral contract cannot be accepted by a promise to perform. It is a "promise for an act."

The language of the offeror's promise must be carefully scrutinized to determine whether it is an offer to create a bilateral or a unilateral contract. If there is any ambiguity as to which it is, it is presumed to be a bilateral contract.

Example Suppose Mary Douglas, the owner of the Chic Dress Shop, says to Peter Jones, a painter, "If you promise to paint my store by July 1, I will pay you $3,000." Peter promises to do so. A bilateral contract was created at the moment Peter promised to paint the dress shop (a promise for a promise). If Peter fails to paint the store, he can be sued for whatever damages result from his breach of contract. Similarly, Peter can sue Mary if she refuses to pay him after he has performed as promised.

Example In the preceding example, if Mary had said, "If you paint my shop by July 1, I will pay you $3,000," the offer would have created a unilateral contract. The offer can be accepted only by the painter's performance of the requested act. If Peter does not paint the shop by July 1, there has been no acceptance, and the painter cannot be sued for damages.

INCOMPLETE OR PARTIAL PERFORMANCE Problems can arise if the offeror in a unilateral contract attempts to revoke an offer after the offeree has begun performance. Generally, an offer to create a unilateral contract can be revoked by the offeror any time prior to the offeree's performance of the requested act. However, the offer cannot be revoked if the offeree has begun or has substantially completed performance.

Example Suppose Alan Matthews tells Sherry Levine that he will pay her $5,000 if she finishes the Boston Marathon. Alan cannot revoke the offer once Sherry starts running the marathon.

> Justice is the end of government. It is the end of civil society. It ever has been, and ever will be pursued, until it be obtained, or until liberty be lost in the pursuit.
>
> James Madison
> *The Federalist No. 51 (1788)*

> A man must come into a court of equity with clean hands.
>
> C. B. Eyre
> *Dering v. Earl of Winchelsea (1787)*

Express and Implied-in-Fact Contracts

An *actual contract* (as distinguished from a quasi-contract, which is discussed later in this chapter) may be either *express* or *implied-in-fact*.

Express contracts are stated in oral or written words. Examples of such contracts include an oral agreement to purchase a neighbor's bicycle and a written agreement to buy an automobile from a dealership.

Implied-in-fact contracts are implied from the conduct of the parties. Implied-in-fact contracts leave more room for questions than express contracts. The following elements must be established to create an implied-in-fact contract:

1. The plaintiff provided property or services to the defendant.
2. The plaintiff expected to be paid by the defendant for the property or services and did not provide the property or services gratuitously.
3. The defendant was given an opportunity to reject the property or services provided by the plaintiff but failed to do so.

In the following case, the court had to decide whether the plaintiffs could sue a defendant for breach of an implied-in-fact contract.

CASE **9.3**
Implied-in-Fact Contract

Wrench LLC v. Taco Bell Corporation

256 F.3d 446, **Web** 200 U.S. App. Lexis 15097 (2001)
United States Court of Appeals for the Sixth Circuit

> " *The district court found that appellants produced sufficient evidence to create a genuine issue of material fact regarding whether an implied-in-fact contract existed between the parties.* "
>
> —Judge Graham

Facts

Thomas Rinks and Joseph Shields created the "Psycho Chihuahua" cartoon character, which they promote, market, and license through their company, Wrench LLC. The Psycho Chihuahua is a clever, feisty, cartoon character dog with an attitude; a self-confident, edgy, cool dog who knows what he wants and will not back down. Rinks and Shields attended a licensing trade show in New York City, where they were approached by two Taco Bell employees, Rudy Pollak, a vice president, and Ed Alfaro, a creative services manager. Taco Bell owns and operates a nationwide chain of fast-food Mexican restaurants. Pollak and Alfaro expressed interest in the Psycho Chihuahua character for Taco Bell advertisements because they thought his character would appeal to Taco Bell's core consumers, males aged 18 to 24. Pollak and Alfaro obtained some Psycho Chihuahua materials to take back with them to Taco Bell's headquarters.

Later, Alfaro contacted Rinks and asked him to create art boards combining Psycho Chihuahua with the Taco Bell name and image. Rinks and Shields prepared art boards and sent them to Alfaro, along with Psycho Chihuahua t-shirts, hats, and stickers. Alfaro showed these materials to Taco Bell's vice president of brand management as well as to Taco Bell's outside advertising agency. Alfaro tested the Psycho Chihuahua marketing concept with focus groups. Rinks suggested to

Alfaro that instead of using the cartoon version of Psycho Chihuahua in its advertisements, Taco Bell should use a live Chihuahua dog manipulated by computer graphic imaging that had the personality of Psycho Chihuahua and a love for Taco Bell food. Rinks and Shields gave a formal presentation of this concept to Taco Bell's marketing department. One idea presented by Rinks and Shields was a commercial in which a male Chihuahua dog passed by a female Chihuahua dog in order to get to Taco Bell food. Taco Bell did not enter into an express contract with Wrench LLC, Rinks, or Shields.

Just after Rinks's and Shields's presentation, Taco Bell hired a new outside advertising agency, Chiat/Day. Taco Bell gave Chiat/Day materials received from Rinks and Shields regarding the Psycho Chihuahua. Three months later, Chiat/Day proposed using a Chihuahua in Taco Bell commercials. One commercial had a male Chihuahua passing up a female Chihuahua to get to a person seated on a bench eating Taco Bell food. Chiat/Day says that it conceived these ideas by itself. In July 1997, Taco Bell aired its first Chihuahua commercial in the United States, and it became an instant success and the basis of its advertising. Taco Bell paid nothing to Wrench LLC or to Rinks and Shields. Plaintiffs Wrench LLC, Rinks, and Shields sued defendant Taco Bell to recover damages for breach of an implied-in-fact contract. On this issue, the District Court agreed with the plaintiffs. The decision was appealed.

Issue

Do the plaintiff's Wrench LLC, Rinks, and Shields state a cause of action for the breach of an implied-in-fact contract?

Language of the Court

The district court found that appellants produced sufficient evidence to create a genuine issue of material fact regarding whether an implied-in-fact contract existed between the parties. On appeal, Taco Bell argues that this conclusion was erroneous, and asserts that the record contains no evidence of an enforceable contract. We agree with the district court's finding that appellants presented sufficient evidence to survive summary judgment on the question of whether an implied-in-fact contract existed under Michigan law.

Decision

The U.S. Court of Appeals held that the plaintiffs had stated a proper cause of action against defendant Taco Bell for breach of an implied-in-fact contract. The Court of Appeals remanded the case for trial.

Law & Ethics Questions

1. What does the doctrine of implied-in-fact contract provide? Explain.

2. **ETHICS** Did Taco Bell act ethically in this case? Did Chiat/Day act ethically in this case?

3. Do you think there was an implied-in-fact contract in this case? If so, what damages should be awarded to the plaintiffs?

Web Exercises

1. **WEB** For the complete opinion of this case, go to *www.prenhall.com/cheesemancases*.

2. **WEB** Visit the website of the U.S. Court of Appeals for the Sixth Circuit, at *www.ca6.uscourts.gov*.

3. **WEB** Visit the website of Taco Bell Corporation, at *www.tacobell.com*. Can you find any reference to the "Psycho Chihuahua" commercial?

4. **WEB** Use *www.google.com* to find an article that discusses the "Psycho Chihuahua" advertising campaign used by Taco Bell. Read it.

ETHICS SPOTLIGHT

"Scrabble" Owner Held Liable on an Implied-in-Fact Contract

> ❝ *Finding that S & R had denied the existence of the contract in bad faith and without probable cause, the district court impose[d] punitive damages on S & R. This factual finding was not clearly erroneous. Indeed defendants have offered no evidence to suggest that they acted in good faith. We therefore affirm the initial $100,000 punitive damage award.* ❞
>
> —Judge Goodwin

Implied-in-fact contracts are implied from the conduct of the parties. Consider the following case. Selchow & Richter Company (S&R) owns the trademark to the famous board game "Scrabble." Mark Landsberg wrote a book on strategy for winning at Scrabble and contracted S&R to request permission to use the Scrabble trademark. In response, S&R requested a copy of Landsberg's manuscript, which he provided. After prolonged negotiations between the parties regarding the possibility of S&R's publication of the manuscript broke off, S&R brought out its own Scrabble strategy book. No express contract was ever entered into between Landsberg and S&R. Landsberg sued S&R for damages for breach of an implied contract.

Was there an implied-in-fact contract between the parties? The U.S. District Court and the U.S. Court of Appeals held that an implied-in-fact contract had been formed between the parties and that the contract was breached by the defendants. The Court of Appeals noted that the law allows for recovery for the breach of an implied-in-fact contract when the recipient of a valuable idea accepts and uses the information without paying for it even though he knows that compensation is expected. The U.S. Court of Appeals noted, "California law allows for recovery for the breach of an implied-in-fact contract when the recipient of a valuable idea accepts the information knowing that compensation is expected, and subsequently uses the idea without paying for it."

Here, the Court of Appeals found (1) that Landsberg's disclosure of his manuscript was confidential and for the limited purpose of obtaining approval for the use of the Scrabble mark, and (2) given Landsberg's express intention to exploit his manuscript commercially, the defendant's use of any portion of it was conditioned on payment. Landsberg was awarded the profits that S&R made on the sale of the book plus $100,000 punitive damages, bringing the total award to $440,300. The U.S. Court of Appeals stated, "Finding that S & R had denied the existence of the contract in bad faith and without probable cause, the district court impose[d] punitive damages on S & R. This factual finding was not clearly erroneous. Indeed defendants have offered no evidence to suggest that they acted in good faith. We therefore affirm the initial $100,000 punitive damage award." *Landsberg v. Selchow & Richter Company*, 802 F.2d 1193, **Web** 1986 U.S. App. Lexis 32453 (United States Court of Appeals for the Ninth Circuit)

Law & Ethics Questions

1. Does the implied-in-fact doctrine provide any useful protections? Explain.

2. **ETHICS** Did Selchow & Richter act ethically in this case?

3. **ETHICS** Does the doctrine of implied-in-fact contract encourage more ethical behavior?

4. **ETHICS** Was the award of punitive damages justified in this case? Why or why not?

Web Exercises

1. **WEB** For the complete opinion of this case, go to *www.prenhall.com/cheesemancases*.

2. **WEB** Visit the website of the United States Court of Appeals for the Ninth Circuit, at *www.ca9.uscourts.gov*.

3. **WEB** Go to the website *www.scrabble.com*, the official world-wide webpage for Scrabble.

4. **WEB** Use *www.google.com* to find an article that discusses strategy for playing Scrabble. Read it.

Quasi-Contracts (Implied-in-Law Contracts)

The equitable doctrine of **quasi-contract**, also called **implied-in-law contract**, allows a court to award monetary damages to a plaintiff for providing work or services to a defendant even though no actual contract existed between the parties. Recovery is generally based on the reasonable value of the services received by the defendant.

The doctrine of quasi-contract is intended to prevent *unjust enrichment* and *unjust detriment*. It does not apply where there is an enforceable contract between the parties. A quasi-contract is imposed where (1) one person confers a benefit on another who retains the benefit and (2) it would be unjust not to require that person to pay for the benefit received.

Example Heather is driving her automobile when she is involved in a serious automobile accident in which she is knocked unconscious. She is rushed to Metropolitan Hospital, where the doctors and other staff perform the necessary medical procedures to save her life. Heather comes out of her coma and, after recovering, is released from the hospital. Subsequently, Metropolitan Hospital sends Heather a bill for its services. The charges are reasonable. Under the doctrine of quasi-contract, Heather is responsible for any charges that are not covered by her insurance coverage.

In the following case, the court found a quasi-contract.

C A S E 9.4

Quasi-Contract

Powell v. Thompson-Powell

Web 2006 Del. C.P. Lexis 10 (2006)
Court of Common Pleas of Delaware

> ❝*A contract implied in law permits recovery of that amount by which the defendant has benefited at the expense of the plaintiff in order to preclude unjust enrichment.*❞
>
> —Judge Trader

Facts

Samuel E. Powell, Jr., and Susan Thompson-Powell, husband and wife, borrowed $37,700 from Delaware Farm Credit and gave a mortgage to Delaware Farm Credit that pledged two pieces of real property as collateral for the loan. The first piece of property was 2.7 acres of land owned as marital property, and the other piece of property was owned by Susan, which she had inherited. Eight years later, Samuel Jr. and Susan defaulted on the mortgage. Samuel Jr. went to his father, Samuel E. Powell, Sr., and orally agreed that if his father would pay the mortgage and the back taxes, he would pay his father back. Samuel Sr. paid off the mortgage and the back taxes owed on the properties. Susan was not a party to this agreement.

Two years later, Samuel Jr. and Susan were divorced. The divorce court ordered that the 2.7 acres of marital real property be sold and the sale proceeds be divided 50 percent to each party. When the property was sold, Samuel Jr. paid Samuel Sr. one-half of the monies he had previously borrowed from his father. Samuel Sr. sued Susan to recover the other half of the money. Susan defended, alleging that she was not a party to the contract between Samuel Jr. and Samuel Sr. and therefore was not bound by it. Samuel Sr. argued that Susan was liable to him for one-half of the money based on the doctrine of quasi-contract.

Issue

Is Susan liable for one-half the money borrowed by Samuel Jr. from Samuel Sr. under the doctrine of quasi-contract?

Language of the Court

The primary issue in this case is whether the plaintiff can recover from Susan Thompson-Powell on the theory of contract implied in law. A contract implied in law permits recovery of that amount by which the defendant has benefited at the expense of the plaintiff in order to preclude unjust enrichment. To claim restitution, the plaintiff must show that the defendant was unjustly enriched and secured a benefit that it would be unconscionable to allow her to retain.

The essential elements of a quasi-contract are a benefit conferred upon the defendant by the plaintiff, appreciation or realization of the benefit by the defendant, and acceptance and retention by the defendant of such benefit under such circumstances that it would be inequitable to retain without paying the value thereof.

In the case before me the plaintiff paid the mortgage of the son and daughter-in-law at a time when the bank was about to foreclose on the mortgage. If the property had been sold at a foreclosure sale, neither Samuel E. Powell, Jr. nor Susan Thompson-Powell would have received any benefit from the sale of the marital property. Additionally, payment of the mortgage protected Susan Thompson-Powell's inherited property. Thus, because of the plaintiff's acts in preserving the real estate from foreclosure Susan Thompson-Powell received a substantial benefit at the plaintiff's expense. Since the retention of the benefit in this case is unjust, she must repay her share of the money advanced by the plaintiff.

Decision

The court held that Samuel E. Powell, Sr., was entitled to recover from Susan Thompson-Powell one-half of the money advanced for her benefit.

Law & Ethics Questions

1. What does the doctrine of quasi-contract provide? Explain.
2. **ETHICS** Was it ethical for Susan Thompson-Powell not to pay back half of the money borrowed from Samuel E. Powell, Sr.?
3. **ETHICS** What is the doctrine of quasi-contract designed to prevent? Explain.

Web Exercises

1. **WEB** For the complete opinion of this case, go to *www.prenhall.com/cheesemancases*.
2. **WEB** Visit the website of the Court of Common Pleas of Delaware, at *www.courts.delaware.gov*.
3. **WEB** Use *www.google.com* to find an article that discusses the doctrine of quasi-contract. Read it.

Formal and Informal Contracts

Contracts may be classified as either *formal* or *informal*. **Formal contracts** are contracts that require a special form or method of creation. The *Restatement (Second) of Contracts* identifies the following types of formal contracts:[4]

- *Negotiable instruments.* **Negotiable instruments**, which include checks, drafts, notes, and certificates of deposit, are special forms of contracts recognized by the UCC. They require a special form and language for their creation and must meet certain requirements for transfer.
- *Letters of credit.* A **letter of credit** is an agreement by the issuer of the letter to pay a sum of money upon the receipt of an invoice and other documents. Letters of credit are governed by the UCC.
- *Recognizances.* In a recognizance, a party acknowledges in court that he or she will pay a specified sum of money if a certain event occurs. A *bail bond* is an example of a recognizance.
- *Contracts under seal.* This type of contract is one to which a seal (usually a wax seal) is attached. Although no state currently requires contracts to be under seal, a few states provide that no consideration is necessary if a contract is made under seal.

All contracts that do not qualify as formal contracts are called **informal contracts** (or **simple contracts**). The term is a misnomer. Valid informal contracts (e.g., leases, sales contracts, service contracts) are fully enforceable and may be sued upon if breached. They are called *informal contracts* only because no special form or method is required for their creation.

Valid, Void, Voidable, and Unenforceable Contracts

Contract law places contracts in the following categories:

1. *Valid contract.* A **valid contract** meets all the essential elements to establish a contract. That is, a valid contract must (1) consist of an agreement between the

parties, (2) be supported by legally sufficient consideration, (3) be between parties with contractual capacity, and (4) accomplish a lawful object. A valid contract is enforceable by at least one of the parties.

2. *Void contract.* A **void contract** has no legal effect. It is as if no contract had ever been created.

> **Example** A contract to commit a crime is void. If a contract is void, neither party is obligated to perform, and neither party can enforce the contract.

3. *Voidable contract.* A **voidable contract** is one in which at least one party has the *option* to void his or her contractual obligations. If the contract is voided, both parties are released from their obligations under the contract. If the party with the option chooses to ratify the contract, both parties must fully perform their obligations.

> **Example** With certain exceptions, contracts may be voided by minors, insane persons, intoxicated persons, persons acting under duress or undue influence or fraud, and in cases involving mutual mistake.

4. *Unenforceable contract.* With an **unenforceable contract**, there is some legal defense to the enforcement of the contract.

> **Example** If a contract is required to be in writing under the Statute of Frauds but is not, the contract is unenforceable. The parties may voluntarily perform a contract that is unenforceable.

Executed and Executory Contracts

A completed contract—that is, one that has been fully performed on both sides—is called an **executed contract**. A contract that has not been performed by both sides is called an **executory contract**. Contracts that have been fully performed by one side but not by the other are classified as executory contracts.

Example Suppose Elizabeth Andrews signs a contract to purchase a new Jaguar automobile from Ace Motors. She has not yet paid for the car, and Ace Motors has not yet delivered it. This is an executory contract. Assume that the car was paid for, but Ace Motors has not yet delivered the car. Here, the contract is executed by Elizabeth but is executory as to Ace Motors. This is an executory contract. Assume that Ace Motors now delivers the car to Elizabeth. The contract has been fully performed by both parties. It is an executed contract.

CONCEPT SUMMARY

Classifications of Contracts

Formation	
	1. **Bilateral contract.** A promise for a promise.
	2. **Unilateral contract.** A promise for an act.
	3. **Express contract.** A contract expressed in oral or written words.
	4. **Implied-in-fact contract.** A contract inferred from the conduct of the parties.
	5. **Quasi-contract.** A contract implied by law to prevent unjust enrichment.
	6. **Formal contract.** A contract that requires a special form or method of creation.
	7. **Informal contract.** A contract that requires no special form or method of creation.

Enforceability	1. **Valid contract.** A contract that meets all the essential elements of establishing a contract.
	2. **Void contract.** No contract exists.
	3. **Voidable contract.** A contract for which a party has the option of voiding or enforcing the contract.
	4. **Unenforceable contract.** A contract that cannot be enforced because of a legal defense.
Performance	1. **Executed contract.** A contract that is fully performed on both sides.
	2. **Executory contract.** A contract that is not fully performed by one or both parties.

Equity

Recall that two separate courts developed in England: the courts of law and the Chancery Courts (or courts of equity). The equity courts developed a set of maxims based on fairness, equality, moral rights, and natural law that were applied in settling disputes. **Equity** was resorted to when (1) an award of money damages "at law" would not be the proper remedy or (2) fairness required the application of equitable principles. Today, in most states of the United States, the courts of law and equity have been merged into one court. In an action "in equity," the judge decides the equitable issue; there is no right to a jury trial in an equitable action. The doctrine of equity is sometimes applied in contract cases.

ETHICS SPOTLIGHT

Equity Saves Contracting Party

❝ *There is only minimal delay in giving notice, the harm to the lessor is slight, and the hardship to the lessee is severe.* ❞

—Judge Abbe

The courts usually interpret a valid contract as a solemn promise to perform. This view of the sanctity of a contract can cause an ethical conflict. Consider the following case.

A landlord leased a motel he owned to lessees for a 10-year period. The lessees had an option to extend the lease for an additional 10 years. To do so, they had to give written notice to the landlord three months before the first ten-year lease expired. The lease provided for forfeiture of all furniture, fixtures, and equipment installed by the lessees, free of any liens, upon termination of the lease.

From almost ten years, the lessees devoted most of their assets and a great deal of their energy to building up the business. During this time, they transformed a disheveled, unrated motel into a AAA three-star operation. With the landlord's knowledge, the lessees made extensive long-term improvements that greatly increased the value of both the property and the business. The landlord knew that the lessees had obtained long-term financing for the improvements that would extend well beyond the first 10-year term of the lease. The landlord also knew

that the only source of income the lessees had to pay for these improvements was the income generated from the motel business. The lessees told the landlord orally in a conversation that they intended to extend the lease.

The lessees had instructed their accountant to exercise the option on time. Despite reminders from the lessees, the accountant failed to give the written notice within three months of the expiration of the lease. As soon as they discovered the mistake, the lessees personally delivered written notice of renewal of the option to the landlord, 13 days too late. The landlord rejected it as late and instituted a lawsuit for unlawful detainer to evict the lessees.

The trial and appellate courts held in favor of the lessees. They rejected the landlord's argument for the strict adherence to the deadline for giving written notice of renewal of the lease. Instead, the courts granted **equitable relief** and permitted the late renewal notice. The court reasoned that "there is only minimal delay in giving notice, the harm to the lessor is slight, and the hardship to the lessee is severe." *Romasanta v. Mitton*, 189 Cal.App.3d 1026, 234

Cal. Rptr. 729, **Web** 1987 Cal. App. Lexis 1428 (Court of Appeal of California)

Law & Ethics Questions

1. **ETHICS** Did the landlord act ethically in this case?
2. **ETHICS** Should the court have applied equity and saved the lessees from their mistake? Or should they have been held to the terms of the lease?

Web Exercises

1. **WEB** For the complete opinion of this case, go to *www.prenhall.com/cheesemancases*.
2. **WEB** Visit the Court of Appeal of California, Second Appellate District, at *www.courtinfo.ca.gov/courts/courtsofappeal*.
3. **WEB** Use *www.google.com* to find an article that discusses the application of equity to contract disputes. Read it.

INTERNATIONAL LAW
The United Nations Convention on Contracts for the International Sale of Goods

The United Nations Convention on Contracts for the International Sale of Goods (CISG) went into effect on January 1, 1988, the climax of more than 50 years of negotiations. The CISG is the work of many countries and several international organizations. There are now approximately 70 signature countries to the CISG. In adopting the CISG, the UN stated the following in its preamble:

Preamble

The State Parties to this Convention, . . .

Considering that the development of international trade on the basis of equality and mutual benefit is an important element in promoting friendly relations among States,

Being of the opinion that the adoption of uniform rules which govern contracts for the international sale of goods and take into account the different social, economic and legal systems would contribute to the removal of legal barriers in international trade and promote the development of international trade,

Have agreed as follows:

The CISG provides legal rules that govern the formation, performance, and enforcement of international contracts entered into between international businesses. Many of its provisions are remarkably similar to those of the United States Uniform Commercial Code (UCC), for example. It incorporates rules from all the major legal systems. It has, accordingly, received widespread support from developed, developing, and Communist countries.

The CISG applies to contracts for the international sale of goods. That is, the buyer and seller must have their places of business in different countries. In addition, either (1) both of the nations must be parties to the convention or (2) the contract must specify that the CISG controls. The contracting parties may agree to exclude (i.e., opt out of) or modify its application.

Web Exercise

1. **WEB** To view the CISG, go to *www.uncitral.org/pdf/english/texts/sales/cisg/CISG.pdf.*
2. **WEB** Use *www.google.com* to find out whether the United States has adopted the CISG.

Singapore

International trade depends on the formation, performance, and enforcement of international contracts.

Chapter Summary

Definition of *Contract*, p. 241

A *contract* is "a promise or a set of promises for the breach of which the law gives a remedy or the performance of which the law in some way recognizes a duty."

Parties to a Contract

The party who makes an offer to enter into a contract is the *offeror*. The party to whom the offer is made is the *offeree*.

Elements of a Contract

1. Agreement
2. Consideration
3. Contractual capacity
4. Lawful object

Defenses to the Enforcement of a Contract

1. Genuineness of assent
2. Writing and form

Form Contracts

Eventually, sellers began using *form contracts* that offered their goods to buyers on a take-it-or-leave-it basis. The majority of contracts in this country today are form contracts.

Sources Of Contract Law, p. 243
The Common Law of Contracts

Developed from early court decisions that became precedent for later decisions. A majority of common law has been developed from state court decisions.

Uniform Commercial Code

Creates a uniform system of commercial law among the 50 states and normally takes precedence over the common law of contracts.

Restatement of the Law of Contracts

This document is advisory only; it is not law.

Theories of Contract Law

1. *Classical law of contracts.* According to this theory; parties were free to negotiate contract terms without government interference.
2. *Modern law of contracts.* According to this theory; parties may negotiate contract terms subject to government regulations.

Classifications of Contracts, p. 247
Bilateral and Unilateral Contracts

A *bilateral contract* is a promise for a promise. A *unilateral contract* is a promise for an act.

Express and Implied-in-Fact Contracts

An *express contract* is a contract expressed in oral or written words. An *implied-in-fact contract* is a contract implied from the conduct of the parties.

Quasi-Contracts (Implied-in-Law Contracts)

A *quasi-contract* is a contract implied by law to prevent unjust enrichment and unjust detriment.

Formal and Informal Contracts

A *formal contract* is a contract that requires a special form or method for creation. An *informal contract* is a contract that requires no special form or method for creation.

Valid, Void, Voidable, and Unenforceable Contracts

Contract law places contracts in the following categories:

1. *Valid contract.* A valid contract meets all the essential elements to establish a contract.
2. *Void contract.* No contract exists.
3. *Voidable contract.* A voidable contract is one where one or both parties have the option of avoiding or enforcing the contract.
4. *Unenforceable contract.* An unenforceable contract is a contract that cannot be enforced because of a legal defense.

Executed and Executory Contracts

A contract that is fully performed on both sides is called an *executed contract.* A contract that is not fully performed by one or both parties is called an *executory contract.*

Equity, p. 253

Equity is a doctrine that permits judges to make decisions based on fairness, equality, moral rights, and natural law.

Test Review Terms and Concepts

Agreement 242
Article 2 (Sales) 243
Article 2A (Leases) 244
Bilateral contract 247
Common law of contracts 243
Consideration 242
Contract 241
Contractual capacity 242
Electronic commerce
  (e-commerce) 247
Equitable relief 253
Equity 253
Executed contract 252
Executory contract 252
Express contract 248
Formal contract 251
Genuineness of assent 242

Informal contract (simple
  contract) 251
Implied-in-fact contract 248
Lawful object 242
Legally enforceable 241
Letter of credit 251
Modern law of contracts 243
Negotiable instrument 251
Objective theory of contracts 244
Offeree 241
Offeror 241
Quasi-contract (implied-in-law
  contract) 250
Reasonable person standard 244
*Restatement of the Law of
  Contracts* 244

*Restatement (Second) of
  Contracts* 244
The United Nations Convention on
  Contracts for the International Sale
  of Goods (CISG) 254
Unenforceable contract 252
Uniform Commercial
  Code (UCC) 243
Uniform Computer Information
  Transactions Act (UCITA) 244
Unilateral contract 247
Valid contract 251
Void contract 252
Voidable contract 252
Writing and form 242

Case Problems

9.1 Bilateral or Unilateral Contract: G. S. Adams, Jr., vice president of the Washington Bank & Trust Co., met with Bruce Bickham. They reached an agreement whereby Bickham agreed to do his personal and corporate banking business with the bank and the bank agreed to loan Bickham money at $7\frac{1}{2}$ percent interest per annum. Bickham would have 10 years to repay the loans. For the next two years, the bank made several loans to Bickham at $7\frac{1}{2}$ percent interest. Adams then resigned from the bank. The bank notified Bickham that general economic changes made it necessary to charge a higher rate of interest on both outstanding and new loans. Bickham sued the bank for breach of contract. Was the contract a bilateral or a unilateral contract? Does Bickham win? *Bickham v. Washington Bank & Trust Company*, 515 So.2d 457, **Web** 1987 La. App. Lexis 10442 (Court of Appeal of Louisiana)

9.2 Implied-in-Fact Contract: For six years, Lee Marvin, an actor, lived with Michelle Marvin. They were not married. At the end of six years, Lee Marvin compelled Michelle Marvin to leave his household. He continued to support her for another year but thereafter refused to provide further support. During their time together, Lee Marvin earned substantial income and acquired property, including motion-picture rights worth over $1 million. Michelle Marvin brought an action against Lee Marvin, alleging that an implied-in-fact contract existed between them and that she was entitled to half of the property they had acquired while living together. She claimed that she had given up a lucrative career as an entertainer and singer to be a full-time companion, homemaker, housekeeper, and cook. Can an implied-in-fact contract result from the conduct of unmarried persons who live together? *Marvin v. Marvin,* 18 Cal.3d 660, 557 P.2d 106, 134 Cal.Rptr. 815, **Web** 1976 Cal. Lexis 377 (Supreme Court of California)

Ethics Issues

9.3 Ethics: The Lewiston Lodge of Elks sponsored a golf tournament at the Fairlawn Country Club in Poland, Maine. For promotional purposes, Marcel Motors, an automobile dealership, agreed to give any golfer who shot a hole-in-one a new Dodge automobile. Fliers advertising the tournament were posted in the Elks Club and sent to potential participants. On the day of the tournament, the new Dodge automobile was parked near the clubhouse with one of the posters conspicuously displayed on the vehicle. Alphee Chenard, Jr., who had seen the promotional literature regarding the hole-in-one offer, registered for the tournament and paid the requisite entrance fee. While playing the thirteenth hole of the golf course, in the presence of the other members of his foursome, Chenard shot a hole-in-one. When Marcel Motors refused to tender the automobile, Chenard sued for breach of contract. Was the contract a bilateral or a unilateral contract? Does Chenard win? Was it ethical for Marcel Motors to refuse to give the automobile to Chenard? *Chenard v. Marcel Motors*, 387 A.2d 596, **Web** 1978 Me. Lexis 911 (Supreme Judicial Court of Maine)

9.4 Ethics: Loren Vranich, a doctor practicing under the corporate name Family Health Care, P.C., entered into a written employment contract to hire Dennis Winkel. The contract provided for an annual salary, insurance benefits, and other employment benefits. Another doctor, Dr. Quan, also practiced with Dr. Vranich. About nine months later, when Dr. Quan left the practice, Vranich and Winkel entered into an oral modification of their written contract whereby Winkel was to receive a higher salary and a profit-sharing bonus. During the next year, Winkel received the increased salary. However, a disagreement arose, and Winkel sued to recover the profit-sharing bonus. Under Montana law, a written contract can be altered only in writing or by an executed oral agreement. Dr. Vranich argued that the contract could not be enforced because it was not in writing. Does Winkel receive the profit-sharing bonus? Did Dr. Vranich act ethically in raising the defense that the contract was not in writing? *Winkel v. Family Health Care, P.C.*, 205 Mont. 40, 668 P.2d 208, **Web** 1983 Mont. Lexis 785 (Supreme Court of Montana)

IRAC Writing Assignment

Read Case A-9 in Appendix A [***Mark Realty, Inc. v. Rogness***]. Read the case and use the IRAC method to prepare a written analysis of the case.

Endnotes

1. *Rebstock v. Birthright Oil & Gas Co.*, 406 So.2d 636, **Web** 1981 La. App. Lexis 5242 (Court of Appeal of Louisiana)
2. *Restatement (Second) of Contracts*, Section 1.
3. *Restatement (Second) of Contracts*, Section 1.
4. *Restatement (Second) of Contracts*, Section 6.

CHAPTER 10

Agreement and Consideration

> ❝ *"When I use a word," Humpty Dumpty said, in rather a scornful tone, "it means just what I choose it to mean—neither more nor less."*
>
> *"The question is," said Alice, "whether you can make words mean so many different things."*
>
> *"The question is," said Humpty Dumpty, "which is to be master— that's all."* ❞

> —LEWIS CARROLL
> Alice's Adventures in Wonderland (1865)

CHAPTER OBJECTIVES

After studying this chapter, you should be able to:

1. Define *offer* and *acceptance*.
2. Define *counteroffer* and describe the effects of counteroffers.
3. Describe how offers are terminated.
4. Define *consideration*.
5. Analyze whether contracts are lacking in consideration.

CHAPTER CONTENTS

- Introduction to Agreement and Consideration
- Agreement
- Offer
- Termination of Offers
- Acceptance
- Consideration
- Contracts Lacking Consideration
- Promissory Estoppel
- Chapter Summary
- Test Review Terms and Concepts
- Case Problems
- Ethics Issues
- IRAC Writing Assignment

    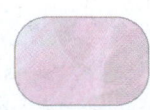

Introduction to Agreement and Consideration

Contracts are voluntary agreements between the parties; that is, one party makes an offer that is accepted by the other party. Without *mutual assent*, there is no contract. Assent may be expressly evidenced by the oral or written words of the parties or implied from the conduct of the parties. This chapter discusses offer and acceptance.

To be enforceable, a contract must be supported by *consideration*, which is broadly defined as something of legal value. It can consist of money, property, the provision of services, the forbearance of a right, or anything else of value. Most contracts that are not supported by consideration are not enforceable. The parties may voluntarily perform a contract that is lacking in consideration. This chapter discusses consideration, promises that lack consideration, and promises that are enforceable without consideration.

Hue, Vietnam

Each country has developed its own contract laws. A company conducting business in a foreign country must have knowledge of that country's contract laws.

Agreement

Agreement is the manifestation by two or more persons of the substance of a contract. It requires an *offer* and an *acceptance*. The process of reaching an agreement usually proceeds as follows. Prior to entering into a contract, the parties may engage in preliminary negotiations about price, time of performance, and such. At some point during these negotiations, one party makes an **offer**. The person who makes the offer is called the **offeror**, and the person to whom the offer is made is called the **offeree**. The offer sets forth the terms under which the offeree is willing to enter into the contract. The offeree has the power to create an agreement by accepting the offer.

Offer

Section 24 of the *Restatement (Second) of Contracts* defines *offer* as "the manifestation of willingness to enter into a bargain, so made as to justify another person in understanding that his assent to that bargain is invited and will conclude it." The following three elements are required for an offer to be effective:

1. The offeror must *objectively intend* to be bound by the offer.
2. The terms of the offer must be definite or reasonably *certain*.
3. The offer must be *communicated* to the offeree.

The making of an offer is shown in Exhibit 10.1.

EXHIBIT 10.1

Offer

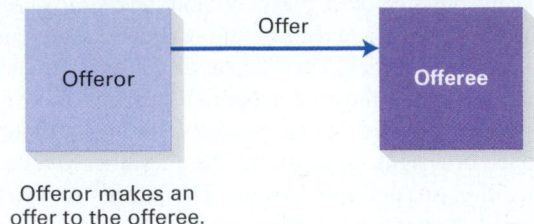

Offeror makes an
offer to the offeree.

A contract is a mutual promise.

William Paley
*The Principles of Moral and
Political Philosophy (1784)*

Objective Intent

The intent to enter into a contract is determined using the **objective theory of contracts**—that is, whether a reasonable person viewing the circumstances would conclude that the parties intended to be legally bound.

Example   The statement "I will buy your building for $2 million" is a valid offer because it indicates the offeror's present intent to contract.

Example   A question such as "Are you interested in selling your building for $2 million?" is not an offer. It is an invitation to make an offer or an invitation to negotiate.

Offers that are made in jest, anger, or undue excitement do not include the necessary objective intent.

Example   Suppose the owner of Company A has lunch with the owner of Company B. In the course of their conversation, Company A's owner exclaims in frustration, "For $2 I'd sell the whole computer division!" An offer such as that cannot result in a valid contract.

Definiteness of Terms

The terms of an offer must be clear enough for the offeree to be able to decide whether to accept or reject the terms of the offer. If the terms are indefinite, the courts cannot enforce the contract or determine an appropriate remedy for its breach.

To be considered definite, an offer (and contract) generally must contain the following terms: (1) identification of the parties, (2) identification of the subject matter and quantity, (3) consideration to be paid, and (4) time of performance. Complex contracts usually state additional terms.

Implied Terms

The common law of contracts required an exact specification of contract terms. If one essential term was omitted, the courts would hold that no contract had been made. This rule was inflexible.

The modern law of contracts is more lenient. The *Restatement (Second) of Contracts* merely requires that the terms of the offer be "reasonably certain."[1] Accordingly, the court can supply a missing term if a reasonable term can be implied.[2] The definition of *reasonable* depends on the circumstances. Terms that are supplied in this way are called **implied terms**.

Generally, time of performance can be implied. Price can be implied if there is a market or source from which to determine the price of the item or service (e.g., the "blue book" for an automobile price, the New York Stock Exchange for a stock price). The parties or subject matter of the contract usually cannot be implied if an item or a service is unique or personal, such as the construction of a house or the performance of a professional sports contract.

In the following case, the Court of Appeals applied the adage "A contract is a contract is a contract."

CASE **10.1**
Contract

Marder v. Jennifer Lopez

450 F.3d 445, **Web** 2006 U.S. App. Lexis 14330 (2006)
United States Court of Appeals for the Ninth Circuit

> **❝***Though in hindsight the agreement appears to be unfair to Marder—she only received $2,300 in exchange for a release of all claims relating to a movie that grossed over $150 million.***❞**
>
> —Judge Pregerson

Facts

The movie *Flashdance* tells a story of a woman construction worker who performs at night as an exotic dancer. She performs an innovative form of dancing that includes a chair dance. Her goal is to obtain formal dance training at a university. The movie is based on the life of Maureen Marder, a nightclub dancer. Paramount Pictures Corporation used information from Marder to create the screenplay for the movie. Paramount paid Marder $2,300, and Marder signed a general release that provides that Marder "releases and discharges Paramount Picture Corporation . . . of and from each and every claim, demand, debt, liability, cost and expense of any kind or character which have risen or are based in whole or in part on any matters occurring at any time prior to the date of this Release." Marder also released Paramount from claims "arising out of or in any way connected with either directly or indirectly, any and all arrangements . . . in connection with the preparation of screenplay material and the production, filming and exploitation of . . . *Flashdance*."

Paramount released the movie *Flashdance*, which grossed over $150 million in domestic box office and is still shown on television and distributed through DVD rentals. Subsequently, Sony Music Entertainment paid Paramount for release of copyright and produced a music video for the Jennifer Lopez song "I'm Glad." The video featured Lopez's performance as a dancer and singer. Marder believed that the video contains re-creations of many well-known scenes from *Flashdance*.

Marder brought a lawsuit in U.S. District Court against Paramount, Sony, and Lopez. Marder sought a declaration that she had rights as a co-author of *Flashdance* and a co-owner with Paramount of the copyright to *Flashdance*. She sued Sony and Lopez for allegedly violating her copyright in *Flashdance*. The District Court dismissed Marder's claims against Paramount, Sony, and Lopez. Marder appealed.

Issue

Was the general release signed by Marder an enforceable contract?

Language of the Court

The Release's language is exceptionally broad and we hold that it is fatal to each of Marder's claims against Paramount. Such a release of "each and every claim" covers all claims within the scope of the language. Accordingly, the law imputes to Marder an intention corresponding to the reasonable meaning of her words and acts. Here, Marder released a broad array of claims relating to any assistance she provided during the creation of a Hollywood movie. Thus, the only reasonable interpretation of the Release is that it encompasses the various copyright claims she asserts in the instant suit.

Though in hindsight the agreement appears to be unfair to Marder—she only received $2,300 in exchange for a release of all claims relating to a movie that grossed over $150 million—there is simply no evidence that her consent was obtained by fraud, deception, misrepresentation, duress, or undue influence.

We also affirm the district court's dismissal of claims against Sony and Lopez. As we held above, under the terms of the Release, Marder cannot sue Paramount to assert a co-ownership in *Flashdance*. It is therefore impossible for her to establish a *prima facie* case of copyright infringement against Sony and Lopez.

Decision

The U.S. Court of Appeals held that the general release signed by Marder was an enforceable contract. The Court of Appeals affirmed the judgment of the District Court that dismissed Marder's complaint against Paramount, Sony, and Lopez.

Law & Ethics Questions

1. What does the adage "A contract is a contract is a contract" mean? Was it applied in this case?

2. **ETHICS** Why did Marder bring this lawsuit? Did she act ethically in bringing this lawsuit? Why or why not?

3. **ETHICS** Do you think Paramount should have paid Marder more money after the movie *Flashdance* became a success?

Web Exercises

1. **WEB** For the complete opinion of this case, go to *www.prenhall.com/cheesemancases*.

2. **WEB** Visit the website of the U.S. Court of Appeals for the Ninth Circuit, at *www.ca9.uscourts.gov*.

3. **WEB** Visit the website of Paramount Pictures Corporation, at *www.paramountpictures.com*. Can you find any reference to the movie *Flashdance*?

4. **WEB** Use *www.google.com* to find a video clip from the movie *Flashdance*.

5. **WEB** Visit the website of Jennifer Lopez, at *www.jenniferlopez.com*.

6. **WEB** Use *www.google.com* to find a video clip of Jennifer Lopez's music video where she dances and sings the song "I'm Glad."

ETHICS SPOTLIGHT

"A Contract Is a Contract Is a Contract"

> "*The disputed agreement transferred plaintiff's copyright in the Mighty Morphin Power Rangers' logo with as much specificity as the law requires.*"
>
> —Judge Kozinski

Mighty Morphin Power Rangers was a phenomenal success as a television series. The Power Rangers battled to save the universe from all sorts of diabolical plots and bad guys. They were also featured in a profitable line of toys and garments bearing the Power Rangers logo. The name and logo of the Power Rangers are known to millions of children and their parents worldwide. The claim of ownership of the logo for the Power Rangers ended up in a battle in a courtroom.

David Dees is a designer who works at d.b.a. David Dees Illustration. Saban Entertainment, Inc. (Saban), which owns the copyright and trademark to Power Rangers figures and the name "Power Ranger," hired Dees as an independent contractor to design a logo for the Power Rangers. The contract signed by the parties was titled "Work-for-Hire/Independent Contractor Agreement." The contract was drafted by Saban with the help of its attorneys; Dees signed the agreement without the representation of legal counsel.

Dees designed the logo currently used for the Power Rangers and was paid $250 to transfer his copyright ownership in the logo. Subsequently, Dees sued Saban to recover damages for copyright and trademark infringement. Saban defended, arguing that Dees was bound by the agreement he had signed.

The trial court agreed with Saban, finding that the "Work-for-Hire/Independent Contractor Agreement" was an enforceable contract between the parties and that Dees had transferred his ownership interests in the logo to Saban. Dees appealed. The Court of Appeals affirmed the judgment for Saban, stating, "The disputed agreement transferred plaintiff's copyright in the Mighty Morphin Power Rangers' logo with as much specificity as the law requires." The Court found that a contract is a contract is a contract, at least in this case. Dees's appeal to the U.S. Supreme Court was denied. *Dees, d/b/a David Dees Illustration v. Saban Entertainment, Inc.*, 131 F.3d 146, **Web** 1997 U.S. App. Lexis 39173 (United States Court of Appeals for the Ninth Circuit)

Law & Ethics Questions

1. Should a contract be enforced as written, even if it is later discovered that one party benefited substantially more than the other party to the contract?

2. **ETHICS** Did Dees act ethically by suing for more money?

Web Exercises

1. **WEB** For the complete opinion of this case, go to *www.prenhall.com/cheesemancases*.

2. **WEB** Visit the website of the U.S. Court of Appeals for the Ninth Circuit, at *www.ca9.uscourts.gov*.

3. **WEB** Use *www.google.com* to find a video clip of the Mighty Morphin Power Rangers.

Communication

An offer cannot be accepted if it is not communicated to the offeree by the offeror or a representative or an agent of the offeror.

Example Suppose Mr. Jones, the CEO of Ace Corporation, wants to sell a manufacturing division to Baker Corporation. He puts the offer in writing, but he does not send it. Assume that Mr. Griswald, the CEO of Baker Corporation, visits Mr. Jones and sees the written offer lying on Jones's desk. Griswald tells his CEO about the offer. Because Mr. Jones never communicated the offer to the CEO of Baker Corporation, there is no offer to be accepted.

Advertisements

Advertisements for the sale of goods, even at specific prices, generally are treated as *invitations to make an offer*.

Example Catalogs, price lists, quotation sheets, offering circulars, and other sales materials are all viewed as a solicitation of an offer, but not as actual offers. This rule is intended to protect advertiser-sellers from the unwarranted breach of contract suits for nonperformance that would otherwise arise if the seller ran out of the advertised goods.

There is one exception to this rule: An advertisement is considered an offer if it is so definite or specific that it is apparent that the advertiser has the present intent to bind himself or herself to the terms of the advertisement.

Example An automobile dealer's advertisement to sell a "previously owned maroon 2004 Lexus 330 SUV, serial no. 3210674, $30,000" is an offer. Because the advertisement identifies the exact automobile for sale, the first person to accept the offer owns the automobile.

In the following case, the Court of Appeals had to decide whether an advertisement was a solicitation of an offer or an offer.

C A S E 10.2
Invitation to Make an Offer

Mesaros v. United States

845 F.2d 1576, **Web** 1988 U.S. App. Lexis 6055
United States Court of Appeals for the Federal Circuit

> ❝ *It is well established that materials such as those mailed to prospective customers by the Mint are no more than advertisements or invitations to deal.* ❞

> —Judge Skelton

Facts

The U.S. Congress directed the Secretary of the Treasury to mint and sell a stated number of specially minted commemorative coins to raise funds to restore and renovate the Statue of Liberty. The U.S. Mint mailed advertising materials to persons, including Mary and Anthony C. Mesaros, husband and wife, that described the various types of coins that were to be issued. Payment could be made by check, money order, or credit card. The materials included an order form. Directly above the space provided on this form for the customer's signature was the following: "YES, Please accept my order for the U.S. Liberty Coins I have indicated." Mary Mesaros forwarded to the mint a credit-card order of $1,675 for certain coins, including the $5 gold coin. All credit-card orders were forwarded by the Mint to Mellon Bank in Pittsburgh, Pennsylvania, for verification, which took a period of time. Meanwhile, cash orders were filled immediately, and orders by check were filled as the checks cleared. The issuance of 500,000 gold coins was exhausted before Mesaros's credit-card order could be filled. The Mint sent a letter to the Mesaroses, notifying them of this fact. The gold coin increased in value by 200 percent within the first few months of 1986. Mary and Anthony C. Mesaros filed a class action lawsuit against the United States, seeking in the alternative either damages for breach of contract or a decree of mandamus ordering the Mint to deliver the gold coins to the plaintiffs. The District Court held for the Mint. The Mesaroses appealed.

Issue

Was the United States Mint's advertisement a solicitation of an offer or an offer?

Language of the Court

The plaintiffs contend that the materials sent to them by the Mint, including the order form, constituted an offer that upon acceptance by the plaintiffs created a binding contract between them and the government whereby the government was bound and obligated to deliver the coins ordered by them. The great weight of authority is against the plaintiffs. It is well established that materials such as those mailed to prospective customers by the Mint are no more than advertisements or invitations to deal. They are mere notices and solicitations for offers that create no power of acceptance in the recipient.

A basic rule of contracts holds that whether an offer has been made depends on the objective reasonableness of the alleged offeree's belief that the advertisement or solicitation was intended as an offer. Generally, it is considered unreasonable for a person to believe that advertisements and solicitations are offers that bind the advertiser. Otherwise, the advertiser could be bound by an excessive number of contracts requiring delivery of goods far in excess of amounts available. That is particularly true in the instant case where the gold coins were limited to 500,000 by the act of Congress.

We conclude that a thorough reading, construction, and interpretation of the materials sent to the plaintiffs by the Mint makes clear that the contention of the plaintiffs that they reasonably believed the materials were intended as an offer is unreasonable as a matter of law. This is especially true in view of the words "YES, Please accept my order . . ." that were printed on the credit-card form, which showed that the credit-card order was an offer from the plaintiffs to the Mint to buy the coins, which offer might or might not be accepted by the Mint. Accordingly, the Mint materials were intended solely as solicitations of offers from customers that were subject to acceptance by the Mint before the Mint would be bound by a contract.

Decision

The Court of Appeals held that the advertising materials sent out by the U.S. Mint were a solicitation to make an offer and not an offer. Therefore, the Mint wins.

Law & Ethics Questions

1. Should an advertisement be treated as an offer instead of as an invitation to make an offer? Why or why not?

2. **ETHICS** Do you think the Mesaroses acted ethically by suing the Mint?

3. Would it cause any problems for businesses if advertisements were considered offers? Explain.

Web Exercises

1. **WEB** For the complete opinion of this case, go to *www.prenhall.com/cheesemancases*.

2. **WEB** Visit the website of the U.S. Court of Appeals for the Federal Circuit, at *www.fedcir.gov*.

3. **WEB** Visit the website of the United States Mint, at *www.usmint.gov*.

4. **WEB** Use *www.google.com* to find an article that discusses U.S. Liberty Coins and their value today. Read it.

Rewards

An offer to pay a **reward** (e.g., for the return of lost property or the capture of a criminal) is an offer to form a unilateral contract. To be entitled to collect the reward, the offeree must (1) have knowledge of the reward offer prior to completing the requested act and (2) perform the requested act.

Example John Anderson accidentally leaves a briefcase containing $500,000 in negotiable bonds on a subway train. He places newspaper ads stating "$5,000 reward for return of briefcase left on a train in Manhattan on January 10, 2010, at approximately 10 A.M. Call 212-555-6789." Helen Smith, who is unaware of the offer, finds the briefcase. She reads the luggage tag containing Anderson's name, address, and telephone number, and she returns the briefcase to him. She is not entitled to the reward money because she did not know about it when she performed the requested act.

Auctions

At an **auction**, the seller offers goods for sale through an auctioneer. Unless otherwise expressly stated, an auction is considered an **auction with reserve**—that is, it is an invitation to make an offer. The seller retains the right to refuse the highest bid and withdraw the goods from sale. A contract is formed only when the auctioneer strikes the gavel down or indicates acceptance by some other means. The bidder may withdraw his or her bid prior to that time.

If an auction is expressly announced to be an **auction without reserve**, the participants reverse the roles: The seller is the offeror, and the bidders are the offerees. The seller must accept the highest bid and cannot withdraw the goods from sale. A seller who sets a minimum bid has to sell the item only if the highest bid is equal to or greater than the minimum bid.

In the following case, the court addressed the issue of an auction.

CASE **10.3**
Auction

Lim v. The.TV Corporation International

99 Cal.App.4th 684, 121 Cal.Rptr.2d 323, **Web** 2002 Cal. App. Lexis 4315 (2002)
Court of Appeal of California

"*Defendant put the name "Golf.tv" up for public auction, and plaintiff bid on that name and no other. That was an offer and acceptance, and formed a contract.*"

—Judge Epstein

Facts

The island nation of Tuvalu was awarded the top-level domain name "tv." Thus, Tuvalu controlled who could use domain names with the suffix "tv" on the Internet. For example, if a person named Jones acquired the suffix tv, her domain name on the Internet would be "jones.tv."

Tuvalu hired The.TV Corporation International, a California corporation doing business under the name dotTV, to sell Internet names bearing the top-level domain name "tv." In April 2000, dotTV posted the name "golf.tv" for sale on its Web site, to be sold to the highest bidder. Je Ho Lim, a resident of South Korea, submitted the highest bid of $1,010 and authorized dotTV to charge his credit card for the amount of the bid. dotTV sent the following e-mail to Lim confirming the sale:

> DotTV—The New Frontier on the Internet
> E-Mail Invoice for Domain Registration
> NAME: Je Ho Lim
> Congratulations!
> You have won the auction for the following domain name:
> DOMAIN NAME: —golf
> SUBSCRIPTION LENGTH: 2 years, starts from activation date
> Amount (US$): $1,010 (first year registration fee)
> Please remember that the annual registration fee increases by 5 annually.
> You have the guaranteed right to renew the registration indefinitely.
> DotTV expects to charge your card and activate the registered domain name by May 15, 2000.
> See ya on the new frontier of the Internet!
> Lou Kerner CEO, dotTV Corporation www.TV

Shortly thereafter, dotTV sent another e-mail to Lim that stated "we have decided to release you from your bid" and that Lim should disregard the prior e-mail because of "an e-mail error that occurred." Later, dotTV publicly offered the domain name "golf.tv" with a beginning bid of $1 million. dotTV claimed that its original e-mail to Lim concerned a different domain name, "—golf," instead of "golf." Lim countered that characters such as two dashes ("—") are not recognized on the Internet and therefore the name "—golf" is an invalid domain name. When dotTV refused to transfer the domain name "golf.tv" to Lim, Lim sued dotTV for breach of contract. The trial court dismissed Lim's case against dotTV. Lim appealed.

Issue

Did Lim properly state a cause of action for breach of contract against dotTV?

Language of the Court

> Defendant put the name "Golf.tv" up for public auction, and plaintiff bid on that name and no other. That was an offer and acceptance, and formed a contract. The distinction between "Golf.tv" and "—Golf.tv" comes from the acceptance e-mail sent by defendant. Certainly the hyphens preceding the name "golf" could not defeat the existence of an already formed contract. Defendant was accepting plaintiff's bid; it plainly was not making a counteroffer, particularly since, according to the pleading, the name "—Golf" did not "compute"; it did not qualify as a domain name. The e-mail must be read as an acknowledgment of plaintiff's winning bid and acceptance of the contract.

Decision

The court of appeals held that plaintiff Lim had properly pleaded a cause of action against defendant dotTV for breach of contract and reinstated Lim's case against dotTV.

Law & Ethics Questions

1. Explain the difference between an auction with reserve and an auction without reserve. Which is presumed if there is no other statement to the contrary?

2. **ETHICS** Did dotTV act ethically in this case? Why do you think that dotTV reneged on its e-mail confirmation to Lim?

3. Are Internet domain names valuable? How do you register an Internet domain name?

Web Exercises

1. **WEB** For the complete opinion of this case, go to *www.prenhall.com/cheesemancases*.

2. **WEB** Visit the website of the court of appeals of California, Second Appellate District, at *www.courtinfo.ca.gov/courts/courtsofappeal*.

3. **WEB** Visit the website of dotTV, at *www.tv*.

4. **WEB** Think up an Internet domain name you would like to have. Go to the Network Solutions website, at *www.networksolutions.com*, and see if that name is available.

CONCEPT SUMMARY

Types of Auctions

TYPE	OFFER
Auction with reserve	No. It is an invitation to make an offer. Because the bidder is the offeror, the seller (the offeree) may refuse to sell the goods. An auction is with reserve unless otherwise stated.
Auction without reserve	Yes. The seller is the offeror and must sell the goods to the highest bidder (the offeree). An auction is without reserve only if it is stipulated as such.

Termination of Offers

An offer may be terminated by the actions of the parties or by operation of laws. The termination of offers is discussed in the following paragraphs.

Revocation of an Offer by the Offeror

Under the common law, an offeror may revoke (i.e., withdraw) an offer any time prior to its acceptance by the offeree. Generally, an offer can be so revoked even if the offeror promised to keep the offer open for a longer time. The **revocation** may be communicated to the offeree by the offeror or by a third party and made by (1) the offeror's express statement (e.g., "I hereby withdraw my offer") or (2) an act of the offeror that is inconsistent with the offer (e.g., selling the goods to another party). Most states provide that a revocation is not effective until it is actually received by the offeree or the offeree's agent.

Offers made to the public may be revoked by communicating the revocation by the same means used to make the offer.

Example If a reward offer for a lost watch was published in two local newspapers each week for four weeks, notice of revocation must be published in the same newspapers for the same length of time. The revocation is effective against all offerees, even those who saw the reward offer but not the notice of revocation.

Rejection of an Offer by the Offeree

An offer is terminated if the offeree **rejects** it. Any subsequent attempt by the offeree to accept the offer is ineffective and is construed as a new offer that the original offeror (now the offeree) is free to accept or reject. A rejection may be evidenced by the offeree's express words (oral or written) or conduct. Generally, a rejection is not effective until it is actually received by the offeror.

Example Harriet Jackson, sales manager of IBM Corporation, offers to sell 1,000 computers to Ted Green, purchasing manager of General Motors Corporation, for $250,000. The offer is made on August 1. Green telephones Jackson to say that he is not interested. This rejection terminates the offer. If Green later decides that he wants to purchase the computers, an entirely new contract must be formed.

Counteroffer by the Offeree

A **counteroffer by the offeree** simultaneously terminates the offeror's offer and creates a new offer.

Example Suppose that Fei Jia says to Harold Brown, "I will sell my house to you for $700,000." Brown says, "I think $700,000 is too high; I will pay you $600,000." Brown has made a counteroffer. The original offer is terminated, and the counteroffer is a new offer that Jia is free to accept or reject.

In the following case, the court found that a counteroffer had been made.

C A S E 10.4
Counteroffer

McLaughlin v. Heikkila

697 N.W.2d 231, **Web** 2005 Minn. App. Lexis 591 (2005)
Court of Appeals of Minnesota

> ❝ *A written offer does not evidence a completed contract and a written acceptance is required.* ❞
>
> —Judge Dietzen

Facts

Wilbert Heikkila listed eight parcels of real property for sale. David McLaughlin submitted written offers to purchase three of the parcels. Three printed purchase agreements were prepared and submitted to Heikkila with three earnest-money checks from McLaughlin. Writing on the purchase agreements, Heikkila changed the price of one parcel from $145,000 to $150,000, the price of another parcel from $32,000 to $45,000, and the price of the third parcel from $175,000 to $179,000.

Heikkila also changed the closing dates on all three of the properties, added a reservation of mineral rights to all three, and signed the purchase agreements.

McLaughlin did not sign the purchase agreements to accept the changes before Heikkila withdrew his offer to sell. McLaughlin sued to compel specific performance of the purchase agreements under the terms of the agreements before Heikkila withdrew his offer. The District Court granted Heikkila's motion to dismiss McLaughlin's claim. McLaughlin appealed.

Issue

Did a contract to convey real property exist between Heikkila and McLaughlin?

Language of the Court

A written offer does not evidence a completed contract and a written acceptance is required. Minnesota has followed the "mirror image rule" in analyzing acceptance of offers. Under that rule, an acceptance must be coextensive with the offer and may not introduce additional terms or conditions. The district court correctly concluded that Heikkila's alterations of the Purchase Agreements constituted a rejection and counteroffer. Heikkila withdrew the counteroffer before McLaughlin provided a written acceptance, as he was entitled to do. Only a written acceptance by McLaughlin of the written terms proposed by Heikkila on the Purchase Agreements would have created a binding contract for the sale of land. Without a written

acceptance and delivery to the other party to the agreement, no contract was formed.

Decision

The court of appeals held that because McLaughlin did not sign or otherwise accept in writing Heikkila's counteroffers, there was no contract for the sale of land between the parties. The court of appeals affirmed the District Court's grant of summary judgment in favor of Heikkila.

Law & Ethics Questions

1. What is a counteroffer? When a counteroffer is made, what happens to the prior offer?
2. **ETHICS** Did McLaughlin have much of a chance to win this lawsuit?
3. **ETHICS** Did Heikkila act ethically in withdrawing his offers in this case?

Web Exercises

1. **WEB** For the complete opinion of this case, go to *www.prenhall.com/cheesemancases*.
2. **WEB** Visit the website of the court of appeals of Minnesota, at *www.courts.state.mn.us*.
3. **WEB** Use *www.google.com* to find an article that discusses counteroffers. Read it.

CONCEPT SUMMARY

Termination of an Offer by Action of the Parties

ACTION	DESCRIPTION
Revocation	The offeror *revokes* (withdraws) the offer any time prior to its acceptance by the offeree.
Rejection	The offeree rejects the offer by his or her words or conduct.
Counteroffer	A counteroffer by the offeree creates a new offer and terminates the offeror's offer.

Destruction of the Subject Matter

An offer terminates if the subject matter of the offer is destroyed through no fault of either party prior to the offer's acceptance. For example, if a fire destroys an office building that has been listed for sale, the offer automatically terminates.

Death or Incompetency of the Offeror or Offeree

The death or incompetancy of either the offeror or the offeree terminates an offer. Notice of the other party's death or incompetence is not a requirement.

Example Suppose that on June 1, Shari Hunter offers to sell her house to Damian Coe for $100,000, provided that he decides on or before June 15. Hunter dies on June 7, before Coe has made up his mind. Because there is no contract prior to her death, the offer automatically terminates on June 7.

Supervening Illegality

If the object of an offer is made illegal prior to the acceptance of the offer, the offer terminates. This situation, which usually occurs when a statute is enacted or a court case is announced that makes the object of the offer illegal, is called a **supervening illegality**.

Example Suppose City Bank offers to loan ABC Corporation $5 million at an 18 percent interest rate. Prior to ABC's acceptance of the offer, the state legislature enacts a statute that sets a usury interest rate of 12 percent. City Bank's offer to ABC Corporation is automatically terminated when the usury statute became effective.

Lapse of Time

An offer expires at the **lapse of time** of an offer. An offer may state that it is effective only until a certain date. Unless otherwise stated, the time period begins to run when the offer is actually received by the offeree and terminates when the stated time period expires.

Example Statements such as "This offer is good for 10 days" or "This offer must be accepted by January 1, 2002" are examples of such notices.

If no time is stated in an offer, the offer terminates after a "reasonable time" dictated by the circumstances. A reasonable time to accept an offer to purchase stock traded on a national stock exchange may be a few moments, but a reasonable time to accept an offer to purchase a house may be a few days. Unless otherwise stated, an offer made face-to-face or during a telephone call usually expires when the conversation ends.

CONCEPT SUMMARY

Termination of an Offer by Operation of Law

ACTION	DESCRIPTION
Destruction of the subject matter	The subject matter of an offer is destroyed prior to acceptance through no fault of either party.
Death or incompetency	Prior to acceptance of an offer, either the offeror or the offeree dies or becomes incompetent.
Supervening illegality	Prior to the acceptance of an offer, the object of the offer is made illegal by statute, regulation, court decision, or other law.
Lapse of time	An offer terminates upon the expiration of a stated time in the offer. If no time is stated, the offer terminates after a "reasonable time."

CONTEMPORARY ENVIRONMENT

Option Contracts

An offeree can prevent the offeror from revoking his or her offer by paying the offeror compensation to keep the offer open for an agreed-upon period of time. This payment is called an **option contract**. In other words, the offeror agrees not to sell the property to anyone but the offeree during the option period. The death or incompetency of either party does not terminate an option contract unless the contract is for the performance of a personal service.

Example Anne Mason offers to sell a piece of real estate to Harold Greenberg for $1 million. Greenberg wants time to make a decision, so he pays Mason $20,000 to keep her offer open to him for six months. At any time during the option period, Greenberg may exercise his option and pay Mason the $1 million purchase price. If Greenberg lets the option expire, however, Mason may keep the $20,000 and sell the property to someone else.

Acceptance

Acceptance is "a manifestation of assent by the offeree to the terms of the offer in a manner invited or required by the offer as measured by the objective theory of contracts."[3] Recall that, generally, (1) unilateral contracts can be accepted only by the offeree's performance of the required act and (2) a bilateral contract can be accepted by an offeree who promises to perform (or, where permitted, by performance of) the requested act.

Who Can Accept an Offer?

Only the offeree has the legal power to accept an offer and create a contract. Third persons usually do not have the power to accept an offer. If an offer is made individually to two or more persons, each has the power to accept the offer. Once one of the offerees accepts the offer, it terminates as to the other offerees. An offer that is made to two or more persons jointly must be accepted jointly.

The acceptance of an offer is illustrated in Exhibit 10.2.

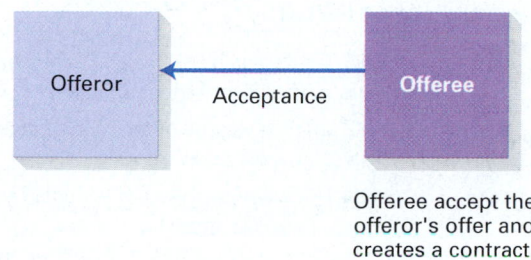

Offeree accept the offeror's offer and creates a contract.

EXHIBIT 10.2

Acceptance of an Offer

Unequivocal Acceptance

The offeree's acceptance must be **unequivocal**. For an acceptance to exist, the offeree must accept the terms as stated in the offer. This is called the **mirror image rule**. Generally, a "grumbling acceptance" is a legal acceptance.

Example A response such as "Okay, I'll take the car, but I sure wish you would make me a better deal" creates an enforceable contract.

An acceptance is equivocal if certain conditions are added to the acceptance.

Example If the offeree responds, "I accept, but only if you repaint the car red." There is no acceptance in this case.

In the following case, the court had to decide whether there had been an acceptance of an offer.

C A S E   **10.5**
Acceptance

Montgomery v. English

902 So.2d 836, **Web** 2005 Fla. App. Lexis 4704 (2005)
Court of Appeal of Florida

> ❝*Florida employs the "mirror image rule" with respect to contracts. Under this rule, in order for a contract to be formed, an acceptance of an offer must be absolute, unconditional, and identical with the terms of the offer.*❞
>
> —Judge Palmer

Facts

Norma English made an offer to purchase a house from Michael and Laurie Montgomery. English included in her offer a request to purchase several items of Montgomerys' personal property. After the Montgomerys received English's offer, they made several changes to the document, including (1) deleting certain items from the personal property section of the offer, (2) deleting a provision regarding latent defects, (3) deleting a provision regarding building inspections, and

(4) adding a specific "AS IS" rider. The Montogomerys signed the counteroffer and delivered it to English. English initialed some, but not all, of the Montgomerys's changes. When the Montgomerys refused to sell the house to English, English sued for specific performance of the contract. The trial court held in favor of English and ordered specific performance. The Montgomerys appealed.

Issue

Was an enforceable contract made between English and the Montgomerys?

Language of the Court

The Montgomerys argue that the trial court erred in denying their motion for summary judgment because the record demonstrated that there had been no meeting of the minds between the parties as to the essential terms of the contract. We agree. Florida employs the "mirror image rule" with respect to contracts. Under this rule, in order for a contract to be formed, an acceptance of an offer must be absolute, unconditional, and identical with the terms of the offer. Applying the mirror image rule to these undisputed facts we hold that, as a matter of law, the parties failed to reach an agreement on the terms of the contract and, therefore, no enforceable contract was created.

Decision

The court of appeals held that no contract had been created between the parties. The court of appeals reversed the trial court's order of specific performance and remanded the case to the trial court with instructions to enter summary judgment in favor of the Montgomerys.

Law & Ethics Questions

1. What does the mirror image rule provide? Explain.
2. **ETHICS** Did the Montgomerys act ethically when they backed out of selling the house?
3. **ETHICS** Did English act ethically by trying to force the sale of the house to her?

Web Exercises

1. **WEB** For the complete opinion of this case, go to *www.prenhall.com/cheesemancases*.
2. **WEB** Visit the website of the court of appeals of Florida, Fifth District, at *www.5dca.org*.
3. **WEB** Use *www.google.com* to find an article that discusses the mirror image rule. Read it.

Silence as Acceptance

Silence usually is not considered acceptance, even if the offeror states that it is. This rule is intended to protect offerees from being legally bound to offers because they failed to respond. Nevertheless, silence *does* constitute acceptance in the following situations:

1. The offeree has indicated that silence means assent.

   Example "If you do not hear from me by Friday, ship the order."

2. The offeree signed an agreement indicating continuing acceptance of delivery until further notification.

   Example Book-of-the-month and CD-of-the-month club memberships are examples of such acceptances.

3. Prior dealings between the parties indicate that silence means acceptance.

   Example A fish wholesaler who delivers 30 pounds of fish to a restaurant each Friday for several years and is paid for the fish can continue the deliveries with expectation of payment until notified otherwise by the restaurant.

4. The offeree takes the benefit of goods or services provided by the offeror even though he or she (a) has an opportunity to reject the goods or services but fails to do so and (b) knows the offeror expects to be compensated.

   Example A homeowner who stands idly by and watches a painter whom she has not hired mistakenly paint her house owes the painter for the work.

> The law has outgrown its primitive stage of formalism when the precise word was the sovereign talisman, and every slip was fatal. It takes a broader view today. A promise may be lacking, and yet the whole writing may be "instinct with an obligation," imperfectly expressed.
>
> Justice Cardozo
> *Wood v. Duff-Gordon (1917)*

CONCEPT SUMMARY

Offer and Acceptance

COMMUNICATION BY OFFEROR	EFFECTIVE WHEN
Offer	Received by offeree
Revocation of offer	Received by offeree
Rejection of offer	Received by offeror
Counteroffer	Received by offeror
Acceptance of offer	Sent by offeree
Acceptance after previous rejection of offer	Received by offeror

Time of Acceptance

Under the common law of contracts, acceptance of a bilateral contract occurs when the offeree *dispatches* the acceptance by an authorized means of communication. This rule is called the **acceptance-upon-dispatch rule**, or, more commonly, the **mailbox rule**. Under this rule, the acceptance is effective when it is dispatched, even if it is lost in transmission. If an offeree first dispatches a rejection and then sends an acceptance, the mailbox rule does not apply to the acceptance.[4]

The problem of lost acceptances can be minimized by expressly altering the mailbox rule. The offeror can do this by stating in the offer that acceptance is effective only upon actual receipt of the acceptance.

Mailbox, Los Angeles, California

The mailbox rule provides that an acceptance is effective when it is dispatched.

Mode of Acceptance

The acceptance must be **properly dispatched**. The acceptance must be properly addressed, packaged in an appropriate envelope or container, and have prepaid postage or delivery charges. Under common law, if an acceptance is not properly dispatched, it is not effective until it is actually received by the offeror.

Generally, an offeree must accept an offer by an *authorized* means of communication. The offer can stipulate that acceptance must be by a specified means of communication (e.g., registered mail, telegram). Such stipulation is called **express authorization**. If the offeree uses an unauthorized means of communication to transmit the acceptance, the acceptance is not effective, even if it is received by the offeror within the allowed time period, because the means of communication was a condition of acceptance.

Most offers do not expressly specify the means of communication required for acceptance. The common law recognizes certain implied means of communication. **Implied authorization** may be inferred from what is customary in similar transactions, usage of trade, or prior dealings between the parties. Section 30 of the *Restatement (Second) of Contracts* permits implied authorization "by any medium reasonable in the circumstances."

The following case brings up many of the elements of offer and acceptance.

CASE 10.6
Counteroffer

Ellefson v. Megadeth, Inc.

Web 2005 U.S. Dist. Lexis 545 (2005)
United States District Court for the Southern District of New York

> "*The issue presented by this motion is reminiscent of a first year law school contracts exam. We begin with the fundamental tenet: to have a valid contract, there must be both an offer and an acceptance.*"
>
> —Judge Buchwald

Facts

David Mustaine and David Ellefson are original members of the heavy metal rock band Megadeth. The band was initially formed in 1983, with Mustaine as the lead guitarist, lead vocalist, and lead songwriter. Ellefson was the band's bassist. In 1990, the parties formed a corporation, Megadeth, Inc., with Mustaine owning 80 percent of the corporation and Ellefson 20 percent. Approximately 13 years later, Ellefson sued Mustaine and Megadeth, Inc., alleging that the defendants (collectively "Mustaine") had defrauded Ellefson out of his share of the corporation's profits.

In October 2003, Ellefson and Mustaine entered into negotiations to settle the case. Both parties were represented by attorneys. Mustaine sent a proposed settlement and general release to Ellefson whereby Mustaine would purchase Ellefson's interest in the corporation and various licensing and recording agreements. The settlement offer was received by Ellefson on April 16, 2004.

Negotiations over the proposed settlement continued uneventfully for the next four weeks. Mustaine imposed a 5:00 P.M. deadline on Friday, May 14, 2004, for completion of the settlement. On May 13, Mustaine e-mailed Ellefson that the offer to Ellefson terminated as of 5:00 P.M. Pacific standard time on Friday, May 14, 2004. The following day, Friday, May 14, the attorneys for both sides traded e-mails proposing changes to the offer. At 4:45 P.M., minutes prior to the expiration of

Mustaine's offer, Mustaine e-mailed Ellefson an execution (read-only) copy of the settlement agreement, reiterated the 5:00 P.M. deadline, and stated that he reserved the right to make further changes to Exhibits A and B the following week. Ellefson signed a copy of the settlement agreement and faxed the signature page to Mustaine. Mustaine alleges that Ellefson's faxed signature page was received before the 5:00 P.M. deadline. Ellefson alleges that his fax was not sent by the 5:00 P.M. deadline.

On Thursday, May 20, 2004, Mustaine sent Ellefson fully executed copies of the settlement agreement by postal mail. On May 24, Ellefson e-mailed Mustaine that he was withdrawing from the negotiations and was withdrawing all proposals. Mustaine responded that there was a signed settlement agreement in place, which Ellefson had faxed on May 14, 2004.

On June 2, 2004, Ellefson received the finalized settlement agreement that had been sent by Mustaine by postal mail on May 20, 2004.

Mustaine argues that there was an enforceable settlement agreement between the parties. Ellefson argues that there was not an enforceable settlement agreement between the parties.

Issue

Was an enforceable settlement agreement reached between the parties?

Language of the Court

The issue presented by this motion is reminiscent of a first year law school contracts exam. We begin with the fundamental tenet: to have a valid contract, there must be both an offer and an acceptance. These critical elements insure that there has been mutual assent by the parties to be bound by the terms of the contract. One party makes an offer to enter into a mutual obligation, and the other party can either accept or reject this offer. However, once the offer has been accepted, the parties have formed a contract and are bound by the terms of that agreement, even if later events make them regret their decisions. In the case at hand, the issue is whether the exchange between Ellefson and Mustaine fulfilled the requirements of offer and acceptance.

Contracts are often formed after receipt of a defective acceptance. This is because an acceptance that does not unequivocally comply with the terms of original offer is considered a counteroffer. Any new terms or modified terms in the defective acceptance are treated as new terms of the counteroffer, which the original offeror may then choose to accept or reject. A late acceptance is a form of defective acceptance, and therefore is considered a counteroffer which the original offeror can decide to either accept or reject. Therefore, in order for a contract to exist after receipt of a late acceptance, the original offeror must accept the offeree's counteroffer.

It is undisputed that Mustaine conditioned his offer to Ellefson on the requirement that it be accepted by Ellefson by 5 P.M. PST on Friday, May 14. Further, there is no evidence to support Mustaine's claim that Ellefson's fax was sent within that deadline; accordingly, Ellefson did not comply with the terms of the offer and no contract was formed upon its receipt. Because Ellefson's acceptance did not fully comply with the terms of the original offer, it was not a valid acceptance and thus is viewed as a counteroffer.

Ellefson asserts that his faxed signature page cannot reasonably be construed as a counteroffer since it was utterly silent as to the terms of the Agreement. We find Ellefson's arguments unpersuasive. Regardless of Ellefson's subjective intent, it is the objective significance of his actions that controls. By faxing a signed signature page to an undisputed, execution version of the Agreement, Ellefson signaled his willingness to be bound by its terms, rather than, as he now claims, a desire to continue negotiations. Upon receipt of this fax, Mustaine could reasonably infer that Ellefson offered to bind himself to the terms of the Agreement (sent to him just minutes earlier) if Mustaine was willing to accept his counteroffer. The fact that the signature page did not contain all of the terms is immaterial, as the terms of the contract are not disputed and were contained in the underlying Agreement. Once Mustaine received the fax, Mustaine was free either to accept or reject Ellefson's counteroffer. While Mustaine could accept or reject Ellefson's counteroffer, Mustaine had to manifest his consent to be bound by the counteroffer. Without such evidence of mutual assent, no contract had been formed.

We do concur with Mustaine's alternative contention that the mailing of the completed contract on May 20, 2004, constituted an acceptance of Ellefson's counteroffer. This act established Mustaine's unequivocal intention to accept Ellefson's counteroffer and be bound by the terms of the Agreement.

Under the mailbox rule, Mustaine's acceptance is considered complete upon mailing. Therefore, Mustaine accepted Ellefson's counteroffer prior to Ellefson's May 24 withdrawal of that offer, and an enforceable contract was formed on May 20, 2004.

Ellefson argues that the Court should reject Mustaine's acceptance because the use of regular U.S. mail was an unreasonable method of acceptance in light of the parties' previous conduct. Prior communications between parties had been almost exclusively by fax or email. Therefore, "it was patently unreasonable for Mustaine to mail a purported acceptance by 'snail mail' without even advising Ellefson that it was mailed." [Ellefson's Memorandum]

Under California law, any reasonable and usual mode of communication may be used to accept an offer unless a specific mode is prescribed. Therefore, in the absence of any specific restriction, defendants' acceptance by mail is reasonable. Having examined all the surrounding circumstances, we find no impediment to Mustaine's acceptance by regular mail. First, the original offer and Ellefson's counteroffer contained no restrictions on the mode of acceptance. Second, the use of fax and email to negotiate the Agreement does not preclude Mustaine from using mail to accept Ellefson's counteroffer by sending a fully-executed hard copy of the Agreement, and Ellefson offers no relevant authority to challenge this proposition.

Mustaine's last offer to Ellefson stated that Mustaine reserved the right to make "further changes pending our finalizing Exhibits A and B and the full execution of the agreement early next week." Ellefson's counteroffer signaled his willingness to comply with these terms, including completion by Mustaine the following week. Therefore Mustaine's mailing of the fully-executed contract the following Thursday was consistent with these terms, and reasonable under the circumstances. We therefore find that an enforceable contract was formed on May 20, 2004, prior to Ellefson's attempted withdrawal.

Decision

The U.S. District Court held that an enforceable settlement agreement had been entered into by the parties. The U.S. District Court granted Mustaine's motion to enforce the settlement agreement against Ellefson.

Law & Ethics Questions

1. What is an offer? What is an acceptance?

2. What does the mailbox rule provide? Explain.

3. Do you think the proper mode of acceptance was used in this case?

4. **ETHICS** Was it ethical for Ellefson to try to revoke his acceptance of the settlement agreement?

5. **ETHICS** Did Mustaine act ethically in this case?

Web Exercises

1. **WEB** For the complete opinion of this case, go to *www.prenhall.com/cheesemancases*.

2. **WEB** Visit the website of the United States District Court for the Southern District of New York, at *www.nysd.uscourts.gov*.

3. **WEB** Visit the website of Megadeth, at *www.megadeth.com*.

4. **WEB** Use *www.google.com* to find a video clip of the band Megadeth.

INTERNET AND TECHNOLOGY
Nondisclosure Agreements

A **nondisclosure agreement**—or NDA, as they are called—swears the signatory to secrecy about confidential ideas, trade secrets, and other nonpublic information revealed by the party proffering the NDA.

NDAs have traditionally been used among lawyers, investment bankers, and others involved in secret takeovers and other large corporate deals. But today many entrepreneurs, particularly those in high-tech industries, are using NDAs. An NDA protects a person who has a great idea (or so he or she thinks) and wants to share it with a potential partner, investor, lawyer, or investment banker but wants an assurance that the recipient of the information will not steal or reveal the information to anyone else.

An NDA is an enforceable contract, so if someone violates it, the disclosing party can sue the breaching party for damages. Bill Gates of Microsoft requires plumbers and other persons who work on his house to sign NDAs. Sabeer Bhatia, founder of Hotmail, collected more then 400 NDAs in two years before selling his company to Microsoft for $400 million.

Although it may not be difficult to get some people to sign NDAs, others balk. Some friends and relatives refuse to sign NDAs thrust on them because they present an aura of distrust. Industry bigwigs—venture capitalists, securities analysts, and successful technology companies—routinely refuse to sign NDAs because they see too many similar ideas and do not want their tongues tied by any single one. NDAs will continue to increase in use, though.

Prague, Czech Republic

International trade is often governed by contracts between businesses or parties from different nations.

Consideration

Consideration must be given before a contract can exist. **Consideration** is defined as something of legal value given in exchange for a promise. Consideration can come in many forms. The most common types consist of either a tangible payment (e.g., money, property) or the performance of an act (e.g., providing legal services). Less usual forms of consideration include the forbearance of a legal right (e.g., accepting an out-of-court settlement in exchange for dropping a lawsuit) and non-economic forms of consideration (e.g., refraining from "drinking, using tobacco, swearing, or playing cards or billiards for money"[5] for a specified time period).

Written contracts are presumed to be supported by consideration. This rebuttable presumption, however, may be overcome by sufficient evidence. A few states provide that contracts made under seal cannot be challenged for lack of consideration.

Requirements of Consideration

Consideration consists of two elements: (1) Something of legal value must be given (e.g., either a legal benefit must be received or legal detriment must be suffered) and (2) there must be a bargained-for exchange. Each of these is discussed in the paragraphs that follow:

1. *Legal value.* Under the modern law of contracts, a contract is considered supported by **legal value** if (1) the promisee suffers a *legal detriment* or (2) the promisor receives a *legal benefit*.

   Example Suppose the Dallas Cowboys contract with a tailor to have the tailor make uniforms for the team. The tailor completes the uniforms, but the team manager thinks the color is wrong and refuses to allow the team to wear them. The tailor has suffered a legal detriment (time spent making the uniforms). Under the modern rule of contracts, there is sufficiency of consideration, and the contract is enforceable.

2. *Bargained-for exchange.* To be enforceable, a contract must arise from a **bargained-for exchange**. In most business contracts, the parties engage in such exchanges. The commercial setting in which business contracts are formed leads to this conclusion.

Gift Promises

Gift promises, also called **gratuitous promises**, are unenforceable because they lack consideration. To change a gift promise into an enforceable promise, the promisee must offer to do something in exchange—that is, consideration—for the promise. A completed gift promise cannot be rescinded for lack of consideration.

Example Suppose Mrs. Colby promised to give her son $10,000 and then rescinded the promise. The son would have no recourse because it was a gift promise that lacked consideration. If, however, Mrs. Colby promised her son $10,000 for getting an "A" in his business law course and the son performed as required, the contract would be enforceable.

Example On May 1, Mr. Smith promises to give his granddaughter $10,000 on June 1. If on June 1, Mr. Smith actually gives the $10,000 to his granddaughter, it is a completed gift promise. Mr. Smith cannot thereafter recover the money from his granddaughter, even if the original promise lacked consideration.

The first case that follows involves an uncompleted gift promise. The second case that follows involves completed gifts.

CASE 10.7
Gift Promise

Alden v. Presley

637 S.W.2d 862, **Web** 1982 Tenn. Lexis 340
Supreme Court of Tennessee

> **❝** *The court of appeals concurred in the finding that there was no gift for failure to deliver.* **❞**

—Judge Fones

Facts

Elvis Presley, a singer of great renown and a man of substantial wealth, became engaged to Ginger Alden. He was generous with the Alden family, paying for landscaping the lawn, installing a swimming pool, and making other gifts. When his fiancée's mother, Jo Laverne Alden, sought to divorce her husband, Presley promised to pay off the remaining mortgage indebtedness on the Alden home, which Mrs. Alden was to receive in the divorce settlement. On August 16, 1977, Presley died suddenly, leaving the mortgage unpaid. When the legal representative of Presley's estate refused to pay the $39,587 mortgage, Mrs. Alden brought an action to enforce Presley's promise. The trial court denied recovery. Mrs. Alden appealed.

Issue

Was Presley's promise to pay the mortgage enforceable?

Language of the Court

In the instant case, the trial court held decedent did make a promise unsupported by consideration to plaintiff, that no gift was consummated for failure of delivery, that plaintiff suffered no detriment as she "wound up much better after her association with Elvis A. Presley than if he had never made any promise to Jo Laverne Alden." The court of appeals concurred in the finding that there was no gift for failure to deliver, holding that delivery is not complete unless complete dominion and control of the gift is surrendered by the donor and acquired by the donee.

Decision

The supreme court held that Presley's promise was a gratuitous executory promise that was not supported by consideration. As such, it was unenforceable against Presley's estate. The court dismissed the case and assessed costs against the plaintiff.

Law & Ethics Questions

1. Should gratuitous promises be enforced? Why or why not?

2. **ETHICS** Was it unethical for the representative of Presley's estate to refuse to complete the gift? Did they have any other choice?

3. Does it make a difference if a gift promise is executed or executory? Explain.

Web Exercises

1. **WEB** For the complete opinion of this case, go to *www.prenhall.com/cheesemancases*.

2. **WEB** Visit the webpage of the supreme court of Tennessee, at *www.tsc.state.tn.us/geninfo/bio/supreme/biosc.htm*.

3. **WEB** Use *www.google.com* to find a brief biography of Elvis Presley. Read it.

4. **WEB** Visit the website of Graceland, the home of Elvis Presley, at *www.elvis.com/graceland*.

5. **WEB** Go to *www.elvis.com* to see a video clip of Elvis Presley singing a song.

CASE 10.8
Gift

Cooper v. Smith

800 N.E.2d 372, **Web** 2003 Ohio App. Lexis 5446
Court of Appeals of Ohio

> **❝** *Many gifts are made for reasons that sour with the passage of time. Unfortunately, gift law does not allow a donor to recover/revoke a gift simply because his or her reasons for giving it have soured.* **❞**

—Judge Harsha

Facts

In May 2001, Lester Cooper suffered serious injuries that caused him to be hospitalized for an extended period of time. While he was hospitalized, Julie Smith, whom Cooper had met the year before, and Janet Smith, Julie's mother, made numerous trips to visit him. Although Julie was married to another man at the time, a romantic relationship developed between Cooper and Julie. While in the hospital, Cooper proposed marriage to Julie, and she accepted. Julie obtained a divorce from her husband in October 2001. Cooper ultimately received an $180,000 settlement for his injuries.

After being released from the hospital, Cooper moved into Janet's house and lived with Janet and Julie. Over the next couple months, Cooper purchased a number of items for Julie, including a diamond engagement ring, a car, a computer, a tanning bed, and horses. On Julie's request, Cooper paid off Janet's car. Cooper also paid for various improvements to Janet's house, such as having a new furnace installed and having wood flooring laid in the kitchen. By December 2001, the settlement money had run out, and Julie had not yet married Cooper. In the summer of 2002, Julie and Cooper had a disagreement, and Cooper moved out of the house. Julie returned the engagement ring to Cooper. Cooper sued Julie and Janet to recover the gifts or the value of the gifts he gave them. The magistrate who heard the case dismissed Cooper's case, and the trial court affirmed the dismissed of the case. Cooper appealed.

Issue

Can Cooper recover the gifts or the value of the gifts he gave to Julie and Janet Smith?

Language of the Court

Unless the parties have agreed otherwise, the donor is entitled to recover the engagement ring (or its value) if the marriage does not occur, regardless of who ended the engagement. While we are willing to imply a condition concerning the engagement ring, we are unwilling to do so for other gifts given during the engagement period. Unlike the engagement ring, the other gifts have no symbolic meaning. Rather, they are merely "tokens of love and affection" which the donor bore for the donee. Many gifts are made for reasons that sour with the passage of time. Unfortunately, gift law does not allow a donor to recover/revoke a gift simply because his or her reasons for giving it have soured.

Generally, a completed gift is absolute and irrevocable. If we were to imply a condition on gifts given during the engagement period, then every gift the donor gave, no matter how small or insignificant, would be recoverable. We believe the best approach is to treat gifts exchanged during the engagement period (excluding the engagement ring) as absolute and irrevocable gifts unless the donor has expressed intent that the gift be conditioned on the subsequent marriage. Cooper offered no evidence establishing that he gave the gifts on the express condition that they be returned to him if the engagement ended. Thus, the gifts are irrevocable gifts and Cooper is not entitled to their return.

Decision

The court of appeals held that the gifts made by Cooper to Julie (other than the engagement ring) and to Janet were irrevocable gifts that he could not recover simply because his engagement with Julie ended. The court of appeals affirmed the judgment of the trial court allowing Julie and Janet Smith to keep these gifts.

Law & Ethics Questions

1. Should the return of an engagement ring and other gifts made during the engagement period be treated differently when the engagement is broken off? Explain.

2. **ETHICS** Did Julie and Janet Smith act ethically in keeping the gifts Cooper had given them? Did Cooper act ethically in trying to get the gifts back?

3. Does the no-fault rule regarding the return of engagement rings upon the termination of an engagement save court expenses? Explain.

Web Exercises

1. **WEB** For the complete opinion of this case, go to *www.prenhall.com/cheesemancases*.

2. **WEB** Visit the website of the court of appeals of Ohio, Fourth District, at *www.4thdistrictappeals.com*.

3. **WEB** Use *www.google.com* to find an article about a gift promise. Read it.

CONTEMPORARY ENVIRONMENT

When Is Consideration Inadequate?

> ❝*Plaintiff expressly testified that "other good and valuable consideration" meant the love and affection plaintiff and James Paul DeLaney had for one another. In Illinois, love and affection do not constitute legal consideration.*❞

—Judge Lorenz

The courts usually do not inquire into the **adequacy of consideration**. Generally, parties are free to agree on the consideration they are willing to pay or receive under a contract. This rule is based on the court's reluctance to inquire into the motives of a party for entering into a contract or to save a party from a "bad deal."

Some states recognize an exception to the general rule that the courts will not examine the sufficiency of consideration. These states permit a party to escape from a contract if the inadequacy of consideration *shocks the conscience of the court*. This standard, which is applied on a case-by-case basis, considers the value of the item or service contracted for, the amount of consideration paid, the relationship of the parties, and other facts and circumstances of the case.

Consider this situation: Mr. and Mrs. James Paul DeLaney were married in January 1953. A few years later, they acquired a painting, allegedly the work of Peter Paul Rubens, titled "The Calydonian Boar Hunt." In 1966, the DeLaneys moved into an apartment building and became friends with Mr. and Mrs. Nicholas T. O'Neill. Mr. Delaney and Mr. O'Neill became close friends. On August 18, 1970, Mr. Delaney purportedly sold the Rubens painting to Mr. O'Neill for $10 and "other good and valuable consideration." A written contract embodying the terms of the agreement was prepared and signed by Mr. DeLaney and Mr. O'Neill. Mrs. DeLaney was not informed of the sale. At the time of the sale, Mr. DeLaney told Mr. O'Neill that the painting was worth at least $100,000. The painting, however, remained with DeLaney and was in storage at the time of this lawsuit. In 1974, Mrs. DeLaney instituted a divorce action against Mr. DeLaney. At that time, she learned of the purported sale of the painting to O'Neill. In the divorce action, Mrs. DeLaney claimed an interest in the painting as marital property. Mr. O'Neill instituted this action, seeking a declaratory judgment regarding title to the painting.

The trial court held in favor of Mrs. DeLaney and voided the sales contract between Mr. DeLaney and Mr. O'Neill. The appellate court affirmed. The courts held that the consideration paid by Mr. O'Neill for the painting "shocked the conscience of the court" and thereby rendered the transfer void. The appellate court stated:

Plaintiff expressly testified that "other good and valuable consideration" meant the love and affection plaintiff and James Paul DeLaney had for one another. In Illinois, love and affection do not constitute legal consideration. Thus, the only remaining valid consideration for the transaction was the tender of $10. A purchase price of $10 for such a valuable work of art is so grossly inadequate consideration as to shock the conscience of this court, as it did the trial court's. To find $10 valid consideration for this painting would be to reduce the requirement of consideration to a mere formality. This we will not do.

Critics of this case argue that the parties should be free to contract based upon what they feel is adequate consideration in the circumstances. Proponents of this case argue that courts should be allowed to examine the adequacy of consideration underlying a contract to prevent unfair contracts. *O'Neill v. DeLaney*, 415 N.E.2d 1260, **Web** 1980 Ill. App. Lexis 4189 (Appellate Court of Illinois)

Law & Ethics Questions

1. What does the doctrine of inadequacy of consideration provide? Explain.
2. **ETHICS** Was it ethical for O'Neill to pay so little for the painting?
3. **ETHICS** Did Mrs. DeLaney have a good lawful cause of action against O'Neill?

Web Exercises

1. **WEB** For the complete opinion of this case, go to *www.prenhall.com/cheesemancases*.
2. **WEB** Visit the website of the appellate court of Illinois, First District, at *www.state.il.us/court/appellatecourt*.
3. **WEB** Use *www.google.com* to find a photo of painting by Peter Paul Rubens called "The Calydonian Boar Hunt." Can you find the value of this painting?

Contracts Lacking Consideration

Some contracts seem as though they are supported by consideration even though they are not. The following types of contracts fall into this category.

Illegal Consideration

A contract cannot be supported by a promise to refrain from doing an illegal act because that is **illegal consideration**. Contracts based on illegal consideration are void.

Example A statement such as "I will burn your house down unless you agree to pay me $10,000" cannot become an enforceable contract. Even if the threatened party agrees to make the payment, the contract is unenforceable and void because it is supported by illegal consideration (arson is unlawful).

Illusory Promises

If parties enter into a contract, but one or both of the parties can choose not to perform their contractual obligations, the contract lacks consideration. Such promises, which are known as **illusory promises** (or **illusory contracts**), are unenforceable.

Example A contract that provides that one of the parties has to perform only if he or she chooses to do so is an illusory contract.

Moral Obligation

Promises made out of a sense of **moral obligation** or honor are generally unenforceable on the ground that they lack consideration. In other words, moral consideration is not treated as legal consideration. Contracts based on love and affection and deathbed promises are examples of such promises. A minority of states hold that moral obligations are enforceable.

Preexisting Duty

A promise lacks consideration if a person promises to perform an act or do something he or she is already under an obligation to do. This is called a **preexisting duty**. The promise is unenforceable because no new consideration has been given.

Example Many states have adopted statutes that prohibit police officers from accepting rewards for apprehending criminals.

In the private sector, the preexisting duty rule often arises when one of the parties to an existing contract seeks to change the terms of the contract during the course of its performance. Such midstream changes are unenforceable: The parties have a preexisting duty to perform according to the original terms of the contract.

Sometimes a party to a contract runs into substantial *unforeseen difficulties* while performing his or her contractual duties. If the parties modify their contract to accommodate these unforeseen difficulties, the modification will be enforced even though it is not supported by new consideration.

Example Suppose a landowner enters into a contract with a contractor who agrees to excavate a hole for the foundation of a major office building. When the excavation is partially completed, toxic wastes are unexpectedly found at the site. Removal of toxic wastes is highly regulated by law and would substantially increase the cost of the excavation. If the landowner agrees to pay the contractor increased compensation to remove the toxic wastes, this modification of the contract is enforceable even though it is unsupported by new consideration.

> There is grim irony in speaking of freedom of contract of those who, because of their economic necessities, give their service for less than is needful to keep body and soul together.
>
> Harlan Fiske Stone
> *Morehead v. N.Y. ex rel. Tipaldo*
> *(1936)*

Past Consideration

In a business setting, problems of **past consideration** often arise when a party to a contract promises to pay additional compensation for work done in the past.

Example Felipe Chavez, who has worked for the Acme Corporation for 30 years, is retiring. The president of Acme says, "Because you were such a loyal employee, Acme will pay you a bonus of $25,000." The corporation refuses to pay the $25,000. Unfortunately for Mr. Chavez, the contract is unenforceable because it is based on past consideration.

The following case the court had to decide whether there was consideration.

C A S E **10.9**
Consideration

In the Matter of Wirth

14 A.D.3d 572, 789 N.Y.S.2d 69, **Web** 2005 N.Y. App. Div. Lexis 424 (2005)
Supreme Court of New York, Appellate Division

❝ The Pledge Agreement further stated: "I acknowledge that Drexel's promise to use the amount pledged by me shall constitute full and adequate consideration for this pledge." ❞

—Judge Schmidt

Facts

Raymond P. Wirth signed a pledge agreement which stated that in consideration of his interest in education, and "intending to be legally bound," he irrevocably pledged and promised to pay Drexel University the sum of $150,000. The pledge agreement provided that an endowed scholarship would be created in Wirth's name. Wirth died two months after signing the pledge but before any money had been paid to Drexel. When Wirth's estate refused to honor the pledge, Drexel sued the estate to collect the $150,000. The estate alleged that the pledge was unenforceable because of lack of consideration. The surrogate court denied Drexel's motion for summary judgment and dismissed Drexel's claim against the estate. Drexel appealed.

Issue

Was the pledge agreement supported by consideration and therefore enforceable against Wirth's estate?

Language of the Court

Pursuant to Pennsylvania's Uniform Written Obligations Act: "A written release or promise, hereafter made and signed by the person releasing or promising, shall not be invalid or unenforceable for lack of consideration, if the writing also contains an additional express statement, in any form or language, that the signer intends to be legally bound." Pursuant to this statute, the Pledge Agreement does not fail for lack of consideration, as the decedent expressly stated his intent to be legally bound by the pledge.

Moreover, even if we were to determine that the decedent, as promisor, anticipated consideration in return for his promise, there was no failure of consideration. The Pledge Agreement, which also was executed by representatives of Drexel, provided that the pledged sum "shall be used by" Drexel to create an endowed scholarship fund in the decedent's name, per the terms of the attached Letter of Understanding. The Pledge Agreement further stated: "I acknowledge that Drexel's promise to use the amount pledged by me shall constitute full and adequate consideration for this pledge."

In our view, pursuant to the terms of the Pledge Agreement, Drexel provided sufficient consideration by expressly accepting the terms of the Pledge Agreement and by promising to establish the scholarship fund in the decedent's name. The fact that the decedent died before the initial gift was transferred into a special account set up by Drexel and therefore the scholarship fund was not yet implemented, did not negate the sufficiency of the promise as consideration to set up the fund.

Decision

The appellate court held that the pledge agreement was supported by consideration and was therefore enforceable against Wirth's estate. The appellate court reversed the decision of the surrogate court and granted Drexel's motion for summary judgment against Wirth's estate.

Law & Ethics Questions

1. What is consideration? What happens if there is lack of consideration supporting a promise? Explain.
2. **ETHICS** Was it ethical for Wirth's estate to try to back out of the pledge agreement that Wirth made before he died?
3. What special statute did Pennsylvania enact that solves the issue of lack of consideration in many contracts? Explain.

Web Exercises

1. **WEB** For the complete opinion of this case, go to *www.prenhall.com/cheesemancases*.
2. **WEB** Visit the website of the supreme court of New York, Appellate Division, Second Department, at *www.courts.state.ny.us/courts/ad2*.
3. **WEB** Visit the website of Drexel University, at *www.drexel.edu*, and Drexel Online, at *www.drexel.com*.
4. **WEB** Use *www.google.com* to find an article that discusses a pledge or gift to your college or university. Read it.

CONCEPT SUMMARY

Promises Lacking Consideration

TYPE OF CONSIDERATION	DESCRIPTION OF PROMISE
Illegal consideration	Promise to refrain from doing an illegal act.
Illusory promise	Promise in which one or both parties can choose not to perform their obligation.
Moral obligation	Promise made out of a sense of moral obligation, honor, love, or affection. Some states enforce these types of contracts.
Preexisting duty	Promise based on the preexisting duty of the promisee to perform. The promise is enforceable if (1) the parties rescind the contract and enter into a new contract or (2) there are unforeseen difficulties.
Past consideration	Promise based on the past performance of the promisee.

CONTEMPORARY ENVIRONMENT
Special Business Contracts

Generally, the courts tolerate a greater degree of uncertainty in business contracts than in personal contracts, under the premise that sophisticated parties know how to protect themselves when negotiating contracts. The law imposes an obligation of good faith on the performance of the parties to requirements and output contracts.

The following paragraphs describe special types of business contracts that specifically allow a greater degree of uncertainty concerning consideration.

Output Contracts

In an **output contract**, the seller agrees to sell all of its production to a single buyer. Output contracts serve the legitimate business purposes of (1) assuring the seller of a buyer for all its output and (2) assuring the buyer of a source of supply for the goods it needs.

> **Example** Organic Foods, Inc., is a company that operates farms that produce organically grown grains and vegetables. Whole Food Markets is a grocery store chain that sells organically grown foods. Whole Food Markets contracts with Organic Foods, Inc., to purchase all the organic foods grown by Organic Foods, Inc., this year. This is an example of an output contract: Organic Foods, Inc., must sell all its output to Whole Foods Market.

Requirements Contracts

A **requirements contract** is one in which a buyer contracts to purchase all the requirements for an item from one seller. Such contracts serve the legitimate business purposes of (1) assuring the buyer of a uniform source of supply and (2) providing the seller with reduced selling costs.

> **Example** The Firestone Tire Company manufactures tires that are used on automobiles. Ford Motor Company manufactures automobiles on which it must place tires before the automobiles can be sold. Ford Motor Company enters into a contract with Firestone Tire Company to purchase all the tires it will need this year from Firestone Tire Company. This is an example of a requirements contract: Ford Motor Company has agreed to purchase all the tires it will need from Firestone Tire Company.

Best-Efforts Contracts

A **best-efforts contract** is a contract that contains a clause that requires one or both of the parties to use their *best efforts* to achieve the objective of the contract. The courts generally have held that the imposition of the best-efforts duty provides sufficient consideration to make a contract enforceable.

> **Example** Real estate listing contracts often require a real estate broker to use his or her best efforts to find a buyer for the listed real estate. Contracts often require underwriters to use their best efforts to sell securities on behalf of their corporate clients.

Settlement of Claims

The law promotes the voluntary settlement of disputed claims. Settlement saves judicial resources and serves the interests of the parties entering into the settlement.

In some situations, one of the parties to a contract believes that he or she did not receive what he or she was due. This party may attempt to reach a compromise with the other party (e.g., by paying less consideration than was provided for in the contract). The compromise agreement is called an **accord**. If the accord is performed, it is called a **satisfaction**. This type of settlement is called an **accord and satisfaction**, or a **compromise**. If the accord is not satisfied, the other party can sue to enforce either the accord or the original contract.

Example Suppose that a contract stipulated that the cost of a computer system that keeps track of inventory, accounts receivable, and so on is $100,000. After it is installed, the computer system does not perform as promised. To settle the dispute, the parties agree that $70,000 is to be paid as full and final payment for the computer. This accord is enforceable even though no new consideration is given because reasonable persons would disagree as to the worth of the computer system that was actually installed.

Promissory Estoppel

The courts have developed the doctrine of **promissory estoppel** or (**detrimental reliance**) to avoid injustice. This doctrine is a broad policy-based doctrine. It is used to provide a remedy to a person who has relied on another person's promise, but that person has withdrawn his or her promise and is not subject to a breach of contract action because one of the two elements discussed in this chapter—agreement or consideration—is lacking.

Courthouse, Santa Barbara, California

Courts are often called upon to enforce contracts between contracting parties.

The doctrine of promissory estoppel *estops* (i.e., prevents) the promisor from revoking his or her promise. Therefore, the person who has detrimentally relied on the promise for performance may sue the promisor for performance or other remedy the court feels is fair to award in the circumstances.

For the doctrine of promissory estoppel to be applied, the following elements must be shown:

1. The promisor made a promise.
2. The promisor should have reasonably expected to induce the promisee to reply on the promise.
3. The promisee actually relied on the promise and engaged in an action or forbearance of a right of a definite and substantial nature.
4. Injustice would result if the promise were not enforced.

> Now equity is no part of the law, but a moral virtue, which qualifies, moderates, and reforms the rigor, hardness, and edge of the law, and is a universal truth.
>
> Lord Cowper
> *Dudley v. Dudley (1705)*

Example XYZ Construction Company, a general contractor, requests bids from subcontractors for work to be done on a hospital building that XYZ plans to submit a bid to build. Bert Plumbing Company submits the lowest bid for the plumbing work, and XYZ incorporates Bert's low bid in its own bid for the general contract. In this example, the doctrine of promissory estoppel prevents Bert from withdrawing its bid. If XYZ is awarded the contract to build the hospital, it could enforce Bert's promise to perform.

INTERNATIONAL LAW
China Adopts New Contract Laws

After 15 years of negotiations, China officially joined the ranks of the World Trade Organization (WTO) in late 2001. In preparation for this, the National People's Congress of China took many steps to assure success, including modernizing the country's legal system. Just two years earlier, China dramatically overhauled its contract laws by enacting the **Unified Contract Law (UCL)**. This new set of laws effectively

wiped out or drastically changed many business and commercial contract laws that had been the standard for many years.

The UCL was designed to provide users with a consistent and easy-to-understand set of statutes that more closely resembled international business contracting principles. This was a necessary step in ensuring that China was accepted into the WTO and helping the country move closer to being the global economic powerhouse it is now becoming.

According to the UCL, the new guidelines exist to "protect contracting parties' legal rights, maintain social economic order, and improve the construction of socialist modernization." The general provisions of the UCL also require that a contract "not interrupt social-economic order or harm public interests" and that the contracting parties be "honest and trustworthy, and respect societal ethics."

The UCL covers all the parts of contract law that should be familiar to Western businesses, including the definitions of *contract*, *acceptance*, *consideration*, *performance*, *breach of contract*, and *remedies*. Even so, there are many aspects of the UCL that differ from U.S. contract law, and anyone doing business in China or with a Chinese company should study it carefully.

Web Exercises

1. **WEB** To learn more about Chinese law, visit the Law Library of Congress guide to China, at *www.loc.gov/law/guide/china.html*.

2. **WEB** To learn more about doing business in China, visit the US-China Business Council's website, at *www.uschina.org*.

Chapter Summary

Agreement, p. 259

1. *Offer.* An offer is a manifestation by one party of a willingness to enter into a contract.
2. *Offeror.* The offeror is the party who makes an offer.
3. *Offeree.* The offeree is the party to whom an offer is made. This party has the power to create an agreement by accepting the terms of the offer.

Offer, p. 259

Objective Intent

The intent to enter into a contract is determined by the *objective theory of contract*—that is, whether a reasonable person viewing the circumstances would conclude that the parties intended to be legally bound.

Definiteness of Terms

The terms of an offer must be definite so that the agreement between the parties can be determined.

Implied Terms

Reasonable terms (e.g., price, time for performance) may be *implied*.

Communication

An offer must be communicated to the offeree by the offeror.

Advertisements

Generally, an advertisement is an invitation to make an offer. However, an advertisement is an offer if it is so definite and specific as to show the advertiser's intent to be bound to the terms of the advertisement.

Rewards

A reward is an offer to create a unilateral contract.

Auctions

There are two types of auctions:

1. *Auction with reserve.* An auction with reserve is an invitation to make an offer. The seller retains the right to refuse the highest bid and withdraw the good from sale.
2. *Auction without reserve.* An auction without reserve is an offer. The seller must accept the highest bid (above the minimum bid). This type of auction must be stipulated.

Termination of Offers, p. 265

Revocation of an Offer by the Offeror

The offeror may *revoke* (withdraw) an offer any time prior to its acceptance by the offeree.

Rejection of an Offer by the Offeree

An offer is terminated if the offeree rejects the offer by his or her words or conduct.

Counteroffer by the Offeree

A counteroffer by the offeree terminates the offeror's offer (and creates a new offer).

Destruction of the Subject Matter

An offer terminates if the subject matter of the offer is destroyed prior to acceptance through no fault of either party.

Death or Incompetency of the Offeror or Offeree

The death or incompetency of either the offeror or the offeree prior to acceptance terminates the offer.

Supervening Illegality

If prior to the acceptance of an offer, the object of the offer is made illegal by statute, regulation, court decision, or other law, the offer terminates.

Lapse of Time

An offer terminates upon the expiration of a stated time in the offer. If no time is stated, the offer terminates after a "reasonable time."

Option Contracts

If an offeree pays the offeror compensation to keep an offer open for an agreed-upon period of time, an *option contract* is created. The offeror cannot sell the property to anyone else during the option period.

Acceptance, p. 269

Acceptance is manifestation of assent by the offeree to the terms of the offer. Acceptance of the offer by the offeree creates a contract.

Rules for Acceptance

1. *Mirror image rule.* Under the common law of contracts, an offeree must accept the terms offered by the offeror to create a contract. Any change in terms by the offeree constitutes a counteroffer, not an acceptance.
2. *Acceptance-upon-dispatch rule.* Unless otherwise provided in the offer, acceptance is effective when it is dispatched by the offeree. This rule is often called the *mailbox rule*.
3. *Proper dispatch rule.* An acceptance must be properly addressed, packaged, and have prepaid postage or delivery charges to be effective when dispatched. Generally, improperly dispatched acceptances are not effective until actually received by the offeror.
4. *Mode of acceptance.* Acceptance must be by the express means of communication stipulated in the offer, or, if no means is stipulated, then by reasonable means in the circumstances.

Consideration, p. 275

Consideration involves a thing of value being given in exchange for a promise. It may be tangible or intangible property, performance of a service, forbearance of a legal right, or another thing of value.

Requirements of Consideration

1. *Legal value.* Something of legal value must be given as consideration. Either (a) the promisee suffers a *legal detriment* or (b) the promisor receives a *legal benefit*.
2. *Bargained-for-exchange.* A contract must arise from a bargained-for exchange.

Gift Promises

Gift promises (or *gratuitous promises*) are unenforceable because they lack consideration.

Contracts Lacking Consideration, p. 278

A number of types of contracts are unenforceable because they lack consideration.

Illegal Consideration

A contract cannot be supported by a promise to refrain from doing an illegal act.

Illusory Promises

If one or both parties to a contract can choose not to perform their contractual duties, the contract lacks consideration.

Moral Obligation

A promise made out of a sense of moral obligation, honor, love, or affection lacks consideration.

Preexisting Duty

A promise to perform an act or do something that a person is already under an obligation to do lacks consideration.

Past Consideration

A promise based on a party's past consideration cannot be the basis for a contract.

Special Contracts

1. *Output contracts.* A contract in which the seller agrees to sell all its production to a single buyer is enforceable if the parties act in good faith.
2. *Requirements contracts.* A contract in which the buyer agrees to purchase all the requirements for an item from a single seller is enforceable if the parties act in good faith.
3. *Best-efforts contracts.* A contract that requires a party to use its best efforts to accomplish the objective of the contract is enforceable.

Settlement of Claims

Accord and satisfaction is a compromise agreement in which the parties agree to settle a contract dispute and do so.

Promissory Estoppel, p. 281

Promissory estoppel is a policy-based equitable doctrine that prevents a promisor from revoking his or her promise even though the promise lacks consideration. The requirements are:

1. The promisor made a promise.
2. The promisor should have reasonably expected to induce the promisee to rely on the promise.
3. The promisee actually relied on the promise and engaged in an action or forbearance of a right of a definite and substantial nature.
4. Injustice would result if the promise were not enforced.

Test Review Terms and Concepts

Case Problems

10.1 Objective Theory of Contracts: While A. H. and Ida Zehmer, husband and wife, were drinking with W. O. Lucy, Mr. Zehmer made a written offer to sell to Lucy a 471-acre farm the Zehmers owned for $50,000. Zehmer contends that his offer was made in jest and that he only wanted to bluff Lucy into admitting that he did not have $50,000. Instead, Lucy appeared to take the offer seriously, offered $5 to bind the deal, and had Mrs. Zehmer sign it. When the Zehmers refused to perform the contract, Lucy brought this action to compel specific performance of the contract. Is the contract enforceable? *Lucy v. Zehmer* 196 Va. 493, 84 S.E.2d 516, **Web** 1954 Va. Lexis 244 (Supreme Court of Virginia)

10.2 Terms of a Contract: Ben Hunt and others operated a farm under the name S.B.H. Farms. Hunt went to McIlory Bank and Trust and requested a loan to build hog houses, buy livestock, and expand farming operations. The bank agreed to loan S.B.H. Farms $175,000, for which short-term promissory notes were signed by Hunt and the other owners of S.B.H. Farms. At that time, oral discussions were held with the bank officer regarding long-term financing of S.B.H.'s farming operations; no dollar amount, interest rate, or repayment terms were discussed. When the owners of S.B.H. Farms defaulted on the promissory notes, the bank filed for foreclosure on the farm and other collateral. S.B.H. Farms counterclaimed for $750,000 damages, alleging that the bank breached its oral contract to provide long-term financing. Was there an oral contract for long-term financing? *Hunt v. McIlory Bank and Trust*, 2 Ark. App. 87, 616 S.W.2d 759, **Web** 1981 Ark. App. Lexis 716 (Court of Appeals of Arkansas)

10.3 Implied Terms: MacDonald Group, Ltd. (MacDonald), is the managing general partner of "Fresno Fashion Square," a regional shopping mall in Fresno, California. The mall has several major anchor tenants and numerous smaller stores and shops, including Edmond's of Fresno, a jeweler. Edmond's signed a lease with MacDonald which provided that "there shall not be more than two jewelry stores" located in the mall. Nine years later, MacDonald sent Edmond's notice that it intended to expand the mall and lease space to other jewelers. The lease was silent as to the coverage of additional mall space. Edmond's sued MacDonald, arguing that the lease applied to mall additions. Who wins? *Edmond's of Fresno v. MacDonald Group, Ltd.*, 171 Cal.App.3d 598, 217 Cal.Rptr. 375, **Web** 1985 Cal. App. Lexis 2436 (Court of Appeal of California)

10.4 Implied Terms: Howard R. Wright hired John W. Cerdes to construct a home for him at a price of $43,150. The contract was silent regarding the time of completion. Construction was not completed after nine months. At that time, Wright obtained an injunction ordering Cerdes to stop work. Wright hired other contractors to complete the building. Cerdes sued Wright for breach of contract, claiming that he was due the contract price. How long should Cerdes have had to complete the house? *Cerdes v. Wright*, 408 So.2d 926, **Web** 1981 La. App. Lexis 5531 (Court of Appeal of Louisiana)

10.5 Reward: Rudy Turilli operated the "Jesse James Museum" in Stanton, Missouri. He contends that the man who was shot, killed, and buried as the notorious desperado Jesse James in 1882 was an impostor and that Jesse James lived for many years thereafter under the alias J. Frank Dalton and last lived with Turilli at his museum until the 1950s. Turilli appeared before a nationwide television audience and stated that he would pay $10,000 to anyone who could prove that his statements were wrong. After hearing this offer, Stella James, a relative of Jesse James, produced affidavits of persons related to and acquainted with the Jesse James family, constituting evidence that Jesse James was killed as alleged in song and legend on April 3, 1882. When Turilli refused to pay the reward, James sued for breach of contract. Who wins? *James v. Turilli*, 473 S.W.2d 757, **Web** 1971 Mo. App. Lexis 585 (Court of Appeals of Missouri)

10.6 Counteroffer: Glende Motor Company (Glende), an automobile dealership that sold new cars, leased premises from certain landlords. One day, fire destroyed part of the leased premises, and Glende restored the leasehold premises. The landlords received payment of insurance proceeds for the fire. Glende sued the landlords to recover the insurance proceeds. Ten days before the trial was to begin, the defendants jointly served on Glende a document titled "Offer to Compromise Before Trial," which was a settlement offer of $190,000. Glende agreed to the amount of the settlement but made it contingent upon the execution of a new lease. The next day, the defendants notified Glende that they were revoking the settlement offer. Glende thereafter tried to accept the original settlement offer. Has there been a settlement of the lawsuit? *Glende Motor Company v. Superior Court*, 159 Cal.App.3d 389, 205 Cal.Rptr. 682, **Web** 1984 Cal. App. Lexis 2435 (Court of Appeal of California)

10.7 Acceptance: Peter Andrus owned an apartment building that he had insured under a fire insurance policy sold by J. C. Durick Insurance (Durick). Two months prior to the expiration of the policy, Durick notified Andrus that the building should be insured for $48,000 (or 80 percent of the building's value), as required by the insurance company. Andrus replied that (1) he wanted insurance to match the amount of the outstanding mortgage on the building (i.e., $24,000) and (2) if Durick could not sell this insurance, he would go elsewhere. Durick sent a new insurance policy in the face amount of $48,000, with the notation that the policy was automatically accepted unless Andrus notified him to the contrary. Andrus did not reply. However, he did not pay the premiums on the policy. Durick sued Andrus to recover these premiums. Who wins? *J. C. Durick Insurance v. Andrus*, 139 Vt. 150, 424 A.2d 249, **Web** 1980 Vt. Lexis 1490 (Supreme Court of Vermont)

10.8 Mailbox Rule: William Jenkins and Nathalie Monk owned a building in Sacramento, California. They leased the building to Tuneup Masters for five years. The lease provided that Tuneup Masters could extend the lease for an additional five years if it gave written notice of its intention to do so by certified or registered mail at least six months prior to the expiration of the term of the lease.

Three days before the expiration of the lease, Larry Selditz, vice president of Tuneup Masters, prepared a letter exercising the option, prepared and sealed an envelope with the letter in it, prepared U.S. Postal Service Form 3800, affixed the certified mail sticker on the envelope, and had his secretary deliver the envelope to the Postal Service annex located on the ground floor of the office building. Postal personnel occupied the annex only between the hours of 9 and 10 A.M. At the end of each day, between 5 and 5:15 P.M., a postal employee picked up outgoing mail. The letter to the landlords was lost in the mail. The landlords thereafter refused to renew the lease and brought an unlawful detainer action against Tuneup Masters. Was the notice renewing the option effective? *Jenkins v. Tuneup Masters*, 190 Cal.App.3d 1, 235 Cal.Rptr. 214, **Web** 1987 Cal. App. Lexis 1475 (Court of Appeal of California)

10.9 Consideration: Clyde and Betty Penley were married. Eighteen years later, Clyde operated an automotive tire business, and Betty owned an interest in a Kentucky Fried Chicken (KFC) franchise. That year, when Betty became ill, she requested that Clyde begin spending additional time at the KFC franchise to ensure its continued operation. Subsequently, Betty agreed that if Clyde would devote full time to the KFC franchise, they would operate the business as a joint enterprise, share equally in the ownership of its assets, and divide its returns equally. Pursuant to this agreement, Clyde terminated his tire business and devoted his full time to the KFC franchise. Twelve years later, Betty abandoned Clyde and denied him any rights in the KFC franchise. Clyde sued to enforce the agreement with Betty. Is the agreement enforceable? *Penley v. Penley*, 314 N.C. 1, 332 S.E.2d 51, **Web** 1985 N.C. Lexis 1706 (Supreme Court of North Carolina)

10.10 Forbearance to Sue: When John W. Frasier died, he left a will that devised certain of his community and separate property to his wife, Lena, and their three children. These devises were more valuable to Lena than just her interest in the community property that she would otherwise have received without the will. The devises to her, however, were conditioned upon the filing of a waiver by Lena of her interest in the community property, and if she failed to file the waiver, she would then receive only her interest in the community property and nothing more. Lena hired her brother, D. L. Carter, an attorney, to represent her. Carter failed to file the waiver on Lena's behalf, thus preventing her from taking under the will. Instead, she received her interest in the community property, which was $19,358 less than she would have received under the will. Carter sent Lena the following letter:

This is to advise and confirm our agreement—that in the event the J. W. Frasier estate case now on appeal is not terminated so that you will receive settlement equal to your share of the estate as you would have done if your waiver had been filed in the estate in proper time, I will make up any balance to you in payments as suits my convenience and will pay interest on your loss at 6 percent.

The appeal was decided against Lena. When she tried to enforce the contract against Carter, he alleged that the contract was not enforceable because it was not supported by valid consideration. Who wins? *Frasier v. Carter*, 92 Idaho 79, 437 P.2d 32, **Web** 1968 Ida. Lexis 249 (Supreme Court of Idaho)

10.11 Past Consideration: A. J. Whitmire and R. Lee Whitmire were brothers. R. Lee Whitmire married Lillie Mae Whitmire. For 4 years, A. J. performed various services for his brother and sister-in-law. During this time, R. Lee and Lillie Mae purchased some land. Fifteen years later, in the presence of Lillie Mae, R. Lee told A. J., "When we're gone, this land is yours" At that time, A. J. had not done any work for R. Lee or Lillie Mae for 16 years, and none was expected or provided in the future. Thirty years later, after both R. Lee and Lillie Mae had died, A. J. filed a claim with the estate of Lillie Mae, seeking specific performance of the earlier promise to give him the land. Does A. J. get the property? *Whitmire v. Watkins*, 245 Ga. 713, 267 S.E.2d 6, **Web** 1980 Ga. Lexis 908 (Supreme Court of Georgia)

10.12 Preexisting Duty: Robert Chuckrow Construction Company (Chuckrow) was employed as the general contractor to build a Kinney Shoe Store. Chuckrow employed Ralph Gough to perform the carpentry work on the store. The contract with Gough stipulated that he was to provide all labor, materials, tools, equipment, scaffolding, and other items necessary to complete the carpentry work. Gough's employees erected 38 trusses at the job site. The next day, 32 of the trusses fell off the building. The reason for the trusses having fallen was unexplained, and evidence showed that it was not due to Chuckrow's fault or a deficiency in the building plans. Chuckrow told Gough that he would pay him to reerect the trusses and continue work. When the job was complete, Chuckrow paid Gough the original contract price but refused to pay him for the additional cost of reerecting the trusses. Gough sued Chuckrow for this expense. Can Gough recover? *Robert Chuckrow Construction Company v. Gough*, 117 Ga. App. 140, 159 S.E.2d 469, **Web** 1968 Ga. App. Lexis 1007 (Court of Appeals of Georgia)

10.13 Promissory Estoppel: Nalley's, Inc. (Nalley's), was a major food distributor with its home office in the state of Washington. Jacob Aronowicz and Samuel Duncan approached Nalley's about the possibility of their manufacturing a line of sliced meat products to be distributed by Nalley's. When Nalley's showed considerable interest, Aronowicz and Duncan incorporated as Major Food Products, Inc. (Major). Meetings to discuss the proposal continued at length with Charles Gardiner, a vice president and general manager of the Los Angeles division of Nalley's. Gardiner delivered a letter to Major, agreeing to become the exclusive Los Angeles and Orange Country distributor for Major's products but stated in the letter "that should we determine your product line is not representative or is not compatible with our operation we are free to terminate our agreement within 30 days." Nalley's was to distribute the full production of products produced by Major.

Based on Gardiner's assurances, Major leased a plant, modified the plant to its specifications, purchased and installed equipment, signed contracts to obtain meat to be processed, and hired personnel. Both Aronowicz and Duncan resigned from their positions at other meat processing companies to devote full time to the project. Financing was completed when Aronowicz and Duncan used their personal fortunes to purchase the stock of Major. Gardiner and other representatives of Nalley's visited Major's plant and expressed satisfaction with the premises. Major obtained the necessary government approvals regarding health standards and immediately achieved full production. Because Nalley's was to pick up the finished products at Major's plant, Nalley's drivers visited Major's plant to acquaint themselves with its operations.

Gardiner sent the final proposal regarding the Nalley's–Major relationship to Nalley's home office for final approval. One week later, Nalley's home office in Washington made a decision not to distribute Major's products. Nalley's refused to give any reason to Major for its decision. No final agreement was ever executed between the parties. Immediate efforts by Major to secure other distribution for its products proved unsuccessful. Further, because Major owned no trucks itself and had no sales organization, it could not distribute the products itself. In less than six months, Major had failed, and Aronowicz's and Duncan's stock in Major was worthless. Major, Aronowicz, and Duncan sued Nalley's for damages under the doctrine of promissory estoppel. Do they win? *Aronowicz v. Nalley's. Inc.*, 30 Cal.App.3d 27, 106 Cal.Rptr. 424, **Web** 1972 Cal. App. Lexis 667 (Court of Appeal of California)

Ethics Issues

10.14 Ethics: Kortney Dempsey took a cruise on a ship operated by Norwegian Cruise Line (Norwegian). In general, suits for personal injuries arising out of maritime torts are subject to a three-year statute of limitations. However, Congress permits this period to be reduced to one year by contract. The Norwegian passenger ticket limited the period to one year. Evidence showed that the cruise line ticket contained the notation "Important Notice" in a bright red box in the bottom-right corner of each of the first four pages of the ticket. The information in the box stated that certain pages of the ticket contain information that "affect[s] important legal rights." In addition, at the top of page 6 of the ticket, where the terms and conditions begin, it is stated in bold letters: "Passengers are advised to read the terms and conditions of the Passenger Ticket Contract set forth below." The clause at issue, which appears on page 8, clearly provides that suits must be brought within one year of injury. More than one year after Dempsey had taken the cruise (but within three years), she filed suit against Norwegian, seeking damages for an alleged injury suffered while on the cruise. Dempsey asserted that the one-year limitations period had not been reasonably communicated to her. Did Dempsey act ethically in suing when she did? Did Norwegian act ethically in reducing the limitations period to one year? Who wins the lawsuit? *Dempsey v. Norwegian Cruise Line*, 972 F.2d 998, **Web** 1992 U.S. App. Lexis 10939 (United States Court of Appeals for the Ninth Circuit)

10.15 Ethics: Genaro Munoz owned property that he leased to Goodwest Rubber Corporation (Goodwest) for five years. The lease granted Goodwest the option to buy the property at a fair market value. Goodwest sought to exercise the option to purchase the property and tendered $80,000 to Munoz. When Munoz rejected this offer, Goodwest filed suit, seeking specific performance of the option agreement. The court was presented with a single issue for review: Was a price designation of "fair market value" definite enough to support an action for specific performance? Do you think Munoz acted ethically in refusing to honor the option? Who wins? *Goodwest Rubber Corp. v. Munoz*, 170 Cal.App.3d 919, 216 Cal.Rptr. 604, **Web** 1985 Cal. App. Lexis 2288 (Court of Appeal of California)

10.16 Ethics: Ocean Dunes of Hutchinson Island Development Corporation (Ocean Dunes) was a developer of condominium units. Prior to the construction, Albert and Helen Colangelo entered into a purchase agreement to buy one of the units and paid a deposit to Ocean Dunes. A provision in the purchase agreement provided:

> If Developer shall default in the performance of its obligations pursuant to this agreement, Purchaser's only remedy shall be to terminate this agreement, whereupon the Deposit shall be refunded to Purchaser and all rights and obligations thereunder shall thereupon become null and void.

The purchase agreement provided that if the buyer defaulted, the developer could retain the buyer's deposit or sue the buyer for damages and any other legal or equitable remedy. When Ocean Dunes refused to sell the unit to the Colangelos, they sued, seeking a decree of specific performance to require Ocean Dunes to sell them the unit. Ocean Dunes alleged that the above-quoted provision prevented the plaintiffs from seeking any legal or equitable remedy. Was the defendant's duty under the contract illusory? Was it ethical for Ocean Dunes to place the provision at issue in the contract? *Ocean Dunes of Hutchinson Island Development Corporation v. Colangelo.* 463 So.2d 437, **Web** 1985 Fla. App. Lexis 12298 (Court of Appeals of Florida)

10.17 Ethics: Red Owl Stores, Inc., a Minnesota corporation with its home office at Hopkins, Minnesota, owns and operates grocery supermarkets and grants franchises to franchisees to also operate such stores. Joseph Hoffman, who operated a bakery with his wife in Wautoma, Wisconsin, was interested in obtaining a Red Owl franchise to operate a grocery store in Wisconsin. Hoffman contacted a representative of Red Owl and had numerous conversations regarding this proposal. Ten months later, Mr. Lukowitz became Red Owl's representative for the territory comprising upper Michigan and most of Wisconsin. Hoffman mentioned to Lukowitz that he had the capital to invest, and Lukowitz assured him that would be sufficient to open a Red Owl franchise.

To gain experience in the grocery store business, and upon the advice of Lukowitz and other Red Owl representatives, Hoffman bought a small grocery store in Wautoma. After three months of operating this store, a Red Owl representative came in and took inventory, checked operations, and found that the store was operating at a profit. Lukowitz advised Hoffman to sell the store to his manager and assured Hoffman that Red Owl would find a larger store for him elsewhere. Although Hoffman was reluctant to sell at that time because it meant losing the summer tourist business, he sold on the assurance that he would be operating a Red Owl store at a new location by the fall. Again, Lukowitz assured Hoffman that the capital he had was sufficient to open a Red Owl franchise.

Red Owl had selected a site in Chilton, Wisconsin, for the proposed store. On Red Owl's insistence, Hoffman obtained an option to purchase the site. Hoffman and his wife rented a house in Chilton. Hoffman met with Lukowitz, who assured him, "Everything is ready to go. Get your money together and we are set." Lukowitz told Hoffman that he must sell his bakery business and building in Wautoma and that this was the only "hitch" in the entire plan. Hoffman sold his bakery building but retained the equipment to be used in the proposed Red Owl store. During the next two months, Red Owl prepared various financial projections for the proposed site. Hoffman met with Lukowitz and the credit manager for Red Owl, who demanded that Hoffman have more capital to invest in the store. Hoffman contacted his father-in-law, who agreed to provide the additional money. A week later, Red Owl sent Hoffman a telegram, demanding that he have more capital to invest. When Hoffman could not raise the additional money, the transaction fell through. Hoffman did not purchase the store site in Chilton and forfeited the option payment. The parties had never entered into a final agreement regarding the franchise.

Hoffman sued Red Owl under the doctrine of promissory estoppel, seeking damages for the money lost on the option payment on the Chilton property and the lease payments on the house in Chilton. Did the representatives of Red Owl Stores, Inc., act ethically in this case? Should the equitable doctrine of promissory estoppel apply in this case? *Hoffman v. Red Owl Stores, Inc.*, 26 Wis.2d 683, 133 N.W.2d 267, **Web** 1965 Wisc. Lexis 1026 (Supreme Court of Wisconsin)

IRAC Writing Assignment

Read **Case A-10** in Appendix A [*Traco, Inc. v. Arrow Glass Co., Inc.*]. Read the case and use the IRAC method to prepare a written analysis of the case.

Endnotes

1. *Restatement (Second) of Contracts*, Section 204.
2. Section 87(2) of the *Restatement (Second) of Contracts* states that an offer which the offeror should reasonably expect to induce action or forbearance of a substantial character on the part of the offeree before acceptance and which does induce such action or forbearance is binding as an option contract to the extent necessary to avoid injustice.
3. *Restatement (Second) of Contracts*, Section 50(1).
4. *Restatement (Second) of Contracts*, Section 40.
5. *Hamer v. Sidwa*, 124 N.Y. 538, 27 N.E. 256, Web 1891 N.Y. Lexis 1396 (Court of Appeal of New York).

CHAPTER 11

Capacity and Legality

> **"***An unconscionable contract is one which no man in his senses, not under delusion, would make, on the one hand, and which no fair and honest man would accept on the other.***"**
>
> —Hume v. United States,
> 132 U.S. 406, 10 S.Ct. 134, 1889 U.S. Lexis 1888 (1889)

CHAPTER OBJECTIVES

After studying this chapter, you should be able to:

1. Define and describe the infancy doctrine.
2. Define *legal insanity* and *intoxication* and explain how they affect contractual capacity.
3. Identify illegal contracts that are contrary to statutes and those that violate public policy.
4. Describe covenants not to compete and exculpatory clauses and identify when they are lawful.
5. Define *unconscionable contracts* and determine when these contracts are unlawful.

CHAPTER CONTENTS

- Introduction to Capacity and Legality
- Minors
- Mentally Incompetent Persons
- Intoxicated Persons
- Legality
- Special Business Contracts

- Unconscionable Contracts
- Chapter Summary
- Test Review Terms and Concepts
- Case Problems
- Ethics Issues
- IRAC Writing Assignment

    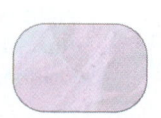

Introduction to Capacity and Legality

Generally, the law presumes that the parties to a contract have the requisite **contractual capacity** to enter into the contract. Certain persons do not have this capacity, however, including minors, insane persons, and intoxicated persons. The common law of contracts and many state statutes protect persons who lack contractual capacity from having contracts enforced against them. The party asserting incapacity or his or her guardian, conservator, or other legal representative bears the burden of proof.

An essential element for the formation of a contract is that the object of the contract be lawful. A contract to perform an illegal act is called an *illegal contract*. Illegal contracts are void. That is, they cannot be enforced by either party to the contract. The term *illegal contract* is a misnomer, however, since no contract exists if the object of the contract is illegal. In addition, courts hold that unconscionable contracts are unenforceable. An unconscionable contract is one that is so oppressive or manifestly unfair that it would be unjust to enforce it.

Capacity to contract and the lawfulness of contracts are discussed in this chapter.

Kewadin Casino, Brevort Township, Michigan

Federal law permits lawful gambling on Native American reservation land if the state permits such gambling.

Minors

Minors do not always have the maturity, experience, or sophistication needed to enter into contracts with adults. Common law defines *minors* as females under the age of 18 and males under the age of 21. In addition, many states have enacted statutes that specify the *age of majority*. The most prevalent age of majority is 18 years of age for both males and females. Any age below the statutory age of majority is called the *period of minority*.

The Infancy Doctrine

To protect minors, the law recognizes the **infancy doctrine**, which gives minors the right to *disaffirm* (or *cancel*) most contracts they have entered into with adults. This right is based on public policy which reasons that minors should be protected from the unscrupulous behavior of adults. In most states, the infancy doctrine is an objective standard. If a person's age is below the age of majority, the court will not inquire into his or her knowledge, experience, or sophistication. Generally, contracts for the necessaries of life, which we discuss later in this chapter, are exempted from the scope of this doctrine.

Under the infancy doctrine, a minor has the option of choosing whether to enforce a contract (i.e., the contract is *voidable* by a minor). The adult party is bound to the minor's decision. If both parties to a contract are minors, both parties have the right to disaffirm the contract.

If performance of the contract favors a minor, the minor will probably enforce the contract. Otherwise, he or she will probably disaffirm the contract. A minor may not affirm one part of a contract and disaffirm another part.

Disaffirmance

A minor can expressly **disaffirm** a contract orally, in writing, or through his or her conduct. No special formalities are required. The contract may be disaffirmed at any time prior to the person's reaching the age of majority plus a "reasonable time." The designation of a reasonable time is determined on a case-by-case basis.

Minor's Duty of Restoration

If a minor's contract is executory and neither party has performed, the minor can simply disaffirm the contract: There is nothing to recover since neither party has given the other party anything of value. If the parties have exchanged consideration and partially or fully performed the contract by the time the minor disaffirms the contract, however, the issue becomes one of what consideration or restitution must be made. The following rules apply:

- *Competent party's duty of restitution.* If the minor has transferred consideration—money, property, or other valuables—to the competent party before disaffirming the contract, that party must place the minor in status quo. That is, the minor must be restored to the same position he or she was in before the minor entered into the contract. This restoration is usually done by returning the consideration to the minor. If the consideration has been sold or has depreciated in value, the competent party must pay the minor the cash equivalent. This action is called the **competent party's duty of restitution**.

- *Minor's duty of restoration.* Generally, a minor is obligated only to return the goods or property he or she has received from the adult in the condition it is in at the time of disaffirmance (subject to several exceptions, discussed later in this chapter), even if the item has been consumed, lost, or destroyed or has depreciated in value by the time of disaffirmance. This rule is called the **minor's duty of restoration**. It is based on the rationale that if a minor had to place the adult in status quo upon disaffirmance of a contract, there would be no incentive for an adult not to deal with a minor.

Example When Sherry is 17 years old (a minor), she enters into a contract to purchase an automobile that costs $10,000 from Bruce, a competent adult. Bruce, who believes that Sherry is an adult and does not ask for verification of her age, delivers ownership of the automobile to Sherry after he receives her payment of $10,000. Subsequently, before Sherry reaches the age of 18 (the age of majority), she is involved in an automobile accident caused by her own negligence. The automobile sustains $7,000 worth of damage in the accident (is now only worth $3,000). Sherry can disaffirm the contract, return the damaged automobile to Bruce, and recover $10,000 from Bruce. In this result, Sherry recovers her entire $10,000 purchase price from Bruce, and Bruce has only a damaged automobile worth $3,000.

The right of a minor to disaffirm his contract is based upon sound public policy to protect the minor from his own improvidence and the overreaching of adults.

Justice Sullivan
Star Chevrolet v. Green (1985)

Minor's Duty of Restitution

Most states provide that the minor must put the adult in status quo upon disaffirmance of a contract if the minor's intentional or grossly negligent conduct caused the loss of value to the adult's property. This rule is called the **minor's duty of restitution**.

Example When Sherry is 17 years old (a minor), she enters into a contract to purchase an automobile that costs $10,000 from Bruce, a competent adult. Bruce, who believes that Sherry is an adult and does not ask for verification of her age, delivers ownership of the automobile to Sherry after he receives her payment of $10,000. Subsequently, before Sherry reaches the age of 18 (the age of majority), she is involved in an automobile accident caused by her own recklessness. The accident happens because Sherry is driving 70 miles per hour in a 45 mile-per-hour traffic zone. The automobile sustains $7,000 worth of damage in the accident (is now only worth $3,000). Sherry can disaffirm the contract and return the damaged automobile to Bruce, but she can recover only $3,000 from Bruce. In this result, Bruce is made whole: He keeps $7,000 of Sherry's money and has a damaged automobile worth $3,000. Sherry has $3,000.

On occasion, minors might misrepresent their age to adults when entering into contracts. Most state laws provide that minors who misrepresent their age must place the adult in status quo if they disaffirm the contract.

Example When Sherry is 17 years old (a minor), she enters into a contract to purchase an automobile that costs $10,000 from Bruce, a competent adult. Bruce, who has doubts that Sherry is an adult, asks Sherry for verification of her age. Sherry produces a driver's license that shows that she is 19 years old. Bruce delivers ownership of the automobile to Sherry after he receives her payment of $10,000. Subsequently, before Sherry reaches the age of 18 (the age of majority), she is involved in an automobile accident caused by another driver's negligence. Sherry is not at fault. The automobile sustains $7,000 worth of damage in the accident (is now only worth $3,000). Sherry can disaffirm the contract and return the damaged automobile to Bruce, but she can recover only $3,000 from Bruce. This is because she lied about her age. In this result, Bruce is made whole: He keeps $7,000 of Sherry's money and has a damaged automobile worth $3,000. Sherry has $3,000.

A few states have enacted statutes that require the minor to make restitution of the reasonable value of the item when disaffirming any contract.

Ratification

If a minor does not disaffirm a contract either during the period of minority or within a reasonable time after reaching the age of majority, the contract is considered ratified (accepted). Hence, the minor (who is now an adult) is bound by the contract; the right to disaffirm the contract is lost. Note that any attempt by a minor to ratify a contract while still a minor can be disaffirmed just as the original contract can be disaffirmed.

The **ratification**, which relates back to the inception of the contract, can be by express oral or written words or implied from the minor's conduct (e.g., after reaching the age of majority, the minor remains silent regarding the contract).

Example When June is 17 years old (a minor), she enters into a contract and purchases a used automobile from Ken, a sane adult, for $10,000. June pays Ken $10,000, and Ken signs over the ownership of the automobile to June. When June reaches the age of 18 (the age of majority), she has not yet disaffirmed the contract. If Jane waits one month after reaching the age of majority and has not yet disaffirmed the contract, then she will be considered to have ratified the contract. She cannot thereafter disaffirm the contract.

The following case presents the issue of whether a minor had ratified a contract when he reached the age of majority.

CASE 11.1
Minor's Contract

Jones v. Free Flight Sport Aviation, Inc.
623 P.2d 370, **Web** 1981 Colo. Lexis 571
Supreme Court of Colorado

> **"***A minor may disaffirm a contract made during his minority within a reasonable time after attaining his majority or he may, after becoming of legal age, by acts recognizing the contract, ratify it.* **"**
>
> —Judge Erickson

Facts

William Michael Jones, a 17-year-old minor, signed a contract with Free Flight Sport Aviation, Inc. (Free Flight), for the use of recreational sky-diving facilities. A covenant not to sue and an exculpatory clause exempting Free Flight from liability were included in the contract. One month later, Jones attained the age of majority (18 years of age). Ten months later, while on a Free Flight skydiving operation, the airplane crashed shortly after takeoff from Littleton Airport. Jones suffered severe personal injuries. Jones filed suit against Free Flight, alleging negligence and willful and wanton misconduct. The trial court granted summary judgment in favor of Free Flight. The Colorado court of appeals affirmed. Jones appealed.

Issue

Did Jones ratify the contract?

Language of the Court

As a matter of public policy, the courts have protected minors from improvident and imprudent contractual commitments by declaring that the contract of a minor is voidable at the election of the minor after he attains his majority. A minor may disaffirm a contract made during his minority within a reasonable time after attaining his majority or he may, after becoming of legal age, by acts recognizing the contract, ratify it.

Affirmance is not merely a matter of intent. It may be determined by the actions of a minor who accepts the benefits of a contract after reaching the age of majority, or who is silent or acquiesces in the contract for a considerable length of time. We conclude that the trial court properly determined that Jones ratified the contract, as a matter of law, by accepting the benefits of the contract when he used Free Flights facilities on October 19, 1974.

Decision

The supreme court of Colorado held that Jones had ratified his contract with Free Flight by continuing, for 10 months after reaching the age of majority, to perform under the contract. Therefore, the covenant not to sue and the exculpatory clause exempting Free Flight from liability to Jones were enforceable. The supreme court affirmed the decision of the trial court and court of appeals in favor of Free Flight.

Law & Ethics Questions

1. Should a person be allowed to disaffirm a contract he or she made as a minor after reaching the age of majority? What is a reasonable length of time after reaching the age of majority to permit disaffirmance?

2. **ETHICS** Did Jones act ethically by suing Free Flight Sport Aviation in this case?

3. Should the covenant not to sue have been enforced here even though Jones was an adult?

Web Exercises

1. **WEB** For the complete opinion of this case, go to *www.prenhall.com/cheesemancases*.

2. **WEB** Visit the website of the supreme court of Colorado, at *www.coloradosupremecourt.com*.

3. **WEB** Use *www.google.com* to find a video clip of someone sky-diving.

Parents' Liability for Their Children's Contracts

Generally, parents owe a legal duty to provide food, clothing, shelter, and other necessaries of life for their minor children. Parents are liable for their children's contracts for necessaries of life if they have not adequately provided such items.

The parental duty of support terminates if a minor becomes *emancipated*. **Emancipation** occurs when a minor voluntarily leaves home and lives apart from his or her parents. The courts consider factors such as getting married, setting up a separate household, or joining the military service in determining whether a minor is emancipated. Each situation is examined on its merits.

Necessaries of Life

Minors are obligated to pay for the **necessaries of life** that they contract for. Otherwise, many adults would refuse to sell these items to them. There is no standard definition of what is a *necessary of life*, but items such as food, clothing, shelter, and medical services are generally understood to fit this category.

Example Goods and services such as automobiles, tools of trade, education, and vocational training have also been found to be necessaries of life in some situations. The minor's age, lifestyle, and status in life influence what is considered necessary. For example, necessaries for a married minor are greater than those for an unmarried minor.

The seller's recovery is based on the equitable doctrine of **quasi-contract** rather than on the contract itself. Under this theory, the minor is obligated only to pay the reasonable value of the goods or services received. Reasonable value is determined on a case-by-case basis.

In the following case, the court found a minor liable for necessaries of life.

CASE 11.2
Necessaries of Life

Yale Diagnostic Radiology v. Estate of Fountain

267 Conn. 351, 838 A.2d 179, **Web** 2004 Conn. Lexis 7 (2004)
Supreme Court of Connecticut

> **❝** *The rule that a minor's contracts are voidable, however, is not absolute. An exception to this rule, eponymously known as the doctrine of necessaries, is that a minor may not avoid a contract for goods or services necessary for his health and sustenance.* **❞**
>
> —Judge Borden

Facts

Harun Fountain, a minor, was shot in the back of the head at point-blank range by a playmate. Fountain required extensive lifesaving medical services from a variety of medical service providers, including Yale Diagnostic Radiology. The expense of the services rendered by Yale to Fountain totaled $17,694. Yale billed Vernetta Turner-Tucker (Tucker), Fountain's mother, for the services. Tucker, however, declared bankruptcy and had Yale's claim against her discharged in bankruptcy. Tucker, on behalf of Fountain, sued the boy who shot Fountain and recovered damages in a settlement agreement. These funds were placed in an estate on Fountain's behalf under the supervision of the probate court.

Yale filed a motion with the probate court for payment of the $17,694 from the estate. The probate court denied the motion. Yale appealed to the trial court, which held in favor of Yale. The trial court held that minors were liable for their necessaries. Fountain's estate appealed.

Issue

Is Fountain's estate liable to Yale under the doctrine of necessaries?

Language of the Court

Connecticut has long recognized the common-law rule that a minor child's contracts are voidable. The rule that a minor's contracts are voidable, however, is not absolute. An exception to this rule, eponymously known as the doctrine of necessaries, is that a minor may not avoid a contract for goods or services necessary for his health and sustenance.

Thus, when a medical service provider renders necessary medical care to an injured minor, two contracts arise: the primary contract between the provider and the minor's parents; and an implied in law contract between the provider and the minor himself. The primary contract between the provider and the parents is based on the parents' duty to pay for their children's necessary expenses, under both common law and statute. The primacy of this contract means that the provider of necessaries must make all reasonable efforts to collect from the parents before resorting to the secondary, implied in law contract with the minor.

The secondary implied in law contract between the medical services provider and the minor arises from equitable considerations, including the law's disfavor of unjust enrichment. Therefore, where necessary medical services are rendered to a minor whose parents do not pay for them, equity and justice demand that a secondary implied in law contract arise between the medical services provider and the minor who has received the benefits of those services. These principles compel the conclusion that, in the circumstances of the present case, the estate of Fountain is liable to plaintiff Yale under the common-law doctrine of necessaries, for the services rendered by Yale to Fountain.

Decision

The supreme court of Connecticut held that under the doctrine of necessaries, Fountain's estate is liable to Yale for the expense of the services rendered to Fountain. The supreme court affirmed the judgment of the trial court in favor of Yale.

Law & Ethics Questions

1. What is the doctrine of necessaries? Explain.

2. What is a parent's legal responsibility for medical services and other necessaries provide to his or her child?

3. **ETHICS** Was it ethical for Fountain's mother not to pay Yale for the medical service rendered to her child? Was it ethical for her to avoid this bill by declaring bankruptcy?

4. **ETHICS** Should Yale have just written off this debt and not pursued Fountain's estate for payment? Why or why not?

Web Exercises

1. **WEB** For the complete opinion of this case, go to *www.prenhall.com/cheesemancases*.

2. **WEB** Visit the website of the supreme court of Connecticut, at *www.jud.state.ct.us*.

3. **WEB** Visit the website of Yale Diagnostic Radiology, at *www.info.med.yale.edu/diagrad*.

4. **WEB** Use *www.google.com* to find an article that discusses minor's contracts. Read it.

CONTEMPORARY ENVIRONMENT
Special Types of Minors' Contracts

The infancy doctrine of the common law of contracts allows minors to disaffirm many contracts they have entered into with adults. Based on public policy, many states have enacted statutes that make certain specified contracts enforceable against minors—that is, minors cannot assert the infancy doctrine against enforcement of these contracts. These usually include contracts for:

- Medical, surgical, and pregnancy care
- Psychological counseling
- Health insurance
- Life insurance
- The performance of duties related to stock and bond transfers, bank accounts, and the like
- Educational loan agreements
- Contracts to support children
- Contracts to enlist in the military
- Artistic, sports, and entertainment contracts that have been entered into with the approval of the court (Many of these statutes require that a certain portion of the wages and fees earned by the minor be put in trust until the minor reaches the age of majority.)

Mentally Incompetent Persons

Mental incapacity may arise because of mental illness, brain damage, mental retardation, senility, and the like. The law protects people suffering from substantial mental incapacity from enforcement of contracts against them because such persons may not understand the consequences of their actions in entering into a contract.

To be relieved of his or her duties under a contract, the law requires a person to have been legally insane at the time of entering into the contract. This state is called **legal insanity**. Most states use the *objective cognitive "understanding" test* to determine legal insanity. Under this test, the person's mental incapacity must render that person incapable of understanding or comprehending the nature of the transaction. Mere weakness of intellect, slight psychological or emotional problems, or delusions does not constitute legal insanity.

The law has developed two standards concerning contracts of mentally incompetent persons: (1) adjudged insane and (2) insane but not adjudged insane.

Adjudged Insane

In certain cases, a relative, a loved one, or another interested party may institute a legal action to have someone declared legally (i.e., adjudged) insane. If after hearing the evidence at a formal judicial or administrative hearing the person is **adjudged insane**, the court will make that person a ward of the court and appoint a guardian to act on that person's behalf. Any contract entered into by a person who has been adjudged insane is *void*. That is, no contract exists. The court-appointed guardian is the only one who has the legal authority to enter into contracts on behalf of the person.

Example Ted, Heather, and Jed are the three surviving relatives of their grandmother, Mabel. For years, Mabel has exhibited substantial mental impairment such that she is incapable of understanding or comprehending the nature of her transactions. The three grandchildren bring a proceeding in family court, asking the court to adjudge Mabel insane. After a hearing in which evidence is introduced, the judge decides that Mabel is permanently insane and issues a judgment saying so. Mabel has now been adjudged insane. The court appoints Heather as guardian. Subsequently, Mabel enters into a contract with Sidell's Siding Company to put new siding on her house. This is a void contract. Only Heather can enter into such contract on behalf of Mabel.

Insane but Not Adjudged Insane

If no formal ruling has been made—that is, if a person is **insane but not adjudged insane**—any contracts entered into by a person who suffers from a mental impairment that makes him or her legally insane are voidable by the insane person. Unless the other party does not have contractual capacity, he or she does not have the option to void the contract.

Example Ted, Heather, and Jed are the three surviving relatives of their grandmother, Mabel. For years, Mabel has exhibited substantial mental impairment such that she is incapable of understanding or comprehending the nature of her transactions. The three grandchildren have never brought a legal proceeding to have Mabel legally declared insane. Mabel enters into a contract with Sidell's Siding Company to put new siding on her house. This is a voidable contract that is voidable only by Mabel. Sidell's Siding Company cannot void the contract; only Mabel can.

Some people have alternating periods of sanity and insanity. Any contracts made by such persons during a lucid interval are enforceable. Contracts made while the person was not legally sane can be disaffirmed.

A person who has dealt with an insane person must place that insane person in status quo if the contract is either void or voided by the insane person. Most states hold that a party who did not know he or she was dealing with an insane person must be placed in status quo upon voidance of the contract. Insane persons are liable in *quasi-contract* to pay the reasonable value for the necessaries of life they receive.

In the following case, the court had to decide whether mental incapacity relieved a person from a contract.

> Insanity vitiates all acts.
>
> Sir John Nicholl
> *Countess of Portsmouth v.*
> *Earl of Portsmouth (1828)*

CASE 11.3
Mental Capacity

Campbell v. Carr

361 S.C. 258, 603 S.E.2d 625, **Web** 2004 S.C. App. Lexis 276 (2004)
Court of Appeals of South Carolina

> **"**This inadequate consideration combined with Carr's weakness of mind, due to her schizophrenia and depression, makes it inequitable to order specific performance.**"**
>
> —Judge Anderson

Facts

Martha M. Carr suffered from schizophrenia and depression. Schizophrenia is a psychotic disorder that is characterized by disturbances in perception, inferential thinking, delusions, hallucinations, and grossly disorganized behavior. Depression is characterized by altered moods and diminished ability to think or concentrate. Carr was taking two prescription drugs for her mental diseases, Haldol and Cogentin.

Carr, a resident of New York, inherited from her mother a 108-acre tract of unimproved land in South Carolina. Carr contacted Raymond C. and Betty Campbell (Campbell), who had leased the property for 30 years, about selling the property to them. Carr asked Campbell how much the property was worth, and Campbell told Carr that the tax assessor's agricultural assessed value of the property was $54,000. Carr and Campbell entered into a written contract for $54,000, which averaged $500 per acre. Campbell paid Carr earnest money. Carr subsequently missed the closing day for the sale of the property, returned the earnest money, and refused to sell the property to Campbell. Campbell sued Carr to obtain a court judgment ordering Carr to specifically perform the contract and sell the property to Campbell. At trial, evidence and expert witness testimony placed the value of the property at $162,000, or $1,500 an acre. Testimony showed that Campbell knew the value of the property exceeded $54,000. The court agreed with Campbell and ordered Carr to specifically perform the contract. Carr appealed.

Issue

Did Carr, because of her mental diseases of schizophrenia and depression, lack the mental capacity to enter into the contract with Campbell?

Language of the Court

An action for specific performance is one in equity. Specific performance should be granted only if there is no adequate remedy at law and specific enforcement of the contract is equitable between the parties. Equity will not decree specific performance unless the contract is fair, just, and equitable.

The consideration stated in the contract between Carr and the Campbells was inadequate. The $54,000 sales price in the contract was significantly below the appraised value of $162,000, the Collateral I.D. report's expected sell value of $129,625 to $145,180, and the Richmond County Tax Assessor's fair market value of $103,700. This inadequate consideration combined with Carr's weakness of mind, due to her schizophrenia and depression, makes it inequitable to order specific performance. The Campbells, as the prospective purchasers, had greater knowledge of the real estate value of the land, having leased the land for thirty years for personal hunting and farming purposes, compared with Carr, who lived in New York, had not visited the property since she was a child, and had no knowledge of the fair market value of the property. Additionally, Carr suffers from mental illness.

Decision

The court of appeals held that Carr's mental diseases of schizophrenia and depression affected her ability to make an informed decision regarding the sale of the property. The court of appeals reversed the trial court's decision ordering specific performance.

Law & Ethics Questions

1. What does the doctrine of incapacity to contract provide? Explain.
2. **ETHICS** Did the Campbells act ethically in this case?
3. **ETHICS** Was it ethical for Carr to withdraw from the contract? Did she have sufficient reason to withdraw from the contract?

Web Exercises

1. **WEB** For the complete decision of this case, go to *www.prenhall.com/cheesemancases*.
2. **WEB** Visit the website of the court of appeals of South Carolina, at *www.judicial.state.sc.us/appeals*.
3. **WEB** Use *www.google.com* to find an article that discusses schizophrenia. Read it.

CONCEPT SUMMARY

Disaffirmance of Contracts Based on Legal Insanity

TYPE OF LEGAL INSANITY	DISAFFIRMANCE RULE
Adjudged insane	Contract is void. Neither party can enforce the contract.
Insane but not adjudged insane	Contract is voidable by the insane person; the competent party cannot void the contract.

Intoxicated Persons

Most states provide that contracts entered into by certain **intoxicated persons** are voidable by those persons. The intoxication may occur because of alcohol or drugs. The contract is not voidable by the other party if that party had contractual capacity.

Under the majority rule, the contract is voidable only if the person was so intoxicated when the contract was entered into that he or she was incapable of understanding or comprehending the nature of the transaction. In most states, this rule holds even if the intoxication was self-induced. Some states allow the person to disaffirm the contract only if the person was forced to become intoxicated or did so unknowingly.

The amount of alcohol or drugs that must be consumed for a person to be considered legally intoxicated to disaffirm contracts varies from case to case. The factors that are considered include the user's physical characteristics and his or her ability to "hold" intoxicants.

A person who disaffirms a contract based on intoxication generally must be returned to the status quo. In turn, the intoxicated person generally must return the consideration received under the contract to the other party and make restitution that returns the other party to status quo. After becoming sober, an intoxicated person can ratify the contracts he or she entered into while intoxicated. Intoxicated persons are liable in *quasi-contract* to pay the reasonable value for necessaries they receive.

In the following case, the court found that a person was not bound to a contact she entered while intoxicated.

> Men intoxicated are sometimes stunned into sobriety.
>
> Lord Mansfield
> *R. v. Wilkes (1770)*

CASE 11.4
Intoxication

Smith v. Williamson

429 So.2d 598, **Web** 1982 Ala. Civ. App. Lexis 1418
Court of Civil Appeals of Alabama

> **❝** *The record further shows that Williamson had consumed a pint of 100-proof vodka and that she remained in an agitated state over the sale of her home.* **❞**
>
> —Judge Bradley

Facts

Carolyn Ann Williamson entered into a contract to sell her house to Mr. and Mrs. Matthews at a time when her house was threatened with foreclosure. Evidence showed that Williamson was an alcoholic. Having read about the threatened foreclosure in the newspaper, attorney Virgil M. Smith appeared at Williamson's home to discuss the matter with her. Williamson told Smith that she expected to receive $17,000 from the sale but had actually received $1,700. On the following day, after drinking a pint of 100-proof vodka, Williamson and her son went to Smith's office, where Smith prepared a lawsuit to have the sale of the house set aside based on Williamson's lack of capacity due to alcoholism. At that time, Smith loaned Williamson $500 and took back a note and mortgage on her house to secure repayment of this amount and his attorneys' fees. Evidence showed that Smith did not allow Williamson's son to read the mortgage. The sale to Mr. and Mrs. Matthews was set aside. Subsequently, Smith began foreclosure proceedings on Williamson's house to recover attorneys' fees and advances. Williamson filed this lawsuit to enjoin the foreclosure. The trial court held that Smith's mortgage was void and permanently enjoined him from foreclosing on Williamson's house. Smith appealed.

Issue

Was Williamson's alcoholism a sufficient mental incapacity to void the mortgage?

Language of the Court

In essence, Smith takes the position that while Williamson had been drinking on the morning that she executed the mortgage to him, the transaction was still valid because she had sufficient capacity to understand the nature of the act, and it was free from fraud and undue influence. To accept Smith's position would require us to ignore certain subtle ironies arising from the facts of this appeal and the nature of the fiduciary relationship between attorney and client.

The record indicates that Williamson executed the note and mortgage on her home to Smith the following morning. The record further shows that Williamson had consumed a pint of 100-proof vodka and that she remained in an agitated state over the sale of her home. To hold that Williamson was incapable of understanding the nature of the transaction with the Matthewses and then to hold that she was able to comprehend the nature of her dealings with Smith would be to reach illogical results, especially in light of the facts presented at trial.

Decision

The court of appeals held that Williamson was not bound to the contract and mortgage with attorney Smith because she was mentally incompetent by reason of intoxication at the time she signed the documents. The court of appeals affirmed the trial court's decision that had held Smith's mortgage void and permanently enjoined him from foreclosing on Williamson's property.

Law & Ethics Questions

1. Should the law protect persons who voluntarily become intoxicated from performing their contracts?

2. **ETHICS** Do you think that attorney Smith acted ethically in this case?

3. Do you think many business deals are entered into after the parties have been drinking? Should these deals be allowed to be voided?

Web Exercises

1. **WEB** For the complete opinion of this case, go to *www.prenhall.com/cheesemancases*.

2. **WEB** Visit the website of the court of civil appeals of Alabama, at *www.judicial.state.al.us*.

3. **WEB** Use *www.google.com* to find a case where someone has been let out of their contract because of intoxication.

Legality

One requirement to have an enforceable contract is that the object of the contract must be lawful. Most contracts that individuals and businesses enter into are **lawful contracts** that are enforceable. These include contracts for the sale of goods, services, real property, and intangible rights; the lease of goods; property leases; licenses; and other contracts.

Some contracts have illegal objects. A contract with an illegal object is *void* and therefore unenforceable. Such contracts are called **illegal contracts**. The following paragraphs discuss various illegal contracts.

Contracts Contrary to Statutes

Both federal and state legislatures have enacted statutes that prohibit certain types of conduct. Penal codes make certain activities crimes; antitrust statutes prohibit certain types of agreements between competitors, and so on. Contracts to perform activities that are prohibited by statute are illegal contracts.

Usury Laws

State **usury laws** set an upper limit on the annual interest rate that can be charged on certain types of loans. The limits vary from state to state. Lenders who charge a higher rate than the state limit are guilty of usury. These laws are intended to protect unsophisticated borrowers from loan sharks and others who charge exorbitant rates of interest.

Most states provide criminal and civil penalties for making usurious loans. Some states require lenders to remit to the borrower the difference between the interest rate charged on the loan and the usury rate. Other states prohibit lenders from collecting any interest on the loan. Still other states provide that a usurious loan is a void contract, permitting the borrower not to have to pay the interest or the principal of the loan to the lender.

Most usury laws exempt certain types of lenders and loan transactions involving legitimate business transactions from the reach of the law. Often, these exemptions include loans made by banks and other financial institutions, loans above a certain dollar amount, and loans made to corporations and other businesses.

Sabbath Laws

Certain states have enacted laws—called **Sabbath laws**, **Sunday laws**, or **blue laws**—that prohibit or limit the carrying on of certain secular activities on Sundays. Except for contracts for the necessaries of life, charitable donations, and such, these laws generally prohibit or invalidate executory contracts that are entered into on Sundays. Many states do not actively enforce these laws. In some states, they have even been found to be unconstitutional.

Contracts to Commit Crimes

As mentioned previously, contracts to commit criminal acts are void. If the object of a contract becomes illegal after a contract is entered into because the government has enacted a statute that makes it unlawful, the parties are discharged from the contract. The contract is not an illegal contract unless the parties agree to go forward and complete it.

Contracts Contrary to Public Policy

Certain contracts are illegal because they are **contrary to public policy**. Such contracts are void. Although *public policy* eludes a precise definition, the courts have held contracts to be contrary to public policy if they have a negative impact on society or interfere with the public's safety and welfare.

Immoral contracts—that is, contracts whose objective is the commission of an act that is considered immoral by society—may be found to be against public policy.

Example A contract that is based on sexual favors has been held to be an immoral contract and void as against public policy. Judges are not free to define morality based on their individual views. Instead, they must look to the practices and beliefs of society when defining immoral conduct.

In the following case, the court had to determine whether a contract violated public policy and was therefore illegal.

CASE **11.5**
Illegal Contract

Flood v. Fidelity & Guaranty Life Insurance Co.

394 So.2d 1311, **Web** 1981 La. App. Lexis 3538
Court of Appeal of Louisiana

> **❝** *Louisiana follows the majority rule that holds, as a matter of public policy, that a beneficiary named in a life insurance policy is not entitled to the proceeds of the insurance if the beneficiary feloniously kills the insured.* **❞**
>
> —Judge Lear

Facts

Ellen and Richard Alvin Flood, who were married, lived in a mobile home in Louisiana. Richard worked as a maintenance man, and Ellen was employed at an insurance agency. Evidence at trial showed that Ellen was unhappy with her marriage. Ellen took out an insurance policy on the life of her husband and named herself as beneficiary. The policy was issued by Fidelity & Guaranty Life Insurance Company (Fidelity). Seven years after the marriage, Richard became unexpectedly ill. He was taken to the hospital, where his condition improved. After a visit at the hospital from his wife, however, Richard died. Ellen was criminally charged with the murder of her husband by poisoning. Evidence showed that six medicine bottles at the couple's home, including Tylenol and paregoric bottles, contained arsenic. The court found that Ellen had fed Richard ice cubes laced with arsenic at the hospital. Ellen was tried and convicted of the murder of her husband. Ellen, as beneficiary of Richard's life insurance policy, requested Fidelity to pay her the benefits. Fidelity refused to pay the benefits and returned all premiums paid on the policy. This suit followed. The District Court held in favor of Ellen Flood and awarded her the benefits of the life insurance policy. Fidelity appealed.

Issue

Was the life insurance policy an illegal contract that is void?

Language of the Court

Louisiana follows the majority rule that holds, as a matter of public policy, that a beneficiary named in a life insurance policy is not entitled to the proceeds of the insurance if the beneficiary feloniously kills the insured.

The genesis of this litigation is the escalating criminal action of Ellen Flood, bent on taking the life of her lawful husband. Our courts have previously adjudicated (1) the issue of the cause of death of Richard Flood, (2) the culprit in that death, and (3) the motives for the death. Under the peculiar circumstances of the case, it was unreasonable of the trial court not to consider and to assign great weight to the mountain of evidence tending to prove Mrs. Flood's scheme to defraud both the insurer, Fidelity, and the insured, Mr. Flood. It is clear to us that the entirety of the transaction here reviewed is tainted with the intendment of Ellen Flood to contravene the prohibitory law.

Life insurance policies are procured because life is, indeed, precarious and uncertain. Our law does not and cannot sanction any scheme that has as its purpose the certain infliction of death for, *inter alia*, financial gain through receipt of the proceeds of life insurance. To sanction this policy in any way would surely shackle the spirit, letter, and life of our laws.

Decision

The court of appeals held that the life insurance policy that Ellen had taken out on the life of her husband was void based on public policy and that Ellen could not recover the life insurance proceeds from the death of her husband, whom she had killed. The court of appeals reversed the decision of the District Court.

Law & Ethics Questions

1. Should Ellen Flood have been allowed to retain the insurance proceeds in this case?

2. **ETHICS** Did Ellen Flood act unethically in this case? Did she act illegally?

3. What would be the economic consequences if persons could recover insurance proceeds for losses caused by their illegal activities (e.g., murder, arson)?

Web Exercises

1. **WEB** For the complete opinion of this case, go to *www.prenhall.com/cheesemancases*.

2. **WEB** Visit the website of the court of appeals of Louisiana, First Circuit, at *www.la-fcca.org*.

3. **WEB** Use *www.google.com* to find an article or case that discusses murder to recover life insurance proceeds. Read it.

Gambling Statutes

All states either prohibit or regulate gambling, wagering, lotteries, and games of chance via **gambling statutes**. States provide various criminal and civil penalties for illegal gambling. There is a distinction between lawful risk-shifting contracts and gambling contracts.

Example If property insurance is purchased on one's own car and the car is destroyed in an accident, the insurance company must pay the claim. This agreement is a lawful risk-shifting contract because the purchaser had an "insurable interest" in the car. Insurance purchased on a neighbor's car would be considered to be gambling, however. The purchaser does not have an insurable interest in the car and is betting only on its destruction.

There are many exceptions to wagering laws. For example, many states have enacted statutes that permit games of chance under a certain dollar amount, bingo games, lotteries conducted by religious and charitable organizations, and the like. Many states also permit and regulate horse racing, harness racing, dog racing, and state-operated lotteries.

Effect of Illegality

Because illegal contracts are void, the parties cannot sue for nonperformance. Further, if an illegal contract is executed, the court will generally leave the parties where it finds them.

Certain situations are exempt from the general rule of the effect of finding an illegal contract. If an exception applies, the innocent party may use the court system to sue for damages or to recover consideration paid under the illegal contract. Persons who can assert an exception are:

1. Innocent persons who were justifiably ignorant of the law or fact that made the contract illegal.

   Example A person who purchases insurance from an unlicensed insurance company may recover insurance benefits from the unlicensed company.

2. Persons who were induced to enter into an illegal contract by fraud, duress, or undue influence.

   Example A shop owner who pays $5,000 "protection money" to a mobster so that his store will not be burned down by the mobster can recover the $5,000.

3. Persons who entered into an illegal contract withdraw before the illegal act is performed.

   Example If the president of New Toy Corporation pays $10,000 to an employee of Old Toy Corporation to steal a trade secret from his employer but reconsiders and tells the employee not to do it before he has done it, the New Toy Corporation may recover the $10,000.

4. Persons who were less at fault than the other party for entering into the illegal contract. At common law, parties to an illegal contract were considered *in pari delicto* (in equal fault). Some states have changed this rule and permit the less-at-fault party to recover restitution of the consideration they paid under an illegal contract from the more-at-fault party.

In the following case, the court had to decide the lawfulness of a contract.

CASE **11.6** *Illegal Contract*	**Ryno v. Tyra** 752 S.W.2d 148, **Web** 1988 Tex. App. Lexis 1646 Court of Appeals of Texas

> **❝** *The trial court could not have compelled Ryno to honor his wager by delivering the BMW to Tyra. However, Ryno did deliver the BMW to Tyra and the facts incident to that delivery are sufficient to establish a transfer by gift of the BMW from Ryno to Tyra.* **❞**
>
> —Judge Farris

Facts

R. D. Ryno, Jr., owned Bavarian Motors, an automobile dealership in Fort Worth, Texas. One day, Lee Tyra discussed purchasing a BMW M-1 from Ryno for $125.000. Ryno then suggested a double-or-nothing coin flip, to which Tyra agreed. If the seller Ryno won the coin flip, Tyra would have to pay $250,000 for the car; if the buyer Tyra won the coin flip, he would get the car for free. When Tyra won the coin flip, Ryno said, "It's yours," and handed Tyra the keys and title to the car. Tyra drove away in the car. This suit ensued as to the ownership of the car. The trial court held in favor of Tyra. Ryno appealed.

Issue

Was there an illegal contract? Who owns the car?

Language of the Court

Ryno complains that the trial court erred in granting Tyra judgment because the judgment enforces a gambling contract. We find there was sufficient evidence to sustain the jury finding that Ryno intended to transfer to Tyra his ownership interest in the BMW at the time he delivered the documents, keys, and possession of the automobile to Tyra. We agree with appellant Ryno that his wager with Tyra was unenforceable. The trial court could not have compelled Ryno to honor his wager by delivering the BMW to Tyra. However, Ryno did deliver the BMW to Tyra and the facts incident to that delivery are sufficient to establish a transfer by gift of the BMW from Ryno to Tyra.

Decision

Tyra, the patron at the car dealership who won the coin toss, owns the car. The court of appeals found that there was an illegal contract and left the parties where it found them—that is, with Tyra in possession of the car. The court of appeals affirmed the trial court's judgment in favor of Tyra.

Law & Ethics Questions

1. Should the court have lent its resources to help Ryno recover the car?
2. **ETHICS** Did Ryno act ethically in this case?
3. What is the moral of this story if you ever win anything in an illegal gambling contract?

Web Exercises

1. **WEB** For the complete opinion of this case, go to *www.prenhall.com/cheesemancases*.
2. **WEB** Visit the website of the court of appeals of Texas, Second District, at *www.2ndcoa.courts.state.tx.us*.
3. **WEB** Use *www.google.com* to find an article about illegal gambling contracts. Read it.

Special Business Contracts

The issue of the lawfulness of contracts applies to several special business contracts. These include contracts that restrain trade; contracts to provide services that require a government license, exculpatory clauses, and covenants not to compete. These contracts are discussed in the following paragraphs.

Contracts in Restraint of Trade

The general economic policy of this country favors competition. At common law, **contracts in restraint of trade**—that is, contracts that unreasonably restrain trade—are held to be unlawful.

Example It would be an illegal restraint of trade if all the bakers in a neighborhood agreed to fix the prices of the bread they sold. The baker's contract would be void.

Licensing Statutes

All states have **licensing statutes** that require members of certain professions and occupations to be licensed by the state in which they practice. Lawyers, doctors, real estate agents, insurance agents, certified public accountants, teachers, contractors, hairdressers, and such are among them. In most instances, a license is granted to a person who demonstrates that he or she has the proper schooling, experience, and moral character required by the relevant statute. Sometimes, a written examination is also required.

Problems arise if an unlicensed person tries to collect payment for services provided to another under a contract. Some statutes expressly provide that unlicensed persons cannot enforce contracts to provide these services. If the statute is silent on the point, enforcement depends on whether it is a *regulatory statute* or a *revenue-raising statute*.

REGULATORY STATUTES Licensing statutes enacted to protect the public are called **regulatory statutes**. Generally, unlicensed persons cannot recover payment for services that a regulatory statute requires a licensed person to provide.

Example State law provides that legal services can be provided only by lawyers who have graduated from law school and passed the appropriate bar exam. Nevertheless, suppose Marie Sweiger, a first-year law student, agrees to draft a will for Randy McCabe for a $150 fee. Because Sweiger is not licensed to provide legal services, she has violated a regulatory statute. She cannot enforce the contract and recover payment from McCabe.

REVENUE-RAISING STATUTES Licensing statutes enacted to raise money for the government are called **revenue-raising statutes**. A person who provides services pursuant to a contract without the appropriate license required by such a statute can enforce the contract and recover payment for services rendered.

Example Suppose a state licensing statute requires licensed attorneys to pay an annual $200 license fee without requiring continuing education or other new qualifications. A licensed attorney who forgets to pay the fee can enforce contracts and recover payment for the legal services he or she renders. The statute merely gathers revenue; protection of the public is not a factor.

ETHICS SPOTLIGHT

An Unlicensed Contractor Gets Dunked

❝The obvious statutory intent is to discourage persons who have failed to comply with the licensing law from offering or providing their unlicensed services for pay.❞

—Justice Eagleson

Hydrotech Systems, Ltd. (Hydrotech), was a New York corporation that manufactured and installed patented equipment to simulate ocean waves. Oasis Waterpark (Oasis) was a California corporation that owned and operated a water-oriented amusement park in Palm Springs, California. Wessman Construction Company, Inc. (Wessman), was Oasis's general contractor at the park.

Wessman contracted with Hydrotech to design and construct a 29,000-square-foot "surfing pool" at the park, using Hydrotech's wave equipment. The total contract price was $850,000. Hydrotech was aware of a California law that requires a contractor to have a California contractor's license to provide construction services in California. The statute stipulates that an unlicensed contractor cannot sue in a California court to recover compensation for work requiring a California contractor's license [California Business and Professional Code Section 7031].

Because it was concerned with the licensing problem, Hydrotech wished only to sell and deliver the equipment and to avoid involvement in the design and construction of the pool. However, Oasis insisted that Hydrotech's unique expertise in design and construction was essential. Oasis induced Hydrotech to provide these services by promising to pay Hydrotech even if the law provided otherwise.

In reliance on these promises, Hydrotech furnished equipment and services in full compliance with the contract. Hydrotech had been paid $740,000 during the course of the contract. When it billed Oasis for the remaining $110,000, Oasis refused to pay. Hydrotech sued Oasis and Wessman for damages in California court for breach of contract and fraud. The defendants moved the court to dismiss the action because Hydrotech did not possess a California contractor's license, as required by law.

The California supreme court agreed with the defendants and ordered Hydrotech's complaint dismissed. The court found that Hydrotech had violated the licensing statute. The supreme court stated: "The obvious statutory intent is to discourage persons who have failed to comply with the licensing law from offering or providing their unlicensed services for pay. Because of the strength and clarity of this policy, it is well settled that Section 7031 applies despite injustice to the unlicensed contractor." *Hydrotech Systems, Ltd. v. Oasis Waterpark*, 52 Cal.3d 988, 277 Cal.Rptr. 517, 803 P.2d 370, **Web** 1991 Cal. Lexis 139 (Supreme Court of California)

Law & Ethics Questions

1. **ETHICS** Did Oasis act unethically by not paying Hydrotech? Explain.

2. **ETHICS** Did Hydrotech act unethically by providing services in California without the proper license? Explain.

Web Exercises

1. **WEB** For the complete opinion of this case, go to *www.prenhall.com/cheesemancases*.

2. **WEB** Visit the website of the supreme court of California, at *www.courtinfo.ca.gov/courts/supreme*.

Exculpatory Clauses

An **exculpatory clause** is a contractual provision that relieves one (or both) of the parties to a contract from tort liability. An exculpatory clause can relieve a party of liability for ordinary negligence. It cannot be used in a situation involving willful conduct, intentional torts, fraud, recklessness, or gross negligence.

Example Exculpatory clauses are often found in leases, sales contracts, ticket stubs to sporting events, parking lot tickets, service contracts, and the like. Such clauses do not have to be reciprocal (i.e., one party may be relieved of tort liability, whereas the other party is not).

Generally, the courts do not favor exculpatory clauses unless both parties have equal bargaining power. The courts are willing to permit competent parties of equal bargaining power to establish which of them bears the risk.

Example Jim Jackson voluntarily enrolled in a parachute jump course and signed a contract containing an exculpatory clause that relieved the parachute center of liability. After receiving proper instruction, he jumped from an airplane. Unfortunately, Jim was injured when he could not steer his parachute toward the target area. He sued the parachute center for damages, but the court enforced the exculpatory clause, reasoning that parachute jumping did not involve an essential service and that there was no decisive advantage in bargaining power between the parties.

Exculpatory clauses that either affect the public interest or result from superior bargaining power are usually found to be void as against public policy. Although the outcome varies with the circumstances of the case, the greater the degree to which the party serves the general public, the greater the chance that the exculpatory clause will be struck down as illegal. The courts will consider such factors as the type of activity involved; the relative bargaining power, knowledge, experience, and sophistication of the parties; and other relevant factors.

In the following case, the court had to decide the legality of an exculpatory clause.

CASE **11.7**
Exculpatory Clause

Zivich v. Mentor Soccer Club, Inc.

696 N.E.2d 201, **Web** 1998 Ohio Lexis 1832
Supreme Court of Ohio

❝ *Yet the threat of liability strongly deters many individuals from volunteering for nonprofit organizations.* ❞

—Judge Sweeney

Facts

Pamela Zivich registered her seven-year-old son, Bryan, to play soccer with the Mentor Soccer Club, Inc. (Club). The Club is a nonprofit organization composed primarily of volunteers in the Mentor, Ohio, area who provide children the opportunity to learn and play soccer. The Club's registration form, which Mrs. Zivich signed, contained the following language:

Recognizing the possibility of physical injury associated with soccer and for the Mentor Soccer Club, and the USYSA [United States Youth Soccer Association] accepting the registrant for its soccer programs and activities, I hereby release, discharge and/or otherwise indemnify the Mentor Soccer Club and the USYSA, its affiliated organizations and sponsors, their employees, and associated personnel, including the owners of the fields and facilities utilized by the Soccer Club, against any claim by or on behalf of the registrant as a result of the registrant's participation in the Soccer Club.

Bryan attended soccer practice with his father, Philip Zivich. During practice, the team participated in an intrasquad scrimmage. After the scrimmage, Bryan jumped onto the soccer goal and was swinging back and forth on it, but the goal was not anchored down. It tipped backward, and Bryan fell. The goal came down on his chest, breaking three of his ribs and his collarbone and severely bruising his lungs. Bryan's parents sued the Club for negligence to recover damages for injuries suffered by Bryan and the loss of consortium for themselves. The Club moved for summary judgment, asserting that the exculpatory agreement signed by Bryan's mother barred the claims. The trial court agreed and granted the Club's summary judgment motion. The court of appeals affirmed. The plaintiffs appealed to the supreme court of Ohio.

Issue

Did the exculpatory agreement signed by Mrs. Zivich on behalf of her son release the Club from liability for the child's claims and the parents' claims?

Language of the Court

It cannot be disputed that volunteers in community recreational activities serve an important function. Organized recreational activities offer children the opportunity to learn valuable life skills. It is here that many children learn how to work as a team and how to operate within an organizational structure. Children also are given the chance to exercise and develop coordination skills. Due in great part to the assistance of volunteers, nonprofit organizations are able to offer these activities at minimal cost. Clearly, without the work of its volunteers, these nonprofit organizations could not exist, and scores of children would be without the benefit and enjoyment of organized sports.

Yet the threat of liability strongly deters many individuals from volunteering for nonprofit organizations. Therefore, faced with the very real threat of a lawsuit, and the potential for substantial damage awards, nonprofit organizations and their volunteers could very well decide that the risks are not worth the effort. Hence, invalidation of exculpatory agreements would reduce the number of activities made possible through the uncompensated services of volunteers and their sponsoring organizations.

Therefore, we conclude that although Bryan, like many children before him, gave up his right to sue for the negligent acts of others, the public as a whole received the benefit of these exculpatory agreements. Because of this agreement, the Club was able to offer affordable recreation and to continue to do so without the risks and overwhelming costs of litigation. Bryan's parents agreed to shoulder the risk. Public policy does not forbid such an agreement. In fact, public policy supports it.

Decision

The supreme court of Ohio held that a parent's signature on an exculpatory agreement on behalf of his or her child releases the other party from liability to the child, the parent who signed the agreement, and the other parent. The supreme court affirmed the decisions of the trial court and court of appeals in favor of Mentor Soccer Club.

Law & Ethics Questions

1. Do exculpatory agreements serve any valid purpose? Should exculpatory agreements be enforceable?

2. **ETHICS** Was it ethical for Mrs. Zivich to sign the exculpatory agreement and then bring this lawsuit?

3. What would have been the consequences if the court had found the exculpatory agreement to be invalid in this case?

Web Exercises

1. **WEB** For the complete opinion of this case, go to *www.prenhall.com/cheesemancases*.

2. **WEB** Visit the website of the supreme court of Ohio, at *www.sconet.state.oh.us*.

3. **WEB** Use *www.google.com* to find an example of an exculpatory clause. Read it.

CONTEMPORARY ENVIRONMENT
Covenants Not to Compete

Entrepreneurs and others often buy and sell businesses. The sale of a business includes its "goodwill," or reputation. To protect this goodwill after the sale, the seller often enters into an agreement with the buyer not to engage in a similar business or occupation within a specified geographic area for a specified period of time following the sale. This agreement is called a **covenant not to compete**, or a **noncompete clause**.

Covenants not to compete that are *ancillary* to a legitimate sale of a business or employment contract are lawful if they are reasonable in three aspects: (1) the line of business protected, (2) the geographic area protected, and (3) the duration of the restriction. A covenant that is found to be unreasonable is not enforceable as written. The reasonableness of covenants not to compete is examined on a case-by-case basis. If a covenant not to compete is unreasonable, the courts may either refuse to enforce it or change it so that it is reasonable. Usually, the courts choose the first option.

Example Suppose Stacy Rogers is a certified public accountant (CPA) with a lucrative practice in San Diego, California. Her business includes a substantial amount of goodwill. When she sells her practice, she agrees not to open another accounting practice in the state of California for a 20-year period. This covenant not to compete is reasonable in the line of business protected but is unreasonable in geographic scope and duration. It will not be enforced by the courts as written. The covenant not to compete would be reasonable and enforceable if it prohibited Rogers only from practicing as a CPA in the city of San Diego for 3 years.

Employment contracts often contain noncompete clauses that prohibit an employee from competing with his or her employer for a certain time period after leaving the employment. These covenants not to compete are also judged using the reasonableness standard.

Unconscionable Contracts

The general rule of freedom of contract holds that if (1) the object of a contract is lawful and (2) the other elements for the formation of a contract are met, the courts will enforce a contract according to its terms. Although it is generally presumed that parties are capable of protecting their own interests when contracting, it is a fact of life that dominant parties sometimes take advantage of weaker parties. As a result, some otherwise lawful contracts are so oppressive or manifestly unfair that they are unjust. To prevent the enforcement of such contracts, the courts developed the equitable **doctrine of unconscionability**, which is based on public policy. A contract found to be unconscionable under this doctrine is called an **unconscionable contract**, or a **contract of adhesion**.

The courts are given substantial discretion in determining whether a contract or contract clause is unconscionable. There is no single definition of *unconscionability*. The doctrine may not be used merely to save a contracting party from a bad bargain.

Elements of Unconscionability

The following elements must be shown to prove that a contract or clause in a contract is unconscionable:

1. The parties possessed severely unequal bargaining power.
2. The dominant party unreasonably used its unequal bargaining power to obtain oppressive or manifestly unfair contract terms.
3. The adhering party had no reasonable alternative.

Unconscionable contracts are sometimes found where there are consumer contracts that takes advantage of uneducated, poor, or elderly people who have been persuaded to enter into unfair contracts. This often involves door-to-door sales and sales over the telephone.

Example Suppose a door-to-door salesperson sells a poor family a freezer full of meat and other foods for $3,000, with monthly payments for 60 months at 20 percent interest. If the retail cost of the freezer and the food retails for $1,000, this contract could be found to be unconscionable.

If the court finds that a contract or contract clause is unconscionable, it may (1) refuse to enforce the contract, (2) refuse to enforce the unconscionable clause but enforce the remainder of the contract, or (3) limit the applicability of any unconscionable clause so as to avoid any unconscionable result. The appropriate remedy depends on the facts and circumstances of each case. Note that because unconscionability is a matter of law, the judge may opt to decide the case without a jury trial.

ETHICS SPOTLIGHT

Unconscionable Contract

> ❝*Considering the terms of the arbitration clause in the light of the commercial context in which it operates and the legitimate needs of the parties at the time it was entered into, we have little difficulty concluding that its terms are so extreme as to appear unconscionable according to the mores and business practices of the time and place.*❞

—Judge Kline

Sometimes contracts favor one party over another party. This unbalance often occurs when the strongest party drafts the contract and presents it to the other party on a take-it-or-leave-it basis. Mere unbalanced contracts are not necessarily illegal, but those that overreach and are too lopsided can be found to be unenforceable under the equitable doctrine of unconscionability. Consider the following case.

Supercuts, Inc., a Delaware corporation, conducts a national hair care franchise business. David E. Lipson was the president of Supercuts. For just over one year, Supercuts employed William N. Stirlen as its vice president and chief financial officer. Stirlen signed an employment agreement that was prepared by Supercuts. The contract provided for Stirlen to receive an annual salary of $150,000, stock options, a bonus plan, a supplemental retirement plan, and a $10,000 signing bonus. The contract was an at-will employment contract, meaning that Stirlen could be terminated without cause at any time.

After beginning work, Stirlen informed Lipson and other corporate officers of various problems and "accounting irregularities" he feared might be in violation of state and federal statutes. Stirlen also expressed concern that the company's decline in profits "was being hidden in the books and from public shareholders." Stirlen provided senior managers with accounting statements outlining the accounting irregularities. After Stirlen brought these issues to Supercuts's outside auditors, Lipson allegedly reprimanded Stirlen and accused him of being a "troublemaker." Lipson also told him that if Stirlen did not reverse his position on these issues, he would no longer be considered a "member of the team." When Stirlen did not comply, Lipson suspended Stirlen from his job; Stirlen was fired the following month.

Stirlen sued Supercuts and Lipson for breach of contract, wrongful termination in violation of public policy, and intentional misrepresentation. The defendants made a motion to the court alleging that the arbitration clause in Stirlen's employment contract required the dispute to be arbitrated. Stirlen countered that the arbitration clause, and other clauses in Supercuts's contract, were unconscionable and therefore unenforceable. The challenged clauses provided that (1) Stirlen would have to submit to final and binding arbitration all disputes concerning the contract, but that Supercuts could go to court on most matters if it sued Stirlen, (2) any damages that could be awarded Stirlen could not exceed the actual damages for breach of contract, and (3) any salary or benefits payable to Stirlen would cease pending the outcome of any action between the parties.

Stirlen argued that the employment contract was so one-sided as to be unconscionable. The court of appeals held that a contract is unconscionable if it "does not fall within the reasonable expectations of the weaker party" or if the contact is "unduly oppressive." Supercuts's attorneys argued that Stirlen was a sophisticated business executive who knew what he was doing when he signed Supercuts's contract.

After weighing all the evidence, the court found that Supercuts's contract was an unconscionable contract—a contract of adhesion—that was unenforceable. The court found Supercuts's contract to be unconscionable in the following ways: Supercuts reserved the right to sue in court but denied this right to Stirlen; Supercuts limited the damages that Stirlen could recover from them in violation of the law; and state law provided that a party could not require another party to waive the ability to sue for fraud, which Supercuts required Stirlen to do. The court also held that Stirlen could proceed with his lawsuit against Supercuts to recover damages. The court concluded: "Considering the terms of the arbitration clause in the light of the commercial context in which it operates and the legitimate needs of the parties at the time it was entered into, we have little difficulty concluding that its terms are so extreme as to appear unconscionable according to the mores and business practices of the time and place." *Stirlen v. Supercuts, Inc.*, 51 Cal.App.4th 1519, 60 Cal.Rptr.2d 138, **Web** 1997 Cal. App. Lexis 13 (Court of Appeal of California)

Law & Ethics Questions

1. What does the doctrine of unconscionability provide? Explain.

2. **ETHICS** Is the doctrine of unconscionability based on ethics principles? Explain.

3. **ETHICS** Did Supercuts act ethically in drafting its employment contract? Should it have been more "fair"?

4. **ETHICS** Did Stirlen act ethically by refusing to be a "team member"?

Web Exercises

1. **WEB** For the complete opinion of this case, go to *www.prenhall.com/cheesemancases*.

2. **WEB** Visit the website of the court of appeals of California, First Appellate District, at *www.courtinfo.ca.gov/courts/courtsofappeal*.

3. **WEB** Visit the website of Supercuts, at *www.supercuts.com*. Can you find this corporation's code of ethics?

Marrakech, Morocco
In many parts of the world, the parties usually engage in negotiations that involve substantial posturing prior to agreeing on a final price.

Chapter Summary

Minors, p. 292
The Infancy Doctrine

Minors under the age of majority may *disaffirm* (cancel) most contracts they have entered into with adults. Such a contract is *voidable* by the minor but not by the adult.

Disaffirmance

Disaffirmance must occur before or within a reasonable time after the minor reaches the age of majority.

Minor's Duty of Restoration

Generally, upon disaffirmance of a contract, a minor owes a duty to return the consideration to the adult in whatever condition it is in at the time of disaffirmance. In addition, if a minor disaffirms a contract, the adult must place the minor in status quo by returning the value of the consideration that the minor paid.

Minor's Duty of Restitution

A minor's duty is to place the adult in status quo by returning the value of the consideration paid by the adult at the time of contracting if the minor (1) misrepresented his or her age or (2) intentionally or with gross negligence caused the loss to the adult's property.

Ratification

If a minor does not disaffirm a contract during the period of minority or within a reasonable time after reaching the age of majority, the contract is *ratified* (accepted).

Parents' Liability for Their Children's Contracts

Generally, parents owe a legal duty to provide food, clothing, shelter, and other necessaries of life for their minor children, and they are liable for their children's contracts for necessaries of life if they have not adequately provided such items. Emancipation occurs when a minor voluntarily leaves home and lives apart from his or her parents. The parents' duty to support the minor terminates upon emancipation.

Necessaries of Life

Minors are obligated to pay the reasonable value for the necessaries of life (e.g., food, clothing, shelter).

Special Types of Minors' Contracts

Many states have enacted statutes that make minors liable on certain types of contracts, such as for medical care, health and life insurance, educational loan agreements, and the like.

Mentally Incompetent Persons, p. 297

Adjudged Insane

Contracts by persons who have been adjudged insane are void. That is, such a contract cannot be enforced by either the sane or insane party.

Insane but Not Adjudged Insane

Contracts by persons who are insane but have not been adjudged insane are *voidable* by the insane person but not by the competent party to the contract.

1. *Duty of restitution.* A person who has dealt with an insane person must place the insane person in status quo by returning the value of the consideration paid by the insane person at the time of contracting. Most states place the same duty on insane persons when they void a contract.
2. *Necessaries of life.* Insane persons are obligated to pay the reasonable value for the necessaries of life.

Intoxicated Persons, p. 299

Contracts by intoxicated persons are voidable by the intoxicated person but not by the competent party to the contract.

1. *Duty of restitution.* Both parties owe a duty to place the other party in status quo by returning the value of the consideration paid by the other party at the time of contracting.
2. *Necessaries of life.* Intoxicated persons are obliged to pay the reasonable value for the necessaries of life.

Legality, p. 301

Contracts Contrary to Statutes

Contracts that violate statutes are illegal, void, and unenforceable.

Usury Laws

Usury laws set the upper limit on the annual interest rate that can be charged on certain types of loans by certain lenders.

Sabbath Laws

Sabbath laws prohibit or limit the carrying on of certain secular activities on Sundays. They are also called *Sunday laws* or *blue laws*.

Contracts to Commit Crimes

Contracts to commit crimes are illegal.

Contracts Contrary to Public Policy

Contracts that violate public policy are illegal, void, and unenforceable. A contract whose objective is the commission of an act that is considered immoral by society is illegal.

Gambling Statutes

Gambling statutes make certain types of gambling illegal.

Effect of Illegality

An illegal contract is void. Therefore, the parties cannot sue for nonperformance. If the contract has been executed, the court will leave the parties where it finds them.

Special Business Contracts, p. 304

Contracts in Restraint of Trade

Contracts that unreasonably restrain trade are illegal contracts.

Licensing Statutes

1. *Regulatory statutes.* These licensing statutes are enacted to protect the public. Unlicensed persons cannot recover payment for providing services that a licensed person is required to provide.
2. *Revenue-raising statutes.* These licensing statutes are enacted to raise money for the government. Unlicensed persons can enforce contracts and recover for rendering services.

Exculpatory Clauses

Contract clauses that relieve one or both of the parties to the contract from tort liability for ordinary negligence are called exculpatory clauses. Exculpatory clauses that affect public interests, that result from superior bargaining power, or that attempt to relieve one party of liability for intentional torts, fraud, recklessness, or gross negligence are illegal. Reasonable exculpatory clauses between parties of equal bargaining power are legal.

Covenants Not to Compete

Covenants not to compete are contracts that provide that a seller of a business or an employee will not engage in a similar business or occupation within a specified geographic area for a specified time following the sale of the business or termination of employment. Also called *noncompete clauses*, they are illegal if they are unreasonable in line of business, geographic area, or time. Reasonable noncompete clauses are legal and enforceable.

Unconscionable Contracts, p. 308

Contracts that are oppressively unfair or unjust are called *unconscionable contracts*, or *contracts of adhesion*.

Elements of Unconscionability

1. The parties possessed severely unequal bargaining power.
2. The dominant party unreasonably used its power to obtain oppressive or manifestly unfair contract terms.
3. The adhering party had no reasonable alternative.

Remedies for Unconscionability

Where a contract or contract clause is found to be unconscionable, the court may do one of the following:
1. Refuse to enforce the contract.
2. Refuse to enforce the unconscionable clause but enforce the remainder of the contract.
3. Limit the applicability of any unconscionable clause so as to avoid any unconscionable result.

Test Review Terms and Concepts

Adjudged insane   297
Competent party's duty of restitution   293
Contract in restraint of trade   304
Contractual capacity   292
Contrary to public policy   302
Covenant not to compete (noncompete clause)   307
Disaffirmance   293
Doctrine of unconscionability   308
Duty of restitution   293
Emancipation   295

Exculpatory clause   306
Gambling statute   303
Illegal contract   301
Immoral contract   302
Infancy doctrine   292
In pari delicto   303
Insane but not adjudged insane   298
Intoxicated persons   299
Lawful contract   301
Legal insanity   297
Licensing statute   305
Minor   292

Minor's duty of restitution   294
Minor's duty of restoration   293
Necessaries of life   296
Quasi-contract   296
Ratification   294
Regulatory statute   305
Revenue-raising statute   305
Sabbath laws (Sunday laws, blue laws)   301
Unconscionable contract (contract of adhesion)   308
Usury law   301

Case Problems

11.1 Infancy Doctrine: James Halbman, Jr., a minor, entered into a contract to purchase an Oldsmobile from Michael Lemke. Halbman paid $1,000 cash and agreed to make weekly payments until the full purchase price was paid. Five weeks later, a connecting rod on the vehicle's engine broke, and Halbman took the car to a garage, where it was repaired at a cost of $637.40. Halbman refused to pay for the repairs, disaffirmed the contract with Lemke, and notified Lemke where the car was located. When Lemke refused to pick up the car and pay the repair bill, the garage legally satisfied its garageman's lien by removing the vehicle's engine. It then towed the car to Halbman's residence. Halbman notified Lemke to remove the car, but Lemke refused to do so. The car was subsequently vandalized, making it worthless and unsalvageable. Halbman sued to disaffirm the contract and recover the consideration from Lemke. Lemke argued that Halbman must make full restitution. Who is correct? *Halbman v. Lemke*, 99 Wis.2d 241, 298 N.W.2d 562, **Web** 1980 Wisc. Lexis 2825 (Supreme Court of Wisconsin)

11.2 Ratification: Charles Edwards Smith, a minor, purchased an automobile from Bobby Floars Toyota (Toyota). Smith executed a security agreement to finance part of the balance due on the purchase price, agreeing to pay off the balance in 30 monthly installments. Smith turned 18, which was the age of majority in his state. Smith made 10 monthly payments after turning 18. He then decided to disaffirm the contract and stopped making the payments. Smith claimed that he could disaffirm the contract entered into when he was a minor. Toyota argued that Smith had ratified the contract since attaining the age of majority. Who is correct? *Bobby Floars Toyota, Inc. v. Smith*, 48 N.C. App. 580, 269 S.E.2d 320, **Web** 1980 N.C. App. Lexis 3263 (Court of Appeals of North Carolina)

11.3 Adjudged Insane: Manzelle Johnson, who had been adjudicated insane, executed a quitclaim and warranty deed conveying real estate she owned to her guardian, Obbie Neal. Neal subsequently conveyed the real estate to James R. Beavers by warranty deed. Charles L. Weatherly, Johnson's present guardian, brought this action seeking a decree of the court that title to the real estate be restored to Johnson because of her inability to contract. Should Johnson be allowed to void the contract? *Beavers v. Weatherly*, 250 Ga. 546, 299 S.E.2d 730, **Web** 1983 Ga. Lexis 581 (Supreme Court of Georgia)

11.4 Intoxication: Betty Galloway, an alcoholic, signed a settlement agreement upon her divorce from her husband, Henry Galloway. Henry, in Betty's absence in court, stated that she had lucid intervals from her alcoholism, had been sober for two months, and was lucid when she signed the settlement agreement. After she retained legal counsel, Betty moved to vacate the settlement agreement. Four months later, Betty was declared incompetent to handle her person and her affairs, and a guardian and conservator was appointed. Betty, through her guardian, sued to have the settlement agreement voided. Who wins? *Galloway v. Galloway*, 281 N.W.2d 804, **Web** 1979 N.D. Lexis 279 (Supreme Court of North Dakota)

11.5 Licensing Statute: The state of Hawaii requires a person who wants to practice architecture to meet certain educational requirements and to pass a written examination before that person is granted a license to practice. After receiving the license, an architect must pay an annual license fee of $15. Ben Lee Wilson satisfied the initial requirements and was granted an architecture license. Four years later, Wilson failed to renew his license by paying the required annual fee. Wilson contracted with Kealakekua Ranch, Ltd., and Gentry Hawaii (defendants) to provide architectural services for the Kealakekua Ranch Center project. Wilson provided $33,994 of architectural services to the defendants. The defendants refused to pay this fee because Wilson did not have an architectural license. Wilson sued to collect his fees. Who wins? *Wilson v. Kealakekua Ranch, Ltd., and Gentry Hawaii*, 57 Haw. 124, 551 P.2d 525, **Web** 1976 Haw. Lexis 119 (Supreme Court of Hawaii)

11.6 Covenant Not to Compete: Gerry Morris owned a silk screening and lettering shop in Tucson, Arizona. Morris entered into a contract to sell the business to Alfred and Connie Gann. The contract contained the following covenant not to compete: "Seller agrees not to enter into silk screening or lettering shop business within Tucson and a 100-mile radius of Tucson, for a period of ten (10) years from the date of this agreement and will not compete in any manner whatsoever with buyers, and seller further agrees that he will refer all business contracts to buyers." Morris opened a silk screening and lettering business in competition with the Ganns and in violation of the noncompete clause. The Ganns brought this action against Morris for breach of contract and to enforce the covenant not to compete. Is the covenant not to compete valid and enforceable in this case? *Gann v. Morris*, 122 Ariz. 517, 596 P.2d 43, **Web** 1979 Ariz. App. Lexis 487 (Court of Appeals of Arizona)

11.7 Exculpatory Clause: Grady Perkins owned the Raleigh Institute of Cosmetology (Institute), and Ray Monk and Rovetta Allen were employed as instructors there. The school trained students to do hair styling and coloring, cosmetology, and other beauty services. The students received practical training by providing services to members of the public under the supervision of the instructors. Francis I. Alston went to the Institute to have her hair colored and styled by a student who was under the supervision of Monk and Allen. Before receiving any services, Alston signed a written release form that released the Institute and its employees from liability for their negligence. While coloring Alston's hair, the student negligently used a chemical that caused Alston's hair to fall out. Alston sued the Institute, Perkins, Monk, and Allen for damages. The defendants asserted that the release form signed by Alston barred her suit. Is the exculpatory clause valid? *Alston v. Monk*, 92 N.C. App. 59, 373 S.E.2d 463, **Web** 1988 N.C. App. Lexis 987 (Court of Appeals of North Carolina)

11.8 Exculpatory Clause: Wilbur Spaulding owned and operated the Jacksonville racetrack at the Morgan Country Fairgrounds, where automobile races were held. Lawrence P. Koch was a flagman at the raceway. One day when Koch arrived at the pit shack at the raceway, he was handed a clipboard on which was a track release and waiver of liability form that released the racetrack from liability for negligence. Koch signed the form and took up his position as flagman. During the first race, the last car on the track lost control and slid off the end of the track, striking Koch. Koch suffered a broken leg and other injuries and was unable to work for 14 months. Koch sued Spaulding for damages for negligence. Spaulding asserted that the release form signed by Koch barred his suit. Is the exculpatory clause valid against Koch? *Koch v. Spaulding*, 174 Ill. App. 3d 692, 529 N.E.2d 19, **Web** 1988 Ill. App. Lexis 1427 (Appellate Court of Illinois)

Ethics Issues

11.9 Ethics: Joe Plumlee owned and operated an ambulance company. He alleged that the law firm Paddock, Loveless & Roach agreed to pay him an up-front fee and a percentage of the law firm's fees generated from personal injury case referrals. When the law firm did not pay Plumlee, he sued to recover damages for breach of contract. Texas law prohibits lawyers from sharing fees with laypersons. [Tex. Penal Code Section 38.12; supreme court of Texas] A disciplinary rule also forbids such activity. [State Bar Rules Art. X, Section 9] The law firm asserted that the contract could not be enforced because it would be an illegal contract. Who wins? Did Plumlee act ethically in this case? If the contract existed, did the lawyers act ethically? *Plumlee v. Paddock, Loveless, and Roach*, 832 S.W.2d 757, Web 1992 Tex. App. Lexis 1544 (Court of Appeals of Texas)

11.10 Ethics: Richard Zientara was friends with Chester and Bernice Kaszuba. All three were residents of Indiana. Bernice, who was employed in an Illinois tavern where Illinois state lottery tickets were sold, had previously obtained lottery tickets for Zientara because Indiana did not have a state lottery. One day, Zientara requested that Kaszuba purchase an Illinois lottery ticket for him. He gave Kaszuba the money for the ticket and the numbers 6–15–16–23–24–37. Kaszuba purchased the ticket, but when it turned out to be the wining combination worth $1,696,800, she refused to give the ticket to Zientara and unsuccessfully tried to collect the money. Zientara filed suit against Kaszuba in Indiana, claiming the ticket and proceeds thereof. Was the contract legal? Did the Kaszubas act ethically in this case? *Kaszuba v. Zientara*, 506 N.E.2d 1, Web 1987 Ind. Lexis 874 (Supreme Court of Indiana)

IRAC Writing Assignment

Read **Case A-11** in Appendix A [*Carnival Leisure Industries, Ltd. V. Aubin*]. Read the case and use the IRAC method to prepare a written analysis of the case.

CHAPTER 12

Genuineness of Assent and Statute of Frauds

> *"A verbal contract isn't worth the paper it's written on."*
>
> —SAMUEL GOLDWYN

CHAPTER OBJECTIVES

After studying this chapter, you should be able to:

1. Explain genuineness of assent.
2. Describe intentional misrepresentation (fraud), duress, and undue influence.
3. List the contracts that must be in writing, according to the Statute of Frauds.
4. Explain the effect of noncompliance with the Statute of Frauds.
5. Describe how the Statute of Frauds is applicable to the sale of goods.

CHAPTER CONTENTS

- Introduction to Genuineness of Assent and Statute of Frauds
- Mistake
- Fraud
- Undue Influence
- Duress
- Statute of Frauds
- Formality of the Writing
- Parol Evidence Rule
- Chapter Summary
- Test Review Terms and Concepts
- Case Problems
- Ethics Issues
- IRAC Writing Assignment

Introduction to Genuineness of Assent and Statute of Frauds

Voluntary *assent* by the parties is necessary to create an enforceable contract. Assent is determined by the relevant facts surrounding the negotiation and formation of the contract. Assent may be manifested in any manner sufficient to show agreement, including express words or conduct of the parties.

A contract may not be enforced if the assent of one or both of the parties to the contract was not genuine or real. Genuine assent may be missing because a party entered into a contract based on mistake, fraudulent misrepresentation, duress, or undue influence. Problems concerning **genuineness of assent** are discussed in this chapter.

Certain types of contracts must be in writing. In addition, other issues regarding the form of a contract may arise, such as the form of signature that is required on a written contract, whether a contract can be created by the integration of several documents, whether any previous oral or written agreements between the parties can be given effect, and how contract language should be interpreted. Issues regarding the writing and formality of contracts are discussed in this chapter.

Hong Kong

International contracts between businesses located in different countries make the global economy possible.

Mistake

A **mistake** occurs where one or both of the parties have an erroneous belief about the subject matter, value, or some other aspect of a contract. Mistakes may be either *unilateral* or *mutual*. The law permits **rescission** of some contracts made in mistake.

Unilateral Mistakes

Unilateral mistakes occur when only one party is mistaken about a material fact regarding the subject matter of the contract. There are three types of situations in which a contract may not be enforced due to such a mistake:

1. One party makes a unilateral mistake of fact, and the other party knew (or should have known) that a mistake was made.
2. A unilateral mistake occurs because of a clerical or mathematical error that is not the result of gross negligence.
3. The mistake is so serious that enforcing the contract would be unconscionable.[1]

In most cases, however, the mistaken party will not be permitted to rescind the contract. The contract will be enforced on its terms.

Example Suppose Trent Anderson wants to purchase a car from a showroom floor. He looks at several models. Although he decides to purchase a car with a sunroof, he does not tell the salesperson about this preference. The model named in the contract he signs does not have this feature, although he believes it does. Anderson's unilateral mistake will not relieve him of his contractual obligation to purchase the car.

In the following case, the court had to decide whether to allow a party out of a contract because of the party's unilateral mistake.

> Words are chameleons, which reflect the color of their environment.
>
> Justice L. Hand
> *Commissioner v. National Carbide Co. (1948)*

CASE 12.1
Unilateral Mistake

Wells Fargo Credit Corporation v. Martin

650 So.2d 531, **Web** 1992 Fla. App. Lexis 9927
Court of Appeal of Florida

> " *We accept the trial court's conclusion that the amount of the sale was grossly inadequate. This inadequacy, however, occurred due to an avoidable, unilateral mistake by an agent of Wells Fargo.* "
>
> —Judge Altenbernd

Facts

Wells Fargo Credit Corporation (Wells Fargo) obtained a judgment of foreclosure on a house owned by Mr. and Mrs. Clevenger. The total indebtedness stated in the judgment was $207,141. The foreclosure sale was scheduled for 11:00 A.M. on July 12, 1991, at the west front door of the Hillsborough County Courthouse.

Wells Fargo was represented by a paralegal, who had attended more than 1,000 similar sales. Wells Fargo's handwritten instruction sheet informed the paralegal to make one bid at $115,000, the tax-appraised value of the property. Because the first "1" in the number was close to the "$," the paralegal misread the bid instruction as $15,000 and opened the bidding at that amount.

Harley Martin, who was attending his first judicial sale, bid $20,000. The county clerk gave ample time for another bid and then announced. "$20,000 going once, $20,000 going twice, sold to Harley . . . " The paralegal screamed, "Stop, I'm sorry. I made a mistake!" The certificate of sale was issued to Martin. Wells Fargo filed suit to set aside the judicial sale based on its unilateral mistake. The trial court held for Martin. Wells Fargo appealed.

Issue

Does Wells Fargo's unilateral mistake constitute grounds for setting aside the judicial sale?

Language of the Court

We accept the trial court's conclusion that the amount of the sale was grossly inadequate. This inadequacy, however, occurred due to an avoidable, unilateral mistake by an agent of Wells Fargo. As between Wells Fargo and a good faith purchaser at the judicial sale, the trial court had the discretion to place the risk of this mistake upon Wells Fargo.

Thus, we affirm the trial court's orders denying relief to Wells Fargo. We are certain that this result seems harsh to Wells Fargo. Nevertheless, Mr. Martin's bid was accepted when the clerk announced "sold." Without ruling that a unilateral mistake by the complaining party could never justify relief, we hold that the trial court had the discretion under these facts to make Wells Fargo suffer the loss.

Decision

The appellate court held that Wells Fargo's unilateral mistake did not entitle it to relief from the judicial sale.

Law & Ethics Questions

1. Should contracts be allowed to be rescinded because of unilateral mistakes? Why or why not?

2. **ETHICS** Did Wells Fargo act ethically in trying to set aside the judicial sale?

3. Do you think mistakes such as the one Wells Fargo made in this case happen very often in business?

Web Exercises

1. **WEB** For the complete opinion of this case, go to *www.prenhall.com/cheesemancases*.

2. **WEB** Visit the website of the court of appeals of Florida, Second District, at *www.2dca.org*.

3. **WEB** Visit the website of Wells Fargo Financial, at *www.wellsfargofinancial.com*.

4. **WEB** Use *www.google.com* to find an article or a case that involves a unilateral mistake.

Mutual Mistakes

Either party may rescind a contract if there has been a **mutual mistake of a past or existing material fact**.[2] A *material fact* is a fact that is important to the subject matter of a contract. An ambiguity in a contract may constitute a mutual mistake of a material fact. An ambiguity occurs where a word or term in the contract is susceptible to more than one logical interpretation. If there has been a mutual mistake, the contract may be rescinded on the ground that no contract has been formed because there has been no "meeting of the minds" between the parties.

In the celebrated case *Raffles v. Wichelhaus*,[3] which has become better known as the case of the good ship *Peerless*, the parties agreed on a sale of cotton that was to be delivered from Bombay by the ship. There were two ships named *Peerless*, however, and each party, in agreeing to the sale, was referring to a different ship. Because the sailing times of the two ships were materially different, neither party was willing to agree to shipment by the other *Peerless*. The court ruled that there was no binding contract because each party had a different ship in mind when the contract was formed.

The courts must distinguish between *mutual mistakes of fact* and *mutual mistakes of value*. A **mutual mistake of value** exists if both parties know the object of the contract but are mistaken as to its value. Here, the contract remains enforceable by either party because the identity of the subject matter of the contract is not at issue. If the rule were different, almost all contracts could later be rescinded by the party who got the "worst" of the deal.

Example Suppose Helen Pitts cleans her attic and finds a painting of a tomato soup can. She has no use for the painting, so she offers to sell it to Qian Huang for $100. Qian, who likes the painting, accepts the offer and pays Helen $100. It is latter discovered that the painting is worth $1,000,000 because it was painted by Andy Warhol. Neither party knew this at the time of contracting. It is a mistake of value. Helen cannot recover the painting.

Fraud

A charge of fraud is such a terrible thing to bring against a man that it cannot be maintained in any court unless it is shown that he had a wicked mind.

M. R. Lord Esher
Le Lievre v. Gould (1732)

A misrepresentation occurs when an assertion is made that is not in accord with the facts.[4] An intentional misrepresentation occurs when one person consciously decides to induce another person to rely and act on a misrepresentation. International misrepresentation is commonly referred to as **fraudulent misrepresentation**, or **fraud**. When fraudulent misrepresentation is used to induce another to enter into a contract, the innocent party's assent to the contract is not genuine, and the contract is voidable by the innocent party.[5] The innocent party can either rescind the contract and obtain restitution or enforce the contract and sue for contract damages.

ETHICS SPOTLIGHT
Proving Fraud

To prove fraud, the following elements must be shown:

1. The wrongdoer made a false representation of material fact.
2. The wrongdoer intended to deceive the innocent party.
3. The innocent party justifiably relied on the misrepresentation.
4. The innocent party was injured.

Each of these elements is discussed in the following paragraphs.

Material Misrepresentation of Fact

A misrepresentation may occur by words (oral or written) or by the conduct of a party. To be actionable as fraud, the misrepresentation must be of a past or existing *material fact*. This means that the misrepresentation must have been a significant factor in inducing the innocent party to enter into the contract. It does not have to have been the sole factor. Statements of opinion or predictions about the future generally do not form the basis for fraud.

Intent to Deceive

To prove fraud, the person making the misrepresentation must have either had knowledge that the representation was false or made it without sufficient knowledge of the truth. This is called **scienter** ("guilty mind"). The misrepresentation must have been made with the **intent to deceive** the innocent party. Intent can be inferred from the circumstances.

Reliance on the Misrepresentation

A misrepresentation is not actionable unless the innocent party to whom the misrepresentation was directed acted on it. Further, an innocent party who acts in **reliance on the misrepresentation** must justify his or her reliance. Justifiable reliance is generally found unless the innocent party knew that the misrepresentation was false or was so extravagant as to be obviously false.

Example Reliance on a statement such as "This diamond ring is worth $10,000, but I'll sell it to you for $100" would not be justified.

Injury to the Innocent Party

To recover damages, the innocent party must prove that the fraud caused economic injury. The measure of damages is the difference between the value of the property as represented and the actual value of the property. This measure of damages gives the innocent party the "benefit of the bargain." In the alternative, the buyer can rescind the contract and recover the purchase price.

Individuals must be on guard in their commercial and personal dealings not to be taken by fraud. Basically, sounding "too good to be true" is a signal that a situation might be fraudulent. Although the law permits a victim of fraud to rescind the contract and recover damages from the wrongdoer, often the wrongdoer cannot be found or the money has been spent.

There are various types of fraud. Some of the most common ones are discussed in the following paragraphs.

Fraud in the Inception

Fraud in the inception, or **fraud in the factum**, occurs if a person is deceived as to the nature of his or her act and does not know what he or she is signing. Contracts involving fraud in the inception are void rather than just voidable.

Example Suppose Heather brings her professor a grade card to sign. The professor signs the front of the grade card. On the back, however, are contract terms that transfer all of the professor's property to Heather. Here, there is fraud in the inception. The contract is void.

Fraud in the Inducement

A great many fraud cases concern **fraud in the inducement**. Here, the innocent party knows what he or she is signing but has been fraudulently induced to enter into the contract. Such contracts are voidable by the innocent party.

Example Suppose Lyle Green tells Candice Young he is forming a partnership to invest in drilling for oil and invites her to invest in this venture. In reality, though, Green intends to use whatever money he receives for his personal expenses, and he absconds with Young's $30,000 investment. Here, there has been fraud in the inducement. Young can rescind the contract and recover the money from Green, if he can be found.

Fraud by Concealment

Fraud by concealment occurs when one party takes specific action to conceal a material fact from another party.[6]

Example Suppose that ABC Blouses, Inc., contracts to buy a used sewing machine from Wear-Well Shirts, Inc. Wear-Well did not show ABC the repair invoices from the sewing machine, even though ABC asked to see them. Relying on the knowledge that the machine was in good condition and never had to be repaired, ABC bought the machine. If ABC discovers that a significant repair record has been concealed, it can sue Wear-Well for fraud.

Silence as Misrepresentation

Generally, neither party to a contract owes a duty to disclose all the facts to the other party. Ordinarily, such silence is not a misrepresentation unless (1) nondisclosure would cause bodily injury or death, (2) there is a fiduciary relationship (i.e., a relationship of trust and confidence) between the contracting parties, or (3) federal and state statutes require disclosure. The *Restatement (Second) of Contracts* specifies a broader duty of disclosure: Nondisclosure is a misrepresentation if it would constitute a failure to act in "good faith."[7]

In the following case, the court found fraud and awarded punitive damages.

CASE 12.2
Fraud

Krysa v. Paine

176 S.W.3d 150, **Web** 2005 Mo. App. Lexis 1680 (2005)
Court of Appeals of Missouri

> *"Punitive damages differ from compensatory damages in that compensatory damages are intended to redress the concrete loss that the plaintiff has suffered by reason of the defendant's wrongful conduct, while the well-established purpose of punitive damages is to inflict punishment and to serve as an example and a deterrent to similar conduct."*

—Judge Ellis

Facts

Frank and Shelly Krysa were shopping for a truck to pull their 18-foot trailer. During the course of their search, they visited Payne's Car Company, a used car dealership owned by Emmett Payne. Kemp Crane, a used car salesman, showed the Krysas around the car lot. The Krysas saw an F-350 truck that they were interested in purchasing. Crane told the Krysas that the truck would tow their trailer, that the truck would make it to 400,000 miles, and that it was "a one-owner trade-in." The Krysas took the truck for a test drive and decided to purchase the truck. The Krysas, who had to borrow some of the money from Mrs. Krysa's mother, paid for the truck and took possession.

Later that day, the Krysas noticed that the power locks did not work on the truck. A few days later, the truck took three hours to start. The heater was not working. Mr. Krysa tried to fix some problems and noticed that the radiator was smashed up, the radiator cap did not have a seal, and the thermostat was missing. Mr. Krysa notice broken glass on the floor underneath the front seats and that the driver's side window had been replaced. Shortly thereafter, Mr. Krysa attempted to tow his trailer, but within two miles, he had his foot to the floor trying to get the truck to pull the trailer. A large amount of smoke was pouring out of the back of the truck. Mr. Krysa also noticed that the truck was consuming a lot of oil. Mr. Krysa obtained a CARFAX report for the truck, which showed that the truck had had 13 prior owners. Evidence proved that the truck was actually two halves of different trucks that had been welded together. An automobile expert told the Krysas not to drive the truck because it was unsafe.

Mr. Krysa went back to the dealership to return the truck and get his money back. Payne told Krysa that he would credit the purchase price of the truck toward the purchase of one of the other vehicles on the lot but that he would not give Krysa his money back. Krysa could not find another vehicle on Payne's used car lot that would suit his needs. The Krysas sued Payne for fraudulent nondisclosure and fraudulent misrepresentation and sought to recover compensatory and punitive damages. The jury returned a verdict for the Krysas and awarded them $18,449 in compensatory damages and $500,000 in punitive damages. Payne appealed the award of punitive damages.

Issue

Did Payne engage in fraudulent nondisclosure, fraudulent misrepresentation, and reckless disregard for the safety of the Krysas and the public to support the award of $500,000 in punitive damages?

Language of the Court

Punitive damages differ from compensatory damages in that compensatory damages are intended to redress the concrete loss that the plaintiff has suffered by reason of the defendant's wrongful conduct, while the well-established purpose of punitive damages is to inflict punishment and to serve as an example and a deterrent to similar conduct. While the damage actually sustained by the Krysas was relatively small and was economic in nature, the record clearly supports a finding that Payne acted indifferently to or in reckless disregard of the safety of the Krysas in selling them a vehicle that he knew or should have known was not safe to drive and that the potential harm to the Krysas was much greater than the harm that was actually incurred.

The evidence also supported a finding that the harm sustained by Krysas was the result of intentional malice, trickery, or deceit, and was not merely an accident. Payne had a significant amount of work done to the vehicle to make it appear to be in good shape. This included, among numerous other repairs, straightening both the bed and cab of the truck. Payne's salesman, Crane, lied to the Krysas on several occasions about the condition of the truck, its origin, and its capabilities. This evidence, in addition to other evidence previously described, sufficiently established that Payne affirmatively misrepresented the condition of the F-350 to the Krysas in an attempt to trick them into buying the vehicle.

In sum, while the harm actually sustained by the Krysas in this case was economic as opposed to physical, Payne's conduct did pose a significant risk to the physical welfare of Respondents and evinced an indifference to or reckless disregard of the health or safety of Krysas and the general public as well. Furthermore, the conduct was consistent with Payne's regular business practices and was not an isolated incident, involved acts of intentional trickery and deceit, and targeted victims that were financially vulnerable. Thus, in society's eyes, viewing the totality of the circumstances, Payne's conduct can only be seen as exhibiting a very high degree of reprehensibility.

Payne contends that the ratio between the actual damages awarded, $18,449.53, and the punitive award, $500,000, is grossly excessive, in that the ratio of punitive to actual damages is approximately 27:1. The initial problem with Payne's argument is that it fails to consider the evidence of the potential harm that could have been sustained by the Krysas. In this case, given the relatively small amount of actual damages awarded, the egregious nature of Payne's acts, Payne's open refusal to alter his behavior, and the magnitude of the potential harm that could have been sustained had the structural problems with the truck not been discovered by the Krysas's expert, the ratio of the punitive to actual damages does not, in and of itself, offend due process.

Decision

The court of appeals found that Payne's fraudulent concealment, fraudulent misrepresentation, and reckless disregard for the safety of the Krysas and the public justified the award of $500,000 of punitive damages to the Krysas.

Law & Ethics Questions

1. What is fraudulent concealment? What is fraudulent misrepresentation?
2. What are punitive damages? Why are they awarded?
3. **ETHICS** Did Payne, the used car dealer, act ethically in this case?
4. **ETHICS** Do you have any apprehension about purchasing a car from a used car dealership? Why or why not?

Web Exercises

1. **WEB** For the complete opinion of this case, go to *www.prenhall.com/cheesemancases*.
2. **WEB** Visit the website of the court of appeals of Missouri, Western District, at *www.courts.mo.gov/page.asp?id=227*.
3. **WEB** Use *www.google.com* to find an article or a case about a fraudulent transaction.

Misrepresentation of Law

Usually, a **misrepresentation of law** is not actionable as fraud. The innocent party cannot generally rescind the contract because each party to a contract is assumed to know the law that applies to the transaction, either through his or her own investigation or by hiring a lawyer. There is one major exception to this rule: The misrepresentation will be allowed as grounds for rescission of the contract if one party to the contract is a professional who should know what the law is and intentionally misrepresents the law to a less sophisticated contracting party.[8]

Innocent Misrepresentation

An **innocent misrepresentation** occurs when a person makes a statement of fact that he or she honestly and reasonably believes to be true even though it is not. Innocent misrepresentation is not fraud. If an innocent misrepresentation has been made, the aggrieved party may rescind the contract but may not sue for damages. Often, innocent misrepresentation is treated as a mutual mistake.

In the following case, the court allowed a contract to be rescinded because of fraud.

CASE **12.3**
Fraud

Wilson v. Western National Life Insurance Company

235 Cal.App.3d 981, 1 Cal.Rptr.2d 157, **Web** 1991 Cal. App. Lexis 1249
Court of Appeal of California

“ *A material misrepresentation or concealment entitles the injured party to rescission.* **”**

—Judge Stone

Facts

Daniel and Doris Wilson were husband and wife. One day, Daniel fainted from a narcotics overdose and was rushed, unconscious, to the hospital. Doris accompanied him. Daniel responded to medication used to counteract a narcotics overdose and recovered. The emergency room physician noted that Daniel had probably suffered from a heroin overdose and that Daniel had multiple puncture sites on his arms. Two months later, an agent for Western National Life Insurance Company

(Western) met with the Wilsons in their home for the purpose of taking their application for life insurance. The agent asked questions and recorded the Wilsons' responses on a written application form. Daniel answered the following questions:

	Yes	No
13. In the past 10 years, have you been treated or joined an organization for alcoholism or drug addiction? If "Yes," explain on the reverse side.		X
17. In the past 5 years, have you consulted or been treated or examined by any physician or practitioner?		X

Both of the Wilsons signed the application form and paid the agent the first month's premium. Under insurance law and the application form, the life insurance policy took effect immediately. Daniel Wilson died from a drug overdose two days later. Western rescinded the policy and rejected Doris Wilson's claim to recover the policy's $50,000 death benefit for Daniel's death, alleging failure to disclose Daniel's heroin overdose incident. Doris sued to recover the death benefits. The trial court granted summary judgment for Western. Doris appealed.

Issue

Was there a concealment of a material fact that justified Western's rescission of the life insurance policy?

Language of the Court

Plaintiff asserts the court erroneously granted summary judgment because Western failed to prove she or decedent made a misrepresentation in the application. We disagree. In her deposition, plaintiff testified neither she nor decedent told Cantrell about decedent's fainting spell or his hospital treatment two months earlier. Thus, there is no question but that they omitted medical information. Knowledge of the true facts by plaintiff and decedent is beyond dispute.

Plaintiff further argues the misrepresentation, if one occurred, was not material. Plaintiff's argument must fail. The trial court properly found the omissions to be material and the evidence supporting its materiality uncontradicted. The trial court had before it evidence from Western that the application would not have been accepted, and decedent would not have been found to be insurable, had he disclosed on the application the episode when he became unconscious from a narcotics overdose.

A material misrepresentation or concealment entitles the injured party to rescission. Concealment, whether intentional or unintentional, entitles the injured party to rescind insurance. Western properly rescinded the insurance contract and its obligation to provide coverage terminated as of the date of application.

Decision

The appellate court held that there was concealment by the Wilsons that warranted rescission of the life insurance policy by Western.

Law & Ethics Questions

1. Should a contract be allowed to be rescinded because of an *innocent* misrepresentation? Why or why not?
2. **ETHICS** Do you think the concealment in this case was intentional or innocent?
3. Do you think there is very much insurance fraud in this country? Explain.

Web Exercises

1. **WEB** For the complete opinion of this case, go to *www.prenhall.com/cheesemancases*.
2. **WEB** Visit the website of the court of appeals of California, at *www.courtinfo.ca.gov/courts/courtsofappeal*.
3. **WEB** Use *www.google.com* to find an article or a case about insurance fraud.

CONCEPT SUMMARY

Types of Misrepresentation

TYPE OF MISREPRESENTATION	LEGAL PARTY MAY: SUE FOR DAMAGES	CONSEQUENCES—INNOCENT FOR RESCIND CONTRACT
Fraud in the inception	Yes	Yes
Fraud in the inducement	Yes	Yes
Fraud by concealment	Yes	Yes
Silence as misrepresentation	Yes	Yes
Misrepresentation of law	Usually no	Usually no
Innocent misrepresentation	No	Yes

Undue Influence

The courts may permit the rescission of a contract based on the equitable doctrine of **undue influence**. Undue influence occurs when one person (the dominant party) takes advantage of another person's mental, emotional, or physical weakness and unduly persuades that person (the servient party) to enter into a contract. The persuasion by the wrongdoer must overcome the free will of the innocent party. A contract that is entered into because of undue influence is voidable by the innocent party.[9] Wills are often challenged as having been made under undue influence.

The following elements must be shown to prove undue influence:

1. A fiduciary or confidential relationship must have existed between the parties.
2. The dominant party must have unduly used his or her influence to persuade the servient party to enter into a contract.

If there is a confidential relationship between persons—such as a lawyer and a client, a doctor and a patient, a psychiatrist and a patient—any contract made by the servient party that benefits the dominant party is presumed to be entered into under undue influence. This rebuttable presumption can be overcome through proper evidence.

Example Mr. Johnson, 70 years old, has a stroke and is partially paralyzed. He is required to use a wheelchair, and he needs constant nursing care. Prior to his stroke, Mr. Johnson had executed a will, leaving his property upon his death equally to his four grandchildren. Edward, a licensed nurse, is hired to care for Mr. Johnson on a daily basis, and Mr. Johnson relies on Edward's care. Edward works for Mr. Johnson for two years before Mr. Johnson passes away. It is discovered that Mr. Johnson had executed a new will three months before he died, leaving all of his property to Edward. If it is shown that Edward used his dominant and fiduciary position to unduly influence Mr. Johnson to change his will, then the will is invalid. If no undue influence is shown, the second will is valid, and Edward will receive the property left to him by Mr. Johnson in the will.

> The meaning of words varies according to the circumstances of and concerning which they are used.
>
> Justice Blackburn
> *Allgood v. Blake* (1873)

ETHICS SPOTLIGHT
Undue Influence

> **❝** *Any species of coercion, whether physical, mental, or moral, which subverts the sound judgment and genuine desire of the individual, is enough to constitute undue influence.* **❞**
>
> —Judge Bownes

Religions obviously have an influence on their members. People who belong to religions often donate money and property to their churches and religious causes. Most religious giving (and church asking) is legitimate. Sometimes there are charges of illegal and unethical conduct, however. Sometimes the charge is undue influence. Consider the following case.

Elizabeth Dayton Dovydenas was born in 1952. As an heir to the Dayton-Hudson department store chain fortune, she was worth approximately $19 million. She married Jonas Dovydenas. When Elizabeth was interested in finding a church to attend, the couple's housekeeper suggested her church, The Bible Speaks (TBS). Elizabeth

and Jonas went to a TBS service, liked what they saw, and left a $500 check in the collection plate.

After this, pastors from TBS contacted them and set up a tea with Carl Stevens, the founder of TBS. Stevens had been a fundamentalist preacher for 26 years. At the first meeting, Stevens asked Elizabeth for money for a counseling center, and she gave him a check for $2,000. Elizabeth became a devout member of TBS. Eventually, Elizabeth met with Stevens alone on a daily basis after Bible classes and attended other functions with him. She abandoned her prior friends and saw little of her family.

One day in the fall of 1984, as she was driving with Stevens, Elizabeth heard a voice telling her to give $1 million to TBS. Elizabeth gave $1 million of Dayton-Hudson stock to TBS. Elizabeth was led to believe that large gifts by her to TBS could affect events on earth. She was also told that she had to obey Stevens because he was the highest authority on earth.

In March 1985, Elizabeth told Stevens that she heard God tell her to give $5 million to TBS in June. Elizabeth had planned a trip to Florida on April 18. Before she left, she was told that a TBS pastor had been detained in Romania and that "they're probably pulling his fingernails out right now." Elizabeth went to Florida but called Stevens on April 21 and told him that she wanted to give the $5 million right away so the pastor would be released. Stevens did not tell her that the pastor had already been released. Elizabeth was cautioned against telling anyone that she had worked a miracle. The gift of $5 million of Dayton-Hudson stock was completed on May 13.

After her relatives tricked Elizabeth away from Stevens, Elizabeth was deprogrammed from her "cult" experience. Elizabeth then sued to rescind her $1 million and $5 million gifts to TBS, alleging that Stevens and TBS had engaged in undue influence. The U.S. District Court agreed and ordered that both gifts be rescinded. On appeal, the U.S. Court of Appeals stated:

> Undue influence, while sometimes susceptible of proof by direct testimony, may be exercised by indirect and secret ways, which are disclosed only in their result. Because undue influence is often practiced in "veiled and secret ways," its existence may be inferred from such factors as disproportionate gifts made under unusual circumstances, the age and health of the donor, and the existence of a confidential relationship
>
> Two other factors are also important. One, attempts by the recipient to isolate the donor from her former friends and relatives can be considered in determining undue influence. Two, a court can also consider that she the donor acted without independent and disinterested advice. Any species of coercion, whether physical, mental, or moral, which subverts the sound judgment and genuine desire of the individual, is enough to constitute undue influence.

The U.S. Court of Appeals reversed as to the $1 million gift, finding no undue influence at the time this gift was made. The U.S. Court of Appeals affirmed that the $5 million gift had been made based on undue influence and must be rescinded. *Dovydenas v. The Bible Speaks*, 869 F.2d 628, **Web** 1989 U.S. App. LEXIS 2895 (United States Court of Appeals for the First Circuit)

Law & Ethics Questions

1. What is undue influence? Is it hard to prove? Explain.

2. **ETHICS** Did Stevens and the other members of TBS act ethically in this case?

3. Should the plaintiff have been saved from her folly? Why or why not?

Web Exercises

1. **WEB** For the complete opinion of this case, go to *www.prenhall.com/cheesemancases*.

2. **WEB** Visit the website of the United States Court of Appeals for the First Circuit, at *www.ca1.uscourts.gov*.

3. **WEB** Use *www.google.com* to find an article that discusses the history of the Dayton-Hudson Corporation. Read it.

4. **WEB** Use *www.google.com* to find an article that discusses what further happened in this story after this case had been decided. Read it.

Duress

Duress occurs when one party threatens to do some wrongful act unless the other party enters into a contract. If a party to a contract has been forced into making the contract, the assent is not voluntary. Such a contract is not enforceable against the innocent party.

Example If someone threatens to harm another person unless that person signs a contract, this is *physical duress*. This contract cannot be enforced against the duressed party.

A threat to commit physical harm or extortion unless someone enters into a contract constitutes duress. So does a threat to bring (or not drop) a criminal lawsuit. Such threats are duress even if the criminal lawsuit is well founded.[10] A threat to bring (or not drop) a civil lawsuit, however, does not constitute duress unless such a suit is frivolous or brought in bad faith.

Economic Duress

The courts have recognized another type of duress—*economic duress*. Economic duress usually occurs when one party to a contract refuses to perform his or her contractual duties unless the other party pays an increased price, enters into a second contract with the threatening party, or the like. The duressed party must prove that he had no alternative but to acquiesce to the other party's threat.

ETHICS SPOTLIGHT
Economic Duress

> **"** *I have a check for you, and you just take it or leave it, this is all you get. If you don't take this, you have got to sue me.* **"**
>
> —General contractor to subcontractor

Economic duress is also called **business compulsion**, **business duress**, and **economic coercion**. The appropriateness of these terms becomes apparent when the facts of the following case are examined.

Ashton Development, Inc. (Ashton), hired Bob Britton, Inc. (Britton), a general contractor, to build a development for it. Britton signed a contract with a subcontractor, Rich & Whillock, Inc. (R&W), to provide grading and excavation work at the project. R&W proceeded with the excavation work and rock removal, which included blasting. After completing all the required work and receiving $109,363 in payments to date, R&W submitted a final bill to Britton for $72,286.

Britton refused to pay this amount. R&W told Britton that it would go "broke" if payment was not received. One month later, Britton presented R&W with an agreement whereby Britton would pay $25,000 upon the signing of the agreement and another $25,000 one month later. When R&W complained of the financial bind it was in, Britton stated: "I have a check for you, and you just take it or leave it, this is all you get. If you don't take this, you have got to sue me." After claiming that it was "blackmail," R&W accepted the $25,000 check. Britton did not pay the other $25,000 until one month later.

After receiving payment, R&W sued Britton for breach of contract. The trial and appellate courts held in favor of R&W, finding that Britton's tactics amounted to economic duress. In applying the doctrine of economic duress to the case, the court stated: "The underlying concern of the economic duress doctrine is the enforcement in the marketplace of certain minimal standards of business ethics." The court found that Britton had acted in bad faith when it refused to pay R&W's final billing and offered instead to pay a compromise amount of $50,000. At the time of its bad faith breach and settlement offer, Britton knew that R&W was a new company over-extended to creditors and subcontractors and faced with imminent bankruptcy if not paid its final billing. Under these circumstances, the court found that the settlement agreement was unenforceable. The court ordered Britton to pay the balance due on the contract to R&W. *Rich & Whillock, Inc. v. Ashton Development, Inc.*, 157 Cal.App.3d 1154, 204 Cal.Rptr. 86, **Web** 1984 Cal. App. Lexis 2272 (Court of Appeal of California)

Law & Ethics Questions

1. What is economic duress? What distinguishes it from just plain hard business tactics?

2. **ETHICS** Did Britton act ethically in this case?

Web Exercises

1. **WEB** For the complete opinion of this case, go to *www.prenhall.com/cheesemancases*.

2. **WEB** Visit the website of the court of appeals of California, at *www.courtinfo.ca.gov/courts/courts of appeal*.

Gitchie Manitou Shores, Lake Huron, Upper Michigan

Contracts that transfer an ownership interest in real property, such as this beachfront property, generally must be in writing under the Statute of Frauds.

Statute Of Frauds

In 1677, the English Parliament enacted a statute called "An Act for the Prevention of Frauds and Perjuries." This act required that certain types of contracts had to be in writing and signed by the party against whom enforcement was sought. Today, every U.S. state has enacted a **Statute of Frauds** that requires certain types of contracts to be in *writing*. This statute is intended to ensure that the terms of important contracts are not forgotten, misunderstood, or fabricated.

Writing Requirement

Although the statutes vary slightly from state to state, most states require the following types of contracts to be in writing[11]:

- Contracts involving interests in land
- Contracts that by their own terms cannot possibly be performed within one year
- Collateral contracts in which a person promises to answer for the debt or duty of another
- Promises made in consideration of marriage
- Contracts for the sale of goods for more than $500
- Real estate agents' contracts
- Agents' contracts where the underlying contract must be in writing
- Promises to write a will
- Contracts to pay debts barred by the statute of limitations or discharged in bankruptcy
- Contracts to pay compensation for services rendered in negotiating the purchase of a business
- Finder's fee contracts

> Statute of Frauds: That unfortunate statute, the misguided application of which has been the cause of so many frauds.
>
> V.C. Bacon
> *Morgan v. Worthington (1878)*

Generally, an *executory contract* that is not in writing even though the Statute of Frauds requires it to be is unenforceable by either party. The Statute of Frauds is usually raised by one party as a defense to the enforcement of the contract by the other party.

If an oral contract that should have been in writing under the Statute of Frauds is already executed, neither party can seek to rescind the contract on the ground of noncompliance with the Statute of Frauds. That is, the contract may be voluntarily performed by the parties.

Generally, contracts listed in the Statute of Frauds must be in writing to be enforceable. There are several equity exceptions to this rule. The contracts that must be in writing pursuant to the Statute of Frauds and the exceptions to this rule are discussed in the following paragraphs.

Contracts Involving Interests in Land

Under the Statute of Frauds, any contract that transfers an ownership interest in **real property** must be in writing to be enforceable. Real property includes the land itself, buildings, trees, soil, minerals, timber, plants, crops, fixtures, and things permanently affixed to the land or buildings. Certain items of personal property that are permanently affixed to the real property are fixtures that become part of the real property.

Example Built-in cabinets in a house are *fixtures* that become part of the real property.

Other contracts that transfer an ownership interest in land must be in writing under the Statute of Frauds. These interests include the following:

- *Mortgages.* Borrowers often give a lender an interest in real property as security for the repayment of a loan. This action must be done through the use of a written **mortgage** or **deed of trust**.

Example Suppose ABC Corporation purchases a factory and borrows part of the purchase price from City Bank. City Bank requires that the factory be used as collateral for the loan and takes a mortgage on the factory. Here, the mortgage must be in writing to be enforceable.

- *Leases.* A **lease** is the transfer of the right to use real property for a specified period of time. Most Statutes of Frauds require leases for a term over one year to be in writing.
- *Life estates.* On some occasions, a person is given a **life estate** in real property. In other words, the person has an interest in the land for the person's lifetime, and the interest will be transferred to another party on that person's death. A life estate is an ownership interest that must be in writing under the Statute of Frauds.
- *Easements.* An **easement** is a given or required right to use another person's land without owning or leasing it. Easements may be either express or implied. Express easements must be in writing to be enforceable, while implied easements need not be written.

Part Performance Exception

If an oral contract for the sale of land or transfer of another interest in real property has been partially performed, it may not be possible to return the parties to their *status quo*. To solve this problem, the courts have developed the equitable doctrine of **part performance**. This doctrine allows the court to order such an oral contract to be specifically performed if performance is necessary to avoid injustice. For this performance exception to apply, most courts require that the purchaser has either paid part of the purchase price and taken possession of the property or made valuable improvements on the land.

The following case involves the doctrine of part performance.

CASE 12.4
Part Performance

Sutton v. Warner

12 Cal.App.4th 415, 15 Cal.Rptr.2d 632, **Web** 1993 Cal. App. Lexis 22
Court of Appeal of California

> "The doctrine of part performance by the purchaser is a well-recognized exception to the Statute of Frauds as applied to contracts for the sale of real property."
>
> —Judge Kline

Facts

Arlene and Donald Warner inherited a one-third interest in a home at 101 Molimo Street in San Francisco. The Warners bought out the other heirs and obtained a $170,000 loan on the property. Donald Warner and Kenneth Sutton were friends. Donald Warner proposed that Sutton and his wife purchase the residence. His proposal included a $15,000 down payment toward the purchase price of $185,000. The Suttons were to pay all the mortgage payments and real estate taxes on the property for five years, and at any time during the five-year period they could purchase the house. All this was agreed to orally. The Suttons paid the down payment and cash payments equal to the monthly mortgage to the Warners. The Suttons paid the annual property taxes on the house. The Suttons also made improvements to the property. Four and one-half years later, the Warners reneged on the sales/option agreement. At that time, the house had risen in value to between $250,000 and $320,000. The Suttons sued for specific performance of the sales agreement. The Warners defended, alleging that the oral promise to sell real estate had to be in writing under the Statute of Frauds and was therefore unenforceable. The trial court applied the equitable doctrine of part performance and ordered specific performance. The Warners appealed.

Issue

Does the equitable doctrine of part performance make this oral contract for the sale of real property enforceable even though the Statute of Frauds may apply?

Language of the Court

The doctrine of part performance by the purchaser is a well-recognized exception to the Statute of Frauds as applied to contracts for the sale of real property. The question here, then, is whether the continued possession of the property by the Suttons and their other actions are sufficiently related to the option contract to constitute part performance. The trial court responded in the affirmative. After entering the oral agreement, the Suttons made a $15,000 down payment and increased their monthly payments to the Warners from the original monthly rental payment to payments in the precise amount of the variable mortgage payments due under the $170,000 loan. They reimbursed the Warners for property taxes in the sum of $800 every six months.

Although it was disputed whether the dollar value of improvements made by the Suttons in reliance upon the oral agreement constituted "substantial" improvements, it is undisputed that many of the improvements—such as painting the interior of the house and the installation of a toilet and entry lamp—were done by the Suttons' own labor. The trial court found that these actions were unequivocally related to the purchase agreement.

The actions taken by the Suttons in reliance upon the oral agreement, when considered together with the Warners' admission that there was an oral agreement of some duration, satisfy both elements of the part performance doctrine.

Decision

The court of appeal held that the doctrine of part performance applied and that the Statute of Frauds did not prevent the enforcement of the oral contract to sell real estate. The court of appeal affirmed the judgment of the trial court that ordered specific performance to the Suttons.

Law & Ethics Questions

1. What purposes are served by the Statute of Frauds? Explain.

2. **ETHICS** Did the Warners act ethically in this case? Did the Statute of Frauds give them a justifiable reason not to go through with the deal?

3. Should important business contracts be put in writing? Why or why not?

Web Exercises

1. **WEB** For the complete opinion of this case, go to *www.prenhall.com/cheesemancases*.

2. **WEB** Visit the website of the court of appeals of California, at *www.courtinfo.ca.gov/courts/courtsofappeal*.

3. **WEB** Use *www.google.com* to find an article about the Statute of Frauds. Read it.

One-Year Rule

According to the Statute of Frauds, an executory contract that cannot be performed by its own terms within one year of its formation must be in writing.[12] This **one-year rule** is intended to prevent disputes about contract terms that may otherwise occur toward the end of a long-term contract. If the performance of the contract is possible within the one-year period, the contract may be oral. The extension of an oral contract might cause the contract to violate the Statute of Frauds.

Example Suppose the owner of a Burger King franchise hires Eugene Daly as a manager for 6 months. This contract may be oral. Assume that after 3 months, the owner and manager agree to extend the contract for an additional 11 months. At the time of the extension, the contract would be for 14 months (the 3 left on the contract plus 11 added by the extension). The modification would have to be in writing because it exceeds the one-year rule.

Guaranty Contracts

A **guaranty contract** occurs when one person agrees to answer for the debts or duties of another person. Guaranty contracts are required to be in writing under the Statute of Frauds.[13]

In a guaranty situation, there are at least three parties and two contracts (see Exhibit 12.1). The first contract, which is known as the **original contract**, or **primary contract**, is between

EXHIBIT 12.1

Guaranty Contract

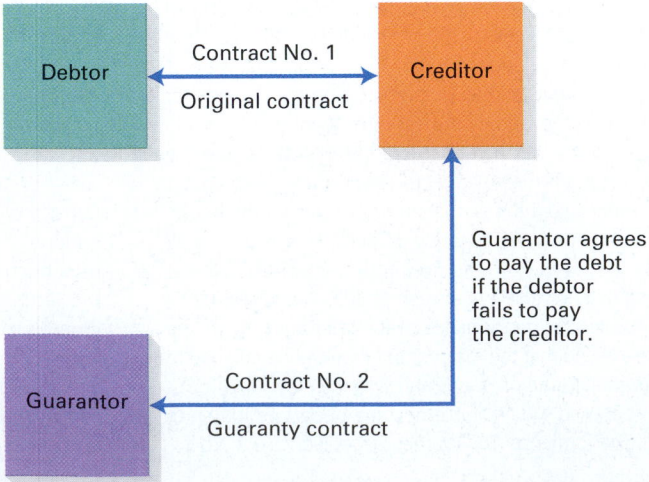

Debtor — Contract No. 1 / Original contract — Creditor

Guarantor agrees to pay the debt if the debtor fails to pay the creditor.

Guarantor — Contract No. 2 / Guaranty contract

the debtor and the creditor. It does not have to be in writing (unless another provision of the Statute of Frauds requires it to be). The second contract, called the *guaranty contract*, is between the person who agrees to pay the debt if the primary debtor does not (i.e., the **guarantor**) and the original creditor. The guarantor's liability is secondary because it does not arise unless the party primarily liable fails to perform.

Example Wei Wang, a recent college graduate, offers to purchase a new automobile on credit from a Mercedes-Benz automobile dealership. Because Wei, a student, does not have a credit history, the dealer will agree to sell the car to her only if there is a guarantor. Wei's father signs the guaranty contract. He becomes responsible for any payments his daughter fails to make.

The Main Purpose Exception

If the main purpose of a transaction and an oral collateral contract is to provide pecuniary (i.e., financial) benefit to the guarantor, the collateral contract is treated like an original contract and does not have to be in writing to be enforced.[14] This exception is called the **main purpose exception**, or **leading object exception**, to the Statute of Frauds. This exception is intended to ensure that the primary benefactor of the original contract (i.e., the guarantor) is answerable for the debt or duty.

Example Suppose Ethel Brand is president and sole shareholder of Brand Computer Corporation, Inc. Assume that (1) the corporation borrows $100,000 from City Bank for working capital, and (2) Ethel orally guarantees to repay the loan if the corporation fails to pay it. City Bank can enforce the oral guaranty contract against Ethel if the corporation does not meet its obligation because the main purpose of the loan was to benefit her as the sole shareholder of the corporation.

Contracts for the Sale of Goods

Section 201 of the Uniform Commercial Code (UCC) is the basic Statute of Frauds provision for sales contracts. It requires that contracts for the sale of goods costing *$500 or more* must be in writing to be enforceable.[15] If the contract price of an original sales contract is below $500, it does not have to be in writing under the **UCC Statute of Frauds**, but if a modification of the contract increases the sales price to $500 or more, the **modification** has to be in writing to be enforceable.[16]

Example Echo enters into an oral contract to sell James her used car for $10,000, with the delivery date to be May 1. When May 1 comes and James tenders $10,000 to Echo, Echo refuses to sell her car to James. The contract will not be enforced against Echo because it was an oral contract for the sale of goods costing $500 or more, and it should have been in writing.

> To break an oral agreement which is not legally binding is morally wrong.
>
> Bava Metzi'a
> *Talmud*

Agents' Contracts

Many state Statutes of Frauds require that **agents' contracts** to sell real property covered by the Statute of Frauds be in writing to be enforceable. The requirement is often referred to as the **equal dignity rule**.

Example Suppose Barney Berkowitz hires Cynthia Lamont, a licensed Century 21 real estate agent, to sell his house. Because a contract to sell real estate must be in writing, pursuant to the Statute of Frauds, the equal dignity rule requires the agents' contract to be in writing as well. Some state Statutes of Frauds expressly list the agents' contracts that must be in writing.

Promises Made in Consideration of Marriage

Under the Statute of Frauds, a unilateral promise to pay money or property in consideration for a promise to marry must be in writing. For example, a **prenuptial agreement**, which is a contract entered into by parties prior to marriage that defines their ownership rights in each other's property, must be in writing.

ETHICS SPOTLIGHT

An Oral Contract Is Not Worth the Paper It's Written On

The Statute of Frauds, which requires certain contracts to be in writing before they are enforceable, is designed to prevent fraud. Entrepreneurs and other businesspersons should know the requirements of the state's Statute of Frauds: otherwise, they may find themselves with an unenforceable oral contract. Consider the following case.

Whitman Heffernan Rhein & Co., Inc. (Whitman), is a company that provides financial advice to firms planning mergers and acquisitions. The Griffin Company (Griffin) was negotiating to purchase Resorts International, Inc., from Donald Trump. Whitman alleged that it entered into an oral contract to provide Griffin with financial and investment advice in connection with the negotiation of the purchase of Resorts International. Once Griffin completed the acquisition of Resorts International from Trump, Whitman requested payment for its services from Griffin. When Griffin did not pay, Whitman sued Griffin to recover payment.

Griffin asserted the New York Statute of Frauds in defense, arguing that Whitman's alleged contract to provide services in negotiating the purchase of a business had to be in writing to be enforceable, and because Whitman's complaint alleged that it was an oral contract, it was not enforceable. The New York court agreed with Griffin and held that the alleged contract was oral and therefore barred by the Statute of Frauds. The court stated:

> New York General Obligation Law §5-701(a)(10) provides that an agreement is void, unless evidenced by a writing signed by

the party to be charged, if the agreement is a contract to pay compensation for services rendered in negotiating the purchase of a business. The term "negotiating" includes assisting in the consummation of the transaction.

The moral of story: Get it in writing! *Whitman Heffernan Rhein & Co., Inc. v. The Griffin Co.*, 557 N.Y.S.2d 342, **Web** 1990 N.Y. App. Div. Lexis 8334 (Supreme Court of New York, Appellate Division)

Law & Ethics Questions

1. What is the purpose of the Statute of Frauds? Explain.

2. Was the legal claim clear in this case?

3. **ETHICS** Does applying the Statute of Frauds ever cause an unfair result? Explain.

Web Exercises

1. **WEB** For the complete opinion of this case, go to *www.prenhall.com/cheesemancases*.

2. **WEB** Visit the website of the supreme court of New York, Appellate Division, First Department, at *www.courts.state.ny.us/courts/ad1*.

3. **WEB** Use *www.google.com* to find an article that discusses your state's Statute of Frauds. Read it.

Promissory Estoppel

The doctrine of **promissory estoppel**, or **equitable estoppel**, is another equitable exception to the strict application of the Statute of Frauds. The version of promissory estoppel in the *Restatement (Second) of Contracts* provides that if parties enter into an oral contract that should be in writing under the Statute of Frauds, the oral promise is enforceable against the promisor if three conditions are met: (1) The promise induces action or forbearance of action by another, (2) the reliance on the oral promise was foreseeable, and (3) injustice can be avoided only by enforcing the oral promise.[17] Where this doctrine applies, the promisor is *estopped* (prevented) from raising the Statute of Frauds as a defense to the enforcement of the oral contract.

ETHICS SPOTLIGHT

Promissory Estoppel

> **❝** *The doctrine of estoppel is proven where one party suffers an unconscionable injury if the Statute of Frauds is asserted to prevent enforcement of oral contracts.* **❞**

—Judge Ballantyne

Bronco Wine Company (Bronco) crushed grapes and sold them for use in bulk wines. It purchased the grapes it needed from various grape growers. Bronco entered into an oral contract with Allied Grape Growers (Allied), a cooperative corporation of many grape growers, to purchase 850 tons of Carnelian grapes from Allied for delivery the next year.

The following year's grape crop was very large, and there was a glut of foreign wines on the market. Thus, the price of grapes and wines decreased substantially. Bronco accepted and paid for one shipment of Carnelian grapes from Allied but refused to accept the rest. By the time Bronco rejected the highly perishable grapes, it was too late for Allied to resell the grapes to another buyer.

Allied sued Bronco to recover damages for breach of contract. Bronco defended, arguing that the Statute of Frauds applied to the Bronco–Allied contract and since the contract was oral, Bronco did not have to perform the contract. Allied argued that the equity doctrine of promissory estoppel applied and excused the writing requirement in this case. The trial court held that the parties' oral contract did not violate the Statute of Frauds because Allied detrimentally relied on Bronco's promise to purchase the grapes. The jury awarded $3.4 million to Allied. Bronco appealed.

The court of appeal applied the doctrine of promissory estoppel and prohibited Bronco from raising the Statute of Frauds against enforcement of its oral promise to buy the grapes from Allied. The court stated:

In California, the doctrine of estoppel is proven where one party suffers an unconscionable injury if the Statute of Frauds is asserted to prevent enforcement of oral contracts. There is substantial evidence that Allied's loss was unconscionable given these facts. The Statute of Frauds should not be used in this instance to defeat the oral agreement reached by the parties in this case.

The court of appeal affirmed the trial court's judgment awarding $3.4 million of damages to Allied. *Allied Grape Growers v. Bronco Wine Company*, 203 Cal.App.3d 432, 249 Cal.Rptr. 872, **Web** 1988 Cal. App. Lexis 699 (Court of Appeal of California)

Law & Ethics Questions

1. Was a contract entered into in this case?

2. **ETHICS** Was it ethical for Bronco to assert the Statute of Frauds to excuse it from performing the oral contract it had agreed to?

3. What does the equity doctrine of promissory estoppel provide?

Web Exercises

1. **WEB** For the complete opinion of this case, go to *www.prenhall.com/cheesemancases*.

2. **WEB** Visit the website of the court of appeal of California, Fifth Appellate District, at *www.courtinfo.ca.gov/courts/courtsofappeal/5thDistrict*.

3. **WEB** Use *www.google.com* to find an article or a case that describes a recent application of the doctrine of promissory estoppel.

Bhutan

Oral contracts are used more in many foreign countries than they are in the United States.

Formality of the Writing

Some written commercial contracts are long, detailed documents that have been negotiated by the parties and drafted and reviewed by their lawyers. Others are preprinted forms with blanks that can be filled in to fit the facts of a particular situation.

Most of the disputes in the world arise from words.

Lord Mansfield, C. J.
Morgan v. Jones (1773)

A written contract does not, however, have to be either drafted by a lawyer or formally typed to be legally binding. Generally, the law only requires a writing containing the essential terms of the parties' agreement.

Example Any writing—including letters, telegrams, invoices, sales receipts, checks, and handwritten agreements written on scraps of paper—can be an enforceable contract under this rule.

Required Signature

The Statute of Frauds and the UCC require a written contract, whatever its form, to be signed *by the party against whom enforcement is sought*. The signature of the person who is enforcing the contract is not necessary. Thus, a written contract may be enforceable against one party but not the other party.

Generally, the signature may appear anywhere on the writing. In addition, it does not have to be a person's full legal name.

Example The person's last name, first name, nickname, initials, seal, stamp, engraving, or other symbol or mark (e.g., an *X*) that indicates the person's intent can be binding. The signature may be affixed by an authorized agent.

Integration of Several Writings

Both the common law of contracts and the UCC permit several writings to be **integrated** to form a single written contract. That is, the entire writing does not have to appear in one document to be an enforceable contract.

Integration may be by an *express reference* in one document that refers to and incorporates another document within it. This procedure is called **incorporation by reference**. Thus, what may often look like a simple one-page contract may actually be hundreds of pages in length.

Example Credit cards, documents to open bank accounts, contracts with colleges and universities, and other contracts often incorporate by express reference such documents as the master agreement between the issuer and cardholders, subsequent amendments to the agreement, and such.

Several documents may be integrated to form a single written contract if they are somehow physically attached to each other to indicate a party's intent to show integration.

Example Attaching several documents together with a staple, paper clip, or some other means may indicate integration. Placing several documents in the same container (e.g., an envelope) may also indicate integration. Such an action is called *implied integration*.

Interpreting Contract Words and Terms

Counsel Randle Jackson: "In the book of nature, my lords, it is written—"
Lord Ellenborough: "—Will you have the goodness to mention the page, sir, if you please."

Lord Campbell
Lives of the Chief Justices (1857)

When contracts are at issue in a lawsuit, courts are often called upon to interpret the meaning of certain contract words or terms. The parties to a contract may define the words and terms used in their contract. Many written contracts contain a detailed definition section—usually called a **glossary**—that defines many of the words and terms used in the contract.

If the parties have not defined the words and terms of a contract, the courts apply the following **standards of interpretation**:

- *Ordinary* words are given their usual meaning according to the dictionary.
- *Technical words* are given their technical meaning, unless a different meaning is clearly intended.
- *Specific terms* are presumed to qualify *general terms*. For example, if a provision in a contract refers to the subject matter as "corn," but a later provision refers to the subject matter as "feed corn" for cattle, this specific term qualifies the general term.
- If both parties are members of the same trade or profession, words will be given their meaning as used in the trade (i.e., *usage of trade*). If the parties do not want trade usage to apply, the contract must indicate that.

- Where a preprinted form contract is used, *typed words* in a contract prevail over *preprinted words. Handwritten words* prevail over both preprinted and typed words.
- If there is an ambiguity in a contract, the ambiguity will be resolved against the party who drafted the contract.

Merger, or Integration, Clause

The parties to a written contract may include a clause which stipulates that the contract is a complete integration and the exclusive expression of their agreement and that parol evidence may not be introduced to explain, alter, contradict, or add to the terms of the contract. This type of clause, called a **merger clause**, or an **integration clause**, expressly reiterates the parol evidence rule.

Parol Evidence Rule

By the time a contract is reduced to writing, the parties usually have engaged in prior or contemporaneous discussions and negotiations or exchanged prior writings. Any oral or written words outside the *four corners* of the written contract are called **parol evidence**. *Parol* means "word."

The **parol evidence rule** was originally developed by courts as part of the common law of contracts. The UCC has adopted the parol evidence rule as part of the law of sales contracts.[18] The parol evidence rule states that if a written contract is a complete and final statement of the parties' agreement (i.e., a *complete integration*), any prior or contemporaneous oral or written statements that alter, contradict, or are in addition to the terms of the written contract are inadmissible in any court proceeding concerning the contract.[19] In other words, a completely integrated contract is viewed as the best evidence of the terms of the parties' agreement.

Exceptions to the Parol Evidence Rule

There are several major exceptions to the general rule excluding parol evidence. Parol evidence may be admitted in court if it:

- Shows that a contract is void or voidable (e.g., evidence that the contract was induced by fraud, misrepresentation, duress, undue influence, or mistake).
- Explains ambiguous language.
- Concerns *a prior course of dealing or course of performance* between the parties or a *usage of trade.*[20]
- *Fills in the gaps* in a contract (e.g., if a price term or time of performance term is omitted from a written contract, the court can hear parol evidence to imply the reasonable price or time of performance under the contract).
- Corrects an obvious clerical or typographical error. The court can **re-form** the contract to reflect the correction.

INTERNATIONAL LAW

Signatures in Foreign Countries

Americans, Europeans, and many others in the world use their personal hand-applied signatures on legal documents. In Japan, China, and other countries of Asia, however, individuals often do not use their hand-applied signatures to sign legal documents. Instead, they follow the age-old tradition of using a stamp as their signature. The stamp is a character or set of characters carved onto the end of a cylinder-shaped piece held in a person's hand. The characters are carved onto one end of the cylinder. The owner places this end in ink and then applies this end to the document to be signed, leaving an imprint that serves as the owner's signature. In Japan this cylinder is called a *hanko*; in China it is called a *chop*. *Hankos* and *chops* are registered with the government. *Hankos* and *chops* can be made of ivory, jade, agate, gold, animal's horn, wood, or even plastic.

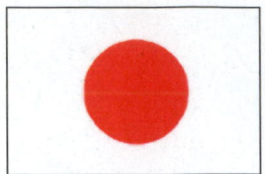

In societies that use personal signatures, if a signature is suspected of being forged, the victim can hire handwriting experts and use modern technology to prove it is not his or her signature. In Japan, China, and other countries where *hankos* and *chops* are used, it is much more difficult to prove forgery because anyone in possession of another's *hanko* or *chop* can apply it. Some people predict the demise of the *hanko* and *chop* because of the possible problem of fraud and the increased use of hand-applied signatures by younger persons in countries used to using the *hanko* and *chop*. Others predict that the rich tradition of using a *hanko* or *chop* will continue.

Beijing, China

Individuals in other countries have different methods for applying their signature to documents.

Chapter Summary

Mistake, p. 316

Unilateral Mistakes

Unilateral mistakes occur when only one party is mistaken about a material fact regarding the subject matter of a contract. The legal consequences are:

1. ***General rule.*** The mistaken party is not permitted to rescind the contract.
2. ***Exceptions.*** The mistaken party can rescind the contract if:
   a. The other party knew or should have known of the mistake and took advantage of it.
   b. The mistake occurred because of a clerical or mathematical error that was not the result of gross negligence.
   c. The mistake is so serious that enforcing the contract would be unconscionable.

Mutual Mistakes

1. ***Mutual mistake of fact.*** If both parties are mistaken about the essence or object of a contract, either party may rescind the contract.
2. ***Mutual mistake of value.*** If both parties know the object of a contract but are mistaken as to its value, neither party may rescind the contract.

Fraud, p. 318

Elements of Fraud

Fraudulent misrepresentation occurs when a person intentionally makes an assertion that is not in accord with the facts. Also called *fraud*. These are the elements of fraud:

1. The wrongdoer made a false representation of material fact.
2. The wrongdoer intended to deceive the innocent party.
3. The innocent party justifiably relied on the misrepresentation.
4. The innocent party was injured.

There are legal consequence if fraudulent misrepresentation is found. The innocent party may do either of the following:

1. Rescind the contract and obtain restitution
2. Enforce the contract and sue for damages

Fraud in the Inception

With fraud in the inception, an innocent person is deceived as to the nature of his or her act. Also called *fraud in the factum*.

Fraud in the Inducement

With fraud in the inducement, the wrongdoer fraudulently induces another party to enter into a contract.

Fraud by Concealment

With this fraud by concealment, the wrongdoer takes specific action to conceal a material fact from the other party.

Silence as Misrepresentation

Silence as misrepresentation is a form of fraud in which the wrongdoer remains silent when he or she is under a legal obligation to disclose a material fact.

Misrepresentation of Law

A professional who should know what the law is may intentionally misrepresent the law to a less sophisticated party.

Innocent Misrepresentation

When a person unintentionally makes an assertion that is not in accord with the facts, the innocent party may rescind the contract but cannot recover damages. Innocent misrepresentation is not fraud.

Undue Influence, p. 323

Undue influence occurs when one person takes advantage of another person's mental, emotional, or physical weakness and unduly persuades that person to enter into a contract. A contract entered into under undue influence cannot be enforced.

1. *Elements of undue influence:*
   a. A fiduciary or confidential relationship existed between the dominant and servient parties.
   b. The dominant party unduly used his or her influence to persuade the servient party to enter into a contract.
2. *Presumption.* If there is a confidential relationship between persons, any contract by the servient party that benefits the dominant party is presumed to have been entered into under undue influence. This position is a *rebuttable presumption*.

Duress, p. 324

Duress occurs when one party threatens to do some wrongful act unless the other party enters into a contract. A contract entered into under duress cannot be enforced. Types of duress:

1. Physical duress
2. Extortion

Economic Duress

Economic duress usually occurs when one party to a contract refuses to perform his or her contractual duties unless the other party pays an increased price, enters into a second contract with the threatening party, or the like. The duressed party must prove that he had no alternative but to acquiesce to the other party's threat.

Statute of Frauds, p. 326
Writing Requirement

A state Statute of Frauds requires that a number of contracts be in writing.

Contracts Involving Interests in Land

According to the Statute of Frauds, contracts for the sale of land, buildings and items attached to land, mortgages, leases for a term of more than one year, and express easements must be in writing.

Part Performance Exception

This exception to the Statute of Frauds permits the specific enforcement of oral contracts for the sale of land when they have been partially performed to avoid injustice.

One-Year Rule

According to the Statute of Frauds, contracts that cannot be performed within one year of their formation must be in writing.

Guaranty Contract

Guranty contracts occur where one person promises to answer for the debts or duties of another person. Also called *collateral contracts*.

Main Purpose Exception

This exception to the Statute of Frauds permits enforcement of oral collateral promises if the main or leading purpose of the collateral promise is to benefit the guarantor.

Contracts for the Sale of Goods

According to Section 201 of the Uniform Commercial Code (UCC), contracts for the sale of goods costing $500 or more must be in writing to be enforceable.

Agents' Contracts

Many state Statutes of Frauds require that agents' contracts to sell real property covered by the Statute of Frauds be in writing to be enforceable.

Promises Made in Consideration of Marriage

Under the Statute of Frauds, a unilateral promise to pay money or property in consideration for a promise to marry (e.g., a prenuptial agreement) must be in writing.

Promissory Estoppel

Promissory estoppel is an equitable doctrine that prevents the application of the Statute of Frauds. It permits the enforcement of oral contracts that should otherwise be in writing under the Statute of Frauds to prevent injustice or unjust enrichment.

Formality of the Writing, p. 331

A written contract does not have to be formal or drafted by a lawyer to be enforceable. Informal contracts, such as handwritten notes, letters, and invoices, are enforceable contracts.

Required Signature

The party against whom enforcement of a contract is sought must have signed the contract. The signature may be the person's full legal name, last name, first name, nickname, initials, or other symbol or mark.

Integration of Several Writings

Several writings may be integrated to form a contract. Integration may be by:
1. *Express reference.* In this case, one document expressly incorporates another document.
2. *Implied reference.* In this case, documents are physically attached by staple or by paper clip or are placed in the same envelop.

Interpreting Contract Words and Terms

The courts have developed the following rules for interpreting contracts:
1. *Ordinary words* are given their usual dictionary meaning.
2. *Technical words* are given their technical meaning, unless a different meaning is clearly intended.
3. Specific terms are presumed to qualify *general terms*.

4. *Typed words* prevail over *preprinted words; handwritten words* prevail over both preprinted and typed words.

5. Ambiguities in a contract are resolved against the party who drafted the contract.

6. Unless otherwise agreed, words will be given their usual meaning in the trade if both parties are members of the same trade.

Merger, or Integration, Clause

A *merger clause*, or an *integration clause*, expressly reiterates the parol evidence rule.

Parol Evidence Rule, p. 333

Parol evidence consists of any oral or written words that are outside the four corners of a written contract. The *parol evidence rule* provides that if a written contract is a complete integration, any prior contemporaneous oral or written statements are inadmissible as evidence to alter or contradict the terms of the written contract.

Exceptions to the Parol Evidence Rule

Parol evidence may be admitted in court to:

1. Prove mistake, fraud, misrepresentation, undue influence, or duress.

2. Explain ambiguous language.

3. Explain a prior course of dealing or course of performance between the parties or a usage of trade.

4. Fill in the gaps in a contract.

5. Correct obvious clerical or typographical errors.

Test Review Terms and Concepts

Agents' contract   329
Deed of trust   326
Duress   324
Easement   327
Economic duress (business compulsion, business duress, economic coercion)   325
Equal dignity rule   329
Fraud by concealment   319
Fraud in the inception (fraud in the factum)   319
Fraud in the inducement   319
Fraudulent misrepresentation (fraud)   318
Genuineness of assent   316
Glossary   332
Guarantor   329
Guaranty contract   328
Incorporation by reference   332
Injury to the innocent party   319
Innocent misrepresentation   321

Integrated   332
Integration of several writings   332
Intent to deceive   319
Lease   327
Life estate   327
Main purpose exception (leading object exception)   329
Material misrepresentation of fact   318
Merger clause (integration clause)   333
Misrepresentation of law   321
Mistake   316
Modification   329
Mortgage   326
Mutual mistake of a past or existing material fact   318
Mutual mistake of value   318
One-year rule   328
Original contract (primary contract)   328

Parol evidence   333
Parol evidence rule   333
Part performance exception   327
Prenuptial agreement   329
Promissory estoppel (equity estoppel)   330
Real property   326
Re-form   333
Reliance on the misrepresentation   319
Rescission   316
Scienter   318
Section 201 of the Uniform Commercial Code (UCC)   329
Silence as misrepresentation   321
Standards of interpretation   332
Statute of Frauds   326
UCC Statute of Frauds   329
Undue influence   323
Unilateral mistake   316

Case Problems

12.1 Unilateral Mistake: Mrs. Chaney died, leaving a house in Annapolis, Maryland. The representative of her estate listed the property for sale with a real estate broker, stating that the property was approximately 15,650 square feet. Drs. Steele and Faust made an offer of $300,000 for the property, which was accepted by the estate. A contract for the sale of the property was signed by all the parties. When a subsequent survey (done before the deed was transferred) showed that the property had an area of 22,047 square feet, the estate requested the buyers to pay more money for the property. When the estate refused to transfer the property to the buyers, they sued for specific performance. Can the estate rescind the contract? *Steele v. Goettee*, 313 Md. 11, 542 A.2d 847, **Web** 1988 Md. Lexis 91 (Court of Appeals of Maryland)

12.2 Unilateral Mistake: The County of Contra Costa, California, held a tax sale in which it offered for sale a vacant piece of property located in the city of El Cerrito. Richard J. Schultz, a carpenter, saw the notice of the pending tax sale and was interested in purchasing the lot to build a house. Prior to attending the tax sale, Schultz visited and measured the parcel, examined the neighborhood and found the houses there to be "very nice," and had a title search done that turned up no liens or judgments against the property. Schultz did not, however, check with the city zoning department regarding the zoning of the property.

Schultz attended the tax sale and, after spirited bidding, won with a bid of $9,100 and received a deed to the property. Within one week of the purchase, Schultz discovered that the city's zoning laws prevented building a residence on the lot. In essence, the lot was worthless, Schultz sued to rescind the contract. Can the contract be rescinded? *Schultz v. County of Contra Costa, California*, 157 Cal.App.3d 242, 203 Cal.Rptr. 760, **Web** 1984 Cal. App. Lexis 2198 (Court of Appeal of California)

12.3 Mutual Mistake: Ron Boskett, a part-time coin dealer, purchased a dime purportedly minted in 1916 at the Denver Mint; he paid nearly $450. The fact that the "D" on the coin signified Denver mintage made the coin rare and valuable. Boskett sold the coin to Beachcomber Coins, Inc. (Beachcomber), a retail coin dealer, for $500. A principal of Beachcomber examined the coin for 15 to 45 minutes prior to its purchase. Soon thereafter, Beachcomber received an offer of $700 for the coin, subject to certification of its genuineness by the American Numismatic Society. When this organization labeled the coin counterfeit, Beachcomber sued Boskett to rescind the purchase of the coin. Can Beachcomber rescind the contract? *Beachcomber Coins, Inc. v. Boskett*, 166 N.J.Super. 442, 400 A.2d 78, **Web** 1979 N.J. Super. Lexis 659 (Superior Court of New Jersey)

12.4 Fraud: Robert McClure owned a vehicle salvage and rebuilding business. He listed the business for sale and had a brochure printed that described the business and stated that the business grossed $581,117 and netted $142,727 the prior year. Fred H. Campbell saw the brochure and inquired about buying the business. Campbell hired a CPA to review McClure's business records and tax returns, but the CPA could not reconcile them with the income claimed for the business in the brochure. When Campbell asked McClure about the discrepancy, McClure stated that the business records did—and tax returns did not—accurately reflect the cash flow or profits of the business because it was such a high-cash operation with much of the cash not being reported to the Internal Revenue Service on tax returns. McClure signed a warranty that stated that the true income of the business was as represented in the brochure.

Campbell bought the business based on these representations. However, the business, although operated in substantially the same manner as when owned by McClure, failed to yield a net income similar to that warranted by McClure. Evidence showed that McClure's representations were substantially overstated. Campbell sued McClure for damages for fraud. Who wins? *Campbell v. McClure*, 182 Cal.App.3d 806, 227 Cal.Rptr. 450, **Web** 1986 Cal. App. Lexis 1751 (Court of Appeal of California)

12.5 Fraud: James L. "Skip" Deupree, a developer, was building a development of townhouses called Point South in Destin, Florida. All the townhouses in the development were to have individual boat slips. Sam and Louise Butner, husband and wife, bought one of the townhouses. The sales contract between Deupree and the Butners provided that a boat slip would be built and was included in the price of the townhouse. The contract stated that permission from the Florida Department of Natural Resources (DNR) had to be obtained to build the boat slips. It is undisputed that a boat slip adds substantially to the value of the property and that the Butners relied on the fact that the townhouse would have a boat slip.

Prior to the sale of the townhouse to the Butners, the DNR had informed Deupree that it objected to the plan to build the boat slips and that permission to build them would probably not be forthcoming. Deupree did not tell the Butners this information but instead stated that there would be "no problem" in getting permission from the state to build the boat slips. The Butners purchased the townhouse. When the DNR would not approve the building of the boat slips for the Butners' townhouse, they sued for damages for fraud, Who wins? *Deupree v. Butner*, 522 So.2d 242, **Web** 1988 Ala. Lexis 55 (Supreme Court of Alabama)

12.6 Innocent Misrepresentation: W. F. Yost, who owned the Red Barn Barbecue Restaurant (Red Barn), listed it for sale. Richard and Evelyn Ramano of Rieve Enterprises, Inc. (Rieve), were interested in buying the restaurant. After visiting and conducting a visual inspection of the premises, Rieve entered into a contract to purchase the assets and equipment of Red Barn, as well as the five-year lease of, and option to buy, the land and the building. Prior to the sale, the restaurant had been cited for certain health violations that Yost had corrected. In the contract of sale, Yost warranted that "the premises will pass all inspections" to conduct the business.

Rieve took possession immediately after the sale and operated the restaurant. After two weeks, when the Board of Health conducted a routine inspection, it cited 52 health code violations and thereupon closed the restaurant. Rieve sued to rescind the purchase agreement. Evidence established that Yost's misrepresentations were innocently made. Can Rieve rescind the contract? *Yost v. Rieve Enterprises, Inc.*, 461 So.2d 178, **Web** 1984 Fla. App. Lexis 16490 (Court of Appeals of Florida)

12.7 Duress: Judith and Donald Eckstein were married and had two daughters. Years later, Judith left the marital abode in the parties' jointly owned Volkswagen van with only the clothes on her back. She did not take the children, who were six and eight years old at the time. She had no funds, and the husband promptly closed the couple's bank account. The wife was unemployed. Shortly after she left, the husband discovered her whereabouts and the location of the van and seized and secreted the van. The husband refused the wife's request to visit or communicate with her children and refused to give her her clothing. He told her that she could see the children and take her clothes only if she signed a separation agreement prepared by his lawyer. The wife contacted Legal Aid but was advised that she did not qualify for assistance.

The wife was directed to go to her husband's lawyer's office. A copy of a separation agreement was given to her to read. The separation agreement provided that the wife (1) give custody of the children to her husband, (2) deed her interest in their jointly owned house to the husband, (3) assign her interest in a jointly owned new Chevrolet van to her husband, and (4) waive alimony, support, maintenance, court costs, attorneys' fees, and any right to inheritance in her husband's estate. By the agreement, she was to receive $1,100 cash, her clothes, the Volkswagen van, and any furniture she desired. The wife testified that her husband told her over an interoffice phone in the lawyer's office that if she did not sign the separation agreement, he would get her for desertion, that she would never see her children again, and that she would get nothing—neither her clothes nor the van—unless she signed the agreement. The wife signed the separation agreement. Immediately thereafter, her clothes were surrendered to her, and she was given $1,100 cash and the keys to the Volkswagen van. The husband filed for divorce. The wife filed an answer seeking to rescind the separation agreement. Can she rescind the separation agreement? *Eckstein v. Eckstein*, 38 Md.App. 506, 379 A.2d 757, **Web** 1978 Md. App. Lexis 324. (Court of Special Appeals of Maryland)

12.8 Undue Influence Conrad Schaneman, Sr., had eight sons and five daughters. He owned an 80-acre farm in the Scotts Bluff area of Nebraska. Conrad was born in Russia and could not read or write English. All of his children had frequent contact with Conrad and helped with his needs. Subsequently, however, his eldest son, Lawrence, advised the other children that he would henceforth manage his father's business affairs. After much urging by Lawrence, Conrad deeded the farm to Lawrence for $23,500. Evidence showed that at the time of the sale, the reasonable fair market value of the farm was between $145,000 and $160,000.

At the time of the conveyance, Conrad was over 80 years old, had deteriorated in health, suffered from heart problems and diabetes, had high and uncontrollable blood sugar levels, weighed almost 300 pounds, had difficulty breathing, could not walk more than 15 feet, and had to have a jackhoist lift him in and out of the bathtub. He was for all purposes an invalid, relying on Lawrence for most of his personal needs,

transportation, banking, and other business matters. After Conrad died, the conservators of the estate brought an action to cancel the deed transferring the farm to Lawrence. Can the conservators cancel the deed? *Schaneman v. Schaneman*, 206 Neb. 113, 291 N.W.2d 412, **Web** 1980 Neb. Lexis 823 (Supreme Court of Nebraska)

12.9 Statute of Frauds: Fritz Hoffman and Fritz Frey contracted the Sun Valley Company (Company) about purchasing a 1.64-acre piece of property known as the "Ruud Mountain Property," located in Sun Valley, Idaho, from the Company. Mr. Conger, a representative of the Company, was authorized to sell the property, subject to the approval of the executive committee of the Company. Conger reached an agreement on the telephone with Hoffman and Frey whereby they would purchase the property for $90,000, payable at 30 percent down, with the balance to be payable quarterly at an annual interest rate of 9.25 percent. The next day, Hoffman sent Conger a letter confirming the conversation.

The executive committee of the Company approved the sale. Sun Valley Realty prepared the deed of trust, note, seller's closing statement, and other loan documents. However, before the documents were executed by either side, Sun Valley Company sold all its assets, including the Ruud Mountain property, to another purchaser. When the new owner refused to sell the Ruud Mountain lot to Hoffman and Frey, they brought this action for specific performance of the oral contract. Who wins? *Hoffman v. Sun Valley Company*, 102 Idaho 187, 628 P.2d 218, **Web** 1981 Ida. Lexis 320 (Supreme Court of Idaho)

12.10 Real Property: Robert Briggs and his wife purchased a home located at 167 Lower Orchard Drive, Levittown, Pennsylvania. They made a down payment and borrowed the balance on a 30-year mortgage. Six years later, when the Briggs were behind on their mortgage payments, they entered into an oral contract to sell the house to Winfield and Emma Sackett if the Sacketts would pay the three months' arrearages on the loan and agree to make the future payments on the mortgage. Mrs. Briggs and Mrs. Sackett were sisters. The Sacketts paid the arrearages, moved into the house, and continued to live there. Fifteen years later, Robert Briggs filed an action to void the oral contract as in violation of the Statute of Frauds and evict the Sacketts from the house. Who wins? *Briggs v. Sackett*, 275 Pa.Super. 13, 418 A.2d 586, **Web** 1980 Pa. Super. Lexis 2034 (Superior Court of Pennsylvania)

12.11 One-Year Contract: Robert S. Ohanian was vice president of sales for the West Region of Avis Rent a Car System, Inc. (Avis). Officers of Avis testified that Ohanian's performance in the West Region was excellent, and, in a depressed economic period, Ohanian's West Region stood out as the one region that was growing and profitable. In the fall of 1980, when Avis's Northeast Region was doing badly, the president of Avis asked Ohanian to take over that region. Ohanian was reluctant to do so because he and his family liked living in San Francisco, and he had developed a good team in the West Region, was secure in his position, and feared the politics of the Northeast Region. Ohanian agreed to the transfer only after the general manager of Avis orally told him "unless you screw up badly, there is no way you are going to get fired—you will never get hurt here in this company." Ohanian did a commendable job in the Northeast Region. Approximately one year later, at the age of 47, Ohanian was fired without cause by Avis. Ohanian sued Avis for breach of the oral lifetime contract. Avis asserted the Statute of Frauds against this claim. Who wins? *Ohanian v. Avis Rent a Car System, Inc.*, 779 F.2d 101, **Web** 1985 U.S. App. Lexis 25456 (United States Court of Appeals for the Second Circuit)

12.12 Guaranty Contract: David Brown met with Stan Steele, a loan officer with the Bank of Idaho (now First Interstate Bank) to discuss borrowing money from the bank to start a new business. After learning that he did not qualify for the loan on the basis of his own financial strength, Brown told Steele that his former employers, James and Donna West of California, might be willing to guarantee the payment of the loan. Steele talked to Mr. West, who orally stated on the telephone that he would personally guarantee the loan to Brown. Based on this guaranty, the bank loaned Brown the money. The bank sent a written guarantee to Mr. And Mrs. West for their signatures, but it was never returned to the bank. When Brown defaulted on the loan, the bank filed suit against the Wests to recover on their guaranty contract. Are the Wests liable? *First Interstate Bank of Idaho, N.A. v. West*, 107 Idaho 851, 693 P.2d 1053, **Web** 1984 Ida. Lexis 600 (Supreme Court of Idaho)

12.13 Guaranty Contract: Six persons, including Benjamin Rosenbloom and Alfred Feiler, were members of the board of directors of the Togs Corporation. A bank agreed to loan the corporation $250,000 if the members of the board would personally guarantee the payment of the loan. Feiler objected to signing the guaranty to the bank because of other pending personal financial negotiations that the contingent liability of the guaranty might adversely affect. Feiler agreed with Rosenbloom and the other board members that if they were held personally liable on the guaranty, he would pay his one-sixth share of that amount to them directly. Rosenbloom and the other members of the board signed the personal guaranty with the bank, and the bank made the loan to the corporation. When the corporation defaulted on the loan, the five guarantors had to pay the loan amount to the bank. When they attempted to collect a one-sixth share from Feiler, he refused to pay, alleging that his oral promise had to be in writing under the Statute of Frauds. Does Feiler have to pay the one-sixth share to the other board members? *Feiler V. Rosenbloom*, 46 Md.App. 297, 416 A.2d 1345, **Web** 1980 Md. App. Lexis 328 (Court of Special Appeals of Maryland)

12.14 Agent's Contract: Paul L. McGirr operated an Enco service station in Los Angeles that sold approximately 25,000 to 35,000 gallons of gasoline per month. McGirr telephoned Gulf Oil Corporation (Gulf) regarding an advertisement for dealers. McGirr met with Theodore Marks, an area representative of Gulf, to discuss the possibility of McGirr's operating a Gulf service station. McGirr asked Marks if Gulf had any good, high-producing units available. Marks replied that he had a station at the corner of Figueroa and Avenue 26 that sold about 200,000 gallons of gasoline per month. Marks told McGirr that this station would not be available for about 90 days because Gulf had to terminate the arrangement with the current operator of the station. Marks told McGirr that he could have the Figueroa station only if he also took a "dog" station on Garvey Avenue. Marks agreed to take this station only if he also was assured he would get the Figueroa station. Marks assured him he would. When McGirr asked Marks for this assurance in writing, Marks stated that he did not have to put it in writing because he was the "kingpin in his territory." So they shook hands on the deal.

McGirr terminated his arrangement with Enco and moved to the Garvey Avenue station. He signed a written lease for the Garvey station, which was signed by Max Reed, Gulf's regional sales manager. Under the Statute of Frauds, the lease for a service station must be in writing. Nothing in writing was ever signed by the parties regarding the Figueroa station. A few months later, Marks was transferred to a different territory, and Gulf refused to lease the Figueroa station to McGirr. McGirr sued Marks and Gulf for breach of an oral contract. Is Marks or Gulf liable? *McGirr v. Gulf Oil Corporation*, 41 Cal.App.3d 246, 115 Cal.Rptr. 902, **Web** 1974 Cal. App. Lexis 783 (Court of Appeal of California)

12.15 Promissory Estoppel: The Atlantic Wholesale Co., Inc. (Atlantic), located in Florence, South Carolina, was in the business of buying and selling gold and silver for customers' accounts. Gary A. Solondz, a New York resident, became a customer of Atlantic and thereafter made several purchases through Atlantic. One day, Solondz telephoned Atlantic and received a quotation on silver bullion. Solondz then bought 300 ounces of silver for a total price of $12,978. Atlantic immediately contracted United Precious Metals in Minneapolis and purchased the silver for Solondz. The silver was shipped to Atlantic, which paid for it.

Atlantic placed the silver in its vault while it waited for payment from Solondz. When Atlantic telephoned Solondz about payment, he told Atlantic to continue to hold the silver in its vault until he decided whether to sell it. Meanwhile, the price of silver had fallen substantially and continued to fall. When Solondz refused to pay for the silver, Atlantic sold it for $4,650, sustaining a loss of $8,328. When Atlantic sued Solondz to recover this loss, Solondz asserted that the Statute of Frauds prevented enforcement of his oral promise to buy the silver. Does the doctrine of promissory estoppel prevent the application of the Statute of Frauds in this case? *Atlantic Wholesale Co., Inc. v. Solondz*, 283 S.C. 36, 320

S.E.2d 720, **Web** 1984 S.C. App. Lexis 555 (Court of Appeals of South Carolina)

12.16 Sufficiency of a Writing: Irving Levin and Harold Lipton owned the San Diego Clippers Basketball Club, a professional basketball franchise. Levin and Lipton met with Philip Knight to discuss the sale of the Clippers to Knight. After the meeting, they all initialed a three-page handwritten memorandum that Levin had drafted during the meeting. The memorandum outlined the major terms of their discussion, including subject matter, price, and the parties to the agreement. Levin and Lipton forwarded to Knight a letter and proposed sale agreement. Two days later, Knight informed Levin that he had decided not to purchase the Clippers. Levin and Lipton sued Knight for breach of contract. Knight argued in defense that the handwritten memorandum was not enforceable because it did not satisfy the Statute of Frauds. Is he correct? *Levin v. Knight*, 865 F.2d 1271, **Web** 1989 U.S. App. Lexis 458 (United States Court of Appeals for the Ninth Circuit)

Ethics Issues

12.17 Ethics: The First Baptist Church of Moultrie, Georgia, invited bids for the construction of a music, education, and recreation building. The bids were to be accompanied by a bid bond of 5 percent of the bid amount. Barber Contracting Company (Barber Contracting) submitted a bid in the amount of $1,860,000. A bid bond in the amount of 5 percent of the bid—$93,000—was issued by The American Insurance Company. The bids were opened by the church, and Barber Contracting's was the lowest bid.

On the next day, Albert W. Barber, the president of Barber Contracting, informed the church that his company's bid was in error and should have been $143,120 higher. The error was caused in totaling the material costs on Barber Contracting's estimate worksheets. The church had not been provided these worksheets. Barber Contracting sent a letter to the church, stating that it was withdrawing its bid. The next day, the church sent a construction contract to Barber Contracting, containing the original bid amount. When Barber Contracting refused to sign the contract and refused to do the work for the original contract price, the church signed a contract with the second-lowest bidder, H & H Construction and Supply Company, Inc., to complete the work for $1,919,272. The church sued Barber Contracting and The American Insurance Company, seeking to recover the amount of the bid bond. Who wins? Did Barber act ethically in trying to get out of the contract? Did the church act ethically in trying to enforce Barber's bid? *First Baptist Church of Moultrie v. Barber Contracting Co.*, 189 Ga.App. 804, 377 S.E.2d 717, **Web** 1989 Ga. App. Lexis 25 (Court of Appeals of Georgia)

12.18 Ethics: Lockheed Missiles & Space Company, Inc. (Lockheed), sent out a request to potential subcontractors, seeking bids for the manufacture of 124 ballast cans for the Trident II nuclear submarines it was building for the U.S. Navy. In February 1989, Lockheed received eight bids, including one from Sulzer Bingham Pumps, Inc. (Sulzer). Sulzer was the lowest bidder, at $6,544,055. The next lowest bid was $10,176,670, and the bids ranged up to $17,766,327. Lockheed itself estimated that the job would cost at least $8.5 million. Lockheed's employees were shocked by Sulzer's bid and thought it was surprisingly low.

Lockheed then inspected Sulzer's Portland facility to evaluate Sulzer's technical capabilities. The inspection revealed that Sulzer would have to make many modifications to its existing facility in order to complete the contract.

Lockheed did not reveal its findings to Sulzer. In addition, it never notified Sulzer that its bid was significantly lower than the next lowest bid and lower than Lockheed's own estimate of the cost of the job as well. Finally, Sulzer was never told that Lockheed suspected the contract could not be completed at the bid price.

Lockheed accepted Sulzer's bid, and Sulzer started work. Nine months later, Sulzer revised its estimate of the cost of the job and asked Lockheed for an additional $2,110,000 in compensation. When Lockheed rejected this request, Sulzer sued Lockheed, asking the court to either increase the price of the contract to $8,645,000 or, alternatively, to rescind its bid. Did Lockheed act ethically in this case by not notifying Sulzer of the suspected mistake? Did Sulzer act ethically by trying to get out of the contract because of its own economic misjudgments? Legally, who wins? *Sulzer Bingham Pumps, Inc. v. Lockheed Missiles & Space Company, Inc.*, 947 F.2d 1362, **Web** 1991 U.S. App. Lexis 24966 (United States Court of Appeals for the Ninth Circuit)

12.19 Ethics: American Broadcasting Company Merchandising, Inc., a subsidiary of American Broadcasting Company, Inc. (collectively "ABC"), entered into a written contract with model Cheryl Tiegs whereby ABC would pay Tiegs $400,000 per year for the right to be the exclusive agent to license the merchandising of goods under her name. When ABC was unsuccessful in attracting licensing arrangements for Tiegs, a representative of ABC contacted Paul Sklar who had previous experience in marketing apparel and licensing labels. Sklar enlisted the help of Mark Blye, and together they introduced ABC and Tiegs to Sears, Roebuck and Company (Sears). This introduction led to an agreement between Sears, ABC, and Tiegs whereby Sears marketed a line of "Cheryl Tiegs" female apparel through Sears department stores and catalog sales. Blye and Sklar sued ABC for a finder's fee for introducing ABC to Sears. Because there was no express written or oral contract between ABC and Blye and Sklar, they alleged that there was an implied-in-fact contract between the parties.

Section 5-701 (a)(10) of the New York Statute of Frauds requires a finder's fee contract of the type in this case to be in writing. Who wins? Did ABC act ethically in this case? *Blye v. American Broadcasting Company Merchandising, Inc.*, 102 A.D.2d 297, 476 N.Y.S.2d 874, **Web** 1984 N.Y. App. Div. Lexis 18341 (Supreme Court of New York)

12.20 Ethics: Adolfo Mozzetti, who owned a construction company, orally promised his son, Remo, that if Remo would manage the family business for their mutual benefit and would take care of him for the rest of his life, he would leave the family home to Remo. Section 2714 of the Delaware Code requires contracts for the transfer of land to be in writing. Section 2715 of the Delaware Code requires testamentary transfers of real property to be in writing. Remo performed as requested; he managed the family business and took care of his father until the father died. The father died, and his will devised the family home to his daughter, Lucia M. Shepard. Remo brought an action to enforce his father's oral promise that the home belonged to him. The daughter argued that the will should be upheld. Who wins? Did the daughter act ethically in trying to defeat the father's promise to leave the property to the son? Did the son act ethically in trying to defeat his father's will? *Shepard v. Mozzetti*, 545 A.2d 621, **Web** 1988 Del. Lexis 217 (Supreme Court of Delaware)

IRAC Writing Assignment

Read **Case A-12** in Appendix A [*Hampton v. Federal Express Corporation*]. Read the case and use the IRAC method to prepare a written analysis of the case.

Endnotes

1. *Restatement (Second) of Contracts*, Section 153.
2. *Restatement (Second) of Contracts*, Section 152.
3. 59 Eng. Rep. 375 (1864).
4. *Restatement (Second) of Contracts*, Section 159.
5. *Restatement (Second) of Contracts*, Sections 163 and 164.
6. *Restatement (Second) of Contracts*, Section 160.
7. *Restatement (Second) of Contracts*, Section 161.
8. *Restatement (Second) of Contracts*, Section 170.
9. *Restatement (Second) of Contracts*, Section 176.
10. *Restatement (Second) of Contracts*, Section 177.
11. *Restatement (Second) of Contracts*, Section 110.
12. *Restatement (Second) of Contracts*, Section 130.
13. *Restatement (Second) of Contracts*, Section 112.
14. *Restatement (Second) of Contracts*, Section 116.
15. UCC Section 2-201(1).
16. UCC Section 2-209(3).
17. *Restatement (Second) of Contracts*, Section 139.
18. UCC Section 2-202.
19. *Restatement (Second) of Contracts*, Section 213.
20. UCC Sections 1-205, 2-202, and 2–208.

C H A P T E R **13**

Third-Party Rights and Discharge

> **"** *An honest man's word is as good as his bond.* **"**
>
> —Don Quixote

Introduction to Third-Party Rights and Discharge

The parties to a contract are said to be in *privity of contract*. Contracting parties have a legal obligation to perform the duties specified in their contract. A party's duty of performance may be discharged by agreement of the parties, excuse of performance, or operation of law. If one party fails to perform as promised, the other party may enforce the contract and sue for breach.

With two exceptions, third parties do not acquire any rights under other people's contracts. The exceptions are (1) *assignees* to which rights are subsequently transferred and (2) *intended third-party beneficiaries* to whom the contracting parties intended to give rights under the contract at the time of contracting.

This chapter discusses the rights of third parties under a contract, conditions to performance, and ways of discharging the duty of performance.

Gateway Arch, St. Louis, Missouri

Many contracts were used in order to complete the construction of the St. Louis Gateway Arch. These included contracts with government agencies, architects, a general contractor, subcontractors, insurance companies, and others.

Assignment of Rights

In many cases, the parties to a contract can transfer their rights under the contract to other parties. The transfer of contractual rights is called an **assignment of rights**, or just an **assignment**.

Form of Assignment

A party who owes a duty of performance is called the *obligor*. A party who is owed a right under a contract is called the *obligee*. An obligee who transfers the right to receive performance is called an **assignor**. The party to whom the right has been transferred is called the **assignee**. The assignee can assign the right to yet another person (called a **subsequent assignee**, or **subassignee**). Exhibit 13.1 illustrates these relationships.

Generally, no formalities are required for a valid assignment of rights. Although the assignor often uses the word *assign*, other words or terms, such as *sell, transfer, convey*, and *give*, are sufficient to indicate intent to transfer a contract right.

Example Suppose a retail clothing store purchases $5,000 worth of goods on credit from a manufacturer. Payment is due in 120 days. Assume that the manufacturer needs cash before the 120-day period expires, so the manufacturer (assignor) sells its right to collect the money to another party (assignee) for $4,000. If the retail store is given proper notice of the assignment, it must pay $5,000 to the assignee.

In the United States, public policy favors a free flow of commerce. Hence, most contract rights are assignable, including sales contracts and contracts for the payment of money. The following paragraphs discuss types of contracts that present special problems for assignment.

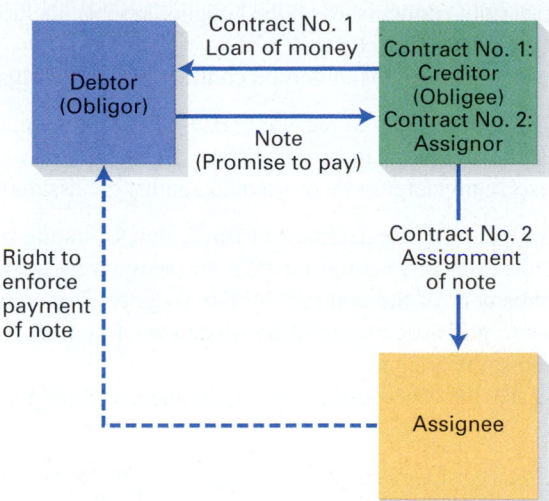

EXHIBIT 13.1

Assignment of a Right

Personal Service Contracts

Contracts for the provision of personal services are generally not assignable.[1]

Example If an artist contracts to paint someone's portrait, the artist cannot send a different artist to do the painting without the prior approval of the person to be painted.

The parties may agree that a **personal service contract** may be assigned.

Example Many professional athletes' contracts contain a clause permitting assignability of the contract.

Assignment of Future Rights

Usually, a person cannot assign a currently nonexistent right that he or she expects to have in the future.

Example Suppose a multimillion-dollar heiress signs a will, leaving all her property to her grandson. The grandson cannot assign his expected right to receive his inheritance.

Contracts Where Assignment Would Materially Alter the Risk

A contract cannot be assigned if the assignment would materially alter the risk or duties of the obligor.

Example Suppose Laura Peters, who has a safe driving record, purchases automobile insurance from an insurance company. Her rights to be insured cannot be assigned to another driver because the assignment would materially alter the risk and duties of the insurance company.

Assignment of Legal Action

Legal actions involving personal rights cannot be assigned.

Example Suppose Donald Matthews is severely injured by Alice Hollyfield in an automobile accident caused by her negligence. Matthews can sue Hollyfield to recover damages for his injuries. He cannot assign his right to sue her to another person.

A legal right that arises out of a breach of contract may be assigned.

Example Suppose Andrea borrows $10,000 from the bank. If she defaults on the loan, the bank may assign the legal rights to collect the money to a collection agency.

Effect of an Assignment of Rights

Where there has been a valid assignment of rights, the assignee "stands in the shoes of the assignor." That is, the assignor is entitled to performance from the obligor. The unconditional

> If a man will improvidently bind himself up by a voluntary deed, and not reserve a liberty to himself by a power of revocation, this court will not loose the fetters he hath put upon himself, but he must lie down under his own folly.
>
> L. C. Lord Nottingham
> *Villers v. Beaumont (1682)*

assignment of a contract right extinguishes all the assignor's rights, including the right to sue the obligor directly for nonperformance.[2]

An assignee takes no better rights under the contract than the assignor had.

Example If the assignor has a right to receive $10,000 from a debtor, the right to receive this $10,000 is all that the assignor can assign to the assignee.

An obligor can assert any defense he or she had against the assignor or the assignee.

Example An obligor can raise the defenses of fraud, duress, undue influence, minority, insanity, illegality of the contract, mutual mistake, or payment by worthless check of the assignor against enforcement of the contract by the assignee. The obligor can also raise any personal defenses (e.g., participation in the assignor's fraudulent scheme) he or she may have directly against the assignee.

In the following case, the court held that an assignment was illegal.

CASE 13.1
Assignment

Accrued Financial Services, Incorporated v. Prime Retail, Incorporated

298 F.3d 291, **Web** 2002 U.S. App. Lexis 15238 (2002) United States Court of Appeals for the Fourth Circuit

> ❝These relationships between AFS and the tenants were essentially lawsuit-mining arrangements under which AFS "mined for" and prosecuted lawsuits with no regard for the informed wishes of the real parties in interest.❞
>
> —Judge Niemeyer

Facts

Accrued Financial Services, Inc. (AFS), is a corporation engaged in the business of conducting lease audits on behalf of tenants in commercial buildings and factory outlet malls. AFS is paid a percentage—usually 40 to 50 percent—of the discrepancy overcharges that it discovers and collects as a result of its audits. The tenant signs a letter of agreement with AFS and assigns all legal causes of action it may have against the landlord to AFS. The assignment grants AFS the authority to file lawsuits in its name against landlords at its discretion. After AFS conducted an audit of Prime Retail, Inc., a landlord, on behalf of tenants that had signed assignment agreements, AFS brought a lawsuit against Prime Retail, asserting various claims of overcharges. The U.S. District Court dismissed the case, finding that the assignment of the tenants' claims to AFS violated public policy and were therefore illegal. AFS appealed.

Issue

Does the assignment by a tenant of its legal claims against a landlord violate public policy, and is it therefore illegal?

Language of the Court

These relationships between AFS and the tenants were essentially lawsuit-mining arrangements under which AFS "mined for" and prosecuted lawsuits with no regard for the informed wishes of the real parties in interest. AFS thus became a promoter of litigation principally for the sake of the fees that it would earn for itself and not for the benefit that it might produce for the tenant, the real party in interest. Under these arrangements, even though the tenant might conclude, after reviewing the facts uncovered, that a lawsuit would imprudently damage the landlord–tenant relationship—or that pursuing aggressive allegations would do more harm than good—the tenant lost the right to control its destiny. Because we see these broad assignments as nothing more than arrangements through which to intermeddle and stir up litigation for the purpose of making a profit, we conclude that they violate Maryland's strong public policy against stirring up litigation and are therefore void and unenforceable in Maryland.

Decision

The U.S. Court of Appeals held that the tenants' assignment of their legal causes of action against Prime Retail to AFS violated public policy and was therefore illegal and void. The Court of Appeals affirmed the decision of the District Court.

Law & Ethics Questions

1. Why did the Court of Appeals find the tenants' assignments of their legal causes of action against Prime Retail to AFS illegal? How can these assignments be distinguished from typical contingency fee arrangements that plaintiffs' lawyers often have with clients?

2. **ETHICS** Did AFS act ethically in this case?

3. What would be the consequences if a party's legal cause of action could be assigned to another party to pursue? Explain.

Web Exercises

1. **WEB** For the complete opinion of this case, go to *www.prenhall.com/cheesemancases*.

2. **WEB** Visit the website of the United States Court of Appeals for the Fourth Circuit, at *www.ca4.uscourts.gov*.

3. **WEB** Use *www.google.com* to find an article about the assignment of a sport celebrity's contract. Read it.

Notice of Assignment

When an assignor makes an assignment of a right under a contract, the assignee is under a duty to notify the obligor that (1) the assignment has been made and (2) performance must be rendered to the assignee. If the assignee fails to notify the obligor of the assignment, the obligor may continue to render performance to the assignor, who no longer has a right to it. The assignee cannot sue the obligor to recover payment because the obligor has performed according to the original contract. The assignee's only course of action is to sue the assignor for damages.

> That what is agreed to be done, must be considered as done.
>
> L. C. Lord Hardwicke
> *Guidot v. Guidot (1745)*

Example Juan borrows $10,000 from Sam. Juan is to pay Sam the principal amount, with 10 percent interest, over three years in 36 equal monthly payments. After 6 months of receiving the proper payments from Juan, Sam assigns this right to receive future payments to Heather. Heather, as the assignee, owes a duty to notify Juan that he is to now make the payments to Heather. If Heather fails to give Juan this notice, Juan will continue to pay Sam. Heather cannot recover from Juan the money that he continued to pay Sam; Heather's only recourse is to recover the money from Sam.

The result changes if the obligor is notified of the assignment but continues to render performance to the assignor. In such situations, the assignee can sue the obligor and recover payment. The obligor will then have to pay twice: once wrongfully to the assignor and then rightfully to the assignee. The obligor's only recourse is to sue the assignor for damages.

Anti-Assignment and Approval Clauses

Some contracts contain **anti-assignment clauses** that prohibit the assignment of rights under the contracts. Such clauses may be used if the obligor does not want to deal with or render performance to an unknown third party. Some contracts contain an **approval clause**. Such clauses require the obligor to approve any assignment. Many states prohibit the obligor from unreasonably withholding approval.

ETHICS SPOTLIGHT

Successive Assignments of the Same Right

An obligee (the party who is owed a performance, money, a right, or another thing of value) has the right to assign a contract right or benefit to another party. If the obligee fraudulently or mistakenly makes successive assignments of the same right to a number of assignees, which assignee has the legal right to the assigned right? To answer this question, the following rules are applied:

- The **American rule** (or **New York rule**) provides that the first assignment *in time* prevails, regardless of notice. Most states follow this rule.

- The **English rule** provides that the first assignee to *give notice* to the obligor (the person who owes the performance, money, duty, or other thing of value) prevails.

- The **possession of tangible token rule** provides that under either the American or English rule, if the assignor makes successive assignments of a contract right that is represented by a tangible token, such as a stock certificate or a savings account passbook, the first assignee who receives delivery of the tangible token prevails over subsequent assignees. However, if the first assignee leaves the tangible token with the assignor, the subsequent assignee prevails. This is because the first assignee could have prevented the problem by having demanded delivery of the tangible token. In other words, physical possession of the tangible token is the pivotal issue.

Delegation of Duties

Unless otherwise agreed, the parties to a contract can generally transfer the performance of their duties under the contract to other parties. This transfer is called the **delegation of duties**, or just **delegation**.

An obligor who transfers his or her duty is called a **delegator**. The party to whom the duty is transferred is the **delegatee**. The party to whom the duty is owed is the **obligee**. Generally, no special words or formalities are required to create a delegation of duties. Exhibit 13.2 illustrates the parties to a delegation of a duty.

Duties That Can and Cannot Be Delegated

Often, contracts are entered into with companies or firms rather than with individuals. In such cases, a firm may designate any of its qualified employees to perform the contract. For example, if a client retains a firm of lawyers to represent her, the firm can delegate the duties under the contract to any qualified member of the firm. If the obligee has a substantial interest in having the obligor perform the acts required by the contract, however, duties may not be transferred.[3] This restriction includes obligations under the following types of contracts:

> "If there's no meaning in it," said the King, "that saves a world of trouble, you know, we needn't try to find any."
>
> Lewis Carroll
> *Alice in Wonderland, Chapter 12*

1. **Personal service contracts calling for the exercise of personal skills, discretion, or expertise.** For example, if P Diddy is hired to give a concert on a college campus, the Dixie Chicks cannot appear in his place. See *www.diddy.com* and *www.dixiechicks.com*.
2. **Contracts whose performance would materially vary if the obligor's duties were delegated.** For example, if a person hires an experienced surgeon to perform a complex surgery, a recent medical school graduate cannot be substituted in the operating room.

Effect of Delegation of Duties

If a delegation is valid, the delegator remains legally liable for the performance of the contract. If the delegatee does not perform properly, the obligee can sue the obligor-delegator for any resulting damages.

The question of the delegatee's liability to the obligee depends on whether there has been an *assumption of duties* or a *declaration of duties*. Where a delegation of duties contains the term *assumption* or other similar language, there is an **assumption of duties** by the delegatee. The delegatee is liable to the obligee for nonperformance. The obligee can sue either the delegator or the delegatee.

If the delegatee has not assumed the duties under a contract, the delegation of duties is called a **declaration of duties**. Here, the delegatee is not legally liable to the obligee for

EXHIBIT 13.2

Delegation of a Duty

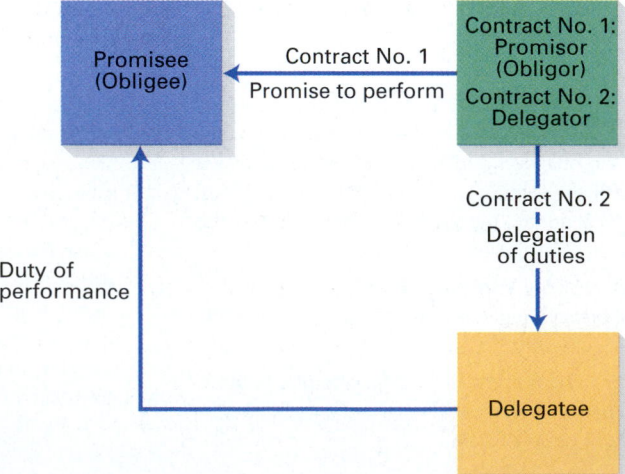

nonperformance. The obligee's only recourse is to sue the delegator. A delegatee who fails to perform his or her duties is liable to the delegator for damages arising from this failure to perform.

Anti-Delegation Clause

The parties to a contract can include an **anti-delegation clause** indicating that the duties cannot be delegated. Anti-delegation clauses are usually enforced. Some courts, however, have held that duties that are totally impersonal in nature—such as the payment of money—can be delegated despite such clauses.

Assignment and Delegation

An **assignment and delegation** occurs when there is a transfer of both rights and duties under a contract. If the transfer of a contract to a third party contains only language of assignment, the modern view holds that there is corresponding delegation of the duties of the contract.[4]

Third-Party Beneficiaries

Third parties sometimes claim rights under others' contracts. Such third parties are either *intended* or *incidental beneficiaries*. Each of these designations is discussed here.

Intended Beneficiaries

When parties enter into a contract, they can agree that the performance of one of the parties should be rendered to or directly benefit a third party. Under such circumstances, the third party is called an **intended third-party beneficiary**. An intended third-party beneficiary can enforce the contract against the party who promised to render performance.[5]

The beneficiary may be expressly named in the contract from which he or she is to benefit or may be identified by another means.

Example There is sufficient identification if a testator of a will leaves his estate to "all my children, equally."

Intended third-party beneficiaries may be classified as either *donee* or *creditor* beneficiaries. These terms are defined in the following sections. The *Restatement (Second) of Contracts* and many state statutes have dropped this distinction, however, and now refer to both collectively as *intended beneficiaries*.[6]

DONEE BENEFICIARIES When a person enters into a contract with the intent to confer a benefit or gift on an intended third party, the contract is called a **donee beneficiary contract**.

Example A life insurance policy with a named beneficiary is an example of a donee beneficiary contract.

The three persons involved in such a contract are:

1. The **promisee** is the contracting party who directs that the benefit be conferred on another.
2. The **promisor** is the contracting party who agrees to confer performance for the benefit of the third person.
3. The **donee beneficiary** is the third person on whom the benefit is to be conferred.

If the promisor fails to perform the contract, the donee beneficiary can sue the promisor directly.

Example Brian Peterson hires a lawyer to draft his will. He directs the lawyer to leave all of his property to his best friend, Jeffrey Silverman. Assume that (1) Peterson dies and (2) the lawyer's negligence in drafting the will causes it to be invalid. Consequently, Peterson's

EXHIBIT 13.3

Donee Beneficiary Contract

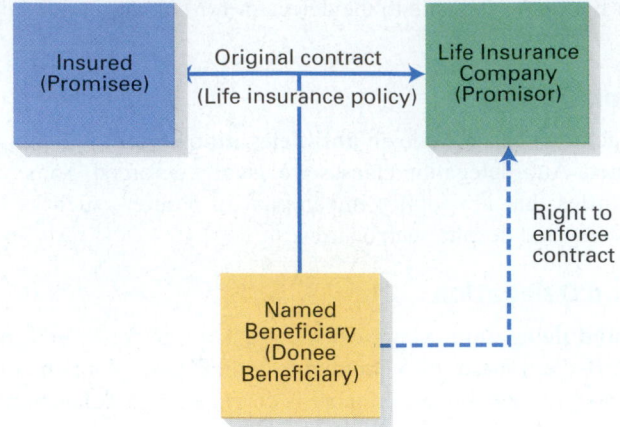

He who derives the advantage ought to sustain the burden.

Legal Maxim

distant relatives receive the property under the state's inheritance statute. Silverman can sue the lawyer for damages because he was the intended donee beneficiary of the will.

Example A mother, the insured, buys a life insurance policy from a life insurance company and names her daughter as the beneficiary to be paid the life insurance proceeds if the mother dies. The daughter is the intended beneficiary of the contract between her mother and the life insurance company. Assume that the mother dies. If the life insurance company refuses to pay the life insurance proceeds to the daughter, the daughter can sue the life insurance company and recover the insurance proceeds (see Exhibit 13.3).

CREDITOR BENEFICIARIES The second type of intended beneficiary is the creditor beneficiary. A **creditor beneficiary contract** usually arises in the following situation:

1. A debtor borrows money from a creditor to purchase some item.
2. The debtor signs an agreement to pay the creditor the amount of the loan plus interest.
3. The debtor sells the item to another party before the loan is paid.
4. The new buyer promises the debtor that he or she will pay the remainder of the loan amount to the creditor.

The creditor is the new intended creditor beneficiary to this second creditor.[7] The parties to the second contract are the original debtor (the promisee), the new party (the promisor), and the original creditor (the **creditor beneficiary**). (See Exhibit 13.4.)

EXHIBIT 13.4

Creditor Beneficiary Contract

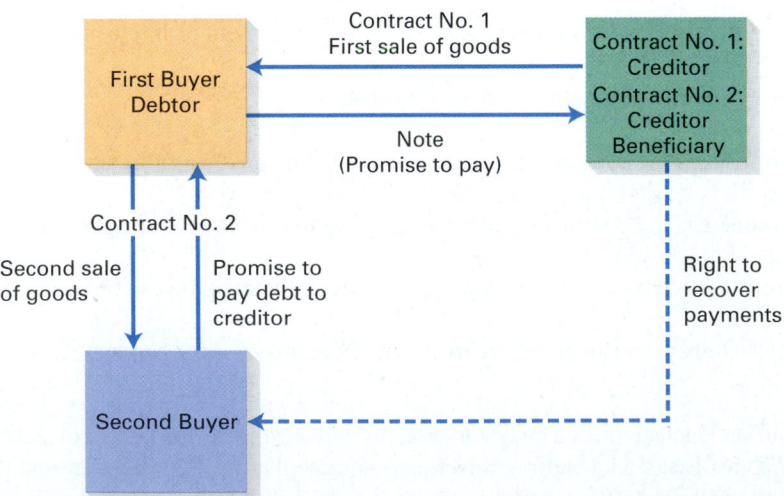

If the promisor fails to perform according to the contract, the creditor beneficiary may either (1) enforce the original contract against the debtor-promisee or (2) enforce the new contract against the promisor. However, the creditor can collect only once.

Example Suppose Big Hotels obtains a loan from City Bank to refurbish a hotel in Atlanta, Georgia. The parties sign a promissory note requiring the loan to be paid off in equal monthly installments over the next 10 years. Before the loan is paid, Big Hotels sells the hotel to ABC Hotels, another chain of hotels. ABC Hotels agrees with Big Hotels to complete the payments due on the City Bank loan. The bank has two options if ABC Hotels fails to pay: It can sue Big Hotels on the promissory note to recover the unpaid loan amount, or it can use its status as a creditor beneficiary to sue ABC Hotels.

Incidental Beneficiaries

In many instances, the parties to a contract unintentionally benefit a third party when the contract is performed. In such situations, the third party is referred to as an **incidental beneficiary**. An incidental beneficiary has no rights to enforce or sue under other people's contracts. Generally, the public and taxpayers are only incidental beneficiaries to contracts entered into by the government on their behalf. As such, they acquire no right to enforce government contracts or to sue parties who breach these contracts.

Example Suppose Heather owns a house on Residential Street. Her neighbor John owns the house next door. Heather contracts with a painting contractor to paint her house. The painting contractor breaches the contract and does not paint Heather's house. Although John may have benefited if Heather's house were painted, he is merely an incidental beneficiary and has no cause of action to sue the painting contractor for not painting Heather's house. Heather, of course, can sue the painting contractor for breach of contract.

Often, the courts are asked to decide whether a third party is an intended or an incidental beneficiary, as in the following case.

CASE 13.2
Third-Party Beneficiary

Bain v. Gillispie

357 N.W.2d 47,
Web 1984 Iowa App. Lexis 1694
Court of Appeals of Iowa

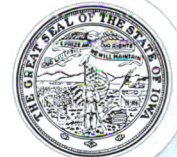

> ❝ *The real test is said to be whether the contracting parties intended that a third person should receive a benefit that might be enforced in the courts.* ❞
>
> —Judge Snell

Facts

James C. Bain, a college basketball referee, had a contract with the Big 10 Basketball Conference (Big 10) to referee various basketball games. During a game that took place on March 6, 1982, Bain called a foul on a University of Iowa player that permitted free throws by a Purdue University player. That player scored the point that gave Purdue a last-minute victory and eliminated Iowa from the Big 10 championship. Some Iowa fans, including John and Karen Gillispie, asserted that the foul call was clearly in error. The Gillispies operated a novelty store in Iowa City that sold University of Iowa sports memorabilia. They filed a complaint against Bain, alleging that his negligent refereeing constituted a breach of his contract with the Big 10 and destroyed a potential market for their products. The Gillispies sought $175,000 in compensatory damages plus exemplary damages. The trial court granted Bain's motion for summary judgment. The Gillispies appealed.

Issue

Were the Gillispies intended beneficiaries of the contract between Bain and the Big 10 Basketball Conference?

Language of the Court

The trial court found that there was no issue of material fact on the Gillispies' claim that they were beneficiaries under Bain's contract with the Big 10. Because the Gillispies would not be privy to the contract, they must be direct beneficiaries to maintain a cause of action, and not merely incidental beneficiaries.

A direct beneficiary is either a donee beneficiary or a creditor beneficiary. Gillispies make no claim that they are creditor beneficiaries of Bain, the Big 10 Athletic Conference, or the University of Iowa. The real test is said to be whether the contracting parties intended that a third person should receive a benefit that might be enforced in the courts. It is clear that the purpose of any promise that Bain might have made was not to confer a gift on Gillispies. Likewise, the Big 10 did not owe any duty to the Gillispies such that they would have been donee beneficiaries. If a contract did exist between Bain and the Big 10, Gillispies can be considered nothing more than incidental beneficiaries and as such are unable to maintain a cause of action. Consequently, there is no genuine issue for trial that could result in Gillispies obtaining a judgment under a contract theory of recovery.

Decision

The appellate court held that the Gillispies were merely incidental beneficiaries of the contract between Bain and the Big 10 Basketball Conference. Therefore, they could not maintain their lawsuit for an alleged breach of that contract. The court of appeals affirmed the judgment of the trial court.

Law & Ethics Questions

1. Should the law allow incidental beneficiaries to recover damages for the breach of other people's contracts? Why or why not?
2. **ETHICS** Did the Gillispies have a legitimate lawsuit in this case?
3. Do third parties have rights under many business contracts? Give some examples.

Web Exercises

1. **WEB** For the complete opinion of this case, go to *www.prenhall.com/cheesemancases*.
2. **WEB** Visit the website of the court of appeals of Iowa, at *www.judicial.state.ia.us/court_of_appeals*.
3. **WEB** Visit the website of the University of Iowa, at *www.uiowa.edu*.
4. **WEB** Use *www.google.com* to find an article that discusses third-party beneficiaries. Read it.

Covenants and Conditions

In contracts, parties make certain promises to each other. These promises may be classified as *covenants* or *conditions*. The difference between the two is discussed in the following paragraphs.

Covenant

A **covenant** is an unconditional promise to perform. Nonperformance of a covenant is a breach of contract that gives the other party the right to sue.

Example   If Medcliff Corporation borrows $100,000 from a bank and signs a promissory note to repay this amount plus 10 percent interest in one year, this promise is a covenant. That is, it is an unconditional promise to perform.

Conditions of Performance

A conditional promise (or qualified promise) is not as definite as a covenant. The promisor's duty to perform (or not perform) arises only if the **condition** does (or does not) occur.[8] It becomes a covenant if the condition is met, however.

Generally, contractual language such as *if, on condition that, provided that, when, after,* and *as soon as* indicates a condition. A single contract may contain numerous conditions that trigger or excuse performance. There are three types of conditions: *conditions precedent, conditions subsequent,* and *concurrent conditions*.

CONDITION PRECEDENT   If a contract requires the occurrence (or nonoccurrence) of an event *before* a party is obligated to perform a contractual duty, there is a **condition precedent**. The happening (or nonhappening) of the event triggers the contract or duty of performance. If the event does not occur, no duty to perform arises because there is a failure of condition.

Example   Suppose Company B offers Joan Andrews a job as an industrial engineer upon her graduation from college. If Andrews graduates, the condition has been met. If the employer refuses to hire Andrews at that time, she can sue the employer for breach of contract. If Andrews does not graduate, however, Company B is not obligated to hire her because there has been a failure of condition.

CONDITION PRECEDENT BASED ON SATISFACTION Some contracts reserve the right to a party to pay for services provided by the other only if the services meet the first party's "satisfaction." The courts have developed two tests—the *personal satisfaction test* and the *reasonable person test*—to examine whether this special form of condition precedent has been met:

1. **Personal satisfaction test.** The **personal satisfaction test** is a *subjective* test that applies if the performance involves personal taste and comfort (e.g., contracts for decorating, tailoring). The only requirement is that the person given the right to reject the contract acts in good faith.

    Example Suppose Gretchen employs an artist to paint her daughter's portrait. Assume that the contract provides that the client does not have to pay for the portrait unless she is satisfied with it. Accordingly, Gretchen may reject the painting if she personally dislikes it, even though a reasonable person would be satisfied with it.

2. **Reasonable person test.** The **reasonable person test** is an *objective* test that is used to judge contracts involving mechanical fitness and most commercial contracts. Most contracts that require the work to meet a third person's satisfaction (e.g., engineer, architect) are judged by this standard.

    Example Suppose a large mail-order catalog business hires someone to install a state-of-the-art computer system that will handle its order-entry and record-keeping functions. The system is installed and operates to industry standards. According to the reasonable person test, the company cannot reject the contract as not meeting its satisfaction.

TIME OF PERFORMANCE AS A CONDITION PRECEDENT Generally, there is a breach of contract if a contract is not performed when due. Nevertheless, if the other party is not jeopardized by the delay, most courts treat the delay as a minor breach and give the nonperforming party additional time to perform. Conversely, if the contract expressly provides that *"time is of the essence"* or similar language, performance by the stated time is an express condition. There is a breach of contract if the contracting party does not perform by the stated date.

> Freedom of contracts begins where equality of bargaining power begins.
>
> Oliver Wendell Holmes, Jr. (1928)

CONDITION SUBSEQUENT A **condition subsequent** exists when a contract provides that the occurrence or nonoccurrence of a specific event automatically excuses the performance of an existing duty to perform.

Example Many employment contracts include a clause that permits the employer to terminate the contract if the employee fails a drug test.

Note that the *Restatement (Second) of Contracts* eliminates the distinction between conditions precedent and conditions subsequent. Both are referred to as "conditions."[9]

CONCURRENT CONDITIONS **Concurrent conditions** arise when the parties to a contract must render performance simultaneously—that is, when each party's absolute duty to perform is conditioned on the other party's absolute duty to perform.

Example Suppose a contract to purchase goods provides that payment is due upon delivery. In other words, the buyer's duty to pay is conditioned on the seller's duty to deliver the goods and vice versa. Recovery is available if one party fails to respond to the other party's performance.

IMPLIED CONDITIONS Any of the previous types of conditions may be further classified as either express or implied conditions. An *express condition* exists if the parties expressly agree on it. An **implied-in-fact-condition** is one that can be implied from the circumstances surrounding a contract and the parties' conduct.

Example A contract in which a buyer agrees to purchase grain from a farmer implies that there are proper street access to the delivery site, proper unloading facilities, and the like.

CONCEPT SUMMARY

Types of Conditions

TYPE OF CONDITION	DESCRIPTION
Condition precedent	A specified event must occur or not occur before a party is obligated to perform contractual duties.
Condition subsequent	The occurrence or nonoccurrence of a specified event excuses the performance of an existing contractual duty to perform.
Concurrent condition	The parties to a contract are obligated to render performance simultaneously. Each party's duty to perform is conditioned on the other party's duty to perform.
Implied condition	An implied-in-fact condition is implied from the circumstances surrounding a contract and the parties' conduct.

Discharge of Performance

A party's duty to perform under a contract may be discharged by *mutual agreement* of the parties, by *impossibility of performance*, or by *operation of law*. These methods of discharge are discussed in the paragraphs that follow.

Discharge by Agreement

In many situations, the parties to a contract mutually decide to discharge their contractual duties. The different types of mutual agreement are discussed in the following paragraphs.

MUTUAL RESCISSION If a contract is wholly or partially executory on both sides, the parties can agree to rescind (i.e., cancel) the contract. **Mutual rescission** requires the parties to enter into a second agreement that expressly terminates the first one. Unilateral rescission of the contract by one of the parties without the other party's consent is not effective. Unilateral rescission of a contract constitutes a breach of that contract.

SUBSTITUTED CONTRACT The parties to a contract may enter into a new contract that revokes and discharges a prior contract. The new contract is called a **substituted contract**. If one of the parties fails to perform his or her duties under a substituted contract, the nonbreaching party can sue to enforce its terms against the breaching party. The prior contract cannot be enforced against the breaching party because it has been discharged.

NOVATION A **novation agreement** (commonly called **novation**) substitutes a third party for one of the original contracting parties. The new substituted party is obligated to perform the contract. All three parties must agree to the substitution. In a novation, the existing party is relieved of liability on the contract.

ACCORD AND SATISFACTION The parties to a contract may agree to settle a contract dispute by an **accord and satisfaction**. The agreement whereby the parties agree to accept something different in satisfaction of the original contract is called an *accord*.[10] The performance of an accord is called a *satisfaction*.

An accord does not discharge the original contract. It only suspends it until the accord is performed. Satisfaction of the accord discharges both the original contract and the accord. If an accord is not satisfied when it is due, the aggrieved party may enforce either the accord or the original contract.

Discharge by Impossibility

Under certain circumstances, the nonperformance of contractual duties is excused—that is, discharged—because of *impossibility of performance*.

Impossibility of performance (or **objective impossibility**) occurs if a contract becomes impossible to perform.[11] The impossibility must be objective impossibility ("it cannot be done") rather than subjective impossibility ("I cannot do it"). The following types of objective impossibility excuse nonperformance:

1. **The death or incapacity of the promisor prior to the performance of a personal service contract.**[12] For example, if a professional athlete dies prior to or during a contract period, his or her contract with the team is discharged.

2. **The destruction of the subject matter of a contract prior to performance.**[13] For example, if a building is destroyed by fire, the lessees are discharged from further performance unless otherwise provided in the lease.

3. **A supervening illegality, which makes performance of the contract illegal.**[14] For example, suppose an art dealer contracts to purchase native art found in a foreign country. The contract is discharged if the foreign country enacts a law forbidding native art from being exported from the country before the contract is performed.

In the following case, the court had to decide if impossibility existed that excused performance.

CASE **13.3**

Impossibility of Performance

Parker v. Arthur Murray, Inc.

295 N.E.2d 487,
Web 1973 Ill. App. Lexis 2760
Appellate Court of Illinois

> **"** *Although neither party to a contract should be relieved from performance on the ground that good business judgment was lacking, a court will not place upon language a ridiculous construction.* **"**
>
> —Judge Stamos

Facts

Ryland S. Parker, a 37-year-old college-educated bachelor, went to the Arthur Murray Studios (Arthur Murray) in Oak Park, Illinois, to redeem a certificate entitling him to three free dancing lessons. At that time, he lived alone in a one-room attic apartment. During the free lessons, the instructor told Parker that he had "exceptional potential to be a fine and accomplished dancer." Parker thereupon signed a contract for more lessons. Parker attended lessons regularly and was praised and encouraged by his instructors despite his lack of progress. Contract extensions and new contracts for additional instructional hours were executed, which Parker prepaid. Each written contract contained the bold-type words, "NON-CANCELLABLE CONTRACT." Two years after having started to take dancing lessons, Parker was severely injured in an automobile accident, rendering him incapable of continuing his dancing lessons. At that time, he had contracted for a total of 2,734 hours of dance lessons, for which he had prepaid $24,812. When Arthur Murray refused to refund any of the money, Parker sued to rescind the outstanding contracts. The trial courts held in favor of Parker and ordered Arthur Murray to return the prepaid contract payments. Arthur Murray appealed.

Issue

Does the doctrine of impossibility excuse Parker's performance of the personal service contracts?

Language of the Court

Plaintiff was granted rescission on the grounds of impossibility of performance. Defendants do not deny that the doctrine of impossibility of performance is generally applicable to the case at bar. Rather they assert that certain contract provisions bring the case within the Restatement's limitation that the doctrine is inapplicable if "the contract indicates a contrary intention." It is contended that such bold-type phrases as "NON-CANCELLABLE CONTRACT," "NON-CANCELLABLE NEGOTIABLE CONTRACT," and "I UNDERSTAND THAT NO REFUNDS WILL BE MADE UNDER THE TERMS OF THIS CONTRACT" manifest the parties' mutual intent to waive their respective rights to invoke the doctrine of impossibility.

This is a construction that we find unacceptable. Courts engage in the construction and interpretation of contracts with the sole aim of determining the intention of the parties. We need rely on no construction aids to conclude that plaintiff never contemplated that by signing a contract with such terms as "NON-CANCELLABLE" and "NO REFUNDS," he was waiving a remedy expressly recognized by Illinois courts. Although neither party to a contract should be relieved from performance on the ground that good business judgment was lacking, a court will not place upon language a ridiculous construction. We conclude that plaintiff did not waive his right to assert the doctrine of impossibility.

Suffice it to say that overwhelming evidence supported plaintiff's contention that he was incapable of continuing his lessons.

Decision

The appellate court held that the doctrine of impossibility of performance excused Parker's performance of the personal service contracts. The appellate court affirmed the trial court's judgment that ordered Arthur Murray to return the prepaid contract payments.

Law & Ethics Questions

1. Should the doctrine of impossibility excuse parties from performance of their contracts? Why or why not?

2. **ETHICS** Did Arthur Murray act ethically in not returning Parker's money?

3. **ETHICS** Did Arthur Murray act ethically by allowing someone to sign up for and prepay for over 2,700 hours of dance lessons?

Web Exercises

1. **WEB** For the complete opinion of this case, go to *www.prenhall.com/cheesemancases*.

2. **WEB** Visit the website of the Appellate Court of Illinois, at *www.state.il.us/court/AppellateCourt/default.asp*.

3. **WEB** Visit the website of Arthur Murray, at *www.arthurmurray.com*.

4. **WEB** Use *www.google.com* to find an article that discusses the doctrine of impossibility of performance. Read it.

FORCE MAJEURE CLAUSES The parties may agree in a contract that certain events will excuse nonperformance of the contract. These clauses are called **force majeure clauses**.

Example Force majeure clauses usually excuse nonperformance caused by natural disasters such as floods, tornadoes, earthquakes, and such. Modern clauses often excuse performance due to labor strikes, shortages of raw materials, and the like.

COMMERCIAL IMPRACTICABILITY Many states recognize the doctrine of **commercial impracticability** as an excuse for nonperformance of contracts. Commercial impracticability excuses performance if an unforeseeable event makes it impractical for the promisor to perform. This doctrine has not yet been fully developed by the courts. It is examined on a case-by-case basis.

Example A utility company enters into a contract to purchase uranium for its nuclear-powered generator from a uranium supplier at a fixed price of $1 million per year for five years. Suppose a new uranium cartel is formed worldwide, and the supplier must pay $3 million for uranium to supply the utility with each year's supply. In this case, the court would likely allow the supplier to rescind its contract with the utility, based on commercial impracticability. Note that it is not impossible for the supplier to supply the uranium.

CONTEMPORARY ENVIRONMENT
Commercial Impracticability

"The focus of impracticability analysis is upon the nature of the agreement and the expectations of the parties."

—Judge Nesbitt

Sometimes, unforeseen circumstances make the performance of a contract highly impracticable or very expensive. Modern contract law, including the Uniform Commercial Code (UCC), recognizes the doctrine of commercial impracticability as excusing nonperformance in certain situations. Consider the following case.

Alimenta (U.S.A.), Inc. (Alimenta), entered into a contract with Cargill, Inc. (Cargill), under which Alimenta would purchase shelled, edible peanuts from Cargill. The peanut crop had been planted in the fields at the time the contract was entered into. Cargill, which had contracts to purchase peanuts from peanut farmers, expected to make $3 million in profit from peanut sales.

Unfortunately, there was a severe drought that year, and the crop yield was substantially reduced. Thus, Cargill could deliver to Alimenta only about 65 percent of the promised peanuts. Cargill delivered the same percentage to all its customers. Alimenta filed suit against Cargill for breach of contract. Cargill asserted that further performance under the contract was excused by the doctrine of commercial impracticability. At trial, the jury rendered a verdict for Cargill. Alimenta appealed.

The Dustrict Court held that the drought in this case was unforeseen. The evidence showed that the shortage of peanuts was unprecedented. In fact, there had been a surplus of domestic peanuts for the preceding 20 years. The trial court found that it was not impossible for Cargill to fully perform the contract. Cargill could have gone into the market and purchased the peanuts, which were selling at a much higher price than contracted for, and delivered the peanuts to Alimenta. Cargill, however, had already suffered a $47 million loss on its peanut contract even without taking this step.

The Court of Appeals affirmed the trial court's ruling in favor of Cargill. The Court held that Cargill was excused from further performance by the doctrine of commercial impracticability. The Court stated that "the focus of impracticability analysis is upon the nature of the agreement and the expectations of the parties" and not on whether it is physically possible for the defendant to perform the contract. *Alimenta (U.S.A.), Inc. v. Cargill, Incorporated*, 861 F.2d 650, **Web** 1988 U.S. App. Lexis 16525 (United States Court of Appeals for the Eleventh Circuit)

Law & Ethics Questions

1. What does the doctrine of commercial impracticability provide? Explain.

2. How does the doctrine of commercial impracticability differ from impossibility of performance?

3. **ETHICS** Did Cargill act ethically in this case? Why or why not?

Web Exercises

1. **WEB** For the complete opinion of this case, go to *www.prenhall.com/cheesemancases*.

2. **WEB** Visit the website for the United States Court of Appeals for the Eleventh Circuit, at *www.ca11.uscourts.gov*.

3. **WEB** Visit the website of Cargill Corporation, at *www.cargill.com*.

4. **WEB** Use *www.google.com* to find the current price of peanuts on a commodities exchange.

Discharge by Operation of Law

Certain legal rules discharge parties from performing contractual duties. These rules are discussed in the following paragraphs:

- **Statutes of limitations.** Every state has a **statute of limitations** that applies to contract actions. Although the time periods vary from state to state, the usual period for bringing a lawsuit based on breach of contract is one to five years. The UCC provides that a cause of action based on a breach of sales or lease contract must be brought within four years after the cause of action accrues [UCC 2-725, 2A-506].

- **Bankruptcy.** Bankruptcy, which is governed by federal law, is a means of allocating the debtor's nonexempt property to satisfy his or her debts. Debtors may also reorganize in bankruptcy. In most cases, the debtor's assets are insufficient to pay all the creditors' claims. In this case, the debtor receives a **discharge** of the unpaid debts. The debtor is then relieved of legal liability to pay the discharged debts.

- **Alteration of the contract.** If a party to a contract intentionally alters the contract materially, the innocent party may opt either to discharge the contract or to enforce it. The contract may be enforced either on its original terms or on the altered terms. A material alteration is a change in price, quantity, or some other important term.

Medina, Fez, Morocco
The negotiation and enforcement of contracts differs in various cultures of the world.

Chapter Summary

Assignment of Rights, p. 344

Assignment is transfer of contractual rights by a party to a contract to a third person.

Form of Assignment

1. *Assignor.* An assignor is a contract party who assigns the contractual rights.
2. *Assignee.* An assignee is a third person to whom contract rights are assigned.

Personal Service Contracts

Contracts for the provision of personal services are generally not assignable.

Assignment of Future Rights

Usually, a person cannot assign a currently nonexistent right that he or she expects to have in the future.

Contracts Where Assignment Would Materially Alter the Risk

A contract cannot be assigned if the assignment would materially alter the risk or duties of the obligor.

Assignment of Legal Action

Legal actions involving personal rights cannot be assigned.

Effect of an Assignment of Rights

The assignee "stands in the shoes of the assignor" and is entitled to performance of the contract by the obligor.

Notice of Assignment

1. *Duty to notify.* The assignee must notify the obligor that (1) the assignment has been made, and (2) performance must be rendered to the assignee.
2. *Failure to give notice.* If the assignee fails to give proper notice to the obligor and the obligor renders performance to the assignor, the assignee's only course of action to recover is from the assignor.

Anti-Assignment and Approval Clauses

An *anti-assignment clause* prohibits the assignment of rights under a contract. An *approval clause* permits assignment of a contract only upon receipt of the obligor's approval.

Successive Assignments of the Same Right

If an obligee makes successive assignments of the same right, one of the following rules (depending on state law) applies:

1. **American rule.** Under this rule, the first assignment in time prevails, regardless of notice. Also called the *New York rule*.
2. **English rule.** Under this rule, the first assignee to give notice to the obligor prevails.
3. **Possession of tangible token rule.** Under either the American or English rule, if the assignor makes successive assignments of a contract right that is represented by a tangible token, the first assignee who receives delivery of the tangible token prevails over subsequent assignees. However, if the first assignee leaves the tangible token with the assignor, the subsequent assignee prevails.

Delegation of Duties, p. 348

Delegation is transfer of contractual duties by a party to a contract to a third person. The *delegator* is the party who transfers his or her contractual duties. The *delegatee* is the third person to whom contractual duties are delegated.

Duties That Can and Cannot Be Delegated

Personal service contracts calling for the exercise of personal skills, discretion, or expertise or contracts whose performance would materially vary if the obligor's duties were delegated.

Effect of Delegation of Duties

The effect of delegation depends on whether there has been:

1. **Assumption of duties.** The delegatee is liable to the obligee for nonperformance. The obligee may sue either the delegatee or the delegator.
2. **Declaration of duties.** The delegatee is not liable to the obligee for non-performance. The obligee can sue only the delegator. The delegatee is liable to the delegator for any damages suffered by the delegator because of the delegatee's nonperformance.

Anti-Delegation Clause

An anti-delegation clause prohibits the delegation of duties under a contract.

Assignment and Delegation

An *assignment and delegation* occurs when there is a transfer of both rights and duties under a contract.

Third-Party Beneficiaries, p. 349

Intended Beneficiaries

An intended beneficiary is a third person who is owed performance under other parties' contract. There are two types of intended beneficiaries:

1. **Donee beneficiary.** This person is to be rendered performance gratuitously under a contract (for example, a beneficiary of a life insurance policy). A donee beneficiary may sue the promisor for nonperformance.
2. **Creditor beneficiary.** A creditor becomes a beneficiary to a contract between the debtor and a third party who agrees to perform the debtor's obligation. If the debt is not paid, the creditor may sue either (1) the debtor under the original contract or (2) the third party as a creditor beneficiary.

Incidental Beneficiaries

An incidental beneficiary is a third person who incidentally receives some benefit under other parties' contract but who has no rights to enforce it or to sue for its nonperformance.

Covenants and Conditions, p. 352

Covenants

Covenants are unconditional promises to perform. Nonperformance of a covenant is a breach of contract that gives the other party the right to sue.

Conditions of Performance

A promisor's duty to perform or not perform arises only if the *condition* does or does not occur. Also called a *qualified promise*. There are several types of conditions:

1. *Condition precedent.* Reserve the right to a party to pay for provided services only if the services meet the party's satisfaction. "Satisfaction" is measured by one or two standards:
   a. Personal satisfaction test. The subjective intent of the decision maker applies if the performance involves personal taste or comfort.
   b. Reasonable person test. The objective intent of a reasonable person in the circumstances applies to contracts involving mechanical fitness or commercial contracts.
2. *Condition subsequent.* This provides that the occurrence or nonoccurrence of a specific event automatically excuses performance under a contract.
3. *Concurrent condition.* This arises when the parties to a contract must render performance simultaneously.
4. *Implied-in-fact condition.* This is a condition that is implied from the circumstances surrounding a contract and the parties' conduct.

Discharge of Performance, p. 354

Discharge by Agreement

1. *Mutual rescission.* The parties mutually agree to rescind an executory contract.
2. *Substituted contract.* The parties enter into a new contract that revokes a prior contract.
3. *Novation.* The parties agree to the substitution of a third party for one of the original parties. The exiting party is relieved of liability, and the entering party is obligated to perform the contract.
4. *Accord and satisfaction.* The parties agree to settle a contract dispute. The *satisfaction* of the *accord* discharges the original contract.

Discharge by Impossibility

1. *Impossibility of performance.* A contract may be objectively impossible to perform because of an event.
2. *Force majeure clause.* The parties may stipulate in a contract what events will excuse performance.
3. *Commercial impracticability.* A contract may be impractical for the promisor to perform because of an event.

Discharge by Operation of Law

1. *Statute of limitations.* If a cause of action based on a breach of sales or lease contract is not brought within the stipulated limitations period after the cause of action, the parties' contractual duties are discharged.
2. *Bankruptcy.* Discharge in bankruptcy relieves the debtor of legal liability to pay the discharged debts.
3. *Alteration of a contract.* If a party to a contract intentionally alters the contract materially, the innocent party may opt either to discharge the contract or enforce it on its original or altered terms.

Test Review Terms and Concepts

Case Problems

13.1 Third-Party Beneficiary: Eugene H. Emmick hired L. S. Hamm, an attorney, to draft his will. The will named Robert Lucas and others (Lucas) as beneficiaries. When Emmick died, it was discovered that the will was improperly drafted, violated state law, and was therefore ineffective. Emmick's estate was transferred pursuant to the state's intestate laws. Lucas did not receive the $75,000 he would have otherwise received had the will been valid. Lucas sued Hamm for breach of the Emmick–Hamm contract to recover what he would have received under the will. Who wins? *Lucas v. Hamm*, 56 Cal.2d 583, 364 P.2d 685, 15 Cal.Rptr. 821, **Web** 1961 Cal. Lexis 321 (Supreme Court of California)

13.2 Third-Party Beneficiary: Angelo Boussiacos hired Demetrios Sofias, a general contractor, to build a restaurant for him. Boussiacos entered into a loan agreement with Bank of America (B of A) whereby B of A would provide the construction financing to build the restaurant. As is normal with most construction loans, the loan agreement provided that loan funds would be periodically disbursed by B of A to Boussiacos at different stages of construction, as requested by Boussiacos. Problems arose in the progress of the construction. When Boussiacos did not pay Sofias for certain work that had been done, Sofias sued B of A for breach of contract to collect payment directly from B of A. Can Sofias maintain the lawsuit against B of A? *Sofias v. Bank of America*, 172 Cal. App. 3d. 583, 218 Cal.Rptr. 388, **Web** 1985 Cal. App. Lexis 2545 (Court of Appeal of California)

13.3 Assignment: William John Cunningham, a professional basketball player, entered into a contract with Southern Sports Corporation, which owned the Carolina Cougars, a professional basketball team. The contract provided that Cunningham was to play basketball for the Cougars for a three-year period. The contract contained a provision that it could not be assigned to any other professional basketball franchise without Cunningham's approval. Subsequently, Southern Sports Corporation sold its assets, including its franchise and Cunningham's contract, to the Munchak Corporation (Munchak). There was no change in the location of the Cougars after the purchase. When Cunningham refused to play for the new owners, Munchak sued to enforce Cunningham's contract. Was Cunningham's contract assignable to the new owner? *Munchak Corporation v. Cunningham*, 457 F.2d 721, **Web** 1972 U.S. App. Lexis 10272 (United States Court of Appeals for the Fourth Circuit)

13.4 Assignment: Berlinger Foods Corporation (Berlinger), pursuant to an oral contract, became a distributor for Häagen-Dazs ice cream. Over the next decade, both parties flourished as the marketing of high-quality, high-priced ice cream took hold. Berlinger successfully promoted the sale of Häagen-Dazs to supermarket chains and other retailers in the Baltimore–Washington, DC, area. Ten years later, the Pillsbury Company acquired Häagen-Dazs. Pillsbury adhered to the oral distribution agreement and retained Berlinger as a distributor for Häagen-Dazs ice cream. Two years later, Berlinger entered into a contract and sold its assets to Dreyers, a manufacturer of premium ice cream that competed with Häagen-Dazs. Dreyers ice cream had previously been sold primarily in the western part of the United States. Dreyers attempted to expand its market to the east by choosing to purchase Berlinger as a means to obtain distribution in the mid-Atlantic region. When Pillsbury learned of the sale, it advised Berlinger that its distributorship for Häagen-Dazs was terminated. Berlinger, which wanted to remain a distributor for Häagen-Dazs, sued Pillsbury for breach of contract, alleging that the oral distribution agreement with Häagen-Dazs and Pillsbury was properly assigned to Dreyers. Who wins? *Berlinger Foods Corporation v. The Pillsbury Company*, 633 F.Supp. 557, **Web** 1986 U.S. Dist. Lexis 26431 (United States District Court for the District of Maryland)

13.5 Anti-Assignment Clause: The city of Vancouver, Washington, contracted with B & B Contracting Corporation (B & B) to construct a well pump at a city-owned water station. The contract contained the following anti-assignment clause: "The contractor shall not assign this contract or any part thereof, or any moneys due or to become due thereunder." The work was not completed on time, and the city withheld $6,510 as liquidated damages from the contract price. B & B assigned the claim to this money to Portland Electric and Plumbing Company (PEPCo). PEPCo, as the assignee, filed suit against the City of Vancouver, alleging that the city had breached its contract with B & B by wrongfully refusing to pay $6,510 to B & B. Can PEPCo maintain the lawsuit against the City of Vancouver? *Portland Electric and Plumbing Company v. City of Vancouver*, 29 Wn. App. 292, 627 P.2d 1350, **Web** 1981 Wash. App. Lexis 2295 (Court of Appeals of Washington)

13.6 Delegation of Duties: C. W. Milford owned a registered Quarterhorse named Hired Chico. Milford sold the horse to Norman Stewart. Recognizing that Hired Chico was a good stud, Milford included the following provision in the written contract that was signed by both parties: "I, C. W. Milford, reserve 2 breedings each year on Hired Chico registration #403692 for the life of this stud horse regardless of whom the horse may be sold to." The agreement was filed with the County Court Clerk of Shelby County, Texas. Stewart later sold Hired Chico to Sam McKinnie. Prior to purchasing the horse, McKinnie read the Milford–Stewart contract and testified that he understood the terms of the contract. When McKinnie refused to grant Milford the stud services of Hired Chico, Milford sued McKinnie for breach of contract. Who wins? *McKinnie v. Milford*, 597 S.W.2d 953, **Web** 1980 Tex. App. Lexis 3345 (Court of Appeals of Texas)

13.7 Condition: Shumann Investments, Inc. (Shumann), hired Pace Construction Corporation (Pace), a general contractor, to build "Outlet World of Pasco Country." In turn, Pace hired OBS Company, Inc. (OBS), a subcontractor, to perform the framing, drywall, insulation, and stucco work on the project. The contract between Pace and OBS stipulated: "Final payment shall not become due unless and until the following conditions precedent to final payment have been satisfied . . . (c) receipt of final payment for subcontractor's work by contractor from owner." When Shumann refused to pay Pace, Pace refused to pay OBS. OBS sued Pace to recover payment. Who wins? *Pace Construction Corporation v. OBS Company, Inc.*, 531 So.2d 737, **Web** 1988 Fla. App. Lexis 4020 (Court of Appeal of Florida)

13.8 Excuse of Condition: Maco, Inc. (Maco), a roofing contractor, hired Brian Barrows as a salesperson. Barrows was assigned a geographic territory and was responsible for securing contracts for Maco within his territory. The employment contract provided that Barrows was to receive a 26 percent commission on the net profits from roofing contracts that he obtained. The contract contained the following provision: "To qualify for payment of the commission, the salesperson must sell and supervise the job; the job must be completed and paid for; and the salesperson must have been in the continuous employment of Maco, Inc., during the aforementioned period." Barrows obtained a $129,603 contract with the Board of Education of Cook County for Maco to make repairs to the roof of the Hoover School in Evanston, Illinois. During the course of the work, Barrows visited the site more than 60 times. Before the work was completed, Maco fired Barrows. Later, Maco refused to pay Barrows the commission when the project was completed and paid for. Barrows sued Maco to recover the commission. Who wins? *Barrows v. Maco, Inc.*, 94 Ill. App. 3d 959, 419 N.E.2d 634, **Web** 1981 Ill. App. Lexis 2371 (Appellate Court of Illinois)

Ethics Issues

13.9 Ethics: Pabagold, Inc. (Pabagold), a manufacturer and distributor of suntan lotions, hired Mediasmith, an advertising agency, to develop an advertising campaign for Pabagold's Hawaiian Gold Pabatan suntan lotion. In the contract, Pabagold authorized Mediasmith to enter into agreements with third parties to place Pabagold advertisements for the campaign and to make payments to these third parties for the Pabagold account. Pabagold agreed to pay Mediasmith for its services and to reimburse it for expenses incurred on behalf of Pabagold. The Pabagold–Mediasmith contract provided for arbitration of any dispute arising under the contract.

Medismith entered into a contract with Outdoor Services, Inc. (Outdoor Services), an outdoor advertising company, to place Pabagold ads on billboards owned by Outdoor Services. Outdoor Services provided the agreed-upon work and billed Mediasmith $8,545 for its services. Mediasmith requested payment of this amount from Pabagold so it could pay Outdoor Services. When Pabagold refused to pay, Outdoor Services filed a demand for arbitration as provided in the Pabagold–Mediasmith contract. Pabagold defended, asserting that Outdoor Services could not try to recover the money because it was not in privity of contract with Pabagold.

Did Pabagold act ethically in refusing to pay Outdoor Services? From a moral perspective, does it matter that Outdoor Services and Pabagold were not in privity of contract? Who wins? *Outdoor Services, Inc. v. Pabagold, Inc.,* 185 Cal.App.3d 676, 230 Cal.Rptr. 73, **Web** 1986 Cal. App. Lexis 2030 (Court of Appeal of California)

13.10 Ethics: Indiana Tri-City Plaza Bowl (Tri-City) leased a building from Charles H. Glueck for use as a bowling alley. The lease provided that Glueck was to provide adequate paved parking for the building. The lease gave Tri-City the right to approve the plans for the construction and paving of the parking lot. When Glueck submitted paving plans to Tri-City, it rejected the plans and withheld its approval. Tri-City argued that the plans were required to meet its personal satisfaction before it had to approve them. Evidence showed that the plans were commercially reasonable in the circumstances. A lawsuit was filed between Tri-City and Glueck. Who wins? Was it ethical for Tri-City to reject the plans? *Indiana Tri-City Plaza Bowl, Inc. v. Estate of Glueck,* 422 N.E.2d 670, **Web** 1981 Ind. App. Lexis 1506 (Court of Appeals of Indiana)

IRAC Writing Assignment

Read **Case A-13** in Appendix A [*Chase Precast Corporation v. John J. Paonessa Company, Inc.*]. Use the IRAC method to prepare a written analysis of the case.

Endnotes

1. *Restatement (Second) of Contracts,* Sections 311 and 318.
2. *Restatement (Second) of Contracts,* Section 317.
3. *Restatement (Second) of Contracts,* Section 318(2).
4. *Restatement (Second) of Contracts,* Section 328.
5. *Restatement (Second) of Contracts,* Section 302.
6. *Restatement (Second) of Contracts,* Section 302(1)(b).
7. *Restatement (Second) of Contracts,* Section 302(1)(a).
8. *The Restatement (Second) of Contracts,* Section 224, defines a *condition* as "an event, not certain to occur, which must occur, unless its nonperformance is excused, before performance under a contract is due."
9. *Restatement (Second) of Contracts,* Section 224.
10. *Restatement (Second) of Contracts,* Section 281.
11. *Restatement (Second) of Contracts,* Section 261.
12. *Restatement (Second) of Contracts,* Section 262.
13. *Restatement (Second) of Contracts,* Section 263.
14. *Restatement (Second) of Contracts,* Section 264.

CHAPTER 14

Remedies for Breach of Traditional and Online Contract

"Contracts must not be sports of an idle hour, mere matters of pleasantry and badinage, never intended by the parties to have any serious effect whatsoever."

—Lord Stowell
Dalrymple v. Dalrymple, (1811)

CHAPTER OBJECTIVES

After studying this chapter, you should be able to:

1. Explain how complete performance discharges contractual duties.
2. Identify inferior performance and the material breach of a contract.
3. Describe compensatory, consequential, and nominal damages.
4. Define the equitable remedies *specific performance*, *reformation*, and *injunction*.
5. Describe torts associated with contracts.

CHAPTER CONTENTS

- Introduction to Remedies for Breach of Traditional and Online Contracts
- Performance and Breach
- Monetary Damages
- Rescission and Restitution
- Equitable Remedies
- Torts Associated with Contracts
- Chapter Summary
- Test Review Terms and Concepts
- Case Problems
- Ethics Issues
- IRAC Writing Assignment

Introduction to Remedies for Breach of Traditional and Online Contracts

There are three levels of performance of a contract: *complete*, *substantial*, and *inferior*. Complete (or strict) performance by a party discharges that party's duties under the contract. Substantial performance constitutes a minor breach of the contract. Inferior performance constitutes a material breach that impairs or destroys the essence of the contract. Various remedies may be obtained by a nonbreaching party if a **breach of contract** occurs— that is, if a contracting party fails to perform an absolute duty owed under a contract.[1]

The most common remedy for a breach of contract is an award of *monetary damages*, often called the "law remedy." If a monetary award does not provide adequate relief, however, the court may order any one of several *equitable remedies*, including specific performance, reformation, and injunction. Equitable remedies are based on the concept of fairness.

This chapter discusses breach of contract and the remedies available to the nonbreaching party.

Tibet

Many areas of the world are trying to preserve historical cultural values while at the same time develop business and trade.

Performance and Breach

If a contractual duty has not been discharged (i.e., terminated) or excused (i.e., relieved of legal liability), the contracting party owes an absolute duty (i.e., covenant) to perform the duty. As mentioned in the chapter introduction, there are three types of performance of a contract: (1) *complete performance*, (2) *substantial performance* (or minor breach), and (3) *inferior performance* (or material breach). These concepts are discussed in the following paragraphs.

> Men keep their agreements when it is an advantage to both parties not to break them.
>
> Solon (c. 600 B.C.)

Complete Performance

Most contracts are discharged by the **complete performance**, or **strict performance**, of the contracting parties. Complete performance occurs when a party to a contract renders performance exactly as required by the contract. A fully performed contract is called an **executed contract**.

Note that **tender of performance** also discharges a party's contractual obligations. *Tender* is an unconditional and absolute offer by a contracting party to perform his or her obligations under the contract.

EXHIBIT 14.1

Remedy Where There Has Been Substantial Performance (Minor Breach)

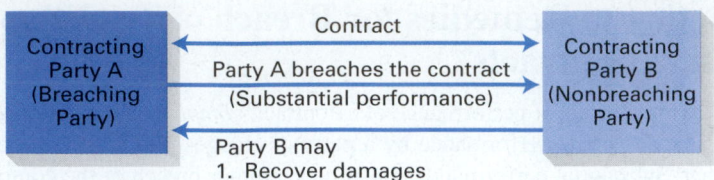

Example Suppose Ashley's Dress Shops, Inc., contracts to purchase dresses from a manufacturer for $25,000. Ashley's has performed its obligation under the contract once it tenders the $25,000 to the manufacturer. If the manufacturer fails to deliver the dresses, Ashley's can sue it for breach of contract.

Substantial Performance: Minor Breach

Substantial performance occurs when there has been a **minor breach** of contract. In other words, it occurs when a party to a contract renders performance that deviates slightly from complete performance. The nonbreaching party may try to convince the breaching party to elevate his or her performance to complete performance. If the breaching party does not correct the breach, the nonbreaching party can sue to recover *damages* by (1) deducting the cost to repair the defect from the contract price and remitting the balance to the breaching party or (2) suing the breaching party to recover the cost to repair the defect if the breaching party has already been paid (see Exhibit 14.1).

> No cause of action arises from a bare promise.
>
> Legal Maxim

Example Suppose Donald Trump contracts with Big Apple Construction Co. to have Big Apple construct an office building for $50 million. The architectural plans call for installation of three-ply windows in the building. Big Apple constructs the building exactly to plan except that it installs two-ply windows. There has been substantial performance. It would cost $300,000 to install the correct windows. If Big Apple agrees to replace the windows, its performance is elevated to complete performance, and Trump must remit the entire contract price. However, if Trump has to hire someone else to replace the windows, he may deduct this cost of repair from the contract price and remit the difference to Big Apple.

Inferior Performance: Material Breach

A **material breach** of a contract occurs when a party renders **inferior performance** of his or her contractual obligations that impairs or destroys the essence of the contract. There is no clear line between a minor breach and a material breach. A determination is made on a case-by-case basis.

Where there has been a material breach of contract, the nonbreaching party may *rescind* the contract and seek restitution of any compensation paid under the contract to the breaching party. The nonbreaching party is discharged from any further performance under the contract.[2] Alternatively, the nonbreaching party may treat the contract as being in effect and sue the breaching party to recover *damages* (see Exhibit 14.2).

Example Suppose a university contracts with a general contractor to build a new three-story building with classroom space for 1,000 students. However, the completed building can support the weight of only 500 students because the contractor used inferior materials.

EXHIBIT 14.2

Remedies Where There Has Been Inferior Performance (Material Breach)

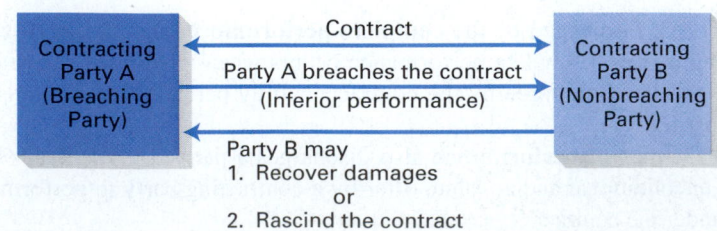

The defect cannot be repaired without rebuilding the entire structure. Because this is a material breach, the university may rescind the contract and require the removal of the building. The university is discharged of any obligations under the contract and is free to employ another contractor to rebuild the building. Alternatively, the university could accept the building and deduct from the contract price damages caused by the defect.

CONCEPT SUMMARY

Types of Performance

TYPE OF PERFORMANCE	LEGAL CONSEQUENCE
Complete performance	The contract is discharged.
Substantial performance (minor breach)	The nonbreaching party may recover damages caused by the breach.
Inferior performance (material breach)	The nonbreaching party may either (1) rescind the contract and recover restitution or (2) affirm the contract and recover damages.

Anticipatory Breach

Anticipatory breach (or **anticipatory repudiation**) of contract occurs when the contracting party informs the other party in advance that he or she will not perform his or her contractual duties when due. This type of material breach can be expressly stated or implied from the conduct of the repudiator. Where there is an anticipatory repudiation, the nonbreaching party's obligations under the contract are discharged immediately. The nonbreaching party also has the right to sue the repudiating party when the anticipatory breach occurs; there is no need to wait until performance is due [UCC 2-610].[3]

In the following case, the court found a breach of contract.

CASE 14.1
Breach of Contract

Chodos v. West Publishing Company, Inc.
292 F.3d 992, **Web** 2002 U.S. App. Lexis 10823 (2002)
United States Court of Appeals for the Ninth Circuit

> "*Because West concedes that the manuscript was of high quality and that it declined to publish it solely for commercial reasons rather than because of any defect in its form and content, we hold as a matter of law that West breached its agreement with Chodos.*"
>
> —Judge Stephen Reinhardt

Facts

Rafael Chodos is a California attorney who specializes in the law of fiduciary duty, which includes a party's obligation to act honestly and with loyalty when performing his or her legal duties to another. Chodos sent a detailed proposal and table of contents to Bancroft-Whitney, the leading publisher of legal texts, to write a treatise on fiduciary duties. The editors at Bancroft-Whitney were enthusiastic about

the proposal and sent Chodos a standard-form "author agreement" that set forth the terms of the publishing contract. Chodos was to be paid 15 percent of the gross revenues from the sales of the treatise. Chodos and Bancroft-Whitney signed the agreement.

For three years, Chodos wrote the manuscript. He significantly limited the time spent on his law practice and spent over 3,600 hours writing the manuscript. During this time, Chodos worked with editors of Bancroft-Whitney in developing and editing the manuscript. Midway thorough this period, West Group purchased Bancroft-Whitney, and the two companies merged. The Bancroft-Whitney editors, now employed by West, continued to work with Chodos on editing and developing the manuscript. Three years after beginning, Chodos submitted the final manuscript to West. West editors suggested changes to the manuscript, which Chodos completed. West sent Chodos a letter, apologizing for delays in publication and assuring him publication would take place within three months.

However, one month after the promised publication date, Chodos received a letter from West's marketing department, stating that West had decided not to publish Chodos's manuscript because it did not "fit with [West's] current product mix" and because of concerns about its "market potential." West admitted, however, that the manuscript was of "high quality" and that its decision was not due to any literary shortcomings of Chodos's work. Chodos filed a lawsuit against West, alleging breach of contract. The U.S. District Court granted summary judgment in favor of West. Chodos appealed.

Issue

Did West Group breach the author agreement it had with Chodos?

Language of the Court

The uncontroverted evidence in this case is that Chodos worked diligently in cooperation with West—indeed with West's encouragement—to produce a work that met the highest professional standard, and that he was successful in that venture. His performance was induced by an agreement that permitted rejection of the completed manuscript only for deficiencies in "form and content." Chodos thus labored to complete a work of high quality with the expectation that, if he did so, it would be published. He devoted thousands of hours of labor to the venture, and passed up substantial professional opportunities, only for West to decide that due to the vagaries of its internal reorganizations and changes in its business strategies or in the national economy or the market for legal treaties, his work, albeit admittedly of high quality, was for naught. It would be inequitable, if not unconscionable, for an author to be forced to bear this considerable burden solely because of his publisher's change of management, its poor planning, or its inadequate financial analyses at the time it entered into the contract, or even because of an unexpected change in the marketplace.

Moreover, to allow a publisher to escape its contractual obligations for these reasons would be directly contrary to both the language and the spirit of the standard Author Agreement.

In sum, we reject the district court's determination that West acted within its discretion afforded it by the Author Agreement when it decided not to publish Chodos's manuscript. Because West concedes that the manuscript was of high quality and that it declined to publish it solely for commercial reasons rather than because of any defect in its form and content, we hold as a matter of law that West breached its agreement with Chodos.

Decision

The U.S. Court of Appeals held as a matter of law that West Group had breached its contract with Chodos. The Court of Appeals reversed the District Court's summary judgment in favor of West, remanded the case to the U.S. District Court to enter summary judgment as to liability in Chodos's favor, and ordered further proceedings consistent with the opinion of the Court of Appeals.

Law & Ethics Questions

1. Should a court enforce the terms of a contract literally? Or should the court give contracts a broad interpretation, as requested by West Group?
2. **ETHICS** Did West Group act ethically in this case? Should it have read Chodos's treatise on fiduciary duty before terminating its contract with Chodos?
3. If West Group wanted to reserve the right to terminate its contract with Chodos based on changes in its own marketing strategy, company reorganization, or changes in the marketplace, how should West have done so? What amount of money should West have paid Chodos?

Web Exercises

1. **WEB** For the complete opinion of this case, go to *www.prenhall.com/cheesemancases*.
2. **WEB** Visit the website of the supreme court of New York, United States Court of Appeals for the Ninth Circuit, at *http://www.ca9.uscourts.gov/*.
3. **WEB** Visit the website of West Group, at *www.westgroup.com*.
4. **WEB** Use *www.google.com* to find an article or case about a breach of a contract. Read it.

Monetary Damages

A nonbreaching party may recover **monetary damages** from a breaching party. Monetary damages are available whether the breach was minor or material. Several types of monetary damages may be awarded. These include *compensatory, consequential, liquidated,* and *nominal damages.*

Compensatory Damages

Compensatory damages are intended to compensate a nonbreaching party for the loss of the bargain. In other words, they place the nonbreaching party in the same position as if the contract had been fully performed by restoring the "benefit of the bargain."

Example Suppose Lederle Laboratories enters into a written contract to employ a manager for three years at a salary of $6,000 per month. Before work is to start, the manager is informed that he or she will not be needed. This is a material breach of contract. Assume that the manager finds another job, but it pays only $5,000 per month. The manager may recover $1,000 per month for 36 months (a total of $36,000) from Lederle Laboratories as compensatory damages. These damages place the manager in the same situation as if the contract with Lederle had been performed.

The amount of compensatory damages that will be awarded for breach of contract depends on the type of contract involved and which party breached the contract. The award of compensatory damages in some special types of contracts is discussed in the following paragraphs.

SALE OF GOODS Compensatory damages for a breach of a sales contract involving goods are governed by the Uniform Commercial Code (UCC). The usual measure of damages for a breach of a sales contract is the difference between the contract price and the market price of the goods at the time and place the goods were to be delivered [UCC 2-708, 2-713].

> It is a vain thing to imagine a right without a remedy: for want of right and want of remedy are reciprocal.
>
> C. J. Holt
> *Ashby v. White (1703)*

Example Suppose Revlon, Inc., contracted to buy a piece of equipment from Greenway Supply Co. for $20,000, and the equipment is not delivered. Revlon then purchases the equipment from another vendor but has to pay $25,000 because the current market price for the equipment has risen. Revlon can recover $5,000—the difference between the market price paid ($25,000) and the contract price ($20,000)—in compensatory damages.

CONSTRUCTION CONTRACTS A construction contract arises when the owner of real property contracts to have a contractor build a structure or do other construction work. The compensatory damages recoverable for a breach of a construction contract vary with the stage of completion the project is in when the breach occurs.

The contractor may recover the profits he or she would have made on the contract if the owner breaches the construction contract before construction begins.

Example Suppose RXZ Corporation contracts to have the Ace Construction Co. build a factory for $1.2 million. It will cost Ace $800,000 in materials and labor to build the factory for RXZ. If RXZ Corporation breaches the contract before construction begins, Ace can recover $400,000 in "lost profit."

> Every unjust decision is a reproach to the law or the judge who administers it. If the law should be in danger of doing injustice, then equity should be called in to remedy it. Equity was introduced to mitigate the rigor of the law.
>
> Lord Denning, M. R.
> *Re Vandervell's Trusts (1974)*

Example Assume in the prior example that Ace Construction Co. had spent $300,000 on materials and labor before RXZ breached the contract. Here, Ace can recover $700,000—$400,000 lost profit plus $300,000 expended on materials and labor.

If the builder breaches a construction contract, either before or during construction, the owner can recover the increased cost above the contract price that he or she has to pay to have the work completed by another contractor.

Example Suppose that in the previous instance Ace Construction Co., which had contracted to build the factory for RXZ for $1.2 million, breached the contract by refusing to build the factory. Assume that RXZ Corporation has to pay $1.5 million to have the same factory built by another contractor. RXZ can recover the increased cost of construction ($300,000) from Ace as compensatory damages.

EMPLOYMENT CONTRACTS An employee whose employer breaches an employment contract can recover lost wages or salary as compensatory damages. If the employee breaches the contract, the employer can recover the costs to hire a new employee plus any increase in salary paid to the replacement.

MITIGATION OF DAMAGES If a contract has been breached, the law places a duty on the innocent nonbreaching party to take reasonable efforts to mitigate (i.e., avoid and reduce) the resulting damages. The extent of **mitigation** required depends on the type of contract involved.

If an employer breaches an employment contract, the employee owes a duty to mitigate damages by trying to find substitute employment. The employee is only required to accept *comparable employment*. The courts consider such factors as compensation, rank, status, job description, and geographic location in determining the comparability of jobs. In the following case, the court had to decide whether jobs were comparable.

CASE 14.2
Mitigation of Damages

Parker v. Twentieth Century Fox Film Corporation
3 Cal.3d 176, 474 P.2d 689, 89 Cal.Rptr. 737, **Web** 1970 Cal. Lexis 199 (1970)
Supreme Court of California

> **"** *The female lead as a dramatic actress in a Western-style motion picture can by no stretch of imagination be considered the equivalent of or substantially similar to the lead in a song-and-dance production.* **"**

—Judge Burke

Facts

Twentieth Century Fox Film Corporation (Fox), a major film production studio, entered into an employment contract with Shirley MacLaine Parker (Parker), an actress. Under the contract, Parker was to play the leading female role in a musical production called *Bloomer Girl*, to be filmed in Los Angeles. In the movie, Parker would be able to use her talents as a dancer and as an actress. The contract provided that Parker was to be paid guaranteed compensation of $53,571.42 per week for 14 weeks, for a total of $750,000. One month before filming was to start, Fox sent Parker a letter, notifying her that it was not going to film *Bloomer Girl*. However, the letter offered Parker the leading female role in a film tentatively titled *Big Country*, which was to be a dramatic western to be filmed in Australia. The compensation Fox offered Parker was identical to that offered for *Bloomer Girl*. Fox gave Parker 1 week to accept. She did not, and the offer expired. Parker sued Fox to recover the guaranteed compensation provided in the *Bloomer Girl* contract. The trial court granted summary judgment to Parker. Fox appealed.

Issue

Was the job that Fox offered Parker in *Big Country* comparable employment that Parker was obligated to accept to mitigate damages?

Language of the Court

The general rule is that the measure of recovery by a wrongfully discharged employee is the amount of salary agreed upon for the period of service, less the amount that the employer affirmatively proves the employee has earned or with reasonable effort might have earned from other employment. However, before projected earnings from other employment opportunities not sought or accepted by the discharged employee can be applied, in mitigation, the employer must show that the other employment was comparable, or substantially similar, to that of which the employee has been deprived, the employee's rejection of or failure to seek other available employment of a different or inferior kind may not be resorted to in order to mitigate damages.

Applying the foregoing rules to the record in the present case, with all intendments in favor of the party opposing the summary judgment motion—here, defendant Fox—it is clear that the trial court correctly ruled that plaintiff's failure to accept defendant's tendered substitute employment could not be applied in mitigation of damages because the offer of the *Big Country* lead was of employment both different and inferior, and that no factual dispute was presented on that issue. The mere circumstances that *Bloomer Girl* was to be a musical review, calling upon plaintiff's talents as a dancer as well as an actress, and was to be produced in the City of Los Angeles, whereas *Big Country* was a straight dramatic role in a Western-type story taking place in an opal mine in Australia, demonstrates the difference in kind between the two employments. The female lead as a dramatic actress in a Western-style motion picture can by no stretch of imagination be considered the equivalent of or substantially similar to the lead in a song-and-dance production.

Decision

The supreme court of California held that the job that Fox offered to Parker in *Big Country* was not comparable employment to the role Fox had contracted Parker to play in *Bloomer Girl*. Therefore, Parker did not fail to mitigate damages by refusing to accept such employment. The supreme court affirmed the trial court's summary judgment in favor of Parker.

Law & Ethics Questions

1. Should nonbreaching parties be under a duty to mitigate damages caused by the breaching party? Why or why not?
2. **ETHICS** Did Fox act ethically in this case? Did Parker?
3. Who is most likely to be able to mitigate damages when there is a breach of an employment contract: (1) the president of a large corporation, (2) a middle manager, or (3) a bank teller?

Web Exercises

1. **WEB** For the complete opinion of this case, go to www.prenhall.com/cheesemancases.
2. **WEB** Visit the website of the supreme court of California, at www.courtinfo.ca.gov/courts/supreme.
3. **WEB** Visit the website of Twentieth Century Fox Film Corporation, at www.foxmovies.com.
4. **WEB** Use www.google.com to find an article that discusses the doctrine of mitigation of damages. Read it.

Consequential Damages

In addition to compensatory damages, a nonbreaching party can sometimes recover **consequential damages**, or **special damages**, from the breaching party. Consequential damages are *foreseeable* damages that arise from circumstances outside a contract. To be liable for consequential damages, the breaching party must know or have reason to know that the breach will cause special damages to the other party.

Example Suppose Soan-Allen Co., a wholesaler, enters into a contract to purchase 1,000 men's suits for $150 each from Fabric Manufacturing Co., a manufacturer. Prior to contracting, the wholesaler tells the manufacturer that the suits will be resold to retailers for $225. The manufacturer breaches the contract by failing to manufacture the suits. The wholesaler cannot get the suits manufactured by anyone else in time to meet his contracts. He or she can recover $75,000 of lost profits on the resale contracts (1,000 suits × $75 profit) as consequential damages from the manufacturer because the manufacturer knew of this special damage to Soan-Allen Co. if it breached the contract.

> The very definition of a good award is that it gives dissatisfaction to both parties.
>
> M. R. Plumer
> *Goodman v. Sayers (1820)*

Liquidated Damages

Under certain circumstances, the parties to a contract may agree in advance to the amount of damages payable upon a breach of contract. These damages are called **liquidated damages**. To be lawful, the actual damages must be difficult or impracticable to determine, and the liquidated amount must be reasonable in the circumstances.[4] An enforceable liquidated damages clause is an exclusive remedy, even if actual damages are later determined to be different.

A liquidated damages clause is considered a **penalty** if actual damages are clearly determinable in advance or if the liquidated damages are excessive or unconscionable. If a liquidated damages clause is found to be a penalty, it is unenforceable. The nonbreaching party may then recover actual damages.

In the following two cases, the court had to decide whether liquidated damages clauses were enforceable.

C A S E 14.3
Liquidated Damages

Uzan v. 845 UN Limited Partnership

10 A.D.3d 230, 778 N.Y.S.2d 171, **Web** 2004 N.Y. App. Div. Lexis 8362 (2004)
Supreme Court of New York, Appellate Division

"In his affidavit Donald Trump stated that he sought 25% down payments from preconstruction purchasers at the Trump World Tower because of the substantial length of time between contract signing and closing, during which period 845 UN had to keep the units off the market, and because of the obvious associated risks."

—Judge Mazzarelli

Facts

The Trump World Tower was a luxury condominium building to be constructed at 845 United Nations Plaza in Manhattan, New York. It would be New York City's highest residential building. 845 UN Limited Partnership (845 UN) began selling condominiums at the building before the building was constructed. Donald Trump is the managing general partner of 845 UN. The condominium offering plan required a nonrefundable down payment of 25 percent of the purchase price. The purchase contract provided that if a purchaser defaulted and did not complete the purchase, 845 UN could keep the 25 percent down payment as liquidated damages.

Cem Uzan and Hakan Uzan, brothers and Turkish billionaires, each contracted to purchase two condominium units on the top floors of the building. Cem and Hakan were both represented by attorneys and took two months of negotiations and many draft purchase agreements in which they obtained special concessions from 845 UN regarding the purchase of their units for a total cost of $32 million. Over the course of two years, while the building was being constructed, the brothers paid the 25 percent nonrefundable down payment of $8 million.

On September 11, 2001, before the building was complete, terrorists attacked New York City by flying two planes into the World Trade Center, the city's two tallest buildings, murdering thousands of people. Thereafter, Cem and Hakan's attorneys delivered a letter to 845 UN stating:

> We believe that our clients are entitled to rescind their Purchase Agreements in view of the terrorist attack which occurred on September 11 and has not abated. In particular, our clients are concerned that the top floors in a "trophy" building, described as the tallest residential building in the world, will be an attractive terrorist target. The situation is further aggravated by the fact that the building bears the name of Donald Trump, perhaps the most widely known symbol of American capitalism. Finally, the United Nations complex brings even more attention to this location.

That day 845 UN sent Cem and Hakan default letters notifying them that they had 30 days to cure their default. Upon the expiration of the cure period, 845 UN terminated the four purchase agreements and kept the 25 percent down payments on the four condominiums as liquidated damages. Cem and Hakan sued 845 UN, alleging that the 25 percent nonrefundable down payment was an unenforceable and unconscionable penalty that should be returned to them. 845 UN defended, arguing that the 25 percent nonrefundable down payment was an enforceable liquidated damages clause. The trial court granted 845 UN partial summary judgment finding that Cem and Hakan had to forfeit a ten percent down payment. 845 UN appealed.

Issue

Is the 25 percent nonrefundable down payment enforceable liquidated damages, or is it an unconscionable and unenforceable penalty?

Language of the Court

In his affidavit Donald Trump stated that he sought 25% down payments from preconstruction purchasers at the Trump World Tower because of the substantial length of time between contract signing and closing, during which period 845 UN had to keep the units off the market, and because of the obvious associated risks. Trump also affirmed that down payments in the range of 20% to 25% are standard practice in the new construction luxury condominium submarket in New York City.

It is clear that plaintiffs are not entitled to a return of any portion of their down payment. Here the 25% down payment was a specifically negotiated element of the contracts. There is no question that this was an arm's length transaction. The parties were sophisticated businesspeople, represented by counsel, who spent two months at the bargaining table before executing the amended purchase agreements. Further, the record evidences that it is customary in the preconstruction luxury condominium industry for parties to price the risk of default at 25% of the purchase price. The purchase agreements included a detailed nonrefundable down payment clause to which plaintiffs' counsel had negotiated a specific amendment. That amendment allowed for the payment of 25% of the purchase price in three installments: 10% at contract, an additional 7 1/2% 12 months later, and a final 7 1/2% 18 months later. Clearly, plaintiffs were fully aware of and accepted the requirement of a nonrefundable 25% down payment for these luxury preconstruction condominiums.

The detailed provision concerning the nonrefundable deposit was integral to the transaction. If plaintiffs were dissatisfied with the 25% nonrefundable down payment provision in the purchase agreements, the time to have voiced objection was at the bargaining table. Because they chose to accept it, they are committed to its terms. Thus, upon plaintiffs' default and failure to cure, defendant was entitled to retain the full 25% down payments.

Decision

The appellate court held that the 25 percent nonrefundable down payment was an enforceable liquidated damages clause and not an unconscionable penalty. The appellate court, as a matter of law, granted 845 UN's motion for summary judgment allowing 845 UN to keep the Cem and Hakan's down payments and dismissed their complaint.

Law & Ethics Questions

1. What are liquidated damages? What purpose is served by liquidated damages? Explain.

2. What is an unconscionable penalty? What are the consequences of finding that a liquidated damages clause is a penalty?

3. **ETHICS** Was it ethical for Cem and Hakan to try to back out of the purchase agreements and get their money back? Do you think they had a good reason to do so?

4. What do you think happened to the prices of high-rise condominiums and apartments in New York City after the terrorist attack?

5. **ETHICS** Was it unethical for Donald Trump and 845 UN not to let Cem and Hakan rescind their purchase agreements and receive back their down payments?

Web Exercises

1. **WEB** For the full opinion of this case, go to
   www.prenhall.com/cheesemancases.

2. **WEB** Visit the website of the supreme court of New York,
   Appellate Division, First Department, at
   www.nycourts.gov/courts/ad1.

3. **WEB** To view a photograph of the Trump World Tower in
   New York City, go to *www.trumpworldtower.com*.

4. **WEB** Use *www.google.com* to find a video of the terrorist
   attack on the World Trade Center in New York City on September
   11, 2001.

CASE **14.4**
Liquidated Damages

California and Hawaiian Sugar Co. v. Sun Ship, Inc.

794 F.2d 1433, **Web** 1986 U.S. App. Lexis 27376
United States Court of Appeals for the Ninth Circuit

> **"***Promising to pay damages of a fixed amount, the parties normally have a much better sense of what damages can occur. Courts must be reluctant to over-rule their judgment.***"**
>
> —Judge Noonan

Facts

The California and Hawaiian Sugar Company (C&H), a California corporation, is an agricultural cooperative owned by 14 sugar plantations in Hawaii. It transports raw sugar to its refinery in Crockett, California. Sugar is a seasonal crop, with about 70 percent of the harvest occurring between April and October. C&H requires reliable seasonal shipping of the raw sugar from Hawaii to California. Sugar stored on the ground or left unharvested suffers a loss of sucrose and goes to waste.

After C&H was notified by its normal shipper that it would be withdrawing its services at a specified date in the future, C&H commissioned the design of a large hybrid vessel—a tug of a catamaran design consisting of a barge attached to the tug. After substantial negotiation, C&H contracted with Sun Ship, Inc. (Sun Ship), a Pennsylvania corporation, to build the vessel for $25,405,000. The contract gave Sun Ship one and three-quarters years to build and deliver the ship to C&H. The contract also contained a liquidated damages clause calling for a payment of $17,000 per day for each day that the vessel was not delivered to C&H after the agreed-upon delivery date. Sun Ship did not complete the vessel until eight and one-half months after the agreed-upon delivery date. Upon delivery, the vessel was commissioned and christened the *Moku Pahu*.

During the season that the boat had not been delivered, C&H was able to find other means of shipping the crop from Hawaii to its California refinery. Evidence established that actual damages suffered by C&H because of the nonavailability of the vessel from Sun Ship were $368,000. When Sun Ship refused to pay the liquidated damages, C&H filed suit to require payment of $4,413,000 in liquidated damages under the contract. The U.S. District Court entered judgment in favor of C&H and awarded the corporation $4,413,000 plus interest. Sun Ship appealed.

Issue

Is the liquidated damages clause enforceable, or is it a penalty clause that is not enforceable?

Language of the Court

Contracts are contracts because they contain enforceable promises, and absent some over-riding public policy, those promises are to be enforced. Where each of the parties is content to take the risk of its turning out in a particular way, why should one be released from the contract, if there were no misrepresentation or other want of fair dealing? Promising to pay damages of a fixed amount, the parties normally have a much better sense of what damages can occur. Courts must be reluctant to over-rule their judgment. Where damages are real but difficult to prove, injustice will be done the injured party if the court substitutes the requirements of judicial proof for the parties own informed agreement as to what is a reasonable measure of damages. The liquidated damage clause here functions in lieu of a court's determination of the consequential damages suffered by C&H.

Proof of this loss is difficult. Whatever the loss, the parties had promised each other that $17,000 per day was a reasonable measure. The court must decline to substitute the requirements of judicial proof for the parties' own conclusion. The court will uphold the parties' bargain.

Decision

The Court of Appeals held that the liquidated damages clause was not a penalty and was therefore enforceable. The Court of Appeals affirmed the judgment of the District Court in favor of C&H.

Law & Ethics Questions

1. Should liquidated damages clauses be enforced, or should nonbreaching parties be allowed to recover only actual damages caused by the breaching party?

2. **ETHICS** Did either party act unethically in this case?

3. Do you think many businesses use liquidated damages clauses? Can you give some examples?

Web Exercises

1. **WEB** For the complete opinion of this case, go to *www.prenhall.com/cheesemancases*.

2. **WEB** Visit the website of the United States Court of Appeals for the Ninth Circuit, at *www.ca9.uscourts.gov*.

3. **WEB** Visit the website of C&H Sugar Company, at *www.chsugar.com*.

4. **WEB** Use *www.google.com* to find information about sugar plantations in Hawaii.

Nominal Damages

A nonbreaching party can sue a breaching party to a contract for nominal damages even if no financial loss resulted from the breach. **Nominal damages** are usually awarded in a small amount, such as $1. Cases involving nominal damages are usually brought on principle.

Example Suppose Mary enters into an employment contract with Microhard Corporation. It is a three-year contract, and Mary is to be paid $100,000 per year. After Mary works for one year, Microhard Corporation fires Mary. The next day, Mary finds a better position at Microsoft Corporation, in the same city, paying $125,000 per year on a two-year contract. Mary has suffered no monetary damages but could bring a civil lawsuit against Microhard Corporation because of its breach and recover nominal damages ($1). Most courts disfavor nominal damage lawsuit because they use valuable court time and resources.

CONCEPT SUMMARY

Types of Monetary Damages

TYPE OF CONDITION	DESCRIPTION
Compensatory	Damages that compensate a nonbreaching party for the loss of a bargain. It places the nonbreaching party in the same position as if the contract had been fully performed.
Consequential	Damages that compensate a nonbreaching party for foreseeable special damages. The breaching party must have known or should have known that these damages would result from the breach.
Liquidated	An agreement by the parties in advance that sets the amount of damages recoverable in case of breach. These damages are lawful if they do not cause a penalty.
Nominal	Damages awarded against the breaching party even though the nonbreaching party has suffered no actual damages because of the breach. A small amount (e.g., $1) is usually awarded.

Enforcement of Remedies

If a nonbreaching party brings a successful lawsuit against a breaching party to a contract, the court will enter a *judgment* in his or her favor. This judgment must then be collected. If the breaching party refuses to pay the judgment, the court may:

- **Issue a writ of attachment.** A **writ of attachment** orders the sheriff or other government officer to seize property in the possession of the breaching party that he or she owns and to sell the property at auction to satisfy the judgment.
- **Issue a writ of garnishment.** A **writ of garnishment** orders that wages, bank accounts, or other property of the breaching party that is in the hands of third parties be paid to the nonbreaching party to satisfy the judgment. Federal and state laws limit the amount of the breaching party's wages or salary that can be garnished.

Rescission and Restitution

Rescission is an action to undo a contract. It is available where there has been a material breach of contract, fraud, duress, undue influence, or mistake. Generally, to rescind a contract, the parties must make **restitution** of the consideration they received under the contract.[5] Restitution consists of returning the goods, property, money, or other consideration received from the other party. If possible, the actual goods or property must be returned. If the goods or property have been consumed or are otherwise unavailable, restitution must be made by conveying a cash equivalent. The rescinding party must give adequate notice of the rescission to the breaching party. Rescission and restitution restore the parties to the positions they occupied prior to the contract.

Example Suppose Filene's Department Store contracts to purchase $100,000 of goods from a sweater manufacturer. The store pays $10,000 as a down payment, and the first $20,000 of goods are delivered. The goods are materially defective, and the defect cannot be cured. This breach is a material breach. Filene's can rescind the contract. The store is entitled to receive its down payment back from the manufacturer, and the manufacturer is entitled to receive the goods back from the store.

In the following case, the court had to decide whether to order the rescission of a contract.

C A S E **14.5** *Rescission of a Contract*	**Hickman v. Bates** 889 So.2d 1249, **Web** 2004 La. App. Lexis 3076 (2004) Court of Appeal of Louisiana	

> 66 *The Court finds that Keith's failure to inform his young, limited, first cousin was intentional and was done to obtain an advantage over her. That is, of divesting her interest in 45 acres in Bienville Parish and 236 acres in Madison Parish for a pittance.* 99
>
> —Judge Caraway

Facts

Patricia Dianne Hickman inherited one-half interests to two pieces of real property when her mother died. One of the properties, in Bienville Parish, Louisiana, contained 45 acres of woodland. The second property, in Madison Parish, Louisiana, contained approximately 236 acres of land and a house. Patricia was 20 years old and had a mental condition that required medication. Patricia, who lived separately from her parents, received a telephone call from her father, Joe Hickman, to come and visit him. Joe was ill with cancer and lived with his sister, Christine Bates, and her husband. Bates and her husband are the parents of Keith Bates, Patricia's first cousin.

The day after Patricia arrived, Joe informed Patricia that an important concern of his was for her to sell her interests in the two pieces of property to Keith Bates and his wife Sheila (Bates). Joe expressed his doubts that Patricia would be able to maintain the properties and his interest in keeping the property in the family. Patricia agreed to sell the properties to Bates for $500. Patricia signed legal documents that had previously been drawn by an attorney prior to her arrival.

Subsequently, through a friend, Patricia sued Bates to rescind the contracts selling her interest in the two pieces of property to them, alleging fraud. Expert testimony at trial valued the Madison Parish property at $259,000 and the Bienville Parish property at $20,700. The trial court found fraud and rescinded the contracts. The trial court did not, however, award Patricia attorneys' fees. Both sides appealed.

Issue

Should the sales contracts be rescinded because of fraud and should Patricia be awarded attorneys fees?

Language of the Court

A contract is formed by the consent of the parties. However, consent may be vitiated by error, fraud, or duress. Fraud is a misrepresentation or a suppression of the truth made with the intention either to obtain an unjust advantage for one party or to cause a loss or inconvenience to the other. Fraud need only be proven by a preponderance of the evidence and may be established by circumstantial evidence.

In its very thorough and well-reasoned oral ruling, the trial court made the following findings of fact concerning its determination of fraud: "The court finds that Patricia's intellectual abilities are limited, both from her lack of education and from her mental condition that requires medicine. Considering her situation, her youth, she was then 20 years old, and her limited abilities, as well as her lack of prior knowledge of the purpose of the visit, and her father's illness, and the fact that she trusted her father and her cousin, the Court finds that Keith had a responsibility to make sure Patricia was informed fully about the transactions and make sure that she understood everything she was doing and the import of everything she was doing, including the fact that she would own nothing, and including the price considerations involved before she signed those documents. The Court finds that Keith's failure to inform his young, limited, first cousin was intentional and was done to obtain an advantage over her. That is, of divesting her interest in 45 acres in Bienville Parish and 236 acres in Madison Parish for a pittance."

We can discern no manifest error in these determinations. Accordingly, we find that the trial court committed no error in rescinding the sales on the ground of fraud. This portion of the judgment is affirmed. We reverse the trial court's ruling denying attorney fees and grant Patricia reasonable attorney fees through the time of this appeal in the amount of $12,000. Costs of this appeal are assessed to defendants-appellants.

Decision

The court of appeals affirmed the trial court's finding of fraud and its judgment rescinding the sales contracts by which Patricia sold her interests in the two properties to Bates. The court of appeals reversed the trial court's denial of an award of attorneys' fees to Patricia and awarded $12,000 in attorneys' fees to Patricia.

Law & Ethics Questions

1. Describe the rescission of a contract.

2. Define *fraud*. Do you think fraud occurred in this case?

3. **ETHICS** Did Patricia's father, Joe Hickman, and her first cousin, Keith Bates, act ethically in this case?

4. **ETHICS** Did Patricia need the court's help in this case?

Web Exercises

1. **WEB** For the complete opinion of this case, go to *www.prenhall.com/cheesemancases*.

2. **WEB** Visit the website of the court of appeals of Louisiana, Second Circuit, at *www.lacoa2.org*.

3. **WEB** Visit the websites of Bienville Parish, Louisiana, at *www.lapage.com/parishes/bienv.htm*, and Madison Parish, Louisiana, at *www.lapage.com/parishes/madis.htm*.

4. **WEB** Use *www.google.com* to find a case in which a contract was rescinded. Read it.

CONTEMPORARY ENVIRONMENT

Must a Wedding Ring Be Returned if the Engagement Is Broken Off?

> **"***The inherent weaknesses in any fault-based system lead us to adopt a no-fault approach to resolution of engagement ring disputes.***"**
>
> —Judge Newman

When a man and woman are in love, the man often asks the woman to marry him and presents her with an engagement ring. But engagements do not always lead to weddings and are sometimes broken off by one of the parties. Who gets the engagement ring? Does the woman get to keep the ring, or can the man recover it? Consider the following case.

Rodger Lindh proposed marriage to Janis Surman and presented her with a diamond ring he purchased for $17,400. She accepted his proposal and ring. Discord developed in their relationship, however. Seven months after the engagement, Rodger called off the engagement. He asked Janis to return the engagement ring, but when she refused, Rodger sued her, seeking recovery of the ring. The Pennsylvania trial court and appellate court applied a no-fault rule and held that Janis must return the ring to Rodger. Janis appealed to the Pennsylvania supreme court.

The Pennsylvania supreme court noted that Janis favored the "fault" rule for deciding who gets the ring in a broken engagement case. Under this rule, if "she" breaks off the engagement, "he" gets the ring back; if "he" breaks off the engagement, "she" gets to keep the ring. Although noting that some states still follow this rule, the Pennsylvania supreme court stated that Pennsylvania would not follow the fault rule. The court noted that the process of determining who is "wrong" and who is "right" is difficult in modern relationships and that this would require parties to aim bitter and unpleasant accusations at each other.

Instead, the Pennsylvania supreme court decided to follow the modern, objective no-fault rule, which holds that an engagement ring must be returned to the donor, no matter who breaks off the engagement. The court stated:

> Courts that have applied no-fault principles to engagement ring cases have borrowed from the policies of their respective legislatures that have moved away from the notion of fault in their divorce statutes. We agree with those jurisdictions that have

looked toward the development of no-fault divorce law for a principle to decide engagement ring cases, and the inherent weaknesses in any fault-based system lead us to adopt a no-fault approach to resolution of engagement ring disputes. We believe that the benefits from the certainty of our rule outweigh its negatives, and that a strict no-fault approach is less flawed than a fault-based theory.

The Pennsylvania supreme court affirmed the judgment of the lower courts, awarding the engagement ring to Rodger. *Lindh v. Surman*, 742 A.2d 643, **Web** 1999 Pa. Lexis 3498 (Supreme Court of Pennsylvania)

Law & Ethics Questions

1. What does the fault rule regarding the return of engagement rings provide? Is there any difficulty in applying this rule? Explain.

2. What does the objective, no-fault, rule regarding the return of engagement rings provide?

3. **ETHICS** Was it ethical for Rodger to sue to get the engagement ring back when he broke off the engagement?

4. **ETHICS** Was it ethical for Janis to keep the engagement ring after the engagement was broken off?

Web Exercises

1. **WEB** For the complete opinion of this case, go to *www.prenhall.com/cheesemancases*.

2. **WEB** Visit the website of the supreme court of Pennsylvania, at *www.courts.state.pa.us/Index/Supreme/indexSupreme.asp*.

3. **WEB** Use *www.google.com* to find your state's law regarding the return of an engagement ring if the engagement is broken off.

Equitable Remedies

Equitable remedies are available if there has been a breach of contract that cannot be adequately compensated through a legal remedy. They are also available to prevent unjust enrichment. The most common equitable remedies are *specific performance*, *reformation*, and *injunction*.

Specific Performance

An award of **specific performance** orders the breaching party to perform the acts promised in a contract. The courts have the discretion to award this remedy if the subject matter of the contract is unique.[6]

Example Specific performance is available to enforce land contracts because every piece of real property is considered to be unique. Works of art, antiques, and items of sentimental value, rare coins, stamps, heirlooms, and such also fit the requirement for uniqueness. Most other personal property does not.

Specific performance of personal service contracts is not granted because the courts would find it difficult or impracticable to supervise or monitor performance of such a contract.

Example Brad contracts with Michael Angelo to paint a life-size portrait of Angie. Subsequently, Michael refuses to paint the painting. Brad cannot sue Michael to paint the painting because specific performance would not be ordered. Brad could sue to recover any payments he has made to Michael.

Example Brad contracts with Michael Angelo to paint a life-size portrait of Angie. Michael paints the painting, but, because he wants to keep his masterpiece, Michael refuses to deliver it to Brad. In this case, Brad can sue for specific performance and recover possession of the unique painting.

In the following case, the court had to decide whether to issue an order of specific performance.

CASE **14.6**
Specific Performance

Alba v. Kaufmann

27 A.D.3d 816, 810 N.Y.S.2d 539, **Web** 2006 N.Y. App. Div. Lexis 2321 (2006)
Supreme Court of New York, Appellate Division

"*The case law reveals that the equitable remedy of specific performance is routinely awarded in contract actions involving real property, on the premise that each parcel of real property is unique.*"

—Judge Crew

Facts

Jean-Claude Kaufmann owned approximately 37 acres of real property located in Rensselaer County, New York. The property is located in a wooded area and is improved with a nineteenth-century farmhouse. Kaufmann and his spouse, Christine Cacace, reside in New York City and use the property as a weekend or vacation home. After Kaufmann and Cacace lost their jobs, their financial situation prompted Kaufmann to list the property for sale for $350,000.

Richard Alba and his spouse (Albas) were shown the property and offered the full asking price. The parties executed a contract for sale, and the Albas paid a deposit, obtained a mortgage commitment, and procured a satisfactory house inspection and title insurance. A date for closing the transaction was set. Prior to closing, Cacace sent the Albas an e-mail indicating that she and Kaufmann had "a change of heart" and no longer wished to go forward with the sale. Albas sent a reply e-mail stating their intent to go forward with the scheduled closing. Cacace responded with another e-mail, informing the Albas that she had multiple sclerosis and alleging that the "remorse and dread" over the impending sale was making her ill. When Kaufmann refused to close, the Albas sued, seeking specific performance and moved for

summary judgment. The supreme court denied the motion. The Albas appealed.

Issue

Was an order of specific performance of the real estate contract warranted in this case?

Language of the Court

There must be a reversal. In order to establish their entitlement to summary judgment, the Albas were required to demonstrate that they substantially performed their contractual obligations and were ready, willing and able to fulfill their remaining obligations, that Kaufmann was able but unwilling to convey the property and that there is no adequate remedy at law. The Albas plainly discharged that burden here. After executing the underlying contract, the Albas paid a deposit, obtained a mortgage commitment, demonstrated that they had the financial wherewithal to purchase what was to be for them a vacation home, obtained a satisfactory home inspection and procured title insurance. In short, the record demonstrates that the Albas were ready, willing and able to close and, but for Kaufmann's admitted refusal to do so, would have consummated the transaction.

As to the remedy the Albas seek, the case law reveals that the equitable remedy of specific performance is routinely awarded in contract actions involving real property, on the premise that each parcel of real property is unique. Although certain defenses do exist including, insofar as is relevant here, unreasonable hardship, the court's discretion to grant or deny specific performance of a contract for the sale of realty is not unlimited; unless the court finds that granting a decree of specific performance would be a drastic or harsh remedy, or work injustice, the court must direct specific performance. Moreover, volitional unwillingness, as distinguished from good faith inability, to meet contractual obligations furnishes neither a ground for cancellation of the contract nor a defense against its specific performance.

Even accepting, for purposes of this discussion, that the alleged exacerbation of Cacace's symptoms is both genuine and causally related to the proposed sale of property, as she is not a party to the contract, her connection to the transaction is simply too attenuated for Kaufmann to claim undue hardship. In our view, permitting a third party who is not a signatory to a real estate contract, such as a spouse or, potentially, a child, sibling or parent, to assert, via the titled owner, an undue hardship claim by voicing objection to or otherwise contending that the proposed sale is simply too much to bear would interject uncertainty and chaos into the otherwise orderly world of contract law. Simply put, permitting a defendant to raise an undue hardship defense under the circumstances present here would place a nearly impossible burden upon potential purchasers of real property, namely, to ascertain whether any of the signatories' relatives had any potential objection to the sale in question.

Decision

The appellate court reversed the supreme court's denial of Alba's motion for summary judgment. The appellate court, as a matter of law, granted the Albas' motion for summary judgment and ordered Kaufmann to specifically perform the real estate contract.

Law & Ethics Questions

1. What does the doctrine of specific performance provide? Explain.
2. **ETHICS** Was it ethical for the seller, Kaufman, to try to back out of the contract?
3. **ETHICS** Should the Alba's knowledge of Cacace's health problems have led them not to sue for specific performance?

Web Exercises

1. **WEB** For the complete opinion of this case, go to *www.prenhall.com/cheesemancases*.
2. **WEB** Visit the website of the supreme court of New York, Appellate Division, Third Department, at *www.courts.state.ny.us/ad3*.
3. **WEB** Use *www.google.com* to find an article or a case in which the doctrine of specific performance has been applied.

Reformation

Reformation is an equitable doctrine that permits the court to rewrite a contract to express the parties' true intentions.

Example Suppose a clerical error is made during the typing of a contract, and both parties sign the contract without discovering the error. If a dispute later arises, the court can reform the contract to correct the clerical error to read as the parties originally intended.

Injunction

An **injunction** is a court order that prohibits a person from doing a certain act. To obtain an injunction, the requesting party must show that he or she will suffer irreparable injury if the injunction is not issued.

Example Suppose a professional football team enters into a five-year employment contract with a "superstar" quarterback. During this five-year period, the quarterback breaches the contract and enters into a contract to play for a competing team. Here, the first team can seek an injunction to prevent the quarterback from playing for the other team.

CONCEPT SUMMARY

Types of Equitable Remedies

TYPE OF EQUITABLE REMEDY	DESCRIPTION
Specific performance	A court orders the breaching party to perform the acts promised in the contract. The subject matter of the contract must be unique.
Reformation	A court rewrites a contract to express the parties' true intentions. This remedy is usually used to correct clerical errors.
Injunction	A court prohibits a party from doing a certain act. Injunctions are available in contract actions only in limited circumstances.

Torts Associated With Contracts

The recovery for breach of contract is usually limited to contract damages. A party who can prove a contract-related **tort**, however, may also recover tort damages. Tort damages include compensation for personal injury, pain and suffering, emotional distress, and possibly punitive damages.

Generally, **punitive damages** are not recoverable for breach of contract. They are recoverable, however, for certain tortious conduct that may be associated with the nonperformance of a contract. These actions include fraud, intentional conduct, and other egregious conduct. Punitive damages are in addition to actual damages and may be kept by the plaintiff. Punitive damages are awarded to punish the defendant, to deter the defendant from similar conduct in the future, and to set an example for others.

The major torts associated with contracts are *intentional interference with contractual relations* and *breach of the implied covenant of good faith and fair dealing*.

Intentional Interference with Contractual Relations

A party to a contract may sue any third person who intentionally interferes with the contract and causes that party injury. The third party does not have to have acted with malice or bad faith. This tort, which is known as the tort of **intentional interference with contractual relations**, usually arises when a third party induces a contracting party to breach a contract with another party. The following elements must be shown:

1. A valid, enforceable contract between the contracting parties
2. Third-party knowledge of this contract
3. Third-party inducement to breach the contract

A third party can contract with the breaching party without becoming liable for this tort if a contracting party has already breached the contract because the third party cannot be held to have induced a preexisting breach.

ETHICS SPOTLIGHT

Interference with a Contract

Ricardo E. Brown, Jr., known as "Kurupt," was an unknown teenage rap singer who lived with his father. In 1989, Lamont Brumfield, a promoter of young rappers, "discovered" Kurupt. Lamont introduced his brother Kenneth Brumfield, who owned a music publishing business, to Kurupt. Beginning in 1990, Lamont produced demos for Kurupt, set up photo shoots, booked him to sing at many clubs, and paid for

Kurupt's clothing and personal and living expenses. Kurupt lived with Lamont after Kurupt's father kicked him out of the house. In 1991, Lamont obtained recording work for Kurupt with the rap group SOS. In November 1991, Kurupt signed an exclusive recording agreement with Lamont's company, an exclusive publishing agreement with Kenneth's company, and a management agreement with Kenneth for an initial term of three years, with an additional option term. These contracts gave Kurupt 7 percent royalties on sales. The Brumfields spent at least $65,000 to support and promote Kurupt, often borrowing money from family and friends to do so.

Andre Young, known as Dr. Dre, invited Lamont, Kenneth, and Kurupt to a picnic, where he introduced them to Marion Knight, the owner of Death Row Records, Inc. The Brumfields and Kurupt made it clear to Dr. Dre and Knight that the Brumfields had exclusive contracts with Kurupt. After Kurupt performed at the picnic, Dr. Dre invited Kurupt to his house to record songs for Dr. Dre's album *Chronic*. In December 1992, *Chronic* was released by Death Row Records, Inc., and sold millions of copies. The Brumfields continued to promote Kurupt and to take care of his living expenses. When Dr. Dre invited Kurupt to go on tour to promote the *Chronic* album, Kurupt told the Brumfields that he was going to visit family in Philadelphia but instead went on tour for four weeks. In 1993, Kurupt worked on another

Death Row Records album. In May 1994, Kenneth exercised his option and renewed his management agreement with Kurupt. Despite the multimillion-dollar profit of the *Chronic* album, the Brumfields were paid nothing by Death Row Records. At the end of 1994, Death Row moved Kurupt out of the condominium he shared with Lamont and into a house. While cleaning out the condominium, Lamont found papers showing that Death Row Records had paid Kurupt advances commencing in April 1993.

The evidence showed that Kurupt had breached the contracts he had with the Brumfields and had earned approximately $1.5 million in royalties from Death Row records for his work on the *Chronic* album and many other albums. The court held that there was evidence that Death Row Records had caused Kurupt to breach these contracts and was therefore liable for the tort of intentional interference with a contract. The court held that defendant Death Row Records, Inc., had committed the tort of intentionally interfering with the contracts that the Brumfields had with rapper Kurupt. The court awarded $5,519,000 to the Brumfields, including $1.5 million in punitive damages to Lamont and $1 million in punitive damages to Kenneth. The judgment of the superior court was upheld by the court of appeals of California. *Brumfield v. Death Row Records, Inc.*, **Web** 2003 Cal. App. Unpub. Lexis 7843 (Court of Appeal of California)

Breach of the Implied Covenant of Good Faith and Fair Dealing

Several states have held that certain contracts contain an **implied covenant of good faith and fair dealing**. Under this covenant, the parties to a contract are not only held to the express terms of the contract but are also required to act in "good faith" and deal fairly in all respects in obtaining the objective of the contract. A breach of this implied covenant is a tort for which tort damages are recoverable. This tort, which is sometimes referred to as the **tort of bad faith**, is an evolving area of the law.

In the following case, the court found a bad faith tort and awarded punitive damages.

C A S E **14.7** *Bad Faith Tort*	**O'Neill v. Gallant Insurance Company** 769 N.E.2d 100, **Web** 2002 Ill. App. Lexis 311 (2002) Appellate Court of Illinois	

> 66 *Where an insurer is pursued for its refusal to settle a claim, "bad faith" lies in an insurer's failure to give at least equal consideration to the insured's interests when the insurer arrives at a decision on whether to settle the claim.* 99
>
> —Judge Clyde L. Kuehn

Facts

On Halloween Day, Christine Narvaez drove her automobile onto the parking lot of a busy supermarket. Narvaez had her two-year-old grandchild with her. The youngster was riding, unconstrained, in a booster seat. Narvaez saw a friend and decided to stop for a brief chat. She parked the car and exited the car, leaving the keys in the ignition and the motor running. The youngster crawled behind the wheel, slipped

the car into gear, and set it in motion. The car struck Marguerite O'Neill, a woman in her eighties, pinned her between the Narvaez car and another car, and slowly crushed the woman's trapped body.

O'Neill was pried loose and airlifted to a hospital trauma center. O'Neill suffered a crushed hip, a broken arm, and four cracked ribs, and she lost more than 40 percent of her blood supply as a result of internal bleeding. She spent one month in the hospital intensive care unit and had to be placed in a nursing home and was deprived of the ability to live independently.

Narvaez carried the $20,000 minimum amount of liability insurance allowed by law. She was insured by Gallant Insurance Company. O'Neill's medical bills totaled $105,000. O'Neill sued Narvaez and her insurance company, Gallant. O'Neill's attorney demanded the policy limit of $20,000 from Gallant in settlement of O'Neill's claim and offered a complete release from liability for Narvaez. Three Gallant insurance adjusters, its claims manager, and the lawyer of the law firm representing Gallant for the case all stated to John Moss, Gallant's executive vice president, that Gallant should accept the settlement offer. Moss rejected their advice and refused to settle the case.

One year later, on the eve of trial. Moss offered to settle for the $20,000 policy limit, but O'Neill then refused. The case went to trial, and the jury returned a verdict against Narvaez of $731,063. Gallant paid $20,000 of this amount, closed its file, and left Narvaez liable for the $711,063 excess judgment. To settle her debt to O'Neill, Narvaez assigned her claims against Gallant to O'Neill. O'Neill then sued Gallant for a bad faith tort for breaching the covenant of good faith and fair dealing that Gallant owed to Narvaez to settle the case. The jury found Gallant liable for a bad faith tort and awarded O'Neill $710,063 ($1,000 short of the judgment in the first trial) in actual damages and $2.3 million in punitive damages. Gallant appealed.

Issue

Was Gallant liable for a bad faith tort?

Language of the Court

Where an insurer is pursued for its refusal to settle a claim, "bad faith" lies in an insurer's failure to give at least equal consideration to the insured's interests when the insurer arrives at a decision on whether to settle the claim. A significant part of the evidence presented against Gallant consisted of the pattern of conduct engaged in by Gallant over the five years leading up to this bad-faith action. O'Neill presented 44 known cases where Gallant's Illinois customers suffered excess judgments after Gallant passed up the opportunity to settle within the policy limits. Most of the excess judgments occurred on John Moss's watch. The dollar amount by which the excess judgments exceeded policy limits totaled $10,849,313.

The jury's finding of bad faith was not against the manifest weight of the evidence. We must side with O'Neill and against Gallant on the extent to which the evidence established the existence of reprehensible conduct on the part of Narvaez's insurance provider. If the term "reprehensible" means shameful, *i.e.*, conduct deserving of severe reproach. Gallant's treatment of Narvaez and others who bought insurance from it was truly reprehensible.

Decision

The appellate court held that Gallant was liable for a bad faith tort and upheld the trial court's judgment awarding O'Neill $710,063 in actual damages and $2.3 million in punitive damages.

Law & Ethics Questions

1. Define the tort of breach of the implied covenant of good faith and fair dealing. Why is it called the "bad faith" tort?
2. **ETHICS** Did Gallant act ethically in this case?
3. **ETHICS** Does the implied covenant of good faith and fair dealing make insurance companies act more ethically toward their customers? Explain.

Web Exercises

1. **WEB** For the complete opinion of this case, go to *www.prenhall.com/cheesemancases*.
2. **WEB** Visit the website of the court of appeals of Illinois, at *www.state.il.us/court/appellatecourt*.
3. **WEB** Use *www.google.com* to find an article or a case that discusses a bad faith tort.

Chapter Summary

Performance and Breach, p. 365

Complete Performance

A party in complete performance renders performance exactly as required by the contract. That party's contractual duties are discharged.

Substantial Performance: Minor Breach

A party in substantial performance renders performance that deviates only slightly from the complete performance specified in the contract. There is a *minor breach*. The nonbreaching party may recover damages caused by the breach.

Inferior Performance: Material Breach

A party in inferior performance fails to perform express or implied contractual duties that impair or destroy the essence of the contract. There is a *material breach*. The nonbreaching party may either (1) rescind the contract and recover restitution or (2) affirm the contract and recover damages.

Anticipatory Breach

In an anticipatory breach, one contracting party informs the other party—by express words or by conduct—that he or she will not perform his or her contractual duties when due. This gives an immediate cause of action to the nonbreaching party to sue for breach of contract. It is also called *anticipatory repudiation*.

Monetary Damages, p. 368

Compensatory Damages

Compensatory damages are intended to compensate a nonbreaching party for the loss of a contract. They restore the "benefit of the bargain" to the nonbreaching party as if the contract had been fully performed.

The law places a duty on a nonbreaching party to take reasonable efforts to avoid or reduce the resulting damages from a breach of contract. To mitigate a breach of an employment contract, the nonbreaching party must only accept "comparable" employment.

Consequential Damages

Consequential damages are foreseeable damages that arise from circumstances outside the contract and of which the breaching party either knew or had reason to know. They are also called *special damages*.

Liquidated Damages

Liquidated damages are damages payable upon breach of contract that are agreed on in advance by the contracting parties. Liquidated damages substitute for actual damages. For a liquidated damages clause to be lawful, the following two conditions must be met:

1. The actual damages must be extremely difficult or impracticable to determine.
2. The liquidated amount must be a reasonable estimate of the harm that would result from the breach.

A liquidated damages clause is considered a *penalty* if actual damages are clearly determinable in advance or the liquidated damages are excessive or unconscionable. A penalty is unenforceable, and the nonbreaching party may recover actual damages.

Nominal Damages

Nominal damages are small damages awarded to a nonbreaching party who has suffered no financial loss because of the defendant's breach of contract. They are usually awarded on principle.

Enforcement of Remedies

If a nonbreaching party brings a successful lawsuit against a breaching party to a contract, the court will enter a *judgment* in his or her favor.

Rescission and Restitution, p. 375

Rescission is an action by a nonbreaching party to undo a contract. It is available upon the material breach of a contract. The parties must make restitution of the consideration they have received from the other party. Rescission and restitution restore the parties to the positions they occupied prior to the contract.

Equitable Remedies, p. 377

Equitable remedies are available if a nonbreaching party cannot be adequately compensated by a legal remedy or to prevent unjust enrichment.

Specific Performance

Specific performance requires the breaching party to perform his or her contractual duties. It is available only if the subject matter of the contract is *unique*.

Reformation

Reformation permits the court to rewrite a contract to express the parties' true intention. It is available to correct clerical and mathematical errors.

Injunction

An injunction is a court order that prohibits a person from doing a certain act. The requesting party must show that he or she will suffer irreparable injury if the injunction is not granted.

Torts Associated With Contracts, p. 380
Intentional Interference with Contractual Relations

The tort of intentional interference with contractual relations arises when a third party intentionally interferes with another party's contract and induces the other party to that contract to breach it, causing the nonbreaching party injury.

Breach of the Implied Covenant of Good Faith and Fair Dealing

The tort of breach of the implied covenant of good faith and fair dealing arises when a party to a contract does not act in good faith or fails to deal fairly in achieving the object of the contract. This duty is implied in only certain contracts (e.g., insurance contracts). It is also called the *tort of bad faith*.

1. *Compensatory damages.* These damages include compensation for personal injury, pain and suffering, emotional distress, and other injuries caused by the defendant's tortious conduct.
2. *Punitive damages.* These damages are recoverable against a defendant for intentional or egregious conduct. They are awarded to punish the defendant, to deter the defendant from similar conduct in the future, and to set an example for others.

Test Review Terms and Concepts

Anticipatory breach (anticipatory repudiation) 367
Breach of contract 365
Compensatory damages 368
Complete performance (strict performance) 365
Consequential damages (special damages) 371
Equitable remedies 377
Executed contract 365
Implied covenant of good faith and fair dealing 381

Inferior performance 366
Injunction 379
Intentional interference with contractual relations 380
Liquidated damages 371
Material breach 366
Minor breach 366
Mitigation of damages 369
Monetary damages 368
Nominal damages 374
Penalty 371
Punitive damages 380

Reformation 379
Rescission 375
Restitution 375
Specific performance 377
Substantial performance 366
Tender of performance 365
Tort 380
Tort of bad faith 381
Writ of attachment 375
Writ of garnishment 375

Case Problems

14.1 Performance: Louis Haeuser, who owned several small warehouses, contracted with Wallace C. Drennen, Inc. (Drennen), to construct a road to the warehouses. The contract price was $42,324. After Drennen completed the work, some cracks appeared in the road, causing improper drainage. In addition, "birdbaths" that accumulated water appeared in the road. When Haeuser refused to pay, Drennen sued to recover the full contract price. Haeuser filed a cross complaint to recover the cost of repairing the road. Who wins? *Wallace C. Drennen, Inc. v. Haeuser*, 402 So.2d 771, **Web** 1981 La. App. Lexis 4453 (Court of Appeal of Louisiana)

14.2 Anticipatory Repudiation: Muhammad Ali (Ali), a professional heavyweight boxer, successfully defended his heavyweight boxing championship of the world by defeating Ken Norton. Shortly after the fight, Ali held a press conference and, as he had done on several occasions before, announced his retirement from boxing. At that time, Ali had beaten every challenger except Duane Bobick, whom he had not yet fought. Subsequently, Madison Square Garden Boxing, Inc. (MSGB), a fight promoter, offered Ali $2.5 million if he would fight Bobick. Ali agreed, stating, "We are back in business again." MSGB and Ali signed a fighters' agreement, and MSGB paid Ali $125,000 advance payment.

The fight was to take place in Madison Square Garden. Three months before the fight was to take place, Ali told MSGB that he was retiring from boxing and would not fight Bobick in February. Must MSGB wait until the date performance is due to sue Ali for breach of contract? *Madison Square Garden Boxing, Inc. v. Muhammad Ali*, 430 F.Supp. 679, **Web** 1977 U.S. Dist. Lexis 16101 (United States District Court for the Northern District of Illinois)

14.3 Damages: Hawaiian Telephone Company entered into a contract with Microform Data Systems, Inc. (Microform), for Microform to provide a computerized assistance system that would handle 15,000 calls per hour with a one-second response time and with a "nonstop" feature to allow automatic recovery from any component failure. The contract called for installation of the host computer no later than mid-February of the next year. Microform was not able to meet the initial installation date, and at that time, it was determined that Microform was at least nine months away from providing a system that met contract specifications. Hawaiian Telephone canceled the contract and sued Microform for damages. Did Microform materially breach the contract to allow recovery of damages? *Hawaiian Telephone Co. v. Microform Data Systems Inc.*, 829 F.2d 919, **Web** 1987 U.S. App. Lexis 13425 (United States Court of Appeals for the Ninth Circuit)

14.4 Damages: Raquel Welch was a movie actress who appeared in about 30 films over a 15-year period. She was considered a sex symbol, and her only serious dramatic role was as a roller derby queen in *Kansas City Bomber*. During that time period, Michael Phillips and David Ward developed a film package based on the John Steinbeck novella *Cannery Row*. Metro-Goldwyn-Mayer Film Company (MGM) accepted to produce the project and entered into a contract with Welch to play the leading female character, a prostitute named Suzy. At 40 years old, Welch relished the chance to direct her career toward more serious roles. Welch was to receive $250,000 from MGM, with payment being divided into weekly increments during filming. Filming began, but three weeks later MGM fired Welch and replaced her with another actress, Debra Winger. Welch sued MGM to recover the balance of $194,444 that remained unpaid under the contract. Who wins? *Welch v. Metro-Goldwyn-Mayer Film Co.*, 207 Cal.App.3d 164, 254 Cal.Rptr. 645, **Web** 1988 Cal. App. Lexis 1202 (Court of Appeal of California)

14.5 Damages: Ptarmigan Investment Company (Ptarmigan), a partnership, entered into a contract with Gundersons, Inc. (Gundersons), a South Dakota corporation in the business of golf course construction. The contract provided that Gundersons would construct a golf course for Ptarmigan for a contract price of $1,294,129. Gundersons immediately started work and completed about one-third of the work by about three months later, when bad weather forced cessation of most work. Ptarmigan paid Gundersons for the work to that date. In the following spring, Ptarmigan ran out of funds and was unable to pay for the completion of the golf course. Gundersons sued Ptarmigan and its individual partners to recover the lost profits that it would have made on the remaining two-thirds of the contract. Can Gundersons recover these lost profits as damages? *Gundersons, Inc. v. Ptarmigan Investment Company*, 678 P.2d 1061, **Web** 1983 Colo. App. Lexis 1133 (Court of Appeals of Colorado)

14.6 Liquidated Damages: H. S. Perlin Company, Inc. (Perlin), and Morse Signal Devices of San Diego (Morse) entered into a contract whereby Morse agreed to provide burglar and fire alarm service to Perlin's coin and stamp store. Perlin paid $50 per month for this service. The contract contained a liquidated damages clause limiting Morse's liability to $250 for any losses incurred by Perlin based on Morse's failure of service. Six years after the burglary system was installed, a burglary occurred at Perlin's store. Before entering the store, the burglars cut a telephone line that ran from the burglar system in Perlin's store to Morse's central location. When the line was cut, a signal indicated the interruption of service at Morse's central station. Inexplicably, Morse took no further steps to investigate the interruption of service at Perlin's store. The burglars stole stamps and coins with a wholesale value of $958,000, and Perlin did not have insurance against this loss. Perlin sued Morse to recover damages. Is the liquidated damages clause enforceable? *H.S. Perlin Company, Inc. v. Morse Signal Devices of San Diego*, 209 Cal.App.3d 1289, 258 Cal.Rptr. 1, **Web** 1989 Cal. App. Lexis 400 (Court of Appeal of California)

14.7 Liquidated Damages: United Mechanical Contractors, Inc. (UMC), an employer, agreed to provide a pension plan for its unionized workers. UMC was to make monthly payments into a pension fund administered by the Idaho Plumbers and Pipefitters Health and Welfare Fund (Fund). Payments were due by the 15th of each month. The contract between UMC and the Fund contained a liquidated damages clause which provided that if payments due from UMC were received later than the 20th of the month, liquidated damages of 20 percent of the required contribution would be assessed against UMC. In one month, the fund received UMC's payment on the 24th. The Fund sued UMC to recover $9,245.23 in liquidated damages. Is the liquidated damages clause enforceable? *Idaho Plumbers and Pipefitters Health and Welfare Fund v. United Mechanical Contractors, Inc.*, 875 F.2d 212, **Web** 1989 U.S. App. Lexis 14528 (United States Court of Appeals for the Ninth Circuit)

14.8 Specific Performance: Liz Claiborne, Inc. (Claiborne), is a large maker of sportswear in the United States and a well-known name in fashion, with sales of over $1 billion per year. Claiborne distributes its products through 9,000 retail outlets in the United States. Avon Products, Inc. (Avon), is a major producer of fragrances, toiletries, and cosmetics, with annual sales of more than $3 billion a year.

Claiborne, which desired to promote its well-known name on perfumes and cosmetics, entered into a joint venture with Avon whereby Claiborne would make available its names, trademarks, and marketing experience, and Avon would engage in the procurement and manufacture of the fragrances, toiletries, and cosmetics. The parties would equally share the financial requirements of the joint venture. During its first year of operation, the joint venture had sales of more than $16 million. In the second year, sales increased to $26 million, making it one of the fastest-growing fragrance and cosmetic lines in the country. One year later, Avon sought to "uncouple" the joint venture. Avon thereafter refused to procure and manufacture the line of fragrances and cosmetics for the joint venture. When Claiborne could not obtain the necessary fragrances and cosmetics from any other source for the fall/Christmas season, Claiborne sued Avon for breach of contract, seeking specific performance of the contract by Avon. Is specific performance an appropriate remedy in this case? *Liz Claiborne, Inc. v. Avon Products, Inc.*, 141 A.D.2d 329, 530 N.Y.S.2d 425, **Web** 1988 N.Y. App. Div. Lexis 6423 (Supreme Court of New York)

14.9 Injunction: Anita Baker, a then-unknown singer, signed a multiyear recording contract with Beverly Glen Music, Inc. (Beverly Glen). Baker recorded for Beverly Glen a record album that was moderately successful. After having some difficulties with Beverly Glen, Baker was offered a considerably more lucrative contract by Warner Communications, Inc. (Warner). Baker accepted the Warner offer and informed Beverly Glen that she would not complete their contract because she had entered into an agreement with Warner. Beverly Glen sued Baker and Warner, and it sought an injunction to prevent Baker from performing as a singer for Warner. Is an injunction an appropriate remedy in this case? *Beverly Glen Music, Inc. v. Warner Communications, Inc.*, 178 Cal.App.3d 1142, 224 Cal.Rptr. 260, **Web** 1986 Cal. App. Lexis 2729 (Court of Appeal of California)

14.10 Intentional Interference with Contractual Relations: Pacific Gas and Electric Company (PG & E) entered into a contract with Placer County Water Agency (Agency) to purchase hydroelectric power generated by the Agency's Middle Fork American River Project. The contract was not terminable until 2013. As energy prices rose during the 1970s, the contract became extremely valuable to PG & E. The price PG & E paid for energy under the contract was much lower than the cost of energy from other sources. Ten year later, Bear Stearns & Company (Bear Stearns), an investment bank and securities underwriting firm, learned of the Agency's power contract with PG & E. Bear Stearns offered to assist the Agency in an effort to terminate the power contract with PG & E in exchange for a share of the Agency's subsequent profits and the right to underwrite any new securities issued by the Agency. Bear Stearns also agreed to pay the legal fees incurred by the Agency in litigation concerning the attempt to get out of the PG & E contract. Who wins and why? *Pacific Gas and Electric Company v. Bear Stearns & Company*, 50 Cal.3d 1118, 791 P.2d 587, 270 Cal.Rptr. 1, **Web** 1990 Cal. Lexis 2119 (Supreme Court of California)

Ethics Issues

14.11 Ethics: Walgreen Company began operating a pharmacy in the Southgate Mall in Milwaukee when the mall opened. It had a lease for a 30-year term that contained an exclusivity clause in which the landlord, Sara Creek Property Company (Sara Creek), promised not to lease space in the mall to anyone else who wanted to operate a pharmacy or a store containing a pharmacy. With 11 years left on the Walgreen–Sara Creek lease, after its anchor tenant went broke, Sara Creek informed Walgreen that it intended to lease the anchor tenant space to Phar-Mor Corporation. Phar-Mor, a "deep discount" chain, would occupy 100,000 square feet, of which 12,000 square feet would be occupied by a pharmacy the same size as Walgreen's. The entrances to the two stores would be within a few hundred feet of each other. Walgreen sued Sara Creek for breach of contract and sought a permanent injunction against Sara Creek's leasing the anchor premises to Phar-Mor. Do the facts of this case justify the issuance of a permanent injunction? Did Sara Creek act ethically in not living up to the contract with Walgreen? *Walgreen Co. v.*

Sara Creek Property Co., 966 F.2d 273, **Web** 1992 U.S. App. Lexis 14847 (United States Court of Appeals for the Seventh Circuit)

14.12 Ethics: Rosina Crisci owned an apartment building in which Mrs. DiMare was a tenant. One day while DiMare was descending a wooden staircase on the outside of the apartment building, she fell through the staircase and was left hanging 15 feet above the ground until she was saved. Crisci had a $10,000 liability insurance policy on the building from the Security Insurance Company (Security) of New Haven, Connecticut. DiMare sued Crisci and Security for $400,000 for physical injuries and psychosis suffered from the fall. Prior to trial, DiMare agreed to take $10,000 in settlement of the case. Security refused this settlement offer. DiMare reduced her settlement offer to $9,000, of which Crisci offered to pay $2,500. Security again refused to settle the case. The case proceeded to trial, and the jury awarded DiMare and her husband $110,000. Security paid $10,000, pursuant to the insurance contract, and Crisci had to pay the difference. Crisci, a widow of 70 years of age, had to sell her assets, became dependent on her relatives, declined in physical health, and suffered from hysteria and suicide attempts. Crisci sued Security for tort damages for breach of the implied covenant of good faith and fair dealing. Did Security act in bad faith? *Crisci v. Security Insurance Company of New Haven, Connecticut*, 66 Cal.App.2d 425, 426 P.2d 173, 58 Cal.Rptr. 13, **Web** 1967 Cal. Lexis 313 (Supreme Court of California)

IRAC Writing Assignment

Read **Case A-14** in Appendix A [*E. B. Harvey & Company, Inc. v. Protective Systems, Inc.*]. Use the IRAC method to prepare a written analysis of the case.

Endnotes

1. *Restatement (Second) of Contracts*, Section 235(2).
2. *Restatement (Second) of Contracts*, Section 241.
3. *Restatement (Second) of Contracts*, Section 253.
4. *Restatement (Second) of Contracts*, Section 356(1).
5. *Restatement (Second) of Contracts*, Section 370.
6. *Restatement (Second) of Contracts*, Section 359.

CHAPTER 15

E-Contracts, Internet Law, and Cyber Crimes

> **"** *Through the use of chat rooms, any person with a phone line can become a town crier with a voice that resonates farther than it could from any soapbox. Through the use of Web pages, mail exploders, and newsgroups, the same individual can become a pamphleteer.* **"**
>
> —JUSTICE STEVENS
> Reno v. American Civil Liberties Union, 521 U.S. 844 (1997)

CHAPTER OBJECTIVES

After studying this chapter, you should be able to:

1. Describe Internet domain names and how domain names are protected by the Anticybersquatting Consumer Protection Act.
2. Define *e-contract* and *software license*.
3. Describe the provisions of the Uniform Computer Information Transactions Act (UCITA).
4. Describe the provisions of the Electronic Signature in Global and National Commerce Act.
5. Describe the federal laws that protect against cyber crimes.

CHAPTER CONTENTS

- Introduction to Internet Law and E-Commerce
- The Internet
- Domain Names
- E-Contracts
- Software and E-Licensing
- Online Privacy
- Cyber Crimes
- Chapter Summary
- Test Review Terms and Concepts
- Case Problems
- Ethics Issues
- IRAC Writing Assignment

   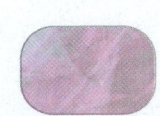 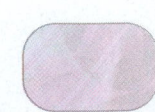

Introduction to Internet Law and E-Commerce

The use of the Internet and the World Wide Web and the sale of goods and services through **electronic commerce**, or **e-commerce** have exploded. Large and small businesses sell goods and services over the Internet through **websites**. Consumers and businesses can purchase almost any good or service they want over the Internet, using such sites as Amazon.com, eBay, and others. Businesses and individuals may register *domain names* to use on the Internet. Anyone who infringes on these rights may be stopped from doing so and is liable for damages.

In addition, software and information may be licensed either by physically purchasing the software or information and installing it on a computer or by merely downloading the software or information directly to a computer.

Many legal scholars and lawyers argued that traditional rules of contract law do not adequately meet the needs of Internet transactions and software and information licensing. These concerns led to an effort to create new contract law for electronic transactions. After much debate, the National Conference of Commissioners on Uniform State Laws developed the *Uniform Computer Information Transactions Act (UCITA)*. This model act provides uniform and comprehensive rules for contracts involving computer information transactions and software and information licenses.

The federal government has also enacted many federal statutes that regulate the Internet and e-commerce. Federal law has been passed that regulates the Internet and protects personal rights while using the Internet. In addition, many new federal criminal statutes have been enacted to protect against cyber crimes.

This chapter covers Internet law, domain names, e-contracts, licensing of software, privacy laws, and criminal laws that regulate the Internet and online commerce.

Internet Law

The development of Internet and electronic commerce has required courts to apply existing law to online commerce transactions and spurred the federal Congress and state legislatures to enact new laws that govern the formation and enforcement of e-contracts and protect Internet users from invasion of privacy and cyber crimes.

The Internet

The **Internet**, or **Net**, is a collection of millions of computers that provide a network of electronic connections between the computers. Hundreds of millions of computers are connected to the Internet. The Internet's evolution helped usher in the Information Age of today. Individuals and businesses use the Internet for communication of information and data.

The World Wide Web

The **World Wide Web** consists of millions of computers that support a standard set of rules for the exchange of information called Hypertext Transfer Protocol (HTTP). Web-based documents are formatted using common coding languages. Businesses and individuals can hook up to the Web by registering with a service such as America Online (AOL).

Individuals and businesses can have their own websites. A website is composed of electronic documents known as webpages. Websites and webpages are stored on servers throughout the world, which are operated by **Internet service providers (ISPs)**. They are viewed by using Web browsing software such as Microsoft Internet Explorer and Netscape Navigator. Each website has a unique online address.

The Web has made it extremely attractive to conduct commercial activities online. Companies such as Amazon.com and eBay are e-commerce powerhouses that sell all sorts of goods and services. Existing brick-and-mortar companies, such as Wal-Mart, Merrill Lynch, and Dell Inc., sell their goods and services online as well. E-commerce over the Web will continue to grow dramatically each year.

INTERNET AND TECHNOLOGY
Free Speech and the Internet

> 66 *Through the use of chat rooms, any person with a phone line can become a town crier with a voice that resonates farther than it could from any soapbox.* 99
>
> —Justice Stevens

In 1997, the U.S. Supreme Court decided *Reno v. American Civil Liberties Union*, a major case involving free-speech rights over the Internet. In the case, the U.S. Supreme Court held that portions of a federal statute enacted by Congress, the Communications Decency Act (CDA), that was designed to protect minors from "indecent transmissions" over the Internet violated the Free Speech Clause of the First Amendment to the U.S. Constitution.

In its decision, the Supreme Court recognized the importance and uniqueness of the Internet and issued an opinion guaranteeing the users of the Internet the highest constitutional free-speech protection. An excerpt of the language from the U.S. Supreme Court's opinion follows:

The Internet is an international network of interconnected computers. The Internet has experienced extraordinary growth. Individuals can obtain access to the Internet from many different sources, generally hosts themselves or entities with a host affiliation. Most colleges and universities provide access for their students and faculty; many corporations provide their employees with access through an office network. Several major national "online services" offer access to their own extensive proprietary networks as well as a link to the much larger resources of the Internet.

Anyone with access to the Internet may take advantage of a wide variety of communication and information retrieval methods. These methods are constantly evolving and difficult to categorize precisely. But, as presently constituted, those most relevant to this case are electronic mail ("e-mail"), automatic mailing list services ("mail exploders," sometimes referred to as "listservs"), "newsgroups," "chat rooms," and the "World Wide Web." All of these methods can be used to transmit text; most can transmit sound, pictures, and moving video images. Taken together, these tools constitute a unique medium—known to its users as "cyberspace"—located in no particular geographical location but available to anyone, anywhere in the world, with access to the Internet.

Each medium of expression may present its own problems. Thus, some of our cases have recognized special justifications for regulation of the broadcast media that are not applicable to other speakers. In these cases, the Court relied on the history of extensive government regulation of the broadcast medium, the scarcity of available frequencies at its inception, and its "invasive" nature. Those factors are not present in cyberspace. Neither before nor after the enactment of the CDA have the vast democratic fora of the Internet been subject to the type of government supervision and regulation that has attended the broadcast industry. Moreover, the Internet is not as "invasive" as radio or television. The District Court specifically found that "communications over the Internet do not invade an individual's home or appear on one's computer screen unbidden. Users seldom encounter content by accident." It also found that "almost all sexually explicit images are preceded by warnings as to the content," and cited testimony that "odds are slim that a user would come across a sexually explicit site by accident."

Unlike the conditions that prevailed when Congress first authorized regulation of the broadcast spectrum, the Internet can hardly be considered a "scarce" expressive commodity. It provides relatively unlimited, low-cost capacity for communication of all kinds. This dynamic, multifaceted category of communication includes not only traditional print and news services, but also audio, video, and still images, as well as interactive, real-time dialogue. Through the use of chat rooms, any person with a phone line can become a town crier with a voice that resonates farther than it could from any soapbox. Through the use of Web pages, mail exploders, and newsgroups, the same individual can become a pamphleteer. As the District Court found, "the content on the Internet is as diverse as human thought."

Systems have been developed to help parents control the material that may be available on a home computer with Internet access. A system may either limit a computer's access to an approved list of sources that have been identified as containing no adult material, it may block designated inappropriate sites, or it may attempt to block messages containing identifiable objectionable features. Although parental control software currently can screen for certain suggestive words or for known sexually explicit sites, it cannot now screen for sexually explicit images. Nevertheless, the evidence indicates that a reasonably effective method by which parents can prevent their children from accessing sexually explicit and other material which parents may believe is inappropriate for their children will soon be available.

The Government may not reduce the adult population to only what is fit for children. The CDA, casting a far darker shadow over free speech, threatens to torch a large segment of the Internet community. Notwithstanding the legitimacy and importance of the congressional goal of protecting children from harmful materials, we agree with the three-judge District Court that the statute abridges "the freedom of speech" protected by the First Amendment.

Reno v. American Civil Liberties Union, 521 U.S. 844, 117 S.Ct. 2329, 138 L.Ed.2d 874, **Web** 1997 U.S. Lexis 4037 (Supreme Court of the United States)

Law & Ethics Questions

1. What did the federal Communications Decency Act (CDA) enacted by Congress try to do?

2. **ETHICS** Should parents be responsible for their children's access to the Internet?

3. Do you agree with the following statement of the U.S. Supreme Court: "The Government may not reduce the adult population to only what is fit for children. The CDA . . . threatens to torch a large segment of the Internet community"?

Web Exercises

1. **WEB** For the complete opinion of this case, go to *www.prenhall.com/cheesemancases*.

2. **WEB** Visit the website of the U.S. Supreme Court, at *www.supremecourtus.gov*. Can you find any documents that relate to this case?

3. **WEB** Visit the website of the attorney general of the United States, at *www.usdoj.gov/ag*. What is the function of the attorney general? Who is the current attorney general?

4. **WEB** Visit the website of the American Civil Liberties Union, at *www.aclu.org*. What is an issue that the ACLU is currently involved in?

E-Mail

Electronic mail, or **e-mail**, is one of the most widely used applications for communication over the Internet. Using e-mail, individuals around the world can instantaneously communicate in electronic writing with one another. Individuals can have e-mail addresses that identify them by unique addresses. E-mail will continue to grow in use in the future as it replaces some telephone and paper correspondence and increases new communication between persons.

In the following case, the court addressed the liability of an ISP.

CASE 15.1

Internet Law

John Doe v. GTE Corporation

347 F.3d 655, **Web** 2003 U.S. App. Lexis 21345 (2003)
United States Court of Appeals for the Seventh Circuit

> **"** *A web host cannot be classified as an aider and abettor of criminal activities conducted through access to the Internet.* **"**
>
> —Judge Easterbrook

Facts

Someone secretly took video cameras into the locker room and showers of the Illinois State football team. Videotapes showing these undressed players were displayed on a website operated by Franco Productions. The Internet name concealed the name of the person responsible. The GTE Corporation, an ISP, provided a high-speed connection and storage space on its server so that the content of the website could be accessed. The nude images passed over GTE's network between Franco Productions and its customers. The football players sued Franco Productions and GTE for monetary damages.

Franco Productions defaulted when it could not be located. Franco Productions was ordered to pay over $500 million in damages, though there is little hope of collection. The U.S. District Court dismissed the case against GTE. The football players appealed.

Issue

Is GTE Corporation, as the ISP, liable for damages to the plaintiff football players?

Language of the Court

The district court's order dismissing the complaint rests on 47 U.S.C. Section 230(c)(1), a part of the federal Communications Decency Act of 1996. This subsection provides: "No provider or user of an interactive computer service shall be treated as the publisher or speaker of any information provided by another information content provider." Just as the telephone company is not liable as an aider and abettor for tapes or narcotics sold by phone, and the Postal Service is not liable for tapes sold (and delivered) by mail, so a web host cannot be classified as an aider and abettor of criminal activities conducted through access to the Internet. GTE is not a "publisher or speaker" as Section 230(c)(1) uses those terms. Therefore, GTE cannot be liable under any state-law theory to the persons harmed by Franco's material.

Decision

The Court of Appeals held that GTE Corporation, as an ISP, was not liable for the nude videos of the football players transmitted over its system by Franco Productions. The Court of Appeals affirmed the District Court's order, dismissing the plaintiff football players' lawsuit against GTE.

Law & Ethics Questions

1. Why do you think Congress enacted Section 230(c)(1) of the Communications Decency Act? Explain.

2. **ETHICS** Did the owner of Franco Productions act ethically in this case?

3. Will the taking and posting on the Internet of unconsented-to photographs of others escalate? Explain.

Web Exercises

1. **WEB** For the complete opinion of this case, go to *www.prenhall.com/cheesemancases*.

2. **WEB** Visit the website of the U.S. Court of Appeals for the Seventh Circuit, at *www.ca7.uscourts.gov*.

3. **WEB** Go to *www.google.com* to find an article that discusses free speech over the Internet. Read it.

Domain Names

Most businesses conduct e-commerce by using websites that can be located on the Internet under domain names. Each website is identified by a unique Internet **domain name**.

Example   The domain name for the publisher of this book is *www.prenhall.com*.

Domain names need to be registered. The first step in registering a domain name is to determine whether any other party already owns the name. For this purpose, InterNIC maintains a "Whois" database that contains the domain names that have been registered. The InterNIC website is located online at *www.internic.net*.

Domain names can be registered at Network Solutions, Inc.'s, website, which is located at *www.networksolutions.com*, as well as at other sites. An applicant must complete a registration form, which can be done online. It costs less than $50 to register a domain name for one year, and the fee may be paid by credit card online.

The most commonly used top-level extensions for domain names are set forth in Exhibit 15.1.

> It will be of little avail to the people, that the laws are made by men of their own choice, if the laws be so voluminous that they cannot be read, or so incoherent that they cannot be understood.
>
> Alexander Hamilton
> *The Federalist Papers (1788)*

EXHIBIT 15.1

Commonly Used Top-Level Extensions for Domain Names

.com	This extension represents the word *commercial* and is the most widely used extension in the world. Most businesses prefer a .com domain name because it is a highly recognized business symbol.
.net	This extension represents the word *network*, and it is most commonly used by ISPs, Web-hosting companies, and other businesses that are directly involved in the infrastructure of the Internet. Some businesses also choose domain names with a .net extension.
.org	This extension represents the word *organization* and is primarily used by nonprofit groups and trade associations.

.info	This extension signifies a resource website. It is an unrestricted global name that may be used by businesses, individuals, and organizations.
.biz	This extension is used for small-business websites.
.us	This extension is for U.S. websites. Many businesses choose this extension, which is a relatively new extension.
.cc	This extension was originally the country code for Coco Keeling Islands, but it is now unrestricted and may be registered by anyone from any country. It is often registered by businesses.
.bz	This extension was originally the country code for Belize, but it is now unrestricted and may be registered by anyone from any country. It is commonly used by small businesses.
.name	This extension is for individuals, who can use it to register personalized domain names.
.museum	This extension enables museums, museum associations, and museum professionals to register websites.
.coop	This extension represents the word *cooperative* and may be used by cooperative associations around the world.
.aero	This extension is exclusively reserved for the aviation community. It enables organizations and individuals in that community to reserve websites.
.pro	This extension is available to professionals, such as doctors, lawyers, and consultants.
.edu	This extension is for educational institutions.

Web Exercises

1. **WEB** Go to *www.networksolutions.com*. See if your name is available with the .com and .name extensions.

2. **WEB** Think up a name that you would like to use for a business. Go to *www.networksolutions.com* and see if this business name is available with the .com extension.

INTERNET AND TECHNOLOGY
The Anticybersquatting Consumer Protection Act

In November 1999, the U.S. Congress enacted, and the president signed, the **Anticybersquatting Consumer Protection Act**.[1] The act was specifically aimed at cybersquatters who register Internet domain names of famous companies and people and hold them hostage by demanding ransom payments from the famous company or person.

In the past, trademark law was of little help in this area, either because the famous person's name was not trademarked or because, even if the name was trademarked, trademark law required distribution of goods or services to find infringement, and most cybersquatters did not distribute goods or services but merely sat on the Internet domain name.

The 1999 act has two fundamental requirements: (1) The name must be famous, and (2) the domain name must have been registered in bad faith. Thus, the law prohibits the act of cybersquatting itself if it is done in *bad faith*.

The first issue in applying the statute is whether the domain name is someone else's famous name. Trademarked names qualify; non-trademarked names—such as those of famous actors, actresses, singers, sports stars, politicians, and such—are also protected. In determining bad faith, the law provides that courts may consider the extent to which the domain name resembles the holder's name or the famous person's name, whether goods or services are sold under the name, the holder's offer to sell or transfer the name, and whether the holder has acquired multiple Internet domain names of famous companies and persons.

The act provides for the issuance of cease-and-desist orders and injunctions by the court. In addition, the law specifies monetary penalties: A plaintiff has the option of seeking statutory damages of between $1,000 and $300,000 in lieu of proving damages. The Anticybersquatting Consumer Protection Act gives owners of trademarks and persons with famous names a weapon to attack the kidnapping of Internet domain names by cyberpirates.

Example The Academy Award–winning actress Julia Roberts won back the domain name *juliaroberts.com* after it had been registered in bad faith by another party. The singer Sting was not so lucky because the word *sting* is generic, allowing someone else to initially register and keep the domain name *sting.com*. Sting was able to acquire the domain name and it is now the artists main page.

In the following case, the court applied the federal anticybersquatting act.

C A S E **15.2**
Domain Name

E. & J. Gallo Winery v. Spider Webs Ltd.

286 F.3d 270, **Web** 2002 U.S. App. Lexis 5928 (2002)
United States Court of Appeals for the Fifth Circuit

❝*Spider Webs has no intellectual property rights or trademark in the name "ernestandjuliogallo," aside from its registered domain name.*❞

—Judge Jolly

Facts

Ernest & Julio Gallo Winery (Gallo) is a famous maker of wines that is located in California. The company registered the trademark "Ernest & Julio Gallo" in 1964 with the U.S. Patent and Trademark Office. The company has spent over $500 million promoting its brand name and has sold more than 4 billion bottles of wine. Its name has taken on a secondary meaning as a famous trademark name. In 1999, Steve, Pierce, and Fred Thumann created Spider Webs Ltd., a limited partnership, to register Internet domain names. Spider Webs registered more than 2,000 Internet domain names, including *www.ernestandjuliogallo .com*. Spider Webs is in the business of selling domain names. Gallo filed suit against Spider Webs Ltd. and the Thumanns, alleging violation of the federal Anticybersquatting Consumer Protection Act (ACPA). The U.S. District Court held in favor of Gallo and ordered Spider Webs to transfer the domain name *www.ernestandjuliogallo.com* to Gallo. Spider Webs Ltd. appealed.

Issue

Did Spider Webs Ltd. and the Thumanns act in bad faith in registering the Internet domain name *www.ernestandjuliogallo.com*?

Language of the Court

Spider Webs does not appeal the holdings that Gallo had a valid registration in its mark, that the mark is famous and distinctive, and that the domain name registered by Spider Webs is identical or confusingly similar to Gallo's mark. However, Spider Webs argues that they did not act with a "bad faith intent to profit," as required by the ACPA.

Spider Webs has no intellectual property rights or trademark in the name "ernestandjuliogallo," aside from its registered domain name. The domain name does not contain the name of Spider Webs or any of the other defendants. Spider Webs had no prior use or any current use of the domain name in connection with the bona fide offering of goods or services. Steve Thumann admitted that the domain name was valuable and that they hoped Gallo would contact them so that they could "assist" Gallo in some way. There is uncontradicted evidence that Spider Webs was engaged in commerce in the selling of domain names and that they hoped to sell this domain name some day.

There was evidence presented that Gallo's mark is distinctive and famous. Further, Gallo registered the mark, which is a family name, thirty-eight years ago, and other courts have found that "'Gallo' has clearly become associated with wine in the United States such that its evolution to 'secondary meaning' status may not be seriously questioned." The circumstances of this case all indicate that Spider Webs knew Gallo had a famous mark in which Gallo had built up goodwill, and that they hoped to profit from this by registering "ernestandjuliogallo.com" and waiting for Gallo to contact them so they could "assist" Gallo. In sum, the factors strongly support a finding of bad faith.

Decision

The U.S. Court of Appeals held that the name "Ernest and Julio Gallo" was a famous trademark name and that Spider Webs Ltd. and the Thumanns acted in bad faith when they registered the Internet domain name *www.ernestandjuliogallo.com*. The U.S. Court of Appeals upheld the U.S. District Court's decision, ordering the defendants to transfer the domain name to plaintiff E. & J. Gallo Winery.

Law & Ethics Questions

1. What does the Anticybersquatting Consumer Protection Act (ACPA) provide? Explain.

2. **ETHICS** Did the defendants act ethically in registering so many Internet domain names? What was the motive of the defendants?

3. How valuable is a company's trademark name? Does the ACPA protect that value? Explain.

Web Exercises

1. **WEB** To find the complete opinion of this case, go to *www.prenhall.com/cheesemancases*.

2. **WEB** Visit the website of the U.S. Court of Appeals for the Fifth Circuit, at *www.ca5.uscourts.gov*.

3. **WEB** Visit the website of the E. & J. Gallo Winery, at *www.ernestandjuliogallo.com*.

INTERNET AND TECHNOLOGY
Armani Outmaneuvered for Domain Name

G. A. Modefine S. A. is the owner of the famous "Armani" trademark, under which it produces and sells upscale and high-priced apparel. The Armani label is recognized worldwide. But Modefine was surprised when it tried to register for the domain name *www.armani.com* and found that it had already been taken. Modefine brought an arbitration action in the **World Intellectual Property Organization (WIPO)**, an international arbitration and mediation center, against the domain name owner to recover the *www.armani.com* domain name. To win, Modefine had to prove that the domain name was identical or confusingly similar to its trademark, the owner who registered the name did not have a legitimate interest in the name, and the owner registered the name in bad faith.

The person who owned the domain name, Anand Ramnath Mani, appeared at the proceeding and defended his ownership rights. The arbitrator found that Modefine's trademark and Mr. Mani's domain name were identical but held that Mr. Mani had a legitimate claim to the domain name. The arbitrator wrote that it is "common practice for people to register domain names which are based upon initials

and a name, acronyms or otherwise variants of their full names." The court rejected Modefine's claim that Mr. Mani's offer to sell the name for $1,935 constituted bad faith. The arbitrator ruled against Modefine and permitted Mr. Mani to own the domain name *www.armani.com*. *G. A. Modefine S. A. v. A. R. Mani*, 2001 WIPO, No. D2001-0537

Law & Ethics Questions

1. **ETHICS** Did Mr. Anand Ramnath Mani have a legitimate reason for having registered the domain name *www.armani.com*?

2. **ETHICS** Did G. A. Modefine S. A., the owner of the "Armani" trademark, have a legitimate claim against to recover the domain name *www.armani.com*? Explain.

Web Exercise

1. **WEB** Go to the website *www.armani.com*. Who owns this website today?

INTERNET AND TECHNOLOGY
Domain Names Sold for Millions

What is a domain name worth? In some case, plenty. Take the case of the domain name *www.business.com*. This name, which was originally registered as a domain name for less than $50, was sold to another purchaser for $150,000 in 1996. Many people at the time thought this was an outrageous sum to pay for a domain name—that is, until the second purchaser turned around and resold the name to ECompanies for $7,500,000.

Other domain names have been sold at high prices, too. For example, the domain name *www.altavista.com* was purchased by Compaq Computer for its Internet search engine. Other domain names sold for high prices include *www.wine.com* for $3 million, *www.bingo.com* for $1.1 million, *www.wallstreet.com* for $1 million, and *www.drugs.com* for $800,000.

The highest price paid for a domain name was paid for the domain name *www.sex.com*. Gary Kremen had purchased the name in 1996 for next to nothing. In 2006, Kremen sold the name to Escom for the record price of $14 million.

As commerce over the Internet increases, unregistered memorable domain names become harder to find. The sale of the better domain names has increased, with multimillion-dollar price tags being paid for the most desirable names—which were originally registered for less than $100.

Web Exercise

1. **WEB** Use *www.google.com* to find an article that discusses the sale of a domain name. What was the domain name, and what price was it sold for?

E-Contracts

E-mail and the Web have exploded as means of personal and business communication. In the business environment, e-mail and the Web are sometimes the methods used to negotiate and agree on contract terms and to send and agree to a final contract. Are e-mail and Web contracts enforceable? Assuming that all the elements to establish a contract are present, an **e-mail contract** or **Web contract** is valid and enforceable. The main problem in a lawsuit seeking to enforce an e-mail or Web contract is evidence, but this problem, which exists in almost all lawsuits, can be overcome by printing out the e-mail or Web contract and its prior e-mail or Web negotiations, if necessary.

INTERNET AND TECHNOLOGY
E-Contracts Writing Requirement

In 2000, the federal government enacted the **Electronic Signature in Global and National Commerce Act (SIGN Act)**. This act is a federal statute enacted by Congress and therefore has national reach. The act is designed to place the world of electronic commerce on a par with the world of paper contracts in the United States.

One of the main features of the SIGN Act is that it recognizes electronic contracts as meeting the writing requirement of the **Statute of Frauds** for most contracts. Statutes of Frauds are state laws that require certain types of contracts to be in writing. The 2000 federal SIGN Act provides that electronically signed contracts cannot be denied effect because they are in electronic form or delivered electronically. The act also provides that record retention requirements are satisfied if the records are stored electronically.

The federal law was passed with several provisions to protect consumers. First, consumers must consent to receiving electronic records and contracts. Second, to receive electronic records, consumers must be able to demonstrate that they have access to the electronic records. Third, businesses must tell consumers that they have the right to receive hard-copy documents of their transaction.

Law & Ethics Questions

1. What do state Statutes of Frauds provide in terms of electronic contracts?

2. What does the federal SIGN Act provide regarding electronic contracts? Explain.

3. **ETHICS** Does the federal SIGN Act promote fraud? Why or why not?

INTERNET AND TECHNOLOGY
E-Signatures

In the past, signatures were hand-applied by the person signing a document. This is no longer always the case. In the electronic commerce world, it is now "What is your mother's maiden name?" "Slide your smart card in the sensor," or "Look into the iris scanner." But are electronic signatures sufficient to form an enforceable contract? In 2000, the federal government stepped into the breach and enacted the Electronic Signature in Global and National Commerce Act (SIGN Act).

The federal SIGN Act recognizes an *electronic signature*, or *e-signature*. The act gives an e-signature the same force and effect as a pen-inscribed signature on paper. The act is technology neutral, however, in that the law does not define or decide which technologies should be used to create a legally binding signature in cyberspace. Loosely defined, a *digital signature* is some electronic method that identifies an individual. The challenge is to make sure that someone who uses a digital signature is the person he or she claims to be. The act provides that a digital signature can basically be verified in one of three ways:

1. By something the signatory knows, such as a secret password, pet's name, and so forth.
2. By something a person has, such as a smart card, which looks like a credit card and stores personal information.
3. By biometrics, which uses a device that digitally recognizes a person's body part, such as fingerprints or the retina or iris of the eye.

The verification of electronic signatures is creating a need for the use of scanners and methods for verifying personal information.

Law & Ethics Questions

1. What is a digital signature?
2. Does the SIGN Act give legal effect to an e-signature?
3. **ETHICS** Does the SIGN Act, by recognizing e-signatures, promote fraud? Why or why not?

Software and E-Licensing

Much of the new cyberspace economy is based on electronic contracts and the licensing of computer information. E-commerce created problems for forming contracts over the Internet, enforcing e-commerce contracts, and providing consumer protection. To address these problems, in 1999 the National Conference of Commissioners on Uniform State Laws (a group of lawyers, judges, and legal scholars) drafted the **Uniform Computer Information Transactions Act (UCITA)**. This model act establishes a uniform and comprehensive set of rules that govern the creation, performance, and enforcement of computer information transactions. A computer information transaction is an agreement to create, transfer, or license computer information or information rights [UCITA 102(a)(11)].

The UCITA does not become law until a state's legislature enacts it as a state statute. Most states have adopted e-commerce and licensing statutes that are similar to many of the provisions of the UCITA as their law for computer transactions and the licensing of software and informational rights. The UCITA will be used as the basis for discussing state laws that affect computer, software, and licensing contracts.

Unless they are preempted by the UCITA, state law and equity principles, including principal and agent law, fraud, duress, mistake, trade secret law, and other state laws, supplement the UCITA [UCITA 114]. Any provisions of the UCITA that are preempted by federal law are unenforceable to the extent of the preemption [UCITA 105(a)].

Licensing

Intellectual property and information rights are extremely important assets of many individuals and companies. Patents, trademarks, copyrights, trade secrets, data, software programs, and such constitute valuable intellectual property and information rights.

The owners of intellectual property and information rights often wish to transfer limited rights in the property or information to parties for specified purposes and limited duration. The agreement that is used to transfer such limited rights is called a **license**, which is defined as follows [UCITA 102(a)(40)]:

> License means a contract that authorizes access to, or use, distribution, performance, modification, or reproduction of, information or information rights, but expressly limits the access or uses authorized or expressly grants fewer than all rights in the information, whether or not the transferee has title to a licensed copy. The term includes an access contract, a lease of a computer program, and a consignment of a copy.

The parties to a license are the licensor and the licensee. The **licensor** is the party who owns the intellectual property or information rights and obligates him- or herself to transfer rights in the property or information to the licensee. The **licensee** is the party who is granted limited rights in or access to the intellectual property of information rights [UCITA 102(a)(41), 102(a)(42)]. A licensing arrangement is illustrated in Exhibit 15.2.

A license grants the contractual rights expressly described in the license and the right to use any information rights within the licensor's control that are necessary to exercise the expressly described rights [UCITA 307(a)].

EXHIBIT 15.2

Licensing Arrangement

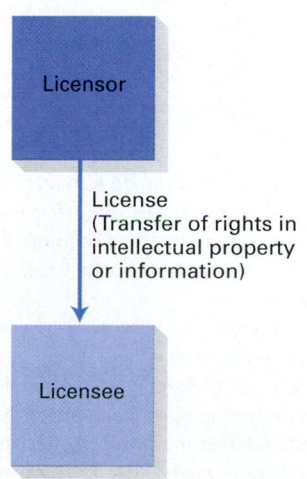

A license can grant the licensee the exclusive rights to use the information. An **exclusive license** means that for the specified duration of the license, the licensor will not grant to any other person rights in the same information [UCITA 307(f)(2)].

INTERNET AND TECHNOLOGY
Click-Wrap Licenses

In the past, most business and consumer contracts consisted of written agreements signed by both parties. With the advent of the Internet, many online contracts no longer fit this traditional mode. Take click-wrap licenses, for example. A **click-wrap license** is a contract used by many software companies to sell their software over the Internet or in physical packages where the software is later installed on a computer.

The software company, which is the licensor, typically displays a series of dialog boxes on the computer screen that state the terms of the agreement before the software is downloaded or installed by the potential licensee. The terms of a software click-wrap license are typically not negotiable, and the licensee (the person who is granted the license) indicates his or her acceptance by clicking on a prompt button on the screen labeled "I accept" or "I agree." Click-wrap licenses contain terms of the agreement, disclaimers of warranties, guarantees for the protection of trademarks and trade secrets, and other provisions that would normally be contained in a paper license. Click-wrap agreements provide a fast, inexpensive, and convenient way for licensors to mass market their software to users without requiring paper contracts or physical signatures.

A question recently presented to the courts is whether click-wrap licenses are enforceable. The courts have held that a party is considered to have manifested his or her consent to enter into a contract by the physical action of using a mouse to click the "I agree" prompt button for the click-wrap license.

The Uniform Computer Information Transactions Act (UCITA) specifically provides that a licensee who has the opportunity to review the terms of the license is bound by those terms if the licensee "manifests assent" before or during the party's initial use of or access to the licensor's software [UCITA 210(a)]. Thus, under the modern e-commerce interpretation of the law of contracts, popular click-wrap licenses are enforceable contracts between software licensors and user licensees.

Law & Ethics Questions

1. What is a click-wrap license? Explain.

2. Have you ever licensed software over the Internet? If so, did you read the click-wrap license before ordering the software?

3. **ETHICS** Should a click-wrap license be enforced against the licensee? Why or why not?

Licensing Agreements

A licensor and a licensee usually enter into a written **licensing agreement** that expressly states the terms of their agreement. Licensing agreements tend to be very detailed and comprehensive contracts. This is primarily because of the nature of the subject matter and the limited uses granted in the intellectual property or informational rights.

INTERNET AND TECHNOLOGY
Counteroffers Ineffectual Against Electronic Agents

In today's e-commerce, many sellers use electronic agents to sell goods and services. An *electronic agent* is any telephonic or computer system that has been established by a seller to accept orders. Voice mail and webpage order systems are examples of electronic agents.

In the past, when humans dealt with each other face to face, by telephone, or in writing, their negotiations might have consisted of an exchange of several offers and counteroffers until agreed-upon terms were reached and a contract was formed. Each new **counteroffer** extinguished the previous offer and became a new viable offer. Most electronic agents do not have the ability to evaluate and accept

counteroffers or to make counteroffers. The UCITA recognizes this limitation and provides that a contract is formed if an individual takes action that causes the electronic agent to cause performance or promise benefits to the individual. Thus, counteroffers are not effective against electronic agents [UCITA 206(a)].

Example "Birdie" is an electronic ordering system for placing orders for electronic information sold by the Green Company, a producer of computer software and electronic information. Freddie Calloway dials the Green Company's toll-free telephone number and orders new software for $1,000, using the Birdie voice mail electronic ordering system.

Freddie enters the product code and description, his mailing address and credit card information, and other data needed to complete the transaction, but at the end of the order states "I will accept this software if, after two weeks of use, I am satisfied with the software." Because Freddie has placed the order with an electronic agent, Freddie has ordered the software, and his counteroffer is ineffectual.

BREACH OF LICENSING AGREEMENTS The parties to a contract for the licensing of information owe a duty to perform the obligations stated in the contract. If a party fails to perform as required, there is a breach of the contract. Breach of contract by one party to a licensing agreement gives the non-breaching party certain rights, including the right to recover damages or other remedies [UCITA 701].

Each party to a licensing agreement expects to receive due performance from the other party. If any reasonable grounds arise prior to the performance date that make one party think that the other party might not deliver performance when due, the aggrieved party may demand adequate assurance of due performance from the other party. Until such assurance is received, the aggrieved party may, if commercially reasonable, suspend performance until assurance is received. Failure to provide assurance within 30 days permits the aggrieved party to repudiate the contract [UCITA 708].

If the licensor tenders a copy that is a material breach of the contract, the nonbreaching party to whom tender is made may either (1) refuse the tender, (2) accept the tender, and (3) accept any commercially reasonable units and refuse the rest [UCITA 704].

If a licensee has accepted tender of a copy where the nonconformity is a material breach, the licensee may later revoke his or her acceptance if (1) acceptance was made because discovery was difficult at the time of tender but was then later discovered or (2) the nonconformity was discovered at the time of tender but the licensor agreed to cure the defect, and the defect has not been reasonably cured [UCITA 707].

> Our legal system faces no theoretical dilemma but a single continuous problem: how to apply to ever changing conditions the never changing principles of freedom.
>
> Earl Warren (1995)

INTERNET AND TECHNOLOGY
Consumers Saved from Electronic Errors

The UCITA provides that a consumer is not bound by their unilateral **electronic errors** if the consumer:

1. Promptly upon learning of the error notifies the licensor of the error.
2. Does not use or receive any benefit from the information or make the information or benefit available to a third party.
3. Delivers all copies of the information to the licensor or destroys all copies of the information, pursuant to reasonable instructions from the licensor.
4. Pays all shipping, reshipping, and processing costs of the licensor [UCITA 217].

The UCITA does not relieve a consumer of his or her electronic error if the other party provides a reasonable method to detect and correct or avoid the error. Thus, many sellers establish methods whereby the buyer must verify the information and purchase order a second time before an electronic order is processed. This procedure strips the consumer of the defense of UCITA Section 217. Section 217 of the UCITA applies only to consumers who make electronic errors in contracting. Electronic errors by non-consumers are handled under the common law of contracts or the Uniform Commercial Code (UCC), whichever applies.

Example Kai, a consumer, intends to order 10 copies of a video game over the Internet from Cybertendo, a video game producer. In fact, Kai makes an error and orders 110 games. The electronic agent that maintains the Cybertendo website's ordering process electronically disburses 110 games. The next morning, Kai discovers his mistake and immediately e-mails Cybertendo, describing the mistake and offering to return or destroy the copies at his expense. When Kai receives the games, he returns the 110 copies unused. Under the UCITA, Kai has no contract obligation for 110 copies but bears the cost of returning them to Cybertendo or destroying them if Cybertendo instructs him to do so. However, if the Cybertendo website's electronic ordering system had asked Kai to confirm his order of 110 copies of the purchase order, and Kai had confirmed the original order of 110 copies, Kai would have had to pay for the 110 copies, even if his confirmation had been in error.

Remedies for Breach of Licensing Agreements

The UCITA provides certain *remedies* to an aggrieved party upon the breach of a licensing agreement. A party may not recover more than once for the same loss, and his or her remedy (other than liquidated damages) may not exceed the loss caused by the breach [UCITA 801]. The UCITA provides that a cause of action must be commenced within one year after the

> You must remember that some things that are legally right are not morally right.
>
> Abraham Lincoln (1840)

breach was or should have been discovered, but not more than five years after the breach actually occurred [UCITA 805]. Remedies are discussed in the following paragraphs.

CANCELLATION OF LICENSING AGREEMENTS If there has been a material breach of a contract that has not been cured or waived, the aggrieved party may cancel the contract. **Cancellation** is effective when the canceling party notifies the breaching party of the cancellation. Upon cancellation, the breaching party in possession or control of copies, information, documentation, or other materials that are the property of the other party must use commercially reasonable efforts to return them or hold them for disposal on instructions from the other party. All obligations that are executory on both sides at the time of cancellation are discharged [UCITA 802(a), 802(b)].

Upon cancellation of a license, the licensor has the right to have all copies of the licensed information returned by the licensee and to prevent the licensee from continuing to use the licensed information.

LICENSOR'S DAMAGES If a licensee breaches a contract, the licensor may recover **licensor's damages**. The licensor may sue and recover from the licensee monetary damages caused by the breach, plus any consequential and incidental damages [UCITA 808]. A licensor can recover *lost profits* caused by the licensee's failure to accept or complete performance of the contract. Lost profits is a proper measure of damages in this case because the licensor has effectively unlimited capability to make access available to others so there will be no license to substitute to reduce damages owed by the breaching licensee.

Example iSuperSoftware.com licenses a master disk of its software program to Distributors, Inc., to make and distribute 10,000 copies of the software. This is a nonexclusive license, and the licensing fee is $1 million. It costs iSuperSoftware.com $15 to produce the disk. If Distributors, Inc., refuses the disk and breaches the contract, iSuperSoftware.com can recover $1 million less $15 as damages for the profits lost on the transaction.

LICENSOR'S RIGHT TO CURE Unlike the common law of contracts, the UCITA provides that a licensor has the **right to cure** a breach of a license in certain circumstances. A breach of contract may be cured if (1) the time of performance of the contract has not expired and the licensor makes conforming performance within the time of performance; (2) the time of performance has expired but the licensor had reasonable grounds to believe the performance would be acceptable, in which case the licensor has a reasonable time to make con-

INTERNET AND TECHNOLOGY
Electronic Self-Help

Just like normal contracts, electronic licenses can be breached by licensees. If such a breach occurs, the licensor can resort to remedies provided in the UCITA. Sections 815 and 816 of the UCITA provide that a licensor can resort to **electronic self-help** if a breach occurs—for example, if the licensee fails to pay the licensing fee. Such electronic self-help can consist of activating disabling bugs and time bombs that have been embedded in the software or information that will prevent the licensee from further using the software or information.

Section 816 provides that a licensor is entitled to use electronic self-help only subject to the following rules:

1. The licensee must specifically agree to the inclusion in the license of self-help as a remedy. There must be a specific self-help option to which the licensee assents.

2. The licensor must give the licensee at least 15 days' notice prior to the disabling action. The notice period allows the licensee to make lawful adjustments to minimize the effects of the licensor's self-help or to seek a judicial remedy to combat the use of the self-help.

3. The licensor may not use self-help if it would cause a breach of the peace, risk personal injury, cause significant damage or injury to information other than the licensee's information, result in injury to the public health or safety, or cause grave harm to national security.

A licensor who violates these provisions and uses self-help improperly is liable for damages. This liability cannot be disclaimed.

forming performance; or (3) the licensor makes conforming performance before the licensee cancels the contract. In all three situations, the licensor must reasonably notify the licensee of the intent to cure [UCITA 703(a)].

LICENSEE'S DAMAGES When a licensor breaches a contract, the licensee may sue and recover monetary damages from the licensor. The amount of the damages depends on the facts of the situation. This is called the **licensee's damages**. Upon the licensor's breach, the licensee may either (1) cover by purchasing other electronic information from another source and recover the difference between the value of the promised performance from the licensor and the cost of cover or (2) not cover and recover the value of the performance from the licensor. **Cover** means engaging in a commercially reasonable substitute transaction. The licensee may obtain an award of consequential and incidental damages in either case. A licensee cannot obtain excessive or double recovery [UCITA 809].

Example Auction.com is an Internet company that operates an online auction service. Auction.com enters into a contract with Microhard, Inc., a software producer, for a site license to use software from Microhard, Inc. Auction.com agrees to pay $500,000 as an initial licensing fee and $10,000 per month for the license duration of three years. Before Auction.com pays any money under the license, Microhard, Inc., breaches the contract and does not deliver the software. Auction.com covers by licensing commercially similar software from another software company for the payment of a $600,000 initial licensing fee and $11,000 per month for the license duration of three years. Under the facts of this case, Auction.com can recover from Microhard, Inc., $100,000 for the increased initial fee and $36,000 for the increased monthly costs for breach of contract.

LIMITATION OF REMEDIES The UCITA provides that the parties to an agreement may limit the remedies available for breach of the contract. This is done by including provisions in the contract. Remedies may be restricted to the return of copies and repayment of the licensing fee or limited to the repair or replacement of the nonconforming copies. Limitations of remedies in licenses subject to the UCITA are enforceable unless they are unconscionable [UCITA 803].

In the following case, the court upheld a limitation-of-remedies clause in a **software license**.

C A S E **15.3**

Remedies

M.A. Mortenson Company, Inc. v. Timberline Software Corporation

93 Wn.App. 819, 970 P.2d 803, **Web** 1999 Wash. App. Lexis 185
Court of Appeals of Washington

> ❝ *We find that Mortenson's installation and use of the software manifested its assent to the terms of the license.* ❞
>
> —Judge Webster

Facts

The Timberline Software Corporation (Timberline) produces software programs that are used by contractors to prepare bids to do work on construction projects. The M.A. Mortenson Company (Mortenson), a contractor, had been using Timberline software for some time without any problem. Timberline introduced an advanced version of its bidding software program called *Precision*. Mortenson, as the licensee, entered into a licensing agreement with Timberline, the licensor, to license the use of the Precision software. Timberline delivered the software to

Mortenson, and a Timberline representative installed the software on Mortenson's computer. The software licensing agreement contained the following terms, which were printed on the outside of the envelope in which the software disks were packaged and on the inside cover of the user's manual, and they also appear on the introductory computer screen each time the software program is executed:

Carefully read the following terms and conditions before using the programs. Use of the programs indicates your acknowledgement that you have read this license, understand it, and agree to be bound by its terms and conditions. If you do not agree to these terms and conditions, promptly return the programs and user manuals to the place of purchase and your purchase price will be refunded. You agree that your use of the program acknowledges that you have read this license, understand it, and agree to be bound by its terms and conditions.

Limitation of remedies and liability; neither Timberline nor anyone else who has been involved in the creation, production or delivery of the programs or user manuals shall be liable to you for any damages of any type, including but not limited to, any lost profits, lost savings, loss of anticipated benefits, or other incidental or consequential damages arising out of the use or inability to use such programs, whether arising out of contract, negligence, strict tort, or under any warranty, or otherwise, even if Timberline has been advised of the possibility of such damages or for any other claim by any other party. Timberline's liability for damages in no event shall exceed the license fee paid for the right to use the programs.

Mortenson used the Precision software and prepared a bid to do contracting work for the Harborview Hospital project. While preparing the bid, the program aborted at least five times before Mortenson's employees finished the bid. Subsequently, Mortenson claimed that its bid was $2 million under what it should have been had the Precision software program worked correctly. Mortenson sued Timberline to recover consequential damages, arguing that the Precision software calculated an inaccurate bid. Timberline defended, alleging that the limitation-of-remedies clause in the software license prevented Mortenson's lawsuit. Mortenson countered that the limitation-of-remedies clause was unconscionable and therefore unenforceable. The trial court granted summary judgment to Timberline and dismissed the lawsuit. Mortenson appealed.

Issue

Was the limitation-of-remedies clause in the Timberline software license unconscionable?

Language of the Court

We hold that the terms of the present license agreement are part of the contract as formed between the parties. We find that Mortenson's installation and use of the software manifested its assent to the terms of the license and that it is bound by all terms of that license that are not found to be illegal or unconscionable.

Considering all the circumstances surrounding the transaction in the case, the limitations clause is not unconscionable. The introductory screen warned that use of the program was subject to a license. This warning placed Mortenson on notice that use of the software was governed by a license. Mortenson had reasonable opportunity to learn and understand the terms of the agreement. The limitations provision was not hidden in a maze of fine print but appeared in all capital letters. Finally such limitations provisions are widely used in the computer software industry.

Decision

The court of appeals held that the limitation-of-remedies clause in the software license was conspicuous and not unconscionable and that it therefore prohibited Mortenson's lawsuit to recover consequential damages from Timberline. The court of appeals affirmed the trial court's grant of summary judgments to Timberline that dismissed the case.

Law & Ethics Questions

1. What does the doctrine of unconscionability provide? Does the doctrine serve any useful purpose?

2. **ETHICS** Did Timberline act ethically when it included a limitation-of-remedies clause in its software license?

3. What would be the business consequences if limitation-of-remedies clauses in software licenses were all held to be *per se* illegal?

Web Exercises

1. **WEB** For the complete opinion of this case, go to *www.prenhall.com/cheesemancases*.

2. **WEB** Visit the website of the court of appeals of Washington, Division I, at *www.courts.wa.gov*.

3. **WEB** Use *www.google.com* to find a software license and determine if it has a limitation-of-remedies clause in it.

Online Privacy

E-mail, computer data, and other electronic communications are sent daily by millions of people using computers and the Internet. Recognizing how the use of computer and electronic communications raise special issues of privacy, the federal government enacted the **Electronic Communications Privacy Act (ECPA)**.

The ECPA makes it a crime to intercept an electronic communication at the point of transmission, while in transit, when stored by a router or server, or after receipt by the intended recipient. An electronic communication includes any transfer of signals, writings, images, sounds, data, or intelligence of any nature. The ECPA makes it illegal to access stored e-mail as well as e-mail in transmission.

The ECPA provides that stored electronic communications may be accessed without violating the law by the following:

1. The party or entity providing the electronic communication service. The primary example would be an employer who can access stored e-mail communications of employees using the employer's service.

Cambodia
The world is connected by the Internet and World Wide Web.

2. Government and law enforcement entities that are investigating suspected illegal activity. Disclosure would be required only pursuant to a validly issued warrant.

The ECPA provides for criminal penalties. In addition, the ECPA provides that an injured party may sue for civil damages for violations of the ECPA.

Law & Ethics Questions

1. What does the Electronic Communications Privacy Act (ECPA) prohibit? Explain.

2. Does the use of electronic communications make it easier to violate privacy rights?

3. **ETHICS** Should one expect to have lessened privacy rights for electronic communications?

Cyber Crimes

The advent of the computer and the Internet created the opportunity for persons to engage in a new form of crimes called *cyber crimes*. New technology has enabled criminals to commit existing crimes using a new medium.

Fraud can now be perpetrated over the Internet. In addition, the Internet has allowed criminals to engage in new crimes. The police, law enforcement agencies, Congress, and the courts have had to address these new cyber crimes. Congress has enacted several new federal statutes that define criminal behavior using computers and the Internet. The courts have had to interpret and apply these new statutes and apply existing criminal statutes to this new medium of crime.

Cyber Law

INTERNET AND TECHNOLOGY

Counterfeit Access Device and Computer Fraud and Abuse Act

The **Counterfeit Access Device and Computer Fraud and Abuse Act** of 1984, as amended, makes it a federal crime to access a computer knowingly to obtain (1) restricted federal government information, (2) financial records of financial institutions, and (3) consumer reports of consumer reporting agencies. The act also makes it a crime to use counterfeit or unauthorized access devices, such as cards or code numbers, to obtain things of value or transfer funds or to traffic in such devices [Public Law 98–473, Title II].

INTERNET AND TECHNOLOGY
Electronic Funds Transfer Act

The **Electronic Funds Transfer Act** regulates the payment and deposit of funds using electronic funds transfers, such as direct deposit of payroll and Social Security checks in financial institutions, transactions using automated teller machines (ATMs), and such. The act makes it a federal crime to use, furnish, sell, or transport a counterfeit, stolen, lost, or fraudulently obtained ATM card, code number, or other device used to conduct electronic funds transfers. The act imposes criminal penalties of imprisonment and the assessment of criminal fines [15 U.S.C. Section 1693].

INTERNET AND TECHNOLOGY
Cyber Identity Fraud

For centuries, some people—for various purposes, mostly financial in nature—have attempted to take the identities of other persons. Today, taking on the identity of another can be extremely lucrative, earning the spoils of another's credit cards, bank accounts, Social Security benefits, and such. The use of new technology—computers and the Internet—has made such "identity fraud" even easier. A victim of such fraud is left with funds stolen, a dismantled credit history, and thousands of dollars in costs trying to straighten out the mess. Identity fraud is the fastest-growing financial fraud in America.

To combat such fraud, Congress passed the **Identity Theft and Assumption Deterrence Act** of 1998. This act criminalizes identity fraud, making it a federal felony punishable with prison sentences ranging from 3 to 25 years. The act also appoints a federal administrative agency, the Federal Trade Commission (FTC), to help victims restore their credit and erase the impact of the imposter. Law enforcement officials suggest the following measures to protect against identity fraud: Never put your Social Security number on any document unless it is legally required, obtain and review copies of your credit report at least twice each year, and use safe passwords (e.g., other than family names and birthdays) on bank accounts and other accounts that require personal identification numbers (PINs).

Law & Ethics Questions

1. What is identity fraud? Explain.
2. How does the Internet make it easier for criminals to commit identity theft?

Web Exercises

1. **WEB** Visit the website of the Federal Trade Commission (FTC), at *www.ftc.gov*. Find information about protecting yourself from identity theft.
2. **WEB** Use *www.google.com* to find an article about a recent identity theft case. Read it.

INTERNET AND TECHNOLOGY
Information Infrastructure Protection Act (IIP Act)

The Internet and Information Age ushered in a whole new world for education, business, and consumer transactions. But what followed was a rash of cyber crimes. Prosecutors and courts wrestled over how to apply existing laws written in a nondigital age to new Internet-related abuses.

In 1996, Congress responded by enacting the **Information Infrastructure Protection Act (IIP Act)**. In this federal law, Congress addresses computer-related crimes as distinct offenses. The IIP Act provides protection for any computer attached to the Internet.

The IIP Act makes it a federal crime for anyone to intentionally access and acquire information from a protected computer without authorization to do so. The IIP Act does not require that the defendant accessed a protected computer for commercial benefit. Thus, persons who transmit a computer virus over the Internet or hackers who trespass into Internet-connected computers may be criminally prosecuted under the IIP Act. Even merely observing data on a protected computer without authorization is sufficient to meet the requirement that the defendant has accessed a protected computer.

Criminal penalties for violating the IIP Act include imprisonment and fines.

The IIP Act gives the federal government a much-needed weapon for directly prosecuting cybercrooks, hackers, and others who enter, steal, destroy, or look at others' computer data without authorization.

Law & Ethics Questions

1. What does the Information Infrastructure Protection Act (IIP Act) provide? Explain.

2. **ETHICS** Is it difficult to get caught violating the IIP Act?

State Criminal Laws

Often, larceny statutes cover only the theft of tangible property. Because computer software, programs, and data are intangible property, they are not covered by some existing state criminal statutes. To compensate for this, many states have either modernized existing laws to include computer crime or amended existing penal codes to make certain abuses of computers criminal offenses. Computer trespass, the unauthorized use of computers, tampering with computers, and the unauthorized duplication of computer-related materials are usually forbidden by these acts [see New York Session Laws, 1986, Chapter 514].

Our growing reliance on computers has made us more aware of the risks associated with losing the data stored on them. As a result, it is likely that the safety of the nation's ever-expanding computer networks will be legislated even more in the future.

INTERNET AND TECHNOLOGY
Computer Hacker Found Guilty of Cyber Crime

In "techie" circles, Kevin D. Mitnick became the underground icon of computer hackers. During a decade's reign, Mitnick terrorized the federal government, universities, and such high-tech companies as Sun Microsystems, Novell Corporation, MCI Communications, Digital Equipment Corporation, and others by breaking into their computer systems. Mitnick used his computer skills to penetrate his victims' computer systems to steal secret information and wreak havoc with their software and data.

Mitnick, a self-taught computer user, has a history of computer-related crime. As a 17-year-old, he was placed on probation for stealing computer manuals from a Pacific Bell Telephone switching center in Los Angeles. Mitnick was next accused of breaking into federal government and military computers. He has also been accused of breaking into the nation's telephone and cellular telephone networks, stealing thousands of data files and trade secrets from corporate targets, obtaining at least 20,000 credit card numbers of some of the country's richest persons, and sabotaging government, university, and private computer systems around the nation. Mitnick was arrested and convicted of computer crimes and served time in prison.

Upon release from prison, Mitnick was put on probation and placed in a medical program to treat his compulsive addiction to computers, which included a court order to not touch a computer or modem. Mitnick dropped out of sight and evaded federal law enforcement officials for several years as he continued a life of computer crime.

Mitnick's next undoing came when he broke into the computer of Tsutomu Shimomura, a researcher at the San Diego Supercomputer Center. Shimomura, a cybersleuth who advises the FBI and major companies on computer and Internet security, made it his crusade to catch the hacker who broke into his computer. Shimomura watched electronically as Mitnick invaded other computers across the country, but he could not physically locate Mitnick because he disguised his whereabouts by breaking into telephone company computers and rerouting all his computer calls. Eventually, Shimomura's patient watching paid off as he traced the electronic burglar to Raleigh, North Carolina. Shimomura flew to Raleigh, where he used a cellular-frequency-direction-finding antenna to locate Mitnick's apartment. The FBI was notified, and an arrest warrant was obtained from a judge at his home. The FBI arrested Mitnick at his apartment. Mitnick was placed in jail without bail, pending the investigation of his case.

Subsequently, Mitnick entered into a plea agreement with federal prosecutors. Mitnick's computer crimes spree has been estimated to have cost his victims hundreds of millions of dollars in losses. Mitnick has not been accused of benefiting financially from his deeds. The U.S. District Court judge sentenced Kevin Mitnick to 46 months in prison, including time served, and ordered him to pay $4,125 in restitution to the companies he victimized. The judge called this a token amount but did not order a larger restitution because she believed Mitnick would not be able to pay more. After serving his time, Mitnick was released from prison. As part of the sentencing, Mitnick cannot use electronic devices, from PCs to cellular telephones, during an additional probationary period following his release from prison. Mitnick is now acting as a consultant to businesses, advising them how to protect themselves from computer hackers.

Law & Ethics Questions

1. What is a computer hacker?

2. Is it a crime to hack into other persons' or entities' computers and either steal important and confidential information or cause damages to the computer system and its contents?

3. **ETHICS** Why do many computer hackers do what they do?

4. Should Mitnick have been given a greater sentence in this case? Why or why not?

Chapter Summary

The Internet, p. 389

The Internet is a collection of millions of computers that provide a network of electronic connections between computers.

The World Wide Web

The Web is an electronic collection of computers that support a standard set of rules for the exchange of information called Hypertext Transfer Protocol (HTTP).

E-Mail

E-mail is electronic written communication between individuals using computers connected to the Internet.

Domain Names, p. 392

A domain name is a unique name that identifies an individual's or a company's website. Domain names are registered by filing the appropriate form with a domain name registration service and paying the appropriate fee.

Anticybersquatting Consumer Protection Act

The Anticybersquatting Consumer Protection Act is a federal statute that permits a court to issue cease-and-desist orders and injunctions and to award monetary damages against anyone who has registered a domain name of a famous name in bad faith.

E-Contracts, p. 396

Contracts may be formed electronically over the Internet using e-mail and the World Wide Web.

The Electronic Signature in Global and National Commerce Act (SIGN Act)

The Electronic Signature in Global and National Commerce Act (SIGN Act) is a federal statute that (1) recognizes electronic contracts as meeting the writing requirement of the Statute of Frauds and (2) recognizes and gives electronic signatures—e-signatures—the same force and effect as pen-inscribed signatures on paper.

Software and E-Licensing, p. 397

Licensing

1. *License.* A license is a contract that transfers limited rights in intellectual property and informational rights.
2. *Licensor.* An owner of intellectual property or informational rights who transfers rights in the property or information to a licensee is called a licensor.
3. *Licensee.* A party who is granted limited rights or access to intellectual property or informational rights owned by a licensor is called a licensee.

Licensing Agreements

A licensing agreement is a detailed and comprehensive written agreement between a licensor and a licensee that sets forth the express terms of their agreement.

The Uniform Computer Information Transactions Act (UCITA)

The Uniform Computer Information Transactions Act (UCITA) is a model act issued by the National Conference of Commissioners on Uniform State Laws that establishes a uniform and comprehensive set of rules that govern the creation, performance, and enforcement of computer information transactions. The UCITA does not become law until a state's legislature enacts it as a state statute.

The following are special provisions of the UCITA:

1. *Counteroffer rule.* Counteroffers are not effective against electronic agents. This is because most electronic agents do not have the ability to evaluate and accept counteroffers or make counteroffers.

2. *Electronic errors.* The UCITA provides that a consumer is not bound by his or her unilateral electronic errors if the consumer:
   a. Promptly upon learning of the error notifies the other party of the error.
   b. Does not use or receive any benefit from the information or make the information or benefit available to a third party.
   c. Delivers all copies of the information to the licensor or destroys all copies of the information pursuant to reasonable instructions from the licensor.
   d. Pays all shipping, reshipping, and processing costs of the licensor.
3. *Electronic self-help.* If an electronic license has been breached by a licensee, the licensor can resort to electronic self-help such as activating disabling bugs and time bombs that have been embedded in the software or information that will prevent the licensee from further using the software or information. A licensor is entitled to use electronic self-help only subject to the following rules:
   a. The licensee must specifically agree to the inclusion in the license of self-help as a remedy.
   b. The licensor must give the licensee at least 15 days' notice prior to the disabling action.
   c. The licensor may not use self-help if it would cause a breach of the peace, risk personal injury, cause significant damage or injury to information other than the licensee's information, result in injury to the public health or safety, or cause grave harm to national security.

Online Privacy, p. 402

The Electronic Communications Privacy Act (ECPA) is a federal statute that makes it a crime to intercept an "electronic communication" at the point of transmission, while in transit, when stored by a router or server, or after receipt by the intended recipient.

Cyber Crimes, p. 403

Cyber crimes are crimes that are committed by using computer technology and the Internet. These crimes may be crimes that already exist or new cyber crimes.

Counterfeit Access Device and Computer Fraud and Abuse Act

The Counterfeit Access Device and Computer Fraud and Abuse Act is a federal statute that makes it a crime to knowingly access a computer to obtain specified information.

Electronic Funds Transfer Act

The Electronic Funds Transfer Act is a federal statute that makes it a crime to use, furnish, sell, or transport a counterfeit, stolen, lost, or fraudulently obtained ATM card, code number, or device used to conduct electronic funds transfers.

Identity Theft and Assumption Deterrence Act

The Identity Theft and Assumption Deterrence Act is a federal statute that makes it a crime to engage in identity theft.

Information Infrastructure Protection Act (IIP Act)

The Information Infrastructure Protection Act (IIP Act) is a federal statute that makes it a crime to intentionally access and obtain information from a protected computer without authorization to do so.

State Criminal Laws

Many states have either modernized existing laws to include computer crime or amended existing penal codes to make certain abuses of computers criminal offenses.

Test Review Terms and Concepts

Case Problems

15.1 Domain Name: Francis Net, a freshman in college and a computer expert, browses websites for hours each day. One day, she thinks to herself, "I can make money registering domain names and selling them for a fortune." She has recently seen an advertisement for Classic Coke, a cola drink produced and marketed by Coca-Cola Company. Coca-Cola Company has a famous trademark on the term *Classic Coke* and has spent millions of dollars advertising this brand and making the term famous throughout the United States and the world. Francis goes to the website *www.networksolutions.com*, an Internet domain name registration service, to see if the Internet domain name *classiccoke.com* has been taken. She discovers that it is available, so she immediately registers the Internet domain name *classiccoke.com* for herself and pays the $70 registration fee with her credit card. Coca-Cola Company decides to register the Internet domain name *classiccoke.com*, but when it checks at Network Solutions, Inc.'s, website, it discovers that Francis Net has already registered the Internet domain name. Coca-Cola Company contacts Francis, who demands $500,000 for the name. Coca-Cola Company sues Francis to prevent Francis from using the Internet domain name *classiccoke.com* and to recover it from her under the federal ACPA. Who wins?

15.2 E-Mail Contract: The Little Steel Company is a small steel fabricator that makes steel parts for various metal machine shop clients. When Little Steel Company receives an order from a client, it must locate and purchase 10 tons of a certain grade of steel to complete the order. The Little Steel Company sends an e-mail message to West Coast Steel Company, a large steel company, inquiring about the availability of 10 tons of the described grade of steel. The West Coast Steel Company replies by e-mail that it has available the required 10 tons of steel and quotes $450 per ton. The Little Steel Company's purchasing agent replies by e-mail that the Little Steel Company will purchase the 10 tons of described steel at the quoted price of $450 per ton. The e-mails are signed electronically by the Little Steel Company's purchasing agent and the selling agent of the West Coast Steel Company. When the steel arrives at the Little Steel Company's plant, the Little Steel Company rejects the shipment, claiming the defense of the Statute of Frauds. The West Coast Steel Company sues the Little Steel Company for damages. Who wins?

15.3 Contract: Einstein Financial Analysts, Inc. (EFA), has developed an electronic database that has recorded the number of plastic pails manufactured and sold in the United States since plastic was first invented. Using this data and a complicated patented software mathematical formula developed by EFA, a user can predict with 100 percent accuracy (historically) how the stock of each of the companies of the Dow Jones Industrial Average will perform on any given day of the year. William Buffet, an astute billionaire investor, wants to increase his wealth, so he enters into an agreement with EFA whereby he is granted the sole right to use the EFA data (updated daily) and its financial model for the next five years. Buffet pays EFA $100 million for the right to the data and mathematical formula. After using the data and software formula for one week, Buffet discovers that EFA has also transferred the right to use the EFA plastic pail database and software formula to his competitor. Buffet sues EFA. What type of arrangement has EFA and Buffet entered into? Who wins?

15.4 License: An Internet firm called Info.com, Inc., licenses computer software and electronic information over the Internet. Info.com has a website, *info.com*, where users can license Info.com software and electronic information. The website is operated by an electronic agent; a potential user enters Info.com's website and looks at available software and electronic information that is available from Info.com Mildred Hayward pulls up the Info.com website on her computer and decides to order a certain type of Info.com software. Hayward enters the appropriate product code and description; her name, mailing address, and credit card information; and other data needed to complete the order for a three-year license at $300 per month; the electronic agent has Hayward verify all the information a second time. When Hayward has completed verifying the information, she types at the end of her order, "I accept this electronic software only if after I have used it for two months I still personally like it." Info.com's electronic agent delivers a copy of the software to Hayward, who downloads the copy of the software onto her computer. Two weeks later, Hayward sends the copy of the software back to *info.com*, stating, "Read our contract: I personally don't like this software; cancel my license." Info.com sues Hayward to recover the license payments for three years. Who wins?

15.5 Electronic Signature: David Abacus uses the Internet to place an order to license software from Inet.License, Inc. (Inet), through Inet's electronic website ordering system. Inet's webpage order form asks David to type in his name, mailing address, telephone number, e-mail address, credit card information, computer location information, and personal identification number. Inet's electronic agent requests that David verify the information a second time before it accepts the order, which David does. The license duration is two years, at a licensing fee of $300 per month. Only after receiving the verification of information does Inet's electronic agent place the order and send an electronic copy of the software program to David's computer, where he installs the new software program. David later refuses to pay the licensing fee due Inet because he claims his electronic signature and information were not authentic. Inet sues David to recover the licensing fee. Is David's electronic signature enforceable against him?

15.6 License: Tiffany Pan, a consumer, intends to order three copies of a financial software program from iSoftware, Inc. Tiffany, using her computer, enters iSoftware's website,

isoftware.com, and places an order with the electronic agent taking orders for the website. The license provides for a duration of three years at $300 per month for each copy of the software program. Tiffany enters the necessary product code and description; her name, mailing address, and credit card information; and other data necessary to place the order. When the electronic order form prompts Tiffany to enter the number of copies of the software program she is ordering, Tiffany mistakenly types in "30." iSoftware's electronic agent places the order and ships 30 copies of the software program to Tiffany. When Tiffany receives the 30 copies of the software program, she ships them back to iSoftware with a note stating, "Sorry, there has been a mistake. I only meant to order 3 copies of the software, not 30." When iSoftware bills Tiffany for the licensing fees for the 30 copies, Tiffany refuses to pay. iSoftware sues Tiffany to recover the licensing fees for 30 copies. Who wins?

15.7 License: Silvia Miofsky licenses a software program from Accura.com, Inc., to sort information from a database to be used in Silvia's financial planning business. The license is for three years, and the licensing fee is $500 per month. The new software program from Accura.com will be run in conjunction with other software programs and databases used by Silvia in her business. The licensing agreement between Accura.com and Silvia, and the label on the software package states that the copy of the licensed software program has been tested by Accura.com and will run without error. Silvia installs the copy of Accura.com's software, but every fifth or sixth time the program is run, it fails to operate properly and shuts down Silvia's computer and other programs. Silvia sends the software, marked *defective*, back to Accura.com. When Accura.com bills Silvia for the unpaid licensing fees for the three years of the license, Silvia refuses to pay. Accura.com sues Silvia to recover the licensing fees under the three-year license. Who wins?

15.8 License: Metatag, Inc., is a developer and distributor of software and electronic information rights over the Internet. Metatag produces a software program called Virtual 4-D Links; a user of the program merely types in the name of a city and address anywhere in the world, and the computer transports the user there and creates a four-dimensional space and a sixth sense unknown to the world before. The software license is nonexclusive, and Metatag licenses its Virtual 4-D Link to millions of users worldwide. Nolan Bates, who has lived alone with his mother too long, licenses the Virtual 4-D Link program for five years for a licensing fee of $350 per month. Bates uses the program for two months before his mother discovers why he has had a smile on his face lately. Bates, upon his mother's urging, returns the Virtual 4-D Link software program to Metatag, stating that he is canceling the license. Metatag sues Bates to recover the unpaid licensing fees. Who wins?

Ethics Issues

15.9 Ethics: BluePeace.org is a new environmental group that has decided that expounding its environmental causes over the Internet is the best and most efficient way to spend its time and money to advance its environmental causes. To draw attention to its websites, BluePeace.org comes up with catchy Internet domain names, such as *macyswearus.org*, *exxonvaldezesseals.org*, and *generalmotorscrashesdummies.org*. The *macyswearus.org* website first shows beautiful women dressed in mink fur coats sold by Macy's department stores and then goes into graphic photos of minks being slaughtered and skinned and made into the coats. The *exxonvaldezesseals.org* website first shows a beautiful, pristine bay in Alaska, with the *Exxon Valdez* oil tanker quietly sailing through the waters, and then it shows photos of the ship breaking open and spewing forth oil and then seals who are gooed with oil, suffocating and dying on the shoreline. The website *generalmotorscrashesdummies.org* shows a General Motors automobile involved in normal crash tests with dummies followed by photographs of automobile accident scenes where adults and children lay bleeding and dying after an accident involving General Motors automobiles. Macy's, Exxon, and General Motors sue BluePeace.org for violating the federal ACPA. Who wins? Has BluePeace.org acted unethically in this case?

15.10 Ethics: Apricot.com is a major software developer that licenses software to be used over the Internet. One of its programs, called Match, is a search engine that searches personal ads on the Internet and provides a match for users for potential dates and possible marriage partners. Nolan Bates subscribes to the Match software program from Apricot.com. The license duration is five years, with a licensing fee of $200 per month. For each subscriber, Apricot.com produces a separate webpage that shows photos of the subscriber and personal data. Bates places a photo of himself with his mother, with the caption, "Male, 30 years old, lives with mother, likes quiet nights at home." Bates licenses the Apricot.com Match software and uses it 12 hours each day, searching for his Internet match. Bates does not pay Apricot.com the required monthly licensing fee for any of the three months he uses the software. After using the Match software but refusing to pay Apricot.com its licensing fee, Apricot.com activates the disabling bug in the software and disables the Match software on Bates' computer. Apricot.com does this with no warning to Bates. It then sends a letter to Bates stating, "Loser, the license is canceled!" Bates sues Apricot.com for disabling the Match software program. Who wins? Did Bates act ethically? Did Apricot.com act ethically?

IRAC Writing Assignment

Read **Case A-15** in Appendix A [*Toys "R" Us, Inc. v. Abir*]. Use the IRAC method to prepare a written analysis of the case.

Endnote

1. 15 U.S.C. Section 1125(d).

UNIT 3

Sales, Leases, and Electronic Contracts

CHAPTER 16

Formation of Sales, Lease, and E-Contracts

> **❝***Commercial law lies within a narrow compass, and is far purer and freer from defects than any other part of the system.* **❞**
>
> —HENRY PETER BROUGHAM
> House of Commons, February 7, 1828

CHAPTER OBJECTIVES

After studying this chapter, you should be able to:

1. Describe the sales contracts that are governed by Article 2 of the UCC.
2. Describe the lease contracts that are governed by Article 2A of the UCC.
3. Apply the basic UCC principles of good faith and reasonableness.
4. Describe the formation of sales and lease contracts.
5. Understand the changes made by Revised Article 2 (Sales) and Revised Article 2A (leases) as they relate to electronic contracts.

CHAPTER CONTENTS

- Introduction to Formation of Sales and Lease Contracts
- Uniform Commercial Code (UCC)
- Article 2 (Sales)
- Article 2A (Leases)
- Formation of Sale, Leases and E-Contracts: Offer
- Formation of Sales and Lease Contracts: Acceptance
- UCC Statute of Frauds
- Chapter Summary
- Test Review Terms and Concepts
- Case Problems
- Ethics Issues
- IRAC Writing Assignment

Introduction to Formation of Sales and Lease Contracts

Most tangible items—such as books, clothing, and tools—are considered *goods*. In medieval times, merchants gathered at fairs in Europe to exchange such goods. Over time, certain customs and rules evolved for enforcing contracts and resolving disputes. These customs and rules, which were referred to as the "Law Merchant," were enforced by "fair courts" established by the merchants. Eventually, the customs and rules of the Law Merchant were absorbed into the common law.

Toward the end of the 1800s, England enacted a statute (the Sales of Goods Act) that codified the common law rules of commercial transactions. In the United States, laws governing the sale of goods also developed. In 1906, the **Uniform Sales Act** was promulgated in the United States, and it was enacted in many states. It was quickly outdated, however, as mass production and distribution of goods developed in the twentieth century.

In 1949, the National Conference of Commissioners on Uniform State Laws promulgated a comprehensive statutory scheme called the *Uniform Commercial Code (UCC)*. The UCC covers most aspects of commercial transactions.

Article 2 (Sales) and *Article 2A (Leases)* of the UCC govern the sale and lease of personal property. These articles are intended to provide clear, easy-to-apply rules that place the risk of loss of the goods on the party most able to either bear the risk or insure against it. The common law of contracts governs if either Article 2 or Article 2A is silent on an issue.

New Revised Article 2 (Sales) and Revised Article 2A (Leases) have been promulgated. These revised articles update many provisions in the existing Articles 2 and 2A, and specifically include provisions that apply to the formation and performance of electronic sales and lease contracts. Where appropriate, the changes made by Revised Article 2 and Revised Article 2A are discussed in the following sales contracts and leases chapters.

This chapter discusses sales, lease, and electronic contracts. Other articles of the UCC are discussed in subsequent chapters.

Rodeo Drive, Beverly Hills, California
Businesses offer a variety of goods for sale based on contracts subject to the Uniform Commercial Code (UCC).

Uniform Commercial Code (UCC)

One of the major frustrations of businesspersons conducting interstate business is that they are subject to the laws of each state in which they operate. To address this problem, in 1949, the National Conference of Commissioners on Uniform State Laws promulgated the **Uniform Commercial Code (UCC)**.

LANDMARK LAW

The Uniform Commercial Code (UCC)

The UCC is a **model act** that has been drafted by the American Law Institute and the National Conference of Commissioners on Uniform State Laws. This model act contains uniform rules that govern commercial transactions. For the UCC, or any part of the UCC, to become law in a state, that state needs to enact the UCC as its commercial law statute. Every state except Louisiana (which has adopted only parts of the UCC) has enacted the UCC or the majority of the UCC as a commercial statute.

The UCC is divided into articles, with each article establishing uniform rules for a particular facet of commerce in this country:

Article 1	General Provisions
Article 2	Sales
Article 2A	Leases
Article 3	Negotiable Instruments
Article 4	Bank Deposits
Article 4A	Funds Transfers
Article 5	Letters of Credit
Article 6	Bulk Transfers and Bulk Sales
Article 7	Warehouse Receipts, Bills of Lading and Other Documents of Title
Article 8	Investment Securities

Article 9	Secured Transactions
Revised Article 9	Secured Transactions

These articles are discussed in the chapters in this section of this book.

The UCC is continually being revised to reflect changes in modern commercial practices and technology. Article 2, which establishes rules that govern the sale of goods, was recently amended. Article 2A was added to govern leases of personal property, and Article 4A was added to regulate the use of wire transfers in the banking system. Articles 3 and 4, which cover the creation and transfer of negotiable instruments and the clearing of checks through the banking system, were substantially amended in 1990. Article 9, which covers secured transactions in personal property, has also been revised.

Web Exercises

1. **WEB** To view the list of articles to the UCC, go to *www.law.cornell.edu/ucc/index.htm*.

2. **WEB** Visit the website of the National Conference of Commissioners on Uniform State Laws, at *www.nccusl.org*.

3. **WEB** Visit the website of the American Law Institute, at *www.ali.org*.

Article 2 (Sales)

All states except Louisiana have adopted some version of **Article 2 (Sales)** of the UCC. Federal courts also apply Article 2 to sales contracts governed by federal law. Article 2 has recently been revised. Some states have adopted this revised article, referred to as *Revised Article 2*.

What Is a Sale?

Article 2 of the UCC applies to transactions in goods [UCC 2-102]. All states have held that Article 2 applies to the sale of goods. A **sale** consists of the passing of title from a seller to a buyer for a price [UCC 2-106(1)].

Example The purchase of a computer is a sale subject to Article 2, whether the computer was paid for by cash, credit card, or another form of consideration (see Exhibit 16.1).

EXHIBIT 16.1

Sales Transaction

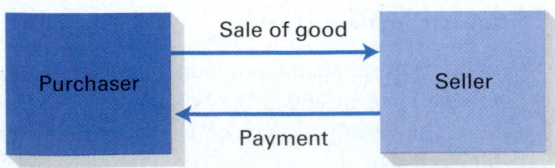

What Are Goods?

Goods are defined as tangible things that are movable at the time of their identification to a contract [UCC 2-105(1)]. **Specially manufactured goods** and the unborn young of animals are examples of goods. Certain items are not considered goods and are not subject to Article 2. They include:

1. Money and intangible items, such as stocks, bonds, and patents, are not tangible goods.
2. Real estate is not a tangible good because it is not movable [UCC 2-105(1)]. Minerals, structures, growing crops, and other things that are severable from real estate may be classified as goods subject to Article 2, however.

   Example The sale and removal of a chandelier in a house is a sale of goods subject to Article 2 because its removal would not materially harm the realty. The sale and removal of the furnace, however, would be a sale of real property because its removal would cause material harm [UCC 2-107(2)].

Goods Versus Services

Contracts for the provision of services—including legal services, medical services, and dental services—are not covered by Article 2. Sometimes, however, a sale involves both the provision of a service and a good in the same transaction. This sale is referred to as a **mixed sale**. Article 2 applies to mixed sales only if the goods are the predominant part of the transaction. The UCC provides no guidance for deciding cases based on mixed sales; therefore, the courts decide these issues on a case-by-case basis, using the common law of contracts.

In the following case, the court had to decide whether a sale was of a good or a service.

CASE 16.1
Good or Service

Brandt v. Boston Scientific Corporation and Sarah Bush Lincoln Health Center

204 Ill.2d 640, 792 N.E.2d 296, 2003 Ill. Lexis 785 (2003)
Supreme Court of Illinois

> **❝** *"Where there is a mixed contract for goods and services, there is a transaction in goods only if the contract is predominantly for goods and incidentally for services.* **❞**
>
> —Justice Garman

Facts

Brenda Brandt was admitted to Sarah Bush Lincoln Health Center (Health Center) to receive treatment for urinary incontinence. During the course of an operation, the doctor surgically implanted a ProteGen Sling (sling) in Brandt. Subsequently, the manufacturer of the sling, Boston Scientific Corporation, issued a recall of the sling because it was causing medical complications in some patients. Brandt suffered serious complications and had the sling surgically removed.

Brandt sued Boston Scientific Corporation and the Health Center for breach of the implied warranty of merchantability included in Article 2 (Sales) of the Uniform Commercial Code (UCC). The Health Center filed a motion with the court to have the case against it dismissed. The Health Center argued that it was a provider of services and not a merchant who sold goods, and because the UCC (Sales) applies to the sale of goods then the Health Center was not covered by the UCC. The trial court agreed with the Health Center, found that the transaction was predominantly the provision of services and not the sale of goods, and dismissed the Brandt's case against the Health Center. The appellate court affirmed the decision. Brandt appealed.

Issue

Was the transaction between Brandt and the Health Center predominantly the provision of services or the sale of goods?

Language of the Court

Article 2 of the UCC imposes the implied warranty of merchantability. To succeed on a claim of breach of implied warranty of merchantability, a plaintiff must allege and prove: (1) a sale of goods (2) by a merchant of those goods, and (3) the goods were not of merchantable quality. Where there is a mixed contract for goods and services, there is a transaction in goods only if the contract is predominantly for goods and incidentally for services.

We now apply the predominant purpose test to the facts of this case. In this case, Brandt's bill from the Health Center reflects that of the $11,174.50 total charge for her surgery, a charge of $1,659.50, or 14.9%, was for the sling and its surgical kit; a charge of $5,428.50, or 48.6%, was for all movable goods, including pharmaceuticals, medical supplies, and sterile supplies. The remainder of the charges were for various services, including the hospital and operating rooms and various kinds of medical testing and treatment. A charge for the implantation of the sling by the surgeon was not included in the bill. A majority of the charges, 51.4%, were for services rather than goods. Only a small fraction of the total charge was for the sling, the goods at issue in this case.

These services, the medical treatment, were the primary purpose of the transaction between Brandt and the Health Center, and the purchase of the sling was incidental to the treatment. Brandt can seek recovery from the manufacturer of the sling.

Decision

The supreme court held that the provision of services, and not the sale of goods, was the predominant feature of the transaction between Brandt and the Health Center and that the Health Center was not liable under Article 2 (Sales) of the UCC. The supreme court affirmed the decision of the trail court and appellate court dismissing Brandt's lawsuit against the Health Center.

Law & Ethics Questions

1. What is a "good"?

2. Where there is a mixed contract for goods and services, what does the predominant purpose test provide?

3. **ETHICS** Why do you think Brandt sued the Health Center for violation of UCC Article 2 (Sales)?

4. Is Boston Scientific Corporation subject to Brandt's UCC Article 2 (Sales) lawsuit? Why or why not?

Web Exercises

1. **WEB** For the complete opinion of this case, go to *www.prenhall.com/cheesemancases*.

2. **WEB** Visit the website of the Supreme Court of Illinois at *www.state.il.us/court*.

3. **WEB** Visit the website of Boston Scientific Corporation at *www.bostonscientific.com*.

4. **WEB** Visit the website of the Sarah Bush Lincoln Health Center at *www.sarahbush.org*.

5. **WEB** Use *www.google.com* to find an article that discusses the use of Article 2 of the UCC in your state. Read it.

Who Is a Merchant?

Generally, Article 2 of the UCC applies to all sales contracts, whether they involve merchants or not. However, Article 2 contains several provisions that either apply only to merchants or impose a greater duty on merchants than on others. UCC 2-104(1) defines a **merchant** as (1) a person who deals in the goods of the kind involved in the transaction or (2) a person who by his or her occupation holds himself or herself out as having knowledge or skill peculiar to the goods involved in the transaction. For example, a sporting goods dealer is a merchant with respect to sporting goods but is not a merchant with respect to selling his lawn mower to a neighbor. The courts disagree as to whether farmers are merchants within this definition.

Article 2A (Leases)

Personal property leases are a billion-dollar industry. Consumer leases of automobiles or equipment and commercial leases of such items as aircraft and industrial machinery fall into this category. In the past, these transactions were governed by a combination of common law principles, real estate law, and reference to Article 2. However, some of these legal rules and concepts do not quite fit lease transactions.

Article 2A (Leases) of the UCC was promulgated in 1987. This article, which is cited as the *Uniform Commercial Code—Leases*, directly addresses personal property leases [UCC 2A-101]. It establishes a comprehensive, uniform law that covers the formation, performance, and default of leases in goods [UCC 2A-102, 2A-103(h)].

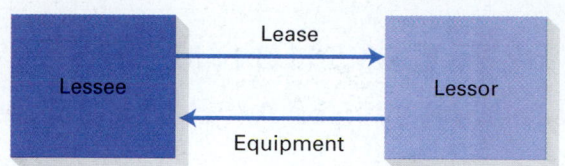

EXHIBIT 16.2

Lease

Article 2A is similar to Article 2. In fact, many Article 2 provisions were changed to reflect leasing terminology and practices that carried over to Article 2A.

Definition of *Lease*

A **lease** is a transfer of the right to the possession and use of the named goods for a set term in return for certain consideration [UCC 2A-103(1)(i)(x)]. The leased goods can be anything from a hand tool leased to an individual for a few hours to a complex line of industrial equipment leased to a multinational corporation for a number of years.

In an ordinary lease, the **lessor** is the person who transfers the right of possession and use of goods under the lease [UCC 2A-103(1)(p)]. The **lessee** is the person who acquires the right to possession and use of goods under a lease [UCC 2A-103(1)(n)].

Example Dow Chemical Company decides to lease robotic equipment to manufacture most of its products. Ingersoll-Rand Corporation, which manufactures robotic equipment, enters into a lease contract to lease robotic equipment to Dow Chemical. Ingersoll-Rand is the lessor, and Dow Chemical is the lessee (see Exhibit 16.2).

Finance Lease

A **finance lease** is a three-party transaction consisting of a lessor, a lessee, and a **supplier** (or vendor). The lessor does not select, manufacture, or supply the goods. Instead, the lessor acquires title to the goods or the right to their possession and use in connection with the terms of the lease [UCC 2A-103(1)(g)].

Example JetBlue Airways, a commercial air carrier, decides to acquire a new airplane. Boeing Company manufactures the airplane JetBlue wants to acquire. To finance the airplane acquisition, JetBlue goes to City Bank, which purchases the airplane from Boeing, and City Bank then leases the airplane to JetBlue. City Bank is the lessor, JetBlue is the lessee, and Boeing is the supplier. City Bank does not take physical delivery of the airplane; the airplane is delivered by Boeing directly to JetBlue (see Exhibit 16.3).

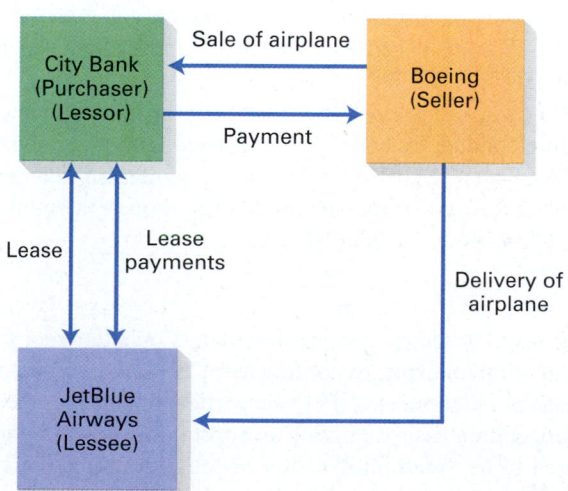

EXHIBIT 16.3

Finance Lease

CONTEMPORARY ENVIRONMENT
Revised Article 2 (Sales) and Revised Article 2A (Leases)

After years of study and debate, in 2003 a **Revised Article 2 (Sales)** and **Revised Article 2A (Leases)** was promulgated by the National Conference of Commissioners on Uniform State Laws and the American Law Institute (together "Commission").

The modifications to Article 2 and Article 2A include changes to provisions that have been controversial in the past, as well as adding new provisions to recognize changes in the commercial environment. The revised Articles 2 and 2A are considered to be the most modern and efficient rules to govern the sales and leases of goods.

In addition, the revised Articles 2 and 2A contain many new provisions and rules that recognize the importance of electronic contracting for the sale and lease of goods. The revised articles provide rules for the creation and enforcement of electronic contracts for the sale and lease of goods.

Since their release in 2003, states have been studying whether to enact Revised UCC Article 2 (Sales) and Revised UCC Article 2A (Leases) as UCC statutes within their states. It is expected that after sufficient study, many states will do so.

This and the following UCC chapters on sales and lease contracts will note the changes and differences that revised Articles 2 and 2A have made to current UCC sales and lease laws.

Automobile

Many automobiles are leased. The provisions of Article 2A of the Uniform Commercial Code (UCC) apply to lease contracts.

Formation of Sale, Leases and E-Contracts: Offer

As with general contracts, the formation of sales and lease contracts requires an offer and an acceptance. The UCC-established rules for each of these elements often differ considerably from common law.

A contract for the sale or lease of goods may be made in any manner sufficient to show agreement, including conduct by both parties that recognizes the existence of a contract [UCC 2-204(1), 2A-204(1)]. Under the UCC, an agreement sufficient to constitute a contract for the sale or lease of goods may be found even though the moment of its making is undetermined [UCC 2-204(2), 2A-204(2)].

Open Terms

Sometimes the parties to a sale or lease contract leave open a major term in the contract. The UCC is tolerant of **open terms**. According to UCC 2-204(3) and 2A-204(3), a contract does not fail because of indefiniteness if (1) the parties intended to make a contract and (2) there is a reasonably certain basis for giving an appropriate remedy. In effect, certain open terms are permitted to be "read into" a sale or lease contract. This rule is commonly referred to as the **gap-filling rule**.

Some examples of terms that are commonly left open are:

- **Open price term.** If a sales contract does not contain a specific price (**open price term**), a "reasonable price" is implied at the time of delivery. The contract may provide that a price is to be fixed by a market rate (e.g., commodities market), as set or recorded by a third person or agency (e.g., a government agency), or by another standard, either upon delivery or on a set date. If the agreed-upon standard is unavailable when the price is to be set, a reasonable price is implied at the time of delivery of the goods [UCC 2-305(1)].

  A seller or buyer who reserves the right to fix a price must do so in good faith [UCC 2-305(2)]. When one of the parties fails to fix an open price term, the other party may opt either (1) to treat the contract as canceled or (2) to fix a reasonable price for the goods [UCC 2-305(3)].

- **Open payment term.** If the parties to a sales contract do not agree on payment terms, payment is due at the time and place at which the buyer is to receive the goods. If delivery is authorized and made by way of document of title, payment is due at the time and place at which the buyer is to receive the document of title, regardless of where the goods are to be received [UCC 2-310].

- **Open delivery term.** If the parties to a sales contract do not agree to the time, place, and manner of delivery of the goods, the place for delivery is the seller's place of business. If the seller does not have a place of business, delivery is to be made at the seller's residence. If identified goods are located at some other place, and both parties know of this fact at the time of contracting, that place is the place of delivery [UCC 2-308].

  Where goods are to be shipped but the shipper is not named, the seller is obligated to make the shipping arrangements. Such arrangements must be made in good faith and within limits of commercial reasonableness [UCC 2-311(2)].

- **Open time term.** If the parties to a sales contract do not set a specific time of performance for any obligation under the contract, the contract must be performed within a reasonable time. If a sales contract provides for successive performance over an unspecified period of time, the contract is valid for a reasonable time [UCC 2-309].

- **Open assortment term.** If the assortment of goods to a sales contract is left open, the buyer is given the option of choosing those goods.

> The foundation of justice is good faith.
>
> Cicero
> *De Officiis, Book 1, Chapter VII*

Example Suppose Macy's contracts to purchase 1,000 dresses from Liz Claiborne, Inc. The contract is silent as to the assortment of colors of the dresses. The buyer may pick the assortment of colors for the dresses from the seller's stock. The buyer must make the selection in good faith and within limits set by commercial reasonableness [UCC 2-311(2)].

CONTEMPORARY ENVIRONMENT

UCC "Firm Offer" Rule

Recall that the common law of contracts allows the offeror to revoke an offer any time prior to its acceptance. The only exception allowed by the common law is an *option contract* (i.e., where the offeree pays the offeror consideration to keep the offer open).

The UCC recognizes another exception, which is called the **firm offer rule**. This rule states that a *merchant* who (1) offers to buy, sell, or lease goods and (2) gives a written and signed assurance on a separate form that the offer will be held open cannot revoke the offer for the time stated or, if no time is stated, for a reasonable time. The

maximum amount of time permitted under this rule is three months [UCC 2-205, 2A-205].

Example On June 1, a merchant-seller offers to sell a Mercedes-Benz to a buyer for $50,000. The merchant-seller signs a written assurance to keep that offer open until August 30. On July 1, the merchant-seller sells the car to another buyer. On August 21, the original offeree tenders $50,000 for the car. The merchant-seller is liable to the original offeree for breach of contract.

Consideration

The formation of sales and lease contracts requires consideration. However, the UCC changes the common law rule that requires the **modification** of a contract to be supported by new consideration. An agreement modifying a sales or lease contract needs no consideration to be binding [UCC 2-209(1), 2A-208(1)].

Modification of a sales or lease contract must be made in good faith [UCC 1-203]. As in the common law of contracts, modifications are not binding if they are obtained through fraud, duress, extortion, and such.

Formation of Sales and Lease Contracts: Acceptance

Both common law and the UCC provide that a contract is created when the offeree (i.e., the buyer or lessee) sends an acceptance to the offeror, not when the offeror receives the acceptance. For example, a contract is made when the acceptance letter is delivered to the post office. The contract remains valid even if the post office loses the letter.

Unless otherwise unambiguously indicated by language or circumstance, an offer to make a sales or lease contract may be accepted in any manner and by any reasonable medium of acceptance [UCC 2-206(1)(a), 2A-206(1)]. Applications of this rule are discussed in the following paragraphs.

Methods of Acceptance

The UCC permits acceptance by any reasonable manner or method of communication.

> Law must be stable and yet it cannot stand still.
>
> Roscoe Pound
> *Interpretations of Legal History*
> *(1923)*

Example A seller sends a telegram to a proposed buyer, offering to sell the buyer certain goods. The buyer responds by mailing a letter of acceptance to the seller. In most circumstances, mailing the letter of acceptance would be considered reasonable. If the goods were extremely perishable or if the market for the goods were very volatile, however, a faster means of acceptance (such as a telegram) might be warranted.

If an order or other offer to buy goods requires prompt or current shipment, the offer is accepted if the seller (1) promptly promises to ship the goods or (2) promptly ships either conforming or nonconforming goods [UCC 2-206(1)(b)]. The shipment of conforming goods signals acceptance of the buyer's offer.

Acceptance of goods occurs after the buyer or lessee has a reasonable opportunity to inspect them and signifies that (1) the goods are conforming, (2) he or she will take or retain the goods in spite of their nonconformity, or (3) he or she fails to reject the goods within a reasonable time after tender or delivery [UCC 2-513(1), 2A-515(1)].

CONTEMPORARY ENVIRONMENT

UCC Permits Additional Terms

Under common law's **mirror image rule**, an offeree's acceptance must be on the same terms as the offer. The inclusion of **additional terms** in the acceptance is considered a **counteroffer** rather than an acceptance. Thus, the offeror's original offer is extinguished.

UCC 2-207(1) is more liberal than the mirror-image rule. It permits definite and timely expression of acceptance or written confirmation to operate as an acceptance even though they contain terms that are additional to or different from the offered terms, unless the acceptance is expressly conditional on assent to such terms. This rule differs for merchants and nonmerchants.

If one or both parties to a sales contract are nonmerchants, any additional terms are considered **proposed additions** to the contract. The proposed additions do not constitute a counteroffer or extinguish

the original offer. If the offeree's proposed additions are accepted by the original offeror, they become part of the contract. If they are not accepted, the sales contract is formed on the basis of the terms of the original offer [UCC 2-207(2)].

Example A salesperson at a Lexus dealership offers to sell a top-of-the-line coupe to a buyer for $64,000. The buyer replies, "I accept your offer, but I would like to have a satellite radio in the car." The satellite radio is a proposed addition to the contract. If the salesperson agrees, the contract between the parties consists of the terms of the original offer plus the additional term regarding the satellite radio. If the salesperson rejects the proposed addition, the sales contract consists of the terms of the original offer because the buyer made a definite expression of acceptance.

Accommodation Shipment

A shipment of nonconforming goods does not constitute an acceptance if the seller reasonably notifies the buyer that the shipment is offered only as an **accommodation** to the buyer [UCC 2-206(1)(b)]. For example, suppose a buyer offers to purchase 500 red candles from a seller. The seller's red candles are temporarily out of stock. The seller sends the buyer 500 green candles and notifies the buyer that these candles are being sent as an accommodation. The seller has not accepted (or breached) the contract. The accommodation is a counteroffer from the seller to the buyer. The buyer is free either to accept or to reject the counteroffer.

CONTEMPORARY ENVIRONMENT
"Battle of the Forms"

When merchants negotiate sales contracts, they often exchange preprinted forms. These "boilerplate" forms usually contain terms that favor the drafter. Thus, an offeror who sends a standard form contract as an offer to the offeree may receive an acceptance drafted on the offeree's own form contract. This scenario—commonly called the **battle of the forms**—raises important questions: Is there a contract? If so, what are its terms? The UCC provides guidance in answering these questions.

Under UCC 2-207(2), If both parties are merchants, any additional terms contained in an acceptance become part of the sales contract unless

(1) the offer expressly limits acceptance to the terms of the offer, (2) the additional terms materially alter the terms of the original contract, or (3) the offeror notifies the offeree that he or she objects to the additional terms within a reasonable time after receiving the offeree's modified acceptance.

The most important point in the battle of the forms is that there is no contract if the additional terms so materially alter the terms of the original offer that the parties cannot agree on the contract. This fact-specific determination is made by the courts on a case-by-case basis.

UCC Statute Of Frauds

The **UCC Statute of Frauds** applies to all sales and lease contracts. All contracts for the sale of goods costing $500 or more and lease contracts involving payments of $1,000 or more must be in writing [UCC 2-201(1), 2A-201(1)]. The writing must be sufficient to indicate that a contract has been made between the parties. Except as discussed in the paragraphs that follow, the writing must be signed by the party against whom enforcement is sought or by his or her authorized agent or broker. If a contract that falls within these parameters is not written, it is unenforceable.

Example A seller orally agrees to sell her computer to a buyer for $550. When the buyer tenders the purchase price, the seller asserts the Statute of Frauds and refuses to sell the computer to him. The seller is correct. The contract must be in writing to be enforceable because the contract price for the computer exceeds $499.99.

Exceptions to the Statute of Frauds

In three situations, a sales or lease contract that would otherwise be required to be in writing is enforceable even if it is not in writing [UCC 2-201(3), 2A-201(4)]:

1. *Specially manufactured goods.* Buyers and lessees often order specially manufactured goods. If a contract to purchase or lease such goods is oral, the buyer or lessee may not assert the Statute of Frauds against the enforcement of the contract if (1) the goods are not suitable for sale or lease to others in the ordinary course of the seller's or the lessor's business and (2) the seller or lessor has made either a substantial beginning of the manufacture of the goods or commitments for their procurement.

2. *Admissions in pleadings or court.* If the party against whom enforcement of an oral sales or lease contract is sought admits in pleadings, testimony, or otherwise in court that a contract for the sale or lease of goods was made, the oral contract is enforceable against that party. However, the contract is only enforceable as to the quantity of goods admitted.

3. *Part acceptance.* An oral sales or lease contract that should otherwise be in writing is enforceable to the extent to which the goods have been received and accepted by the buyer or lessee.

Example A lessor orally contracts to lease 100 personal computers to a lessee. The lessee accepts the first 20 computers tendered by the lessor. This action is part acceptance. The lessee refuses to take delivery of the remaining 80 computers. Here, the lessee must pay for the 20 computers she originally received and accepted. The lessee does not have to accept or pay for the remaining 80 computers.

CONTEMPORARY ENVIRONMENT
UCC Written Confirmation Rule

It both parties to an oral sales or lease contract are merchants, the Statute of Frauds requirement can be satisfied if (1) one of the parties to an oral agreement sends a written confirmation of the sale or lease within a reasonable time after contracting and (2) the other merchant does not give written notice of an objection to the contract within 10 days after receiving the confirmation. This situation is true even though the party receiving the written confirmation has not signed it. The only stipulations are that the confirmation be sufficient and that the party to whom it was sent has reason to know its contents [UCC 2-201(2)].

Example A merchant-seller in Chicago orally contracts by telephone to sell goods to a merchant-buyer in Phoenix for $25,000. Within a reasonable time after contracting, the merchant-seller sends a sufficient written confirmation to the buyer. The buyer, who has reason to know the contents of the confirmation, fails to object to the contents of the confirmation in writing within 10 days after receiving it. The Statute of Frauds has been met, and the buyer cannot thereafter raise it against enforcement of the contract.

When Written Modification Is Required

Oral modification of a contract is not enforceable if the parties agree that any modification of the sales or lease contract must be signed in writing [UCC 2-209(2), 2A-208(2)]. In the absence of such an agreement, oral modifications to sales and lease contracts are binding if they do not violate the Statute of Frauds.

If the oral modification brings the contract within the Statute of Frauds, it must be in writing to be enforceable.

Example A lessor and lessee enter into an oral lease contract for the lease of goods at a rent of $450. Subsequently, the contract is modified to raise the rent to $550. Because the modified contract rent is more than $499.99, the contract comes under the UCC Statute of Frauds, and the modification must be in writing to be enforceable.

ETHICS SPOTLIGHT
A Chicken Farmer Gets Plucked

The Statute of Frauds was designed to prevent fraud, but sometimes people try to use it to back out of an oral sales contract. Consider the following case.

Perdue Farms, Inc., sells dressed poultry under the brand name "Perdue Roasters." Motts, Inc., of Mississippi entered into an oral contract with Perdue to purchase 1,500 boxes of roasters from Perdue at a stated price. Motts was to pick up the roasters at Perdue's Maryland plant. Motts entered into a contract to resell the roasters to Dairyland, Inc. Motts sent a letter to Perdue, confirming the oral agreement. Perdue received the confirmation and did not object to it. When a Mott's truck arrived at Perdue's Maryland plant to pick up the roasters, Perdue informed the Motts drivers that the roasters would not be loaded unless complete payment was made before delivery. Under previous contracts between the parties, payment was due seven days after delivery. Perdue informed Motts that the roasters would not be sold to Motts on credit. Perdue then sold the roasters directly to Dairyland.

Motts sued Perdue to recover damages for breach of the sales contract. Perdue denied liability, arguing that the contract had to be in writing under the UCC Statute of Frauds because it was over $500. Motts argued that the situation fell under the written confirmation rule exception to the UCC Statute of Frauds.

The District Court agreed with Motts. UCC-2-201(2) binds merchants to oral sales contracts if one sends the other a confirmation letter that is not objected to within 10 days after its receipt. Both parties in this case were merchants, and Perdue did not object within 10 days to the confirmation letter Motts sent. The Court denied Perdue the Statute of Frauds defense and made the Motts confirmation letter enforceable against Perdue. *Perdue Farms, Inc. v. Motts, Inc. of Mississippi*, 25 UCC Rep.Serv. 9. 1978 U.S. Dist. LEXIS 18215.

Law & Ethics Questions

1. What does the UCC Statute of Frauds provide?

2. What does the UCC written confirmation rule provide? Explain.

3. **ETHICS** Did Perdue act ethically in this case? Why do you think Perdue did not want to meet its agreement with Motts?

Web Exercises

1. **WEB** For the compete opinion of this case, go to *www.prenhall.com/cheesemancases*.

2. **WEB** Visit the website of Perdue Farms, Inc., at *www.perdue.com*.

3. **WEB** Use *www.google.com* to find an article that discusses the UCC Statute of Frauds. Read it.

Parol Evidence Rule

The **parol evidence rule** states that when a sales or lease contract is evidenced by a writing that is intended to be a final expression of the parties' agreement or a confirmatory memorandum, the terms of the writing may not be contradicted by evidence of (1) a prior oral or written agreement or (2) a contemporaneous oral agreement (i.e., parol evidence) [UCC 2-202, 2A-202]. This rule is intended to ensure certainty in written sales and lease contracts.

Occasionally, the express terms of a written contract are not clear on their face and must be interpreted. In such cases, reference may be made to certain sources outside the contract. These sources are construed together when they are consistent with each other. If that is unreasonable, they are considered in descending order of priority [UCC 2-208(2), 2A-207(2)]:

1. *Course of performance.* The previous conduct of the parties regarding the contract in question.
2. *Course of dealing.* The conduct of the parties in prior transactions and contracts.
3. *Usage of trade.* Any practice or method of dealing that is regularly observed or adhered to in a place, a vocation, a trade, or an industry.

Example A cattle rancher contracts to purchase corn from a farmer. The farmer delivers feed corn to the rancher. The rancher rejects this corn and demands delivery of corn that is fit for human consumption. Ordinarily, usage of trade would be the first source of interpretation of the word *corn*. If the parties had prior dealings, though, the usage of the term in their prior dealings would become the primary source of interpretation.

CONCEPT SUMMARY

Comparison of Contract Law and the Law of Sales

TOPIC	COMMON LAW OF CONTRACT	UCC LAW OF SALES
Definiteness	Contract must contain all the material terms of the parties' agreement.	The UCC gap-filling rule permits terms to be implied if the parties intended to make a contract [UCC 2-204].
Irrevocable offers	Option contracts.	Option contracts. Firm offers by merchants to keep an offer open are binding up to three months without any consideration [UCC 2-205].
Counteroffers	Acceptance must be a mirror image of the offer. A counteroffer rejects and terminates the offer.	Additional terms of an acceptance become part of the contract if (1) they do not materially alter the terms of the offer and (2) the offeror does not object within a reasonable time after reviewing the acceptance [UCC 2-207].
Statute of Frauds	Writing must be signed by the party against whom enforcement is sought.	Writing may be enforced against a party who has not signed it if (1) both parties are merchants, (2) one party sends a written confirmation of oral agreement within a reasonable time after contracting, and (3) the other party does not give written notice of objection within 10 days after receiving the confirmation [UCC 2-201].
Modification	Consideration is required.	Consideration is not required [UCC 2-209].

INTERNET AND TECHNOLOGY

Revised Article 2 (Sales) and Article 2A (Leases) Recognizes the Importance of Electronic Contracting

Revised Article 2 (Sales) and **Revised Article 2A (Leases)** contain provisions that recognize the importance of electronic contracting in sales and lease transactions. The revised articles contain new definitions that apply to sales and lease contracts. Some of the new definitions for electronic commerce and their implications are discussed below.

■ "Electronic" means relating to technology having electrical, digital, magnetic, wireless, optical, electromagnetic, or similar capabilities [Revised UCC 2-103(1)(f), Revised UCC 2A-103(1)(h)]. This term, as used throughout revised Articles 2 and 2A, extends many of the provisions and rules of the UCC to cover electronic contracting of sales and lease contracts.

■ "Electronic agent" means a computer program or an electronic or other automated means used independently to initiate an action or respond to electronic records or performances in whole or in part, without review or action by an individual [Revised UCC 2-103(1)(g), Revised UCC 2A-103(1)(i)]. This definition, as used in many of the provisions of UCC Article 2 and 2A, allows

for the contracting for the sale and lease of goods over the Internet using websites to order or lease goods.

■ "Electronic record" means a record created, generated, sent, communicated, received, or stored by electronic means [Revised UCC 2-103(1)(h), Revised UCC 2A-103(1)(j)]. This term is often used in revised Articles 2 and 2A to replace the word "writing" and thus recognizes that UCC contracts and other information may be sent or stored by electronic means rather than in tangible writings.

■ "Record" means information that is inscribed on tangible medium or that is stored in an electronic or other medium and is retrievable in perceivable form [Revised UCC 2-103(1)(m), Revised UCC 2A-103(1)(cc)]. The term "record" is now used in many of the provisions of revised Article 2 and 2A in place of the term "writing" and thus further recognizes the importance of electronic contracting.

These terms are used throughout the provisions of Revised Article 2 (Sales) and Revised Article 2A (Leases). These definitions expand the coverage of the provisions of UCC Article 2 and Article 2A to electronic contracting of sales and lease contracts.

INTERNATIONAL LAW

Letters of Credit in International Trade

The major risks in any business transaction involving the sale of goods are (1) that the seller will not be paid after delivering the goods and (2) that the buyer will not receive the goods after paying for them. These risks are especially acute in international transactions, where the buyer and seller may not know each other, the parties are dealing at long distance, and the judicial systems of the parties' countries may not have jurisdiction to decide a dispute if one arises. The irrevocable **letter of credit** has been developed to manage these risks in international sales. The function of a letter of credit is to substitute the credit of a recognized international bank for that of the buyer.

An irrevocable letter of credit works this way. Suppose a buyer in one country and a seller in another country enter into a contract for the sale of goods. The buyer goes to his or her bank and pays the bank a fee to issue a letter of credit in which the bank agrees to pay the amount of the letter (which is the amount of the purchase price of the goods) to the seller's bank if certain conditions are met. These conditions are usually the delivery of documents indicating that the seller has placed the goods in the hands of a shipper. The buyer is called the **account party**, the bank that issues the letter of credit is called the **issuing bank**, and the seller is called the **beneficiary** of the letter of credit.

The issuing bank then forwards the letter of credit to a bank that the seller has designated in his or her country. This bank, which is called the

correspondent, or **confirming bank**, relays the letter of credit to the seller. Now that the seller sees that he or she is guaranteed payment, he or she makes arrangements to ship the goods and receives a **bill of lading** from the carrier proving so. The seller then delivers these documents to the confirming bank. The confirming bank examines the documents, and if it finds them in order, it pays the seller and forwards the documents to the issuing bank. By this time, the buyer has usually paid the amount of the purchase price to the issuing bank (unless an extension of credit has been arranged), and the issuing bank then charges the buyer's account. The issuing bank forwards the bill of lading and other necessary documents to the buyer, who then picks up the goods from the shipper when they arrive.

If the documents (e.g., bill of lading, proof of insurance) conform to the conditions specified in the letter of credit, the issuing bank must pay the letter of credit. If the account party does not pay the issuing bank, the issuing bank's only recourse is to sue the account party to recover damages.

Article 5 (Letters of Credit) of the Uniform Commercial Code governs letters of credit unless otherwise agreed by the parties. The International Chamber of Commerce has promulgated the **Uniform Customs and Practices for Documentary Credits (UCP)**, which contains rules governing the formation and performance of letters of credit. Although the UCP is neither a treaty nor a legislative enactment, most banks incorporate the terms of the UCP in letters of credit they issue.

Hong Kong
Businesses worldwide enter into sales and lease contracts. The parties usually agree in their contracts as to which country's contract law applies to the contract.

Chapter Summary

Uniform Commercial Code (UCC), p. 413

The Uniform Commercial Code (UCC) is a model act that contains uniform rules that govern commercial transactions. Most states have enacted all or part of the UCC as their commercial law statute.

Article 2 (Sales), p. 414

What Is a Sale?

Article 2 of the UCC applies to transactions in goods.

What Are Goods?

Goods are tangible things that are movable at the time of their identification in a sales contract.

Goods Versus Services

Contracts for the provision of services—including legal services, medical services, and dental services—are not covered by Article 2.

Who Is a Merchant?

Article 2 applies to all sales contracts, whether they involve merchants or not. The UCC defines a *merchant* as (1) a person who deals in the goods of the kind involved in the transaction or (2) a person who by his or her occupation holds himself or herself out as having knowledge or skill peculiar to the goods involved in the transaction.

Article 2A (Leases), p. 416

Article 2A of the UCC applies to personal property leases of goods.

Definition of Lease

A lease is a transfer of the right to the possession and use of the named goods for a set term in return for certain consideration. These are the parties to a lease:

1. *Lessor.* A person who transfers the right of possession and use of goods is a lessor.
2. *Lessee.* A person who acquires the right to possession and use of goods is a lessee.

Finance Lease

A finance lease is a three-party transaction of the lessor, the lessee, and the supplier of the leased goods. The parties to a finance lease are:

1. *Lessor.* The lessor acquires title to the goods from the supplier and leases the goods to the lessee. The lessor is often a bank or another creditor.
2. *Lessee.* The lessee is the person who acquires the right to possession and use of the goods.
3. *Supplier.* The supplier is the third party who supplies the goods. The supplier usually sells the goods to the lessor.

Formation of Sale, Leases and E-Contracts: Offer, p. 418

Open Terms

If the parties leave open a major term in a sales or lease contract, the UCC permits the following terms to be read into the contract:

1. Price term
2. Payment term
3. Delivery term
4. Time term
5. Assortment term
   This is commonly called the *gap-filling rule*.

UCC Firm Offer Rule

The firm offer rule is a UCC rule which says that a merchant who (1) makes an offer to buy, sell, or lease goods and (2) assures the other party in a separate writing that the offer will be held open cannot revoke the offer for the time stated or, if no time is stated, for a reasonable time.

Consideration

The formation of sales and lease contracts requires consideration. An agreement modifying a sales or lease contract needs no consideration to be binding.

Formation of Sales and Lease Contracts: Acceptance, p. 420

Methods of Acceptance

The UCC permits acceptance by any reasonable manner or method of communication.

Additional Terms Permitted

The UCC permits an acceptance of a sales contract to contain additional terms and still to act as an acceptance rather than a counteroffer in certain circumstances. The following UCC rules apply:

1. *One or both parties are nonmerchants.* The additional terms are considered proposed additions to the contract. If the offeree's proposed terms are accepted by the offeror, they become part of the contract. If they are not accepted, the sales contract is formed on the basis of the terms of the original offer.
2. *Both parties are merchants.* The additional terms contained in the acceptance become part of the sales contract *unless* (1) the offer expressly limits the acceptance to the terms of the offer, (2) the additional terms materially alter the original contract, or (3) the offerer notifies the offeree that he or she objects to the additional terms within a reasonable time after receiving the offeree's modified acceptance. There is no contract if the additional terms so materially alter the terms of the original offer that the parties cannot agree on the contract.

Accommodation Shipment

An accommodation shipment is a shipment that a seller offers to a buyer as a replacement for the original shipment when the original shipment cannot be filled. The buyer may either accept or reject this shipment.

UCC Statute of Frauds, p. 421

The UCC Statute of Frauds requires contracts for the sale of goods costing $500 or more and lease contracts involving payments of $1,000 or more to be in writing.

Exceptions to the Statute of Frauds

The UCC recognizes the following exceptions to the Statute of Frauds where a sales or lease contract that is required to be in writing is enforceable even though it is not in writing:

1. *Specially manufactured goods.* In these contracts, the goods are not suitable for sale or lease to others in the ordinary course of business, and the seller or lessor has made either a substantial beginning of manufacture of the goods or commitments for their procurement.

2. *Admissions in pleadings or court.* A party admits in pleadings, testimony, or otherwise in court that he or she has entered into a contract.
3. *Part acceptance.* An oral sales or lease contract is enforceable to the extent to which the goods have been received and accepted by the buyer or lessee.

UCC Written Confirmation Rule

If both parties to an oral sales or lease contract are merchants, the Statute of Frauds requirements are satisfied if (1) one of the parties sends a *written confirmation* of the sale to the other within a reasonable time after contracting and (2) the other merchant does not give written notice of an objection to the contract within 10 days after receiving the confirmation.

When Written Modification Is Required

Oral modification of a contract is not enforceable if the parties agree that any modification of the sales or lease contract must be signed in writing. In the absence of such an agreement, oral modifications to sales and lease contracts are binding if they do not violate the Statute of Frauds.

Parol Evidence Rule

The parol evidence rule states that when a sales or lease contract is evidenced by a writing that is intended to be a final expression of the parties' agreement or a confirmatory memorandum, the terms of the writing may not be contradicted by evidence of (1) a prior oral or written agreement or (2) a contemporaneous oral agreement (i.e., parol evidence).

Test Review Terms and Concepts

Accommodation shipment 420	Firm offer rule 419	Parol evidence rule 423
Account party 424	Gap-filling rule 418	Part acceptance 421
Additional terms 420	Goods 415	Proposed additions 420
Article 2 (Sales) 414	Issuing bank 424	Sale 414
Article 2A (Leases) 416	Lease 417	Specially manufactured
Article 5 (Letters of Credit) 424	Lessee 417	goods 415
Battle of the forms 421	Lessor 417	Supplier 417
Beneficiary 424	Letter of credit 424	UCC Statute of Frauds 421
Bill of lading 424	Merchant 416	UCC written confirmation rule 427
Correspondent (confirming	Mirror image rule 420	Uniform Commercial
bank) 424	Mixed sale 415	Code (UCC) 413
Counteroffer 420	Model act 414	Uniform Customs and Practices for
Course of dealing 423	Modification 419	Documentary Credits (UCP) 424
Course of performance 423	Open price term 419	Uniform Sales Act 413
Finance lease 417	Open term 418	Usage of trade 420

Case Problems

16.1 Merchant: Mark Hemphill was a football player at Southern Illinois State University. As a member of the team, Hemphill was furnished with a uniform and helmet. He was injured while playing football for the school. Hemphill claimed that his helmet was defective and contributed to his injuries. Hemphill's attorneys suggested that he sue the university's athletic director, Sayers, and the head football coach, Shultz. The attorneys told Hemphill that he may be able to recover for his injuries based on several provisions of the Uniform Commercial Code. The attorneys specifically suggested that he use the UCC provisions that impose cer-

tain obligations upon merchants. Hemphill brought suit against Sayers and Shultz. Does Article 2 apply to this case? *Hemphill v. Sayers*, 552 F.Supp. 685, **Web** 1982 U.S. Dist. Lexis 16240 (United States District Court for the Southern District of Illinois)

16.2 Good or Service: Mr. Gulash lived in Shelton, Connecticut. He wanted an above-ground swimming pool installed in his backyard. Gulash contacted Stylarama, Inc. (Stylarama), a company specializing in the sale and construction of pools. The two parties entered into a contract that called for Stylarama to "furnish all labor and materials to construct a Wavecrest brand pool, and furnish and install a pool with vinyl liners." The total cost for materials and labor was $3,690. There was no breakdown in the contract of costs between labor and materials. After the pool was installed, its sides began bowing out, the 2″ by 4″ wooden supports for the pool rotted and misaligned, and the entire pool became tilted. Gulash brought suit, alleging that Stylarama had violated several provisions of Article 2 of the UCC. Is this transaction one involving goods, making it subject to Article 2? *Gulash v. Stylarama*, 33 Conn. Supp. 108, 364 A.2d 1221, **Web** 1975 Conn. Super. Lexis 209 (Superior Court of Connecticut)

16.3 Unconscionable Contract: Jane Wilson leased a Toyota pickup truck from World Omni Leasing, Inc. (Omni). Wilson had experience in business and had signed contracts before. In the past, Wilson had read the contracts before signing them. When signing the contract for the lease of the truck, however, Wilson did not take the opportunity to read the lease. However, she signed a statement declaring that she had read and understood the lease. The lease contained a provision that made Wilson responsible for payments on the truck even if the truck was destroyed. Several months after leasing the truck, Wilson was involved in a two-vehicle collision. The pickup truck was destroyed. Omni demanded to be paid for the balance of the lease. Wilson refused, claiming that the lease was unconscionable. Is the lease unconscionable? *Wilson v. World Omni Leasing, Inc.*, 540 So.2d 713, **Web** 1989 Ala. Lexis 41 (Supreme Court of Alabama)

16.4 Statute of Frauds: St. Charles Cable TV (St. Charles) was building a new cable television system in Louisiana. It contacted Eagle Comtronics, Inc. (Eagle), by phone and began negotiating to buy descrambler units for its cable system. These units would allow St. Charles's customers to receive the programs they had paid for. Although no written contract was ever signed, St. Charles ordered several thousand descramblers. The descramblers were shipped to St. Charles, along with a sales acknowledgment form. St. Charles made partial payment for the descramblers before discovering that some of the units were defective. Eagle accepted a return of the defective scramblers. St. Charles then attempted to return all the descramblers, asking that they be replaced by a newer model. When Eagle refused to replace all the old descramblers, St. Charles stopped paying Eagle. Eagle sued St. Charles, claiming that no valid contract existed between the parties. Is there a valid sales contract? *St. Charles Cable TV v. Eagle Comtronics, Inc.*, 687 F.Supp. 820, **Web** 1988 U.S. Dist. Lexis 4566 (United States District Court for the Southern District of New York)

16.5 Firm Offer: Gordon Construction Company (Gordon) was a general contractor in the New York City area. Gordon planned on bidding for the job of constructing two buildings for the Port Authority of New York. In anticipation of its own bid, Gordon sought bids from subcontractors. E. A. Coronis Associates (Coronis), a fabricator of structured steel, sent a signed letter to Gordon. The letter quoted a price for work on the Port Authority project and stated that the price could change, based on the amount of steel used. The letter contained no information other than the price Coronis would charge for the job. One month later, Gordon was awarded the Port Authority project. Four days later, Coronis sent Gordon a telegram, withdrawing its offer. Gordon replied that it expected Coronis to honor the price that it had previously quoted to Gordon. When Coronis refused, Gordon sued. Gordon claimed that Coronis was attempting to withdraw a firm offer. Who wins? *E. A. Coronis Associates v. Gordon Construction Co.*, 90 N.J. Super. 69, 216 A.2d 246, **Web** 1966 N.J. Super. Lexis 368 (Superior Court of New Jersey)

16.6 Battle of the Forms: Dan Miller was a commercial photographer who had taken a series of photographs that had appeared in the *New York Times*. *Newsweek* magazine wanted to use the photographs. When a *Newsweek* employee named Dwyer phoned Miller, he was told that 72 images were available. Dwyer said that he wanted to inspect the photographs and offered a certain sum of money for each photo *Newsweek* used. The photos were to remain Miller's property. Miller and Dwyer agreed to the price and the date for delivery. *Newsweek* sent a courier to pick up the photographs. Along with the photos, Miller gave the courier a delivery memo that set out various conditions for the use of the photographs. The memo included a clause that required *Newsweek* to pay $1,500 each if any of the photos were lost or destroyed. After *Newsweek* received the package, it decided it no longer needed Miller's work. When Miller called to have the photos returned, he was told that they had all been lost. Miller demanded that *Newsweek* pay him $1,500 each for the 72 lost photos. Assuming that the court finds Miller and *Newsweek* to be merchants, are the clauses in the delivery memo part of the sales contract? *Miller v. Newsweek, Inc.*, 660 F.Supp. 852, **Web** 1987 U.S. Dist. Lexis 4338 (United States District Court for the District of Delaware)

16.7 Open Terms: Alvin Cagle was a potato farmer in Alabama who had had several business dealings with the H. C. Schmieding Produce Co. (Schmieding). Several months before harvest, Cagle entered into an oral sales contract with Schmieding. The contract called for Schmieding to pay the market price at harvest time for all the red potatoes that Cagle grew on his 30-acre farm. Schmieding asked that the potatoes be delivered during the normal harvest months. As Cagle began harvesting his red potatoes, he contacted Schmieding to arrange delivery. Schmieding told the farmer that no contract had been formed because the terms of the agreement were too indefinite. Cagle demanded that Schmieding buy his crop. When Schmieding refused, Cagle sued to have the contract enforced. Has a valid sales contract been formed? *H. C. Schmieding Produce Co. v. Cagle*, 529 So.2d 243, **Web** 1988 Ala. Lexis 284 (Supreme Court of Alabama)

16.8 Statute of Frauds: Collins was a sales representative of Donzi Marine Corp. (Donzi), a builder of light speedboats. Collins met Wallach, the owner of a retail boat outlet, at a marine trade show. Collins offered him a Donzi dealership, which would include the right to purchase and then market Donzi speedboats. Wallach tendered a check for $50,000 to Collins. Collins accepted the check, but neither party ever signed a written contract. Wallach ordered several boats. Donzi terminated the dealership because it had found another boat dealer willing to pay more for the franchise. Wallach sued Donzi for breach of contract. Is the contract enforceable under the UCC? *Wallach Marine Corp. v. Donzi Marine Corp.*, 675 F.Supp. 838, **Web** 1987 U.S. Dist. Lexis 11762 (United States District Court for the Southern District of New York)

Ethics Issues

16.9 Ethics: Kurt Perschke was a grain dealer in Indiana. Perschke phoned Ken Sebasty, the owner of a large wheat farm, and offered to buy 14,000 bushels of wheat for $1.95 per bushel. Sebasty accepted the offer. Perschke said that he could send a truck for the wheat on a date six months later. On the day of the phone call, Perschke's office manager sent a memorandum to Sebasty, stating the price and quantity of wheat that had been contracted for. One month before the scheduled delivery, Perschke called Sebasty to arrange for the loading of the wheat. Sebasty stated that no contract had been made. When Perschke brought suit, Sebasty claimed that the contract was unenforceable because of the Statute of Frauds. Was it ethical for Sebasty to raise the Statute of Frauds as a defense? Assuming that both parties are merchants, who wins the suit? *Sebasty v. Perschke*, 404 N.E.2d 1200, **Web** 1980 Ind. App. Lexis 1489 (Court of Appeals of Indiana)

16.10 Ethics: Alex Abatti was the sole owner of A&M Produce Company (A&M), a small farming company located in California's Imperial Valley. Although Abatti had never grown tomatoes, he decided to do so. He sought the advice of FMC Corporation (FMC), a large diversified manufacturer of farming and other equipment, as to what kind of equipment he would need to process the tomatoes. An FMC representative recommended a certain type of machine, which A&M purchased from FMC pursuant to a form sales contract provided by FMC. Within the fine print, the contract contained one clause that disclaimed any warranty liability by FMC and a second clause that stated that FMC would not be liable for consequential damages if the machine malfunctioned.

A&M paid $10,680 down toward the $32,041 purchase price, and FMC delivered and installed the machine. A&M immediately began experiencing problems with the machine. It did not process the tomatoes quickly enough. Tomatoes began piling up in front of the belt that separated the tomatoes for weight-sizing. Overflow tomatoes had to be sent through the machine at least twice, causing damage to them. Fungus spread through the damaged crop. Because of these problems, the machine had to be continually started and stopped, which significantly reduced processing speed.

A&M tried on several occasions to get additional equipment from FMC, but on each occasion, its request was rejected. Because of the problems with the machine, A&M closed its tomato operation. A&M finally stated, "Let's call the whole thing off," and offered to return the machine if FMC would refund A&M's down payment. When FMC rejected this offer and demanded full payment of the balance due, A&M sued to recover its down payment and damages. It alleged breach of warranty caused by defect in the machine. In defense, FMC pointed to the fine print of the sales contract, stating that the buyer waived any rights to sue it for breach of warranty or to recover consequential damages from it.

Was it ethical for FMC to include waiver of liability and waiver of consequential damage clauses in its form contract? Did A&M act ethically in signing the contract and then trying to get out from under its provisions? Legally, are the waiver clauses so unconscionable as to not be enforced? *A&M Produce Co. v. FMC Corp.*, 135 Cal.App.3d 473, 186 Cal.Rptr. 114, **Web** 1982 Cal. App. Lexis 1922 (Court of Appeal of California)

IRAC Writing Assignment

Read **Case A-16** in Appendix A [*Cafazzo v. Central Medical Health Services, Inc.*]. Use the IRAC method to prepare a written analysis of the case.

CHAPTER 17

Performance of Sales, Leases, and E-Contracts

"A lawyer without history or literature is a mechanic, a mere working mason: if he possesses some knowledge of these, he may venture to call himself an architect."

—SIR WALTER SCOTT
Guy Mannering, Chapter 37 (1815)

CHAPTER OBJECTIVES

After studying this chapter, you should be able to:

1. Identify when title to goods passes in shipment and destination contracts.
2. Define terms related to shipment and delivery.
3. Describe who bears the risk of loss when goods are lost or damaged in shipment.
4. Identify who bears the risk of loss when goods are stolen and resold.
5. Define *good faith purchaser for value* and *buyer in the ordinary course of business*.

CHAPTER CONTENTS

Introduction to Performance of Sales and Lease Contracts

Under common law, the rights and obligations of the buyer, the seller, and third parties were determined based on who held technical title to the goods. Article 2 of the Uniform Commercial Code (UCC) establishes precise rules for determining the *passage of title* in sales contracts. Other provisions of Article 2 apply, irrespective of title, except as otherwise provided [UCC 2-401].

Common law placed the *risk of loss* to goods on the party who held title to the goods. Article 2 of the UCC rejects this notion and adopts concise rules for risk of loss that are not tied to title. It also gives the parties to the sales contract the right to *insure* the goods against loss if they have an "insurable interest" in the goods. Title, risk of loss, and insurable interest are discussed in this chapter.

Lighthouse, Straits of Mackinac, Michigan

Common carriers, such as freighters and other ships that carry goods for others, are independent contractors. Risk of loss of goods depends on the shipping terms used in the shipping contract.

Cyber Law

INTERNET AND TECHNOLOGY

Revised Article 2 (Sales) and Revised Article 2A (Leases) Establish Rules for Electronic Contracts and Signatures

Written contracts and written signatures are given effect by Article 2 (Sales) and Article 2A (Leases) of the UCC. The UCC has also established rules for written communications concerning contracts for the sale and lease of goods. Revised Article 2 (Sales) and Revised Article 2A (Leases) add new rules regarding the recognition of signatures and communications concerning electronic contracts. Several of these rules are discussed below.

- A record or signature may not be denied legal effect or enforcement solely because it is in electronic form [Revised UCC 2-211(1), Revised UCC 2A-222(1)]. This provision states that electronic contracts and electronic signatures are to be given legal effect and can be enforced against contracting parties.

- An electronic record or electronic signature is attributable to a person if it was the act of the person or the person's electronic agent [Revised UCC 2-212, Revised UCC 2A-223]. This provision permits a person to conduct business himself or through electronic agents using electronic records and electronic signatures.

- If the receipt of an electronic communication has a legal effect, it has that effect even if no individual is aware of its receipt [Revised UCC 2-213(1), Revised UCC 2A-224(1)]. This rule acknowledges legal effect of electronic communications that are received by electronic agents such as Internet websites.

- Receipt of an electronic acknowledgment of an electronic communication establishes that the communication was received but, in itself, does not establish that the content sent corresponds to the content received [Revised UCC 2-213(2), Revised UCC 2A-224(2)]. Thus, an electronic acknowledgment of the receipt of an electronic communication proves that the electronic communication was received. This acknowledgment does not, in itself, establishment what the content of the electronic communication was, however. That must come from other evidence.

The previous rules place electronic signatures on par with written signatures. These rules also establish special rules regarding the receipt of electronic communications.

Identification and Passage of Title

The identification of goods is rather simple. It means distinguishing the goods named in a contract from the seller's or lessor's other goods. The seller or lessor retains the risk of loss of the goods until he or she identifies them in a sales or lease contract. Further, UCC 2-401(1) and 2-501 prevent title to goods from passing from the seller to the buyer unless the goods are identified in the sales contract. In a lease transaction, title to the leased goods remains with the lessor or a third party. It does not pass to the lessee.

The identification of goods and the passage of title are discussed in the following paragraphs.

Identification of Goods

Identification of goods can be made at any time and in any manner explicitly agreed to by the parties to a contract. In the absence of such an agreement, the UCC mandates when identification occurs [UCC 2-501(1), 2A-217].

Already existing goods are identified when the contract is made and names the specific goods sold or leased.

Example A piece of farm machinery, a car, or a boat is identified when its serial number is listed on a sales or lease contract.

Goods that are part of a larger mass of goods are identified when the specific merchandise is designated.

Example If a food processor contracts to purchase 150 cases of oranges from a farmer who has 1,000 cases of oranges, the buyer's goods are identified when the seller explicitly separates or tags the 150 cases.

Future goods are goods not yet in existence. For example, unborn young animals (such as unborn cattle) are identified when the young are conceived. Crops to be harvested are identified when the crops are planted or otherwise become growing crops. Future goods other than crops and unborn young are identified when the goods are shipped, marked, or otherwise designated by the seller or lessor as the goods to which the contract refers.

Passage of Title

Once the goods that are the subject of a contract exist and have been identified, title to the goods may be transferred from the seller to the buyer. Article 2 of the UCC establishes precise rules for determining the **passage of title** in sales contracts. (As mentioned earlier, lessees do not acquire title to the goods they lease.)

Under UCC 2-401(1), **title** to goods passes from the seller to the buyer in any manner and on any conditions explicitly agreed upon by the parties. If the parties do not agree to a specific time, title passes to the buyer when and where the seller's performance with reference to the physical delivery is completed. This point in time is determined by applying the rules discussed in the following paragraphs [UCC 2-401(2)].

Shipment and Destination Contracts

A **shipment contract** requires the seller to ship the goods to the buyer via a common carrier. The seller is required to (1) make proper shipping arrangements and (2) deliver the goods into the carrier's hands. Title passes to the buyer at the time and place of shipment [UCC 2-401(2)(a)].

A **destination contract** requires the seller to deliver the goods either to the buyer's place of business or to another destination specified in the sales contract. Title passes to the buyer when the seller tenders delivery of the goods at the specified destination [UCC 2-401(2)(b)].

Delivery of Goods Without Moving Them

Sometimes a sales contract authorizes goods to be delivered without requiring the seller to move them. In other words, the buyer might be required to pick up goods from the seller. In such situations, the time and place of the passage of title depends on whether the seller is to deliver a **document of title** (i.e., a warehouse receipt or bill of lading) to the buyer. If a document of title is required, title passes when and where the seller delivers the document to the buyer [UCC 2-401(3)(a)].

Example If the goods named in a sales contract are located at a warehouse, title passes when the seller delivers to the buyer a warehouse receipt representing the goods.

If (1) no document of title is needed and (2) the goods are identified at the time of contracting, title passes at the time and place of contracting [UCC 2-401(3)(b)]. For example, if the buyer signs a sales contract to purchase bricks from the seller, and the contract stipulates that the buyer will pick up the bricks at the seller's place of business, title passes when the contract is signed by both parties. This situation is true even if the bricks are not picked up until a later date.

Risk of Loss: No Breach of Sales Contract

In the case of sales contracts, common law placed the risk of loss of goods on the party who had title to the goods. Article 2 of the UCC rejects this notion and allows the parties to a sales contract to agree among them who will bear the risk of loss if the goods subject to the contract are lost or destroyed. If the parties do not have a specific agreement concerning the assessment of the risk of loss, the UCC mandates who will bear the risk.

Carrier Cases: Movement of Goods

Unless otherwise agreed, goods that are shipped via carrier (e.g., railroad, ship, truck) are considered to be sent pursuant to a *shipment contract* or a *destination contract*. Absent any indication to the contrary, sales contracts are presumed to be shipment contracts rather than destination contracts.

SHIPMENT CONTRACTS A *shipment contract* requires the seller to ship goods conforming to the contract to a buyer via a carrier. The risk of loss passes to the buyer when the seller delivers the conforming goods to the carrier. The buyer bears the risk of loss of the goods during transportation [UCC 2-509(1)(a)].

Shipment contracts are created in two ways. The first requires the use of the term *shipment contract*. The second requires the use of one of the following delivery terms: F.O.B., F.A.S., C.I.F., or C. & F.

DESTINATION CONTRACTS A sales contract that requires the seller to deliver conforming goods to a specific destination is a *destination contract*. Such a contract requires the seller to bear the risk of loss of the goods during their transportation. Thus, with the exception of a no-arrival, no-sale contract, the seller is required to replace any goods lost in transit. The buyer does not have to pay for destroyed goods. The risk of loss does not pass until the goods are tendered to the buyer at the specified destination [UCC 2-509(1)(b)].

Unless otherwise agreed, destination contracts are created in two ways. The first method requires the use of the term *destination contract*. The alternative method requires the use of the following delivery terms: F.O.B. *place of destination*, ex-ship, or no-arrival, no-sale contract.

CONTEMPORARY ENVIRONMENT
Shipping Terms

The following are commonly used shipping terms:

- **F.O.B. (free on board)** *point of shipment* (e.g., F.O.B. Anchorage, Alaska) requires the seller to arrange to ship goods and put the goods in the carrier's possession. The seller bears the expense and risk of loss until this is done [UCC 2-319(1)(a)].

- **F.A.S. (free alongside)** or **F.A.S. (vessel)** *port of shipment* (e.g., *The Gargoyle*, New Orleans) requires the seller to deliver and tender the goods alongside the named vessel or on the dock designated and provided by the buyer. The seller bears the expense and risk of loss until this is done [UCC 2-319(2)(a)].

- **C.I.F. (cost, insurance, and freight)** and **C. & F. (cost and freight)** are pricing terms that indicate the cost for which the seller is responsible. These terms require the seller to bear the expense and the risk of loss of loading the goods on the carrier [UCC 2-320(1)(3)].

- **F.O.B.** *place of destination* (e.g., F.O.B. Miami, Florida) requires the seller to bear the expense and risk of loss until the goods are tendered to the buyer at the place of destination [UCC 2-319(1)(b)].

- **Ex-ship (from the carrying vessel)** requires the seller to bear the expense and risk of loss until the goods are unloaded from the ship at its port of destination [UCC 2-322(1)(b)].

- **No-arrival, no-sale contract** requires the seller to bear the expense and risk of loss of the goods during transportation. However, the seller is under no duty to deliver replacement goods to the buyer because there is no contractual stipulation that the goods will arrive at the appointed destination [UCC 2-324(a)(b)].

Noncarrier Cases: No Movement of Goods

Sometimes a sales contract stipulates that the buyer is to pick up the goods at either the seller's place of business or another specified location. This type of arrangement raises a question: Who bears the risk of loss if the goods are destroyed or stolen after the contract date and before the buyer picks up the goods from the seller? The UCC provides two different rules for this situation. One applies to *merchant-sellers* and the other to *nonmerchant-sellers* [UCC 2-509(3)].

MERCHANT-SELLER If the seller is a merchant, the risk of loss does not pass to the buyer until the goods are received. In other words, a merchant-seller bears the risk of loss between the time of contracting and the time the buyer picks up the goods.

Example On June 1, Tyus Motors, a merchant, contracts to sell a new automobile to a consumer. Tyus Motors keeps the car for a few days after contracting to prep it. During this period, the car is destroyed by fire. Under the UCC, Tyus Motors bears the risk of loss because of its merchant status.

NONMERCHANT-SELLER Nonmerchant-sellers pass the risk of loss to the buyer upon "tender of delivery" of the goods. Tender of delivery occurs when the seller (1) places or holds the goods available for the buyer to take delivery and (2) notifies the buyer of this fact.

Example On June 1, a nonmerchant contracts to sell his automobile to his next-door neighbor. Delivery of the car is tendered on June 3, and the buyer is notified of this. The buyer tells the seller he will pick up the car "in a few days." The car is destroyed by fire before the buyer picks it up. In this situation, the buyer bears the risk of loss because (1) the seller is a nonmerchant and (2) delivery was tendered on June 3. If the car were destroyed on June 2—that is, before delivery was tendered—the seller would bear the risk of loss.

Goods in the Possession of a Bailee

Goods sold by a seller to a buyer are sometimes in the possession of a **bailee** (e.g., a warehouse). If such goods are to be delivered to the buyer without the seller moving them, the risk of loss passes to the buyer when (1) the buyer receives a negotiable document of title (such as a warehouse receipt or bill of lading) covering the goods, (2) the bailee acknowledges the buyer's right to possession of the goods, or (3) the buyer receives a nonnegotiable document of title or other written direction to deliver *and* has a reasonable time to present the document or direction to the bailee and demand the goods. If the bailee refuses to honor the document or direction, the risk of loss remains on the seller [UCC 2-509(2)].

Risk of Loss: Conditional Sales

Sellers often entrust possession of goods to buyers on a trial basis. These transactions are classified as *sales on approval*, *sales or returns*, and *consignment* transactions [UCC 2-326].

Sale on Approval

In a **sale on approval**, there is no sale unless and until the buyer accepts the goods. A sale on approval occurs when a merchant (e.g., a computer store) allows a customer to take the goods (e.g., an Apple computer) home for a specified period of time (e.g., three days) to

> The law is not a series of calculating machines where definitions and answers come tumbling out when the right levers are pushed.
>
> William O. Douglas
> *The Dissent, A Safeguard of Democracy (1948)*

see if they fit the customer's needs. The prospective buyer may use the goods to try them out during this time.

Acceptance of the goods occurs if the buyer (1) expressly indicates acceptance, (2) fails to notify the seller of rejection of the goods within the agreed-upon trial period (or, if no time is agreed upon, a reasonable time), or (3) uses the goods inconsistently with the purpose of the trial (e.g., the customer resells the computer to another person).

The goods are not subject to the claims of the buyer's creditors until the buyer accepts them. In a sale on approval, the risk of loss and title to the goods remain with seller. They do not pass to the buyer until acceptance [UCC 2-327(1)].

Sale or Return

In a **sale or return** contract, the seller delivers goods to a buyer with the understanding that the buyer may return them if they are not used or resold within a stated period of time (or within a reasonable time, if no specific time is stated). The sale is considered final if the buyer fails to return the goods within the specified time or a reasonable time if no time is specified. The buyer has the option of returning all the goods or any commercial unit of the goods.

Example Suppose a fashion designer delivers 10 dresses to a fashion boutique on a sale or return basis. The boutique pays $10,000 ($1,000 per dress). If the boutique does not resell the dresses within three months, it may return the unsold garments to the designer. Say that at the end of three months, the boutique has sold 4 of the dresses. The boutique may return the remaining 6 dresses to the designer and recover the compensation paid for the returned dresses.

In a sale or return contract, the risk of loss and title to the goods pass to the buyer when the buyer takes possession of the goods.

Example In the previous example, if the dresses were destroyed while they were at the boutique, the boutique owner would be responsible for paying the designer for them [UCC 2-327(2)].

Goods sold pursuant to a sale or return contract are subject to the claims of the buyer's creditors while the goods are in the buyer's possession.

Consignment

In a **consignment**, a seller (the **consignor**) delivers goods to a buyer (the **consignee**) to sell them. The consignee is paid a fee if he or she sells the goods on behalf of the consignor. A consignment is treated as a sale or return under the UCC. Whether the goods are subject to the claims of the buyer's creditors usually depends on whether the seller files a financing statement as required by Article 9 of the UCC. If the seller files a financing statement, the goods are subject to the claims of the seller's creditors. If the seller fails to file such statement, the goods are subject to the claims of the buyer's creditors [UCC 2-326(3)].

In the following case, the court had to assess risk of loss in a conditional sale situation.

C A S E **17.1**

Conditional Sale

Prewitt v. Numismatic Funding Corporation

745 F.2d 1175, **Web** 1984 U.S. App. Lexis 17926
United States Court of Appeals for the Eighth Circuit

> " *Under the provisions of the UCC relating to risk of loss, as adopted in Missouri, the risk of loss remains with the seller.* "
>
> —Judge Bright

Facts

Numismatic Funding Corporation (Numismatic), with its principal place of business in New York, sells rare and collector coins by mail throughout the United States. Frederick R. Prewitt, a resident of St. Louis, Missouri, responded to Numismatic's advertisement in *The Wall Street Journal*. Prewitt received several shipments of coins from Numismatic via the mails. These shipments were "on approval" for 14 days. Numismatic gave no instructions as to the method for returning unwanted coins. Prewitt kept and paid for several coins and returned the others to Numismatic, fully insured, via FedEx. Numismatic mailed Prewitt 28 gold and silver coins worth over $60,000 on a 14-day approval. Thirteen days later, Prewitt returned all the coins via certified mail and insured them for the maximum allowed, $400. Numismatic never received the coins. Prewitt brought this action seeking a declaratory judgment as to his nonliability. Numismatic filed a counterclaim. The District Court awarded Prewitt a declaratory judgment of nonliability. Numismatic appealed.

Issue

Who bears the risk of loss, Prewitt or Numismatic?

Language of the Court

The trial court determined, and the parties do not dispute, that the delivery of coins between seller Numismatic and buyer Prewitt constituted a sale "on approval." Under the provisions of the UCC relating to risk of loss, as adopted in Missouri, the risk of loss remains with the seller.

Appellant Numismatic contends that the parties impliedly agreed to shift the risk of loss to Prewitt. It argues that an agreement by Prewitt to assume the risk of loss arose by implication from the prior course of dealing between the parties in which Prewitt had returned coins fully insured via Federal Express. The trial court found that Numismatic shipped the coins to Prewitt through the U.S. Postal Service and that no instructions on the method of return were ever given by Numismatic. In light of this finding, and the absence of any specific evidence in the record

indicating that the parties had agreed upon a method of return, we reject Numismatic's contention that there was an understanding between the parties that Prewitt would return the coins fully insured via Federal Express.

Decision

The Court of Appeals held that the transaction in question was a sale on approval and that under UCC 2-327(1), Numismatic, the owner of the coins, bore the risk of their loss during the return shipment from Prewitt. The Court of Appeals affirmed the decision of the District Court.

Law & Ethics Questions

1. Do you agree with how the UCC assesses risk of loss in sale on approval transactions?

2. **ETHICS** Should Prewitt have fully insured the coins before sending them back to Numismatic?

3. How could Numismatic have protected its interests in this case?

Web Exercises

1. **WEB** For the complete opinion of this case, go to *www.prenhall.com/cheesemancases*.

2. **WEB** Visit the website of the U.S. Court of Appeals for the Eighth Circuit, at *www.ca8.uscourts.gov*.

3. **WEB** Use *www.google.com* to find an article that discusses conditional sales. Read it.

Risk of Loss: Breach of Sales Contract

The risk of loss rules just discussed apply where there is no breach of contract. Separate risk of loss rules apply to situations involving breach of a sales contract [UCC 2-510].

Seller in Breach

A seller breaches a sales contract if he or she tenders or delivers nonconforming goods to the buyer. If the goods are so nonconforming that the buyer has the right to reject them, the risk of loss remains on the seller until (1) the defect or nonconformity is cured or (2) the buyer accepts the nonconforming goods.

> Laws are not masters but servants, and he rules them who obeys them.
>
> Henry Ward Beecher
> *Proverbs from Plymouth Pulpit*
> *(1887)*

Example A buyer orders 1,000 talking dolls from a seller. The contract is a shipment contract, which normally places the risk of loss during transportation on the buyer. The seller ships nonconforming dolls that cannot talk. The goods are destroyed in transit. The seller bears the risk of loss because he breached the contract by shipping nonconforming goods.

Buyer in Breach

A buyer breaches a sales contract if he or she (1) refuses to take delivery of conforming goods, (2) repudiates the contract, or (3) otherwise breaches the contract. A buyer who breaches a sales contract before the risk of loss would normally pass to him or her bears the risk of loss of any goods identified in the contract. The risk of loss rests on the buyer for only a commercially reasonable time. The buyer is only liable for any loss in excess of insurance recovered by the seller.

Risk of Loss: Lease Contracts

The parties to a lease contract may agree as to who will bear the risk of loss of the goods if they are lost or destroyed. If the parties do not so agree, the UCC supplies the following risk of loss rules:

1. In the case of an ordinary lease, the risk of loss is retained by the lessor. If the lease is a finance lease, the risk of loss passes to the lessee [UCC 2A-219].
2. If a tender of delivery of goods fails to conform to the lease contract, the risk of loss remains with the lessor or supplier until cure or acceptance [UCC 2A-220(1)(a)].

CONTEMPORARY ENVIRONMENT
Insuring Against Loss of Goods

To protect against financial loss that would occur if goods were damaged, destroyed, lost, or stolen, the parties to sales and lease contracts should purchase insurance against such loss. If the goods are then lost or damaged, the insured party receives reimbursement from the insurance company for the loss.

To purchase insurance, a party must have an *insurable interest* in the goods. A seller has an insurable interest in goods as long as he or she retains title or has a security interest in the goods. A lessor retains an insurable interest in the goods during the term of the lease. A buyer or lessee obtains an insurable interest in the goods when they are identified in the sales or lease contract. Both the buyer and seller, or the lessee and lessor, can have an insurable interest in the goods at the same time [UCC 2-501, 2A-218].

To obtain and maintain proper insurance coverage on goods, a contacting party should:

- Determine the value of goods subject to the sales or lease contract.
- Purchase insurance from a reputable insurance company to cover the goods subject to the contract.
- Maintain the insurance by paying the premiums when they are due.
- Immediately file the proper claim and supporting documentation with an insurance company if the goods are damaged, destroyed, lost, or stolen.

Sales by Nonowners

Sometimes people sell goods even though they do not hold valid title to them. The UCC anticipated many of the problems this situation could cause and established rules concerning the title, if any, that could be transferred to the purchasers.

Void Title and Lease: Stolen Goods

In a case in which a buyer purchases goods or a lessee leases goods from a thief who has stolen them, the purchaser does not acquire title to the goods and the lessee does not acquire any leasehold interest in the goods. This is called **void title**. The real owner can reclaim the goods from the purchaser or lessee [UCC 2-403(1)].

Example Suppose someone steals a truckload of Sony television sets that are owned by Sears. The thief resells the televisions to City-Mart, which does not know that the goods were stolen. If Sears finds out where the televisions are, it can reclaim them. Because the thief had no title to the goods, title was not transferred to City-Mart. City-Mart's only recourse is against the thief, if he or she can be found.

Voidable Title: Sales or Lease of Goods to Good Faith Purchasers for Value

A seller or lessor has **voidable title** to goods if the goods were obtained by fraud, if a check is later dishonored, or if he or she impersonates another person. A person with voidable title to goods can transfer good title to a **good faith purchaser for value** or a

good faith subsequent lessee. A good faith purchaser or lessee for value is someone who pays sufficient consideration or rent for the goods to the person he or she honestly believes has good title to those goods [UCC 1-201(44)(d), 2-201(1)]. The real owner cannot reclaim goods from such a purchaser [UCC 2-403(1)].

Example Suppose a person buys a Rolex watch from his neighbor for nearly fair market value. It is later discovered that the seller obtained the watch from a jewelry store with a "bounced check." The jewelry store cannot reclaim the watch because the second purchaser purchased the watch in good faith and for value.

Suppose that instead, the purchaser bought the watch from a stranger for far less than fair market value. It is later discovered that the seller obtained the watch from a jewelry store by fraud. The jewelry store can reclaim the watch because the second purchaser was not a good faith purchaser for value.

Entrustment Rule

UCC 2-403(2) holds that if an owner **entrusts** the possession of his or her goods to a merchant who deals in goods of that kind, the merchant has the power to transfer all rights (including title) in the goods to a **buyer in the ordinary course of business**. The real owner cannot reclaim the goods from this buyer.

Example Kim Jones brings her computer to The Computer Store to be repaired. The Computer Store both sells and services computers. Jones leaves (entrusts) her computer at the store until it is repaired. The Computer Store sells her computer to Harold Green. Green, a buyer in the ordinary course of business, acquires title to the computer. Jones cannot reclaim the computer from Green. Her only recourse is against The Computer Store.

The **entrustment rule** also applies to leases. If a lessor entrusts the possession of his or her goods to a lessee who is a merchant who deals in goods of that kind, the merchant-lessee has the power to transfer all the lessor's and lessee's rights in the goods to a buyer or sublessee in the ordinary course of business [UCC 2A-305(2)].

In the following case, the court had to decide whether a purchaser was a buyer in the ordinary course of business.

C A S E **17.2**

Buyer in the Ordinary Course of Business

Lindholm v. Brant

Web 2005 Conn. Super. Lexis 2366 (2005)
Superior Court of Connecticut

> ❝*Any entrusting of possession of goods to a merchant who deals in goods of that kind gives him power to transfer all rights of the entruster to a buyer in ordinary course of business.* ❞

—Judge Rogers

Facts

In 1962, Andy Warhol, a famous artist, created a silkscreen on canvas titled "Red Elvis." Red Elvis consists of 36 identical faces of Elvis Presley with a red background and is approximately 5.75 feet in height and 4.35 feet in width. Kerstin Lindholm was an art collector who, for 30 years, had been represented by Anders Malmberg, an art dealer. In 1987, with the assistance and advice of Malmberg, Lindholm purchased "Red Elvis" for $300,000

In 1996, the Guggenheim Museum in New York City decided to sponsor an Andy Warhol Exhibition (Exhibition). The staff of the Guggenheim contacted Malmberg to see if Lindholm was willing to lend "Red Elvis" to the Exhibition. Lindholm agreed and Red Elvis was placed in the Exhibition. When the Exhibition was completed in 2000, Malmberg told Lindholm that he could place "Red Elvis" on loan to the Louisiana Museum in Denmark if Lindholm agreed. By letter dated March 20, 2000, Lindholm agreed and gave permission to Malmberg to obtain possession of "Red Elvis" from the Guggenheim Museum and place it on loan to the Louisiana Museum. Instead of placing "Red Elvis" on loan to the Louisiana Museum, Malmberg, claiming ownership to "Red Elvis," immediately contracted to sell "Red Elvis" to Peter M. Brant, an art collector, for $2.9 million. Brant had his lawyer do a UCC lien search and search of the Art Loss Registry related to "Red Elvis." These searches revealed no claims or liens against "Red Elvis."

Brant paid $2.9 million to Malmberg and received an invoice of sale and possession of "Red Elvis." Subsequently, Lindholm discovered the fraud. Lindholm brought a civil lawsuit in the State of Connecticut against Brant to recover "Red Elvis." Brant argued that he was a buyer in the ordinary course of business because he purchased "Red Elvis" from an art dealer to whom Lindholm had entrusted "Red Elvis" and therefore he had a claim that was superior to Lindholm's claim of ownership.

Issue

Was Brant a buyer in the ordinary course of business who had a claim of ownership to "Red Elvis" that was superior to that of the owner Lindholm?

Language of the Court

The Brant defendants have pleaded a special defense to all counts that Brant is a buyer in the ordinary course pursuant to Conn. Gen. Stat. Sections 42a-2-403(2) and (3). A person with voidable title has power to transfer a good title to a good faith purchase for value. Any entrusting of possession of goods to a merchant who deals in goods of that kind gives him power to transfer all rights of the entruster to a buyer in ordinary course of business. "Entrusting" includes any delivery and any acquiescence in retention of possession regardless of any condition expressed between the parties to the delivery or acquiescence and regardless of whether the procurement of the entrusting or the possessor's disposition of the goods have been such as to be larcenous under the criminal law.

That statutory provision sets forth the circumstances in which an innocent, good faith purchaser of goods who acquires them from a dealer in goods of that kind has a right to the goods superior to the rights of the owner/entruster of the goods. This special defense requires the Brant defendants to show that Brant was a buyer in the ordinary course.

K. Lindholm's March 20, 2000 letter constituted an entrustment of Red Elvis to a merchant, Malmberg. Once K. Lindholm entrusted Red Elvis to Malmberg she gave him the power to transfer all of her rights as the entruster to a buyer in the ordinary course. Plaintiff's expert, Hoffeld, admitted that the Art Loss Registry is the best recognized mechanism for determining whether a piece of art is stolen. Accordingly, it was reasonable in investigating title for Brant to search the Art Loss Registry and the UCC liens to determine if there were any claims on Red Elvis.

Neither Brant nor his attorneys were focused on the possibility that Malmberg was simply stealing the painting from K. Lindholm. Based on Brant's lawyer's failure to identify to Brant that this might be an outright theft by Malmberg and based on Malmberg's excellent reputation in the art world as well as the fact that the Guggenheim released the painting to Malmberg, it was reasonable for Brant to believe that Malmberg had title to the painting when Malmberg physically delivered the painting to the agreed-upon bonded warehouse.

After considering all of the evidence, the court finds that pursuant to Conn. Gen. Stat. Section 42a-2-403 Brant took good title to Red Elvis. Specifically, Brant purchased Red Elvis from Malmberg in good faith and in the ordinary course of business. Brant honestly believed Malmberg owned Red Elvis when he purchased the painting from him. Brant also observed reasonable commercial standards of fair dealing in the art industry when he purchased Red Elvis from Malmberg. Accordingly, because Brant has proven his special defense of being a buyer in the ordinary course, judgment will enter in favor of the defendants on all counts.

Decision

The court held that Brant was a buyer in the ordinary course of business who obtained ownership to Red Elvis when he purchased the stolen Red Elvis from Malmberg. The court held that Brant's claim of ownership as a buyer in the ordinary course of business was superior to Lindholm's claim of ownership because Lindholm had entrusted "Red Elvis" to an art dealer who sold the stolen "Red Elvis" to Brant.

Law & Ethics Questions

1. What does the rule of ordinary buyer in the course of business provide regarding the purchase of stolen property? Explain.

2. Did Lindholm entrust "Red Elvis" to Malmberg, an art dealer? What could be the consequence of entrusting property to a merchant who sells the type of property that is entrusted to him?

3. **ETHICS** Did Malmberg act ethically in this case? Did he act criminally?

4. **ETHICS** Did Lindholm act ethically in bringing this case to try to recover "Red Elvis" from Brant?

Web Exercises

1. **WEB** For the complete opinion of this case, go to *www.prenhall.com/cheesemancases*.

2. **WEB** Visit the website of the Superior Court of Connecticut, at *www.jud.state.ct.us/external/super*.

3. **WEB** Use *www.google.com* to find a short biography of Andy Warhol. Read it.

4. **WEB** Visit the website of the Guggenheim Museum in New York City, at *www.guggenheim.org*.

5. **WEB** Use *www.google.com* to find a picture of "Red Elvis."

CONCEPT SUMMARY

Passage of Title by Nonowner Third Parties

TYPE OF TRANSACTION	TITLE POSSESSED BY SELLER	INNOCENT PURCHASER	PURCHASER ACQUIRES TITLE TO GOODS
Goods acquired by theft are resold.	Void title	Good faith purchaser for value	No. Original owner may reclaim the goods.
Goods acquired by fraud or dishonored check are resold.	Voidable title	Good faith purchaser for value	Yes. Purchaser takes goods, free of claim of original owner.
Goods entrusted by owner to merchant who deals in that type of good are resold.	No title	Buyer in the ordinary course of business	Yes. Purchaser takes goods, free of claim of original owner.
Creditor possesses security interest in goods that are sold.	Good title	Buyer in the ordinary course of business	Yes. Purchaser takes goods, free of creditor's security interest.

INTERNATIONAL LAW
International Trade Terms

Trade abbreviations, such as F.O.B., C.I.F., etc., are widely used in international contracts. The most widely used trade terms are those published by the International Chamber of Commerce. Called *Incoterms*, they are well known throughout the world. Their use in international sales is encouraged by trade councils, courts, and international lawyers. The United Nations Convention on Contracts for the International Sale of Goods (CISG) allows parties to incorporate trade terms of their choosing.

Parties who adopt the *Incoterms* or any other trade terms in their international contracts should make sure they express their desire clearly. For example, a contract might refer to F.O.B. (*Incoterms 1990*) or C.I.F. (*U.S. UCC*).

London

International contracts usually contain shipping and risk of loss terms.

Chapter Summary

Identification and Passage of Title, p. 432

Identification of Goods

Identification distinguishes the goods named in a contract from the seller's or lessor's other goods.

Passage of Title

1. *Passage of title by agreement.* Title to goods of a sales contract passes from the seller to the buyer in any manner and on any conditions explicitly agreed upon by the parties.
2. *Passage of title where there is no agreement.* If the parties have no agreement as to the passage of title, title passes according to the UCC rules.
3. *Passage of title in lease contracts.* Title to the leased goods remains with the lessor or a third party. Title does not pass to the lessee.

Shipment and Destination Contracts

1. *Shipment contract.* A shipment contract requires the seller to ship the goods to the buyer via a common carrier. Title passes to the buyer at the time and place of shipment.
2. *Destination contract.* A destination contract requires the seller to deliver the goods to the buyer's place of business or other designated destination. Title passes to the buyer when the seller tenders delivery of the goods at the specified destination.

Delivery of Goods Without Moving Them

If a sales contract authorizes goods to be delivered without requiring the seller to move them, title passes at the time and place of contracting, unless a document of title is required, in which case title passes when the seller delivers the document of title to the buyer.

Risk of Loss: No Breach of Sales Contract, p. 433

The parties to a sales contract may agree among themselves as to who will bear the risk of loss of goods if they are lost or destroyed. If the parties to a sales contract do not have a specific agreement concerning the assessment of risk of loss, the UCC mandates who will bear the risk.

Carrier Cases: Movement of Goods

1. *Shipment contract.* With a shipment contract, the risk of loss passes to the buyer when the seller delivers conforming goods to a carrier. The buyer bears the risk of loss during transportation.
2. *Destination contract.* With a destination contract, the risk of loss does not pass to the buyer until the goods are tendered to the buyer at the designated destination. The seller bears the risk of loss during transportation.

Shipping Terms

Sales contracts often contain the following shipping terms:
1. F.O.B. (free on board) *point of shipment*
2. F.A.S. (free alongside) or F.A.S. (vessel) *port of shipment*
3. C.I.F. (cost, insurance, and freight) and C. & F. (cost and freight)
4. F.O.B. *place of destination*
5. Ex-ship (from the carrying vessel)
6. No-arrival, no-sale contract

Noncarrier Cases: No Movement of Goods

If a buyer is to pick up the goods from the seller's place of business or other specified location, the following UCC rules apply:
1. *Merchant-seller.* If the seller is a merchant, the risk of loss does not pass to the buyer until the goods are received by the buyer. The merchant-seller bears the risk of loss between the time of contracting and the time the buyer picks up the goods.
2. *Nonmerchant-seller.* If the seller is a nonmerchant, risk of loss passes to the buyer upon tender of delivery of the goods by the seller (i.e., the seller holds the goods available for the buyer to take delivery).

Goods in the Possession of a Bailee

If goods are to be delivered to the buyer without the seller moving them, the risk of loss passes to the buyer when (1) the buyer receives a negotiable document of title, (2) the bailee acknowledges the buyer's right to possession of the goods, or (3) the buyer receives a nonnegotiable document of title or other written direction to deliver *and* has a reasonable time to present the document or direction to the bailee and demand the goods.

Risk of Loss: Conditional Sales, p. 434

When a seller entrusts goods to a buyer on a trial basis, a number of UCC rules for risk of loss apply.

Sale on Approval

Sale on approval occurs when a merchant allows a customer to take the goods for a specified period of time to try the goods. There is no sale unless and until the buyer accepts the goods. The risk of loss remains with the seller and does not transfer to the buyer until acceptance.

Sale or Return

With a sale or return contract, a seller delivers goods to a buyer with the understanding that the buyer may return them if they are not used or resold during a stated period of time. The risk of loss passes to the buyer when the buyer takes possession of the goods.

Consignment

Consignment occurs when a seller (*consignor*) delivers goods to a buyer (*consignee*) to sell them. The risk of loss passes to the consignee when the consignee takes possession of the goods.

Risk of Loss: Breach Of Sales Contract, p. 436

If there has been a *breach of a sales contract*, the UCC rules concerning risk of loss apply.

Seller in Breach

If a seller breaches a sales contract by tendering or delivering nonconforming goods, the risk of loss to the goods remains with the seller until (1) the defect or nonconformity is cured or (2) the buyer accepts the nonconforming goods.

Buyer in Breach

If a buyer breaches a sales contract by refusing to take delivery of conforming goods or repudiating the contract before the risk of loss would normally transfer to him or her, the buyer bears the risk of loss of any goods identified in the contract for a reasonable commercial time.

Risk of Loss: Lease Contracts, p. 437

The parties to a lease contract may agree as to who will bear the risk of loss of the goods if they are lost or destroyed. If the parties do not have an agreement concerning the assessment of risk of loss, the following UCC rules for risk of loss apply:
1. In the case of an ordinary lease, the risk of loss is retained by the lessor. If the lease is a finance lease, the risk of loss passes to the lessee.
2. If a tender of delivery of goods fails to conform to the lease contract, the risk of loss remains with the lessor or supplier until cure or acceptance.

Sales by Nonowners, p. 437

If a person sells goods that he or she does not hold valid title to, the buyer acquires rights in the goods under the UCC.

Void Title and Lease: Stolen Goods

A thief acquires no title to goods he or she steals. A person who purchases stolen goods does not acquire title to the goods. Any such title is call *void title*. The real owner can reclaim the goods from the purchaser. The purchaser's recourse is to recover from the thief.

Voidable Title: Sales or Lease of Goods to Good Faith Purchasers for Value

If goods are obtained by fraud, with a check that is later dishonored, or through impersonation of another person, the perpetrator acquires *voidable title* to the goods. If the perpetrator sells or leases the goods to a *good faith purchaser or lessee for value*—a person who pays sufficient consideration or rent for the goods and honestly believes that the seller or lessor has good title to the goods—the buyer or lessee acquires good title to the goods. The real owner's recourse is against the perpetrator who acquired the goods from him or her.

Entrustment Rule

If an owner entrusts possession of his or her goods to a merchant who deals in goods of that kind (e.g., for repair) and the merchant sells those goods to a *buyer in the ordinary course of business* (e.g., a customer of the merchant), the buyer acquires title to the goods. The real owner's recourse is against the merchant who sold his or her goods. This rule is called the *entrustment rule*.

Test Review Terms and Concepts

Bailee 434	Document of title 433	Good faith subsequent lessee 438
Buyer in breach	Entrust 438	Identification of goods 432
Buyer in the ordinary course of business 438	Entrustment rule 438	No-arrival, no-sale contract 434
C. & F. (cost and freight) 434	Ex-ship (from the carrying vessel) 434	Noncarrier cases 434
C.I.F. (cost, insurance, and freight) 434	F.A.S. (free alongside) or F.A.S. (vessel) *port of shipment* 433	Passage of title 432
Conditional sale 434	F.O.B. *place of destination* 434	Sale on approval 434
Consignee 435	F.O.B. (free on board) *point of shipment* 433	Sale or return 435
Consignment 435	Future goods 432	Seller in breach 436
Consignor 435	Good faith purchaser for value 437	Shipment contract 432
Destination contract 432		Title 432
		Void title 437
		Voidable title 437

Case Problems

17.1 Identification of Goods: The Big Knob Volunteer Fire Company (Fire Co.) agreed to purchase a fire truck from Hamerly Custom Productions (Hamerly), which was in the business of assembling various component parts into fire trucks. Fire Co. paid Hamerly $10,000 toward the price two days after signing the contract. Two weeks later, it gave Hamerly $38,000 more toward the total purchase price of $53,000. Hamerly bought an engine chassis for the new fire truck on credit from Lowe and Meyer Garage (Lowe and Meyer). After installing the chassis, Hamerly painted the Big Knob Fire Department's name on the side of the cab. Hamerly never paid for the engine chassis, and the truck was repossessed by Lowe and Meyer. The Fire Co. sought to recover the fire truck from Lowe and Meyer. Although the Fire Co. was the buyer of a fire truck, Lowe and Meyer questioned whether any goods had ever been identified in the contract. Were they? *Big Knob Volunteer Fire Co. v. Lowe and Meyer Garage*, 338 Pa. Super. 257, 487 A.2d 953, **Web** 1985 Pa. Super. Lexis 5540 (Superior Court of Pennsylvania)

17.2 Passage of Title: New England Yacht Sales (Yacht Sales) sold a yacht to Robert Pease. Pease paid for the yacht in full, and Yacht Sales delivered to him a marine bill of sale. The marine bill of sale stated that Yacht Sales was transferring "all of its right, title, and interest" in the yacht to Pease.

The yacht never left the Connecticut shipyard that Yacht Sales rented. During the winter, Yacht Sales did repair work on the yacht. In the spring, Yacht Sales delivered the yacht to Pease in Rhode Island. At issue in this case was when the sales tax was due to the state of Connecticut—October 18, 1980, or May 8, 1981. When did the title actually pass? *New England Yacht Sales v. Commissioner of Revenue Services*, 198 Conn. 624, 504 A.2d 506, **Web** 1986 Conn. Lexis 719 (Supreme Court of Connecticut)

17.3 Stolen Goods: John Torniero was employed by Michaels Jewelers, Inc. (Michaels). During the course of his employment, Torniero stole pieces of jewelry, including several diamond rings, a sapphire ring, a gold pendant, and several loose diamonds. Over a period of several months, Torniero sold individual pieces of the stolen jewelry to G&W Watch and Jewelry Corporation (G&W). G&W had no knowledge of how Torniero obtained the jewels. Torniero was arrested when Michaels discovered the thefts. After Torniero admitted that he had sold the stolen jewelry to G&W, Michaels attempted to recover it from G&W. G&W claimed title to the jewelry as a good faith purchaser for value. Michaels challenged G&W's claim to title in court. Who wins? *United States v. Michaels Jewelers, Inc.*, 42 UCC Rep.Serv. 141, **Web** 1985 U.S. Dist. Lexis 15142 (United States District Court for the District of Connecticut)

17.4 Passage of Title: J. A. Coghill owned a Rolls Royce Corniche automobile, which he sold to a man claiming to be Daniel Bellman. Bellman gave Coghill a cashier's check for $94,500. When Coghill tried to cash the check, his bank informed him that the check had been forged. Coghill reported the vehicle as stolen. Subsequently, Barry Hyken responded to a newspaper ad listing a Rolls Royce Corniche for sale. Hyken went to meet the seller of the car, the man who claimed to be Bellman, in a parking lot. When Hyken asked why the car was advertised as a 1980 model when it was in fact a 1979, Bellman replied that it was a newspaper mistake. Hyken agreed to pay $62,000 for the car. When Hyken asked to see Bellman's identification, Bellman provided documents with two different addresses. Bellman explained that he was in the process of moving. Although there seemed to be some irregularities in the title documents to the car, Hyken took possession anyway. Three weeks later, the Rolls Royce Corniche was seized by the police. Hyken sued to get it back. Who wins? *Landshire Food Service, Inc. v. Coghill*, 709 S.W.2d 509, **Web** 1986 Mo. App. Lexis 3961 (Court of Appeals of Missouri)

17.5 Passage of Title: Cherry Creek Dodge, Inc. (Cherry Creek), sold a 1985 Dodge Ramcharger to Executive Leasing of Colorado (Executive Leasing). Executive Leasing, which was in the business of buying and selling cars, paid for the Dodge with a draft. Cherry Creek maintained a security interest in the car until the draft cleared. The same day that Executive Leasing bought the Dodge, it sold the car to Bruce and Peggy Carter. The Carters paid in full for the Dodge with a cashier's check, and the vehicle was delivered to them. The Carters had no knowledge of the financial arrangement between Executive Leasing and Cherry Creek. The draft that Executive Leasing gave Cherry Creek was worthless. Cherry Creek attempted to recover the vehicle from the Carters. Who wins? *Cherry Creek Dodge, Inc. v. Carter*, 733 P.2d 1024, **Web** 1987 Wyo. Lexis 408 (Supreme Court of Wyoming)

17.6 Entrustment Rule: Fuqua Homes, Inc. (Fuqua), is a manufacturer of prefabricated houses. MMM was a partnership created by two men named Kirk and Underhill. MMM operated as a dealer of prefabricated homes. On seven occasions before the disputed transactions occurred, MMM had ordered homes from Fuqua. MMM was contacted by Kenneth Ryan, who wanted to purchase a 55-foot modular home. MMM called Fuqua and ordered a prefabricated home that met Ryan's specifications. Fuqua delivered the home to MMM and retained a security interest in it until MMM paid the purchase price. MMM installed the house on Ryan's property and collected full payment from Ryan. Kirk and Underhill then disappeared, taking Ryan's money with them. Fuqua was never paid for the prefabricated home it had manufactured. Ryan had no knowledge of the dealings between MMM and Fuqua. Fuqua claimed title to the house based upon its security interest. Who has title to the home? *Fuqua Homes, Inc. v. Evanston Bldg. & Loan Co.*, 52 Ohio App. 2d 399, 370 N.E.2d 780, **Web** 1977 Ohio App. Lexis 6968 (Court of Appeals of Ohio)

17.7 Risk of Loss: All America Export-Import Corp. (All America) placed an order for several thousand pounds of yarn with A.M. Knitwear (Knitwear). On June 4, All America sent Knitwear a purchase order. The purchase order stated the terms of the sale, including language that stated that the price was F.O.B. the seller's plant. A truck hired by All America arrived at Knitwear's plant. Knitwear turned the yarn over to the carrier and notified All America that the goods were now on the truck. The truck left Knitwear's plant and proceeded to a local warehouse. Sometime during the night, the truck was hijacked, and all the yarn was stolen. All America had paid for the yarn by check but stopped payment on it when it learned that the goods had been stolen. Knitwear sued All America, claiming that it must pay for the stolen goods because it bore the risk of loss. Who wins? *A. M. Knitwear v. All America, Etc.*, 41 N.Y.2d 14, 359 N.E.2d 342, 390 N.Y.S.2d 832, **Web** 1976 N.Y. Lexis 3201 (Court of Appeals of New York)

17.8 Risk of Loss: Mitsubishi International Corporation (Mitsubishi) entered into a contract with Crown Door Company (Crown) that called for Mitsubishi to sell 12 boxcar loads of plywood to Crown. According to the terms of the contract, Mitsubishi would import the wood from Taiwan and deliver it to Crown's plant in Atlanta. Mitsubishi had the wood shipped from Taiwan to Savannah, Georgia. At Savannah, the plywood was loaded onto trains and hauled to Atlanta. When the plywood arrived in Atlanta, it was discovered that the railroad had been negligent in loading the train. The negligent loading had caused the cargo to shift during the trip, and the shifting had caused extensive damage to the wood. Who bore the risk of loss? *Georgia Port Authority v. Mitsubishi International Corporation*, 156 Ga. App. 304, 274 S.E.2d 699, **Web** 1980 Ga. App. Lexis 2952 (Court of Appeals of Georgia)

17.9 Risk of Loss: Martin Silver ordered two rooms of furniture from Wycombe, Meyer & Co., Inc. (Wycombe), a manufacturer and seller of custom-made furniture. On February 23, 1982, Wycombe sent invoices to Silver, advising him that the furniture was ready for shipment. Silver tendered payment in full for the goods and asked that one room of furniture be shipped immediately and that the other be held for shipment on a later date. Before any instructions were received as to the second room of furniture, it was destroyed in a fire. Silver and his insurance company attempted to recover the money he had paid for the destroyed furniture. Wycombe refused to return the payment, claiming that the risk of loss was on Silver. Who wins? *Silver v. Wycombe, Meyer & Co., Inc.*, 124 Misc. 2d 717, 477 N.Y.S.2d 288, **Web** 1984 N.Y. Misc. Lexis 3319 (Civil Court of the City of New York)

17.10 Insurable Interest: Donald Hayward signed a sales contract with Dry Land Marina, Inc. (Dry Land).

The contract was for the purchase of a 30-foot Revel Craft Playmate Yacht for $10,000. The contract called for Dry Land to install a number of options on Hayward's yacht and then deliver it to him. Before taking delivery of the yacht, Hayward signed a security agreement in favor of Dry Land and a promissory note.

Several weeks later, a fire swept through Dry Land's showroom. Hayward's yacht was among the goods destroyed in the fire. Who had an insurable interest in the yacht? *Hayward v. Potsma*, 31 Mich. App. 720, 188 N.W.2d 31, **Web** 1971 Mich. App. Lexis 2150 (Court of Appeals of Michigan)

Ethics Issues

17.11 Ethics: Raceway Auto Auction (Raceway), New York, sold an Oldsmobile automobile to Triangle Auto Sales (Triangle). Triangle paid for the car with a check. Raceway delivered possession of the car to Triangle. Thereafter, Triangle's check bounced because of insufficient funds. In the meantime, Triangle sold the car to Campus Auto Sales (Campus), Rhode Island, which sold it to Charles Motor Co., Inc. (Charles), Rhode Island, which sold it to Lee Oldsmobile-Cadillac, Inc. (Lee Oldsmobile), Maine, which sold it to Stephanie K. LeBlanc of Augusta, Maine. When Triangle's check bounced, Raceway reported the car as stolen. Four months after she purchased the car, Stephanie was stopped by the Maine police, who seized the car. To maintain good relations with its customer, Lee Oldsmobile paid Raceway to obtain the certificate of title to the automobile and then sued Charles to recover. Did Triangle Auto Sales act ethically in this case? Did Charles Motor Co. obtain valid title to the automobile? *Lee Oldsmobile-Cadillac, Inc. v. Labonte*, 30 UCC Rep.Serv. 74, **Web** 1980 R.I. Super. Lexis 190 (Superior Court of Rhode Island)

17.12 Ethics: Executive Financial Services, Inc. (EFS), purchased three tractors from Tri-County Farm Company (Tri-County), a John Deere dealership owned by Gene Mohr and James Loyd. The tractors cost $48,000, $19,000, and $38,000. EFS did not take possession of the tractors but instead left the tractors on Tri-County's lot. EFS leased the tractors to Mohr-Loyd Leasing (Mohr-Loyd), a partnership between Mohr and Loyd, with the understanding and representation by Mohr-Loyd that the tractors would be leased out to farmers. Instead of leasing the tractors, Tri-County sold them to three different farmers. EFS sued and obtained judgment against Tri-County, Mohr-Loyd, and Mohr and Loyd personally for breach of contract. Because that judgment remained unsatisfied, EFS sued the three farmers who bought the tractors to recover the tractors from them. Did Mohr and Loyd act ethically in this case? Who owns the tractors, EFS or the farmers? *Executive Financial Services, Inc. v. Pagel*, 238 Kan. 809, 715 P.2d 381, **Web** 1986 Kan. Lexis 290 (Supreme Court of Kansas)

IRAC Writing Assignment

Read **Case A-17** in Appendix A [*Burnett v. Purtell*]. Use the IRAC method to prepare a written analysis of the case.

CHAPTER 18

Remedies for Breach of Sales, Leases, and E-Contracts

> **❝***Trade and commerce, if they were not made of Indian rubber, would never manage to bounce over the obstacles which legislators are continually putting in their way.* **❞**
>
> —HENRY D. THOREAU
> Resistance to Civil Government (1849)

CHAPTER OBJECTIVES

After studying this chapter, you should be able to:

1. Describe the performance of sales and lease contracts.
2. List and describe the seller's remedies for the buyer's breach of a sales contract.
3. List and describe the buyer's remedies for the seller's breach of a sales contract.
4. List and describe the lessor's remedies for the lessee's breach of a lease contract.
5. List and describe the lessee's remedies for the lessor's breach of a lease contract.

CHAPTER CONTENTS

- Introduction to Remedies for Breach of Sales and Lease Contracts
- Seller's and Lessor's Performance
- Buyer's and Lessee's Performance
- Seller's and Lessor's Remedies
- Buyer's and Lessee's Remedies
- Additional Performance Issues
- Chapter Summary
- Test Review Terms and Concepts
- Case Problems
- Ethics Issues
- IRAC Writing Assignment

   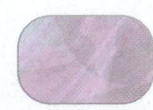 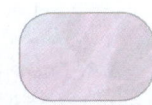

Introduction to Remedies for Breach of Sales and Lease Contracts

Usually, the parties to a sales or lease contract owe a duty to perform the **obligations** specified in their agreement [UCC 2-301, 2A-301]. The seller's or lessor's general obligation is to transfer and deliver the goods to the buyer or lessee. The buyer's or lessee's general obligation is to accept and pay for the goods.

When one party **breaches** a sales or lease contract, the UCC provides the injured party with a variety of prelitigation and litigation remedies. These remedies are designed to place the injured party in as good a position as if the breaching party's contractual obligations were fully performed [UCC 1-106(1), 2A-401(1)]. The best remedy depends on the circumstances of the particular case.

The performance of obligations and remedies available for breach of sales and lease contracts are discussed in this chapter.

Russia

Sales and lease contracts between companies from different countries should specify what commercial law applies to the contract and its performance.

Seller's and Lessor's Performance

The seller's or lessor's basic obligation is the **tender of delivery**, or the transfer and delivery of goods to the buyer or lessee in accordance with a sales or lease contract [UCC 2-301]. Tender of delivery requires the seller or lessor to (1) put and hold conforming goods at the buyer's or lessee's disposition and (2) give the buyer or lessee any notification reasonably necessary to enable delivery of goods. The parties may agree as to the time, place, and manner of delivery. If there is no special agreement, tender must be made at a reasonable hour, and the goods must be kept available for a reasonable period of time.

Example The seller cannot telephone the buyer at 12:01 A.M. and say that the buyer has 15 minutes to accept delivery [UCC 2-503(1), 2A-508(1)].

Unless otherwise agreed or unless the circumstances permit either party to request delivery in lots, the goods named in a contract must be tendered in a single delivery. Payment of a sales contract is due upon tender of delivery unless an extension of credit between the parties has been arranged. If the goods are rightfully delivered in lots, the payment is apportioned for each lot [UCC 2-307]. Lease payments are due in accordance with the terms of the lease contract.

Place of Delivery

Many sales and lease contracts state where the goods are to be delivered. Often, the contract will say that the buyer or lessee must pick up the goods from the seller or lessor. If the contract does not expressly state the **place of delivery**, the UCC stipulates place of delivery on the basis of whether a carrier is involved.

Noncarrier Cases

Unless otherwise agreed, the place of delivery is the seller's or lessor's place of business. If the seller or lessor has no place of business, the place of delivery is the seller's or lessor's residence. If the parties have knowledge at the time of contracting that identified goods are located in some other place, that place is the place of delivery.

Example If parties contract regarding the sale of wheat that is located in a silo, the silo is the place of delivery [UCC 2-308].

Sometimes the goods are in the possession of a bailee (e.g., a warehouse) and are to be delivered without being moved. In such cases, tender of delivery occurs when the seller either (1) tenders to the buyer a negotiable document of title covering the goods, (2) produces acknowledgment from the bailee of the buyer's right to possession of the goods, or (3) tenders a nonnegotiable document of title or a written direction to the bailee to deliver the goods to a buyer. The seller must deliver all such documents in correct form [UCC 2-503(4), 2-503(5)].

Carrier Cases

Unless the parties have agreed otherwise, if delivery of goods to a buyer is to be made by carrier, the UCC establishes different rules for *shipment contracts* and *destination contracts*. These rules are described in the paragraphs that follow.

SHIPMENT CONTRACTS Sales contracts that require the seller to send the goods to the buyer, but not to a specifically named destination, are called **shipment contracts**. Under such contracts, the seller must do all the following [UCC 2-504]:

1. Put the goods in the carrier's possession and contract for the proper and safe transportation of the goods.
2. Obtain and promptly deliver or tender in correct form any documents (a) necessary to enable the buyer to obtain possession of the goods, (b) required by the sales contract, or (c) required by usage of trade.
3. Promptly notify the buyer of the shipment.

The buyer may reject the goods if a material delay or loss is caused by the seller's failure to make a proper contract for the shipment of goods or properly notify the buyer of the shipment.

Example If a shipment contract involves perishable goods and the seller fails to ship the goods via a refrigerated carrier, the buyer may rightfully reject the goods if they spoil during transit.

DESTINATION CONTRACTS A sales contract that requires the seller to deliver goods to the buyer's place of business or another specified destination is a **destination contract**. Unless otherwise agreed, destination contracts require delivery to be tendered at the buyer's place of business or other location specified in the sales contract. Delivery must occur at a reasonable time, in a reasonable manner, and with proper notice to the buyer. Appropriate documents of title must be provided by the seller to enable the buyer to obtain the goods from the carrier [UCC 2-503].

Perfect Tender Rule

A seller or lessor is under a duty to deliver conforming goods. If the goods or tender of delivery fails in any respect to conform to the contract, the buyer or lessee may opt either (1) to reject the whole shipment, (2) to accept the whole shipment, or (3) to reject part and accept part of the shipment. This option is referred to as the **perfect tender rule** [UCC 2-601, 2A-509].

Example A sales contract requires the seller to deliver 100 shirts to a buyer. When the buyer inspects the delivered goods, it is discovered that 99 shirts conform to the contract, and 1 shirt does not conform. Pursuant to the perfect tender rule, the buyer may reject the entire shipment. If a buyer accepts nonconforming goods, the buyer may seek remedies against the seller.

Exceptions to the Perfect Tender Rule

The UCC alters the perfect tender rule in the following situation:

1. *Agreement of the parties.* The parties to a sales or lease contract may agree to limit the effect of the perfect tender rule. For example, they may decide that (1) only the defective or nonconforming goods may be rejected, (2) the seller or lessor may replace nonconforming goods or repair defects, or (3) the buyer or lessee will accept nonconforming goods with appropriate compensation from the seller or lessor.
2. *Substitution of carriers.* The UCC requires the seller to use a commercially reasonable substitute if (1) the agreed-upon manner of delivery fails or (2) the agreed-upon type of carrier becomes unavailable [UCC 2-614(1)].

   Example A sales contract specifies delivery of goods by Mac Trucks, Inc., a common carrier, but a labor strike prevents delivery by this carrier. The seller must use any commercially reasonable substitute (such as another truck line or the rails). The buyer cannot reject the delivery because there is a substitute carrier. Unless otherwise agreed, the seller bears any increased cost of the substitute performance.

> The buyer needs a hundred eyes, the seller not one.
>
> George Herbert
> *Jacula Prudentum (1651)*

Cure

The UCC gives a seller or lessor who delivers nonconforming goods an opportunity to **cure** the nonconformity. Although the term *cure* is not defined by the UCC, it generally means an opportunity to repair or replace defective or nonconforming goods [UCC 2-508, 2A-513].

A cure may be attempted if the time for performance has not expired and the seller or lessor notifies the buyer or lessee of his or her intention to make a conforming delivery within the contract time.

Example A lessee contracts to lease a BMW 850i automobile from a lessor for delivery July 1. On June 15, the lessor delivers a BMW 740i to the lessee, and the lessee rejects it as nonconforming. The lessor has until July 1 to cure the nonconformity by delivering the BMW 850i specified in the contract.

A cure may also be attempted if the seller or lessor had reasonable grounds to believe the delivery would be accepted. The seller or lessor may have a further reasonable time to substitute a conforming tender.

Example A buyer contracts to purchase 100 red dresses from a seller for delivery July 1. On July 1, the seller delivers 100 blue dresses to the buyer. In the past, the buyer has accepted different-colored dresses than those ordered. This time, though, the buyer rejects the blue dresses as nonconforming. The seller has a reasonable time after July 1 to deliver conforming red dresses to the buyer.

In the following case, a seller attempted to cure a defective delivery.

CASE 18.1
Cure

Joc Oil USA, Inc. v. Consolidated Edison Company of New York, Inc.
443 N.E.2d 932, 457 N.Y.S.2d 458, **Web** 1982 N.Y. Lexis 3846
Court of Appeals of New York

> 66 *Therefore, prior to delivery and at the time Joc Oil made its offer to cure by tendering a new conforming shipment, it had cause to believe that the original shipment would have been accepted by the buyer 'with or without money allowance.'* 99
>
> —Judge Fuchsberg

Facts

Joc Oil USA, Inc. (Joc Oil), contracted to purchase low-sulfur fuel oil from an Italian oil refinery. The Italian refinery issued a certificate to Joc Oil, indicating that the sulfur content of the oil was 0.50 percent. Joc Oil entered into a sales contract to sell the oil to Consolidated Edison Company of New York, Inc. (Con Ed). Con Ed agreed to pay an agreed-upon price per barrel for oil not to exceed 0.50 percent sulfur. When the ship delivering the oil arrived, it discharged the oil into three Con Ed storage tanks. A report issued by Con Ed stated that the sulfur content of the oil was 0.92 percent. Joc Oil then made an offer to cure the defect by substituting a conforming shipment of oil that was already on a ship that was to arrive within two weeks. Con Ed rejected Joc Oil's offer to cure. Joc Oil sued Con Ed for breach of contract. The trial court held that under the circumstances of this case, Joc Oil had the right to cure the defect in delivery and that Con Ed breached the contract by refusing to permit this cure. The court entered judgment against Con Ed and awarded Joc Oil $1,385,512 in damages plus interest and the costs of this action. The appellate division court affirmed the judgment. Con Ed appealed.

Issue

Did Joc Oil have a right to cure the defect in the delivery?

Language of the Court

Joc Oil had "reasonable grounds to believe" that the original shipment would be "acceptable" to Con Ed. Moreover, although Joc Oil had no predelivery knowledge of the 0.92% sulfur content disclosed after delivery, it would still have believed that such a shipment would have been acceptable to Con Ed based upon its prior knowledge of Con Ed purchase and use practices during this period of oil scarcity and volatile pricing. Prior to delivery and at the time Joc Oil made its offer to cure by tendering a new conforming shipment, it had cause to believe that the original shipment would have been accepted by the buyer "with or without money allowance" [UCC 2-508(2)].

Decision

The court of appeals held that Joc Oil had made a reasonable and timely offer to cure that was improperly rejected by Con Ed. The court of appeals affirmed the prior court's judgment awarding Joc Oil $1,385,512 in damages plus interest and costs.

Law & Ethics Questions

1. Should the law recognize the right to cure a defective tender of goods? Why or why not?

2. **ETHICS** Did Con Ed act ethically in this case? Did Joc Oil?

3. Why do you think Con Ed rejected Joc Oil's offer to cure the defect in delivery? Explain.

Web Exercises

1. **WEB** For the complete opinion of this case, go to *www.prenhall.com/cheesemancases*.

2. **WEB** Visit the website of the court of appeals of New York, at *www.nycourts.gov/ctapps*.

3. **WEB** Visit the website of Consolidated Edison Company of New York, at *www.coned.com*.

4. **WEB** Use *www.google.com* to find an article that discusses the UCC's rule concerning curing a defective delivery of a good. Read it.

Installment Contracts

An **installment contract** is a contract that requires or authorizes goods to be delivered and accepted in separate lots. Such a contract must contain a clause that states "each delivery in a separate lot" or equivalent language.

Example A contract in which the buyer orders 100 shirts, to be delivered in four equal installments of 25 items, is an installment contract.

The UCC alters the perfect tender rule with regard to installment contracts. The buyer or lessee may reject the entire contract only if the nonconformity or default with respect to any installment or installments substantially impairs the value of the entire contract. The buyer or lessee may reject any nonconforming installment if the value of the installment is impaired and the defect cannot be cured. Thus, in each case, the court must determine whether the nonconforming installment impairs the value of the entire contract or only that installment [UCC 2-612, 2A-510].

Destruction of Goods

The UCC provides that if goods identified in a sales or lease contract are totally destroyed without the fault of either party before the risk of loss passes to the buyer or the lessee, the contract is void. Both parties are then excused from performing the contract.

If the goods are only partially destroyed, the buyer or lessee may inspect the goods and then choose either to treat the contract as void or to accept the goods. If the buyer or lessee opts to accept the goods, the purchase price or rent will be reduced to compensate for damages [UCC 2-613, 2A-221].

> This is the kind of order which makes the administration of justice stink in the nostrils of commercial men.
>
> A. L. Smith
> *L. J. Graham v. Sutton,*
> *Carden & Company (1897)*

Example A buyer contracts to purchase a sofa from a seller. The seller agrees to deliver the sofa to the buyer's home. The truck delivering the sofa is hit by an automobile, and the sofa is totally destroyed. Because the risk of loss has not passed to the buyer, the contract is voided, and the buyer does not have to pay for the sofa.

ETHICS SPOTLIGHT

Good Faith and Reasonableness

Generally, the common law of contracts only obligates the parties to perform according to the express terms of their contract. There is no breach of contract unless the parties fail to meet these terms.

Recognizing that certain situations may develop that are not expressly provided for in a contract or that strict adherence to the terms of a contract without doing more may not be sufficient to accomplish the contract's objective, the Uniform Commercial Code (UCC) adopts two broad principles that govern the performance of sales and lease contracts: *good faith* and *reasonableness*.

UCC 1-203 states, "Every contract or duty within this Act imposes an obligation of good faith in its performance or enforcement." Although both parties owe a duty of good faith in the performance of a sales or lease contract, merchants are held to a higher standard of good faith than nonmerchants. Nonmerchants are held to the subjective standard of honesty in fact, whereas merchants are held to the objective standard of fair dealing in the trade [UCC 2-103(1)(b)].

The words *reasonable* and *reasonably* are used throughout the UCC to establish the duties of performance by the parties to sales and lease contracts. For example, unless otherwise specified, the parties must act within a "reasonable" time [UCC 1-204(1)(2)]. As another example, if a seller does not deliver the goods as contracted, the buyer may make "reasonable" purchases to cover (i.e., obtain substitute performance) [UCC 2-712(1)]. The term *commercial reasonableness* is used to establish certain duties of merchants under the UCC. Articles 2 and 2A of the UCC do not specifically define the terms *reasonable* and *commercial reasonableness*. Instead, these terms are defined by reference to the course of performance or the course of dealing between the parties, usage of trade, and such.

Note that the concepts of good faith and reasonableness extend to the "spirit" of the contract as well as the contract terms. The underlying theory is that the parties are more apt to perform properly if their conduct is to be judged against these principles. This is a major advance in the law of contracts.

Law & Ethics Questions

1. **ETHICS** Do the UCC concepts of *good faith* and *reasonableness* enhance ethical conduct?

2. Should the concept of *good faith* be implied in every contract? Why or why not?

Buyer's and Lessee's Performance

Once the seller or lessor has properly tendered delivery, the buyer or lessee is obligated to accept and pay for the goods in accordance with the sales or lease contract. If there is no agreement, the provisions of the UCC control.

Right of Inspection

Unless otherwise agreed, the buyer or lessee has the **right to inspect** goods that are tendered, delivered, or identified in a sales contract prior to accepting or paying for them. If the goods are shipped, the inspection may take place after their arrival. If the inspected goods do not conform to the contract, the buyer or lessee may reject them without paying for them [UCC 2-513(1), 2A-515(1)].

The parties may agree as to the time, place, and manner of inspection. If there is no such agreement, the inspection must occur at a reasonable time and place and in a reasonable manner. Reasonableness depends on the circumstances of the case, common usage of trade, prior course of dealing between the parties, and such. If the goods conform to the contract, the buyer pays for the inspection. If the goods are rejected for nonconformance, the cost of inspection can be recovered from the seller [UCC 2-513(2)].

Buyers who agree to **C.O.D. (cash on delivery)** deliveries are not entitled to inspect the goods before paying for them. In certain sales contracts (e.g., cost, insurance, and freight [C.I.F.] contracts), payment is due from the buyer upon receipt of documents of title, even if the goods have not yet been received. In such a case, the buyer is not entitled to inspect the goods before paying for them [UCC 2-513(3)].

Payment

> A proceeding may be perfectly legal and may yet be opposed to sound commercial principles.
>
> L. J. Lindley
> *Verner v. General and Commercial Trust (1894)*

Goods that are accepted must be paid for [UCC 2-607(1)]. Unless the parties to a contract agree otherwise, payment is due from a buyer when and where the goods are delivered, even if the place of delivery is the same as the place of shipment. Buyers often purchase goods on credit extended by the seller. Unless the parties agree to other terms, the credit period begins to run from the time the goods are shipped [UCC 2-310]. A lessee must pay lease payments in accordance with the lease contract [UCC 2A-516(1)].

The goods can be paid for in any manner currently acceptable in the ordinary course of business (check, credit card, or the like) unless the seller demands payment in cash or unless the contract names a specific form of payment. If the seller requires cash payment, the buyer must be given an extension of time necessary to procure the cash. If the buyer pays by check, payment is conditional on the check being honored (paid) when it is presented to the bank for payment [UCC 2-511].

Acceptance

Acceptance occurs when the buyer or lessee takes any of the following actions after a reasonable opportunity to inspect the goods: (1) signifies to the seller or lessor in words or by conduct that the goods are conforming or that the buyer or lessee will take or retain the goods despite their nonconformity or (2) fails to effectively reject the goods within a reasonable time after their delivery or tender by the seller or lessor. Acceptance also occurs if a buyer acts inconsistently with the seller's ownership rights in the goods.

Example Acceptance occurs if the buyer resells the goods delivered by the seller [UCC 2-606(1), 2A-515(1)].

Buyers and lessees may only accept delivery of a "commercial unit." A commercial unit is a unit of goods that commercial usage deems is a single whole for purpose of sale. Thus, it may be a single article (such as a machine), a set of articles (such as a suite of furniture or an assortment of sizes), a quantity (such as a bale, a gross, or a carload), or any other unit treated in use or in the relevant market as a single whole. Acceptance of a part of any commercial unit is acceptance of the entire unit [UCC 2-606(2), 2A-515(2)].

Revocation of Acceptance

A buyer or lessee who has accepted goods may subsequently revoke his or her acceptance if (1) the goods are nonconforming, (2) the nonconformity substantially impairs the value of the goods to the buyer or lessee, and (3) one of the following factors is shown: (a) the seller's or lessor's promise to timely cure of the nonconformity is not met, (b) the goods were accepted before the nonconformity was discovered and the nonconformity was difficult to discover, or (c) the goods were accepted before the nonconformity was discovered and the seller or lessor assured the buyer or lessee that the goods were conforming.

Revocation of acceptance is not effective until the seller or lessor is so notified. In addition, the revocation must occur within a reasonable time after the buyer or lessee discovers or should have discovered the grounds for the revocation. The revocation, which must be of a lot or commercial unit, must occur before there is any substantial change in the condition of the goods (e.g., before perishable goods spoil) [UCC 2-608(1), 2A-517(1)].

Seller's and Lessor's Remedies

Various remedies are available to sellers and lessors if a buyer or lessee breaches a contract. These remedies are discussed in the paragraphs that follow.

Right to Withhold Delivery

Delivery of goods may be withheld if the seller or lessor is in possession of them when the buyer or lessee breaches the contract. The **right to withhold delivery** is available if the buyer or lessee wrongfully rejects or revokes acceptance of the goods, fails to make a payment when due, or repudiates the contract. If part of the goods under the contract have been delivered when the buyer or lessee materially breaches the contract, the seller or lessor may withhold delivery of the remainder of the affected goods [UCC 2-703(a), 2A-523(1)(c)].

A seller or lessor who discovers that the buyer or lessee is insolvent before the goods are delivered may refuse to deliver as promised unless the buyer or lessee pays cash for the goods [UCC 2-702(1), 2A-525(1)]. Under the UCC, a person is insolvent when he or she (1) ceases to pay his or her debts in the ordinary course of business, (2) cannot pay his or her debts as they become due, or (3) is insolvent within the meaning of the federal bankruptcy law [UCC 1-201(23)].

Right to Stop Delivery of Goods in Transit

Often, sellers and lessors employ common carriers and other bailees (e.g., warehouses) to hold and deliver goods to buyers and lessees. The goods are considered to be *in transit* while they are in possession of these carriers or bailees. A seller or lessor that learns of the buyer's or lessee's insolvency while the goods are in transit has the **right to stop delivery of the goods transit**, regardless of the size of the shipment.

Essentially, the same remedy is available if the buyer or lessee repudiates the contract, fails to make payment when due, or otherwise gives the seller or lessor some other right to withhold or reclaim the goods. In these circumstances, however, the delivery can be stopped only if it constitutes a carload, a truckload, a planeload, or a larger express or freight shipment [UCC 2-705(1), 2A-526(1)].

The seller or lessor must give sufficient notice to allow the bailee, by reasonable diligence, to prevent delivery of the goods. After receipt of notice, the bailee must hold and deliver the goods according to the directions of the seller or lessor. The seller is responsible for all expenses borne by the bailee in stopping the goods [UCC 2-705(3), 2A-526(3)].

Goods may be stopped in transit until the buyer or lessee obtains possession of the goods or the carrier or other bailee acknowledges that it is holding the goods for the buyer or lessee [UCC 2-705(2), 2A-526(2)].

Right to Reclaim Goods

In certain situations, a seller or lessor may demand the return of the goods it sold or leased that are already in the possession of the buyer or lessee. In a sale transaction, the seller or lessor has the **right to reclaim goods** in two situations. If the goods are delivered in a credit sale and the seller then discovers that the buyer was insolvent, the seller has 10 days within which to demand that the goods be returned [UCC 2-507(2)]. If the buyer misrepresented his or her solvency in writing within three months before delivery [UCC 2-702(2)] or paid for goods in a cash sale with a check that bounces [UCC 2-507(2)], the seller may reclaim the goods at any time.

A lessor may reclaim goods in the possession of the lessee if the lessee is in default of the contract [UCC 2A-525(2)].

To exercise a right of reclamation, the seller or lessor must send the buyer or lessee a written notice demanding return of the goods. The seller or lessor may not use self-help to reclaim the goods if the buyer or lessee refuses to honor his or her demand. Instead, appropriate legal proceedings must be instituted.

Right to Dispose of Goods

If a buyer or lessee breaches or repudiates a sales or lease contract before the seller or lessor has delivered the goods, the seller or lessor may resell or release the goods and recover damages from the buyer or lessee [UCC 2-703(d), 2-706(1), 2A-523(1)(e), 2A-527(1)]. The **right to dispose of goods** also arises if the seller or lessor has reacquired the goods after stopping them in transit.

The disposition of the goods by the seller or lessor must be made in good faith and in a commercially reasonable manner. The goods may be disposed of as a unit or in parcels in a public or private transaction. The seller or lessor must give the buyer or lessee reasonable notification of his or her intention to dispose of goods unless the goods threaten to quickly decline in value or are perishable. The party who buys or leases the goods in good faith for value takes the goods, free of any rights of the original buyer or lessee [UCC 2-706(5), 2A-527(4)].

The seller or lessor may recover any damages incurred on the disposition of the goods. In the case of a sales contract, damages are defined as the difference between the disposition price and the original contract price. In the case of a lease contract, damages are the difference between the disposition price and the rent the original lessee would have paid.

The profit does not revert to the original buyer or lessee if the seller or lessor disposes of the goods at a higher price than the buyer or lessee contracted to pay. The seller or lessor may also recover any **incidental damages** (reasonable expenses incurred in stopping delivery, transportation charges, storage charges, sales commission, and the like [UCC 2-710, 2A-530]) incurred on the disposition of the goods [UCC 2-706(1), 2A-527(2)].

Example   A buyer contracts to purchase a racehorse for $20,000. When the seller tenders delivery, the buyer refuses to accept the horse or pay for it. The seller, in good faith, and in a commercially reasonable manner, resells the horse to a third party for $17,000. Incidental expenses of $500 are incurred on the resale. The seller can recover $3,500 from the original buyer: the $3,000 difference between the resale price and the contract price and $500 for the incidental expenses.

UNFINISHED GOODS   Sometimes a sales or lease contract is breached or repudiated before the goods are finished. In a case of **unfinished goods**, the seller or lessor may choose either (1) to cease manufacturing the goods and resell them for scrap or salvage value or (2) to complete the manufacture of the goods and resell, release, or otherwise dispose of them to another party [UCC 2-704(2), 2A-524(2)]. The seller or lessor may recover damages from the breaching buyer or lessee.

Right to Recover the Purchase Price or Rent

In certain circumstances, the UCC provides that a seller or lessor may sue the buyer or lessee to recover the purchase price or rent stipulated in the sales or lease contract.

The seller or lessor has the **right to recover the purchase price or rent** in the following situations:

1. The buyer or lessee accepts the goods but fails to pay for them when the price or rent is due.
2. The buyer or lessee breaches the contract after the goods have been identified in the contract and the seller or lessor cannot resell or dispose of them.
3. The goods are damaged or lost after the risk of loss passes to the buyer or lessee [UCC 2-709(1), 2A-529(1)].

To recover the purchase price or rent, the seller or lessor must hold the goods for the buyer or lessee. If resale or other disposition of the goods becomes possible prior to the collection of the judgment, however, the seller or lessor may resell or dispose of them. In such situations, the net proceeds of any disposition must be credited against the judgment [UCC 2-709(2), 2A-529(2), 2A-529(3)]. The seller or lessor may also recover incidental damages from the buyer or lessee.

Right to Recover Damages for Breach of Contract

If a buyer or lessee repudiates a sales or lease contract or wrongfully rejects tendered goods, the seller or lessor may sue to **recover the damages** caused by the buyer's or lessee's breach. Generally, the amount of damages is calculated as the difference between the contract price (or rent) and the market price (or rent) of the goods at the time and place the goods were to be delivered to the buyer or lessee plus incidental damages [UCC 2-708(1), 2A-528(1)].

If the preceding measure of damage will not put the seller or lessor in as good a position as performance of the contract would have, the seller or lessor can seek to **recover any lost profits** that would have resulted from the full performance of the contract plus an allowance for reasonable overhead and incidental damages [UCC 2-708(2), 2A-528(2)].

Right to Cancel a Contract

A seller or lessor has the **right to cancel a contract** if the buyer or lessee breaches that contract by rejecting or revoking acceptance of the goods, failing to pay for the goods, or repudiating all or any part of the contract. The cancellation may refer only to the affected goods or to the entire contract if the breach is material [UCC 2-703(f), 2A-523(1)(a)].

A seller or lessor who rightfully cancels a sales or lease contract by notifying the buyer or lessee is discharged of any further obligations under that contract. The buyer's or lessee's duties are not discharged, however. The seller or lessor retains the right to seek damages for the breach [UCC 2-106(4), 2A-523(3)].

CONTEMPORARY ENVIRONMENT
Lost Volume Seller

Should a seller be permitted to recover the profits it lost on a sale to a defaulting buyer if the seller sold the goods to another buyer? It depends. If the seller had only one item or a limited number of items and could produce no more, the seller cannot recover lost profits from the defaulting buyer. This is because the seller made those profits on the sale of the item to the new buyer. If, however, the seller could have produced more of the item, the seller is a **lost volume seller**. In this situation, the seller can make the profit from the sale of the item to the new buyer and sue the defaulting buyer to recover the profit it would have made from this sale. This is because the seller would have realized profits from two sales—the sale to the first buyer who defaulted and the second sale to the new buyer.

CONCEPT SUMMARY

Seller's and Lessor's Remedies

POSSESSION OF GOODS AT THE TIME OF THE BUYER'S BREACH	SELLER'S OR LESSOR'S REMEDIES

Goods in the possession of the seller	1. Withhold delivery of the goods [UCC 2-703(a), 2A-523(1)(c)].
	2. Demand payment in cash if the buyer is insolvent [UCC 2-702(1), 2A-525(1)].
	3. Resell or release the goods and recover the difference between the contract or lease price and the resale or release price [UCC 2-706, 2A-527].
	4. Sue for breach of contract and recover as damages either of the following:
	   a. The difference between the market price and the contract price [UCC 2-708(1), 2A-528(1)]
	   b. Lost profits [UCC 2-708(2), 2A-528(2)]
	5. Cancel the contract [UCC 2-703(f), 2A-523(1)(a)].

Goods in the possession of a carrier or bailee	1. Stop goods in transit [UCC 2-705(1), 2A-526(1)].
	   a. Carload, truckload, planeload, or larger shipment if the buyer is solvent.
	   b. Any size shipment if the buyer is insolvent.

Goods in the possession of the buyer	1. Sue to recover the purchase price or rent [UCC 2-709(1), 2A-525(1)].
	2. Reclaim the goods [UCC 2-507(2), 2A-525(2)].
	   a. The seller delivers goods in cash sale, and the buyer's check is dishonored.
	   b. The seller delivers goods in a credit sale, and the goods are received by an insolvent buyer.

Buyer's and Lessee's Remedies

The UCC provides a variety of remedies to a buyer or lessee upon the seller's or lessor's breach of a sales or lease contract. These remedies are discussed in the following paragraphs.

Right to Reject Nonconforming Goods or Improperly Tendered Goods

If the goods or the seller's or lessor's tender of delivery fails to conform to a sales or lease contract in any way, the buyer or lessee may (1) reject the whole, (2) accept the whole, or (3) accept any commercial unit and reject the rest. If the buyer or lessee chooses to reject the goods, he or she must identify defects that are ascertainable by reasonable inspection. Failure to do so prevents the buyer or lessee from relying on those defects to justify the rejection if the defect could have been cured by a seller or lessor who was notified in a timely manner [UCC 2-601, 2A-509]. Nonconforming or improperly tendered goods must be rejected within a reasonable time after their delivery or tender. The seller or lessor must be notified of the rejection. The buyer or lessee must hold any rightfully rejected goods with reasonable care for a reasonable time [UCC 2-602(2), 2A-512(1)].

If the buyer or lessee is a merchant and the seller or lessor has no agent or place of business at the market where the goods are rejected, the merchant-buyer or merchant-lessee must follow any reasonable instructions received from the seller or lessor with respect to the rejected goods [UCC 2-603, 2A-511]. If the seller or lessor gives no instructions and the rejected goods are perishable or will quickly decline in value, the buyer or lessee may make reasonable efforts to sell them on the seller's or lessor's behalf [UCC 2-604, 2A-512].

Any buyer or lessee who rightfully rejects goods is entitled to reimbursement from the seller or lessor for reasonable expenses incurred in holding, storing, reselling, shipping, and otherwise caring for the rejected goods.

Right to Recover Goods from an Insolvent Seller or Lessor

If a buyer or lessee makes partial or full payment for goods before they are received and the seller or lessor becomes insolvent within 10 days after receiving the first payment, the buyer or lessee has the **right to recover the goods** from the seller or lessor. To do so, the buyer or lessee must tender the unpaid portion of the purchase price or rent due under the sales or lease contract. Only conforming goods that are identified in the contract may be recovered [UCC 2-502, 2A-522]. This remedy is often referred to as **capture**.

Right to Obtain Specific Performance

If goods are unique or the remedy at law is inadequate, a buyer or lessee has the **right to obtain specific performance** of a sales or lease contract. A decree of **specific performance** orders the seller or lessor to perform the contract. Specific performance is usually used to obtain possession of works of art, antiques, rare coins, and other unique items [UCC 2-716(1), 2A-521(1)].

Example A buyer enters into a sales contract to purchase a specific Rembrandt painting from a seller for $10 million. When the buyer tenders payment, the seller refuses to sell the painting to the buyer. The buyer may bring an equity action to obtain a decree of specific performance from the court, ordering the seller to sell the painting to the buyer.

Right to Cover

A buyer or lessee has the **right to cover** by purchasing or renting substitute goods if the seller or lessor fails to make delivery of the goods or repudiates the contract or if the buyer or lessee rightfully rejects the goods or justifiably revokes their acceptance. The buyer's or lessee's cover must be made in good faith and without unreasonable delay. If the exact commodity is not available, the buyer or lessee may purchase or lease any commercially reasonable substitute.

A buyer or lessee who rightfully covers may sue the seller or lessor to recover as damages the difference between the cost of cover and the contract price or rent. The buyer or lessee may also recover incidental and consequential damages, less expenses saved (such as delivery costs) [UCC 2-712, 2A-518]. The UCC does not require a buyer or lessee to cover when a seller or lessor breaches a sales or lease contract. Failure of the buyer or lessee to cover does not bar the buyer from other remedies against the seller.

Right to Replevy Goods

A buyer or lessee has the **right to replevy (recover) goods** from a seller or lessor who is wrongfully withholding them. The buyer or lessee must show that he or she was unable to cover or that attempts at cover will be unavailing. Thus, the goods must be scarce, but not unique. **Replevin** actions are available only as to goods identified in a sales or lease contract [UCC 2-716(3), 2A-521(3)].

Example On January 1, IBM contracts to purchase monitors for computers from a seller for delivery on June 1. IBM intends to attach the monitors to a new computer that will be introduced on June 30. On June 1, the seller refuses to sell the monitors to IBM because it can get a higher price from another buyer. IBM tries to cover but cannot. IBM may successfully replevy the monitors from the seller.

Right to Cancel a Contract

If a seller or lessor fails to deliver conforming goods or repudiates the contract, or if the buyer or lessee rightfully rejects the goods or justifiably revokes acceptance of the goods, the buyer or lessee may cancel the sales or lease contract. The contract may be canceled with respect to the affected goods, or, if there is a material breach, the whole contract may be canceled. A buyer or lessee who rightfully cancels a contract is discharged from any further obligations on the contract and retains his or her rights to other remedies against the seller or lessor [UCC 2-711(1), 2A-508(1)(a)].

Right to Recover Damages for Nondelivery or Repudiation

If a seller or lessor fails to deliver the goods or repudiates the sales or lease contract, the buyer or lessee may recover **damages**. The measure of damages is the difference between the contract price (or original rent) and the market price (or rent) at the time the buyer or lessee learned of the breach. Incidental and consequential damages, less expenses saved, can also be recovered [UCC 2-713, 2A-519].

Example Fresh Foods Company contracts to purchase 10,000 bushels of soybeans from Sunshine Farms for $5 per bushel. Delivery is to occur on August 1. On August 1, the market price of soybeans is $7 per bushel. Sunshine Farms does not deliver the soybeans. Fresh Foods decides not to cover and to do without the soybeans. Fresh Foods sues Sunshine for market value minus the contract price damages. It can recover $20,000 ($7 market price minus $5 contract price multiplied by 10,000 bushels) plus incidental damages less expenses saved because of Sunshine's breach. Fresh Foods cannot recover consequential damages because it did not attempt to cover.

Right to Recover Damages for Accepted Nonconforming Goods

A buyer or lessee may accept nonconforming goods from a seller or lessor. Even with acceptance, the buyer or lessee still has the **right to recover damages for accepted nonconforming goods** and any loss resulting from the seller's or lessor's breach. Incidental and consequential damages may also be recovered. The buyer or lessee must notify the seller or lessor of the nonconformity within a reasonable time after the breach was or should have been discovered. Failure to do so bars the buyer or lessee from any recovery. If the buyer or lessee accepts nonconforming goods, he or she may deduct all or any part of damages resulting from the breach from any part of the purchase price or rent still due under the contract [UCC 2-714(1), 2A-516(1)].

Example A retail clothing store contracts to purchase 100 designer dresses for $100 per dress from a seller. The buyer pays for the dresses prior to delivery. After the dresses are delivered, the buyer discovers that 10 of the dresses have flaws in them. The buyer may accept these nonconforming dresses and sue the seller for reasonable damages resulting from the nonconformity.

CONCEPT SUMMARY

Buyer's and Lessee's Remedies

SITUATION	BUYER'S OR LESSEE'S REMEDY
Seller or lessor refuses to deliver the goods or delivers nonconforming goods that the buyer or lessee does not want.	1. Reject nonconforming goods [UCC 2-601, 2A-509]. 2. Revoke acceptance of nonconforming goods [UCC 2-608, 2A 517(1)]. 3. Cover [UCC 2-712, 2A-518]. 4. Sue for breach of contract and recover damages [UCC 2-713, 2A-519]. 5. Cancel the contract [UCC 2-711(1), 2A-508(1)(a)].
Seller or lessor tenders nonconforming goods and the buyer or lessee accepts them.	1. Sue for ordinary damages [UCC 2-714(1), 2A-516(1)]. 2. Deduct damages from the unpaid purchase or rent price [UCC 2-714(1), 2A-516(1)].
Seller or lessor refuses to deliver the goods and the buyer or lessee wants them.	1. Sue for specific performance [UCC 2-716(1), 2A-521(1)]. 2. Replevy the goods [UCC 2-716(3), 2A-521(3)]. 3. Recover the goods from an insolvent seller or lessor [UCC 2-502, 2A-522].

INTERNET AND TECHNOLOGY

Revised Article 2 (Sales) and Revised Article 2A (Leases) Recognize the Formation and Enforcement of Electronic Contracts

Revised Article 2 (Sales) and **Revised Article 2A (Leases)** expressly provide for the formation and enforcement of electronic contracts for the sale and lease of goods. Several of the important new provisions that apply to the creation, performance, and enforcement of electronic sales and lease contracts are discussed below.

- A contract for the sale of goods may be made by the interaction of electronic agents and the interaction of an electronic agent and an individual [Revised UCC 2-204(1), Revised UCC 2A-204(1)]. This important provision provides for the formation of contracts using the Internet and websites.

- A contract may be formed by the interaction of electronic agents of the parties, even if no individual was aware of or reviewed the electronic agents' actions or the resulting terms and agreements [Revised UCC 2-204(4)(a), Revised UCC 2A-204(4)(a)]. This provision recognizes that many Internet and web contracts are entered into electronically without an individual reviewing the transaction.

- A contract may be formed by the interaction of an electronic agent and an individual acting on the individual's own behalf or for another person. A contract is formed if the individual is free to refuse to take or makes a statement, and the individual has reason to know that the actions or statement will (i) cause the electronic agent to complete the transaction or performance, or (ii) indicate acceptance of an offer, regardless of other expressions or actions by the individual to which the electronic agent cannot react [Revised UCC 2-204(4)(b), Revised

UCC 2A-204(4)(b)]. This provision recognizes that when purchases are made over the Internet and from websites, a contract is formed when the purchaser or leasee places his or her order and knows that the electronic ordering system will complete the sale or lease on the terms offered by the website. The purchaser or leasee cannot later argue that he or she offered terms different than those provided on the electronic site of the seller or leasor.

- A contract may not be denied legal effect or enforceability solely because an electronic record was used in its formation [Revised UCC 2-211(2), Revised UCC 2A-222(2)]. This provision is extremely important because it recognizes that contracts may be formed electronically and that these electronic contracts are as enforceable as written contracts.

- A contract formed by the interaction of an individual and an electronic agent does not include terms provided by the individual if the individual has reason to know that the agent could not react to the terms provided [Revised UCC 2-211(4), Revised UCC 2A-222(4)]. This provision recognizes that most Internet websites offer goods for sale or lease on the terms provided, and that electronic websites are incapable of negotiating the terms of the sale or lease with the purchaser or leasee.

These provisions of Revised Article 2 (Sales) and Revised Article 2A (Leases) provide for the formation, performance, and enforceability of electronic contracts. These provisions recognize the importance of electronic contracting in today's commercial environment.

Additional Performance Issues

UCC Articles 2 (Sales) and 2A (Leases) contain several other provisions that affect the parties' performance of a sales or lease contract. These provisions are discussed in the following paragraphs.

Assurance of Performance

Each party to a sales or lease contract expects that the other party will perform his or her contractual obligations. If one party to a contract has reasonable grounds to believe that the other party either will not or cannot perform his or her contractual obligations, an adequate **assurance of performance** may be demanded in writing. If it is commercially reasonable, the party making the demand may suspend his or her performance until adequate assurance of due performance is received from the other party [UCC 2-609, 2A-401].

Example A buyer contracts to purchase 1,000 bushels of wheat from a farmer. The contract requires delivery on September 1. In July, the buyer learns that floods have caused substantial crop loss in the area of the seller's farm. The farmer receives the buyer's written demand for adequate assurance on July 15. The farmer fails to give adequate assurance of performance. The buyer may suspend performance and treat the sales contract as having been repudiated.

Anticipatory Repudiation

Occasionally, a party to a sales or lease contract repudiates the contract before his or her performance is due under the contract. If the repudiation impairs the value of the contract to the aggrieved party, it is called **anticipatory repudiation**. Mere wavering on performance does not meet the test for anticipatory repudiation.

If an anticipatory repudiation occurs, the aggrieved party can (1) await performance by the repudiating party for a commercially reasonable time (e.g., until the delivery date or shortly thereafter) or (2) treat the contract as having been breached at the time of the anticipatory repudiation, which gives the aggrieved party an immediate cause of action. In either case, the aggrieved party may suspend performance of his or her obligations under the contract [UCC 2-610, 2A-402].

An anticipatory repudiation may be retracted before the repudiating party's next performance is due if the aggrieved party has not (1) canceled the contract, (2) materially changed his or her position (e.g., purchased goods from another party), or (3) otherwise indicated that the repudiation is considered final. The retraction may be made by any method that clearly indicates the repudiating party's intent to perform the contract [UCC 2-611, 2A-403].

Statute of Limitations

The UCC **statute of limitations** provides that an action for breach of any written or oral sales or lease contract must commence within four years after the cause of the action accrues. The parties may agree to reduce the limitations period to one year, but they cannot extend it beyond four years.

Agreements Affecting Remedies

> Convenience is the basis of mercantile law.
>
> Lord Mansfield
> *Medcalf v. Hall (1782)*

The parties to a sales or lease contract may agree on remedies in addition to or in substitution for the remedies provided by the UCC.

Example   The parties may limit the buyer's or lessee's remedies to repair and replace defective goods or parts or to the return of the goods and repayment (refund) of the purchase price or rent. The remedies agreed upon by the parties are in addition to the remedies provided by the UCC unless the parties expressly provide that they are exclusive. If an exclusive remedy fails in its essential purpose (e.g., there is an exclusive remedy of repair but there are no repair parts available), any remedy may be had, as provided in the UCC.

The UCC permits parties to a sales or lease contract to establish in advance the damages that will be paid upon a breach of the contract. Such preestablished damages, called **liquidated damages**, substitute for actual damages. In a sales or lease contract, liquidated damages are valid if they are reasonable in light of the anticipated or actual harm caused by the breach, the difficulties of proof of loss, and the inconvenience or nonfeasibility of otherwise obtaining an adequate remedy [UCC 2-718(1), 2A-504].

ETHICS SPOTLIGHT

Unconscionable Contracts

UCC Article 2 (Sales) and Article 2A (Leases) have adopted the equity doctrine of **unconscionability**. Under this doctrine, a court may determine as a matter of law that a contract is unconscionable. To prove unconscionability, there must be proof that the parties had substantially unequal bargaining power, that the dominant party misused its power in contracting, and that it would be manifestly unfair or oppressive to enforce the contract. This sometimes happens where a dominant party uses a preprinted form contract and the terms of the contract are unfair or oppressive.

If a court finds that a contract or any clause in a contract is unconscionable, the court may refuse to enforce the contract, or it may enforce the remainder of the contract without the unconscionable clause, or it may so limit the application of any unconscionable clause as to avoid any unconscionable result [UCC 2-302, 2A-108].

Unconscionability is sometimes found in a consumer lease if the consumer has been induced by unconscionable conduct to enter into the lease. The doctrine of unconscionability also applies to online contracts.

Law & Ethics Questions

1. **ETHICS** Does the doctrine of unconscionability encourage ethical behavior? Explain.

2. Is the doctrine of unconscionability necessary? Explain.

Myanmar

Many goods sold in the United States by American companies are made in foreign countries. Why do U.S. companies do this? Do foreign workers receive the same protection as American workers?

Chapter Summary

Seller's and Lessor's Performance, p. 447

Tender of delivery requires the seller or lessor to (1) put and hold *conforming goods* at the buyer's or lessee's disposition and (2) give the buyer or lessee any notification reasonably necessary to enable the buyer or lessee to take delivery of the goods.

Place of Delivery

The parties may agree in a sales or lease contract as to the place of delivery. If there is no agreement in the contract as to place of delivery, several UCC rules apply.

Noncarrier Cases

The place of delivery is the seller's or lessor's place of business, unless the seller or lessor has no place of business, in which case the place of delivery is the seller's or lessor's residence.

Carrier Cases

1. ***Shipment contracts.*** A shipment sales contract requires the seller to send goods to the buyer by carrier. Delivery occurs when the seller puts the goods in the carrier's possession.
2. ***Destination contracts.*** A destination sales contract requires the seller to deliver the goods to the buyer's place of business or other destination. Delivery occurs when the goods reach this destination.

Perfect Tender Rule

The seller or lessor is under a duty to deliver *conforming goods* to the buyer or lessee. If the goods or tender of delivery fails in any respect to conform to the contract, the buyer or lessee may opt to (1) reject the whole shipment, (2) accept the whole shipment, or (3) reject part and accept part of the shipment.

Exceptions to the Perfect Tender Rule

The UCC recognizes the following exceptions to the perfect tender rule:

1. *Agreement of the parties.* The parties may agree to limit the effect of the perfect tender rule.
2. *Substitution of carriers.* A seller must use a commercially reasonable substitute if the agreed-upon manner of deliver fails or the agreed-upon type of carrier becomes unavailable.

Cure

A seller or lessor who delivers nonconforming goods has the opportunity to *cure* the nonconformity by repairing or replacing defective or nonconforming goods if the time for performance has not expired and the seller or lessor notifies the buyer or lessee of his or her intention to make a conforming delivery within the contract time.

Installment Contracts

The buyer or lessee may reject any nonconforming installment if the value of the installment is impaired and the defect cannot be cured. The buyer or lessee may reject the entire contract upon the tender of a nonconforming installment only if the nonconformity substantially impairs the value of the entire contract.

Destruction of Goods

If goods identified in the contract are totally destroyed without fault of either party before the risk of loss passes to the buyer or lessee, the seller or lessor is excused from performance.

Good Faith and Reasonableness

The UCC has adopted the following broad principles that govern the performance of sales and lease contracts:

1. *Good faith.* Parties to a sales or lease contract must perform their contract obligations in *good faith.*
2. *Reasonableness.* Many UCC provisions require parties to take *reasonable* steps or to act *reasonably* in performing contract obligations.
3. *Commercial reasonableness.* Some provisions of the UCC require merchants to use *commercial reasonableness* in the performance of their contract obligations.

Buyer's and Lessee's Performance, p. 451

Right of Inspection

Unless otherwise agreed, the buyer or lessee has the right to inspect goods that are tendered, delivered, or identified in a sales or lease contract prior to accepting or paying for them.

Payment

Goods that are accepted by the buyer or lessee must be paid for in accordance with the terms of the sales or lease contract. Unless otherwise agreed, payment or rent is due when and where the goods are delivered.

Acceptance

Acceptance occurs when the buyer or lessee takes one of the following actions:

1. Signifies in words or by conduct that the goods are conforming or that the goods will be taken or retained despite their nonconformity.
2. Fails to reject the goods within a reasonable time after their delivery by the seller or lessor.
3. Acts inconsistently with the seller's ownership rights in the goods.

Buyers and lessees may only accept delivery of a *commercial unit.*

Revocation of Acceptance

A buyer or lessee who has accepted goods may subsequently revoke his or her acceptance if (1) the goods are nonconforming, (2) the nonconformity substantially impairs the value of the goods to the buyer or lessee, and (3) one of the following factors is shown:

1. The seller's or lessor's promise to reasonably cure the nonconformity is not met.
2. The goods were accepted before the nonconformity was discovered and the nonconformity was difficult to discover.
3. The goods were accepted before the nonconformity was discovered and the seller or lessor assured the buyer or lessee that the goods were conforming.

Seller's and Lessor's Remedies, p. 453

Right to Withhold Delivery

Delivery of goods may be withheld if a seller or lessor discovers that the buyer or lessee is insolvent before the goods are delivered. If the seller or lessor discovers that the buyer or lessee is insolvent, he or she may refuse to deliver the goods unless payment is rendered in cash.

Right to Stop Delivery of Goods in Transit

If goods are in transit or in a bailee's possession, a seller or lessor may stop delivery (1) of a carload, a truckload, or a planeload of goods if the buyer or lessee repudiates the contract, fails to make a payment when due, or otherwise breaches the contract or (2) of any size shipment if the buyer or lessee becomes insolvent.

Right to Reclaim Goods

A seller or lessor may reclaim goods in the possession of the buyer or lessee if:

1. The goods are delivered in a credit sale and the seller then discovers that the buyer was insolvent.
2. The buyer misrepresented his or her solvency in writing within three months before delivery or paid for goods in a cash sale with a check that bounces.

Right to Dispose of Goods

If a buyer or lessee breaches or repudiates a sales or lease contract before the seller or lessor has delivered the goods, the seller or lessor may resell or release the goods and recover damages from the buyer or lessee. Damages are calculated as the difference between the disposition price or rent and the original contract price or rent.

Right to Recover the Purchase Price or Rent

If a buyer or lessee accepts goods but fails to pay for them when the contract price or rent is due, the seller or lessor may sue to recover the contracted-for purchase price or rent from the buyer or lessee.

Right to Recover Damages for Breach of Contract

If a buyer or lessee repudiates a sales or lease contract, the seller or lessor may sue to recover the damages caused by the breach. Damages are calculated as the difference between the original contract price (or rent) and the market price (or rent) of the goods at the time and place the goods were to be delivered, or lost profits.

Right to Cancel a Contract

A seller or lessor may cancel a sales or lease contract if the buyer or lessee breaches the contract. The seller or lessor is discharged of any further obligations under the canceled contract.

Buyer's and Lessee's Remedies, p. 456

Right to Reject Nonconforming Goods or Improperly Tendered Goods

If goods or a seller's or lessor's tender of delivery fails to conform to a sales or lease contract in any way, the buyer or lessee may (1) reject the whole, (2) accept the whole, or (3) accept any commercial unit and reject the rest.

Right to Recover Goods from an Insolvent Seller or Lessor

If a buyer or lessee makes partial or full payment for goods before they are received and the seller or lessor becomes insolvent within 10 days after receiving the first payment, the buyer or lessee may recover the goods from the seller or lessor.

Right to Obtain Specific Performance

If the goods in a contract are unique or the remedy at law is inadequate, a buyer or lessee may obtain a decree of specific performance that orders the seller or lessor to perform the sales or lease contract.

Right to Cover

If a seller or lessor fails to make delivery of goods or repudiates a sales or lease contract or if the buyer or lessee rightfully rejects the goods or justifiably revokes their acceptance, the buyer or lessee may cover by purchasing or renting substitute goods from another party. The buyer or lessee may recover from the seller or lessor damages calculated as the difference between the cost of cover and the original contract price or rent.

Right to Replevy Goods

A buyer or lessee may replevy (recover) scarce goods from a seller or lessor who is wrongfully withholding them.

Right to Cancel a Contract

A buyer or lessee may cancel a sales or lease contract if the seller or lessor fails to deliver conforming goods or repudiates the contract or if the buyer or lessee rightfully rejects the goods or justifiably revokes acceptance of the goods. The buyer or lessee is discharged from any further obligations under the canceled contract.

Right to Recover Damages for Nondelivery or Repudiation

If a seller or lessor fails to deliver the goods or repudiates a sales or lease contract, the buyer or lessee may recover damages from the seller or lessor. Damages are calculated as the difference between the contract price (or original rent) and the market price (or rent) at the time the buyer or lessee learned of the breach.

Right to Recover Damages for Accepted Nonconforming Goods

If a buyer or lessee accepts nonconforming goods from a seller or lessor, the buyer or lessee may recover as damages any loss resulting from the seller's or lessor's breach or deduct damages from unpaid purchase price or rent.

Deduct damages from unpaid purchase price or rent.

If a seller or lessor breaches the sales or lease contract and the buyer or lessee accepts nonconforming goods, the buyer or lessee may deduct all or any part of the damages resulting from the breach from any part of the price or rent still due under the sales or lease contract [UCC 2-714(1), 2A-516(1)].

Additional Performance Issues, p. 459

Assurance of Performance

If one party to a sales or lease contract has reasonable grounds to believe that the other party either will not or cannot perform his or her contractual obligations, he or she may demand in writing an adequate assurance of performance from the other party. The party making the demand may suspend his or her performance until adequate assurance of performance is received.

Anticipatory Repudiation

Anticipatory repudiation occurs when a party to a sales or lease contract repudiates the contract before his or her performance is due. The aggrieved party can (1) await performance when due or (2) treat the contract as having been breached at the time of the anticipatory repudiation.

Statute of Limitations

The UCC provides that an action for breach of any written or oral sales or lease contract must commence within four years after the cause of action accrues. The parties may agree to reduce the limitations period to one year, but they cannot extend it beyond four years.

Agreements Affecting Remedies

The parties to a sales or lease contract may agree on remedies in addition to or in substitution for the remedies provided by Article 2 or 2A of the UCC. The parties to a sales or lease contract may establish in advance the damages that will be paid upon a breach of the contract.

Unconscionable Contracts

If a sales or lease contract or any clause in it is *unconscionable*, the court may either refuse to enforce the contract or limit the application of the unconscionable clause.

Test Review Terms and Concepts

Case Problems

18.1 Nonconforming Goods: The Jacob Hartz Seed Company, Inc. (Hartz), bought soybeans for use as seed from E. R. Coleman. Coleman certified that the seed had an 80 percent germination rate. Hartz paid for the beans and picked them up from a warehouse in Card, Arkansas. After the seed was transported to Georgia, a sample was submitted for testing to the Georgia Department of Agriculture. When the department reported a germination level of only 67 percent, Coleman requested that the seed be retested. The second set of tests reported a germination rate of 65 percent. Hartz canceled the contract after the second test, and Coleman reclaimed the seed. Hartz sought a refund of the money it had paid for the seed, claiming that the soybeans were nonconforming goods. Who wins? *Jacob Hartz Seed Co. v. Coleman*, 271 Ark. 756, 612 S.W.2d 91, **Web** 1981 Ark. Lexis 1153 (Supreme Court of Arkansas)

18.2 Right to Cure: Connie R. Grady purchased a new Chevrolet Chevette from Al Thompson Chevrolet (Thompson). Grady gave Thompson a down payment on the car and financed the remainder of the purchase price through General Motors Acceptance Corporation (GMAC). Grady picked up the Chevette. The next day, the car broke down and had to be towed back to Thompson. Grady picked up the repaired car one day later. The car's performance was still unsatisfactory in that the engine was hard to start, the transmission slipped, and the brakes had to be pushed to the floor to function. Two weeks later, Grady again returned the Chevette for servicing. When she picked up the car that evening, the engine started, but the engine and brake warning lights came on. This pattern of malfunction and repair continued for another two months. Grady wrote a letter to Thompson, revoking the sale. Thompson repossessed the Chevette. GMAC sued Grady to recover its money. Grady sued Thompson to recover her down payment. Thompson claimed that Grady's suit was barred because the company was not given adequate opportunity to cure. Who wins? *General Motors Acceptance Corp. v. Grady*, 27 Ohio App. 3d 321, 501 N.E.2d 68, **Web** 1985 Ohio App. Lexis 10353 (Court of Appeals of Ohio)

18.3 Revocation of Acceptance: Roy E. Farrar Produce Company (Farrar) was a packer and shipper of tomatoes in Rio Arribon County, New Mexico. Farrar contacted Wilson, an agent and salesman for International Paper Company (International), and ordered 21,500 tomato boxes for $.64 per box. The boxes were to each hold between 20 and 30 pounds of tomatoes for shipping. When the boxes arrived at Farrar's plant, 3,624 of them were immediately used to pack tomatoes. When the boxes were stacked, they began to collapse and crush the tomatoes contained within them. The produce company was forced to repackage the tomatoes and store the unused tomato boxes. Farrar contacted International and informed it that it no longer wanted the boxes because they could not perform as promised. International claimed that Farrar had accepted the packages and must pay for them. Who wins? *International Paper Co. v. Farrar*, 102 N.M. 739, 700 P.2d 642, **Web** 1985 N.M. Lexis 2000 (Supreme Court of New Mexico)

18.4 Commercial Impracticality: Charles C. Campbell was a farmer who farmed some 600 acres in the vicinity of Hanover, Pennsylvania. In the spring, Campbell entered into a contract with Hostetter Farms, Inc. (Hostetter), a grain dealer with facilities in Hanover. The sales agreement called for Campbell to sell Hostetter 20,000 bushels of No. 2 yellow corn at $1.70 per bushel. Delivery was made five months later, in the fall. Unfortunately, the summer was an unusually rainy one, and Campbell could not plant part of his crop because of the wet ground. After the corn was planted, part of the crop failed due to the excessive rain. As a result, Campbell delivered only 10,417 bushels. Hostetter sued Campbell for breach of contract. Campbell asserted the defense of commercial impracticability. Who wins? *Campbell v. Hostetter Farms, Inc.*, 251 Pa. Super. 232, 380 A.2d 463, **Web** 1977 Pa. Super. Lexis 2699 (Superior Court of Pennsylvania)

18.5 Right to Reclaim Goods: Archer Daniels Midland Company (Archer) sold ethanol for use in gasoline. Archer sold 80,000 gallons of ethanol on credit to Charter International Oil Company (Charter). The ethanol was shipped to Charter's facility in Houston. Charter became insolvent sometime during that period. Archer sent a written notice to Charter, demanding the return of the ethanol. At the time Charter received the reclamation demand, it had only 12,000 gallons of ethanol remaining at its Houston facility. When Charter refused to return the unused ethanol, Archer sued to recover the ethanol. Who wins? *Archer Daniels Midland v. Charter International Oil Company*, 60 B.R. 854, **Web** 1986 U.S. Dist. Lexis 25828 (United States District Court for the Middle District of Florida)

18.6 Right to Resell Goods: Meuser Material & Equipment Company (Meuser) was a dealer in construction equipment. Meuser entered into an agreement with Joe McMillan for the sale of a bulldozer to McMillan. The agreement called for Meuser to deliver the bulldozer to McMillan's residence in Greeley, Colorado. McMillan paid Meuser with a check. Before taking delivery, McMillan stopped payment on the check. Meuser entered into negotiations with McMillan in an attempt to get McMillan to abide by the sales agreement. During this period, Meuser paid for the upkeep of the bulldozer. When it became apparent that further negotiations would be fruitless, Meuser began looking for a new buyer. Fourteen months after the original sale was supposed to have taken place, the bulldozer was resold for less than the original contract price. Meuser sued McMillan to recover the difference between the contract price and the resale price as well as for the cost of upkeep on the bulldozer for 14 months. Who wins? *McMillan v. Meuser Material & Equipment Company*, 260 Ark. 422, 541 S.W.2d 911, **Web** 1976 Ark. Lexis 1814 (Supreme Court of Arkansas)

18.7 Right to Recover Purchase Price: C. R. Daniels, Inc. (Daniels), entered into a contract for the design and sale of grass catcher bags for lawn mowers to Yazoo Manufacturing Company, Inc. (Yazoo). Daniels contracted to design grass catcher bags that would fit the "S" series mower made by Yazoo. Yazoo provided Daniels with a lawn mower to design the bag. After Yazoo approved the design of the bags, it issued a purchase order for 20,000 bags. Daniels began to ship the bags. After accepting 8,000 bags, Yazoo requested that the shipments stop. Officials of Yazoo told Daniels that it would resume accepting shipments in a few months. Despite several attempts, Daniels could not get Yazoo to accept delivery of the remaining 12,000 bags. Daniels sued Yazoo to recover the purchase price of the grass bags still in its inventory. Who wins? *C. R. Daniels, Inc. v. Yazoo Mfg. Co., Inc.*, 641 F.Supp. 205, **Web** 1986 U.S. Dist. Lexis 23550 (United States District Court for the Southern District of Mississippi)

18.8 Right to Recover Lost Profits: Saber Energy, Inc. (Saber), entered into a sales contract with Tri-State Petroleum Corporation (Tri-State). The contract called for Saber to sell Tri-State 110,000 barrels of gasoline per month for six months. Saber was to deliver the gasoline through the colonial pipeline in Pasadena, Texas. The first 110,000 barrels were delivered on time. On August 1, Saber was informed that Tri-State was canceling the contract. Saber sued Tri-State for breach of contract and sought to recover its lost profits as damages. Tri-State admitted its breach but claimed that lost profits is an inappropriate measure of damages. Who wins? *Tri-State Petroleum Corporation v. Saber Energy, Inc.* 845 F.2d 575, **Web** 1988 U.S. App. Lexis 6819 (United States Court of Appeals for the Fifth Circuit)

18.9 Specific Performance: Dr. and Mrs. Sedmak (Sedmaks) were collectors of Chevrolet Corvettes. The Sedmaks saw an article in *Vette Vues* magazine concerning a new limited-edition Corvette. The limited edition was designed to commemorate the selection of the Corvette as the official pace car of the Indianapolis 500. Chevrolet was manufacturing only 6,000 of these pace cars. The Sedmaks visited Charlie's Chevrolet, Inc. (Charlie's), a local Chevrolet dealer. Charlie's was to receive only one limited-edition car, which the sales manager agreed to sell to the Sedmaks for the sticker price of $15,000. When the Sedmaks went to pick up and pay for the car, they were told that because of the great demand for the limited edition, it was going to be auctioned to the highest bidder. The Sedmaks sued the dealership for specific performance. Who wins? *Sedmak v. Charlie's Chevrolet, Inc.*, 622 S.W.2d. 694, **Web** 1981 Mo. App. Lexis 2911 (Court of Appeals of Missouri)

18.10 Right to Cover: Kent Nowlin Construction, Inc. (Nowlin), was awarded a contract by the state of New Mexico to pave a number of roads. After Nowlin was awarded the contract, it entered into an agreement with Concrete Sales & Equipment Rental Company, Inc. (C&E). C&E was to supply 20,000 tons of paving material to Nowlin. Nowlin began paving the roads, anticipating C&E's delivery of materials. On the delivery date, however, C&E shipped only 2,099 tons of paving materials. Because Nowlin had a deadline to meet, the company contracted with Gallup Sand and Gravel Company (Gallup) for substitute material. Nowlin sued C&E to recover the difference between the higher price it had to pay Gallup for materials and the contract price C&E had agreed to. C&E claims that it is not responsible for Nowlin's increased costs. Who wins? *Concrete Sales & Equipment Rental Company, Inc. v. Kent Nowlin Construction, Inc.*, 106 N.M. 539, 746 P.2d 645, **Web** 1987 N.M. Lexis 3808 (Supreme Court of New Mexico)

Ethics Issues

18.11 Ethics: Ruby and Carmen Ybarra purchased a new double-wide mobile home from Modern Trailer Sales, Inc. (Modern). Modern delivered the mobile home to the Ybarras. A few days after delivery, portions of the floor began to rise and bubble, creating an unsightly and troublesome situation for the Ybarras. The Ybarras complained to Modern about the floor as soon as they discovered the defects. Modern sent repairmen to cure the defective floor on at least three occasions, but each time they were unsuccessful. The Ybarras continued to complain about the defects. The Ybarras continued to rely on Modern's assurances that it was able and willing to repair the floor. After four years of complaints, the Ybarras sued to revoke their acceptance of the sales contract. Did the Ybarras properly revoke their acceptance of the sales contract? Did Modern act ethically in this case? Did the Ybarras? *Ybarras v. Modern Trailer Sales, Inc.*, 94 N.W. 249, 609 P.2d 331, **Web** 1980 N.M. Lexis 2676 (Supreme Court of New Mexico)

18.12 Ethics:s Allsopp Sand and Gravel (Allsopp) and Lincoln Sand and Gravel (Lincoln) were both in the business of supplying sand to construction companies. In March 1986, Lincoln's sand dredge became inoperable. To continue in business, Lincoln negotiated a contract with Allsopp to purchase sand over the course of a year. The contract called for the sand to be loaded on Lincoln's trucks during Allsopp's regular operating season (March through November). Loading at other times was to be done by "special arrangement." By November 1986, Lincoln had taken delivery of one-quarter of the sand it had contracted for. At that point, Lincoln requested that several trucks of sand be loaded in December. Allsopp informed Lincoln that it would have to pay extra for this special arrangement. Lincoln refused to pay extra, pointing out that the sand was already stockpiled at Allsopp's facilities. Allsopp also offered to supply an employee to supervise the loading. Negotiations between the parties broke down, and Lincoln informed Allsopp that it did not intend to honor the remainder of the contract. Allsopp sued Lincoln. Was it commercially reasonable for Lincoln to demand delivery of sand during December? Did Lincoln act ethically in this case? *Allsopp Sand and Gravel v. Lincoln Sand and Gravel*, 171 Ill. App. 3d 532, 525 N.E.2d 1185, **Web** 1988 Ill. App. Lexis 939 (Appellate Court of Illinois)

IRAC Writing Assignment

Read **Case A-18** in Appendix A [*LNS-Investment Company, Inc. v. Phillips 66 Company*]. Use the IRAC method to prepare a written analysis of the case.

CHAPTER 19

Warranties and Product Liability

> *When a manufacturer engages in advertising in order to bring his goods and their quality to the attention of the public and thus to create consumer demand, the representations made constitute an express warranty running directly to a buyer who purchases in reliance thereon. The fact that the sale is consummated with an independent dealer does not obviate the warranty.*
>
> —JUSTICE FRANCIS
> Henningsen v. Bloomfield Motors, Inc.

CHAPTER OBJECTIVES

After studying this chapter, you should be able to:

1. Identify and describe express warranties.
2. Describe the implied warranty of merchantability and the implied warranty of fitness for a particular purpose.
3. Identify warranty disclaimers and determine when they are unlawful.
4. Define the doctrine of *strict liability*.
5. Describe defects in manufacture, design, and failure to warn.

CHAPTER CONTENTS

- Introduction to Warranties and Product Liability
- Express Warranties
- Implied Warranties
- Warranty Disclaimers
- Product Liability
- Strict Liability

- Defective Products
- Defenses to Product Liability
- Chapter Summary
- Test Review Terms and Concepts
- Case Problems
- Ethics Issues
- IRAC Writing Assignment

    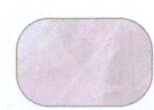

Introduction to Warranties and Product Liability

The doctrine of *caveat emptor*—"let the buyer beware"—governed the law of sales and leases for centuries. Finally, the law recognized that consumers and other purchasers and lessees of goods needed greater protection. Article 2 of the Uniform Commercial Code (UCC), which has been adopted in whole or in part by 50 states, establishes certain **warranties** that apply to the sale of goods. Article 2A of the UCC, which has been adopted in many states, establishes warranties that apply to lease transactions.

Warranties are the buyer's or lessee's assurance that the goods meet certain standards. Warranties, which are based on contract law, may be either *expressly* stated or *implied* by law. If the seller or lessor fails to meet a warranty, the buyer or lessee can sue for breach of warranty. Sales and lease warranties are discussed in this chapter.

If a product defect causes injury to purchasers, lessees, users, or bystanders, the injured party may be able to recover for his or her injuries under certain tort doctrines. These tort doctrines include negligence, misrepresentation, and the modern theory of strict liability. The liability of manufacturers, sellers, lessors, and others for injuries caused by defective products is commonly referred to as **product liability**. The various tort principles that permit injured parties to recover damages caused by defective products are discussed in this chapter.

Santa Monica, California

The law implies a warranty that the food restaurants serve is fit for human consumption.

Express Warranties

Express warranties, which are the oldest form of warranty, are created when a seller or lessor affirms that the goods he or she is selling or leasing meet certain standards of quality, description, performance, or condition [UCC 2-313(1), 2A-210(1)]. Express warranties can be either written, oral, or inferred from the seller's conduct.

It is not necessary to use formal words such as *warrant* or *guarantee* to create an express warranty. Express warranties can be made by mistake because the seller or lessor does not have to specifically intend to make the warranty [UCC 2-313(2), 2A-210(2)].

Sellers and lessors are not required to make express warranties. Generally, express warranties are made to entice consumers and others to buy or lease their products. That is why these warranties are often in the form of advertisements, brochures, catalogs, pictures, illustrations, diagrams, blueprints, and so on.

An express warranty is created when a seller or lessor indicates that the goods will conform to:

1. All *affirmations of fact or promise* made about them (for example, statements such as "This car will go 100 miles per hour" or "This house paint will last at least five years").
2. Any *description* of them (for example, terms such as *Idaho potatoes* and *Michigan cherries*).
3. Any *model* or *sample* of them (for example, a model oil-drilling rig or a sample of wheat taken from a silo).

Basis of the Bargain

> Warranties are favored in law, being a part of a man's assurance.
>
> Coke First Institute

Buyers and lessees can recover for breach of an express warranty if the warranty was a contributing factor—not necessarily the sole factor—that induced the buyer to purchase the product or the lessee to lease the product. This is known as the **basis of the bargain** [UCC 2-313(1), 2A-210(1)]. The UCC does not define the term *basis of the bargain*, so this test is broadly applied by the courts. Generally, all statements by the seller or lessor prior to or at the time of contracting are presumed to be part of the basis of the bargain unless good reason is shown to the contrary. Postsale statements that modify the contract are part of the basis of the bargain.

Generally, a retailer is liable for the express warranties made by manufacturers of goods it sells. A manufacturer is not liable for express warranties made by wholesalers and retailers unless the manufacturer authorizes or ratifies a warranty.

Statements of Opinion

Many express warranties arise during the course of negotiations between a buyer and a seller (or lessor and lessee). The seller's or lessor's **statements of opinion** (i.e., **puffing**) or commendation of the goods does not create an express warranty [UCC 2-313(2)]. It is often difficult to determine whether the seller's statement is an affirmation of fact (which creates an express warranty) or a statement of opinion (which does not create a warranty). An affirmation of the *value* of goods does not create an express warranty [UCC 2-313(2)].

Example A used car salesperson's saying "This is the best used car available in town" does not create an express warranty because it is an opinion and mere puffing. However, a statement such as "This car has been driven only 20,000 miles" is an express warranty because it is a statement of fact. Statements such as "This painting is worth a fortune" or "Others would gladly pay $20,000 for this car" do not create an express warranty because these are a statement of value and a statement of fact.

In the following case, the court had to decide whether an express warranty had been created.

CASE 19.1
Express Warranty

Daughtrey v. Ashe

243 Va. 73, 413 S.E.2d 336, **Web** 1992 Va. Lexis 152
Supreme Court of Virginia

> **"** *The trial judge found that the diamonds were of a grade substantially less than v.v.s.* **"**
>
> —Judge Whiting

Facts

W. Hayes Daughtrey consulted Sidney Ashe, a jeweler, about the purchase of a diamond bracelet as a Christmas present for his wife. Ashe showed Daughtrey a diamond bracelet that he had for sale for $15,000. When Daughtrey decided to purchase the bracelet, Ashe completed and signed an appraisal form that stated that the diamonds were "H color and v.v.s. quality." (V.v.s. is one of the highest ratings in a jeweler's quality classification.) After Daughtrey paid for the bracelet, Ashe put the bracelet and the appraisal form in a box. Daughtrey gave the bracelet to his wife as a Christmas present. One year later, when another jeweler looked at the bracelet, Daughtrey discovered that the diamonds were of substantially lower grade than v.v.s. Daughtrey filed a specific performance suit against Ashe to compel him to replace the bracelet with one mounted with v.v.s. diamonds or pay appropriate damages. The trial court denied relief for breach of warranty. Daughtrey appealed.

Issue

Was an express warranty made by Ashe regarding the quality of the diamonds in the bracelet?

Language of the Court

We consider whether Ashe's statement of the grade of the diamonds was an express warranty. The Court contends that Ashe's statement of the grade of the diamonds is a mere opinion and, thus, cannot qualify as an express warranty.

It is not necessary to the creation of an express warranty that the seller use formal words such as "warrant" or "guarantee" or that he have a specific intention to make a warranty. Here, Ashe did more than give a mere opinion of the value of the goods; he specifically described them as diamonds of "H color and v.v.s. quality." Ashe did not qualify his statement as a mere opinion. And, if one who has superior knowledge makes a statement about the goods sold and does not qualify the statement as his opinion, the statement will be treated as a statement of fact. The trial judge found that the diamonds were of a grade substantially less than v.v.s.

Given these considerations, we conclude that Ashe's description of the goods was more than his opinion; rather, he intended it to be a statement of a fact. Therefore, the court erred in holding that the description was not an express warranty.

Decision

The appellate court held that an express warranty had been created. The trial court's decision was reversed, and the case was remanded for a determination of appropriate damages to be awarded to Daughtrey.

Law & Ethics Questions

1. What is the remedy when an express warranty has been breached? Is the remedy sufficient?

2. **ETHICS** Did Ashe act ethically in denying that his statement created an express warranty?

3. Do businesses have to make express warranties? Why do businesses make warranties about the quality of their products?

Web Exercises

1. **WEB** For the complete opinion of this case, go to *www.prenhall.com/cheesemancases*.

2. **WEB** Visit the website of De Beers International, at *www.debeers.com*. Find the rating system for the quality of diamonds.

3. **WEB** Visit the website of the supreme court of Virginia, at *www.courts.state.va.us*.

4. **WEB** Use *www.google.com* to find an article about the De Beers monopoly and the mining of diamonds. Read it.

Damages Recoverable for Breach of Warranty

Where there has been a breach of warranty, the buyer or lessee may sue the seller or lessor to recover **compensatory damages**. The amount of recoverable compensatory damages is generally equal to the difference between (1) the value of the goods as warranted and (2) the actual value of the goods accepted at the time and place of acceptance [UCC 2-714(2), 2A-508(4)]. A purchaser or lessee can recover for personal injuries that are caused by a breach of warranty.

Example Suppose a used car salesperson warrants that a used car has been driven only 20,000 miles. If true, that would make the car worth $10,000. The salesperson gives the buyer a "good deal" and sells the car for $8,000. Unfortunately, the car was worth only $4,000 because it was actually driven 100,000 miles. The buyer discovers the breach of warranty and sues the salesperson for damages. The buyer can recover $6,000 ($10,000 warranted value minus $4,000 actual value). The contract price ($8,000) is irrelevant to this computation.

Example Suppose Frances Gordon purchases new tires for her car, and the manufacturer expressly warrants the tires against blowout for 50,000 miles. Suppose one of the tires blows out after being used only 20,000 miles, causing severe injury to Ms. Gordon. She can recover personal injury damages from the manufacturer because of the breach of warranty.

Implied Warranties

In addition to express warranties made by a manufacturer or seller, the law sometimes implies warranties in the sale or lease of goods. Implied warranties are not expressly stated in the sales or lease contract but instead are implied by law. The most common forms of implied warranties are the *implied warranty of merchantability*, the *implied warranty of fitness for human consumption*, and the *implied warranty of fitness for a particular purpose*. These warranties are discussed in the following paragraphs.

Implied Warranty of Merchantability

If the seller or lessor of a good is a merchant with respect to goods of that kind, the sales contract contains an **implied warranty of merchantability** unless it is properly disclaimed [UCC 2-314(1), 2A-212(1)]. This warranty requires that the following standards to be met:

- **The goods must be fit for the ordinary purposes for which they are used.** For example, a chair must be able to safely perform the function of a chair. If a normal-sized person sits in a chair that has not been tampered with, and the chair collapses, there has been a breach of the implied warranty of merchantability. If, however, the same person is injured because he or she uses the chair as a ladder and it tips over, there is no breach of implied warranty because serving as a ladder is not the ordinary purpose of a chair.
- **The goods must be adequately contained, packaged, and labeled.** For example, the implied warranty of merchantability applies to the milk bottle as well as to the milk inside the bottle.
- **The goods must be of an even kind, quality, and quantity within each unit.** All the goods in a carton, package, or box must be consistent.
- **The goods must conform to any promise or affirmation of fact made on the container or label.** The goods must be capable of being used safely in accordance with the instructions on the package or label.
- **The quality of the goods must pass without objection in the trade.** Other users of the goods should not object to their quality.
- **Fungible goods must meet a fair average or middle range of quality.** For example, to be classified as a certain grade, grain or ore must meet the average range of quality of that grade.

Note that the implied warranty of merchantability does not apply to sales or leases by nonmerchants or casual sales.

Example The implied warranty of merchantability applies to the sale of a lawn mower that is sold by a merchant who is in the business of selling lawn mowers. It does not apply when one neighbor sells a lawn mower to another neighbor.

The following case raised the issue of implied warranty of merchantability.

C A S E **19.2**

Implied Warranty of Merchantability

Denny v. Ford Motor Company

87 N.Y.2d 248, 662 N.E.2d 730, 639 N.Y.S.2d 250, **Web** 1995 N.Y. Lexis 4445
Court of Appeals of New York

❝ *The law implies a warranty by a manufacturer that places its product on the market that the product is reasonably fit for the ordinary purpose for which it was intended.* ❞

—Judge Titone

Facts

Nancy Denny purchased a Bronco II, a small utility vehicle that was manufactured by Ford Motor Company. Denny testified that she purchased the Bronco for use on paved city and suburban streets and not for off-road use. On June 9, 1986, when Denny was driving the vehicle on a paved road, she slammed on the brakes in an effort to avoid a deer that had walked directly into her motor vehicle's path. The Bronco II rolled over, and Denny was severely injured. Denny sued Ford Motor Company to recover damages for breach of the implied warranty of merchantability.

Denny alleged that the Bronco II presented a significantly higher risk of occurrence of rollover accidents than did ordinary passenger vehicles. Denny introduced evidence at trial that showed that the Bronco II had a low stability index because of its high center of gravity, narrow tracks, and shorter wheelbase, as well as the design of its suspension system. Ford countered that the Bronco II was intended as an off-road vehicle and was not designed to be used as a conventional passenger automobile on paved streets. The trial court found Ford liable and awarded Denny $1.2 million in damages. Ford appealed.

Issue

Did Ford Motor Company breach the implied warranty of merchantability?

Language of the Court

> Plaintiff introduced a Ford marketing manual that predicted many buyers would be attracted to the Bronco II because utility vehicles were suitable to "contemporary lifestyles" and were "considered fashionable" in some suburban areas. According to this manual, the sales presentation of the Bronco II should take into account the vehicle's "suitability for commuting and for suburban and city driving." Additionally, the vehicle's ability to switch between two-wheel and four-wheel drive would "be particularly appealing to women who may be concerned about driving in snow and ice with their children." Plaintiff testified that the perceived safety benefits of its four-wheel drive capacity was what attracted her to the Bronco II. She was not at all interested in its off-road use.
>
> The law implies a warranty by a manufacturer that places its product on the market that the product is reasonably fit for the ordinary purpose for which it was intended. If it is, in fact, defective and not reasonably fit to be used for its intended purpose, the warranty is breached. Plaintiff's proof focused on the sale of the Bronco II for suburban driving and everyday road travel. Plaintiff also adduced proof that the Bronco II's design characteristics made it unusually susceptible to rollover accidents when used on paved roads. All of this evidence was useful in showing that routine highway and street driving was the "ordinary purpose" for which the Bronco II was sold and that it was not "fit"—or safe—for that purpose. Thus, under the evidence in this case, a rational fact finder could have concluded that the vehicle was not safe for the "ordinary purpose" of daily driving for which it was marketed and sold.

Decision

The court of appeals held that Ford had breached the implied warranty of merchantability and upheld the jury award for the plaintiff.

Law & Ethics Questions

1. What is an implied warranty of merchantability? Explain.
2. What is the public policy underlying an implied warranty?
3. **ETHICS** Did Ford act ethically in defending that the Bronco II was sold only as an off-road vehicle? Was this argument persuasive?
4. What are the business implications of this decision? Do you think that utility vehicles such as the Bronco II have a higher rollover danger than normal passenger automobiles?

Web Exercises

1. **WEB** For the complete opinion of this case, go to *www.prenhall.com/cheesemancases*.
2. **WEB** Visit the website of Ford Motor Company, at *www.ford.com*. Does Ford still make a Bronco class of vehicle?
3. **WEB** Visit the website of the court of appeals of New York, at *www.nycourts.gov/ctapps*.
4. **WEB** Use *www.google.com* to find an article about the rollover problem of Ford Bronco vehicles. Read it.

Implied Warranty of Fitness for Human Consumption

The common law implied a special warranty—the **implied warranty of fitness for human consumption**—to food products. The UCC incorporates this warranty, which applies to food and drink consumed on or off the seller's premises, within the implied warranty of merchantability. Restaurants, grocery stores, fast-food outlets, and vending-machine operators are all subject to this warranty. States use one of the following two tests in determining whether there has been a breach of the implied warranty of fitness for human consumption:

- **Foreign substance test.** Under the **foreign substance test**, a food product is unmerchantable if a foreign object in that product causes injury to a person.

Example The warranty would be breached if an injury were caused by a nail in a cherry pie. If the same injury were caused by a cherry pit in the pie, the pie would not be unmerchantable.

■ **Consumer expectation test.** The majority of states have adopted the modern **consumer expectation test** to determine the merchantability of food products.

Example Under this implied warranty, if a person is injured by a chicken bone while eating fried chicken, the injury is not actionable. However, the implied warranty would be breached if a person were injured by a chicken bone while eating a chicken salad sandwich. This is because a consumer would expect that the food preparer would have removed all bones from the chicken.

Implied Warranty of Fitness for a Particular Purpose

The UCC contains an implied **warranty of fitness for a particular purpose**. This implied warranty is breached if the goods do not meet the buyer's or lessee's expressed needs. The warranty applies to both merchant and nonmerchant sellers and lessors.

The warranty of fitness for a particular purpose is implied at the time of contracting if [UCC 2-315, 2A-213]:

1. The seller or lessor has reason to know the particular purpose for which the buyer is purchasing the goods or the lessee is leasing the goods.
2. The seller or lessor makes a statement that the goods will serve this purpose.
3. The buyer or lessee relies on the seller's or lessor's skill and judgment and purchases or leases the goods.

Example Susan Logan wants to buy lumber to build a house, so she goes to Winter's lumber yard. Logan describes to Winter the house she intends to build. She also tells Winter that she is relying on him to select the right lumber. Winter selects the lumber, and Logan buys it and builds the house. Unfortunately, the house collapses because the lumber was not strong enough to support it. Logan can sue Winter for breach of the implied warranty of fitness for a particular purpose.

The following case raises the issue of implied warranty of fitness for a particular purpose.

CASE 19.3
Implied Warranty of Fitness for a Particular Purpose

Mack Massey Motors, Inc. v. Garnica

814 S.W.2d 167, **Web** 1991 Tex. Lexis 1814
Court of Appeals of Texas

> **"***A claim of warranty of fitness requires that goods serve their particular purpose.***"**
>
> —Judge Fuller

Facts

Felicitas Garnica sought to purchase a vehicle capable of towing a 23-foot Airstream trailer she had on order. She went to Mack Massey Motors, Inc. (Massey Motors), to inquire about purchasing a Jeep Cherokee that was manufactured by Jeep Eagle. After Garnica explained her requirements to the sales manager, he called the Airstream dealer concerning the specifications of the trailer Garnica was purchasing. The sales manager advised Garnica that the Jeep Cherokee could do the job of pulling the trailer. After purchasing the vehicle, Garnica claimed that it did not have sufficient power to pull the trailer. She brought the Jeep Cherokee back to Massey

Motors several times for repairs for a slipping transmission. Eventually, she was told to go to another dealer. The drive shaft on the Jeep Cherokee twisted apart at 7,229 miles. Garnica sued Massey Motors and Jeep Eagle for damages, alleging breach of the implied warranty of fitness for a particular purpose. The jury returned a verdict in favor of Garnica. Massey Motors and Jeep Eagle appealed.

Issue

Did the defendants make and breach an implied warranty of fitness for a particular purpose?

Language of the Court

In the instant case, the service provided by Massey Motors' sales staff included undertaking the responsibility of checking with the Airstream dealer and thereafter representing that the Jeep Cherokee, with an automatic transmission, was suitable for pulling the Airstream. Massey Motors' sales manager testified he knew the intended purpose for Mrs. Garnica's use of the proposed vehicle and that he undertook to investigate the specifications of the Airstream. After having undertaken the inquiry, he recommended the Jeep Cherokee as being suitable for the purposes Mrs. Garnica was seeking—that of towing the Airstream trailer she had on order.

A claim of warranty of fitness requires that goods serve their particular purpose. The evidence supported the jury determination that the Jeep Cherokee simply was exceeding its towing capacity and that Massey Motors had misrepresented the fact that this was the proper vehicle suitable for towing the Airstream trailer. In light of Massey Motors' superior knowledge and expertise concerning Mrs. Garnica's inquiry and reliance, the evidence was sufficient to support the jury's finding.

Decision

The appellate court held that Massey Motors had made and breached an implied warranty of fitness for a particular purpose but that Jeep Eagle had not.

Law & Ethics Questions

1. Should the law recognize the implied warranty of fitness for a particular purpose? Or should buyers be held to know their own requirements?

2. **ETHICS** Did Massey Motors act unethically in this case?

3. Do you think damages should have been awarded in this case?

Web Exercises

1. **WEB** For the complete opinion of this case, go to *www.prenhall.com/cheesemancases*.

2. **WEB** Visit the website of DaimlerChrysler Motors, at *www.daimlerchrysler.com*. Does the company still sell Jeep vehicles?

3. **WEB** Visit the website of Airstream, Inc., at *www.airstream.com*. Look for an Airstream that is 23 feet long, the size of the Airstream in this case.

4. **WEB** Visit the website of the court of appeals of Texas, Eight Circuit, at *www.8thcoa.courts.state.tx.us*.

5. **WEB** Use *www.google.com* to find an article that discusses the safety of Jeep vehicles. Read it.

CONCEPT SUMMARY

Express and Implied Warranties of Quality

TYPE OF WARRANTY	HOW CREATED	DESCRIPTION
Express warranty	Made by the seller or lessor.	Affirms that the goods meet certain standards of quality, description, performance, or condition [UCC 2-313(1), 2A-210(1)].
Implied warranty of merchantability	Implied by law if the seller or lessor is a merchant.	Implies that the goods: 1. Are fit for the ordinary purposes for which they are used. 2. Are adequately contained, packaged, and labeled. 3. Are of an even kind, quality, and quantity within each unit. 4. Conform to any promise or affirmation of fact made on the container or label. 5. Pass without objection in the trade. 6. Meet a fair, average, or middle range of quality for fungible goods [UCC 2-314(1), 2A-212(1)].
Implied warranty of fitness for a particular purpose	Implied by law.	Implies that the goods are fit for the purpose for which the buyer or lessee acquires the goods if: 1. The seller or lessor has reason to know the particular purpose for which the goods will be used. 2. The seller or lessor makes a statement that the goods will serve that purpose. 3. The buyer or lessee relies on the statement and buys or leases the goods [UCC 2-315, UCC 2A-213].

Warranty Disclaimers

Warranties can be **disclaimed**, or limited. If an *express warranty* is made, it can be limited only if the **warranty disclaimer** and the warranty can be reasonably construed with each other.

All implied warranties of quality may be disclaimed by expressions such as *as is*, *with all faults*, or other language that makes it clear to the buyer that there are no implied warranties. This type of disclaimer is often included in sales contracts for used products. If the preceding language is not used, disclaimers of the *implied warranty of merchantability* must specifically mention the term *merchantability*. These disclaimers may be oral or written.

The *implied warranty of fitness for a particular purpose* may be disclaimed in general language, without specific use of the term *fitness*.

Example Language such as "There are no warranties that extend beyond the description on the fact hereof" is sufficient to disclaim the fitness warranty. The disclaimer must be in writing.

Conspicuous Display of Disclaimer

Written disclaimers must be conspicuously displayed to be valid. The courts construe **conspicuous** as noticeable to a reasonable person [UCC 2-316, 2A-214].

Example A heading printed in uppercase letters or a typeface that is larger or in a different style than the rest of the body of a sales or lease contract is considered to be conspicuous. Different-color type is also considered conspicuous.

INTERNET AND TECHNOLOGY
Warranty Disclaimers in Software Licenses

Most software companies license their software to users. A software license is a complex contract that contains the terms of the license. Most software licenses contain warranty disclaimer and limitation on liability clauses that limit the licensor's liability if the software malfunctions. Disclaimer of warranty and limitation on liability clauses that are included in a typical software license appear below.

SOFTWARE.COM, INC.
LIMITATION AND WAIVERS OF WARRANTIES,
REMEDIES, AND CONSEQUENTIAL DAMAGES

Limited Warranty.   Software.com, Inc. warrants that (a) the software will perform substantially in accordance with the accompanying written materials for a period of 90 days from the date of receipt, and (b) any hardware accompanying the software will be free from defects in materials and workmanship under normal use and service for a period of one year from the date of the receipt. Any implied warranties on the software and hardware are limited to 90 days and one (1) year, respectively. Some states do not allow limitations on duration of an implied warranty, so the above limitation may not apply to you.

Customer Remedies.   Software.com, Inc.'s entire liability and your exclusive remedy shall be, at Software.com, Inc.'s option, either (a) return of the price paid or (b) repair or replacement of the software or hardware that does not meet Software.com, Inc.'s Limited Warranty and that is returned to Software.com, Inc. with a copy of your receipt. This Limited Warranty is void if failure of the software or hardware has resulted from accident, abuse, or misapplication. Any replacement software will be warranted for the remainder of the original warranty or 30 days, whichever is longer. These remedies are not available outside the United States of America.

No Other Warranties.   Software.com, Inc. disclaims all other warranties, either express or implied, including but not limited to implied warranties of merchantability and fitness for a particular purpose, with respect to the software, the accompanying written materials, and any accompanying hardware. This Limited Warranty gives you specific legal rights. You may have others, which vary from state to state.

No Liability for Consequential Damages.   In no event shall Software.com, Inc. or its suppliers be liable for any damages whatsoever (including, without limitation, damages for loss of business profits, business interruption, loss of business information, or other pecuniary loss) arising out of the use of or inability to use this Software.com, Inc. product, even if Software.com, Inc. has been advised of the possibility of such damages. Because some states do not allow the exclusion or limitation of liability for consequential or incidental damages, the above limitation may not apply to you.

LANDMARK LAW
Magnuson-Moss Warranty Act Protects Consumers

In 1975, Congress enacted the **Magnuson-Moss Warranty Act**, which covers written warranties relating to *consumer* products.[1] This federal act is administered by the Federal Trade Commission (FTC). Commercial and industrial transactions are not governed by the act. The act does not require a seller or lessor to make express written warranties. However, persons who do make such warranties are subject to the provisions of the act. If the warrantor chooses to make an express warranty, the Magnuson-Moss Warranty Act requires that the warranty be labeled as either "full" or "limited."

To qualify as a **full warranty**, the warrantor must guarantee free repair or replacement of the defective product. The warrantor must indicate whether there is a time limit on the full warranty (e.g., "full 36-month warranty"). In a **limited warranty**, the warrantor limits the scope of a full warranty in some way (e.g., a return of the purchase price or replacement or such). The fact that the warranty is full or limited must be conspicuously displayed. The disclosures must be in "understandable language."

A consumer may bring a civil action against a defendant for violating the provisions of the act. A successful plaintiff can recover damages, attorneys' fees, and other costs incurred in bringing the action. The act authorizes warrantors to establish an informal dispute resolution procedure. The procedure must be conspicuously described in the written warranty. Aggrieved consumers must assert their claims through this procedure before they can take legal action.

The act does not create any implied warranties. It does, however, modify the state law of implied warranties in one crucial respect: Sellers or lessors who make express written warranties relating to consumer products are forbidden from disclaiming or modifying the implied warranties of merchantability and fitness for a particular purpose. A seller or lessor may set a time limit on implied warranties, but this time limit must correspond to the duration of any express warranty.

Law & Ethics Questions

1. What is the underlying purpose of the Magnuson-Moss Warranty Act? Explain.

2. **ETHICS** Do you think that the Magnuson-Moss Warranty Act will cause sellers of products to consumers to act more ethically? Why or why not?

Web Exercise

1. **WEB** Use *www.google.com* to find an article that discusses the protections to consumers afforded by the Magnuson-Moss Warranty Act. Read it.

In the following case, the court addressed the issue of break of an express warranty.

CASE 19.4
Magnuson-Moss Warranty Act

Milicevic v. Fletcher Jones Imports, Ltd. and Mercedes-Benz USA

402 F.3d 912, 2005 U.S. App. Lexis 4905 (2005)
United States Court of Appeals for the Ninth Circuit

> **"** *I feel like I am stranded. I cannot feel comfortable to take the car on a trip. I do not feel comfortable to drive because I don't know what next will come. Every day is a new problem.* **"**
>
> —Marina Milicevic, Consumer

Facts

Marina Milicevic purchased a new Mercedes-Benz S-500 automobile from Fletcher Jones Imports, Ltd., a car dealership, for $98,722. The automobile had been imported into the United States by Mercedes-Benz USA (Fletcher Jones and Mercedes-Benz are collectively referred to as Mercedes). Mercedes advertised the car as the "best car in the world." Mercedes made a new car limited express warranty that warranted to the owner that only authorized Mercedes-Benz Centers would make any repairs or replacements necessary to correct defects in material or workmanship for the duration of the warranty.

From day one, the car exhibited a number of aesthetic and mechanical problems. Within the first seven months, the following repairs were made: all four brake rotors were warped and required replacement at 6,000 miles; after locking Milicevic out of the car, the remote entry system was replaced; the motor for the passenger side window was replaced; the passenger side mirror was replaced;

and the rear window seal and molding were unsuccessfully repaired three times. All repairs were covered and paid for under the Mercedes-Benz limited warranty. By the end of seven months, the car had spent 55 days at Fletcher Jones' repair shop. The rear window deformity and the problem with the brakes were never corrected.

At that point, Milicevic notified Mercedes that she wanted Mercedes to replace the car or take the car back and reimburse her for the purchase price. When Mercedes did not respond, Milicevic sued Mercedes-Benz and Fletcher Jones for breach of an express limited warranty, to rescind the purchase of the automobile, and to recover the value of the car, damages, and attorneys' fees. Milicevic testified at trial: "I feel like I am stranded. I cannot feel comfortable to take the car on a trip. I do not feel comfortable to drive because I don't know what next will come. Every day is a new problem."

The U.S. district court found that the defendants had breached the written warranty between the parties. Milicevic was awarded $93,423—the purchase price of the car, including taxes and fees, less an amount that represented her reasonable use of the automobile. The court also awarded Milicevic costs and attorneys' fees. The defendants appealed.

Issue

Was there a breach of the express warranty made by Mercedes that would permit Milicevic to rescind the purchase of the Mercedes-Benz automobile and recover the value of the car and damages?

Language of the Court

As defined in the Magnuson-Moss Warranty Act, a written warranty is a writing made by the supplier of a product relating to the nature of the material or workmanship of the product, which warranty promises that the product is defect free or will meet a certain level of performance for a given period of time, or a writing in which the supplier agrees to refund, repair, replace, or take other remedial action in the event that the product fails to meet its specifications. Here, Mercedes supplied such a limited written warranty which by its terms "warrants to the original and each subsequent owner of a new Mercedes-Benz passenger car that any authorized Mercedes-Benz Center will make any repairs or replacements necessary to correct defects in material or workmanship" at no charge for parts or labor.

The district court did not clearly err in finding that two significant nonconformities—the rear window seal and the brakes—were not corrected. Milicevic testified the brakes still did not work properly. The district court also found that all of the defects, conditions and nonconformities complained of by Milicevic, which Fletcher Jones was unable to repair, were covered by Mercedes-Benz's said warranty. Thus, when Mercedes failed to correct the defects in the rear window seal and brakes, Mercedes breached the terms of its limited written warranty. Having made out a claim for relief under the Magnuson-Moss Warranty Act, Milicevic may be awarded reasonable costs and attorneys' fees.

Decision

The U.S. court of appeals affirmed the U.S. district court's judgment that found that Mercedes had breached the express limited warranty, thus permitting Milicevic to rescind the contract and recover the value of the car, damages, costs, and attorneys' fees.

Law & Ethics Questions

1. What is an express limited warranty? Explain.
2. What types of contracts are covered by the Magnuson-Moss Warranty Act?
3. What remedies and damages were awarded Milicevic? Could damages for emotional distress have been awarded to Milicevic? Why or why not?
4. **ETHICS** Did Mercedes-Benz or Fletcher Jones act ethically in this case? Why do you think they fought this case to the appellate level? What do you think their legal fees were?
5. **ETHICS** Based on the facts of this case, what do you think Mercedes-Benz and Fletcher Jones should have done? Explain.

Web Exercises

1. **WEB** For the complete opinion of this case, go to *www.prenhall.com/cheesemancases*.
2. **WEB** Visit the website of the U.S. Court of Appeals for the Ninth Circuit at *www.ca9.uscourts.gov*.
3. **WEB** Visit the website of Mercedes-Benz at *www.mbusa.com* and *www.mercedes-benz.com*. Can you find any information about any express warranties made by Mercedes-Benz?
4. **WEB** Go to *www.google.com*. Find an article that discusses a consumer's problems with a new car purchase.

Product Liability

The law provides that persons injured by products, and heirs of persons killed by products, may bring tort actions to recover for damages. The plaintiff may rely on several traditional tort theories, including negligence and material misrepresentation of the defendant. In addition, in certain circumstances, a plaintiff can assert the relatively modern tort doctrine of strict liability. If a violation of strict liability has been found, the plaintiff may recover compensatory damages and also may be able to recover punitive damages if the defendant's conduct has been reckless or intentional.

Sault Ste. Marie, Michigan
The sellers of goods, including food, can be held liable under the tort doctrines of negligence, misrepresentation, and strict liability for injuries caused by the products they sell.

Negligence

A person injured by a defective product may bring an action for **negligence** against the negligent party. To be successful, the plaintiff must prove that the defendant breached a duty of due care to the plaintiff and thereby caused the plaintiff's injuries. In other words, the plaintiff must prove that the defendant was at fault for causing the plaintiff's injuries.

Example Failure to exercise due care includes failing to assemble the product carefully, negligent product design, negligent inspection or testing of the product, negligent packaging, failure to warn of the dangerous propensities of the product, and such. It is important to note that in a negligence lawsuit, only a party who was actually negligent is liable to the plaintiff.

The plaintiff and the defendant do not have to be in privity of contract.[2] For example, in the landmark case *MacPherson v. Buick Motor Co.*,[3] the court held that an injured consumer could recover damages from the manufacturer of a product even though the consumer was not in a contract with the manufacturer from which he had purchased the product. The plaintiff generally bears the difficult burden of proving that the defendant was negligent.

Example Assume that the purchaser of a motorcycle is injured in an accident. The accident occurred because a screw was missing from the motorcycle. How does the buyer prove who was negligent? Was it the manufacturer, which left the screw out during the assembly of the motorcycle? Was it the retailer, who negligently failed to discover the missing screw while preparing the motorcycle for sale? Was it the mechanic, who failed to replace the screw after repairing the motorcycle? Negligence remains a viable, yet difficult, theory on which to base a product liability action.

Misrepresentation

A buyer or lessee who is injured because a seller or lessor fraudulently misrepresented the quality of a product can sue the seller for the tort of **intentional misrepresentation,** or **fraud.** Recovery is limited to persons who were injured because they relied on the misrepresentation.

Intentional misrepresentation occurs when a seller or lessor either (1) affirmatively misrepresents the quality of a product or (2) conceals a defect in it. Because most reputable manufacturers, sellers, and lessors do not intentionally misrepresent the quality of their products, fraud is not often used as the basis for product liability actions.

Strict Liability

In the landmark case *Greenman v. Yuba Power Products, Inc.*,[4] the California supreme court adopted the **doctrine of strict liability in tort** as a basis for product liability actions. Most states have now adopted this doctrine as a basis for product liability actions. The doctrine of strict liability removes many of the difficulties for the plaintiff associated with other theories of product liability. This section examines the scope of the strict liability doctrine.

Liability Without Fault

Unlike negligence, strict liability does not require the injured person to prove that the defendant breached a duty of care. **Strict liability** is **liability without fault**. A seller can be found strictly liable even though he or she has exercised all possible care in the preparation and sale of his or her product.

The doctrine of strict liability applies to sellers and lessors of products who are engaged in the business of selling and leasing products. Casual sales and transactions by nonmerchants are not covered. Thus, a person who sells a defective product to a neighbor in a casual sale is not strictly liable if the product causes injury.

Strict liability applies only to products, not services. In hybrid transactions involving both services and products, the dominant element of the transaction dictates whether strict liability applies.

Example In a medical operation that requires a blood transfusion, the operation would be the dominant element, and strict liability would not apply.

Strict liability may not be disclaimed.

Liability of All in the Chain of Distribution

All parties in the **chain of distribution** of a defective product are *strictly liable* for the injuries caused by that product. Thus, all manufacturers, distributors, wholesalers, retailers, lessors, and subcomponent manufacturers may be sued under the doctrine of strict liability in tort. This view is based on public policy. Lawmakers presume that sellers and lessors will insure against the risk of a strict liability lawsuit and spread the cost to their consumers by raising the prices of products.

Example Suppose a subcomponent manufacturer produces a defective tire and sells it to a truck manufacturer. The truck manufacturer places the defective tire on one of its new-model trucks. The truck is distributed by a distributor to a retail dealer. Ultimately, the retail dealer sells the truck to a buyer. The defective tire causes an accident in which the buyer is injured. All the parties in the tire's chain of distribution can be sued by the injured party; in this case, the liable parties are the subcomponent manufacturer, the truck manufacturer, the distributor, and the retailer.

A defendant who has not been negligent but who is made to pay a strict liability judgment can bring a separate action against the negligent party in the chain of distribution to recover its losses. In the preceding example, for instance, the retailer could sue the manufacturer to recover the strict liability judgment assessed against it.

Exhibit 19.1 compares the doctrines of negligence and strict liability.

FIGURE 19.1

Negligence and Strict Liability Compared

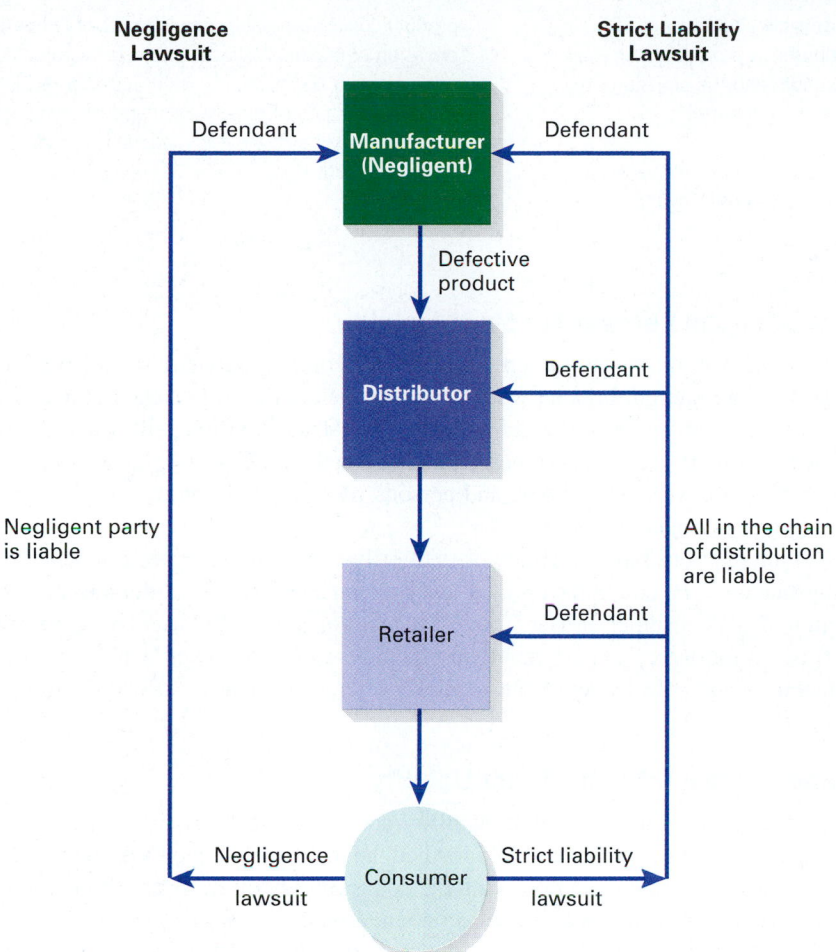

Negligence Lawsuit — Strict Liability Lawsuit

Defendant → **Manufacturer (Negligent)** ← Defendant

Defective product

Distributor ← Defendant

Negligent party is liable

All in the chain of distribution are liable

Retailer ← Defendant

Negligence lawsuit ← **Consumer** → Strict liability lawsuit

Defective product causes injury

CONTEMPORARY ENVIRONMENT

Strict Liability in the *Restatement of Torts*

Restatement (Second) of Torts

The most widely recognized articulation of the doctrine of strict liability in tort is found in *Section 402A* of the ***Restatement (Second) of Torts***, which provides:

1. One who sells any product in a defective condition unreasonably dangerous to the user or consumer or to his property is subject to liability for physical harm thereby caused to the ultimate user or consumer, or to his property, if
   a. the seller is engaged in the business of selling such a product, and
   b. it is expected to and does reach the user or consumer without substantial change in the condition in which it is sold.

2. The rule stated in Subsection (1) applies although
   a. the seller has exercised all possible care in the preparation and sale of his product, and

   b. the user or consumer has not bought the product from or entered into any contractual relation with the seller.

Restatement (Third) of Torts

In 1997, the American Law Institute (ALI) adopted the ***Restatement (Third) of Torts: Product Liability***. This new *Restatement* includes the following definition of *defect*:

A product is defective when, at the time of sale or distribution, it contains manufacturing defect, is defective in design, or is defective because of inadequate instructions or warnings.

A product:

   a. contains a manufacturing defect when the product departs from its intended design even though all possible care was exercised in the preparation and marketing of the product;

   b. is defective in design when the foreseeable risks of harm posed by the product could have been reduced or avoided by the adoption of a reasonable alternative design by the seller or other distributor, or a predecessor in the commercial chain of distribution, and the omission of the alternative design renders the product not reasonably safe;

c. is defective because of inadequate instructions or warnings when the foreseeable risks of harm posed by the product could have been reduced or avoided by the provision of reasonable instructions or warnings by the seller or other distributor, or a predecessor in the commercial chain of distribution, and the omission of the instructions or warnings renders the product not reasonably safe.

Parties Who Can Recover for Strict Liability

Because strict liability is a tort doctrine, privity of contract between the plaintiff and the defendant is not required. In other words, the doctrine applies even if the injured party had no contractual relations with the defendant. Under strict liability, sellers and lessors are liable to the ultimate user or consumer. Users include the purchaser or lessee, family members, guests, employees, customers, and persons who passively enjoy the benefits of the product (e.g., passengers in automobiles).

Most jurisdictions have judicially or statutorily extended the protection of strict liability to bystanders. The courts have stated that bystanders should be entitled to even greater protection than a consumer or user. This is because consumers and users have the opportunity to inspect for defects and to limit their purchases to articles manufactured by reputable manufacturers and sold by reputable retailers, whereas bystanders do not have the same opportunity.

Damages Recoverable for Strict Liability

The damages recoverable in a strict liability action vary by jurisdiction. Damages for personal injuries are recoverable in all jurisdictions that have adopted the doctrine of strict liability, although some jurisdictions limit the dollar amount of the award. Property damage is recoverable in most jurisdictions, but economic loss (e.g., lost income) is recoverable in only a few jurisdictions. *Punitive damages*, which are monetary damages awarded to punish the defendant, are generally allowed if the plaintiff can prove that the defendant either intentionally injured him or her or acted with reckless disregard for his or her safety.

Defective Products

To recover for strict liability, the injured party must first show that the product that caused the injury was somehow *defective*. (Remember that the injured party does not have to prove who caused the product to become defective.) Plaintiffs can allege multiple **product defects** in one lawsuit. A product can be found to be defective in many ways. The most common types of defects are *defects in manufacture*, *defects in design*, *defects in packaging*, and *failure to warn*. These defects are discussed in the following paragraphs.

Defect in Manufacture

A **defect in manufacture** occurs when the manufacturer fails to (1) properly assemble a product, (2) properly test a product, or (3) adequately check the quality of a product.

Example American Ladder Company designs, manufactures, and sells ladders. A worker at American Ladder Company fails to put one of the screws in a ladder the company is manufacturing; this screw would support one of the steps of the ladder. The ladder is sold to Weingard Distributor, a wholesaler, which sells it to Reynolds Hardware Store, which sells the ladder to Heather, a consumer. When Heather is on the ladder, painting her house, the step of the ladder breaks because of the missing screw, and Heather falls and is injured. The missing screw is an example of a defect in manufacture. Under the doctrine of strict liability, American Ladder Company, Weingard Distributor, and Reynolds Hardware Store are liable to Heather.

The following case is a classic example involving a defect in manufacture.

CASE 19.5
Defect in Manufacture

Shoshone Coca-Cola Bottling Company v. Dolinski
82 Nev. 439, 420 P.2d 855, **Web** 1966 Nev. Lexis 260 (1966)
Supreme Court of Nevada

> **"***In the case at hand, Shoshone contends that insufficient proof was offered to establish that the mouse was in the bottle of "Squirt" when it left Shoshone's possession.***"**
>
> —Judge Thompson

Facts

Leo Dolinski purchased a bottle of Squirt, a soft drink, from a vending machine at a Sea and Ski plant, his place of employment. Dolinski opened the bottle and consumed part of its contents. He immediately became ill. Upon examination, it was found that the bottle contained the decomposed body of a mouse, mouse hair, and mouse feces. Dolinski visited a doctor and was given medicine to counteract nausea. Dolinski suffered physical and mental distress from consuming the decomposed mouse and thereafter possessed an aversion to soft drinks. The Shoshone Coca-Cola Bottling Company (Shoshone) had manufactured and distributed the Squirt bottle. Dolinski sued Shoshone, basing his lawsuit on the doctrine of strict liability. The state of Nevada had not previously recognized the doctrine of strict liability. However, the trial court adopted the doctrine of strict liability, and the jury returned a verdict in favor of the plaintiff. Shoshone appealed.

Issue

Should the state of Nevada judicially adopt the doctrine of strict liability? If so, was there a defect in the manufacture of the Squirt bottle that caused the plaintiff's injuries?

Language of the Court

In our view, public policy demands that one who places upon the market a bottled beverage in a condition dangerous for use must be held strictly liable to the ultimate user for injuries resulting from such use, although the seller has exercised all reasonable care.

Our acceptance of strict tort liability against the manufacturer and distributor of a bottled beverage does not mean that the plaintiff is relieved of the burden of proving a case. He must still establish that his injury was caused by a defect in the product and that such defect existed when the product left the hands of the defendant.

In the case at hand, Shoshone contends that insufficient proof was offered to establish that the mouse was in the bottle of "Squirt" when it left Shoshone's possession. The plaintiff

offered the expert testimony of a toxicologist who examined the bottle and contents on the day the plaintiff drank from it. It was his opinion that the mouse "had been dead for a long time" and that the dark stains (mouse feces) that he found on the bottom of the bottle must have been there before the liquid was added. The jury apparently preferred the latter evidence that traced cause to the defendant.

Decision

The supreme court of Nevada adopted the doctrine of strict liability and held that the evidence supported the trial court's finding that there was a defect in manufacture. The supreme court affirmed the trial court's decision in favor of plaintiff Dolinski.

Law & Ethics Questions

1. Should the courts adopt the theory of strict liability? Why or why not?
2. **ETHICS** Was it ethical for Shoshone to argue that it was not liable to Dolinski?
3. **ETHICS** Should all parties in the chain of distribution of a defective product—even parties that are not responsible for the defect—be held liable under the doctrine of strict liability? Or should liability be based only on fault?

Web Exercises

1. **WEB** For the complete opinion of this case, go to *www.prenhall.com/cheesemancases*.
2. **WEB** Visit the website of PepsiCo, at *www.pepsico.com*. Can you find any information on the manufacture of Squirt soda?
3. **WEB** Visit the website of the supreme court of Nevada, at *www.nvsupremecourt.us*.
4. **WEB** Use *www.google.com* to find an article about strict liability as it applies to product defects. Read it.

Defect in Design

A **defect in design** can support a strict liability action. Design defects include toys that are designed with removable parts that could be swallowed by children, machines and appliances designed without proper safeguards, and trucks and other vehicles designed without warning devices to let people know that the vehicle is backing up.

In evaluating the adequacy of a product's design, the courts apply a risk-utility analysis and consider the gravity of the danger posed by the design, the likelihood that injury will occur, the availability and cost of producing a safer alternative design, the social utility of the product, and other factors.

In the following two cases, that courts had to decide whether there was a design defect.

CASE 19.6
Defect in Design

Lakin v. Senco Products, Inc.

144 Ore.App. 52, 925 P.2d 107, **Web** 1996 Ore. App. Lexis 1466
Court of Appeals of Oregon

> *Thus, it was foreseeable—indeed, highly likely given the SN325's recoil and 'bump fire' potential—that serious injury could occur to someone when the nail gun double fired.*
>
> —Judge Haselton

Facts

Senco Products, Inc. (Senco), manufactures and markets a variety of pneumatic nail guns, including the SN325 nail gun, which discharges 3.25-inch nails. The SN325 uses special nails designed and sold by Senco. The SN325 will discharge a nail only if two trigger mechanisms are activated; that is, the user must both squeeze the nail gun's finger trigger and press the nail gun's muzzle against a surface, activating the bottom trigger, or safety. The SN325 can fire up to nine nails per second if the trigger is continuously depressed and the gun is bounced along the work surface, constantly reactivating the muzzle safety/trigger.

John Lakin was using a Senco SN325 nail gun to help build a new home. When attempting to nail two-by-fours under the eaves of the garage, Lakin stood on tiptoe and raised a two-by-four over his head. As he held the board in position with his left hand and the nail gun in his right hand, he pressed the nose of the SN325 up against the board, depressed the safety, and pulled the finger trigger to fire the nail into the board. The gun fired the first nail and then, in a phenomenon known as "double firing," immediately discharged an unintended second nail that struck the first nail. The gun recoiled violently backward toward Lakin and, with Lakin's finger still on the trigger, came into contact with his cheek. That contact activated the safety/trigger, causing the nail gun to fire a third nail. This third nail went through Lakin's cheekbone and into his brain.

The nail penetrated the frontal lobe of the right hemisphere of Lakin's brain, blocked a major artery, and caused extensive tissue damage. Lakin was unconscious for several days and ultimately underwent multiple surgeries. He suffers permanent brain damage and is unable to perceive information from the left hemisphere of the brain. He also suffers partial paralysis of the left side of his body. Lakin has undergone a radical personality change and is prone to violent outbursts. He is unable to obtain employment. Lakin's previously warm and loving relationship with his wife and four children has been permanently altered. He can no longer live with his family and instead resides in a supervised group home for brain-injured persons. Lakin and his wife sued Senco for strict liability based on design defect. The trial court found Senco liable and awarded $5,323,413 to Lakin, $876,000 to his wife, and $4 million in punitive damages against Senco. Senco appealed.

Issue

Is Senco liable to Lakin for strict liability based on a design defect in the SN325 that allowed it to double fire?

Language of the Court

The evidence disclosed that the SN325 double-fired once in every 15 firings. Defendant rushed the SN325's production in order to maintain its position in the market, modifying an existing nail gun model so that it could shoot longer nails, without engaging in additional testing to determine whether the use of longer nails in that model would increase the prevalence of double fire. A reasonable juror could plausibly infer that conscious profit/market share motives underlay the failure to engage in adequate product research, development, and testing.

After reviewing the entire record, we conclude that the amount of damages awarded was within the range that a rational juror would be entitled to award. Before John Lakin's injury, defendant knew from numerous complaints that it was highly probably that the SN325 would "double fire." Thus, it was foreseeable—indeed, highly likely given the SN325's recoil and "bump fire" potential—that serious injury could occur to someone when the nail gun double fired.

Decision

The court of appeals applied a risk-utility analysis and held that the SN325 was defectively designed. The court affirmed the award of damages to Lakin and his wife.

Law & Ethics Questions

1. Do you think the utility served by the nine-nails-per-second SN325 outweighed its risk of personal injury?

2. **ETHICS** Did Senco act in conscious disregard of safety factors when it designed, manufactured, and sold the SN325 nail gun?

3. **ETHICS** Do you think the award of punitive damages was warranted in this case?

Web Exercises

1. **WEB** For the complete opinion of this case, go to *www.prenhall.com/cheesemancases*.

2. **WEB** Visit the website of Senco Products, Inc., at *www.senco.com*. Can you find descriptions of the nail guns it now sells?

3. **WEB** Visit the website of the court of appeals of Oregon, at *www.ojd.state.or.us/courts/coa*.

4. **WEB** Use *www.google.com* to find an article about the dangers of using nail guns. Read it.

C A S E   19.7

Design Defect

Higgins v. Intex Recreation Corporation

123 Wn.App. 821, 99 P.3d 421, **Web** 2004 Wash. App. Lexis 2424 (2004)
Court of Appeals of Washington

> **66** *Now, the ride down a snow-covered hill backward at 30 miles per hour may be a thrill. But it has very little social value when compared to the risk of severe injury.* **99**
>
> —Judge Sweeney

Facts

Intex Recreation designed and sold the Extreme Sno-Tube II. This snow tube is ridden by a user down snow-covered hills and can reach a speed of 30 miles per hour. The snow tube has no steering device, and therefore a rider may end up spinning and going down a hill backward.

Dan Falkner bought an Extreme Sno-Tube II and used it for sledding the same day. During Falkner's second run, the tube rotated him backward about one-quarter to one-third of the way down the hill. A group of parents, including Tom Higgins, stood near the bottom of the hill. Higgins saw seven-year old Kyle Potter walking in the path of Falkner's speeding Sno-Tube. Higgins ran and grabbed Potter to save him from harm, but while doing so, the Sno-Tube hit Higgins and threw him into the air. Higgins landed on his forehead, which snapped his head back. The impact severed Higgins's spinal cord and left him quadriplegic.

Higgins sued Intex for damages based on strict liability. Evidence was introduced at trial that showed that the Sno-Tube could rotate while going down hill and that it had no guiding mechanism and no steering device. Evidence also showed that Intex made a Sno-Boggan that went just as fast but did not rotate because of ridges on the bottom of the device. The jury found a design defect in the Sno-Tube and held Intex liable for 35 percent of Higgins's damages.

Issue

Was the Extreme Sno-Tube II defectively designed, thus supporting the judgment against Intex?

Language of the Court

There are two tests for determining whether a product is defective. The risk-utility test requires a showing that the likelihood and seriousness of harm outweigh the burden on the manufacturer to design a product that would have prevented that harm and would not have impaired the product's usefulness. The consumer-expectation test requires a showing that the product is more dangerous than the ordinary consumer would expect. This test focuses on the reasonable expectation of the consumer.

A plaintiff can satisfy its burden of proving an alternative design by showing that another product more safely serves the same function as the challenged product. There is evidence in this record from which a jury could conclude that the placement of ribs or ridges on the bottom of the Sno-Tube, like those used on Intex's Sno-Boggan, would keep the rider from facing downhill. The rider could then see obstacles and direct the tube. All this could be done without sacrificing speed. This is enough to prove an alternative safer design. Now, the ride down a snow-covered hill backward at 30 miles per hour may be a thrill. But it has very little social value when compared to the risk of severe injury. We do not think the Sno-Tube is a product that is necessary regardless of the risks involved to the user. We find ample evidence to support this verdict, applying the risk-utility test.

We next take up Intex's assertion that the tube was not unsafe to an extent beyond that which would be contemplated by the ordinary consumer. Again, we find ample evidence in this record to support the Higgins's assertion to the contrary. And a reasonable jury could easily infer that the average consumer may expect the Sno-Tube to rotate. But he or she might not expect that it would continue in a backward position. Here, the Sno-Tube is inexpensive. But so is Intex's Sno-Boggan. And the Sno-Boggan provides a fast ride but not a blind high-speed ride. A jury could then find that a reasonable consumer would expect that a snow sliding product would not put him or her in a backward, high-speed slide. We find ample evidence in favor of the plaintiffs applying the consumer-expectation test.

Decision

The court of appeals held that the Sno-Tube was defectively designed and affirmed the judgment in favor of Higgins against Intex.

Law & Ethics Questions

1. What is a design defect? Explain.
2. What does the risk-utility test require? What does the consumer-expectation test require?
3. **ETHICS** Should Intex have placed a ridge on the bottom of the Sno-Tube or equipped it with a steering device to make it safer?
4. Would you have found for or against Intex in this case? Explain.

Web Exercises

1. **WEB** For the complete opinion of this case, go to *www.prenhall.com/cheesemancases*.
2. **WEB** Visit the website of Intex Recreation Corporation, at *www.intexcorp.com*. Does the company still sell that type of snow-tube devices?
3. **WEB** Visit the website of the court of appeals of Washington, at *www.courts.wa.gov*.
4. **WEB** Use *www.google.com* to find an article about the dangers of snow tubing. Read it.

Crashworthiness Doctrine

Often, when an automobile is involved in an accident, the driver or passengers are not injured by the blow itself. Instead, they are injured when their bodies strike something inside their own automobile (e.g., the dashboard, the steering wheel). This is commonly referred to as the "second collision." The courts have held that automobile manufacturers are under a duty to design automobiles to take into account the possibility of this second collision. This is called the **crashworthiness doctrine**. Failure to design an automobile to protect occupants from foreseeable dangers caused by a second collision subjects the manufacturer and dealer to strict liability.

ETHICS SPOTLIGHT

Design Defect in Pool Equipment

Lorenzo Peterson was swimming in a swimming pool with a friend at an apartment complex. Lorenzo watched as his friend swam to the bottom of the pool, slid an unattached drain cover away, and then slid it back. Lorenzo thought his friend had hidden something inside the drain, so he swam to the bottom of the pool. Lorenzo slid the drain cover aside and stuck his arm inside the drain. The 300 to 400 pounds of pull of the drain pump held Lorenzo trapped underwater. At least seven people tried to free Lorenzo to no avail. When the police arrived, they broke down the door to the pool equipment room and turned off the drain pump.

Lorenzo was trapped underwater for 12 minutes, which left him irreversibly brain damaged. Lorenzo, through his relatives, sued Sta-Rite Industries, Inc., the manufacturer of the drain, under the doctrine of strict liability to recover damages for Lorenzo's injuries. The plaintiff alleged that the underwater pool drain was defectively designed because it did not contain a shut-off mechanism. Evidence at trial showed that Sta-Rite's drain covers are designed to screw down, but often a drain cover becomes loose. Further evidence showed that there had been more than 20 prior suction-entrapment accidents involving Sta-Rite's drain covers and pumps.

Previously, experts had designed a pool drain pump with a mechanism that would automatically shut off a pool drain pump when it detected that it was pulling more than it should. Sta-Rite did not install such safety features on its drain pumps, however. After hearing the evidence, including seeing a video of a typical day in the life of Lorenzo after the accident, the jury took less than two hours to return a verdict against Sta-Rite. The jury found that a design defect existed in Sta-Rite's pool drain equipment and awarded Lorenzo $32 million for past and future medical expenses and $72 million for pain and suffering. *Sta-Rite Industries, Inc. v. Peterson*, 837 So.2d 988, **Web** 2003 Fla. App. Lexis 1673 (Court of Appeal of Florida, 2003)

Law & Ethics Questions

1. **ETHICS** Do you think Sta-Rite acted unethically in this case? Why or why not?
2. **ETHICS** Was the award of $104 million in this case warranted? Explain

Web Exercises

1. **WEB** For the complete opinion of this case, go to *www.prenhall.com/cheesemancases*.
2. **WEB** Visit the website of Sta-Rite Industries, at *www.starite.com*. Can you locate any information about the safety of its products.
3. **WEB** Visit the website of the court of appeals of Florida, *www.flcourts.org*.
4. **WEB** Use *www.google.com* to find an article about someone being injured in a pool accident. Read it.

Failure to Warn

Certain products are inherently dangerous and cannot be made any safer and still accomplish the task for which they are designed. For example, certain useful drugs cause side effects, allergies, and other injuries to some users. Many machines and appliances include dangerous moving parts that, if removed, would defeat the purpose of the machine or appliance. Manufacturers and sellers of such products are under a *duty to warn* users about such a product's dangerous propensities.

A proper and conspicuous warning placed on such a product insulates the manufacturer and others in the chain of distribution from strict liability. **Failure to warn** of these dangerous propensities is a defect that will support a strict liability action.

Example The Universal Drug Corporation develops a new drug that has tremendous success in preventing and treating a certain type of cancer. The drug, however, has a 3 percent probability of causing an increased risk of heart disease in patients who take the drug. The drug cannot be made any safer and still have its cancer treatment effects. The Universal Drug Corporation owes a duty to warn potential users of its drug of these heart-related risks. If it fails to do so and a user suffers a heart attack due to use of the drug, the Universal Drug Corporation would be held strictly liable for failure to warn.

In the following three cases, the court had to decide whether there was a design defect and if so, was there a failure to warn of the defect.

CASE 19.8
Design Defect

Karlsson v. Ford Motor Company

140 Cal.App.4th 1202, 45 Cal.Rptr.3d 265, **Web** 2006 Cal. App. Lexis 976 (2006)
Court of Appeal of California

> **"** *This is a chance for you to say, 'Hey Ford, if you know about a problem that is taking place, than do something about it.'* **"**
>
> —Plaintiff's Lawyer

Facts

Five-year-old Johan Karlsson was riding in a Ford Windstar minivan with his mother, uncle, and four siblings. The Windstar minivan was designed and manufactured by Ford Motor Company. The Windstar had three rows of seating and provided combination lap belt and shoulder harnesses for all the seats but one—the center seat of the rear third row bench, where Johan was seated. Instead of the so-called three-point harness worn by the others, Johan was provided only a lap belt.

The Karlssons were driving on Interstate 5, when the driver of the tractor-trailer in front of them dozed off and rear-ended a truck in front of him. A 15-ton steel coil fell off of the tractor-trailer and struck the Karlssons' minivan. The six Karlssons who were wearing the shoulder harnesses were injured but made full recoveries. Johan suffered severe spinal injuries and was left a paraplegic.

The tractor-trailer was owned by TransContinental Transport (TCT). Johan sued TCT and Ford Motor Company. Johan settle with TCT for $10 million. Johan sued Ford to recover damages for strict liability, alleging design defect and failure to warn. The jury awarded Johan

over $30 million in economic damages, pain and suffering, and punitive damages. Ford appealed.

Issue

Was there a design defect in the Windstar minivan, and did Ford fail to warn of the defect?

Language of the Court

Johan's injuries were consistent with something physicians call seat belt syndrome, when a passenger restrained by only a lap belt jackknives over at the waist due to the force of the collision. Had Johan been wearing a three-point restraint, his injuries would have been no more severe than the other occupants of the Windstar. Johan's mother testified that she adjusted Johan's lap belt for him before starting the trip, making sure it fit snugly and rested on his hips.

The jury in this case was instructed on the theories of: (1) design defect under the risk-benefit approach; and (2) failure to warn. Under the design defect theory, Johan argued to the jury that Ford could have and should have installed a seat belt in the rear bench center seat that included some type of shoulder harness. Under the failure to warn theory, Johan argued to the jury that Ford did not adequately warn of the need to wear the lap belt properly, or of the magnitude of the harm that might follow as a result. Ford's primary defense was that the collision was a severe one and that Johan's seat belt was not properly adjusted.

The one comment to which Ford raised an objection came at the very end of Johan's rebuttal argument. After Johan's lawyer said, "This is your chance that maybe companies won't try to destroy . . . ," Ford counsel cut him off with an objection. That objection was overruled, and Johan's lawyer then said, "This is a chance for you to say, 'Hey Ford, if you know about a problem that is taking place, than do something about it.' " Johan's lawyer concluded his argument soon after.

Decision

The court of appeals affirmed the trial court's judgment in favor of plaintiff Johan Karlsson against Ford Motor Company

Law & Ethics Questions

1. What is a design defect? Explain.

2. What constitutes failure to warn? Explain.

3. **ETHICS** Did Ford Motor Company act ethically in this case?

Web Exercises

1. **WEB** For the complete opinion of this case, go to *www.prenhall.com/cheesemancases*.

2. **WEB** Visit the website of Ford Motor Company, at *www.ford.com*. To learn about Ford vehicles, including minivans, go to *www.fordvehicles.com*.

3. **WEB** Visit the website of the California court of appeals, at *www.courtinfo.ca.gov/courts/courtsofappeal*. Click on "2nd District" link.

4. **WEB** Use *www.google.com* to find an article that discusses strict liability. Read it.

CASE 19.9
Failure to Warn

Crosswhite v. Jumpking, Inc.

411 F.Supp.2d 1228, **Web** 2006 U.S. Dist. Lexis 6285 (2006)
United States District Court for the District of Oregon

> **❝***Plaintiff must present evidence that the trampoline was defectively designed. The burden of proof that the product was defective at the time it left the hands of the particular seller is upon the injured plaintiff.***❞**
>
> —Judge Aiken

Facts

One day, Gary Crosswhite was jumping on a trampoline with another boy. The trampoline was owned by Jack and Misty Urbach. The 14-foot round-shaped "backyard" trampoline was manufactured by Jumpking, Inc. While on the trampoline, Crosswhite attempted a back flip and accidentally landed on his head and neck. The force of the fall caused a fracture in Crosswhite's spine, resulting in paraplegia. Crosswhite was 16 years old at the time of the injury.

Crosswhite filed a lawsuit in U.S. District Court against Jumpking to recover damages for strict liability based on design defect and failure to warn of the danger of using the trampoline. Defendant Jumpking filed a motion for summary judgment.

Issue

Is defendant Jumpking liable for strict liability to Crosswhite based on either defect in design or failure to warn?

Language of the Court

Plaintiff must present evidence that the trampoline was defectively designed. The burden of proof that the product was defective at the time it left the hands of the particular seller is upon the injured plaintiff; and unless evidence can be produced which will support the conclusion that it was then defective the burden will not be sustained. Plaintiff has not submitted any evidence to meet this burden. There can be no dispute that an ordinary consumer buys and uses a trampoline to jump on it, and a design that allows for such activity is exactly that which is contemplated by an ordinary consumer or user of a trampoline. Plaintiff's complaint against the defendant seems to be that all trampolines are defectively designed and should be banned from the marketplace. Given Oregon's objective standard and the facts that plaintiff was a 16-year-old, with a 3.6 grade point average in high school, with over six years experience with trampolines, I find that plaintiff was capable of appreciating the risks associated with jumping and performing flips on a trampoline.

Defendant's trampoline is manufactured with nine warning labels that are affixed to various trampoline components. In addition to these nine warning labels, defendant also provides a large laminated warning placard that is designed to be attached by the consumer to the metal frame near the ladder upon which jumpers mount the trampoline. Defendant further provides consumers with a detailed User Manual and a videotape that instructs both users and supervisors about safe and responsible trampoline use. However, defendant did affix those warnings to the trampoline as well as on a large warning placard attached to the trampoline at the point of entry or mounting. Specifically, warnings attached to the trampoline frame leg stated:

!Warning

Do not land on head or neck. Paralysis or death can result, even if you land in the middle of the trampoline mat (bed). To reduce the chance of landing on your head or neck, do not do flips.

!Warning

Only one person at a time on the trampoline. Multiple jumpers increase the chances of loss of control, collision, and falling off. This can result in a broken head, neck, back or leg.

I find that defendant's warnings were adequate as a matter of law.

Decision

The U.S. District Court held that there was no design defect or failure to warn by defendant Jumpking. The District Court granted summary judgment to Jumpking and dismissed the plaintiff's lawsuit.

Law & Ethics Questions

1. Do you think there was a defect in the design of the trampoline? Why or why not?

2. Do you think there was a failure to warn about the dangers of using the trampoline? Why or why not?

3. **ETHICS** With the inherent dangers of using a trampoline, should all trampolines be barred from the marketplace? Why or why not?

Web Exercises

1. **WEB** For the complete opinion of this case, go to *www.prenhall.com/cheesemancases*.

2. **WEB** Go to the website of Jumpking, Inc., at *www.jumpking.com* and view what a trampoline looks like.

3. **WEB** Visit the website of the U.S. District Court for Oregon, at *www.ord.uscourts.gov*.

4. **WEB** Use *www.google.com* to find an article about someone else being injured using a trampoline. Read it.

CASE 19.10
Failure to Warn

Glenn v. Overhead Door Corporation

935 So.2d 1074, **Web** 2006 Miss. App. Lexis 60 (2006)
Court of Appeals of Mississippi

> *"Jolie could have easily avoided exposing Brittany to dangerous levels of carbon monoxide by not leaving her in a car unattended for an extended period of time with the engine running and the garage door down."*
>
> —Judge Chandler

Facts

Jolie Glenn placed her three-year-old daughter, Brittany, in a car with the engine running while it was parked in her garage with the garage door closed. Glenn went back into the house, sat down, and fell asleep. When she awoke, she realized that Brittany was not with her. Jolie went into the garage and saw that the garage door was closed. Brittany was in the car and had died as a result of carbon monoxide poisoning. Overhead Door Corporation had manufactured the garage door and the garage door opener used by Jolie to open and close the garage door.

Malcolm Glenn, Jolie's ex-husband and Brittany's father, sued Overhead Door for strict liability, alleging design defect and failure to warn. Glenn argued that Overhead Door should have designed its garage door opener with a sensor that would determine when carbon monoxide had gotten too high in a garage and then alert the car owner. Glenn also alleged that Overhead Door had failed to warn a user of its garage door opener that if the car was left running and the garage door was closed, carbon monoxide could build up to dangerous levels in the garage. The trial court granted summary judgment to Overhead Door.

Issue

Was Overhead Door liable for strict liability for either design defect or failure to warn?

Language of the Court

Jolie could have easily avoided exposing Brittany to dangerous levels of carbon monoxide by not leaving her in a car unattended for an extended period of time with the engine running and the garage door down. Proving that a manufacturer did not warn of some potential danger does not, by itself, create an issue of fact. In order to create a triable issue regarding failure to warn, the plaintiff must show that the user was ignorant of the danger warned against. Manufacturers and distributors have no duty to warn of dangers that are open and obvious or if the hazard associated with the product is common knowledge to the ordinary observer or consumer.

Malcolm argues that there is a genuine issue as to whether Overhead Door should have warned of the dangers of carbon monoxide poisoning because Jolie Glenn testified that it never crossed her mind that her daughter could die from carbon monoxide poisoning. However, she did testify that she knew a person should never leave a child unattended in a car with the engine running. She also testified that she knew and appreciated the danger of [**11] carbon monoxide poisoning and that she knew the garage door would not open automatically. She needed no other warning.

Decision

The court of appeals held that Overhead Door was not strictly liable for design defect or failure to warn. The court of appeals affirmed the trial court's grant of summary judgment in favor of Overhead Door.

Law & Ethics Questions

1. Do you think there was a design defect in this case? Explain.
2. Do you think there was a failure to warn in this case? Explain.
3. **ETHICS** Was it ethical for the plaintiff in this case to sue Overhead Door based on the facts of this case?
4. **ETHICS** Did Overhead Door owe a duty to design its garage door opener with a sensor to alert of high levels of carbon monoxide? Why or why not?
5. **ETHICS** Did Overhead Door owe a duty to warn the owners of its garage doors and garage door openers of the danger of carbon monoxide poisoning? Why or why not?

Web Exercises

1. **WEB** For the complete opinion of this case, go to *www.prenhall.com/cheesemancases*.
2. **WEB** Visit the website of the court of appeals of Mississippi, at *www.mssc.state.ms.us*.
3. **WEB** Visit the website of Overhead Door Corporation, at *www.overheaddoor.com*. Does the company sell any garage door openers with sensors on them to detect levels of carbon monoxide poisoning?
4. **WEB** Use *www.google.com* to find an article about the safety of garage doors and garage door openers. Read it.

Defect in Packaging

Manufacturers owe a duty to design and provide safe packages for their products. This duty requires manufacturers to provide packages and containers that are tamperproof or that clearly indicate if they have been tampered with. Certain manufacturers, such as drug manufacturers, owe a duty to place their products in containers that cannot be opened by children. A manufacturer's failure to meet this duty—a **defect in packaging**—subjects the manufacturer and others in the chain of distribution of the product to strict liability.

In the following case, the court had to decide whether there was defective packaging.

| CASE 19.11 *Defect in Packaging* | **Elsroth v. Johnson & Johnson** 700 F.Supp. 151, **Web** 1998 U.S. Dist. Lexis 13167 United States District Court for the Southern District of New York |  |

" We return, however, to the fundamental premise: no packaging can boast of being tamperproof. "

—Judge Goettel

Facts

Harriet Notarnicola purchased a box of Extra-Strength Tylenol capsules from a Bronxville, New York, grocery store owned by The Great Atlantic & Pacific Tea Co. (A&P). The Tylenol was manufactured by McNeil Consumer Products Co., a division of McNeilab, Inc. (McNeil), under the name Johnson & Johnson. Diane Elsroth was visiting her boyfriend, Michael Notarnicola, for a week at the home of Michael's parents. Late one night, Diane complained of a headache. Michael went to the kitchen, opened the box and plastic container of Extra-Strength Tylenol purchased by his mother at the A&P store, and returned with two capsules and a glass of water for Diane. A short time after ingesting the capsules, Diane retired. Her dead body was found the next day. The medical examiner concluded that the Tylenol capsules ingested by Diane had been contaminated by a lethal does of potassium cyanide. The murder remains unsolved, but evidence shows that the Tylenol bottle had been tampered with after the product left the manufacturer's control. An unknown third party purchased the Tylenol, breached the packaging, substituted cyanide for some of the medicine contained in several of the gelatin capsules, somehow resealed the container and box in such a way that the tampering was not readily detectable, and placed the contaminated box on the shelf of the A&P, store. John Elsroth, administrator of Diane's estate, brought this strict liability action against McNeil and A&P, seeking $1 million in compensatory damages and $92 million in punitive damages.

Issue

Was there a defect in packaging that would support an action for strict liability?

Language of the Court

Following issuance of the rule, the makers of Tylenol have marketed the product in tamper-resistant packaging with the following features: (1) a foil seal glued to the mouth of the container or bottle, (2) a "shrink seal" around the neck and cap of the container, and (3) a sealed box (the end flaps of which are glued shut) in which the product and container are placed. As one McNeil official put it, tampering by "the Rembrandt kind of criminals" could not be prevented by this type of packaging. McNeil was also operating under the constraint, as recognized by the Food and Drug Administration (FDA), that no packaging could prevent this kind of "exotic" tampering—tamperproof packaging is not possible.

The packaging alternative designed by McNeil employed not one, not two, but three of the tamper-resistant features. When all of these factors are thrown into the mix, we find, as a matter of law, that under a utility/risk analysis this packaging was in a condition reasonably contemplated by the ultimate consumer and was not unreasonably dangerous for its intended use. If there are better tamper-resistant features available that would be feasible for use here, plaintiff has not described them. We return, however, to the fundamental premise: no packaging can boast of being tamperproof.

Decision

The Court held that there was not a defect in packaging. The defendants are not therefore strictly liable for Ms. Elsroth's death.

Law & Ethics Questions

1. Should manufacturers be forced to make tamperproof packaging for their products? Is this possible? What would be the expense?

2. **ETHICS** Did any of the parties in the case act unethically? Explain.

3. **ETHICS** Do you think the plaintiff's seeking $92 million in punitive damages was warranted?

Web Exercises

1. **WEB** For the complete opinion of this case, go to *www.prenhall.com/cheesemancases*.

2. **WEB** Visit the website of Johnson & Johnson, at *www.jnj.com*.

3. **WEB** Visit the website of the U.S. District Court for the Southern District of New York, at *www.nysd.uscourts.gov*.

4. **WEB** Use *www.google.com* to find an article about the liability of manufacturers for failing to provide safe packaging. Read it.

Failure to Provide Adequate Instructions

Sellers are responsible to provide adequate instructions for the safe assembly and use of the products they sell.

Failure to provide adequate instructions for the safe assembly and use of a product is a defect that subjects the manufacturer and others in the chain of distribution to strict liability.

Other defects include inadequate testing of products, inadequate selection of component parts or materials, and improper certification of the safety of a product. The concept of "defect" is an expanding area of the law.

London, England

Most industrialized countries and many other countries have well-developed product liability law based on negligence, but few have adopted the doctrine of strict liability.

Punitive Damages

In product liability cases, a court can award **punitive damages** if it finds that the defendant's conduct was committed with intent or reckless disregard for human life. Punitive damages are meant to punish the defendants and to send a message to the defendant (and other companies) that such behavior will not be tolerated. However, with large punitive damage awards making the headlines, companies began asking themselves when are punitive damages too much. The U.S. Supreme Court has addressed this issue.

In the following case, the Supreme Court was asked to overturn a large award of punitive damages.

CASE **19.12**

Punitive Damages

U.S. SUPREME COURT
Philip Morris USA v. Williams

127 S.Ct. 1057, 166 L.Ed.2d 940,
Web 2007 U.S. Lexis 1332 (2007)
Supreme Court of the United States

> "*In our view, the Constitution's Due Process Clause forbids a State to use a punitive damages award to punish a defendant for injury that it inflicts upon nonparties or those whom they directly represent, i.e., injury that it inflicts upon those who are, essentially, strangers to the litigation.*"

—Justice Breyer

Facts

Jesse Williams was a heavy cigarette smoker. He favored Marlboro brand cigarettes, which are produced by Philip Morris USA. Jesse Williams died because of his cigarette smoking. Williams's personal representative sued Philip Morris, alleging that the company had engaged in deceit and had knowingly led Williams to believe that cigarette smoking was safe.

At trial, the jury held that Philip Morris had engaged in deceit. The jury awarded $821,000 in compensatory damages and $79.5 million in punitive damages. In reaching its decision on punitive damages, the jury was permitted to consider harm caused to others who were not parties to the lawsuit. The trial court judge held that the $79.5 million in punitive damages was excessive and reduced it to $32 million. Both sides appealed.

The Oregon court of appeals rejected Philip Morris's arguments and restored the $79.5 million jury award. The Oregon supreme court denied review. The case was appealed to the U.S. Supreme Court.

Issue

Did the Oregon court unconstitutionally punish the defendant Philip Morris USA by allowing the jury to consider harm to non-party victims when awarding punitive damages to the plaintiff?

Language of the U.S. Supreme Court

In our view, the Constitution's Due Process Clause forbids a State to use a punitive damages award to punish a defendant for injury that it inflicts upon nonparties or those whom they directly represent, i.e., injury that it inflicts upon those who are, essentially, strangers to the litigation. For one thing, the Due Process Clause prohibits a State from punishing an individual without first providing that individual with an opportunity to present every available defense. A defendant threatened with punishment for injuring a nonparty victim has no opportunity to defend against the charge, by showing, for example in a case such as this, that the other victim was not entitled to damages because he or she knew that smoking was dangerous or did not rely upon the defendant's statements to the contrary.

To permit punishment for injuring a nonparty victim would add a near standardless dimension to the punitive damages equation. How many such victims are there? How seriously were they injured? Under what circumstances did injury occur? The trial will not likely answer such questions as to nonparty victims. The jury will be left to speculate. And the fundamental due process concerns to which our punitive damages cases refer—risks of arbitrariness, uncertainty and lack of notice—will be magnified. We can find no authority supporting the use of punitive damages awards for the purpose of punishing a defendant for harming others.

Respondent argues that she is free to show harm to other victims because it is relevant to a different part of the punitive damages constitutional equation, namely, reprehensibility. That is to say, harm to others shows more reprehensible conduct. Philip Morris, in turn, does not deny that a plaintiff may show harm to others in order to demonstrate reprehensibility. Nor do we. Evidence of actual harm to nonparties can help to show that the conduct that harmed the plaintiff also posed a substantial risk of harm to the general public, and so was particularly reprehensible. A jury may not go further than this and use a punitive damages verdict to punish a defendant directly on account of harms it is alleged to have visited on nonparties.

Decision

The U.S. Supreme Court held that the Oregon court had applied the wrong standard in permitting the jury to award $79.5 million of punitive damages against Philip Morris. The Supreme Court remanded the case so that the Oregon court could apply the correct standard stated by the U.S. Supreme Court in determining an award of punitive damages against Philip Morris.

Law & Ethics Questions

1. What does the constitutional doctrine of due process provide? Explain.

2. **ETHICS** Does Philip Morris act ethically in selling cigarettes that knowingly cause cancer and other diseases and early death to many smokers?

3. What are the purposes of allowing the award of punitive damages? Do you think punitive damages have a deterrent effect?

4. **ETHICS** Do you think that the award of $79.5 million of punitive damages was warranted in this case? How much, if any, would you have awarded?

5. **ETHICS** Does Philip Morris USA act socially responsibly enough by trying to dissuade people from smoking? Should it have this burden at all? Explain.

Web Exercises

1. **WEB** For the complete opinion of this case, go to *www.prenhall.com/cheesemancases*.

2. **WEB** Visit the website of Philip Morris USA, at *www.philipmorrisusa.com*. Does the company still sell the Marlboro brand of cigarettes?

3. **WEB** Visit the website of the U.S. Supreme Court, at *www.supremecourtus.gov*. Can you find any documents related to this case?

4. **WEB** Use *www.google.com* to find an article that discusses the dangers of smoking. Read it.

5. **WEB** Use *www.google.com* to find an advertisement for the Marlboro brand of cigarettes.

Defenses to Product Liability

Defendants in strict liability or negligence actions may raise several defenses to the imposition of liability. These defenses are discussed in the paragraphs that follow.

Generally Known Dangers

Certain products are inherently dangerous and are known to the general population to be so. Sellers are not strictly liable for failing to warn of **generally known dangers**.

Example It is a known fact that guns shoot bullets. Manufacturers of guns do not have to place a warning on the barrel of a gun warning of this generally known danger.

Government Contractor Defense

Many defense and other contractors manufacture products (e.g., rockets, airplanes) to government specification. Most jurisdictions recognize a **government contractor defense** to product liability actions. To establish this defense, a government contractor must prove that (1) the precise specifications for the product were provided by the government, (2) the product conformed to those specifications, and (3) the contractor warned the government of any known defects or dangers of the product.

Example Assume that an airplane manufacturer becomes a government contractor when it is hired to manufacture a fighter airplane to specifications provided by the U.S. Air force. If the airplane proves defective because of its designs, crashes, and causes injury, the manufacturer can escape liability by asserting the government contractor defense if the manufacturer either did not know of the defect or knew of the defect and warned the government of the defect.

Assumption of the Risk

Theoretically, the traditional doctrine of **assumption of the risk** is a defense to a product liability action. For this defense to apply, the defendant must prove that (1) the plaintiff knew and appreciated the risk and (2) the plaintiff voluntarily assumed the risk. In practice, the defense assumption of the risk is narrowly applied by the courts.

Misuse of the Product

Sometimes users are injured when they misuse a product. If a user brings a product liability action, the defendant-seller may be able to assert **misuse of the product** as a defense. Whether the defense is effective depends on whether the misuse was foreseeable. The seller is relieved of product liability if the plaintiff has **abnormally misused** the product—that is, if there has been an **unforeseeable misuse** of the product. However, the seller is liable if there has been a **foreseeable/misuse** of the product. This reasoning is intended to provide an incentive for manufacturers to design and manufacture safer products.

Correction of a Product Defect

A manufacturer that produces a defective product and later discovers said defect must (1) notify purchasers and users of the defect and (2) correct the defect. Most manufacturers faced with this situation recall the defective product and either repair the defect or replace the product.

The seller must make reasonable efforts to notify purchasers and users of the defect and the procedure to correct it. Reasonable efforts normally consist of sending letters to known purchasers and users and placing notices in newspapers and magazines of general circulation. If a user ignores the notice and fails to have the defect corrected, the seller may raise this as a defense against further liability with respect to the defect. Many courts have held that reasonable notice is effective even against users who did not see the notice.

Supervening Event

For a seller to be held strictly liable, the product it sells must reach the consumer or user "without substantial change" in its condition. Under the doctrine of **supervening event,** or **intervening event**, the original seller is not liable if the product is materially altered or modified after it leaves the seller's possession and the alteration or modification causes an injury. A supervening event absolves all prior sellers in the chain of distribution from strict liability.

Example A manufacturer produces a safe piece of equipment. It sells the equipment to a distributor, which removes a safety guard from the equipment. The distributor sells it to a retailer, who sells it to a buyer. The buyer is injured because of the removal of the safety guard. The manufacturer can raise the defense of supervening event against the imposition of liability. However, the distributor and retailer are strictly liable for the buyer's injuries.

ETHICS SPOTLIGHT
General Motors Liable for Design Defect

❝We're just like numbers. Statistics. That's something that is wrong.❞

—Juror

On Christmas Eve, Patricia Anderson was driving her Chevrolet Malibu automobile, which was manufactured by the General Motors Corporation (GM), home from church. Her four young children, ages one through nine, and a neighbor, were also in the car. The Chevy Malibu was stopped at a stoplight at 89th Place and Figueroa Street in Los Angeles when a drunken driver plowed his car into the back of the Malibu at 50 to 70 mph. The Malibu burst into flames as its gas tank ruptured and ignited. Although no one died in the crash, the occupants of the Malibu were severely burned. Many required substantial and multiple skin grafts.

The two injured women and four injured children sued GM for product liability. They alleged that the fuel tank of the Chevy Malibu was defectively designed and placed too close to the rear bumper. GM countered that the tragic accident was the fault of the drunken driver who struck the Malibu. The accident victims produced evidence which showed that GM knew that the car's fuel tank design was unsafe but had not changed the design because of cost. The Chevy Malibu was one of GM's A-Class cars, which also included the Pontiac Grand Am, the Oldsmobile Cutlass, and the Chevrolet Monte Carlo, all of which had similar fuel tank designs. The plaintiffs produced GM memos that said it would cost GM $8.59 per vehicle to produce and install a safer fuel tank design but that it would cost the company only an estimated $2.40 per car to not fix the cars and pay damages to injured victims.

After a 10-week trial, the jurors returned a verdict of $107 million in compensatory damages to the plaintiffs for injuries, disfigurement, and pain and suffering caused to them by the accident. The jury then tacked on $4.9 billion as punitive damages to punish GM. This was the largest amount ever awarded in a personal injury lawsuit. After the trial, one juror stated: "We're just like numbers. Statistics. That's something that is wrong."

GM asked the trial judge to throw out the trial. GM claimed that the jury was prejudiced by repetitive personal attacks on GM as a "soulless company" and its lawyers as "hired guns" who consumed "cappuccinos and designer muffins." GM did not convince the judge that such animosity influenced the jury.

In its posttrial motions, GM argued that the award of damages, specifically the $4.9 billion in punitive damages, was the result of bias and prejudice of the jury and asked the trial court judge to reduce the award of damages. The trial court judge let the compensatory damage award stand but reduced the award of punitive damages to $1 billion (Anderson v. General Motors).

Law & Ethics Questions

1. **ETHICS** Did GM's "cost–benefit" memos have much bearing on the outcome of the lawsuit? Explain.

2. **ETHICS** Do you think GM deserved to be punished with punitive damages? Was the amount of punitive damages awarded appropriate? Explain.

Web Exercises

1. **WEB** Visit the website of General Motors Corporation, at *www.gm.com*.

2. **WEB** Use *www.google.com* to find an article that discusses a case of strict liability where punitive damages were awarded. Read it.

Statute of Limitations and Statute of Repose

Most states have **statutes of limitations** that require an injured person to bring an action within a certain number of years from the time he or she was injured by a defective product. This limitation period varies from state to state. Failure to bring an action within the appropriate time relieves the defendant of liability.

In most jurisdictions, the statute of limitations does not begin to run until the plaintiff suffers an injury. This subjects sellers and lessors to exposure for an unspecified period of time because a defective product may not cause an injury for years, or even decades, after it was sold.

Some states have enacted **statutes of repose**. Statues of repose limit the seller's liability to a certain number of years from the date when the product was first sold. The period of repose varies from state to state.

CONCEPT SUMMARY

Statute of Limitation and Statute of Repose

STATUTE	BEGINS TO RUN
Statute of limitations	When the plaintiff suffers injury
Statute of repose	When the product is first sold

Contributory Negligence and Comparative Fault

Sometimes a person who is injured by a defective product is negligent and contributes to his or her own injuries. The defense of **contributory negligence** bars an injured plaintiff from recovering from the defendant in a negligence action. However, this doctrine generally does not bar recovery in strict liability actions.

Many states have held that the doctrine of **comparative fault** applies to strict liability actions. Under this doctrine, a plaintiff who is contributorily negligent for his or her injuries is responsible for a *proportional share* of the damages. In other words, the damages are apportioned between the plaintiff and the defendant.

Example Suppose an automobile manufacturer produces a car with a hidden defect and a consumer purchases the car from an automobile dealer. Assume that the consumer is injured in an automobile accident in which the defect is found to be 75 percent responsible for the accident and the consumer's own reckless driving is found to be 25 percent responsible. The plaintiff suffers $1 million worth of injuries. Under the doctrine of *contributory negligence*, the plaintiff would recover nothing from the defendants. Under the doctrine of *comparative negligence*, the plaintiff would recover $750,000 from the defendants.

CONCEPT SUMMARY

Contributory Negligence and Comparative Fault

DOCTRINE	DESCRIPTION
Contributory negligence	A person who is partially responsible for causing his or her own injuries may not recover anything from the manufacturer or seller of a defective product that caused the remainder of the person's injuries.
Comparative fault	A person who is partially responsible for causing his or her own injuries is responsible for a proportional share of the damages. The manufacturer or seller of the defective product is responsible for the remainder of the plaintiff's damages.

Chapter Summary

Express Warranties, p. 469

An express warranty is an affirmation by a seller or lessor that the goods he or she is selling or leasing meet certain standards of quality, description, performance, or condition.

Basis of the Bargain

Buyers and lessees can recover for breach of an express warranty if the warranty was a contributing factor—not necessarily the sole factor—that induced the buyer to purchase the product or the lessee to lease the product.

Statements of Opinion

Many express warranties arise during the course of negotiations between a buyer and a seller (or lessor and lessee). The seller's or lessor's *statements of opinion* (i.e., *puffing*) or commendation of the goods does not create an express warranty [UCC 2-313(2)].

Damages Recoverable for Breach of Warranty

Where there has been a breach of warranty, the buyer or lessee may sue the seller or lessor to recover *compensatory damages*. The amount of recoverable compensatory damages is generally equal to the difference between (1) the value of the goods as warranted and (2) the actual value of the goods accepted at the time and place of acceptance [UCC 2-714(2), 2A-508(4)]. A purchaser or lessee can recover for personal injuries that are caused by a breach of warranty.

Implied Warranties, p. 472

Implied Warranty of Merchantability

The implied warranty of merchantability is implied by law in sales and lease transactions. It requires that goods:

1. Be fit for the ordinary purposes for which they are used.
2. Be adequately contained, packaged, and labeled.
3. Be of an even kind, quality, and quantity within each unit.
4. Conform to any promise or affirmation of fact made on the container or label.
5. Pass without objection in the trade.
6. Meet a fair or middle range of quality if the goods are fungible.

Implied Warranty of Fitness for Human Consumption

The implied warranty of fitness for human consumption is a warranty implied by law that food products are fit for human consumption. States apply one of the following two tests:

1. *Foreign substance test.* A food is unmerchantable if a foreign object in the food caused the plaintiff's injury.
2. *Consumer expectation test.* A food is unmerchantable if an object in the food that a consumer would not expect to be there caused the plaintiff's injury. The UCC incorporates this warranty within the implied warranty of merchantability.

Implied Warranty of Fitness for a Particular Purpose

The implied warranty of fitness for a particular purpose is a warranty by a seller or lessor that goods will meet the buyer's or lessee's expressed needs.

Warranty Disclaimers, p. 476

1. *Express warranties.* Express warranties can be limited if the warranty and disclaimer can be reasonably construed with each other.
2. *Implied warranties.* An implied warranty can be disclaimed by expressions like *as is*, *with all faults*, or such language. If the preceding language is not used, disclaimers of the *implied warranty of merchantability* must specifically mention the term *merchantability*. These disclaimers may be oral or written. The *implied warranty of fitness for a particular purpose* may be disclaimed in general language, without specific use of the term *fitness*.

Conspicuous Display of Disclaimer

Written disclaimers must be conspicuously displayed to be enforceable.

Magnuson-Moss Warranty Act

The Magnuson-Moss Warranty Act is a federal statute that covers written warranties that apply to consumer products.

1. *Full and limited warranties.* If the warrantor makes an express warranty, the warranty must be labeled *full* or *limited*:
    a. *Full warranty.* A full warranty guarantees free repair or replacement of a defective product. A time limit may be placed on the warranty.

    b. *Limited warranty.* A limited warranty limits the scope of a full warranty in some way (e.g., return of the purchase price).

    2. *Limitation on disclaiming implied warranties.* If a seller or lessor makes an express warranty, he or she cannot disclaim or modify the implied warranties of merchantability and fitness for a particular purpose. A time limit may be placed on implied warranties but must correspond to the duration of the express warranty.

Product Liability, p. 478

Negligence

A seller or lessor breaches his or her duty of due care by producing a defective product that causes injury to the plaintiff. Privity of contract between the seller or lessor and the plaintiff is not required.

Misrepresentation

In some cases, a seller or lessor may fraudulently misrepresent the quality of a product, and the plaintiff may rely on the misrepresentation and be injured thereby.

Strict Liability, p. 480

Liability Without Fault

A manufacturer or seller who sells a defective product is liable to the ultimate user who is injured thereby.

Liability of All in the Chain of Distribution

All in the chain of distribution are liable, irrespective of fault. This is sometimes called *vertical liability*.

Parties Who Can Recover for Strict Liability

Because strict liability is a tort doctrine, privity of contract between the plaintiff and the defendant is not required. In other words, the doctrine applies even if the injured party had no contractual relations with the defendant.

Damages Recoverable for Strict Liability

The damages recoverable in a strict liability action vary by jurisdiction. Damages for personal injuries are recoverable in all jurisdictions that have adopted the doctrine of strict liability, although some jurisdictions limit the dollar amount of the award. Property damage is recoverable in most jurisdictions, but economic loss (e.g., lost income) is recoverable in only a few jurisdictions

Defective Products, p. 482

Defect in Manufacture

A defect in manufacture occurs when the manufacturer fails to properly assemble a product, test, or adequately check the quality of a product.

Defect in Design

A defect in design can support a strict liability action. Design defects are considered products designed without proper safeguards.

Crashworthiness Doctrine

The Crashworthiness Doctrine states that the failure of an automobile manufacturer to design an automobile to protect occupants from foreseeable dangers caused by a second collision subjects both the manufacturer and dealer to strict liability.

Failure to Warn

The failure to warn consumers of the dangerous propensities of a product is a defect that will support a strict liability action.

Defect in Packaging

A defect in packaging subjects the manufacturer and others in the chain of distribution of the product to strict liability.

Failure to Provide Adequate Instructions

Sellers are responsible to provide adequate instructions for the safe assembly and use of the products they sell.

Punitive Damages

Punitive damages are awarded if the court finds that the defendant's conduct was committed with intent or reckless disregard for human life. These damages are meant to punish and to send a message to the defendant (and other companies) that such behavior will not be tolerated.

Defenses to Product Liability, p. 493

A manufacturer or seller is not liable for damages caused by a product it manufactures or sells if one of several defenses applies.

Generally Known Dangers

A manufacturer or seller is not liable for failing to warn about inherent dangers in products that are known to the general population.

Government Contractor Defense

A manufacturer is not liable if it produces a product to government specifications and warns the government of any known defects in the specific design.

Assumption of the Risk

A manufacturer or seller is not liable if the plaintiff knew and appreciated the risk and voluntarily assumed the risk.

Misuse of the Product

1. *Abnormal misuse.* The manufacturer or seller is not liable for injuries caused by the abnormal misuse of the product by the plaintiff. Also called *unforeseeable misuse*.
2. *Foreseeable misuse.* The manufacturer or seller is liable for injuries caused by the foreseeable misuse of a product. The manufacturer must design products to be safe for foreseeable misuses.

Correction of a Product Defect

A manufacturer or seller is not liable if it learns about a defect in a product it has sold and notifies purchasers and users of the defect and corrects the defect.

Supervening Event

A manufacturer or seller is not liable if the product was materially altered or modified after it left the seller's possession and the alteration or modification caused an injury. Also called *intervening event*.

Statute of Limitations and Statute of Repose

1. *Statute of limitations.* An injured person must bring a product liability lawsuit within a specified period of time after being injured by a defective product.
2. *Statute of repose.* A person must bring a product liability lawsuit within a specified period of time after a defective product was first purchased or leased.

Contributory Negligence and Comparative Fault

1. *Contributory negligence.* Under this doctrine, a person who is partially responsible for causing his or her own injuries may not recover anything from the manufacturer or seller of a defective product that caused the remainder of the person's injuries.
2. *Comparative negligence.* Under this doctrine, a person who is partially responsible for causing his or her own injuries is responsible for a proportional share of the damages. The manufacturer or seller of the defective product is responsible for the remainder of the plaintiff's damages. Also called *comparative fault*.

Test Review Terms and Concepts

Abnormal misuse (unforeseeable misuse)   494
Assumption of the risk   494
Basis of the bargain   470
Chain of distribution   480
Comparative fault   496
Compensatory damages   471
Conspicuous   476
Consumer expectation test   474
Contributory negligence   496
Crashworthiness doctrine   486
Defect in design   483
Defect in manufacture   482
Defect in packaging   490
Disclaim   476
Doctrine of strict liability in tort   480
Express warranty   469
Failure to provide adequate instructions   491

Failure to warn   487
Foreign substance test   473
Foreseeable misuse   494
Full warranty   477
Generally known dangers   493
Government contractor defense   493
Greenman v. Yuba Power Products, Inc.   480
Implied warranty of fitness for human consumption   473
Implied warranty of fitness for a particular purpose   474
Implied warranty of merchantability   472
Intentional misrepresentation (fraud)   479
Liability without fault   480
Limited warranty   477
MacPherson v. Buick Motor Co.   479

Magnuson-Moss Warranty Act   477
Misrepresentation   479
Misuse of the product   494
Negligence   479
Product defect   482
Product liability   469
Punitive damages   492
Restatement (Second) of Torts   481
Restatement (Third) of Torts: Product Liability   481
Statements of opinion (puffing)   470
Statute of limitations   495
Statute of repose   495
Strict liability   480
Supervening event (intervening event)   494
Warranty   469
Warranty disclaimer   476

Case Problems

19.1 Warranty of Title: When James Redmond wanted to purchase an automobile, he spoke to a salesman at Bill Branch Chevrolet, Inc. (Bill Branch). The salesman offered to sell Redmond a blue Chevrolet Caprice for $6,200. The car was to be delivered to Redmond's residence. Redmond gave the salesman $1,000 cash and received a receipt in return. The next day, the salesman delivered the car to Redmond, and Redmond paid the remaining amount due. The salesman gave Redmond a printed sales contract that reflected the payments made, with no balance due. One month later, Redmond called Bill Branch and asked for the title papers to the car. Redmond was told that the car had been reported stolen prior to the sale and that he could not receive title until he contacted Bill Branch's insurance company. Redmond sued Bill Branch Chevrolet, Inc. Is Bill Branch liable? *Bill Branch Chevrolet v. Redmond,* 378 So.2d 319, **Web** 1980 Fla. App. Lexis 15413 (Court of Appeal of Florida)

19.2 Express Warranty: Gloria Crandell purchased a used Coronado clothes dryer from Larkin and Jones Appliance Company (Larkin and Jones). The dryer, which was displayed on the sales floor, had a tag affixed to it that described the machine as a "quality reconditioned unit" that was "tag tested" and "guaranteed." In addition to these written statements, a salesman assured Crandell that the dryer carried a 90-day guarantee for "workmanship, parts, and labor." Crandell bought the dryer because of the guarantee and the low price. Two weeks after the machine was delivered, Crandell asked her son to put a blanket in the dryer to dry. Twenty minutes later, she noticed smoke pouring into her bedroom. By the time Crandell reached the laundry room, the machine was engulfed in flames. A defect in the clothes dryer had caused the fire. Crandell sued Larkin and Jones for breach of an express warranty. Is there an express warranty? *Crandell v. Larkin and Jones Appliance Company,* 334 N.W.2d 31, **Web** 1983 S.D. Lexis 326 (Supreme Court of South Dakota)

19.3 Statement of Fact or Opinion: Jack Crothers went to Norm's Auto Sales (Norm's) to buy a used car. Maurice Boyd, a salesman at Norm's, showed Crothers a Dodge automobile. While running the car's engine, Boyd told Crothers that the Dodge "had a rebuilt carburetor" and "was a good runner." After listening to the sales pitch, Crothers bought the car. As Crothers was driving the Dodge the next day, the car suddenly went out of control and crashed into a tree. Crothers was seriously injured. The cause of the crash was an obvious defect in the Dodge's accelerator linkage. Crothers sued Norm's. Who wins? *Crothers v. Norm's Auto Sales,* 384 N.W.2d 562, **Web** 1986 Minn. App. Lexis 4202 (Court of Appeals of Minnesota)

19.4 Implied Warranty of Merchantability: Geraldine Maybank took a trip to New York City to visit her son and her two-year-old grandson. She borrowed her daughter's camera for the trip. Two days before leaving for New York, Maybank purchased a package of G. T. E. Sylvania Blue Dot flashcubes at a Kmart store, owned by the S. S. Kresge Company. On the carton of the package were words to the effect that each bulb was safety coated. Upon arriving in New York, Maybank decided to take a picture of her grandson. She opened the carton of flashcubes and put one on the camera. When Maybank pushed down the lever to take a picture, the flashcube exploded. The explosion knocked her glasses off and caused cuts to her left eye. Maybank was hospitalized for eight days. Maybank sued S. S. Kresge Company. Who wins? *Maybank v. S. S. Kresge Company*, 46 N.C.App. 687, 266 S.E.2d 409, **Web** 1980 N.C. App. Lexis 2927 (Court of Appeals of North Carolina)

19.5 Implied Warranty of Fitness for Human Consumption: Tina Keperwas went to a Publix Supermarket (Publix) in Florida and bought a can of Doxsee brand clam chowder. Keperwas opened the can of soup and prepared it at home. While eating the chowder, she bit down on a clamshell and injured one of her molars. Keperwas filed suit against Publix and Doxsee for breach of an implied warranty. In the lawsuit, Keperwas alleged that the clam chowder "was not fit for use as food, but was defective, unwholesome, and unfit for human consumption" and "was in such condition as to be dangerous to life and health." At the trial, Doxsee's general manager testified as to the state-of-the-art methods Doxsee uses in preparing its chowder. Are Publix and Doxsee liable for the injury to Keperwas's tooth? *Keperwas v. Publix Supermarkets. Inc.*, 534 So.2d 872, **Web** 1988 Fla. App. Lexis 5306 (Court of Appeal of Florida)

19.6 Disclaimer of Warranty: Automatic Sprinkler Corporation of America (Automatic Sprinkler) wished to purchase a dry chemical fire protection system from Ansul Company (Ansul). An Ansul representative gave Automatic Sprinkler a proposal on the company's behalf. The proposal was a document five pages long. Each page included printed information describing the fire extinguisher system. Only the fifth and last page had printing on the back. The information on the back of page 5 contained a limited five-year warranty that covered only the replacement of defective parts. The limited warranty concluded with this statement: "This warranty is in lieu of all other warranties express or implied."

Automatic Sprinkler purchased the system and installed it in a client's building. Several years later, a fire broke out in the building, and the Ansul fire extinguisher system failed to discharge. Automatic Sprinkler sued Ansul for a breach of an implied warranty of merchantability. Ansul claimed that all warranties except the limited five-year warranty were disclaimed. Is Ansul's disclaimer enforceable? *Insurance Company of North America v. Automatic Sprinkler*, 67 Ohio St.2d 91, 423 N.E.2d 151, **Web** 1981 Ohio Lexis 554 (Supreme Court of Ohio)

19.7 Disclaimer of Warranty: Cole Energy Development Company (Cole Energy) wanted to lease a gas compressor for use in its business of pumping and selling natural gas and began negotiating with the Ingersoll-Rand Company (Ingersoll-Rand). On December 5, 1983, the two parties entered into a lease agreement for a KOA gas compressor. The lease agreement contained a section labeled "WARRANTIES." Part of the section read:

There are no Implied Warranties of Merchantability or Fitness for a Particular Purpose Contained Herein.

The gas compressor that was installed failed to function properly. As a result, Cole Energy lost business. Cole Energy sued Ingersoll-Rand for the breach of an implied warranty of merchantability. Is Ingersoll-Rand liable? *Cole Energy Development Company v. Ingersoll-Rand Company*, 678 F.Supp. 208, **Web** 1988 U.S. Dist. Lexis 923 (United States District Court for the Central District of Illinois)

19.8 Disclaimer of Warranty: Edward Cate owned and operated an automotive repair shop. Cate wanted to purchase a set of automotive lifts (i.e., the devices used to elevate vehicles for repair work). Cate purchased a set of Rotary Brand lifts, manufactured by Dover Corporation (Dover). The contract for the lifts contained a five-year written warranty covering the repair of all defective parts returned to the factory. The warranty section of the contract, printed in black ink, also contained a separate paragraph stating:

This warranty is exclusive and in lieu of all other warranties express or implied including any implied warranty of merchantability or implied warranty of fitness for a particular purpose.

The entire warranty section was framed by double blue lines, and the word "Warranty" was printed in solid blue letters. After the lifts were installed in Cate's shop, they began to malfunction. Cars would suddenly fall off the lifts. Dover's employees made several unsuccessful repair attempts. Rather than sending the lifts back to the factory, Cate sued Dover for breach of implied warranty of merchantability. Who wins? *Cate v. Dover Corporation*, 776 S.W.2d 680, **Web** 1989 Tex. App. Lexis 2086 (Court of Appeals of Texas)

19.9 Strict Liability: Jeppesen and Company produces charts that graphically display approach procedures for airplanes landing at airports. These charts are drafted from tabular data supplied by the Federal Aviation Administration (FAA), a federal agency of the U.S. government. By law, Jeppesen cannot construct charts that include information different from that supplied by the FAA. One day, the pilot of an airplane owned by World Airways was on descent to land at the Cold Bay, Alaska, airport. The pilot was using an instrument approach procedure chart published by Jeppesen. The airplane crashed into a mountain near Cold Bay, killing all six crew members and destroying the aircraft. Evidence showed that the FAA data did not include the mountain. The heirs of the deceased crew members and World Airways brought a strict liability action against Jeppesen. Does the doctrine of strict liability apply to this case? Is Jeppesen liable? *Brocklesby v. Jeppesen and Company*, 767 F.2d 1288, **Web** 1985 U.S. App. Lexis 21290 (United States Court of Appeals for the Ninth Circuit)

19.10 Failure to Warn: The Emerson Electric Co. manufactures and sells a product called the Weed Eater XR-90. The Weed Eater is a multipurpose weed-trimming and brush-cutting device. It consists of a handheld gasoline-powered engine connected to a long drive shaft, at the end of which can be attached various tools for cutting weeds and brush. One such attachment is a 10-inch circular sawblade capable of cutting through growth up to 2 inches in diameter. When this sawblade is attached to the Weed Eater, approximately 270 degrees of blade edge are exposed when in use. The owner's manual contained the following warning: "Keep children away. All people and pets should be kept at a safe distance from the work area, at least 30 feet, especially when using the blade." Donald Pearce, a 13-year-old boy, was helping his uncle clear an overgrown yard. The uncle was operating a Weed Eater XR-90 with the circular sawblade attachment. When Pearce stooped to pick up something off the ground about 6 to 10 feet behind and slightly to the left of where his uncle was operating the Weed Eater, the sawblade on the Weed Eater struck something near the ground. The Weed Eater kicked back to the left and cut off Pearce's right arm to the elbow. Pearce, through his mother, Charlotte Karns, sued Emerson to recover damages under strict liability. Is Emerson liable? *Karns v. Emerson Electric Co.*, 817 F.2d 1452, **Web** 1987 U.S. App. Lexis 5608 (United States Court of Appeals for the Tenth Circuit)

19.11 Crashworthiness Doctrine: One night Verne Prior, while driving on U.S. 101 under the influence of alcohol and drugs at a speed of 65 to 85 miles per hour, crashed his automobile into the left rear of a Chevrolet station wagon stopped on the shoulder of the freeway because of a flat tire. Christine Smith was sitting in the passenger seat of the parked car when the accident occurred. In the crash, the Chevrolet station wagon was knocked into a gully, where its fuel tank ruptured. The vehicle caught fire, and Smith suffered severe burn injuries. The Chevrolet station wagon was manufactured by General Motors Corporation. Evidence showed that the fuel tank was located in a vulnerable position in the back of the station wagon, outside the crossbars of the frame. Evidence further showed that if the fuel tank had been located underneath the body of the station wagon, between the crossbars of the frame, it would have been well protected in the collision. Smith sued General Motors for strict liability. Was the Chevrolet station wagon a defective product? *Smith v. General Motors Corporation*, 42 Cal.App.3d 1, 116 Cal.Rptr. 575, **Web** 1974 Cal. App. Lexis 1199 (Court of Appeal of California)

19.12 Failure to Warn: Virginia Burke purchased a bottle of "Le Domaine" champagne that was manufactured by Almaden Vineyards, Inc. At home, she removed the wine seal from the top of the bottle but did not remove the plastic cork. She set the bottle on the counter, intending to serve it in a few minutes. Shortly thereafter, the plastic cork spontaneously ejected from the bottle, ricocheted off the wall, and struck Burke in the left lens of her eyeglasses, shattering the lens and driving pieces of glass into her eye. The champagne bottle did not contain any warning of this danger. Evidence showed that Almaden had previously been notified of the spontaneous ejection of the cork from its champagne bottles. Burke sued Almaden to recover damages for strict liability. Is Almaden liable? *Burke v. Almaden Vineyards, Inc.*, 86 Cal.App.3d 768, 150 Cal.Rptr. 419, **Web** 1978 Cal. App. Lexis 2123 (Court of Appeal of California)

19.13 Assumption of Risk: Lillian Horn was driving her Chevrolet station wagon, which was designed and manufactured by General Motors Corporation, down Laurel Canyon Boulevard in Los Angeles, California. Horn swerved to avoid a collision when a car coming toward her crossed the centerline and was coming at her. In doing so, her hand knocked the horn cap off the steering wheel, which exposed the area underneath the horn cap, including three sharp prongs that had held the horn cap to the steering wheel. A few seconds later, when her car hit an embankment, Horn's face was impaled on the three sharp exposed prongs, causing her severe facial injuries. Horn sued General Motors for strict liability. General Motors asserted the defense of assumption of the risk against Horn. Who wins? *Horn v. General Motors Corporation*, 17 Cal.3d 359, 551 P.2d 398, 131 Cal.Rptr. 78, **Web** 1976 Cal. Lexis 283 (Supreme Court of California)

19.14 Misuse: The Wilcox-Crittendon Company manufactured harnesses, saddles, bridles, leads, and other items commonly used for horses, cattle, and other ranch and farm animals. One such item was a stallion or cattle tie, a five-inch-long iron hook with a one-inch ring at one end. The tongue on the ring opened outward to allow the hook to be attached to a rope or another object. In 1964, a purchasing agent for United Airlines, who was familiar with this type of hook because of earlier experiences on a farm, purchased one of these hooks from Keystone Brothers, a harness and saddlery wares outlet located in San Francisco, California. Four years later, on March 28, 1968, Edward Dosier, an employee of United Airlines, was working to install a new grinding machine at a United Airlines maintenance plant. As part of the installation process, Dosier attached the hook to a 1,700-pound counterweight and raised the counterweight into the air. While the counterweight was suspended in the air, Dosier reached under the counterweight to retrieve a missing bolt. The hook broke, and the counterweight fell and crushed Dosier's arm. Dosier sued Wilcox-Crittendon for strict liability. Who wins? *Dosier v. Wilcox-Crittendon Company*, 45 Cal.App.3d 74, 119 Cal.Rptr. 135, **Web** 1975 Cal. App. Lexis 1665 (Court of Appeal of California).

Ethics Issues

19.15 Ethics: Brian Keith, an actor, attended a boat show in Long Beach, California. At the boat show, Keith obtained sales literature on a sailboat called the "Island Trader 41" from a sales representative of James Buchanan, a seller of sailboats. One sales brochure described the vessel as "a picture of sure-footed seaworthiness." Another brochure called the sailboat "a carefully well-equipped and very seaworthy live-aboard vessel." One month later, Keith purchased an Island Trader 41 sailboat from Buchanan for a total purchase price of $75,610. After delivery of the sailboat, a dispute arose in regard to the seaworthiness of the vessel. Keith sued Buchanan for breach of warranty. Buchanan defended, arguing that no warranty had been made. Is it ethical for Buchanan to try to avoid being held accountable for statements of quality about the product that were made in the sales brochures given Keith? Should sales "puffing" be considered to create an express warranty? Why or why not? Who wins this case? *Keith v. Buchanan*, 173 Cal.App.3d 13, 220 Cal.Rptr. 392, **Web** 1985 Cal. App. Lexis 2603 (Court of Appeal of California)

19.16 Ethics: Peter Troy, president and owner of Troy's Custom Smoking Co., Inc. (Troy's), contacted Peter Bader, president of Swan Island Sheet Metal Works, Inc. (Swan Island), and asked Bader if Swan Island could manufacture two stainless steel gas-burner crab cookers for Troy's. Troy explained to Bader the planned use of the cooker and some of the special needs a crab cooker must satisfy—that is, a crab is cooked by dropping it into boiling water, allowing the water to recover to a rolling boil, and boiling the crab for 10 minutes. If the recovery time exceeds 10 minutes, or if the cooker cannot sustain a rolling boil, the crab is immersed too long in hot water, and the finished product is unpalatable. Troy and Bader were equally unknowledgeable about gas-burner cookers, but Bader assured Troy that he would hire an expert to assist in manufacturing a crab cooker to meet Troy's needs.

Bader sent Troy a brochure illustrating the type of burner the expert had selected to meet Troy's needs. Troy ordered the cooker, which was delivered to Troy's Beaverton, Oregon, store. Within a week or two after delivery, Troy complained to Swan Island concerning the cooker's performance. The cooker cooked too slowly, and the pilot light and burner were difficult to light and keep lit. Swan Island attempted but could not correct the defects. For four months,

Troy's cooked crab in the Swan Island cooker. Because of the poor performance of the cooker, Troy's ruined a substantial amount of crab and had to obtain cooked crab from another outlet to serve its customers. Troy's notified Swan Island to pick up the crab cooker. Swan Island sued Troy's to recover the purchase price of the cooker. Troy's filed a counterclaim against Swan Island to rescind the contract and recover damages. Did Swan Island breach an implied warranty of fitness for a particular purpose? Did Swan Island act ethically in denying liability in this case? *Swan Island Sheet Metal Works, Inc. v. Troy's Custom Smoking Co., Inc.*, 49 Ore. App. 469, 619 P.2d 1326, **Web** 1980 Ore. App. Lexis 3731 (Court of Appeals of Oregon)

19.17 Ethics: Celestino Luque lived with his cousins Harry and Laura Dunn in Millbrae, California. The Dunns purchased a rotary lawn mower from Rhoads Hardware. The lawn mower was manufactured by Air Capital Manufacturing Company and was distributed by Garehime Corporation. Neighbors asked Luque to mow their lawn. While Luque was cutting the lawn, he noticed a small carton in the path of the lawn mower. Luque left the lawn mower in a stationary position with its motor running and walked around the side of the lawn mower to remove the carton. As he did so, he slipped on the wet grass and fell backward. Luque's left hand entered the unguarded hole of the lawn mower and was caught in its revolving blade, which turns at 175 miles per hour and 100 revolutions per second. Luque's hand was severely mangled and lacerated. The word *Caution* was printed above the unguarded hole on the lawn mower. Luque sued Rhoads Hardware, Air Capital, and Garehime Corporation for strict liability. The defendants argued that strict liability does not apply to *patent* (obvious) defects. Was it ethical for the defendants to argue that they were not liable for patent defects? Would patent defects ever be corrected if the defendants' contention was accepted by the court? Who wins? *Luque v. McLean, Trustee*, 8 Cal.3d 136, 501 P.2d 1163, 104 Cal.Rptr. 443, **Web** 1972 Cal. Lexis 245 (Supreme Court of California)

IRAC Writing Assignment

Read **Case A-19** in Appendix A [*Johnson v. Chicago Pneumatic Tool Company*]. Use the IRAC method to prepare a written analysis of the case.

Endnotes

1. 15 U.S.C. Sections 2301–2312.
2. *Restatement (Second) of Torts*, Section 395.
3. 217 N.Y.382, 111 N.E. 1050, **Web** 1916 N.Y. Lexis 1324 (Court of Appeals of New York).
4. 59 Cal.2d 57, 377 P.2d 897, 27 Cal.Rptr. 697, **Web** 1963 Cal. Lexis 140 (Supreme Court of California).

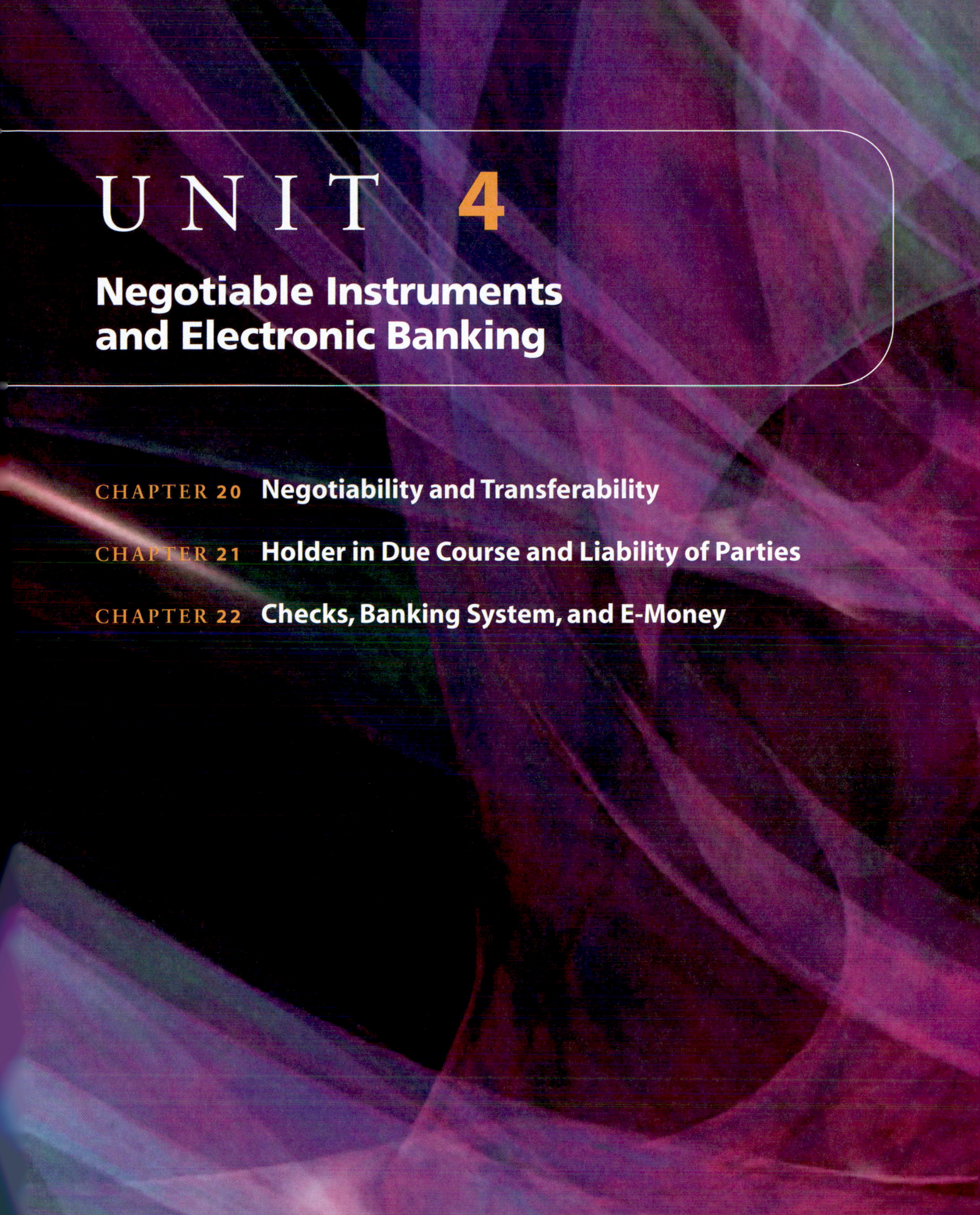

UNIT 4

Negotiable Instruments and Electronic Banking

CHAPTER 20

Negotiability and Transferability

"The great object of the law is to encourage commerce."

—JUDGE CHAMBRE
Beale v. Thompson (1803)

CHAPTER OBJECTIVES

After studying this chapter, you should be able to:

1. Distinguish between negotiable and nonnegotiable instruments.
2. Describe drafts and checks and identify the parties to these instruments.
3. Describe promissory notes and certificates of deposit and identify the parties to these instruments.
4. Describe how negotiable instruments are indorsed and transferred.
5. Distinguish between blank, special, qualified, and restrictive indorsements.

CHAPTER CONTENTS

- Introduction to Negotiability and Transferability
- Negotiable Instruments
- Types of Negotiable Instruments
- Creating a Negotiable Instrument
- Unconditional Promise or Order to Pay
- Nonnegotiable Contracts and Assignment
- Transfer by Negotiation
- Indorsement
- Chapter Summary
- Test Review Terms and Concepts
- Case Problems
- Ethics Issues
- IRAC Writing Assignment

Introduction to Negotiability and Transferability

Negotiable instruments (or **commercial paper**) are important for the conduct of business and personal affairs. In this country, modern commerce could not continue without them. Examples of negotiable instruments include checks (such as the one that may have been used to pay for this book) and promissory notes (such as the one executed by a borrower of money to pay for tuition). The term **instrument** means negotiable instrument [UCC 3-104(b)]. These terms are often used interchangeably. The types and creation of negotiable instruments are discussed in this chapter.

Once created, a negotiable instrument can be transferred to subsequent parties by *negotiation*. This is accomplished by placing an *indorsement* on the instrument. There are several types of indorsements, each with its own requirements and effect. This chapter discusses the negotiation of an instrument and types of indorsements.

China

Negotiable instruments support both domestic and international commerce.

Negotiable Instruments

To qualify as a negotiable instrument, a document must meet certain requirements established by Article 3 of the Uniform Commercial Code (UCC). If these requirements are met, a transferee who qualifies as a *holder in due course* (HDC) takes the instrument free of many defenses that can be asserted against the original payee. In addition, the document is considered an ordinary contract that is subject to contract law.

The concept of *negotiation* is important to the law of negotiable instruments. The primary benefit of a negotiable instrument is that it can be used as a substitute for money. As such, it must be freely transferable to subsequent parties. Technically, a negotiable instrument is negotiated when it is originally issued. The term *negotiation*, however, is usually used to describe the transfer of negotiable instruments to subsequent transferees.

Functions of Negotiable Instruments

Negotiable instruments serve the following functions:

1. **Substitute for money.** Merchants and consumers often do not carry cash for fear of loss or theft. Further, it would be almost impossible to carry enough cash for large purchases (e.g., a car, a house). Thus certain forms of negotiable instruments—for example, checks—serve as *substitutes for money*.
2. **Act as credit devices.** Some forms of negotiable instruments extend credit from one party to another.

Example A seller may sell goods to a customer on a customer's promise to pay for the goods at a future time, or a bank may lend money to a buyer who signs a note promising to repay the money. Both of these examples represent *extensions of credit*. Without negotiable instruments, the "credit economy" of the United States and other modern industrial countries would not be possible.

3. *Act as record-keeping devices.* Negotiable instruments often serve as *record-keeping devices.*

Example Banks may return canceled checks to checking-account customers each month. These act as a record-keeping device for the preparation of financial statements, tax returns, and the like.

LANDMARK LAW
Revised Article 3 (Negotiable Instruments) of the UCC

Although negotiable instruments have been used in commerce since medieval times, the English law courts did not immediately recognize their validity. To compensate for this failure, the merchants developed rules governing their use. These rules, which were enforced by local private merchant courts, became part of what was called the **Law Merchant**. Eventually, in 1882, England enacted the Bills of Exchange Act, which codified the rules of the Law Merchant.

In 1886, the National Conference of Commissioners of Uniform State Laws promulgated the **Uniform Negotiable Instruments Law (NIL)** in the United States. By 1920, all of the states had enacted the NIL as law, but the rapid development of commercial paper soon made the law obsolete.

Article 3 (Commercial Paper) of the UCC, which was promulgated in 1952, established rules for the creation of, transfer of, enforcement of, and liability on negotiable instruments. All the states and the District of Columbia have replaced the NIL with Article 3 of the UCC.

In 1990, the American Law Institute and the National Conference of Commissioners on Uniform State Laws repealed Article 3 and replaced it with **Revised Article 3 of the UCC**. The new article, which is called "Negotiable Instruments" instead of "Commercial Paper," is a comprehensive revision of Article 3. Revised Article 3 is used as the basis for this and the following chapters on negotiable instruments.

Types of Negotiable Instruments

Revised Article 3 recognizes four kinds of instruments: (1) drafts, (2) checks, (3) promissory notes, and (4) certificates of deposit. Each of these is discussed in the following paragraphs.

Drafts

A **draft**, which is a three-party instrument, is an unconditional written order by one party (the **drawer**) that orders a second party (the **drawee**) to pay money to a third party (the **payee**) [UCC 3-104(e)]. The drawee must be obligated to pay the drawer money before the drawer can order the drawee to pay this money to a third party (the payee).

For the drawee to be liable on a draft, the drawee must accept the drawer's written order to pay it. Acceptance is usually shown by the written word *accepted* on the face of the draft, along with the drawee's signature and the date. The drawee is called the **acceptor** of the draft because his or her obligation changes from that of having to pay the drawer to that of having to pay the payee. After the drawee accepts the draft, it is returned to the drawer or the payee. The drawer or the payee, in turn, can freely transfer it as a negotiable instrument to another party.

Example Mary Owens owes Hector Martinez $1,000. Martinez writes out a draft that orders Owens to pay this $1,000 to Cindy Choy. Owens agrees to this change of obligation and accepts the draft. Martinez is the drawer, Owens is the drawee, and Choy is the payee.

A draft can be either a time draft or a sight draft. A **time draft** is payable at a designated future date. Language such as "pay on January 1, 2008" or "pay 120 days after date" creates a time draft (see Exhibit 20.1).

A **sight draft** is payable on sight. A sight draft is also called a **demand draft**. Language such as "on demand pay" or "at sight pay" creates a sight draft.

EXHIBIT 20.1

Time Draft

Payee

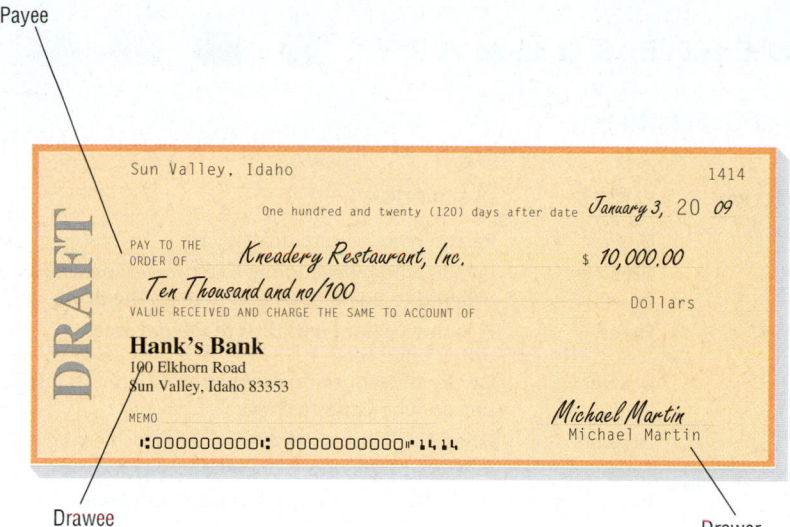

Drawee

Drawer

A draft can be both a time and a sight draft. Such a draft would provide that it is payable at a stated time after sight. This type of draft is created by language such as "payable 90 days after sight."

A **trade acceptance** is a sight draft that arises when credit is extended with the sale of goods. In this type of draft, the seller is both the drawer and the payee. The buyer to whom credit is extended is the drawee. Even though only two actual parties are involved, it is considered a three-party instrument because three legal positions are involved.

Checks

A **check** is a distinct form of draft. It is unique in that it is drawn on a financial institution (the drawee) and is payable on demand [UCC 3-104(f)]. In other words, a check is an order to pay (see Exhibit 20.2). Most businesses and many individuals have checking accounts at financial institutions.

Like other drafts, a check is a three-party instrument. A customer who has a checking account and writes (draws) a check is the **drawer**. The financial institution upon which the check is written is the **drawee**. And the party to whom the check is written is the **payee**.

In addition to traditional checks, there are several forms of special checks, including certified checks, cashier's checks, and traveler's checks. These special checks are discussed later in the book.

EXHIBIT 20.2

Check

Payee

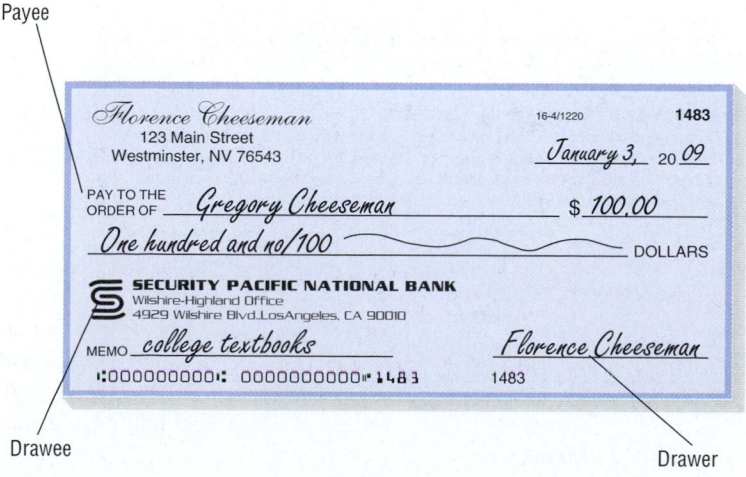

Drawee

Drawer

CONCEPT SUMMARY

Types of Orders to Pay

ORDER TO PAY	PARTIES	DESCRIPTION
Draft	Drawer	Person who issues a draft.
	Drawee	Person who owes money to a drawer; person who is ordered to pay a draft and accepts the draft.
	Payee	Person to whom a draft is made payable.
Check	Drawer	Owner of a checking account at a financial institution; person who issues a check.
	Drawee	Financial institution where drawer's checking account is located; party who is ordered to pay a check.
	Payee	Person to whom a check is made payable.

Promissory Notes

A **promissory note** (or **note**) is an unconditional written promise by one party to pay money to another party [UCC 3-104(e)]. It is a two-party instrument (see Exhibit 20.3), not an order to pay. Promissory notes usually arise when one party borrows money from another. The note is evidence of (1) the extension of credit and (2) the borrower's promise to repay the debt.

A party who makes a promise to pay is the **maker** of a note (i.e., the borrower). The party to whom the promise to pay is made is the **payee** (i.e., the lender). A promissory note is a negotiable instrument that the payee can freely transfer to other parties.

The parties are free to design the terms of a note to fit their needs. Notes can be payable at a specific time (**time notes**) or on demand (**demand notes**). Notes can be made payable to a named payee or to "bearer." They can be payable in a single payment or in installments. The latter are called **installment notes**. Most notes require the borrower to pay interest on the principal.

Lenders sometimes require the maker of a note to post security for the repayment of the note. This security, which is called **collateral**, may be in the form of automobiles, houses,

EXHIBIT 20.3

Promissory Note

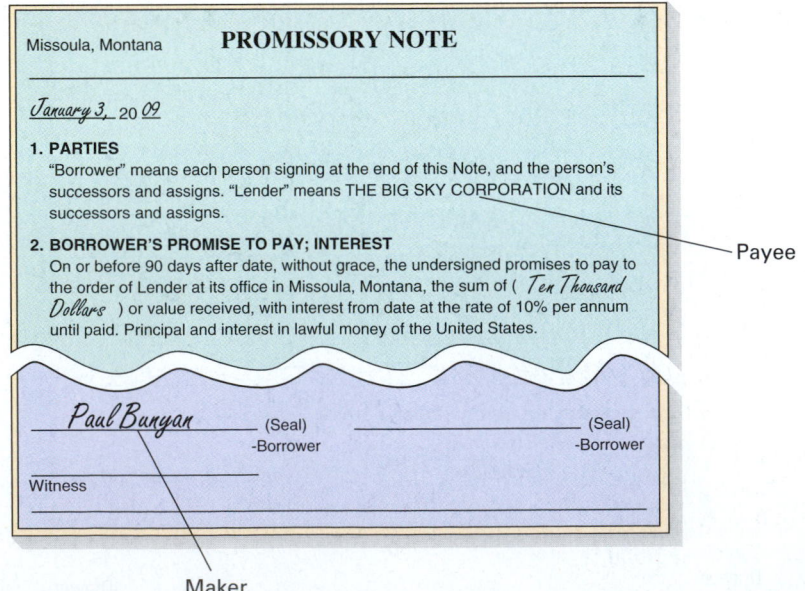

Promissory Note

securities, or other property. If the maker fails to repay the note when it is due, the lender can foreclose and take the collateral as payment for the note. Notes are often named after the security that underlies the note. For example, notes that are secured by real estate are called **mortgage notes**, and notes that are secured by personal property are called **collateral notes**.

Automobile

The purchaser of an automobile often borrows money from a bank or other lender to purchase the vehicle. The borrower signs a promissory note promising to repay the loan. The promissory note quali-fies as a negotiable instrument.

Certificates of Deposit

A **certificate of deposit (CD)** is a special form of note that is created when a depositor deposits money at a financial institution in exchange for the institution's promise to pay back the amount of deposit plus an agreed-upon rate of interest upon the expiration of a set time period agreed upon by the parties [UCC 3-104(j)].

The financial institution is the borrower (the **maker**), and the depositor is the lender (the **payee**). A CD is a two-party instrument (see Exhibit 20.4). Note that a CD is a promise to pay, not an order to pay.

Payee

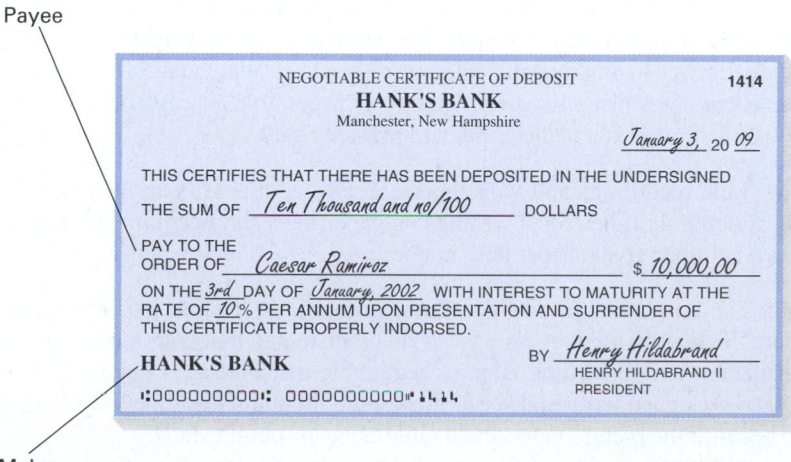

Maker

EXHIBIT 20.4

Certificate of Deposit

Unlike a regular passbook savings account, a CD is a negotiable instrument. CDs under $100,000 are commonly referred to as **small CDs**. CDs of $100,000 or more are usually called **jumbo CDs**.

CONCEPT SUMMARY

Types of Promises to Pay

PROMISE TO PAY	PARTIES	DESCRIPTION
Promissory note	Maker	Party who issues a promissory note; this is usually the borrower.
	Payee	Party to whom a promissory note is made payable; this is usually the lender.
Certificate of deposit (CD)	Maker	Financial institution that issues a CD.
	Payee	Party to whom a CD is made payable; this is usually the depositor.

Creating a Negotiable Instrument

According to UCC 3-104(a), a negotiable instrument must:

- Be in writing.
- Be signed by the maker or drawer.
- Be an unconditional promise or order to pay.
- State a fixed amount of money.
- Not require any undertaking in addition to the payment of money.
- Be payable on demand or at a definite time.
- Be payable to order or to bearer.

These requirements must appear on the *face* of the instrument. If they do not, the instrument does not qualify as negotiable. Each of these requirements is discussed in the paragraphs and sections that follow.

Writing

A negotiable instrument must be (1) in writing and (2) permanent and portable. Often the requisite writing is on a preprinted form, but typewritten, handwritten, or other tangible agreements are also acceptable [UCC 1-201(46)]. In addition, the instrument can be a combination of different kinds of writing. For example, a check is often a preprinted form on which the drawer handwrites the amount of the check, the name of the payee, and the date of the check. Oral promises do not qualify as negotiable instruments because they are not clearly transferable in a manner that will prevent fraud.

Example Tape recordings and videotapes are not negotiable instruments because they are not considered writings. Most writings on paper meet the **permanency requirement**, although a writing on tissue paper does not because of its impermanence.

Example The courts have held that writings on objects besides paper (e.g., baseballs, shirts) meet this requirement. A promise or an order to pay that is written in snow or sand is not permanent and, therefore, is not a negotiable instrument. A photograph of such a writing that was signed by the maker or drawer would qualify as a negotiable instrument, however, because the picture meets the requirements of permanence.

The **portability requirement** is intended to ensure free transfer of the instrument.

Example A promise to pay chiseled in a California redwood tree would not qualify as a negotiable instrument because the tree is not freely transferable in commerce. Writing the same promise or order to pay on a small block of wood could qualify as a negotiable instrument, however.

The best practice is to place a written promise or order to pay on traditional paper. This method ensures that the permanency and portability requirements are met so that transferees will readily accept the instrument.

Signed by the Maker or the Drawer

The UCC **signature requirement** requires that a negotiable instrument must be *signed* by the maker if it is a note or CD and by the drawer if it is a check or draft. The maker or drawer is not liable on the instrument unless his or her signature appears on it. The signature can be placed on the instrument by the maker or drawer or by an authorized agent [UCC 3-401(a)]. Although the signature of the maker, drawer, or agent can be located anywhere on the face of the negotiable instrument, it is usually placed in the lower-right corner.

The UCC broadly defines **signature** as any symbol executed or adopted by a party with a present intent to authenticate writing [UCC 1-201(39)]. A signature is made by the use of any name, including a trade or assumed name, or by any word or mark used in lieu of a written signature [UCC 3-401(b)].

Example The requisite signature can be the maker's or drawer's formal name (Henry Richard Cheeseman), informal name (Hank Cheeseman), initials (HRC), or nickname (The Big Cheese). Any other symbol or device (e.g., an *X*, a thumbprint) adopted by the signer as his or her signature also qualifies. The signer's intention to use the symbol as his or her signature is controlling. Typed, printed, lithographed, rubber-stamped, and other mechanical means of signing instruments are recognized as valid by the UCC.

CONTEMPORARY ENVIRONMENT
Authorized Representative's Signature

A maker or drawer can appoint an *agent* to sign a negotiable instrument on his or her behalf. For example, corporations and other organizations use agents, usually corporate officers or employees, to sign the corporation's negotiable instruments. Individuals can also appoint agents to sign their negotiable instruments.

A maker or drawer is liable on a negotiable instrument signed by an authorized agent. The agent is not personally liable on the negotiable instrument if his or her signature properly unambiguously discloses (1) his or her agency status and (2) the identity of the maker or drawer [UCC 3-402(b)]. In the case of an organization, the agent's signature is proper if the organization's name is preceded or followed by the name of the authorized agent.

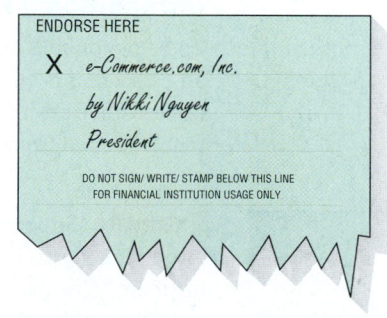

Unconditional Promise or Order to Pay

To be a negotiable instrument under the requirements of UCC 3-104, a writing must contain either an **unconditional order to pay** (draft or check) or an **unconditional promise to pay** (note or CD). The term *unconditional*, which is discussed in the following paragraphs, is key.

Order to Pay

To be negotiable, a *draft* or *check* must contain the drawer's unconditional **order to pay** a payee. An order is a direction for the drawee to pay and must be more than an authorization or a request to pay. The language of the order must be precise and contain the word *pay*.

Example The printed word *pay* on a check is a proper order that is sufficient to make a check negotiable. The order can be in a courteous form, such as "please pay" or "kindly pay." A mere request or acknowledgment, such as "I wish you would pay," is not sufficient because it lacks a direction to pay.

An order to pay a draft or check must identify the drawee who is directed to make the payment. The name of the drawee's financial institution that is preprinted on a check is sufficient. The order can be directed to one or more parties jointly, such as "to A *and* B," or in the alternative, such as "to A *or* B." The order cannot, however, be in succession, such as "to A, and if she does not pay, then to B."

Promise to Pay

To be negotiable, a *promissory note* must contain the maker's unconditional and affirmative **promise to pay**. The mere acknowledgment of a debt is not sufficient to constitute a negotiable instrument. In other words, an implied promise to pay is not negotiable, but an expressly stated promise to pay is negotiable.

Example The statement "I owe you $100" is merely an I.O.U. It acknowledges a debt, but it does not contain an express promise to repay the money. If the I.O.U. used language such as "I promise to pay" or "the undersigned agrees to pay," however, a negotiable instrument would be created because the note would contain an affirmative obligation to pay.

CDs are an exception to this rule. CDs do not require an express promise to pay because the bank's acknowledgment of the payee's bank deposit and other terms of the CD clearly indicate the bank's promise to repay the certificate holder. Nevertheless, most CDs contain an express promise to pay.

Unconditional Promise or Order

To be negotiable, a promise or order must be **unconditional** [UCC 3-104(a)]. A promise or an order that is **conditional** on another promise or event is not negotiable because the risk of the other promise or event not occurring would fall on the person who held the instrument. A conditional promise is subject to normal contract law.

Example Suppose American Airlines buys a $10 million airplane from Boeing Aircraft. American signs a promissory note that promises to pay Boeing if it is "satisfied" with the airplane. This promise is a conditional promise. The condition—that American is satisfied with the airplane—destroys the negotiability of the note.

A promise or an order is conditional and, therefore, not negotiable if it states (1) an express condition to payment, (2) that the promise or order is subject to or governed by another writing, or (3) the rights or obligations with respect to the promise or order are stated in another writing. The mere reference to another writing does not make a promise or order conditional [UCC 3-106(a)].

Example Dow Chemical purchases equipment from Illinois Tool Works and signs a sales contract. Dow Chemical borrows the purchase price from Citibank and executes a promissory note evidencing this debt and promising to repay the borrowed money plus interest. The note contains the following reference: "sales contract—purchase of equipment." This reference does not affect the negotiability of the note. The note would not be negotiable, however, if the reference stated, "This note hereby incorporates by this reference the terms of the sales contract between Dow Chemical and Illinois Tool Works of this date."

A promise or an order remains unconditional even though it refers to another writing for description of rights to collateral, prepayment, or acceleration (for example, "See collateral agreement dated January 15, 2004").

A promise or an order may also stipulate that payment is limited to a particular fund or source. (for example, "Payable out of the proceeds of the Tower Construction Contract") [UCC 3-106(b)].

In the following case, the court had to decide whether a negotiable instrument had been created.

CASE 20.1
Negotiable Instrument

FFP Marketing Company, Inc. v. Long Lane Master Trust IV
169 S.W.3d 402, **Web** 2005 Tex. App. Lexis 5277 (2005)
Court of Appeals of Texas

> **"** *Because the promissory notes in this case are not negotiable instruments, the Code does not govern their enforcement; contract law does.* **"**

—Judge Dauphinot

Facts

FFP Operating Partners, L.P. (FFP Operating), operates a number of convenience stores and gas stations. FFP Operating executed 31 promissory notes in favor of Franchise Mortgage Acceptance Company (FMAC). In connection with the notes, FFP Marketing Company, Inc. (FFP Marketing), executed guaranties of payment in favor of FMAC for all 31 notes. Loan and security agreements were also executed in connection with all 31 transactions. The promissory notes incorporated by reference the loan, security, and guaranty agreements, which included waivers, consents, and acknowledgments. Bay View Mortgage Acceptance Corporation (Bay View) became a successor in interest to FMAC with respect to the promissory notes, guaranties, and associated loan documents and, in turn, assigned all of its interests to Long Lane Master Trust IV (LLMT).

FFP Operating failed to make payments on the notes. LLMT gave notice to FFP Operating of the default, accelerated the obligations under the promissory notes, and demanded payment. The notes went unpaid. The outstanding principal of the notes was $13,212,199, with unpaid interest of $1,488,899. LLMT filed suit against FFP Operating and FFP Marketing. LLMT filed a motion for summary judgment on its claim of default under the 31 promissory notes and guaranties for the amount due. FFP Operating declared bankruptcy and was nonsuited from this case. The trial court entered summary judgment in favor of LLMT against FFP Marketing. FFP Marketing appealed.

Issue

Are the 31 promissory notes negotiable instruments that can be enforced against FFP Marketing?

Language of the Court

The Texas version of the Uniform Commercial Code ("the Code") recognizes that the holder of a negotiable instrument has the right to enforce the instrument whether or not he is the instrument's lawful owner. Under the Code, the "holder" of a financial instrument is "the person in possession of a negotiable instrument that is payable either to bearer or to an identified person that is the person in possession." However, to be subject to the Code's governance, a promissory note must be a negotiable instrument. A promissory note is a negotiable instrument subject to the Code if it is a written unconditional promise to pay a sum certain in money, upon demand or at a definite time, and is payable to order or to bearer. The negotiability of an instrument is a question of law.

In the case before us, both the Long Lane notes broadly define the maker's liability to include obligations found outside the four corners of the instruments. The presence of this definition in the notes defeats the sum certain requirement because one cannot determine from the face of each note the extent of the maker's liability. The notes fail the requirement for an unconditional promise because each note specifically "incorporates by reference" the terms of other documents, requiring one to examine those documents to determine if they place conditions on payment. Although a promise is not made conditional by reference to a separate writing for information regarding rights and obligations with respect to collateral, here, as security for each note's payment and performance, each note incorporates by reference the terms of both the loan and indenture agreements executed in conjunction with the transaction.

Each note also incorporates by reference the waivers, consents, and acknowledgments of the maker found in other loan documents. Thus, each note is governed by the terms of another writing, requiring one to look outside the note to determine if payment is conditional or if the terms of that document alter the rights with respect to payment. Accordingly, we conclude that the notes in this case are not negotiable instruments. Because the promissory notes in this case are not negotiable instruments, the Code does not govern their enforcement; contract law does.

Decision

The court of appeals decided that the 31 promissory notes were not negotiable instruments because they were conditional on obligations contained in other documents, and therefore the provisions of the Uniform Commercial Code regarding negotiable instruments did not apply in this case. The court of appeals reversed the decision of the trial court and remanded the case to be tried on the merits of the case using contract law.

Law Ethics Questions

1. Why does the UCC require that a negotiable instrument not be conditional on obligations contained in other agreements? Explain.

2. Why did the court decide the promissory notes in this case were not negotiable instruments?

3. What is the consequence of finding that the notes were not promissory notes and were contracts? Explain.

4. **ETHICS** Did any of the parties in this case act unethically?

Web Exercises

1. **WEB** For the complete opinion of this case, go to *www.prenhall.com/cheesemancases*.

2. **WEB** Visit the website of the court of appeals of Texas, Second Circuit, at *www.2ndcoa.courts.state.tx.us*.

3. **WEB** Use *www.google.com* to find an article or a case where promissory notes or other documents were found not to be negotiable instruments.

CONTEMPORARY ENVIRONMENT
Payable to Order or to Bearer

Because negotiable instruments are primarily intended to act as a substitute for money, they must be freely transferable to other persons or entities. The UCC requires that negotiable instruments be either **payable to order** or **payable to bearer** [UCC 3-104(a)(1)]. Promises or orders to pay that do not meet this requirement are not negotiable. They may, however, be assignable under contract law.

Order Instruments

An instrument is an **order instrument** if it is payable (1) to the order of an identified person or (2) to an identified person or orders [UCC 3-109(b)].

> **Example** An instrument that states "payable to the order of IBM" or "payable to IBM or order" is negotiable. It would not be negotiable if it stated either "payable to IBM" or "pay to IBM" because it is not payable to *order*.

An instrument can be payable to the order of the maker, the drawer, the drawee, the payee, two or more payees together, or, alternatively, to an office, an officer by his or her title, a corporation, a partnership, an unincorporated association, a trust, an estate, or another legal entity. A party to which an instrument is payable may be identified in any way, including by name, identifying number, office, or account number. An instrument is payable to the party intended by the signer of the instrument even if that party is identified in the instrument by a name or other identification that is not that of the intended party [UCC 3-110].

> **Example** An instrument made "payable to the order of Lovey" is negotiable. The identification of "Lovey" may be determined by evidence. On the other hand, an instrument made "payable to the order of my loved ones" is not negotiable because the payees are not ascertainable with reasonable certainty.

Bearer Instruments

A **bearer instrument** is payable to anyone in physical possession of the instrument who presents it for payment when it is due. The person in possession of the instrument is called the **bearer**. Bearer paper results when the drawer or maker does not make the instrument payable to a specific payee.

> **Example** An instrument is payable to bearer when any of the following language is used: "payable to the order of bearer," "payable to bearer," "payable to Xerox or bearer," "payable to cash," or "payable to the order of cash." In addition, any other indication that does not purport to designate a specific payee creates bearer paper [UCC 3-109(a)]. For example, an instrument "payable to my dog Fido" creates a bearer instrument.

Fixed Amount of Money

To be negotiable, an instrument must contain a promise or an order to pay a **fixed amount of money** [UCC 3-104(a)]. The fixed amount requirement ensures that the value of the instrument can be determined with certainty. The principal amount of the instrument must appear on the face of the instrument.

An instrument does not have to be payable with interest, but if it is, the amount of interest being charged may be expressed as either a *fixed* or *variable* rate. The amount or rate of interest may be stated or described in the instrument or may require reference to information not contained in the instrument. If an instrument provides for interest but the amount of interest cannot be determined from the description, interest is payable at the judgment rate (legal rate) in effect at the place of payment of the instrument [UCC 3-112].

Example A note that contains a promise to pay $10,000 in one year at a stated rate of 10 percent interest is a negotiable instrument because the value of the note can be determined at any time. A note that contains a promise to pay in goods or services is not a negotiable instrument because the value of the note would be difficult to determine at any given time.

Payable in Money

UCC 3-104(a) provides that the fixed amount of a negotiable instrument must be **payable in money**. The UCC defines **money** as a "medium of exchange authorized or adopted by a domestic or foreign government as part of its currency" [UCC 1-201(24)].

Example An instrument that is "payable in $10,000 U.S. currency" is a negotiable instrument.

Instruments that are fully or partially payable in a medium of exchange other than money are not negotiable.

Example An instrument that is "payable in $10,000 U.S. gold" is not negotiable.

Although the stated amount is a fixed amount, it is not payable in a medium of exchange of the U.S. government.

Example Instruments that are payable in diamonds, commodities, goods, services, stocks, bonds, and such do not qualify as negotiable instruments.

> Bad money drives out good money.
>
> Sir Thomas Gresham (1560)

CONTEMPORARY ENVIRONMENT

Variable Interest Rate Loan

Many lending institutions offer **variable interest rate loans**. These loans tie the interest rate to some set measure, such as a major bank's prime rate (e.g., Citibank's prime) or another well-known rate (e.g., the Freddie Mac rate). Thus, the interest changes during the life of the loan. Some lenders make loans that are fixed for a period of time (i.e., the first seven years) and become variable for the remaining period of the loan.

Revised Article 3 of the UCC expressly provides that variable interest rate notes are negotiable instruments. UCC 3-112(b) provides: "Interest may be stated in an instrument as a fixed or variable amount of money or it may be expressed as a fixed or variable rate or rates." UCC 3-112(b) also provides that the amount or rate of interest may be determined by reference to information not contained in the instrument.

Not Require Any Undertaking in Addition to the Payment of Money

To qualify as a negotiable instrument, a promise or an order to pay cannot state any other undertaking by the person promising or ordering payment to do any act in addition to the payment of money [UCC 3-104(a)(3)].

Example If a note required the maker to pay a stated amount of money *and* perform some type of service, it would not be negotiable.

A promise or an order may include authorization or power to protect collateral, dispose of collateral, and waive any law intended to protect the obligee.

In the following case, the court had to decide whether a negotiable instrument had been created.

CASE 20.2
Unconditional Promise

Deeks v. United States

Web 2005 U.S. App. Lexis 21605 (2005)
United States Court of Appeals for the Federal Circuit

> "We also reject Deek's contention that the Willett Document is a "bill of credit" or some negotiable instrument, as the text reveals neither an intent that it be circulated as money, nor an unconditional promise to pay a certain sum."
>
> —Judge Lourie

Facts

Andre Deeks possesses a handwritten document prepared in 1792 by Colonial Marinus Willett, a military officer of the United States of America, that evidences a 1781 agreement between the colonel and 60 members of the Oneida tribe of Native Americans, who were promised blankets in exchange for their assistance during the Revolutionary War. The United States government had never made good on its promise. Deeks filed a complaint against the U.S. government, alleging that the Willett Document was a negotiable instrument and that Deeks was due an estimated $3 million. The U.S. Court of Federal Claims dismissed Deeks's complaint. Deeks appealed.

Issue

Is the 1792 Willett Document a negotiable instrument?

Language of the Court

Deek's arguments are unavailing, and his accusations against the trial court and the government are wholly without merit. We agree with the trial court that the statute of limitations for bringing suit to enforce an agreement dating back to 1781 has long run. We also reject Deek's contention that the Willett Document is a "bill of credit" or some negotiable instrument, as the text reveals neither an intent that it be circulated as money, nor an unconditional promise to pay a certain sum.

Decision

The Court of Appeals held that the Willett Document was not a negotiable instrument and that the statute of limitations had run on a contract claim. The Court of Appeals affirmed the trial court's decision dismissing Deeks's complaint.

Law & Ethics Questions

1. What element that is necessary for there to be a negotiable instrument was missing from the Willett Document? Explain.

2. What would have been the outcome if the Willett Document had been found to be a negotiable instrument?

3. **ETHICS** Do you think Deeks had any chance of winning his case?

Web Exercises

1. **WEB** For the complete opinion of this case, go to *www.prenhall.com/cheesemancases*.

2. **WEB** Visit the website of the U.S. Court of Appeals for the Federal Circuit, at *www.fedcir.gov*.

3. **WEB** Use *www.google.com* to find an article that discusses the Willett Document. Read it.

Payable on Demand or at a Definite Time

For an instrument to be negotiable, it is necessary to know when the maker, drawee, or acceptor is required to pay it. UCC 3-104(a)(2) requires the instrument to be either **payable on demand** or **payable at a definite time**, as noted on the face of the instrument.

PAYABLE ON DEMAND Instruments that are payable on demand are called **demand instruments**. Demand instruments are created by (1) language such as "payable on demand," "payable at sight," or "payable on presentment" or (2) silence regarding when payment is due [UCC 3-108(a)].

By definition, checks are payable on demand [UCC 3-104(f)]. Other instruments, such as notes, CDs, and drafts, can be, but are not always, payable on demand.

PAYABLE AT A DEFINITE TIME Instruments that are payable at a definite time are called **time instruments**. UCC 3-108(b) and 3-108(c) states that an instrument is payable at a definite time if it is payable:

1. At a fixed date (for example, "Payable on January 1, 2010").
2. On or before a stated date (for example, "Payable on or before January 1, 2010"). In this case, the maker or drawee has the option of paying the note before—but not after—the stated maturity date.
3. At a fixed period after sight (for example, "Payable 60 days after sight"). Drafts often contain this type of language. The holder must formally present this type of instrument for acceptance so that the date of sight can be established.
4. At a time readily ascertainable when the promise or order is issued (for example, "Payable 60 days after January 1, 2010").

Instruments that are payable upon an uncertain act or event are not negotiable.

Example Suppose Sarah Smith's father executes a promissory note stating, "I promise to pay to the order of my daughter, Sarah, $100,000 on the date she marries Bobby Boggs." This note is nonnegotiable because the act and date of marriage are uncertain.

Prepayment, Acceleration, and Extension Clauses

The inclusion of prepayment, acceleration, or extension clauses in an instrument does not affect its negotiability. Such clauses are commonly found in promissory notes.

A **prepayment clause** permits the maker to pay the amount due prior to the due date of the instrument. An **acceleration clause** allows the payee or holder to accelerate payment of the principal amount of an instrument, plus accrued interest, upon the happening of an event (e.g., default). An **extension clause** is the opposite of an acceleration clause: It allows the date of maturity of an instrument to be extended to some time in the future.

CONCEPT SUMMARY

Formal Requirements for a Negotiable Instrument

REQUIREMENT	DESCRIPTION
Writing	Writing must be permanent and portable. Oral or implied instruments are nonnegotiable [UCC 3-104(d)].
Signed by maker or drawer	Signature must appear on the face of the instrument. It may be any mark intended by the signer to be his or her signature. Signature may be by anauthorized representative [UCC 3-104(a)].
Unconditional promise or order to pay	Instrument must be an unconditional promise or order to pay [UCC 3-104(a)]. Permissible notations listed in UCC 3-106(a) do not affect the instrument's negotiability. If payment is conditional on the performance of another agreement, the instrument is nonnegotiable.
Fixed amount of money	1. *Fixed amount*. The amount required to discharge an instrument must be on the face of the instrument [UCC 3-104(a)]. The amount may include payment of interest and costs of collection. Revised Article 3 provides that variable interest rate notes are negotiable instruments.
	2. *In money*. The amount must be payable in U.S. or foreign country's currency. If payment is to be made in goods, services, or non-monetary items, the instrument is nonnegotiable [UCC 3-104(a)].

Cannot require any undertaking in addition to the payment of money	A promise or an order to pay cannot state any other undertaking to do an act in addition to the payment of money [UCC 3-104(a)(3)]. A promise or an order may include authorization or power to protect collateral, dispose of collateral, waive any law intended to protect the obligee, and the like.
Payable on demand or at a definite time	1. *Payable on demand.* Payable at sight, upon presentation, or when no time for payment is stated [UCC 3-108(a)].
	2. *Payable at a definite time.* Payable at a definite date or before a stated date, a fixed period after a stated date, or at a fixed period after sight [UCC 3-108(b), 3-108(c)]. An instrument payable only upon the occurrence of an uncertain act or event is nonnegotiable.

INTERNATIONAL LAW

Negotiable Instruments Payable in Foreign Currency

The UCC expressly provides that an instrument may state that it is payable in foreign money [UCC 3-107].

Example An instrument "payable in 10,000 yen in Japanese currency" is a negotiable instrument that is governed by Article 3 of the UCC.

Unless the instrument states otherwise, an instrument that is payable in foreign currency can be satisfied by the equivalent in U.S. dollars, as determined on the due date. The conversion rate is the current bank-offered spot rate at the place of payment on the due date. The instrument can expressly provide that it is payable only in the stated foreign currency. In that case, the instrument cannot be paid in U.S. dollars.

Nonnegotiable Contracts and Assignment

If a promise or an order to pay does not meet one of the previously discussed requirements of negotiability, it is a **nonnegotiable contract**. As such, it is not subject to the provisions of UCC Article 3. A promise or an order that conspicuously states that it is not negotiable or is not subject to Article 3 is not a negotiable instrument [UCC 3-104(d)]. It is therefore a nonnegotiable contract.

A nonnegotiable contract is not rendered either nontransferable or nonenforceable. A nonnegotiable contract can be enforced under normal contract law. If the maker or drawer of a nonnegotiable contract fails to pay it, the holder of the contract can sue the nonperforming party for breach of contract.

Assignment

An **assignment** is the transfer of rights under a contract. It transfers the rights of the transferor (**assignor**) to the transferee (**assignee**). Because normal contract principles apply, the assignee acquires only the rights that the assignor possessed. Thus, any defenses to the enforcement of the contract that could have been raised against the assignor can also be raised against the assignee.

An assignment occurs when a nonnegotiable contract is transferred. In the case of a negotiable instrument, assignment occurs when the instrument is transferred but the transfer fails to qualify as a negotiation under Article 3. In this case, the transferee is an *assignee* rather than a *holder*.

Money speaks sense in a language all nations understand.

Aphra Behn
The Rover

Example Party A and Party B enter into a contract whereby Party A owes Party B something of value (i.e., money). Party A (assignor) assigns this right to Party C (assignee). It is later learned, however, that Party B had engaged in fraud in enticing Party A to enter into the contract. When Party C tries to enforce the contract against Party A to collect the

EXHIBIT 20.5

Assignment

money that Party A owes, Party A can raise the defense it has against Party B (i.e., Party B's fraud) against Party C. The result: Party A does not have to pay Party C because of Party B's fraud. Party A can sue Party B to get her money back; Party C can sue Party B to recover any money he paid to Party B to obtain the right to collect the money from Party A, which is now not collectable (see Exhibit 20.5).

Transfer by Negotiation

Negotiation is the transfer of a negotiable instrument by a person other than the issuer. The person to whom the instrument is transferred becomes the holder [UCC 3-201(a)]. The **holder** receives at least the rights of the transferor and may acquire even greater rights than the transferor if he or she qualifies as a holder in due course (HDC) [UCC 3-302]. An HDC has greater rights because he or she is not subject to some of the defenses that could otherwise have been raised against the transferor.

The proper method of negotiation depends on whether the instrument is order paper or bearer paper, as discussed in the following paragraphs.

Negotiating Order Paper

An instrument that is payable to a specific payee or indorsed to a specific indorsee is **order paper**. Order paper is negotiated by delivery with the necessary indorsement [UCC 3-201(b)]. Thus, for order paper to be negotiated, there must be delivery and indorsement.

Example Sam Bennett receives a weekly payroll check from his employer, Ace Plumbing Corporation. Bennett takes the check to a local store, signs the back of the check (indorsement), gives the check to the cashier (delivery), and receives cash from the check. Bennett has negotiated the check to the store. Delivery and indorsement have occurred.

Negotiating Bearer Paper

An instrument that is not payable to a specific payee or indorsee is **bearer paper**. Bearer paper is negotiated by *delivery*; indorsement is not necessary [UCC 3-201(b)]. Substantial risk is associated with the loss or theft of bearer paper.

Example Suppose Mary draws a check "pay to cash" and gives it to Peter. There has been a negotiation because Mary delivered a bearer instrument (the check) to Peter. Subsequently, Carmen steals the check from Peter. There has not been a negotiation because the check was not voluntarily delivered. That Carmen physically possesses the check is irrelevant. The negotiation is complete, however, if Carmen delivers the check to an innocent third party. The party is a holder and may qualify as an HDC with all the rights in the check [UCC 3-302]. If the holder is an HDC, Peter's only recourse is to recover against Carmen.

CONTEMPORARY ENVIRONMENT
Converting Order and Bearer Paper

An instrument can be converted from order paper to bearer paper and vice versa many times until the instrument is paid [UCC 3-109(c)]. The deciding factor is the type of indorsement placed on the instrument at the time of each subsequent transfer. For example, follow the indorsements in the example shown here to determine whether order or bearer paper has been created.

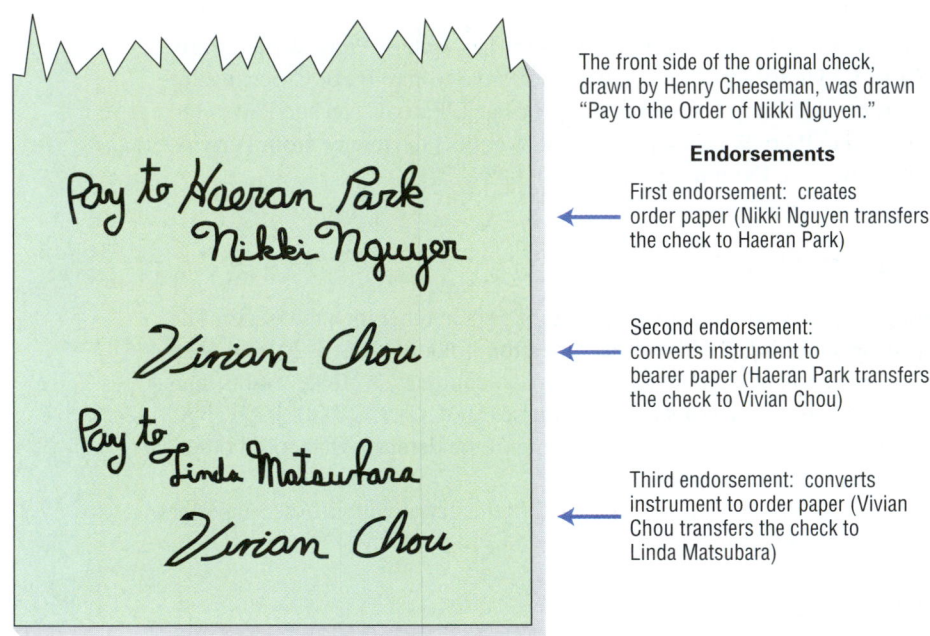

The front side of the original check, drawn by Henry Cheeseman, was drawn "Pay to the Order of Nikki Nguyen."

Endorsements

First endorsement: creates order paper (Nikki Nguyen transfers the check to Haeran Park)

Second endorsement: converts instrument to bearer paper (Haeran Park transfers the check to Vivian Chou)

Third endorsement: converts instrument to order paper (Vivian Chou transfers the check to Linda Matsubara)

Indorsement

An **indorsement** is the signature of a signer (other than as a maker, a drawer, or an acceptor) that is placed on an instrument to negotiate it to another person. The signature may (1) appear alone, (2) name an individual to whom the instrument is to be paid, or (3) be accompanied by other words [UCC 3-204(2)]. The person who indorses an instrument is called the **indorser**. If the indorsement names a payee, this person is called the **indorsee**.

Example Nikki Choy receivers a $500 check for her birthday. She can transfer the check to anyone merely by signing her name on the back of the check. Suppose she indorses it "pay to Rob Dewey." Choy is the indorser; Rob Dewey is the indorsee.

Indorsements are usually placed on the reverse side of the instrument, such as on the back of a check (see Exhibit 20.6). If there is no room on the instrument, the indorsement may be written on a separate piece of paper called an **allonge**. The allonge must be affixed (e.g., stapled, taped) to the instrument [UCC 3-204(a)].

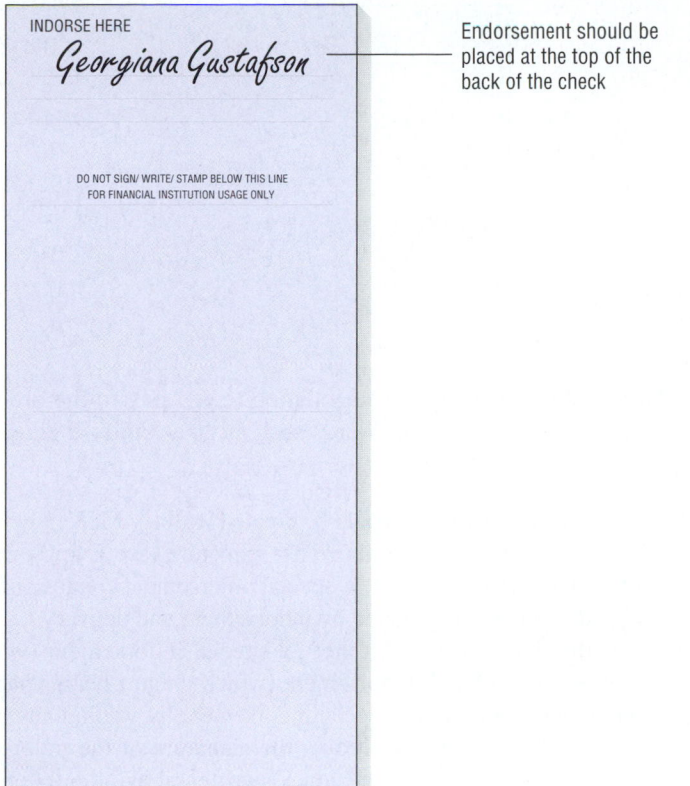

EXHIBIT 20.6

Placement of an Indorsement

Indorsements are required to negotiate order paper, but they are not required to negotiate bearer paper [UCC 3-201(b)]. For identification purposes and to impose liability on the transferor, however, the transferee often requires the transferor to indorse the bearer paper at negotiation.

Types of Indorsements

There are four categories of indorsements:

1. Blank indorsement
2. Special indorsement
3. Qualified indorsement
4. Restrictive indorsement

These types of indorsements are discussed in the following paragraphs.

BLANK INDORSEMENT A **blank indorsement** does not specify a particular indorsee. It may consist of a mere signature [UCC 3-205(b)].

Example Suppose Harold Green draws a check "pay to the order of Victoria Rudd" and delivers the check to Victoria. Victoria indorses the check in blank by writing her signature on the back of the check (see Exhibit 20.7).

Order paper that is indorsed in blank becomes bearer paper. As mentioned earlier, bearer paper can be negotiated by delivery; indorsement is not required.

Example If Victoria Rudd loses the check she indorsed in blank and Mary Smith finds it, Mary Smith can deliver it to another person without indorsing it. Thus, the lost check can be presented for payment or negotiated to another holder.

SPECIAL INDORSEMENT A **special indorsement** contains the signature of the indorser and specifies the person (indorsee) to whom the indorser intends the instrument to be

EXHIBIT 20.7

Blank Indorsement

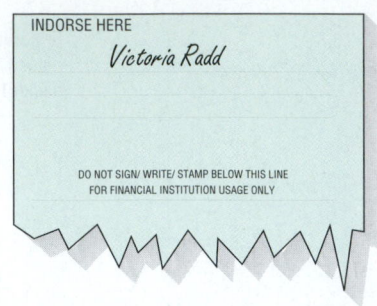

payable [UCC 3-205(a)]. Words of negotiation (e.g., "pay to the order of …") are not required for a special indorsement. Words such as "pay Emily Ingman" are sufficient to form a special indorsement.

Example   A special indorsement would be created if Betsy McKenny indorsed her check and then wrote "pay to Dan Jones" above her signature (see Exhibit 20.8). The check is negotiated when Betsy gives it to Dan. A special indorsement creates *order paper*. As mentioned earlier, order paper is negotiated by indorsement and delivery.

To prevent the risk of loss from theft, a special indorsement (which creates order paper) is preferred over a blank indorsement (which creates bearer paper). A holder can convert a blank indorsement into a special indorsement by writing any contract consistent with the character of the indorsement over the signature of the indorser in blank [UCC 3-205(c)]. Words such as "pay to John Jones" written above the indorser's signature are enough to convert bearer paper to order paper.

QUALIFIED INDORSEMENT   Generally, an indorsement is a promise by the indorser to pay the holder or any subsequent indorser the amount of the instrument if the maker, drawer, or acceptor defaults on it. This promise is called an **unqualified indorsement**. Unless otherwise agreed, the order and liability of the indorsers is presumed to be the order in which they indorse the instrument [UCC 3-415(a)].

Example   Cindy draws a check payable to the order of John. John (indorser) indorses the check and negotiates it to Steve (indorsee). When Steve presents the check for payment, there are insufficient funds in Cindy's account to pay the check. John, as an **unqualified indorser**, is liable on the check. John can recover from Cindy.

The UCC permits **qualified indorsements**—that is, indorsements that disclaim or limit liability on the instrument. A **qualified indorser** does not guarantee payment of the instrument if the maker, drawer, or acceptor defaults on it. A qualified indorsement is created by placing a notation such as "without recourse" or other similar language that disclaims liability as part of the indorsement [UCC 3-415(b)]. A quantified indorsement protects only the indorser who wrote it on the instrument. Subsequent indorsers must also

EXHIBIT 20.8

Special Indorsement

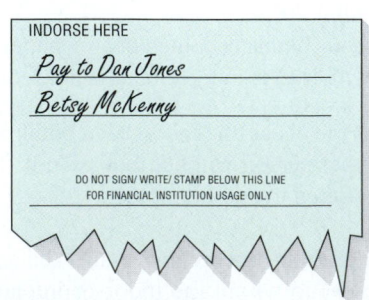

EXHIBIT 20.9

Qualified Indorsements

place a qualified indorsement on the instrument to be protected from liability. An instrument containing a qualified indorsement can be further negotiated.

Qualified indorsements are often used by persons signing instruments in a representative capacity.

Example Suppose an insurance company that is paying a claim makes out a check payable to the order of the attorney representing the payee. The attorney can indorse the check to his client (the payee) with the notation "without recourse." This notation ensures that the attorney is not liable as an indorser if the insurance company fails to pay the check.

A qualified indorsement can be either a special qualified indorsement or a blank qualified indorsement. A *special qualified indorsement* creates order paper that can be negotiated by indorsement and delivery. A *blank qualified indorsement* creates bearer paper that can be further negotiated by delivery without indorsement (see Exhibit 20.9).

RESTRICTIVE INDORSEMENT Most indorsements are *nonrestrictive*. **Nonrestrictive indorsements** do not have any instructions or conditions attached to the payment of the funds.

Example An indorsement is nonrestrictive if the indorsee merely signs his signature to the back of an instrument or includes a notation to pay a specific indorsee ("pay to Sam Smith").

Occasionally, an indorser includes some form of instruction in an indorsement. This instruction is called a **restrictive indorsement**. A restrictive indorsement restricts the indorsee's rights in some manner. An indorsement that purports to prohibit further negotiation of an instrument does not destroy the negotiability of the instrument.

Example A check that is indorsed "pay to Sarah Stein only" can still be negotiated to other transferees. Because of its ineffectiveness, this type of restrictive indorsement is seldom used.

UCC 3-206 recognizes the following types of restrictive indorsements:

- ■ *Indorsement for deposit or collection.* An indorser can indorse an instrument so as to make the indorsee his collecting agent. Such indorsement—called an **indorsement for deposit or collection**—is often done when an indorser deposits a check or other instrument for collection at a bank. Words such as *for collection*, *for deposit only*, and *pay any bank* create this type of indorsement. Banks use this type of indorsement in the collection process.
- ■ *Indorsement in trust.* An indorsement can state that it is for the benefit or use of the indorser or another person.

Example Checks are often indorsed to attorneys, executors of estates, real estate agents, and other fiduciaries in their representative capacity for the benefit of clients, heirs, or others. These indorsements are called **indorsements in trust** or **agency indorsements** (see Exhibit 20.10). The indorser is not personally liable on the instrument if there is a proper trust or agency indorsement.

An indorsee who does not comply with the instructions of a restrictive indorsement is liable to the indorser for all losses that occur because of such noncompliance.

EXHIBIT 20.10

Trust Indorsement

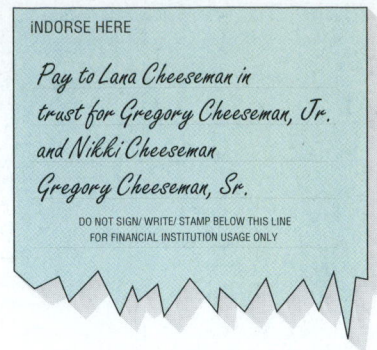

INDORSE HERE

Pay to Lana Cheeseman in trust for Gregory Cheeseman, Jr. and Nikki Cheeseman

Gregory Cheeseman, Sr.

DO NOT SIGN/ WRITE/ STAMP BELOW THIS LINE
FOR FINANCIAL INSTITUTION USAGE ONLY

Example Suppose a check is drawn "payable to Anne Spencer, Attorney, in trust for Joseph Watkins." If Spencer indorses the check to an automobile dealer in payment for a car that she purchases personally, the automobile dealer (indorsee) has not followed the instructions of the restrictive indorsement. He is liable to Joseph Watkins for any losses that arise because of his noncompliance with the restrictive indorsement.

CONCEPT SUMMARY

Types of Indorsements

TYPE OF INDORSEMENT	DESCRIPTION
Blank	Does not specify a particular indorsee (e.g., /s/MaryJones). This indorsement creates bearer paper.
Special	Specifies the person to whom the indorser intends the instrument to be payable (e.g., "Pay to the order of John Smith" /s/Mary Jones). This indorsement creates order paper. (If it is not payable to order [e.g., "Pay to John Smith" /s/MaryJones], it can be converted to order paper [e.g., "Pay to the order of Fred Roe" /s/John Smith].)
Unqualified	Does not disclaim or limit liability. The indorsee is liable on the instrument if it is not paid by the maker, acceptor, or drawer.
Qualified	Disclaims or limits the liability of the indorsee. There are two types: 1. Special qualified indorsement (e.g., "Pay to the order of John Smith, without recourse" /s/MaryJones). 2. Blank qualified indorsement (e.g., "Without recourse" /s/MaryJones).
Nonrestrictive	No instructions or conditions are attached to the payment of funds (e.g., "Pay to John Smith or order" /s/MaryJones).
Restrictive	Conditions or instructions restrict the indorsee's rights. There are four types: 1. Conditional indorsement (e.g., "Pay to John Smith if he completes construction of my garage by June 1, 2004" /s/MaryJones). 2. Indorsement prohibiting further indorsement (e.g., "Pay to John Smith only" /s/MaryJones). 3. Indorsement for deposit or collection (e.g., "For deposit only" /s/MaryJones). 4. Indorsement in trust (e.g., "Pay to John Smith, trustee" /s/MaryJones).

Misspelled or Wrong Name

Where the name of the payee or indorsee is misspelled in a negotiable instrument, the payee or indorsee can indorse the instrument in the misspelled name, the correct name, or both.

Example If Susan Worth receives a check payable to "Susan Wirth," she can indorse the check "Susan Wirth," "Susan Worth," or both. A person paying or taking the instrument for value or collection may require a signature in both the misspelled and the correct versions [UCC3-204(d)].

> A negotiable bill or note is a courier without luggage.
>
> Chief Justice Gibson,
> California Supreme Court

CONTEMPORARY ENVIRONMENT
Multiple Payees or Indorsees

Drawers, makers, and indorsers often make checks, promissory notes, and other negotiable instruments payable to two or more payees or indorsees. The question then arises: Can the instrument be negotiated by the signature of one payee or indorsee, or are all of their signatures required to negotiate the instrument?

Section 3-110(d) of Revised Article 3 of the UCC and cases that have interpreted that section establish the following rules:

■ If an instrument is *payable jointly* using the word *and* (for example, "Pay to Shou-Yi Kang *and* Min-Wer Chen"), both persons' indorsements are necessary to negotiate the instrument.

■ If the instrument is *payable in the alternative* using the word *or* (for example, "Pay to Shou-Yi Kang *or* Min-Wer Chen"), either person's indorsement alone is sufficient to negotiate the instrument.

■ If a *virgule*—a slash mark—is used, courts have held that the instrument is payable in the alternative. Thus, if a virgule is used (for example, "Pay to Shou-Yi Kang/Min-Wer Chen"), either person may individually indorse and negotiate the instrument.

Chapter Summary

Negotiable Instruments, p. 507

Article 3 of the UCC governs the creation of, transfer of, enforcement of, and liability on negotiable instruments.

Functions of Negotiable Instruments

A negotiable instrument is a:
1. Substitute for money.
2. Credit device.
3. Record-keeping device.

Types of Negotiable Instruments, p. 508
Drafts

A draft is an unconditional written order by one party (the drawer) that orders a second party (the drawee) to pay money to a third party (the payee). The drawee must owe money to the drawer for the drawer to issue a draft ordering the money to be paid to the payee.
1. *Drawer.* The party who writes the order for a draft.
2. *Drawee.* The party who must pay the money stated in a draft. The drawee is also called the acceptor.
3. *Payee.* The party who receives the money from a draft.
4. *Types of drafts:*
   a. *Time draft.* A draft payable at a designated future date.
   b. *Sight draft.* A draft payable on sight. Also called a demand draft.

     c. Trade acceptance. A sight draft that arises when credit is extended (by a seller to a buyer) with the sale of goods. The seller is both the drawer and the payee, and the buyer is the drawee.

Checks

A check is a form of draft drawn on a financial institution (the drawee) and payable on demand. The checking account holder (the drawer) orders the financial institution (the drawee) to pay money to a third party (the payee).

1. *Drawer.* The checking account holder and writer of a check.
2. *Drawee.* The financial institution where the drawer has his or her checking account and pays the money to the payee.
3. *Payee.* The party to whom a check is written.
4. *Types of checks:*
   a. Ordinary checks
   b. Special checks:
      i. Certified checks
      ii. Cashier's checks
      iii. Traveler's checks

Promissory Notes

A promissory note is an unconditional written promise by one party (the maker) to pay money to another party (the payee). Promissory notes are also called notes:

1. *Maker.* The party who makes a promise to pay (the borrower).
2. *Payee.* The party to whom a promise to pay is made (the lender).
3. *Types of promissory notes:*
   a. *Time note.* A note payable at a specific time.
   b. *Demand note.* A note payable on demand.
   c. *Installment note.* A note paid in more than one installment.
   d. *Mortgage note.* A note secured by real estate.
   e. *Collateral note.* A note secured by personal property.

Certificates of Deposit

A CD is a special form of note that is created when a depositor (the payee) deposits money at a financial institution (the maker) in exchange for the institution's promise to pay back the amount of the deposit plus an agreed-upon rate of interest upon the expiration of a set time period agreed upon by the parties.

1. *Maker.* The financial institution (the borrower).
2. *Payee.* The depositor (the lender).
3. *Types of CDs:*
   a. *Small CD.* A CD under $100,000.
   b. *Jumbo CD.* A CD of $100,000 or more.

Creating a Negotiable Instrument, p. 512

A negotiable instrument must:

1. Be in writing.
2. Be signed by the maker or drawer.
3. Be an unconditional promise or order to pay.
4. State a fixed amount of money.
5. Not require any undertaking in addition to the payment of money.
6. Be payable on demand or at a definite time.
7. Be payable to order or to bearer.

Writing

A negotiable instrument must be in writing; oral promises or orders do not qualify as negotiable instruments.

1. *Permanency requirement.* The writing must be in a permanent state, such as written on ordinary paper.
2. *Portability requirement.* The writing must be able to be easily transported between areas.

Signed by the Maker or the Drawer

1. *Signature.* A negotiable instrument must be signed by the maker if it is a note or CD and by the drawer if it is a draft or check.
2. *Type of signature.* Any symbol executed or adopted by the maker or drawer with a present intent to authenticate a writing qualifies as his or her signature. This signature can be a formal name, an informal name, initials, a nickname, or any symbol or device.
3. *Signature of authorized agent.* A maker or drawer can appoint an agent to sign a negotiable instrument on his or her behalf. Liability of the parties:
   a. *Maker or drawer.* The maker or drawer is liable on a negotiable instrument signed by an authorized agent.
   b. *Agent.* An agent is not personally liable on a negotiable instrument if his or her signature discloses his or her agency status and the identity of the maker or drawer. An agent who fails to meet these requirements is personally liable on the instrument.

Unconditional Promise or Order to Pay, p. 513

Order to Pay

A drawer's order to pay must be an unconditional order to a drawee to pay a payee.

Promise to Pay

A maker's promise to pay must be an unconditional and affirmative undertaking to repay the debt evidenced by the note or CD.

Unconditional Promise or Order

Promises to pay and orders to pay must be unconditional in order to be negotiable. A promise or an order that is conditional on another promise or event is not negotiable. A promise or an order is conditional if:

1. It states an express condition to payment.
2. It states that the promise or order is subject to or governed by another writing.
3. The rights or obligations with respect to the promise or order are stated in another writing.

A promise or an order remains unconditional if it merely references another writing or refers to another writing for rights as to collateral, prepayment, or acceleration.

Payable to Order or to Bearer

A negotiable instrument must be payable to order or to bearer.

1. *Order instruments.* An order instrument is payable to the order of an identified person or to an identified person or order. The term order must be included in the instrument; otherwise, it is not negotiable. For example, an instrument that states "payable to the order of IBM" or "payable to IBM or order" is negotiable; a writing that states "payable to IBM" or "pay to IBM" is not negotiable.
2. *Bearer instruments.* A bearer instrument is payable to anyone in physical possession of the instrument. An instrument is payable to bearer when any of the following language is used: "payable to bearer," "payable to the order of bearer," "payable to IBM or bearer," "payable to cash," or "payable to the order of cash." The person in possession of a bearer instrument is called the bearer.

Fixed Amount of Money

The value of an instrument must be able to be determined with certainty. An instrument does not have to provide for the payment of interest, but if it does, interest may be expressed as a fixed or variable amount or rate. The amount or rate of interest may be determined by reference to information not contained in the instrument (e.g., a bank's prime rate or a government index).

Payable in Money

The fixed amount must be payable in money, which is any medium of exchange authorized or adopted by a domestic or foreign government. Instruments that are payable in gold, diamonds, commodities, goods, services, stocks, bonds, and such do not qualify as negotiable instruments.

Not Require Any Undertaking in Addition to the Payment of Money

A promise or an order cannot require the person promising or ordering payment to do any act in addition to the payment of money. A note that requires such additional undertaking (e.g., the provision of a service) is not negotiable.

Payable on Demand or at a Definite Time

A negotiable instrument must be payable either on demand or at a definite time.
1. *Payable on demand.* An instrument may be payable on demand, at sight, or on presentment or may be silent regarding when payment is due. This is called a demand instrument.
2. *Payable at a definite time.* An instrument is payable at a definite time if it is payable:
   a. At a fixed date.
   b. On or before a stated date.
   c. At a fixed period after sight.
   d. At a time readily ascertainable when the promise or order is issued.

Prepayment, Acceleration, and Extension Clauses

The following clauses in an instrument do not affect its negotiability:
1. *Prepayment clause.* A clause that permits a maker or drawee to pay an instrument prior to its due date.
2. *Acceleration clause.* A clause that allows the payee or holder to accelerate payment of an instrument upon the happening of an event.
3. *Extension clause.* A clause that allows the maturity of an instrument to be extended to some time in the future.

Nonnegotiable Contracts and Assignment, p. 520

A writing that fails to qualify as a negotiable instrument is a nonnegotiable contract. Nonnegotiable contracts are subject to normal contract law rather than Revised Article 3 of the UCC. Once issued, negotiable instruments can be transferred by assignment or negotiation. The rights acquired by transferees differ according to the method of transfer.

Assignment

Assignment is transfer of rights that the transferor (assignor) has in a contract to a transferee (assignee). Ordinary contracts, writings that do not qualify as negotiable instruments, and negotiable instruments that are not transferred by negotiation can be transferred by assignment. An assignor is the transferor in an assignment situation. An assignee is the transferee in an assignment situation. The transferee acquires only the rights that the transferor had and is subject to all the defenses that can be raised against the transferor.

Transfer by Negotiation, p. 521

Negotiation involves a transfer of a negotiable instrument by a person other than the issuer to a person who becomes a holder. *Negotiation* is a term signifying that a negotiable instrument has met certain requirements in being transferred. A transferor is a person who transfers a negotiable instrument by negotiation. A holder is a person who receives a negotiable instrument by negotiation. The holder receives at least the rights of the transferor and may acquire even greater rights than the transferor if he or she qualifies as a holder in due course (HDC).

Negotiating Order Paper

Order paper (an instrument payable to a specific payee or indorsee) is negotiated by delivery and indorsement. That is, the transferor signs (indorses) the instrument, with or without other notation, and delivers the instrument to the holder.

Negotiating Bearer Paper

Bearer paper (an instrument that is not payable to a specific payee) is negotiated by delivery; indorsement is not required. There is substantial risk associated with the loss or theft of bearer paper.

Converting Order and Bearer Paper

Negotiable instruments can be converted from order paper to bearer paper by the holder indorsing the instrument without naming a specific payee. An instrument can be converted from bearer paper to order paper by the holder indorsing the instrument and naming a specific payee.

Indorsement, p. 522

An indorsement is the signature of the signer (other than as a maker, a drawer, or an acceptor) that is placed on an instrument to negotiate it to another person—for example, a holder singing the back of a check. An indorsement may be a signature alone (creating bearer paper), be accompanied by the name of a specific payee (creating order paper), or be accompanied by other words (e.g., "without recourse").

1. *Indorser.* An indorser is a person who indorses a negotiable instrument.
2. *Indorsee.* An indorsee is a person to whom a negotiable instrument is indorsed.
3. *Allonge.* An indorsement is usually placed on the reverse side of a negotiable instrument. If there is no room on an instrument, the indorsement may be placed on a separate sheet of paper called an allonge that is firmly affixed to the instrument.
4. *Instruments requiring indorsement.* Indorsements are required to negotiate order paper (indorsement and delivery required). Indorsements are not required to negotiate bearer paper (only delivery is required).

Types of Indorsements

1. *Blank Indorsements.* A blank indorsement is an indorsement that does not specify a particular indorser, which occurs when an indorser merely signs an instrument without naming a payee. This indorsement creates bearer paper.
2. *Special Indorsements.* A special indorsement is an indorsement that specifies a named payee, which occurs when the indorser signs an instrument and names a particular indorsee. This indorsement creates order paper.
3. *Qualified indorsement.* An unqualified indorsement does not disclaim or limit the liability of the indorser. An unqualified indorser is liable to pay any holder or subsequent indorser if the maker, drawer, or acceptor does not pay the instrument. This indorsement disclaims or limits the liability of the indorser. A qualified indorser is not liable to pay any holder or subsequent indorser if the maker, drawer, or acceptor does not pay the instrument. A qualified indorsement is done by adding the words without recourse or similar language that disclaims liability.
4. *Restrictive indorsement.* A nonrestrictive indorsement is an indorsement that has no instructions or conditions attached to the payment of the funds. This indorsement occurs when the indorser signs his or her signature to the instrument (either naming a specific payee or not) but does not add any specific condition or instruction concerning the payment of the money. A restrictive indorsement is an indorsement that

contains some sort of instruction from the indorser. The UCC recognizes the following restrictive indorsements:

a. **Conditional indorsement.** An indorsement that conditions the payment of an instrument upon the happening or nonhappening of a specified event.

b. **Indorsement for deposit or collection.** An indorsement that makes the indorsee the indorser's collection agent (e.g., indorsement "for deposit only").

c. **Indorsement in trust.** An indorsement which states that it is for the benefit or use of the indorser or another person.

An indorsement that purports to prohibit further negotiation of a negotiable instrument (e.g., "pay to Sarah Smith only") is ineffective and does not destroy the negotiability of the instrument.

Misspelled or Wrong Name

If the name of the payee or indorsee is misspelled or is wrong, the payee or indorsee can indorse the instrument in the misspelled or wrong name, the correct name, or both.

Multiple Payees or Indorsees

An instrument that is payable to two or more persons with *and* between their names is payable jointly. All their indorsements are required to negotiate the instrument.

Test Review Terms and Concepts

Case Problems

20.1 Type of Negotiable Instrument: Marcus Wiley, James Tate, and James Irby were partners engaged in buying and selling used cars under the trade name Wiley, Tate & Irby. Over an extended period of time, the partnership sold a number of automobiles to Billy Houston, a sole proprietor doing business as Houston Auto Sales. In connection with each purchase, Houston executed and delivered to the partnership a negotiable instrument drawn on the Peoples Bank and Trust Company of Tupelo, Mississippi. Upon delivery of each negotiable instrument, the automobiles were delivered to Houston. Each of the instruments involved in these transactions contained a number of variations in text and form. However, each of them was similar in that each was drawn on a bank, signed by the maker, and contained an unconditional order to pay a sum certain on the demand of the payee. What type of negotiable instruments were involved in these transactions? *Wiley v. Peoples Bank and Trust Company*, 438 F.2d 513, **Web** 1971 U.S. App. Lexis 11917 (United States Court of Appeals for the Fifth Circuit)

20.2 Note: Sandra McGuire and her husband entered into a contract to purchase the inventory, equipment, accounts receivable, and name of "Becca's Boutique" from Pascal and Rebecca Tursi. Becca's Boutique was a clothing store that was owned as a sole proprietorship by the Tursis. The McGuires agreed to purchase the store for $75,000, with a down payment of $10,000 and the balance to be paid at a specified date in the future. The promissory note signed by the McGuires read: "For value received, Thomas J. McGuire and Sandra A. McGuire, husband and wife, do promise to pay to the order of Pascal and Rebecca Tursi the sum of $65,000." Is the note an order to pay or a promise to pay? *P. P. Inc. v. McGuire*, 509 F. Supp. 1079, **Web** 1981 U.S. Dist. Lexis 17984 (United States District Court for the District of New Jersey)

20.3 Negotiable Instrument: William H. Bailey, M.D., executed a note payable to California Dreamstreet, a joint venture that solicited investments for a cattle breeding operation. Bailey's promissory note read: "Dr. William H. Bailey hereby promises to pay to the order of California Dreamstreet the sum of $329,800." Four years later, Dreamstreet negotiated the note to Cooperatieve Centrale Raiffeisen-Boerenleenbank B.A. (Cooperatieve), a foreign bank. A default occurred, and Cooperatieve filed suit against Bailey to recover on the note. Was the note executed by Bailey a negotiable instrument? *Cooperatieve Centrale Raiffeisen-Boerenleenbank B.A. v. Bailey*, 710 F.Supp. 737, **Web** 1989 U.S. Dist. Lexis 4488 (United States District Court for the Central District of California)

20.4 Bearer or Order Instrument: Broadway Management Corporation (Broadway) owned and operated the American Nursing Center. Conan Briggs had received services from the center and had executed an instrument to pay for those services. The instrument read, in relevant part, "Ninety days after date, I, we, or either of us, promises to pay to the order of $3,498.45." Briggs refused to pay on the note. Broadway claimed that this note was bearer paper and as such was payable to the holder. Briggs claimed that the note was order paper and was therefore payable only to a named payee. Can Broadway collect on this note as its bearer? *Broadway Management Corporation v. Briggs*, 30 Ill. App. 3d 403, 332 N.E.2d 131, **Web** 1975 Ill. App. Lexis 2625 (Appellate Court of Illinois)

20.5 Formal Requirements: Mr. Higgins operated a used car dealership in the state of Alabama. Higgins purchased a Chevrolet Corvette. He paid for the car with a draft on his account at the First State Bank of Albertville. Soon after, Higgins resold the car to Mr. Holsonback. To pay for the car, Holsonback signed a check that was printed on a standard-sized envelope. The reason the check was printed on an envelope is that this practice made it easier to transfer title and other documents from the seller to the buyer. The envelope on which the check was written contained a certificate of title, a mileage statement, and a bill of sale. Does a check printed on an envelope meet the formal requirements to be classified as a negotiable instrument under the UCC? *Holsonback v. First State Bank of Albertville*, 394 So.2d 381, **Web** 1980 Ala. Civ. App. Lexis 1208 (Court of Civil Appeals of Alabama)

20.6 Unconditional Promise: M. S. Horne executed a $100,000 note in favor of R. C. Clark. The note stipulated that it could not be transferred, pledged, or assigned without Horne's consent. Along with the note, Horne signed a letter authorizing Clark to use the note as collateral for a loan. Clark pledged the note as collateral for a $50,000 loan from First State Bank of Gallup (First State). First State telephoned Horne to confirm that Clark could pledge the note, and Horne indicated that it was okay. Clark eventually defaulted on the loan. First State attempted to collect on the note, but Horne refused to pay. Did the restriction written on Horne's promissory note cause it to be nonnegotiable despite the letter of authorization? *First State Bank of Gallup v. Clark and Horne*, 91 N.M. 117, 570 P.2d 1144, **Web** 1977 N.M. Lexis 1093 (Supreme Court of New Mexico)

20.7 Demand Instrument: In July 1977, Stewart P. Blanchard borrowed $50,000 from Progressive Bank & Trust Company (Progressive) to purchase a home. As part of the transaction, Blanchard signed a note secured by a mortgage. The note provided for a 10 percent annual interest rate. Under the terms of the note, payment was "due on demand, if no demand is made, then $600 monthly" beginning at a specified date. Blanchard testified that he believed Progressive could demand immediate payment only if he failed to make the monthly installments. After one year, Blanchard received notice that the rate of interest on the note would rise to 11 percent. Despite the notice, Blanchard continued to make $600 monthly payments. One year later, Progressive notified Blanchard that the interest rate on the loan would be increased to 12.75 percent. Progressive requested that Blanchard sign a form consenting to the interest rate adjustment. When Blanchard refused to sign the form, Progressive demanded immediate payment of the note balance. Progressive sued Blanchard to enforce the terms of the note. Was the note a demand instrument? *Blanchard v. Progressive Bank & Trust Company*, 413 So.2d 589, **Web** 1982 La. App. Lexis 7213 (Court of Appeal of Louisiana)

20.8 Order to Pay: Sana Travel Services, Ltd. (Sana), is a travel agency located in New York. Sana was negotiating with Al-Bank Turismo, a Brazilian company, to secure additional business in that country. To expedite negotiations, one of Sana's directors, Attaullah Paracha, made out a check for $33,000 payable to the order of "Jamil Ahmed Kahn, Al-Bank Turismo." On the check Paracha wrote "Just to hold for the security of future business." Paracha then sent the check to Kahn in Brazil. Kahn, Al-Bank's owner, indorsed the check and sold it to Jurandi Carador, a Brazilian citizen. Carador then arranged for the check to be presented to the National Bank of Pakistan, Sana's New York bank. When the bank received the check, it telephoned Sana, which directed the bank to dishonor the check. Sana claims that the notation on the check "Just to hold" rendered the instrument conditional and made it a nonnegotiable instrument. Was the check a negotiable instrument? *Carador v. Sana Travel Services, Ltd.*, 876 F.2d 890, **Web** 1989 U.S. App. Lexis 10488 (United States Court of Appeals for the Second Circuit)

20.9 Reference to Another Document: J. Monte Williamson was the owner of a 16.65% interest in Lake Manor Associates, a partnership. Williamson agreed to sell his interest to H. Louis Salomonsky and Tiffany H. Armstrong in exchange for shares of a certain stock valued at $15 per share and a non-interest-bearing note in the amount of $4,000 for the balance. The notes were executed and contained the following notation: "For value received, the undersigned promises to pay to the order of J. Monte Williamson the principal sum of $4,000 payable as set forth in that certain agreement, an executed copy of which is attached hereto."

The agreement referred to in the notes listed conditions that had to be met to cause the notes to become due. Five years after the notes were executed, Salomonsky and Armstrong claimed that because the notes were negotiable instruments, the statute of limitations on the enforcement of the notes has run. Are these notes negotiable instruments? *Salomonsky v. Kelly*, 232 Va. 261, 349 S.E.2d 358, **Web** 1986 Va. Lexis 253 (Supreme Court of Virginia)

20.10 Reference to Another Agreement: Holly Hill Acres, Ltd. (Holly Hill), purchased land from Rogers and Blythe. As part of its consideration, Holly Hill gave Rogers and Blythe a promissory note and purchase money mortgage. The note read, in part, "This note with interest is secured by a mortgage on real estate made by the maker in favor of said payee. The terms of said mortgage are by reference made a part hereof." Rogers and Blythe assigned this note and mortgage to Charter Bank of Gainesville (Charter Bank) as security in order to obtain a loan from the bank. Within a few months, Rogers and Blythe defaulted on their obligation to Charter Bank. Charter Bank sued to recover on Holly Hill's note and mortgage. Did the reference to the mortgage in the note cause it to be nonnegotiable? *Holly Hill Acres, Ltd. v. Charter Bank of Gainesville*, 314 So.2d 209, **Web** 1975 Fla. App. Lexis 13715 (Court of Appeals of Florida)

20.11 Indorsement: Charles Pribus owed $126,500 to Ford and Mary Williams (Williams). At Pribus's request, his mother, Helen Pribus, executed a promissory note for $126,500 in favor of Williams. Within a few months, Williams bought Philip L. Bush's option to purchase an apartment complex in Texas. As partial payment for the option, Williams gave Bush the promissory note they had received from Helen Pribus. A letter, which was signed by Williams, was stapled to the note. It read: "For valuable consideration, the undersigned do hereby assign the attached note to Philip L. Bush." There was sufficient space on the note itself to write an indorsement and the words contained in the letter. When Bush went to collect on the note, Helen Pribus refused to pay. Bush sued Pribus to enforce the note. Was the note properly indorsed? *Pribus v. Bush*, Rep 118 Cal.App.3d 1003, 173 Cal.Rptr. 747, **Web** 1981 Cal. App. Lexis 1724 (Court of Appeal of California)

20.12 Indorsement: Wilson was the office manager of Palmer and Ray Dental Supply Company of Abilene, Inc. (Dental Supply). Each workday, James Frank Ray, the president of Dental Supply, would take the checks received from customers and place them on Wilson's desk. Wilson was authorized to (1) indorse these checks through the use of a rubber stamp reading "Palmer & Ray Dental Supply, Inc., of Abilene, Box 2894, 3110 B.N. 1st, Abilene, Texas 79603" and (2) deposit the indorsed checks into the company's account at the First National Bank of Abilene (First National Bank). After several years of working at Dental Supply, Wilson began to embezzle money from the company. Her scheme involved indorsing the checks made payable to Dental Supply with the rubber stamp and drawing cash on them instead of making a deposit. The bank cashed these checks without requiring any further indorsement. Is the bank liable? *Palmer & Ray Dental Supply of Abilene, Inc, v.*

First National Bank of Abilene, 477 S.W.2d 954, **Web** 1972 Tex. App. Lexis 2071 (Court of Civil Appeals of Texas)

20.13 Order or Bearer Paper: Samuel C. Mazilly wrote a personal check that was drawn on Calcasieu-Marine National Bank of Lake Charles, Inc. (CMN Bank). The check was made payable to the order of Lee St. Mary and was delivered to him. St. Mary indorsed the check in blank and delivered it to Leland H. Coltharp, Sr., in payment for some livestock. Coltharp accepted the check and took it to the City Savings Bank & Trust Company (City Savings) to deposit it. He indorsed the check as follows: "Pay to the order of City Savings Bank & Trust Company, DeRidder, Louisiana." City Savings accepted the check and forwarded it to CMN Bank for payment. The check never arrived at CMN Bank. Some unknown person stole the check while it was in transit and presented it directly to CMN Bank for payment. The teller at CMN Bank cashed the check without indorsement of the person who presented it. At the time CMN Bank accepted the check, was it order or bearer paper? *Caltharp v. Calcasieu-Marine National Bank of Lake Charles, Inc.*, 199 So.2d 568, **Web** 1967 La. App. Lexis 5203 (Court of Appeal of Louisiana)

20.14 Taking for Value: Betty Ellis and her then husband W. G. Ellis executed and delivered to the Standard Finance Company (Standard) a promissory note in the amount of $2,800. After receiving the note, Standard issued a check to the couple for $2,800. The check was made payable to "W. G. Ellis and Betty Ellis." The check was cashed after both parties indorsed it. Shortly thereafter, the Ellises were divorced. Mrs. Ellis claims that (1) she never saw or used the money and (2) Standard understood that all the money went to her ex-husband. W. G. Ellis was declared bankrupt. When the note became due four years later, Betty Ellis refused to pay it. Standard sued her, seeking payment as a holder in due course. She claimed that Standard is not a holder in due course in regard to her because she never received consideration for the note and, therefore, Standard did not take the note for value. Who wins? *Standard Finance Company, Ltd. v. Ellis*, 3 Haw. App. 614, 657 P.2d 1056, **Web** 1983 Haw. App. Lexis 83 (Intermediate Court of Appeals of Hawaii)

Ethics Issues

20.15 Ethics: Mullins Enterprises, Inc. (Mullins), was a business operating in the state of Kentucky. To raise capital, Mullins obtained loans from Corbin Deposit Bank & Trust Company (Corbin). During the course of four years, Corbin made eight loans to Mullins. Mullins executed a promissory note setting out the amount of the debt, the dates and times of installment payments, and the date of final payment and delivered it to the bank each time a loan was made. The notes were signed by an officer of Mullins. Several years later, a dispute arose between Mullins and Corbin as to the proper interpretation of the language contained in the notes. The bank contended that the notes were demand notes. Mullins claimed that the notes were time instruments. Did Corbin or Mullins act unethically in this case? Or was this just a legal dispute? Who wins? *Corbin Deposit Bank & Trust Co. v. Mullins Enterprises, Inc.*, 641 S.W.2d 760, **Web** 1982 Ky. App. Lexis 264 (Court of Appeals of Kentucky)

20.16 Ethics: Mike J. Rogers, owner of Arkansas Parts and Equipment Company (Arkansas Parts), invited Paul Mollenhour to be an officer of the business. Rogers wanted Mollenhour to join the business because his strong financial position would allow Rogers to more easily secure operating financing. With Mollenhour's assistance, Arkansas Parts secured financing. Arkansas Parts executed a revolving credit note with State First National Bank of Texarkana (State First) in the amount of $150,000. The note was signed as follows:

/s/Mike Rogers

Mike Rogers, Individually

/s/Dave Mollenhour, V. Pres.

Dave Mollenhour, Individually

EQUIPMENT CO., INC.

by: /s/Mike Rogers

Mike Rogers, President

by: /s/Dave Mollenhour, V. Pres.

Dave Mollenhour, Vice President and Secretary

The note stipulated that the parties were jointly and severally obligated to State First. After Arkansas Parts defaulted on the note, State First sued Arkansas Parts and Rogers and Mollenhour, individually. Mollenhour claimed that he is not liable because his signature indicated his representative capacity. Who wins? Did Mollenhour act ethically in this case? *Mollenhour v. State First National Bank of Texarkana*, 27 Ark. App. 176, 769 S.W.2d 28, **Web** 1989 Ark. App. Lexis 197 (Court of Appeals of Arkansas)

20.17 Ethics Murray Walter, Inc. (Walter, Inc.), was the general contractor for the construction of a waste treatment plant in New Hampshire. Walter, Inc., contracted with H. Johnson Electric, Inc. (Johnson Electric), to install the electrical system in the treatment plant. Johnson Electric purchased its supplies for the project from General Electric Supply (G.E. Supply). Walter, Inc., issued a check payable to "Johnson Electric and G.E. Supply" in the amount of $54,900, drawn on its account at Marine Midland Bank (Marine Midland). Walter, Inc., made the check payable to both the subcontractor and its material supplier, to be certain that the supplier was paid by Johnson Electric. Despite this precautionary measure, Johnson Electric negotiated the check without G.E. Supply's indorsement, and the check was paid by Marine Midland. Johnson Electric never paid G.E. Supply. G.E. Supply then demanded payment from Walter, Inc. When Walter, Inc., learned that Marine Midland had paid the check without G.E. Supply's indorsement, it demanded to be reimbursed. When Marine Midland refused, Walter, Inc., sued Marine Midland to recover for the check. Was Johnson Electric's indorsement sufficient to legally negotiate the check to Marine Midland Bank? Did any party act unethically in this case? *Murray Walter, Inc. v. Marine Midland Bank*, 103 A.D.2d 466, 480 N.Y.S.2d 631, **Web** 1984 N.Y. App. Div. Lexis 19962 (Supreme Court of New York)

IRAC Writing Assignment

Read **Case A-20** in Appendix A [*Federal Deposit Insurance Corporation v. Woodside Construction, Inc.*]. Use the IRAC method to prepare a written analysis of the case.

Holder in Due Course and Liability of Parties

> **"***If one wants to know the real value of money, he needs but to borrow some from his friends.***"**
>
> —CONFUCIUS
> Analects (c. 500 B.C.)

CHAPTER OBJECTIVES

After studying this chapter, you should be able to:

1. Describe the signature liability of makers, drawees, drawers, acceptors, and accommodation parties.
2. List the transfer and presentment warranties and describe the liability of parties for breaching them.
3. Define *holder in due course* and identify universal defenses that can be asserted against a holder in due course.
4. Describe the Federal Trade Commission rule that prohibits the holder in due course rule in consumer transactions.
5. Describe how parties are discharged from liability on negotiable instruments.

CHAPTER CONTENTS

- Introduction to Holder in Due Course and Liability of Parties
- Holder in Due Course (HDC)
- Requirements for HDC Status
- Signature Liability
- Forged Indorsement
- Warranty Liability

- Defenses
- Discharge
- Chapter Summary
- Test Review Terms and Concepts
- Case Problems
- Ethics Issues
- IRAC Writing Assignment

Introduction to Holder in Due Course and Liability of Parties

Recall that the primary purpose of commercial paper is to act as a substitute for money. For this to occur, the holder of a negotiable instrument must qualify as a *holder in due course (HDC)*. Commercial paper held by an HDC is virtually as good as money because HDCs take an instrument free of all claims and most defenses that can be asserted by other parties. Several defenses, called *universal defenses*, can be raised against the payment of an instrument to the HDC. This chapter discusses the rules of holders in due course.

If payment is not made on a negotiable instrument when it is due, the holder can use the court system to enforce the instrument. Various parties, including both signers and non-signers, may be liable on it. Some parties are primarily liable on an instrument, while others are secondarily liable. Accommodation parties (i.e., guarantors) can also be held liable. This chapter discusses the liability of parties to pay a negotiable instrument and the discharge of liability on a negotiable instrument.

Islamic Mosque, Uzbekistan

Negotiable instruments are used as payments for international trade among businesses from different countries.

Holder in Due Course (HDC)

Two of the most important concepts of the law of negotiable instruments are those of *holder* and *holder in due course*. A **holder** is a person in possession of an instrument that is payable to bearer or an identified person who is in possession of an instrument payable to that person [UCC 1-201(20)]. The holder of a negotiable instrument has the same rights as an assignee of an ordinary nonnegotiable contract. That is, the holder is subject to all the claims and defenses that can be asserted against the transferor.

The concept of holder in due course is unique to the area of negotiable instruments. A **holder in due course (HDC)** is a holder who takes an instrument for value, in good faith, and without notice that it is defective or overdue. An HDC takes a negotiable instrument free of all claims and most defenses that can be asserted against the transferor of the instrument. Only *universal defenses*—and not *personal defenses*—may be asserted against an HDC. (Defenses are discussed later in this chapter). Thus, an HDC can acquire greater rights than a transferor.

Example John purchases an automobile from Shannen. At the time of sale, Shannen tells John that the car has had only one previous owner and has been driven only 20,000 miles. John, relying on these statements, purchases the car. He pays 10 percent down and signs a promissory note to pay the remainder of the purchase price, with interest, in 12 equal monthly installments. Shannen transfers the note to Patricia. Then John discovers that the car has actually had four previous owners and has been driven 100,000 miles. If Patricia were a holder (but not an HDC) of the note, John could assert Shannen's fraudulent representations against enforcement of the note by Patricia. John could rescind the note and refuse to pay Patricia. Patricia's only recourse would be against Shannen.

If Patricia qualified as an HDC, however, the result would be different. John could not assert Shannen's fraudulent conduct against enforcement of the note by Patricia because this type of fraud is a personal defense that cannot be raised against an HDC. Therefore, Patricia could enforce the note against John. John's only recourse would be against Shannen, if she could be found.

Requirements for HDC Status

To qualify as an HDC, a transferee must meet the requirements established by the Uniform Commercial Code (UCC): The person must be the *holder* of a negotiable instrument that was taken (1) for value; (2) in good faith; (3) without notice that it is overdue, dishonored, or encumbered in any way; and (4) bearing no apparent evidence of forgery, alterations, or irregularity [UCC 3-302]. These requirements are discussed in the paragraphs that follow. Exhibit 21.1 illustrates the HDC doctrine.

Taking for Value

Under the UCC **taking for value requirement**, the holder must have *given value* for the negotiable instrument in order to qualify as an HDC [UCC 3-302(a)(2)(i)].

Example Suppose Ted draws a check "payable to the order of Mary Smith" and delivers the check to Mary. Mary indorses it and gives it as a gift to her daughter. Mary's daughter cannot qualify as an HDC because she has not given value for it. The purchaser or a limited interest in a negotiable instrument is an HDC only to the extent of the interest purchased.

Under the UCC, value has been given if the holder [UCC 3-303]:

1. Performs the agreed-upon promise.
2. Acquires a security interest in or lien on the instrument.
3. Takes the instrument in payment of or as security for an antecedent claim.
4. Gives a negotiable instrument as payment.
5. Gives an irrevocable obligation as payment.

If a person promises to perform but has not yet done so, no value has been given, and he or she is not an HDC.

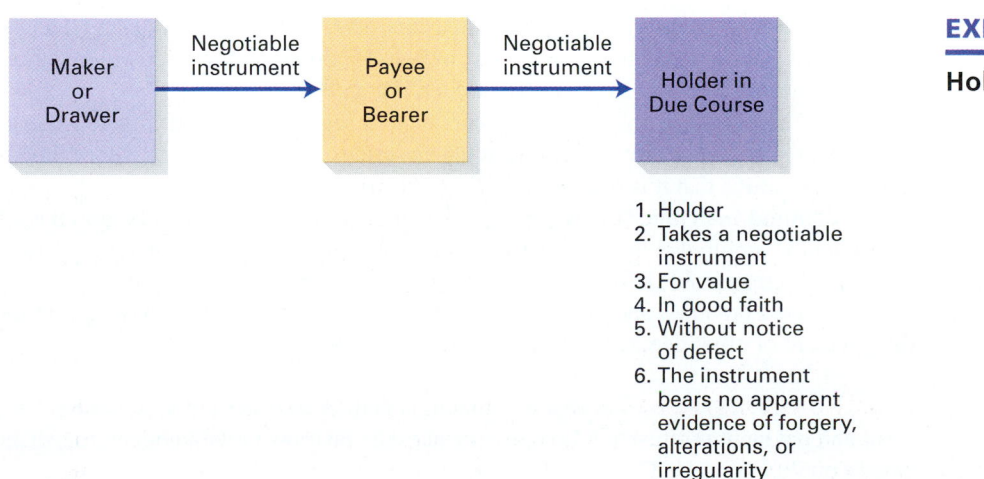

EXHIBIT 21.1

Holder in Due Course

Example Karen executes a note payable to Fred for $3,000 for goods she had purchased from him. Fred transfers the note to Amy for her promise to pay the note in 90 days. Before Amy pays the note, Karen discovers that the goods she purchased from Fred are defective. Karen can raise this defect against enforcement of the note by Amy because no value has yet been given for the note. If Amy had already paid for the note, she would qualify as an HDC, and Karen could not raise the issue of defect against enforcement of the note by Amy.

Taking in Good Faith

Under the UCC **taking in good faith requirement**, a holder must *take* an instrument in *good faith* to qualify as an HDC [UCC 3-302(a)(2)(ii)]. *Good faith* means honesty in fact in the conduct or transaction concerned [UCC 1-201(19)]. Honesty in fact is a subjective test that examines the holder's actual belief. A holder's subjective belief can be inferred from the circumstances.

Example If a holder acquires an instrument from a stranger under suspicious circumstances and at a deep discount, it could be inferred that the holder did not take the instrument in good faith. A naïve person who acquired the same instrument at the same discount, however, may be found to have acted in good faith and thereby qualify as an HDC. Each case must be reviewed individually.

Note that the good faith test applies only to the holder. It does not apply to the transferor of the instrument.

Example Suppose a thief steals a negotiable instrument and transfers it to Harry. Harry does not know that the instrument is stolen. Harry meets the good faith test and qualifies as an HDC.

Taking Without Notice of Defect

Under the UCC **taking without notice of defect requirement**, a person cannot qualify as an HDC if he or she has notice that the instrument is defective in any of the following ways [UCC 3-302(a)(2)]:

- It is overdue.
- It has been dishonored.
- It contains an unauthorized signature or has been altered.
- There is a claim to it by another person.
- There is a defense against it.

OVERDUE INSTRUMENTS If a **time instrument** is not paid on its expressed due date, it becomes overdue the next day. When an instrument is not paid when due, there is some defect to its payment.

Example Suppose a promissory note is due June 15, 2009. To qualify as an HDC, a purchaser must acquire the note by 11:59 P.M. on June 15, 2009. A purchaser who acquires the note on June 16, 2009, or later is only a holder, not an HDC.

Often, a debt is payable in installments or in a series of notes. If a maker misses an installment payment or fails to pay one note in a series of notes, the purchaser of the instruments is on notice that it is overdue [UCC 3-304(b)].

A **demand instrument** is payable on demand. A purchaser cannot be an HDC if the instrument is acquired either (1) after demand or (2) at an unreasonable length of time after its issue. A "reasonable time" for presenting a check for payment is presumed to be 90 days. Business practices and the circumstances of the case determine a reasonable time for the payment of other demand instruments [UCC 3-304(a)].

DISHONORED INSTRUMENTS An instrument is **dishonored** when it is presented for payment and payment is refused. A holder who takes the instrument with notice of its dishonor cannot qualify as an HDC.

Example A person who takes a check that has been marked by the payer bank "payment refused—not sufficient funds" cannot qualify as an HDC.

RED LIGHT DOCTRINE A holder cannot qualify as an HDC if he or she has notice that an instrument contains an unauthorized signature or has been altered or that there is any adverse claim against or defense to its payment. This rule is commonly referred to as the **red light doctrine**.

Notice of a defect is given when the holder (1) has actual knowledge of the defect, (2) has received a notice or notification of the defect, or (3) has reason to know from the facts and circumstances that the defect exists [UCC 1-201(25)]. The filing of a public notice does not of itself constitute notice unless the person actually reads the public notice [UCC 3-302(b)].

No Evidence of Forgery, Alteration, or Irregularity

The UCC has a **no evidence of forgery, alteration, or irregularity requirement**. Under this rule, a holder does not qualify as an HDC if at the time the instrument was issued or negotiated to the holder, it bore apparent evidence of forgery or alteration or was otherwise so irregular or incomplete as to call into question its authenticity [UCC 3-302(a)(1)].

Clever and undetectable forgeries and alterations are not classified as obvious irregularities. Determining whether a forgery or an alteration is apparent and whether the instrument is so irregular or incomplete that its authenticity should be questioned are issues of fact that must be decided on a case-by-case basis.

Payee as an HDC

Payees generally do not meet the requirements for being HDCs because they know about any claims or defenses against the instrument. In a few situations, however, a payee who does not have such knowledge would qualify as an HDC.

Example Suppose Kate purchases an automobile from Jake for $5,000. Jake owes Sherry Smith $5,000 from another transaction. Jake has Kate make out the $5,000 check for the automobile "payable to the order of Sherry Smith." Jake gives the check to Sherry. The car Jake sold to Kate is defective, and she wants to rescind the purchase. Sherry (payee), who did not have notice of the defect in the car, is an HDC. As such, Sherry can enforce the check against Kate. Kate's only recourse is to recover from Jake.

CONTEMPORARY ENVIRONMENT

Shelter Principle

A holder who does not qualify as a holder in due course in his or her own right becomes a holder in due course if he or she acquires the instrument through a holder in due course. This is called the **shelter principle**.

Example Jason buys a used car from Debbie. He pays 10 percent down and signs a negotiable promissory note promising to pay Debbie the remainder of the purchase price, with interest, in 36 equal monthly installments. At the time of sale, Debbie materially misrepresented the mileage of the automobile. Later, Debbie negotiates the note to Eric, who has no notice of the misrepresentation. Eric, an HDC, negotiates the note to Jaime. Assume that Jaime does not qualify as an HDC in her own right. She becomes an HDC, however, because she acquired the note through an HDC (Eric). Jaime can enforce the note against Jason.

To qualify as an HDC under the shelter principle, the following rules apply:

- The holder does not have to qualify as an HDC in his or her own right.

- The holder must acquire the instrument from an HDC or be able to trace his or her title back to an HDC.

- The holder must not have been a party to a fraud or an illegality affecting the instrument.

- The holder cannot have notice of a defense or claim against the payment of the instrument.

Signature Liability

A person cannot be held contractually liable on a negotiable instrument unless his or her signature appears on it [UCC 3-401(a)]. Therefore, this type of liability is often referred to as **signature liability**, or **contract liability**. A signature on a negotiable instrument identifies who is obligated to pay it. If it is unclear who the signer is, parol evidence can identify the signer. This liability does not attach to bearer paper because no indorsement is needed.

Signers of instruments sign in many different capacities, including as makers of notes and certificates of deposit, drawers of drafts and checks, drawees who certify or accept checks and drafts, indorsers who indorse instruments, agents who sign on behalf of others, and accommodation parties. The location of the signature on an instrument generally determines the signer's capacity. A signature in the lower-right corner of a check indicates that the signer is the drawer of the check. A signature in the lower-right corner of a promissory note indicates that the signer is the maker of the note. The signature of the drawee named in a draft on the face of the draft or another location on the draft indicates that the signer is an acceptor of the draft.

Most indorsements appear on the back or reverse side of an instrument. Unless the instrument clearly indicates that such a signature is made in some other capacity, it is presumed to be that of the indorser.

Every party that signs a negotiable instrument (except qualified indorsers and agents that properly sign the instrument) is either primarily or secondarily liable on the instrument. The following discussion outlines the particular liability of signers.

Signature Defined

The **signature** on a negotiable instrument can be any name, word, or mark used in lieu of a written signature [UCC 3-401(b)]. In other words, a signature is any symbol that is (1) handwritten, typed, printed, stamped, or made in almost any other manner and (2) executed or adopted by a party to authenticate a writing [UCC 1-201(39)]. This rule permits trade names and other assumed names to be used as signatures on negotiable instruments.

The unauthorized signature of a person on an instrument is ineffective as that person's signature. It is effective as the signature of the unauthorized signer in favor of an HDC, however. A person who forges a signature on a check may be held liable to an HDC. An unauthorized signature may be ratified [UCC 3-403(a)].

Primary Liability

Makers of promissory notes and certificates of deposit have **primary liability** for the instruments. Upon signing a promissory note, the maker unconditionally promises to pay the amount stipulated in the note when it is due. A maker is absolutely liable to pay the instrument, subject only to certain universal defenses. The holder need not take any action to give rise to this obligation. Generally, the maker is obligated to pay a note according to its original terms. If the note was incomplete when it was issued, the maker is obligated to pay the note as completed, as long as he or she authorized the terms as they were filled in [UCC 3-412].

A draft or a check is an order from a drawer to pay the instrument to a payee (or other holder) according to its terms. No party is primarily liable when the draft or check is issued because such instruments are merely orders to pay. Thus, a drawee who refuses to pay a draft or a check is not liable to the payee or holder. If there has been a wrongful dishonor of the instrument, the drawee may be liable to the drawer for certain damages.

On occasion, a drawee is requested to accept a draft or check. Acceptance of a draft occurs when the drawee writes the word *accepted* across the face of the draft. The acceptor— that is, the drawee—is primarily liable on the instrument. A check, which is a special form of draft, is accepted when it is certified by a bank. The bank's certification discharges the drawer and all prior indorsers from liability on the check. Note that the bank may choose to refuse to certify the check without liability. The issuer of a cashier's check is also primarily liable on the instrument [UCC 3-411].

In the following case, the court held that a co-maker was primarily liable on a promissory note.

CASE 21.1
Signature Liability

Grand Island Production Credit Assn. v. Humphrey

388 N.W.2d 807, **Web** 1986 Neb. Lexis 1185
Supreme Court of Nebraska

> ❝*Mrs. Humphrey admits that she signed the promissory note and the supplemental agreement. Consequently, as a co-maker of the note, she is jointly and severally liable for the obligations of the note.*❞

— Judge Krivosha

Facts

The Grand Island Production Credit Association (Grand Island) is a federally chartered credit union. Carl M. and Beulah C. Humphrey, husband and wife, entered into a loan arrangement with Grand Island for a $50,000 line of credit. Mr. and Mrs. Humphrey signed a line of credit promissory note that provided, in part, "As long as the Borrower is not in default, the Association will lend to the Borrower, and the Borrower may borrow and repay and reborrow at any time from date of said 'Line of Credit' Promissory Note in accordance with the terms thereof and prior to maturity thereof, up to an aggregate maximum amount of principal at any one time outstanding of $50,000."

Mr. Humphrey borrowed money against the line of credit to purchase cattle. Two months later, Mrs. Humphrey went to Grand Island's office and told the loan officer that she had left Mr. Humphrey and filed for a divorce. She told the loan officer not to advance any more money to Mr. Humphrey for cattle purchases. When the Humphreys failed to pay the outstanding balance on the line of credit, Grand Island sued Mr. and Mrs. Humphrey to recover the unpaid balance of $13,936.71. A default judgment was entered against Mr. Humphrey. The district court held Mrs. Humphrey not liable for the full outstanding balance. Grand Island appealed.

Issue

Was Mrs. Humphrey a co-maker of the line of credit promissory note and, therefore, primarily liable for the outstanding principal balance of the note, plus interest?

Language of the Court

Under the provisions of Neb. UCC § 3-413(1), the maker of a note engages that he or she will pay the instrument according to its tenor at the time of his or her engagement. Mrs. Humphrey admits that she signed the promissory note and the supplemental agreement. Consequently, as a co-maker of the note, she is jointly and severally liable for the obligations of the note. If Mrs. Humphrey was to be relieved of this obligation, it was a matter that she needed to arrange and take up with her husband in the divorce action. No such arrangement could, however, be binding upon Grand Island, which entered into this transaction in reliance upon the promise of both Mr. Humphrey and Mrs. Humphrey that they would be liable and would pay the amounts so advanced. The fact of the pending divorce was irrelevant.

Decision

The state supreme court held that Mrs. Humphrey was a co-maker on the line of credit promissory note and was therefore primarily liable to Grand Island in the amount of $13,936.71 plus interest. The supreme court reversed the district court's decision.

Law & Ethics Questions

1. Should family problems, such as the separation and divorce action in this case, take precedence over the commercial law rules of the UCC? Why or why not?

2. **ETHICS** Was it ethical for Mrs. Humphrey to deny liability on the promissory note in this case?

3. What would have been the economic effects if the district court's decision had been upheld in this case?

Web Exercises

1. **WEB** For the complete opinion of this case, go to *www.prenhall.com/cheesemancases*.

2. **WEB** Visit the website of the supreme court of Nebraska, at *www.supremecourt.ne.gov*.

3. **WEB** Use *www.google.com* to find an article that discusses the liability of a co-maker on a promissory note. Read it.

Secondary Liability

Under the UCC's *indorsers' liability* rules, drawers of checks and drafts and unqualified indorsers of negotiable instruments have **secondary liability** on the instruments. This liability is similar to that of a guarantor of a simple contract. It arises when the party primarily liable on the instrument defaults and fails to pay the instrument when due.

If an unaccepted draft or check is dishonored by the drawee or acceptor, the drawer is obliged to pay it according to its terms, either when it is issued or, if incomplete when issued, when it is properly completed [UCC 3-414(a)].

Example Elliot draws a check on City Bank "payable to the order of Phyllis Jones." When Phyllis presents the check for payment, City Bank refuses to pay it. Phyllis can collect the amount of the check from Elliot because Elliot—the drawer—is secondarily liable on the check when it is dishonored.

UNQUALIFIED INDORSERS **Unqualified indorsers** have secondary liability on negotiable instruments. In other words, they must pay any dishonored instrument to the holder or to any subsequent indorser according to its terms, when issued or properly completed. Unless otherwise agreed, indorsers are liable to each other in the order in which they indorsed the instrument [UCC 3-415(a)].

Example Dara borrows $10,000 from Todd and signs a promissory note promising to pay Todd this amount plus interest in one year. Todd indorses the note and negotiates it to Frank. Frank indorses the note and negotiates it to Linda. Dara refuses to pay the note when it is presented for payment by Linda. Because Frank became secondarily liable on the note when he indorsed it to Linda, he must pay the note to her. He can then require Todd to pay the note because Todd (as payee) became secondarily liable on the note when he indorsed it to Frank. Todd can then enforce the note against Dara. Linda could have skipped over Frank and required the payee, Todd, to pay the note. In this instance, Frank would have been relieved of any further liability because he indorsed the instrument after the payee.

QUALIFIED INDORSERS **Qualified indorsers** (i.e., indorsers who indorse instruments "without recourse" or similar language that disclaims liability) are not secondarily liable on an instrument because they have expressly disclaimed liability [UCC 3-415(b)]. The drawer can disclaim all liability on a draft (but not a check) by drawing the instrument "without recourse." In this instance, the drawer becomes a qualified drawer [UCC 3-414(e)]. Many payees, however, will not accept a draft or check that has been drawn without recourse.

REQUIREMENTS FOR IMPOSING SECONDARY LIABILITY A party is secondarily liable on a negotiable instrument only if the following requirements are met:

1. *The instrument is properly presented for payment.* **Presentment** is a demand for acceptance or payment of an instrument made upon the maker, acceptor, drawee, or other payer by or on behalf of the holder. Presentment may be made by any commercially reasonable means, including oral, written, or electronic communication. Presentment is effective when it is received by the person to whom presentment is made [UCC 3-501].
2. *The instrument is dishonored.* An instrument is *dishonored* when acceptance or payment of the instrument is refused or cannot be obtained from the party required to accept or pay the instrument within the prescribed time after presentment is duly made [UCC 3-502].
3. *Notice of the dishonor is timely given to the person to be held secondarily liable on the instrument.* A secondarily liable party cannot be compelled to accept or pay an instrument unless proper **notice of dishonor** has been given. Notice may be given by any commercially reasonable means. The notice must reasonably identify the instrument and indicate that it has been dishonored. Return of an instrument given to a bank for collection is sufficient notice of dishonor. Banks must give notice of dishonor before midnight of the next banking day following the day that presentment is made. Others must give notice of dishonor within 30 days following the day on which the person receives notice of dishonor [UCC 3-503].

CONTEMPORARY ENVIRONMENT
Accommodation Party

The party who signs an instrument for the purpose of lending his or her name (and credit) to another party to the instrument is the **accommodation party**. The accommodation party, who may sign an instrument as maker, drawer, acceptor, or indorser, is obliged to *pay* the instrument in the capacity in which he or she signs [UCC 3-419(a) and 3-419(b)]. An accommodation party who pays an instrument can recover reimbursement from the accommodated party and enforce the instrument against him or her [UCC 3-419(e)].

There are two types of liability of an accommodation party:

1. **Guarantee of payment.** The accommodation party may sign an instrument guaranteeing either payment or collection. An accommodation party who signs an instrument **guaranteeing payment** is *primarily liable* on the instrument. That is, the debtor can seek payment on the instrument directly from the accommodation maker without first seeking payment from the maker.

   Example Sonny, a college student, wants to purchase an automobile on credit from ABC Motors. He does not have a sufficient income or credit history to justify the extension of credit to him alone. Sonny asks his mother to cosign the note to ABC Motors, which she does. Sonny's mother is an accommodation maker and is primarily liable on the note.

2. **Guarantee of collection.** An accommodation party may sign an instrument **guaranteeing collection** rather than payment of an instrument. In this situation, the accommodation party is only *secondarily liable* on the instrument. To reserve this type of liability, the signature of the accommodation party must be accompanied by words indicating that he or she is guaranteeing collection rather than payment of the obligation.

An accommodation party who guarantees collection is obliged to pay the instrument only if (1) execution of judgment against the other party has been returned unsatisfied, (2) the other party is insolvent or in an insolvency proceeding, (3) the other party cannot be served with process, or (4) it is otherwise apparent that payment cannot be obtained from the other party [UCC 3-419(d)].

CONCEPT SUMMARY

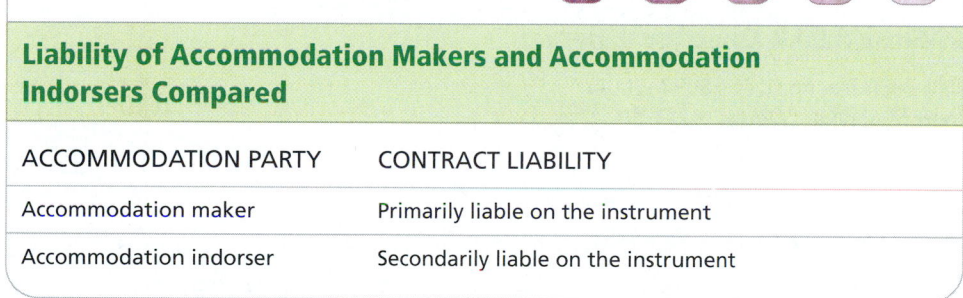

Liability of Accommodation Makers and Accommodation Indorsers Compared

ACCOMMODATION PARTY	CONTRACT LIABILITY
Accommodation maker	Primarily liable on the instrument
Accommodation indorser	Secondarily liable on the instrument

Agent's Signature

A person may either sign a negotiable instrument him- or herself or authorize a representative to sign the instrument on his or her behalf [UCC 3-401(a)]. The representative is the **agent**, and the represented person is the **principal**. The authority of an agent to sign an instrument is established under general agency law. No special form of appointment is necessary.

AUTHORIZED SIGNATURE If an authorized agent signs an instrument with either the principal's name or the agent's own name, the principal is bound as if the signature were made on a simple contract. It does not matter whether the principal is identified in the instrument [UCC 3-402(2)].

Example Suppose Anderson was the agent for Puttkammer. The following signatures on a negotiable instrument would bind Puttkammer on the instrument:

1. Puttkammer, by Anderson, agent
2. Puttkammer
3. Puttkammer, Anderson
4. Anderson

> A trader is trusted upon his character, and visible commerce; that credit enables him to acquire wealth.
>
> Lord Mansfield
> *Worseley v. Demattos (1758)*

An authorized agent's personal liability on an instrument he or she signs on behalf of a principal depends on the information disclosed in the signature. The agent has no liability if the signature shows unambiguously that it is made on behalf of a principal who is identified in the instrument [UCC 3-402(b)(1)].

Example Signature number 1 above ("Puttkammer, by Anderson, agent") satisfies this requirement.

If the authorized agent's signature does not show unambiguously that the signature was made in a representative capacity and the agent cannot prove that the original parties did not intend him or her to be liable, the agent is liable (1) to an HDC who took the instrument without notice that the agent was not intended to be liable on the instrument and (2) to any other person other than an HDC [UCC 3-402(b)(2)].

Example Signature number 2 above ("Puttkammer") shows such a signature. Signatures number 3 above ("Puttkammer, Anderson") and 4 ("Anderson") place the agent at risk of personal liability to an HDC that does not have notice that the agent was not intended to be liable on the instrument. To avoid liability to a non-HDC for these signatures, the agent would have to prove that the third-party non-HDC did not intend to hold the agent liable on the instrument.

There is one exception to these rules: If an agent signs his or her name as the drawer of a check without indicating the agent's representative status and the check is payable from the account of the principal who is identified on the check, the agent is not liable on the check [UCC 3-402(c)].

In the following case, the court had to decide if officers of a corporation were liable on the corporation's negotiable instruments.

CASE **21.2**

Signature of Representative

S. Mansukhlal & Company v. Husein

Web 2004 Tex. App. Lexis 8097 (2004)
Court of Appeals of Texas

> **❝** *If the form of the signature shows unambiguously that the signature is made on behalf of the represented person who is identified in the instrument, the representative is not liable on the instrument.* **❞**
>
> —Judge Anderson

Facts

S. Mansukhlal & Company (Company) sold $200,000 worth of goods on credit to Griffen, Inc. The goods were delivered to Griffen. When Griffen began having financial difficulties and was unable to pay the full value of the goods, upon Company's request, Griffen issued 10 negotiable instruments in favor of Company. The instruments were signed by Muhammad Husein and Sultana Husein, who were officers and directors of Griffen.

Nine of the 10 instruments were dishonored by Griffen's bank for insufficient funds. Company sued Griffen to recover on the instruments, but Griffen filed for bankruptcy. Company then sued Muhammad and Sultana, alleging that they were personally liable on the instruments. Muhammad and Sultana defended, arguing that they were not personally liable on the instruments because they signed the instruments in their representative capacities as officers and directors of Griffen. The trial court held that Muhammad and Sultana signed the Griffen negotiable instruments in their representative capacity and were therefore not personally liable on the instruments. The trial court entered a take-nothing judgment against Company. Company appealed.

The negotiable instruments have the appearance of a standard issued check, in that each is numbered in the upper-right corner, each bears the name of Griffen, Inc., along with its address and telephone number, each contains account numbers listed on the bottom of the document, and each is payable "to the order" of "State Bank of India A/C: S. Mansukhlal & Co." In addition, on the bottom right of each instrument, the following appears: "Griffen, Inc. Per [signatures of Muhammad Husein and Sultana Husein].

Issue

Are Muhammad and Sultana personally liable on Griffen, Inc.'s negotiable instruments?

Language of the Court

Company contends this language is insufficient to prove appellees were authorized on behalf of Griffen, Inc. to sign the instruments and therefore appellees should be held personally liable. Section 3.402 of the Code—which applies to all instruments, including checks and notes—governs the effect of a signature by an authorized representative. The relevant portion of that section includes the following: "(b) If a representative signs the name of the representative to an instrument and the signature is an authorized signature of the represented person, the following rules apply: (1) If the form of the signature shows unambiguously that the signature is made on behalf of the represented person who is identified in the instrument, the representative is not liable on the instrument."

In order for subsection 3.402(b)(1) to apply the appellees' signature must be authorized and the signature must show unambiguously that it is made on behalf of Griffen. Here, the form of the signature contained on the instruments unambiguously shows appellees signed the instruments on behalf of Griffen, Inc. as an authorized agent. Appellant Company argues that because the instruments state "authorized signature" and do not identify appellees by title, authorization is not shown. This distinction, however, is immaterial because the instrument unambiguously refers to appellees' status as an authorized agent of Griffen.

Decision

The court of appeals affirmed the judgment of the trial court which held that Muhammad and Sultana Husein signed the negotiable instruments of Griffen, Inc., in their representative capacities and were therefore not personally liable on the negotiable instruments.

Law & Ethics Questions

1. Why should corporate officers and directors make sure that they sign the corporation's negotiable instruments in their representative capacities? What are the consequences if an officer fails to identify his or her representative capacity on the negotiable instruments he or she signs?

2. **ETHICS** Did S. Mansukhlal & Company act ethically in suing Muhammad and Sultana Husein personally?

3. **ETHICS** Did Muhammad and Sultana Husein act ethically when they signed the negotiable instruments when they knew that Griffen was having financial difficulties?

Web Exercises

1. **WEB** For the complete opinion of this case, go to *www.prenhall.com/cheesemancases*.

2. **WEB** Visit the website of the court of appeals of Texas, Fourteenth District, at *www.14thcoa.courts.state.tx.us*.

3. **WEB** Use *www.google.com* to find an article about negotiable instruments not being paid when due. Read it.

UNAUTHORIZED SIGNATURE An **unauthorized signature** is a signature made by a purported agent without authority from the purported principal. Such a signature arises if (1) a person signs a negotiable instrument on behalf of a person for whom he or she is not an agent or (2) an authorized agent exceeds the scope of his or her authority. An unauthorized signature by a purported agent does not act as the signature of the purported principal. The purported agent is liable to any person who in good faith pays the instrument or takes it for value [UCC 3-403(a)]. The purported principal is liable if he or she ratifies the unauthorized signature [UCC 3-403(a)].

Example A purported agent signs a contract and promissory note to purchase a building for a purported principal. Suppose that the purported principal likes the deal and accepts it. She has ratified the transaction and is liable on the note.

Forged Indorsement

Article 3 of the UCC establishes certain rules for assessing liability when a negotiable instrument has been paid over a **forged indorsement**. With few exceptions, unauthorized indorsements are wholly inoperative as the indorsement of the person whose name is signed [UCC 3-401(a)]. Where an indorsement on an instrument has been forged or is unauthorized, the general rule is that the loss falls on the party who first takes the forged instrument after the forgery.

Example Suppose Andy draws a check payable to the order of Mallory. Leslie steals the check from Mallory, forges Mallory's indorsement, and cashes the check at a liquor store. The liquor store is liable. Andy, the drawer, is not. The liquor store can recover from Leslie, the forger (if she can be found).

There are two exceptions to this rule: where a drawer or maker bears the loss and where an indorsement is forged. The rules governing these circumstances—the imposter rule and the fictitious payee rule—are discussed in the following special business ethics discussions.

ETHICS SPOTLIGHT
Imposter Rule

Impersonating a Payee

For purposes of the imposter rule, an *imposter* is someone who impersonates a payee and induces the maker or drawer to issue an instrument in the payee's name and give the instrument to the imposter. If the imposter forges the indorsement of the named payee, the drawer or maker is liable on the instrument to any person who, in good faith, pays the instrument or takes it for value or for collection [UCC 3-404(a)]. This rule is called the **imposter rule**.

> **Example** Suppose Fred purchases goods by telephone from Cynthia. Fred has never met Cynthia. Beverly goes to Fred and pretends to be Cynthia. Fred draws a check payable to the order of Cynthia and gives the check to Beverly, believing her to be Cynthia. Beverly forges Cynthia's indorsement and cashes the check at a liquor store. Under the imposter rule, Fred is liable and the liquor store is not because Fred was in the best position to have prevented the forged indorsement.

Posing as an Agent

The imposter rule does not apply if the wrongdoer poses as the agent of the drawer or maker.

> **Example** Suppose in the preceding example that Beverly lied to Fred and said that she was Cynthia's agent. Believing this, Fred draws the check payable to the order of Cynthia and gives it to Beverly. Beverly forges Cynthia's indorsement and cashes the check at a liquor store. Here, the store is liable because the imposter rule does not apply. The liquor store may recover from Beverly, if she can be found.

Law & Ethics Questions

1. What does the imposter rule provide? Explain. Who is liable under the imposter rule? What is the public policy underlying the imposter rule?
2. **ETHICS** Does an imposter act ethically?
3. What are the consequences of someone posing as an agent of a drawer or maker? Explain.
4. **ETHICS** Has the person who poses as an agent for the drawer or maker acted ethically?

ETHICS SPOTLIGHT
Fictitious Payee Rule

A drawer or maker is liable on a forged or unauthorized indorsement under the **fictitious payee rule**. This rule applies when a person signing as or on behalf of a drawer or maker intends the named payee to have no interest in the instrument or when the person identified as the payee is a fictitious person [UCC 3-404(b)].

> **Example** Marcia is the treasurer of the Weld Corporation. As treasurer, Marcia makes out and signs the payroll checks for the company. Marcia draws a payroll check payable to the order of her neighbor Harold Green, who does not work for the company. Marcia does not intend Harold to receive this money. She indorses Harold's name on the check and names herself as the indorsee. She cashes the check at a liquor store. Under the fictitious payee rule, Weld Corporation is liable because it was in a better position than the liquor store to have prevented the fraud.

The fictitious payee rule also applies if an agent or employee of the drawer or maker supplies the drawer or maker with the name of a fictitious payee [UCC 3-405(c)].

> **Example** Elizabeth is an accountant for the Baldridge Corporation. She is responsible for drawing up a list of employees who are to receive payroll checks. The treasurer of Baldridge Corporation actually signs the checks. Elizabeth places the name "Annabelle Armstrong" (a fictitious person) on the list. Baldridge Corporation issues a payroll check to this fictitious person. Elizabeth indorses the instrument "Annabelle Armstrong" and names herself as indorsee. She cashes the check at a liquor store. Under the fictitious payee rule, Baldridge Corporation is liable; the liquor store is not.

Law & Ethics Questions

1. What does the fictitious payee rule provide? Explain.
2. What is the public policy underlying the fictitious payee rule?
3. **ETHICS** Does a fictitious payee act ethically?

Warranty Liability

In addition to signature liability, transferors can be held liable for breaching certain **implied warranties** when negotiating instruments. **Warranty liability** is imposed whether or not the transferor signed the instrument. Note that a transferor makes an implied warranty; implied warranties are not made when the negotiable instrument is originally issued.

There are two types of implied warranties: *transfer warranties* and *presentment warranties*. Transfer and presentment warranties shift the risk of loss to the party who was in the best position to prevent the loss. This party is usually the one who dealt face-to-face with the wrongdoer. These implied warranties are discussed in the paragraphs that follow.

Transfer Warranties

Any passage of an instrument other than its issuance and presentment for payment is considered a *transfer*. Any person who transfers a negotiable instrument for consideration makes the following five warranties to the transferee. If the transfer is by indorsement, the transferor also makes these warranties to any subsequent transferee [UCC 3-416(a)]:

1. The transferor has good title to the instrument or is authorized to obtain payment or acceptance on behalf of one who does have good title.
2. All signatures are genuine or authorized.
3. The instrument has not been materially altered.
4. No defenses of any party are good against the transferor.
5. The transferor has no knowledge of any insolvency proceeding against the maker, the acceptor, or the drawer of an unaccepted instrument.

Transfer warranties cannot be disclaimed with respect to checks, but they can be disclaimed with respect to other instruments. An indorsement that states "without recourse" disclaims the transfer warranties [UCC 3-419(c)].

A transferee who took the instrument in good faith may recover damages for breach of transfer warranty from the warrantor equal to the loss suffered. The amount recovered cannot exceed the amount of the instrument plus expenses and interest [UCC 3-416(b)].

Example Jill issues a $1,000 note to Adam. Adam cleverly raises the note to $10,000 and negotiates the note to Nick. Nick indorses the note and negotiates it to Matthew. When Matthew presents the note to Jill for payment, she has to pay only the original amount of the note, $1,000. Matthew can collect the remainder of the note ($9,000) from Nick, based on a breach of the transfer warranty. If Nick, is lucky, he can recover the $9,000 from Adam.

Presentment Warranties

Any person who presents a draft or check for payment or acceptance makes the following **presentment warranties** to a drawee or an acceptor who pays or accepts the instruments in good faith [UCC 3-417(a)]:

1. The presenter has good title to the instrument or is authorized to obtain payment or acceptance of the person who has good title.
2. The instrument has not been materially altered.
3. The presenter has no knowledge that the signature of the maker or drawer is unauthorized.

A drawee who pays an instrument may recover damages for breach of presentment warranty from the warrantor. The amount that can be recovered is limited to the amount paid by the drawee less the amount the drawee received or is entitled to receive from the drawer because of the payment plus expenses and interest [UCC 3-147(b)].

Example Suppose Maureen draws a $1,000 check on City Bank "payable to the order of Paul." Paul cleverly raises the check to $10,000 and indorses and negotiates the check to Neal. Neal presents the check for payment to City Bank. As the presenter of the check, Neal makes the presentment warranties of UCC 3-417(1) to City Bank. City Bank pays the check as altered ($10,000) and debits Maureen's account. When Maureen discovers the alteration, she demands that the bank recredit her account, which the bank does. City Bank can recover against the presenter (Neal), based on breach of the presentment warranty that the instrument was not altered when it was presented. Neal can recover against the wrongdoer (Paul), based on breach of the transfer warranty that the instrument was not altered.

Defenses

The creation of negotiable instruments may give rise to defenses against their payment. Many of these defenses arise from the underlying transactions. There are two general types of defenses: universal defenses and personal defense. An HDC (or a holder through an HDC) takes an instrument free from personal defenses but not universal defenses. Personal and universal defenses can be raised against a normal holder of a negotiable instrument. These types of defenses are discussed in the paragraphs that follow.

Universal Defenses

Universal defenses (also called **real defenses**) can be raised against both holders and HDCs [UCC 3-305(b)]. If a universal defense is proven, the holder or HDC cannot recover on the instrument. Universal defenses are discussed in the following paragraphs.

MINORITY Infancy, or **minority**, is a universal defense to a negotiable instrument to the extent that it is a defense to a simple contract [UCC 3-305(a)(1)(i)]. In most states, a minor who does not misrepresent his or her age can disaffirm contracts, including negotiable instruments. Usually, minors must pay the reasonable value of necessaries of life.

EXTREME DURESS **Extreme duress** is a universal defense against the enforcement of a negotiable instrument by a holder or an HDC [UCC 3-305(a)(1)(ii)]. Extreme duress usually requires some form of force or violence (e.g., a promissory note signed at gunpoint). Ordinary duress is a personal defense (discussed later in this chapter).

MENTAL INCAPACITY Adjudicated **mental incompetence** is a universal defense that can be raised against holders and HDCs [UCC 3-305(a)(1)(ii)]. A person adjudicated mentally incompetent cannot issue a negotiable instrument; the instrument is void from is inception. Nonadjudicated mental incompetence, which is usually only a personal defense, is discussed later in this chapter.

ILLEGALITY If an instrument arises out of an illegal transaction, the **illegality** is a universal defense if the law declares the instrument void [UCC 3-305(a)(1)(ii)].

Example Assume that a state's law declares gambling to be illegal and gambling contracts to be void. Gordon wins $1,000 from Jerry in an illegal poker game. He signs a promissory note promising to pay Gordon this amount plus interest in 30 days. Gordon negotiates this note to Dawn, an HDC. When Dawn presents the note to Jerry for payment, Jerry can raise the universal defense of illegality against the enforcement of the note. Dawn's recourse is against Gordon. If the law makes an illegal contract voidable instead of void, it is only a personal defense. (This situation is discussed later in this chapter.)

DISCHARGE IN BANKRUPTCY Bankruptcy law is intended to relieve debtors of burdensome debts, including obligations to pay negotiable instruments. Thus, **discharge in bankruptcy** is a universal defense against the enforcement of a negotiable instrument by a holder or an HDC [UCC 3-305(a)(1)(iv)].

Example Suppose Hunt borrows $10,000 from Amy and signs a note promising to pay Amy this amount plus interest in one year. Amy negotiates the note to Richard, an HDC. Before the note is due, Hunt declares bankruptcy and receives a discharge of his unpaid debts. Richard cannot thereafter enforce the note against Hunt, but he can recover against Amy.

FRAUD IN THE INCEPTION **Fraud in the inception** (also called the **fraud in the factum** or **fraud in the execution**) is a universal defense against the enforcement of a negotiable instrument by a holder or an HDC [UCC 3-305(a)(1)(iii)]. It occurs when a person is deceived into signing a negotiable instrument, thinking that it is something else.

> One cannot help regretting that where money is concerned it is too much the rule to overlook moral obligations.
>
> Malins, V.C.
> *Ellis v. Houston (1878)*

Example Suppose Sam, a door-to-door salesman, convinces Lance, an illiterate consumer, to sign a document purported to be an agreement to use a plasma TV set on a 90-day trial basis. In actuality, the document is a promissory note in which Lance has agreed to pay $5,000 for the plasma TV set. Sam negotiates the note to Stephanie, an HDC. Lance can raise the universal defense of fraud in the inception against the enforcement of the note by Stephanie. Stephanie, in turn, can recover from Sam.

A person is under a duty to use reasonable efforts to ascertain what he or she is signing. The court inquires into a person's age, experience, education, and other factors before allowing fraud in the inception to be asserted as a universal defense to defeat an HDC. Fraud in the inducement (discussed later) is only a personal defense.

FORGERY Another universal defense to the payment of a negotiable instrument is **forgery**. The unauthorized signature of a maker, a drawer, or an indorser is wholly inoperative as that of the person whose name is signed unless that person either ratifies it or is precluded from denying it. In the latter case, a person can be estopped from raising the defense of forgery if his or her negligence substantially contributes to the forgery. A forged signature operates as the signature of the forger. Thus, the forger is liable on the instrument [UCC 3-403(a)].

MATERIAL ALTERATION An instrument that has been fraudulently and materially altered cannot be enforced by an ordinary holder. **Material alteration** consists of adding to any part of a signed instrument, removing any part of a signed instrument, making changes in the number or relations of the parties, or completing an incomplete instrument without the authority to do so.

Under the UCC rule that words control figures, correcting the figure on a check to correspond to the written amount on the check is not a material alteration [UCC 3-118(c)]. If an alteration is not material, the instrument can be enforced by any holder in the original amount for which the drawer wrote the check [UCC 3-407(b)].

Material alteration of a negotiable instrument is only a partial defense against an HDC. Subsequent HDCs can enforce any instrument, including an altered instrument, according to its original terms, if the alteration is not apparent. An obvious change puts the holder on notice of the alteration and disqualifies him or her as an HDC [UCC 3-407(c)].

CONCEPT SUMMARY

Universal Defenses

DEFENSE	EFFECT
Universal defenses:	Universal defenses can be raised against a holder in due course.
1. Minority	A minor who does not misrepresent his or her age can disaffirm negotiable instruments.
2. Extreme duress	If the use of force or violence was used to issue or have issued a negotiable instrument, then it is unenforceable.
3. Mental incapacity	A person adjudicated mentally incompetent cannot issue a negotiable instrument; the instrument is void from is inception.
4. Illegality	If an instrument arises out of an illegal transaction it is unenforceable.
5. Discharge in bankruptcy	Bankruptcy law allow for obligations to pay negotiable instruments to be discharged and therefore unenforceable.
6. Fraud in the inception	If a person is deceived into signing a negotiable instrument, thinking that it is something else, it is unenforceable.
7. Forgery	The unauthorized signature of a maker, a drawer, or an indorser is wholly inoperative as that of the person whose name is signed.
8. Material alteration	An instrument that has been fraudulently and materially altered cannot be enforced by an ordinary holder.

Personal Defenses

Although **personal defenses** cannot be raised against an HDC, they can be raised against enforcement of a negotiable instrument by an ordinary holder. Personal defenses are discussed in the paragraphs that follow.

BREACH OF CONTRACT **Breach of contract** is one of the most common defenses raised by a party to a negotiable instrument. This personal defense is effective only against an ordinary holder.

Example When Brian purchases a used car on credit from Karen, he signs a note promising to pay Karen the $10,000 purchase price plus interest, in 36 equal monthly installments. The sales agreement warrants that the car is in perfect working condition. A month later, the car's engine fails; the cost of repair is $3,000. Brian, the maker of the note, can raise breach of warranty as a defense against enforcement of the note by Karen.

The outcome would be different if Karen negotiated the promissory note to Max (an HDC) immediately after the car was sold to Brian. Max would be an HDC, and Brian could not raise the breach of warranty defense against him. Max could enforce the note against Brian. Brian's only recourse would be to seek recovery for breach of warranty from Karen.

FRAUD IN THE INDUCEMENT **Fraud in the inducement** occurs when a wrongdoer makes a false statement (i.e., misrepresentation) to another person to lead that person to enter into a contract with the wrongdoer. Negotiable instruments often arise out of such transactions. Fraud in the inducement is a personal defense that is not effective against HDCs. It is effective against ordinary holders, however.

Example Morton represents to investors that he will accept funds to drill for oil and that the investors will share in the profits from the oil wells. He plans to use these funds himself, however. Relying on Morton's statements, Mimi draws a $50,000 check payable to him. Morton absconds with the funds. Because Morton is an ordinary holder, Mimi can raise the personal defense of fraud in the inducement and, if she stops payment on the check before Morton receives payment, not pay the check.

Example If Morton had negotiated the check to Tim, an HDC, Tim could enforce the check against Mimi. Because personal defenses are not effective against Tim (an HDC), Mimi's only recourse is to recover against the wrongdoer (Morton), if he can be found.

OTHER PERSONAL DEFENSES The following personal defenses can be raised against enforcement of a negotiable instrument by an ordinary holder:

1. Mental illness that makes a contract voidable instead of void (usually a nonadjudicated mental illness)
2. Illegality of a contract that makes the contract voidable instead of void
3. Ordinary duress or undue influence [UCC 3-305(a)(1)(ii)]
4. Discharge of an instrument by payment or cancellation [UCC 3-602, 3-604]

> The great source of the flourishing state of this kingdom is its trade, and commerce, and paper currency, guarded by proper regulations and restrictions, is the life of commerce.
>
> Justice Ashhurst
> *Jordaine v. Lashbrooke (1798)*

CONCEPT SUMMARY

Personal Defenses

DEFENSE	EFFECT
Personal defenses:	Personal defenses cannot be raised against a holder in due course, only against ordinary holders.
1. Breach of contract	If there is a breach of contract, the negotiable instrument may be deemed unenforceable against an ordinary holder.
2. Fraud in the inducement	Occurs when a wrongdoer makes a false statement to another person to lead that person to enter into a contract with the wrongdoer. Only effective against ordinary holders, however.
3. Mental illness that makes a contract voidable instead of void (usually a nonadjudicated mental illness)	If found to make a contract void then the negotiable instrument is unenforceable.
4. Illegality of a contract that makes the contract voidable instead of void	If a contract is found to be illegal then the negotiable instrument is unenforceable.
5. Ordinary duress or undue influence [UCC 3-305(a)(1)(ii)]	If a person is wrongfully influenced or threatened to enter into a negotiable instrument it is unenforceable.
6. Discharge of an instrument by payment or cancellation	If an instrument is discharged by payment or cancellation it is unenforceable.

LANDMARK LAW
FTC Rule Limits HDC Status

In certain situations, the HDC rule can cause a hardship for the consumer.

Example Greg, a consumer, purchases a stereo on credit from Lou's Stereo. He signs a note promising to pay the purchase price plus interest to Lou's Stereo in 12 equal monthly installments. Lou's Stereo immediately negotiates the note at a discount to City Bank for cash. City Bank is an HDC. The stereo is defective. Greg would like to stop paying on it, but the HDC rule prevents him from asserting any personal defenses against City Bank. Under the UCC, Greg's only recourse is to sue Lou's Stereo. However, this is often an unsatisfactory result because Greg has no leverage against Lou's Stereo, and bringing a court action is expensive and time-consuming.

To correct this harsh result, the Federal Trade Commission (FTC), a federal administrative agency in charge of consumer protection, adopted the **FTC rule**, which eliminates HDC status with regard to negotiable instruments arising out of certain *consumer* credit transactions [16 C.F.R. 433.2 (1987)]. This federal law takes precedence over any state's UCC.

Thus, sellers of goods and services are prevented from separating the consumer's duty to pay the credit and the seller's duty to perform. This subjects the HDC of a consumer credit instrument to *all* the defenses and claims of the consumer.

Example In the prior example, Greg can raise the defect in the stereo as a defense against enforcement of the promissory note by City Bank, an HDC.

The FTC rules applies to consumer credit transactions in which (1) the buyer signs a sales contract that includes a promissory note, (2) the buyer signs an installment sales contract that contains a waiver of defenses clause, and (3) the seller arranges consumer financing with a third-party lender. Note that payment for goods and services with a check is not covered by this rule because it is not a credit transaction.

The FTC rule requires that the following clause be included in bold type in covered consumer credit sales and installment contracts:

Notice. Any holder of this consumer credit contract is subject to all claims and defenses which the debtor could assert against the seller of the goods or services obtained pursuant hereto or with the proceeds hereof. Recovery hereunder by the debtor shall not exceed amounts paid by the debtor hereunder.

A consumer creditor may assert the FTC rule to prevent enforcement of a note that arose from a covered transaction. The FTC can impose monetary fines for violations.

Discharge

The UCC specifies when and how certain parties are **discharged** (relieved) from liability on negotiable instruments. Generally, all parties to a negotiable instrument are discharged from liability if (1) the party primarily liable on the instrument pays it in full to the holder of the instrument or (2) a drawee in good faith pays an unaccepted draft or check in full to the holder. When a party other than a primary obligor (e.g., an indorser) pays a negotiable instrument, that party and all subsequent parties to the instrument are discharged from liability [UCC 3-602].

The holder of a negotiable instrument can discharge the liability of any party to the instrument by **cancellation** [UCC 3-604]. Cancellation can be accomplished by (1) any manner apparent on the face of the instrument or the indorsement (e.g., writing "canceled" on the instrument) or (2) destruction or mutilation of a negotiable instrument with the intent of eliminating the obligation.

Intentionally striking out the signature of an indorser cancels that party's liability on the instrument and the liability of all subsequent indorsers. Prior indorsers are not discharged from liability. The instrument is not canceled if it is destroyed or mutilated by accident or by an unauthorized third party. The holder can bring suit to enforce the destroyed or mutilated instrument.

A party to a negotiable instrument sometimes posts collateral as security for the payment of the obligation. Other parties (e.g., holders, indorsers, accommodation parties) look to the credit standing of the party primarily liable on the instrument, the collateral (if any) that is posted, and the liability of secondary parties for the payment of the instrument when it is due. A holder owes a duty not to impair the rights of others when seeking recourse against the liable parties or the collateral. Thus, a holder who either (1) releases an obligor from liability or (2) surrenders the collateral without the consent of the parties who would benefit thereby discharges those parties from their obligation on the instrument [UCC 3-605(e)]. This discharge is called **impairment of the right of recourse**.

Red Square, Moscow, Russia
Negotiable instruments facilitate international trade.

Chapter Summary

Holder in Due Course, p. 538

1. *Holder.* A holder is a person who is in possession of a negotiable instrument that is drawn, issued, or indorsed to that person or his or her order, or to bearer, or in blank. A holder has the same rights as the assignee of an ordinary contract. A holder is subject to all claims and defenses that can be asserted against the transferor.

2. *Holder in due course (HDC).* An HDC is a holder who takes a negotiable instrument for value, in good faith, and without notice that it is defective or overdue. An HDC takes a negotiable instrument free of all claims and most defenses that can be asserted against the transferor. Thus, an HDC can acquire greater rights than a transferor.

Requirements for HDC Status, p. 539

To qualify as an HDC, a transferee must be a holder and take the negotiable instrument:

1. For value
2. In good faith
3. Without notice that it is overdue, dishonored, or encumbered in any way
4. With no apparent evidence of forgery, alteration, or irregularity

Taking for Value

Value has been given for a negotiable instrument if a holder:

1. Performs the agreed-upon promise.
2. Acquires a security interest in or lien on the instrument.
3. Takes the instrument in payment of or as security for an antecedent claim.
4. Gives a negotiable instrument as payment.
5. Gives an irrevocable obligation as payment.

Taking in Good Faith

A holder must take an instrument in good faith to qualify as an HDC. Good faith means honesty in the conduct or transaction. The holder's subjective belief can be inferred from the circumstances.

Taking Without Notice of Defect

A person cannot qualify as an HDC if he or she has notice that the instrument is defective in any of the following ways:

1. It is overdue.
2. It has been dishonored.
3. It contains an unauthorized signature or has been altered.
4. There is a claim to it by another person.
5. There is a defense against it.

No Evidence of Forgery, Alteration, or Irregularity

A holder cannot become an HDC to an instrument that is apparently forged or altered or is so otherwise irregular or incomplete as to call into question its authenticity.

Payee as an HDC

If a payee who does not know of any claims of defense against an instrument then they qualify as an HDC.

Signature Liability, p. 542

A person cannot be held contractually liable on a negotiable instrument unless his or her signature appears on the instrument. Signature liability is also called *contract liability*. A person can sign an instrument in the capacity of:

1. A maker of notes and certificates of deposit
2. A drawer of drafts and checks
3. A drawee who certifies or accepts checks and drafts
4. An indorser who indorses instruments
5. An agent who signs on behalf of others
6. An accommodation party

Every party that signs a negotiable instrument (except qualified indorsers and agents that properly sign the instrument) is either primarily or secondarily liable on the instrument.

Signature *Defined*

The signature on a negotiable instrument can be any name, word, or mark used in lieu of a written signature. A signature may be (a) handwritten, typed, stamped, or made in almost any other manner and (b) executed or adopted by a party to authenticate a writing.

Primary Liability

Primary liability is absolute liability of certain signers to pay a negotiable instrument, subject to certain universal defenses. The following signers have *primary liability* to pay a negotiable instrument:

1. Makers of promissory notes and certificates of deposit
2. Acceptorsof drafts and checks (e.g., a bank that certifies a check)

Secondary Liability

Secondary liability is liability on a negotiable instrument that is imposed on a party only when the party primarily liable on the instrument defaults and fails to pay the instrument when due.

1. ***Parties who have secondary liability.*** The following signers have secondary liability to pay a negotiable instrument:
   a. Drawers of a draft or check if the draft or check is dishonored by the drawee or acceptor.
   b. Unqualified indorsers if the primary obligor fails to pay the instrument.
2. ***Qualified indorsers.*** Qualified indorsers (i.e., indorsers who indorse instruments "without recourse" or similar language that disclaims liability) are not secondarily liable on the instrument.
3. ***Requirements for imposing secondary liability.*** Parties are secondarily liable on a negotiable instrument only if the following requirements are met:
   a. *The instrument is properly presented for payment.* Presentment is a demand for acceptance or payment of an instrument made upon the maker, acceptor, drawee, or other payer by or on behalf of the holder.
   b. *The instrument is dishonored.* Dishonor occurs when acceptance or payment of an instrument is refused or cannot be obtained from the party required to accept or pay the instrument within the prescribed time after presentment is duly made.
   c. *Notice of dishonor is timely given to the person to be held secondarily liable on the instrument. Notice of dishonor may* be given by any commercially reasonable means.

Accommodation Party

An accommodation occurs when a party signs a negotiable instrument to lend his or her name (and credit) to another party to the instrument. The accommodation party is the party who signs an instrument and lends his or her name (and credit) to another party to the instrument. The accommodated party is the party to whom an accommodation party lends his or her name (and credit) on a negotiable instrument. An accommodation party may sign an instrument guaranteeing either *payment* or *collection*:

1. ***Guarantee of payment.*** In this form of accommodation, the accommodation party *guarantees payment* of a negotiable instrument. The accommodation party is *primarily liable* on the instrument with the accommodated party. For example, an *accommodation maker* is primarily liable on a promissory note he or she signs. The debtor can seek payment from the accommodation maker without first seeking payment from the maker.
2. ***Guarantee of collection.*** In this form of accommodation, the accommodation party *guarantees collection* of a negotiable instrument. The accommodation party is secondarily liable on the instrument. For example, an *accommodation indorser* is secondarily liable on a check he or she indorses. The holder cannot seek payment from the accommodation indorser unless he or she first seeks to recover payment from the primary obligor and is unsuccessful. To reserve this type of liability, the accommodation party's signature must be accompanied by words indicating that he or she is guaranteeing collection rather than payment of the obligation.

Agent's Signature

An agent is a person who has been authorized to sign a negotiable instrument on behalf of another person. A principal is a person who authorizes an agent to sign a negotiable instrument on his or her behalf.

1. ***Authorized signature.*** An authorized signature is an agent's signature on a negotiable instrument that is authorized by the principal.

   a. *Principal's liability.* A principal is liable on a negotiable instrument signed on his or her behalf by an authorized agent if either the name of the principal or the name of the agent (or both) appears on the instrument.

   b. *Agent's liability:*

      i. *Unambiguous signature.* An authorized agent is not personally liable on a negotiable instrument he or she signs on behalf of a principal if the signature shows unambiguously that it is made on behalf of a principal who is identified in the instrument.

      ii. *Ambiguous signature.* An authorized agent is personally liable to the following parties on a negotiable instrument if the signature does not show unambiguously that it is made in a representative capacity or the principal is not identified in the instrument:

         a. To an HDC who took the instrument without notice that the agent was not intended to be liable on the instrument

         b. To any other person other than an HDC unless the agent proves that the original parties did not intend the agent to be liable on the instrument

An agent who signs a check from the account of a principal who is identified on the check without indicating the agent's representative capacity is not personally liable on the check.

  2. *Unauthorized signature.* An unauthorized signature is a signature made by a purported agent on behalf of a purported principal without the purported principal's authority.

   a. *Liability of the purported principal.* An unauthorized signature by a purported agent does not act as the signature of the purported principal. The purported principal is not liable on the instrument.

   b. *Liability of the purported agent.* The purported agent is liable to any person who in good faith pays the instrument or takes it for value.

Forged Indorsement, p. 547

Forged indorsements are wholly inoperative as the indorsement of the person whose name is signed [UCC 3-401(a)]. Where an indorsement on an instrument has been forged or is unauthorized, the general rule is that the loss falls on the party who first takes the forged instrument after the forgery.

Warranty Liability, p. 549

The law implies certain warranties on transferors of negotiable instruments. There are two types of implied warranties: Transfer warranties and presentment warranties.

Transfer Warranties

Transfer means any passage of an instrument other than its issuance and presentment for payment. Any person who transfers a negotiable instrument for consideration makes the following five warranties to the transferee:

  1. The transferor has good title to the instrument or is authorized to obtain payment or acceptance on behalf of one who does have good title.

  2. All signatures are genuine or authorized.

  3. The instrument has not been materially altered.

  4. No defenses of any party are good against the transferor.

  5. The transferor has no knowledge of any insolvency proceeding against the maker, or acceptor, or the drawer of an unaccepted instrument.

A transferee who takes an instrument in good faith may recover damages for *breach of transfer warranty* from the warrantor equal to the loss suffered. The amount cannot exceed the amount of the instrument plus expenses and interest.

Presentment Warranties

Presentment is the demand for acceptance or payment of an instrument made upon the maker, acceptor, drawee, or other party by or on behalf of the holder. Any person who presents a draft or check for payment or acceptance makes the following three warranties to a drawee or an acceptor who in good faith pays or accepts the instrument:

1. The presenter has good title to the instrument or is authorized to obtain payment or acceptance of the person who has good title.
2. The instrument has not been materially altered.
3. The presenter has no knowledge that the signature of the maker or drawer is unauthorized.

A drawee who pays an instrument may recover damages for breach of presentment warranty from the warrantor. The amount that can be recovered is limited to the amount paid by the drawee less the amount the drawee received or is entitled to receive from the drawer because of the payment plus expenses and interest.

Defenses, p. 550

The creation of negotiable instruments may give rise to a defense against payment of the instrument. There are two types of defenses: universal and personal.

Universal Defenses

Universal, or real, defenses are defenses against the enforcement of a negotiable instrument that can be raised against both holders and HDCs. Universal defenses include the following:

1. **Minority.** In most states, minors who do not misrepresent their age can disaffirm contracts, including negotiable instruments.
2. **Extreme duress.** A person who has signed a negotiable instrument under extreme duress (e.g., because of force or violence or threat of force or violence) may raise duress as a defense of the enforcement of the instrument.
3. **Mental incapacity.** An instrument that was signed by a person who has been adjudicated mentally incompetent is void.
4. **Illegality.** If an instrument arises out of an illegal transaction, the illegality is a universal defense if the law declares the instrument void.
5. **Discharge in bankruptcy.** If an obligor's duty to pay a negotiable instrument has been discharged in bankruptcy, that person is relieved of the obligation to pay the instrument.
6. **Fraud in the inception.** Fraud in the inception, also called *fraud in the factum* or *fraud in the execution*, occurs when a person is deceived into signing a negotiable instrument thinking that it is something else. This a universal defense against enforcement of an instrument.
7. **Forgery.** In forgery, the unauthorized signature of a maker, a drawer, or an indorser is wholly inoperative as that of the person whose name is signed. Forgery is a universal defense unless the person whose name has been signed ratifies it or is precluded from raising the defense (e.g., his or her negligence substantially contributed to the forgery).
8. **Material alteration.** Material alteration of a negotiable instrument is a partial defense against an HDC. An HDC can enforce an altered instrument according to its original tenor but not to the raised amount.

Personal Defenses

Personal defenses are defenses against the enforcement of a negotiable instrument that can be raised against holders but cannot be raised against HDCs. Personal defenses include:

1. **Breach of contract.** The breach of contract by one of the original parties at the time of contracting can be raised against the enforcement of an instrument by a holder. This defense is not effective against an HDC, however.
2. **Fraud in the inducement.** This type of fraud occurs when a wrongdoer makes a false representation to another person to lead that person to enter into a contract with the wrongdoer. This type of fraud may be raised as a defense against a holder but not against an HDC.

3. *Other personal defenses.* The following additional personal defenses can be raised against enforcement of a negotiable instrument by an ordinary holder but not against an HDC:
   a. Mental illness that makes the contract voidable instead of void (usually a nonadjudicated mental illness)
   b. Illegality of a contract that makes the contract voidable instead of void
   c. Ordinary duress or undue influence
   d. Discharge of an instrument by payment or cancellation

FTC Rule Limits HDC Status

A consumer credit transaction is a transaction in which a consumer purchases goods or services on credit and signs a negotiable instrument (note) agreeing to pay the remainder of the purchase price. The Federal Trade Commission (FTC) has adopted a rule that eliminates HDC status with regard to negotiable instruments that arise out of certain consumer credit transactions. All defenses and claims that can be raised by the consumer purchaser against holders can also be raised against HDCs. Thus, both personal and universal defenses can be raised against an HDC in this situation.

Discharge, p. 554

Discharge involves actions or events that relieve certain parties from liability on negotiable instruments. The three methods of discharge are:

1. *Payment.* Generally, all parties to an instrument are discharged from liability if (a) the party primarily liable on the instrument pays it in full to the holder or (b) the drawee pays an unaccepted draft or check in full to the holder.
2. *Cancellation.* Cancellation of the instrument discharges the liability of any party to the instrument. Cancellation can be accomplished by (a) any manner apparent on the face of the instrument or the indorsement (e.g., writing "canceled" on the instrument) or (b) destroying or mutilating the instrument with the intent of eliminating the obligation.
3. *Impairment of the right of recourse.* Certain parties (holders, accommodation parties) are discharged from liability on an instrument if the holder (a) releases an obligor from liability or (b) surrenders collateral without the consent of the parties who would benefit by it.

Test Review Terms and Concepts

Case Problems

21.1 Holder in Due Course: National Financial Services (National) issued a check to Patrick J. Doherty for $62,812.36. The check was drawn on National's account at the Bank of New England. The next day, Doherty took the check to his bank, the M & I Marshall & Ilsley Bank (M & I), and properly indorsed it. The bank gave Doherty $1,350 in cash and deposited the remainder of the funds into his checking account at the bank. As soon as the check was deposited, M & I froze these funds to help offset a $90,000 overdraft in Doherty's account. When Doherty learned of this action, he contacted National and asked them to stop payment on the check. Although National agreed to do so, it refused to issue a new check until the original check was returned. In the meantime, M & I forwarded the check for payment to the Bank of New England. The Bank of New England returned the check to M & I, stamped "payment stopped." When M & I received the dishonored check, it sent it to Doherty, who forwarded it to National. National then issued Doherty a new check. M & I sued National to recover on the first check. M & I claims it was a holder in due course and that National could not stop payment on the check. Who wins? *M & I Marshall & Ilsley Bank v. National Financial Services Corporation*, 704 F.Supp. 890, **Web** 1989 U.S. Dist. Lexis. 1233 (United States District Court for the Eastern District of Wisconsin)

21.2 Holder in Due Course: Royal Insurance Company Ltd. (Royal) issued a draft in the amount of $12,000 payable through the Morgan Guaranty Trust Company (Morgan Guaranty). The draft was made payable to Gary E. Terrell in settlement of a claim in an insurance policy for fire damage to premises located at 3031 North 11th Street, Kansas City, Kansas. On May 9, the attorney for Mr. and Mrs. Louis Wexler notified Royal that Terrell's clients had an insurable interest in the damaged property. As a result, Royal immediately stopped payment on the draft. On the same day, the draft was indorsed by Gary E. Terrell and deposited in his account at the UAW-CIO Local #31 Federal Credit Union (Federal). Over the next two days, Terrell withdrew $9,000 from this account. Immediately upon receiving the draft, Federal indorsed it and forwarded it to Morgan Guaranty for payment. The draft was returned to Federal on May 14, with the notation "payment stopped." When Royal refused to pay Federal the amount of the draft, Federal sued. The basis of the suit was whether Federal was a holder in due course. Who wins? *UAW-CIO Local #31 Federal Credit Union v. Royal Insurance Company, Ltd.*, 594 S.W.2d 276, **Web** 1980 Mo. Lexis 446 (Supreme Court of Missouri)

21.3 Principal's Liability: John Smith was the corporate secretary for Carriage House Mobile Homes, Inc. (Carriage House). Smith signed a series of checks totaling $13,900 made payable to Danube Carpet Mills (Danube). The checks were in payment for carpet ordered by Carriage House. Each check was signed in the following manner: "Carriage House Mobile homes, Inc., General Account, By: /s/John Smith." When Danube presented the checks for payment to the drawee bank, the First State Bank of Phil Campbell, Alabama (First State Bank), payment was refused. The reason for the refusal was that the checks were drawn against uncollected funds. The holder of these checks, Southeastern Financial Corporation, sued Smith and Carriage House to recover the $13,900. Who is liable on the checks? *Southeastern Financial Corporation v. Smith*, 397 F.Supp. 649, **Web** 1975 U.S. Dist. Lexis 12624 (United States District Court for the District of Alabama)

21.4 Drawer's Liability: Carlisle Distributing Company, Inc. (Carlisle), owed William Paladino $10,000. To pay this debt, Carlisle delivered a $10,000 check drawn on an Arkansas bank made payable to Paladino. Paladino indorsed the check and delivered it to Wildman Stores, Inc. (Wildman), as security for an $8,000 loan he had received from that company. Seventeen months after receiving the check, Wildman presented it for payment at the bank upon which it had been drawn. The payer bank dishonored the check due to insufficient funds. Wildman informed Carlisle of the dishonor and demanded payment of the $10,000. Carlisle refused Wildman's demand. Wildman sued Carlisle to collect the $10,000. The statute of limitations for enforcing a negotiable instrument in Arkansas is five years. Who wins? *Wildman Stores, Inc. v. Carlisle Distributing Co., Inc.*, 15 Ark. App. 11, 688 S.W.2d 748, **Web** 1985 Ark. App. Lexis 1926 (Court of Appeals of Arkansas)

21.5 Maker's Liability: James Wright met with Jones, the president of The Community Bank (Community Bank), to request a loan of $7,500. Because Wright was already obligated on several existing loans, he was informed that his request would have to be reviewed by the bank's loan committee. Jones suggested that this delay could be avoided if the loan were made to Mrs. Wright. Wright asked his wife to go to the bank and "indorse" a note for him. Mrs. Wright went to the bank and spoke to Jones. Although she claims that Jones told her that she was merely indorsing the note, the language of the note clearly indicated that she would be liable in the case of default. Mrs. Wright signed the instrument in its lower-right corner. Wright did not sign the instrument. The $7,500 was deposited directly into Wright's business account. The Wrights were subsequently separated. Following the separation, Mrs. Wright received notice that she was in default on the note. The notice indicated that she was solely obligated to repay the instrument. Is Mrs. Wright obligated to repay the note? *The Community Bank v. Wright*, 221 Va. 172, 267 S.E.2d 158, **Web** 1980 Va. Lexis 229 (Supreme Court of Virginia)

21.6 Accommodation Party: Dr. Michael P. Cooper and his wife Georgia moved to Oakley, Kansas. Dr. Cooper was a chiropractor and intended to establish a practice in Oakley. In order to obtain funds to purchase equipment and remodel an office, Dr. Cooper approached the Farmers Bank of Oakley (Farmers Bank). Farmers Bank agreed to loan Cooper $5,000 if the bank received some sort of security for the money. Dr. Cooper offered professional equipment, household items, and his automobile as collateral. The president of Farmers Bank decided that these items were not enough to secure the loan completely. When Dr. Cooper learned of the bank's decision, he asked his father, Paul A. Cooper, to cosign the loan. Paul Cooper agreed to do so, and a promissory note was executed to the bank. The note was signed by Michael P. Cooper, Georgia Cooper, and Paul A. Cooper. When the note was in default, the bank sued Paul A. Cooper to recover on the note. Who wins? *Farmers State Bank of Oakley v. Cooper*, 227 Kan. 547, 608 P.2d 929, **Web** 1980 Kan. Lexis 262 (Supreme Court of Kansas)

21.7 Transfer Warranties: David M. Fox was a distributor of tools manufactured and sold by Matco Tools Corporation (Matco). Cox purchased tools from Matco using a credit line that he repaid as the tools were sold. The credit line was secured by Cox's Matco tool inventory. In order to expedite payment on Cox's line of credit, Matco decided to authorize Cox to deposit any customer checks that were made payable to "Matco Tools" or "Matco" into Cox's own account. Matco's controller sent Cox's bank, Pontiac State Bank (Pontiac), a letter stating that Cox was authorized to make such deposits. Several years later, some Matco tools were stolen from Cox's inventory. The Travelers Indemnity Company (Travelers), which insured Cox against such a loss, sent Cox a settlement check in the amount of $24,960. The check was made payable to "David M. Cox and Matco Tool Co." Cox indorsed the check and deposited it in his account at Pontiac. Pontiac forwarded the check through the banking system for payment by the drawee bank. Cox never paid Matco for the destroyed tools. Matco sued Pontiac for accepting the check without the proper indorsements. Is Pontiac liable? *Matco Tools Corporation v. Pontiac State Bank.* 614 F.Supp. 1059, **Web** 1985 U.S. Dist. Lexis 17234 (United States District Court for the Eastern District of Michigan)

21.8 Presentment Warranties: John Waddell Construction Company (Waddell) maintained a checking account at the Longview Bank & Trust Company (Longview Bank).

Waddell drafted a check from this account made payable to two payees, Engineered Metal Works (Metal Works) and E. G. Smith Construction (Smith Construction). The check was sent to Metal Works, which promptly indorsed the check and presented it to the First National Bank of Azle (Bank of Azle) for payment. The Bank of Azle accepted the check with only Metal Works's indorsement and credited Metal Works's account. The Bank of Azle subsequently presented the check to Longview Bank through the Federal Reserve System. Longview Bank accepted and paid the check. When Waddell received the check along with its monthly checking statements from Longview Bank, a company employee noticed the missing indorsement and notified Longview Bank. Longview Bank returned the check to the Bank of Azle, and the Bank of Azle's account was debited the amount of the check at the Federal Reserve. Did the Bank of Azle breach its warranty of good title? *Longview Bank & Trust Company v. First National Bank of Azle*, 750 S.W.2d 297, **Web** 1988 Tex. App. Lexis 1377 (Court of Appeals of Texas)

21.9 Authorized Agent's Liability: Richard G. Lee was the president of Village Homes, Inc. (Village Homes). Village Homes had several loans from Farmers & Merchants National Bank of Hattan, North Dakota (Farmers Bank), that were in default. Lee and Farmers Bank worked out an arrangement to consolidate the delinquent loans and replace them with a new loan. The new loan would be secured by a promissory note. The parties drafted a note in the amount of $85,000 with a 17 percent annual interest rate. Lee signed the note without indicating that he was signing as an agent of Village Homes. The name "Village Homes, Inc." did not appear on the note. Six months after the note was signed, Village Homes defaulted on it. Farmers Bank sued Lee, seeking to hold him personally liable for the note. Who wins? *Farmers & Merchants National Bank of Hattan, North Dakota v. Lee*, 333 N.W.2d 792, **Web** 1983 N.D. Lexis 289 (Supreme Court of North Dakota)

21.10 Liability of Accommodation Makers: John Valenti wanted to operate an Amoco service station. He contracted with American Oil Company (Amoco), the licensor of Amoco service stations, to lease a service station and become a dealer of Amoco products. The documents that made up the lease agreement included a promissory note and guaranty. Because Valenti had no established credit history, Amoco required that his father be a cosigner. Both Valentis signed the lease and note. After about one year, the younger Valenti abandoned the operation. Amoco sued both Valentis to recover on the note and guaranty. The suit against the son was dropped when Amoco learned that he had no assets from which to satisfy a judgment. The father claimed that Amoco could not go after him because it was not suing his son. Who wins? *American Oil Company v. Valenti*, 179 Conn. 349, 426 A.2d 305, **Web** 1979 Conn. Lexis 973 (Supreme Court of Connecticut)

21.11 Imposter Rule: Allan Q. Mowatt was employed as a bookkeeper at the law firm of McCarthy, Kenney & Reidy,

P.C. The law firm maintained a primary checking account at First National Bank of Boston (Bank of Boston) and two smaller accounts at other banks to pay operating expenses. One of the law firm's secondary accounts, with Union Bank of Lowell, was under the name Clement McCarthy, the name of the firm's senior partner. It was funded by checks drawn on the Bank of Boston account and payable to "Clement McCarthy." The checks used to fund the secondary account were signed by any of four attorneys who had check-writing authority. When either of the two accounts was running low, Mowatt would make a check payable to "Clement McCarthy" and have it signed by one of the authorized attorneys. In addition to drawing checks needed to fund the secondary account, Mowatt began making out extra checks on the Bank of Boston account payable to Clement McCarthy. Mowatt would explain that the extra checks were needed to maintain funds in the secondary accounts. Mowatt then forged the indorsement of Clement McCarthy to the extra checks and deposited them into his own bank account. Who is liable for the loss caused by this forgery? *McCarthy, Kenney & Reidy, P.C. v. First National Bank of Boston*, 402 Mass. 630, 524 N.E.2d 390, **Web** 1988 Mass. Lexis. 173 (Supreme Judicial Court of Massachusetts)

21.12 Fraud in the Factum: John Wade was employed by Mike Fazzari. Fazzari was an immigrant who was unable to speak or read English. Wade prepared a promissory note in the amount of $400. The instrument was payable at the Glen National Bank, Watkins Glen, New York. Wade took the note to Fazzari and told him that the document was a statement of wages earned by Wade during the course of his employment. Fazzari signed the instrument after Wade told him it was necessary for income tax purposes. Fazzari was not in debt to Wade, and there was no consideration given for the note. Four months later, the note was presented to the First National Bank of Odessa by Wellington Doane, a customer of the bank and an indorsee of the payee, Wade. Doane indorsed the check in blank and accepted a $400 cashier's check in exchange for the note. Fazzari and Glen National Bank refused payment of the note. Can the First National Bank of Odessa enforce payment of the note as a holder in due course? *First National Bank of Odessa v. Fazzari*, 10 N.Y.2d 394, 179 N.E.2d 493, 223 N.Y.S. 2d 483, **Web** 1961 N.Y. Lexis 857 (Court of Appeals of New York)

21.13 Fraud in the Inducement: J. H. Thompson went to the Central Motor Company (Central), an automobile dealership, to purchase a car. With the assistance of Central's sales manager, Ed Boles, Thompson selected an automobile.

Boles drew up a loan agreement that stipulated 35 monthly installments and a final installment of $5,265. Under this agreement, Thompson would be charged an annual interest rate of 8 percent. Boles assured Thompson that when the $5,265 installment became due, he would be allowed to sign a second note to cover that amount. Thompson was told that the interest rate on this second note would also be 8 percent. With this assurance, Thompson signed the original loan agreement and note and made all the payments except the final one. When Thompson went to Central to sign the second note, he was told that the interest rate on the second installment note would be 12 percent, not 8 percent. Thompson refused to sign the second note or make the balloon payment on the original note. Instead, he returned the car. Central was able to sell the car, but it sued Thompson to recover a deficiency judgment. Who wins? *Central Motor Company v. J. H. Thompson*, 465 S.W. 2d 405, **Web** 1971 Tex. App. Lexis 2634 (Court of Civil Appeals of Texas)

21.14 Federal Trade Commission Rule: Warren and Kristina Mahaffey were approached by a salesman from the Five Star Solar Screens Company (Five Star). The salesman offered to install insulation in their home at a cost of $5,289. After being told that the insulation would reduce their heating bills by 50 percent, the Mahaffeys agreed to the purchase. To pay for the work, the Mahaffeys executed a note promising to pay the purchase price with interest, in installments. The note, which was secured by a deed of trust on Warren and Kristina Mahaffeys' home, contained the following language: "Notice: Any holder of this consumer credit contract is subject to all claims and defenses which the debtor could assert against the seller of goods or services obtained pursuant hereto or with the proceeds thereof." Several days after Five Star finished working at the home, it sold the installment note to Mortgage Finance Corporation (Mortgage Finance).

There were major defects in the way the insulation was installed in Warren and Kristina Mahaffeys' home. Large holes were left in the walls, and heater blankets and roof fans were never delivered, as called for by the purchase contract. Because of these defects, Warren and Mahaffey refused to make the payments due on the note. Mortgage Finance instituted foreclosure proceedings to collect the money owed. Can Warren and Mahaffey successfully assert the defense of breach of contract against the enforcement of the note by Mortgage Finance? *Mahaffey v. Investor's National Security Company*, 103 Nev. 615, 747 P.2d 890, **Web** 1987 Nev. Lexis 1875 (Supreme Court of Nevada)

Ethics Issues

21.15 Ethics: Anthony and Dolores Angelini entered into a contract with Lustro Aluminum Products, Inc. (Lustro). Under the contract, Lustro agreed to replace exterior veneer on the Angelini home with Gold Bond Plasticrylic avocado

siding. The cash price for the job was $3,600, and the installment plan price was $5,363.40. The Angelinis chose to pay on the installment plan and signed a promissory note as security. The note's language provided that it would not mature until 60 days after a certificate of completion was signed. Ten days after the note was executed, Lustro assigned it for consideration to General Investment Corporation (General), an experienced home improvement lender. General was aware that Lustro (1) was nearly insolvent at the time of the assignment and (2) had engaged in questionable business practices in the past. Lustro never completed the installation of siding at the Angelini home. General demanded payment of the note from the Angelinis as a holder in due course. Who wins? Did General act ethically in this case? *General Investment Corporation v. Angelini*, 58 N. J. 396, 278 A.2d 193, **Web** 1971 N. J. Lexis 263 (Supreme Court of New Jersey)

21.16 Ethics: Marvin L. Rose was an experienced real estate developer. One of his projects was Rosewood, a tract of land located in Illinois. To finance this project, Rose and his wife obtained two loans from Belleville National Bank for the aggregate amount of $879,000. The Roses executed promissory notes to the bank for each loan. The Roses claim that officers of the bank led them to believe that the two loans were five-year-term notes with fixed interest rates. Despite this, each note stipulated that it was payable "on demand or if no demand be made, due and payable five (5) years after date." The Roses claim that they were not aware of this language because they did not read the documents. A year and a half after the notes were executed, the bank informed the Roses that they must renew the loans, or the notes would be called. The Roses now claim that their signatures were obtained by fraud in the inception because they thought they were signing term notes and not demand notes. Who wins? Did the bank act ethically? Did the Roses act ethically? *Belleville National Bank v. Rose*, 119 Ill. App. 3d 56, 456 N.E.2d 281, **Web** 1983 Ill. App. Lexis 2435 (Appellate Court of Illinois)

IRAC Writing Assignment

Read **Case A-21** in Appendix A [*Kedzie & 103rd Currency Exchange, Inc. v. Hodge*].
Use the IRAC method to prepare a written analysis of the case.

CHAPTER 22

Checks, Banking System, and E-Money

> **"** *Bankers have no right to establish a customary law among themselves, at the expense of other men.* **"**
>
> —JUSTICE FOSTER
> Hankey v. Trotman, (1746)

CHAPTER OBJECTIVES

After studying this chapter, you should be able to:

1. Describe the difference between certified, cashier's, and traveler's checks.
2. Describe the system of processing and collecting checks through the banking system.
3. Identify when a bank engages in a wrongful dishonor of a check.
4. Describe electronic fund transfer systems.
5. Define *commercial wire transfer* and describe the use of wire transfers in commerce.

CHAPTER CONTENTS

- Introduction to Checks, Banking System, and E-Money
- The Bank–Customer Relationship
- Ordinary Checks
- Special Types of Checks
- Honoring Checks
- Forged Signatures and Altered Checks
- The Collection Process
- Commercial Wire Transfers
- Chapter Summary
- Test Review Terms and Concepts
- Case Problems
- Ethics Issues
- IRAC Writing Assignment

Introduction to Checks, Banking System, and E-Money

*C*hecks are the most common form of negotiable instrument used in this country. More than 70 billion checks are written annually. Checks act both as substitutes for money and as record-keeping devices, but they do not serve a credit function. In addition, billions of dollars are transferred each day by *wire transfer* between businesses and banks. This chapter discusses the various forms of checks, the procedure for paying and collecting on checks through the banking system, the duties and liabilities of banks and other parties in the collection process, and the process of electronic fund transfers.

Hong Kong, China

Hong Kong is one of the world's great banking centers.

The Bank–Customer Relationship

When a customer makes a deposit into a bank, a **creditor–debtor relationship** is formed. The customer is the creditor, and the bank is the debtor. In effect, the customer is loaning money to the bank.

A **principal–agent relationship** is created if (1) the deposit is a check that the bank must collect for the customer or (2) the customer writes a check against his or her account. The customer is the principal, and the bank is the agent. The bank is obligated to follow the customer's order to collect or pay the check. The rights and duties of a bank and a checking account and wire transfer customer are contractual. The signature card and other bank documents signed by the customer form the basis of the contract.

The Uniform Commercial Code Banking Provisions

Various articles of the Uniform Commercial Code (UCC) establish rules for creating, collecting, and enforcing checks and wire transfers. These articles are:

- **Article 3 (Negotiable Instruments)** establishes the requirements for finding a negotiable instrument. Because a check is a negotiable instrument, the provisions of Article 3 apply. **Revised Article 3** was promulgated in 1990. The provisions of Revised Article 3 serve as the basis of the discussion of Article 3 in this chapter.
- **Article 4 (Bank Deposits and Collections)** establishes the rules and principles that regulate bank deposit and collection procedures for checking accounts offered by

commercial banks, NOW (negotiable orders of withdrawal) accounts, and other check-like accounts offered by savings and loan associations, savings banks, credit unions, and other financial institutions. Article 4 controls when the provisions of Articles 3 and 4 conflict [UCC 4-102(a)]. Article 4 was substantially amended in 1990. The amended Article 4 serves as the basis of the discussion of Article 4 in this chapter.

■ **Article 4A (Funds Transfers)** establishes rules that regulate the creation and collection of and liability for wire transfers. Article 4A was added to the UCC in 1989.

Ordinary Checks

Most adults and businesses have at least one checking account at a bank. A customer opens a checking account by going to a bank, completing the necessary forms (including a signature card), and making a *deposit* to the account. The bank issues *checks* to the customer. The customer then uses the checks to purchase goods and services.

Parties to a Check

UCC 3-104(f) defines a **check** as an order by the drawer to the drawer bank to pay a specified sum of money from the drawer's checking account to the named payee (or holder). There are three parties to an **ordinary check**:

1. *Drawer.* The **drawer** is the customer who maintains the checking account and writes (draws) checks against the account.
2. *Drawee (or payer bank).* The **drawee** is the bank on which a check is drawn.
3. *Payee.* The **payee** is the party to whom a check is written.

Example The Kneadery Restaurant, Inc., has a checking account at Mountain Bank. Mike Mortin, the president of the Kneadery Restaurant, Inc., writes a check for $1,000 from this account payable to Sun Valley Bakery to pay for food supplies. The Kneadery Restaurant, Inc., is the drawer, Mountain Bank is the drawee, and Sun Valley Bakery is the payee (see Exhibit 22.1).

Indorsement of a Check

The payee is the *holder* of a check. As such, the payee has the right to either (1) demand payment of the check or (2) *indorse* the check to another party by signing the back of the check. This latter action is called **indorsement** of a check. The payee is the **indorser**, and

EXHIBIT 22.1

Ordinary Check

the person to whom the check is indorsed is the **indorsee**. The indorsee in turn becomes a holder who can either demand payment of the check or indorse it to yet another party. Any subsequent holder can demand payment of the check or further transfer the check [UCC 3-204(a)].

Example Referring to the previous example, the Sun Valley Bakery may either present the Kneadery Restaurant's check to Mountain Bank for payment or indorse the check to another party. Assume that Sun Valley Bakery indorses the check to the Flour Company in payment for flour; Sun Valley Bakery is the indorser, and the Flour Company is the indorsee. The Flour Company may either present the check for payment or indorse it to another party, and so on.

INTERNET AND TECHNOLOGY
Electronic Fund Transfer Systems

Computers and electronic technology have made it possible for banks to offer electronic payment and collection systems to bank customers. This technology is collectively referred to as **electronic fund transfer systems (EFTS)**. EFTS is supported by contracts among and between customers, banks, private clearinghouses, and other third parties. The most common forms of EFTS are discussed in the following paragraphs.

Automated Teller Machines

An **automated teller machine (ATM)** is an electronic machine that is located either on a bank's premises or at some other convenient location, such as a shopping center or supermarket. These devices are connected online to the bank's computers. Each bank customer is issued a secret personal identification number (PIN) to access his or her bank accounts through ATMs.

ATMs are commonly used when the bank is not open. They are also used as an alternative means of conducting banking when the bank is open. They are used to withdraw cash from bank accounts, cash checks, make deposits to checking or savings accounts, and make payments owed to the bank.

Point-of-Sale Terminals

Many banks issue *debit cards* to customers. Debit cards replace checks in that customers can use them to make purchases. No credit is extended. Instead, the customer's bank account is immediately debited for the amount of a purchase.

Debit cards can be used only at merchants that have **point-of-sale (POS) terminals** at the checkout counters. These terminals are connected online to the bank's computers. To make a purchase, a customer inserts a debit card into the terminal for the amount of the purchase. If there are sufficient funds in the customer's account, the transaction will debit the customer's account and credit the merchant's account for the amount of the purchase. If there are insufficient funds in the customer's account, the purchase is rejected unless the customer has overdraft protection. Some POS terminals allow for the extension of credit in the transaction. Gasoline station POS terminals are one example. At many POS terminals, customers can also obtain cash back above the amount of their purchase.

Direct Deposits and Withdrawals

Many banks provide the service of paying recurring payments and crediting recurring deposits on behalf of customers. These payments are commonly for utilities, insurance premiums, mortgage payments, and the like. Social Security checks, wages, and dividend and interest checks are examples of recurring deposits. To provide this service, the customer's bank and the payee's bank must belong to the same clearinghouse.

Pay-by-Internet

Many banks permit customers to pay bills from their bank accounts by using personal computers and the Internet. To do so, a customer must enter his or her PIN and account name or number, the amount of the bill to be paid, and the account number of the payee to whom the funds are to be transferred. Internet banking is expected to increase dramatically in the future.

Special Types of Checks

If a payee fears there may be insufficient funds in the drawer's account to pay a check when it is presented for payment or that the drawer has stopped payment of the check, the payee may be unwilling to accept an ordinary check from the drawer. However, the payee might be willing to accept a **bank check**—that is, a certified check, a cashier's check, or a traveler's check. These types of checks are usually considered "as good as cash" because the bank is solely or primarily liable for payment. These forms of checks are discussed in the following paragraphs.

EXHIBIT 22.2

Certified Check

Certified Checks

When a bank *certifies a check*, it agrees in advance to (1) accept the check when it is presented for payment and (2) pay the check out of funds set aside from the customer's account and either placed in a special certified check account or held in the customer's account. Certified checks do not become stale. Thus, they are payable at any time from the date they are issued.

A check is **certified** when the bank writes or stamps the word *certified* across the face of an ordinary check. The certification should also contain the date and the amount being certified and the name and title of the person at the bank who certifies the check (see Exhibit 22.2). Note that a bank is not obligated to certify a check. A bank's refusal to do so is not a dishonor of a check [UCC 3-409(d)].

LIABILITY ON A CERTIFIED CHECK Either the drawer or the payee (or holder) can present a check to the drawee's bank for certification. If the drawee's bank certifies the check, the drawer is discharged from liability on the check, regardless of who obtained the certification [UCC 3-414(c)]. The holder must recover from the certifying bank. The obligated bank can be held liable for the amount of the check, expenses, and loss of interest resulting from non-payment. If the bank refuses to pay after receiving notice of particular circumstances giving rise to such damages, it can also be held liable for consequential damages [UCC 3-413].

Problems may arise if a certified check was altered (e.g., the amount of the check was increased). If the alteration occurred before the check was certified, the certifying bank is liable for the certified amount. If the check was altered after certification, the bank is liable for only the certified amount, not the raised amount. The drawer cannot stop payment on a certified check. Because certification constitutes acceptance of the check, the certifying bank can revoke its certification only in limited circumstances [UCC 3-413].

Cashier's Checks

A person can purchase a **cashier's check** from a bank by paying the bank the amount of the check plus a fee for issuing the check. Usually, a specific payee is named. The purchaser does not have to have a checking account at the bank. The check is a noncancellable negotiable instrument upon issue.

A cashier's check is a two-party check for which (1) the issuing bank serves as both the drawer and the drawee and (2) the holder serves as payee [UCC 3-104(g)]. The bank, which has been paid for the check, guarantees its payment. When the check is presented for payment, the bank debits its own account [UCC 3-412]. (See Exhibit 22.3 for a sample cashier's check.)

EXHIBIT 22.3

Cashier's Check

EXHIBIT 22.4

Traveler's Check

An obligated bank that wrongfully refuses to pay a cashier's check is liable to the person asserting the right to enforce the check for expenses, loss of interest resulting from nonpayment, and consequential damages [UCC 3-411].

Traveler's Checks

Traveler's checks are so named because individuals often purchase them to use as a safe substitute for cash while on vacations or other trips. They may be issued by banks or by companies other than banks (e.g., American Express). A traveler's check is a two-party instrument, where the issuing bank serves as both the drawer and the drawee. It is drawn by the bank upon itself.

Traveler's checks may be purchased in many denominations, including $10, $20, $50, and $100. Unlike cashier's checks, traveler's checks are issued without a named payee. The checks have two signature blanks. The purchaser signs one blank when the traveler's checks are issued. The purchaser enters the payee's name and signs the second blank when he or she uses a check to purchase goods or services. A traveler's check is not a negotiable instrument until it is signed the second time [UCC 3-104(i)] (see Exhibit 22.4).

Purchasers of traveler's checks do not have to have a checking account at the issuing bank. The purchaser pays the bank the amount of the checks to be issued. When a traveler's check is presented for payment, the bank debits its own account. Most banks charge a fee for this service, but some banks merely earn interest on the "float" while the checks are not written. If a traveler's check is stolen or lost prior to its use, the purchasers can stop payment on the check. Payment cannot be stopped once the check has been negotiated.

INTERNET AND TECHNOLOGY
Bank Debit Cards

Computers have made it much easier and faster for banks and their customers to conduct banking transactions. For example, bank customers can now use **debit cards** to pay for goods and services. When a bank customer uses a debit card to pay, the money is immediately deducted electronically from his or her bank account. There is no extension of credit as there is when a credit card is used: using a debit card is like writing an electronic check.

Congress enacted the **Electronic Fund Transfer Act** [15 U.S.C. Section 1693 *et seq.*] to regulate consumer electronic fund transfers. The Federal Reserve Board, which is empowered to enforce the provisions of the act, adopted **Regulation E** to further interpret it. Regulation E has the force of law. The Electronic Fund Transfer Act and Regulation E establish the following consumer rights:

1. **Unsolicited cards.** A bank can send unsolicited EFTS debit cards to a consumer only if the cards are not valid for use. Unsolicited cards can be validated for use by a consumer's specific request.

2. **Lost or stolen debit cards.** Debit cards are sometimes lost or stolen. If a customer notifies the issuer bank within 2 days of learning that his or her debit card has been lost or stolen, the customer is liable for only $50 for unauthorized use. If a customer does not notify the bank within this 2-day period, the customer's liability increases to $500. If the customer fails to notify the bank within 60 days after an unauthorized use appears on the customer's bank statement, the customer can be held liable for more than $500. Federal law allows states to impose a lesser liability on customers for lost or stolen debit cards.

3. **Evidence of transaction.** Other than for a telephone transaction, a bank must provide a customer with a written receipt of a transaction made through a computer terminal. This receipt is prima facie evidence of the transaction.

4. **Bank statements.** A bank must provide a monthly statement to an electronic funds transfer customer at the end of the month in which the customer conducts a transaction. Otherwise, a quarterly statement must be provided to the customer. The statement must include the date and amount of the transfer, the name of the retailer, the location or identification of the terminal, and the fees charged for the transaction. Bank statements must also contain the address and telephone number where inquiries or errors can be reported.

Banks are required to disclose the foregoing information to their customers. A bank is liable for wrongful dishonor when it fails to pay an electronic fund transfer when there are sufficient funds in the customer's account to do so.

Honoring Checks

When a customer opens a checking account at a bank, the customer impliedly agrees to keep sufficient funds in the account to pay any checks written against it. Thus, when the drawee bank receives a properly drawn and payable check, the bank is under a duty to **honor** the check and charge (debit) the drawer's account the amount of the check [UCC 4-401(a)].

Stale Checks

Occasionally, payees or other holders in possession of a check fail to present the check immediately to the payer bank for payment. A check that has been outstanding for more than six months is considered stale, and the bank is under no obligation to pay it. A bank that pays a **stale check** in good faith may charge the drawer's account [UCC 4-404].

Incomplete Checks

Drawers sometimes write checks that omit certain information, such as the amount of the check or the payee's name, either on purpose or by mistake. In such cases, the payee or any holder can complete the check, and the payer bank that in good faith makes payment on the completed check can charge the customer's account the amount of the completed check unless it has notice that the completion was improper [UCC 3-407(c), 4-401(d)(2)]. The UCC places the risk of loss of an incomplete item on the drawer.

> The love of money is the root of all evil.
>
> I Timothy 6:10
> *The Bible*

Example Suppose Richard, who owes Sarah $500, draws a check payable to Sarah on City Bank. Richard signs the check but leaves the amount blank. Sarah fraudulently fills in $1,000 and presents the check to City Bank, which pays it. City Bank can charge Richard's account $1,000. Richard's only recourse is to sue Sarah. If Richard had telephoned the bank to tell them that he owed Sarah only $500, however, City Bank would be liable for paying any greater amount to Sarah.

Death or Incompetence of a Drawer

Checks may be paid against the accounts of deceased customers or customers who have been adjudicated incompetent until the bank has actual knowledge of such condition and had reasonable opportunity to act on the information. In the case of a deceased customer, the bank may pay or certify checks drawn on the deceased customer's account on or prior to the date of death for 10 days after the date of death. This rule applies unless a person claiming an interest in the account, such as an heir or a taxing authority, orders the bank to stop payment. A bank that pays such a check when it should not have is liable for the amount improperly paid [UCC 4-405].

Postdated Checks

On occasion, a drawer of a check does not want a check he or she writes to be cashed until sometime in the future. This is called a **postdated check**. Under UCC 4-401(c), to require a bank to abide by a postdated check, the drawer must take the following steps:

1. The drawer must postdate the check to some date in the future.
2. The drawer must give *separate written notice* to the bank, describing the check with reasonable certainty and notifying the bank not to pay the check until the date on the check.

If these steps are taken and the bank pays the check before its date, the bank is liable to the drawer for any losses resulting from its act.

Example On May 1, Gion writes a check to Tina and postdates the check June 1. Suppose Gion sent a separate written notice to his bank, notifying the bank of this fact. If Tina cashes the check on May 2, and Gion's bank pays the check, the bank is liable to Gion if Gion suffers any loss.

Stop-Payment Orders

A **stop-payment order** is an order by a drawer of a check to the payer bank not to pay or certify a check. Only the drawer can order a stop-payment order. If the signature of more than one person is required to draw on an account, any of these persons may stop payment on the account. The bank must be given a reasonable opportunity to act on a stop-payment order. The order is ineffectual if the bank has already accepted or certified the check.

A stop-payment order can be given orally or in writing. An *oral order* is binding on the bank for only 14 calendar days, unless confirmed in writing during this time. A *written order* is effective for six months. It can be renewed in writing for additional six-month periods [UCC 4-403].

If the payer bank fails to honor a valid stop-payment order, it must recredit the customer's account. The bank is subrogated to the rights of the drawer. In addition, the bank is liable only for the actual damages suffered by the drawer. The drawer must prove the fact and amount of loss resulting from the payment of a check on which a stop-payment order was issued.

Example Suppose Karen buys a car from Silvio. She pays for the car by drawing a $10,000 check on City Bank, payable to the order of Silvio. Karen thinks the car is defective and stops payment on the check. If City Bank mistakenly pays Silvio over the stop-payment order, it is liable and must recredit Karen's account. If it is determined that the car is not defective, however, City Bank does not have to recredit Karen's account because Karen has suffered no actual loss; she owes Silvio for the car.

Overdrafts

If the drawer does not have enough money in his or her account when a properly payable check is presented for payment, the payer bank can either (1) dishonor the check or (2) honor the check and create an overdraft in the drawer's account [UCC 4-401(a)]. The bank notifies the drawer of the dishonor and returns the check to the holder, marked "insufficient funds." The holder often resubmits the check to the bank, hoping that the drawer has deposited more money into the account and the check will clear. If the check does not clear, the holder's recourse is against the drawee of the check.

If the bank chooses to pay the check even though there are insufficient funds in the drawer's account, it can later charge the drawer's account for the amount of the **overdraft** [UCC 4-401(a)] because there is an implied promise that the drawer will reimburse the bank for paying checks the drawer orders the bank to pay. If the drawer does not fulfill this commitment, the bank can sue him or her to recover payment for the overdrafts and overdraft fees. A bank cannot charge interest on the amount of the overdraft without the drawer's permission. Therefore, many banks offer optional overdraft protection to their customers.

Wrongful Dishonor

If the bank does not honor a check when there are sufficient funds in a drawer's account to pay a properly payable check, it is liable for **wrongful dishonor**. The payer bank is liable to the drawer for damages proximately caused by the wrongful dishonor as well as for consequential damages, damages caused by criminal prosecution, and such. A payee or holder cannot sue the bank for damages caused by the wrongful dishonor of a drawer's check. The only recourse for the payee or holder is to sue the drawer to recover the amount of the check [UCC 4-402].

CONTEMPORARY ENVIRONMENT
Federal Currency Reporting Law

The Federal Currency Reporting Law requires financial institutions and other entities (e.g., retailers, car and boat dealers, antique dealers, jewelers, travel agencies, real estate brokers) to file a **Currency Transaction Report (CTR)** with the Internal Revenue Service (IRS), reporting:

- The receipt in a single transaction or a series of related transactions of cash in an amount greater than $10,000. "Cash" is not limited to currency but includes cashier's checks, bank drafts, traveler's checks, and money orders (but not ordinary checks) [26 U.S.C. Section 60501].

- Suspected criminal activity by bank customers involving a financial transaction of $1,000 or more in funds [12 C.F.R. Section 21.11(b)(3)].

The law also stipulates that it is a crime to structure or assist in structuring any transaction for the purpose of evading these reporting requirements [31 U.S.C. Section 5324]. Financial institutions and entities may be fined for negligent violations of the currency reporting requirements. Fines may be levied for a pattern of negligent violations. Willful failure to file reports may subject the violator to civil money penalties, charges of aiding and abetting the criminal activity, and prosecution for violating the money-laundering statutes.

Law & Ethics Questions

1. What does the Federal Currency Reporting Law require?

2. **ETHICS** Why was the Federal Currency Reporting Law enacted? Explain.

Web Exercises

1. **WEB** Use *www.google.com* to find an article that discusses the reasons the federal currency reporting law was enacted. Read it.

2. **WEB** Use *www.google.com* to find an article that discusses a violation of the federal currency reporting law. Read it.

Forged Signatures and Altered Checks

Major problems associated with checks are that (1) signatures are sometimes forged and (2) the check itself may have been altered prior to presentment for payment. The UCC rules that apply to these situations are discussed in the following paragraphs. These rules apply to all types of negotiable instruments but are particularly important concerning checks.

Forged Signature of the Drawer

When a check is presented to the payer bank for payment, the bank is under a duty to verify the drawer's signature. This is usually done by matching the signature on the signature card on file at the bank to the signature on the check.

A check with a *forged drawer's signature* is called a **forged instrument**. A forged signature is wholly inoperative as the signature of the drawer. The check is not properly payable because it does not contain an order of the drawer. The payer bank cannot charge the customer's account if it pays a check over the forged signature. If the bank has charged the customer's account, it must recredit the account, and the forged check must be dishonored [UCC 3-401].

The bank can recover from the party who presented the check to it for payment only if that party had knowledge that the signature of the drawer on the check was unauthorized [UCC 3-417(a)(3)]. The forger is liable on the check because the forged signature acts as the forger's signature [UCC 3-403(a)]. Although the payer bank can sue the forger, the forger usually cannot be found or is judgment-proof.

Example Suppose Gregory has a checking account at Country Bank. Lana steals a check, completes it, and forges Gregory's signature. She indorses it to Mike, who knows that Gregory's signature has been forged. Mike indorses it to Barbara, who is innocent and does not know of the forgery. Barbara presents it to Country Bank, the payer bank, which pays the check. Country Bank may recover from the original forger, Lana, and from Mike, who knew of the forgery. It cannot recover from Barbara because she did not have knowledge of the forgery.

The following case involved counterfeit checks and forged signatures.

CASE **22.1**
Forged Checks

Triffin v. Pomerantz Staffing Services, LLC

370 N.J.Super. 301, 851 A.2d 100,
Web 2004 N.J. Super. Lexis 228 (2004)
Superior Court of New Jersey

> **❝** *We conclude that only the malefactor can be held liable on a forged or counterfeit instrument.* **❞**
>
> —Judge Fisher

Facts

Friendly Check Cashing Corporation was presented with 18 counterfeit checks in amounts ranging between $380 and $398, purported to have been issued by Pomerantz Staffing Services, LLC, on its bank account at Bank of New York. Each check bore Pomerantz's full name and address and a facsimile signature of "Gary Pomerantz." Also printed on the face of each check was a warning "The Back of this Check has Heat Sensitive Ink to Confirm Authenticity." Without examining the checks as suggested by this warning, Friendly cashed the checks, which the bank returned unpaid and stamped "COUNTERFEIT" and "DO NOT PRESENT AGAIN."

Friendly assigned any causes of action to plaintiff Robert J. Triffin, who filed a lawsuit against Pomerantz to recover on the counterfeit forged checks. The trial court granted Pomerantz's motion for summary judgment. Triffin appealed.

Issue

Is Pomerantz liable on the counterfeit forged checks?

Language of the Court

We start with the signatures on the face of the checks, which purport to have been made by Pomerantz. Pomerantz claimed, and plaintiff did not dispute, that it did not sign the checks, which also did not come from its check stock. A signature may be made manually or by means of a device or machine, and by use of any name, including a trade or assumed name, or by a word, mark, or symbol executed or adopted by a person with present intention to authenticate writing. Since the emphasis is not on the manner in which a symbol, representing a signature, is made, but is on the signer's present intention to authenticate the writing, it is clear that a forged signature cannot convey the intention of the drawer to authenticate the writing.

We conclude that only the malefactor can be held liable on a forged or counterfeit instrument; that is, as the statute expressly states, the unauthorized signature is ineffective "except as the signature of the unauthorized signor." The forgery does not operate as the ostensible drawer's signature. Since some malefactor signed Pomerantz's name on these checks, then that malefactor can be held liable, but not Pomerantz. Accordingly, it was undisputed that the forged signatures were unauthorized and could not impose liability on Pomerantz for these counterfeit checks.

Decision

The superior court held that Pomerantz was not liable on the counterfeit forged checks. The superior court affirmed the trial court's grant of summary judgment to Pomerantz.

Law & Ethics Questions

1. What are counterfeit checks?
2. **ETHICS** Did the counterfeiter and forger of the checks act unethically in this case? Did the counterfeiter and forger commit a crime?
3. Did Triffin have a good cause of action in this case?

Web Exercises

1. **WEB** For the complete opinion of this case, go to *www.prenhall.com/cheesemancases*.
2. **WEB** Visit the website of the superior court of New Jersey, Appellate Division, at *www.judiciary.state.nj.us/appdivlindex.htm*.
3. **WEB** Use *www.google.com* to find an article or a case involving checks that were counterfeited.

Altered Checks

Sometimes a check is altered before it is presented for payment. This is an unauthorized change in the check that modifies the legal obligation of a party [UCC 3-407(a)]. The payer bank can dishonor an **altered check** if it discovers the alteration.

If the payer bank pays the altered check, it can charge the drawer's account for the **original tenor** of the check but not the altered amount [UCC 3-407(c), 4-401(d)(1)].

If the payer bank has paid the altered amount, it can recover the difference between the altered amount and the original tenor from the party who presented the altered check for payment. This is because the presenter of the check for payment and each prior transferor *warrant* that the check has not been altered [UCC 3-417(a)(2)]. This is called the **presentment warranty**. If there has been an alteration, each party in the chain of collection can recover from the preceding transferor based on a breach of this warranty. The ultimate loss usually falls on the party that first paid the altered check because that party was in the best position to identify the alteration. The forger is liable for the altered amount—if he or she can be found and is not judgement-proof.

> A banker so very careful to avoid risk would soon have no risk to avoid.
>
> Lord MacNaghten
> *Bank of England v. Vaglliano Brothers (1891)*

Example Father draws a $100 check on City Bank made payable to his daughter. The daughter alters the check to read "$1,000" and cashes the check at a liquor store. The liquor store presents the check for payment to City Bank. City Bank pays the check. Father is liable only for the original tenor of the check ($100), and City Bank can charge the father's account this amount. City Bank is liable for the $900 difference, but it can recover this amount from the liquor store for breach of presentment warranty. The liquor store can seek to recover the $900 from the daughter.

CONTEMPORARY ENVIRONMENT
Receipt of Bank Statement

If the same wrongdoer engages in a *series of forgeries* or *alterations* on the same account, the customer must report that to the payer bank within a reasonable period of time, not exceeding 30 calendar days from the date that the bank statement was made available to the customer [UCC 4-406(d)(2)]. The customer's failure to do so discharges the bank from liability on all similar forged or altered checks after this date and prior to notification.

The drawer's failure to report a forged or altered check to the bank within *one year* of receiving the bank statement and canceled checks containing it relieves the bank of any liability for paying the instrument [UCC 4-406(3)]. Thus, the payer bank is not required after this time to recredit the customer's account for the amount of the forged or altered check, even if the customer later discovers the forgery or alteration.

In the following case, the court held against a checking account holder who had not reviewed its bank statements in time to catch a series of forgeries by an employee.

CASE **22.2**
Bank Statements

Spacemakers of America, Inc. v. SunTrust Bank

271 Ga.App. 335, 609 S.E.2d 683, **Web** 2005 Ga. App. Lexis 43 (2005)
Court of Appeals of Georgia

> ❝In this case, the undisputed evidence showed that Spacemakers hired as a bookkeeper a twice-convicted embezzler who was on probation, then delegated the entire responsibility of reviewing and reconciling its bank statements to her while failing to provide any oversight on these essential tasks. ❞
>
> —Judge Ellington

Facts

Spacemakers of America, Inc., employed Jenny Triplett as its bookkeeper. Spacemakers did not inquire as to any prior criminal record or conduct a criminal background check of Triplett. If it had, it would have discovered that Triplett was on probation for 13 counts of forgery and had been convicted of theft by deception. All convictions were the result of Triplett forging checks of previous employers.

Spacemakers hired Triplett as a bookkeeper and delegated to her sole responsibility from maintaining the company's checkbook, reconciling the checkbook with monthly bank statements, and preparing financial reports. Triplett also handled the company's accounts payable and regularly presented checks to Dennis Rose, the president of Spacemakers, so he could sign them.

On January 20, 2000, just weeks after starting her job at Spacemakers, Triplett forged Rose's signature on a check for $3,000 made payable to her husband's company, "Triple M Entertainment Group," which was not a vendor for Spacemakers. By the end of the first full month of employment, Triplett had forged 5 more checks totaling $22,320, all payable to Triple M. Over the next nine months, Triplett forged 59 more checks totaling approximately $475,000. All checks were drawn against Spacemakers's bank account at SunTrust Bank. No one except Triplett reviewed the company's bank statements.

On October 13, 2000, a SunTrust loss prevention employee visually inspected a $30,670 check. She became suspicious of the signature and called Rose. The SunTrust employee faxed a copy of the check to Rose, which was made payable to "Triple M." Rose knew that Triple M was not one of the company's vendors, and a Spacemakers employee reminded Rose that Triplett's husband owned Triple M. Rose immediately called the police, and Triplett was arrested.

Spacemakers sent a letter to SunTrust Bank, demanding that the bank credit $523,106 to its account for the forged checks. The bank refused, contending that Spacemakers's failure to provide the bank with timely notice of the forgeries barred Spacemakers's claim. Spacemakers sued SunTrust for negligence and unauthorized payment of forged items. The trial court granted SunTrust's motion for summary judgment. Spacemakers appealed.

Issue

Did Spacemakers's failure to uncover the forgeries and failure to provide SunTrust with timely notice of the forgeries bar its claim against SunTrust?

Language of the Court

Spacemakers claims the trial court erred in applying Georgia Commercial Code OCGA Section 11-4-406 to the facts of this case. This rule imposes upon a bank customer the duty to promptly examine its monthly statements and notify the bank of any unauthorized transaction. If the customer fails to report the first forged item within 30 days, it is precluded from recovering for that transaction and for any additional items forged by the same wrongdoer. The underlying justification for this provision is simple: one of the most serious consequences of the failure of a customer to timely examine its statement is that it gives the wrongdoer the opportunity to repeat his misdeeds. Clearly, the customer is in the best position to discover and report small forgeries before the same wrongdoer is emboldened and attempts a lager misdeed.

In this case, the undisputed evidence showed that Spacemakers hired as a bookkeeper a twice-convicted embezzler who was on probation, then delegated the entire responsibility of reviewing and reconciling its bank statements to her while failing to provide any oversight on these essential tasks. The bookkeeper started forging checks within weeks of taking control of the company's checkbook and, by the end of January 2000, had forged six checks totaling $25,320. Triplett made all of the checks payable to her husband's company, which had never been a Spacemakers vendor. There is every reason to believe that, if Spacemakers had simply reviewed its bank statement for January 2000, it would have discovered the forgeries. More importantly, it would have been able to timely notify the bank of its discovery and avoided its subsequent losses of almost $475,000. Clearly, Spacemakers' extensive and unnecessary loss due to forgery is precisely the scenario that the duties created by OCGA Section 11-4-406 were designed to prevent. Accordingly, we find that Spacemakers is precluded as a matter of law from asserting claims based upon the forgeries in this case.

Decision

The court of appeals held that Spacemakers had failed to give timely notice to SunTrust Bank as required by the Georgia Uniform Commercial Code and was therefore barred from recovering the value of the forged checks from SunTrust. The court of appeals affirmed the trial court's grant of summary judgment to SunTrust.

Law & Ethics Questions

1. What is a bank account holder's duty regarding reviewing bank statements? Explain.

2. Could Spacemakers have prevented the forgeries in this case?

3. **ETHICS** Did Triplett act ethically in this case? Would Spacemakers have hired her if it had known her prior history?

4. **ETHICS** Should Spacemakers have sued SunTrust to try to recover its losses from the forgeries?

Web Exercises

1. **WEB** For the complete opinion of this case, go to *www.prenhall.com/cheesemancases*.

2. **WEB** Visit the website of the court of appeals of Georgia, at *www.gaappeals.us*.

3. **WEB** Visit the website of SunTrust Bank, at *www.suntrust.com*.

4. **WEB** Use *www.google.com* to find an article or a case involving a bookkeeper, a financial officer, or another employee forging checks of his or her employer. Read it.

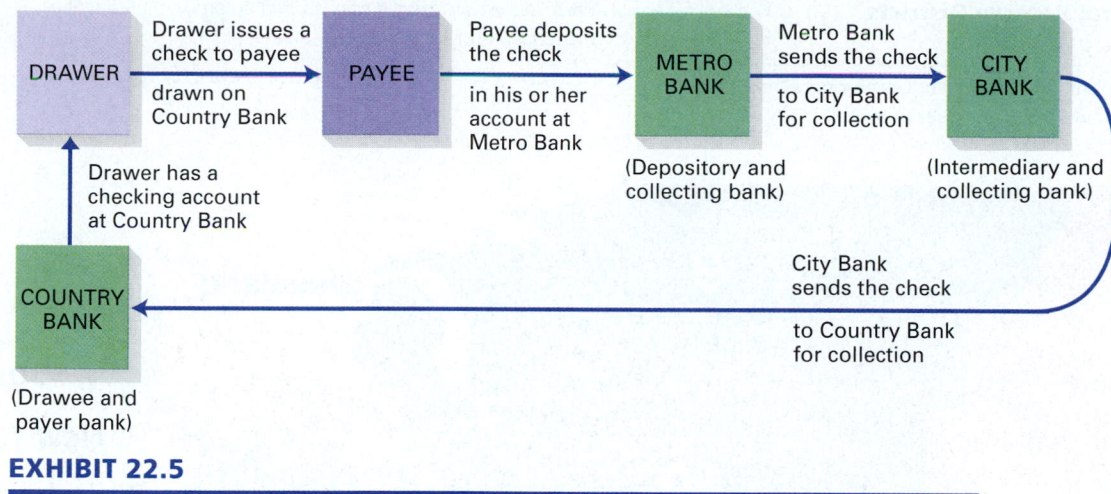

EXHIBIT 22.5

Check Collection Process

The Collection Process

A bank is under a duty to accept deposits into a customer's account. This includes collecting checks that are drawn on other banks and made payable or indorsed to the depositor. The collection process, which may involve several banks, is governed by Article 4 of the UCC.

When a payee or holder receives a check, he or she can either go to the drawer's bank (the **payer bank**) and present the check for payment in cash or—as is more common—deposit the check into a bank account at his or her own bank, called the **depository bank**. (The depository bank may also serve as the payer bank if both parties have accounts at the same bank.)

The depository bank must present the check to the payer bank for collection. At this point in the process, the Federal Reserve System (discussed next) and other banks may be used in the collection of a check. The depository bank and these other banks are called **collecting banks**. Banks in the collection process that are not the depository or payer bank are called **intermediary banks**. A bank can have more than one role during the collection process [UCC 4-105]. The **check collection process** is illustrated in Exhibit 22.5.

C O N T E M P O R A R Y   E N V I R O N M E N T

The Federal Reserve System

The **Federal Reserve System**, which consists of 12 regional Federal Reserve banks located in different geographic areas of the country, assists banks in the collection of checks. Rather than send a check directly to another bank for collection, member banks may submit paid checks to the Federal Reserve banks for collection.

Most banks in this country have accounts at the regional Federal Reserve banks. The Federal Reserve banks debit and credit the accounts of these banks daily to reflect the collection and payment of checks. Banks pay the Federal Reserve banks a fee for this service. In large urban areas, private clearinghouses may provide a similar service [UCC 4-110, 4-213(a)].

The Federal Reserve Board

The Twelve Federal Reserve Districts

Web Exercises

1. **WEB** Visit the website of the Board of Governors of the Federal Reserve System, at *www.federalreserve.gov*.

2. **WEB** Use *www.google.com* to find an article that describes the functions of the Federal Reserve. Read it.

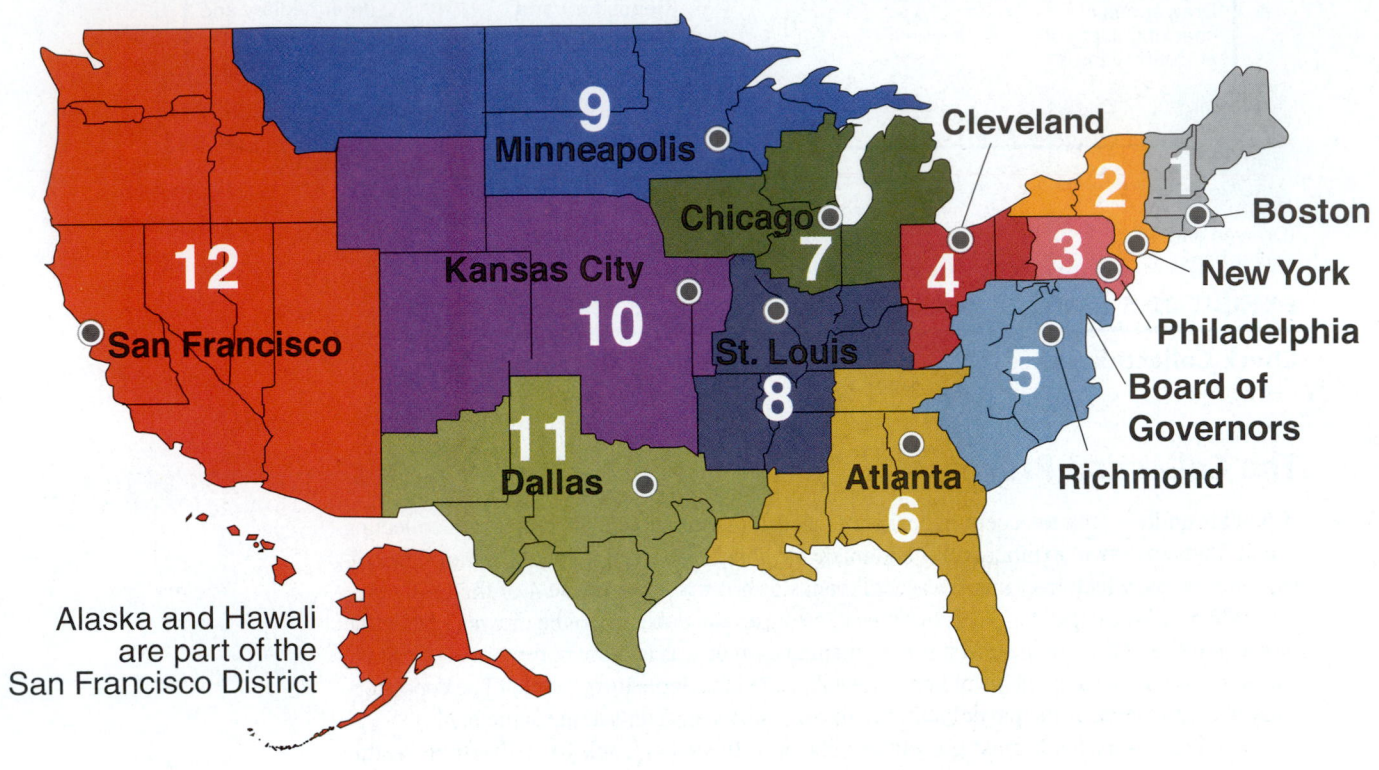

Alaska and Hawaii are part of the San Francisco District

Deferred Posting

The **deferred posting rule** applies to all banks in the collection process. This rule allows banks to fix an afternoon hour of 2:00 P.M. or later as a cutoff hour for the purpose of processing checks. Any check or deposit of money received after this cutoff hour is treated as being received on the next banking day [UCC 4-108]. Saturdays, Sundays, and holidays are not banking days unless the bank is open to the public for carrying on substantially all banking functions [UCC 4-104(a)(3)].

Provisional Credits

When a customer deposits a check into a checking account for collection, the depository bank does not have to pay the customer the amount of the check until the check "clears"—that is, until final settlement occurs. The depository bank may **provisionally credit** the customer's account. Each bank in the collection process provisionally credits the account of the prior transferor [UCC 4-201(a)]. If the check is dishonored by the payer bank (e.g., for insufficient funds, a stop-payment order, or a closed account), the check is returned to the payee or holder, and the provisional credits are reversed. The collecting bank must either return the check to the prior transferor or notify that party within a reasonable time that provisional credit is being revoked. If the collecting bank fails to do this, it is liable for any losses caused by its delay [UCC 4-214].

Depository banks often allow their customers to withdraw the funds prior to final settlement. If the bank later learns that a check was dishonored, it can debit the customer's account for the amount withdrawn. If this is not possible (e.g., the payee or holder does not have sufficient funds in his or her account or has closed the account), the depository bank can sue the customer to recover the funds.

Final Settlement

A check is finally paid when the payer bank (1) pays the check in cash, (2) settles for the check without having a right to revoke the settlement, or (3) fails to dishonor the check within certain statutory time periods. These time periods are discussed in the following paragraphs.

When a check is finally settled, the provisional credits along the chain of collecting banks "firm up" and become **final settlements** [UCC 4-215(a)].

"ON US" CHECKS If the drawer and the payee or holder have accounts at the *same* bank, the depository bank is also the payer bank. The check is called an **"on us" item** when it is presented for payment by the payee or holder. In this case, the bank has until the opening of business on the second banking day following the receipt of the check to dishonor it. If it fails to do so, the check is considered paid. The payee or holder can withdraw the funds at this time [UCC 4-215(e)(2)].

Example Christine and Jim both have checking accounts at Country Bank. On Tuesday morning, Christine deposits a $1,000 check from Jim into her account. Country Bank issues a provisional credit to Christine's account for this amount. On Thursday morning when the bank opens for business, the check is considered honored.

"ON THEM" CHECKS If the drawer and the payee or holder have accounts at *different* banks, the payer and depository bank are not the same bank. In this case, the check is called an **"on them" item**.

Each bank in the collection process, including the payer bank, but excepting the collecting bank, must take proper action on the check prior to its "midnight deadline." The **midnight deadline** is the midnight of the next banking day following the banking day on which the bank received an "on them" check for collection [UCC 4-104(a)(10)]. Collecting banks are permitted to act within a reasonably longer time, but the bank then has the burden of establishing the timeliness of its action [UCC 4-202(b)].

This deadline is of particular importance to the payer bank: If the payer bank does not dishonor a check by its midnight deadline, the bank is *accountable* (liable) for the face amount of the check. It does not matter whether the check is properly payable or not [UCC 4-302(a)].

Example If on Wednesday morning, a payer bank receives an "on them" check drawn on an account at the bank, it has until midnight of the next banking day, Thursday, to dishonor the check. If it does not, the check is considered paid by the bank. This deadline does not apply to "on us" checks, which clear when the bank opens on the second business day following receipt of the checks (unless they are dishonored).

Instead of depositing an "on them" check for collection, a depositor can physically present the check for payment at the payer bank. This is called **presentment across the counter**. In this case, the payer bank has until the end of that banking day to dishonor the check. If it fails to do so, it must pay the check [UCC 4-301(a)].

DEPOSIT OF CASH A deposit of cash to an account becomes available for withdrawal at the opening of the next banking day following the deposit [UCC 4-215(a)].

The "Four Legals" That Prevent Payment of a Check

Sometimes the payer bank receives some form of notice that affects the payment of a check that has been presented for collection and is in the process of being *posted*. The following types of notices or actions—known as the **four legals**—effectively prevent payment of the check:

1. Receipt of a notice affecting the account, such as a notice of the customer's death, adjudgment of incompetence, or bankruptcy.
2. Receipt of service of a court order or other legal process that "freezes" the customer's account, such as a writ of garnishment.
3. Receipt of a stop-payment order from the drawer.

4. The payer bank's exercise of its right of setoff against the customer's account (i.e., notice to pay a debt the customer owes to the bank).

If one of these four legals is received before the payer bank has finished its process of posting, the check cannot be paid contrary to the legal notice or action. However, the account is not affected if the check was paid or the process of posting was completed before the notice was received. The *process of posting* is considered completed when (1) the responsible bank officer has made a decision to pay the check and (2) the proper book entry has been made to charge the drawer's account the amount of the check.

CONTEMPORARY ENVIRONMENT
Failure to Examine Bank Statements in a Timely Manner

Ordinarily, banks send their checking account customers monthly statements of account. The canceled checks usually accompany the statement, although banks are not required to send them. If the canceled checks are not sent to the customer, the statement of account must provide sufficient information to allow the customer to identify the checks paid (e.g., check number, amount, date of payment) [UCC 4-406(a)]. In addition, if the checks are not returned to the customer, the bank must retain either the original checks or legible copies for seven years. A customer may request a check or a copy of it during this period [UCC 4-406(b)].

The customer owes a duty to examine the statements (and canceled checks, if received) promptly and with reasonable care to determine whether any payment was not authorized because of alteration of a check or a forged signature. The customer must promptly notify the bank of unauthorized payments [UCC 4-406(c)]. The customer is liable if the payer bank suffers a loss because of the customer's failure to perform these duties [UCC 4-406(d)(1)].

Most banks provide images of checks online.

Liability of Collecting Banks for Their Own Negligence

The collecting bank owes a **duty of ordinary care** in presenting and sending a check for collection, sending notices of dishonor, and taking other actions in the collection process. Failure to do so constitutes *negligence*. A collecting bank that takes proper action on a check prior to its midnight deadline is deemed to have exercised ordinary care. A bank is liable only for losses caused by its own negligence [UCC 4-202].

In the following case, a defendant was found criminally guilty for check fraud.

CASE 22.3
Criminal Forgery

State of Tennessee v. Heck

Web 2004 Tenn. Crim. App. Lexis 614 (2004)
Court of Criminal Appeals of Tennessee

❝ *The defendant presentence report reveals she has more than one hundred prior convictions including many of the same offenses involved in the case at bar.* **❞**

—Judge Riley

Facts

The state of Tennessee prosecuted Lisa Darlene Heck of several counts of criminal check forgery. Heck pled guilty to five counts of forgery over $500 and one count of forgery over $1,000. Heck had issued checks to numerous victims while representing herself as "Christy L. Richer" and using false identification. Heck testified that she graduated from high school and obtained an associate's degree in hospitality management. Heck has two children but does not have custody of either. Heck served a total of four years' confinement for prior convictions and had violated the terms of prior sentences of probation on several occasions. Heck testified that she has essentially lived her life by stealing money and assuming the identities of others. She apologized to the court for her actions. At the conclusion of the sentencing hearing, the trial court ordered that Heck serve a four-year sentence in jail followed by a four-year period of probation. Heck appealed.

Issue

Did the trial court err in imposing the sentence on Heck?

Language of the Court

The defendant contends the trial court erred in imposing incarceration. We disagree. Under the Sentencing Act, sentences which involve confinement are to be based on the following considerations contained in the Tennessee Code: (A) confinement is necessary to protect society by restraining a defendant who has a long history of criminal conduct; (B) confinement is necessary to avoid depreciating the seriousness of the offense or confinement is particularly suited to provide an effective deterrence to others likely to commit similar offenses; or (C) measures less restrictive than confinement have frequently or recently be applied unsuccessfully to the defendant.

The defendant presentence report reveals she has more than one hundred prior convictions including many of the same offenses involved in the case at bar. Furthermore, the defendant has violated the terms of prior sentences of probation on three occasions. We conclude the trial court properly denied alternative sentencing based upon the defendant's long history of criminal conduct and the unsuccessful application of measures less restrictive than confinement.

Decision

The court of criminal appeals affirmed the trial court's judgment that imposed on Heck a four-year prison sentence followed by a four-year probation period.

Law & Ethics Questions

1. Is forgery of checks a crime?
2. Do you think that the sentence imposed in this case was reasonable? Why or why not?
3. **ETHICS** Do you think Heck will change her ways after serving her incarceration period?

Web Exercises

1. **WEB** For the complete opinion of this case, go to *www.prenhall.com/cheesemancases*.
2. **WEB** Visit the website of the court of criminal appeals of Tennessee at Knoxville, at *www.tsc.state.tn.us*.
3. **WEB** Use *www.google.com* to find an article or case that discusses criminal forgery of checks. Read it.

INTERNATIONAL LAW
Hiding Money in Offshore Banks

Little did Christopher Columbus know in 1503 when he sailed past the Cayman Islands in the Caribbean that these tiny islands would become a bastion of international finance in the late twentieth and early twenty-first centuries. These tiny islands of 35,000 people host about 600 banks with over $500 million in deposits. Why is so much money being hoarded there? The answer: Bank secrecy laws.

Every nation has banking laws, but all banking laws are not equal. What the Cayman Islands banking law provides is confidentiality. In most instances, no party other than the depositor has the right to know the identity of the depositor, account number, or amount in the account. In fact, most accounts are held in the name of trusts instead of the depositor's actual name. This bank secrecy law has attracted many persons to park their (sometimes ill-gotten) gains in Cayman Islands banks. Often the bank is usually no more than a lawyer's office.

Switzerland was once the primary location for depositing money that did not want to be found. After some pressure from the United States and other countries, however, Switzerland entered into memorandums of understanding agreeing to cooperate with criminal investigations by these countries and to help uncover money deposited in Switzerland made through securities frauds and other crimes. Therefore, Switzerland has lost some of its luster as an international money hideout.

Switzerland has been replaced by other places offering even more secret bank secrecy laws. The Cayman Islands is now the "Switzerland of the Caribbean." There are several other bank secrecy hideouts around the world, including The Bahamas in the Caribbean, the country of Liechtenstein in Europe, the Isle of Man off of Great Britain, and the micro-island of Niue in the South Pacific. These tiny countries and islands follow the adage "Write a good law, and they will come."

Law & Ethics Questions

1. Can each country have its own banking laws?
2. What do bank secrecy laws that have been enacted in many countries provide? Why do countries enact bank secrecy laws?
3. **ETHICS** Who do you think uses banks in countries with bank secrecy laws? Explain.

Web Exercises

1. **WEB** Use *www.google.com* to find an article that discusses the bank secrecy laws of The Bahamas. Read it.
2. **WEB** Use *www.google.com* to find an article that discusses the bank secrecy laws of the Cayman Islands. Read it.
3. **WEB** Use *www.google.com* to find an article that discusses the bank secrecy laws of the Cook Islands. Read it.
4. **WEB** Use *www.google.com* to find an article that discusses the bank secrecy laws of the Isle of Man. Read it.

Commercial Wire Transfers

Commercial wire transfers, or **wholesale wire transfers**, are electronic transfers of funds from a bank to another party. They are often used to transfer payments between businesses and financial institutions. For example, a customer of a bank may request the bank to pay another party by wiring funds (money) to that party's bank account.

Trillions of dollars per day are transferred over the two principal wire payment systems—the **Federal Reserve wire transfer network (Fedwire)** and the **Clearing House Interbank Payments System (CHIPS)**. A wire transfer often involves a large amount of money (multimillion-dollar transactions are commonplace). The benefits of using wire transfers are their speed—most transfers are completed on the same day— and low cost. Banks sometimes require a customer to pay for a fund transfer in advance. On other occasions, however, a bank will extend credit to a customer and pay for the fund transfer. The customer is liable to pay the bank for any properly paid fund transfer.

Web Exercises

1. **WEB** Visit the website of the Clearing House Interbank Payment System (CHIPS), at *www.chips.org*.
2. **WEB** Visit the website of the Federal Reserve Board, at *www.federalreserve.gov*.

INTERNET AND TECHNOLOGY
Article 4A (Funds Transfers)

UCC Article 4A (Funds Transfers), which was promulgated in 1989, governs commercial wire transfers. Most states have adopted this article. Where adopted, Article 4A governs the rights and obligations between parties to a fund transfer unless they have entered into a contrary agreement. Article 4A applies only to *commercial* electronic fund transfers; consumer electronic fund transfers subject to the Electronic Fund Transfer Act are not subject to Article 4A.

Fund transfers are not complex transactions.

Example Suppose Diebold Corporation wants to pay Bethlehem Steel for supplies it purchased. Instead of delivering a negotiable instrument such as a check to Bethlehem, Diebold instructs its bank to wire the funds to Bethlehem's bank, with instructions to credit Bethlehem's account. Diebold's order is called a *payment order*, Diebold is the *originator* of the wire transfer, and Bethlehem is the *beneficiary*. Diebold's bank is called the *originator's bank*, and Bethlehem's bank is called *beneficiary's bank*. In more complex transactions, there may be one or more additional banks, known as *intermediary banks*, between the originator's bank and the beneficiary's bank [UCC 4A-103(a)].

If a receiving bank mistakenly pays a greater amount to the beneficiary than ordered, the originator is liable for only the amount he or she instructed to be paid. The receiving bank that erred has the burden of recovering any overpayment from the beneficiary [UCC 4A-303(a)]. If a wrong beneficiary is paid, the originator is not obliged to pay his or her payment order. The bank that issued the erroneous payment order has the burden of recovering the payment from the improper beneficiary [UCC 4A-303(c)].

Fund Transfer Procedures

Banks and customers usually establish security procedures (e.g., codes, identifying numbers, words) to prevent unauthorized electronic payment orders. To protect the bank from liability for unauthorized payment orders, the security procedure must be commercially reasonable. If the bank verifies the authenticity of a payment order by complying with such a security procedure and pays the order, the customer is bound to pay the order, even if it was not authorized [UCC 4A-202]. The customer is not liable if it can prove that the unauthorized order was not initiated by an employee or another agent or by a person who obtained that information from a source controlled by the customer [UCC 4A-203].

Japan
Commercial wire transfers facilitate international trade between businesses located in different countries.

Chapter Summary

The Bank–Customer Relationship, p. 566

1. *Creditor–debtor relationship.* This relationship occurs when a customer (the *depositor*) deposits money into his or her account at a financial institution. In effect, the customer is loaning money to the financial institution. The customer is the creditor, and the financial institution is the debtor.

2. *Principal–agent relationship.* This relationship occurs when a customer writes a check against his or her checking account or deposits a check into his or her account for collection by the financial institution. The customer is the principal, and the financial institution is the agent.

The Uniform Commercial Code Banking Provisions

The following articles of the Uniform Commercial Code (UCC) govern the creation, collection, and enforcement of checks and wire transfers:

1. *Article 3.* This article sets forth the requirements for creating negotiable instruments including checks. Revised Article 3 was promulgated in 1990.

2. *Article 4.* This article establishes rules and principles that regulate the deposit and collection of checks by the banking system.

3. *Article 4A.* This article establishes rules and principles regulating the creation and collection of and liability for wire transfers. This article was promulgated in 1989.

Ordinary Checks, p. 567

A check is an order by a checking account holder (the drawer) to the financial institution at which the account is located (the drawee) to pay a named person (the payee) the amount of the check.

Parties to a Check

1. *Drawer.* The drawer is the checking account holder and writer of a check.
2. *Drawee.* The drawee is the financial institution on which a check is drawn.
3. *Payee.* The payee is the party to whom a check is written.

Indorsement of a Check

The indorsement of a check is necessary for the payee to sign the check over to another party.

Special Types of Checks, p. 568

Bank checks are special types of checks for which the bank is solely or primarily liable. Bank checks include certified checks, cashier's checks, and traveler's checks. These bank checks are considered "as good as cash" because the issuing bank has guaranteed their payment.

Certified Checks

A bank agrees in advance (certifies) to accept and pay a certified check when it is presented for payment. The issuer or holder takes an ordinary check to the bank, and the bank writes "certified" on the check. The bank sets aside funds from the issuer's account to pay the check when it is presented for payment.

Cashier's Checks

A person pays a bank the amount of a cashier's check and a fee, and the bank guarantees that it will pay the check when it is presented for payment. The person purchasing a cashier's check does not have to have a checking account at the bank.

Traveler's Checks

A traveler's check is a form of check sold by banks and other issuers. The purchaser of a traveler's check signs it at the time of purchase. When the check is used to purchase goods or services, the purchaser again signs the check and fills in the payee's name. Purchasers of traveler's checks do not have to have an account at the issuing bank.

Honoring Checks, p. 571

When a drawee bank receives a properly drawn check and there are sufficient funds in the drawer's account to pay the check, the bank must honor the check and pay it.

Stale Checks

A check that has been outstanding for more than six months before it is presented for payment is stale. A bank is under no obligation to pay a stale check. A bank that pays a stale check in good faith may charge the drawer's account.

Incomplete Checks

A check that omits certain information, such as the amount of the check or the payee's name is incomplete. A bank may pay an incomplete check as completed by the payee as long as it acts in good faith and without notice that the completion was improper.

Death or Incompetence of a Drawer

1. *Death of drawer.* A bank may pay or certify checks drawn on a deceased customer's account for 10 days after receiving actual notice of the customer's death, unless a person claiming an interest in the account (e.g., heir, taxing authority) stops payment on the checks.
2. *Incompetence of drawer.* A bank may pay checks of a customer adjudicated incompetent until the bank has received actual notice of the customer's adjudication of incompetence.

Postdated Checks

A postdated check is dated with a date in the future. A bank may pay a postdated check and charge the drawer's account, even though payment is made before the date on the check unless the drawer has given the bank separate notice (notice in addition to the date on the check) stating not to pay the postdated check until its date and describing the check with reasonable certainty. Oral notice is good for 14 days, and written notice is good for six months, which may be renewed for additional six-month periods. A bank that pays a post-dated check over such notice is liable for damages resulting therefrom.

Stop-Payment Orders

A stop-payment order is an order by a drawer of a check to the payer bank not to pay or certify a check. An oral stop-payment order is binding on the bank for only 14 days; a written stop-payment order is binding for six months and may be renewed for additional six-month periods. If the payer bank fails to honor a stop-payment order and pays the check, it must recredit the customer's account the amount paid. The bank is subrogated to the rights of the drawer.

Overdrafts

When a check is presented for payment and there are insufficient funds in the drawer's account to pay the check, the payer bank may either (1) dishonor the check or (2) honor the check and create an overdraft in the drawer's account. The bank can later charge the drawer's account the amount of the overdraft or sue the drawer to recover this amount.

Wrongful Dishonor

Wrongful dishonor occurs when a payer bank dishonors a drawer's properly payable check when it is presented for payment even though there are sufficient funds in the account to honor the check. The payer bank is liable to the drawer for damages proximately caused by the wrongful dishonor of a check plus consequential damages and damages caused by criminal prosecution.

Forged Signatures and Altered Checks, p. 573

Forged Signature of the Drawer

A forged instrument is a check on which the drawer's signature has been forged.

1. *Drawer.* A forged signature is wholly inoperative as the signature of the drawer. Therefore, the drawer is not liable on a forged instrument, and the bank cannot charge the drawer's account the amount paid. If the bank has charged the drawer's account, the account must be recredited.
2. *Forger.* The forger is liable on the check because the forged signature acts as the forger's signature.
3. *Prior transferors.* Prior transferors who had knowledge that the signature of a drawer was forged are liable on the forged instrument.
4. *Payer bank.* A payer bank that has charged the drawer's account for a forged instrument must seek recovery from the forger and prior transferors who had knowledge of the forged signature. The ultimate loss for the payment of a forged check usually falls on the payer bank (unless it can recover from the forger).

Altered Checks

An altered check is a check that has been altered without authorization of the drawer that modifies the legal obligation of a party.

1. *Drawer.* If a payer bank pays an altered check, it can charge the drawer's account the *original tenor* (original amount) of the check. The drawer is not liable for the altered amount.
2. *Forger.* The person who altered the check is liable on the check for the amount above the original tenor.
3. *Prior transferors.* The presenter of the check for payment and all prior transferors warrant that the check has not been altered. This is called a presentment warranty. The payer bank can recover from the presenter for breach of this warranty, and each

party in the chain of collection can recover from the preceding transferor based on the breach of this warranty. The ultimate loss usually falls on the party that first paid the altered check (unless that party can recover from the forger).

4. *Payer bank.* The payer bank can recover from the presenter of the altered check, any prior transferor, or the forger.

The Collection Process, p. 577

1. *Bank's duty to accept deposits.* A bank owes a duty to accept deposits into a customer's account. This includes collecting checks that are drawn on other banks and made payable or indorsed to the customer.

2. *Collection process.* If a customer deposits a check drawn on another bank into his or her account at a bank, his or her bank may send the check directly to the payer bank or through other banks until it is received by the payer bank for payment.

3. *Banks in the collection process.* The banks that may be involved in the collection process are:

   a. *Depository bank.* The bank at which the payee or holder has an account and deposits a check into this account to be collected.

   b. *Payer bank.* The bank where the drawer has a checking account and that will pay the check if properly payable. (The payer bank and depository bank are the same bank if the drawer and the payee or holder have accounts at the same bank.)

   c. *Collecting bank.* Any bank in the collection process other than the payer bank. The depository bank is also a collecting bank.

   d. *Intermediary bank.* A bank in the collection process other than the depository and payer banks.

The Federal Reserve System

A series of 12 regional Federal Reserve banks assist banks in the collection of checks. The Federal Reserve banks act as collecting banks by debiting and crediting the accounts of banks at the Federal Reserve banks daily to reflect the collection and payment of checks.

Deferred Posting

1. *Deferred posting rule.* This rule allows banks to fix an afternoon hour of 2:00 P.M. or later as a cutoff hour for the purpose of processing checks. Any check or deposit received after this cutoff hour is treated as being received the next banking day.

2. *Banking days.* Banking days are days that a bank is open to the public for carrying on substantially all banking functions.

Provisional Credit

Provisional credit occurs when a bank in the collection process credits a customer's account with the amount of a deposited check before the check has cleared by final settlement. If a deposited check does not clear (e.g., for insufficient funds, stop-payment order), all provisional credits may be reversed.

Final Settlement

Final settlement occurs when the payer bank either (1) pays the check in cash, (2) settles for the check without having a right to revoke the settlement, or (3) fails to dishonor the check within certain statutory time periods. When a check is finally settled, all provisional credits "firm up" and become final settlements. Article 4 of the UCC establishes the following statutory deadlines for collecting and payer banks to act on checks:

1. *"On us" check.* An "on us" check is a check that is presented for payment where the drawer and payee or holder have accounts at the same bank. That is, the payer bank is also the depository bank. In this case, the bank has until the opening for business on the second banking day following the receipt of the check to dishonor it. If it fails to do so, the check is considered paid.

2. ***"On them" check.*** An "on them" check is a check that is presented for payment where the drawer and payee or holder have accounts at different banks. That is, the payer bank and the depository bank are different banks. In this case, each bank in the collection process, including the payer bank, must take proper action on the check (particularly the payer bank to dishonor the check) prior to its "midnight deadline." The midnight deadline is the midnight of the next banking day following the banking day on which the bank received the "on them" check for collection.

3. ***Presentment across the counter.*** This occurs when a payee or holder physically presents an "on them" check for payment at the payer bank rather than using the collection process. In this case, the payer bank has until the end of that banking day to dishonor the check. If it fails to do so, it must pay the check.

4. ***Deposit of cash.*** A deposit of cash to an account becomes available for withdrawal at the opening of the next banking day following the deposit.

The "Four Legals" That Prevent Payment of a Check

Four notices or actions can prevent the payment of a check if they are received by the payer bank before it has finished its process of posting the check for payment:

1. Receipt of a notice affecting the account, such as a notice of the customer's death, adjudgment of incompetence, or bankruptcy.

2. Receipt of service of a court order or other legal process that "freezes" the customer's account, such as a writ of garnishment.

3. Receipt of a stop-payment order from the drawer.

4. The payer bank's exercise of its right of setoff against the customer's account.

Failure to Examine Bank Statements in a Timely Manner

1. ***Duty to examine bank statements.*** A bank customer owes a duty to examine bank statements (and canceled checks, if received) promptly and with reasonable care to determine if any payment was not authorized because of the forged signature of the customer or alteration of a check. The customer must notify the bank of unauthorized payments.

2. ***Failure to examine bank statements.*** A customer who fails to examine bank statements promptly and reasonably and notify the bank of unauthorized payments is liable for any losses suffered by the bank because of this failure.

3. ***Series of forgeries or alterations.*** If the same wrongdoer engages in a series of forgeries or alterations on the same account, the customer must report that to the payer bank within a reasonable period of time, not exceeding 30 calendar days from the date that the bank statement was made available to the customer. The customer's failure to do so discharges the bank from liability on all similar forged or altered checks after this date and prior to notification.

Liability of Collecting Banks for Their Own Negligence

1. ***Duty of ordinary care.*** Collecting banks are required to exercise ordinary care in presenting for and sending checks for collection.

2. ***Liability for negligence.*** A collecting bank that fails to exercise ordinary care in the collection of checks is negligent. A collecting bank is liable for losses caused by its negligence in the collection process.

Commercial Wire Transfers, p. 582

A commercial wire transfer involves the transfer of funds electronically by wire between business and financial institutions.

1. ***Wire payment systems.*** The two principal wire payment systems in this country are the Federal Reserve wire transfer network (Fedwire) and the Clearing House Interbank Payments Systems (CHIPS).

2. ***Article 4A of the UCC.*** This article of the UCC governs the creation of, transfer, and collection of and liability for commercial wire transfers.

Test Review Terms and Concepts

Case Problems

22.1 Cashier's Check: Dr. Graham Wood purchased a cashier's check in the amount of $6,000 from Central Bank of the South (Bank). The check was made payable to Ken Walker and was delivered to him. Eleven months later, Bank's branch manager informed Wood that the cashier's check was still outstanding. Wood subsequently signed a form requesting that payment be stopped and a replacement check issued. He also agreed to indemnify Bank for any damages resulting from the issuance of the replacement check. Bank issued a replacement check to Wood. Seven months later, Walker deposited the original cashier's check in his bank, which was paid by Bank. Bank requested that Woods repay the bank $6,000. When he refused, Bank sued Woods to recover this amount. Who wins? *Wood v. Central Bank of the South*, 435 So.2d 1287, **Web** 1982 Ala. Civ. App. Lexis 1362 (Court of Civil Appeals of Alabama)

22.2 Overdraft: Louise Kalbe maintained a checking account at the Pulaski State Bank (Bank) in Wisconsin. Kalbe made out a check for $7,260, payable in cash. Thereafter, she misplaced it but did not report the missing check to the bank or stop payment on it. One month later, some unknown person presented the check to a Florida bank for payment. The Florida bank paid the check and sent it to the Bank for collection. Bank paid the check even though it created a $6,542.12 overdraft in Kalbe's account. Bank requested Kalbe pay this amount. When she refused, Bank sued Kalbe to collect the overdraft. Who wins? *Pulaski State*

Bank v. Kalbe, 122 Wis.2d 663, 364 N.W.2d 162, **Web** 1985 Wisc. App. Lexis 3034 (Court of Appeals of Wisconsin)

22.3 Wrongful Dishonor: Larry J. Goodwin and his wife maintained a checking and savings account at City National Bank of Fort Smith (Bank). Bank also had a customer named Larry K. Goodwin. Two loans of Larry K. Goodwin were in default. Bank mistakenly took money from Larry J. Goodwin's checking account to pay the loans. At the end of the month, the Goodwins received written notice that four of their checks, which were written to merchants, had been dishonored for insufficient funds. When the Goodwins investigated, they discovered that their checking account balance was zero, and the bank had placed their savings account on hold. After being informed of the error, Bank promised to send letters of apology to the four merchants and to correct the error. Bank, however, subsequently "bounced" several other checks of the Goodwins. Eventually, Bank notified all the parties of its error. One month later, the Goodwins closed their accounts at Bank and were paid the correct balances due. They sued the bank for consequential and punitive damages for wrongful dishonor. Who wins? *City National Bank of Fort Smith v. Goodwin*, 301 Ark. 182, 783 S.W.2d 335, **Web** 1990 Ark. Lexis 49 (Supreme Court of Arkansas)

22.4 Stale Check: Charles Ragusa & Son (Ragusa), a partnership consisting of Charles and Michael Ragusa, issued a check in the amount of $5,000, payable to Southern Masonry, Inc.

(Southern). The check was drawn on Community State Bank (Bank). Several days later, Southern informed Ragusa that the check had been lost. Ragusa issued a replacement check for the same amount and sent it to Southern, and that check was cashed. At the same time, Ragusa gave a verbal stop-payment order to Bank regarding the original check. Three years later, the original check was deposited by Southern into its account at the Bank of New Orleans. When the check was presented to Bank, it paid it and charged $5,000 against Ragusa's account. The partnership was not made aware of this transaction until one month later, when it received its monthly bank statement. Ragusa demanded that Bank recredit its account $5,000. When Bank refused to do so, Ragusa sued. Who wins? *Charles Ragusa & Son v. Community State Bank*, 360 So.2d 231, **Web** 1978 La. App. Lexis 3435 (Court of Appeal of Louisiana)

22.5 Postdated Check: David Siegel maintained a checking account with the New England Merchants National Bank (Bank). On September 14, Siegel drew and delivered a $20,000 check payable to Peter Peters. The check was dated November 14. Peters immediately deposited the check in his own bank, which forwarded it for collection. On September 17, Bank paid the check and charged it against Siegel's account. Siegel discovered that the check had been paid when another of his checks was returned for insufficient funds. Siegel informed Bank that the check to Peters was postdated November 14 and requested that the bank return the $20,000 to his account. When Bank refused, Siegel sued for wrongful debit of his account. Must Bank recredit Siegel's account? *Siegel v. New England Merchants National Bank*, 386 Mass. 672, 437 N.E.2d 218, **Web** 1982 Mass. Lexis 1559 (Supreme Judicial Court of Massachusetts)

22.6 Stop Payment: Dynamite Enterprises, Inc. (Dynamite), a corporation doing business in Florida, maintained a checking account at Eagle National Bank of Miami (Bank). Dynamite drew a check on this account, payable to one of its business associates. Before the check had been cashed or deposited, Dynamite issued a written stop-payment order to Bank. Bank informed Dynamite that it would not place a stop-payment order on the check because there were insufficient funds in the account to pay the check. Several weeks later, the check was presented to Bank for payment. By this time, sufficient funds had been deposited in the account to pay the check. Bank paid the check and charged Dynamite's account. When Dynamite learned that the check had been paid, it requested Bank to recredit its account. When Bank refused, Dynamite sued to recover the amount of the check. Who wins? *Dynamite Enterprises, Inc. v. Eagle National Bank of Miami*, 517 So.2d 112, **Web** 1987 Fla. App. Lexis 11791 (Court of Appeals of Florida)

22.7 Examining Bank Statements: Mr. Gennone maintained a checking account at Peoples National Bank & Trust Company of Pennsylvania (Bank). Gennone noticed that he was not receiving his bank statements and canceled checks. When Gennone contacted Bank, he was informed that the statements had been mailed to him. Bank agreed to hold future statements so that he could pick them up in person. Gennone picked up the statements but did not reconcile the balance of the account. As a result, it was not until two years later that he discovered that beginning over one year earlier his wife had forged his signature on 25 checks. Gennone requested Bank to reimburse him for the amount of these checks. When Bank refused, Gennone sued Bank to recover. Who wins? *Gennone v. Peoples National Bank & Trust Co.*, 9 U.C.C. Rep.Serv. 707, **Web** 1971 Pa. Dist. & Cnty. Dec. Lexis 551, 51 Pa. D. & C.2d 529 (Common Pleas Court of Montgomery County, Pennsylvania)

22.8 Deferred Posting: Dr. Robert L. Pracht received a check in the amount of $6,571.25 from Northwest Feedyards in payment for three loads of corn. The check was drawn on a checking account at Oklahoma State Bank (Bank). Pracht also maintained an account at Bank. On Friday, Pracht indorsed the check and gave it to an associate to deposit to Pracht's account at the bank. When the associate arrived at the bank around 3:00 P.M., he discovered that the bank's doors were locked. After gaining the attention of a bank employee, the associate was allowed into the bank, where he gave the check and deposit slip to a teller. Because the bank's computer had shut down at 3:00 P.M., the teller put the check aside. The associate testified that several bank employees were working at their desks as he left the bank. The bank was not open on Saturday or Sunday. Three days later, Bank dishonored the check due to insufficient funds. Pracht sued to recover the amount of the check from Bank. Who wins? *Pracht v. Oklahoma State Bank*, 1979 OK 43, 592 P.2d 976, **Web** 1979 Okla. Lexis 209 (Supreme Court of Oklahoma)

22.9 Right of Setoff: States Steamship Company (States Steamship) drew a check for $35,948 on its checking account at Crocker National Bank (Crocker). The check was made payable to Nautilus Leasing Services, Inc. (Nautilus). Nautilus deposited the check in its account at Chartered Bank of London, which forwarded the check to Crocker for collection. The check was received at Crocker's processing center at 8:00 A.M. on Friday.

At the time the check was presented for payment, States Steamship was indebted to Crocker for loans in the amount of $2 million. These loans were payable on demand. Previously, States Steamship was in severe financial difficulty and was conducting merger negotiations with another steamship company. On Monday morning, Crocker learned that these merger negotiations had broken down and demanded immediate payment of the $2 million. Crocker then seized the $1,726,032 in States Steamship's checking account at the bank. This action left State Steamship's account with a zero balance. State Steamship's check to Nautilus, as well as other checks that had been presented for payment, were returned unpaid. Nautilus sued Crocker to recover the amount of the check. Who wins? *Nautilus Leasing Services, Inc. v. Crocker National Bank*, 147 Cal. App. 3d 1023, 195 Cal.Rptr. 478, **Web** 1983 Cal. App. Lexis 2257 (Court of Appeal of California)

Ethics Issues

22.10 Ethics: Actors Equity, a union that represents 37,000 stage actors, sought to hire a new comptroller. A man named Nicholas Scotti applied for the position and submitted an extensive resume, showing that he was currently employed by Paris Maintenance Company as its comptroller. Scotti also stated that he had held various financial positions with Equitable Life Assurance Society and the Investors Funding Corporation. Officers of Actors Equity interviewed Scotti and offered him the job. No attempt was made to verify Scotti's background or prior employment history.

Actors Equity maintained a checking account at the Bank of New York. During the first six months as comptroller, Scotti forged the signature of the appropriate company employee on four Actors Equity checks totaling $100,000. The checks were made payable to N. Piscotti and were cashed by Scotti and paid by the Bank of New York. The forged signatures were of professional quality. After Scotti resigned as comptroller, the forgeries were discovered. Subsequent investigation revealed that Scotti's real name was Piscotti, that the information on his resume was false, and that he had an extensive criminal record. Actors Equity sued the drawee bank to recover the $100,000. Did Scotti act ethically in this case? Should Actors Equity have sued the bank to recover on the forged checks? Who wins? *Fireman's Fund Insurance Co. v. The Bank of New York*, 146 A.D.2d 95, 539 N.Y.S.2d 339, **Web** 1989 N.Y. App. Div. Lexis 4172 (Supreme Court of New York)

22.11 Ethics: Golden Gulf, Inc. (Golden Gulf), opened a checking account at AmSouth Bank, N.A. (AmSouth). Golden Gulf entered into a subscription agreement wherein Albert M. Rossini agreed to pay $250,000 for stock in the company. Rossini tendered a check drawn on the Mark Twain Bank in Kansas City, Missouri, to Golden Gulf for that amount. Golden Gulf deposited the check in its checking account at AmSouth on August 30, 1988. Three days later, Golden Gulf contacted AmSouth and asked if the funds were "available." AmSouth said the funds were available for use. Golden Gulf requested AmSouth to wire transfer the funds to it in New York for use in that state. AmSouth complied with the request. Five days later, AmSouth received notice from the Mark Twain Bank that Rossini's check would not be paid due to insufficient funds. On September 8, 1988, AmSouth notified Golden Gulf that the check had been dishonored. AmSouth revoked the credit it had given to Golden Gulf's account, resulting in an overdraft of $248,965.69. AmSouth sued to recover this amount. Did Golden Gulf act ethically in this case? Did AmSouth extend a provisional or final settlement to Golden Gulf's account? *Golden Gulf, Inc. v. AmSouth Bank, N.A.*, 565 So.2d 114, **Web** 1990 Ala. Lexis 436 (Supreme Court of Alabama)

IRAC Writing Assignment

Read **Case A-22** in Appendix A [*First American Bank and Trust v. Rishoi*]. Use the IRAC method to prepare a written analysis of the case.

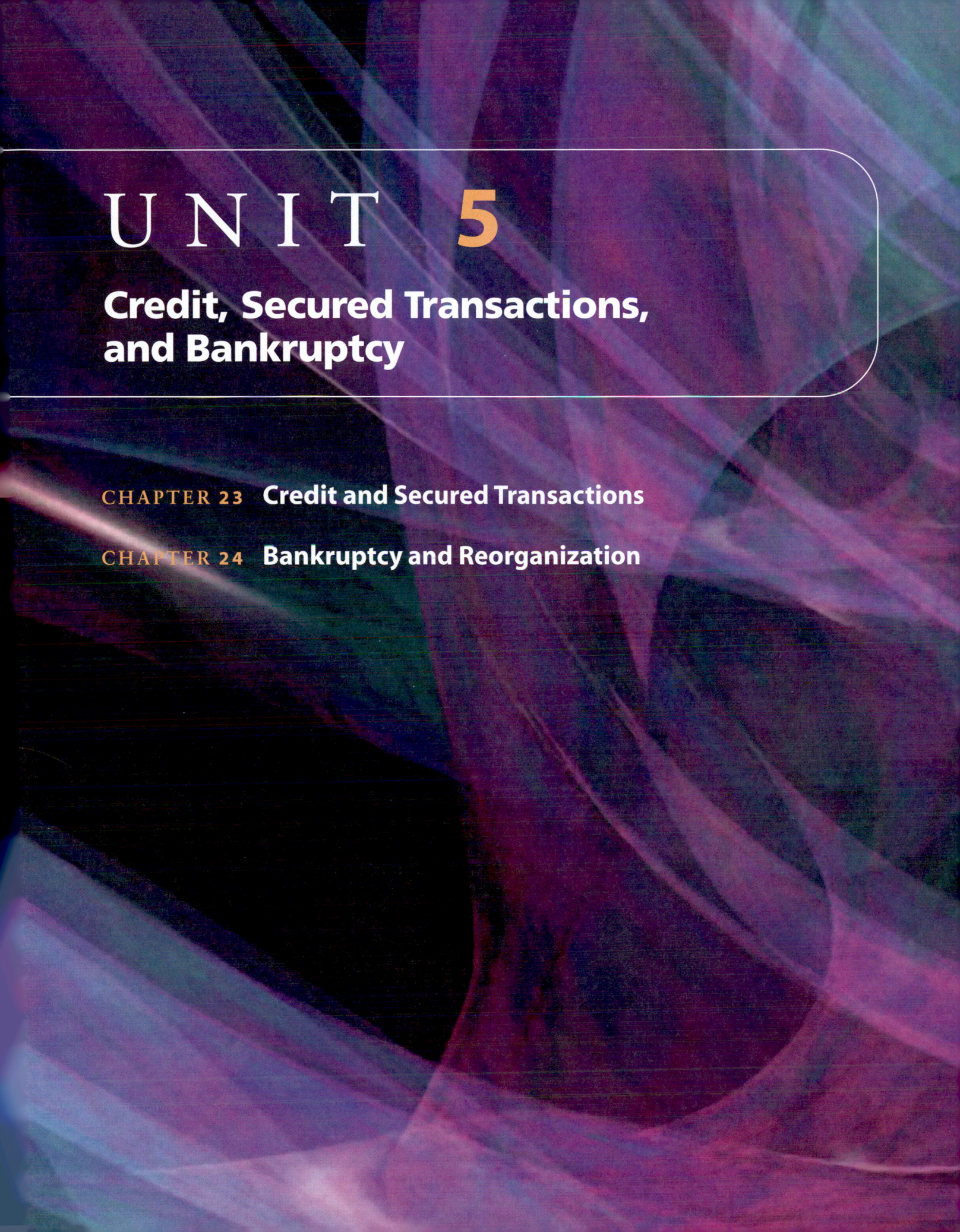

UNIT 5

Credit, Secured Transactions, and Bankruptcy

CHAPTER 23

Credit and Secured Transactions

"Creditors have better memories than debtors."

—BENJAMIN FRANKLIN
Poor Richard's Almanack (1758)

CHAPTER OBJECTIVES

After studying this chapter, you should be able to:

1. Distinguish between unsecured and secured credit.
2. Describe security interests in real property, such as mortgages and deeds of trust.
3. Describe the scope of Revised Article 9 of the UCC.
4. Describe how a security interest in personal property is created and the perfection of a security interest.
5. Describe the protections afforded by federal law to debtors from abusive, deceptive, and unfair practices.

CHAPTER CONTENTS

   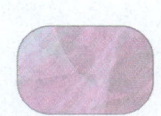 

Introduction to Credit and Secured Transactions

The U.S. economy is a **credit** economy. Consumers borrow money to make major purchases (e.g., homes, automobiles, appliances) and use credit cards (e.g., Visa, Master Card) to purchase goods and services at clothing stores, restaurants, and other businesses. Businesses use credit to purchase equipment, supplies, and other goods and services. In a credit transaction, the borrower is the *debtor*, and the lender is the *creditor*.

Because lenders are sometimes reluctant to lend large sums of money simply on the borrower's promise to repay, many of them take a *security interest* in either the item purchased or some other property of the debtor. The property in which the security interest is taken is called *collateral*. If the debtor does not pay the debt, the creditor can foreclose on and recover the collateral.

A lender who is unsure whether a debtor will have sufficient income or assets to repay a loan may require another person to guarantee payment. If the borrower fails to repay the loan, that person is responsible for paying it. This responsibility is called *suretyship*. The federal government has enacted several major statutes that protect debtors from abusive, deceptive, and unfair credit practices.

This chapter discusses types of credit, security interests in real property, secured transactions in personal property, suretyship, and debtor protection laws.

Victorian Cottage, Mackinac Island, Michigan

A bank or another creditor that lends money to a borrower to purchase a house usually takes back a mortgage that makes the house security (collateral) for the loan.

Unsecured and Secured Credit

Credit may be extended on either an *unsecured* or a *secured* basis. The following paragraphs discuss these types of credit.

Debtor and Creditor

In a transaction involving the extension of credit, there are two parties. The party extending the credit, the lender, is called the **creditor**. The party borrowing the money, the borrower, is called the **debtor** (see Exhibit 23.1).

Example Prima goes to Urban Bank and borrows $100,000. In this case, Prima is the debtor, and Urban Bank is the creditor.

EXHIBIT 23.1

Debtor and Creditor

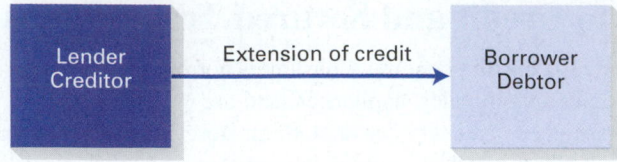

Unsecured Credit

Unsecured credit does not require any security (collateral) to protect the payment of the debt. Instead, the creditor relies on the debtor's promise to repay the principal (plus any interest) when it is due. If the debtor fails to make the payments, the creditor may bring legal action and obtain a judgment against him or her. If the debtor is *judgment-proof* (i.e., has little or no property or no income that can be garnished), the creditor may never collect.

Secured Credit

To minimize the risk associated with extending unsecured credit, a creditor may require a security interest in the debtor's property (collateral). The collateral secures payment of the loan. This type of credit is called **secured credit**. Security interests may be taken in real, personal, intangible, and other property.

If the debtor fails to make the payments when due, the collateral may be repossessed to recover the outstanding amount. Generally, if the sale of the collateral is insufficient to repay the loan (plus interest), the creditor may bring a lawsuit against the debtor to recover a deficiency judgment for the difference.

Example Douglas purchases a new automobile from Mina Motors, an automobile dealership. Douglas pays $5,000 cash as a down payment and borrows $25,000 from Mina Motors to cover the rest of the purchase price. The loan is for three years, with equal monthly payments. Mina Motors takes a security interest in the automobile, which becomes collateral for the loan. Suppose Douglas later fails to pay his loan payments. Mina Motors can repossess the automobile and sell it to another buyer. If there is $20,000 remaining unpaid on the loan, and Mina Motors sells the used automobile to another buyer for 16,000, it can go to court and get a deficiency judgment against Douglas for $4,000. Mina Motors can then try to recover the $4,000 from Douglas.

CONTEMPORARY ENVIRONMENT

Unsecured Credit Versus Secured Credit

“*In this case and so many others, Klondike's rights in the goods have become subject to a superior lien.*”

—Judge Baynes

Generally, a creditor would rather be a secured creditor than an unsecured creditor because of the extra protection and priority status the secured position gives the creditor. The following case shows why. Sunstate Dairy & Food Products Co. (Sunstate) distributed dairy products in Florida. It had the following two debts among its other debts:

1. Sunstate borrowed money from Barclays Business Credit, Inc. (Barclays), and signed a security agreement granting Barclays a continuing security interest in and lien upon substantially all of

Sunstate's personal property, including all of Sunstate's inventory, equipment, accounts receivable, and general intangibles then existing or thereafter acquired. Barclays perfected its security interest by filing a financing statement with the proper state government authorities.

2. Fifteen months later, Sunstate purchased $49,512 of Klondike ice cream bars from Isaly Klondike Company (Klondike) on credit. Klondike did not take a security interest in the ice cream bars.

One week after purchasing the Klondike bars, Sunstate filed for bankruptcy. At that time, Sunstate owed Barclays $10,050,766, and $47,731 worth of unpaid-for Klondike bars remained in Sunstate's possession. Barclays and Klondike fought over the Klondike bars. Klondike filed a motion with the court, seeking to reclaim the Klondike bars. Barclays sought to enforce its security agreement against Sunstate and recover the Klondike bars in Sunstate's possession.

The court sided with Barclays because it was a secured creditor with a perfected security interest. The court found that Klondike, as an unsecured creditor, had no legal right to reclaim the Klondike bars. The U.S. Bankruptcy Court stated, "In this case and so many others, Klondike's rights in the goods have become subject to a superior lien."

Klondike was merely one of many unsecured general creditors that would receive but pennies on the dollar in Sunstate's bankruptcy. Klondike learned a costly lesson: It is better to be a secured creditor than an unsecured creditor. *In the Matter of Sunstate Dairy & Food Products Company*, 145 B.R. 341, **Web** 1992 Bankr. Lexis 1496 (United States Bankruptcy Court for the Middle District of Florida)

Law & Ethics Questions

1. What is the difference between secured credit and unsecured credit? Explain.

2. **ETHICS** Was it ethical for the debtor, Sunstate Dairy & Food Products Company, to not pay its debt to Klondike?

Web Exercises

1. **WEB** Visit the website of the United States Bankruptcy Court for the Middle District of Florida, at *www.flmb.uscourts.gov*.

2. **WEB** To read a history of the Isaly Klondike Company and Klondike bar, go to *www.icecreamusa.com/klondike/history*.

Security Interest in Real Property

Owners of real estate can create security interests in their property. This occurs if an owner borrows money from a lender and pledges real estate as security for repayment of the loan.

Mortgage

A person who owns a piece of real property has an ownership interest in that property. A property owner who borrows money from a creditor may use his or her real estate as collateral for repayment of the loan. This type of collateral arrangement, known as a **mortgage**, is a *two-party instrument*. The *owner-debtor* is the **mortgagor**, and the *creditor* is the **mortgagee**. The parties to a mortgage are illustrated in Exhibit 23.2.

Example Suppose General Electric purchases a manufacturing plant for $10 million, pays $2 million cash as a down payment, and borrows the remaining $8 million from City Bank. To secure the loan, City Bank requires General Electric to give it a mortgage on the plant. If General Electric defaults on the loan, the bank may take action under state law to foreclose on the property.

Note and Deed of Trust

Some states' laws provide for the use of a *deed of trust* and *note* in place of a mortgage. The **note** is the instrument that evidences the borrower's debt to the lender; the **deed of trust** is the instrument that gives the creditor a security interest in the debtor's property that is pledged as collateral.

A deed of trust is a *three-party instrument*. Under it, legal title to the real property is placed with a **trustee** (usually a trust corporation) until the amount borrowed has been paid. The *owner-debtor* is called the **trustor**. Although legal title is vested in the trustee, the trustor has full legal rights to possession of the real property. The *creditor* is called the **beneficiary**. Exhibit 23.3 illustrates the relationship between the parties.

When the loan is repaid, the trustee files a *written reconveyance* with the county recorder's office, which transfers title to the real property to the borrower-debtor. If the

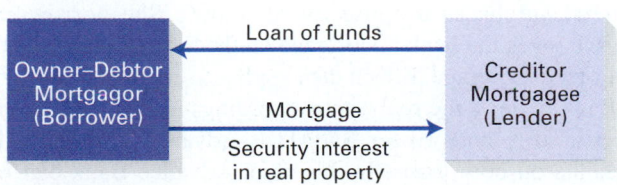

EXHIBIT 23.2

Mortgage

EXHIBIT 23.3

Note and Deed of Trust

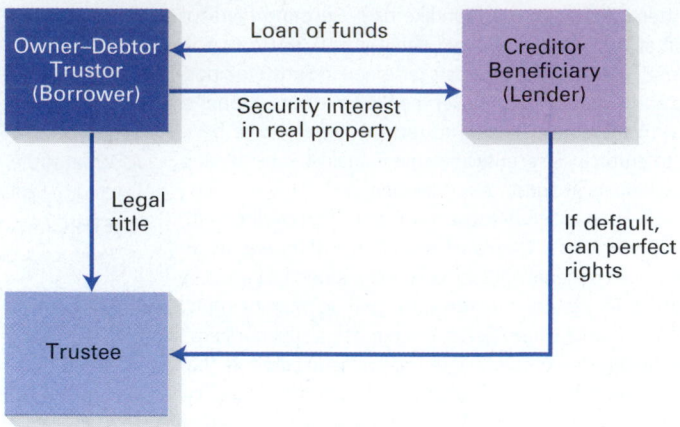

loan is not repaid, the trustee can deed the property to the lender-creditor beneficiary or sell the property through foreclosure proceeding, depending on state law.

> Debt is the prolific mother of folly and of crime.
>
> Benjamin Disraeli
> *Henrietta Temple (1837)*

Example Gregory purchases a house and obtains a loan from City Bank. Gregory signs a *note* that evidences his debt to City Bank. Gregory also signs a *deed of trust* that gives City Bank a security interest in the house; that is, the house becomes collateral for the loan. The deed of trust names Commercial Trust Company as the trustee, and Commercial Trust Company owns legal title to the house. If Gregory pays the loan, Commercial Trust Company will transfer title to the house to Gregory. If Gregory does not repay the loan, however, Commercial Trust Company can transfer title to the house to City Bank or institute foreclosure proceedings, whichever is provided by state law.

Recording Statute

Most states have enacted **recording statutes** that require a mortgage or deed of trust to be recorded in the county recorder's office in the county in which the real property is located. This record gives potential lenders or purchasers of real property the ability to determine whether there are any existing liens (mortgages) on the property.

The nonrecordation of a mortgage or deed of trust does not affect either the legality of the instrument between the mortgagor and the mortgagee or the rights and obligations of the parties. In other words, the mortgagor is obligated to pay the amount of the mortgage according to the terms of the mortgage, even if the document is not recorded. However, an improperly recorded document is not effective against either (1) subsequent purchasers of the real property or (2) other mortgagees or lienholders who have no notice of the prior mortgages.

> By no means run in debt.
>
> George Herbert
> *The Temple (1633)*

Example Suppose Debbie Brown purchases a house for $500,000. She borrows $400,000 from Country Bank and gives the bank a mortgage on the house for this amount. Country Bank fails to record the mortgage. Brown contracts to sell the house to Edward Johnson. Johnson reviews the real estate recordings and finds no mortgage against the property. The deed transferring ownership of the property from Brown to Johnson is recorded. Johnson pays $600,000 cash to Brown for the house. Brown defaults on her loan from Country Bank. In this case, Country Bank cannot foreclose on the real property because it failed to record the mortgage. Johnson owns the house free of Country Bank's mortgage. The bank's only recourse is to sue Brown to recover the amount of the loan.

Suppose Eileen purchases a house for $500,000. She borrows $400,000 from Boulevard Bank and gives the bank a mortgage on the house for this amount. Boulevard Bank fails to record the mortgage. Eileen then applies to borrow $400,000 from Advance Bank. Advance Bank reviews the real estate recordings and finds no mortgage recorded against the property, so it lends Eileen $400,000. Advance Bank records its mortgage. Later, Eileen defaults on both loans. In this case, Advance Bank can foreclose on the house because it had recorded its mortgage. Boulevard Bank, even though it made the first loan to Eileen, does not get the house and can only sue Eileen to recover the unpaid loan.

In the following case, the court had to determine the priority of mortgages on the same real property.

C A S E 23.1
Recording Statute

Bank of South Palm Beaches v. Stockton, Whatley, Davin & Company

473 So.2d 1358, **Web** 1985 Fla. App. Lexis 14742
Court of Appeals of Florida

> **❝** *The very act of recording a mortgage in compliance with the Florida recording statute constitutes constructive notice to all subsequent mortgagees.* **❞**
>
> —Judge Hurley

Facts

Stockton, Whatley, Davin & Company (SWD) loaned $448,200 to Castle Builders Construction Company (Castle Builders). This loan was secured by a promptly recorded mortgage on two parcels of land. Thereafter, several additional creditors, including the Bank of South Palm Beaches, lent Castle Builders various sums that were secured by duly recorded mortgages on the same two parcels of land. South Palm Beaches Bank's secured note from Castle Builders was in the amount of $77,500. Eventually, Castle Builders fell behind in its payments on the loan from SWD and asked SWD for additional loan funds in the amount of $150,000. SWD was willing to advance the additional money but only on the condition that the other creditors agreed to subordinate their security interests to SWD's new loans. The other creditors agreed to do so, and subordination agreements were duly executed and recorded. Apparently, through an oversight of SWD, however, it never procured a subordination agreement from South Palm Beaches Bank. SWD advanced the $150,000 to Castle Builders, with most of the proceeds being applied to pay the amount owed to SWD on the initial loan. The deed of trust was modified to show this increase in the loan and was properly recorded. Castle Builders defaulted on the SWD loans, and SWD initiated foreclosure proceedings. South Palm Beaches Bank was brought into the action. The trial court held that SWD had first lien priority regarding its entire loan to Castle Builders. South Palm Beaches Bank appealed.

Issue

Did the modification loan from SWD have lien priority over the loans from South Palm Beaches Bank?

Language of the Court

In an apparent attempt to reach the fairest result, the trial court disregarded the "first in time" maxim and ruled that SWD's interest was superior to that of South Palm Beaches Bank, notwithstanding the fact that the bank's interest was recorded first. The very act of recording a mortgage in compliance with the Florida recording statute constitutes constructive notice to all subsequent mortgagees.

It is not disputed that the bank's mortgage securing the $77,500 note from Castle Builders was recorded in compliance with the Florida recording statute and before SWD either recorded or entered into the modification agreement with Castle Builders. SWD therefore had constructive knowledge of the bank's prior interest. Consequently, the bank's mortgage securing the $77,500 note had lien priority over funds advanced to Castle Builders pursuant to the mortgage modification agreement.

Decision

The court of appeals held that South Palm Beaches Bank's mortgage had priority because it was recorded prior to SWD's loan. The court of appeals reversed the judgment of the trial court.

Law & Ethics Questions

1. What does the "first in time to record" rule provide? Would any other rule work in this case?

2. **ETHICS** Did SWD act ethically in arguing that its second note took priority over South Palm Beaches Bank's previously recorded note?

3. What is a subordination agreement? What are the economic consequences of a creditor agreeing to subordinate its loan to another loan?

Web Exercises

1. **WEB** For the complete opinion of this case, go to *www.prenhall.com/cheesemancases*.

2. **WEB** Visit the website of the court of appeals of Florida, Fourth District, at *www.4dca.org*.

3. **WEB** Use *www.google.com* to find an article that describes the recording statute in your state. Where do mortgages or notes have to be recorded?

Foreclosure

If a mortgagor defaults on a mortgage, the mortgagee can declare the entire debt due and payable immediately. This right can be enforced through a procedure called **foreclosure**. Issues relating to foreclosure are discussed in the following paragraphs.

FORECLOSURE SALE All states permit **foreclosure sales**. Under this method, the debtor's defaulting may trigger a legal court action for foreclosure. Any party having an interest in the property—including owners of the property and other mortgagees or lienholders—must be named as defendants. If the mortgagee's case is successful, the court will issue a judgment that orders the real property to be sold at a judicial sale. The procedures for a foreclosure action and sale are mandated by state statute. Any surplus must be paid to the mortgagor.

Example Suppose Christine borrows $500,000 from Country Bank to buy a house. Christine (mortgagor) gives a mortgage to Country Bank (mortgagee), making the house collateral to secure the loan. Later, Christine defaults on the loan. Country Bank can foreclose on the property and follow applicable state law to sell the house at a judicial sale. If the house sells for $575,000, the bank keeps $500,000 and must remit $75,000 to Christine. Most state statutes permit the mortgagee-lender to recover the costs of the foreclosure and judicial sale from the sale proceeds before remitting the surplus to the mortgagor-borrower.

POWER OF SALE Most states permit foreclosure by **power of sale**, although this must be expressly conferred in the mortgage or deed of trust. Under a power of sale, the procedure for that sale is contained in the mortgage or deed of trust itself. No court action is necessary. Some states have enacted statutes that establish the procedure for conducting the sale. Such a sale must be by auction for the highest price obtainable. Any surplus must be paid to the mortgagor.

Deficiency Judgment

Some states permit a mortgagee to bring a separate legal action to recover a deficiency from the mortgagor. If the mortgagee is successful, the court will award a **deficiency judgment** that entitles the mortgagee to recover the amount of the judgment from the mortgagor's property.

Several states have enacted statutes that prohibit deficiency judgments regarding certain types of mortgages, such as loans for the original purchase of residential property. These statutes are called **antideficiency statutes**.

Example Assume that a house is located in a state that has an antideficiency statute. Kaye buys the house, puts $200,000 down, and borrows $600,000 of the $800,000 purchase price from a bank, which takes a mortgage on the property to secure the loan. Suppose that Kaye defaults, and when the bank forecloses on the property, it is worth only $500,000. The bank cannot recover the $100,000 deficiency from Kaye because the state has an antideficiency statute.

Right of Redemption

The common law and many state statutes give the mortgagor the right to redeem real property after default and before foreclosure. This right, which is called the **right of redemption**, requires the mortgagor to pay the full amount of the debt—that is, principal, interest, and other costs—incurred by the mortgagee because of the mortgagor's default. Redemption of a partial interest is not permitted. Upon redemption, the mortgagor receives title to the property, free and clear of the mortgage debt.

Some states allow the mortgagor to redeem real property only for a specified period (usually six months or one year) after foreclosure. This is called the *statutory period of redemption*. If this right exists, the deed to the real property is not delivered to the purchaser at the foreclosure sale until after the statutory period of redemption has expired.

Most state laws provide that any party in interest—such as a second mortgage holder or another lienholder—may redeem the property during the redemption period.

Land Sales Contract

Most states permit the transfer and sale of real property pursuant to a **land sales contract**. Here, the owner of real property agrees to sell the property to a purchaser, who agrees to pay the purchase price to the owner-seller over an agreed-upon period of time. Often, making such a loan is referred to as "carrying the paper."

Land sales contracts are often used to sell undeveloped property, farms, and the like. Under such contracts, the seller retains title to the property until the purchaser pays the purchase price (plus interest). During the period of the contract, the purchaser (1) has the legal right to possession and use of the property and (2) is responsible for the payment of insurance, taxes, and such.

If the purchaser defaults, the seller may declare a forfeiture and retake possession of the property. Many states provide a statutory procedure that must be followed to foreclose on a land sales contract. These procedures are often simpler, less time-consuming, and less expensive than foreclosure on a mortgage or deed of trust. Many states give the debtor the right to redeem the real property within a specified statutory period.

CONTEMPORARY ENVIRONMENT
Mechanic's Lien

Owners of real property often hire contractors and laborers (e.g., painters, plumbers, roofers, bricklayers, furnace installers) to make improvements to that property. The contractors and laborers expend the time to provide their services as well as money to provide the materials for the improvements. Their investments are protected by state statutes that permit them to file a **mechanic's lien** against the improved real property.

When a lien is properly filed, the real property to which the improvements have been made becomes security for the payment of these services and materials. In essence, the lienholder has the equivalent of a mortgage on the property. If the owner defaults, the lienholder may foreclose on the lien, sell the property, and satisfy the debt plus interest and costs out of the proceeds of the sale. Any surplus must be paid to the owner-debtor.

Generally, the lien must be foreclosed on during a specific period of time (commonly six months to two years) from the date the lien is filed. Mechanic's liens are usually subject to the debtor's right of redemption.

Procedure for Obtaining a Mechnic's Lien

Although the procedures for obtaining a mechanic's lien vary from state to state, the following requirements generally must be met:

1. The lienholder must file a *notice of lien* with the county recorder's office in the county in which the real property subject to the lien is located.

2. The notice must state the amount of the claim, the name of the claimant, the name of the owner of the real property, and a description of the real property.

3. The notice must be filed within a specified time period (commonly 30 to 120 days) after the services have been performed or materials have been delivered.

4. Notice of the lien must be given to the owner of the real property.

Lien Release

Most state statutes permit an owner of real property to have contractors, subcontractors, laborers, and material persons who have provided services or materials to a real property project to sign a written **release of lien** contract (also called a **lien release**) attesting to the receipt of payment and releasing any lien they might otherwise assert against the property. A lien release can be used by the property owner to defeat a statutory lienholder's attempt to obtain payment.

Example Suppose Travis Company, which owns an undeveloped piece of property, hires Mason Corporation, a general contractor, to build a warehouse on the lot. Mason builds the warehouse and hires Rouse Company, a roofer, as a subcontractor to put the roof on the warehouse. When the warehouse is complete, Travis pays Mason the full contract price for the warehouse but fails to obtain a release of lien from Rouse. Mason does not pay Rouse. Rouse files a mechanic's lien against the warehouse and demands payment from Travis. Here, Travis must pay Rouse for the roofing work; if he does not, Rouse may foreclose on the warehouse, have it sold, and satisfy the debt out of the proceeds of the sale. Travis ends up paying twice for the roofing work. Travis's only recourse is to sue Mason.

Example Suppose that Travis obtained a lien release from Rouse before or at the time Travis paid Mason, the general contractor. If Mason failed to pay the subcontractor Rouse, Rouse could not file a lien against Travis's house. In this situation, Rouse's only recourse is to sue Mason.

Latvia

Banks and creditors in the countries of the former Soviet Union provide financing for the purchase of real estate.

Secured Transactions: Revised Article 9 of the UCC

Individuals and businesses purchase or lease various forms of tangible and intangible **personal property**. *Tangible personal property* includes equipment, vehicles, furniture, computers, clothing, jewelry, and such. *Intangible personal property* includes securities, patents, trademarks, and copyrights.

Personal property is oftentimes sold on credit. This means the purchaser-debtor has borrowed money from a lender-creditor to purchase the personal property. Sometimes a lender will extend ***unsecured credit*** to a debtor to purchase personal property. In this case, the creditor takes no interest in any collateral to secure the loan but looks to the credit standing of the debtor to repay the loan. If the debtor defaults on the loan, the creditor must sue the debtor to try to recover the unpaid loan amount.

In some credit transactions, particularly those involving large or expensive items, a creditor may agree to extend credit only if the purchaser pledges some personal property as collateral for the loan. This is called ***secured credit***. If the debtor defaults on the loan, the creditor may seek to recover the collateral under a lawful foreclosure action.

> Creditor: One of a tribe of savages dwelling beyond the Financial Straits and dreaded for their desolating excursions.
>
> Ambrose Bierce
> *The Devil's Dictionary (1911)*

CONTEMPORARY ENVIRONMENT
Revised Article 9—Secured Transactions

Article 9 (Secured Transactions) of the Uniform Commercial Code (UCC) governs secured transactions in personal property. Where personal property is used as collateral for a loan or extension of credit, a resulting secured transaction is governed by Article 9 of the UCC.

After years of study and debate, a **Revised Article 9 (Secured Transactions)**, as promulgated by the National Conference of Commissioners on Uniform State Laws and the American Law Institute (together "Commission"), became effective in 2001.

Revised Article 9 includes modern and efficient rules to govern secured transactions in personal property. Revised Article 9 includes

changes to provisions that have been controversial in the past, as well as adding new provisions to recognize changes in the commercial environment.

In addition, Revised Article 9 contains many new provisions and rules that recognize the importance of electronic commerce. Revised Article 9 provides rules for the creation, filing, and enforcement of electronic secured transactions.

Since its release in 2001, all states have enacted Revised Article 9 (Secured Transactions) as the UCC statute within their states. The following material in this chapter that covers secured transactions is based on the provisions of Revised Article 9.

Secured Transaction

When a creditor extends credit to a debtor and takes a security interest in some personal property of the debtor, it is called a **secured transaction**. The **secured party** is the seller, lender, or other party in whose favor there is a security interest. If the debtor defaults and does not repay the loan, generally the secured party can foreclose and recover the collateral.

Definitions Important to Secured Transactions

Revised Article 9 contains definitions that are important for understanding secured transactions. Some of the most important definitions are described below.

1. *Debtor* – A person that has an ownership or other interest in the collateral and owes payment of a secured obligation [Revised UCC 9-102(a)(28)].

   Example A farmer who purchases a large John Deere tractor from a retail dealer on credit and gives the secured creditor an interest in the collateral is the debtor.

2. *Secured party* – A person in whose favor a security interest is created or provided under a security agreement [Revised UCC 9-102(a)(72)].

   Example In the previous example, the John Deere retail dealer is the secured creditor. (The secured party can be the seller (e.g., the John Deere retail dealer), another lender (e.g., a bank), or buyer of accounts (e.g., an investor that purchases the security interest)).

3. *Security interest* – An interest in the collateral, such as personal property or fixtures, which secures payment or performance of an obligation [UCC 1-201(b)(35)].

   Example In the previous example, the debtor-farmer gave the retail dealer-secured creditor a security interest in the John Deere tractor.

4. *Security agreement* – An agreement that creates or provides for a security interest [Revised UCC 9-102(a)(73)].

   Example In the prior example, when the farmer purchased the John Deere tractor from the retail dealer on credit, the retail dealer may require, as a condition of the sale, that the farmer sign a security agreement giving the retail dealer a secured interest in the tractor. If this is done, and the farmer defaults on the payments, the John Deere retail dealer can foreclose on its security agreement and recover the tractor.

5. *Collateral* – The property that is subject to a security agreement [Revised UCC 9-102(a)(12)].

   Example In the previous example, the John Deere tractor is the collateral for the security agreement.

6. *Financing statement* – The record of an initial financing statement or filed record relating to the initial financing statement [Revised UCC 9-102(a)(39)]. This is **Form UCC 1 (UCC Financing Statement)**. The financing statement is usually filed with the appropriate state office to give public notice of the secured party's security interest in the collateral.

   Example In the previous example, if the retail dealer (the secured creditor) files a financing statement, it has given public notice of its secured interest in the collateral, the John Deere tractor.

Two-Party Secured Transaction

Exhibit 23.4 illustrates a **two-party secured transaction**. Such transactions occur, for example, when a seller sells goods to a buyer on credit and retains a security interest in the goods.

EXHIBIT 23.4

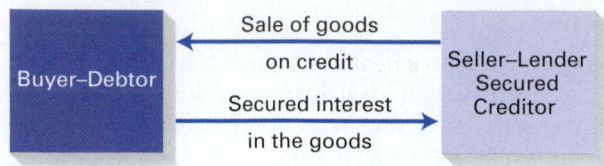

Example Mechanical Company manufactures and sells equipment used by oil companies to drill for oil. The Big Oil Company purchases equipment from Mechanical Company on credit, with Oil Company signing a note promising to pay for the equipment within 90 days. The contract provides that Mechanical Company retains a security interest in the equipment. Mechanical Company is the secured creditor, and Oil Company is the buyer-debtor in this two-party secured transaction. Mechanical Company delivers the equipment to Oil Company. If Oil Company fails to pay for the equipment within the time specified, Mechanical Company can recover the collateral, the equipment.

Three-Party Secured Transaction

Exhibit 23.5 illustrates a **three-party secured transaction**. This type of situation occurs when a seller sells goods to a buyer who has obtained financing from a third-party lender (e.g., bank) that takes a security interest in the goods sold.

Example Contractor Company manufactures and sells equipment used by road construction companies to build highways. Road Company purchases equipment from Contractor Company, but to do so, Road Company borrows the money from City Bank. Road Company signs a note promising to repay the loan from City Bank within one year. The contract provides that City Bank retains a security interest in the equipment. Contractor Company is the seller, City Bank is the secured creditor, and Road Company is the buyer-debtor in this three-party secured transaction. Road Company pays Contractor Company, and Contractor Company delivers the equipment to Road Company. If Road Company fails to pay for the equipment within the time specified, City Bank can recover the collateral, the equipment.

Personal Property Subject to a Security Agreement

A security interest may be given in various types of personal property that becomes **collateral** for the loan [Revised UCC 9-102(a)(12)]. Personal property that may be given as security is listed in Exhibit 23.6.

EXHIBIT 23.5

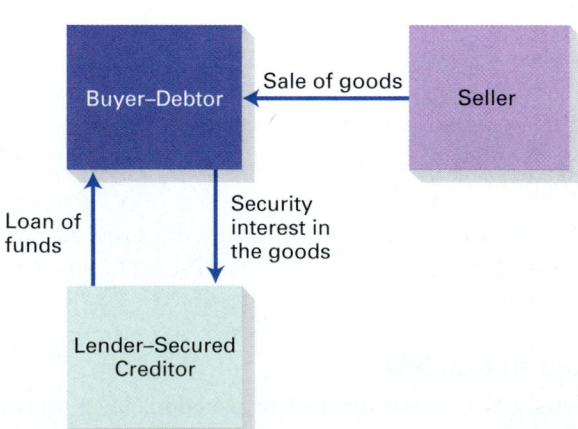

EXHIBIT 23.6

Types of Collateral

1. **Tangible Personal Property**   All things that are movable when a security interest attaches [Revised UCC 9-102(a)(44)]. This includes:
   1. **Accessions** that are goods that are physically united with other goods in such a manner that the identity of the original goods is not lost [Revised UCC 9-102(a)(1)].

      Example GPS system that is installed in an automobile.

   2. **Consumer goods** bought or used primarily for personal, family, or household purposes [Revised UCC 9-102(a)(23)].

      Examples Household televisions, furniture, and furnishings.

   3. **Equipment** bought or used primarily for business [Revised UCC 9-102(a)(33)].

      Examples Business trucks, moving cranes, and assembly line equipment.

   4. **Farm products**, including crops, aquatic goods, livestock, and supplies produced in a farming operations [Revised UCC 9-102(a)(34)].

      Examples Wheat, fish, cattle, milk, apples, and unborn calves.

   5. **Inventory** held for sale or lease, including work in progress and materials [Revised UCC 9-102(a)(48)].

      Example Raw materials used in production of goods.

2. **Intangible Personal Property**   Nonphysical personal property. This includes:
   1. **Accounts** that includes a right to payment of a monetary obligation (a) for personal or real property sold, leased, licensed, assigned, or otherwise disposed of, (b) services rendered or to be rendered, (c) policies of insurance, (d) secondary obligations incurred, (e) energy provided, (f) use of hire of a vessel under charter, (g) arising out of the use of a credit or charge card, (h) winnings in a state-operated or state-sponsored lottery, and (i) health-care-insurance receivables [Revised UCC 9-102(a)(1)].
   2. **Chattel paper**, which is a record that evidences both a monetary obligation and a security interest in specific goods and software used in the goods [Revised UCC 9-102(a)(11)].

      Example A security agreement. **Tangible chattel paper** is inscribed on a tangible medium [Revised UCC 9-102(a)(78)]. **Electronic chattel paper** is evidenced by information stored in an electronic medium [Revised UCC 9-102(a)(31)].

   3. **Deposit accounts** [Revised UCC 9-102(a)(29)].

      Examples Demand, time, savings, passbook, or similar account maintained at a bank.

   4. **General intangibles**, which means any personal property (other than exceptions listed in Revised UCC 9-102(a)(42)) payment intangibles, and software [Revised UCC 9-102(a)(42)].

      Examples Patents, copyrights, royalties, and the like.

   5. **Instruments,** which include negotiable instruments and any other writing that evidences a right to the payment of a monetary obligation that can ordinarily be transferred [Revised UCC 9-102(a)(47)].

      Examples Checks, notes, stocks, bonds, and other investment securities [Revised UCC 9-102(a)

   Revised Article 9 of the UCC does not apply to transactions involving real estate mortgages, landlord's liens, artisan's or mechanic's liens, liens on wages, judicial liens, and the like. These types of liens are usually covered by other laws.

Creating and Perfecting a Security Interest

Revised Article 9 sets forth the requirements that must be met to create a security interest in personal property. These requirements are discussed in the following paragraphs.

Security Agreement

Unless the creditor has possession of the collateral, there must be a **security agreement**. A security agreement means an agreement that creates or provides for a security interest [Revised UCC 9-102(a)(73)]. To be valid, the **security agreement** must (1) clearly describe the collateral so that it can be readily identified, (2) contain the debtor's promise to repay the creditor, including terms of repayment (e.g., the interest rate, time of payment), (3) set forth the creditor's rights upon the debtor's default, and (4) be signed by the debtor.

Example Suppose Ashley borrows $1,000 from Chris and gives Chris her gold ring as security for the loan. This agreement does not have to be in writing because the creditor is in possession of the collateral. This oral security agreement is enforceable. If Ashley retained possession of the ring, however, a written security interest describing the collateral (the ring) signed by Ashley would be required.

Attachment

The debtor must have a current or future legal right in or the right to possession of the collateral. For example, a debtor may give a creditor a security interest in goods currently owned or in the possession of the debtor or in goods to be later acquired by the debtor. A debtor who does not have ownership or possessory rights to property cannot give a security interest in that property.

If these requirements are met, the rights of the secured party attach to the collateral. **Attachment** means that the creditor has an enforceable security interest against the debtor and can satisfy the debt out of the designated collateral (subject to the priority rules discussed later in this chapter) [Revised UCC 9-203(a)].

The Floating-Lien Concept

A security agreement may provide that the security interest attaches to property that was not originally in the possession of the debtor when the agreement was executed. This interest is usually referred to as a **floating lien**. A floating lien can attach to after-acquired property, sale proceeds, and future advances. These are discussed in the following paragraphs.

AFTER-ACQUIRED PROPERTY Many security agreements contain a clause that gives the secured party a security interest in **after-acquired property** of the debtor. After-acquired property is property that the debtor acquires after the security agreement is executed [Revised UCC 9-204(a)].

Example Manufacturing Corporation borrows $100,000 from First Bank and gives the bank a security interest in both its current and after-acquired inventory. If Manufacturing Corporation defaults on its loan to First Bank, the bank can claim any available original inventory as well as enough after-acquired inventory to satisfy its secured claim.

SALE PROCEEDS Unless otherwise stated in a security agreement, if a debtor sells, exchanges, or disposes of collateral subject to such an agreement, the secured party automatically has the right to receive the **proceeds** of the sale, exchange, or disposition [Revised UCC 9-102(a)(64), 9-203(f), 9-315(a)].

Example Zip, Inc., is a retail automobile dealer. To finance its inventory of new automobiles, Zip borrows money from First Bank and gives the bank a security interest in the inventory. Zip sells an automobile subject to the security agreement to Phyllis, who signs an installment sales contract, agreeing to pay Zip for the car in 24 equal monthly installments.

If Zip defaults on its payment to First Bank, the bank is entitled to receive the remaining payments from Phyllis.

FUTURE ADVANCES Often, debtors establish a continuing or revolving line of credit at a bank. Certain personal property of the debtor is designated as collateral for future loans from the line of credit. A maximum limit that the debtor may borrow is set, but the debtor can draw against the line of credit at any time. Any **future advances** made against the line of credit are subject to the security interest in the collateral. A new security agreement does not have to be executed each time a future advance is taken against the line of credit [Revised UCC 9-204(c)].

Example E-Corporation establishes a $1 million line of credit with Urban Bank. E-Corporation pledges its patent for an e-imager as collateral for the line of credit. This means that E-Corporation can draw on this line of credit (i.e., borrow money) any time it needs money. For example, E-Corporation immediately borrows $100,000. At a later date, E-Corporation decides to draw $500,000 against the line of credit. The new $500,000 loan is secured by the patent on the e-imager; a new security agreement does not have to be executed to create this security interest.

Perfecting a Security Interest

The concept of **perfection of a security interest** establishes the right of a secured creditor against other creditors who claim an interest in the collateral. Perfection is a legal process. The three main methods of perfecting a security interest under the UCC are (1) perfection by filing a financing statement, (2) perfection by possession of collateral, and (3) perfection by a purchase money security interest in consumer goods. These three main methods of perfecting a security interest are discussed in the following paragraphs.

PERFECTION BY FILING A FINANCING STATEMENT Often, a creditor's physical possession of collateral is impractical because it would deprive the debtor of use of the collateral (e.g., farm equipment, industrial machinery, consumer goods). At other times, it is simply impossible (e.g., accounts receivable). Filing a **financing statement** in the appropriate government office is the most common method of perfecting a creditor's security interest in such collateral [Revised UCC 9-501]. The person who files the financing statement should request the filing officer to note on his or her copy of the document the file number, date, and hour of filing. A financing statement covering fixtures is called a *fixture filing*. A filing can be electronically filed [Revised UCC 9-102(a)(18)].

A uniform financing statement form, UCC Form I, is used in all states [Revised UCC 9-521(a)]. The UCC Form I Financing Statement is shown in Exhibit 23.7.

Example Star Flyer Corporation manufactures and sells small airplanes. Sky Company, Inc., which operates a flying lesson school, purchases a specific airplane from Star Flyer Corporation on credit. The credit agreement requires Sky Company, Inc., to make equal monthly installment payments for three years until the purchase price (plus interest) is paid. Star Flyer Corporation files a financing statement with the appropriate state office that designates its security interest in the airplane. When the financing statement is properly filed and recorded, it is notice to the world of Star Flyer Corporation's security interest in the airplane.

Financing statements are available for review by the public. They serve as constructive notice to the world that a creditor claims an interest in a property. Financing statements are effective for five years from the date of filing [Revised UCC 9-515(a)]. A *continuation statement* may be filed up to six months prior to the expiration of the financing statement's five-year term. Such statements are effective for a new five-year term. Succeeding continuation statements may be filed [Revised UCC 9-515(d) and (e)].

To be enforceable, a financing statement must contain (1) the name of the debtor or a representative of the secured party, the name and address of the secured party and the collateral covered by the financing statement [Revised UCC 9-502(a)]. The secured party can file the security agreement as a financing statement.

A financing statement that provides only the debtor's trade name does not sufficiently provide the name of the debtor [Revised UCC 9-503(c)].

EXHIBIT 23.7

UCC Financing Statement

UCC FINANCING STATEMENT AMENDMENT

FOLLOW INSTRUCTIONS (front and back) CAREFULLY

A. NAME & PHONE OF CONTACT AT FILER [optional]

B. SEND ACKNOWLEDGMENT TO (Name and Address)

THE ABOVE SPACE IS FOR FILING OFFICE USE ONLY

1a. INTIAL FINANCING STATEMENT FILE.

1b. This FINANCING STATEMENT AMENOMENT is to be filled [for record] (for recorded) in the REAL ESTATE RECORDS.

2. ☐ **TERMINATION:** Effectiveness of the Financing Statement identified above is terminated with respect to security Interest(s) of the Secured Party authorizing this Temination Statement.

3. ☐ **CONTINUATION:** Effectiveness of the Financing Statement identified above with respect to security interest(s) of the Secured Party authorizing this Continuation Statement is continued for the additional period provided by applicable law.

4. ☐ **ASSIGNMENT** (full or partial: Give name of assignee in item 7a or 7b and address of assignee in item 7c and else give name of assignee in item 9.

5. AMENDMENT (PARTY INFORMATION): This Amendment affects ☐ Debtor or ☐ Securied Part of record. Check only one of these two boxes.

Also check one of the following three boxes and provide appropriate Information in items 6 and/or 7.

☐ CHANGE name and/or address. Give current record name in item 6a or 6b, also give now name (if name change) in item 7a or 7b, and/or new address (if address change) in item 7c.
☐ DELETE name: Give record name to be deleted in item 6a or 6b.
☐ ADD name: Complete item 7a or 7b, and also item 7c also complete items 7d-7c (if applicable)

6. CURRENT RECORD INFORMATION:

6a ORGANIZATION'S NAME			
OR 6b INDIVIDUAL'S LAST NAME	FIRST NAME	MIDDLE NAME	SUFFIX

7. CHANGED (NEW) OR ADDED INFORMATION:

7a ORGANIZATION'S NAME			
OR 6b INDIVIDUAL'S LAST NAME	FIRST NAME	MIDDLE NAME	SUFFIX
7c. MAILING ADDRESS	CITY	STATE	POSTAL CODE	COUNTRY

7d. TAX ID # 3SN OR EIN	ADD'L INFO RE ORGANIZATION DEBTOR	7e. TYPE OF ORGANIZATION	7f. JURISDICTION OF ORGANIZATION	Tg. ORGANIZATIONAL ID #, If any ☐ NONE

8. AMENDMENT (COLLATERAL CHANGE): check only one box.

Describe collateral ☐ deleted or ☐ added, or give entire ☐ reslated collateral description, or describe collateral ☐ assigned

9. NAME OF SECURED PARTY OF RECORD AUTHORIZING THIS AMENDMENT (name of assigner, if this is an Assignment). If this is an Amendment authorized by a Debtor which adds collateral or add the authorizing Debtor. or if this is a Termination authorized by a Debtor, check here ☐ and enter name of **DEBTOR** authorizing this Amendment.

9a. ORGANIZATION'S NAME			
OR 9b. INDIVIDUAL'S LAST NAME	FIRST NAME	MIDDLE NAME	SUFFIX

10. OPTIONAL FILTER FREFERENCE DATA.

FILING OFFICE COPY—NATIONAL UCC FINANCING STATEMENT AMENDMENT (FORM UCC3) (REV. 07/29/98)

Example Plains States Corporation, the legal name of the corporation, operates a farm equipment sales dealership under the trade name "Farmer Mary's Store." Plain States Corporation sells a large piece of farm equipment, on credit, to Fanny Farmer who operates a farm. Plain States Corporation files a financing statement but places its trade name, "Farmer Mary's Store" on the financing statement rather that its corporate name Plain States Corporation. This filing is defective.

State law specifies where the financing statement must be filed. A state may choose either the secretary of state or the county clerk in the county of the debtor's residence or, if the debtor is not a resident of the state, in the county where the goods are kept or in another county office or both. Most states require financing statements covering farm equipment, farm products, accounts, and consumer goods to be filed with the county clerk [Revised UCC 9-501].

In the following case, the court found that there was a defective filing of a financing statement.

C A S E **23.2**

Financing Statement

In re Greenbelt Cooperative, Inc.

124 B.R. 465, **Web** 1991 Bankr. Lexis 233
United States Bankruptcy Court for the District of Maryland

> **❝**A creditor should only be required to search under the legal name of a debtor to obtain notice of a security interest or to be put on notice to inquire further.**❞**
>
> —Judge Derby

Facts

Greenbelt Cooperative, Inc. (Greenbelt), was a consumer-owned cooperative engaged in the retail furniture business. Greenbelt operated under the trade name "SCAN Furniture," and it was well known among consumers by that name. Greenbelt leased forklifts, racking, and other equipment from Raymond Leasing Corporation (Raymond) and executed an equipment lease and security agreement giving Raymond a security interest in the equipment. At the conclusion of the lease term, Greenbelt could purchase the equipment for $1. Raymond filed a financing statement covering the equipment in the proper state government office. Raymond listed "SCAN Furniture" as the debtor on the financing statement. One and one-half years later, Greenbelt filed for bankruptcy in U.S. Bankruptcy Court. The bankruptcy trustee made a motion to avoid Raymond's claimed security interest in the equipment, alleging that Greenbelt had not properly filed a financing statement concerning the equipment because it had named the wrong party in the financing statement.

Issue

Did Raymond properly identify the debtor on the financing statement?

Language of the Court

This court concludes a Maryland court would apply a rule which requires that a financing statement be filed either under the legal name of the debtor or under a name which is substantially similar to the legal name of the debtor. A creditor should only be required to search under the legal name of a debtor to obtain notice of a security interest or to be put on notice to inquire further. Such a rule follows the weight of authority, it makes commercial sense, and it promotes uniformity. A filing under SCAN would not be found by those looking for security interests in the assets of Greenbelt Cooperative, Inc. Consequently, Raymond's financing statement was not sufficient to perfect its security interest in the debtor's assets against the claims of others.

Decision

The U.S. Bankruptcy Court held that Raymond had failed to identify the actual debtor in its financing statement. The Bankruptcy Court voided Raymond's lien on the equipment.

Law & Ethics Questions

1. Should creditors searching financing records be required to search for financing statements filed under the debtor's trade names as well as its legal name? Why or why not?

2. In this case, was the filing of the financing statement under the wrong name an error that could have easily been prevented?

3. **ETHICS** Was it ethical for Raymond to argue that there was a proper filing of the financing statement in this case?

Web Exercises

1. **WEB** For the complete opinion of this case, go to *www.prenhall.com/cheesemancases*.

2. **WEB** Visit the website of the United States Bankruptcy Court for the District of Maryland, at *www.mdb.uscourts.gov*.

3. **WEB** Use *www.google.com* to find an example of a filing statement.

PERFECTION BY POSSESSION OF COLLATERAL No financing statement has to be filed if the creditor has physical **possession of the collateral**. The rationale behind this rule is that if someone other than the debtor is in possession of the property, a potential creditor is on notice that another may claim an interest in the debtor's property. A secured creditor who holds the debtor's property as collateral must use reasonable care in its custody and preservation [Revised UCC 9-310, 9-312(b), 9-313].

Example Suppose Karen borrows $3,000 from Alan and gives her motorcycle to him as security for the loan. Alan does not file a financing statement. Another creditor obtains a judgment against Karen. This creditor cannot recover the motorcycle from Alan. Even though Alan has not filed a financing statement, his security interest in the motorcycle is perfected because he has possession of the motorcycle.

PERFECTION BY A PURCHASE MONEY SECURITY INTEREST IN CONSUMER GOODS
Sellers and lenders often extend credit to consumers to purchase consumer goods. **Consumer goods** include furniture, television sets, home appliances, and other goods used primarily for personal, family, or household purposes.

A creditor who extends credit to a consumer to purchase a consumer good under a written security agreement obtains a **purchase money security interest** in the consumer good. This agreement automatically perfects the creditor's security interest at the time of the sale. The creditor does not have to file a financing statement or take possession of the goods to perfect his or her security interest. This interest is called **perfection by attachment**, or the **automatic perfection rule** [Revised UCC 9-309(1)].

Two types of consumer goods are excepted from this rule: Financing statements must be filed to perfect a security interest in motor vehicles, trailers, boats and fixtures.

Example Assume that Marcia buys a $3,000 high-definition plasma television for her home on credit extended by the seller, Circuit City. Circuit City requires Marcia to sign a security agreement. Circuit City has a purchase money security interest in the television that is automatically perfected at the time of the credit sale. Now suppose Marcia borrowed the money from Country Bank to buy the television for cash from Circuit City. If the bank requires Marcia to sign a security agreement, its security interest in the television is automatically perfected at the time Marcia buys the television from Circuit City.

In the following case, the court had to decide whether a purchase money security interest in a consumer good had been created.

CASE 23.3
Purchase Money Security Interest

In re Phillips

55 B.R. 663, **Web** 1985 Bankr. Lexis 4762
United States Bankruptcy Court for the Western District of Virginia

> **"** *If the computer goods were classified as "consumer goods," the secured creditor would not have to file a financing statement to have a perfected security interest in the collateral.* **"**

—Judge Pearson

Facts

Charlene T. Phillips and her husband, Jacob, owned the Village Variety 5 & 10 Store in Bloomfield, Virginia. Charlene was also employed as a computer science teacher at the Wytheville Community College. Charlene entered into a retail installment contract to purchase an IBM computer and other equipment from Holdren's, Inc. (Holdren's). The contract, which was also a security agreement, provided for total payment of $3,175.68 in equal monthly installments of $132.32. Charlene testified that she told the salesperson at Holdren's that she was purchasing the computer equipment for use in her teaching assignments and for use at the variety store. She received a special discount price given to teachers. Holdren's did not file a financing statement regarding the computer equipment. Holdren's immediately assigned the installment contract to Creditway of America (Creditway). Six months after the purchase of the computer, Mr. and Mrs. Phillips filed a petition for Chapter 7 liquidation bankruptcy. The balance due and owing on the computer was $2,597.79. Creditway filed a motion with the U.S. Bankruptcy Court to recover the computer and equipment, alleging that the computer and other equipment were consumer goods and that the secured party obtained a perfected purchase money security interest in the goods and was not required to file a financing statement to perfect its security interest in the goods.

Issue

Are the computer and other equipment "consumer goods" in which the secured party obtained a perfected purchase money security interest?

Language of the Court

If the computer goods were classified as "consumer goods," the secured creditor would not have to file a financing statement to have a perfected security interest in the collateral. In this case, however, the court classified the goods as "equipment" because the goods were purchased for business purposes. Such classification required the secured creditor to file a financing statement to perfect its security interest, which it did

not do. The secured creditor holds an unperfected security interest in the collateral.

Decision

The Bankruptcy Court held that the secured creditor did not have a perfected purchase money security interest in the collateral because the collateral was equipment, not consumer goods. The Court denied the secured creditor's motion to recover the collateral.

Law & Ethics Questions

1. Should purchase money security interests be given priority over other security interests? Why or why not?

2. **ETHICS** Was there any unethical conduct in this case?

3. Are secured creditors who perfect their security interests always guaranteed of being able to be fully paid from the collateral upon default by the debtor?

Web Exercises

1. **WEB** For the complete opinion of this case, go to *www.prenhall.com/cheesemancases*.

2. **WEB** Visit the website of the United States Bankruptcy Court for the Western District of Virginia, at *www.vawb.uscourts.gov*.

3. **WEB** Use *www.google.com* to find an article that discusses perfection of a security interest by a purchase money security interest in consumer goods. Read it.

CONCEPT SUMMARY

Methods for Perfecting a Security Interest

PERFECTION METHOD	HOW CREATED
Financing statement	Creditor files a financing statement with the appropriate government office.
Possession of collateral	Creditor obtains physical possession of the collateral.
Purchase money security interest	Creditor extends credit to a debtor to purchase consumer goods and obtains a security interest in the goods.

Termination Statement

When a secured consumer debt is paid, the secured party must file a **termination statement** with each filing officer with whom the financing statement was filed. The termination statement must be filed within one month after the debt is paid or 20 days after receipt of the debtor's written demand, whichever occurs first [Revised UCC 9-513(b)]. In all other cases, the secured party must either file a termination statement with each filing officer with whom the financing statement has been filed or send the termination statement to the debtor within 20 days of receipt of a written demand by the debtor [Revised UCC 9-513(c)]. If the affected secured party fails to file or send the termination statement as required, the secured party is liable for any other losses caused to the debtor.

Store Window, Brentwood, California

Businesses often purchase goods on credit from suppliers. To secure the loan, a supplier often takes a security interest in personal property, such as the inventory in this store.

Priority of Claims

Often, two or more creditors claim an interest in the same collateral or property. The priority of the claims is determined according to (1) whether the claim is unsecured or secured and (2) the time at which secured claims were attached or were perfected.

UCC Rules for Determining Priority

The UCC establishes the following rules for determining **priority of claims** of creditors:

1. *Secured versus unsecured claims.* A creditor who has the only secured interest in the debtor's collateral has priority over unsecured interests.
2. *Competing unperfected security interests.* If two or more secured parties claim an interest in the same collateral but neither has a perfected claim, the first to attach has priority [Revised UCC 9-322(a)(3)].
3. *Perfected versus unperfected claims.* If two or more secured parties claim an interest in the same collateral but only one has perfected his or her security interest, the perfected security interest has priority [Revised UCC 9-322(a)(2)].
4. *Competing perfected security interests.* If two or more secured parties have perfected security interests in the same collateral, the first to perfect (e.g., by filing a financing statement or taking possession of the collateral) has priority [Revised UCC 9-322(a)(1)].
5. *Perfected secured claims in fungible, commingled goods.* If a security interest in goods is perfected but the goods are later commingled with other goods in which there are perfected security interests and the goods become part of a product or mass and lose their identity, the security interests rank equally according to the ratio that the cost of goods to which each interest originally attached bears to the cost of the total product or mass [Revised UCC 9-336].

Exceptions to the Perfection-Priority Rule

Perfection does not always protect a secured party from third-party claims. As discussed in the paragraphs that follow, the UCC recognizes several exceptions to the perfection-priority rule. These exceptions are discussed in the following paragraphs.

> We are either debtors or creditors before we have had time to look around.
>
> Johann Wolfgang Von Goethe
> *Elective Affinities, Book II (1808)*

PURCHASE MONEY SECURITY INTEREST: INVENTORY AS COLLATERAL In certain circumstances, a perfected purchase money security interest prevails over perfected nonpurchase money security interests in after-acquired property. The order of perfection is irrelevant. If the collateral is inventory, the perfected purchase money security interest prevails if the purchase money secured party gives written notice of the perfection to the perfected nonpurchase money secured party [Revised UCC 9-324(b)].

Example Toy Shops, Inc., a retailer, borrows money from First Bank for working capital. In return, First Bank gets a security interest in all of Toy Shops's current and after-acquired inventory. First Bank perfects its security interest by filing a financing statement. Later, Toy Shops purchases new inventory on credit from Mattel, a toy manufacturer. Mattel perfects its purchase money security interest by filing a financing statement. It notifies First Bank of this fact prior to delivery of the new inventory. Toy Shops defaults on its loans. Mattel's lien has priority.

PURCHASE MONEY SECURITY INTEREST: NONINVENTORY AS COLLATERAL If the collateral is something other than inventory, a perfected purchase money security interest prevails over a perfected nonpurchase money security interest in after-acquired property if it is perfected when the debtor receives possession or within 20 days after the debtor receives possession of the collateral [Revised UCC 9-324(a)].

Example On September 1, Matco, a manufacturer, borrows money for working capital from First Bank and gives First Bank a security interest in its current and after-acquired equipment. First Bank perfects its security interest by filing a financing statement. On September 8, Matco purchases a new piece of equipment on credit from Allegheny Industries, an equipment manufacturer. On September 20, Allegheny perfects its purchase money security interest by filing a financing statement. Matco defaults on its loans. Here, Allegheny's perfected purchase money security interest prevails because the lien was perfected within 20 days after the debtor received the collateral. If Allegheny had waited until September 29 to perfect its purchase money security interest, First Bank would have prevailed.

BUYERS IN THE ORDINARY COURSE OF BUSINESS A **buyer in the ordinary course of business** who purchases goods from a merchant takes the goods free of any perfected or unperfected security interest in the merchant's inventory, even if the buyer knows of the existence of the security interest. This rule is necessary because buyers would be reluctant to purchase goods if a merchant's creditors could recover the goods if the merchant defaulted on loans owed to secured creditors [Revised UCC 9-320(a), 1-201(9)].

A buyer in the ordinary course of business means a person that buys goods in good faith, without knowledge that the sale violates the rights of another person in the goods, and in the ordinary course from a person in the business of selling goods of that kind.

Example Suppose Central Car Sales, Inc. (Central), a new car dealership, finances all its inventory of new automobiles at First Bank. First Bank takes a security interest in Central's inventory of cars and perfects this security interest. Kim, a buyer in the ordinary course of business, purchases a car from Central for cash. The car cannot be recovered from Kim even if Central defaults on its payments to the bank.

SECONDHAND CONSUMER GOODS Buyers of **secondhand consumer goods** take the goods free of security interest if they do not have actual or constructive knowledge about the security interest, give value, and buy the goods for personal, family, or household purposes. The filing of a financing statement by a creditor provides constructive notice of the security interest [Revised UCC 9-320(b)].

> Words pay no debts.
>
> William Shakespeare
> *Troilus and Cressida, Act III*

Example Suppose Anne purchases a microwave oven on credit from Stearns, a retailer, to be used for household purposes. Pursuant to a security agreement, Stearns acquires an automatically perfected purchase money security interest in the oven. Suppose Stearns does not file a financing statement. Anne sells the microwave oven to her neighbor, Jeff, for cash. Anne defaults on her loan payments to Stearns. Stearns cannot recover the microwave oven from Jeff. Note, however, that Stearns could recover the oven from Jeff if it had filed a financing statement prior to the sale to Jeff.

Revised Article 9 (Secured Transactions) contains provisions that recognize the importance of electronic records. The revised article contains new definitions that apply to secured transactions in personal property. Some of the definitions for electronic commerce and their implications are discussed below.

- "Record" means information that is inscribed on tangible medium, or which is stored in an electronic or other medium and is retrievable in perceivable form [Revised UCC 9-102(a)(69)]. The term "record" is now used in many of the provisions of Revised Article 9 in place of the term "writing" and thus further recognizes the importance of electronic commerce.

- "Electronic chattel paper" means chattel paper evidenced by a record or records consisting of information stored in an electronic medium [Revised UCC 9-102(a)(31)]. This includes records initially created and executed in electronic form or a tangible writing that is converted to electronic form, for example, creating electronic images of a signed writing.

- "Financing statement" means a record composed of an initial financing statement and any filed record relating to the initial financing statement [Revised UCC 9-102(a)(39)]. Thus, financing statements may be in electronic form, and filed and stored as an electronic record.

These provisions of Revised Article 9 (Secured Transactions) recognize the importance of electronic transactions and records used in today's commercial environment.

Default and Remedies

Article 9 of the UCC defines the rights, duties, and remedies of the secured party and the debtor in the event of **default**. The term *default* is not defined. Instead, the parties are free to define it in their security agreement. Failure to make scheduled payments when due, bankruptcy of the debtor, breach of the warranty of ownership as to the collateral, and other such events are commonly defined in the security agreement as default.

Upon default by the debtor, the secured party may reduce his or her claim to judgment, foreclose, or otherwise enforce his or her security interest by any available judicial procedure [Revised UCC 9-601(a)]. The UCC provides the secured party with the remedies discussed in the following paragraphs.

Taking Possession of the Collateral

Most secured parties seek to cure a default by **taking possession of the collateral**. This taking is usually done by **repossessing** the goods from the defaulting debtor. A secured party may reposes the collateral pursuant to judicial process, or without judicial process if the self-help repossession of the collateral is without breach of the peace [Revised UCC 9-609(b)].

After repossessing the goods, the secured party can either (1) retain the collateral or (2) sell, lease, license, or otherwise dispose of it and satisfy the debt from the proceeds of the sale or disposition. There is one caveat: The secured party must act in good faith, with commercial reasonableness, and with reasonable care to preserve the collateral in his or her possession [Revised UCC 9-603, 9-610(a), 9-620].

Example Western Drilling, Inc., purchases a piece of oil-drilling equipment on credit from Haliburton, Inc. Haliburton files a financing statement covering its security interest in the equipment. If Western Drilling fails to make the required payments, Haliburton can foreclose on its lien and repossess the equipment.

Retention of Collateral

A secured creditor who repossesses collateral may propose to **retain the collateral** in satisfaction of the debtor's obligation. Notice of the proposal must be sent to the debtor unless he or she has signed a written statement renouncing this right. In the case of consumer goods, no other notice need be given. Otherwise, notice of the proposal must be sent to any other secured party who has given written notice of a claim of interest in the collateral [Revised UCC 9-620(a)].

A secured creditor may not retain the collateral (and must dispose of the collateral) in the following two situations:

1. ***Written objection.*** A secured creditor must dispose of the collateral if it receives a written objection to the proposal from a person entitled to receive notice within 20 days after the notice was sent [Revised UCC 9-602, 9-603, 9-610, 9-613].
2. ***Consumer goods.*** A secured creditor must dispose of the collateral if the debt involves consumer goods, and the debtor has paid 60 percent of the cash price or loan. In this case, the secured creditor must dispose of the goods within 90 days after taking possession of them. A consumer may renounce his or her rights under this section [Revised UCC 9-620(e) and (f)].

A secured creditor may retain the collateral as satisfaction of the debtor's obligation if neither of the preceding two situations prevents this action.

Disposition of Collateral

A secured party who chooses not to retain the collateral may sell, lease, or otherwise dispose of it in its current condition or following any commercially reasonable preparation or processing. **Disposition of the collateral** may be by public or private proceedings. The method, manner, time, place, and terms of the disposition must be commercially reasonable [Revised UCC 9-610].

The secured party must notify the debtor in writing about the time and place of any public or private sale or any other intended disposition of the collateral unless the debtor has signed a statement renouncing or modifying his on her rights to receive such notice. In the case of consumer goods, no other notification need be sent. In other cases, the secured party must send notice to any other secured party from whom the secured party has received written notice of a claim of an interest in the collateral. Notice of the sale or disposition is not required if the collateral is perishable or threatens to decline steadily in value or is of a type customarily sold on a recognized market. Disposition discharges the security interest under which it is made as well as any subordinate security interests or liens [Revised UCC 9-602(7), 9-603, 9-610, 9-613].

Proceeds from the Disposition of Collateral

The proceeds from a sale, a lease, or another disposition of collateral must be applied in the following order [Revised UCC 9-608]:

1. Reasonable expenses of retaking, holding, and preparing the collateral for sale, lease, or other disposition are paid first. Attorneys' fees and other legal expenses may be paid if provided for in the security agreement and not prohibited by law.
2. Satisfaction of the balance of the indebtedness owed by the debtor to the secured party is made next.
3. Satisfaction of subordinate (junior) security interests whose written notifications of demand have been received before distribution of the proceeds is completed. The secured party may require subordinate security interests to furnish reasonable proof of his or her interest.
4. The debtor is entitled to receive any surplus that remains.

Deficiency Judgment

Unless otherwise agreed, if the proceeds from the disposition of collateral are not sufficient to satisfy the debt to the secured party, the debtor is personally liable to the secured party for the deficiency. The secured party may bring an action to recover a *deficiency judgment* against the debtor [Revised UCC 9-608(a)(4)]. If the underlying transaction was a sale of accounts, chattel paper, payment intangibles, or promissory notes, the debtor is not entitled to any surplus, and the obligor is not liable for any deficiency [Revised UCC 9-608(b)].

Example Sean borrows $15,000 from First Bank to purchase a new automobile. He signs a security agreement giving First Bank a purchase money security interest in the automobile. Sean defaults after making payments that reduce the debt to $13,250. First Bank repossesses the automobile and sells it at a public auction for $11,000. The selling expenses and sales commission are $1,250. This amount is deducted from the proceeds. The remaining $9,750 is applied to the $13,250 balance of the debt. Sean remains personally liable to First Bank for the $3,500 deficiency.

Redemption Rights

A debtor or another secured party may redeem the collateral before the priority lienholder has disposed of it, entered into a contract to dispose of it, or discharged the debtor's obligation by exercising a right to retain the collateral. The right of redemption may be accomplished by payment of all obligations secured by the collateral, all expenses reasonably incurred by the secured party in retaking and holding the collateral, and any attorneys' fees and other legal expenses provided for in the security agreement and not prohibited by law [Revised UCC 9-623].

Relinquishing the Security Interest and Proceeding to Judgment on the Underlying Debt

Instead of repossessing the collateral, a secured creditor may relinquish his or her security interest in the collateral and proceed to **judgment** against the debtor to recover the underlying debt. This course of action is rarely chosen unless the value of the collateral has been reduced below the amount of the secured interest and the debtor has other assets from which to satisfy the debt [Revised UCC 9-601(a)].

Example Suppose Jack borrows $100,000 from First Bank to purchase a piece of equipment, and First Bank perfects its security interest in the equipment for this amount. Jack defaults on the loan. If the equipment has gone down in value to $60,000 at the time of default but Jack has other personal assets to satisfy the debt, it may be in the bank's best interest to relinquish its security interest, sue Jack, and proceed to judgment on the underlying debt.

Cumulative Remedies

The rights and remedies provided by Revised UCC 9-601(a) are cumulative and may be exercised simultaneously [Revised UCC 9-601(c)]. Thus, the secured party is not required to elect one of the previously discussed remedies. Instead, if one remedy is unsuccessful, the secured party can move on to the next.

Example If the secured creditor obtains a judgment against the debtor but the debtor has no money to pay the judgment, the secured creditor can proceed to take possession of the collateral.

CONTEMPORARY ENVIRONMENT

Artisan's Liens

If a worker in the ordinary course of business furnishes services or materials to someone with respect to goods and receives a lien on the goods by statute, this **artisan's lien** prevails over all other security interests in the goods unless a statutory lien provides otherwise. Thus, such liens are often called *super-priority liens*. An artisan's lien is possessory, that is, the artisan must be in possession of the property in order to affect this artisan's lien.

Example Suppose Janice borrows money from First Bank to purchase an automobile. First Bank has a purchase money security interest in the

car and files a financing statement. The automobile is involved in an accident, and Janice takes the car to Joe's Repair Shop (Joe's) to be repaired. Joe's retains an artisan's lien on the car for the amount of the repair work. When the repair work is completed, Janice refuses to pay. She also defaults on her payments to First Bank. If the car is sold to satisfy the liens, the artisan's lien is paid in full from the proceeds before First Bank is paid anything.

Surety and Guaranty Arrangements

Sometimes a creditor refuses to extend credit to a debtor unless a third person agrees to become liable on the debt. The third person's credit becomes the security for the credit extended to the debtor. This relationship may be either a *surety arrangement* or a *guaranty arrangement*. These arrangements are discussed in the following paragraphs.

Surety Arrangement

In a strict **surety arrangement**, a third person—known as the **surety**, or **co-debtor**—promises to be liable for the payment of another person's debt. A person who acts as a surety is commonly called an **accommodation party**, or **cosigner**. Along with the principal debtor, the surety is *primarily liable* for paying the principal debtor's debt when it is due.

The principal debtor does not have to be in default on the debt, and the creditor does not have to have exhausted all its remedies against the principal debtor before seeking payment from the surety.

Example Ivy, a college student, wants to purchase a new BMW automobile. She goes to Auto Dealer and finds exactly the car she wants, and she wants to finance the car. Auto Dealer will not sell the car to Ivy on credit based on her own credit standing. Auto Dealer requires Ivy to find a cosigner on the purchase and credit contract. Ivy asks her mother to cosign on the agreement. When Ivy's mother signs as a cosigner, she is now a surety. Ivy's mother is equally bound by the contract with Ivy. Ivy's mother is *primarily liable* with Ivy on the loan. Usually, if Ivy does not pay, Auto Dealer will immediately bring legal action against Ivy's mother for payment. Auto Dealer does not have to sue Ivy first.

Guaranty Arrangement

In a **guaranty arrangement**, a third person (the **guarantor**) agrees to pay the debt of the principal debtor if the debtor defaults and does not pay the debt when it is due. In this type of arrangement, the guarantor is *secondarily liable* on the debt. In other words, the guarantor is obligated to pay the debt only if the principal debtor defaults and the creditor have attempted unsuccessfully to collect the debt from the debtor.

Example Ivan, a college student, wants to purchase a new computer, printer, and other electronic equipment on credit from Electronics Retail, Inc. Electronics will not sell the computer and other equipment to Ivan unless he can get someone to guarantee the payment. Ivan asks his roommate, Edward, to guarantee the payment. Edward agrees, and he is placed on the credit agreement as a guarantor. Edward is *secondarily liable*: If Ivan fails to make the necessary payment, Electronics must first attempt unsuccessfully to recover the payments from Ivan before taking legal action against Edward to recover payment.

In the following case, the court had to decide whether there was a surety or guaranty contract.

C A S E **23.4**
Surety

General Motors Acceptance Corporation v. Daniels

492 A.2d 1306, **Web** 1985 Md. Lexis 596
Court of Appeals of Maryland

> "*Seymoure signed the contract on the line on the contract designated 'Co-Buyer.'*"
> —Judge Cole

Facts

John Daniels agreed to purchase a used automobile from Lindsay Cadillac Company (Lindsay Cadillac). Because John had a poor credit rating, his brother, Seymoure, agreed to cosign with him. General Motors Acceptance Corporation (GMAC), a company engaged in the business of financing automobiles, agreed to finance the purchase. Seymoure accompanied John to Lindsay Cadillac. John signed the contract on the line designated "Buyer." Seymoure signed the contract on the line designated "Co-Buyer." One year later, GMAC declared the contract in default. After attempting to locate the automobile for several months, GMAC brought this action against the Daniels brothers. Because service of process was never affected upon the purchaser John, the case proceeded to trial only against Seymoure. The trial court found that Seymoure had entered into a guaranty contract and that Seymoure was not liable because GMAC had not yet proceeded against John. GMAC appealed.

Issue

Was the contract Seymoure signed a guaranty or surety contract?

Language of the Court

If the contract Seymoure signed was a guaranty contract, he would have been only secondarily liable on his brother's loan. This situation was not true in this case, however, because Seymoure signed the contract on the line on the contract designated "Co-Buyer." The contract clearly stated that all buyers agreed to be jointly and severally liable for the purchase of the vehicle. Seymoure executed the same contract as his brother, thereby making himself a party to the original contract. These facts establish the existence of a surety contract upon which Seymoure became primarily liable.

Decision

The court of appeals held that Seymoure had signed a surety contract and thus agreed to be primarily liable with his brother John for the purchase of the automobile. GMAC was therefore not required to proceed against John first before proceeding against Seymoure. The court of appeals reversed the decision of the trial court and held that Seymoure was a surety co-buyer primarily liable to GMAC for the car loan he made with his brother, John.

Law & Ethics Questions

1. How do guaranty and surety contracts differ? Explain.
2. **ETHICS** Did Seymoure act ethically in trying to avoid liability for his brother's loan?
3. As a lender, would you rather have a third party sign as a surety or guarantor?

Web Exercises

1. **WEB** For the complete opinion of this case, go to *www.prenhall.com/cheesemancases*.
2. **WEB** Visit the website of the court of appeals of Maryland, at *www.courts.state.md.us/coappeals*.
3. **WEB** Use *www.google.com* to find a case in which a guarantor or surety had to pay on a primary borrower's defaulted loan.

Defenses of a Surety or Guarantor

Generally, the defenses the principal debtor has against the creditor may also be asserted by a surety or guarantor. For example, if credit has been extended for the purchase of a piece of machinery that proves to be defective, the debtor and surety both can assert the defect as a defense to liability. The defenses of fraudulent inducement to enter into the surety or guaranty agreement and duress may also be cited as personal defenses to liability. The surety or guarantor cannot assert the debtor's incapacity (i.e., minority or insanity) or bankruptcy as a defense against liability. The surety's or guarantor's own incapacity or bankruptcy may be asserted, however.

CONCEPT SUMMARY

Surety and Guaranty Contracts

TYPE OF ARRANGEMENT	PARTY	LIABILITY
Surety contract	Surety	Primarily liable. The surety is a co-debtor who is liable to pay the debt when it is due.
Guaranty contract	Guarantor	Secondarily liable. The guarantor is liable to pay the debt if the debtor defaults and does not pay the debt when it is due.

Debtor-Protection Law

> Debtors are liars.
>
> George Herbert
> *Jacula Prudentum* (1651)

Creditors have been known to engage in various abusive, deceptive, and unfair practices when dealing with consumer-debtors. To protect consumer-debtors from such practices, the federal government has enacted a comprehensive scheme of laws concerning the extension and collection of credit. These laws are discussed in the following sections.

Truth-in-Lending Act

In 1968, Congress enacted the **Truth-in-Lending Act (TILA)** as part of the Consumer Credit Protection Act (CCPA).[1] The TILA, as amended, requires creditors to make certain disclosures to debtors in consumer transactions (e.g., retail installment sales, automobile loans) and real estate loans on the debtor's principal dwelling.

The TILA covers only creditors who regularly (1) extend credit for goods or services to consumers or (2) arrange such credit in the ordinary course of their business. Consumer credit is defined as credit extended to natural persons for personal, family, or household purposes.

Regulation Z

The TILA is administered by the Federal Reserve Board, which has authority to adopt regulations to enforce and interpret the act. **Regulation Z**, which sets forth detailed rules for compliance with the TILA, was adopted under this authority.[2] The TILA and Regulation Z require the creditor to disclose the following information to the consumer-debtor:

- Cash price of the product or service
- Down payment and trade-in allowance
- Unpaid cash price
- Finance charge, including interest, points, and other fees paid for the extension of credit
- Annual percentage rate (APR) of the finance charges
- Charges not included in the finance charge (such as appraisal fees)
- Total dollar amount financed
- Date the finance charge begins to accrue
- Number, amounts, and due dates of payments
- A description of any security interest
- Penalties to be assessed for delinquent payments and late charges
- Prepayment penalties
- Comparative costs of credit (optional)

The uniform disclosures required by the TILA and Regulation Z are intended to help consumers shop for the best credit terms.

In the following case, the U.S. Supreme Court had to decide if the TILA had been violated.

C A S E **23.5** *Truth-in-Lending Act*	**U.S. SUPREME COURT** **Household Credit Services, Inc. and MBNA America Bank, N.A. v. Pfennig** 541 U.S. 232, 124 S.Ct. 1741, 158 L.Ed.2d 450, **Web** 2004 U.S. Lexis 3051 (2004) Supreme Court of the United States

> ❝*TILA's disclosure provisions seek to ensure meaningful disclosure of credit terms.*❞
>
> —Justice Thomas

Facts

Sharon Pfennig holds a credit card issued by MBNA America Bank, N.A. (MBNA). Although the credit card agreement set Pfennig's credit limit at $2,000, she was able to make charges exceeding that limit, subject to a $29 "over-limit fee" for each month in which the balance exceeded $2,000. Pfennig was charged this fee for exceeding her credit limit.

Regulation Z, a regulation adopted by the Federal Reserve Board, expressly does not require an over-limit fee to be included in the calculation of the "finance charge" that is required by the TILA to be disclosed to debtors. MBNA did disclose the $29 over-limit fee on each monthly statement received by Pfennig, however. Pfennig brought a class action lawsuit against MBNA seeking civil damages, alleging that MBNA violated the Truth-in-Lending Act (TILA) by not including the over-limit fee in the calculation of the "finance charge." The U.S. District Court dismissed Pfennig's complaint. The U.S. Court of Appeals reversed. MBNA appealed to the U.S. Supreme Court.

Issue

Is the Federal Reserve Board's Regulation Z, which explicitly excludes over-limit fees from the definition of *finance charge*, a reasonable interpretation of the TILA?

Language of the Court

Congress enacted the Truth-in-Lending Act (TILA) in order to promote the "informed use of credit" by consumers. To that end, TILA's disclosure provisions seek to ensure meaningful disclosure of credit terms. Further, Congress delegated expansive authority to the Federal Reserve Board (Board) to enact appropriate regulations to advance this purpose. We granted certiorari to decide whether the Board's Regulation Z, which specifically excludes fees imposed for exceeding a credit limit (over-limit fees) from the definition of "finance charge," is an unreasonable interpretation of the TILA.

Congress has specifically designated the Board and staff as the primary source for interpretation and application of truth-in-lending law. Whenever Congress has explicitly left a gap for the agency to fill, the agency's regulation is given controlling weight unless it is arbitrary, capricious, or manifestly contrary to the statute. TILA itself does not explicitly address whether over-limit fees are included within the definition of "finance charge."

Because over-limit fees, regardless of a creditor's particular billing practice, are imposed only when a consumer exceeds his credit limit, it is perfectly reasonable to characterize an over-limit fee not as a charge imposed for obtaining an extension of credit over a consumer's credit limit, but rather as a penalty for violating the credit agreement.

Decision

The U.S. Supreme Court held that the Board's Regulation Z that excluded over-limit fees from the definition of *finance charge* set forth in the TILA is a reasonable interpretation of the TILA. The Supreme Court reversed the judgment of the U.S. Court of Appeals.

Law & Ethics Questions

1. Why does the TILA require finance charges to be disclosed to consumer-debtors?
2. **ETHICS** Do you think that MBNA should have disclosed the over-limit fee to credit card holders in advance? Why or why not?
3. Do you think that there are very many "hidden fees" in credit card and bank lending?

Web Exercises

1. **WEB** For the complete opinion of this case, go to *www.prenhall.com/cheesemancases*.
2. **WEB** Visit the website of the U.S. Supreme Court, at *www.supremecourtus.gov*, and try to find documents that relate to this case.
3. **WEB** Use *www.google.com* to find a recent case of consumer fraud in lending.

Consumer Leasing Act

Consumers often opt to lease consumer products, such as automobiles, rather than purchase them. The **Consumer Leasing Act (CLA)** extended the TILA's coverage to lease terms in consumer leases.[3] The CLA applies to lessors who engage in leasing or arranging leases for consumer goods in the ordinary course of their business. Casual leases (such as leases between consumers) are not subject to the CLA. Creditors who violate the CLA are subject to the civil and criminal penalties provided in the TILA.

Fair Credit and Charge Card Disclosure Act

The **Fair Credit and Charge Card Disclosure Act** of 1988[4] amended the TILA to require disclosure of credit terms on credit- and charge-card solicitations and applications. The regulations adopted under the act require that any direct written solicitation to a consumer display, in tabular form, the following information: (1) the APR, (2) any annual membership fee, (3) any minimum or fixed finance charge, (4) any transaction charge for use of the card for purchases, and (5) a statement that charges are due when the periodic statement is received by the debtor.

Equal Credit Opportunity Act

The **Equal Credit Opportunity Act (ECOA)** was enacted in 1975.[5] The ECOA, as amended, prohibits discrimination in the extension of credit based on sex, marital status, race, color, national origin, religion, age, or receipt of income from public assistance programs. The ECOA applies to all creditors who extend or arrange credit in the ordinary course of their business, including banks, savings and loan associations, automobile dealers, real estate brokers, credit-card issuers, and the like.

The creditor must notify the applicant within 30 days regarding the action taken on a credit application. If the creditor takes an *adverse action* (i.e., denies, revokes, or changes the credit terms), the creditor must provide the applicant with a statement containing the specific reasons for the action. If a creditor violates the ECOA, the consumer may bring a civil action against the creditor and recover actual damages (including emotional distress and embarrassment).

Fair Credit Reporting Act

In 1970, Congress enacted the **Fair Credit Reporting Act (FCRA)** as Title VI of the TILA.[6] This act protects consumers who are subjects of a **credit report** by setting out guidelines for consumer reporting agencies—that is, credit bureaus that compile and sell credit reports for a fee. A consumer may request the following information at any time: (1) the nature and substance of all the information in the consumer's credit file, (2) the sources of this information, and (3) the names of recipients of his or her credit report.

If a consumer challenges the accuracy of pertinent information contained in the credit file, the agency may be compelled to reinvestigate. If the agency cannot find an error despite the consumer's complaint, the consumer may file a 100-word written statement of his or her version of the disputed information. If a consumer reporting agency or user violates the FCRA, the injured consumer may bring a civil action against the violator and recover actual damages. The FCRA also provides for criminal penalties.

Fair Debt Collection Practices Act

In 1977, Congress enacted the **Fair Debt Collection Practices Act (FDCPA)**.[7] This act protects consumer-debtors from abusive, deceptive, and unfair practices used by *debt collectors*. The FDCPA expressly prohibits debt collectors from using certain practices: (1) harassing, abusive, or intimidating tactics (e.g., threats of violence and obscene or abusive language), (2) false or misleading misrepresentations (e.g., posing as a police officer or an attorney), and (3) unfair or unconscionable practices (e.g., threatening the debtor with imprisonment).

In some circumstances, the debt collector may not contact the debtor. These situations include the following:

1. At any inconvenient time. The FDCPA provides that convenient hours are between 8:00 A.M. and 9:00 P.M. unless this time is otherwise inconvenient for the debtor (e.g., the debtor works a night shift and sleeps during the day).
2. At inconvenient places, such as at a place of worship or social events.
3. At the debtor's place of employment if the employer objects to such contact.
4. If the debtor is represented by an attorney.
5. If the debtor gives a written notice to the debt collector that he or she refuses to pay the debt or does not want the debt collector to contact him or her again.

The FDCPA limits the contact that a debt collector may have with third persons other than the debtor's spouse or parents. Such contact is strictly limited. Unless the court has given its approval, third parties can be consulted only for the purpose of locating a debtor. They can be contacted only once. A debt collector may not inform a third person that a consumer owes a debt that is in the process of collection. A debtor may bring a civil action against a debt collector for intentionally violating the FDCPA.

CONTEMPORARY ENVIRONMENT
Collection Remedies

When a debt is past due, the creditor may bring a legal action against the debtor. If the creditor is successful, the court will award a judgment against the debtor. The judgment will state that the debtor owes the creditor a specific sum of money. The amount usually consists of principal and interest past due on the debt, other costs resulting from the debtor's default, and court costs. The most common collection remedies are:

1. **Attachment.** Attachment is a prejudgment court order that permits the seizure of a debtor's property while the lawsuit is pending. To obtain a *writ of attachment*, a creditor must follow the procedures of state law, give the debtor notice, and post a bond with the court.

2. **Execution.** Execution is a postjudgment court order that permits the seizure of the debtor's property that is in the possession of the debtor. Certain property is exempt from levy (e.g., tools of trade, clothing, homestead exemption). A *writ of execution* is a court order directing the sheriff to seize the debtor's property

and authorizing a judicial sale of that property. The proceeds are used to pay the creditor the amount of the final judgment. Any surplus must be paid to the debtor.

3. **Garnishment.** Garnishment is a postjudgment court order that permits the seizure of a debtor's property that is in the possession of third parties. The creditor (also known as the *garnishor*) must go to court to seek a *writ of garnishment*. The third person is called the *garnishee*. Common garnishees are employers who possess wages due a debtor, banks in possession of funds belonging to the debtor, and other third parties in the possession of property of the debtor. To protect debtors from abusive and excessive garnishment actions by creditors, Congress enacted Title III of the Consumer Credit Protection Act. This law allows debtors who are subject to a writ of garnishment to retain the greater of (1) 75 percent of their weekly disposable earnings (after taxes) or (2) an amount equal to 30 hours of work paid at federal minimum wage. State law limitations on garnishment control are more stringent than federal law.

Chapter Summary

Unsecured and Secured Credit, p. 593
Debtor and Creditor

In a transaction involving the extension of credit, there are two parties: The party extending the credit, the lender, is called the creditor, and the party borrowing the money, the borrower, is called the debtor.

Unsecured Credit

Unsecured credit does not require any security (collateral) to protect the payment of the loan. If the debtor does not pay the loan, the creditor may bring a legal action and obtain a judgment against the debtor. The debtor is called judgment-proof if he or she has no money to pay the judgment.

Secured Credit

Secured credit requires security (collateral) that secures the payment of the loan. The property that is pledged as security for a loan is called collateral.

Security Interest in Real Property, p. 595
Mortgage

1. *Mortgage.* A mortgage is an instrument that represents a security interest in real property.
2. *Mortgagor.* A mortgagor is an owner-debtor who pledges his or her real property as security for a loan.
3. *Mortgagee.* A mortgagee is a creditor who holds a security interest in the owner-debtor's real property.

Note and Deed of Trust

Some states use a note and deed of trust as an alternative to a mortgage. A note is an instrument that evidences the debt. A deed of trust is an instrument that gives the creditor a security interest in the owner-debtor's real property.

Recording Statute

A statute that requires a mortgage or deed of trust to be recorded in the county recorder's office in the county in which the real property is located.

Foreclosure

Foreclosure is a method whereby if a mortgagor defaults on the payment on a mortgage, the mortgagee can declare the entire debt due and proceed to acquire title to the property that is collateral for the loan.

Deficiency Judgment

If, after foreclosure of the property, there is a deficiency owing, the mortgagee can sue the mortgagor to recover the amount of the deficiency. Some states have enacted anti-deficiency statutes that prohibit a mortgagee from recovering a deficiency owed on a loan.

Right of Redemption

The mortgagor right to redeem real property after default and before foreclosure. Requires the mortgagor to pay the full amount of the debt—that is, principal, interest, and other costs—incurred by the mortgagee because of the mortgagor's default.

Land Sales Contract

The owner of real property agrees to sell the property to a purchaser, who agrees to pay the purchase price to the owner-seller over an agreed-upon period of time.

Mechanic's Lien

A mechanic's lien is given by law to contractors and laborers on real property they made improvement on until the amount they are owed is paid.

Secured Transactions: Revised Article 9 of the UCC, p. 600
Article 9 of the UCC

Article 9 of the Uniform Commercial Code governs secured transactions in personal property.

Revised Article 9 of the UCC

Once adopted as state law to replace Article 9 of the UCC, Revised Article 9, effective July 1, 2001, governs transactions in personal property.

Secured Transaction

Secured transactions are created when a creditor makes a loan to a debtor in exchange for the debtor's pledge of personal property as security.
1. *Two-party secured transaction.* In this type of transaction, a seller sells goods to a buyer on credit and retains a security interest in the goods.
2. *Three-party secured transaction.* In this type of transaction, a seller sells goods to a buyer who has obtained financing from a third-party lender (e.g., bank) that takes a security interest in the goods sold.

Creating and Perfecting a Security Interest, p. 604
Requirements for Creating a Security Interest
1. Requirements
   a. Written security agreement
   b. Value given to the debtor
   c. Debtor has rights in collateral
   If these requirements are met, the rights of the secured creditor attach to the collateral.

Tangible Personal Property Subject to a Security Agreement

1. Accessions
2. Consumer goods
3. Equipment
4. Farm products
5. Inventory

Intangible Personal Property Subject to a Security Agreement

1. Accounts
2. Chattel Paper
3. Deposit accounts
4. General intangibles
5. Instruments

Security Agreement

Unless the creditor has possession of the collateral, there must be a written security agreement.

Attachment

With attachment, the creditor has an enforceable security interest against the debtor and can satisfy the debt out of the designated collateral.

The Floating-Lien Concept

A floating lien occurs when a security agreement provides that the security interest attaches to personal property that was not originally in the possession of the debtor when the agreement was executed. This property may include:

1. *After-acquired property.* Property acquired after a security agreement is executed.
2. *Sale proceeds.* Proceeds from the sale, exchange, or disposal of collateral subject to a security agreement.
3. *Future advances.* Personal property of a debtor that is designated as collateral for future loans taken against a line of credit.

Perfection of a Security Interest

Perfection of a security interest establishes the right of the secured creditor against other creditors who claim an interest in the collateral. The UCC provides the following three methods of perfecting a security interest:

1. *Perfection by Filing a Financing Statement.* If the creditor files a financing statement with the appropriate government recording office, this statement puts the world on notice of the creditor's security interest in the property. This method is the most common form of perfecting a security interest.
2. *Perfection by Possession of Collateral.* If the creditor has physical possession of the collateral, no financing statement has to be filed. This method is the least common form of perfecting a security interest.
3. *Perfection by a Purchase Money Security Interest in Consumer Goods.* A creditor (seller or lender) who extends credit to a consumer to purchase a consumer good under a written security agreement obtains a purchase money security interest in the goods. This agreement automatically perfects the creditor's security interest at the time of the sale. The creditor does not have to file a financing statement to perfect his or her security interest. This method is called perfection by attachment or the automatic perfection rule.

Termination Statement

A termination statement is a document that a secured creditor must file within a specified number of days after a secured consumer debt has been paid. This statement must be filed where the original financing statement was filed.

Priority of Claims, p. 610

UCC Rules for Determining Priority

The UCC establishes the following rules for determining priority among conflicting claims of creditors to the collateral:

1. *Secured versus unsecured claims.* Secured claims have priority over unsecured claims.
2. *Competing unperfected secured claims.* The first claim to attach has priority.
3. *Perfected versus unperfected claims.* The perfected claim has priority.
4. *Competing perfected secured claims.* The first to perfect has priority.
5. *Perfected secured claims in fungible, commingled goods.* The security interests rank equally according to the ratio that the cost of goods to which each interest originally attached bears to the cost of the total product or mass.

Exceptions to the Perfection-Priority Rule

Perfection does not always protect a secured creditor from third-party claims. The UCC recognizes the following exceptions to the perfection-priority rule:

1. *Purchase money security interest: Inventory as collateral.* A perfected purchase money security interest in inventory prevails over a perfected nonpurchase money security interest in after acquired property.
2. *Purchase money security interest: Noninventory as collateral.* A perfected purchase money security interest in noninventory prevails over a perfected nonpurchase money security interest in after-acquired property if it was perfected before or within 10 days after the debtor receives possession of the collateral.
3. *Buyers in the ordinary course of business.* A buyer in the ordinary course of business who purchases goods from a merchant takes the goods free of any perfected or unperfected security interest in the merchant's inventory, even if the buyer knows of the existence of the security interest.
4. *Secondhand consumer goods.* Buyers of secondhand consumer goods take the goods free of security interests if they do not have actual or constructive knowledge about the security interest, give value, and buy the goods for personal, family, or household purposes.

Default and Remedies, p. 612

The parties may define the actions or inactions that cause default under an agreement. These actions usually include failure to make scheduled payments when due, bankruptcy of the debtor, and breach of other terms of the agreement. Article 9 of the UCC provides a secured creditor with certain remedies upon the debtor's default.

Taking Possession of the Collateral

The secured creditor can use self-help to take physical possession of the collateral as long as it does not cause a breach of peace.

Retention of the Collateral

The creditor has the right to retain any repossessed collateral to satisfy the debtor's obligation. Notice of the proposal must be sent to the debtor unless he or she has signed a written statement renouncing this right.

Disposition of Collateral

A secured party who chooses not to retain the collateral may sell, lease, or otherwise dispose of it in its current condition or following any commercially reasonable preparation or processing.

Proceeds from the Disposition of Collateral

The proceeds from a sale, a lease, or another disposition of collateral must be applied in the following order, (1) Reasonable expenses of retaking, holding, and preparing the collateral for sale, lease, or other disposition, (2) satisfaction of the balance of the indebtedness owed by the debtor to the secured party, (3) satisfaction of subordinate (junior) security interests whose written notifications of demand have been received before distribution of the proceeds is completed, and (4) the debtor is entitled to receive any surplus that remains.

Deficiency Judgment

If the proceeds from the disposition of the collateral are not sufficient to satisfy the debt, the secured party may obtain a deficiency judgment against the debtor, holding the debtor personally liable for the difference.

Redemption Rights

The debtor may redeem the collateral within a statutorily stipulated period of time after repossession by payment of all obligations owed on the debt and all expenses reasonably incurred by the secured creditor in repossessing and holding the collateral.

Relinquishing the Security Interest and Proceeding to Judgment on the Underlying Debt

Instead of repossessing the collateral, a secured creditor may relinquish his or her security interest in the collateral and proceed to judgment against the debtor to recover the underlying debt. This course of action is usually taken only when the value of the collateral has been reduced below the amount of the secured interest and the debtor has other assets from which to satisfy the debt.

Artisan's Liens

Liens are given by law to artisans on personal property they made repairs or improvements on until the amount they are owed is paid. Artisan's liens for services or materials provided prevail over all other security interests in goods unless a statute provides otherwise.

Surety and Guaranty Arrangements, p. 615

Surety and guaranty arrangements both occur when a creditor refuses to extend credit to a debtor without further security and a third person agrees to provide that security by agreeing to become liable on the debt.

Surety Arrangement

In a strict surety arrangement, a third party—called the surety, or co-debtor—promises to be liable for another person's debt. The surety is primarily liable for payment of the debt when it is due, along with the principal debtor. The creditor does not have to attempt to collect the debt from the principal debtor before demanding payment from the surety.

Guaranty Arrangement

In a guaranty arrangement, a third party—called the guarantor—agrees to pay the debt of the principal debtor if the debtor defaults and does not pay the debt when it is due. The guarantor is secondarily liable and has to pay the debt only if the creditor has attempted unsuccessfully to collect the debt from the debtor.

Defenses of a Surety or Guarantor

Generally, the defenses the principal debtor has against the creditor may also be asserted by a surety or guarantor.

Debtor-Protection Law, p. 616

Truth-in-Lending Act

The Truth-in-Lending Act (TILA) is a federal statute that requires creditors to make certain disclosures to consumer-debtors in most consumer credit transactions and real estate loans on the debtor's principal dwelling.

Regulation Z

The Federal Reserve Board adopted Regulation Z to enforce and interpret the TILA.

Consumer Leasing Act

The Consumer Leasing Act (CLA) is a federal statute that requires lessors to make disclosures to lessees in most consumer lease transactions.

Fair Credit and Charge Card Disclosure Act

The Fair Credit and Charge Card Disclosure Act is a federal statute that requires disclosure of certain credit terms to credit card holders.

Equal Credit Opportunity Act

The Equal Credit Opportunity Act (ECOA) is a federal statute that prohibits discrimination in the extension of credit based on the applicant's sex, marital status, race, color, national origin, religion, age, or receipt of income from public assistance programs. The ECOA requires a creditor to notify a consumer-debtor of the reasons for an adverse action on a credit application.

Fair Credit Reporting Act

The Fair Credit Reporting Act (FRCA) is a federal statute that regulates credit reporting agencies and establishes a procedure for a consumer-debtor to have errors in credit reports corrected. The act permits a consumer-debtor to place a 100-word written statement in his or her credit report file concerning any unresolved dispute. This information must be conveyed to anyone seeking a credit report on the debtor.

Fair Debt Collection Practices Act

The Fair Debt Collection Practices Act (FDCPA) is a federal statute that protects consumer-debtors from abusive, deceptive, and unfair practices used by debt collectors. The FDCPA prohibits or limits a creditor from making certain contact with third parties and the debtor concerning a debt it is trying to collect.

Collection Remedies

If a creditor sues a debtor or obtains a judgment against a debtor, the creditor can use the following collection remedies to recover from the debtor.

1. **Attachment.** This is a prejudgment court order that permits the seizure of the debtor's property while the lawsuit is pending. The creditor must follow the procedures established by state law, give the debtor notice, and post a bond with the court.
2. **Execution.** This is a postjudgment court order that permits the seizure of the debtor's property that is in the possession of the debtor. Certain property is exempt from levy (e.g., homestead exemption).
3. **Garnishment.** This is a postjudgment court order that permits the seizure of the debtor's property in the possession of third parties (e.g., wages to be paid to the debtor by his or her employer). Garnishment is subject to limitations established by federal and state law.

Test Review Terms and Concepts

Accommodation party (cosigner) 615
Accounts 603
After-acquired property 604
Antideficiency statute 598
Article 9 (Secured Transactions)
  of the Uniform Commercial Code
  (UCC) 600
Artisan's lien 614
Attachment 604
Beneficiary 595
Buyer in the ordinary course
  of business 611
Chattel paper 603
Collateral 602
Consumer goods 608

Consumer Leasing Act (CLA) 618
Credit 593
Creditor 593
Credit report 619
Debtor 593
Deed of trust 595
Default 612
Deficiency judgment 598
Disposition of collateral 613
Equal Credit Opportunity Act
  (ECOA) 619
Fair Credit and Charge Card
  Disclosure Act 619
Fair Credit Reporting Act
  (FCRA) 619

Fair Debt Collection Practices Act
  (FDCPA) 619
Financing statement 601
Floating lien 604
Foreclosure 598
Foreclosure sale 598
Future advance 605
General intangibles 603
Goods 603
Guarantor 615
Guaranty arrangement 615
Instruments 603
Judgment 614
Land sales contract 599
Mechanic's lien 599

Case Problems

23.1 Mechanic's Lien: Ironwood Exploration, Inc. (Ironwood), owned a lease on oil and gas property located in Duchesne County, Utah. Ironwood contracted to have Lantz Drilling and Exploration Company, Inc. (Lantz), drill an oil well on the property. Thereafter, Lantz rented equipment from Graco Fishing and Rental Tools, Inc. (Graco), for use in drilling the well. Graco billed Lantz for these rentals, but Lantz did not pay. Graco filed a notice of a mechanic's lien on the well in the amount of $19,766. Ironwood, which had paid Lantz, refused to pay Graco. Graco sued to foreclose on its mechanic's lien. Who wins? *Graco Fishing and Rental Tools, Inc. v. Ironwood Exploration, Inc.*, 766 P.2d 1074, 98 Utah Adv. Rep. 28, **Web** 1988 Utah Lexis 125 (Supreme Court of Utah)

23.2 Foreclosure: Atlantic Ocean Kampgrounds, Inc. (Atlantic), borrowed $60,000 from Camden National Bank (Camden National) and executed a note and mortgage on property located in Camden, Maine, securing that amount. Maine permits strict foreclosure. Atlantic defaulted on the loan, and Camden commenced strict foreclosure proceedings pursuant to state law. After the one-year period of redemption, Camden National sold the property to a third party in an amount in excess of the mortgage and costs of the foreclosure proceeding. Atlantic sued to recover the surplus from Camden National. Who wins? *Atlantic Ocean Kampgrounds, Inc. v. Camden National Bank*, 473 A.2d 884, **Web** 1984 Me. Lexis 666 (Supreme Judicial Court of Maine)

23.3 Redemption: Elmer and Arletta Hans, husband and wife, owned a parcel of real property in Illinois. They borrowed $100,000 from First Illinois National Bank (First Illinois) and executed a note and mortgage to First Illinois, making the real estate security for the loan. The security agreement authorized First Illinois to take possession of the property upon the occurrence of a default and required the Hanses to execute a quitclaim deed in favor of First Illinois.

The state of Illinois recognizes the doctrine of redemption. When the Hanses defaulted on the loan, First Illinois filed a lawsuit, seeking an order requiring the Hanses to immediately execute a quitclaim deed to the property. Must the Hanses execute the quitclaim deed before the foreclosure sale? *First Illinois National Bank v. Hans*, 143 Ill. App. 3d 1033, 493 N.E.2d 1171, **Web** 1986 Ill. App. Lexis 2287 (Appellate Court of Illinois)

23.4 Financing Statement: C&H Trucking, Inc. (C&H), borrowed $19,747.56 from S&D Petroleum Company, Inc. (S&D). S&D hired Clifton M. Tamsett to prepare a security agreement naming C&H as the debtor and giving S&D a security interest in a new Mack truck. The security agreement prepared by Tamsett declared that the collateral also secured:

any other indebtedness or liability of the debtor to the secured party direct or indirect, absolute or contingent, due or to become due, now existing or hereafter arising, including all future advances or loans which may be made at the option of the secured party.

Tamsett failed to file a financing statement or the executed agreement with the appropriate government office. C&H subsequently paid off the original debt, and S&D continued to extend new credit to C&H. Two years later, when C&H owed S&D over $17,000, S&D learned that (1) C&H was insolvent, (2) the Mack truck had been sold, and (3) Tamsett had failed to file the security agreement. Does S&D have a security interest in the Mack truck? Is Tamsett liable to S&D? *S&D Petroleum Company, Inc. v. Tamsett*, 144 A.D.2d 849, 534 N.Y.S.2d 800, **Web** 1988 N.Y. App. Div. Lexis 11258 (Supreme Court of New York)

23.5 Priority of Security Agreements: World Wide Tracers, Inc. (World Wide), sold certain of its assets and properties, including equipment, furniture, uniforms, accounts receivable, and contract rights, to Metropolitan Protection, Inc. (Metropolitan). To secure payment of the purchase price, Metropolitan executed a security agreement and financing statement in favor of World Wide. The agreement, which stated that "all of the property listed on Exhibit A (equipment, furniture, and fixtures) together with any property of the debtor acquired after" the agreement was executed was collateral, was filed with the Minnesota secretary of state.

One and one-half years later, State Bank (Bank) loaned money to Metropolitan, which executed a security agreement and financing statement in favor of Bank. Bank filed the financing statement with the Minnesota secretary of state's office on March 3, 1982. The financing statement contained the following language describing the collateral:

All accounts receivable and contract rights owned or hereafter acquired. All equipment now owned and hereafter acquired, including but not limited to, office furniture and uniforms.

When Metropolitan defaulted on its agreement with World Wide six months later, World Wide brought suit, asserting its alleged security agreement in Metropolitan's accounts receivable. Bank filed a counterclaim, asserting its perfected security interest in Metropolitan's accounts receivable. Who wins? *World Wide Tracers, Inc. v. Metropolitan Protection, Inc.*, 384 N.W.2d 442, **Web** 1986 Minn. Lexis 753 (Supreme Court of Minnesota)

23.6 Floating Lien: On March 17, 1973, Joseph H. Jones and others (debtors) borrowed money from Columbus Junction State Bank (Bank) and executed a security agreement in favor of Bank. Bank perfected its security interest by filing financing statements covering "equipment, farm products, crops, livestock, supplies, contract rights, and all accounts and proceeds thereof" with the Iowa secretary of state. Four years and 10 months later, Bank filed a continuation statement with the Iowa secretary of state. Four years and 10 months later, Bank filed a second continuation statement with the Iowa secretary of state. Two years later, the debtors filed for Chapter 7 liquidation bankruptcy. The bankruptcy trustee collected $10,073 from the sale of the debtors' crops and an undetermined amount of soybeans harvested on farmland owned by the debtors. The bankruptcy trustee claimed the funds and soybeans on behalf of the bankruptcy estate. Bank claimed the funds and soybeans as a perfected secured creditor. Who wins? *In re Jones*, 79 B.R. 839, **Web** 1987 Bankr. Lexis 1825 (United States Bankruptcy Court for the Northern District of Iowa)

23.7 Sale Proceeds: Murphy Oldsmobile, Inc. (Murphy), operated an automobile dealership that sold new and used automobiles. General Motors Acceptance Corporation (GMAC) loaned funds to Murphy to finance the purchase of new automobiles as inventory. The loan was secured by a duly perfected security agreement in all existing and after-acquired inventory and the proceeds therefrom. Section 9-306 of the New York UCC provides that a security interest in collateral continues in "identifiable proceeds." During the first week of May 1980, Murphy received checks and drafts from the sale of the secured inventory in the amount of $97,888, which it deposited in a general business checking account at Norstar Bank (Bank). During that week, Murphy defaulted on certain loans it had received from Bank. Bank exercised its right of setoff and seized the funds on deposit in Murphy's checking account. GMAC sued to enforce its security claim against these funds. Who wins? *General Motors Acceptance Corporation v. Norstar Bank, N.A.*, 141 Misc. 2d 349, 532 N.Y.S.2d 685, **Web** 1988 N.Y. Misc. Lexis 595 (Supreme Court of New York)

23.8 Priority of Security Interests: Clyde and Marlys Trees, owners of the Wine Shop, Inc., borrowed money from the American Heritage Bank & Trust Company (Bank). They personally and on behalf of the corporation executed a promissory note, security agreement, and financing statement to Bank. Bank properly filed a security agreement and financing statement naming the Wine Shop's inventory, stock in trade, furniture, fixtures, and equipment "now owned or hereafter to be acquired" as collateral. The Trees also borrowed money from a junior lienholder, whose promissory note was secured by the same collateral. The Wine Shop subsequently defaulted on both notes. Without informing Bank, the junior lienholder took over the assets of the Wine Shop and transferred them to a corporation, O&E, Inc. Fearing that its security interest would not be adequately protected, Bank filed a motion to enforce its security interest. Can Bank enforce its security interest even though the collateral was transferred to another party? *American Heritage Bank & Trust Company v. O&E, Inc.*, 40 Colo. App. 306, 576 P.2d 566, **Web** 1978 Colo. App. Lexis 667 (Court of Appeals of Colorado)

23.9 Priority of Security Interests: Paul High purchased various items of personal property and livestock from William and Marilyn McGowen. To secure the purchase price, High granted the McGowens a security interest in the personal property and livestock. Two and one-half months later, High borrowed $86,695 from Nebraska State Bank (Bank) and signed a promissory note granting Bank a security interest in all his farm products, including but not limited to all his livestock. Bank immediately perfected its security agreement by filing a financing statement with the county clerk in Dakota County, Nebraska. The McGowens perfected their security interest by filing a financing statement and security agreement with the county clerk three months after the Bank filed its financing statement. Three years later, High defaulted on the obligations owed to the McGowens and Bank. Whose security interest has priority? *McGowen v. Nebraska State Bank*, 229 Neb. 471, 427 N.W.2d 772, **Web** 1988 Neb. Lexis 290 (Supreme Court of Nebraska)

23.10 Purchase Money Security Interest: Prior Brothers, Inc. (PBI), began financing its farming operations through Bank of California, N.A. (Bank). Bank's loans were secured by PBI's equipment and after-acquired property. Bank immediately filed a financing statement perfecting its security interest. Two years later, PBI contacted the International Harvester dealership in Sunnyside, Washington, about the purchase of a new tractor. A retail installment contract for a model 1066 International Harvester tractor was executed. PBI took delivery of the tractor "on approval," agreeing that if it decided to purchase the tractor, it would inform the dealership of its intention and would send a $6,000 down payment. The dealership received a $6,000 check. The dealership immediately filed a financing statement concerning the tractor. Subsequently, when PBI went into receivership, the dealership filed a complaint, asking the court to declare that its purchase money security interest in the tractor had priority over Bank's security interest. Does it? *In the Matter of Prior Brothers, Inc.*, 29 Wn. App. 905, 632 P.2d 522, **Web** 1981 Wash. App. Lexis 2507 (Court of Appeals of Washington)

23.11 Purchase Money Security Interest: Sandwich State Bank (Sandwich) made a general farm loan to David Klotz and Hinckley Grain Company. The loan was secured by the assets of Klotz's farm and after-acquired property. Sandwich filed a financing statement with the Kane County Recorder to perfect its security interest. Sandwich filed the necessary continuation statements so its security interest remained in effect up to and during the time of trial. Eleven years after Sandwich State Bank made its loan, DeKalb Bank (DeKalb) loaned Klotz funds for the particular purpose of purchasing certain cattle. DeKalb immediately filed a financing statement to perfect its security interest in the cattle. The cattle in question were all purchased using funds loaned to Klotz by DeKalb. When Klotz defaulted on its loan to DeKalb, DeKalb sued to enforce its security interest and to recover possession of the cattle. Does DeKalb's security interest have priority over Sandwich's security interest? *DeKalb Bank v. Klotz*, 151 Ill. App. 3d 638, 502 N.E.2d 1256, **Web** 1986 Ill. App. Lexis 3351 (Appellate Court of Illinois)

23.12 Buyer in the Ordinary Course of Business: Heritage Ford Lincoln Mercury, Inc. (Heritage), was in the business of selling new cars. Heritage entered into an agreement with Ford Motor Credit Company (Ford) whereby Ford extended a continuing line of credit to Heritage to purchase vehicles. Heritage granted Ford a purchase money security interest in all motor vehicles it owned and thereafter acquired and in all proceeds from the sale of such motor vehicles. Ford immediately filed its financing statement with the secretary of state. When the dealership experienced financial trouble, two Heritage officers decided to double finance certain new cars by issuing dealer papers to themselves and obtaining financing for two new cars from First National Bank & Trust Company of El Dorado (Bank). The loan proceeds were deposited in the dealership's account to help its financial difficulties. The cars were available for sale. When the dealership closed its doors and turned over the car inventory to Ford, Bank alleged that it had priority over Ford because the Heritage officers were buyers in the ordinary course of business. Who wins? *First National Bank and Trust Company of El Dorado v. Ford Motor Credit Company*, 231 Kan. 431, 646 P.2d 1057, **Web** 1982 Kan. Lexis 280 (Supreme Court of Kansas)

23.13 Artisan's Lien: Ozark Financial Services (Ozark) loaned money to Lonnie and Patsy Turner to purchase a tractor truck unit. The Turners signed a security agreement giving Ozark a security interest in the tractor truck. Ozark properly filed a financing statement giving public notice of its security interest. Two months later, the Turners took the truck to Pete & Sons Garage, Inc. (Pete & Sons), for repairs. When the Turners arrived to pick up the truck, they could not pay for the repairs. Pete & Sons returned the truck to the Turners upon their verbal agreement that if they did not pay for the repairs, they would return the truck to Pete & Sons. The Turners did not pay Pete & Sons for the repair services and defaulted on the loan payments due Ozark. Ozark brought an action to recover the truck under its security agreement. Pete & Sons asserted that it had a common law artisan's lien on the truck for the unpaid repair services that it claimed took priority over Ozark's security interest. Who wins? *Ozark Financial Services v. Turner*, 735 S.W.2d 374, **Web** 1987 Mo. App. Lexis 4273 (Court of Appeals of Missouri)

Ethics Issues

23.14 Ethics: Sally Fitch obtained a loan from Buffalo Federal Savings and Loan Association (Buffalo Federal). She signed a promissory note for $130,000 with interest at 17 percent. The loan was secured with a real estate mortgage on property owned by Fitch located in Johnson County, Wyoming. Wyoming does not have an antideficiency statute. Four years later, Fitch was in default on the note. When she was unable to pay the loan to current status, Buffalo Federal sent her a notice of foreclosure. After publication of proper public notice, the sheriff conducted the sale as advertised on the steps of the Johnson County Courthouse. The property sold for a high bid of $66,000. Buffalo Federal applied the $66,000 to the $150,209 balance on the note and sued Fitch to recover a judgment for the deficiency of $84,209. Who wins? Do antideficiency statutes serve any social purpose? *Fitch v. Buffalo Federal Savings and Loan Association*, 751 P.2d 1309, **Web** 1988 Wyo. Lexis 27 (Supreme Court of Wyoming)

23.15 Ethics: Jessie Lynch became seriously ill and needed medical attention. Her sister, Ethel Sales, took her to the Forsyth Memorial Hospital in North Carolina for treatment. Lynch was admitted for hospitalization. Sales signed Lynch's admission form, which included the following section:

The undersigned, in consideration of hospital services being rendered or to be rendered by Forsyth County Memorial Hospital Authority, Inc., in Winston-Salem, N.C., to the above patient, does hereby guarantee payment to Forsyth County Hospital Authority, Inc., on demand all charges for said services and incidentals incurred on behalf of such patient.

Lynch received the care and services rendered by the hospital until her discharge over 30 days later. The total bill during her hospitalization amounted to $7,977. When Lynch refused to pay the bill, the hospital instituted an action against Lynch and Sales to recover the unpaid amount. Is Sales liable? Did Sales act ethically in denying liability? Did she have a choice when she signed the contract? *Forsyth County Memorial Hospital Authority, Inc.*, 82 N.C. App. 265, 346 S.E.2d 212, **Web** 1986 N.C. App. Lexis 2432 (Court of Appeals of North Carolina)

23.16: Ethics: Elizabeth Valentine purchased a home in Philadelphia, Pennsylvania. She applied for and received a home loan from Salmon Building and Loan Association (Salmon) for the purpose of paneling the cellar walls and redecorating the house. Salmon took a security interest in the house as collateral for the loan. Although Salmon gave Valentine a disclosure document, nowhere on the document were finance charges disclosed. The document did notify Valentine that Salmon had a security interest in the house. Over two years later, Valentine sued Salmon (which had since merged with Influential Savings and Loan Association) to rescind the loan. Who wins? Did Salmon act ethically in this case? *Valentine v. Influential Savings and Loan Association*, 572 F.Supp. 36, **Web** 1983 U.S. Dist. Lexis 15884 (United States District Court for the Eastern District of Pennsylvania)

Irac Writing Assignment

Read **Case A-23** in Appendix A [*Davenport v. Chrysler Credit Corporation*]. Use the IRAC method to prepare a written analysis of the case.

Endnotes

1. 15 U.S.C. Section 1601 *et seq.*
2. 12 C.F.R. 226.
3. 15 U.S.C. Section 1667 *et seq.*
4. 15 U.S.C. Section 1637.
5. 15 U.S.C. Section 1691.
6. 15 U.S.C. Section 1681 *et seq.*
7. 15 U.S.C. Section 1692.

CHAPTER 24

Bankruptcy and Reorganization

"A trifling debt makes a man your debtor, a large one makes him your enemy."

—SENECA
Epistulae Morales and Lucilium, Letters 63–65

CHAPTER OBJECTIVES

After studying this chapter, you should be able to:

1. Identify and describe the major changes to federal bankruptcy law made by the Bankruptcy Abuse Prevention and Consumer Protection Act of 2005.
2. Describe a Chapter 7 liquidation bankruptcy and the means test for filing for Chapter 7 bankruptcy.
3. Describe a Chapter 13 adjustment of debts of an individual with regular income.
4. Describe how businesses are reorganized in Chapter 11 bankruptcy.
5. Describe a Chapter 12 adjustment of debts of a family farmer or fisherman with regular income.

CHAPTER CONTENTS

- Introduction to Bankruptcy and Reorganization
- Bankruptcy Law
- Bankruptcy Procedure
- Bankruptcy Estate
- Chapter 7—Liquidation
- Chapter 13—Adjustment of Debts of an Individual with Regular Income
- Chapter 11—Reorganization
- Chapter 12—Family Farmer and Family Fisherman Bankruptcy
- Special Forms of Bankruptcy
- Chapter Summary
- Test Review Terms and Concepts
- Case Problems
- Ethics Issues
- IRAC Writing Assignment

Introduction to Bankruptcy and Reorganization

The extension of credit from creditors to debtors in commercial and personal transactions is important to the viability of the U.S. and world economies. On occasion, however, borrowers become overextended and are unable to meet their debt obligations. The goal of bankruptcy laws is to balance the rights of debtors and creditors and provide methods for debtors to be relieved of some debt in order to obtain a "fresh start."

The founders of our country thought that the plight of debtors was so important that they included a provision in the U.S. Constitution, giving Congress the authority to establish uniform federal bankruptcy laws. Congress enacted bankruptcy laws pursuant to this power. Prior to 2005, the most recent overhaul of federal bankruptcy law occurred in 1978. The 1978 law was structured to make it easier for debtors to be relieved of much of their debt by declaring bankruptcy; it was deemed "debtor friendly" because it allowed many debtors to escape their unsecured debts.

After a decade of lobbying by credit card companies and banks, Congress enacted the *Bankruptcy Abuse Prevention and Consumer Protection Act of 2005*. The 2005 act makes it much more difficult for debtors to escape their debts under federal bankruptcy law. The 2005 act, which has been criticized by consumer groups for being too "creditor friendly," has been praised by many businesses, banks, and credit card issuers.

This chapter discusses federal bankruptcy law, including how the provisions of the Bankruptcy Abuse Prevention and Consumer Protection Act of 2005 have changed bankruptcy law.

Family Farm, Idaho

Chapter 12 of the federal Bankruptcy Code contains special provisions for reorganizing family farmers and family fishermen.

Bankruptcy Law

Article I, section 8, clause 4 of the U.S. Constitution provides that "The Congress shall have the power . . . to establish . . . uniform laws on the subject of bankruptcies throughout the United States." Bankruptcy law is exclusively federal law; there are no state bankruptcy laws. Congress enacted the original federal Bankruptcy Act in 1878. The Bankruptcy Code is contained in Title 11 of the *United States Code* (U.S.C.).

LANDMARK LAW

Bankruptcy Abuse Prevention and Consumer Protection Act of 2005

Other the years, Congress adopted various bankruptcy laws. Federal bankruptcy law was completely revised by the **Bankruptcy Reform Act of 1978** [11 U.S.C. Sections 101–1330]. The 1978 act substantially changed—and eased—the requirements for filing bankruptcy. The 1978 act made it easier for debtors to rid themselves of unsecured debt, primarily by filing for Chapter 7 liquidation bankruptcy. By 2005, more than 1 million debtors were filing for Chapter 7 liquidation bankruptcy each year.

For over a decade before 2005, credit card companies, commercial banks, and other businesses lobbied Congress to pass a new bankruptcy act that would reduce the ability of some debtors to relieve themselves of unwanted debt through bankruptcy. In response, Congress enacted the **Bankruptcy Abuse Prevention and Consumer Protection Act of 2005** [P.L. 109-8, 119 Stat. 23 (April 20, 2005)]. The 2005 act substantially amended federal bankruptcy law, making it much more difficult for debtors to escape unwanted debt through bankruptcy.

Federal bankruptcy law, as amended, is called the **Bankruptcy Code**. The Bankruptcy Code establishes procedures for filing for bankruptcy, resolving creditors' claims, and protecting debtors' rights.

The changes made by the 2005 act are integrated throughout this chapter.

Types of Bankruptcy

The Bankruptcy Code is divided into chapters. Chapters 1, 3, and 5 set forth definitions and general provisions that govern case administration. The provisions of these chapters generally apply to all forms of bankruptcy.

Four special chapters of the Bankruptcy Code provide different types of bankruptcy under which individual and business debtors may be granted remedy. The four types of bankruptcies, and the filing fees established by the 2005 act, are:

Chapter	Type of Bankruptcy	Filing Fee
Chapter 7	Liquidation	$ 200
Chapter 11	Reorganization	$1,000
Chapter 12	Adjustment of Debts of a Family Farmer or Fisherman with Regular Income	$ 200
Chapter 13	Adjustment of Debts of an Individual with Regular Income	$ 150

These types of bankruptcies are covered in detail in this chapter. Several special forms of bankruptcy covered in the Bankruptcy Code are also described in this chapter.

"Fresh Start"

The primary purpose of federal bankruptcy law is to grant different forms of relief to debtors from overly burdensome debt while at the same time protecting some of the rights of creditors. The granting of bankruptcy gives debtors a **fresh start** by freeing them of some legal responsibility for past debts. Prior to the 2005 act, debtors were more likely to obtain an almost complete fresh start under Chapter 7 liquidation bankruptcy. With the changes made by the 2005 act, however, a debtor may sometimes only obtain a partial fresh start because the debtor may have to pay more of his or her pre-petition bankruptcy debts out of post-petition earnings than required prior to the 2005 act.

Federal bankruptcy law is designed to accomplish the following: (1) protect debtors from abusive activities by creditors in collecting debts; (2) prevent certain creditors from obtaining an unfair advantage over other creditors; (3) protect creditors from actions of the debtor that would diminish the value of the bankruptcy estate; (4) provide for the speedy, efficient, and equitable distribution of the debtor's nonexempt property to creditors; (5) require debtors to repay debts if they have the means to do so; and (6) preserve existing business relationships.

Bankruptcy Courts

Congress created a system of federal **bankruptcy courts**. These special courts are necessary because the number of bankruptcies would overwhelm the federal districts courts. The bankruptcy courts are part of the federal court system, and one bankruptcy court is attached to each of the 94 U.S. District Courts located across the country. The Bankruptcy Reform Act of 2005 increased the number of bankruptcy judges to handle the increasing number and complexity of bankruptcy cases.

Bankruptcy judges are specialists who hear bankruptcy proceedings. Pursuant to the 2005 act, bankruptcy judges are appointed by the U.S. Circuit Court of Appeals for the circuit in which the bankruptcy court district is located. Bankruptcy judges are appointed for 14-year terms. The relevant District Court has jurisdiction to hear appeals from bankruptcy court. However, a Bankruptcy Appellate Panel Service, which is composed of bankruptcy judges of the relevant district, can hear and decide appeals if the parties consent.

Bankruptcy judges decide *core proceedings* regarding bankruptcy issues (e.g., allowing creditor claims, deciding preferences, confirming plans of reorganization). *Noncore* proceedings involving the debtor (e.g., personal injury lawsuits, divorce proceedings, criminal cases, other civil cases) are heard and decided by the relevant state or federal court.

Web Exercise

1. **WEB** Go to *www.uscourts.gov/bankruptcycourts.html*. Click on "94 federal judicial districts" and find the location of the U.S. bankruptcy court that serves your area.

U.S. Trustee

Federal law establishes the office of **U.S. trustee**. A U.S. trustee is a federal government official who has the responsibility of handling and supervising many of the administrative tasks associated with a bankruptcy case.[1] A U.S. trustee is empowered to perform many of the tasks that the bankruptcy judge previously performed. One such task is the appointment of interim trustees to take control of a debtor's assets prior to a permanent trustee being elected by the creditors and the supervision of trustees in Chapter 7, 11, 12, and 13 cases. Each U.S. trustee is under the general supervision of the U.S. attorney general. The U.S. trustee must notify the U.S. attorney general of any action that may constitute a crime in a bankruptcy case.

Bankruptcy Procedure

The Bankruptcy Code requires that certain procedures be followed for the commencement and prosecution of a bankruptcy case. The Bankruptcy Code provides procedures and requirements for filing petitions for bankruptcy, defines the bankruptcy estate, provides certain protections to debtors during the course of bankruptcy, and establishes the rights of creditors. These issues are discussed in the following paragraphs.

Pre-Petition and Post-Petition Counseling

The 2005 act added a new provision that requires an individual filing for bankruptcy to receive **pre-petition counseling** and **post-petition counseling**. A debtor must receive pre-petition credit counseling within 180 days prior to filing his or her petition for bankruptcy. This includes counseling on types of credit, the use of credit, and budget analysis. The counseling is to be provided by nonprofit credit counseling agencies approved by the U.S. trustee.

In addition, the 2005 act requires that before an individual debtor receives a discharge in a Chapter 7 or Chapter 13 bankruptcy, the debtor must attend a personal financial management course approved by the U.S. trustee. This course is designed to provide the debtor with information on responsible use of credit and personal financial planning.

The pre-petition credit counseling and the post-petition financial management counseling may be provided in person, over the telephone, or on the Internet. Individuals unable to receive such services due to disability, impairment, or active military duty in a combat zone are excused from these requirements.

Filling a Bankruptcy Petition

A bankruptcy case is commenced when a **petition** is filed with the bankruptcy court. Two types of petitions can be filed:

1. *Voluntary petition.* A **voluntary petition** is filed by the debtor. A voluntary petition can be filed by the debtor in Chapter 7 (liquidation), Chapter 11 (reorganization), Chapter 12 (family farmer or fisherman), and Chapter 13 (adjustment of debts) bankruptcy cases. The petition has to state that the debtor has debts.
2. *Involuntary petition.* An **involuntary petition** is filed by a creditor or creditors and places the debtor into bankruptcy. An involuntary petition can be filed in Chapter 7 (liquidation) and Chapter 11 (reorganization) cases; an involuntary petition cannot be filed in Chapter 12 (family farmer or fisherman) or Chapter 13 (adjustment of debts) cases.

   An involuntary petition must allege that the debtor is not paying his or its debts as they become due. If the debtor has 12 or more creditors, the petition must be signed by at least 3 of them. If there are fewer than 12 creditors, any creditor can sign the petition. The creditor or creditors who sign the petition must have valid unsecured claims of at least $12,300 in aggregate.

   Form B1, a voluntary petition for bankruptcy, appears as Exhibit 24.1.

Schedules

An individual debtor must submit the following schedules upon filing a voluntary petition; all forms must be sworn under oath and signed by the debtor:

1. List of secured and unsecured creditors, with addresses
2. List of all property owned
3. Statement of the financial affairs of the debtor
4. Statement of the debtor's monthly income
5. Current income and expenses
6. Evidence of payments received from employers within 60 days prior to the filing of the petition

EXHIBIT 24.1

Form B1: Voluntary Petition for Bankruptcy

(Official Form 1) (12/03)

FORM B1	United States Bankruptcy Court District of _____	Voluntary Petition

Name of Debtor (if individual, enter Last, First, Middle):	Name of Joint Debtor (Spouse) (Last, First, Middle):
All Other Names used by the Debtor in the last 6 years (include married, maiden, and trade names):	All Other Names used by the Joint Debtor in the last 6 years (include married, maiden, and trade names):
Last four digits of Soc. Sec. No./Complete EIN or other Tax I.D. No. (if more than one, state all):	Last four digits of Soc. Sec.No./Complete EIN or other Tax I.D. No. (if more than one, state all):
Street Address of Debtor (No. & Street, City, State & Zip Code):	Street Address of Joint Debtor (No. & Street, City, State & Zip Code):
County of Residence or of the Principal Place of Business:	County of Residence or of the Principal Place of Business:
Mailing Address of Debtor (if different from street address):	Mailing Address of Joint Debtor (if different from street address):

Location of Principal Assets of Business Debtor
(if different from street address above):

Information Regarding the Debtor (Check the Applicable Boxes)

Venue (Check any applicable box)

☐ Debtor has been domiciled or has had a residence, principal place of business, or principal assets in this District for 180 days immediately preceding the date of this petition or for a longer part of such 180 days than in any other District.

☐ There is a bankruptcy case concerning debtor's affiliate, general partner, or partnership pending in this District.

Type of Debtor (Check all boxes that apply)		**Chapter or Section of Bankruptcy Code Under Which the Petition is Filed** (Check one box)
☐ Individual(s) ☐ Corporation ☐ Partnership ☐ Other _____	☐ Railroad ☐ Stockbroker ☐ Commodity Broker ☐ Clearing Bank	☐ Chapter 7 ☐ Chapter 11 ☐ Chapter 13 ☐ Chapter 9 ☐ Chapter 12 ☐ Sec. 304 - Case ancillary to foreign proceeding

Nature of Debts (Check one box)

☐ Consumer/Non-Business   ☐ Business

Filing Fee (Check one box)

☐ Full Filing Fee attached

☐ Filing Fee to be paid in installments (Applicable to individuals only) Must attach signed application for the court's consideration certifying that the debtor is unable to pay fee except in installments. Rule 1006(b). See Official Form No. 3.

Chapter 11 Small Business (Check all boxes that apply)

☐ Debtor is a small business as defined in 11 U.S.C. § 101

☐ Debtor is and elects to be considered a small business under 11 U.S.C. § 1121(e) (Optional)

Statistical/Administrative Information (Estimates only)

☐ Debtor estimates that funds will be available for distribution to unsecured creditors.

☐ Debtor estimates that, after any exempt property is excluded and administrative expenses paid, there will be no funds available for distribution to unsecured creditors.

THIS SPACE IS FOR COURT USE ONLY

Estimated Number of Creditors	1-15	16-49	50-99	100-199	200-999	1000-over		
	☐	☐	☐	☐	☐	☐		

Estimated Assets	$0 to $50,000	$50,001 to $100,000	$100,001 to $500,000	$500,001 to $1 million	$1,000,001 to $10 million	$10,000,001 to $50 million	$50,000,001 to $100 million	More than $100 million
	☐	☐	☐	☐	☐	☐	☐	☐

Estimated Debts	$0 to $50,000	$50,001 to $100,000	$100,001 to $500,000	$500,001 to $1 million	$1,000,001 to $10 million	$10,000,001 to $50 million	$50,000,001 to $100 million	More than $100 million
	☐	☐	☐	☐	☐	☐	☐	☐

7. Copy of the debtor's federal income tax return for the most recent year ending prior to the filing of the petition

In addition, an individual debtor must file a certificate stating that he or she has received the required pre-petition credit counseling.

ETHICS SPOTLIGHT
Attorney Certification

The 2005 act places a new burden on attorneys who represent debtors in bankruptcy. The 2005 act requires an attorney to certify the accuracy of the information contained in the bankruptcy petition and the schedules, under penalty of perjury. If there are any factual discrepancies, the attorney is subject to monetary fines and sanctions. Many attorneys may no longer represent debtors in bankruptcy because of this rule.

If an attorney represents a debtor in bankruptcy, the attorney has to conduct a thorough investigation of the debtor's financial position and schedules to determine the accuracy of the information contained in the petition and schedules. The attorney may also require that accountants, appraisers, and other investigators be hired to help establish the accuracy of the information.

The new **attorney certification** requirement could add significantly to the cost of filing for bankruptcy. The debtor has to pay the attorney for the additional time necessary to conduct the investigation and pay for accountants, appraisers, and other professionals to help verify the accuracy of the information.

Law & Ethics Questions

1. What are the attorney certification requirements?
2. **ETHICS** Will the attorney certification requirements encourage ethical behavior by debtors filing for bankruptcy? Explain

Order for Relief

The filing of either a voluntary petition or an unchallenged involuntary petition constitutes an **order for relief**. If the debtor challenges an involuntary petition, a trial is held to determine whether an order for relief should be granted. If an order is granted, the case is accepted for further bankruptcy proceedings. In the case of an involuntary petition, the debtor must file the same schedules filed by voluntary petition debtors.

Meeting of the Creditors

Within a reasonable time after the court grants an order for relief (not less than 10 days or more than 30 days), the court must call a **meeting of the creditors** (also called the **first meeting of the creditors**). The bankruptcy judge cannot attend the meeting. The debtor must appear and submit to questioning, under oath, by creditors. Creditors may ask questions regarding the debtor's financial affairs, disposition of property prior to bankruptcy, possible concealment of assets, and such. The debtor may have an attorney present at this meeting.

Proof of Claim and Proof of Interest

A creditor must file a **proof of claim** stating the amounts of his or her claim against the debtor. The document for this statement is provided by the court. The proof of claim must be timely filed, which generally means within six months of the first meeting of the creditors. A secured creditor whose claim exceeds the value of the collateral may submit a proof of claim and become an unsecured claimant as to the difference. An equity security holder (e.g., a shareholder of a corporation) must file a **proof of interest**.

The proof of claim or proof of interest must be allowed by the court before a creditor or an equity security holder is permitted to participate in the bankruptcy estate. Any party of interest may object to a claim or an interest. If an objection to a claim or an interest is raised, the court holds a hearing to determine the validity and amount of the claim or interest.

Bankruptcy Trustee

A **trustee** must be appointed in the following types of bankruptcy cases: Chapter 7 (liquidation), Chapter 12 (family farmer or family fisherman), and Chapter 13 (adjustment of debts). A trustee may be appointed in a Chapter 11 (reorganization) case upon a showing of fraud, dishonesty, incompetence, or gross mismanagement of the affairs of the debtor by current management.

Trustees, who are often lawyers, accountants, or business professionals, are entitled to receive reasonable compensation for their services and reimbursement for expenses. Once appointed, the trustee becomes the legal representative of the debtor's estate. Generally, the trustee is empowered to:

- Take immediate possession of the debtor's property.
- Protect domestic-support creditors (e.g., former spouse, children of the debtor), a duty added by the 2005 act.
- Review all materials filed by the debtor.
- Separate secured and unsecured property.
- In a Chapter 7 case, file a statement as to whether the case is presumed to be an abuse under the new means test established by the 2005 act.
- Set aside exempt property.
- Investigate the debtor's financial affairs.
- Employ professionals (e.g., attorneys, accountants, appraisers) to assist in the administration of the case.
- Examine proof of claims.
- Defend, bring, and maintain lawsuits on behalf of the estate.
- Invest the property of the estate.
- Sell or otherwise dispose of property of the estate.
- Distribute the proceeds of the estate.
- Make reports to the court, creditors, debtor, and other parties of interest regarding the administration of the estate.

Automatic Stay

The filing of a voluntary or an involuntary petition automatically stays—that is, suspends—certain legal actions by creditors against the debtor or the debtor's property. This is called an **automatic stay**. The stay, which applies to collection efforts of both secured and unsecured creditors, is designed to prevent a scramble for the debtor's assets in a variety of court proceedings. The following creditor actions are stayed:

- Instituting or maintaining legal actions to collect pre-petition debts
- Enforcing judgments obtained against the debtor
- Obtaining, perfecting, or enforcing liens against property of the debtor
- Nonjudicial collection efforts, such as self-help activities (e.g., repossession of an automobile)

Actions to recover domestic support obligations (e.g., alimony, child support), the dissolution of a marriage, and child custody cases are not stayed in bankruptcy. An automatic stay does not preclude efforts by creditors against co-debtors and guarantors of the bankrupt debtor's debts unless the co-debtor is also in bankruptcy. Criminal actions against the debtor are not stayed. The court also has authority to issue injunctions preventing creditor activity not covered by the automatic stay provision.

RELIEF FROM STAY A secured creditor may petition the court for **relief from stay**, which usually occurs in situations involving depreciating assets where the secured property is not adequately protected during the bankruptcy proceeding. If this situation is found, the court may grant relief from stay. In the alternative, the court may provide adequate protection rather than grant relief from stay. In such cases, the court may (1) order cash payments equal to the amount of the depreciation, (2) grant an additional or a replacement lien, or (3) grant an "indubitable equivalent" (e.g., a guarantee from a solvent party).

Discharge

In Chapter 7 (liquidation), Chapter 11 (reorganization), Chapter 12 (family farmer and family fisherman), and Chapter 13 (adjustment of debts) bankruptcies, if the requirements are met, the court grants the debtor a **discharge** of all or some of his, her, or its debts. When discharge is granted, the debtor is relieved of responsibility to pay the discharged debts. In other words, the debtor is no longer legally liable to pay the discharged debts. Discharge is one of the primary reasons a debtor files for bankruptcy. The specifics of discharge under each type of bankruptcy are discussed in this chapter.

EXCEPTIONS TO DISCHARGE The following debts are not dischargeable in bankruptcy; the dollar limits are those established by the 2005 act:

- Claims for income or gross receipts taxes owed to federal, state, or local governments accrued within three years prior to the filing of the petition for bankruptcy, or for such taxes for any period where the debtor made a fraudulent return or willfully attempted to evade or defeat such tax, and property taxes accrued within one year prior to filing the petition for bankruptcy.
- Certain fines and penalties payable to federal, state, and local governmental units.
- Claims based on the debtor's liability for causing willful or malicious injury to a person or property.
- Claims arising from fraud, larceny, or embezzlement by the debtor while acting in a fiduciary capacity.
- Domestic support obligations and alimony, maintenance, and child support payments resulting from a divorce decree or separation agreement.
- Unscheduled claims.
- Claims based on the consumer-debtor's purchase of luxury goods or services of more than $500 from a single creditor on or within 90 days of the order for relief. This is a rebuttable presumption that may be challenged by the debtor by proving that the expenses were incurred to support the debtor or dependants and are therefore not luxuries.
- Cash advances in excess of $750 obtained by a consumer-debtor by use of a revolving line of credit or credit cards on or within 70 days of the order for relief. This is also a rebuttable presumption.
- Judgments and consent decrees against the debtor for liability incurred as a result of the debtor's operation of a motor vehicle, vessel, or aircraft while legally intoxicated.
- A debt that would result in a benefit to the debtor that outweighs the detrimental consequences to a spouse, former spouse, or child of the debtor.
- An amount owed to a pension, profit-sharing, or stock bonus plan and loans owed to employee retirement plans.

Creditors who have nondischargeable claims against the debtor may participate in the distribution of the bankruptcy estate. The creditor may pursue the nondischarged balance against the debtor after bankruptcy.

> I will pay you some, and, as most debtors do, promise you indefinitely.
>
> William Shakespeare
> *Henry IV, Part 11 (1597)*

CONTEMPORARY ENVIRONMENT
Reaffirmation Agreement

A debtor and a creditor can enter into a **reaffirmation agreement** whereby the debtor agrees to pay the creditor for a debt that is dischargeable in bankruptcy. This might occur if the debtor wishes to repay a debt to a family member, to a bank, or to another party. A reaffirmation agreement must be entered into before discharge is granted. A reaffirmation agreement must be filed with the court. Approval by the court is required if the debtor is not represented by an attorney. If the debtor is represented by an attorney, the attorney must certify that the debtor voluntarily entered into the reaffirmation agreement and that the debtor understands the consequences of the agreement. Even if the debtor is represented by an attorney, court approval is required if the agreement will cause undue hardship on the debtor or his or her family.

Bankruptcy Estate

The **bankruptcy estate** is created upon the commencement of a bankruptcy case. It includes all the debtor's legal and equitable interests in real, personal, tangible, and intangible property, wherever located, that exist when the petition is filed, and all interests of the debtor and the debtor's spouse in community property. Certain *exempt property* (which is discussed later in this section) is not part of the bankruptcy estate.

Gifts, inheritances, life insurance proceeds, and property from divorce settlements that the debtor is entitled to receive within 180 days after the petition is filed are part of the bankruptcy estate. Earnings from property of the estate—such as rents, dividends, and interest payments—are property of the estate.

Earnings from services performed by an individual debtor are not part of the bankruptcy estate in a Chapter 7 liquidation bankruptcy. However, the 2005 act provides that a certain amount of post-petition earnings from services performed by the debtor that are earned for up to five years after the order for relief may be required to be paid as part of the completion of Chapter 12 (family farmer or family fisherman), Chapter 11 (reorganization), and Chapter 13 (adjustment of debts) cases. These repayment plans are discussed later in this chapter.

Exempt Property

Because the Bankruptcy Code is not designed to make the debtor a pauper, certain property is exempt from the bankruptcy estate. The debtor may retain exempt property. **Exempt property** is property of the debtor that he or she can keep and that does not become part of the bankruptcy estate. The creditors cannot claim this property.

The Bankruptcy Code establishes a list of property and assets that the debtor can claim as exempt property. The federal exemptions, with the dollar limits established by the 2005 act, are listed in Exhibit 24.2.[2] Federal exemptions are adjusted every three years to reflect changes in the consumer price index:

EXHIBIT 24.2

Federal Exemptions from the Bankruptcy Estate

1. Interest up to $18,450 in equity in property used as a residence and burial plots (called the "homestead exemption")
2. Interest up to $2,950 in value in one motor vehicle
3. Interest up to $475 per item in household goods and furnishings, wearing apparel, appliances, books, animals, crops, or musical instruments, up to an aggregate value of $9,850 for all items
4. Interest in jewelry up to $1,225
5. Interest in any property the debtor chooses (including cash) up to $975, plus up to $9,250 of any unused portion of the homestead exemption
6. Interest up to $1,850 in value in implements, tools, or professional books used in the debtor's trade
7. Any unmatured life insurance policy owned by the debtor
8. Professionally prescribed health aids
9. Many government benefits, regardless of value, including Social Security benefits, welfare benefits, unemployment compensation, veteran's benefits, disability benefits, and public assistance benefits
10. Certain rights to receive income, including domestic support payments (e.g., alimony and child support), certain pension benefits, profit sharing, and annuity payments
11. Interests in wrongful death benefits and life insurance proceeds to the extent necessary to support the debtor or his or her dependants
12. Personal injury awards up to $18,450
13. Retirement funds that are in a fund or an account that is exempt from taxation under the Internal Revenue Code, except that an exemption for individual retirement accounts (IRAs) shall not exceed $1 million for an individual unless the interests of justice require this amount to be increased

Poor bankrupt.

William Shakespeare
Romeo and Juliet (1595)

State Exemptions

The Bankruptcy Code permits states to enact their own exemptions. States that do so may (1) give debtors the option of choosing between federal and state exemptions or (2) require debtors to follow state law. The exemptions available under state law are often more liberal than those provided by federal law.

The following two cases involve the issue of whether certain property is exempt from the bankruptcy estate.

CASE 24.1
Exempt Property

In re Lebovitz

344 B.R. 556, **Web** 2006 Bankr. Lexis 1044 (2006)
United States Bankruptcy Court for the Western District of Tennessee

> **"** *The Debtor urges the court to read into the Tennessee statutes an absolute exemption for wedding rings.* **"**
>
> —Judge Latta

Facts

Dr. Morris Lebovitz and Kerrye Hill Lebovitz, husband and wife, were residents of the state of Tennessee. Dr. Lebovitz filed for bankruptcy protection as a result of illness. Mrs. Lebovitz (Debtor) filed for bankruptcy because she had cosigned on a large loan with Dr. Lebovitz. The Debtor is the owner of the following pieces of jewelry: a Tiffany 5-carat diamond engagement ring (purchase price $40,000–$50,000), a pair of diamond stud earrings of approximately 1 carat each, a diamond drop necklace of approximately 1 carat, and a Cartier watch. All these items were gifts from Dr. Lebovitz.

Tennessee has chosen to opt out of the federal bankruptcy exemption provisions and has adopted its own bankruptcy exemption provisions. Tennessee does not provide for an exemption for jewelry. Tennessee does provide for an exemption for "necessary and proper wearing apparel." Debtor claimed that her jewelry was necessary and proper wearing apparel and was therefore exempt property from the bankruptcy estate. The bankruptcy trustee filed an objection to the claim of exemption.

Issue

Does jewelry qualify as necessary and proper wearing apparel and therefore exempt property from the bankruptcy estate?

Language of the Court

The Debtor argues that she should be able to exempt all of her jewelry as wearing apparel because the wearing apparel exemption provided by Tennessee law is unlimited in amount, the items are worn by the Debtor regularly, have sentimental value to her because they were given to her by her husband, and were not purchased for investment. The Trustee responds that the Debtor is not entitled to claim her jewelry as exempt because the items are neither necessary nor proper wearing apparel for a bankruptcy debtor. As difficult as this case is given

the unfortunate illness of Dr. Lebovitz that led to the filing, the Trustee is correct. Whether the Debtor's jewelry is valued at its wholesale value or retail value, the items constitute luxury items. The court finds the items to constitute luxury items, not necessary or proper wearing apparel. The Debtor urges the court to read into the Tennessee statutes an absolute exemption for wedding rings. As sympathetic as that position seems, the court cannot substitute its judgment for that of the Tennessee legislature.

Decision

The U.S. bankruptcy court held that the debtor's luxury jewelry did not qualify as necessary and proper wearing apparel and was therefore not exempt property from the Debtor's bankruptcy estate. The U.S. bankruptcy court granted the trustee's motion for turnover of the property to be included in the bankruptcy estate.

Law & Ethics Questions

1. What is the consequence of property being held to be exempt from the bankruptcy estate?

2. Should engagement and wedding rings be considered exempt property? Why or why not?

3. **ETHICS** Did the debtor have much of a chance to win the lawsuit?

Web Exercises

1. **WEB** For the complete opinion of this case, go to *www.prenhall.com/cheesemancases*.

2. **WEB** Visit the website of the U.S. Bankruptcy Court for the Western District of Tennessee, at *www.tnwb.uscourts.gov*.

3. **WEB** Use *www.google.com* to find out whether your state has adopted exemptions from the bankruptcy estate. If it has, compare the state exemptions to the federal exemptions list in Exhibit 24.2.

C A S E 24.2

Exempt Property

U.S. SUPREME COURT CASE
Rousey v. Jacoway
544 U.S. 320, 125 S.Ct. 1561, 161 L.Ed.2d 563,
Web 2005 U.S. Lexis 2933 (2005)
Supreme Court of the United States

> 66 *The Bankruptcy Code permits debtors to exempt certain property from the bankruptcy estate, allowing them to retain those assets rather than divide them among their creditors.* 99

—Justice Thomas

Facts

Richard and Betty Jo Rousey were formerly employed at Northrup Grumman Corporation. At the termination of their employment, they took lump-sum distributions from their employer-sponsored pension plans. Each of the Rouseys deposited this lump sum into an individual retirement account (IRA). Subsequently, the Rouseys rolled over distributions received from other retirement plans into their IRAs.

IRA contributions receive favorable tax treatment. The Internal Revenue Code defers taxation of the money placed in IRAs and income earned from these sums until the assets are withdrawn. The money from an IRA may be taken, or begin to be taken, after the account holder reaches the age of 59½. Withdrawals made before 59½ are subject to a 10 percent tax penalty. The money from an IRA must be taken, or begin to be taken, when the account holder reaches the age of 70½.

Several years after establishing their IRAs, the Rouseys filed a joint Chapter 7 bankruptcy petition with the U.S. bankruptcy court. In the schedules and statements accompanying their petition, the Rouseys sought to shield their IRAs from creditors by claiming them as property exempt from the bankruptcy estate. The bankruptcy court appointed Jill R. Jacoway as the Chapter 7 trustee. Jacoway objected to the Rouseys' claim for the exemption of their IRAs from the bankruptcy estate and moved for turnover of these funds to the trustee. The U.S. bankruptcy court held that the IRAs were not exempt property and granted Jacoway's motion. The U.S. Court of Appeals affirmed. The Rouseys appealed to the U.S. Supreme Court.

Issue

Can debtors exempt IRAs from their bankruptcy estate?

Language of the Court

The Bankruptcy Code permits debtors to exempt certain property from the bankruptcy estate, allowing them to retain those assets rather than divide them among their creditors. The Rouseys sought to shield portions of their IRAs from their creditors by claiming them as exempt from the bankruptcy estate pursuant to 11 U.S.C. Section 522(d)(10). This exemption provides that a debtor may withdraw from the bankruptcy estate his "right to receive—(E) a payment under a stock bonus, pension, profitsharing, annuity, or similar plan or contract on account of illness, disability, death, age, or length of service, to the extent reasonably necessary for the support of the debtor and any dependent of the debtor."

The Rouseys contend that IRAs are similar to stock bonus, pension, profitsharing, or annuity plans or contracts, in that they have the same primary purpose, namely, enabling Americans to save for their retirement. Jacoway counters that IRAs are unlike the listed plans because those plans provide deferred compensation, whereas IRAs allow complete access to deposited funds and are therefore not deferred at all. We agree with the Rouseys that IRAs are similar to the plans specified in the statute. Those plans, like the Rouseys' IRAs, provide a substitute for wages and are not mere savings accounts. The Rouseys' IRAs are therefore similar plans or contracts within the meaning of Section 522(d)(10)(E).

Decision

The U.S. Supreme Court held that IRAs qualify as exempt property from the debtor's bankruptcy estate and are not subject to reach by the creditors. The U.S. Supreme Court reversed the judgment of the U.S. Court of Appeals and remanded the case for further proceedings consistent with its opinion.

Law & Ethics Questions

1. How is exempt property treated in bankruptcy? Explain.
2. What is the public policy for the Bankruptcy Code to shield pension plans and IRAs from inclusion in a debtor's bankruptcy estate? Is anyone hurt by this policy?
3. **ETHICS** Was it ethical for the Rouseys to keep the money in their IRAs when their creditors were not getting fully paid?

Web Exercises

1. **WEB** For the complete opinion of this case, go to *www.prenhall.com/cheesemancases*.
2. **WEB** Visit the website of the U.S. Supreme Court, at *www.supremecourtus.gov* and try to find documents that relate to this case.
3. **WEB** Use *www.google.com* to find an article that discusses exempt property in bankruptcy. Read it.

Homestead Exemption

The federal Bankruptcy Code permits homeowners to claim a **homestead exemption** of $18,450 in their principal residence. Many states require the debtor to file a *Declaration of Homestead* prior to bankruptcy. This document is usually filed in the county recorder's office in the county in which the real property is located. If the debtor's equity in the property (i.e., the value above the amount of mortgages and liens) exceeds the exemption limits, the trustee may sell the property to realize the excess value for the bankruptcy estate.

Example Assume that a debtor owns a principal residence worth $500,000 that is subject to a $400,000 mortgage and the debtor therefore owns $100,000 of equity in the property. The debtor files a petition for Chapter 7 liquidation bankruptcy. The trustee may sell the home, pay off the mortgage, pay the debtor $18,450 (applying the federal exemption), and use the remaining proceeds of $81,550 for distribution to the debtor's creditors.

ETHICS SPOTLIGHT

2005 Act Limits the Homestead Exemption

The Bankruptcy Code's federal homestead exemption is $18,450. Homestead exemptions under many state laws are usually higher than the federal exemption. Most states exempt between $20,000 and $100,000 of equity in a debtor's principal residence from the bankruptcy estate.

The largest exemptions are provided by Florida and Texas. Florida and Texas have no dollar amount limit on their homestead exemptions, although they do limit the size of the real property that qualifies for the homestead exemption. These states have been known as "debtor's havens" for wealthy debtors who have filed for bankruptcy. Prior to the 2005 act, many wealthy debtors from other states moved their money into principal residences in Florida and Texas to benefit from these generous homestead exemptions.

The 2005 act limits abusive homestead exemptions. The 2005 act provides the following restrictions on homestead exemptions:

1. A debtor may not exempt an amount greater than $125,000 if the property was acquired by the debtor within 1,215 days (approximately three years and four months) before the petition for bankruptcy is filed. This limit does not apply to a family farmer or to an interest transferred from a previous principal residence acquired prior to the 1,215-day period to another principal residence in the same state.

2. A debtor may not exempt an amount greater than $125,000 if the debtor has been convicted of a felony for bankruptcy fraud, securities fraud, or criminal, intentional, willful, or reckless

misconduct that caused serious physical injury or death to another in the preceding five years prior to filing a petition for bankruptcy.

Example Assume that a debtor owns a principal residence in Florida that he acquired 10 years ago. The equity in the property is $3 million. If the debtor files for Chapter 7 liquidation bankruptcy, the entire $3 million is shielded as exempt property. Now assume that the debtor owns a principal residence in Florida that has an equity value of $3 million, but that the property was acquired only two years prior to filing the petition in bankruptcy. In this case, the debtor can shield only $125,000 as a homestead exemption under the 2005 act because the property was acquired within 1,215 days prior to filing the petition.

Law & Ethics Questions

1. **ETHICS** Why did the states of Florida and Texas adopt generous homestead exemptions for a debtor's bankruptcy estate?

2. **ETHICS** Will the 2005 limits on homestead exemptions reduce abusive bankruptcy behavior by wealthy debtors?

Web Exercise

1. **WEB** Use *www.google.com* to find what the homestead exemption is in your state. Compare your state's homestead exemption to the federal homestead exemption.

Voidable Transfers

The Bankruptcy Code prevents debtors from making fraudulent and preferential transfers of property during certain time periods prior to bankruptcy that would unfairly benefit the debtor or some creditors at the expense of other creditors. Such payments or transfers can be voided by the court, and the recovered property or its equivalent value is placed in the bankruptcy estate for the benefit of the creditors. If a transfer is voided, a bona fide good faith purchaser must receive the value he or she paid for the property. The following paragraphs discuss preferential and fraudulent transfers that may be voided by the bankruptcy trustee.

PREFERENTIAL TRANSFERS The Bankruptcy Code gives the bankruptcy court the power to void certain **preferential transfers** of the debtor's property made by the debtor. To be subject to voidance, a transfer of property or an occurrence of an obligation must fall in either of two time periods: (1) to or with any party on or within 90 days of filing the petition or (2) to or with an insider between 90 days and one year of filing the petition. Insiders are defined as relatives, partners, partnerships, officers and directors of a corporation, corporations, and others who have a relationship with the debtor.

To void a preferential transfer of an interest of the debtor in property, the bankruptcy court must find that (1) the transfer was made to or for the benefit of a creditor, (2) the transfer was made for an *antecedent* (preexisting) debt, (3) the creditor to whom the transfer was made would receive more from the transfer than it would from a Chapter 7 liquidation of the debtor, and (4) the debtor was insolvent at the time of the transfer. Insolvency means that the debtor's debts exceed the value of the debtor's property. The Bankruptcy Code presumes that a debtor is insolvent on or within the 90 days prior to filing the petition; after 90 days of the petition, the court must determine whether the debtor was insolvent.

Example Assume that five months prior to filing a petition for bankruptcy, a debtor purchases $30,000 of equipment on unsecured credit from a supplier. Within 90 days of filing the petition, the debtor still owes the $30,000 to this creditor, and the payment is not due for another 120 days after the petition has been filed. Suppose that the debtor pays this creditor $30,000 before filing the petition. In the debtor's Chapter 7 liquidation case, however, this creditor would receive only $5,000. This payment is a voidable preferential payment because it was made within 90 days of filing the petition, when the debtor is presumed to be insolvent, was made to pay an antecedent debt, and gives the creditor more than it would receive in Chapter 7 liquidation.

Example Assume that Glen borrows $100,000 from his sister, Ida. This is an unsecured debt. Subsequently, Glen is insolvent and owes $500,000 of unsecured debt, including the $100,000 he borrowed from Ida. On this day, Glen grants his sister Ida a $100,000 mortgage on his house in which he has $100,000 in equity. This converts Ida from being an unsecured creditor to being a secured creditor. Nine months later, while still owing the $400,000 to his unsecured creditors and $100,000 secured credit to Ida, Glen files a petition for bankruptcy. If Ida was an unsecured creditor, she would receive only $10,000 in a bankruptcy proceeding. The mortgage on Glen's house in favor of Ida is a preferential lien that can be voided by the bankruptcy court. This is because the mortgage was made within one year of filing the petition, was made when the debtor was insolvent, was made to an insider, was made to pay an antecedent debt, and gives the creditor, Ida, more than she would receive in Chapter 7 liquidation. Without this preferential mortgage, Ida would be an unsecured creditor equal to Glen's other unsecured creditors. The court will void Glen's mortgage in favor of Ida and make her an unsecured creditor again.

There are exceptions to preferential transfer avoidance rules. The following debts may be paid by the debtor without being voided as preferential payments: (1) transfers for current consideration (e.g., equipment purchased for cash), (2) credit payments made in the ordinary course of business or financial affairs of the debtor (e.g., supplies purchased on credit and paid for within the normal payment terms, such as within 30 days after purchase), (3) payments of up to $600 by a consumer-debtor to a creditor, (4) payment of up to $5,000 by a debtor for debts that are not primarily consumer debts (e.g., a business debt), or (5) transfers that were bona fide payments of debts for domestic support obligations.

An otherwise preferential transfer cannot be voided if the transfer was made as a part of an alternative repayment schedule between the debtor and a creditor that was created and approved by a nonprofit budgeting and credit counseling agency.

> It is the policy of the law that the debtor be just before he be generous.
>
> Justice Finch
> *Hearn 45 St. Corp.v. Jano (1940)*

ETHICS SPOTLIGHT
Fraudulent Transfers Before Bankruptcy

The 2005 act gives the bankruptcy court the power to void certain **fraudulent transfers** of a debtor's property and obligations incurred by the debtor within two years of filing a petition for bankruptcy. To void a transfer or an obligation, the court must find that (1) the transfer was made or the obligation was incurred by the debtor with the actual intent to hinder, delay, or defraud a creditor or (2) the debtor received less than a reasonable equivalent in value. In addition, either the debtor must have been insolvent on the date the transfer was made or the obligation must have been incurred or the transfer or obligation must have been beyond the debtor's ability to pay.

Example Assume that Kathy owes her unsecured creditors $100,000. On February 9, Kathy knows that she is insolvent. Kathy owns a Mercedes-Benz automobile that is worth $55,000. On February 9, Kathy sells her Mercedes-Benz automobile to her friend, Wei, for

$35,000. Wei is a bona fide purchaser who does not know of Kathy's financial situation. On July 1, Kathy files for Chapter 7 liquidation bankruptcy while still owing the $100,000 to her unsecured creditors. The court can void Kathy's sale of her automobile to Wei as a fraudulent transfer because it occurred within two years of the petition, Kathy received less than a reasonable equivalent in value, and Kathy was insolvent at the time of the sale. Because Wei was a bona fide purchaser, the court must repay Wei the purchase price of $35,000 to recover the automobile from her.

Law & Ethics Questions

1. What does the fraudulent transfer rule provide? Explain.

2. **ETHICS** Do you think there are many fraudulent transfers by debtors prior to their filing of bankruptcy petitions?

OTHER FRAUDULENT TRANSFERS The 2005 act provides that transfers to or for the benefit of an insider under an employment contract and not in the ordinary course of business made within two years of the filing of a petition are voidable by the court. The 2005 act stipulates that transfers made to charitable or religious organizations by a debtor within two years of the filing of a petition are not voidable if they do not exceed 15 percent of the gross annual income of the debtor for the year in which the contribution was made and the debtor did not intend to hinder, delay, or defraud a creditor.

In recent years, many persons have established self-settled *living trusts* and have transferred their assets to these trusts. The owners and transferors usually designate themselves as trustees for the trust and make decisions regarding the investment and use of trust assets. The transferors-trustees usually name themselves as beneficiaries of the trust and therefore receive trust income and will receive the trust assets if the trust is terminated. In essence, the transferor-trustee-beneficiary has placed his or her assets in a legal entity—the living trust—but still has complete control over the trust assets. Living trusts are usually established to avoid probate upon the death of the beneficiary.

The 2005 act provides that any transfer of assets by a debtor to a living trust can be voided if (1) the transfer was made within 10 years before the filing of the petition of the debtor for bankruptcy, (2) the transfer was made to a self-settled trust, (3) the debtor is the beneficiary of the trust, and (4) the debtor made the transfer with the actual intent to hinder, delay, or defraud a creditor to which the debtor was or became indebted.

Transfers made within 10 years before the date of the filing of a petition that are made in anticipation of any money judgment, settlement, civil penalty, or criminal fine incurred because of a violation of securities laws or because of fraud, deceit, or manipulation in a fiduciary capacity can be voided.

Chapter 7—Liquidation

Chapter 7 liquidation bankruptcy (also called **straight bankruptcy**) is a familiar form of bankruptcy.[3] In this type of bankruptcy proceeding, the debtor is permitted to keep a substantial portion of his or her assets (exempt assets); the debtor's nonexempt property is sold for cash, and the cash is distributed to the creditors; and any of the debtor's unpaid debts are discharged. The debtor's future income, even if he or she became rich, cannot be reached to pay the discharged debt. Thus, a debtor would be left to start life anew, without the burden of his or her pre-petition debts. Prior to the 2005 act, filing for Chapter 7 bankruptcy almost became part of many persons' financial planning.

The 2005 act substantially restricts the ability of many debtors to obtain a Chapter 7 liquidation bankruptcy. The 2005 act added the *median income test* and the dollar-based *means test* that must be met before a debtor is permitted to obtain a discharge of debts under Chapter 7. If these tests are not met, the 2005 act provides that the debtor's Chapter 7 proceeding may be dismissed or converted to a Chapter 13 or Chapter 11 bankruptcy proceeding, with the debtor's consent.

The purpose of the 2005 act's changes to Chapter 7 is to force many debtors out of Chapter 7 liquidation bankruptcy and into Chapter 13 debt adjustment bankruptcy, which requires debtors to pay some of their future income over a five-year period to pay off pre-petition debts. Thus, the 2005 act reduces the number of debtors who can escape their pre-petition debts entirely.

Chapter 7 Procedure

Any person, including an individual, partnership, corporation, and other business entity, may be a debtor in a Chapter 7 proceeding. Voluntary and involuntary petitions may be filed. Most Chapter 7 filings are voluntarily filed by individuals.

Upon the filing of a Chapter 7 case, the U.S. trustee appoints an interim trustee. A meeting of the creditors is then held, and the creditors may elect a permanent trustee at the meeting. The duty of a Chapter 7 trustee is to collect the nonexempt property of the bankruptcy estate, sell or otherwise dispose of such property, collect the money received, pay the money to the creditors and other claimants, and close the estate as quickly as possible. The trustee must act in the best interests of the parties of interest, including the debtor, secured creditors, and unsecured creditors.

The 2005 Act's Changes to Chapter 7

Prior to the 2005 act, there was a presumption in favor of granting the relief sought by the debtor under Chapter 7. Relief could be denied if the court found *substantial abuse* of Chapter 7. However, because this was rarely found, most debtors were granted relief and a fresh start, free of their pre-petition unsecured debt.

One of the primary purposes for the enactment of the 2005 act was to make it more difficult for individual debtors to qualify for Chapter 7 liquidation bankruptcy. To do so, the 2005 act established new *simple abuse* rules and a means test to determine whether a debtor should be granted relief under Chapter 7. If a debtor fails this test, a presumption of an **abusive filing** arises, and the Chapter 7 case can be dismissed or, with the debtor's consent, converted to a Chapter 11 or Chapter 13 case.

Thus, the goal of the 2005 act is to deny Chapter 7 discharge to debtors who have the means to pay some of their unsecured debt from post-petition earnings and to steer most of those debtors into filing for Chapter 13 bankruptcy, where they have to use a portion of their post-petition earnings to pay some of their pre-petition unsecured debt.

Abusive Chapter 7 Filing

Section 707(b) of the 2005 act provides that the bankruptcy court, after notice and hearing, may dismiss a Chapter 7 liquidation case filed by an individual debtor whose debts are primarily consumer debts if the court finds that granting Chapter 7 relief to the debtor would be an abuse of Chapter 7. Consumer debt means debt incurred for personal, family, or household purposes.

Abuse is objectively determined by applying the median income test and means test established by the 2005 act. Within 10 days after the first meeting of the creditors, the trustee must file a statement with the bankruptcy court about whether the debtor's Chapter 7 case is an abusive filing.

Median Income Test

The first step with regard to the **median income test** is to determine whether the debtor's income either exceeds or is below the **state's median family income** for a family the same size as the debtor's family. A state's **median income** is defined as that income where half of the state's families have income above that figure and half of the state's families have incomes below that figure. Exhibit 24.3 sets forth the median incomes for four-person families, by state, published by the U.S. Census Bureau.

EXHIBIT 24.3

Median Income for Four-Person Families, By State (Estimates for the 2004–2005 U.S. Census Bureau)

STATE	MEDIAN INCOME	STATE	MEDIAN INCOME
(U.S. Average	$65,093)	Montana	$49,124
Alabama	55,448	Nebraska	63,625
Alaska	72,110	Nevada	63,005
Arizona	58,206	New Hampshire	79,339
Arkansas	48,353	New Jersey	87,412
California	67,814	New Mexico	45,867
Colorado	71,559	New York	69,354
Connecticut	86,001	North Carolina	56,712
Delaware	72,680	North Dakota	57,092
District of Columbia	56,067	Ohio	66,066
Florida	58,605	Oklahoma	50,216
Georgia	62,294	Oregon	61,570
Hawaii	71,320	Pennsylvania	68,578
Idaho	53,376	Rhode Island	71,098
Illinois	72,368	South Carolina	56,433
Indiana	65,009	South Dakota	59,272
Iowa	64,341	Tennessee	55,401
Kansas	64,215	Texas	54,554
Kentucky	53,198	Utah	62,032
Louisiana	50,529	Vermont	65,876
Maine	59,596	Virginia	71,697
Maryland	82,363	Washington	69,130
Massachusetts	82,561	West Virginia	46,169
Michigan	68,602	Wisconsin	69,010
Minnesota	76,773	Wyoming	56,065
Mississippi	46,570		
Missouri	64,128		

Example If a state's median income for a family of four is $65,000, then half of the state's four-member families have incomes above $65,000, and half of the state's four-member families have incomes below $65,000.

A family's income is calculated by adding the family's income for the six months prior to the petition, dividing by 6 to get the average monthly income for this six-month period, and then multiplying by 12 to determine the family's annual income.

If the debtor's family income is at or below the state's median income, there is no presumption of abuse, and the means test does not apply. The debtor may proceed with his or her Chapter 7 case and be granted discharge of his or her unsecured debts. Thus, it is important to note that for debtors at or below the state's median income, the 2005 act makes no changes in the ability to obtain Chapter 7 relief (see Exhibit 24.4).

EXHIBIT 24.4

Median Income Test

	If a family has a median income that is higher than the state's median family income, the 2005 act requires that the "means test" be applied to see if the debtor qualifies for Chapter 7 bankruptcy.
Median Family Income for a Family of Four in the State	_____
	If a family has a median income that is at or lower than the state's median family income, under the 2005 Act, there is no presumption of abuse, the means test does not apply, and the debtor may file for Chapter 7 bankruptcy (as long as the other requirements are met).

Means Test

The 2005 act makes major changes for debtors whose family income exceeds the state's median income. If the debtor's family income is above the state's median income, a new means test applies. If a debtor's family income exceeds the state's median income, any party of interest, including the trustee and creditors, may file a motion with the court to have the debtor's Chapter 7 case dismissed.

The **means test** is a new, complicated calculation that establishes, by law, a bright-line test to determine whether the debtor has the means to pay pre-petition debts out of post-petition income. If it is found by this calculation that the debtor has the means to pay some of his or her pre-petition debts out of post-petition income, the debtor is denied relief under Chapter 7. The debtor's Chapter 7 proceeding is dismissed unless the debtor approves that his or her case be converted to a Chapter 11 or Chapter 13 proceeding. The following paragraphs discuss the means test.

CALCULATING THE MEANS TEST Under the means test, a debtor's current monthly income is calculated by adding the debtor's past six months' income (minus certain deductions) and dividing by 6. This figure is then reduced by certain monthly expenditures to get a "net amount." The 2005 act, however, does not allow the debtor to use his or her actual current expenses but instead uses objective amounts established by Internal Revenue Service (IRS) standards. These national standards establish allowances for food, clothing, personal care, and entertainment. Regional standards apply for transportation costs, and county standards apply for housing costs. Deductions are also allowed for post-petition domestic support payments, charitable contributions up to 15 percent of gross income, and school expenses up to $1,500 per child per year.

Once the net amount is calculated (average current monthly income minus allowed expenses and deductions), this net amount is multiplied by 60 (representing 60 months, or five years). Then this amount is subtracted from the state's median income for five years. The 2005 act then places the debtor into one of the following three categories, depending on the result of the calculation:

1. *Net amount less than $6,000.* If the debtor's net amount is less than $6,000 over five years (i.e., less than $100 per month), abuse is not presumed, and the debtor is eligible for Chapter 7 relief.

   Example Assume that Sam's net amount is $80 per month, which is $4,800 over five years. Because $4,800 is less than $6,000, abuse is not presumed, and Sam is eligible for Chapter 7 relief.

2. *Net amount between $6,000 and $9,999.* If the debtor's net amount is between $6,000 and $9,999 for five years (i.e., $100 to $166.66 per month), the 2005 act establishes two possible outcomes: (a) If the debtor's net amount is sufficient to pay at least 25 percent of his or her unsecured debt, Chapter 7 relief is denied, or (b) if the debtor's net amount is insufficient to pay 25 percent of his or her unsecured debt, Chapter 7 relief is granted.

   Example Assume that Amy's net amount is $7,500 over five years (i.e., $125 per month). If Amy's unsecured debt is $24,000, she can pay over 25 percent of her unsecured debt, or $6,000, from the $7,500 available. Abuse is presumed, and Amy is not eligible for Chapter 7 relief.

   Example Assume that Amy's net amount is $7,500 over five years (i.e., $125 per month). If Amy's unsecured debt is $40,000, she cannot pay 25 percent of her debt, which is $10,000, from the $7,500 available. Abuse is not presumed, and Amy is eligible for Chapter 7 relief.

3. *Net amount $10,000 or more.* If the debtor's net amount is $10,000 or more over five years (i.e., equal to or greater than $166.67 per month), abuse is presumed, and the debtor is not eligible for Chapter 7 relief.

Example Assume that Beth's net amount is $200 per month, which is $12,000 over five years. Because $12,000 is greater than $10,000, abuse is presumed, and Beth is not eligible for Chapter 7 relief.

Exhibit 24.5 summarizes the means test.

Even if a debtor qualifies for Chapter 7 relief under the median income and means tests, the court can still deny relief if the court determines that the debtor filed the Chapter 7 petition in bad faith or because of the **"totality of the circumstances"** of the debtor's financial situation. This determination is made on a case-by-case basis.

The trustee, a creditor, or any other party of interest can request the court to dismiss the debtor's Chapter 7 case if abuse is found. The court can convert the case to a Chapter 11 or Chapter 13 case, with the debtor's approval. In practice, although the court can dismiss the Chapter 7 case if abuse is found, in the majority of the cases, the debtor agrees to convert the case to a Chapter 13 proceeding ("adjustment of debts of an individual with regular income"). Chapter 13 requires a debtor to pay some of his or her unsecured debt for a five-year period out of his or her post-petition earnings. Chapter 13 bankruptcy is discussed later in this chapter.

Statutory Distribution of Property

If a debtor qualifies for a Chapter 7 liquidation bankruptcy, the *nonexempt property* of the bankruptcy estate must be distributed to the debtor's secured and unsecured creditors pursuant to statutory priority established by the Bankruptcy Code. The

EXHIBIT 24.5

Means Test

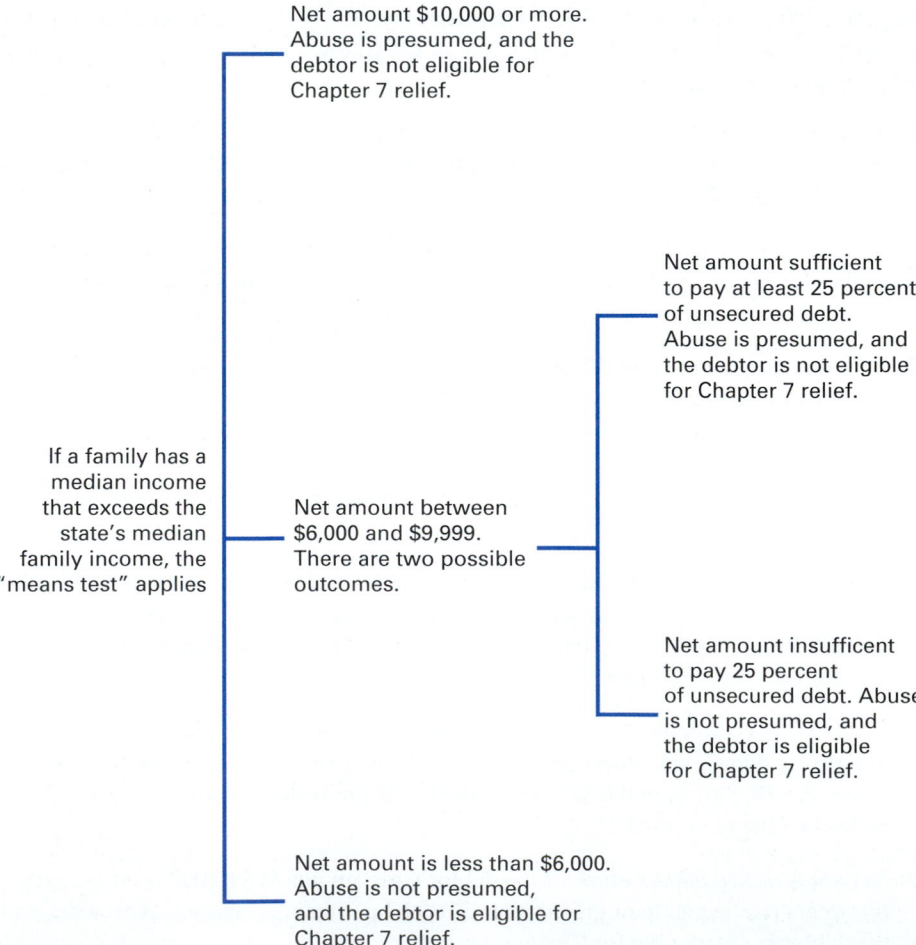

If a family has a median income that exceeds the state's median family income, the "means test" applies

Net amount $10,000 or more. Abuse is presumed, and the debtor is not eligible for Chapter 7 relief.

Net amount between $6,000 and $9,999. There are two possible outcomes.

Net amount sufficient to pay at least 25 percent of unsecured debt. Abuse is presumed, and the debtor is not eligible for Chapter 7 relief.

Net amount insufficent to pay 25 percent of unsecured debt. Abuse is not presumed, and the debtor is eligible for Chapter 7 relief.

Net amount is less than $6,000. Abuse is not presumed, and the debtor is eligible for Chapter 7 relief.

distribution of property to secured and unsecured debtors is discussed in the following paragraphs.

SECURED CREDITOR CLAIMS The claims of secured creditors to the debtor's nonexempt property have priority over the claims of unsecured creditors. Two situations can result:

1. *Oversecured secured creditor.* If the value of the collateral securing the secured loan exceeds the secured interest, the secured creditor is an *oversecured creditor*. In this case, the property is usually sold, the secured creditor is paid the amount of its secured interest (i.e., principal and accrued principal and interest), and reasonable fees and costs resulting from the debtor's default. The excess becomes available to satisfy the claims of the debtor's unsecured creditors. Sometimes the secured creditor is awarded the property but must remit the difference between the market value of the property and the amount of its interest to the trustee for distribution to the unsecured creditors.

   Example Assume that Edwin obtains a loan of $200,000 from City Bank to purchase a piece of investment real estate that is worth $240,000. The real estate is given as security for the loan. Several years later, when the value of the real estate is $220,000, Edwin files and qualifies for Chapter 7 relief. Edwin still owes $185,000 of the loan amount at the time of bankruptcy. In this case, City Bank will probably be awarded the real estate but must pay the bankruptcy estate $35,000 (i.e., the $220,000 market value of the real estate minus $185,000 loan amount still owed).

2. *Undersecured secured creditor.* If the value of the collateral securing the secured loan is less than the secured interest, the secured creditor is an *undersecured creditor*. In this case, the property is usually awarded to the secured creditor. The secured creditor then becomes an unsecured creditor as to the amount still owed to it, which consists of unpaid principal and interest and reasonable fees and costs of the debtor's default.

   Example Assume that Page obtains a loan of $200,000 from City Bank to purchase a piece of investment real estate that is worth $240,000. The real estate is given as security for the loan. Several years later, when the value of the real estate has declined to $150,000, Page files and qualifies for Chapter 7 relief. Page still owes $175,000 of the loan amount at the time of bankruptcy. In this case, City Bank will be awarded the real estate and becomes an unsecured creditor with a claim of $25,000 (i.e., the $175,000 loan amount still owed minus $150,000 market value of the real estate).

SECURED PERSONAL PROPERTY The 2005 act added a new provision regarding **secured personal property**. Under the 2005 act, if personal property of an individual debtor secures a claim or is subject to an unexpired lease (e.g., an automobile lease) and is not exempt property, the debtor must either (1) surrender the personal property, (2) redeem the property by paying the secured lien in full, or (3) assume the unexpired lease.

Example Assume that Gee leases an automobile on a three-year lease. Gee files for and qualifies for Chapter 7 relief while she still has two years to go on the automobile lease, with a total amount of $12,000 to pay. Gee has three choices. First, she can surrender the personal property to the secured creditor, and the rules regarding oversecured and undersecured creditors apply. Second, Gee can redeem the automobile by paying the $12,000 in full. Third, Gee can assume the unexpired lease, which will not be discharged in her Chapter 12 case, and make the payments in the future, in accordance with the original lease terms.

> Small debts are like small shot; they are rattling on every side, and can scarcely be escaped without a wound: great debts are like cannon; of loud noise, but little danger.
>
> Samuel Johnson
> *Letter to Joseph Simpson (1759)*

PRIORITY UNSECURED CREDITOR CLAIMS Unsecured claims are to be satisfied out of the bankruptcy estate in the order of their statutory priority, as established by the Bankruptcy Code. The statutory **priority of unsecured claims**, including the changes made by the 2005 act, is set forth in Exhibit 24.6. Because both individuals and businesses can be granted Chapter 7 relief, some items on this list apply primarily to individual debtors, while other items on this list apply primarily to business debtors. Each class must be paid in full before any lower class is paid anything. If a class cannot be paid in full, the claims of that class are paid pro rata (proportionately).

NONPRIORITY UNSECURED CREDITOR CLAIMS After the priority claims have been paid, the *nonpriority* unsecured creditors are paid. In most Chapter 7 bankruptcies, the **nonpriority unsecured claims** usually receive little, if anything, in the bankruptcy proceeding. If there is any balance remaining after the allowed claims of the creditors are satisfied, it is returned to the debtor. This, too, is an unlikely event.

Chapter 7 Discharge

In a Chapter 7 bankruptcy, the property of the estate is sold, and the proceeds are distributed to satisfy allowed claims. The remaining unpaid debts that the debtor incurred prior to the date of the order for relief are discharged. *Discharge* means that the debtor is no longer legally responsible for paying those claims. Only individual debtors may be granted discharge. The major benefit of a **Chapter 7 discharge** is that it is granted quite soon after the petition is filed. The individual debtor is not responsible for paying pre-petition debts out of post-petition income, as would be required in other forms of bankruptcy.

The 2005 act stipulates that a debtor can be granted Chapter 7 relief only after eight years following a Chapter 7 or Chapter 11 relief and only after six years following Chapter 12 or Chapter 13 relief. Discharge is not available to partnerships, limited liability companies, and corporations. These entities must liquidate under state law before or upon completion of a Chapter 7 proceeding.

EXHIBIT 24.6

Priority of Unsecured Creditor Claims

1. Unsecured claims for domestic support obligations owed to a spouse, former spouse, or child of the debtor.
2. Fees and expenses of administering the estate, including court costs, trustee fees, attorneys' fees, appraisal fees, and other costs of administration.
3. In an involuntary bankruptcy, secured claims of "gap" creditors who sold goods or services on credit to the debtor in the ordinary course of the debtor's business between the date of the filing of the petition and the date of the appointment of the trustee or issuance of the order for relief (whichever occurred first).
4. Unsecured claims for wages, salary, commissions, severance pay, and sick leave pay earned by the debtor's employees within 180 days immediately preceding the filing of the petition, up to $10,000 per employee.
5. Unsecured claims for contributions to employee benefit plans based on services performed within 180 days immediately preceding the filing of the petition, up to $10,000 per employee.
6. Farm producers and fishermen against debtors who operate grain storage facilities or fish storage or processing facilities, respectively, up to $4,925 per claim.
7. Unsecured claims for cash deposited by a consumer with the debtor prior to the filing of the petition in connection with the purchase, lease, or rental of property or the purchases of services that were not delivered or provided by the debtor, up to $2,225 per claim.
8. Unsecured claims for unpaid income and gross receipts taxes owed to governments incurred during the three years preceding the bankruptcy petition and unpaid property taxes owed to governments incurred within one year preceding the bankruptcy petition.
9. Commitment by the debtor to maintain the capital of an insured depository institution such as a commercial bank or savings bank.
10. Claims against the debtor for personal injuries or death caused by the debtor while he or she was intoxicated from using alcohol or drugs.

Example Suppose that at the time that Eric is granted Chapter 7 relief, he still owes $50,000 of unsecured debt that there is no money in the bankruptcy estate to pay. This debt is composed of credit card debt, an unsecured loan from a friend, and unsecured credit from a department store. This $50,000 of unsecured credit is discharged. This means that Eric is relieved of this debt and is not legally liable for its repayment. The unsecured creditors must write off this debt.

In the following case, the U.S. Supreme Court ruled that a debt was dischargeable in bankruptcy.

C A S E **24.3**

Discharge

U.S. SUPREME COURT CASE
Kawaauhau v. Geiger

523 U.S. 57, 118 S.Ct. 974, 140 L.Ed.2d 90, **Web** 1998
U.S. Lexis 1595
Supreme Court of the United States

> **"***The debt is dischargeable.***"**

—Justice Ginsburg

Facts

Margaret Kawaauhau sought treatment from Dr. Paul Geiger for a foot injury. Dr. Geiger examined Kawaauhau and admitted her to the hospital to attend to the risks of infection. Although Dr. Geiger knew that intravenous penicillin would have been a more effective treatment, he prescribed oral penicillin, explaining that he thought that his patient wished to minimize the cost of her treatment. Dr. Geiger then departed on a business trip, leaving Kawaauhau in the care of other physicians. When Dr. Geiger returned, he discontinued all antibiotics because he believed that the infection had subsided. Kawaauhau's condition deteriorated over the next few days, requiring the amputation of her right leg below the knee. Kawaauhau and her husband sued Dr. Geiger for medical malpractice. The jury found Dr. Geiger liable and awarded the Kawaauhaus $355,000 in damages. Dr. Geiger, who carried no malpractice insurance, filed for bankruptcy in an attempt to discharge the judgment. The U.S. bankruptcy court denied discharge, and the U.S. District Court agreed. The U.S. Court of Appeals reversed and allowed Dr. Geiger discharge of the damage award he owed the Kawaauhaus in his bankruptcy. The Kawaauhaus appealed to the U.S. Supreme Court.

Issue

Is a debt arising from a medical malpractice judgment that is attributable to negligent or reckless conduct dischargeable in bankruptcy?

Language of the U.S. Supreme Court

The Bankruptcy Code provides that a debt "for willful and malicious injury by the debtor to another" is not dischargeable. The question before us is whether a debt arising from a medical malpractice judgment, attributable to negligent or reckless conduct, falls within this statutory exception. We hold that it does

not and that the debt is dischargeable. Had Congress meant to exempt debts resulting from unintentionally inflicted injuries, it might have selected an additional word or words, i.e., "reckless" or "negligent," to modify injury.

Decision

The U.S. Supreme Court ruled that a medical malpractice judgment based on negligent or reckless conduct—and not willful conduct—is dischargeable in bankruptcy. The U.S. Supreme Court affirmed the decision of the U.S. Court of Appeals.

Law & Ethics Questions

1. What public policy is promoted by denying discharge for "willful" injurious conduct?
2. **ETHICS** Was it ethical for Dr. Geiger not to carry malpractice insurance?
3. **ETHICS** Was it ethical for Dr. Geiger to file for bankruptcy to avoid paying the judgment to the Kawaauhaus?
4. Who is hurt and who is helped by this decision? Do you think this is a fair result?

Web Exercises

1. **WEB** For the complete opinion of this case, go to *www.prenhall.com/cheesemancases*.
2. **WEB** Visit the website of the U.S. Supreme Court, at *www.supremecourtus.gov* and try to find documents that relate to this case.
3. **WEB** Use *www.google.com* to find an article that discusses the Bankruptcy Abuse Prevention and Consumer Protection Act of 2005. Read it.

Acts That Bar Discharge

Any party of interest may file an objection to the discharge of a debt. The court then holds a hearing. Discharge of unsatisfied debts is denied if the debtor:

- Made false representations about his or her financial position when he or she obtained an extension of credit.
- Transferred, concealed, removed, or destroyed property of the estate with the intent to hinder, delay, or defraud creditors within one year before the date of the filing of the petition.
- Falsified, destroyed, or concealed records of his or her financial condition.
- Failed to account for any assets.
- Failed to submit to questioning at the meeting of the creditors (unless excused).
- Failed to complete an instructional course concerning personal financial management, as required by the 2005 act (unless excused).

If a discharge is obtained through fraud of the debtor, any party of interest may bring a motion to have the bankruptcy revoked. The bankruptcy court may revoke a discharge within one year after it is granted.

> Beggars can never be bankrupt.
>
> Thomas Fuller
> *Gnomologia (1732)*

CONTEMPORARY ENVIRONMENT
Discharge of Student Loans

Upon graduation from college and professional schools, many students have borrowed money to have paid tuition and living expenses. At this point in time, when the students might have large student loans and very few assets, a student might be inclined to file for bankruptcy in an attempt to have his or her student loans discharged.

To prevent such abuse of bankruptcy law, Congress amended the Bankruptcy Code to make it more difficult for students to have their student loans discharged in bankruptcy. Student loans are defined by the Bankruptcy Code to include loans made by or guaranteed by governmental units. The 2005 act added student loans made by nongovernmental commercial institutions, such as banks, as well as

fund for scholarships, benefits, or stipends granted by educational institutions.

The Bankruptcy Code now states that student loans can be discharged in bankruptcy only if the nondischarge would cause an "undue hardship" to the debtor and his or her dependants. Undue hardship is construed strictly and would be difficult for a debtor to prove unless he or she could show severe physical or mental disability or that he or she is unable to pay for the basic necessities of food or shelter for his or her family.

Cosigners (e.g., parents who guarantee their child's student loan) must also meet the heightened undue hardship test to discharge their obligation.

Chapter 13—Adjustment of Debts of an Individual With Regular Income

Chapter 13, which is called **adjustment of debts of an individual with regular income**, is a rehabilitation form of bankruptcy for individuals.[4] Chapter 13 permits a qualified debtor to propose a plan to pay all or a portion of the debts he or she owes in installments over a specified period of time, pursuant to the requirements of Chapter 13. The bankruptcy court supervises the debtor's plan for the payment.

The debtor has several advantages under Chapter 13. These include avoiding the stigma of Chapter 7 liquidation, retaining more property than is exempt under Chapter 7, and incurring less expenses than in a Chapter 7 proceeding. The creditors have advantages too: They may recover a greater percentage of the debts owed them than they would recover under a Chapter 7 bankruptcy.

Chapter 13 petitions are usually filed by individual debtors who do not qualify for Chapter 7 liquidation bankruptcy and by homeowners who want to protect nonexempt equity in their residence. Chapter 13 enables debtors to catch up on secured credit loans, such as home mortgages, and avoid repossession and foreclosure.

Filing the Petition

A Chapter 13 proceeding can be initiated only through the voluntary filing of a petition by an individual debtor with regular income. A creditor cannot file an involuntary petition to institute a Chapter 13 case.

An *individual with regular income* means an individual whose income is sufficiently stable and regular to enable such individual to make payments under a Chapter 13 plan. Regular income may be from any source, including wages, salary, commissions, income from investments, Social Security, pension income, or public assistance. The debts of the individual debtor must be primarily consumer debt. *Consumer debt* means debts incurred by an individual for personal, family, or household purposes.

The debtor must allege that he or she is (1) insolvent or (2) unable to pay his or her debts when they become due. The petition must state that the debtor desires to effect an extension or a composition of debts, or both. An *extension* provides for a longer period of time for the debtor to pay his or her debts. A *composition* provides for the reduction of debts. The petition must be filed in good faith.

> Debt rolls a man over and over, binding him hand and foot, and letting him hang upon the fatal mesh until the long-legged interest devours him.
>
> Henry Ward Beecher

Limitations on Who Can File for Chapter 13 Bankruptcy

The 2005 act establishes dollar limits on the secured and unsecured debt that a debtor may have in order to qualify to file for Chapter 13 bankruptcy. Only an individual with regular income alone or with his or her spouse who owes individually or with his or her spouse (1) noncontingent, liquidated, unsecured debts of less than $307,675 and (2) secured debts of less than $922,975 may file a petition for Chapter 13 bankruptcy. Individual debtors who exceed these dollar limits do not qualify for Chapter 13 bankruptcy. Sole proprietorships, because they are owned by individuals, may file for Chapter 13.

Chapter 13 Procedures

When (or shortly after) the petition is filed, the debtor must file a list of creditors, assets, and liabilities with the court. The court then schedules a meeting of creditors. Prior to one day before the meeting of the creditors; a Chapter 13 debtor must have filed all tax returns due for a four-year period prior to the filing of the petition for bankruptcy. The court may extend this period if the debtor can prove that the filings have not been made because of circumstances beyond the control of the debtor. The debtor must appear at the meeting of the creditors.

Creditors may submit proof of claims, which are allowed or disallowed by the court. No creditor committees are appointed, but the court must appoint a trustee upon confirmation of the plan.

The U.S. trustee must appoint a trustee in a Chapter 13 case. In addition to the normal duties of a trustee, in a Chapter 13 case, the trustee may appear in court and be heard concerning the confirmation of a Chapter 13 plan, and the trustee may assist the debtor in the performance of the plan.

An automatic stay goes into place after the order for relief. The stay stops creditors from commencing or continuing any civil action to collect all or part of a consumer debt from the debtor. In a Chapter 13 case, the automatic stay is also effective against the co-debtor. The court can grant a relief from the stay if the creditor's interest would be irreparably harmed by the continuation of the stay.

Property of the Estate

The property of a Chapter 13 estate consists of all nonexempt property of the debtor at the commencement of the case and nonexempt property acquired after the commencement of the case but before the case is closed. In addition, the property of the estate includes earnings and future income earned by the debtor after the commencement of the case but before the case is closed. This ensures that pre-petition creditors receive payments from the debtor's post-petition earnings and income.

The debtor remains in possession of all of the property of the estate during the completion of the plan except as otherwise provided by the plan. If the debtor is self-employed, the debtor may continue to operate his or her business. In the alternative, the court may order that a trustee operate the business, if necessary.

Chapter 13 Plan of Payment

The debtor's **plan of payment** must be filed not later than 90 days after the order for relief. The debtor must file information about his or her finances, including a budget of estimated income and expenses during the period of the plan. The plan may designate a class or classes of nonpriority unsecured claims. The plan may, however, treat consumer debt differently than other secured claims.

The 2005 act establishes rules as to the length of a plan under Chapter 13. The Chapter 13 plan may be either up to three years or up to five years, based on the following calculation:

- If the debtor's or debtor's and spouse's monthly income multiplied by 12 is less than the state's median income for the year for the same size family of up to four members (plus $525 per month for each member in excess of four members), the plan period may not exceed three years, unless the court approves a period of up to five years for cause.
- If the debtor's or debtor's and spouse's monthly income multiplied by 12 is equal to or more than the state's median income for the year for the same size family of up to four members (plus $525 per month for each member in excess of four members), the plan period may not be longer than five years.

Modification of the Rights of Creditors

A Chapter 13 plan of payment may modify the rights of unsecured creditors and some secured creditors. Any objections they have may be voiced at the confirmation hearing held by the court. The modifications of creditors' rights permitted under a Chapter 13 plan of payment are discussed in the following paragraphs.

SECURED CREDITORS The plan must be submitted to secured creditors for acceptance. The plan is confirmed as to a secured creditor if that creditor accepts the plan. If a secured creditor does not accept the plan, the court may still confirm the plan if (1) the plan permits the secured creditor to retain its lien until the payment of the underlying debt or discharge and the value of the plan's distribution to the creditor is equal to the creditor's secured interest or (2) the debtor surrenders the property securing the claim to the secured creditor. A Chapter 13 plan must provide holders of claims secured by personal property adequate protection during the plan period.

If the debtor has a purchase money security interest in a motor vehicle acquired for personal use within 910 days preceding the filing date or a purchase money security interest in other personal property that was acquired within one year preceding the filing date, the debtor must pay the secured and unsecured portions (if any) of the claim in full. If the debtor does not, the creditor can foreclose on its lien and recover the vehicle.

Example Suppose Emmett purchased a personal automobile 700 days prior to filing a petition for Chapter 13 bankruptcy and borrowed $20,000 from the dealer at the time of purchase. If at the time of bankruptcy Emmett still owed $16,000 debt, he would have to pay this amount in full under his Chapter 13 plan, or the creditor could recover the vehicle.

UNSECURED CREDITORS The plan is confirmed as to an unsecured creditor if that creditor accepts the plan. If an unsecured creditor objects to the plan, the court may still confirm the plan if (1) the plan proposes to pay the objecting unsecured creditor the amount of his or her claim or (2) the debtor agrees to commit all of his or her disposable income during the plan period to pay his or her unsecured creditors.

Disposable income is defined as current monthly income less amounts reasonably necessary to be expended for the maintenance or support of the debtor and the dependants of the debtor. Expenses include amounts necessary to pay domestic support obligations and charitable donations that do not exceed 15 percent of the debtor's gross income for the year the charitable donations are made. If a debtor earns more than the median income of the state, his or her expenses are determined by the objective IRS standards.

Example Suppose a debtor earns $3,800 per month, which is less than the median income of the state. Suppose that $3,000 is reasonably necessary to support the debtor and his or her family. If the $800 per month disposable income is committed to pay pre-petition unsecured debts, the court may confirm the plan even if the debts of the unsecured creditors are substantially modified under the plan.

Confirmation of a Chapter 13 Plan of Payment

The court can confirm a Chapter 13 plan of payment if the prior requirements are met and if (1) the plan was proposed in good faith, (2) the plan passes the feasibility test (e.g., the debtor must be able to make the proposed payments), (3) the plan is in the best interests of the creditors (i.e., the present value of the payments must equal or exceed the amount that the creditors would receive in a Chapter 7 liquidation proceeding), (4) the debtor has paid all domestic support obligations owed, and (5) the debtor has filed all applicable federal, state, and local tax returns.

The debtor must begin making the planned installment payments to the trustee within 30 days after the plan is filed or the order of relief, whichever is earlier. These interim payments must continue until the plan is confirmed or denied. If the plan is denied, the trustee must return the interim payments to the debtor, less any administrative costs. If the plan is confirmed, the debtor must continue making the required payments to the trustee. The trustee is responsible for remitting these payments to the creditors. The trustee is paid for administering the plan. Payments under the plan must be made in equal monthly installments.

A Chapter 13 plan may be modified if the debtor's circumstances materially change. For example, if the debtor's income subsequently decreases, the court may decrease the debtor's payments under the plan. If an interested party objects to the modification, the court must hold a hearing to determine whether it should be approved.

Chapter 13 Discharge

The court grants an order discharging the debtor from all unpaid unsecured debts covered by the plan after all the payments required under the plan are completed (which could be up to three years or up to five years). This is called a **Chapter 13 discharge**. The debtor must certify that all domestic support payments have been paid before discharge is granted. Most unpaid taxes are not discharged. Prior to the 2005 act, student loans could be discharged under Chapter 13. The 2005 act changed this and provides that student loans can only be discharged upon proving undue hardship.

A debtor cannot be granted Chapter 13 discharge if the debtor has received discharge under Chapter 7, 11, or 12 within the prior four-year period or Chapter 13 relief within the prior two-year period of the order for relief in the current Chapter 13 case.

Chapter 11—Reorganization

Chapter 11 of the Bankruptcy Code provides a method for reorganizing a debtor's financial affairs under the supervision of the bankruptcy court.[5] The goal of Chapter 11 is to reorganize the debtor with a new capital structure so that it emerges from bankruptcy as a viable concern. This option, which is referred to as **reorganization bankruptcy**, is often in the best interests of the debtor and its creditors.

Chapter 11 Reorganization Proceeding

Chapter 11 is available to individuals, partnerships, corporations, other business entities, nonincorporated associations, and railroads. It is not available to commercial banks, savings banks, credit unions, insurance companies, stockbrokers, or commodities brokers. The majority of Chapter 11 proceedings are filed by corporations that want to reorganize their capital structure by receiving discharge of a portion of their debts, obtain relief from burdensome contracts, and emerge from bankruptcy as a going concern. Much of the following discussion applies to business reorganizations.

A Chapter 11 petition may be filed voluntarily by the debtor or involuntarily by its creditors. The principles discussed earlier in this chapter regarding the filing of petitions, the first meeting of the creditors, the entry of the order for relief, automatic stay, and relief from stay also apply to Chapter 11 proceedings.

The court can dismiss a Chapter 11 case or convert a case to a Chapter 7 liquidation case upon the request of the debtor or any party of interest if the court finds that it would be in the best interests of the parties to do so.

Debtor-in-Possession

In most Chapter 11 cases, the debtor is left in place to operate the business during the reorganization proceeding. In such cases, the debtor is called a **debtor-in-possession**. The court may appoint a trustee to operate the debtor's business only upon a showing of cause, such as fraud, dishonesty, or gross mismanagement of the affairs of the debtor by current management. Even if a trustee is not appointed, however, the court may appoint an examiner to investigate the debtor's financial affairs.

The debtor-in-possession or trustee is empowered to operate the debtor's business during the bankruptcy proceeding. This power includes authority to enter into contracts, purchase supplies, incur debts, and so on. Some suppliers accept only cash for their goods or services during this time, whereas others extend credit. Credit extended by post-petition unsecured creditors in the ordinary course of business is given automatic priority as an administrative expense in bankruptcy. Further, upon notice and hearing, the court may create a secured interest by granting a post-petition unsecured creditor a lien on the debtor-in-possession's property.

Creditors' Committees

After an order for relief is granted, the court appoints a **creditors' committee** composed of representatives of the class of unsecured claims. The court may also appoint a committee of secured creditors and a committee of equity holders. Generally, the parties holding the seven largest creditor claims or equity interests are appointed to their requisite committees. Committee members owe a fiduciary duty to represent the interest of the class. Committees may appear at bankruptcy court hearings, participate in the negotiation of a plan of reorganization, assert objections to proposed plans of reorganization, and the like. Committees can employ attorneys, accountants, appraisers, investment bankers, and other professionals.

Automatic Stay in Chapter 11

The filing of a Chapter 11 petition stays (suspends) actions by creditors to recover the debtor's property. This **automatic stay** suspends certain legal actions against the debtor or the debtor's property, including the ability of creditors to foreclose on assets given as collateral for their loans to the debtor. This automatic stay is extremely important to a business trying to reorganize under Chapter 11 because the debtor needs to keep its assets to stay in business.

CONTEMPORARY ENVIRONMENT

UAL Corporation's Chapter 11 Bankruptcy

UAL Corporation, the parent company of United Airlines, filed for Chapter 11 reorganization bankruptcy. At the time of filing the petition, UAL owned or leased airplanes, equipment, trucks and other vehicles, docking space at airports, warehouses, office space, and other assets. In many cases, UAL had borrowed the money to purchase or lease these assets. Most of the lenders took back mortgages or security interests in the assets for which they had loaned money to UAL to purchase or lease. In addition, UAL also owed unsecured creditors money that it could not repay, and it had unexpired executory contracts and unexpired leases that it also could not pay.

If UAL was not in bankruptcy and defaulted on its secured loans or leases, the secured creditors could use state law and foreclose on their security interests and recover these assets as collateral. UAL would be left without most of its major assets that it would need to operate its business. When UAL filed for Chapter 11 bankruptcy, however, the automatic stay of federal bankruptcy law went into effect and prevented the secured creditors from using state law to foreclose on UAL's assets. Therefore, UAL was able to continue to operate its business while it reorganized under bankruptcy law protection.

Under bankruptcy court protection, UAL proposed a plan of reorganization that would decrease its unsecured debts to a proportion of what they were prior to filing for bankruptcy. UAL also examined its executory contracts and unexpired leases; it kept those that were beneficial to the company's survival and rejected those it believed would be detrimental to the company's survival in the future. Bitter disputes to reduce the pay and benefits of UAL's labor unions resulted. Eventually, the disputes with the pilots' union, the flight attendants' union, the maintenance workers' union, and other unions were resolved.

When UAL emerged from Chapter 11 bankruptcy, it still had most of its assets. The secured creditors had to be paid any arrearages that UAL owed to them. The secured creditors remained secured creditors during and after the bankruptcy reorganization. UAL's unsecured credit was substantially reduced, and the unpaid portion was discharged. Also, UAL was able to reject the executory contracts and unexpired leases that it did not want, and it renegotiated terms of other contracts, such as its labor union contracts.

The decline, insolvency, and eventual restructuring of UAL provide an example of how a company—in this case a very large corporation—can use the protection of bankruptcy law to reinvent itself into a going concern.

Excerpts from UAL's disclosure statement appear as Exhibit 24.7.

Law & Ethics Questions

1. Explain some of the provisions in Chapter 11 bankruptcy that UAL used to restructure itself as a going concern.

2. **ETHICS** Is it ethical for a debtor to use bankruptcy law to relieve itself of its obligations to creditors?

Web Exercises

1. **WEB** Visit the website of the United Airlines, at *www.united.com*.

2. **WEB** Use *www.google.com* to find an article that discusses UAL's disputes with its unions during its Chapter 11 restructuring. Did the unions lose much in the way of pay and benefits?

> IN THE UNITED STATES BANKRUPTCY COURT
> FOR THE NORTHERN DISTRICT OF ILLINOIS
> EASTERN DIVISION
>
> | | | |
> |---|---|---|
> | In re: |) | Chapter 11 |
> | |) | |
> | UAL Corporation, *et al.*, |) | |
> | |) | Case No. 02-B-48191 |
> | Debtors.[1] |) | (Jointly Administered) |
> | |) | Honorable Eugene R. Wedoff |
>
> DISCLOSURE STATEMENT FOR REORGANIZING DEBTORS' JOINT PLAN OF REORGANIZATION PURSUANT TO CHAPTER 11 OF THE UNITED STATES BANKRUPTCY CODE
>
> ARTICLE I.
> SUMMARY
>
> UAL Corporation ("UAL") is a holding company whose principal, wholly-owned subsidiary is United Air Lines, Inc. ("United"). United's operations, which consist primarily of the transportation of persons, property, and mail throughout the U.S. and abroad, accounted for most of UAL's revenues and expenses in 2004. United is one of

EXHIBIT 24.7

Excerpts from a Disclosure Statement

(continued)

EXHIBIT 24.7

(continued)

the largest scheduled passenger airlines in the world with over 1,500 daily departures to more than 120 destinations in 26 countries and two U.S. territories. Through United's global route network, United serves virtually every major market around the world, either directly or through the Star Alliance, which is the world's largest airline network. In addition to the Star Alliance, United provides regional service into United's domestic hubs through marketing relationships with "United Express®" carriers. In 2004, United added a new low-fare brand, called Ted, designed to serve select leisure markets and to more effectively compete with low-fare carriers.

On December 9, 2002 (the "Petition Date"), UAL, United, and 26 other direct and indirect wholly-owned subsidiaries filed voluntary petitions for relief under Chapter 11 of the United States Bankruptcy Code (the "Bankruptcy Code") in the United States Bankruptcy Court for the Northern District of Illinois, Eastern Division (the "Bankruptcy Court"). The foregoing entities are sometimes referred to collectively as the "Debtors."

The Purpose of the Plan

The Debtors have concluded, after careful review of their current business operations, their prospects as ongoing business enterprises, and the estimated recoveries of Creditors in various liquidation scenarios, that the recovery of Holders of Allowed Claims will be maximized by the Debtors' continued operation as a going concern. The Debtors believe that their businesses and assets have significant value that would not be realized in a liquidation scenario, either in whole or in substantial part. According to the liquidation analysis described herein (the "Liquidation Analysis") and the other analyses prepared by the Debtors and their advisors, the value of the Debtors' Estates is considerably greater as a going concern than if they were liquidated.

Accordingly, the Debtors believe that the Plan provides the best recoveries possible for the Holders of Allowed Claims and strongly recommend that, if you are entitled to vote, you vote to accept the Plan. The Debtors believe that any alternative to Confirmation of the Plan, such as liquidation or attempts by another party in interest to file a plan or reorganization, could result in significant delays, litigation, and additional costs.

Executory Contracts and Unexpired Leases

Another major benefit of Chapter 11 bankruptcy is that the debtor is given the opportunity to accept or reject certain executory contracts and unexpired leases. **Executory contracts** and **unexpired leases** are contracts or leases that have not been fully performed.

Example A contract to purchase or supply goods at a later date is an executory contract; a 20-year office lease that has 8 years left until it is completed is an unexpired lease. Other executory contracts and unexpired leases may include consulting contracts, contracts to purchase or provide services, equipment leases, warehouse leases, and such.

Under the Bankruptcy Code, the debtor-in-possession (or trustee) in a Chapter 11 proceeding is given authority to assume or reject executory contracts. In general, the debtor rejects unfavorable executory contracts and assumes favorable executory contracts. Court approval is necessary to reject an executory contract. The debtor is not liable for damages caused by the rejection of executory contracts and unexpired leases in bankruptcy. Note that executory contracts and unexpired leases may also be rejected in Chapter 7, Chapter 12, and Chapter 13 proceedings.

Example Suppose Import Corporation files for Chapter 11 reorganization bankruptcy. After a review of its executory contracts and unexpired leases, the corporation identifies the following unfavorable executory contracts and unexpired leases: a contract to purchase goods from a supplier that has 2 years left, a contract to deliver services to a customer that has 1 year left, a lease for office space that has 10 years left, and an equipment lease for trucks that has 3 years left. Import Corporation can reject all these contracts and leases, with the court's approval. Import Corporation is not liable for any damages caused by its rejection of these executory contracts and unexpired leases.

Labor Union and Retiree Benefits Contracts

Debtors that file for Chapter 11 reorganization sometimes have collective bargaining agreements with labor unions that require the payment of agreed-upon wages and other benefits to union member-employees for some agreed-upon period in the future. Debtors also often have contracts to pay union and nonunion retired employees and their dependants' medical, surgical, hospitalization, dental, and death benefits (retiree benefits). The Bankruptcy Code requires that the following multistep process be followed:

1. The debtor makes a proposal to the union or representative that sets forth its proposed modifications.
2. The debtor meets with the union or representative to discuss the proposal and confers in good faith in an attempt to reach a mutually satisfactory modification.
3. The union or representative refuses to accept the proposal without good cause.

In a Chapter 11 case, union members and union retirees are represented by the responsible labor union. The court appoints a committee to represent nonunion retirees.

The debtor and the representatives of the union members and retirees can voluntarily agree to modify the union collective bargaining agreement and retiree benefits. If such an agreement is not reached, the debtor can petition the bankruptcy court to reject the collective bargaining agreement and to modify retiree benefits.

If these steps have been taken, the court holds a hearing. The court may order the rejection of the collective bargaining agreement or modification of retiree benefits if it finds that the "balance of equities" favors rejection or modification and that rejection or modification is necessary to the reorganization.

Chapter 11 Plan of Reorganization

The debtor has the exclusive right to file a **plan of reorganization** with the bankruptcy court within the first 120 days after the date of the order for relief. Under the 2005 act, this period may be extended up to 18 months from the date of the order for relief. The debtor has the right to obtain creditor approval of the plan within 180 days after the date of the order. If the debtor fails to do so, any party of interest (e.g., a trustee, a creditor, an equity holder) may propose a plan up to 20 months from the date of the order. In other words, the original 180-day period cannot be extended beyond 20 months.

The plan of reorganization sets forth the proposed new financial structure of the debtor. This includes the portion of the unsecured debts proposed to be paid by the debtor and the unsecured debt the debtor proposes to be discharged. The plan must specify the executory contracts and unexpired leases that the debtor proposes to reject that have not previously been rejected in the bankruptcy proceeding. The plan also designates how equity holders are proposed to be treated, describes any new equity investments that are proposed to be made in the debtor, and includes other relevant information.

The debtor must supply the creditors and equity holders with a *disclosure statement* that contains adequate information about the proposed plan of reorganization so that they can make an informed judgment about the plan.

CONTEMPORARY ENVIRONMENT

Prepackaged Bankruptcy

In most cases, a debtor business and its creditors know that the business is heading for Chapter 11 bankruptcy. In some cases, the debtor and creditors negotiate the terms of a proposed plan of reorganization before the bankruptcy petition is filed. This is done through negotiation and can be accomplished only with creditor approval. This type of bankruptcy is called a "prepackaged bankruptcy."

In order for a prepackaged bankruptcy to work, the debtor and its creditors pre-negotiate the terms of the plan of Chapter 11 reorganization. It is therefore necessary to get the good faith cooperation of the debtors and its creditors to negotiate the prepackaged terms for Chapter 11 bankruptcy. It is necessary to get the necessary approvals of the shareholders of the debtor and the approval of the creditors. These approvals are filed along with the bankruptcy petition.

The general idea in preparing a plan before filing for bankruptcy is to shorten and simplify the bankruptcy process in order to save the company and its creditor money. The savings is due to the minimization of legal fees for both the company and creditors. Prepackaging is expected to minimize the disruption of the company's business and lessen the damage to its goodwill with its creditors. With a prepackaged bankruptcy, it is hoped that the debtor and its creditors will continue their relationship in the future.

Confirmation of a Chapter 11 Plan of Reorganization

There must be **confirmation of a Chapter 11 plan of reorganization** by the bankruptcy court for the debtor to be reorganized under Chapter 11. The bankruptcy court confirms a plan of reorganization under the **acceptance method** if (1) the plan is in the best interests of the creditors because the creditors would receive at least what they would receive in a Chapter 7 liquidation bankruptcy, (2) the plan is feasible (that is, the new reorganized company is likely to succeed), and (3) each class of creditors accepts the plan (i.e., at least one-half the number of creditors who represent at least two-thirds of the dollar amount of the debt vote to accept the plan).

If a class of creditors does not accept the plan, the plan can still be confirmed by the court, using the Bankruptcy Code's **cram-down provision**. In order for the court to confirm a plan over the objection of a class of creditors, at least one class of creditors must have voted to accept the plan, the plan must be in the best interests of the creditors, the plan must be feasible, the plan must not discriminate unjustly against any creditors, and the plan must be fair and equitable.

The plan must provide for the payment in full of unpaid income, gross receipts, employment, and excise taxes incurred by the debtor within three years prior to the date of the petition and property taxes incurred within one year prior to the date of the petition. The plan may provide that these payments be made in equal installments over not more than five years.

Example Suppose that the BigDotCom Corporation has financial difficulties and has filed for Chapter 11 reorganization. At the time of filing for Chapter 11, the corporation has $100 million of secured credit, $100 million of unsecured credit, and common stockholders whose equity securities are now worthless. The corporation files a plan of reorganization whereby (1) the corporation keeps the secured assets for the business, pays the secured creditors any arrearages owed, and has the secured creditors retain their secured interests in the secured assets; (2) reduces unsecured debt by $45 million and discharges $55 million of unsecured debt; (3) eliminates the interests of the equity holders; (4) rejects specified executory contracts and unexpired leases; (5) eliminates several unprofitable product lines; (6) provides for the payment of required unpaid taxes, and (7) accepts the investment of $30 million in capital from an investment bank that wants to invest in the corporation. If this plan is approved by the court, $55 million of the corporation's unsecured debt is discharged. The corporation emerges from Chapter 11 as a reorganized going concern.

Individuals Filing for Chapter 11 Reorganization

Individuals may file for Chapter 11 reorganization bankruptcy. The 2005 act establishes several special rules that apply when individuals apply for Chapter 11 reorganization. The property of the estate is the same as that which would be included in the estate under a Chapter 7 or Chapter 13 proceeding, as well as all property acquired by the debtor between the time the bankruptcy was commenced and when the case is closed. An individual must file a plan of reorganization. The 2005 act requires that the plan provide for the payment to creditors of a portion of the debtor's earnings from personal services earned after the commencement of the case, as necessary to complete the plan.

If an unsecured creditor objects to an individual debtor's plan, the court can cram down the plan over the objection of the creditor if (1) the plan pays the discounted value of the claim to the creditor or (2) the value of the property to be distributed under the plan is not less than the disposable income of the debtor during the five-year period from the date that the first payment is due under the plan. An individual debtor's Chapter 11 plan can be modified at any time to reflect a change in the debtor's circumstances.

When the debtor has completed the required payments under the plan, the court grants discharge of any unpaid debts to the debtor. The court may grant discharge to a debtor who has not completed plan payments if modification of the plan is not practicable and the amount paid to the unsecured creditors has been as much as the creditor would have received in a Chapter 7 liquidation case.

CONTEMPORARY ENVIRONMENT

Small Business Bankruptcy

Large firms that reorganize under Chapter 11 of the Bankruptcy Code have the resources to hire lawyers, investment bankers, and other professionals to assist them in the time-consuming and expensive Chapter 11 reorganization process. Smaller firms often do not have the resources or the luxury of the time that is necessary to use a typical Chapter 11 proceeding.

To address this problem, the Bankruptcy Code permits a "small business," defined as one with total debts of less than $2 million, to use a simpler and fast-track form of Chapter 11 reorganization bankruptcy. **Small business bankruptcy** provides an efficient and cost-saving method for smaller businesses to reorganize under Chapter 11. Debtors whose primary activity is owning or operating real property or a debtor that is a member of an affiliated group with over $2 million in debt cannot file for small business bankruptcy.

The debtor must attach its most recent financial statements and tax returns to its petition or be excused by the court from doing so. The debtor, through its senior management, must attend interviews, conferences, and a meeting of the creditors. A trustee is appointed unless the court excuses this requirement. During the bankruptcy proceeding, the debtor must file information regarding its profitability, cash flow, expenses, tax returns, and other financial information.

The Bankruptcy Code provides for a fast-track processing of a small business case. A small business debtor has 180 days after the order for relief to file its plan of reorganization. If the debtor does not file a plan, any creditor or other party of interest may submit a plan up to 300 days after the order of relief. The bankruptcy court must confirm a small business debtor's plan of reorganization within 45 days after the plan is filed, as long as the plan meets the requirements of Chapter 11. The court can extend all the time periods for cause.

Chapter 12—Family Farmer and Family Fisherman Bankruptcy

Beginning in 1986, family farmers were permitted to file for bankruptcy reorganization under Chapter 12 of the Bankruptcy Code. Chapter 12 was only a temporary part of Bankruptcy Code, however, and it needed to be periodically reenacted by Congress to remain law. The 2005 act made Chapter 12 a permanent part of the Bankruptcy Code and added family fisherman as debtors who could seek reorganization under its provisions. The 2005 act established special definitions and rules that allow family farmers and family fisherman to file for bankruptcy reorganization under **Chapter 12—adjustment of debts of a family farmer or fisherman with regular income**.[6]

Family Farmer

Chapter 12 defines a **family farmer** as either of the following:

1. An individual or an individual and spouse whose total debt does not exceed $3,273,000, which is at least 50 percent related to farming operations and whose gross income for the preceding taxable year or each of the second and third preceding taxable years was at least 50 percent earned from farming operations
2. A corporation or partnership that is at least 50 percent owned by one family or one family and its relatives, and such family or relatives conduct the farming operation, more than 80 percent of the assets of the business are related to the farming operation, and the business's total debt does not exceed $3,273,000 and is at least 50 percent related to the farming operation

Family Fisherman

Chapter 12 defines a **family fisherman** as either of the following:

1. An individual or an individual and spouse whose total debt does not exceed $1,500,000 and is at least 80 percent related to the commercial fishing operation and whose gross income for the preceding taxable year was at least 50 percent earned from the commercial fishing operation
2. A corporation or partnership that is at least 50 percent owned by one family or one family and its relatives, and such family or its relatives conduct the commercial

fishing operation, more than 80 percent of the assets of the business are related to the commercial fishing operation, and the business's total debt does not exceed $1,500,000 and is at least 80 percent related to the commercial fishing operation

Procedure and Estate

Under Chapter 12, the debtor may file a voluntary petition. Creditors cannot, however, file involuntary petitions. After a debtor files for Chapter 12 bankruptcy, a trustee is appointed. The family farmer or family fisherman is a debtor-in-possession who remains in possession of the property of the estate and is permitted to operate the farming or commercial fishing operation unless cause, such as fraud, dishonesty, or gross mismanagement, is proven.

Upon the filing of the petition, an automatic stay goes into place against creditors' actions (e.g., foreclosure proceedings) against the debtor. A secured creditor can petition the court for relief from the stay if the creditor's security interest would be irreparably harmed by the stay.

In addition to the property normally included in a bankruptcy proceeding, the bankruptcy estate in a Chapter 12 case also includes (1) property that the debtor acquires after the commencement of the case and before the reorganization plan is completed and (2) earnings from services performed by the debtor after the commencement of the case and before the reorganization plan is completed.

The debtor can convert a Chapter 12 reorganization case to a Chapter 7 liquidation case at any time.

Chapter 12 Plan of Reorganization

A family farmer or family fisherman debtor must file a plan of reorganization within 90 days of the order for relief. Generally, the plan may provide for payments to creditors over a period no longer than three years, but the court can increase the period to up to five years, based on a showing of cause. The plan of reorganization must be confirmed by the court before it becomes operable.

The plan of reorganization can modify the rights of secured creditors and unsecured creditors. The plan may treat claims for an individual debtor's consumer debt differently than other unsecured debt.

SECURED CLAIMS Chapter 12 provides certain protections for secured creditors. A debtor's plan can be confirmed as to a secured creditor if (1) the holder of the claim has accepted the plan, (2) the debtor surrenders the property securing the claim to the secured creditor, or (3) the plan provides that the secured creditor retains the mortgage or lien securing the claim and the plan distributes property to the secured creditor that is not less than the allowed amount of the claim.

PRIORITY UNSECURED CLAIMS As discussed previously in this chapter, Section 507 of the Bankruptcy Code defines certain unsecured claims as priority claims and designates their priority of payment in a bankruptcy proceeding. The debtor and an unsecured creditor can voluntarily agree to the terms for the settlement of an unsecured creditor's priority claim. This can take the form of reducing the amount of the claim or extending the time period for the payment of the claim.

If no such agreement is reached, the plan of reorganization must (1) provide for the full payment of the claim in deferred cash payments or (2) provide for less than full payment of the claim if the plan provides that all of the debtor's projected disposable income for the plan period is applied to make payments under the plan.

NONPRIORITY UNSECURED CLAIMS The debtor and an unsecured creditor can voluntarily agree to the terms for the settlement of an unsecured creditor's nonpriority claim. If no agreement is reached, the plan can modify the claims of unsecured creditors as necessary to accomplish the reorganization. This includes reducing the amount of the claim as well as extending the period to pay the claim.

EXECUTORY CONTRACTS A Chapter 12 plan can provide for the assumption or rejection of executory contracts and unexpired leases.

Example Suppose a family farmer is obligated under a contract to sell his harvested grain for the next three years to a buyer. The debtor can assume this contract or reject this contract, depending on what is in his or her best interests. If the debtor rejects the contract, the buyer cannot sue the debtor to recover damages.

CONFIRMATION OF A CHAPTER 12 PLAN The bankruptcy court holds a hearing regarding the **confirmation of a Chapter 12 plan**. Creditors can appear at the hearing and object to the plan. If the requirements previously discussed are met, the bankruptcy court must confirm a plan if:

- The plan has been proposed in good faith
- The plan is in the best interests of each of the allowed unsecured claims because the plan pays each unsecured claim at least what such claim would have received under Chapter 7 liquidation bankruptcy
- The plan is feasible—that is, the debtor will be able to make the payments specified in the plan

The debtor must submit all or such portion of the debtor's future earnings or other future income to the trustee as is necessary for the completion of the plan

CRAM-DOWN PROVISION If a priority or nonpriority unsecured creditor objects to a Chapter 12 plan, the court can cram down the plan over the objecting unsecured creditors if the plan provides any of the following: (1) The unsecured creditor is paid the discounted present value of his or her claim, (2) the debtor's projected disposable income received in the plan period is applied to make payments under the plan, or (3) the value of the property to be distributed under the plan is not less than the disposable income of the debtor during the plan period.

Chapter 12 Discharge

When a family farmer or family fisherman debtor has completed making all payments required by the plan (which is usually three years but could be up to five years), the bankruptcy court grants the debtor discharge of all debts provided for by the plan. This is called a **Chapter 12 discharge**. For example, if the Chapter 12 plan calls for the debtor to pay 55 percent of the outstanding unsecured debt to the unsecured creditors, and this amount has been paid by the debtor during the plan period, the court grants discharge of the unpaid 45 percent of this unsecured debt.

The court may grant discharge to a debtor who has not completed payments under the plan if modification of the plan is not practicable, the debtor's failure to complete the required payments is due to circumstances for which the debtor is not accountable, and the amount paid to the unsecured creditors has been as much as the creditor would have received in a Chapter 7 liquidation bankruptcy.

ETHICS SPOTLIGHT
Bankruptcy Fraud

Most of the time, bankruptcy law is used for legitimate purposes, and the information provided by the debtor and creditors is true and complete. However, sometimes debtors or creditors abuse bankruptcy law and commit fraudulent acts in a bankruptcy proceeding.

Federal law makes it a crime for any person to devise, intend to devise, or execute a scheme or an artifice to commit fraud by filing a voluntary or involuntary petition for bankruptcy, filing a fraudulent document, or making a false or fraudulent claim in connection with a bankruptcy case [18 U.S.C. Section 157]. A person convicted of bankruptcy fraud may be fined and imprisoned for up to five years. Each case is independently examined by the court.

Section 802 of the **Sarbanes-Oxley Act**, a federal statute enacted to address business fraud, makes it a crime for anyone to knowingly alter, falsify, conceal, or make a false entry in any document with the intent to obstruct or influence the investigation of any bankruptcy case. A violation is punishable by fine or imprisonment for not more than 20 years, or both.

Law & Ethics Questions

1. **ETHICS** Do you think much bankruptcy fraud occurs? Give several examples.
2. **ETHICS** Will the new provisions of the 2005 act help prevent bankruptcy fraud? Explain.

Special Forms of Bankruptcy

The Bankruptcy Code and other federal laws include provisions that permit special forms of bankruptcy. Some of these special forms of bankruptcy are:

- **■** *Railroad reorganization.* Chapter 11 of the Bankruptcy Code provides special requirements and provisions for the reorganization of railroads.[7] The bankruptcy court is directed to consider the public interest in approving the reorganization of railroads and the abandonment of railroad lines.
- **■** *Municipality adjustment of debts.* Chapter 9 of the Bankruptcy Code provides for a proceeding for adjusting the debts of a municipality.[8] Under Chapter 9, cities, towns, counties, sewage and water districts, and other local governmental units can file for bankruptcy and reorganize their debts.
- **■** *Stockbroker and commodities broker liquidation.* Chapter 7 of the Bankruptcy Code provides special requirements and provisions for the liquidation bankruptcy of stockbrokers[9] and commodities brokers.[10] This includes provisions for the treatment of customer accounts, protection of clients' property, and processing of claims.
- **■** *Commercial banks, savings banks, and credit unions.* The Bankruptcy Code does not provide for the bankruptcy of commercial banks, savings banks, or credit unions. The bankruptcy proceedings of commercial banks, savings banks, and credit unions are handled by federal governmental agencies that oversee the operation of these financial institutions.

INTERNATIONAL LAW
British Bankruptcy Law

Many of our country's forefathers were debtors fleeing the harsh laws of Britain and European countries where debtors were often sent to debtors' prisons or were required to work off the debt owed to creditors. When this country was founded, the right to declare bankruptcy was considered just as important as the right to free speech, and both rights were included in the U.S. Constitution. Even today, U.S. bankruptcy law treats debtors more leniently than the bankruptcy laws of other countries.

Consider the case of bankruptcy reorganization laws in Britain versus those in the United States for handling the reorganization of bankrupt companies. British law banishes lawyers from the reorganization process and puts it in the hands of specially licensed accountants. When a firm files for reorganization bankruptcy in Britain, an administrative order is issued. The order permits the creditors of the troubled company to appoint a team of bankruptcy accountants to handle the company's reorganization.

British law assumes that the company's misfortune is not a result of bad luck but is based on mismanagement by the company's officers and directors. Consequently, the bankruptcy accountants are empowered to remove the firm's existing management and take over control of its operations. The accountants then orchestrate the reorganization and sale of the company's assets. Many U.S. bankruptcy lawyers allege that British bankruptcy law tramples too hard on debtors' rights. Proponents of the British system argue that it is faster, cheaper, and more efficient than a bankruptcy reorganization under Chapter 11 of the U.S. Bankruptcy Code. They assert that the British system does not coddle debtors and make lawyers rich, as the U.S. bankruptcy system does.

Chapter Summary

Bankruptcy Law, p. 631

Bankruptcy Abuse Prevention and Consumer Protection Act of 2005

The Bankruptcy Reform Act of 1978 is a federal act that substantially changed federal bankruptcy law. This act made it easier for debtors to file for bankruptcy and have their unpaid debts discharged. The 1978 act was often referred to as being debtor friendly. The Bankruptcy Abuse Prevention and Consumer Protection Act of 2005 is a federal act that substantially amended federal bankruptcy law. This act makes it more difficult for debtors to file for bankruptcy and have their unpaid debts discharged. *Bankruptcy code* is the name given to federal bankruptcy law, as amended.

Types of Bankruptcy

1. Chapter 7: Liquidation
2. Chapter 11: Reorganization
3. Chapter 12: Adjustment of debts of a family farmer or fisherman with regular income
4. Chapter 13: Adjustment of debts of an individual with regular income.

"Fresh Start"

The goal of federal bankruptcy law is to grant a debtor relief from some of his or her burdensome debts while protecting creditors by requiring the debtor to pay more of his or her debts than would otherwise have been required prior to the 2005 act.

Bankruptcy Courts

Bankruptcy courts are special federal courts that hear and decide bankruptcy cases. Bankruptcy courts have exclusive jurisdiction to hear bankruptcy cases. A bankruptcy court is attached to each federal district court. Bankruptcy judges are appointed for 14-year terms.

U.S. Trustee

A U.S. trustee is a federal government official who is responsible for handling and supervising many of the administrative tasks of a bankruptcy case.

Bankruptcy Procedure, p. 634

Pre-Petition and Post-Petition Counseling

The 2005 act added a new provision that requires an individual filing for bankruptcy to receive pre-petition and post-petition credit and financial counseling.

Filling a Bankruptcy Petition

The filing of a petition commences a bankruptcy case.
1. *Voluntary petition.* A voluntary petition is filed by a debtor.
2. *Involuntary petition.* An involuntary petition is filed by a creditor or creditors.

Schedules

An individual debtor must submit a number of schedules upon filing a voluntary petition; all forms must be sworn under oath and signed by the debtor.

Attorney Certification

The 2005 act requires the attorney to certify the accuracy of the information contained in the bankruptcy petition and the schedules, under penalty of perjury.

Order for Relief

An order for relief designates that the bankruptcy court has accepted a case for further proceedings.

Meeting of the Creditors

The debtor must appear at the meeting of the creditors and answer questions asked by the creditors. Also called the *first meeting of the creditors.*

Proof of Claim and Proof of Interest

Unsecured creditors must file proof of claim, stating the amount of their claims against the debtors. Equity security holders must file proof of interest, stating the amount of their interest against the debtor.

Bankruptcy Trustee

A trustee is elected in certain bankruptcies. Once appointed, a trustee becomes the legal representative of the debtor's estate.

Automatic Stay

The filing of a bankruptcy petition *stays* (suspends) certain legal actions against the debtor or the debtor's property. A secured creditor may petition the court for a relief from stay in situations in which the creditor is not adequately protected during the bankruptcy proceeding.

Discharge

An order of the court that relieves a debtor of his or her legal liability to pay his or her debts that were not paid in the bankruptcy proceeding. The debtor's legal obligation to pay discharged debts is terminated. The Bankruptcy Code stipulates that certain debts are not dischargeable.

Reaffirmation Agreement

A reaffirmation agreement is an agreement entered into by a debtor with a creditor prior to discharge whereby the debtor agrees to pay the creditor a debt that would otherwise be discharged in bankruptcy.

Bankruptcy Estate, p. 639

The bankruptcy estate includes all the debtor's legal and equitable interests in real, personal, tangible, and intangible property at the time the petition if filed. It includes gifts, inheritances, life insurance proceeds, and property from divorce settlements that the debtor is entitled to receive within 180 days after the petition is filed.

Exempt Property

The Bankruptcy Code permits the debtor to retain certain property that does not become part of the bankruptcy estate. Exemptions are stipulated in federal and state law.

State Exemptions

The bankruptcy code allows for state's to enact their own exemptions. Debtor's are allowed to chose from either state or federal exemptions.

Homestead Exemption

The debtor is permitted to retain some equity in his or her home. The 2005 act limits abusive homestead exemptions.

Voidable Transfers

The following transfers and preferences are voidable by the court:
1. *Preferential transfer within 90 days before bankruptcy.* Transfer is for an antecedent debt and gives the creditor more than he or she would receive in bankruptcy.
2. *Preferential liens within 90 days before bankruptcy.* Transfer is for an antecedent debt, and the creditor receives more because of this lien than he or she would as an unsecured creditor in bankruptcy.
3. *Preferential transfer to an insider within one year before bankruptcy.* The transferee is an "insider" (e.g., relative, business associate), and the creditor is insolvent.
4. *Fraudulent transfer within two years before bankruptcy.* The debtor transfers property with the intent to hinder, delay, or defraud creditors.

5. ***Fraudulent transfer to a trust within ten years before bankruptcy*** The 2005 act voids transfers of property by a debtor to a living trust made with the intent to hinder, delay, or defraud creditors.

Chapter 7—Liquidation, p. 644

In Chapter 7 bankruptcy, also called *liquidation bankruptcy*, the debtor's nonexempt property is sold for cash, the cash is distributed to the creditors, and any unpaid debts are discharged.

Chapter 7 Procedure

Any person, including an individual, partnership, corporation, and other business entity, may be a debtor in a Chapter 7 proceeding. Voluntary and involuntary petitions may be filed. Most Chapter 7 filings are voluntarily filed by individuals.

The 2005 Act's Changes to Chapter 7

In a Chapter 7 filing that is found to be an abuse of Chapter 7 liquidation bankruptcy, the court can dismiss the case or convert the case to a Chapter 13 or Chapter 11 proceeding, with the debtor's consent.

Median Income Test

For any size family, a state's median income is income where half of the state's families of the same size have incomes above this figure and half of the state's families of this size have incomes less than this figure. The median income test is a test that determines whether a debtor's median family income exceeds or is equal to or below the state median income.

1. If the debtor's median family income is at or below the state's family median income, the debtor can receive Chapter 7 relief.
2. If the debtor's median family income exceeds the state's median family income, then the "means test" applies to determine if the debtor can receive Chapter 7 relief.

Means Test

The means test is a complicated test that applies to a debtor whose family income exceeds the state's median income for families of the same size to determine whether the debtor qualifies for Chapter 7 relief.

Statutory Distribution of Property

Nonexempt property of the bankruptcy estate is distributed to the creditors in the following statutory priority:

1. ***Secured creditors.*** Either a secured creditor obtains the collateral or the collateral is sold and the secured creditor is paid. If the value of the collateral exceeds the secured interest, the excess becomes available to pay other creditors. If the value of the collateral is less than the secured interest, the secured creditor becomes an unsecured creditor to the difference.
2. ***Unsecured creditors.*** Unsecured creditors are paid in the priority established by the Bankruptcy Code. Each class must be paid in full before any lower class is paid anything. If a class cannot be paid in full, the claims of that class are paid *pro rata* (proportionately).

Chapter 7 Discharge

After the nonexempt property is distributed, the remaining unpaid claims of the debtor are *discharged*, and the debtor's legal obligation to pay these unpaid debts is terminated. Discharge is available only to individuals. The Bankruptcy Code stipulates that certain debts are not dischargeable.

Acts That Bar Discharge

A bankruptcy court may deny discharge of debts if the debtor has engaged in prohibited conduct.

Discharge of Student Loans

A student loan may be discharged after it is due only if nondischarge would cause an *undue hardship* on the debtor or his or her family.

Chapter 13—Adjustment of Debts of an Individual with Regular Income, p. 652

Chapter 13, also called *consumer debt adjustment*, is a rehabilitation form of bankruptcy that permits bankruptcy courts to supervise the debtor's plan for the repayment of unpaid debts by installment.

Filing the Petition

A Chapter 13 proceeding can be initiated only through the voluntary filing of a petition by an individual debtor with regular income.

Limitations on Who Can File for Chapter 13 Bankruptcy

The 2005 act establishes limitations on the amount of unsecured and secured debt a debtor can have to file for Chapter 13 bankruptcy.

Chapter 13 Procedures

A permanent trustee is appointed by the court. The debtor makes payments to the trustee, who is responsible for remitting payments to the creditors.

Property of the Estate

The property of a Chapter 13 estate consists of all nonexempt property of the debtor at the commencement of the case and nonexempt property acquired after the commencement of the case but before the case is closed.

Chapter 13 Plan of Payment

The debtor must file a plan of payment. The plan period is either up to three years or up to five years, depending on the debtor's income.

Modification of the Rights of Creditors

A plan may be modified if the debtor's circumstances materially change.

Confirmation of a Chapter 13 Plan of Payment

The court can confirm a Chapter 13 plan of payment if all of the Chapter 13 requirements are met and if (1) the plan was proposed in good faith, (2) the plan passes the feasibility test, (3) the plan is in the best interests of the creditors, (4) the debtor has paid all domestic support obligations owed, and (5) the debtor has filed all applicable federal, state, and local tax returns.

Chapter 13 Discharge

The court grants an order discharging the debtor from all unpaid debts covered by the plan only after all the payments required under the plan are completed.

Chapter 11—Reorganization, p. 655

Chapter 11 bankruptcy provides a method for reorganizing the debtor's financial affairs under the supervision of the bankruptcy court.

Chapter 11 Reorganization Proceeding

The requirements of filing of a petition, the first meeting of the creditors, the entry for the order of relief, and automatic stay apply to Chapter 11 proceedings.

Debtor-in-Possession

In most Chapter 11 cases, the debtor is left in place to operate the business during the reorganization proceeding. In such cases, the debtor is called a debtor-in-possession. The court may appoint a trustee to operate the debtor's business only upon a showing of cause, such as fraud, dishonesty, or gross mismanagement of the affairs of the debtor by current management.

Creditors' Committees

The court appoints a committee of unsecured creditors (usually the creditors holding the seven largest claims). The court may also appoint committees of secured creditors and equity holders. Committees participate in the bankruptcy proceeding and in the negotiation of a plan of reorganization.

Automatic Stay in Chapter 11

The filing of a bankruptcy petition stays (suspends) certain legal actions against the debtor or the debtor's property. A secured creditor may petition the court for a relief from stay in situations in which the creditor is not adequately protected during the bankruptcy proceeding.

Executory Contracts and Unexpired Leases

The debtor-in-possession (or trustee) may assume or reject executory contracts and unexpired leases. A special procedure has been established for rejecting union collective bargaining agreements.

Labor Union and Retiree Benefits Contracts

In a Chapter 11 case, union members and union retirees are represented by the responsible labor union. The court appoints a committee to represent nonunion retirees. The debtor and the representatives of the union members and retirees can voluntarily agree to modify the union collective bargaining agreement and retiree benefits. If such an agreement is not reached, the debtor can petition the bankruptcy court to reject the collective bargaining agreement and to modify retiree benefits.

Chapter 11 Plan of Reorganization

A Chapter 11 plan of reorganization sets forth the debtor's proposed new capital structure. The debtor has the exclusive right to file a plan within the first 120 days after the date of the order for relief. The debtor must supply the creditors and equity holders with a disclosure statement that contains adequate information about the proposed plan of reorganization.

Confirmation of a Chapter 11 Plan of Reorganization

A plan of reorganization must be confirmed by the bankruptcy court before it becomes effective. Confirmation may be by either of the following methods:
1. *The acceptance method.* This type of confirmation requires each class of creditors to accept the plan.
2. *The cram-down provision.* This type of confirmation permits the bankruptcy court to confirm a plan over the objection of a class of creditors.

Upon confirmation of a plan of reorganization, the debtor is granted a discharge of all claims not included in the plan. The debtor's legal obligation to pay the discharged debts is terminated.

Individuals Filing for Chapter 11 Reorganization

Individuals may file for Chapter 11 reorganization bankruptcy. The 2005 act requires that the plan provide for the payment to creditors of a portion of the debtor's earnings from personal services earned after the commencement of the case, as necessary to complete the plan.

Small Business Bankruptcy

The Bankruptcy Reform Act of 1994 provides a less costly and faster procedure for small businesses to file, maintain, and emerge from a Chapter 11 bankruptcy proceeding.

Chapter 12—Family Farmer and Family Fisherman Bankruptcy, p. 661

Chapter 12 is a rehabilitation form of bankruptcy that provides a method for reorganizing a family farmer debtor's or family fisherman debtor's financial affairs under the supervision of the bankruptcy court.

Family Farmer

The Bankruptcy Code defines a family farmer as a debtor whose total debts do not exceed a certain amount, whose operations are primarily related to farming operations, and whose gross income is primarily related to farming operations.

Family Fisherman

The Bankruptcy Code defines a family fisherman as a debtor whose total debts do not exceed a certain amount, whose operations are primarily related to fishing operations, and whose gross income is primarily related to fishing operations.

Procedure and Estate

Under Chapter 12 only voluntary petitions may be filed. In Chapter 12, the family farmer or family fisherman is a debtor-in-possession who remains in possession of the property of the estate and is permitted to operate the farming or commercial fishing operation unless cause, such as fraud, dishonesty, or gross mismanagement, is proven.

Chapter 12 Plan of Reorganization

A plan of reorganization can only be filed by a farmer-debtor or fisherman-debtor. The plan of reorganization can modify the rights of secured creditors and unsecured creditors.

Chapter 12 Discharge

A discharge in a Chapter 12 case is granted to a family farmer or family fisherman debtor after the debtor's plan of payment is completed (which is usually three years but could be up to five years).

Special Forms of Bankruptcy, p. 664

The Bankruptcy Code provides for special bankruptcy rules for:
1. Railroad reorganization
2. Municipality adjustment of debts
3. Stockbroker and commodities broker liquidation
4. Commercial banks, savings banks, and credit unions

Test Review Terms and Concepts

Case Problems

24.1 Petition: Daniel E. Beren, John M. Elliot, and Edward F. Mannino formed Walnut Street Four, a general partnership, to purchase and renovate an office building in Harrisburg, Pennsylvania. They borrowed more than $200,000 from Hamilton Bank to purchase the building and begin renovation. Disagreements among the partners arose when the renovation costs exceeded their estimates. When Beren was unable to obtain assistance from Elliot and Mannino regarding obtaining additional financing, the partnership quit paying its debts. Beren filed an involuntary petition to place the partnership into Chapter 7 bankruptcy. The other partners objected to the bankruptcy filing. At the time of the filing, the partnership owed debts of more than $380,000 and had approximately $550 in the partnership bank account. Should the petition for involuntary bankruptcy be granted? *In re Walnut Street Four*, 106 B.R. 56, **Web** 1989 Bankr. Lexis 1806 (United States Bankruptcy Court for the Middle District of Pennsylvania)

24.2 Bankruptcy Estate: Bill K. and Marilyn E. Hargis, husband and wife, filed a Chapter 11 bankruptcy proceeding. More than 120 days after the bankruptcy petition was filed, Bill died. His life was insured for $700,000. His wife was the beneficiary of the policy. The bankruptcy trustee moved to recover the $700,000 as property of the bankruptcy estate. Who gets the insurance proceeds? *In re Hargis*, 887 F.2d 77, **Web** 1989 U.S. App. Lexis 16246 (United States Court of Appeals for the Fifth Circuit)

24.3 Automatic Stay: James F. Kost filed a voluntary petition for relief under Chapter 11 of the Bankruptcy Code. First Interstate Bank of Greybull (First Interstate) held a first mortgage on the debtor's residence near Basin, Wyoming. Appraisals and other evidence showed that the house was worth $116,000. The debt owed to First Interstate was almost $103,000 and was increasing at the rate of $32.46 per day. The debtor had only an 11.5 percent equity cushion in the property. Further evidence showed that the (1) Greybull/Basin area was suffering from tough economic times, (2) there were more than 90 homes available for sale in the area, (3) the real estate market in the area was declining, (4) the condition of the house was seriously deteriorating and the debtor was not financially able to make the necessary improvements, and (5) the insurance on the property had lapsed. First Interstate moved for a relief from stay so that it could foreclose on the property and sell it. Should

the motion be granted? *In re Kost*, 102 B.R. 829, **Web** 1989 U.S. Dist. Lexis 8316 (United States District Court for the District of Wyoming)

24.4 Fraudulent Transfer: Peter and Geraldine Tabala (Debtors), husband and wife, purchased a house in Clarkstown, New York. They purchased a Carvel ice cream business for $70,000 with a loan obtained from People's National Bank. In addition, the Carvel Corporation extended trade credit to Debtors. Two years after getting the bank loan, Debtors conveyed their residence to their three daughters, ages 9, 19, and 20, for no consideration. Debtors continued to reside in the house and to pay maintenance expenses and real estate taxes due on the property. On the date of transfer, Debtors owed obligations in excess of $100,000. Five months after conveying their residence to their daughters, Debtors filed a petition for Chapter 7 bankruptcy. The bankruptcy trustee moved to set aside Debtors' conveyance of their home to their daughters as a fraudulent transfer. Who wins? *In re Tabala*, 11 B.R. 405, **Web** 1981 Bankr. Lexis 3663 (United States Bankruptcy Court for the Southern District of New York)

24.5 Preferential Payment: Air Florida System, Inc. (Air Florida), an airline company, filed a voluntary petition to reorganize under Chapter 11 of the Bankruptcy Code. Within 90 days prior to the commencement of the case, Air Florida paid $13,575 to Compania Panamena de Aviacion, S.A. (COPA), in payment of an antecedent debt. This payment enabled COPA to receive more than it would have received if Air Florida had been liquidated under Chapter 7. Is the payment to COPA an avoidable preferential transfer? *In re Jet Florida System, Inc. f/k/a Air Florida System, Inc.*, 105 B.R. 137, **Web** 1989 Bankr. Lexis 1629 (United States Bankruptcy Court for the Southern District of Florida)

24.6 Plan of Reorganization: Richard P. Friese (Debtor) filed a voluntary petition for Chapter 11 bankruptcy. Debtor filed a plan of reorganization that divided his creditors into three classes. The first class, administrative creditors, were to be paid in full. The second class, unsecured creditors, were to receive 50 percent on their claims. The IRS was the third class; it was to receive $20,000 on confirmation and the balance in future payments. No creditors voted to accept the plan. The unsecured creditors were impaired because their legal, equitable, and contractual rights were being altered. Can the bankruptcy court confirm Debtor's plan of reorganization? *In re Friese*, 103 B.R. 90, **Web** 1989 Bankr. Lexis 1309 (United States Bankruptcy Court for the Southern District of New York)

24.7 Consumer Debt Adjustment: Manuel Guadalupe (Debtor) was a tool and die machinist who was employed at Elco Industries for more than five years. He accumulated more then $19,000 in unsecured debt, including deficiencies owed after secured creditors repossessed a van (leaving a deficiency of $1,066) and a car (leaving a deficiency of $3,130). Shortly after the second automobile was repossessed, Debtor borrowed approximately $19,000 from Elco Credit Union to purchase a four-wheel-drive Chevrolet Blazer. The $472 monthly payment was to be taken directly from Debtor's earnings.

Subsequently, Debtor filed a voluntary petition for Chapter 13 consumer debt adjustment. The schedule listed total secured debts of $22,132, which included the debt for the Blazer, furniture, and a camcorder. Total unsecured debt was $19,575, which included $2,160 owed to General Finance Corporation (General). Debtor's budget projected that $700 per month would be left over for funding the Chapter 13 plan after his monthly expenses were deducted from his $25,000 gross income. Secured creditors were to be paid in full; unsecured creditors would receive 10 percent of their claims. General objected to the plan. Should Debtor's Chapter 13 plan be confirmed? *In re Reyes*, 106 B.R. 155, **Web** 1989 Bankr. Lexis 1731 (United States Bankruptcy Court for the Northern District of Illinois)

24.8 Student Loan: Donald Wayne Doyle (Debtor) obtained a guaranteed student loan to enroll in a school for training truck drivers. Due to his impending divorce, Debtor never attended the program. The first monthly installment of approximately $50 to pay the student loan became due. Two weeks later, Debtor filed a voluntary petition for Chapter 7 bankruptcy.

Debtor was a 29-year-old man who earned approximately $1,000 per month at an hourly wage of $7.70 as a truck driver, a job that he had held for 10 years. Debtor resided on a farm where he performed work in lieu of paying rent for his quarters. Debtor was paying monthly payments of $89 on a bank loan for his former wife's vehicle, $200 for his truck, $40 for health insurance, $28 for car insurance, $120 for gasoline and vehicular maintenance, $400 for groceries and meals, and $25 for telephone charges. In addition, a state court had ordered Debtor to pay $300 per month to support his children, ages four and five. Debtor's parents were assisting him by buying him $130 of groceries per month. Should Debtor's student loan be discharged in bankruptcy? *In re Doyle*, 106 B.R. 272, **Web** 1989 Bankr. Lexis 1772 (United States Bankruptcy Court for the Northern District of Alabama)

24.9 Preference Rule: ZZZZ Best Co., Inc. (Debtor), borrowed $7 million from Union Bank. Seven months later, Debtor filed a voluntary petition under Chapter 7 (liquidation). During the preceding 90-day period, Debtor had made two interest payments on its loan to Union Bank totaling $100,000. The trustee of Debtor's estate filed a complaint against Union Bank to recover those interest payments as preferential transfers made within 90 days of the bankruptcy filing. Can payments on long-term debt qualify as payments within the ordinary course of business exception to the 90-day preference rule? *Union Bank v. Wolas*, 502 U.S. 151, 112 S.Ct. 527, 116 L.Ed.2d 514, **Web** 1991 U.S. Lexis 7174 (Supreme Court of the United States)

Ethics Issues

24.10 Ethics: Scott Greig Keebler (Debtor) became indebted, and his debts exceeded his assets. The Internal Revenue Service (IRS) had levied his wages for nonpayment of taxes. Debtor was healthy and capable of earning a substantial income. Evidence showed that Debtor did not try his best to pay his debts, lived an affluent lifestyle, and determined not to pay his principal creditors. Debtor voluntarily quit his job and filed a voluntary petition for Chapter 7 bankruptcy. The petition stated that he was unemployed. Shortly after filing for bankruptcy, the petitioner resumed work. Was it ethical for Keebler to be able to file for Chapter 7 bankruptcy? *In re Keebler*, 106 B.R. 662, **Web** 1989 Bankr. Lexis 1919 (United States Bankruptcy Court for the District of Hawaii)

24.11 Ethics: The Record Company, Inc. (The Record Company), entered into a purchase agreement to buy certain retail record stores from Bummbusiness, Inc. (Bummbusiness). All assets and inventory were included in the deal. The Record Company agreed to pay Bummbusiness $20,000 and to pay the $380,000 of trade debt owed by the stores. In exchange, Bummbusiness agreed not to compete with the new buyer for two years within a 15-mile radius of the stores and to use its best efforts to obtain an extension of the due dates for the trade debt. The Record Company began operating the stores but shortly thereafter filed a petition for Chapter 11 bankruptcy. At the time of the bankruptcy filing, (1) The Record Company owed Bummbusiness $10,000 and owed the trade debt of $380,000, and (2) Bummbusiness was obligated not to compete with The Record Company. Can The Record Company reject the purchase agreement? Was it ethical for The Record Company to try to reject the purchase agreement? *In re The Record Company*, 8 B.R. 57, **Web** 1981 Bankr. Lexis 5157 (United States Bankruptcy Court for the Southern District of Indiana)

IRAC Writing Assignment

Read **Case A-24** in Appendix A [*Dewsnup v. Timm*]. Use the IRAC method to prepare a written analysis of the case.

Endnotes

1. 28 U.S.C. Sections 586–589b.
2. 11 U.S.C. Section 522(d).
3. 11 U.S.C. Sections 701–784.
4. 11 U.S.C. Sections 1301–1330.
5. 11 U.S.C. Sections 1101–1174.
6. 11 U.S.C. Sections 1201–1231.
7. 11 U.S.C. Sections 1161–1174.
8. 11 U.S.C. Sections 901–946.
9. 11 U.S.C. Sections 741–753.
10. 11 U.S.C. Sections 761–767.

UNIT 6

Business Organizations and Investor Protection

CHAPTER 25

Agency Relationships

"Let every eye negotiate for itself, and trust no agent."

—WILLIAM SHAKESPEARE
Much Ado About Nothing (1598)

CHAPTER OBJECTIVES

After studying this chapter, you should be able to:

1. Define *agency* and describe how express and implied agencies are created.
2. Identify and describe the principal's liability for the tortious conduct of an agent.
3. Describe the principal's and agent's liability on third-party contracts.
4. Define and apply the doctrine of *apparent agency*.
5. Define a principal–independent contractor relationship and describe the liability for tortious conduct of independent contractors.

CHAPTER CONTENTS

- Introduction to Agency Relationships
- Agency
- Formation of an Agency
- Tort Liability to Third Parties
- Contract Liability to Third Parties
- Independent Contractor
- Termination of an Agency
- Chapter Summary
- Test Review Terms and Concepts
- Case Problems
- Ethics Issues
- IRAC Writing Assignment

Introduction to Agency Relationships

If businesspeople had to personally conduct all their business, the scope of their activities would be severely curtailed. Partnerships would not be able to operate; corporations could not act through managers and employees; and sole proprietorships would not be able to hire employees. The use of agents (or agency), which allows one person to act on behalf of another, solves this problem.

There are many examples of agency relationships, including a salesperson who sells goods for a store, an executive who works for a corporation, a partner who acts on behalf of a partnership, an attorney who is hired to represent a client, and a real estate broker who is employed to sell a house. Agency is governed by a large body of common law known as **agency law**. The formation and termination of agencies is discussed in this chapter.

Principals and agents owe certain duties to each other and are liable to each other for breaching these duties. When acting for the principal, an agent often enters into contracts and otherwise deals with third parties. Agency law has established certain rules that make principals, agents, and independent contractors liable to third persons for contracts and tortious conduct. This chapter discusses the liability of principals, agents, and independent contractors to each other and to third parties.

Logo, Prentice Hall Publishing Company

Prentice Hall is a leading publisher of business and business law textbooks. Prentice Hall's contract with the author of this book creates an independent contractor status between the two parties.

Web Exercises

1. **WEB** Visit the website of Prentice Hall, at *www.prenhall.com*.

2. **WEB** Pearson, an international media company, owns Prentice Hall. Visit the website of Pearson, at *www.pearson.com*.

Agency

Agency relationships are formed by the mutual consent of a principal and an agent. Section 1(1) of the *Restatement (Second) of Agency* defines *agency* as a fiduciary relationship "which results from the manifestation of consent by one person to another that the other shall act in his behalf and subject to his control, and consent by the other so to act." The *Restatement (Second) of Agency* is the reference source for the rules of agency. A party who employs another person to act on his or her behalf is called a **principal**. A party who agrees to act on behalf of another is called an **agent**. The principal–agent relationship is commonly referred to as an **agency**. This relationship is depicted in Exhibit 25.1.

EXHIBIT 25.1

Principal–Agent
Relationship

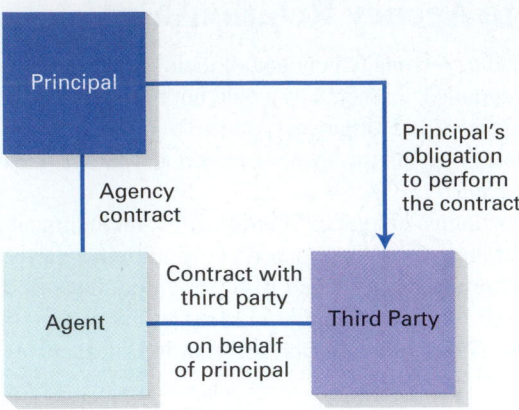

Persons Who Can Initiate an Agency Relationship

Any person who has the capacity to contract can appoint an agent to act on his or her behalf. Generally, persons who lack **contractual capacity**, such as insane persons and minors, cannot appoint agents. However, the court can appoint a legal guardian or another representative to handle the affairs of insane persons, minors, and others who lack capacity to contract. With court approval, these representatives can enter into enforceable contracts on behalf of the persons they represent.

An agency can be created only to accomplish a lawful purpose. Agency contracts that are created for illegal purposes or are against public policy are void and unenforceable.

Example A principal cannot hire an agent to kill another person.

Some agency relationships are prohibited by law.

Example Unlicensed agents cannot be hired to perform the duties of certain licensed professionals (e.g., doctors, lawyers).

Principal–Agent Relationship

A **principal–agent relationship** is formed when an employer hires an employee and gives that employee authority to act and enter into contracts on his or her behalf. The extent of this authority is governed by any express agreement between the parties and implied from the circumstances of the agency.

Example The president of a corporation usually has the authority to enter into major contracts on the corporation's behalf, and a supervisor on the corporation's assembly line may have the authority only to purchase the supplies necessary to keep the line running.

Employer–Employee Relationship

An **employer–employee relationship** exists when an employer hires an employee to perform some form of physical service.

Example A welder on General Motors Corporation's assembly line is employed in an employer–employee relationship because he performs a physical task.

An employee is not an agent unless he or she is specifically empowered to enter into contracts on the principal employer's behalf. Employees may only enter into contracts that are within the scope of their employment.

Example The welder in the previous example is not an agent because he cannot enter into contracts on behalf of General Motors Corporation. If the company empowered him to enter into contracts, he would become an agent.

> ## CONCEPT SUMMARY
>
> ### Kinds of Employment Relationships
>
> | TYPE OF RELATIONSHIP | DESCRIPTION |
> | --- | --- |
> | Principal–agent | The agent has authority to act on behalf of the principal, as authorized by the principal and implied from the agency. An employee is often the agent of his employer. |
> | Employer–employee | The employer has the right to control the physical conduct of the employee. |

Principal–Independent Contractor Relationship

Principals often employ outsiders—that is, persons and businesses that are not employees—to perform certain tasks on their behalf. These persons and businesses are called **independent contractors**.

Example Doctors, dentists, consultants, stockbrokers, architects, certified public accountants, real estate brokers, and plumbers are examples of those in professions and trades who commonly act as independent contractors. An independent contractor who is a professional, such as a lawyer, is called a *professional agent*.

A principal can authorize an independent contractor to enter into contracts. Principals are bound by the authorized contracts of their independent contractors. For example, if a client authorizes an attorney to settle a case within a certain dollar amount and the attorney does so, the settlement agreement is binding.

Formation of an Agency

An agency and the resulting authority of an agent can arise in any of these four ways: express agency, implied agency, apparent agency, and agency by ratification. These types of agencies are discussed in the paragraphs that follow.

Express Agency

Express agency is the most common form of agency. In an express agency, the agent has the authority to contract or otherwise act on the principal's behalf, as expressly stated in the agency agreement. In addition, the agent may also possess certain implied or apparent authority to act on the principal's behalf (as discussed later in this chapter).

Express agency occurs when a principal and an agent expressly agree to enter into an agency agreement with each other. Express agency contracts can be either oral or written, unless the Statute of Frauds stipulates that they must be written. For example, in most states, a real estate broker's contract to sell real estate must be in writing.

If a principal and an agent enter into an **exclusive agency contract**, the principal cannot employ any agent other than the exclusive agent. If the principal does so, the exclusive agent can recover damages from the principal. If an agency is not an exclusive agency, the principal can employ more than one agent to try to accomplish a stated purpose. When multiple agents are employed, the agencies with all the agents terminate when any one of the agents accomplishes the stated purpose.

Web Exercises

1. **WEB** Use *www.google.com* to determine what Bill Gates's official position is at Microsoft Corporation. Is he an agent of the corporation?

2. **WEB** Use *www.google.com* to find out who is the president of Yahoo! Corporation. Is that person an agent of the corporation?

3. **WEB** Select a company. Use *www.google.com* to find out who the chief financial officer (CFO) of the corporation is. Is that person an agent of the company?

4. **WEB** Use *www.google.com* to find the names of the president and the provost of your university or college. Are these people agents of your educational institution?

In the following case, the court had to decide whether an agency had been created.

CASE 25.1
Agency

Bosse v. Brinker Restaurant Corporation, d.b.a. Chili's Grill and Bar

Web 2005 Mass. Super. Lexis 372 (2005)
Superior Court of Massachusetts

> **"** *The evidence is insufficient to create a genuine issue whether Chili's appointed or authorized the patron to act as a posse to conduct the chase.* **"**
>
> —Judge Sikora

Facts

Brendan Bosse and Michael Griffin were a part of a group of four teenagers eating a meal at a Chili's restaurant in Dedham, Massachusetts. Chili's is owned by Brinker Restaurant Corporation (collectively "Chili's"). The cost of the meal was $56. The teenagers decided not to pay. They went out of the building, got in their car, and drove away, heading northward up Route 1.

A patron of the restaurant saw the teenagers leave without payment. He followed them in his white sport-utility vehicle (SUV). The teenagers saw him following them. A high-speed chase ensued through Dedham side streets. The patron used his cell phone to call the Chili's manager. The manager called 911 and reported the incident and the location of the car chase. The teenagers' car collided with a cement wall, and Bosse and Griffin were seriously injured. The Chili's patron drove past the crash scene and was never identified.

Bosse and Griffin sued Chili's for compensatory damages for their injuries. The plaintiffs argued that the patron was an agent of Chili's, and therefore Chili's was liable to the plaintiffs, based on the doctrine of *respondeat superior*, which holds a principal liable for the acts of its agents. Chili's filed a motion for summary judgment, arguing that the patron was not its agent.

Issue

Was the restaurant patron who engaged in the high-speed car chase an agent of Chili's?

Language of the Court

The plaintiffs sue under the theory of respondeat superior. They contend that the Chili's patron converted to a Chili's servant; that he conducted the chase as an agent of the restaurant; and that the restaurant should be liable for the consequences of his negligent or reckless pursuit. An agency relationship will require three elements. Most obviously, Chili's must have consented to the

action of the patron on its behalf. Second, Chili's must have retained control, or the right of control, over the physical conduct of the patron in the performance of the pursuit. Third, the conduct of the agent must serve the benefit or further the interest of the principal.

The evidence is insufficient to create a genuine issue whether Chili's appointed or authorized the patron to act as a posse to conduct the chase. No information indicates any preliminary communication between the patron and restaurant manager. The events were spontaneous and fast breaking. No member of Chili's house staff joined in the pursuit. The plaintiffs argue that Chili's effectively assented to an agency relationship by acceptance of the patron's reconnaissance reports during the course of the chase; and by failure to instruct him to break off the chase. That circumstance is not enough. The patron need not have been an agent to engage in that conduct. He was pursuing petty crime. Chili's was reporting the petty crime to the police. No information indicates that Chili's had any effective control over the patron. The dominant purpose of Chili's relay of the patron's reports to the police appears to have been the public interest in the apprehension of petty criminals and not the private recovery of the unpaid bill.

Decision

The superior court held that the restaurant patron who engaged in the high-speed chase in which the plaintiffs were injured was not the agent of Chili's restaurant. The superior court granted summary judgment to Chili's.

Law & Ethics Questions

1. What does the doctrine of *respondeat superior* provide? Explain.

2. Did the elements exist to make the restaurant patron an agent of Chili's restaurant? Explain.

3. **ETHICS** Why do you think the plaintiffs sued Chile's? Do you think it was ethical if they based their decision on their probability of collecting against Chili's?

Web Exercises

1. **WEB** For the complete opinion of this case, go to www.prenhall.com/cheesemancases.

2. **WEB** Visit the website of the superior court of Massachusetts at Suffolk, at www.mass.gov/courts/courtsandjudges/courts/superiorcourt/index.html.

3. **WEB** Visit the website of Chili's Grill & Bar, at www.chilis.com.

4. **WEB** Use www.google.com to find an article or a case in which an agency was not found.

CONTEMPORARY ENVIRONMENT
Power of Attorney

A **power of attorney** is one of the most formal types of express agency agreements. It is often used to give an agent the power to sign legal documents, such as deeds to real estate, on behalf of the principal. There are two kinds of powers of attorney: **general power of attorney**, which confers broad powers on the agent to act in any matters on the principal's behalf; and **special power of attorney**, which limits the agent to those acts specifically enumerated in an agreement. The agent is called an **attorney-in-fact** even though he

or she does not have to be a lawyer. Powers of attorney must be written. Usually, they must also be notarized.

Web Exercises

1. **WEB** Use www.google.com to find a general power of attorney that is effective in your state.

2. **WEB** Use www.google.com to find a special power of attorney that is effective in your state.

Implied Agency

In many situations, a principal and an agent do not expressly create an agency. Instead, the agency is implied from the conduct of the parties. This type of agency is referred to as an **implied agency**. The extent of the agent's authority is determined from the facts and circumstances of the particular situation. Implied authority can be conferred by either industry custom, prior dealing between the parties, the agent's position, acts deemed necessary to carry out the agent's duties, and other factors the court deems relevant. Implied authority cannot conflict with express authority or with stated limitations on express authority.

INCIDENTAL AUTHORITY Often, even an express agency agreement does not provide enough detail to cover contingencies that may arise in the future regarding the performance of the agency. In this case, the agent possesses certain implied authority to act. This implied authority is sometimes referred to as **incidental authority**.

Certain emergency situations may arise in the course of an agency. If the agent cannot contact the principal for instructions, the agent has implied emergency powers to take all actions reasonably necessary to protect the principal's property and rights.

An agent's scope of authority was at issue in the following case.

CASE 25.2	Edgewater Motels, Inc. v. Gatzke and Walgreen Company
Agency	277 N.W.2d 11, **Web** 1979 Minn. Lexis 1381
	Supreme Court of Minnesota

“ *After careful consideration of the issue we are persuaded by the reasoning of the courts that hold that smoking can be an act within an employee's scope of employment.* ”

—Judge Scott

Facts

Arlen Gatzke (Gatzke) was a district manager for the Walgreen Company (Walgreen). Gatzke was sent to Duluth, Minnesota, to supervise the opening of a new Walgreen store. In Duluth, Gatzke stayed at the Edgewater Motel (Edgewater). While in Duluth, Gatzke was "on call" 24 hours a day to other Walgreen stores located in his territory. About midnight one evening, Gatzke, after working 17 hours that day, went with several other Walgreen employees to a restaurant and bar to drink. Within one hour's time. Gatzke had consumed three doubles and one single brandy Manhattan. About 1:30 A.M., he went back to the Edgewater Motel and filled out his expense report. Soon thereafter, a fire broke out in Gatzke's motel room. Gatzke escaped, but the fire spread and caused extensive damage to the motel. Evidence showed that Gatzke smoked two packs of cigarettes a day. An expert fire reconstruction witness testified that the fire started from a lit cigarette in or next to the wastepaper basket in Gatzke's room. Edgewater sued Gatzke and Walgreen. The damage to the Edgewater Motel was $330,360. The jury returned a verdict against defendants Gatzke and Walgreen. The court granted Walgreen's posttrial motion for judgment notwithstanding the verdict. Plaintiff Edgewater and defendant Gatzke appealed.

Issue

Was Gatzke's act of smoking within his "scope of employment," making his principal, the Walgreen Company, vicariously liable for his negligence?

Language of the Court

After careful consideration of the issue we are persuaded by the reasoning of the courts that hold that smoking can be an act within an employee's scope of employment. It seems only logical to conclude that an employee does not abandon his employment as a matter of law while temporarily acting for his personal comfort when such activities involve only slight deviations from work that are reasonable under the circumstances. We hold that an employer can be held vicariously liable for his employee's negligent smoking of a cigarette if he was otherwise acting in the scope of his employment at the time of the negligent act.

The record contains a reasonable basis from which a jury could find that Gatzke was involved in serving his employer's interests at the time he was at the bar. Gatzke testified that, while at the restaurant and bar, he discussed the operation of the newly opened Walgreen's store with other Walgreen employees. Additionally, the record indicates that Gatzke was an executive type of employee who had no set working hours. He considered himself a 24-hour-a-day man; his room at the Edgewater Motel was his "office away from home." It was therefore also reasonable for the jury to determine that the filling out of his expense account was done within authorized time and space limits of his employment.

Decision

The supreme court of Minnesota held that Gatzke's negligent act of smoking was within the scope of his employment while acting as an employee of the Walgreen Company. The supreme court reinstated the jury's verdict awarding damages to plaintiff Edgewater Motels, Inc.

Law & Ethics Questions

1. **ETHICS** Should smoking cigarettes be held to be within an employee's scope of employment? Why or why not?

2. **ETHICS** Do employers owe a duty to police the personal habits of their employees?

3. **ETHICS** Because of the dangers of smoking, would employers be justified in hiring only nonsmokers as employees?

Web Exercises

1. **WEB** For the complete opinion of this case, go to *www.prenhall.com/cheesemancases*.

2. **WEB** Visit the website of the supreme court of Minnesota, at *www.mncourts.gov/?page=550*.

3. **WEB** Visit the website of Duluth, Minnesota, at *www.visitduluth.com*.

4. **WEB** Use *www.google.com* to find an article that discusses the formation of an agency. Read it.

Apparent Agency

Apparent agency (or **agency by estoppel**) arises when a principal creates the appearance of an agency that in actuality does not exist. Where an apparent agency is established, the principal is estopped from denying the agency relationship and is bound to contracts entered into by the apparent agent while acting within the scope of the apparent agency. Note that the principal's actions—not the agent's—create an apparent agency.

Example Suppose Georgia Pacific, Inc., interviews Albert Iorio for a sales representative position. Mr. Iorio, accompanied by Jane Franklin, the national sales manager, visits retail stores located in the open sales territory. While visiting one store, Jane tells the store manager, "I wish I had more sales reps like Albert." Nevertheless, Albert is not hired. If Albert later enters into contracts with the store on behalf of Georgia Pacific and Jane has not controverted the impression of Albert she left with the store manager, the company will be bound to the contract.

ETHICS SPOTLIGHT
Apparent Agency

❝The uniformity of signs, design and color schemes easily lead the public to believe that each motor lodge is under common ownership or conforms to common standards, and the jury could find they are intended to do so.❞

—Judge Orfinger

Franchising has become a major form of conducting business in the United States. In a franchise agreement, one company (called the franchisor) licenses another company (called the franchisee) to use its trade name, trademarks and service marks, and trade secrets. Many fast-food restaurants, gasoline stations, motels and hotels, and other businesses operate in this fashion.

The franchisor and franchisee are independently owned businesses. A principal–agent relationship usually is not created by the franchise. If no express or implied agency is created, the franchisor would not normally be civilly liable for the tortious conduct (e.g., negligence) of the franchisee. Liability could be imposed on the franchisor, however, if an apparent agency were shown. Consider the following case.

Howard Johnson International (HJ) operates a chain of hotels, motels, and restaurants across the United States. Approximately 75 percent of the HJ motor lodges are owned and operated by franchisees that are licensed by HJ to do business under the "Howard Johnson" trade name and trademarks. The rest are company owned.

Orlando Executive Park, Inc. (OEP), is a corporate franchisee that owns and operates an HJ motor lodge franchise in Orlando, Florida. The motor lodge is part of a large complex known as "Howard Johnson's Plaza," located off Interstate 4. The motor lodge contains approximately 300 guest rooms in six separate buildings.

P.D.R. (name withheld by the court), a 35-year-old married woman and mother of a small child, worked as a supervisor for a restaurant chain. Her work occasionally required her to travel and stay overnight in Orlando. On October 22, 1975, P.D.R. stopped to stay at the HJ motor lodge in Orlando. At approximately 9:30 P.M., P.D.R. registered for her previously reserved room at the lodge. The registration form did not inform her that the hotel was an HJ franchisee. P.D.R. parked her car in the motor lodge parking lot and proceeded with her suitcase to her ground-floor room in Building A, which was located directly behind the registration office. P.D.R. then went back to her car to get some papers. After obtaining the papers from her car, P.D.R. returned to Building A. As she proceeded down an interior hallway of the building toward her room, she was accosted by a man she had previously seen standing behind the registration office. The man struck her in the throat and neck and choked her until she became semiconscious. When P.D.R. fell to the floor, her assailant sat on top of her and stripped her of her jewelry. He then dragged her down the hallway and beneath a secluded stairway, where he brutally beat her. The assailant then disappeared into the might and has never been identified.

P.D.R. suffered serious physical and psychological injury, including memory loss, mental confusion, and an inability to tolerate and communicate with people. P.D.R. suffers permanent injury that requires expensive, long-term medical and psychiatric treatment. P.D.R. brought a tort action against OEP and HJ and sought actual and punitive damages against both of them.

Negligence of the Independent Contractor

The jury had little trouble finding that OEP had breached its duty of care and was liable. Evidence showed that other criminal activity had occurred previously on the premises but that OEP failed to warn guests, including P.D.R., of the danger. In fact, OEP management actively discouraged criminal investigations by the sheriff's deputies, thus minimizing any deterrent effect they may have had. Further evidence showed that the dark and secluded stairwell area where P.D.R. was dragged was a security hazard that should have been boarded up or better lit.

Liability of the Principal

The jury also found HJ liable to P.D.R. under the doctrine of apparent agency. The appellate court stated: "While OEP might not be HJ's agent for all purposes, the signs, national advertising, uniformity of building design and color schemes allow the public to assume that this and other similar motor lodges are under the same ownership. An HJ official testified that it was the HJ marketing strategy to appear as a 'chain that sells a product across the nation.'" The court continued, "There was sufficient evidence for the jury to reasonably conclude that HJ represented to the traveling public that it could expect a particular level of service at a Howard Johnson Motor Lodge. The uniformity of signs, design and color schemes easily lead the public to believe that each motor lodge is under common ownership or conforms to common standards, and the jury could find they are intended to do so." The appellate court upheld an award of $750,000 compensatory damages against OEP and HJ jointly. *Orlando Executive Park, Inc. v. P.D.R.*, 402 So.2d 442, **Web** 1981 Fla. App. Lexis 20565 (Court of Appeal of Florida)

Law & Ethics Questions

1. Should the doctrine of apparent agency be recognized by law?

2. Should the Howard Johnson have been found liable in this case? Explain.

3. **ETHICS** Is it ethical for a franchisor to have its system of franchise outlets contain the franchisor's name but then try to avoid liability of its franchisees? Explain.

1. **WEB** For the complete opinion of this case, go to *www.prenhall.com/cheesemancases*.

2. **WEB** Visit the website of the court of appeals of Florida, Fifth District, at *www.5dca.org*.

3. **WEB** Visit the website of Howard Johnson International, at *www.hojo.com*. Can you find any information about franchise opportunities?

4. **WEB** Use *www.google.com* to find an article or a case that discusses the doctrine of apparent agency. Read it.

Agency by Ratification

Agency by ratification occurs when (1) a person misrepresents himself or herself as another's agent when in fact he or she is not and (2) the purported principal ratifies (accepts) the unauthorized act. In such cases, the principal is bound to perform, and the agent is relieved of any liability for misrepresentation.

Example Bill Levine sees a house for sale and thinks his friend Sherry Maxwell would want it. Bill Levine enters into a contract to purchase the house from the seller and signs the contract "Bill Levine, agent for Sherry Maxwell." Because Bill is not Sherry Maxwell's agent, she is not bound to the contract. However, if Sherry agrees to purchase the house, there is an agency by ratification. The ratification "relates back" to the moment Bill Levine entered into the contract. Upon ratification of the contract, Sherry Maxwell is obligated to purchase the house.

CONCEPT SUMMARY

Formation of Agency Relationships

TYPE OF AGENCY	FORMATION	ENFORCEMENT OF THE CONTRACT
Express	Authority is expressly given to the agent by the principal.	Principal and third party are bound to the contract.
Implied	Authority is implied from the conduct of the parties, custom and usage of trade, or act incidental to carrying out the agent's duties.	Principal and third party acts are bound to the contract.
Apparent	Authority is created when the principal leads a third party to believe that the agent has authority.	Principal and third party are bound to the contract.
By ratification	Acts of the agent are committed outside the scope of his or her authority.	Principal and third party are not bound to the contract unless the principal ratifies the contract.

Principal's Duty of Compensation

A principal owes a **duty to compensate** an agent for services provided. Usually, the agency contract (whether written or oral) specifies the compensation to be paid. The principal must pay this amount either upon the completion of the agency or at some other mutually agreeable time.

If there is no agreement as to the amount of compensation, the law implies a promise that the principal will pay the agent the customary fee paid in the industry. If the compensation cannot be established by custom, the principal owes a duty to pay the reasonable value of the agent's services.

There is no duty to compensate a gratuitous agent. However, gratuitous agents who agree to provide their services free of charge may be paid voluntarily.

Certain types of agents traditionally perform their services on a **contingency-fee basis**. Under this type of arrangement, the principal owes a duty to pay the agent the agreed-upon contingency fee only if the agency is completed.

Example Real estate brokers, finders, lawyers, and salespersons often work on a contingency-fee basis.

Principal's Duties of Reimbursement and Indemnification

In carrying out an agency, an agent may spend his or her own money on the principal's behalf. Unless otherwise agreed, the principal owes a **duty to reimburse** the agent for all such expenses if they were (1) authorized by the principal, (2) within the scope of the agency, and (3) necessary to discharge the agent's duties in carrying out the agency.

Example A principal must reimburse an agent for authorized business trips taken on the principal's behalf.

A principal also owes a **duty to indemnify** the agent for any losses the agent suffers because of the principal. This duty usually arises where an agent is held liable for the principal's misconduct.

Example Suppose an agent enters into an authorized contract with a third party on the principal's behalf, the principal fails to perform on the contract, and the third party recovers a judgment against the agent. The agent can recover indemnification of this amount from the principal.

Principal's Duty of Cooperation

Unless otherwise agreed, the principal owes a **duty to cooperate** with and assist the agent in the performance of the agent's duties and the accomplishment of the agency. For example, unless otherwise agreed, a principal who employs a real estate agent to sell her house owes a duty to allow the agent to show the house to prospective purchasers during reasonable hours.

Agent's Duty of Performance

An agent who enters into a contract with a principal has two distinct obligations: (1) to perform the lawful duties expressed in the contract and (2) to meet the standards of reasonable care, skill, and diligence implicit in all contracts. Collectively, these duties are referred to as the agent's **duty of performance**.

Normally, an agent is required to render the same standard of care, skill, and diligence that a fictitious reasonable agent in the same occupation would render in the same locality and under the same circumstances.

Example A general medical practitioner in a rural area would be held to the standard of a reasonable general practitioner in rural areas. The standard might be different for a general medical practitioner in a big city. In some professions, such as accounting, a national standard of performance (such as the "generally accepted accounting principles") is imposed. If an agent holds himself or herself as possessing higher-than-customary skills, the agent will be held to that higher standard of performance. For example, a lawyer who claims to be a specialist in securities law will be held to a reasonable specialist-in-securities-law standard.

An agent who does not perform his or her express duties or fails to use the standard degree of care, skill, or diligence is liable to the principal for breach of contract. An agent who has negligently or intentionally failed to perform properly is also liable in tort.

Agent's Duty of Notification

In the course of an agency, the agent usually learns information that is important to the principal. This information may come from third parties or other sources. The agent's duty to notify the principal of such information is called the **duty of notification**. The agent is liable to the principal for any injuries resulting from a breach of this duty.

IMPUTED KNOWLEDGE Most information learned by an agent in the course of an agency is **imputed** to the principal. This means that the principal is assumed to know what the agent knows. This is so even if the agent does not tell the principal certain relevant information.

Agent's Duty of Accountability

Unless otherwise agreed, an agent owes a duty to maintain an accurate accounting of all transactions undertaken on the principal's behalf. This **duty of accountability** includes keeping records of all property and money received and expended during the course of the agency. A principal has a right to demand an accounting from the agent at any time, and the agent owes a legal duty to make the accounting. This duty also requires the agent to (1) maintain a separate account for the principal and (2) use the principal's property in an authorized manner.

Any property, money, or other benefit received by the agent in the course of an agency belongs to the principal. For example, all secret profits received by an agent are the property of the principal. If an agent breaches the agency contract, the principal can sue the agent to recover damages caused by breach. The court can impose a *constructive trust* on any secret profits on property purchased with secret profits for the benefit of the principal.

Agent's Duty of Loyalty to the Principal

Because the agency relationship is based on trust and confidence, an agent owes the principal a **duty of loyalty** in all agency-related matters. Thus, an agent owes a fiduciary duty not to act adversely to the interests of the principal. If this duty is breached, the agent is liable to the principal. The most common types of breaches of loyalty by an agent are discussed in the following paragraphs.

SELF-DEALING Agents are generally prohibited from undisclosed **self-dealing** with the principal.

Example A real estate agent who is employed to purchase real estate for a principal cannot secretly sell his or her own property in the transaction. However, the deal is lawful if the principal agrees to buy the property after the agent discloses his or her ownership.

USURPING AN OPPORTUNITY An agent cannot **usurp an opportunity** that belongs to the principal.

Example A third-party offer to an agent must be conveyed to the principal. The agent cannot appropriate the opportunity for himself or herself unless the principal rejects it after due consideration. Opportunities to purchase real estate, businesses, products, ideas, and other property are subject to this rule.

COMPETING WITH THE PRINCIPAL Agents are prohibited from **competing with the principal** during the course of an agency unless the principal agrees. The reason for this rule is that an agent cannot meet his or her duty of loyalty when his or her personal interests conflict with the principal's interests. If the parties have not entered into an enforceable covenant-not-to-compete, an agent is free to compete with the principal when the agency has ended.

MISUSE OF CONFIDENTIAL INFORMATION In the course of an agency, the agent often acquires confidential information about the principal's affairs (e.g., business plans, technological innovations, customer lists, trade secrets). The agent is under a legal duty not to disclose or misuse such information either during or after the course of the agency. There is no prohibition against using general information, knowledge, or experience acquired during the course of the agency.

DUAL AGENCY An agent cannot meet a duty of loyalty to two parties with conflicting interests. **Dual agency** occurs when an agent acts for two or more different principals in the same transaction. This practice is generally prohibited unless all the parties involved in the transaction agree to it. If an agent acts as an undisclosed dual agent, he or she must forfeit all compensation received in the transaction. Some agents, such as middlemen and finders, are not considered dual agents. This is because they only bring interested parties together; they do not take part in any negotiations.

Grand Hotel, Mackinac Island, Michigan

This hotel, as the employer, is liable for injuries caused by the negligent acts of its employees that are committed while the employees are acting within their scope of employment.

Tort Liability to Third Parties

A principal and an agent are each personally liable for their own tortious conduct. The principal is liable for the tortious conduct of an agent who is acting within the scope of his or her authority. The agent, however, is liable for the tortious conduct of the principal only if he or she directly or indirectly participates in or aids and abets the principal's conduct.

The courts have applied a broad and flexible standard in interpreting scope of authority in the context of employment. Although other factors may also be considered, the courts rely on the following factors to determine whether an agent's conduct occurred within the scope of his or her employment:

- Was the act specifically requested or authorized by the principal?
- Was it the kind of act that the agent was employed to perform?
- Did the act occur substantially within the time period of employment authorized by the principal?
- Did the act occur substantially within the location of employment authorized by the employer?
- Was the agent advancing the principal's purpose when the act occurred?

Where liability is found, tort remedies are available to the injured party. These remedies include recovery for medical expenses, lost wages, pain and suffering, emotional distress, and, in some cases, punitive damages. As discussed in the following paragraphs, the three main sources of **tort liability** for principals and agents are negligence, intentional torts, and misrepresentation.

Negligence

Principals are liable for the negligent conduct of agents acting within the scope of their employment. This liability is based on the common law doctrine of *respondeat superior* ("let the master answer"), which, in turn, is based on the legal theory of **vicarious liability**

(liability without fault). In other words, the principal is liable because of his or her employment contract with the negligent agent, not because the principal was personally at fault.

The doctrine of **negligence** rests on the principle that if someone (i.e., the principal) expects to derive certain benefits from acting through others (i.e., an agent), that person should also bear the liability for injuries caused to third persons by the negligent conduct of an agent who is acting within the scope of his or her employment.

In the following case, the court had to decide whether an employer was liable for the negligent conduct of an employee.

CASE 25.3
Negligence

Keating v. Goldick and Lapp Roofing and Sheet Metal Company, Inc.

Web 2004 Del. Super. Lexis 102 (2004)
Superior Court of Delaware

> 66 *There comes a point in every litigation where common sense will make some conclusions obvious.* 99

—Judge Carpenter

Facts

Lapp Roofing and Sheet Metal Company, Inc., is an Ohio corporation headquartered in Dayton, Ohio. The company provides construction services in several states. Lapp Roofing sent James Goldick and other Lapp Roofing employees to work on a roofing project in Wilmington, Delaware. Lapp Roofing's company policy prohibited employees from driving company vehicles for personal purposes. Lapp Roofing entrusted Goldick, as job foreman, with a white Ford van to transport the workers to the job site and to provide transportation to meals and other necessities.

While in Wilmington, Goldick and another Lapp Roofing employee, James McNees, went to Gators Bar and Restaurant. Goldick, after eating and drinking for several hours, was ejected from the bar. Shortly thereafter, Goldick drove the company van onto the curb in front of the bar, striking two people in the parking lot and seven individuals on the curb outside the bar. Subsequently, the police stopped the van and apprehended Goldick. Goldick was arrested and pleaded guilty to criminal assault charges. Christopher M. Keating and the other injured individuals filed a personal injury lawsuit against Goldick and Lapp Roofing. Lapp Roofing defended, alleging that it was not liable because Goldick's negligent conduct was committed outside the scope of his employment.

Issue

Was Goldick's negligent conduct committed within the scope of his employment for Lapp Roofing?

Language of the Court

There comes a point in every litigation where common sense will make some conclusions obvious. If the injured plaintiffs were not involved in this litigation and were simply asked whether they believe that an individual who used an employer's truck late at night to go to a bar and consume alcohol was acting within the scope of that employer's employment, they would without hesitation say no. Logic and common sense would lead any reasonable person to the same conclusion.

One could argue that sending a work crew from Ohio with only a work truck as transportation would be sufficient deviation. To a degree, the court agrees this allows the range of covered conduct to be explained. Obviously a crew who is assigned for several days or weeks to a remote location will need to utilize the company vehicle to get meals or other necessities associated with that stay. Therefore, if this event had occurred as the employees were leaving Happy Harry's after they obtained a needed prescription or from Denny's Restaurant after a meal, the court believes these foreseeable and logical consequences of a lengthy stay away from home would bring the conduct within the scope of employment under the dual purpose rationale.

However, no reasonable person could conclude this limitation on available transportation would provide the mechanism to expand the coverage to a drunken brawl that occurred after hours and was unassociated with the employee's work or associated with his stay. Such conduct is so adverse to the employer that no conceivable benefit could be derived. It is completely unrelated to the employer's business and does not advance the work for which the employees were sent to this location. Here, Goldick used the van to go drinking with another employee and drove the van in the parking lot and on the curb injuring various individuals. No jury could reasonably conclude that Goldick's conduct was actuated, even in part, by a purpose to serve his employer. This incident did not occur during working hours and Goldick decided to go to Gators and become intoxicated for purely personal reasons and not to serve Lapp Roofing's interests whatsoever.

Decision

The superior court held that Goldick was not acting within the course and scope of his employment when his negligent conduct occurred. The superior court granted summary judgment to Lapp Roofing on this issue.

Law & Ethics Questions

1. Why was Lapp Roofing found not liable in this case? Explain.

2. If the negligent conduct would have occurred when Goldick was driving to a restaurant for a meal, would the decision have been the same?

3. **ETHICS** Did Lapp Roofing act ethically in denying liability for the negligent conduct of one of its employees?

Web Exercises

1. **WEB** For the complete opinion of this case, go to *www.prenhall.com/cheesemancases*.

2. **WEB** Visit the website of the superior court of Delaware, New Castle, at *www.courts.delaware.gov/Courts/Superior%20Court*.

3. **WEB** Use *www.google.com* to find an article or a case that imposes liability on an employer for negligent conduct of its employee. Read it.

FROLIC AND DETOUR Agents sometimes do things during the course of their employment to further their own interests rather than the principal's. For example, an agent might take a detour to run a personal errand while on assignment for the principal. This is commonly referred to as a **frolic and detour**. Negligence actions stemming from frolic and detour are examined on a case-by-case basis. Agents are always personally liable for their tortious conduct in such situations. Principals are generally relieved of liability if the agent's frolic and detour is substantial. However, if the deviation is minor, the principal is liable for the injuries caused by the agent's tortious conduct.

Example A salesperson stops home for lunch while on an assignment for his principal. While leaving his home, the agent hits and injures a pedestrian with his automobile. The principal would be liable if the agent's home were not too far out of the way from the agent's assignment. However, the principal would not be liable if an agent who is supposed to be on assignment to Los Angeles flies to San Francisco to meet a friend and is involved in an accident. The facts and circumstances of each case determine its outcome.

In the following case involves the frolic and detour rule.

CASE **25.4**
Frolic and Detour

Siegenthaler v. Johnson Welded Products, Inc.

2006 Ohio 5588, **Web** 2006 Ohio App. Lexis 5616 (2006)
Court of Appeals of Ohio

> "No reasonable finder of fact could find from this evidence that Spires was subject to the direction and control of Johnson Welded Products as to the operation of his truck at the time of the collision, while he was on his way to a friend's house for lunch."
>
> —Judge Fain

Facts

Jesse Spires was employed as a welder by Johnson Welded Products, Inc. Johnson Welded Products provides a lunchroom equipped with microwave, refrigerator, and vending machine for sandwiches, snacks, and drinks. Spires worked a shift that ran from 3:15 P.M. until 12:15 A.M. One day at work, Spires was on his way to a friend's house for lunch during his lunch break, driving his own pickup truck, when he collided with Donald Siegenthaler, who was riding a motorcycle. The collision, which was the result of Spires's negligence, caused injury to Siegenthaler.

Siegenthaler sued Johnson Welded Products, alleging that Spires was an agent of Johnson Welded Products at the time of the accident and that Johnson Welded Products was vicariously liable under the doctrine of *respondeat superior*. Johnson Welded Products argued that

Spires was on personal business when he caused the accident. The trial court granted Johnson Welded Products's motion for summary judgment. Siegenthaler appealed.

Issue

Was Spires an agent of Johnson Welded Products, acting within the scope of his employment, at the time of the accident that injured Siegenthaler?

Language of the Court

Under the doctrine of respondeat superior, an employer will be held liable for the negligent act of its employee if the employee was acting within the course and scope of his employment. No reasonable finder of fact could find from this evidence that Spires was subject to the direction and control of Johnson Welded Products as to the operation of his truck at the time of the collision, while he was on his way to a friend's house for lunch.

There is nothing in this record to suggest that Spires's contract of employment with Johnson Welded Products purported to give Johnson Welded Products the right to control the manner in which Spires would drive his own vehicle to or from work, and the only reasonable inference is that Johnson Welded Products had no right to control Spires's conduct in that matter. We can see no reason why Johnson Welded Products would have any desire to control the manner in which its employees drive to or from work.

Decision

The court of appeals held that Spires was not acting within his scope of employment when he collided with and injured Siegenthaler. The court of appeals affirmed the trial court's grant of summary judgment to Johnson Welded Products.

Law & Ethics Questions

1. What does the doctrine of *respondeat superior* provide? Explain.
2. What does the doctrine of frolic and detour provide? Explain.
3. How important is the element of control in determining whether an employee is acting within the scope of his or her employment?
4. Could Siegenthaler recover from Spires? If so, under what legal theory?
5. **ETHICS** Did Siegenthaler act ethically in bringing this case against Johnson Welded Products?

Web Exercises

1. **WEB** For the complete opinion of this case, go to *www.prenhall.com/cheesemancases*.
2. **WEB** Visit the website of the court of appeals of Ohio, Second Appellate District, Clark County, at *www.sconet.state.oh.us/District_Courts/Districts/dc02.asp*.
3. **WEB** Use *www.google.com* to find an article or a case that discusses the doctrine of frolic and detour. Read it.

COMING AND GOING RULE Under the common law, a principal is generally not liable for injuries caused by its agents and employees while they are on their way to or from work. This so-called **coming and going rule** applies even if the principal supplies the agent's automobile or other transportation or pays for gasoline, repairs, and other automobile operating expenses. This rule is quite logical. Because principals do not control where their agents and employees live, they should not be held liable for tortious conduct of agents on their way to and from work.

In the following case, the court applied the coming and going rule.

CASE 25.5
Coming and Going Rule

American National Property and Casualty Company v. Farah

2006 Ohio 5519, **Web** 2006 Ohio App. Lexis 5496 (2006)
Court of Appeals of Ohio

> **"**Therefore, the trial court applied the coming and going rule and determined that Morgenstern was not in the course of his company's business at the time of the accident.**"**
>
> —Judge Klatt

Facts

Daniel J. Morgenstern was a licensed chiropractor and owned and was the sole shareholder of Daniel J. Morgenstern, D.C., Inc., d.b.a. Morning Star Chiropractic. He treats patients in an office located in Gahanna, Ohio. One day when he did not have any scheduled appointments, he planned on meeting his wife at her sister's house. Around 11:00 A.M., Morgenstern drove to a restaurant for lunch. After having lunch, he headed toward his sister-in-law's house. On the way, he stopped at a grocery store in Columbus, Ohio. After leaving the store, his lunch began to "weigh a little heavy" on his stomach, so he decided to go to his office to take some nutrients for his stomach. On the way, Morgenstern collided with Ayan Farah's automobile. Farah was seriously injured as a result of the collision. Farah sued Morgenstern personally as well as his company, alleging that Morgenstern's negligence caused her injuries and that the company was vicariously liable.

American National Property and Casualty Company (ANPAC) insured Morgenstern personally for $250,000 for liability and insured the company for $1 million for liability. ANPAC filed a declaratory judgment action to resolve its insurance liability. ANPAC conceded that Morgenstern's $250,000 personal liability automobile insurance policy provided Farah with coverage. ANPAC argued, however, that its $1 million commercial automobile policy on the company did not cover Farah because Morgenstern was not acting in the scope of his employment when the accident happened. ANPAC argued that the coming and going rule protected it from liability. The trial court agreed with ANPAC and entered judgment in favor of ANPAC. Farah appealed.

Issue

Did the coming and going rule protect the company, and therefore ANPAC, from liability to Farah?

Language of the Court

In determining whether an employee has a fixed place of employment, and therefore is subject to the coming and going rule, courts have focused on when and where the employee commences his substantial employment duties. If an employee commences substantial employment duties only after arriving at a specific and identifiable work place designated by the employer, the employee has a fixed place of employment and the coming and going rule applies. In the case at bar, the trial court found that Morgenstern has a fixed place of employment. Therefore, the trial court applied the coming and going rule and determined that Morgenstern was not in the course of his company's business at the time of the accident. Consequently, there was no coverage under the company's commercial policy. We agree.

In the normal context, an employee's commute to a fixed work site bears no meaningful relation to his employment contract and serves no purpose of the employer's business. Morgenstern was driving to his office primarily because he did not feel well. Simply because he was listening to an audiotape

of his lecture notes at the time of the accident does not change the fundamental character of the drive to his office. In conclusion, Morgenstern was driving to his Gahanna office at the time of the accident. That office was a fixed place of employment for Morgenstern. Thus, under the coming and going rule, he was not in the course of his company's business when he collided with appellant. Accordingly, ANPAC's commercial policy does not provide Morgenstern with coverage.

Decision

The court of appeals held that Morgenstern was not acting within the course of the company's business when he collided with Farah, and that the coming and going rule applied. The court of appeals affirmed the trial court's judgment, which held that ANPAC's $1 million commercial policy insuring the company was not available to Farah's claims.

Law & Ethics Questions

1. What does the coming and going rule provide? Explain.
2. What is the public policy that supports the coming and going rule?
3. Why did the injured victim, Farah, want Morgenstern to be found to be acting in the scope of the company's employment when the accident happened?
4. Did Morgenstern want to be found to have been acting within the scope of his company's employment when the accident happened? Why or why not?
5. **ETHICS** Was it unethical for ANPAC to deny coverage on its commercial insurance policy?

Web Exercises

1. **WEB** For the complete opinion of this case, go to *www.prenhall.com/cheesemancases.*
2. **WEB** Visit the website of the court of appeals of Ohio, Tenth Appellate District, Franklin County, at *www.franklincountyohio.gov/appeals.*
3. **WEB** Visit the website of the American National Property and Casualty Company, at *www.anpac.com.*
4. **WEB** Use *www.google.com* to find an article or a case that discusses the coming and going rule. Read it.

DUAL-PURPOSE MISSION Sometimes, principals request that agents run errands or conduct other acts on their behalf while the agent or employee is on personal business. In this case, the agent is on a **dual-purpose mission**. That is, he or she is acting partly for himself or herself and partly for the principal. Most jurisdictions hold both the principal and the agent liable if the agent injures someone while on such a mission.

Example Suppose a principal asks an employee to drop off a package at a client's office on the employee's way home. If the employee negligently injures a pedestrian while on this dual-purpose mission, the principal is liable to the pedestrian.

Intentional Torts

Intentional torts include such acts as assault, battery, false imprisonment, and other intentional conduct that causes injury to another person. A principal is not liable for the intentional torts of agents and employees that are committed outside the principal's scope of business.

For example, if an employee attends a sporting event after working hours and gets into a fight with another spectator at the event, the employer is not liable.

However, a principal is liable under the doctrine of vicarious liability for intentional torts of agents and employees committed within the agent's scope of employment. The courts generally apply one of the following tests in determining whether an agent's intentional torts were committed within the agent's scope of employment:

- ■ *Motivation test.* Under the **motivation test**, if the agent's motivation in committing an intentional tort is to promote the principal's business, the principal is liable for any injury caused by the tort. However, if an agent's motivation in committing the intentional tort is personal, the principal is not liable, even if the tort takes place during business hours or on business premises. For example, a principal is not liable if his agent was motivated by jealousy to beat up someone on the job who dated her boyfriend.
- ■ *Work-related test.* Some jurisdictions have rejected the motivation test as too narrow. These jurisdictions apply the **work-related test** instead. Under this test, if an agent commits an intentional tort within a work-related time or space—for example, during working hours or on the principal's premises—the principal is liable for any injuries caused by the agent's intentional torts. Under this test, the agent's motivation is immaterial.

In the following two cases, the court had to determine whether an employer was liable for an agent's intentional tort.

CASE 25.6
Intentional Tort

Desert Cab Inc. v. Marino

823 P.2d 898, **Web** 1992 Nev. Lexis 6
Supreme Court of Nevada

> ❝ *A finding that Edwards committed a wrongful act by attacking Marino is a prerequisite to imposing liability upon Desert Cab.* ❞
>
> —Judge Mowbray

Facts

Maria Marino, a cab driver with Yellow-Checkered Cab Company (Yellow Cab), and James Edwards, a cab driver with Desert Cab Inc. (Desert Cab), parked their cabs at the taxicab stand at the Sundance Hotel and Casino in Las Vegas to await fares. Marino's cab occupied the first position in the line, and Edwards's cab occupied the third. As Marino stood alongside her cab conversing with the driver of another taxi, Edwards began verbally harassing her from inside his cab. When Marino approached Edwards to inquire as to the reason for the harassment, a verbal argument ensued. Edwards jumped from his cab, grabbed Marino by her neck and shoulders, began choking her, and threw her in front of his taxicab. A bystander pulled Edwards off Marino and escorted her back to her cab. Marino sustained injuries that rendered her unable to work for a time. Edwards was convicted of misdemeanor assault and battery. Marino brought a personal injury action against Desert Cab. The jury found Desert Cab liable and awarded Marino $65,000. Desert Cab appealed.

Issue

Is Desert Cab liable for the intentional tort of its employee?

Language of the Court

The district court admitted into evidence the judgment of Edwards' misdemeanor assault and battery conviction. The court found this evidence to conclusively prove Edwards' civil liability to Marino. Edwards' judgment of conviction provides conclusive evidence of his civil liability to Marino.

A finding that Edwards committed a wrongful act by attacking Marino is a prerequisite to imposing liability upon Desert Cab. In order to find Desert Cab liable, Marino still had to establish that Desert Cab was "responsible" for Edwards' conduct. Desert Cab could be found "responsible" only if Marino proved that the attack arose out of the course and scope of Edwards' employment with Desert Cab. We affirm the judgment of the district court.

Decision

The appellate court held that Desert Cab was liable for the intentional tort committed by its employee.

Law & Ethics Questions

1. Should employers be held liable for the intentional torts of their employees?
2. **ETHICS** Did Desert Cab act ethically in denying liability?
3. Should employers give prospective employees psychological examinations to determine whether they have any dangerous propensities?

Web Exercises

1. **WEB** For the complete opinion of this case, go to *www.prenhall.com/cheesemancases*.
2. **WEB** Visit the website of the supreme court of Nevada, at *www.nvsupremecourt.us*.
3. **WEB** Use *www.google.com* to find an article that discusses an employer's liability for the intentional tort of an agent. Read it.

CASE 25.7
Intentional Tort

Massey v. Starbucks Corporation

Web 2004 U.S. Dist. Lexis 12993 (2004)
United States District Court for the Southern District of New York

> ❝*Thus, if the Starbucks employees had assaulted Massey in order to remove her from the premises so that they could close the store on time, they could have been acting within the scope of employment.*❞
>
> —Judge Scheindlin

Facts

Kenya Massey and her fiancée, Raymond Rodriquez, entered a Starbucks coffee shop in Manhattan, New York City. The couple ordered two beverages from Starbucks employee Okang Wilson and paid for the drinks. When Massey and Rodriquez moved toward the seating area while waiting for their drinks to be prepared, Karen Morales, the shift supervisor at the store, told Massey and Rodriquez that they could not sit down because the store was closing. Massey asked Morales what time the store closed, and Morales told her that it closed at 10:00. Massey pointed at a large digital clock across the street that read 9:52. Morales responded that it was 10:00 according to her watch and that she was closing the store.

Massey, who had not yet received her drinks, informed Morales that when she received her drinks, she and Rodriquez intended to sit and enjoy them at Starbucks. Morales instructed Starbucks employee Louis Suriel to cancel Massey's beverage order and refund Massey's money. Massey asked to speak with a manager. Morales identified herself as the manager and told Massey to "get a life." Massey insisted she was not leaving until she could file a complaint about Morales's behavior.

At that point, Starbucks employee Melissa Polanco became involved in the argument. She told Massey, "I get off at ten o'clock, and we can go outside." Rodriquez suggested to Massey that they leave voluntarily, and Massey agreed. Suriel apologized to them as Morales, Polanco, and Wilson held the door open for Massey and

Rodriquez as they exited. The couple walked away from the store while Massey and the employees yelled profanities at each other.

As Massey continued to walk away, Polanco ran after and caught her and punched Massey in the face. Morales then jumped on Massey's back. Massey and Morales fell into a snow bank on the sidewalk, and a physical altercation ensued. A pedestrian passerby finally separated Massey and Morales. Massey's face was bleeding when she got up.

Massey pressed criminal charges against Morales and Polanco the next morning. Morales and Polanco each pleaded guilty to assault. All three Starbucks employees who were involved in the altercation—Morales, Polanco, and Wilson—were terminated by Starbucks. Massey sued Starbucks for damages for the injuries she suffered. Starbucks moved for summary judgment, alleging that the employees were not acting within the scope of their employment when they assaulted Massey.

Issue

Were the Starbucks employees acting within their scope of employment when they assaulted Massey?

Language of the Court

Massey contends that because her assault was sparked by a dispute concerning whether the store should close, the employees were acting in an employment capacity even when they chased Massey down the street. Massey fails to consider that she suffered no damages as a result of the dispute, but only as a result of the assault. Thus, the question for this court is not whether employees were acting within the scope of their employment when they first began arguing with Massey. Rather, the question is whether they were acting within the scope of their employment when they assaulted her. Massey urges this court to view both the dispute and the ensuing assault as one event, centering around the closing of the store. However, several facts lead me to conclude that while the dispute may have started when the employees were acting within the scope of employment; it ended in an assault that was clearly outside of that scope.

First, when Polanco ran after Massey, there was no question that the store was closed and that Massey would not be returning that night. Thus, the employees could not have been motivated by a desire to close the store when they assaulted Massey. Second, Polanco told Massey that she "gets off at ten" at which point they could "go outside." The employees thereby differentiated between the dispute and the subsequent assault, their professional obligations and their personal animosity. Third, the employees made a point of waiting until Massey had left the store before they assaulted her. By holding the door open for Massey and Rodriquez while they exited, the employees indicated to Massey that their roles as employees were different from their roles as assailants.

New York courts have held employers vicariously liable for the intentional torts committed by employees only where the employees intended those actions to benefit their employer. Thus, if the Starbucks employees had assaulted Massey in order to remove her from the premises so that they could close the store on time, they could have been acting within the scope of employment. If that were the case, it would not matter whether the employees' actions were actually in Starbucks's interest, so long as the employees were at least partly motivated by a desire to do their job.

In this case, the employees did not assault Massey as part of their job. They did not attack Massey on the sidewalk to remove her from the store at closing time, or for any other employment-related purpose. In fact, the employees deliberately waited until Massey had voluntarily left the store before they assaulted her. Morales, Polanco, and Wilson were not acting overzealously in executing their assigned tasks. This assault was not the result of poor employee judgment; rather, it was an act committed for purely personal means.

Decision

The U.S. District Court held that the Starbucks employees Morales, Polanco, and Wilson were not acting within the scope of their employment when they assaulted Massey. The U.S. District Court granted Starbucks's motion for summary judgment.

Law & Ethics Questions

1. What is an intentional tort? Explain.

2. When is an employer liable for the intentional torts of its employees?

3. **ETHICS** Did the Starbucks employees act responsibly in this case?

4. **ETHICS** Was plaintiff Massey part of the problem in this case?

Web Exercises

1. **WEB** For the complete opinion of this case, go to *www.prenhall.com/cheesemancases*.

2. **WEB** Visit the website of the U.S. District Court for the Southern District of New York, at *www.nysd.uscourts.gov*.

3. **WEB** Use *www.google.com* to find an article or a case in which an employer has been found liable for an intentional tort of its employee. Read it.

Misrepresentation

Intentional misrepresentations are also known as **fraud** or **deceit**. They occur when an agent makes statements that he or she knows are not true. An **innocent misrepresentation** occurs when an agent negligently makes a misrepresentation to a third party.

A principal is liable for the intentional and innocent misrepresentations made by an agent acting within the scope of employment. The third party can either (1) rescind the contract with the principal and recover any consideration paid or (2) affirm the contract and recover damages.

Example Assume that (1) a car salesman is employed to sell the principal's car and (2) the principal tells the agent that the car was repaired after it was involved in a major accident. If the agent intentionally tells the buyer that the car was never involved in an accident, the agent has made an intentional misrepresentation. Both the principal and the agent are liable for this misrepresentation.

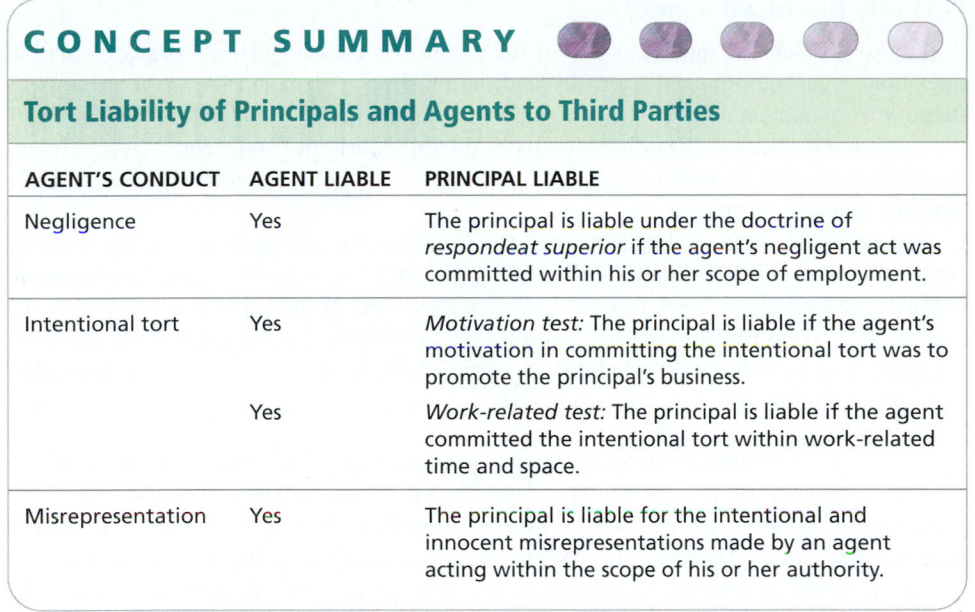

CONCEPT SUMMARY

Tort Liability of Principals and Agents to Third Parties

AGENT'S CONDUCT	AGENT LIABLE	PRINCIPAL LIABLE
Negligence	Yes	The principal is liable under the doctrine of *respondeat superior* if the agent's negligent act was committed within his or her scope of employment.
Intentional tort	Yes	*Motivation test:* The principal is liable if the agent's motivation in committing the intentional tort was to promote the principal's business.
	Yes	*Work-related test:* The principal is liable if the agent committed the intentional tort within work-related time and space.
Misrepresentation	Yes	The principal is liable for the intentional and innocent misrepresentations made by an agent acting within the scope of his or her authority.

Contract Liability to Third Parties

A principal who authorizes an agent to enter into a contract with a third party is liable on the contract. Thus, the third party can enforce the contract against the principal and recover damages from the principal if the principal fails to perform it.

The agent can also be held liable on the contract in certain circumstances. Imposition of such liability depends on whether the agency is classified as fully disclosed, partially disclosed, or undisclosed.

Fully Disclosed Agency

A **fully disclosed agency** results if a third party entering into a contract knows (1) that the agent is acting as an agent for a principal and (2) the actual identity of the principal.[1] The third party has the requisite knowledge if the principal's identity is disclosed to the third party by either the agent or some other source.

In a fully disclosed agency, the contract is between the principal and the third party. Thus, the principal, who is called a **fully disclosed principal**, is liable on the contract. The agent, however, is not liable on the contract because the third party relied on the principal's credit and reputation when the contract was made. An agent is liable on the contract if he or she guarantees that the principal will perform the contract.

The agent's signature on a contract entered into on the principal's behalf is important. It can establish the agent's status and, therefore, his or her liability. For instance, in a fully disclosed agency, the agent's signature must clearly indicate that he or she is acting as an agent for a specifically identified principal. Examples of proper signatures include "Allison Adams, agent for Peter Perceival," "Peter Perceival, by Allison Adams, agent," and "Peter Perceival, by Allison Adams."

Example Poran Kawamara decides to sell her house and hires Mark Robbins, a real estate broker, to list and sell the house for a price of $1 million. They agree that Mark will disclose the existence of the agency and the identity of the principal to interested third parties. This is a fully disclosed agency. Mark shows the house to Heather, a prospective buyer, and discloses to Heather that he is acting as an agent for Poran. Heather makes an offer for the house at the $1 million asking price. Mark signs the contract with Heather on behalf of Poran by signing "Mark Robbins, agent for Poran Kawamara." Poran is liable on the contract with Heather, but Mark is not liable on the contract with Heather.

Partially Disclosed Agency

A **partially disclosed agency** occurs if the agent discloses his or her agency status but does not reveal the principal's identity and the third party does not know the principal's identity from another source. The nondisclosure may be because (1) the principal instructs the agent not to disclose his or her identity to the third party or (2) the agent forgets to tell the third party the principal's identity. In this kind of agency, the principal is called a partially disclosed principal.

In a partially disclosed agency, both the principal and the agent are liable on third-party contracts.[2] This is because the third party must rely on the agent's reputation, integrity, and credit because the principal is unidentified. If the agent is made to pay the contract, the agent can sue the principal for indemnification. The third party and the agent can agree to relieve the agent's liability. A partially disclosed agency can be created either expressly or by mistake.

Example Assume that a principal employs an agent to purchase a business on its behalf. The principal and agent expressly agree that the agent will disclose the existence of the agency to third parties but will not disclose the identity of the principal. The agent finds a business that is for sale, and he discloses to the seller that he is acting as an agent but does not disclose the identity of the principal. The seller agrees to sell the business, and the agent signs "Allison Adams, agent." Here, there is a partially disclosed agency. The principal is liable on the contract with the third-party seller; the agent is also liable on the contract with the third-party seller.

Example Suppose a principal and an agent agree that the agent will represent the principal to purchase a business and that the agent will disclose the existence of the agency and the identity of the principal to third parties; this is a fully disclosed agency. Suppose the agent finds a suitable business for the principal and contracts to purchase the business on behalf of the principal, but the agent mistakenly signs the contract with the third party "Allison Adams, agent." This is a partially disclosed agency that occurs because of mistake. The principal is liable on the contract with the third party, and the agent is also liable.

Undisclosed Agency

An **undisclosed agency** occurs when the third party is unaware of either the existence of an agency or the principal's identity. The principal is called an **undisclosed principal**. Undisclosed agencies are lawful. They are often used when the principal feels that the terms of the contract would be changed if his or her identity were known. For example, a wealthy person may use an undisclosed agency to purchase property if he thinks that the seller would raise the price of the property if his identity were revealed.

In an undisclosed agency, both the principal and the agent are liable on the contract with the third party. This is because the agent, by not divulging that he or she is acting as an agent, becomes a principal to the contract. The third party relies on the reputation and credit of the agent in entering into the contract. If the principal fails to perform the contract, the third party can recover against the principal or the agent. If the agent is made to pay the contract, he or she can recover indemnification from the principal. An undisclosed agency can be created either expressly or by mistake.

Example Assume that The Walt Disney Company wants to open a new theme park in Chicago but needs to first acquire land for the park. Disney employs an agent to work on its behalf to acquire the needed property, with an express agreement that the agent will not disclose the existence of the agency to a third-party seller. If a seller agrees to sell the needed land and the agent signs her name "Allison Adams," without disclosing the existence of the agency, it is an undisclosed agency. Disney is liable on the contract with the third-party seller, and so is the agent.

Example Suppose instead that Disney hires an agent to purchase land on its behalf and they agree that the agent will represent Disney in a fully disclosed agency—that is, the agent is to disclose the existence of the agency and the identity of the principal to the third-party seller. If the agent locates a third-party seller who is willing to enter into a contract to sell the land but the agent mistakenly signs the contract "Allison Adams," without disclosing the agency to the third party, it is an undisclosed agency. Disney is liable on the contract with the third-party seller, and the agent is also liable.

Agent Exceeding the Scope of Authority

An agent who enters into a contract on behalf of another party impliedly warrants that he or she has the authority to do so. This is called the agent's **implied warranty of authority**. If the agent exceeds the scope of his or her authority, the principal is not liable on the contract unless the principal **ratifies** it. The agent, however, is liable to the third party for breaching the implied warranty of authority. To recover, the third party must show (1) reliance on the agent's representation and (2) ignorance of the agent's lack of status.

Example Suppose Sam, Sara, Satchel, Samantha, and Simone form a rock band called SSSSS. SSSSS is just a voluntary association without any legal status. Sam enters into a contract with Rocky's Musical Instruments to purchase instruments and equipment for the band on credit and signs the contract, "Sam, for SSSSS." When SSSSS fails to pay the debt, Rocky's can sue Sam and recover. Sam must pay the debt because he breached his implied warranty of authority when he acted as an agent for a **nonexistent principal**; that is, the purported principal was not a legal entity on which liability could be imposed.

In the following cases, the court had to decide whether a fully disclosed agency had been created.

| C A S E **25.8**
Fully Disclosed Agency | **Collette v. Unique Vacations, Inc.**

2004 Mass. App. Div. 59, **Web** 2004 Mass. App. Div. Lexis 19 (2004)
State of Massachusetts, Appellate Division |  |

> ❝*Unique would not have become a party to any contract made with the Collettes because its principal, Sandals, was disclosed.*❞
>
> —Judge Greco

Facts

Heather Kelly Collette and Kevin Collette visited the Vacation Outlet at Filene's Basement Department Store, where they reviewed vacation packages operated by Sandals Resorts in Jamaica. The Sandals brochure contained a "Blue Chip Hurricane Guarantee" by Sandals that promised a free replacement vacation with round-trip airfare if a hurricane interrupted a customer's stay. The Collettes relied on this guarantee and booked their honeymoon trip to Sandals resorts in Jamaica. The honeymooners were to stay seven days in Jamaica, with their stay split between two Sandals resorts, one at Negril and the other at Montego Bay. The Collettes paid Vacation Outlet for their trip.

Sandals Resorts used Unique Vacations, Inc., to book all of its reservations. Sandals did not provide booking services itself. Unique Vacations was a separate company, and Sandals had no ownership interest in the company. Unique Vacations was identified as the Sandals booking agent in the brochure that the Collettes had read. The

Vacation Outlet booked the Collettes' stay at the Sandals resorts. The Collettes had no interaction with Unique Vacations while making their reservations or during their stay in Jamaica.

The Collettes arrived in Jamaica for their honeymoon. However, Hurricane Mitch hit the island, and because of the hurricane, the Collettes were unable to use many of the facilities at Negril. Three of the four restaurants were closed, and many resort activities were not available. Also, the Collettes were not able to go to the second resort at Montego Bay. Upon their return home, the Collettes contacted Sandals to obtain the guaranteed replacement vacation. Dissatisfied with the result of their contact with Sandals, the Collettes sued Unique Vacations and Vacation Outlet for breach of contract and violation of the Massachusetts Consumer Protection Act; the Collettes did not sue Sandals, and the complaint against Vacation Outlet was dismissed by the court. The Collettes alleged that Unique Vacations was Sandals' agent and as such was therefore liable to them. The trial court found against Unique Vacations and awarded the Collettes $3,922 on their breach of contract claim, treble damages for violation of the Consumer Protection Act, and $26,843 in attorneys' fees. Unique Vacations appealed this decision.

Issue

Is Unique Vacations, Inc., an agent of Sandals that is liable to the Collettes based on the Sandals hurricane guarantee?

Language of the Court

Unique would not have become a party to any contract made with the Collettes because its principal, Sandals, was disclosed. Moreover, there was no evidence that Unique played any role in formulating or offering the "Blue Chip Hurricane Guarantee," that the Collettes dealt directly with Unique in making their decision to go to Sandals, or that they even discussed the "Hurricane Guarantee" with anyone from Unique.

The evidence in the record before us was insufficient to permit the trial judge to disregard the separate corporate identities of Sandals and Unique. The Collettes could never have been deceived by Unique or about Unique's role in their vacation plans. They went to the Vacation Outlet to book a Sandals vacation. It was at the Vacation Outlet that they learned of the "Hurricane Guarantee." They never dealt with Unique, never discussed the Guarantee with anyone from Unique, and had no reason to be aware of the mechanics of the reservation process or to be concerned about it.

Decision

The appellate court held that Unique was a disclosed agent of Sandals and therefore was not liable on the hurricane guarantee made by

Sandals to the Collettes. The appellate court reversed and vacated the trial court's judgment in favor of the Collettes and ordered judgment for Unique.

Law & Ethics Questions

1. What is a fully disclosed agency? What party or parties are liable if the principal breaches a contract with a third person if the name of the principal has been fully disclosed by the agent?

2. Do you think that Sandals Resorts would have been liable in this case if the Collettes had named it as a defendant in this case? Why or why not?

3. **ETHICS** Did any party act unethically in this case? Explain.

4. **ETHICS** Do you think consumers are at a disadvantage in trying to sue for breach of contracts by larger companies? Explain.

Web Exercises

1. **WEB** For the complete opinion of this case, go to *www.prenhall.com/cheesemancases*.

2. **WEB** Visit the website of the state of Massachusetts, Appellate Division, Northern District, at *www.mass.gov/courts/ courtsandjudges/courts/appealscourt*.

3. **WEB** Visit the website of Sandals Resorts, at *www.sandals.com*. Find photos of the two resorts that the Collettes were to stay at on their honeymoon.

4. **WEB** Visit the website *www.jamaica.com* for further information on that country.

CONCEPT SUMMARY

Contract Liability of Principals and Agents to Third Parties

TYPE OF AGENCY	PRINCIPAL LIABLE	AGENT LIABLE
Fully disclosed	Yes	No, unless the agent (1) acts as a principal or (2) guarantees the performance of the contract
Partially disclosed	Yes	Yes, unless the third party relieves the agent's liability
Undisclosed	Yes	Yes
Nonexistent	No, unless the principal ratifies the contract	Yes, the agent is liable for breaching the implied warranty of authority.

Independent Contractor

Principals often employ outsiders—that is, persons and businesses that are not employees—to perform certain tasks on their behalf. These persons and businesses are called **independent contractors**. For example, lawyers, doctors, dentists, consultants, stockbrokers, architects, certified public accountants, real estate brokers, and plumbers are examples of people who commonly act as independent contractors. The party that employs an independent contractor is called a *principal*.

Example Jamie is a lawyer who has her own law firm and specializes in real estate law. Raymond, a real estate developer, hires Jamie to represent him in the purchase of land. Raymond is the principal, and Jamie is the independent contractor.

A principal–independent contractor relationship is depicted in Exhibit 25.2.

Factors for Determining Independent Contractor Status

Section 2 of the *Restatement (Second) of Agency* defines *independent contractor* as "a person who contracts with another to do something for him who is not controlled by the other nor subject to the other's right to control with respect to his physical conduct in the performance of the undertaking." Independent contractors usually work for a number of clients, have their own offices, hire employees, and control the performance of their work.

The crucial factor in determining whether someone is an independent contractor or an employee is the **degree of control** that the principal has over the agent. Critical factors in determining independent contractor status include:

- Whether the worker is engaged in a distinct occupation or an independently established business
- The length of time the agent has been employed by the principal
- The amount of time that the agent works for the principal
- Whether the principal supplies the tools and equipment used in the work
- The method of payment, whether by time or by the job
- The degree of skill necessary to complete the task
- Whether the worker hires employees to assist him or her
- Whether the employer has the right to control the manner and means of accomplishing the desired result

If an examination of these factors shows that the principal asserts little control, the person is an independent contractor. Substantial control indicates an employer–employee relationship. Labeling someone an independent contractor is only one factor in determining whether independent contractor status exists.

Liability for an Independent Contractor's Contracts

A principal can authorize an independent contractor to enter into contracts. Principals are bound by the authorized contracts of their independent contractors. For example, suppose a client hires a lawyer as an independent contractor to represent her in a civil lawsuit against a defendant to recover monetary damages. If the client authorizes the lawyer to settle a case within a certain dollar amount and the lawyer does so, the settlement agreement is binding.

If an independent contractor enters into a contract with a third party on behalf of the principal without express or implied authority from the principal to do so, the principal is not liable on the contract.

Liability for an Independent Contractor's Torts

Generally, a principal is not liable for the torts of its independent contractors. Independent contractors are personally liable for their own torts. The rationale behind this rule is that principals do not control the means by which the results are accomplished.

Example Qixia hires Harold, a lawyer and an independent contractor, to represent her in a court case. While driving to the courthouse to represent Qixia at trial, Harold negligently causes an automobile accident in which Mildred is severely injured. Harold is liable to Mildred because he caused the accident. Qixia is not liable to Mildred because Harold was an independent contractor when he caused the accident.

In the following case, the court applied these factors in order to determine whether an injured worker was an employee or an independent contractor.

EXHIBIT 25.2

Principal–Independent Contractor Relationship

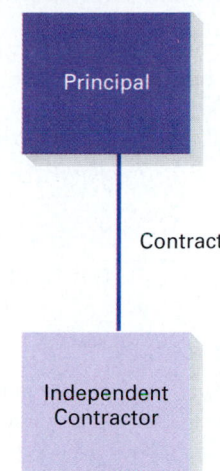

CASE 25.9
Independent Contractor

Torres v. Reardon

3 Cal.App.4th 831, 5 Cal.Rptr.2d 52, **Web** 1992 Cal. App. Lexis 198
Court of Appeal of California

> ❝ *The evidence establishes as a matter of law that Torres was not an employee of the Reardons, but was an independent contractor at the time he was injured.* ❞
>
> —Judge Croskey

Facts

Jose Torres was a self-employed gardener, doing business under the name Jose Torres Gardening Service. For four years, Torres performed weekly general gardening services at several homes in Torrance, California, including the home of Michael and Ona Reardon (Reardons). One day, the Reardons employed Torres to trim a 70-foot-tall tree located in their front yard. At 11:00 A.M. on the morning on the scheduled day, Torres arrived at the Reardons' home with one helper. The Reardons were not at home. David Boice, Reardons' next-door neighbor, cautioned Torres to take care in cutting a large branch 25 feet from the ground that overhung the roof of Boice's house.

When Torres was ready to cut the branch, Boice came outside to hold a rope that was tied to the branch, with the intention of pulling the branch away from his house as it fell. Torres positioned himself on the branch next to the trunk and began to cut at a point just beyond where he was standing. According to Torres, Boice pulled on the rope when Torres was not expecting a pull. As a result, Torres's chain saw "kicked back," and Torres fell from the tree, landing on his back. Torres was rendered a paraplegic as a result of his fall.

Torres sued the Reardons to recover for his injuries, alleging that they were his employer and he was their employee and therefore could recover from them for failing to provide him with workers' compensation insurance. The Reardons countered this argument by saying that Torres was an independent contractor to whom they were not liable. The trial court agreed with the Reardons and granted their motion for summary judgment. Torres appealed.

Issue

Was Torres an employee or an independent contractor?

Language of the Court

Uncontradicted evidence established that: (1) Torres performed services for the Reardons, including both general gardening services and the special project of trimming the Reardons' tree, in the course of his independently established business, Jose Torres Gardening Service, a business in which he customarily engaged; (2) it appears that Torres supplied the equipment to be used in the job; (3) Torres was not hired by the day or hour, but contracted with the Reardons to produce the specified result of trimming the tree for the specified price of $350, a price quoted by Torres and accepted by the Reardons; (4) the work that Torres contracted to perform was not work ordinarily done in the course of the Reardons' business, but was maintenance work done on their home; (5) Torres had a substantial investment in his gardening business, including a truck and equipment; (6) Torres had employees who assisted him both in his general gardening business and in the tree trimming project. The evidence establishes as a matter of law that Torres was not an employee of the Reardons, but was an independent contractor at the time he was injured.

Decision

The court of appeals held that Torres was an independent contractor and that the Reardons were not liable to him. The court of appeals affirmed the summary judgment in favor of the Reardons.

Law & Ethics Questions

1. Suppose that Torres had negligently cut the branch and it had fallen on Boice and injured him. Could Boice have recovered damages from Torres? from the Reardons?

2. **ETHICS** Did Torres act ethically in suing the Reardons? Why do you think he sued them?

3. Can businesses reduce their liability exposure by hiring more independent contractors and fewer employees to do jobs?

Web Exercises

1. **WEB** For the complete opinion of this case, go to *www.prenhall.com/cheesemancases*.

2. **WEB** Visit the website of the court of appeals of California, Second Appellate District, Division Three, at *www.courtinfo.ca.gov/courts/courtsofappeal/2ndDistrict*.

3. **WEB** Use *www.google.com* to find an article or a case that discusses the elements that distinguish an agent from an independent contractor. Read it.

EXCEPTIONS IN WHICH A PRINCIPAL IS LIABLE FOR THE TORTS OF AN INDEPENDENT CONTRACTOR There are two exceptions in which the law imposes liability on a principal for the tortious conduct of an independent contractor he or she has hired:

- *Inherently dangerous activities.* Principals cannot avoid strict liability for **inherently dangerous activities** assigned to independent contractors. For example, the use of explosives, clearing of land by fire, crop dusting, and such involve special risks that are shared by the principal.
- *Negligence in the selection of an independent contractor.* A principal who hires an unqualified or knowingly dangerous person as an independent contractor is liable if that person injures someone while on the job.

ETHICS SPOTLIGHT

Principal Liable for Repo Man's Tort

> ❝*The issue in this case is whether a secured creditor may avoid liability for breaches of the peace by using an independent contractor.*❞

—Judge Mauzy

Yvonne Sanchez borrowed money from MBank El Paso (MBank) to purchase an automobile. She gave MBank a security interest in the vehicle to secure the loan. When Sanchez defaulted on the loan, MBank hired El Paso Recovery Service, an independent contractor, to repossess the automobile. The two men who were dispatched to Sanchez's house found the car parked in the driveway and hooked it to a tow truck. Sanchez demanded that they cease their efforts and leave the premises, but the men nonetheless continued with the repossession. Before the men could tow the automobile into the street, Sanchez jumped into the car, locked the doors, and refused to leave. The men towed the car at a high rate of speed to the repossession yard. They parked the car in the fenced repossession yard, with Sanchez inside, and padlocked the gate. Sanchez was left in the repossession lot with a Doberman Pinscher guard dog loose in the yard. Later, she was rescued by the police. The law prohibits the repossession of a vehicle if a breach of peace would occur. Sanchez filed suit against MBank, alleging that it was liable for the tortious conduct of El Paso Recovery Service. The trial court granted summary judgment to MBank, but the court of appeals reversed. MBank appealed.

The Supreme Court of Texas held that MBank, the principal, was liable for the tortious conduct of El Paso Recovery Service, an independent contractor. The court held that the act of repossessing an automobile from a defaulting debtor is an inherently dangerous activity and

a nondelegable duty. The court concluded that El Paso Recovery Service had breached the peace in repossessing the car from Sanchez and caused her physical and emotional harm. The court held that MBank, the principal, could not escape liability by hiring an independent contractor to do this task. The court found MBank liable to Sanchez. *MBank El Paso, N.A. v. Sanchez*, 836 S.W.2d 151, **Web** 1992 Tex. Lexis 97 (Supreme Court of Texas)

Law & Ethics Questions

1. **ETHICS** Did the independent contractor act responsibly in this case?
2. Should the principal bank have been held liable in this case? Why or why not?

Web Exercises

1. **WEB** For the complete opinion of this case, go to *www.prenhall.com/cheesemancases*.
2. **WEB** Visit the website of the supreme court of Texas, at *www.supreme.courts.state.tx.us*.
3. **WEB** Use *www.google.com* to find an article that discusses how an employer can be held liable for the torts of its independent contractor. Read it.

Termination of an Agency

An agency contract is similar to other contracts in that it can be terminated either by an act of the parties or by operation of law. These different methods of termination are discussed next. Note that once an agency relationship is terminated, the agent can no longer represent the principal or bind the principal to contracts.

Termination by Acts of the Parties

The parties to an agency contract can terminate the agency contract by agreement or by their actions. The four methods of **termination of an agency relationship by acts of the parties** are:

1. *Mutual agreement.* As with any other contract, the parties to an agency contract can mutually agree to terminate their agreement. By doing so, the parties relieve each other of any further rights, duties, obligations, or powers provided for in the agency contract. Either party can propose the termination of an agency contract.

2. *Lapse of time.* Agency contracts are often written for a specific period of time. The agency terminates when the specified time period elapses. If the agency contract does not set forth a specific termination date, the agency terminates after a reasonable time has elapsed. The courts often look to the custom of an industry in determining the reasonable time for the termination of the agency.

   Example Suppose that the principal and agent enter into an agency contract "beginning January 1, 2008, and ending December 31, 2011." The agency automatically terminates on December 31, 2011.

3. *Purpose achieved.* A principal can employ an agent for the time it takes to accomplish a certain task, purpose, or result. Such agencies automatically terminate when they are completed.

   Example Suppose a principal employs a licensed real estate broker to sell his house. The agency terminates when the house is sold and the principal pays the broker the agreed-upon compensation.

4. *Occurrence of a specified event.* An agency contract can specify that the agency exists until a specified event occurs. The agency terminates when the specified event happens.

   Example If a principal employs an agent to take care of her dog until she returns from a trip, the agency terminates when the principal returns from the trip.

Notification Required at the Termination of an Agency

If an agency is terminated by agreement between the parties, the principal is under a duty to give certain third parties notification of the termination. Unless otherwise required, the notice can be from the principal or some other source (e.g., the agent). If an agency terminates by operation of law, there is no duty to notify third parties about the termination, however.

The termination of an agency extinguishes an agent's actual authority to act on the principal's behalf. However, if the principal fails to give the proper notice of termination to a third party, the agent still has apparent authority to bind the principal to contracts with these third parties. If this happens, the contract is enforceable against the principal. The principal's only recourse is against the agent to recover damages caused by these unauthorized contracts.

The following notification requirements must be met:

- *Parties who dealt with the agent.* Direct notice of termination must be given to all persons with whom the agent dealt. Although the notice may be either written or oral, it is better practice to give written notice.
- *Parties who have knowledge of the agency.* The principal must give direct or constructive notice to any third party who has knowledge of the agency but with whom the agent has not dealt. Direct notice is often in the form of a letter. Constructive notice usually consists of placing a notice of the termination of the agency in a newspaper serving the relevant community. This notice is effective even against persons who do not see it.

■ *Parties who have no knowledge of the agency.* Generally, a principal is not obligated to give notice of termination to strangers who have no knowledge of the agency. However, a principal who has given the agent written authority to act but fails to recover the writing upon termination of the agency may be liable to strangers who later rely on this writing and deal with the agent. The laws of most states provide that this liability can be avoided by giving constructive notice (e.g., newspaper announcement) of the termination of the agency.

CONTEMPORARY ENVIRONMENT
Agency Coupled with an Interest

An **agency coupled with an interest** is a special type of agency relationship that is created for the agent's benefit. This type of agency is **irrevocable** by the principal (i.e., the principal cannot terminate it). An agency coupled with an interest is commonly used in security agreements to secure loans. An agency coupled with an interest is not terminated by the death or incapacity of either the principal or the agent. It terminates only when the agent's obligations are performed. However, the parties can expressly agree that an agency coupled with an interest is terminated.

Example Heidi Norville owns a piece of real estate. She goes to Wells Fargo Bank to obtain a loan on the property. The bank makes the loan but requires her to sign a security agreement (e.g., a mortgage) pledging the property as collateral for the loan. The security agreement contains a clause that appoints that bank as Ms. Norville's agent and permits the bank to sell the property and recover the amount of the loan from the sale proceeds if she defaults on her payments. This agency is irrevocable by Ms. Norville, the principal.

Termination by Operation of Law

Agency contracts can be **terminated by operation of law** as well as by agreement. The five methods of terminating an agency relationship by operation of law are:

1. **Death.** The death of either the principal or the agent terminates an agency relationship. This rule is based on the old legal principle that because a dead person cannot act, no one can act for him or her. Note that an agency terminates even if one party is unaware of the other party's death. An agent's actions that take place after the principal's death do not bind the principal's estate.

2. **Insanity.** The insanity of either the principal or the agent generally terminates an agency relationship. A few states have modified this rule to provide that a contract entered into by an agent on behalf of an insane principal is enforceable if (1) the insane person has not been adjudged insane, (2) the third party does not have knowledge of the principal's insanity at the time of contracting, and (3) the enforcement of the contract will prevent injustice.

3. **Bankruptcy.** An agency relationship is terminated if the principal is declared bankrupt. Bankruptcy requires the filing of a petition for bankruptcy under federal bankruptcy law. With few exceptions, neither the appointment of a state court receiver nor the principal's financial difficulties or insolvency terminates the agency relationship. The agent's bankruptcy usually does not terminate an agency unless the agent's credit standing is important to the agency relationship.

4. **Changed circumstances.** An agency terminates when there is an unusual change in circumstances that would lead the agent to believe that the principal's original instructions should no longer be valid.

    Example Suppose a principal employs a licensed real estate agent to sell a farm for $100,000. The agent thereafter learns that oil has been discovered on the property and makes it worth $1 million. The agency terminates because of this change in circumstances.

5. **War.** The outbreak of a war between the principal's country and the agent's country terminates an agency relationship between the parties. Such an occurrence usually makes the performance of the agency contract impossible.

Termination by Impossibility

An agency relationship terminates if a situation arises that makes its fulfillment impossible. The following circumstances can lead to **termination by impossibility**:

1. *The loss or destruction of the subject matter of the agency.* For example, assume that a principal employs an agent to sell his horse, but the horse dies before it is sold. The agency relationship terminates at the moment the horse dies.
2. *The loss of a required qualification.* For example, suppose a principal employs a licensed real estate agent to sell her house, and the real estate agent's license is revoked. The agency terminates at the moment the license is revoked.
3. *A change in the law.* For example, suppose a principal employs an agent to trap alligators. If a law is passed that makes trapping alligators illegal, the agency contract terminates when the law becomes effective.

Wrongful Termination of an Agency or Employment Contract

Generally, agency and employment contracts that do not specify a definite time for their termination can be terminated at will by either the principal or the agent, without liability to the other party. When a principal terminates an agency contract, it is called a **revocation of authority**. When an agent terminates an agency, it is called a **renunciation of authority**.

Unless an agency is irrevocable, both the principal and the agent have individual power to unilaterally terminate any agency contract. Note that having the power to terminate an agency agreement is not the same as having the right to terminate it. The unilateral termination of an agency contract may be wrongful. If the principal's or agent's termination of an agency contract breaches the contract, the other party can sue for damages for **wrongful termination**.

Example A principal employs a licensed real estate agent to sell his house. The agency contract gives the agent an exclusive listing for three months. After one month, the principal unilaterally terminates the agency. The principal has the power to do so, and the agent can no longer act on behalf of the principal. However, because the principal did not have the right to terminate the contract, the agent can sue him and recover damages (i.e., lost commission) for wrongful termination.

Chapter Summary

Agency, p. 677

Agency is a fiduciary relationship that results from the manifestation of consent by one person to act on behalf of another person, with that person's consent. A principal is a party who employs another person to act on his or her behalf. An agent is a party who agrees to act on behalf of another person.

Persons Who Can Initiate an Agency Relationship

Any person who has the capacity to contract can appoint an agent to act on his or her behalf. Persons who lack contractual capacity, such as insane persons and minors, cannot appoint agents.

Principal–Agent Relationship

In a principal–agent relationship, an employer hires an employee and authorizes the employee to enter into contracts on the employer's behalf.

Employer–Employee Relationship

In an employer–employee relationship, an employer hires an employee to perform some form of physical service. An employee is not an agent unless the principal authorizes him or her to enter into contracts on the principal's behalf.

Principal–Independent Contractor Relationship

Principals often employ outsiders—that is, persons and businesses that are not employees—to perform certain tasks on their behalf. These persons and businesses are called independent contractors. The crucial factor in determining whether someone is an independent contractor or an employee is the degree of control that the principal has over the agent.

Formation of an Agency, p. 679

Express Agency

In an express agency, the principal and agent expressly agree in words to enter into an agency agreement. The agency contract may be oral or written, unless the Statute of Frauds requires it to be in writing.

Implied Agency

In an implied agency, the agency is implied (inferred) from the conduct of the parties.

Apparent Agency

Apparent agency arises when a principal creates the appearance of an agency that in actuality does not exist. Also called *agency by estoppel* or *ostensible agency*.

Agency by Ratification

Agency by ratification occurs when a person misrepresents him- or herself as another's agent when he or she is not and the purported principal ratifies (accepts) the unauthorized act.

Principal's Duty of Compensation

A principal must pay the agent the agreed-upon compensation. If there is no agreement, the principal must pay what is customary in the industry or, if there is no custom, the reasonable value of the services.

Principal's Duties of Reimbursement and Indemnification

A principal must reimburse an agent for all expenses paid that were authorized by the principal, within the scope of the agency, and necessary to discharge the agent's duties. The principal must indemnify the agent for any losses suffered because of the principal's misconduct.

Principal's Duty of Cooperation

A principal must cooperate with and assist the agent in the performance of the agent's duties and the accomplishment of the agency.

Agent's Duty of Performance

An agent must perform the lawful duties expressed in the agency contract with reasonable care, skill, and diligence.

Agent's Duty of Notification

An agent owes a duty to notify the principal of any information he or she learns that is important to the agency. Information learned by the agent in the course of the agency is imputed to the principal.

Agent's Duty of Accountability

An agent must maintain an accurate accounting of all transactions undertaken on the principal's behalf. A principal may demand an accounting from the agent at any time.

Agent's Duty of Loyalty to the Principal

An agent owes a duty not to act adversely to the interests of the principal. The most common breaches of loyalty are:

1. *Self-dealing.* The agent cannot deal with the principal unless his or her position is disclosed and the principal agrees to deal with the agent.
2. *Usurping an opportunity.* An agent cannot usurp (take) an opportunity belonging to the principal as his or her own.

3. *Competing with the principal.* An agent is prohibited from competing with the principal during the course of an agency unless the principal agrees.

4. *Misuse of confidential information.* An agent is under a legal duty not to disclose or misuse confidential information learned within the course of an agency.

5. *Dual agency.* An agent cannot act on behalf of two different principals in the same transaction unless the principals agree.

Tort Liability to Third Parties, p. 687

A principal is liable for the tortious conduct of an agent who is acting within the scope of his or her authority. Liability is imposed for misrepresentation, negligence, and intentional torts.

Negligence

A principal is liable for the negligent conduct of agents acting within the scope of their employment. Special negligence doctrines include:

1. *Frolic and detour.* A principal is generally relieved of liability if the agent's negligent act occurred on a substantial frolic and detour from the scope of employment.

2. *Coming and going rule.* A principal is not liable if the agent's tortious conduct occurred while on the way to or from work.

3. *Dual-purpose mission.* If an agent is acting on his or her own behalf and on behalf of the principal, the principal is generally liable for the agent's tortious conduct.

Intentional Torts

States apply one of the following rules to determine liability for intentional torts:

1. *Motivation test.* The principal is liable if the agent's intentional tort was committed to promote the principal's business.

2. *Work-related test.* The principal is liable if the agent's intentional tort was committed within a work-related time or space.

Agents are personally liable for their own tortious conduct.

Misrepresentation

A principal is liable for intentional and innocent misrepresentations made by an agent acting within the scope of his or her employment.

Contract Liability to Third Parties, p. 695

Fully Disclosed Agency

In a fully disclosed agency, the third party entering into the contract knows that the agent is acting for a principal and knows the identity of the principal. The principal is liable on the contract; the agent is not liable on the contract.

Partially Disclosed Agency

In a partially disclosed agency, the third party knows that the agent is acting for a principal but does not know the identity of the principal. Both the principal and the agent are liable on the contract.

Undisclosed Agency

In an undisclosed agency, the third party does not know that the agent is acting for a principal. Both the principal and the agent are liable on the contract.

Agent Exceeding the Scope of Authority

An agent who enters into a contract on behalf of another party impliedly warrants that he or she has the authority to do so. If the agent exceeds the scope of his or her authority, the principal is not liable on the contract.

Independent Contractor, p. 698

In a principal–independent contractor relationship, a principal employs a person who is not an employee of the principal. The independent contractor has authority only to enter into contracts authorized by the principal.

Factors for Determining Independent Contractor Status

The crucial factor in determining whether someone is an independent contractor or an employee is the degree of control that the principal has over the agent.

Liability for an Independent Contractor's Contracts

A principal can authorize an independent contractor to enter into contracts and are bound by the authorized contracts of their independent contractors. If an independent contractor enters into a contract with a third party on behalf of the principal without express or implied authority from the principal to do so, the principal is not liable on the contract.

Liability for an Independent Contractor's Torts

Generally, principals are not liable for the tortious conduct of independent contractors. Exceptions to the rule are for:

1. Inherently dangerous activities
2. Negligence in selecting an independent contractor

Independent contractors are personally liable for their own torts.

Termination of an Agency, p. 701

Termination by Acts of the Parties

The following acts of the parties terminate agency contracts:

1. *Mutual agreement.* The parties may mutually agree to terminate an agency contract.
2. *Lapse of time.* An agency contract terminates when the stipulated time period of the agency expires.
3. *Purpose achieved.* An agency contract terminates when the stipulated purpose of the agency is achieved.
4. *Occurrence of a specified event.* An agency contract terminates when the stipulated event occurs.

Notification Required at the Termination of an Agency

If an agency is terminated by agreement between the parties, the principal must notify third parties as follows:

1. *Parties who dealt with the agent.* Direct notice must be given to these parties.
2. *Parties who have knowledge of the agency.* Direct or constructive (e.g., public notice in newspapers) notice must be given to these parties.
3. *Parties who have no knowledge of the agency.* No notice needs to be given to these parties.

If the proper notice of termination of an agency is not given, the agent has apparent authority to bind the principal to contracts. The principal and agent both have the power to terminate an agency at any time. After termination, the agent can no longer act on behalf of the principal. The terminating party may not, however, have had the right to terminate the agency and may be held liable for damages caused by wrongful termination of the agency.

Agency Coupled with an Interest

An agency coupled with an interest is a special type of agency that is irrevocable by the principal. This type of agency is commonly used in security interests to secure loans.

Termination by Operation of Law

Agency contracts can be terminated by operation of law. This includes the following methods:

1. *Death.* An agency contract terminates when either the principal or the agent dies.
2. *Insanity.* An agency contract terminates when either the principal or the agent is insane.
3. *Bankruptcy.* An agency contract terminates when the principal is bankrupt.
4. *Changed circumstances.* An agency contract terminates when an unusual circumstance would lead the agent to believe that the principal's original instructions are no longer valid.
5. *War.* An agency contract terminates when war breaks out between the principal's country and the agent's country.

Termination by Impossibility

An agency relationship terminates if a situation arises that makes its fulfillment impossible. Such situations include the loss or destruction of the subject matter of the agency, the loss of a required qualification, and a change in the law.

Wrongful Termination of an Agency or Employment Contract

If an agency is for an agreed-upon term or purpose, the unilateral termination of the agency contract by either the principal or the agent constitutes the wrongful termination of the agency. The breaching party is liable to the other party for damages caused by the breach.

Test Review Terms and Concepts

Agency   677
Agency by ratification   684
Agency coupled with an interest   703
Agency law   677
Agent   677
Apparent agency (agency by
    estoppel)   682
Attorney-in-fact   681
Coming and going rule   690
Competing with the principal   686
Contingency-fee basis   685
Contractual capacity   678
Degree of control   699
Dual agency   686
Dual-purpose mission   691
Duty of accountability   686
Duty of loyalty   686
Duty of notification   685
Duty of performance   685
Duty to compensate   684
Duty to cooperate   685
Duty to indemnify   685
Duty to reimburse   685
Employer–employee
    relationship   678

Exclusive agency contract   679
Express agency   679
Frolic and detour   689
Fully disclosed agency   695
Fully disclosed principal   695
General power of attorney   681
Implied agency   681
Implied warranty of authority   697
Imputed knowledge   686
Incidental authority   681
Independent contractor   679
Inherently dangerous activity   701
Innocent misrepresentation   694
Intentional misrepresentation (fraud
    or deceit)   694
Intentional tort   691
Irrevocable agency   703
Lapse of time   702
Misuse of confidential
    information   686
Motivation test   692
Mutual agreement   702
Negligence   688
Nonexistent principal   697
Occurrence of a specified event   702

Partially disclosed agency   696
Partially disclosed principal   696
Power of attorney   681
Principal   677
Principal–agent relationship   678
Principal–independent contractor
    relationship   679
Purpose achieved   702
Ratify   697
Renunciation of authority   704
Respondeat superior   687
Revocation of authority   704
Self-dealing   686
Special power of attorney   681
Termination by acts of the
    parties   702
Termination by impossibility   704
Termination by operation of law   703
Tort liability   687
Undisclosed agency   696
Undisclosed principal   696
Usurping an opportunity   686
Vicarious liability   687
Work-related test   692
Wrongful termination   704

Case Problems

25.1 Creation of an Agency: Renaldo, Inc., doing business as Baker Street, owned and operated a nightclub in Georgia. On the evening in question, plaintiff Ginn became "silly drunk" at the nightclub and was asked by several patrons and the manager to leave the premises. The police were called, and Ginn left the premises. When Ginn realized that his jacket was still in the nightclub, he attempted to reenter the premises. He was met at the door by the manager, who refused him admittance. When Ginn persisted, an unidentified patron, without the approval of the manager, pushed Ginn, who lost his balance and fell backward. To break his fall, Ginn put his hand against the door jamb. The unidentified patron slammed the door on Ginn's hand and held it shut

for several minutes. Ginn, who suffered severe injuries to his right hand, sued the nightclub for damages. Was the unidentified patron an agent of the nightclub? *Ginn v. Renaldo, Inc.*, 183 Ga. App. 618, 359 S.E.2d 390, **Web** 1987 Ga. App. Lexis 2023 (Court of Appeals of Georgia)

25.2 Independent Contractor: Mercedes Connolly and her husband purchased airline tickets and a tour package for a tour to South Africa from Judy Samuelson, a travel agent doing business as International Tours of Manhattan. Samuelson sold tickets for a variety of airline companies and tour operators, including African Adventurers, which was the tour operator for the Connollys' tour. Mercedes fell while trying to cross a 6-inch-deep stream while the tour group was on a walking tour to see hippopotami in a river at a game reserve. In the process, she injured her left ankle and foot. She sued Samuelson for damages. Is Samuelson liable? *Connolly v. Samuelson*, 671 F.Supp. 1312, **Web** 1987 U.S. Dist. Lexis 8308 (United States District Court for the District of Kansas)

25.3 Contract Liability: Leroy Behlman and 18 other football fans from Connecticut and New York decided to attend the Super Bowl football game in New Orleans. They entered into contracts with Octagon Travel Center, Inc. (Octagon), a tour operator, and paid $399 each for transportation, lodging, and a ticket to the Super Bowl football game. They purchased the tour package through Universal Travel Agency, Inc. (Universal), a travel agency that acts as a broker for a number of airline companies and tour operators. The individual contracts, however, were between the football fans and Octagon. When they arrived in New Orleans, no tickets to the Super Bowl were forthcoming. Upon returning, they sued Universal for breach of contract. Is Universal liable? *Behlman v. Universal Travel Agency, Inc.*, 4 Conn. App. 688, 496 A.2d 962, **Web** 1985 Conn. App. Lexis 1092 (Appellate Court of Connecticut)

25.4 Power of Attorney: As a result of marital problems, Howard R. Bankerd "left for the west," and Virginia Bankerd, his wife, continued to reside in their jointly owned home. Before his departure, Howard executed a power of attorney to Arthur V. King, which authorized King to "convey, grant, bargain, and/or sell" Howard's interest in the property. For the ensuing decade, Howard lived in various locations in Nevada, Colorado, and Washington but rarely contacted King. Howard made no payments on the mortgage, for taxes, or for maintenance or upkeep of the home.

Nine years later, Virginia, who was nearing retirement, requested King to exercise his power of attorney and transfer Howard's interest in the home to her. King's attempts to locate Howard were unsuccessful. He believed that Howard, who would then be 69 years of age, might be dead. King gifted Howard's interest in the property to Virginia, who sold the property for $62,500. Four years later, Howard returned and filed suit against King, alleging breach of trust and fiduciary duty. Is King liable? *King v. Bankerd*, 303 Md. 98, 492 A.2d 608, **Web** 1985 Md. Lexis 589 (Court of Appeals of Maryland)

25.5 Apparent Agency: Robert Bolus was engaged in various businesses in which he sold and repaired trucks. He decided to build a truck repair facility in Bartonsville, Pennsylvania. Bolus contacted United Penn Bank (Bank) to obtain financing for the project and was referred to Emmanuel Ziobro, an assistant vice president. Ziobro orally agreed that Bank would provide funding for the project. He did not tell Bolus that he only had express authority to make loans of up to $10,000. After extending $210,000 in loans to Bolus, Bank refused to provide further financing. When

Bolus defaulted on the loan, Bank pressed judgment against Bolus. Bank sought to recover Bolus's assets in payment for the loan. Bolus sued Bank for damages for breach of contract. Who wins? *Bolus v. United Penn Bank*, 363 Pa. Super. 247, 525 A.2d 1215, **Web** 1987 Pa. Super. Lexis 7258 (Superior Court of Pennsylvania)

25.6 Imputed Knowledge: Iota Management Corporation entered into a contract to purchase the Bel Air West Motor Hotel in the City of St. Louis from Boulevard Investment Company. The agreement contained the following warranty: "Seller has no actual notice of any substantial defect in the structure of the Hotel or in any of its plumbing, heating, air-conditioning, electrical, or utility systems."

When the buyer inspected the premises, no leaks in the pipes were visible. Iota purchased the hotel for $2 million. When Iota removed some of the walls and ceilings during remodeling, it found evidence of prior repairs to leaking pipes and ducts, as well as devices for catching water (e.g., milk, cartons, cookie sheets, buckets). The estimate to repair these leaks was $500,000. Evidence at trial showed that Cecil Lillibridge, who was Boulevard's maintenance supervisor for the four years prior to the motor hotel's sale, had actual knowledge of these problems and had repaired some of the pipes. Iota sued Boulevard to rescind the contract. Is Boulevard liable? *Iota Management Corporation v. Boulevard Investment Company*, 731 S.W.2d 399, **Web** 1987 Mo. App. Lexis 4027 (Court of Appeals of Missouri)

25.7 Fiduciary Duty: After Francis Pusateri retired, he met with Gilbert J. Johnson, a stockbroker with E. F. Hutton & Co., Inc., and informed Johnson that he wished to invest in tax-free bonds and money market accounts. Pusateri opened an investment account with E. F. Hutton and checked a box stating that his objective was "tax-free income and moderate growth." During the course of a year, Johnson churned Pusateri's account to make commissions and invested Pusateri's funds in volatile securities and options. Johnson kept telling Pusateri that his account was making money, and the monthly statement from E. F. Hutton did not indicate otherwise. The manager at E. F. Hutton was aware of Johnson's activities but did nothing to prevent them. When Johnson left E. F. Hutton, Pusateri's account—which had been called the "laughing-stock" of the office—had shrunk from $196,000 to $96,880. Pusateri sued E. F. Hutton for damages. Is E. F. Hutton liable? *Pusateri v. E. F. Hutton & Co., Inc.*, 180 Cal.App.3d 247, 225 Cal.Rptr. 526, **Web** 1986 Cal. App. Lexis 1502 (Court of Appeal of California)

25.8 Fiduciary Duty: Boettcher DTC Building Joint Venture (Boettcher) owned an office building in which it leased space to tenants. Harmon Wilfred, an independent leasing agent, contacted Boettcher on behalf of Landmark Associates (Landmark), which was interested in leasing office space in the Boettcher building. Wilfred represented Boettcher as a special agent in the transaction. Landmark executed a 68-month lease with Boettcher. Boettcher paid

Wilfred a commission. Shortly thereafter, Landmark began negotiating with Boettcher for additional lease space. Landmark also contacted Wilfred to inquire about the availability of lease space in other buildings. When Wilfred found lease space for Landmark in another office building, Landmark vacated its premises at the Boettcher building and defaulted on its lease agreement. Boettcher sued Wilfred for damages, alleging that Wilfred had violated his fiduciary duty to Boettcher. Who wins? *Boettcher DTC Building Joint Venture v. Wilfred*, 762 P.2d 788, **Web** 1988 Colo. App. Lexis. 323 (Court of Appeals of Colorado)

25.9 Duty of Loyalty: Peter Shields was the president and a member of the board of directors of Production Finishing Corporation for seven years. The company provided steel polishing services. It did most, if not all, of the polishing work in the Detroit area, except for that of the Ford Motor Company. (Ford did its own polishing.) On a number of occasions, Shields discussed with Ford, on behalf of Production Finishing, the possibility of providing Ford's steel polishing services. When Shields learned that Ford was discontinuing its polishing operation, he incorporated Flat Rock Metal and submitted a confidential proposal to Ford which provided that he would buy Ford's equipment and provide polishing services to Ford. It was not until he resigned from Production Finishing that he informed the board of directors that he was pursuing the Ford business himself. Production Finishing sued Shields. Did Shields breach his fiduciary duty of loyalty to Production Finishing? *Production Finishing Corporation v. Shields*, 158 Mich. App. 479, 405 N.W.2d 171, **Web** 1987 Mich. App. Lexis 2379 (Court of Appeals of Michigan)

25.10 Independent Contractor: The Butler Telephone Company, Inc. (Butler), contracted with the Sandidge Construction Company to lay 18 miles of telephone cable in a rural area. In the contract, Butler reserved the right to inspect the work for compliance with the terms of the contract. Butler did not control how Sandidge performed the work. Johnnie Carl Pugh, an employee of Sandidge, was killed on the job when the sides to an excavation in which he was working caved in on top of him. Evidence disclosed that the excavation was not properly shored or sloped and that it violated general safety standards. Pugh's parents and estate brought a wrongful death action against Butler. Is Butler liable? *Pugh v. Butler Telephone Company, Inc.*, 512 So.2d 1317, **Web** 1987 Ala. Lexis 4468 (Supreme Court of Alabama)

25.11 Personal Guaranty: Sebastian International, Inc., entered into a five-year lease for a building in Chadsworth, California. Just over two years later, with the consent of the master lessors, Sebastian sublet the building to West Valley Grinding, Inc. In conjunction with the execution of the sublease, the corporate officers of West Valley, including Kenneth E. Peck, each signed a guaranty of lease, personally ensuring the payment of West Valley's rental obligations. The guaranty contract referred to Peck in his individual capacity; however, on the signature line, he was identified as "Kenneth Peck, Vice President." Eight months later, West Valley went out of business, leaving 24 months remaining on the sublease. After unsuccessful attempts to secure another subleasee, Sebastian surrendered the leasehold back to the master lessors and brought suit against Peck to recover the unpaid rent. Peck argued that he was not personally liable because his signature was that of an agent for a disclosed principal and not that of a principal himself. Who wins? *Sebastian International, Inc. v. Peck*, 195 Cal.App.3d 803, 240 Cal.Rptr. 911, **Web** 1987 Cal. App. Lexis 2237 (Court of Appeal of California)

25.12 Contract Liability: G. Elvin Grinder of Marbury, Maryland, was a building contractor who, for years, did business as an individual and traded as "Grinder Construction." Grinder maintained an open account, on his individual credit, with Bryans Road Building & Supply Co., Inc. Grinder would purchase materials and supplies from Bryans on credit and later pay the invoices. G. Elvin Grinder Construction, Inc., a Maryland corporation, was formed, with Grinder personally owning 52 percent of the stock of the corporation. Grinder did not inform Bryans that he had incorporated, and he continued to purchase supplies on credit from Bryans under the name "Grinder Construction." Five years later, after certain invoices were not paid by Grinder, Bryans sued Grinder personally to recover. Grinder asserted that the debts were owed by the corporation. Bryans amended its complaint to include the corporation as a defendant. Who is liable to Bryans? *Grinder v. Bryans Road Building & Supply Co., Inc.*, 290 Md. 687, 432 A.2d 453, **Web** 1981 Md. Lexis 246 (Court of Appeals of Maryland)

25.13 Dual Agency: Chemical Bank was the primary bank for Washington Steel Corporation. As an agent for Washington Steel, Chemical Bank expressly and impliedly promised that it would advance the best interests and welfare of Washington Steel. During the course of the agency, Washington Steel provided the bank with comprehensive and confidential financial information, other data, and future business plans.

At some point during the agency, TW Corporation and others approached Chemical Bank to request a loan of $7 million to make a hostile tender offer for the stock of Washington Steel. Chemical Bank agreed and became an agent for TW. Management at Chemical Bank did not disclose to Washington Steel its adverse relationship with TW, did not request Washington Steel's permission to act as an agent for TW, and directed employees of the bank to conceal from Washington Steel the bank's involvement with TW. After TW commenced its public tender offer, Washington Steel filed suit, seeking to obtain an injunction against Chemical Bank and TW. Who wins? *Washington Steel Corporation v. TW Corporation*, 465 F.Supp. 1100, **Web** 1979 U.S. Dist. Lexis 14391 (United States District Court for the Western District of Pennsylvania)

25.14 Tort Liability: Ray Johnson and his eight-year-old son, David, were waiting for a "walk" sign before crossing a street in downtown Salt Lake City. A truck owned by Newspaper Agency Corporation (NAC) and operated by its employee, Donald Rogers, crossed the intersection and jumped the curb, killing David and injuring Ray. Before reporting for work on the evening of the accident, Rogers had consumed approximately seven mixed drinks containing vodka and had chugalugged a 27-ounce drink containing two minibottles of tequila. His blood alcohol content after the accident was .18 percent.

Evidence showed that the use of alcohol and marijuana was widespread at NAC and that the company made no effort to curtail such use. Evidence further showed that NAC vehicles were returned with beer cans in them and that on one occasion, an NAC supervisor who had observed drivers smoking marijuana had told the drivers to "do it on the road." Ray Johnson sued Rogers and NAC for the wrongful death of his child, David, and physical injury to Ray. Is NAC liable? *Johnson v. Rogers*, 763 P.2d 771, 90 Utah Adv. Rep. 3, **Web** 1988 Utah Lexis 81 (Supreme Court of Utah)

25.15 Tort Liability: Intrastate Radiotelephone, Inc., was a public utility that supplied radiotelephone utility service to the general public for radiotelephones, pocket pagers, and beepers. Robert Kranhold, an employee of Intrastate, was authorized to use his personal vehicle on company business. One morning, when Kranhold was driving his vehicle to Intrastate's main office, he negligently struck a motorcycle being driven by Michael S. Largey, causing severe and permanent injuries to Largey. The accident occurred at the intersection where Intrastate's main office is located. Evidence showed that Kranhold acted as a consultant to Intrastate, worked both in and out of Intrastate's offices, had no set hours of work, often attended meetings at Intrastate's offices, and went to Intrastate's offices to pick things up or drop things off. Largey sued Intrastate for damages. Is Intrastate liable? *Largey v. Radiotelephone, Inc.*, 136 Cal.App.3d 660, 186 Cal.Rptr. 520, **Web** 1982 Cal. App. Lexis 2049 (Court of Appeal of California)

25.16 Tort Liability: Donnie Joe Jackson hired Ted Green to do some remodeling work on his house. Jackson never paid Green for his work, and a dispute arose as to how much was owed to Green. Jackson worked at the Higgenbotham-Bartlett Lumber Company, a lumberyard where Green often purchased lumber and supplies. During the course of the following year, when Green went to the lumberyard to do business, Jackson verbally accosted him on at least three separate occasions. Each time, Green left the lumberyard. Green, accompanied by his son, made two trips to the facility. On the first trip, Jackson and Green had a verbal altercation. On the second trip, Jackson hit Green, knocking him unconscious and causing injuries. Green sued Jackson's employer for damages. Is the lumber company liable for the intentional tort of its agent? *Green v. Jackson*, 674 S.W.2d 395, **Web** 1984 Tex. App. Lexis 5592 (Court of Appeals of Texas)

Ethics Issues

25.17 Ethics: The Hagues, husband and wife, owned a 160-acre tract that they decided to sell. They entered into a listing agreement with Harvey C. Hilgendorf, a licensed real estate broker, which gave Hilgendorf the exclusive right to sell the property for a period of 12 months. The Hagues agreed to pay Hilgendorf a commission of 6 percent of the accepted sale price if a bona fide buyer was found during the listing period.

By letter five months later, the Hagues terminated the listing agreement with Hilgendorf. Hilgendorf did not acquiesce to the Hagues' termination, however. One month later, Hilgendorf presented an offer to the Hagues from a buyer willing to purchase the property at the full listing price. The Hagues ignored the offer and sold the property to another buyer. Hilgendorf sued the Hagues for breach of the agency agreement. Did the Hagues act ethically in this case? Who wins the lawsuit? *Hilgendorf v. Hague*, 293 N.W.2d 272, **Web** 1980 Iowa Sup. Lexis 882 (Supreme Court of Iowa)

25.18 Ethics: Elizabeth Krempasky, who was 82 years old, owned a house and four certificates of deposit (CDs) at a bank. In her will, Krempasky devised her estate to her niece, Lydia Vrablova Wanamaker. Krempasky died while a patient at a hospital. Wanamaker, who was appointed executrix of the decedent's estate, could not find the CDs. Upon further inquiry, she discovered that the name of Anna A. Parana, an acquaintance of Krempasky's, had been added to the CDs on the day of the decedent's death. Evidence showed that (1) Parana prepared the forms necessary to authorize the bank to add her name to the CDs, (2) the decedent signed the forms on the day of her death sometime before dying at 2:45 P.M., and (3) Parana presented the authorization forms to the bank sometime between 3:00 P.M. and 4:00 P.M. on the same day. A transfer of CDs to joint tenancy is not effective until the bank officially makes the transfer on its records, which it did because it did not have notice of Krempasky's death. Wanamaker, as executrix of the decedent's estate, filed a petition requesting that the CDs be ordered returned to the decedent's estate. Was Anna Parana an agent of Elizabeth Krempasky? Did Parana act ethically in this case? *Estate of Krempasky*, 348 Pa. Super. 128, 501 A.2d 681, **Web** 1985 Pa. Super. Lexis 10545 (Superior Court of Pennsylvania)

25.19 Ethics: William Venezio, a real estate broker, conducted his business under the trade name King Realty and had properly filed the required name certificate in the Schenectady County clerk's office. King Realty entered into a contract to purchase property located in the town of Rotterdam, Schenectady County, from Ermino Bianchi. Venezio signed the end of the contract "King Realty for Customer." Four days later, King Realty entered into a contract to sell the property to Mario Attanasio. However, Bianchi refused to sell the property to King Realty, alleging that because the original contract had failed to adequately identify the purchaser, there was not a binding contract. Venezio, d.b.a. King Realty, brought an action for specific performance against Bianchi. Was it ethical for Bianchi to try to back out of the contract? Can King Realty, as an agent for a partially disclosed principal, enforce the contract against Bianchi? *Venezio v. Bianchi*, 124 A.D.2d 933, 508 N.Y.S.2d 349, **Web** 1986 N.Y. App. Div. Lexis 62252 (Supreme Court of New York)

25.20 Ethics: National Biscuit Company (Nabisco) is a corporation that produces and distributes cookies and other food products to grocery stores and other outlets across the nation. Nabisco hired Ronnell Lynch as a cookie salesman-trainee, and eventually assigned Lynch to his own sales territory. Lynch's duties involved making sales calls, taking orders, and making sure that shelves of stores in his territory were stocked with Nabisco products. During the first two months, Nabisco received numerous complaints from store owners in Lynch's territory that Lynch was overly aggressive and was taking shelf space for Nabisco products that was reserved for competing brands.

One day, after being in his territory for two months, Lynch visited a grocery store that was managed by Jerome Lange. Lynch was there to place previously delivered merchandise on the store's shelves. An argument developed between Lynch and Lange. Lynch became very angry and started swearing. Lange told Lynch to stop swearing or leave the store because children were present. Lynch became uncontrollably angry and went behind the counter and dared Lange to fight. When Lange refused to fight, Lynch proceeded to viciously assault and batter Lange, causing severe injuries. When Lange sued Nabisco, Nabisco denied liability. Was it ethical for Nabisco to deny liability in this case? Do you think the prior complaints against Lynch had any effect on the decision reached in this case? Is Nabisco liable for the intentional tort (assault and battery) of its employee Ronnell Lynch? *Lange v. National Biscuit Company*, 297 Minn. 399, 211 N.W.2d 783, **Web** 1973 Minn. Lexis 1106 (Supreme Court of Minnesota)

IRAC Writing Assignment

Read **Case A-25** in Appendix A [*District of Columbia v. Howell*]. Use the IRAC method to prepare a written analysis of the case.

Endnotes

1. *Restatement (Second) of Agency*, Section 4.
2. *Restatement (Second) of Agency*, Section 321.

CHAPTER **26**

Sole Proprietorships and General and Limited Partnerships

❝*There are a great many of us who will adhere to that ancient principle that we prefer to be governed by the power of laws, and not by the power of men.*❞

—WOODROW WILSON
Speech, September 25, 1912

CHAPTER OBJECTIVES

After studying this chapter, you should be able to:

1. Define *sole proprietorship* and describe the liability of a sole proprietor.
2. Define *general partnership* and describe how general partnerships are formed.
3. Explain the contract liability and tort liability of general partners.
4. Define *limited partnership* and describe the process of forming a limited partnership.
5. Identify and describe the liability of general and limited partners.

CHAPTER CONTENTS

Introduction to Sole Proprietorships and General and Limited Partnerships

A person who wants to start a business must decide whether the business should operate as one of the major forms of business organization—*sole proprietorship*, *general partnership*, *limited partnership*, *limited liability partnership*, *limited liability company*, and *corporation*—or under some other available legal business form. The selection depends on many factors, including the ease and cost of formation, the capital requirements of the business, the flexibility of management decisions, government restrictions, the extent of personal liability, tax considerations, and the like.

This chapter discusses **entrepreneurship**, sole proprietorships, general partnerships, and limited partnerships. Corporations, limited liability companies, limited liability partnerships, franchising, and other forms of business are discussed in following chapters.

Windmills Near Palm Springs, California

Many businesses, such as these windmills, are operated as limited partnerships.

Entrepreneurship

An **entrepreneur** is a person who forms and operates a new business. An entrepreneur may start a business by him- or herself or cofound a business with others. Most businesses started by entrepreneurs are small, although some grow into substantial organizations. For example, Bill Gates started Microsoft Corporation, which grew into the giant software and Internet company. Michael Dell started Dell Computers as a mail-order business; it has become a leader in computer sales. Every day, entrepreneurs in this country and elsewhere around the world create new businesses that hire employees, provide new products and services, and contribute to the growth of economies of countries.

Entrepreneurial Forms of Conducting Business

Entrepreneurs contemplating starting a business have many options when choosing the legal form in which to conduct the business. Each of these forms of business has advantages and disadvantages for the entrepreneurs. The major forms for conducting businesses and professions are:

> It is when merchants dispute about their own rules that they invoke the law.
>
> Judge Brett
> *Robinson v. Mollett (1875)*

1. Sole proprietorship
2. General partnership
3. Limited partnership
4. Limited liability partnership
5. Limited liability company
6. Corporation

Certain requirements must be met to form and operate each of these forms of business.

Web Exercises

1. **WEB:** Use *www.google.com* to find an article that discusses the founder of Dell Computers. Visit the Dell website, at *www.dell.com*.
2. **WEB:** Use *www.google.com* to find an article that discusses the founders of YouTube. Visit the YouTube website, at *www.youtube.com*.
3. **WEB:** Use *www.google.com* to find an article that discusses the founders of Starbucks. Visit the Starbucks website, at *www.starbucks.com*.
4. **WEB:** Use *www.google.com* to find an article that discusses the founders of MySpace.com. Visit the MySpace.com website, at *www.myspace.com*.
5. **WEB:** Use *www.google.com* to find an article that discusses the founders of Microsoft Corporation. Visit the Microsoft website, at *www.microsoft.com*.

University of Southern California Campus

Many of today's students will become tomorrow's entrepreneurs.

Sole Proprietorship

A **sole proprietorship** is the simplest form of business organization. The owner of the business, the **sole proprietor**, is the business. There is no separate legal entity. Sole proprietorships are the most common form of business organization in the United States. Many small businesses—and a few large ones—operate in this way.

There are several major advantages to operating a business as a sole proprietorship. They include the following:

1. Forming a sole proprietorship is easy and does not cost a lot.
2. The owner has the right to make all management decisions concerning the business, including those involving hiring and firing employees.
3. The sole proprietor owns all of the business and has the right to receive all of the business's profits.
4. A sole proprietorship can be easily transferred or sold if and when the owner desires to do so; no other approval (such as from partners or shareholders) is necessary.

There are important disadvantages to this business form, too. For example, the sole proprietor's access to the capital is limited to personal funds plus any loans he or she can obtain, and the sole proprietor is legally responsible for the business's contracts and the torts he or she or any of his or her employees commit in the course of employment.

Creation of a Sole Proprietorship

It is easy to create a sole proprietorship. There are no formalities, and no federal or state government approval is required. Some local governments require all businesses, including sole proprietorships, to obtain licenses to do business within the city. If no other form of business organization is chosen, the business is by default a sole proprietorship.

Web Exercises

1. **WEB:** Use *www.google.com* to find an article that discusses a specific sole proprietorship. Read it.

2. **WEB:** Use *www.google.com* to find an article about operating a sole proprietorship in your state. Read it.

CONTEMPORARY ENVIRONMENT
d.b.a.—"Doing Business As"

A sole proprietorship can operate under the name of the sole proprietor or a *trade name*. For example, the author of this book can operate a sole proprietorship under the name "Henry R. Cheeseman" or under a trade name such as "The Big Cheese." Operating under a trade name is commonly designated as **d.b.a. (doing business as)** (e.g., Henry R. Cheeseman, doing business as "The Big Cheese").

Most states require all businesses that operate under a trade name to file a **fictitious business name statement** (or **certificate of trade name**) with the appropriate government agency. The statement must contain the name and address of the applicant, the trade name, and the address of the business. Most states also require notice of the trade name to be published in a newspaper of general circulation serving the area in which the applicant does business.

These requirements are intended to disclose the real owner's name to the public. Noncompliance can result in a fine. Some states prohibit violators from maintaining lawsuits in the state's courts.

Web Exercises

1. **WEB:** Use *www.google.com* to find an article that discusses the use of a d.b.a. name. Read it.

2. **WEB:** Use *www.google.com* to find the requirements that must be met in your state to obtain a d.b.a. name.

Personal Liability of Sole Proprietors

A sole proprietor bears the risk of loss of the business; that is, the owner will lose his or her entire capital contribution if the business fails. In addition, the sole proprietor has *unlimited personal liability* (see Exhibit 26.1). Therefore, creditors may recover claims against the business from the sole proprietor's personal assets (e.g., home, automobile, bank accounts).

Example Suppose Kathan Perek opens a clothing store called "The Clothing Store" and operates it as a sole proprietorship. Perek files the proper statement and publishes the necessary notice of the use of the trade name. Perek contributes $25,000 of his personal funds to the business and borrows $100,000 in the name of the business from a bank. Assume that after several months, Perek closes the business because it is unsuccessful. At the time it is closed, the business has no assets, owes the bank $100,000, and owes rent, trade credit, and other debits of $25,000. Here, Perek is personally liable to pay the bank and all the debts from his personal assets.

EXHIBIT 26.1

Sole Proprietorship

Debt or
obligation owed

Sole
Proprietorship → Third
Party

Capital investment

Sole
Proprietor
(Owner)

Personal liability
for sole proprietorship's
debts and obligations

In the following case, the court had to decide the liability of a sole proprietor.

C A S E   26.1
Sole Proprietorship

Vernon v. Schuster, d/b/a Diversity Heating and Plumbing

179 Ill.2d 338, 688 N.E.2d 1172, **Web** 1997 Ill. Lexis 482
Supreme Court of Illinois

> ❝ *It is well settled that a sole proprietorship has no legal identity separate from that of the individual who owns it.* ❞
>
> —Judge Freeman

Facts

James Schuster was a sole proprietor doing business as (d.b.a.) "Diversity Heating and Plumbing." Diversity Heating was in the business of selling, installing, and servicing heating and plumbing systems. George Vernon and others (Vernon) owned a building that needed a new boiler. Vernon hired Diversity Heating to install a new boiler in the building. Diversity Heating installed the boiler and gave a warranty that the boiler would not crack for 10 years. Four years later, James Schuster died. On that date, James's son, Jerry Schuster, inherited his father's business and thereafter ran the business as a sole proprietorship under the d.b.a "Diversity Heating and Plumbing." One year later, the boiler installed in Vernon's building broke and could not be repaired. Vernon demanded that Jerry Schuster honor the warranty and replace the boiler. When Jerry Schuster refused to do so, Vernon had the boiler replaced at a cost of $8,203 and sued Jerry Schuster to recover this amount for breach of warranty. The trial court dismissed Vernon's complaint, but the appellate court reinstated the case. Jerry Schuster appealed to the supreme court of Illinois.

Issue

Is Jerry Schuster liable for the warranty made by his father?

Language of the Court

Common identity of ownership is lacking when one sole proprietorship succeeds another. It is well settled that a sole proprietorship has no legal identity separate from that of the individual who owns it. The sole proprietor may do business under a fictitious name if he or she chooses. However, doing business under another name does not create an entity distinct from the person operating the business. The individual who does business as a sole proprietor under one or several names remains one person, personally liable for all his or her obligations. There is generally no continuity of existence because on the death of the sole proprietor, the sole proprietorship obviously ends.

In this case, therefore, it must be remembered that "Diversity Heating" has no legal existence. Diversity Heating was only a pseudonym for James Schuster. Once he died, Diversity Heating ceased to exist. Now, Diversity Heating is only a pseudonym for the defendant, Jerry Schuster. Once sole proprietor James Schuster died, he could not be the same sole proprietor as defendant Jerry Schuster who became a sole proprietor after his father's death. James Schuster and Jerry Schuster, one succeeding the other, cannot be the same entity. Even though defendant Jerry Schuster inherited Diversity Heating from his father, defendant would not have continued his father's sole proprietorship, but rather would have started a new sole proprietorship.

Decision

The Illinois supreme court held that Jerry Schuster, as a sole proprietor, was not liable for the warranty previously made by his father, who was also a sole proprietor. The supreme court reversed the decision of the appellate court.

Law & Ethics Questions

1. Is a sole proprietorship a separate legal entity? Explain.

2. Do you think many businesses are run as sole proprietorships? What are the benefits and detriments of doing so?

3. **ETHICS** Did Jerry Schuster act unethically by failing to honor the warranty made by his father?

Web Exercises

1. **WEB:** For the complete opinion of this case, go to *www.prenhall.com/cheesemancases*.

2. **WEB:** Visit the website of the supreme court of Illinois, at *www.state.il.us/court/SupremeCourt*.

3. **WEB:** Use *www.google.com* to find an article that discusses the benefits and detriments of conducting business as a sole proprietor. Read it.

General Partnership

General, or *ordinary, partnerships* have been recognized since ancient times. The English common law of partnerships governed early U.S. partnerships. The individual states expanded the body of partnership law.

A **general partnership**, or partnership, is a voluntary association of two or more persons for carrying on a business as co-owners for profit. The formation of a partnership creates certain rights and duties among partners and with third parties. These rights and duties are established in the partnership agreement and by law. **General partners**, or **partners**, are personally liable for the debts and obligations of the partnership (see Exhibit 26.2).

EXHIBIT 26.2

General Partnership

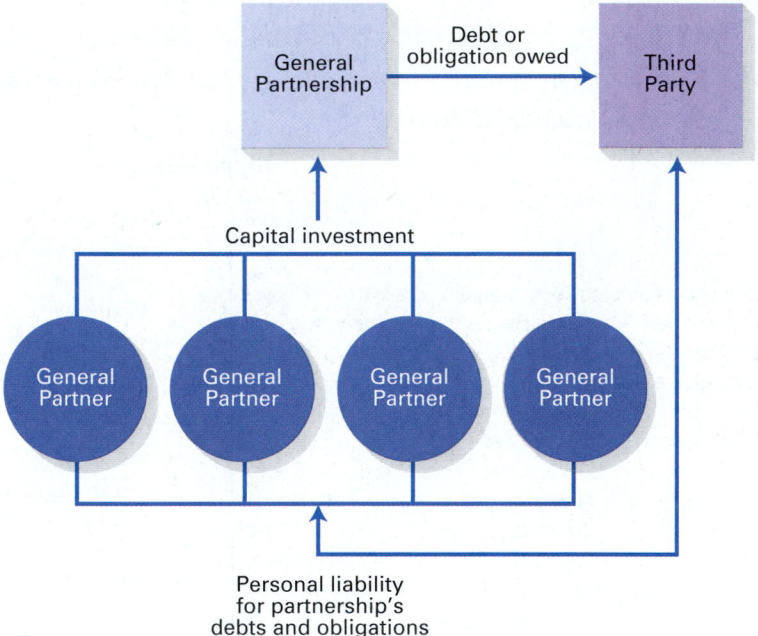

LANDMARK LAW
Uniform Partnership Act (UPA)

In 1914, the National Conference of Commissioners on Uniform State Laws (a group of lawyers, judges, and legal scholars) promulgated the **Uniform Partnership Act (UPA)**. The UPA codifies partnership law. Its goal was to establish consistent partnership law that was uniform throughout the Unites States. The UPA has been adopted in whole or in part by 48 states, the District of Columbia, Guam, and the Virgin Islands. Because it is so important, the UPA forms the basis of the study of general partnerships in this chapter.

The UPA covers most problems that arise in the formation, operation, and dissolution of ordinary partnerships. Other rules of law or equity govern if there is no applicable provision of the UPA [UPA Section 5].

The UPA adopted the *entity theory* of partnership, which considers partnerships as separate legal entities. As such, partnerships can hold title to personal and real property, transact business in the partnership name, and the like.

General Partnership Name

An ordinary partnership can operate under the names of any one or more of the partners or under a fictitious business name. If the partnership operates under a fictitious name, it must file a *fictitious business name statement* with the appropriate government agency and publish a notice of the name in a newspaper of general circulation where the partnership does business. The name selected by the partnership cannot indicate that it is a corporation (e.g., it cannot contain the term *Inc.*) and cannot be similar to the name used by any existing business entity.

Web Exercises

1. **WEB:** Use *www.google.com* to find an article about a specific general partnership. Read it.

2. **WEB:** Use *www.google.com* to find the requirements that must be met in your state to form a general partnership.

3. **WEB:** Use *www.google.com* to find a website that sells documents online to form a general partnership in your state. How much does this service cost?

Formation of a General Partnership

A business must meet four criteria to qualify as a partnership under the UPA [UPA Section 6(1)]. It must be (1) an association of two or more persons (2) carrying on a business (3) as co-owners (4) for profit. Partnerships are voluntary associations of two or more persons. All partners must agree to the participation of each co-partner. A person cannot be forced to be a partner or to accept another person as a partner. The UPA definition of *person* includes natural persons, partnerships (including limited partnerships), corporations, and other associations. A business—a trade, an occupation, or a profession—must be carried on. The organization or venture must have a profit motive in order to qualify as a partnership, even though the business does not actually have to make a profit.

> The partner of my partner is not my partner.
>
> *Legal maxim*

A general partnership may be formed with little or no formality. Co-ownership of a business is essential to create a partnership. The most important factor in determining co-ownership is whether the parties share the business's profits and management responsibility.

Receipt of a share of business profits is *prima facie* evidence of a partnership because nonpartners usually are not given the right to share in the business's profits. No inference of the existence of a partnership is drawn if profits are received in payment of (1) a debt owed to a creditor in installments or otherwise; (2) wages owed to an employee; (3) rent owed to a landlord; (4) an annuity owed to a widow, widower, or representative of a deceased partner; (5) interest owed on a loan; or (6) consideration for the sale of goodwill of a business [UPA Section 7]. An agreement to share losses of a business is strong evidence of a partnership.

The right to participate in the management of a business is important evidence for determining the existence of a partnership, but it is not conclusive evidence because the right to participate in management is sometimes given to employees, creditors, and others. It is compelling evidence of the existence of a partnership if a person is given the right to share in profits, losses, and management of a business.

The General Partnership Agreement

The agreement to form a partnership may be oral, written, or implied from the conduct of the parties. It may even be created inadvertently. No formalities are necessary, although a few states require general partnerships to file certificates of partnership with an appropriate government agency. Partnerships that exist for more than one year or are authorized to deal in real estate must be in writing under the Statute of Frauds.

It is good practice for partners to put their partnership agreement in writing. A written document is important evidence of the terms of the agreement, particularly if a dispute arises among the partners.

A written partnership agreement is called a **partnership agreement,** or **articles of partnership**. The parties can agree to almost any terms in their partnership agreement, except terms that are illegal. The articles of partnership can be short and simple or long and complex. If the agreement fails to provide for an essential term or contingency, the provisions of the UPA control. Thus, the UPA acts as a gap-filling device to the partners' agreement.

In the following case, the court had to decide whether a partnership had been created.

CASE **26.2**
General Partnership

Vohland v. Sweet

433 N.E. 2d 860, **Web** 1982 Ind. App. Lexis 1145
Court of Appeals of Indiana

> "*There is evidence from which it can be inferred that the parties intended to do the things that amount to the formation of a partnership, regardless of how they may later characterize the relationship.*"
>
> —Judge Neal

Facts

When he was a youngster, Norman E. Sweet began working for Charles Vohland as an hourly employee at a garden nursery owned by Vohland. Upon completion of military service, Sweet resumed his former employment. Three years later, Charles Vohland retired, and his son Paul Vohland (Vohland) commenced what became known as Vohland's Nursery, the business of which was landscape gardening. Vohland purchased the interests of his brothers and sisters in the nursery. At that time, Sweet's status changed: He was to receive a 20 percent share of the net profit of the business after all expenses were paid, including labor, supplies, plants, and other expenses. Sweet contributed no capital to the enterprise. The compensation was paid on an irregular basis; every several weeks, Vohland and Sweet would sit down, compute the income received and expenses paid, and Sweet would be issued a check for 20 percent of the balance. No Social Security or income taxes were withheld from Sweet's checks.

Vohland and Sweet did not enter into a written agreement. No partnership income tax returns were filed by the business. Sweet's tax returns declared that he was a self-employed salesman. He paid self-employment Social Security taxes. Vohland handled all the finances and books of the nursery and borrowed money from the bank solely in his own name for business purposes. Vohland made most of the sales for the business. Sweet managed the physical aspects of the nursery, supervised the care of the nursery stock, and oversaw the performance of the contracts for customers. Sweet testified that Vohland told him:

"He was going to take me in and that I wouldn't have to punch a time clock anymore, that I would be on a commission basis and that I would be—have more of an interest in the business if I had an interest in the business. He referred to it as a 'piece of the action.'"

Vohland denied making this statement. Sweet brought an action for dissolution of the alleged partnership and for an accounting. He sought payment for 20 percent of the business's inventory. The trial court held in favor of Sweet and awarded him $58,733. Vohland appealed.

Issue

Did Vohland and Sweet enter into a general partnership?

Language of the Court

"Commission" was used to refer to Sweet's share of the profits, and the receipt of a share of the profits is *prima facie* evidence of a partnership. Though evidence is conflicting, there is evidence that the payments were not wages, but a share of the profit of a partnership. It can readily be inferred from the evidence most favorable to support the judgment that the parties intended a community of interest in any increment in the value of the capital and in the profit. Absence of contribution to capital is not controlling, and contribution of labor and skill will suffice. There is evidence from which it can be inferred that the parties intended to do the things that amount to the formation of a partnership, regardless of how they may later characterize the relationship.

Decision

The court of appeals held that a general partnership had been created between Vohland and Sweet. The court of appeals affirmed the decision of the trial court in favor of Sweet.

Law & Ethics Questions

1. Do you think a partnership was formed in this case? Should all partnership agreements be required to be in writing?

2. **ETHICS** Do you think either party acted unethically in this case?

3. What are some of the consequences of founding a general partnership?

Web Exercises

1. **WEB:** For the complete opinion of this case, go to *www.prenhall.com/cheesemancases*.

2. **WEB:** Visit the website of the court of appeals of Indiana, at *www.state.in.us/judiciary/appeals*.

3. **WEB:** Use *www.google.com* to find an article that discusses the benefits and detriments of operating a business as a general partnership. Read it.

Right to Participate in Management

In the absence of an agreement to the contrary, all partners have equal rights in the conduct and **management of the partnership business**. In other words, each partner has one vote, regardless of the proportional size of his or her capital contribution or share in the partnership's profits. Under the UPA, a simple majority decides most ordinary partnership matters [UPA Section 18]. If the vote is tied, the action being voted on is considered to be defeated. The partners may agree to modify the majority rule by delegating management responsibility to a committee of partners or to a managing partner.

General Partners' Rights to Share in Profits

Unless otherwise agreed, the UPA mandates that a partner has the right to an equal share in the partnership's profits and losses [UPA Section 18(a)]. Partnership agreements often provide that profits and losses are to be allocated in proportion to the partners' capital contributions. The right to share in the profits of the partnership is considered to be the right to share in the earnings from the investment of capital.

Taxation of partnerships. Partnerships do not pay federal income taxes instead the income and losses of partnership flow onto individual partners' federal income tax returns.

Example Suppose LeAnn Pearson and Mark Butler form a partnership. Pearson contributes $75,000 capital, and Butler contributes $25,000 capital. They do not have an agreement as to how profits or losses are to be shared. Assume that the partnership makes $100,000 in profits. Under the UPA, Pearson and Butler share the profits equally— $50,000 each.

Where a partnership agreement provides for the sharing of profits but is silent as to how losses are to be shared, losses are shared in the same proportion as profits. The reverse is not true, however. If a partnership agreement provides for the sharing of losses but is silent as to how profits are to be shared, profits are shared equally.

Expressly providing how profits and losses are to be shared by partners can increase the benefits to partners. For example, partners with high incomes from other sources can benefit most from the losses generated by a partnership.

Right to Compensation and Reimbursement

Unless otherwise agreed, the UPA provides that no partner is entitled to remuneration for his or her performance in the partnership's business [UPA Section 18(f)]. Under this rule, partners are not entitled to receive a salary for providing services to the partnership unless agreed to by the partners.

Under the UPA, it is implied that partners will devote full time and service to the partnership. Thus, unless otherwise agreed, income earned by partners from providing services elsewhere belongs to the partnership [UPA Section 21].

Partners sometimes incur personal travel, business, and other expenses on behalf of the partnership. A partner is entitled to **indemnification** (i.e., reimbursement) for such expenditures if they are reasonably incurred in the ordinary and proper conduct of the business [UPA Section 18(b)].

Right to Return of Loans and Capital

A partner who makes a loan to the partnership becomes a creditor of the partnership. The partner is entitled to repayment of the loan, but this right is subordinated to the claims of creditors who are not partners [UPA Section 40(b)]. The partner is also entitled to receive interest from the date of the loan.

Upon termination of a partnership, the partners are entitled to have their capital contributions returned to them [UPA Section 18(a)]. However, this right is subordinated to the rights of creditors, who must be paid their claims first [UPA Section 40(b)].

Right to Information

Each partner has the right to demand true and full information from any other partner of all things affecting the partnership [UPA Section 20]. The corollary to this rule is that each partner has a duty to provide such information upon the receipt of a reasonable demand. The partnership books (financial records, tax records, and such) must be kept at the partnership's principal place of business [UPA Section 19]. The partners have an absolute right to inspect and copy these records.

Duty of Loyalty

Partners are in a *fiduciary relationship* with one another. As such, they owe each other a **duty of loyalty**. This duty is imposed by law and cannot be waived. If there is a conflict between partnership interests and personal interests, the partner must choose the interest of the partnership. Some basic forms of breach of loyalty involve:

1. *Self-dealing.* **Self-dealing** occurs when a partner deals personally with the partnership, such as buying or selling goods or property to the partnership. Such actions are permitted only if full disclosure is made and consent of the other partners is obtained.

   Example Suppose a partnership in which Dan is a partner is looking for a piece of property on which to build a new store. Dan owns a desirable piece of property. To sell the property to the partnership, Dan must first disclose his ownership interest and receive his partners' consent.

2. *Usurping a partnership opportunity.* A partner who is offered an opportunity on behalf of the partnership cannot take the opportunity for himself or herself. In other words, if a third party offers an opportunity to a partner in his or her partnership status (e.g., the opportunity to purchase a business), the partner cannot take the opportunity for him- or herself before offering it to the partnership. If the partnership rejects the opportunity, the partner is free to pursue the opportunity.

3. *Competing with the partnership.* A partner may not **compete with the partnership** without the permission of the other partners. For example, a partner in a partnership that operates an automobile dealership cannot open a competing automobile dealership without his or her co-partners' permission.

4. *Secret profits.* Partners may not make **secret profits** from partnership business. For example, a partner may not keep a kickback from a supplier.

5. *Breach of confidentiality.* Partners owe a duty to keep partnership information (e.g., trade secrets, customer lists) confidential.

6. *Misuse of property.* Partners owe a duty not to use partnership property for personal use.

A partner who breaches the duty of loyalty must disgorge any profits made from the breach to the partnership. In addition, the partner is liable for any damages caused by the breach.

> It has been uniformly laid down in this Court, as far back as we can remember, that good faith is the basis of all mercantile transactions.
>
> Judge Buller
> *Salomons v. Nissen* (1788)

Duty of Care

A partner must use reasonable care and skill in transacting partnership business. The **duty of care** calls for the partners to use the same level of care and skill that a reasonable business manager in the same position would use in the same circumstances. Breach of the duty of care is *negligence*. A partner is liable to the partnership for any damages caused by his or her negligence. The partners are not liable for honest errors in judgment.

Example Suppose Tina, Eric, and Brian form a partnership to sell automobiles. Tina, who is responsible for ordering inventory, orders large, expensive cars. Assume that a war breaks out in the Middle East that interrupts the supply of oil to the United States. The demand for large cars drops substantially, and the partnership cannot sell its inventory. Tina is not liable because the duty of care was not breached. The situation might have been different if the war had broken out before the order was placed.

Duty to Inform

Partners owe a **duty to inform** their co-partners of all information they possess that is relevant to the affairs of the partnership [UPA Section 20]. Even if a partner fails to do so, the other partners are *imputed* with knowledge of all notices concerning any matters relating to partnership affairs. Knowledge is also imputed regarding information acquired in the role of partner that affects the partnership and should have been communicated to the other partners [UPA Section 12].

Example Suppose Ted and Diane are partners. Ted knows that a piece of property owned by the partnership contains dangerous toxic wastes but fails to inform Diane of this fact. Even though Diane does not have actual knowledge of this fact, it is imputed to her.

Duty of Obedience

The **duty of obedience** requires the partners to adhere to the provisions of the partnership agreement and the decisions of the partnership. A partner who breaches this duty is liable to the partnership for any damages caused by the breach.

Example Jodie, Bart, and Denise form a partnership to develop real property. Their partnership agreement specifies that acts of the partners are limited to those necessary to accomplish the partnership's purpose. Suppose Bart, acting alone, loses $100,000 of partnership funds in commodities trading. Bart is personally liable to the partnership for the lost funds because he breached the partnership agreement.

CONTEMPORARY ENVIRONMENT

Right to an Accounting

Partners are not permitted to sue the partnership or other partners at law. Instead, they are given the right to bring an **action for an accounting** against other partners. An action for an accounting is a formal judicial proceeding in which the court is authorized to (1) review the partnership and the partners' transactions and (2) award each partner his or her share of the partnership assets [UPA Section 24]. It results in a money judgment for or against partners, according to the balance struck.

Liability of General Partners

Partners must deal with third parties in conducting partnership business. This often includes entering into contracts with third parties on behalf of the partnership. Partners, employees, and agents of the partnership sometimes injure third parties while conducting partnership business. Partners of a general partnership have personal liability for the contracts and torts of the partnership. Contract and tort liability of partnerships and their partners is discussed in the following paragraphs.

Tort Liability

While acting on partnership business, a partner or an employee of the partnership may commit a tort that causes injury to a third person. This tort could be caused by a negligent act, a breach of trust (such as embezzlement from a customer's account), a breach of fiduciary duty, defamation, fraud, or another intentional tort. The partnership is liable if the act is committed while the person is acting within the ordinary course of partnership business or with the authority of his or her co-partners.

Under the UPA, partners are **jointly and severally liable** for torts and breaches of trust [UPA Section 15(a)]. This is so even if a partner did not participate in the commission of the act. This type of liability permits a third party to sue one or more of the partners separately. Judgment can be collected only against the partners who are sued. The partnership and partners who are made to pay tort liability may seek indemnification from the partner who committed the wrongful act. A release of one partner does not discharge the liability of other partners.

Example Suppose Nicole, Jim, and Maureen form a partnership. Assume that Jim, while on partnership business, causes an automobile accident that injures Kurt, a pedestrian. Kurt suffers $100,000 in injuries. Kurt, at his option, can sue Nicole, Jim, or Maureen separately, or any two of them, or all of them.

The court applied the doctrine of joint and several liabilities in the following case.

CASE **26.3**

Tort Liability of General Partners

Zuckerman v. Antenucci

124 Misc.2d 971, 478 N.Y.S.2d 578, **Web** 1984 N.Y. Misc. Lexis 3283
Supreme Court of New York

> " *A partnership is liable for the tortious act of a partner, and a partner is jointly and severally liable for tortious acts chargeable to the partnership.* "
>
> —Judge Leviss

Facts

Jose Pena and Joseph Antenucci were both medical doctors who were partners in a medical practice. Both doctors treated Elaine Zuckerman during her pregnancy. Her son, Daniel Zuckerman, was born with severe physical problems. Elaine, as Daniel's mother and natural guardian, brought a medical malpractice suit against both doctors. The jury found that Pena was guilty of medical malpractice but that Antenucci was not. The amount of the verdict totaled $4 million. The trial court entered judgment against Pena but not against Antenucci. The plaintiffs made a posttrial motion for judgment against both defendants.

Issue

Is Antenucci jointly and severally liable for the medical malpractice of his partner, Pena?

Language of the Court

A partnership is liable for the tortious act of a partner, and a partner is jointly and severally liable for tortious acts chargeable

to the partnership. When a tort is committed by the partnership, the wrong is imputable to all of the partners jointly and severally, and an action may be brought against all or any of them in their individual capacities or against the partnership as an entity. Therefore, even though the jury found that defendant Antenucci was not guilty of any malpractice in his treatment of the patient, but that defendant Pena, his partner, was guilty of malpractice in his treatment of the patient, they were then both jointly and severally liable for the malpractice committed by defendant Pena by operation of law.

Decision

The court held that both partners were jointly and severally liable for the judgment. The supreme court reversed the decision of the trial court and held that Antenucci was liable for the tort of his partner Pena.

Law & Ethics Questions

1. What is joint and several liability? How does it differ from joint liability?

2. **ETHICS** Is it ethical for a partner to deny liability for torts of other partners?

3. What types of insurance should a partnership purchase? Why?

Web Exercises

1. **WEB:** For the complete opinion of this case, go to *www.prenhall.com/cheesemancases*.

2. **WEB:** Visit the website of the supreme court of New York, Trial Term, Queens County, at *www.courts.state.ny.us/courts/nyc/supreme/index.shtml*.

3. **WEB:** Use *www.google.com* to find an article or a case that discusses tort liability of general partners. Read it.

Contract Liability

As a legal entity, a partnership must act through its agents—that is, its partners. Contracts entered into with suppliers, customers, lenders, or others on the partnership's behalf are binding on the partnership.

Under the UPA, partners are **jointly liable** for the contracts and debts of the partnership [UPA Section 15(b)]. This means that a third party who sues to recover on a partnership contract or debt must name all the partners in the lawsuit. If such a lawsuit is successful, the plaintiff can collect the entire amount of the judgment against any or all of the partners. If the third party's suit does not name all the partners, the judgment cannot be collected against any of the partners or the partnership assets. Similarly, releasing any partner from the lawsuit releases them all.

A partner who is made to pay more than his or her proportionate share of contract liability may seek indemnification from the partnership and from those partners who have not paid their share of the loss.

In the following case, the court found partners jointly liable on a partnership contract.

CASE 26.4

Contract Liability of General Partners

Edward A. Kemmler Memorial Foundation v. Mitchell

62 Ohio.St. 494, 584 N.E.2d 695, **Web** 1992 Ohio Lexis 205
Supreme Court of Ohio

> **“***Every partner is an agent of the partnership.***”**
>
> —Judge Brown

Facts

Clifford W. Davis and Dr. William D. Mitchell formed a general partnership to purchase and operate rental properties for investment purposes. The general partnership purchased a parcel of real property from the Edward A. Kemmler Memorial Foundation (Foundation) on credit. Davis signed a $150,000 promissory note to the Foundation as "Cliff W. Davis, Partner." Prior to executing the note, Davis and Mitchell entered into an agreement that provided that only Davis, and not Mitchell, would be personally liable on the note to the Foundation. They did not inform the Foundation of this side agreement, however. When the partnership defaulted on the note, the Foundation sued the partnership and both partners to recover on the note. Mitchell asserted in defense that the side agreement with Davis relieved him of personal liability. The trial court found Davis and Mitchell jointly liable. The appellate court reversed, excusing Mitchell from liability. The Foundation appealed.

Issue

Are both general partners, Davis and Mitchell, jointly liable on the note?

Language of the Court

Every partner is an agent of the partnership for the purpose of its business, and the act of every partner, including the execution in the partnership name of any instrument, for apparently carrying on in the usual way the business of the partnership of which he is a member binds the partnership, unless the partner so acting has in fact no authority to act for the partnership in the particular matter, and the person with whom he is dealing has knowledge of the fact that he has no such authority.

Thus, if a promissory note is executed in the name of the partnership, the partnership is bound, unless a contradictory agreement between the partners is known to the parties with whom they are dealing. The trial court found that the Foundation had no knowledge of the agreement between Davis and Mitchell regarding Mitchell's liability for the note.

Decision

The supreme court of Ohio held that both partners were jointly liable on the note. The supreme court reversed the decision of the appellate court.

Law & Ethics Questions

1. What is joint liability? Should one general partner be liable to pay a judgment against the partnership?

2. **ETHICS** Should Davis and Mitchell have notified the Foundation of their side agreement?

3. Is it financially dangerous to be a partner in a general partnership? Explain.

Web Exercises

1. **WEB:** For the complete opinion of this case, go to *www.prenhall.com/cheesemancases*.

2. **WEB:** Visit the website of the supreme court of Ohio, at *www.sconet.state.oh.us*.

3. **WEB:** Use *www.google.com* to find an article that discusses contract liability of general partners. Read it.

Liability of Incoming Partners

A new partner who is admitted to a partnership is liable for the existing debts and obligations (*antecedent debts*) of the partnership only to the extent of his or her capital contribution. The **incoming partner** is personally liable for debts and obligations incurred by the partnership after becoming a partner.

Example Bubble.com is a general partnership with four partners. On May 1, Frederick is admitted as a new general partner by investing a $100,000 capital contribution. As of May 1, Bubble.com owes $800,000 of debt. After Frederick becomes a partner, the general partnership borrows $1 million of new debt. If the general partnership goes bankrupt and out of business still owing both debts, Frederick's capital contribution of $100,000 will go toward paying the $800,000 of existing debt owed by the partnership when he joined the partnership, but he is not personally liable for this debt. However, Frederick is personally liable for the $1 million of unpaid debt that the partnership borrowed after he became a partner.

Dissolution of a General Partnership

The duration of a partnership can be a fixed term (e.g., five years) or until a particular undertaking is accomplished (e.g., until a real estate development is completed), or it can be an unspecified term. A partnership with a fixed duration is called a **partnership for a term**. A partnership with no fixed duration is called a **partnership at will**.

The **dissolution** of a partnership is "the change in the relation of the partners caused by any partner ceasing to be associated in the carrying on of the business" [UPA Section 29]. A partnership that is formed for a specific time (e.g., five years) or purpose (e.g., the completion of a real estate development) dissolves automatically upon the expiration of the time or the accomplishment of the objective. Any partner of a partnership at will (i.e., one without a stated time or purpose) may rightfully withdraw and dissolve the partnership at any time.

Unless a partnership is continued, the **winding up** of the partnership follows its dissolution. The process of winding up consists of the liquidation (sale) of partnership assets and the distribution of the proceeds to satisfy claims against the partnership. The surviving partners have the right to wind up the partnership. If a surviving partner performs the winding up, he or she is entitled to reasonable compensation for his or her services [UPA Section 18(f)].

Wrongful Dissolution

A partner has the *power* to withdraw and dissolve the partnership at any time, whether it is a partnership at will or a partnership for a term. A partner who withdraws from a partnership at will has the *right* to do so and is therefore not liable for dissolving the partnership.

A partner who withdraws from a partnership for a term prior to the expiration of the term does not have the right to dissolve the partnerships. The partner's action causes a **wrongful dissolution** of the partnership. The partner is liable for damages caused by the wrongful dissolution of the partnership.

Example Ashley, Vivi, Qixia, and Tina form a general partnership called "Four Divas Clothing" to operate an upscale women's clothing store. The partnership has a stated term of five years. After one year, Ashley decides to quit the partnership. Because Ashley has the power to quit the partnership, when she does so, the four-partner partnership dissolves. Ashley does not have the right to quit the partnership, and her action causes the wrongful dissolution of the partnership. She is liable for any damages caused by her wrongful dissolution of the partnership.

Notice of Dissolution

The dissolution of a partnership terminates the partners' actual authority to enter into contracts or otherwise act on behalf of the partnership. **Notice of dissolution** must be given to certain third parties. The degree of notice depends on the relationship of the third party with the partnership [UPA Section 35]:

1. Third parties who have actually dealt with the partnership must be given *actual notice* (verbal or written) of dissolution or have acquired knowledge of the dissolution from another source.
2. Third parties who have not dealt with the partnership but have knowledge of it must be given either actual or *constructive notice* of dissolution. Constructive notice consists of publishing a notice of dissolution in a newspaper of general circulation serving the area where the business of the partnership was regularly conducted.
3. Third parties who have not dealt with the partnership and do not have knowledge of it do not have to be given notice.

If proper notice is not given to a required third party after the dissolution of a partnership, and a partner enters into a contract with the third party, liability may arise on the grounds of *apparent authority*.

Distribution of Assets

After partnership assets have been liquidated and reduced to cash, the proceeds are distributed to satisfy claims against the partnership. The debts are satisfied in the following order [UPA Section 40(b)]:

1. Creditors (except partners who are creditors)
2. Creditor-partners
3. Capital contributions
4. Profits

The partners can agree to change the priority of distribution of assets among themselves. If the partnership cannot satisfy its creditors' claims, the partners are personally liable for the partnership's debts and obligations [UPA Sections 40(d), 40(f)].

After the proceeds are distributed, the partnership automatically terminates. Termination ends the legal existence of the partnership [UPA Section 30].

Continuation of a General Partnership After Dissolution

The surviving, or remaining, partners have the right to continue a partnership after dissolution. It is good practice for the partners of a partnership to enter into a *continuation agreement* that expressly sets forth the events that allow for **continuation of the partnership**, the amount to be paid **outgoing partners**, and other details.

When a partnership is continued, the old partnership is dissolved, and a new partnership is created. The new partnership is composed of the remaining partners and any new partners admitted to the partnership. The creditors of the old partnership become creditors of the new partnership and have equal status with the creditors of the new partnership [UPA Section 41].

Liability of Outgoing Partners

The dissolution of a partnership does not of itself discharge the liability of outgoing partners for existing partnership debts and obligations.

Example If a partnership consisting of four partners is dissolved, each partner is personally liable for debts and obligations of the partnership that exist at the time of dissolution.

Example If a partnership is dissolved because a partner leaves the partnership and the partnership is continued by the remaining partners, the outgoing partner is personally liable for the debts and obligations of the partnership at the time of dissolution. The outgoing partner is not liable for any new debts and obligations incurred by the partnership after the dissolution, as long as proper notification of his or her withdrawal from the partnership has been given to the creditor.

CONTEMPORARY ENVIRONMENT
Right of Survivorship

A partner is a co-owner with the other partners of the specific partnership property as a *tenant in partnership* [UPA Section 25(1)]. This is a special legal status that exists only in a partnership. Upon the death of a partner, the deceased partner's right in specific partnership property vests in the remaining partner or partners; it does not pass to his or her heirs or next of kin. This is called the **right of survivorship**. Upon the death of the last surviving partner, the rights in specific partnership property vest in the deceased partner's legal representative [UPA Section 25(2)(C)]. The *value* of the deceased partner's interest in the partnership passes to his or her beneficiaries or heirs upon his or her death, however.

Example Jaime, Harold, Shou-Ju, and Jesus form a general partnership to operate a new restaurant. After their first restaurant is successful, they expand until the partnership owns 100 restaurants. At that time, Jaime dies. None of the partnership assets transfer to Jaime's heirs: for example, they do not get 25 of the restaurants. Instead, under the right of survivorship, they inherit Jaime's ownership interest, and his heirs now have the right to receive Jaime's one-quarter of the partnership's profits each year.

INTERNATIONAL LAW
General Partnerships Outside the United States

In England, partnership law is virtually identical to that of the United States. In both countries, which follow the *English model*, a partnership is an association of two or more persons carrying on business with the intent to make a profit. In both countries, general partners are personally liable for the debts and obligations of the general partnership.

In France and Germany, which are civil law countries, a partnership is called a "company" (*société* in French and *Gesellschaft* in German). In both France and Germany, the owners have full personal liability for the actions of these companies.

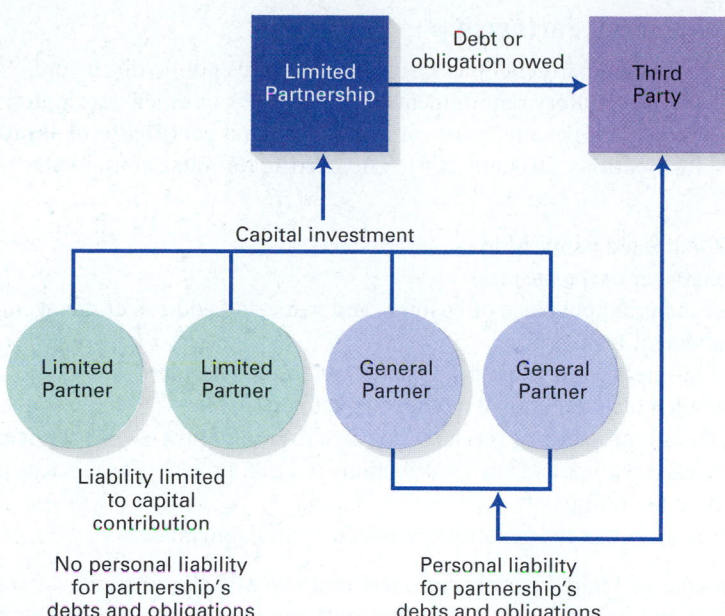

EXHIBIT 26.3

Limited Partnership

Limited Partnership

A **limited partnership** has two types of partners: (1) **general partners**, who invest capital, manage the business, and are personally liable for partnership debts, and (2) **limited partners**, who invest capital but do not participate in management and are not personally liable for partnership debts beyond their capital contributions (see Exhibit 26.3).

A limited partnership must have one or more general partners and one or more limited partners [RULPA Section 101(7)]. There are no upper limits on the number of general or limited partners allowed in a limited partnership. Any person may be a general or limited partner. This includes natural persons, partnerships, limited partnerships, trusts, estates, associations, and corporations. A person may be both a general and a limited partner in the same limited partnership.

The Revised Uniform Limited Partnership Act , RULPA, permits a corporation to be the sole general partner of a limited partnership. Where this is permissible, it affects the liability of the limited partnership. This is because the limited partners are liable only to the extent of their capital contributions, and the corporation acting as general partner is liable only to the extent of its assets.

L A N D M A R K   L A W

The Revised Uniform Limited Partnership Act

In 1916, the National Conference of Commissioners on Uniform State Laws, a group composed of lawyers, judges, and legal scholars, promulgated the **Uniform Limited Partnership Act (ULPA)**. The ULPA contains a uniform set of provisions for the formation, operation, and dissolution of limited partnerships. Most states originally enacted this law.

In 1976, the National Conference of Commissioners on Uniform State Laws promulgated the **Revised Uniform Limited Partnership**

Act (RULPA), which provides a more modern, comprehensive law for the formation, operation, and dissolution of limited partnerships. This law supersedes the ULPA in the states that have adopted it. The RULPA provides the basic foundation for the discussion of limited partnership law in the following text.

Certificate of Limited Partnership

The creation of a limited partnership is formal and requires public disclosure. The entity must comply with the statutory requirements of the RULPA or other state statutes. Under the RULPA, two or more persons must execute and sign a **certificate of limited partnership** [RULPA Sections 201 and 206]. The certificate must contain the following information:

1. Name of the limited partnership
2. General character of the business
3. Address of the principal place of business and name and address of the agent to receive service of legal process
4. Name and business address of each general and limited partner
5. Latest date on which the limited partnership is to dissolve
6. Amount of cash, property, or services (and description of property or services) contributed by each partner and any contributions of cash, property, or services promised to be made in the future
7. Any other matters that the general partners determine to include

The certificate of limited partnership must be filed with the secretary of state of the appropriate state and, if required by state law, with the county recorder in the county or counties in which the limited partnership carries on business. The limited partnership is formed when the certificate of limited partnership is filed.

Amendments to the Certificate of Limited Partnership

A limited partnership must keep its certificate of limited partnership current by filing necessary certificates of amendment at the same offices where the certificate of limited partnership is filed [RULPA Section 202(a)]. Such amendments are filed to apprise creditors and others of current information regarding the limited partnership and its partners. The certificate of amendment must be filed within 30 days of the occurrence of the following events:

1. A change in a partner's capital contribution
2. The admission of a new partner
3. The withdrawal of a partner
4. The continuation of the business after a judicial decision dissolving the limited partnership after the withdrawal of the last general partner

Name of the Limited Partnership

> It is the privilege of a trader in a free country, in all matters not contrary to law, to regulate his own mode of carrying it on according to his own discretion and choice.
>
> B. Alderson
> *Hilton v. Eckersly (1855)*

The firm name of a limited partnership may not include the surname of a limited partner unless (1) it is also the surname of a general partner or (2) the business was carried on under that name before the admission of the limited partner [RULPA Section 102(2)]. A limited partner who knowingly permits his or her name to be used in violation of this provision becomes liable as a general partner to any creditors who extend credit to the partnership without actual knowledge of his or her true status [RULPA Section 303(d)].

Other restrictions on the name of a limited partnership are that (1) the name cannot be the same as or deceptively similar to the names of corporations or other limited partnerships, (2) states can designate words that cannot be used in limited partnership names, and (3) the name must contain, without abbreviation, the words *limited partnership* [RULPA Section 102].

Capital Contributions

Under the RULPA, the capital contributions of general and limited partners may be in cash, property, services rendered, or promissory notes or other obligations to contribute cash or property or to perform services [RULPA Section 501]. A partner or creditor of a limited partnership may bring a lawsuit to enforce a partner's promise to make a contribution [RULPA Section 502(a)].

Web Exercises

1. **WEB:** Use *www.google.com* to find an article about a specific limited partnership. Read it.

2. **WEB:** Use *www.google.com* to find the requirements that must be met in your state to form a limited partnership.

3. **WEB:** Use *www.google.com* to find a website that sells documents online to form a limited partnership in your state. How much does this service cost?

Defective Formation

Defective formation occurs when (1) a certificate of limited partnership is not properly filed, (2) there are defects in a certificate that is filed, or (3) some other statutory requirement for the creation of a limited partnership is not met. If there is a substantial defect in the creation of a limited partnership, persons who thought they were limited partners can find themselves liable as general partners.

Partners who erroneously but in good faith believe they have become limited partners can escape liability as general partners by either (1) causing the appropriate certificate of limited partnership (or certificate of amendment) to be filed or (2) withdrawing from any future equity participation in the enterprise and causing a certificate showing this withdrawal to be filed. Nevertheless, the limited partner remains liable to any third party who transacts business with the enterprise before either certificate is filed if the third person believed in good faith that the partner was a general partner at the time of the transaction [RULPA Section 304].

Limited Partnership Agreement

Although not required by law, the partners of a limited partnership often draft and execute a **limited partnership agreement** (also called the **articles of limited partnership**) that sets forth the rights and duties of the general and limited partners; the terms and conditions regarding the operation, termination, and dissolution of the partnership; and so on. Where there is no such agreement, the certificate of limited partnership serves as the articles of limited partnership.

It is good practice to establish voting rights in a limited partnership agreement or certificate of limited partnership. The limited partnership agreement can provide which transactions must be approved by which partners (i.e., general, limited, or both). General and limited partners may be given unequal voting rights.

Exhibit 26.4 contains a sample limited partnership agreement.

Share of Profits and Losses

A limited partnership agreement may specify how profits and losses from the limited partnership are to be allocated among the general and limited partners. If there is no such agreement, the RULPA provides that profits and losses from a limited partnership are shared on the basis of the value of the partner's capital contribution [RULPA Section 503]. A limited partner is not liable for losses beyond his or her capital contribution.

Example Suppose there are four general partners, each of whom contributes $50,000 in capital to the limited partnership, and four limited partners, each of whom contributes $200,000 capital. The total amount of contributed capital is $1 million. The limited partnership agreement does not stipulate how profits and losses are to be allocated. Assume that the limited partnership makes $3 million in profits. Under the RULPA, each general partner would receive $150,000 profit, and each limited partner would receive $600,000.

Example Suppose instead that the limited partnership loses $3 million. Under the RULPA, each limited partner would suffer a loss of $200,000 (up to his or her capital contribution), while each general partner would suffer a personal loss of $500,000 (after his or her capital of $50,000 each is used to pay the debt).

EXHIBIT 26.4

Sample Limited Partnership Agreement

LIMITED PARTNERSHIP AGREEMENT

---

1. Introduction. This agreement of Limited Partnership dated January 2, 2008 by and between John Weston, Wai Chan, and Susan Martinez (General Partners) and Shari Berkowitz, Raymond Wong, and Harold Johnson (Limited Partners).

The General Partners and Limited Partners agree to form a Limited Partnership (Partnership) pursuant to the provisions of the California Revised Limited Partnership Act on the terms and conditions hereinafter set forth.

2. Name of Partnership. The name of the Partnership shall be "The Wilshire Investment Company, a California Limited Partnership." The business of the Partnership shall be conducted in that name.

3. Principal Place of Business. The principal office of the Partnership shall be at 4000 Wilshire Boulevard, Los Angeles, California 90010 or at such other place within California as may be determined from time to time by the General Partners.

4. Purpose of the Partnership. The Partnership shall be engaged in the business of buying, selling, and developing commercial and industrial real estate and such activities as are related or incidental thereto.

5. Agent for Service of Process. The name of the agent for service of process is Frederick Friendly, whose address is 2500 Century Park East, Suite 600, Los Angeles, California 90067.

6. Term of Partnership. The term of the Partnership shall commence on the date on which the Partnership's Certificate of Limited Partnership is filed by the Secretary of State of California and shall continue until it terminates in accordance with the provisions of this Agreement.

7. Certificate of Limited Partnership. The General Partners shall immediately execute a Certificate of Limited Partnership and cause that Certificate to be filed in the office of the secretary of state of California. The General Partners shall also record a certified copy of the Certificate in the office of the county recorder of every county in which the Partnership owns real property.

8. Members of the Partnership.

(a) The names and addresses of each original General Partner is as follows:

Name	Address
John Weston	500 Ocean Boulevard, Los Angeles, California
Wai Chan	700 Apple Road, Seattle, Washington
Susan Martinez	800 Palm Drive, Miami, Florida

(b) The names and addresses of each original Limited Partner is as follows:

Name	Address
Shari Berkowitz	700 Apple Street, New York, New York
Raymond Wong	900 Flower Avenue, San Francisco, California
Harold Johnson	300 Oil Field Road, Houston, Texas

9. General Partners' Capital Contributions. The General Partners shall make the following contributions to the Partnership's capital no later than January 2, 2000.

Cash

John Weston	$ 60,000

Property

Wai Chan	$ 30,000
Susan Martinez	$ 30,000

No interest will be paid on any balances in the General Partners' capital accounts.

10. Limited Partners' Capital Contributions. The Limited Partners shall make the following contributions to the Partnership's capital no later than January 2, 2000.

Cash

Shari Berkowitz	$100,000
Raymond Wong	$ 50,000
Harold Johnson	$ 50,000

No interest will be paid on any balances in the General Partners' capital accounts.

11. Additional Capital Contributions from Limited Partners. The General Partners may call for additional cash contributions to the Partnership's capital from the Limited Partners. The aggregate of all additional contributions made by the Limited Partners pursuant to this Paragraph shall not exceed 100 percent of the original capital contributions made by them pursuant to Paragraph 10 of this Agreement. Notice of the call shall be made by registered mail, return receipt requested, and shall be deemed made when posted. The Limited Partners's additional capital contribution must be made no later than 60 days following the call.

12. Division of Profits. Each Partner shall receive the following share of the net profits of the Partnership:

Partner	Percent
General Partners:	
John Weston	30%
Wai Chan	15%
Susan Martinez	15%
Limited Partners:	
Shari Berkowitz	20%
Raymond Wong	10%
Harold Johnson	10%

13. Sharing of Losses. Each Partner shall bear a share of the losses of the Partnership equal to the share of the profits to which he is entitled. The share of the losses of each Partner shall be charged against his contribution to the capital of the Partnership.

The Limited Partners will not be liable for any Partnership debts or losses beyond the amounts to be contributed to them pursuant to Paragraphs 10 and 11 of this Agreement.

After giving effect to the share of losses chargeable against the capital contributions of Limited Partners, the remaining Partnership losses shall be borne by the General Partners in the same proportions in which, between themselves, they are to share profits.

14. Management of Partnership. The General Partners shall have the sole and exclusive control of the Limited Partnership.

The General Partners shall have an equal voice in the management of the Partnership, and each shall devote his or her full time to the conduct of the Partnership's business.

The General Partners shall have the power and authority to take such action from time to time as they may deem to be necessary, appropriate, or convenient in connection with the management and conduct of the business and affairs of the Partnership, including, without limitation, the power to

(a) Acquire property, including real and personal property.

(b) Dispose of Partnership property.

(c) Borrow or lend money.

(continued)

EXHIBIT 26.4

(Continued)

(d) Make, deliver, or accept commercial paper.

(e) Pledge, mortgage, encumber, or grant a security interest in the Partnership properties as security for repayment of loans.

(f) Take any and all other action permitted by law that is customary in or reasonably related to the conduct of the Partnership business or affairs.

15. Limited Partners Not to Manage Business. The Limited Partners will not manage the business of the Partnership or assist in its management.

16. Partnership Books and Records. The Partnership books of account will be kept in accordance with generally accepted accounting principles. The books and supporting records will be maintained at the Partnership's principal office and will be examined by the Partnership's certified public accountants at least annually. The Partnership's fiscal year shall start on January 1 and close on December 31.

17. General Partner's Salaries. The General Partners shall each receive a salary of $60,000 per annum, payable in monthly installments, as compensation for managing the Partnership. No increases shall be made in the General Partners' salaries without the written consent of a majority of the Limited Partners.

18. Admission of New General Partners. No new General Partners will be admitted to the Partnership without the written consent of all the General Partners and Limited Partners as to both his or her admission and the terms on which the new General Partner is admitted.

19. Admission of New Limited Partners. No new Limited Partners will be admitted to the Partnership without the written consent of all the General Partners and Limited Partners as to both his or her admission and the terms on which the new Limited Partner is admitted.

20. No Sale or Assignment of, or Granting Lien on Partnership Interest by General Partner. Without the written consent of all the General Partners and Limited Partners, no General Partner shall assign, mortgage, or give a security interest in his or her Partnership interest.

21. Right of Limited Partner to Assign Partnership Interest or Substitute New Limited Partner. Upon 30 days' written notice to the General Partners, a Limited Partner can assign his or her interest in the Partnership's profits to a third party. Such assignment shall not constitute a substitution of the third party as a new Limited Partner in the place of the assignor. A Limited Partner may substitute a third party in his or her place as a new Limited Partner only with the consent in writing of all the General Partners and Limited Partners.

22. Effect of Death, Disability, or Retirement of a General Partner. The death, retirement, or permanent disability of a General Partner (the withdrawing General Partner) that makes it impossible for him or her to carry out his or her duties under this Agreement shall terminate the Partnership.

If a General Partner survives, the remaining General Partners may continue the Partnership business and may purchase the interest of the withdrawing General Partner in the assets and goodwill of the Partnership. The remaining General Partners have the option, exercisable by them at any time within 30 days after the date on which the withdrawing General Partner ceases to be a General Partner, to purchase the withdrawing General Partner's interest by paying to the person legally entitled thereto the value of that interest as shown on the lst regular accounting of the Partnership preceding the date on which the General Partner ceased to be General Partner, together with the full unwithdrawn portion of the withdrawing General Partner's interest by paying to the person legally entitled thereto the value of that interest as shown on the last regular accounting of the Partnership preceding the date on which the General Partner ceased to be General Partner, together with the full unwithdrawn portion of the withdrawing General Partner's distributive share of any net profits earned by the Partnership between the date of that accounting and the date on which the withdrawing General Partner ceased to be a General Partner of the Partnership.

23. Duties of Remaining Purchasing General Partners. Upon the purchase of a withdrawing General Partner's interest, the remaining General Partners shall assume all obligations of the Partnership and shall hold the withdrawing General Partner, the personal representative and estate of the withdrawing General Partner, and the property of the withdrawing General Partner free and harmless from all liability for those obligations.

The remaining General Partners shall immediately amend the Certificate of Limited Partnership and shall file such amendment with the office of the Secretary of State, and shall cause to be prepared, filed, served, and published all other notices required by law to protect the withdrawing General Partner or the personal representative and estate of the withdrawing General Partner from all liability for the future obligations of the Partnership business.

24. Effect of Death of Limited Partner or Substitution of Limited Partner. The death of a Limited Partner or the substitution of a new Limited Partner for a Limited Partner shall not affect the continuity of the Partnership of the conduct of its business.

25. Voluntary Dissolution. A General Partner may terminate the Partnership at any time upon 120 days written notice to each Limited Partner. Upon termination of the Partnership, it shall be liquidated in accordance with Paragraph 26 of this Agreement.

26. Liquidation of Partnership. If the Partnership is liquidated, its assets, including its goodwill and name, shall be sold in the manner designed to produce the greatest return. The proceeds of the liquidation shall be distributed in the following order:

(a) To creditors of the Partnership including Partners who are creditors to the extent permitted by law, in satisfaction of liabilities of the Partnership

(b) To Partners in payment of the balances in their income accounts

(c) To Partners in payment of the balances in their capital accounts

(d) To Partners in payment of the remainder of the proceeds

27. Certificate of Dissolution. Upon dissolution of the Partnership, the General Partners shall execute and file in the office of the secretary of state a Certificate of Dissolution. If dissolution occurs after a sole General Partner ceases to be General Partner, the Limited Partners conducting the winding up of the Partnership's affairs shall file the Certificate of Dissolution.

28. Entire Agreement. This Agreement contains the entire understanding among the Partners and supersedes any prior written or oral agreements between them respecting the subject matter contained herein. There are no representations, agreements, arrangements, or understandings, oral or written, between and among the Partners relating to the subject matter of this Agreement that are not fully expressed herein.

29. Controlling Law. This Agreement shall be interpreted under the law of the State of California. Further, each Partner consents to the jurisdiction of the courts of the State of California.

30. Service of Notices. Service of notice upon the Partnership will be made by registered or certified mail, return receipt requested, addressed to the Partnership's principal place of business.

Service of notice upon any or all Partners will be made by registered mail, return receipt requested, addressed to the addresses given in this Agreement or such other addresses as a Partner may from time to time give to the Partnership.

31. Severability. If any provisions of this agreement shall be declared by a court of competent jurisdiction to be invalid, void, or unenforceable, the remaining provisions shall continue in full force and effect.

32. Arbitration of Disputes. Any controversy concerning this Agreement will be settled by arbitration according to the rules of the American Arbitration Association, and judgment upon the award may be entered and enforced in any court.

_____   _____
General Partner   Limited Partner

_____   _____
General Partner   Limited Partner

> It is the spirit and not the form of law that keeps justice alive.
>
> Earl Warren
> *The Law and the Future* (1955)

Right to Information

Upon reasonable demand, each limited partner has the right to obtain from the general partners true and full information regarding the state of the business, the financial condition of the limited partnership, and so on [RULPA Section 305]. In addition, the limited partnership must keep the following records at its principal office:

1. A copy of the certificate of limited partnership and all amendments thereto
2. A list of the full names and business addresses of each partner
3. Copies of effective written limited partnership agreements
4. Copies of federal, state, and local income tax returns
5. Copies of financial statements of the limited partnership for the three most recent years

Admission of New Partners

Once a limited partnership has been formed, a new limited partner can be added only upon the written consent of all partners, unless the limited partnership agreement provides otherwise. New general partners can be admitted only with the specific written consent of each partner [RULPA Section 401]. A limited partnership agreement cannot waive the right of partners to approve the admission of new general partners. The admission is effective when an amendment of the certificate of limited partnership reflecting that fact is filed [RULPA Section 301].

Foreign Limited Partnerships

A limited partnership is a **domestic limited partnership** in the state in which it is organized. It is a **foreign limited partnership** in all other states. Under the RULPA, the law of the state in which the entity is organized governs its organization, its internal affairs, and the liability of its limited partners [RULPA Section 901].

Before transacting business in a foreign state, a foreign limited partnership must file an application for registration with the secretary of state. If the application conforms with law, a **certificate of registration** permitting the foreign limited partnership to transact business will be issued. [RULPA Section 902].

Once registered, a foreign limited partnership may use the courts of the foreign state to enforce contracts and other rights. Failure to register neither impairs the validity of any act or contract of the unregistered foreign limited partnership nor prevents it from defending itself in any proceeding in the courts of the foreign state. However, unregistered foreign limited partnerships may not initiate litigation in the foreign jurisdiction. The limited partner's status is not affected by whether the limited partnership is registered or unregistered. For example, if a foreign limited partnership has failed to register in a foreign state and causes an injury to someone in that state, the limited partners are not personally liable [RULPA Section 907].

CONTEMPORARY ENVIRONMENT
Master Limited Partnership

One of the major drawbacks for investors who are limited partners in a limited partnership is that their investment usually is not liquid because there is no readily available market for buying and selling limited partnership interests.

Large limited partnerships can choose to be **master limited partnerships (MLPs)**. An MLP is a limited partnership whose limited partnership interests are traded on organized securities exchanges such as the New York Stock Exchange. MLPs are often created by corporations that transfer certain corporate assets (such as real estate) to an MLP and then sell limited partnership interests to the public. The corporation usually remains as the general partner. Some MLPs are formed to make original investments.

There are tax benefits to owning a limited partnership interest in an MLP rather than owning corporate stock. MLPs pay no income tax; partnership income and losses flow directly onto the individual partners' income tax returns. Profit and other distribution of MLPs also avoid the double taxation of corporate dividends.

Liability of General and Limited Partners

The general partners of a limited partnership have **unlimited liability** for the debts and obligations of the limited partnerships. Thus, general partners have unlimited **personal liability** for the debts and obligations of the limited partnership. This liability extends to debts that cannot be satisfied with the existing capital of the limited partnership.

Generally, limited partners have **limited liability** for the debts and obligations of the limited partnership. Limited partners are liable only for the debts and obligations of the limited partnership up to their capital contributions, and they are not personally liable for the debts and obligations of the limited partnership.

Example Gertrude and Gerald are the general partners of a limited partnership called Real Estate Development, Ltd. Lin, Leopold, Lonnie, and Lawrence are limited partners of the limited partnership and have each invested $100,000 in the limited partnership. Real Estate Development, Ltd., borrows $2 million from City Bank. After six months, the limited partnership goes bankrupt, still owing City Bank $2 million. In this case, the four limited partners each lose their $100,000 capital investment but are not personally liable for the $2 million debt owed by the limited partnership to City Bank. The four general partners, however, are each personally liable to City Bank for the limited partnership's unpaid $2 million loan to City Bank.

Participation in Management

Under partnership law, general partners have the right to manage the affairs of the limited partnership. On the other hand, as a trade-off for limited liability, limited partners give up their right to participate in the control and management of the limited partnership. This means, in part, that limited partners have no right to bind the partnership to contracts or other obligations.

Under the RULPA, a limited partner is liable as a general partner if his or her participation in the control of the business is substantially the same as that of a general partner, but the limited partner is liable only to persons who reasonably believed him or her to be a general partner [RULPA Section 303(a)].

Permissible Activities of Limited Partners

The RULPA clarifies the types of activities that a limited partner may engage in without losing his or her limited liability. These activities include [RULPA Sections 303(b), 303(c)]:

1. Being an agent, an employee, or a contractor of the limited partnership or a general partner
2. Being a consultant or an advisor to a general partner regarding the limited partnership
3. Acting as a surety for the limited partnership
4. Approving or disapproving an amendment to the limited partnership agreement
5. Voting on the following partnership matters:
   a. The dissolution and winding up of the limited partnership
   b. The sale, transfer, exchange, lease, or mortgage of substantially all of the assets of the limited partnership
   c. The incurrence of indebtedness by the limited partnership other than in the ordinary course of business
   d. A change in the nature of the business of the limited partnership
   e. The removal of a general partner

Example Laura is an investor limited partner in a limited partnership. At some time after she becomes a limited partner, Laura does not think that the general partners are doing a very good job at managing the affairs of the limited partnership, so she participates in the management of the limited partnership. While doing so, a bank loans $1 million to the limited partnership, believing that Laura is a general partner because of her involvement in the management of the limited partnership. If the limited partnership defaults on the $1 million loan owed to the bank, Laura will be treated as a general partner and be held personally liable for the loan along with the general partners of the limited partnership.

Example Assume that in the previous example, the general partners of the limited partnership vote to make Laura, a limited partner, president of the limited partnership. Laura therefore has two distinct relationships with the limited partnership: first as an investor limited partner and second as a manager (president) of the limited partnership. In this case, Laura can lawfully participate in the management of the limited partnership without losing the limited liability shield granted by her limited partner status.

Liability on Personal Guarantee

On some occasions when limited partnerships apply for an extension of credit from a bank, a supplier, or another creditor, the creditor will not make the loan based on the limited partnership's own credit history or ability to repay the credit. The creditor may require a limited partner to personally guarantee the repayment of the loan in order to extend credit to the limited partnership. If a limited partner personally guarantees a loan made by a creditor to the limited partnership and the limited partnership defaults on the loan, the creditor may enforce the **personal guarantee** and recover payment from the limited partner who personally guaranteed the repayment of the credit.

CONCEPT SUMMARY

Liability of Partners of a Limited Partnership

General rule	Limited partners are not individually liable for the obligations or conduct of the partnership beyond the amount of their capital contribution.
Exceptions to the general rule	Limited partners are individually liable for the debts, obligations, and tortious acts of the partnership in three situations:

1. *Defective formation.* There has not been substantial compliance in good faith with the statutory requirements to create a limited partnership. *Exception:* Persons who erroneously believed themselves to be limited partners either (1) caused the appropriate certificate of limited partnership or amendment thereto to be filed or (2) withdrew from any future equity participation in the profits of the partnership and caused a certificate of withdrawal to be filed.

2. *Participation in management.* The limited partner participated in the management and control of the partnership. *Exception:* The limited partner was properly employed by the partnership as a manager or an executive.

3. *Personal guarantee.* The limited partner signed an enforceable personal guarantee to guarantee the performance of the limited partnership.

ETHICS SPOTLIGHT

Limited Partner Liable on Personal Guarantee

> **"** *Stover had every reason to know that his unqualified signature on the documents would bind his personal credit as that of the general partner.* **"**
>
> —Judge Shangler

Many small businesses, including limited partnerships, attempt to borrow money from banks or obtain credit from suppliers. Often these lenders require owners of partnerships and other small businesses to personally guarantee that they will repay the loan if the partnership or business does not. Consider the following case.

Linnane Magnavox Home Entertainment Center was a limited partnership that was organized under the laws of Kansas. Paul T. Linnane was the sole general partner, and Richard Gale Stover was the limited partner. Stover was the "silent partner" who provided capital for the limited partnership. Stover took no part in the day-to-day management or control of the limited partnership. The limited partnership wanted to enter into a contract with General Electric Credit Corporation (GE Credit) whereby GE Credit would provide financing to the limited partnership. GE Credit refused to grant the credit to the limited partnership unless Stover, the limited partner, signed as the guarantor of the credit. It was not until Stover personally signed the credit agreement as the guarantor that GE Credit extended credit to the limited partnership.

When the limited partnership defaulted on the payment of the debt and Paul Linnane, the general partner, was adjudicated bankrupt, GE Credit sued Stover to recover the debt. The court of appeals held that Stover, the limited partner, was liable to pay the debts of the limited partnership to GE Credit. The court stated:

> The question for decision was whether, for the purpose of the extension of credit to Linnane Magnavox, Stover put his personal assets at stake and GE Credit was therefore induced to extend its credit to the partnership. The evidence before the trial court was that GE Credit would have not extended credit to Linnane Magnavox had not Stover signed the credit agreement. Stover had every reason to know that his unqualified signature on the documents would bind his personal credit as that of the general partner.

The court of appeals held that Stover was liable on his personal guarantee to GE Credit. *General Electric Credit Corporation v. Stover*, 708 S.W.2d 355, **Web** 1986 Mo. App. Lexis 3931 (Court of Appeals of Missouri)

Law & Ethics Questions

1. What is a personal guarantee? Why do lenders and other creditors often require personal guarantees?
2. **ETHICS** Was it ethical for Stover to try to get out from his personal guarantee?

Web Exercises

1. **WEB:** For the complete opinion of this case, go to *www.prenhall.com/cheesemancases*.
2. **WEB:** Visit the website of the court of appeals of Missouri, Western District, at *www.courts.mo.gov/page.asp?id=227*.
3. **WEB:** Use *www.google.com* to find an article or a case in which a person has been found liable on a personal guarantee. Read it.
4. **WEB:** Use *www.google.com* to find a copy of a personal guarantee.

Dissolution of a Limited Partnership

A limited partnership may be dissolved and its affairs wound up just like a general partnership. The RULPA establishes rules for the dissolution and winding up of limited partnerships. Upon the dissolution and the commencement of the winding up of a limited partnership, a **certificate of cancellation** must be filed by the limited partnership with the secretary of state of the state in which the limited partnership is organized [RULPA Section 203].

Causes of Dissolution

Under the RULPA, the following four events cause the dissolution of a limited partnership [RULPA Section 801]:

1. The end of the life of the limited partnership, as specified in the certificate of limited partnership—that is, at the end of a set time period or the completion of a project.
2. The written consent of all general and limited partners.
3. The withdrawal of a general partner. Withdrawal includes the retirement, death, bankruptcy, adjudged insanity, or removal of a general partner or the assignment by a general partner of his or her partnership interest. If a corporation or partnership is a

general partner, the dissolution of the corporation or partnership is considered withdrawal.

4. The entry of a *decree of judicial dissolution*, which may be granted to a partner whenever it is not reasonably practical to carry on the business in conformity with the limited partnership agreement [RULPA Section 802] (e.g., if the general partners are deadlocked over important decisions affecting the limited partnership).

A limited partnership is not dissolved upon the withdrawal of a general partner if (1) the certificate of limited partnership permits the business to be carried on by the remaining general partner or partners or (2) within 90 days of the withdrawal, all partners agree in writing to continue the business (and select a general partner or partners, if necessary) [RULPA Section 801].

Winding Up

A limited partnership must *wind up* its affairs upon dissolution. Unless otherwise provided in the limited partnership agreement, the partnership's affairs may be wound up by the general partners who have not acted wrongfully or, if there are none, the limited partners. Any partner may petition the court to wind up the affairs of a limited partnership [RULPA Section 803]. A partner who winds up the affairs of a limited partnership has the same rights, powers, and duties as a partner winding up a general partnership.

Distribution of Assets

After the assets of a limited partnership have been liquidated, the proceeds must be distributed. The RULPA provides the following order of distribution of partnership assets upon the winding up of a limited partnership [RULPA Section 804]:

1. *Creditors* of the limited partnership, including partners who are creditors (except for liabilities for distributions)
2. *Partners* with respect to:
   a. Unpaid distributions
   b. Capital contributions
   c. The remainder of the proceeds

The partners may provide in the limited partnership agreement for a different distribution among the partners, but the creditors must retain their first priority.

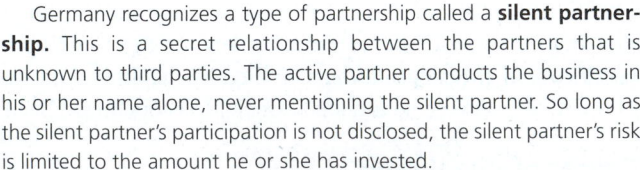

INTERNATIONAL LAW
Limited Partnerships Outside the United States

The limited partnership form of business is recognized outside the United States. As in the United Sates, at least one partner must be a general partner, and at least one partner must be a limited partner. Limited partners have limited liability for the debts and obligations of the partnership. In France, limited partners can participate in the internal administration of the limited partnership. In Germany, they can participate in the internal administration as well as deal with third parties on behalf of the limited partnership.

Germany recognizes a type of partnership called a **silent partnership.** This is a secret relationship between the partners that is unknown to third parties. The active partner conducts the business in his or her name alone, never mentioning the silent partner. So long as the silent partner's participation is not disclosed, the silent partner's risk is limited to the amount he or she has invested.

Chapter Summary

Entrepreneurship, p. 714

An entrepreneur is a person who forms and operates a new business.

Entrepreneurial Forms of Conducting Business

Entrepreneurs may choose to conduct business using any of the following forms:
1. Sole proprietorship
2. General partnership
3. Limited partnership
4. Limited liability partnership (LLP)
5. Limited liability company (LLC)
6. Corporation

Certain requirements must be met to form and operate each of these forms of business.

Sole Proprietorship, p. 715

Sole proprietorship is a form of business in which the owner and the business are one. The business is not a separate legal entity.

Creation of a Sole Proprietorship

To create a sole proprietorship, there are no formalities, and no federal or state government approval is required.

d.b.a.—Doing Business As

A sole proprietorship can operate under the name of the sole proprietor or a trade name. Operating under a trade name is commonly designated as a *d.b.a.* (doing business as). If a trade name is used, a fictitious business name statement must be filed with the appropriate state government office.

Personal Liability of Sole Proprietors

A sole proprietor is personally liable for the debts and obligations of the sole proprietorship.

General Partnership, p. 718

A general partnership is an association of two or more persons to carry on as co-owners of a business for profit.

Uniform Partnership Act (UPA)

The Uniform Partnership Act (UPA) is a model act that codifies partnership law. Most states have adopted all or part of the UPA. The UPA adopted the entity theory of partnerships, which holds that partnerships are separate legal entities that can hold title to personal and real property, transact business in the partnership name, and the like.

General Partnership Name

A general partnership can operate under the names of any one or more of the partners or under a fictitious business name.

Formation of a General Partnership

A business must meet four criteria to qualify as a partnership under the UPA [UPA Section 6(1)]. It must be (1) an association of two or more persons (2) carrying on a business (3) as co-owners (4) for profit.

The General Partnership Agreement

A partnership agreement establishes a general partnership. It sets forth the terms of the partnership. It is good practice to have a written partnership agreement that the partners sign. In some states, general partnerships must file a certificate of partnership with the appropriate state government agency.

Right to Participate in Management

In the absence of an agreement to the contrary, all partners have equal rights in the conduct and management of the partnership business.

General Partners' Rights to Share in Profits

Unless otherwise agreed, the UPA mandates that a partner has the right to an equal share in the partnership's profits and losses [UPA Section 18(a)].

Right to Compensation and Reimbursement

Unless otherwise agreed, the UPA provides that no partner is entitled to remuneration for his or her performance in the partnership's business [UPA Section 18(f)]. A partner is entitled to indemnification (i.e., reimbursement) for such expenditures if they are reasonably incurred in the ordinary and proper conduct of the business [UPA Section 18(b)].

Right to Return of Loans and Capital

A partner who makes a loan to the partnership becomes a creditor of the partnership. The partner is entitled to repayment of the loan, but this right is subordinated to the claims of creditors who are not partners [UPA Section 40(b)].

Upon termination of a partnership, the partners are entitled to have their capital contributions returned to them [UPA Section 18(a)]. However, this right is subordinated to the rights of creditors, who must be paid their claims first [UPA Section 40(b)].

Right to Information

Each partner has the right to demand true and full information from any other partner of all things affecting the partnership [UPA Section 20].

Duty of Loyalty

Partners are in a fiduciary relationship with one another. If there is a conflict between partnership interests and personal interests, the partner must choose the interest of the partnership.

Duty of Care

The duty of care calls for the partners to use the same level of care and skill that a reasonable business manager in the same position would use in the same circumstances.

Duty to Inform

Partners owe a duty to inform their co-partners of all information they possess that is relevant to the affairs of the partnership [UPA Section 20].

Duty of Obedience

The duty of obedience requires the partners to adhere to the provisions of the partnership agreement and the decisions of the partnership.

Right to an Accounting

An action for an accounting is a formal judicial proceeding in which the court is authorized to (1) review the partnership and the partners' transactions and (2) award each partner his or her share of the partnership assets [UPA Section 24].

Liability of General Partners, p. 723

Tort Liability

1. *Tort.* A tort occurs when a partner causes injury to a third party by his or her negligent act, breach of trust, breach of fiduciary duty, or intentional tort.
2. *Partnership liability.* The partnership is liable to third persons who are injured by torts committed by a partner while he or she is acting within the ordinary course of partnership business.

3. *Joint and several liability of partners.* Partners are personally liable for torts committed by partners acting on partnership business. This liability is joint and several. This means that the plaintiff can sue one or more of the partners separately. If successful, the plaintiff can recover the entire amount of the judgment from any or all of the defendant-partners.

Contract Liability

1. *Partners' contract authority.* A contract entered into by a partner with a third party on behalf of a partnership is binding on the partnership.
2. *Ratification.* The partners can decide to ratify an unauthorized contract. The ratification binds the partnership to the contract from the time of execution.
3. *Partnership liability.* A partnership is liable for the contracts entered into on its behalf by partners acting with express, implied, or apparent authority, or where unauthorized contracts have been ratified by the partners.

Liability of Incoming Partners

A new partner who is admitted to a partnership is liable for the existing debts and obligations (antecedent debts) of the partnership only to the extent of his or her capital contribution. The new partner is personally liable for debts and obligations incurred by the partnership after becoming a partner.

Dissolution of a General Partnership, p. 726

The dissolution of a partnership is a change in the relationship of the partners caused by any partner ceasing to be associated in the carrying on of the business.

Wrongful Dissolution

Wrongful dissolution occurs when a partner withdraws from a partnership without having the right to do so at the time. The partner is liable for damages caused by the wrongful dissolution of the partnership.

Notice of Dissolution

1. *Notice of dissolution to partners.* Notice of dissolution must be given to all partners. If a partner who has not received notice of dissolution enters into a contract on behalf of the partnership in the course of partnership business, the contract is binding on all the partners.
2. *Notice of dissolution to third parties.* The following notice must be given to third parties when a partnership has been dissolved other than by operation of law:
   a. *Actual notice.* Actual notice must be given to third parties who have actually dealt with the partnership.
   b. *Constructive notice.* Constructive notice must be given to third parties who have not dealt with the partnership but have knowledge of it. Constructive notice is given by publishing a notice of dissolution in a newspaper of general circulation serving the area where the business of the partnership is conducted.
   c. *No notice.* Parties who have not dealt with the partnership and do not have knowledge of it do not have to be given notice.

Distribution of Assets

After partnership assets have been liquidated and reduced to cash, the proceeds are distributed to satisfy claims against the partnership. The debts are satisfied in the following order [UPA Section 40(b)]:

1. Creditors (except partners who are creditors)
2. Creditor-partners
3. Capital contributions
4. Profits

Continuation of a General Partnership After Dissolution

The surviving, or remaining, partners have the right to continue a partnership after dissolution. When a partnership is continued, the old partnership is dissolved, and a new partnership is created.

1. *Continuation agreement.* This document expressly sets forth the events that allow for continuation of the partnership, the amount to be paid to outgoing partners, and other details.
2. *Creditors' status.* The creditors of the old partnership become creditors of the new partnership and have equal status with the creditors of the new partnership.

Liability of Outgoing Partners

An outgoing partner is liable for existing partnership debts unless the creditor, other partners, and the outgoing partner enter into an agreement that expressly relieves the outgoing partner of liability to the creditor.

Right of Survivorship

A partner is a co-owner with the other partners of the specific partnership property as a *tenant in partnership* [UPA Section 25(1)]. This is a special legal status that exists only in a partnership. Upon the death of a partner, the deceased partner's right in specific partnership property vests in the remaining partner or partners; it does not pass to his or her heirs or next of kin.

Limited Partnership, p. 729

Limited partnership is a special form of partnership that has both limited and general partners:

1. *General partners.* General partners in a limited partnership invest capital, manage the business, and are personally liable for partnership debts.
2. *Limited partners.* Limited partners in a limited partnership invest capital but do not participate in management and are not personally liable for partnership debts beyond their capital contributions.

A corporation may be the sole general partner of a limited partnership. Shareholders of corporations are liable only up to their capital contributions.

The Revised Uniform Limited Partnership Act

1. *Uniform Limited Partnership Act (ULPA).* This 1916 model act contains a uniform set of provisions for the formation, operation, and dissolution of limited partnerships.
2. *Revised Uniform Limited Partnership Act (RULPA).* This 1976 revision of the ULPA provides a more modern, comprehensive law for the formation, operation, and dissolution of limited partnerships.

Certificate of Limited Partnership

This certificate is a document that two or more persons must execute and sign that establishes a limited partnership. The certificate of limited partnership must be filed with the secretary of state of the appropriate state.

Amendments to the Certificate of Limited Partnership

The certificate of amendment must be filed within 30 days of the occurrence of the following events:

1. A change in a partner's capital contribution
2. The admission of a new partner
3. The withdrawal of a partner
4. The continuation of the business after a judicial decision dissolving the limited partnership after the withdrawal of the last general partner

Name of the Limited Partnership

The firm name of a limited partnership may not include the surname of a limited partner unless (1) it is also the surname of a general partner or (2) the business was carried on under that name before the admission of the limited partner [RULPA Section 102(2)].

Capital Contributions

Under the RULPA, the capital contributions of general and limited partners may be in cash, property, services rendered, or promissory notes or other obligations to contribute cash or property or to perform services [RULPA Section 501]. A partner or creditor of a limited partnership may bring a lawsuit to enforce a partner's promise to make a contribution [RULPA Section 502(a)].

Defective Formation

Defective formation occurs when a certificate of limited partnership is not properly filed, there are defects in a certificate that is filed, or some other statutory requirement for the creation of a limited partnership is not met. A limited partner may be held liable as a general partner if the limited partnership is defectively formed.

Limited Partnership Agreement

This document sets forth the rights and duties of general and limited partners; the terms and conditions regarding the operation, termination, and dissolution of the partnership; and so on.

Share of Profits and Losses

Unless otherwise agreed, profits and losses from a limited partnership are shared on the basis of the value of a partner's capital contributions. A limited partner is not liable for losses beyond his or her capital contribution. The limited partnership agreement may specify how profits and losses are to be allocated among the general and limited partners.

Right to Information

Upon reasonable demand, each limited partner has the right to obtain from the general partners true and full information regarding the state of the business, the financial condition of the limited partnership, and so on [RULPA Section 305].

Admission of New Partners

Once a limited partnership has been formed, a new limited partner can be added only upon the written consent of all partners, unless the limited partnership agreement provides otherwise. New general partners can be admitted only with the specific written consent of each partner [RULPA Section 401].

Foreign Limited Partnerships

A limited partnership is a *domestic limited partnership* in the state in which it is organized. It is a *foreign limited partnership* in all other states. Under the RULPA, the law of the state in which the entity is organized governs its organization, its internal affairs, and the liability of its limited partners [RULPA Section 901].

Liability of General and Limited Partners, p. 735

General partners of a limited partnership have unlimited personal liability for the debts and obligations of the limited partnership. Limited partners of a limited partnership are liable for the debts and obligations of the limited partnership only up to their capital contributions.

Participation in Management

Limited partners have no right to participate in the management of a partnership. A limited partner is liable as a general partner if his or her participation in the control of the business is substantially the same as that of a general partner, but the limited partner is liable only to persons who reasonably believed him or her to be a general partner.

Permissible Activities of Limited Partners

Permissible activities of a Limited Partnership include [RULPA Sections 303(b), 303(c)]:

1. Being an agent, an employee, or a contractor of the limited partnership or a general partner
2. Being a consultant or an advisor to a general partner regarding the limited partnership
3. Acting as a surety for the limited partnership
4. Approving or disapproving an amendment to the limited partnership agreement
5. Voting on the following partnership matters:
   a. The dissolution and winding up of the limited partnership
   b. The sale, transfer, exchange, lease, or mortgage of substantially all of the assets of the limited partnership
   c. The incurrence of indebtedness by the limited partnership other than in the ordinary course of business
   d. A change in the nature of the business of the limited partnership
   e. The removal of a general partner

Liability on Personal Guarantee

If a limited partner personally guarantees a loan made by a creditor to the limited partnership and the limited partnership defaults on the loan, the creditor may enforce the personal guarantee and recover payment from the limited partner who personally guaranteed the repayment of the credit.

Dissolution of a Limited Partnership, p. 737

The RULPA establishes rules for the dissolution and winding up of limited partnerships. Upon the dissolution and the commencement of the winding up of a limited partnership, the limited partnership must file a certificate of cancellation with the secretary of state of the state in which the limited partnership is organized.

Causes of Dissolution

The following four events cause the dissolution of a limited partnership:

1. The end of the life of the limited partnership.
2. The written consent of all general and limited partners.
3. The withdrawal of a general partner.
4. The entry of a decree of judicial dissolution.

Winding Up

A limited partnership must wind up its affairs upon dissolution. Any partner may petition the court to wind up the affairs of a limited partnership. A partner who winds up the affairs of a limited partnership has the same rights, powers, and duties as a partner winding up a general partnership.

Distribution of Assets

Assets are distributed in the following order upon the winding up of a limited partnership:

1. Creditors of the limited partnership, including partners who are creditors.
2. Partners with respect to unpaid distributions, capital contributions, and the remainder of the proceeds.

The partners may provide in the limited partnership agreement for a different distribution among the partners, but the creditors must retain their first priority.

Test Review Terms and Concepts

Case Problems

26.1   General Partnership: Thomas Smithson, a house builder and small-scale property developer, decided that a certain tract of undeveloped land in Franklin, Tennessee, would be extremely attractive for development into a subdivision. Smithson contacted the owner of the property, Monsanto Chemical Company, and was told that the company would sell the property at the "right price."

Smithson did not have the funds with which to embark unassisted in the endeavor, so he contacted Frank White, a co-owner of the Andrews Realty Company, and two agents of the firm, Dennis Devrow and Temple Ennis. Smithson showed them a sketch map with the proposed layout of the lots, roads, and so forth. Smithson testified that they all orally agreed to develop the property together, and in lieu of a financial investment, Smithson would oversee the engineering of the property. Subsequently, H. R. Morgan was brought into the deal to provide additional financing.

Smithson later discovered that White had contacted Monsanto directly. When challenged about this, White assured Smithson that he was still "part of the deal" but refused to put the agreement in writing. White, Devrow, Ennis, and Morgan purchased the property from Monsanto. They then sold it to H.A.H. Associates, a corporation, for a $184,000 profit. When they refused to pay Smithson, he sued to recover an equal share of the profits. Was a partnership formed between Smithson and the defendants? *Smithson v.*

White, **Web** 1988 Tenn. App. Lexis 221 (Court of Appeals of Tennessee)

26.2   General Partnership: Richard Filip owned Trans Texas Properties. Tracy Peoples was an employee of the company. In order to obtain credit to advertise in the *Austin American–Statesman* newspaper, which was owned by Cox Enterprises, Inc., Peoples completed a credit application that listed Jack Elliot as a partner in Trans Texas. Evidence showed that Elliot did not own an interest in Trans Texas and did not consent to or authorize Peoples to make this representation to Cox. Cox made no effort to verify the accuracy of the representation and extended credit to Trans Texas. When Trans Texas defaulted on payments owed Cox, Cox sued both Filip and Elliot to recover the debt. Is Elliot liable? *Cox Enterprises, Inc. v. Filip and Elliot,* 538 S.W.2d 836, **Web** 1976 Tex. App. Lexis 2947 (Court of Civil Appeals of Texas)

26.3   Tort Liability: Charles Fial and Roger J. Steeby entered into a partnership called Audit Consultants to perform auditing services. Pursuant to the agreement, they shared equally the equity, income, and profits of the partnership. Originally, they performed the auditing services themselves, but as business increased, they engaged independent contractors to do some of the audit work. Fial's activities generated approximately 80 percent of the partnership's revenues. Unhappy with their agreement to divide the profits equally, Fial wrote a letter to Steeby seven years later, dissolving the partnership.

Fial asserted that the clients should be assigned based on who brought them into the business. Fial formed a new business called Audit Consultants of Colorado, Inc. He then terminated the original partnership's contracts with many clients and put them under contract with his new firm. Fial also terminated the partnership's contracts with the independent-contractor auditors and signed many of these auditors with his new firm. The partnership terminated about 11 months after Fial wrote the letter to Steeby. Steeby brought an action against Fial, alleging breach of fiduciary duty and seeking a final accounting. Who wins? *Steeby v. Fial*, 765 P.2d 1081, **Web** 1988 Colo. App. Lexis 409 (Court of Appeals of Colorado)

26.4 Fiduciary Duty: Edgar and Selwyn Husted, attorneys, formed Husted and Husted, a law partnership. Herman McCloud, who was the executor of his mother's estate, hired them as attorneys for the estate. When taxes were due on the estate, Edgar told McCloud to make a check for $18,000 payable to the Husted and Husted Trust Account and that he would pay the IRS from this account. There was no Husted and Husted Trust Account. Instead, Edgar deposited the check into his own personal account and converted the funds to his own personal use. When Edgar's misconduct was uncovered, McCloud sued the law firm for conversion of estate funds. Is the partnership liable for Edgar's actions? *Husted v. McCloud*, 436 N.E.2d 341, **Web** 1982 Ind. App. Lexis 1244 (Court of Appeals of Indiana)

26.5 Tort Liability: Thomas McGrath was a partner in the law firm Tarbenson, Thatcher, McGrath, Treadwell & Schoonmaker. One day, at approximately 4:30 P.M., McGrath went to a restaurant-cocktail establishment in Kirkland, Washington. From that time until about 1:00 A.M., he imbibed considerable alcohol while socializing and discussing personal and firm-related business. After 11:00 P.M., McGrath did not discuss firm business but continued to socialize and drink until approximately 1:45 A.M., when he and Fredrick Hayes, another bar patron, exchanged words. Shortly thereafter, the two encountered each other outside, and after another exchange, McGrath shot Hayes. Hayes sued McGrath and the law firm for damage. Who is liable? *Hayes v. Tarbenson, Thatcher, McGrath, Treadwell & Schoonmaker*, 50 Wn. App. 505, 749 P.2d 178, **Web** 1988 Wash. App. Lexis 27 (Court of Appeals of Washington)

26.6 Notice of Dissolution: Leonard Sumter, Sr., entered into a partnership agreement with his son, Michael T. Sumter, to conduct a plumbing business in Shreveport, Louisiana, under the name Sumter Plumbing Company. The father, on behalf of the partnership, executed a credit application with Thermal Supply of Louisiana, Inc., for an open account to purchase supplies on credit. For the next four years, the Sumters purchased plumbing supplies from Thermal on credit and paid their bills without fail. Both partners and one

employee signed for supplies at Thermal. In May 1980, the partnership was dissolved, and all outstanding debts to Thermal were paid in full. The Sumters did not, however, notify Thermal that the partnership had been dissolved.

A year later, the son decided to reenter the plumbing business. He used the name previously used by the former partnership, listed the same post office address for billing purposes, and hired the employee of the former partnership who signed for supplies at Thermal. The father decided not to become involved in this venture. The son began purchasing supplies on credit from Thermal on the open credit account of the former partnership. Thermal was not informed that the son was opening a new business. When the son defaulted on payments to Thermal, it sued the original partnership to recover the debt. Is the father liable for these debts? *Thermal Supply of Louisiana, Inc. v. Sumter*, 452 So.2d 312, **Web** 1984 La. App. Lexis 8975 (Court of Appeal of Louisiana)

26.7 Liability of General Partners: Pat McGowan, Val Somers, and Brent Robertson were general partners of Vermont Place, a limited partnership formed for the purpose of constructing duplexes on an undeveloped tract of land in Fort Smith, Arkansas. The general partners appointed McGowan and his company, Advance Development Corporation, to develop the project, including contracting with materials people, mechanics, and other suppliers. None of the limited partners took part in the management or control of the partnership.

Eight months later, Somers and Robertson discovered that McGowan had not been paying the suppliers. They removed McGowan from the partnership and took over the project. The suppliers sued the partnership to recover the money owed them. The partnership assets were not sufficient to pay all their claims. Who is liable to the suppliers? *National Lumber Company v. Advance Development Corporation*, 293 Ark. 1, 732 S.W.2d 840, **Web** 1987 Ark. Lexis 2225 (Supreme Court of Arkansas)

26.8 Liability of Limited Partners: Union Station Associates of New London (USANL) was a limited partnership formed under the laws of Connecticut. Allen M. Schultz, Anderson Nolter Associates, and the Lepton Trust were limited partners. The limited partners did not take part in the management of the partnership. The National Railroad Passenger Association (NRPA) entered into an agreement to lease part of a railroad facility from USANL. NRPA sued USANL for allegedly breaching the lease and also named the limited partners as defendants. Are the limited partners liable? *National Railroad Passenger Association v. Union Station Associates of New London*, 643 F.Supp. 192, **Web** 1986 U.S. Dist. Lexis 22190 (United States District Court for the District of Columbia)

26.9 Liability of Limited Partners: 8 Brookwood Fund (Brookwood) was a limited partnership that was formed to invest in securities. The original certificate of limited partnership, which was filed with the Westchester County, New York, clerk listed Kenneth Stein as the general partner and

Barbara Stein as the limited partner. Within the next four months, additional investors joined Brookwood as limited partners. However, no certificate amending the original certificate was filed to reflect the newly admitted limited partners. The newly added partners conducted themselves at all times as limited partners.

The partnership purchased securities on margin (i.e., it borrowed a percentage of the purchase price of the securities) from the securities firms of Sloate, Weisman, Murray & Co., Inc. (Sloate), and Bear Stearns & Co., Inc. (Bear Stearns). One day, the stock market crashed, causing many of the securities that Brookwood had purchased to go down in value. The securities firms made margin calls on Brookwood to pay more money to cover the losses. When the margin calls were not met, Sloate and Bear Stearns immediately initiated arbitration proceedings to recover the balance of $1,849,183 allegedly due after Brookwood's accounts were liquidated. Nine days later, Brookwood filed a certificate amending the original certificate of limited partnership to reflect the recently added limited partners.

Upon receiving the notice of arbitration, the recently added limited partners renounced their interest in the profits of the limited partnership. Can these limited partners be held individually liable for the partnership debts owed to Sloate and Bear Stearns? *8 Brookwood Fund v. Bear Stearns & Co., Inc.*, 148 A.D.2d 661, 539 N.Y.S.2d 411, **Web** 1989 N.Y. App. Div. Lexis 4208 (Supreme Court of New York)

26.10 Liability of Limited Partners: Virginia Partners, Ltd. (Virginia Partners), a limited partnership organized under the laws of Florida, conducted business in Kentucky but failed to register as a foreign limited partnership, as required by Kentucky law. Robert Day was tortiously injured in Garrard County, Kentucky, by a negligent act of Virginia Partners. At the time of the accident, Day was a bystander observing acid being injected into an abandoned oil well by Virginia Partners. The injury occurred when a polyvinyl chloride (PVC) valve failed, causing a hose to rupture from its fitting and spray nitric acid on Day, severely injuring him. Day sued Virginia Partners and its limited partners to recover damages. Are the limited partners liable? *Virginia Partners, Ltd. v. Day*, 738 S.W.2d 837, **Web** 1987 Ky. App. Lexis 564 (Court of Appeals of Kentucky)

26.11 Liability of Partners: Raugust-Mathwig, Inc., a corporation, was the sole general partner of a limited partnership. Calvin Raugust was the major shareholder of this corporation. The three limited partners were (1) Cal-Lee Trust, (2) W.J. Mathwig, Inc., and (3) W.J. Mathwig, Inc., and Associates. All three of the limited partners were valid corporate entities. Although the limited partnership agreement was never executed and a certificate of limited partnership was not filed with the state, the parties opened a bank account and began conducting business.

John Molander, an architect, entered into an agreement with the limited partnership to design a condominium complex and professional office building to be located in Spokane, Washington. The contract was signed on behalf of the limited partnership by its corporate general partner. Molander provided substantial architectural services to the partnership, but neither project was completed because of a lack of financing. Molander sued the limited partnership, its corporate general partner, the corporate limited partners, and Calvin Raugust individually to recover payments allegedly due him. Against whom can Molander recover? *Molander v. Raugust-Mathwig, Inc.*, 44 Wn. App. 53, 722 P.2d 103, **Web** 1986 Wash. App. Lexis 2992 (Court of Appeals of Washington)

26.12 Limited Partnership: The Courts of the Phoenix was a limited partnership that owned a building that housed several racquetball and handball courts. William Reich was its general partner. Charter Oaks Fire Insurance Company (Charter Oaks) issued a fire insurance policy that insured the building. One day, a fire caused extensive damage to the building. When the Chicago fire department found evidence of arson, Charter Oaks denied the partnership's $1.7 million-plus insurance claim. It reasoned that Reich had either set the fire or had arranged to have it set in order to liquidate a failing investment. Can the limited partnership recover on the fire insurance policy? *Courts of the Phoenix v. Charter Oaks Fire Insurance Company*, 560 F. Supp. 858, **Web** 1983 U.S. Dist. Lexis 17792 (United States District Court for the Northern District of Illinois)

26.13 Removal of General Partner: The Aztec Petroleum Corporation (Aztec) was the general partner of a limited partnership. The partnership agreement provided that it could be amended by a vote of 70 percent of the limited partnership units. Over 70 percent of these units voted to amend the partnership agreement to provide that a vote of 70 percent of the limited partnership units could remove the general partner and replace it with another general partner. Prior to this amendment, there had been no provision for the removal and substitution of a general partner. Texas law requires unanimous approval of new partners unless the partnership agreement provides otherwise.

When a vote was held, over 70 percent of the limited partnership units voted to remove Aztec as the general partner and replace it with the MHM Company. Aztec challenged its removal. Who wins? *Aztec Petroleum Corporation v. MHM Company*, 703 S.W.2d 290, **Web** 1985 Tex. App. Lexis 12879 (Court of Appeals of Texas)

26.14 Limited Partner's Interest: When the Chrysler Credit Corporation (Chrysler Credit) extended credit to Metro Dodge, Inc. (Metro Dodge), Donald P. Peterson signed an agreement guaranteeing to pay the debt if Metro Dodge did not pay. When Metro Dodge failed to pay, Chrysler Credit sued Peterson on the guarantee and obtained a judgment of $350,000 against him. After beginning collection efforts, Chrysler Credit learned through discovery that Peterson owned four limited partnership units in Cedar Riverside Properties, a limited partnership. Can Chrysler Credit charge Peterson's limited partnership interests? *Chrysler Credit Corporation v. Peterson*, 342 N.W.2d 170, **Web** 1984 Minn. App. Lexis 2976 (Court of Appeals of Minnesota)

Ethics Issues

26.15 Ethics: Harriet Hankin, Samuel Hankin, Moe Henry Hankin, Perch P. Hankin, and Pauline Hankin, and their spouses, for many years operated a family partnership composed of vast real estate holdings. Some of the properties included restaurants, industrial buildings, shopping centers, golf courses, a motel chain, and hundreds of acres of developable ground, estimated to be worth $72 million. Because of family disagreement and discontent, the Hankin family agreed to dissolve the partnership. When they could not agree on how to liquidate the partnership assets, Harriet and Samuel (collectively called Harriet) initiated an equity action.

Based on assurances from Moe and Perch that they would sell the partnership assets as quickly as possible and at the highest possible price, the court appointed them as liquidators of the partnership during the winding-up period. Based on similar assurances, the court again appointed them liquidators for the partnership. But two years later, only enough property had been sold to retire the debt of the partnership. Evidence showed that Moe and Perch had not aggressively marketed the remaining properties and that Moe wished to purchase some of the properties for himself at a substantial discount from their estimated value. Six years and three appeals to the superior court later, Harriet brought an action seeking the appointment of a receiver to liquidate the remaining partnership assets.

Did the winding-up partners breach their fiduciary duties? Should the court appoint a receiver to liquidate the remaining partnership assets? Did Moe Henry Hankin act ethically in this case? *Hankin v. Hankin*, 507 Pa. 603, 493 A.2d 675, **Web** 1985 Pa. Lexis 337 (Supreme Court of Pennsylvania)

26.16 Ethics: John Gilroy, an established commercial photographer in Kalamazoo, Michigan, had a small contractual clientele of schools for which he provided student portrait photographs. Robert Conway joined Gilroy's established business, and they formed a partnership called "Skylight Studios." Both partners solicited schools with success, and gross sales, which were $40,000, increased every year and amounted to over $200,000 six years later.

Conway notified Gilroy that the partnership was dissolved. Gilroy discovered that Conway had closed up the partnership's place of business and opened up his own business, had purchased equipment and supplies in preparation for opening his own business and charged them to the partnership, had taken with him the partnership's employees and

most of its equipment, had personally taken over business of some customers by telling them the partnership was being dissolved, and had withdrawn partnership funds for personal use. Gilroy sued Conway for an accounting, alleging that Conway had converted partnership assets. Did Conway act ethically in this case? Who wins? *Gilroy v. Conway*, 151 Mich. App. 628, 391 N.W.2d 419, **Web** 1986 Mich. App. Lexis 2633 (Court of Appeals of Michigan)

26.17 Ethics: Robert K. Powers and Lee M. Solomon were among other limited partners of the Cosmopolitan Chinook Hotel (Cosmopolitan), a limited partnership. Cosmopolitan entered into a contract to lease and purchase neon signs from Dwinell's Central Neon (Dwinell's). The contract identified Cosmopolitan as a "partnership" and was signed on behalf of the partnership, "R. Powers, President." At the time the contract was entered into, Cosmopolitan had taken no steps to file its certificate of limited partnership with the state, as required by limited partnership law. The certificate was not filed with the state until several months after the contract was signed. When Cosmopolitan defaulted on payments due under the contract, Dwinell's sued Cosmopolitan and its general and limited partners. Did the limited partners act ethically in denying liability on the contract? Are the limited partners liable? *Dwinell's Central Neon v. Cosmopolitan Chinook Hotel*, 21 Wn. App. 929, 587 P.2d 191, **Web** 1978 Wash. App. Lexis 2735 (Court of Appeals of Washington)

26.18 Ethics: The Second Montclair Company was a limited partnership organized under the laws of Alabama to develop an office building in Birmingham called Montclair II. Joseph Cox, Sr., and F&S were general partners, each owning a one-third interest in the limited partnership. Eleven limited partners owned equal shares of the remaining one-third interest. Cox was president of Cox Realty and Development Company (Cox Realty), which had its offices in Montclair II. Cox Realty managed Montclair II under a written agreement with the limited partnership. Evidence showed that Cox used assets of the limited partnership for personal use. F&S sued Cox, seeking dissolution and liquidation of the limited partnership and damages. Did Cox act ethically in this case? Should the limited partnership be dissolved? Should damages be awarded? *Cox v. F&S*, 489 So.2d 516, **Web** 1986 Ala. Lexis 3448 (Supreme Court of Alabama)

IRAC Writing Assignment

Read **Case A-26** in Appendix A [*Catalina Mortgage Company, Inc. v. Monier*]. Use the IRAC method to prepare a written analysis of the case.

CHAPTER 27

Corporate Formation and Financing

> **"**A corporation is an artificial being, invisible, intangible, and existing only in the contemplation of law. Being the mere creature of the law, it possesses only those properties which the charter of its creation confers upon it, either expressly or as incidental to its very existence. These are such as supposed best calculated to effect the object for which it was created. Among the most important are immortality, and, if the expression may be allowed, individuality; properties by which a perpetual succession of many persons are considered as the same, and may act as a single individual.**"**
>
> —CHIEF JUSTICE JOHN MARSHALL, U.S. SUPREME COURT
> Dartmouth College v. Woodward, 4 Wheaton 518, 636 (1819)

CHAPTER OBJECTIVES

After studying this chapter, you should be able to:

1. Define *corporation* and list the major characteristics of a corporation.
2. Describe the process of forming a corporation.
3. Describe promoter's liability.
4. Define *common stock* and *preferred stock*.
5. Define *S corporation* and describe the tax benefits of this form of corporation.

CHAPTER CONTENTS

    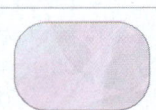

Introduction to Corporate Formation and Financing

Corporations are the most dominant form of business organization in the United States, generating over 85 percent of the country's gross business receipts. Corporations range in size from one owner to thousands of owners. Owners of corporations are called *shareholders*.

Corporations were first formed in medieval Europe. Great Britain granted charters to certain trading companies from the 1500s to the 1700s. The English law of corporations applied in most of the colonies until 1776. After the Revolutionary War, the states of the United States developed their own corporations law.

Originally, corporate charters were individually granted by state legislatures. In the late 1700s, however, the states began enacting *general corporation statutes* that permitted corporations to be formed without the separate approval of the legislature. Today, most corporations are formed pursuant to general corporations laws of the states.

The formation and financing of corporations are discussed in this chapter.

The Great Wall, China

Commercial opportunities for multinational corporations will increase as new markets open up around the world.

Nature of the Corporation

Corporations can only be created pursuant to the laws of the state of incorporation. These laws—commonly referred to as **corporations codes**—regulate the formation, operation, and dissolution of corporations. The state legislature may amend its corporate statute at any time. Such changes may require a corporation's articles of incorporation to be amended.

The courts interpret state corporation statutes to decide individual corporate and shareholder disputes. As a result, a body of common law has evolved concerning corporate and shareholder rights and obligations.

The Corporation as a Legal "Person"

A corporation is a separate **legal entity** (or **legal person**) for most purposes. Corporations are treated, in effect, as artificial persons created by the state that can sue or be sued in their own names, enter into and enforce contracts, hold title to and transfer property, and be found civilly and criminally liable for violations of law. Because corporations cannot be put in prison, the normal criminal penalty is the assessment of a fine, loss of a license, or other sanction.

Corporations have unique characteristics, as discussed in the paragraphs that follow.

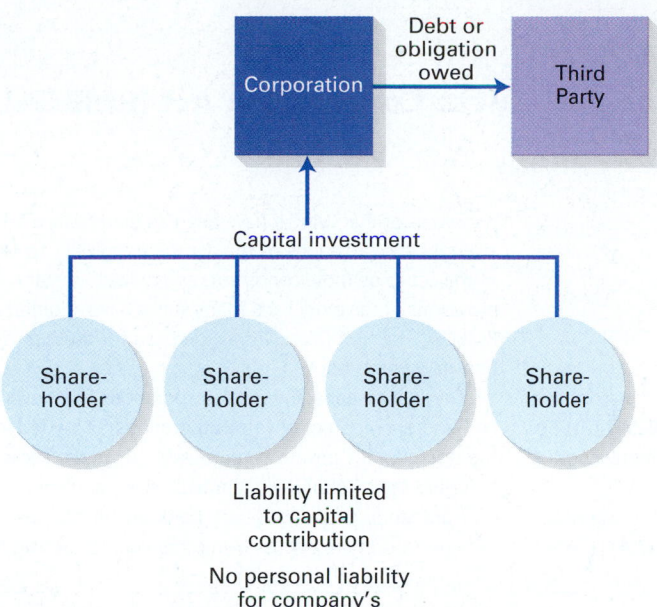

EXHIBIT 27.1

Corporation

LIMITED LIABILITY OF SHAREHOLDERS As separate legal entities, corporations are liable for their own contracts and debts. Generally, the shareholders have only **limited liability**. That is, they are liable only to the extent of their capital contributions and do not have personal liability for the corporation's contracts and debts (see Exhibit 27.1).

Example Tina, Vivi, and Qixia form IT.com, Inc., a corporation, and each contributes $100,000 capital. The corporation borrows $1 million from State Bank. One year later, IT.com, Inc., goes bankrupt and defaults on the $1 million loan owed to State Bank. At that time, IT.com, Inc., has only $50,000 cash left, which State Bank recovers. Tina, Vivi, and Qixia each lose their $100,000 capital contribution. However, Tina, Vivi, and Qixia are not personally liable for the $950,000 still owed to State Bank. State Bank must absorb this loss.

FREE TRANSFERABILITY OF SHARES Corporate shares are freely transferable by the shareholder by sale, assignment, pledge, or gift unless they are issued pursuant to certain exemptions from securities registration. Shareholders may agree among themselves on restrictions on the transfer of shares. National securities markets, such as the New York Stock Exchange and NASDAQ, have been developed for the organized sale of securities.

Web Exercises

1. **WEB** Go to the website of the New York Stock Exchange (NYSE), at *www.nyse.com*. What types of securities are traded on the NYSE?

2. **WEB** Go to the website of NASDAQ, at *www.nasdaq.com*. What types of securities are traded on NASDAQ?

PERPETUAL EXISTENCE Corporations exist in perpetuity unless a specific duration is stated in a corporation's articles of incorporation. The existence of a corporation can be voluntarily terminated by the shareholders. A corporation may be involuntarily terminated by the corporation's creditors if an involuntary petition for bankruptcy against the corporation is granted. The death, insanity, or bankruptcy of a shareholder, a director, or an officer of a corporation does not affect its existence.

CENTRALIZED MANAGEMENT The *board of directors* makes policy decisions concerning the operation of a corporation. The members of the board of directors are elected by the shareholders. The directors, in turn, appoint corporate *officers* to run the corporation's day-to-day operations. Together, the directors and the officers form the *corporate management*.

LANDMARK LAW
Revised Model Business Corporation Act (RMBCA)

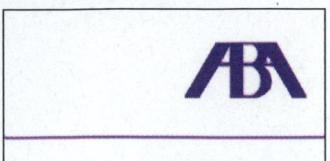

The Committee on Corporate Laws of the American Bar Association first drafted the **Model Business Corporation Act (MBCA)** in 1950. The model act was intended to provide a uniform law regulating the formation, operation, and termination of corporations.

In 1984, the committee completely revised the MBCA and issued the **Revised Model Business Corporation Act (RMBCA)**. Certain provisions of the RMBCA have been amended since 1984. The RMBCA arranges the provisions of the act more logically, revises the language of the act to be more consistent, and makes substantial changes in the provisions of the model act. Many states have adopted all or part of the RMBCA. The RMBCA serves as the basis for the discussion of corporations law in this book.

There is no general federal corporations law governing the formation and operation of private corporations. Many federal laws regulate the operation of private corporations, however. These include federal securities laws, labor laws, antitrust laws, consumer protection laws, environmental protection laws, bankruptcy laws, and the like. These federal statutes are discussed in other chapters in this book.

Public and Private Corporations

Government-owned corporations (or **public corporations**) are formed to meet a specific governmental or political purpose. For example, most cities and towns are formed as corporations, as are most water, school, sewage, and park districts. Local government corporations are often called *municipal corporations*.

Private corporations are formed to conduct privately owned business. They are owned by private parties, not by the government. Most corporations fall into this category.

Web Exercises

1. **WEB** Go to the website of the Tennessee Valley Authority (TVA), at *www.tva.gov*. The TVA is an example of a government-owned (or public) corporation. What is the purpose of the TVA?

2. **WEB** Go to the website of Microsoft Corporation, at *www.microsoft.com*. Microsoft is an example of a private corporation owned by private parties, its shareholders.

Profit and Not-for-Profit Corporations

Private corporations can be classified as either for profit or not-for-profit. **Profit corporations** are created to conduct a business for profit and can distribute profits to shareholders in the form of dividends. Most private corporations fit this definition.

Not-for-profit corporations are formed for charitable, educational, religious, or scientific purposes. Although not-for-profit corporations may make a profit, they are prohibited by law from distributing this profit to their members, directors, or officers. About a dozen states have enacted the **Model Nonprofit Corporation Act**, which governs the formation, operation, and termination of not-for-profit corporations. All other states have their own individual statutes that govern the formation, operation, and dissolution of such corporations.

Web Exercises

1. **WEB** Choose a for-profit corporation you are familiar with and use *www.google.com* to find the website for that corporation. What products or services does that corporation sell?

2. **WEB** Select a not-for-profit charitable institution you are familiar with and use *www.google.com* to find that institution's website. What is the purpose of that institution?

Publicly Held and Closely Held Corporations

Publicly held corporations have many shareholders. Often, they are large corporations with hundreds or thousands of shareholders whose shares are traded on organized securities markets. IBM Corporation and General Motors Corporation are examples of publicly held corporations. The shareholders rarely participate in the management of such corporations.

A **closely held** (or **close**) **corporation** is one whose shares are owned by a few shareholders who are often family members, relatives, or friends. Frequently, the shareholders are involved in the management of the corporation. The shareholders sometimes enter into buy-and-sell agreements that prevent outsiders from becoming shareholders.

Web Exercises

1. **WEB** Choose a large publicly held corporation that you are familiar with and use *www.google.com* to look up that company's website.

2. **WEB** Choose a small business in your neighborhood. Use *www.google.com* to try to find a website for that business.

Professional Corporations

Professional corporations are formed by professionals such as lawyers, accountants, physicians, and dentists. The abbreviations *P.C.* (professional corporation), *P.A.* (professional association), and *S.C.* (service corporation) often identify professional corporations. Shareholders of professional corporations are often called *members*. Generally, only licensed professionals may become members.

All states permit the incorporation of professional corporations, although some states allow only designated types of professionals to incorporate. Professional corporations have normal corporate attributes and are formed like other corporations.

Members of a professional corporation are not usually liable for the torts committed by the corporation's agents or employees. Some states impose liability on members for the malpractice of other members of the corporation.

> The corporation is, and must be, the creature of the state, into its nostrils the state must breathe the breath of a fictitious life for otherwise it would be no animated body but individualistic dust.
>
> Frederic William Maitland
> *Introduction to Political Theories of the Middle Ages (1900)*

Domestic, Foreign, and Alien Corporations

A corporation is a **domestic corporation** in the state in which it is incorporated. It is a **foreign corporation** in all other states and jurisdictions.

Example Suppose a corporation is incorporated in Texas and does business in Montana. The corporation is a domestic corporation in Texas and a foreign corporation in Montana.

A state can require a foreign corporation to *qualify* to conduct intrastate commerce within the state. Where a foreign corporation is required to qualify to do intrastate commerce in a state, it must obtain a *certificate of authority* from the state [RMBCA Section 15.01(a)] . This requires the foreign corporation to file certain information with the secretary of state, pay the required fees, and appoint a registered agent for service of process.

Conduct that usually constitutes "doing business" includes maintaining an office to conduct intrastate business, selling personal property in intrastate business, entering into contracts involving intrastate commerce, using real estate for general corporate purposes, and the like. Activities that are generally *not* considered doing business within the state include maintaining, defending, or settling a lawsuit or an administrative proceeding; maintaining bank accounts; effectuating sales through independent contractors; soliciting orders through the mail; securing or collecting debts; transacting any business in interstate commerce; and the like [RMBCA Sections 15.01(b), 15.01(c)].

Conducting intrastate business in a state in which it is not qualified subjects a corporation to fines. In addition, the corporation cannot bring a lawsuit in the state, although it can defend itself against lawsuits and administrative proceedings brought by others [RMBCA Section 15.02].

An **alien corporation** is a corporation that is incorporated in another country. In most instances, alien corporations are treated as foreign corporations.

Example The Ford Motor Company, a major manufacture of automobiles and other vehicles, is incorporated in Delaware. It is a domestic corporation in Delaware. The Ford Motor Company conducts business in Michigan, where its headquarters offices are located, and it distributes vehicles in all of the 49 states other than Delaware. The Ford Motor Company is a foreign corporation in these other states. The Lenovo Corporation, a corporation incorporated in China, does business in the United States. The Lenovo Corporation is an alien corporation in the states in which it does business in the United States.

Web Exercises

1. **WEB** Visit the website of the Ford Motor Company, at *www.ford.com*.
2. **WEB** Visit the website of the Lenovo Corporation, at *www.lenovo.com*.

CONCEPT SUMMARY

Types of Corporations

TYPE OF CORPORATION	DESCRIPTION
Domestic	A corporation is a domestic corporation in the state in which it is incorporated.
Foreign	A corporation is a foreign corporation in states other than the one in which it is incorporated.
Alien	A corporation is an alien corporation in the United States if it is incorporated in another country.

Incorporation Procedures

Corporations are creatures of statute. Thus, the organizers of a corporation must comply with the state's corporations code to form a corporation. The procedure for *incorporating* a corporation varies somewhat from state to state. The procedure for incorporating a corporation is discussed in the following paragraphs.

Selecting a State for Incorporating a Corporation

A corporation can be incorporated in only one state, even though it can do business in all other states in which it qualifies to do business. In choosing a state for incorporation, the incorporators, directors, and/or shareholders must consider the corporations law of the states under consideration.

For the sake of convenience, most corporations (particularly small ones) choose the state in which the corporation will be doing most of its business as the state for incorporation. Large corporations generally opt to incorporate in the state with the laws that are most favorable to the corporation's internal operations (e.g., Delaware).

Web Exercises

1. **WEB** Use *www.google.com* to find a website that contains the corporations law of your state. Read it.
2. **WEB** Use *www.google.com* to find an article that discusses the advantages of large corporations incorporating in the state of Delaware. Read it.
3. **WEB** Use *www.google.com* to find an article that discusses the advantages of corporations incorporating in the state of Nevada. Read it.

CONTEMPORARY ENVIRONMENT
Selecting a Corporate Name

When starting a new corporation, the organizers must choose a name for the entity. To ensure that the name selected is not already being used by another business, the organizers should do the following [RMBCA Section 4.01]:

- Choose a name (and alternative names) for the corporation. The name must contain the words *corporation*, *company*, *incorporated*, or *limited* or an abbreviation of one of these words (i.e., *Corp.*, *Co.*, *Inc.*, *Ltd.*).

- Make sure the name chosen does not contain any word or phrase that indicates or implies that the corporation is organized for any purpose other than those stated in the articles of incorporation. For example, a corporate name cannot contain the word *Bank* if it is not authorized to conduct the business of banking.

- Determine whether the name selected is federally trademarked by another company and is therefore unavailable for use. Trademark lawyers and specialized firms can conduct trademark searches for a fee.

- Determine whether the chosen name is similar to other non-trademarked names and is therefore unavailable for use. Lawyers and specialized firms can conduct such searches for a fee.

- Determine whether the name selected is available as a domain name on the Internet. If the domain name is already owned by another person or business, the new corporation cannot use this domain name to conduct e-commerce over the Internet. Therefore, it is advisable to select another corporate name.

Web Exercises

1. **WEB** Use *www.google.com* to find the website for the state government agency in your state that is responsible for assigning corporate names.

2. **WEB** Choose a name you would like to have for a corporation and use *www.google.com* to see if that name is available.

3. **WEB** Go to the website of the U.S. Patent and Trademark Office, at *www.uspto.gov*. Click on "Trademarks" and then "Search TM Database" and check to see if the name you have chosen has been trademarked.

INTERNET AND TECHNOLOGY
Domain Name

Most large corporations trademark their corporate names as well as the major brand names of their products and services. In addition, since the advent of the Internet, these corporations usually register the **domain name** of their trademarks and service marks to promote and conduct business over the World Wide Web. One such corporation that did so was Ticketmaster Corporation, which registered the name "Ticketmaster" as a mark with the U.S. Patent and Trademark Office and also registered the domain name *ticketmaster.com.*

Subsequently, a person named Brown registered three domain names—*urn2ticketmaster.com*, *urn2ticketmaster.net*, and *urn2 ticketmaster.org*. Ticketmaster Corporation brought an arbitration proceeding against Brown in the World Intellectual Property Organization (WIPO), alleging a violation of the Uniform Domain Name Dispute Resolution Procedure (UDRP), by which all domain name registrants agree to abide. To recover or cancel a domain name under UDRP, the petitioner must prove that (1) the challenged domain name is identical or confusingly similar to its trademark or service mark, (2) the registrant of the domain name has no legitimate interest in the name, and (3) the domain name was registered in *bad faith*.

The arbitrator first found that the three domain names registered by Brown were confusingly similar to Ticketmaster's service mark and that the addition of the prefix "urn2" (pronounced "you are into") did nothing to reduce the domain names' similarity or confusion to

Ticketmaster's famous mark. Second, the arbitrator held that Brown had no legitimate interest in the domain names. Third, the arbitrator found that Brown had acted in bad faith in registering the domain names. The arbitrator noted that Brown had offered to sell *urn2ticketmaster.com* to Ticketmaster Corporation and had made no use of any of the names. Accordingly, the arbitrator ordered that the three domain names to be cancelled. *Ticketmaster Corporation v. Brown*, WIPO, No. D2001-0716 (2001).

Law & Ethics Questions

1. What is a domain name? How is a domain name valuable to a corporation? Explain.

2. **ETHICS** Did Brown act ethically in this case? Explain.

3. **ETHICS** Had Brown registered the domain names in bad faith?

Web Exercises

1. **WEB** Visit the website of Ticketmaster, at *www.ticketmaster.com*.

2. **WEB** Visit the website of World Intellectual Property Organization (WIPO), at *www.wipo.int*. Can you find information about the arbitration procedures provided by the WIPO?

3. **WEB** Use *www.google.com* to find an article that discusses someone registering as a domain name for someone else's trademark in bad faith.

4. **WEB** Visit the website of Network Solutions, at *www.networksolutions.com*. Pick out a name that you would like to get as a domain name. Check the availability of that domain name.

Incorporators

One or more persons, partnerships, domestic or foreign corporations, or other associations may act as **incorporators** of a corporation [RMBCA Section 2.01]. An incorporator's primary duty is to sign the articles of incorporation. Incorporators often become shareholders, directors, or officers of the corporation.

ETHICS SPOTLIGHT

Promoters' Liability

A **promoter** is a person who organizes and starts a corporation, finds the initial investors to finance the corporation, and so on. Promoters often enter into contracts on behalf of a corporation prior to its actual incorporation. **Promoters' contracts** include leases, sales contracts, contracts to purchase property, employment contracts, and the like. **Promoters' liability** and corporations' liability on promoters' contracts follows these rules:

- If the corporation never comes into existence, the promoters have joint personal liability on the contract unless the third party specifically exempts them from such liability.

- If the corporation is formed, it becomes liable on a promoters' contract only if it agrees to become bound to the contract. A resolution of the board of directors binds the corporation to a promoter's contract.

- Even if the corporation agrees to be bound to the contract, the promoter remains liable on the contract unless the parties enter into a novation. A *novation* is a three-party agreement in which the corporation agrees to assume the contract liability of the promoter with the consent of the third party. After a novation, the corporation is solely liable on the promoter's contract.

Law & Ethics Questions

1. What is promoter's liability? Explain.

2. **ETHICS** Is it ethical for a promoter to try to avoid liability on a promoter's contract?

Articles of Incorporation

The **articles of incorporation** (or **corporate charter**) is the basic governing document of a corporation. It must be drafted and filed with, and approved by, the state before the corporation can be officially incorporated. Under the RMBCA, the articles of incorporation must include [RMBCA Section 2.02(a)]:

1. The name of the corporation
2. The number of shares the corporation is authorized to issue
3. The address of the corporation's initial registered office and the name of the initial registered agent
4. The name and address of each incorporator

The articles of incorporation may also include provisions concerning (1) the period of duration (which may be perpetual), (2) the purpose or purposes for which the corporation is organized, (3) limitation or regulation of the powers of the corporation, (4) regulation of the affairs of the corporation, or (5) any provision that would otherwise be contained in the corporation's bylaws.

Exhibit 27.2 illustrates sample articles of incorporation.

AMENDING THE ARTICLES OF INCORPORATION The articles of incorporation can be amended to contain any provision that could have been lawfully included in the original document [RMBCA Section 10.01]. Such an amendment must show that (1) the board of directors adopted a *resolution* recommending the amendment and (2) the shareholders voted to approve the amendment [RMBCA Section 10.03]. The board of directors of a corporation may approve an amendment to the articles of incorporation without shareholder approval if the amendment does not affect rights attached to shares [RMBCA Section 10.02]. After the

EXHIBIT 27.2

Articles of Incorporation

**ARTICLES OF INCORPORATION
OF
THE BIG CHEESE CORPORATION**

ONE: The name of this corporation is:

THE BIG CHEESE CORPORATION

TWO: The purpose of this corporation is to engage in any lawful act or activity for which a corporation may be organized under the General Corporation Law of California other than the banking business, the trust company business, or the practice of a profession permitted to be incorporated by the California Corporations Code.

THREE: The name and address in this state of the corporation's initial agent for service of process is:

Nikki Nguyen, Esq.
1000 Main Street
Suite 800
Los Angeles, California 90010

FOUR: This corporation is authorized to issue only one class of shares which shall be designated common stock. The total number of shares it is authorized to issue is 1,000,000 shares.

FIVE: The names and addresses of the persons who are appointed to act as the initial directors of this corporation are:

Shou-Yi Kang	100 Maple Street Los Angeles, California 90005
Frederick Richards	200 Spruce Road Los Angeles, California 90006
Jessie Qian	300 Palm Drive Los Angeles, California 90007
Richard Eastin	400 Willow Lane Los Angeles, California 90008

SIX: The liability of the directors of the corporation from monetary damages shall be eliminated to the fullest extent possible under California law.

SEVEN: The corporation is authorized to provide indemnification of agents (as defined in Section 317 of the Corporations Code) for breach of duty to the corporation and its stockholders through bylaw provisions or through agreements with the agents, or both, in excess of the indemnification otherwise permitted by Section 317 of the Corporations Code, subject to the limits on such excess indemnification set forth in Section 204 of the Corporations Code.

IN WITNESS WHEREOF, the undersigned, being all the persons named above as the initial directors, have executed these Articles of Incorporation.

Dated: January 1, 2008

shareholders approve an amendment, the corporation must file *articles of amendment* with the secretary of state of the state of incorporation [RMBCA Section 10.06].

Web Exercises

1. **WEB** To view the articles of incorporation of Microsoft Corporation, go to *www.microsoft.com/about/companyinformation/corporategovernance/articlesincorp.mspx*.

2. **WEB** To view the articles of incorporation of Harley-Davidson, Inc., go to *www.harley-davidson.com/en_US/media/downloads/Foundation/Articles_of_Incorporation.pdf*.

3. **WEB** To view the articles of incorporation of General Motors Corporation, go to *http://www.secinfo.com/d17xw.621.d.htm#87d*.

4. **WEB** Select a corporation and then use *www.google.com* to see if you can find its articles of incorporation online.

5. **WEB** Use *www.google.com* to find a company that sells incorporation packages to incorporate a corporation in your state. How much does this service cost?

Corporate Status

The RMBCA provides that corporate existence begins when the articles of incorporation are filed. The secretary of state's filing of the articles of incorporation is *conclusive proof* that the incorporations satisfied all conditions of incorporation. After that, only the state can bring a proceeding to cancel or revoke the incorporation or involuntarily dissolve the corporation. Third parties cannot thereafter challenge the existence of the corporation or raise, assert their lack of existence as a corporation as a defense against the corporation [RMBCA Section 2.03]. The corollary to this rule is that failure to file articles of incorporation is conclusive proof of the nonexistence of a corporation.

Purpose of a Corporation

A corporation can be formed for any lawful purpose. Many corporations include a **general-purpose clause** in their articles of incorporation. Such a clause allows the corporation to engage in any activity permitted by corporations law. A corporation may choose to limit its purpose or purposes by including a **limited-purpose clause** in the articles of incorporation [RMBCA Section 3.01]. For example, a corporation may be organized "to engage in the business of real estate development."

Registered Agent

The articles of incorporation must identify a **registered office** with a designated **registered agent** (either an individual or a corporation) in the state of incorporation [RMBCA Section 5.01]. The registered office does not have to be the same as the corporation's place of business. A statement of change must be filed with the secretary of state of the state of incorporation if either the registered office or the registered agent is changed.

The registered agent is empowered to accept service of process on behalf of the corporation.

Example If someone is suing a corporation, the complaint and summons are served on the registered agent. If no registered agent is named or the registered agent cannot be found at the registered office with reasonable diligence, service may be made by mail or alternative means [RMBCA Section 5.04].

Corporate Bylaws

In addition to the articles of incorporation, corporations are governed by their **bylaws**. Either the incorporators or the initial directors can adopt the bylaws of the corporation. The bylaws are much more detailed than are the articles of incorporation. Bylaws may contain any provisions for managing the business and affairs of the corporation that are not inconsistent with law or the articles of incorporation [RMBCA Section 2.06]. They do not have to be filed with any government official. The bylaws are binding on the directors, officers, and shareholders of the corporation.

The bylaws govern the internal management structure of the corporation. For example, they typically specify the time and place of the annual shareholders' meeting, how special meetings of shareholders are called, the time and place of annual and monthly board of directors' meetings, how special meetings of the board of directors are called, the notice required for meetings, the quorum necessary to hold a shareholders' or board of directors' meeting, the required vote necessary to enact a corporate matter, the corporate officers and their duties, the committees of the board of directors and their duties, where the records of the corporation are kept, directors' and shareholders' inspection rights of corporate records, the procedure for transferring shares of the corporation, and such.

Sample provisions of corporate bylaws are set forth in Exhibit 27.3.

The board of directors has the authority to amend the bylaws unless the articles of incorporation reserve that right for the shareholders. The shareholders of the corporation have the absolute right to amend the bylaws even though the board of directors may also amend the bylaws [RMBCA Section 10.20].

EXHIBIT 27.3

Bylaws

**BYLAWS
OF
THE BIG CHEESE CORPORATION**

ARTICLE I   Offices

Section 1. Principal Executive Office.   The corporation's principal executive office shall be fixed and located at such place as the Board of Directors (herein called the "Board") shall determine. The Board is granted full power and authority to change said principal executive office from one location to another.

Section 2. Other Offices.   Branch or subordinate offices may be established at any time by the Board at any place or places.

ARTICLE II   Shareholders

Section 1. Annual Meetings.   The annual meetings of shareholders shall be held on such date and at such time as may be fixed by the Board. At such meetings, directors shall be elected and any other proper business may be transacted.

Section 2. Special Meetings.   Special meetings of the shareholders may be called at any time by the Board, the Chairman of the Board, the President, or by the holders of shares entitled to cast not less than ten percent of the votes at such meeting. Upon request in writing to the Chairman of the Board, the President, any Vice President or the Secretary by any person (other than the Board) entitled to call a special meeting of shareholders, the officer forthwith shall cause notice to be given to the shareholders entitled to vote that a meeting will be held at a time requested by the person or persons calling the meeting, not less than thirty-five nor more than sixty days after the receipt of the request. If the notice is not given within twenty days after receipt of the request, the persons entitled to call the meeting may give the notice.

Section 3. Quorum.   A majority of the shares entitled to vote, represented in person or by proxy, shall constitute a quorum at any meeting of shareholders. If a quorum is present, the affirmative vote of a majority of the shares represented and voting at the meeting (which shares voting affirmatively also constitute at least a majority of the required quorum) shall be the act of the shareholders, unless the vote of a greater number or voting by classes is required by law or by the Articles, except as provided in the following sentence. The shareholders present at a duly called or held meeting at which a quorum is present may continue to do business until adjournment, notwithstanding the withdrawal of enough shareholders to leave less than a quorum, if any action taken (other than adjournment) is approved by at least a majority of the shares required to constitute a quorum.

ARTICLE III   Directors

Section 1. Election and term of office.   The directors shall be elected at each annual meeting of the shareholders, but if any such annual meeting is not held or the directors are not elected thereat, the directors may be elected at any special meeting of shareholders held for that purpose. Each director shall hold office until the next annual meeting and until a successor has been elected and qualified.

Section 2. Quorum.   A majority of the authorized number of directors constitutes a quorum of the Board for the transaction of business. Every act or decision done or made by a majority of the directors present at a meeting duly held at which a quorum is present shall be regarded as the act of the Board, unless a greater number be required by law or by the Articles. A meeting at which a quorum is initially present may continue to transact business notwithstanding the withdrawal of directors, if any action taken is approved by at least a majority of the required quorum for such meeting.

Section 3. Participation in Meetings by Conference Telephone.   Members of the Board may participate in a meeting through use of conference telephone or similar communications equipment, so long as all members participating in such meeting can hear one another.

Section 4. Action Without Meeting.   Any action required or permitted to be taken by the Board may be taken without a meeting if all members of the board shall individually or collectively consent in writing to such action. Such consent or consents shall have the same effect as a unanimous vote of the Board and shall be filed with the minutes of the proceedings of the Board.

Web Exercises

1. **WEB** To view the bylaws of Microsoft Corporation, go to
   www.microsoft.com/about/companyinformation/corporategovernance/bylaws.mspx.

2. **WEB** To view the bylaws of Harley-Davidson, Inc., go to *http://investor.harley-davidson.com/CorporateGovernance.cfm?locale=en_US&bmLocale=en_US*.

3. **WEB** To view the bylaws of General Motors Corporation, go to
   http://www.secinfo.com/d17×w.u4.htm.

4. **WEB** Select a corporation and then use *www.google.com* to see if you can find its bylaws online.

Corporate Seal

Most corporations adopt a **corporate seal** [RMBCA Section 3.02(2)]. Generally, the seal is a design that contains the name of the corporation and the date of incorporation. It is imprinted by the corporate secretary on certain legal documents (e.g., real estate deeds) that are signed by corporate officers or directors. The seal is usually affixed by a metal stamp.

Organizational Meeting

An **organizational meeting** of the initial directors of a corporation must be held after the articles of incorporation are filed. At this meeting, the directors must adopt the bylaws, elect corporate officers, and transact such other business as may come before the meeting [RMBCA Section 2.05]. The last category includes such matters as accepting share subscriptions, approving the form of the stock certificate, authorizing the issuance of the shares, ratifying or adopting promoters' contracts, authorizing the reimbursement of promoters' expenses, selecting a bank, choosing an auditor, forming committees of the board of directors, fixing the salaries of officers, hiring employees, authorizing the filing of applications for government licenses to transact the business of the corporation, and empowering corporate officers to enter into contracts on behalf of the corporation. Exhibit 27.4 contains sample corporate resolutions from an organizational meeting of a corporation.

CONTEMPORARY ENVIRONMENT

S Corporations

A C corporation is a corporation that does not qualify to or does not elect to be taxed as an S corporation. Any corporation with more than 75 shareholders is automatically a C corporation. A C corporation must pay federal income tax at the corporate level. In addition, if a C corporation distributes its profits to shareholders in the form of dividends, the shareholders must pay personal income tax on the dividends. This causes *double taxation*: one tax paid at the corporate level and another paid at the shareholder level.

Congress enacted the **Subchapter S Revision Act** [26 U.S.C. Sections 6242 *et seq.*] to allow some corporations and their shareholders to avoid double taxation by electing to be S corporations.

If a corporation elects to be taxed as an **S corporation**, it pays no federal income tax at the corporate level. As in a partnership, the corporation's income or loss flows to the shareholders' individual income tax returns. Thus, this election is particularly advantageous if (1) the corporation is expected to have losses that can be offset against other income of the shareholders or (2) the corporation is expected to make profits and the shareholders' income tax brackets are lower than the corporation's. Profits are taxed to the shareholders even if the income is not distributed. The shares retain other attributes of the corporate form, including limited liability.

Election to be an S Corporation

Corporations that meet the following criteria can elect to be taxed as S corporations:

1. The corporation must be a domestic corporation.

2. The corporation cannot be a member of an affiliated group of corporations.

3. The corporation can have no more than 75 shareholders.

4. Shareholders must be individuals, estates, or certain trusts. Corporations and partnerships cannot be shareholders.

5. Shareholders must be citizens or residents of the United States. Nonresident aliens cannot be shareholders.

6. The corporation cannot have more than one class of stock. Shareholders do not have to have equal voting rights.

An S corporation election is made by filing form 2553 with the Internal Revenue Service (IRS). The election can be rescinded by shareholders who collectively own at least a majority of the shares of the corporation. However, if the election is rescinded, another S corporation election cannot be made for five years.

Web Exercises

1. **WEB** To view IRS form 2553, go to *www.irs.gov/pub/irs-pdf/f2553.pdf*.

2. **WEB** To read the instructions for preparing IRS form 2553, go to *www.irs.gov/instructions/i2553/ch01.html*.

3. **WEB** Use *www.google.com* to find an article that discusses the benefits and drawbacks of S corporations.

Financing the Corporation

A corporation needs to finance the operation of its business. The most common way to do this is by selling *equity securities* and *debt securities*. **Equity securities** (or **stocks**) represent ownership rights in the corporation. Equity securities can be *common stock* and *preferred stock*. These are discussed in the following paragraphs.

Common Stock

Common stock is an equity security that represents the residual value of a corporation. Common stock has no preferences. That is, creditors and preferred shareholders must receive their required interest and dividend payments before common shareholders receive anything. Common stock does not have a fixed maturity date. If the corporation is liquidated, the creditors and preferred shareholders are paid the value of their interests first, and

EXHIBIT 27.4

Minutes of an Organizational Meeting

MINUTES OF FIRST MEETING
OF
BOARD OF DIRECTORS
OF
THE BIG CHEESE CORPORATION
January 2, 2008
10:00 A.M.

The Directors of said corporation held their first meeting on the above date and at the above time pursuant to required notice.

The following Directors, constituting a quorum of the Board of Directors, were present at such meeting:

> Shou-Yi Kang
> Frederick Richards
> Jessie Quian
> Richard Eastin

Upon motion duly made and seconded, Show-Yi was unanimously elected Chairman of the meeting and Frederick Richards was unanimously elected Secretary of the meeting.

1. Articles of Incorporation and Agent for Service of Process

The Chairman stated that the Articles of Incorporation of the Corporation were filed in the office of the California Secretary of State. The Chairman presented to the meeting a certified copy of the Articles of Incorporation. The Secretary was directed to insert the copy in the Minute Book. Upon motion duly made and seconded, the following resolution was unanimously adopted:

> RESOLVED, that the agent named as the initial agent for service of process in the Articles of Incorporation of this corporation is here by confirmed as this corporation's agent for the purpose of service of process.

2. Bylaws

The matter of adopting Bylaws for the regulation of the affairs of the corporation was next considered. The Secretary presented to the meeting a form of Bylaws, which was considered and discussed. Upon motion duly made and seconded, the following recitals and resolutions were unanimously adopted:

> WHEREAS, there has been presented to the directors a form of Bylaws for the regulation of the affairs of this corporation; and
>
> WHEREAS, it is deemed to be in the best interests of this corporation that said Bylaws be adopted by this Board of Directors as the Bylaws of this corporation;
>
> NOW, THEREFORE, BE IT RESOLVED, that Bylaws in the form presented to this meeting are adopted and approved as the Bylaws of this corporation until amended or repealed in accordance with applicable law.
>
> RESOLVED FURTHER, that the Secretary of this corporation is authorized and directed to execute a certificate of the adoption of said Bylaws and to enter said Bylaws as so certified in the Minute Book of this corporation, and to see that a copy of said Bylaws is kept at the principal executive or business office of this corporation in California.

3. Corporate Seal

The secretary presented for approval a proposed seal of the corporation. Upon motion duly made and seconded, the following resolution was unanimously adopted:

> RESOLVED, that a corporate seal is adopted as the seal of this corporation in the form of two concentric circles, with the name of this corporation between the two circles and the state and date of incorporation within the inner circle.

4. Stock Certificate

The Secretary presented a proposed form of stock certificate for use by the corporation. Upon motion duly made and seconded, the following resolution was unanimously adopted:

> RESOLVED, that the form of stock certificate presented to this meeting is approved and adopted as the stock certificate of this corporation.

The secretary was instructed to insert a sample copy of the stock certificate in the Minute Book immediately following these minutes.

5. Election of officers

The Chairman announced that it would be in order to elect officers of the corporation. After discussion and upon motion duly made and seconded, the following resolution was unanimously adopted:

> RESOLVED, that the following persons are unanimously elected to the offices indicated opposite their names

Title	Name
Chief Executive Officer	Shou-Yi Kang
President	Frederick Richards
Secretary and Vice President	Jessie Quian
Treasurer	Richard Eastin

There being no further business to come before the meeting, on motion duly made, seconded and unanimously carried, the meeting was adjourned.

the common shareholders are paid the value of their interests (if any) last. Corporations may issue different classes of common stock [RMBCA Sections 6.01(a), 6.01(b)].

Persons who own common stock are called **common stockholders**. A common stockholder's investment in the corporation is represented by a **common stock certificate**. Common stockholders have the right to elect directors and to vote on mergers and other important matters. In return for their investment, common stockholders receive **dividends** declared by the board of directors.

PAR VALUE AND NO PAR SHARES Common shares are sometimes categorized as either par or no par. *Par share* is a value assigned to common shares by the corporation, usually in the articles of incorporation, which sets the lowest price at which the shares may be issued by the corporation. It does not affect the market value of the shares. Most shares that are issued by corporations are *no par shares*. No par shares are not assigned a par value. The RMBCA has eliminated the concept of par value.

Preferred Stock

Preferred stock is an equity security that is given certain *preferences and rights over common stock* [RMBCA Section 6.01(c)]. The owners of preferred stock are called **preferred stockholders**. Preferred stockholders are issued *preferred stock certificates* to evidence their ownership interest in the corporation.

Preferred stock can be issued in classes or series. One class of preferred stock can be given preference over another class of preferred stock. Like common stockholders, preferred stockholders have limited liability. Preferred stockholders generally are not given the right to vote for the election of directors or such. However, they are often given the right to vote if there is a merger or if the corporation has not made the required dividend payments for a certain period of time (e.g., three years).

Preferences of preferred stock must be set forth in the articles of incorporation. Preferred stock may have any or all of the preferences or rights that are discussed in the following paragraphs.

DIVIDEND PREFERENCE A **dividend preference** is the right to receive a **fixed dividend** at set periods during the year (e.g., quarterly). The dividend rate is usually a set percentage of the initial offering price.

Example Suppose a stockholder purchases $10,000 of a preferred stock that pays an 8 percent dividend annually. The stockholder has the right to receive $800 each year as a dividend on the preferred stock.

LIQUIDATION PREFERENCE The right to be paid before common stockholders if the corporation is dissolved and liquidated is called a **liquidation preference**. A liquidation preference is normally a stated dollar amount.

Example A corporation issues a preferred stock that has a liquidation preference of $200. This means that if the corporation is dissolved and liquidated, the holder of each preferred share will receive at least $200 before the common shareholders receive anything. Note that because the corporation must pay its creditors first, there may be insufficient funds to pay this preference.

CUMULATIVE DIVIDEND RIGHT Corporations must pay a preferred dividend if they have the earnings to do so. **Cumulative preferred stock** provides that any missed dividend payments must be paid in the future to preferred shareholders before the common shareholders can receive any dividends. The amount of unpaid cumulative dividends is called dividend *arrearages*. Usually, arrearages can be accumulated for only a limited period of time (e.g., three years). With **noncumulative preferred stock**, there is no right of accumulation. In other words, the corporation does not have to pay any missed dividends.

RIGHT TO PARTICIPATE IN PROFITS **Participating preferred stock** allows the stockholder to participate in the profits of the corporation along with the common stockholders. Participation is in addition to the fixed dividend paid on preferred stock. The terms of participation vary widely. Usually, the common stockholders must be paid a certain amount of dividends before participation is allowed. **Nonparticipating preferred stock** does not give the holder a right to participate in the profits of the corporation beyond the fixed dividend rate. Most preferred stock falls into this category.

CONVERSION RIGHT **Convertible preferred stock** permits the stockholders to convert their shares into common stock. The terms and exchange rate of the conversion are established when the shares are issued. The holders of convertible preferred stock usually exercise this option if the corporation's common stock significantly increases in value. Preferred stock without a conversion feature is called **nonconvertible preferred stock**. Nonconvertible stock is more common.

This list of preferences and rights is not exhaustive [RMBCA Section 6.01(d)]. Corporations may establish other preferences and rights for preferred stock.

Redeemable Preferred Stock

Redeemable preferred stock (or **callable preferred stock**) permits a corporation to redeem (i.e., buy back) the preferred stock at some future date. The terms of the redemption are established when the shares are issued. Corporations usually redeem the shares when the current interest rate falls below the dividend rate of the preferred shares. Preferred stock that is not redeemable is called **nonredeemable preferred stock**. Nonredeemable stock is more common.

Authorized, Issued, and Outstanding Shares

The number of shares provided for in the articles of incorporation is called **authorized shares** [RMBCA Section 6.01]. The shareholders may vote to amend the articles of incorporation to increase this amount. Authorized shares that have been sold by the corporation are called **issued shares**. Not all authorized shares have to be issued at the same time. Authorized shares that have not been issued are called **unissued shares**. The board of directors can vote to issue unissued shares at any time without shareholder approval.

A corporation is permitted to repurchase its own shares [RMBCA Section 6.31]. Repurchased shares are commonly called **treasury shares**. Treasury shares cannot be voted by the corporation, and dividends are not paid on these shares. Treasury shares can be reissued by the corporation. The shares that are in shareholder hands, whether originally issued or reissued treasury shares, are called **outstanding shares**. Only outstanding shares have the right to vote [RMBCA Section 6.03].

CONCEPT SUMMARY

Types of Shares

TYPE OF SHARE	DESCRIPTION
Authorized	Shares authorized in the corporation's articles of incorporation.
Issued	Shares sold by the corporation.
Treasury	Shares repurchased by the corporation. These shares do not have the right to vote.
Outstanding	Issued shares minus treasury shares. These shares have the right to vote.

Consideration to Be Paid for Shares

The RMBCA allows shares to be issued in exchange for any benefit to the corporation, including cash, tangible property, intangible property, promissory notes, services performed, contracts for services performed, or other securities of the corporation. In the absence of fraud, the judgment of the board of directors or shareholders as to the value of consideration received for shares is conclusive [RMBCA Sections 6.21(b), 6.21(c)].

CONTEMPORARY ENVIRONMENT
Stock Options and Stock Warrants

A corporation can grant stock options (options) and stock warrants (warrants) that permit parties to purchase common or preferred shares at a certain price for a set time [RMBCA Section 6.24].

A **stock option** gives the recipient the right to purchase shares of the corporation from the corporation at a stated price (called the *striking price*) for a specified period of time (called the *option period*). If the profitability of the corporation and the market value of its securities increase during the option period, the holder of the option is likely to *exercise the option*—that is, purchase the shares subject to the option. Stock options are nontransferable.

Corporations commonly grant stock options to top-level managers. Stock options are often issued to attract executive talent to work for the corporation. Shareholders sometimes criticize their corporations for being too generous in granting stock options.

A **stock warrant** is a stock option that is evidenced by a certificate. Warrants are commonly issued in conjunction with other securities. A warrant holder can exercise the warrant and purchase the common stock at the strike price any time during the warrant period. Warrants can be transferable or nontransferable.

Debt Securities

A corporation often raises funds by issuing debt securities [RMBCA Section 3.02(7)]. **Debt securities** (also called **fixed income securities**) establish a debtor–creditor relationship in which the corporation borrows money from the investor to whom the debt security is issued. The corporation promises to pay interest on the amount borrowed and to repay the principal at some stated maturity date in the future. The corporation is the *debtor*, and the holder is the *creditor*. The three classifications of debt securities are:

1. *Debenture.* A **debenture** is a *long-term* (often 30 years or more), *unsecured* debt instrument that is based on a corporation's general credit standing. If the corporation encounters financial difficulty, unsecured debenture holders are treated as general creditors of the corporation (i.e., they are paid only after the secured creditors' claims are met).
2. *Bond.* A **bond** is a *long-term* debt security that is *secured* by some form of *collateral* (e.g., real estate, personal property). Thus, bonds are the same as debentures except that they are secured. Secured bondholders can foreclose on the collateral in the event of nonpayment of interest, principal, or other specified events.
3. *Note.* A **note** is a *short-term* debt security with a maturity of five years or less. Notes can be either *unsecured* or *secured*. They usually do not contain a conversion feature. They are sometimes made redeemable.

INDENTURE AGREEMENT The terms of a debt security are commonly contained in a contract between the corporation and the holder; this contract is known as an **indenture agreement** (or simply an **indenture**). The indenture generally contains the maturity date of the debt security, the required interest payment, the collateral (if any), conversion rights into common or preferred stock, call provisions, any restrictions on the corporation's right to incur other indebtedness, the rights of holders upon default, and such. It also establishes the rights and duties of the indenture trustee. Generally, a trustee is appointed to represent the interest of the debt security holders. Bank trust departments often serve in this capacity.

CONCEPT SUMMARY

Debt Instruments

DEBT INSTRUMENT	DESCRIPTION
Debenture	A *long-term, unsecured* debt instrument that is based on a corporation's general credit rating.
Bond	A *long-term* debt security that is *secured* by some form of property. The property securing the bond is called *collateral*. In the event of nonpayment of interest or principal or other specified events, bondholders can foreclose on and obtain the collateral.
Note	A *short-term* debt instrument with a maturity of five years or less. Notes can be either unsecured or secured.

CONTEMPORARY ENVIRONMENT

Close Corporation

Many of the formal rules in state corporation statutes are designed to govern the management of large, publicly held corporations. These rules may not be relevant for regulating the management of *close corporations*—that is, corporations formed by entrepreneurs with few shareholders who often work for the corporation and manage its day-to-day operations.

The **Model Statutory Close Corporation Supplement (Supplement)** was added to the RMBCA to permit entrepreneurial corporations to choose to be close corporations. Only corporations with 50 or fewer shareholders may elect statutory close corporation (SCC) status. To choose this status, two-thirds of the shares of each class of shares of the corporation must approve the election. The articles of incorporation must contain a statement that the corporation is a statutory close corporation, and the share certificates must conspicuously state that the shares have been issued by a statutory close corporation.

A close corporation may dispense with some of the formalities of operating a corporation. For example, if all the shareholders approve, a close corporation may operate without a board of directors, and the articles of incorporation should contain a statement to that effect. The powers and affairs of the corporation are then managed by the shareholders. A close corporation need not adopt bylaws if the provisions required by law to be contained in bylaws are contained in the articles of incorporation or a shareholders' agreement. The corporation need not hold annual shareholders' meetings unless one or more shareholders demand in writing that such meetings be held. The shareholders may enter into a shareholders' agreement about how the corporation will be managed. In effect, the shareholders can treat the corporation as a partnership for governance purposes [Supp. Section 20(b)(3)]. Selecting statutory close corporation status does not affect the limited liability of shareholders [Supp. Section 25].

Corporate Powers

A corporation has the same basic rights to perform acts and enter into contracts as a physical person [RMBCA Section 3.02]. The express and implied powers of a corporation are discussed in the following paragraphs.

Express Powers

A corporation's **express powers** are found in (1) the U.S. Constitution, (2) state constitutions, (3) federal statutes, (4) state statutes, (5) articles of incorporation, (6) bylaws, and (7) resolutions of the board of directors. Corporation statutes normally state the express powers granted to the corporation.

Generally, a corporation has the power to purchase, own, lease, sell, mortgage, or otherwise deal in real and personal property; make contracts; lend money; borrow money; incur liabilities; issue notes, bonds, and other obligations; invest and reinvest funds; sue and be sued in its corporate name; make donations for the public welfare or for charitable, scientific, or educational purposes; and the like. RMBCA Section 3.02 provides a list of express corporate powers.

Corporations formed under general incorporation laws cannot engage in certain businesses, such as banking, insurance, or operating public utilities. A corporation must obtain a corporate charter under special incorporation statutes and receive approval of special government administrative agencies before engaging in these businesses.

Implied Powers

Neither the governing laws nor the corporate documents can anticipate every act necessary for a corporation to carry on its business. **Implied powers** allow a corporation to exceed its express powers in order to accomplish its corporate purpose.

Example A corporation has the implied power to open a bank account, reimburse its employees for expenses, engage in advertising, purchase insurance, and the like.

Ultra Vires Act

An act by a corporation that is beyond its express or implied powers is called an ***ultra vires* act**. The following remedies are available if an *ultra vires* act is committed:

1. Shareholders can sue for an injunction to prevent the corporation from engaging in the act.
2. The corporation (or the shareholders, on behalf of the corporation) can sue the officers or directors who caused the act for damages.
3. The attorney general of the state of incorporation can bring an action to enjoin the act or to dissolve the corporation [RMBCA Section 3.04].

Dissolution and Termination of Corporations

The life of a corporation may be terminated voluntarily or involuntarily. The methods for dissolving and terminating corporations are discussed in the following paragraphs.

Voluntary Dissolution

A corporation can be voluntarily dissolved. If the corporation has not commenced business or issued any shares, it may be dissolved by a vote of the majority of the incorporators or initial directors [RMBCA Section 14.01]. After that, the corporation can be voluntarily dissolved if the board of directors recommends dissolution and a majority of shares entitled to vote (or a greater number, if required by the articles of incorporation or bylaws) votes for dissolution as well [RMBCA Section 14.02]. For a **voluntary dissolution** to be effective, **articles of dissolution** must be filed with the secretary of state of the state of incorporation. A corporation is dissolved upon the effective date of the articles of dissolution [RMBCA Section 14.03].

Administrative Dissolution

The secretary of state can obtain **administrative dissolution** of a corporation if (1) it failed to file an annual report, (2) it failed for 60 days to maintain a registered agent in the state, (3) it failed, for 60 days after a change of its registered agent, to file a statement of such change with the secretary of state, (4) it did not pay its franchise fee, or (5) the period of duration stated in the corporation's articles of incorporation has expired [RMBCA Section 14.20]. Administrative dissolution is simple. If the corporation does not cure the default within 60 days of being notified of it, the secretary of state issues a *certificate of dissolution* that dissolves the corporation [RMBCA Section 14.21].

Judicial Dissolution

A corporation can be involuntarily dissolved by a judicial proceeding. **Judicial dissolution** can be instituted by the attorney general of the state of incorporation if the corporation (1) procured its articles of incorporation through fraud or (2) exceeded or abused the authority conferred on it by law [RMBCA Section 14.30(1)]. If a court judicially dissolves a corporation, it enters a *decree of dissolution* that specifies the date of dissolution [RMBCA Section 14.33].

Winding Up, Liquidation, and Termination

A dissolved corporation continues its corporate existence but may not carry on any business except as required to **wind up** and **liquidate** its business and affairs [RMBCA Section 14.05].

In a voluntary dissolution, the liquidation is usually carried out by the board of directors. If the dissolution is involuntary or the dissolution is voluntary but the directors refuse to carry out the liquidation, a court-appointed receiver carries out the winding up and liquidation of the corporation [RMBCA Section 14.32].

Termination occurs only after the winding up of the corporation's affairs, the liquidation of its assets, and the distribution of the proceeds to the claimants. The liquidated assets are paid to claimants according to the following priority: (1) expenses of liquidation and creditors according to their respective liens and contract rights, (2) preferred shareholders according to their liquidation preferences and contract rights, and (3) common stockholders.

The dissolution of a corporation does not impair any rights or remedies available against the corporation or its directors, or officers, or shareholders for any right or claim existing or incurred prior to dissolution.

Chapter Summary

Nature of the Corporation, p. 750

A corporation is a legal entity created pursuant to the laws of the state of incorporation. State statutes govern the formation, operation, and dissolution of corporations.

The Corporation as a Legal "Person"

A corporation is a separate legal entity—an *artificial person*—that can own property, sue and be sued, enter into contracts, and such. Characteristics of corporations:

1. *Limited liability of shareholders.* Shareholders are liable for the debts and obligations of the corporation only to the extent of their capital contributions.
2. *Free transferability of shares.* Shares of a corporation are freely transferable by shareholders unless they are expressly restricted.
3. *Perpetual existence.* A corporations exist in perpetuity unless a specific duration is stated in the corporation's articles of incorporation.
4. *Centralized management.* The board of directors of a corporation makes policy decisions for the corporation. Corporate officers appointed by the board of directors run the corporation's day-to-day operations. Together, the directors and officers form the corporation's management.

Revised Model Business Corporation Act (RMBCA)

1. *Model Business Corporation Act (MBCA).* This model act, drafted in 1950, was intended to provide a uniform law for the regulation of corporations.
2. *Revised Model Business Corporation Act (RMBCA).* The RMBCA is a revision of the MBCA promulgated in 1984 that arranges the provisions of the model act more logically, revises the language to be more consistent, and makes substantial changes that modernize the provisions of the act.

Public and Private Corporations

1. *Public corporation.* A public corporation is a corporation formed to meet a specific governmental or political purpose. Also called a *government-owned* corporation. Municipal corporations (i.e., cities) are an example.
2. *Private corporation.* A private corporation is a corporation formed to conduct privately owned business. It may be large or small.

Profit and Not-for-Profit Corporations

1. *Profit corporation.* A profit corporation is created to conduct a business for profit that can distribute profits to shareholders in the form of dividends.
2. *Not-for-profit corporation.* A not-for-profit corporation is formed to operate charitable institutions, colleges, universities, and other not-for-profit entities. These corporations have no shareholders.

Publicly Held and Closely Held Corporations

1. *Publicly held corporation.* A publicly held corporation has many shareholders, and its securities are often traded on national stock exchanges. General Motors Corporation is an example.
2. *Closely held corporation.* A closely held corporation is owned by one or a few shareholders. Examples are family-owned corporations. They are also called *close corporations*.

Professional Corporations

Professional corporations are formed by lawyers, doctors, and other professionals. Shareholders of professional corporations are usually called *members*. Members must be licensed to practice the profession for which the corporation is formed.

Domestic, Foreign, and Alien Corporations

1. *Domestic corporation.* A domestic corporation is a corporation in the state in which it is incorporated.
2. *Foreign corporation.* A foreign corporation is a corporation in any state other than the one in which it is incorporated. A domestic corporation often transacts business in states other than its state of incorporation; hence, it is a foreign corporation in these states. A foreign corporation must obtain a certificate of authority from these other states to transact intrastate business there.
3. *Alien corporation.* An alien corporation is a corporation that is incorporated in another country. Alien corporations are treated as foreign corporations for most purposes.

Incorporation Procedures, p. 754

Incorporation is the process of incorporating (forming) a new corporation. Corporations are creatures of statute; they can be formed only if certain statutory formalities contained in the state's corporations code are followed.

Selecting a State for Incorporating a Corporation

A corporation can be incorporated in only one state, although it can conduct business in other states.

Selecting a Corporate Name

A corporate name selected for a new corporation must be distinguishable from existing corporate names. A corporate name may be reserved for a limited period of time while the corporation is being formed.

Incorporators

Incorporators are the person or persons, partnerships, or corporations who are responsible for incorporating a new corporation.

Promoters' Liability

1. *Promoter.* A promoter is a person who organizes and starts a corporation, negotiates and enters into contracts in advance of formation, finds the initial investors to finance the corporation, and so forth.
2. *Promoters' contracts.* A promoter enters into a promoter's contract on behalf of a proposed corporation prior to its incorporation. These contracts often include leases, sales contracts, contracts to purchase property, and so forth.
3. *Liability of promoters for promoters' contracts.* Promoters are personally liable for promoters' contracts unless the corporation ratifies the contract as its own once it is

formed and the corporation, the promoter, and the third party with whom the contract is made enter into a *novation* agreement that expressly releases the promoter from liability.

Articles of Incorporation

The articles of incorporation is the basic governing document of a corporation. This document must be filed with the secretary of state of the state of incorporation. It is a public document. It is also called the *corporate charter*.

1. ***Information to be set forth in the articles of incorporation.*** The corporations code of each state sets out the information that must be included in a corporation's articles of incorporation. Additional information may be included in the articles of incorporation, as deemed necessary or desirable by the incorporators.
2. ***Amending the articles of incorporation.*** The articles of incorporation can be amended to contain any provision that could have been lawfully included in the original articles of incorporation. After an amendment is approved by the shareholders, the corporation must file articles of amendment with the secretary of state in the state in which it is incorporated.

Corporate Status

The filing of articles of incorporation is conclusive proof that a corporation exists. After that, only the state can challenge the status of the corporation; third parties cannot. Failure to file articles of incorporation is conclusive proof that the corporation does not exist, and the state and third parties may challenge the existence of the corporation.

Purpose of a Corporation

A corporation can be formed for "any lawful purpose." A corporation can limit its purposes by including in the articles of incorporation a limited-purpose clause that stipulates the purposes and activities the corporation can engage in.

Registered Agent

A new corporation must designate a person or corporation that is empowered to accept service of process on behalf of the corporation. A new designation must be made annually.

Corporate Bylaws

Bylaws are a detailed set of rules that the board of directors adopts after a corporation is formed that contains provisions for managing the business and affairs of the corporation. This document does not have to be filed with the secretary of state.

Corporate Seal

A corporate seal is a design that contains the name of the corporation and the date of incorporation. It is imprinted by the corporate secretary on certain legal documents, using a metal stamp containing the design.

Organizational Meeting

The initial directors of a corporation must hold an organizational meeting after the articles of incorporation are filed. At this meeting, the directors adopt the bylaws, elect corporate officers, ratify promoters' contracts, adopt a corporate seal, and transact such other business as may come before the meeting. Minutes are the written recording of the actions taken by the directors at the organizational and other directors' meetings.

S Corporations

An S corporation is a corporation that has elected to be taxed as an S corporation for federal income tax purposes. An S corporation pays no federal income tax at the corporate level, and the S corporation's income or loss flows to the shareholders and must be reported on the shareholders' individual income tax returns. A corporation must meet certain requirements to elect to be an S corporation.

Financing the Corporation, p. 760

Equity securities represent the ownership rights to the corporation. They are also called *stocks*. Equity securities consist of common stock and preferred stock.

Common Stock

Common stock is a type of equity security that represents the residual value of the corporation. Common stock has no preferences, and its shareholders are paid dividends and assets upon liquidation only after creditors and preferred shareholders have been paid.

1. *Common stockholder.* A common stockholder is a person who owns common stock.
2. *Common stock certificate.* A common stock certificate represents the common shareholder's investment in the corporation.
3. *Par value.* A par value is assigned by the corporation to common shares that sets the lowest price at which the shares may be issued by the corporation. *No par* shares are not assigned a par value. The RMBCA has eliminated the concept of par value.

Preferred Stock

Preferred stock is a type of equity security that is given certain preferences and rights over common stock. A preferred stockholder is a person who owns preferred stock. A preferred stock certificate represents a preferred stockholder's investment in a corporation. Preferred stock may have any or all of the following preferences or rights:

1. *Dividend preference.* This preference gives the right to receive a fixed dividend at stipulated periods during the year (e.g., quarterly).
2. *Liquidation preference.* This preference gives the right to be paid a stated dollar amount if the corporation is dissolved and liquidated. The corporation must pay its creditors first, however.
3. *Cumulative dividend right.* Cumulative preferred stock is stock that provides that any missed dividend payments must be paid in the future to the preferred shareholders before the common shareholders can receive any dividends.
4. *Right to participate in profits.* Participating preferred stock is preferred stock that allows the stockholder to participate in the profits of the corporation along with the common stockholders on an expressly stated basis.
5. *Conversion right.* Convertible preferred stock is preferred stock that permits stockholders to convert their shares into common stock at a stipulated conversion price.

Redeemable Preferred Stock

Redeemable preferred stock may be bought back by the corporation at a specified price at some future date. This stock is also called *callable preferred stock.*

Authorized, Issued, and Outstanding Shares

1. *Authorized shares.* The articles of incorporation provides for a particular number of shares. The shareholders may amend the articles of incorporation to increase the number of authorized shares.
2. *Issued shares.* Issued shares are authorized shares that have been sold by the corporation.
3. *Unissued shares.* Unissued shares are authorized shares that have not been sold by the corporation.
4. *Treasury shares.* Treasury shares are issued shares that have been repurchased by the corporation. They may be resold by the corporation.
5. *Outstanding shares.* Outstanding shares are shares that are in shareholder hands, whether originally issued or reissued treasury shares. Only outstanding shares have the right to vote.

Consideration to Be Paid for Shares

Shares may be issued in exchange for any benefit to the corporation, including cash, tangible property, intangible property, promissory notes, services performed, contracts for services to be performed, or other securities of the corporation.

Stock Options and Stock Warrants

1. *Stock option.* A stock option is a nontransferable right to purchase shares of the corporation from the corporation at a stated price for a specific period of time.
   a. *Striking price.* The striking price is the stated price at which a stock may be bought at a future date.
   b. *Option period.* The option period is the specified period of time for exercising a stock option.
   c. *Exercising the option.* Exercising the option is the act of purchasing the shares subject to the option by the holder of the option. Stock options are usually granted to the management of a corporation.
2. *Stock warrant.* A stock warrant is a stock option that is represented by a certificate. Stock warrants are commonly issued in conjunction with another security. Warrants may be transferable or nontransferable.

Debt Securities

Debt securities establish a debtor–creditor relationship in which the corporation borrows money from the investor to whom the debt security is issued.

1. *Debenture.* A debenture is a long-term, unsecured debt instrument that is based on the corporation's general credit rating.
2. *Bond.* A bond is a long-term debt security that is secured by some form of property. The property securing the bond is called collateral. In the event of nonpayment of interest or principal or other specified events, bondholders can foreclose on and obtain the collateral.
3. *Note.* A note is a short-term debt instrument with a maturity of five years or less. Notes can be either unsecured or secured.
4. *Indenture agreement.* The indenture agreement is the contract between the corporation and debt security holders that contains the terms of the agreement between the corporation and the holders.

Corporate Powers, p. 765

Express Powers

A corporation has the express powers granted to it by the U.S. Constitution, state constitutions, federal statutes, state statutes (particularly the state's corporation code), articles of incorporation, bylaws, and resolutions of the board of directors.

Implied Powers

Implied powers allow a corporation to accomplish its corporate purpose.

Ultra Vires Acts

Ultra vires acts are acts by a corporation that are beyond its express or implied powers. The following remedies are available if an *ultra vires* act is committed:

1. Shareholders can sue for an injunction to prevent the corporation from engaging in the act.
2. The corporation (or shareholders, on behalf of the corporation) can sue the officers and directors who caused the act for damages.
3. The attorney general of the state of incorporation can bring an action to enjoin the act or to dissolve the corporation.

Dissolution and Termination of Corporations, p. 766

Voluntary Dissolution

Voluntary dissolution is dissolution of a corporation by the incorporators or initial directors if the corporation has not begun business or issued shares and by the majority vote of shareholders if the corporation has begun business or issued shares. The articles of dissolution is a document that is filed with the secretary of state of the state of incorporation when a corporation is voluntarily dissolved.

Administrative Dissolution

Administrative dissolution is involuntary dissolution of a corporation that is ordered by the secretary of state if the corporation has failed to comply with certain procedures required by law (e.g., failure to pay franchise tax). The certificate of dissolution is a document that is filed by the secretary of state when a corporation is administratively dissolved.

Judicial Dissolution

Judicial dissolution is dissolution of a corporation by a court proceeding instituted by:
1. *The state.* If the corporation procured its articles of incorporation through fraud or exceeded or abused the authority conferred upon it by law, the state may order its dissolution.
2. *Decree of dissolution.* This is an order issued by the court when a corporation has been judicially dissolved.

Winding Up, Liquidation, and Termination

1. *Winding up and liquidation.* A dissolved corporation's assets are collected, liquidated, and distributed to creditors, shareholders, and other claimants.
2. *Termination.* The ending of a corporation occurs only after the winding up of the corporation's affairs, the liquidation of its assets, and the distribution of the proceeds and property to the claimants.

Test Review Terms and Concepts

Case Problems

27.1 Legal Entity: Jeffrey Sammak was the owner of a contracting business known as Senaco. Sammak decided to enter the coal reprocessing business. Sammak attended the "Coal Show" in Chicago, Illinois, at which he met representatives of the Deister Co., Inc. (Deister). Deister was incorporated under the laws of Pennsylvania. Sammak began negotiating with Deister to purchase equipment to be used in his coal reprocessing business. Deister sent Sammak literature guaranteeing a certain level of performance for the equipment. Sammak purchased the equipment. After the equipment was installed, Sammak became dissatisfied with its performance. Sammak believed that Deister breached an express warranty and wanted to sue. Can a suit be brought against a corporation such as Deister? *Blackwood Coal v. Deister Co., Inc.*, 626 F.Supp. 727, **Web** 1985 U.S. Dist. Lexis 12767 (United States District Court for the Eastern District of Pennsylvania)

27.2 Limited Liability of Shareholders: Joseph M. Billy was an employee of the USM Corporation (USM), a publicly held corporation. Billy was at work when a 4,600-pound ram from a vertical boring mill broke loose and crushed him to death. Billy's widow brought suit against USM, alleging that the accident was caused by certain defects in the manufacture and design of the vertical boring mill and the two moving parts directly involved in the accident, a metal lifting arm and the 4,600-pound ram. If Mrs. Billy's suit is successful, can the shareholders of USM be held personally liable for any judgment against USM? *Billy v. Consolidated Mach. Tool. Corp.*, 51 N.Y.2d 152, 412 N.E.2d 934, 432 N.Y.S.2d 879, **Web** 1980 N.Y. Lexis 2638 (Court of Appeals of New York)

27.3 Corporation: William O'Donnel and Vincent Marino worked together as executives of a shipping container repair company known as Marine Trailers. Marine Trailers's largest customer was American Export Lines (American Export). When American Export became unhappy with the owners of Marine Trailers, it let O'Donnel and Marino know that if they formed their own company, American Exports would give them its business. O'Donnel and Marino decided to take American Exports's suggestion, and they bought the majority of shares of a publicly traded corporation known as Marine Repair Services, Inc. (Repair Services). O'Donnel and Marine operated Repair Services as a container repair company at the Port of New York. The company prospered, expanding to five other states and overseas. O'Donnel and Marino's initial $12,000 investment paid off. Ten years after buying the company, each man was earning over $150,000 a year in salary alone. What type of corporation is Repair Services? *O'Donnel v. Marine Repair Service, Inc.*, 530 F.Supp. 1199, **Web** 1982 U.S. Dist. Lexis 10456 (United States District Court for the Southern District of New York)

27.4 Corporation: Hutchinson Baseball Enterprises, Inc. (Hutchinson, Inc.), was incorporated under the laws of

Kansas. Among the purposes of the corporation, according to its bylaws, were to "promote, advance, and sponsor baseball, which shall include Little League and Amateur baseball, in the Hutchinson, Kansas, area." The corporation was involved in a number of activities, including leasing a field for American Legion teams, furnishing instructors as coaches for Little League teams, conducting a Little League camp, and leasing a baseball field to a local junior college for a nominal fee. Hutchinson, Inc., raised money through ticket sales to amateur baseball games, concessions, and contributions. Any profits were used to improve the playing fields. Profits were never distributed to the corporation's directors or members. What type of corporation is Hutchinson, Inc.? *Hutchinson Baseball Enterprises, Inc. v. Commissioner of Internal Revenue*, 696 F.2d 757, **Web** 1982 U.S. App. Lexis 23179 (United States Court of Appeals for the Tenth Circuit)

27.5 Corporation: Elmer Balvik and Thomas Sylvester formed a partnership, named Weldon Electric, for the purpose of engaging in the electrical contracting business. Balvik contributed $8,000 and a vehicle worth $2,000, and Sylvester contributed $25,000 to the partnership's assets. The parties operated the business as a partnership for several years and then decided to incorporate. Stock was issued to Balvik and Sylvester in proportion to their partnership ownership interests, with Sylvester receiving 70 percent and Balvik receiving 30 percent of the stock. Balvik and his wife and Sylvester and his wife were the four directors of the corporation. Sylvester was elected president of the corporation. Balvik was vice president. The corporation's bylaws stated that "sales of shares of stock by any shareholder shall be as set forth in a 'Buy Sell Agreement' entered into by the shareholders." What type of corporation is Weldon Electric? *Balvik v. Sylvester*, 411 N.W.2d 383, **Web** 1987 N.D. Lexis 392 (Supreme Court of North Dakota)

27.6 Corporation: Leo V. Mysels was the president of Florida Fashions of Interior Design, Inc. (Florida Fashions). Florida Fashions, which was a Pennsylvania corporation, had never registered to do business in the state of Florida. While acting in the capacity of a salesman for the corporation, Mysels took an order for goods from Francis E. Barry. The transaction took place in Florida. Barry paid Florida Fashions for the goods ordered. When Florida Fashions failed to perform its obligations under the sales agreement, Barry brought suit in Florida. What type of corporation was Florida Fashions in regard to the state of Pennsylvania and to the state of Florida? Can Florida Fashions defend itself in a lawsuit? *Mysels v. Barry*, 332 So.2d 38, **Web** 1976 Fla. App. Lexis 14344 (Court of Appeal of Florida)

27.7 Promoters' Liability: The Homes Corporation (Homes), a closely held corporation whose sole stockholders were Jerry and Beverly Ann Allen, purchased 10 acres of real estate near Kahaluu on the island of Oahu, Hawaii. Homes made a down payment of $50,000. The Allens intended to obtain approval for a planned unit development (PUD) from the city and county of Honolulu and then develop the property with some 60 condominium townhouses. To further this project, the Allens sought an outside investor. Herbert Hadley, a real estate developer from Texas, decided to join the Allens' project. The two parties entered an agreement whereby a new Hawaiian corporation would be formed to build the condominiums, with Handley owning 51 percent of the corporation's stock and the Allens the remaining 49 percent. The two parties began extensive planning and design of the project. They also took out a $69,500 loan from the Bank of Hawaii. After a year had gone by, Handley informed the Allens that he was no longer able to advance funds to the project. Soon thereafter, the city and county denied their PUD zoning application. The new corporation was never formed. Who is liable for the failed condominium project's contractual obligations? *Handley v. Ching*, 2 Haw. App. 166, 627 P.2d 1132, **Web** 1981 Haw. App. Lexis 192 (Intermediate Court of Appeals of Hawaii)

27.8 Promoters' Contracts: Martin Stern, Jr., was an architect who worked in Nevada. Nathan Jacobson asked Stern to draw plans for Jacobson's new hotel/casino, the Kings Castle at Lake Tahoe. Stern agreed to take on the project and immediately began preliminary work. At this time, Stern dealt directly with Jacobson, who referred to the project as "my hotel." One month later, Stern wrote to Jacobson, detailing, among other things, the architect's services and fee. The two men subsequently discussed Stern's plans and set Stern's fee at $250,000. Three months later, Jacobson formed Lake Enterprises, Inc. (Lake Enterprises), a Nevada corporation of which Jacobson was the sole shareholder and president. Lake Enterprises was formed for the purpose of owning the new casino. During this period, Stern was paid monthly by checks drawn on an account belonging to another corporation controlled by Jacobson. Stern never agreed to contract with any of these corporations and always dealt exclusively with Jacobson. When Stern was not paid the full amount of his architectural fee, he sued Jacobson to recover. Jacobson claimed that he was not personally liable for any of Stern's fee because a novation had taken place. Who wins? *Jacobson v. Stern*, 96 Nev. 56, 605 P.2d 198, **Web** 1980 Nev. Lexis 522 (Supreme Court of Nevada)

27.9 Preferred Stock: Commonwealth Edison Co. (Commonwealth Edison), through its underwriters, sold 1 million shares of preferred stock at an offering price of $100 per share. Commonwealth Edison wanted to issue the stock with a dividend rate of 9.26 percent, but its major underwriter, First Boston Corporation (First Boston), advised that a rate of 9.44 percent should be paid. According to First Boston, a shortage of investment funds existed, and a higher dividend rate was necessary for a successful stock issue. Commonwealth Edison's management was never happy with the high dividend rate being paid on this preferred stock. Nine months later, Commonwealth Edison's vice chairman was quoted in the report of the annual meeting of the corporation as saying "we were disappointed at the 9.44 percent dividend rate on the preferred stock we sold last August, but we expect to refinance it when market conditions make it feasible." Commonwealth Edison, pursuant to the terms under which the stock was sold, bought back the 1 million shares of preferred stock at a price of $110 per share. What type of preferred stock is this? *The Franklin Life Insurance Company v. Commonwealth Edison Company*, 451 F.Supp. 602, **Web** 1978 U.S. Dist. Lexis 17604 (United States District Court for the Southern District of Illinois)

27.10 Debt Security: United Financial Corporation of California (United Financial) was incorporated in the state of Delaware. United Financial owned the majority of a California savings and loan association as well as three insurance agencies. The next year, the original investors in United Financial decided to capitalize on an increase in investor interest in savings and loans. The first public offering of United Federal stock was made. The stock was sold as a unit, with 60,000 units being offered. Each unit consisted of two shares of United Financial stock and one $100, 5 percent interest-bearing debenture bond. This initial offering was a success. It provided $7.2 million to the corporation, of which $6.2 million was distributed as a return of capital to the original investors. What is the difference between the stock offered for sale by United Financial and the debenture bonds? *Jones v. H.F. Ahmanson & Company*, 1 Cal. 3d 93, 460 P.2d 464, 81 Cal.Rptr. 592, **Web** 1969 Cal. Lexis 195 (Supreme Court of California)

Ethics Issues

27.11 Ethics: John A. Goodman was a real estate salesman in the state of Washington. Goodman sold to Darden, Doman & Stafford Associates (DDS), a general partnership, an apartment building that needed extensive renovation. Goodman represented that he personally had experience in renovation work. During the course of negotiations on a renovation contract, Goodman informed the managing partner of DDS that he would be forming a corporation to do the work. A contract was executed in August between DDS and

"Building Design and Development (In Formation), John A. Goodman, President." The contract required the renovation work to be completed by October 15. Goodman immediately subcontracted the work, but the renovation was not completed on time. DDS also found that the work that was completed was of poor quality. Goodman did not file the articles of incorporation for his new corporation until November 1. The partners of DDS sued Goodman to hold him liable for the renovation contracts. Goodman denied personal liability. Was it ethical for Goodman to deny liability? Is Goodman personally liable? *Goodman v. Darden, Doman & Stafford Associates*, 100 Wn.2d 476, 670 P.2d 648, **Web** 1983 Wash. Lexis 1776 (Supreme Court of Washington)

27.12 Ethics: Pursuant to a public offering, Knoll International, Inc. (Knoll), issued debentures to investors. The debentures bore interest at 8 1/8 percent, matured in 30 years, and were subordinated, convertible into common stock at the rate of each $19.20 of principal amount for one share of common stock, and redeemable. Section 8.08 of the indenture agreement provided that no debenture holder could sue unless the holders of 35 percent of the debentures requested the trustee to sue. The indenture also gave the trustee the authority to amend the indenture agreement.

Knoll was controlled through a series of subsidiaries by Knoll International Holdings, Inc. (Holdings), which, in turn, was controlled by Marshall S. Cogan. Four years later, Knoll merged into Holdings and paid its common shareholders $12 cash per share. Knoll and the indenture trustee executed a supplemental indenture that provided that each debenture holder would receive $12 cash for each $19.20 principal amount of debentures. Simons, a debenture holder who did not own 35 percent of the debentures, brought a suit against Knoll and Cogan. Does Knoll International, Inc., or Cogan owe a fiduciary duty to the debenture holders? Did Cogan breach an ethical duty to the debenture holders? *Simons v. Cogan*, 542 A.2d 785, **Web** 1987 Del. Ch. Lexis 520 (Court of Chancery of Delaware)

IRAC Writing Assignment

Read **Case A-27** in Appendix A [*Johnson v. Dodgen*]. Use the IRAC method to prepare a written analysis of the case.

CHAPTER **28**

Corporate Governance and the Sarbanes-Oxley Act

> **❝***Corporation: An ingenious device for obtaining individual profit without individual responsibility.***❞**
>
> —AMBROSE BIERCE
> The Devil's Dictionary (1911)

CHAPTER OBJECTIVES

After studying this chapter, you should be able to:

1. Describe the functions of shareholders, directors, and officers in managing the affairs of a corporation.
2. Describe a director's and an officer's duty of care and the business judgment rule.
3. Describe a director's and an officer's duty of loyalty and how this duty is breached.
4. Define *piercing the corporate veil*, or *alter ego doctrine*.
5. Describe how the Sarbanes-Oxley Act affects corporate governance.

CHAPTER CONTENTS

- Introduction to Corporate Shareholders, Directors, and Officers
- Shareholders
- Board of Directors
- Corporate Officers
- Liability of Directors and Officers
- Criminal Liability
- Sarbanes-Oxley Act
- Chapter Summary
- Test Review Terms and Concepts
- Case Problems
- Ethics Issues
- IRAC Writing Assignment

Introduction to Corporate Shareholders, Directors, and Officers

Shareholders, directors, and officers have different rights in managing a corporation. The shareholders elect the directors and vote on other important issues affecting the corporation. The directors are responsible for making policy decisions and employing officers. The officers are responsible for the corporation's day-to-day operations.

As a legal entity, a corporation can be held liable for the acts of its directors and officers and for authorized contracts entered into on its behalf. The directors and officers of a corporation have certain rights and owe certain duties to the corporation and its shareholders. A director or an officer who breaches any of these duties can be held personally liable to the corporation, to its shareholders, or to third parties. Insurance is available against certain of these losses. Except in a few circumstances, shareholders do not owe a fiduciary duty to other shareholders or the corporation.

This chapter discusses the rights, duties, and liability of corporate shareholders, directors, and officers.

Japan

Multinational corporations have grown to immense size and power in recent years. For example, the Mitsubishi Group of Japan operates subsidiary corporations in many nations of the world.

Shareholders

A corporation's **shareholders** own the corporation (see Exhibit 28.1). Nevertheless, they are not agents of the corporation (i.e., they cannot bind the corporation to any contracts), and the only management duties they have is the right to vote on matters such as the election of directors and the approval of fundamental changes in the corporation.

Shareholders' Meetings

Annual shareholders' meetings are held to elect directors, choose an independent auditor, or take other actions. These meetings must be held at the times fixed in the bylaws [RMBCA Section 7.01]. If a meeting is not held within either 15 months of the last annual meeting or 6 months after the end of the corporation's fiscal year, whichever is earlier, a shareholder may petition the court to order the meeting held [RMBCA Section 7.03].

Special shareholders' meetings may be called by the board of directors, the holders of at least 10 percent of the voting shares of the corporation, or any other person authorized to do so by the articles of incorporation or bylaws (e.g., the president) [RMBCA Section 7.02]. Special meetings may be held to consider important or emergency issues, such as a merger or consolidation of the corporation with one or more other corporations, the removal of directors, amendment of the articles of incorporation, or dissolution of the corporation.

EXHIBIT 28.1

Shareholders

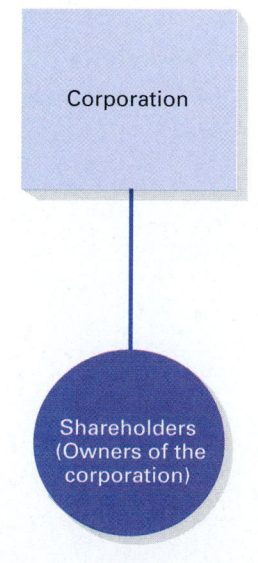

Any act that can be taken at a **shareholders' meeting** can be taken without a meeting if all the corporate shareholders sign a written consent approving the action [RMBCA Section 7.04].

NOTICE OF SHAREHOLDERS' MEETINGS A corporation is required to give the shareholders written notice of the place, day, and time of annual and special meetings. For a special meeting, the purpose of the meeting must also be stated. Only matters stated in the **notice of a meeting** can be considered at the meeting. The notice, which must be given not less than 10 days or more than 50 days before the date of the meeting, may be given in person or by mail [RMBCA Section 7.05]. If the required notice is not given or is defective, any action taken at the meeting is void.

Proxies

Shareholders do not have to attend a shareholders' meeting to vote. Shareholders may vote by *proxy*; that is, they can appoint another person (the proxy) as their agent to vote at the shareholders' meeting. The proxy may be directed exactly how to vote the shares or may be authorized to vote the shares at his or her discretion. Proxies may be in writing or posted online. The written document itself is called the **proxy** (or **proxy card**). Unless otherwise stated, a proxy is valid for 11 months [RMBCA Section 7.22].

Voting Requirements

At least one class of shares of a corporation must have voting rights. The Revised Model Business Corporation Act (RMBCA) permits corporations to grant more than one vote per share to some classes of stock and less than one vote per share to others [RMBCA Section 6.01].

Only those shareholders who own stock as of a set date may vote at a shareholders' meeting. This date, which is called the **record date**, is set forth in the corporate bylaws. The record date may not be more than 70 days before the shareholders' meeting [RMBCA Section 7.07].

The corporation must prepare a **shareholders' list** that contains the names and addresses of the shareholders as of the record date and the class and number of shares owned by each shareholder. This list must be available for inspection at the corporation's main office [RMBCA Section 7.20].

Quorum and Vote Required

Unless otherwise provided in the articles of incorporation, if a majority of shares entitled to vote are represented at a meeting in person or by proxy, there is a **quorum** to hold the meeting. Once a quorum is present, the withdrawal of shares does not affect the quorum of the meeting [RMBCA Sections 7.25(a), 7.25(b)].

The affirmative *vote* of the majority of the *voting* shares represented at a shareholders' meeting constitutes an act of the shareholders for actions other than for the election of directors [RMBCA Section 7.25(c)].

Example Suppose there are 20,000 shares of a corporation outstanding. Assume that a shareholders' meeting is duly called to amend the articles of incorporation and that 10,001 shares are represented at the meeting. A quorum is present because a majority of the shares entitled to vote are represented. Suppose that 5,001 shares are voted in favor of the amendment. The amendment passes. In this example, just over 25 percent of the shares of the corporation bind the other shareholders to the action taken at the shareholders' meeting.

Straight (Noncumulative) Voting

Unless otherwise stated in a corporation's articles of incorporation, voting for the election of directors is by the **straight voting**, or **noncumulative voting**, method. This voting method is quite simple: Each shareholder votes the number of shares he or she owns on candidates for each of the positions open for election. Thus, a majority shareholder can elect the entire board of directors.

Example Assume that a corporation has 10,000 outstanding shares. Erin Caldwell owns 5,100 shares (51 percent), and Michael Rhodes owns 4,900 shares (49 percent). Suppose that three directors of the corporation are to be elected. Caldwell casts 5,100 votes each for her chosen candidates. Rhodes votes 4,900 shares for each of his chosen candidates, who are different from those favored by Caldwell. Each of the three candidates whom Caldwell voted for wins, with 5,100 votes.

> The law does not permit the stockholders to create a sterilized board of directors.
>
> Judge Collin
> *Manson v. Curtis (1918)*

CONTEMPORARY ENVIRONMENT

Cumulative Voting

A corporation's articles of incorporation may provide for **cumulative voting** for the election of directors. Under this method, a shareholder can accumulate all of his or her votes and vote them all for one candidate or split them among several candidates. This means that each shareholder is entitled to multiply the number of shares he or she owns by the number of directors to be elected and cast the product for a single candidate or distribute the product among two or more candidates [RMBCA Section 7.28]. Cumulative voting gives a minority shareholder a better opportunity to elect someone to the board of directors.

Example Suppose Lisa Monroe owns 1,000 shares. Assume that four directors are to be elected to the board. Under cumulative voting, Monroe can multiply the number of shares she owns by the number of directors to be elected. She can take the resulting number of votes (4,000) and cast them all for one candidate or split them.

Examples of cumulative voting are set forth in Exhibit 28.2.

EXHIBIT 28.2

Cumulative Voting

Formula for Cumulative Voting. A shareholder can use the following formula to determine whether or not he or she owns a sufficient number of shares to elect a director to the board of directors using cumulative voting:

$$\frac{S \times T}{D + 1} + 1 = X$$

where X is the number of shares needed by a shareholder to elect a director to the board, S is the number of shares that actually vote at the shareholders' meeting, T is the number of directors the shareholder wants to elect, and D is the number of directors to be elected at the shareholders' meeting.

Example 1 Suppose there are 9,000 outstanding shares of a corporation. Shareholder 1 owns 1,000 shares, shareholder 2 owns 4,000 shares, and shareholder 3 owns 4,000 shares. Assume nine directors are to be elected to the board of directors. All the shares are voted. Under cumulative voting, does shareholder 1 have enough votes to elect a director to the board? The answer is yes:

$$\frac{9,000 \times 1}{9 + 1} + 1 = 901$$

Example 2 If a board of directors is divided into classes and elected by staggered elections, the ability of a minority shareholder to elect a director to the board is diminished. Suppose in Example 1 that the corporation staggered the election of the board of directors so that three directors are elected each year to serve three-year terms. How many shares would a shareholder have to own to elect a director to the board?

$$\frac{9,000 \times 1}{3 + 1} + 1 = 2,251$$

Because of the staggered election of the board of directors, shareholder 1 (who owns 1,000 shares) would not be able to elect a director to the board without the assistance of another shareholder.

Supramajority Voting Requirement

The articles of incorporation or the bylaws of a corporation can require a greater than majority of shares to constitute a quorum or the vote of the shareholders [RMBCA Section 7.27]. This is called a **supramajority voting requirement** (or **supermajority**). Such votes are often required to approve mergers, consolidation, the sale of substantially all the assets of a corporation, and such. To add a supramajority voting requirement, the amendment must be adopted by the number of shares of the proposed increase. For example, increasing a majority voting requirement to an 80 percent supramajority voting requirement would require an 80 percent affirmative vote.

Voting Trusts

Sometimes shareholders agree in advance as to how their shares will be voted. A **voting trust** is an arrangement whereby shareholders transfer their stock certificates to a trustee. Legal title to these shares is held in the name of the trustee. In exchange, *voting trust certificates* are issued to the shareholders. The trustee of the voting trust is empowered to vote the shares held by the trust. The trust may either specify how the trustee is to vote the shares or authorize the trustee to vote the shares at his or her discretion. The members of the trust retain all other incidents of ownership of the stock.

A voting trust agreement must be in writing and cannot exceed 10 years. It must be filed with the corporation and is open to inspection by shareholders of the corporation [RMBCA Section 7.30].

Shareholder Voting Agreements

Two or more shareholders may enter into an agreement that stipulates how they will vote their shares for the election of directors or other matters that require shareholder vote. **Shareholder voting agreements** are not limited in duration and do not have to be filed with the corporation. They are specifically enforceable [RMBCA Section 7.31]. Shareholder voting agreements can be either revocable or irrevocable [RMBCA Section 7.22(d)].

Right of First Refusal

Generally, shareholders have the right to transfer their shares. Shareholders may enter into agreements with one another to prevent unwanted persons from becoming owners of the corporation [RMBCA Section 6.27]. A **right of first refusal** is an agreement that shareholders enter into whereby they grant each other the right of first refusal to purchase shares they are going to sell. A selling shareholder must offer his or her shares for sale to the other parties to the agreement before selling them to anyone else. If the shareholders do not exercise their right of first refusal, the selling shareholder is free to sell his or her shares to another party. A right of first refusal may be granted to the corporation as well.

Buy-and-Sell Agreement

Shareholders sometimes inter into a **buy-and-sell agreement** that requires selling shareholders to sell their shares to the other shareholders or to the corporation at the price specified in the agreement. The price of the shares is normally determined by a formula that considers, among other factors, the profitability of the corporation. The purchase of shares of a deceased shareholder pursuant to a buy-and-sell agreement is often funded by proceeds from life insurance.

Preemptive Rights

The articles of incorporation can grant shareholders preemptive rights. **Preemptive rights** give existing shareholders the option of subscribing to new shares being issued by the corporation in proportion to their current ownership interests [RMBCA Section 6.30]. Such a purchase can prevent a shareholder's interest in the corporation from being *diluted*.

Shareholders are given a reasonable period of time (such as 30 days) to exercise their preemptive rights. If a shareholder does not exercise his or her preemptive rights during this time, shares can then be sold to anyone.

Example Suppose that the ABC Corporation has 10,000 outstanding shares and that Linda Norton owns 1,000 shares (10 percent). Assume that the corporation plans to raise more capital by issuing another 10,000 shares of stock. With preemptive rights, Norton must be offered the option to purchase 1,000 of the 10,000 new shares before they are offered to the public. If she does not purchase them, her ownership in the corporation will be diluted from 10 percent to 5 percent.

Right to Receive Information and Inspect Books and Records

Shareholders have the right to be informed about the affairs of the corporation. A corporation must furnish its shareholders with an **annual financial statement** that contains a balance sheet, an income statement, and a statement of changes in shareholder equity [RMBCA Section 16.20].

Shareholders have an absolute *right to inspect* the shareholders' list, the articles of incorporation, the bylaws, and the minutes of shareholders' meetings held within the past three years. To inspect accounting and tax records, minutes of board of directors' and committee meetings, and minutes of shareholders' meetings held more than three years in the past, a shareholder must demonstrate a "proper purpose," such as deciding how to vote in a shareholder election, identifying fellow shareholders to communicate with them regarding corporate matters, investigating the existence of corporate mismanagement or improper action, and the like [RMBCA Section 16.02].

Dividends

Profit corporations operate to make a profit. The objective of the shareholders is to share in those profits, either through capital appreciation, the receipt of dividends, or both. **Dividends** are paid at the discretion of the board of directors [RMBCA Section 6.40]. The directors are responsible for determining when, where, how, and how much will be paid in dividends. They may opt to retain the profits in the corporation to be used for corporate purposes instead of as dividends. This authority cannot be delegated to a committee of the board of directors or to officers of the corporation.

When a corporation declares a dividend, it sets a date, usually a few weeks prior to the actual payment, that is called the *record date*. Persons who are shareholders on that date are entitled to receive the dividend, even if they sell their shares before the payment date. Once declared, a cash or property dividend cannot be revoked. Shareholders can sue to recover declared but unpaid dividends.

STOCK DIVIDENDS Corporations may use additional shares of stock as a dividend. **Stock dividends** are not a distribution of corporate assets. They are paid in proportion to the existing ownership interests of shareholders, so they do not increase a shareholder's proportionate ownership interest.

Example Suppose Betty owns 1,000 shares (10 percent) of the 10,000 outstanding shares of the ABC Corporation. If the ABC Corporation declares a stock dividend of 20 percent, Betty will receive a stock dividend of 200 shares. She now owns 1,200 shares—or 10 percent—of a total of 12,000 outstanding shares.

Derivative Lawsuits

If a corporation is harmed by someone, the directors of the corporation have the authority to bring an action on behalf of the corporation against the offending party to recover damages or other relief. If the corporation fails to bring the lawsuit, shareholders have the right to bring the lawsuit on behalf of the corporation. This is called a **derivative action**, or **derivative lawsuit** [RMBCA Section 7.40].

A shareholder can bring a derivative action if he or she (1) was a shareholder of the corporation at the time of the act complained of; (2) fairly and adequately represents the interests of the corporation; and (3) made a written demand upon the corporation to take suitable actions and either the corporation rejected the demand or 90 days have expired from the date of the demand.

To bring a derivative lawsuit, a shareholder usually must make a written demand upon the corporate directors to bring the lawsuit, and if the directors fail to bring the suit, then the shareholder may pursue the lawsuit on behalf of the corporation. Oftentimes, the third party who has damaged the corporation is one or more of the corporation's own directors or officers. For example, board members or officers, or both, may have committed fraud or otherwise stolen property from or misused property of the corporation. In this case, the written demand will be excused.

A derivative lawsuit will be dismissed by the court if either a majority of independent directors or a panel of independent persons appointed by the court determines that the lawsuit is not in the best interests of the corporation. This decision must be reached in good faith and only after conducting a reasonable inquiry.

If a shareholder's derivative action is successful, any award goes into the corporate treasury. The plaintiff-shareholder is entitled to recover payment for reasonable expenses, including attorneys' fees, incurred in bringing and maintaining the derivative action. Any settlement of a derivative action requires court approval.

In the following case, the U.S. Supreme Court decided that demand on the board of directors was excused in a derivative lawsuit.

CASE 28.1
Derivative Lawsuit

UNITED STATES SUPREME COURT
Kamen v. Kemper Financial Services, Inc.

500 U.S. 90, 111 S.Ct. 1711, 114 L.Ed.2d 152,
Web 1991 U.S. Lexis 2782
Supreme Court of the United States

> *Demand typically is deemed to be futile when a majority of the directors have participated in or approved the alleged wrongdoing.*
>
> —Justice Marshall

Facts

Jill S. Kamen was a shareholder of Cash Equivalent Fund, Inc. (Fund), a mutual fund that employed Kemper Financial Services, Inc. (Kemper), as its investment advisor. Kamen brought a derivative lawsuit on behalf of Fund against Kemper, alleging that Kemper violated fiduciary duties owed to Fund as imposed by the Investment Company Act of 1940 (Act), a federal statute. Kamen did not make a demand on Fund's board of directors to sue Kemper any earlier. She alleged that it would have been futile to do so because the directors were acting in a conspiracy with Kemper. The Act was silent as to the rule concerning derivative actions under the Act. The trial court granted Kemper's motion to dismiss the lawsuit. The Court of Appeals adopted a "universal demand rule" as part of the federal common law and affirmed. This rule requires that a shareholder always make a demand on the directors of a corporation before bringing a derivative lawsuit. Kamen appealed to the U.S. Supreme Court.

Issue

Should federal law adopt the universal demand rule for bringing derivative actions?

Language of the U.S. Supreme Court

The presumption that state law should be incorporated into federal common law is particularly strong in areas in which private parties have entered legal relationship with the expectation that their rights and obligations would be governed by state law standards. Corporation law is one such area. Corporations are creatures of state law, state law which is the font of corporate directors' powers. Consequently, we conclude that gaps in federal statutes bearing on the allocation of governing power within the corporation should be filled with state law.

The purpose of requiring a precomplaint demand is to protect the directors' prerogative to take over the litigation or to oppose it. Thus, the demand requirement implements the basic principle of corporate governance that the decisions of a corporation—including the decision to initiate litigation—should be made by the board of directors or the majority of shareholders. To the extent that a jurisdiction recognizes the futility exception to demand, the jurisdiction places a limit upon the directors' usual power to control the initiation of corporate litigation. Demand typically is deemed to be futile when a majority of the directors have participated in or approved the alleged wrongdoing. Superimposing a rule of universal demand over the corporate doctrine of these States would clearly upset the balance that they have struck between the power of the individual shareholder and the power of the directors to control corporate litigation.

Decision

The U.S. Supreme Court refused to adopt the universal demand rule as federal common law but instead held that federal law should follow the appropriate state law concerning demands in derivative lawsuits if a federal statute is silent as to this issue. The U.S. Supreme Court reversed the decision of the U.S. Court of Appeals that had dismissed Kamen's lawsuit against Kemper.

Law & Ethics Questions

1. Which do you think is the better rule: the universal demand rule or the futility exception rule? Why?

2. **ETHICS** Should Kamen have given the directors of Fund the opportunity to have sued Kemper before she did?

3. **ETHICS** Do you think directors often engage in fraudulent conduct that harms the rights of shareholders?

4. **ETHICS** Do you think that the possibility of derivative lawsuits makes directors and officers act more ethically?

Web Exercises

1. **WEB** For the complete opinion of this case, go to *www.prenhall.com/cheesemancases*.

2. **WEB** Visit the website of the U.S. Supreme Court, at *www.supremecourtus.gov* and try to find documents that relate to this case.

3. **WEB** Use *www.google.com* to find an article that discusses a recent derivative lawsuit. Read it.

Piercing the Corporate Veil

Shareholders of a corporation generally have **limited liability** (i.e., they are liable for the debts and obligations of the corporation only to the extent of their capital contribution), and they are not personally liable for the debts and obligations of the corporation. However, if a shareholder or shareholders dominate a corporation and misuse it for improper purposes, a court of equity can *disregard the corporate entity* and hold the shareholders of a corporation personally liable for the corporation's debts and obligations. This doctrine is commonly referred to as **piercing the corporate veil**. It is often resorted to by unpaid creditors who are trying to collect from shareholders a debt owed by the corporation. The piercing the corporate veil doctrine is also called the **alter ego doctrine** because the corporation becomes the *alter ego* of the shareholder.

Courts will pierce the corporate veil if (1) the corporation has been formed without sufficient capital (i.e., *thin capitalization*) or (2) separateness has not been maintained between the corporation and its shareholders (e.g., commingling of personal and corporate assets, failure to hold required shareholders' meetings, failure to maintain corporate records and books). The courts examine this doctrine on a case-by-case basis.

The piercing the corporate veil doctrine was raised in the following case.

C A S E   28.2
Piercing the Corporate Veil

Northeast Iowa Ethanol, LLC v. Drizin

Web 2006 U.S. Dist. Lexis 4828
United States District Court for the Northern District of Iowa

> ❝ *If capital is illusory or trifling compared with the business to be done and the risk of loss, this is a ground for denying the separate entity privilege.* ❞
>
> —Judge Jarvey

Facts

Local farmers in Manchester, Iowa, decided to build an ethanol plant in the Manchester area. An ethanol plant produces ethanol and feed grain which can be sold at a profit exceeding that of the sale of grain. After many meetings, the local farmers invested $2,365,000 for the project. The farmers formed Northeast Iowa Ethanol, LLC (Northeast Iowa), to hold the money and develop the project. William Ethanol Service agreed to invest $1 million, and North Central Construction agreed to invest $500,000. In all, $3,865,000 was raised for the construction of the ethanol plant. The funds were placed in an escrow account. The project needed another $20 million, for which financing needed to be secured.

Jerry Drizin formed Global Syndicate International, Inc. (GSI), a Nevada corporation with $250 capital. GSI was formed for the purpose of assisting Northeast Iowa raise the additional financing for the project. Traditional financing from banks was not available for such a project, so Drizin looked for other sources of money. Drizin talked Northeast Iowa into transferring money to a bank in south Florida to serve as security for a possible loan. Drizin commingled those funds with his own personal funds. Through an array of complex transfers orchestrated by Drizin, all of the funds of Northeast Iowa were stolen. Drizin invested some funds in a worthless gold mine and lost the rest of the money in other worthless investments.

Plaintiff Northeast Iowa sued Drizin for civil fraud to recover its funds. Drizin defended, arguing that GSI was liable but that he was not liable because he was but a shareholder of GSI. The plaintiffs alleged that the doctrine of piercing the corporate veil applied and that Drizin was therefore personally liable for the funds.

Issue

Does the doctrine of piercing the corporate veil apply in this case, thus allowing the plaintiffs to pierce the corporate veil of GSI and reach shareholder Drizin for liability for civil fraud?

Language of the Court

In every financial scam like that perpetrated on the plaintiff here, there comes a point at which the victim must make an exceedingly quick decision and seemingly, the entire fate of the project depends on taking that leap of faith. From that point on, very bad things follow and only time will tell what they are.

Generally a corporation is a distinct entity from its shareholders. This distinction usually insulates shareholders from personal liability for corporate debts. However, this protection is not absolute. Personal liability may be imposed upon shareholders in "exceptional circumstances." The corporate veil may be pierced, for example, where the corporation is a mere shell, serving no legitimate business purpose, and used primarily as an intermediary to perpetuate fraud or promote injustice. Factors used in Iowa law to support finding exceptional circumstances are:

1. the corporation is undercapitalized;
2. the corporation lacks separate books;
3. its finances are not kept separate from individual finances, or individual obligations are paid by the corporation;
4. the corporation is used to promote fraud or illegality;
5. corporate formalities are not followed; or
6. the corporation is a mere sham

This list is not meant to be exhaustive. Concerns for justice and equity can also be taken into account by a court in determining whether to pierce the corporate veil.

If a corporation lacks substantial capital such that it would not be able to meet its debts, this is a ground for denying the privilege of separate entity. If capital is illusory or trifling compared with the business to be done and the risk of loss, this is a ground for denying the separate entity privilege. Secondly, if corporate funds are not segregated, there is a strong inference that they are being used by the shareholders for their individual purposes. A major corporate officer cannot avoid liability by emulating the three fabled monkeys, "hearing, seeing and speaking no evil."

Without question, this case presents the "exceptional circumstance" warranting the piercing of GSI's corporate veil and finding Mr. Drizin personally liable for GSI's misdeeds, as the sole purpose of establishing GSI was to perpetuate fraud. GSI engaged in no legitimate business transactions whatsoever. The $250.00 initial capitalization of GSI is, in fact, "trifling compared with the business to be done and the risk of loss." GSI had no errors and omissions insurance. Mr. Drizin used GSI's accounts as his own, constantly transferring money from the GSI escrow account to his personal accounts for "reimbursement" and to other accounts for "safekeeping" and "diversification." And now, GSI is a defunct corporation. Justice and equity call for piercing the corporate veil.

Drizin's actions with respect to plaintiff's money were both outrageous and malicious. As a result of Drizin's tortious conduct, good people were hurt. The evidence is clear, convincing, and satisfactory that punitive damages are appropriate in this case to punish Drizin and to deter others from engaging in similar conduct.

Decision

The U.S. District Court held that the corporate veil of GSI could be pierced to reach its shareholder Drizin. The Court awarded the plaintiff compensatory damage of $3.8 million and punitive damages of $7.6 million against Drizin.

Law & Ethics Questions

1. What is civil fraud? What are the elements that define civil fraud?

2. What does the doctrine of piercing the corporate veil provide? Explain.

3. **ETHICS** Did Drizin act ethically in this case?

4. **ETHICS** Did the owners of Northeast Iowa have any responsibility for the losses they suffered in this case? Explain.

5. Do you think that the plaintiff Northeast Iowa will recover on its $11.4 million judgment in this case?

Web Exercises

1. **WEB** For the complete opinion of this case, go to *www.prenhall.com/cheesemancases*.

2. **WEB** Visit the website of the U.S. District Court for the Northern District of Iowa, at *www.iand.uscourts.gov*.

3. **WEB** For information about using ethanol as a fuel, visit the website of Renewable Fuels Association, at *www.ethanolrfa.org*.

4. **WEB** Use *www.google.com* to find an article that describes the benefits of ethanol as a fuel. Read it.

INTERNET AND TECHNOLOGY LAW
Corporation Codes Recognize Electronic Communications

Most state corporations codes have been amended to permit the use of electronic communications to shareholder and among directors. For example, the Delaware General Corporation law recognizes the following uses of electronic technology:

- Delivery of notices to stockholders may be made electronically if the stockholder consents to the delivery of notices in this form.

- Proxy solicitation for shareholder votes may be made by electronic transmission.

- The shareholder list of a corporation that must be made available during the 10 days prior to a stockholder meeting may be made available either at the principal place of business of the corporation or by posting the list on an electronic network.

- Stockholders who are not physically present at a meeting may be deemed present, participate in, and vote at the meeting by electronic communication; a meeting may be held solely by electronic communication, without a physical location.

- The election of directors of the corporation may be held by electronic transmission.

- Directors' actions by unanimous consent may be taken by electronic transmission.

The use of electronic transmissions, electronic networks, and communications by e-mail will make the operation and administration of corporate affairs more efficient.

Web Exercises

1. **WEB** Use *www.google.com* to find an article that discusses your state's corporations law. Read it.

2. **WEB** Use *www.google.com* to find an article that discusses a state's corporation code that permits electronic transmissions and communications between directors and shareholders of a corporation. Read it.

ETHICS SPOTLIGHT
Controlling Shareholder's Breach of Fiduciary Duty

Shareholders usually do not owe a fiduciary duty to their fellow shareholders. However, many courts have held that a controlling shareholder does owe a fiduciary duty to monitor shareholders. A controlling shareholder is one who owns a sufficient number of shares to control the corporation effectively. This may or may not be majority ownership.

The courts have held that controlling shareholders breach their fiduciary duty to minority shareholders if they:

- Sell assets of the corporation and thereby cause an unusual loss to the minority shareholders.

- Sell corporate assets to themselves at less than fair market value.

- Sell controlling interest in the corporation to someone they know intends to loot the corporation and does.

- Take other action that oppresses the minority shareholders.

The courts examine each case on its particular facts.

Law & Ethics Questions

1. **ETHICS** Should controlling shareholders be held to a fiduciary duty to other shareholders? Why or why not?

2. Should all shareholders owe a fiduciary duty to each other? Discuss.

Board of Directors

The **board of directors** of a corporation is elected by the shareholders of the corporation. The board of directors is responsible for formulating the *policy decisions* that affect the management, supervision, control, and operation of the corporation (see Exhibit 28.3) [RMBCA Section 8.01]. Such policy decisions include deciding the business or businesses in which the corporation should be engaged, selecting and removing the top officers of the corporation, determining the capital structure of the corporation, declaring dividends, and the like.

The board may initiate certain actions that require shareholders' approval. These actions are initiated when the board of directors adopts a *resolution* that approves a transaction and recommends that it be submitted to the shareholders for a vote. Examples of

EXHIBIT 28.3

Board of Directors

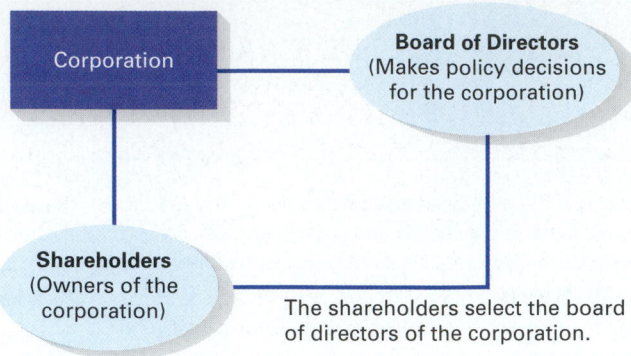

The shareholders select the board of directors of the corporation.

such transactions include mergers, sale of substantially all of the corporation's assets outside the course of ordinary business operations, amendment of the articles of incorporation, and voluntary dissolution of the corporation.

Corporate directors are required to have access to the corporation's books and records, facilities, and premises, as well as any other information that affects the operation of the corporation. This right of inspection is absolute. It cannot be limited by the articles of incorporation, the bylaws, or board resolution.

Compensating Directors

Originally, it was considered an honor to serve as a director. No payment was involved. Today, directors are often paid an annual retainer and an attendance fee for each meeting attended. Unless otherwise provided in the articles of incorporation, the directors are permitted to fix their own compensation [RMBCA Section 8.11].

Selecting Directors

Boards of directors are typically composed of inside and outside directors. An **inside director** is a person who is also an officer of the corporation. For example, the president of the corporation often sits as a director of the corporation.

An **outside director** is a person who sits on the board of directors of a corporation but is not an officer of that corporation. Outside directors are often officers and directors of other corporations, bankers, lawyers, professors, and others. Outside directors are often selected for their business knowledge and expertise.

There are no special qualifications that a person must meet to be elected a director of a corporation. A director need not be a resident of the state of incorporation or a shareholder of the corporation. The articles of incorporation or bylaws may prescribe qualifications for directors, however [RMBCA Section 8.02].

A board of directors can consist of one or more individuals. The number of initial directors is fixed by the articles of incorporation. This number can be amended in the articles of incorporation or the bylaws. The articles of incorporation or bylaws can establish a variable range for the size of the board of directors. The exact number of directors within the range may be changed from time to time by the board of directors or the shareholders [RMBCA Section 8.03].

CONCEPT SUMMARY

Classification of Directors

CLASSIFICATION	DESCRIPTION
Inside director	A person who is also an officer of the corporation
Outside director	A person who is not an officer of the corporation

Term of Office

The term of a director's office expires at the next annual shareholders' meeting following his or her election, unless terms are staggered [RMBCA Section 8.05]. The RMBCA allows boards of directors that consist of nine or more members to be divided into two or three classes (each class to be as nearly equal in number as possible) that are elected to serve *staggered terms* of two or three years [RMBCA Section 8.06]. The specifics of such an arrangement must be outlined in the articles of incorporation.

Example Suppose a board of directors consists of nine directors. The board can be divided into three classes of three directors each, each class to be elected to serve a three-year term. Only three directors of the nine-member board would come up for election each year. This nine-member board could also be divided into two classes of five and four directors, each class to be elected to two-year terms.

Vacancies on a board of directors can occur because of death, illness, the resignation of a director before the expiration of his or her term, or an increase in the number of positions on the board. Such vacancies can be filled by the shareholders or the remaining directors [RMBCA Section 8.10].

Meetings of the Board of Directors

The directors of a corporation can act only as a board. They cannot act individually on the corporation's behalf. Every director has the right to participate in any meeting of the board of directors. Each director has one vote. Directors cannot vote by proxy.

Regular meetings of the board of directors are held at the times and places established in the bylaws. Such meetings can be held without notice. The board can call *special meetings* as provided in the bylaws [RMBCA Section 8.20(a)]. They are usually convened for such reasons as issuing new shares, considering proposals to merge with other corporations, adopting maneuvers to defend against hostile takeover attempts, and the like.

The board of directors may act without a meeting if all the directors sign written consents that set forth the actions taken. The RMBCA permits meetings of the board to be held via conference calls [RMBCA Section 8.20(b)].

Quorum and Voting Requirement

A simple majority of the number of directors established in the articles of incorporation or bylaws usually constitutes a *quorum* for transacting business. However, the articles of incorporation and the bylaws may increase this number. If a quorum is present, the approval or disapproval of a majority of the quorum binds the entire board. The articles of incorporation or the bylaws can require a greater than majority of directors to constitute a quorum or the vote of the board [RMBCA Section 8.24].

> The director is really a watch-dog, and the watch-dog has no right, without the knowledge of his master, to take a sop from a possible wolf.
>
> L. J. Bowen
> *Re The North Australian Territory Co. Ltd. (1891)*

CONTEMPORARY ENVIRONMENT
Committees of the Board of Directors

In the current complex business world, the demands on directors have increased. To help handle this increased workload, boards of directors have turned to creating **committees** of their members to handle specific duties. Board members with special expertise or interests are appointed to the various committees.

Unless the articles of incorporation or bylaws provide otherwise, the board of directors may create committees of the board and delegate certain powers to those committees [RMBCA Section 8.25]. All members of these committees must be directors. An act of a committee pursuant to delegated authority is the act of the board of directors.

Committees commonly appointed by the board of directors include:

- **Executive committee.** The **executive committee** has authority to (1) act on certain matters on behalf of the board during the interim period between board meetings and (2) conduct preliminary investigations of proposals on behalf of the full board. Most members of the committee are inside directors because it is easiest for them to meet to address corporate matters.

- **Audit committee.** The **audit committee** hires independent public accountants and supervises the audit of the financial records of the corporation.

- **Nominating committee.** The **nominating committee** nominates the management slate of directors to be submitted for shareholder vote.

- **Compensation committee.** The **compensation committee** approves management compensation, including salaries, bonuses, stock option plans, fringe benefits, and such.

- **Investment committee.** The **investment committee** is responsible for investing and reinvesting the funds of the corporation.

- **Litigation committee.** The **litigation committee** reviews and decides whether to pursue requests by shareholders for the corporation to sue persons who have allegedly harmed the corporation.

The following powers cannot be delegated to committees but must be exercised by the board itself: (1) declaring dividends, (2) initiating actions that require shareholders' approval, (3) appointing members to fill vacancies on the board, (4) amending the bylaws, (5) approving a plan of merger that does not require shareholder approval (short-form merger), and (6) authorizing the issuance of shares.

ETHICS SPOTLIGHT

Sarbanes-Oxley Act Imposes Duties on Audit Committee

During the late 1990s and early 2000s, many corporations engaged in accounting fraud to report inflated earnings or to conceal losses. It was often management who perpetrated this accounting fraud, which was not detected by the board of directors. Sometimes members of the board of directors conspired or participated in the accounting fraud. In response, Congress enacted the federal *Sarbanes-Oxley Act* of 2002. This act placed certain responsibilities on a corporation's audit committee.

A public company must have an audit committee. Members of the audit committee must be members of the board of directors and must be independent—that is, not employed or receive compensation from the company or any of its subsidiaries for services other than as a board member and member of the audit committee. These board members are called *outside* board members because they are not employees (e.g., president, CEO) of the corporation. At least one member of the audit committee must be a financial expert, based on either education or prior experience, so as to understand generally accepted accounting principles, preparation of financial statements, and audit committee functions.

The audit committee is responsible for the appointment of, payment of compensation for, and oversight of public accounting firms employed to audit the company. The audit committee must preapprove all audit and permissible non-audit services to be performed by a public accounting firm. The audit committee has authority to employ independent legal counsel and other advisors.

The act requires public companies to establish and maintain adequate internal controls and procedures for financial reporting. The act requires a public company to prepare an assessment of the effectiveness of its internal quality controls at the end of each fiscal year. These internal audits are supervised by the audit committee.

Law & Ethics Questions

1. What is the purpose of the Sarbanes-Oxley Act? Explain.

2. What is an audit committee? What is its purpose? Who may be members of the audit committee?

3. **ETHICS** Will the requirement of having only independent outside directors on the audit committee help prevent accounting frauds? Explain.

4. **ETHICS** Do you think there is very much fraud by boards of directors in managing corporations? Explain.

Web Exercises

1. **WEB** Use *www.google.com* to find an article that discusses the Sarbanes-Oxley Act. Read it.

2. **WEB** Use *www.google.com* to find an article that discusses a member of a corporate board of directors found liable for fraud. Read it.

Corporate Officers

The board of directors has the authority to appoint the officers of the corporation. The **corporate officers** are elected by the board of directors at such time and by such manner as prescribed in the corporation's bylaws. The directors can delegate certain management authority to the officers of the corporation (see Exhibit 28.4).

At a minimum, most corporations have the following officers: a president, one or more vice presidents, a secretary, and a treasurer. The bylaws or the board of directors can authorize duly appointed officers the power to appoint assistant officers. The same individual may simultaneously hold more than one office in the corporation [RMBCA Section 8.40]. The duties of each officer are specified in the bylaws of the corporation.

An officer of a corporation may be removed by the board of directors. The board only has to determine that the best interests of the corporation will be served by such removal

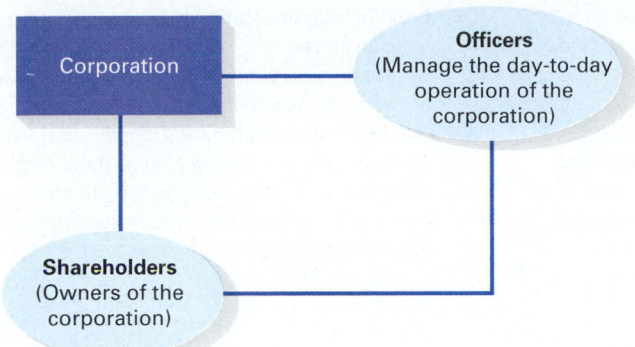

EXHIBIT 28.4

Corporate Officers

[RMBCA Section 8.43(b)]. Officers who are removed in violation of an employment contract can sue the corporation for damages.

Agency Authority of Officers

Officers and agents of a corporation have such authority as may be provided in the bylaws of the corporation or as determined by resolution of the board of directors [RMBCA Section 8.41]. As agents, the authority of officers to bind a corporation to contracts is derived from express authority, implied authority, and apparent authority.

A corporation can *ratify* an unauthorized act of a corporate officer or agent. For example, suppose an officer acts outside the scope of his or her employment and enters into a contract with a third person. If the corporation accepts the benefits of the contract, it has ratified the contract and is bound by it. Officers are liable on an unauthorized contract if the corporation does not ratify it.

CONCEPT SUMMARY

Management of a Corporation

GROUP	FUNCTION
Shareholders	Owners of the corporation. They vote on the directors and other major actions to be taken by the corporation.
Board of directors	Responsible for making policy decisions and employing the major officers for the corporation. It also makes recommendations regarding actions to be taken by the shareholders.
Officers	Responsible for the day-to-day operation of the corporation, including acting as agents for the corporation, hiring other officers and employees, and the like.

CONTEMPORARY ENVIRONMENT

Indemnification and D&O Insurance Protection

Directors and officers of corporations are sometimes personally named in lawsuits that involve actions they have taken on behalf of the corporation. Such lawsuits are often brought by disgruntled shareholders or third parties who claim they have suffered damages because of the director's or officer's negligence or other conduct.

Directors and officers can protect themselves against personal liability by making sure the corporation does the following:

■ **Purchase directors' and officers' liability insurance (D&O insurance).** Corporations can purchase **D&O insurance** from private insurance companies by paying an annual premium for the insurance. The insurance company is required to defend a corporate director or officer who has been sued in his or her corporate capacity. The insurance company is also required, subject to the terms of the insurance coverage, to pay the litigation costs incurred in defending the lawsuit (e.g., attorneys' fees, court costs) and any judgments or settlement costs. Most D&O policies contain deductible clauses and maximum coverage limits [RMBCA Section 8.57].

■ **Provide indemnification.** Corporations may provide that directors and officers who are sued in their corporate capacities will be indemnified by the corporation for the costs of the litigation as well as any judgments or settlements stemming from the lawsuit. **Indemnification** means that the corporation—and not the director or officer personally—pays these costs. The RMBCA provides that a court may order indemnification if a director or an officer is found to be fairly and reasonably entitled to such indemnification [RMBCA Sections 8.54, 8.56(1)].

Liability of Directors and Officers

A corporation's directors and officers owe the **fiduciary duties** of trust and confidence to the corporation and its shareholders. More specifically, they owe the (1) *duty of obedience*, (2) *duty of care*, and (3) *duty of loyalty*. These duties are discussed in detail in the paragraphs that follow.

Duty of Obedience

The directors and officers of a corporation must act within the authority conferred upon them by the state corporations code, the articles of incorporation, the corporate bylaws, and the resolutions adopted by the board of directors. This duty is called the **duty of obedience**. Directors and officers who either intentionally or negligently act outside their authority are personally liable for any resultant damages caused to the corporation or its shareholders.

Example Suppose its articles of incorporation authorizes a corporation to invest in real estate only. If a corporate officer invests corporate funds in the commodities markets, the officer is liable to the corporation for any losses suffered.

Duty of Care

The **duty of care** requires corporate directors and officers to use *care and diligence* when acting on behalf of the corporation. To meet this duty, the directors and officers must discharge their duties (1) in good faith, (2) with the care that an *ordinary prudent person* in a like position would use under similar circumstances, and (3) in a manner they reasonably believe to be in the best interests of the corporation [RMBCA Sections 8.30(a), 8.42(a)].

A director or an officer who breaches this duty of care is personally liable to the corporation and its shareholders for any damages caused by the breach. Such breaches, which are normally caused by **negligence**, often involve a director's or an officer's failure to (1) make a reasonable investigation of a corporate matter, (2) attend board meetings on a regular basis, (3) properly supervise a subordinate who causes a loss to the corporation through embezzlement and such, or (4) keep adequately informed about corporate affairs. Breaches are examined by the courts on a case-by-case basis.

ETHICS SPOTLIGHT

Outside Directors Relieved of Liability for Ordinary Negligence

In the past, being made a member of a board of directors of a corporation was considered to be an honor. Many persons outside the company, such as lawyers, doctors, businesspeople, professors, and others, were asked to sit on boards because of their knowledge, expertise, or contacts. Meetings were held once a month and usually did not take a lot of time, and votes were often just a formality to "rubber stamp" management's preordained decisions.

Things changed as an explosion of lawsuits against boards of directors occurred, brought by disgruntled shareholders, bondholders, and others. Under normal corporate laws, directors are personally liable for their intentional or negligent conduct that causes harm to others. Most of these lawsuits alleged that directors were negligent in one regard or another, and juries often agreed.

Inside directors—directors who are also executives of the corporation—remained on boards because of their vested interests, and their liability as officers would remain anyway. But "outside directors"—the directors from outside the company—began fleeing from corporations and refusing to accept nominations to boards of directors. The honor of sitting on a board of directors became a liability, and all of a board member's personal assets—house, investments, and bank accounts—were at risk.

In response to this situation, the Delaware legislature enacted a statute which provided that an outside director of a Delaware corporation cannot be held liable for ordinary negligence. Thus, this statute overrode the common law of negligence as it applied to outside directors. The law was hailed as a landmark, and many major corporations that were not already incorporated in Delaware abandoned their current states of incorporation and reincorporated there.

Many other states have enacted similar statutes. The RMBCA contains a similar provision [RMBCA Section 2.02(b)(4)]. The main features of these statutes are that they:

- Apply to outside directors but not to inside directors.
- Relieve liability for ordinary negligence but not for intentional conduct, recklessness, or gross negligence.
- Do not apply to violations of federal and state securities law.

Law & Ethics Questions

1. Should outside directors be relieved of ordinary negligence liability? Why or why not?
2. **ETHICS** Do you think outside directors will act more or less carefully if they are relieved of liability for ordinary negligence?
3. Will more persons be willing to serve as outside directors of corporations under the new law?

THE BUSINESS JUDGMENT RULE The determination of whether a corporate director or officer has met his or her duty of care is measured as of the time the decision is made; the benefit of hindsight is not a factor. Therefore, the directors and officers are not liable to the corporation or its shareholders for honest mistakes of judgment. This is called the **business judgment rule**. Were it not for the protection afforded by the business judgment rule, many high-risk but socially desirable endeavors might not be undertaken.

Example Suppose that after conducting considerable research and investigation, the directors of a major automobile company decide to produce a large and expensive SUV vehicle. Three years later, when the SUV is introduced to the public for sale, few of the SUVs are sold because of the public's interest in buying smaller, less expensive automobiles caused by a recession in the economy and an increase in gasoline prices. Because this was an honest mistake of judgment on the part of corporate management, their judgment is shielded by the business judgment rule.

RELIANCE ON OTHERS Corporate directors and officers are usually unable to personally investigate every corporate matter brought to their attention. Under the RMBCA, directors and officers are entitled to rely on information, opinions, reports, or statements, including financial statements and other financial data, prepared or presented by [RMBCA Sections 8.30(b), 8.42(b)]:

- Officers and employees of the corporation whom a director believes are reliable and competent in the matter presented
- Lawyers, public accountants, and other professionals as to any matters that a director believes to be within their professional or expert competence
- A committee of the board of directors upon which a director does not serve as to matters within the committee's designated authority and which committee a director reasonably believes to merit confidence

A director is not liable if such information is false, misleading, or otherwise unreliable unless he or she has knowledge that would cause such reliance to be unwarranted [RMBCA

Sections 8.30(c), 8.42(c)]. The degree of an officer's reliance on such sources is more limited than that given to directors because they are more familiar with corporate operations.

DISSENT TO DIRECTORS' ACTION On some occasions, individual directors may oppose the action taken by the majority of the board of directors. To avoid liability for such action, the dissenting director must either resign from the board or register his or her **dissent**. Dissent may be registered by (1) entering it in the minutes of the meeting, (2) filing a written dissent with the secretary before the adjournment of the meeting, or (3) forwarding a written dissent by registered mail to the secretary immediately following the adjournment of the meeting [RMBCA Section 8.24(d)]. A dissenting director who has not attended the meeting must follow the latter course of action to register his or her dissent.

The court had to decide whether directors were protected by the business judgment rule in the following case.

C A S E **28.3**
Duty of Care

Smith v. Van Gorkom

488 A.2d 858,
Web 1985 Del. Lexis 421
Supreme Court of Delaware

❝*In the specific context of a proposed merger of a domestic corporation, a director has a duty, along with his fellow directors, to act in an informed and deliberate manner in determining whether to approve an agreement of merger.*❞

—Judge Horsey

Facts

Trans Union Corporation (Trans Union) was a publicly traded, diversified holding company that was incorporated in Delaware. Its principal earnings were generated by its railcar leasing business. Jerome W. Van Gorkom was a Trans Union officer for more than 24 years, its chief executive officer for more than 17 years, and the chairman of the board of directors for 2 years. Van Gorkom, a lawyer and certified public accountant, owned 75,000 shares of Trans Union. He was approaching 65 years of age and mandatory retirement. Trans Union's board of directors was composed of 10 members—5 inside directors and 5 outside directors.

Van Gorkom decided to meet with Jay A. Pritzker, a well-known corporate takeover specialist and a social acquaintance of Van Gorkom's, to discuss the possible sale of Trans Union to Pritzker. Van Gorkom met Pritzker at Pritzker's home on Saturday. He did so without consulting Trans Union's board of directors. At this meeting, Van Gorkom proposed a sale of Trans Union to Pritzker at a price of $55 per share. The stock was trading at about $38 in the market. On Monday, Pritzker notified Van Gorkom that he was interested in the $55 cash-out merger proposal. Van Gorkom, along with two inside directors, privately met with Pritzker on Tuesday and Wednesday. After meeting with Van Gorkom on Thursday, Pritzker notified his attorney to begin drafting the merger documents.

On Friday, Van Gorkom called a special meeting of Trans Union's board of directors for the following day. The board members were not told the purpose of the meeting. At the meeting, Van Gorkom disclosed the Pritzker offer and described its terms in a 20-minute presentation. Neither the merger agreement nor a written summary of the terms of agreement was furnished to the directors. No valuation study as to the value of Trans Union was prepared for the meeting. After two hours, the board voted in favor of the cash-out merger with Pritzker's company at $55 per share for Trans Union's stock. The board also voted not to solicit other offers. The merger agreement was executed by Van Gorkom during Saturday evening at a formal social event he hosted for the opening of the Chicago Lyric Opera's season. Neither he nor any other director read the agreement prior to its signing and delivery to Pritzker.

Trans Union's board of directors recommended the merger be approved by its shareholders and distributed proxy materials to the shareholders stating that the $55 per share price for their stock was fair. In the meantime, Trans Union's board of directors took steps to dissuade two other possible suitors who showed an interest in purchasing Trans Union. On February 10, 1981, 69.9 percent of the shares of Trans Union stock was voted in favor of the merger. The merger was consummated. Alden Smith and other Trans Union shareholders sued Van Gorkom and the other directors for damages. The plaintiffs alleged that the defendants were negligent in their conduct in selling Trans Union to Pritzker. The Delaware court of chancery held in favor of the defendants. The plaintiffs appealed.

Issue

Did Trans Union's directors breach their duty of care?

Language of the Court

In the specific context of a proposed merger of a domestic corporation, a director has a duty, along with his fellow directors, to act in an informed and deliberate manner in determining whether to approve an agreement of merger. The directors (1) did not adequately inform themselves as to Van Gorkom's role in forcing the sale of the company and in establishing the per share purchase price; (2) they were uninformed as to the intrinsic value of the company and (3) given these circumstances, at a minimum, they were grossly negligent in approving the sale of the company upon two hours' consideration, without prior notice, and without the exigency of a crisis or emergency.

Without any documents before them concerning the proposed transaction, the members of the board were required to rely entirely upon Van Gorkom's 20-minute oral presentation of the proposal. No written summary of the terms of the merger was presented; the directors were given no documentation to support the adequacy of $55 price per share for sale of the company; and the board had before it nothing more than Van Gorkom's statement of his understanding of the substance of an agreement that he admittedly had never read, or that any member of the board had ever seen. Thus, the record compels the conclusion that the board lacked valuation information to reach an informed business judgment as to the fairness of $55 per share for sale of the company. We conclude that Trans Union's board was grossly negligent in that it failed to act with informed reasonable deliberation in agreeing to the Pritzker merger proposal.

Decision

The supreme court of Delaware held that the defendant directors had breached their duty of care. The supreme court reversed the judgment of the court of chancery and remanded the case to the court of chancery to conduct an evidentiary hearing to determine the fair value of the shares represented by the plaintiffs' class. If that value was higher than $55 per share, the difference was to be awarded to the plaintiffs as damages.

Law & Ethics Questions

1. Describe the fiduciary duty of care owed by directors and officers.

2. What does the business judgment rule provide? Is this a good rule? Explain.

3. **ETHICS** Do you think Van Gorkom and the other directors had the shareholders' best interests in mind? Explain.

4. **ETHICS** What type of liability exposure is there for being a member of a board of directors? Explain.

Web Exercises

1. **WEB** For the complete opinion of this case, go to *www.prenhall.com/cheesemancases*.

2. **WEB** Visit the website of the supreme court of Delaware, at *http://courts.delaware.gov/Courts/SupremeCourt*.

3. **WEB** Use *www.google.com* to find an article that discusses the duty of care owed by officers of a corporation. Read it.

4. **WEB** Use *www.google.com* to find an article that discusses the Delaware corporations code. Read it.

ETHICS SPOTLIGHT

Disney Board of Directors Did Not Breach Duty of Care

> ❝ *This argument is best understood against the backdrop of the presumptions that cloak director action being reviewed under the business judgment standard.* ❞
>
> —Justice Jacobs

The business judgment rule was designed to protect corporate officers and directors from being second-guessed by judges and juries for making business decisions they thought were in the best interests of the corporation. How far, however, does the business judgment rule go in protecting board members? Consider the following case.

Michael D. Eisner was the chairman of the board and chief executive officer of the Walt Disney Company (Disney). In a move to make Disney even more "Hollywood" and move into the digital age, Eisner recruited and hired his friend Michael S. Ovitz to serve as Disney's president. At the time, Ovitz was head of Creative Artists Agency (CAA), a firm of talent agents, and was known as the "most powerful man in Hollywood." To entice Ovitz away from CAA, Disney's board of directors unanimously approved a five-year employment contract with Ovitz. All parties signed. Ovitz was appointed president and was nominated and elected to Disney's board.

The employment contract provided for Ovitz to receive an annual salary of $1 million, a discretionary bonus determined by the board, and options to purchase (at a discount price) and exercise 1 million shares of Disney's common stock each year for five years. The contract contained a severance package that included the following provisions: (1) that Disney could terminate Ovitz for "good cause"—which was defined as gross negligence or malfeasance in the execution of his duties—without liability and (2) that if Disney terminated Ovitz without good cause or if Ovitz resigned from Disney with the consent of the board, he would get his remaining salary payments, and 3 million of his options on Disney stock would immediately vest upon his separation from the company. At the time of signing the severance package, no Disney board member bothered to quantify the benefits Ovitz would receive if his employment was terminated before the expiration of the five-year term.

Ovitz began his term as Disney's president amid media hype, but within a year, Ovitz was unhappy with his role at Disney, and the Disney board of directors did not think Ovitz's employment was working out very well. Ovitz began looking for alternative employment. Ovitz sent a letter to Eisner, stating his desire to leave Disney only 14 months after having joined Disney, and Eisner consented to Ovitz's request for a non-fault termination. The next day, Disney's board agreed, and Ovitz left Disney. His severance pay package—which included salary, bonus, and 3 million stock options—was worth $140 million.

Several Disney shareholders brought a derivative lawsuit against the Disney board of directors, alleging that they had breached their fiduciary duty to the shareholders. The shareholders argued that the Disney board should have terminated Ovitz for "good cause" instead of agreeing to the nonfault termination and severance pay package. The Disney directors defended, arguing that the business judgment rule protected their largess. Because Disney is incorporated in Delaware, Delaware's courts were given the opportunity to decide the case. In deciding in favor of the Disney directors, the trial court judge stated:

> The Board made a business decision to grant Ovitz a Non-Fault Termination. Plaintiffs may disagree with the Board's judgment as to how this matter should have been handled. But where, as here, there is no reasonable doubt as to the disinterest of or absence of fraud by the Board, mere disagreement cannot serve as grounds for imposing liability based on alleged breaches of fiduciary duty and waste.

After almost nine years of trials and appeals, the Delaware supreme court applied the business judgment rule, agreed with the trial court's reasoning, and decided the case in favor of the Disney board. In its decision, the Delaware supreme court stated

This argument is best understood against the backdrop of the presumptions that cloak director action being reviewed under the business judgment standard. Our law presumes that "in making a business decision the directors of a corporation acted on an informed basis, in good faith, and in the honest belief that the action taken was in the best interests of the company."

In re Walt Disney Company Derivative Litigation, 906 A.2d 27, 2006 Del. Lexis 307 (Supreme Court of Delaware, 2006)

Law & Ethics Questions

1. What does the business judgment rule provide? What is the purpose of the business judgment rule?

2. **ETHICS** Did the board of directors of Disney act in the best interests of the shareholders in this case? Why or why not?

Web Exercises

1. **WEB** For the complete opinion of this case, go to *www.prenhall.com/cheesemancases*.

2. **WEB** Visit the website of the supreme court of Delaware, at *http://courts.delaware.gov/Courts/SupremeCourt*.

3. **WEB** Visit the website of The Walt Disney Company, at *http://corporate.disney.go.com*. Can you locate a code of ethics for the company?

4. **WEB** Use *www.google.com* to find an article that discusses the business judgment rule. Read it.

Duty of Loyalty

The **duty of loyalty** requires directors and officers to subordinate their personal interests to those of the corporation and its shareholders. Justice Benjamin Cardozo defined this duty of loyalty as follows:

> [A corporate director or officer] owes loyalty and allegiance to the corporation—a loyalty that is undivided and an allegiance that is influenced by no consideration other than the welfare of the corporation. Any adverse interest of a director [or officer] will be subjected to a scrutiny rigid and uncompromising. He may not profit at the expense of his corporation and in conflict with its rights; he may not for personal gain divert unto himself the opportunities that in equity and fairness belong to the corporation.
>
> Many forms of conduct permissible in a workaday world for those acting at arm's length are forbidden to those bound by fiduciary ties. Not honesty alone, but the punctilio of an honor the most sensitive, is then the standard of behavior. As to this there has developed a tradition that is unbending and inveterate.[1]

If a director or an officer breaches his or her duty of loyalty and makes a secret profit on a transaction, the corporation can sue the director or officer to recover the secret profit. Some of the most common breaches of the duty of loyalty are discussed in the following paragraphs.

USURPING A CORPORATE OPPORTUNITY Directors and officers may not personally usurp (steal) a corporate opportunity for themselves. **Usurping a corporate opportunity** constitutes a violation of a director's or an officer's duty of loyalty. If usurping is proven, the corporation can (1) acquire the opportunity from the director or officer and (2) recover any profits made by the director or officer.

The following elements must be shown to prove usurping:

1. The opportunity was presented to the director or officer in his or her corporate capacity.
2. The opportunity is related to or connected with the corporation's current or proposed business.

3. The corporation has the financial ability to take advantage of the opportunity.

4. The corporate officer or director took the corporate opportunity for him- or herself.

However, the director or officer is personally free to take advantage of a corporate opportunity if it was fully disclosed and presented to the corporation and the corporation rejected it.

Example Suppose Heather works as the president of YBox.com, a company that develops and sells video games. Nerd Sue, an electronic genius and gamer, develops the video game *SpiderGirl*. Sue takes this game to Heather and offers the game to Heather as president of YBox.com. Instead of bringing the opportunity to YBox.com's board of directors, Heather pays Sue's asking price and purchases *SpiderGirl* for herself. Heather leaves YBox.com and forms her own company to distribute *SpiderGirl* video game. This would be an example of usurping a corporate opportunity.

SELF-DEALING Under the RMBCA, a contract or transaction with a corporate director or officer is voidable by the corporation if it is unfair to the corporation [RMBCA Section 8.31]. Contracts of a corporation to purchase property from, sell property to, or make loans to corporate directors or officers where the directors or officers have not disclosed their interest in the transaction are often voided under this standard. In the alternative, the corporation can affirm the contract and recover any profits from the **self-dealing** employee. Contracts or transactions with corporate directors or officers are enforceable if their interest in the transaction has been disclosed to the corporation and the disinterested directors or the shareholders have approved the transaction.

> It appears to me that the atmosphere of the temple of Justice is polluted by the presence of such things as companies.
>
> L. J. James
> *Wilson v. Church (1879)*

Example Suppose Peter works for Big-Mart Corporation, a corporation that has superstores that sell everything known to humankind. Peter's job is to locate future sites for Big-Mart stores. Peter finds a piece of real estate that would make a great site for a Big-Mart store. Peter tells his mother-in-law to purchase the property from its current owner, which she does. Peter has a secret agreement with his mother-in-law to split the profits when she sells the property to Big-Mart. Peter, without disclosing his interest in the property, recommends the site to Big-Mart, which then purchases the property from Peter's mother-in-law. The mother-in-law splits the profits with Peter. This is an example of self-dealing. Big-Mart can void the contract and get its money back, or it can affirm the contract and recover the secret profits made on the transaction.

COMPETING WITH THE CORPORATION Directors and officers cannot engage in activities that **compete with the corporation** unless full disclosure is made and a majority of the disinterested directors or shareholders approve the activity. The corporation can recover any profits made by nonapproved competition and any other damages caused to the corporation.

Example Josh works as a real estate broker for Century 22 Corporation, a real estate brokerage company. In his capacity at Century 22, Josh represents proposed sellers or buyers of homes in their home sales and purchases. The money he earns on every Century 22 transaction is split 50 percent to Josh and 50 percent to Century 22. A home buyer comes to Josh to list her house for sale. Josh, without getting Century 22's permission and failing to list the house with Century 22, sells the house personally and pockets 100 percent of the commission. This would be an example of competing with the corporation.

MAKING A SECRET PROFIT If a director or an officer breaches his or her duty of loyalty and **makes a secret profit** on a transaction, the corporation can sue the director or officer to recover the secret profit.

Example Suppose Maxine Chambers is the purchasing agent for the Roebolt Corporation. Her duties require her to negotiate and execute contracts to purchase office supplies and equipment for the corporation. Assume that Bruce Nevel, a computer salesperson, pays Chambers a $10,000 kickback to purchase computers needed by the Roebolt Corporation. The Roebolt Corporation can sue and recover the $10,000 secret profit from Chambers.

CONCEPT SUMMARY

Fiduciary Duties of Corporation Directors and Officers

DUTY	DESCRIPTION	VIOLATION
Duty of obedience	Duty to act within the authority	Acts outside the corporate officer's or director's authority.
Duty of care	Duty to use care and diligence when acting on behalf of the corporation. This duty is discharged if an officer or a director acts: 1. In good faith 2. With the care that an ordinary prudent person in a like position would use under similar circumstances 3. In a manner he or she reasonably believes to be in the best interests of the corporation	Acts of negligence and mismanagement. Such acts include failure to: 1. Make a reasonable investigation of a corporate matter 2. Attend board meetings on a regular basis 3. Properly supervise a subordinate who causes a loss to the corporation 4. Keep adequately informed about corporate matters 5. Take other actions necessary to discharge duties
Duty of loyalty	Duty to subordinate personal interests to those of the corporation and its shareholders.	Acts of disloyalty. Such acts include unauthorized: 1. Self-dealing with the corporation 2. Usurping of a corporate opportunity 3. Competition with the corporation 4. Making of secret profit that belongs to the corporation

CONTEMPORARY ENVIRONMENT
State Constituency Statutes

Under the traditional business judgment rule, directors of a corporation owe a fiduciary duty to act on an informed basis, with reasonable care, and in good faith. Historically, this duty has been rigidly and exclusively owed to the corporation and its shareholders and to no others. Under this classical theory of the corporation, the rights of other constituents—such as employees, bondholders and creditors, suppliers, and customers—exist by contract, period.

Today this view has been moderated. Corporate directors and officers, although mindful of their primary duty to the shareholders of the corporation, also consider the rights of other constituents of the corporation when making corporate decisions. In fact, more than 30 states have enacted **constituency statutes** that allow directors to consider constituents other than shareholders when making decisions. For example, Minnesota adopted the following statute:

> In discharging the duties of the position of director, a director may, in considering the best interests of the corporation, consider the interests of the corporation's employees, customers, suppliers, and creditors, the economy of the state and nation, community and societal considerations, and the long-term as

well as short-term interests of the corporation and its shareholders, including the possibility that these interests may be best served by the continued independence of the corporation. [Minn. Stat. Section 302A.251(5)]

Constituency statutes recognize the complex nature of the modern corporation and the modern view that shareholders are not the only "owners" of corporations. These statutes acknowledge the rights of a variety of participants, including employees, managers, suppliers, distributors, customers, and the local communities in which corporations are located. Most constituency statutes are permissive, not mandatory. That is, directors may take into account nonstockholder interests but are not required to do so.

Law & Ethics Questions

1. What do state constituency statutes provide? Why do state legislatures enact constituency statutes?

2. **ETHICS** Do constituency statutes make corporate boards of directors more socially responsible? Explain.

Criminal Liability

Corporate directors, officers, employees, and agents are personally liable for the crimes they commit while acting on behalf of the corporation. Criminal law sanctions include fines and imprisonment.

Under the law of agency, a corporation is liable for the crimes committed by its directors, officers, employees, or agents while acting within the scope of their employment. Because a corporation cannot be placed in prison, the criminal penalty imposed on a corporation is usually the assessment of a monetary fine or the loss of some legal privilege (such as a license).

Many states' attorney generals have aggressively pursued criminal cases against corporate officers and directors in recent years. The attorney general of New York has been a leading force in bringing cases against fraudulent officers and directors. The U.S. Department of Justice brings criminal cases against officers and directors for violating federal statutes, such as securities law, racketeering laws, and other federal statutes.

Sarbanes-Oxley Act

During the late 1990s and early 2000s, the U.S. economy was wracked by a number of business and accounting scandals. Companies such as Enron, Tyco, and Worldcom engaged in fraudulent conduct, leading to many corporate officers being convicted of financial crimes. Many of these companies went bankrupt, causing huge losses to their shareholders, employees, and creditors. Boards of directors were complacent, not keeping a watchful eye over the conduct of their officers and employees.

In response, Congress enacted the federal **Sarbanes-Oxley Act** of 2002. This act establishes far-reaching rules regarding corporate governance. The goals of the Sarbanes-Oxley Act are to improve corporate governance rules, eliminate conflicts of interest, and instill confidence in investors and the public that management will run public companies in the best interests of all constituents.

ETHICS SPOTLIGHT

Sarbanes-Oxley Act Improves Corporate Governance

The Sarbanes-Oxley Act has changed the rules of corporate governance in important respects. Several major provisions of the act regarding corporate governance are discussed in the following paragraphs.

CEO and CFO Certification

The CEO and CFO of a public company must file a statement accompanying each annual and quarterly report, certifying that the signing officer has reviewed the report, based on the officer's knowledge that the report does not contain any untrue statement of a material fact or omit to state a material fact that would make the statement misleading and that the financial statement and disclosures fairly present, in all material aspects, the operation and financial condition of the company. A knowing and willful violation is punishable by up to 20 years in prison and a fine of not more than $5 million.

Reimbursement of Bonuses and Incentive Pay

If a public company is required to restate its financial statements because of material noncompliance with financial reporting requirements, the CEO and CFO must reimburse the company for any bonuses, incentive pay, or securities trading profits made because of the noncompliance.

Prohibition on Personal Loans

The act prohibits public companies from making personal loans to their directors or executive officers.

Tampering with Evidence

The act makes it a crime for any person to knowingly alter, destroy, mutilate, conceal, or create any document to impair, impede, influence, or obstruct any federal investigation. A violation is punishable by up to 20 years in prison and a monetary fine.

Bar from Acting as an Officer or a Director

The Securities and Exchange Commission (SEC), a federal government agency, may issue an order prohibiting any person who has committed securities fraud from acting as an officer or a director of a public company.

Although the Sarbanes-Oxley Act applies only to public companies, private companies and nonprofit organizations are also influenced by the act's accounting and corporate governance rules.

Law & Ethics Questions

1. What does the new CEO and CFO certification requirement require?

2. **ETHICS** Will the CEO and CFO certification requirement reduce corporate fraudulent conduct? Explain.

3. **ETHICS** Was there an opportunity for fraud when corporations were permitted to make loans to their own officers? Explain.

4. **ETHICS** Will the Sarbanes-Oxley Act encourage more ethical behavior by corporate officers and directors?

Web Exercises

1. **WEB** Choose a corporation. Use *www.google.com* to find that company's website and then find the company's code of ethics.

2. **WEB** Use *www.google.com* to find an article that discusses a recent breach of the duty of loyalty by a corporate officer. Read it.

Chapter Summary

Shareholders, p. 777

Shareholders of a corporation own the corporation.

Shareholders' Meetings

1. *Annual shareholders' meeting.* A meeting of the shareholders of a corporation must be held annually by the corporation to elect directors and vote on other matters.

   2. *Special shareholders' meeting.* A meeting of shareholders may be called to consider and vote on important or emergency matters, such as a proposed merger or amending the articles of incorporation.

   3. *Notice of shareholders' meetings.* The corporation must notify shareholders of the place, day, and time of annual and special shareholder meetings. If the required notice is not given or is defective, any action taken at the meeting is void.

Proxies

   1. *Proxy.* Shareholders may appoint another person (the *proxy*) as their agent to vote their shares at shareholders' meetings.

   2. *Proxy card.* A proxy card is a written document that a shareholder signs that authorizes another person to vote his or her shares at a shareholders' meeting.

Voting Requirements

   1. *Record date.* The record date is a date specified in the corporate bylaws that determines whether a shareholder may vote at a shareholders' meeting. Only persons who are shareholders on the record date are permitted to vote at the meeting.

   2. *Shareholders' list.* This list contains the names and addresses of the shareholders as of the record date and the class and number of shares owned by each shareholder. This list must be made available to all shareholders.

Quorum and Vote Required

   1. *Quorum.* A quorum is the required number of shares that must be represented in person or by proxy to hold a shareholders' meeting. The RMBCA establishes a majority of outstanding shares as a quorum.

   2. *Vote required for elections other than for directors.* The affirmative vote of the majority of the voting shares represented at a shareholders' meeting constitutes an act of the shareholders for actions other than for the elections of directors.

Straight (Noncumulative) Voting

Unless otherwise stated, each shareholder votes the number of shares he or she owns on candidates for each of the positions open for election. The candidate or candidates with the most votes win the open position or positions.

Cumulative Voting

The articles of incorporation may provide for cumulative voting. Under this method, a shareholder is entitled to multiply the number of shares he or she owns by the number of directors to be elected and cast the product for a single candidate or distribute the product among two or more candidates.

Supramajority Voting Requirement

The articles of incorporation or bylaws can require a greater than majority of shares to constitute quorum or the vote of the shareholders (e.g., 80 percent). Also called *supermajority*.

Voting Trusts

In a voting trust arrangement, participating shareholders transfer their shares to a trustee, who is empowered to vote the shares held by the trust. Shareholders are issued voting trust certificates that evidence their interest in the trust.

Shareholder Voting Agreements

An agreement is made between two or more shareholders, who determine how they will vote their shares. Voting agreements are enforceable.

Right of First Refusal

Shareholders have the right to transfer their shares. Shareholders can enter into a right of first refusal. This agreement requires the selling shareholder to offer his or her shares for sale to the other parties to the agreement before selling them to anyone else.

Buy-and-Sell Agreement

A buy-and-sell agreement requires selling shareholders to sell their shares to the other shareholders or to the corporation at the price specified in the agreement.

Preemptive Rights

Preemptive rights give existing shareholders the option of subscribing to new shares being issued by the corporation in proportion to their current ownership interest.

Right to Receive Information and Inspect Books and Records

A corporation must furnish its shareholders with an annual financial statement that contains a balance sheet, an income statement, and a statement of changes in shareholder equity. Shareholders have the absolute right to inspect the shareholders' list, the articles of incorporation, the bylaws, and the minutes of shareholders' meetings held within the past three years. They have the right to inspect accounting and tax records, minutes of board of directors and committee meetings, and minutes of shareholders' meetings held more than three years in the past if they demonstrate a proper purpose.

Dividends

1. *Directors' authority to pay dividends.* The board of directors has the discretion to pay dividends to shareholders.
2. *Record date.* When a corporation declares a dividend, it sets a date, usually a few weeks prior to the actual payment, that establishes the record date for payment of the dividend. Shareholders as of that date will be paid the dividend.
3. *Stock dividends.* Additional shares of stock may be issued to the shareholders as a dividend. They are paid in proportion to the existing ownership interests of shareholders, so they do not increase a shareholder's proportionate ownership interest.

Derivative Lawsuits

A shareholder may bring a derivative lawsuit on behalf of the corporation against an offending party who has injured the corporation when the directors of the corporation fail to bring the suit. The shareholder must make a written demand upon the corporation to bring the lawsuit, and before the shareholder can bring the suit, the corporation must either reject the demand or let 90 days expire without the corporation bringing the requested lawsuit.

Piercing the Corporate Veil

Shareholders of corporations generally have limited liability; that is, they are liable for the debts and obligations of the corporation only to the extent of their capital contribution to the corporation. Courts can disregard the corporate entity and hold shareholders personally liable for the debts and obligations of the corporation if (a) the corporation has been formed without sufficient capital (thin capitalization) or (b) separateness has not been maintained between the corporation and its shareholders. Also called the *alter ego doctrine.*

Board of Directors, p. 785

1. *Board of directors.* The board is a panel of decision makers for the corporation, the members of which are elected by the shareholders.
2. *Policy decisions.* The directors of a corporation are responsible for formulating the policy decisions that affect the corporation, such as deciding what business to engage in, determining the capital structure of the corporation, and selecting and removing top officers of the corporation.
3. *Resolutions.* The board of directors can adopt and recommend to shareholders a resolution that approves a transaction that requires shareholder vote.
4. *Right of Inspection.* Corporate directors have an *absolute right* to have access to the corporation's books, records, facilities, premises, and any other information affecting the operation of the corporation.

Compensating Directors

Directors are usually paid an annual retainer and an attendance fee for each meeting attended.

Selecting Directors

1. *Inside director.* An inside director is a member of the board of directors who is also an officer of the corporation.

2. *Outside director.* An outside director is a member of the board of directors who is not an officer of the corporation.
3. *Qualifications.* There are no qualifications to serve as a director unless the articles of incorporation or bylaws prescribe qualifications.
4. *Number of directors.* A board of directors can consist of one or more individuals. The articles of incorporation fix the number of initial directors. This number can be amended by the articles of incorporation or bylaws.
5. *Variable range.* The articles of incorporation or bylaws can establish a variable range for the size of the board of directors. The exact number of directors within the range may be changed from time to time by the board or directors or the shareholders.

Term of Office

1. *Annual term.* The term of a director's office expires at the next annual shareholders' meeting following his or her election unless terms are staggered.
2. *Staggered terms.* If a board of directors consists of nine or more members, it may be divided into two or three classes (each class to be as nearly equal in number as possible), and classes can be elected to serve staggered terms of two or three years.
3. *Vacancies.* Vacancies on a board of directors can be filled by the shareholders or the remaining directors.

Meetings of the Board of Directors

A regular meeting of the board of directors is held at the time and place scheduled in the bylaws. A special meeting of the board of directors may be convened to discuss an important or emergency matter, such as a proposed merger or a hostile takeover attempt. The board of directors may act without a meeting if all the directors sign written consents that set forth the action taken. The board of directors may meet via conference call if all the directors can hear and participate in the call.

Quorum and Voting Requirement

1. *Quorum.* A simple majority of the number of directors established in the articles of incorporation or bylaws constitutes a quorum for transacting business.
2. *Vote.* The approval or disapproval of a majority of the quorum binds the entire board.
3. *Supramajority vote.* The articles of incorporation or bylaws may require a greater than majority of directors to constitute quorum or the vote of the board.

Committees of the Board of Directors

Unless the articles of incorporation or bylaws provide otherwise, the board of directors may create committees of its members and delegate certain powers to those committees. The most common committees are:

1. *Executive committee.*
2. *Audit committee.*
3. *Nominating committee.*
4. *Compensation committee.*
5. *Investment committee.*
6. *Litigation committee.*

Sarbanes-Oxley Act Imposes Duties on Audit Committee

The audit committee is responsible for the appointment of, payment of compensation for, and oversight of public accounting firms employed to audit the company. The audit committee must preapprove all audit and permissible non-audit services to be performed by a public accounting firm. The audit committee has authority to employ independent legal counsel and other advisors.

Corporate Officers, p. 788

Officers are employees of a corporation who are appointed by the board of directors to manage the day-to-day operations of the corporation. Unless an employment contract provides otherwise, any officer of a corporation may be removed by the board of directors.

Agency Authority of Officers

Officers and agents of a corporation have express, implied, and apparent authority to bind the corporation to contracts with third parties.

Indemnification and D&O Insurance Protection

1. *Indemnification.* A corporation must indemnify (pay back) any director or officer for litigation expenses incurred in a lawsuit won by the director or officer. The corporation may indemnify a director or officer who loses a lawsuit as long as the director or officer was not adjudged liable to the corporation or did not improperly obtain personal benefit for himself or herself in the challenged transaction.
2. *D&O Insurance.* Corporations can purchase *directors' and officers' liability insurance (D&O insurance)* that pays the cost to defend litigation against directors and officers and pays any judgment or settlement of the lawsuit.

Directors and officers may not be paid insurance or indemnification for intentional conduct that harmed third parties.

Liability of Directors and Officers, p. 790

Corporate directors and officers owe the fiduciary duties of trust and confidence to the corporation and its shareholders. They owe the duties of obedience, care, and loyalty.

Duty of Obedience

Directors and officers of a corporation have a duty to act within the authority conferred upon them by the state corporations code, the articles of incorporation, the corporate bylaws, and the resolutions adopted by the board of directors.

Duty of Care

Corporate directors and officers have a duty to use care and diligence when acting on behalf of the corporation. This duty is discharged if they perform their duties (a) in good faith, (b) with the care that an ordinary prudent person in a like position would use under similar circumstances, and (c) in a manner they reasonably believe to be in the best interests of the corporation.

1. *Negligence.* Negligence is the failure of a corporate director or officer to exercise the duty of care when conducting the corporation's business.
2. *Business judgment rule.* This rule says that directors and officers are not liable to the corporation or its shareholders for honest mistakes of judgment.
3. *Reliance on others.* Directors and officers may rely on information and reports prepared by competent and reliable officers and employees, lawyers, public accountants, other professionals, and committees of the board of directors as long as such reliance is warranted.
4. *Dissent to directors' action.* When an individual director opposes the action taken by the majority of the board of directors, he or she should register his or her dissent by (a) entering it in the minutes of the meeting, (b) filing a written dissent with the secretary before the adjournment of the meeting, or (c) forwarding a written dissent by registered mail to the secretary immediately following the adjournment of the meeting if the director has not attended the meeting.

Duty of Loyalty

Directors and officers have a duty not to act adversely to the interests of the corporation and to subordinate their personal interests to those of the corporation and its shareholders. The following are common examples of breaches of the duty of loyalty:

1. *Usurping a corporate opportunity.* A director or an officer may not personally usurp (steal) an opportunity that belongs to the corporation. The corporation can acquire the opportunity from the director or officer and recover any profits made by the director or officer.
2. *Self-dealing.* The corporation may void any transaction with a director or an officer if it is unfair to the corporation. Such transactions usually involve undisclosed self-dealing by a director or an officer with the corporation.

3. *Competing with the corporation.* Directors and officers may not compete with their corporation unless the competitive activity has been fully disclosed to the corporation and approved by a majority of disinterested directors or shareholders.

4. *Secret profits.* The corporation can sue and recover any secret profits made by an officer's or a director's breach of his or her duty of loyalty.

Criminal Liability, p. 797

1. *Liability of directors and officers.* Corporate directors and officers are personally liable for the crimes they commit while acting on behalf of the corporation. Criminal sanctions include fines and imprisonment.

2. *Liability of the corporation.* Under the law of agency, a corporation is liable for the crimes committed by its directors and officers while acting within the scope of their authority. Criminal sanctions include monetary fines and loss of legal privileges (e.g., loss of a license).

Sarbanes-Oxley Act, p. 798

The Sarbanes-Oxley Act of 2002 is a federal statute enacted by Congress to improve corporate governance rules, establish independence between public accounting firms and the public companies they audit, and eliminate conflicts of interest.

Sarbanes-Oxley Act Improves Corporate Governance

1. *CEO and CFO certification.* The CEO and CFO of a public company must file a statement accompanying each annual and quarterly report, certifying that the signing officer has reviewed the report and certifying that, based on the officer's knowledge, the report:

   a. Does not contain any untrue statement of a material fact or omit to state a material fact that would make the statement misleading.

   b. Fairly presents, in all material aspects, the operation and financial condition of the company.

   A knowing and willful violation is punishable for up to 20 years in prison and a fine of not more than $5 million.

2. *Reimbursement of bonuses and incentive pay.* The CEO and CFO must reimburse the company for any bonuses, incentive pay, or securities trading profits if the company is required to restate its financial statements because of material noncompliance with financial reporting requirements.

3. *Prohibition on personal loans.* Public companies cannot make personal loans to their directors or executive officers.

4. *Tampering with evidence.* It is a crime for any person to tamper with evidence to impede, influence, or obstruct any federal investigation. A violation is punishable for up to 20 years in prison and a monetary fine.

5. *Bar from acting as an officer or a director.* The Securities and Exchange Commission may issue an order prohibiting any person who has committed securities fraud from acting as an officer or a director of a public company.

Test Review Terms and Concepts

Annual financial statement   781
Annual shareholders' meeting   777
Audit committee   787
Board of directors   785
Business judgment rule   791
Buy-and-sell agreement   780
Committees   787
Compensation committee   788
Competing with the corporation   795
Constituency statute   796

Corporate officers   788
Criminal liability   797
Cumulative voting   779
Derivative action (derivative lawsuit)   781
Directors' and officers' liability insurance (D&O insurance)   789
Dissent   792
Dividends   781
Duty of care   790

Duty of loyalty   794
Duty of obedience   790
Executive committee   787
Fiduciary duties   790
Indemnification   790
Inside director   786
Investment committee   788
Limited liability   783
Litigation committee   788
Making a secret profit   795

Case Problems

28.1 Shareholders' Meeting: Ocilla Industries, Inc. (Ocilla), owned 40 percent of the stock of Direct Action Marketing, Inc. (Direct Action). Direct Action was a New York corporation that specialized in the marketing of products through billing inserts. Ocilla helped place Howard Katz and Joseph Esposito on Direct Action's five-member board of directors. A dispute between Ocilla and the two directors caused Ocilla to claim that Katz and Esposito wanted excess remuneration in exchange for leaving the board at the end of their terms. As a result, no shareholders' meeting was held for one and one-half years. Under the Model Business Corporations Act, can Ocilla compel Direct Action to hold the meeting earlier? *Ocilla Industries, Inc. v. Katz*, 677 F.Supp. 1291, **Web** 1987 U.S. Dist. Lexis 12741 (United States District Court for the Eastern District of New York)

28.2 Special Shareholders' Meeting: Jack C. Schoenholtz was a shareholder and member of the board of directors of Rye Psychiatric Hospital Center, Inc. (Rye Hospital). Four years after the hospital was incorporated, a split had developed among the board of directors concerning the operation of the facility. Three directors stood on one side of the dispute, and three directors on the other. In an attempt to break the deadlock, Schoenholtz, who owned over 10 percent of the corporation's voting stock, asked the corporation's secretary to call a special meeting of the shareholders. In response, the secretary sent a notice to the shareholders, stating that a special meeting of the shareholders would be held "for the purpose of electing directors." The meeting was held as scheduled. Some stockholders brought suit, claiming that the special shareholders' meeting was not called properly. Who wins? *Rye Psychiatric Hospital Center, Inc. v. Schoenholtz*, 101 A.D.2d 309, 476 N.Y.S.2d 339, **Web** 1984 N.Y. App. Div. Lexis 17818 (Supreme Court of New York)

28.3 Proxy: George Gibbons, William Smith, and Gerald Zollar were all shareholders in GRG Operating, Inc. (GRG). Zollar contributed $1,000 of his own funds so that the corporation could begin to do business. In exchange for this contribution, Gibbons and Smith both granted Zollar the right to vote their shares of GRG stock. They gave Zollar a signed form that stated that "Gibbons and Smith, for a period of 10 years from the date hereof, appoint Zollar as their proxy. This proxy is solely intended to be an irrevocable proxy." A year after the agreement was signed, Gibbons and Smith wanted to revoke their proxies. Can they? *Zollar v. Smith*, 710 S.W.2d 155, **Web** 1986 Tex. App. Lexis 12900 (Court of Appeals of Texas)

28.4 Right to Inspect Records: Helmsman Management Services, Inc. (Helmsman), became a 25 percent stockholder of A&S Consultants, Inc. (A&S), a Delaware corporation. Helmsman paid $50,000 for its interest in A&S. At the time of the stock purchase, Helmsman was also a customer of A&S, paying the company for the use of a computer software program. Since his investment, Helmsman verified A&S's billings by a periodic review of certain of A&S's books and records. Three years later, Helmsman conducted a review of A&S's records over a six-day period. The review showed that A&S had never paid any dividends on the stock held by Helmsman and that Helmsman had never received notice of A&S's stockholder meetings. Suspecting that A&S was being mismanaged, Helmsman sent a letter to A&S, asking to inspect all of A&S's records. The letter stated several purposes for the inspection, including to (1) determine the reasons for nonpayment of dividends and (2) gain information to be used in determining how to vote in stockholders' elections. Under the Model Business Corporations Act, should Helmsman's request be honored? *Helmsman Management Services, Inc. v. A & S Consultants, Inc.*, 525 A.2d 160, **Web** 1987 Del. Ch. Lexis 397 (Court of Chancery of Delaware)

28.5 Dividends: Gay's Super Markets, Inc. (Super Markets), was a corporation formed under the laws of the state of Maine. Hannaford Bros. Company held 51 percent of the corporation's common stock. Lawrence F. Gay and his brother Carrol were both minority shareholders in Super Markets. Lawrence Gay was also the manager of the corporation's store at Machias, Maine. One day, he was dismissed from his job. At the meeting of Super Markets's board of directors, a decision was made not to declare a stock dividend for the prior year. The directors cited expected losses from increased competition and the expense of opening a new store as reasons for not paying a dividend. Lawrence Gay claims that the reason for not paying a dividend was to force him to sell his shares in Super Markets. Lawrence sued to force the corporation to declare a dividend. Who wins? *Gay v. Gay's Super Markets, Inc.*, 343 A.2d 577, **Web** 1975 Me. Lexis 391 (Supreme Judicial Court of Maine)

28.6 Duty of Loyalty: Edward Hellenbrand ran a comedy club known as the Comedy Cottage in Rosemont, Illinois. The business was incorporated, with Hellenbrand and his wife as the corporation's sole shareholders. The corporation leased the premises in which the club was located. Hellenbrand hired Jay Berk as general manager of the club. Two years later, Berk was made vice president of the corporation and given 10 percent of its stock. Hellenbrand experienced health problems and moved to Nevada, leaving Berk to manage the daily affairs of the business. Four years later, the ownership of the building where the Comedy Cottage was located changed hands. Shortly thereafter, the club's lease on the premises expired. Hellenbrand instructed Berk to negotiate a new lease. Berk arranged a month-to-month lease but had the lease agreement drawn up in his name instead of that of the corporation. When Hellenbrand learned of Berk's move, he fired him. Berk continued to lease the building in his own name and opened his own club there, known as the Comedy Company, Inc. Hellenbrand sued Berk for an injunction to prevent Berk from leasing the building. Who wins? *Comedy Cottage, Inc. v. Berk*, 145 Ill.App.3d 355, 495 N.E.2d 1006, **Web** 1986 Ill. App. Lexis 2486 (Appellate Court of Illinois)

28.7 Duty of Loyalty: Lawrence Gaffney was the president and general manager of Ideal Tape Company (Ideal). Ideal, which was a subsidiary of Chelsea Industries, Inc. (Chelsea), was engaged in the business of manufacturing pressure-sensitive tape. Gaffney recruited three other Ideal executives to join him in starting a tape manufacturing business. The four men remained at Ideal for the two years it took them to plan the new enterprise. During this time, they used their positions at Ideal to travel around the country to gather business ideas, recruit potential customers, and purchase equipment for their business. At no time did they reveal to Chelsea their intention to open a competing business. The new business was incorporated as Action Manufacturing Company (Action). When executives at Chelsea discovered the existence of the new venture, Gaffney and the others resigned from Chelsea. Chelsea sued them for damages. Who wins? *Chelsea Industries, Inc. v. Gaffney*, 389 Mass. 1, 449 N.E.2d 320, **Web** 1983 Mass. Lexis 1413 (Supreme Judicial Court of Massachusetts)

28.8 Indemnification: William G. Young was a director of Pool Builders Supply, Inc. (Pool Builders). Pool Builders experienced financial difficulties and was forced to file for bankruptcy. Eddie Lawson was appointed the receiver for the creditors of the corporation. Lawson believed that Young had mismanaged the corporation. Lawson filed a suit against Young and Pool Builders, alleging that Young had used Pool Builders personally to obtain money, goods, and property from creditors on the credit of the corporation. Lawson's suit also alleged that Young had attempted to convert corporate assets for his own use. Young defended the suit for himself and the corporation. At trial, the judge found insufficient evidence to support Lawson's charges, and the suit was dismissed. Young then sought to have Pool Builders pay the legal fees he had incurred while defending the suit. Can Young recover this money from the corporation? *Lawson v. Young*, 21 Ohio App.3d 190, 486 N.E.2d 1177, **Web** 1984 Ohio App. Lexis 12678 (Court of Appeals of Ohio)

28.9 Derivative Shareholder Lawsuit: Four brothers— Monnie, Mechel, Merko, and Sam Dotlich—formed a partnership to run a heavy equipment rental business. One decade later, the company had been incorporated as Dotlich Brothers, Inc. Each brother owned 25 percent of the corporation's stock, and each served on the board of directors. During the course of its operation, the business acquired a 56-acre tract of land in Speedway, Indiana. This land was held in the name of Monnie Dotlich. Each of the brothers was aware of this agreement. The corporation also had purchased six other pieces of property, all of which were held in Monnie's name. Sam Dotlich was not informed that Monnie was the record owner of these other properties. Sam discovered this irregularity and requested that the board of directors take action to remedy the situation. When the board refused to do so, Sam initiated a lawsuit on behalf of the corporation. Can Sam bring this lawsuit? *Dotlich v. Dotlich*, 475 N.E.2d 331, **Web** 1985 Ind. App. Lexis 2233 (Court of Appeals of Indiana)

28.10 Piercing the Corporate Veil: M. R. Watters was the majority shareholder of several closely held corporations, including Wildhorn Ranch, Inc. (Wildhorn). All these businesses were run out of Watters's home in Rocky Ford, Colorado. Wildhorn operated a resort called the Wildhorn Ranch Resort in Teller County, Colorado. Although Watters claimed that the ranch was owned by the corporation, the deed for the property listed Watters as the owner. Watters paid little attention to corporate formalities, holding corporate meetings at his house, never taking minutes of those meetings, and paying the debts of one corporation with the assets of another. During August 1986, two guests of Wildhorn Ranch Resort drowned while operating a paddleboat at the ranch. The family of the deceased guests sued for damages. Can Watters be held personally liable? *Geringer v. Wildhorn Ranch, Inc.*, 706 F.Supp. 1442, **Web** 1988 U.S. Dist. Lexis 15701 (United States District Court for the District of Colorado)

Ethics Issues

28.11 Ethics: Alfred S. Johnson, Inc. (Corporation), was incorporated by Alfred S. Johnson, who owned 70 shares of the corporation. Two employees of the corporation, James DeBaun and Walter Stephens, owned 20 and 10 shares, respectively. When Johnson died 10 years later, his will created a testamentary trust in which his 70 shares were placed. Johnson's will named First Western Bank and Trust Company (Bank) trustee for the trust. Several years later, Bank decided to sell the 70 shares but did not tell anyone associated with Corporation of its decision. An appraisal was obtained that valued the corporation at $326,000 as a going concern.

Three years later, Raymond J. Mattison submitted an offer to purchase the 70 shares for $250,000, payable as $50,000 in securities of companies Mattison owned and the $200,000 balance over a five-year period. Bank obtained a Dun & Bradstreet report that showed several outstanding tax liens against Mattison. Bank accepted Mattison's explanation that they were not his fault. At the time, Mattison owed Bank a judgment for fraud. Bank was also aware that Mattison owed unpaid debts and that several entities in which he was involved were insolvent. Bank did not investigate these matters. If it had, the public records of Los Angeles County would have revealed 38 unsatisfied judgments against Mattison and his entities, totaling $330,886, 54 pending lawsuits claiming damages of $373,588, and 18 tax liens aggregating $20,327. Bank agreed to sell the 70 shares to Mattison and accepted the assets of Corporation as security for the repayment of the $200,000 balance. As part of the transaction, Bank required Mattison to agree to have Corporation give its banking business to Bank.

At the time of sale, Corporation was a successful going business with a bright future. It had cash of $76,000 and other liquid assets of over $120,000. Its net worth was about $220,000. Corporation was profitable, and its trend of earnings indicated a pattern of growth. Mattison immediately implemented a systematic scheme to loot Corporation. He (1) diverted $73,000 in corporate cash to himself and a shell company he owned, (2) caused Corporation to assign all its assets, including accounts receivable, to the shell company, (3) diverted all corporate mail to a post office box and extracted incoming checks to Corporation, (4) refused to pay corporate creditors on time or at all, (5) issued payroll checks without sufficient corporate funds, and (6) removed Corporation's books and records. One year later, hopelessly insolvent, Corporation shut down operations and was placed in receivership. At that time, its debts exceeded its assets by over $200,000. DeBaun's and Stephens's shares were worthless. They sued Bank for damages, alleging that Bank, as the majority shareholder of Corporation, had breached its fiduciary duty to the minority shareholders.

Did Bank have knowledge of the dangerous situation in which it placed Corporation? Did Bank, as the controlling shareholder of Corporation, breach its fiduciary duty to the minority shareholders? *DeBaun v. First Western Bank and Trust Co.*, 46 Cal.App.3d 686, 120 Cal.Rptr. 354, **Web** 1975 Cal. App. Lexis 1801 (Court of Appeal of California)

28.12 Ethics: Jon-T Chemicals, Inc. (Chemicals), was an Oklahoma corporation engaged in the fertilizer and chemicals business. John H. Thomas was its majority shareholder and its president and board chairman. Chemicals incorporated Jon-T Farms, Inc. (Farms), as a wholly owned subsidiary to engage in the farming and land-leasing business. Chemicals invested $10,000 to establish Farms. All the directors and officers of Farms were directors and officers of Chemicals, and Thomas was its president and board chairman. In addition, Farms used officers, computers, and accountants of Chemicals without paying a fee, and Chemicals paid the salary of Farms's only employee. Chemicals made regular informal advances to pay Farms's expenses. These payments reached $7.5 million by January 1975.

Thomas and Farms engaged in a scheme whereby they submitted fraudulent applications for agricultural subsidies from the federal government under the Uplands Cotton Program. As a result of these applications, the Commodity Credit Corporation, a government agency, paid over $2.5 million in subsidies to Thomas and Farms. After discovering the fraud, the federal government obtained criminal convictions against Thomas and Farms. In a separate civil action, the federal government obtained a $4.7 million judgment against Thomas and Farms, finding them jointly and severally liable for the tort of fraud. Farms declared bankruptcy, and Thomas was unable to pay the judgment. Because Thomas and Farms were insolvent, the federal government sued Chemicals to recover the judgment. Was Farms the alter ego of Chemicals, permitting the United States to pierce the corporate veil and recover the judgment from Chemicals? Did Thomas act ethically in this case? *United States of America v. Jon-T Chemicals, Inc.*, 768 F.2d 686, **Web** 1985 U.S. App. Lexis 21255 (United States Court of Appeals for the Fifth Circuit)

IRAC Writing Assignment

Read **Case A-28** in Appendix A [*United States v. WRW Corporation*]. Use the IRAC method to prepare a written analysis of the case.

Endnotes

1. Meinhard v. Salmon, 249 N.Y. 458, 164 N.E. 545, Web 1928 N.Y. Lexis 830 (Court of Appeals of New York)

CHAPTER 29

Corporate Acquisitions and Multinational Corporations

> **❝**To supervise wisely the great corporations is well; but to look backward to the days when business was polite pillage and regard our great business concerns as piratical institutions carrying letters of marque and reprisal is a grave error born in the minds of little men. When these little men legislate they set the brakes going uphill. **❞**
>
> —ELBERT HUBBARD
> Notebook, page 16

CHAPTER OBJECTIVES

After studying this chapter, you should be able to:

1. Describe the process for soliciting proxies from shareholders and engaging in proxy contests.
2. Define *shareholder proposal* and identify when a shareholder can include a proposal in proxy materials.
3. Describe the process for approving a merger or share exchange.
4. Define *tender offer* and describe poison pills, white knight mergers, greenmail, and other defensive maneuvers to prevent hostile takeover.
5. Examine the use of multinational corporations in conducting international business.

CHAPTER CONTENTS

   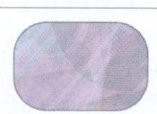 

Introduction to Corporate Acquisitions and Multinational Corporations

During the course of its existence, a corporation may go through certain *fundamental changes*. A corporation must seek shareholder approval for many changes. This requires the solicitation of votes or proxies from shareholders. Persons who want to take over the management of a corporation often conduct proxy contests to try to win over shareholder votes.

Corporations often engage in acquisitions of other corporations or businesses. This may occur by friendly merger or consolidation or by hostile tender offer. In defense, a corporation may erect certain barriers or impediments to a hostile takeover.

Multinational corporations are often used to conduct international business around the world. This is done through a variety of business arrangements.

This chapter discusses fundamental changes to a corporation, including the solicitation of proxies, mergers and consolidations, hostile tender offers, and defensive strategies of corporations. This chapter also examines the use of multinational corporations in conducting international business.

Mandalay, Myanmar

Many companies in the United States and other countries do not do business in or with companies from Myanmar. This is because of alleged human rights violations by the military government of Myanmar.

Proxy Solicitation and Proxy Contests

Corporate shareholders have the right to vote on the election of directors, mergers, charter amendments, and the like. They can exercise their power to vote either in person or by proxy [RMBCA Section 7.22]. Voting by proxy is common in large corporations with thousands of shareholders located across the country and around the world.

A *proxy* is a written document (often called a **proxy card**) that is completed and signed by the shareholder and sent to the corporation. The proxy authorizes another person—the proxy holder—to vote the shares at the shareholders' meeting as directed by the shareholder. The proxy holder is often a director or an officer of the corporation. Exhibit 29.1 shows a proxy card.

Federal Proxy Rules

Section 14(a) of the Securities Exchange Act of 1934 gives the Securities and Exchange Commission (SEC) the authority to regulate the solicitation of proxies.[1] The federal proxy rules promote full disclosure. In other words, management or any other

EXHIBIT 29.1

Proxy

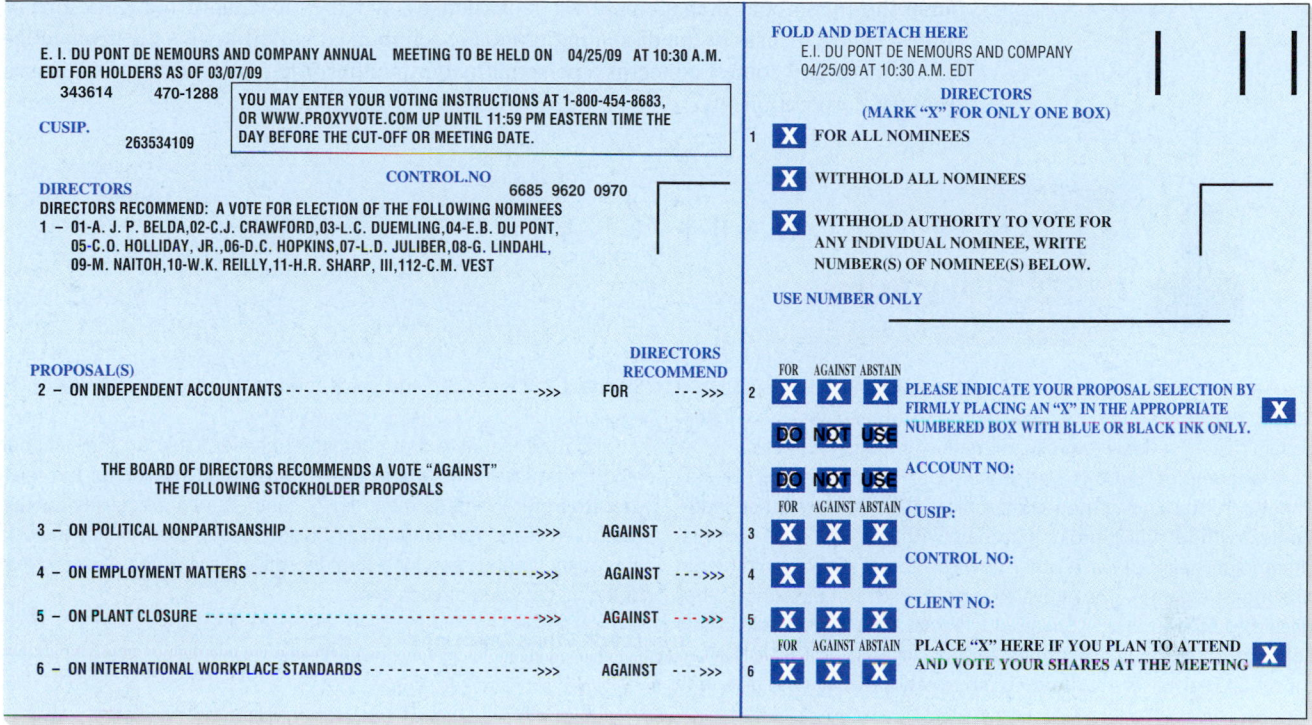

party soliciting proxies from shareholders must prepare a **proxy statement** that fully describes (1) the matter for which the proxy is being solicited, (2) who is soliciting the proxy, and (3) any other pertinent information.

A copy of the proxy, the proxy statement, and all other solicitation material must be filed with the SEC at least 10 days before the materials are sent to the shareholders. If the SEC requires additional disclosures, the solicitation can be held up until these disclosures are made.

Antifraud Provision

Section 14(a) of the Securities Exchange Act of 1934 is an **antifraud provision** that prohibits material misrepresentations or omissions of a material fact in the proxy materials. Known false statements of facts, reasons, opinions, or beliefs in proxy solicitation materials are actionable. Violations of this rule can result in civil and criminal actions by the SEC and the Justice Department, respectively. The courts have implied a private cause of action under this provision. Thus, shareholders who are injured by a material misrepresentation or omission in proxy materials can sue the wrongdoer and recover damages. The court can also order a new election if a violation is found.

Proxy Contests

Shareholders sometimes oppose the actions taken by the **incumbent directors** and management. These **insurgent shareholders** may challenge the incumbent management in a **proxy contest**, in which both sides solicit proxies from the other shareholders. The side that receives the greatest number of votes wins the proxy contest. Such contests are usually held with regard to the election of directors.

Management must either (1) provide a list of shareholders to the dissenting group or (2) mail the proxy solicitation materials of the challenging group to the shareholders.

REIMBURSEMENT OF EXPENSES In a proxy contest, both sides usually spend considerable amounts of money on legal expenses, media campaigns, mailers, telephone solicitations, and the like. If a proxy contest involves an issue of policy, the corporation must reimburse the incumbent management for its expenses, whether it wins or loses the proxy contest. The expenses of the dissenting group are reimbursed only if it wins the proxy contest. If the proxy contest concerns a personal matter, neither side may recover its expenses from the corporation.

CONTEMPORARY ENVIRONMENT

SEC Proxy Rules

The Securities Exchange Commission (SEC), the federal administrative agency empowered to administer federal securities laws, has adopted certain rules that apply to proxy solicitation and proxy contests.

A shareholder who is not seeking proxy voting authority may engage in oral and written communications with any other shareholder without filing proxy materials with the SEC. For example, shareholders can ask each other how the corporation should be run or suggest changes. They have to register with the SEC only if they decide to solicit proxies. Shareholders who own more than $5 million of the company's securities are not covered by this rule. They must still register any written communication to shareholders with the SEC.

SEC rules requires companies seeking proxies to "unbundle" the propositions set for shareholder vote so that the shareholders can vote on each separate issue. Previous proxy rules allowed companies to bundle the propositions and present them as one package for a single shareholder vote. This tactic prevented shareholders from considering the merits of individual propositions.

SEC rules require all companies to include performance charts in their annual reports. These charts must compare the company's stock performance to that of a general index of companies, such as the Standard & Poor's 500, and companies in its peer group index (e.g., retailers).

SEC rules mandate that companies provide tables in their annual reports that succinctly summarize executive compensation for the chief executive officer and its most highly compensated executives for the past three years. The tables must disclose salary, stock options, stock appreciation rights, and long-term incentive plans of these executives, including the value of each item.

Law & Ethics Questions

1. What is a proxy? Explain.

2. What is a proxy contest? Why is a proxy contest fought?

3. **ETHICS** Do you think that the incumbent management has an advantage in a proxy contest? Why or why not?

Web Exercises

1. **WEB** Visit the website of the Securities Exchange Commission (SEC), at *www.sec.gov*.

2. **WEB** Use *www.google.com* to find an article that discusses a recent proxy contest. Who won?

Shareholder Resolutions

At times, shareholders may wish to submit issues for a vote to other shareholders. The Securities Exchange Act of 1934 and SEC rules adopted thereunder permit a shareholder to submit a resolution to be considered by other shareholders if (1) the shareholder owned at least 1,000 shares of the corporation's stock for at least two years and (2) the resolution does not exceed 550 words. Such **shareholder resolutions** are usually made when the corporation is soliciting proxies from its shareholders.

If management does not oppose a resolution, it may be included in the proxy materials issued by the corporation. Even if management is not in favor of a resolution, a shareholder has a right to have the shareholder resolution included in the corporation's proxy materials if it (1) relates to the corporation's business, (2) concerns a *policy issue* (and not the day-to-day operations of the corporation), and (3) does not concern the payment of dividends. The SEC rules on whether a resolution can be submitted to shareholders.

Example Shareholder resolutions have been presented concerning protecting the environment, reducing global warming, preventing the overcutting of the rain forests in Brazil, and prohibiting U.S. corporations from purchasing goods manufactured in developing countries under poor working conditions, including the use of forced and child labor.

Most shareholder resolutions have a slim chance of being enacted because large-scale investors usually support management. They can, however, cause a corporation to change the way it does business. For example, to avoid the adverse publicity such issues can create, some corporations voluntarily adopt the changes contained in shareholder resolutions. Others negotiate settlements with the sponsors of resolutions to get the measures off the agenda before the annual shareholders' meetings.

ETHICS SPOTLIGHT

Shareholder Resolution

The E. I. du Pont de Nemours and Company (DuPont), organized under the laws of the state of Delaware, is one of the largest chemical and consumer products companies in the world. As such, DuPont has manufacturing and production facilities located in many foreign countries. Several of these countries have been criticized because child labor and forced labor are alleged to be used to produce goods in those countries.

At its annual meeting, the International Brotherhood of Teamsters General Fund, owner of shares of DuPont common stock, proposed the following shareholder resolution to the shareholders of DuPont:

Stockholder Proposal on International Workplace Standards

RESOLVED: *That the Board of Directors of E. I. du Pont de Nemours and Company (Du Pont) shall adopt, implement and enforce the workplace Code of Conduct (Code) as based on the International Labor Organization's (ILO) Conventions on workplace human rights, which include:*

- *No use of child labor.*
- *No discrimination or intimidation in employment.*
- *All workers have the right to form and join unions and to bargain collectively.*
- *No use of forced labor.*

Stockholder's (Teamster's) Statement in support of the proposal:
The Teamsters, in support of its proposal, provided the following statement in Du Pont's annual Proxy Statement submitted to Du Pont shareholders.

As a global institution, Du Pont and its international operations and sourcing arrangements are exposed to sundry risks. Adoption of this proposal manages the risk of being a party to serious human rights violations in the workplace. Du Pont operates or has business relationships in a number of countries, including China, Indonesia, and Thailand, where the U.S. State Department, Amnesty International, and Human Rights Watch indicate law and public policy do not adequately protect human rights. To wit: Forced labor, illegal child labor, and violence against women.

The success of Du Pont's operations depends on consumer and governmental good will. Brand name is a significant asset. Du Pont benefits from adopting and enforcing the Code ensuring that it isn't associated with human rights violations. This protects Du Pont's brand names and its relationships with customers and the numerous governments under which Du Pont operates and with which it does business.

Position of the Board of Directors in Opposition to the Proposal

In response, Du Pont included the following statement in the Proxy Statement, recommending that Du Pont shareholders vote against the shareholder resolution.

Du Pont is committed to conducting its business affairs with the highest ethical standards, and works diligently to be a respected corporate citizen throughout the world. The company has had in place for many years an Ethics Policy, Mission Statement and Code of Business Conduct addressing many of the issues covered in the standards proposed for adoption. These corporate policies are applicable to all employees in all Du Pont businesses around the world.

The company is supportive of the general intent of the proposal and similar international workplace standards suggested by other organizations for adoption. The company reviews on an ongoing basis codes offered by other organizations, and examines its own policies and practices in light of the provisions of the proposed codes. The company also meets with advocates of codes to explore issues of mutual concern. These efforts will continue. The company therefore believes adoption of the proposed code is unnecessary.

The shareholder resolution for the adoption of International Workplace Standards was defeated by an overwhelming majority of DuPont shareholders at the annual meeting.

Law & Ethics Questions

1. What is a shareholder resolution? Explain.

2. **ETHICS** Why do you think the International Brotherhood of Teamsters introduced this shareholder resolution?

3. **ETHICS** Do you think the reasons DuPont asserted for recommending that its shareholders vote against the proposal were legitimate? Explain.

4. Why do shareholders submit shareholder resolutions for a vote of the shareholders when they know that the shareholder resolutions will probably not pass?

Web Exercises

1. **WEB** Visit the website of E. I. du Pont de Nemours and Company, at *www.dupont.com*. Can you find its most current proxy statement?

2. **WEB** Visit the website of the International Brotherhood of Teamsters, at *www.teamsters.org*. What are some of the issues that the Teamsters are concerned about?

3. **WEB** Use *www.google.com* to find a recent article that discusses a shareholder resolution. Read it.

Mergers and Acquisitions

Corporations may agree to friendly acquisitions or combinations of one another. This may be by (1) merger, (2) consolidation, (3) share exchange, or (4) sale of assets. These types of combinations are discussed in the following paragraphs.

Mergers

A **merger** occurs when one corporation is absorbed into another corporation and ceases to exist. The corporation that continues to exist is called the **surviving corporation**. The other corporation, which ceases to exist, is called the **merged corporation** [RMBCA Section 11.01]. The surviving corporation gains all the rights, privileges, powers, duties, obligations, and liabilities of the merged corporation. Title to property owned by the merged corporation transfers to the surviving corporation, without formality or deeds. The shareholders of the merged corporation receive stock or securities of the surviving corporation or other consideration, as provided in the plan of merger.

Example Suppose that Corporation A and Corporation B merge and it is agreed that Corporation A will absorb Corporation B. Corporation A is the surviving corporation. Corporation B is the merged corporation. A symbolic representation of this merger is A + B = A (see Exhibit 29.2).

Consolidations

A **consolidation** occurs when two or more corporations combine to form an entirely new corporation (i.e., there is no surviving corporation). The two consolidated corporations are called *merged corporations* and cease to exist. The new corporation is called the *consolidated corporation*. The articles of incorporation of the new corporation replace the articles of incorporation of the component corporations.

Example Suppose that Corporation A and Corporation B consolidate to form a new organization called Corporation C. A symbolic representation of this combination is A + B = C (see Exhibit 29.3).

EXHIBIT 29.2

Merger

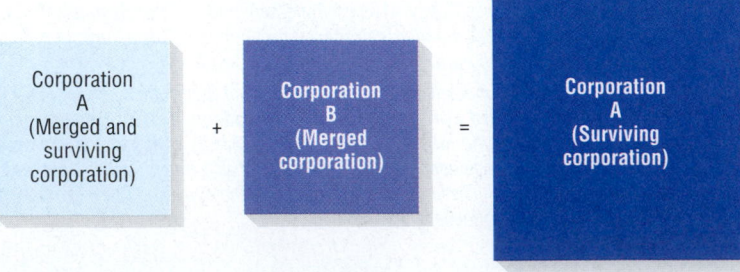

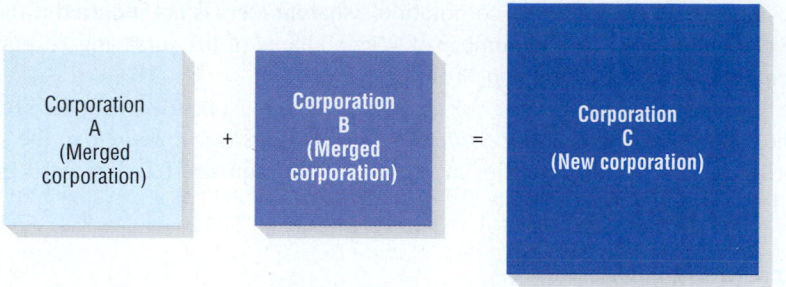

EXHIBIT 29.3

Consolidation

The new corporation accedes to all the rights, privileges, powers, duties, obligations, and liabilities of the constituent corporations. Title to property owned by the component corporations transfers to the new corporation, without any formality. The shareholders receive stock or other securities in the consolidated corporation or other agreed-upon consideration. Today, consolidations are not used very often because it is generally advantageous for one of the corporations to survive.

Share Exchanges

One corporation can acquire all the shares of another corporation through a **share exchange**. In a share exchange, both corporations retain their separate legal existence. After the exchange, one corporation (the *parent corporation*) owns all the shares of the other corporation (the *subsidiary corporation*) [RMBCA Section 1102]. Such exchanges are often used to create holding company arrangements (e.g., bank or insurance holding companies).

Example Suppose that Corporation A wants to acquire Corporation B. Assume that Corporation A offers to exchange its shares for those of Corporation B and that Corporation B's shareholders approve of the transaction. After the share exchange, Corporation A owns all the stock of Corporation B. Corporation A is the parent corporation, and Corporation B is the wholly owned subsidiary of Corporation A (see Exhibit 29.4).

Required Approvals for a Merger or Share Exchange

An ordinary merger or share exchange requires (1) the recommendation of the board of directors of each corporation and (2) an affirmative vote of the majority of shares of each corporation that is entitled to vote [RMBCA Section 11.03]. The articles of incorporation or corporate bylaws can require the approval of a *supramajority*, such as 80 percent of the voting shares.

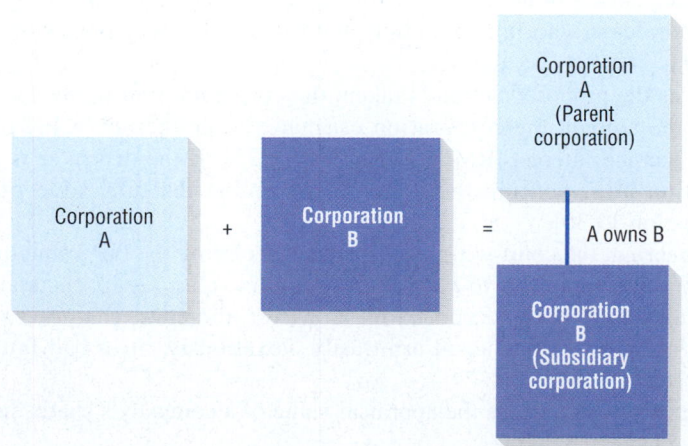

EXHIBIT 29.4

Share Exchange

The approval of the surviving corporation's shareholders is not required if the merger or share exchange increases the number of voting shares of the surviving corporation by 20 percent or less [RMBCA Section 11.03(g)].

The approved *articles of merger or share exchange* must be filed with the secretary of state. The state normally issues a *certificate of merger or share exchange* to the surviving corporation after all the formalities are met and the requisite fees are paid [RMBCA Section 11.05].

Short-Form Mergers

If one corporation (called the *parent corporation*) owns 90 percent or more of the outstanding stock of another corporation (known as the *subsidiary corporation*), a **short-form merger** procedure may be followed to merge the two corporations. A short-form merger procedure is simpler than an ordinary merger because neither the approval of the shareholders of either corporation nor the approval of the board of directors of the subsidiary corporation is needed. All that is required is the approval of the board of directors of the parent corporation [RMBCA Section 11.04].

Sale or Lease of Assets

A corporation may sell, lease, or otherwise dispose of all or substantially all of its property in other than the usual and regular course of business. Such a **sale or lease of assets** requires (1) the recommendation of the board of directors and (2) an affirmative vote of the majority of the shares of the selling or leasing corporation that is entitled to vote (unless greater vote is required) [RMBCA Section 12.02]. This rule prevents the board of directors from selling all or most of the assets of the corporation without shareholder approval.

Dissenting Shareholder Appraisal Rights

Specific shareholders sometimes object to a proposed ordinary or short-form merger, share exchange, or sale or lease of all or substantially all of the property of a corporation, even though the transaction received the required approvals. Objecting shareholders are provided a statutory right to dissent and obtain payment of the fair value of their shares [RMBCA Section 13.02]. This is referred to as a **dissenting shareholder appraisal right**, or an **appraisal right**. Shareholders have no other recourse unless the transaction is unlawful or fraudulent.

A corporation must notify shareholders of the existence of their appraisal rights before a transaction can be voted on [RMBCA Section 13.20]. To obtain appraisal rights, a dissenting shareholder must (1) deliver written notice of his or her intent to demand payment of his or her shares to the corporation before the vote is taken and (2) not vote his or her shares in favor of the proposed action [RMBCA Section 13.23]. The shareholder must deposit his or her share certificates with the corporation [RMBCA Section 13.23]. Shareholders who fail to comply with these statutory procedures lose their appraisal rights.

As soon as the proposed action is taken, the corporation must pay each dissenting shareholder the amount the corporation estimates to be the fair value of his or her shares, plus accrued interest [RMBCA Section 13.25]. If the dissenter is dissatisfied, the corporation must petition the court to determine the fair value of the shares [RMBCA Section 13.30].

After a hearing, the court will issue an order declaring the fair value of the shares. Appraisers may be appointed to help determine this value. Court costs and appraisal fees are usually paid by the corporation. However, the court can assess these costs against the dissenters if they acted arbitrarily, vexatiously, or in bad faith [RMBCA Section 13.31].

The court had to determine the appraisal value of a company's shares in the following case.

CASE 29.1

Dissenting Shareholder Appraisal Rights

In the Matter of the Appraisal of Shell Oil Company

607 A.2d 1213,
Web 992 Del. Lexis 193
Supreme Court of Delaware

> **" *Valuation is an art rather than a science.* "**
>
> —Judge Walsh

Facts

Royal Dutch Petroleum Company (Royal Dutch), a large natural resource conglomerate, owned 94.6 percent of the stock of Shell Oil Company (Shell). The remaining shares of Shell were held by minority, public shareholders. Royal Dutch effectuated a short-form merger with Shell and offered $60 cash per share for the outstanding shares of Shell that it did not own. After the merger was complete, 1,005,001 shares had not accepted the offer and qualified for appraisal rights. The Delaware chancery court conducted an appraisal hearing. The parties offered extensive evidence through expert witnesses. These experts gave the following estimated per-share values for Shell's shares:

Valuation Method	Shell's Expert	Shareholders' Expert
Liquidation value	$57	$100
Comparative value	$60	$106
Market value	$43–$45	$92–$143

Liquidation value was the estimated value if Shell were dissolved and its assets sold. Comparative value was an estimate based on a price reflected by prices in similar transactions in the oil and gas industry. Market value was an estimated price that Shell shares would sell for without the effect of merger speculation.

The chancery court determined that the fair value was $71.20 per share. It further held that the shareholders were entitled to 10 percent interest on that amount from the date of the merger to the date of payment. Both parties appealed.

Issue

What price should Shell be required to pay its minority shareholders who demanded appraisal rights?

Language of the Court

After reviewing the valuation evidence in its effort to fix the fair value of Shell stock on the date of the merger, the Court of Chancery expressed some dissatisfaction with the lack of objectivity in the presentations. The court noted that it was "obvious that the dynamics of this litigation and the economic interest of the parties contributed to the wide differences in the expert opinions."

Valuation is an art rather than a science. So too is the weighing of evidence in the appraisal process. More than anything else, this emphasizes the broad discretion which the Court of Chancery must have in fixing values. The Vice Chancellor's conclusions are amply supported by the record and the product of an orderly and logical deductive process. We therefore decline to disturb them.

Decision

The supreme court of Delaware affirmed the award granted by the chancery court.

Law & Ethics Questions

1. Should the law provide dissenting shareholder appraisal rights? Why or why not?

2. **ETHICS** Do you think expert witnesses act objectively?

3. **ETHICS** Is there a temptation for a company to "lowball" the cash-out price offered to shareholders in a merger? Explain.

Web Exercises

1. **WEB** For the complete opinion of this case, go to *www.prenhall.com/cheesemancases*.

2. **WEB** Visit the website of the supreme court of Delaware, at *http://courts.delaware.gov/Courts/SupremeCourt*.

3. **WEB** Visit the website of Shell Oil Company, at *www.shell.com*.

4. **WEB** Use *www.google.com* to find an article or a case that discusses the valuation of stock in a merger or an acquisition. Read it.

ETHICS SPOTLIGHT

Golden Parachutes

The term *golden parachute* has been coined to describe the large severance payments that top executives receive when they leave their employ at a corporation. They are called "golden" because of their lucrative nature. They are called "parachutes" because they are "pulled" when an executive leaves or is fired from a company that has been taken over.

Golden parachutes are long-term employment contracts. They usually provide that all cash payments and stock options due under the contract become due and payable immediately upon the occurrence of the trigger—the takeover of the company.

Example Suppose that a company enters into a three-year employment contract with its president and agrees to pay a $1 million salary annually and grant options to purchase 10,000 shares of the company stock at $10 per share. The contract includes a golden parachute clause in the event of a takeover. Suppose the company is taken over in a $15-per-share tender offer. The president can "pull" his or her parachute and demand $3 million in salary as well as making $1.5 million profit by exercising his stock options.

Two benefits of golden parachutes are often cited. First, they are necessary to lure talented executives and keep them from looking for other positions when a takeover of the company is pending. Second, they act as an antitakeover device, protecting a company from hostile takeovers. Both of these reasons have been challenged as a cover-up for the real reason for golden parachutes: top executives' greed.

Law & Ethics Questions

1. Do you think top executives' compensation is too high? Explain.

2. **ETHICS** Are golden parachutes a legitimate compensation scheme, or are they an egregious example of management greed?

Tender Offers

Recall that a merger, a consolidation, a share exchange, and a sale of assets all require the approval of the board of directors of the corporation whose assets or shares are to be acquired. If the board of directors of the target corporation does not agree to a merger or an acquisition, the acquiring corporation can make a **tender offer** for the shares directly to the shareholders of the **target corporation**. The shareholders each make an individual decision about whether to sell their shares to the **tender offeror** (see Exhibit 29.5). Such offers are often referred to as *hostile tender offers*.

The tender offeror's board of directors must approve the offer, although the shareholders do not have to approve. The offer can be made for all or a portion of the shares of the target corporation.

In a tender offer, the tendering corporation and the target corporation retain their separate legal status. However, a successful tender offer is sometimes followed by a merger of the two corporations.

EXHIBIT 29.5

Tender Offer

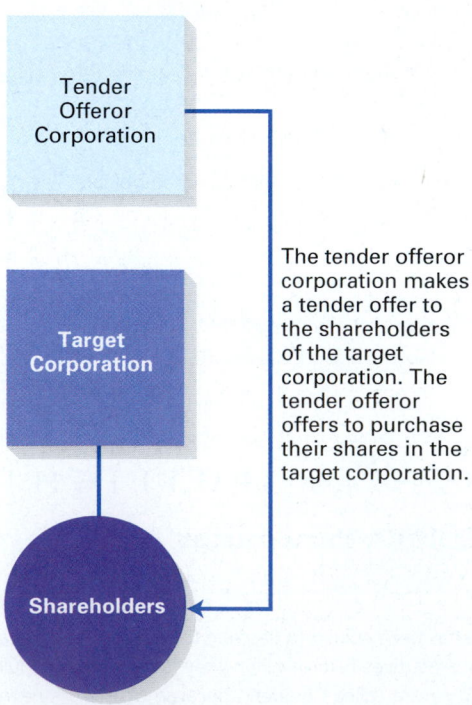

The tender offeror corporation makes a tender offer to the shareholders of the target corporation. The tender offeror offers to purchase their shares in the target corporation.

The Williams Act

Prior to 1968, tender offers were not federally regulated. However, securities that were issued in conjunction with such offers had to be registered with the SEC or qualify for an exemption from registration. Tender offers made with cash were not subject to any federal disclosure requirements.

In 1968, Congress enacted the **Williams Act** as an amendment to the Securities Exchange Act of 1934.[2] This act specifically regulates all tender offers, whether they are made with securities, cash, or other consideration, and it establishes certain disclosure requirements and antifraud provisions.

Tender Offer Rules

The Williams Act does not require a tender offeror to notify either the management of the target company or the SEC until the offer is made.[3] Detailed information regarding the terms, conditions, and other information concerning the tender offer must be disclosed at that time.

Tender offers are governed by the following rules:

1. The offer cannot be closed before 20 business days after the commencement of the tender offer.
2. The offer must be extended for 10 business days if the tender offeror increases the number of shares it will take or the price it will pay for the shares.
3. The **fair price rule** stipulates that any increase in price paid for shares tendered must be offered to all shareholders, even those who have previously tendered their shares.
4. The **pro rata rule** holds that the shares must be purchased on a pro rata basis if too many shares are tendered.

A shareholder who tenders his or her shares has the absolute right to withdraw them at any time prior to the closing of the tender offer. The dissenting shareholder appraisal rights are not available.

Antifraud Provision

Section 14(e) of the Williams Act prohibits fraudulent, deceptive, and manipulative practices in connection with a tender offer.[4] Violations of this section may result in civil charges brought by the SEC or criminal charges brought by the Justice Department. The courts have implied a private civil cause of action under Section 14(e). Therefore, a shareholder who has been injured by a violation of Section 14(e) can sue the wrongdoer for damages.

CONTEMPORARY ENVIRONMENT
Leveraged Buyout

Many tender offerors do not have the hundreds of millions or billions of dollars necessary to purchase the stock from the shareholders of the target corporation. Instead, the tender offeror relies on the fact that the money can be raised from creditors. Many tender offers are not possible without such loans. Because of the use of borrowed money, these acquisitions are called **leveraged buyouts (LBOs)**.

A typical LBO works as follows. The tender offeror identifies a potential target and then contacts a large commercial bank and an investment banker. For a large fee, the commercial bank agrees to supply some of the funds necessary to make the initial acquisition. The bank will be paid off at a later date, after the acquisition is successful.

Most of the rest of the purchase price comes from money raised by the investment banker by selling **junk bonds** of the acquiring firm to investors. Junk bonds are risky bonds that pay a higher rate of interest than normal corporate bonds. Generally, the buyers are banks, pension funds, investment pools, and wealthy individuals. The tender offeror pays the investment banker a huge fee for raising this money. With the borrowed money in hand, the tender offeror commences its hostile tender offer for the shares of the target corporation.

After the tender offer is completed, the tender offeror usually merges with the target corporation. The resulting entity is a highly leveraged corporation. The tender offeror usually sells off some of the assets to pay the bank loans, fees, and other expenses of the takeover.

Fighting a Tender Offer

The incumbent management of the target of a hostile tender offer may not want the corporation taken over by the tender offeror. Therefore, it may engage in various activities to impede and defeat the tender offer. Incumbent management may use some of the following strategies and tactics in defending against hostile tender offers:

1. *Persuasion of shareholders.* Media campaigns are often organized to convince shareholders that the tender offer is not in their best interests.
2. *Delaying lawsuits.* Lawsuits may be filed, alleging that the tender offer violates securities laws, antitrust laws, or other laws. The time gained by this tactic gives management the opportunity to erect or implement other defensive maneuvers.
3. *Selling a crown jewel.* Such assets as profitable divisions or real estate that are particularly attractive to outside interests—that is, **crown jewels**—may be sold. This tactic makes the target corporation less attractive to the tender offeror.
4. *Adopting a poison pill.* **Poison pills** are defensive strategies that are built into the target corporation's articles of incorporation, corporate bylaws, or contracts and leases. For example, contracts and leases may provide that they will expire if the ownership of the corporation changes hands. These tactics make the target corporation more expensive to the tender offeror.
5. *White knight merger.* **White knight mergers** are mergers with friendly parties—that is, parties that promise to leave the target corporation and/or its management intact.
6. *Pac-Man tender offer.* With a **Pac-Man (or reverse) tender offer**, the target corporation makes a tender offer on the tender offeror. Thus, the target corporation tries to purchase the tender offeror.
7. *Issuing additional stock.* Placing additional stock on the market increases the number of outstanding shares that the tender offeror must purchase in order to gain control of the target corporation.
8. *Creating an employee stock ownership plan (ESOP).* A company may create an **employee stock ownership plan (ESOP)** and place a certain percentage of the corporation's securities (e.g., 15 percent) in it. The ESOP is then expected to vote the shares it owns against the potential acquirer in a proxy contest or tender offer because the beneficiaries (i.e., the employees) have a vested interest in keeping the company intact.
9. *Flip-over and flip-in rights plans.* These plans provide that existing shareholders of the target corporation may convert their shares for a greater amount (e.g., twice the value) of shares of the acquiring corporation (*flip-over rights plan*) or debt securities of the target company (*flip-in rights plan*). Rights plans are triggered if the acquiring firm acquires a certain percentage (e.g., 20 percent) of the shares of the target corporation. They make it more expensive for the acquiring firm to take over the target corporation.
10. *Greenmail and standstill agreements.* Most tender offerors purchase a block of stock in the target corporation before making an offer. Occasionally, the tender offeror will agree to give up its tender offer and agree not to purchase any further shares if the target corporation agrees to buy back the stock at a premium over fair market value. This payment is called **greenmail**. The agreement of the tender offeror to abandon its tender offer and not purchase any additional stock is called a **standstill agreement**.

There are many other strategies and tactics that target companies initiate and implement in defending against a tender offer.

> The usual trade and commerce is cheating all round by consent.
>
> Thomas Fuller
> *Gnomologia (1732)*

Business Judgment Rule

The members of the board of directors of a corporation owe a *fiduciary duty* to the corporation and its shareholders. This duty, which requires the board to act carefully and honestly, is truly tested when a tender offer is made for the stock of the company. That is because shareholders and others then ask whether the board's initiation and implementation or defensive measures were taken in the best interests of the shareholders or to protect the board's own interests and jobs.

The legality of defensive strategies is examined using the **business judgment rule**. This rule protects the decisions of a board of directors that acts on an informed basis, in good faith, and in the honest belief that the action taken was in the best interests of the corporation and its shareholders.[5] In the context of a tender offer, the defensive measures chosen by the board must be reasonable in relation to the threat posed.[6]

In the following case, the court found that certain defensive tactics by a target corporation violated the law.

CASE 29.2
Tender Offer

Paramount Communications, Inc. v. QVC Network, Inc.

637 A.2d 34,
Web 1994 Del. Lexis 57
Supreme Court of Delaware

> **"** *Paramount must be put on the block and auctioned to the highest bidder.* **"**
>
> —Judge Veasey

Facts

Viacom, Inc. (Viacom), and Paramount Communications, Inc. (Paramount), announced a friendly merger agreement. Basically, Viacom was taking over Paramount. Viacom controlled national cable networks, including Showtime and The Movie Channel. Paramount's holdings included Paramount Pictures, the Simon & Schuster publishing company, Madison Square Garden, the New York Knicks basketball team, and the New York Rangers hockey team. Both sides touted the synergism of the marriage of these two companies into a media colossus.

Five days later, QVC Network, Inc. (QVC), a rival cable operator, made a $90-per-share hostile bid for Paramount that topped Viacom's merger offer. Paramount's board of directors, which did not want Paramount to be taken over by QVC, adopted the following anti-takeover strategies:

1. A **no-shop provision** whereby the Paramount board guaranteed Viacom that it would not investigate QVC's offer or meet with QVC.

2. A **lockup option** that granted Viacom (but not QVC) the right to buy 23.7 million shares of Paramount at $69.14 each if a bidder other than Viacom bought Paramount.

3. An agreement to drop certain poison pill defenses as to Viacom but not as to QVC. (Thus, Viacom could pursue its acquisition of Paramount, but QVC could not.)

QVC sued Paramount in Delaware chancery court, alleging that these tactics violated the fiduciary duty of the Paramount board of directors to the corporation and its shareholders. The Delaware chancery court agreed with QVC that Paramount's defensive strategies were unlawful. Paramount appealed.

Issue

Do the defensive tactics that Paramount's board of directors adopted violate their fiduciary duties?

Language of the Court

The Delaware Supreme Court ruled as follows:

1. The no-shop provision was unlawful, and the Paramount directors had a duty to continue their search for the best value available to its shareholders.

2. The less-than-fair-market-value lockup option stock purchase plan was an illegal transfer of corporate wealth to Viacom at the expense of Paramount shareholders.

3. The poison pills that Paramount had erected must be dismantled for QVC and any other bidder as they had been dismantled for Viacom.

4. Paramount must be put on the block and auctioned to the highest bidder.

Decision

The Delaware supreme court invalidated Paramount's no-shop provision and lockup option. The court held that once a Delaware corporation has put itself "in play," it must remove all poison pills as to all possible bidders and put itself up for auction to be purchased by the highest bidder.

Note: After escalating bids from both Viacom and QVC, the five-month saga ended when Viacom won the right to buy Paramount with a $10-plus-billion bid.

Law & Ethics Questions

1. Can the management of a target company fight a tender offer? Explain.

2. **ETHICS** Did the board of directors of Paramount act in their shareholders' best interests by adopting the defensive maneuvers?

3. **ETHICS** Does a no-shop option work in the best interests of a company's shareholders? Explain.

4. **ETHICS**   What effect would the less-than-fair-market-value lockup option stock purchase plan offered to Viacom by Paramount's directors have on the shareholders of Paramount? Explain.

5. Are many corporations safe from being taken over by tender offerors?

Web Exercises

1. **WEB**   For the complete opinion of this case, go to *www.prenhall.com/cheesemancases*.

2. **WEB**   Visit the website of Paramount Pictures, at *www.paramount.com*.

3. **WEB**   Visit the website of QVC Network, Inc., at *www.qvc.com*.

4. **WEB**   Visit the website of Viacom, Inc., at *www.viacom.com*.

5. **WEB**   Use *www.google.com* to find an article about a recent tender offer. Was it successful?

ETHICS SPOTLIGHT

"Just Say No" Defense

❝*The corporation law does not operate on the theory that directors are obligated to follow the wishes of a majority of shares. In fact, directors, not shareholders, are charged with the duty to manage the firm.*❞

—Judge Horsey

Time, Inc. (Time), was a publishing company that published *People*, *Money*, *Sports Illustrated*, and other magazines and newspapers; it also owned cable television and pay television channels. Warner Communications, Inc. (Warner), was a communications company that produced and sold movies, television programs, and records, and it also owns cable stations. After years of negotiations, Time and Warner agreed to a merger. Based on the agreed-upon ratio of exchange, Time shareholders were to receive $120 in stock of the new TimeWarner for each share of Time stock they owned. The shareholders' meetings to vote on the merger were set.

Paramount Communications, Inc. (Paramount), was a film production and distribution company. For years, it had been looking for an acquisition in the publishing and communications industry. Two weeks before the Time shareholders were to vote on the planned merger with Warner, Paramount announced a hostile tender offer for Time's shares at $175 per share.

Time, which was obviously going to lose the shareholder vote, canceled the proposed merger with Warner and made a friendly tender offer to acquire 50 percent of Warner's stock for $70 per share. This acquisition would make Time too big for Paramount to take over. In addition, the vote of Time shareholders would not be required. Time had other defensive maneuvers in place as well.

Paramount sued Time, alleging that the refusal of Time's management to dismantle the poison pills and put Time on the block violated their fiduciary duty. In defense, Time argued that the merger of Time and Warner was in the best interests of Time shareholders over the long run and that the long-term benefits of the combination of Time and Warner and their cultures would create synergism that would pay off in the future; Paramount's tender offer offered only one-time short-term profits.

The Delaware court applied the business judgment rule and sided with Time. The court held that the projected long-term benefits to Time shareholders justified Time's management's refusal to dismantle the poison pills. The court stated: "The corporation law does not operate on the theory that directors are obligated to follow the wishes of a majority of shares. In fact, directors, not shareholders, are charged with the duty to manage the firm." Thus, incumbent management of a target corporation can "just say no" to a tender offer, as long as it can show that it is acting in the long-term interests of the shareholders. *Paramount Communications, Inc. v. Time, Inc.*, 571 A.2d 1140, **Web** 1989 Del. Lexis 917 (Supreme Court of Delaware)

Law & Ethics Questions

1. What does the "just say no" defense upheld by the supreme court of Delaware provide? Explain.

2. **ETHICS**   Is it ethical for a board of directors of a corporation to go against the wishes of its shareholders?

Web Exercises

1. **WEB**   For the complete opinion of this case, go to *www.prenhall.com/cheesemancases*.

2. **WEB**   Visit the website of the supreme court of Delaware, at *http://courts.delaware.gov/Courts/SupremeCourt*.

3. **WEB**   Visit the website of TimeWarner, at *www.timewarner.com*.

4. **WEB**   Visit the website of Paramount Pictures, at *www.paramount.com*.

5. **WEB**   Use *www.google.com* to find an article that discusses a tender offer. Read it.

State Antitakeover Statutes

Many states have enacted **antitakeover statutes** that are aimed at protecting corporations that are either incorporated in or do business within the state from hostile takeovers. Many of these state statutes have been challenged as being unconstitutional because they violate the Williams Act and the Commerce and Supremacy Clauses of the U.S. Constitution.

In the following case, the U.S. Supreme Court held that a state antitakeover statute was constitutional.

C A S E 29.3 *State Antitakeover Statute*	**U.S. SUPREME COURT** **CTS Corporation v. Dynamics Corporation of America** 481 U.S. 69, 107 S.Ct. 1637, 95 L.Ed.2d. 67, **Web** 1987 U.S. Lexis 1811 Supreme Court of the United States

> " *The desire of the Indiana legislature to protect shareholders of Indiana corporations from this type of coercive offer does not conflict with the Williams Act. Rather, it furthers the federal policy of investor protection.* "
>
> —Justice Powell

Facts

Indiana enacted the Control Share Acquisitions Chapter. This act covers corporations that (1) are incorporated in Indiana and have at least 100 shareholders, (2) have their primary place of business or substantial assets in Indiana, and (3) have either 10 percent of their shareholders in Indiana or 10 percent of their shares owned by Indiana residents. The act provides that if an entity acquires 20 percent or more of the voting shares of a covered corporation, the acquirer loses voting rights to these shares unless a majority of the disinterested shareholders of the acquired corporation vote to restore such voting rights. The acquirer can request that such vote be held within 50 days after its acquisition. If the shareholders do not restore the voting rights, the target corporation may redeem the shares from the acquirer at fair market value, but it is not required to do so.

Dynamics Corporation of America (Dynamics), a Delaware corporation, announced a tender offer for 1 million shares of CTS Corporation, an Indiana corporation covered by the act. The purchase of these shares would have brought Dynamics's voting interest in CTS to 27.5 percent. Dynamics sued in federal court, alleging that Indiana's Control Share Acquisitions Chapter was unconstitutional. The U.S. District Court held for Dynamics. The Court of Appeals affirmed. CTS appealed.

Issue

Does the Indiana Control Share Acquisitions Chapter conflict with the Williams Act or violate the Commerce Clause of the U.S. Constitution by unduly burdening interstate commerce?

Language of the U.S. Supreme Court

It is entirely possible for entities to comply with both the Williams and the Indiana acts. The statute now before the court protects the independent shareholder against the contending parties. Thus, the Indiana act furthers a basic purpose of the Williams Act, placing investors on an equal footing with the takeover bidder. The Indiana act operates on the assumption that independent shareholders faced with tender offers often are at a disadvantage. By allowing such shareholders to vote as a group, the act protects them from the coercive aspects of some tender offers. Under the Indiana act, the shareholders as a group could reject the offer although individual shareholders might be inclined to accept it. The desire of the Indiana legislature to protect shareholders of Indiana corporations from this type of coercive offer does not conflict with the Williams Act. Rather, it furthers the federal policy of investor protection.

Decision

The U.S. Supreme Court held that the Indiana Control Share Acquisitions Chapter neither conflicted with the Williams Act nor violated the Commerce Clause of the U.S. Constitution. The Supreme Court reversed the decision of the Court of Appeals.

Law & Ethics Questions

1. Should states be permitted to adopt antitakeover statutes? Why or why not? Whom do you think these statutes actually protect?
2. **ETHICS** Is it ethical for a target corporation's management to assert a state antitakeover statute?
3. What are the economic effects of a state antitakeover statute?

Web Exercises

1. **WEB** For the complete opinion of this case, go to *www.prenhall.com/cheesemancases*.
2. **WEB** Visit the website of the U.S. Supreme Court, at *www.supremecourtus.gov* and try to find documents that pertain to this case.
3. **WEB** Visit the website of CTS Corporation, at *www.ctscorp.com*.
4. **WEB** Use *www.google.com* to find an article that discusses a state's antitakeover statute. How does it differ from the one in this case?

INTERNATIONAL LAW
The Exon-Florio Law

The **Exon-Florio Law** of 1988 [50 U.S.C. 2170], as amended, mandates the president of the United States to suspend, prohibit, or dismantle the acquisition of U.S. businesses by foreign investors if there is credible evidence that the foreign investor might take action that threatens to impair the "national security."

The act applies to mergers, acquisitions, takeovers, stock purchases, asset purchases, joint ventures, and proxy contests that would result in foreign control of U.S. businesses engaged in interstate commerce in the United States. The U.S. business could be a corporation, a partnership, a sole proprietorship, or another business. The size of the U.S. operation is irrelevant.

Exon-Florio and the regulations adopted thereunder do not define the term *national security*. The Treasury Department has interpreted the term broadly to include not only defense contractors but also technology and other businesses. The term *control* includes any investment exceeding 10 percent ownership in a U.S. business by a foreign investor.

When a foreign investor proposes to acquire an interest in a U.S. business, it may voluntarily notify the U.S. government of its intention. If the president of the United States finds a threat to the national security, the acquisition may be prohibited. If the foreign investor does not notify the U.S. government and completes the acquisition, it remains indefinitely subject to divestment if the president subsequently

determines that the acquisition threatens the national security. The president's decision is not subject to judicial review.

Web Exercises

1. **WEB** Use *www.google.com* to find an article that discusses the acquisition of a U.S. company by a foreign company. Read it.

2. **WEB** Use *www.google.com* to find an article about a U.S. company's acquisition of a company in a foreign country. Read it.

3. **WEB** Use *www.google.com* to find an article that discusses the application of the Exon-Florio Law to a proposed acquisition of a U.S. company by a foreign entity. Read it.

Singing Sand Mountains, Xin Jiang Autonomous Region, China

The Exon-Florio Law permits the president of the United States to prohibit certain mergers that impair the "national security."

Multinational Corporations

In the past, the size, power, and range of activities of corporations were limited. This changed at the beginning of the twentieth century, when corporations won the right to own stock in each other. National corporate networks soon followed. Eventually, parent corporations, mostly American, expanded these networks overseas by setting up subsidiary corporations under the laws of other countries. These *international networks* (or *multinational enterprises*) are made up of companies of different nationalities that constitute a single economic unit connected by shareholding, managerial control, or contractual agreement.

The simplest international operating structure is one that subcontracts with independent firms in the host country to carry out sales or purchases. *National multinational* firms that establish wholly owned branches and subsidiaries overseas are somewhat more complex. *International multinational* firms are even more complicated; they are made up of two or more parents from different countries that co-own operating businesses in two or more countries.

The Ford Motor Company is an example of a national multinational firm. Organized in the United States at the beginning of the twentieth century, Ford has always viewed the entire world as its market. The company's policy is for the U.S. parent to own and control all of its overseas subsidiaries, so the U.S. parent entirely owns Ford's 10 European subsidiaries. The Mitsubishi Companies is another example of this organizational format. It is actually made up of several Japanese companies that use joint directors' meetings to coordinate their activities in Japan and overseas.

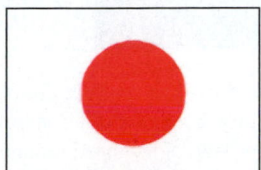

The Royal Dutch/Shell Group of companies is an example of an international multinational corporation. In 1907, the Dutch and British parents each formed a wholly owned holding company in their respective countries. Each then transferred the ownership of the operating subsidiary to the holding company and exchanged shares in the holding companies. The Dutch parent held 60 percent of each holding company, and the British parent held 40 percent. In addition, the management and operation of the two companies were organized to function as a single economic unit.

Unilever, Dunlop-Pirelli, and VFW-Fokker are also international multinational corporations.

Web Exercises

1. **WEB** Visit the website of The Ford Motor Company, at *www.ford.com*. Find information about the company's operation in foreign countries.
2. **WEB** Visit the website of the Mitsubishi Companies, at *www.mitsubishi.com*. Find information about its worldwide operations.
3. **WEB** Visit the website of Royal Dutch/Shell Group, at *www.shell.com*. Find information about its worldwide operations.
4. **WEB** Select a company that you are interested in. Use *www.google.com* to find the company's website. Is the company engaged in international operations?

INTERNATIONAL LAW
International Branch Office

A corporation can conduct business in another country by using a **branch office**. A branch office is not a separate legal entity but is merely an office of the corporation. As such, the corporation is liable for the contracts of the branch office and is also liable for the torts committed by personnel of the branch office. There is no liability shield between the corporation and the branch office.

Example Ford Motor Company, a U.S. corporation incorporated under the laws of Delaware, opens a branch office in Delhi, India, to sell its automobiles there. If an employee at the branch office in India negligently injures an Indian citizen in India while on a test drive, Ford Motor Company in the United States is wholly liable for the injured person's damages.

International Branch Office

Conducting International Business Using a Branch Office

Corporation A (in Country A)

No limited liability shield—Corporation A in Country A is liable for the tort and contract liabilities of its branch office in Country B.

Branch Office (in Country B)

The branch office is not a separate legal entity.

INTERNATIONAL LAW
International Subsidiary Corporation

A corporation can conduct business in another country by using a **subsidiary corporation**. The subsidiary corporation is organized under the laws of the foreign country. The **parent corporation** usually owns all or the majority of the subsidiary corporation. A subsidiary corporation is a separate legal entity. Therefore, the parent corporation is not liable for the contracts of or torts committed by the subsidiary corporation. There is a liability shield between the parent corporation and the subsidiary corporation.

Example Ford Motor Company, a U.S. corporation incorporated under the laws of Delaware, forms a subsidiary corporation called Ford.India Corporation, an Indian corporation formed under the laws of India, to sell automobiles in India. Ford Motor Company is the parent corporation, and Ford.India Corporation is the subsidiary corporation. If an employee of Ford.India Corporation negligently injures an Indian citizen while on a test drive, only Ford.India Corporation is liable; Ford Motor Company in the United States is not liable aside from the fact that it may lose its capital contribution in Ford.India Corporation.

International Subsidiary Corporation

Conducting International Business Using a Subsidiary Corporation

Corporation A (in Country A)

Limited liability shield—Corporation A in Country A is not liable for the tort and contract liabilities of its subsidiary corporation in Country B except up to its capital contribution in Corporation B.

Corporation B (in Country B)

Corporation B is a separate legal entity.

Chapter Summary

Proxy Solicitation and Proxy Contests, p. 808

1. *Proxy.* Shareholders can exercise their rights to vote on the election of directors, mergers, charter amendments, and the like either in person or by proxy.
2. *Proxy card.* A proxy card is a written document signed by a shareholder that authorizes another person to vote the shareholder's shares.

Federal Proxy Rules

Section 14(a) is a provision of the Securities Exchange Act of 1934 that authorizes the Securities and Exchange Commission to regulate the solicitation of proxies.

1. *Solicitation of proxies.* Solicitation of proxies occurs when management or others seek to obtain proxies from a corporation's shareholders.
2. *Proxy statement.* A proxy statement is a written document that management and others who are soliciting shareholder proxies must give to shareholders. The statement must fully describe (a) the matter for which the proxy is being solicited, (b) who is soliciting the proxy, and (c) any other pertinent information.
3. *Filing with the SEC.* Proxy statements must be filed with the SEC at least 10 days before the materials are sent to shareholders.

Antifraud Provision

Section 14(a) of the 1934 Securities Exchange Act prohibits misrepresentations or omissions of a material fact in proxy materials. The SEC, the U.S. Justice Department, shareholders, and others may sue the wrongdoer.

Proxy Contests

Proxy contests occur when opposing factions of shareholders and managers solicit proxies from other shareholders. The side that receives the greatest number of votes wins the proxy contest.

1. **Opposing groups:**
   a. *Incumbent group.* This is the management-sponsored slate of proposed directors.
   b. *Insurgent group.* This is the slate of proposed directors sponsored by the group that is challenging the incumbent group.
2. **Reimbursement of expenses.** In a proxy contest that involves a *policy issue*, the corporation pays the expenses of the incumbent management, whether the corporation wins or loses the proxy contest. If the insurgent group wins the proxy contest, the corporation must reimburse its expenses, too. If the proxy contest concerned a *personal matter*, neither side may recover its expenses from the corporation.

SEC Proxy Rules

The Securities Exchange Commission (SEC), the federal administrative agency empowered to administer federal securities laws, has adopted certain rules that apply to proxy solicitation and proxy contests.

Shareholder Resolutions, p. 810

Shareholder resolutions are submitted by a shareholder or group of shareholders to be considered and voted by the corporation's shareholders. Most shareholder resolutions concern social issues (e.g., protection of the environment, discontinuation of the manufacture and sale of dangerous products).

1. **Inclusion in proxy materials.** If management does not oppose a proposal, it may be included in the proxy materials issued by the corporation. If management opposes a shareholder resolution, the SEC rules on whether the proposal must be submitted to the shareholders in the corporation's proxy materials.
2. **Requirements.** To be included in the corporation's proxy materials, a shareholder resolution must (a) relate to the corporation's business, (b) concern policy issues (and not the day-to-day operations of the corporation), and (c) not concern the payment of dividends.

Mergers and Acquisitions, p. 812

Mergers, consolidations, and share exchanges are friendly combinations of corporations.

Mergers

A merger occurs when one corporation is absorbed into another corporation and ceases to exist. The corporation that continues to exist after a merger is called the surviving corporation. The corporation that is absorbed in the merger and ceases to exist as a separate entity is called the merged corporation.

Consolidations

A consolidation occurs when two or more corporations combine to form an entirely new corporation. The new corporation is called the consolidated corporation.

Share Exchanges

A share exchange occurs when one corporation acquires all the shares of another corporation while both corporations retain their separate legal existence. The corporation that owns the shares of the other corporation is called the parent corporation. The corporation that is owned by the other corporation is called the subsidiary corporation.

Required Approvals for a Merger or Share Exchange

An ordinary merger or share exchange requires (a) the recommendation of the board of directors of each corporation and (b) an affirmative vote of the majority of shares of each corporation that are entitled to vote (unless a greater vote is required).

1. **No shareholder vote required.** The approval of the surviving corporation's shareholders is not required if a merger or share exchange increases the number of voting shares of the surviving corporation by 20 percent or less.

2. *Articles of merger or share exchange.* This document must be filed with the secretary of state when a merger or share exchange is completed.

Short-Form Mergers

A short-form merger is a merger between a parent corporation and a subsidiary corporation where the parent corporation owns 90 percent or more of the subsidiary corporation. Only the approval of the board of directors of the parent corporation is required to effectuate a short-form merger. The votes of the shareholders of either corporation and the board of directors of the subsidiary corporation are not required.

Sale or Lease of Assets

The sale, lease, or disposition by a corporation of all or substantially all its assets not in the usual and regular course of business requires (a) the recommendation of the board of directors and (b) an affirmative vote of the majority of the shares of the selling or leasing corporation that are entitled to vote (unless a greater vote is required).

Dissenting Shareholder Appraisal Rights

Shareholders who object to a proposed merger, share exchange, or sale or lease of all or substantially all the property of a corporation have a statutory right to have their shares valued by the court and receive cash payment of this value from the corporation.

1. ***Procedures.*** A corporation must notify shareholders of their appraisal rights. To obtain appraisal rights, a shareholder must (a) deliver written notice to the corporation of his or her intent to demand payment of his or her shares before the vote is taken and (b) not vote his or her shares in favor of the proposed action.
2. ***Fair value.*** If a shareholder does not accept the value offered by the corporation, the court will determine the fair value of the shares. The court may hire appraisers to assist in making this determination. Costs of this proceeding are usually borne by the corporation.

Tender Offers, p. 816

A tender offer is an offer that an acquirer makes directly to a target corporation's shareholders in an effort to acquire the target corporation or control of the target corporation.

1. ***Tender offeror.*** The tender offeror is the party that makes a tender offer.
2. ***Target corporation.*** The target corporation is the corporation that is proposed to be acquired in a tender offer situation.

The Williams Act

The Williams Act is a federal statute that regulates all tender offers. The Securities and Exchange Commission is empowered to administer the Williams Act.

Tender Offer Rules

1. ***Notification.*** A tender offeror does not have to notify the SEC or the target corporation's management until the tender offer is made.
2. ***Completion.*** A tender offer cannot be closed before 20 business days after the commencement of the offer.
3. ***Extension.*** A tender offer must be extended for 10 business days if the tender offeror increases the number of shares it will take or the price it will pay for the shares.
4. ***Fair price rule.*** This rule stipulates that any increase in price paid for shares tendered must be offered to all shareholders, even those who have previously tendered their shares.
5. ***Pro rata rule.*** This rule provides that shares must be purchased on a pro rata basis if too many shares are tendered.
6. ***Withdrawal rights.*** Shareholders who tender their shares have an absolute right to withdraw them at any time prior to the closing of the tender offer.

Antifraud Provision

Section 14(e) of the Williams Act prohibits fraudulent, deceptive, and manipulative practices in connection with a tender offer.

Leveraged Buyout

Many tender offerors do not have the hundreds of millions or billions of dollars necessary to purchase the stock from the shareholders of the target corporation. Instead, the tender offeror relies on the fact that the money can be raised from creditors. Many tender offers are not possible without such loans. Because of the use of borrowed money, these acquisitions are called **leveraged buyouts (LBOs)**.

Fighting a Tender Offer

The management of the target corporation often takes one or more of the following steps to try to defeat a hostile tender offer:

1. Persuade the shareholders not to tender their shares.
2. File delaying lawsuits (e.g., antitrust lawsuits).
3. Sell a crown jewel (e.g., a valuable asset that the tender offeror is particularly interested in acquiring).
4. Adopt a poison pill (e.g., contract provisions that make contracts and leases expire).
5. Find a white knight to purchase the corporation in a friendly acquisition.
6. Conduct a Pac-Man tender offer (i.e., a reverse tender offer to acquire the tender offeror).
7. Issue additional stock to friendly parties.
8. Create an employee stock ownership plan (ESOP) and issue stock to the ESOP.
9. Adopt flip-over and flip-in rights plans that make it more expensive for the tender offeror to acquire shares.
10. Pay greenmail by purchasing the shares held by the tender offeror at a premium or obtain a standstill agreement whereby the offeror agrees not to purchase shares of the target corporation for a stipulated period of time.

The management of the target corporation may engage in other strategies and tactics that make it more difficult for a tender offeror to complete its tender offer.

Business Judgment Rule

The actions of the management of a target corporation in fighting a tender offer are judged by the business judgment rule. A defensive measure must be reasonable in relation to the threat posed. The business judgment rule protects the decisions of a board of directors that acts on an informed basis, in good faith, and in the honest belief that the action taken was in the best interests of the corporation and its shareholders.

State Antitakeover Statutes, p. 821

Statutes enacted by state legislatures are aimed at protecting corporations that are either incorporated in or doing business within the state from hostile takeovers. State antitakeover statutes are lawful if they do not conflict with the federal Williams Act or unduly burden interstate commerce in violation of the Commerce Clause of the U.S. Constitution.

The Exon-Florio Law

The **Exon-Florio Law** of 1988 [50 U.S.C. 2170], as amended, mandates the president of the United States to suspend, prohibit, or dismantle the acquisition of U.S. businesses by foreign investors if there is credible evidence that the foreign investor might take action that threatens to impair the "national security."

Multinational Corporations, p. 822

A multinational corporation operates in more than one country.

International Branch Office

A branch office is not a separate legal entity but is merely an office of a corporation. As such, the corporation is liable for the contracts of a branch office and is also liable for the torts committed by personnel of the branch office. There is no liability shield between the corporation and the branch office.

International Subsidiary Corporation

An international subsidiary corporation is organized under the laws of the foreign country. The parent corporation usually owns all or the majority of the subsidiary corporation. A subsidiary corporation is a separate legal entity. Therefore, the parent corporation is not liable for the contracts of or torts committed by the subsidiary corporation. There is a liability shield between the parent corporation and the subsidiary corporation.

Test Review Terms and Concepts

Antifraud provision   809
Antitakeover statute   821
Branch office   823
Business judgment rule   819
Consolidation   812
Crown jewel   818
Dissenting shareholder appraisal right
  (appraisal right)   814
Employee stock ownership plan
  (ESOP)   818
Exon-Florio Law   822
Fair price rule   817
Greenmail   818
Incumbent director   809
Insurgent shareholder   809

Junk bond   817
Leveraged buyout (LBO)   817
Lockup option   819
Merged corporation   812
Merger   812
Multinational corporation   808
No-shop provision   819
Pac-Man (or reverse) tender offer   818
Parent corporation   824
Poison pill   818
Pro rata rule   817
Proxy card   808
Proxy contest   809
Proxy solicitation   808
Proxy statement   809

Sale or lease of assets   814
Section 14(a) of the Securities
  Exchange Act of 1934   808
Section 14(e) of the Williams Act   817
Share exchange   813
Shareholder resolution   810
Short-form merger   814
Standstill agreement   818
Subsidiary corporation   824
Surviving corporation   812
Target corporation   816
Tender offer   816
Tender offeror   816
White knight merger   818
Williams Act   817

Case Problems

29.1 Proxy in Disclosure: Western Maryland Company (Western) was a timbering and mining concern. A substantial portion of its stock was owned by CSX Minerals (CSX), its parent corporation. The remaining shares were owned by several minority shareholders, including Sanford E. Lockspeiser. Western's stock was not publicly traded. The board of directors of Western voted to merge the company with CSX. Western distributed to the minority shareholders a proxy statement which stated that CSX would vote for the merger and recommended approval of the merger by the other shareholders. The proxy materials disclosed Western's natural resource holdings in terms of acreage of minerals and timber. It also stated real property values as carried on the company's books—that is, a book value of $17.04 per share. It included an opinion of the First Boston Corporation, an investment banking firm, that the merger was fair to shareholders; First Boston did not undertake an independent evaluation of Western's physical assets. Lockspeiser sued, alleging that the proxy materials were misleading because they did not state tonnage of Western's coal reserves, timber holdings in board feet, and actual value of Western's assets. Did Lockspeiser state a claim for relief? *Lockspeiser v. Western Maryland Company*, 768 F.2d 558, **Web** 1985 U.S. App. Lexis 20476 (United States Court of Appeals for the Fourth Circuit)

29.2 Proxy Contest: The Medfield Corporation (Medfield) was a publicly held corporation engaged in operating hospitals and other health care facilities. Medfield established a date for its annual shareholders' meeting, at which time the board of directors would be elected. In its proxy statement, management proposed the incumbent slate of directors. A group known as the Medfield Shareholders Committee nominated a rival slate of candidates and also solicited proxies. Medfield sent proxy solicitation material to shareholders that:

1. Failed to disclose that Medfield had been overpaid more than $1.8 million by Blue Cross and this amount was due and owing Blue Cross.
2. Failed to disclose that Medicare funds were being withheld because of Medfield's nonpayment.
3. Failed to adequately disclose self-dealing by one of the directors with Medfield who owned part of a laboratory used by Medfield.
4. Failed to disclose that Medfield was attempting to sell two nursing homes.
5. Impugned the character, integrity, and personal reputation of one of the rival candidates by stating that he had previously been found liable for patent infringement when, in fact, the case had been reversed on appeal.

At the annual meeting, the incumbent slate of directors received 50 percent of the votes cast, against 44 percent of the insurgent slate of directors. The Gladwins, who owned voting stock, sued to have the election overturned. Who wins?

Gladwin v. Medfield Corporation, 540 F.2d 1266, **Web** 1976 U.S. App. Lexis 6548 (United States Court of Appeals for the Fifth Circuit)

29.3 Proxy Contest: The Fairchild Engine and Airplane Corporation (Fairchild) was a privately held corporation whose management proposed the incumbent slate of directors for election at its annual shareholders' meeting. An insurgent slate of directors challenged the incumbents for election to the board. After the solicitation of proxies and a hard-fought proxy contest, the insurgent slate of directors was elected. Evidence showed that the proxy contest was waged over matters of corporate policy and for personal reasons. The old board of directors had spent $134,000 out of corporate funds to wage the proxy contest. The insurgents had spent $127,000 of their personal funds in their successful proxy contest and sought reimbursement from Fairchild for this amount. The payment of these expenses was ratified by a 16-to-1 majority vote of the stockholders. Mr. Rosenfeld, an attorney who owned 25 of the 2,300,000 outstanding shares of the corporation, filed an action to recover the amounts already paid by the corporation and to prevent any further payments of these expenses. Who wins? *Rosenfeld v. Fairchild Engine and Airplane Corporation*, 309 N.Y. 168, 128 N.E.2d 291, **Web** 1955 N.Y. Lexis 947 (Court of Appeals of New York)

29.4 Shareholder Resolution: The Medical Committee for Human Rights (Committee), a nonprofit corporation organized to advance concerns for human life, received a gift of shares of Dow Chemical (Dow) stock. Dow manufactured napalm, a chemical defoliant that was used during the Vietnam Conflict. Committee objected to the sale of napalm by Dow primarily because of its concerns for human life. Committee owned sufficient shares for a long enough time to propose a shareholders' resolution as long as it met the other requirements to propose such a resolution. Committee proposed that the following resolution be included in the proxy materials circulated by management for the annual shareholders' meeting:

> RESOLVED, that the shareholders of the Dow Chemical company request that the Board of Directors, in accordance with the law, consider the advisability of adopting a resolution setting forth an amendment to the composite certificate of incorporation of the Dow Chemical Company that the company shall not make napalm.

Dow's management refused to include the requested resolution in its proxy materials. Committee sued, alleging that its resolution met the requirements to be included in the proxy materials. Who wins? *Medical Committee for Human Rights v. Securities and Exchange Commission*, 139 U.S. App. D.C. 226, 432 F.2d 659, **Web** 1970 U.S. App. Lexis 8284 (United States Court of Appeals for the District of Columbia Circuit)

29.5 Merger: The board of directors of Plant Industries, Inc. (Plant), under the guidance of Robert B. Bregman, the chief executive officer of the corporation, embarked on a course of action that resulted in the sale of several unprofitable subsidiaries. Bregman then engaged in a course of action to sell Plant National (Quebec) Ltd., a subsidiary that constituted Plant's entire Canadian operations. This was a profitable subsidiary that comprised over 50 percent of Plant's assets, sales, and profits. Do Plant's shareholders have to be accorded voting and appraisal rights regarding the sale of this subsidiary? *Katz v. Bregman*, 431 A.2d 1274, **Web** 1981 Del. Ch. Lexis 449 (Court of Chancery of Delaware)

29.6 Dissenting Shareholder Appraisal Rights: Over a period of several years, the Curtiss-Wright Corporation (Curtiss-Wright) purchased 65 percent of the stock of Dorr-Oliver Incorporated (Dorr-Oliver). Curtiss-Wright's board of directors decided that a merger with Dorr-Oliver would be beneficial to Curtiss-Wright. The board voted to approve a merger of the two companies and to pay $23 per share to the stockholders of Dorr-Oliver. The Dorr-Oliver board and 80 percent of Dorr-Oliver's shareholders approved the merger. The merger became effective. John Bershad, a minority shareholder of Dorr-Oliver, voted against the merger but thereafter tendered his 100 shares and received payment of $2,300. Bershad subsequently sued, alleging that the $23 per share paid to Dorr-Oliver shareholders was grossly inadequate. Can Bershad obtain minority shareholder appraisal rights? *Bershad v. Curtiss-Wright Corporation*, 535 A.2d 840, **Web** 1987 Del. Lexis 1313 (Supreme Court of Delaware)

29.7 Tender Offer: Mobil Corporation (Mobil) made a tender offer to purchase up to 40 million outstanding common shares of stock in Marathon Oil Company (Marathon) for $85 per share in cash. It further stated its intentions to follow the purchase with a merger of the two companies. Mobil was primarily interested in acquiring Marathon's oil and mineral interests in certain properties, including the Yates Field. Marathon directors immediately held a board meeting and determined to find a white knight. Negotiations developed between Marathon and United States Steel Corporation (U.S. Steel). Two weeks later, Marathon and U.S. Steel entered into an agreement whereby U.S. Steel would make a tender offer for 30 million common shares of Marathon stock at $125 per share, to be followed by a merger of the two companies.

The Marathon–U.S. Steel agreement was subject to the following two conditions: (1) U.S. Steel was given an irrevocable option to purchase 10 million authorized but unissued shares of Marathon common stock for $90 per share (or 17 percent of Marathon's outstanding shares), and (2) U.S. Steel was given an option to purchase Marathon's interest in oil and mineral rights in Yates Field for $2.8 billion (Yates Field option). The Yates Field option could be exercised only if U.S. Steel's offer did not succeed and if a third party gained control of Marathon. Evidence showed that Marathon's interest in the Yates Field was worth up to $3.6 billion. Marathon did not give Mobil either of these two options. Mobil sued, alleging that these two options violated Section 14(e) of the Williams Act. Who wins? *Mobil Corporation v. Marathon Oil Company*, 669 F.2d 366, **Web** 1981 U.S. App. Lexis 14958 (United States Court of Appeals for the Sixth Circuit)

29.8 Tender Offer: The Fruehauf Corporation (Fruehauf) is engaged in the manufacture of large trucks and industrial vehicles. The Edelman group (Edelman) made a cash tender offer for the shares of Fruehauf for $48.50 per share. The stock had sold in the low $20-per-share range a few months earlier. Fruehauf's management decided to make a competing management-led leveraged buyout (MBO) tender offer for the company in conjunction with Merrill Lynch. The MBO would be funded using $375 million borrowed from Merrill Lynch, $375 million borrowed from Manufacturers Hanover Bank, and $100 million contributed by Fruehauf. The total equity contribution to the new company under the MBO would be only $25 million: $10 million to $15 million from management and the rest from Merrill Lynch. In return for their equity contributions, management would receive between 40 and 60 percent of the new company.

Fruehauf's management agreed to pay $30 million to Merrill Lynch for brokerage fees that Merrill Lynch could keep even if the deal did not go through. Management also agreed to a no-shop clause whereby they agreed not to seek a better deal with another bidder. Incumbent management received better information about the goings-on. They also gave themselves golden parachutes that would raise the money for management's equity position in the new company.

Edelman informed Fruehauf's management that it could top their bid, but Fruehauf's management did not give them the opportunity to present their offer. Management's offer was accepted. Edelman sued, seeking an injunction. Did Fruehauf's management violate the business judgment rule? *Edelman v. Fruehauf Corporation*, 798 F.2d 882, **Web** 1986 U.S. App. Lexis 27911 (United States Court of Appeals for the Sixth Circuit)

29.9 Flip-Over Defense: Household International, Inc. (Household), was a diversified holding company with its principal subsidiaries engaged in financial services, transportation, and merchandising. The board of directors of Household adopted a 48-page "Rights Plan" by a 14-to-2 vote. Basically, the plan provided that Household common stockholders were entitled to the issuance of one irrevocable right per common share if any party acquired 20 percent of Household's shares. The right permitted Household shareholders to purchase $200 of the common stock of the tender offeror for $100. In essence, this forced any party interested in taking over Household to negotiate with Household's directors. Dyson-Kissner-Moran Corporation (DKM), which was interested in taking over Household, filed suit, alleging that this flip-over rights plan violated the business judgment rule. Who wins? *Moran v. Household International, Inc.*, 500 A.2d 1346, **Web** 1985 Del. Lexis 557 (Supreme Court of Delaware)

29.10 State Antitakeover Statute: The state of Wisconsin enacted an antitakeover statute that protects corporations that are incorporated in Wisconsin and have their headquarters, substantial operations, or 10 percent of their shares of shareholders in the state. The statute prevents any party that acquires a 10 percent interest in a covered corporation from engaging in a business combination (e.g., merger) with the covered corporation for three years unless approval of the management is obtained in advance of the combination. Wisconsin firms cannot opt out of the law. This statute effectively eliminates hostile leveraged buyouts because buyers must rely on the assets and income of the target company to help pay off the debt incurred in effectuating the takeover.

Universal Foods (Universal) was a Wisconsin corporation covered by the statute. Amanda Acquisition Corporation (Amanda) commenced a cash tender offer for up to 75 percent of the stock of Universal. Universal asserted the Wisconsin law. Is Wisconsin's antitakeover statute lawful? *Amanda Acquisition Corporation v. Universal Foods*, 877 F.2d 496, **Web** 1989 U.S. App. Lexis 9024 (United States Court of Appeals for the Seventh Circuit)

Ethics Issues

29.11 Ethics: MCA, Inc. (MCA), a corporate holding company, owned 92 percent of the stock of Universal Pictures Company (Universal) and 100 percent of the stock of Universal City Studios, Inc. (Universal City). These two subsidiaries merged pursuant to Delaware's short-form merger statute. The minority shareholders of Universal were offered $75 per share for their shares. Francis I. Du Pont & Company and other minority shareholders (Plaintiffs)

rejected the offer and then perfected their dissenting shareholder appraisal rights. The appraiser filed a final report in which he found the value of Universal stock to be $91.47 per share. Both parties filed exceptions to this report.

The parties' ultimate disagreement was over the value of the stock. Plaintiffs submitted that the true value was $131.89 per share; the defendant said it was $52.36. The computations were as follows:

Plaintiffs' Valuation			
Value Factor	Value	Weight	Result
Earnings	$129.12	70%	$ 90.38
Market	144.36	20	28.87
Assets	126.46	10	12.64
Value per share			**$131.89**

Defendant's Valuation			
Earnings	$51.93	70%	$ 36.35
Dividends	41.66	20	8.33
Assets	76.77	10	7.68
Value per share			**$ 52.36**

Appraiser's Valuation			
Earnings	$92.89	80%	$ 74.31
Assets	85.82	20	17.16
Value per share			**$ 91.47**

The defendant took exception to the appraiser's failure to find that, in the years prior to merger, the industry was declining and that Universal was ranked near its bottom. And it argued that Universal was in the business of producing and distributing feature motion pictures for theatrical exhibition. It contended that such business, generally, was in a severe decline at the time of merger and that Universal, in particular, was in a vulnerable position because it had failed to diversify, its feature films were of low commercial quality, and, unlike other motion picture companies, substantially all of its film library had already been committed to distributors for television exhibition. In short, defendant pictures Universal was a weak "wasting asset" corporation in a sick industry with poor prospects for revival.

The stockholders saw a different company. They said that Universal's business was indeed the production and distribution of feature films, but not merely for theatrical exhibition. They argued that there was a dramatic increase in the television market for such feature films at the time of the merger. This market, they contended, gave great new value to a fully amortized film library and significantly enhanced the value of Universal's current and future productions. Thus, they painted a portrait of a well-situated corporation in a rejuvenated industry.

Did the parties act ethically in arriving at their proposed values of the company? What is the value of the minority shareholders' shares of Universal Pictures Company? *Francis I. Du Pont & Company v. Universal City Studios, Inc.*, 312 A.2d 344, **Web** 1973 Del. Ch. Lexis 123 (Court of Chancery of Delaware)

29.12 Ethics: Realist, Inc. (Realist), was a Delaware corporation with its principal place of business in Wisconsin. In March 1988, Royal Business Group, Inc. (Royal), a New Hampshire corporation, acquired 8 percent of the outstanding voting stock of Realist. Royal sent a series of letters to Realist, declaring its intention to acquire all of Realist's outstanding shares at an above-market premium. Realist repulsed Royal's overtures. Unbeknownst to Royal, Realist began negotiations to acquire Ammann Laser Technik AG (Ammann), a company based in Switzerland.

Royal instituted a proxy contest and nominated two candidates for the two Realist directorships to be filed at the annual shareholders' meeting. Realist and Royal both submitted proxy statements to Realist's shareholders.

The insurgent Royal nominees prevailed. Realist announced that it had acquired Ammann. This acquisition made Realist much less attractive as a takeover target. Royal immediately withdrew its offer to acquire Realist and sued Realist to recover the $350,000 it had spent in connection with the proxy contest. Royal alleged that Realist had engaged in fraud in violation of Section 14(a) of the Securities Exchange Act of 1934 by failing to disclose its secret negotiations with Ammann in its proxy materials. The basis of Royal's complaint was that if Realist had disclosed that it intended to acquire Ammann, Royal would not have engaged in the costly proxy contest. Is Realist liable to Royal? Did Realist act unethically in seeking to acquire Ammann to thwart Royal's takeover attempt? *Royal Business Group, Inc. v. Realist, Inc.*, 933 F.2d 1056, **Web** 1991 U.S. App. Lexis 10389 (United States Court of Appeals for the First Circuit)

IRAC Writing Assignment

Read **Case A-29** in Appendix A [*Neal v. Alabama By-Products Corporation*]. Use the IRAC method to prepare a written analysis of the case.

Endnotes

1. 15 U.S.C. Section 78n(a).
2. 15 U.S.C. Sections 78n(d) and (e).
3. Section 13(d) of the Securities Exchange Act of 1934 requires that any party that acquires 5 percent or more of any equity security of a company registered with the SEC must report the acquisition to the SEC and disclose its intentions regarding the acquisition. This is public information.
4. 15 U.S.C. Section 78n(e).
5. *Smith v. Van Gorkom*, 488 A.2d 858, **Web** 1985 Del. Lexis 421 (Supreme Court of Delaware)
6. *Unocal Corporation v. Mesa Petroleum Company*, 493 A.2d 946, **Web** 1985 Del. Lexis 482 (Supreme Court of Delaware)

C H A P T E R 30

Limited Liability Companies and Limited Liability Partnerships

> **"**_Justice is the end of government. It is the end of civil society. It ever has been, and ever will be pursued, until it be obtained, or until liberty be lost in the pursuit._**"**
>
> —JAMES MADISON
> The Federalist, No. 51 (1788)

CHAPTER OBJECTIVES

After studying this chapter, you should be able to:

1. Define _limited liability company_ (_LLC_) and limited liability partnership (LLP).
2. Describe the process of organizing an LLC and LLP.
3. Describe the limited liability shield provided by an LLC and LLP.
4. Compare member-managed LLCs and manager-managed LLCs.
5. Determine when members and managers owe fiduciary duties of loyalty and care to an LLC.

CHAPTER CONTENTS

- Introduction to Limited Liability Companies and Limited Liability Partnerships
- Limited Liability Company (LLC)
- LLC Members' Limited Liability
- Formation of an LLC
- Management of an LLC

- Dissolution of an LLC
- Limited Liability Partnership (LLP)
- Chapter Summary
- Test Review Terms and Concepts
- Case Problems
- Ethics Issues
- IRAC Writing Assignment

Introduction to Limited Liability Companies and Limited Liability Partnerships

Owners may choose to operate a business as a *limited liability company* (*LLC*). The use of LLCs as a form of conducting business in the United States is of rather recent origin. In 1977, Wyoming was the first state in the United States to enact legislation creating an LLC as a legal form for conducting business. This new form of business received little attention until the early 1990s, when several more states enacted legislation to allow the creation of LLCs. The evolution of LLCs then grew at blinding speed, with all the states having enacted LLC statues by 1998. Most LLC laws are quite similar, although some differences do exist between these state statutes.

An LLC is an unincorporated business entity that combines the most favorable attributes of general partnerships, limited partnerships, and corporations. An LLC may elect to be taxed as a partnership, the owners can manage the business, and the owners have limited liability. Many entrepreneurs who begin new businesses choose the LLC as their legal form for conducting business.

Most states have enacted laws that permit certain types of professionals, such as accountants, lawyers, and doctors, to operate as *limited liability partnerships* (*LLPs*). The owners of an LLP have limited liability.

The formation and operation of LLCs and LLPs, and the liability of their owners, are discussed in this chapter.

London, England

The limited liability company form of business is used in the United States and countries of Europe and Latin America.

Limited Liability Company (LLC)

Limited liability companies (LLCs) are creatures of state law, not federal law. An LLC can only be created pursuant to the laws of the state in which the LLC is being organized. These statutes, commonly referred to as **limited liability company codes**, regulate the formation, operation, and dissolution of LLCs. The state legislature may amend its LLC statute at any time. The courts interpret state LLC statutes to decide LLC and member disputes.

An LLC is a separate *legal entity* (or legal person) distinct from its members [ULLCA Section 201]. LLCs are treated as artificial persons who can sue or be sued, enter into and enforce contracts, hold title to and transfer property, and be found civilly and criminally liable for violations of law.

In 1995, the National Conference of Commissioners on Uniform State Laws (a group of lawyers, judges, and legal scholars) issued the **Uniform Limited Liability Company Act (ULLCA)**. The ULLCA codifies LLC law. Its goal is to establish comprehensive LLC law that is uniform throughout the United States. The ULLCA covers most problems that arise in the formation, operation, and termination of LLCs. The ULLCA is not law unless a state adopts it as its LLC statute. Many states have adopted all or part of the ULLCA as their LLC law. Because it is so important, the ULLCA forms the basis of the study of limited liability companies in this chapter.

Taxation of LLCs

> Morality cannot be legislated, but behavior can be regulated. Judicial decrees may not change the heart, but they can restrain the heartless.
>
> Martin Luther King, Jr.
> *Strength to Love (1963)*

Under the Internal Revenue Code and regulations adopted by the Internal Revenue Service (IRS), for federal income tax purposes, an LLC is taxed as a partnership unless it elects to be taxed as a corporation. Thus, an LLC is not taxed at the entity level, but its income or losses "flow through" to the members' individual income tax returns. This avoids double taxation. Most LLCs accept the default status of being taxed as a partnership instead of electing to be taxed as a corporation.

Powers of an LLC

An LLC has the same powers as an individual to do all things necessary or convenient to carry on its business or affairs. These include the power to own and transfer personal property; sell, lease, and mortgage real property; make contracts and guarantees; borrow and lend money; issue notes and bonds; sue and be sued; and take other actions to conduct the affairs and business of the LLC [ULLCA Section 112].

Steven Spielberg, Jeffrey Katzenberg, and David Geffen formed DreamWorks SKG, which is a major movie and recording Production Company. Spielberg's fame and money came from directing films, Katzenberg had been a leading executive at Disney, and Geffen had built and sold a major record company. These multimillionaire multimedia giants combined their talents to form a formidable entertainment company.

DreamWorks was formed as a Delaware LLC. The organizers chose to create an LLC because it is taxed as a partnership, and the profits (or losses) flow directly to the owners, but as in a corporation, the owners are protected from personal liability beyond their capital contributions.

CLASS	INVESTMENTS
A	Outside investors. Class A stock was sold to big investors with over $20 million to invest. Microsoft's cofounder, Paul Allen, purchased $500 million of Class A stock. Class A investors got seats on the board of directors.
S	Outside investors. Class S stock was issued for smallish, "strategic" investments with other companies for cross-marketing purposes.
E	Employees. Employees were granted the right to participate in an employee stock purchase plan.

DreamWorks issued several classes of interests. The three principals put up $100 million ($33.3 million each) for "SKG" stock, which grants the principals 100 percent voting control and 67 percent of the firm's profits. In addition, each principal has multiyear employment contracts plus other benefits.

DreamWorks raised the other $900 million of its $1 billion capital from other investors, who were to receive one-third of future profits. The other investors were issued the following classes of stock:

Web Exercises

1. **WEB** Visit the website of DreamWorks, at *www.dreamworks.com*.

2. **WEB** Use *www.google.com* to find information on whether your state permits LLCs.

LLC Members' Limited Liability

The owners of LLCs are usually called **members**. The general rule is that members are not personally liable to third parties for the debts, obligations, and liabilities of an LLC beyond their capital contribution. Members are said to have **limited liability** (see Exhibit 30.1). The debts, obligations, and liabilities of an LLC, whether arising from contracts, torts, or otherwise, are solely those of the LLC [ULLCA Section 303(a)].

Example Jasmin, Shou-Yi, and Vanessa form an LLC, and each contributes $25,000 in capital. The LLC operates for a period of time, during which it borrows money from banks and purchases goods on credit from suppliers. After some time, the LLC experiences financial difficulty and goes out of business. If the LLC fails with $500,000 in debts, each of the members will lose her capital contribution of $25,000 but will not be personally liable for the rest of the unpaid debts of the LLC.

The failure of an LLC to observe the usual company formalities is not grounds for imposing personal liability on the members of the LLC [ULLCA Section 303(b)]. For example, if the LLC does not keep minutes of the company's meetings, the members do not become personally liable for the LLC's debts.

In the following case, the court addressed the issue of the limited liability of a member of an LLC.

> The great can protect themselves, but the poor and humble require the arm and shield of the law.
>
> Andrew Jackson

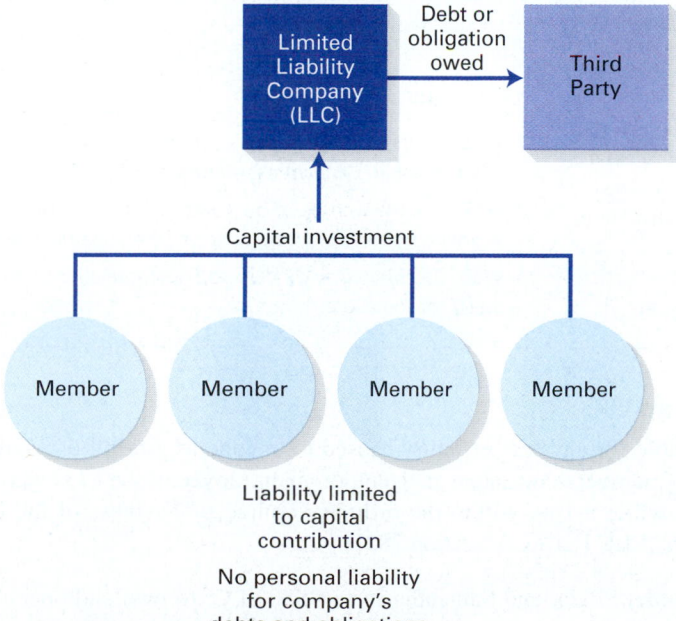

EXHIBIT 30.1

Limited Liability Company (LLC)

CASE 30.1

Limited Liability Company

Page v. Roscoe, LLC

128 N.C.App. 678, 497 S.E.2nd 422,
Web 1998 N.C. App. Lexis 169 Court of Appeals of North Carolina

> *"A person who is a member or manager, or both, of a limited liability company is not liable for the obligations of a limited liability company solely by reason of being a member or manager or both."*
>
> —Judge Walker

Facts

Dale C. Bone was a member of Roscoe, LLC, an LLC organized under the laws of North Carolina. Roscoe, LLC, purchased 2 acres of land near the town of Apex, North Carolina. Apex approved Roscoe, LLC's plan to construct and operate a propane gas bulk storage and distribution facility on the land. This use was permitted under Apex's zoning ordinance. Daylene Page and other homeowners in the area sued Roscoe, LLC, and Dale C. Bone, alleging that the gas storage facility, if constructed, would constitute a nuisance. After the trial court denied the plaintiffs' motion to obtain a preliminary injunction against construction of the facility, the plaintiffs dismissed the lawsuit. Subsequently, Bone sued the plaintiffs for sanctions to recover attorneys' fees he had spent in defending against the plaintiffs' lawsuit. Bone alleged that he should have not been named a defendant in the lawsuit because he was a member of Roscoe, LLC, and would have had no personal liability in the lawsuit. The trial court ordered the plaintiffs to pay Bone's attorneys' fees. The plaintiffs appealed.

Issue

Were the sanctions warranted against the plaintiffs for naming an individual member of an LLC in the lawsuit they brought against the LLC?

Language of the Court

We do find that the allegations against Bone individually are not well-grounded in law. N.C.Gen.Stat. § 57C-3-30 (1993) provides in pertinent part:

a. A person who is a member or manager, or both, of a limited liability company is not liable for the obligations of a limited liability company solely by reason of being a member or manager or both, and does not become so by participating, in whatever capacity, in the management or control of the business.

b. A member of a limited liability company is not a proper party to proceedings by or against a limited liability company.

Therefore, under the above statute, it was improper to name an individual member of a limited liability company as a party defendant. The naming of Bone as an individual defendant was not well-grounded in law.

Decision

The court of appeals held that Bone, as a member of Roscoe, LLC, was not liable as a matter of law for the acts of the LLC and was therefore improperly named as a defendant in the lawsuit filed by the plaintiffs. The plaintiffs were held liable for sanctions and were required to pay Bone's attorneys' fees that he expended in defending against the plaintiffs' lawsuit. The court of appeals affirmed the trial court's judgment in favor of Bone.

Law & Ethics Questions

1. Should members of an LLC be released from personal liability for the debts and obligations incurred by the LLC?

2. **ETHICS** Did the plaintiff homeowners act ethically in naming Bone as a defendant? Why do you think they named Bone as a defendant?

3. Is this case a good precedent for businesspersons wishing to conduct business as LLCs?

Web Exercises

1. **WEB** For the complete opinion of this case, go to *www.prenhall.com/cheesemancases*.

2. **WEB** Visit the website of the court of appeals of North Carolina, at *www.nccourts.org/courts/appellate/appeal/default.asp*.

3. **WEB** Use *www.google.com* to find information about forming an LLC in your state.

Liability of an LLC

An LLC is liable for any loss or injury caused to anyone as a result of a wrongful act or omission by a member, a manager, an agent, or an employee of the LLC who commits the wrongful act while acting within the ordinary course of business of the LLC or with authority of the LLC [ULLCA Section 302].

Example Sable, Silvia, and Samantha form SSS, LLC, to own and operate a business. Each member contributes $10,000 capital. While on LLC business, Sable drives her automobile and accidentally hits and injures Damon. Damon can recover damages for his injuries from Sable personally because she committed the negligent act. Damon can also recover damages from SSS, LLC, because Sable was acting within the scope of the ordinary business of the LLC when the accident occurred. Silvia and Samantha have limited liability only up to their capital contributions in SSS, LLC.

Liability of Managers

Managers of LLCs are not personally liable for the debts, obligations, and liabilities of the LLC they manage [ULLCA Section 303(a)].

Example An LLC that does real estate development hires Sarah Goldstein, a nonmember, to be its president. While acting within the scope of her LLC authority, Sarah signs a loan agreement whereby the LLC borrows $1 million from a bank to complete the construction of an office building. If the LLC subsequently suffers financial difficulty and defaults on the bank loan, Sarah is not personally responsible for the loan. The LLC is liable for the loan, but Sarah is not because she is the manager of the LLC.

In the following case, the court enforced a personal guarantee against a manager of an LLC.

C A S E **30.2** *Limited Liability* *Company*	**Creative Resource Management, Inc. v. Soskin** **Web** 1998 Tenn. App. Lexis 788 Court of Appeals of Tennessee	

> ❝ *The words "I personally guarantee any and all payments payable as represented and outlined in this agreement" reflect indisputably a guarantee by someone.* ❞
>
> —Judge Cain

Facts

Nashville Pro Hockey, LLC, was a limited liability company organized under the laws of Tennessee. The LLC owned and operated the Nashville Nighthawks, a minor league professional hockey team. Nashville Pro Hockey, LLC, contracted with Creative Resource Management, Inc. (CRM), whereby CRM, for fees and other consideration, would provide employee leasing services to Nashville Pro Hockey, LLC. The contract was signed by Barry Soskin, the president of Nashville Pro Hockey, LLC. A paragraph in the contract provided: "By affixing my hand and seal to this agreement, I personally guarantee any and all payments payable as represented and outlined in this agreement."

Nashville Pro Hockey, LLC, failed, owing CRM $29,626. CRM sued Nashville Pro Hockey, LLC, and Barry Soskin to recover the unpaid compensation. Soskin defended, alleging that his signature on the contract was in his representative capacity only and not in his individual capacity as a guarantor. The trial court agreed and granted summary judgment to Soskin. CRM appealed.

Issue

Did Soskin's signature on the contract constitute a personal guarantee for the payment of the debt of Nashville Pro Hockey, LLC, to CRM?

Language of the Court

This case concerns a contract which contains personal guarantee language in the body of the contract. The words "I personally guarantee any and all payments payable as represented and outlined in this agreement" reflect indisputably a guarantee by someone. Soskin insists that he signed only as a representative of the limited liability company. CRM insists that his signature imposes personal liability upon him. The stark fact is that the words "I personally guarantee" are meaningless if applied to Nashville Pro Hockey, LLC and not to Barry Soskin individually. Since the words "I personally guarantee" cannot refer to Nashville Pro Hockey, LLC and retain any meaning at all in the context of this agreement, they must of necessity reflect the personal guarantee of Barry Soskin.

Decision

The court of appeals held that Soskin was a guarantor and that he was liable to repay the money owed to CRM by Nashville Pro Hockey, LLC. The court of appeals reversed the judgment of the trial court and granted summary judgment to CRM.

Law & Ethics Questions

1. In this case, a contracting party, CRM, was able to break the limited liability shield of an LLC and have a manager of the LLC personally guarantee its contract with the LLC. Are tort victims of negligent conduct of an LLC's employees and agents granted the same benefit?
2. **ETHICS** Did Soskin act ethically in arguing that he was not liable on the contract? Was the language of the contract clear?
3. What purpose do personal guarantees serve in business transactions?

Web Exercises

1. **WEB** For the complete opinion of this case, go to *www.prenhall.com/cheesemancases*.
2. **WEB** View the website of the court of appeals of Tennessee, at *www.tsc.state.tn.us/geninfo/bio/appeals/biotca.htm*.
3. **WEB** Use *www.google.com* to find an article that discusses the liability of owners of an LLC. Read it.

Liability of Tortfeasors

A person who intentionally or unintentionally (negligently) causes injury or death to another person is called a **tortfeasor**. A tortfeasor is personally liable to persons he or she injures and to the heirs of persons who die because of his or her conduct. This rule applies to members and managers of LLCs. Thus, if a member or a manager of an LLC negligently causes injury or death to another person, he or she is personally liable to the injured person or the heirs of the deceased person.

Formation of an LLC

Most LLCs are organized to operate businesses, real estate developments, and such. Certain professionals, such as accountants, lawyers, and doctors, cannot operate practices as LLCs; instead, they can operate practices as limited liability partnerships (LLPs).

An LLC can be organized in only one state, even though it can conduct business in all other states. When choosing a state for organization, the members should consider the LLC codes of the states under consideration. For the sake of convenience, most LLCs, particularly small ones, choose as the state of organization the state in which the LLC will be doing most of its business.

When starting a new LLC, the organizers must choose a name for the entity. The name must contain the words *limited liability company* or *limited company* or the abbreviation *L.L.C.*, *LLC*, *L.C.*, or *LC*. *Limited* may be abbreviated as *Ltd.*, and *company* may be abbreviated as *Co*. [ULLCA Section 105(a)].

Articles of Organization

Because LLCs are creatures of statute, certain formalities must be taken and statutory requirements must be met to form an LLC.

Under the ULLCA, an LLC may be organized by one or more persons. Some states require at least two members to organize an LLC. In states where an LLC may be organized by only one member, sole proprietors can obtain the benefit of the limited liability shield of an LLC.

An LLC is formed by delivering **articles of organization** to the office of the secretary of state of the state of organization for filing. If the articles are in proper form, the secretary of state will file the articles. The existence of an LLC begins when the articles of organization are filed. The filing of the articles of organization by the secretary of state is conclusive proof that the organizers have satisfied all the conditions necessary to create the LLC [ULLCA Section 202].

Under the ULLCA, the articles of organization of an LLC must set forth [ULLCA Section 203]:

1. The name of the LLC
2. The address of the LLC's initial office
3. The name and address of the initial agent for service of process
4. The name and address of each organizer
5. Whether the LLC is a term LLC and, if so, the term specified

EXHIBIT 30.2

Articles of Organization

> **ARTICLES OF ORGANIZATION**
> **FOR FLORIDA LIMITED LIABILITY COMPANY**
>
> **ARTICLE I - NAME**
> The name of the Limited Liability Company is
> iCitrusSystems.com
>
> **ARTICLE II - ADDRESS**
> The mailing address and street address of the principal office of the Limited Liability
> Company is
>
> 3000 Dade Boulevard
> Suite 200
> Miami Beach, Florida 33139
>
> **ARTICLE III - DURATION**
> The period of duration for the Limited Liability Company shall be
> 50 years
>
> **ARTICLE IV - MANAGEMENT**
> The Limited Liability Company is to be managed by a manager and the name and
> address of such manager is
>
> Susan Escobar
> 1000 Collins Avenue
> Miami Beach, Florida 33141
>
> _____
> Thomas Blandford
>
> _____
> Pam Rosales

6. Whether the LLC is to be a manager-managed LLC and, if so, the name and address of each manager
7. Whether one or more of the members of the LLC are to be personally liable for the LLC's debts and obligations

The articles of organization may set forth provisions from the members' operating agreement and any other matter not inconsistent with law. A sample articles of organization document is set forth in Exhibit 30.2. The articles of organization may be amended at any time by filing *articles of amendment* with the secretary of state [ULLCA Section 204].

Duration of an LLC

An LLC is an **at-will LLC** (i.e., with no specified term) unless it is designated as a **term LLC** and the duration of the term is specified in the articles of organization [ULLCA Section 203(a)(5)]. The duration of a term LLC may be specified in any manner that sets forth a specific and final date for the dissolution of the LLC.

Example Periods specified as "50 years from the date of filing of the articles of organizations end "the period ending January 1, 2050" are valid to create a term LLC.

Capital Contribution to an LLC

A member's capital contribution to an LLC may be in the form of money, personal property, real property, other tangible property, intangible property (e.g., a patent), services performed, contracts for services to be performed, promissory notes, or other agreements to contribute cash or property [ULLCA Section 401].

A member's obligation to contribute capital is not excused by the member's death, disability, or other inability to perform. If a member cannot make the required contribution of property or services, he or she is obligated to contribute money equal to the value of the promised contribution. The LLC or any creditor who extended credit to the LLC in reliance on the promised contribution may enforce the promised obligation [ULLCA Section 402].

Certificate of Interest

An LLC's operating agreement may provide that a member's ownership interest may be evidenced by a **certificate of interest** issued by the LLC [ULLCA Section 501(c)]. The certificate of interest acts the same as a stock certificate issued by a corporation.

Operating Agreement

Members of an LLC may enter into an **operating agreement** that regulates the affairs of the company and the conduct of its business and governs relations among the members, managers, and company [ULLCA Section 103(a)]. The operating agreement may be amended by the approval of all members unless otherwise provided in the agreement. The operating agreement and amendments may be oral but are usually written.

Conversion of an Existing Business to an LLC

Many LLCs are formed by entrepreneurs to start new businesses. In addition, an existing business may want to convert to an LLC to obtain its tax benefits and limited liability shield. General partnerships, limited partnerships, and corporations may be converted to LLCs if the following requirements are met [ULLCA Section 902]:

1. An **agreement of conversion** is drafted that sets forth the terms of the conversion.
2. The terms of the conversion are approved by all the parties or by the number or percentage of owners required for conversion.
3. Articles of organization of the LLC are filed with the secretary of state. The articles must state that the LLC was previously another form of business and the prior business's name.

The conversion takes effect when the articles of organization are filed with the secretary of state or at any later date specified in the articles of organization. When the conversion takes effect, all property owned by the prior business vests in the LLC, and all debts, obligations, and liabilities of the prior business become those of the LLC [ULLCA Section 903].

Dividing an LLC's Profits and Losses

Unless otherwise agreed, the ULLCA mandates that a member has the right to an equal share in the LLC's profits [ULLCA Section 405(a)]. This is a default rule that the members can override by agreement and is usually a provision in their operating agreement.

Example In many instances, the members may not want the profits of the LLC to be shared equally. This would normally occur if the capital contributions of the members were unequal. If the members want the profits divided in the same proportion as their capital contributions, that should be specified in the operating agreement.

> There shall be one law for the native and for the stranger who sojourns among you.
>
> Moses
> *Exodus 12:49*

Example Lilly and Harrison form an LLC. Lilly contributes $75,000 capital, and Harrison contributes $25,000 capital. They do not have an agreement as to how profits are to be shared. If the LLC makes $100,000 in profits, under the ULLCA, Lilly and Harrison will share the profits equally—$50,000 each. To avoid this outcome, Lilly and Harrison should agree in their operating agreement how they want the profits to be divided.

Losses from an LLC are shared equally unless otherwise agreed. Sometimes members will not want to divide losses equally and maybe not even in the same way as their capital contributions. If the LLC has chosen to be taxed as a partnership, the losses from an LLC flow to the members' individual income tax returns. Losses from an LLC can sometimes be offset against members' gains from other sources. Therefore, the members may want to agree to divide the losses so that the members who can use them to offset other income will receive a greater share of the losses.

Profits and losses from an LLC do not have to be distributed in the same proportion.

Example A member who has the right to a 10 percent share of profits may be given the right to receive 25 percent of the LLC's losses.

Distributional Interest

A member's ownership interest in an LLC is called a **distributional interest**. A member's distributional interest in an LLC is personal property and may be transferred in whole or in part [ULLCA Section 501(b)]. Unless otherwise provided in the operating agreement, a transfer of an interest in an LLC does not entitle the transferee to become a member of the LLC or to exercise any right of a member. A transfer entitles the transferee to receive only distributions from the LLC to which the transferor would have been entitled [ULLCA Section 502]. A transferee of a distributional interest becomes a member of the LLC if it is so provided in the operating agreement or if all the other members of the LLC consent [ULLCA Section 503(a)].

Example Cleveland, Heather, and Archibald are members of the Boston Tea Party, LLC; each owns a one-third interest in the LLC, and the members agree to divide the distributions equally in one-third portions. The LLC's operating agreement does not provide that a transferee of a distributional interest will become a member. Cleveland sells his one-third interest to Theodore. The members do not consent to allow Theodore to become a member. The LLC makes $99,999 in profits. Theodore is entitled to receive one-third of the distributions ($33,333). Theodore is not a member of the LLC, however.

A transferee who transfers his or her distributional interest is not released from liability for the debts, obligations, and liabilities of the LLC [ULLCA Section 503(c)].

CONTEMPORARY ENVIRONMENT

Why Operate a Business as a Limited Liability Company (LLC)?

Why should an LLC be used instead of an S corporation or a partnership? S corporations and partnerships are subject to many restrictions and adverse consequences that do not exist with an LLC. Some differences are:

- S corporations cannot have shareholders other than estates, certain trusts, and individuals (who cannot be nonresident aliens). S corporations can have no more than 75 shareholders and one class of stock and may not own more than 80 percent of another corporation. LLCs have no such restrictions.

- In a general partnership, the partners are personally liable for the obligations of the partnership. Members of LLCs have limited liability.

- A limited partnership must have at least one general partner who is personally liable for the obligations of the partnership (although this partner can be a corporation). Limited partners are precluded from participating in the management of the business. An LLC provides limited liability to all members, even though they participate in management of the business.

Management of an LLC

An LLC can be either a **member-managed LLC** or a **manager-managed LLC**. An LLC is a member-managed LLC unless it is designated as a manager-managed LLC in its articles of organization [ULLCA Section 203(a)(b)]. The distinctions between these two are:

- *Member-managed LLC.* In this type of LLC, the members of the LLC have the right to manage the LLC.
- *Manager-managed LLC.* In this type of LLC, the members designate a manager or managers to manage the LLC, and by doing so, they delegate their management rights to the manager or managers, designated manager or managers have the authority to manage the LLC, and the members no longer have the right to manage the LLC.

A manager may be a member of an LLC or a nonmember.

Whether an LLC is a member-managed or manager-managed LLC has important consequences on the right to bind the LLC to contracts and on determining the fiduciary duties owed by members to the LLC. These important distinctions are discussed in the paragraphs that follow.

Member-Managed LLC

In a member-managed LLC, each member has equal rights in the management of the business of the LLC, regardless of the size of his or her capital contribution. Any matter relating to the business of the LLC is decided by a majority vote of the members [ULLCA Section 404(a)].

Example Allison, Jaeson, Stacy, Lan-Wei, and Ivy form North West.com, LLC. Allison contributes $100,000 capital, and the other four members each contributes $25,000 capital. When deciding whether to add another line of products to the business, Stacy, Lan-Wei, and Ivy vote to add the line, and Allison and Jaeson vote against it. The line of new products is added to the LLC's business because three members voted yes while two members voted no. It does not matter that the two members who voted no contributed $125,000 in capital collectively versus $75,000 in capital contributed by the three members who voted yes.

Manager-Managed LLC

In a manager-managed LLC, the members and nonmembers who are designated managers control the management of the LLC. The members who are not managers have no rights to manage the LLC unless otherwise provided in the operating agreement. In a manager-managed LLC, each manager has equal rights in the management and conduct of the company's business. Any matter relating to the business of the LLC may be exclusively decided by the managers by a majority vote of the managers [ULLCA Section 403(b)].

A manager must be appointed by a vote of a majority of the members; managers may also be removed by a vote of the majority of the members [ULLCA Section 404(b)(3)].

Certain actions cannot be delegated to managers but must be voted on by all members of the LLC. These include (1) amending the articles of organization, (2) amending the operating agreement, (3) admitting new members, (4) consenting to dissolve the LLC, (5) consenting to merge the LLC with another entity, and (6) selling, leasing, or disposing of all or substantially all of the LLC's property [ULLCA Section 404(c)].

> Laws too gentle are seldom obeyed; too severe, seldom executed.
>
> Benjamin Franklin
> *Poor Richard's Almanack (1756)*

CONCEPT SUMMARY

Management of an LLC

TYPE OF LLC	DESCRIPTION
Member-managed LLC	The members do not designate managers to manage the LLC. The LLC is managed by its members.
Manager-managed LLC	The members designate certain members or nonmembers to manage the LLC. The LLC is managed by the designated managers; nonmanager members have no right to manage the LLC.

Compensation and Reimbursement

A nonmanager member of an LLC is not entitled to remuneration for services performed for the LLC (except for winding up the business of the LLC). Managers of an LLC, whether they are members or not, are paid compensation and benefits as specified in their employment agreements with the LLC [ULLCA Section 403(d)].

An LLC is obligated to reimburse members and managers for payments made on behalf of the LLC (e.g., business expenses) and to indemnify members and managers for liabilities incurred in the ordinary course of LLC business or in the preservation of the LLC's business or property [ULLCA Section 403(a)].

Agency Authority to Bind an LLC to Contracts

The designation of an LLC as member managed or manager managed is important in determining who has authority to bind the LLC to contracts. The following rules apply:

- *Member-managed LLC.* In a member-managed LLC, all members have agency authority to bind the LLC to contracts.

  Example If Theresa, Artis, and Yolanda form a member-managed LLC, each one of them can bind the LLC to a contract with a third party such as a supplier, purchaser, or landlord.

- *Manager-managed LLC.* In a manager-managed LLC, the managers have authority to bind the LLC to contracts, but nonmanager members cannot bind the LLC to contracts.

  Example Alexis, Derek, Ashley, and Sadia form an LLC. They designate the LLC as a manager-managed LLC and name Alexis and Ashley as the managers. Alexis, a manager, enters into a contract to purchase goods from a supplier for the LLC. Derek, a nonmanager member, enters into a contract to lease equipment on behalf of the LLC. The LLC is bound to the contract entered into by Alexis, a manager, but is not bound to the contract entered into by Derek, a nonmanager member.

An LLC is bound to contracts that members or managers have properly entered into on its behalf in the ordinary course of business [ULLCA Section 301].

> It is the spirit and not the form of law that keeps justice alive.
>
> Earl Warren
> *The Law and the Future (1955)*

CONCEPT SUMMARY

Agency Authority to Bind an LLC to Contracts

TYPE OF LLC	AGENCY AUTHORITY
Member-managed LLC	All members have agency authority to bind the LLC to contracts.
Manager-managed LLC	The managers have authority to bind the LLC to contracts; the nonmanager members cannot bind the LLC to contracts.

Duty of Loyalty Owed to an LLC

A member of a member-managed LLC and a manager of a manager-managed LLC owe a *fiduciary* **duty of loyalty** to the LLC. This means that these parties must act honestly in their dealings with the LLC. The duty of loyalty includes the duty not to usurp the LLC's opportunities, make secret profits, secretly deal with the LLC, secretly compete with the LLC, or represent any interests adverse to those of the LLC [ULLCA Section 409(b)].

Example Ester, Yi, Maria, and Enrique form the member-managed LLC Big.Business.com, LLC, which conducts online auctions over the Internet. Ester secretly starts a competing business to conduct online auctions over the Internet. Ester is liable for breaching her duty of loyalty to the LLC with Yi, Maria, and Enrique. Ester is liable for any secret profits she made, and her business will be shut down.

Now suppose that instead, Ester, Yi, Maria, and Enrique designated their LLC as a manager-managed LLC and named Ester and Yi managers. In this case, only the managers owe a duty of loyalty to the LLC, but nonmanager members do not. Therefore, Ester and Yi, the named managers, could not compete with the LLC; Maria and Enrique, nonmanager members, could compete with the LLC without any legal liability.

Limited Duty of Care Owed to an LLC

A member of a member-managed LLC and a manager of a manager-managed LLC owe a *fiduciary* **duty of care** to the LLC not to engage in (1) a known violation of law, (2) intentional conduct, (3) reckless conduct, or (4) grossly negligent conduct that injures the LLC. A member of a member-managed LLC or a manager of a manager-managed LLC are liable to the LLC for any damages the LLC incurs because of such conduct.

This duty is a *limited duty of care* because it does not include ordinary negligence. Thus, if a covered member or manager commits an *ordinarily negligent* act that is not grossly negligent, he or she is not liable to the LLC.

Example Charlene is a member of a member-managed LLC. While engaging in LLC business, Charlene is driving an automobile and accidentally hits Zubin, a pedestrian, and severely injures him. Under agency theory, Zubin sues the LLC and recovers $1 million in damages. If the court determines that Charlene was ordinarily negligent when she caused the accident—for example, she was driving the speed limit and did not see Zubin because the sun was in her eyes—she will not be liable to the LLC for any losses caused to the LLC by her ordinary negligence. If instead the court determines that Charlene was driving 65 mph in a 35 mph zone and thus was grossly negligent, Charlene is liable to the LLC for the $1 million it was ordered to pay Zubin.

No Fiduciary Duty Owed by a Nonmanager Member

A member of a manager-managed LLC who is not a manager owes no fiduciary duty of loyalty or care to the LLC or its other members [ULLCA Section 409(h)(1)]. Basically, a non-manager member of a manager-managed LLC is treated equally to a shareholder in a corporation.

Example Felicia is a member of a 30-person manager-managed LLC that is engaged in buying, developing, and selling real estate. Felicia is not a manager of the LLC but is just a member-owner. If a third party approaches Felicia with the opportunity to purchase a large and valuable piece of real estate that is ripe for development, and the price is below fair market value, Felicia owes no duty to offer the opportunity to the LLC. She may purchase the piece of real estate for herself without violating any duty to the LLC.

Dissolution of an LLC

Unless the operating agreement provides otherwise, a member has the *power* to withdraw from an LLC, whether it is an at-will LLC or a term LLC [ULLCA Section 602(a)]. The disassociation of a member from an at-will LLC is not wrongful unless the power to withdraw is eliminated in the operating agreement [ULLCA Section 602(b)]. The disassociation of a member from a term LLC before the expiration of the specified term is wrongful. A member who wrongfully disassociates him- or herself from an LLC is liable to the LLC and to the other members for any damages caused by his or her **wrongful disassociation** [ULLCA Section 602(c)].

A member's disassociation from an LLC terminates that member's right to participate in the management of the LLC, act as an agent of the LLC, or conduct the LLC's business [ULLCA Section 603(b)(3)]. Disassociation also terminates the disassociating member's duties of loyalty and care to the LLC [ULLCA Section 603(b)(3)].

Payment of Distributional Interest

If a member disassociates from an at-will LLC without causing a wrongful disassociation, the LLC must purchase the disassociated member's *distributional interest* [ULLCA Section 701(a)(1)]. The price and terms of a distributional interest may be fixed in the operating agreement [ULLCA Section 701(c)]. If the price is not agreed upon in the operating agreement, the LLC must pay the fair market value of the distributional interest.

If a member disassociates him- or herself from a term LLC, the LLC must only purchase the disassociating member's distributional interest on the expiration of the specified term of the LLC [ULLCA Section 701(a)(2)]. Any damages caused by wrongful withdrawal must be offset against the purchase price [ULLCA Section 701(f)].

Notice of Disassociation

For two years after a member disassociates him- or herself from an LLC that continues in business, the disassociating member has apparent authority to bind the LLC to contracts in the ordinary course of business except to parties who either (1) know of the disassociation or (2) are given notice of the disassociation [ULLCA Section 703].

An LLC can give *constructive notice* of a member's disassociation by filing a **statement of disassociation** with the secretary of state, stating the name of the LLC and the name of the member disassociated from the LLC [ULLCA Section 704]. This notice is effective against any person who later deals with the disassociated member, whether the person was aware of the notice or not.

Example William, Jesse, and Sandy are members of a member-managed LLC that operates an automobile dealership. Jesse disassociates from the LLC. The LLC fails to file a statement of disassociation with the secretary of state. Although Jesse has no express agency authority to bind the LLC to contracts because she is no longer a member of the LLC, Jesse has apparent authority to bind the LLC to contracts in the ordinary course of business for two years after the disassociation or until the LLC files a statement of disassociation with the secretary of state.

Continuation of an LLC

At the expiration of the term of a term LLC, some of its members may want to continue the LLC. At the expiration of its term, a term LLC can be continued in two situations. First, the members of the LLC may vote prior to the expiration date to continue the LLC for an additional specified term. This requires the unanimous vote of all of the members and the filing of an amendment to the articles of organization with the secretary of state, stating this fact. Second, absent the unanimous vote to continue the term LLC, the LLC may be continued as an at-will LLC by a simple majority vote of the members of the LLC [ULLCA Section 411(b)].

Winding Up an LLC's Business

If an LLC is not continued, the LLC is wound up. The *winding up* of an LLC is the process of preserving and selling the assets of the LLC and distributing the money and property to creditors and members.

The assets of the LLC must be applied to first pay off the creditors; thereafter, the surplus amount is distributed to the members in equal shares, unless the operating agreement provides otherwise [ULLCA Section 806]. It is good practice for members to specify in the operating agreement how distributions will be made to members.

INTERNATIONAL LAW
Limited Liability Companies in Foreign Countries

The United States did not invent the LLC as a form of business. An LLC form of business has been used in different countries of the world for a long time. The **limitada**, a form of business used in Latin America, has many similarities to the LLC. *Limitadas* have been used in Argentina, Brazil, Mexico, and other Latin American countries for a century. These entities share the features of limited liability of owners and centralized management with the LLC. On the European continent, an equivalent form of business to the LLC has existed for centuries. In Spain it was called the **sociedad de responsibilidades limitada**. Modern European LLCs provide for limited liability of owners and centralized management. Germany was one of the last European countries to add the LLC as a form of business—one century ago. In England, an antecedent to the LLC, called the *stock company*, was developed around 1555. These companies, while technically partnerships, had limited liability of owners, free transferability of ownership interests, and centralized management similar to those of modern LLCs.

Limited Liability Partnership (LLP)

Many states have enacted legislation to permit the creation of **limited liability partnerships (LLPs)**. In an LLP, there does not have to be a general partner who is personally liable for the debts and obligations of the partnership. Instead, *all* partners are limited partners who stand to lose only their capital contribution if the partnership fails. None of the partners is personally liable for the debts and obligations of the partnership beyond his or her capital contribution (see Exhibit 30.3).

In most states, the law restricts the use of LLPs to certain types of professionals, such as accountants, lawyers, and doctors. Nonprofessionals cannot use the LLP form of partnership.

LLPs enjoy the "flow-through" tax benefit of other types of partnerships—that is, there is no tax paid at the partnership level, and all profits and losses are reported on the individual partners' income tax returns.

Example Suppose Shou-Yi, Patricia, Ricardo, and Namira, all lawyers, form an LLP called "Shou-Yi, Namira LLP" to provide legal services. While providing legal services to the LLP's client Multi Motors, Inc., Patricia commits legal malpractice (negligence). This malpractice causes Multi Motors, Inc., a huge financial loss. In this case, Multi Motors, Inc., can sue and recover against Patricia, the negligent party, and against Shou-Yi, Namira LLP. Shou-Yi, Ricardo, and Namira can lose their capital contribution in Shou-Yi, Namira LLP but are not personally liable for the damages caused to Multi Motors, Inc. Patricia is personally liable to Multi Motors, Inc., because she was the negligent party.

Articles of Partnership

LLPs must be created formally by filing **articles of partnership** with the secretary of state of the state in which the LLP is organized. This is a public document. The LLP is a **domestic LLP** in the state in which it is organized. The LLP law of the state governs the operation of the LLP. An LLP may do business in other states, however. To do so, the LLP must register as a **foreign LLP** in any state in which it wants to conduct business.

EXHIBIT 30.3

Limited Liability Partnership (LLP)

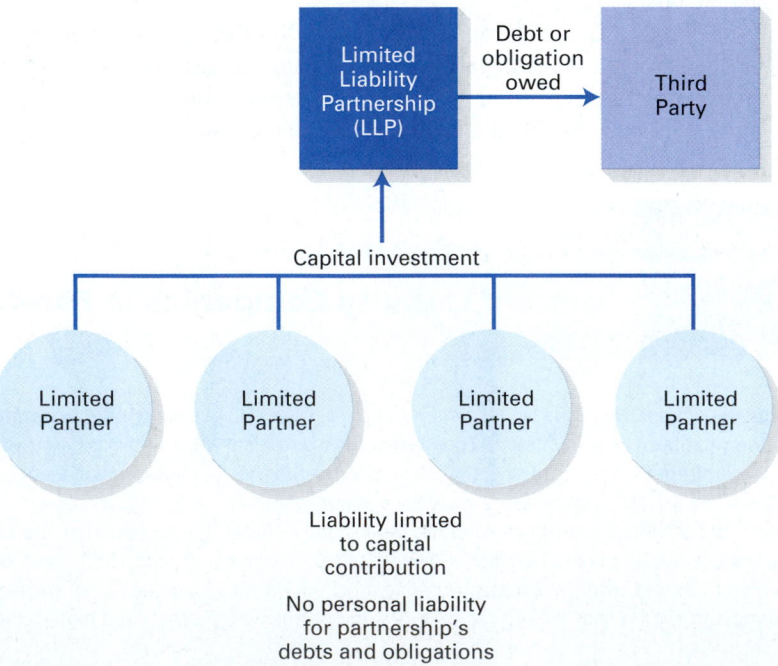

LLP Liability Insurance

In most states, LLP law restricts the use of the LLPs to certain types of professionals, such as accountants and lawyers. Many state laws require LLPs to carry a minimum of $1 million of liability insurance that covers negligence, wrongful acts, and misconduct by partners or employees of the LLP. This requirement guarantees that injured third parties will have compensation to recover for their injuries and is a quid pro quo for permitting partners to have limited liability.

CONTEMPORARY ENVIRONMENT

Accounting Firms Operate as LLPs

Prior to the advent of the limited liability partnership (LLP) form of doing business, accounting firms operated as general partnerships. As such, the general partners were personally liable for the debts and obligations of the general partnership. In large accounting firms, this personal liability was rarely imposed because the partnership usually carried sufficient liability insurance to cover most awards to third-party plaintiffs in lawsuits.

Under this system, when accounting firms were hit with large court judgments, the partners were personally liable. Many lawsuits were brought in conjunction with the failure of large commercial banks and other large firms that accountants had audited. Many of these firms failed because of fraud by their major owners and officers. The shareholders and creditors of these failed companies sued the auditors, alleging that the auditors had been negligent in not catching the fraud. Many

juries agreed and awarded large awards against the accounting firms. Sometimes an accounting firm's liability insurance was not enough to cover a judgment, thus imposing personal liability on partners.

In response, state legislatures created a new form of business, the LLP. This entity was particularly created for accountants, lawyers, and other professionals to offer their services under an umbrella of limited liability. The partners of an LLP have limited liability up to their capital contribution; the partners do not have personal liability for the debts and liabilities of the LLP, however.

Once LLPs were permitted by law, all of the Big Four accounting firms changed their status from general partnerships to LLPs. The signs and letterhead of each Big Four accounting firm prominently announce that the firm is an LLP. Many accounting firms other than the Big Four have also changed over to LLP status, as have many law firms.

Chapter Summary

Limited Liability Company (LLC), p. 833

An LLC is a special form of unincorporated business entity that combines the tax benefits of a partnership and limited liability attribute of a corporation.

The Uniform Limited Liability Company Act

The Uniform Limited Liability Company Act (ULLCA) is a model act that provides comprehensive and uniform rules for the formation, operation, and dissolution of LLCs.

Taxation of LLCs

For federal income tax purposes, an LLC is taxed as a partnership unless it elects to be taxed as a corporation.

Powers of an LLC

An LLC has the same powers as an individual to do all things necessary or convenient to carry on its business or affairs [ULLCA Section 112].

LLC Members' Limited Liability, p. 835

Members are liable for an LLC's debts, obligations, and liabilities only to the extent of their capital contributions. Members are not personally liable for the debts, obligations, and liabilities of the LLC.

Liability of an LLC

An LLC is liable for any loss or injury caused to anyone as a result of a wrongful act or omission by a member, a manager, an agent, or an employee of the LLC who commits the wrongful act while acting within the ordinary course of business of the LLC or with authority of the LLC.

Liability of Managers

Managers of LLCs are not personally liable for the debts, obligations, and liabilities of the LLC they manage. A member is personally liable for the debts of an LLC if he or she personally guarantees the repayment of the LLC's debts.

Liability of Tortfeasors

A tortfeasor is a person who intentionally or unintentionally (negligently) causes injury or death to another person. A member or manager of an LLC who intentionally or unintentionally (negligently) causes injury or death to another person is personally liable to the injured person or the heirs of a deceased person.

Formation of an LLC, p. 838

The name of an LLC must contain the words *limited liability company* or *limited company* or the abbreviation *L.L.C.*, *LLC*, *L.C.*, or *LC*. *Limited* may be abbreviated as *Ltd.*, and *company* may be abbreviated as *Co.*

Articles of Organization

The articles of organization is a document that owners of an LLC must execute, sign, and file with the secretary of state of the appropriate state to form an LLC.

Duration of an LLC

An LLC is an *at-will LLC* unless it is designated as a *term LLC* and the duration of the term is specified in the articles of organization.

Capital Contribution to an LLC

A member's capital contribution to an LLC may be in the form of money, personal property, real property, other tangible property, intangible property (e.g., a patent), services performed, contracts for services to be performed, promissory notes, or other agreements to contribute cash or property [ULLCA Section 401]. The LLC or any creditor who extended credit to the LLC in reliance on the promised contribution may enforce the promised obligation [ULLCA Section 402].

Certificate of Interest

The certificate of interest evidences a member's ownership interest in an LLC.

Operating Agreement

An operating agreement is an agreement between members that governs the affairs and business of the LLC and relations among members, managers, and the LLC.

Conversion of an Existing Business to an LLC

An agreement of conversion is a document that sets forth the terms for converting general partnerships, limited partnerships, and corporations to an LLC.

Dividing an LLC's Profits and Losses

Unless otherwise agreed, the ULLCA mandates that a member has the right to an equal right to share in an LLC's profits and losses. Members may agree in an operating agreement how profits and losses of an LLC will be shared by the members.

Distributional Interest

Distributional interest is a member's ownership interest in an LLC. This interest is personal property that may be transferred in whole or in part.

Management of an LLC, p. 841

Member-Managed LLC

In a member-managed LLC, the members have not designated managers to manage the LLC. A member-managed LLC is managed by its members.

Manager-Managed LLC

In a manager-managed LLC, the members have designated certain members or nonmembers to manage the LLC. A manager-managed LLC is managed by the designated managers; nonmanager members have no right to manage the LLC.

Compensation and Reimbursement

A nonmanager member of an LLC is not entitled to remuneration for services performed for the LLC (except for winding up the business of the LLC). Managers of an LLC, whether they are members or not, are paid compensation and benefits. An LLC is obligated to reimburse members and managers for payments made on behalf of the LLC (e.g., business expenses) and to indemnify members and managers for liabilities incurred in the ordinary course of LLC business.

Agency Authority to Bind an LLC to Contracts

1. *Member-managed LLC.* In a member-managed LLC, all members have agency authority to bind the LLC to contracts.
2. *Manager-managed LLC.* In a manager-managed LLC, the managers have authority to bind the LLC to contracts; The nonmanager members cannot bind the LLC to contracts.
3. *Liability for contracts.* An LLC is bound to contracts that members or managers have properly entered into on its behalf in the ordinary course of business or that the LLC has authorized.

Duty of Loyalty Owed to an LLC

A member of a member-managed LLC and a manager of a manager-managed LLC owe a duty of care to the LLC. This means that these parties must act honestly in their dealings with the LLC. These parties are liable to the LLC for any secret profits made by them and damages caused to the LLC by a violation of their duty of loyalty.

Limited Duty of Care Owed to an LLC

A member of a member-managed LLC and a manager of a manager-managed LLC owe a duty of care to the LLC not to engage in a known violation of law, intentional conduct, reckless conduct, or grossly negligent conduct that injures the LLC. A covered member or manager is liable to the LLC for any damages the LLC suffers because of such breaches of the duty of care. A covered member or manager is not liable to the LLC for damages caused to the LLC because of his or her ordinary negligence.

No Fiduciary Duty Owed by a Nonmanager Member

A member of a manager-managed LLC who is not a manager owes no fiduciary duty of loyalty or care to the LLC.

Dissolution of an LLC, p. 844

Unless the operating agreement provides otherwise, members have the power to withdraw from both at-will and term LLCs. The disassociation of a member from a term LLC before the expiration of the specified term is wrongful. The disassociation of a member from an at-will LLC is not wrongful unless the power to withdraw is eliminated in the operating agreement.

Payment of Distributional Interest

A member who wrongfully disassociates himself or herself from an LLC is liable to the LLC and to the other members for any damages caused by his or her wrongful disassociation.

Notice of Disassociation

The statement of disassociation, filed with the secretary of state, states the name of the member disassociated from the LLC. This statement is constructive notice that is effective against persons, whether those persons are aware of the notice or not. A disassociated member has apparent authority to bind an LLC to contracts in the ordinary course of business for two years after disassociation, unless either the other party knew of the disassociation or constructive notice of the disassociation was given.

Continuation of an LLC

At the expiration of a term LLC, the LLC can be continued by all or some of its members.

Winding Up an LLC's Business

If an LLC is not continued, an LLC's business is wound up. This consists of preserving and selling the assets of the LLC and distributing the money and property to creditors and members. After dissolution and winding up, an LLC may terminate its existence by filing articles of termination with the secretary of state.

Limited Liability Partnership, p. 845

An LLP is a relatively new form of business in which there does not have to be a general partner who is personally liable for debts and obligations of the partnership. All partners are limited partners and stand to lose only their capital contributions should the partnership fail. LLPs are formed by accountants and other professionals, as allowed by LLP law. The partners are the owners of an LLP. An LLP does not pay federal income taxes unless it elects to do so. If an LLP is taxed as a partnership, the income and losses of the LLP flow onto individual partners' federal income tax returns.

Articles of Partnership

In order to form an LLP, the partners of the LLP must execute, sign, and file articles of partnership with the secretary of state of the state in which the LLP organizes.

LLP Liability Insurance

Many state laws require LLPs to carry a minimum of $1 million of liability insurance that covers negligence, wrongful acts, and misconduct by partners or employees of the LLP.

Test Review Terms and Concepts

Case Problems

30.1 Liability of Members: Harold, Jasmine, Caesar, and Yuan form Microhard.com, LLC, a limited liability company, to sell computer hardware and software over the Internet. Microhard.com, LLC, hires Heather, a recent graduate of the University of Chicago and a brilliant software designer, as an employee. Heather's job is to design and develop software that will execute a computer command when the computer user thinks of the next command he or she wants to execute on the computer. Using Heather's research, Microhard.com, LLC, develops the Third Eye software program that does this. Microhard.com, LLC, sends Heather to the annual Comdex computer show in Las Vegas, Nevada, to unveil this revolutionary software. Heather goes to Las Vegas, and while there, she rents an automobile to get from the hotel to the computer show and to meet interested buyers at different locations in Las Vegas. While Heather is driving from her hotel to the site of the Comdex computer show, she negligently causes an accident in which she runs over Harold Singer, a pedestrian.

Singer, who suffers severe personal injuries, sues Microhard.com, LLC, Heather, Harold, Jasmine, Caesar, and Yuan to recover monetary damages for his injuries. Who is liable?

30.2 Liability of Members: Isabel, Koshi, and Winchester each contribute $50,000 capital to form a limited liability company called Fusion Restaurant, LLC, which operates an upscale restaurant that serves "fusion" cuisine, combining foods from cultures around the world. Fusion Restaurant, LLC, as a business, borrows $1 million from Melon Bank for operating capital. Isabel, Koshi, and Winchester are so busy cooking, serving, and running the restaurant that they forget to hold members' meetings, keep minute books, or otherwise observe any usual company formalities for the entire first year of business. After this one year of hard work, Fusion Restaurant, LLC, suffers financial difficulties and defaults on the $1 million bank loan from Melon Bank. Melon Bank sues Fusion Restaurant, LLC, Isabel, Koshi, and Winchester to recover the unpaid bank loan. Who is liable?

30.3 Personal Guarantee: Tran, Donald, and Elvira form a limited liability company called Real Estate Developers, LLC. Each of the three owners contributes $50,000 capital to the LLC, and the LLC then purchases a 400-acre parcel of vacant land 75 miles from Chicago, Illinois. Real Estate Developers, LLC, wants to build a tract of homes on the site. The owners of Real Estate Developers, LLC, go to City Bank and ask to borrow $100 million to complete the development and construction of the homes. City Bank agrees to make the loan, but only if Donald agrees to personally guarantee the LLC's loan and give security for the loan by pledging his 12-story penthouse in Manhattan, worth $100 million, as collateral for the loan. Donald agrees and signs the personal guarantee that pledges his penthouse as collateral for the loan; City Bank makes the $100 million loan to the LLC. Real Estate Developers, LLC, makes regular interest payments on the loan for one year and then defaults on the loan, with $100 million still owed to City Bank. At the time of default, Real Estate Developers, LLC's only asset is the 400-acre parcel of land that is still worth $150,000. City Bank sues Real Estate Developers, LLC, Tran, Donald, and Elvira to recover the amount of the unpaid loan. Who is liable to City Bank?

30.4 Member-Managed LLC: Jennifer, Martin, and Edsel form a limited liability company called Big Apple, LLC, to operate a bar in New York City. Jennifer, Martin, and Edsel are member-managers of the LLC. One of Jennifer's jobs as a member-manager is to drive the LLC's truck and pick up certain items of supply for the bar each Wednesday. On the way back to the bar one Wednesday after picking up the supplies for that week, Jennifer negligently runs over a pedestrian, Tilly Tourismo, on a street in Times Square. Tilly is severely injured and sues Big Apple, LLC, Jennifer, Martin, and Edsel to recover monetary damages for her injuries. Who is liable?

30.5 Contract Liability: Maria, Richard, and Dakota form a limited liability company called Ummmmm, LLC, to operate a spa in Santa Fe, New Mexico. Each member contributes $100,000 in capital to start the LLC. Ummmmm, LLC, is a member-managed LLC. Maria enters into a contract on behalf of the LLC in which she contracts to have a new hot tub installed at the spa by Hot Tubs, Inc., for $80,000. Hot Tubs, Inc., installs the hot tub and sends a bill for $80,000 to Ummmmm, LLC. When Ummmmm, LLC, fails to pay the bill, Hot Tub, Inc., sues Ummmmm, LLC, to recover the unpaid $80,000. Is Ummmmm, LLC, liable?

30.6 Manager-Managed LLC: Juan, Min-Yi, and Chelsea form Unlimited, LLC, a limited liability company that operates a chain of women's retail clothing stores that sell eclectic women's clothing. The company is a manager-managed LLC, and Min-Yi has been designated in the articles of organization filed with the secretary of state as the manager of Unlimited, LLC. Min-Yi sees a store location on Rodeo Drive in Beverly Hills, California, that she thinks would be an excellent location for an Unlimited Store. Min-Yi enters into a five-year lease on behalf of Unlimited, LLC, with Landlord, Inc., the owner of the store building, to lease the store at $100,000 rent per year. While visiting Chicago, Chelsea sees a store location on North Michigan Avenue in Chicago that she thinks is a perfect location for an Unlimited store. Chelsea enters into a five-year lease on behalf of Unlimited, LLC, with Real Estate, Inc., the owner of the store building, to lease the store location at $100,000 rent per year. Is Unlimited, LLC, bound to either of these leases?

30.7 Division of Profits: Donna, Arnold, Jose, and Won-Suk form a limited liability company called Millennium Foods, LLC, to operate an organic foods grocery store in Portland, Oregon. Donna and Arnold each contribute $25,000 capital, Jose contributes $50,000, and Won-Suk contributes $100,000. The LLC's articles of organization are silent as to how profits and losses of the LLC are to be divided. The organic foods grocery store is an immediate success, and Millennium Foods, LLC, makes $200,000 profit the first year. Jose and Won-Suk want the profits distributed based on the amount of the members' capital contribution. Arnold and Donna think the profits should be distributed equally. Who is correct?

30.8 Distributional Interest: Daniel is one of five members of Blue Note, LLC, a limited liability company that operates a jazz club in New Orleans, Louisiana. The LLC's operating agreement provides that Daniel has the right to receive 20 percent of the LLC's profits. Daniel also owns another business as a sole proprietorship and has taken out a $100,000 loan from River Bank to operate this other business. Daniel defaults on his loan from River Bank, and River Bank sues Daniel and obtains a charging order against Daniel's ownership interest in Blue Note, LLC. What rights does River Bank have with regard to Blue Note, LLC, and Daniel's interest in Blue Note, LLC?

30.9 Duty of Loyalty: Ally is a member and a manager of the manager-managed limited liability company called Movers & You, LLC, a moving company. The main business of Movers & You, LLC, is moving large corporations from old office space to new office space in other buildings. After Ally has been a member-manager of Movers & You, LLC, for several years, she decides to join her friend Lana and form another LLC, called Lana & Me, LLC. This new LLC provides moving services that move large corporations from old office space to new office space. Ally becomes a member-manager of Lana & Me, LLC, while retaining her member-manager position at Movers & You, LLC. Ally does not disclose her new position at Lana & Me, LLC, to the other members or managers of Movers & You, LLC. Several years later, the other members of Movers & You, LLC, discover Ally's other ownership and management position at Lana & Me, LLC. Movers & You, LLC, sues Ally to recover damages for her working for Lana & Me, LLC. Is Ally liable?

30.10 Duty of Care: Jonathan is a member of a member-managed limited liability company called Custom Homes, LLC. Custom Homes, LLC, is hired by an owner of a piece of vacant land located on Hilton Head Island, South Carolina, to build a new custom home on the site. Custom Homes, LLC, begins work on the house. Jonathan is responsible for making sure that flashing warning lights are placed in front of the house while it is being constructed to mark open holes in the ground and other dangerous conditions. One night Jonathan leaves the site and forgets to place a flashing warning light marking a hole in front of the house that the LLC is building. That night, Candy, a neighbor who lives in one of the houses in the housing tract where the new house is being built, takes her dog for a walk. As Candy is walking by the unmarked area in front of the new house, she falls into the hole and is severely injured. Candy sues Custom Homes, LLC, to recover damages for her injuries. The jury finds that Jonathan had been ordinarily negligent when he failed to place the flashing warning lights to mark the hole that Candy fell in and awards Candy $1 million for her injuries. Custom Homes, LLC, pays Candy the $1 million and then sues Jonathan to recover the $1 million. Is Jonathan liable?

Ethics Issues

30.11 Ethics: Angela, Yoko, Cherise, and Serena want to start a new business that designs and manufactures toys for children. At a meeting in which the owners want to decide what type of legal form to use to operate the business, Cherise states:

> We should use a limited liability company to operate our business because this form of business provides us, the owners, with a limited liability shield, which means that if the business gets sued and loses, we the owners are not personally liable to the injured party except up to our capital contribution in the business.

The others agree and form a limited liability company called Fuzzy Toys, LLC, to conduct the member-managed business. Each of the four owners contributes $50,000 as her capital contribution to the LLC. Fuzzy Toys, LLC, purchases $800,000 of liability insurance from Allied Insurance Company and starts business. Fuzzy Toys, LLC, designs and produces "Heidi," a new toy doll and female action figure. The new toy doll is an instant success, and Fuzzy Toys, LLC, produces and sells millions of these female action figures. After a few months, however, the LLC starts getting complaints that one of the parts of the female action figure is breaking off quite regularly, and some children are swallowing the part. The concerned member-managers of Fuzzy Toys, LLC, issue an immediate recall of the female action figure, but before all of the dolls are returned for a refund, Catherine, a seven-year-old child, swallows the toy's part and is severely injured. Catherine, through her mother, sues Fuzzy Toys, LLC, Allied Insurance Company, Angela, Yoko, Cherise, and Serena to recover damages for product liability. At the time of suit, Fuzzy Toys, LLC, has $200,000 of assets. The jury awards Catherine $10 million for her injuries. Who is liable to Catherine and for how much? How much does Catherine recover? Did Angela, Yoko, Cherise, and Serena act ethically in setting up their toy business as an LLC? Explain.

30.12 Ethics: Christopher, Melony, Xie, and Ruth form iNet.com, LLC, a limited liability company. The four members are all Ph.D. scientists who have been working together in a backyard garage to develop a handheld wireless device that lets you receive and send e-mail, surf the Internet, use a word processing program that can print to any printer in the world, view cable television stations, and keep track of anyone you want anywhere in the world and let you zoom in on the person being tracked without that person knowing you are doing so. This new device, called Eros, costs only $29 but makes the owners $25 profit per unit sold. The owners agree that they will buy a manufacturing plant and start producing the unit in six months. Melony, who owns a one-quarter interest in iNet.com, LLC, decides she wants "more of the action" and soon, so she secretly sells the plans and drawings for the new Eros unit to a competitor for $100 million. The competitor comes out with exactly the same device, called Zeus, in one month and beats iNet.com, LLC, to the market. The LLC, which later finds out about Melony's action, suffers damages of $100 million because of Melony's action. Is Melony liable to iNet.com, LLC? Explain. Did Melony act ethically in this case?

IRAC Writing Assignment

Read **Case A-30** in Appendix A [*Water, Waste, and Land, Inc. v. Preferred Income Investors, L.L.C.*]. Use the IRAC method to prepare a written analysis of the case.

Franchises and Special Forms of Business

> **❝** *It has been uniformly laid down in this Court, as far back as we can remember, that good faith is the basis of all mercantile transactions.* **❞**
>
> —JUDGE BULLER
> Salomons v. Nisson (1788)

CHAPTER OBJECTIVES

After studying this chapter, you should be able to:

1. Define *franchise* and describe the various forms of franchises.
2. Describe the rights and duties of the parties to a franchise agreement.
3. Identify the contract tort liability of franchisors and franchisees.
4. Define *licensing* and describe how trademarks and intellectual property are licensed.
5. Describe how international franchising, joint ventures, and strategic alliances are used in global commerce.

CHAPTER CONTENTS

- Introduction to Franchises and Special Forms of Business
- Franchise
- Liability of Franchisor and Franchisee
- Licensing
- Joint Venture
- Strategic Alliance
- Chapter Summary
- Test Review Terms and Concepts
- Case Problems
- Ethics Issues
- IRAC Writing Assignment

Introduction to Franchises and Special Forms of Business

Franchising is an important method for distributing goods and services to the public. Originally pioneered by the automobile and soft drink industries, franchising today is used in many other forms of business. The 700,000-plus franchise outlets in the United States account for over 25 percent of retail sales and about 15 percent of the gross domestic product (GDP).

Special forms of business are used in domestic and international commerce. *Licensing* permits one business to use another business's trademarks, service marks, trade names, and other intellectual property in selling goods or services. *Joint ventures* allow two or more businesses to combine their resources to pursue a single project or transaction. *Strategic alliances* are often used to enter foreign markets.

This chapter discusses franchises, licensing, joint ventures, and strategic alliances used in domestic and international commerce.

Franchising

Franchising is a major form of business in the United States.

Franchise

A **franchise** is established when one party (the **franchisor**, or **licensor**) licenses another party (the **franchisee**, or **licensee**) to use the franchisor's trade name, trademarks, commercial symbols, patents, copyrights, and other property in the distribution and selling of goods and services. Generally, the franchisor and the franchisee are established as separate corporations. The term *franchise* refers to both the agreement between the parties and the franchise outlet.

There are several advantages to franchising. For example, the franchisor can reach lucrative new markets, the franchisee has access to the franchisor's knowledge and resources while running an independent business, and consumers are assured of uniform product quality.

A typical franchise arrangement is illustrated in Exhibit 31.1.

Types of Franchises

There are four basic forms of franchises: (1) *distributorship franchise*, (2) *processing plant franchise*, (3) *chain-style franchise*, and (4) *area franchise*. They are discussed in the following paragraphs.

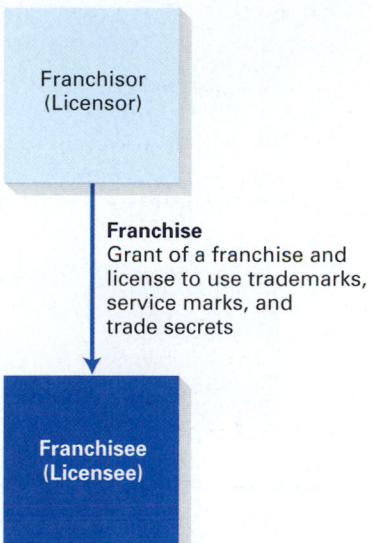

EXHIBIT 31.1

Franchise

DISTRIBUTORSHIP FRANCHISE In a **distributorship franchise**, the franchisor manufactures a product and licenses a retail dealer to distribute the product to the public.

Example The Ford Motor Company manufactures automobiles and franchises independently owned automobile dealers (franchisees) to sell them to the public.

PROCESSING PLANT FRANCHISE In a **processing plant franchise**, the franchisor provides a secret formula or the like to the franchisee. The franchisee then manufactures the product at its own location and distributes it to retail dealers.

Example The Coca-Cola Corporation, which owns the secret formulas for making Coca-Cola and other soft drinks, licenses regional bottling companies to manufacture and distribute soft drinks under the "Coca-Cola" and other brand names.

CHAIN-STYLE FRANCHISE In a **chain-style franchise**, the franchisor licenses the franchisee to make and sell its products or services to the public from a retail outlet serving an exclusive geographic territory. Most fast-food franchises use this form.

Example The Pizza Hut Corporation franchises independently owned restaurant franchises to make and sell pizzas to the public under the "Pizza Hut" name.

AREA FRANCHISE In an **area franchise**, the franchisor authorizes the franchisee to negotiate and sell franchises on behalf of the franchisor. The area franchisee is called a **subfranchisor** (see Exhibit 31.2). An area franchise is granted for a certain designated geographic area, such as a state, a region, or another agreed-upon area. Area franchises are often used when a franchisor wants to enter a market in another country.

Example If Starbucks wanted to enter the country of Vietnam to operate its coffee shops, it could grant an area franchise to a Vietnamese company, which would then choose the individual franchisees in that country.

State Disclosure Laws

Most states have enacted franchise laws that require franchisors to register and deliver disclosure documents to prospective franchisees. State franchise administrators developed a uniform disclosure document called the **Uniform Franchise Offering Circular (UFOC)**.

The UFOC and state laws require a franchisor to make specific presale disclosures to prospective franchisees. Information that must be disclosed includes a description of the

EXHIBIT 31.2

Area Franchise

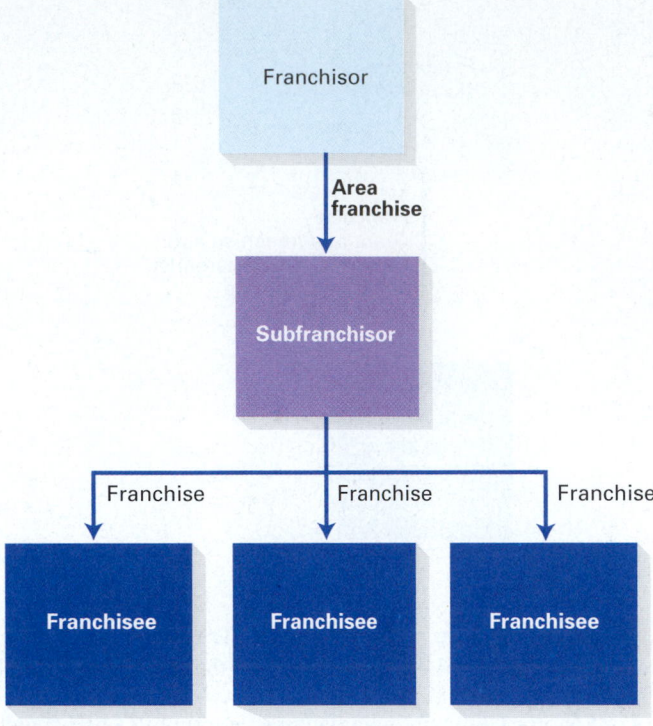

franchisor's business, balance sheets and income statements of the franchisor for the preceding three years, material terms of the franchise agreement, any restrictions on the franchisee's territory, grounds for termination of the franchise, and other relevant information.

FTC Franchise Rule

The **Federal Trade Commission (FTC)**, a federal administrative agency, has adopted the **FTC franchise rule**. The FTC rule requires franchisors to make full presale disclosure nationwide to prospective franchisees.[1] The FTC does not require the registration of the disclosure document prior to its use. The UFOC satisfies both state regulations and the FTC. The FTC rule requires the disclosures discussed in the following paragraphs.

DISCLOSURE OF SALES OR EARNINGS PROJECTIONS BASED ON ACTUAL DATA If a franchisor makes sales or earnings projections for a potential franchise location that are based on the actual sales, income, or profit figures of an existing franchise, the franchisor must disclose the following:

- The number and percentage of its actual franchises that have obtained such results.
- A cautionary statement in at least 12-point boldface type that reads, "Caution: Some outlets have sold (or earned) this amount. There is no assurance you'll do as well. If you rely upon our figures, you must accept the risk of not doing so well."

DISCLOSURE OF SALES OR EARNINGS PROJECTIONS BASED ON HYPOTHETICAL DATA If a franchisor makes sales or earnings projections based on hypothetical examples, the franchisor must disclose the following:

- The assumptions underlying the estimates.
- The number and percentage of actual franchises that have obtained such results.
- A cautionary statement in at least 12-point boldface print that reads, "Caution: These figures are only estimates of what we think you may earn. There is no assurance you'll do as well. If you rely upon our figures, you must accept the risk of not doing so well."

CONTEMPORARY ENVIRONMENT
FTC Franchise Notice

The FTC requires that the following statement, called the **FTC notice**, appear in at least 12-point boldface type on the cover of a franchisor's required disclosure statement to prospective franchisees:

> **To protect you, we've required your franchisor to give you this information.**
>
> **We haven't checked it, and don't know if it's correct. It should help you make up your mind. Study it carefully. While it includes some information about your contract, don't rely on it alone to understand your contract. Read all of your contract carefully. Buying a franchise is a complicated investment. Take your time to decide. If**

possible, show your contract and this information to an adviser, like a lawyer or an accountant. If you find anything you think may be wrong or anything important that's been left out, you should let us know about it. It may be against the law. There may also be laws on franchising in your state. Ask your state agencies about them.

If a franchisor violates FTC disclosure rules, the wrongdoer is subject to an injunction against further franchise sales, civil fines, and an FTC civil action on behalf of injured franchisees to recover damages from the franchisor that were caused by the violation.

Trademarks

A franchisor's ability to maintain the public's perception of the quality of the goods and services associated with its trade name, **trademarks**, and **service marks** is the essence of its success. The **Lanham Trademark Act**[2] provides for the registration of trademarks and service marks with the federal **Patent and Trademark Office** in Washington, DC, by franchisors and others. Most franchisors license the use of their trade names, trademarks, and service marks and prohibit their franchisees from misusing these marks. Anyone who uses a mark without authorization may be sued for *trademark infringement*. The trademark holder can sue to recover damages and obtain an injunction prohibiting further unauthorized use of the mark.

Example The McDonald's Corporation, a major franchisor of fast-food restaurants, licenses to franchisees the rights to use its trademarks, such as "McDonald's," "Big Mac," "Chicken McNuggets," "Quarter Pounder," "McChicken," "McBacon," "McFeast," "I'm Lovin' It," "Ronald McDonald," the McDonald's Golden Arches, and such.

Web Exercises

1. **WEB** Visit the website of McDonald's Corporation, at *www.mcdonalds.com*. What famous trademarks can you find?

2. **WEB** Visit the website of KFC, a major franchiser of fast-food restaurants, at *www.kfc.com*. What famous trademarks can you find?

3. **WEB** Visit the website of Baskin-Robbins, a franchisor of retail ice cream stores, at *www.baskinrobbins.com*. What famous trademarks can you find?

ETHICS SPOTLIGHT
Häagen-Dazs Ice Cream Franchise

Franchise agreements are detailed documents that are carefully drafted to spell out the rights and duties of the parties. A franchisee must be careful to read and understand the terms of the agreement, as the following case demonstrates.

Reuben Mattus developed a "super premium" ice cream and named it "Häagen-Dazs" to give the product a Scandinavian flair. Mattus began selling Häagen-Dazs ice cream in prepackaged pints to small stores and delicatessens in the New York metropolitan area. Sales

of the product were expanded into some grocery stores and other retail outlets.

Twenty years later, Mattus's daughter, Doris Mattus-Hurley, opened the first "Häagen-Dazs Shoppe" in Brooklyn Heights, New York. After this shop prospered, Mattus-Hurley began franchising other shops to independent franchisees throughout the country. Häagen-Dazs ice cream is manufactured, distributed, and franchised through a variety of corporate entities (collectively referred to as "Häagen-Dazs"). The franchise agreement grants a limited license to the franchisee to operate a single shop under the Häagen-Dazs trademark at a specific location for a specified term ranging from 5 to 12 years. The franchisee agrees to purchase all its ice cream from the franchisor at prices set by Häagen-Dazs.

Seven years after Häagen-Dazs Company began granting franchises, the Pillsbury Company (Pillsbury), a diversified international food and restaurant company headquartered in Minneapolis, Minnesota, purchased the Häagen-Dazs Company, including its franchise operations. The franchise agreements were assigned to Pillsbury as part of the sale. Pillsbury decided that it could maximize sales of Häagen-Dazs ice cream by expanding sales through methods of distribution that did not involve franchisees. Pillsbury substantially increased sales of Häagen-Dazs products to national grocery store chains, convenience stores such as 7-Eleven, and other retail outlets.

This change severely harmed sales at existing franchises. Franchisees located in many states sued Pillsbury, alleging breach of the franchise agreement. The plaintiffs claimed that the defendant breached the franchise agreement by distributing Häagen-Dazs ice cream through nonfranchised outlets that were not "upscale" and through mass distribution of prepackaged pints that competed with franchise outlet sales.

The U.S. District Court held that the express terms of the franchise agreement had not been violated. The franchise agreement expressly reserved the right of the franchisor to distribute Häagen-Dazs products "through not only Häagen-Dazs Shoppes, but through any other distribution method, which may from time to time be established." The Court held that this language gave Pillsbury the right to aggressively distribute prepackaged pints of Häagen-Dazs ice cream through nonfranchise outlets even though that distribution adversely affected retail sales by franchisees. The District Court granted Pillsbury's motion for summary judgment. *Carlock v. Pillsbury Company*, 719 F.Supp. 791, **Web** 1989 U.S. Dist. Lexis 9370 (United States District Court for the District of Minnesota)

Law & Ethics Questions

1. **ETHICS** Even though the express terms of the franchise agreement allowed Pillsbury to distribute Häagen-Dazs ice cream through nonfranchise outlets, do you think Pillsbury acted ethically in doing so?

2. **ETHICS** Should franchise agreements include an implied covenant that requires a franchisor to act in good faith when dealing with franchisees? Would that have helped the franchisees in this case?

Web Exercises

1. **WEB** For the complete opinion of this case, go to *www.prenhall.com/cheesemancases*.

2. **WEB** Visit the website of the U.S. District Court of Minnesota, at *www.mnd.uscourts.gov*.

3. **WEB** Visit the website of Pillsbury Company, at *www.pillsbury.com*. Can you find any information about Häagen-Dazs franchising.

4. **WEB** Use *www.google.com* to find an article that discusses Häagen-Dazs franchise opportunities. Read it.

5. **WEB** Use *www.google.com* to find a photo of a Häagen-Dazs franchise outlet.

Trade Secrets

Franchisors are often owners of **trade secrets**, including product formulas, business plans and models, and other ideas. Franchisors license and disclose many of their trade secrets to franchisees. The misappropriation of a trade secret is called *unfair competition*. The holder of the trade secret can sue the offending party for damages and obtain an injunction to prohibit further unauthorized use of the trade secret.

Example The formula for the Coca-Cola soft drink is a highly protected trade secret.

Web Exercises

1. **WEB** Visit the website of the Coca-Cola Corporation, at *www.cocacola.com*. Can you find any information about the protection of its trade secrets?

2. **WEB** Use *www.google.com* to find an article that discusses the protection of the famous Coca-Cola formula. Read it.

3. **WEB** Use *www.google.com* to find an article that discusses the protection of any important trade secret. Read it.

The Franchise Agreement

A prospective franchisee must apply to the franchisor for a franchise. The application often includes detailed information about the applicant's previous employment, financial and educational history, credit status, and so on. If an applicant is approved, the parties enter into a **franchise agreement** that sets forth the terms and conditions of the franchise. Although some states permit oral franchise agreements, most have enacted a Statute of Frauds that requires franchise agreements to be in writing. To prevent unjust enrichment, the courts occasionally enforce oral franchise agreements that violate the Statute of Frauds.

Franchise agreements do not usually have much room for negotiation. Generally, the agreement is a standard form contract prepared by the franchisor. Franchise agreements cover the following topics:

1. *Quality control standards.* The franchisor's most important assets are its name and reputation. The quality control standards set out in the franchise agreement—such as the franchisor's right to make periodic inspections of the franchisee's premises and operations—are intended to protect these assets. Failure to meet the proper standards can result in loss of the franchise.
2. *Training requirements.* Franchisees and their personnel are usually required to attend training programs either on site or at the franchisor's training facilities.
3. *Covenant not to compete.* Covenants not to compete prohibit franchisees from competing with the franchisor during a specific time and in a specified area after the termination of the franchise. Unreasonable (overextensive) covenants not to compete are void.
4. *Arbitration clause.* Most franchise agreements contain an arbitration clause which provides that any claim or controversy arising from the franchise agreement or an alleged breach thereof is subject to arbitration. The U.S. Supreme Court has held such clauses to be enforceable.[3]
5. *Other terms and conditions.* Capital requirements are included in the agreement. They may include restrictions on the use of the franchisor's trade name, trademarks, and logo; standards of operation; duration of the franchise; record-keeping requirements; sign requirements; hours of operation; prohibition as to the sale or assignment of the franchise; conditions for the termination of the franchise; and other specific terms pertinent to the operation of the franchise and the protection of the parties' rights.

Sample provisions from a franchise agreement are set forth in Exhibit 31.3.

Web Exercises

1. **WEB** Use *www.google.com* to find a copy of the McDonald's Corporation franchise agreement.
2. **WEB** Use *www.google.com* to find a copy of the KFC franchise agreement.

Franchise Fees

Franchise fees payable by the franchisee are usually stipulated in the franchise agreement. The franchisor may require the franchisee to pay any or all of the following fees:

1. *Initial license fee.* An **initial license fee** is a lump-sum payment for the privilege of being granted a franchise.
2. *Royalty fees.* A **royalty fee** is a fee for the continued use of the franchisor's trade name, property, and assistance that is often computed as a percentage of the franchisee's gross sales.
3. *Assessment fee.* An **assessment fee** is a fee for such things as advertising and promotional campaigns and administrative costs, billed either as a flat monthly or annual fee or as a percentage of gross sales.
4. *Lease fees.* **Lease fees** are payment for any land or equipment leased from the franchisor, billed either as a flat monthly or annual fee or as a percentage of gross sales or other agreed-upon amount.
5. *Cost of supplies.* **Cost of supplies** involves payment for supplies purchased from the franchisor.

Termination of a Franchise

Most franchise agreements permit a franchisor to terminate the franchise "for cause." For example, the continued failure of a franchisee to pay franchise fees or meet legitimate quality control standards would be deemed just cause. Unreasonably strict application of

EXHIBIT 31.3

Sample Provisions from a Franchise Agreement

FRANCHISE AGREEMENT

Agreement, this 2nd day of January, 2008, between ALASKA PANCAKE HOUSE, INC., an Alaska corporation located in Anchorage, Alaska (hereinafter called the Company) and PANCAKE SYRUP COMPANY, INC., a Michigan corporation located in Detroit, Michigan (hereinafter called the Franchisee), for one KLONDIKE PANCAKE HOUSE restaurant to be located in the City of Mackinac Island, Michigan.

RECITALS

A. The Company is the owner of proprietary and other rights and interests in various service marks, trademarks, and trade names used in its business including the trade name and service mark "KLONDIKE PANCAKE HOUSE."

B. The Company operates and enfranchises others to operate restaurants under the trade name and service mark "KLONDIKE PANCAKE HOUSE" using certain recipes, formulas, food preparation procedures, business methods, business forms, and business policies it has developed. The Company has also developed a body of knowledge pertaining to the establishment and operation of restaurants. The Franchisee acknowledges that he does not presently know these recipes, formulas, food preparation procedures, business methods, or business policies, nor does the Franchisee have these business forms or access to the Company's body of knowledge.

C. The Franchisee intends to enter the restaurant business and desires access to the Company's recipes, formulas, food preparation procedures, business methods, business forms, business policies, and body of knowledge pertaining to the operation of a restaurant. In addition, the Franchisee desires access to information pertaining to new developments and techniques in the Company's restaurant business.

D. The Franchisee desires to participate in the use of the Company's rights in its service marks and trademarks in connection with the operation of one restaurant to be located at a site approved by the Company and the Franchisee.

E. The Franchisee understands that information received from the Company or from any of its officers, employees, agents, or franchisees is confidential and has been developed with a great deal of effort and expense. The Franchisee acknowledges that the information is being made available to him so that he may more effectively establish and operate a restaurant.

F. The Company has granted, and will continue to grant others, access to its recipes, formulas, food preparation procedures, business methods, business forms, business policies, and body of knowledge pertaining to the operation of restaurants and information pertaining to new developments and techniques in its business.

G. The Company has and will continue to license others to use its service marks and trademarks in connection with the operation of restaurants at Company-approved locations.

H. The Franchise Fee and Royalty constitute the sole consideration to the Company for the use by the Franchisee of its body of knowledge, systems, and trademark rights.

I. The Franchisee acknowledges that he received the Company's franchise offering prospectus at or prior to the first personal meeting with a Company representative and at least ten (10) business days prior to the signing of this Agreement and that he has been given the opportunity to clarify provisions he did not understand and to consult with an attorney or other professional advisor. Franchisee represents he understands and agrees to be bound by the terms, conditions, and obligations of this Agreement.

J. The Franchisee acknowledges that he understands that the success of the business to be operated by him under this Agreement depends primarily upon his efforts and that neither the Company nor any of its agents or representatives have made any oral, written, or visual representations or projections of actual or potential sales, earnings, or net or gross profits. Franchisee understands that the restaurant operated under this Agreement may lose money or fail.

AGREEMENT

Acknowledging the above recitals, the parties hereto agree as follows:

1. Upon execution of this Agreement, the Franchisee shall pay to the Company a Franchise Fee of $30,000 that shall not be refunded in any event.

2. The Franchisee shall also pay to the Company, weekly, a Royalty equal to eight (8%) percent of the gross sales from each restaurant that he operates throughout the term of this Agreement. "Gross sales" means all sales or revenues derived from the Franchisee's location exclusive of sales taxes.

3. The Company hereby grants to the Franchisee:

   a. Access to the Company's recipes, formulas, food preparation procedures, business methods, business forms, business policies, and body of knowledge pertaining to the operation of a restaurant.

   b. Access to information pertaining to new developments and techniques in the Company's restaurant business.

   c. License to use of the Company's rights in and to its service marks and trademarks in connection with the operation of one restaurant to be located at a site approved by the Company and the Franchisee.

4. The Company agrees to:

   a. Provide a training program for the operator of restaurants using the Company's recipes, formulas, food preparation procedures, business methods, business forms, and business policies. The Franchisee shall pay all transportation, lodging, and other expenses incurred in attending the program. The Franchisee must attend the training program before opening his restaurant.

   b. Provide a Company Representative that the Franchisee may call upon for consultation concerning the operation of his business.

   c. Provide the Franchise with a program of assistance that shall include periodic consultations with a Company Representative, publish a periodical advising of new developments and techniques in the Company's restaurant business, and grant access to Company personnel for consultations concerning the operation of his business.

5. The Franchisee agrees to:

   a. Begin operation of a restaurant within 365 days. The restaurant will be at a location found by the Franchisee and approved by the Company. The Company or one of its designees will lease the premises and sublet them to the Franchisee at cost. The Franchisee will then construct and equip his unit in accordance with Company specifications contained in the Operating Manual. Upon written request from the Franchisee, the Company will grant a 180-day extension that is effective immediately upon receipt of the request. Under certain circumstances, and at the sole discretion of the Company, the Company may grant additional time in which to open the business. In all instances, the location of each unit must be approved by the Company and the Franchisee. If the restaurant is not operating within 365 days, or within any approved extensions, this Agreement will automatically expire.

   b. Operate his business in compliance with applicable laws and governmental regulations. The Franchisee will obtain at his expense, and keep in force, any permits, licenses, or other consents required for the leasing, construction, or operation of his business. In addition, the Franchisee shall operate his restaurant in accordance with the Company's Operation Manual, which may be amended from time to time as a result of experience, changes in the law, or changes in the marketplace. The Franchisee shall refrain from conducting any business or selling any products other than those approved by the Company at the approved location.

   c. Be responsible for all costs of operating his unit, including but not limited to, advertising, taxes, insurance, food products, labor, and utilities. Insurance shall include, but not be limited to, comprehensive liability insurance including products liability coverage in the minimum amount of $1,000,000. The Franchisee shall keep these policies in force for the mutual benefit of the parties. In addition, the Franchisee shall save the Company harm from any claim of any type that arises in connection with the operation of his business.

a just cause termination clause constitutes wrongful termination. A single failure to meet a quality control standard, for example, is not cause for termination.

Termination-at-will clauses in franchise agreements are generally held to be void on the grounds that they are unconscionable. The rationale for this position is that the franchisee has spent time, money, and effort developing the franchise.

If a franchise is terminated without just cause, the franchisee can sue the franchisor for **wrongful termination**. The franchisee can then recover damages caused by the unlawful termination and recover the franchise.

Breach of the Franchise Agreement

A lawful franchise agreement is an enforceable contract. Each party owes a duty to adhere to and perform under the terms of the franchise agreement. If the agreement is breached, the aggrieved party can sue the breaching party for rescission of the agreement, restitution, and damages.

In the following case, the court held that a franchisor had properly terminated a franchisee.

C A S E 31.1 *Termination of a Franchise*	**Dunkin' Donuts of America, Inc. v. Middletown Donut Corporation** 495 A.2d 66, **Web** 1985 N.J. Lexis 2369 Supreme Court of New Jersey

> **❝** *A franchisee who gets caught with his hand in the proverbial cookie jar (or doughnut box, as the case may be) must suffer the known consequences.* **❞**
>
> —Judge Clifford

Facts

Dunkin' Donuts of America, Inc. (Dunkin' Donuts), is a franchisor that licenses franchised donuts shops throughout the United States. Gerald Smothergill, through two corporations, entered into franchise and lease agreements with Dunkin' Donuts to operate Dunkin' Donuts franchise shops in Middletown and West Long Branch, New Jersey. Smothergill paid $115,000 for the two franchises. Under each franchise agreement, Smothergill was required to keep accurate sales records, pay a basic franchise fee of 4.9 percent of gross sales, and pay an advertising fee of 2 percent of gross sales. The lease agreements were conditioned on Smothergill's remaining a franchisee in good standing under the franchise agreements.

Subsequently, Dunkin' Donuts notified Smothergill that his franchise agreements were being terminated due to his intentional underreporting of gross sales. The termination notice provided an opportunity for Smothergill to cure the breach by making prompt payment of the amounts due. Smothergill made no attempt to cure and refused to abandon his Dunkin' Donuts shops. Dunkin' Donuts sued to enforce its claimed right of termination and to collect damages. The trial court permitted Dunkin' Donuts to terminate the franchise agreements. Smothergill appealed.

Issue

Was the franchise agreements properly terminated "for cause" by Dunkin' Donuts?

Language of the Court

At the conclusion of the trial, the trial court found as fact that Smothergill had been guilty of substantial, intentional, and long-continued underreporting of gross sales at both of his Dunkin' Donuts stores. The court determined that Smothergill had failed to keep the financial records that were required under the franchise agreements and that the failure to keep records was not the result of carelessness or incompetence. Rather, Smothergill's delinquency in recordkeeping was part of a deliberate effort to underreport sales, which in turn would result in the underpayment of franchise fees, underpayment of advertising fund fees, underpayment of rental override charges, and evasion of federal and state taxes. In short, the trial court found as a fact that Smothergill was "guilty of unconscionable cheating."

Dunkin' Donuts, as franchisor of a sizeable network of New Jersey franchises, has a real and legitimate interest in maintaining the integrity of its system. Other Dunkin' Donuts franchisees also have an interest in promoting honest reporting because a percentage of their reported gross sales are pooled in a common advertising fund that benefits all. To the extent that a franchisee such as Smothergill underreports gross sales, he cheats not only the franchisor but all other franchisees as well. Upon signing the Dunkin' Donuts franchise agreement, both franchisor and franchisee were aware of the rules of the game.

Those rules seem fair. A franchisee who gets caught with his hand in the proverbial cookie jar (or doughnut box, as the case may be) must suffer the known consequences.

Decision

The supreme court of New Jersey held that Smothergill intentionally breached the franchise agreements and that Dunkin' Donuts had properly terminated Smothergill as a franchisee. The supreme court affirmed the trial court's decision allowing Dunkin' Donuts to terminate the franchise agreements.

Law & Ethics Questions

1. Should franchisors be permitted to terminate franchises at will? Or is the rule that permits franchisors to terminate franchises "for cause" a better rule? Explain.

2. **ETHICS** Did Smothergill act ethically in this case?

3. **ETHICS** Do you think many franchisees "cheat" when franchise royalty fees are based on gross sales?

Web Exercises

1. **WEB** For the complete opinion of this case, go to *www.prenhall.com/cheesemancases*.

2. **WEB** Visit the website of the supreme court of New Jersey, at *www.judiciary.state.nj.us/supreme/index.htm*.

3. **WEB** Visit the website of Dunkin' Donuts, at *www.dunkindonuts.com*. Can you find any information about obtaining a Dunkin' Donuts franchise?

4. **WEB** Use *www.google.com* to find a picture of a Dunkin' Donuts shop.

ETHICS SPOTLIGHT

Franchisee's Fraud Caught

Baskin-Robbins Ice Cream Company (Baskin-Robbins) is a franchisor that has established a system of more than 2,700 franchise ice cream retail stores nationwide. The franchisees agree to purchase ice cream in bulk only from Baskin-Robbins or an authorized Baskin-Robbins source, to sell only Baskin-Robbins ice cream under the "Baskin-Robbins" trademarks, and to keep specific business hours. Franchisees agree to pay ice cream invoices to Baskin-Robbins when due. If ice cream invoices are not paid within seven days of delivery of the ice cream, payment by certified check is required. If such check is not received, prepayment in cash is then required. If Baskin-Robbins must institute a lawsuit for a breach of the franchise agreement, the franchisee is required to pay all costs incurred by Baskin-Robbins if it is successful in the lawsuit.

Baskin-Robbins entered into a standard franchise agreement with D&L Ice Cream Company, Inc., (D&L), granting it a franchise to operate a retail ice cream store in Brooklyn, New York. During the course of the franchise, D&L consistently failed to maintain proper business hours and failed to pay ice cream invoices when due. Baskin-Robbins properly invoked its right to require payment by certified check. When such payment was not received, Baskin-Robbins required prepayment in cash for ice cream deliveries. In response, D&L purchased bulk ice cream from other manufacturers and sold it in its store under the "Baskin-Robbins" trademarks. Upon discovering this fact, Baskin-Robbins sent a notice of termination to D&L. D&L ignored the notice and continued to operate the Baskin-Robbins store and sell other brands of ice cream

in cups and containers bearing the Baskin-Robbins trademarks. Baskin-Robbins sued D&L for trademark infringement.

The court stated that the sale by a franchised licensee of unauthorized products—that is, products outside the scope of the license—is likely to confuse the public into believing that such products are in fact manufactured or authorized by the trademark owner, when in fact they are not. The court concluded that D&L had engaged in trademark infringement. The court held that Baskin-Robbins was entitled to a permanent injunction, to recover outstanding monies owed by D&L, to all profits made by D&L as a result of the trademark infringement, and to full costs and attorneys' fees incurred in connection with this litigation. *Baskin-Robbins Ice Cream Co. v. D&L Ice Cream Co., Inc.*, 576 F.Supp. 1055, **Web** 1983 U.S. Dist. Lexis 11057 (United States District Court for the Eastern District of New York)

Law & Ethics Questions

1. **ETHICS** Did D&L act ethically in this case?

2. Do you think there was trademark infringement in this case?

Web Exercises

1. **WEB** For the complete opinion of this case, go to *www.prenhall.com/cheesemancases*.

2. **WEB** Visit the website of the U.S. District Court for the Eastern District of New York, at *www.nyed.uscourts.gov*.

INTERNATIONAL LAW
International Franchising

The international market presently offers a great opportunity for U.S. franchisors to expand their businesses. Many U.S. franchisors view international expansion as their number-one priority. However, in addition to providing lucrative new markets, international franchising also poses difficulties and risks.

The expansion into other countries through franchising means that U.S. franchisors can expand internationally without the huge capital investments that would be required if they tried to penetrate those markets with company-owned stores or branches. In addition, a foreign franchisee will know things about the cultural and business traditions of the foreign country that the franchisor will not. Consequently, the franchisee will be better able to serve the consumers and customers in the particular market.

Foreign franchising is not without difficulties, however. For example, the host country's laws may differ from U.S. laws. Foreign cultures may also require different advertising, marketing, and promotional approaches. In addition, the franchisor may be subjecting itself to government regulation in the host country. Finally, different dispute settlement procedures may be in place that will have to be used if there is a dispute between the U.S. franchisor and the foreign franchisee. Many U.S. companies are entering China or expanding existing operations there. China provides an enormous opportunity for the expansion of franchises.

In addition to U.S. franchisors' expanding to other countries, foreign franchisors also view the United States as a potential market. This will provide an opportunity for U.S. entrepreneurs to become franchisees for foreign franchisors.

Web Exercises

1. **WEB** Use *www.google.com* to find an article that discusses how McDonald's Corporation expanded its operations into China. Has the expansion been successful? Use *www.google.com* to find a photo of a McDonald's fast-food restaurant in China.

2. **WEB** Use *www.google.com* to find an article that discusses how KFC expanded its operations into China. Has the expansion been successful? Use *www.google.com* to find a photo of a KFC fast-food restaurant in China.

3. **WEB** Use *www.google.com* to find an article that discusses how Starbucks expanded its operations into France. Has the expansion been successful? Use *www.google.com* to find a photo of a Starbucks coffee shop in Paris, France.

Tokyo, Japan

Franchisers are expanding into other countries using area franchises and other forms of joint ventures and strategic alliances.

Liability of Franchisor and Franchisee

If properly organized and operated, the franchisor and franchisee are separate legal entities. Therefore, the franchisor deals with the franchisee as an *independent contractor.*

Franchisees are liable on their own contracts and are liable for their own torts (e.g., negligence). Franchisors are liable for their own contracts and torts. Generally, neither party is liable for the contracts or torts of the other.

Example Suppose that McDonald's Corporation, a fast-food restaurant franchisor, grants a restaurant franchise to Tina Corporation. Tina Corporation opens the franchise restaurant. One day, a customer at the franchise spills a chocolate shake on the floor. The employees at the franchise fail to clean up the spilled shake, and one hour later, another customer slips on the spilled shake and suffers severe injuries. The injured customer can recover damages from the franchisee, Tina Corporation, because it was negligent. It cannot recover damages from the franchisor, McDonald's Corporation.

Now suppose that McDonald's Corporation, the franchisor, grants a franchise to Gion Corporation, the franchisee. McDonald's Corporation enters into a loan agreement with City Bank, whereby it borrows $100 million. Gion Corporation, the franchisee, is not liable on the loan. McDonald's Corporation, the franchisor and debtor, is liable on the loan.

In the first case that follows, the court found the franchisee directly liable for its own negligent conduct. In the second case that follows, the court imposed liability on a franchisor for its own negligent conduct.

CASE 31.2

Franchisee Liability

Cislaw v. Southland Corporation

4 Cal.App.4th 1284, 6 Cal.Rptr.2d 386, **Web** 1992 Cal. App. Lexis 375
Court of Appeal of California

> **"** *In this field of franchise agreements, the question of whether the franchisee is an independent contractor or an agent is ordinarily one of fact, depending on whether the franchisor exercises complete or substantial control over the franchisee.* **"**
>
> —Judge Sonenshine

Facts

The Southland Corporation (Southland) owns the "7-Eleven" trademark and licenses franchisees to operate convenience stores using this trademark. Each franchise is independently owned and operated. The franchise agreement stipulates that the franchisee is an independent contractor who is authorized to make all inventory, employment, and operational decisions for the franchise.

Timothy Cislaw, 17 years old, died of respiratory failure on May 10, 1984. His parents filed a wrongful death action against the franchise and Southland, alleging that Timothy's death resulted from his consumption of Djarum Specials (clove cigarettes) sold at a Costa Mesa, California, 7-Eleven franchise store. The Costa Mesa 7-Eleven was franchised to Charles Trujillo and Patricia Colwell-Trujillo. After answering the complaint, Southland moved for summary judgment, arguing that it was not liable for the alleged tortious conduct of its franchisee because the franchisee was an independent contractor. The plaintiffs alleged that the franchisee was Southland's agent and therefore Southland was liable for its agent's alleged negligence of selling the clove cigarettes to their son. The trial court granted Southland's motion. The Cislaws appealed.

Issue

Was the Costa Mesa franchisee an agent of Southland?

Language of the Court

In this field of franchise agreements, the question of whether the franchisee is an independent contractor or an agent is ordinarily one of fact, depending on whether the franchisor exercises complete or substantial control over the franchisee. The agreement recites that the franchisees are independent contractors, and two provisions give the Trujillos the right to make all inventory, employment and operational decisions.

Colwell-Trujillo said that, as provided under the franchise agreement, she exercised "full and complete control over" the store's employees and "any and all labor relations," including "hiring, firing, disciplining, compensation and work schedules."

She attested, "I could purchase whatever inventory I chose and from whomever I wanted and I did so." Colwell-Trujillo stated. "Southland had no control over my decision to sell or not sell clove cigarettes at the store. It was my sole decision to sell clove cigarettes. In no way did Southland ever advertise, promote or merchandise the clove cigarettes sold in my store."

Decision

The court of appeals held that the Costa Mesa 7-Eleven franchise was not an agent of Southland but was an independent contractor. The court of appeals affirmed the judgment of the trial court.

Law & Ethics Questions

1. Should franchisors be automatically held liable for the tortious conduct of their franchisees? Why or why not?

2. **ETHICS** Did the Cislaws act ethically in suing Southland?

3. How careful must a franchisor be to retain enough control to protect the quality of the goods and services sold by its franchisees but not to retain too much control so as to become liable for the actions of its franchisees?

Web Exercises

1. **WEB** For the complete opinion of this case, go to www.prenhall.com/cheesemancases.

2. **WEB** Visit the website of the court of appeals of California, Fourth Appellate District, at www.appellatelaw.net/ca/coa4.htm.

3. **WEB** Visit the website of the 7-Eleven convenience stores, at www.7-eleven.com. Can you find any information on becoming a 7-Eleven franchisee?

4. **WEB** Use www.google.com to find an article that discusses the liability of franchisors for tortious injuries. Read it.

CASE **31.3**

Franchisor Liability

Martin v. McDonald's Corporation

572 N.E.2d 1073, **Web** 1991 Ill. App. Lexis 715
Court of Appeals of Illinois

> **❝***The trial court correctly determined that McDonald's Corporation had a duty to protect plaintiffs Laura Martin, Maureen Kincaid, and Therese Dudek from harm.***❞**
>
> —Judge McNulty

Facts

McDonald's Corporation (McDonald's) is a franchisor that licenses franchisees to operate fast-food restaurants and to use McDonald's trademarks and service marks. One such franchise, which was located in Oak Forest, Illinois, was owned and operated by McDonald's Restaurants of Illinois, the franchisee.

Recognizing the threat of armed robbery at its franchises, especially in the time period immediately after closing, McDonald's established an entire corporate division to deal with security problems at franchises. McDonald's prepared a manual for restaurant security operations and required its franchisees to adhere to these procedures.

Jim Carlson was the McDonald's regional security manager for the area in which the Oak Forest franchise was located. Carlson visited the Oak Forest franchise on October 31, to inform the manager of security procedures. He specifically mentioned these rules: (1) No one should throw garbage out the backdoor after dark, and (2) trash and grease were to be taken out the side glass door at least one hour prior to closing. During his inspection, Carlson noted that the locks had to be changed at the restaurant and an alarm system needed to be installed for the backdoor. Carlson never followed up to determine whether these security measures had been taken.

On the evening of November 29, a six-woman crew, all teenagers, was working to clean up and close the Oak Forest restaurant. Laura Martin, Therese Dudek, and Maureen Kincaid were members of that crew. A person later identified as Peter Logan appeared at the back of the restaurant with a gun. He ordered the crew to open the safe and get him the money and then ordered them into the refrigerator. In the course of moving the crew into the refrigerator, Logan shot and killed Martin and assaulted Dudek and Kincaid. Dudek and Kincaid suffered severe emotional distress from the assault.

Evidence showed that Logan had entered the restaurant through the backdoor. Trial testimony proved that the work crew used the backdoor exclusively, both before and after dark, and emptied garbage and grease through the backdoor all day and all night. In addition, there was evidence that the latch on the backdoor did not work properly. Evidence also showed that the crew had not been instructed about the use of the backdoor after dark, the crew had never received copies of the McDonald's security manual, and the required warning about not using the backdoor after dark had not been posted at the restaurant.

Martin's parents, Dudek, and Kincaid sued McDonald's to recover damages for negligence. The trial court awarded damages of $1,003,445 to the Martins for the wrongful death of their daughter and awarded $125,000 each to Dudek and Kincaid. McDonald's appealed.

Issue

Is McDonald's liable for negligence?

Language of the Court

The trial court correctly determined that McDonald's Corporation had a duty to protect plaintiffs Laura Martin, Maureen Kincaid, and Therese Dudek from harm. Although it did not specifically state that such duty was "assumed," there is ample support in case law and the facts of this case to support a determination that McDonald's Corporation voluntarily assumed a duty to provide security to plaintiffs and protect them from harm.

Once McDonald's Corporation assumed the duty to provide security and protection to plaintiffs, it had the obligation to perform this duty with due care and competence, and any failure to do so would lead to a finding of breach of duty. Accordingly, there was ample evidence for the jury to determine that McDonald's had breached its assumed duty to plaintiffs.

Decision

The appellate court held that McDonald's was negligent for not following up and making sure that the security deficiencies it had found at the Oak Forest franchise had been corrected. The appellate court affirmed the judgment of the trial court, holding McDonald's liable.

Law & Ethics Questions

1. Should businesses be held liable for criminal actions of others? Why or why not?

2. **ETHICS** Should McDonald's have denied liability in this case?

3. What is the benefit to a franchisor of establishing and requiring its franchisees to adhere to security rules? Is there any potential detriment? Explain.

Web Exercises

1. **WEB** For the complete opinion of this case, go to *www.prenhall.com/cheesemancases*.

2. **WEB** Visit the website of the court of appeals of Illinois, at *www.state.il.us/court*.

3. **WEB** Visit the website of McDonald's Corporation, at *www.mcdonalds.com*. Can you find any information on becoming a McDonald's franchisee?

4. **WEB** Use *www.google.com* to find an article that discusses the liability of McDonald's Corporation for a tort committed at one of its franchisees.

Apparent Agency

If a franchisee is the *actual* or *apparent agent* of the franchisor, the franchisor is responsible for the torts and contracts the franchise committed or entered into within the scope of the agency.

Actual agency is created when a franchisor expressly or implicitly makes a franchisee its agent. The franchisor is liable for the contracts entered into and torts committed by the franchisee while the franchisee is acting within the scope of the agency. Franchisors very seldom appoint franchisees as their agents.

Apparent agency is created when a franchisor leads a third person into believing that the franchisee is its agent. For example, a franchisor and franchisee who use the same trade name and trademarks and make no effort to inform the public of their separate legal status may find themselves in such a situation. However, mere use of the same name does not automatically make a franchisor liable for the franchisee's actions. The court's decision of whether an apparent agency has been created depends on the facts and circumstances of the case.

In the following case, the court found that a franchisee was the apparent agent of the franchisor, thereby making the franchisor liable for the tortious conduct of the franchisee.

CASE 31.4
Apparent Agency

Holiday Inns, Inc. v. Shelburne

576 So.2d 322, **Web** 1991 Fla. App. Lexis 585
District Court of Appeal of Florida

> ❝ *Clearly, on the question of reliance, the jury had a right to conclude that appellees believed exactly what Holiday Inns, Inc. wanted them to believe—that the Fort Pierce Holiday Inn and its Rodeo Bar were part of Holiday Inn's system.* ❞
>
> —Judge Hersey

Facts

Holiday Inns, Inc. (Holiday Inns), is a franchisor that licenses franchisees to operate hotels using its trademarks and service marks. Holiday Inns licensed Hospitality Venture to operate a franchised hotel in Fort Pierce, Florida. The Rodeo Bar, which had a reputation as the "hottest bar in town," was located in the hotel.

The Fort Pierce Holiday Inn and Rodeo Bar did not have sufficient parking, so security guards posted in the Holiday Inn parking lot required Rodeo Bar patrons to park in vacant lots that surrounded the hotel but that were not owned by the hotel. The main duty of the guards was to keep the parking lot open for hotel guests. Two unarmed security guards were on duty on the night in question. One guard was drinking on the job, and the other was an untrained temporary fill-in.

The record disclosed that although the Rodeo Bar had a capacity of 240 people, the bar regularly admitted 270 to 300 people, with 50 to 75 people waiting outside. Fights occurred all the time in the bar and the parking lots, and often there were three or four fights a night. Police reports involving 58 offenses, including several weapons charges and battery and assault charges, had been filed during the previous 18 months.

On the night in question, the two groups involved in the altercation did not leave the Rodeo Bar until closing time. According to the record, these individuals exchanged remarks as they moved toward their respective vehicles in the vacant parking lots adjacent to the Holiday Inn. Ultimately, a fight erupted. The evidence shows that during the course of physical combat, Mr. Carter shot David Rice, Scott Turner, and Robert Shelburne. Rice died from his injuries.

Rice's heirs, Turner, and Shelburne sued the franchisee. Hospitality Venture, and the franchisor, Holiday Inns, for damages. The trial court found Hospitality Venture negligent for not providing sufficient security to prevent the foreseeable incident that took the life of Rice and injured Turner and Shelburne. The court also found that Hospitality Venture was the apparent agent of Holiday Inns and therefore Holiday Inns was vicariously liable for its franchisee's tortious conduct. Turner was awarded $3,825,000 for his injuries, Shelburne received $1 million, and Rice's interests were awarded $1 million. Hospitality Venture and Holiday Inns appealed.

Issue

Are the franchisee and the franchisor liable?

Language of the Court

There was testimony that Holiday Inns, Inc. gave Hospitality Venture, the franchisee, use of the Holiday Inns, Inc. logo and made the franchisee part of the corporation's reservation system. In fact, Holiday Inns, Inc.'s standard sign was displayed in front of the Fort Pierce Holiday Inn in order to draw customers through name recognition. Clearly, this evidence shows that Holiday Inns, Inc. represented to the public that this particular hotel was a part of the national chain of Holiday Inns and that it could find a certain level of service and safety at its hotel and bar.

Clearly, on the question of reliance, the jury had a right to conclude that appellees believed exactly what Holiday Inns, Inc. wanted them to believe—that the Fort Pierce Holiday Inn and its Rodeo Bar were part of Holiday Inn's system. For these reasons, the evidence supported the jury's finding that Hospitality Venture was the apparent agent of Holiday Inns, Inc. and was acting within the scope of its apparent authority.

Decision

The court of appeals held that the franchisee was negligent and that the franchisee was the apparent agent of the franchisor. The court of appeals affirmed the judgment of the trial court.

Law & Ethics Questions

1. What does the doctrine of apparent agency provide?

2. **ETHICS** Did Hospitality Venture act ethically in denying liability? Did Holiday Inns act ethically in denying liability?

3. Why do you think the plaintiffs included Holiday Inns as a defendant in their lawsuit? Do you think the damages that were awarded were warranted?

Web Exercises

1. **WEB** For the complete opinion of this case, go to *www.prenhall.com/cheesemancases*.

2. **WEB** Visit the website of the district court of appeals of Florida, at *www.4dca.org*.

3. **WEB** Visit the website of Holiday Inn, at *www.holiday-inn.com*. Using this site, can you find any information on the Fort Pierce, Florida, Holiday Inn?

4. **WEB** Use *www.google.com* to find an article that discusses the liability of Holiday Inn for a tort committed at one of its franchisees. Read it.

Licensing

Licensing is an important business arrangement in both domestic and international markets. **Licensing** occurs when one business or party that owns trademarks, service marks, trade names, and other intellectual property (the **licensor**) contracts to permit another business or party (the **licensee**) to use its trademarks, service marks, trade names, and other intellectual property in the distribution of goods, services, software, and digital information. A licensing arrangement is illustrated in Exhibit 31.4.

Example The Walt Disney Company owns the merchandising rights to "Winnie the Pooh" stories and all the characters associated with the Winnie the Pooh stories. The Walt Disney Company enters into an agreement whereby it permits the Beijing Merchandising

EXHIBIT 31.4

Licensing

Licensor

License
Grant of permission
to use trademarks,
service marks, trade
names, and other
intellectual property

Licensee

Company, a business formed under Chinese law, to manufacture and distribute a line of clothing, children's toys, and other items bearing the likeness of the Winnie the Pooh characters. This is a license. The Walt Disney Company is the licensor, and the Beijing Merchandising Company is the licensee.

INTERNATIONAL LAW
Pokémon Licensing

The Japanese company Nintendo's animated Pokémon creatures have been a huge hit in Japan. In this role-playing game, children manipulate Pokémon characters with different stated strengths and weaknesses in a variant of the rock, paper, scissors game. The several hundred cute, gender-neutral characters, with such names as Pikachu, Piyo Piyo, Dalki, and Dragon Ball, show up in TV cartoons and video games and on playing cards, book bags, and thousands of other items. Japanese children are crazy about acquiring the next Pokémon character.

But would American children buy into the oddly animated creatures and their interactive games? Nintendo had doubts and did not want to take the exporting risk directly. Up stepped Alfred Kahn and Thomas Kenney, both prior toy company executives, who formed 4Kids Entertainment, Inc., a U.S. Company. They approached Nintendo about bringing the Pokémon games and characters to the United States through the concept of licensing. After much negotiation, Nintendo agreed that 4Kids would be its licensing agent in the United States.

4Kids syndicated a Pokémon TV series, with episodes dubbed in English. Within four months, Pokémon was the top-rated syndicated kids' program in the United States. After this TV success, Nintendo released the first Pokémon video games in the United States, followed by trading cards, comic books, home videos, and compact discs. 4Kids

has signed more than 100 licensing deals for Pokémon, including deals with Hasbro toy company as its master toy licensee and TimeWarner for the Pokémon TV series. The Pokémon craze reached a fever pitch in the United States as it had in Japan.

The Pokémon invasion of the United States has reaped a plethora of royalties for Nintendo and its local entrepreneurs. With Pokémon sales exceeding $1 billion in the United States, 4Kids has earned up to $75 million, making its owners multimillionaires.

Web Exercises

1. **WEB** Use *www.google.com* to find likenesses of several Pokémon characters.

2. **WEB** Use *www.google.com* to find an article that discusses a licensing agreement. Read it.

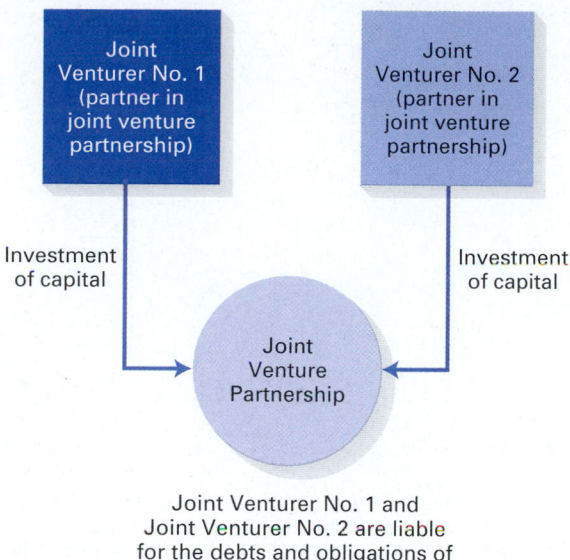

EXHIBIT 31.5

**Joint Venture
Partnership**

Joint Venturer No. 1 and
Joint Venturer No. 2 are liable
for the debts and obligations of
the joint venture partnership

Joint Venture

A **joint venture** is an arrangement in which two or more business entities combine their
resources to pursue a single project or transaction. The parties to a joint venture are called
joint venturers. Joint ventures resemble partnerships, except that partnerships are usually
formed to pursue ongoing business operations rather than to focus on a single project or
transaction.

Unless otherwise agreed, joint venturers have equal rights to manage a joint venture.
Joint venturers owe each other the fiduciary duties of loyalty and care. If a joint venturer
violates these duties, it is liable for the damages the breach causes.

Joint Venture Partnership

If a joint venture is operated as a partnership, then each joint venturer is considered a partner of the joint venture. This is called a **joint venture partnership** (see Exhibit 31.5). In a
joint venture partnership, each joint venturer is liable for the debts and obligations of the
joint venture partnership.

Example Suppose a new oil field is discovered in northern Canada. Two large oil companies, ChevronTexaco Corp. and ConocoPhillips Corp., would each like to drill for oil there,
but neither one has sufficient resources to do so alone. They join together to form a joint
venture partnership, and each contributes $100 million capital to the joint venture. If the
joint venture fails and the joint venture owes $1 billion to its creditors, which it cannot pay,
ChevronTexaco Corp. and ConocoPhillips Corp. are each responsible for the joint venture's unpaid debts and obligations. This is because they are partners in the joint venture.

Joint Venture Corporation

In pursuing a joint venture, joint venturers often form a corporation to operate the joint
venture. This is called a **joint venture corporation** (see Exhibit 31.6.). The joint venturers
are shareholders of the joint venture corporation. The joint venture corporation is liable for
its own debts and obligations. The joint venturers are liable for the debts and obligations
of the joint venture corporation only up to their capital contributions to the joint venture
corporation.

EXHIBIT 31.6

**Joint Venture
Corporation**

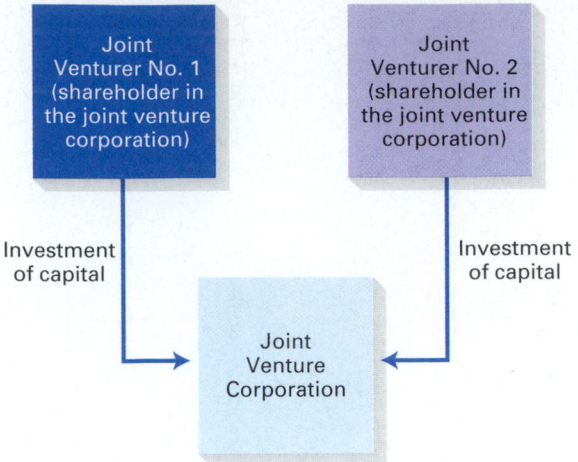

Joint Venturer No. 1 and Joint Venturer No. 2
are liable for the debts and obligations
of the joint venture corporation only up to their capital
contributions to the joint venture corporation

Example Suppose in the prior example that ChevronTexaco Corp. and ConocoPhillips Corp. formed a third corporation, called Canadian Imperial Corp., to operate the joint venture. ChevronTexaco and ConocoPhillips each contributes $100 million capital to Canadian Imperial Corp., and each becomes a shareholder of Canadian Imperial Corp. If the joint venture fails and Canadian Imperial Corp. owes $1 billion to its creditors, which it cannot pay, ChevronTexaco and ConocoPhillips each loses its $100 million capital contribution but is not liable for any further unpaid debts or obligations of Canadian Imperial Corp.

INTERNATIONAL LAW

A Starbucks U.S.–Chinese International Joint Venture

Starbucks has been a tremendous success in the United States. Beginning with a single outlet in Seattle, Washington, Starbucks Coffee Company has expanded Starbucks shops across the United States. The company expanded in the United States through company-owned stores.

When Starbucks wanted to enter overseas markets, however, it realized it could not expand solely through company-owned outlets. This was because (1) government restrictions in some countries prohibit 100 percent ownership of a business by a foreign investor and (2) the company lacked the business expertise and cultural knowledge necessary to enter many foreign markets. To enter foreign markets, Starbucks turned to joint ventures. For example, Starbucks is expanding its operations in China by using a 50–50 joint venture with Shanghai President Coffee Corporation, a Chinese company.

Web Exercises

1. **WEB** Visit the website of Starbucks Corporation, at *www.starbucks.com*.

2. **WEB** Use *www.google.com* to find an article that discusses the Starbucks–Shanghai President Coffee Corporation joint venture in China. Read it.

3. **WEB** Use *www.google.com* to find an article that discusses the joint ventures Starbucks has made in other countries.

Strategic Alliance

A **strategic alliance** is an arrangement between two or more companies in the same industry in which they agree to ally themselves to accomplish a designated objective. A strategic alliance allows the companies to reduce risks, share costs, combine technologies, and extend their markets. For example, companies often enter into strategic alliances when they decide to expand internationally into foreign countries.

Strategic alliances do not have the same protection as mergers, joint ventures, or franchising, and sometimes they are dismantled. Consideration must always be given to the fact that a strategic alliance partner is also a potential competitor.

INTERNET AND TECHNOLOGY
Strategic Internet Alliances in China

Leading Internet companies in the United States have eyed the China market for its tremendous growth potential. But China prohibits complete ownership of Internet companies in China by foreigners. In addition, the legendary Chinese "connections" method of conducting business places another hurdle in the way of foreign companies wishing to do business there. So what is the main way to tap into this Internet market? Strategic alliances.

A major strategic alliance by U.S. companies in China was their tie-in with and investment in China.com. China.com is a Chinese-language Web portal backed by investments by U.S. companies TimeWarner, Inc., Sun Microsystems, and Nortel Networks. China.com became China's largest Internet company when it went public. Intel Corp., another major U.S. company, has aligned itself with Sohu.com, a Chinese Internet company located in Beijing. CMGI Inc., a U.S. Internet holding company, has joined with Pacific Century Cyber-Works (PCCW), a Hong Kong company, to sell Web content and e-commerce services to the exploding Chinese Internet market from its base in Hong Kong. The Chinese government has permitted these strategic alliances.

Based on the communist government's rules in China and a culture that favors business connections, U.S. Internet companies will continue to enter the Chinese Internet market through strategic alliances with Chinese Internet firms. These strategic alliances bring together the expertise of all the parties.

Web Exercises

1. **WEB** Visit the website of China.com, at *www.english.china.com*.
2. **WEB** Use *www.google.com* to find another example of strategic alliances between companies of different countries.

Beijing, China

Foreign markets offer substantial growth opportunities for franchisors.

Chapter Summary

Franchise, p. 854

A franchise is established when one party licenses another party to use the franchisor's trade name, trademarks, commercial symbols, patents, copyrights, and other property in the distribution and selling of goods and services.

1. **Franchisor.** The franchisor is the party who does the licensing in a franchise arrangement. Also called the *licensor*.
2. **Franchisee.** The franchisee is the party who is licensed by the franchisor in a franchise arrangement. Also called the *licensee*.

Types of Franchises

1. *Distributorship franchise.* In this type of franchise, the franchisor manufactures a product and licenses a retail franchisee to distribute the product to the public.
2. *Processing plant franchise.* In this type of franchise, the franchisor provides a secret formula or process to the franchisee, and the franchisee manufactures the product and distributes it to retail dealers.
3. *Chain-style franchise.* In this type of franchise, the franchisor licenses the franchisee to make and sell its products or distribute its services to the public from a retail outlet serving an exclusive territory.
4. *Area franchise.* In this type of franchise, the franchisor authorizes the franchisee to negotiate and sell franchises on behalf of the franchisor in designated areas. The area franchisee is called a *subfranchisor*.

State Disclosure Laws

Many states have enacted statutes that require franchisors to make specific presale disclosures to prospective franchisees. Some states use a uniform disclosure document called the Uniform Franchise Offering Circular (UFOC).

FTC Franchise Rule

The FTC requires franchisors to make presale disclosures to prospective franchisees. If a franchisor uses actual or hypothetical sales or income data in its sales materials, the franchisor must disclose assumptions underlying any estimates and how many franchises have obtained such results, and it must provide a mandated cautionary statement.

Trademarks

1. *Trademarks and service marks.* A distinctive mark, symbol, name, word, motto, or device may identify the goods or services of a particular franchisor.
2. *Licensing of marks.* A franchisor licenses the use of its trademarks and service marks to its franchisees in the franchise agreement.
3. *Trademark infringement.* Anyone who uses a mark without authorization from the franchisor may be sued for trademark infringement. The franchisor can recover damages and obtain an injunction prohibiting further unauthorized use of the mark.

Trade Secrets

Trade secrets are ideas, formulas, and methods of doing business that make a franchise successful but do not qualify for trademark, patent, or copyright protection. Anyone who steals and uses a franchisor's trade secret is liable for misappropriation of a trade secret. The franchisor can recover damages and obtain an injunction prohibiting further unauthorized use of the trade secret.

The Franchise Agreement

A franchise agreement is an agreement that a franchisor and franchisee enter into that sets forth the terms and conditions of the franchise. Common terms in a franchise agreement include:

1. Quality control standards
2. Training requirements
3. Covenant not to compete
4. Arbitration clause
5. Other terms and conditions

Franchise Fees

A franchisee may be required to pay any or all of the following franchise fees to the franchisor:

1. *Initial license fee.* This is a lump-sum payment for the privilege of being granted a franchise.
2. *Royalty fee.* This is a fee for the continued use of the franchisor's trade name, property, and assistance, and it is often computed as a percentage of the franchisee's gross sales.

3. *Assessment fee.* This is a fee for such things as advertising and promotional campaigns, administrative costs, and the like, billed either as a flat monthly fee or annual fee or as a percentage of gross sales.
4. *Lease fees.* These fees are payment for any land or equipment leased from the franchisor, billed either as a flat monthly or annual fee or as a percentage of gross sales or other agreed-upon amount.
5. *Cost of supplies.* These fees are payment for supplies purchased from the franchisor.

Termination of a Franchise

Most franchise agreements and state and federal laws permit a franchisor to terminate the franchise "for cause" (e.g., nonpayment of franchise fees by the franchisee, continued failure of the franchisee to meet quality control standards).

1. *Termination at will.* Most state and federal laws regulating franchising prohibit franchisors from terminating franchises at will. This prevents a franchisor from taking advantage of the good will developed at the franchise location by the franchisee.
2. *Wrongful termination.* If a franchisor terminates a franchise agreement without just cause, the franchisee can sue the franchisor for wrongful termination. The franchisee can recover damages caused by the wrongful termination and recover the franchise.

Breach of the Franchise Agreement

If a franchisee breaches the franchise agreement and is found liable they may be required to pay all costs incurred by the franchisor.

Liability of Franchisor and Franchisee, p. 864

1. *Liability.* Franchisors and franchisees are liable for their own contracts and torts.
2. *Independent contractor.* An independent contractor is a separately organized and operated business that is not the agent of another party with which it does business. This is the typical franchisor–franchisee arrangement. There is no agency relationship, so neither party is liable for the other's contracts or torts.

Actual Agency

This arrangement occurs where a franchisor expressly or implicitly by its conduct makes a franchisee its agent. The franchisor is liable for the contracts entered into and torts committed by the franchisee while acting within the scope of the agency.

Apparent Agency

Apparent agency arises when a franchisor creates the appearance that a franchisee is its agent when in fact an actual agency does not exist. The franchisor is liable for the contracts entered into and torts committed by the franchisee acting as an apparent agent.

Licensing, p. 867

1. *License.* In a licensing arrangement, the owner of trademarks, service marks, trade names, and other intellectual property grants another party the right to use these in the manufacture and sale of goods, services, software, or digital information.
2. *Licensor.* The licensor is the party who grants a license.
3. *Licensee.* The licensee is the party to whom a license is granted.

Joint Venture, p. 869

A joint venture is an arrangement whereby two or more business entities combine their resources to pursue a single project or transaction. A joint venturer is a party to a joint venture.

Joint Venture Partnership

If a joint venture is operated as a partnership, then each joint venturer is considered a partner of the joint venture. Each joint venturer is liable for the debts and obligations of the joint venture partnership.

Joint Venture Corporation

The joint venturers are shareholders of the joint venture corporation and are liable for the debts and obligations of the joint venture corporation only up to their capital contributions to the joint venture corporation. The joint venture corporation is liable for its own debts and obligations.

Strategic Alliance, p. 870

A strategic alliance is an arrangement between two or more companies in the same industry whereby they agree to accomplish a designated objective. A company may use strategic alliances to enter a foreign market.

Test Review Terms and Concepts

Apparent agency   866
Area franchise   855
Assessment fee   859
Breach of the franchise
   agreement   861
Chain-style franchise   855
Cost of supplies   859
Distributorship franchise   855
Federal Trade Commission
   (FTC)   856
Franchise   854
Franchise agreement   858
Franchisee (licensee)   854

Franchisor (licensor)   854
FTC franchise rule   856
FTC notice   857
Initial license fee   859
Joint venture   869
Joint venture corporation   869
Joint venture partnership   869
Joint venturer   869
Lanham Trademark Act   857
Lease fees   859
Licensee   867
Licensor   867
Licensing   867

Patent and Trademark
   Office   857
Processing plant
   franchise   855
Royalty fee   859
Service marks   857
Strategic alliance   870
Subfranchisor   855
Trademarks   857
Trade secrets   858
Uniform Franchise Offering
   Circular (UFOC)   855
Wrongful termination   861

Case Problems

31.1 Franchise Agreement: H&R Block, Inc. (Block), is a franchisor that licenses franchisees to provide tax preparation services to customers under the "H&R Block" service mark. June McCart was granted a Block franchise at 900 Main Street, Rochester, New York. For seven years, her husband, Robert, was involved in the operation of a Block franchise in Rensselaer, New York. After that, he assisted June in the operation of her Block franchise. All the McCarts' income during the time in question came from the Block franchises.

The Block franchise agreement that June signed contained a provision whereby she agreed not to compete (1) in the business of tax preparation (2) within 250 miles of the franchise (3) for a period of two years after the termination of the franchise. Robert did not sign the Rochester franchise agreement. Two years later, June wrote a letter to Block, giving notice that she was terminating the franchise. Shortly thereafter, the McCarts sent a letter to people who had been clients of the Rochester Block office, informing them that June was leaving Block and that Robert was opening a tax preparation service in which June would assist him. Block granted a new franchise in Rochester to another franchisee. It sued the McCarts to enforce the covenant not to compete against them. Who wins? *McCart v. H&R Block, Inc.*, 470

N.E.2d 756, **Web** 1984 Ind. App. Lexis 3039 (Court of Appeals of Indiana)

31.2 Franchise Agreement: Libby-Broadway Drive-In, Inc. (Libby), is a corporation licensed to operate a McDonald's fast-food franchise restaurant by the McDonald's System, Inc. (McDonald's). Libby was granted a license to operate a McDonald's in Cleveland, Ohio, and was granted an exclusive territory in which McDonald's could not grant another franchise. The area was described as "bound on the north by the south side of Miles Avenue, on the west and south side by Turney Road, on the east by Warrensville Center Road." McDonald's granted a franchise to another franchisee to operate a McDonald's restaurant on the west side of Turney Road. Libby sued McDonald's, alleging a breach of the franchise agreement. Is McDonald's liable? *Libby-Broadway Drive-In, Inc. v. McDonald's System, Inc.*, 72 Ill. App. 3d 806, 391 N.E.2d 1, **Web** 1979 Ill. App. Lexis 2698 (Appellate Court of Illinois)

31.3 Franchisor Disclosure: My Pie International, Inc. (My Pie), an Illinois corporation, was a franchisor that licensed franchisees to open pie shops under its trademark name. My Pie licensed 13 restaurants throughout the country, including one owned by Dowmont, Inc. (Dowmont), in

Glen Ellyn, Illinois. The Illinois Franchise Disclosure Act requires a franchisor that desires to issue franchises in the state to register with the state or qualify for an exemption from registration and to make certain disclosures to prospective franchisees. My Pie granted the license to Dowmont without registering with the state of Illinois or qualifying for an exemption from registration and without making the required disclosures to Dowmont. Dowmont operated its restaurant as a "My Pie" franchise for four years, and after that, it operated it under the name "Arnold's." Dowmont paid franchise royalty fees for the four years. My Pie sued Dowmont for breach of the franchise agreement to recover royalties it claimed were due from Dowmont. Dowmont filed a counterclaim seeking to rescind the franchise agreement and recover the royalties it paid to My Pie. Who wins? *My Pie International, Inc. v. Dowmont, Inc.*, 687 F.2d 919, **Web** 1982 U.S. App. Lexis 16537 (United States Court of Appeals for the Seventh Circuit)

31.4 Tort Liability: Georgia Girl Fashions, Inc. (Georgia Girl), was a franchisor that licensed franchisees to operate women's retail clothing stores under the "Georgia Girl" trademark. Georgia Girl granted a franchise to a franchisee to operate a store on South Cobb Drive in Smyrna, Georgia. Georgia Girl did not supervise or control the day-to-day operations of the franchisee. Melanie McMullan entered the store to exchange a blouse that she had previously purchased at the store. When she found nothing that she wished to exchange the blouse for, she began to leave the store. At that time, she was physically restrained and accused of shoplifting the blouse. McMullan was taken to the local jail, where she was held until her claim of prior purchase could be verified. The store then dropped the charges against her, and she was released from jail. McMullan filed an action against the store owner and Georgia Girl to recover damages for false imprisonment. Is Georgia Girl liable? *McMullan v. Georgia Girl Fashions, Inc.*, 180 Ga. App. 228, 348 S.E.2d 748, **Web** 1986 Ga. App. Lexis 2093 (Court of Appeals of Georgia)

31.5 Tort Liability: The Seven-Up Company (Seven-Up) is a franchisor that licenses local bottling companies to manufacture, bottle, and distribute soft drinks using the "7-Up" trademark. The Brooks Bottling Company (Brooks) is a Seven-Up franchisee that bottles and sells 7-Up soft drinks to stores in Michigan. Under the franchise agreement, the franchisee is required to purchase the 7-Up syrup from Seven-Up, but it can purchase its bottles, cartons, and other supplies from independent suppliers if Seven-Up approves the design of these articles.

Brooks used cartons designed and manufactured by Olinkraft, Inc., using a design that Seven-Up had approved. Sharon Proos Kosters, a customer at a Meijers Thrifty Acre Store in Holland, Michigan, removed a cardboard carton containing six glass bottles of 7-Up from a grocery store shelf, put it under her arm, and walked toward the checkout counter. As she did so, a bottle slipped out of the carton, fell on the floor, and exploded, causing a piece of glass to strike

Kosters in her eye as she looked down; she was blinded in that eye. Evidence showed that the 7-Up carton was designed to be held from the top and was made without a strip on the side of the carton that would prevent a bottle from slipping out if held underneath. Kosters sued Seven-Up to recover damages for her injuries. Is Seven-Up liable? *Kosters v. Seven-Up Company*, 595 F.2d 347, **Web** 1979 U.S. App. Lexis 15945 (United States Court of Appeals for the Sixth Circuit)

31.6 Trademark: The Kentucky Fried Chicken Corporation (KFC) is the franchisor of Kentucky Fried Chicken restaurants. Franchisees must purchase equipment and supplies from manufacturers approved in writing by KFC. Equipment includes cookers, fryers, ovens, and the like; supplies include carry-out boxes, napkins, towelettes, and plastic eating utensils known as "sporks." These products are not trade secrets. KFC may not "unreasonably withhold" approval of any suppliers who apply and whose goods are tested and found to meet KFC's quality control standards. The 10 manufacturers who went through KFC's approval process were approved. KFC also sells supplies to franchisees in competition with these independent suppliers. All supplies, whether produced by KFC or the independent suppliers, must contain "Kentucky Fried Chicken" trademarks.

Upon formation, Diversified Container Corporation (Diversified) began manufacturing and selling supplies to KFC franchisees without applying for or receiving KFC's approval. All the items sold by Diversified contained KFC trademarks. Diversified represented to franchisees that its products met "all standards" of KFC and that it sold "approved supplies." Diversified even affixed KFC trademarks to the shipping boxes in which it delivered supplies to franchisees. Evidence showed that Diversified's products did not meet the quality control standards set by KFC. KFC sued Diversified for trademark infringement. Who wins? *Kentucky Fried Chicken Corporation v. Diversified Container Corporation*, 549 F.2d 368, **Web** 1977 U.S. App. Lexis 14128 (United States Court of Appeals for the Fifth Circuit)

31.7 Trademark: Ramada Inns, Inc. (Ramada Inns), is a franchisor that licenses franchisees to operate motor hotels using the "Ramada Inns" trademarks and service marks. In August, the Gadsden Motor Company (Gadsden), a partnership, purchased a motel in Attalla, Alabama, and entered into a franchise agreement with Ramada Inns to operate it as a Ramada Inns motor hotel. Five years later, the motel began receiving poor ratings from Ramada Inns inspectors, and Gadsden fell behind on its monthly franchise fee payments. Despite prodding from Ramada Inns, the motel never met Ramada Inns's operational standards again. One year later, Ramada Inns properly terminated the franchise agreement, citing quality deficiencies and Gadsden's failure to pay past-due franchise fees. The termination notice directed Gadsden to remove any materials or signs identifying the motel as a Ramada. Gadsden continued using Ramada Inns's signage, trademarks, and service marks inside and outside the motel.

In September, Ramada Inns sued Gadsden for trademark infringement. Who wins? *Ramada Inns, Inc. v. Gadsden Motel Company*, 804 F.2d 1562, **Web** 1986 U.S. App. Lexis 34279 (United States Court of Appeals for the Eleventh Circuit)

31.8 Termination of a Franchise: Kawasaki Motors Corporation (Kawasaki), a Japanese corporation, manufactures motorcycles that it distributes in the United States through its subsidiary, Kawasaki Motors Corporation, U.S.A. (Kawasaki USA). Kawasaki USA is a franchisor that grants franchises to dealerships to sell Kawasaki motorcycles. Kawasaki USA granted the Kawasaki Shop of Aurora, Inc. (Dealer), a franchise to sell Kawasaki motorcycles in Aurora, Illinois. The franchise changed locations twice. Both moves were within the five-mile exclusive territory granted Dealer in the franchise agreement.

Dealer did not obtain Kawasaki USA's written approval for either move, as required by the franchise agreement. Kawasaki USA acquiesced to the first move but not the second. At the second new location, Dealer also operated Honda and Suzuki motorcycle franchises and was negotiating to operate a Yamaha franchise. The Kawasaki franchise agreement expressly permitted multiline dealerships. Kawasaki USA objected to the second move, asserting that Dealer had not received written approval for the move, as required by the franchise agreement. Evidence showed, however, that the real reason Kawasaki objected to the move was because it did not want its motorcycles to be sold at the same location as other manufacturers' motorcycles. Kawasaki terminated Dealer's franchise. Dealer sued Kawasaki USA for wrongful termination. Who wins? *Kawasaki Shop of Aurora, Inc. v. Kawasaki Motors Corporation, U.S.A.*, 188 Ill. App. 3d 664, 544 N.E.2d 457, **Web** 1989 Ill. App. Lexis 1442 (Appellate Court of Illinois)

Ethics Issues

31.9 Ethics: Southland Corporation (Southland) owns the "7-Eleven" trademark and licenses franchisees throughout the country to operate 7-Eleven stores. The franchise agreement provides for fees to be paid to Southland by each franchisee based on a percentage of gross profits. In return, franchisees receive a lease of premises, a license to use the 7-Eleven trademark and trade secrets, advertising merchandise, and bookkeeping assistance. Vallerie Campbell purchased an existing 7-Eleven store in Fontana, California, and became a Southland franchisee. The franchise was designated #13974 by Southland. As part of the purchase, she applied to the state of California for transfer of the beer and wine license from the prior owner. Southland also executed the application. California approved the transfer and issued the license to "Campbell Vallerie Southland #13974."

An employee of Campbell's store sold beer to Jesse Lewis Cope, a minor who was allegedly intoxicated at the time. After drinking the beer, Cope drove his vehicle and struck another vehicle. Two occupants of the other vehicle, Denise Wickham and Tyrone Crosby, were severely injured, and a third occupant, Cedrick Johnson, was killed. Johnson (through his parents), Wickham, and Crosby sued Southland—but not Campbell—to recover damages. Is Southland legally liable for the tortious acts of its franchisee? Is it morally responsible? *Wickham v. The Southland Corporation*, 168 Cal.App.3d 49, 213 Cal.Rptr. 825, **Web** 1985 Cal. App. Lexis 2070 (Court of Appeal of California)

31.10 Ethics: The Kentucky Fried Chicken Corporation (KFC), with its principal place of business in Louisville, Kentucky, is the franchisor of KFC restaurants. KFC's registered trademarks and service marks include "Kentucky Fried Chicken," "It's Finger Lickin' Good," and the portrait of Colonel Harlan Sanders. KFC grants licenses to its franchisees to use these marks in connection with the preparation and sale of "Original Recipe Kentucky Fried Chicken." Original Recipe Kentucky Fried Chicken, which is sold only by KFC franchisees, is prepared by a special cooking process featuring the use of a secret recipe seasoning known as "KFC Seasonings." This blend of seasoning was developed by KFC's founder, Colonel Harlan Sanders. As a condition of each franchise agreement, KFC requires that its franchisees use only KFC Seasoning in connection with the preparation and sale of Kentucky Fried Chicken.

KFC Seasoning is a trade secret. To make the seasoning, KFC has entered into contracts with two spice blenders, the John W. Sexton Company, Inc. (Sexton), and Strange Company (Strange). Each of these companies blends approximately one-half the spices of KFC Seasoning; neither has knowledge of the complete formulation of KFC Seasoning, and both entered into secrecy agreements to maintain the confidentiality of their formulations. After the seasoning is blended by Sexton and Strange, it is mixed together and sold directly to all KFC franchisees. KFC does not receive a royalty or other economic benefit from the sale of KFC Seasoning. KFC's relationship with Sexton and Strange has existed for more than 25 years; no other companies are licensed to blend KFC Seasoning.

Marion-Kay Company, Inc. (Marion-Kay), was a spice blender engaged in the manufacture of chicken seasoning known as "Marion-Kay Seasoning." Marion-Kay requested permission from KFC to sell its seasoning products to KFC franchisees. KFC refused the request. Four years later, KFC learned that Marion-Kay was supplying some KFC franchisees with Marion-Kay seasoning and demanded it cease this practice. When Marion-Kay refused, KFC sued it for interference with contractual relations. Marion-Kay filed a counterclaim, alleging violation of antitrust law. Who wins? Was KFC justified in preventing Marion-Kay from blending its seasonings? Did Marion-Kay act ethically in selling seasoning to KFC franchisees? *KFC Corporation v. Marion-Kay Company, Inc.*, 620 F.Supp. 1160, **Web** 1985 U.S. Dist. Lexis 14766 (United States District Court for the Southern District of Indiana)

IRAC Writing Assignment

Read **Case A-31** in Appendix A [***Little v. Howard Johnson Company***]. Use the IRAC method to prepare a written analysis of the case.

Endnote

1. 16 CFR Part 436.
2. 15 U.S.C. Section 1114 *et seq.*
3. *Southland Corporation v. Keating*, 465 U.S. 1, 104 S.Ct. 852, 79 L.Ed.2d 1, **Web** 1984 U.S. Lexis 2 (Supreme Court of the United States).

CHAPTER 32

Investor Protection and Online Securities Transactions

> **"**Fraud is infinite in variety: sometimes it is audacious and unblushing: sometimes it pays a sort of homage to virtue, and then it is modest and retiring: it would be honesty itself, if it could only afford it.**"**
>
> —LORD MACNAGHTEN
> Reddaway v. Banham (1896)

CHAPTER OBJECTIVES

After studying this chapter, you should be able to:

1. Describe the procedure for going public and how securities are registered with the Securities and Exchange Commission.
2. Describe the requirements for qualifying for private placement, intrastate, and small offering exemptions from registration.
3. Describe insider trading that violates Section 10(b) of the Securities Exchange Act of 1934.
4. Describe the liability of tippers and tippees for insider trading.
5. Describe short-swing profits that violate Section 16(b) of the Securities Exchange Act of 1934.

CHAPTER CONTENTS

- Introduction to Investor Protection and Online Securities Transactions
- Definition of *Security*
- The Securities and Exchange Commission (SEC)
- The Securities Act of 1933: Going Public
- Private Transactions Exempt from Registration
- The Securities Exchange Act of 1934: Trading in Securities
- Short-Swing Profits
- State Securities Laws
- Chapter Summary
- Test Review Terms and Concepts
- Case Problems
- Ethics Issues
- IRAC Writing Assignment

    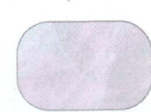

Introduction to Investor Protection and Online Securities Transactions

Prior to the 1920s and 1930s, the securities markets in this country were not regulated by the federal government. Securities were sold to investors with little, if any, disclosure. Fraud in these transactions was common.

Following the stock market crash of 1929, Congress enacted a series of statutes designed to regulate securities markets. The *Securities Act of 1933* requires disclosure by companies and others who wish to issue securities to the public. The *Securities Exchange Act of 1934* was enacted to prevent fraud in the subsequent trading of securities, including insider trading. Securities are now sold online, and the SEC regulates the sale of securities online.

The federal and state securities statutes are designed to require disclosure of information to investors and prevent fraud. This chapter discusses federal and state securities laws and regulations that provide investor protection, as well as the sale of securities online.

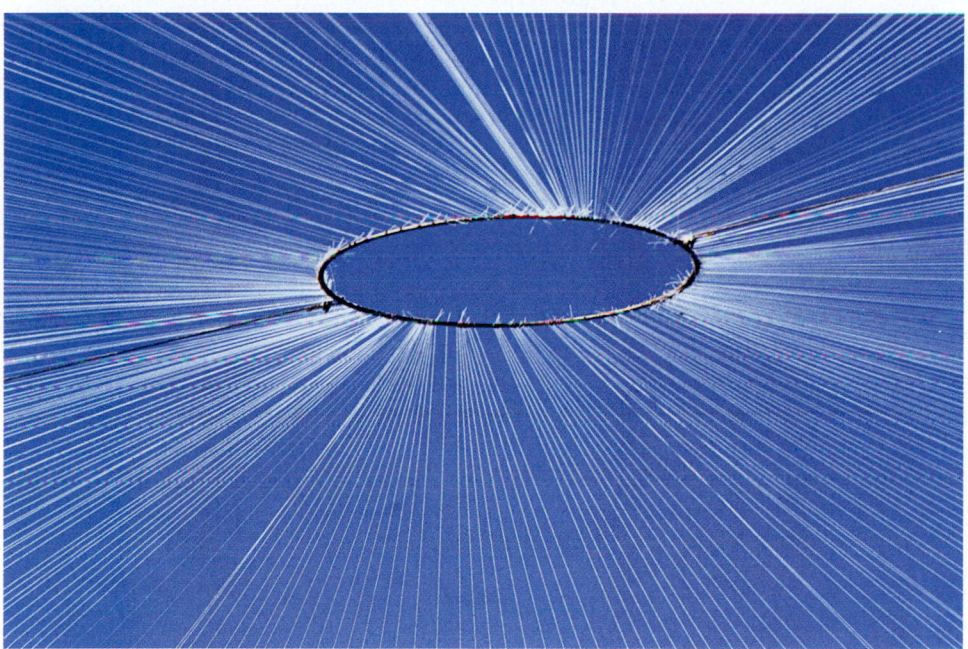

"Blue Sky" Laws

State securities laws are often referred to as "blue-sky" laws because they help prevent investors from purchasing a piece of the blue sky.

Definition of *Security*

Congress has enacted the Securities Act of 1933, the Securities Exchange Act of 1934, and several other securities statutes to regulate the issuance and sale of securities. For these federal statutes to apply, however, a **security** must first be found. Federal securities laws define securities as:

1. ***Common securities.*** Interests or instruments that are commonly known as securities (e.g., common stock, preferred stock, bonds, debentures, warrants).
2. ***Statutorily defined securities.*** Interests or instruments that are expressly mentioned in securities acts (e.g., preorganization subscription agreements; interests in oil, gas, and mineral rights; deposit receipts for foreign securities).
3. ***Investment contracts.*** An **investment contract** is any contract whereby an investor invests money or other consideration in a common enterprise and expects to make a profit from the significant efforts of others. Limited partnership interests, pyramid sales schemes, and investments in farm animals accompanied by care agreements have been found to be securities under this test, which is known as the **Howey test**.[1]

In the following case, the U.S. Supreme Court held that a financial scheme constituted a security subject to federal securities laws.

<table>
<tr><td>

CASE **32.1**

Definition of Security

</td><td>

U.S. SUPREME COURT

Securities and Exchange Commission v. Edwards

540 U.S. 389, 124 S.Ct. 892, 157 L.Ed.2d 813,
Web 2004 U.S. Lexis 659
Supreme Court of the United States

</td><td>

</td></tr>
</table>

> 66 *"Opportunity doesn't always knock, sometimes it rings." (ETS Payphones promotional brochure). And sometimes it hangs up. So it did for the 10,000 people who invested a total of $300 million in the payphone sale-and-leaseback arrangement touted by respondent Edwards under that slogan.* 99
>
> —Justice O'Connor

Facts

Charles Edwards was the chairman, chief executive officer (CEO), and sole shareholder of ETS Payphones, Inc. (ETS). ETS sold payphones to the public via independent distributors. The payphones were sold to buyers in a $7,000 package deal, consisting of a payphone site lease, a five-year leaseback by ETS, and an agreement whereby ETS would install the equipment at the site, arrange for connection and long-distance telephone service, collect coin revenues, and maintain and repair the payphones. Under the ETS contract, each payphone investor was guaranteed to receive $82 per month on his or her investment. ETS guaranteed to refund the full purchase price at the end of the lease. ETS enrolled more than 10,000 people in the payphone program, and they invested over $300 million.

In actuality, the payphone program did not generate enough revenues for ETS to make the guaranteed monthly payments. After ETS defaulted on hundreds of millions of dollars of payments to investors, it filed for bankruptcy. The Securities and Exchange Commission (SEC) brought a civil action against Edwards and ETS, alleging that the defendants had failed to register the payphone sale-and-leaseback arrangement with the SEC as a "security" prior to selling the phones to the public and had committed securities fraud. The U.S. District Court held that the payphone arrangement constituted a "security" and was therefore subject to federal securities laws. The U.S. Court of Appeals reversed, finding no security because the sale-and-leaseback arrangement provided for a fixed rate of return rather than capital appreciation or participation in the earnings of the enterprise. The SEC appealed to the U.S. Supreme Court.

Issue

Is the payphone sale-and-leaseback arrangement that guaranteed a fixed rate of return a security and therefore subject to federal securities laws?

Language of the U.S. Supreme Court

"Opportunity doesn't always knock, sometimes it rings." (ETS Payphones promotional brochure). And sometimes it hangs up. So it did for the 10,000 people who invested a total of $300 million in the payphone sale-and-leaseback arrangement touted by respondent Edwards under that slogan. Congress' purpose in enacting the securities laws was to regulate *investments*, in whatever form they are made and by whatever name they are called. To that end, it enacted a broad definition of "security" to encompass virtually any instrument that might be sold as an investment.

There is no reason to distinguish between promises of fixed returns and promises of variable returns. In both cases, the investing public is attracted by representations of investment income as purchasers were in this case by ETS' invitation to "watch the profits add up." Moreover, investments pitched as low risk (such as those offering a guaranteed fixed return) are particularly attractive to individuals more vulnerable to investment fraud, including older and less sophisticated investors. Under the reading respondent Edwards advances, unscrupulous marketers of investments could evade the securities laws by picking a rate of return to promise. We will not read into the securities laws a limitation not compelled by the language that would so undermine the laws' purposes. We hold that an investment scheme promising a fixed rate of return can be an "investment contract" and thus a "security" subject to the federal securities laws.

Decision

The U.S. Supreme Court held that an investment arrangement that offers a fixed rate of return is a security subject to the provisions of federal securities laws. The Supreme Court reversed the decision of the Court of Appeals and remanded the case for further proceedings, based on violations of securities laws and securities fraud.

Law & Ethics Questions

1. If a financial arrangement that guaranteed a fixed rate of return were not found to be a security, what would be the result for society? Explain.

2. **ETHICS** Did Edwards act ethically in this case? Is there any evidence that he acted fraudulently? Explain.

3. **ETHICS** If Edwards had had to disclose the truth about his and ETS's investment scheme, would many people have invested? Explain.

Web Exercises

1. **WEB** For the complete opinion of this case, go to *www.prenhall.com/cheesemancases*.

2. **WEB** Visit the website of the U.S. Supreme Court, at *www.supremecourtus.gov*, and try to find documents that relate to this case.

3. **WEB** Visit the website of the Securities and Exchange Commission, at *www.sec.gov*.

4. **WEB** Use *www.google.com* to find an article or a case that describes a security fraud. Read it.

CONCEPT SUMMARY

Definition of *Security*

TYPE OF SECURITY	DEFINITION
Common securities	Interests or instruments that are commonly known as securities, such as common stock, preferred stock, debentures, and warrants.
Statutorily defined securities	Interests and instruments that are expressly mentioned in securities acts as being securities, such as interests in oil, gas, and mineral rights.
Investment contracts	A flexible standard for defining a security. Under the Howey test, a security exists if an investor invests money in a common enterprise and expects to make a profit from the significant efforts of others.

The Securities and Exchange Commission (SEC)

The Securities Exchange Act of 1934 created the **Securities and Exchange Commission (SEC)** and empowered it to administer federal securities laws. The SEC is an administrative agency composed of five members who are appointed by the president. The major responsibilities of the SEC are:

1. Adopting rules (also called regulations) that further the purpose of the federal securities statutes. These rules have the force of law.
2. Investigating alleged securities violations and bringing enforcement actions against suspected violators. This may include a recommendation of criminal prosecution. Criminal prosecutions of violations of federal securities laws are brought by the U.S. Department of Justice.
3. Regulating the activities of securities brokers and advisors. This includes registering brokers and advisors and taking enforcement action against those who violate securities laws.

Web Exercises

1. **WEB** Visit the website of the Securities and Exchange Commission (SEC), at *www.sec.gov*.
2. **WEB** Go to *www.sec.gov/edgar.shtml* to see the SEC's electronic filings and forms system (called EDGAR).
3. **WEB** Use *www.google.com* to find an article about an action brought by the SEC against defendants for securities fraud. Read it.

The Securities Act of 1933: Going Public

The **Securities Act of 1933** primarily regulates the issuance of securities by corporations, limited partnerships, other businesses, and individuals.[2] **Section 5 of the Securities Act of 1933** requires securities offered to the public through the use of the mails or any facility of interstate commerce to be registered with the SEC by means of a registration statement and an accompanying prospectus.

The business or party selling the securities to the public is called the **issuer**. The issuer may be a relatively new company (e.g., Google, Inc.) selling securities to the public through an **initial public offering (IPO)**, or it may be an established company (e.g., Microsoft Corporation) selling new securities to the public. Many issuers of securities employ **investment bankers**, which are independent securities companies, to sell their securities to the public. Issuers pay a fee to investment bankers for this service.

Registration Statement

A covered issuer must file a written **registration statement** with the SEC. The issuer's lawyer normally prepares the statement, with the help of the issuer's management, accountants, and underwriters.

A registration statement must contain descriptions of (1) securities being offered for sale; (2) the registrant's business; (3) the management of the registrant, including compensation, stock options and benefits, and material transactions with the registrant; (4) pending litigation, (5) how the proceeds from the offering will be used; (6) government regulation; (7) the degree of competition in the industry; and (8) any special risk factors. In addition, a registration statement must be accompanied by financial statements certified by public accountants.

Registration statements usually become effective 20 business days after they are filed, unless the SEC requires additional information to be disclosed. A new 20-day period begins each time the registration statement is amended. At the registrant's request, the SEC may "accelerate the *effective date*" (i.e., not require the registrant to wait 20 days after the last amendment is filed).

The SEC does not pass judgment on the merits of the securities offered. It decides only whether the issuer has met the disclosure requirements.

Web Exercises

1. **WEB** Google. Inc. went public in an initial public offering (IPO). Visit *www.google-ipo.com* for the basic facts of this IPO.

2. **WEB** Use *www.google.com* to find an article that discusses the Google, Inc., IPO. Read it.

3. **WEB** To review Google, Inc.'s registration statement, go to *http://www.sec.gov/Archives/edgar/data/1288776/000119312504073639/ds1.html/*.

Prospectus

A **prospectus** is a written disclosure document that must be submitted to the SEC along with the registration statement. A prospectus is used as a selling tool by the issuer. It is provided to prospective investors to enable them to evaluate the financial risk of an investment.

A prospectus must contain the following language in capital letters and boldface (usually red) type:

THESE SECURITIES HAVE NOT BEEN APPROVED OR DISAPPROVED BY THE SECURITIES AND EXCHANGE COMMISSION OR ANY STATE SECURITIES COMMISSION NOR HAS THE SECURITIES AND EXCHANGE COMMISSION OR ANY STATE SECURITIES COMMISSION PASSED UPON THE ACCURACY OR ADEQUACY OF THIS PROSPECTUS. ANY REPRESENTATION TO THE CONTRARY IS A CRIMINAL OFFENSE.

Web Exercises

1. **WEB** Use *www.google.com* to find an article that discusses any special features of the Google, Inc., IPO. Read it.

2. **WEB** To review the preliminary prospectus of Google, Inc., go to *www.sec.gov/Archives/edgar/data/1288776/000119312504142742/ds1a.htm*.

E T H I C S   S P O T L I G H T

"Plain English" Disclosure in Securities Offerings

Nonlawyers have always been frustrated by the legalese that lawyers use in contracts, court documents, and regulatory disclosures. There has been no wider use of arcane legal language than in prospectuses offering securities for sale to the public. These documents, which are supposed to provide relevant information to potential investors before they invest in company stock and securities, are usually barely skimmed, let alone read, by potential investors.

The SEC decided to change this practice in 1998 when it adopted a "plain English" rule for securities offerings. Under this rule, issuers of securities must use plain English language on the cover page, in the summary, and in the risk factors sections of their prospectuses. Issuers must now use:

- Active voice
- Short sentences
- "Everyday" words
- Bulleted lists for complex information
- No legal jargon or highly technical terms
- No multiple negatives

The plain English rule has required a major cultural change by issuers, underwriters, and securities lawyers, who are used to using complicated and confusing language. The SEC has stated that it will not be the "grammar police" but will instead focus on the clarity of disclosures to potential investors by issuers. The SEC hopes that its new rule will encourage issuers to use plain English throughout the entire prospectus. [Regulation C Rule 421(d)]

Law & Ethics Questions

1. **ETHICS** Why was the "plain English" rule adopted? Explain.
2. Do you think that most investors read and understand the information provided in a prospectus?

Limitations on Activities During the Registration Process

Section 5 of the Securities Act of 1933 limits the types of activities that an issuer, an underwriter, and a dealer may engage in during the registration process. These limitations are divided into three time periods: the *prefiling period*, the *waiting period*, and the *posteffective period*. These periods are discussed in the following paragraphs.

PREFILING PERIOD The **prefiling period** begins when the issuer first contemplates issuing the securities and ends when the registration statement is filed. During this time, the issuer cannot either sell or offer to sell the securities. The issuer also cannot *condition the market* for the upcoming securities offering. This rule makes it illegal for an issuer to engage in a public relations campaign (e.g., newspaper and magazine articles and advertisements) that touts the prospects of the company and the planned securities issue. However, sending annual reports to shareholders and making public announcements of factual matters (such as the settlement of a strike) are permissible because they are considered normal corporate disclosures. See Exhibit 32.1 for the cover page of a preliminary prospectus.

EXHIBIT 32.1

Cover Page of the Preliminary Prospectus of Google, Inc.

Thomas Weisel Partners LLC

Table of Contents

TABLE OF CONTENTS

	Page
Prospectus Summary	1
Risk Factors	4
Special Note Regarding Forward-Looking Statements	26
Letter from the Founders	27
Auction Process	34
How to Participate in the Auction for our IPO	42
Use of Proceeds	44
Dividend Policy	44
Cash and Capitalization	44
Dilution	46
Selected Consolidated Financial Data	48
Management's Discussion and Analysis of Financial Condition and Results of Operations	50
Business	73
Management	87
Certain Relationships and Related Party Transactions	100
Principal and Selling Stockholders	102

You should rely only on the information contained in this prospectus. We have not authorized anyone to provide you with information that is different from that contained in this prospectus. We are offering to sell, and seeking offers to buy, shares of our Class A common stock only in jurisdictions where offers and sales are permitted. The information in this prospectus is complete and accurate only as of the date of the front cover regardless of the time of delivery of this prospectus or of any sale of shares. Except where the context requires otherwise, in this prospectus, the "Company," "Google," "we," "us" and "our" refer to Google Inc., a Delaware corporation, and, where appropriate, its subsidiaries.

We have not undertaken any efforts to qualify this offering for offers to individual investors in any jurisdiction outside the U.S.; therefore, individual investors located outside the U.S. should not expect to be eligible to participate in this offering.

Until,   2004, 25 days after the date of this offering, all dealers that effect transactions in our shares, whether or not participating in this offering, may be required to deliver a prospectus. This is in addition to the dealers' obligation to deliver a prospectus when acting as underwriters and with respect to their unsold allotments or subscriptions.

Table of Contents

PROSPECTUS SUMMARY

This summary highlights information contained elsewhere in this prospectus and does not contain all of the information you should consider in making your investment decision. You should read this summary together with the more detailed information, including our financial statements and the related notes, elsewhere in this prospectus. You should carefully consider, among other things, the matters discussed in "Risk Factors."

Google Inc.

Google is a global technology leader focused on improving the ways people connect with information. Our innovations in web search and advertising have made our web site a top Internet destination and our brand one of the most recognized in the world. We maintain the world's largest online index of web sites and other content, and we make this information freely available to anyone with an Internet connection. Our automated search technology helps people obtain nearly instant access to relevant information from our vast online index.

We generate revenue by delivering relevant, cost-effective online advertising. Businesses use our AdWords program to promote their products and services with targeted advertising. In addition, the thousands of third-party web sites that comprise our Google Network use our Google AdSense program to deliver relevant ads that generate revenue and enhance the user experience. Advertisers in our AdWords program pay us a fee each time a user clicks on one of their ads displayed either on our web sites or on the web sites of Google Network members that participate in our AdSense program. When a user clicks on an ad displayed on a web site of a Google Network member, we retain only a small portion of the advertiser fee, while most of the fee is paid to the Google Network member.

Our mission is to organize the world's information and make it universally accessible and useful. We believe that the most effective, and ultimately the most profitable, way to accomplish our mission is to put the needs of our users first. We have found that offering a high-quality user experience leads to increased traffic and strong word-of-mouth promotion. Our dedication to putting users first is reflected in three key commitments we have made to our users:

■ We will do our best to provide the most relevant and useful search results possible, independent of financial incentives. Our search results will be objective and we will not accept payment for inclusion or ranking in them.
■ We will do our best to provide the most relevant and useful advertising. Whenever someone pays for something, we will make it clear to our users. Advertisements should not be an annoying interruption.
■ We will never stop working to improve our user experience, our search technology and other important areas of information organization.

We believe that our user focus is the foundation of our success to date. We also believe that this focus is critical for the creation of long-term value. We do not intend to compromise our user focus for short-term economic gain.

Corporate Information

We were incorporated in California in September 1998. In August 2003, we reincorporated in Delaware. Our principal executive offices are located at 1600 Amphitheatre Parkway, Mountain View, California 94043, and our telephone number is (650) 623-4000. We maintain a number of web sites including www.google.com. The information on our web sites is not part of this prospectus.

Google® is a registered trademark in the U.S. and several other countries. Our unregistered trademarks include: AdSense, AdWords, Blogger, Froogle, Gmail, I'm Feeling Lucky and PageRank. All other trademarks, trade names and service marks appearing in this prospectus are the property of their respective holders.

WAITING PERIOD The **waiting period** begins when the registration statement is filed with the SEC and continues until the registration statement is declared effective.

The issuer is encouraged to condition the market during this time. Thus, the issuer may (1) make oral offers to sell (including face-to-face and telephone conversations), (2) distribute a *preliminary prospectus* (usually called a red herring), which contains most of the information to be contained in the final prospectus except for price, (3) distribute a *summary prospectus*, which is a summary of the important terms contained in the prospectus, and

(4) publish *tombstone ads* in newspapers and other publications. Unapproved writings (which are considered illegal offers to sell) as well as actual sales are prohibited during the waiting period.

POSTEFFECTIVE PERIOD The **posteffective period** begins when the registration statement becomes effective and runs until the issuer either sells all the offered securities or withdraws them from sale. Thus, the issuer and its underwriter and dealers may close the offers received prior to the effective date and solicit new offers and sales.

INTERNET AND TECHNOLOGY
Going Public over the Internet

The SEC permits companies to issue securities over the Internet. The same federal securities laws that regulate the traditional issuance of securities also apply to the issuance of securities using the Internet. One company's Internet initial public offering (IPO) follows:

Running sideways (left margin): *The information in this prospectus is not complete and may be changed. We may not sell these securities until the registration statement filed with the Securities and Exchange Commission is effective. This prospectus is not an offer to sell these securities and is not soliciting an offer to buy these securities in any state where the offer or sale is not permitted.*

SUBJECT TO COMPLETION, DATED DECEMBER 21, 2000

PEET'S COFFEE & TEA, INC.

3,300,000 Shares
of Common Stock

This is our initial public offering and no public market currently exists for our shares. We expect that the public offering price will be between $10.00 and $14.00 per share. This price may not reflect the market price of our shares after this offering.

THE OFFERING	PER SHARE	TOTAL
Public Offering Price	$	$
Underwriting Discount	$	$
Proceeds to Peet's	$	$
Proceeds to Selling Shareholders	$	$

Of the 3,300,000 shares being offered, we are selling 2,500,000 shares and the selling shareholders identified in this prospectus are selling 800,000 shares. We will not receive any of the proceeds from the sale of shares by the selling shareholders. We have granted the underwriters the right to purchase up to 182,623 additional shares from us and 312,377 additional shares from the selling shareholders within 30 days to cover any over-allotments. The underwriters expect to deliver shares of common stock to purchasers on   , 2001.

Proposed Nasdaq National Market Symbol: PEET

OPENIPO: The method of distribution being used by the underwriters in this offering differs somewhat from that traditionally employed in firm commitment underwritten public offerings. In particular, the public offering price and allocation of shares will be determined primarily by an auction process conducted by the underwriters and other securities dealers participating in this offering. A more detailed description of this process, known as an OpenIPO, is included in "Plan of Distribution."

THIS OFFERING INVOLVES A HIGH DEGREE OF RISK. YOU SHOULD PURCHASE SHARES ONLY IF YOU CAN AFFORD A COMPLETE LOSS OF YOUR INVESTMENT. SEE "RISK FACTORS" BEGINNING ON PAGE 5.

NEITHER THE SECURITIES AND EXCHANGE COMMISSION NOR ANY STATE SECURITIES COMMISSION HAS APPROVED OR DISAPPROVED OF THESE SECURITIES OR DETERMINED IF THIS PROSPECTUS IS TRUTHFUL OR COMPLETE. ANY REPRESENTATION TO THE CONTRARY IS A CRIMINAL OFFENSE.

WR HAMBRECHT + CO

Pacific Growth Equities, Inc.

The date of this prospectus is   , 2001

Web Exercises

1. **WEB** Use *www.google.com* to find an article about a security offering that was made over the Internet. Read it.

2. **WEB** Use *www.google.com* to find electronic documents used to make a recent security offering over the Internet.

Prior to or at the time of confirming a sale or sending a security to a purchaser, the issuer (or its representative) must deliver a *final prospectus* (also called a *statutory prospectus*) to the investor. Failure to do so is a violation of Section 5. Tombtone ads are often used during this period.

The investor may rescind his or her purchase if the issuer violates any of the prohibitions on activities during these periods. If an underwriter or a dealer violates any of these prohibitions, the SEC may issue sanctions, including the suspension of securities licenses.

Sale of Unregistered Securities

Sale of securities that should have been registered with the SEC but were not violates the Securities Act of 1933. Investors can rescind their purchase and recover damages. The U.S. government can impose criminal penalties on any person who willfully violates the Securities Act of 1933.

Regulation A Offerings

Regulation A permits issuers to sell up to $5 million of securities to the public during a 12-month period, pursuant to a simplified registration process. Such offerings may have an unlimited number of purchasers who do not have to be accredited investors. Issuers with offerings exceeding $100,000 must file an **offering statement** with the SEC. The offering statement requires less disclosure than a registration statement and is less costly to prepare. Investors must be provided with an offering circular prior to the purchase of securities. There are no resale restrictions on the securities.

CONTEMPORARY ENVIRONMENT
Small Corporate Offering Registration Form (SCOR)

Small businesses often need to raise capital and must find public investors to buy company stock. In 1992, after years of investigation, the SEC amended Regulation A by adopting the **Small Corporate Offering Registration Form (SCOR)**. The SCOR form—**Form U-7**—is a question-and-answer disclosure form that small businesses can complete and file with the SEC if they plan on raising $1 million or less from the public issue of securities. An issuer must answer the questions on Form U-7, which then becomes the offering circular that must be given to prospective investors.

Form U-7 questions are so clearly and specifically drawn that they can be answered by the issuer without the help of an expensive securities lawyer. The SCOR questions require the issuer to develop a business plan that states specific company goals and how it plans to reach them. SCOR is limited to domestic businesses. The SCOR offering cannot exceed $1 million, and the offering price of the common stock or its equivalent may not be less than $5 per share. SCOR offerings are a welcome addition for entrepreneur-owners who want to raise money through a small public offering.

Private Actions

Private parties who have been injured by violations of the Securities Act of 1933 have recourse against the violator under the following two sections:

1. **Section 12 of the Securities Act of 1933** imposes *civil liability* on any person who violates the provisions of Section 5 of the act. Violations include selling securities pursuant to an unwarranted exemption and making misrepresentations concerning the offer or sale of securities. The purchaser's remedy for a violation of Section 12 is either to rescind the purchase or to sue for damages.
2. **Section 11 of the Securities Act of 1933** provides for civil liability for damages when a registration statement on its effective date misstates or omits a material fact.

Liability under Section 11 is imposed on those who (1) intentionally defraud investors or (2) are negligent in not discovering the fraud. Thus, the issuer, certain corporate officers (e.g., chief executive officer, chief financial officer, chief accounting officer), directors, signers of the registration statement, underwriters, and experts (e.g., accountants who certify financial statements and lawyers who issue legal opinions that are included in a registration statement) may be liable.

All defendants except the issuer may assert a **due diligence defense** against the imposition of Section 11 liability. If this defense is proven, the defendant is not liable. To establish a due diligence defense, the defendant must prove that after reasonable investigation, he or she had reasonable grounds to believe and did believe that, at the time the registration statement became effective, the statements contained therein were true and there was no omission of material facts.

SEC Actions

The SEC may (1) issue a *consent order* whereby a defendant agrees not to violate securities laws in the future but does not admit to having violated securities laws in the past, (2) bring an action in federal district court to obtain an *injunction*, or (3) request the court to grant ancillary relief, such as *disgorgement of profits* by the defendant.

Criminal Liability

Section 24 of the Securities Act of 1933 imposes *criminal liability* on any person who *willfully* violates either the act or the rules and regulations adopted thereunder.[3] A violator may be fined or imprisoned for up to five years, or both. Criminal actions are brought by the Department of Justice.

The following is a classic case in which the court imposed civil liability for a violation of the Securities Act of 1933.

C A S E **32.2**

Issuance of Securities

Escott v. BarChris Construction Corporation

283 F.Supp. 643,
Web 1968 U.S. Dist. Lexis 3853
United States District Court for the Southern District of New York

66 *Accountants should not be held to a standard higher than that recognized in their profession. Berardi's review did not come up to that standard.* 99

—Justice McLean

Facts

BarChris Construction Corporation (BarChris), a company primarily engaged in the construction and sale of bowling alleys, was in need of additional financing. To raise working capital, BarChris decided to issue debentures to investors. It filed a registration statement, including a prospectus, with the SEC. After two amendments, the registration statement became effective. Peat, Marwick, Mitchell & Co. (Peat, Marwick), a public accounting firm, audited the financial statements of the company that were included in the registration statement and prospectus. The debentures were sold, and investors were provided a final prospectus concerning the debentures. Unbeknownst to the investors, however, the registration statement and prospectus contained the following material misrepresentations and omissions of material fact:

1. Current assets on the balance sheet were overstated by $609,689 (15 percent).

2. Contingent liabilities were understated by $618,853 (42 percent).

3. Sales for the most recent quarter were overstated by $519,810 (32 percent).

4. Gross profits for the most recent quarter were overstated by $230,755 (92 percent).

5. The backlog of orders was overstated by $4,490,000 (186 percent).

6. Loans to officers of BarChris of $386,615 were not disclosed.

7. Customer delinquencies and BarChris's potential liability thereto of $1,350,000 were not disclosed.

8. The use of the proceeds of the debentures to pay old debts was not disclosed.

One year later, BarChris was failing financially, and it filed a petition for protection to be reorganized under federal bankruptcy law. BarChris defaulted on interest payments due to be paid on the debentures to investors. Barry Escott and other purchasers of the debentures brought a civil action against the executive officers, directors, and the outside accountants of BarChris. The plaintiffs alleged that the defendants had violated Section 11 of the Securities Act of 1933 by submitting misrepresentations and omissions of material facts in the registration statement filed with the SEC.

Issue

Are the defendants liable for violating Section 11, or have they proved their due diligence defense?

Language of the Court

I turn now to the question of whether defendants have proved their due diligence defenses.

Russo Russo was, for all intents and purposes, the chief executive officer of BarChris. He was a member of the executive committee. He was familiar with all aspects of the business. He was thoroughly aware of BarChris's stringent financial condition. In short, Russo knew all the relevant facts. He could not have believed that there were no untrue statements or material omissions in the prospectus. Russo has no due diligence defenses.

Vitolo and Pugliese They were the founders of the business. Vitolo was president and Pugliese was vice president. Vitolo and Pugliese each are men of limited education. It is not hard to believe that for them the prospectus was difficult reading, if indeed they read it at all. But whether it was or not is irrelevant. The liability of a director who signs a registration statement does not depend upon whether or not he read it or, if he did, whether or not he understood what he was reading. And in any case, there is nothing to show that they made any investigation of anything that they may not have known about or understood. They have not proved their due diligence defenses.

Trilling Trilling was BarChris's controller. He signed the registration statement in that capacity, although he was not a director. He was a comparatively minor figure in BarChris. He was not considered an executive officer. Trilling may well have been unaware of several of the inaccuracies in the prospectus. But he must have known of some of them. As a financial officer, he was familiar with BarChris's finances and with its books of account. Trilling did not sustain the burden of proving his due diligence defenses.

Peat, Marwick Peat, Marwick's work was in general charge of a member of the firm, Cummings, and more immediately in charge of Peat, Marwick's manager, Logan. Most of the actual work was performed by a senior accountant, Berardi, who has junior assistants, one of whom was Kennedy. Berardi was then about 30 years old. He was not yet a CPA. He had had no previous experience with the bowling industry. This was his first job as a senior accountant. He could hardly have been given a more difficult assignment.

Berardi made the S–1 review. He devoted a little over two days to it. He did not discover any of the errors or omissions pertaining to the state of affairs, all of which were material. In conducting the S–1 review, Berardi did not examine any important financial records other than the trial balance. He asked questions, he got answers that he considered satisfactory, and he did nothing to verify them.

Accountants should not be held to a standard higher than that recognized in their profession. Berardi's review did not come up to that standard. He did not take some of the steps that Peat, Marwick's written program prescribed. He did not spend an adequate amount of time on a task of this magnitude. Most important of all, he was too easily satisfied with glib answers to his inquiries. There were enough danger signals to require some further investigation on his part. Generally accepted accounting standards required such further investigation under these circumstances. Peat, Marwick has not established its due diligence defense.

Decision

The District Court held that the defendants had failed to prove their due diligence defense.

Law & Ethics Questions

1. Should defendants in a Section 11 lawsuit be permitted to prove a due diligence defense to the imposition of liability? Or should liability be strictly imposed?

2. **ETHICS** Who do you think committed the fraud in this case? Did any of the other defendants act unethically?

3. Who do you think bore the burden of paying the judgment in this case?

Web Exercises

1. **WEB** For the complete opinion of this case, go to *www.prenhall.com/cheesemancases*.

2. **WEB** Visit the website of the U.S. District Court, Southern District of New York, at *www.nysd.uscourts.gov*.

3. **WEB** Use *www.google.com* to find an article that discusses liability imposed for fraud in the sale of securities. Read it.

ETHICS SPOTLIGHT

Sarbanes-Oxley Act Erects a Wall Between Investment Bankers and Security Analysis

Investment banking is a service provided by many securities firms, whereby they assist companies in **going public** when issuing shares to the public and otherwise selling securities. The securities firms are paid lucrative fees for providing investment banking services in assisting companies to sell their securities and finding customers to purchase these securities. These same securities firms often provide securities analysis, whereby they provide investment advice, recommending securities listed on the stock exchanges and other securities to be purchased by the public.

In the late 1990s and early 2000s, many conflicts of interest were uncovered. Investment bankers and securities analysts of the same firm shared information, and the analysts were paid or pressured by the securities firms to write glowing reports of companies from which the investment bankers of the firm were earning fees.

Congress sought to remedy this problem by enacting Section 501 of the **Sarbanes-Oxley Act** of 2002. Section 501 established rules for separating the investment banking and securities advice functions of securities firms, thus eliminating many conflicts of interest:

- Securities firms must establish structural and institutional "walls" between their investment banking and securities analysis areas.

These walls must protect analysts from review, pressure, and oversight by persons employed by the investment banking area of the securities firm.

- Securities analysts must disclose in each research report or public appearance any conflicts of interest that are known or should have been known to exist at the time of publication or public appearance.

The SEC is empowered to adopt rules to enforce the provisions of Section 501.

Law & Ethics Questions

1. **ETHICS** Why did investment bankers of securities firms put pressure on analysts to issue positive reports on certain companies? Was this conduct ethical?

2. **ETHICS** Do you think Section 501 will prevent such conduct in the future? Why or why not?

Private Transactions Exempt from Registration

Certain *transactions* in securities are **exempt** from registration. Exempt transactions are subject to the antifraud provisions of the federal securities laws. Therefore, the issuer must provide investors with adequate information—including annual reports, quarterly reports, proxy statements, financial statements, and so on—even though a registration statement is not required. The exempt transactions are discussed in the paragraphs that follow.

Non-issuer Exemption

Non-issuers, such as average investors, do not have to file a registration statement prior to reselling securities they have purchased. This is because the Securities Act of 1933 exempts from registration securities transactions not made by an issuer, an underwriter, or a dealer. For example, an investor who owns shares of IBM can resell those shares to another at any time without having to register with the SEC.

Intrastate Offerings

The purpose of the **intrastate offerings exemption** is to permit local businesses to raise from local investors capital to be used in the local economy without the need to register with the SEC.[4] There is no limit on the dollar amount of capital that can be raised pursuant to an intrastate offering exemption. An issuer can qualify for this exemption in only one state.

Three requirements must be met to qualify for this exemption:[5]

1. The issuer must be a resident of the state for which the exemption is claimed. A corporation is a resident of the state in which it is incorporated.
2. The issuer must be doing business in that state. This requires that 80 percent of the issuer's assets be located in the state, 80 percent of its gross revenues be derived from the state, its principal office be located in the state, and 80 percent of the proceeds of the offering be used in the state.
3. The purchasers of the securities must all be residents of that state.

Web Exercises

1. **WEB** Use *www.google.com* to find an article that discusses the intrastate offering exemption. Read it.

2. **WEB** Use *www.google.com* to find an article about a recent intrastate offering. Read it.

Private Placements

An issue of securities that does not involve a public offering is exempt from the registration requirements.[6] This exemption—known as the **private placement exemption**—allows issuers to raise capital from an unlimited number of accredited investors without having to register the offering with the SEC.[7] There is no dollar limit on the amount of securities that can be sold pursuant to this exemption.

An **accredited investor** may be:[8]

1. Any natural person (including spouse) who has a net worth of at least $1 million.
2. Any natural person who has had an annual income of at least $200,000 for each of the previous two years and reasonably expects to make $200,000 income in the current year.
3. Any corporation, partnership, or business trust with total assets in excess of $5 million.
4. Insiders of the issuers, such as executive officers and directors of corporate issuers and general partners of partnership issuers.
5. Certain institutional investors, such as registered investment companies, pension plans, colleges and universities, and the like.

No more than 35 *nonaccredited investors* may purchase securities pursuant to a private placement exemption. Nonaccredited investors must be sophisticated investors, however, either through their own experience and education or through representatives (e.g., accountants, lawyers, and business managers). General selling efforts, such as advertising to the public, are not permitted.

Web Exercises

1. **WEB** Use *www.google.com* to find an article that discusses private placements. Read it.
2. **WEB** Use *www.google.com* to find an article about a recent private placement offering. Read it.

Small Offerings

Securities offerings that do not exceed a certain dollar amount are exempt from registration.[9] Rule 504 exempts from registration the sale of securities not exceeding $1 million during a 12-month period. The securities may be sold to an unlimited number of accredited and unaccredited investors, but general selling efforts to the public are not permitted. This is called the **small offering exemption**.

Web Exercises

1. **WEB** Use *www.google.com* to find an article that discusses the small offering exemption. Read it.
2. **WEB** Use *www.google.com* to find an article about a recent small offering. Read it.

CONTEMPORARY ENVIRONMENT

Rule 144A: Qualified Institutional Investors

To establish a more liquid and efficient secondary market in unregistered securities, the SEC adopted **Rule 144A**. This rule permits *qualified institutional investors*—defined as institutions that own and invest at least $100 million in securities—to buy unregistered securities without being subject to the holding periods of Rule 144. This rule is designed to create an institutional market in unregistered securities as well as to permit foreign issuers to raise capital from sophisticated investors in this country without making registration process disclosures.

Resale Restrictions

Securities sold pursuant to the intrastate, private placement, or small offering exemptions are called **restricted securities** because they cannot be resold for a limited period of time after their initial issue. The following restrictions apply:

- **Rule 147** stipulates that securities sold pursuant to an intrastate offering exemption cannot be sold to nonresidents for a period of nine months.

■ **Rule 144** provides that securities sold pursuant to the private placement or small offering exemption must be held for one year from the date when the securities are last sold by the issuer. After that time, investors may sell the greater of (1) 1 percent of the outstanding securities of the issuer or (2) the average weekly volume of trading in the securities (i.e., the four-week moving average) in any three-month period. Information about the issuer must be available to the public. Generally, all restrictions are lifted after two years.

Preventing Transfer of Restricted Securities

To protect the nontransferability of restricted shares, the issuer must:

1. Require the investors to sign an *affidavit* stating that they are buying the securities for investment, acknowledging that they are purchasing restricted securities, and promising not to transfer the shares in violation of the restriction.
2. Place a *legend* on the stock certificate describing the restriction.
3. Notify the *transfer agent* not to record a transfer of the securities that would violate the restriction.

If the issuer has taken these precautions, it will not lose its exemption from registration even if isolated transfers of stock occur in violation of the restricted periods. If these precautions are not taken, the issuer may lose its exemption from registration. In that event, it has sold unregistered securities in violation of Section 5, and all purchasers are permitted to rescind their purchases of the securities.

CONTEMPORARY ENVIRONMENT

Securities Exempt from Registration

Certain *securities* are exempt from registration. Once a security is exempt, it is exempt forever. It does not matter how many times the security is transferred. Exempt securities include:

1. Securities issued by any government in the United States (e.g., municipal bonds issued by city governments).

2. Short-term notes and drafts that have a maturity date that does not exceed nine months (e.g., commercial paper issued by corporations).

3. Securities issued by nonprofit issuers, such as religious institutions, charitable institutions, and colleges and universities.

4. Securities of financial institutions (e.g., banks and savings associations) that are regulated by the appropriate banking authorities.

5. Securities issued by common carriers (railroads and trucking companies) that are regulated by the Interstate Commerce Commission (ICC).

6. Insurance and annuity contracts issued by insurance companies.

7. Stock dividends and stock splits.

8. Securities issued in a corporate reorganization in which one security is exchanged for another security.

The Securities Exchange Act of 1934: Trading in Securities

Unlike the Securities Act of 1933, which regulates the original issuance of securities, the **Securities Exchange Act of 1934** primarily regulates subsequent trading.[10] It provides for the registration of certain companies with the SEC, the continuous filing of periodic reports by these companies to the SEC, and the regulation of securities exchanges, brokers, and dealers. It also contains provisions that assess civil and criminal liability on violators of the 1934 act and rules and regulations adopted thereunder.

Section 10(b) and Rule 10b-5

Section 10(b) is one of the most important sections in the entire 1934 act. It prohibits the use of manipulative and deceptive devices in contravention of the rules and regulations prescribed by the SEC.

Pursuant to its rule-making authority, the SEC has adopted **Rule 10b-5**, which provides:

It shall be unlawful for any person, directly or indirectly, by use of any means or instrumentality of interstate commerce or of the mails, or of any facility of any national securities exchange,

a. to employ any device, scheme, or artifice to defraud,
b. to make any untrue statement of a material fact or to omit to state a material fact necessary in order to make the statements made, in light of the circumstances under which they were made, not misleading, or
c. to engage in any act, practice, or course of business that operates or would operate as a fraud or deceit upon any person, in connection with the purchase or sale of any security.

Rule 10b-5 is not restricted to purchases and sales of securities of reporting companies.[11] All transfers of securities, whether made on a stock exchange, in the over-the-counter market, in a private sale, or in connection with a merger, are subject to this rule.[12] The U.S. Supreme Court has held that only conduct involving **scienter** (intentional conduct) violates Section 10(b) and Rule 10b-5. Negligent conduct is not a violation.[13]

Section 10(b) and Rule 10b-5 require reliance by the injured party on the misstatement. However, many sales and purchases of securities occur in open-market transactions (e.g., over stock exchanges) where there is no direct communication between the buyer and the seller.

Insider Trading

One of the most important purposes of Section 10(b) and Rule 10b-5 is to prevent **insider trading**. Insider trading occurs when a company employee or company advisor uses material nonpublic information to make a profit by trading in the securities of the company. This practice is considered illegal because it allows insiders to take advantage of the investing public.

In the *Matter of Cody, Roberts & Co.*[14] the SEC announced that the duty of an insider who possesses material nonpublic information is to either (1) abstain from trading in the securities of the company or (2) disclose the information to the person on the other side of the transaction before the insider purchases the securities from or sells the securities to him or her.

Insiders

For purposes of Section 10(b) and Rule 10b-5, **insiders** are defined as (1) officers, directors, and employees at all levels of a company; (2) lawyers, accountants, consultants, and other agents and representatives who are hired by the company on a temporary and non-employee status to provide services or work to the company; and (3) others who owe a fiduciary duty to the company.

Example The Widget Corporation has its annual audit done by its outside CPAs, Ernest & Old, CPAs. Peter is one of the CPAs who conduct the audit. The audit discloses that the Widget Corporation's profits have doubled since last year, and Peter rightfully discloses this fact to Martha, the chief financial officer (CFO) of Widget Corporations. Both Martha and Peter are *insiders*. The earnings information is definitely *material*, and it is *nonpublic* until the corporation publicly announces its earnings in two days. Prior to the earnings information being made public, Peter and Martha buy stock in Widget Corporation at $100 per share. After the earnings information is made public, the stock of Widget Corporation increases to $150 per share. Both Peter and Martha are liable for

> He will lie sir, with such volubility that you would think truth were a tool.
>
> William Shakespeare
> *All's Well That Ends Well (1604)*

insider trading in violation of Section 10(b) and Rule 10b-5 because they traded in the securities of Widget Corporation while in possession of inside information.

The following is a classic case of insider trading.

C A S E **32.3**

Insider Trading

Securities and Exchange Commission v. Texas Gulf Sulphur Company

401 F.2d 833,
Web 1968 U.S. App. Lexis 5797
United States Court of Appeals for the Second Circuit

❝ *The insiders here were not trading on an equal footing with the outside investors.* **❞**

—Judge Waterman

Facts

Texas Gulf Sulphur Co. (TGS), a mining company, drilled an exploratory hole—Kidd 55—near Timmins, Ontario. Assay reports showed that the core from this drilling proved to be remarkably high in copper, zinc, and silver. TGS kept the discovery secret, camouflaged the drill site, and diverted drilling efforts to another site to allow TGS to acquire land around Kidd 55. TGS stock traded at $18 per share.

Eventually, rumors of a rich mineral strike began circulating. On Saturday, the *New York Times* published an unauthorized report of TGS drilling efforts in Canada and its rich mineral strike. On Sunday, officers of TGS drafted a press release that was issued that afternoon. The press release appeared in morning newspapers of general circulation on Monday. It read in pertinent part: "The work done to date has not been sufficient to reach definite conclusions and any statement as to size and grade of ore would be premature and possibly misleading."

The rumors persisted. Three days later, at 10:00 A.M., TGS held a press conference for the financial media. At the time of the press conference, TGS stock was trading at $37 per share. At this press conference, which lasted about 10 minutes, TGS disclosed the richness of the Timmins mineral strike and that the strike should run to at least 25 million tons in ore. Several officers, directors, and other employees of TGS who had knowledge of the mineral strike at Timmins traded in the stock of TGS during the five-month period prior to the public announcement. After the announcement, the stock was selling at $58.

The SEC brought an action against several of these executives for insider trading in violation of Section 10(b) of the Securities Exchange Act of 1934. The SEC sought to rescind their stock purchases. The District Court held against most of these executives, who then appealed.

Issue

Are the defendant executives liable for engaging in insider trading?

Language of the Court

The insiders here were not trading on an equal footing with the outside investors. They alone were in a position to evaluate the probability and magnitude of what seemed from the outset to be a major ore strike.

Crawford Crawford telephoned his orders to his Chicago broker about midnight on [the day before the announcement] and again at 8:30 in the morning of [the day of the announcement] with instructions to buy at the opening of the Midwest Stock Exchange that morning. The trial court's finding that "he sought to, and did, 'beat the news,'" is well documented by the record. Before insiders may act upon material information, such information must have been effectively disclosed in a manner sufficient to ensure its availability to the investing public. Particularly here, where a formal announcement to the entire financial news media had been promised in a prior official release known to the media, all insider activity must await dissemination of the promised official announcement.

Coates Coates was absolved by the court below because his telephone order was placed shortly before 10:20 A.M. on [the day of the announcement], which was after the announcement had been made even though the news could not be considered already a matter of public information. This result seems to have been predicated upon a misinterpretation of dicta in *Cady Roberts*, where the SEC instructed insiders to "keep out of the market until the established procedures for public release of the information are carried out instead of hastening to execute transactions in advance of, and in frustration of, the objectives of the release." The reading of a news release, which prompted Coates into action, is merely the first step in the process of dissemination required for compliance with the regulatory objective of providing all investors with an equal opportunity to make informed investment judgments. Assuming that the contents of the official release could instantaneously be acted upon, at the minimum Coates should have waited until the news could reasonably have been expected to appear over the media of widest circulation, rather than hastening to ensure an advantage to himself and his broker son-in-law.

Decision

The Court of Appeals held that the executives in this case had engaged in illegal insider trading.

Law & Ethics Questions

1. Should insider trading be illegal? Why or why not?

2. **ETHICS** Did the inside executives act ethically in this case?

3. **ETHICS** Is insider trading easy to detect? Do you think insider trading is very prevalent?

4. How can businesses protect against their employees engaging in insider trading? Explain.

Web Exercises

1. **WEB** For the complete opinion of this case, go to *www.prenhall.com/cheesemancases*.

2. **WEB** Visit the website of the U.S. Court of Appeals of the Second Circuit, at *www.ca2.uscourts.gov*.

3. **WEB** Visit the website of the Securities and Exchange Commission (SEC), at *www.sec.gov*.

4. **WEB** Use *www.google.com* to find an article that discusses an act of insider trading. Read it.

Misappropriation Theory

The courts have developed laws to address trading in securities by insiders who possess inside information. But sometimes the persons who possess inside information about a company is not an employee or a temporary insider to that company. Instead, this party is an outsider. However, if the outsider has misappropriated the information in violation of his or her fiduciary duty, it violates Section 10(b) and Rule 10b-5. This rule, called the **misappropriation theory**, was approved in the following U.S. Supreme Court decision.

CASE 32.4

Misappropriation Theory

U.S. SUPREME COURT
United States v. O'Hagan

521 U.S. 642, 117 S.Ct. 2199, 138 L.Ed.2d 724,
Web 1997 U.S. Lexis 4033
Supreme Court of the United States

> ❝*The misappropriation theory outlaws trading on the basis of nonpublic information by a corporate "outsider" in breach of a duty owed not to a trading party, but to the source of the information.*❞
>
> —Justice Ginsburg

Facts

James O'Hagan was a partner in the law firm Dorsey & Whitney in Minneapolis, Minnesota. Grand Metropolitan PLC (Grand Met), a company based in London, England, hired Dorsey & Whitney to represent it in a secret tender offer for the stock of the Pillsbury Company, headquartered in Minneapolis. While this transaction was still secret, O'Hagan began purchasing call options for Pillsbury stock. Each call option gave O'Hagan the right to purchase 100 shares of Pillsbury stock at a specified price. O'Hagan continued to purchase call options for two months, and he became the largest holder of call options for Pillsbury stock. O'Hagan also purchased 5,000 shares of Pillsbury common stock at $39 per share. These purchases were all made while Grand Met's proposed tender offer for Pillsbury remained secret to the public. When Grand Met publicly announced its tender offer one month later, Pillsbury stock increased to nearly $60 per share. O'Hagan sold his Pillsbury call options and common stock, making a profit of more than $4.3 million.

The U.S. Department of Justice charged O'Hagan with criminally violating Section 10(b) and Rule 10b-5. Because this was not a case of classic insider trading because O'Hagan did not trade in the stock of his law firm's client, Grand Met, the government alleged that O'Hagan was liable under the misappropriation theory for trading in Pillsbury stock by engaging in deceptive conduct by misappropriating the secret information about Grand Met's tender offer from his employer, Dorsey & Whitney, and from its client, Grand Met. The District Court found O'Hagan guilty and sentenced him to 41 months in prison. The Eighth Circuit Court of Appeals reversed, finding that liability under Section 10(b) and Rule 10b-5 cannot be based on the misappropriation theory. The government appealed to the U.S. Supreme Court.

Issue

Can a defendant be criminally convicted of violating Section 10(b) and Rule 10b-5 based on the misappropriation theory?

Language of the U.S. Supreme Court

The "misappropriation theory" holds that a person commits fraud "in connection with" a securities transaction, and thereby violates Section 10(b) and Rule 10b-5, when he misappropriates confidential information for securities trading purposes, in breach of a duty owed to the source of the information. Under this theory, a fiduciary's undisclosed, self-serving use of a principal's information to purchase or sell securities, in breach of a duty of loyalty and confidentiality, defrauds the principal of the exclusive use of that information.

The classical theory targets a corporate insider's breach of duty to shareholders with whom the insider transacts; the misappropriation theory outlaws trading on the basis of nonpublic information by a corporate "outsider" in breach of a duty owed not to a trading party, but to the source of the information. The misappropriation theory comports with Section 10(b)'s language, which requires deception "in connection with the purchase or sale of any security."

Decision

The U.S. Supreme Court held that a defendant can be criminally convicted of violating Section 10(b) and Rule 10b-5 under the misappropriation theory. The U.S. Supreme Court reversed the decision of the Court of Appeals, which had held otherwise.

Law & Ethics Questions

1. Should the misappropriation theory be recognized as a basis for criminal liability under Section 10(b) and Rule 10b-5? Do you agree with the Supreme Court's decision?
2. **ETHICS** If the Supreme Court had upheld the circuit court's decision, would ethics alone be enough to prevent persons like O'Hagan from trading on secret information?
3. **ETHICS** Will the securities markets be more or less honest because of the Supreme Court's ruling in this case?

Web Exercises

1. **WEB** For the complete opinion of this case, go to *www.prenhall.com/cheesemancases*.
2. **WEB** Visit the website of the U.S. Supreme Court, at *www.supremecourtus.gov*, and try to find documents that relate to this case.
3. **WEB** Visit the website of the U.S. Department of Justice, at *www.usdoj.gov*.
4. **WEB** Use *www.google.com* to find an article that describes the misappropriation theory. Read it.

Tipper–Tippee Liability

A person who discloses material nonpublic information to another person is called a **tipper**. A person who receives such information is known as a **tippee**. A tippee is liable for acting on material information that he or she knew or should have known was not public. The tipper is liable for the profits made by the tippee. If the tippee tips other persons, both the tippee (who is now a tipper) and the original tipper are liable for the profits made by these remote tippees. The remote tippees are liable for their own trades if they knew or should have known that they possessed material inside information.

In the following case, the court found insider trading and tippee liability.

C A S E **32.5**
Insider Trading and Tipping

United States of America v. Bhagat

436 F.3d 1140,
Web 2006 U.S. App. Lexis 3008 (2006)
United States Court of Appeals for the Ninth Circuit

> **"** To convict Bhagat of tipping Gill, the government was required to prove that the tipper, Bhagat, provided the tippee, Gill, with material, inside information, prior to the tippee's purchase of stock. **"**
>
> —Judge Rawlinson

Facts

The Nvidia Corporation was a Silicon Valley, California, manufacturer of graphics processors and media communications devices. On a Sunday, Nvidia entered into a contract with Microsoft Corporation to develop and manufacture a 3-D graphics processor for Microsoft's new video game console, the Xbox. At 11:04 P.M. that night, Nvidia's president and CEO sent an e-mail message to all Nvidia employees, announcing the contract. The e-mail said that Nvidia had obtained the contract from Microsoft. The e-mail revealed that Microsoft would prepay Nvidia $200 million and predicted that the Xbox contract would generate about $2 billion for the company over the next five years.

On Monday, at 9:15 A.M., Nvidia's vice president of marketing sent an e-mail to all Nvidia employees titled "xbox shhhhh" that said "keep xbox news quiet. Not a word to anyone outside of our walls. Microsoft plans to make the news public this Friday." Other e-mails imposed a trading blackout on the purchase of Nvidia stock by its employees. Atul Bhagat worked as an engineer for Nvidia. Bhagat arrived at work on Monday, midmorning. Evidence proved that all of the e-mails concerning the Microsoft contract were on his computer when he arrived for work. Twenty minutes after arriving for work, Bhagat purchased a large quantity of Nvidia stock—his largest purchase in nearly three years.

The Securities and Exchange Commission (SEC), a federal administrative agency, conducted an investigation of trading in Nvidia's stock. Bhagat told federal government investigators that he did not read the company's e-mails until 40 minutes after he purchased the stock and that he purchased the stock based on the general strength of the company. Less than one-half hour after Bhagat made his purchase, his friend Mamat Gill purchased Nvidia's stock. This was Gill's largest purchase of the year. Evidence showed that Bhagat sent Gill an e-mail the day after Gill purchased the Nvidia stock, containing a link to an Internet article discussing Nvidia and the Xbox.

The U.S. Department of Justice brought criminal charges against Bhagat, alleging insider trading and tipping. At trial, the government, which did not have any direct evidence of the alleged crimes, asked the jury to infer Bhagat's actions from the circumstantial evidence presented at trial. The jury at the U.S. District Court found Bhagat guilty on all charges. Bhagat appealed.

Issue

Is the defendant Bhagat guilty of the crimes of insider trading and tipping?

Language of the Court

To convict Bhagat of insider trading, the government was required to prove that he traded stock on the basis of material, nonpublic information. The government offered significant evidence to support the jury's conclusion that Bhagat was aware of the confidential X-Box information before he executed his trades. The X-Box e-mails were sent prior to his purchase. The e-mails were found on his computer. Bhagat was at his office for several hours prior to executing his trade, which provided him the opportunity to read his e-mails. Finally, Bhagat took virtually no action to divest himself of the stock or to inform his company that he had violated the company's trading blackout. The fact that this evidence was all circumstantial does not lessen its sufficiency to support a guilty verdict.

To convict Bhagat of tipping Gill, the government was required to prove that the tipper, Bhagat, provided the tippee, Gill, with material, inside information, prior to the tippee's

purchase of stock. Viewing the evidence in the light most favorable to the prosecution, we cannot say that no reasonable trier of fact could have found Bhagat guilty. Bhagat and Gill were friends; Gill purchased stock shortly after Bhagat; and Gill's purchase was his largest purchase of the year.

Sufficient evidence supported Bhagat's convictions on all counts.

Decision

The U.S. Court of Appeals affirmed the judgment of the U.S. District Court that had found Bhagat guilty of insider trading and tipping in violation of federal securities laws.

Law & Ethics Questions

1. What elements are necessary to prove the crime of insider trading? Explain.

2. What elements are necessary to prove the crime of tipping? Explain.

3. What is the difference between direct evidence and circumstantial evidence?

4. Is circumstantial evidence sufficient to convict a person of the crimes of insider trading and tipping?

5. **ETHICS** Did Bhagat act unethically by purchasing stock of his employer?

6. **ETHICS** Did Bhagat act ethically in tipping his friend to purchase stock in Nvidia?

7. **ETHICS** Do you think you would have traded on the inside information if you had been in Bhagat's situation? Explain.

Web Exercises

1. **WEB** For the complete opinion of this case, go to *www.prenhall.com/cheesemancases*.

2. **WEB** Visit the website of the U.S. Court of Appeals for the Ninth Circuit, at *www.ca9.uscourts.gov*.

3. **WEB** Visit the website of the U.S. Department of Justice, at *www.usdoj.gov*.

4. **WEB** Visit the website of the Securities and Exchange Commission (SEC), at *www.sec.gov*.

5. **WEB** Visit the website of Microsoft Corporation, at *www.microsoft.com*.

6. **WEB** Use *www.google.com* to find information about the Xbox.

7. **WEB** Visit the website of Nvidia Corporation, at *www.nvidia.com*.

Private Actions

Although Section 10(b) and Rule 10b-5 do not expressly provide for a private right of action, courts have implied such a right. Generally, a private plaintiff may seek rescission of the securities contract or recover damages (e.g., disgorgements of the illegal profits by the defendants). Private securities fraud claims must be brought within two years after discovery or five years after the violation occurs, whichever is shorter.

> Fraud includes the pretense of knowledge when knowledge there is none.
>
> Chief Justice Cardozo
> *Ultramares Corp. v. Touche* (1931)

SEC Actions

The SEC may investigate suspected violations of the Securities Exchange Act of 1934 and the rules and regulations adopted thereunder. The SEC may enter into *consent orders* with defendants, seek *injunctions* in federal District Court, or seek court orders requiring defendants to *disgorge* illegally gained profits.

In 1984, Congress enacted the **Insider Trading Sanctions Act**,[15] which permits the SEC to obtain a *civil penalty* of up to three times the illegal profits gained or losses avoided on insider trading. The fine is payable to the U.S. Treasury.

Criminal Liability

Section 32 of the Securities Exchange Act of 1934 makes it a criminal offense to willfully violate the provisions of the act or the rules and regulations adopted thereunder.[16] Under the Sarbanes-Oxley Act of 2002, a person who willfully violates the Securities Exchange Act of 1934 can be fined up to $5 million or imprisoned for up to 25 years, or both. A corporation or another entity may be fined up to $2.5 million.

Sarbanes-Oxley Act

Under the Sarbanes-Oxley Act the SEC may issue an order prohibiting any person who has committed securities fraud from acting as an officer or a director of a public company.

ETHICS SPOTLIGHT

Fair Disclosure to All

Prior to 2000, publicly held companies routinely announced crucial earnings and other significant information to securities analysts and other Wall Street insiders before making the information public. This meant that the analysts and others on Wall Street could profit from the information before it was made available to the general public. They did this by purchasing securities of the disclosing companies on good news and selling securities on bad news, before others could act. The SEC felt that this so-called "front running" gave an unfair advantage to the investment professionals.

In 2000, the SEC adopted **Regulation Fair Disclosure (Reg FD)**, which prohibits companies from leaking important information to securities professionals before the information is disclosed to the public. Reg FD forces companies, by law, to reveal sensitive information to the general public at the same time that the information is released to stock analysts. Reg FD has taken away a lucrative advantage that the Wall Street professionals had over the general investing public.

Law & Ethics Questions

1. **ETHICS** Was it ethical for securities professionals to "front run" by trading securities before the public had the same information?

2. Do the fair disclosure rules level the playing field? Explain.

Short-Swing Profits

Section 16(a)

Section 16(a) of the Securities Exchange Act of 1934 defines any person who is an executive officer, a director, or a 10 percent shareholder of an equity security of a reporting company as a *statutory insider* for Section 16 purposes. Statutory insiders must file reports with the SEC, disclosing their ownership and trading in the company's securities.[17] These reports must be filed with the SEC and made available on the company's website within two days after the trade occurs.

Section 16(b)

Section 16(b) of the Securities Exchange Act of 1934 requires that any profits made by a statutory insider on transactions involving **short-swing profits**—that is, trades involving equity securities occurring within six months of each other—belong to the corporation.[18]

The corporation may bring a legal action to recover these profits. Involuntary transactions, such as forced redemption of securities by the corporation or an exchange of securities in a bankruptcy proceeding, are exempt. Section 16(b) is a strict liability provision. Generally, no defenses are recognized. Neither intent nor the possession of inside information need be shown.

Example Rosanne is the president of a corporation and a statutory insider who does not possess any inside information. On February 1, she purchases 1,000 shares of her employer's stock at $10 per share. On June 1, she sells the stock for $14 per share. The corporation can recover the $4,000 profit because the trades occurred within six months of each other. Rosanne would have to wait until after August 1 to sell the securities.

Law & Ethics Questions

1. What do Section 16(a) and Section 16(b) require?

2. **ETHICS** Do you think Section 16(a) and Section 16(b) make corporate directors and policy-making officers act more ethically?

SEC Section 16 Rules

The SEC has adopted the following rules under Section 16:

- It clarifies the definition of *officer* to include only executive officers who perform policy-making functions. This would include the president, the chief executive officer, the vice presidents in charge of business units or divisions, the principal financial officer, the principal accounting officer, and the like. Officers who run day-to-day operations but are not responsible for policy decisions are not included.

- It relieves insiders of liability for transactions that occur within six months before becoming an insider. For example, if a non-insider buys shares of his or her company January 15, becomes an insider March 15, and sells the shares May 15, the January 15 purchase is not matched against the May 15 sale.

- It continues the rule that insiders are liable for transactions that occur within six months of the last transaction engaged in while an insider. For example, if an insider buys shares in his or her company April 30 and leaves the company May 15, this purchase must be matched against any sale of the company's shares that occurs on or before October 30.

CONCEPT SUMMARY

Section 10(b) and Section 16(b) Compared

ELEMENT	SECTION 10(B) AND RULE 10B-5	SECTION 16(B)
Covered securities	All securities.	Securities required to be registered with the SEC under the 1934 act.
Inside information	Defendant made a misrepresentation or traded on inside (or perhaps misappropriated) information.	Short-swing profits recoverable whether or not they are attributable to misappropriation or inside information.
Recovery	Belongs to the injured purchaser or seller.	Belongs to the corporation.

State Securities Laws

Most states have enacted securities laws. These laws, which are often called *blue-sky laws*, generally require the registration of certain securities and provide exemptions from registration. They also contain broad antifraud provisions. The **Uniform Securities Act** has been adopted by many states. This act is drafted to coordinate **state securities laws** with federal securities laws.

Web Exercises

1. **WEB** Use *www.google.com* to find an article that discusses blue-sky laws. Read it.
2. **WEB** Use *www.google.com* to find an article that discusses your state's securities laws. Read it.

INTERNATIONAL LAW
Chinese Bank Launches World's Largest IPO

In late 2006, Industrial and Commercial Bank of China (ICBC) issued shares to the public in the world's largest IPO. The bank raised over US$19 billion in a dual listing on the Hong Kong and Shanghai, China, stock exchanges. The IPO of 50 billion shares at 39 cents each was oversubscribed. The IPO made available only about 15 percent of ICBC's total shares.

One year prior to the IPO, Goldman Sachs purchased 6 percent of the bank's stock for about $3 billion. Other strategic alliance pre-IPO shares were sold to American Express, Royal Bank of Scotland, and Allianz AG of Germany. After the pre-IPO sales and IPO, the central government of China would control 72.5 percent of the bank's shares.

The IPO of China's largest bank was a tremendous success. Prior to the pre-IPO sales to strategic partners and the IPO, ICBC was a state-owned bank, meaning that the Chinese government owned and operated the bank. A few years ago, about one-third of ICBC's loans were past due, stemming from poor lending practices and corruption. Prior to the IPO, the Chinese government stepped in, infused cash into the bank, and transferred many bad loans out of the bank.

In the year prior to ICBC's IPO, two other Chinese state-owned banks, the Bank of China and China Reconstruction Bank, issued shares to the public, raising a combined $20 billion. These two Chinese IPOs rank in the world's top 10 IPOs.

Web Exercises

1. **WEB** Visit the website of the Industrial and Commercial Bank of China (ICBC), at *www.icbc.com.cn*.
2. **WEB** Visit the website of the Hong Kong Stock Market, at *www.hkex.com.hk*.
3. **WEB** Visit the website of the Shanghai Stock Market, at *www.sse.com.cn*.
4. **WEB** Use *www.google.com* to find an article about a recent IPO by a foreign company in another country. Read it.

Beijing, China

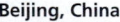

Foreign securities markets have developed in many countries. Each country has its own securities laws. For example, China is developing securities laws to regulate its developing securities markets.

CONTEMPORARY ENVIRONMENT
Commodities Regulation

Commodities include grains (e.g., wheat, soybeans, oats), animals (e.g., cattle, hogs), animal products (e.g., pork bellies), foods (e.g., sugar, coffee), metals (e.g., gold, silver), and oil. A **commodities futures contract** is an agreement to buy or sell a specific amount and type of commodity at some future date, at a price established at the time of contracting. For example, a futures contract may be to sell 5,000 bushels of a specified grain on August 31 at $5.00 per bushel. Standardized terms are established for futures contracts (e.g., quantity and quality of the commodity, time and place of delivery). Thus, the contracts can be bought and sold on the commodities exchanges just as stocks and bonds are bought and sold on securities exchanges. Farmers, ranchers, food processors, milling companies, mineral producers, oil companies, and investors often buy and sell futures contracts

Commodities exchanges have been established at different locations across the country where commodity futures contracts can be bought and sold by food producers, farmers, and speculators. The major commodity exchanges are:

- The Chicago Board of Trade (CBOT)
- The Chicago Mercantile Exchange (CME)
- The Commodity Exchange of New York (COMEX)
- Kansas City Board of Trade (KBOT)
- New York Mercantile Exchange (NYME)
- New York Futures Exchange (NYF)

The federal **Commodity Exchange Act (CEA)** of 1936, as amended, regulates the trading of commodity futures contracts. The **Commodity Futures Trading Commission (CFTC)**, a federal administrative agency, has the authority to regulate trading in commodities futures contracts, to adopt regulations, conduct investigations, bring administrative proceedings against suspected violators, and impose civil fines. Suspected criminal violations can be referred to the Justice Department for criminal action.

Web Exercises

1. **WEB** Visit the website of the Commodity Futures Trading Commission (CFTC), at *www.cftc.gov*.

2. **WEB** Visit the website of the Chicago Board of Trade (CBOT), at *www.cbot.com*.

3. **WEB** Visit the website of New York Mercantile Exchange (NYME), at *www.nymex.com*.

4. **WEB** Use *www.google.com* to find the price of a futures contract for pork bellies.

Chapter Summary

Definition of *Security*, p. 879

A security must be found before federal securities laws apply. A security is defined as:
1. *Common securities.* Common securities are interests or instruments that are commonly known as securities, such as common stock, preferred stock, debentures, and warrants.
2. *Statutorily defined securities.* Statutorily defined securities are interests and instruments that are expressly mentioned in securities acts as being securities, such as interests in oil, gas, and mineral rights.
3. *Investment contracts.* An investment contract is a flexible standard for defining a security. Under the Howey test, a security exists if an investor invests money in a common enterprise and expects to make a profit from the significant efforts of others.

The Securities and Exchange Commission (SEC), p. 881

Created in 1934, the SEC is a federal administrative agency empowered to administer federal securities laws. The SEC can adopt rules and regulations to interpret and implement federal securities.

The Securities Act of 1933: Going Public, p. 881

The Securities Act of 1933 is a federal statute that primarily regulates the *issuance* of securities by corporations, partnerships, associations, and individuals. Section 5 of the 1933 act requires an issuer to register its securities with the SEC prior to selling them to the public if the securities or transaction does not qualify for an exemption from registration.

Registration Statement

The registration statement is a document that an issuer of securities files with the SEC to register its securities. It must contain information about the issuer, the securities to be issued, and other relevant information.

Prospectus

A prospectus is a written disclosure document that is submitted to the SEC with the registration statement. It is distributed to prospective investors to enable them to evaluate the financial risk of the investment.

Limitations on Activities During the Registration Process

1. *Prefiling period.* This period begins when the issuer first contemplates issuing securities and ends when the registration statement is filed with the SEC. During this period, the issuer cannot offer to sell securities, sell securities, or condition the market.
2. *Waiting period.* This period begins when the registration statement is filed with the SEC and ends when the registration statement becomes effective. During this time, the issuer cannot sell securities or use unapproved writing to offer to sell the securities. The issuer may make oral offers, distribute preliminary and summary prospectuses, and publish tombstone ads.
3. *Posteffective period.* This period begins when the registration statement becomes effective and runs until the issuer either sells all of the offered securities or withdraws them from sale. The issuer may offer to sell and sell the securities during this period. The issuer must deliver a final prospectus (statutory prospectus) to a purchaser prior to or at the time of confirming the sale or sending the security to the purchaser.

Sale of Unregistered Securities

Securities that should have been registered with the SEC but violates the Securities Act of 1933. Investors can rescind their purchase and recover damages. The U.S. government can impose criminal penalties on any person who willfully violates the Securities Act of 1933.

Regulation A Offerings

Regulation A permits an issuer to sell up to $5 million of securities to the public during a 12-month period pursuant to a simplified registration process.

Small Corporate Offering Registration Form (SCOR)

The Small Corporate Offering Registration Form (SCOR) is a regulation that permits businesses to sell up to $1 million of securities to the public pursuant to a simplified registration process. Form U-7 is a question-and-answer disclosure form that a business can complete and file with the SEC to sell securities pursuant to SCOR.

Private Actions

Private parties who have been injured by a violation of the 1933 act may sue the violator to rescind the securities contract or recover damages. The plaintiff may sue under:
1. *Section 12.* This provision of the 1933 act imposes civil liability on any person who violates the provisions of Section 5 of the act (e.g., sells unregistered securities).
2. *Section 11.* This provision of the 1933 act imposes civil liability on persons who intentionally defraud investors by making misrepresentations or omissions of material facts in the registration statement or are negligent in not discovering the fraud.

   a. *Due diligence defense*. This is a defense to a Section 11 action that, if proven, makes the defendant not liable. It requires the defendant to have made a reasonable investigation and had reasonable grounds to believe and did believe that the statements made in the registration statement were true.

SEC Actions

The SEC may seek the following remedies:

1. **Consent order.** The SEC may issue a consent order whereby a defendant agrees not to violate securities laws in the future but does not admit to violating securities laws in the past.
2. **Injunction.** The SEC may bring an action in federal District Court to obtain an injunction.
3. **Disgorgement of profits.** The SEC may request the court to order the defendant to disgorge illegally gained profits.

Criminal Liability

Section 24 of the 1933 act imposes criminal liability on any person who willfully violates either the act or the rules and regulations adopted thereunder. Criminal actions are brought by the U.S. Justice Department.

Private Transactions Exempt from Registration, p. 890

The following *transactions* are exempt from the SEC registration process: non-issuer transactions, intrastate offerings, private placements, and small offerings.

Non-issuer Exemption

Securities transactions *not* by an issuer, an underwriter, or a dealer are exempt from SEC registration. This covers normal purchases of securities by investors.

Intrastate Offerings

A local business can issue securities without dollar limit without registering with the SEC if the following requirements are met:

1. The issuer is a resident of the state (e.g., the corporation is incorporated in the state).
2. The issuer is doing business in the state, which requires that:
   a. 80 percent of the issuer's assets are located in the state.
   b. 80 percent of the issuer's gross revenues are derived from the state.
   c. The issuer's principal office is located in the state.
   d. 80 percent of the proceeds of the offering will be used in the state.
3. The purchasers of the securities are all residents of the state.

Private Placements

An issue of securities that does not involve a public offering is exempt from SEC registration. There is no dollar limit on the amount of securities that can be issued pursuant to this exemption. Securities can be sold to any number of accredited investors but to no more than 35 nonaccredited investors. Accredited investors include:

1. Any natural person (including spouse) who has a net worth of at least $1 million.
2. Any natural person who has had an annual income of at least $200,000 for each of the previous two years and reasonably expects to make $200,000 income in the current year.
3. Any corporation, partnership, or business trust with total assets in excess of $5 million.
4. Insiders of the issuers, such as executive officers and directors of corporate issuers and general partners of partnership issuers.
5. Certain institutional investors, such as registered investment companies, pension plans, colleges and universities, and the like.

Small Offerings

An offering of securities that does not exceed $1 million during a 12-month period is exempt from SEC registration. The securities may be sold to any number of purchasers.

Rule 144A: Qualified Institutional Investors

Rule 144A is an SEC rule that permits qualified institutional investors—defined as institutions—that own and invest at least $100 million in securities—to buy unregistered securities without being subject to the holding periods of Rule 144.

Resale Restrictions

Securities sold pursuant to the intrastate, private placement, or small offering exemptions are called restricted securities.

1. *Rule 147.* This SEC rule stipulates that securities sold pursuant to an intrastate offering exemption cannot be sold to nonresidents for a period of nine months.
2. *Rule 144.* This SEC rule stipulates that securities sold pursuant to the private placement or small offering exemption must be held for two years; limited sales may be made between years two and three, and unlimited sales are permitted thereafter.

Preventing Transfer of Restricted Securities

To prevent the illegal transfer of restricted securities, the issuer must take the following precautions:

1. *Affidavit.* The issuer must require investors to sign an affidavit stating that they are buying the securities for investment and promising not to transfer the restricted securities until the restrictions no longer apply.
2. *Legend.* The issuer must place a legend on the stock certificate describing the restriction.
3. *Transfer agent.* The issuer must appoint and notify the transfer agent not to record a transfer of the securities that would violate the restriction.

Securities Exempt from Registration

The following securities are exempt from the SEC registration process:

1. Securities issued by any government in the United States (e.g., municipal bonds issued by city governments)
2. Short-term notes and drafts that have a maturity date that does not exceed nine months (e.g., commercial paper issued by corporations)
3. Securities issued by nonprofit issuers, such as religious institutions, charitable institutions, and colleges and universities
4. Securities of financial institutions (e.g., banks, savings associations) that are regulated by the appropriate banking authorities
5. Securities issued by common carriers (e.g., railroads, trucking companies) that are regulated by the Interstate Commerce Commission (ICC)
6. Insurance and annuity contracts issued by insurance companies
7. Stock dividends and stock splits
8. Securities issued in a corporate reorganization in which one security is exchanged for another security

Securities Exchange Act of 1934: Trading in Securities, p. 892

The Securities Exchange Act of 1934 is a federal statute that primarily regulates the trading of securities.

Section 10(b) and Rule 10b-5

1. *Section 10(b).* This provision of the 1934 act prohibits the use of manipulative and deceptive devices in the purchase or sale of securities in contravention of the rules and regulations prescribed by the SEC.
2. *Rule 10b-5.* This rule adopted by the SEC clarifies the reach of Section 10(b) against deceptive and fraudulent activities in the purchase and sale of securities.
3. *Scienter.* Only conduct involving scienter (intentional conduct) violates Section 10(b) and Rule 10b-5. Negligent conduct is not a violation.

Insider Trading

Insider trading occurs when an insider makes a profit by purchasing shares of a commodity prior to public release of favorable information or selling shares of the corporation prior to public disclosure of unfavorable information. Insider trading violates Section 10(b) and Rule 10b-5.

Insiders

Insiders for Section 10(b) and Rule 10b-5 purposes include all employees of a company, independent contractors hired by the company on a temporary basis to provide services or work to the company, and others who owe a fiduciary duty to the company.

Misappropriation Theory

The misappropriation theory is a rule that imposes liability under Section 10(b) and Rule 10b-5 on an outsider who misappropriates information about a company in violation of his or her fiduciary duty and then trades in the securities of that company.

Tipper–Tippee Liability

1. *Tipper.* A tipper is a person who discloses material nonpublic information to another person. A tipper is liable for his or her own profits and the profits made by the tippee.
2. *Tippee.* A tippee is a person who receives material nonpublic information from a tipper. A tippee is liable for acting on material information received from a tipper if he or she knew or should have known that the information was not public. The tippee must disgorge profits made on the tip.

Private Actions

A private plaintiff has an implied right under Section 10(b) and Rule 10b-5 to sue to rescind the securities contract or recover damages from a defendant who has engaged in manipulative and deceptive practices that have caused the plaintiff injury.

SEC Actions

The SEC may enter into consent orders with defendants, seek injunctions in federal District Court, or seek orders requiring defendants to disgorge illegally gained profits.

Criminal Liability

Section 32 of the 1934 act imposes criminal liability on any person who willfully violates the 1934 act or the rules and regulations adopted thereunder. Criminal actions are brought by the U.S. Justice Department.

Sarbanes-Oxley Act

The Sarbanes-Oxley Act provides various securities regulations. Under this act the SEC my prevent a person who is involved in securities fraud from serving as an officer of a corporation.

Short-Swing Profits, p. 898

Section 16(a) of the Securities Exchange Act of 1934 defines a statutory insider for Section 16 purposes as any person who is an executive officer, a director, or a 10-percent shareholder of an equity security of a reporting company.

Section 16(b)

Short-swing profits are profits made by statutory insiders on trades involving equity securities that occur within six months of each other. Section 16(b) is a provision of the 1934 act which requires that any profits made by a statutory insider on transactions involving short-swing profits belong to the corporation.

SEC Section 16 Rules

The SEC's Section 16 rules clarify the persons and transactions subject to Section 16 short-swing profit rules.

State Securities Laws, p. 899

Most states have enacted securities laws that regulate the issuance and trading of securities. These acts are often patterned after, and are designed to coordinate with, federal securities laws. The Uniform Securities Act, which is a model state securities act, has been adopted by many states.

Test Review Terms and Concepts

Accredited investor   891

Commodities futures
   contract   901

Commodity Exchange
   Act (CEA)   901

Commodity Futures Trading
   Commission (CFTC)   901

Due diligence defense   888

Exempt   890

Form U-7   887

Going public   889

Howey test   879

Initial public offering (IPO)   881

Insiders   893

Insider Trading Sanctions Act   898

Insider trading   893

Intrastate offering exemption   890

Investment bankers   881

Investment contract   879

Issuer   881

Misappropriation theory   895

Non-issuer exemption   890

Offering statement   887

Posteffective period   886

Prefiling period   883

Private actions   897

Private placement exemption   890

Prospectus   882

Registration statement   882

Regulation A   887

Regulation Fair Disclosure
   (Reg FD)   898

Resale restrictions   891

Restricted securities   891

Rule 10b-5   893

Rule 144   892

Rule 144A   891

Rule 147   891

Sarbanes-Oxley Act   890

Scienter   893

SEC actions   888

Section 5 of the Securities Act
   of 1933   881

Section 10(b)   893

Section 11 of the Securities Act
   of 1933   887

Section 12 of the Securities Act
   of 1933   887

Section 24 of the Securities Act of
   1933   888

Section 16(a) of the Securities
   Exchange Act of 1934   898

Section 16(b) of the Securities
   Exchange Act of 1934   898

Section 32 of the Securities Exchange
   Act of 1934   898

Securities Act of 1933   881

Securities and Exchange
   Commission (SEC)   881

Securities Exchange Act of
   1934   892

Security   879

Short-swing profits   898

Small Corporate Offering
   Registration Form (SCOR)   887

Small offering exemption   891

State securities laws   899

Tippee   896

Tipper   896

Tipper–tippee liability   896

Uniform Securities Act   899

Waiting period   885

Case Problems

32.1 Definition of *Security*: Dare To Be Great, Inc. (Dare), was a Florida corporation that was wholly owned by Glenn W. Turner Enterprises, Inc. Dare offered self-improvement courses aimed at improving self-motivation and sales ability. In return for an investment of money, the purchaser received certain tapes, records, and written materials. In addition, depending on the level of involvement, the purchaser had the opportunity to help sell the Dare courses to others and to receive part of the purchase price as a commission. There were four different levels of involvement.

The task of salespersons was to bring prospective purchasers to "Adventure Meetings." The meetings, which were conducted by Dare people and not the salespersons, were conducted in a preordained format that included great enthusiasm, cheering and charming, exuberant handshaking, standing on chairs, and shouting. The Dare people and the salespersons dressed in modern, expensive clothes, displayed large sums of cash, drove new expensive automobiles, and engaged in "hard-sell" tactics to induce prospects to sign their name and part with their money. In actuality, few Dare purchasers ever attained the wealth promised. The tape recordings and materials distributed by Dare were worthless. Is this sales scheme a "security" that should have been registered with the SEC? *Securities and Exchange Commission v. Glenn W. Turner Enterprises, Inc.,* 474 F.2d

476, **Web** 1973 U.S. App. Lexis 11903 (United States Court of Appeals for the Ninth Circuit)

32.2 Definition of *Security*: The Farmer's Cooperative of Arkansas and Oklahoma (Co-Op) was an agricultural cooperative that had approximately 23,000 members. To raise money to support its general business operations, the Co-Op sold promissory notes to investors that were payable upon demand. The Co-Op offered the notes to both members and nonmembers, advertised the notes as an "investment program" and offered an interest rate higher than that available on savings accounts at financial institutions. More than 1,600 people purchased the notes, worth a total of $10 million. Subsequently, the Co-Op filed for bankruptcy. A class of holders of the notes filed suit against Ernst & Young, a national firm of certified public accountants that had audited the Co-Op's financial statements, alleging, that Ernst & Young had violated Section 10(b) of the Securities Exchange Act of 1934. Are the notes issued by the Co-Op "securities"? *Reeves v. Ernst & Young,* 494 U.S. 56, 110 S.Ct. 945, 108 L.Ed.2d 47, **Web** 1990 U.S. Lexis 1051 (Supreme Court of the United States)

32.3 Intrastate Offering Exemption: The McDonald Investment Company was a corporation organized and incorporated in the state of Minnesota. The principal and only place of business from which the company conducted operations was located in Rush City, Minnesota. More than 80 percent of the company's assets were located in Minnesota, and more than 80 percent of its income was derived from Minnesota. McDonald sold securities to Minnesota residents only. The proceeds from the sale were used entirely to make loans and other investments in real estate and other assets located outside the state of Minnesota. The company did not file a registration statement with the SEC. Does this offering qualify for an intrastate offering exemption from registration? *Securities and Exchange Commission v. McDonald Investment Company*, 343 F.Supp. 343, **Web** 1972 U.S. Dist. Lexis 13547 (United States District Court for the District of Minnesota)

32.4 Transaction Exemption: Continental Enterprises, Inc., had 2,510,000 shares of stock issued and outstanding. Louis E. Wolfson and members of his immediate family and associates owned in excess of 40 percent of those shares. The balance was in the hands of approximately 5,000 outside shareholders. Wolfson was Continental's largest shareholder and the guiding spirit of the corporation, who gave direction to and controlled the company's officers. During the course of five months, without public disclosure, Wolfson and his family and associates sold 55 percent of their stock through six brokerage houses. Wolfson and his family and associates did not file a registration statement with the SEC with respect to these sales. Do the securities sales by Wolfson and his family and associates qualify for an exemption for registration as a sale "not by an issuer, an underwriter, or a dealer"? *United States v. Wolfson*, 405 F.2d 779, **Web** 1968 U.S. App. Lexis 4342 (United States Court of Appeals for the Second Circuit)

32.5 Insider Trading: Chiarella worked as a "markup man" in the New York composing room of Pandick Press, a financial printer. Among the documents that Chiarella handled were five secret announcements of corporate takeovers. The tender offerors had hired Pandick Press to print the offers, which would later be made public when the tender offers were made to the shareholders of the target corporations. When the documents were delivered to Pandick Press, the identities of the acquiring and target corporations were concealed by blank spaces or false names. The true names would not be sent to Pandick Press until the night of the final printing.

Chiarella was able to deduce the names of the target companies before the final printing. Without disclosing this knowledge, he purchased stock in the target companies and sold the shares immediately after the takeover attempts were made public. Chiarella realized a gain of $30,000 in the course of 14 months. The federal government indicted Chiarella for criminal violations of Section 10(b) of the

Securities Exchange Act of 1934. Is Chiarella guilty? *Chiarella v. United States*, 445 U.S. 222, 100 S.Ct. 1108, 63 L.Ed.2d 348, **Web** 1980 U.S. Lexis 88 (Supreme Court of the United States)

32.6 Section 10(b): Leslie Neadeau was the president of T.O.N.M. Oil & Gas Exploration Corporation (TONM). Charles Lazzaro was a registered securities broker employed by Batemen Eichler, Hill Richards, Inc. (Bateman Eichler). The stock of TONM was traded in the over-the-counter market. Lazzaro made statements to potential investors that he had "inside information" about TONM, including that (1) vast amounts of gold had been discovered in Surinam and that TONM had options on thousands of acres in the gold-producing regions of Surinam; (2) the discovery was "not publicly known, but would be subsequently announced"; and (3) when this information was made public, TONM stock, which was then selling from $1.50 to $3.00 per share, would increase to $10.00 to $15.00 within a short period of time and might increase to $100.00 per share within a year.

The potential investors contacted Neadeau at TONM, and he confirmed that the information was not public knowledge. In reliance on Lazzaro's and Neadeau's statements, the investors purchased TONM stock. The "inside information" turned out to be false, and the shares declined substantially below the purchase price. The investors sued Lazzaro, Bateman Eichler, Neadeau, and TONM, alleging violations of Section 10(b) of the Securities Exchange Act of 1934. The defendants asserted that the plaintiffs' complaint should be dismissed because they participated in the fraud. Who wins? *Bateman Eichler, Hill Richards, Inc. v. Berner*, 472 U.S. 299, 105 S.Ct. 2622, 86 L.Ed.2d 215, **Web** 1985 U.S. Lexis 95 (Supreme Court of the United States)

32.7 Insider Trading: Donald C. Hoodes was the chief executive officer of the Sullair Corporation. As an officer of the corporation, he was regularly granted stock options to purchase stock of the company at a discount. On July 20, Hoodes sold 6,000 shares of Sullair common stock for $38,350. On July 31, Sullair terminated Hoodes as an officer of the corporation. On August 20, Hoodes exercised options to purchase 6,000 shares of Sullair stock that cost Hoodes $3.01 per share ($18,060) at the time they were trading at $4.50 per share ($27,000). Hoodes did not possess material nonpublic information about Sullair when he sold or purchased the securities of the company. The corporation brought suit against Hoodes to recover the profits Hoodes made on these trades. Who wins? *Sullair Corporation v. Hoodes*, 672 F.Supp. 337, **Web** 1987 U.S. Dist. Lexis 10152 (United States District Court for the Northern District of Illinois)

Ethics Issues

32.8 Ethics: Stephen Murphy owned Intertie, a California company that was involved in financing and managing cable television stations. Murphy was both an officer of the

corporation and chairman of the board of directors. Intertie would buy a cable television station, make a small cash down payment, and finance the remainder of the purchase price. It would then create a limited partnership and sell the cable station to the partnership for a cash down payment and a promissory note in favor of Intertie. Finally, Intertie would lease the station back from the partnership. Intertie purchased more than 30 stations and created an equal number of limited partnerships, from which it received more than $7.5 million from approximately 400 investors.

Evidence showed that most of the limited partnerships were not self-supporting but that this fact was not disclosed to investors. Intertie commingled partnership funds, taking funds generated from the sale of new partnership offerings to meet debt service obligations of previously sold cable systems; Intertie also used funds from limited partnerships that were formed but that never acquired cable systems. Intertie did not keep any records regarding the qualifications of investors to purchase the securities and also refused to make its financial statements available to investors.

Intertie suffered severe financial difficulties and eventually filed for bankruptcy. The limited partners suffered substantial losses. Did each of the limited partnership offerings alone qualify for the private placement exemption from registration? Should the 30 limited partnership offerings be integrated? *Securities and Exchange Commission v. Murphy*, 626 F.2d 633, **Web** 1980 U.S. App. Lexis 15483 (United States Court of Appeals for the Ninth Circuit)

32.9 Ethics: R. Foster Winans, a reporter for the *Wall Street Journal*, was one of the writers of the "Heard on the Street" column, a widely read and influential column in the *Journal*. This column frequently included articles that discussed the prospects of companies listed on national and regional stock exchanges and the over-the-counter market. David Carpenter worked as a news clerk at the *Journal*. The *Journal* had a conflict of interest policy that prohibited employees from using nonpublic information learned on the job for their personal benefit. Winans and Carpenter were aware of this policy.

Kenneth P. Felis and Peter Brant were stockbrokers at the brokerage house of Kidder Peabody. Winans agreed to provide Felis and Brant with information that was to appear in the "Heard" column in advance of its publication in the *Journal*. Generally, Winans would provide this information to the brokers the day before it was to appear in the *Journal*. Carpenter served as a messenger between the parties. Based on this advance information, the brokers bought and sold securities of companies discussed in the "Heard" column. During 1983 and 1984, prepublication trades of approximately 27 "Heard" columns netted profits of almost $690,000. The parties used telephones to transfer information. The *Wall Street Journal* is distributed by mail to many of its subscribers.

Eventually, Kidder Peabody noticed a correlation between the "Heard" column and trading by the brokers. After an SEC investigation, criminal charges were brought against defendants Winans, Carpenter, and Felis in U.S. District Court. Brant became the government's key witness. Winans and Felis were convicted of conspiracy to commit securities, mail, and wire fraud. Carpenter was convicted of aiding and abetting the commission of securities, mail, and wire fraud. The defendants appealed their convictions. Can the defendants be held criminally liable for conspiring to violate, and aiding and abetting the violation of, Section 10(b) and Rule 10b-5 of securities law? Did Winans act ethically in this case? Did Brant act ethically by turning government's witness? *United States v. Carpenter*, 484 U.S. 19, 108 S.Ct. 316, 98 L.Ed.2d 275, **Web** 1987 U.S. Lexis 4815 (Supreme Court of the United States)

IRAC Writing Assignment

Read **Case A-32** in Appendix A [*Lampf, Pleva, Lipkind, Prupis & Petigrow v. Gilbertson*]. Use the IRAC method to prepare a written analysis of the case.

Endnotes

1. *Securities and Exchange Commission v. W. J. Howery Co.*, 328 U.S. 293, 66 S. Ct. 1100, 90 L.Ed. 1244, **Web** 1946 U.S. Lexis 3159 (Supreme Court of the United States).
2. 15 U.S.C. Sections 77a–77aa.
3. 15 U.S.C. Section 77x.
4. Securities Act of 1933, Section 3(a)(11).
5. SEC Rule 147.
6. Securities Act of 1933, Section 4(2).
7. SEC Rule 506.
8. SEC Rule 501.
9. Securities Act of 1933, Section 3(b).
10. 15 U.S.C. Sections 78a–78mm.
11. Litigation instituted pursuant to Section 10(b) and Rule 10b-5 must be commenced within one year after the discovery of the violation and within three years after such violation. *Lampf,*

Pleva, Lipkind, Prupis & Petigrow v. Gilbertson, 501 U.S. 350, 111 S.Ct. 2773, 115 L.Ed.2d 321, **Web** 1991 U.S. Lexis 3629 (Supreme Court of the United States).

12. The U.S. Supreme Court has held that the sale of a business is a sale of securities that is subject to Section 10(b). *See Gould v. Ruefenacht*, 471 U.S. 701, 105 S.Ct. 2308, 85 L.Ed.2d 708, **Web** 1985 U.S. Lexis 21 (Supreme Court of the United States), where 50 percent of a business was sold, and *Landreth Timber Co. v. Landreth*, 471 U.S. 681, 105 S.Ct. 2297, 85 L.Ed.2d 692, **Web** 1985 U.S. Lexis 20 (Supreme Court of the United States), where 100 percent of a business was sold.

13. *Ernst & Ernst v. Hochfelder*, 425 U.S. 185, 96 S.Ct. 1375, 47 L.Ed.2d 668, **Web** 1976 U.S. Lexis 2 (Supreme Court of the United States).

14. 40 SEC 907 Section (1961).

15. 15 U.S.C. Sections 78ff.

16. P.L. 98–376.

17. 15 U.S.C. Section 78l.

18. 15 U.S.C. Section 78p(b).

UNIT 7

Government Regulation
and Employment Law

CHAPTER 33

Antitrust Law

> ❝ *While competition cannot be created by statutory enactment, it can in large measure be revived by changing the laws and forbidding the practices that killed it, and by enacting laws that will give it heart and occasion again. We can arrest and prevent monopoly.* ❞
>
> —WOODROW WILSON
> Speech, August 7, 1912

CHAPTER OBJECTIVES

After studying this chapter, you should be able to:

1. Describe the enforcement of federal antitrust laws.
2. Describe the horizontal and vertical restraints of trade that violate Section 1 of the Sherman Act.
3. Identify acts of monopolization that violate Section 2 of the Sherman Act.
4. Explain how the lawfulness of mergers is examined under Section 7 of the Clayton Act.
5. Apply Section 5 of the Federal Trade Commission Act to antitrust cases.

CHAPTER CONTENTS

- Introduction to Antitrust Law
- Federal Antitrust Laws
- Restraints of Trade: Section 1 of the Sherman Act
- Monopolization: Section 2 of the Sherman Act
- Mergers: Section 7 of the Clayton Act
- Tying Arrangements: Section 3 of the Clayton Act
- Price Discrimination: Section 2 of the Clayton Act
- Unfair Methods of Competition: Section 5 of the Federal Trade Commission Act
- Exemptions from Antitrust Laws
- State Antitrust Laws
- Chapter Summary
- Test Review Terms and Concepts
- Case Problems
- Ethics Issues
- IRAC Writing Assignment

   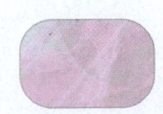 

Introduction to Antitrust Law

The U.S. economic system was built on the theory of freedom of competition. After the Civil War, however, the U.S. economy changed from a rural and agricultural economy to an industrialized and urban one. Many large industrial trusts were formed during this period. These arrangements resulted in a series of monopolies in basic industries such as oil and gas, sugar, cotton, and whiskey.

Because the common law could not deal effectively with these monopolies, Congress enacted a comprehensive system of **antitrust laws** to limit anticompetitive behavior. Almost all industries, businesses, and professions operating in the United States were affected. Although many states have also enacted antitrust laws, most actions in this area are brought under federal law.

This chapter discusses antitrust laws.

Oriole Park, Baltimore, Maryland

In 1922, the U.S. Supreme Court held that professional baseball was exempt from antitrust laws because baseball was not engaged in interstate commerce.

Federal Antitrust Laws

The *Sherman Act*, enacted in 1890, made certain restraints of trade and monopolistic acts illegal. Both the **Clayton Act** and the **Federal Trade Commission Act (FTC Act)** were enacted in 1914. The Clayton Act regulates mergers and prohibits certain exclusive dealing arrangements. The FTC Act prohibits unfair methods of competition. The *Robinson-Patman Act*, which prohibits price discrimination, was enacted in 1930.

Antitrust Enforcement

The federal antitrust statutes are broadly drafted to reflect the government's enforcement policy and to allow it to respond to economic, business, and technological changes. Each administration that occupies the White House adopts an enforcement policy for antitrust laws. From the 1940s through the 1970s, antitrust enforcement was quite stringent. During the 1980s, government enforcement of antitrust laws was more relaxed. During the 2000s, antitrust enforcement increased.

Federal antitrust laws provide for both government and private lawsuits.

> The notion that a business is clothed with a public interest and has been devoted to the public use is little more than a fiction intended to beautify what is disagreeable to the sufferers.
>
> J. Holmes
> *Tyson & Bro-United Theatre Ticket Offices v. Banton (1927)*

Government Actions

The federal government is authorized to bring actions to enforce federal antitrust laws. Government enforcement of federal antitrust laws is divided between the **Antitrust Division of the Department of Justice** and the **Bureau of Competition of the FTC**.

The Sherman Act is the only major antitrust act with *criminal* sanctions. Intent is the prerequisite for criminal liability under this act. Penalties for individuals include fines and prison terms; corporations may be fined.[1]

The government may seek *civil* damages, including treble damages, for violations of antitrust laws.[2] Broad remedial powers allow the courts to order a number of civil remedies, including orders for divestiture of assets, cancellation of contracts, liquidation of businesses, licensing of patents, and such. Private parties cannot intervene in public antitrust actions brought by the government.

Web Exercises

1. **WEB** Visit the website of the Federal Trade Commission (FTC), at *www.ftc.gov*. Click on "Competition."

2. **WEB** Visit the website of the United States Department of Justice, at *www.usdoj.gov*. Click on "DOJ Agencies" and click on "Antitrust Division."

Private Actions

Section 4 of the Clayton Act permits any person who suffers antitrust injury in his or her "business or property" to bring a *private civil action* against the offenders.[3] Consumers who have to pay higher prices because of an antitrust violation have recourse under this provision.[4] To recover damages, plaintiffs must prove that they suffered *antitrust injuries* caused by the prohibited act. The courts have required that consumers must have dealt *directly* with the alleged violators to have standing to sue; indirect injury resulting from higher prices being "passed on" is insufficient.

Successful plaintiffs may recover **treble damages** (i.e., triple the amount of the damages), plus reasonable costs and attorneys' fees. Damages may be calculated as lost profits, an increase in the cost of doing business, or a decrease in the value of tangible or intangible property caused by the antitrust violation. This rule applies to all violations of

People of the same trade seldom meet together, even for merriment and diversion, but that the conversation ends in a conspiracy against the public, or in some contrivance to raise prices.

Adam Smith
The Wealth of Nations (1776)

the Sherman Act, the Clayton Act, and the Robinson-Patman Act. Only actual damages—not treble damages—may be recovered for violations of the FTC Act.

A private plaintiff has four years from the date on which an antitrust injury occurred to bring a private civil treble-damages action. Only damages incurred during this four-year period are recoverable. This statute is *tolled* (i.e., does not run) during a suit by the government.

Effect of a Government Judgment

A government judgment against a defendant for an antitrust violation may be used as *prima facie* evidence of liability in a private civil treble-damages action. Antitrust defendants often opt to settle government-brought antitrust actions by entering a plea of **nolo contendere** in a criminal action or a **consent decree** in a government civil action. These pleas usually subject the defendant to penalty without an admission of guilt or liability.

Section 16 of the Clayton Act permits the government or a private plaintiff to obtain an injunction against anticompetitive behavior that violates antitrust laws.[5] Only the FTC may obtain an injunction under the FTC Act.

Web Exercises

1. **WEB** Use *www.google.com* to find an article or a case that discusses a plea of *nolo contendere* in a criminal antitrust action. Read it.

2. **WEB** Use *www.google.com* to find an article or a case that discusses a consent decree in a government civil antitrust action. Read it.

Restraints of Trade: Section 1 of the Sherman Act

In 1890, Congress enacted the **Sherman Act**. The purpose of the act was to out-law anticompetitive behavior. The Sherman Act has been called the "Magna Carta of free enterprise."[6] **Section 1 of the Sherman Act** is intended to prohibit certain concerted anticompetitive activities. It provides:

> Every contract, combination in the form of trust or otherwise, or conspiracy, in restraint of trade or commerce among the several states, or with foreign nations, is hereby declared to be illegal. Every person who shall make any contract or engage in any combination or conspiracy hereby declared to be illegal shall be deemed guilty of a felony.[7]

In other words, Section 1 outlaws *contracts, combinations*, and *conspiracies* in restraint of trade. Thus, it applies to unlawful conduct by two or more parties. The agreement may be written, oral, or inferred from the conduct of the parties. The two tests the U.S. Supreme Court has developed for determining the lawfulness of a restraint—the *rule of reason* and the *per se rule*—are discussed in the following paragraphs.

Rule of Reason

If Section 1 of the Sherman Act were read literally, it would prohibit almost all contracts. In the landmark case ***Standard Oil Company of New Jersey v. United States***,[8] the Supreme Court adopted the **rule of reason** standard for analyzing Section 1 cases. This rule holds that only *unreasonable restraints of trade* violate Section 1 of the Sherman Act. Reasonable restraints are lawful. The courts examine the following factors in applying the rule of reason:

- The pro- and anticompetitive effects of the challenged restraint
- The competitive structure of the industry
- The firm's market share and power

■ The history and duration of the restraint
■ Other relevant factors

Per Se Rule

The Supreme Court adopted the **per se rule**, which is applicable to restraints of trade that are considered inherently anticompetitive. No balancing of pro- and anticompetitive effects is necessary in such cases: The restraint is automatically in violation of Section 1 of the Sherman Act. When a restraint is characterized as a *per se* violation, no defenses or justifications for the restraint will save it, and no further evidence need be considered. Restraints that are not characterized as *per se* violations are examined using the rule of reason.

CONCEPT SUMMARY

Restraints of Trade: Section 1 of the Sherman Act

RULE	DESCRIPTION
Rule of reason	Requires a balancing of pro- and anticompetitive effects of the challenged restraint. Restraints that are found to be unreasonable are unlawful and violate Section 1 of the Sherman Act. Restraints that are found to be reasonable are lawful and do not violate Section 1 of the Sherman Act.
Per se rule	Applies to restraints that are inherently anticompetitive. No justification for the restraint is permitted. Such restraints automatically violate Section 1 of the Sherman Act.

Horizontal Restraints of Trade

A **horizontal restraint of trade** occurs when two or more competitors at the *same level of distribution* enter into a contract, combination, or conspiracy to restrain trade (see Exhibit 33.1). Many horizontal restraints fall under the *per se* rule; others are examined under the rule of reason. The most common forms of horizontal restraint are discussed in the following paragraphs.

PRICE-FIXING Horizontal **price-fixing** occurs when the competitors in the same line of business agree to set the price of goods or services they sell. Price-fixing is defined as raising, depressing, fixing, pegging, or stabilizing the price of a commodity or service. Illegal price-fixing includes setting minimum or maximum prices or fixing the quantity of a product or service to be produced or provided. Although most price-fixing agreements occur between sellers, an agreement among buyers to set the price they will pay for goods or services is also price-fixing. The plaintiff bears the burden of proving a price-fixing agreement.

Price-fixing is a *per se violation* of Section 1 of the Sherman Act. No defenses or justifications of any kind—such as "the price-fixing helps consumers or protects competitors from ruinous competition"—can prevent the *per se* rule from applying.

EXHIBIT 33.1

Horizontal Restraint of Trade

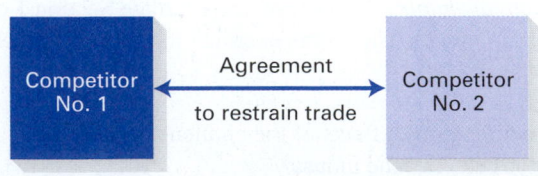

Example If the three largest automobile manufacturers agreed among themselves as to what prices to charge automobile dealers for this year's models, this would be sellers' illegal *per se* price-fixing.

Example If the three largest automobile manufacturers agreed among themselves as to what price they would pay to purchase tires from tire manufactures, this would be buyers' illegal *per se* price-fixing.

In the following case, the U.S. Supreme Court found illegal price-fixing.

C A S E **33.1**

Price-Fixing

U.S. SUPREME COURT
Federal Trade Commission v. Superior Court Trial Lawyers Association

493 U.S. 411, 110 S.Ct. 768, 107 L.Ed.2d 851,
Web 1990 U.S. Lexis 638
Supreme Court of the United States

> ❝ *The horizontal arrangement among these competitors was unquestionably a "naked restraint" on price and output.* ❞

—Justice Stevens

Facts

In the District of Columbia (District), lawyers in private practice are appointed to represent indigent defendants in misdemeanor cases and some felony cases. These private attorneys are paid pursuant to District's Criminal Justice Act (CJA) fee schedule. Most appointments went to approximately 100 lawyers called "CJA regulars," who handled more than 25,000 cases each year. These lawyers derived almost all of their income from representing indigents. The CJA regulars belonged to the Superior Court Trial Lawyers Association (SCTLA), which was a professional organization and not a labor union. The SCTLA unsuccessfully tried to persuade District to increase CJA rates. Subsequently, about 100 CJA lawyers resolved not to accept any new cases if legislation providing for an increase in fees was not passed. When the legislation was not enacted, most CJA regulars refused to accept new assignments. As anticipated, their action had a severe impact on District's criminal justice system. Within 10 days, District's criminal justice system was on the brink of collapse.

The Federal Trade Commission (FTC) filed a complaint against SCTLA, alleging that SCTLA's actions restrained trade constituted price-fixing in violation of federal antitrust law. FTC found that there was *per se* price-fixing and held against SCTLA. The U.S. Court of Appeals held that there was no price-fixing and vacated the FTC order. The FTC appealed to the U.S. Supreme Court.

Issue

Did the actions of SCTLA constitute price-fixing and a *per se* violation of Section 1 of the Sherman Act?

Language of the U.S. Supreme Court

Prior to the boycott CJA lawyers were in competition with one another, each deciding independently whether and how often to offer to provide services to the District at CJA rates. The agreement among the CJA lawyers was designed to obtain higher prices for their services and was implemented by a concerted refusal to serve the only customer in the market for the particular services that CJA regulars offered. This constriction of supply is the essence of price-fixing.

The horizontal arrangement among these competitors was unquestionably a "naked restraint" on price and output. The social justifications preferred for respondents' restraint of trade thus do not make it any less unlawful. The statutory policy underlying the Sherman Act precludes inquiry into the question whether competition is good or bad. No matter how altruistic the motives of respondents may have been, it is undisputed that their immediate objective was to increase the price that they would be paid for their services. The per se rules are, of course, the product of judicial interpretations of the Sherman Act, but the rules nevertheless have the same force and effect as any other statutory commands.

Decision

The U.S. Supreme Court held that the SCTLA lawyers' horizontal agreement to fix prices was a *per se* violation of Section 1 of the Sherman Act. The U.S. Supreme Court reversed the judgment of the U.S. Court of Appeals and remanded the case for further proceeding.

Law & Ethics Questions

1. **ETHICS** Do you think that *per se* rules are necessary? Or should the courts be required to examine fully the pro- and anticompetitive effects of an activity to determine whether it violates Section 1 of the Sherman Act?
2. **ETHICS** Do you think the CJA lawyers were acting altruistically in this case? Did District act ethically by keeping CJA rates low and refusing to increase them?

3. **ETHICS** Should professionals be subject to antitrust laws? Why or why not?

Web Exercises

1. **WEB** For the complete opinion of this case, go to *www.prenhall.com/cheesemancases*.

2. **WEB** Visit the website of the U.S. Supreme Court, at *www.supremecourtus.gov*, and try to find documents that relate to this case.

3. **WEB** Use *www.google.com* to find an article that discusses a recent case of price-fixing. Read it.

ETHICS SPOTLIGHT

The Department of Justice Flunks the Ivy League Schools

For years, the administrators of the Ivy League schools (Brown, Columbia, Cornell, Dartmouth, Harvard, Princeton, the University of Pennsylvania, and Yale) and Massachusetts Institute of Technology (MIT) met annually to trade information about student applicants seeking admission and scholarships at their universities. The universities than divided up the applicants and agreed to offer scholarships to the students they thought would attend their schools; they did not offer scholarships to those less likely to attend. The schools defended this practice as preventing "overlap"—that is, certain students getting scholarship offers from many schools and other applicants receiving no scholarship offers.

The U.S. Department of Justice sued the universities, alleging that they engaged in the horizontal restraint of trade of price-fixing, in violation of Section 1 of the Sherman Act.

The Department of Justice lawyers pointed to what they learned in Economics 101 and asserted that this collegiate cartel was no different from any other cartel: It denied customers (students) the right to "comparison shop" just as they would for other services.

The eight Ivy League schools agreed to settle the case with the Department of Justice. Under the terms of the consent decree, the schools agreed not to share financial aid information or discuss future tuition levels with other schools. MIT chose to fight the case in court and lost. The court found MIT guilty of price-fixing and enjoined the challenged practices. *United States v. Brown University*, 5 F.3d 658, **Web** 1993 U.S. App. Lexis 23895 (United States Court of Appeals for the Third Circuit)

Law & Ethics Questions

1. **ETHICS** Do you think the schools acted ethically in this case? What did they intend to accomplish by their agreement?

2. Did their "overlap" argument justify the universities' actions?

Web Exercises

1. **WEB** For the complete opinion of this case, go to *www.prenhall.com/cheesemancases*.

2. **WEB** Visit the website of the U.S. Court of Appeals for the Third Circuit, at *www.ca3.uscourts.gov*.

3. **WEB** Visit the website of Brown University, at *www.brown.edu*.

DIVISION OF MARKETS Competitors who agree that each will serve only a designated portion of the market are engaging in a **division of markets** (or **market sharing**), which is a *per se* violation of Section 1 of the Sherman Act. Each market segment is considered a small monopoly served only by its designated "owner." Horizontal market-sharing arrangements include division by geographic territory, customers, and products.

Example Suppose that three national breweries agreed among themselves that each one would be assigned one-third of the country as its geographic "territory," and each agreed not to sell beer in the other two companies' territories. This would be a *per se* illegal geographic division of markets.

Now suppose that the three largest sellers of media software agreed that each could only sell media software to one designated media software purchaser and not to any other media software purchasers. This would be a *per se* illegal product division of markets.

In the following case, the U.S. Supreme Court had to decide if there was an unlawful division of markets.

CASE 33.2
Division of Markets

U.S. SUPREME COURT
Palmer v. BRG of Georgia, Inc.
498 U.S. 46, 111 S.Ct. 401, 112 L.Ed.2d 349,
Web 1990 U.S. Lexis 5901
Supreme Court of the United States

> ❝*Each agreed not to compete in the other's territories. Such agreements are anticompetitive. Thus, the agreement between HBJ and BRG was unlawful on its face.*❞
>
> —Chief Justice Rehnquist

Facts

Harcourt Brace Jovanovich Legal and Professional Publications (HBJ) was the nation's largest provider of bar review materials and lecture services. HBJ began offering a Georgia bar review course in direct competition with BRG of Georgia, Inc. (BRG), the only other main provider of bar review services in the state. Subsequently, HBJ and BRG entered into an agreement whereby BRG was granted an exclusive license to market HBJ bar review materials in Georgia in exchange for paying HBJ $100 per student enrolled by BRG in the course. HBJ agreed not to compete with BRG in Georgia, and BRG agreed not to compete with HBJ outside of Georgia. Immediately after the agreement, the price of BRG's course was increased from $150 to $400. Jay Palmer and other law school graduates who took the BRG bar review course in preparation for the Georgia bar exam sued BRG and HBJ, alleging a violation of Section 1 of the Sherman Act. The U.S. District Court found that there was no division of markets and held in favor of the defendants. The U.S. Court of Appeals affirmed the judgment. The plaintiffs appealed to the U.S. Supreme Court.

Issue

Did the BRG–HBJ agreement constitute a division of markets and a *per se* violation of Section 1 of the Sherman Act?

Language of the U.S. Supreme Court

The revenue-sharing formula in the agreement between BRG and HBJ, coupled with the price increase that took place immediately after the parties agreed to cease competing with each other, indicates that this agreement was formed for the purpose and with the effect of raising the price of the bar review course.

Here, HBJ and BRG had previously competed in the Georgia market; under their allocation agreement, BRG received that market, while HBJ received the remainder of the United States. Each agreed not to compete in the other's territories. Such agreements are anticompetitive. Thus, the agreement between HBJ and BRG was unlawful on its face.

Decision

The U.S. Supreme Court held that the agreement between BRG and HBJ constituted a division of markets and as such was a *per se* violation of Section 1 of the Sherman Act. The U.S. Supreme Court reversed the judgment of the U.S. Court of Appeals and remanded the case for further proceedings.

Law & Ethics Questions

1. Should the division of markets be considered a *per se* violation of Section 1 of the Sherman Act? Or should the rule of reason apply?
2. **ETHICS** Did BRG and HBJ act ethically in this case? Should the defendants, as bar review providers, have been aware of the antitrust law that prohibits division of markets?
3. Why do you think BRG and HBJ entered into this agreement?

Web Exercises

1. **WEB** For the complete opinion of this case, go to *www.prenhall.com/cheesemancases*.
2. **WEB** Visit the website of the U.S. Supreme Court, at *www.supremecourtus.gov*, and try to find documents that relate to this case.
3. **WEB** Use *www.google.com* to find an article that discusses a recent case of a division of markets. Read it.

GROUP BOYCOTTS A **group boycott** (or **refusal to deal**) occurs when two or more competitors at one level of distribution agree not to deal with others at a different level of distribution. Although in the past the U.S. Supreme Court held that group boycotts were *per se* illegal, recent Supreme Court decisions have held that only certain group boycotts are *per se* illegal; others are to be examined under the rule of reason. Nevertheless, most group boycotts are found to be illegal.

Example A boycott would occur if a group of television manufacturers agreed not to sell their products to certain discount retailers (see Exhibit 33.2).

Example A boycott would occur if a group of rental car companies agreed not to purchase Chrysler automobiles for their fleets (see Exhibit 33.3).

EXHIBIT 33.2

**Group Boycott
by Sellers**

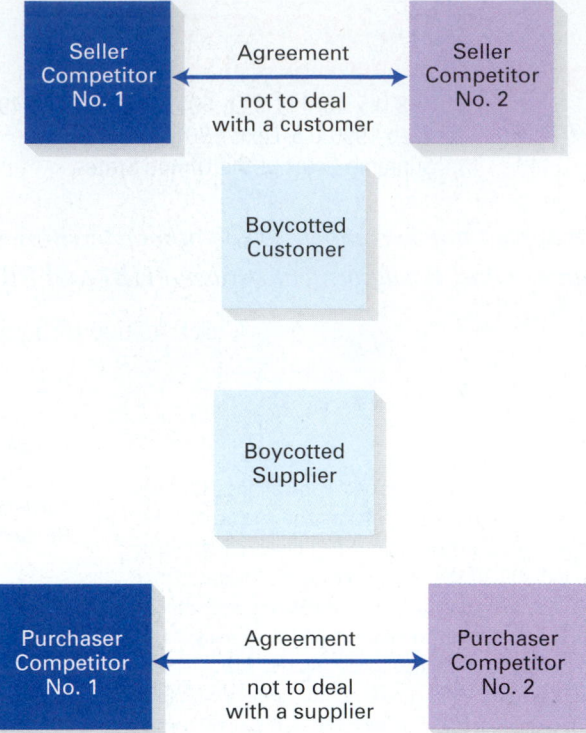

EXHIBIT 33.3

**Group Boycott
by Purchasers**

In the following case, the U.S. Supreme Court held that group boycotts are not always *per se* illegal.

C A S E **33.3**
Group Boycott

U.S. SUPREME COURT

NYNEX Corporation v. Discon, Incorporated

525 U.S. 128, 119 S.Ct. 493, 142 L.Ed.2d 510,
Web 1998 U.S. Lexis 8080
Supreme Court of the United States

❝*We conclude no boycott-related per se rule applies.*❞

—Justice Breyer

Facts

The NYNEX Corporation owned New York Telephone, a provider of local telephone services on the East Coast of the United States. NYNEX also owned the Material Enterprises Company (Material), an entity that purchased services for the removal of old switching equipment and other obsolete telephone equipment from New York Telephone's physical locations. For years, Material contracted with Discon Incorporated, an independent company, to provide this equipment removal services. After several years, Material did not renew Discon's contract and instead contracted with AT&T to provide these removal services. Discon, which went out of business, sued NYNEX, Material, New York Telephone, and AT&T for engaging in a group boycott not to deal with Discon, an alleged *per se* violation of Section 1 of the Sherman Act. The U.S. District Court dismissed Discon's complaint. The U.S. Court of Appeals affirmed. The U.S. Supreme Court granted review.

Issue

Did the conduct of the defendants amount to a horizontal agreement that constituted a *per se* group boycott violation of Section 1 of the Sherman Act?

Language of the U.S. Supreme Court

We conclude no boycott-related *per se* rule applies. Our conclusion rests in large part upon precedent, for precedent limits the *per se* rule in the boycott context to cases involving horizontal agreements among direct competitors.

Decision

The U.S. Supreme Court held that a *per se* violation of Section 1 of the Sherman Act requires a horizontal agreement to not deal with another party. The Supreme Court held that the antitrust rule that group boycotts are illegal *per se* did not apply to a single buyer's (Material's) decision to purchase from one supplier rather than another supplier.

Law & Ethics Questions

1. Describe a *per se* illegal group boycott. Why did the Supreme Court find one did not exist in this case?
2. **ETHICS** Was there anything unethical about Material's decision not to renew its contract with Discon? Would your answer be

different if Material knew that such a decision would put Discon out of business?
3. Should businesses be allowed to make exclusive decisions about who to deal with without facing antitrust?

Web Exercises

1. **WEB** For the complete opinion of this case, go to *www.prenhall.com/cheesemancases*.
2. **WEB** Visit the website of the U.S. Supreme Court, at *www.supremecourtus.gov*, and try to find documents that relate to this case.
3. **WEB** Use *www.google.com* to find an article that discusses a recent group boycott case. Read it.

OTHER HORIZONTAL AGREEMENTS Some agreements entered into by competitors at the same level of distribution—including trade association activities and rules, exchange of non-price information, participation in joint ventures, and the like—are examined using the rule of reason. Reasonable restraints are lawful; unreasonable restraints violate Section 1 of the Sherman Act.

Vertical Restraints of Trade

A **vertical restraint of trade** occurs when two or more parties on *different levels of distribution* enter into a contact, combination, or conspiracy to restrain trade (see Exhibit 33.4). The Supreme Court has applied both the *per se* rule and the rule of reason in determining the legality of vertical restraints of trade under Section 1 of the Sherman Act. The most common forms of vertical restraint are discussed in the following paragraphs.

RESALE PRICE MAINTENANCE **Resale price maintenance** (or **vertical price-fixing**) occurs when a party at one level of distribution enters into an agreement with a party at another level to adhere to a price schedule that either sets or stabilizes prices. Setting *minimum* resale prices is a *per se* violation of Section 1 of the Sherman Act as an unreasonable restraint of trade.[9]

Example Integral Camera Corporation manufactures digital cameras and sets a *minimum* price below which the cameras cannot be sold by retailers to consumers (e.g., the cameras cannot be sold for less than $1,000 to consumers by retailers). This constitutes *per se* illegal minimum resale price maintenance.

NON-PRICE VERTICAL RESTRAINTS The legality of **non-price vertical restraints** of trade under Section 1 of the Sherman Act is examined using the rule of reason.[10] Non-price restraints are unlawful under this analysis if their anticompetitive effects outweigh their procompetitive effects. Non-price vertical restraints include situations in which a manufacturer assigns exclusive territories to retail dealers or limits the number of dealers that may be located in a certain territory.

In the following case, the Supreme Court had to decide whether the setting of a *maximum* resale price was a *per se* violation of Section 1 of the Sherman Act.

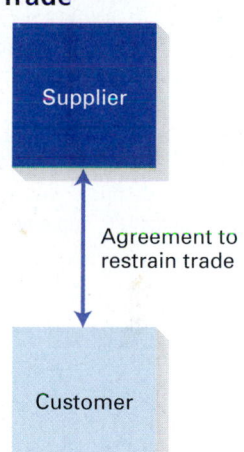

EXHIBIT 33.4

Vertical Restraint of Trade

CASE **33.4**
Resale Price Maintenance

U.S. SUPREME COURT
State Oil Company v. Khan
522 U.S. 3, 118 S.Ct. 275, 139 L.Ed.2d 199,
Web 1997 U.S. Lexis 6705
Supreme Court of the United States

> ❝ *We find it difficult to maintain that vertically-imposed maximum prices could harm consumers or competition to the extent necessary to justify their* per se *invalidation.* ❞

—Justice O'Connor

Facts

Barkat U. Khan and his corporation entered into an agreement with State Oil Company to lease and operate a gas station and convenience store owned by State Oil. The agreement provided that Khan would obtain his station's gasoline supply from State Oil. The agreement provided that Khan could charge any price for the gasoline he sold to the station's customers, but if the price charged was higher than State Oil's "suggested retail price," the excess was to be rebated to State Oil; Khan could choose to sell gasoline for less than State Oil's suggested retail price. Khan sued State Oil, alleging that the maximum resale price required by State Oil was a *per se* violation of Section 1 of the Sherman Act. The U.S. District Court entered summary judgment for State Oil. The U.S. Court of Appeals reversed, holding that the maximum resale price set by State Oil was a *per se* violation of Section 1. The U.S. Court of Appeals cited a previous U.S. Supreme Court case—*Albrecht v. Herald Co.*, 390 U.S. 145 (1968)—which held that the setting of maximum resale prices was a *per se* violation of Section 1. State Oil appealed to the U.S. Supreme Court.

Issue

Is the setting of a maximum resale price by a supplier a *per se* violation of Section 1 of the Sherman Act?

Language of the U.S. Supreme Court

We find it difficult to maintain that vertically-imposed maximum prices could harm consumers or competition to the extent necessary to justify their *per se* invalidation. Although we have acknowledged the possibility that maximum pricing might mask minimum pricing, we believe that such conduct can be appropriately recognized and punished under the rule of reason. Indeed, both courts and antitrust scholars noted that *Albrecht's* rule may actually harm consumers and manufacturers. After reconsidering *Albrecht's* rationale and the substantial criticism the decision has received, we conclude that there is insufficient economic justification for *per se* invalidation of vertical maximum price fixing.

In overruling *Albrecht*, we of course do not hold that all vertical maximum price fixing is *per se* lawful. Instead, vertical maximum price fixing, like the majority of commercial arrangements subject to the antitrust laws, should be evaluated under the rule of reason. In our view, rule-of-reason analysis will effectively identify those situations in which vertical maximum price fixing amounts to anticompetitive conduct.

Decision

The U.S. Supreme Court reversed *Albrecht*. The Supreme Court held that the setting of a maximum resale price is not a *per se* violation of Section 1 of the Sherman Act but, instead, its legality would be analyzed using the rule of reason test. The Supreme Court remanded the case for trial using the new rule of reason standard.

Law & Ethics Questions

1. How often do you think the U.S. Supreme Court reverses itself? Do you think it should have done so in this case?
2. **ETHICS** Was the State Oil contract that set a maximum resale price in this case lawful under the rule of reason standard?
3. How will this decision affect suppliers and the retailers they sell to? Explain.

Web Exercises

1. **WEB** For the complete opinion of this case, go to *www.prenhall.com/cheesemancases*.
2. **WEB** Visit the website of the U.S. Supreme Court, at *www.supremecourtus.gov*, and try to find documents that relate to this case.
3. **WEB** Use *www.google.com* to find an article that discusses a recent example of resale price maintenance. Read it.

Defenses to Section 1 of the Sherman Act

The courts have recognized several defenses to alleged violations of Section 1 of the Sherman Act. These defenses, which are discussed in the following paragraphs, are unilateral refusal to deal, conscious parallelism, and the *Noerr* doctrine.

UNILATERAL REFUSAL TO DEAL The U.S. Supreme Court has held that a firm can unilaterally choose not to deal with another party without being liable under Section 1 of the

Sherman Act. A **unilateral refusal to deal** is not a violation of Section 1 because there is no concerted action with others. This rule was announced in *United States v. Colgate & Co.* and is therefore often referred to as the **Colgate doctrine**.[11]

Example If Louis Vuitton, a maker of expensive women's clothing, shoes, handbags, and accessories, refuses to sell its merchandise to Wal-Mart stores, this is a lawful unilateral refusal to deal.

CONSCIOUS PARALLELISM If two or more firms act the same, but no concerted action is shown, there is no violation of Section 1 of the Sherman Act. This doctrine is often referred to as **conscious parallelism**. Thus, if two competing manufacturers of a similar product both separately reach an independent decision not to deal with a retailer, there is no violation of Section 1 of the Sherman Act. The key is that each of the manufacturers acted on its own.

Example If Louis Vuitton, Gucci, and Chanel, makers of expensive women's clothing, shoes, handbags, and accessories, each independently make a decision not to sell their products to Wal-Mart, this is lawful conscious parallelism. There is no violation of Section 1 of the Sherman Act because the parties did not agree with one another in making their decisions.

In the following case, the U.S. Supreme Court found that conscious parallelism existed.

***NOERR* DOCTRINE** The *Noerr* **doctrine** holds that two or more persons may petition the executive, legislative, or judicial branch of the government or administrative agencies to enact laws or to take other action without violating the antitrust laws. The rationale behind this doctrine is that the right to petition the government has precedence because it is guaranteed by the Bill of Rights.[12]

Example General Motors and Ford collectively petition Congress to pass a law that would limit the import of foreign automobiles into this country. This is lawful activity under the *Noerr* doctrine.

There is an exception to this doctrine. Under the *"sham" exception*, petitioners are not protected if their petition or lawsuit is baseless—that is, if a reasonable petitioner or litigant could not realistically expect to succeed on the merits of the petition or lawsuit. If the protection of the *Noerr* doctrine is lost, an antitrust action may be maintained against the parties who asserted its protection.

CASE **33.5**
Conscious Parallelism

U.S. SUPREME COURT

Bell Atlantic Corporation v. Twombly

127 S.Ct. 1955,
Web 2007 U.S. Lexis 5901 (2007)
Supreme Court of the United States

> ❝*Even 'conscious parallelism,' a common reaction of firms in a concentrated market that recognize their shared economic interests and their interdependence with respect to price and output decisions is not in itself unlawful.*❞
>
> —Justice Souter

Facts

Over 20 years ago, the federal government ordered the divesture of the American Telephone & Telegraph Company's (AT&T's) monopoly over telephone services in this country. AT&T was split into regional service monopolies called "incumbent local exchange carriers" (ILECs). Subsequently, Congress enacted the Telecommunications Act of 1996 which required ILECs, by law, to share their networks and telephone lines with competitors. A group of companies known as "competitive local exchange carriers" (CLECs) developed, which purchased telephone and other services at wholesale rates from ILECs and then resold the services to customers in competition with ILECs. The ILECs and CLECs battled each other in court to determine what network elements the ILECs had to share with the CLECs. Each ILEC chose not to compete as a CLEC in another ILEC's territory.

William Twombly brought a class action lawsuit against Bell Atlantic Corporation and the other ILECs, alleging that the ILECs engaged in parallel conduct that inhibited the growth of upstart CLECs, thus causing inflated charges for local telephone and high-speed Internet services. The plaintiffs alleged that this conduct constituted an illegal conspiracy in violation of Section 1 of the Sherman Act. The U.S. District Court dismissed the plaintiffs' complaint for failure to state a claim upon which relief could be granted. The U.S. District Court held that the plaintiffs' allegation of the defendants' conscious parallelism did not constitute a conspiracy in violation of Section 1 of the Sherman Act. The U.S. Court of Appeals reversed, letting the case proceed against the defendants. Bell South and the other defendants appealed to the U.S. Supreme Court.

Issue

Can a Sherman Act Section 1 complaint survive a motion to dismiss when it alleges that major telecommunications providers engaged in parallel conduct unfavorable to competition?

Language of the U.S. Supreme Court

Because Section 1 of the Sherman Act does not prohibit all unreasonable restraints of trade but only restraints effected by a contract, combination, or conspiracy, the crucial question is whether the challenged anticompetitive conduct stems from independent decision or from an agreement, tacit or express. Even "conscious parallelism," a common reaction of firms in a concentrated market that recognize their shared economic interests and their interdependence with respect to price and output decisions is not in itself unlawful.

When we look for plausibility in this complaint, we agree with the district court that plaintiffs' claim of conspiracy in restraint of trade comes up short. To begin with, the complaint leaves no doubt that plaintiffs rest their Section 1 claim on descriptions of parallel conduct and not on any independent allegation of actual agreement among the ILECs. The nub of the complaint, then, is the ILECs' parallel behavior, consisting of steps to keep the CLECs out and manifest disinterest in becoming CLECs themselves.

We think that nothing contained in the complaint invests either the action or inaction alleged with a plausible suggestion of conspiracy. We agree with the district court that nothing in the complaint intimates that the resistance to the upstarts was anything more that the natural, unilateral reaction of each ILEC intent on keeping its regional dominance. There is no reason to infer that the companies had agreed among themselves to do what was only natural anyway. As the district court said, "each ILEC has reason to want to avoid dealing with CLECs" and "each ILEC would attempt to keep CLECs out, regardless of the actions of the other ILECs." Because the plaintiffs here have not nudged their claims across the line from conceivable to plausible, their complaint must be dismissed.

Decision

The U.S. Supreme Court held that the plaintiffs' allegation of conscious parallelism was not sufficient to support a conspiracy claim of a violation of Section 1 of the Sherman Act. The U.S. Supreme Court reversed the judgment of the U.S. Court of Appeals and dismissed the plaintiffs' complaint against the defendants. The Supreme Court remanded the case for further proceedings consistent with its opinion.

Law & Ethics Questions

1. What does a violation of Section 1 of the Sherman Act require? Explain.
2. What is conscious parallelism? Does it violate Section 1 of the Sherman Act? Why or why not?
3. **ETHICS** Did the plaintiffs have much of a chance of winning this case? Explain.
4. **ETHICS** Did the ILECs act ethically in trying to fight the CLECs' sharing of their networks?

Web Exercises

1. **WEB** For the complete opinion of this case, go to *www.prenhall.com/cheesemancases*.
2. **WEB** Visit the website of the U.S. Supreme Court, at *www.supremecourtus.gov*, and try to find documents that relate to this case.
3. **WEB** Use *www.google.com* to find an article or a case that discusses the concept of conscious parallelism. Read it.

ETHICS SPOTLIGHT
Trade Association Activities

Trade associations are organizations that industry members form in order to promote the industry, provide education to members, formulate rules for self-regulation of the industry, and conduct lobbying and other activities. Trade associations usually hold annual and other meetings that industry members attend.

At trade association meetings, there is often a tendency to discuss information about the industry, companies, competitors, customers,

suppliers, products, pricing, and other information that could lead to charges of antitrust violations. To avoid antitrust problems, attendees should avoid sharing and discussing certain information with each other. Here are some pointers:

■ Do not discuss or exchange price information about sales to customers.

- Do not discuss contract terms about customers or suppliers.
- Do not discuss with competitors the possibility of limiting competition with them.
- Do not discuss price information about suppliers.
- Do not discuss reasons for not selling to certain customers.
- Do not discuss reasons for not buying products or services from certain suppliers.
- Do not share information about product development with competitors.
- Do not agree to share or split customers or geographic areas.
- Do not agree to operate only during agreed-upon hours.

Law & Ethics Questions

1. What is the purpose of a trade association annual or periodic meeting?
2. **ETHICS** Why might competitors wish to share sensitive information about customer or supplier pricing with each other?

Web Exercise

1. **WEB** Use *www.google.com* to find an article about a trade association convention that will be held in Las Vegas, Nevada. Read it.
2. **WEB** Visit the website of Las Vegas, Nevada, the number-one destination of trade shows and conventions in the country, at *www.lasvegas.com*. Can you find any information about holding trade shows or industry conventions in Las Vegas?

Monopolization: Section 2 of the Sherman Act

By definition, monopolies have the ability to affect the price of goods and services. **Section 2 of the Sherman Act** was enacted in response to widespread concern about the power generated by this type of anticompetitive activity. Section 2 of the Sherman Act prohibits the act of monopolization. It provides:

> Every person who shall monopolize, or attempt to monopolize, or combine or conspire with any other person or persons, to monopolize any part of the trade or commerce among the several States, or with foreign nations, shall be deemed guilty of a felony.[13]

Proving that a defendant is in violation of Section 2 means proving that the defendant (1) possesses monopoly power in the relevant market and (2) engaged in a willful act of monopolization to acquire or maintain that power. Each of these elements is discussed in the following paragraphs.

Defining the Relevant Market

Identifying the **relevant market** for a Section 2 action requires defining the relevant product or service market and geographic market. The definition of the relevant market often determines whether the defendant has monopoly power. Consequently, this determination is often litigated.

The **relevant product or service market** generally includes substitute products or services that are reasonably interchangeable with the defendant's products or services. Defendants often try to make their market share seem smaller by arguing for a broad definition of the product or service market. Plaintiffs, on the other hand, usually argue for a narrow definition.

Example If the Anheuser-Busch Corporation, which is the largest beer producer in the United States, is sued by the government for violating Section 2 of the Sherman Act, the government would argue that the relevant product market is beer sales. Anheuser-Busch, on the other hand, would argue that the relevant product market is sales of all alcoholic beverages, or even of all drinkable beverages.

The **relevant geographic market** is usually defined as the area in which the defendant and its competitors sell the product or service. This may be a national, regional, state, or local area, depending on the circumstances.

Example If the Coca-Cola Corporation is sued by the government for violating Section 2 of the Sherman Act, the relevant geographic market would be the nation. If the largest owner of automobile dealerships in south Florida were sued for violating Section 2, the geographic market would be the counties of south Florida.

Monopoly Power

For an antitrust action to be sustained, the defendant must possess **monopoly power** in the relevant market. Monopoly power is defined by the courts to be the power to control prices or exclude competition. The courts generally apply the following guidelines: Market share above 70 percent is monopoly power; market share under 20 percent is not monopoly power. Otherwise, the courts generally prefer to examine the facts and circumstances of each case before making a determination about monopoly power.

Willful Act of Monopolizing

Section 2 of the Sherman Act outlaws the **act of monopolizing**, not monopolies. Any act that otherwise violates any other antitrust law (such as illegal restraints of trade in violation of Section 1 of the Sherman Act) is an act of monopolizing that violates Section 2. When coupled with monopoly power, certain otherwise lawful acts have been held to constitute acts of monopolizing.

Predatory pricing—that is, pricing below average or marginal cost—that is intended to drive out competition has been held to violate Section 2.[14]

In the following case, the U.S. Supreme Court had to decide whether an act of monopolization had occurred.

CASE 33.6
Monopolization

U.S. SUPREME COURT
Weyerhaeuser v. Ross-Simmons Hardwood Lumber Company, Inc.

127 S.Ct. 1069, 166 L.Ed.2d 911,
Web 2007 U.S. Lexis 1333 (2007)
Supreme Court of the United States

“*If all goes as planned, the predatory bidder will reap monopolistic profits that will offset any losses suffered in bidding up input prices.*”

—Justice Thomas

Facts

Weyerhaeuser Company is a large corporation that produces hardwood lumber in the Pacific Northwest. Weyerhaeuser purchases alder sawlogs that are processed at its lumber mills. Weyerhaeuser entered this market by acquiring an existing lumber company in 1980. As of 2001, Weyerhaeuser operated six hardwood lumber mills in the Pacific Northwest and purchased approximately 65 percent of the alder logs available for sale in the region. Weyerhaeuser invested more than $75 million in capital in these hardwood mills. Weyerhaeuser uses state-of-the-art technology, including sawing equipment, to increase the amount of lumber recovered from each log. Logs represent up to 75 percent of a sawmill's total costs.

Ross-Simmons Hardwood Lumber Company, Inc., began operating a hardwood lumber sawmill in the state of Washington in 1962. From 1998 to 2001, the price of alder sawlogs increased while prices for finished hardwood lumber fell. This caused profit margins to fall. Ross-Simmons suffered heavy losses and shut down its sawmill in May 2001.

Ross-Simmons blamed Weyerhaeuser for driving it out of business by bidding up input costs of alder logs. Ross-Simmons filed an antitrust lawsuit against Weyerhaeuser, alleging that it had engaged in buy-side predatory bidding that amounted to monopolization in violation of Section 2 of the Sherman Act. The jury returned a $26 million verdict against Weyerhaeuser. The verdict was trebled to approximately $79 million. The Court of Appeals affirmed the verdict against Weyerhaeuser. Weyerhaeuser appealed to the U.S. Supreme Court.

Issue

Is Weyerhaeuser liable for buy-side predatory bidding that constitutes monopolization in violation of Section 2 of the Sherman Act?

Language of the U.S. Supreme Court

In *Brooke Group Ltd. v. Brown & Williamson Tobacco Corp.,* 509 U.S. 209, 113 S.Ct. 2578, **Web** 1993 U.S. Lexis 4245 (1993), we considered what a plaintiff must show on a claim of predatory pricing under Section 2 of the Sherman Act. In a typical predatory-pricing scheme, the predator reduces the sale price of its product (its output) to below cost, hoping to drive competitors out of business. Then, with competition vanquished, the predator raises output prices to a supracompetitive level. For the scheme to make economic sense, the losses suffered from pricing goods below cost must be recouped (with interest) during the supracompetitive-pricing stage of the scheme.

A predatory bidder ultimately aims to exercise the monopsony power gained from bidding up input prices. To that end, once the predatory bidder has caused competing bidders to exit the market for purchasing inputs, it will seek to restrict its input purchases below the competitive level, thus reducing the unit price for the remaining inputs it purchases. If all goes as planned, the predatory bidder will reap monopsonistic profits that will offset any losses suffered in bidding up input prices.

A predatory-bidding plaintiff also must prove that the defendant has a dangerous probability of recouping the losses incurred in bidding up input prices through the exercise of monopsony power. Absent proof of likely recoupment, a strategy of predatory bidding makes no economic sense because it would involve short-term losses with no likelihood of offsetting long-term gains. Ross-Simmons has conceded that it has not satisfied the Brooke Group standard. Therefore, its predatory-bidding theory of liability cannot support the jury's verdict.

Decision

The U.S. Supreme Court held that Ross-Simmons had failed to prove that Weyerhaeuser had engaged in predatory-bidding necessary to find a violation of Section 2 of the Sherman Act. The Supreme Court vacated the judgment of the Court of Appeals and remanded the case for further proceedings consistent with its opinion.

Law & Ethics Questions

1. What is predatory pricing? What is predatory bidding? How do they differ from one another?
2. **ETHICS** Do you think that Ross-Simmons had a legitimate claim against Weyerhaeuser? Why or why not?
3. **ETHICS** Did Weyerhaeuser, by investing more capital in state-of-the-art technology, breach any duty of ethics if doing so is what drove Ross-Simmons out of business? Explain.

Web Exercises

1. **WEB** For the complete opinion of this case, go to www.prenhall.com/cheesemancases.
2. **WEB** Visit the website of the U.S. Supreme Court, at www.supremecourtus.gov, and try to find documents that relate to this case.
3. **WEB** Visit the website of Weyerhaeuser Company, at www.weyerhaeuser.com.
4. **WEB** Use www.google.com to find an article that discusses the logging industry in the Pacific Northwest. Read it.

CONCEPT SUMMARY

Monopolization: Section 2 of the Sherman Act

ELEMENT	DESCRIPTION
Relevant product or service market	The market that includes substitute products or services that are reasonably interchangeable with the defendant's products or services.
Relevant geographic market	The geographic area in which the defendant and its competitors sell the product or service.
Monopoly power	The power to control prices or exclude competition. If the defendant does not possess monopoly power, it cannot be held liable for monopolization. If the defendant possesses monopoly power, the court will determine whether the monopolist has engaged in an act of monopolizing.
Act of monopolizing	The defendant's engagement in a willful act of monopolizing trade or commerce in the relevant market.

Defenses to Monopolization

Only two narrow defenses to a charge of monopolizing have been recognized: (1) *innocent acquisition* (e.g., acquisition because of superior business acumen, skill, foresight, or industry) and (2) *natural monopoly* (e.g., a small market that can support only one competitor, such as a small-town newspaper). If a monopoly that fits into one of these categories exercises its power in a predatory or exclusionary way, the defense is lost.

A monopoly granted either to an individual or to a trading company has the same effect as a secret in trade or manufacture. The monopolists, by keeping the market constantly understocked, by never fully supplying the effectual demand, sell their commodities much above the natural price, and raise their emoluments greatly above their natural rate.

Adam Smith
The Wealth of Nations (1776)

Attempts and Conspiracies to Monopolize

Firms that *attempt* or *conspire* to monopolize a relevant market may be found liable under Section 2 of the Sherman Act. A single firm may be found liable for monopolizing or attempting to monopolize. Two or more firms may be found liable for conspiring to monopolize.

INTERNET AND TECHNOLOGY
United States v. Microsoft Corporation

In less than 40 years, Microsoft Corporation has grown from a startup company into the world's largest software company, whose products touch the lives of virtually everyone who uses a personal computer. Microsoft dominates the software market with its Windows operating system, which is used on most of the world's personal computers.

Netscape, a competing company, developed its Navigator Internet web browser and controlled over 80 percent of that market. Microsoft began a campaign to defeat Netscape. Microsoft developed its own browser, called *Explorer*, and attached it to its Windows operating system for free. Microsoft warned Apple, a manufacturer of personal computers, that it would cancel Microsoft's all-important Microsoft's Office Software unless Apple used Explorer; Apple capitulated and made Explorer its web browser. Microsoft muscled AOL into offering Explorer in return for a small placement on the Windows desktop if it would not offer Netscape anywhere on its online service. AOL agreed. Microsoft gave Compaq, a maker of personal computers, a reduced price for Windows in return for placing a Microsoft icon for the Explorer web browser on Compaq's computers. Microsoft was alleged to have used "bundling" of its software products with its operating systems to eliminate competitors from the software marketplace.

After investigating, the U.S. government and 19 states sued Microsoft in a civil antitrust case. After a nine-month trial and four months of failed settlement negotiations, the U.S. District Court held that Microsoft had used predatory and anticompetitive conduct to illegally maintain its monopoly in the Windows operating system in violation of Section 2 of the Sherman Act. The judge issued an order that prohibited Microsoft from engaging in such conduct in the future and ordered that Microsoft be split into two separate companies, one company to own the operating systems such as Windows, and a second company to own software, Internet browsers, and other computer applications.

Microsoft appealed. On appeal, the U.S. Court of Appeals upheld the finding that Microsoft had engaged in monopolization in violation of Section 2, but it ruled that Microsoft did not have to be broken up. The case was remanded for further proceedings.

A new U.S. District Court judge ordered Microsoft Corporation to refrain from engaging in coercive practices and to make some of the code for its operating systems available to other software companies under reasonable licensing arrangement so that they could design their software to be used in conjunction with Microsoft's operating system. The court stated:

WHEREAS, this Final Judgment does not constitute any admission by any party regarding any issue of fact or law;

WHEREAS, Microsoft agrees to be bound by the provisions of this Final Judgment pending its approval by the Court;

Microsoft shall not retaliate against an OEM by altering Microsoft's commercial relations with that OEM, or by withholding newly introduced forms of non-monetary Consideration (including but not limited to new versions of existing forms of non-monetary Consideration) from that OEM, because it is known to Microsoft that the OEM is or is contemplating:

1. developing, distributing, promoting, using, selling, or licensing any software that competes with Microsoft Platform Software or any product or service that distributes or promotes any Non-Microsoft Middleware;
2. Shipping a Personal Computer that (a) includes both a Windows Operating System Product and a non-Microsoft Operating System, or (b) will boot with more than one Operating System; or
3. Exercising any of the options or alternatives provided for under this Final Judgment.

Many commentators believe that Microsoft basically "won" this case. *United States v. Microsoft Corporation*, **Web** 2002 U.S. Dist. Lexis 22864 (United States District Court for the District of Columbia)

Law & Ethics Questions

1. What is "bundling" of products? How can this hinder competition? Explain.
2. **ETHICS** Did Microsoft act ethically when it engaged in coercive tactics?
3. **ETHICS** In this settlement, did Microsoft admit to any wrongdoing?

Web Exercises

1. **WEB** For the complete opinion of this case, go to *www.prenhall.com/cheesemancases*.
2. **WEB** Visit the website of the United States District Court for the District of Columbia, at *www.dcd.uscourts.gov*.
3. **WEB** Visit the website of Microsoft Corporation, at *www.microsoft.com*. Can you find Microsoft's code of ethics?
4. **WEB** Use *www.google.com* to find an article that discusses this antitrust lawsuit against Microsoft Corporation. Read it.

CONCEPT SUMMARY

The Sherman Act

SECTION	DESCRIPTION
1	Prohibits contracts, combinations, and conspiracies in restraint of trade. To violate Section 1, the restraint must be found to be unreasonable under either of two tests: (1) rule of reason or (2) *per se* rule. A violation requires the concerted action of two or more parties.
2	Prohibits the act of monopolizing and attempts or conspiracies to monopolize. This act can be violated by the conduct of one firm.

Mergers: Section 7 of the Clayton Act

In the late 1800s and early 1900s, *mergers* led to increased concentration of wealth in the hands of a few wealthy individuals and large corporations. In response, in 1914, Congress enacted **Section 7 of the Clayton Act**, which gave the federal government the power to prevent anticompetitive mergers. Originally, Section 7 of the Clayton Act applied only to stock mergers. The Celler-Kefauver Act, which was enacted in 1950, widened Section 7's scope to include asset acquisitions.

Today, Section 7 applies to all methods of external expansion, including technical mergers, consolidations, purchases of assets, subsidiary operations, joint ventures, and other combinations.

Section 7 of the Clayton Act provides that it is unlawful for a person or business to acquire stock or assets of another "where in any line of commerce or in any activity affecting commerce in any section of the country, the effect of such acquisition may be substantially to lessen competition, or to tend to create a monopoly."[15] In determining whether a merger is lawful under Section 7 of the Clayton Act, the courts must examine the elements discussed in the following paragraphs.

Line of Commerce

Determining the **line of commerce** that will be affected by a merger involves defining the relevant *product or service market*. Traditionally, the courts have done this by applying the functional interchangeability test. Under this test, the relevant line of commerce includes products or services that consumers use as substitutes. If two products are substitutes for each other, they are considered part of the same line of commerce.

Example Suppose a price increase for regular coffee causes consumers to switch to Sanka (decaffeinated coffee). The two products are part of the same line of commerce because they are interchangeable.

Section of the Country

Defining the relevant **section of the country** consists of determining the relevant *geographic market*. The courts traditionally identify this market as the geographic area that will feel the direct and immediate effects of the merger. It may be a local, state, or regional market; the entire country; or some other geographic area.

Example Anheuser-Busch and the Miller Brewing Company, two brewers, sell beer nationally. If Anheuser-Busch and the Miller Brewing Company plan to merge, the relevant section of the country is the nation.

Example Anheuser-Busch is a brewer that sells beer nationally. Upper Stream Brewery is a local brewery that only sells beer in the Upper Peninsula of Michigan. If Anheuser-Busch intends to acquire Upper Stream Brewery, the relevant section of the country is the Upper Peninsula of Michigan.

Probability of a Substantial Lessening of Competition

After the relevant product or service and geographic market have been defined, the court must determine whether a merger or an acquisition is likely to **substantially lessen competition** or create a monopoly. If the court feels that a merger is likely to do either, it may prevent the merger. Section 7 tries to prevent potentially anticompetitive mergers before they occur. It deals in probabilities; an actual showing of the lessening of competition is not required.

CONCEPT SUMMARY

Merger: Section 7 of the Clayton Act

ELEMENT	DESCRIPTION
Line of commerce	The market that will be affected by a merger. It includes products or services that consumers use as substitutes for those produced or sold by the merging firms.
Section of the country	The geographic market that will be affected by a merger.
Probability of a substantial lessening of competition	A probability of a substantial lessening of competition after a merger, in which case the merger may be prohibited. The statute deals with probabilities; a showing of actual lessening of competition is not required.

Types of Mergers

In applying Section 7, mergers are generally classified as one of the following: *horizontal merger*, *vertical merger*, *market extension merger*, or *conglomerate merger*. These are discussed in the paragraphs that follow.

HORIZONTAL MERGERS A **horizontal merger** is a merger between two or more companies that compete in the same business and geographic market. The merger of two grocery store chains that serve the same geographic market fits this definition. Such mergers are subjected to strict review under Section 7 because they clearly result in an increase in concentration in the relevant market.

Example General Motors Corporation and Ford Motor Company are two of the largest automobile, SUV, and truck manufacturers. If General Motors Corporation and Ford Motor Company tried to merge, this would be a horizontal merger. This merger would most likely violate Section 7.

In the landmark case *United States v. Philadelphia National Bank*,[16] the U.S. Supreme Court adopted the *presumptive illegality test* for determining the lawfulness of horizontal mergers. This test finds horizontal mergers presumptively illegal under Section 7 if (1) the merged firm would have a 30 percent or more market share in the relevant market and (2) the merger would cause an increase in concentration of 33 percent or more in the relevant market. This presumption is rebuttable—that is, the defendants may overcome it by introducing evidence that shows that the merger does not violate Section 7.

This test is not the only criterion for evaluating the lawfulness of a merger. The court must also examine factors such as the trend toward concentration in the relevant market, the past history of the firms involved, the aggressiveness of the merged firms, the economic efficiency of the proposed merger, and consumer welfare.

VERTICAL MERGERS A **vertical merger** is a merger that integrates the operations of a supplier and a customer. In examining the legality of vertical mergers, the courts usually consider such factors as the past history of the firms, the trend toward concentration in the industries involved, the barriers to entry, the economic efficiencies of the merger, and the elimination of potential competition caused by the merger.

Example If Prentice Hall Publishing, a textbook publisher, acquired a paper mill, this would be a **backward vertical merger**. If a book publisher such as Simon & Schuster acquired a retail bookstore chain such as Barnes & Noble it would be a **forward vertical merger**.

Vertical mergers do not create an increase in market share because the merging firms serve different markets. They may, however, cause anticompetitive effects such as *foreclosing* competitors from either selling goods or services to or buying them from the merged firm.

Example Assume that a furniture manufacturer acquires a chain of retail furniture stores. The merger is unlawful if it is likely that the merged firm will not buy furniture from other manufacturers or sell furniture to other retailers.

MARKET EXTENSION MERGERS A **market extension merger** is a merger between two companies in similar fields whose sales do not overlap. The merger may expand the acquiring firm's geographic or product market. The legality of market extension mergers is examined under Section 7 of the Clayton Act.

A merger between two regional brewers that do not sell beer in the same geographic area is called a **geographic market extension merger**. A merger between sellers of similar products, such as a soft drink manufacturer and an orange juice producer, is called a **product market extension merger**.

CONGLOMERATE MERGERS **Conglomerate mergers** are mergers that do not fit into any other category. That is, they are mergers between firms in unrelated businesses.

Example If an oil company such as ExxonMobil merged with a clothing retailer such as Neiman-Marcus, the result would be a conglomerate merger.

The *unfair advantage theory* holds that a conglomerate merger may not give the acquiring firm an unfair advantage over its competitors in finance, marketing, or expertise. This rule is intended to prevent wealthy companies from overwhelming the competition in a given market.

Example Wal-Mart Stores, Inc., a giant discount warehouse store and one of the largest and wealthiest companies in the world, may be prevented from acquiring Polo Ralph Lauren Corporation, a high-end clothing manufacturer and retailer, under the unfair advantage theory.

Defenses to Section 7 Actions

There are two primary defenses to Section 7 actions. These defenses can be raised even if the merger would otherwise violate Section 7. The defenses are:

1. *The failing company doctrine.* According to the **failing company doctrine**, a competitor may merge with a failing company if (1) there is no other reasonable alternative for the failing company, (2) no other purchaser is available, and (3) the assets of the failing company would completely disappear from the market if the anticompetitive merger were not allowed to go through.
2. *The small company doctrine.* The courts have permitted two or more small companies to merge without liability under Section 7 if the merger allows them to compete more effectively with a large company. This is called the **small company doctrine**.

Premerger Notification

In 1976, premerger notification rules were enacted pursuant to the **Hart-Scott-Rodino Antitrust Improvement Act**.[17] These rules require certain firms to notify the FTC and the Department of Justice of any proposed merger. This gives those agencies time to investigate and challenge any mergers they deem anticompetitive. If a merger is reportable, the parties must file the notification form and wait 30 days. If within the waiting period the government sues, the suit is entitled to expedited treatment in the courts.

Tying Arrangements: Section 3 of the Clayton Act

Section 3 of the Clayton Act prohibits tying arrangements that involve sales and leases of goods (tangible personal property).[18] **Tying arrangements** are vertical trade restraints that involve the seller's refusal to sell a product (the *tying* item) to a customer unless the customer purchases a second product (the *tied* item). Section 1 of the Sherman Act (restraints of trade) forbids tying arrangements involving goods, services, intangible property, and real property.

The defendant must be shown to have had sufficient economic power in the tying product market to restrain competition in the tied product market.

A tying arrangement is lawful if there is some justifiable reason for it. For example, the protection of quality control coupled with a trade secret may make a tying arrangement lawful.

Example Suppose that a manufacturer makes one patented product and one unpatented product. An illegal tying arrangement occurs if the manufacturer refuses to sell the patented product to a buyer unless the buyer also purchases the unpatented product.

Example Coca-Cola Company owns the right to the formula for the syrup to make Coca-Cola, which is a trade secret. Suppose that Coca-Cola requires its distributors to purchase the syrup to make Coca-Cola from it. The tying product is the Coca-Cola franchise distributorship, and the tied product is the syrup. Here, the tying arrangement is lawful because a trade secret is involved, and quality control must be preserved.

Price Discrimination: Section 2 of the Clayton Act

Businesses in the U.S. economy survive by selling their goods and services at prices that allow them to make a profit. Sellers often offer favorable terms to their preferred customers. **Price discrimination** occurs if a seller does this without just cause. The rules regarding this type of unlawful trade practices are found in **Section 2 of the Clayton Act**, which is commonly referred to as the **Robinson-Patman Act**. **Section 2(a) of the Robinson-Patman Act** contains the following basic prohibition against price discrimination in the sale of goods:

> It shall be unlawful for any person engaged in commerce, either directly or indirectly, to discriminate in price between different purchases of commodities of like grade and quality, where either or any of the purchases involved in such discrimination are in commerce, where the effect of such discrimination may be substantially to lessen competition or tend to create a monopoly in any line of commerce, or to injure, destroy, or prevent competition with any person who either grants or knowingly receives the benefit of such discrimination, or with customers of either of them.[19]

Section 2 does not apply to the sale of services, real estate, intangible property, securities, leases, consignments, or gifts. Mixed sales (i.e., those involving both services and commodities) are controlled based on the dominant nature of the transaction.

Direct Price Discrimination

To prove a violation of Section 2(a) of the Robinson-Patman Act, the following elements of **direct price discrimination** must be shown:

- *Sales to two or more purchasers.* To violate Section 2(a), the price discrimination must involve sales to at least two different purchasers at approximately the same time. It is legal to make two or more sales of the same product to the same purchaser at different prices. The Robinson-Patman act requires that the discrimination occur "in commerce."
- *Commodities of like grade and quality.* A Section 2(a) violation must involve goods of "like grade and quality." To avoid this rule, sellers sometimes try to differentiate identical or similar products by using brand names. Nevertheless, as one court stated, "Four roses under any other name would still swill the same."[20]
- *Injury.* To recover damages, the plaintiff must have suffered actual injury because of the price discrimination. The injured party may be the purchaser who did not receive the favored price (*primary line injury*), that party's customers to whom the lower price could not be passed along (*secondary line injury*), and so on down the line (*tertiary line injury*).

A plaintiff who has not suffered injury because of the price discrimination cannot recover.

Example Assume that a wholesaler sells the same-type Michelin tires to one automobile repair and tire shop at a lower price than to another repair and tire shop. If the second tire shop cannot purchase the same-type Michelin tires at this or a lower price, it has a good case of price discrimination against the wholesaler. If the second tire shop could have purchased comparable Michelin tires elsewhere at the lower price, it cannot recover for price discrimination.

Indirect Price Discrimination

Because direct forms of price discrimination are readily apparent, sellers of goods have devised sophisticated ways to provide discriminatory prices to favored customers. Favorable credit terms, freight charges, and such are examples of **indirect price discrimination** that violate the Robinson-Patman Act.

Defenses to Price Discrimination

The Robinson-Patman Act establishes three statutory defenses to Section 2(a) liability: cost justification, changing conditions, and meeting the competition. These defenses are discussed in the following paragraphs.

COST JUSTIFICATION Section 2(a) provides that a seller's price discrimination is not unlawful if the price differential is due to "differences in the cost of manufacture, sale, or delivery" of the product. This is called the **cost justification defense**. For example, quantity or volume discounts are lawful to the extent that they are supported by cost savings. Sellers may classify buyers into various broad groups and compute an average cost of selling to the group. The seller may then charge members of different groups different prices without being liable for price discrimination. The seller bears the burden of proving this defense.

Example If Procter & Gamble can prove that bulk shipping rates make it less costly to deliver 10,000 boxes of Tide than lesser quantities, it may charge purchasers accordingly. However, Procter & Gamble may not simply lower its price per-box because the buyer is a good customer.

CHANGING CONDITIONS Price discrimination is not unlawful, under Section 2(a), if it is in response to "changing conditions in the market for or the marketability of the goods." For example, the price of goods can be lowered to subsequent purchasers to reflect the deterioration of perishable goods (e.g., fish), obsolescence of seasonable goods (e.g., winter coats sold in the spring), a distress sale pursuant to court order, or discontinuance of a business. This is called the **changing conditions defense**.

MEETING THE COMPETITION   The **meeting the competition defense** to price discrimination is stipulated in **Section 2(b) of the Robinson-Patman Act**[21] This defense holds that a seller may lawfully engage in price discrimination to meet a competitor's price.

Example   Assume that Rockport sells its "Pro Walker" shoe nationally at $100 per pair, while the Great Lakes Shoe Co. (Great Lakes), which produces and sells a comparable walking shoe, sells its product only in Michigan and Wisconsin. If Great Lakes sells its walking shoes at $75 per pair, Rockport can do the same in Michigan and Wisconsin. Rockport does not have to reduce the price of the shoe in the other 48 states. The seller can only meet, not beat, the competitor's price, however.

Unfair Methods of Competition: Section 5 of the Federal Trade Commission Act

In 1914, Congress enacted the *FTC Act* and created the FTC. **Section 5 of the FTC Act** prohibits "**unfair methods of competition** and unfair or deceptive acts or practices" in or affecting commerce.[22]

Section 5, which is broader than the other antitrust laws, covers conduct that (1) violates any provision of the Sherman Act or the Clayton Act, (2) violates the "spirit" of those acts, (3) fills the gaps of those acts, and (4) offends public policy; is immoral, oppressive, unscrupulous, or unethical; or causes substantial injury to competitors or consumers.

The FTC is exclusively empowered to enforce the FTC Act. It can issue interpretive rules, general statements of policy, trade regulation rules, and guidelines that define unfair or deceptive practices, and it can conduct investigations of suspected antitrust violations. It can also issue cease-and-desist orders against violators. These orders are appealable to federal court. The FTC Act provides for a private civil cause of action for injured parties. Treble damages are not available.

Exemptions From Antitrust Laws

Certain industries and businesses are exempt from federal antitrust laws. The three categories of exemptions are statutory exemptions, implied exemptions, and state action exemptions. These are discussed in the following paragraphs.

Statutory Exemptions

Certain statutes expressly exempt some forms of business and other activities from the reach of antitrust laws. **Statutory exemptions** include labor unions,[23] agricultural cooperatives,[24] export activities of American companies,[25] and insurance business that is regulated by a state.[26] Other federal statutes exempt railroad, utility, shipping, and securities industries from most antitrust laws.

Implied Exemptions

The federal courts have implied several exemptions from antitrust laws. Examples of **implied exemptions** include professional baseball (but not other professional sports) and airlines.[27] The airline exemption was granted on the ground that railroads and other forms of transportation were expressly exempt. The Supreme Court has held that professionals such as lawyers do not qualify for an implied exemption from antitrust laws.[28] The Supreme Court strictly construes implied exemptions from antitrust laws.

State Action Exemptions

The U.S. Supreme Court has held that economic regulations mandated by state law are exempt from federal antitrust laws. The **state action exemption** extends to businesses that must comply with these regulations.

Example States may set the rates that public utilities (e.g., gas, electric, and cable television companies) may charge their customers. The states that set these rates and the companies that must abide by them are not liable for price-fixing in violation of federal antitrust law.

LANDMARK CASE
Baseball's Grand Slam Against Antitrust Laws

> ❝*The business is giving exhibitions of base ball, which are purely state affairs.* ❞
>
> —Justice Holmes

It was 1922. Babe Ruth was slamming home runs as the New York Yankees of the American League won the World Series of baseball. But that year, the most important home run in baseball was hit at the U.S. Supreme Court. The opposing team—the U.S. government—struck out. Here is the story.

The American League and the National League were the dominant professional baseball leagues of the day, with such teams as the New York Giants, Boston Red Sox, and Chicago Cubs drawing millions of fans in metropolitan markets throughout the country. Seeing these leagues' success, an upstart league called the Federal League began fielding teams in competing and other metropolitan markets.

To eliminate this competition, the National League induced some of the Federal League clubs to leave the league and purchased other Federal League teams. The lone remaining Federal League team sued the National League, alleging that it had conspired to wreck the Federal League in violation of federal antitrust laws. The trial court agreed with the plaintiff, but the appeals court and the Supreme Court did not.

The Supreme Court justices held that the "national pastime" was exempt from antitrust laws because there was no interstate commerce involved in the National League's activities. Because of the finding of no interstate commerce, federal antitrust laws did not apply, and the

merit of the case was never decided. *Federal Baseball Club of Baltimore, Inc. v. National League of Professional Baseball Clubs*, 259 U.S. 200, 42 S.Ct. 465, 66 L.Ed. 898, **Web** 1922 U.S. Lexis 2475 (Supreme Court of the United States, 1922).

In 1972, the U.S. Supreme Court refused to overturn its ruling reached in 1922 in the *Federal Baseball* case. *Flood v. Kuhn*, 407 U.S. 258, 92 S.Ct. 2099, 32 L.Ed.2d 728, **Web** 1972 U.S. Lexis 138 (Supreme Court of the United States, 1972). In his decision, Justice Blackmun cited a portion of "He Never Heard of Casey," from Grantland Rice (*New York Herald Tribune*, June 1, 1926, p. 23):

Ten million never heard of Keats, or Shelley, Burns or Poe;

But they know "the air was shattered by the force of Casey's blow";

They never heard of Shakespeare, nor of Dickens, like as not,

But they know the somber drama from old Mudville's haunted lot.

Under the modern broad definition of *interstate commerce*, the decision to exempt baseball from antitrust laws does not comport with a modern reading of the Interstate Commerce Clause. In fact, other professional sports have not been accorded a similar exemption from antitrust laws.

State Antitrust Laws

Most states have enacted antitrust statutes. These statutes are usually patterned after the federal antitrust statutes. They often contain the same language as well. State antitrust laws are used to attack anticompetitive activity that occurs in intrastate commerce. When federal antitrust laws are laxly applied, plaintiffs often bring lawsuits under state antitrust laws.

Art Center, Paris, France

The European Union (EU) has enacted and enforces very strong antitrust laws. The EU antitrust authorities have denied mergers of multinational companies that had been previously approved by antitrust authorities in the United States.

Chapter Summary

Federal Antitrust Laws, p. 913

Congress has enacted a series of laws to limit anticompetitive behavior in business. Federal antitrust laws include:

1. *Sherman Act.* This act, enacted in 1890, made certain restraints of trade and monopolistic acts illegal.
2. *Clayton Act.* This act, enacted in 1914, regulates mergers and prohibits certain exclusive dealing arrangements.
3. *Federal Trade Commission (FTC) Act.* This act, enacted in 1914, prohibits unfair methods of competition.
4. *Robinson-Patman Act.* This act, enacted in 1930, prohibits price discrimination.

Antitrust Enforcement

Each administration adopts an enforcement policy for antitrust laws. Antitrust laws are enforced more stringently at some times than at other times.

Government Actions

Federal antitrust laws provide the following penalties:

1. *Criminal sanctions.* Criminal penalties may be assessed for violations of the Sherman Act.

CHAPTER 33 • ANTITRUST LAW **937**

2. *Civil penalties.* The federal government may seek civil damages, including treble damages, for violations of federal antitrust laws. Courts may issue orders for divestiture of assets, cancellation of contracts, and other remedies.

Private Actions

Section 4 of the Clayton Act provides that anyone injured in his or her business or property by the defendant's violation of any federal antitrust law (except the FTC Act) may bring a civil action and recover from the defendant treble damages plus reasonable costs and attorneys' fees.

Effect of a Government Judgment

A government judgment against a defendant for an antitrust violation may be used as *prima facie* evidence of liability in a private, civil treble-damages action. A plea of *nolo contendere* or a consent decree cannot be used as evidence in a subsequent private, civil antitrust action.

Restraints of Trade: Section 1 of the Sherman Act, p. 915

Section 1 of the Sherman Act prohibits contracts, combinations, or conspiracies that cause unreasonable restraints of trade. It requires concerted activity between two or more parties. The courts apply one of the following two tests in determining the lawfulness of a restraint of trade.

Rule of Reason

The rule of reason requires a balancing of pro- and anticompetitive effects of the restraint. Restraints found to be unreasonable are unlawful, violating Section 1 of the Sherman Act.

Per Se *Rule*

The *per se* rule is applied to restraints that are inherently anticompetitive. No justification for the restraint is permitted.

Horizontal Restraints of Trade, p. 916

Horizontal restraint of trade occurs when two or more competitors at the same level of distribution enter into a contract, combination, or conspiracy to restrain trade.

Price-Fixing

With price-fixing, competitors in the same line of business agree to set the price of the goods or services they sell. This is a *per se* restraint of trade violation.

Division of Markets

In a division of markets, competitors agree that each will serve only a designated portion of a market. Also called *market sharing*. This is a *per se* restraint of trade violation.

Group Boycotts

In a group boycott, competitors agree not to deal with others at another level of distribution (e.g., customer, supplier). Most group boycotts are examined using the rule of reason.

Other Horizontal Agreements

Horizontal agreements besides price-fixing, division of markets, and group boycotts are examined using the rule of reason.

Vertical Restraints of Trade

Vertical restraint of trade occurs when two or more parties on different levels of distribution enter into a contract, combination, or conspiracy to restrain trade. Vertical restraints include:

1. *Resale price maintenance.* Resale price maintenance occurs when a party at one level of distribution (e.g., a manufacturer) requires a party at another level of distribution (e.g., a retailer) to sell a good or service at a designated price. Also called *vertical price fixing*. This is a *per se* restraint of trade violation.
2. *Non-price vertical restraints.* Non-price vertical restraints of trade are examined using the rule of reason.

Defenses to Section 1 of the Sherman Act

The following defenses may be raised against an alleged violation of Section 1 of the Sherman Act:

1. *Unilateral refusal to deal.* A party may unilaterally refuse to deal with another party. This does not violate Section 1 because there has been no concerted action.
2. *Conscious parallelism.* This occurs when two or more firms act the same but without concerted action; they reached their decisions independently.
3. *The Noerr doctrine.* Two or more parties may petition the executive, legislative, or judicial branches of government to enact laws or take other action. The *Noerr* doctrine does not protect petitioners or plaintiffs if their petition or lawsuit is without merit.

Monolpolization: Section 2 of the Sherman Act, p. 925

Section 2 of the Sherman Act prohibits the act of monopolizing and attempts, combinations, and conspiracies to monopolize trade or commerce in a relevant market. The following elements are necessary to prove a defendant is in violation of Section 2 of the Sherman Act.

Defining the Relevant Market

The relevant market is defined as:

1. *Relevant product or service market.* This market includes substitute products or services that are reasonably interchangeable with the defendant's products or services.
2. *Relevant geographic market.* This is the geographic area in which the defendant and its competitors sell the product or service.

Monopoly Power

The defendant must possess monopoly power in the relevant market. This is defined as the power to control prices or exclude competition.

Willful Act of Monopolizing

For an antitrust action to be sustained, the defendant must have engaged in a willful act of monopolizing. Mere possession of a monopoly is not enough.

Defenses to Monopolization

The following defenses may be raised against an alleged violation of Section 2 of the Sherman Act:

1. *Innocent acquisition.* A monopoly may be acquired through superior skill, foresight, or industry.
2. *Natural monopoly.* A monopoly may be thrust upon the defendant (e.g., the only newspaper in a small town).

Attempts and Conspiracies to Monopolize

Firms that attempt or conspire to monopolize a relevant market may be found liable under Section 2 of the Sherman Act.

Mergers: Section 7 of the Clayton Act, p. 929

Section 7 of the Clayton Act prohibits acquisitions that may substantially lessen competition in any line of commerce in any section of the country. The following elements are necessary to prove a violation of Section 7 of the Clayton Act.

Line of Commerce

The line of commerce is defined as the market that will be affected by a merger. It includes products or services that consumers use as substitutes for those produced or sold by the merging firms.

Section of the Country

The section of the country is the geographic market that will be affected by a merger. It includes the area that will feel the direct and immediate impact of the merger.

Probability of a Substantial Lessening of Competition

If the court determines that a merger would have a probability of a substantial lessening of competition, the merger may be prohibited. The statute deals with probabilities: A showing of actual lessening of competition is not required.

Types of Mergers

1. *Horizontal mergers.* A horizontal merger is a merger between two or more firms that compete in the same business and geographic market; it is a merger between competitors at the same level of distribution.
2. *Vertical mergers.* A vertical merger is a merger between firms at different levels of distribution that integrates the operations of a supplier and a customer.
3. *Market extension mergers.* A market extension merger is a merger of two firms in similar fields whose sales do not overlap.
   a. *Geographic market extension mergers.* A geographic market extension merger is a merger of two firms that sell the same product or service but in different geographic markets.
   b. *Product market extension mergers.* A product market extension merger is a merger of two firms that sell similar products or services in the same geographic market.
4. *Conglomerate mergers.* A conglomerate merger is a merger of firms in totally unrelated businesses. Conglomerate mergers may be challenged under unfair advantage theory. A merger may not give the acquiring firm an unfair advantage over its competitors in finance, marketing, or expertise.

Defenses to Section 7 Actions

The following defenses may be raised against a violation of Section 7 of the Clayton Act:
1. *Failing company doctrine.* A competitor may merge with a failing company if (1) there is no other reasonable alternative for the failing company, (2) no other purchaser is available, and (3) the assets of the failing company would completely disappear from the market if the anticompetitive merger were not allowed to go through.
2. *Small company doctrine.* Two or more small companies may merge if the merger allows them to compete more effectively with a large company.

Premerger Notification

The Hart-Scott-Rodino Antitrust Improvement Act is a federal act that requires certain firms to notify the FTC and Justice Department in advance of a proposed merger. Unless the government challenges the proposed merger within 30 days, the merger may proceed.

Tying Arrangements: Section 3 of the Clayton Act, p. 932

A tying arrangement occurs when a seller refuses to sell a product (the tying product) to a customer unless the customer purchases a second product (the tied product). Section 3 of the Clayton Act prohibits tying arrangements involving sales and leases of goods. Section 1 of the Sherman Act prohibits tying arrangements involving goods, services, intangible property, and real property.

Price Discrimination: Section 2 of the Clayton Act, p. 932

Section 2 of the Clayton Act is commonly referred to as the Robinson-Patman Act. It prohibits price discrimination and discriminatory fees, payments, and services. The act applies only to products, not services.

Direct Price Discrimination

Section 2(a) of the Clayton Act prohibits a seller from discriminating in price between two or more different purchasers of commodities of like grade and quality where the effect may be to substantially lessen competition. Direct price discrimination is unlawful.

Indirect Price Discrimination

Favorable credit terms, freight charges, and such are examples of indirect price discrimination that violate the Robinson-Patman Act.

Cost Justification

Differences in the cost of maintenance, sale, or delivery of a product to different purchasers can justify cost discrimination.

Changing Conditions

A seller is allowed to respond to changing conditions in the market (e.g., deterioration of perishable goods).

Meeting the Competition

Section 2(b) permits a seller to have a lower price in one market than in another market to meet the price of a competitor in the lower-priced market.

Unfair Methods of Competition: Section 5 of the Federal Trade Commission Act, p. 934

Sections 5 of the FTC Act prohibits unfair methods of competition and unfair or deceptive acts or practices. Section 5 covers conduct that violates any provision of the Sherman Act or the Clayton Act, violates the "spirit" of those acts, fills the gaps of those acts, and causes substantial injury to competitors or consumers.

Exemptions from Antitrust Law, p. 934

Statutory Exemptions

Statutes expressly exempt from federal antitrust laws labor unions; agricultural cooperatives; export activities of U.S. companies; insurance business regulated by states; and railroad, utility, shipping, and securities industries.

Implied Exemptions

The courts have held that certain industries, including professional baseball and airlines, are implicitly exempt from federal antitrust laws.

State Action Exemptions

Activities of businesses that are mandated by state law are exempt from federal antitrust laws.

State Antitrust Laws, p. 936

Most states have enacted state antitrust laws that attack anticompetitive activity that occurs in intrastate commerce.

Test Review Terms and Concepts

Case Problems

33.1 Price-Fixing: The Maricopa County Medical Society (Society) is a professional association that represents doctors of medicine, osteopathy, and podiatry in Maricopa County, Arizona. The society formed the Maricopa Foundation for Medical Care (Foundation), a nonprofit Arizona corporation. Approximately 1,750 doctors, who represent 70 percent of the practitioners in the country, belong to the foundation. The foundation acts as an insurance administrator between its member doctors and insurance companies that pay patients' medical bills.

The foundation established a maximum fee schedule for various medical services. The member doctors agreed to abide by this fee schedule when providing services to patients. The state of Arizona brought this action against the Society and the Foundation and its members, alleging price-fixing in violation of Section 1 of the Sherman Act. Who wins? *Arizona v. Maricopa County Medical Society*, 457 U.S. 332, 102 S.Ct. 2466, 73 L.Ed.2d 48, **Web** 1982 U.S. Lexis 5 (Supreme Court of the United States)

33.2 Division of Market: Topco Associates, Inc., was founded in the 1940s by a group of small, local grocery store chains to act as a buying cooperative for the member stores. In this capacity, Topco procured and distributed to its members more than 1,000 different food and related items. Topco did not itself own any manufacturing or processing facilities, and the items it procured were shipped directly from the manufacturer or packer to Topco members. Topco members agreed to sell only Topco brand products within an exclusive territory. The United States sued Topco and its members, alleging a violation of Section 1 of the Sherman Act. Who wins? *United States v. Topco Associates, Inc.*, 405 U.S. 596, 92 S.Ct. 1126, 31 L.Ed.2d 515, **Web** 1972 U.S. Lexis 167 (Supreme Court of the United States)

33.3 Tying Arrangement: Mercedes-Benz of North America (MBNA) was the exclusive franchiser of Mercedes-Benz dealerships in the United States. MBNA's franchise agreements required each dealer to establish a customer service department for the repair of Mercedes-Benz automobiles and for dealers to purchase Mercedes-Benz replacement parts from MBNA. At least eight independent wholesale distributors, including Metrix Warehouse, Inc., sold replacement parts for Mercedes-Benz automobiles.

Because they were precluded from selling parts to Mercedes-Benz dealers, these parts distributors sold their replacement parts to independent garages that specialized in the repair of Mercedes-Benz automobiles. Evidence showed that Metrix sold replacement parts for Mercedes-Benz automobiles of equal quality and at a lower price than those sold by MBNA. Metrix sued MBNA, alleging a tying agreement violation of Section 1 of the Sherman Act. Who wins? *Metrix Warehouse, Inc. v. Mercedes-Benz of North America, Inc.*, 828 F.2d 1033, **Web** 1987 U.S. App. Lexis 12341 (United States Court of Appeals for the Fourth Circuit)

33.4 Resale Price Maintenance: The Union Oil Company was a major oil company that operated a nationwide network of franchised service station dealers that sold Union Oil gasoline and other products throughout the United States. The franchise dealers leased their stations from Union Oil; they also signed a franchise agreement to purchase gasoline and other products on assignment from Union Oil. Both the lease and the franchise agreement were one-year contracts that Union Oil could cancel if a dealer did not adhere to the contract. The franchise agreement provided that all dealers must adhere to the retail price of gasoline as set by Union Oil. The retail price fixed by Union Oil for gasoline during the period in question was 29.9 cents per gallon. Simpson, a franchised dealer, violated this provision in the franchise agreement and sold gasoline at 27.9 cents per gallon to meet competitive prices. Because of this, Union Oil canceled Simpson's lease and franchise agreement. Simpson sued Union Oil, alleging a violation of Section 1 of the Sherman Act. Who wins? *Simpson v. Union Oil Company*, 377 U.S. 13, 84 S.Ct. 1051, 12 L.Ed.2d 98, **Web** 1964 U.S. Lexis 2378 (Supreme Court of the United States)

33.5 Monopolization: The International Business Machine Corporation (IBM) manufactured entire computer systems, including mainframes and peripherals, and provided software and support services to customers. IBM both sold and leased computers. Greyhound Computer Corporation, Inc., was a computer leasing company that bought older computers from IBM and then leased them to businesses. Thus, Greyhound was both a customer and a competitor of IBM. Prior to 1963, IBM sold its second-generation equipment at a 10 percent discount per year, up to a maximum of 75 percent. Thus, equipment on the market for several years could be purchased at a substantial discount from its original cost.

IBM's market share of this leasing market was 82.5 percent. The portion of the leasing market not controlled by IBM was dispersed among many companies, including Greyhound. IBM officials became concerned that the balance between sales and leases was turned too heavily toward sales and that the rapid increase in leasing companies occurred because of their ability to purchase second-generation computers from IBM at a substantial discount. In 1963, IBM reduced the annual discount to 5 percent per year, with a maximum of 35 percent. In 1964, the discount was changed to 12 percent after the first year, with no further discounts. Greyhound sued IBM, alleging that IBM engaged in monopolization in violation of Section 2 of the Sherman Act. Who wins? *Greyhound v. International Business Machine Corporation*, 559 F.2d 488, **Web** 1977 U.S. App. Lexis 11957 (United States Court of Appeals for the Ninth Circuit)

33.6 Merger: The Lipton Tea Co. was the second-largest U.S. producer of herbal teas, controlling 32 percent of the national market. Lipton announced that it would acquire Celestial Seasonings, the largest U.S. producer of herbal teas, which controlled 52 percent of the national market. R.C. Bigelow, Inc., the third-largest producer of herbal teas, with 13 percent of the national market, brought an action, alleging that the merger would violate Section 7 of the Clayton Act and seeking an injunction against the merger. What type of merger was proposed? What was the relevant market? Should the merger be enjoined? *R. C. Bigelow, Inc., v. Unilever, N.V.*, 867 F.2d 102, **Web** 1989 U.S. App. Lexis 574 (United States Court of Appeals for the Second Circuit)

33.7 Antitrust Injury: The Brunswick Corporation was the second-largest manufacturer of bowling equipment in the United States. In the late 1950s, the bowling industry expanded rapidly. Brunswick's sales of lanes, automatic pinsetters, and ancillary equipment to bowling alley operators rose accordingly. Because the equipment required a major capital expenditure by bowling center operators, Brunswick required a cash down payment and extended credit for the rest of the purchase price. It took a security interest in the equipment.

Brunswick's sales dropped in the early 1960s, when the bowling industry went into a sharp decline. In addition, many of the bowling center operators defaulted on their loans. By the end of 1964, Brunswick was in financial difficulty. It met with limited success when it foreclosed on its security interests and attempted to lease or sell the repossessed equipment and bowling centers. To avoid complete loss, Brunswick started running those centers that would provide a positive cash flow. This made Brunswick the largest operator of bowling centers in the country, with more than five times as many bowling centers as its next largest competitor. Because the bowling industry was so deconcentrated, however, Brunswick controlled fewer than 2 percent of the bowling centers in the country.

Pueblo Bowl-O-Mat, Inc., operated three bowling centers in markets where Brunswick had repossessed bowling centers and began operating them. Pueblo Bowl sued Brunswick, alleging that Brunswick had violated Section 7 of the Clayton Act. Pueblo Bowl alleged that it had suffered injury in the form of lost profits that it would have made had Brunswick allowed the bowling centers to go bankrupt, and it requested treble damages. Is Brunswick liable? *Brunswick Corporation v. Pueblo Bowl-O-Mat, Inc.*, 429 U.S. 477, 97 S.Ct. 690, 50 L.Ed.2d 701, **Web** 1977 U.S. Lexis 37 (Supreme Court of the United States)

33.8 Price Discrimination: Corn Products Refining Company manufactured corn syrup, or glucose (a principal ingredient of low-priced candy), at two plants, one located in Chicago, Illinois, and the other in Kansas City, Missouri. Corn Products sold glucose at the same retail price to all purchasers but charged separately for freight charges. Instead of charging actual freight charges, Corn Products charged every purchaser the price it would have cost for the glucose to be shipped from Chicago, even if the glucose was shipped from its Kansas City plant. This "base point pricing" system created a favored price zone for Chicago-based purchasers and put them in a better position to compete for business. The FTC sued Corn Products, alleging that it was engaging in price discrimination in violation of Section 2(a) of the Robinson-Patman Act. Was it? *Corn Products Refining Company v. Federal Trade Commission*, 324 U.S. 726, 65 S.Ct. 961, 89 L.Ed. 1320, **Web** 1945 U.S. Lexis 2749 (Supreme Court of the United States)

Ethics Issues

33.9 Ethics: E. I. du Pont de Nemours & Co. (Du Pont) is a manufacturer of chemicals, paints, finishes, fabrics, and other products. General Motors Corporation is a major manufacturer of automobiles. During the period 1917–1919, Du Pont purchased 23 percent of the stock of General Motors. Du Pont became a major supplier of finishes and fabrics to General Motors.

Du Pont's commanding position as a General Motors supplier was not achieved until shortly after its purchase of a sizable block of General Motors stock in 1917. The company's interest in buying into General Motors was stimulated by John J. Raskob, Du Pont's treasurer, and Pierre S. du Pont, Du Pont's president, who acquired personal holdings of General Motors stock in 1914. General Motors had been organized six years earlier by William C. Durant to acquire the previously independent automobile manufacturing companies Buick, Cadillac, Oakland, and Oldsmobile. Durant later brought in Chevrolet, organized by Durant when he was temporarily out of power, during 1910–1915, and a bankers' group controlled General Motors. In 1915, when Durant and the bankers deadlocked on the choice of a board of directors, they resolved the deadlock by an agreement under which Pierre S. du Pont was named chairman of the General Motors board, and Pierre S. du Pont, Raskob, and two nominees of Mr. du Pont were named neutral directors. By 1916, Durant settled his differences with the bankers and resumed the presidency and his controlling position in General Motors. He prevailed upon Pierre S. du Pont and Raskob to continue their interest in General Motors's affairs, which both did as members of the finance committee, working closely with Durant in matters of finances and operations and plans for future expansion.

Raskob foresaw the success of the automobile industry and the opportunity for great profit in a substantial purchase of General Motors stock. On December 19, 1917, Raskob submitted a treasurer's report to the Du Pont finance committee, recommending a purchase of General Motors stock in the amount of $25 million. That report made it clear that more than just a profitable investment was contemplated. A major consideration was that an expanding General Motors would provide a substantial market needed by the burgeoning Du Pont organization. Raskob's summary of reasons in support of the purchase included this statement: "Our interest in the General Motors Company will undoubtedly secure for us the entire Fabrikoid, Pyralin (celluloid), paint and varnish business of those companies, which is a substantial factor."

General Motors was the colossus of the giant automobile industry. It accounted annually for upward of two-fifths of the total sales of automotive vehicles in the nation. Expressed in percentages, Du Pont supplied 67 percent of General Motors's requirements for finishes in 1946 and 68 percent in 1947. In fabrics, Du Pont supplied 52.3 percent of requirements in 1946 and 38.5 percent in 1947. Because General Motors accounted for almost one-half of the automobile industry's annual sales, its requirements for automotive finishes and fabrics must have represented approximately one-half of the relevant market for these materials.

In 1949, the United States brought an antitrust action against Du Pont, alleging violation of Section 7 of the Clayton Act and seeking the divestiture of Du Pont's ownership of stock in General Motors. Did Du Pont's ownership of 23 percent of the stock of General Motors constitute a vertical merger that gave Du Pont illegal preferences over competitors in the sale of finishes and fabrics to General Motors in violation of Section 7 of the Clayton Act? Did the du Ponts act ethically in this case? *United States v. E. I. du Pont de Nemours & Co.*, 353 U.S. 586, 77 S.Ct. 872, 1 L.Ed.2d 1057, **Web** 1957 U.S. Lexis 1755 (Supreme Court of the United States)

33.10 Ethics: Falls City Industries, Inc. (Falls City), was a regional brewer located in Nebraska. It sold its Falls City brand beer in 13 states, including Indiana and Kentucky. In Indiana, Falls City sold its beer to Vanco Beverage, Inc., a beer wholesaler located in Vanderburgh County. In Kentucky, Falls City sold its beer to wholesalers located in Henderson County. The two counties are directly across from each other and are separated only by the Indiana–Kentucky state line. A four-lane interstate highway connects the two counties. When other brewers raised their wholesale prices in Indiana, Falls City also raised its prices. Falls City also raised its wholesale prices in Kentucky, but less than it raised its prices in Indiana. Vanco brought a treble-damages action against Falls City, alleging that Falls City had engaged in price discrimination in violation of Section 2(a) of the Robinson-Patman Act by raising prices less in Kentucky than in Indiana. Does the meeting-the-competition defense protect Falls City Industries from liability for price discrimination? Did Falls City act unethically in this case? *Falls City Industries, Inc. v. Vanco Beverage, Inc.*, 460 U.S. 428, 103 S.Ct. 1282, 75 L.Ed.2d 174, **Web** 1983 U.S. Lexis 148 (Supreme Court of the United States)

IRAC Writing Assignment

Read **Case A-33** in Appendix A [*Texaco Inc. v. Hasbrouck, dba Rick's Texaco*]. Use the IRAC method to prepare a written analysis of the case.

Endnotes

1. Antitrust Amendments Act of 1990, P.L. 101–588.
2. Antitrust Amendments Act of 1990, P.L. 101–588.
3. 15 U.S.C. Section 15.
4. *Reiter v. Sonotone Corporation*, 442 U.S. 330, 99 S.Ct. 2326, 60 L.Ed.2d 931, **Web** 1979 U.S. Lexis 108 (Supreme Court of the United States).
5. 15 U.S.C. Section 26.
6. Justice Marshall, *United States v. Topco Associates, Inc.*, 405 U.S. 596, 92 S.Ct. 1126, 31 L.Ed.2d 515, **Web** 1972 U.S. Lexis 167 (Supreme Court of the United States).
7. 15 U.S.C. Section 1.
8. 221 U.S. 1, 31 S.Ct. 502, 55 L.Ed. 619, **Web** 1911 U.S. Lexis 1725 (Supreme Court of the United States). The Court found that Rockefeller's oil trust violated the Sherman Act and ordered the trust broken up into 30 separate companies.
9. *Dr. Miles Medical Co. v. John D. Park & Sons, Co.*, 220 U.S. 373, 31 S.Ct. 376, 55 L.Ed. 502, **Web** 1911 U.S. Lexis 1685 (Supreme Court of the United States).
10. *Continental T.V., Inc. v. GTE Sylvania, Inc.*, 433 U.S. 36, 97 S.Ct. 2549, 53 L.Ed.2d 568, **Web** 1977 U.S. Lexis 134 (Supreme Court of the United States), reversing *United States v. Arnold Schwinn & Co.*, 388 U.S. 365, 87 S.Ct. 1856, 18 L.Ed.2d 1249, **Web** 1967 U.S. Lexis 2965 (Supreme Court of the United States).
11. 250 U.S. 300, 39 S.Ct. 465, 63 L.Ed. 992, **Web** 1919 U.S. Lexis 1748 (Supreme Court of the United States).
12. This doctrine is the result of two U.S. Supreme Court decisions: *Eastern R.R. President's Conference v. Noerr Motor Freight, Inc.*, 365 U.S. 127, 81 S.Ct. 523, 5 L.Ed.2d 464, **Web** 1961 U.S. Lexis 2128 (Supreme Court of the United States), and *United Mine Workers v. Pennington*, 381 U.S. 657, 85 S.Ct. 1585, 14 L.Ed.2d 626, **Web** 1965 U.S. Lexis 2207 (Supreme Court of the United States).
13. 15 U.S.C. Section 2.
14. *William Inglis & Sons Baking Company v. ITT Continental Baking Company, Inc.*, 668 F.2d 1014, **Web** 1982 U.S. App. Lexis 21926 (United States Court of Appeals for the Ninth Circuit).
15. 15 U.S.C. Section 18.
16. 374 U.S. 321, 83 S.Ct. 1715, 10 L.Ed.2d 915, **Web** 1963 U.S. Lexis 2413 (Supreme Court of the United States).
17. 15 U.S.C. Section 18(a).
18. 15 U.S.C. Section 14.
19. 15 U.S.C. Section 13(a).
20. *Hartley & Parker, Inc. v. Florida Beverage Corp.*, 307, F.2d 916, 923, **Web** 1962 U.S. App. Lexis 4196 (United States Court of Appeals for the Fifth Circuit).
21. 15 U.S.C. Section 13(b).
22. 15 U.S.C. Section 45.
23. Section 6 of the Clayton Act, 15 U.S.C. Section 17; the Norris-LaGuardia Act of 1932, 29 U.S.C. Sections 101–155; and the National Labor Relations Act of 1935, 29 U.S.C. Section

141 *et seq.* Labor unions that conspire or combine with nonlabor groups to accomplish a goal prohibited by federal antitrust law lose their exemption.

24. Capper-Volstrand Act of 1922, 7 U.S.C. Section 291; and Cooperative Marketing Act of 1926, 15 U.S.C. Section 521.
25. Webb-Pomerene Act, 15 U.S.C. Sections 61–65.
26. McCarran-Ferguson Act of 1945, 15 U.S.C. Sections 1011–1015.
27. *Community Communications Co., Inc. v. City of Boulder*, 455 U.S. 40, 102 S.Ct. 835, 70 L.Ed.2d 810, **Web** 1982 U.S. Lexis 65 (Supreme Court of the United States).
28. *Goldfarb v. Virginia State Bar*, 421 U.S. 773, 95 S.Ct. 2004, 44 L.Ed.2d 572, **Web** 1975 U.S. Lexis 13 (Supreme Court of the United States).

CHAPTER 34

Consumer Protection and Environmental Law

> **❝** *I should regret to find that the law was powerless to enforce the most elementary principles of commercial morality.* **❞**
>
> —LORD HERSCHELL
> Reddaway v. Banham (1896)

CHAPTER OBJECTIVES

After studying this chapter, you should be able to:

1. Describe government regulation of food, drugs, cosmetics, and medicinal devices.
2. Explain the coverage of consumer protection laws.
3. Identify and describe unfair and deceptive business practices.
4. Describe the protections afforded by the Clean Air Act, the Clean Water Act, and other environmental protection laws.
5. Describe how the Endangered Species Act protects endangered and threatened species and their habitats.

CHAPTER CONTENTS

   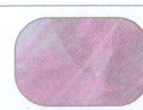 

Introduction to Consumer Protection and Environmental Law

Originally, sales transactions in this country were guided by the principle of *caveat emptor* ("let the buyer beware"). To promote the safety of foods, cosmetics, drugs, products, and services, and to prohibit abusive, unfair, and deceptive selling practices, federal and state governments have enacted a variety of statutes that regulate the behavior of businesses that deal with consumers. These laws are collectively referred to as **consumer protection laws**. This chapter examines consumer protection laws.

In producing and consuming products, businesses and consumers generate air pollution, water pollution, and hazardous and toxic wastes that cause harm to the environment and to human health. Pollution has now reached alarming rates in this country and the rest of the world. In response, federal and state governments have enacted **environmental protection laws** to contain the levels of pollution and to clean up hazardous waste sites in this country. This chapter examines environmental laws that are applicable to businesses and individuals.

Harbor, St. Ignace, Michigan

The federal and state governments have enacted many statutes to protect the water, air, and the environment from pollution.

Web Exercise

1. **WEB** Visit the website of St. Ignace, Michigan, at *www.stignace.com*.

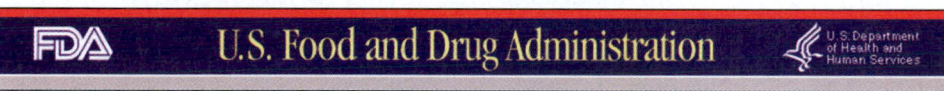

Food, Drug, and Cosmetic Safety

The federal **Food, Drug, and Cosmetic Act (FDCA or FDC Act)** was enacted in 1938.[1] This act, as amended, regulates the testing, manufacture, distribution, and sale of foods, drugs, cosmetics, and medicinal products and devices in the United States. The **Food and Drug Administration (FDA)** is the federal administrative agency empowered to enforce the FDCA.

Before certain food additives, drugs, cosmetics, and medicinal devices can be sold to the public, they must receive FDA approval. An applicant must submit an application to the FDA that contains relevant information about the safety and uses of the product. The FDA, after considering the evidence, will either approve or deny the application.

The FDA can seek search warrants and conduct inspections; obtain orders for the seizure, recall, and condemnation of products; seek injunctions; and turn over suspected criminal violations to the U.S. Department of Justice for prosecution.

Web Exercises

1. **WEB** Visit the website of the Food and Drug Administration, at *www.fda.gov*.

2. **WEB** Use *www.google.com* to find an article that discusses food safety. Read it.

Regulation of Food

The FDCA prohibits the shipment, distribution, or sale of **adulterated food**. Food is deemed adulterated if it consists in whole or in part of any "filthy, putrid, or decomposed substance" or if it is otherwise "unfit for food." Note that food does not have to be entirely pure to be distributed or sold—it only has to be unadulterated.

The FDCA also prohibits **false and misleading labeling** of food products. In addition, it mandates affirmative disclosure of information on food labels, including the name of the food, the name and place of the manufacturer, a statement of ingredients, and nutrition content. A manufacturer may be held liable for deceptive labeling or packaging.

The United States Department of Agriculture (USDA) is a federal administrative agency that is responsible for regulating meat, poultry, and other food products. The USDA conducts inspections of food processing and storage facilities, and can initiate legal proceedings against violators. The USDA initiated a proceeding in the following case.

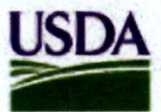

United States Department of Agriculture

Web Exercise

1. **WEB** Visit the website of the U.S. Department of Agriculture, at *www.usda.gov*.

2. **WEB** Use *www.google.com* to find a website that shows a meat-packing plant.

CASE **34.1**
Adulterated Food

United States of America v. LaGrou Distribution Systems, Incorporated

466 F.3d 585,
Web 2006 U.S. App. Lexis 25986 (2006)
United States Court of Appeals for the Seventh Circuit

> **❝** *The conditions at LaGrou's cold storage warehouse at 2101 Pershing Road in Chicago were enough to turn even the most enthusiastic meat-loving carnivore into a vegetarian.* **❞**

—Judge Bauer

Facts

LaGrou Distribution Systems, Incorporated, operated a cold storage warehouse and distribution center in Chicago, Illinois. The warehouse stored raw, fresh, and frozen meat, poultry, and other food products that were owned by customers who paid LaGrou to do so. Over 2 million pounds of food went into and out of the warehouse each day.

The warehouse had a rat problem for a considerable period of time. LaGrou workers consistently found rodent droppings and rodent-gnawed products, and they caught rats in traps throughout the warehouse on a daily basis. The manager of the warehouse and the president of LaGrou were aware of this problem and discussed it weekly. The problem became so bad that workers were assigned to "rat

patrols" to search for rats and to put out traps to catch rats. At one point, the rat patrols were trapping as many as 50 rats per day. LaGrou did not inform its customers of the rodent infestation. LaGrou would throw out products that had been gnawed by rats but tell the customer that the product was thrown out because of warehouse damage such as torn boxes and forklift mishaps. LaGrou employees, as a joke, would write "MM" for Mickey Mouse on products that was infested.

One day, a food inspector for the United States Department of Agriculture (USDA) went to the LaGrou warehouse and discovered the rat problem. The following morning, 14 USDA inspectors and representatives of the federal Food and Drug Administration (FDA) arrived at the warehouse to begin an extensive investigation. The inspectors found the extensive rat infestation and the contaminated meat. The contaminated meat could transmit bacterial, viral, parasitic, and fungal pathogens, including *E. coli* and *Salmonella*, which could cause severe illness in human beings.

The USDA ordered the warehouse shut down. Eight million pounds of the 22 million pounds of meat, poultry, and other food products stored at the warehouse was found to be adulterated and was destroyed. The remaining product was required to be treated with strict decontamination procedures. The U.S. government brought charges against LaGrou for violating federal food safety laws. The U.S. District Court ordered LaGrou to pay restitution of $8.2 million to customers who lost product and to pay a $2 million fine, and it sentenced LaGrou to a five-year term of probation. LaGrou appealed.

Issue

Did LaGrou knowingly engage in the improper storage of meat, poultry, and other food products in violation of federal food safety laws?

Language of the Court

The conditions at LaGrou's cold storage warehouse at 2101 Pershing Road in Chicago were enough to turn even the most enthusiastic meat-loving carnivore into a vegetarian. According to Dr. Bonnie Rose, the USDA microbiologist who testified, LaGrou's warehouse was the "worst case" she had seen in her 28 years with the USDA. The inspectors found and photographed the following conditions at the Pershing Road warehouse: rat droppings and rat nesting material throughout the warehouse, including next to and on product; rodent-gnawed meat, poultry, and other food products; live rodent sightings; blood from meat product on the floor mixed with rodent droppings and rat tail marks; dirt and debris on meat product; potential rodent access points, including open sewer drains and openings under doors; holes in ceilings, walls, and floors; ice buildup on the ceilings directly above stored product and water dripping from the ceilings onto the product; mold and filth on the walls and ceilings; several inoperable bathrooms, which forced warehouse workers to use broken toilets and "flush" them with buckets of water; and raw sewage and standing water on the floors.

The instructions in this case explained that in order to convict LaGrou, the jury had to find that an authorized agent or employee of LaGrou knowingly stored products under insanitary conditions. Since 1999, LaGrou's President, managers, and several employees were aware of the unsanitary conditions in the Pershing Road warehouse. LaGrou was aware of the rodent infestation from formal reports, such as from the ASI and McCloud, LaGrou's pest control company, and from informal reports, such as LaGrou employee rat patrols and the employees' necessary sorting of rat-infested product from supposedly clean product. A crucial charge in these three offenses is that LaGrou knowingly stored these products under unsanitary conditions, which states the requisite mens rea for the charges.

Decision

The U.S. Court of Appeals held that LaGrou had knowingly engaged in the improper storage of meat, poultry, and other food products in violation of federal food safety laws. The Court of Appeals affirmed the judgment of the District Court, except that it reduced the fine from $2 million to $1.5 million.

Law & Ethics Questions

1. What is the USDA? What is the purpose of the USDA?
2. **ETHICS** Did LaGrou management knowingly engage in improper storage of food products?
3. **ETHICS** Do you think that the penalties imposed on LaGrou were sufficient? Why or why not?

Web Exercises

1. **WEB** For the complete opinion of this case, go to *www.prenhall.com/cheesemancases*.
2. **WEB** Visit the website of the U.S. Supreme Court, at *www.supremecourtus.gov*, and try to find documents that relate to this case.
3. **WEB** Visit the website of the U.S. Department of Agriculture, at *www.usda.gov*.
4. **WEB** Visit the website of LaGrou Distribution Systems, Incorporated, at *www.lagrou.com*.
5. **WEB** Use *www.google.com* to find an article about adulterated food at food storage and processing facilities. Read it.

CONTEMPORARY ENVIRONMENT
Food Safety of Peanut Butter

You take a big bite of a peanut butter sandwich and savor the taste. It has been processed by a food manufacturer and inspected by the federal government, so you think it is pure peanut butter. Not necessarily. Under federal FDA guidelines, peanut butter may contain up to 30 insect fragments per 3 ounces and still be considered "safe" for human consumption.

The FDA has set ceilings, or "action levels," for certain contaminants, or "defects," as the FDA likes to call them, for various foods. Several of these action levels are:

- Golden raisins—35 fly eggs per 8 ounces
- Popcorn—two rodent hairs per pound
- Shelled peanuts—20 insects per 100 pounds
- Canned mushrooms—20 maggots per 3.5 ounces
- Tomato juice—10 fly eggs per 3.5 ounces

The FDA can mount inspections and raids to enforce its action levels. If it finds that the federal tolerance system has been violated, it can seize the offending food and destroy it at the owner's expense.

The courts have upheld the presence of some contamination in food as lawful under the federal FDCA. For example, in one case, the court found that 28 insect parts in 9 pounds of butter did not violate the act. The court stated, "Few foods contain no natural or unavoidable defects. Even with modern technology, all defects in foods cannot be eliminated." *United States v. Capital City Foods, Inc.*, 345 F.Supp. 277, **Web** 1972 U.S. Dist. Lexis (United States District Court for the District of North Dakota)

Web Exercises

1. **WEB** Visit the website *www.peanutbutter.com/nutrition.asp*. Does this website discuss the FDA rules allowing certain contaminants in peanut butter?

2. **WEB** Use *www.google.com* to find an article or a website that discusses lawsuits regarding the injuries caused by eating peanut butter.

Food Labeling

In 1990, Congress passed a sweeping truth-in-labeling law called the **Nutrition Labeling and Education Act**. This statute requires food manufacturers and processors to provide nutrition information on most foods and prohibits them from making scientifically unsubstantiated health claims.

The law requires the more than 20,000 food labels found on grocery store shelves to disclose the number of calories derived from fat and the amount of dietary fiber, saturated fat, cholesterol, and a variety of other substances. The law applies to packaged foods as well as fruits, vegetables, and raw seafood. Meat, poultry, and egg products, which are regulated by the Department of Agriculture, are exempt from the act.

The FDA announced final regulations to implement the act. The regulations require food processors to provide uniform information about serving sizes and nutrients on labels of the food products they sell and establish standard definitions for *light*, *low fat*, *natural*, and other terms routinely bandied about by food processors.

Tibet

Areas of the world have differing ways of producing food for people and animals.

Regulation of Drugs

The FDCA gives the FDA the authority to regulate the testing, manufacture, distribution, and sale of **drugs**. The **Drug Amendment to the FDCA**,[2] enacted in 1962, gives the FDA broad powers to license new drugs in the United States. After a new drug application is filed, the FDA holds a hearing and investigates the merits of the application. This process can take many years. The FDA may withdraw approval of any previously licensed drug.

This law requires all users of prescription and nonprescription drugs to receive proper directions for use (including the method and duration of use) and adequate warnings about any related side effects. The manufacture, distribution, or sale of adulterated or misbranded drugs is prohibited.

The possible regulation of a drug was at issue in the following case.

CASE **34.2**

Regulation of a Drug

U.S. SUPREME COURT

Food and Drug Administration v. Brown & Williamson Tobacco Corporation

529 U.S. 120, 20 S.Ct. 1291, 146 L.Ed.2d 121,
Web 2000 U.S. Lexis 2195 (2000)
Supreme Court of the United States

> " *The agency has amply demonstrated that tobacco use, particularly among children and adolescents, poses perhaps the single most significant threat to public health in the United States.* "
>
> —Justice O'Connor

Facts

The Food and Drug Administration (FDA) is a federal administrative agency empowered to administer the Food, Drug, and Cosmetic Act (FDC Act). Pursuant to this act, the FDA can regulate "drugs" and medical "devices." Based on its perceived power under the FDA Act, the FDA enacted a rule regulating tobacco products. The rule:

1. Prohibits the sale of cigarettes and smokeless tobacco to persons younger than 18.
2. Requires retailers to verify through photo identification the age of all purchasers younger than 27.
3. Prohibits the sale of cigarettes in quantities smaller than 20.
4. Prohibits the distribution of free samples.
5. Prohibits sales through self-service displays and vending machines except in adult-only locations.
6. Requires that print advertising appear in black-and-white, text-only format.
7. Prohibits outdoor advertising within 1,000 feet of any public school or playground.
8. Prohibits the distribution of any promotional items, such as t-shirts or hats, bearing the manufacturer's brand.
9. Prohibits a manufacturer from sponsoring any athletic, musical, artistic, or other social or cultural event using its brand name.
10. Requires that the statement "A Nicotine-Delivery Device for Persons 18 or Older" appear on all tobacco products.

A group of tobacco manufacturers and advertisers filed a lawsuit in U.S. District Court, asserting that the FDA did not have authority to regulate tobacco as a "drug" or "device" that delivered nicotine to the body. The District Court certified the issue to the Court of Appeals, which held that the FDC Act did not grant the FDA power to regulate tobacco products. The plaintiffs appealed to the U.S. Supreme Court.

Issue

Does the Food, Drug, and Cosmetic Act grant the Food and Drug administration authority to regulate tobacco products as a "drug" or "device"?

Language of the U.S. Supreme Court

Regardless of how serious the problem an administrative agency seeks to address, however, it may not exercise its authority in a manner that is inconsistent with the administrative structure that Congress enacted into law. Congress has foreclosed the removal of tobacco products from the market. A provision of the United States Code currently in force states that "the marketing of tobacco constitutes one of the greatest basic industries of the United States with ramifying activities which directly affect interstate and foreign commerce at every point, and stable conditions therein are necessary to the general welfare." More importantly, Congress has directly addressed the problem of tobacco and health through legislation on six occasions since 1965. See Federal Cigarette Labeling and Advertising Act (FCLAA), Public Health Cigarette Smoking Act of 1969, Alcohol and Drug Abuse Amendments of 1983, Comprehensive Smoking Education Act, Comprehensive Smokeless Tobacco Health Education Act of 1986, and Alcohol, Drug Abuse, and Mental Health Administration Reorganization Act. When Congress enacted these statutes, the adverse health consequences of tobacco use were well known, as were nicotine's pharmacological effects. Nonetheless, Congress stopped well short of ordering a ban. Instead, it has generally regulated the labeling and advertisement of tobacco products.

Considering the FDC Act as a whole, it is clear that Congress intended to exclude tobacco products from the FDA's jurisdiction. A fundamental precept of the FDC Act is that any product regulated by the FDA—but not banned—must be safe for its intended use. Consequently, if tobacco products were within the FDA's jurisdiction, the FDC Act would require the FDA to remove them from the market entirely. But a ban would contradict Congress' clear intent as expressed in its more recent, tobacco-specific legislation. The inescapable conclusion is that there is no room for tobacco products within the FDC Act's regulatory scheme.

By no means do we question the seriousness of the problem that the FDA has sought to address. The agency has amply demonstrated that tobacco use, particularly among children and adolescents, poses perhaps the single most significant threat to public health in the United States. Nonetheless, no matter how important, conspicuous, and controversial the issue, an administrative agency's power to regulate in the public interest must always be grounded in a valid grant of authority from Congress. And, in our anxiety to effectuate the congressional purpose of protecting the public, we must take care not to extend the scope of the statute beyond the point where Congress indicated it would stop. Reading the FDC Act as a whole, as well as in conjunction with Congress' subsequent tobacco-specific legislation, it is plain that Congress has not given the FDA the authority that it seeks to exercise here.

Decision

The U.S. Supreme Court held that the FDA does not have authority under the Food, Drug, and Cosmetic Act to regulate tobacco products as a "drug" or "device." It affirmed the judgment of the Court of Appeals.

Law & Ethics Questions

1. Did the FDA exceed its delegated authority under the FDC Act by enacting its tobacco products rules?
2. Did the cigarette companies come out ahead by the result reached in this lawsuit?
3. **ETHICS** Do you think that the cigarette companies have "bought off" Congress? Explain your answer.
4. **ETHICS** Do the state and federal governments have a stake in cigarette product sales? What economic effects would a ban on cigarette sales cause to state and federal governments?

Web Exercises

1. **WEB** For the complete opinion of this case, go to *www.prenhall.com/cheesemancases*.
2. **WEB** Visit the website of the U.S. Supreme Court, at *www.supremecourtus.gov*, and try to find documents that relate to this case.
3. **WEB** Visit the website of the federal Food and Drug Administration, at *www.fda.gov*.
4. **WEB** Visit the website *www.bwdocs.com*. What types of documents are posted on this website?
5. **WEB** Use *www.google.com* to find an article about the health risks of smoking and the difficulty of giving up smoking. Read it.

ETHICS SPOTLIGHT

Safety Warnings About Viagra

The anti-impotency drug Viagra is prescribed by doctors to male patients who cannot have or have trouble getting erections, and it helps such men have intercourse. The drug became successful and is now used by millions of men worldwide. In the United States, the Food and Drug Administration (FDA) approved the drug for use by the general public.

After hundreds of deaths of men taking the drug were reported, the FDA investigated and found that men with certain health predispositions may be at risk of death if they take Viagra. Therefore, the FDA required Pfizer, Inc., the manufacturer of Viagra, to place labels on Viagra containers, warning individuals with the following conditions to be careful when taking the drug:

- Men who have had a heart attack or an irregular heartbeat in the past six months
- Men who have a history of cardiac failure or coronary artery disease that caused angina
- Men who have significant high or low blood pressure

By requiring the new warnings, the FDA hopes men consider these risk factors before taking Viagra.

Law & Ethics Questions

1. Are there risks in taking many of the prescription drugs on the market today? Can you describe one such drug?
2. **ETHICS** In applying a cost–benefit analysis to the development and marketing of a drug, when is a point reached at which the cost (in injuries, side effects, and deaths) exceeds the benefits to society? Explain.

Web Exercise

1. **WEB** Visit the website of Pfizer Pharmaceutical Company, the manufacturer of Viagra, at *www.pfizer.com*.

Regulation of Cosmetics

The FDA's definition of **cosmetics** includes substances and preparations for cleansing, altering the appearance of, and promoting the attractiveness of a person. Eye shadow and other facial makeup products are examples of cosmetics subject to FDA regulation. Ordinary household soap is expressly exempt from this definition.

The FDA has issued regulations that require cosmetics to be labeled, to disclose ingredients, and to contain warnings if they are carcinogenic (cancer-causing) or otherwise dangerous to a person's health. The manufacture, distribution, or sale of adulterated or misbranded cosmetics is prohibited. The FDA may remove from commerce any cosmetics that contain unsubstantiated claims of preserving youth, increasing virility, growing hair, and such.

Regulation of Medicinal Devices

In 1976, Congress enacted the **Medicinal Device Amendment to the FDCA**.[3] This amendment gives the FDA authority to regulate medicinal devices, such as heart pacemakers, kidney dialysis machines, defibrillators, surgical equipment, and other diagnostic, therapeutic, and health devices. The mislabeling of such devices is prohibited. The FDA is empowered to remove "quack" devices from the market.

Cattle Pasture

The United States Department of Agriculture (USDA), a federal administrative agency, administers and enforces numerous federal statutes that regulate the safety of agricultural and food products.

INTERNATIONAL LAW

United Nations Biosafety Protocol for Genetically Altered Foods

In many countries, the food is not genetically altered. However, many food processors in the United States and elsewhere around the world genetically modify some foods by adding genes from other organisms to help crops grow faster or ward off pests. In the past, food processors did not notify consumers that they were purchasing genetically modified agricultural products. Although the companies insist that genetically altered foods are safe, consumers and many countries began to demand that such foods be clearly labeled so that buyers could decide for themselves.

The most concerned countries in the world regarding this issue were in Europe. Led by Germany, many European countries wanted to require genetically engineered food products to be labeled as such and be transported separately from nonaltered agricultural products. Some European countries wanted genetically altered foods to be banned completely. The United States, a major exporter of agricultural products and the leader in the development of biotech foods, argued that these countries were using this issue to erect trade barriers to keep U.S.-produced food products out of their countries, in violation of international trade treaties and conventions administered by the World Trade Organization (WTO), which had reduced or eliminated many international trade restrictions.

In January 2000, a compromise was reached when 138 countries, including the United States, agreed to the United Nations–sponsored **Biosafety Protocol**. After much negotiation, the countries agreed that all genetically engineered foods would be clearly labeled with the phrase "May contain living modified organisms." This allows consumers to decide on their own whether to purchase such altered food products. In addition, the boxes and containers in which such goods are shipped must also be clearly marked as containing genetically altered food products.

Web Exercises

1. **WEB** Visit the website *www.bio.org*. Whose website is this? What is the purpose of this website?

2. **WEB** Use *www.google.com* to find a website that discusses whether the United States should have joined the United Nations–sponsored Biosafety Protocol.

Product Safety

In 1972, Congress enacted the **Consumer Product Safety Act (CPSA)**[4] and created the **Consumer Product Safety Commission (CPSC)**. The CPSC is an independent federal administrative agency empowered to (1) adopt rules and regulations to interpret and enforce the CPSA, (2) conduct research on the safety of consumer products, and (3) collect data regarding injuries caused by consumer products.

Because the CPSC regulates potentially dangerous consumer products, it issues product safety standards for consumer products that pose unreasonable risk of injury. If a consumer product is found to be imminently hazardous—that is, if its use can cause an unreasonable risk of death or serious injury or illness—the manufacturer can be required to recall, repair, or replace the product or take other corrective action. Alternatively, the CPSC can seek injunctions, bring actions to seize hazardous consumer products, seek civil penalties for knowing violations of the act or of CPSA rules, and seek criminal penalties for knowing and willful violations of the act or of CPSC rules. A private party can sue for an injunction to prevent violations of the act or of CPSC rules and regulations.

Certain consumer products, including motor vehicles, boats, aircraft, and firearms, are regulated by other government agencies.

Web Exercises

1. **WEB** Visit the website of the Consumer Product Safety Commission (CPSC), at *www.cpsc.gov*. Can you find any product that the CPSC has recently recalled?

2. **WEB** Use *www.google.com* to find a recent product that the CPSC has taken off the market because it violated safety rules.

ETHICS SPOTLIGHT
Lemon Laws

In the past, consumers who purchased automobiles and other vehicles that developed nagging mechanical problems had to try to convince the dealer or manufacturer to correct the problems. If a problem was not corrected, the consumer's only recourse was to seek redress through costly and time-consuming litigation. Today, most states have enacted **lemon laws**, which give consumers a new weapon in this battle.

Lemon laws provide a procedure for consumers to follow to correct recurring problems in vehicles. Lemon laws establish an administrative procedure that is less formal than a court proceeding. Most of these laws require that an arbitrator decide the dispute between a consumer and a car dealer. Lemon laws stipulate that if the dealer or manufacturer does not correct a recurring defect in a vehicle within a specified number of tries (e.g., four tries) within a specified period of time (e.g., two years), the purchaser can rescind the purchase and recover a full refund of the vehicle's purchase price.

To properly invoke a state's lemon law, a consumer should take the following steps:

1. Notify the car dealer immediately of any mechanical or other problems that appear in the vehicle.

2. Take the vehicle back to the dealer for the statutory number of times to give the dealer the opportunity to correct the defect.

3. File a claim with the appropriate state agency, seeking arbitration of the claim if the defect is not corrected during the number of times and time period established by the state's lemon law.

4. Attend the arbitration hearing and present evidence to substantiate the claim that the vehicle suffered from a defect that was not corrected by the dealer or manufacturer within the statutorily prescribed period.

Law & Ethics Questions

1. **ETHICS** In general, do you think automobile dealerships are very scrupulous?

2. **ETHICS** Are lemon laws needed to protect consumers?

Web Exercise

1. **WEB** Use *www.google.com* to find out whether your state has a lemon law.

Unfair and Deceptive Practices

The **Federal Trade Commission Act (FTC Act)** was enacted in 1914.[5] The **Federal Trade Commission (FTC)** was created the following year. The FTC is empowered to enforce the FTC Act as well as other federal consumer protection statutes.

Section 5 of the FTC Act, as amended, prohibits *unfair and deceptive practices*. It has been used extensively to regulate business conduct. This section gives the FTC the authority to bring an administrative proceeding to attack a deceptive or unfair practice. If, after a public administrative hearing, the FTC finds a violation of Section 5, it may order a cease-and-desist order, an affirmative disclosure to consumers, corrective advertising, or the like. The FTC may sue in state or federal court to obtain compensation on behalf of consumers. The decision of the FTC may be appealed to federal court.

Web Exercises

1. **WEB** Visit the website of the Federal Trade Commission, at *www.ftc.gov*.
2. **WEB** Visit the website of the Office of Consumer Protection of the FTC, at *www.ftc.gov/bcp/consumer.shtm*. What kind of information is provided on this website?

False and Deceptive Advertising

Advertising is false and deceptive under Section 5 of the FTC Act if it (1) contains misinformation or omits important information that is likely to mislead a "reasonable consumer" or (2) makes an unsubstantiated claim (e.g., "This product is 33 percent better than our competitor's"). Proof of actual deception is not required. Statements of opinion and "sales talk" (e.g., "This is a great car") do not constitute false and deceptive advertising.

BAIT AND SWITCH **Bait and switch** is a type of deceptive advertising under Section 5 of the FTC Act. It occurs when a seller advertises the availability of a low-cost discounted item (the "bait") to attract customers to its store. Once the customers are in the store, however, the seller pressures them to purchase more expensive merchandise (the "switch"). The FTC states that a bait and switch occurs if the seller refuses to show consumers the advertised merchandise, discourages employees from selling the advertised merchandise, or fails to have adequate quantities of the merchandise available.

Door-to-Door Sales

Some salespersons sell merchandise and services door-to-door. In some situations, these salespersons use aggressive sales tactics to overcome a consumer's resistance to the sale. To protect consumers from ill-advised decisions, many states have enacted laws that give the consumer a certain number of days to rescind (cancel) a door-to-door sales contract. The usual period is three days. The consumer must send a required notice of cancellation to the seller. An FTC regulation requires the salesperson to permit cancellation of the contract within the stipulated time.

The following is a classic case of false and deceptive advertising.

C A S E **34.3**

Deceptive Advertising

U.S. SUPREME COURT

Federal Trade Commission v. Colgate-Palmolive Company

380 U.S. 374, 85 S.Ct. 1035, 13 L.Ed.2d 904,
Web 1965 U.S. Lexis 2300 (1965)
Supreme Court of the United States

❝We agree with the FTC that the undisclosed use of Plexiglas in the present commercial was a material deceptive practice.❞

—Chief Justice Warren

Facts

The Colgate-Palmolive Co. (Colgate) manufactured and sold a shaving cream called "Rapid Shave." Colgate hired Ted Bates & Company (Bates), an advertising agency, to prepare television commercials designed to show that Rapid Shave could shave the toughest beards. With Colgate's consent, Bates prepared a television commercial that included the sandpaper test. The announcer informed the audience, "To prove Rapid Shave's super-moisturizing power, we put it right from the can onto this tough, dry sandpaper. And off in a stroke."

While the announcer was speaking, Rapid Shave was applied to a substance that appeared to be sandpaper, and immediately a razor was shown shaving the substance clean. Evidence showed that the substance resembling sandpaper was in fact a simulated prop or "mock-up" made of Plexiglas to which sand had been glued. The Federal Trade Commission (FTC) issued a complaint against Colgate and Bates, alleging a violation of Section 5 of the FTC Act. The FTC held against the defendants. The Court of Appeals reversed. The FTC appealed to the U.S. Supreme Court.

Issue

Did the defendants engage in false and deceptive advertising in violation of Section 5 of the FTC Act?

Language of the U.S. Supreme Court

We agree with the FTC that the undisclosed use of Plexiglas in the present commercial was a material deceptive practice. Respondents claim that it will be impractical to inform the viewing public that it is not seeing an actual test, experiment or demonstration, but we think it inconceivable that the ingenious advertising world will be unable, if it so desires, to conform to the FTC's insistence that the public be not misinformed.

If it becomes impossible or impracticable to show simulated demonstrations on television in a truthful manner, this indicates that television is not a medium that lends itself to this type of commercial. Similarly unpersuasive is respondents' objection that the FTC's decision discriminates against sellers whose product claims cannot be verified on television without the use of stimulation. All methods of advertising do not equally favor every seller. If the inherent limitations of a method do not permit its use in the way a seller desires, the seller cannot by material misrepresentation compensate for those limitations.

Decision

The U.S. Supreme Court held that Colgate and Bates had engaged in false and deceptive advertising. The Supreme Court reversed the decision of the Court of Appeals and remanded the case for further proceeding.

Law & Ethics Questions

1. **ETHICS** Does the government owe a duty to protect consumers from false and misleading business practices?
2. **ETHICS** Did Colgate and Bates act ethically in this case? Do you think the viewing public believed the commercial?
3. **ETHICS** Do you think many companies engage in false and deceptive advertising? Can you think of any examples?

Web Exercises

1. **WEB** For the complete opinion of this case, go to *www.prenhall.com/cheesemancases*.
2. **WEB** Visit the website of the U.S. Supreme Court, at *www.supremecourtus.gov*, and try to find documents that relate to this case.
3. **WEB** Visit the website of Colgate-Palmolive Company, at *www.colgate.com*.
4. **WEB** Use *www.google.com* to find an article about a case of false and deceptive advertising. Read it.

ETHICS SPOTLIGHT

Kraft No Longer the "Big Cheese"

> **❝***Kraft's arguments lack merit. . . . [The FTC] rationally concluded that a 30% exaggeration of calcium content was a nutritionally significant claim that would affect consumer purchasing decisions.* **❞**
>
> —Judge Flaum

Kraft, Inc., the king of cheese producers in the United Sates, makes and sells Singles American Pasteurized Process Cheese slices (Singles) that can be used on sandwiches and for other purposes. When Kraft's dominant position in this market began to be eroded by imitation cheese slices made from vegetable oil and other products, Kraft designed a new advertising campaign to tout the health benefits of its Singles. In its campaign, Kraft advertised that (1) a slice of its Singles contained the same amount of calcium as 5 ounces of milk and (2) its Singles contained more calcium than most imitation slices.

The Federal Trade Commission (FTC) filed charges against Kraft, claiming that neither of these statements was true. The FTC found that although Kraft uses 5 ounces of milk in making each Kraft Single, about one-third of the calcium contained in the milk is lost during processing. The FTC also found that most imitation slices contain the same amount of calcium as Kraft Singles. The FTC held that Kraft's advertisements constituted unfair and deceptive advertising in violation of Section 5 of the Federal Trade Commission Act because they were likely to mislead consumers. The FTC ordered Kraft to cease and desist from making these misrepresentations. The Court of Appeals upheld the FTC's order. The court stated, "Kraft's arguments lack merit. The FTC found solid evidence that consumers placed great importance on calcium consumption and from this reasonably inferred that a claim quantifying the calcium in Kraft Singles would be material to consumers. It rationally concluded that a 30% exaggeration of calcium content was a nutritionally significant claim that would affect consumer purchasing decisions." *Kraft, Inc. v. Federal Trade Commission*, 970 F.2d 311, **Web** 1992 U.S. App. Lexis 17575 (United States Court of Appeals for the Seventh Circuit)

Law & Ethics Questions

1. **ETHICS** Were the claims made by Kraft truthful?
2. **ETHICS** Why do you think Kraft made these claims?

Web Exercises

1. **WEB** Visit the website of Kraft Foods, at *www.kraft.com*. Can you find any information about Kraft Singles?
2. **WEB** Use *www.google.com* to find an article that discusses a company's false advertising of a product or service. Read it.

Environmental Protection

In the 1970s, the federal government began enacting statutes to protect our nation's air and water from pollution, to regulate hazardous wastes, and to protect wildlife. In many instances, states enacted their own environmental laws that now coexist with federal law. These laws provide both civil and criminal penalties. *Environmental protection* is one of the most important, and costly, issues facing business and society today.

> Good government is an empire of laws.
>
> John Adams
> *Thoughts on Government (1776)*

Environmental Protection Agency

In 1970, Congress created the **Environmental Protection Agency (EPA)** to coordinate the implementation and enforcement of the federal environmental protection laws. The EPA has broad rule-making powers to adopt regulations to advance the laws that it is empowered to administer. The agency also has adjudicative powers to hold hearings, make decisions, and order remedies for violations of federal environmental laws. In addition, the EPA can initiate judicial proceedings in court against suspected violators of federal environmental laws.

Web Exercise

1. **WEB** Visit the website of the U.S. Environmental Protection Agency, at *www.epa.gov*. Click on "Climate Change." What type of information appears on this page?

Environmental Impact Statement

The **National Environmental Policy Act (NEPA)** became effective January 1, 1970.[6] The NEPA mandates that the federal government consider the "adverse impact" of proposed legislation, rule making, or other federal government action on the environment before the action is implemented.

The NEPA and rules adopted thereunder require that an **environmental impact statement (EIS)** must be prepared for any proposed legislation or major federal action that significantly affects the quality of the human environment. The purpose of the EIS is to provide enough information about the environment to enable the federal government to determine the feasibility of the project. The EIS is also used as evidence in court whenever a federal action is challenged as violating the NEPA or other federal environmental protection laws. Examples of actions that require an EIS include proposals to build new federally funded highways, to license nuclear plants, and the like.

The EIS must (1) describe the affected environment, (2) describe the impact of the proposed federal action on the environment, (3) identify and discuss alternatives to the proposed action, (4) list the resources that will be committed to the action, and (5) contain a cost–benefit analysis of the proposed action and alternative actions. Expert professionals, such as engineers, geologists, and accountants, may be consulted during the preparation of an EIS.

Once an EIS is prepared, it is subject to public review, and the public has 30 days to submit comments to the EPA. After the comments have been received and reviewed, the EPA will issue an order that states whether the proposed federal action may proceed. Decisions of the EPA are appealable to the appropriate U.S. Court of Appeals.

Most states and many local governments have enacted laws that require an EIS to be prepared regarding proposed state and local government action as well as private development.

Web Exercise

1. **WEB** Use *www.google.com* to find an EIS that has been filed regarding a proposed government project in your state.

Air Pollution

One of the major problems facing the United States is **air pollution**. The **Clean Air Act** was enacted in 1963 to assist states in dealing with air pollution. The act was amended in 1970 and 1977 and, most recently, by the **Clean Air Act Amendments** of 1990.[7] The Clean Air Act, as amended, provides comprehensive regulation of air quality in this country.

Sources of Air Pollution

Substantial amounts of air pollution are emitted by **stationary sources** (e.g., industrial plants, oil refineries, public utilities). The Clean Air Act requires states to identify major stationary sources and develop plans to reduce air pollution from these sources. Automobile and other vehicle emissions are one of the major sources of air pollution in his country. In an effort to control emissions from these **mobile sources of air pollution**, the Clean Air Act requires air pollution controls to be installed on motor vehicles. Emission standards have been set for automobiles, trucks, buses, motorcycles, and airplanes. In addition, the Clean Air Act authorizes the EPA to regulate air pollution caused by fuel and fuel additives.

National Ambient Air Quality Standards

The Clean Air Act directs the EPA to establish **national ambient air quality standards (NAAQS)** for certain pollutants. These standards are set at two different levels: primary (to protect human beings) and secondary (to protect vegetation, matter, climate, visibility, and economic values). Specific standards have been established for carbon monoxide, nitrogen oxide, sulfur oxide, ozone, lead, and particulate matter.

Although the EPA establishes air quality standards, the states are responsible for their enforcement. The federal government has the right to enforce these air pollution standards if the states fail to do so. Each state is required to prepare a **state implementation plan (SIP)** that sets out how the state plans to meet the federal standards. The EPA has divided each state into **air quality control regions (AQCRs)**. Each region is monitored to ensure compliance.

Web Exercise

1. **WEB** Use *www.google.com* to find an article or a website that discusses national ambient air quality standards (NAAQS) set for your state or region.

Nonattainment Areas

Regions that do not meet air quality standards are designated **nonattainment areas**. A nonattainment area is classified into one of five categories—marginal, moderate, serious, severe, and extreme—based on the degree to which it exceeds the ozone standard. Deadlines are established for areas to meet the attainment level. States must submit compliance plans that (1) identify major sources of air pollution and require them to install pollution control equipment, (2) institute permit systems for new stationary sources, and (3) implement inspection programs to monitor mobile sources. States that fail to develop or implement approved plans are subject to the following sanctions: loss of federal highway funds and limitations on new sources of emissions (e.g., the EPA can prohibit the construction of a new pollution-causing industrial plant in the nonattainment area).

The Clean Air Act was at issue in the following case.

CASE 34.4
Air Pollution

U.S. SUPREME COURT

Whitman, Administrator of Environmental Protection Agency v. American Trucking Association

531 U.S. 457, 121 S.Ct. 903, 149 L.Ed.2d 1,
Web 2001 U.S. Lexis 1952 (2001)
Supreme Court of the United States

> 66 *The EPA, based on the information about health effects contained in the technical criteria documents, is to identify the maximum airborne concentration of a pollutant that the public health can tolerate.* 99
>
> —Justice Scalia

Facts

Section 109 of the federal Clean Air Act requires the administrator of the EPA, a federal administrative agency, to set NAAQS for air pollutants. Section 109 instructs the EPA to set NAAQS at levels "to protect the public health" with "an adequate margin of safety." Pursuant to Section 109, the EPA issued new standards for ozone and particular matter emitted from the operation of trucks. The American Trucking Association sued the EPA, arguing that the EPA must consider the cost caused to trucking firms before issuing the NAAQS. The EPA argued that it did not have to do so under the statute. The U.S. District Court held for the American Trucking Association, but the U.S. Court of Appeals held for the EPA on this issue. The U.S. Supreme Court granted review.

Issue

Under Section 109 of the federal Clean Air Act, must the EPA consider the cost imposed on trucking firms before setting NAAQS for ozone and particulate matter emissions from trucks?

Language of the U.S. Supreme Court

Section 109 instructs the EPA to set primary ambient air quality standards "the attainment and maintenance of which are requisite to protect the public health" with "an adequate margin of safety." This text does not permit the EPA to consider costs in setting the standards. The language is absolute. The EPA, based on the information about health effects contained in the technical criteria documents, is to identify the maximum airborne concentration of a pollutant that the public health can tolerate, decrease the concentration to provide an adequate margin of safety, and set the standard at that level. Nowhere are the costs of achieving such a standard made part of that initial calculation.

Respondent argues many more factors than air pollution affect public health. In particular, the economic cost of implementing a very stringent standard might produce losses sufficient to offset the health gains achieved in cleaning the air—for example, by closing down whole industries and thereby impoverishing the workers and consumers dependent upon those industries. That is unquestionably true. Accordingly, to prevail in their present challenge, respondent must show a textual commitment of authority to the EPA to consider costs in setting NAAQS under Section 109. Congress does not alter the fundamental details of a regulatory scheme.

Decision

The U.S. Supreme Court held that the statutory language of Section 109 of the Clean Air Act does not require the EPA to consider the cost to trucking firms for implementing the NAAQS set by the EPA. The Supreme Court affirmed the decision of the Court of Appeals in favor of the EPA.

Law & Ethics Questions

1. Do you think the statutory language of Section 109 was clear in this case?
2. **ETHICS** Would the "public health" be compromised under the trucking firms' argument? Why did the trucking firms resist the NAAQS set by the EPA?
3. What are the economic consequences of the Supreme Court's ruling? Explain.

Web Exercises

1. **WEB** For the complete opinion of this case, go to *www.prenhall.com/cheesemancases*.
2. **WEB** Visit the website of the U.S. Supreme Court, at *www.supremecourtus.gov*, and try to find documents that relate to this case.
3. **WEB** Visit the website of the American Trucking Association, at *www.trucklines.com*.
4. **WEB** Use *www.google.com* to find an article that discusses the health problems associated with air pollution. Read it.

CONTEMPORARY ENVIRONMENT
Indoor Air Pollution

According to officials of the EPA, the air inside some buildings may be 100 times more polluted than outside air. Doctors increasingly attribute a wide range of symptoms to **indoor air pollution**, or **sick building syndrome**. Indoor air pollution has two primary causes. In an effort to reduce dependence on foreign oil, many recently constructed office buildings have been overly insulated and built with sealed windows and no outside air ducts. As a result, no fresh air enters many workplaces. This lack of fresh air can cause headaches, fatigue, and dizziness among workers.

The other chief cause of sick building syndrome, which is believed to affect up to one-third of U.S. office buildings, is hazardous chemicals and construction materials. In the office, these include everything from asbestos to noxious fumes omitted from copy machines, carbonless paper, and cleaning fluids. In the home, radon, an odorless gas that is emitted from the natural breakdown of uranium in soil, poses a particularly widespread danger. Radon gas damages and may destroy lung tissue. The costs of eliminating these conditions can be colossal.

Experts predict that sick building syndrome is likely to spawn a flood of litigation and that a wide range of parties will be sued. Manufacturers, employers, home sellers, builders, engineers, and architects will increasingly be forced to defend themselves against tort and breach of contract actions filed by homeowners, employees, and others affected by indoor air pollution. Insurance companies will undoubtedly be drawn into costly lawsuits stemming from indoor air pollution.

Web Exercise

1. **WEB** Use *www.google.com* to find a website that discusses the dangers of indoor air pollution. Read it.

Water Pollution

Water pollution affects human health, recreation, agriculture, and business. Pollution of waterways by industry and humans has caused severe ecological and environmental problems, including making water sources unsafe for human consumption, fish, birds, and animals. The federal government has enacted a comprehensive scheme of statutes and regulations to prevent and control water pollution.

In 1948, Congress enacted the **Federal Water Pollution Control Act (FWPCA)** to regulate water pollution. This act has been amended several times. As amended, it is simply referred to as the **Clean Water Act**.[8] This act is administered by the EPA.

Pursuant to the Clean Water Act, the EPA has established water quality standards that define which bodies of water can be used for public drinking water, recreation (e.g., swimming), propagation of fish and wildlife, and agricultural and industrial uses.

States are primarily responsible for enforcing the provisions of the Clean Water Act and EPA regulations adopted thereunder. If a state fails to do so, the federal government may enforce the act.

Point Sources of Water Pollution

The Clean Water Act authorizes the EPA to establish water pollution control standards for **point sources of water pollution** (i.e., mines, manufacturing plants, paper mills, electric utility plants, municipal sewage plants, other stationary sources of water pollution). Dischargers of pollutants are required to keep records, maintain monitoring equipment, and keep samples of discharges.

The U.S. Supreme Court addressed an issue related to water pollution in the following case.

CASE **34.5**
Water Pollution

U.S. SUPREME COURT
Friends of the Earth, Incorporated v. Laidlaw Environmental Services (TOC), Inc.
528 U.S. 167, 120 S.Ct. 693, 145 L.Ed.2d 610,
Web 2000 U.S. Lexis 501 (2000)
Supreme Court of the United States

“*It can scarcely be doubted that, for a plaintiff who is injured or faces the threat of future injury due to illegal conduct ongoing at the time of suit, a sanction that effectively abates that conduct and prevents its recurrence provides a form of redress.*”

—Justice Ginsburg

Facts

Laidlaw Environmental Services (TOC), Inc., operated a hazardous waste incinerator facility in Roebuck, South Carolina, where it discharged wastes into the North Tyger River. Between 1987 and 1995, Laidlaw discharged wastes into the river that exceeded the mercury limits allowed at the site. Mercury is a dangerous pollutant. The South Carolina Department of Health and Environmental Control (DHEC) sued Laidlaw. Laidlaw, which had gained an economic benefit of over $1 million by making these illegal discharges, reached a settlement with the DHEC whereby it paid $100,000 in penalties.

The Friends of the Earth, Incorporated (FOE), and other environmental groups brought a lawsuit against Laidlaw, seeking to obtain civil penalties permitted in civil citizens' lawsuits under the federal Clean Water Act. Laidlaw argued that FOE could not sue because Laidlaw had already reached a settlement with the state of South Carolina. The U.S. District Court held for FOE and ordered Laidlaw to pay $405,800 in civil penalties and ordered a hearing to determine the amount of attorneys' fees to be awarded to FOE. Laidlaw appealed, and the Court of Appeals reversed. FOE appealed to the U.S. Supreme Court.

Issue

Does settlement with a state for environmental violations make moot a civil citizens' lawsuit under the federal Clean Water Act?

Language of the U.S. Supreme Court

It can scarcely be doubted that, for a plaintiff who is injured or faces the threat of future injury due to illegal conduct ongoing at the time of suit, a sanction that effectively abates that conduct and prevents its recurrence provides a form of redress. Civil penalties can fit that description. To the extent that they encourage defendants to discontinue current violations and deter them from committing future ones, they afford redress to citizen plaintiffs who are injured or threatened with injury as a consequence of ongoing unlawful conduct.

Decision

The U.S. Supreme Court held that defendant Laidlaw was subject to the Friends of the Earth's civil-citizen lawsuit for damages under the Clean Water Act even though Laidlaw had previously been sued and reached a settlement with the state of South Carolina. The Supreme Court remanded the case for a determination of the attorneys' fees to be awarded to Friends of the Earth.

Law & Ethics Questions

1. Should citizens be permitted to bring lawsuits to enforce environmental laws? Or should only the governments have this power?
2. **ETHICS** Did Laidlaw act ethically in this case? Explain.
3. **ETHICS** Do you think that Laidlaw came out ahead financially in its settlement with the state of South Carolina? Explain.

Web Exercises

1. **WEB** For the complete opinion of this case, go to *www.prenhall.com/cheesemancases*.
2. **WEB** Visit the website of the U.S. Supreme Court, at *www.supremecourtus.gov*, and try to find documents that relate to this case.
3. **WEB** Use *www.google.com* to find a website that discusses the activities of Friends of the Earth. What does the article discuss?
4. **WEB** Use *www.google.com* to find an article that discusses water pollution in your state. Read it.

Thermal Pollution

The Clean Water Act expressly forbids **thermal pollution** because the discharge of heated waters or materials into the nation's waterways may upset the ecological balance; decrease the oxygen content of water; and harm fish, birds, and other animals that use the waterways.[9] Sources of thermal pollution (e.g., electric utility companies, manufacturing plants) are subject to the provisions of the Clean Water Act and regulations adopted by the EPA.

Wetlands

Wetlands are defined as areas that are inundated or saturated by surface water or ground water that support vegetation typically adapted for life in saturated soil conditions. Wetlands include swamps, marshes, bogs, and similar areas that support birds, animals, and vegetative life. The Clean Water Act forbids the filling or dredging of wetlands unless a permit has been obtained from the **Army Corps of Engineers (Corps)**. The Corps is empowered to adopt regulations and conduct administrative proceedings to enforce the act.

Safe Drinking Water Act

The **Safe Drinking Water Act**,[10] which was enacted in 1974 and amended in 1986, authorizes the EPA to establish national primary drinking water standards (setting the minimum quality of water for human consumption). The act also prohibits the dumping of wastes into wells used for drinking water. The states are primarily responsible for enforcing the act. If a state fails to do so, the federal government can enforce the act.

The following case involved the definition of *navigable waters* under the Clean Water Act.

CASE 34.6
Water Pollution

U.S. SUPREME COURT
Solid Waste Agency of Northern Cook County, Illinois v. United States Army Corps of Engineers

531 U.S. 159, 121 S.Ct. 675, 148 L.Ed.2d 576,
Web 2001 U.S. Lexis 640 (2001)
Supreme Court of the United States

> ❝*Congress passed the Clean Water Act for the stated purpose of restoring and maintaining the chemical, physical, and biological integrity of the Nation's waters.*❞
>
> —Chief Justice Rehnquist

Facts

Section 404 of the federal Clean Water Act (CWA) regulates the discharge of dredged or fill material into *navigable waters*. The U.S. Army Corps of Engineers (Corps) is authorized to enforce this statute and to issue permits for discharge of dredged or fill material into navigable waters in the United States. The Solid Waste Agency of Northern Cook County, Illinois (Agency), a consortium of 23 suburban Chicago cities and villages, located a 533-acre parcel of real property that was a closed sand and gravel pit mining operation as a proposed disposal site for baled nonhazardous solid waste. Long since abandoned, the old mining site had permanent and seasonal water ponds of varying size and depth that served several species of migrating birds. The ponds were not connected to any water tributary but were filled by rain water and melting snow. When the Corps refused to issue a permit, the Agency sued the Corps, arguing that the Corps had no jurisdiction over the site because it did not contain any *navigable waters*. The District Court held for the Corps, and the Court of Appeals affirmed. The U.S. Supreme Court granted review.

Issue

Does the gravel and sand pit contain navigable waters that give the Army Corps of Engineers jurisdiction over the site?

Language of the U.S. Supreme Court

Congress passed the Clean Water Act for the stated purpose of restoring and maintaining the chemical, physical, and biological integrity of the Nation's waters. Relevant here, Section 404 authorizes the U.S. Army Corps of Engineers to regulate the discharge of fill material into "navigable waters," which the statute defines as "the waters of the United States, including the territorial seas." The Corps has interpreted these words to cover the abandoned gravel pit at issue here because it is used as habitat for migratory birds. We thus decline the Corps's invitation to hold that isolated ponds, some only seasonal, wholly located within Illinois, fall under Section 404's definition of "navigable waters" because they serve as habitat for

migratory birds. As counsel for the Corps conceded at oral argument, such a ruling would assume that the use of the word *navigable* in the statute does not have any independent significance.

Decision

The U.S. Supreme Court held that the ponds located on the sand and gravel pit are not *navigable waters* as defined by Section 404 of the Clean Water Act. Therefore, the U.S. Army Corps of Engineers does not have authority or jurisdiction over these ponds. The U.S. Supreme Court reversed the judgment of the Court of Appeals.

Law & Ethics Questions

1. Do you think that the U.S. Supreme Court properly interpreted the term *navigable waters* as used in Section 404 of the Clean Water Act?
2. **ETHICS** Did the petitioner Solid Waste Agency act ethically in placing a waste disposal site on an area where the habitat of several migrating birds could be destroyed?
3. In the United States, has a proper balance been struck between the protection of the environment and the ability of businesses to operate without too much burden from these laws? Explain.

Web Exercises

1. **WEB** For the complete opinion of this case, go to *www.prenhall.com/cheesemancases*.
2. **WEB** Visit the website of the U.S. Supreme Court, at *www.supremecourtus.gov*, and try to find documents that relate to this case.
3. **WEB** Visit the website of the U.S. Army Corps of Engineers, at *www.usace.army.mil*. What is the mission of the Army Corps of Engineers?
4. **WEB** Use *www.google.com* to find an article that discusses the plant and animal life in wetlands. Read it.

Ocean Protection

The **Marine Protection, Research, and Sanctuaries Act**,[11] enacted in 1972, extends environmental protection to the oceans. It (1) requires a permit for dumping wastes and other foreign materials into ocean waters and (2) establishes marine sanctuaries in ocean waters as far seaward as the edge of the Continental Shelf and in the Great Lakes and their connecting waters.

The Clean Water Act authorizes the U.S. government to clean up oil spills and spills of other hazardous substances in ocean waters within 12 miles of the shore and on the Continental Shelf and to recover the cleanup costs from responsible parties.

In the past, there have been several major oil spills from oil tankers in ocean waters off the coast of the United States. These oil spills caused significant damage to sea life, animal life, and human life, as well as to their habitats. In response, Congress enacted the federal **Oil Pollution Act** of 1990,[12] which is administered by the U.S. Coast Guard. This act requires the oil industry to adopt procedures and contingency plans to readily respond to and clean up oil spills. A tanker owner-operator must prove that it is fully insured to cover any liability that may occur from an oil spill. The act also requires oil tankers to have double hulls by 2015.

ETHICS SPOTLIGHT
Illegal Dumping of Pollutants

> 66*There was absolutely no acceptance of responsibility in this case. No remorse whatsoever was shown by Irby.*99

—Judge Murnaghan

Mark Irby was plant manager of a wastewater treatment plant. The record shows that Irby ordered employees of the plant to bypass the treatment system after hours and to discharge approximately 500,000 gallons of raw, untreated sewage and partially treated sludge sewage at least twice a week for two years into the Reedy River. The District Court found that these discharges caused environmental damage. Irby was charged with criminal violation of the Clean Water Act. The jury convicted him of six criminal violations of the act, and the Court sentenced him to the maximum allowable jail sentence of 33 months. Irby challenged his sentence.

The Court of Appeals held that Irby exercised decision-making authority in directing the employees of the wastewater treatment plant to discharge the untreated sewage into the Reedy River. The court also held that the offense resulted in an ongoing, continuous, and repetitive discharge of pollutants into the environment, thus justifying the imposition of the 33 months of jail time. The Court stated, "There was absolutely no acceptance of responsibility in this case. No remorse whatsoever was shown by Irby." *United States v. Irby*, **Web** 1991 U.S. App. Lexis 21687 (United States Court of Appeals for the Fourth Circuit)

Law & Ethics Questions

1. **ETHICS** Did Irby act ethically in this case?

2. **ETHICS** What is the incentive for businesses and organizations to avoid environmental laws?

INTERNATIONAL LAW
European Union Adopts Tough Environmental Law

The United States is not the only country in the world facing environmental challenges and doing something about it. The **European Union (EU)** is a regional organization that has 27 members in Europe. In 2006, after years of debate, the EU adopted the world's most stringent law aimed at protecting the environment from thousands of toxic chemicals. The legislation, called the **Registration, Evaluation, and Authorization of Chemicals (REACH)**, will replace existing national laws and provide uniform environmental rules throughout the EU. A new European Chemicals Agency located in Helsinki, Finland, will become the central regulatory agency to administer the new law.

The new law regulates about 30,000 toxic substances that affect people and the environment. It either bans or restricts the 1,500 most hazardous chemicals. REACH requires industries to register chemicals and submit health and safety data. The law also requires that the most hazardous chemicals be replaced with safer alternatives. The new law will be phased in over an 11-year period.

The new EU environmental legislation will have far-reaching effects on industries and products worldwide. Any company wishing to sell or distribute chemicals or products containing chemicals in nations of the EU must meet the stringent restrictions established by REACH.

Web Exercise

1. **WEB** Visit the website of the European Union (EU), at
   http://userpage.chemie.fu-berlin.de/adressen/eu.html.

Toxic Substances and Hazardous Waste

Many chemicals used for agriculture, industry, and mining contain **toxic substances** that cause cancer, birth defects, and other health-related problems in human beings, as well as injury or death to birds, fish, other animals, and vegetation. Many chemical compounds that are used in the manufacture of products are toxic (e.g., PCBs, asbestos). Hundreds of new chemicals and chemical compounds that may be toxic are discovered each year.

Wastes, which often contain hazardous substances that can harm the environment or pose a danger to human health, are generated by agriculture, mining, industry, other businesses, and households. Wastes consist of garbage, sewage, industrial discharges, old equipment, and such. The mishandling and disposal of **hazardous wastes** can cause air, water, and land pollution.

Toxic Substances Control

In 1976, Congress enacted the **Toxic Substances Control Act**[13] and gave the EPA authority to administer the act. The act requires the EPA to identify **toxic air pollutants** that cause serious illness or death to humans. So far, more than 200 chemicals have been listed as toxic, including asbestos, mercury, vinyl chloride, benzene, beryllium, and radionuclides.

The act requires the EPA to establish standards for toxic chemicals and requires stationary sources to install equipment and technology to control emissions of toxic substances. EPA standards for toxic substances are set without regard to economic or technological feasibility. The act requires manufacturers and processors to test new chemicals to determine their effects on human health and the environment and to report the results to the EPA before they can be marketed.

The EPA may limit or prohibit the manufacture and sale of toxic substances, and it can remove them from commerce if it finds that they pose an imminent hazard or an unreasonable risk of injury to human health or the environment. The EPA also requires special labeling of toxic substances.

Insecticides, Fungicides, and Rodenticides

Farmers and ranchers use chemical pesticides, herbicides, fungicides, and rodenticides to kill insects, weeds, and pests. Evidence shows that the use of some of these chemicals on food, and their residual accumulation in soil, poses health hazards. In 1947, Congress enacted the **Insecticide, Fungicide, and Rodenticide Act**, which gave the federal government authority to regulate pesticides and related chemicals. This act, which was substantially amended in 1972,[14] is administered by the EPA. Under the act, pesticides must be registered with the EPA before they can be sold. The EPA may suspend the registration of a registered pesticide that it finds poses an imminent danger or emergency.

Hazardous Waste

The disposal of hazardous wastes sometimes causes **land pollution**. In 1976, Congress enacted the **Resource Conservation and Recovery Act (RCRA)**,[15] which regulates the disposal of new hazardous wastes. This act, which has been amended several times, authorizes the EPA to regulate facilities that generate, treat, store, transport, and dispose of hazardous wastes. States have primary responsibility for implementing the standards established by the act and EPA regulations.

The act defines *hazardous waste* as a solid waste that may cause or significantly contribute to an increase in mortality or serious illness or pose a hazard to human health or the environment if improperly managed. The EPA has designated substances that are toxic, radioactive, or corrosive or that ignite as hazardous and can add to the list of hazardous wastes as needed.

The EPA also establishes standards and procedures for the safe treatment, storage, disposal, and transportation of hazardous wastes. Under the act, the EPA is authorized to regulate underground storage facilities, such as underground gasoline tanks.

LANDMARK LAW

Superfund

In 1980, Congress enacted the **Comprehensive Environmental Response, Compensation, and Liability Act (CERCLA)**, which is commonly called the **Superfund** [42 U.S.C. Sections 9601–9675]. The act, which was significantly amended in 1986, is administered by the EPA. The act gave the federal government a mandate to deal with hazardous wastes that have been spilled, stored, or abandoned. The Superfund provides for the creation of a government fund to finance the cleanup of hazardous waste sites (hence the name *Superfund*). The fund is financed through taxes on chemicals, feedstocks, motor fuels, and other products that contain hazardous substances.

The Superfund requires the EPA to (1) identify sites in the United States where hazardous wastes have been disposed, stored, abandoned, or spilled and (2) rank these sites regarding the severity of the risk. When it ranks the sites, the EPA considers factors such as the types of hazardous waste, the toxicity of the wastes, the types of pollution (air, water, land, or other pollution), the number of people potentially affected by the risk, and other factors. The hazardous waste sites with the highest ranking are put on the National Priority List. The sites on this list receive first consideration for cleanup. The EPA has the authority to clean up hazardous priority or nonpriority sites quickly to prevent fire, explosion, contamination of drinking water, and other imminent danger.

The EPA can order a responsible party to clean up a hazardous waste site. If that party fails to do so, the EPA can clean up the site and recover the cost of the cleanup. The Superfund imposes strict liability—that is, liability without fault. The EPA can recover the cost of the cleanup from (1) the generator who deposited the wastes, (2) the transporter of the wastes to the site, (3) the owner of the site at the time of the disposal, and (4) the current owner and operator of the site. The Superfund permits states and private parties who clean up hazardous waste sites to seek reimbursement from the fund.

Law & Ethics Questions

1. What does the Superfund law provide? Explain.

2. **ETHICS** What is strict liability? Is it ethical for the government to recover from an owner of a polluted real estate site even though the owner did not cause the pollution?

Nuclear Waste

Nuclear-powered fuel plants create radioactive wastes that maintain a high level of *radioactivity*. Radioactivity can cause injury and death to humans and other life and can also cause severe damage to the environment. Accidents, human error, faulty construction, and such can all be causes of **radiation pollution**.

The **Nuclear Regulatory Commission (NRC)**, which was created by Congress in 1977, licenses the construction and opening of commercial nuclear power plants. It continually monitors the operation of nuclear power plants and may close a plant if safety violations are found.

The EPA is empowered to set standards for radioactivity in the environment and to regulate the disposal of radioactive waste. The EPA also regulates thermal pollution from nuclear power plants and emissions from uranium mines and mills.

The **Nuclear Waste Policy Act** of 1982[16] mandates that the federal government select and develop a permanent site for the disposal of nuclear wastes.

INTERNATIONAL LAW
Kyoto Protocol

For decades, scientists have been concerned that **greenhouse gases**—particularly from carbon dioxide created by burning coal, oil, and gas—are causing a global warming effect and creating a hole in the ozone layer around the earth. In 1997, after much debate, the countries of the world met in Kyoto, Japan, and proposed the **Kyoto Protocol**, an international treaty to reduce greenhouse gases. The deal almost fell apart; but in 2001, 178 countries agreed to abide by the rules of the Kyoto Protocol.

The Kyoto Protocol calls for the reduction of greenhouse gases worldwide to 5.2 percent below 1990 levels, with this goal to be reached by 2012. The protocol originally set targets for 39 industrialized countries; however, developing nations are not covered by the initial emission control standards. The protocol calls for member nations to create a $400 million fund to help developing nations adopt technology to reduce greenhouse gases. The United States was not a signatory to the Kyoto Protocol but instead chose to adopt its own laws to control greenhouse gas emissions.

Law & Ethics Questions

1. What is global warming? In your opinion, is this a very great problem? Explain.

2. **ETHICS** Was it ethical for the United States not to become a signatory to the Kyoto Protocol? Why did the United States not want to be bound by the Kyoto Protocol?

Web Exercise

1. **WEB** Use *www.google.com* to find an article that discusses the problems of global warming. Read it.

Monterey, California

Endangered species of birds, fish, reptiles, and other animals are protected by federal and state environmental laws.

Endangered Species

Many species of animals are endangered or threatened with extinction. The reduction of certain species of wildlife may be caused by environmental pollution, real estate development, or hunting. The **Endangered Species Act** was enacted in 1973.[17] The act, as amended, protects *endangered* and *threatened* species of animals. The secretary of the interior is empowered to declare a form of wildlife as endangered or threatened. The act requires the EPA and the Department of Commerce to designate *critical habitats* for each endangered and threatened species. Real estate and other development in these areas is prohibited or severely limited. The secretary of commerce is empowered to enforce the provisions of the act as to marine species.

In addition, the Endangered Species Act, which applies to both government and private persons, prohibits the taking of any endangered species. *Taking* is defined as an act intended to "harass, harm, pursue, hunt, shoot, wound, kill, trap, capture, or collect" an endangered animal.

Numerous other federal laws protect wildlife. These include (1) the Migratory Bird Treaty Act, (2) the Bald Eagle Protection Act, (3) the Wild Free-Roaming Horses and Burros Act, (4) the Marine Mammal Protection Act, (5) the Migratory Bird Conservation Act, (6) the Fishery Conservation and Management Act, (7) the Fish and Wildlife Coordination Act, and (8) the National Wildlife Refuge System. Many states have enacted statutes that protect and preserve wildlife.

The following is a classic case of the application by the U.S. Supreme Court of the Endangered Species Act.

CASE **34.7**
Endangered Species

U.S. SUPREME COURT
Tennessee Valley Authority v. Hill, Secretary of the Interior
437 U.S. 153, 98 S.Ct.2279, 57 L.Ed.2d 117,
Web 1978 U.S. Lexis 33
Supreme Court of the United States

> " *Examination of the language, history, and structure of the legislation under review here indicates beyond doubt that Congress intended endangered species to be afforded the highest of priorities.* "

—Chief Justice Burger

Facts

The Tennessee Valley Authority (TVA) is a wholly owned public corporation of the United States. It operates a series of dams, reservoirs, and water projects that provide electric power, irrigation, and flood control to areas in several southern states. In 1967, with appropriations from Congress, the TVA began construction of the Tellico Dam on the Little Tennessee River. When completed, the dam would impound water covering 16,500 acres, thereby converting the river's shallow, fast-flowing waters into a deep reservoir over 30 miles in length. Construction of the dam continued until 1977, when it was completed.

In 1973, a University of Tennessee ichthyologist found a previously unknown species of perch called the *Percina tanasi*—or "snail darter"—in the Little Tennessee River. After further investigation, it was determined that approximately 10,000 to 15,000 of these 3-inch, tannish-colored fish existed in the river's waters that would be flooded by the operation of the Tellico Dam. The snail darter is not found anywhere else in the world. It feeds exclusively on snails and requires substantial oxygen, both supplied by the fast-moving waters of the Little Tennessee River. The impounding of the water behind the Tellico Dam would destroy the snail darter's food and oxygen supplies, thus causing its extinction. Evidence was introduced showing that the TVA could

not, at that time, successfully transplant the snail darter to any other habitat.

Also in 1973, Congress enacted the Endangered Species Act. This act authorizes the secretary of the interior to declare species of animal life endangered and to identify the critical habitats of these creatures. When a species or its habitat is so listed, Section 7 of the act mandates that the secretary take such action as is necessary to ensure that actions of the federal government do not jeopardize the continued existence of such endangered species. The secretary declared the snail darter an endangered species and the area that would be affected by the Tellico Dam its critical habitat.

Congress continued to appropriate funds for the construction of the dam, which was completed at a cost of over $100 million. In 1976, a regional association of biological scientists, a Tennessee conservation group, and several individuals filed an action seeking to enjoin the TVA from closing the gates of the dam and impounding the water in the reservoir on the grounds that those actions would violate Section 7 of the act by causing the extinction of the snail darter. The District Court held in favor of the TVA. The Court of Appeals reversed and remanded with instructions to the District Court to issue a permanent injunction halting the operation of the Tellico Dam. The TVA appealed to the U.S. Supreme Court.

Issue

Would the TVA be in violation of the Endangered Species Act if it operated the Tellico Dam?

Language of the U.S. Supreme Court

It may seem curious to some that the survival of a relatively small number of 3-inch fish among all the countless millions of species extant would require the permanent halting of a virtually completed dam for which Congress has expended more than $100 million. We conclude, however, that the explicit provisions of the Endangered Species Act required precisely this result.

One would be hard pressed to find a statutory provision whose terms were any plainer than those in Section 7 of the Endangered Species Act. Its very words affirmatively command all federal agencies to ensure that actions authorized, funded, or carried out by them do not jeopardize the continued existence of an endangered species or result in the destruction or modification of habitat of such species. This language admits no exception. Nonetheless, petitioner TVA urges that the Act cannot reasonably be interpreted as applying to a federal project that was well under way when Congress passed the Endangered Species Act of 1973. To sustain that position, however, we would be forced to ignore the ordinary meaning of plain language.

Examination of the language, history, and structure of the legislation under review here indicates beyond doubt that Congress intended endangered species to be afforded the highest of priorities. As it was passed, the Endangered Species Act of 1973 represented the most comprehensive legislation for the preservation of endangered species ever enacted by any nation. Virtually all dealings with endangered species, including taking, possession, transportation, and sale, were prohibited.

Decision

The U.S. Supreme Court held that the Endangered Species Act prohibited the impoundment of the Little Tennessee River by the Tellico Dam. The Supreme Court affirmed the decision of the Court of Appeals that enjoined the operation of the dam. Eventually, after substantial research and investigation, it was determined that the snail darter could live in another habitat that was found for it. After the snail darter was removed, at government expense, to this new location, the TVA was permitted to close the gates of the Tellico Dam and begin its operation.

Law & Ethics Questions

1. Should the law protect endangered species? Why or why not?
2. **ETHICS** Did the TVA act ethically in this case by completing construction of the dam?
3. Do you think the cost of constructing the Tellico Dam ($100 million) should have been considered by the Court in reaching its decision?

Web Exercises

1. **WEB** For the complete opinion of this case, go to *www.prenhall.com/cheesemancases*.
2. **WEB** Visit the website of the U.S. Supreme Court, at *www.supremecourtus.gov*, and try to find documents that relate to this case.
3. **WEB** To view a photo of the dam at issue in this case, visit the website of the Tennessee Valley Authority (TVA), at *www.tva.gov*. What is the purpose of the TVA?
4. **WEB** Use *www.google.com* to find an article that discusses the snail darter and its protection from extinction. Can you find a photograph of a snail darter?

ETHICS SPOTLIGHT

Smog Swapping

Businesses have long thought that the enforcement of environmental laws was too burdensome and cumbersome, whereas environmentalists argue that current laws have not brought about sufficient reductions in pollution. Today, the "command and control" environmental regulation—the amount of pollution a plant can produce—is giving way to a market-based trading scheme. It is hoped that the new scheme will reduce pollution without unduly burdening businesses.

The Clean Air Act Amendments of 1990 include a program that allows companies to trade sulfur dioxide emissions (which are responsible for acid rain). Under this plan, companies still face strict quotas for reducing such emissions, but they are free to satisfy their limits by buying pollution credits from other companies.

Example Say that Company A uses all of its 2,000-pound limit, and it wants to add equipment that would increase the amount of emissions it produces. Company B also has a 2,000-pound limit, but it uses only 1,500 pounds. Company A can buy pollution credits from Company B. The credits are deducted in pounds of pollution allowed per day. For every 1.2 pounds of pollution eliminated by the selling company, the program allows the creation of only 1 pound of pollution by the buying company. This system is designed to reduce overall pollution. Trades cannot happen until the EPA certifies the pollution credits for sale.

The Southern California Air Quality Management District (AQMD), where the air pollution levels exceed federal health standards more than 180 days each year, has also adopted an extensive market-based trading program. The program covers the three pollutants most responsible for smog: sulfur oxide, nitrogen oxide, and reactive organic gas.

Markets are developing for the trading of pollution credits. For example, the Chicago Board of Trade will offer futures contracts on pollution credits. Manufacturers, refiners, utilities, and speculators would buy and sell pollution credits on these markets. Companies that buy credits can lock in pollution rights for the future.

Law & Ethics Questions

1. What is the public policy underlying the allowance of smog swapping?

2. **ETHICS** Is it ethical for a company that wants to pollute more than its allowed amount to purchase pollution credits on the open market to allow this excessive pollution?

Web Exercise

1. **WEB** Use *www.google.com* to find a website where carbon dioxide futures are traded.

State Environmental Protection Laws

Many state and local governments have enacted statutes and ordinances to protect the environment.

Example Most states require that an EIS or a report be prepared for any proposed state action. In addition, under their police power to protect the "health, safety, and welfare" of their residents, many states require private industry to prepare EISs for proposed developments.

Some states have enacted special environmental statutes to protect unique areas within their boundaries. For example, Florida has enacted laws to protect the Everglades, and California has enacted laws to protect its Pacific Ocean coastline.

Tibet, China

Environmental laws of all the countries of the world will protect the environment from excess pollution.

Chapter Summary

Food, Drug, and Cosmetic Safety, p. 947

1. *Federal Food, Drug, and Cosmetic Act (FDCA).* This federal statute regulates the testing, manufacture, distribution, and sale of foods, food additives, drugs, cosmetics, and medicinal products.
2. *Federal Food and Drug Administration (FDA).* This federal administrative agency is empowered to interpret and enforce the federal Food, Drug, and Cosmetic Act and other federal consumer protection laws. The FDA has the power to approve or deny applications by private companies to distribute drugs, food additives, and medicinal devices to the public.

Regulation of Food

The FDA prohibits the shipment, distribution, or sale of adulterated or misbranded food, drugs, cosmetics, or medicinal devices.

Food Labeling

The Nutrition Labeling and Education Act is a federal statute that requires food manufacturers and processors to provide nutritional information on food products and prohibits the making of scientifically unsubstantiated health claims.

Regulation of Drugs

The FDCA gives the FDA the authority to regulate the testing, manufacture, distribution, and sale of drugs. The Drug Amendment to the FDCA, enacted in 1962, gives the FDA broad powers to license new drugs in the United States.

Regulation of Cosmetics

The FDA's definition of cosmetics includes substances and preparations for cleansing, altering the appearance of, and promoting the attractiveness of a person. The FDA has issued regulations that require cosmetics to be labeled, to disclose ingredients, and to contain warnings if they are carcinogenic (cancer-causing) or otherwise dangerous to a person's health

Regulation of Medicinal Devices

In 1976, Congress enacted the Medicinal Device Amendment to the FDCA. This amendment gives the FDA authority to regulate medicinal devices, such as heart pacemakers, kidney dialysis machines, defibrillators, surgical equipment, and other diagnostic, therapeutic, and health devices.

United Nations Biosafety Protocol for Genetically Altered Foods

This United Nations–sponsored protocol requires signatory countries to place the label "May contain living modified organisms" on all genetically engineered foods.

Product Safety, p. 954

1. *Consumer Product Safety Act (CPSA).* This federal statute regulates the safety of consumer products. It created the Consumer Product Safety Commission.
2. *Consumer Product Safety Commission (CPSC).* The CPSC is a federal administrative agency that is empowered to:
   a. Interpret and enforce the Consumer Product Safety Act.
   b. Conduct research on safety.
   c. Collect data regarding injuries.

Unfair and Deceptive Practices, p. 955

1. *Federal Trade Commission (FTC).* This federal administrative agency is empowered to enforce the FTC Act and other federal consumer protection statutes.
2. *Section 5 of the Federal Trade Commission Act (FTC Act).* This federal statute prohibits unfair and deceptive practices, including false and deceptive advertising, abusive sales tactics, consumer fraud, and other unfair business practices.

False and Deceptive Advertising

Advertising is false and deceptive under Section 5 of the FTC Act if it (1) contains misinformation or omits important information that is likely to mislead a "reasonable consumer" or (2) makes an unsubstantiated claim.

Door-to-Door Sales

Many states have enacted laws that give the consumer a certain number of days to rescind (cancel) a door-to-door sales contract. The usual period is three days.

Environmental Protection, p. 957

Federal and state governments have enacted environmental protection statutes to control pollution and to penalize those who violate these statutes.

Environmental Protection Agency

The Environmental Protection Agency (EPA) is a federal administrative agency that is empowered to implement and enforce federal environmental protection statutes. The EPA can adopt regulations to interpret and enforce the laws it is authorized to administer.

Environmental Impact Statement

1. *Environmental Impact Statement (EIS).* An EIS is a document that must be prepared for all proposed legislation or major federal action that significantly affects the quality of the human environment. The EIS must (1) describe the affected environment, (2) describe the impact of the proposed federal action on the environment, (3) identify and discuss alternatives to the proposed action, (4) list the resources that will be committed to the action, and (5) contain a cost–benefit analysis of the proposed action and alternative actions.
2. *National Environmental Policy Act (NEPA).* This federal statute mandates that the federal government consider the adverse impact a federal government action would have on the environment before the action is implemented.

Air Pollution, p. 958

Air pollution is caused by factories, homes, vehicles, and the like. The Clean Air Act is a federal statute, enacted in 1963 and amended several times, that regulates air pollution.

Sources of Air Pollution

1. *Stationary sources.* Stationary sources are sources of air pollution such as industrial plants, oil refineries, and public utilities.
2. *Mobile sources.* Mobile sources are sources of air pollution such as automobiles, trucks, buses, motorcycles, and airplanes.

National Ambient Air Quality Standards

The national ambient air quality standards (NAAQS) are standards for certain pollutants set by the EPA to protect (1) human beings (primary) and (2) vegetation, matter, climate, visibility, and economic values (secondary).

1. *State implementation plan (SIP).* An SIP is a document issued by a state that explains how the state plans to meet federal air pollution standards.
2. *Air quality control regions (AQCRs).* AQCRs are divisions by the EPA of each state into geographical areas that are monitored to ensure compliance with federal air pollution standards.

Nonattainment Areas

Nonattainment areas are regions that do not meet federal air quality standards. Each is classified into one of five categories—marginal, moderate, serious, severe, and extreme—based on the degree to which it exceeds federal air quality standards. States that fail to develop or implement approved plans to correct deficiencies are subject to sanctions.

Water Pollution, p. 960

Water pollution is pollution of lakes, rivers, oceans, and other bodies of water. The Clean Water Act is a federal statute that regulates water pollution.

Point Sources of Water Pollution

Point sources of water pollution are sources of water pollution such as paper mills, manufacturing plants, electric utility plants, and sewage plants. Point sources are required to install pollution-control equipment.

Thermal Pollution

Thermal pollution involves heated water or material being discharged into waterways and upsetting the ecological balance and decreases the oxygen content. Thermal pollution is subject to the provisions of the Clean Water Act.

Wetlands

Wetlands are areas that are inundated or saturated by surface or groundwater that support vegetation typically adapted for life in such conditions. The Clean Water Act forbids the filling or dredging of wetlands unless a permit has been obtained from the Army Corps of Engineers.

Safe Drinking Water

The Safe Drinking Water Act of 1974 authorizes the EPA to establish national minimum quality of water standards for human consumption. States are primarily responsible for enforcing the act. If a state fails to do so, the federal government can enforce the act.

Ocean Protection

The Marine Protection, Research, and Sanctuaries Act of 1972 is a federal statute that extends environmental protection to oceans. It requires a permit for dumping wastes and other foreign materials into ocean waters. The Clean Water Act authorizes the U.S. government to clean up oil spills and spills of other hazardous substances in ocean waters within 12 miles of the shore and on the Continental Shelf.

Toxic Substances and Hazardous Waste, p. 964

Toxic substances are chemicals used for agricultural, industrial, and mining uses that cause injury to humans, birds, animals, fish, and vegetation. The Toxic Substances Control Act is a federal statute that requires manufacturers and processors to test new chemicals to determine their effect on human health and the environment before the EPA will allow them to be marketed. The EPA requires special labeling of toxic substances.

Insecticides, Fungicides, and Rodenticides

The federal Insecticide, Fungicide, and Rodenticide Act requires pesticides, herbicides, fungicides, and rodenticides to be registered with the EPA. The EPA may deny, suspend, or cancel registration.

Hazardous Waste

Hazardous waste is solid waste that may cause or significantly contribute to an increase in mortality or serious illness, or pose a hazard to human health or the environment, if improperly managed. Pollution of the land is generally caused by hazardous waste being disposed of in an improper manner. The Resource Conservation and Recovery Act is a federal statute that authorizes the EPA to regulate facilities that generate, treat, store, transport, and dispose of hazardous wastes.

Superfund

The Comprehensive Environmental Response, Compensation, and Liability Act (CERCLA), also called the Superfund, is a federal statute that gives the federal government a mandate to deal with hazardous wastes that have been spilled, stored, or abandoned. This act is commonly called the Superfund.

1. *Hazardous waste sites.* The Superfund requires the EPA to identify sites in the United States where hazardous wastes have been disposed, stored, spilled, or abandoned and to rank these sites regarding the severity of the risk.
2. *Superfund.* The act created a fund to finance the cleanup of hazardous waste sites (hence the name Superfund).

3. *Liability for cleanup costs.* The EPA can order a responsible party to clean up a hazardous waste site. If that party fails to do so, the EPA can clean up the site and recover the cost of the cleanup from the responsible parties.

Nuclear Waste

Nuclear waste is radioactive waste generated by nuclear-powered fuel plants.

1. *Radioactive pollution.* Emissions from radioactive wastes can cause injury and death to humans and other life and can cause severe damage to the environment.

2. *Nuclear Regulatory Commission (NRC).* The NRC is a federal agency that licenses the construction and opening of commercial nuclear power plants. The NRC may deny or revoke a license.

Endangered Species, p. 966

The Endangered Species Act is a federal statute that protects endangered and threatened species of animals. The act requires the EPA to designate critical habits for each endangered and threatened species. The act prohibits the taking (e.g., hunting, trapping, harming) of any endangered species.

State Environmental Protection Laws, p. 969

Many states and local governments have enacted statutes and ordinances to protect the environment.

Test Review Terms and Concepts

Case Problems

34.1 Food Regulation: Barry Engel owned and operated the Gel Spice Co., Inc. (Gel Spice), which specialized in the importation and packaging of various food spices for resale. All the spices Gel Spice imported were unloaded at a pier in New York City and taken to a warehouse on McDonald Avenue. Storage and repackaging of the spices took place in the warehouse. During three years, the McDonald Avenue warehouse was inspected four times by investigators from the Food and Drug Administration (FDA). The investigators found live rats in bags of basil leaves, rodent droppings in boxes of chili peppers, and mammalian urine in bags of sesame seeds. The investigators produced additional evidence which showed that spices packaged and sold from the warehouse contained insects, rodent excreta pellets, rodent hair, and rodent urine. The FDA brought criminal charges against Engel and Gel Spice. Are they guilty? *United States v. Gel Spice Co., Inc.,* 601 F.Supp. 1205, *Web* 1984 U.S. Dist. Lexis 21041 (United States District Court for the Eastern District of New York)

34.2 Regulation of Drugs: Dey Laboratories, Inc. (Dey), was a drug manufacturer operating in the state of Texas. Dey scientists created an inhalant known as ASI. The only active ingredient in ASI was atropine sulfate. The inhalant was sold to physicians, who then prescribed the medication for patients suffering from asthma, bronchitis, and other pulmonary diseases. Dey filed a new drug application with the Food and Drug Administration (FDA). Four months later, Dey was advised that its application would not be approved. In spite of the lack of FDA approval, Dey began marketing ASI. The United States filed a complaint for forfeiture of all ASI manufactured by Dey. The inhalant was seized, and Dey sued to have the FDA's seizure declared illegal. Who wins? *United States v. Atropine Sulfate 1.0 Mg. (Article of Drug),* 843 F.2d 860, *Web* 1988 U.S. App Lexis 5817 (United States Court of Appeals for the Fifth Circuit)

34.3 Cosmetics Regulation: FBNH Enterprises, Inc. (FBNH), was a distributor of a product known as "French Bronze Tablets." The purpose of the tablets was to allow a person to achieve an even tan without exposure to the sun. When ingested, the tablets imparted color to the skin through the use of various ingredients, one of which is canthaxanthin, a coloring agent. Canthaxanthin had not been approved for use by the Food and Drug Administration (FDA) as a coloring additive. The FDA became aware that FBNH was marketing the tablets and that each contained 30 milligrams of canthaxanthin. The FDA filed a lawsuit seeking the forfeiture and condemnation of eight cases of the tablets in the possession of FBNH. FBNH challenged the government's right to seize the tablets. Who wins? *United States v. Eight Unlabeled Cases of an Article of Cosmetic,* 888 F.2d 945, *Web* 1989 U.S. App. Lexis 15589 (United States Court of Appeals for the Second Circuit)

34.4 Drug Regulation: Joseph Wahba had a prescription filled at Zuckerman's Pharmacy (Zuckerman's) in Brooklyn, New York. The prescription was for Lomotil, a drug used to counteract stomach disorders. The pharmacy dispensed 30 tablets in a small, plastic container unequipped with a "childproof" cap. Joseph took the medicine home, where it was discovered by Wahba's two-year-old son, Mark. Mark opened the container and ingested approximately 20 pills before Mark's mother saw him and stopped him. She rushed him to a hospital but, despite the efforts of the doctors, Mark lapsed into a coma and died. The Wahbas sued H&N Prescription Center, Inc., the company that owns Zuckerman's, for damages. Who wins? *Wahba v. H&N Prescription Center, Inc.,* 539 F.Supp. 352, *Web* 1982 U.S. Dist. Lexis 12327 (United States District Court for the Eastern District of New York)

34.5 Environmental Impact Statement: The U.S. Forest Service is responsible for managing the country's national forests for recreational and other purposes. This includes issuing special use permits to private companies to operate ski areas on federal lands. Sandy Butte is a 6,000-foot mountain located in the Okanogan National Forest in Okanogan County, Washington. Sandy Butte, like the Methow Valley it overlooks, is a pristine, unspoiled, sparsely populated area located within the North Cascades National Park. Large populations of mule deer and other animals exist in the park.

Methow Recreation, Inc. (MRI), applied to the Forest Service for a special use permit to develop and operate its proposed Early Winters Ski Resort on Sandy Butte and a 1,165-acre parcel of private land it had acquired adjacent to the national forest. The proposed development would make use of approximately 3,900 acres of Sandy Butte to provide up to 16 ski lifts capable of accommodating 10,500 skiers at one time. Is an environmental impact statement required? *Robertson v. Methow Valley Citizens Council,* 490 U.S. 332, 109 S.Ct. 1835, 104 L.Ed.2d 351, *Web* 1989 U.S. Lexis 2160 (Supreme Court of the United States)

34.6 Clean Air Act: Pilot Petroleum Associates, Inc., and various affiliated companies distributed gasoline to retail gasoline stations in the state of New York. Pilot owned some of these stations and leased them out to individual operators who were under contract to purchase gasoline from Pilot. The EPA took samples of gasoline from five different service stations to which Pilot had sold unleaded gasoline. These samples showed that Pilot had delivered "unleaded gasoline that contained amounts of lead in excess of that permitted by the Clean Air Act and EPA regulations." The United States brought criminal charges against Pilot for violating the act and EPA regulations and sought fines from Pilot. Who wins? *United States v. Pilot Petroleum Associates, Inc.,* 712 F.Supp. 1077, *Web* 1989 U.S. Dist.

Lexis 6119 (United States District Court for the Eastern District of New York)

34.7 Rule Making: Placer mining is a method used to mine for gold in the streambeds of Alaska. The miner removes soil, mud, and clay from the streambed, places it in an on-site sluice box, and separates the gold from the other matter by forcing water through the pay dirt. The water in the sluice box is discharged into the stream, causing aesthetic and water-quality impacts on the water both in the immediate vicinity and downstream. Toxic metals, including arsenic, cadmium, lead, zinc, and copper, are found in higher concentrations in streams where mining occurs than in streams where there is no mining.

After public notice and comment, the EPA issued rules that require placer miners to use the best practical control technology (BPCT) to control discharges of nontoxic pollutants and the best available control technology (BACT) to control discharges of toxic pollutants. The BACT standard requires miners to construct settling ponds and recycle water through these ponds before discharging the water into the streambed. This method requires substantial expenditure. The Alaska Miners Association challenged the EPA's rule making. Who wins? *Rybachek v. U.S. Environmental Protection Agency*, 904 F.2d 1276, *Web* 1990 U.S. App. Lexis 7833 (United States Court of Appeals for the Ninth Circuit)

34.8 Wetlands: Leslie Salt Company owned a 153-acre tract of undeveloped land south of San Francisco. The property abutted the San Francisco National Wildlife Refuge and was approximately one-quarter mile from Newark Slough, a tidal arm of the San Francisco Bay. Originally, the property was pastureland. The first change occurred in the early 1900s when Leslie's predecessors constructed facilities to manufacture salt on the property. They excavated pits and created large, shallow, watertight basins on the property. Salt production on the property was stopped in 1959. The construction of a sewer line and public roads on and around the property created ditches and culverts on the property. Newark Slough is connected to the property by these culverts, and tidewaters reach the property. Water accumulates in the ponds, ditches, and culverts, providing wetland vegetation to wildlife and migratory birds. Fish live in the ponds on the property. Over 25 years later, Leslie started to dig a ditch to drain the property and began construction to block the culvert that connected the property to the Newark Slough. The Army Corps of Engineers issued a cease-and-desist order against Leslie. Leslie challenged the order. Who wins? *Leslie Salt Co. v. United States*, 896 F.2d 354, *Web* 1990 U.S. App. Lexis 1524 (United States Court of Appeals for the Ninth Circuit)

34.9 Clean Water Act: The Reserve Mining Company (Reserve) owned and operated a mine in Minnesota that was located on the shores of Lake Superior and produced hazardous waste. In 1947, Reserve obtained a permit from the state of Minnesota to dump its wastes into Lake Superior. The permits prohibited discharges that would "result in any clouding or discoloration of the water outside the specific discharge zone" or "result in any material adverse affects on public water supplies." Reserve discharged its wastes into Lake Superior for years. Evidence showed that the discharges caused discoloration of surface waters outside the zone of discharge and contained carcinogens that adversely affected public water supplies. The United States sued Reserve for engaging in unlawful water pollution. Who wins? *United States v. Reserve Mining Co.*, 543 F.2d 1210, *Web* 1976 U.S. App. Lexis 6503 (United States Court of Appeals for the Eighth Circuit)

34.10 Hazardous Waste: Douglas Hoflin was the director of the Public Works Department for Ocean Shores, Washington. During a period of seven years, the department purchased 3,500 gallons of paint for road maintenance. As painting jobs were finished, the 55-gallon drums that had contained the paint were returned to the department's yard. Paint contains hazardous substances such as lead. When 14 of the drums were discovered to still contain unused paint, Hoflin instructed employees to haul the paint drums to the city's sewage treatment plant and bury them. The employees dug a hole on the grounds of the treatment plant and dumped the drums in. Some of the drums were rusted and leaking. The hole was not deep enough, so the employees crushed the drums with a front-end loader to make them fit. The refuse was then covered with sand. Almost two years later, one of the city's employees reported the incident to state authorities, who referred the matter to the EPA. Investigation showed that the paint had contaminated the soil. The United States brought criminal charges against Hoflin for aiding and abetting the illegal dumping of hazardous waste. Who wins? *United States v. Hoflin*, 880 F.2d 1033, *Web* 1989 U.S. App. Lexis 10169 (United States Court of Appeals for the Ninth Circuit)

34.11 Nuclear Waste: Metropolitan Edison Company owns and operates two nuclear-fueled power plants at Three Mile Island near Harrisburg, Pennsylvania. Both power plants were licensed by the NRC after extensive proceedings and investigations, including the preparation of the required environmental impact statements. When one of the power plants was shut down for refueling, the other plant suffered a serious accident that damaged the reactor. The governor of Pennsylvania recommended an evacuation of all pregnant women and small children, and many area residents did leave their homes for several days. As it turned out, no dangerous radiation was released.

People Against Nuclear Energy (PANE), an association of area residents who opposed further operation of the nuclear power plants at Three Mile Island, sued to enjoin the plants from reopening. They argued that the reopening of the plants would cause severe psychological health damage to persons living in the vicinity and serious damage to the stability and cohesiveness of the community. Are these reasons sufficient to prevent the reopening of the nuclear power plants? *Metropolitan Edison Co. v. People Against Nuclear Energy*, 460 U.S. 766, 103 S.Ct. 1556, 75 L.Ed.2d 534, *Web* 1983 U.S. Lexis 21 (Supreme Court of the United States)

34.12 Endangered Species: The red-cockaded woodpecker is a small bird that lives almost exclusively in old pine forests throughout the southern United States. Its survival depends on a very specialized habitat of pine trees that are at least 30, if not 60, years old, in which they build nests and forage for insects. The population of this bird decreased substantially as pine forests were destroyed by clear-cutting. The secretary of the interior has named the red-cockaded woodpecker an endangered species.

The Forest Service, which is under the authority of the secretary of agriculture, manages federal forests and is charged with duties to provide recreation, protect wildlife, and provide timber. To accomplish the charge of providing timber, the Forest Service leases national forest lands to private companies for lumbering. When the Forest Service proposed to lease several national forests in Texas, where the red-cockaded woodpecker lives, to private companies for lumbering, the Sierra Club sued. The Sierra Club sought to enjoin the Forest Service from leasing these national forests for lumbering. Who wins? *Sierra Club v. Lyng, Secretary of Agriculture*, 694 F.Supp. 1260, *Web* 1988 U.S. Dist. Lexis 9203 (United States District Court for the Eastern District of Texas)

Ethics Issues

34.13 Ethics: Charles of the Ritz Distributing Corporation (Ritz) was a New York corporation engaged in the sale and distribution of a product called "Rejuvenescence Cream." The extensive advertising campaign that accompanied the sale of the cream placed emphasis upon the supposed rejuvenating powers of the products. The ads claimed that the cream would bring to the user's "skin quickly the clear radiance" and "the petal-like quality and texture of youth." Another advertisement claimed that the product would "restore natural moisture necessary for a live, healthy skin" with the result that "Your face need not know drought years." The Federal Trade Commission (FTC) learned of the ads and asked several experts to investigate the claimed benefits of Rejuvenescence Cream. The experts reported to the FTC that it is impossible for an external application of cosmetics to overcome skin conditions that result from physiological changes occurring with the passage of time. The FTC issued a cease-and-desist order with regard to the advertising. Ritz appealed the FTC's decision to a federal court. Did Ritz act ethically in making its advertising claims? Who wins? *Charles of the Ritz Distributing Corp. v. FTC*, 143 F.2d 676, *Web* 1944 U.S. App. Lexis 3172 (United States Court of Appeals for the Second Circuit)

34.14 Ethics: Leon A. Tashof operated a store known as the New York Jewelry Company. The store was located in an area that served low-income consumers, many of whom had low-paying jobs and had no bank or charge accounts. About 85 percent of the store's sales were made on credit. The store advertised eyeglasses "from $7.50 complete," including "lenses, frames and case." Tashof advertised this sale extensively on radio and in newspapers. Evidence showed that of the 1,400 pairs of eyeglasses sold by the store, fewer than 10 were sold for $7.50; the rest were more expensive glasses. The Federal Trade Commission sued Tashof for engaging in "bait and switch" marketing. Was Tashof's conduct ethical? Who wins? *Tashof v. Federal Trade Commission*, 141 U.S. App. D.C. 274,

437 F.2d 707, *Web* 1970 U.S. App. Lexis 5809 (United States Court of Appeals for the District of Columbia Circuit)

34.15 Ethics: The state of Michigan owns approximately 57,000 acres of land that comprise the Pigeon River County State Forest in southwestern Michigan. Shell Oil Company applied to the Michigan Department of Natural Resources (DNR) for a permit to drill 10 exploratory oil wells in the forest. Roads had to be constructed to reach the proposed drill sites. Evidence showed that the only sizable elk herd east of the Mississippi River annually used the forest as its habitat and returned to this range every year to breed. Experts testified that elk avoid roads, even when there is no traffic, and that the construction of the roads and wells would destroy the elk's habitat. Michigan law prohibits activities that adversely affect natural resources. The West Michigan Environmental Action Council sued the DNR, seeking to enjoin the DNR from granting the drilling permits to Shell. Did Shell Oil Company act socially responsibly in this case? Who wins? *West Michigan Environmental Action Council, Inc. v. Natural Resources Commission*, 405 Mich. 741, 275 N.W.2d 538, *Web* 1979 Mich. Lexis 347 (Supreme Court of Michigan)

34.16 Ethics: Riverside Bayview Homes, Inc. (Riverside), owned 80 acres of low-lying marshland (wetlands) near the shores of Lake St. Clair in Macomb County, Michigan. Riverside began to place fill materials on its property as part of its preparations for construction of a housing development. Riverside did not obtain a permit from the Army Corps of Engineers. Upon discovery of Riverside's activities, the Corps sued, seeking to enjoin Riverside from discharging a pollutant (fill) onto wetlands. Is the subject property subject to the Corps of Engineers permit system? Did Riverside Bayview Homes act ethically in this case? *United States v. Riverside Bayview Homes, Inc.*, 474 U.S. 121, 106 S.Ct. 455, 88 L.Ed.2d 419, *Web* 1985 U.S. Lexis 145 (Supreme Court of the United States)

IRAC Writing Assignment

Read **Case A-34** in Appendix A [*FMC Corporation v. United States Department of Commerce*]. Use the IRAC method to prepare a written analysis of the case.

Endnotes

1. 21 U.S.C. Section 301.
2. 21 U.S.C. Section 321.
3. 21 U.S.C. Section 360(c) *et seq.*
4. 15 U.S.C. Section 2051.
5. 15 U.S.C. Sections 41–51.
6. 42 U.S.C. Sections 4321–4370d.
7. 42 U.S.C. Sections 7401–7671q.
8. 33 U.S.C. Sections 1251–1367.
9. 33 U.S.C. Section 1254(t).
10. 21 U.S.C. Section 349 and Sections 300f–300j-25.
11. 16 U.S.C. Section 1431 *et seq.*; 33 U.S.C. Sections 1401–1445.
12. 33 U.S.C. Sections 2701–2761.
13. 15 U.S.C. Sections 2601–2692.
14. 7 U.S.C. Sections 135 *et seq.*
15. 42 U.S.C. Sections 6901–6986.
16. 42 U.S.C. Sections 10101–10270.
17. 16 U.S.C. Sections 1531–1544.

CHAPTER 35

Employment, Worker Protection, and Labor Law

"Strong responsible unions are essential to industrial fair play. Without them the labor bargain is wholly one-sided."

—LOUIS D. BRANDEIS (1935)

CHAPTER OBJECTIVES

After studying this chapter, you should be able to:

1. Explain how state workers' compensation programs work and describe the benefits available.
2. Describe employers' duty to provide safe working conditions under the Occupational Safety and Health Act.
3. Describe the minimum wage and overtime pay rules of the Fair Labor Standards Act.
4. Describe how a union is organized and describe the process of collective bargaining.
5. Describe employees' rights to strike and picket.

CHAPTER CONTENTS

Introduction to Employment, Worker Protection, and Labor Law

Before the Industrial Revolution, the doctrine of laissez-faire governed the employment relationship in this country. Generally, this meant that employment was subject to the common law of contracts and agency law. In most instances, employees and employers had somewhat equal bargaining power.

This changed dramatically when the country became industrialized in the late 1800s. For one thing, large corporate employers had much more bargaining power than their employees. For another, the issues of child labor, unsafe working conditions, long hours, and low pay caused concern. Both federal and state legislation were enacted to protect workers' rights. Today, employment law is a mixture of contract law, agency law, and government regulation.

This chapter discusses employment law, worker safety, immigration law, and workers' privacy law.

Mackinac Bridge, Michigan

Workers on this bridge are covered by workers' compensation, occupational safety, and other labor and worker protection laws.

Workers' Compensation

Many types of employment are dangerous, and each year, many workers are injured on the job. Under common law, employees who were injured on the job could sue their employers for negligence. This time-consuming process placed the employee at odds with his or her employer. In addition, there was no guarantee that the employee would win the case. Ultimately, many injured workers—or the heirs of deceased workers—were left uncompensated.

Workers' compensation acts were enacted by states in response to the unfairness of that result. These acts create an administrative procedure for workers to receive compensation for injuries that occur on the job. First, the injured worker files a claim with the appropriate state government agency (often called the workers' compensation board or commission). Next, that entity determines the legitimacy of the claim. If the worker disagrees with the agency's findings, he or she may appeal the decision through the state court system. Workers' compensation benefits are paid according to preset limits established by statute or regulation. The amounts that are recoverable vary from state to state.

Workers' Compensation Insurance

States usually require employers to purchase insurance from private insurance companies or state funds to cover workers' compensation claims. Some states permit employers to self-insure if they demonstrate that they have the ability to pay workers' compensation claims. Many large companies self-insure. Workers can sue their employers in court to recover damages for employment-related injuries if the employer does not carry **workers' compensation insurance** or does not self-insure if permitted to do so.

Employment-Related Injury

For an injury to be compensable under workers' compensation, the claimant must prove that the injury arose out of and in the course of his or her employment. An accident that occurs while an employee is actively working is clearly within the scope of this rule. Accidents that occur at a company cafeteria or while on a business lunch for an employer are covered. Accidents that happen while the employee is at an off-premises restaurant during his or her personal lunch hour are not covered. Many workers' compensation acts include stress as a compensable **employment-related injury**.

Exclusive Remedy

Workers' compensation is an **exclusive remedy**. Thus, workers cannot sue their employers in court for damages. There is one exception to this rule: If an employer intentionally injures a worker, the worker can collect workers' compensation benefits and sue the employer. Workers' compensation acts do not bar injured workers from suing responsible third parties to recover damages.

The following cases involve workers' compensation issues.

CASE **35.1** *Workers' Compensation*	**Medrano v. Marshall Electrical Contracting Inc.** 173 S.W.3d 333, **Web** 2005 Mo. App. Lexis 1088 (2005) Court of Appeals of Missouri	

> **"** *In determining that Medrano's accidental death arose out of and in the course of his employment with MEC, the Commission relied on the mutual benefit doctrine.* **"**
>
> —Judge Hardwick

Facts

Immar Medrano was employed as a journeyman electrician by Marshall Electrical Contracting, Inc. (MEC), in Marshall, Missouri. Medrano attended an electrician apprenticeship night class at a community college in Sedalia, Missouri. MEC paid Medrano's tuition and book fees. Attendance at the course required Medrano to drive 70 miles round-trip. One night when Medrano was driving home from the class, a drunk driver crossed the centerline of U.S. Highway 65 and collided head-on with Medrano's automobile. Medrano died in the accident. His wife and two children filed a workers' compensation claim for death benefits against MEC. After a hearing, an administrative law judge (ALJ) denied the claim, determining that Medrano's death did not arise out of nor within the course and scope of his employment. The Labor & Industrial Relations Commission (Commission) reversed the ALJ's decision, found the Medrano was acting within the course and scope of his employment when he was killed, and awarded death benefits to Medrano's family. MEC appealed.

Issue

Was Medrano acting within the course and scope of his employment when he was killed in the automobile accident?

Language of the Court

In determining that Medrano's accidental death arose out of and in the course of his employment with MEC, the Commission relied on the mutual benefit doctrine. The doctrine holds that an injury suffered by an employee while performing an act for the mutual benefit of the employer and the employee is usually compensable. MEC argues that it received no benefit from Medrano's attendance at the apprenticeship class and, thus, the Commission erred in determining the death claim was compensable. However, our review of the entire record indicates there is substantial and competent evidence to support the Commission's finding that the classroom instruction was beneficial to Medrano and his employer.

Mike Mills, the owner and president of MEC, testified at the administrative hearing: "The training made the employees more valuable to MEC by improving the quality of service to customers." The record is sufficient to show that MEC derived substantial benefit from having its employees travel from Marshall to Sedalia to fully participate in the apprenticeship program. MEC encouraged employees to attend the classroom instruction and covered the costs of tuition. Even though employees like Medrano obtained personal benefits in formalizing their education, MEC mutually benefited from the program as a convenient way for MEC to train its employees and ultimately provide a better quality of service to its customers.

Decision

The court of appeals upheld the Commission's finding that Medrano was acting within the course and scope of his employment when he was fatally injured in the car crash. The court of appeals affirmed the Commission's award of workers' compensation death benefited to Medrano's family.

Law & Ethics Questions

1. What is workers' compensation? Explain.

2. What does the mutual benefit doctrine provide? Explain.

3. **ETHICS** Was it ethical for MEC to argue that it did not owe workers' compensation benefits to Medrano's surviving family?

4. What would have been the outcome of the case if the court had found that Medrano was not acting within the course and scope of his employment when he was fatally injured in the car crash?

Web Exercises

1. **WEB** For the complete opinion of this case, go to *www.prenhall.com/cheesemancases*.

2. **WEB** Visit the website of the Missouri Labor and Industrial Relations Commission, at *www.dolir.mo.gov*.

3. **WEB** Visit the website of the court of appeals of Missouri, Western District, at *www.courts.mo.gov/page.asp?id=227*.

4. **WEB** Use *www.google.com* to find the agency that hears workers' compensation cases in your state.

CASE 35.2
Scope of Employment

Smith v. Workers' Compensation Appeals Board

191 Cal.App.3d 127, 236 Cal.Rptr. 248,
Web 1987 Cal. App. Lexis 1587
Court of Appeal of California

> *"Teachers were evaluated on whether they shared equally in the sponsorship or the supervision of out-of-classroom student activities, and decedent had been commended for his participation in this area."*
>
> —Judge Ballantyne

Facts

Ronald Wayne Smith was employed by Modesto High School as a temporary math instructor. In addition, he coached the girls' baseball and basketball teams. The contract under which he was employed stated that he "may be required to devote a reasonable amount of time to other duties" in addition to instructional duties. The teachers in the school system were evaluated once a year regarding both instructional duties and non-instructional duties, including "sponsorship or the supervision of out-of-classroom student activities."

The high school's math club holds an annual end-of-year outing. A picnic was scheduled to be held at the Modesto Reservoir. The students invited their math teachers, including Smith, to attend. The food was paid for by math club members' dues. Smith attended the picnic with his wife and three children. One of the students brought along a windsurfer. Smith watched the students as they used it before and after the picnic. When Smith tried it himself, he fell and was seriously injured. He died shortly thereafter. Mrs. Smith filed a claim for workers' compensation benefits, to which the employer objected. The workers' compensation judge denied benefits, and the Workers' Compensation Appeals Board affirmed the denial of benefits. Mrs. Smith appealed.

Issue

Was Smith engaged in employment-related activities when the accident occurred?

Language of the Court

In the instant case, decedent was a temporary instructor at Modesto High. As such, he was more vulnerable to pressure or suggestion that he participate in extracurricular activities to better his chances of being rehired. The math club was an official school club. Notices of meetings to plan the picnic appeared in the school bulletin. The food for the event was paid for out of the math club funds. The school was more than minimally involved in the picnic. Teachers were encouraged to involve themselves in extracurricular activities of the school, thus conferring the benefit of better teacher–student relationships. More importantly, teachers were evaluated on whether they shared equally in the sponsorship or the supervision of out-of-classroom student activities, and decedent had been commended for his participation in this area.

Respondent argues that if this court finds that decedent's attendance at the picnic was required by his employment, then his activities in using the windsurfer were outside the course and scope of his employment. Because attendance at the picnic was an implied requirement of decedent's employment, his accident that resulted from his engaging in the recreational activities that were part and parcel of the picnic's "entertainment" is causally connected to his employment.

Decision

The court of appeals held that the decedent's accident was causally connected to his employment for purposes of awarding workers' compensation benefits to his heirs. The court of appeals reversed the decision of the Workers' Compensation Appeals Board and remanded the case for further proceedings.

Law & Ethics Questions

1. Should workers' compensation benefits be awarded only for accidents that occur at the job site? Why or why not?

2. **ETHICS** Did the employer act ethically in objecting to the payment of benefits in this case?

3. How costly is workers' compensation for businesses? Do you think that many fraudulent workers' compensation claims are filed?

Web Exercises

1. **WEB** For the complete opinion of this case, go to *www.prenhall.com/cheesemancases*.

2. **WEB** Visit the website of the court of appeals of California, Fifth Appellate District, at *www.courtinfo.ca.gov/courts/courtsofappeal/5thDistrict*.

3. **WEB** Use *www.google.com* to find a discussion of a case in which workers' compensation benefits were in dispute.

CASE 35.3
Dual-Purpose Mission

Cochran Electric Company, Inc. v. Mahoney

129 Wn.App. 687, 121 P.3d 747,
Web 2005 Wash. App. Lexis 2450 (2005)
Court of Appeals of Washington

> **❝** *The dual purpose exception may apply when an employee is injured in transit to or from a location off the employer's premises when the employee's presence at that location served both a business and personal purpose.* **❞**
>
> —Judge Cox

Facts

Neil Mahoney worked as a service electrician for Cochran Electric Company, Inc. Cochran provided Mahoney with a service van to drive to and from scheduled job sites. Service electricians were responsible for getting their assigned vans serviced. On a day that Mahoney was not scheduled to work, he drove the service van to the Cochran office to submit some paperwork. He then dropped off the van at a local garage for service. Mahoney had brought his bicycle in the van for the trip home. As he biked home from the garage, an automobile struck Mahoney. Mahoney suffered severe injuries from which he subsequently died.

Susan Mahoney, Neil's widow, filed a claim with the Washington State Department of Labor and Industries (L&I) to recover survivor benefits under Washington's Industrial Insurance Act (Act). The L&I held that the accident did not occur in the course of employment and denied benefits. The Board of Industrial Insurance Appeals Board (Board) reversed and awarded workers' compensation benefits to Neil's widow. The superior court affirmed the Board's award of benefits. Cochran appealed.

Issue

Was Mahoney acting within the course of his employment at the time that the accident occurred?

Language of the Court

Cochran argues that if Mahoney had been traveling to work when injured, his claim would be precluded by the "going and coming" rule. The rule excluding off-premises injuries during the journey to and from work does not apply if the making of the journey, or the special degree of urgency under which it is made, is in and of itself a substantial part of the service for which the worker is employed. This principle, that is, that the journey is an inherent part of the service, explains the recognized exceptions to the going and coming rule. Thus, one such recognized exception is the "special errand" rule. Here, taking the van for servicing, leaving it, and returning home were all part of a special errand for Cochran's benefit. The trouble and time of making the journey was sufficient to bring the entire trip within the course of employment.

Cochran asserts that Mahoney is not covered under the Act because the bike ride was undertaken solely for his own purposes. It argues that the Board erred when it applied the "dual purpose" exception to the going and coming rule. The dual purpose exception may apply when an employee is injured in transit to or from a location off the employer's premises when the employee's presence at that location served both a business and personal purpose. We conclude that the Board did not err in applying the dual purpose exception in this case.

Decision

The court of appeals held that Mahoney was acting within the course of his employment when the accident occurred. The court of appeals upheld the judgment of the superior court that awarded death benefits to Neil Mahoney's widow.

Law & Ethics Questions

1. What does the going and coming rule provide? Explain.

2. What does the special errand exception to the going and coming rule provide? Explain.

3. What does the dual-purpose exception to the going and coming rule provide? Explain.

4. **ETHICS** Did Cochran Electric Company, Neil Mahoney's employer, act ethically in denying workers' compensation death benefits to Mahoney's widow?

Web Exercises

1. **WEB** For the complete opinion of this case, go to *www.prenhall.com/cheesemancases*.

2. **WEB** Visit the website of the court of appeals of Washington, Division One, at *www.courts.wa.gov*.

3. **WEB** Visit the website of the Washington Department of Labor and Industries, at *www.lni.wa.gov*.

4. **WEB** Use *www.google.com* to find a case in your state in which workers' compensation benefits were awarded.

CASE 35.4
Frolic

Simmons v. Bob Mears Wholesale Florist

167 S.W.3d 222,
Web 2005 Mo. App. Lexis 1050 (2005)
Court of Appeals of Missouri

> 66*Simmons was on an alcohol related frolic, which was entirely personal. He was in violation of Employer's policy.*99
>
> —Judge Prewitt

Facts

Harry Simmons was employed by Bob Mears Wholesale Florist (Mears) and handled sale accounts in Arkansas and Missouri. One day, Simmons drove to Mountain Home, Arkansas, in his employer's vehicle. After visiting customers in Mountain Home, Simmons stopped at a liquor store and picked up a half-pint of Jack Daniels whiskey before leaving at 1:30 P.M. that afternoon. Simmons drove toward Forsyth, Missouri, where he had customers. En route, Simmons stopped at a pull-off on Highway 125 to drink the whiskey. This detour lasted 30 minutes.

Simmons drove back onto the highway. At 3:25 P.M., Simmons's vehicle left Highway 76, tore down 75 feet of fencing, struck a tree, and caught on fire. The police report indicated that Simmons was asleep at the time of the accident. When Simmons was admitted to the hospital, a physician determined that he suffered from alcohol intoxication.

Simmons suffered a broken pelvis, a broken fibula, burns and cuts over his legs, nerve damage to his elbow, a concussion, a broken nose, and injuries to his left shoulder.

Simmons filed a claim for workers' compensation for his injuries. Mears, his employer, and Florist Mutual Insurance Company (Insurance Company), which provided workers' compensation to Mears, denied liability. The administrative law judge (ALJ) found that Simmons was acting within the course of his employment at the time of the accident and awarded workers' compensation benefits. The Labor & Industrial Relations Commission (Commission) concluded that Simmons was involved in an alcohol-related frolic and that the accident did not arise in the course of his employment. The Commission denied workers' compensation benefits to Simmons. Simmons appealed.

Issue

Was Simmons acting within the course of his employment at the time he was injured in the automobile accident?

Language of the Court

Simmons was on an alcohol related frolic, which was entirely personal. He was in violation of Employer's policy. He was not in a location that he would travel to return to the warehouse in Springfield nor was he headed in the correct direction to continue to Forsyth. He left the course of his employment and had not returned to the course of his employment when the accident occurred.

In response to cross-examination, Simmons agreed that his work day ended at one o'clock p.m. He said it was "vaguely possible" that his trip to Forsyth was to "goof off." Simmons admitted he never took Highway 76 as a part of his regular route to Forsyth. Simmons agreed it would be inappropriate to "call upon a retailer" with alcohol on his breath.

Injuries have been held compensable where an employee's acts were reasonably incidental to commencement of employee's work and were also for the benefit of the employer. Based upon the evidence on the record, the Commission was justified in finding that Simmons' actions were a personal "frolic" with no benefit to Employer and outside the course of employment.

Decision

The court of appeals affirmed the Commission's decision that Simmons was not acting within the course of his employment at the time of the accident but was instead engaged in a personal frolic. The court of appeals affirmed the Commission's denial of workers' compensation benefits to Simmons.

Law & Ethics Questions

1. Define *acting within the course of employment*.
2. What is a "frolic" from the course of employment? Explain.
3. **ETHICS** Was it ethical for Simmons to seek workers' compensation based on the facts of this case?
4. Do you think the court should have awarded Simmons workers' compensation benefits in this case? Why or why not?

Web Exercises

1. **WEB** For the complete opinion of this case, go to *www.prenhall.com/cheesemancases*.
2. **WEB** Visit the website of the court of appeals of Missouri, Southern District, at *www.courts.mo.gov/page.asp?id=208*.
3. **WEB** Visit the website of the Missouri Labor and Industrial Relations Commission, at *www.dolir.mo.gov*.
4. **WEB** Use *www.google.com* to find an article or a case in which workers' compensation benefits were denied.

Occupational Safety

In 1970, Congress enacted the **Occupational Safety and Health Act**[1] to promote safety in the workplace. Virtually all private employers are within the scope of the act, but federal, state, and local governments are exempt. Industries regulated by other federal safety legislation are also exempt.[2] The act also established the **Occupational Safety and Health Administration (OSHA)**, a federal administrative agency within the Department of Labor that is empowered to enforce the act. The act imposes record-keeping and reporting requirements on employers and requires them to post notices in the workplace, informing employees of their rights under the act.

OSHA is empowered to adopt rules and regulations to interpret and enforce the Occupational Safety and Health Act. OSHA has adopted thousands of regulations to enforce the safety standards established by the act.

Specific Duty Standards

Many of the OSHA standards address safety problems of a **specific duty** nature. For example, OSHA standards establish safety requirements for equipment (e.g., safety guards), set maximum exposure levels to hazardous chemicals, regulate the location of machinery, establish safety procedures for employees, and the like.

General Duty Standards

The Occupational Safety and Health Act imposes a **general duty** on an employer to provide a work environment free from recognized hazards that are causing or are likely to cause death or serious physical harm to his employees. This is so even if no specific regulation applies to the situation.

OSHA is empowered to inspect places of employment for health hazards and safety violations. If a violation is found, OSHA can issue a *written citation* that requires the employer to abate or correct the situation. Contested citations are reviewed by the Occupational Safety & Health Review Commission. Its decision is appealable to the Court of Appeals for the Federal Circuit. Employers who violate the act, OSHA rules and regulations, or OSHA citations are subject to both civil and criminal penalties.

Web Exercise

1. **WEB** Visit the website of the Occupational Safety and Health Administration (OSHA), at *www.osha.gov*.

2. **WEB** Use *www.google.com* to find a recent safety issue that OSHA is involved in.

ETHICS SPOTLIGHT

Company Violates OSHA's Safety Rule

> **❝** *The purpose of the safety devices listed in the regulation is to provide fall protection, and a roof cannot provide fall protection if workers must operate along the perimeter.* **❞**
>
> —Judge Thornberry

Corbesco, Inc. (Corbesco), an industrial roofing and siding installation company, was hired to put metal roofing and siding over the skeletal structure of five aircraft hangars at Chennault Air Base in Louisiana. Corbesco assigned three of its employees to work on the partially completed flat roof of Hangar B, a large single-story building measuring 60 feet high, 374 feet wide, and 574 feet long. Soon after starting work, one of the workers, Roger Matthew, who was on his knees installing insulation on the roof, lost his balance and fell 60 feet to the concrete below. He was killed by the fall.

The next day, an Occupational Safety and Health Administration (OSHA) compliance officer cited Corbesco for failing to install a safety net under the work site. The officer cited an OSHA safety standard that requires that safety nets be provided when workers are more than 25 feet above the ground. Corbesco argued that the flat roof on which the employees were working served as a "temporary floor," and therefore it was not required to install a safety net. An administrative law judge (ALJ) of the Occupational Safety & Health Review Commission (Commission) held that Corbesco had committed a serious violation of the Occupational Safety and Health Act (Act) by failing to install a safety net at the work site. Corbesco appealed.

The U.S. Court of Appeals rejected Corbesco's argument. The Court of Appeals held that Corbesco had notice that it was required to install safety nets under its crew while they were working on the edge of a flat roof some 60 feet above a concrete floor. The Court of Appeals stated, "Moreover, we do not believe that the Commission has abused

its discretion by determining that a flat roof cannot be a temporary floor. The purpose of the safety devices listed in the regulation is to provide fall protection, and a roof cannot provide fall protection if workers must operate along the perimeter." The Court of Appeals held that Corbesco had violated OSHA's rules by not providing a safety net below its employees who were working more than 25 feet above the ground. *Corbesco, Inc. v. Dole, Secretary of Labor*, 926 F.2d 422, 1991 U.S. App. 3369 (United States Court of Appeals for the Fifth Circuit)

Law & Ethics Questions

1. Why are occupational safety laws enacted? Would just letting employees sue their employers for injuries caused by unsafe working conditions accomplish the same result?

2. **ETHICS** Did Corbesco act ethically in arguing that the flat roof created a temporary floor that relieved it of the duty to install a safety net?

Web Exercises

1. **WEB** Visit the OSHA website, at *www.osha.gov*. Can you find any safety rules that OSHA has enacted?

2. **WEB** Visit the website of the Occupational Safety & Health Review Commission, at *www.oshrc.gov*. What is the function of the Commission?

Fair Labor Standards Act (FLSA)

In 1938, Congress enacted the **Fair Labor Standards Act (FLSA)** to protect workers.[3] The FLSA applies to private employers and employees engaged in the production of goods for interstate commerce. The **U.S. Department of Labor** is empowered to enforce the FLSA. Private civil actions are also permitted under the FLSA.

Web Exercises

1. **WEB** Visit the website of the U.S. Department of Labor, at *www.dol.gov*.

2. **WEB** Using the U.S. Department of Labor website, at *www.dol.gov*, find an issue that the U.S. Department of Labor has been involved in recently.

Child Labor

The FLSA forbids the use of oppressive child labor and makes it unlawful to ship goods produced by businesses that use oppressive child labor. The Department of Labor has adopted the following regulations that define lawful child labor: (1) Children under the age of 14 cannot work except as newspaper deliverers; (2) children ages 14 and 15 may work limited hours in nonhazardous jobs approved by the Department of Labor (e.g., restaurants, gasoline stations); and (3) children ages 16 and 17 may work unlimited hours in nonhazardous jobs. The Department of Labor determines which occupations are hazardous (e.g., mining, roofing, working with explosives). Children who work in agricultural employment and child actors and performers are exempt from these restrictions. Persons age 18 and older may work at any job, whether it is hazardous or not.

The FLSA establishes minimum wage and overtime pay requirements for workers. Managerial, administrative, and professional employees are exempt from the act's wage and hour provisions.

Minimum Wage

The federal **minimum wage** is set by Congress and can be changed. As of 2007, it was set at $5.15 per hour. The Department of Labor permits employers to pay less than the minimum wage to students and apprentices. An employer may reduce the minimum wage by an amount equal to the reasonable cost of food and lodging provided to employees.

Some states have enacted minimum wage laws that set minimum wages at a rate higher than the federal rate. Some cities have enacted minimum wage requirements, usually called "living wage" laws, which also set higher minimum wage rates than the federal level.

Web Exercises

1. **WEB** Use *www.google.com* to find out if the federal minimum wage rate has been changed since 2007.

2. **WEB** Go to the website *www.dol.gov/esa/minwage/america.htm*. What is the minimum wage for your state?

Overtime Pay

Under the FLSA, an employer cannot require nonexempt employees to work more than 40 hours per week unless they are paid **overtime pay** of one-and-a-half times their regular pay for each hour worked in excess of 40 hours. Each week is treated separately.

Example If an employee works 50 hours one week and 30 hours the next, the employer owes the employee 10 hours of overtime pay for the first week.

In the following case, the U.S. Supreme Court was called upon to interpret the Fair Labor Standards Act.

CASE **35.5**

Fair Labor Standards Act

U.S. SUPREME COURT

IBP, Inc. v. Alvarez

546 U.S. 21, 126 S.Ct. 514, 163 L.Ed.2d 288,
Web 2005 U.S. Lexis 8373 (2005)
Supreme Court of the United States

> *"The relevant text describes the workday as roughly the period from "whistle to whistle.""*

—Justice Stevens

Facts

IBP, Inc., is a large producer of fresh beef, pork, and related products. At its plant in Pasco, Washington, it employed approximately 178 workers in its slaughter division and 800 line workers. All workers must wear gear such as outer garments, hardhats, earplugs, gloves, aprons, leggings, and boots. Those who use knives must wear additional protective equipment. IBP requires employees to store their equipment and tools in company locker rooms, where the workers don and doff their equipment and protective gear.

The pay of production workers is based on time spent cutting and bagging meat. Pay begins with the first piece of meat and ends with the last piece of meat. IBP pays for four minutes of clothes-changing time. IBP employees filed a class action lawsuit against IBP to recover compensation for preproduction and postproduction work, including time spent donning and doffing protective gear and time walking between the locker room and the production floor before and after their assigned shifts. The employees alleged that IBP violated the Fair Labor Standards Act (FLSA).

The U.S. District Court held that the donning and doffing of protective gear and the walking time between the locker room and the production floor were compensable time and awarded $3 million in damages. The U.S. Court of Appeals agreed with the District Court's ultimate conclusions. IBP appealed. On appeal, IBP did not challenge the District Court's holding regarding payment for donning and doffing of protective gear, but it did challenge the District Court's decision to require payment of compensation to workers for the time spent walking between the locker room and the production area. The U.S. Supreme Court granted a writ of certiorari to hear the appeal.

Issue

Is the time spent by employees walking between the locker room and production area compensable under the Fair Labor Standards Act?

Language of the U.S. Supreme Court

The Department of Labor has adopted the continuous workday rule, which means that the "workday" is generally defined as the period between the commencement and completion on the same workday of an employee's principal activity or activities. The relevant text describes the workday as roughly the period from "whistle to whistle."

In 1955, we were confronted with the question whether workers in a battery plant had a statutory right to compensation for the time incident to changing clothes at the beginning of the shift and showering at the end, where they must make extensive use of dangerously caustic and toxic materials, and are compelled by circumstances, including vital considerations of health and hygiene, to change clothes and to shower in facilities which state law requires their employers to provide. After distinguishing changing clothes and showering under normal conditions and stressing the important health and safety risks associated with the production of batteries, the Court endorsed the court of appeals' conclusion that these activities were compensable under the FLSA. *Steiner v. Mitchell*, 350 U.S. 247, 76 S.Ct. 330, 100 L.Ed. 267, **Web** 1956 U.S. Lexis 1743 (Supreme Court of the United States)

We hold that any activity that is integral and indispensable to a principal activity is itself a principal activity. Moreover, during a continuous workday, any walking time that occurs after the beginning of the employee's first principal activity and before the end of the employee's last principal activity is covered by the FLSA.

Decision

The U.S. Supreme Court held that the time spent by employees walking between the locker room and the production areas of the plant were compensable under the Fair Labor Standards Act.

Law & Ethics Questions

1. When does an employee's workday begin and end? What does the reference to "whistle-to-whistle" mean?
2. Why do you think IBP, Inc., fought so hard against the workers' demands?
3. **ETHICS** Did IBP act ethically in not paying for the workers' time spent walking to and from the locker room and the production areas? Explain.

Web Exercises

1. **WEB** For the full opinion of this case, go to *www.prenhall.com/cheesemancases*.
2. **WEB** Visit the website of the U.S. Supreme Court, at *www.supremecourtus.gov*. Can you find any documents related to this case? If so, what are they?
3. **WEB** Use *www.google.com* to find a website or an article that shows a photograph of the inside of a meat-packing plant.

ETHICS SPOTLIGHT
Microsoft Violates Employment Law

> *It is our conclusion that Microsoft either exercised, or retained the right to exercise, direction over the services performed. This control establishes an employer–employee relationship.*

—Judge Schwarzer

Microsoft Corporation is the world's largest provider of computer operating systems, software programs, and Internet browsers. The company has grown into one of the largest corporations in the United States, making one of its founders, Bill Gates, the richest person in the world. But the company has been caught nickel-and-diming some of its workers. The situation was brought to light by an Internal Revenue Service (IRS) investigation.

Microsoft is headquartered in the state of Washington. In addition to having regular employees, Microsoft used the services of other workers, classified as *independent contractors* (called *freelancers*) and temporary agency employees (called *temps*). Most of these special employees worked full time for Microsoft, doing jobs that were identical to jobs performed by Microsoft's regular employees. Microsoft paid the special employees by check as outside workers. The IRS conducted an employment tax examination and determined that Microsoft had misclassified these special workers as independent contractors and that the workers in these positions needed to be reclassified as employees for federal tax purposes.

But the IRS investigation was not the end of the story. Plaintiff Donna Vizcaino and other freelancers sued Microsoft in a class action lawsuit, alleging that they were denied employment benefits, especially employee stock options that were paid to regular employees. Microsoft contributed 3 percent of an employee's salary to the stock option plan. The U.S. Court of Appeals agreed with the plaintiffs, citing the Internal Revenue Code that requires such stock option plans to be available to all employees. The Court of Appeals stated, "It is our conclusion that Microsoft either exercised, or retained the right to exercise, direction over the services performed. This control establishes an employer–employee relationship." Thus, Microsoft's attempt to define certain full-time employees as freelancers and temps was rebuffed by the courts. *Vizcaino v. United States District Court for the Western District of Washington*, 173 F.3d 713, **Web** 1999 U.S. App. Lexis 9057 (United States Court of Appeals for the Ninth Circuit)

Law & Ethics Questions

1. **ETHICS** Did Microsoft act ethically in this case?

2. Why did Microsoft classify full-time workers as freelancers and temps? Explain.

Web Exercises

1. **WEB** Visit the website of the U.S. Court of Appeals for the Ninth Circuit, at *www.ce9.uscourts.gov*.

2. **WEB** Visit the website of Microsoft Corporation, at *www.microsoft.com*.

Other Worker Protection Laws

In addition to the statutes already discussed in this chapter, the federal government has enacted many other statutes that regulate the employment relationship. These include the Consolidated Omnibus Budget Reconciliation Act (COBRA), the Family and Medical Leave Act, the Employee Retirement Income Security Act (ERISA), and immigration laws. These federal statutes are discussed in the following paragraphs.

Consolidated Omnibus Budget Reconciliation Act (COBRA)

The **Consolidated Omnibus Budget Reconciliation Act (COBRA)** of 1985 [26 U.S.C. Sections 1161–1169] provides that an employee of a private employer or the employee's beneficiaries must be offered the opportunity to continue his or her group health insurance after the voluntary or involuntary termination of a worker's employment or the loss of coverage due to certain qualifying events defined in the law. The employer must notify covered employees and their beneficiaries of their rights under COBRA. To continue coverage, a person must pay the required group rate premium. Government employees are subject to parallel provisions found in the Public Health Service Act.

CONTEMPORARY ENVIRONMENT
Family and Medical Leave Act

In February 1993, Congress enacted the **Family and Medical Leave Act** [29 U.S.C. Sections 2601, 2611–2619, 2651–2654]. This act guarantees workers unpaid time off from work for medical emergencies. The act, which applies to companies with 50 or more workers as well as federal, state, and local governments, covers about half of the nation's workforce. To be covered by the act, an employee must have worked for the employer for at least one year and have performed more than 1,250 hours of service during the previous 12-month period.

Covered employers are required to provide up to 12 weeks of unpaid leave during any 12-month period due to:

1. The birth of and care for a child

2. The placement of a child with an employee for adoption or foster care

3. A serious health condition that makes the employee unable to perform his or her duties

4. Care for a spouse, child, or parent with a serious health problem

Leave because of the birth of a child or the placement of a child for adoption or foster care cannot be taken intermittently unless the employer agrees. Other leaves may be taken on an intermittent basis. The employer may require medical proof of claimed serious health conditions.

An eligible employee who takes leave must, upon returning to work, be restored to either the same or an equivalent position with equivalent employment benefits and pay. The restored employee is not entitled to the accrual of seniority during the leave period, however. A covered employer may deny restoration to a salaried employee who is among the highest-paid 10 percent of that employer's employees if the denial is necessary to prevent "substantial and grievous economic injury" to the employer's operations.

Employee Retirement Income Security Act (ERISA)

Employers are not required to establish pension plans for their employees. If they do, however, they are subject to the record-keeping, disclosure, and other requirements of the **Employee Retirement Income Security Act (ERISA).**[4] ERISA is a complex act designed to prevent fraud and other abuses associated with private pension funds. Federal, state, and local government pension funds are exempt from its coverage. ERISA is administered by the Department of Labor and the IRS.

Among other things, ERISA requires pension plans to be in writing and to name a pension fund manager. The plan manager owes a fiduciary duty to act as a "prudent person" in managing the fund and investing its assets. No more than 10 percent of a pension fund's assets can be invested in the securities of the sponsoring employer.

Vesting occurs when an employee has a nonforfeitable right to receive pension benefits. First, ERISA provides for immediate vesting of each employee's own contributions to the plan. Second, it requires employers' contributions to be either (1) completely forfeitable for a set period of up to five years and totally vested after that (*cliff vesting*) or (2) gradually vested over a seven-year period and completely vested after that time.

Immigration Laws

The **Immigration Reform and Control Act of 1986 (IRCA)**[5] and the Immigration Act of 1990[6] are administered by the **U.S. Immigration and Customs Enforcement**. These acts make it unlawful for employers to hire illegal immigrants. Employers are required to inspect documents of prospective employees and determine that they are either U.S. citizens or otherwise qualified to work in the country (e.g., have proper work visas).

Employers must maintain records and post in the workplace notices of the contents of the law. Violators are subject to both civil and criminal penalties.

Web Exercises

1. **WEB** Visit the website of the U.S. Immigration and Customs Enforcement (ICE), at *www.ice.gov*.

2. **WEB** Using the *www.ice.gov*, can you find a recent topic or issue that the ICE is involved with?

CONTEMPORARY ENVIRONMENT
Drug Testing and Polygraph Tests

Drug testing of employees or prospective employees by private and public employers has increased dramatically in the past decade. Employers see drug testing as a way to increase productivity and decrease liability exposure. Job applicants and employees often view drug testing as an invasion of privacy. Although the courts have not been totally consistent in deciding drug testing cases, several trends have emerged.

Generally, preemployment drug screening has been upheld by the courts. Because job applicants have a lower expectation of privacy than incumbent employees, legal challenges are less likely. Drug testing of incumbent employees by private employers is usually upheld where the employer either has a reasonable suspicion that an employee is impaired or drug testing is required after an accident has occurred.

The **Employee Polygraph Protection Act** of 1988 [29 U.S.C. Sections 2001–2009], a federal statute, prohibits most private employers from using polygraph lie detector tests to screen job applicants and employees. Federal and state governments are not covered by the act. Polygraph tests may also be used by employers in matters dealing with national defense (e.g., certain defense contractors) and security services that hire employees who protect the public health and safety (e.g., guards at electric power plants).

The act requires private employers that are permitted to use polygraph testing to follow certain procedures, including giving notice to the person to be tested, using licensed examiners, and prohibiting certain questions (e.g., those relating to the religion or sexual behavior of the subject).

Government Programs

The U.S. government has established several programs that provide benefits to workers and their dependants. Two of these programs, unemployment compensation and Social Security, are discussed in the following paragraphs.

Unemployment Compensation

In 1935, Congress established an **unemployment compensation** program to assist workers who were temporarily unemployed. Under the **Federal Unemployment Tax Act (FUTA)**[7] and state laws enacted to implement the program, employers are required to pay unemployment contributions (taxes). The tax rate and unemployment wage level are subject to change. Employees do not pay unemployment taxes.

State governments administer unemployment compensation programs under general guidelines set by the federal government. Each state establishes its own eligibility requirements and the amount and duration of the benefits. To collect benefits, applicants must be able and available for work and seeking employment. Workers who have been let go because of bad conduct (e.g., illegal activity, drug use on the job) or who voluntarily quit work without just cause are not eligible to receive benefits.

Web Exercise

1. **WEB** Use *www.google.com* to find out what unemployment benefits are available in your state.

Social Security

In 1935, Congress established the federal **Social Security** system to provide limited retirement and death benefits to certain employees and their dependents. The Social Security system is administered by the **Social Security Administration**. Today, Social Security benefits include (1) retirement benefits, (2) survivors' benefits to family members of

deceased workers, (3) disability benefits, and (4) medical and hospitalization benefits (Medicare).

Under the **Federal Insurance Contributions Act (FICA)**,[8] employees must make contributions (pay taxes) into the Social Security fund. An employee's employer must pay a matching amount. Social Security does not operate like a savings account. Instead, current contributions are used to fund current claims. The employer is responsible for deducting employees' portions from their wages and remitting the entire payment to the IRS.

Under the **Self-Employment Contributions Act**,[9] self-employed individuals must pay Social Security contributions, too. The amount of taxes self-employed individuals must pay is equal to the combined employer–employee amount.

Failure to submit Social Security taxes subjects the violator to interest payments, penalties, and possible criminal liability. Social Security taxes may be changed by act of Congress.

Web Exercises

1. **WEB** Visit the website of the Social Security Administration, at *www.ssa.gov*.
2. **WEB** Using *www.ssa.gov/online*, search for the SS-5 form. What is this form used for?

Washington, DC

In the United States, federal labor laws protect the rights of workers to form and join unions and to engage in peaceful strikes and picketing.

Labor Law

In the 1880s, few laws protected workers against employment abuses. Workers reacted by organizing unions in an attempt to gain bargaining strength. Unlike unions in many European countries, unions in the United States did not form their own political party. By the early 1900s, employers used violent tactics against workers who were trying to organize into unions. The courts generally sided with employers in such disputes.

The **American Federation of Labor (AFL)** was formed in 1886, under the leadership of Samuel Gompers. Only skilled craft workers such as silversmiths and artisans were allowed to belong. In 1935, John L. Lewis formed the **Congress of Industrial Organizations (CIO)**. The CIO permitted semiskilled and unskilled workers to become members. In 1955, the AFL and CIO combined to form the **AFL-CIO**. Individual unions (such as the United Auto Workers and United Steel Workers) may choose to belong to the AFL-CIO, but not all unions opt to join.

Today, approximately 10 percent of private-sector wage and salary workers belong to labor unions. Many government employees also belong to unions.

> Management and union may be likened to that serpent of the fables who on one body had two heads that fighting with poisoned fangs, killed themselves.
>
> Peter Drucker
> *The New Society (1951)*

Web Exercises

1. **WEB** Visit the website of the AFL-CIO, at *www.aflcio.org*.

2. **WEB** Using *www.aflcio.org*, find a political issue that the AFL-CIO has taken a position on.

LANDMARK LAW
Federal Labor Union Statutes

In the early 1900s, members of the labor movement lobbied Congress to pass laws to protect their rights to organize and bargain with management. During the Great Depression of the 1930s, several statutes that were enacted gave workers certain rights and protections. Other statutes have been added since then. The major federal statutes in this area are:

- **Norris-LaGuardia Act.** Enacted in 1932, the **Norris-LaGuardia Act** stipulates that it is legal for employees to organize [29 U.S.C. Sections 101–110, 113–115].

- **National Labor Relations Act (NLRA).** The **National Labor Relations Act (NLRA)**, also known as the Wagner Act, was enacted in 1935 [29 U.S.C. Sections 151–169]. The NLRA establishes the right of employees to form, join, and assist labor organizations; to bargain collectively with employers; and to engage in concerted activity to promote these rights.

- **Labor-Management Relations Act.** In 1947, Congress enacted the **Labor-Management Relations Act (the Taft-Hartley Act)** [29 U.S.C. Section 141 *et seq*.]. This act (1) expands the activities that labor unions can engage in, (2) gives employers the right to engage in free-speech efforts against unions prior to a union election, and (3) gives the president of the United States the right to seek an injunction (for up to 80 days) against a strike that would create a national emergency.

- **Labor-Management Reporting and Disclosure Act.** In 1959, Congress enacted the **Labor-Management Reporting and Disclosure Act (the Landrum-Griffin Act)** [29 U.S.C. Section 401 *et seq*.]. This act regulates internal union affairs and establishes the rights of union members.

- **Railway Labor Act.** The **Railway Labor Act** of 1926, as amended in 1934, covers employees of railroad and airline carriers [45 U.S.C. Sections 151–162 and 181–188].

National Labor Relations Board (NLRB)

The National Labor Relations Act created the **National Labor Relations Board (NLRB)**. The NLRB is an administrative body composed of five members appointed by the president and approved by the Senate. The NLRB oversees union elections, prevents employers and unions from engaging in illegal and unfair labor practices, and enforces and interprets certain federal labor laws. The decisions of the NLRB are enforceable in court.

Web Exercise

1. **WEB** Visit the website of the National Labor Relations Board (NLRB), at *www.nlrb.gov*. What is the stated purpose of the NLRB?

ETHICS SPOTLIGHT
Internal Union Affairs

Unions may adopt **internal union rules** to regulate the operation of the union, acquire and maintain union membership, and the like. The undemocratic manner in which many unions were formulating these rules prompted Congress in 1959 to enact **Title I of the Landrum-Griffin Act**. Title I, which is often referred to as **labor's bill of rights**, gives each union member equal rights and privileges to nominate candidates for union office, vote in elections, and participate in membership meetings. It further guarantees union members the right of free speech and assembly, provides for due process (notice and hearing), and permits union members to initiate judicial or administrative action.

A union may discipline members for participating in certain activities, including (1) walking off the job in a nonsanctioned strike, (2) working for wages below union scale, (3) spying for an employer, and (4) any other unauthorized activity that has an adverse economic impact on the union. A union may not punish a union member for participating in a civic duty, such as testifying in court against the union.

Law & Ethics Questions

1. Why was labor's bill of rights passed?

2. **ETHICS** Do you think that there has been much fraud in the use of labor union members' dues in the past?

Web Exercises

1. **WEB** Visit the website of the International Brotherhood of Teamsters, at *www.teamster.org*. What types of workers belong to this union?

2. **WEB** Use *www.google.com* to find an article that discusses where the money first came from to build Las Vegas, Nevada.

Organizing a Union

Section 7 of the NLRA gives employees the right to join together to form a union. Section 7 provides that employees shall have the right to self-organize; to form, join, or assist labor organizations; to bargain collectively through representatives of their own choosing; and to engage in other concerted activities for the purpose of collective bargaining or other mutual aid protection.

The group that the union is seeking to represent—which is called the **appropriate bargaining unit**, or **bargaining unit**—must be defined before the union can petition for an election. This group can be the employees of a single company or plant, a group within a single company (e.g., maintenance workers at all of a company's plants), or an entire industry (e.g., nurses at all hospitals in the country). Managers and professional employees may not belong to unions formed by employees whom they manage.

Types of Union Elections

If it can be shown that at least 30 percent of the employees in a bargaining unit are interested in joining or forming a union, the NLRB can be petitioned to investigate and set an election date. The following types of elections are possible:

- ■ *Contested election.* Most union elections are contested by the employer. The NLRB is required to supervise all **contested elections**. A simple majority vote (over 50 percent) wins the election. For example, if 51 of 100 employees vote for the union, the union is certified as the bargaining agent for all 100 employees.
- ■ *Consent election.* If management does not contest an election, a **consent election** may be held without NLRB supervision.
- ■ *Decertification election.* If employees no longer want to be represented by a union, a **decertification election** will be held. Such elections must be supervised by the NLRB.

Union Solicitation on Company Property

If union solicitation is being conducted by employees, an employer may restrict solicitation activities to the employees' free time (e.g., coffee breaks, lunch hours, before and after work). The activities may also be limited to nonworking areas such as the cafeteria, rest room, or parking lot. Off-duty employees may be barred from union solicitation on company premises, and nonemployees (e.g., union management) may be prohibited from soliciting on behalf of the union anywhere on company property. Employers may dismiss employees who violate these rules.

An exception to this rule applies if the location of the business and the living quarters of the employees place the employees beyond the reach of reasonable union efforts to communicate with them. This so-called **inaccessibility exception** applies to logging camps, mining towns, company towns, and the like.

In the following case, the U.S. Supreme Court addressed the issue of whether an employer had to allow nonemployee union organizers on its property.

CASE 35.6
Organizing a Labor Union

U.S. SUPREME COURT
Lechmere, Inc. v. National Labor Relations Board

502 U.S. 527, 112 S.Ct. 841, 117 L.Ed.2d 79,
Web 1992 U.S. Lexis 555
Supreme Court of the United States

> ❝*In practice, nonemployee organizational trespassing had generally been prohibited except where "unique obstacles" prevented nontresspassory methods of communication with the employees.*❞
>
> —Justice Thomas

Facts

Lechmere, Inc. (Lechmere), owned and operated a retail store in the Lechmere Shopping Plaza in Newington, Connecticut. Thirteen smaller stores were located between the Lechmere store and the parking lot, which was owned by Lechmere. The United Food and Commercial Workers Union, AFL-CIO (Union), attempted to organize Lechmere's 200 employees, none of whom belonged to a union. After a full-page advertisement in a local newspaper drew little response, nonemployee Union organizers entered Lechmere's parking lot and began placing handbills on windshields of cars parked in the employee section of the parking lot. Lechmere's manager informed the organizers that Lechmere prohibited solicitation or handbill distribution of any kind on the property and asked them to leave. They did so, and Lechmere personnel removed the handbills. Union organizers renewed their handbill effort in the parking lot on several subsequent occasions, but each time, they were asked to leave, and the handbills were removed. Union filed a grievance with the NLRB. The NLRB ruled in favor of Union and ordered Lechmere to allow handbill distribution in the parking lot. The Court of Appeals affirmed this decision. Lechmere appealed to the U.S. Supreme Court.

Issue

May a store owner prohibit nonemployee union organizers from distributing leaflets in a shopping mall parking lot owned by the store?

Language of the U.S. Supreme Court

In practice, nonemployee organizational trespassing had generally been prohibited except where "unique obstacles" prevented

nontresspassory methods of communication with the employees. The inaccessibility exception is a narrow one. It does not apply wherever nontrespassory access to employees may be cumbersome or less-than-ideally effective, but only where the location of a plant and the living quarters of the employees place the employees beyond the reach of reasonable union efforts to communicate with them.

Although the employees live in a large metropolitan area (Greater Hartford), that fact does not in itself render them "inaccessible." Their accessibility is suggested by the union's success in contacting a substantial percentage of them directly, via mailings, phone calls, and home visits. In this case, other alternative means of communication were readily available. Thus, signs (displayed, for example, from the public grassy strip adjoining Lechmere's parking lot) would have informed the employees about the union's organizational efforts. Access to employees, not success in winning them over, is the critical issue.

Decision

The U.S. Supreme Court held that under the facts of this case, Lechmere could prohibit nonemployee union organizers from distributing leaflets to employees in the store's parking lot. The Supreme Court reversed the decision of the Court of Appeals.

Law & Ethics Questions

1. Should property rights take precedence over a union's right to organize employees?

2. **ETHICS** Is it ethical for an employer to deny union organizers access to company property to conduct their organization efforts? Is it ethical for union organizers to demand this as a right?

3. What implications does this case have for business? Was the decision in this case a pro- or anti-business decision?

Web Exercises

1. **WEB** For the complete opinion of this case, go to *www.prenhall.com/cheesemancases*.

2. **WEB** Visit the website of the U.S. Supreme Court, at *www.supremecourtus.gov*, and try to find documents that relate to this case.

3. **WEB** Visit the website of the United Food and Commercial Workers Union, AFL-CIO, at *www.ufcw.org*. What are some of the types of employees who make up the membership of this union?

4. **WEB** Use *www.google.com* to find an article that discusses a recent attempt of a union to organize an employer's employees. Read it.

Illegal Interference with an Election

Section 8(a) of the NLRA makes it an **unfair labor practice** for an employer to interfere with, coerce, or restrain employees from exercising their statutory right to form and join unions. Threats of loss of benefits for joining the union, statements such as "I'll close this plant if a union comes in here," and the like are unfair labor practices. Also, an employer may not form a company union.

Section 8(b) of the NLRA prohibits unions from engaging in unfair labor practices that interfere with a union election. Coercion, physical threats, and such are unfair labor practices.

Where an unfair labor practice has been found, the NLRB (or the courts) may issue a cease-and-desist order or an injunction to restrain unfair labor practices and may set aside an election and order a new election.

The following is a classic case in which the U.S. Supreme Court found that an employer had engaged in an unfair labor practice.

CASE 35.7
Labor Union Election

U.S. SUPREME COURT
National Labor Relations Board v. Exchange Parts Company
375 U.S. 405, 84 S.Ct. 457, 11 L.Ed.2d 435,
Web 1964 U.S. Lexis 2263
Supreme Court of the United States

> "*The danger inherent in well-timed increases in benefits is the suggestion of a "fist inside a velvet glove."*"
>
> —Justice Harlan

Facts

Exchange Parts Co. (Exchange Parts) was engaged in the business of rebuilding automobile parts in Fort Worth, Texas. Its employees were not represented by a union. The International Brotherhood of Boilermakers, Iron Shipbuilders, Blacksmiths, Forgers and Helpers, AFL-CIO (Union), advised Exchange Parts that it was going to conduct a campaign to organize the workers at the plant. After obtaining sufficient support from members of the appropriate bargaining unit, Union petitioned the NLRB to set an election date. After completing its investigation, the NLRB issued an order setting an election date. Three weeks prior to the election date, Exchange Parts held a dinner for its employees at which management announced a new company benefit allowing employees to have an extra holiday (their birthday). Two weeks before the election date, Exchange Parts sent a letter to its employees that announced new increased wages for overtime pay and an extended vacation plan for employees. Union subsequently lost the election. Union filed a complaint with the NLRB, and the NLRB held in favor of Union and ordered a new election. The Court of Appeals reversed. The NLRB appealed to the U.S. Supreme Court.

Issue

Is it an unfair practice for an employer to confer new economic benefits on its employees on the eve of a union election?

Language of the U.S. Supreme Court

The broad purpose of Section 8(a) is to establish the right of employees to organize for mutual aid without employer interference. We have no doubt that it prohibits not only intrusive threats but also conduct immediately favorable to employees that is undertaken with the express purpose of impinging upon their freedom of choice for or against unionization and is reasonably calculated to have that effect. The danger inherent in well-timed increases in benefits is the suggestion of a "fist inside a velvet glove." Employees are not likely to miss the inference that the source of benefits now conferred is also the source from which future benefits must flow and which may dry up if it is not obliged.

We cannot agree with the court of appeals that enforcement of the NLRB's order will have the ironic result of discouraging benefits for labor. The beneficence of an employer is likely to be ephemeral if prompted by a threat of unionization that is subsequently removed. Insulating the right of collective organization from calculated goodwill of this sort deprives employees of little that has lasting value.

Decision

The U.S. Supreme Court held that an employer's conferral of benefits on employees on the eve of a union election in an attempt to affect the outcome of that election is an unfair labor practice. The Supreme Court reversed the decision of the Court of Appeals.

Law & Ethics Questions

1. Should a company be prohibited from taking away (or giving) economic benefits in its fight with a union?
2. **ETHICS** Was it ethical for the employer in this case to increase employee benefits on the eve of the union election?
3. Do you think the employer's conduct in this case constituted a "fist in a velvet glove"? Were the benefits conferred in this case likely to be ephemeral?

Web Exercises

1. **WEB** For the complete opinion of this case, go to *www.prenhall.com/cheesemancases*.
2. **WEB** Visit the website of the U.S. Supreme Court, at *www.supremecourtus.gov*, and try to find documents that relate to this case.
3. **WEB** Visit the website of the International Brotherhood of Boilermakers, at *www.boilermakers.org*.
4. **WEB** Use *www.google.com* to search to see if the professors or other employees of your university or college are unionized.

Collective Bargaining

Once a union has been elected, the employer and the union discuss the terms of employment of union members and try to negotiate a contract that embodies these terms. The act of negotiating is called **collective bargaining**, and the resulting contract is called a **collective bargaining agreement**. The employer and the union must negotiate with each other in good faith. Among other things, this prohibits making take-it-or-leave-it proposals.

The subjects of collective bargaining are classified as follows:

- *Compulsory subjects.* Wages, hours, and other terms and conditions of employment are **compulsory subjects of collective bargaining**. Fringe benefits, health benefits, retirement plans, work assignments, safety rules, and the like are included in this category.
- *Illegal subjects.* Subjects such as closed shops and discrimination are **illegal subjects of collective bargaining** and may not be negotiated.
- *Permissive subjects.* Subjects that are not compulsory or illegal are **permissive subjects of collective bargaining**. These include such issues as the size and composition of the supervisory force, location of plants, corporate reorganizations, and the like. These subjects may be bargained for if the company and union agree to do so.

Union Security Agreements

To obtain the greatest power possible, elected unions sometimes try to install a **union security agreement**. There are two types of security agreements:

- *Union shop.* Under a **union shop** agreement, an employee must join the union within a certain time period (e.g., 30 days) after being hired. Employees who do not join must be discharged by the employer upon notice from the union. Union members pay union dues to the union. Union shops are lawful.

■ *Agency shop.* Under an **agency shop** agreement, employees do not have to become union members, but they do have to pay an agency fee (an amount equal to dues) to the union. Agency shops are lawful.

Upon proper notification by the union, union and agency shop employers are required to (1) deduct union dues and agency fees from employees' wages and (2) forward these dues to the union.

The following case involves the legality of a union security clause.

C A S E **35.8**
Union Security Clause

U.S. SUPREME COURT
Marquez v. Screen Actors Guild, Inc.
525 U.S. 33, 119 S.Ct 292, 142 L.Ed.2d 242,
Web 1998 U.S. Lexis 7110
Supreme Court of the United States

> ❝*The membership that may be required as a condition of employment is whittled down to its financial core.*❞

—Justice O'Connor

Facts

The Screen Actors Guild (SAG) is a labor union that represents performers in the entertainment industry. Lakeside Productions, an entertainment production company, signed a collective bargaining agreement with SAG making SAG the exclusive union for performers that Lakeside hired for its productions. The collective bargaining agreement contained a standard "union security clause" providing that any performer who worked for Lakeside must be a member of SAG. Naomi Marquez, a part-time actress, auditioned for a one-line role in a TV episode to be filmed by Lakeside and won the part. When Marquez did not pay the $500 membership fee to SAG, Lakeside hired another actress for the part. Marquez sued SAG and Lakeside, alleging that the union security clause was unlawful. The district court held for the defendants, and the Court of Appeals affirmed. The U.S. Supreme Court granted certiorari to hear the appeal.

Issue

Does the union security clause negotiated between Lakeside Productions and SAG violate federal labor law?

Language of the U.S. Supreme Court

Section 8(a)(3) of the National Labor Relations Act (NLRA) permits unions and employers to negotiate an agreement that requires union "membership" as a condition of employment for all employees. Although Section 8(a)(3) states that unions may negotiate a clause requiring "membership" in the union, an employee can satisfy the membership condition merely by paying to the union an amount equal to the union's initiation fees and dues. In other words, the membership that may be required as a condition of employment is whittled down to its financial core.

Section 8(a)(3) does not permit unions to exact dues or fees from employees for activities that are not germane to collective bargaining, grievance adjustment, or contract administration. Section 8(a)(3) permits unions and employers to require only that employees pay the fees and dues necessary to support the union's activities as the employees' exclusive bargaining representative.

Decision

The U.S. Supreme Court held that the union security clause negotiated between Lakeside Productions and SAG was lawful under federal labor law. The U.S. Supreme Court affirmed the judgment of the Court of Appeals.

Law & Ethics Questions

1. What does an exclusive union security clause provide? Under this agreement, must a worker join a labor union? Explain.
2. **ETHICS** Did SAG and Lakeside act ethically in this case?
3. Do the decisions of the U.S. Supreme Court regarding union security agreements prevent the "free rider" problem? Explain.

Web Exercises

1. **WEB** For the complete opinion of this case, go to *www.prenhall.com/cheesemancases*.
2. **WEB** Visit the website of the U.S. Supreme Court, at *www.supremecourtus.gov*, and try to find documents related to this case.
3. **WEB** Visit the website of the Screen Actors Guild (SAG), at *www.sag.org*. Find out how to become a member.
4. **WEB** Use *www.google.com* to find an article that discusses the most recent collective bargaining contract of the SAG. Read it.

CONTEMPORARY ENVIRONMENT
State Right-to-Work Laws

In 1947, Congress amended the Taft-Hartley Act by enacting Section 14(b), which provides: "Nothing in this Act shall be construed as authorizing the execution or application of agreements requiring membership in a labor organization as a condition of employment in any State or Territory in which such execution or application is prohibited by State or Territorial Law." In other words, states can enact **right-to-work laws**—either by constitutional amendment or statute—that outlaw union and agency shops.

If a state enacts a right-to-work law, individual employees cannot be forced to join a union or pay union dues and fees even though a union has been elected by other employees. Right-to-work laws are often enacted by states to attract new businesses to a nonunion and low-wage environment. Unions vehemently oppose the enactment of right-to-work laws because they substantially erode union power.

Today, the following 22 states have enacted right-to-work laws:

Alabama	Arkansas
Arizona	Florida
Georgia	North Dakota
Idaho	Oklahoma
Iowa	South Carolina
Kansas	South Dakota
Louisiana	Tennessee
Mississippi	Texas
Nebraska	Utah
Nevada	Virginia
North Carolina	Wyoming

The remedies for violation of right-to-work laws vary from state to state but usually include damages to persons injured by the violation, injunctive relief, and often criminal penalties.

Strikes and Picketing

The NLRA gives union management the right to recommend that the union call a **strike** if a collective bargaining agreement cannot be reached. Before there can be a strike, though, a majority vote of the union's members must agree to the action. In order to support a strike, union members often picket at their employer's place of business. Picketing and strikes are discussed in the following paragraphs.

Picketing

Striking union members often engage in **picketing** in support of their strike. Picketing usually takes the form of the striking employees and union representatives walking in front of the employer's premises carrying signs announcing their strike. Picketing is used to put pressure on an employer to settle a strike. The right to picket is implied from the NLRA.

Picketing is lawful unless it (1) is accompanied by violence, (2) obstructs customers from entering the employer's place of business, (3) prevents nonstriking employees from entering the employer's premises, or (4) prevents pickups and deliveries at the employer's place of business. An employer may seek an injunction against unlawful picketing.

Secondary Boycott Picketing

Unions sometimes try to bring pressure against an employer by picketing the employer's suppliers or customers. Such **secondary boycott picketing** is lawful only if it is product picketing (i.e., if the picketing is against the primary employer's product). The picketing is illegal if it is directed against the neutral employer instead of the struck employer's product.

Example Suppose the apple pickers' union in the state of Washington goes on strike against its primary employers, the apple growers. Picketing the apple orchards may do little to draw attention of the strike to the public. Therefore, members of the apple pickers' union may picket grocery stores in metropolitan areas that sell Washington apples. If the signs the picketers carry ask shoppers at the grocery stores not to buy Washington apples, the secondary boycott is lawful. However, it is unlawful if the signs ask customers not to shop at the grocery stores.

In the following case, the court had to decide whether a secondary boycott had occurred.

CASE 35.9
Secondary Boycott

Kentov, Regional Director, National Labor Relations Board v. Sheet Metal Workers' International Association Local 15, AFL-CIO

418 F.3d 1259, **Web** 2005 U.S. App. Lexis 16461 (2005)
United States Court of Appeals for the Eleventh Circuit

> **" *Here, the Union representatives patrolled for approximately two hours near the entrance of the hospital, carrying a large coffin and accompanied by a Union representative dressed as the grim reaper complete with a large sickle.* "**
>
> —Judge Kravitch

Facts

The Sheet Metal Workers' International Association Local 15, AFL-CIO (Union) had a labor dispute with Massey Metals, Inc. (Massey), and Workers Temporary Staffing (WTS), which supplied nonunion labor employees to Massey and whom Massey used on its various construction projects. The Brandon Regional Medical Center (Hospital) employed Massey as the metal fabricator and installation contractor for a construction project at the Hospital.

One day, the Union staged a mock funeral procession in front of the Hospital. The procession consisted of four Union representatives acting as pallbearers and carrying a large coffin back and forth on the sidewalk near the entrance to the Hospital. Another Union representative accompanied the procession dressed as the "Grim Reaper." The Union broadcast somber funeral music over loudspeakers mounted on a flatbed trailer that was positioned nearby. Four other Union representatives distributed handbills to persons entering and leaving the Hospital that stated, "Going to Brandon Regional Hospital Should Not be a Grave Decision." The procession lasted approximately two hours and was videotaped.

Rochelle Kentov, the regional director of the National Labor Relations Board (NLRB), immediately filed a petition for a temporary injunction against the Union's mock funeral. The NLRB alleged that the Union's mock funeral procession at the Hospital constituted an illegal secondary boycott picketing. The U.S. District Court agreed with the NLRB and issued an injunction against the Union, prohibiting such mock funeral processions at the Hospital. The Union appealed.

Issue

Did the mock funeral procession by the Union at the hospital constitute an illegal secondary boycott picketing?

Language of the Court

We examine whether there is reasonable cause to believe that the Union violated the National Labor Relations Act (NLRA),

which prohibits secondary boycotts. This provision aims to prohibit a union that has a labor dispute with one employer (the primary employer) from exerting pressure on another neutral employer (the secondary employer), where the union's conduct is calculated to force the secondary employer to cease doing business with the primary employer. The NLRA implements the dual congressional objectives of preserving the right of labor organizations to bring pressure to bear on offending employers in primary labor disputes and of shielding unoffending employers and others from pressures in controversies not their own.

Here, the Union representatives patrolled for approximately two hours near the entrance of the hospital, carrying a large coffin and accompanied by a Union representative dressed as the grim reaper complete with a large sickle. During the procession, the Union played somber funeral music from large speakers. This activity could reasonably be expected to discourage persons from approaching the hospital. One of the Union's objectives in staging the procession was to exert pressure on the hospital to cease doing business with the non-union contractors, with whom the Union had a primary labor dispute. Under these facts, we hold that there is reasonable cause to believe that the Union violated the NLRA.

Decision

The U.S. Court of Appeals agreed with the U.S. District Court that the Union's mock funeral procession at the Hospital constituted an illegal secondary boycott picketing. The U.S. Court of Appeals affirmed the judgment of the U.S. District Court that banned the Union from further engaging in such activity at the Hospital.

Law & Ethics Questions

1. What is secondary boycott picketing?

2. Why does the National Labor Relations Act (NLRA) make secondary boycott picketing illegal? Explain.

3. What was the purpose of the Union holding a mock funeral procession at the hospital?

4. **ETHICS** Was the Union's conduct ethical in this case?

Web Exercises

1. **WEB** For the complete opinion of this case, go to *www.prenhall.com/cheesemancases*.

2. **WEB** Visit the website of the U.S. Court of Appeals for the Eleventh Circuit, at *www.ca11.uscourts.gov*.

3. **WEB** Visit the website of the Sheet Metal Workers' International Association, at *www.smwia.org*. What is a current political issue that the union is interested in?

4. **WEB** Use *www.google.com* to find a drawing or picture of the Grim Reaper.

5. **WEB** Go to the website *www.americanrightsatwork.org*. What is the purpose of this website?

No private business monopoly, producer organization or cartel wields the market (and physical) power or commands the discipline over its members which many unions have achieved.

Gottfried Haberler
Economic Growth and Stability (1974)

Illegal Strikes

Several types of strikes have been held to be illegal and are not protected by federal labor law. The following are **illegal strikes**:

- *Violent strikes.* In **violent strikes**, striking employees cause substantial damage to property of the employer or a third party. Courts usually tolerate a certain amount of isolated violence before finding that the entire strike is illegal.
- *Sit-down strikes.* In **sit-down strikes**, striking employees continue to occupy the employer's premises. Such strikes are illegal because they deny the employer's statutory right to continue its operations during the strike.
- *Partial or intermittent strikes.* In **partial or intermittent strikes**, employees strike part of the day or workweek and work the other part. This type of strike is illegal because it interferes with the employer's right to operate its facilities at full operation.
- *Wildcat strikes.* In **wildcat strikes**, individual union members go on strike without proper authorization from the union. The courts have recognized that a wildcat strike becomes lawful if it is quickly ratified by the union.
- *Strikes during the 60-day cooling-off period.* It is illegal for a strike to begin during the mandatory 60-day **cooling-off period**. This time is designed to give the employer and the union time to negotiate a settlement of the union grievances and avoid a strike. Any strike without a proper 60-day notice is illegal.
- *Strikes in violation of a no-strike clause.* It is illegal for a strike to take place in violation of a negotiated **no-strike clause**, under which an employer gives economic benefits to the union and, in exchange, the union agrees that no strike will be called for a set time.

Illegal strikers may be discharged by the employer, with no rights to reinstatement.

Crossover and Replacement Workers

Individual members of a union do not have to honor a strike. They may (1) choose not to strike or (2) return to work after joining the strikers for a time. Employees who choose either of these options are known as **crossover workers**.

Once a strike begins, the employer may continue operations by using management personnel and hiring **replacement workers** to take the place of the striking employees. Replacement workers can be hired on either a temporary or permanent basis. If replacement workers are given permanent status, they do not have to be dismissed when the strike is over.

Employer Lockout

If an employer reasonably anticipates a strike by some of its employees, it may prevent those employees from entering the plant or premises. This is called an **employer lockout**.

Example In 2004, when the owners of professional hockey teams that belong to the National Hockey League (NHL) anticipated a strike by the professional hockey players' union, the owners locked out the players. The team owners and the union could not reach an agreement, so the 2004–2005 season was cancelled.

ETHICS SPOTLIGHT

Plant Closing Act

Often, a company would choose to close a plant without giving its employees prior notice of the closing. To remedy this situation, in 1988, Congress enacted the **Worker Adjustment and Retraining Notification (WARN) Act**, also called the **Plant Closing Act** [29 U.S.C. Section 2102]. The act, which covers employers with 100 or more employees, requires employers to give their employees 60 days' notice before engaging in certain plant closings or layoffs.

If the employees are represented by a union, the notice must be given to the union; if they are not, the notice must be given to the employees individually.

The act covers the following actions:

- **Plant closings.** A plant closing is a permanent or temporary shutdown of a single site that results in a loss of employment of 50 or more employees during any 30-day period.

- **Mass layoffs.** A mass layoff is a reduction of 33 percent of the employees or at least 50 employees during any 30-day period.

An employer is exempted from having to give such notice if:

1. The closing or layoff is caused by business circumstances that were not reasonably foreseeable as of the time that the notice would have been required.

2. The business was actively seeking capital or business that, if obtained, would have avoided or postponed the shutdown and the employer in good faith believed that giving notice would have precluded it from obtaining the needed capital or business.

Law & Ethics Questions

1. What does the WARN Act provide? Explain.

2. **ETHICS** Was the WARN Act enacted to prevent unethical conduct by business? Explain.

Chapter Summary

Workers' Compensation, p. 979

Workers' compensation acts are state statutes that create an administrative procedure for workers to receive payments for job-related injuries.

Workers' Compensation Insurance

Most states require employers to carry private or government-sponsored workers' compensation insurance. Some states permit employers to self-insure.

Employment-Related Injury

For an injury to be compensable under workers' compensation, a claimant must prove that the injury arose out of and in the course of his or her employment.

Exclusive Remedy

Workers' compensation is an exclusive remedy. Thus, workers cannot sue their employers to recover damages for job-related injuries.

1. *Exceptions to the exclusive-remedy rule.* Workers may recover damages from their employers for job-related injuries if the employer does not provide workers' compensation and intentionally causes the worker's injuries.
2. *Lawsuits against third parties.* Workers' compensation acts do not bar injured workers from suing responsible third parties to recover damages (e.g., the manufacturer of a defective machine that caused a worker's injuries).

Occupational Safety, p. 984

The Occupational Safety and Health Act is a federal statute that requires employers to provide safe working conditions. The Occupational Safety and Health Administration

(OSHA) is a federal administrative agency that administers and enforces the Occupational Safety and Health Act.

Specific Duty Standards

Specific duty standards are safety standards for specific equipment (e.g., lathe) or a specific industry (e.g., mining).

General Duty Standards

General duty standards impose a general duty on employers to provide safe working conditions.

Fair Labor Standards Act (FLSA), p. 986

The federal Fair Labor Standards Act (FLSA) protects workers.

Child Labor

The FLSA forbids the use of illegal child labor. The U.S. Department of Labor defines illegal child labor.

Minimum Wage

The minimum wage is set by Congress and can be changed. The minimum wage as of 2007 is $5.15 per hour.

Overtime Pay

An employer cannot require employees to work more than 40 hours per week unless it pays them 1.5 times their regular pay for each hour worked in excess of 40 hours.

Other Worker Protection Laws, p. 988

Consolidated Omnibus Budget Reconciliation Act (COBRA)

COBRA is a federal statute that requires an employer to offer an employee or the employee's beneficiaries the opportunity to continue health benefits (upon payment of the premium) after termination of employment due to dismissal or death.

Family and Medical Leave Act

The Family and Medical Leave Act is a federal statute that guarantees covered workers unpaid time off from work for the birth or adoption of a child, serious health problems of the worker, and serious health problems of a spouse, child, or parent.

Employee Retirement Income Security Act (ERISA)

ERISA governs the establishment and administration of private pension programs to prevent fraud and other abuses.

Immigration Laws

The Immigration Reform and Control Act and the Immigration Act prohibit employers from employing illegal immigrants. Employers must require workers to prove that they are U.S. citizens or have proper work visas to work in this country.

Government Programs, p. 990

Unemployment Compensation

State and federal programs pay compensation to unemployed persons who meet certain qualifying standards. Employers are required to pay unemployment compensation payments to the government to fund the program. Unemployment is authorized by the Federal Unemployment Tax Act (FUTA) and state laws.

Social Security

Social Security is a federal government program that provides limited retirement, disability, and medical and hospitalization to covered employees and their dependents. Employers and employees pay taxes to fund the program.

Labor Law, p. 992

Federal Labor Union Statutes

Federal labor statutes include:

1. *Norris-LaGuardia Act.* This act made it legal for employees to organize.
2. *National Labor Relations Act.* This act established the right of employees to form, join, and assist labor unions. Also called the *Wagner Act* or *NLRA*.
3. *Labor-Management Relations Act.* This act expanded the activities labor unions could engage in, gave employers free speech rights to oppose unionization, and gave the president the right to seek injunctions against strikes that would create a national emergency. Also called the *Taft-Hurley Act*.
4. *Labor-Management Reporting and Disclosure Act.* This act gives union members the right to nominate candidates for union offices and vote in union elections. Also called the *Landrum-Griffin Act*.
5. *Railway Labor Act.* This act governs union rights of railroad and airline employees.

National Labor Relations Board (NLRB)

The NLRB is a federal administrative agency empowered to administer federal labor law, oversee union elections, and decide labor disputes.

Internal Union Affairs

Title I of the Landrum-Griffin Act, commonly called *labor's bill of rights*, gives each union member equal rights and privileges to nominate candidates for union office, vote in union elections, and participate in membership meetings.

Organizing a Union, p. 993

1. *Section 7 of the NLRA.* Section 7 of the NLRA gives employees the right to join together and form a union.
2. *Appropriate bargaining unit.* An appropriate bargaining unit is a group of employees that a union is seeking to represent.

Types of Union Elections

1. *Contested election.* Management may contest a union. The NLRB must supervise this type of election.
2. *Consent election.* In a consent election, management does not contest the union election.
3. *Decertification election.* This is an election to determine if the employees want to reject a union as their representative. The NLRB must supervise the election.

Union Solicitation on Company Property

An employer may restrict solicitation activities to the employees' free time (e.g., breaks, lunch hours, before and after work). An employer may prohibit solicitation on company property unless the employees cannot otherwise be contacted.

Illegal Interference with an Election

1. *Section 8(a) of the NLRA.* This section makes it an unfair labor practice for an employer to interfere with, coerce, or restrain employees from exercising their right to form and join unions.
2. *Section 8(b) of the NLRA.* This section makes it an unfair labor practice for a union to interfere with a union election.

Collective Bargaining

Collective bargaining is a process whereby a union and an employer negotiate the terms and conditions of employment for the covered employee union members. A collective bargaining agreement is a contract resulting from collective bargaining.

1. *Compulsory subjects.* Compulsory subjects of collective bargaining are wages, hours, and other terms and conditions of employment (e.g., vacations, medical benefits).

2. *Illegal subjects.* Illegal subjects of collective bargaining are subjects that may not be negotiated (e.g., discrimination).
3. *Permissive subjects.* Permissive subjects of collective bargaining are not compulsory or illegal (e.g., closing of plants).

Union Security Agreements

1. *Union shop.* A union shop is an establishment where an employee must join a union within a certain number of days after being hired.
2. *Agency shop.* In an agency shop, employees do not have to join the union but must pay an agency fee equal to union dues.

State Right-to-Work Laws

States may enact statutes that make union shops and agency shops illegal. In such a case, individual employees may choose not to join the union.

Strikes and Picketing, p. 998

A strike is a cessation of work by union members in order to obtain economic benefits, to correct an unfair labor practice, or to preserve their work. The NLRA gives union employees the right to strike.

Picketing

Striking employees and union organizers may picket—that is, walk around the employer's premises, usually carrying signs, notifying the public of their grievance against the employer. Picketing is illegal if it is accompanied by violence or obstructs customers, nonstriking workers, or suppliers from entering the employer's premises.

Secondary Boycott Picketing

A secondary boycott is picketing conducted at a third party's premises. Product picketing against the products of the struck employer is lawful. Picketing directed against the neutral employer is illegal.

Illegal Strikes

1. *Violent strike.* In this type of strike, striking employees cause substantial damage to the employer's or a third party's property.
2. *Sit-down strike.* In this type of strike, employees occupy and refuse to leave the employer's premises.
3. *Partial or intermittent strike.* In this type of strike, employees strike for only parts of each day or week.
4. *Wildcat strike.* A wildcat strike is a strike that is not sanctioned by the union.
5. *Strike during the 60-day cooling-off period.* In this type of strike, the union has not given the employer at least 60 days' prior notice of the strike.
6. *Strike in violation of a no-strike clause.* This type of strike violates a no-strike clause in a collective bargaining agreement.

Crossover and Replacement Workers

A crossover worker is an employee who does not honor a strike who either (1) chooses not to strike or (2) returns to work after joining strikers for a time. A replacement worker is a person who is hired to take the place of a striking worker. The employer may offer replacement workers permanent positions.

Employer Lockout

An employer may lock employees out of its premises if it reasonably anticipates a strike.

Plant Closing Act

The Worker Adjustment and Retraining Notification (WARN) Act is a federal law that requires employers with 100 or more employees to give their employees 60 days' notice before engaging in certain plant closings or layoffs. Also called the *Plant Closing Act*.

Test Review Terms and Concepts

Case Problems

35.1 Workers' Compensation: John B. Wilson was employed by the city of Modesto, California, as a police officer. He was a member of the special emergency reaction team (SERT), a tactical unit of the city's police department that is trained and equipped to handle highly dangerous criminal situations. Membership in SERT is voluntary for police officers. No additional pay or benefits are involved. To be a member of SERT, each officer is required to pass physical tests four times a year. One such test requires members to run two miles in 17 minutes. Other tests call for minimum numbers of push-ups, pull-ups, and sit-ups. Officers who do not belong to SERT are not required to undergo these physical tests. One day, Wilson completed his patrol shift, changed clothes, and drove to the Modesto Junior College track. While running there, he injured his left ankle. Wilson filed a claim for workers' compensation benefits, which was contested by his employer. Who wins? *Wilson v. Workers' Compensation Appeals Board*, 196 Cal.App.3d 902, 239

Cal.Rptr. 719, **Web** 1987 Cal. App. Lexis 2382 (Court of Appeal of California)

35.2 Workers' Compensation: Joseph Albanese was employed as a working foreman by Atlantic Steel Company, Inc., for approximately 17 years. His duties included the supervision of plant employees. The business was sold to a new owner. One year later, after the employees voted to unionize, friction developed between Albanese and the workers. Part of the problem was caused by management's decision to eliminate overtime work, which required Albanese to go out into the shop and prod the workers to expedite the work.

Additional problems resulted from the activities of Albanese's direct supervisor, the plant manager. On one occasion, the manager informed Albanese that the company practice of distributing Thanksgiving turkeys was to be discontinued. The following year, the manager told Albanese that the company did not intend to give the workers a Christmas bonus. The plant manager also informed Albanese that he did not intend to pay overtime wages to any worker. On each occasion, after Albanese relayed the information to the workers, the plant manager reversed his own decision.

After the last incident, Albanese became distressed and developed chest pains and nausea. When the chest pains became sharper, he went home to bed. Albanese did not work thereafter. He experienced continuing pain, sweatiness, shortness of breath, headaches, and depression. Albanese filed a claim for workers' compensation based on stress. The employer contested the claim. Who wins? *Albanese's Case*, 378 Mass. 14, 389 N.E.2d 83, **Web** 1979 Mass. Lexis 795 (Supreme Judicial Court of Massachusetts)

35.3 Occupational Safety: Getty Oil Company (Getty) operates a separation facility where it gathers gas and oil from wells and transmits them to an outgoing pipeline under high pressure. Getty engineers designed and produced a pressure vessel, called a fluid booster, which was to be installed to increase pressure in the system. Robinson, a Getty engineer, was instructed to install the vessel. Robinson picked up the vessel from the welding shop without having it tested. After he completed the installation, the pressure valve was put into operation. When the pressure increased from 300 to 930 pounds per square inch, an explosion occurred. Robinson died from the explosion, and another Getty employee was seriously injured. The secretary of labor issued a citation against Getty for violating the general duty provision for worker safety contained in the Occupational Safety and Health Act. Getty challenged the citation. Who wins? *Getty Oil Company v. Occupational Safety and Health Review Commission*, 530 F.2d 1143, **Web** 1976 U.S. App. Lexis 11640 (United States Court of Appeals for the Fifth Circuit)

35.4 ERISA: United Artists is a Maryland corporation doing business in the state of Texas. United Pension Fund (Plan) is a defined-contribution employee pension benefit plan sponsored by United Artists for its employees. Each employee has his or her own individual pension account, but Plan's assets are pooled for investment purposes. Plan is administered by a board of trustees. During a period of nine years, seven of the trustees used Plan to make a series of loans to themselves. The trustees did not (1) require the borrowers to submit written applications for the subject loans, (2) assess the prospective borrowers' ability to repay the loans, (3) specify a period in which the loans were to be repaid, or (4) call in the loans when they remained unpaid. The trustees also charged less than fair market value interest rates for the loans. The secretary of labor sued the trustees, alleging that they had breached their fiduciary duty in violation of ERISA. Who wins? *McLaughlin v. Rowley*, 698 F.Supp. 1333, **Web** 1988 U.S. Dist. Lexis 12674 (United States District Court for the Northern District of Texas)

35.5 Drug Testing: Air traffic controllers are federal government employees who are responsible for directing commercial and private air traffic in this country. They are subject to regulation by the secretary of transportation (Secretary). Secretary adopted a regulation that provides for postaccident urinalysis drug testing of air traffic controllers responsible for the airspace in which an airplane accident has occurred. The National Air Traffic Controllers Association, MEBA/NNU, AFL-CIO, sued, alleging that such drug testing was an unreasonable search and seizure in violation of the Fourth Amendment to the U.S. Constitution. Who wins? *National Air Traffic Controllers Assn., MEBA/NNU, AFL-CIO v. Burnley*, 700 F.Supp. 1043, **Web** 1988 U.S. Dist. Lexis 15884 (United States District Court for the Northern District of California)

35.6 Unemployment Benefits: Devon Overstreet, who worked as a bus driver for the Chicago Transit Authority (CTA) for over six years, took sick leave for six weeks. Because she had been on sick leave for more than seven days, CTA required her to take a medical examination. The blood and urine analysis indicated the presence of cocaine. A second test confirmed this finding. The CTA suspended her and placed her in the employee assistance program for substance abuse for not less than 30 days, with a chance of reassignment to a nonoperating job if she successfully completed the program. The program is an alternative to discharge and is available at the election of the employee. Overstreet filed for unemployment compensation benefits. CTA contested her claim. Who wins? *Overstreet v. Illinois Department of Employment Security*, 168 Ill.App. 3d 24, 522 N.E.2d 185, **Web** 1988 Ill. App. Lexis 269 (Appellate Court of Illinois)

35.7 Unfair Labor Practice: The Teamsters Union (Teamsters) began a campaign to organize the employees at a Sinclair Company (Sinclair) plant. When the president of Sinclair learned of the Teamsters' drive, he talked with all of his employees and emphasized the results of a long strike 13 years earlier that he claimed "almost put our company out of business," and he expressed worry that the employees were forgetting the "lessons of the past." He emphasized that Sinclair was on "thin ice" financially, that the Teamsters' "only weapon is to strike," and that a strike "could lead to the closing of the plant" because Sinclair had manufacturing facilities elsewhere. He also noted that because of the employees' ages and the limited usefulness of their skills, they might not be able to find reemployment if they lost their jobs. Finally, he sent literature to the employees stating that "the Teamsters Union is a strike happy outfit" and that they were under "hoodlum control," and included a cartoon showing the preparation of a grave for Sinclair and other headstones containing the names of other plants allegedly victimized by unions. The Teamsters lost the election 7 to 6 and then filed an unfair labor practice charge with the NLRB. Did Sinclair violate labor law? *N.L.R.B. v. Gissel Packing Co.*, 395 U.S. 575, 89 S.Ct.

1918, 23 L.Ed.2d 547, **Web** 1969 U.S. Lexis 3172 (Supreme Court of the United States)

35.8 Right-to-Work Law: Mobile Oil Corporation (Mobile) had its headquarters in Beaumont, Texas. It operated a fleet of eight oceangoing tankers that transported its petroleum products from Texas to ports on the East Coast. A typical trip on a tanker from Beaumont to New York took about five days. No more than 10 to 20 percent of the seamen's work time was spent in Texas. The 300 or so seamen who were employed to work on the tankers belonged to the Oil, Chemical & Atomic Workers International Union, AFL-CIO (Union), which had an agency shop agreement with Mobile. The state of Texas enacted a right-to-work law. Mobile sued Union, claiming that the agency shop agreement was unenforceable because it violated the Texas right-to-work law. Who wins? *Oil, Chemical & Atomic Workers International Union, AFL-CIO v. Mobile Oil Corp.*, 426 U.S. 407, 96 S.Ct. 2140, 48 L.Ed.2d 736, **Web** 1976 U.S. Lexis 106 (Supreme Court of the United States)

35.9 Plant Closing: Arrow Automotive Industries, Inc. (Arrow), was engaged in the remanufacture and distribution of automobile and truck parts. All its operating plants produced identical product lines. Arrow was planning to open a new facility in Santa Maria, California. The employees at the Arrow plant in Hudson, Massachusetts, were represented by the United Automobile, Aerospace, and Agricultural Implement Workers of America (Union). The Hudson plant had a history of unprofitable operations. Union called a strike when the existing collective bargaining agreement expired and a new agreement could not be reached. After several months, the board of directors of Arrow voted to close the striking plant. The closing gave Arrow a 24 percent increase in gross profits and freed capital and equipment for the new Santa Maria plant. In addition, the existing customers of the Hudson plant could be serviced by the Spartanburg plant, which was being underutilized. Union filed an unfair labor practice claim with the NLRB. Does Arrow have to bargain with Union over the decision to close a plant? What would have to be done if the Plant Closing Act applied to this situation? *Arrow Automotive Industries, Inc. v. N.L.R.B.*, 853 F.2d 223, **Web** 1988 U.S. App. Lexis 10091 (United States Court of Appeals for the Fourth Circuit)

35.10 Illegal Strike: The employees of the Shop Rite Foods, Inc. (Shop Rite), warehouse in Lubbock, Texas, elected the United Packinghouse, Food and Allied Workers (Union), as its bargaining agent. Negotiations for a collective bargaining agreement began. Three months later, when an agreement had not yet been reached, Shop Rite found excessive amounts of damage to merchandise in its warehouse and concluded that it was being intentionally caused by dissident employees as a pressure tactic to secure concessions from Shop Rite. Shop Rite notified the Union representative that employees caught doing such acts would be terminated; the Union representative in turn notified the employees.

A Shop Rite manager observed an employee in the flour section—where he had no business being—making quick motions with his hands. The manager found several bags of flour that had been cut. The employee was immediately fired. Another employee (a fellow Union member) led about 30 other employees in an immediate walkout. The company discharged these employees and refused to rehire them. The employees filed a grievance with the NLRB. Can they get their jobs back? *N.L.R.B. v. Shop Rite Foods, Inc.*, 430 F.2d 786, **Web** 1970 U.S. App. Lexis 7613 (United States Court of Appeals for the Fifth Circuit)

35.11 Employer Lockout: The American Ship Building Company (American) operated a shipyard in Chicago, Illinois, where it repaired Great Lakes ships during the winter months, when freezing on the Great Lakes rendered shipping impossible. The workers at the shipyard were represented by several unions. The unions notified American of their intention to seek modification of the current collective bargaining agreement when it expired three months later. On five previous occasions, agreements had been preceded by strikes (including illegal strikes) that were called just after the ships had arrived in the shipyard for repairs so that the unions increased their leverage in negotiations with the company.

Based on this history, American displayed anxiety as to the unions' strike plans and possible work stoppage. On the day that the collective bargaining agreement expired, after extended negotiations, American and the unions reached an impasse in their collective bargaining. In response, American decided to lay off most of the workers at the shipyard. It sent them the following notice: "Because of the labor dispute which has been unresolved, you are laid off until further notice." The unions filed unfair labor practice charges with the NLRB. Are American's actions legal? *American Ship Building Company v. N.L.R.B.*, 380 U.S. 300, 85 S.Ct. 955, 13 L.Ed.2d 855, **Web** 1965 U.S. Lexis 2310 (Supreme Court of the United States)

35.12 Replacement Workers: The union (Union) member-employees of the Erie Resistor Company (Company) struck Company over the terms of a new collective bargaining agreement that was being negotiated between Company and Union. Company continued production operations during the strike by hiring new hires and crossover union members who were persuaded to abandon the strike and come back to work. Company promised all replacement workers superseniority. This would take the form of adding 20 years to the length of a worker's actual service for the purpose of future layoffs and recalls. Many union members accepted the offer. Union filed an unfair labor practice charge with the NLRB. Is Company's offer of the superseniority lawful? *N.L.R.B. v. Erie Resistor Co.*, 373 U.S. 221, 83 S.Ct. 1139, 10 L.Ed.2d 308, **Web** 1963 U.S. Lexis 2492 (Supreme Court of the United States)

35.13 Secondary Boycott: Safeco Title Insurance Company (Safeco) was a major insurance company that underwrote title insurance for real estate in the state of Washington. Five local title companies acted as insurance brokers that exclusively sold Safeco insurance. Local 1001 of the Retail Store Employees Union, AFL-CIO (Union), was elected as the bargaining agent for certain Safeco employees. When negotiations between Safeco and Union reached an impasse, the employees went on strike. Union did not confine its picketing to Safeco's office in Seattle but also picketed each of the five local title companies. The picketers carried signs declaring that Safeco had no contract with Union and distributed handbills asking consumers to support the strike by canceling their Safeco insurance policies. The local title companies filed a complaint with the NLRB. Is the picketing of the neutral title insurance companies lawful? *N.L.R.B. v. Retail Store Employees Union, Local 1001, Retail Clerks International Association, AFL-CIO*, 447 U.S. 607, 100 S.Ct. 2372, 65 L.Ed.2d 377, **Web** 1980 U.S. Lexis 133 (Supreme Court of the United States)

Ethics Issues

35.14 Ethics: Jeffrey Glockzin was an employee of Nordyne, Inc. (Nordyne), which manufactured air-conditioning units. Sometimes Glockzin worked as an assembly line tester. The job consisted of attaching one of two wire leads with bare metal alligator-type clips leading from the testing equipment to each side of the air-conditioning unit. When the tester turned on a toggle switch, the air-conditioning unit was energized. Once a determination was made that the air-conditioning unit was working properly, the toggle switch would be turned off and the wire leads removed. One day, while testing an air-conditioning unit, Glockzin grabbed both alligator clips at the same time. He had failed to turn off the toggle switch, however. Glockzin received a 240-volt electric shock, causing his death. His heirs sued Nordyne for wrongful death and sought to recover damages for an intentional tort. Nordyne made a motion for summary judgment, alleging that workers' compensation benefits were the exclusive remedy for Glockzin's death. Does the "intentional tort" exception to the rule that workers' compensation is the exclusive remedy for a worker's injury apply in this case? Did Nordyne's management violate its ethical duty by not providing safer testing equipment? *Glockzin v. Nordyne, Inc.*, 815 F.Supp. 1050, **Web** 1992 U.S. Dist. Lexis 8059 (United States District Court for the Western District of Michigan)

35.15 Ethics: Whirlpool Corporation (Whirlpool) operated a manufacturing plant in Marion, Ohio, for the production of household appliances. Overhead conveyors transported appliance components throughout the plant. To protect employees from objects that occasionally fell from the conveyors, Whirlpool installed a horizontal wire-mesh guard screen approximately 20 feet above the plant floor. The mesh screen was welded to angle-iron frames suspended from the building's structural steel skeleton.

Maintenance employees spent several hours each week removing objects from the screen, replacing paper spread on the screen to catch grease drippings from the materials on the conveyors, and performing occasional maintenance work on the conveyors. To perform these duties, maintenance employees were usually able to stand on the iron frames, but sometimes they found it necessary to step onto the wire-mesh screen itself. Several employees had fallen partly through the screen. One day, a maintenance employee fell to his death through the guard screen.

The next month, two maintenance employees, Virgil Deemer and Thomas Cornwell, met with the plant supervisor to voice their concern about the safety of the screen. Unsatisfied with the supervisor's response, two days later, they met with the plant safety director and voiced similar concerns. When they asked him for the name, address, and telephone number of the local OSHA office, he told them they "had better stop and think about" what they were doing. The safety director then furnished them with the requested information, and later that day, one of the men contacted the regional OSHA office and discussed the guard screen.

The next day, Deemer and Cornwell reported for the night shift at 10:45 P.M. Their foreman directed the two men to perform their usual maintenance duties on a section of the screen. Claiming that the screen was unsafe, they refused to carry out the directive. The foreman sent them to the personnel office, where they were ordered to punch out without working or being paid for the remaining six hours of the shift. The two men subsequently received written reprimands, which were placed in their employment files.

The secretary of labor filed suit, alleging that Whirlpool's actions constituted discrimination against the two men in violation of the Occupational Safety and Health Act. Did Whirlpool act ethically in this case? Can employees engage in self-help under certain circumstances under OSHA regulations? *Whirlpool Corporation v. Marshall, Secretary of Labor*, 445 U.S. 1, 100 S.Ct. 883, 63 L.Ed.2d 154, **Web** 1980 U.S. Lexis 81 (Supreme Court of the United States)

35.16 Ethics: The International Association of Machinists and Aerospace Workers, AFL-CIO (Union), began soliciting the employees of Whitcraft Houseboat Division, North American Rockwell Corp. (Whitcraft), to organize a union. For three days, Whitcraft management dispersed congregating groups of employees. During these three days, production was down almost 50 percent. On the third day,

Whitcraft adopted the following no-solicitation rule and mailed a copy to each employee and posted it around the workplace:

> As you well know working time is for work. No one will be allowed to solicit or distribute literature during our working time, that is, when he or she should be working. Anyone doing so and neglecting his work or interfering with the work of another employee will be subject to discharge.

Two days later, a manager of Whitcraft found that two employees of the company were engaged in union solicitation during working hours in a working area. Whitcraft discharged them for violating the no-solicitation rule. Is their discharge lawful? Did Whitcraft act ethically in discharging the employees? *Whitcraft Houseboat Division, North American Rockwell Corporation v. International Association of Machinists and Aerospace Workers*, AFL-CIO, 195 N.L.R.B. 1046 (N.L.R.B.), **Web** 1972 NLRB Lexis 1117.

35.17 Ethics: Most musicians belonged to the American Federation of Musicians (Union), which represented more than 200,000 members in the United States. Union was divided into separate local unions (Locals) that represented the members from a certain geographic area. Gamble Enterprises, Inc. (Gamble), owned and operated the Palace Theater in Akron, Ohio, which staged the performances of local and traveling musicians.

Union adopted the following rule: "Traveling members cannot, without the consent of a Local, play any presentation performance unless a local house orchestra is also employed." This meant that the theater owner might have to pay two bands or orchestras. Gamble's refusal to abide by this rule caused Union to block the appearances of traveling bands and orchestras. Gamble filed an unfair labor practice charge with the NLRB. Is the Union rule lawful? *N.L.R.B. v. Gamble Enterprises, Inc.*, 345 U.S. 117, 73 S.Ct. 560, 97 L.Ed. 864, **Web** 1953 U.S. Lexis 2620 (Supreme Court of the United States)

IRAC Writing Assignment

Read **Case A-35** in Appendix A [*Wiljef Transportation, Inc. v. National Labor Relations Board*]. Use the IRAC method to prepare a written analysis of the case.

Endnotes

1. 29 U.S.C. Sections 553, 651–678.
2. For example, the Railway Safety Act and the Coal Mine Safety Act regulate workplace safety of railway workers and coal miners, respectively.
3. 29 U.S.C. Sections 201–206.
4. 29 U.S.C. Sections 1001 *et seq.*
5. 29 U.S.C. Section 1802.
6. 8 U.S.C. Sections 1101 *et seq.*
7. 26 U.S.C. Sections 3301–3310.
8. 26 U.S.C. Sections 3101–3125.
9. 26 U.S.C. Sections 1401–1403.

CHAPTER 36

Equal Opportunity in Employment

> **"***What people have always sought is equality of rights before the law. For rights that were not open to all equally would not be rights.***"**

—CICERO
De officilis, Book II, Chapter XII

CHAPTER OBJECTIVES

After studying this chapter, you should be able to:

1. Describe the scope of coverage of Title VII of the Civil Rights Act of 1964.
2. Identify race, color, and national origin discrimination that violate Title VII.
3. Identify sex discrimination—including sexual harassment—that violates Title VII.
4. Describe the scope of coverage of the Age Discrimination in Employment Act.
5. Describe the protections afforded by the Americans with Disabilities Act of 1990.

CHAPTER CONTENTS

- Introduction to Equal Opportunity in Employment
- Title VII of the Civil Rights Act of 1964
- Equal Pay Act
- Age Discrimination in Employment Act
- Americans with Disabilities Act
- Affirmative Action
- State and Local Government Antidiscrimination Laws
- Chapter Summary
- Test Review Terms and Concepts
- Case Problems
- Ethics Issues
- IRAC Writing Assignment

Introduction to Equal Opportunity in Employment

Under common law, employers could terminate an employee at any time and for any reason. In this same vein, employers were free to hire and promote anyone they chose without violating the law. This often created unreasonable hardship on employees and erected employment barriers to certain minority classes.

Starting in the 1960s, Congress began enacting a comprehensive set of federal laws that eliminated major forms of employment **discrimination**. These laws, which were passed to guarantee **equal employment opportunity** to all employees and job applicants, have been broadly interpreted by the federal courts, particularly the U.S. Supreme Court. States have also enacted antidiscrimination laws.

This chapter discusses federal and state **equal opportunity in employment** laws.

> Racial discrimination in any form and in any degree has no justifiable part whatever in our democratic way of life. It is unattractive in any setting but it is utterly revolting among a free people who have embraced the principles set forth in the Constitution of the United States.
>
> Judge Murphy, dissenting opinion
> *Korematsu v. U.S. (1944)*

Disabled Person's Parking Space

Title I of the Americans with Disabilities Act (ADA) requires employers to make reasonable accommodations for individuals with disabilities that do not cause undue hardship to the employer.

Title VII of the Civil Rights Act of 1964

Prior to the passage of major federal antidiscrimination laws in the 1960s, much discrimination in employment existed in this country. In the 1960s, Congress enacted several major federal statutes that outlawed employment discrimination against members of certain classes. These federal laws were instrumental in providing equal opportunity in employment in this country. One of the main statutes is *Title VII of the Civil Rights Act of 1964*.

LANDMARK LAW
Title VII of the Civil Rights Act of 1964

After substantial debate, Congress enacted the **Civil Rights Act of 1964**. **Title VII of the Civil Rights Act** (called the **Fair Employment Practices Act**) was intended to eliminate job discrimination based on the following *protected classes*: *race*, *color*, *national origin*, *sex*, and *religion*.

As amended by the **Equal Employment Opportunity Act of 1972**, Section 703(a)(2) of Title VII provides, in pertinent part, that:

It shall be an unlawful employment practice for an employer

(1) to fail or refuse to hire or to discharge any individual, or otherwise to discriminate against any individual with respect to his compensation, terms, conditions, or privileges of employment, because of such individual's race, color, religion, sex, or national origin; or

(2) to limit, segregate, or classify his employees or applicants for employment in any way which would deprive or tend to deprive any individual of employment opportunities or otherwise adversely affect his status as an employee, because of such individual's race, color, religion, sex, or national origin.

Scope of Coverage of Title VII

Title VII of the Civil Rights Act of 1964 applies to (1) employers with 15 or more employees, (2) all employment agencies, (3) labor unions with 15 or more members, (4) state and local governments and their agencies, and (5) most federal government employment. Native American tribes and tax-exempt private clubs are expressly excluded from coverage [42 U.S.C. Section 2000e *et seq.*; other portions of the Civil Rights Act of 1964 prohibit discrimination in housing, education, and other facets of life].

Title VII prohibits discrimination in hiring, decisions regarding promotion or demotion, payment of compensation and fringe benefits, availability of job training and apprenticeship opportunities, referral systems for employment, decisions regarding dismissal, work rules, and any other "term, condition, or privilege" of employment. Any employee of covered employers, including undocumented aliens [*Equal Employment Opportunity Commission v. Tortilleria "La Mejor,"* 758 F.Supp. 585, **Web** 1991 U.S. Dist. Lexis 5754 (United States District Court for the Eastern District of California)], may bring actions for employment discrimination under Title VII.

Title VII prohibits two major forms of employment discrimination: disparate-treatment discrimination and disparate-impact discrimination.

Disparate-Treatment Discrimination

Disparate-treatment discrimination occurs when an employer treats a specific *individual* less favorably than others because of that person's race, color, national origin, sex, or religion. In such situations, the complainant must prove that (1) he or she belongs to a Title VII protected class, (2) he or she applied for and was qualified for the employment position, (3) he or she was rejected despite this, and (4) the employer kept the position open and sought applications from persons with the complainant's qualifications [*McDonnell Douglas v. Green*, 411 U.S. 792, 93 S.Ct. 1817, 36 L.Ed.2d 668, **Web** 1973 U.S. Lexis154 (Supreme Court of the United States)].

Example A member of a minority race applies for a promotion to a position advertised as available at his company. The minority applicant, who is qualified for the position, is rejected by the company, which hires a nonminority applicant for the position. The minority applicant sues under Title VII. He has a *prima facie* case of illegal discrimination. The burden of proof shifts to the employer to prove a nondiscriminatory reason for its decision. If the employer offers a reason, such as saying that the minority applicant lacked sufficient experience, the burden shifts back to the minority applicant to prove that this was just a *pretext* (not the real reason) for the employer's decision.

Disparate-Impact Discrimination

Disparate-impact discrimination occurs when an employer discriminates against an entire protected *class*. Many disparate-impact cases are brought as class action lawsuits. Often, this type of discrimination is proven through statistical data about the employer's employment practices. The plaintiff must demonstrate a *causal link* between the challenged practice and the statistical imbalance. Showing a statistical disparity between the percentages of protected class employees versus the percentage of the population that the protected class makes within the surrounding community is not enough, by itself, to prove discrimination.

Example Disparate-impact discrimination occurs when an employer adopts a work rule that is neutral on its face but is shown to cause an adverse impact on a protected class. If an employer has a rule that all applicants for an executive position must be at least 5'8" tall, this looks like a neutral rule because it applies to both males and females. However, because this rule is unrelated to the performance of an executive position and eliminates many more females than males from being hired or promoted to an executive position, it is disparate-impact sex discrimination in violation of Title VII.

Intentional Discrimination

In a case involving intentional discrimination, the aggrieved party can recover compensatory damages. A court can award punitive damages against an employer in a case involving an employer's malice or reckless indifference to federally protected rights. The sum of compensatory and punitive damages is capped at different amounts of money, depending on the size of the employer.

Equal Employment Opportunity Commission (EEOC)

> God . . . hath made of one blood all nations of men for to dwell on the face of the earth.
>
> The Bible
> *Acts 17:26*

The **Equal Employment Opportunity Commission (EEOC)** is the federal agency responsible for enforcing most federal antidiscrimination laws. The members of the EEOC are appointed by the U.S. president. The EEOC is empowered to conduct investigations, interpret the statutes, encourage conciliation between employees and employers, and bring suit to enforce the law. The EEOC can also seek injunctive relief.

To bring an action under Title VII, a private complainant must first file a complaint with the EEOC within 180 days or 300 days (depending on the state) of the alleged discrimination.[1] The EEOC is given the opportunity to sue the employer on the complainant's behalf. If the EEOC chooses not to bring suit, it will issue a **right to sue letter** to the complainant. This gives the complainant the right to sue the employer.

Remedies for Violations of Title VII

A successful plaintiff in a Title VII action can recover back pay and reasonable attorneys' fees. The courts also have broad authority to grant equitable remedies. For instance, the courts can order reinstatement, grant fictional seniority, and issue injunctions to compel the hiring or promotion of protected minorities.

In the following case, the U.S. Supreme Court had to decide whether a complaint of employment discrimination would be permitted to go to trial.

CASE **36.1**
Equal Employment Opportunity Commission

U.S. SUPREME COURT
Ledbetter v. The Goodyear Tire & Rubber Company, Inc.

127 S. Ct. 2162; 167 L. Ed. 2d 982; 75 U.S.L.W. 4359
Web 2007 U.S. Lexis 6295
Supreme Court of the United States

❝*The EEOC filing deadline protects employers from the burden of defending claims arising from employment decisions that are long past.*❞

—Justice Alito

Facts

Lilly Ledbetter worked for The Goodyear Tire & Rubber Company, Inc. (Goodyear), at its Gadsden, Alabama, plant for 20 years. During this time, salaried employees at the plant were given or denied raises based on their supervisors' evaluation of their performance. After 20 years of employment, Ledbetter filed a formal charge with the Equal Employment Opportunity Commission (EEOC), alleging acts of sex discrimination. Ledbetter took immediate early retirement. Ledbetter then sued Goodyear for Title VII pay discrimination. The U.S. District Court allowed the case to go to trial, at which evidence was introduced that during the course of her employment, Ledbetter had been discriminated against. The jury returned a verdict in favor of Ledbetter and awarded her back pay and damages.

On appeal, Goodyear contended that Ledbetter's pay discrimination claim was time barred with respect to all pay decisions made prior to 180 days before she filed her claim with the EEOC. During this time period, Goodyear had made only two nondiscriminatory pay decisions that denied Ledbetter raises. The U.S. Court of Appeals held that Ledbetter was time barred from raising any previous allegations of employment discrimination. Ledbetter appealed to the U.S. Supreme Court.

Issue

Does the rule requiring a claimant to file a claim of employment discrimination with the EEOC within 180 days of the alleged discriminatory conduct bar Ledbetter's lawsuit against Goodyear alleging pay discrimination during her 20 years of employment with Goodyear?

Language of the U.S. Supreme Court

Title VII of the Civil Rights Act of 1964 makes it an unlawful employment practice to discriminate against any individual with respect to his compensation because of such individual's sex. An individual wishing to challenge an employment practice under

this provision must first file a charge with the EEOC. Such a charge must be filed within a specified period (either 180 or 300 days, depending on the State) after the alleged unlawful employment practice occurred, and if the employee does not submit a timely EEOC charge, the employee may not challenge that practice in court.

Ledbetter's attempt to take the intent associated with the prior pay decisions and shift it to the last pay decision is unsound. It would shift intent from one act (the act that consummates the discriminatory employment practice) to a later act that was not performed with bias or discriminatory motive. The effect of this shift would be to impose liability in the absence of the requisite intent.

The EEOC filing deadline protects employers from the burden of defending claims arising from employment decisions that are long past. Certainly, the 180-day EEOC charging deadline is short by any measure, but by choosing what are obviously quite short deadlines Congress clearly intended to encourage the prompt processing of all charges of employment discrimination. This short deadline reflects Congress' strong preference for the prompt resolution of employment discrimination allegations through voluntary conciliation and cooperation.

Decision

The U.S. Supreme Court held that the 180-day period for filing Title VII employment discrimination claim with the EEOC was lawfully applied and was not met in this case. The U.S. Supreme Court affirmed the judgment of the U.S. Court of Appeals that held in favor of Goodyear.

Law & Ethics Questions

1. What is the 180-filing period? Explain.
2. Is the 180-day filing period to report employment discrimination to the EEOC too short? Do you think the reporting period should be increased?

3. **ETHICS** Was it ethical for Goodyear to avoid paying back pay and damages to Ledbetter because she had not timely filed her claim of discrimination with the EEOC?

4. **ETHICS** Had Ledbetter waited way too long to file a claim of discrimination against Goodyear?

Web Exercises

1. **WEB** For the complete opinion of this case, go to *www.prenhall.com/cheesemancases*.

2. **WEB** Visit the website of the U.S. Supreme Court, at *www.supremecourtus.gov*, and try to find documents that relate to this case.

3. **WEB** Visit the website of the Goodyear Tire & Rubber Company, at *www.goodyear.com*.

4. **WEB** Visit the website of the Equal Employment Opportunity Commission (EEOC), at *www.eeoc.gov*. Find the procedure for filing a charge of employment discrimination with the EEOC.

Rights matter most when they are claimed by unpopular minorities.

J. Michael Kirby
Sydney Morning Herald
(November 30, 1985)

Race, Color, and National Origin Discrimination

Title VII of the Civil Rights Act of 1964 was primarily enacted to prohibit employment discrimination based on *race, color, and national origin. Race* refers to broad categories such as African American, Caucasian, Asian, and Native American. *Color* refers to the color of a person's skin. *National origin* refers to the country of a person's ancestors or cultural characteristics. Discrimination by an employer based on race, color, or national origin violates Title VII.

Example Widget Corporation has a job opening for its chief executive officer (CFO) position. The employer receives applications for this position from many persons, including Joe Thomas, who is an African American. Mr. Thomas is the best-qualified applicant for the job. If Widget Corporation does not hire Mr. Thomas because of his race, the company has engaged in race discrimination in violation of Title VII.

Example Widget Corporation has a position for chief operations officer (COO) open. Several persons from within the company apply for a promotion to this position. Gloria Rodriquez, whose national origin is Mexico, is one of the applicants. Gloria has a Ph.D. in information sciences, 10 years' work experience, and has been with the company for 5 years in the capacity of operations manager. Although Gloria is the best-qualified person for the position, Gloria is not promoted because of her Hispanic heritage, and a less qualified person is promoted. The company has engaged in national origin discrimination in violation of Title VII.

Example The Widget Corporation has a position open for financial analyst. The two best-qualified applicants for the position are both African American. If the company decides to hire the applicant with the lighter skin color over the applicant with the darker skin color, this is an example of illegal discrimination based on color.

The first case that follows demonstrates race discrimination. The second case that follows demonstrates national origin discrimination.

CASE **36.2**

Race Discrimination

National Association for the Advancement of Colored People, Newark Branch v. Town of Harrison, New Jersey

907 F.2d 1408, **Web** 1990 U.S. App. Lexis 11793
United States Court of Appeals for the Third Circuit

> **"** *Thus, Harrison's facially neutral residency requirements have been shown to have a disproportionate impact upon black persons.* **"**
>
> —Judge Cowen

Facts

The town of Harrison, New Jersey (Harrison), adopted Ordinance 747, which stipulated that "all officers and employees of the Town shall, as a condition of employment, be bona fide residents of the Town." Because of the implementation of this ordinance for years, none of the 51 police officers, 55 firefighters, or 80 nonuniformed employees of the town was black. Although Harrison is a small primarily white community located in Hudson County, New Jersey, it is clearly aligned with Essex County to the west and is considered an extension of the city of Newark, which it abuts. Adjacent counties are within an easy commute of Harrison. Only 0.2 percent of Harrison's population is black. Several blacks who were members of the National Association for the Advancement of Colored People, Newark Branch (NAACP), applied for employment with Harrison but were rejected because they did not meet the residency requirement. The NAACP sued Harrison for race discrimination in violation of Title VII. The U.S. District Court dismissed the plaintiff's complaint. The NAACP appealed.

Issue

Does the residency requirement of the town of Harrison violate Title VII of the Civil Rights Act of 1964?

Language of the Court

The geographical area from which Harrison draws employees includes its own county of Hudson as well as Bergen, Essex, and Union counties. These four counties have a total civilian labor force of 1,353,555 of which 214,747 are black. By reason of the geographical location and the flow of transportation facilities, Harrison could reasonably be viewed as functionally a component of the city of Newark and a part of Essex County. Newark's population is approximately 60% black. Essex County's civilian labor force totals 391,612 of which 130,397 (or 33.3%) are black. It would be hard to conclude that among the very substantial number of black workers in the four-county labor market there are not large numbers of persons qualified to serve as police officers, firefighters, clerk typists, and laborers.

For all practical purposes, Harrison has no black residents. Thus, to limit employment or applications for employment to residents effectively excludes black persons from employment by the municipality. There is strong evidence that, if the residency requirement were removed, qualified black persons would seek positions with Harrison's municipal government. Thus, Harrison's facially neutral residency requirements have been shown to have a disproportionate impact upon black persons.

Decision

The U.S. Court of Appeals held that the plaintiffs had established that the ordinance constituted disparate-impact race discrimination in violation of Title VII of the Civil Rights Act of 1964. The Court of Appeals issued an injunction against enforcement of the ordinance.

Law & Ethics Questions

1. Would the same residency requirement rule cause disparate-impact discrimination if it were adopted by New York City or Los Angeles? Explain.

2. **ETHICS** Did the town of Harrison act ethically when it adopted the residency requirements?

3. Could a private business impose a residency requirement on its employees?

Web Exercises

1. **WEB** For the complete opinion of this case, go to *www.prenhall.com/cheesemancases*.

2. **WEB** Visit the website of the U.S. Court of Appeals for the Third Circuit, at *www.ca3.uscourts.gov*.

3. **WEB** Visit the website of the National Association for the Advancement of Colored People, at *www.naacp.org*. What is an issue on which the NAACP has taken a position?

4. **WEB** Use *www.google.com* to find an article that discusses race discrimination in the workplace. Read it.

C A S E **36.3**

National Origin Discrimination

Rivera v. Baccarat, Inc.

10 F.Supp.2d 318,
Web 1998 U.S. Dist. Lexis 9099
United States District Court for the Southern District of New York

> 66 *Accent and national origin are obviously inextricably intertwined in many cases.* 99
>
> —Judge Francis

Facts

Irma Rivera is a Hispanic woman who was born in Puerto Rico. She began working for Baccarat, Inc. (Baccarat), a distributor of fine crystal, as a sales representative in its retail store in Manhattan. Eight years later, Rivera was the top sales representative at the Baccarat store. J. D. Watts, the store's manager, stated that Rivera was "one of the best salespeople I have encountered in my 15 years in quality tabletop and gift retailing."

Jean Luc Negre became the new president of Baccarat, with ultimate authority for personnel decisions. Subsequently, Negre angrily told Rivera that he did not like her attitude and that he did not want her to speak Spanish on the job. Six months later, Dennis Russell, the chief financial officer of Baccarat, notified Rivera that Negre had made a decision to terminate her. Rivera pressed Russell to tell her why she was being fired. According to Rivera, he replied, "Irma, he doesn't want Hispanics." Negre also terminated Ivette Brigantty, another Hispanic sales representative. The store retained its non-Hispanic salesperson. Rivera sued Baccarat for national origin discrimination in violation of Title VII of the Civil Rights Act.

Issue

Did Baccarat engage in unlawful national origin discrimination?

Language of the Court

Under Equal Opportunity Commission regulations, national origin discrimination includes the denial of employment opportunity because an individual has the linguistic characteristics of a national origin group. Accent and national origin are obviously inextricably intertwined in many cases. Thus, unless any employee's accent materially interferes with her job performance, it cannot legally be the basis for an adverse employment action.

In this case, Ms. Rivera testified that during her one face-to-face meeting with Mr. Negre, he specifically stated that he did not like her accent. While Baccarat characterizes this as a single stray remark insufficient to support a finding of discriminatory intent, its probative values, if credited, is substantial. It is a statement by the president of the company who himself made the decision to terminate Ms. Rivera. Mr. Negre's criticism of Ms. Rivera's accent, his statement that he did not want Hispanic sale employees, and the fact that two Hispanic sales representatives were discharged while the non-Hispanic salesperson was retained all buttress the jury's finding of liability.

Decision

The U.S. District Court held that Baccarat had engaged in national origin discrimination in violation of Title VII. The Court awarded Ms. Rivera $104,373 in damages, attorneys' fees of $102,437, and prejudgment interest.

Law & Ethics Questions

1. Why did Congress include national origin discrimination under Title VII? How does it differ from race discrimination?
2. **ETHICS** Did the president of Baccarat act ethically in this case?
3. Do you think national origin discrimination is very prevalent in business?

Web Exercises

1. **WEB** For the complete opinion of this case, go to *www.prenhall.com/cheesemancases*.
2. **WEB** Visit the website of the U.S. District Court for the Southern District of New York, at *www.nysd.uscourts.gov*.
3. **WEB** Visit the website of Baccarat, Inc., at *www.baccarat.fr*.
4. **WEB** Use *www.google.com* to find an article that discusses national origin discrimination in the workplace. Read it.

Sex Discrimination

Although the prohibition against **sex discrimination** applies equally to men and women, the overwhelming majority of Title VII sex discrimination cases are brought by women. The old airline practice of ignoring the marital status of male flight attendants but hiring only single female flight attendants is an example of such discrimination.

In 1978, the **Pregnancy Discrimination Act** was enacted as an amendment to Title VII.[2] This amendment forbids employment discrimination because of "pregnancy, childbirth, or related medical conditions." Thus, a work rule that prohibits the hiring of pregnant women violates Title VII.

In the following case, the court found sex discrimination in violation of Title VII.

C A S E **36.4**

Sex Discrimination

Barbano v. Madison County, New York

922 F.2d 139, **Web** 1990 U.S. App. Lexis 22494
United States Court of Appeals for the Second Circuit

> ❝ *His questioning Barbano about whether she would get pregnant and quit was also discriminatory.* ❞
>
> —Judge Feinberg

Facts

The position of director of the Madison County Veterans Service Agency became vacant. The Madison County Board of Supervisors (Board) appointed a committee of five men to hold interviews. Maureen E. Barbano applied for the position and was interviewed by the committee. Upon entering the interview, Barbano heard someone say, "Oh, another woman." When the interview began, Donald Greene, a committee member, said he would not consider "some woman" for the position. He then asked Barbano personal questions about her plans on having a family and whether her husband would object to her transporting male veterans. Barbano said the questions were irrelevant and discriminatory. No committee member asked Barbano any substantive questions. Ultimately, the Board acted on the committee's recommendation and hired a male candidate. Barbano sued Madison County for sex discrimination in violation of Title VII. The U.S. District Court held in favor of Barbano and awarded her $55,000 in back pay, prejudgment interest, and attorneys' fees. Madison County appealed.

Issue

Did the Madison County Board of Supervisors engage in sex discrimination in violation of Title VII?

Language of the Court

There is little doubt that Greene's statements during the interview were discriminatory. He said he would not consider "some woman" for the position. His questioning Barbano about whether she would get pregnant and quit was also discriminatory, since it was unrelated to a bona fide occupational qualification. Similarly, Greene's questions about whether Barbano's husband would mind if she had to "run around the country with men," and that he would not want his wife to do it, were discriminatory.

Given the discriminatory tenor of the interview, and the acquiescence of the other Committee members to Greene's line of questioning, it follows that the trial court judge could find that those present at the interview, and not merely Greene, discriminated against Barbano. The record before us supports the district court's finding that the Board discriminated in making the hiring decision.

Decision

The U.S. Court of Appeals held that the defendant, Madison County, had engaged in sex discrimination in violation of Title VII. The Court of Appeals affirmed the District Court's decision that awarded damages to plaintiff Barbano.

Law & Ethics Questions

1. Why are questions concerning family obligations made illegal by Title VII?

2. **ETHICS** Was Greene's conduct morally reprehensible?

3. What actions should employers take to make sure their interviewers and other personnel understand Title VII and other antidiscrimination laws?

Web Exercises

1. **WEB** For the complete opinion of this case, go to *www.prenhall.com/cheesemancases*.

2. **WEB** Visit the website of the U.S. Court of Appeals for the Second Circuit, at *www.ca2.uscourts.gov*.

3. **WEB** Visit the website of Madison County, New York, at *www.madisoncounty.org*.

4. **WEB** Use *www.google.com* to find an article that discusses sex discrimination in the workplace. Read it.

Sexual Harassment

In the modern work environment, co-workers sometimes become sexually interested or involved with each other voluntarily. On other occasions, though, a co-worker's sexual advances are not welcome.

Refusing to hire or promote someone unless he or she has sex with the manager or supervisor is sex discrimination that violates Title VII. Other forms of conduct, such as lewd remarks, touching, intimidation, posting of indecent materials, and other verbal or physical conduct of a sexual nature constitute **sexual harassment** and violate Title VII.[3]

To determine what conduct creates a hostile work environment, the Supreme Court has stated:

We can say that whether an environment is "hostile" or "abusive" can be determined only by looking at all the circumstances. These may include the frequency of the discriminatory conduct; its severity; whether it is physically threatening or humiliating, or a mere offensive utterance; and whether it unreasonably interferes with an employee's work performance.[4]

In the following two cases, the U.S. Supreme Court decided legal issues concerning hostile work environment lawsuits.

CASE 36.5
Hostile Work Environment

U.S. SUPREME COURT
Harris v. Forklift Systems Incorporated

510 U.S. 17, 114 S.Ct. 367, 126 L.Ed.2d 295,
Web 1993 U.S. Lexis 7155
Supreme Court of the United States

> ❝*The very fact that the discriminatory conduct was so severe or pervasive that it created a work environment abusive to employees because of their race, gender, religion, or national origin offends Title VII's broad rule of workplace equality.*❞
>
> —Justice O'Connor

Facts

Teresa Harris worked as a manager at Forklift Systems Incorporated (Forklift), an equipment rental company, for two and one-half years. Charles Hardy was Forklift's president. Throughout Harris's time at Forklift, Hardy often insulted her because of her sex and made her the target of unwanted sexual innuendos. Hardy told Harris on several occasions, in the presence of other employees, "You're a woman, what do you know?" and "We need a man as the rental manager"; at least once, he told her she was "a dumb ass woman." Again in front of others, he suggested that the two of them "go to the Holiday Inn to negotiate Harris's raise." He made sexual innuendos about Harris's and other women's clothing.

Six weeks before Harris quit her job, Harris complained to Hardy about his conduct. Hardy said he was surprised that Harris was offended, claimed he was only joking, and apologized. He also promised he would stop, and based on this assurance, Harris stayed on the job. But two weeks later, Hardy began anew. While Harris was arranging a deal with one of Forklift's customers, he asked her, again in front of other employees. "What did you do, promise the guy some sex Saturday night?" One month later, Harris collected her paycheck and quit.

Harris then sued Forklift, claiming that Hardy's conduct had created an abusive work environment for her because of her gender. The U.S. District Court held that because Harris had not suffered severe psychological injury, she could not recover. The U.S. Court of Appeals affirmed. Harris appealed to the U.S. Supreme Court.

Issue

Must conduct, to be actionable as abusive work environment sexual harassment, seriously affect the victim's psychological well-being?

Language of the U.S. Supreme Court

When the workplace is permeated with discriminatory intimidation, ridicule, and insult that is sufficiently severe or pervasive to alter the conditions of the victim's employment and create an abusive working environment, Title VII is violated.

A discriminatorily abusive work environment, even one that does not seriously affect employees' psychological well-being, can and often will detract from employees' job performance, discourage employees from remaining on the job, or keep them from advancing in their careers. The very fact that the discriminatory conduct was so severe or pervasive that it created a work environment abusive to employees because of their race, gender, religion, or national origin offends Title VII's broad rule of workplace equality.

Certainly Title VII bars conduct that would seriously affect a reasonable person's psychological well-being, but the statute is not limited to such conduct. So long as the environment would reasonably be perceived, and is perceived, as hostile or abusive, there is no need for it also to be psychologically injurious.

Decision

The U.S. Supreme Court held that Title VII does not require a victim to prove that the challenged conduct seriously affected her psychological well-being in order to bring a Title VII lawsuit. The Supreme Court reversed the decision of the U.S. Court of Appeals and remanded the case to the U.S. District Court for further proceedings.

Law & Ethics Questions

1. What is sexual harassment? How does it differ from sex discrimination?
2. What is a hostile work environment? Is it easy to determine whether a work environment is hostile?
3. **ETHICS** What penalty should be assessed against Hardy for his conduct?
4. **ETHICS** What steps can a businesses take to eliminate sexual harassment on the job?

Web Exercises

1. **WEB** For the complete opinion of this case, go to *www.prenhall.com/cheesemancases*.
2. **WEB** Visit the website of the U.S. Supreme Court, at *www.supremecourtus.gov*, and try to find documents that relate to this case.
3. **WEB** Visit the website of Forklift Systems Incorporated, at *www.forkliftsystems.com*.
4. **WEB** Use *www.google.com* to find an article that discusses a recent case involving hostile work enviornment. Read it.

CASE **36.6**
Sexual Harassment

U.S. SUPREME COURT

Pennsylvania State Police v. Suders

542 U.S. 129, 124 S.Ct. 2342, 159 L.Ed.2d 204,
Web 2004 U.S. Lexis 4176 (2004)
Supreme Court of the United States

> **"** *Essentially, Suders presents a "worse case" harassment scenario, harassment ratcheted up to the breaking point.* **"**
>
> —Justice Ginsburg

Facts

The Pennsylvania State Police (PSP) hired Nancy Drew Suders as a police communications operator for the McConnellsburg barracks. Suders's supervisors were Sergeant Eric D. Easton, station commander at the McConnellsburg barracks, Patrol Corporal William D. Baker, and Corporal Eric B. Prendergast. Those three supervisors subjected Suders to a continuous barrage of sexual harassment that ceased only when she resigned from the force. Easton would bring up the subject of people having sex with animals each time Suders entered his office. He told Prendergast, in front of Suders, that young girls should be given instruction in how to gratify men with oral sex. Easton also would sit down near Suders, wearing spandex shorts, and spread his legs apart. Baker repeatedly made an obscene gesture in Suders's presence by grabbing his genitals and shouting out a vulgar comment inviting oral sex. Baker made this gesture as many as 5 to 10 times per night throughout Suders's employment at the barracks. Further, Baker would rub his rear end in front of her and remark "I have a nice ass, don't I?"

Five months after being hired, Suders contacted Virginia Smith-Elliot, PSP's equal opportunity officer, stating that she was being harassed at work and was afraid. Smith-Elliot's response appeared to Suders to be insensitive and unhelpful. Two days later, Suders resigned from the force. Suders sued PSP, alleging that she had been subject to sexual harassment and constructively discharged and forced to resign. The U.S. District Court held that although the evidence was sufficient for a jury to conclude that Suders's supervisors had engaged in sexual harassment, PSP was not vicariously liable for the supervisors' conduct. The U.S. District Court granted PSP's motion for summary judgment. The U.S. Court of Appeals reversed and remanded the case for trial on the merits against PSP. PSP appealed to the U.S. Supreme Court.

Issue

Can an employer be held vicariously liable when the sexual harassment conduct of its employees is so severe that the victim of the harassment resigns?

Language of the U.S. Supreme Court

To establish hostile work environment, plaintiffs like Suders must show harassing behavior sufficiently severe or pervasive to alter the conditions of their employment. The very fact that the discriminatory conduct was so severe or pervasive that it created a work environment abusive to employees because of their gender offends Title VII's broad rule of workplace equality. Beyond that, we hold, to establish "constructive discharge," the plaintiff must make a further showing: She must show that the abusive working environment became so intolerable that her resignation

qualified as a fitting response. An employer may defend against such a claim by showing both (1) that it had installed a readily accessible and effective policy for reporting and resolving complaints of sexual harassment, and (2) that the plaintiff unreasonably failed to avail herself of that employer-provided preventive or remedial apparatus. This affirmative defense will not be available to the employer, however, if the plaintiff quits in reasonable response to an employer-sanctioned adverse action officially changing her employment status or situation, for example, a humiliating demotion, extreme cut in pay, or transfer to a position in which she would face unbearable working conditions.

Essentially, Suders presents a "worse case" harassment scenario, harassment ratcheted up to the breaking point. Harassment so intolerable as to cause a resignation may be effected through co-worker conduct, unofficial supervisory conduct, or official company acts. Unlike an actual termination, which is always effected through an official act of the company, a constructive discharge need not be. A constructive discharge involves both an employee's decision to leave and precipitating conduct.

Decision

The U.S. Supreme Court agreed with the U.S. Court of Appeals that Suders's case presented genuine issues of material fact concerning Suders's hostile work environment and constructive discharge claims. The Supreme Court remanded the case for further proceedings consistent with its opinion.

Law & Ethics Questions

1. What is vicarious liability? Explain.
2. What is constructive discharge? Explain.
3. **ETHICS** Did Suders's supervisors act responsibly in this case?
4. **ETHICS** Do you think very much sexual harassment occurs in the workplace?

Web Exercises

1. **WEB** For the complete opinion of this case, go to *www.prenhall.com/cheesemancases*.
2. **WEB** Visit the website of the U.S. Supreme Court, at *www.supremecourtus.gov*, and try to find documents that relate to this case.
3. **WEB** Visit the website of Pennsylvania State Police, at *www.psp.state.pa.us*. Locate employment opportunities with the force.
4. **WEB** Use *www.google.com* to find an article that discusses a recent case involving a sexual harassment. Read it.

Same-Sex Discrimination

For years, it was unclear whether same-sex sexual harassment and **same-sex discrimination** in employment were actionable under Title VII. In 1998, in *Omcale v. Sundowner Offshore Services, Incorporated*,[5] the U.S. Supreme Court held that same-sex discrimination and harassment violated Title VII. Many state and local antidiscrimination laws outlaw same-sex discrimination and harassment in the workplace.

Example Suppose two members of the same gender work for an employer. One is the supervisor of the other. If the supervisor engages in sexual harassment of the employee of the same gender, this would violate Title VII.

CONTEMPORARY ENVIRONMENT
Employer's Defense to a Charge of Sexual Harassment

In two cases, *Faragher v. City of Boca Raton* and *Burlington Industries, Inc. v. Ellerth*, female plaintiffs sued their employers, proving that their supervisors had engaged in unconsented physical touching and verbal sexual harassment. In both cases, the female employee quit her job and sued her employer for sexual harassment in violation of Title VII. In the first case, the employer had never disseminated a policy against sexual harassment to its employees. The U.S. District Court held in favor of the female employee. In the second case, the employer had disseminated its policy against sexual harassment to its employees and had put into place a complaint system that the female employee did not use. In this case, the U.S. District Court granted summary judgment to the company. After appeals, the U.S. Supreme Court accepted these two cases for review.

The U.S. Supreme Court, in both of these decisions, held that an employer is not strictly liable for sexual harassment. The Supreme Court held that an employer may raise an **affirmative defense** against liability by proving two elements:

1. The employer exercised reasonable care to prevent, and promptly correct, any sexual harassing behavior.
2. The plaintiff employee unreasonably failed to take advantage of any preventive or corrective opportunities provided by the employer or to otherwise avoid harm.

The defendant employer has the burden of proving this affirmative defense. In determining whether the defense has been proven, a court must consider (1) whether the employer has an anti-harassment policy, (2) whether the employer had a complaint mechanism in place,

(3) whether employees were informed of the anti-harassment policy and complaint procedure, and (4) other factors that the court deems relevant. *Faragher v. City of Boca Raton*, 524 U.S. 775, 118 S.Ct. 2275, 141 L.Ed.2d 662, **Web** 1998 U.S. Lexis 4216 (Supreme Court of the United States), and *Burlington Industries, Inc. v. Ellerth*, 524 U.S. 742, 118 S.Ct. 2257, 141 L.Ed.2d 633, **Web** 1998 U.S. Lexis 4217 (Supreme Court of the United States)

Law & Ethics Questions

1. **ETHICS** Should an employer be accorded the defense allowed by these cases? Why or why not?
2. **ETHICS** Should employees be required to use the company's complaint system before being allowed to win a hostile environment discrimination lawsuit?

Web Exercises

1. **WEB** For the complete opinion of *Faragher v. City of Boca Raton*, go to *www.prenhall.com/cheesemancases*.
2. **WEB** For the complete opinion of *Burlington Industries, Inc. v. Ellerth*, go to *www.prenhall.com/cheesemancases*.
3. **WEB** Use *www.google.com* to find the sexual harassment policy of your college or university.
4. **WEB** Choose a company. Use *www.google.com* to find that company's sexual harassment policy and the procedures for reporting violations of the policy.

INTERNET AND TECHNOLOGY
E-Mails That Cause Sexual Harassment

The use of e-mail in business has dramatically increased efficiency and information sharing among employees. Managers and workers alike can communicate with each other, send documents, and keep each other apprised of business developments. In many organizations, e-mail has replaced the telephone as the most-used method of communication and has eliminated the need for many meetings. This is a boon for business. But the downside is that e-mail has increased the exposure of businesses to sexual and racial harassment lawsuits. For example, the largest settlement regarding a sexual harassment case arose from e-mail.

E-mail often sets the social tone of an office and has been permitted to be slightly ribald. At some point, however, e-mail conduct becomes impermissible and crosses the line to actionable sexual or racial harassment. The standard of whether e-mail creates an illegal hostile work environment is the same as that for measuring harassment in any other context: The offensive conduct must be severe and cannot consist of isolated or trivial remarks and incidents. And, as in other harassment cases, an employer may raise a defense if it meets two required elements: (1) The employer exercised reasonable care to prevent and correct the behavior and (2) the plaintiff employee unreasonably failed to take advantage of any preventive or corrective opportunities provided by the employer or to avoid the harm.

E-mail differs from many other incidents of harassment because it is subtle and insidious. Unlike paper pin-up calendars in plain view, an employer does not readily see e-mail messages. Obscenity pulled off the Internet or scanned into a computer can be sent as an attachment to an e-mail message. Because e-mail is hidden, to detect offensive messages, employers must take action to review e-mail messages on its network. Courts have generally held that an employee does not have an expectation of privacy of e-mail. Stored e-mail is the property of the employer, which may review it freely. Employers can also use software to scan and filter e-mail messages that contain any of a predefined list of objectionable words or phrases or certain "to" or "from" headers. Employers can also use software programs to scan graphics and block X-rated pictures.

E-mail has increased the possibility of sexual or racial harassment on the job, and it has also become a smoking gun that undermines a company's attempt to defend such cases. Therefore, employers must adopt policies pertaining to the use of e-mail by their employees and make their employees aware that certain e-mail messages constitute sexual or racial harassment and violate the law. Employers should make periodic inspections and audits of stored e-mail to ensure that employees are complying with the company's anti-harassment policies.

Religious Discrimination

Title VII prohibits employment discrimination based on a person's religion. Religions include traditional religions, other religions that recognize a supreme being, and religions based on ethical or spiritual tenets. Many **religious discrimination** cases involve a conflict between an employer's work rule and an employee's religious beliefs (e.g., when an employee is required to work on his or her religious holiday).

The right of an employee to practice his or her religion is not absolute. Under Title VII, an employer is under a duty to *reasonably accommodate* the religious observances, practices, or beliefs of its employees if doing so does not cause an *undue hardship* on the employer. The courts must apply these general standards to specific fact situations. In making their decisions, the courts must consider such factors as the size of the employer, the importance of the employee's position, and the availability of alternative workers.

Title VII expressly permits religious organizations to give preference in employment to individuals of a particular religion. For example, if a person applies for a job with a religious organization but does not subscribe to its religious tenets, the organization may refuse to hire that person.

Example The Big Computer Company has 2,000 employees who work at its main manufacturing plant. The plant works three shifts per day, seven days per week. David Berkowitz, an employee, is Jewish and wishes to celebrate the holy day of Yom Kippur. Yom Kippur falls on one of the days David is scheduled to work. Yom Kippur, however, requires work restrictions for Jews. With as many employees as Big Computer Company has working at its plant, it would be a reasonable accommodation for the company to give David and other Jews the day off and require other workers to take their shifts. This would not cause an undue hardship for the company.

Defenses to a Title VII Action

Title VII and case law recognize several defenses to a charge of discrimination under Title VII. These include merit, seniority, and bona fide occupational qualification (BFOQ). These defenses are discussed in the following paragraphs.

MERIT Employers can select or promote employees based on *merit*. Merit decisions are often based on work, educational experience, and professionally developed ability tests. To be lawful under Title VII, such a requirement must be job related.

Example Requiring a person to pass a typing test to be hired as a typist would be lawful. Requiring a person to pass a college-level English composition test to be employed as a maintenance worker would violate Title VII.

SENIORITY Many employers maintain *seniority* systems that reward long-term employees. Higher wages, fringe benefits, and other preferential treatment (e.g., choice of working hours and vacation schedule) are examples of such rewards. Seniority systems provide an incentive for employees to stay with the company. Such systems are lawful if they are not the result of intentional discrimination.

BONA FIDE OCCUPATIONAL QUALIFICATION (BFOQ) Discrimination based on protected classes (other than race or color) is permitted if it is shown to be a **bona fide occupational qualification (BFOQ)**. To be legal, a BFOQ must be both *job related* and a *business necessity*.

Example Allowing only women to be locker room attendants in a women's gym is a valid BFOQ. Prohibiting males from being managers or instructors at the same gym would not be a BFOQ.

As the following U.S. Supreme Court case shows, BFOQ exceptions are narrowly interpreted by the courts.

C A S E **36.7**

Bona Fide Occupational Qualification

U.S. SUPREME COURT

International Union, United Automobile, Aerospace and Agricultural Implement Workers of America, UAW v. Johnson Controls, Inc.

499 U.S. 187, 111 S.Ct. 1196, 113 L.Ed.2d 158,
Web 1991 U.S. Lexis 1715
Supreme Court of the United States

❝*The bias in Johnson Controls' policy is obvious. Fertile men, but not fertile women, are given a choice as to whether they wish to risk their reproductive health for a particular job.*❞

—Justice Blackmun

Facts

Johnson Controls, Inc. (Johnson Controls), manufactures batteries. Lead is the primary ingredient in the manufacturing process. Exposure to lead entails health risks, including risk of harm to a fetus carried by a female employee. To protect unborn children from such risk, Johnson Controls adopted an employment rule that prevented pregnant women and women of childbearing age from working at jobs involving lead exposure. Only women who were sterilized or could prove they could not have children were not affected by the rule. Consequently, most female employees were relegated to lower-paying clerical jobs at the company. Several female employees filed a class action suit, challenging Johnson Controls's fetal-protection policy as sex discrimination in violation of Title VII. The U.S. District Court held that the policy was justified as a bona fide occupational qualification (BFOQ) and granted summary judgment to Johnson Controls; the U.S. Court of Appeals affirmed the judgment. The plaintiffs appealed to the U.S. Supreme Court.

Issue

Is Johnson Controls's fetal-protection policy a BFOQ?

Language of the U.S. Supreme Court

The bias in Johnson Controls' policy is obvious. Fertile men, but not fertile women, are given a choice as to whether they

wish to risk their reproductive health for a particular job. Johnson Controls' fetal-protection policy explicitly discriminates against women on the basis of their sex. The policy excludes women with childbearing capacity from lead-exposed jobs and so creates a facial classification based on gender.

The bona fide occupational qualifications (BFOQ) defense is written narrowly, and this Court has read it narrowly. We have no difficulty concluding that Johnson Controls cannot establish a BFOQ. Fertile women, as far as appears in the record, participate in the manufacture of batteries as efficiently as anyone else. Johnson Controls' professed moral and ethical concerns about the welfare of the next generation do not suffice to establish a BFOQ of female sterility. Decisions about the welfare of future children must be left to the parents who conceive, bear, support, and raise them rather than to the employers who hire those parents.

Decision

The U.S. Supreme Court held that Johnson Controls's fetal-protection policy was not a BFOQ. Instead, it was sex discrimination in violation of Title VII. The Supreme Court reversed the decision of the U.S. Court of Appeals and remanded the case for further proceedings.

Law & Ethics Questions

1. Should any BFOQ exceptions to Title VII actions be permitted? Why or why not?
2. **ETHICS** Did Johnson Controls's moral and ethical concerns about the welfare of the next generation justify its actions?
3. Does Johnson Controls have any tort liability to children who are born injured by exposure to lead? How can Johnson Controls limit such liability?

Web Exercises

1. **WEB** For the complete opinion of this case, go to *www.prenhall.com/cheesemancases*.

2. **WEB** Visit the website of the U.S. Supreme Court, at *www.supremecourtus.gov*, and try to find documents that relate to this case.
3. **WEB** Visit the website of Johnson Controls, at *www.jci.com*. Locate employment opportunities with this company.
4. **WEB** Visit the website of the union United Automobile Workers (UAW), at *www.uaw.org*. What is one of the political issues that the UAW is concerned about?
5. **WEB** Use *www.google.com* to find an article that discusses a recent case involving a bona fide occupational qualification (BFOQ). Read it.

CONCEPT SUMMARY

Title VII of the Civil Rights Act

Covered employers and employment decisions	1. **Employers.** Employers with 15 or more employees for 20 weeks in the current or preceding year, all employment agencies, labor unions with 15 or more members, state and local governments, and most federal agencies. 2. **Employment decisions.** Decisions regarding hiring; promotion; demotion; payment of salaries, wages, and fringe benefits; dismissal; job training and apprenticeships; work rules; or any other term, condition, or privilege of employment. Decisions to admit partners to a partnership are also covered.
Protected classes	1. **Race.** A broad class of individuals with common characteristics (e.g., African American, Caucasian, Asian, Native American). 2. **Color.** The color of a person's skin (e.g., light-skinned person, dark-skinned person). 3. **National origin.** A person's country of origin or national heritage (e.g., Italian, Hispanic). 4. **Sex.** A person's sex, whether male or female. Includes sexual harassment and discrimination against females who are pregnant. 5. **Religion.** A person's religious beliefs. An employer has a duty to reasonably accommodate an employee's religious beliefs if doing so does not cause an undue hardship on the employer.
Types of discrimination	1. **Disparate-treatment discrimination.** Discrimination against a specific individual because that person belongs to a protected class. 2. **Disparate-impact discrimination.** Discrimination in which an employer discriminates against a protected class. A neutral-looking employment rule that causes discrimination against a protected class is disparate-impact discrimination.
Defenses	1. **Merit.** Job-related experience, education, or unbiased employment test. 2. **Seniority.** Length of time an employee has been employed by the employer. Intentional discrimination based on seniority is unlawful. 3. **Bona fide occupational qualification (BFOQ).** Discrimination based on sex, religion, or national origin is permitted if it is a valid BFOQ for the position. Qualification based on race or color is not a permissible BFOQ.

Remedies

1. **Equitable remedy.** The court may order the payment of back pay, issue an injunction awarding reinstatement, grant fictional seniority, or order some other equitable remedy.

2. **Damages.** The court can award compensatory damages in cases of intentional discrimination. The court can award punitive damages in cases involving an employer's malice or reckless indifference to federally protected rights.

Forbidden City, Beijing, China

Foreign nationals employed in foreign countries by U.S.-controlled companies are not covered by Title VII; U.S. citizens employed by U.S.-controlled companies in foreign countries are covered by Title VII, however.

LANDMARK LAW
Civil Rights Act of 1866

The **Civil Rights Act of 1866** was enacted after the Civil War. **Section 1981** of this act states that all persons "have the same right . . . to make and enforce contracts . . . as is enjoyed by white persons" [42 U.S.C. Section 1981]. This law was enacted to give African Americans, just freed from slavery, the same right to contract as whites. Section 1981 expressly prohibits racial discrimination; it has also been held to forbid discrimination based on national origin.

Employment decisions are covered by Section 1981 because the employment relationship is contractual. Although most racial and national origin employment discrimination cases are brought under Title VII, there are two reasons that a complainant would bring an action under Section 1981: (1) A private plaintiff can bring an action without going through the procedural requirements of Title VII, and (2) there is no cap on the recovery of compensatory or punitive damages.

Law & Ethics Questions

1. What does Section 1981 of the Civil Rights Act of 1866 provide?

2. **ETHICS** Why was Section 1981 of the Civil Rights Act of 1866 enacted? Explain.

Equal Pay Act

Discrimination often takes the form of different pay scales for men and women performing the same job. The **Equal Pay Act** of 1963 protects both sexes from pay discrimination based on sex.[6] This act covers all levels of private-sector employees and state and local government employees. Federal workers are not covered, however.

The act prohibits disparity in pay for jobs that require *equal skill* (i.e., equal experience), *equal effort* (i.e., mental and physical exertion), *equal responsibility* (i.e., equal supervision and accountability), or *similar working conditions* (e.g., dangers of injury, exposure to the elements). To make this determination, the courts examine the actual requirements of jobs to determine whether they are equal and similar. If two jobs are determined to be equal and similar, an employer cannot pay disparate wages to members of different sexes.

By what justice can an association of citizens be held together when there is no equality among the citizens?

Cicero
De Republica De Legibus J
XXXII 49

Employees can bring a private cause of action against an employer for violating the Equal Pay Act. Back pay and liquidated damages are recoverable. In addition, the employer must increase the wages of the discriminated-against employee to eliminate the unlawful disparity of wages. The wages of other employees may not be lowered.

Criteria That Justify a Differential in Wages

The Equal Pay Act expressly provides four criteria that justify a differential in wages. These defenses include payment systems that are based on:

- Seniority
- Merit (as long as there is some identifiable measurement standard)
- Quantity or quality of product (commission, piecework, or quality-control–based payment systems are permitted)
- "Any factor other than sex" (including shift differentials, i.e., night versus day shifts)

The employer bears the burden of proving these defenses.

Example Mary and Peter, who both meet the educational requirements for a particular entry-level job, are both hired as staff accountants by a company and will be performing exactly the same duties at their job. If the company pays Peter a salary that is 20 percent higher than Mary's salary, this would be a violation of the Equal Pay Act.

Example Peter, a college graduate, has been working for a company for five years as a staff accountant. Mary, a new college graduate with no experience, is hired by the company as a staff accountant, with the same job duties and responsibilities as Peter. Peter is paid a 20 percent higher salary than Mary. This differential is justified based on seniority and therefore does not violate the Equal Pay Act.

Age Discrimination in Employment Act

Some employers have discriminated against employees and prospective employees based on their age. Primarily, employers have often refused to hire older workers. The **Age Discrimination in Employment Act (ADEA)**, which prohibits certain *age discrimination* practices, was enacted in 1967.[7]

The ADEA covers nonfederal employers with at least 20 employees, labor unions with at least 25 members, and all employment agencies. State and local government employees except those in policy-making positions are covered, as are employees of certain sectors of the federal government.

The ADEA prohibits age discrimination in all employment decisions, including hiring, promotions, payment of compensation, and other terms and conditions of employment. The **Older Workers Benefit Protection Act (OWBPA)** amended the ADEA to prohibit age discrimination with regard to employee benefits. Employers cannot use employment advertisements that discriminate against applicants covered by the ADEA. The same defenses that are available in a Title VII action are also available in an ADEA action.

Protected Age Categories

Originally, the ADEA prohibited employment discrimination against persons between the ages of 40 and 65. Later, its coverage was extended to persons up to age 70. Further amendments completely eliminated an age ceiling, so the ADEA now applies to employees who are 40 and older. As a result, covered employers cannot establish mandatory retirement ages for their employees.

Because persons under 40 are not protected by the ADEA, an employer can maintain an employment policy of hiring only workers who are 40 years of age or older without violating the ADEA. However, an employer cannot maintain an employment practice whereby it hires only persons 50 years of age and older because that would discriminate against persons aged 40 to 49.

The ADEA is administered by the EEOC. Private plaintiffs can also sue under the ADEA. A successful plaintiff in an ADEA action can recover back wages, attorneys' fees, and equitable relief, including hiring, reinstatement, and promotion. Where a violation of the ADEA is found, the employer must raise the wages of the discriminated-against employee. It cannot lower the wages of other employees.

Example The General Corporation has an opening for its chief financial officer (CFO) position. The company receives several applications for the position. The two best and equally qualified applicants are Wendy and Alicia, which have similar educational experience. Wendy, who is 57 years old, has 20 years' experience as a CFO of another company. Alicia, who is 30 years old, has 5 years' experience as a CFO at another company. The board of directors of General Company believes these two candidates are equally qualified but hires Alicia because of her younger age. One of the board members at the meeting states, "We need younger blood at this position. Alicia is too old for the rigors of this position." This would be a violation of the ADEA.

Example The General Corporation has an opening for its controller position. The company receives several applications for the position. The two best and equally qualified applicants are Alan and Gregory. They both have similar educational experience. Alan, who is 47 years old, has 20 years' experience as the controller of another company. Gregory, who is 30 years old, has 5 years' experience as a controller at another company. The board of directors of General Company believes these two candidates are equally qualified but hires Alan. One of the board members at the meeting states, "We need older blood at this position. Gregory is too young for this position." This would not be a violation of the ADEA because the company can discriminate against applicants who are younger than 40 years of age without violating the ADEA. (Caution: Some state laws protect workers of all ages from age discrimination.)

In the following case, the U.S. Supreme Court addressed a legal issue involving age discrimination.

C A S E **36.8**
Age Discrimination

U.S. SUPREME COURT
General Dynamics Land Systems, Inc. v. Cline
540 U.S. 581, 124 S.Ct. 1236, 157 L.Ed.2d 1094,
Web 2004 U.S. Lexis 1623 (2004)
Supreme Court of the United States

"*The enemy of 40 is 30, not 50.*"

—Justice Souter

Facts

General Dynamics Land Systems, Inc., and the United Automobile Workers (UAW), a labor union, entered into a collective bargaining agreement that eliminated the company's obligation to provide health benefits to employees who subsequently retired, except to the current workers who were at least 50 years old. Dennis Cline, a General Dynamics employee and member of the UAW, was over 40 but younger than 50, and thus he lost the right to the benefits when he retired. Cline sued General Dynamics, alleging that because he was over 40 years old, the company engaged in age discrimination against him in violation of the federal Age Discrimination in Employment Act (ADEA) when it eliminated benefits for employees who were under 50 years of age. The U.S. District Court dismissed the case. The U.S. Court of Appeals reversed, holding that the ADEA protected a younger

covered employee from discrimination in favor of an older covered employee. General Dynamics appealed to the U.S. Supreme Court.

Issue

Does the ADEA protect a younger covered employee from an employer's employment rule that discriminates in favor of older covered employees?

Language of the U.S. Supreme Court

The record is devoid of any evidence that younger workers were suffering at the expense of their elders, let alone that a social problem required a federal statute to place a younger worker in parity with an older worker. This same, idiomatic sense of the statutory phrase is confirmed by the statute's restriction of the protected class to those 40 and above. If Congress had been worrying about protecting the younger against the older, it would not likely have ignored everyone under 40. The enemy of 40 is 30, not 50. Thus, the 40-year threshold makes sense as identifying a class requiring protection against preference for their juniors, not as defining a class that might be threatened by favoritism toward seniors. We see the text, structure, purpose, and history of the ADEA, along with its relationship to other federal statutes, as showing that the statute does not mean to stop an employer from favoring an older employee over a younger one.

Decision

The U.S. Supreme Court held that the ADEA does not prohibit an employer from favoring a covered older employee over a younger covered employee. The Supreme Court reversed the decision of the U.S. Court of Appeals.

Law & Ethics Questions

1. What does the Age Discrimination in Employment Act (ADEA) provide? What age group does the ADEA protect?
2. Why did General Dynamics come up with the rule that allowed benefits to be retained by workers 50 and older but eliminated those benefits for workers who were under 50 years of age? Explain.
3. **ETHICS** Did General Dynamics act ethically in eliminating the benefits of workers under 50 but preserving the benefits for workers who were 50 and older?
4. Do you think older workers are more expensive than younger workers? Explain.
5. **ETHICS** Do you think very much age discrimination occurs in business?

Web Exercises

1. **WEB** For the complete opinion of this case, go to *www.prenhall.com/cheesemancases*.
2. **WEB** Visit the website of the U.S. Supreme Court, at *www.supremecourtus.gov*, and try to find documents that relate to this case.
3. **WEB** Visit the website of General Dynamics Land Systems, Inc., at *www.gdls.com*. What type of business is this company engaged in?
4. **WEB** Visit the website of the United Automobile Workers (UAW), at *www.uaw.org*. What is one of the political issues that the UAW is concerned about?
5. **WEB** Use *www.google.com* to find an article that discusses a recent case involving age discrimination. Read it.

ETHICS SPOTLIGHT

"You're Overqualified for the Job"

> **"** *For those individuals in the protected age group, such a reason may often be simply a code word for too old.* **"**
>
> —Judge Cardamone

Preview Subscription Television, Inc. (Preview), a subsidiary of Time Incorporated (Time), hired Thomas Taggart as a print production manager for Preview's magazine *Guide*. Taggart was 58 years old at the time and had more than 30 years' experience in the printing industry. Seven months later, Time notified Preview employees that Preview would be dissolved and, though not guaranteed jobs, the employees were told they would receive special consideration for other positions at Time.

Taggart applied for 32 positions in various divisions at Time and its subsidiaries, including *Sports Illustrated*, *People Magazine*, *Life*, *Money*, and *Discover* magazines. Although Taggart interviewed for many of these openings, he was not offered employment. Time explained this by saying that Taggart was "overqualified" for many of the positions. Time hired less qualified, younger applicants for many of the positions for which Taggart was rejected.

Taggart sued Time for age discrimination in violation of the Age Discrimination in Employment Act (ADEA). The U.S. District Court granted Time's motion for summary judgment. Taggart appealed. The

U.S. Court of Appeals held that an employer's proffered reason for not hiring an applicant for a position because he was overqualified is a circumstance from which a reasonable juror could infer discriminatory animus. The U.S. Court of Appeals stated:

> This is an appeal in an age discrimination suit. It seems that often an old employee who is cashiered never has the right combination of credentials to fit into the existing openings. He or she is found to be underqualified, unable to stand pressure, difficult to work with and the like. The principal reason advanced by the employer during this litigation for refusing to hire appellant was because he was "overqualified." For those individuals in the protected age group, such a reason may often be simply a code word for too old.

The court noted that Taggart was over 40 years old and belonged to the protected age group. The fact that Taggart was found to be overqualified for some of the jobs he applied for at Time supported his allegation that he was capable of performing the jobs. Further, Time hired persons younger than he for those jobs. Thus, Taggart established a *prima facie* case of age discrimination. The U.S. Court of Appeals reversed and remanded the case for further proceedings. *Taggart v. Time Incorporated*, 924 F.2d 43, 1991 U.S. App. 1227 (United States Court of Appeals for the Second Circuit)

Law & Ethics Questions

1. **ETHICS** Did Time Incorporated act ethically in adopting the "you are overqualified" reason for not hiring Taggart?

2. Do you think older workers have a harder time finding employment than younger persons and therefore need the protection of the ADEA?

3. Should persons younger than 40 years of age be covered by the ADEA, too? Why or why not?

Web Exercises

1. **WEB** For the complete opinion of this case, go to *www.prenhall.com/cheesemancases*.

2. **WEB** Visit the website of the U.S. Court of Appeals for the Second Circuit, at *www.ca2.uscourts.gov*.

3. **WEB** Use *www.google.com* to find out whether your state has enacted an age discrimination law. If so, what age group does it cover?

Americans with Disabilities Act

The **Americans with Disabilities Act (ADA)**,[8] which was signed into law July 26, 1990, is the most comprehensive piece of civil rights legislation since the Civil Rights Act of 1964. The ADA imposes obligations on employers and providers of public transportation, telecommunications, and public accommodations to accommodate individuals with disabilities.

LANDMARK LAW

Americans with Disabilities Act

Title I of the ADA prohibits employment discrimination against qualified individuals with disabilities in regard to job application procedures, hiring, compensation, training, promotion, and termination. Title I covers employers with 15 or more employees. The United States, corporations wholly owned by the United States, and bona fide tax-exempt private membership clubs are exempt from Title I coverage.

Title I requires an employer to make reasonable accommodations to individuals with disabilities that do not cause undue hardship to the employer. **Reasonable accommodations** may include making facilities readily accessible to individuals with disabilities, providing part-time or modified work schedules, acquiring equipment or devices, modifying examination and training materials, and providing qualified readers or interpreters.

Employers are not obligated to provide accommodations that would impose an **undue burden**—that is, actions that would require significant difficulty or expense. The EEOC and the courts consider factors such as the nature and cost of accommodation, the overall financial resources of the employer, and the employer's type of operation. Obviously, what may be a significant difficulty or expense for a small employer may not be an undue hardship for a large employer.

Qualified Individual with a Disability

> All about me may be silence and darkness, yet within me, in the spirit, is music and brightness, and color flashes through all my thoughts.
>
> Helen Keller
> *The Open Door (1957)*

A **qualified individual with a disability** is a person who, with or without reasonable accommodation, can perform the essential functions of the job that person desires or holds. A disabled person is someone who (1) has a physical or mental impairment that substantially limits one or more of his or her major life activities, (2) has a record of such impairment, or (3) is regarded as having such impairment. Mental retardation, paraplegia, schizophrenia, cerebral palsy, epilepsy, diabetes, muscular dystrophy, multiple sclerosis, cancer, infection with HIV (human immunodeficiency virus), and visual, speech, and hearing impairments are covered under the ADA. A current user of illegal drugs or an alcoholic who uses alcohol or is under the influence of alcohol at the workplace is not covered. However, recovering alcoholics and former users of illegal drugs are protected.

Forbidden Conduct

Title I of the ADA limits an employer's ability to inquire into or test for an applicant's disabilities. Title I forbids an employer from asking a job applicant about the existence, nature, and severity of a disability. An employer may, however, inquire about the applicant's ability to perform job-related functions. Preemployment medical examinations are forbidden before a job offer. Once a job offer has been made, an employer may require a medical examination and may condition the offer on the examination results, as long as all entering employees are subject to such an examination. The information must be kept confidential.

Procedure and Remedies

Title I of the ADA is administered by the EEOC. An aggrieved individual must first file a charge with the EEOC, which may take action against the employer or permit the individual to pursue a private cause of action. Relief can take the form of an injunction, hiring or reinstatement (with back pay), payment of attorneys' fees, and recovery of compensatory and punitive damages (subject to the same caps as Title VII damages).

In the following two cases, the U.S. Supreme Court was called upon to interpret and apply the ADA.

C A S E **36.9**

Disability Discrimination

U.S. SUPREME COURT

PGA Tour, Inc. v. Martin

532 U.S. 661, 121 S.Ct. 1879, 149 L.Ed.2d 904,
Web 2001 U.S. Lexis 4115 (2001)
Supreme Court of the United States

> *As an initial matter, we observe that the use of carts is not itself inconsistent with the fundamental character of the game of golf.*
>
> —Justice Stevens

Facts

The PGA Tour, Inc., is a nonprofit entity that sponsors professional golf tournaments. The PGA has adopted a set of rules that apply to its golf tour. One rule requires golfers to walk the golf course during PGA-sponsored tournaments. Casey Martin is a talented amateur golfer who won many high school and university golf championships. Martin has been afflicted with Klippel-Trenaunay-Weber Syndrome, a degenerative circulatory disorder that obstructs the flow of blood from his right leg to his heart. The disease is progressive and has atrophied his right leg. Walking causes Martin pain, fatigue, and anxiety, with significant risk of hemorrhaging.

When Martin turned professional, he qualified for the PGA Tour. He made a request to use a golf cart while playing in PGA tournaments. When the PGA denied his request, Martin sued the PGA for violation of the Americans with Disabilities Act (ADA) for not making reasonable accommodations for his disability. The U.S. District Court sided with Martin and ordered the PGA to permit Martin to use a golf cart. The U.S. Court of Appeals affirmed the judgment in favor of Martin. The PGA appealed to the U.S. Supreme Court.

Issue

Does the ADA require the PGA Tour, Inc., to accommodate Casey Martin, a disabled professional golfer, by permitting him to use a golf cart while playing in PGA-sponsored golf tournaments?

Language of the U.S. Supreme Court

As an initial matter, we observe that the use of carts is not itself inconsistent with the fundamental character of the game of golf. From early on, the essence of the game has been shot-making—using clubs to cause a ball to progress from the teeing ground to a hole some distance away with as few strokes as possible. Golf carts started appearing with increasing regularity on American golf courses in the 1950s. Today they are everywhere. And they are encouraged. For one thing, they often speed up play, and for another, they are great revenue producers.

The force of petitioner PGA Tour's argument is, first of all, mitigated by the fact that golf is a game in which it is impossible to guarantee that all competitors will play under exactly the same conditions or that an individual's ability will be the sole determinant of the outcome. For example, changes in the weather may produce harder greens and more head winds for the tournament leader than for his closest pursuers. A lucky bounce may save a shot or two. Whether such happenstance events are more or less probable than the likelihood that a golfer afflicted with Klippel-Trenaunay-Weber Syndrome would one day qualify for the PGA Tour, they at least demonstrate that pure chance may have a greater impact on the outcome of elite golf tournaments than the fatigue resulting from the enforcement of the walking rule.

Decision

The U.S. Supreme Court held that the ADA requires that the PGA Tour, Inc., accommodate Casey Martin, a disabled professional golfer, by allowing him to use a golf cart while competing in PGA-sponsored professional golf tournaments. The Supreme Court affirmed the judgment of the U.S. Court of Appeals.

Law & Ethics Questions

1. Do you agree with U.S. Supreme Court's decision? Will the decision open a floodgate of similar lawsuits?
2. **ETHICS** Was Casey Martin just asking for "fairness," or was he asking for an advantage when competing in professional golf tournaments?

3. Is the PGA Tour a lucrative business? Will the Supreme Court's ruling have any effect on the revenues generated by the PGA Tour?

Web Exercises

1. **WEB** For the complete opinion of this case, go to *www.prenhall.com/cheesemancases*.
2. **WEB** Visit the website of the U.S. Supreme Court, at *www.supremecourtus.gov*, and try to find documents that relate to this case.
3. **WEB** Visit the website of the PGA Tour, at *www.pgatour.com*.

C A S E 36.10
Disability Discrimination

U.S. SUPREME COURT
Sutton v. United Airlines, Inc.
527 U.S. 471, 119 S.Ct. 2139, 144 L.Ed.2d 450,
Web 1999 U.S. Lexis 4371
Supreme Court of the United States

> ❝*With respect to the disability definition, our decision turns on whether disability is to be determined with or without reference to corrective measures.*❞
>
> —Justice O'Connor

Facts

Karen Sutton and Kimberly Hinton (petitioners), twin sisters, applied to United Airlines, Inc., for employment as commercial airline pilots. They met United's education and experience requirements and the Federal Aviation Administration (FAA) certification qualifications. Both of the petitioners have severe myopia, with uncorrected visual acuity of 20/200 or worse and 20/400 or worse. Each of the petitioners has vision that is 20/20 or better with the use of corrective lens. Without corrective lens, neither of the petitioners can see to conduct activities such as driving a vehicle, watching television, or shopping in public stores, but with corrective lens, both function identically to persons without similar impairment. United rejected the petitioners' employment applications because they did not meet United's minimum visual requirement of uncorrected visual acuity of 20/100 or better. Petitioners filed a charge of disability discrimination against United for allegedly violating the Americans with Disabilities Act (ADA). The U.S. District Court dismissed petitioners' complaint, and the U.S. Court of Appeals affirmed the judgment. Petitioners appealed to the U.S. Supreme Court.

Issue

Are the petitioners disabled within the meaning of the ADA?

Language of the U.S. Supreme Court

With respect to the disability definition, our decision turns on whether disability is to be determined with or without reference

to corrective measures. Petitioners maintain that whether an impairment is substantially limiting should be determined without regard to corrective measures. United, in turn, maintains that an impairment does not substantially limit a major life activity if it is corrected. We conclude that United is correct. Looking at ADA as a whole, it is apparent that if a person is taking measures to correct for, or mitigate, a physical or mental impairment, the effects of those measures—both positive and negative—must be taken into account when judging whether that person is "substantially limited" in a major life activity and thus "disabled" under the ADA.

The ADA defines a "disability" as "a physical or mental impairment that substantially limits one or more of the major life activities" of an individual. A person whose physical or mental impairment is corrected by medication or other measures does not have an impairment that presently substantially limits a major life activity. To be sure, a person whose physical or mental impairment is corrected by mitigating measures still has an impairment, but if the impairment is corrected it does not substantially limit a major life activity.

Decision

The U.S. Supreme Court held that *disability* under the Americans with Disabilities Act (ADA) does not include persons with corrected conditions, such as petitioners' corrected vision. The Supreme Court concluded that the petitioners' complaint was properly dismissed.

Law & Ethics Questions

1. Does the Americans with Disabilities Act promote an important social policy? Do you think a federal law was needed to effectuate this policy?
2. **ETHICS** Did United Airlines act ethically in this case?
3. What would have been the economic implications for business if the Supreme Court had held in the petitioners' favor?

Web Exercises

1. **WEB** For the complete opinion of this case, go to *www.prenhall.com/cheesemancases*.
2. **WEB** Visit the website of the U.S. Supreme Court, at *www.supremecourtus.gov*, and try to find documents that relate to this case.
3. **WEB** Visit the website of United Airlines, Inc., at *www.united.com*.

ETHICS SPOTLIGHT

Obesity Treated as a Disability

> **❝***In a society that all too often confuses "slim" with "beautiful" or "good," morbid obesity can present formidable barriers to employment.***❞**
>
> —Judge Selya

For eight years, Bonnie Cook worked as an institutional attendant at the Ladd Center, a residential facility for retarded persons that was operated by the Rhode Island Department of Mental Health, Retardation, and Hospitals (MHRH). Ms. Cook voluntarily left the position, leaving behind a spotless work record. Two years later, Ms. Cook reapplied for the identical position. Despite passing the routine physical examination, the MHRH refused to hire Ms. Cook because she stood 5' 20" and weighed more than 320 pounds. The director of the hospital testified that Ms. Cook was not hired because he believed that her obesity compromised her ability to evacuate patients in case of an emergency and put her at increased risk of being absent and developing serious ailments that would increase her likelihood of filing a workers' compensation claim.

Ms. Cook filed suit against MHRH for violating federal disability law. The U.S. District Court found that Ms. Cook's obesity did not prevent or impede her from doing the job she applied for. The District Court found that MHRH had perceived her to have a disability, when in fact she did not. The District Court held that MHRH had violated federal disability law. The jury awarded Ms. Cook $100,000 in damages.

The U.S. Court of Appeals agreed with the U.S. District Court and held that obesity is a protected category under federal disability law. The Court stated, "In a society that all too often confuses 'slim' with 'beautiful' or 'good,' morbid obesity can present formidable barriers to employment." The Court of Appeals upheld the award of $100,000 in damages to Ms. Cook. *Cook v. State of Rhode Island, Department of Mental Health, Retardation, and Hospitals*, 10 F.3d 17, 1993 U.S. App. 30060 (United States Court of Appeals for the First Circuit)

Law & Ethics Questions

1. What is a perceived disability? Explain.
2. **ETHICS** Did MHRH act ethically in this case?

Web Exercises

1. **WEB** For the complete opinion of this case, go to *www.prenhall.com/cheesemancases*.
2. **WEB** Visit the website of the U.S. Court of Appeals for the First Circuit, at *www.ca1.uscourts.gov*.

Affirmative Action

Employers often adopt **affirmative action** plans which provide that certain job preferences will be given to members of minority racial and ethnic groups, females, and other protected-class applicants when an employer makes an employment decision. Such plans can be voluntarily adopted by employers, undertaken to settle a discrimination action, or ordered by the courts.

To be lawful, an affirmative action plan must be *narrowly tailored* to achieve some *compelling interest*. Employment quotas based on a specified number or percentage of minority applicants or employees are unlawful. If a person's minority status is only one factor of many factors considered is an employment decision, that decision will usually be considered lawful.

Affirmative action plans are often controversial. Proponents of such plans argue that the plans are necessary to address imbalances in the workforce and to remedy past discrimination against protected classes. Some argue that affirmative action plans cause work hardship on other employees.

Reverse Discrimination

Title VII not only applies to members of minority groups but also protects members of majority classes from discrimination. Lawful affirmative action plans have an effect on members of majority classes. The courts have held that this effect is not actionable by the members of the majority class who are affected.

The courts have held, however, that if an affirmative action plan is based on preestablished numbers or percentage quotas for hiring or promoting minority applicants, then it causes illegal **reverse discrimination**. In this case, the members of the majority class may sue under Title VII and recover damages and other remedies for reverse discrimination. Very few reverse discrimination cases are successful.

CONTEMPORARY ENVIRONMENT
Affirmative Action and Reverse Discrimination

Affirmative action has been used to make up for past discrimination against minority classes. To be lawful, an affirmative action plan must be narrowly tailored to achieve a compelling interest. Making up for past discrimination against minority classes would be a compelling interest. However, the affirmative action plan must also be narrowly tailored—that is, not overly aggressive in accomplishing its stated goal.

When affirmative plans are overly broad, they may tend to cause *reverse discrimination*. Reverse discrimination lawsuits are brought by persons of a majority class who believe that they have been discriminated against because of affirmative action program that grants an unlawful preference in hiring to persons of minority classes.

Consider the case of an affirmative action plan implemented by the city of Birmingham, Alabama, to ensure the promotion of black firefighters. The case began over 20 years ago, when black firefighters sued the city for discrimination because it had only a few black firefighters and none in supervisory positions. After a lawsuit, the city agreed to promote white and black firefighters to the rank of lieutenant on a 1-to-1 basis until the number of blacks equaled the 28 percent of the surrounding county's workforce that was black. Because of this affirmative action program, years later, the target was reached. Thus, the affirmative action plan was successful in accomplishing its goal of making up for past discrimination.

However, when the city continued this quota system after the stated goal was reached, several white firefighters challenged the city's affirmative action plan. The white firefighters lost in U.S. District Court. The U.S. Court of Appeals reversed, finding that the city's affirmative action plan violated the Equal Protection Clause of the Constitution and Title VII because it was no longer narrowly tailored to achieve a compelling

interest. The Court of Appeals stated, "In our view, the City decree fails under Title VII because the indefinitely-lasting, arbitrarily-selected 50% figure for annual black promotions to fire lieutenant unnecessarily trammels the rights of non-black firefighters by unduly restricting their promotional opportunities through establishment of an arbitrary fixed quota." The U.S. Supreme Court denied review of this case.

Thus, employers must walk a fine line in establishing and maintaining affirmative action plans. If an affirmative action plan is narrowly tailored and serves a compelling interest, it will be held to be lawful. If an affirmative action plan is too broad, or if a compelling interest does not exist, it may be found to constitute reverse discrimination. *Bennett v. Arrington, Mayor of the City of Birmingham, Alabama*, 20 F.3d 1525, 1994 U.S. App. 10262 (United States Court of Appeals for the Eleventh Circuit)

Law & Ethics Questions

1. What is affirmative action? When is affirmative action lawful?
2. What is reverse discrimination?

Web Exercises

1. **WEB** For the complete opinion of this case, go to *www.prenhall.com/cheesemancases*.
2. **WEB** Visit the website of the U.S. Court of Appeals for the Eleventh Circuit, at *www.ca11.uscourts.gov*.
3. **WEB** Use *www.google.com* to find an article that discusses why affirmative action programs are necessary to make up for past discrimination. Read it.

State and Local Government Antidiscrimination Laws

Many state and local governments have adopted laws that prevent discrimination in employment. These **state and local governments antidiscrimination laws** usually include classes protected by federal equal opportunity laws as well as classes of persons not protected by federal laws.

INTERNATIONAL LAW
United Nations Treaty to Protect the Rights of the Disabled

In 2006, the General Assembly of the United Nations (UN) adopted a convention to protect the rights of disabled persons worldwide. The convention, called the **Convention in the Rights of Persons with Disabilities**, requires countries to protect disabled people from exploitation and abuse and to protect the rights of disabled people in education, work, and health care. The convention advocates keeping disabled persons in their communities rather than segregating them, as many countries now do. It is estimated that there are 600 million disabled people worldwide that would be covered by the convention. Excerpts from the convention are presented here:

Preamble

The States Parties to the present Convention,

a. Recalling the principles proclaimed in the Charter of the United Nations which recognize the inherent dignity and worth and the equal and inalienable rights of all members of the human family as the foundation of freedom, justice and peace in the world, . . .

c. Reaffirming the universality, indivisibility, interdependence and interrelatedness of all human rights and fundamental freedoms and the need for persons with disabilities to be guaranteed their full enjoyment without discrimination, …

h. Recognizing also that discrimination against any person on the basis of disability is a violation of the inherent dignity and worth of the human person, …

p. Concerned about the difficult conditions faced by persons with disabilities who are subject to multiple or aggravated forms of discrimination on the basis of race, colour, sex, language, religion, political or other opinion, national, ethnic, indigenous or social origin, property, birth, age or other status, . . .

y. Convinced that a comprehensive and integral international convention to promote and protect the rights and dignity of persons with disabilities will make a significant contribution to redressing the profound social disadvantage of persons with disabilities and promote their participation in the civil, political, economic, social and cultural spheres with equal opportunities, in both developing and developed countries, . . .

Article 1—Purpose

The purpose of the present Convention is to promote, protect and ensure the full and equal enjoyment of all human rights and fundamental freedoms by all persons with disabilities, and to promote respect for their inherent dignity.

Persons with disabilities include those who have long-term physical, mental, intellectual or sensory impairments which in interaction with various barriers may hinder their full and effective participation in society on an equal basis with others.

The convention was adopted by the General Assembly of the United Nations, which consists of the 192 member nations of the United Nations. A country's lawmakers must ratify the convention before it becomes effective in that country.

Web Exercises

1. **WEB** Visit the website of the United Nations, at *www.un.org*.

2. **WEB** To view the convention, go to *www.un.org/disabilities/convention/conventionfull.shtml*.

3. **WEB** To learn about various organizations that serve disabled individuals, visit *www.access-board.gov/links/disability.htm*.

Chapter Summary

Title VII of the Civil Rights Act of 1964, p. 1011

Title VII of the Civil Rights Act of 1964 is a federal statute that prohibits job discrimination based on the race, color, religion, sex, or national origin of the job applicant.

1. *Scope of Coverage of Title VII:*

   a. *Employers subject to Title VII.* Employers with 15 or more employees for at least 20 weeks in the current or preceding year, all employment agencies, labor unions with 15 or more members, state and local governments, and most federal agencies are subject to Title VII.

   b. *Employment decisions subject to Title VII.* Decisions regarding hiring; promotion; demotion; payment of salaries, wages, and fringe benefits; job training and apprenticeships; work rules; and any other "term, condition, or privilege of employment" are subject to Title VII.

2. *Forms of Title VII Actions:*

   a. Disparate-treatment discrimination. This type of discrimination occurs when an employer treats a specific individual less favorably than others because of that person's race, color, national origin, sex, or religion. To be successful, the complainant must prove that he or she belongs to a Title VII protected class, he or she applied for and was qualified for the employment position, he or she was rejected despite these qualifications, and the employer kept the position open and sought applications from persons with the complainant's qualifications.

   b. Disparate-impact discrimination. This type of discrimination occurs when an employer discriminates against an entire protected class. It may be proven using statistical data that demonstrate a causal link between the challenged practice and the statistical imbalance. Neutral employment rules that have an adverse impact on a protected class constitute disparate-impact discrimination.

Equal Employment Opportunity Commission (EEOC)

The EEOC is a federal administrative agency responsible for administering, interpreting, and enforcing most federal equal employment opportunity (antidiscrimination) laws. The following is the procedure for bringing a Title VII action:

1. *Complaint.* A private complainant must file a complaint with the EEOC. The EEOC has the opportunity to sue the employer on the complainant's behalf.
2. *Right to sue letter.* If the EEOC chooses not to bring suit, it will issue a right to sue letter that authorizes the complainant to sue the employer.

Remedies for Violations of Title VII

A successful plaintiff in a Title VII action can recover back pay, compensatory and punitive damages (subject to certain caps, based on the size of the defendant employer), reasonable attorneys' fees, and equitable remedies such as reinstatement, fictional seniority, and injunctions.

Race, Color, and National Origin Discrimination

1. *Race.* Race is a broad class of individuals with common physical characteristics (e.g., black, Caucasian, Asian, Native American).
2. *Color.* Color refers to the color of a person's skin (e.g., light-skinned person, dark-skinned person).
3. *National origin.* National origin is a person's country of origin or national heritage (e.g., Italian, Hispanic).

Sex Discrimination

Sex refers to a person's sex, whether male or female. The Pregnancy Discrimination Act of 1978 amended Title VII to forbid employment discrimination because of "pregnancy, childbirth, or related medical conditions."

Sexual Harassment

Sexual harassment is lewd remarks, touching, intimidation, posting of pin-ups, and other verbal or physical conduct of a sexual nature that occurs on the job. Sexual harassment that creates a hostile work environment violates Title VII.

Same-Sex Discrimination

In 1998, in *Omcale v. Sundowner Offshore Services, Incorporated*, the U.S. Supreme Court held that same-sex discrimination and harassment violated Title VII. Many state and local antidiscrimination laws outlaw same-sex discrimination and harassment in the workplace.

Religious Discrimination

Religious discrimination is discrimination solely because of a person's religious beliefs or practices. An employer has a duty to reasonably accommodate an employee's religious beliefs if doing so does not cause an undue hardship on the employer.

Defenses to a Title VII Action

1. *Merit.* Merit includes job-related experiences, education, or unbiased employment tests.
2. *Seniority.* Seniority is the length of time an employee has been employed by the employer. Intentional discrimination based on seniority is unlawful.
3. *Bona fide occupational qualification (BFOQ).* Employment discrimination based on the sex, religion, or national origin of an applicant is permitted if it is a bona fide occupational qualification (BFOQ) for the position. To be legal, a BFOQ must be job related and a business necessity. BFOQ exceptions are narrowly interpreted by the courts.

Civil Rights Act of 1866

The Civil Rights Act of 1866, enacted after the Civil War, states that all persons "have the same right . . . to make and enforce contracts . . . as is enjoyed by white persons." Section 1981 of the act prohibits race and national origin discrimination concerning employment contracts. A successful plaintiff can recover back pay, equitable remedies, compensatory and punitive damages, and reasonable attorneys' fees. The act places no monetary caps on compensatory and punitive damages.

Equal Pay Act, p. 1024

The Equal Pay Act is a federal statute that forbids pay discrimination for the same job based on the sex of the employee performing the job. There cannot be pay disparity based on sex for jobs that require equal skill, equal effort, equal responsibility, and similar working conditions.

Criteria That Justify a Differential in Wages

The Equal Pay Act stipulates that the following four criteria justify a differential in wages: seniority, merit, quantity or quality of work (commission, piecework, or quality control–based pay systems), and any factor other than sex (e.g., night versus day shifts).

Age Discrimination in Employment Act, p. 1025

The Age Discrimination in Employment Act (ADEA) is a federal statute that prohibits employment discrimination against applicants and employees who are 40 years of age or older.

1. *Older Workers Benefit Protection Act (OWBPA).* This federal statute amended the ADEA to prohibit age discrimination with respect to employment benefits.
2. *Defenses.* The same defenses that are available in a Title VII action are also available in an ADEA action.
3. *Remedies.* A successful plaintiff can recover back wages, attorney's fees, and equitable relief, including hiring, reinstatement, and promotion.

Protected Age Categories

The ADEA prohibits employment discrimination against persons above the age of 40. Covered employers cannot establish mandatory retirement ages for their employees.

Americans with Disabilities Act, p. 1028

The Americans with Disabilities Act (ADA) of 1990 is a federal statute that imposes obligations on employers and providers of public transportation, telecommunications, and public accommodations to accommodate individuals with disabilities.

1. *Title I of the ADA.* This federal law prohibits employment discrimination against qualified individuals with disabilities.
2. *Reasonable accommodation.* Title I requires employers to make reasonable accommodations to accommodate employees with disabilities that do not cause undue hardship to the employer.

Qualified Individual with a Disability

A qualified individual with a disability is a person who (1) has a physical or mental impairment that substantially limits one or more of his or her major life functions, (2) has a record of such impairment, or (3) is regarded as having such impairment.

Forbidden Conduct

Title I forbids an employer from asking a job applicant about the existence, nature, and severity of a disability. An employer may inquire about the applicant's ability to perform job-related functions. Pre-employment medical examinations are forbidden, but once a job offer has been made, an employer may require a medical examination and may condition the offer on the examination results, as long as all entering employees are subject to such an examination.

Procedure and Remedies

A successful plaintiff can recover back pay, compensatory and punitive damages (subject to certain caps, based on the size of the defendant employer), reasonable attorneys' fees, and equitable remedies, such as hiring, reinstatement, or promotion.

Affirmative Action, p. 1031

Affirmative action is a policy which provides that certain job preferences will be given to minority or other protected-class applicants when an employer makes an employment decision. To be lawful, an affirmative action plan must be narrowly tailored to achieve some compelling interest.

Reverse Discrimination

Reverse discrimination is discrimination against a person who is a member of a group that is usually thought of as a majority.

State and Local Government Antidiscrimination Laws, p. 1032

Many state and local governments have adopted laws that prevent discrimination in employment.

Test Review Terms and Concepts

Affirmative action   1031
Affirmative defense   1020
Age Discrimination in Employment
   Act (ADEA)   1025
Americans with Disabilities Act   1028
Bona fide occupation qualification
   (BFOQ)   1022
Civil Rights Act of 1866   1024
Civil Rights Act of 1964   1011
Color discrimination   1014
Convention in the Rights of Persons
   with Disabilities   1033
Discrimination   1011
Disparate-impact discrimination   1012
Disparate-treatment
   discrimination   1012

Equal employment opportunity   1011
Equal Employment Opportunity Act
   of 1972   1011
Equal Employment Opportunity
   Commission (EEOC)   1012
Equal opportunity in
   employment   1011
Equal Pay Act   1024
National origin discrimination   1014
Older Workers Benefit Protection Act
   (OWBPA)   1025
Pregnancy Discrimination
   Act   1016
Qualified individual with a
   disability   1028
Race discrimination   1014

Reasonable accommodations   1028
Religious discrimination   1021
Reverse discrimination   1032
Right to sue letter   1012
Same-sex discrimination   1020
Section 1981 of the Civil Rights Act
   of 1866   1024
Sex discrimination   1016
Sexual harassment   1017
State and local government
   antidiscrimination laws   1032
Title I of the ADA   1028
Title VII of the Civil Rights Act of
   1964 (Fair Employment Practices
   Act)   1011
Undue burden   1028

Case Problems

36.1 Equal Pay Act: For years, New York law prevented females from working at night. Therefore, Corning Glass Works employed male workers for night inspection jobs and female workers for day inspection jobs. Males working the night shift were paid higher wages than were females who worked the day shift. When the federal Equal Pay Act was enacted, Corning began hiring females for night shift jobs, but it instituted a "red circle" wage rate that permitted previously hired male night shift workers to continue to receive higher wages than newly hired night shift workers. Does this violate the Equal Pay Act? *Corning Glass Works v. Brennan, Secretary of Labor*, 417 U.S. 188, 94 S.Ct. 2223, 41 L.Ed.2d 1, **Web** 1974 U.S. Lexis 62 (Supreme Court of the United States)

36.2 Sex Discrimination: The Los Angeles Department of Water and Power maintains a pension plan for its employees that is funded by both employer and employee contributions. The plan pays men and women retirees' pensions with the same monthly benefits. However, because statistically women on average live several years longer than men, female employees are required to make monthly contributions to the pension fund that are 14.84 percent higher than the contributions required of male employees. Because employee contributions are withheld from paychecks, a female employee takes home less pay than a male employee earning the same salary. Does this practice violate Title VII? *City of Los Angeles Department of Water and Power v. Manhart*, 435 U.S. 702, 98 S.Ct. 1370, 55 L.Ed.2d 657, **Web** 1978 U.S. Lexis 23 (Supreme Court of the United States)

36.3 Hostile Work Environment: Shirley Huddleston became the first female sales representative of Roger Dean Chevrolet, Inc. (RDC), in West Palm Beach, Florida. Shortly after she began working at RDC, Philip Geraci, a fellow sales representative, and other male employees began making derogatory comments to and about her, expelled gas in her presence, and called her derogatory names. Many of these remarks were made in front of customers. The sales manager of RDC participated in the harassment. On several occasions, Huddleston complained about this conduct to RDC's general manager. Was Title VII violated? *Huddleston v. Roger Dean Chevrolet, Inc.*, 845 F.2d 900, **Web** 1988 U.S. App. Lexis 6823 (United States Court of Appeals for the Eleventh Circuit)

36.4 Religious Discrimination: Trans World Airlines (TWA), an airline, operated a large maintenance and overhaul base for its airplanes in Kansas City, Missouri. Because of its essential role, the stores department at the base operated 24 hours per day, 365 days per year. The employees at the base were represented by the International Association of Machinists and Aerospace Workers (Union). TWA and Union entered into a collective bargaining agreement that included a seniority system for the assignment of jobs and shifts.

TWA hired Larry Hardison to work as a clerk in the stores department. Soon after beginning work, Hardison joined the Worldwide Church of God, which does not allow its members to work from sunset on Friday until sunset on Saturday and on certain religious holidays. Hardison, who had the second lowest seniority within the stores department, did not have enough seniority to observe his Sabbath regularly. When Hardison asked for special consideration, TWA offered to allow him to take his Sabbath off if he could switch shifts with another employee-union member. None of the other employees would do so. TWA refused Hardison's request for a four-day workweek because it would have had to either hire and train a part-time worker to work on Saturdays or incur the cost of paying overtime to an existing full-time worker on Saturdays. Hardison sued TWA for religious discrimination in violation of Title VII. Did TWA's actions violate Title VII? *Trans World Airlines v. Hardison*, 432 U.S. 63, 97 S.Ct. 2264, 53 L.Ed.2d 113, **Web** 1977 U.S. Lexis 115 (Supreme Court of the United States)

36.5 Bona Fide Occupational Qualification: At the age of 60, Manuel Fragante emigrated from the Philippines to Hawaii. In response to a newspaper ad, Fragante applied for an entry-level civil service clerk job with the City of Honolulu's Division of Motor Vehicles and Licensing. The job required constant oral communication with the public, either at the information counter or on the telephone. Fragante scored the highest of 731 test takers on a written examination that tested word usage, grammar, and spelling. As part of the application process, two civil service employees who were familiar with the demands of the position interviewed Fragante. They testified that his accent made it difficult to understand him. Fragante was not hired for the position, which was filled by another applicant. Fragante sued, alleging national origin discrimination in violation of Title VII. Who wins? *Fragante v. City and County of Honolulu*, 888 F.2d 591, **Web** 1989 U.S. App. Lexis 2636 (United States Court of Appeals for the Ninth Circuit)

36.6 Age Discrimination: Walker Boyd Fite was an employee of First Tennessee Production Credit Association for 19 years. He had attained the position of vice president–credit. During the course of his employment, he had never received an unsatisfactory review. On December 26, 1983, at the age of 57, Fite was hospitalized with a kidney stone. On January 5, 1984, while Fite was recovering at home, an officer of First Tennessee called to inform him that he had been retired as of December 31, 1983. A few days later, Fite received a letter stating that he had been retired because of poor job performance. Fite sued First Tennessee for age discrimination. Who wins? *Fite v. First Tennessee Production Credit Association*, 861 F.2d 884, **Web** 1988 U.S. App. Lexis 14759 (United States Court of Appeals for the Sixth Circuit)

Ethics Issues

36.7 Ethics: Dianne Rawlinson, 22 years old, was a college graduate whose major course of study was correctional psychology. After graduation, she applied for a position as a correctional counselor (prison guard) with the Alabama Board of Corrections. Her application was rejected because she failed to meet the minimum 120-pound weight requirement of an Alabama statute that also established a height minimum of 5 feet 2 inches. In addition, the Alabama Board of Corrections adopted Administrative Regulation 204, which established gender criteria for assigning correctional counselors to maximum-security prisons for "contact positions." These are correctional counselor positions that require continual close physical proximity to inmates. Under this rule, Rawlinson did not qualify for contact positions with male prisoners in Alabama maximum-security prisons. Rawlinson brought a class action lawsuit against Dothard, who was the director of the Department of Public Safety of Alabama. Does either the height–weight requirement or the contact position rule constitute a bona fide occupational qualification that justifies the sexual discrimination in this case? Does society owe a duty of social responsibility to protect women from dangerous job positions? Or is this "romantic paternalism"? *Dothard, Director, Department of Public Safety of Alabama v. Rawlinson*, 433 U.S. 321, 97 S.Ct. 2720, 53 L.Ed.2d 786, **Web** 1977 U.S. Lexis 143 (Supreme Court of the United States)

36.8 Ethics: Rita Machakos, a white female, worked for the Civil Rights Division (CRD) of the Department of Justice. During her employment, she was denied promotion to certain paralegal positions. In each instance, the individual selected was a black female. Evidence showed that the CRD maintained an institutional and systematic discrimination policy that favored minority employees over white employees. Machakos sued the CRD for race discrimination under Title VII. Who wins? *Machakos v. Attorney General of the United States*, 859 F.2d 1487, **Web** 1988 U.S. App. Lexis 14672 (United States Court of Appeals for the District of Columbia Circuit)

IRAC Writing Assignment

Read **Case A-36** in Appendix A [*Robinson v. Jacksonville Shipyards, Inc.*]. Use the IRAC method to prepare a written analysis of the case.

Endnotes

1. In some states, the complaint must be filed with the appropriate state agency rather than the EEOC.
2. 42 U.S.C. Section 2000e(K).
3. *Meritor Savings Bank v. Vinson*, 477 U.S. 57, 106 S.Ct. 2399, 91 L.Ed.2d 49, **Web** 1986 U.S. Lexis 108 (Supreme Court of the United States).
4. *Harris v. Forklift Systems, Inc.*, 510 U.S. 17, 114 S.Ct. 367, 126 L.Ed.2d 295, **Web** 1993 U.S. Lexis 7155 (Supreme Court of the United States).
5. 523 U.S. 75, 118 S.Ct. 998, 140 L.Ed.2d 201, **Web** 1998 U.S. Lexis 1599 (Supreme Court of the United States).
6. 29 U.S.C. Section 206(d).
7. 29 U.S.C. Sections 621–634.
8. 42 U.S.C. Section 1201 *et seq*.

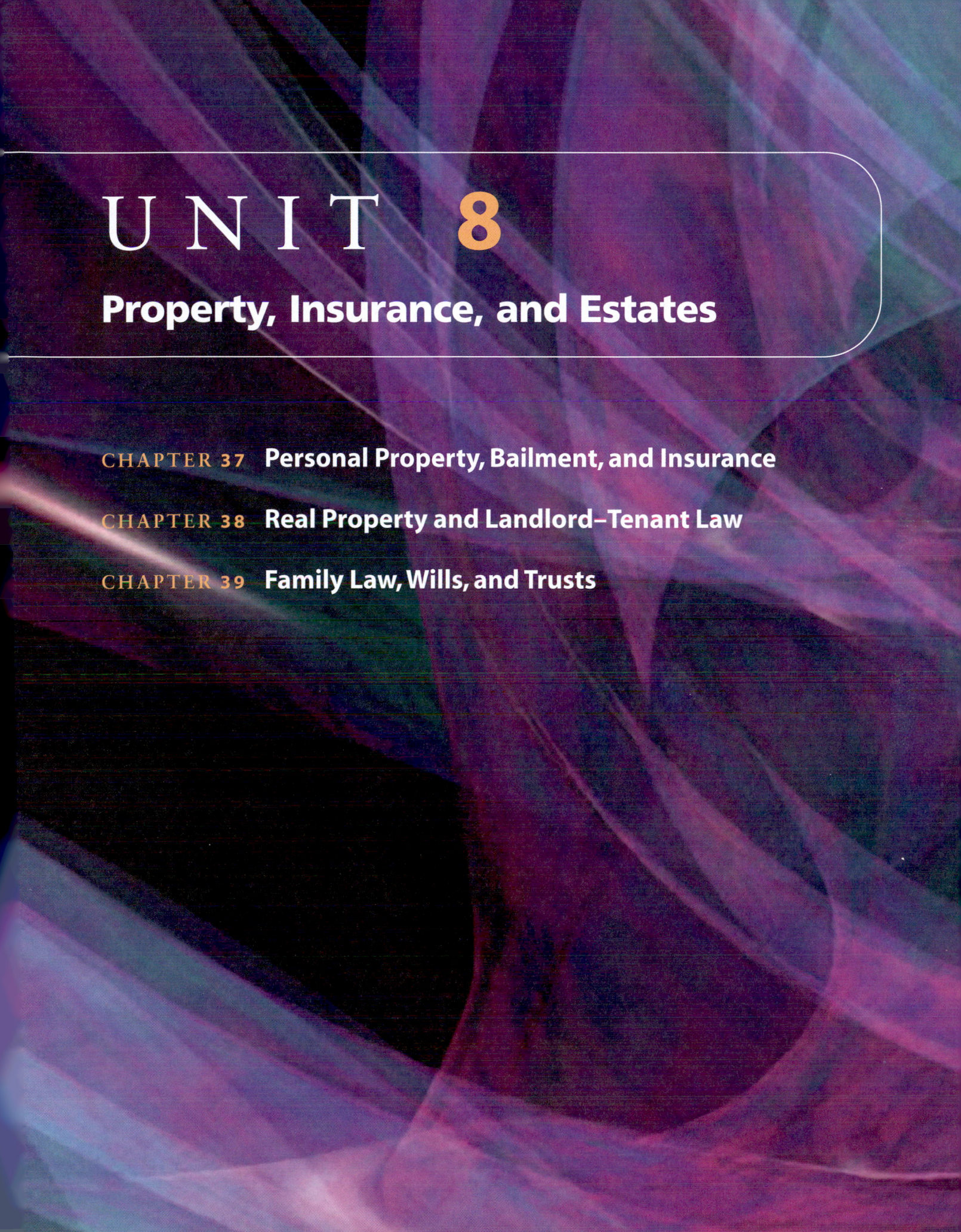

UNIT 8

Property, Insurance, and Estates

C H A P T E R   37

Personal Property, Bailment, and Insurance

"Property and law are born and must die together."

—JEREMY BENTHAM
Principles of the Civil Code, I Works 309

CHAPTER OBJECTIVES

After studying this chapter, you should be able to:

1. Define *personal property* and the methods for acquiring and transferring ownership in personal property.
2. Describe and apply rules regarding ownership rights in mislaid, lost, and abandoned property.
3. Describe the elements for creating a bailment and explain the liability of bailees for lost, damaged, or destroyed goods.
4. Describe an insurance contract and define *insurable interest*.
5. List and describe the various types of life, health, disability, and business insurance.

CHAPTER CONTENTS

- Introduction to Personal Property, Bailment, and Insurance
- Personal Property
- Mislaid, Lost, and Abandoned Personal Property
- Bailment
- Insurance
- Chapter Summary
- Test Review Terms and Concepts
- Case Problems
- Ethics Issues
- IRAC Writing Assignment

   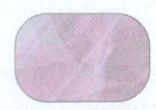 

Introduction to Personal Property, Bailment, and Insurance

Private ownership of property forms the foundation of our economic system. Therefore, a comprehensive body of law has been developed to protect property rights. The law protects the rights of property owners to use, sell, dispose of, control, and prevent others from trespassing on their rights.

This chapter first discusses the kinds of *personal property*, methods of acquiring ownership in personal property, and property rights in mislaid, lost, and abandoned property. The next part of this chapter discusses *bailment*, situations in which possession of (but not title to) personal property is delivered to another party for transfer, safekeeping, or some other purpose.

Insurance is a means for persons and businesses to protect themselves against the risk of loss. For example, a business may purchase fire insurance to cover its buildings. If there is a fire and the property is damaged, the insurance company will pay for all or part of the loss, depending on the policy. Similarly, an individual who purchases automobile insurance may be reimbursed by the insurer if his or her car is stolen. Insurance is crucial to personal, business, and estate planning.

This chapter covers the formation of an insurance contract, types of insurance, defenses of insurance companies to liability, and other topics of insurance law.

Bicycle Shop, Mackinac Island, Michigan

These bicycles are an example of tangible personal property.

Personal Property

There are two kinds of property: *real property* and *personal property*. Real property includes land and property that is permanently attached to it. For example, minerals, crops, timber, and buildings that are attached to land are generally considered real property. **Personal property** (sometimes referred to as *goods* or *chattels*) consists of everything that is not real property. Real property can become personal property if it is removed from the land. For example, a tree that is part of a forest is real property; a tree that is cut down is personal property.

Personal property that is permanently affixed to land or buildings is called a *fixture*. Such property, which includes things like heating systems and storm windows, is categorized as real property. Unless otherwise agreed, fixtures remain with a building when it is sold. Personal property (e.g., furniture, pictures, other easily portable household items) may be removed by the seller prior to sale.

Personal property can be either tangible or intangible. **Tangible property** includes physically defined property, such as goods, animals, and minerals. **Intangible property** represents rights that cannot be reduced to physical form, such as stock certificates, certificates of deposit, bonds, and copyrights.

Real and personal property may be owned by one person or by more than one person. If property is owned concurrently by two or more persons, there is concurrent ownership.

Personal property may be acquired or transferred with a minimum of formality. Commerce would be severely curtailed if the transfer of such items were difficult. The methods for acquiring ownership in personal property are possession or capture, purchase, production, gift, will, inheritance, accession, confusion, and divorce. These methods are discussed in the following paragraphs.

Possession or Capture

A person can acquire ownership in unowned personal property by *taking possession* of it or *capturing* it. The most notable unowned objects are things in their natural state.

Example People who obtain the proper fishing license acquire ownership of all the fish they catch. This type of property acquisition was important when this country was being developed. In today's urbanized society, however, there are few unowned objects, and this method of acquiring ownership in personal property has become less important.

Purchase

The most common method of acquiring title to personal property is by *purchasing* the property from its owner.

Example Urban Concrete Corporation owns a large piece of equipment. City Builders, Inc., purchases the equipment from Urban Concrete for $50,000. Urban Concrete signs over the title to the equipment to City Builders. City Builders is now the owner of the equipment.

Production

Production is a common method of acquiring ownership in personal property. A manufacturer that purchases raw materials and produces a finished product owns that product.

Example Cheetah Motor Company manufactures automobiles. The company purchases many of the parts that go into the manufacture of the automobiles from subcontractors. For example, Cheetah purchases the steel to make parts of the car from Subcontractor No. 1, the engine from Subcontractor No. 2, the seats from Subcontractor No. 3, the tires from Subcontractor No. 4, and many other parts of the automobile from other subcontractors. Cheetah assembles the parts it makes and the parts it acquires from subcontractors to produce its famous Cheetah brand automobile. Cheetah Motor Company owns the produced automobiles.

Gift

A **gift** is a voluntary transfer of property without consideration. The lack of consideration is what distinguishes a gift from a purchase. The person making a gift is called the **donor**. The person who receives the gift is called the **donee**. There are three elements of a valid gift:

1. *Donative intent.* For a gift to be effective, the donor must have intended to make a gift. **Donative intent** can be inferred from the circumstances or language used by the donor. The courts also consider such factors as the relationship of the parties, the size of the gift, and the mental capacity of the donor.
2. *Delivery.* **Delivery** must occur for there to be a valid gift. Although *physical delivery* is the usual method of transferring personal property, it is sometimes impracticable.

In such circumstances, *constructive delivery* (or *symbolic delivery*) is sufficient. For example, if the property being gifted is kept in a safe-deposit box, physically giving the key to the donee is enough to signal the gift. Most intangible property is transferred by written conveyance (e.g., conveying a stock certificate represents a transfer of ownership in a corporation).

3. *Acceptance.* **Acceptance** is usually not a problem because most donees readily accept gifts. In fact, the courts presume acceptance unless there is proof that the gift was refused. Nevertheless, a person cannot be forced to accept an unwanted gift.

GIFT *INTER VIVOS* AND GIFT *CAUSA MORTIS* A gift made during a person's lifetime that is an irrevocable present transfer of ownership is a **gift *inter vivos***. A **gift *causa mortis*** is a gift made in contemplation of death. A gift *causa mortis* is established when (1) the donor makes a gift in anticipation of approaching death from some existing sickness or peril and (2) the donor dies from such sickness or peril without having revoked the gift. A gift *causa mortis* can be revoked by the donor up until the time he or she dies. A gift *causa mortis* takes precedence over a prior conflicting will.

Example Suppose Sandy is a patient in a hospital. She is to have a major operation from which she may not recover. Prior to going into surgery, Sandy removes her diamond ring and gives it to her friend Pamela, stating, "In the event of my death, I want you to have this." This gift is a gift *causa mortis*. If Sandy dies from the operation, the gift is effective, and Pamela owns the ring. If Sandy lives, the requisite condition for the gift (her death) has not occurred; therefore, the gift is not effective, and Sandy can recover the ring from Pamela.

In the following case, the court had to determine whether a gift of a valuable painting had been made.

CASE 37.1
Gift

Gruen v. Gruen
68 N.Y.2d 48, 496 N.E.2d 869, 505 N.Y.S.2d 849,
Web 1986 N.Y. Lexis 19366
Court of Appeals of New York

> **"** *The letters unambiguously establish that Victor Gruen intended to make a present gift of title to the painting at that time.* **"**
>
> —Judge Simons

Facts

Victor Gruen was a successful architect. Victor purchased a painting titled *Schloss Kammer am Attersee II* by a noted Austrian modernist, Gustav Klimt, and paid $8,000 for the painting. Four years after acquiring the painting, Victor wrote a letter to his son Michael, then an undergraduate student at Harvard University, giving the painting to Michael but reserving a life estate in the painting. The letter stated:

> Dear Michael:
>   The 21st birthday, being an important event in life, should be celebrated accordingly. I therefore wish to give you as a present the oil painting by Gustav Klimt of Schloss Kammer which now hangs in the New York living room.

> Happy birthday again.
> Love,
> [Signed] Victor

Because Victor retained a life interest in the painting, Michael never took possession of the painting. Victor died 17 years later. The painting was appraised at $2.5 million. When Michael requested the painting from his stepmother, Kemija Gruen, she refused to turn it over to him. Michael sued to recover the painting. The trial court held in favor of the stepmother. The appellate division reversed and awarded the painting to Michael. The stepmother appealed.

Issue

Did Victor Gruen make a valid gift *inter vivos* of the Klimt painting to his son Michael?

Language of the Court

An *inter vivos* gift requires that the donor intends to make an irrevocable present transfer of ownership. The evidence is all but conclusive that Victor intended to transfer ownership of the painting to plaintiff but to retain a life estate in it and that he did, therefore, effectively transfer a remainder interest in the painting to plaintiff at that time. The letters unambiguously establish that Victor Gruen intended to make a present gift of title to the painting at that time.

In order to have a valid inter vivos gift, there must be a delivery of the gift, either by a physical delivery of the subject of the gift or a constructive or symbolic delivery. What Victor Gruen gave plaintiff was not all rights to the Klimt painting, but only title to it with no right of possession until his death.

Decision

The appellate court held that Victor Gruen had made a valid gift *inter vivos* of the Klimt painting to his son Michael. The court affirmed the judgment of the appellate division awarding the painting to Victor's son Michael.

Law & Ethics Questions

1. Should a donor who makes a gift *inter vivos* be required to relinquish physical possession of the property to the donee?

2. **ETHICS** Did the stepmother act unethically in refusing to turn the painting over to Michael? Explain.

3. What could Victor Gruen have done to make his donative intent more clear? Explain.

Web Exercises

1. **WEB** For the complete opinion of this case, go to *www.prenhall.com/cheesemancases*.

2. **WEB** Visit the website of the court of appeals of New York, at *www.courts.state.ny.us/ctapps*.

3. **WEB** Use *www.google.com* to find a picture of the painting *Schloss Kammer am Attersee II* by Gustav Klimt. Can you find a recent value of this painting?

UNIFORM GIFT TO MINORS ACT All states have adopted in whole or part the **Uniform Gift to Minors Act** or the **Revised Uniform Gift to Minors Act**. These laws establish procedures for adults to make irrevocable gifts of money and securities to minors. Gifts of money can be made by depositing the money in an account in a financial institution, with the donor or another trustee (such as another adult or bank) as custodian for the minor. Gifts of securities can be made by registering the securities in the name of a trustee as custodian for the minor. The laws give custodians broad discretionary powers to invest the money or securities for the benefit of the minor.

Will or Inheritance

Title to personal property is frequently acquired by **will** or **inheritance**. If the person who dies has a valid will, the property is distributed to the **beneficiaries**, pursuant to the provisions of that will. If a person dies without having executed a will, the property is distributed to the **heirs** as provided in the relevant state's inheritance statute.

Example Henry is an older man whose wife has predeceased him. Henry has executed a will, leaving his property as follows: his baseball card collection to his son, Andy, a painting by Andy Warhol to his daughter Ida, and a diamond ring he owns to his daughter Michelle. His will leaves the remaining property of his estate to his granddaughter Vivi. When Henry's estate is probated and the property distributed, Andy owns the baseball card collection, Ida owns the Warhol painting, Michelle owns the diamond ring, and Vivi owns the rest of Henry's property.

Example Henry, whose wife has predeceased him, has three children, Andy, Ida, and Michele, and a granddaughter, Vivi. When Henry dies, he has no will. Therefore, his property will be distributed pursuant to the state's inheritance statute. In this situation, most inheritance statutes will require Henry's property to be distributed equally to his three children. His granddaughter Vivi will receive nothing. Some of Henry's property might have to be sold to pay his three surviving children their equal share.

Accession

Accession occurs when the value of personal property increases because it is added to or improved by natural or manufactured means.

Example Accession that occurs naturally belongs to the owner. Suppose a colt that is born to a mare belongs to Julie. Pursuant to accession, Julie owns the newborn colt.

If an improvement was made wrongfully, the owner acquires title to the improved property and does not have to pay the improver for the value of the improvements.

Example Suppose a thief steals a car and puts a new engine in it. The owner is entitled to recover the car as improved and does not have to pay the thief for the improvements.

If an improvement was mistakenly made by an improver and the improvement can be easily separated from the original article, the improver must remove the improvement and pay any damages caused by such removal.

Example A builder who puts the wrong door on a house must replace that door with the correct door at his own cost.

If an improvement was mistakenly made by an improver and the improvement cannot be removed from the original article, the owner owns title to the improved property and does not have to pay the improver for the improvement.

Example If a builder misreads blueprints and extends an addition to a building farther than the owner has contracted for, the owner of the building is entitled to keep the improvement at no extra cost.

Confusion

Confusion occurs if two or more persons commingle *fungible goods* (i.e., goods that are exactly alike, such as the same grade of oil, grains, or cattle). Title to goods can be acquired by confusion. The owners share ownership in the commingled goods in proportion to the amount of goods contributed. It does not matter whether the goods were commingled by agreement or by accident. If goods are wrongfully or intentionally commingled without permission, the innocent party acquires title to them.

Example If three farmers voluntarily agree to store the same amount of Grade B winter wheat in a silo, each of them owns one-third. When the grain is sold, the profits are divided into three parts; if the silo burns to the ground, each suffers one-third of the loss.

Divorce

When a marriage is dissolved by a divorce, the parties obtain certain rights in the property of the marital estate. Often, a settlement of property rights is reached. If not, the court must decide the property rights of the spouses.

Example Beth and James, who were married, obtain a divorce. In the property settlement, Beth receives property that includes such personal property as jewelry, furniture, and an automobile. Beth owns this personal property. If James receives personal property consisting of a painting, an SUV, and a motorcycle, this personal property belongs to James.

Mislaid, Lost, and Abandoned Personal Property

Often, people find another person's personal property. Ownership rights to the property differ, depending on whether the property was mislaid, lost, or abandoned. The following paragraphs discuss these legal rules.

Mislaid Property

Property is **mislaid** when its owner voluntarily places the property somewhere and then inadvertently forgets it. It is likely that the owner will return for the property upon realizing that it was misplaced.

Only a ghost can exist without material property.

Ayn Rand
Atlas Shrugged (1957)

Laws are always useful to persons of property, and hurtful to those who have none.

Jean-Jacques Rousseau
Du Contrat Social (1761)

Personal property has no locality.

Lord Loughborough C.J.
Sill v. Worswick (1971)

The owner of the premises where the property is mislaid is entitled to take possession of the property against all except the rightful owner. This right is superior to the rights of the person who finds it. Such possession does not involve a change of title. Instead, the owner of the premises becomes an involuntary bailee of the property (bailments are discussed later in this chapter) and owes a duty to take reasonable care of the property until it is reclaimed by the owner.

Example Suppose Felicity is on a business trip and stays in a hotel during her trip. Felicity accidentally leaves her diamond engagement ring in the hotel room she has stayed in and checks out of the hotel. The engagement ring is mislaid property, and the hotel has a duty to return it to Felicity, its rightful owner.

Lost Property

Property is considered **lost property** when its owner negligently, carelessly, or inadvertently leaves it somewhere. The finder obtains title to such property against the whole world except the true owner. The lost property must be returned to its rightful owner, whether he or she discovers the loser's identity or the loser finds him or her. A finder who refuses to return the property is liable for the tort of conversion and the crime of larceny. Many states require the finder to conduct a reasonable search (e.g., place advertisements in newspapers) to find the rightful owner.

Example If a commuter finds a laptop computer on the floor of a subway station in New York City, the computer is considered lost property. The finder can claim title to the computer against the whole world except the true owner. If the true owner discovers that the finder has her computer, she may recover it from the finder. If there is identification of the owner on the computer (e.g., name, address, and telephone number), the finder owes a duty to contact the rightful owner and give back the computer.

Abandoned Property

Property is classified as **abandoned property** if (1) an owner discards the property with the intent to relinquish his or her rights in it or (2) an owner of mislaid or lost property gives up any further attempts to locate it. Anyone who finds abandoned property acquires title to it. The title is good against the whole world, including the original owner.

Example Property left at a garbage dump is abandoned property. It belongs to the first person who claims it.

ETHICS SPOTLIGHT
Estray Statute

Most states have enacted **estray statutes** that permit a finder of *mislaid* or *lost* property to clear title to the property if:

1. The finder reports the found property to the appropriate government agency and then turns over possession of the property to this agency.
2. Either the finder or the government agency posts notices and publishes advertisements describing the lost property.
3. A specified time (usually a year or a number of years) has passed without the rightful owner's reclaiming the property.

Many state estray statutes provide that the government receive a portion of the value of the property. Some statutes provide that title cannot be acquired in found property that is the result of illegal activity.

For example, title has been denied to finders of property and money deemed to have been used for illegal drug purchases.

Law & Ethics Questions

1. **ETHICS** Does an estray statute encourage ethical behavior? Explain.

Web Exercise

1. **WEB** Use *www.google.com* to find the estray statute or other law in your state that applies to finding of property. If there is an estray statute, what requirements must be met, and how long is the waiting period?

The following two cases involve lost or mislaid property.

C A S E **37.2**

Estray Statute

Willsmore v. Township of Oceola, Michigan

106 Mich.App. 671, 308 N.W.2d 796,
Web 1981 Mich. App. Lexis 2993
Court of Appeals of Michigan

> "*The Lost Goods Act provides certainty of title to property by eventually vesting clear title after a set period of time. It encourages honesty in finders.* "
>
> —Judge Corsiglia

Facts

While hunting on unposted and unoccupied property in Oceola Township, Michigan, Duane Willsmore noticed an area with branches arranged in a crisscross pattern. When he kicked aside the branches and sod, he found a watertight suitcase in a freshly dug hole. Willsmore informed the Michigan State Police of his find. A state trooper and Willsmore together pried open the suitcase and discovered $383,840 in cash. The state police took custody of the money, which was deposited in an interest-bearing account. Michigan's "Lost Goods Act" provides that the finder and the township in which the property was found must share the value of the property if the finder publishes required notices and the true owner does not claim the property within one year.

Willsmore published the required notices and brought a declaratory judgment action seeking a determination of the ownership of the money. Thomas Powell, the owner of the land on which the suitcase was found, claimed he was the owner of the suitcase. After Powell incorrectly named the amount of money in the suitcase, he asserted his Fifth Amendment right not to testify at his deposition and at trial. The trial court awarded the money equally to Willsmore and the Township of Oceola. Powell appealed.

Issue

Who is the owner of the lost briefcase and its contents?

Language of the Court

It is a universally accepted fundamental principle of property law that the true owner, assuming he presented himself within the one-year statute of limitations of the Lost Goods Act, would be entitled to the money before any other party in this case.

Voluntarily, and perhaps wisely, claimant Powell did not present himself at trial. At Powell's deposition, virtually the only answer he would give was the bald assertion that he was the true owner of the money. When asked the sum of money in the suitcase, his answer was incorrect. When faced with questions about how he obtained the money and hid it, claimant Powell had the right to assert his constitutional privilege to remain silent. However, the court not only had the right, but also the

duty, to conclude from such silence that claimant Powell did not carry his burden of proof. Claimant Powell's claim as true owner fails as a matter of law. The trial court was justified in granting a directed verdict against claimant Powell, claiming as the true owner.

The Lost Goods Act provides certainty of title to property by eventually vesting clear title after a set period of time. It encourages honesty in finders. The public obtains a portion of the benefit of a find through receipt of one-half of the value by the township. The finder receives an award for his honesty by receiving one-half of the value of the property plus costs.

Decision

The court of appeals held that Willsmore and the Township of Oceola were the owners of the briefcase and its contents. The court of appeals affirmed the judgment of the trial court and ordered that Willsmore and the township each receive one-half the proceeds of the find after Willsmore's costs were deducted.

Law & Ethics Questions

1. What is an estray statute? What is the public policy underlying an estray statute?

2. **ETHICS** If you had found the suitcase, would you have turned it in to the government?

3. Should the government be entitled to half the find? Why or why not?

Web Exercises

1. **WEB** For the complete opinion of this case, go to *www.prenhall.com/cheesemancases*.

2. **WEB** Visit the website of the court of appeals of Michigan, at *www.courtofappeals.state.mi.us*.

3. **WEB** Use *www.google.com* to find a case concerning the ownership of found personal property.

CASE **37.3**
Mislaid Property

Franks v. Kazi

88 Ark.App. 243, 197 S.W.3d 5,
Web 2004 Ark. App. Lexis 771 (2204)
Court of Appeals of Arkansas

> *"The place where money or property is found is an important factor in the determination of the question of whether it was lost or mislaid."*
>
> —Judge Griffen

Facts

Alex Franks was a guest staying at a Comfort Inn in Searcy, Arkansas, while he was working on a highway project. Franks found a bundle of money in plain view in the left part of the left drawer in the dresser in his room. Franks notified the hotel manager, who notified the police. The police took custody of the money and discovered that the carefully wrapped bundle contained $14,200 cash—46 $100 bills and 480 $20 bills. Franks sued to recover the cash. J.K. Kazi, the owner of the hotel, joined the lawsuit, also claiming the money. Franks argued that the money was lost property and therefore he, as the finder, was entitled to the money. Kazi argued that the money was mislaid property and that he, as the owner of the premises on which the money was found, was entitled to the money. The trial court held that the money had been mislaid and awarded the money to Kazi, the hotel owner. Franks appealed.

Issue

Was the money mislaid or lost property?

Language of the Court

Mislaid property is property that is intentionally put into a certain place and later forgotten. Mislaid property is presumed to have been left in the custody of the owner or occupier of the premises upon which it is found. A finder of mislaid property acquires no ownership rights in it, and, where such property is found upon another's premises, the finder is required to turn it over to the owner of the premises. The owner of such premises becomes a gratuitous bailee by operation of law, with a duty to use ordinary care to return it to the owner and is absolutely liable for a misdelivery. The place where money or property is

found is an important factor in the determination of the question of whether it was lost or mislaid. To reason by analogy, if one leaves a wallet in a drawer, there is no greater reason to believe it was lost rather than intentionally placed there and forgotten. Similarly, here, as the trial court found, the fact that the money was placed in the drawer supports a finding that the property was not abandoned or lost, but was mislaid.

Decision

The court of appeals held that the money was mislaid property. The court of appeals affirmed the trial court's judgment awarding the money to Kazi, the hotel owner.

Law & Ethics Questions

1. What is lost property? Who is entitled to lost property that is found?

2. What is mislaid property? Who is entitled to lost property that is found?

3. **ETHICS** Did Franks have much of a chance to win this case?

Web Exercises

1. **WEB** For the complete opinion of this case, go to *www.prenhall.com/cheesemancases*.

2. **WEB** Visit the website of the court of appeals of Arkansas, at *www.courts.state.ar.us/coa*.

3. **WEB** Use *www.google.com* to find an article that discusses lost and mislaid property.

CONCEPT SUMMARY

Mislaid, Lost, and Abandoned Property

TYPE OF PROPERTY	OWNERSHIP RIGHTS
Mislaid property	The owner of the premises where property is mislaid is entitled to possession but does not acquire title. He or she holds the property as an involuntary bailee until the owner reclaims it.
Lost property	The finder acquires title to the property against the whole world except the true owner; the owner may reclaim his or her property from the finder.
Abandoned property	The finder acquires title to the property, even against its original owner.

CONTEMPORARY ENVIRONMENT
Treasure Trove on the *SS Central America*

On Saturday, September 12, 1857, the *SS Central America*, a luxurious steamship that made frequent trips between New York and Panama, lost a desperate three-day battle to keep itself afloat. It sank 169 miles off the coast of South Carolina. The ship carried 587 passengers, many of whom were returning from California, where they had recovered gold from newly discovered mines. Only 166 passengers survived. Insurance companies paid claims of $1.2 million (1857 value) for gold coins and bricks that sank with the ship.

For nearly 130 years, the *SS Central America* lay peacefully in the icy waters off the East Coast. While many dreamed of finding the ship and its cargo, which was estimated to be worth up to $1 billion in today's market, no one knew exactly where to look. In 1981, Thomas G. Thompson, an Ohio-based scientist and entrepreneur, raised money for an expedition called the Columbus–America Discovery Group (Columbus Group) to recover the sunken ship by submerging a 5,000-pound robot, with a video camera attached to its arm, into the water. The exploration of the Atlantic Ocean began in 1986, and the following year, the Columbus group located the *SS Central America* on the ocean floor off the South Carolina coast, with its undisturbed cargo of thousands of rare gold coins and even rarer gold bars.

When the jubilant Thompson and crew returned to port, they were greeted by more than just well-wishers. Representatives of several insurance companies immediately claimed that some of the *SS Central America*'s loot belonged to them as compensation for the claims they had paid 130 years earlier. Eventually, after over a decade of lawsuits, the U.S. courts applied the **Law of Salvage** and awarded the Columbus group approximately 90 percent of the value of the gold coins and other valuables found on the *SS Central America*, with the insurance companies being awarded the rest.

Web Exercises

1. **WEB** Use *www.google.com* to find an article that discusses the history of the *SS Central America*. Read it.

2. **WEB** Use *www.google.com* to find pictures or drawings of the *SS Central America*. Read it.

3. **WEB** Use *www.google.com* to find out if you can purchase any of the gold coins found on the *SS Central America*.

Bailment

A **bailment** occurs when the owner of personal property delivers his or her property to another person, either to be held, stored, or delivered or for some other purpose. In a bailment, the owner of the property is the **bailor**. The party to whom the property is delivered for safekeeping, storage, or delivery (e.g., warehouse, common carrier) is the **bailee** (see Exhibit 37.1). The law of bailment establishes the rights, duties, and liabilities of parties to a bailment.

A bailment is different from a sale or a gift because title to the goods does not transfer to the bailee. Instead, the bailee must follow the bailor's directions concerning the goods.

Example Suppose Hudson Corporation is relocating offices and hires American Van Lines to move its office furniture and equipment to the new location. American Van Lines (the bailee) must follow Hudson's (the bailor's) instructions regarding delivery.

Elements Necessary to Create a Bailment

Three elements are necessary to create a bailment:

1. ***Personal property.*** *Only personal property* can be bailed. The property can be *tangible* (e.g., automobiles, jewelry, animals) or *intangible* (e.g., stocks, bonds, promissory notes).

EXHIBIT 37.1

Bailment

2. *Delivery of possession.* Delivery of possession involves two elements: (1) The bailee must have exclusive control over the personal property, and (2) the bailee must knowingly accept the personal property.

Example No bailment is created if a patron goes into a restaurant and hangs her coat on an unattended coat rack because other patrons have access to the coat.

Example A bailment is created if a patron checks her coat with a checkroom attendant because the restaurant has assumed exclusive control over the coat. If valuable property was left in the pocket of the coat, there would be no bailment of that property because the checkroom attendant did not knowingly accept it.

Most bailments are created by *physical delivery*. For example, a bailment is created if Great Lakes Shipping, Inc., delivers a vessel to Marina Repairs, Inc., for repairs. *Constructive delivery* can create a bailment, too. For example, there has been constructive delivery of an automobile if the owner gives someone the keys and registration to his car.

3. *Bailment agreement.* The creation of a bailment does not require any formality. A bailment may be either express or implied. Most *express bailments* can be either written or oral. Under the Statute of Frauds, however, a **bailment agreement** must be in writing if it is for more than one year. An example of an *implied bailment* is the finding and safeguarding of lost property.

In the following two cases, the court had to decide whether bailments had been created.

CASE 37.4
Bailment

Sisters of Charity of the Incarnate Word v. Meaux

122 S.W.3d 428,
Web 2003 Tex. App. Lexis 10189 (2003)
Court of Appeals of Texas

> "*A bailee has the duty to exercise ordinary care over the goods and is therefore responsible for the bailor's goods.*"
>
> —Judge Amidei

Facts

The Sisters of Charity of the Incarnate Word, d/b/a/ St. Elizabeth Hospital of Beaumont, operates a health and wellness center. Phil Meaux was a paying member of the health center. The rules of the center, which Meaux had been given, state, "The Health & Wellness Center is not responsible for lost or stolen items." A sign stating "We cannot assure the safety of your valuables" was posted at the check-in desk. The wellness center furnished a lock and key to each member but had a master key to open lockers in case a member forgot or lost his or her key.

One day, Meaux went to the wellness center and placed his clothes, an expensive Rolex watch, and a money clip with $400 cash in the locker assigned him. Upon returning from swimming, Meaux discovered that his locker had been pried open, and his watch and money had been stolen by some unknown person. Meaux sued the Sisters of Charity, alleging that a bailment had been created between him and the Sisters and that the Sisters, as bailee, were negligent and therefore liable to him for the value of his stolen property. The trial court held in

favor of Meaux and awarded him $19,500 as the value of the stolen property, plus interest and attorneys' fees. The Sisters of Charity appealed.

Issue

Was a bailment created between Meaux and the Sisters of Charity?

Language of the Court

A bailee has the duty to exercise ordinary care over the goods and is therefore responsible for the bailor's goods. In contrast, a lease is a transfer of interest in and possession of property for a prescribed period of time in exchange for an agreed consideration called rent. The lessor has the duty of ordinary care in maintaining the premises it controls, but does not have a duty to exercise care regarding the lessee's property stored on the premises. The lessor is therefore not responsible for the property of the lessee. As between the owner of premises and the owner of personal property left in a locker on the premises when exclusive possession thereof has not been delivered and control and dominion of the property is dependant in no degree upon the co-operation of the owner of the premises, a landlord and tenant relationship is created. Having failed to establish either the delivery and acceptance of exclusive possession in the defendant, or defendant's specific knowledge of articles entrusted to him, plaintiff has failed to establish the necessary elements of bailment. There was no evidence of a bailment agreement.

Decision

The court of appeals held that a landlord–tenant agreement, and not a bailment, had been created between Meaux and the Sisters of Charity. The court held that the Sisters of Charity were not liable for Meaux's loss. The court of appeals reversed the trial court's judgment in favor of Meaux and rendered a decision in favor of the Sisters of Charity.

Law & Ethics Questions

1. What is the difference between a bailment and a landlord–tenant relationship? Explain.

2. **ETHICS** Did Meaux act ethically in arguing that a bailment had been created in this case?

3. Do you think the fact that the Sisters of Charity had a public rule that it was "not responsible" for the loss of items had much bearing on the outcome of this case?

Web Exercises

1. **WEB** For the complete opinion of this case, go to *www.prenhall.com/cheesemancases*.

2. **WEB** Visit the website of the court of appeals of Texas, Ninth District, at *www.9thcoa.courts.state.tx.us*.

3. **WEB** Use *www.google.com* to find an article that discusses the creation of a bailment. Read it.

C A S E 37.5
Bailment

Ziva Jewelry, Inc. v. Car Wash Headquarters, Inc.

897 So.2d 1011,
Web 2004 Ala. Lexis 238 (2004)
Supreme Court of Alabama

> ❝ *Thus, Ziva Jewelry cannot claim that CWH knew or that it should have reasonably foreseen or expected that it was taking responsibility for over $850,000 worth of jewelry when it accepted Smith's vehicle for the purpose of washing it.* ❞
>
> —Judge Stuart

Facts

Ziva Jewelry, Inc., is a jewelry wholesaler. Stewart Smith was employed by Ziva Jewelry as a traveling sales representative. In connection with the employment, Smith drove his own vehicle to meet clients and attend trade shows. Smith testified that he knew that thieves are aware of jewelry trade shows and sometimes follow jewelry sales representatives, looking for an opportunity to steal the jewelry in the possession of the sales representatives and that they are most likely to strike when the car carrying the jewelry is unattended. Smith's practice was to keep the jewelry in the trunk of his vehicle while he was traveling on business. He kept the trunk padlocked and kept the only key to the padlock on the key ring with his ignition key.

One day, when Smith was traveling from a jewelry trade show, he stopped at Rain Tunnel Car Wash, owned by Car Wash Headquarters, Inc. (CWH). At Rain Tunnel, the driver leaves his or her vehicle with employees of the car wash, and the vehicle is sent through a wash "tunnel." Upon completion of the car wash cycle, an employee drives the vehicle to another area of the car-wash premises to be hand dried. Once the vehicle is dried, the driver is signaled to retrieve the vehicle.

Smith left his car and the keys with a car-wash employee. Jewelry worth $850,000 was locked in the trunk of the vehicle. Smith watched the car as it went through the car wash tunnel. He watched as an employee dried the vehicle. As Smith was standing at the counter waiting to pay the cashier, he saw the employee wave a flag indicating that the vehicle was ready for Smith. The employee then walked away from the vehicle. While Smith was standing at the cashier counter, someone jumped into Smith's vehicle and sped off. When Smith's vehicle was recovered about 15 minutes later by the police, the jewelry was gone.

Ziva Jewelry sued CWH to recover the value of the jewelry, alleging that a bailment had been created between Ziva and CWH and that CWH, as the bailee, was negligent in protecting the bailed goods. CWH defended, arguing that no bailment was created and therefore it was not liable for the loss of Ziva's stolen jewelry. The trial court held that no bailment had been created and entered summary judgment for CWH. Ziva Jewelry appealed.

Issue

Was a bailment created between Ziva Jewelry and CWH?

Language of the Court

A bailment is defined as the delivery of personal property by one person to another for a specific purpose, with a contract, express or implied, that the trust shall be faithfully executed, and the property returned or duly accounted for when the special purpose is accomplished, or kept until the bailor reclaims it. In order for a bailment to exist the bailee must have voluntarily assumed the custody and possession of the property for another.

In this case, Ziva Jewelry cannot establish that CWH expressly or impliedly agreed to take responsibility for the jewelry hidden inside Smith's trunk. Ziva Jewelry acknowledges that the jewelry was not plainly visible; that its presence was not made known to the car-wash employees; and that there was no reason that the employees should have expected expensive jewelry to be in the trunk of Smith's vehicle. Thus, Ziva Jewelry cannot claim that CWH knew or that it should have reasonably foreseen or expected that it was taking responsibility for over $850,000 worth of jewelry when it accepted Smith's vehicle for the purpose of washing it. Thus, there is no evidence indicating that CWH expressly or impliedly accepted responsibility for the jewelry in the trunk of Smith's vehicle. Without express or implied acceptance by the purported bailee, a bailment cannot arise.

Decision

The supreme court held that no bailment had been created between Ziva Jewelry and CWH. The supreme court affirmed the trial court's ruling that granted summary judgment to CWH.

Law & Ethics Questions

1. What is a bailment? What is required for a bailment to be created?
2. Why was a bailment not created in this case? Explain.
3. **ETHICS** Did Ziva Jewelry have a good chance of winning this case? Why or why not?
4. Do you think Smith was negligent in this case?

Web Exercises

1. **WEB** For the complete opinion of this case, go to *www.prenhall.com/cheesemancases*.
2. **WEB** Visit the website of the supreme court of Alabama, at *www.judicial.state.al.us/supreme.cfm*.
3. **WEB** Use *www.google.com* to find an article or a case about a bailment that was created.

Bailment for the Sole Benefit of the Bailor

A **bailment for the sole benefit of the bailor** is a **gratuitous bailment** that benefits only the bailor. This ordinary bailment arises when the bailee is requested to care for the bailor's property as a favor. The bailee owes only a **duty of slight care** to protect the bailed property—that is, he or she owes a duty not to be grossly negligent in caring for the bailed goods.

Example The Watkins family is going on vacation and asks the neighbors, the Smiths, to feed its dog, which is allowed to run free. The Smiths diligently feed the dog, but the dog runs away and does not return. The Smiths are not liable for the loss of the dog.

Bailment for the Sole Benefit of the Bailee

A **bailment for the sole benefit of the bailee** is a *gratuitous bailment* that solely benefits the bailee. This ordinary bailment arises when a bailee requests to use the bailor's property for personal reasons. In this situation, the bailee owes a **duty of great care** (or **utmost care**) to protect the bailed property—that is, he or she owes a duty not to be slightly negligent in caring for the bailed goods.

Example Suppose Mitch borrows Courtney's lawn mower (free of charge) to mow his own lawn. Mitch is the bailee, and Courtney is the bailor. This bailment is for the sole benefit of the bailee. Suppose Mitch, while mowing his lawn, leaves the lawn mower in his front yard while he goes into his house to answer the telephone. While he is gone, the lawn mower is stolen. Here, Mitch will be held liable to Courtney for the loss of the lawn mower because Mitch breached his duty of great care to protect the lawn mower.

Mutual Benefit Bailment

A **mutual benefit bailment** is a bailment that *benefits both parties*. The bailee owes a *duty of reasonable care* (or *ordinary care*) to protect the bailed goods. This means that the bailee is liable for any goods that are lost, damaged, or destroyed because of his or her negligence.

Example Suppose ABC Garment Co. delivers goods to Lowell, Inc., a commercial warehouser, for storage. A fee is charged for this service. ABC Garments Co. receives the benefit of having its goods stored, and Lowell, Inc., receives the benefit of being paid compensation for storing the goods. In this example, Lowell, Inc. (the bailee), owes a duty of ordinary care to protect the goods.

CONCEPT SUMMARY

Ordinary Bailment

TYPE OF BAILMENT	DUTY OF CARE OWED BY BAILEE	BAILEE LIABLE TO BAILOR FOR
For the sole benefit of the bailor	Slight	Gross negligence
For the sole benefit of the bailee	Great	Slight negligence
For the mutual benefit of the bailor and bailee	Ordinary	Ordinary negligence

Duration and Termination of Bailments

A bailment generally expires at a specified time or when a certain purpose is accomplished. A **bailment for a fixed term** terminates at the end of the term or sooner, by mutual consent of the parties. A party who terminates a bailment in breach of the bailment agreement is liable to the innocent party for damages resulting from the breach. Bailments without a fixed term are called **bailments at will**. A bailment at will can be terminated at any time by either party. Gratuitous bailees can generally terminate a fixed-term bailment prior to expiration of the term.

Upon termination of a bailment, the bailee is legally obligated to do as the bailor directs with the property. Unless otherwise agreed, the bailee is obligated to return the identical goods bailed. Where commingled *fungible goods* are involved (e.g., grain), identically equivalent goods may be returned by the bailee.

Warehouse Company

A **warehouser**, or **warehouse company**, is a bailee engaged in the business of storing property for compensation. Warehousers are subject to the rights, duties, and liability of an ordinary bailee. As such, they owe a *duty of reasonable care* to protect the bailed property in their possession from harm or loss [UCC 7-204(1), 7-403(1)]. Warehousers are liable only for loss or damage to the bailed property caused by their own negligence. They are not liable for loss or damage caused to bailed goods by another person's negligence or conduct. Warehousers can limit the dollar amount of their liability if they offer the bailor the opportunity to increase the liability limit for the payment of an additional charge.

WAREHOUSE RECEIPT A **warehouse receipt** is a document of title issued by a warehouse company that is engaged in the business of storing goods for hire, such as a warehouse company or a storage company [UCC 1-201(45)]. The warehouse receipt that is issued to the bailor is often a preprinted form drafted by the warehouse company. Warehouse receipts include the date of issue, a description of the goods or of the packages containing them, the location of the warehouse where the goods are stored, and other terms relating to the bailment. A warehouse company has a **lien** on the goods in its possession for necessary expenses incurred in storing and handling the goods. If the charges are not paid, the warehouse company may sell the goods at a public or private auction and apply the proceeds to pay the charges. Any excess proceeds must be held for the persons who had the right to demand delivery of the goods.

Common Carrier

Common carriers offer transportation services to the general public. For example, commercial airlines, railroads, public trucking companies, public pipeline companies, and such are common carriers. The delivery of goods to a common carrier creates a mutual benefit bailment. The person shipping the goods is the **shipper** or **consignor** (the bailor). The transportation company is called the **common carrier** (the bailee). The person to whom the goods are to be delivered is called the **consignee**.

Example Purchasing Company signs a contract to purchase specified goods from Selling Company. Selling Company contracts with United Airlines to transport the goods to Purchasing Company. In this scenario, Selling Company, which is shipping the goods, is the bailor (shipper or consignor); United Airlines, the transportation company, is the bailee (common carrier); and Purchasing Company, to whom the goods are to be delivered, is the consignee.

Common carriers are held to a **duty of strict liability** [UCC 7-301(1)] Thus, if the goods are lost, damaged, destroyed, or stolen, the common carrier is liable even if it was not at fault for the loss. Common carriers are not liable for the loss, damage, or destruction of goods caused by (1) an act of God (e.g., a tornado), (2) an act of a public enemy (e.g., a terrorist activity), (3) an order of the government (e.g., statutes, court decisions, government regulations), (4) an act of the shipper (e.g., improper packaging), or (5) the inherent nature of the goods (e.g., perishability).

Common carriers can limit their liability to a stated dollar amount by expressly stating that in the bailment agreement. Federal law requires common carriers who take advantage of such limitation to offer shippers the opportunity to pay a premium and declare a higher value for the goods [UCC 7-309(2)].

BILL OF LADING A **bill of lading** is a document of title that is issued by a carrier-bailee to the bailor when goods are received for transportation. A carrier has a lien on the goods in its possession covered by a bill of lading for necessary charges and expenses. If the charges are not paid, the carrier can sell the goods at public or private sale and apply the proceeds to pay the charges. Any excess proceeds must be held for the person who had the right to demand delivery of the goods [UCC 7-308(1)].

Innkeeper

An **innkeeper** is the owner of a facility that provides lodging to the public for compensation (e.g., hotel, motel). Under the common law, innkeepers are held to a *strict liability standard* regarding loss caused to the personal property of transient guests. Permanent lodgers are not subject to this rule.

However, almost all states have enacted **innkeepers' statutes** that change the common law and limit the liability of innkeepers. These statutes allow innkeepers to avoid liability for loss caused to guests' property if a safe is provided in which the guests' valuable property may be kept and the guests are aware of the safe's availability. Most state laws also allow innkeepers to limit the dollar amount of their liability by notifying their guests of this limit (e.g., by posting a notice on each guest room door).

Example Hospitality Hotel, Inc., operates a hotel. The hotel is located in a state that has an innkeepers' statute that (1) eliminates a hotel's liability for guests' property not placed in the safe located at the hotel's registration desk and (2) limits a hotel's liability to $500 for any guest's property stored in the hotel's safe. The hotel has proper notices posted at the registration counter and in guests' rooms, notifying guests of these limitations on liability. Suppose Gion, a guest at the hotel, leaves expensive jewelry and cameras in his room when he temporarily leaves the hotel. Upon return, Gion's jewelry and cameras have been stolen. Because of the innkeepers' statute, the hotel is not liable for Gion's loss. Suppose instead that Gion had taken items to the hotel's registration desk and had the hotel place them in the hotel's safe. If the items had been stolen from the hotel's safe, the innkeepers' statute would have limited the hotel's liability to $500.

CONCEPT SUMMARY

Special Bailments

TYPE OF BAILEE	LIABILITY	LIMITATION ON LIABILITY
Warehouse company	Ordinary negligence	May limit the dollar amount of liability by offering the bailor the right to declare a higher value for the bailed goods for an additional charge.
Common carrier	Strictly liable except for: 1. Act of God 2. Act of a public enemy 3. Order of the government 4. Act of the shipper 5. Inherent nature of the goods	May limit the dollar amount of liability by offering the bailor the right to declare a higher value for the bailed goods for an additional charge.
Innkeeper	Strictly liable	State innkeepers' statutes limit the liability of an innkeeper for others' negligence.

Insurance

Insurance is defined as a contract whereby one party undertakes to indemnify another against loss, damage, or liability arising from a contingent or unknown event. It is a means of transferring and distributing risk of loss. The risk of loss is *pooled* (i.e., spread) among all the parties (or **insureds**) who pay premiums to a particular insurance company. The insurance company—also called the **insurer**, or **underwriter**—is then obligated to pay insurance proceeds to those members of the pool who experience losses.

> *An insurance policy is like old underwear. The gaps in its cover are only shown by accident.*
>
> David Yates

An insurance contract is called a **policy**. The money paid to the insurance company is called a **premium**. Premiums are based on an estimate of the number of parties within the pool who will suffer the risks insured against. The estimate is based on past experience.

Insurance policies are often sold by insurance agents or brokers. An *insurance agent* usually works exclusively for one insurance company and is an agent of that company. An *insurance broker* is an independent contractor who represents a number of insurance companies. The broker is the agent of the insured. Some insurance is sold directly by the insurer to the insured (e.g., by direct mail).

The **McCarran-Ferguson Act**[1] which was enacted by the federal government, gave the regulation of insurance to the states.

Insurable Interest

Anyone who would suffer a pecuniary (monetary) loss from the destruction of real or personal property has an **insurable interest** in that property. If the insured does not have an insurable interest in the property being insured, the contract is treated as a wager and cannot be enforced.

Ownership creates an insurable interest. In addition, mortgagees, lienholders, and tenants have an insurable interest in property. The insurable interest in property must exist at the time of loss.

In the case of life insurance, a person must have a close family relationship or an economic benefit from the continued life of another to have an insurable interest in that person's life. Thus, spouses, parents, children, and sisters and brothers may insure each others' lives. Other more remote relationships (e.g., aunts, uncles, cousins) require additional proof of an economic interest (e.g., proof of support). The insurable interest must exist when the life insurance policy is issued but need not exist at the time of death.

A person may insure his or her own life and name anyone as the **beneficiary**. The named beneficiary or beneficiaries receive the proceeds from the life insurance policy when the insured dies. The beneficiary does not have to have an insurable interest in the insured's life.

Insurance Policy

An insurance contract, called an **insurance policy**, is governed by the law of contracts. Most policies are prepared on standardized forms. Some states even make that a requirement. Often, state statutes mandate that specific language be included in different types of insurance contracts. These statutes concern coverage for certain losses, how limitations on coverage must be stated in the contract, and the like. The insurance coverage is in place once the insurance policy is issued.

If both the insurer and the insured agree, an insurance policy may be modified. Modification is usually done either by adding an **endorsement** to the policy or by the execution of a document called a **rider**.

In most instances, an insured can cancel an insurance policy at any time. An insurer may cancel an insurance policy for nonpayment of premiums. Many insurance policies provide a *grace period* during which an insured may pay an overdue premium. The insurance usually remains in effect during the grace period.

Duties of Insured and Insurer

The parties to an insurance contract are obligated to perform the duties imposed by the contract. The insured owes the following duties: (1) to pay the premiums stipulated by the policy, (2) to notify the insurer after the occurrence of an insured event within the time period stated in the policy or within a reasonable time, and (3) to cooperate with the insurer in investigating claims made against the insurer.

The insurer owes two primary duties. First, the insurer owes a *duty to defend* against any suit brought against the insured that involves a claim within the coverage of the policy. Thus, the insurer must provide and pay for the lawyers and court costs necessary to defend the lawsuit. Second, the insurer owes the *duty to pay* legitimate claims up to the policy limit. Insurers who wrongfully refuse to perform these duties are liable for damages.

Deductible Clause

Many insurance policies, such as automobile insurance and medical insurance policies, contain **deductible clauses**. A deductible clause provides that insurance proceeds are payable only after the insured has paid a certain amount of the damage or loss. For example, typical deductibles for automotive collision insurance are $500 and $1,000.

Example Suppose that an insured has a $50,000 automobile collision policy with a $1,000 deductible, and his or her car suffers $10,000 damages in an accident. The insured must pay the first $1,000; the insurer will pay the remaining $9,000.

Exclusions from Coverage

Most insurance policies include certain **exclusions from coverage**. For example, standard fire insurance policies often exclude coverage for damage caused by the storage of explosives or flammable liquids unless a special premium is paid for this coverage. Many medical insurance policies exclude coverage for preexisting undisclosed medical conditions.

Coinsurance Clause

A **coinsurance clause** requires an insured to pay a percentage of the cost of an insured loss. These clauses are sometimes structured as **copay clauses**, in which case the insured must pay a flat amount rather than a percentage.

Example Some medical insurance policies require the insured to pay a stated percentage of medical costs. Thus, if a medical insurance policy has 10% coinsurance and an insured's medical bills are $50,000, the insurance company will pay $45,000, and the insured will have to pay $5,000.

Misrepresentation and Concealment

Insurance companies may require applicants to disclose certain information to help determine whether they will insure the risk and to calculate the premium. The insurer may avoid liability on a policy (1) if its decision is based on a material misrepresentation on the part of the applicant or (2) if the applicant concealed material information from the insurer. This rule applies whether the misrepresentation was intentional or not intentional.

Many states have enacted **incontestability clauses** that prevent insurers from contesting statements made by insureds in applications for insurance after the passage of a stipulated number of years (the typical length of time is two to five years).

An incontestability clause was at issue in the following case.

| C A S E **37.6** _Incontestability Clause_ | **Amex Life Assurance Company v. Slome Capital Corp.**
14 Cal.4th 1231, 60 Cal.Rptr.2d 898, 930 P.2d 1264,
Web 1997 Cal. Lexis 404
Supreme Court of California |  |

> **❝** _The beneficiaries should be assured they will receive the expected benefits, and not a lawsuit, upon the insured's death._ **❞**
>
> —Judge Chin

Facts

Jose Morales applied for a life insurance policy from Amex Life Assurance Company (Amex). Morales knew he was HIV (human immunodeficiency virus) positive, but he lied on the application form and denied having AIDS (acquired immune deficiency syndrome). As part of the application process, Amex required Morales to have a medical examination. A paramedic working for Amex met a man claiming to be Morales and took blood and urine samples from him. On his application, Morales had listed his height as 5 feet 6 inches and his weight as 147 pounds. The examiner registered the man taking the examination as 5 feet 10 inches tall, weighing 172 pounds, and appearing to be "older than the stated age." The blood samples tested HIV negative. Amex issued Morales a life insurance policy; the policy included a two-year incontestability clause, as required by state law. All premiums were paid.

Two years and one month after the life insurance policy was issued, Morales died of AIDS-related causes. When Morales's life insurance policy was presented to Amex for payment, Amex refused to pay, alleging that Morales had engaged in fraud and had had an imposter take his physical examination for him. The trial court denied Amex's summary judgment motion. The court of appeals held that the incontestability clause prevented Amex from denying coverage. Amex appealed.

Issue

Does the two-year incontestability clause prevent Amex from raising the insured's fraud as a reason not to pay the life insurance proceeds?

Language of the Court

Amex argues it insured, if anyone, the person who appeared for the medical examination, not Morales, and that to the extent the policy purported to insure Morales, it was void from the beginning. But imposter fraud is similar to other frauds the incontestability clause covers. When the named insured applies

for the policy, and the premiums are faithfully paid for over two years, the beneficiaries should be assured they will receive the expected benefits, and not a lawsuit, upon the insured's death. The incontestability clause requires the insurer to investigate fraud before it issues the policy or within two years afterwards. The insurer may not accept the premiums for two years and investigate a possible defense only after the beneficiaries file a claim. Here, with minimal effort, Amex could have discovered the fraud at the outset, as it did finally from information available before it issued the policy.

Decision

The supreme court held that the incontestability clause prevented Amex from denying coverage. The supreme court affirmed the judgment of the court of appeals, ordering Amex to pay the proceeds of Morales's life insurance policy.

Law & Ethics Questions

1. Should the law contain incontestability clauses? What public policy is served by these clauses?

2. **ETHICS** Did Morales act ethically in this case? Should unethical conduct be rewarded?

3. Who pays the cost of insurance fraud? Explain.

Web Exercises

1. **WEB** For the complete opinion of this case, go to _www.prenhall.com/cheesemancases_.

2. **WEB** Visit the website of the supreme court of California, at _www.courtinfo.ca.gov/courts/supreme_.

3. **WEB** Use _www.google.com_ to find a recent case of insurance fraud.

Life Insurance

Life insurance is really "death insurance" because the insurer is normally obligated to pay a specified sum of money upon the death of the insured. Some life insurance policies provide for the payment of all or a portion of the proceeds to the insured before death if he or she is suffering from a terminal illness. This allows the insured to pay for medical and other costs associated with the illness.

There are four parties to a life insurance contract:

1. The *insurance company* issues the policy.
2. The *owner* of the policy is the person who contracts with the insurance company and pays the premiums.
3. The *insured* is the person whose life is insured.
4. The *beneficiary* is the person who is to receive the insurance proceeds when the insured dies.

The owner of the policy has the power to name the beneficiary of the insurance proceeds. Most life insurance contracts permit the owner to change beneficiaries. If no beneficiary is named, the proceeds go to the insured's estate.

Often, the owner and the insured are the same person. For example, an owner may take out an insurance policy on his or her own life. The owner and beneficiary may also be the same person.

Example A son may take out an insurance policy on his father's life and name himself as the beneficiary. In this case, the father is the insured and the son is both the beneficiary and the owner of the policy.

A life insurance policy where the insured takes out life insurance on her own life and names a beneficiary is illustrated in Exhibit 37.2.

SUICIDE CLAUSE Life insurance policies usually contain **suicide clauses**, which state that if the insured commits suicide within a certain period after taking out a life insurance policy on himself or herself, the insurance company does not have to pay the life insurance proceeds to the named beneficiary. The usual time period for the validity of a suicide clause in two years.

If the insured commits suicide before the specified date, the insurance company does not have to pay the policy proceeds but must refund the premiums paid to the deceased insured's estate. If the insured commits suicide after the specified date, the insurance

EXHIBIT 37.2

Life Insurance

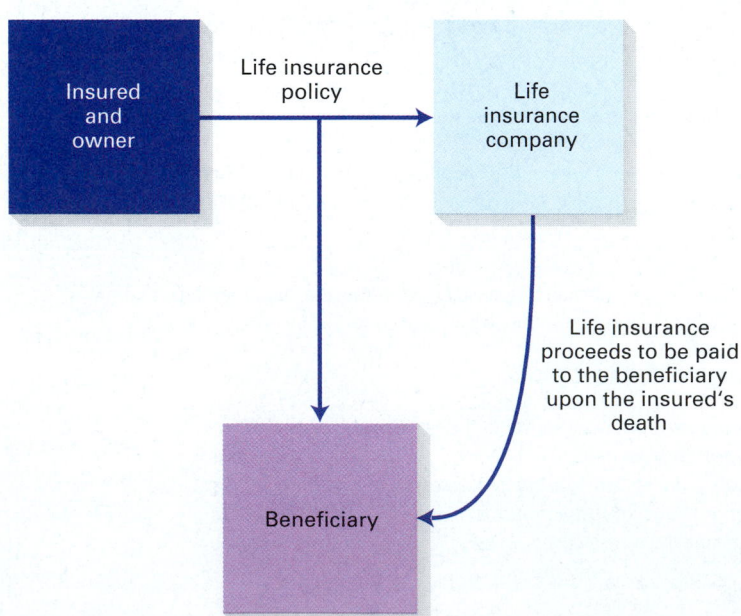

company must pay the life insurance proceeds to the insured's designated beneficiary or, if there is none, to the deceased insured's estate.

The following case is an example of the application of a suicide clause in a life insurance policy.

CASE 37.7
Suicide Clause

Needleman v. John Hancock Life Insurance Company

Web 2006 U.S. Dist. Lexis 14850
United States District Court for the Northern District of Texas

> **❝** *Defendant, therefore, did not breach its contract or policy of insurance when it denied Plaintiffs' claim for benefits on the Policy pursuant to the suicide exclusion clause.* **❞**
>
> —Judge Lindsay

Facts

Michael Needleman purchased a $4 million life insurance policy from John Hancock Life Insurance Company (John Hancock). The policy contained a two-year suicide clause that denied coverage if Needleman died of suicide during this period. About one year later, Needleman experienced certain business losses and suffered hip and knee injuries. As a result, Needleman became depressed. He sought help from a doctor, who prescribed antidepression medicine. Needleman also saw a psychiatrist. Mrs. Needleman asked a friend who was a psychologist to speak with Needleman. As a result of the meeting, the psychologist advised Mrs. Needleman to lock up the guns in the house. Mrs. Needleman locked the guns in the study.

One day Mrs. Needleman arrived home at approximately 4:00 P.M. to find Mr. Needleman sitting in an empty bathtub holding a .357 Magnum revolver to his head. Mr. Needleman, who was crying, told her, "I wanted to do this before you got home." Mrs. Needleman sat in the bathroom with her husband for approximately 45 minutes as Mr. Needleman pointed the gun at his head and his chest. The gun discharged, and Needleman shot himself in the chest. Needleman was taken to a hospital, where he was pronounced dead. The police report stated that the cause of death was suicide. The autopsy ruled the death a suicide.

Needleman's $4 million life insurance policy was presented for payment. John Hancock refused payment because Mr. Needleman's death had occurred 14½ months after the life insurance policy had been issued, which was within the two-year period of the suicide clause. Members of Needleman's family sued John Hancock to recover the $4 million. The family alleged that Needleman's death was caused by accident when his finger slipped and caused the gun to discharge. The family also argued that Needleman's death was induced by the antidepression drugs that he was taking, which impaired his judgment.

Issue

Did Mr. Needleman commit suicide, which would prevent the payment of the life insurance proceeds pursuant to the two-year suicide clause in the life insurance policy?

Language of the Court

The evidence in this case necessarily establishes that Needleman intended the actions that took his life. Needleman got into a bathtub with the gun. He alternately held the gun to his head and his chest. When Needleman held the gun to his head, his finger was on the trigger. When he held the gun to his chest, both thumbs were on the trigger, or inside the trigger guard. One of the most telling facts is that Needleman told his wife, "I wanted to do this before you got home." Thus, the court determines that Needleman committed the acts that took his life; he intended to commit those acts; his actions would be regarded as suicide in a sane person; and therefore, Plaintiffs are excluded by the suicide clause in the Policy from recovering the death benefits, regardless of whether Needleman realized or was capable of realizing that his actions would cause his death, and regardless of whether he was capable of entertaining an intention to kill himself. Defendant, therefore, did not breach its contract or policy of insurance when it denied Plaintiffs' claim for benefits on the Policy pursuant to the suicide exclusion clause.

Decision

The U.S. District Court held that the two-year suicide clause in the John Hancock life insurance policy justified the nonpayment of the life insurance proceeds to surviving members of Mr. Needleman's family. The U.S. District Court granted summary judgment to John Hancock.

Law & Ethics Questions

1. What does a suicide clause provide?

2. Why do life insurance companies include short-term suicide clauses in their contracts? Explain.

3. **ETHICS** Did the plaintiffs have much of a chance at winning this case?

Web Exercises

1. **WEB** For the complete opinion of this case, go to *www.prenhall.com/cheesemancases*.

2. **WEB** Visit the website of the U.S. District Court for the Northern District of Texas, at *www.txnd.uscourts.gov*.

3. **WEB** Use *www.google.com* to find a case in which a suicide clause in a life insurance policy was enforced.

Health Insurance

A person who is injured or sick may have to have medical treatment, surgery, or hospital care. **Health insurance** may be purchased to help cover the costs of such medical care. Health insurance usually covers only a portion of the costs of medical care. Many insurance companies also offer dental insurance.

Disability Insurance

A person who is injured or becomes sick may not be able to continue gainful employment. **Disability insurance**, which provides a monthly income to an insured who is disabled and cannot work, may be purchased to protect the insured against such an eventuality. The monthly benefits are usually based on the degree of disability.

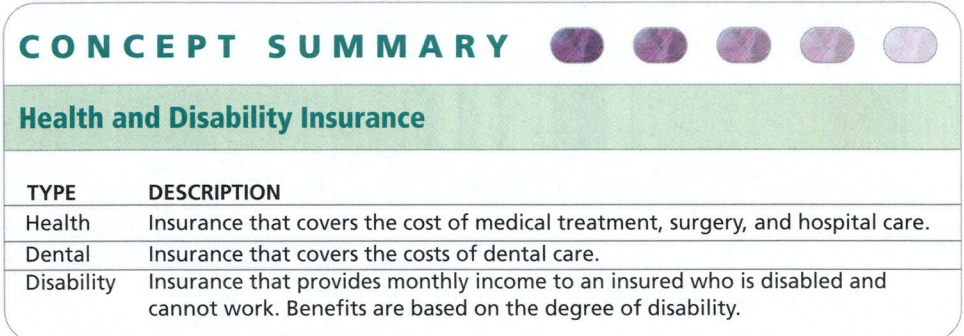

CONCEPT SUMMARY

Health and Disability Insurance

TYPE	DESCRIPTION
Health	Insurance that covers the cost of medical treatment, surgery, and hospital care.
Dental	Insurance that covers the costs of dental care.
Disability	Insurance that provides monthly income to an insured who is disabled and cannot work. Benefits are based on the degree of disability.

Fire and Homeowners' Insurance

Two major forms of insurance are available for residences: *a standard fire insurance policy* and a *homeowners' policy*. Such insurance is often required on real property that is mortgaged. Renters may also purchase insurance policies. These types of policies are discussed in the paragraphs that follow.

STANDARD FIRE INSURANCE POLICY A standard fire insurance policy protects real and personal property against loss resulting from fire and certain related perils. It does not, however, provide liability insurance for personal injury.

Most states require insurance companies to use a **standard fire insurance form** as the standard fire insurance policy. This standard policy protects the homeowner from loss caused by fire, lightning, smoke, and water damage. The coverage of a standard policy can be enlarged by adding *riders* or *endorsements* to the policy. Riders are often added to cover damage caused by windstorms, rainstorms, hail, explosions, theft, and liability. Additional coverage requires the payment of increased premiums.

Most standard fire insurance policies exclude coverage for loss caused by enemy attack, civil war, revolution, landslides, and floods. In the case of property located in a designated flood area, a separate flood insurance policy is required.

Most policies limit recovery to damage caused by *hostile fires* (e.g., fire caused by faulty electrical wiring) and not *friendly fires* (e.g., damage caused by a fire contained in a fireplace). No personal liability coverage is provided.

Most modern fire insurance policies provide **replacement cost insurance**. That is, the insurance will pay the cost to replace the damaged or destroyed property up to the policy limits (and subject to coinsurance). The insurer has the right to either pay the insured for the loss or pay to have the property restored or replaced.

HOMEOWNERS' POLICY A **homeowners' policy** is a comprehensive insurance policy that includes coverage for the real and personal risks covered by a fire insurance policy and also includes personal liability insurance.

A homeowners' policy covers (1) the dwelling, (2) any appurtenant structures (e.g., garage and storage building), and (3) personal property (e.g., furniture and clothing). A homeowners' policy also provides protection for losses caused by theft, whether the items are taken from the home or workplace or taken while traveling.

PERSONAL LIABILITY COVERAGE Personal liability coverage homeowners' policy provides comprehensive *personal liability insurance* for the insured and members of his or her family. The insurer must pay property damage, personal injuries, and medical expenses to persons injured on the insured's property (e.g., a guest slips on the sidewalk) and to persons injured by the insured or members of the insured's immediate family away from the insured's property (e.g., while golfing).

PERSONAL ARTICLES FLOATER An insured may wish to obtain insurance for specific valuable items (e.g., jewelry, works of art, furs). This is accomplished by adding a **personal articles floater**, or **personal effects floater**, to a homeowners' policy. The insured must submit a list of the items he or she wants covered, along with a statement of the value of each item, to the insurance company. The insurance company will charge an increased premium based on the articles insured. A personal articles floater provides coverage for loss or damage to the articles while traveling.

RENTERS' INSURANCE Renters may purchase insurance to cover loss or damage to their possessions. A **renters' insurance policy** covers a renter's possessions against the same perils as a homeowners' broad-form policy and provides personal liability coverage.

CONCEPT SUMMARY

Fire and Homeowners' Insurance

TYPE	DESCRIPTION
Standard fire insurance policy	Insurance that protects real and personal property against loss resulting from fire, lightning, smoke, water damage, and related perils. Most policies limit recovery to damage caused by *hostile fires* (e.g., fire caused by faulty electrical wiring) and not *friendly fires* (e.g., damage caused by a fire contained in a fireplace). No personal liability coverage is provided.
Homeowners' policy	A comprehensive insurance policy that includes coverage for the risks covered by a standard fire insurance policy as well as personal liability insurance. It includes coverage for property damage, personal injury, and medical expenses of persons injured on the insured's property.
Personal Liability Coverage	Insurance for the insured and members of his or her family. The insurer must pay property damage, personal injuries, and medical expenses to persons injured on the insured's property (e.g., a guest slips on the sidewalk) and to persons injured by the insured or members of the insured's immediate family away from the insured's property (e.g., while golfing).
Personal articles floater	Insurance that covers specific valuable items (e.g., jewelry, works of art, furs) that are usually excluded from standard fire and homeowners' policies.
Renters' insurance	Insurance that covers loss and damage to renters' possessions and provides personal liability coverage. Insures against the same perils as a homeowners' policy.

Title Insurance

Owners of real property may purchase **title insurance** to ensure that they have clear title to the property. Mortgagees and other lienholders can purchase title insurance on property on which they have a lien.

Title insurance protects against defects in titles and liens or encumbrances that are not disclosed on the title insurance policy. An owner or a mortgagee pays only one premium for title insurance, usually at closing. Each new owner or mortgagee who wants this coverage must purchase a new title insurance policy. Mortgagees sometimes require a debtor to purchase such a policy as a prerequisite for making a loan.

CONTEMPORARY ENVIRONMENT
Mold Eats Away at Insurers' Profits

When the residents of a home become seriously ill and doctors cannot find the cause of their illness, what may have caused the illness? Possibly mold. Thousands of sick homeowners and residents are having their homes tested for mold, and thousands of cases have been found. Mold usually develops when there have been leaks of water in a house or an apartment. Mold grows on water-soaked wood, stucco, and other building materials.

Whose headache is mold? Definitely that of the homeowner or resident. But it is also a problem for the insurance company that wrote the homeowners' insurance policy covering the home or residence. Thousands of claims have been filed against insurance companies concerning mold-related damages. The claims not only include the cost of removing the mold and making the home livable again but also include claims for the personal suffering caused by the mold-related illnesses, pain and suffering, and other damages. The illnesses related to mold include sore throats, asthma, respiratory problems, and even memory loss.

Mold is fast becoming one of the most costly problems for the insurance industry as the number of lawsuits grows all over the country. Juries have awarded many multimillion-dollar judgments in toxic-mold verdicts. Some experts estimate that toxic-mold liability is in the billions of dollars and may exceed the asbestosis liability paid for by the insurance industry.

Automobile Insurance

Several types of automobile insurance policies include both property and liability insurance. Many states require proof of automobile insurance before license plates are issued. The basic types of automobile insurance policies are discussed in the paragraphs that follow.

COLLISION INSURANCE An owner of an automobile may purchase **collision insurance** that insures his or her car against risk of loss or damage. This form of property insurance pays for damages caused if the car is struck by another car. The coverage is in effect whether the insured's car is moving or standing still. For example, if another motorist hits the insured's automobile while it is parked on the street, collision insurance would pay for the damages. Usually the premium is less if the policy has a deductible.

COMPREHENSIVE INSURANCE **Comprehensive insurance** is a form of property insurance that insures an automobile from loss or damage due to causes other than collision, such as fire, theft, explosion, windstorm, hail, falling objects, earthquakes, floods, hurricanes, vandalism, and riot. Many insureds purchase both collision and comprehensive insurance when they insure their automobiles against damage.

Los Angeles, California

Automobile accidents are a primary cause of injury and death in the United States. Most states require automobile owners to carry automobile insurance. The required amount is often low, however.

LIABILITY INSURANCE Automobile **liability insurance** covers damages that the insured causes to third parties, including both bodily injury and property damage. The limits of liability insurance are usually stated in three numbers, such as 200/500/50. This limits the insurer's obligation to pay insurance proceeds arising from one accident to $200,000 for bodily injury to one person, $500,000 for total bodily injury to all persons injured, and $50,000 for property damage. States often require insureds to carry minimum liability insurance specified by statute.

A basic automobile liability policy protects the insured when driving his or her own automobile. The owner, however, may wish to expand coverage by adding (1) an *omnibus* or *other-driver clause*, which protects the owner when someone else drives the car with his or her permission, and (2) a *D.O.C. (drive-other coverage)*, which protects the insured while driving other automobiles (e.g., rental cars). Some omnibus clauses extend coverage to third parties who drive automobiles with permission from a person to whom the owner gave permission to drive the car. Additional premiums are charged for this coverage.

MEDICAL PAYMENT COVERAGE An owner can obtain a **medical payment coverage** policy that covers medical expenses incurred by him- or herself, other authorized drivers of the car, and passengers in the car who are injured in an automobile accident. Coverage includes payments for reasonable medical, surgical, and hospital services.

UNINSURED MOTORIST COVERAGE Usually, people injured in an automobile accident look to the insurer of the party at fault to recover for their personal injury. But what if the person who is at fault has no insurance? An owner of an automobile may purchase **uninsured motorist coverage** that provides coverage to the driver and passengers who are injured by an uninsured motorist or a hit-and-run driver. Certain states require uninsured motorist coverage to be included in automobile insurance policies.

CONTEMPORARY ENVIRONMENT
No-Fault Automobile Insurance

Until fairly recently, most automobile insurance coverage in this country was based on the principle of "fault," whereby a party injured in an accident relied on the insurance of the at-fault party to pay for his or her injuries. This system led to substantial litigation, but many accident victims were unable to recover because the at-fault party had either inadequate insurance or no insurance at all.

To remedy this problem, more than half of the states have enacted legislation that mandates **no-fault insurance** for automobile accidents. Under this system, a driver's insurance company pays for any injuries or death he or she suffered in an accident, no matter who caused the accident. No-fault insurance assures the insureds that coverage is available if they are injured in an automobile accident.

No-fault insurance policies provide coverage for medical expenses and lost wages. Pain and suffering are sometimes covered. No-fault insurance usually covers the insured, members of the insured's immediate family, authorized drivers of the automobile, and passengers.

CONCEPT SUMMARY

Automobile Insurance

TYPE	DESCRIPTION
Collision	Property insurance that covers the insured's vehicle against risk of loss or damage when it is struck by another vehicle.
Comprehensive	Property insurance that covers the insured's vehicle against risk of loss or damage from causes other than collision, such as fire, theft, explosion, hail, windstorm, falling objects, earthquakes, floods, hurricanes, vandalism, and riots.

TYPE	DESCRIPTION
Liability	Insurance that covers damage and loss that the insured causes to third parties. This includes both bodily injury and property damage. States often require individuals to carry minimum liability insurance, specified by statute. Additional coverage may be purchased: Other-driver coverage is liability coverage that protects the owner of a vehicle when someone else drives his or her vehicle with his or her permission, and drive-other coverage is liability coverage that protects the insured while driving other vehicles.
Medical payment	Insurance that covers medical expenses incurred by the owner, passengers, and other authorized drivers of his or her car who are injured in an automobile accident.
Uninsured motorist	Insurance that provides coverage to the driver and passengers of a vehicle who are injured by an uninsured motorist or a hit-and-run driver.
No-fault	Insurance required in some states whereby the driver's insurance company pays for any injuries or death the driver suffers in an accident, no matter who caused the accident.

Umbrella Insurance Policy

Liability coverage under most insurance policies, such as automobile and homeowners' insurance, is usually limited to a certain dollar amount. Insureds who want to increase their liability beyond the original coverage can purchase an **umbrella policy**. Coverage under an umbrella policy is usually at least $1 million and often reaches $5 million. An umbrella policy pays only if the basic policy limits have been exceeded. An insurer will issue an umbrella policy only if a stipulated minimum amount of basic coverage has been purchased by the insured.

Example Suppose an insured purchases automobile liability insurance that pays up to $500,000 per accident and an umbrella policy with an additional $3 million of coverage. If the insured's negligence causes an automobile accident in which injuries to other persons total $2 million, the basic automobile policy will pay the first $500,000, and the umbrella policy will pay the remaining $1.5 million.

Business Insurance

Businesses usually purchase automobile insurance, property and casualty insurance, liability insurance, and other types of insurance previously discussed in this chapter. In addition, businesses often purchase insurance to cover risks uniquely applicable to conducting business. These types of business insurance are discussed in the following paragraphs.

BUSINESS INTERRUPTION INSURANCE When a business is severely damaged or destroyed by fire or some other peril, it usually takes time to repair or reconstruct the damaged property. During this time, the business loses money. A business can purchase a **business interruption insurance** policy that will reimburse it for any revenues lost during such a period.

Example Suppose a retail store that is covered by business interruption insurance is destroyed by fire, and it takes nine months to rebuild the store. During this nine-month period, the owner of the store will be paid the insurance proceeds provided in the business interruption insurance policy to cover the lost revenues the store would have made had it been in business.

WORKERS' COMPENSATION INSURANCE Employees are sometimes injured while working within the scope of their employment. All states have enacted legislation that compensates employees for such injuries. Employers may purchase **workers' compensation insurance** to cover this risk. Many states require companies to purchase this form of insurance.

Under a workers' compensation system, an injured worker submits a claim to the appropriate workers' compensation court or administrative agency for a determination of payment for loss. In most instances, the injured employee cannot sue his or her employer for liability because the workers' compensation award is the exclusive remedy.

Example Suppose Mary is injured while working on an assembly line of an automobile manufacturer and loses the use of one of her arms. Assume that the manufacturer has purchased appropriate workers' compensation insurance. In this case, Mary can pursue her claim and be awarded money for her injury from workers' compensation insurance. Mary cannot, however, sue her employer in court to recover tort damages in a normal court action.

KEY-PERSON LIFE INSURANCE In many small businesses, such as partnerships, limited liability companies, and close corporations, the death of one of the owners may cause a loss to the business. To compensate for such loss, the business often purchases **key-person life insurance** on owners and other important persons who work for the business. The business pays the premiums for the key-person life insurance policies. Upon the death of the insured person, the proceeds of the key-person life insurance are paid to the business.

Sometimes key-person life insurance is used to fund buy–sell agreements among the owners of the business. Thus, if an insured owner dies, the insurance proceeds are paid to the deceased's beneficiaries, and the deceased's interest in the business then reverts to either the other owners or the business, according to the terms of the buy–sell agreement.

DIRECTORS' AND OFFICERS' LIABILITY INSURANCE Most large and medium corporations carry **directors' and officers' liability insurance (D&O insurance)** to protect directors and officers from liability for the actions they take on behalf of the corporation. Smaller companies tend to forgo this type of insurance because of the expense involved.

Example Suppose that the iDot Computer Corporation has purchased D&O insurance. Assume that the shareholders of the corporation sue the board of directors, alleging that the directors were negligent in not catching a fraud perpetrated by management, thus causing a loss to the shareholders. If the court finds that the directors were negligent, the D&O insurance will pay the award and court costs.

PROFESSIONAL MALPRACTICE INSURANCE Professionals—such as attorneys, accountants, physicians, dentists, architects, and engineers—are liable for injuries resulting from their negligence in practicing their professions. These professionals can purchase **professional malpractice insurance** to insure against liability. Premiums for malpractice insurance are often quite high.

Example Ms. Jones, Ms. Chen, and Ms. Smith form the law firm Jones, Chen, and Smith. The law firm purchases professional malpractice insurance. Assume that Ms. Smith is negligent and fails to file legal documents with the court that causes the client's case to be dismissed. The client successfully sues the law firm for malpractice. In this case, the professional malpractice insurance will cover the client's award, up to its policy limits.

PRODUCT LIABILITY INSURANCE Manufacturers and sellers of products can be held liable for injuries caused by defective products. These businesses may purchase **product liability insurance** specifically to insure against this risk.

Example Suppose the Children's Toy Company purchases product liability insurance. The company produces a toy that is defectively designed and causes injury to a child using the toy. The child sues the company for product liability. The court finds the company liable and issues a judgment for monetary damages against the company. In this case, the company's product liability insurance would pay the judgment up to the policy limit of the insurance.

Airplane

Airline companies purchase substantial property and liability insurance to cover the possibility of accidents.

Chapter Summary

Personal Property, p. 1041

Personal property consists of everything that is not real property. It is sometimes referred to as goods or chattels. Types of personal property:

1. *Tangible property.* Tangible property is physically defined property such as goods, animals, and minerals.
2. *Intangible property.* Intangible property is rights that cannot be reduced to physical form, such as stock certificates, bonds, and copyrights.

Possession or Capture

A person can take possession of or capture unowned property, such as wild animals.

Purchase

A person can purchase property from its rightful owner.

Production

A person can produce a finished product from raw materials and supplies.

Gift

A gift is a voluntary transfer of property by its owner to a donee without consideration.

1. *Elements to create a valid gift:*
   a. *Donative intent.* The donor must have intended to make a gift. This intent can be inferred from the circumstances.
   b. *Delivery.* Delivery of the personal property must be made to the donee by physical delivery or, where impracticable, by constructive (or symbolic) delivery.
   c. *Acceptance.* The donee must accept the gift. Donees are free to reject gifts that they do not want.
2. *Gift* **Inter Vivos** *and Gift* **Causa Mortis:**
   a. *Gifts* **inter vivos.** These gifts are made during a donor's lifetime and are irrevocable present transfers of ownership.
   b. *Gifts* **causa mortis.** These gifts are made in anticipation of death. A gift causa mortis is established if the donor makes a gift in anticipation of approaching death from an existing illness or peril and the donor dies from such illness or peril without having revoked the gift.

3. *Uniform Gift to Minors Act.* These laws establish procedures for adults to make irrevocable gifts of money and securities to minors.

Will or Inheritance

Gifts are made to beneficiaries named in a will. Heirs are stipulated in an inheritance statute.

Accession

Accession occurs when the value of personal property increases because it is added to or improved by natural or manufactured means.

Confusion

Where fungible goods are commingled, the owners share title to the commingled goods in proportion to the amount of goods contributed.

Divorce

When a marriage is dissolved by a divorce, the parties obtain certain rights in the property of the marital estate.

Mislaid, Lost, and Abandoned Personal Property, p. 1045

Mislaid Property

Mislaid property is personal property that an owner voluntarily places somewhere and then inadvertently forgets. The owner of the premises where the property is mislaid does not acquire title to the property but has the right of possession against all except the rightful owner. The rightful owner can reclaim the property.

Lost Property

Lost property is personal property that an owner leaves somewhere because of negligence or carelessness. The finder obtains title to the property against the whole world except the true owner. The rightful owner can reclaim the property.

Abandoned Property

Abandoned property is personal property that an owner has discarded or mislaid or lost property that the owner gives up any further attempt to locate. The finder acquires title to the property. The prior owner cannot reclaim the property.

Estray Statute

Estray statutes are state statutes that permit a finder of mislaid or lost property to obtain title to the property. To obtain clear title, the finder must:
1. Report the find to the appropriate government agency and turn over possession of the property to the agency.
2. Post and publish required notices.
3. Wait the statutorily required time (e.g., one year) without the rightful owner claiming the property.

Bailment, p. 1049

Bailment occurs when the owner of personal property delivers the property to another person to be held, stored, or delivered, or for some other purpose. Parties to a bailment:
1. ***Bailor.*** The bailor is the owner of the property.
2. ***Bailee.*** The bailee is the party to whom the property is delivered.

Elements Necessary to Create a Bailment

Three elements are necessary to create a bailment:
1. ***Personal property.*** Only personal property can be bailed.
2. ***Delivery of possession.*** The bailee must knowingly accept the property and have exclusive control over it.
3. ***Bailment agreement.*** There must be a bailment agreement. Express bailments may be oral or written unless required to be in writing by the Statute of Frauds. A bailment may be implied from the circumstances.

Bailment for the Sole Benefit of the Bailor

A bailment for the sole benefit of the bailor arises when the bailee is requested to care for the bailor's property as a favor. The bailee owes a duty of slight care—that is, the bailee is liable for gross negligence.

Bailment for the Sole Benefit of the Bailee

A gratuitous bailment arises when the bailee uses the bailor's property for personal reasons without paying compensation. The bailee owes a duty of great care (or utmost care) and is liable for even slight negligence.

Mutual Benefit Bailment

A mutual benefit bailment arises when both parties benefit from the bailment. This includes commercial bailments. The bailee owes a duty of reasonable care (or ordinary care) and is liable for ordinary negligence.

Duration and Termination of Bailments

1. *Bailment for a fixed term.* This type of bailment terminates at the end of a stipulated term. It may be terminated prior to the end of the term by mutual assent of the bailor and bailee.
2. *Bailments at will.* They are bailments without a fixed term. They may be terminated at any time by either party.

Warehouse Company

Warehouse companies engage in the business of storing property for compensation. Warehouse companies owe a duty of reasonable care (or ordinary care) to protect the bailed goods from loss or damage. A warehouse receipt is issued by a warehouse company to the bailor when goods are received by the warehouse company for storage.

Common Carrier

Common carriers are companies that offer transportation services to the public, such as airlines, railroads, and trucking firms. The cosignor is the person shipping the goods, the bailor. The common carrier is the transportation company, the bailee. The cosignee is the party to whom the goods are to be delivered. Common carriers owe a duty of strict liability; that is, if the goods are lost, damaged, destroyed, or stolen, the common carrier is liable even if the loss or damage was not its fault.

A bill of lading is a document of title that is issued by a common carrier to the bailor when goods are received by the common carrier for transportation.

Innkeeper

An innkeeper is the owner of a facility that provides lodging to the public for compensation (e.g., hotel, motel). Under the common law, innkeepers owe a duty of strict liability regarding loss caused to guests' property. Innkeepers' statutes are laws that limit the liability of innkeepers for loss or damage to guests' property. The innkeeper must post required notices to be covered by the law.

Insurance, p. 1055

Insurance is a contract whereby one party (insurer) undertakes to indemnify another party (insured) against loss, damage, or liability arising from a contingent or unknown event. Insurance is based on the concept of risk pooling—that is, transferring and distributing the risk of loss among a large number of persons (insureds).

1. *Insured.* The insured is the person who purchases insurance to cover a risk.
2. *Insurer.* The insurance company (or underwriter) is obligated to pay insurance proceeds if an insured risk occurs.
3. *Agent.* An agent is a party who sells insurance exclusively for one insurance company.
4. *Broker.* A broker is a party who is an independent contractor and sells insurance for a number of insurance companies.
5. *Policy.* A policy is an insurance contract between an insured and an insurer.

6. *Premium.* The premium is the money the insured is obligated to pay the insurer for insurance coverage.
7. *McCarran-Ferguson Act.* The federal McCarran-Ferguson Act gave the regulation of insurance to the states.

Insurable Interest

A person must have an insurable interest in anything he or she insures. That is, the person must benefit from the preservation of the life, health, property, or other interest that is insured.

Insurance Policy

Insurance contracts are governed by the law of contracts and statutes enacted to regulate the insurance contract. The insurer and insured may modify an insurance contract by adding an endorsement to the policy or executing a document called a rider. A grace period is a time period during which an insured may pay an overdue premium and during which the insurance remains in effect.

Duties of Insured and Insurer

Duties of the insured:
1. Pay premiums stipulated in the policy.
2. Notify the insurer after the occurrence of an insured event.
3. Cooperate with the insurer in the investigation of claims.

Duties of the insurer:
1. Defend against suits brought against the insured that involve a claim within the coverage of the policy.
2. Pay legitimate claims up to the policy limit.

Deductible Clause

A deductible clause requires insureds to pay a certain amount of the loss before the insurer is obligated to pay.

Exclusions from Coverage

An exclusions from coverage clause stipulates exclusions from insurance coverage (e.g., preexisting conditions).

Coinsurance Clause

A coinsurance clause requires an insured to pay a percentage of the cost of an insured loss.

Misrepresentation and Concealment

Insureds sometimes misrepresent or conceal material information prior to the running of the incontestability period. Incontestability statutes prohibit insurers from contesting statements made by insureds after the passage of a stipulated number of years.

Life Insurance

Life insurance is really "death insurance" because the insurer is normally obligated to pay a specified sum of money upon the death of the insured. The owner of the policy has the power to name the beneficiary of the insurance proceeds. A suicide clause states that if an insured commits suicide within a time period specified in a life insurance contract, the life insurance company does not have to pay the proceeds of the life insurance policy.

Health Insurance

Health insurance is insurance that covers the cost of medical treatment, surgery, and hospital care. Many insurance companies also offer dental insurance.

Disability Insurance

Disability insurance provides monthly income to an insured who is disabled and cannot work. Benefits are based on the degree of disability.

Fire and Homeowners' Insurance

Insurance that covers damage or destruction to residences.

1. *Standard fire insurance policy.* Insurance that protects real and personal property against loss resulting from fire, lightning, smoke, water damage, and related perils. Most policies limit recovery to damage caused by hostile fires (e.g., fire caused by faulty electrical wiring) and not friendly fires (e.g., damage caused by a fire contained in a fireplace). No personal liability coverage is provided.

2. *Homeowners' policy.* Comprehensive insurance policy that includes coverage for the risks covered by a standard fire insurance policy as well as personal liability insurance. It includes coverage for property damage, personal injury, and medical expenses of persons injured on the insured's property.

3. *Personal liability coverage homeowners' policy.* Insurance policy that provides comprehensive personal liability insurance for the insured and members of his or her family. The insurer must pay for property damage, personal injuries, and medical expenses to persons injured on the homeowner's premises or by the homeowner or members of his or her family.

4. *Personal articles floater.* Insurance that covers specific valuable items (e.g., jewelry, works of art, furs) that are usually excluded from standard fire and homeowners' policies.

5. *Renters' insurance.* Insurance that covers loss and damage to renters' possessions and provides personal liability coverage. Insures against the same perils as a homeowners' policy.

Title Insurance

Owners of real property may purchase title insurance to ensure that they have clear title to the property. Title insurance protects against defects in title and liens or encumbrances that are not disclosed on the title insurance policy.

Automobile Insurance

1. *Collision insurance.* Property insurance that covers the insured's vehicle against risk of loss or damage when it is struck by another vehicle.

2. *Comprehensive insurance.* Property insurance that covers the insured's vehicle against risk of loss or damage from causes other than collision, such as fire, theft, explosion, hail, windstorm, falling objects, earthquakes, floods, hurricanes, vandalism, and riots.

3. *Liability insurance.* Insurance that covers damage and loss that the insured causes to third parties. Other-driver coverage is liability coverage that protects the owner of a vehicle when someone else drives his or her vehicle with his or her permission, and drive-other coverage is liability coverage that protects the insured while driving other vehicles.

4. *Medical payment coverage.* Insurance that covers medical expenses incurred by the owner, passengers, and other authorized drivers of his or her car who are injured in an automobile accident.

5. *Uninsured motorist coverage.* Insurance that provides coverage to the driver and passengers of a vehicle who are injured by an uninsured motorist or a hit-and-run driver.

6. *No-fault automobile coverage.* Insurance required in some states whereby the driver's insurance company pays for any injuries or death the driver suffers in an accident, no matter who caused the accident.

Umbrella Insurance Policy

Liability coverage under most insurance policies, such as automobile and homeowners' insurance, is usually limited to a certain dollar amount. Insureds who want to increase their liability beyond the original coverage can purchase an umbrella policy. An umbrella policy pays only if the basic policy limits of other insurance have been exceeded.

Business Insurance

Businesses usually purchase automobile insurance, property and casualty insurance, and liability insurance. In addition, businesses often purchase insurance to cover risks uniquely applicable to conducting business.

1. *Business interruption insurance.* When a business is severely damaged or destroyed by fire or some other peril, business interruption insurance will reimburse it for any revenues lost while the business property is being rebuilt.
2. *Workers' compensation insurance.* Insurance that compensates employees who are injured while working within the scope of their employment.
3. *Key-person life insurance.* Life insurance that cover owners and other important persons who work for the business and is paid to the business if a covered person dies. The business usually pays the premiums for a key-person life insurance policy.
4. *Directors' and officers' liability insurance (D&O insurance).* Insurance that protects directors and officers of a business from liability for the actions they take on behalf of the corporation.
5. *Professional malpractice insurance.* Insurance that covers attorneys, accountants, physicians, dentists, architects, and other professionals from liability for injuries resulting from their negligence in practicing their profession.
6. *Product liability insurance.* Insurance that manufacturers and sellers of products can purchase to protect themselves from liability for injuries caused by defective products.

Test Review Terms and Concepts

Case Problems

37.1 Gift: For 12 years, Theodore Alexander Buder's father made substantial gifts to his minor grandchildren. Theodore Buder and his wife divorced during this period. The cash gifts, typically in the form of checks made directly payable to the children, were given to Buder with the understanding that he would safeguard the money and invest it on behalf of the children. Buder invested various amounts of the children's money in "blue chip" stocks traded over the New York and American stock exchanges. Buder also invested substantial sums of the children's money in speculative penny stocks. The stocks were purchased in Buder's name as custodian for the children, as required by the Uniform Gifts to Minors Act (UGMA). At one point, almost half of the children's money was invested in penny stocks. All the penny stocks except one suffered substantial losses. Buder's ex-wife, Sartore, sued him, alleging that he had breached his fiduciary duty owed to the children under the UGMA. She sought to recover the funds lost by Buder's investment of the children's funds in penny stocks. Who wins? *Buder v. Sartore*, 774 P.2d 1383, **Web** 1989 Colo. Lexis 227 (Supreme Court of Colorado)

37.2 Lost Property: Danny Lee Smith and his brother, Jeffrey Allen Smith, found a 16-foot fiberglass boat lying beside the roadway in Mobile County, Alabama. Seeing two sheriff's deputies, they stopped them to discuss the boat. Over the Smiths' objections, the deputies impounded the boat. The Smiths made it clear that if the true owner of the boat was not found, they wanted the boat. The true owner did not claim the boat. Mobile County claimed the boat and wanted to auction it off for sale to raise money for county recreational programs. The Smiths claimed the boat as finders. Alabama did not have an estray statute that applied to the situation. Who gets the boat? *Smith v. Sheriff Purvis*, 474 So.2d 1131, **Web** 1985 Ala. Civ. App. Lexis 1280 (Court of Civil Appeals of Alabama)

37.3 Abandoned Property: Police officers of the city of Miami, Florida, responded to reports of a shooting at the apartment of Carlos Fuentes. Fuentes had been shot in the neck and shoulder, and shortly after the police arrived, he was removed to a hospital. In an ensuing search of the apartment, the police found assorted drug paraphernalia, a gun, and cash in the amount of $58,591. The property was seized, taken to the police station, and placed in custody. About nine days later, the police learned that Fuentes had been discharged from the hospital. All efforts by police to locate Fuentes and his girlfriend, a co-occupant of Fuentes's apartment, were unsuccessful. Neither Fuentes nor his girlfriend ever came forward to claim any of the items taken by the police from his apartment. About four years later, James W. Green and Walter J. Vogel, the owners of the apartment building in which Fuentes was a tenant, sued the city of Miami to recover the cash found in Fuentes's apartment.

The state of Florida intervened in the case, also claiming an interest in the money. Who wins? *State of Florida v. Green*, 456 So.2d 1309, **Web** 1984 Fla. App. Lexis 15340 (Court of Appeal of Florida)

37.4 Bailment: James D. Merritt leased a storage locker from Nationwide Warehouse Co., Ltd. (Nationwide), and agreed to pay a monthly fee to lease the locker. Merritt placed various items in the leased premises but never informed Nationwide as to the nature or quantity of articles stored therein. Merritt was free to store or remove whatever he wished without consultation with, permission from, or notice to Nationwide. Merritt locked the leased premises with his own lock and key. Nationwide was not furnished with a key. Subsequently, certain personal property belonging to Merritt disappeared from the storage space. Merritt sued Nationwide to recover damages of $5,275. Was a bailment created between Merritt and Nationwide? *Merritt v. Nationwide Warehouse Co., Ltd.*, 605 S.W.2d 250, **Web** 1980 Tenn. App. Lexis 338 (Court of Appeals of Tennessee)

37.5 Lost Goods: Clarence Williams took his wife's fur coat to Debonair Cleaners for cleaning and storage. The clerk told him that the cleaner was experienced in such matters and that the charge would be 3 percent of the stated value of the coat. Williams stated that the coat was worth $13,000, and the clerk gave Williams a claim check and informed Williams that the total fee for storage would be $390, to be paid when the coat was retrieved. That evening, Williams related the substance of his conversation with the clerk to his wife, America, and gave her the claim check. Approximately eight months later, America Williams went to Debonair Cleaners to retrieve her coat. She presented the claim check to the clerk, who, after searching the premises for the coat, told her that it could not be located. Williams was informed that the coat had probably been stolen during a break-in and burglary. Williams sued Debonair Cleaners to recover the value of the coat. Who wins? *Mahallati v. Williams*, 479 A.2d 300, **Web** 1984 D.C. App. Lexis 419 (District of Columbia Court of Appeals)

37.6 Gratuitous Bailment: Marsha Hamilton and Andrea Morris were guests at a dinner party attended by approximately 25 people. The party began about 7:00 P.M. and ended at approximately 1:00 A.M. Alcoholic beverages were served throughout the evening. At approximately 11:30, while working in the kitchen, Hamilton removed her watch and placed it on the counter. About midnight, Hamilton left the kitchen and went outside. After about 15 minutes, she became ill and fled to the bathroom. Shortly after Hamilton left the kitchen, Morris saw the watch on the counter and, fearing for its safety, picked it up and carried it in her hand as she looked for Hamilton. When Hamilton came out of the bathroom, she and her fiancé left the party. Morris was unable to find Hamilton and could not recall precisely what she did with the watch. She testified that she either gave it to Hamilton's fiancé or put it somewhere in the host's house for safekeeping. Hamilton's fiancé testified that Morris did not give him the watch. The next day, Hamilton discovered that she did not have her watch, but in a search of the host's home, the watch was not recovered. Hamilton sued Morris for damages. Who wins? *Morris v. Hamilton*, 225 Va. 372, 302 S.E.2d 51, **Web** 1983 Va. Lexis 231 (Supreme Court of Virginia)

37.7 Parking Lot's Liability: Allright, Inc., was a parking lot operated in Houston, Texas. Kirkland Strauder drove his automobile to a Houston Allright parking lot and placed it in a row of cars to be parked by the attendant. When Strauder returned two hours later to reclaim his car, it could not be found. Strauder reported the car stolen. Allright could not explain the loss of the car, which was found weeks later, wrecked and stripped. Strauder sued Allright, Inc., for damages. Who wins? *Allright, Inc. v. Strauder*, 679 S.W.2d 81, **Web** 1984 Tex. App. Lexis 6006 (Court of Appeals of Texas)

37.8 Disclaimer of Liability: Joseph Conboy, his wife, and a group of friends convened in Manhattan, New York, for a party at a club where patrons dance to recorded music. The Conboy party checked their coats, 14 in all, with the coatroom attendant. After paying a $0.75 charge per coat, they received seven check stubs. A small sign in the coatroom stated "Liability for lost property in this coat/check room is limited to $100 per loss of misplaced article." Conboy testified that he did not notice it when he checked his coat and that the coatroom attendant did not call his attention to the sign. At the end of the evening, Conboy and the other guests of the party attempted to reclaim their coats. Conboy's one-month-old $1,350 leather coat was missing. Conboy sued the club for damages. Is the disclaimer of liability enforceable? *Conboy v. Studio 54, Inc.*, 113 Misc.2d 403, 449 N.Y.S.2d 391, **Web** 1982 N.Y. Misc. Lexis 3309 (Civil Court of the City of New York)

37.9 Exclusion: Richard Usher's home was protected by a homeowners' policy issued by National American Insurance Company of California. The policy included personal liability insurance. A provision in the policy read: "Personal liability and coverage do not apply to bodily injury or property damage arising out of the ownership, maintenance, use, loading, or unloading of a motor vehicle owned or operated by, or rented or loaned to any insured." Usher parked a Chevrolet van he owned in his driveway. He left the van's side door open while he loaded the van in preparation for a camping trip. While Usher was inside his house, several children, including two-year-old Graham Coburn, began playing near the van. One of the children climbed into the driver's seat and moved the shift lever from *park* to *reverse*. The van rolled backward, crushing Coburn and killing him. Coburn's parents sued Usher for negligence. Is the accident covered by Usher's homeowners' policy? *National American Insurance Company of California v. Coburn*, 209 Cal.App.3d 914, 257 Cal.Rptr. 591, **Web** 1989 Cal. App. Lexis 356 (Court of Appeal of California)

37.10 Insurance Premiums: Mutual Life Insurance Company of New York (Mutual Life) issued a $100,000 life insurance policy on the life of 65-year-old Alex Brecher. In consideration for the policy, Brecher agreed to pay an annual insurance premium of $7,830 in 12 monthly installments. Brecher provided a written request and authorization to have the insurance company withdraw the premiums directly from his checking account at Citibank. The insurance company's first attempt to do so was returned unpaid. Mutual Life and Brecher were informed that one of Brecher's creditors had placed a restraining order on the bank account. Mutual Life sent Brecher a returned check notice, advising him that the withdrawal had been dishonored by his bank and that to keep the policy in force, the unpaid premiums would have to be paid before August 28. Mutual Life received Brecher's check for the outstanding amounts on August 26. When Mutual Life tried to cash the check, which was drawn on the Citibank account, the bank returned it unpaid, marked "refer to maker." Brecher made no further attempts to pay the insurance premiums. He died on September 18. His widow, the beneficiary of the life insurance policy, filed a claim to recover $100,000 from Mutual Life. When Mutual Life refused to pay, the widow sued. Who wins? *Brecher v. Mutual Life Insurance Company of New York*, 120 A.D.2d 423, 501 N.Y.S.2d 879, **Web** 1986 N.Y. App. Div. Lexis 56512 (Supreme Court of New York)

37.11 Automobile Insurance: Jowenna Surber owned a Mercedes-Benz automobile that she insured through an insurance broker, Mid-Century Insurance Company (Mid-Century). Mid-Century secured a policy for Surber with the Farmers Insurance Company (Farmers). Surber gave permission to her friend, Bruce Martin, to use the car. Martin held a valid California driver's license. Surber did not receive any compensation for allowing Martin to use the car. While driving the car, Martin was involved in a collision with another vehicle, driven by Loretta Haynes, who suffered severe injuries. Martin admitted that his negligence was the cause of the accident. Surber's policy stipulates that the policy covers "you or any family member or any person using your insured car." Is Farmers liable to Haynes? *Mid-Century Insurance Company v. Haynes*, 218 Cal.App.3d 737, 267 Cal.Rptr. 248, **Web** 1990 Cal. App. Lexis 219 (Court of Appeal of California)

37.12 Automobile Insurance: Antonio Munoz and Jacinto Segura won some money from two unidentified men in a craps game in a Los Angeles park. When Munoz and Segura left the park in Segura's car, the two men followed them in another car. They chased Segura's car for several miles and then pulled beside it on a freeway. The men in the other car fired several gunshots at Segura's car, killing Munoz. At the time he was killed, Munoz had an automobile insurance policy issued by Nationwide Mutual Insurance Company (Nationwide). A provision in the policy covered damages from "an accident arising out of the use of an uninsured vehicle." Munoz's widow and child filed a claim with Nationwide to recover for Munoz's death. Nationwide rejected the claim. Who wins? *Nationwide Mutual Insurance Company v. Munoz*, 199 Cal.App.3d 1076, 245 Cal.Rptr. 324, **Web** 1988 Cal. App. Lexis 259 (Court of Appeal of California)

37.13 Malpractice Insurance: Donald Barker, a wealthy Oregon resident, went to the law firm of Winokur, Schoenberg, Maier, Hamerman & Knudson to have his estate planned. An attorney at the firm repeatedly told Barker that he could convey half of his $20-million estate to his wife tax free under Oregon's marital deduction. Barker had his will drawn based upon the law firm's advice. It was not until after Barker died three years later that Barker's family learned that Oregon does not recognize the marital deduction. As a result, the will's beneficiaries were subject to significant estate taxes. The beneficiaries sued the law firm for negligence, and the case was settled for $2 million. At the time Barker was being advised by the law firm, it had a professional malpractice insurance policy with the Travelers Insurance Company (Travelers) that covered "all sums which the insured shall become legally obligated to pay as damages because of any act or omission of the insured arising out of the performance of professional services for others in the insured's capacity as a lawyer." The policy expired one year prior to Barker's death. Is Travelers liable for the $2 million settlement? *Travelers Insurance Company v. National Union Fire Insurance Company of Pittsburgh*, 207 Cal.App.3d 1390, 255 Cal.Rptr. 727, **Web** 1989 Cal. App. Lexis 130 (Court of Appeal of California)

Ethics Issues

37.14 Ethics: When Dr. Arthur M. Edwards died, leaving a will disposing of this property, he left the villa-type condominium in which he lived, its "contents," and $10,000 to his stepson, Ronald W. Souders. Edwards left the residual of his estate to other named legatees. In administering the estate, certain stock certificates, passbook savings accounts, and other bank statements were found in Edwards's condominium. Souders claimed that these items belonged to him because they were "contents" of the condominium. The other legatees opposed Souders's claim, alleging that the disputed property was intangible property and not part of the contents of the condominium. The value of the property was as follows: condominium, $138,000; furniture in condominium, $4,000; stocks, $377,000; and passbook and other bank accounts, $124,000. Who is entitled to the stocks and bank accounts? Do you think Souders acted ethically in this case? *Souders v. Johnson*, 501 So.2d 745, **Web** 1987 Fla. App. Lexis 6579 (Court of Appeal of Florida)

37.15 Ethics: Darryl Kulwin was employed by Nova Stylings, Inc. (Nova), as a jewelry salesman. In that capacity, he traveled throughout the country, carrying with him jewelry owned and manufactured by Nova to show to prospective buyers. Kulwin was visiting Panoria Ruston, who was a guest registered with the Red Roof Inn in Overland Park, Kansas. Ruston and Kulwin met at the Red Roof Inn and later made plans to leave to go to dinner. Kulwin asked Ruston to make arrangements with the desk clerk to leave his sample case in the office of the Red Roof Inn while they went out to dinner. Ruston asked the clerk if she could leave the bag in the manager's office of the Red Roof Inn, and the clerk agreed. Ruston advised the clerk that the contents of the case were valuable but did not describe the contents of the bag.

Kansas Statute Section 36-402(b) provides:

No hotel or motel keeper in this state shall be liable for the loss of, or damage to, merchandise for sale or samples belonging to a guest, lodger, or boarder unless the guest, lodger, or boarder upon entering the hotel or motel, shall give notice of having merchandise for sale or samples in his possession, together with an itemized list of such property, to the hotel or motel keeper, or his authorized agent or clerk in the registration office of the hotel or motel office.

No hotel or motel keeper shall be liable for any loss of such property designated in this subsection (b), after notice an itemized statement having been given and delivered as aforesaid, in an amount in excess of two hundred fifty dollars ($250), unless such hotel or motel keeper, by specific agreement in writing, individually, or by an authorized agent or clerk in charge of the registration office of the hotel or motel, shall voluntarily assume liability for a larger amount with reference to such property. The hotel or motel keeper shall not be compelled to receive such guests, lodgers, or boarders with merchandise for sale or samples.

The inn posted the proper notice of the provisions of this act in all of the guests' rooms, including that of Ruston. An unidentified person obtained access to the manager's office and removed the case from the office. Nova sued Red Roof Inns for the alleged value of the jewelry, $650,000. Is Red Roof Inns liable? Did either party act unethically in this case? *Nova Stylings v. Red Roof Inns, Inc.*, 242 Kan. 318, 747 P.2d 107, **Web** 1987 Kan. Lexis 469 (Supreme Court of Kansas)

37.16 Ethics: A federal regulation adopted pursuant to the Resource Conservation and Discovery Act required certain manufacturers to insure against pollution hazards. Advanced Micro Devices, Inc. (AMD), a company covered by the regulation, purchased the required insurance from Great American Surplus Lines Insurance Company (Great American). Before issuing the policy, Great American asked AMD to disclose any preexisting conditions that could give rise to a claim. AMD warranted that there were none. AMD made this statement despite the existence of a prior company memorandum written by AMD's environmental supervisor. The memo warned that toxic waste was escaping from an underground steel tank in AMD's acid neutralization system "C" and that AMD was "far from being in compliance" with environmental laws. Great American issued the insurance policy. One year later, the government ordered AMD to undertake a $1.5 million cleanup of the toxic contaminants surrounding the steel tank in system "C." AMD filed a claim for this amount with Great American, which refused to pay. AMD sued. Who wins? Did AMD's management act ethically in this case? *Advanced Micro Devices, Inc. v. Great American Surplus Lines Insurance Company*, 199 Cal.App.3d 791, 245 Cal.Rptr. 44, **Web** 1988 Cal. App. Lexis 226 (Court of Appeal of California)

IRAC Writing Assignment

Read **Case A-37** in Appendix A [*Michigan Mutual Insurance Company v. Marriot Corporation*]. Use the IRAC method to prepare a written analysis of the case.

Endnote

1. 5 U.S.C. Sections 1011–1015.

CHAPTER 38

Real Property and Landlord–Tenant Law

> **"**_Without that sense of security which property gives, the land would still be uncultivated._**"**
>
> —FRANCOIS QUESNAY
> Maximes, IV

CHAPTER OBJECTIVES

After studying this chapter, you should be able to:

1. List and describe the different interests in real property.
2. Explain how ownership interests in real property can be transferred.
3. Explain how a landlord–tenant relationship is created and describe the various types of tenancy.
4. Describe the landlord's and tenant's duties and the tort liability of landlords and tenants.
5. Describe the various forms of land use regulation.

CHAPTER CONTENTS

- Introduction to Real Property and Landlord–Tenant Law
- Real Property
- Estates in Land
- Concurrent Ownership
- Future Interests
- Transfer of Ownership of Real Property
- Nonpossessory Interests
- Landlord–Tenant Relationship
- Zoning
- Civil Rights Acts and Real Estate
- Eminent Domain and the "Taking" of Real Property
- Chapter Summary
- Test Review Terms and Concepts
- Case Problems
- Ethics Issues
- IRAC Writing Assignment

   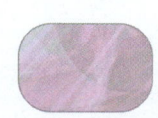 

Introduction to Real Property and Landlord–Tenant law

Property is an instrument of humanity. Humanity is not an instrument of property.

Woodrow Wilson
Speech (1912)

Property and ownership rights in *real property* play an important part in the U.S. society and economy. The concept of real property is concerned with the legal rights to the property rather than the physical attributes of the tangible land. Thus, real property includes some items of personal property that are affixed to real property (e.g., fixtures) and other rights (e.g., minerals, air).

Individuals and families own or rent houses, farmers and ranchers own or lease farmland and ranches, and businesses own or lease commercial and office buildings. In addition, over half of the population rents their homes, and many businesses lease office space, stores, manufacturing facilities, and other commercial property. The parties to a *landlord–tenant relationship* have certain legal rights and duties that are governed by a mixture of real estate and contract law.

Although the United States has the most advanced private property system in the world, the ownership and possession of real estate are not free from government regulation. Pursuant to constitutional authority, federal, state, and local governments have enacted myriad laws that regulate the ownership, possession, lease, and use of real property. These laws include zoning laws, building codes, anti-discrimination laws, and the like. The government may also take private property for public use, assuming that certain requirements are met and just compensation is paid to the owner.

This chapter covers the law concerning the ownership and transfer of real property, landlord–tenant relationships, and the government regulation of real estate.

Cottages, Mackinac Island, Michigan
A person's house is often his or her most valuable asset.

Real Property

Property is usually classified as either real or personal property. **Real property** is immovable or attached to immovable land or buildings, whereas personal property is movable. The various types of real property are described in the following paragraphs.

Land and Buildings

Land is the most common form of real property. A landowner usually purchases the **surface rights** to the land—that is, the right to occupy the land. The owner may use, enjoy, and develop the property as he or she sees fit, subject to any applicable government regulation.

Buildings constructed on land are real property. Houses, apartment buildings, manufacturing plants, and office buildings constructed on land are real property. Such things as radio towers and bridges are usually considered real property as well.

Subsurface Rights

The owner of land possesses **subsurface rights**, or **mineral rights**, to the earth located beneath the surface of the land. These rights can be very valuable. Gold, uranium, oil, or natural gas may lie beneath the surface of the land. Theoretically, mineral rights extend to the center of the earth. In reality, mines and oil wells usually extend only several miles into the earth. Subsurface rights may be sold separately from surface rights.

Plant Life and Vegetation

Plant life and vegetation growing on the surface of land are considered real property. Such vegetation includes both natural plant life (e.g., trees) and cultivated plant life (e.g., crops). When land is sold, any plant life growing on the land is included unless the parties agree otherwise. Plant life that is severed from the land is considered personal property.

Fixtures

Certain personal property is so closely associated with real property that it becomes part of the realty. Such items are called **fixtures**. Kitchen cabinets, carpet, and doorknobs are fixtures, but throw rugs and furniture are personal property.

Unless otherwise provided, if a building is sold, the fixtures are included in the sale. If the sale agreement is silent as to whether an item is a fixture, the courts make their determination on the basis of whether the item can be removed without causing substantial damage to the realty.

CONTEMPORARY ENVIRONMENT
Air Rights

Common law provided that the owners of real property owned that property from the center of the earth to the heavens. This rule has been eroded by modern legal restrictions such as land use regulation laws, environmental protection laws, and air navigation requirements. Even today, however, the owners of land may sell or lease air space parcels above their land.

An **air space parcel** is the air space above the surface of the earth of an owner's real property. Air space parcels are valuable property rights, particularly in densely populated metropolitan areas where building property is scarce.

Example Many developments have been built in air space parcels in New York City. More developments are expected to be built in air space parcels in the future.

Estates in Land

A person's ownership right in real property is called an **estate in land** (or **estate**). An estate is defined as the bundle of *legal rights* that the owner has to possess, use, and enjoy the property. The type of estate that an owner possesses is determined from the deed, will, lease, or other document that transferred the ownership rights to him or her.

Freehold Estate

A **freehold estate** is an estate in which the owner has a *present possessory interest* in the real property; that is, the owner may use and enjoy the property as he or she sees fit, subject to any applicable government regulation or private restraint. There are three types of freehold estates: two *estates in fee—fee simple absolute (or fee simple)* and *fee simple defeasible (or qualified fee)*—and *life estate*. These are discussed in the following paragraphs.

FEE SIMPLE ABSOLUTE (OR FEE SIMPLE) A **fee simple absolute** (or **fee simple**) is an estate in fee that is the highest form of ownership of real property because it grants the owner the fullest bundle of legal rights that a person can hold in real property. It is the type of ownership most people connect with "owning" real property. A fee simple owner has the right to exclusively possess and use his or her property to the extent that the owner has not transferred any interest in the property (e.g., by lease).

If a person owns real property in fee simple, his or her ownership:

- Is infinite in duration (fee)
- Has no limitation on inheritability (simple)
- Does not end upon the happening of any event (absolute)

Example Mary owns a fee simple absolute (or fee simple) in a piece of real property. This means that there are no limitations on her ownership rights. Mary owns this property while she is alive, with no conditions on her ownership rights, and she can transfer the property by will to a named beneficiary or beneficiaries when she dies.

FEE SIMPLE DEFEASIBLE (OR QUALIFIED FEE) A **fee simple defeasible** (or **qualified fee**) grants the owner all the incidents of a fee simple absolute except that it may be taken away if a specified *condition* occurs or does not occur.

Example A conveyance of property to a church "as long as the land is used as a church or for church purposes" creates a qualified fee. The church has all the rights of a fee simple absolute owner except that its ownership rights are terminated if the property is no longer used for church purposes.

LIFE ESTATE A **life estate** is an interest in real property that lasts for the life of a specified person, usually the grantee. For example, a conveyance of real property "to Anna for her life" creates a life estate. A life estate may also be measured by the life of a third party, which is called *estate pour autre vie* (for example, "To Anna for the life of Benjamin"). A life estate may be defeasible (for example, "To John for his life but only if he continues to occupy this residence").

Upon the death of the named person, the life estate terminates, and the property reverts to the grantor or the grantor's estate or other designated person.

Example Say that a life estate in real property has been granted to Joseph. When Joseph dies, the life estate is terminated. The ownership of the property reverts to the person who is given ownership rights upon the death of the person who held the life estate.

A life tenant is treated as the owner of the property during the duration of the life estate. He or she has the right to possess and use the property except to the extent that it would cause permanent *waste* of the property. A life tenant may sell, transfer, or mortgage his or her estate in the land. However, the mortgage cannot exceed the duration of the life estate. A life tenant is obligated to keep the property in repair and to pay property taxes.

CONCEPT SUMMARY

Freehold Estates

ESTATE	DESCRIPTION
Fee simple absolute	Is the highest form of ownership of real property. Ownership (1) is infinite in duration, (2) has no limitation on inheritability, and (3) does not end upon the occurrence or nonoccurrence of an event.
Fee simple defeasible	Grants the owner all the incidents of a fee simple absolute except that it may be taken away if a specified condition occurs or does not occur.
Life estate	Is an interest in property that lasts for the life of a specified person. A life estate terminates upon the death of the named person and reverts back to the grantor or his or her estate or other designated person.

Concurrent Ownership

Two or more persons may own a piece of real property. This is called **co-ownership**, or **concurrent ownership**. The following forms of co-ownership are recognized: *joint tenancy, tenancy in common, tenancy by the entirety, community property, condominiums,* and *cooperatives.*

Joint Tenancy

To create a joint tenancy, words that clearly show a person's intent to create a joint tenancy must be used. Language such as "Marsha Leest and James Leest, as joint tenants" is usually sufficient. The most distinguished feature of a **joint tenancy** is the co-owners' *right of survivorship.* This means that upon the death of one of the **co-owners** (or **joint tenants**), the deceased person's interest in the property automatically passes to the surviving joint tenants. Any contrary provision in the deceased's will is ineffective.

Example Jones, one of four people who own a piece of property in joint tenancy, executes a will leaving all of his property to a university, Jones dies. The surviving joint tenants—not the university—acquire his interest in the piece of property. Each joint tenant has a right to sell or transfer his or her interest in the property, but such conveyance terminates the joint tenancy. The parties then become tenants in common.

Tenancy in Common

In a **tenancy in common**, the interests of a surviving *tenant in common* pass to the deceased tenant's estate and not to the co-tenants. A tenancy in common may be created by express words (for example, "Ian Cespedes and Joy Park, as tenants in common"). Unless otherwise agreed, a tenant in common can sell, give, devise, or otherwise transfer his or her interest in the property without the consent of the other co-owners.

Example Lopez, who is one of four tenants in common who own a piece of property, has a will that leaves all his property to his granddaughter. When Lopez dies, the granddaughter receives his interest in the tenancy in common, and the granddaughter becomes a tenant in common with the other three owners.

Tenancy by the Entirety

Tenancy by the entirety is a form of co-ownership of real property that can be used only by married couples. This type of tenancy must be created by express words (for example, "Harold Jones and Maude Jones, husband and wife, as tenants by the entirety). A surviving spouse has the right of survivorship.

Tenancy by the entirety is distinguished from a joint tenancy because neither spouse may sell or transfer his or her interest in the property without the other spouse's consent. Only about half of the states recognize tenancy by the entirety.

Community Property

Nine states—Arizona, California, Idaho, Louisiana, Nevada, New Mexico, Texas, Washington, and Wisconsin—recognize a form of co-ownership known as **community property**. This method of co-ownership applies only to married couples. It is based on the notion that a husband and wife should share equally in the fruits of the marital partnership. Under these laws, each spouse owns an equal one-half share of the *income* both spouses earned during the marriage and one-half of the *assets acquired by this income during the marriage*, regardless of who earns the income. Property that is acquired through gift or inheritance either before or during marriage remains **separate property**. Interest payments, dividends, and appreciation of separate property received or accrued during marriage is also separate property.

When a spouse dies, the surviving spouse automatically receives one-half the community property. The other half passes to the heirs of the deceased spouse as directed by will or by state intestate statute if there is no will.

During the marriage, neither spouse can sell, transfer, or gift community property without the consent of the other spouse. Upon a divorce, each spouse has a right to one-half the community property.

The location of the real property determines whether community property law applies. If a married couple who lives in a non-community property state purchases real property located in a community property state, community property laws apply to that property.

Example Elma is a successful brain surgeon who makes $500,000 income per year. She meets and marries Brad, a struggling actor who makes $10,000 per year. When Elma gets married, she owns $1 million of real estate and $2 million in securities, which she retains as her separate property. Brad has no separate property when he and Elma are married. After three years, Elma and Brad get a divorce. Assume that Elma has made $500,000 and Brad has made $10,000 each of the three years of their marriage, their living expenses were $110,000 per year, and they have $1,200,000 of earned income saved in a bank account. During the marriage, Elma's real estate has increased in value to $1.5 million, and her securities have increased in value to $3 million. Upon divorce, Elma receives her $1.5 million in real estate and $3 million in securities as her separate property. If they live in a state that recognizes community property, Elma and Brad each receive $600,000 from the community property bank account.

CONCEPT SUMMARY

Concurrent Ownership

FORM OF OWNERSHIP	RIGHT OF SURVIVORSHIP	TENANT MAY UNILATERALLY TRANSFER HIS OR HER INTEREST
Joint tenancy	Yes, deceased tenant's interest automatically passes to co-tenants.	Yes, tenant may transfer his or her interest without the consent of co-tenants. Transfer severs joint tenancy.
Tenancy in common	No, deceased tenant's interest passes to his or her estate.	Yes, tenant may transfer his or her interest without the consent of co-tenants. Transfer does not sever tenancy in common.
Tenancy by the entirety	Yes, deceased tenant's interest automatically passes to his or her spouse.	No, neither spouse may transfer his or her interest without the other spouse's consent.
Community property	Yes, when a spouse dies, the surviving spouse automatically receives one-half of the community property. The other half passes to the heirs of the deceased spouse, as directed by a valid will or by state intestate statute if there is no will.	No, neither spouse may transfer his or her interest without the other spouse's consent.

Condominium

Condominiums are a common form of ownership in multiple-dwelling buildings. Purchasers of a condominium (1) have title to their individual units and (2) own the common areas (e.g., hallways, elevators, parking areas, recreational facilities) as tenants in common with the other owners. Owners may sell or mortgage their units without the permission of the other owners. Owners are assessed monthly fees for the maintenance of common areas. In addition to being used for dwelling units, the condominium form of ownership is often used for office buildings, boat docks, and such.

Cooperative

A **cooperative** is a form of co-ownership of a multiple-dwelling building in which a corporation owns the building, and the residents own shares in the corporation. Each cooperative owner leases a unit in the building from the corporation under a renewable, long-term, proprietary lease. Individual residents may not secure loans with the units they occupy. The corporation may borrow money on a blanket mortgage, and each shareholder is jointly and severally liable on the loan. Usually, cooperative owners may not sell their shares or sublease their units without the approval of the other owners.

In the following case, the court had to decide how to split the proceeds from the sale of real property owned by co-owners.

| C A S E **38.1**
Real Property | **Cunningham v. Hastings**

556 N.E.2d 12,
Web 1990 Ind. App. Lexis 764
Court of Appeals of Indiana |  |

❝ *Once a joint tenancy relationship is found to exist between two people in a partition action, it is axiomatic that each person owns a one-half interest.* **❞**

—Judge Baker

Facts

Warren R. Hastings and Joan L. Cunningham, who were unmarried, purchased a house together. Hastings paid a $45,000 down payment toward the purchase price out of his own funds. The deed referred to Hastings and Cunningham as "joint tenants with the right of survivorship." Hastings and Cunningham occupied the property jointly. After their relationship ended, Hastings took sole possession of the property. Cunningham filed a complaint seeking partition of the real estate. Based on its determination that the property could not be split, the trial court ordered it to be sold. The trial court further ordered that the sale proceeds be paid to Hastings to reimburse him for his down payment and that the remainder of the proceeds be divided equally between Hastings and Cunningham. Cunningham appealed, alleging that Hastings should not have been given credit for the down payment.

Issue

Is Cunningham entitled to an equal share of the proceeds of the sale of the real estate?

Language of the Court

The parties do not dispute that the unequivocal language of the deed created a joint tenancy in the real estate. The determination of the parties' interests in the present case is simple. There are only two parties involved in the joint tenancy. Once a joint tenancy relationship is found to exist between two people in a partition action, it is axiomatic that each person owns a one-half interest. Based on this reasoning, we find that the trial court erred in allowing Hastings a $45,000 credit for the purchase price he paid. Regardless of who provided the money to purchase the land, the creation of a joint tenancy relationship entitles each party to an equal share of the proceeds of the sale upon partition. Equitable adjustments to cotenants' equal shares are allowed when the cotenants hold the property as tenants in common, not when they hold as joint tenants. The deed in the case before us unequivocally states that the parties held the property as joint tenants, not as tenants in common. The equitable adjustment of their equal shares, therefore, was improper.

Decision

The court of appeals held that Cunningham was entitled to an equal share of the proceeds of the sale because she and Hastings owned the property as joint tenants. The court of appeals reversed the trial court's judgment and remanded the case to the trial court, with instructions to order the entire proceeds of the sale to be divided equally between Cunningham and Hastings.

Law & Ethics Questions

1. Should the law recognize so many different forms of ownership of real property? Do you think most people understand the legal consequences of taking title in the various forms?
2. **ETHICS** Did Cunningham act ethically in demanding one-half the value of the down payment even though she did not contribute to it?
3. Could Hastings have protected the $45,000 he paid for the down payment? If so, how could he have done it?

Web Exercises

1. **WEB** For the complete opinion of this case, go to *www.prenhall.com/cheesemancases*.
2. **WEB** Visit the website of the court of appeals of Indiana, at *www.in.gov/judiciary/appeals*.
3. **WEB** Use *www.google.com* to find an article that discusses the ownership of property by joint tenancy. Read it.

Future Interests

A person may be given the right to possess property in the *future* rather than in the present. This right is called a **future interest**. The two forms of future interests are *reversion* and *remainder*.

Reversion

A **reversion** is a right of possession that returns to the *grantor* after the expiration of a limited or contingent estate. Reversions do not have to be expressly stated because they arise automatically by law.

Example If a grantor conveys property "to M. R. Harrington for life," the grantor has retained a reversion in the property. That is, when Harrington dies, the property reverts to the grantor or, if he or she is not living, then to his or her estate.

Remainder

If the right of possession returns to a *third party* upon the expiration of a limited or contingent estate, it is called a **remainder**. The person who is entitled to the future interest is called a **remainder beneficiary**.

Example A conveyance of property "to Joe for life, remainder to Meredith" is a vested remainder. The only contingency to Meredith's possessory interest is Joe's death.

CONCEPT SUMMARY

Future Interests

FUTURE INTEREST	DESCRIPTION
Reversion	Right to possession of real property returns to the grantor after the expiration of a limited or contingent estate.
Remainder	Right to possession of real property goes to a third person upon the expiration of a limited or contingent estate.

Transfer of Ownership of Real Property

Ownership of real property may be transferred from one person to another. Title to real property may be transferred by sale; tax sale; gift, will, or inheritance; and adverse possession. The different methods of transfer provide different degrees of protection to the transferee.

Sale of Real Estate

A **sale**, or **conveyance**, is the most common method for transferring ownership rights in real property. An owner may offer his or her real estate for sale either by himself or herself or by using a real estate broker. Once a buyer has been located and the parties have negotiated the terms of the sale, a **real estate sales contract** is executed by the parties. The Statute of Frauds in most states requires this contract to be in writing.

The seller delivers a deed to the buyer, and the buyer pays the purchase price at the **closing**, or **settlement**. Unless otherwise agreed, it is implied that the seller is conveying fee simple absolute title to the buyer. If either party fails to perform, the other party may sue for breach of contract and obtain either monetary damages or specific performance.

DEEDS **Deeds** are used to convey real property by sale or gift. The seller or donor is called the **grantor**. The buyer or recipient is called the **grantee**. A deed may be used to transfer a fee simple absolute interest in real property or any lesser estate (e.g., life estate).

State laws recognize different types of deeds that provide different degrees of protection to grantees. A **warranty deed** (i.e., a deed in which the grantor warrants that he or she has sold title to the real property) contains the greatest number of warranties and provides the most protection to grantees. A **quitclaim deed** (i.e., a deed in which the grantor transfers only whatever interest he or she has in the real property) provides the least amount of protection because only the grantor's interest is conveyed.

RECORDING STATUTES Every state has a **recording statute** which provides that copies of deeds and other documents concerning interests in real property (e.g., mortgages, liens, easements) may be filed in a government office, where they become public records open to viewing by the public. Recording statutes are intended to prevent fraud and to establish certainty in the ownership and transfer of property. Instruments are usually filed in the **county recorder's office** of the county in which the property is located. A fee is charged to record an instrument.

Persons interested in purchasing property or lending on property should check these records to determine whether the grantor or borrower actually owns the property in question and whether any other parties (e.g., lienholders, mortgages, easement holders) have an interest in the property. The recordation of a deed is not required to pass title from the grantor to the grantee. Recording the deed gives **constructive notice** to the world of the owner's interest in the property.

Example First National Bank makes a loan to Mary Smith to purchase a house, and the bank takes back a mortgage, making the house security for the repayment of the loan. If Mary does not make her payments as required, the bank can foreclose on the property. At the time of making the loan, First National Bank records the mortgage in the proper county recorder's office. When Mary tries to borrow more money on the house from Second National Bank, Second National Bank checks the county recorder's office and finds the recorded mortgage of First National Bank. Suppose Second National Bank makes a second loan to Mary and takes a mortgage on the house. If Mary defaults on these loans, First National Bank has priority in foreclosing on the property to recover payment for its loan.

Example First National Bank makes a loan to Mary Smith to purchase a house, and the bank takes back a mortgage, making the house security for the repayment of the loan. If Mary does not make her payments as required, the bank can foreclose on the property. At the time of making the loan, First National Bank fails to record the mortgage in the proper county recorder's office. When Mary tries to borrow more money on the house from Second National Bank, Second National Bank checks the county recorder's office and finds no recorded mortgage. Suppose Second National Bank makes the loan to Mary, takes back a mortgage on the house, and records the mortgage in the proper county recorder's office. If Mary defaults on these loans, Second National Bank has priority in foreclosing on the property to recover payment for its loan because it recorded its loan.

QUIET TITLE ACTION A party who is concerned about his or her ownership rights in a parcel of real property can bring a **quiet title action**, which is a lawsuit to have a court determine the extent of those rights. Public notice of the hearing must be given so that anyone claiming an interest in the property may appear and be heard. After the hearing, the judge declares who has title to the property; that is, the court "quiets title" by its decision.

Example Jacob owns the legal title to a piece of real estate. Before purchasing the property, Jacob had a survey done, and the surveyor marked the legal lot lines of the property. Relying on this information, Jacob purchased the property. Michelle, a neighbor who owns property that abuts Jacob's property on one side, claims that the lot line should be an old fence that was constructed 50 years ago. The fence is 20 feet over the survey line on

Jacob's property. If the fence line is considered the lot line, Jacob losses 20 feet of his property for the length of the property on Mary's side. Jacob can bring a quiet title action in court to have the court determine what should be the lot line between the two properties.

In the following case, the court had to decide whether a recording statute had been properly complied with.

C A S E 38.2
Recording Statute

The Howard Savings Bank v. Brunson

244 N.J.Super. 571, 582 A.2d 1305,
Web 1990 N.J. Super Lexis 436
Superior Court of New Jersey

> ❝*Where a loss must be borne by one of two innocent parties, equity will impose the loss on the party whose first act would have prevented the loss.*❞
>
> —Judge Margolis

Facts

Burl Brunson purchased a parcel of real property in Newark, New Jersey. The deed for the property was properly recorded and indexed by the county recorder. Subsequently, Brunson borrowed $50,000 from The Howard Savings Bank, secured by a mortgage that was properly recorded; however, the county recorder did not list the mortgage in its index for recorded documents. Brunson sold the property to Jesus and Celeste Ijalba and executed and delivered a deed for the property to them. This deed was properly recorded and indexed at the county recorder's office. Jesus and Celeste Ijalba borrowed money from Chrysler First Financial Services Corporation, secured by a mortgage on the property that was properly recorded and indexed at the county recorder's office. Subsequently, Howard Savings Bank's mortgage from two years earlier was finally indexed by the county recorder. Three months later, Howard Savings Bank brought a foreclosure action on the property for Brunson's default on its loan and claimed that its mortgage had priority over the Ijalbas' deed and Chrysler First Financial's mortgage. The Ijalbas and Chrysler First Financial argued that Howard Savings Bank's mortgage did not have priority because it was not indexed, and therefore when they conducted their title search, Howard Savings Bank's mortgage did not appear in the index. The Ijalbas and Chrysler First Financial filed motions for summary judgment.

Issue

Was Howard Savings Bank's mortgage on the property properly recorded and indexed so as to give notice of its existence to subsequent parties?

Language of the Court

The fundamental purpose of the Recording Act is to provide notice to subsequent parties in interest and the protection of purchasers and encumbrancers of real property against undisclosed titles and liens. A rule prohibiting title searchers from depending upon the alphabetical index would unduly hinder the commercial transactions in the State: lengthy title searches would cost more and would cause unreasonably long closings; potential purchasers, mortgagors and lenders would hesitate to be involved in commercial transactions where they could not be confident that a reasonable search of the record would reveal prior interests or where they feared being held liable for a clerk's misindexing error; and the cost of title insurance would increase.

Obviously, one effect of finding a duty in the mortgagee to see that his instrument is properly indexed will be that the mortgagee will be required to conduct "run down" searches or to employ some other similar mechanism for ensuring that his interest is properly indexed. Yet such a practice is seen as making good business sense anyway. Furthermore, placing the burden upon the mortgagee to ensure that the requisite notice has been given is not out of step with the equitable maxim that where a loss must be borne by one of two innocent parties, equity will impose the loss on the party whose first act would have prevented the loss.

Decision

The court held that Howard Saving Bank's mortgage was not properly recorded as to give the necessary notice to subsequent parties because it was not indexed. The court granted the defendant's motion for summary judgment.

Law & Ethics Questions

1. What are the purposes of recording and indexing statutes?

2. **ETHICS** Did any party act unethically in this case?

3. Howard Savings Bank, the Ijalbas, and Chrysler First Financial were innocent parties in this case. Do you think the law placed the risk of loss on the right party in this case? Explain.

Web Exercises

1. **WEB** For the complete opinion of this case, go to *www.prenhall.com/cheesemancases*.

2. **WEB** Visit the website of the superior court of New Jersey, at *www.judiciary.state.nj.us*.

3. **WEB** Use *www.google.com* to find the procedure for recording deeds and mortgages in your area.

MARKETABLE TITLE A grantor has the obligation to transfer **marketable title**, or **good title**, to the grantee. Marketable title means that the title is free from any encumbrances, defects in title, or other defects that are not disclosed but would affect the value of the property. The three most common ways of assuring marketable title are as follows:

- *Attorney's opinion.* An attorney examines an **abstract of title** (i.e., a chronological history of the chain of title and encumbrances affecting the property) and renders an opinion concerning the status of the title. The attorney may be sued for any losses caused by his or her negligence in rendering the opinion.
- *Torrens system.* The **Torrens system** is a method of determining title to real property in a judicial proceeding at which everyone claiming an interest in the property may appear and be heard. After the evidence is heard, the court issues a **certificate of title** to the person who is determined to be the rightful owner.
- *Title insurance.* The best way for a grantee to be sure that he or she has obtained marketable title is to purchase **title insurance** from an insurance company. The title insurer must reimburse the insured for any losses caused by undiscovered defects in the title. Each time a property is transferred or refinanced, a new title insurance policy must be obtained.

Tax Sale

If an owner of real property fails to pay property taxes, the government may obtain a *lien* on the property for the amount of the taxes. If the taxes remain unpaid for a statutory period of time, the government may sell the property at a **tax sale** to satisfy the lien. Any excess proceeds are paid to the taxpayer. The buyer receives title to the property.

Many states provide a **period of redemption** after a tax sale during which the taxpayer may redeem the property by paying the unpaid taxes and penalties. In these states, the buyer at a tax sale does not receive title to the property until the period of redemption has passed.

Gift, Will, or Inheritance

> The right of property enables an industrious man to reap where he has sown.
>
> Anonymous

Ownership of real property may be transferred by **gift**. The gift is made when the deed to the property is delivered by the donor to the donee or to a third party to hold for the donee. No consideration is necessary.

Example Suppose a grandfather wants to give his farm to his granddaughter. To do so, he only has to execute a deed and give the deed to her or to someone to hold for her, such as her parents.

Real property may also be transferred by **will**.

Example A person may leave a piece of real estate to his best friend by will when he dies. This transfer does not require the transfer of a deed during the testator's lifetime. A deed will be issued to the beneficiary when the will is probated. If a person dies without a valid will, his or her property is distributed to the heirs pursuant to the applicable state intestacy statute.

Adverse Possession

> Good fences make good neighbors.
>
> Robert Frost
> *"Mending Wall" (1914)*

In most states, a person who wrongfully possesses someone else's real property obtains title to that property if certain statutory requirements are met. This is called **adverse possession**. Property owned by federal and state governments is not subject to adverse possession.

Under the doctrine of adverse possession, the transfer of the property is involuntary and does not require the delivery of a deed. To obtain title under adverse possession, the wrongful possession must be:

- *For a statutorily prescribed period of time.* In most states, this period is between 10 and 20 years.
- *Open, visible, and notorious.* The adverse possessor must occupy the property so as to put the owner on notice of the possession.

- *Actual and exclusive.* The adverse possessor must physically occupy the premises. The planting of crops, grazing of animals, or building of a structure on the land constitutes physical occupancy.
- *Continuous and peaceful.* The occupancy must be continuous and uninterrupted for the required statutory period. Any break in normal occupancy terminates the adverse possession. This means that the adverse possessor may leave the property to go to work, to the store, on a vacation, and such. The adverse possessor cannot take the property by force from an owner.
- *Hostile and adverse.* The possessor must occupy the property without the express or implied permission of the owner. Thus, a lessee cannot claim title to property under adverse possession.

If the elements of adverse possession are met, the adverse possessor acquires clear title to the land. However, title is acquired only as to the property actually possessed and occupied during the statutory period, and not the entire tract.

Example An adverse possessor who occupies 1 acre of a 200,000-acre ranch for the statutory period of time acquires title only to the 1 acre.

In the following two cases, the court had to decide whether the elements for adverse possession had been met.

C A S E **38.3**
Adverse Possession

Witt v. Miller

845 S.W.2d 665,
Web 1993 Mo. App. Lexis 20
Court of Appeals of Missouri

> **❝** *Hostility does not imply animosity.* **❞**
>
> —Judge Gaertner

Facts

Edward and Mary Shaughnessey purchased a 16-acre tract in St. Louis County, Missouri. Subsequently, they subdivided 12 acres into 18 lots offered for sale and retained possession of the remaining 4-acre tract. Thirteen years later, Charles and Elaine Witt purchased lot 12, which is adjacent to the 4-acre tract. The Witts constructed and moved into a house on their lot. The next year, they cleared an area of land that ran the length of their property and extended 40 feet onto the 4-acre tract. The Witts constructed a pool and a deck, planted a garden, made a playground for their children, set up a dog run, and built a fence along the edge of the property line, which included the now-disputed property. Neither the Witts nor the Shaughnesseys realized that the Witts had encroached on the Shaughnesseys' property.

Twenty years later, the Shaughnesseys sold the 4-acre tract to Thomas and Rosanne Miller. When a survey showed the Witts' encroachment, the Millers demanded that the Witts remove the pool and cease using the property. When the Witts refused to do so, the Millers sued to quiet title. The Witts defended, arguing that they had obtained title to the disputed property by adverse possession. The trial court held that there was no adverse possession and ruled in favor of the Millers. The Witts appealed.

Issue

Had the elements for adverse possession been met?

Language of the Court

We address the element of "hostile possession." Hostility does not imply animosity. There is no substantial evidence to support the finding that plaintiffs' possession was not hostile. Plaintiffs testified that they intended to possess the disputed property as their own because they believed it was part of lot 12. That intent manifests itself in plaintiffs' actions which include clearing the area, maintaining the area, planting grass and a garden, erecting a fence, installing playground equipment and a dog run, and building an above ground pool with a deck.

The evidence established plaintiffs' claim to title of the disputed property under adverse possession. The trial court's decision was not supported by substantial evidence and erroneously declared the law.

Decision

The court of appeals held that the Witts had proven the necessary elements for adverse possession under state law. The Witts' occupation of the land was open and notorious, actual and exclusive, hostile and adverse, and continuous and peaceful, and it had occurred for over the statutory period of 10 years. The court of appeals reversed the decision of the trial court and issued an order quieting title to the disputed property in the Witts' favor.

Law & Ethics Questions

1. What does the doctrine of adverse possession provide? What elements need to be proven?

2. **ETHICS** Did the Witts act ethically in claiming title to someone else's land? Should they be allowed to benefit from their own mistake?

3. What should owners of property do to protect themselves from adverse possession claims? Explain.

Web Exercises

1. **WEB** For the complete opinion of this case, go to *www.prenhall.com/cheesemancases*.

2. **WEB** Visit the website of the court of appeals of Missouri, Eastern District, at *www.courts.mo.gov/page.asp?id+261*.

3. **WEB** Use *www.google.com* to find the requirements for adverse possession in your state.

CASE 38.4
Adverse Possession

Johnson v. Asfaw and Tanus

Web 2005 Wash. App. Lexis 2167 (2005)
Court of Appeals of Washington

> " *The disseisor must unfurl his flag on the land, and keep it flying, so that the owner may see, if he will, that an enemy has invaded his domains, and planted the standard of conquest.* "
>
> —Judge Ellington

Facts

The Sauder family purchased a home in Burien, Washington. The adjacent property was undeveloped and overgrown and was landlocked except for a narrow strip of land running to the street, described as the access strip. The Sauders planted six rhododendrons in the access strip. Ten years later, Samuel Asfaw and Trisna Tanus purchased the Sauders' property. One year later, Jack Johnson purchased the undeveloped adjacent lot with the intention of building a house. He planned to use the access strip for a driveway because it provided the only street access to the property.

Johnson filed an action to quiet title to the access strip. Asfaw and Tanus counter-claimed, seeking title to the land occupied by the rhododendrons through adverse possession. The trial court granted summary judgment quieting title in Johnson. Asfaw and Tanus appealed.

Issue

Had the elements of adverse possession been met?

Language of the Court

The law presumes that possession is in the holder of legal title. A party claiming ownership by adverse possession must show possession for at least ten years that is open and notorious, actual and uninterrupted, and hostile. The disseisor must unfurl his flag on the land, and keep it flying, so that the owner may see, if he will, that an enemy has invaded his domains, and planted the standard of conquest.

The Sauders planted six rhododendrons in the access strip. The planting was random, in an area that is heavily wooded and includes ferns and brush. The Sauders did not clear the land around the shrubs, did not plant a lawn, did not mow or store

wood, did not maintain the area around the shrubs, and made no other use of the land. The mere presence of rhododendrons in northwest woods is not advertisement of another's claim on the land. In view of the wooded and natural state of the access strip, random planting and minimal upkeep of a small number of rhododendrons is not an open and notorious use, and therefore does not constitute actual possession of the land.

Decision

The court of appeals held that the elements of adverse possession had not been met in this case. The court of appeals affirmed the judgment of the trial court that had quieted title to the disputed property.

Law & Ethics Questions

1. What is a quiet title action? Explain.

2. **ETHICS** Did Asfaw and Tanus act ethically in claiming title to the property?

3. If Asfaw and Tanus had won the case, what would have been the consequences for Johnson?

Web Exercises

1. **WEB** For the complete opinion of this case, go to *www.prenhall.com/cheesemancases*.

2. **WEB** Visit the website of the court of appeals of Washington, Division One, at *www.courts.wa.gov*.

3. **WEB** Use *www.google.com* to find the procedure for quieting title in your state.

Nonpossessory Interests

A person may own a **nonpossessory interest** in another's real estate. Three nonpossessory interests—*easement*, *license*, and *profit*—are discussed in the following paragraphs.

Easement

An **easement** is an interest in land that gives the holder the right to make limited use of another's property without taking anything from it. Typical easements are common driveways, party walls, and rights-of-way. Easements may be expressly created by *grant* (where an owner gives another party an easement across his or her property) or *reservation* (where an owner sells land that he or she owns but reserves an easement on the land). Easement can also be implied by (1) *implication*, where an owner subdivides a piece of property with a well, path, road, or other beneficial appurtenant that serves the entire parcel, or by (2) *necessity*—for example, where "landlocked" property has an implied easement across surrounding property to enter and exit the landlocked property. Easements can also be created by *prescription*—that is, adverse possession.

There are two types of easements: easements appurtenant and easements in gross. These are described in the following paragraphs.

EASEMENTS APPURTENANT An **easement appurtenant** is created when the owner of one piece of land is given an easement over an adjacent piece of land. The land over which the easement is granted is called the **servient estate**. The land that benefits from the easement is called the **dominant estate**. Adjacent land is defined as two estates that are in proximity to each other but do not necessarily abut each other. An appurtenant easement runs with the land.

Example If an owner sells the servient estate, the new owner acquires the benefit of the easement. If an owner sells the dominant estate, the buyer purchases the property subject to the easement.

EASEMENTS IN GROSS An **easement in gross** authorizes a person who does not own adjacent land the right to use another person's land. An easement in gross is a personal right because it does not depend on the easement holder owning adjacent land. Thus, there is no dominant estate. Examples of easements in gross include those granted to run power, telephone, and cable television lines across an owner's property. Commercial easements in gross run with the land.

The easement holder owes a duty to maintain and repair the easement. The owner of the estate can use the property as long as doing so does not interfere with the easement.

Example If a piece of property is subject to an easement for an underground pipeline, the owner of the property could graze cattle or plant crops on the land above the easement, subject to the easement holder's right to repair the pipeline.

In the following case, the court had to decide whether an easement had been created.

CASE **38.5**
Easement

Walker v. Ayres
Web 1993 Del. Lexis 105
Supreme Court of Delaware

" *An implied easement was created by the severance which landlocked Bluff Point.* "

—Judge Moore

Facts

Elizabeth Star Ayres and Clara Louise Quillen owned in fee simple absolute a tract of land in Sussex County known as "Bluff Point." The tract was surrounded on three sides by Rehoboth Bay and was landlocked on the fourth side by land owned by Irvin C. Walker. At one time, the two tracts were held by a common owner. In 1878, Bluff Point was sold in fee simple absolute apart from the other holdings, thereby landlocking the parcel. A narrow dirt road, which traversed Walker's land, connected Bluff Point to a public road and was its only means of access to Bluff Point. Ayres and Quillen sought an easement to use this road, and Walker objected. This lawsuit ensued. The trial court granted an easement to Ayres and Quillen. Walker appealed.

Issue

Should Ayres and Quillen's estate be granted an easement against Walker's estate?

Language of the Court

Based upon our review of the record, we conclude that the factual findings of the trial court are clearly sustainable. There is ample evidence in the record to support the finding that the two tracts originated from the unified holdings of one owner, and that an implied easement was created by the severance which landlocked Bluff Point. The record also sufficiently supports the finding that navigable access to Bluff Point was not feasible.

Decision

The supreme court held that an implied easement had been created. The supreme court affirmed the trial court's judgment that granted Ayres and Quillen an easement to use the road that traversed Walker's property.

Law & Ethics Questions

1. Should easements be recognized by the law? Why or why not?
2. **ETHICS** Did Walker act ethically in denying the easement? Did Ayres and Quillen act ethically in seeking to use Walker's property?
3. Does an easement increase or decrease the value of the servient estate? of the dominant estate?

Web Exercises

1. **WEB** For the complete opinion of this case, go to *www.prenhall.com/cheesemancases*.
2. **WEB** Visit the website of the supreme court of Delaware, at *www.courts.delaware.gov*.
3. **WEB** Use *www.google.com* to find a recent case regarding an easement dispute.

License

A **license** grants a person the right to enter upon another's property for a specified and usually short period of time. The person granting the license is called the **licensor**; the person receiving the license is called the **licensee**.

Example A ticket to a movie theater or sporting event that grants the holder the right to enter the premises for the performance is a common license. A license does not transfer any interest in the property. A license is a personal privilege that may be revoked by the licensor at any time.

Profit

A *profit-à-prendre* (or **profit**) gives the holder the right to remove something from another's real property. Profits usually involve the right to remove gravel, minerals, grain, or timber from another's property.

CONCEPT SUMMARY

Nonpossessory Interests

NONPOSSESSORY INTEREST	DESCRIPTION
Easement appurtenant	Is an easement over a servient estate that benefits a dominant estate. The easement runs with the land.
Easement in gross	Is an easement that grants a person a right to use another's land. It is a personal right that does not run with the land.

| License | Grants a person the right to enter upon another's real property for a specified event or time (e.g., for a concert). |
| Profit | Grants the holder the right to remove something from another's real property (e.g., timber, grain). |

Inle Lake, Myanmar
Many countries do not have well-developed real estate laws or standards. This house on the Inle Lake in Myanmar is built on stilts.

EXHIBIT 38.1

Landlord–Tenant Relationship

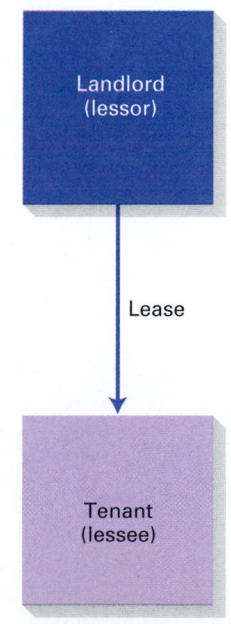

Owner-landlord owns title to the real property

Landlord (lessor)

Lease

Tenant (lessee)

Tenant acquires a nonfreehold estate in the real property that gives the tenant a right to possession of the property

Landlord–Tenant Relationship

A **landlord–tenant relationship** is created when the owner of a freehold estate (i.e., an estate in fee or a life estate) transfers a right to exclusively and temporarily possess the owner's property. The tenant receives a *nonfreehold estate* in the property; that is, the tenant has a right to possession of the property but not title to the property.

The tenant's interest in the property is called a **leasehold estate**, or **leasehold**. The owner who transfers the leasehold estate is called the **landlord**, or **lessor**. The party to whom the leasehold estate is transferred is called the **tenant**, or **lessee**. A landlord–tenant relationship is illustrated in Exhibit 38.1

Lease

A rental agreement between a landlord and a tenant is called a **lease**. Leases can generally be either oral or written, but most Statutes of Frauds require that leases for periods of time longer than one year be in writing. A lease must contain the essential terms of the parties' agreement. A lease is often a form contract that is prepared by the landlord and presented to the tenant. This practice is particularly true of residential leases. Other leases are negotiated between the parties. For example, Bank of America's lease of a branch office would be negotiated with the owner of the building.

There are four types of *tenancies*: (1) *tenancy for years*, (2) *periodic tenancy*, (3) *tenancy at will*, and (4) *tenancy at sufferance*. They are described in the following paragraphs.

TENANCY FOR YEARS A **tenancy for years** is created when a landlord and a tenant agree on a specific duration for a lease. Any lease for a stated period—no matter how long or short—is called a tenancy for years. Examples of such arrangements include office space leased in a high-rise office building on a 30-year lease and a cabin leased for a summer. A tenancy for years terminates automatically, without notice, upon the expiration of the stated term.

PERIODIC TENANCY A **periodic tenancy** is created when a lease specifies intervals at which payments are due but does not specify how long the lease is for. A lease that states, "Rent is due on the first day of the month" establishes a periodic tenancy. Many such leases are created by implication. A periodic tenancy may be terminated by either party at the end of any payment interval, but adequate notice of the termination must be given. Under common law, the notice period equaled the length of the payment period. That is, a month-to-month tenancy required a one-month notice of termination.

TENANCY AT WILL A lease that may be terminated at any time by either party creates a **tenancy at will**. A tenancy at will may be created expressly (e.g., "to tenant as long as landlord wishes") but is more likely to be created by implication. Most states have enacted statutes requiring minimum advance notice for the termination of a tenancy at will. The death of either party terminates a tenancy at will.

TENANCY AT SUFFERANCE A **tenancy at sufferance** is created when a tenant retains possession of property after the expiration of another tenancy or a life estate without the owner's consent. That is, the owner suffers the **wrongful possession** of his or her property by the holdover tenant. This is not a true tenancy but merely the possession of property without right. Technically, a tenant at sufferance is a trespasser. A tenant at sufferance is liable for the payment of rent during the period of sufferance. Most states require an owner to go through certain legal proceedings, called *eviction proceedings* or *unlawful detainer actions*, to evict a holdover tenant. A few states allow owners to use self-help to evict a holdover tenant as long as force is not used.

CONCEPT SUMMARY

Types of Tenancies

TYPES OF TENANCY	DESCRIPTION
Tenancy for years	Continues for the duration of the lease and terminates automatically without requiring notice. It does not terminate upon the death of either party.
Periodic tenancy	Continues from payment interval to payment interval. It may be terminated by either party with adequate notice. It does not terminate upon the death of either party.
Tenancy at will	Continues at the will of the parties and may be terminated by either party at any time with adequate notice. It terminates upon the death of either party.
Tenancy at sufferance	Arises when a tenant wrongfully occupies real property after the expiration of another tenancy or life estate. It continues until the owner either evicts the tenant or holds him or her over for another term. It terminates upon the death of the tenant.

Soho, New York City
Many people rent apartments from landlords. The landlord and tenant owe each other certain duties.

Landlord's Duty to Deliver Possession

A lease grants the tenant **exclusive possession** of the leased premises until (1) the term of the lease expires or (2) the tenant defaults on the obligations under the lease. The landlord is obligated to deliver possession of the leased premises to the tenant on the date the lease term begins. A landlord may not enter leased premises unless the right is specifically reserved in the lease.

Landlord's Duty Not to Interfere with the Tenant's Right to Quiet Enjoyment

The law implies a **covenant of quiet enjoyment** in all leases. Under this covenant, the landlord may not interfere with the tenant's quiet and peaceful possession, use, and enjoyment of the leased premises. The covenant is breached if the landlord, or anyone acting with the landlord's consent, interferes with the tenant's use and enjoyment of the property. This interference is called **wrongful eviction**, or **unlawful eviction**. It may occur if the landlord actually evicts a tenant by physically preventing him or her from possessing or using the leased premises or if the landlord constructively evicts the tenant by causing the leased premises to become unfit for their intended use (e.g., by failing to provide electricity). If the landlord refuses to cure the defect after a reasonable time, a tenant who has been constructively evicted may (1) sue for damages and possession of the premises or (2) treat the lease as terminated, vacate the premises, and cease paying rent. The landlord is not responsible for wrongful acts of third persons that were done without his or her authorization.

Landlord's Duty to Maintain the Leased Premises

At common law, the doctrine of *caveat lessee*—"lessee beware"—applied to leases. The landlord made no warranties about the quality of leased property and had no duty to repair it. The tenant took the property "as is." Modern real estate law, however, imposes certain statutory and judicially implied duties on landlords to repair and maintain leased premises.

States and local municipalities have enacted statutes called **building codes**, or **housing codes**. These statutes impose specific standards on property owners to maintain and repair leased premises. They often provide certain minimum standards regarding heat, water, light, and other services. Depending on the statute, violators may be subject to fines by the government, loss of their claim for rent, and imprisonment for serious violations.

Tenant's Duty to Pay Rent

A commercial or residential tenant owes a duty to pay the agreed-upon amount of **rent** for the leased premises to the landlord at the agreed-upon time and terms. Generally, rent is payable in advance (e.g., on the first day of the month for use that month), although the lease may provide for other times and methods for payment. Reasonable late charges may be assessed on rent that is overdue. In a *gross lease*, the tenant pays a gross sum to the landlord. The landlord is responsible for paying the property taxes and assessments on the property.

Several of the most common commercial rental arrangements are:

- *Net lease.* In a **net lease** arrangement, the tenant is responsible for paying rent and property taxes.
- *Double net lease.* In a **double net lease** arrangement, the tenant is responsible for paying rent, property taxes, and utilities.
- *Net, net, net lease (or triple net lease).* In a **net, net, net lease (triple net lease)** arrangement, the tenant is responsible for paying rent, property taxes, utilities, and insurance.

Upon nonpayment of rent, the landlord is entitled to recover possession of the leased premises from the tenant. This may require the landlord to *evict* the tenant. Most states provide a summary procedure called **unlawful detainer action** that a landlord can bring to evict a tenant. The landlord may also sue to recover the unpaid rent from the tenant. The more modern rule requires the landlord to make reasonable efforts to *mitigate damages* (i.e., to make reasonable efforts to re-lease the premises).

CONCEPT SUMMARY

Tenant's Duty to Pay Rent

RENTAL AGREEMENT	DESCRIPTION
Gross lease	The tenant pays a stated sum to the landlord. The landlord is responsible for paying property taxes and assessments on the property.
Net lease	The tenant is responsible for paying rent and property taxes.
Double net lease	The tenant is responsible for paying rent, property taxes, and utilities.
Triple net lease	The tenant is responsible for paying rent, property taxes, utilities, and insurance.

Tenant's Duty Not to Use Leased Premises for Illegal or Nonstipulated Purposes

A tenant may use leased property for any lawful purposes permitted by the lease. Leases often stipulate that the leased premises can be used only for specific purposes. If the tenant uses the leased premises for unlawful purposes (e.g., operating an illegal gambling casino) or nonstipulated purposes (e.g., operating a restaurant in a residence), the landlord may terminate the lease, evict the tenant, and sue for damages.

Tenant's Duty Not to Commit Waste

A tenant is under a **duty not to commit waste** to the leasehold. Waste occurs when the tenant causes substantial and permanent damage to the leased premises that decreases the value of the property and the landlord's reversionary interest in it. Waste does not include ordinary wear and tear. The landlord can recover damages from the tenant for waste.

Example It would be waste if the floor of the premises buckled because a tenant permitted heavy equipment to be placed on the premises. It would not be waste if the paint chipped from the walls because of the passage of time.

Tenant's Duty Not to Disturb Other Tenants

A tenant owes a duty not to disturb the use and enjoyment of the leased premises by other tenants in the same building. A landlord may evict a tenant who interferes with the quiet enjoyment of other tenants.

Example A tenant in an apartment building breaches this duty if he or she disturbs the sleep of other tenants by playing loud music throughout the night.

Implied Warranty of Habitability

The courts of many jurisdictions hold that an **implied warranty of habitability** applies to residential leases for their duration. This warranty provides that the leased premises must be fit, safe, and suitable for ordinary residential use.

Example Unchecked rodent infestation, leaking roofs, unworkable bathroom facilities, and the like have been held to breach the implied warranty of habitability. On the other hand, a small crack in a wall or some paint peeling from a door does not breach this warranty.

State statutes and judicial decisions provide various remedies that can be used if a landlord's failure to maintain or repair leased premises affects the tenant's use or enjoyment of the premises. Generally, the tenant may (1) withhold from his or her rent the amount by which the defect reduced the value of the premises to him or her, (2) repair the defect and deduct the cost of repairs from the rent due for the leased premises, (3) cancel the lease if the failure to repair constitutes constructive eviction, or (4) sue for damages in the amount by which the landlord's failure to repair the defect reduced the value of the leasehold.

In the following case, the court found a breach of the implied warranty of habitability.

> Property has its duties as well as its rights.
>
> Benjamin Disraeli
> *Sybil, Book II, Chapter XI (1845)*

C A S E 38.6
Implied Warranty of Habitability

Solow v. Wellner
150 Misc.2d 642, 569 N.Y.S.2d 882,
Web 1991 N.Y. Misc. Lexis 169
Civil Court of the City of New York

❝ *The premises are to be maintained in accordance with the reasonable expectations of the tenant.* **❞**

—Judge York

Facts

The defendants are approximately 80 tenants of a 300-unit luxury apartment building on the upper east side of Manhattan. The monthly rents in the all-glass-enclosed building, which won several architectural awards, were very high. The landlord brought a summary proceeding against the tenants to recover rent when they engaged in a rent strike in protest against what they viewed as deteriorating conditions and services. Among other things, the evidence showed that during the period in question, the elevator system made tenants and their guests wait interminable lengths of time, the elevators skipped floors and opened on the wrong floors, a stench emanated from garbage stored near the garage and mice appeared in that area, fixtures were missing in public areas, water seeped into mailboxes, the air conditioning in the lobby was inoperative, and air conditioners in individual units leaked. The defendant-tenants sought abatement of rent for breach of the implied warranty of habitability.

Issue

Did the landlord breach the implied warranty of habitability?

Language of the Court

In determining whether the warranty of fitness has been breached, this jurisdiction has adopted the "reasonable expectation" test. This means that the premises are to be maintained in accordance with the reasonable expectations of the tenant. Certain amenities not necessarily life threatening, but consistent with the nature of the bargain—air conditioning would be an example—fall under the protection of this branch of the warranty. Predictability and reliability of services is another factor.

In applying this branch of the warranty to this case, we start with the obvious expectations of this uniquely designed all-glass-enclosed building on Manhattan's fashionable Upper East Side. Add to this the comparatively high rents exacted for these apartments and one would have to assume that the expectations of the tenants encompassed more than the minimal amenities. While the warranty certainly entitled them to freedom from conditions threatening their life, health and safety, their higher rents justified increased expectations of a well-run,

impeccably clean building of consistent and reliable services. These expectations were reasonably enhanced by the brochure they received, which was also incorporated into the lease, with its promises of security, air conditioning in the public areas and panoramic views. The promises and expectations fell far short of the reality. The warranty in the public areas was breached.

Decision

The court held that the landlord had breached the implied warranty of habitability. The court abated the rent of each of the tenants individually, in total allowing the landlord to recover only 22 percent of the amount he sued for. The court ordered the landlord to pay the tenants' attorneys' fees.

Law & Ethics Questions

1. What is the implied warranty of habitability? Explain.

2. **ETHICS** Did the landlord act ethically in not correcting the defects in the building? Did the tenants act ethically in engaging in a rent strike?

3. Was the remedy the court ordered appropriate in this case?

Web Exercises

1. **WEB** For the complete opinion of this case, go to *www.prenhall.com/cheesemancases*.

2. **WEB** Visit the website of the New York City civil court, at *www.courts.state.ny.us/courts/nyc/civil/nyadmin.shtml*.

3. **WEB** Use *www.google.com* to find an article that discusses the implied warranty of habitability. Read it.

Premises Liability

A tenant owes a *duty of reasonable care* to persons who enter upon leased premises. If a tenant's negligence causes injury to a third person, the tenant is liable in tort for any damages sustained by the injured person. For example, a tenant who leaves a skateboard on the steps is liable for the injuries caused to a visitor who trips on it.

Landlords owe a *duty of reasonable care* to tenants and third parties not to negligently cause them injury. This duty is based on the foreseeability standard of ordinary negligence actions. A landlord who breaches this duty is liable to the injured tenant or third party for tort damages.

The liability of landlords and tenants to persons injured on their premises is called **premise liability**. The following case illustrates premise liability.

C A S E **38.7**
Premise Liability

Feld v. Merriam

314 Pa.Super. 414, 461 A.2d 225,
Web 1983 Pa. Super Lexis 3092
Superior Court of Pennsylvania

66 *We hold that in all areas of the leasehold, particularly in the areas under his control, the landlord is under a duty to provide adequate security to protect his tenants from the foreseeable criminal actions of third persons.* 99

—Judge Cirillo

Facts

Cedarbrook was a complex of approximately 1,000 apartment units located on a 36-acre tract of land in Cheltenham, Pennsylvania, owned by John W. Merriam. Vehicles could enter the grounds through two entrances, each of which was staffed by security guards. Automobiles parked in garages located beneath each apartment building. The parking facility under Building No. 1 had spaces for 160 cars. Access to the garages could be gained through two open entrances. The garages were not well lit. Over a five-year period, the crime rate in Cedarbrook had risen. During the three-month period preceding the criminal incident at issue in this case, 21 separate incidents of criminal activity, including robberies, burglaries at apartments, car thefts, and an assault on a tenant, were reported.

One night, at approximately 9:00 P.M., Samuel and Peggy Feld, tenants in Building No. 1, drove into the Cedarbrook complex and parked their car in the garage. After getting out of their car, they walked toward the pedestrian exit. Three armed men emerged from behind a parked car, accosted them, and robbed them at gunpoint. They then raped Mrs. Feld. Following the incident, Mrs. Feld began psychotherapy to help alleviate her severe emotional distress. Her psychiatrist testified that she would never recover from the emotional trauma of the event. Following the incident, Mr. Feld was constantly in a fearful, nervous, and agitated state. At the time of trial, he was still unable to discuss the details of the criminal episode with anyone. Although the Felds' marriage deteriorated, they remained together out of compassion for each other.

Mr. and Mrs. Feld sued Cedarbrook for damages. The jury returned a verdict that awarded $2 million compensatory damages to Mrs. Feld, $1 million compensatory damages to Mr. Feld, and $1.5 million punitive damages to each of them. Cedarbrook appealed.

Issue

Is Cedarbrook liable for the criminal attack on the Felds?

Language of the Court

We hold that in all areas of the leasehold, particularly in the areas under his control, the landlord is under a duty to provide adequate security to protect his tenants from the foreseeable criminal actions of third persons. In order to establish a *prima facie* case of negligence against a landlord for his failure to provide adequate security, a plaintiff must present evidence showing that the landlord had notice of criminal activity that posed risk of harm to his tenants, that he had the means to take precautions to protect the tenant against this risk of harm, and that his failure to do so was the proximate cause of the tenant's injuries.

Cedarbrook contends that since it did not have prior notice of sexual assaults occurring on the Cedarbrook grounds, it cannot be held liable under the facts of the instant case. We disagree. In the instant case, sufficient evidence was presented to show that Cedarbrook was aware of criminal activity on the Cedarbrook grounds. From this evidence, the jury could have concluded that Cedarbrook had sufficient notice that criminal conduct by third parties was likely to endanger the safety of its tenants. Two experts testified that the security provided by Cedarbrook did not conform to the accepted standard in buildings of the same class. From this evidence the jury could have logically concluded that Cedarbrook acted unreasonably in failing to implement a more effective security plan.

Decision

The appellate court affirmed the trial court's judgment in favor of the Felds except for the punitive damages awarded to Mr. Feld, which it reduced to $750,000.

Law & Ethics Questions

1. Should a landlord be held liable for the criminal activities of third parties? Why or why not?

2. **ETHICS** Did the landlord act ethically in not providing better security? Did the tenants act ethically in suing the landlord for the criminal actions of third parties?

3. Do you think the damage awards were excessive in this case? Were the punitive damages warranted?

Web Exercises

1. **WEB** For the complete opinion of this case, go to *www.prenhall.com/cheesemancases*.

2. **WEB** Visit the website of the superior court of Pennsylvania, at *www.superior.court.state.pa.us*.

3. **WEB** Use *www.google.com* to find an article that discusses premises liability. Read it.

Transfer of Rights to Leased Property

Landlords may sell, gift, devise, or otherwise transfer their interests in leased property. For example, a landlord can sell either the right to receive rents, his or her reversionary interest, or both. If complete title is transferred, the property is subject to the existing lease. The new landlord cannot alter the terms of the lease (e.g., raise the rent) during the term of the lease unless the lease so provides.

The tenant's right to transfer possession of the leased premises to another depends on the terms of the lease. Many leases permit the tenants to *assign* or *sublease* their rights in the property. Assignment and subleases are discussed in the following paragraphs.

ASSIGNMENT OF A LEASE If a tenant transfers all of his or her interests under a lease, it is an **assignment**. The original tenant is the **assignor**, and the new tenant is the **assignee** (see Exhibit 38.2). Under an assignment, the assignee acquires all the rights that the

> The right of property has not made poverty, but it has powerfully contributed to make wealth.
>
> J. R. McCulloch
> *Principles of Political Economy*

EXHIBIT 38.2

Assignment of a Lease

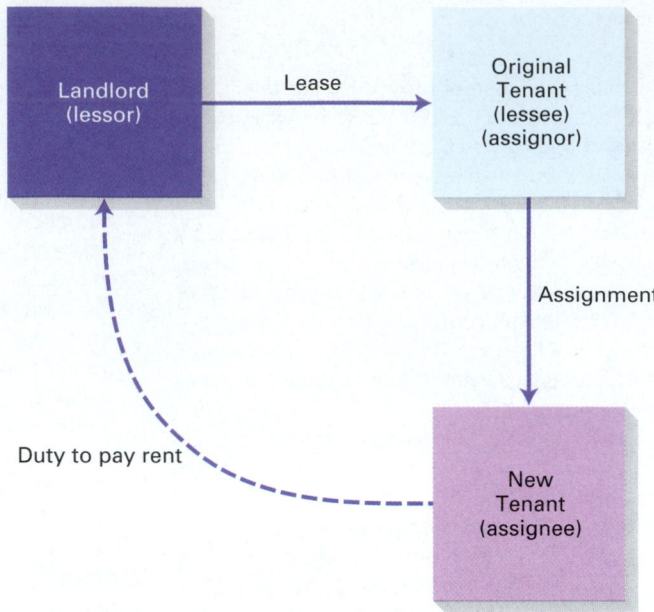

assignor had under the lease. The assignee is obligated to perform the duties that the assignor had under the lease. That is, the assignee must pay the rent and perform other covenants contained in the original lease.

The assignor remains responsible for his or her obligations under the lease unless specifically released from doing so by the landlord. If the landlord recovers from the assignor, the assignor has a course of action to recover from the assignee. Many leases contain a provision prohibiting a lessee from assigning a lease without the lessor's consent.

Example Real Estate Investment Corporation (REIC) owns a warehouse that it leases to American Import Corp. Assume that American Import Corp. assigns its lease on the warehouse to China Export, Inc. American Import Corp. is the assignor, and China Export, Inc., is the assignee. China Export, Inc., owes a duty to pay rent to REIC. If China Export, Inc., does not pay the rent, REIC can sue American Import Corp. to recover the unpaid rent unless the assignment relieves American Import Corp. of this duty.

SUBLEASE If a tenant transfers only some of his or her rights under a lease, it is a **sublease**. The original tenant is the **sublessor**, and the new tenant is the **sublessee** (see Exhibit 38.3). The sublessor is not released from his or her obligations under the lease unless specifically released by the landlord.

Subleases differ from assignments in important ways. In a sublease, no legal relationship is formed between the landlord and the sublessee. Therefore, the sublessee does not acquire rights under the original lease. For example, a sublessee would not acquire the sublessor's option to renew a lease. Further, the landlord cannot sue the sublessee to recover rent payments or enforce duties under the original lease.

In most cases, tenants cannot assign or sublease their leases without the landlord's consent. This right protects the landlord from the transfer of the leasehold to someone who might damage the property or not have the financial resources to pay the rent. Most states, either by statute or by judicial decision, hold that the owner's consent cannot be unreasonably withheld.

Example Apartment Company, Inc., owns an apartment building. As the landlord, it leases an apartment unit to Yi Hong Jia, the tenant. Assume that Yi Hong subleases the apartment to Felix Martinez. Yi Hong is the sublessor, and Felix is the sublessee. Felix owes a duty to pay the rent to Yi Hong, who owes a duty to pay the rent to Apartment Company, Inc. If Felix does not pay the rent to Yi Hong, Yi Hong still must pay the rent to

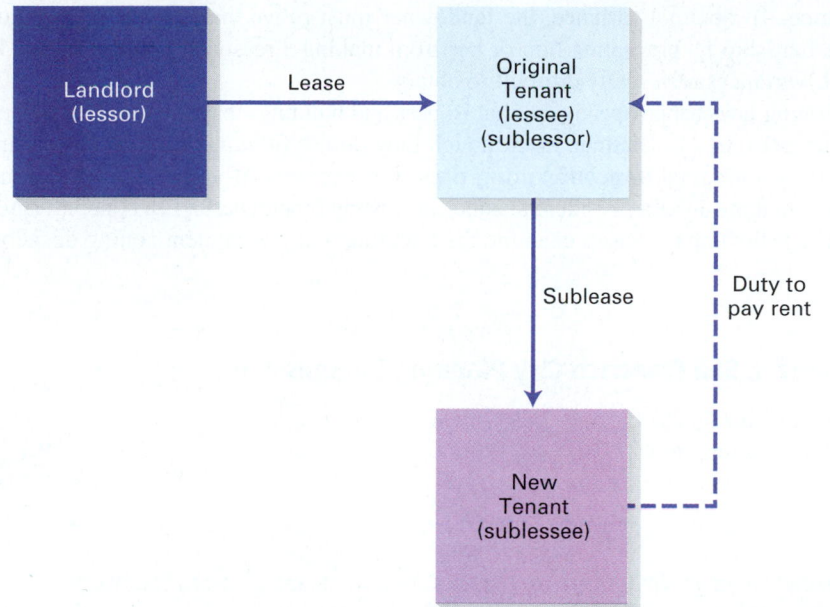

EXHIBIT 38.3

Sublease

Apartment Company, Inc. If Apartment Company, Inc., does not receive the rent, it can sue Yi Hong, the original tenant, to recover the rent. Yi Hong, the sublessor, can sue Felix, the sublessee, to recover any unpaid rent.

CONTEMPORARY ENVIRONMENT

Rent Control

Many local communities across the country have enacted **rent control ordinances** that stipulate the amount of rent a landlord can charge for residential housing. Most of these ordinances fix the rent at a specific amount and provide for minor annual increases. Although many communities have adopted rent control ordinances, New York City has the most famous one.

Landlords, of course, oppose rent control, arguing that rent control ordinances are merely a "regulatory tax" that transfers wealth from landowners to tenants. Tenants and proponents of rent control say that it is necessary to create affordable housing, particularly in high-rent urban areas. The U.S. Supreme Court has upheld the use of rent control. *Yee v. City of Escondido, California*, 503 U.S. 519, 112 S.Ct. 1522, 118 L.Ed.2d 153, **Web** 1992 U.S. Lexis 2115 (Supreme Court of the United States)

Zoning

Most counties and municipalities have enacted **zoning ordinances** to regulate land use. Zoning ordinances generally (1) establish use districts within the municipality (i.e., areas are generally designated residential, commercial, or industrial); (2) restrict the height, size, and location of buildings on a building site; and (3) establish aesthetic requirements or limitations for the exterior of buildings.

A **zoning commission** usually formulates zoning ordinances, conducts public hearings, and makes recommendations to the city council, which must vote to enact an ordinance. Once a zoning ordinance is enacted, the zoning ordinance commission enforces it. If landowners believe that a zoning ordinance is illegal or that it has been unlawfully applied to them or their property, they may institute a court proceeding seeking judicial review of the ordinance or its application.

An owner who wishes to use his or her property for a use different from that permitted under a current zoning ordinance may seek relief from the ordinance by obtaining a

variance. To obtain a variance, the landowner must prove that the ordinance causes an undue hardship by preventing him or her from making a reasonable return on the land as zoned. Variances are usually difficult to obtain.

Zoning laws act prospectively; that is, uses and buildings that already exist in the zoned area are permitted to continue even though they do not fit within new zoning ordinances. Such uses are called **nonconforming uses.** For example, if a new zoning ordinance is enacted, making an area a residential zone, an existing funeral parlor is a nonconforming use.

The following two cases examine the lawfulness of government zoning decisions.

C A S E   38.8
Zoning

Guinnane v. San Francisco City Planning Commission

209 Cal.App.3d 732, 257 Cal.Rptr. 742,
Web 1989 Cal.App. Lexis 377
Court of Appeal of California

> **“** *In particular, the Commission is directed to protect the character and stability of residential areas.* **”**

—Judge Racanelli

Facts

Roy Guinnane purchased four vacant lots located on Edgehill Way in San Francisco. One year later, the city of San Francisco designated an area, including Guinnane's property, as "Edgehill Woods." Two years later, the city adopted a resolution to exercise its discretionary review power over proposed development in the Edgehill Woods area. Guinnane filed an application for a building permit to construct a four-story, 6,000-square-foot house with five bedrooms, five baths, and parking for two cars on one of his lots. Although the proposed building met the specifications of other zoning laws and building codes, the San Francisco Planning Commission disapproved the application because the proposed structure was "not in character" with other homes in the neighborhood. The board of permit appeals agreed. Guinnane appealed.

Issue

Is the aesthetic zoning by the city of San Francisco lawful?

Language of the Court

The basic standard guiding the Planning Commission in discharging its function is the promotion of the public health, safety, peace, morals, comfort, convenience, and general welfare. In particular, the Commission is directed to protect the character and stability of residential areas. Under the Municipal Code, any city department may exercise its discretion in deciding whether to approve any application; and in doing so, it may consider the effect of the proposed project upon the surrounding properties.

We conclude that both the Planning Commission and the Board of Permit Appeals are authorized to exercise independent discretionary review of a building permit application, the final authority being reposed in the board. Further, we conclude that such review is not confined to a determination whether the applicant has complied with the city's zoning ordinances and building codes.

Decision

The court of appeals held that San Francisco's aesthetic zoning ordinance was lawful because it was enacted pursuant to the city's police power to protect its residents' health, safety, and welfare. The court of appeals upheld the board's judgment denying Guinnane's application for a building permit.

Law & Ethics Questions

1. Should a city have zoning authority over the aesthetics of an area? Why or why not?
2. **ETHICS** Is it ethical for a property owner to build a structure that does not comport with the character of the area?
3. Do zoning ordinances affect the value of real property?

Web Exercises

1. **WEB** For the complete opinion of this case, go to *www.prenhall.com/cheesemancases*.
2. **WEB** Visit the website of the court of appeals of California, First Appellate District, Division One, at *www.courtinfo.ca.gov/courts/courtsofappeal*.
3. **WEB** Use *www.google.com* to find an article that discusses the zoning laws in your area. Read it.

CASE **38.9**

Zoning

Stratosphere Gaming Corporation, D/B/A Stratosphere Resort & Casino v. City of Las Vegas, Nevada

120 Nev. 523, 96 P.3d 756,
Web 2004 Nev. Lexis 73 (2004)
Supreme Court of Nevada

> ❝ *The City Council must ensure that the development "contributes" to the City's long-term attractiveness and to public safety, health and general welfare.* ❞
>
> —Judge Shearing

Facts

The Stratosphere Resort & Casino (Stratosphere) in Las Vegas, Nevada, applied to the City of Las Vegas for a site development plan review to construct a proposed ride located on Las Vegas Boulevard South in Las Vegas. The proposed roller-coaster-type ride would consist of a steel structure rising 510 feet on the east side of the existing Stratosphere tower. A passenger car would ascend the 510 feet and then free-fall 204 feet, reaching a maximum speed of 93 miles per hour. The passenger car would then ascend a 325-foot tower that would be built on the Stratosphere property across from the Stratosphere tower. The ride would be located in a permitted C-2 (General Commercial) zoning district and would not require a zoning variance to be built.

The Las Vegas Planning Commission held a public meeting on the application for the proposed ride. The Commission received 670 protests against the proposed ride. At the public hearing, opponents argued that the proposed ride was in proximity to residential neighborhoods and that it would create increased traffic and noise. The Planning Commission failed to approve the application by a 2–2 vote. The Las Vegas City Council then considered the proposed ride and denied Stratosphere's application by a 6–0 vote. Stratosphere appealed to the district court, seeking a declaration that it had a vested right to build the proposed ride because the location was within a properly zoned area. The district court ruled against Stratosphere. Stratosphere appealed.

Issue

Did the Las Vegas City Council have discretionary power to reject Stratosphere's application to build the proposed thrill ride even though the ride would be located in a properly zoned location?

Language of the Court

The City Council's review of a site development plan is governed by section 19.18.050(A), which states that the purpose of the review process is to ensure that the development plan:

1. Is consistent with the General Plan, this Title, the Design Standards Manual, the Landscape, Wall and Buffer Standards and other regulations, plans and policies of the City;

2. Contributes to the long term attractiveness of the City;

3. Contributes to the economic vitality of the community by ensuring compatibility of development throughout the community; and

4. Contributes to the public safety, health and general welfare.

In the context of governmental immunity, we have defined a "discretionary act" as "an act that requires a decision requiring personal deliberation and judgment." The language used in section 19.18.050 clearly indicates a discretionary act on the part of the City Council. The ordinance uses numerous terms that require the City Council to exercise personal deliberation and judgment. For example, the City Council must ensure that the development "contributes" to the City's long-term attractiveness and to public safety, health and general welfare, is "compatible" with development in the area, and is not "unsightly, undesirable or obnoxious in appearance."

Decision

The supreme court held that the Las Vegas City Council lawfully used its discretionary power when it denied Stratosphere's application to build the thrill ride.

Law & Ethics Questions

1. Should a zoning commission or city council have the discretion to deny a petition to build a structure that meets the general zoning laws of the area in which it is to be built?

2. Should other parties' interests (e.g., those of neighboring businesses or residential areas) be considered when making decisions to approve building permits?

3. **ETHICS** Is it ethical for parties to assert the "not in my backyard" position in opposition to a proposed development when zoning laws would otherwise permit the proposed development?

Web Exercises

1. **WEB** For the complete opinion of this case, go to *www.prenhall.com/cheesemancases*.

2. **WEB** Visit the website of the supreme court of Nevada, at *www.nvsupremecourt.us*.

3. **WEB** Visit the website of the Stratosphere Resort & Casino in Las Vegas, at *www.stratospherehotel.com*.

Civil Rights Acts and Real Estate

Federal and state laws guarantee civil rights in the purchase, sale, and leasing of real estate, and the use of public property. Several major federal statutes that regulate real estate are the *Civil Rights Act*, the *Fair Housing Act*, and *Title III of the Americans with Disabilities Act*. These federal statutes are discussed in the following paragraphs.

Civil Rights Act

Federal and state governments have enacted statutes that prohibit discrimination in the sale and rental of real property. The **Civil Rights Act**, a federal statute, prohibits racial discrimination in the transfer of real property, including housing, commercial, and industrial property.[1] The act prohibits private and public discrimination and permits lawsuits to recover damages and obtain injunctions against offending conduct.

Many states and local communities have also enacted statutes and ordinances that prohibit discrimination in the sale or lease of real property. These laws usually prohibit discrimination based on race, color, national origin, sex, or religion but also often prohibit discrimination based on other protected classes, such as age, sexual preference, and receipt of government assistance.

Fair Housing Act

The **Fair Housing Act**, a federal statute, makes it unlawful for a party to refuse to rent or sell a dwelling to any person because of his or her race, color, national origin, sex, or religion.[2] The act also prohibits discrimination by real estate brokers, mortgage lenders, and advertisers concerning the sale or rental of real property. The law does not apply to the following: (1) a person who owns a building of four or fewer units and occupies one of the units and leases the others and (2) a person who leases a single-family dwelling and does not own more than three single-family dwellings. To qualify for either exemption, the lessor cannot use a real estate broker or advertise in a discriminating manner.

Title III of the Americans with Disabilities Act

The **Americans with Disabilities Act (ADA)**, a federal statute, became effective on January 26, 1992.[3] The ADA is a broad civil rights statute that prohibits discrimination against disabled individuals in employment, public services, public accommodations and services, and telecommunications. **Title III of the ADA** prohibits discrimination on the basis of disability in places of public accommodation operated by private entities. The U.S. Department of Justice is empowered to issue regulations that interpret and enforce the ADA.

Title III of the ADA applies to public accommodations and commercial facilities such as motels, hotels, restaurants, theaters, recreation facilities, colleges and universities, department stores, retail stores, and office buildings. It does not generally apply to residential facilities (single-and multifamily housing).

Title III requires covered facilities to be designed, constructed, and altered in compliance with specific accessibility requirements established by regulations issued pursuant to the ADA. This includes constructing ramps to accommodate wheelchairs, installing railings next to steps, placing signs written in Braille in elevators and at elevator call buttons, and so on.

New construction must be built in such a manner as to be readily accessible to and usable by disabled individuals. Any alterations made to existing buildings must be made so that the altered portions of the building are readily accessible to disabled individuals to the maximum extent feasible. With respect to existing buildings, architectural barriers must be removed if such removal is readily achievable. In determining when an action is readily achievable, the factors to be considered include the nature and cost of the action, the financial resources of the facility, and the type of operations of the facility.

Property is the most ambiguous of categories. It covers a multitude of rights which have nothing in common except that they are exercised by persons and enforced by the state.

R. H. Tawney
The Acquisitive Society,
Chapter V (1921)

The ADA provides for both private right of action and enforcement by the attorney general. Individuals may seek injunctive relief and monetary damages, while the attorney general may seek equitable relief and civil fines for any violation.

Building owners, managers, architects, and others involved in the design, construction, ownership, and management of public accommodations and commercial buildings must be knowledgeable about and comply with the provisions of Title III of the ADA.

In the following case, the court had to determine whether the ADA had been violated

---

C A S E **38.10**
Disabilities Act

United States of America v. Cinemark USA, Inc.

348 F.3d 569,
Web 2003 U.S. App. Lexis 22757 (2003)
United States Court of Appeals for the Sixth Circuit

> **"** *The regulation thus is plain in its requirement that the wheelchair lines of sight be similar, or at least roughly similar, to those of other patrons.* **"**
>
> —Judge Rogers

Facts

Title III of the Americans with Disabilities Act (ADA) requires that public accommodations must be "readily accessible to and usable by individuals with disabilities." The U.S. Department of Justice (DOJ) is empowered to adopt regulations to enforce the ADA. The DOJ adopted Standard 4.33.3 for movie theaters, which provides:

> Wheelchair areas shall be an integral part of any fixed seating plan and shall be provided so as to provide people with physical disabilities a choice of admission prices and lines of sight comparable to those for members of the general public. They shall adjoin an accessible route that also serves as a means of egress in case of emergency. At least one companion fixed seat shall be provided next to each wheelchair seating area. When the seating capacity exceeds 300, wheelchair spaces shall be provided in more than one location. Readily removable seats may be installed in wheelchair spaces when the spaces are not required to accommodate wheelchair users.

Cinemark USA, Inc., owns and operates movie theaters throughout the United States. Cinemark has constructed "stadium-style" movie theaters. The theaters have stadium-style seating configuration, with the rows of seats rising at a relatively steep grade to provide better "sight lines" for movie patrons. The stadium-style seating is inaccessible for wheelchair-using patrons. For wheelchair-using patrons, the theaters provide a flat area in front of the screen where these patrons do not have the same sight line to the screen as non-wheelchair-using patrons. The United States sued Cinemark, alleging that the seating arrangement in Cinemark stadium-style theaters violated Standard 4.33.3 and Title III of the ADA. The U.S. District Court granted summary judgment to Cinemark. The United States appealed.

Issue

Does Cinemark's wheelchair seating arrangement in its stadium-style theaters violate Standard 4.33.3 and Title III of the ADA?

Language of the Court

The regulation at issue appears plainly to require that wheelchair patrons have something more than a merely unobstructed view in seating adjacent to other patrons. While we agree that "line of sight" can be defined as unobstructed view, the regulation requires more than "lines of sight" for wheelchair patrons. It requires comparable lines of sight. The regulation thus is plain in its requirement that the wheelchair lines of sight be similar, or at least roughly similar, to those of other patrons. Viewing angles are truly the only operative way of measuring whether the line of sight offered by a seat is "comparable" to those offered to the general public.

The thrust of Title III's mandate leads us to conclude that the term "lines of sight comparable to those for members of the general public" requires that wheelchair users be afforded comparable viewing angles to those provided for the general public. Only then will wheelchair users have "equal enjoyment" with the general public. Under the district court's interpretation, a wheelchair-using patron could be relegated to the worst seats in the theater so long as the disabled patron still had an "unobstructed view" of the screen. This does not comport with the "full and equal enjoyment" language of Title III.

Decision

The U.S. Court of Appeals ruled that Title III of the ADA and the DOJ's Standard 4.33.3 required Cinemark to provide "lines of sight" for wheelchair-using patrons "comparable" to those offered to the general public and that its current seating configuration for wheelchair-using patrons violated the law. The U.S. Court of Appeals reversed the judgment of the U.S. District Court and remanded the case for further proceedings consistent with its opinion.

Law & Ethics Questions

1. What are the goals underlying the Americans with Disabilities Act (ADA)?

2. **ETHICS** Did Cinemark act socially responsible in this case? Explain.

3. Do the requirements of the ADA and regulations adopted thereunder add significant costs to businesses?

Web Exercises

1. **WEB** For a complete opinion of this case, go to *www.prenhall.com/cheesemancases*.

2. **WEB** Visit the website of the U.S. Court of Appeals for the Sixth Circuit, at *www.ca6.uscourts.gov*.

3. **WEB** Visit the website of Cinemark Theaters, at *www.cinemark.com*.

4. **WEB** Use *www.google.com* to find an article that discusses Title III of the Americans with Disabilities Act. Read it.

Eminent Domain and the "Taking" of Real Property

The government may use its power of **eminent domain** to acquire private property for public purposes. However, the **Due Process Clause** of the Fifth Amendment to the U.S. Constitution (and state constitutions, where applicable) requires that the government only take property for "public use." The government must allow the owner of the property to make a case for keeping the property.

The **Just Compensation Clause** of the Fifth Amendment to the U.S. Constitution requires the government to compensate the property owner (and possibly others, such as lessees) when it exercises the power of eminent domain. Anyone who is not satisfied with the compensation offered by the government can bring an action to have the court determine the compensation to be paid.

Example Assume that ITT Corporation owns a large piece of property, with the intention of erecting a 10-story commercial building at some future time. The current zoning laws permit this building. Now suppose the government wants to build a new highway that passes through the property owned by ITT. The government can use its power of eminent domain to acquire the property for this public use. There has been a "taking," so the government must pay ITT just compensation.

Example Assume that ITT Corporation owns a large piece of property, with the intention of erecting a 10-story commercial building at some future time. Suppose that the government enacts a zoning law that restricts buildings in the area to five stories. Although ITT would suffer a substantial economic loss, the zoning law, nevertheless, would probably not constitute a "taking" that required the payment of compensation.

In the following case, the U.S. Supreme Court decided a major "takings" case.

CASE **38.11**
"Taking"

U.S. SUPREME COURT

Kelo v. City of New London, Connecticut

545 U.S. 469, 125 S.Ct. 2655, 162 L.Ed.2d 439
Web 2005 U.S. Lexis 5011 (2005)
Supreme Court of the United States

❝*The concept of the public welfare is broad and exclusive. The values it represents are spiritual as well as physical, aesthetic as well as monetary.*❞

—Justice Stevens

Facts

The City of New London is located in southeastern Connecticut, at the junction of the Thames River and Long Island Sound. The city has suffered decades of economic decline, including the closing of the federal military base in the Fort Trumbull area of the city. The city's unemployment was nearly double that of the state's, and the city's population of 24,000 was the lowest since 1920.

To try to remedy the situation, state and local officials targeted the City of New London for economic revitalization. The government created the New London Development Corporation (NLDC) to assist the city in planning economic redevelopment. The NLDC finalized an integrated redevelopment plan for 90 acres in the Fort Trumbull area of the city. The redevelopment plan included a waterfront conference hotel, restaurants, stores, a marina, 80 new residences, and office buildings. These projects were to be constructed and owned by private developers and parties selected by the city. The stated purposes were to make the city more attractive, create jobs, and increase tax revenue.

The city purchased most of the land needed for the redevelopment from private owners. When Susette Kelo and other homeowners in the redevelopment district (collectively Kelo) refused to sell their properties, the NLDC initiated eminent domain actions to take their properties. The properties themselves were well kept and were not blighted. Kelo defended, arguing that the taking violated the "public use" requirement of the Fifth Amendment to the U.S. Constitution. The state trial court held for Kelo. The state supreme court held that the taking of private property by the NLDC was valid. Kelo appealed to the U.S. Supreme Court.

Issue

Does the city's decision to take property for the purpose of economic development satisfy the "public use" requirement of the Fifth Amendment to permit Kelo's property to be taken by eminent domain?

Language of the U.S. Supreme Court

The disposition of this case therefore turns on the question whether the City's development plan serves a "public purpose." Without exception, our cases have defined this concept broadly. The concept of the public welfare is broad and exclusive. The values it represents are spiritual as well as physical, aesthetic as well as monetary. It is within the power of the legislature to determine that the community should be beautiful as well as healthy, spacious as well as clean, well-balanced as well as carefully patrolled.

Those who govern the City were not confronted with the need to remove blight in the Fort Trumbull area, but their determination that the area was sufficiently distressed to justify a program of economic rejuvenation is entitled to our deference. The City has carefully formulated an economic development plan that it believes will provide appreciable benefits to the community, including—but by no means limited to—new jobs and increased tax revenue. As with other exercises in urban planning and development, the City is endeavoring to coordinate a variety of commercial,

residential, and recreational uses of land, with the hope that they will form a whole greater than the sum of its parts. To effectuate this plan, the City has invoked a state statute that specifically authorizes the use of eminent domain to promote economic development. Given the comprehensive character of the plan, the thorough deliberation that preceded its adoption, and the limited scope of our review, it is appropriate for us to resolve the challenges of the individual owners, not on a piecemeal basis, but rather in light of the entire plan. Because that plan unquestionably serves a public purpose, the takings challenged here satisfy the public use requirement of the Fifth Amendment.

Just as we decline to second-guess the City's considered judgments about the efficacy of its development plan, we also decline to second-guess the City's determinations as to what lands it needs to acquire in order to effectuate the project. It is not for the courts to oversee the choice of the boundary line nor to sit in review on the size of a particular project area. Once the question of the public purpose has been decided, the amount and character of land to be taken for the project and the need for a particular tract to complete the integrated plan rests in the discretion of the legislative branch. In affirming the City's authority to take petitioners' properties, we do not minimize the hardship that condemnations may entail, notwithstanding the payment of just compensation.

Decision

The U.S. Supreme Court held that the City of New London's decision to take property through the power of eminent domain for the purpose of economic development satisfied the "public use" requirement of the Fifth Amendment. The U.S. Supreme Court affirmed the state supreme court's decision permitting the taking of Kelo's property.

Law & Ethics Questions

1. What is eminent domain? Explain.
2. What does the "public use" requirement in the Fifth Amendment to the U.S. Constitution provide? Explain.
3. **ETHICS** Was the City of New London acting socially responsible when it tried to take Kelo's property?
4. **ETHICS** What are the ramifications of the U.S. Supreme Court's decision in this case? Explain.

Web Exercises

1. **WEB** For a complete opinion of this case, go to *www.prenhall.com/cheesemancases*.
2. **WEB** Visit the website of the Supreme Court of the United States, at *www.supremecourtus.gov*, and try to find documents that relate to this case.
3. **WEB** Visit the website of the City of New London, Connecticut, at *www.ci.new-london.ct.us*. Can you find any information about the redeveloped area?
4. **WEB** Use *www.google.com* to find an article that discusses the *Kelo* case. Read it.

Chapter Summary

Real Property, p. 1077

Real property is immovable. It includes land, buildings, subsurface rights, air rights, plant life, and fixtures.

Land and Buildings

Land is the most common form of real property. Buildings constructed on land are real property.

Subsurface Rights

The owner of land possesses *subsurface rights*, or *mineral rights*, to the earth located beneath the surface of the land. Subsurface rights may be sold separately from surface rights.

Plant Life and Vegetation

Plant life and vegetation growing on the surface of land are considered real property. When land is sold, any plant life growing on the land is included unless the parties agree otherwise. Plant life that is severed from the land is considered personal property.

Fixtures

Fixtures are personal property that is so closely associated with real property that it becomes part of the realty.

Air Rights

The owners of land may sell or lease air space parcels above their land.

Estates in Land, p. 1078
Freehold Estate

Freehold estates are estates in which the owner has a present possessory interest in the real property.
  1. *Estate in fee:*
     a. *Fee simple absolute* (or *fee simple*). This is the highest form of ownership.
     b. *Fee simple defeasible* (or *qualified fee*). This is an estate that ends if a specified condition occurs.
  2. *Life estate.* This is an interest in real property that lasts for the life of a specified person. It is called an *estate pour autre vie* if the time is measured by the life of a third person.

Concurrent Ownership, p. 1080

In concurrent ownerships, two or more persons jointly own real property.

Joint Tenancy

With joint tenancy, owners may transfer their interests without the consent of co-owners. Transfer severs the joint tenancy. Under the right of survivorship, the interest of a deceased owner passes to his or her co-owners.

Tenancy in Common

With tenancy in common, owners may transfer their interests without the consent of co-owners. Transfer does not sever the tenancy in common. Interest of a deceased owner passes to his or her estate.

Tenancy by the Entirety

The tenancy by the entirety form of co-ownership can be used only by a married couple. Neither spouse may transfer his or her interest without the other spouse's consent. A surviving spouse has the right of survivorship.

Community Property

The community property form of co-ownership applies only to a married couple. Neither spouse may transfer his or her interest without the other spouse's consent. When a spouse dies, the surviving spouse automatically receives one-half the community property.

Condominium

Condominium owners have title to their individual units and own the common areas as tenants in common. Owners may transfer their interests without the consent of other owners.

Cooperative

With a cooperative, a corporation owns the building, and the residents own shares of the corporation. Usually, owners may not transfer their shares without the approval of the other owners.

Future Interests, p. 1083

A future interest is a right to possess real property in the future rather than currently.

Reversion

With reversion, the right to possession returns to the grantor after the expiration of a limited or contingent estate.

Remainder

With remainder, the right to possession goes to a third person after the expiration of a limited or contingent estate. The third person is called a remainder beneficiary.

Transfer of Ownership of Real Property, p. 1083

Sale of Real Estate

An owner may sell his or her property to another for consideration.

1. *Deeds.* Instrument used to convey real property by sale or gift:

   a. *Warranty deed.* This type of deed provides the most protection to the grantee because the grantor makes warranties against defect in title.

   b. *Quitclaim deed.* This type of deed provides the least amount of protection to the grantee because the grantor transfers only the interest he or she has in the property.

2. *Recording Statutes.* Recording statutes permit copies of deeds and other documents concerning interests in real property (e.g., mortgages, liens) to be filed in a government office, where they become public record. This puts third parties on notice of recorded interests.

3. *Marketable Title.* A marketable title is free from any undisclosed encumbrances, defects in title, or other defects. Methods of assuring marketable title:

   a. *Attorney's opinion.* An attorney renders an opinion concerning the status of the title.

   b. *Torrens system.* A court issues a certificate of title to the rightful owner of the property.

   c. *Title insurance.* A title insurer agrees to reimburse the insured for losses caused by undiscovered defects in title.

Tax Sale

The government may obtain a lien on property for nonpayment of taxes and sell the property at a tax sale to a buyer. The buyer takes the title subject to the taxpayer's right of redemption.

Gift, Will, or Inheritance

Owners may give their property to another during their lifetime or leave their property by will to a beneficiary when they die. If a person dies without a will, his or her property is distributed to the heirs pursuant to state intestacy statutes.

Adverse Possession

A person who occupies another's property acquires title to the property if the occupation has been:
1. For a statutory period of time (in many states, 10 to 20 years)
2. Open, visible, and notorious
3. Actual and exclusive
4. Continuous and peaceful
5. Hostile and adverse

Nonpossessory Interests, p. 1089

Easement

An easement is an interest in land that gives the holder the right to make limited use of another's property without taking anything from it (e.g., driveways, party walls).
1. *Easement appurtenant.* With this type of easement, an owner of land is given an easement over an adjacent piece of land.
2. *Easement in gross.* This type of easement authorizes a person who does not own adjacent land the right to use another's land.

License

A license is a right to enter upon another's property for a specified and usually short period of time (e.g., ticket to a sporting event).

Profit

Profit gives the holder the right to remove something from another's real property.

Landlord–Tenant Relationship, p. 1091

A landlord–tenant relationship is created when an owner of a freehold estate transfers a right to another to exclusively and temporarily possess the owner's property.

Lease

A lease is a rental agreement between a landlord and a tenant that contains the essential terms of the parties' agreement. There are four types of tenancy:
1. *Tenancy for years.* This is tenancy for a specified period of time.
2. *Periodic tenancy.* This is tenancy for a period of time determined by the payment interval.
3. *Tenancy at will.* This is tenancy that may be terminated at any time by either party.
4. *Tenancy at sufferance.* This is tenancy created by the wrongful possession of property.

Landlord's Duty to Deliver Possession

A landlord is obligated to deliver possession of the leased premises to the tenant on the date the lease term begins.

Landlord's Duty Not to Interfere with the Tenant's Right to Quiet Enjoyment

A landlord may not interfere with the tenant's quiet and peaceful possession, use, and enjoyment of the leased premises.

Landlord's Duty to Maintain the Leased Premises

A landlord owes contractual and statutory duties to repair and maintain the leased premises. The leased premises must be fit, safe, and suitable for ordinary residential use.

Tenant's Duty to Pay Rent

A tenant owes a duty to pay the agreed-upon rent to the landlord. Reasonable late charges may be assessed on overdue rent. A gross lease requires the tenant to pay a stated sum to the landlord. The landlord is responsible for paying property taxes and assessments on the property. Common commercial rental arrangements are:

1. *Net lease.* The tenant is responsible for paying rent and property taxes.
2. *Double net lease.* The tenant is responsible for paying rent, property taxes, and utilities.
3. *Net, net, net lease (triple net lease).* The tenant is responsible for paying rent, property taxes, utilities, and insurance.

Tenant's Duty Not to Use Leased Premises for Illegal or Nonstipulated Purposes

A tenant may not use leased premises for any illegal or nonstipulated uses.

Tenant's Duty Not to Commit Waste

A tenant may not commit waste to the leased premises.

Tenant's Duty Not to Disturb Other Tenants

A tenant may not disturb the use and enjoyment of the premises by other tenants.

Implied Warranty of Habitability

The warranty of habitability is implied by law in residential leases. It provides that leased premises must be fit, safe, and suitable for ordinary residential use.

Transfer of Rights to Leased Property

1. *Assignment of a lease.* Landlords may transfer their ownership interests in leased property. The tenant becomes a tenant of the new owner.
2. *Sublease.* Subject to the terms of the lease, tenants may assign or sublease the leased premises to a third party. The original tenant is not relieved of obligations under the lease.

Zoning, p. 1099

Zoning ordinance are laws adopted by local governments that restrict the use of property, set building standards, and establish architectural requirements.

1. *Variance.* A variance permits an owner to make a nonzoned use of his or her property. A variance requires permission from a zoning board.
2. *Nonconforming use.* A nonconforming use is a nonzoned use that is permitted (grandfathered in) when an area is rezoned.

Civil Rights Acts and Real Estate, p. 1102

Civil Rights Act

The Civil Rights Act is a federal statute that prohibits racial discrimination in the transfer of real property.

Fair Housing Act

The Fair Housing Act is a federal statute that makes it unlawful for a party to refuse to rent or sell a dwelling to any person because of his or her race, color, national origin, sex, or religion.

Title III of the Americans with Disabilities Act

Title III of the ADA prohibits discrimination on the basis of disability in places of public accommodation operated by private entities.

Eminent Domain and the "Taking" of Real Property, p. 1104

Eminent domain is the power and process by which the government acquires private property for public purposes. The Just Compensation Clause of the U.S. Constitution mandates that the government compensate the property owner and possibly others just compensation when the government exercises its power of eminent domain and takes property for government purposes.

Test Review Terms and Concepts

Abstract of title   1086
Adverse possession   1086
Air space parcel   1078
Americans with Disabilities Act
   (ADA)   1102
Assignee   1097
Assignment   1097
Assignor   1097
Attorney's opinion   1086
Building codes (housing
   codes)   1094
Buildings   1077
Certificate of title   1086
Civil Rights Act   1102
Closing (settlement)   1083
Community property   1080
Condominium   1081
Constructive notice   1084
Cooperative   1082
Co-owners
   (joint tenants)   1080
Co-ownership (concurrent
   ownership)   1080
County recorder's office   1084
Covenant of quiet enjoyment   1093
Deed   1084

Dominant estate   1089
Double net lease   1094
Due Process Clause   1104
Duty not to commit waste   1095
Easement   1089
Easement appurtenant   1089
Easement in gross   1089
Eminent domain   1104
Estate in land (estate)   1078
Estate pour autre vie   1079
Exclusive possession   1093
Fair Housing Act   1102
Fee simple absolute
   (fee simple)   1078
Fee simple defeasible
   (qualified fee)   1079
Fixtures   1078
Freehold estate   1078
Future interest   1083
Gift   1086
Grantee   1084
Grantor   1084
Implied warranty of
   habitability   1095
Joint tenancy   1080
Just Compensation Clause   1104

Land   1077
Landlord (lessor)   1091
Landlord–tenant
   relationship   1091
Lease   1091
Leasehold estate
   (leasehold)   1091
License   1050
Licensee   1050
Licensor   1050
Life estate   1079
Marketable title
   (good title)   1086
Net lease   1094
Net, net, net lease (triple net
   lease)   1094
Nonconforming use   1100
Nonpossessory interest   1089
Period of redemption   1086
Periodic tenancy   1092
Plant life and vegetation   1078
Premise liability   1096
Profit-à-prendre (profit)   1050
Quiet title action   1084
Quitclaim deed   1084
Real estate sales contract   1083

Case Problems

38.1 Subsurface Rights: In 1883, Isaac McIlwee owned 100 acres of land in Valley Township, Guernsey Country, Ohio. In that year, he sold the property to Akron & Cambridge Coal Company (Akron & Cambridge) in fee simple but reserved in fee simple "the surface of all said lands" to himself. Over the years, the interests in the land were transferred to many different parties. On hundred years after McIlwee's transfer of an interest in the property to Akron & Cambridge, the Mid-Ohio Coal Company owned the rights originally transferred to Akron & Cambridge, and Peter and Irene Minnich owned the rights reserved by Isaac McIlwee in 1883. The Minniches claim they possess subsurface rights to the property except for coal rights. Who wins? *Minnich v. Guernsey Savings and Loan Company*, 36 Ohio App.3d 54, 521 N.E.2d 489, **Web** 1987 Ohio App. Lexis 10497 (Court of Appeals of Ohio)

38.2 Life Estate and Remainder: Baudilio Bowles died testate. His will devised to his sister, Julianita B. Vigil, "one-half of any income, rents, or profits from any real property located in Bull Creek or Colonias, New Mexico." The will contained another clause that left to his children "my interest in any real property owned by me at the time of my death, located in Bull Creek and/or Colonias, San Miguel County." The property referred to in both devises is the same property. Julianita died before the will was probated. Her heirs claim a one-half ownership interest in the real property. Bowles's children asserted that they owned all his property. Who wins? *In the Matter of the Estate of Bowles*, 107 N.M. 739, 764 P.2d 510, **Web** 1988 N.M. App. Lexis 93 (Court of Appeals of New Mexico)

38.3 Reversion: W.E. and Jennie Hutton conveyed land they owned to the Trustees of Schools of District Number One of the Town of Allison, Illinois (School District), by warranty deed "to be used for school purpose only; otherwise to revert to Grantor." The School District built a school on the site, commonly known as Hutton School. The Huttons conveyed the adjoining farmland and their rever-sionary interest in the school site to the Jacqmains, who in turn conveyed their interest to Herbert and Betty Mahrenholz. The 1.5-acre site sits in the middle of Mahrenhoz's farmland. Over 30 years after School District built the school, the School District discontinued holding regular classes at Hutton School. Instead, it used the school building to warehouse and store miscellaneous school equipment, supplies, unused desks, and the like. Mahrenholz filed suit to quiet title to the school property to themselves. Who wins? *Mahrenholz v. County Board of School Trustees of Lawrence Country*, 188 Ill.App.3d 260, 544 N.E.2d 128, **Web** 1989 Ill. App. Lexis 1445 (Appellate Court of Illinois)

38.4 Community Property: Daniel T. Yu and his wife, Bernice, owned a house and two lots as community property. Yu entered into an agreement with Arch, Ltd. (Arch), whereby he agreed to exchange these properties for two office buildings owned by Arch. Yu signed the agreement, but his wife did not. At the date set for closing, Arch performed its obligations under the agreement, executed all documents, and was prepared to transfer title to its properties to Yu. Yu, however, refused to perform his obligations under the agreement. Evidence showed that the office buildings had decreased in value from $800,000 to $700,000 from the date of the agreement to the date set for closing. Arch sued Yu to recover damages for breach of contract. Who wins? *Arch, Ltd. v. Yu*, 108 N.M. 67, 766 P.2d 911, **Web** 1988 N.M. Lexis 330 (Supreme Court of New Mexico)

38.5 Easement in Gross: John L. Yutterman died and left one piece of property, located in Fort Smith, Arkansas, to his two sons and two daughters. Each child received approximately one-fourth of the property in fee simple. A 40-foot driveway divided the property. Concerning the driveway, Yutterman's will provided as follows: "Further, a specific condition of this will and of these devises is that the forty (40) foot driveway from Free Ferry Road, three hundred (300) feet Northward, shall be kept open for the common use of the devisees in this will." Subsequently, one of the daughters wanted to sell her property to a third party. If the third party purchases the property, will that party have an easement to use the driveway? *Merriman v. Yutterman*, 291 Ark. 207, 723 S.W.2d 823, **Web** 1987 Ark. Lexis 1934 (Supreme Court of Arkansas)

38.6 Adverse Possession: Joseph and Helen Naab purchased a tract of land in a subdivision of Williamstown, West Virginia. At the time of purchase, there were both a house and a small concrete garage on the property. Evidence showed that the garage had been erected sometime prior to 20 years earlier by one of the Naabs' predecessors in title. Two years after the Naabs bought their property, Roger and Cynthia Nolan purchased a lot contiguous to that owned by the Naabs. The following year, the Nolans had their property surveyed. The survey indicated that one corner of the Naabs' garage encroached 1.22 feet onto the Nolans' property and the other corner encroached 0.91 feet over the property line. The Nolans requested that the Naabs remove the garage from their property. When the Naabs refused, a lawsuit ensued. Who wins? *Naab v. Nolan*, 174 W. Va. 390, 327 S.E.2d 151, **Web** 1985 W.Va. Lexis 476 (Supreme Court of Appeals of West Virginia)

38.7 Constructive Eviction: T&W Building Company (Landlord) entered into a five-year lease agreement with Merrillville Sport & Fitness, Inc. (Tenant), to lease space in a building to be used as a sports and fitness center. The lease provided that Landlord was to keep the heating and cooling plant "in good order, repair, and condition" and was to commence required repairs as soon as reasonably practicable after receiving written notice of problems. Tenant complained of several problems throughout the first year of its tenancy. First, the heating system did not work properly, causing the premises to be extremely cold, particularly in the winter months. Second, there was no water on many occasions. Third, there was only one plug installed on the premises. Landlord failed to rectify the problems. As a result, Tenant lost members. It gave notice and vacated the premises within one year of signing the lease. Tenant and Landlord ended up in a lawsuit regarding the lease. Who wins? *T&W Building Co. v. Merrillville Sport & Fitness, Inc.*, 529 N.E.2d 865, **Web** 1988 Ind. App. Lexis 805 (Court of Appeals of Indiana)

38.8 Implied Warranty of Habitability: Sharon Love entered into a written lease agreement with Monarch Apartments for apartment 4 at 441 Winfield in Topeka, Kansas. Shortly after moving in, she experienced serious problems with termites. Her walls swelled, clouds of dirt came out, and when she checked on her children one night, she saw termites flying around the room. She complained to Monarch, which arranged for the apartment to be fumigated. When the termite problem persisted, Monarch moved Love and her children to apartment 2. Upon moving in, Love noticed that roaches crawled over the walls, ceilings, and floors of the apartment. She complained, and Monarch called an exterminator, who sprayed the apartment. When the roach problem persisted, Love vacated the premises. Did Love lawfully terminate the lease? *Love v. Monarch Apartments*, 13 Kan.App.2d 341, 771 P.2d 79, **Web** 1989 Kan. App. Lexis 219 (Court of Appeals of Kansas)

38.9 Lease: Susan Nylen, Elizabeth Lewis, and Julie Reed, students at Indiana University, signed a rental agreement as cosigners to lease an apartment from Park Doral Apartments. The rental term was from August 26 until August 19 of the following year. The lessees agreed to pay a monthly rent for the apartment. The tenants paid a security deposit, constituting prepayment of rent for the last month of the lease term. At the end of the fall semester, Reed moved out of the apartment and refused to pay any further rent. Nylen and Lewis remained in possession of the apartment, paying only two-thirds of the total rent due for the month for several months. Nylen and Lewis made a full payment of the rent for March and then vacated the apartment. The landlord, who was unable to re-lease the apartment during the lease term, sued Reed, Nylen, and Lewis for the unpaid rent. Who wins? *Nylen v. Park Doral Apartments*, 535 N.E.2d 178, **Web** 1989 Ind. App. Lexis 185 (Court of Appeals of Indiana)

38.10 Tort Liability: William Long, d/b/a Hoosier Homes, owned an apartment building in Indianapolis, Indiana. He rented a second-story apartment to Marvin Tardy. Almedia McLayea visited Tardy with her one-month-old nephew, Garfield Dawson. As McLayea was leaving the apartment, she walked down the stairway, carrying Dawson in an infant seat. As she came down 4 steps to a landing, which led to a flight of 10 stairs, she caught her heel on a stair, slipped, and fell forward. There was no handrail along the stairway (as required by law) by which she could break her fall. Instead, her shoulder struck a window at the landing, the window broke, the rotted screen behind it collapsed, and Dawson fell through the opening to the ground below. He sustained permanent injuries, including brain damage. Dawson (through his mother) sued the landlord to recover damages for negligence. Who wins? *Dawson v. Long*, 546 N.E.2d 1265, **Web** 1989 Ind. App. Lexis 1225 (Court of Appeals of Indiana)

38.11 Tort Liability: Luis and Barbara Chavez leased a house they owned in Arizona to Michael and Terry Diaz. The lease provided that no pets were to be kept on the premises without prior written approval of the landlords. The Diazes, without the landlords' consent or knowledge, kept a Pit Bull and another dog, which was half Pit Bull and half Rottweiler, at the leased premises. Two weeks later, the Diazes' two dogs escaped from the backyard and attacked and injured Josephine Gibbons. Gibbons sued the landlords for damages. Are the landlords liable? Are the tenants liable? *Gibbons v. Chavez*, 160 Ariz. 73, 770 P.2d 377, **Web** 1988 Ariz. App. Lexis 373 (Court of Appeals of Arizona)

38.12 Zoning: The city of Ladue is one of the wealthy suburban residential areas of metropolitan St. Louis. The homes in the city are considerably more expensive than those in surrounding areas and consist of homes of traditional design such as colonial, French provincial, and English. The city set up an architectural board to approve plans for buildings that "conform to certain minimum architectural standards of appearance and conformity with surrounding structures, and that unsightly, grotesque, and unsuitable structures, detrimental to the stability of value and the welfare of surrounding property, structures, and residents, and to the general welfare and happiness of the community, be avoided." The owner of a lot in the city submitted a plan to build a house of ultramodern design. It was pyramid-shaped, with a flat top and triangular-shaped windows and doors. Although the house plans met other city zoning ordinances and building codes, the architectural board rejected the owner's petition for a building permit based on aesthetic reasons. The owner sued the city. Who wins? *State of Missouri v. Berkeley*, 458 S.W.2d 305, **Web** 1970 Mo. Lexis 902 (Supreme Court of Missouri)

38.13 Zoning: The town of Hempstead, New Hampshire, enacted a zoning ordinance "in order to retain the beauty and countrified atmosphere of the town, and to promote health, safety, morals, order, convenience, peace, prosperity, and general welfare of its inhabitants." To preserve abutting property owners' views and light, the ordinance limits the homes in the town to one-and-one-half stories. In violation of the ordinance, John M. Alexander built a shell of a second story and a new roof on his house. After the town ordered him to halt construction and denied him permission to occupy the second floor, he applied for a variance. Should the variance be granted? *Alexander v. Town of Hempstead*, 129 N.H. 278, 525 A.2d 276, **Web** 1987 N.H. Lexis 171 (Supreme Court of New Hampshire)

Ethics Issues

38.14 Ethics: Victor and Phyllis Garber acquired a piece of real property by warranty deed. The deed was recorded. The property consisted of 80 acres enclosed by a fence that had been in place for over 50 years. The enclosed area was used to graze cattle and produce hay. Ten years later, William and Herbert Doenz acquired a piece of real property adjacent to the Garbers' and employed a surveyor to locate their land's boundaries. As a result of the survey, it was discovered that the shared fence was 20 to 30 feet inside the deed line on the Doenz property. The amount of property between the old fence and the deed line was 3.01 acres. The Doenzes removed the old fence and constructed a new fence along the deed line. The Garbers brought suit to quiet title. Did the Doenzes act ethically in removing the fence? Did the Garbers act ethically in claiming title to property that originally belonged with the adjacent property? Did the Garbers acquire title to the property between the fence and the deed through adverse possession? *Doenz v. Garber*, 665 P.2d 932, **Web** 1983 Wyo. Lexis 339 (Supreme Court of Wyoming)

38.15 Ethics: Moe and Joe Rappaport (tenants) leased space in a shopping mall owned by Bermuda Avenue Shopping Center Associates, L.P. (landlord), to use as an indoor golf arcade. The lease was signed, and the tenants were given possession of the leased premises. The tenants were not told by the landlord of the extensive renovations planned for the mall. For one month, the golf arcade was busy and earned a net profit. However, at the end of the month, renovation of the mall began in front of the arcade. According to the tenants, their store sign was taken down, there was debris and dust in front of the store, the sidewalks and parking spaces in front of the store were taken away, and their business "died." The tenants closed their arcade approximately one month later and sued the landlord for damages. The landlord counterclaimed, seeking to recover lost rental income. Did the landlord act ethically in not explaining the planned renovations to the tenants? Did the tenants act ethically in terminating the lease? Were the tenants constructively evicted from the leased premise? *Bermuda Avenue Shopping Center Associates v. Rappaport*, 565 So.2d 805, **Web** 1990 Fla. App. Lexis 5354 (Court of Appeal of Florida)

38.16 Ethics: The Middleton Tract consisted of approximately 560 acres of land located in the Santa Cruz Mountains in San Mateo County, California. The land, which had once been owned by William H. Middleton, had been subdivided into 80 parcels of various shapes and sizes that were owned by various parties. The original deeds of conveyance from Middleton to purchasers contained certain restrictive covenants. One covenant limited use of the land exclusively for "residential purposes." Most of the land consists of thickly wooded forest with redwood and Douglas fir trees. The Holmeses, who owned parcels totaling 144 acres, proposed to engage in commercial logging activities on their land. The plaintiffs, who owned other parcels in the tract, sued the Holmeses, seeking an injunction against such commercial activities. Who wins? *Greater Middleton Assn. v. Holmes Lumber Co.*, 222 Cal.App.3d 980, 271 Cal.Rptr. 917, **Web** 1990 Cal. App. Lexis 816 (Court of Appeal of California)

IRAC Writing Assignment

Read **Case A-38** in Appendix A [***Walker v. Quillen***]. Use the IRAC method to prepare a written analysis of the case.

Endnotes

1. 42 U.S.C. Section 1971 *et seq.*
2. 42 U.S.C. Section 360 *et seq.*
3. 42 U.C.C. Section 1201 *et seq.*

CHAPTER 39

Family Law, Wills, and Trusts

> **"** *When you have told someone you have left him a legacy, the only decent thing to do is to die at once.* **"**
>
> —SAMUEL BUTLER

CHAPTER OBJECTIVES

After studying this chapter, you should be able to:

1. Define *marriage* and enumerate the legal requirements of marriage.
2. Define *divorce* and describe how assets are distributed upon the termination of marriage.
3. List and describe the requirements for making a valid will.
4. Identify how property is distributed under intestacy statutes if a person dies without a will.
5. Define *trust, living trust, living will*, and *health care directive* and identify the parties to these instruments.

CHAPTER CONTENTS

   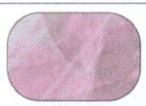 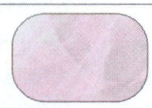

Introduction to Family Law, Wills, and Trusts

Family law and domestic relations is a broad area of the law, involving marriage, prenuptial agreements, dissolution of marriage, division of property upon dissolution of marriage, spousal and child support, child custody, and other family law issues. This chapter covers in detail the family law and domestic relations issues.

Wills and trusts are means of transferring property. *Wills* transfer property upon a person's death. They permit people to state exactly where they want their property to go when they die. If a person dies *intestate*—that is, without a will—the deceased's property is distributed to relatives according to state statute. The property escheats (goes) to the state if there are no relatives.

Trusts are used to transfer property that is to be held and managed for the benefit of another person or persons. Although trusts are created during one's lifetime, they may be worded to become effective only upon the trustor's (or grantor's) death. A *living trust* is a special type of trust used for estate planning. This chapter discusses the use of wills and trusts to transfer and protect property.

Henry Benjamin and Florence Lorraine Cheeseman

The author's parents, who celebrated 50 years of marriage.

Premarriage Issues

Prior to marriage, several legal issues may arise. These include promises to marry, engagement, and prenuptial agreements.

Promise to Marry

In the nineteenth century, many courts recognized an action for breach of a **promise to marry**. This would usually occur if a man proposed marriage, the woman accepted, and then the man backed out before the marriage took place. The lawsuit was based on a breach-of-contract theory. Today, most courts do not recognize a breach of a promise-to-marry lawsuit. The denial of such lawsuits is based on current social norms. If the potential groom backs out late, after many of the items for the pending marriage were purchased or contracted for (e.g., flowers, rental of a reception hall), he may be responsible for paying these costs, however.

Engagement

As a prelude to getting married, many couples go through a period of time known as **engagement**. The engagement usually begins when the male proposes marriage to the female, and if the female accepts, he gives her an engagement ring (usually a diamond ring). The engagement period runs until the wedding is held or the engagement is broken off. If the couple get married, they often exchange wedding band rings at the marriage ceremony.

Sometimes the engagement is broken off prior to the wedding. Then the issue becomes: Who gets the engagement ring if the engagement is broken off? Some states follow a **fault rule**, which works as follows:

- If the prospective groom breaks off the engagement, the prospective bride gets to keep the engagement ring.
- If the prospective bride breaks off the engagement, she must return the engagement ring to the prospective groom.

The fault rule is sometimes difficult to apply. Questions often arise as to who broke off the engagement, which then requires a trial to decide the issue.

The modern rule and trend is to abandon the fault rule and adopt an **objective rule**: If the engagement is broken off, the prospective bride must return the engagement ring, regardless of who broke off the engagement. This objective rule is clear and usually avoids litigation unless the female refuses to return the ring.

CONTEMPORARY ENVIRONMENT
Prenuptial Agreement

In today's society, many spouses sign prenuptial agreements in advance of their marriage. **Prenuptial agreements**—also called **premarital agreements**—are contracts that specify how property will be distributed upon termination of the marriage or death of a spouse. To be enforced, a prenuptial agreement must be in writing.

Prenuptial agreements are often used where both parties to a marriage have their own careers and have accumulated assets prior to the marriage, or if one of the spouses has significant assets prior to the marriage. Prenuptial agreements are also often used where there are children from a prior marriage and the agreement guarantees that these children will receive a certain share of the assets of the remarrying spouse if he or she dies or the marriage is terminated.

For a prenuptial agreement to be enforceable, each party must make full disclosure of all his or her assets and liabilities, and each party should be represented by his or her own attorney. Prenuptial agreements must be voluntarily entered into, without threats or undue pressure. They must provide for the fair distribution of assets and must not be unconscionable. Generally, courts will enforce a properly negotiated prenuptial agreement even if the agreement provides for an unequal distribution of assets and eliminates financial support of a spouse in case the marriage is terminated.

Courts will not enforce a prenuptial agreement in the following circumstances:

- One of the parties was not represented by an attorney.
- One of the parties failed to make full disclosure of his or her assets and liabilities.

- The agreement was entered into at the "last moment," immediately prior to the marriage.
- The terms of the agreement are unfair or unconscionable.
- The agreement violates public policy (e.g., if a party is forced to live on government assistance if the agreement is enforced).

Sometimes the parties enter into an agreement during the marriage, setting forth the distribution of property upon death or termination of the marriage. This is called an **antenuptial agreement**. The courts apply the same standards for enforceability as to prenuptial agreements.

Law & Ethics Questions

1. What is a prenuptial agreement? What purpose does a prenuptial agreement serve?
2. **ETHICS** Is there anything unethical about requiring the other party to sign a prenuptial agreement before getting married?

Web Exercises

1. **WEB** Use *www.google.com* to find an article about a recent situation in which a prenuptial agreement was used. Read it.
2. **WEB** Use *www.google.com* to find an online copy of a prenuptial agreement.

Marriage

Each state has marriage laws that recognize a legal union between a man and a woman. **Marriage** confers certain legal rights and duties on the spouses, as well as on the children born of the marriage. A couple wishing to marry must meet the legal requirements established by the state in which they are to be married. The following paragraphs discuss the legal rights and duties of spouses.

Marriage Requirements

State law establishes certain requirements that must be met before two people can be married. Most states require that the parties be a man and a woman. The parties must be of a certain age (usually 18 years of age). States will permit younger persons to be married if they have the consent of their parents or if they are emancipated from their parents. *Emancipation* means that the person is not supported by his or her parents and provides for himself or herself.

All states provide that persons under a certain age, such as 14 or 15 years of age, cannot be married. States also prohibit marriages between persons who are closely related, usually by blood. A brother cannot marry his sister or half-sister. Cousins may marry in some states. Another requirement of marriage is that neither party is currently married to someone else.

Web Exercise

1. **WEB** Use *www.google.com* to find the requirements to get married in your state.

Marriage License

In order for two people to be legally married, certain legal procedures must be followed. State law requires that the parties obtain a **marriage license** issued by the state. Marriage licenses are usually obtained at the county clerk's office. Some states require that the parties take a blood test prior to obtaining a license. This is to determine if the parties have certain diseases, particularly sexually transmitted diseases.

Some states require that, in addition to a marriage license, there must be some sort of *marriage ceremony*. This ceremony is usually held in front of a justice of the peace or similar government officer, or at a church, temple, or synagogue, in front of a minister, priest, or rabbi. At the ceremony, the parties exchange wedding vows, in which they make a public statement that they will take each other as wife and husband.

After the wedding ceremony, the marriage license is recorded. Some states require a waiting period between the time the marriage license is obtained and when the wedding ceremony takes place.

Financial Support

Most states require a spouse to financially support the other spouse and their children during their marriage. This includes providing for the necessities such as food, shelter, clothing, and medical care. A spouse is obligated only up to the level he or she is able to provide. In some states this duty exists even if the spouses are living apart. The spouses are free to agree on additional duties in separate contracts. Contracts to provide sex violate public policy and therefore are illegal.

Common Law Marriage

Several states recognize a form of marriage called a **common law marriage**. A common law marriage is one in which the parties have not obtained a valid marriage license, nor have they participated in a legal marriage ceremony. Instead, a common law marriage is recognized if the following requirements are met: (1) The parties are eligible to marry, (2) the parties voluntarily intend to be husband and wife, (3) the parties must live together, and (4) the parties hold themselves out as husband and wife.

There are several misconceptions about common law marriages. First, cohabitation is not sufficient in and of itself to establish a common law marriage. Second, the length of time the parties live together is not sufficient alone to establish a common law marriage. For example, couples who immediately live together and intend a common law marriage have one, whereas couples who live together a long time but do not intend a common law marriage do not have one.

When a state recognizes a common law marriage and the necessary requirements are met to establish one, the couple has a legal and formal marriage. All the rights and duties of a normal licensed marriage apply. As such, a court decree of divorce must be obtained to end a common law marriage.

Web Exercise

1. **WEB** Use *www.google.com* to find information about whether your state acknowledges common law marriages. If so, what requirements must be met?

CONTEMPORARY ENVIRONMENT
Same-Sex Marriage

Many couples of the same sex cohabit as if they are married couples. These same-sex couples have fought legal battles in many states to have the law changed to recognize **same-sex marriage**. These couples argue that the Equal Protection Clause of the U.S. Constitution and state constitutions require that their unions be accorded the same legal recognition as a marriage union between a man and a woman. The state of Massachusetts has granted equal rights for gay couples to get married. Several other states have provided that gay partners can enter into "civil unions" that grant gay partners rights similar to those of heterosexual marriage partners.

Under the Full Faith and Credit Clause of the U.S. Constitution, states are required to recognize and give full faith and credit to the laws of other states. Thus, if one or a few states were to legally recognize same-sex marriages, homosexual couples would go to those states to get married and then return to their home state and demand that their marriage be recognized. Many states adopted statutes stating that same-sex marriages obtained in other states would not be recognized as legal in their state.

In 1996, Congress enacted the federal **Defense of Marriage Act (DOMA)** [28 U.S.C. Section 1738C], which bars same-sex couples from enjoying federal benefits (e.g., Social Security benefits due the spouse in a married couple). This federal act also provides that states cannot be forced to recognize same-sex marriages performed in other states.

The battle between the sides that want and do not want same-sex marriages to be recognized as legal will continue for years to come. Most of these battles will be fought in state courts and legislatures. There is also lobbying by both sides to enact more federal laws that weigh in on this issue.

Parents and Children

In many instances, a major purpose of marriage is to have children. Couples who have children have certain legal rights and duties that develop from their parental status.

Parents' Rights and Duties

Parents have the obligation to provide food, shelter, clothing, medical care, and other necessities to their children until a child reaches the age of 18 or until **emancipation**. A child becomes emancipated if he or she leaves the parents and voluntarily lives on his or her own. The law imposes certain duties on parents as well. A parent must see to it that the child attends school up until 16 or 18 years of age, depending on the state, unless the child is home-schooled. Parents may be legally responsible for a child beyond the age of majority if the child has a disability.

Parents also have the right to control the behavior of a child. Parents have the right to select the schools for their children and the religion they will practice. Parents have the right to use corporal punishment (physical punishment) as long as it does not rise to the level of child abuse. For example, mild slapping or spanking is legally permitted.

Child neglect occurs when a parent fails to provide a child with the necessities of life or other basic needs. The state may remove a child, either temporarily or permanently, from situations of child neglect. A parent's refusal to obtain medical care for a child can be punished as a crime.

Paternity Actions

If there is any question as to whom the father of a child is, a **paternity action** may be filed in court to determine the true identity of the father. The majority of these actions are filed by a mother against a man whom the mother claims to be the father of the child. This often is done to seek financial assistance from the father for the child's upbringing.

Paternity lawsuits are sometimes brought by the government where the mother is receiving welfare payments. In these cases, the government seeks to recover the financial assistance payments made to the mother and to establish the father's financial responsibility in the future. Sometimes a paternity action is brought by a male to prove that he is not the father of a child.

Sometimes a father will bring a paternity action to establish that he is the biological father of a child. This is usually done when the father seeks to obtain legal rights, such as custody or visitation rights, concerning the child. Most states have a **father's registry** where a male may register as the father of a child. This requires that the father be notified of planned adoption of the child so he may appear and oppose the adoption.

In most states, the law presumes that the husband of a wife who bears a child is the legal father of the child. In about half the states, a husband who believes that he is not the father can bring a lawsuit to prove that he is not the father. The other states do not permit such actions.

A male can be proven to be or not to be the father of a child through DNA testing. A male may prove that he is not the father of a child if he had no access to the mother at the time of pregnancy or if he is impotent or had a vasectomy prior to the pregnancy.

Parent's Liability for a Child's Wrongful Act

Generally, parents are not liable for their children's negligent acts. For example, if a child negligently injures another child while they are playing, the parents of the child who caused the injury are not liable. Parents are liable if their negligence caused their child's act.

> Law cannot stand aside from the social changes around it.
>
> William J. Brennan, Jr.

Example   If a parent lets a child who does not have a driver's license drive an automobile and the child-driver injures someone, the parents are liable.

About half of the states have enacted child liability statutes that make the parents financially liable for the intentional torts of their children. This liability is usually limited to a specified dollar amount, such as $5,000.

CONTEMPORARY ENVIRONMENT
Surrogacy

A relatively new area of the law has to do with reproductive medicine. This includes the areas of **surrogacy** and fertilized embryos. Several cases highlight the legal questions that arise.

In the famous Baby M case, **In re Baby M** [109 N.J. 396, 537 A. 2d 1227, **Web** 1988 N.J. Lexis 1 (Supreme Court of New Jersey)], William and Elizabeth Stern contracted with Mary Beth Whitehead whereby Ms. Whitehead was artificially inseminated with Mr. Stern's sperm and agreed to give the baby to the Sterns when it was born, at which time Mrs. Stern would adopt the baby. Ms. Whitehead was compensated $10,000 by the Sterns.

When the baby was born, Ms. Whitehead decided to keep the baby. The Sterns sued Ms. Whitehead for breach of contract. The New Jersey Supreme Court held that the **surrogacy contract** violated public policy and could not be enforced because it represented baby selling. The court decided, however, that it was in the child's best interests

to place the baby in the Sterns' custody but awarded visitation rights to Ms. Whitehead.

In another case, **Anna J. v. Mark C.** [12 Cal.App.4th 977, 286 Cal.Rptr 369, **Web** 1991 Cal. App. Lexis 1162 (Court of Appeal of California)], a contract was executed whereby a fertilized embryo formed from the husband's sperm and the wife's egg was implanted in the womb of a surrogate mother. When the non-biological surrogate mother refused to turn over the baby to the biological parents, the biological parents sued. In this case, the court enforced the contract and ruled in favor of the biological parents. The court held that the surrogate mother had no legal rights concerning the child she had borne.

As these cases suggest, surrogate parenting is an unsettled area of the law. As medical science expands, so must the law in delineating the rights and duties of biological and surrogate parents of children born using advanced medical technology.

Adoption

Adoption occurs when a person becomes the legal parent of a child who is not his or her biological child. Thus, a married couple can adopt a child together, a single parent can adopt a child, and a spouse can adopt the child of his or her new spouse.

The process for adoption is complicated and is regulated by state law. Basically, the procedure for adoption consists of the following requirements:

- All procedures of the state law for adoption are met.
- The biological parents' legal rights as parents are terminated by legal decree or death.
- A court formally approves the adoption.

The two main ways by which persons can become adoptive parents are *agency adoptions* and *independent adoptions*

AGENCY ADOPTION An **agency adoption** occurs when a person adopts a child from a social service organization of a state. The state often obtains jurisdiction over children who are born out of wedlock and whose biological parents give up the children for adoption by terminating their parental rights. The state may also obtain jurisdiction over a child if the child has been permanently removed from parents who are judged unsuitable to be parents or where parents are deceased and no relative wants or qualifies to become the child's parents.

In the past, the identity of the biological parents of adopted children was kept confidential in an agency adoption. Currently, many states allow for disclosure of the identity of the biological parents in certain circumstances. Usually, the court will notify the other side—either the child or the biological parent—that the other wishes to meet with them. If both sides consent, the meeting will be arranged.

In many cases today, *open adoption* procedures are being used. In these cases, the biological and adoptive parents are introduced prior to the adoption. The biological parents may screen the prospective adoptive parents to ensure that the adoptive parents are suitable for the child. In many instances, the adoptive and biological parents remain in contact with each other, and the biological parents are given visitation rights to see the child.

INDEPENDENT ADOPTION An **independent adoption** occurs when there is a private arrangement between the biological and adoptive parents. Often, an intermediary, such as a lawyer, doctor, or private adoption agency, introduces the two parties. The biological parents and the adoptive parents enter into a private arrangement for adoption of the child. Adoptive parents usually pay intermediaries a fee for their services, as well as paying the costs of the adoption.

Many divorced people who have children remarry. Often, a new stepparent formally adopts the child or children of his or her new spouse. To do so, the other biological parent of the child must relinquish his or her legal rights concerning the child. This can be done voluntarily or by order of the court if it is in the best interests of the child.

COURT APPROVAL OF ADOPTION In both agency adoptions and independent adoptions, the court must approve the adoption before it is legal. The court will consider the home environment, financial resources, and family stability of the adoptive parents, as well as their religious beliefs, ages, and other factors. The decision of the court will be based on the best interests of the child. Although preference is usually given to couples, single parents can adopt children. States vary as to whether they permit homosexual couples to adopt children.

Once the court approves an adoption, the adoptive couple is subject to a probation period, which is usually six months or one year. During this time, government social workers will investigate whether the adoptive parents are properly caring for the adopted child. If they are not, the court can remove the child from the adoptive parents.

Foster Care

A child may become the responsibility of the state under several circumstances. The first is if a child's parents or parent dies and there are no relatives to take the child or no other arrangements have been made for the care of the child. Another situation occurs if the state institutes a proceeding to remove a child from the parents' or parent's custody because the parent is unfit to care for the child or because the child is in danger (e.g., from child abuse).

Today, the primary means of caring for children under the state's jurisdiction is to place children in **foster care**. This is usually a temporary arrangement. The state pays the foster family for the care given to the foster child. This temporary arrangement will be terminated if the child is returned to his or her biological parents or if the child is legally adopted. Sometimes the foster parents will legally adopt a child who has been placed in their care.

Web Exercise

1. **WEB** Use *www.google.com* to find the government agency that administers the foster care program in your state.

Marriage Termination

Once a state has recognized the marital status of a couple, only the state can terminate this marital status. This is so even if the couple separate and live apart from one another. As long as they are married, they continue to have certain legal rights and duties to one another. The law recognizes two methods for legally terminating a marriage: *annulment* and *divorce*.

Annulment

An **annulment** is an order of the court declaring that a marriage did not exist. The order invalidates the marriage. Annulments are rarely granted now that most states recognize no-fault divorces.

Certain grounds must be asserted to obtain a legal annulment. One ground is that the parties lacked capacity to consent. For example, an annulment may be granted if (1) one of the parties was a minor and had not obtained his or her parents' consent to marry, (2) one of the parties was mentally incapacitated at the time of marriage, (3) one of the parties was intoxicated at the time of the marriage, and (4) the marriage was never consummated. Marriage can also be annulled if the parties are too closely related to one another or there was bigamy (one of the parties was already married). A marriage can also be annulled if there was duress or fraud leading to the marriage (e.g., one of the parties declared that he or she could conceive children when the person knew in fact that he or she could not).

Many annulments are sought because of a person's religion. A Roman Catholic cannot be remarried in the church if he or she is divorced. An annulment would allow for a subsequent marriage in the church. A person may also be required to go through a procedure to seek an annulment from the church. A legal annulment and a religious annulment are two separate and distinct procedures.

The law considers children born of a marriage that is annulled to be legitimate. When a marriage is annulled, issues of child support, child custody, spousal support, and property settlement must be agreed upon by the couple or decided by the court.

Divorce

The most common option used by married partners to terminate their marriage is divorce. **Divorce** is a legal proceeding whereby the court issues a decree that legally orders a marriage terminated.

Traditionally, a married person who sought a divorce had to prove that the other person was *at fault* for causing a major problem with continuing the marriage. Grounds for granting a divorce consisted of adultery, physical or emotional abuse, abandonment, substance or alcohol abuse, or insanity.

Beginning in the 1960s, states began to recognize **no-fault divorce**. A spouse wishing to obtain a divorce merely had to assert *irreconcilable differences* with his or her spouse. In a no-fault divorce, neither party is blamed for the divorce. Today, every state recognizes no-fault divorce. A spouse may still decide to assert that the other party was at fault for causing the divorce in those states that consider fault when deciding how to divide marital assets and award spousal support.

DIVORCE PROCEEDINGS A divorce proceeding is commenced by a spouse filing a **petition for divorce** with the proper state court. The petition must contain required information, such as the names of the spouses, date and place of marriage, names of minor children, and the reason for the divorce. The petition must be served on the other spouse. This spouse then has a certain period of time (usually 20 to 30 days) to file an answer to the petition.

If the spouses do not reach a settlement of the issues involved in the divorce—such as property division, custody of the children, and spousal and child support—the case will go to trial. The parties are permitted to conduct discovery, which includes taking depositions and obtaining the production of documents. If the case goes to trial, each side is permitted to call witnesses, including expert witnesses (e.g., financial experts), to testify on his or her behalf. Both parties are also allowed to introduce evidence that will support their claims.

Many states require a certain waiting period from the date a divorce petition is filed to the date the court grants a divorce. A typical waiting period is six months. The public policy for this waiting period is to give the parties time for reconciliation. After the waiting period has passed, a court will enter a **decree of divorce**, which is a court order terminating the marriage. The parties are then free to marry again. The decree of divorce may be granted even if the other issues concerning the divorce, such as the division of property or support payments, have not yet been settled or tried.

If there is a showing that one partner is likely to injure the other spouse, a court may issue a **restraining order**. This places limitations on the ability of the dangerous partner to go near the innocent partner.

PRO SE DIVORCE In a *pro se* **divorce**, the parties do not have to hire lawyers to represent them but may represent themselves in the divorce proceeding. Most states permit *pro se*—commonly called "do-it-yourself"—divorces. If there are substantial assets at stake in the divorce, or if there are other complicated issues involving child custody, child support, or spousal support, the parties usually hire lawyers to represent them in the divorce proceeding.

SETTLEMENT AGREEMENT Approximately 90 percent of divorce cases are settled between the parties prior to trial. The parties often engage in negotiations to try to settle a divorce lawsuit in order to save the time and expense of a trial and to reach an agreement that is acceptable to each side. These negotiations are usually conducted between the parties with the assistance of each of their attorneys.

Some divorcing parties use mediation to try to reach a settlement of the issues involved in terminating their marriage. Some states have mandatory mediation before divorcing couples can use the court to try the case. In *mediation*, a neutral third party—often an attorney, a retired judge, or another party—acts as a *mediator* between the parties. A mediator is not empowered to make a decision but, instead, acts as a go-between and facilitator to try to help the parties reach an acceptable settlement of the issues. Mediation is often successful because it forces the parties to consider all facets of the case, even the position of the opposing side.

If a settlement is reached, a **settlement agreement** will be drafted, usually by the attorneys. After being signed by the parties, the settlement agreement will be presented to the court. The court will accept the terms of the settlement agreement if the judge believes that the settlement is fair and that the rights of the parties and minor children are properly taken care of. If a case is not settled, the case will then go to trial.

Division of Assets

Upon termination of a marriage, the parties may own certain assets, including property owned prior to marriage, gifts and inheritances received during marriage, and assets purchased with income earned during marriage. In most cases, the parties reach a settlement as to how these assets are to be divided. If no settlement agreement is reached, the court will order the division of assets.

Separate Property

In most states, each spouse's separate property will be awarded to the spouse who owns the separate property. **Separate property** includes property owned by a spouse prior to the marriage, as well as inheritances and gifts received during the marriage. In most states, upon the termination of a marriage, each spouse is awarded his or her separate property.

However, if separate property is commingled with marital property during the course of the marriage, or if the owner of the separate property changes title to the separate property by placing the other spouse's name on title to the property (e.g., real estate), the separate property is then considered marital property.

Marital Property

Marital property consists of property acquired during the course of the marriage using income earned by the spouses during the marriage and separate property that has been converted to marital property.

There are two major legal theories that different states adhere to when dividing marital assets upon the termination of a marriage. These are the theories of *equitable distribution* and *community property*.

EQUITABLE DISTRIBUTION   In states that follow the rule of **equitable distribution**, the court may order the *fair distribution* of property. The fair distribution of property does not necessarily mean the equal distribution of property. In determining the fair distribution of property, the court may consider factors such as:

- Length of the marriage
- Occupation of each spouse
- Standard of living during the marriage
- Wealth and income-earning ability of each spouse
- Which party is awarded custody of the children
- Health of the individuals
- Other factors relevant to the case

In most states, the house is usually awarded to the parent who is granted custody of the children. A court may order the house to be sold and the proceeds divided fairly between the individuals.

COMMUNITY PROPERTY   Under the doctrine of **community property**, all property acquired during the marriage using income earned during the marriage is considered marital property. It does not matter which spouse earned the income or which spouse earned the higher income. Money placed in pension funds, stock options, the value of businesses, the value of professional licenses, and such, are considered community property.

In community-property states, marital property is divided *equally* between the individuals. This does not necessarily mean that each piece of property is sold and the proceeds divided equally between the individuals. Usually each asset of the marital asset is valued using appraisers and expert witnesses. The court then awards the property to the spouses. If one spouse is awarded the house, the other spouse is awarded other property of equal value.

CONCEPT SUMMARY

Division of Marital Assets

LAW	DESCRIPTION
Equitable distribution	Marital property is fairly distributed. This does not necessarily mean equal distribution of the property.
Community property	Marital property is divided *equally* between the parties.

Division of Debts

Individuals often have debts that must be divided upon termination of the marriage. How these debts are divided depends on the type of debt and on state law. In most states, each spouse is personally liable for his or her own premarital debts, and the other spouse is not liable for these debts. This is because the debt was incurred prior to the marriage. Student loans are a good example of these types of debts.

Debts that are incurred during the marriage for necessities and other joint needs, including shelter, clothing, automobiles, medical expenses, and such, are **joint marital debts** and are the joint responsibility of each spouse. The court may equally distribute these debts upon termination of the marriage. Spouses are jointly liable for taxes incurred during their marriage. If a debt is not paid by the spouse to whom the court has distributed the debt, the third-party creditor may recover payment of the debt from the other spouse, however. This individual's only recourse is to recover the amount paid from his or her prior spouse.

Upon the termination of a marriage, it is wise for the individuals to notify prior creditors that they will no longer be responsible for the other's debts. This is particularly true if the individuals have joint credit cards.

In the following two cases, the courts had to decide if certain property was marital or separate property.

> Our legal system faces no theoretical dilemma but a single continuous problem: how to apply to ever changing conditions the never changing principles of freedom.
>
> Earl Warren

CASE 39.1
Marital Property

Giha v. Giha

609 A.2d 945,
Web 1992 R.I. Lexis 133
Supreme Court of Rhode Island

> **❝***Therefore, since the husband won the $2.4 million lottery prize during the existence of the parties' marriage, we conclude that the prize is a marital asset and is subject to the equitable-distribution statute.* **❞**
>
> —Judge Fay

Facts

Nagib Giha (husband) filed a complaint for divorce from Nelly Giha (wife) on the grounds of irreconcilable differences. On May 20, the parties reached an agreement for the disposition of their property which provided that they would divide equally the net proceeds from the sale of their marital assets. There was a statutory waiting period before the divorce was final. On December 25, the husband learned that he had won $2.4 million in the Massachusetts MEGABUCKS state lottery. The husband kept this fact secret. After the waiting period was over, the family court entered its final judgment on April 27 of the following year, legally severing the parties' marriage. Six months later, the husband claimed his lottery prize. When the ex-wife learned of the lottery winnings, she sued to recover her portion of the lottery prize. She alleged that the lottery prize was a marital asset because her husband had won it before their divorce was final. The trial court dismissed her complaint. The wife appealed.

Issue

Was the $2.4 million lottery prize personal property of the marital estate?

Language of the Court

We have established that the parties to a divorce action remain as husband and wife until the entry of the final decree of divorce. In the present case the husband won the lottery prize four months before the Family Court entered its final judgment. The parties remained as husband and wife until the entry of the final judgment. Because the parties' marriage remained in effect throughout the waiting period, so did the property rights each spouse had in the property acquired by the other spouse during that period. Therefore, since the husband won the $2.4 million lottery prize during the existence of the parties' marriage, we conclude that the prize is a marital asset and is subject to the equitable-distribution statute. We conclude that the parties to a divorce action have a continuing duty to provide information about changes in their financial condition until the entry of a final judgment of divorce.

Decision

The supreme court of Rhode Island held that the parties remained husband and wife until the entry of final judgment of divorce. Therefore, the lottery prize was a marital asset. The supreme court reversed the decision of the trial court and remanded the case for a division of the lottery prize.

Law & Ethics Questions

1. Why was a lottery prize considered marital property in this case?

2. **ETHICS** Did the husband act ethically in this case?

3. Can couples who are getting married agree on what property is marital property and what property is their separate property in advance of marriage? Explain.

Web Exercises

1. **WEB** For the complete opinion of this case, go to *www.prenhall.com/cheesemancases*.

2. **WEB** Visit the website of the supreme court of Rhode Island, at *www.courts.state.ri.us*.

3. **WEB** Use *www.google.com* to find an article that discusses a recent dispute about the ownership of lottery winnings. Read it.

CASE 39.2
Separate Property

In the Matter of the Marriage of Joyner

196 S.W.3d 883,
Web 2006 Tex. App. Lexis 5691 (2006)
Court of Appeals of Texas

> **"***Belinda Joyner filed for divorce from Thomas Joyner. The day after the final hearing, Thomas purchased a winning lottery ticket worth $2,080,000.***"**
>
> —Judge Carter

Facts

Belinda Ann Joyner filed for divorce from Thomas Stephen Joyner. The parties engaged in three mediation sessions to negotiate the settlement of property disputes. After the end of their third mediation session, the parties signed a mediated settlement agreement that delineated and partitioned their property. The lawyers for each of the parties also signed the agreement. Subsequently, the parties appeared in court for the final hearing, to argue a few personal property issues that remained, which included a ring and a broach that had been given to Thomas by his mother. The court clearly and explicitly decided which party should have ownership of these items. Although Belinda argued that she should have them because Thomas had made them gifts to their daughter earlier, the court awarded Thomas's mother's rings and broach to Thomas. The judge then stated: "You've elected not to make yourself a gift of these items to your daughter. And that's your prerogative. You have every legal right to do so. And it may be that—your divorce is granted—so I'll now say—your former wife has made all this up."

The day after the final hearing, Thomas purchased a lottery ticket. He won the lottery worth $2,080,000. The judge subsequently signed the final decree of divorce. Belinda filed a motion claiming that the divorce had never been finalized and that she was still married to Thomas because the judge had not yet signed the final decree of divorce. Belinda argued the $2,080,000 lottery winnings should be divided equally with her. Thomas alleged that the divorce was final and that the $2,080,000 was his separate property and was his and his only. The trial court agreed with Thomas and awarded him the money. Belinda appealed.

Issue

Was the $2,080,000 lottery winning separate property that Thomas may keep, or was it community property that needed to be divided equally between Thomas and Belinda?

Language of the Court

Belinda Joyner filed for divorce from Thomas Joyner. The day after the final hearing, Thomas purchased a winning lottery ticket worth $2,080,000. The issue in this case is whether the trial court's actions constituted an oral rendition of judgment on the Joyners' divorce. A judgment is rendered when the court makes an announcement, either in writing or orally in open court, of its decision on the matter submitted for adjudication. Once a judgment is rendered by oral pronouncement, the entry of a written judgment is purely a ministerial act. In order to be an official judgment, the trial court's oral pronouncement must indicate intent to render a full, final, and complete judgment at that point in time.

In this case, the words granting a divorce are undeniably there. The statement by the trial court was made in open court while officiating as the presiding judge after all evidence had been presented and in the presence of all parties and attorneys. During the process of ruling on some personal property items, the court then stated, "You've elected not to make yourself a gift of these items to your daughter. And that is your prerogative. You have every legal right to do so. And it may be that—your divorce is granted—so I'll now say—your former wife has made all this up." We interpret that as a clear statement granting the divorce. The trial court then referred to Belinda as "your former wife." Once a couple is divorced, they can no longer accumulate community property, for there is no longer a community.

Decision

The court of appeals held that the Joyners' divorce was final when the trial court made its oral pronouncement of such. The court of appeals affirmed the judgment of the trial court that awarded the $2,080,000 lottery prize to Thomas as his separate property.

Law & Ethics Questions

1. What is the difference between separate and community property? Explain.
2. **ETHICS** Did Melinda act ethically in this case?
3. **ETHICS** Did Thomas act ethically in this case?

Web Exercises

1. **WEB** For the complete opinion of this case, go to *www.prenhall.com/cheesemancases*.
2. **WEB** Visit the website of the court of appeals of Texas that decided this case, at *www.6thcoa.courts.state.tx.us*.
3. **WEB** Use *www.google.com* to find an article that discusses the difference between separate and marital property. Read it.

Spousal Support, Child Support, and Child Custody

When a marriage is terminated, spousal support and child support may be awarded. In addition, custody of the children must be decided. These issues are discussed in the following paragraphs.

Spousal Support

In some cases in which a marriage is terminated, a court may award **spousal support**—also called **alimony**—to one of the divorced spouses. The other divorced spouse is usually ordered to pay the alimony in monthly payments. The parties may agree to the amount of alimony to be paid. If an agreement is not reached, the court will determine whether the payment of alimony is warranted and, if so, the amount of alimony to be paid. In the past, alimony has usually been awarded to the female. Today, with the female often earning more than the male, the male has been awarded alimony in some cases.

Alimony is usually awarded for a specific period of time. This is called **temporary alimony**, or **rehabilitation alimony**. This alimony is designed to provide the receiving individual with payment for a limited time during which the individual can obtain the necessary education or job skills necessary to enter the job force. Alimony is also awarded in cases in which a parent, usually the female, is needed to care for a disabled child and must remain home to care for the child. The amount of alimony is based on the needs of the individual who will receive the alimony and the income and ability of the other individual to pay.

Spousal support payments usually terminate if the former spouse dies, remarries, or otherwise becomes self-sufficient. Spousal support awards may be modified by the court if circumstances change. This usually occurs if the paying individual loses his or her job or his or her income decreases, or if the receiving individual's income increases. A party wishing to have a spousal support award changed must petition the court to *modify* the award of spousal support.

The award of **permanent alimony**—sometimes called **lifetime alimony**—is usually awarded only if the individual to receive the alimony is of an older age and if that individual has been a homemaker who has little opportunity to obtain job skills to enter the workplace. Permanent alimony must be paid until the individual receiving it dies or remarries.

Child Support

The non-custodial parent is obligated to contribute to the expenses of paying for the financial support of his or her natural and adopted children. This includes a child's costs for food, shelter, clothing, medical expenses, and other necessities of life. This payment is called **child support**. The custodial and non-custodial parents may agree to the amount of child support. If they do not, the court will determine the amount of child support to be paid.

In awarding child support, the court may consider several factors, including the number of children, needs of the children, net income of the parents, standard of living of the children prior to termination of the marriage, any special medical or other needs of the children, and other factors the court deems relevant. The duty to pay child support usually continues until a child reaches the age of majority or graduates from high school, or emancipates himself or herself by voluntarily choosing to live on his or her own.

To help in the determination of child support, about half of the states have adopted formulas for computing the amount of child support. These formulas are usually based on a percentage of the non-custodial parent's income. A court is permitted to deviate from the formula if a child has special needs, such as if the child has a disability or requires special educational assistance.

An award of child support may be *modified* if conditions change. For example, an award of child support may be decreased if the non-custodial parent loses his or her job. The amount of child support may also be modified if the child's needs change, such as if the child needs special care because of a disability. The parent wishing to obtain modification of child support must petition the court to change the award of child support.

ETHICS SPOTLIGHT
Family Support Act

In the past, many non-custodial parents failed to pay child support when due. This often required long and expensive legal procedures by the custodial parent to obtain child support payments. To remedy this situation, the federal government enacted the **Family Support Act** [Public Law 100-485]. This federal law, effective in 1994, provides that all original or modified child support orders require automatic wage withholding from a non-custodial parent's income. The Family Support Act was designed primarily to prevent non-custodial parents from failing to pay required support payments.

Assume that a court order requires a non-custodial parent to pay 25 percent of his or her gross monthly income for child support. In this case, the court will order the non-custodial parent's employer to deduct this amount from that parent's income and send a check in that amount to the custodial parent. The non-custodial parent receives a check for the remainder of his or her income.

Law & Ethics Questions

1. **ETHICS** What is the goal of the federal Family Support Act? Explain.
2. **ETHICS** Do you think that there are many deadbeat parents who do not pay child support as ordered by the court?

Web Exercises

1. **WEB** Use *www.google.com* to find an article that discusses the problem of parents failing to pay court-ordered child support. Read it.
2. **WEB** Use *www.google.com* to find a recent case in which the Family Support Act was enforced.

Child Custody

When a couple terminates their marriage and they have minor unemancipated children, the issue of who is legally and physically responsible for raising the children must be decided, either by settlement or by the court. The legal term **custody** is used to describe who has legal responsibility for raising a child. Child custody is one of the most litigated issues of a divorcing couple.

Traditionally, the court almost always granted custody of a child to the mother. Today, with fathers taking a more active role in childrearing, and with many mothers working, this is not always the case. In child custody disputes where both parents want custody of a child, the courts will determine what is in the *best interests of the child* in awarding custody. The following are some of the factors that a court will consider:

- The ability of each parent to provide for the emotional needs of the child.
- The ability of each parent to provide for the needs of the child, such as education.
- The ability of each parent to provide for a stable environment for the child.
- The ability of each parent to provide for the special needs of a child if the child has a disability or requires special care.
- The desire of each parent to provide for the needs of the child.
- The wishes of the child. This factor is given more weight the older the child is.
- The religion of each parent.
- Other factors the court deems relevant.

The awarding of custody is not permanent. Custody may be altered by the court if circumstances change.

The parent who is awarded custody has **legal custody** of the child and is called the **custodial parent**. This usually includes physical custody of the child. The custodial parent has the right to make day-to-day decisions and major decisions concerning the child's education, religion, and other such matters.

The court will not award custody to a parent, and sometimes not to either parent, if it is in the child's best interest not to be awarded to a parent, or if there has been child abuse, or because of other such extenuating circumstances. In such cases, the court may award custody to other relatives, such as grandparents, or place the child in a foster home.

JOINT CUSTODY Most states now permit joint custody of a child. **Joint custody** means that both parents are responsible for making major decisions concerning the child, such as his or her education, religion, and other major matters.

Parents are sometimes awarded *joint physical custody* of the child as well. This means that the child spends a certain portion of time being raised by each parent. For example, the child may spend every other week with each parent, or the child may spend weekdays with one parent and weekends with the other parent. These arrangements are awarded only if the child's best interests are served, such as the child remains in the same school while in the physical custody of each parent.

VISITATION RIGHTS If the parents do not have joint custody of a child, the non-custodial parent is usually awarded **visitation rights**. This means that the non-custodial parent is given the right to visit the child for limited periods of time, as determined in a settlement agreement or by the court.

If the court is concerned about the safety of a child, the court may grant only supervised visitation rights to a non-custodial parent. This means that a court-appointed person must be present during the non-custodial parent's visitation with the child. This is usually done if there has been a history of child abuse or there is a strong possibility that the non-custodial parent may kidnap the child.

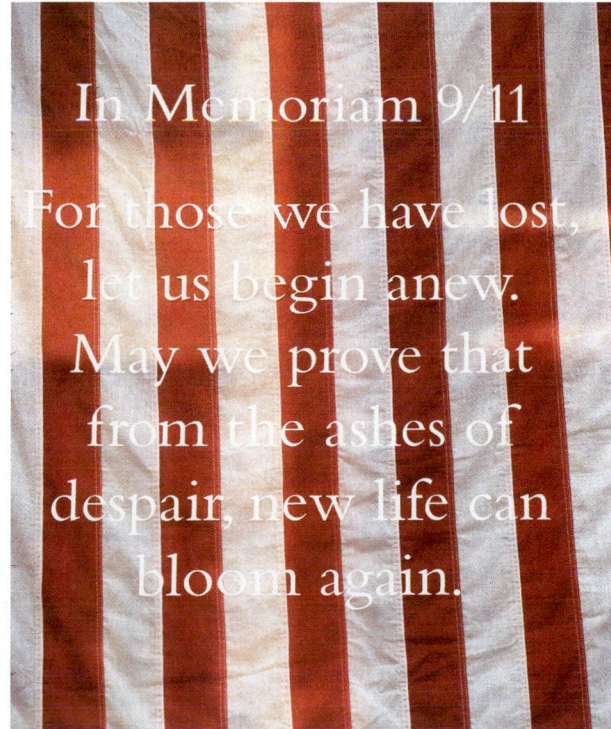

New York City

It is wise for a person to have a valid will that designates how his or her property will be distributed upon his or her death.

Wills

A **will** is a declaration of how a person wants his or her property to be distributed upon his or her death. It is a testamentary deposition of property. The person who makes the will is called the **testator** or **testatrix**. The persons designated in the will to receive the testator's property are called **beneficiaries** (see Exhibit 39.1).

EXHIBIT 39.1

Parties to a Will

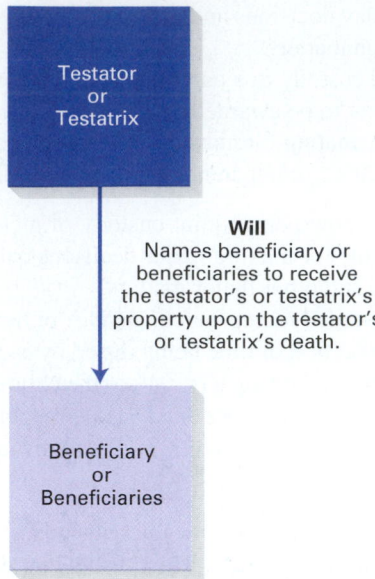

Requirements for Making a Will

Every state has a **Statute of Wills** that establishes the requirements for making a valid will in that state. These requirements are:

- *Testamentary capacity.* The testator must have been of legal age and "sound mind" when the will was made. The courts determine **testamentary capacity** on a case-by-case basis. The legal age for executing a will is set by state statute.
- *Writing.* Wills must be in writing to be valid (except for dying declarations, discussed later in this chapter). The writing may be formal or informal. Although most wills are typewritten, they can be handwritten (see the later discussion of holographic wills). The writing may be on legal paper, other paper, scratch paper, envelopes, napkins, or the like. A will may incorporate other documents by reference.
- *Testator's signature.* Wills must be signed. Most jurisdictions require the **testator's signature** to appear at the end of the will. This step is to prevent fraud that could occur if someone added provisions to the will below the testator's signature. For example, courts have held that initials (*R.K.H.*), a nickname (*Buffy*), title (*mother*), and even an *X* is a valid signature on a will if it can be proven that the testator intended it to be his or her signature.

Attestation by Witnesses

Wills must be **attested** to by mentally competent witnesses. Although state law varies, most states require two or three witnesses. The witnesses do not have to reside in the jurisdiction in which the testator is domiciled. Most jurisdictions stipulate that interested parties (e.g., a beneficiary under the will, the testator's attorney) cannot be witnesses. If an interested party has attested to a will, state law either voids any clauses that benefit such person or voids the entire will.

Witnesses usually sign a will following the signature of the testator. These signatures are called the **attestation clause**. Most jurisdictions require that each witness attest to the will in the presence of the other witnesses.

A will that meets the requirements of the Statute of Wills is called a **formal will**. A sample will is shown in Exhibit 39.2.

Codicil

A will cannot be amended by merely striking out existing provisions and adding new ones. Adding **codicils** is the legal way to change an existing will. A codicil is a separate document that must be executed with the same formalities as a will. In addition, it must incorporate by reference the will it is amending. The codicil and the will are then read as one instrument.

EXHIBIT 39.2

Will

Last Will and Testament of Florence Winthorpe Blueblood

I, FLORENCE WINTHORPE BLUEBLOOD, presently residing at Boston, County of Suffolk, Massachusetts, being of sound and disposing mind and memory, hereby make, publish, and declare this to be my Last Will and Testament.

FIRST. I hereby revoke any and all Wills and Codicils previously made by me.

SECOND. I direct that my just debts and funeral expenses be paid out of my Estate as soon as practicable after my death.

THIRD. I am presently married to Theodore Hannah Blueblood III.

FOURTH. I hereby nominate and appoint my husband as the Personal Representative of this my Last Will and Testament. If he is unable to serve as Personal Representative, then I nominate and appoint Mildred Yardly Winthorpe as Personal Representative of this my Last Will and Testament. I direct that no bond or other security be required to be posted by my Personal Representative.

FIFTH. I hereby nominate and appoint my husband as Guardian of the person and property of my minor children. In the event that he is unable to serve as Guardian, then I nominate and appoint Mildred Yardly Winthorpe Guardian of the person and property of my minor children. I direct that no bond or other security be required to be posted by any Guardian herein.

SIXTH. I give my Personal Representative authority to exercise all the powers, rights, duties, and immunities conferred upon fiduciaries under law with full power to sell, mortgage, lease, invest, or reinvest all or any part of my Estate on such terms as he or she deems best.

SEVENTH. I hereby give, devise, and bequeath my entire estate to my husband, except for the following specific bequests:

I give my wedding ring to my daughter, Hillary Smythe Blueblood.
I give my baseball card collection to my son, Theodore Hannah Blueblood IV.
In the event that either my above-named daughter or son predeceases me, then and in that event, I give, devise, and bequeath my deceased daughter's or son's bequest to my husband.

EIGHTH. In the event that my husband shall predecease me, then and in that event, I give, devise and bequeath my entire estate, with the exception of the bequests in paragraph SEVENTH, to my beloved children or grandchildren surviving me, per stirpes.

NINTH. In the event I am not survived by my husband or any children or grandchildren, then and in that event, I give, devise, and bequeath my entire estate to Harvard University.

IN WITNESS WHEREOF, I, Florence Winthorpe Blueblood, the Testatrix, sign my name to this Last Will and Testament this 3rd day of January, 2006.

Florence Winthorpe Blueblood
(Signature)

Signed, sealed, published and declared by the above-named Testatrix, as and for her Last Will and Testament, in the presence of us, who at her request, in her presence, and in the presence of one another, have hereunto subscribed our names as attesting witnesses, the day and year last written above.

Witness	Address
Norm Peterson	100 Beacon Hill Rd Boston, Massachusetts
Clifford Claven	200 Minute Man Drive Boston, Massachusetts
Rebecca Howe	300 Charles River Place Boston, Massachusetts

Revoking a Will

A will may be **revoked** by acts of the testator. A will is revoked if the testator intentionally burns, tears, obliterates, or otherwise destroys it. A properly executed **subsequent will** revokes a prior will if it specifically states that it is the testator's intention to do so. If the second will does not expressly revoke the prior will, the wills are read together. If any will provisions are inconsistent, the provisions in the second will control.

Wills can also be revoked by operation of law. For example, divorce or annulment revokes disposition of property to the former spouse under a will. The remainder of the will is valid. The birth of a child after a will has been executed does not revoke the will but does entitle the child to receive his or her share of the parents' estate, as determined by state statute.

INTERNET AND TECHNOLOGY
Videotaped Wills

Many acrimonious will contests involve written wills. The contesters allege such things as mental incapacity of the testator at the time the will was made, undue influence, fraud, or duress. Although a written will speaks for itself, the mental capacity of the testator and the voluntariness of his or her actions cannot be determined from the writing alone.

To prevent unwarranted will contests, a testator can use a **videotaped will** to supplement a written will. Videotaping a will that can withstand challenges by disgruntled relatives and alleged heirs involves a certain amount of planning.

The following procedures should be followed. A written will should be prepared to comply with the state's Statute of Wills. The video session should not begin until after the testator has become familiar with the document. The video should begin with the testator reciting the will verbatim. Next, the lawyer should ask the testator questions to demonstrate the testator's sound mind and understanding of the implications of his or her actions. The execution ceremony—the signing of the will by the testator and the attestation by the witnesses—should be the last segment on the film. The videotape should then be stored in a safe place.

With the testator's actions crystallized on videotape, a judge or jury will be able to determine the testator's mental capacity at the time the will was made and the voluntariness of his or her **testamentary gifts**. In addition, fraudulent competing wills will fall in the face of such proof.

Law & Ethics Questions

1. What are the purposes of having a will signing videotaped and recorded?

2. **ETHICS** Does having a will signing videotaped prevent unethical conduct in the future? Explain.

Web Exercises

1. **WEB** Use *www.google.com* to find an article that discusses a testator or testatrix having his or her will signing videotaped. Read it.

2. **WEB** Use *www.google.com* to find a service in your area that will videotape a will signing.

Joint and Mutual Wills

If two or more testators execute the same instrument as their will, the document is called a **joint will**. A joint will may be held invalid as to one testator but not the other(s).

Mutual wills, or **reciprocal wills**, arise where two or more testators execute separate wills that make testamentary dispositions of their property to each other on the condition that the survivor leave the remaining property on his or her death as agreed by the testators. The wills are usually separate instruments with reciprocal terms. Because of their contractual nature, mutual wills cannot be unilaterally revoked after one of the parties has died.

Special Types of Wills

The law recognizes several types of wills that do not meet all the requirements discussed previously. The special types of wills admitted by the courts include:

- *Holographic wills.* **Holographic wills** are entirely handwritten and signed by the testator. The writing may be in ink, pencil, crayon, or some other medium. Many states recognize the validity of such wills even though they are not witnessed.
- *Nuncupative wills.* **Nuncupative wills** are oral wills that are made before witnesses. Such wills are usually valid only if they are made during the testator's last illness. They are sometimes called **dying declarations**, or **deathbed wills**.

Exhibit 39.3 sets forth excerpts from the will of Anna Nicole Smith.

Simultaneous Deaths

Sometimes people who would inherit property from each other die simultaneously. If it is impossible to determine who died first, the question becomes one of inheritance. The **Uniform Simultaneous Death Act**, a model act adopted by many states, provides that each deceased person's property is distributed as though he or she survived.

Example Suppose a husband and wife make wills that leave their entire estate to each other. Assume that the husband and wife are killed simultaneously in an airplane crash. Here, the husband's property would go to his relatives, and the wife's property would go to her relatives.

EXHIBIT 39.3

Excerpts from the Will of Anna Nicole Smith

WILL OF VICKIE LYNN MARSHALL

I, VICKIE LYNN MARSHALL, also known as Vickie Lynn Smith, and Vickie Lynn Hogan, and Anna Nicole Smith, a resident of Los Angeles county, California, declare that this is my Will. I revoke all prior Wills and Codicils. I hereby dispose of all property that I am entitled to dispose of by will and exercise all general powers of appointment that I am entitled to exercise. I have not entered into a contract to make or not revoke a Will.

ARTICLE I FAMILY DECLARATIONS AND STATUTORY DISINHERITANCES

I am unmarried. I have one child DANIEL WAYNE SMITH. I have no predeceased children nor predeceased children leaving issue.

Except as otherwise provided in this will, I have intentionally omitted to provide for my spouse and other heirs, including future spouses and children and other descendants now living and those hereafter born or adopted, as well as existing and future stepchildren and foster children.

ARTICLE II DISPOSITION OF ESTATE

All of the property of my estate (the "residue"), after payment of any taxes or other expenses of my estate as provided below, including property subject to a power of appointment exercised hereby, shall be distributed to HOWARD STERN, Esq., to hold in trust for my child under such terms as he and a court of competent jurisdiction may declare, such that my children are distributed sufficient sums for the heath, education, and support according to their accustomed manner of living from either the income or principal of the trust until age twenty-five; and are at that time given one-third of all of the income of the trust and one-third of the principal of the trust as then constituted; and at thirty are given one-half of the income from the trust and one-half of the principal of the trust as then constituted; and at thirty-five are given all of the principal of the trust. If, in the discretion of the Trustee, the amount remaining in the Trust is too small to efficiently administer, he may give all of the corpus of the trust to my child at once.

Law & Ethics Questions

1. Anna Nicole Smith had another child after this will was made, but she did not change this will. Why do you think Anna Nicole Smith disinherited future children?

2. **ETHICS** Why do you think Anna Nicole Smith provided that her assets would be distributed to her son in increments, with the last distribution to be made when he reached the age of 35? Was this good planning?

Web Exercises

1. **WEB** Use *www.google.com* to find the will of Anna Nicole Smith online.

2. **WEB** Use *www.google.com* to find a recent article concerning the court battle for the assets of Anna Nicole Smith's estate. Read it.

Undue Influence

A will may be found to be invalid if it was made as a result of **undue influence** on the testator. Undue influence can be inferred from the facts and circumstances surrounding the making of a will.

Example If an 85-year-old woman leaves all her property to the lawyer who drafted her will and ignores her blood relatives, the court is likely to presume undue influence.

Undue influence is difficult to prove by direct evidence, but it may be proved by circumstantial evidence. The court considers elements such as the following to determine the presence of undue influence include:

- The benefactor and beneficiary are involved in a relationship of confidence and trust.
- The will contains substantial benefit to the beneficiary.
- The beneficiary caused or assisted in effecting execution of the will.
- There was an opportunity to exert influence.
- The will contains an unnatural disposition of the testator's property.
- The bequests constitute a change from a former will.
- The testator was highly susceptible to the undue influence.

> The power of making a will is an instrument placed in the hands of individuals for the prevention of private calamity.
>
> Jeremy Bentham
> *Principles of the Civil Code (1748)*

In the following two cases, the court had to decide if there had been undue influence in a will contest.

CASE 39.3
Undue Influence

Medlock v. Mitchell

Web 2006 Ark. App. Lexis 320 (2006)
Court of Appeals of Arkansas

> **"** *There must be a malign influence resulting from fear, coercion, or any other cause which deprives the testator of his free agency in disposing of his property.* **"**

— Judge Hart

Facts

Richard Mitchell executed a will leaving his estate equally to two of his children, Mark and Michelle. Four months later, Richard married Glenda Kay. On the same day, Richard created a revocable living trust. The trust was to terminate 10 years after Richard's death. Upon termination of the trust, the trust corpus was to be distributed to Mark and Michelle. Five years later, Richard was diagnosed with terminal lung cancer. Three months later, he executed another will, leaving his entire $3.5 million estate to Kay. Richard died two months later.

Michelle filed her father's earlier will for probate. Kay filed Richard's most recent will for probate, arguing that Richard's earlier will had been revoked by the most recent will. Michelle responded that her father's most recent will was invalid because of Richard's incompetence at the time it was executed and was a product of undue influence by Kay. Kay died pending trial, and her son Jerald pursued the lawsuit. The trial court found that there was a confidential relationship between Richard and Kay, and therefore the burden shifted to Jerald to prove that there was no undue influence in the making of Richard's last will.

After hearing numerous witnesses, the trial court held that Jerald had not rebutted the presumption of undue influence, and judgment was ordered to probate the earlier will leaving all of Richard's property to his children Mark and Michelle. Jerald appealed.

Issue

Has Jerald rebutted the presumption of undue influence?

Language of the Court

Whether two individuals have a confidential relationship is a question of fact. We cannot say that the trial court clearly erred in finding under the facts of the case that a confidential relationship existed between Kay and Richard, either because of their confidential relationship as husband and wife and Richard's terminal illness or because Kay had Richard's durable power of attorney. It is the combination of both confidential relationships that gives rise to a presumption of undue influence in the present case. We affirm on this point.

It is not enough that a confidential relationship exist in order to void a testamentary instrument; there must be a malign influence resulting from fear, coercion, or any other cause which deprives the testator of his free agency in disposing of his property. Undue influence on a testator may be inferred from the

facts and circumstances. First, we consider the fact that Richard was in the hospital in a weakened state at the time the instruments were prepared. This could indicate undue influence. According to Michelle, during Richard's hospitalization, Kay indicated that she wanted Richard's will changed, suggesting that Kay was the driving force behind the changes. By her own testimony, Kay admitted to being present when Richard discussed the will and amendments to the trust with the Attorney Pierces, another possible sign of undue influence. She was also present at the execution of the will and the trust amendments, another factor indicating undue influence if other factors are present.

A will may also be invalidated for undue influence under certain circumstances where a person makes false statements and accusations to a testator concerning the natural objects of his bounty. Here, the trial court specifically found that Kay's statements to Richard that Mark broke into the office and wanted Richard taken off of life support precipitated the changes to the will and trust.

Decision

The court of appeals held that given the facts of the case, Jerald was required to rebut the presumption of Kay's undue influence, which he failed to do. The court of appeals affirmed the judgment of the trial court that enforced Richard's prior will that left his estate to his two children, Mark and Michelle.

Law & Ethics Questions

1. What does the doctrine of undue influence provide? Explain.

2. What is the result if a confidential relationship is found between the person making a will and the beneficiary of the will? Explain. Is this important?

3. **ETHICS** Do you think Kay acted ethically in this case?

Web Exercises

1. **WEB** For the complete opinion of this case, go to *www.prenhall.com/cheesemancases*.

2. **WEB** Visit the website of the court of appeals of Arkansas, at *http://courts.state.ar.us/*.

3. **WEB** Go to *www.google.com* to find a recent situation involving undue influence in the making of a will.

C A S E **39.4**

Undue Influence

In re Estate of James Allen Hendrix

Web 2006 Wash. App. Lexis 1526 (2006)
Court of Appeals of Washington

> **❝***The evidence to establish undue influence must be clear, cogent, and convincing. The burden on a will contestant to prove undue influence is thus daunting.***❞**

—Judge Coleman

Facts

James Allen Hendrix (Al) and Lucille Jeter were married, and their child Jimi was born in November 1942. Another son, Leon, was born to Lucille in January 1948. Although Al was listed on Leon's birth certificate as his father, Al told many people that Leon was not his biological child. Al and Lucille divorced in 1951, and Al was granted custody of Jimi and Leon. Leon was placed in a series of foster homes but continued contact with Al and Jimi. Al worked as a gardener, supporting his family on modest means. Al had dropped out of high school in the seventh grade. In 1966, Al married Ayako Jinka, who was known as June. June had five children from another marriage. One of these children, named Janie, was 5 years old when Al married June.

In 1960, at the age of 18, Jimi joined the Armed Forces and never lived at home again. Jimi played the electric rock guitar. Jimi was discharged from the military, and after several years, he formed the Jimi Hendrix Experience. In 1967, the rock band rocketed to international stardom behind Jimi's innovative music and dazzling showmanship. In 1968, Jimi met June and Janie for the first time. After a brief four-year reign as a superstar, Jimi died in 1970 of a drug overdose. Jimi Hendrix remains a music icon because of his excellent guitar playing and electrifying performances. Jimi died without a will, so his entire estate was distributed under New York's intestate statute to Al, since Lucille had predeceased Jimi. The current and future value of Jimi's music and legacy were worth between $50 and $100 million.

Leon married in 1974, and he and his wife had six children. Leon separated from his wife. Leon had not been steadily employed since 1979, but worked intermittently as a musician and an artist. Leon had a history of drug abuse. In 1999, Al and Leon reached an agreement that required Leon to undergo a 90-day inpatient drug treatment program. Leon was dismissed from the program because of a conflict with his counselor.

In 1993, Al signed a will, drafted by attorney Jonathan Whetzel, naming June, Leon, Janie, and Leon's and Janie's respective children beneficiaries. In 1994, Al executed a new will, also drafted by attorney Whetzel. This will left 38 percent of Al's estate to June, 38 percent to Jamie, and 24 percent to Leon and his children. In the summer of 1996, two of Leon's children were charged with unrelated criminal felony offenses. During this time, Leon hired an attorney to represent him. Leon alleged that Al had breached a prior promise to give his children $7000,000, and that he would go to the media with the story unless Al paid him $3 million.

In April 1997, Al signed a codicil to his will, with the following result: Janie's share of Al's estate increased from 38 percent to 47.72 percent, Leon's share dropped from 24 percent to 0, and other beneficiaries were left the rest of his estate. In April 2002, Al died after a long illness. On the day Al died, Leon's lawyer sent a letter to Al's lawyers, threatening legal action relating to Al's estate. Four months later, Leon filed lawsuits against Janie and Al's estate, alleging that Janie had engaged in undue influence over Al and that Al's codicil should be voided.

The trial court held that there was a presumption of undue influence but that Janie had presented factual evidence that rebutted this presumption. Leon appealed.

Issue

Did Janie engage in undue influence over Al when he signed the codicil to his will?

Language of the Court

To vitiate a will there must be something more than mere influence. There must have been an undue influence at the time of the testamentary act, which interfered with the free will of the testator and prevented the exercise of judgment and choice. The evidence to establish undue influence must be clear, cogent, and convincing. The burden on a will contestant to prove undue influence is thus daunting.

Certain facts and circumstances bearing upon the execution of a will may be of such nature and force as to raise a suspicion, varying in its strength, against the validity of the testamentary instrument. The most important of such facts are (1) that the beneficiary occupied a fiduciary or confidential relation to the testator; (2) that the beneficiary actively participated in the preparation or procurement of the will; and (3) that the beneficiary received an unusually or unnaturally large part of the estate. Added to these may be other considerations, such as the age or condition of health and mental vigor of the testator, the nature or degree of relationship between the testator and the beneficiary, the opportunity for exerting an undue influence, and the naturalness or unnaturalness of the will.

The combination of facts shown by the evidence in a particular case may be of such suspicious nature as to raise a presumption of undue influence and, in the absence of rebuttal evidence, may even be sufficient to overthrow the will. We believe and hold that the facts in this case did raise a presumption of undue influence, and that the presumption was of such strength as to impose upon the proponent the duty to come forward with evidence sufficient at least to balance the scales and restore the equilibrium of evidence touching the validity of the will.

The trial court found that there was enough evidence to raise the presumption of undue influence, but that Janie successfully rebutted the presumption by providing evidence of ample countervailing justifications for Al not to have provided for Leon and Leon's children in his will. There is evidence in the record that Al met with his estate planning attorneys alone many times, and the attorneys explained the estate plan to Al numerous times. Al signed his will on videotape, acknowledging that he was not leaving a bequest to Leon other than Jimi's gold record and that he was very satisfied with his will. Janie was not present during this signing and had not been present during most of the will drafting meetings. All of these provide substantial evidence to support the court's conclusion that Janie successfully rebutted the presumption of undue influence.

Decision

The court of appeals affirmed the trial court's judgment which held that Jamie had rebutted the presumption of undue influence. The court of appeals held that Al's will and codicil were valid.

Law & Ethics Questions

1. Define *undue influence*. Is it an easy concept to define?

2. **ETHICS** Do you think there was undue influence in this case? Explain.

3. **ETHICS** Were there significant reasons Al would disinherit his son Leon?

4. What would have been the result in this case if the court had voided Al's codicil? Explain.

Web Exercises

1. **WEB** For the complete opinion of this case, go to *www.prenhall.com/cheesemancases*.

2. **WEB** Use *www.google.com* to find a video clip of the music of Jimi Hendrix.

3. **WEB** Visit the website of the court of appeals of Washington, at *www.courts.wa.gov/courts*.

4. **WEB** Use *www.google.com* to find an article that discusses the life of Jimi Hendrix. Read it.

Probate

When a person dies, his or her property must be collected, debts and taxes paid, and the remainder of the estate distributed to the beneficiaries of the will or the heirs under the state intestacy statute. This process is called **settlement of the estate**, or **probate**. The process and procedures for settling an estate are governed by state statute. A specialized state court, called the **probate court**, usually supervises the administration and settlement of an estate.

A *personal representative* must be appointed to administer an estate during its settlement phase. If the testator's will names the personal representative, that person is called an *executor* or *executrix*. If no one is named or if the decedent dies intestate, the court will appoint an *administrator* or *administratrix*. Usually, this party is a relative of the deceased or a bank. An attorney is usually appointed to help administer the estate and to complete the probate.

Testamentary Gifts

A gift of real estate by will is called a **devise**. A gift of personal property by will is called a **bequest**, or **legacy**. Gifts in wills can be specific, general, or residuary:

- *Specific gifts.* **Specific gifts** in a will are gifts of specifically named pieces of property.

  Example A gift of a ring, a boat, or a piece of real estate in a will is a specific gift.

- *General gifts.* **General gifts** are gifts that do not identify the specific property from which the gift is to be made.

  Example A gift of $100,000 to a named beneficiary is an example of a general gift. The cash can come from any source in the decedent's estate.

- *Residuary gifts.* **Residuary gifts** are gifts that are established by a **residuary clause** in a will.

  Example A clause in a will that states "I give my daughter the rest, remainder, and residual of my estate" is an example of a residuary gift. This clause means that any portion of the estate left after the debts, taxes, and specific and general gifts have been paid belongs to the decedent's daughter.

A person who inherits property under a will or an intestacy statute takes the property subject to all the outstanding claims against it (e.g., liens, mortgages). A person can **renounce** an inheritance and often does where the liens or mortgages against the property exceed the value of the property.

Lineal Descendants

A testator's will can state that property is to be left to his or her **lineal descendants** (children, grandchildren, great-grandchildren, etc.) either *per stirpes* or *per capita*. The differences between these two methods are discussed in the following paragraphs.

PER STIRPES DISTRIBUTION Pursuant to ***per stirpes* distribution**, the lineal descendants *inherit by representation of their parent*; that is, they split what their deceased parent would have received. If their parent is not deceased, they receive nothing.

Example Suppose Anne dies without a surviving spouse, and she had three children, Bart, Beth, and Bruce. Bart, who survives his mother, has no children. Beth has one child, Carla, and they both survive Anne. Bruce, who predeceased his mother, had two children, Clayton and Cathy; and Cathy, who predeceased Anne, had two children, Deborah and Dominic, both of whom survive Anne.

If Anne leaves her estate to her lineal descendants *per stirpes*, Bart and Beth each get one-third, Carla receives nothing because Beth is alive, Clayton gets one-sixth, and Deborah and Dominic each get one-twelfth. See Exhibit 39.4.

EXHIBIT 39.4

Per Stirpes Distribution

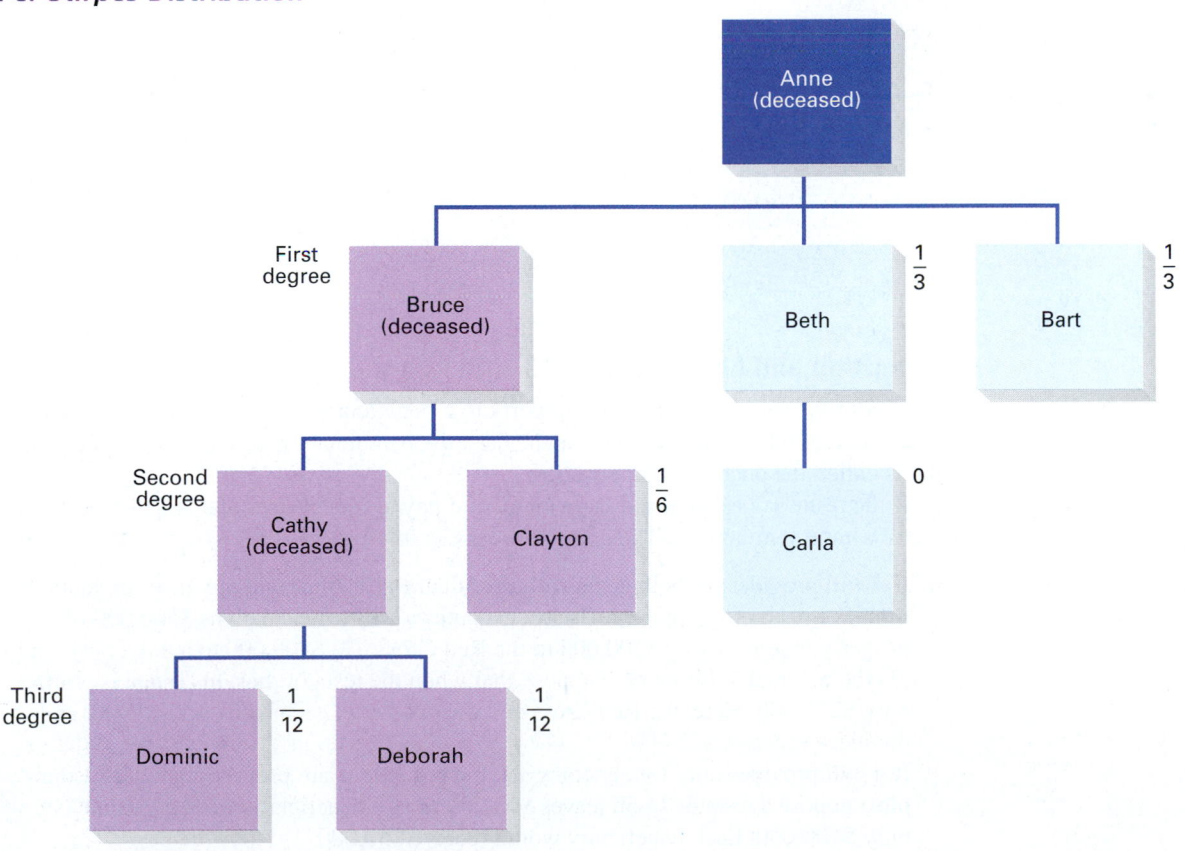

PER CAPITA **DISTRIBUTION** Pursuant to ***per capita*** distribution, the lineal descendants *equally share the property of the estate.* That is, children of the testator share equally with grandchildren, great-grandchildren, and so forth.

Example Suppose the facts are the same as in the previous example, except that Anne leaves her estate to her lineal descendants *per capita.* In this case, all the surviving lineal descendants—Bart, Beth, Carla, Clayton, Deborah, and Dominic—share equally in the estate. That is, they each get one-sixth of Anne's estate. See Exhibit 39.5.

EXHIBIT 39.5

Per Capita Distribution

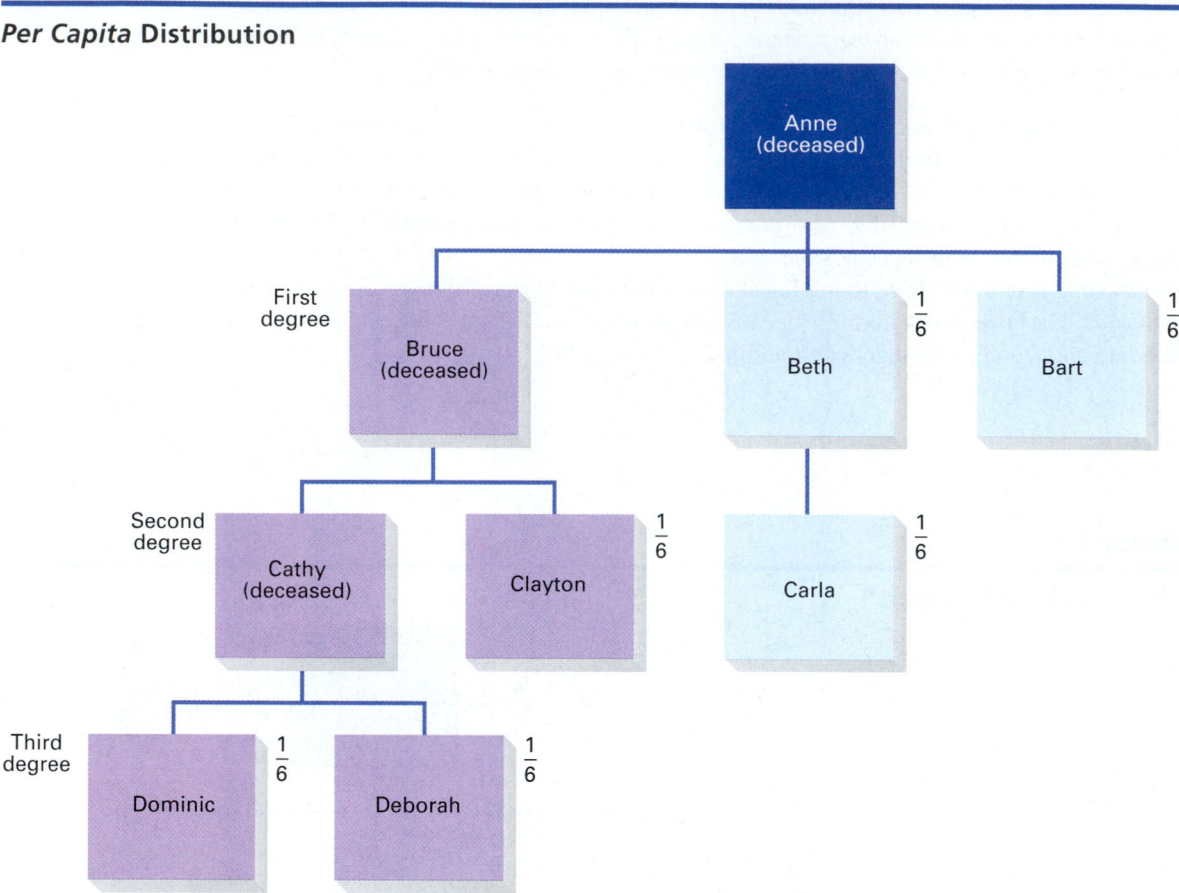

Ademption and Abatement

If a testator leaves a specific gift of property to a beneficiary, but the property is no longer in the estate of the testator when he or she dies, the beneficiary receives nothing. This doctrine is called the doctrine of **ademption**.

If the testator's estate is not large enough to pay all the devises and bequests, the doctrine of **abatement** applies. The doctrine works as follows:

■ If a will provides for both general and residuary gifts, the residuary gifts are abated first. For example, suppose a testator executes a will when he owns $500,000 of property that leaves (1) $100,000 to the Red Cross, (2) $100,000 to a university, and (3) the residual to his niece. Suppose that when the testator dies, his estate is worth only $225,000. Here, the Red Cross and the university each receive $100,000, and the niece receives $25,000.

■ If a will provides only for general gifts, the reductions are proportionate. For example, suppose a testator's will leaves $75,000 to two beneficiaries, but the estate is only $100,000. Each beneficiary would receive $50,000.

In the following case, the court held that a specific bequest failed because of ademption.

CASE 39.5
Ademption

Opperman v. Anderson

782 S.W.2d 8,
Web 1989 Tex.App. Lexis 3175
Court of Appeals of Texas

> **"** *The intention of the testator must be ascertained at the time the will was executed and from the four corners of the will.* **"**
>
> —Judge Biery

Facts

Ethel M. Ramchissel executed a will that made the following bequests: (1) one-half of the stock she owned in Pabst Brewing Company (Pabst) to Mary Lee Anderson, (2) all of the stock she owned in Houston Natural Gas Corporation (Houston Natural Gas) to Ethel Baker and others (Baker), and (3) the residual and remainder of her estate to Boysville, Inc.

Later, the following events happened. First, in response to an offer by G. Heilman Brewing Company to purchase Pabst, Ramchissel sold all of her Pabst stock and placed the cash proceeds in a bank account to which no other funds were added. Second, pursuant to a merger agreement between Internorth, Inc., and Houston Natural Gas, Ramchissel converted her Houston Natural Gas stock to cash and placed the cash in a bank account to which no other funds were added. When Ramchissel died about 3½ years after making her will, her will was admitted into probate. The probate court awarded the money in the two bank accounts to Anderson and Baker, respectively. An appeal ensued.

Issue

Were the bequests to Anderson and Baker specific bequests that were adeemed when the stock was sold?

Language of the Court

Ademption is the doctrine by which a specific bequest becomes inoperative because of the disappearance of its subject matter from a testator's estate during his or her lifetime. A specific bequest is one comprised of specific articles of the testator's estate distinguished from all others of the same kind. Because ademption applies only to specific bequests, courts must make a preliminary determination of whether a bequest is specific or general. The intention of the testator must be ascertained at the time the will was executed and from the four corners of the will. We conclude that Ramchissel clearly intended the gifts of stock at issue be specific bequests subject to ademption. We find that ademption occurred when specific shares of stock described were sold prior to the testatrix's death.

Decision

The court of appeals held that the bequests of stock at issue in this case were specific bequests that were adeemed when the stock was sold and converted to cash. Therefore, the cash proceeds of these stock sales did not pass to Anderson and Baker but instead passed to Boysville, Inc., pursuant to the residuary clause of Ramchissel's will.

Law & Ethics Questions

1. Should the doctrine of ademption be recognized by law? What other solution would there be?

2. **ETHICS** Do you think the result reached in this case was fair or what Ramchissel intended?

3. Explain the difference between ademption and abatement.

Web Exercises

1. **WEB** For the compete opinion of this case, go to *www.prenhall.com/cheesemancases*.

2. **WEB** Visit the website of the court of appeals of Texas that decided this case, at *www.4thcoa.courts.state.tx.us*.

3. **WEB** Using *www.google.com*, find an article about a will contest alleging undue influence. Read it.

Intestate Succession

If a person dies without a will—that is, **intestate**—or if his or her will fails for some legal reason, the property is distributed to his or her relatives pursuant to the state's **intestacy statute**.

Relatives who receive property under these statutes are called **heirs**. Although intestacy statutes differ from state to state, the general rule is that the deceased's real property is distributed according to the intestacy statute of the state where the real property is located, and the deceased's personal property is distributed according to the intestacy statute of the state where the deceased had his or her permanent residence.

Intestacy statutes usually leave the deceased's property to his or her heirs in this order: spouse, children, lineal heirs (e.g., grandchildren, parents, brothers and sisters), collateral heirs (e.g., aunts, uncles, nieces, nephews), and other next of kin (e.g., cousins). If the deceased has no surviving relatives, then the deceased's property **escheats** (goes) to the state. In-laws do not inherit under most intestacy statutes. If a child dies before his or her parents, the child's spouse does not receive the child's inheritance.

To avoid the distribution of an estate as provided in an intestacy statute, a person should have a properly written, signed, and witnessed will that distributes the estate property as the testator wishes.

CONCEPT SUMMARY

Comparison of Dying With and Without a Valid Will

SITUATION	PARTIES WHO RECEIVE DECEASED'S PROPERTY
Deceased dies with a valid will	Beneficiaries named in the will.
Deceased dies without a valid will	Heirs set forth in the applicable state intestacy statute. If there are no heirs, the deceased's property escheats to the state.

Trusts

> Disinherit: The prankish action of the ghosts in cutting the pockets out of trousers.
>
> Frank McKinney Hubbard
> *The Roycroft Dictionary (1923)*

A **trust** is a legal arrangement under which one person (the **settlor**, **trustor**, or **transferor**) delivers and transfers legal title to property to another person, bank, or other entity (the **trustee**), to be held and used for the benefit of a third person or entity (the **beneficiary**). The property and assets held in trust are called the **trust corpus**, or **trust res**. The trust has legal title to the trust corpus, and the beneficiary has equitable title. Unlike wills, trusts are not public documents, so property can be transferred in privacy. Exhibit 39.6 shows the parties to a trust.

EXHIBIT 39.6

Trust

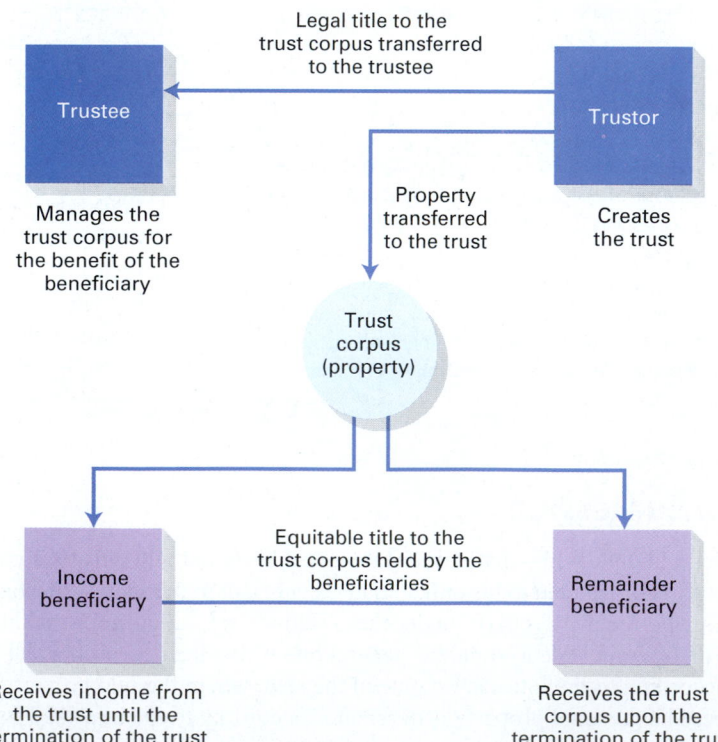

A trust can be created and becomes effective during a trustor's lifetime, or it can be created during a trustor's lifetime to become effective upon the trustor's death.

During the existence of a trust, the trustee collects money owed to the trust, pays taxes and necessary expenses of the trust, makes investment decisions, pays the income to the income beneficiary, and keeps necessary records of transactions.

Beneficiaries

Trusts often provide that any trust income is to be paid to a person or an entity called the **income beneficiary**. The person or entity to receive the trust corpus upon the termination of the trust is called the **remainder beneficiary**. The income beneficiary and the remainder beneficiary can be the same person or different persons. The designated beneficiary can be any identifiable person, animal (such as a pet), charitable organization, or other institution or cause that the settlor chooses. There can be multiple income and remainder beneficiaries. An entire class of persons—for example, "my grandchildren"—can be named.

A trust can allow the trustee to invade (use) the trust corpus for certain purposes. These purposes can be named (e.g., "for the beneficiary's college education"). The trust agreement usually specifies how the receipts and expenses of the trust are to be divided between the income beneficiary and the remainder beneficiary.

Generally, the trustee has broad management powers over the trust property. Thus the trustee can invest the trust property to preserve its capital and make it productive. The trustee must follow any restrictions on investments contained in the trust agreement or state statute.

Express Trust

An **express trust** is voluntarily created by the settlor. It is usually written. The written agreement is called a *trust instrument*, or *trust agreement*. Express trusts fall into two categories. The first is an ***inter vivos* trust** that is created while the settlor is alive. The settlor transfers legal title of property to a named trustee to hold, administer, and manage for the benefit of named beneficiaries. The second is a **testamentary trust** that is created by will. In other words, the trust comes into existence when the settlor dies. If the will that establishes the trust is found to be invalid, the trust is also invalid.

Example Suppose Grandmother creates a trust and places assets in the trust that consist of stocks, bonds, bank accounts, and an apartment building. In the trust document, Grandmother designates her daughter to receive the income from the trust (e.g., dividends, interest, and rental income) until the daughter dies, and upon the daughter's death, the trust corpus is to be divided equally among Grandmother's three granddaughters. Grandmother names Country Bank the trustee. This is a testamentary trust. Grandmother is the trustor, Country Bank is the trustee, the daughter is the income beneficiary, and the three granddaughters are the remainder beneficiaries.

Constructive Trust

A **constructive trust** is an equitable trust that is implied by law to avoid fraud, unjust enrichment, and injustice. In constructive trust arrangements, the holder of the actual title to property (i.e., the trustee) holds the property in trust for its rightful owner.

> A constructive trust is the formula through which the conscience of equity finds expression.
>
> Judge Cardozo
> *Beatty v. Guggenheim Exploration Co. (1919)*

Example Suppose Thad and Kaye are partners. Assume that Kaye embezzles partnership funds and uses the stolen funds to purchase a piece of real estate. In this case, the court can impose a constructive trust under which Kaye (who holds actual title to the land) is considered a trustee who is holding the property in trust for Thad, its rightful owner.

Resulting Trust

A **resulting trust** is implied from the conduct of the parties. For example, suppose Henry is purchasing a piece of real estate but cannot attend the closing. He asks his brother, Gregory, to attend the closing and take title to the property until he can return. In this case, Gregory holds the title to the property as trustee for Henry until he returns.

Special Types of Trusts

Trusts may be created for special purposes. Three types of special trusts are fairly common:

- *Charitable trusts.* A **charitable trust** is created for the benefit of a segment of society or society in general. A trust that is created for the construction and maintenance of a public park is an example of a charitable trust.
- *Spendthrift trusts.* A **spendthrift trust** is designed to prevent a beneficiary's personal creditors from reaching his or her trust interest. All control over the trust is removed from the beneficiary. Personal creditors still can go after trust income that is paid to the beneficiary, however.
- *Totten trusts.* A **totten trust** is created when a person deposits money in a bank account in his or her own name and holds it as a trustee for the benefit of another person. A totten trust is a tentative trust because (a) the trustee can add or withdraw funds from the account, and (b) the trust can be revoked at any time prior to the trustee's death or prior to completing delivery of the funds to the beneficiary.

Termination of a Trust

A trust is irrevocable unless the settlor reserves the right to revoke it. Most trusts fall into the first category. Usually, a trust either contains a specific termination date or provides that it will terminate upon the occurrence of an event (e.g., when the remainder beneficiary reaches a certain age). Upon termination, the trust corpus is distributed as provided in the trust agreement.

Living Trusts

Living trusts have become a popular method for holding property during a person's lifetime and distributing the property upon that person's death. A living trust works as follows. During his or her life, a person establishes a living trust, which is a legal entity used for estate planning. A living trust is also referred to as a **grantor's trust**, or a **revocable trust**. The person who creates the trust is called the **grantor** (or the **trustor**).

Benefits of a Living Trust

The primary purpose of using a living trust is to avoid *probate* associated with using a will. If a person dies with a will, the will must be probated so the deceased's assets can be properly distributed according to the will. A probate judge is named to oversee the probate process, and all documents, including the will, are public record. A living trust, on the other hand, is private. When the grantor dies, the assets are owned by the living trust and are therefore not subject to probate proceedings. In addition, if real property is owned in more than one state and a will is used, then ancillary probate must be conducted in the other state. If a living trust is used, ancillary probate is avoided.

Living trusts are often promoted for claimed benefits that do not exist. The true facts are that a living trust:

- Does not reduce estate taxes any more than a will.
- Does not reduce the grantor's income taxes. All the income earned by the trust is attributed to the grantor, who must pay income taxes on the earnings just as if the trust did not exist.
- Does not avoid creditors. Thus, creditors can obtain liens against property in the trust.
- Is subject to property division upon divorce.
- Is usually not less expensive to create than a will. Both require payments to lawyers and usually to accountants and other professionals to draft and probate a will or draft and manage a living trust.
- Does not avoid controversies upon the grantor's death. Like wills, living trusts can be challenged for lack of capacity, undue influence, duress, and other legal grounds.

> The law relating to public policy cannot remain immutable, it must change with the passage of time. The wind of change blows on it.
>
> L. J. Danckwerts
> *Nagle v. Feilden (1966)*

Funding and Operation of a Living Trust

To fund a living trust, the grantor transfers title to his or her property to the trust. This property is called the *trust corpus*. Bank accounts, stock certificates, real estate, personal property, intangible property, and other property owned by the grantor must be retitled to the trust's name. For example, the grantor must execute deeds transferring title to real estate to the trust. Once property is transferred to the trust, the trust is considered funded. A living trust is revocable during the grantor's lifetime. Thus, a grantor can later change his or her mind and undo the trust and retake title of the property in his or her own name.

A living trust names a *trustee* who is responsible for maintaining, investing, buying, or selling trust assets. The trustee is usually the grantor. Thus, the grantor who establishes the trust does not lose control of the property placed in the trust and may manage and invest trust assets during his or her lifetime. The trust should name a *successor trustee* to replace the grantor-trustee if the grantor becomes incapacitated or too ill to manage the trust.

Beneficiaries

A living trust names a **beneficiary** or **beneficiaries** who are entitled to receive income from the living trust while it is in existence and to receive the property of the trust when the grantor dies. Usually the grantor is the **income beneficiary**, who receives the income from the trust during his or her lifetime. Upon the death of the grantor, assets of the trust are distributed to the **remainder beneficiary** or beneficiaries named in the trust. The designated trustee has the fiduciary duties of identifying assets, paying creditors, paying income and estate taxes, transferring assets to named beneficiaries, and rendering an accounting.

Pour-Over Will

A **pour-over will** is necessary to distribute any property acquired in the name of the grantor after a living trust is established or any property that was not transferred to the trust in the first place. The pour-over will transfers this property to the trust upon the grantor's death, and it is then distributed to the named beneficiaries of the trust. A pour-over will is subject to probate and is therefore public. A pour-over will is usually created at the same time that a living trust is established.

A living trust is a legitimate planning tool for many people. A person should seek professional advice from, and have a living trust, pour-over will, and other necessary documents drafted by an attorney.

Kathmandu, Nepal

Different countries and cultures around the world have various rituals for honoring their deceased loved ones and transferring property upon death. In some cultures, property is often left to the eldest son.

Living Will and Health Care Directive

Technological breakthroughs have greatly increased the life span of human beings. This same technology, however, permits life to be sustained long after a person is "brain dead." Some people say they have a right to refuse life-extending treatment. Others argue that human life must be preserved at all costs. In 1990, the U.S. Supreme Court was called upon to decide the **right to die** issue. In the ***Cruzan v. Director, Missouri Department of Health***[1] case, the U.S. Supreme Court acknowledged that the right to refuse medical treatment is a personal liberty protected by the Due Process Clause of the U.S. Constitution. The Court stated that this interest must be expressed through clear and convincing proof that the patient did not want to be sustained by artificial means.

The clear message of the Supreme Court's opinion is that people who do not want their lives prolonged indefinitely by artificial means should sign a **living will** that stipulates their wishes before catastrophe strikes and they become unable to express it themselves because of an illness or an accident. The living will should state which life-saving measures the signor does and does not want. In addition, the signor can specify that he or she wants any such treatments withdrawn if doctors determine that there is no hope of a meaningful recovery. A living will provides clear and convincing proof of a patient's wishes with respect to medical treatment.

In a living will or in a separate document, usually called a **health care directive**, or **health care proxy**, the maker should name someone, such as a spouse or another relative or trusted party, to be his or her **health care agent** to make all health care decisions in accordance with his or her wishes in the living will. An alternative person should also be named in case the originally designated health care agent is unable or chooses not to serve in that capacity.

Example A well-known example of a case in which a person did not have a living will and health care proxy was the Terri Schiavo case. In February 1990, Terri collapsed and was placed on life support systems. For 15 years, Terri remained in a vegetative state. Her husband wanted Terri to be taken off life support systems, but her parents did not. After years of legal battles that included more than 50 trial and appellate court hearings, in April 2005, the Florida supreme court ordered Terri to be taken off life support systems. Days later, she died. Much of the legal battle concerned what Terri's intention would have been about staying on or being removed from life support systems. If Terri had had a living will and health care proxy, her intentions would have been clear.

Web Exercises

1. **WEB** Use *www.google.com* to find an article that discusses a living will and health care directive. Read it.

2. **WEB** Use *www.google.com* to locate online a living will and health care directive that is effective in your state.

The Right to Die

One legal issue that has been prominent in the news is whether an individual has the right to choose to die when he or she is terminally ill and has less than a certain time to live. Many persons in the United States support this right to die, while others are against having such a law.

The state of Oregon presented this choice to its residents in a ballet measure. The Oregon Death with Dignity Act passed by a 51 percent to 49 percent margin and became law in Oregon. In the following case, the U.S. Supreme Court was called upon to decide the legality of this state law when the federal government asserted that an existing federal law prohibited the Oregon law.

CASE 39.6
Death with Dignity Law

U.S. SUPREME COURT
Gonzales, Attorney General v. Oregon
546 U.S. 243, 126 S.Ct. 904, 163 L.Ed.2d 748,
Web 2006 U.S. Lexis 767 (2006)
Supreme Court of the United States

> "*Americans are engaged in an earnest and profound debate about the morality, legality, and practicality of physician-assisted suicide.*"
>
> —Justice Kennedy

Facts

In 1994, the State of Oregon became the first state to legalize assisted suicide when voters approved a ballet measure enacting the Oregon Death With Dignity Act (ODWDA) [Oregon Revised Statute Section 127.800 *et seq.*]. The Oregon law exempts from civil or criminal liability state-licensed physicians who, in compliance with the safeguards in ODWDA, dispense or prescribe a lethal dose of drugs upon the request of a terminally ill patient.

For Oregon residents to be eligible to request a prescription under ODWDA, they must receive a diagnosis from their attending physician that they have an incurable and irreversible disease that, within reasonable medical judgment, will cause death within six months. Attending physicians must also determine whether a patient has made a voluntary request, ensure that a patient's choice is informed, and refer patients to counseling if they might be suffering from a psychological disorder or depression causing impaired judgment. A second consulting physician must examine the patient and the medical record and confirm the attending physician's conclusions. Oregon physicians may dispense or issue a prescription for the requested drug but may not administer it. Physicians who dispense medication pursuant to ODWDA must also be registered with both the state's Board of Medical Examiners and the federal Drug Enforcement Administration (DEA).

The drugs Oregon physicians prescribe pursuant to ODWDA are regulated under a federal statute, the Controlled Substances Act (CSA) [21 U.S.C. Section 801 *et seq.*]. The CSA allows covered drugs to be available only by written prescription from a registered physician. To prevent the diversion of controlled substances, the physician must obtain a registration from the U.S. Attorney General. The Attorney General may deny, suspend, or revoke this registration if the physician's registration would be "inconsistent with the public interest."

On November 9, 2001, the U.S. attorney general issued an interpretive rule announcing his intent to restrict the use of controlled substances for physician-assisted suicide. The U.S. attorney general ruled that assisting suicide is not a legitimate medical purpose and that prescribing or dispensing federally controlled substances to assist suicide violates the federal CSA. The interpretive rule also stated that a physician who prescribed controlled substances for assisted suicides violated the public interest and would be subject to suspension or revocation of his or her medical license.

In response, the state of Oregon, joined by a physician, a pharmacist, and some terminally ill patients, all from Oregon, challenged the interpretive rule in federal court. The U.S. District Court entered a permanent injunction against the federal government's enforcement of the interpretive rule. The U.S. Court of Appeals agreed and held the interpretive rule invalid. The U.S. attorney general appealed to the U.S. Supreme Court.

Issue

Does the U.S. attorney general have the statutory power pursuant to the federal Controlled Substances Act to issue the interpretive rule criminalizing medical practices authorized by the state of Oregon law?

Language of the U.S. Supreme Court

Americans are engaged in an earnest and profound debate about the morality, legality, and practicality of physician-assisted suicide. The dispute before us is in part a product of this political and moral debate, but its resolution requires an inquiry familiar to the courts: interpreting a federal statute to determine whether Executive action is authorized by, or otherwise consistent with, the enactment.

In deciding whether the CSA can be read as prohibiting physician-assisted suicide, we look to the statute's text and design. The statute and our case law amply support the conclusion that Congress regulates medical practice insofar as it bars doctors from using their prescription-writing powers as a means to engage in illicit drug dealing and trafficking as conventionally understood. Beyond this, however, the statute manifests no intent to regulate the practice of medicine generally. The silence is understandable given the structure and limitations of federalism, which allow States great latitude under their police powers to legislate as to the protection of the lives, limbs, health, comfort, and quiet of all persons. Oregon's regime is an example of the state regulation of medical practice that the CSA presupposes. Rather than simply decriminalize assisted suicide, ODWDA limits its exercise to the attending physicians of terminally ill patients, physicians who must be licensed by Oregon's Board of Medical Examiners.

The Government, in the end, maintains that the prescription requirement delegates to a single Executive officer the power to effect a radical shift of authority from the States to the Federal Government to define general standards of medical practice in every locality. The text and structure of the CSA show that Congress did not have this far-reaching intent to alter the federal-state balance and the congressional role in maintaining it.

Decision

The U.S. Supreme Court held that the federal Controlled Substances Act did not authorize the U.S. attorney general to issue the interpretive rule in this case. The Supreme Court affirmed the judgment of the Court of Appeals which held that the interpretive rule was invalid and permanently enjoined from enforcement. Thus, the Oregon Death With Dignity Act can be administered as written.

Law & Ethics Questions

1. What did the Oregon Death With Dignity Act provide? Explain.
2. What does the federal Controlled Substances Act provide? Explain.
3. What did the U.S. attorney general's interpretive rule provide? Explain.
4. **ETHICS** Do you think it is morally right for a terminally ill patient to request physician-assisted suicide? Explain.

Web Exercises

1. **WEB** For the complete opinion of this case, go to *www.prenhall.com/cheesemancases*.
2. **WEB** Visit the website of the state of Oregon, at *www.oregon.gov*.
3. **WEB** Visit the website of the U.S. Supreme Court, at *www.supremecourtus.gov*, and try to find documents that relate to this case.
4. **WEB** Use *www.google.com* to find an article that discusses assisted-suicide laws. Read it.

Chapter Summary

Premarriage Issues, p. 1116

Promise to Marry

A promise by one person to marry is made to another person. The courts usually do not enforce such promises as contracts.

Engagement

An engagement is a period of time that begins when one person asks another person to marry him or her and ends when the parties get married or terminate their engagement. If a party ends the engagement, states apply one of the following rules regarding the return of the engagement ring:

1. *Fault rule.* If the prospective groom breaks off the engagement, the prospective bride may keep the ring. If the prospective bride breaks off the engagement, the ring must be returned to the prospective groom.
2. *Objective rule.* If the engagement is broken off, the prospective bride must return the ring to the prospective groom irrespective as to which party broke off the engagement.

Prenuptial Agreement

A prenuptial agreement is a contract entered into by prospective spouses prior to marriage that specifies how property will be distributed upon termination of the marriage or the death of a spouse. An antenuptial agreement is a contract entered into by prospective spouses during marriage that specifies how property will be distributed upon termination of the marriage or death of a spouse.

Marriage, p. 1117

Marriage has traditionally been defined as a legal union between a male and a female that confers certain duties and rights upon the spouses. Some states permit the marriage of spouses of the same sex.

Marriage Requirements

In order for a couple to be married they must meet the following requirements:

1. The parties must be of at least 18 years of age. States will permit younger persons to be married if they have the consent of their parents or if they are emancipated from their parents. All states provide that persons under a certain age, such as 14 or 15 years of age, cannot be married.

2. The parties may not be closely, usually related by blood. Cousins may marry in some states.
3. Neither party is currently married to someone else.

Marriage License

A marriage license is a legal document issued by the state which certifies that two people are married. A marriage ceremony is held before a designated government official, or at a church, temple, synagogue, or other place of worship before a minister, priest, or rabbi. At the ceremony, the parties exchange wedding vows.

Financial Support

Most states require a spouse to financially support the other spouse and their children during their marriage, only up to the level he or she is able to provide. This includes providing for the necessities such as food, shelter, clothing, and medical care.

Common Law Marriage

Several states recognize common law marriage, wherein two people who have not been officially married are considered married if certain requirements are met, such as living together for a specified period of time.

Same-Sex Marriage

Same-sex marriage is a marriage between two people of the same sex. Several states permit same-sex marriage. Some other states permit civil unions between persons of the same sex.

Parents and Children, p. 1119

Parents' Rights and Duties

Parents have the obligation to provide food, shelter, clothing, medical care, and other necessities to their children until a child reaches the age of 18 or until emancipation. Emancipation occurs if a child leaves the parents and voluntarily lives on his or her own. The child then is responsible for providing his or her livelihood.

Paternity Action

A paternity action is a legal proceeding in which the court identifies the biological father of a child.

Parent's Liability for a Child's Wrongful Act

Generally, parents are not liable for their children's negligent acts. Parents are liable if their negligence caused their child's act.

Surrogacy

Surrogacy is a situation in which a woman agrees to be artificially inseminated with the sperm of a male and to give the baby up to the sperm donor (and his spouse, if he has a spouse) upon the birth of the child. The contract between the birth mother and the father (and spouse) is called a surrogacy agreement.

Adoption

Adoption occurs when a person becomes the legal parent of a child who is not his or her biological child.
1. *Agency adoption.* In an agency adoption, a person adopts a child from a social organization of a state. In an open adoption, the biological mother is introduced to the adoptive parent or parents prior to the adoption.
2. *Independent adoption.* In an independent adoption, the biological mother or parents enter into a private arrangement with the adoptive parent or parents for the adoption of a child.

Foster Care

Foster care is an arrangement in which a child is placed temporarily with a foster family. The state government pays the foster family a fee for caring for the foster child.

Marriage Termination, p. 1122

Annulment

An annulment is an order of the court declaring that a marriage did not exist.

Divorce

A divorce is an order of the court that terminates a marriage. The court issues a decree of divorce that terminates the marriage. A no-fault divorce is a divorce recognized by the law of a state where neither party is blamed for the divorce; the petitioning party merely has to assert irreconcilable differences.

1. **Divorce proceedings.** A divorce proceeding is commenced by a spouse filing a petition for divorce with the proper state court. The petition must be served on the other spouse. This spouse then has a certain period of time (usually 20 to 30 days) to file an answer to the petition. If the spouses do not reach a settlement of the issues involved in the divorce the case will go to trial. If the case goes to trial, each side is permitted to call witnesses and introduce evidence that will support their claims.

   Many states require a certain waiting period from the date a divorce petition is filed to the date the court grants a divorce. A typical waiting period is six months. After the waiting period has passed, a court will enter a decree of divorce, which is a court order terminating the marriage. The parties are then free to marry again.

2. **Pro se divorce.** *Pro se* denotes a divorce proceeding in which the parties do not hire an attorney but instead represent themselves in the divorce action.

3. **Settlement agreement.** Prior to going to court, the parties sometimes settle their divorce voluntarily. The settlement agreement is a written document signed by the divorcing parties that evidences their agreement to settle property rights and other issues of their divorce.

Division of Assets, p. 1123

Separate Property

Separate property is the property owned by a spouse prior to marriage, as well as inheritances and gifts received by the spouse during the marriage.

Marital Property

Marital property is the property acquired during the course of marriage using income earned during the marriage, plus property that has been converted into marital property. States use one of the following methods for the division of property:

1. **Equitable (fair) distribution.** In some states, the court orders equitable (fair) distribution of marital property to the divorcing spouses. This does not necessarily mean the equal distribution of marital property.

2. **Community property.** In some states, the court orders an equal distribution of marital property to the divorcing spouses.

Division of Debts

Joint marital debts incurred during the marriage are the joint responsibility of divorcing spouses. The court may distribute these debts to the individual divorcing spouses, but if a spouse does not pay the debt, the creditor can seek payment form the other divorced spouse.

Spousal Support, Child Support, and Child Custody, p. 1127

Spousal Support

Spousal support is an amount of money ordered by a court to be paid by one divorcing spouse to another divorcing spouse for a period of time during and after the divorce is final. Also called alimony, of which there are two types:

1. *Temporary alimony.* An amount ordered by the court to be paid to one divorcing spouse to the other divorcing spouse for a limited period of time. Also called *rehabilitation alimony.*
2. *Permanent alimony.* An amount ordered by the court to be paid to one divorcing spouse to the other divorcing spouse until the receiving spouse dies or remarries. Sometimes called *lifetime alimony.*

Child Support

Child support consists of payments made by the non-custodial parent to help with the financial support of his or her children.

Family Support Act

The Family Support Act is a federal statute that provides for the automatic withholding of child support payments from a non-custodial parent's income.

Child Custody

The awarding of child custody to a parent is based on the best interests of the child. The parent awarded custody is called the custodial parent. The other parent is called the non-custodial parent.

1. *Joint custody.* Joint custody means that both divorcing parents are responsible for making major decisions concerning the child. Joint physical custody means that the child of divorcing parents spends a certain amount of time being raised by each parent.
2. *Visitation rights.* Visitation rights confer to the non-custodial parent the right to visit his or her child for limited periods of time.

Wills, p. 1129

A will is a declaration of how a person wants his or her property to be distributed upon his or her death. Parties to a will:

1. *Testator or testatrix.* This is the person who makes a will.
2. *Beneficiary.* A beneficiary is a person designated in the will to receive the testator's property. There may be multiple beneficiaries.
3. *Executor or executrix.* This is the person named in a will to administer the testator's estate during the settlement of the estate.

Requirements for Making a Will

A Statute of Wills is a state statute that establishes the requirements for making a valid will. The normal requirements for making a will are:

1. *Testamentary capacity.* The testator must have been of legal age and "sound mind" when his or her will was made.
2. *Writing.* A will must be in writing, except for certain special wills.
3. *Testator's signature.* A will must be signed by the testator.

Attestation by Witnesses

A will must be attested to by the stipulated number of mentally competent and uninterested witnesses.

Codicil

Adding a codicil is a legal way to change an existing will. A codicil must be executed with the same formalities as a will.

Revoking a Will

A will is revoked if the testator intentionally burns, tears, obliterates, or otherwise destroys it. A properly executed subsequent will revokes a prior will if it specifically states that it is the testator's intention to do so. If the second will does not expressly revoke the prior will, the wills are read together. If any will provisions are inconsistent, the provisions in the second will control. Wills can also be revoked by operation of law.

Joint and Mutual Wills

1. *Joint will.* Two or more testators may execute the same instrument as their will. This is called a joint will.
2. *Mutual, or reciprocal, will.* Two or more testators may execute separate wills that leave property in favor of the other on condition that the survivor leave the remaining property on his or her death as agreed by the testators.

Special Types of Wills

1. *Holographic will.* A holographic will is entirely handwritten and signed by the testator. Most states recognize the validity of these wills even though they are not witnessed.
2. *Nuncupative will.* Nuncupative wills are oral wills that are made by dying persons before witnesses. Many states recognize these oral wills. Also called a *dying declaration* or a *deathbed will.*

Simultaneous Deaths

The Uniform Simultaneous Death Act provides that if people who would inherit property from each other die simultaneously, each deceased person's property is distributed as though he or she had survived.

Undue Influence

A will may be found to be invalid if it was made under undue influence, where one person takes advantage of another person's mental, emotional, or physical weakness and unduly persuades that person to make a will.

Probate

Probate is the process of collecting a deceased person's property, paying their debts and taxes, and distributing the remainder of the estate to the beneficiaries of the will or the heirs under the state intestacy statute.

Testamentary Gifts

1. *Specific gift.* A specific gift is a gift of a specifically mentioned piece of property (e.g., a ring).
2. *General gift.* A general gift is a gift that does not identify the specific property from which the gift is to be made (e.g., gift of cash).
3. *Residuary gift.* A residuary gift is a gift of the remainder of the testator's estate after the debts, taxes, and specific and general gifts have been paid.

Lineal Descendants

1. **Per stirpes** *distribution.* With this type of distribution, lineal descendants inherit by representation of their parent—that is, they split what their deceased parent would have received.
2. **Per capita** *distribution.* With this type of distribution, lineal descendants equally share the property of the estate without regard to degree.

Ademption and Abatement

1. *Ademption.* Under ademption, if a testator leaves a specific gift but the property is no longer in the estate when the testator dies, the beneficiary of that gift receives nothing.
2. *Abatement.* Under abatement, if the testator's estate is insufficient to pay the stated gifts, the gifts are abated (reduced) in the following order: (1) residuary gifts and then (2) general gifts, proportionately.

Intestate Succession, p. 1139

1. ***Intestacy statutes.*** These state statutes stipulate how a deceased's property will be distributed if he or she dies without leaving a will or if the will fails for some legal reason.
2. ***Heirs.*** Heirs are relatives who receive property under an intestacy statute.
3. ***Escheat.*** Intestacy statutes provide that if there are no heirs, the deceased's property escheats (goes) to the state.

Trusts, p. 1140

A trust is a legal arrangement whereby one person delivers and transfers legal title to property to another person to be held and used for the benefit of a third person. The trust corpus (or trust res) is property that is held in trust. Parties to a trust:

1. ***Settlor.*** A settlor is a person who establishes a trust. Also called a *trustor* or *transferor*.
2. ***Trustee.*** A trustee is a person to whom legal title of the trust assets is transferred. The trustee is responsible for managing the trust assets as established by the trust and law.

Beneficiaries

A beneficiary is a person for whose benefit a trust is created. A beneficiary holds equitable title to the trust assets. There can be multiple beneficiaries, including:

1. ***Income beneficiary.*** This is a person to whom trust income is to be paid.
2. ***Remainder beneficiary.*** This is a person who is entitled to receive the trust corpus upon the termination of the trust.

Express Trust

An express trust is voluntarily created by the settlor. There are two types of express trusts, the first is an int*er vivos* trust that is created while the settlor is alive. The settlor transfers legal title of property to a named trustee to hold, administer, and manage for the benefit of named beneficiaries. The second is a testamentary trust that is created by will.

Constructive Trust

A constructive trust is an equitable trust that is implied by law to avoid fraud, unjust enrichment, and injustice.

Resulting Trust

A resulting trust is implied from the conduct of the parties.

Special Types of Trusts

- ***Charitable trusts.*** A charitable trust is created for the benefit of a segment of society or society in general.
- ***Spendthrift trusts.*** A spendthrift trust is designed to prevent a beneficiary's personal creditors from reaching his or her trust interest. All control over the trust is removed from the beneficiary.
- ***Totten trusts.*** A totten trust is created when a person deposits money in a bank account in his or her own name and holds it as a trustee. A totten trust is a tentative trust because (a) the trustee can add or withdraw funds from the account, and (b) the trust can be revoked at any time prior to the trustee's death or prior to completing delivery of the funds to the beneficiary.

Termination of a Trust

A trust is irrevocable unless the settlor reserves the right to revoke it. Usually, a trust either contains a specific termination date or provides that it will terminate upon the occurrence of an event. Upon termination, the trust corpus is distributed as provided in the trust agreement.

Living Trusts, p. 1142

A living trust is a legal entity used for estate planning. Also called a *grantor's trust* or a *revocable trust*. The trust corpus (or trust res) is property that is held in trust. Parties to a living trust:

1. *Grantor.* The person who creates a trust and funds the trust with assets. Also called the *grantor* or *trustor*.
2. *Trustee.* The party who is responsible for maintaining, investing, buying, or selling trust assets. The trustee is usually the grantor.

Benefits of a Living Trust

A living trust is private. When the grantor dies, the assets are owned by the living trust and are therefore not subject to probate proceedings. In addition, if real property is owned in more than one state ancillary probate is avoided.

Funding and Operation of a Living Trust

To fund a living trust, the grantor transfers title to his or her property to the trust. This property is called the *trust corpus*. A living trust names a *trustee* who is responsible for maintaining, investing, buying, or selling trust assets.

Beneficiaries

1. *Income beneficiary.* The party or parties who are entitled to receive income from a living trust during his or her lifetime. The income beneficiary is usually the grantor.
2. *Remainder beneficiary.* The party or parties who, upon the death of the grantor, are awarded the assets of the trust.

Pour-Over Will

A type of will that is necessary to distribute any property of the grantor that is not in the living trust.

Living Will and Health Care Directive, p. 1144

1. *Living will.* A living will is a document signed by a person that stipulates his or her wishes to not have his or her life prolonged by artificial means.
2. *Health care directive.* A health care directive is a direction in a living will (or in a separate document) that names and authorizes a health care agent to make medical and health care decisions for the maker if the maker is unable to.
3. *Health care agent.* A health care agent is a person named in a living will or other document to make health care decisions for the maker of the living will or other document in accordance with the maker's wishes.

The Right to Die

The right to die is a personal liberty protected by the U.S. Constitution.

Test Review Terms and Concepts

Case Problems

39.1 Marital Assets: George Neville and Tina Neville were married. At the time, George was 31 years old and a practicing attorney; Tina was a 23-year-old medical student. After 7 years, Tina became a licensed physician. Soon after, George filed for divorce from Tina because she was having an adulterous affair with another doctor. At the time of the divorce, George was earning $55,000 per year practicing law; Tina was earning $165,000 per year as a physician.

The divorce was filed in Mississippi, where the couple lived. Mississippi follows the doctrine of equitable distribution. George sought to have Tina's medical license and medical practice valued as an ongoing business, and he claimed a portion of the value. The court refused George's request and instead applied the doctrine of equitable distribution and awarded him rehabilitative alimony of $1,400 per month for 120 months. The aggregate amount of the alimony was $168,000. George appealed this award, alleging on appeal that Tina's medical license and practice should be valued, and he should receive a portion of this value. Under the doctrine of equitable distribution, was the trial court's award

fair, or should George win on appeal? *Neville v. Neville*, 734 So.2d 352, **Web** 1999 Miss. App. Lexis 68 (Court of Appeals of Mississippi)

39.2 Marital Assets: Ronald R. and Edith Johnston were married and had three sons ranging in age from 12 to 16 when the parties separated. Edith filed for divorce the same year. The Johnstons owned a primary residence worth $186,000, with no mortgage on it. Ronald was a successful entrepreneur. He owned Depot Distributors, Inc., a business involved in selling and installing bathroom cabinets. He also owned several other businesses. Ronald's income was $543,382, $820,439, $1,919,713, and $1,462,712 in the four years leading up to the divorce. Ronald invested much of his income in commercial and residential real estate, which was held in his name only. At the time of the divorce trial, the real estate was valued at $11,790,000 and was subject to mortgages of $4,966,343.

After their separation, Ronald engaged in certain transfers of property and distributions of property, in violation of the court's order, that obfuscated his income and net worth.

The trial court judge therefore accepted Edith's appraisals of the value of the real estate. The trial court judge applied the equitable distribution doctrine of Massachusetts and awarded Edith real estate totaling $2,446,000, the family residence, and alimony of $1,200 per month. The trial court judge awarded Ronald real estate valued at $9,314,000 subject to mortgages of $4,966,343, for a net value of $4,347,657. The judge characterized this as a roughly 60–40 split of the real estate (i.e., 60 percent for Ronald and 40 percent for Edith). Ronald appealed the split of real estate and the award of alimony as violating the equitable distribution doctrine. Under the doctrine of equitable distribution, was the trial court's award fair, or should Ronald win on appeal? *Johnston v. Johnston*, 38 Mass.App.Ct. 531, 649 N.E.2d 799, **Web** 1995 Mass. App. Lexis 429 (Appeals Court of Massachusetts)

39.3 Child Custody: Randolph J. Schweinberg and Sandra Faye Click were married. Thirteen years later, Sandra Click moved out of the couple's home, and the couple was divorced the same year. At the time of the divorce, the couple had two minor children, Randolph II and Russell. Randolph II had cerebral palsy and walked with difficulty. The children lived with Randolph after Sandra moved out. Randolph was a sergeant in the United States Air Force, stationed in South Carolina; he considered Florida as his permanent home, however.

In the divorce proceeding, the court awarded custody of the two minor children to Randolph. The two children were doing well in school, and the court found that Randolph II needed the emotional support provided by his brother Russell. Sandra was permitted visitation rights to see the children. Sandra later married a new husband, who had previously been convicted of lewd and lascivious behavior on a female child and was under court supervision for 15 years.

Sandra petitioned the court to modify the custody order to grant her custody of the two minor children. The trial court granted the petition and awarded custody to Sandra. Randolph appealed the trial court's decision. Under the best interests test, should Randolph or Sandra be awarded custody of the two minor children? *Schweinberg v. Click* 627 So.2d 548, **Web** 1993 Fla. App. Lexis 11660 (Court of Appeal of Florida)

39.4 Will: Martha Jansa executed a will naming her two sons as executors and leaving all her property to them. The will was properly signed and attested to by witnesses. Thereafter, Martha died. When Martha's safe-deposit box at a bank was opened, the original of this will was discovered, along with two other instruments that were dated after the will. One was a handwritten document that left her home to her grandson, with the remainder of her estate to her two sons; this document was not signed. The second document was a typed version of the handwritten one; this document was signed by Martha but was not attested to by witnesses. Which of the three documents should be admitted to pro-

bate? *In re Estate of Jansa*, 670 S.W.2d 767, **Web** 1984 Tex. App. Lexis 5503 (Court of Appeals of Texas)

39.5 Mental Capacity: Everett Clark met with William Wham, an attorney, to discuss the preparation of a will. Clark, who had never married and who lived with his sister, was to return the following day to execute his will. Clark was hospitalized that evening with a perforated ulcer. He underwent surgery on March 19. Subsequent to the surgery, and until the time of his death, he was in intensive care and unable to communicate verbally. On March 23, Clark's cousin John Bailey retrieved the will prepared by Wham and took it to attorney Frank Walker to have him finalize it. Walker testified that he took the will to the hospital on March 25. Immediately prior to the execution of the will, Walker asked Clark a few questions. Walker testified that Clark knew what he was doing. Dorothy Smith, an attesting witness, testified that Clark could not talk but answered her questions by nodding yes or no. She asked Clark "if he knew me and if he knew we were all there and he shook his head yes." She testified that he also shook his head yes to the question "Is this your will and testament?" "Is John Bailey your cousin?" and "Do you want to leave everything to John Bailey?" Clark signed the will with an *X*. On March 26, Clark passed into a coma and died. Bailey introduced the will into probate, but another relative of Clark's challenged it. Is the will valid? *Bailey v. Bailey*, 203 Ill.App.3d 1017, 561 N.E.2d 367, **Web** 1990 Ill. App. Lexis 1541 (Appellate Court of Illinois)

39.6 Lineal Descendants: In October 1973, Mr. and Mrs. Pate executed separate wills that followed a common plan in disposing of their respective estates. Each will provided for the establishment of trusts with a life estate to their son Billy, and upon his death, the estate was to be distributed "in equal shares *per stirpes* to my natural born grandchildren." Mr. and Mrs. Pate had two sons, Billy and Wallace. Billy's first marriage ended in divorce without children. Billy's second marriage also ended in divorce without children, although his second wife had a daughter by her previous marriage. Billy married again, and to the time of this action, no children had been born to his 32-year-old wife. Wallace first married in 1952. Of that marriage five children were born, each before the time that the Pates made their wills. After that marriage ended in divorce, Wallace married his present wife. There were no children of the second marriage, but there were stepchildren by Wallace's second wife. One of Wallace's daughters had two children by her marriage. Mr. Pate died on November 9, 1979, leaving an estate of $1.6 million. Mrs. Pate died on October 21, 1983, leaving an estate of $6.7 million. Who inherits the estate? *Pate v. Ford*, 293 S.C. 268, 360 S.E.2d 145, **Web** 1987 S.C. App. Lexis 363 (Court of Appeals of South Carolina)

39.7 Ademption: Mrs. Mildred D. Potter executed a will which provided that her residence in Pompano Beach, Florida, was to go to her daughter and an equivalent amount of cash to her son upon her death. Evidence showed that Mrs. Potter's intent was to treat the daughter and son equally in the distribution of her estate. When she died, her will was admitted into probate. At the time, she still possessed her home in Pompano Beach. Unfortunately, there were insufficient assets to pay Mrs. Potter's son the equivalent amount of cash. Can the son share in the value of the house so that his inheritance is equal to his sister's? *In re Estate of Potter*, 469 So.2d 957, **Web** 1985 Fla. App. Lexis. 14338 (Court of Appeal of Florida)

39.8 Will: During his first marriage to Miriam Talbot, Robert Mirkil Talbot executed a will in multiple originals that bequeathed his entire estate to Miriam, or if she should predecease him, to his friend J. Barker Killgore. After his first wife's death, Robert married Lois McClen Mills. After consulting a Louisiana intestacy chart, the Talbots determined that if Robert died, Lois would receive Robert's entire estate because he had no descendants, surviving parents, or siblings. However, Lois did have descendants. Lois wanted to leave Robert a portion of her estate. Robert and his new wife went to an attorney to execute the new wife's will. While there, the attorney took Robert aside and showed him his prior will that made Killgore the contingent beneficiary. The attorney asked Robert if he wanted to leave his estate to his new wife, and Robert answered "yes." Robert then tore the old will in half in the attorney's presence. After leaving the attorney's office, Robert and Lois went shopping for furnishings for their new house. That night, Robert became short of breath and was taken to a hospital, where he died. Killgore retrieved a multiple original of Robert's 1981 will and petitioned to have it probated. Lois opposed the petition. Who wins? *Succession of Talbot*, 530 So.2d 1132, **Web** 1988 La. Lexis 1597 (Supreme Court of Louisiana)

39.9 Intestate: Mr. and Mrs. Campbell were out in a small boat on Hyatt Lake near Ashland, Oregon. The boat capsized near the middle of the lake sometime in the afternoon. No one saw the capsizing or either of the Campbells in the water. The deputy sheriff was called to the lake about 5 o'clock, after the Campbells' boat was found. Numerous people searched the shoreline and lake, but the Campbells were not located by nightfall. The body of Mrs. Campbell was found the next morning. The body of Mr. Campbell was found four days later. The pathologists who conducted the autopsies testified that both Mr. and Mrs. Campbell died of drowning but could not determine the exact time of death. Both parties died intestate. Mr. Campbell was survived by three sisters and a brother, and Mrs. Campbell was survived by a daughter and son from a prior marriage. Who inherits the Campbells' property? *In re Estate of Campbell*, 56 Ore.App. 222, 641 P.2d 610, **Web** 1982 Ore. App. Lexis 2448 (Court of Appeals of Oregon)

39.10 Murder: Dr. Duncan R. Danforth, a 75-year-old man of substantial means, married 21-year-old Loretta Ollison. Immediately following the ceremony, the newlyweds went to a lawyer's office, where Danforth executed a newly prepared will naming Ollison a principal beneficiary of his estate. Four days later, Danforth was murdered by Michael Stith, Ollison's lover. In a criminal trial, Ollison was convicted of conspiracy to commit murder and was sentenced to 10 years in prison. Can Ollison recover under the will or take her elective share of the estate under the state's intestate statute? *In re the Estate of Danforth*, 705 S.W.2d 609, **Web** 1986 Mo. App. Lexis 3757 (Court of Appeals of Missouri)

Ethics Issues

39.11 Ethics: Mrs. Barbara Chadwick filed for divorce in Pennsylvania from Mr. H. Beatty Chadwick. During an equitable distribution conference, Mr. Chadwick informed the divorce court that he had transferred more than $2.5 million of the marital estate to pay an alleged debt he owed to Maison Blanche, Ltd., a Gibraltar partnership. It was later discovered that the principals of Maison Blanche had transferred $995,726 to a bank account in Switzerland in Mr. Chadwick's name and had purchased $869,106 of insurance annuity contracts in Mr. Chadwick's name. Mr. Chadwick redeemed these annuity contracts and received the money. In addition, $550,000 in stock certificates in Mr. Chadwick's name had been "lost."

The divorce court ordered Mr. Chadwick to return the $2,502,000 to an account under the jurisdiction of the court. When Mr. Chadwick refused, the court held Mr. Chadwick in civil contempt of court and ordered him jailed. During a seven-year period of incarceration, Mr. Chadwick applied 14 times to be released from prison, and each request was denied. Mr. Chadwick filed another request to be released from prison, alleging that he should be released because it was unlikely that he would comply with the divorce court's order to turn over the money and that, therefore, the civil contempt order had lost its coercive effect. The District Court agreed and granted Mr. Chadwick's petition to be released from prison. The government appealed the case to the U.S. Court of Appeals. Did Mr. Chadwick act ethically in this case? Should Mr. Chadwick be released from prison? *Chadwick V. Janecka, Warden*, 312 F.3d 597, **Web** 2002 U.S. App. Lexis 25263 (United States Court of Appeals for the Third Circuit)

39.12 Ethics: Homer and Edna Jones, husband and wife, executed a joint will that provided "We will and give to our survivor, whether it be Homer Jones or Edna Jones, all property and estate of which the first of us that dies may be seized and possessed. If we should both die in a common catastrophe, or upon the death of our survivor, we will and give all property and estate then remaining to our children, Leonida Jones Eschman, daughter, Sylvia Marie Jones, daughter, and Grady V. Jones, son, share and share alike."

When Homer died 18 years later, Edna Jones received his entire estate under the will. Two years later, Edna executed a new will that left a substantially larger portion of the estate to her daughter, Sylvia Marie Jones, than to the other two children. Edna Jones died in 1982. Edna's daughter introduced her mother's will for probate. The other two children introduced the earlier joint will for probate. Did Edna act ethically in this case? Who wins? *Jones v. Jones*, 718 S.W.2d 416, **Web** 1986 Tex. App. Lexis 8929 (Court of Appeals of Texas)

39.13 Ethics: Wilmer Breeden, an active socialist, was a very wealthy individual. When he died, his will designated the bulk of his estate to be placed in the Breeden-Schmidt Foundation. This testamentary trust was to be administered by the trustees named in Breeden's will, and the funds of the foundation were to be distributed "to persons, entities and causes advancing the principles of socialism and those causes related to socialism. This shall include, but not be limited to, subsidizing publications, establishing and conducting reading rooms, supporting radio, television and the newspaper media and candidates for public office." Breeden's nephew and niece petitioned the court to have the trust provision declared invalid and the estate residue given to them as intestate heirs. Did the language in Breeden's will create a valid testamentary charitable trust? Did the nephew and niece act ethically in this case? *In re Estate of Breeden*, 208 Cal.App.3d 981, 256 Cal.Rptr. 813, **Web** 1989 Cal. App. Lexis 215 (Court of Appeal of California)

IRAC Writing Assignment

Read **Case A-39** in Appendix A [*In re Estate of Vallerius*]. Use the IRAC method to prepare a written analysis of the case.

Endnotes

1. 497 U.S. 261, 110 S.Ct. 2841, 11 L.Ed.2d 224, Web 1990 U.S. Lexis 3301 (Supreme Court of the United States).

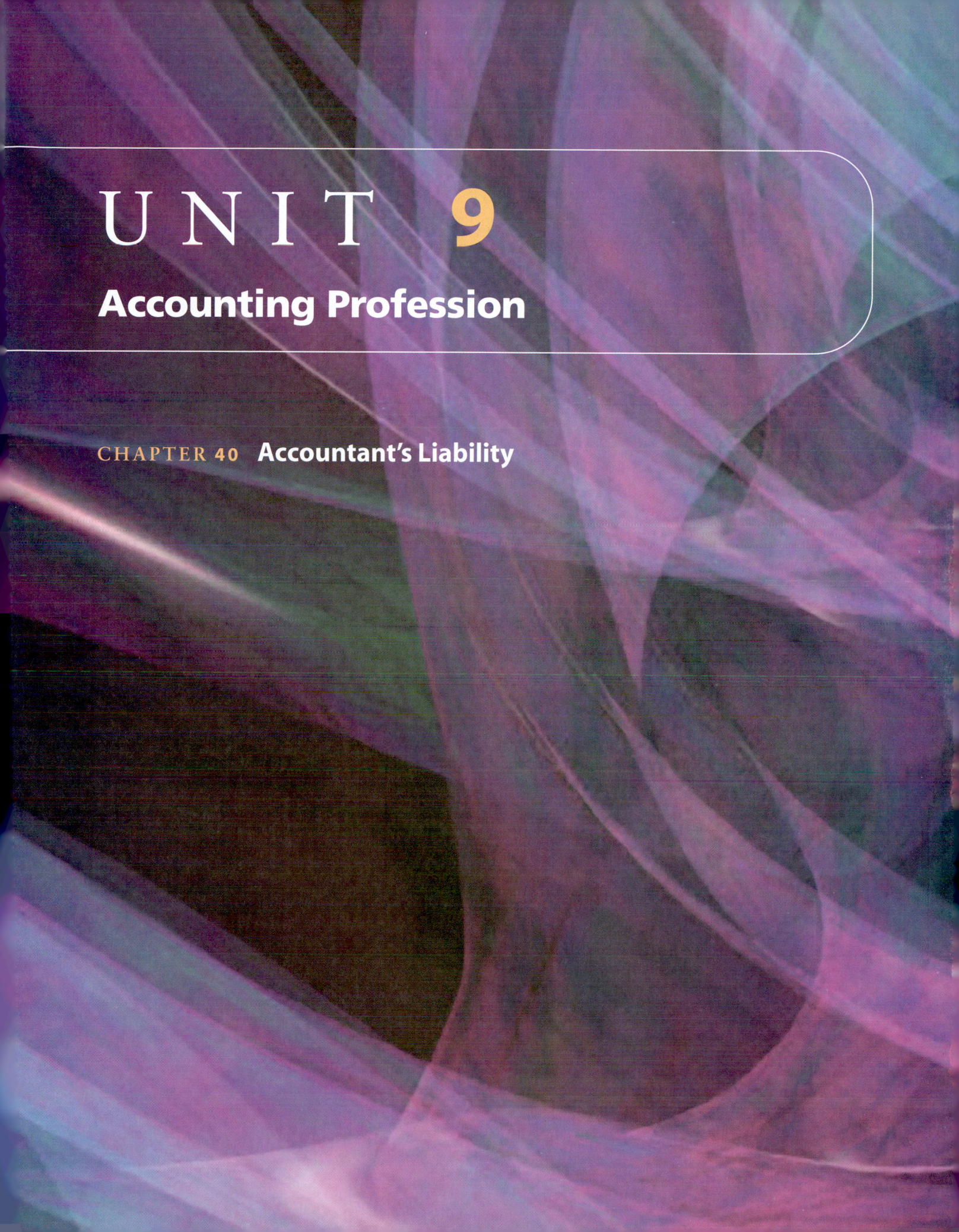

UNIT 9

Accounting Profession

CHAPTER 40 **Accountant's Liability**

CHAPTER 40

Accountant's Liability

In our complex society the accountant's certificate and the lawyer's opinion can be instruments for inflicting pecuniary loss more potent than the chisel or the crowbar.

—JUSTICE BLACKMAN
Dissenting Opinion, Ernst & Ernst v. Hochfelder, (1976)

CHAPTER OBJECTIVES

After studying this chapter, you should be able to:

1. Describe an accountant's liability to his or her client for breach of contract and fraud.
2. Describe an accountant's liability to third parties under the *Ultramares* doctrine.
3. Describe an accountant's liability to third parties under the *Restatement (Second) of Torts* and the foreseeability standard.
4. Describe an accountant's civil liability and criminal liability under federal securities laws.
5. Describe the duties of accountants under the Sarbanes-Oxley Act.

CHAPTER CONTENTS

   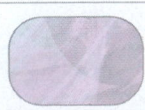 

Introduction to Accountant's Liability

Although accountants provide a wide variety of services to corporations and other businesses, their primary functions are (1) auditing financial statements and (2) rendering opinions about those audits. Accountants also prepare unaudited financial statements for clients, render tax advice, prepare tax forms, and provide consulting and other services to clients.

Audits generate the majority of litigation against accountants. Lawsuits against accountants are based on the common law (e.g., breach of contract, misrepresentation, and negligence) or on violation of certain statutes (particularly federal securities laws). Accountants can be held liable both to clients and to third parties. This chapter examines the legal liability of accountants.

Times Square, New York City

Public accountants provide audit and other services to public corporations and other businesses. NASDAQ is an automated quotation system for publicly traded companies.

Public Accounting

The term *accountant* applies to persons who perform a variety of services, including bookkeepers, tax preparers, and so on. The term **certified public accountant (CPA)** applies to accountants who meet certain educational requirements, pass the CPA examination, and have a certain number of years of audit experience. A person who is not certified is generally referred to as a **public accountant**.

Web Exercises

1. **WEB** Use *www.google.com* to find the requirements that must be met to become a certified public accountant (CPA) in your state.

2. **WEB** Use *www.yahoo.com* to find the companies that provide CPA review services in your state.

CONTEMPORARY ENVIRONMENT
"Big Four" Accounting Firms

There are thousands of public accounting firms in the United States. The four largest accounting firms in the United States, which have worldwide operations, are PricewaterhouseCoopers, Deloitte Touche Tohmatsu, Ernst & Young, and KPMG. These four accounting firms are often referred to as "Big Four" accounting firms.

Web Exercises

1. **WEB** Visit the website of PricewaterhouseCoopers, at *www.pwc.com*.

2. **WEB** Visit the website of Deloitte Touche Tohmatsu, at *www.deloitte.com*.

3. **WEB** Visit the website of Ernst & Young, at *www.ey.com*.

4. **WEB** Visit the website of KPMG, at *www.kpmg.com*.

5. **WEB** Use *www.google.com* to find the website of an accounting firm in your state.

Accounting Standards and Principles

Certified public accountants must comply with two uniform standards of professional conduct. They are (1) **generally accepted accounting principles (GAAPs)**, which are standards for the preparation and presentation of financial statements,[1] and (2) **generally accepted auditing standards (GAASs)**, which specify the methods and procedures that must be used to conduct audits.[2]

Web Exercises

1. **WEB** For a description of generally accepted accounting principles (GAAPs), go to *www.fasab.gov/accepted.html*.

2. **WEB** For a description of generally accepted auditing standards (GAASs), go to *www.aicpa.org/download/members/div/auditstd/AU-00150.pdf*.

Audits

Audit can be defined as a verification of a company's books and records. Pursuant to federal securities laws, state laws, and stock exchange rules, an audit must be performed by an independent CPA. The CPA must review the financial records, check their accuracy, and otherwise investigate the financial position of the company.

The auditor must also (1) conduct a sampling of inventory to verify the figures contained in the client's financial statements and (2) verify information from third parties (contracts, bank accounts, real estate, accounts receivable, etc.). An accountant's failure to follow GAASs when conducting audits constitutes negligence.

CONTEMPORARY ENVIRONMENT
Auditor's Opinions

After an audit is complete, the auditor must render an **opinion** about how fairly the financial statements of the client company represent the company's financial position, results of operations, and change in financial position. The auditor's opinion may be unqualified, qualified, or adverse. Alternatively, the auditor may offer a disclaimer of opinion. Most auditors give unqualified opinions. The various types of opinions are described in the following paragraphs.

Unqualified Opinion

An **unqualified opinion** represents an auditor's finding that the company's financial statements fairly represent the company's financial position, the results of its operations, and the changes in its financial position for the period under audit, in conformity with consistently applied generally accepted accounting principles. This is the most favorable opinion an auditor can give.

Qualified Opinion

A **qualified opinion** states that the financial statements are fairly represented except for (or subject to) a departure from generally accepted accounting principles, a change in accounting principles, or a material uncertainty. The exception, departure, or uncertainty is noted in the auditor's opinion.

Adverse Opinion

An **adverse opinion** determines that the financial statements do not fairly represent the company's financial position, results of operations, or changes in financial position in conformity with generally accepted accounting principles. This type of opinion is usually issued when an auditor determines that a company has materially misstated certain items on its financial statements.

Disclaimer of Opinion

A **disclaimer of opinion** expresses the auditor's inability to draw a conclusion as to the accuracy of the company's financial records. This opinion is generally issued when the auditor lacks sufficient information about the financial records to issue an overall opinion.

The issuance of other than an *unqualified opinion* can have substantial adverse effects on the company audited.

Example A company that receives an opinion other than an unqualified opinion may not be able to sell its securities to the public, merge with another company, or obtain loans from banks. The Securities and Exchange Commission (SEC) has warned publicly held companies against "shopping" for a favorable opinion.

Limited Liability Partnership (LLP)

Most public accounting firms are organized and operated as **limited liability partnerships (LLPs)**. In this form of partnership, all the partners are limited partners who lose only their capital contribution in the LLP if the LLP fails. The limited partners are not personally liable for the debts and obligations of the LLP (see Exhibit 40.1). A limited partner whose negligent or intentional conduct causes injury is personally liable for his or her own conduct.

Example Suppose Alicia, Min-Wei, Holly, Won Suk, and Florence, each a certified public accountant (CPA), form an LLP called "Min-Wei Florence, LLP." While working on an audit for Min-Wei Florence LLP's client Microhard Corporation, Holly commits accounting malpractice (negligence) and fails to detect an accounting fraud at Microhard. Because of the fraud, Microhard goes bankrupt, and its shareholders lose their entire investment. In this case, the shareholders of Microhard Corporation can sue and recover against Holly, the negligent party, and against Min-Wei Florence LLP. Alicia, Min-Wei, Won Suk, and Florence can lose their capital contribution in Min-Wei Florence LLP but are not personally liable for the losses suffered by Microhard's shareholders. Holly is personally liable to the shareholders of Microhard Corporation because she was the negligent party.

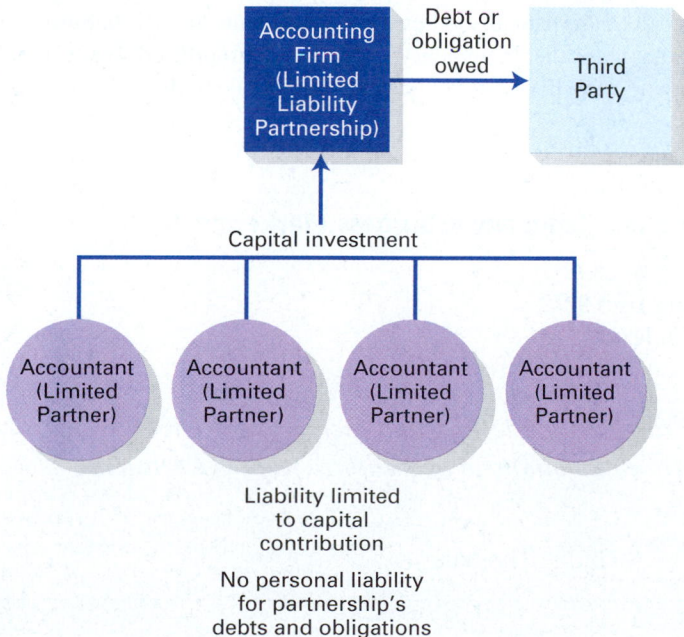

EXHIBIT 40.1

Accounting Firm LLP

Liability of Accountants to their Clients

Accountants are employed by their clients to perform certain accounting services. Under the *common law*, accountants may be found liable to the clients who hire them under several legal theories, including breach of contract, fraud, and negligence.

Breach of Contract

The terms of an **engagement** are specified when an accountant and a client enter into a contract. An accountant who fails to perform may be sued for damages caused by the **breach of contract**. Generally, the courts consider damages to be the expenses the client incurs in securing another accountant to perform the needed services as well as any fines or penalties incurred by the client for missed deadlines, lost opportunities, and such.

Fraud

Where an accountant has been found liable for actual or constructive **fraud**, the client may recover any damages proximately caused by that fraud. Punitive damages may be awarded in cases of actual fraud. **Actual fraud** is defined as intentional misrepresentation or omission of a material fact that is relied on by the client and causes the client damage. Such cases are rare. **Constructive fraud** occurs when the accountant acts with "reckless disregard" for the truth or the consequence of his or her actions. This type of fraud is sometimes categorized as "gross negligence."

Negligence

Accountants owe a duty to use *reasonable care*, *knowledge*, *skill*, and *judgment* when providing auditing and other accounting services to a client. In other words, an accountant's actions are measured against those of a "reasonable accountant" in similar circumstances. The development of GAAPs, GAASs, and other uniform accounting standards have generally made this a national standard.

An accountant who fails to meet this standard may be sued for **negligence** (also called **accountant malpractice**). For example, an accountant who does not comply with GAASs when conducting an audit and thereby fails to uncover a fraud or embezzlement by an employee of the company being audited can be sued for damages arising from this negligence. If the audit turns up a suspicious transaction or entry, the accountant is under a duty to investigate it and to inform the client of the results of the investigation.

Violations of GAAPs or GAASs are *prima facie* evidence of negligence, although compliance does not automatically relieve the accountant of such liability. Accountants can also be held liable for their negligence in preparing **unaudited financial statements**.

In the following case, the court held accountants liable to their client for malpractice.

CASE 40.1
Malpractice

Greenstein, Logan & Company v. Burgess Marketing, Inc.

744 S.W.2d 170,
Web 1987 Tex. App. Lexis 9279
Court of Appeals of Texas

" *The evidence from these experts was both legally and factually sufficient to support the finding that the failure to perform the audits in accordance with GAASs was negligence.* "

—Judge Thomas

Facts

Burgess Marketing, Inc. (Burgess Marketing), whose principal owner is Jack Burgess, sells gasoline and other fuels in central Texas through convenience stores it owns or leases. Greenstein, Logan & Company (Greenstein, Logan), certified public accountants (CPAs), had performed Burgess Marketing's annual audit for 15 years. For the last 3 of those years, Burgess Marketing's controller had underaccrued and underpaid the company's federal excise tax. Greenstein, Logan failed to discover these errors during its annual audits. Evidence showed that Greenstein, Logan had not complied with generally accepted auditing standards in conducting these audits.

Burgess Marketing fired Greenstein, Logan and employed Patillo, Brown & Hill (Patillo, Brown) as its accountants. Patillo, Brown's investigation revealed that Burgess Marketing owed approximately $1,177,000 in delinquent excise taxes, and not $137,473 as shown on the audited financial statements prepared by Greenstein, Logan. Instead of a net profit and a positive net worth, as shown on these statements, Burgess Marketing actually had been operating at a substantial monthly deficit, was bankrupt, and had a negative net worth of $1.7 million. At the time of trial, the company's total liability for federal excise taxes, including interest and penalties, was approximately $2.7 million. The Internal Revenue Service (IRS) levied a tax lien for this amount against Burgess Marketing's assets and against Burgess individually. Burgess and Burgess Marketing sued Greenstein, Logan and six of its partners for accounting malpractice. The jury found the defendants liable for accountant malpractice and awarded $3.5 million in damages to the plaintiffs. The defendants appealed.

Issue

Is Greenstein, Logan liable to Burgess Marketing for accounting malpractice?

Language of the Court

Stanley Scott, a professor of accounting at Southern Methodist University, reviewed Burgess Marketing's ledgers, journals and financial statements, as well as Greenstein, Logan's audit work papers, and explained to the jury in detail how Greenstein, Logan had departed from the GAASs during the audits. He described their work on the two audits as such a "flagrant, violent violation of the generally accepted auditing standards" that he felt compelled to testify against them. Dr. Bill Thomas, the head of Baylor University's accounting department, agreed that Greenstein, Logan had not complied with the GAASs while performing the two audits. Dr. Thomas was Greenstein, Logan's own accounting expert. Scott and Thomas both said that the tax delinquency would have been easily discovered during the audits if Greenstein, Logan had only adhered to the GAASs. The evidence from these experts was both legally and factually sufficient to support the finding that the failure to perform the audits in accordance with GAASs was negligence.

Decision

The court affirmed the jury's finding of accounting malpractice by Greenstein, Logan and its partners.

Law & Ethics Questions

1. Should accountants be held liable to their clients for negligence?
2. **ETHICS** Did Greenstein, Logan act ethically in this case?
3. Should accountants purchase malpractice insurance? Why or why not?

Web Exercises

1. **WEB** For the complete opinion of this case, go to *www.prenhall.com/cheesemancases*.
2. **WEB** View the website of the court of appeals of Texas, Tenth District, at *www.10thcoa.courts.state.tx.us*.
3. **WEB** Use *www.google.com* to find an article that discusses accountant's malpractice. Read it.

Liability of Accountants to Third Parties

Many lawsuits against accountants involve liability of accountants to third parties. The plaintiffs are third parties (e.g., shareholders and bondholders, trade creditors, banks) who relied on information supplied by the auditor. There are three major rules of liability that a state may adopt in determining whether an accountant is liable in negligence to third parties: (1) the *Ultramares* doctrine, (2) Section 552 of the *Restatement (Second) of Torts*, and (3) the foreseeability standard. These rules are discussed in the paragraphs that follow.

The *Ultramares* Doctrine

The landmark case that initially defined the liability of accountants to third parties was ***Ultramares Corporation v. Touche***.[3] In that case, Touche Niven & Co. (Touche), a national firm of certified public accountants, was employed by Fred Stern & Co. (Stern), to conduct an audit of the company's financial statements. Touche was negligent in conducting the audit and did not uncover over $700,000 of accounts receivable that were based on fictitious sales and other suspicious activities. Touche rendered an unqualified opinion and provided 32 copies of the audited financial statements to Stern. Stern gave one copy to

Ultramares Corporation (Ultramares). Ultramares made a loan to Stern on the basis of the information contained in the audited statements. When Stern failed to repay the loan, Ultramares brought a negligence action against Touche.

In his now-famous opinion, Judge Cardozo held that an accountant could not be held liable for negligence unless the plaintiff was in either in *privity of contract* or a *privity-like relationship* with the accountant. Judge Cardozo wrote:

> If liability for negligence exists, a thoughtless slip or blunder, the failure to detect a theft or forgery beneath the cover of deceptive entries may expose accountants to a liability in an indeterminate amount for an indeterminate time to an indeterminate class. The hazards of a business conducted on these terms are so extreme as to enkindle doubt whether a flaw may not exist in the implication of a duty that exposes to these consequences.

For this purpose, a relationship would occur where a client employed an accountant to prepare financial statements to be used by a third party for a specific purpose. For example, if (1) a client employs an accountant to prepare audited financial statements to be used by the client to secure a bank loan and (2) the accountant is made aware of this special purpose, the accountant is liable for any damages incurred by the bank because of a negligently prepared report. The ***Ultramares* doctrine** remains the majority rule for accountants' liability in this country.

In the following case, the court reaffirmed the *Ultramares* doctrine and held accountants not liable to third-party plaintiffs.

CASE 40.2
Ultramares Doctrine

Credit Alliance Corporation v. Arthur Andersen & Co.

65 N.Y.2d 536, 493 N.Y.S.2d 435,
Web 1985 N.Y. Lexis 15157
Court of Appeals of New York

> **"** *The facts as alleged by plaintiffs fail to demonstrate the existence of a relationship between the parties sufficiently approaching privity.* **"**
>
> —Judge Jasen

Facts

L. B. Smith, Inc., of Virginia (Smith) was a Virginia corporation engaged in the business of selling, leasing, and servicing heavy construction equipment. It was a capital-intensive business that regularly required debt financing. Arthur Andersen & Co. (Andersen), a large national firm of certified public accountants, was employed to audit Smith's financial statements. Andersen audited Smith's financial statements for two years. During this period of time, Andersen issued unqualified opinions concerning Smith's financial statements. Without Andersen's knowledge, Smith gave copies of its audited financial statements to Credit Alliance Corporation (Credit Alliance). Credit Alliance, in reliance on these financial statements, extended over $15 million of credit to Smith to finance the purchase of capital equipment through installment sales and leasing arrangements.

The audited financial statements overstated Smith's assets, net worth, and general financial position. In performing the audits, Andersen was negligent and failed to conduct investigations in accordance with generally accepted auditing standards. Because of this negligence, Andersen failed to discover Smith's precarious financial condition. The next year, Smith filed a petition for bankruptcy. Smith defaulted on obligations owed Credit Alliance in an amount exceeding $8.8 million. Credit Alliance brought this action against Andersen for negligence. The trial court denied Andersen's motion to dismiss. The appellate division affirmed. Andersen appealed.

Issue

Is Anderson liable under the *Ultramares* doctrine?

Language of the Court

Upon examination of *Ultramares*, certain criteria may be gleaned. Before accountants may be held liable in negligence to noncontractual parties who rely to their detriment on inaccurate financial reports, certain prerequisites must be satisfied, (1) the accountants must have been aware that the financial reports were to be used for a particular purpose or purposes, (2) in the furtherance of which a known party or parties was intended to rely, and (3) there must have been some conduct on the part of the accountants linking them to that party or parties, which evinces the accountants' understanding of that party or parties' reliance.

In the appeal we decide today, application of the foregoing principles presents little difficulty. The facts as alleged by plaintiffs fail to demonstrate the existence of a relationship between the parties sufficiently approaching privity. While the allegations in the complaint state that Smith sought to induce plaintiffs to extend credit, no claim is made that Andersen was being employed to prepare the reports with that particular purpose in mind. Moreover, there is no allegation that Andersen had any direct dealings with plaintiffs, had specifically agreed with Smith to prepare the report for plaintiffs' use or according to plaintiffs' requirements, or had specifically agreed with Smith to provide plaintiffs with a copy or actually did so. Indeed there is simply no allegation of any word or action on the part of Andersen directed to plaintiffs or anything contained in Andersen's retainer agreement with Smith that provided the necessary link between them.

Decision

The court of appeals held that the state should follow the *Ultramares* doctrine in examining the liability of accountants to third parties for negligence. The court reversed the lower court's decision and dismissed Credit Alliance's cause of action for negligence against defendant Andersen.

Law & Ethics Questions

1. Do you agree with the *Ultramares* doctrine? Or should a different standard be used for assessing accountants' liability?

2. **ETHICS** Should an accountant's ethical duty parallel the *Ultramares* doctrine?

3. Do you think accountants favor the *Ultramares* doctrine of liability to third parties?

Web Exercises

1. **WEB** For the complete opinion of this case, go to *www.prenhall.com/cheesemancases*.

2. **WEB** Visit the website of the court of appeals of New York, at *www.courts.state.ny.us/ctapps*.

3. **WEB** Use *www.google.com* to find an article that discusses an accountant's liability to his or her client. Read it.

Section 552 of the *Restatement (Second) of Torts*

Section 552 of the *Restatement (Second) of Torts* provides a broader standard for holding accountants liable to third parties for negligence than the *Ultramares* doctrine. Under the *Restatement* standard, an accountant is liable for his or her negligence to any member of *a limited class of intended users* for whose benefit the accountant has been employed to prepare the client's financial statements or to whom the accountant knows the client will supply copies of the financial statements. In other words, the accountant does not have to know the specific name of the third party. Many states have adopted this standard.

Example Suppose a client employs an accountant to prepare financial statements to be used to obtain investors for the company. The accountant is negligent in preparing these statements and overstates the company's earnings. If the company provides copies of the financial statements to potential investors, the accountant may be held liable to any investor who relies on the information in the financial statements, purchases securities in the company, and is injured thereby. This is so even though the accountant does not know the identity of these investors when the financial statements are prepared.

In the following case, the court held that accountants were not liable to third-party plaintiffs under the *Restatement* standard.

C A S E **40.3** *Restatement (Second)* *of Torts*	**Industrial Loan Thrift Guaranty Corporation** **of Iowa v. Reese & Company, P.C.** 422 N.W.2d 178, **Web** 1988 Iowa Sup. Lexis 84 Supreme Court of Iowa

❝ *We believe the position announced in Section 552 may be accepted to the extent that it extends the right to recover for negligence to persons whose benefit and guidance the accountant knows the information is intended.* ❞

—Judge Larson

Facts

First Security Acceptance Corporation (First Security) was an industrial loan company organized under the laws of the state of Iowa. Reese & Company, P.C., which was owned by Bill M. Reese, C.P.A., was First Security's auditor. Reese prepared audited financial statements for First Security for eight years. Reese knew that the statements were being filed by First Security with the Iowa state auditor, as required by law. The Industrial Loan Thrift Guaranty Corporation (Guaranty Corporation) was established by the state of Iowa to insure depository-type accounts at industrial loan corporations that qualified for membership. First Security applied for membership and submitted its financial statements for the previous eight years to support its application. After examining the financial reports, Guaranty Corporation made a decision to admit First Security as a member. However, Reese did not know that the financial statements he prepared would be submitted by First Security to Guaranty Corporation.

The next year, First Security became insolvent, and Guaranty Corporation had to pay the investors who lost money on thrift certificates issued by First Security. Guaranty Corporation sued Reese & Co., P.C., and Reese to recover damages for accounting malpractice, alleging that First Security's audited financial statements overstated the financial health of the company. The trial court granted Reese's motion for summary judgment. Guaranty Corporation appealed.

Issue

Is Reese liable for accounting malpractice under Section 552 of the *Restatement (Second) of Torts*?

Language of the Court

We believe the position announced in Section 552 may be accepted to the extent that it extends the right to recover for negligence to persons whose benefit and guidance the accountant *knows* the information is intended, especially when the party to be benefited is identified before the statement or report is submitted by the accountant.

In the present case, the plaintiff Guaranty Corporation suggests that it would fall within the coverage of such a rule—when the reports were filed with the auditor, it should have been foreseen by Reese that another agency such as the Guaranty Corporation would use them. We do not agree. The end and aim of the report in the present case could be said to be an assistance to First Security in the internal management of its affairs and to allow it to comply with Iowa law by filing copies with the state auditor. It cannot reasonably be said, however, that the end and aim of the report was to allow use by filing with an entity such as the Guaranty Corporation. Under these circumstances, it would not be reasonable to assume that other parties beyond First Security and the auditor would be intended users of the information.

Decision

The state supreme court held that Guaranty Corporation was not within the class of parties identifiable by Reese at the time the audits were made or a member of the class intended by Reese to be a user under the *Restatement* rule. The court affirmed the trial court's dismissal of the plaintiff's action.

Law & Ethics Questions

1. Do you think the *Restatement* rule is better than the *Ultramares* doctrine in assessing accountants' liability to third parties?

2. **ETHICS** Did the accountant act ethically in denying liability in this case?

3. Are accountants often sued as "deep pockets"? Explain.

Web Exercises

1. **WEB** For the complete opinion of this case, go to *www.prenhall.com/cheesemancases*.

2. **WEB** Visit the website of the supreme court of Iowa, at *www.judicial.state.ia.us/Supreme_Court*.

3. **WEB** Use *www.google.com* to find a recent article that discusses accountant's liability to third parties. Read it.

The Foreseeability Standard

A few states have adopted a broad rule known as the **foreseeability standard** for holding accountants liable to third parties for negligence. Under this standard, an accountant is liable to any foreseeable user of the client's financial statements. The accountant's liability does not depend on his or her knowledge of the identity of either the user or the intended class of users.

Example Suppose a corporation makes a tender offer for the shares of a target corporation whose financial statements have been audited by a CPA. If the CPA negligently prepared the financial statements and the tender offeror relied on them to purchase the target corporation, the accountant is liable for injuries suffered by the tender offeror.

CONCEPT SUMMARY

Accountants' Negligence Liability to Third Parties

LEGAL THEORY	TO WHOM LIABLE
Ultramares doctrine	Any person in *privity of contract* or a privity-like relationship with the accountant.
Section 552 of the *Restatement (Second) of Torts*	Any member of a *limited class* of intended users for whose benefit the accountant has been employed to prepare the client's financial statements or whom the accountant knows will be supplied copies of the client's financial statements.
Foreseeability standard	Any *foreseeable user* of the client's financial statements.

Fraud

If an accountant engages in *actual* or *constructive fraud*, a third party who relies on the accountant's fraud and is injured thereby may bring a tort action against the accountant to recover damages.

Example Salvo Retailers, Inc. (Salvo), applies for a bank loan, but the bank requires audited financial statements of the company before making the loan. Salvo hires a CPA to do the audit, and the CPA falsifies the financial position of the company. The bank extends the loan to Salvo, and the loan is not repaid. The bank can recover its losses from the CPA who committed fraud.

Breach of Contract

Third parties usually cannot sue accountants for breach of contract because the third parties are merely incidental beneficiaries who do not acquire any rights under the accountant–client contract. That is, they are not in **privity of contract** with the accountants.

Example An accountant contracts to perform an audit for Kim Manufacturing Company (Kim) but then fails to do so. A supplier to Kim cannot sue the accountant. This is because the supplier is not in privity of contract with the accountant.

> Like a gun that fires at the muzzle and kicks over at the breach, a cheating transaction hurts the cheater as much as the man cheated.
>
> Henry Ward Beecher
> *Proverbs from Plymouth Pulpit*
> *(1887)*

ETHICS SPOTLIGHT

Accountant's Duty to Report Client's Illegal Activity

In the course of conducting an audit of a client company's financial statements, an accountant could uncover information about the client's illegal activities. In 1995, Congress added **Section 10A to the Securities Exchange Act of 1934**. Section 10A imposes duties on auditors to detect and report illegal acts committed by their clients. Under Section 10A, an *illegal act* is defined as an "act or omission that violates any law, or any rule or regulation having the force of law." Section 10A imposes the following reporting requirements on accountants [15 U.S.C. Section 78j-1]:

- Unless an illegal act is "clearly inconsequential," the auditor must inform the client's management and audit committee of the illegal act.

- If management fails to take timely and appropriate remedial action, the auditor must report the illegal act to the client's full board of directors if (a) the illegal act will have a material effect on the client's financial statements and (b) the auditor expects to issue a nonstandard audit report or intends to resign from the audit engagement.

- Once the auditor reports the illegal act to the board of directors, the board of directors must inform the Securities and Exchange Commission (SEC) of the auditor's conclusion within one business day; if the client fails to do so, the auditor must notify the SEC on the next business day.

Law & Ethics Questions

1. **ETHICS** Should accountants report illegal activities of their clients without the law requiring them to do so?

2. **ETHICS** Should accountants report unethical conduct of clients that is not considered illegal conduct? Why or why not?

Liability of Accountants for Violations of Securities Laws

Accountants can be held liable for violating various federal and state securities laws. This section examines the civil and criminal liability of accountants under these statutes.

Section 11(a)

The Securities Act of 1933 requires that before corporations and other businesses sell securities to the public, the issuer must file a registration statement with the Securities and Exchange Commission (SEC). Accountants are often employed to prepare and certify financial statements that are included in the registration statements filed with the SEC. Accountants are considered experts, and the financial statements they prepare are considered an *expertised portion* of the registration statement.

Section 11(a) of the Securities Act of 1933 imposes civil liability on accountants and others for (1) making misstatements or omissions of material facts in a registration statement or (2) failing to find such misstatements or omissions.[4] Accountants can be held liable for fraud or negligence under Section 11(a) if the financial statements they prepare for a registration statement contain such errors.

Accountants can, however, assert a **due diligence defense** to liability. An accountant avoids liability if he or she had, after reasonable investigation, reasonable grounds to believe and did believe, at the time the registration statement became effective, that the statements made therein were true and there was no omission of a material fact that would make the statements misleading.

Example While conducting an audit, the accountants fail to detect a fraud in the financial statements. The accountants' unqualified opinion is included in the registration statement and prospectus for the offering. An investor purchases the securities and suffers a loss when the fraud is uncovered. The investor can sue the makers of the misrepresentations for fraud and the accountants for negligence.

The plaintiff may recover the difference between the price he or she paid for the security and the value of the security at the time of the lawsuit (or at the time the security was sold, if it was sold prior to the lawsuit). The plaintiff does not have to prove that he or she relied on the misstatement or omission. Privity of contract is irrelevant.

Section 10(b) and Rule 10b-5

Section 10(b) of the Securities Exchange Act of 1934 prohibits any manipulative or deceptive practice in connection with the purchase or sale of any security.[5] **Rule 10b-5** makes it unlawful for any person, by the use or means or instrumentality of interstate commerce, to employ any device or artifice to defraud; to make misstatements or omissions of material fact; or to engage in any act, practice, or course of conduct that would operate as a fraud or deceit upon any person in connection with the purchase or sale of any security.[6]

The scope of these antifraud provisions is quite broad, and the courts have implied a civil private cause of action. Thus, plaintiffs injured by a violation of these provisions can sue the offending party for monetary damages. Only purchasers and sellers of securities can sue under Section 10(b) and Rule 10b-5. Privity of contract is irrelevant.

Accountants are often defendants in Section 10(b) and Rule 10b-5 actions. The U.S. Supreme Court has decided that only intentional conduct and recklessness of accountants and others, but not ordinary negligence, violates Section 10(b) and Rule 10b-5.[7]

Section 18(a)

Section 18(a) of the Securities Exchange Act of 1934 imposes civil liability on any person who makes false or misleading statements of material fact in any application, report, or document filed with the SEC.[8] Because accountants often file reports and other documents with the SEC on behalf of clients, they can be found liable for violating this section.

Like Section 10(b), Section 18(a) requires a showing of fraud or reckless conduct on the part of the defendant. Thus, the plaintiffs in a Section 18(a) action must prove that they relied on the misleading statement and that it affected the price of the security. Negligence is not actionable.

There are two ways an accountant or another defendant can defeat the imposition of liability under Section 18(a). First, the defendant can show that he or she acted in *good faith*. Second, he or she can show that the plaintiff had knowledge of the false or misleading statement when the securities were purchased or sold.

CONTEMPORARY ENVIRONMENT
Private Securities Litigation Reform Act of 1995

The **Private Securities Litigation Reform Act of 1995**, a federal statute, changed the liability of accountants and other securities professionals in the following ways:

- The act imposes pleading and procedural requirements that make it more difficult for plaintiffs to bring class action securities lawsuits.

- The act replaces **joint and several liability** of defendants (where one party of several at-fault parties could be made to pay all of a judgment) with **proportionate liability**. This new rule limits a defendant's liability to its *proportionate* degree of fault. It therefore relieves accountants from being the "deep pocket" defendant except up to their degree of fault. The only exception to this rule—where joint and several liability is still imposed—is if the defendant acted knowingly [15 U.S.C. Section 78u-4(g)].

Example Consider a case involving plaintiffs who are victims of a securities fraud perpetrated by a firm, and they suffer $1 million in damages. If the accountants for the firm are found to be 25 percent liable, the accountants are only required to pay their proportionate share in damages—$250,000. If the accountants knowingly participated in the fraud, they would be jointly and severally liable for the entire $1 million in damages, however.

Law & Ethics Questions

1. What is joint and several liability? Explain.

2. What is proportionate liability? How does it differ from joint and several liability?

3. **ETHICS** Is joint and several liability fair? Why or why not?

Web Exercises

1. **WEB** Use *www.google.com* to find an article that discusses class action securities lawsuits. Read it.

2. **WEB** Use *www.google.com* to find an article that discusses the changes made by the Private Securities Litigation Reform Act of 1995. Read it.

Criminal Liability of Accountants

Many statutes impose criminal penalties on accountants who violate their provisions. These criminal statutes are discussed in the following paragraphs.

Section 24

Section 24 of the Securities Act of 1933 makes it a criminal offense for any person to (1) willfully make any untrue statement of material fact in a registration statement filed with the SEC, (2) omit any material fact necessary to ensure that the statements made in the registration statement are not misleading, or (3) willfully violate any other provision of the Securities Act of 1933 or rule or regulation adopted thereunder. Because accountants prepare the financial reports included in the registration statements, they are subject to criminal liability for violating this section. Penalties for a violation of this statute include fines, imprisonment, or both.[9]

Section 32(a)

Section 32(a) of the Securities Exchange Act of 1934 makes it a criminal offense for any person willfully and knowingly to make or cause to be made any false or misleading statement in any application, report, or other document required to be filed with the SEC pursuant to the Securities Exchange Act of 1934 or any rule or regulation adopted thereunder. Because accountants often file reports and documents with the SEC on behalf of clients, they are subject to this rule. Insider trading also falls within the parameters of this section.

Upon conviction under Section 32(a), an individual may be fined, imprisoned, or both. A corporation or other entity may be fined. A person cannot be imprisoned under Section 32(a) unless he or she had knowledge of the rule or regulation violated.[10]

If the SEC finds evidence of fraud or other willful violation of federal securities laws, or other federal law (such as mail and wire fraud statutes), the matter may be referred to the U.S. Department of Justice, with a recommendation that the suspected offending party be criminally prosecuted. The Department of Justice determines whether actual criminal charges will be brought.

Criminal Liability Regarding Tax Preparation

The **Tax Reform Act of 1976** imposes criminal liability on accountants and other who prepare federal tax returns.[11] The act specifically imposes the following penalties: (1) fines for the negligent understatement of the tax liability, (2) fines for the willful understatement of a client's tax liability, and (3) fines for an individual and imprisonment, and fines for a corporation, for aiding and assisting in the preparation of a false tax return. Accountants who have violated these provisions can be enjoined from further federal income tax practice.

Racketeer Influenced and Corrupt Organizations Act (RICO)

Accountants and other professionals can be named as defendants in lawsuits that assert violations of the **Racketeer Influenced and Corrupt Organizations Act (RICO)**[12] Because securities fraud falls under the definition of racketeering activity, the government often brings a RICO allegation in conjunction with a securities fraud allegation.

Persons injured by a RICO violation can bring a private *civil* action against the violator and recover treble (triple) damages, but only if the defendant has been criminally convicted in connection with the securities fraud.[13] A third-party independent contractor (e.g., an outside accountant) must have participated in the operation or management of the enterprise to be liable for civil RICO.[14]

State Securities Laws

Most states have enacted securities laws that are often patterned after federal securities laws. State securities laws provide for a variety of civil and criminal penalties for violations of these laws. Many states have enacted all or part of the **Uniform Securities Act**. *Section 101* of this act makes it a criminal offense for accountants and others to willfully falsify financial statements and other reports.

ETHICS SPOTLIGHT
The Demise of Andersen

In 2000, the Enron Corporation was the sixth-largest corporation in America. Its main business was brokering energy between buyers and sellers, as well as investing in and constructing energy ventures. The cost of Enron stock reached $90 per share. About one year later, Enron's shares were worth less than 50 cents each, and the company filed for bankruptcy. The stockholders of Enron saw their share value wiped out.

Enron's employees, who had their pension funds invested in Enron stock through an employee stock ownership fund, saw their dreams of a comfortable retirement collapse. Others—including bondholders, suppliers, banks and other creditors—also suffered huge losses.

What caused the collapse of this once mighty corporation? The discovery of false accounting records of the corporation that showed that the company was making huge profits, when in reality it was suffering from huge losses. Enron used a multitude of partnerships it owned to borrow money from banks, and then the money was distributed to Enron. The debt showed up on the partnerships' balance sheets but did not appear as debt on Enron's balance sheet. Instead, on Enron's balance sheet, the money from the partnerships was booked as investments. This practice went undetected for years. Eventually, the bubble burst, and the accounting fraud came to light.

Andersen LLP, one of what used to be the "Big Five" accounting firms in the United States, had been Enron's auditor for years. Andersen was making over $2 million per month for providing auditing and other services to Enron. During the course of the sham accounting practices at Enron, Andersen did not catch or did not "red-flag" such accounting tactics, but turned a blind eye to the practice. When the Enron accounting fraud was discovered, Andersen became a target of government investigation, too.

In the summer of 2001, the Securities and Exchange Commission (SEC), a federal government agency, notified Andersen that it was investigating the Enron affair. Several of the partners at Andersen's Houston, Texas, office, which was responsible for the Enron audit, immediately ordered the shredding of thousands of documents connected to the Enron audit. After this fact was leaked to the press and the SEC, a court issued an injunction preventing Andersen from shredding any more documents. But the damage was done: Thousands of pertinent documents relating to Andersen's involvement in the Enron fraud had been destroyed.

The U.S. Department of Justice filed a criminal complaint against Andersen, and a grand jury issued an indictment against the firm. Andersen began to unravel. Foreign accounting firms that operated as licensees using the Andersen name jumped ship and joined other accounting firms. Andersen's tax practice and consulting services were sold to other accounting firms as well, leaving only Andersen's core business, its auditing practice. But many auditing customers quickly terminated Andersen as their auditor. After months of negotiating with the Justice Department, Andersen signed a consent decree agreeing that it had violated the law.

Andersen also faced hundreds of civil lawsuits from shareholders, creditors, and others hurt by the Enron debacle. The allegations in these civil lawsuits ranged from negligence to misrepresentation. Eventually, Andersen could hold out no longer and went out of business. Many of its partners and associates found jobs at the other major accounting firms and elsewhere. But the damage was done: One of America's premiere accounting firms was dragged down with Enron's fraudulent accounting practices. *United States v. Andersen* (2002)

Law & Ethics Questions

1. Did Andersen act negligently in conducting the audits of Enron? Explain.
2. **ETHICS** Did Andersen employees act ethically in shredding important audit documents.

Web Exercises

1. **WEB** Use *www.google.com* to find an article that discusses the demise of the Enron Corporation. Read it.
2. **WEB** Use *www.google.com* to find an article that discusses the history and demise of Andersen LLP. Read it.

Sarbanes-Oxley Act

During the late 1990s and early 2000s, many corporations in the United States engaged in fraudulent accounting in order to report inflated earnings or to conceal losses. Many public accounting firms that were hired to audit the financial statements of these companies conspired with the companies to conceal this fraudulent conduct.

In response, Congress enacted the federal **Sarbanes-Oxley Act of 2002**.[15] This act imposes new rules that affect public accountants. The goals of these rules are to improve financial reporting, eliminate conflicts of interest, and provide government oversight of accounting and audit services. Several major provisions of the act that addresses accounting issues are discussed in the following paragraphs.

Establishment of the Public Company Accounting Oversight Board

The act creates the Public Company Accounting Oversight Board, which consists of five financially literate members who are appointed by the SEC for five-year terms. Two of the members must be CPAs, and three must not be CPAs. The SEC has oversight and enforcement authority over the board. The board has the authority to adopt rules concerning auditing, accounting quality control, independence, and ethics of public companies and public accountants.

Public Accounting Firms Registering with the Board

In order to audit a public company, a public accounting firm must register with the board. Registered accounting firms that audit more than 100 public companies annually are subject to inspection and review by the board once a year; all other public accounting firms must be audited by the board every three years. The board may discipline public accountants and accounting firms and order sanctions for intentional or reckless conduct, including suspending or revoking registration with the board, placing temporary limitations on activities, and assessing civil money penalties.

Separation of Audit and Nonaudit Services

The act makes it unlawful for a registered public accounting firm to simultaneously provide audit and certain nonaudit services to a public company. If a public accounting firm audits a public company, the accounting firm may not provide the following nonaudit services to the client: (1) bookkeeping services; (2) financial information systems; (3) appraisal or valuation services; (4) internal audit services; (5) management functions; (6) human resources services; (7) broker, dealer, or investment services; (8) investment banking services; (9) legal services; or (10) any other services the board determines. A certified public accounting firm may provide tax services to audit clients if such tax services are preapproved by the audit committee of the client.

AUDIT REPORT SIGN-OFFS Each audit by a certified public accounting firm is assigned an audit partner of the firm to supervise the audit and approve the audit report. The act requires that a second partner of the accounting firm review and approve audit reports prepared by the firm. All audit papers must be retained for at least seven years. The lead audit partner and reviewing partner must rotate off an audit every five years.

PROHIBITED EMPLOYMENT Any person who is employed by a public accounting firm that audits a client cannot be employed by that client as the chief executive officer (CEO), chief financial officer (CFO), controller, chief accounting officer, or equivalent position for a period of one year following the audit.

Law & Ethics Questions

1. What is the Public Company Accounting Oversight Board?
2. **ETHICS** Do you think that the Sarbanes-Oxley Act will encourage more transparency and honesty by accountants?

Web Exercises

1. **WEB** Visit the website of the Public Company Accounting Oversight Board (PCAOB), at *www.pcaobus.org*. What is the mission of this board?
2. **WEB** Use *www.google.com* to find an article that discusses the function of the Public Company Accounting Oversight Board. Read it.
3. **WEB** Use *www.google.com* to find an article that discusses the provisions of the Sarbanes-Oxley Act that separate audit and nonaudit services provided by public accountants. Read it.

Accountant's Privilege and Work Papers

In the course of conducting audits and providing other services to clients, accountants obtain information about their clients and prepare work papers. Sometimes clients are sued in court, and the court seeks information about the client from the accountant. The following paragraphs discuss the law that applies to these matters.

Accountant–Client Privilege

Sometimes clients of accountants are sued in court. About 20 states have enacted statues that create an **accountant–client privilege**. In these states, an accountant cannot be called as a witness against a client in a court action. The majority of the states follow the common law, which provides that an accountant may be called at court to testify against his or her client.

The U.S. Supreme Court has held that there is no accountant–client privilege under federal law.[16] Thus, an accountant could be called as a witness in cases involving federal securities laws, federal mail or wire fraud, federal RICO, or other federal criminal statutes.

Accountants' Work Papers

Accountants often generate substantial internal *work papers* as they perform their services. These papers often include plans for conducting audits, work assignments, notes regarding the collection of data, evidence as to the testing of accounts, notes concerning the client's internal controls, notes reconciling the accountant's report and the client's records, research, comments, memorandums, explanations, opinions, information regarding the affairs of the client, and so on.

Some state statutes provide **work product immunity**, which means an **accountant's work papers** cannot be discovered in a court case against the accountant's client. Most states do not provide this protection, and an accountant's work papers can be discovered. Federal law allows for discovery of an accountant's work papers in a federal case against the accountant's client.

In the following case, the U.S. Supreme Court was called upon to determine how far the government can go to obtain work product of accountants concerning its client.

CASE **40.4**
Accountant's Work Papers

U.S. SUPREME COURT
United States v. Arthur Young & Co.
465 U.S. 805, 104 S.Ct. 1495, 79 L.Ed.2d 826,
Web 1984 U.S. Lexis 43
Supreme Court of the United States

"*By certifying the public reports that collectively depict a corporation's financial status, the independent auditor assumes a public responsibility transcending any employment relationship with the client.*"

—Justice Burger

Facts

Arthur Young & Co. (Young) is a national firm of certified public accountants. The Amerada Hess Corp. (Amerada) employed Young to audit its financial statements, including an evaluation of Amerada's reserves for contingent liabilities. During the course of the audit, Young generated certain work papers, memorandums, and documents (work papers) related to the evaluation of Amerada's contingent liabilities.

The Internal Revenue Service (IRS) began a routine audit of Amerada's corporate income tax liability for the previous three tax years. When the audit revealed that Amerada had made questionable payments from a "special disbursement account," the IRS instituted a criminal investigation of Amerada's tax returns. In that process, the IRS issued an administrative summons to Young that required Young to make its tax accrual work papers generated during the audit of Amerada available to the IRS. Amerada instructed Young not to comply with the IRS summons. The IRS brought this action against Young to obtain the tax accrual work papers. Amerada intervened in the lawsuit. The District Court ruled in favor of the IRS. The Court of Appeals reversed. The IRS appealed.

Issue

Is there a federal accountant–client privilege that protects work papers in the possession of independent accountants from discovery by the IRS?

Language of the U.S. Supreme Court

We do not find persuasive the argument that a work product immunity for accountants' tax accrual work papers is a fitting analogue to the attorney work product doctrine. The attorney work product doctrine was founded upon the private attorney's role as the client's confidential advisor and advocate, a loyal representative whose duty it is to present the client's case in the most favorable possible light.

An independent certified accountant performs a different role. By certifying the public reports that collectively depict a corporation's financial status, the independent auditor assumes a public responsibility transcending any employment relationship with the client. The independent public accountant performing this special function owes ultimate allegiance to the corporation's creditors and stockholders, as well as to the investing public. This "public watchdog" function demands that the accountant maintain total independence from the client at all times and requires complete fidelity to the public trust. To insulate from disclosure a certified public accountant's interpretations of the client's financial statement would be to ignore the significance of the accountant's role as a disinterested analyst charged with public obligations. Thus, the independent auditor's obligation to serve the public interest assures that the integrity of the securities markets will be preserved, without the need for a work product immunity for accountants' tax accrual work papers.

Decision

The Supreme Court held that the work product of accountants is not privileged from disclosure and must be disclosed pursuant to a validly issued IRS administrative summons. The Court reversed the judgment of the Court of Appeals.

Law & Ethics Questions

1. Do you think that there should be an accountant–client privilege similar to the attorney–client privilege? Why or why not?
2. **ETHICS** Did Amerada act ethically when it instructed Young not to disclose its work product to the IRS?
3. Is it more dangerous for a company to tell information to its accountant than to its lawyer?

Web Exercises

1. **WEB** For the complete opinion of this case, go to *www.prenhall.com/cheesemancases*.
2. **WEB** Visit the website of the U.S. Supreme Court, at *www.supremecourtus.gov*, and try to find documents that relate to this case.
3. **WEB** Use *www.google.com* to find an article that discusses whether your state recognizes the accountant-client privilege. Read it.
4. **WEB** Use *www.google.com* to find an article that discusses the work product immunity of accountants. Read it.

Chapter Summary

Public Accounting, p. 1159
Accounting Standards and Principles

1. *Generally accepted accounting principals (GAAPs).* GAAPs are standards for the preparation and presentation of financial statements.
2. *Generally accepted auditing standards (GAASs).* GAASs specify method and procedures to be used to conduct audits.

Audits

An audit is a verification of a company's books and records.

Auditor's Opinions

1. *Unqualified opinion.* This type of opinion states that the company's financial statements fairly represent the company's financial.
2. *Qualified opinion.* This type of opinion states that the company's financial statements are fairly represented except for a departure from generally accepted accounting standards.
3. *Adverse opinion.* This type of opinion states that the company's financial statements do not fairly represent the company's financial position.
4. *Disclaimer of opinion.* This type of opinion expresses the auditor's inability to draw a conclusion as to the accuracy of the company's financial records.

Limited Liability Partnership (LLP)

A limited liability partnership (LLP) is the legal form many accounting firms use to organize. An LLP provides partners with limited liability.

Liability of Accountants to Their Clients, p. 1162
Breach of Contract

A breach of contract occurs when an accountant fails to perform based on the terms of engagement. An accountant may be sued for damages caused by the breach of contract. Generally, the courts consider damages to be the expenses the client incurs in securing another accountant to perform the needed services as well as any fines or penalties incurred by the client for missed deadlines, lost opportunities, and such.

Fraud

Where an accountant has been found liable for actual or constructive fraud, the client may recover any damages proximately caused by that fraud. Punitive damages may be awarded in cases of actual fraud.

Negligence

Accountants owe a duty to use reasonable care, knowledge, skill, and judgment when providing auditing and other accounting services to a client. An accountant who fails to meet this standard may be sued for negligence.

Liability of Accountants to Third Parties, p. 1163

The Ultramares Doctrine

The *Ultramares* doctrine states that an accountant is not liable for negligence to a third party unless the third party was either in privity of contract or a privity-like relationship with the accountant.

Section 552 of the Restatement (Second) of Torts

Section 552 of the *Restatement (Second) of Torts* is a doctrine which states that an accountant is liable for his or her negligence to any member of a *limited class of intended users* for whose benefit the accountant has been employed to prepare the client's financial statements or to whom the accountant knows the client will supply copies of the financial statements.

The Foreseeability Standard

The foreseeability standard is a doctrine which states that an accountant is liable to any foreseeable user of the client's financial statements.

Fraud

A third party who relies on the accountant's fraud and is injured thereby may bring an action against the accountant to recover damages.

Breach of Contract

Third parties usually cannot sue accountants for breach of contract because the third parties are merely incidental beneficiaries.

Accountant's Duty to Report Client's Illegal Activity

Section 10A of the Securities Exchange Act of 1934 imposes duties on auditors to detect and report illegal acts committed by their clients.

Liability of Accountants for Violations of Securities Laws, p. 1168

Section 11(a)

Section 11(a) of the Securities Act of 1933 imposes civil liability on accountants for making misstatements or omissions of material facts in a registration statement or failing to find such misstatements or omissions.

Section 10(b) and Rule 10b-5

Section 10(b) of the Securities Act of 1933 imposes civil liability on accountants who engage in a manipulative or deceptive practices in connection with the purchase or sale of any security.

Rule 10b-5 makes it unlawful for any person, by the use or means or instrumentality of interstate commerce, to employ any device or artifice to defraud.

Section 18(a)

Section 18(a) of the Securities Exchange Act of 1034 imposes civil liability on accountants who make false or misleading statements of material fact in any application, report, or document filed with the Securities and Exchange Commission (SEC).

Private Securities Litigation Reform Act of 1995

The Private Securities Litigation Reform Act of 1995 is a federal securities act that makes it more difficult for plaintiffs to bring class action securities lawsuits, and imposes proportional liability for violations of securities laws.

Criminal Liability of Accountants, p. 1170

Section 24

Section 24 of the Securities Act of 1933 makes it a criminal offense for an accountant to willfully make an untrue statement of material fact in a registration statement filed with the Securities and Exchange Commission (SEC).

Section 32(a)

Section 32(a) of the Securities Exchange Act of 1934 makes it a criminal act for an accountant to willfully and knowingly make or cause to be made any false or misleading statement in any application, report, or other document required to be filed with the Securities and Exchange Commission (SEC).

Criminal Liability Regarding Tax Preparation

The Tax Reform Act of 1976 imposes criminal liability on accountants for aiding or assisting in the preparation of a false tax return.

Racketeer Influenced and Corrupt Organizations Act (RICO)

The Racketeer Influenced and Corrupt Organizations Act (RICO) imposes criminal penalties on persons convicted of racketeering. The Act also imposes civil treble damages against defendants if they have been previously been criminally convicted of securities fraud.

State Securities Laws

Many states have enacted securities laws that provide for criminal and civil liability for violators.

Sarbanes-Oxley Act, p. 1171

Establishment of the Public Company Accounting Oversight Board

The Sarbanes-Oxley Act established the Public Company Accounting Oversight Board (PCAOB).

Public Accounting Firms Registering with the Board

The Sarbanes-Oxley Act requires accounting firms that audit public companies to register with the PCAOB.

Separation of Audit and Nonaudit Services

The Sarbanes-Oxley Act makes it unlawful for a registered public accounting firm to simultaneously provide audit and certain nonaudit services to a public company.

Accountant's Privilege and Work Papers, p. 1173

Accountant–Client Privilege

In many states, an accountant can raise this privilege and cannot be called as a witness against a client. The other states permit an accountant to be called as a witness against his or her client. The federal government does not recognize the accountant–client privilege, and an accountant can therefore be called as a witness against his client in a federal proceeding.

Accountants' Work Papers

Some states provide work product immunity, which means than an accountant's work papers cannot be discovered in a court case against the accountant's client. Other states and federal law allow for discovery of an accountant's work papers in actions against the accountant's client.

Test Review Terms and Concepts

Case Problems

40.1 Audit Opinion: Stephens Industries, Inc. (Stephens), agreed to purchase the stock of Colorado Rent-A-Car, Inc. (Rent-A-Car), subject to an audit of the car rental company by Haskins and Sells (Haskins & Sells), a national accounting and CPA firm. When Haskins & Sells conducted the audit, it found that the accounts receivable records were so poorly maintained that the figures could not be reconciled. Haskins & Sells issued a qualified opinion which clearly stated that the account receivable had not been audited. The purchase agreement between Stephens and Rent-A-Car stated that the accounts receivable had not been adjusted to reflect the fact that they could not be collected. Stephens later sued Haskins & Sells regarding the audit of accounts receivable. Does the qualified opinion protect the accountants from liability? *Stephens Industries, Inc. v. Haskins and Sells*, 438 F.2d 357, **Web** 1971 U.S. App. Lexis 11628 (United States Court of Appeals for the Tenth Circuit)

40.2 Auditor's Liability to Third Party: Michael H. Clott was chairman and chief executive officer of First American Mortgage Company, Inc. (FAMCO), which originated loans and sold them to investors, including E. F. Hutton Mortgage Corp. (Hutton). FAMCO employed Ernst & Whinney, a national CPA firm, to conduct audits of its financial statements. Hutton received a copy of the financial statements with an unqualified certification by Ernst & Whinney. Hutton bought more than $100 million of loans from FAMCO. As a result of massive fraudulent activity by Clott, which was undetected by Ernst & Whinney during its audit, many of the loans purchased by Hutton proved to be worthless. Ernst & Whinney had no knowledge of Clott's activities. Hutton's own negligence contributed to most of the losses it suffered. Hutton sued Ernst & Whinney for fraud and negligence. Is Ernst & Whinney liable? *E. F. Hutton Mortgage Corporation v. Pappas*, 690 F.Supp. 1465, **Web** 1988 U.S. Dist. Lexis 6444 (United States District Court for the District of Maryland)

40.3 Auditor's Liability: Guarente-Harrington Associates was a limited partnership formed for the purpose of investing in securities. There were 2 general partners and 40 limited partners. The partnership agreement provided that no partner could withdraw any part of his or her interest in the partnership except at the end of the fiscal year and with not less than 30 days' prior notice. Arthur Andersen & Co. (Arthur Andersen), a national CPA firm, was hired to audit the books of the limited partnership. In certifying the financial statements of the partnership and preparing its tax returns, Arthur Andersen failed to report that the general partners had withdrawn $2 million of their $2.6 million capital investment at times other than at the end of the fiscal year and without proper notice. The partnership suffered losses because of this lack of capital. Shelby White, a limited partner, sued Arthur Andersen for accounting malpractice. Is Arthur Andersen liable under the *Ultramares* doctrine? *White v. Guarente*, 43 N.Y.2d 356, 372 N.E.2d 315, 401 N.Y.S.2d 474, **Web** 1977 N.Y. Lexis 2470 (Court of Appeals of New York)

40.4 Accountant's Liability to Third Party: Giant Stores Corporation (Giant) hired Touche Ross & Co. (Touche), a national CPA firm, to conduct audits of the company's financial statements for two years. Touche gave an unqualified opinion for both years. Touche was unaware of any specific use of the audited statements by Giant. After receiving copies of these audited financial statements from Giant, Harry and Barry Rosenblum (Rosenblums) sold their retail catalog showroom business to Giant in exchange for 80,000 shares of Giant stock.

One year later, a major fraud was uncovered at Giant that caused its bankruptcy. Because of the bankruptcy, the stock that the Rosenblums received became worthless. In conducting Giants' audits, Touche had failed to uncover that Giant did not own certain assets that appeared on its financial statements and that Giant had omitted substantial amounts of accounts payable from its records. The Rosenblums sued Touche for accounting malpractice. Is Touche liable for accounting malpractice under any of the three negligence theories discussed in this chapter? *H. Rosenblum, Inc. v. Adler*, 93 N.J. 324, 461 A.2d 138, **Web** 1983 N.J. Lexis 2717 (Supreme Court of New Jersey)

40.5 *Ultramares* **Doctrine:** Texscan Corporation (Texscan) was a corporation located in Phoenix, Arizona. The company was audited by Coopers & Lybrand (Coopers), a national CPA firm that prepared audited financial statements for the company. The Lindner Fund, Inc., and the Lindner Dividend Fund, Inc. (Lindner Funds), were mutual funds that invested in securities of companies. After receiving and reviewing the audited financial statements of Texscan, Lindner Funds purchased securities in the company. Thereafter, Texscan suffered financial difficulties, and Lindner Funds suffered substantial losses on its investment. Lindner Funds sued Coopers, alleging that Coopers was negligent in conducting the audit and preparing Texscan's financial statements. Can Coopers be held liable to Lindner Funds for accounting malpractice under the *Ultramares* doctrine, Section 552 of the *Restatement (Second) of Torts*, or the foreseeability standard? *Lindner Fund v. Abney*, 770 S.W.2d 437, **Web** 1989 Mo. App. Lexis 490 (Court of Appeals of Missouri)

40.6 Section 10(b): The Firestone Group, Ltd. (Firestone), a company engaged in real estate development, entered into a contract to sell nursing homes it owned to a buyer. The buyer paid a $30,000 deposit to Firestone and promised to pay the remainder of the $28 million purchase price in the future. The profit on the sale, if consummated, would have been $2 million.

To raise capital, Firestone planned on issuing $7.5 million of securities to investors. Firestone hired Laventhol, Krekstein, Horwath & Horwath (Laventhol), a national CPA firm, to audit the company for the fiscal year. When Laventhol proposed to record the profit from the sale of the nursing homes as unrealized gross profit, Firestone threatened to withdraw its account from Laventhol. Thereafter, Laventhol decided to recognize $235,000 as profit and to record the balance of $1,795,000 as "deferred gross profit." This was done even though, during the course of the audit, Laventhol learned that there was no corporate resolution approving the sale, the sale transaction was not recorded in the minutes of the corporation, and the buyer had a net worth of only $10,000. Laventhol also failed to verify the enforceability of the contracts.

Gerald M. Herzfeld and other investors received copies of the audited financial statements and invested in the securities issued by Firestone. Later, when the buyer did not purchase the nursing homes, Firestone declared bankruptcy. Herzfeld and the other investors lost most of their investment. Herzfeld sued Laventhol for securities fraud in violation of Section 10(b) of the Securities Exchange Act of 1934. Is Laventhol liable? *Herzfeld v. Laventhol, Krekstein, Horwath & Horwath*, 540 F.2d 27, **Web** 1976 U.S. App. Lexis 8008 (United States Court of Appeals for the Second Circuit)

40.7 Accountant–Client Privilege: For five years, Chaple, an accountant licensed by the state of Georgia, provided accounting services to Roberts and several corporations in which Roberts was an officer and shareholder (collectively called Roberts). During this period, Roberts provided Chaple with confidential information, with the expectation that this information would not be disclosed to third parties. Georgia statutes provide for an accountant–client privilege. When the IRS began investigating Roberts, Chaple, voluntarily and without being subject to a subpoena, released some of this confidential information about Roberts to the IRS. Roberts sued Chaple, seeking an injunction to prevent further disclosure, requesting return of all information in Chaple's possession, and seeking monetary damages. Who wins? *Roberts v. Chaple*, 187 Ga.App. 123, 369 S.E.2d 482, **Web** 1988 Ga. App. Lexis 554 (Court of Appeals of Georgia)

Ethics Issues

40.8 Ethics: The archdiocese of Miami established a health and welfare plan to provide medical coverage for its employees. The archdiocese purchased a stop-loss insurance policy from Lloyd's of London (Lloyd's), which provided insurance against losses that exceeded the basic coverage of the plan. The archdiocese employed Coopers & Lybrand (Coopers), a national firm of CPAs, to audit the health plan every year for 12 years.

The audit program required Coopers to obtain a copy of the current stop-loss policy and record any changes. After 2 years, Coopers neither obtained a copy of the policy nor verified the existence of the Lloyd's insurance. Nevertheless,

Coopers repeatedly represented to the trustees of the archdiocese that the Lloyd's insurance policy was in effect, when in fact it had been canceled. During this period of time, Dennis McGee, an employee of the archdiocese, had embezzled funds that were to be used to pay premiums on the Lloyd's policy. The archdiocese sued Coopers for accounting malpractice and sought to recover the funds stolen by McGee. Did Coopers act ethically in this case? Is Coopers liable? *Coopers & Lybrand v. Trustees of the Archdiocese of Miami*, 536 So.2d 278, **Web** 1988 Fla. App. Lexis 5348 (Court of Appeal of Florida)

40.9 Ethics: Milton Mende purchased the Star Midas Mining Co., Inc., for $6,500. This Nevada corporation was a shell corporation with no assets. Mende changed the name of the corporation to American Equities Corporation (American Equities) and hired Bernard Howard to prepare certain accounting reports so that the company could issue securities to the public. In preparing the financial accounts, Howard (1) made no examination of American Equities's books, (2) falsely included an asset of over $700,000 on the books, which was a dormant mining company that had been through insolvency proceedings, (3) included in the profit and loss statement companies that Howard knew American Equities did not own, and (4) recklessly stated as facts things of which he was ignorant. The United States sued Howard for criminal conspiracy in violation of federal securities laws. Is Howard criminally liable? *United States v. Howard*, 328 F.2d 854, **Web** 1964 U.S. App. Lexis 6343 (United States Court of Appeals for the Second Circuit)

IRAC Writing Assignment

Read **Case A-40** in Appendix A [*United States v. Natelli*]. Use the IRAC method to prepare a written analysis of the case.

Endnotes

1. GAAPs are official standards promulgated by the Financial Accounting Standards Board (FASB). GAAPs also include unofficial pronouncements, interpretations, research studies, textbooks, and the like.
2. GAASs are issued by the Auditing Standards Committee of the American Institute of Certified Public Accountants (AICPA).
3. 255 N.Y. 170, 174 N.E. 441, **Web** 1931 N.Y. Lexis 660 (Court of Appeals of New York).
4. 15 U.S.C. Section 77k(a).
5. 15 U.S.C. Section 78j(b).
6. 17 C.F.R. Section 240.10b-5.
7. *Ernst & Ernst v. Hochfelder*, 425 U.S. 185, 96 S.Ct. 1375, 47 L.Ed.2d 668, **Web** 1976 U.S. Lexis 2 (Supreme Court of the United States).
8. 15 U.S.C. Section 78r(a).
9. 15 U.S.C. Section 77x.
10. 15 U.S.C. Section 78ff.
11. 26 U.S.C. Sections 7206(1),7206(2).
12. 18 U.S.C. Sections 1961–1968.
13. Private Securities Litigation Reform Act of 1995.
14. *Reves v. Ernst & Young*, 507 U.S. 170, 113 S.Ct. 1163, 122 L.Ed.2d 525, **Web** 1993 U.S. Lexis 1940 (Supreme Court of the United States).
15. Public Law No. 107-204, 16 Statute 745, also known as the Public Company Accounting Reform and Investor Protection Act of 2002.
16. *Couch v. U.S.*, 409 U.S. 322, 93 S.Ct. 611, 34 L.Ed.2d 548, **Web**, 1973 U.S. Lexis 23 (Supreme Court of the United States).

UNIT 10

Global Environment

CHAPTER 41   International and World Trade Law

CHAPTER 41

International and World Trade Law

> *International law, or the law that governs between nations, has at times, been like the common law within states, a twilight existence during which it is hardly distinguishable from morality or justice, till at length the imprimatur of a court attests its jural quality.*
>
> —JUSTICE CARDOZO
> New Jersey v. Delaware, (1934)

CHAPTER OBJECTIVES

After studying this chapter, you should be able to:

1. Describe the federal government's power under the Foreign Commerce and Treaty Clauses of the U.S. Constitution.
2. List and describe the sources of international law.
3. Describe the functions and governance of the United Nations.
4. Describe the North American Free Trade Agreement (NAFTA) and other regional economic organizations.
5. Describe the World Trade Organization (WTO) and explain how its dispute resolution procedure works.

CHAPTER CONTENTS

- Introduction to International and World Trade Law
- The United States and Foreign Affairs
- Sources of International Law
- United Nations
- Regional International Organizations
- World Trade Organization (WTO)
- National Courts Decide International Disputes
- Chapter Summary
- Test Review Terms and Concepts
- Case Problems
- Ethics Issues
- IRAC Writing Assignment

Introduction to International and World Trade Law

International law, important to both nations and businesses, has many unique features. First, there is no single legislative source of international law. All countries of the world and numerous international organizations are responsible for enacting international law. Second, there is no single world court that is responsible for interpreting international law. There are, however, several courts and tribunals that hear and decide international legal disputes of parties that agree to appear before them. Third, there is no world executive branch that can enforce international law. Thus, nations do not have to obey international law enacted by other countries or international organizations. Because of these uncertainties, some commentators question whether international law is really law.

As technology and transportation bring nations closer together and American and foreign firms increase their global activities, international law will become even more important to governments and businesses. This chapter introduces the main concepts of international law and discusses the sources of international law and the organizations responsible for its administration.

Nepal

Many countries of the world are not democracies like the United States. The Kingdom of Nepal, for example, is a monarchy.

The United States and Foreign Affairs

The U.S. Constitution divides the power to regulate the internal affairs of this country between the federal and state governments. On the international level, however, the Constitution gives most of the power to the federal government. Two constitutional provisions establish this authority: the Foreign Commerce Clause and the Treaty Clause.

Foreign Commerce Clause

Article I, Section 8, clause 3 of the U.S. Constitution—the **Foreign Commerce Clause**—vests Congress with the power "to regulate commerce with foreign nations." The Constitution does not vest exclusive power over foreign affairs in the federal government, but any state or local law that unduly burdens foreign commerce is unconstitutional as a violation of the Foreign Commerce Clause.

Example General Motors Corporation and the Ford Motor Company, two of America's largest automobile manufactures, are headquartered in the state of Michigan. The state of Michigan, in order to reduce the sales of foreign-made automobiles in the state, enacts a state law that imposes a 50 percent tax on foreign-made automobiles sold in the state but does not imposes this tax on American-made automobiles sold in the state. This tax violates the Foreign Commerce Clause because it unduly burdens foreign commerce.

Example   General Motors Corporation and the Ford Motor Company, two of America's largest automobile manufactures, are headquartered in the state of Michigan. The state of Michigan, in order to protect the environment, enacts a state tax that places a 20 percent tax on all automobile sales made in the state. This tax does not violate the Foreign Commerce Clause because it does not treat foreign commerce any differently than domestic commerce.

Treaty Clause

Article II, Section 2, clause 2 of the U.S. Constitution—the **Treaty Clause**—states that the president "shall have power, by and with the advice and consent of the Senate, to make treaties, provided two-thirds of the senators present concur."

Under the Treaty Clause, only the federal government may enter into treaties with foreign nations. Under the Supremacy Clause of the Constitution, treaties become part of the "law of the land," and conflicting state or local law is void. The president is the agent of the United States in dealing with foreign countries.

Example   The federal government of the United States can enter into a treaty with the country of China whereby the two countries agree to reduce trade barriers between the two countries. However, the state of California cannot enter into a treaty with the country of China that reduces trade barriers between the state of California and China.

Cambodia

The federal government of the United States is authorized to enter into treaties with foreign countries and to regulate foreign commerce.

Sources of International Law

The **sources of international law** are those things that international tribunals rely on in deciding international disputes. **Article 38(1) of the Statute of the International Court of Justice** lists the following four sources of international law: *treaties and conventions, custom, general principles of law*, and *judicial decisions and teachings*. Most courts rely on the hierarchy suggested by this list; that is, treaties and conventions are turned to before custom, and so on. These sources of law are discussed in the following paragraphs.

Treaties and Conventions

Treaties and conventions are the equivalents of legislation at the international level. A **treaty** is an agreement or a contract between two or more nations that is formally signed by an authorized representative and ratified by the supreme power of each nation. *Bilateral treaties* are between two nations; *multilateral treaties* involve more than two nations.

Conventions are treaties that are sponsored by international organizations, such as the United Nations. Conventions normally have many signatories.

Treaties and conventions address such matters as human rights, foreign aid, navigation, commerce, and the settlement of disputes. Most treaties are registered with and published by the United Nations.

Custom

Custom between nations is an independent source of international law. Custom describes a practice followed by two or more nations when dealing with each other. Custom may be found in official government statements, diplomatic correspondence, policy statements, press releases, speeches, and the like. Two elements must be established to show that a practice has become a custom:

1. Consistent and recurring action by two or more nations over a considerable period of time
2. Recognition that the custom is binding—that is, followed because of legal obligation rather than courtesy

International customs evolve as more, technology, forms of government, political parties, and other factors change throughout the world. Customs that have been recognized for some period of time are often codified in treaties.

General Principles of Law

Courts and tribunals that decide international disputes frequently rely on **general principles of law** that are recognized by civilized nations. These are principles of law that are common to the *national* law of the parties to the dispute. They may be derived from constitutions, statutes, regulations, common law, or other sources of national law. In some cases, however, the countries' laws may differ concerning the matter in dispute.

Judicial Decisions and Teachings

A fourth source of law to which international tribunals can refer is **judicial decisions and teachings** of the most qualified scholars of the various nations involved in the dispute. Although international courts are not bound by the doctrine of *stare decisis* and may decide each case on its own merits, the courts often refer to their own past decisions for guidance. Court decisions of national courts do not create precedent for international courts.

Web Exercise

1. **WEB** Select a country and then use *www.google.com* to find an article that discusses that country's legal system.

United Nations

One of the most important international organizations is the **United Nations (UN)**, which was created by a multilateral treaty on October 24, 1945.[1] Most countries of the world are members of the UN. The goals of the UN, which is headquartered in New York City, are to maintain peace and security in the world, promote economic and social cooperation, and protect human rights (see Exhibit 41.1).

The UN is governed by the General Assembly, the Security Council, and the Secretariat, which are discussed in the following paragraphs.

General Assembly

> Only when the world is civilized enough to keep promises will we get any kind of international law.
>
> Julius Henry Cohen

The **General Assembly** is composed of all member nations. As the legislative body of the UN, it adopts resolutions concerning human rights, trade, finance and economics, and other matters within the scope of the UN Charter. Although resolutions have limited force, they are usually enforced through persuasion and the use of economic and other sanctions.

EXHIBIT 41.1

Charter of the United Nations (Selected Provisions)

Our respective Governments, through representatives assembled in the city of San Francisco, who have exhibited their full powers found to be in good and due form, have agreed to the present Charter of the United Nations and do hereby establish an international organization to be known as the United Nations.

Chapter 1. Purposes and Principles

Article 1 The Purposes of the United Nations are:

(1) To maintain international peace and security, and to that end: to take effective collective measures for the prevention and removal of threats to the peace, and for the suppression of acts of aggression or other breaches of the peace, and to bring about by peaceful means, and in conformity with the principles of justice and international law, adjustment or settlement of international disputes or situations which might lead to a breach of the peace;

(2) To develop friendly relations among nations based on respect for the principle of equal rights and self-determination of peoples, and to take other appropriate measures to strengthen universal peace;

(3) To achieve international co-operation in solving international problems of an economic, social, cultural, or humanitarian character, and in promoting and encouraging respect for human rights and for fundamental freedoms for all without distinction as to race, sex, language, or religion; and

(4) To be a centre for harmonizing the actions of nations in the attainment of these common ends.

Security Council

The **Security Council** is composed of 15 member nations, 5 of which are permanent members (China, France, Russia, the United Kingdom, and the United States), and 10 other countries chosen by the members of the General Assembly to serve two-year terms. The council is primarily responsible for maintaining international peace and security and has authority to use armed forces.

Secretariat

The **Secretariat** administers the day-to-day operations of the UN. It is headed by the *secretary-general*, who is elected by the General Assembly. The secretary-general may refer matters that threaten international peace and security to the Security Council and use his office to help solve international disputes.

Web Exercises

1. **WEB** Visit the website of the United Nations, at *www.un.org*.

2. **WEB** Visit the website of the Security Council, at *www.un.org/Docs/sc*.

3. **WEB** Visit the website *www.un.org/sg*. Who is the current secretary-general? What country is this person from?

Bhutan

Even the smallest countries of the world, such as Bhutan, a Buddhist nation in Asia, are members of the United Nations.

UN Agencies

The UN is composed of various autonomous agencies that deal with a wide range of economic and social problems. These include the **United Nations Educational, Scientific, and Cultural Organization (UNESCO)**, the **United Nations International Children's Emergency Fund (UNICEF)**, the International Monetary Fund (IMF), the World Bank, and the **International Fund for Agricultural Development (IFAD)**.

Web Exercises

1. **WEB** Visit the website of UNESCO, at *www.unesco.org*. What purposes does this agency serve?

2. **WEB** Visit the website of UNICEF, at *www.unicef.org*. What purposes does this agency serve?

3. **WEB** Visit the website of IFAD, at *www.ifad.org*. What purposes does this agency serve?

INTERNATIONAL LAW
International Monetary Fund (IMF)

The **International Monetary Fund (IMF)**, an agency of the United Nations, was established by treaty in 1945 to help promote the world economy following the Great Depression of the 1930s and the end of World War II in 1945. The IMF comprises more than 180 countries that are each represented on the board of directors, which makes the policy decisions of the IMF. The day-to-day operations of the IMF are run by the executive committee, which is composed of the United States, the United Kingdom, Japan, Germany, France, China, Russia, Saudi Arabia, and 16 elected countries other than those already named. The IMF is funded by monetary contributions of member nations, assessed based on the size of each nation's economy. The IMF's headquarters is located in Washington, DC.

The primary function of the IMF is to promote sound monetary, fiscal, and macroeconomic policies worldwide by providing assistance to needy countries. The IMF responds to financial crises around the globe. It does so by providing short-term loans to member countries to help them weather problems caused by unstable currencies, to balance payment problems, and to recover from the economic policies of past governments. The IMF examines a country's economy as a whole and its currency accounts, inflation, balance of payments with other countries, employment, consumer and business spending, and other factors to determine whether the country needs assistance. For example, the IMF has played a financial role in helping eastern and central European countries recover since the collapse of the Soviet Union. In return for the financial assistance, a country must agree to meet certain monetary, fiscal, employment, inflation, and other goals established by the IMF.

Web Exercises

1. **WEB** Visit the website of the International Monetary Fund (IMF), at *www.imf.org*.

2. **WEB** At *www.imf.org*, find a description of the functions of the IMF.

3. **WEB** Use *www.google.com* to find an article that discusses recent assistance that the IMF has provided to a country. Read it.

International Monetary Fund

Morocco

The primary function of the IMF is to promote sound monetary, fiscal, and macroeconomic policies worldwide by providing assistance to countries.

INTERNATIONAL LAW
World Bank

The **World Bank** is a United Nations agency that comprises more than 180 member nations. The World Bank is financed by contributions from developed countries, with the United States, the United Kingdom, Japan, Germany, and France being its main contributors. The World Bank has employees located in its headquarters in Washington, DC, and regional offices elsewhere throughout the world. Each member country is represented on a board of governors that meets to determine how the bank's funds will be distributed. The executive directors, comprising directors from the 5 largest donor countries and 19 directors elected by the other countries, is responsible for the conduct of the bank's general operations.

The World Bank provides money to developing countries to fund projects for humanitarian purposes and to relieve poverty. The World Bank provides funds to build roads, construct dams and build other water projects, establish hospitals and provide medical assistance, develop agriculture, and provide humanitarian aid. The World Bank provides outright grants of funds to developing countries for such projects, and it makes long-term low-interest-rate loans to those countries. The bank routinely grants debt relief for these loans.

The World Bank
IBRD & IDA: Working for a World Free of Poverty

Web Exercises

1. **WEB** Visit the website of the World Bank, at *www.worldbank.org*.

2. **WEB** At *www.worldbank.org*, find the description of the functions of the World Bank.

3. **WEB** Use *www.google.com* to find an article that discusses recent assistance that the World Bank has provided to a country. Read it.

Laos

The World Bank provides money to developing countries to fund projects for humanitarian purposes and to relieve poverty.

THE INTERNATIONAL COURT OF JUSTICE The **International Court of Justice (ICJ)**, also called the **World Court**, is located in The Hague, the Netherlands. It is the judicial branch of the UN. Only nations, not individuals or businesses, may have cases decided by this court. The ICJ may hear cases that nations refer to it as well as cases involving treaties and the UN Charter. A nation may seek redress on behalf of an individual or a business that has a claim against another country. The ICJ is composed of 15 judges who serve nine-year terms; not more than 2 judges may be from the same nation. A nation that is a party to a dispute before the ICJ may appoint 1 judge on an ad hoc basis for that case.

Web Exercise

1. **WEB** Visit the website of the International Court of Justice, at *www.icj-cij.org*.

Regional International Organizations

There are several significant regional organizations whose members have agreed to work together to promote peace and security as well as economic, social, and cultural development. The most important of these organizations are discussed in the following paragraphs.

European Union

The European Union (EU) is a regional trade bloc comprised of countries of western and eastern Europe. The EU treaty creates open borders for trade by providing for the free flow of capital, labor, goods, and services among member nations.

European Union

One of the most important international regional organizations is the **European Union (EU)**, formerly called the *European Community*, or *Common Market*. The EU, which was created in 1957, is composed of many countries of western and eastern Europe, including Austria, Belgium, Bulgaria, Cyprus (the Greek part), Czech Republic, Denmark, Estonia, Finland, France, Germany, Greece, Hungary, Ireland, Italy, Latvia, Lithuania, Luxembourg, Malta, the Netherlands, Poland, Portugal, Romania, Slovakia, Slovenia, Spain, Sweden, and the United Kingdom of Great Britain and Northern Ireland. The EU represents more than 500 million people and a gross community product that exceeds that of the United States, Canada, and Mexico combined.

The EU's *Council of Ministers* is composed of representatives from each member country, who meet periodically to coordinate efforts to fulfill the objectives of the treaty. The council votes on significant issues and changes to the treaty. Some matters require unanimity, whereas others require only a majority vote. The member nations have surrendered substantial sovereignty to the EU. The *EU Commission*, which is independent of its member nations, is charged to act in the best interests of the union. The member nations have delegated substantial powers to the commission, including authority to enact legislation and to take enforcement actions to ensure member compliance with the treaty.

The EU treaty creates open borders for trade by providing for the free flow of capital, labor, goods, and services among member nations. Under the EU, customs duties have been eliminated among member nations. Common customs tariffs have been established for EU trade with the rest of the world. A single monetary unit, the **euro**, and a common monetary policy have been introduced. An EU central bank, equivalent to the U.S. Federal Reserve Board, has been established.

A unanimous vote of existing EU members is needed to admit a new member. Other nonmember European countries are expected to apply for and be admitted as members of the EU.

A map of the EU is shown in Exhibit 41.2.

Web Exercises

1. **WEB** Visit the website of the European Union (EU), at *http://europa.eu/index_ns_en.htm*.

2. **WEB** Use *www.google.com* to find an article that discusses the advantages of the European Union. Read it.

3. **WEB** Use *www.google.com* to find an article about the euro currency.

4. **WEB** Use *finance.yahoo.com* to find the current exchange rate of the euro to the U.S. dollar.

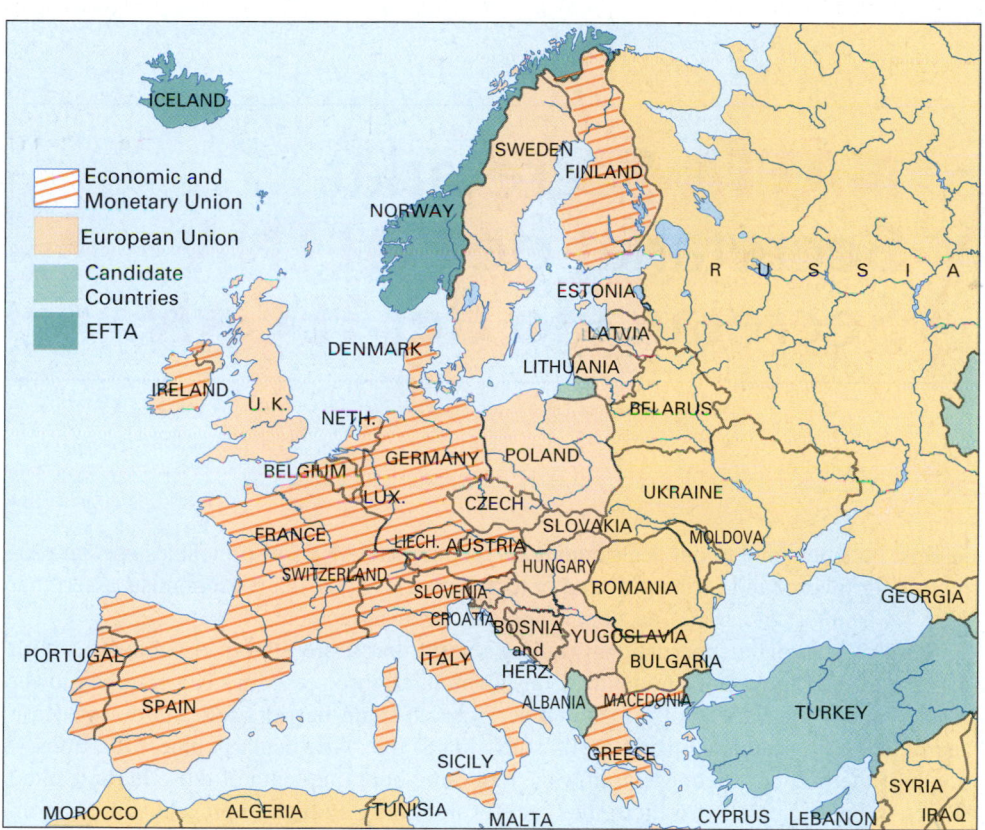

EXHIBIT 41.2

Map of European Union (EU) Countries as of 2007

North American Free Trade Agreement (NAFTA)

In 1990, Mexico asked the United States to set up a two-country trade pact. Negotiations between the two countries began. Canada joined the negotiations, and on August 12, 1992, the **North American Free Trade Agreement (NAFTA)** was signed by the leaders of the three countries. The treaty creates a free-trade zone stretching from the Yukon to the Yucatan, bringing together more than 400 million people in the three countries.

NAFTA eliminates or reduces most of the duties, tariffs, quotas, and other trade barriers between Mexico, the United States, and Canada. Agriculture, automobiles, computers, electronics, energy and petrochemicals, financial services, insurance, telecommunications, and many other industries are affected. The treaty contains a safety valve: A country can reimpose tariffs if an import surge from one of the other nations hurts its economy or workers. Like other regional trading agreements, NAFTA allows the bloc to discriminate

> When Kansas and Colorado have a quarrel over the water in the Arkansas River they don't call out the National Guard in each state and go to war over it. They bring a suit in the Supreme Court of the United States and abide by the decision. There isn't a reason in the world why we cannot do that internationally.
>
> Harry S. Truman
> *Speech (1945)*

Canada

The parties to the North American Free Trade Agreement (NAFTA) are Canada, Mexico, and the United States of America.

against outsiders and to cut deals among its members. NAFTA also includes special protection for favored industries with a lot of lobby muscle. Thus, many economists assert that NAFTA is not a "free trade" pact but a *managed trade* agreement.

NAFTA forms a supernational trading region that more effectively competes with Japan and the European Community. Consumers in all three countries began to pay lower prices on a wide variety of goods and services as trade barriers fell and competition increased. Critics contend that NAFTA shifted U.S. jobs—particularly blue-collar jobs—south of the border, where Mexican wage rates are about one-tenth of those in the United States. Environmentalists criticize the pact for not doing enough to prevent and clean up pollution in Mexico.

A map of NAFTA is shown in Exhibit 41.3.

Web Exercises

1. **WEB** Visit the website of the NAFTA Secretariat, at *www.nafta-sec-alena.org*. What does this organization do?

2. **WEB** Use *www.google.com* to find an article that discusses the advantages and disadvantages of NAFTA. Read it.

Asian Economic Communities

In 1967, the **Association of Southeast Asian Nations (ASEAN)** was created. The countries that belong to ASEAN are Brunei Darussalam, Cambodia, Indonesia, Laos, Malaysia, Myanmar, Philippines, Singapore, Thailand, and Vietnam. This is a cooperative association of diverse nations.

EXHIBIT 41.3

Map of North American Free Trade Agreement (NAFTA) Countries

Two of the world's largest countries, Japan and China, do not belong to any significant economic community. Although not a member of ASEAN, Japan has been instrumental in providing financing for the countries that make up that organization. China also works closely with the countries of ASEAN and is a potential member of ASEAN.

Web Exercise

1. **WEB** Visit the website of ASEAN, at *www.aseansec.org*.

> My nationalism is intense internationalism. I am sick of the strife between nations or religions.
>
> Gandhi

Organization of the Petroleum Exporting Countries (OPEC)

One of the most well-known economic organizations is the **Organization of the Petroleum Exporting Countries (OPEC)**. OPEC consists of oil-producing and exporting countries from Africa, Asia, the Middle East, and South America. The member nations are Algeria, Angola, Indonesia, Iran, Iraq, Kuwait, Libya, Nigeria, Qatar, Saudi Arabia, United Arab Emirates (UAE), and Venezuela. OPEC sets quotas on the output of oil production by member nations.

Web Exercise

1. **WEB** Visit the website of OPEC, at *www.opec.org*.

Other Regional Economic Organizations

Countries of Latin America and the Caribbean have established several regional organizations to promote economic development and cooperation. Mexico, the largest industrialized country in Latin America and the Caribbean, has entered into a free trade agreement with all the countries of Central America as well as Chile, Colombia, and Venezuela. Other regional economic organizations include countries of Central America and South America. Several regional economic communities have been formed in Africa as well.

> We need to have the spirit of science in international affairs, to make the conduct of international affairs the effort to find the right solution, the just solution of international problems, not the effort by each nation to get the better of other nations, to do harm to them when it is possible.
>
> Linus Carl Pauling
> *No More War (1958)*

INTERNATIONAL LAW
Central America Free Trade Agreement

After years of negotiations, the United States and several Central American countries formed the **Central America Free Trade Agreement (CAFTA)**. The agreement originally encompassed the United States and the Central American countries of Costa Rica, El Salvador, Guatemala, Honduras, and Nicaragua. The Dominican Republic subsequently joined CAFTA, which is now commonly called **DR-CAFTA**. This agreement lowered tariffs and reduced trade restrictions among the member nations. The United States has bilateral trade agreements with several other Central American countries that are not members of DR-CAFTA.

The formation of DR-CAFTA is seen as a stepping stone toward the creation of the **Free Trade Area of the Americas (FTAA)**, which would be an ambitious free trade agreement that would encompass most of the counties of Central America, North America, and South America. The negotiation of the FTAA is difficult because of the different interests of the countries that would be members.

World Trade Organization (WTO)

In 1995, the **World Trade Organization (WTO)** was created as part of the Uruguay Round of trade negotiations on the *General Agreement on Tariffs and Trade (GATT)*. GATT is a multilateral treaty that establishes trade agreements and limits tariffs and trade restrictions among its 150 member nations.

The WTO is an international organization whose headquarters is located in Geneva, Switzerland. WTO members have entered into many trade agreements among themselves, including international agreements on investments, sale of goods, provision of services, intellectual property, licensing, tariffs, subsidies, and the removal of trade barriers.

The WTO, which has been referred to as the "Supreme Court of Trade," has become the world's most important trade organization. The WTO has jurisdiction to enforce the most important and comprehensive trade agreements in the world among its more than 130 member nations. Many herald the WTO as a much-needed world court that can peaceably solve trade disputes among nations.

Web Exercises

1. **WEB** Visit the website of the World Trade Organization (WTO), at *www.wto.org*.

2. **WEB** Use *www.google.com* to find a website that contains information that is in opposition to the WTO.

INTERNATIONAL LAW
China Joins the WTO

For almost 60 years, China and the United States have pursued divergent paths. China became the world's largest communist country and the United States the leading democracy. China maintained its agricultural base, while the United States pursued industrialization. Most of China's businesses were state owned, while those in the United States were privately owned under a capitalist system. For over a decade, these two countries engaged in on-again, off-again trade negotiations. Then in November 1999, they formed a landmark trade pact. In exchange for being granted the right to import most goods and services into the United States, China, which had substantially restricted imports into its country, agreed to open its markets to foreign goods and services.

The China–U.S. trade agreement was a prelude to China's trade agreements with other countries. These trade agreements supported China's application to join the WTO. In 2002, China became a member of the WTO, making it a full partner in the world's trading system.

China's entry into the WTO is not without critics. In the United States, labor unions complain that U.S. manufacturing jobs will be lost to China, while environmentalists complain that little is being done to protect the environment from an industrialized economy the size of China's. In China, workers at state-owned enterprises might lose their jobs to foreign capitalist companies that can produce goods and services more efficiently, and China's already impoverished farmers may be harmed by cheap farm products imported from other countries.

Beijing, China

China, the world's largest country, is a member of the World Trade Organization (WTO).

INTERNATIONAL LAW
Vietnam Joins the WTO

During the late 1960s and early 1970s, the United States engaged in a military action to aid South Vietnam in its struggle against Communist North Vietnam. The might of the United States was unable to defeat the guerilla warfare of the Communists, and the United States abandoned Vietnam. The Communists unified North and South Vietnam into one county. The war left visible scars: Millions of Vietnamese soldiers and civilians on both sides died or were wounded, and 50,000 U.S. soldiers died and hundreds of thousands were wounded.

Vietnam and the United States remained enemies for the rest of the century. The two countries eventually opened diplomatic relations, and in 2000, they signed a trade pact. The United States reduced tariffs on Vietnamese imports, and Vietnam did the same for U.S. imports.

Vietnam agreed to phase in the entry of U.S. service industries, such as distribution, legal, accounting, and engineering services. The new trade pact gives Vietnam much easier access to the rich U.S. consumer marketplace, and it gives U.S. companies entry into the Vietnamese marketplace, for both the manufacture and sale of goods.

In 2007, with the backing of the United States and other existing members of the World Trade Organization (WTO), Vietnam was admitted as the 150th member of the WTO. As a member of the WTO, Vietnam has agreed to impose the rule of law and to abide by international trade rules and restrictions. With admission into the WTO, Vietnam, still a socialist country, became one of the world's newest capitalist recruits.

Vietnam

Vietnam became the 150th member of the World Trade Organization.

WTO Dispute Resolution

One of the primary functions of the WTO is to hear and decide trade disputes between member nations. Before the creation of the WTO, GATT governed trade disputes between signatory nations. This system was inadequate because any member nation that was found to have violated any GATT trade agreement could itself veto any sanctions imposed by GATT's governing body. The WTO solved this problem by adopting a "judicial" mode of dispute resolution to replace GATT's more politically based one.

A member nation that believes that another member nation has breached one of these agreements can initiate a proceeding to have the WTO hear and decide the dispute. The dispute is first heard by a three-member **WTO panel**, which issues a "panel report." The members of the panel are professional judges from member nations. The report, which is the decision of the panel, contains the panel's findings of fact and law, and it orders a remedy if a violation has been found. The report is then referred to the **WTO dispute-settlement body**. This body is required to adopt the panel report unless the body, by consensus, agrees not to adopt it. Because each member nation has a representative on this settlement body, it can be presumed that panel reports will automatically be adopted because the winning nation in the dispute will almost assuredly vote to adopt it. This is a radical change from the former GATT settlement procedure. Under GATT, unanimity was required to enforce a panel report, and the losing party usually voted to block the implementation of a panel's findings against it. One of the most important features of the WTO is the elimination of this blocking power of member nations.

There is a **WTO appellate body** to which a party can appeal a decision of the dispute-settlement body. This appeals court is composed of seven professional justices selected from member nations. Appeals are heard by panels composed of three members of the appellate body. Appeals are limited to issues of law, not fact. The entire dispute proceeding is completed within 9 months when a panel report is not appealed and within 12 months when there is an appeal. A shortened period is available if the parties agree or if there is an urgent matter that must be decided quickly.

If a violation of a trade agreement is found, the general report and appellate decision can order the offending nation to cease from engaging in the violating practice and to pay damages to the other party. If the offending nation refuses to abide by the order, the WTO can order retaliatory trade sanctions (e.g., tariffs) by other member nations against the non-complying nation.

Web Exercise

1. **WEB** Use *www.google.com* to find an article about a recent trade dispute decided by the WTO. Read it.

INTERNATIONAL LAW
WTO Rules Against the United States

The number-one plaintiff in cases brought against countries before the World Trade Organization (WTO) has been the United States. This country has initiated and won cases against Japan, Brazil, and the European Union (EU) to knock down subsidies and other measures instituted by these countries to protect their industries from open trade. But in a recent case, the tables were turned on the United States, which lost an important case brought against it in the WTO by the EU.

The U.S. Tax Code provided that if U.S. companies ran the paperwork concerning the export of goods to Europe through the tax-haven countries in the Caribbean, then the goods would not be subject to U.S. export tax. The goods could be shipped directly from the United States to their destination in Europe, however, and still qualify for this tax saving, as long as paperwork (which is basically digital) was routed through the Caribbean counties. The EU brought an action before the WTO against the United States, alleging that this tax break was an illegal export subsidy that violated WTO free-trade rules. After a hearing, the WTO ruled that the United States had engaged in a subtle and lucrative export subsidy that violated WTO trade laws. The WTO ordered the United States to dismantle this favorable tax subsidy. This ruling by the WTO is its most significant to date, repealing hundreds of millions of dollars of tax breaks sneakily given by the U.S. government to Microsoft Corporation, Boeing Company, and other large U.S. exporters.

INTERNATIONAL LAW
Nationalization of Private Property

When a company invests capital in a foreign country in plant, equipment, bank accounts, and such, it runs the risk that that country may **nationalize** (seize) its assets. International law recognizes the right of nations to nationalize private property owned by foreigners and residents. Nationalization of assets occurs more often in underdeveloped or developing countries than in developed countries. Sometimes when private property is nationalized, the owner of the property is paid just compensation by the government that seized the property. Other times, however, the government that nationalizes the property pays nothing for the property.

When a foreign government nationalizes property, there are few legal remedies available to the owners of the nationalized property. The government of the owners of the property that has been nationalized by another country may try to recover payment through diplomatic means, but this is often not successful. The U.S. government and several private companies offer political risk insurance that covers loss from the uncompensated nationalization of private property.

National Courts Decide International Disputes

The majority of cases involving international law disputes are heard by **national courts** of individual nations. This is primarily the case for commercial disputes between private litigants that do not qualify to be heard by international courts. Some countries have specialized courts that hear international commercial disputes. Other countries permit such disputes to proceed through their regular court systems. In the United States, commercial disputes between U.S. companies and foreign governments or parties may be brought in U.S. District Court.

Judicial Procedure

A party seeking judicial resolution of an international dispute faces several problems, including which nation's courts will hear the case and what law should be applied to the case. Jurisdiction is often a highly contested issue. Absent an agreement providing otherwise, a case involving an international dispute will be brought in the national court of the plaintiff's home country.

Many international contracts contain a **choice of forum clause** (or **forum-selection clause**) that designates which nation's court has jurisdiction to hear a case arising out of a contract. In addition, many contracts also include a **choice of law clause** that designates which nation's laws will be applied in deciding the case. Absent these two clauses, and without the parties agreeing to these matters, an international dispute may never be resolved.

CONCEPT SUMMARY

International Contract Clauses

CLAUSE	DESCRIPTION
Forum-selection	A clause that designates the judicial or arbitral forum that will hear and decide a case.
Choice of law	A clause that designates the law to be applied by the court or arbitrator in deciding a case.

Act of State Doctrine

A general principle of international law is that a country has absolute authority over what transpires *within* its own territory. In furtherance of this principle, the **act of state doctrine** states that judges of one country cannot question the validity of an act committed by another country within that other country's own borders. In *United States v. Belmont*,[2] the U.S. Supreme Court declared, "Every sovereign state must recognize the independence of every other sovereign state; and the courts of one will not sit in judgment upon the acts of the government of another, done within its own territory." This restraint on the judiciary is justified under the doctrine of separation of powers and permits the executive branch of the federal government to arrange affairs with foreign governments.

Example Suppose the country of North Korea outlaws the practice of all religions in that country. Paul, a Christian who is a citizen of, and living in, the United States, disagrees with North Korea's law. Paul brings a lawsuit against North Korea in a U.S. District Court located in the state of Idaho, arguing to the court that the North Korean law should be declared illegal. The U.S. District Court will apply the act of state doctrine and dismiss Paul's lawsuit again North Korea. The U.S. District Court will rule that North Korea's law is an act of that state (country) and that a U.S. court does not have authority to hear and decide Paul's case.

In the following two cases, the courts were called upon to apply the act of state doctrine.

C A S E **41.1** *Act of State Doctrine*	**Glen v. Club Mediterranee, S.A.** 450 F.3d 1251, **Web** 2006 U.S. App. Lexis 13400 (2006) United States Court of Appeals for the Eleventh Circuit

> ❝*The act of state doctrine is a judicially-created rule of decision that precludes the courts of this country from inquiring into the validity of the public acts a recognized foreign sovereign power committed within its own territory.*❞
>
> —Judge Cox

Facts

Prior to the Communist revolution in Cuba, Elvira de la Vega Glen and her sister, Ana Maria de la Vega Glen, were Cuban citizens and residents who jointly owned beachfront property on the Penninsula de Hicacos in Varadero, Cuba. On or about January 1, 1959, in conjunction with Fidel Castro's Communist revolution, the Cuban government expropriated the property without paying the Glens. Also in 1959, the sisters fled Cuba. Ana Maria de la Vega Glen died and passed any interest she had in the Varadero beach property to her nephew Robert M. Glen.

In 1997, Club Mediterranee, S.A. and Club Mediterranee Group (Club Med) entered into a joint venture with the Cuban government to develop the property. Club Med constructed and operated a five-star luxury hotel on the property that the Glens had owned. The Glens sued Club Med in a U.S. District Court located in the state of Florida. The Glens alleged that the original expropriation of their property by the Cuban government was illegal and that Club Med had trespassed on their property and had been unduly enriched by its joint venture with the Cuban government to operate a hotel on their expropriated property. The Glens sought to recover the millions of dollars in profits earned by Club Med from its alleged wrongful occupation and use of the Glens' expropriated property. The U.S. District Court held that the act of state doctrine barred recovery by the Glens and dismissed the Glens' claims against Club Med. The Glens appealed.

Issue

Does the act of state doctrine bar recovery by the Glens?

Language of the Court

The act of state doctrine is a judicially-created rule of decision that precludes the courts of this country from inquiring into the validity of the public acts a recognized foreign sovereign power committed within its own territory. The doctrine prevents any court in the United States from declaring that an official act of a foreign sovereign performed within its own territory is invalid. It requires that the acts of foreign sovereigns taken within their own jurisdictions shall be deemed valid. The act of state doctrine is a product of judicial concern for separation of powers, a result of the judiciary's recognition that it is the province of the executive and legislative branches to establish and pursue foreign policy and that judicial determinations regarding the validity of the acts of foreign sovereigns might negatively affect those policies.

The validity of the Cuban government's act of expropriation is directly at issue in this litigation. The act of state doctrine is properly applied to claims, like the Glens', that necessarily require U.S. courts to pass on the legality of the Cuban government's expropriation of property within Cuba from then-Cuban citizens. Because the act of state doctrine requires the courts deem valid the Cuban government's expropriation of the real property at issue in this case, the Glens cannot maintain their claims for trespass and unjust enrichment against Club Med.

Decision

The U.S. Court of Appeals applied the act of state doctrine and affirmed the judgment of the U.S. District Court that dismissed the Glens' claim against Club Med.

Law & Ethics Questions

1. What is the expropriation of property by a government? How does this differ from the nationalization of property by a government?

2. What does the act of state doctrine provide? Explain.

3. **ETHICS** Did the Cuban government act ethically when it expropriated the Glens' property?

4. **ETHICS** Did Club Med act ethically when it entered into a joint venture with the Cuban government to develop the property that had been expropriated from the Glens?

Web Exercises

1. **WEB** For the complete opinion of this case, go to *www.prenhall.com/cheesemancases*.

2. **WEB** Visit the website of the U.S. Court of Appeals for the Eleventh Circuit, at *www.ca11.uscourts.gov*.

3. **WEB** Visit the website of Club Med, at *www.clubmed.com*.

4. **WEB** Visit the website of the government of Cuba, at *www.cubagov.cu*.

5. **WEB** Use *www.google.com* to find an article that discusses Fidel Castro and the Communist revolution in Cuba. Read it.

6. **WEB** Visit the website at *www.stateofcuba.com*. What is the purpose of this website?

CASE 41.2
Act of State Doctrine

U.S. SUPREME COURT
W. S. Kirkpatrick & Co., Inc. v. Environmental Tectonics Corporation, International

493 U.S. 400, 110 S.Ct. 701, 107 L.Ed.2d 816,
Web 1990 U.S. Lexis 486
Supreme Court of the United States

“*The act of state doctrine does not establish an exception for cases and controversies that may embarrass foreign governments.*”

—Justice Scalia

Facts

Harry Carpenter, a U.S. citizen and chairman of the board and chief executive officer of W. S. Kirkpatrick & Co., Inc. (Kirkpatrick), learned that the Republic of Nigeria was interested in contracting for the construction of an aeromedical center at Kaduna Air Force Base in Nigeria. He made arrangements with Benson "Tunde" Akindale, a Nigerian citizen, whereby Akindale would help secure the contract for Kirkpatrick by paying bribes to Nigerian officials. In accordance with the plan, the contract was awarded to a wholly owned subsidiary of Kirkpatrick; Kirkpatrick paid the agreed-upon funds to Akindale, which were dispersed as bribes to Nigerian officials. Environmental Tectonics Corporation, International (Environmental), an unsuccessful bidder for the Kaduna contract, learned of the bribes and informed the U.S. embassy in Lagos, Nigeria. In a criminal action, Carpenter and Kirkpatrick pleaded guilty to violating the U.S. Foreign Corrupt Practices Act. Environmental then brought this civil action against Carpenter, Kirkpatrick, and Akindale seeking damages under federal and state racketeering and antitrust laws. The District Court held that the action was barred by the act of state doctrine and dismissed the complaint. The Court of Appeals reversed, holding that Environment's lawsuit was not barred by the act of state doctrine and that Environmental could proceed with its lawsuit. The defendants appealed to the U.S. Supreme Court.

Issue

Does the act of state doctrine bar the plaintiff's civil suit against the defendants?

Language of the U.S. Supreme Court

In every case in which we have held the act of state doctrine applicable, the relief sought or the defense interposed would have required a court in the United States to declare invalid the official act of a foreign sovereign performed within its own territory. In the present case, by contrast, neither the claim nor any asserted defense requires a determination that Nigeria's contract with Kirkpatrick was, or was not, effective. Act of state issues arise only when a court must decide—that is, when that outcome of the case turns upon—the effect of official action by a foreign sovereign. When that question is not in the case, neither is the act of state doctrine. That is the situation here.

The short of the matter is this: Courts in the United States have the power, and ordinarily the obligation, to decide cases and controversies properly presented to them. The act of state doctrine does not establish an exception for cases and controversies that may embarrass foreign governments, but merely requires that, in the process of deciding, the acts of foreign sovereigns taken within their own jurisdictions shall be deemed valid. That doctrine has no application to the present case because the validity of no foreign sovereign act is at issue.

Decision

The Supreme Court held that the act of state doctrine did not apply to the case and therefore did not bar plaintiff Environmental's civil lawsuit against the defendants. The U.S. Supreme Court affirmed the judgment of the U.S. Court of Appeals that allowed Environmental to proceed with its lawsuit.

Law & Ethics Questions

1. Should the United States follow the act of state doctrine?
2. **ETHICS** Did Carpenter act ethically in obtaining the contract with the Nigerian government?

3. What implications does the act of state doctrine have for business? Explain.

Web Exercises

1. **WEB** For the complete opinion of this case, go to *www.prenhall.com/cheesemancases*.
2. **WEB** Visit the website of the U.S. Supreme Court, at *www.supremecourtus.gov*, and try to find documents that relate to this case.
3. **WEB** Use *www.google.com* to find an article that discusses a recent application of the act of state doctrine.

Doctrine of Sovereign Immunity

One of the oldest principles of international law is the **doctrine of sovereign immunity**. Under this doctrine, *countries* are granted immunity from suits in courts in other countries. For example, if a U.S. citizen wanted to sue the government of China in a U.S. court, he or she could not (subject to certain exceptions).

Originally, the United States granted absolute immunity to foreign governments from suits in U.S. courts. In 1952, the United States switched to the principle of *qualified immunity*, or *restricted immunity*, which was eventually codified in the **Foreign Sovereign Immunities Act (FSIA)** of 1976.[3] This act now exclusively governs suits against foreign nations in the United States, whether in federal or state court. Most Western nations have adopted the principle of restricted immunity. Other countries still follow the doctrine of absolute immunity.

EXCEPTIONS TO THE SOVEREIGN IMMUNITIES ACT The FSIA provides that a foreign country is not immune from lawsuits in U.S. courts in the following two situations:

1. The foreign country has waived its immunity, either explicitly or by implication.
2. The action is based on a commercial activity carried on in the United States by the foreign country or carried on outside the United States but causing a direct effect in the United States.

What constitutes "commercial activity" is the most litigated aspect of the FSIA. If it is commercial activity, the foreign sovereign is subject to suit in the United States; if it is not, the foreign sovereign is immune from suit in this country.

Example The president of the country of Argentina is visiting the United States on a diplomatic mission to meet with the president of the United States to discuss political and economic issues. Suppose that while in Washington, DC, the president of Argentina negligently injures a U.S. citizen. The doctrine of sovereign immunity protects the president of Argentina from being sued by the injured party in state or federal courts in the United States.

Example If the country of Argentina sells bonds to investors in the United States to raise money, then Argentina is involved in commercial activity in the United States. If Argentina defaults and does not pay the U.S. investors back their money, the investors can sue Argentina in U.S. courts under the commercial activity exception to the doctrine of sovereign immunity to recover the unpaid money.[4]

In the following case, the U.S. Supreme Court applied the doctrine of sovereign immunity.

CASE 41.3
Doctrine of Sovereign Immunity

U. S. SUPREME COURT
Republic of Argentina v. Weltover, Inc.

504 U.S. 607, 112 S.Ct. 2160, 119 L.Ed.2d 394,
Web 1992 U.S. Lexis 3542
Supreme Court of the United States

> 66 *When a foreign government acts, not as regulator of a market, but in the manner of a private player within it, the foreign sovereign's actions are "commercial" within the meaning of the FSIA.* 99
>
> —Justice Scalia

Facts

In an attempt to stabilize its currency, Argentina and its central bank, Banco Central (collectively Argentina), issued bonds called "Bonods." The bonds, which were sold to investors worldwide, provided for repayment in U.S. dollars through transfers on the London, Frankfurt, Zurich, and New York markets at the bondholder's election. Argentina lacked sufficient foreign exchange to retire the bonds when they matured. Argentina unilaterally extended the time for payment and offered bondholders substitute instruments as a means of rescheduling the debts. Two Panamanian corporations and a Swiss bank refused the rescheduling and insisted that full payment be made in New York. When Argentina did not pay, they brought a breach of contract action against Argentina in U.S. District Court in New York. Argentina moved to dismiss, alleging that it was not subject to suit in U.S. courts under the federal Foreign Sovereign Immunities Act (FSIA). The plaintiffs asserted that the "commercial activity" exception to the act applied, subjecting Argentina to suit in U.S. court. The District Court denied Argentina's motion for dismissal, and the Court of Appeals affirmed, thus permitting the plaintiffs to sue Argentina in U.S. court. Argentina appealed to the U.S. Supreme Court.

Issue

Does the doctrine of sovereign immunity prevent the plaintiffs from suing Argentina in a U.S. court?

Language of the U.S. Supreme Court

When a foreign government acts, not as regulator of a market, but in the manner of a private player within it, the foreign sovereign's actions are "commercial" within the meaning of the FSIA. Thus, a foreign government's issuance of regulations limiting foreign currency exchange is a sovereign activity, because such authoritative control of commerce cannot be exercised by a private party; whereas a contract to buy army boots or even bullets is a "commercial" activity, because private companies can similarly use sales contracts to acquire goods.

The commercial character of the Bonods is confirmed by the fact that they are in almost all respects garden-variety debt instruments: They may be held by private parties; they are nego-

tiable and may be traded on the international market; and they promise a future stream of cash income. We conclude that Argentina's issuance of the Bonods was a "commercial activity" under the FSIA. We have little difficulty concluding that Argentina's unilateral rescheduling of the maturity dates on the Bonods had a "direct effect" in the United States.

Decision

The Supreme Court held that Argentina's issuance of the bonds was a commercial activity that had a direct effect in the United States. Therefore, the commercial activity exception to the Sovereign Immunities Act applied, which allowed the plaintiffs to sue Argentina in a U.S. court.

Law & Ethics Questions

1. Should the United States recognize the doctrine of absolute sovereign immunity or qualified immunity? Explain.
2. **ETHICS** Did the government of Argentina act ethically in not paying the bonds when due and unilaterally rescheduling the debt?
3. Is there more risk for investors who invest in obligations of foreign countries than in obligations of the U.S. government?

Web Exercises

1. **WEB** For the complete opinion of this case, go to *www.prenhall.com/cheesemancases*.
2. **WEB** Visit the website of the U.S. Supreme Court, at *www.supremecourtus.gov*, and try to find documents that relate to this case.
3. **WEB** Use *www.google.com* to find an article that discusses a recent application of the doctrine of sovereign immunity. Read it.

CONCEPT SUMMARY

Act of State and Sovereign Immunity Doctrines Compared

DOCTRINE	DESCRIPTION
Act of state	A doctrine that states that an act of a government in its *own country* is not subject to suit in a foreign country's courts.
Sovereign immunity	A doctrine that states that an act of a government in a *foreign country* is not subject to suit in the foreign country. Some countries provide absolute immunity, and other countries (such as the United States) provide limited immunity.

International Arbitration

As an alternative to litigation, the parties to an international contract may agree that any dispute that arises between them regarding the transaction will be decided by mandatory arbitration. **Arbitration** is a nonjudicial method of dispute resolution whereby a neutral third party decides the case. The parties agree to be bound by the arbitrator's decision. Generally, arbitration is faster, less expensive, less formal, and more private than litigation.

An **arbitration clause** should specify the arbitrator or the means of selecting the arbitrator. Several organizations conduct **international arbitration**, including the American Arbitration Association, the International Chamber of Commerce, the International Center for the Settlement of Investment Disputes, and the United Nations Commission on International Trade Law. International arbitrators are usually businesspeople or lawyers experienced in worldwide commercial transactions. An arbitration clause should also specify the law to be applied by the arbitrator. Arbitration clauses are appearing in an increasing number of international contracts.

An arbitrator issues an *award*, not a judgment. An arbitrator does not have the power to enforce the award it renders. Therefore, if the losing party refuses to pay the award, the winning party must petition a court to enforce the award. More than 50 countries that conduct the bulk of worldwide commercial transactions are signatories to the **United Nations Convention on the Recognition and Enforcement of Foreign Arbitral Awards**.[5] The United States adopted the convention in 1970 and amended the Federal Arbitration Act to reflect this international law.[6] The recipient of an arbitral award subject to the convention can attach property of the loser that is located in any country that is a signatory to the convention.

INTERNATIONAL LAW
Jewish Law and the Torah

Jewish law, which has existed for centuries, is a complex legal system based on ideology and theology of the Torah. The Torah prescribes comprehensive and integrated rules of religious, political, and legal life that together form Jewish thought. Jewish law is decided by rabbis who are scholars of the Torah and other Jewish scriptures. Rabbinic jurisprudence, known as **Halakhah**, is administered by rabbi-judges sitting as the **Beis Din**, Hebrew for the "house of judgment." As a court, the *Beis Din* has roots that go back 3,000 years.

Today, Jews are citizens of countries worldwide. As such, they are subject to the criminal and civil laws of their host countries. But Jews, no matter where they live, abide by the principles of the Torah in many legal matters, such as marriage, divorce, inheritance, and other family matters. Thus, the legal principles embedded in the Torah coexist with the secular laws of Jews' home countries.

The rabbinical judges tend to be actively involved in cases. True to its roots, the *Beis Din* is more a search for the truth than it is an adversarial process.

Israel

INTERNATIONAL LAW
Islamic Law and the Koran

Approximately 20 percent of the world's population is Muslim. Islam is the principal religion of Afghanistan, Algeria, Bangladesh, Egypt, Indonesia, Iran, Iraq, Jordan, Kuwait, Libya, Malaysia, Mali, Mauritania, Morocco, Niger, North Yemen, Oman, Pakistan, Qatar, Saudi Arabia, Somalia, South Yemen, Sudan, Syria, Tunisia, Turkey, and the United Arab Emirates. *Islamic law* (or **Shari'a**) is the only law in Saudi Arabia. In other Islamic countries, the *Shari'a* forms the basis of family law but coexists with other laws.

The Islamic law system is derived from the Koran, the Sunnah (decisions and sayings of the prophet Muhammad), and reasonings by Islamic scholars. By the tenth century A.D., Islamic scholars had decided that no further improvement of the divine law could be made, closed the door of *ijtihad* (independent reasoning), and froze the evolution of Islamic law at that point. Islamic law prohibits *riba*, or the making of unearned or unjustified profit. Making a profit from the sale of goods or the provision of services is permitted. The most notable consequence of *riba* is that the payment of interest on loans is forbidden. To circumvent this result, the party with the money is permitted to purchase the item and resell it to the other party at a profit or to advance the money and become a trading partner who shares in the profits of the enterprise.

Today, Islamic law is primarily used in the areas of marriage, divorce, and inheritance and, to a limited degree, in criminal law. To resolve the tension between *Shari'a* and the practice of modern commercial law, the *Shari'a* is often ignored in commercial transactions.

Uzbekistan

INTERNATIONAL LAW
Hindu Law—*Dharmasastra*

Over 20 percent of the world's population is Hindu. Most Hindus live in India, where they make up 80 percent of the population. Others live in Burma, Kenya, Malaysia, Pakistan, Singapore, Tanzania, and Uganda. *Hindu law* is a religious law. As such, individual Hindus apply this law to themselves, regardless of their nationality or place of domicile.

Classical Hindu law rests neither on civil codes nor on court decisions but on the works of private scholars that were passed along for centuries by oral tradition and eventually were recorded in the *smitris* (law books). Hindu law—called ***dharmasastra*** in Sanskrit, that is, the doctrine of proper behavior—is linked to the divine revelation of Veda

(the holy collection of Indian religious songs, prayers, hymns, and sayings written between 2000 and 1000 B.C.). Most Hindu law is concerned with family matters and the law of succession.

After India became a British colony, British judges applied a combination of Hindu law and common law in solving cases. This Anglo-Hindu law, as it was called, was ousted when India gained its independence. In the mid-1950s, India codified Hindu law by enacting the Hindu Marriage Act, the Hindu Minority and Guardianship Act, the Hindu Succession Act, and the Hindu Adoptions and Maintenance Act. Outside India, Anglo-Hindu law applies in most other countries populated by Hindus.

Nepal

INTERNATIONAL LAW
Holocaust Victims Recover Payment from Swiss Banks

> *"I have no quarrel with the settlement. I do not say it is fair, because fairness is a relative term. No amount of money can possibly be fair under those circumstances."*
>
> —Ernest Lobet, a survivor of the Holocaust

During World War II, the German Nazi regime engaged in years of persecution of Jews, including genocide, slave labor, and a wholesale and systematic looting of personal and business property of the Jewish victims. World War II ended in 1945 when the Allies defeated Germany and its Axis collaborators. During World War II, the European country of Switzerland remained neutral.

Switzerland has been a financial center to Europe for centuries. It is famous for its bank secrecy laws; that is, Swiss law protects the names

and other information of depositors. Before and during the war, many Swiss banks held money and other property of Jews throughout Europe. And during the war, the Swiss banks obtained new clients—the Nazis—who stole their Jewish victims' property and placed it with the Swiss banks for safekeeping.

Over 50 years later, a series of class-action lawsuits were filed in U.S. District Court by the survivors of the Holocaust and their heirs against Union Bank of Switzerland and many other Swiss banks. The plaintiffs alleged that during World War II, the Swiss banks knowingly retained, concealed, and laundered the money and assets of Holocaust victims stolen by the Nazis. The lawsuits also alleged that Swiss banks did not pay money back to the Jewish survivors or to the heirs of the deceased victims that was on deposit at the banks once World War II was over.

After substantial negotiations, the plaintiffs reached a settlement with the defendant Swiss banks. The defendants dropped their defense that the claims were time-barred and agreed to pay $1.25 billion into a settlement fund. In exchange, the plaintiffs agreed to release all further claims against the banks. The District Court judge approved the settlement agreement. Ernest Lobet, a survivor of the Holocaust, commented about the settlement:

I have no quarrel with the settlement. I do not say it is fair, because fairness is a relative term. No amount of money can possibly be fair under those circumstances, but I'm quite sure it is the very best that could be done by the groups that negotiated for the settlement. The world is not perfect and the people that negotiated I'm sure tried their very best, and I think they deserve our cooperation and that they be supported and the settlement be approved.

A procedure was established for the plaintiffs to make claims against the settlement fund. *In re Holocaust Victim Asset Litigation*, 105 F.Supp.2d 139, **Web** 2000 U.S. Dist. Lexis 10721 (United States District Court for the Eastern District of New York, 2000)

Chapter Summary

The United States and Foreign Affairs, p. 1183

Two provisions in the U.S. Constitution establish the federal government's authority to regulate international affairs: the Foreign Commerce Clause and the Treaty Clause.

Foreign Commerce Clause

The Foreign Commerce Clause vests Congress with the power "to regulate commerce with foreign nations."

Treaty Clause

The Treaty Clause gives the president the authority to enter into treaties with foreign nations, subject to a two-thirds vote of the Senate.

Sources of International Law, p. 1185
Treaties and Conventions

Treaties are agreements between nations that are formally ratified by the supreme power of each signatory nation. Conventions are treaties that are sponsored by international organizations (e.g., the United Nations).

Custom

A custom is a practice followed by two or more nations over a period of time when dealing with each other.

General Principles of Law

General principles of law are common to the nations of the parties involved in a dispute.

Judicial Decisions and Teachings

Judicial decisions of national courts and teachings of the most qualified legal scholars of the nations of the parties involved in a dispute are sources of international law.

United Nations, p. 1186

The United Nations (UN) is an international organization headquartered in New York City. Most countries of the world are members of the UN. Its goals are to maintain peace and security in the world, promote economic and social cooperation, and protect human rights.

General Assembly

The General Assembly is composed of all member nations. As the legislative body of the UN, it adopts resolutions concerning human rights, trade, finance and economics, and other matters within the scope of the UN Charter.

Security Council

The Security Council is composed of 15 member nations, 5 of which are permanent members (China, France, Russia, the United Kingdom, and the United States), and 10 other countries chosen by the members of the General Assembly to serve two-year terms. The council is primarily responsible for maintaining international peace and security and has authority to use armed forces.

Secretariat

The Secretariat administers the day-to-day operations of the UN. It is headed by the *secretary-general*, who is elected by the General Assembly.

UN Agencies

The UN is composed of various autonomous agencies that deal with a wide range of economic and social problems, including the United Nations Educational, Scientific, and Cultural Organization (UNESCO), the United Nations International Children's Emergency Fund (UNICEF), the International Monetary Fund (IMF), the World Bank, and the International Fund for Agricultural Development (IFAD).

Regional International Organizations, p. 1190

European Union

The European Union, which was created in 1957, is composed of many countries of western and eastern Europe.

North American Free Trade Agreement (NAFTA)

On August 12, 1992, the North American Free Trade Agreement (NAFTA) was signed by the leaders of Canada, the United States and Mexico. The treaty creates a free-trade zone stretching from the Yukon to the Yucatan.

Asian Economic Communities

In 1967, the Association of Southeast Asian Nations (ASEAN) was created and is a cooperative association of diverse nations.

Organization of the Petroleum Exporting Countries (OPEC)

OPEC consists of oil-producing and exporting countries from Africa, Asia, the Middle East, and South America. OPEC sets quotas on the output of oil production by member nations.

Other Regional Economic Organizations

Countries of Latin America and the Caribbean have established several regional organizations to promote economic development and cooperation.

World Trade Organization (WTO), p. 1194

The WTO is an international organization headquartered in Geneva, Switzerland. Many countries of the world are members. Its goals are to limit tariff and trade restrictions and provide a mechanism for resolving trade disputes among its member nations.

WTO Dispute Resolution

One of the primary functions of the WTO is to hear and decide trade disputes between member nations. The dispute is first heard by a three-member WTO panel, which issues a "panel report." The members of the panel are professional judges from member nations.

National Courts Decide International Disputes, p. 1198

Judicial Procedure

National courts are limited by two principles of judicial restraint: the act of state doctrine and the doctrine of sovereign immunity.

Act of State Doctrine

The act of state doctrine states that judges of one country cannot question the validity of an act committed by another country within that other country's borders.

Doctrine of Sovereign Immunity

The doctrine of sovereign immunity states that countries are granted immunity from suits in courts in other countries. Some countries provide for absolute immunity, and other countries (such as the United States) provide qualified or restricted immunity. The United States provides that a foreign country is not immune from lawsuits in U.S. court if:

1. The foreign country has waived its immunity.
2. The foreign country has engaged in commercial activity in the United States or outside the United States that causes a direct effect in the United States.

International Arbitration

Arbitration is a nonjudicial method of dispute resolution whereby a neutral third party decides the case. Arbitration clauses are included in many international contracts that require arbitration of disputes arising from the contract.

Test Review Terms and Concepts

Case Problems

41.1 Act of State Doctrine: Prior to 1918, the Petrograd Metal Works, a Russian corporation, deposited a large sum of money with August Belmont, a private banker doing business in New York City under the name August Belmont & Co. (Belmont). In 1918, the Soviet government nationalized the corporation and appropriated all its property and assets wherever situated, including the deposit account with Belmont. As a result, the deposit became the property of the Soviet government. In 1933, the Soviet government and the United States entered into an agreement to settle claims and counterclaims between them. As part of the settlement, it was agreed that the Soviet government would take no steps to enforce claims against American nationals (including Belmont) and assigned all such claims to the United States.

The United States brought an action against the executors of Belmont's estate to recover the money originally deposited with Belmont by Petrograd Metal Works. Who owns the money? *United States v. Belmont*, 301 U.S. 324, 57 S.Ct. 758, 81 L.Ed. 1134, **Web** 1937 U.S. Lexis 293 (Supreme Court of the United States)

41.2 Act of State Doctrine: Banco Nacional de Costa Rica is a bank wholly owned by the government of Costa Rica. It is subject to the rules and regulations adopted by the minister of finance and the central bank of Costa Rica. The bank borrowed $40 million from a consortium of private banks located in the United Kingdom and the United States. The bank signed promissory notes agreeing to repay the principal plus interest on the loan in four equal installments due on July 30, August 30, September 30, and October 30 of the following year. The money was to be used to provide export financing of sugar and sugar products from Costa Rica. The loan agreements and promissory notes were signed in New York City, and the loan proceeds were tendered to the bank there.

The bank paid the first installment on the loan. The bank did not, however, make the other three installment payments and defaulted on the loan. The lending banks sued the bank in U.S. District Court in New York to recover the unpaid principal and interest. The bank alleged in defense that the minister of finance and the central bank of Costa Rica issued a decree forbidding the repayment of loans by the bank to private lenders, including the lending banks in this case. The action was taken because Costa Rica was having trouble servicing debts to foreign creditors. The bank alleged that the act of state doctrine prevented the plaintiffs from recovering on their loans to the bank. Who wins? *Libra Bank Limited v. Banco Nacional de Costa Rica*, 570 F.Supp. 870, **Web** 1983 U.S. Dist. Lexis 14677 (United States District Court for the Southern District of New York)

41.3 Forum-Selection Clause: Zapata Off-Shore Company is a Houston, Texas–based American corporation that engages in drilling oil wells throughout the world. Unterweser Reederei, GMBH, is a German corporation that provides ocean shipping and towing services. Zapata requested bids from companies to tow its self-elevating drilling rig *Chaparral* from Louisiana to a point off Ravenna, Italy, in the Adriatic Sea, where Zapata had agreed to drill certain wells. Unterweser submitted the lowest bid and was requested to submit a proposed contract to Zapata, which it did. The contract submitted by Unterweser contained the following provision: "Any dispute arising must be treated before the London Court of Justice." Zapata executed the contract without deleting or modifying this provision.

Unterweser's deep sea tug *Bremen* departed Venice, Louisiana, with the *Chaparral* in tow, bound for Italy. While the flotilla was in international waters in the middle of the Gulf of Mexico, a severe storm arose. The sharp roll of the *Chaparral* in Gulf waters caused portions of it to break off and fall into the sea, seriously damaging the *Chaparral*. Zapata instructed the *Bremen* to tow the *Chaparral* to Tampa, Florida, the nearest port of refuge, which it did. Zapata filed suit against Unterweser and the *Bremen* in U.S. District Court in Florida, alleging negligent towing and breach of contract. The defendants asserted that suit could be brought only in the London Court of Justice. Who is correct? *M/S Bremen and Unterweser Reederei, GMBH v. Zapata Off-Shore Company*, 407 U.S. 1, 92 S.Ct. 1907, 32 L.Ed.2d 513, **Web** 1972 U.S. Lexis 114 (Supreme Court of the United States)

41.4 International Arbitration: Alberto-Culver Company is an American company that is incorporated in Delaware and has its principal office in Illinois. It manufactures and distributes toiletries and hair care products in the United States and other countries. Fritz Scherk owned three interrelated businesses organized under the laws of Germany and Liechtenstein that were engaged in the manufacture of toiletries. After substantial negotiations, in February 1969, Alberto-Culver entered into a contract with Scherk to purchase his three companies, along with all rights held by these companies to trademarks in cosmetic goods. The contract contained a number of express warranties whereby Scherk guaranteed the sole and unencumbered ownership of these trademarks. The contract also contained a clause that provided that "any controversy or claim that shall arise out of this agreement or breach thereof" was to be referred to arbitration before the International Chamber of Commerce in Paris, France. The transaction closed in Geneva, Switzerland.

Nearly one year later, Alberto-Culver allegedly discovered that the trademark rights purchased under the contract were subject to substantial encumbrances that threatened to give other parties superior rights to the trademarks and to restrict or preclude Alberto-Culver's use of them. Alberto-Culver sued Scherk in U.S. District Court in Illinois, alleging fraudulent misrepresentation in violation of Section 10(b) of the federal Securities Exchange Act of 1934. Scherk asserted in defense that the case was subject to mandatory arbitration in Paris. Who is correct? *Scherk v. Alberto-Culver Co.*, 417 U.S. 506, 94 S.Ct. 2449, 41 L.Ed.2d 270, **Web** 1974 U.S. Lexis 73 (Supreme Court of the United States)

Ethics Issues

41.5 Ethics: Bank of Jamaica is wholly owned by the government of Jamaica. Chisholm & Co. was a Florida corporation owned by James Henry Chisholm, a Florida resident. The United States Export–Import Bank (Eximbank) provided financial services and credit insurance to export and import companies. The Bank of Jamaica and Chisholm & Co. agreed that Chisholm & Co. would arrange lines of credit from various banks and procure $50 million of credit insurance from Eximbank to be available to aid Jamaican importers. Chisholm & Co. was to be paid commissions for its services.

Chisholm & Co. negotiated and arranged for $50 million of credit insurance from Eximbank and lines of credit from Florida National Bank, Bankers Trust Company, and Irving Trust Company. Chisholm also arranged meetings between the Bank of Jamaica and the U.S. banks. Unbeknownst to Chisholm & Co., the Bank of Jamaica went directly to Eximbank to exclude Chisholm & Co. from the Jamaica program and requested that the credit insurance be issued solely in the name of the Bank of Jamaica. As a result, Chisholm & Co.'s Eximbank insurance application was not considered. The Bank of Jamaica also obtained lines of credit from other companies and paid them commissions. Chisholm & Co. sued the Bank of Jamaica in U.S. District Court in Miami, Florida, alleging breach of contract and seeking damages. The Bank of Jamaica filed a motion to dismiss the complaint, alleging that its actions were protected by sovereign immunity. Who wins? Did the Bank of Jamaica act ethically in trying to avoid its contract obligations? *Chisholm & Co. v. Bank of Jamaica*, 643 F.Supp. 1393, **Web** 1986 U.S. Dist. Lexis 20789 (United States District Court for the Southern District of Florida)

41.6 Ethics: Nigeria, an African nation, while in the midst of a boom period due to oil exports, entered into $1 billion of contracts with various countries to purchase huge quantities of Portland cement. Nigeria was going to use the cement to build and improve the country's infrastructure. Several of the contracts were with American companies, including Texas Trading & Milling Corporation (Texas Trading). Nigeria substantially overbought cement, and the country's docks and harbors became clogged with ships waiting to unload. Unable to accept delivery of the cement it had bought, Nigeria repudiated many of its contracts, including the one with Texas Trading. When Texas Trading sued Nigeria in a U.S. District Court to recover damages for breach of contract, Nigeria asserted in defense that the doctrine of sovereign immunity protected it from liability. Who wins? *Texas Trading & Milling Corp. v. Federal Republic of Nigeria*, 647 F.2d 300, **Web** 1981 U.S. App. Lexis 14231 (United States Court of Appeals for the Second Circuit)

IRAC Writing Assignment

Read **Case A-41** in Appendix A [*OHG v. Kolodny*]. Use the IRAC method to prepare a written analysis of the case.

Endnotes

1. The Charter of the United Nations was entered into force October 24, 1945, and it was adopted by the United States October 24, 1945 (59 Stat. 1031, T.S. 993, 3 Bevans 1153, 1976 Y.B.U.N. 1043).
2. 301 U.S. 324, 57 S.Ct. 758, 81 L.Ed. 1134, **Web** 1937 U.S. Lexis 293 (Supreme Court of the United States).
3. 28 U.S.C. Sections 1602–1611.
4. *Republic of Argentina v. Weltover, Inc.*, 504 U.S. 607, 112 S.Ct. 2160, 119 L.Ed.2d 394, **Web** 1992 U.S. Lexis 3542 (Supreme Court of the United States).
5. 21 U.S.T. 2517, T.I.A.S. 6997.
6. 9 U.S.C. Section 201–208.

Appendix A   Case Appendix

CASE A.1
Anheuser-Busch, Incorporated vs. Schmoke,

Mayor of Baltimore City, 63 F. 3d 1305 (1995)
United States Court of Appeals, Fourth Circuit
Niemeyer, Circuit Judge

In January 1994, Baltimore exercised the authority granted it by the state and enacted Ordinance 288 prohibiting the outdoor advertising of alcoholic beverages in certain locations in Baltimore City. It also includes an exception permitting such advertising in certain commercially and industrially zoned areas of the City. By its terms, the ordinance was to become effective February 5, 1994. Before enacting the ordinance, the Baltimore City Council conducted public hearings, receiving testimony and previously conducted studies detailing the adverse effects of alcohol consumption on minors and the correlation between underage drinking and the advertising of alcoholic beverages.

The City Council found that alcoholic beverages are the second most heavily advertised products in America (after cigarettes), and that outdoor billboards are a "unique and distinguishable" medium of advertising that subjects the public to involuntary and unavoidable forms of solicitation. The City Council noted that children are exposed to the advertising of alcoholic beverages "simply by walking to school or playing in their neighborhood" and that children's "attitudes favorable to alcohol are significantly related to their exposure to alcohol advertisements." Attempting to tailor its ban, the City Council allowed advertising of alcoholic beverages in commercial and industrial areas, stating that it was "narrowly focus[ing] its efforts on those advertisements which most directly affect minors where they live, attend school, attend church and engage in recreational activities."

On January 14, 1994, several weeks before the ordinance was to become effective, Anheuser-Busch, Inc., filed suit in federal court, facially challenging the constitutionality of the ordinance under the First Amendment. Anheuser-Busch is the nation's largest brewer of beers and malt beverages, producing approximately 15 different brands, including Budweiser, Michelob, and Busch. They advertise in all media, including outdoor billboards and displays. In addition to contending that there is no correlation between alcoholic beverage advertising and underage drinking, Anheuser-Busch asserts that the purpose of its advertising is "to solidify brand loyalty and increase market share by shifting adult beer drinkers from other brands to the advertised brand of beer."

Following a hearing, the district court issued an opinion upholding the constitutionality of the ordinance [(*Anheuser-Busch, Inc. v. Mayor and City Council*, 855 F.Supp. 811 (D.Md.1994)]. The court held the ordinance constitutional after concluding that it "directly advances the City's asserted interest in promoting the welfare and temperance of minors" and is "narrowly tailored" to that end.

On appeal, Anheuser-Busch argues that the ordinance is unconstitutional on its face because (1) it does not directly and materially advance the government's interest in promoting temperance of minors and (2) it is not narrowly tailored to serve that purpose. They also argue that, as applied, the ordinance would impermissibly restrict their noncommercial speech.

We find that it was reasonable for the Baltimore City Council to have concluded that Ordinance 288's regulation of the outdoor advertising of alcoholic beverages directly and materially advances Baltimore's interest in promoting the welfare and temperance of minors. The City Council found that outdoor advertising is a unique and distinct medium which subjects the public to involuntary and unavoidable solicitation, and that children, simply by walking to school or playing in their neighborhood, are exposed daily to this advertising. The City Council pointed to its legislative finding that the majority of research studies show a definite correlation between alcoholic beverage advertising and underage drinking.

We simply do not believe that the liquor industry spends a billion dollars a year on advertising solely to acquire an added market share at the expense of competitors. We hold, as a matter of law, that prohibitions against the advertising of alcoholic beverages are reasonably related to reducing the sale and consumption of those beverages and their attendant problems. The entire economy of the industries that bring these challenges is based on the belief that advertising increases sales.

It is readily acknowledged that limitations on outdoor advertising of alcoholic beverages designed to protect minors also reduce the opportunities for adults to receive advertised information. And adults, who constitute a majority of the population, are the object of the government's legislation. But it also appears that no less restrictive means may be available to advance the government's interest. Anheuser-Busch argues that Baltimore could just as effectively advance its goal of promoting the welfare and temperance of minors by increasing enforcement of existing laws prohibiting sales to, and possession of alcoholic beverages by, minors, or by implementing and encouraging educational programs on the dangers of alcohol. These approaches might indeed prove beneficial in reducing underage drinking, but they do not provide an alternative to the approach selected by the City of curbing the enticement to consume alcoholic beverages. In the face of a problem as significant as that which the City seeks to address, the City must be given some reasonable latitude.

The problem of underage drinking is a most serious one that contributes significantly to a variety of social problems. Baltimore was faced with statistics showing that fully one-half of all deaths of minors were alcohol-related, and 40 to 50 percent of juveniles who drowned or had diving accidents had consumed alcohol immediately prior to the incident. The City Council found that alcohol is overwhelmingly and consistently the most widely used "drug" at all adolescent age levels. It pointed to data which showed that over half of all twelfth graders, 40 percent of tenth graders, and over a quarter eighth graders reported that they consumed alcohol within the past 30 days. Widespread underage drinking was also found to be a major factor in crime. One-third of all juvenile males arrested said they had consumed alcohol within the previous 72 hours, and nearly 40 percent of all youths in adult correctional facilities reported drinking alcohol before committing their crimes.

Through outdoor advertising, children are involuntarily and unavoidably confronted daily with the advertised message. Billboards are "seen without the exercise of choice or volition," and viewers have the message "thrust upon them by all the arts and devices that skill can produce." The City argues that the only means to address this problem is to ban such advertising in locations where children generally walk and play. Such a ban still permits adults to receive advertising messages and information from signs in commercial areas of the City and through the numerous other media to which adults are constantly exposed.

In summary, Baltimore City's regulation of stationary outdoor "advertising that advertises alcoholic beverages" in certain locations directly and materially advances a substantial governmental interest in promoting the welfare and temperance of minors who are involuntarily and unavoidably exposed to such advertisements. While the means selected of limiting the location of such outdoor advertising is not a perfect "fit" with the governmental objective, it nevertheless falls well within the range tolerated by the First Amendment for the regulation of commercial speech.

For the reasons stated, we affirm the judgment of the district court, upholding Baltimore City Ordinance 288 against a facial constitutional challenge under the First Amendment.

AFFIRMED.

CASE A.2
Lee v. Weismen, 120 L.Ed. 2d 467,

112 S.Ct. 2649 (1992)
United States Supreme Court
Kennedy, Justice (joined by Blackmun, Stevens, O'Conner, and Souter)

Deborah Weisman graduated from Nathan Bishop Middle School, a public school in Providence, at a formal ceremony in June 1989. She was about 14 years old. For many years it has been the policy of the Providence school committee and the Superintendent of Schools to permit principals to invite members of the clergy to give invocations and benedictions at middle school and high school graduations. Many, but not all, of the principals elected to include prayers as part of the graduation ceremonies. Acting for himself and his daughter, Deborah's father, Daniel Weisman, objected to any prayers at Deborah's middle school graduation, but to no avail. The school principal, petitioner Robert E. Lee, invited a rabbi to deliver prayers at the graduation exercises for Deborah's class. Rabbi Leslie Gutterman, of the Temple Beth El in Providence, accepted.

It has been the custom of Providence school officials to provide invited clergy with a pamphlet entitled "Guidelines for Civic Occasions," prepared by the National Conference of Christians and Jews. The Guidelines recommended that public prayers at nonsectarian civic ceremonies be composed with "inclusiveness and sensitivity," though they acknowledge that "prayer of any kind may be inappropriate on some civic occasions." The principal gave Rabbi Gutterman the pamphlet before the graduation and advised him the invocation and benediction should be non-sectarian.

Deborah's graduation was held on the premises of Nathan Bishop Middle School on June 29, 1989. Four days before the ceremony, Daniel Weisman, in his individual capacity as a Providence taxpayer and as next friend of Deborah, sought a temporary restraining order in the United States District Court for the District of Rhode Island to prohibit school offices from including an invocation or benediction in the graduation ceremony. The court denied the motion for lack of adequate time to consider it. Deborah and her family attended the graduation, where the prayers were recited. In July 1989, Daniel Weisman filed an amended complaint seeking a permanent injunction barring petitioners, various officials of the Providence public schools, from inviting the clergy to deliver invocations and benedictions at future graduations.

The case was submitted on stipulated facts. The district court held that petitioners' practice of including invocations and benedictions in public school graduations violated the Establishment Clause of the First Amendment, and it enjoined petitioners from continuing the practice. The court applied the three-part Establishment Clause test. Under that test, to satisfy the Establishment Clause a governmental practice must (1) reflect a clearly secular purpose, (2) have a primary effect that neither advances nor inhibits religion, and (3) avoid excessive government entanglement with religion. On appeal, the United States Court of Appeals for the First Circuit affirmed.

These dominant facts mark and control the confines of our decision: State officials direct the performance of a formal religious exercise at promotional and graduation ceremonies for secondary schools. Even for those students who object to the religious exercise, their attendance and participation in the state-sponsored religious activity are in a fair and real sense obligatory, though the school district does not require attendance as a condition for receipt of the diploma.

The controlling precedents as they relate to prayer and religious exercise in primary and secondary public schools compel the holding here that the policy of the city of Providence is an unconstitutional one. It is beyond dispute that, at a minimum, the Constitution guarantees that government may not coerce anyone to support or participate in religion or its exercise, or otherwise act in a way which "establishes a state religion or religious faith, or tends to do so."

We are asked to recognize the existence of a practice of nonsectarian prayer within the embrace of what is known as the Judeo-Christian tradition, prayer which is more acceptable than one which, for example, makes explicit references to the God of Israel, or to Jesus Christ, or to a patron saint. If common ground can be defined which permits once conflicting faiths to express the shared conviction that there is an ethnic and a morality which transcend human invention, the sense of community and purpose sought by all decent societies might be advanced. But though the First Amendment does not allow the government to stifle prayers which aspire to these ends, neither does it permit the government to undertake that task for itself.

The sole question presented is whether a religious exercise may be conducted at a graduation ceremony in circumstances where, as we have found, young graduates who object are induced to conform. No holding by this Court suggests that a school can persuade or compel a student to participate in a religious exercise. That is being done here, and it is forbidden by the Establishment Clause of the First Amendment.

For the reasons we have stated, the judgment of the court of appeals is AFFIRMED.

Scalia, Justice (joined by Rehnquist, White, and Thomas) dissenting, expressed the view that (1) the establishment of religion clause should not have been interpreted so as to invalidate a longstanding American tradition of nonsectarian prayer at public school graduations, (2) graduation invocations and benedictions involve no psychological coercion of students to participate in religious exercises, (3) the only coercion that is forbidden by the establishment of religion clause is that which is backed by a threat of penalty, and (4) the middle school principal did not direct or control the content of the prayers in question, and thus there was no pervasive government involvement with religious activity.

CASE A.3

Peoples Trust Company of Bergen County v. Kozuck

98 N.J. Super. 235; 236 A.2d 630; 1967 N.J. Super. Lexis 389
Superior Court of New Jersey, Law Division
Botter, Judge

Defendants Saul and Elaine Kozuck, husband and wife, contest service of process in this action. Plaintiff sued on a promissory note signed by defendants Defendants denied liability on the note, contending that the due date was improperly filled in by plaintiff bank. The issues as to service of process and liability on the note were both submitted to the jury, and the jury returned a verdict in favor of plaintiff. However, the court had reserved decision under *R.R. 4:51-2(a)* on defendants' motion for judgment in which defendants contended that service of process was defective as a matter of law. The summons and complaint were left outside defendants' home by the sheriff's officer after Mrs. Kozuck had appeared in the window but refused to answer the door and receive the papers.

John Zimmerman testified for plaintiff. He is a process server in the sheriff's office of Essex County. On January 4, 1967 he went to defendants' home to serve the summons and complaint. He testified that he rang the bell; that he heard a woman open a window upstairs and ask, "Who's there?"; that he asked, "Are you Mrs. Kozuck?", and that the woman answered, "Yes." He testified he said that he was from the sheriff's office and had a summons and complaint in the case of *Peoples Trust Company versus Saul and Elaine Kozuck*. He said the woman then denied that she was Mrs. Kozuck and that when she started to close the window he told her he would leave the papers in the mailbox. He testified that when she closed the window he tried to get her attention again, rang the doorbell, but she did not answer. He testified he left the papers in a mailbox when the door was not opened.

Mrs. Kozuck testified she was housecleaning on the second floor when the doorbell rang. She went to the window and asked who was there. She testified that a male voice called up and said "he had papers from the Peoples Trust." Further, that she told the man Mrs. Kozuck wasn't home and that she was not Mrs. Kozuck. She testified that the man said he would leave the papers outside and he then left. She also testified there was no mailbox outside the house. However, she looked outside about half an hour later and found the papers on the stoop. At first she testified that she did not want to answer the door because she was not dressed and there was danger in opening the door for a stranger. However, she later admitted she knew that the Peoples Trust Company was trying to collect money on notes she and her husband had signed, and that is why she did not want to go downstairs and receive the papers.

The issue is whether, as a matter of law, service of process can validly be effected in the manner testified to by Zimmerman. *R.R. 4:4-4(a)* provides that service may be made upon an individual "by delivering a copy of the summons and complaint to him personally; or by leaving a copy thereof at his dwelling house or usual place of abode with some competent member of his family of the age of 14 years or over then residing therein. . . ." The question here is whether leaving the summons and complaint outside the house was "delivery" to Mrs. Kozuck "personally" or a "leaving with" Mrs. Kozuck for her husband within the meaning of *R.R. 4:4-4(a)*.

Due process requires that the method of service be reasonably calculated to give notice to a defendant of the proceedings against him. It is generally held that when a summons is offered to someone, he cannot avoid service by refusing physically to accept the summons if he is informed that service of process is being attempted.

The rule means that a person within the jurisdiction has an obligation to accept service of process when service is attempted reasonably. In *Slaght v. Robbins*, defendant refused "to remain and hear the summons read to him." The court upheld the service, saying that a defendant cannot take advantage of "his own improper conduct." Similarly, the court upheld service in *Walkoczy v. Bowers*, where defendant closed the door and refused to accept a summons offered to him. See also *Borden v. Borden*, where the summons was attached to the door handle after defendant pushed the process server out of the doorway upon learning of his intention to make service. The Wisconsin Supreme Court, citing *Slaght v. Robbins*, said it is proper in these circumstances to make service by depositing the process in an appropriate place in the presence of defendant or where it is likely to come into his possession.

New York courts have expressly declared that a person within the jurisdiction has an obligation to accept service of process. *Application of Joseph Barbara, Sr.* In *Barbara*, service of a subpoena taped to a door was upheld against a person who refused to come to the door but was observed in his house and advised of the attempted service by a "bull horn" and other means used by the server.

Service of process may be effectuated even if the process server does not see the person being served, where the defendant identified himself but refused to open the door to his apartment and the server left the papers in the vestibule. Also, service may validly be made upon a person who misidentifies himself and refuses to accept the process, where the court upheld service on a defendant who denied that he was the person sought.

The jury verdict establishes that personal service was made in the manner contended by plaintiff. Such service is valid and could not be avoided by Mrs. Kozuck's refusal to open the door and accept the papers, or by her denying her true identity. The judgment entered on the jury's verdict will stand.

CASE A.4

Gnazzo v. G.D. Searle & Co.,

973 F.2d 136 (1992)
U.S. Court of Appeals for the Second Circuit
Pierce, Circuit Judge

On November 11, 1974, Gnazzo had a CU-7 intrauterine device (IUD) inserted in her uterus for contraceptive purposes. The IUD was developed, marketed, and sold by G.D. Searle & Co. (Searle). When Gnazzo's deposition was taken, she stated that her doctor had informed her that "the insertion would hurt, but not for long," and that she "would have uncomfortable and probably painful periods of the first three to four months." On October 11, 1975, Gnazzo found it necessary to return to her physician due to excessive pain and cramping. During this visit she was informed by her doctor that he thought she had Pelvic Inflammatory Disease (PID). She recalled that he stated that the infection was possibly caused by venereal disease or the use of the IUD. The PID was treated with antibiotics and cleared up shortly thereafter. Less than one year later, Gnazzo was again treated for an IUD-associated infection. This infection was also treated with antibiotics. Gnazzo continued using the IUD until it was finally removed in December of 1977.

Following a laparoscopy in March of 1989, Gnazzo was informed by a fertility specialist that she was infertile because of PID-induced adhesions resulting from her prior IUD use. Subsequent to this determination, and at the request of her then-attorneys, Gnazzo completed a questionnaire dated May 11, 1989. In response to the question, "when and why did you first suspect that your IUD had caused you any harm?", Gnazzo responded "sometime in 1981" and explained: "I was married in April 1981 so I stopped using birth control so I could get pregnant—nothing ever happened (of course) then I started hearing and reading about how damaging IUDs could be. I figured that was the problem, however, my marriage started to crumble so I never pursued the issue."

On May 4, 1990, Gnazzo initiated the underlying action against Searle. In an amended complaint, she alleged that she had suffered injuries as a result of her use of the IUD developed by Searle. Searle moved for summary judgment on the ground that Gnazzo's claim was time-barred by Connecticut's three-year statute of limitations for product liability actions. Searle argued, inter alia, that Gnazzo knew in 1981 that she had suffered harm caused by her IUD. Gnazzo contended that her cause of action against Searle accrued only when she learned from the fertility specialist that the IUD had caused her PID and subsequent infertility.

In a ruling dated September 18, 1991, the district court granted Searle's motion for summary judgment on the ground that Gnazzo's claim was time-barred by the applicable statute of limitations. In reaching this result, the court determined that Connecticut law provided no support for Gnazzo's contention that she should not have been expected to file her action until she was told of her infertility and the IUD's causal connection. This appeal followed.

On appeal, Gnazzo contends that the district court improperly granted Searle's motion for summary judgment because a genuine issue of material fact exists as to when she discovered, or reasonably should have discovered, her injuries and their causal connection to the defendant's alleged wrongful conduct. Summary judgment is appropriate when there is no genuine issue as to any material fact and the moving party is entitled to judgment as a matter of law. We consider the record in the light most favorable to the non-movant. However, the non-movant "may not rest upon the mere allegations of denials of her pleading, but must set forth specific facts showing that there is a genuine issue for trial."

Under Connecticut law, a product liability claim must be brought within "three years from the date when the injury is first sustained or discovered in the exercise of reasonable care should have been discovered." In Connecticut, a cause of action accrues when a plaintiff suffers actionable harm. Actionable harm occurs when the plaintiff discovers or should discover, through the exercise of reasonable care, that he or she has been injured and that the defendant's conduct caused such injury.

Gnazzo contends that "the mere occurrence of a pelvic infection or difficulty in becoming pregnant does not necessarily result in notice to the plaintiff of a cause of action." Thus, she maintains that her cause of action did not accrue until 1989 when the fertility specialist informed her both that she was infertile and that this condition resulted from her previous use of the IUD.

Under Connecticut law, however, "the statue of limitations begins to run when the plaintiff discovers some form of actionable

harm, not the fullest manifestation thereof." Therefore, as Gnazzo's responses to the questionnaire indicate, she suspected "sometime in 1981" that the IUD had caused her harm because she had been experiencing trouble becoming pregnant and had "started hearing and reading about how damaging IUDs could be and had figured that was the problem." Thus, by her own admission, Gnazzo had recognized, or should have recognized, the critical link between her injury and the defendant's causal connection to it. In other words, she had "discovered or should have discovered through the exercise of reasonable care, that she had been injured and that Searle's conduct caused such injury." However, as Gnazzo acknowledged in the questionnaire, she did not pursue the "issue" at the time because of her marital problems. Thus, even when viewed in the light most favorable to Gnazzo, the non-moving party, we are constrained to find that she knew by 1981 that she had "some form of actionable harm." Consequently, by the time she commenced her action in 1990, Gnazzo was time-barred by the Connecticut statute of limitations.

Since we have determined that Gnazzo's cause of action commenced in 1981, we need not address Searle's additional contention that Gnazzo's awareness in 1975 of her PID and her purported knowledge of its causal connection to the IUD commenced the running of the Connecticut statute of limitations at that time.

We are sympathetic to Gnazzo's situation and mindful that the unavoidable result we reach in this case is harsh. Nevertheless, we are equally aware that "it is within the Connecticut General Assembly's constitutional authority to decide when claims for injury are to be brought. Where a plaintiff has failed to comply with this requirement, a court may not entertain the suit." The judgment of the district court is AFFIRMED.

CASE A.5
Braun v. Soldier of Fortune Magazine, Inc.

968 F.2nd 1110 (1992)
United States Court of Appeals for the Eleventh Circuit
Anderson, Circuit Judge

In January 1985, Michael Savage submitted a personal service advertisement to Soldier of Fortune (SOF). After several conversations between Savage and SOF's advertising manager, Joan Steel, the following advertisement ran in the June 1985 through March 1986 issues of SOF:

GUN FOR HIRE: 37-year-old professional mercenary desires jobs. Vietnam Veteran. Discrete [*sic*] and very private. Body guard, courier, and other special skills. All jobs considered. Phone (615) 436-9785 (days) or (615) 436-4335 (nights), or write: Rt. 2, Box 682 Village Loop Road, Gatlinburg, TN 37738.

Savage testified that, when he placed the ad, he had no intention of obtaining anything but legitimate jobs. Nonetheless, Savage stated that the overwhelming majority of the 30 to 40 phone calls a week he received in response to his ad sought his participation in criminal activity such as murder, assault, and kidnapping. The ad also generated at least one legitimate job as a bodyguard, which Savage accepted.

In late 1984 or early 1985, Bruce Gastwirth began seeking to murder his business partner, Richard Braun. Gastwirth enlisted the aid of another business associate, John Horton Moore, and together they arranged for at least three attempts on Braun's life, all of which were unsuccessful. Responding to Savage's SOF ad, Gastwirth and Moore contacted him in August 1985 to discuss plans to murder Braun. On August 26, 1985, Savage, Moore, and another individual, Sean Trevor Doutre, went to Braun's suburban Atlanta home. As Braun and his 16-year-old son Michael were driving down the driveway, Doutre stepped in front of Braun's car and fired several shots into the car with a MAC 11 automatic pistol. The shots hit Michael in the thigh and wounded Braun as well. Braun managed to roll out of the car, but Doutre walked over to Braun and killed him by firing two more shots into the back of his head as he lay on the ground.

On March 31, 1988, appellees Michael and Ian Braun filed this diversity against appellants in the United States District Court for the Middle District of Alabama, seeking damages for the wrongful death of their father. Michael Braun also filed a separate action seeking recovery for the personal injuries he received at the time of his father's death. The district court consolidated these related matters.

Trial began on December 3, 1990. Appellees contended that, under Georgia law, SOF was liable for their injuries because SOF negligently published a personal service advertisement that created an unreasonable risk of the solicitation and commission of violent criminal activity, including murder. To show that SOF knew of the likelihood that criminal activity would result from placing an ad like Savage's, appellees introduced evidence of newspaper and magazine articles published prior to Braun's murder which described links between SOF and personal service ads and a number of criminal convictions including murder, kidnapping, assault, extortion, and attempts thereof. Appellees also presented evidence that, prior to SOF's acceptance of Savage's ad, law enforcement officials had contacted SOF staffers on two separate occasions in connection with investigations of crimes.

In his trial testimony, SOF president Robert K. Brown denied having any knowledge of criminal activity associated with SOF's personal service ads at any time prior to Braun's murder in August 1985. Both Jim Graves, a former managing editor of SOF, and Joan Steel, the advertising manager who accepted Savage's advertisement, similarly testified that they were not aware of other crimes connected with SOF ads prior to running Savage's ad. Steel further testified that she had understood the "Gun for Hire" in Savage's ad to refer to a "bodyguard or protection service-type thing," rather than to any illegal activity.

The jury returned a verdict in favor of appellee and awarded compensatory damages on the wrongful death claim in the amount of $2,000,000. The jury also awarded appellee Michael Braun $375,000 in compensatory damages and $10,000,000 in punitive damages for his personal injury claim.

To prevail in an action for negligence in Georgia, a party must establish the following elements:

(1) A legal duty to conform to a standard of conduct raised by the law for the protection of others against unreasonable risks of harm, (2) a breach of this standard, (3) a legally attributable causal connection between the conduct and the resulting injury, and (4) some loss or damage flowing to the plaintiff's legally protected interest as a result of the alleged breach of the legal duty. To the extent that SOF denies that a publisher owes any duty to the public when it publishes personal service ads, its position is clearly inconsistent with Georgia law. We believe, however, that the crux of SOF's argument is not that it had no duty to the public, but that, as a matter of law, there is a risk to the public when a publisher prints an "unreasonable" advertisement if the ad openly solicits criminal activity.

SOF further argues that imposing liability on publishers for the advertisements they print indirectly threatens core, noncommercial speech to which the Constitution accords its full protection. Supreme Court cases discussing the limitations the First Amendment places on state defamation law indicate that there is no constitutional infirmity in Georgia law holding publishers liable under a negligence standard with respect to the commercial advertisements they print. Past Supreme Court decisions indicate, however, that the negligence standard that the First Amendment permits is a "modified" negligence standard. The Court's decisions suggest that Georgia law may impose tort liability on publishers for injury caused by the advertisements they print only if the ad on its face, without the need to investigate, makes it apparent that there is a substantial danger of harm to the public.

We conclude that the First Amendment permits a state to impose upon a publisher liability for compensatory damages for negligently publishing a commercial advertisement where the ad on its face, and without the need for investigation, makes it apparent that there is a substantial danger of harm to the public. The absence of a duty requiring publishers to investigate the advertisements they print and the requirement that the substance of the ad itself must warn the publisher of a substantial danger of harm to the public guarantee that the burden placed on publishers will not impermissibly chill protected commercial speech.

Our review of the language of Savage's ad persuades us that SOF had a legal duty to refrain from publishing it. Savage's advertisement (1) emphasized the term "Gun for Hire," (2) described Savage as a "professional mercenary," (3) stressed Savage's willingness to keep his assignments confidential and "very private," (4) listed legitimate jobs involving the use of a gun-bodyguard and courier-followed by a reference to Savage's "other special skills," and (5) concluded by stating that Savage would consider "all jobs." The ad's combination of sinister terms makes it apparent that there was a substantial danger of harm to the public. The ad expressly solicits all jobs requiring the use of a gun. When the list of legitimate jobs—i.e., bodyguard and courier—is followed by "other special skills" and "all jobs considered," the implication is clear that the advertiser would consider illegal jobs. We agree with the district court that "the language of this advertisement is such that, even though couched in terms not explicitly offering criminal services, the publisher could recognize the offer of criminal activity as readily as its readers obviously did." We find that the jury had ample grounds for finding that SOF's publication of Savage's ad was the proximate cause of Braun's injuries.

For the foregoing reasons, we AFFIRM the district court's judgment.

CASE A.6
Schalk v. Texas,

823 S.W.2d 633 (1991)
Court of Criminal Appeals of Texas
Miller, Judge

Appellants Schalk and Leonard are former employees of Texas Instruments (hereafter TI). Both men have doctoral degrees and specialized in the area of speech research at TI. Schalk resigned his position with TI in April 1983 to join a newly developed company, Voice Control Systems (hereafter VCS). In February 1985, Leonard resigned from TI and joined VCS. Several TI employees eventually joined the ranks of VCS. Speech research was the main thrust of the research and development performed by VCS. In fact, VCS was a competitor of TI in this field. In April 1985, Sam Kuzbary, then employed with VCS and a former TI employee, noticed some information which he believed to be proprietary to TI stored in the memory of the computer he was using at VCS. Kuzbary contacted TI and agreed to serve as "informant" for them.

He then searched the premises of VCS and photographed materials which he recognized from his employment with TI. A TI internal investigation revealed that a few hours prior to Schalk's and Leonard's departures from TI, each appellant, utilizing TI computers, copied the entire contents of the directories respectively assigned to them. This information included computer programs which TI claimed to be its trade secrets. Officials of TI then contacted the Dallas District Attorney's office. A search of the premises of VCS resulted in the seizure of computer tapes containing the alleged TI trade secret programs from appellant's offices. Appellants were arrested.

We granted review to consider, first, whether the evidence was sufficient to establish that the computer programs named in the indictments were trade secrets, and second, to determine whether the items listed in the search warrant were sufficiently described so as to preclude a general exploratory search.

Having determined that computer programs are proper subjects for trade secret litigation under Texas civil and criminal law, we now look to the case *sub judice* to determine whether the programs which appellants copied and took with them to VCS are trade secrets as defined by §31.05 of the Penal Code.

§31.05 Theft of trade secrets:

(a) For the purposes of this section:

(4) "Trade secret" means the whole or any part of any scientific or technical information, design, process, procedure, formula, or improvement that has value and that the owner has taken measures to prevent from becoming available to persons other than those selected by the owner to have access for limited purposes.

Appellants claimed on appeal that the programs did not meet the statutory trade secrets criteria because they alleged their former employer TI failed to take "measures to prevent [the information] from becoming available to persons other than those selected by the owner." We note, as did the court of appeals, that the statute sets no standards for degree of sufficiency of the "measures" taken. Specifically, appellants pointed to considerable disclosure of speech research information, citing the "academic environment" of the laboratory in which they worked as encouraging the sharing of information, rather than maintaining secrecy. Appellants also claimed that TI policy favored protection of its research and development efforts through the patent process, as opposed to trade secret designation. Further, appellants allege that the programs that are the subject of the instant case were not listed in the TI register of trade secrets and that TI was lax in implementing its standard procedures with regard to notifying employees of trade secrets within the company. The precise issue before us in the case *sub judice* is one of the first impression in Texas, to wit: what constitutes requisite "measures" to protect trade secret status?

We now determine whether the information disclosed with TI's permission or encouragement, such as published articles, seminar papers, speeches given at public meetings, information provided to government agencies, etc., was so extensive as to destroy any trade secret status that may have existed regarding the computer software which is the subject of the instant indictments. It is axiomatic that the core element of a trade secret must be that it remain a secret. However, absolute secrecy is not required.

A trade secret can exist in a combination of characteristics and components, each of which, by itself, is in the public domain, but the unified process and operation of which, in unique combination, affords a competitive advantage and is a protectable secret. We find based on the record in this case that the limited disclosure made by TI in regard to the speech research lab activities merely described the application and configuration of the certain elements of the software but did not reveal the actual composition of the programs. The measures used by TI to secure its premises to prevent unauthorized personnel from admission to or exposure to its proprietary research data were reasonable under the circumstances.

We need not decide today whether any one of the preventive measures listed, standing alone, is factually sufficient to support trade secret status. We do find that the combination of employment agreements, strict plant security, restricted computer access, the nonauthorization of disclosure of the subject programs and the general nondisclosure of those programs by TI and its employees served to support trade secret status of the computer programs that are the subject of the instant indictments. Appellants neither requested nor received permission to copy the files containing these programs. The unauthorized copying of the article representing a trade secret constitutes an offense under V.T.C.A. Penal Code §31.05(b)(2).

Therefore we AFFIRM the court of appeals' ruling that the subject programs are trade secrets.

CASE A.7

Feist Publications, Inc. v. Rural Telephone Service Co., Inc.,

499 U.S. 340, 111 S.Ct. 1282, 113 L.Ed.2d 358 (1991)
United States Supreme Court
O'Connor, Justice

Rural Telephone Service Company is a certified public utility that provides telephone service to several communities in northwest Kansas. It is subject to a state regulation that requires all telephone companies operating in Kansas to issue annually an updated telephone directory. Accordingly, as a condition of its monopoly franchise, Rural publishes a typical telephone directory, consisting of white pages and yellow pages. The white pages list in alphabetical order the names of Rural's subscribers, together with their towns and telephone numbers. The yellow pages list Rural's business subscribers alphabetically by category and feature classified advertisements of various sizes. Rural distributes its directory free of charge to its subscribers, but earns revenue by selling yellow pages advertisements.

Feist Publications, Inc., is a publishing company that specializes in area-wide telephone directories. Unlike a typical directory, which covers only a particular calling area, Feist's area-wide directories cover a much larger geographical range, reducing the need to call directory assistance or consult multiple directories. The Feist directory that is the subject of this litigation covers 11 different telephone service areas in 15 counties and contains 46,878 white pages listings—compared to Rural's approximately 7,700 listings.

Of the 11 telephone companies, only Rural refused to license its listings to Feist. Rural's refusal created a problem for Feist, as omitting these listings would have left a gaping hole in its area-wide directory, rendering it less attractive to potential yellow pages advertisers. Unable to license Rural's white pages listings, Feist used them without Rural's consent.

Rural sued for copyright infringement in the District Court for the District of Kansas, taking the position that Feist, in compiling its own directory, could not use the information contained in Rural's white pages. The district court granted summary judgment to Rural, explaining that "courts have consistently held that telephone directories are copyrightable" and citing a string of lower court decisions. In an unpublished opinion, the Court of Appeals for the Tenth Circuit affirmed "for substantially the reasons given by the district court."

This case concerns the interaction of two well-established propositions. The first is that facts are not copyrightable; the other, that compilations of facts generally are. The key to resolving the tension lies in understanding why facts are not copyrightable. The *sine qua non* of copyright is originality. To qualify for copyright protection, a work must be original to the author. Original, as the term is used in copyright, means only that the work was independently created by the author (as opposed to copied from other works), and that it possesses at least some minimal degree of creativity.

Originality is a constitutional requirement. The source of Congress's power to enact copyright laws is Article 1, §8. C1. 8, of the Constitution, which authorizes Congress to "secure for limited Times to Authors . . . the exclusive Right to their respective Writings." It is this bedrock principle of copyright that mandates the law's seemingly disparate treatment of facts and factual compilations. No one may claim originality as to facts. This is because facts do not owe their origin to an act of authorship. The distinction is one between creation and discovery: the first person to find and report a particular fact has not created the fact; he or she has merely discovered its existence.

If the selection and arrangement of facts are original, these elements of the work are eligible for copyright protection. No matter how original the format, however, the facts themselves do not become original through association.

There is no doubt that Feist took from the white pages of Rural's directory a substantial amount of factual information. At a minimum, Feist copied the names, towns, and telephone numbers of 1,309 of Rural's subscribers. Not all copying, however, is copyright infringement, two elements must be proven: (1) ownership of a valid copyright, and (2) copying of constituent elements of the work that are original. The first element is not at issue here: Feist appears to concede that Rural's directory, considered as a whole, is subject to a valid copyright because it contains some foreword text, as well as original material in its yellow pages advertisements.

The question is whether Rural has proven the second element. In other words, did Feist, by taking 1,309 names, towns, and telephone numbers from Rural's white pages, copy anything that was "original" to Rural? Certainly, the raw data does not satisfy the originality requirement. Rural may have been the first to discover and report the names, towns, and telephone numbers of its subscribers, but this data does not "owe its origin" to Rural. The question that remains is whether Rural selected, coordinated, or arranged these copyrightable facts in an original way. The selection, coordination, and arrangement of Rural's white pages do not satisfy the minimum constitutional standards for copyright protection. Rural's selection of listings could not be more obvious: it publishes the most basic information—name, town, and telephone number—about each person who applies to it for telephone service. This is "selection" of a sort, but it lacks a modicum of creativity necessary to transform mere selection into copyrightable expression. Rural extended sufficient effort to make the white pages directory useful, but insufficient creativity to make it original.

The judgment of the court of appeals is REVERSED.

CASE A.8
Ramirez v. Plough, Inc.

15 Cal. App. 4th 1110, 12 Cal. Rptr. 2d 423 (1992)
Court of Appeal of California
Thaxter, Judge

Jorge Ramirez, a minor, by his guardian ad litem Rosa Rivera, appeals from a summary judgment in favor of Plough, Inc. Appellant sued Plough alleging negligence, product liability, and fraud. The action sought damages for injuries sustained in March 1986 when Jorge, who was then four months old, contracted Reye's Syndrome after ingesting St. Joseph Aspirin for Children (SJAC). Plough marketed and distributed SJAC.

Reye's syndrome is a serious disease of unknown cause characterized by severe vomiting, lethargy, or irritability which may progress to delirium or coma. The disease generally strikes children or teenagers who are recovering from a mild respiratory tract infection, influenza, chicken pox, or other viral illnesses. The mortality rate of the disease is high, and permanent brain damage occurs in many cases. As a result of contracting Reye's Syndrome, appellant suffered catastrophic injuries including quadriplegia, blindness, and profound mental retardation.

In the early 1980s, there was significant scientific debate concerning the cause of Reye's syndrome. Several state studies suggested a statistical association between the ingestion of aspirin and the disease. In December 1982, the federal government acknowledged the debate. After considering the state studies and their critics, the federal government rejected a proposal which would require a warning label and instead, undertook an independent study. Apparently, Plough participated in efforts to influence government officials and agencies to reject the label proposal which Plough considered premature.

In December 1985, the Food and Drug Administration (FDA) requested that aspirin manufacturers voluntarily place a label on aspirin products warning consumers of the possible association between aspirin and Reye's Syndrome. Plough voluntarily complied and begin including a warning and insert in SJAC packaging. On June 5, 1986, the Reye's Syndrome warning became mandatory.

In March 1986, SJAC labeling bore the following warning: "Warning: Reye's Syndrome is a rare but serious disease which can follow flu or chicken pox in children and teenagers. While the cause of Reye's Syndrome is unknown, some reports claim aspirin may increase the risk of developing this disease. Consult a doctor before use in children or teenagers with flu or chicken pox." In addition, the SJAC package insert included the following statement: "The symptoms of Reye's Syndrome can include persistent vomiting, sleepiness and lethargy, violent headaches, unusual behavior, including disorientation, combativeness, and delirium. If any of these symptoms occur, especially following chicken pox or flu, call your doctor immediately, even if your child has not taken any medication. Reye's Syndrome is Serious, so Early Detection and Treatment are Vital."

Rosa Rivera purchased SJAC on March 12, 1986, and administered it to appellant who was suffering from what appeared to be a cold or upper respiratory infection. She gave appellant the aspirin without reading the directions or warnings appearing on the SJAC packaging. The packaging was in English and Ms. Rivera can speak and understand only Spanish. She did not seek to have the directions or warnings translated from English to Spanish, even though members of her household spoke English.

The trial court granted Plough's motion for summary judgment on the grounds that "there is no duty to warn in a foreign language and there is no causal relationship between plaintiff's injury and defendant's activities."

It is undisputed SJAC was marketed and intended for the treatment of minor aches and pains associated with colds, flu, and minor viral illnesses. The SJAC box promised "fast, effective relief of fever and minor aches and pains of colds." Both parties accept the premise that Plough had a duty to warn consumers that the use of SJAC after a viral infection or chicken pox could lead to Reye's Syndrome, an illness with serious, possibly fatal, consequences. In March 1986, federal regulations requiring a Reye's Syndrome warning had been promulgated and were final, although not yet effective. The FDA had previously solicited voluntary labeling. In response to the request for voluntary labeling, Plough started packaging SJAC with explicit warnings of the risks of Reye's Syndrome. The scientific community had already confirmed and documented the relationship between Reye's Syndrome and the use of aspirin after a viral illness. There is no doubt Plough had a duty to warn of the Reye's Syndrome risk.

The question thus is whether the warning given only in English was adequate under the circumstances. Respondent argues that as a matter of law it has no duty to place foreign-language warnings on products manufactured to be sold in the United States and that holding manufacturers liable for failing to do so would violate public policy.

While the constitutional, statutory, regulatory, and judicial authorities relied on by respondent may reflect a public policy recognizing the status of English as an official language, nothing compels the conclusion that a manufacturer of a dangerous or defective product is immunized from liability when an English-only warning does not adequately inform non-English literate persons likely to use the product.

Plough's evidence showed that over 148 foreign languages are spoken in the United States and over 23 million Americans speak a language other than English in their homes. That evidence plainly does not prove that Plough used reasonable care in giving an English-only warning. Plough, then, resorts to arguing that the burden on manufacturers and society of requiring additional warnings is so "staggering" that the courts should preclude liability as a matter of law. We are not persuaded.

Certainly the burden and costs of giving foreign-language warnings is one factor for consideration in determining whether a manufacturer acted reasonably in using only English. The importance of that factor may vary from case to case depending upon other circumstances, such as the nature of the product, marketing efforts directed to segments of the population unlikely to be English-literate, and the actual and relative size of the consumer market which could reasonably be expected to speak or read only a certain foreign language. Plough presented no evidence from which we can gauge the extent of the burden under the facts of this case.

Ramirez submitted evidence that Plough knew Hispanics were an important part of the market for SJAC and that Hispanics often maintain their first language rather than learn English. SJAC was advertised in the Spanish media, both radio and television. That evidence raises material questions of fact concerning the foreseeability of purchase by a Hispanic not literate in English and the reasonableness of not giving a Spanish-language warning. If Plough has evidence conclusively showing that it would have been unreasonable to give its label warning in Spanish because of the burden, it did not present that evidence below.

Given the triable issues of material fact, if we accepted Plough's arguments in this case in effect we would be holding that failure to warn in a foreign language is not negligence, regardless of the circumstances. Such a sweeping grant of immunity should come from the legislative branch of government, not the judicial. In deciding that Plough did not establish its right to judgment as a matter of law, we do not hold that manufacturers are required to warn in languages other than English simply because it may be foreseeable that non-English literate persons are likely to use their products. Our decision merely recognizes that under some circumstances the standard of due care may require such warning.

Because the evidence shows triable issues of material fact and because Plough did not establish its immunity from liability as a matter of law, its motion for summary judgment should have been denied.

CASE A.9
Mark Realty, Inc. v. Rogness,

418 So.2d 373 (1982)
District Court of Appeal of Florida
Cowart, Judge

Tilman A. Rogness, owner, entered into four separate agreements with Mark Realty, Inc., a real estate broker. They were entitled "exclusive right of sale" and gave the broker, for a stated period of time, the exclusive right to sell the property for a certain stated price and on certain terms. The broker sued on the four agreements for brokerage commissions, alleging that during the time provided in the agreements the owner had conveyed the four properties. The owner's answer alleged affirmative defenses to the effect that the owner had "canceled, revoked and terminated" the brokerage agreements before the properties were sold and that the broker had never performed under the agreements.

The trial judge construed the brokerage agreements to constitute mere offers to enter into unilateral contracts under which the broker would be entitled to a commission only if he performed by "finding a purchaser of the above property." If the documents in question are merely offers limited to acceptance by performance only, the trial judge's analysis and conclusion would be correct.

We cannot agree that the documents were only offers for a unilateral contract. The documents illustrate what has been termed "the usual practice" in the making of bargains. One party indicates what he will do and what he requires in exchange and the other then agrees. These documents, when first executed by the owner and tendered to the broker, constituted offers which, when accepted by the broker by his execution, constituted contracts. The contract is bilateral because it contains mutual promises made in exchange for each other by each of the two contracting parties.

The most common recurring brokerage transaction is one in which the owner employs a broker to find a purchaser able and willing to buy, on terms stated in advance by the owner, and in which the owner promises to pay a specific commission for the service. Such a transaction as this is an offer by the owner of a unilateral contract, an offered promise to pay by the owner, creating in the broker a power of accepting the offer by actual rendition of the requested services. The only contemplated contract between the owner and broker is a unilateral contract—a promise to pay a commission for services rendered. Such an offer of a promise to pay a commission for services rendered is revocable by the owner by notice before the broker has rendered any part of the requested service. On the other hand, the transaction between the owner and the broker can be a bilateral contract. An owner who puts his land in the hands of a broker for sale usually clearly promises to pay a commission but the broker rarely promises in return that he will produce a purchaser, although he often promises, expressly or impliedly, that he will make certain efforts to do so. If the parties have thus made mutual promises, the transaction no longer has the status of an unaccepted offer—there is an existing bilateral contract and neither party has a power of revocation. During the term of such a contract the owner may withdraw any power the owner has given the broker to contract with a third party in the owner's name, but this is not a revocation of the contract between the owner and the broker and normally such action constitutes a breach of the brokerage contract.

In this case, the broker promised to inspect the property, to list the property with a multiple listing service, to advertise the property in the local newspaper or other media, to furnish information to inquiring cooperating brokers and prospective purchasers, to show the property, to make efforts to find a purchaser, to "make an earnest and continued effort to sell," and to direct the concentrated efforts of his organization in bringing about a sale.

In the instant case, the contract clearly provided that the brokerage commission would be paid "whether the purchaser be secured by you or me, or by any other person." Thus the contract granted the broker an exclusive right of sale and the trial court erred in construing the agreement as an offer of a unilateral contract revocable at will at any time prior to performance.

The final judgment is REVERSED.

CASE A.10
Traco, Inc. v. Arrow Glass Co., Inc.,

814 S.W.2d 186 (1991)
Court of Appeals of Texas
Chapa, Justice

This is a construction dispute stemming from a quotation given by Traco, Inc., a Three Rivers Aluminum Company, a material supplier of preengineered aluminum and glass sliding doors and windows, to Arrow Glass Company, Inc., a subcontractor, in connection with the USAA Towers project in San Antonio, Texas. Arrow initially brought suit against Traco on the theories of promissory, estoppel and negligence for Traco's failure to supply aluminum and glass sliding doors at the quoted price. After a bench trial, the trial court held for Arrow solely under the theory of promissory estoppel and awarded Arrow judgment against Traco for damages in the amount of $75,843.38, plus attorneys' fees and prejudgment interest.

The facts of this case reflect that on or about October 9, 1986, construction bids were due for the USAA Towers, a $49,000,000 retirement housing project located near Fort Sam Houston, Texas. There were numerous suppliers, subcontractors, and general contractors bidding to obtain work on this project including the appellant, Traco, and the appellee, Arrow.

On bid day, a representative for Arrow received a telephone call from Dale Ferrar of Traco. Mr. Ferrar told Bill Morris, the general manager of Arrow Glass, that Traco was a very large window and sliding glass and aluminum door manufacturer in Pennsylvania. Mr. Ferrar offered its A-2 aluminum and glass sliding doors, as an alternate product substitution, to Arrow, which was bidding that portion of the project. However, after some discussion of the required specifications, the parties realized that

Traco's doors would have to be modified in order to comply with the project specifications. Arrow declined to use Traco's bid and, instead, submitted its original bid, using a different supplier of doors. At approximately noon on bid day, Mr. Ferrar phoned Mr. Morris, quoting a new price for the doors which included a modification of the frame depth which, supposedly, enabled the doors to comply with the specifications. At this time, Mr. Morris informed Mr. Ferrar that his bid was low and asked him to recheck his figures. Mr. Ferrar explained that because of Traco's size and the fact that it could manufacture its products under one roof, Traco could sell the project for that amount. Mr. Ferrar also indicated that Traco was seeking a high profile project to represent Traco in the San Antonio area.

After receiving these assurances, Mr. Morris told Mr. Ferrar that he was going to use Traco's bid. Mr. Morris then phoned the contractors to whom he had originally submitted his bid, and deducted $100,000 in reliance upon Traco's bid. Mr. Morris later told Mr. Ferrar that he had received favorable responses from three or four general contractors, and that it appeared Arrow would get the project. Mr. Morris advised Mr. Ferrar that if Arrow obtained the project, then Traco would be awarded the contract on the doors.

The oral quote by Traco was followed with a written bid confirmation on the next day, which reflected the product that would be supplied and the price agreed upon by the parties. The confirmation also included the 1-¼" frame extended at a cost of $27,860, which, allegedly, brought the doors into compliance with the project specifications.

Sometime in November, long after Mr. Morris had relied upon Mr. Ferrar's representations in submitting his bid, Mr. Morris began hearing rumors that there was a problem with the doors. Mr. Morris contacted Mr. Ferrar, who admitted that there was a problem with the doors meeting the architect's wind load deflection requirement in the specifications. Shortly after learning of this problem, Mr. Morris received a second quote from Traco, wherein Traco offered its A-3 doors, which were a more expensive, heavy grade commercial door that met the deflection requirement, for a price of $304,300. After receiving this bid, Morris objected to the price and demanded that Traco deliver doors meeting the project specifications at the original price quoted. Traco refused and when it became obvious that Arrow would not be able to use Traco's product, Mr. Morris contracted with another supplier who had bid on the project.

The record clearly reflects the following: that it was Traco that initially contacted Arrow and offered to do a certain specific act, i.e., supply the sliding doors required; that Mr. Ferrar phoned Mr. Morris on several occasions and discussed, among other things, the fact that the doors which Traco wished to bid would not comply with the specifications without some modification; and, that Mr. Ferrar assured Mr. Morris that the doors could be modified to comply with the specifications. Thus, under the present facts, Traco's bid gave Arrow "a right to expect or claim the performance of some particular thing"; specifically, Traco's bid constituted a promise to supply sliding doors meeting the project specifications at a specified price.

Appellant initially argues that the trial court erred in rendering judgment for Arrow because Traco's bid was revocable and properly withdrawn 30 days after it was made. Appellant primarily relies upon the argument that its sliding doors are goods as defined by the Texas Business and Commerce Code. Nevertheless, appellant's arguments ignore the appellee's basic contention and legal theory under which this suit was brought. Appellee sought relief under the equitable doctrine of promissory estoppel, on the premise that appellant's promises, by way of its *oral* bid, caused appellee to substantially rely to its detriment. The appellee relied to its detriment when it reduced its bid based on a telephone conversation with the appellant, prior to the time appellant's confirmation letter was sent or received. We must now resolve whether the equitable theory of promissory estoppel applies to bid construction cases and, if so, whether this doctrine applies under the specific facts of this case. While no Texas case has previously applied the theory of promissory estoppel in a bid construction case, other jurisdictions have consistently applied this doctrine under similar facts, recognizing the necessity for equity in view of the lack of other remedies.

The Texas Supreme Court, in emphasizing that the underlying function of the theory of promissory estoppel is to promote equity, has stated that: "The Vital principal is that he who by his language or conduct leads another to do what he would not otherwise have done, shall not subject such person to loss or injury by disappointing the expectations, upon which he acted. This remedy is always so applied as to promote the ends of justice." Clearly promissory estoppel is "a rule of equity" applied to prevent injustice. As is true in most, if not all, bid construction cases, the present situation does not involve a contract. Therefore, were we to hold that promissory estoppel does not exist in bid construction cases, this would necessarily mean that, notwithstanding any language or conduct by the subcontractor which leads the general contractor to do that which he would not otherwise have done and, thereby, incur loss or injury, the general contractor would be denied all relief. This proposition is untenable and conflicts with the underlying premise of promissory estoppel.

Section 90 of the STATEMENT (SECOND) OF CONTRACTS (1981) states the principle of promissory estoppel as follows: "A promise which the promisor should reasonably expect to induce action or forbearance on the part of the promisee or a third person and which does induce such action or forbearance is binding if injustice can be avoided only by enforcement of the promise." Accordingly, the requirements of promissory estoppel are: "(1) a promise, (2) foreseeability of reliance thereon by the promisor, and (3) substantial reliance by the promisee to his detriment." In order to invoke the doctrine of estoppel, all the necessary elements of estoppel must be present and the failure to establish even one of these elements is fatal to the claimant's cause of action.

Appellant insists, however, that because Traco was not an approved manufacturer and bid its doors as an alternate, that by its nature, Traco's bid was conditional and, therefore, promissory estoppel cannot lie. We fail to see how a bid for a specific door at a specific price, which was submitted in response to solicitations that detailed project specifications, is contingent, or somehow not final, merely because the wrong door was bid upon. The appellant's failure to receive the architect's approval was not due to new specifications but was caused by the appellant's failure to regard those specifications originally required when the appellant offered its doors. Appellant's point is rejected.

Notwithstanding the existence of this promise, the appellant argues that appellee could not have justifiably and reasonably relied upon appellant's bid because: Traco was not an approved manufacturer and bid its A-2 doors as an alternate and, further, Traco's bid was lower than the other suppliers who bid upon the contract.

Because of the withdrawal of Traco's bid, Arrow was compelled to seek another supplier of doors at a much greater cost; clearly, this constituted an injustice to the appellee. Additionally,

appellee's reliance upon appellant's bid was reasonable in view of the appellant's attempts to modify its doors, and Mr. Ferrar's assurances that the doors, as modified, would meet the project specifications.

We hold that the controlling findings of fact support the promissory estoppel theory.

The judgment is AFFIRMED.

CASE A.11
Carnival Leisure Industries, Ltd. v. Aubin,

938 F.2d 624 (1991)
United States Court of Appeals, Fifth Circuit
Garwood, Circuit Judge

During a January 1987 visit to the Bahamas, George J. Aubin, a Texas resident, visited Cable Beach Hotel and Casino (the Casino), which was owned and operated by Carnival Leisure Industries, Ltd. (Carnival Leisure). While gambling at the Casino, Aubin received markers or chips from the Casino and the Casino received drafts drawn on Aubin's bank accounts in Texas. Aubin spent all of the markers provided on gambling, although he could also have spent them on food, beverages, souvenirs, or lodging at the Casino. Aubin ultimately gambled and lost $25,000, having given the Casino the same amount in bank drafts.

Carnival Leisure was unable to cash the bank drafts because Aubin had subsequently directed his bank to stop payment. Carnival Leisure sued Aubin in the United States District Court for the Southern District of Texas to enforce the debt. The district court granted Carnival Leisure's motion for summary judgment against Aubin in the amount of $25,000 and attorney's fees and costs. Carnival Leisure claimed that the debt was enforceable under Texas law because public policy had changed and now favored enforcement of gambling debts. The district court agreed. Aubin raised on appeal only the issue of whether public policy in Texas continues to prevent the enforcement of gambling debts.

Carnival Leisure claims, however, that since 1973 the public policy of Texas toward gambling and the legality of gambling debts has changed. Although gambling is generally proscribed in Texas, there has been an exception for the "social" gambler since 1973. The Texas legislature enacted the Bingo Enabling Act in 1981, the Texas Racing Act in 1986, and the Charitable Raffle Enabling Act in 1989. Provisions were added to the Texas Penal Code excepting these three activities from its general proscription against gambling.

The enactment of statutes legalizing some forms of gambling admittedly evidences some dissipation or narrowing of public disapproval of gambling. However, such statutes hardly introduce a judicially cognizable change in public policy with respect to gambling generally. The social gambling permitted is confined to private places where no one receives any benefit other than his personal winnings and all participants are subject to the same risks, a categorically vastly different kind of activity from the sort involved here. The racing, bingo, and raffling exceptions are narrow, strictly regulated exceptions to a broad public policy in Texas against most forms of gambling. Further, the kind of gambling engaged in here is not of the sort permitted by any of these exceptions.

Even if gambling legislation in Texas were evidence sufficient to warrant judicial notice of a shift in public policy with respect to legalized gambling, such a shift would not be inconsistent with a continued public policy disfavoring gambling on credit. Although Aubin could have used the loaned markers for nongambling purposes at the Casino, it is undisputed that they were in fact used exclusively for gambling. Aubin's gambling debt therefore fits squarely within the terms of the public policy of Texas prohibiting enforcement of gambling debts owed to gambling participants incurred for the purpose of gambling.

We hold that the public policy in Texas against gambling on credit prevents enforcement of a debt incurred for the purpose of gambling and provided by a participant in the gambling activity. The district court's grant of summary judgment in favor of Carnival Leisure is accordingly REVERSED and this case is remanded to the district court for further proceedings consistent with this opinion.

CASE A.12
Hampton v. Federal Express Corporation,

917 F.2d 1119 (1990)
United States Court of Appeals, Eighth Circuit
Re, Chief Judge

In March 1988, Carl Gerome Hampton, a 13-year-old cancer patient at Children's Memorial Hospital in Omaha, Nebraska, was awaiting a bone marrow transplant. A transplant operation was scheduled at the University of Iowa Hospital in Iowa City, Iowa, where five potential bone marrow donors had been found. On March 21, 1988, in order to match Carl with the most suitable donor, five samples of Carl's blood were sent by the shipper, the Children's Memorial Hospital in Omaha, to Dr. Nancy Goeken, at the Veterans Administration Medical Center in Iowa City. The shipper, the Children's Memorial Hospital, entered into a contract with the carrier, Federal Express, for the transport of the blood samples.

In a paragraph entitled "Damages or Loss," the contract of carriage, set forth in the airbill, stated: "We are liable for no more than $100 per package in the event of physical loss or damage, unless you fill in a higher Declared Value to the left and document higher actual loss in the event of a claim. We charge 30 cents for each additional $100 of declared value up to the maximum shown in our Service Guide." The reverse side of the airbill contains several paragraphs, entitled "Limitations On Our Liability," which state that: "Our liability for loss or damage to your package is limited to your actual damages or $100, whichever is less, unless you pay for and declare a higher authorized value." It is not disputed that the blood samples were never received by Dr. Goeken; that Carl Hampton, the infant cancer patient, never obtained a bone marrow transplant; and that he died on May 19, 1988. Alleging causes of action for personal injury, wrongful death, and loss of services, Carl Jerry Hampton, individually and on behalf of his deceased son, Carl Gerome Hampton, filed suit in the United States District Court for the Western District of Missouri, seeking $3,081,000 in damages. The district court granted Federal Express's motion for partial summary judgment, and entered judgment in favor of Hampton for $100. Hampton appealed from judgment of the district court.

We have held that, under federal common law, "a common carrier may not exempt itself from liability for its negligence; however, a carrier may limit its liability" [*Hopper Furs, Inc. v. Emery Air Freight Corp.*, 749 F.2d 1261, 1264 (8th Cir. 1984)].

In this case, the contract entered into by the shipper, the Children's Memorial Hospital, with the carrier, Federal Express, clearly limited the liability of the carrier to $100, and provided the shipper with an opportunity to declare a higher value.

Furthermore, it is not disputed that the shipper never declared a higher value for the blood samples. Hence, the liability of the carrier would be limited to $100. Clearly, Federal Express had no knowledge of Hampton, and did not know that the package contained blood samples. It is equally clear that the shipper, Children's Memorial Hospital, did not declare a value higher than $100 for the package. Under these circumstances, Federal Express could not reasonably foresee any injury to Hampton, or the nature and extent of the injury.

Since, on the facts presented, the nature and extent of damages suffered by plaintiff Hampton were not reasonably foreseeable to the carrier, Federal Express, we AFFIRM the judgment of the district court granting Federal Express's motion for partial summary judgment.

CASE A.13
Chase Precast Corporation v. John J. Paonessa Co., Inc.,

409 Mass. 371, 566 N.E. 2d 603 (1991)
Supreme Judicial Court of Massachusetts
Lynch, Justice

This appeal raises the question whether the doctrine of frustration of purpose may be a defense in a breach of contract action in Massachusetts, and, if so, whether it excuses the defendant John J. Paonessa Company, Inc. (Paonessa), from performance.

The claim of the plaintiff, Chase Precast Corporation (Chase), arises from the cancellation of its contracts with Paonessa to supply median barriers in a highway construction project of the Commonwealth. Chase brought an action to recover its anticipated profit on the amount of the media barriers called for by its supply contracts with Paonessa but not produced. Paonessa brought a cross action against the Commonwealth for indemnification in the event if should be held liable to Chase. After a jury-waived trial, a Superior Court judge ruled for Paonessa on the basis of impossibility of performance. Chase and Paonessa cross-appealed. The appeals court affirmed, noting that the doctrine of frustration of purpose more accurately described the basis of the trial judge's decision than the doctrine of impossibility. We agree. We allowed Chase's application for further appellate review and we now affirm.

The pertinent facts are as follows. In 1982, the Commonwealth, through the Department of Public Works (department), entered into two contracts with Paonessa for resurfacing and improvements to two stretches of Route 128. Part of each contract called for replacing a grass median strip between the north- and southbound lanes with concrete resurfacing and precast concrete median barriers. Paonessa entered into two contracts with Chase under which Chase was to supply, in the aggregate, 25,800 linear feet of concrete median barriers according to the specifications of the department for highway construction. The quantity and type of barriers to be supplied were specified in two purchase orders prepared by Chase.

The highway reconstruction began in the spring of 1983. By late May, the department was receiving protests from angry residents who objected to use of the concrete barriers and removal of the grass median strip. Paonessa and Chase became aware of the protest around June 1. On June 6, a group of about 100 citizens filed an action in the Superior Court to stop installation of the concrete barriers and other aspects of the work. On June 7, anticipating modification by the department, Paonessa notified Chase by letter to stop producing concrete barriers for the projects. Chase did so upon receipt of letter the following day. On June 17, the department and the citizen's group entered into a settlement which provided, in part, that no additional concrete median barriers would be installed. On June 23, the department deleted the permanent concrete median barriers item from its contract with Paonessa.

Before stopping production on June 8, Chase had produced approximately one-half of the concrete median barriers called for by its contracts with Paonessa, and had delivered most of them to the construction sites. Paonessa paid Chase for all that it had produced, at the contract price. Chase suffered no out-of-pocket expense as a result of cancellation of the remaining portion of barriers.

This court has long recognized and applied the doctrine of impossibility as a defense to an action of breach of contract. Under that doctrine, "where from the nature of the contract it appears that the parties must from the beginning have contemplated the continued existence of some particular specified thing as the foundation of what was to be done, then, in the absence of any warranty that the thing shall exist . . . the parties shall be excused . . . when[cb] performance becomes impossible from the accidental perishing of the thing without the fault of either party."

On the other hand, although we have referred to the doctrine of frustration of purpose in a few decisions, we have never clearly defined it. Other jurisdictions have explained the doctrine as follows: when an event neither anticipated nor caused by either party, the risk of which was not allocated by the contract, destroys the object or purpose of the contract, thus destroying the value of performance, the parties are excused from further performance.

In *Mishara Construction Co.*, we called frustration of purpose a "companion rule" to the doctrine of impossibility. Both doctrines concern the effect of supervening circumstances upon the rights and duties of the parties. The difference lies in the effect of the supervening event. Another definition of frustration of purpose is found in the Restatement (Second) of Contracts §265 (1981). "Where, after a contract is made, a party's principal purpose is substantially frustrated without his fault by the occurrence of an event the nonoccurrence of which was a basic assumption on which the contract was made, his remaining duties to render performance are discharged, unless the language or the circumstances indicate the contrary."

Paonessa bore no responsibility for the department's elimination of the median barriers from the projects. Therefore, whether it can rely on the defense of frustration turns on whether elimination of the barriers was a risk allocated by the contracts to Paonessa. The question is, given the commercial circumstances in which the parties dealt: "Was the contingency which developed one which the parties could reasonably be thought to have foreseen as a real possibility which could affect performance? Was it one of that variety of risks which the parties were tacitly assigning to the promisor by their failure to provide for it explicitly? If it was, performance will be required. If it could not be considered, performance is excused."

The record supports the conclusion that Chase was aware of the department's power to decrease quantities of contract items. The judge found that Chase had been a supplier of median barriers to the department in the past. The provision giving the department the power to eliminate items or portions thereof was standard in its contracts. The judge's finding that all parties were well aware that lost profits were not an element of damage in either of the public works projects in issue further supports the conclusion that Chase was aware of the department's power to decrease

quantities, since the term prohibiting claims for anticipated profit is part of the same sentence in the standard provision as that allowing the engineer to eliminate items or portions of work. In this case, even if the parties were aware generally of the department's power to eliminate contract items, the judge could reasonably have concluded that they did not contemplate the cancellation for a major portion of the project of such a widely used item as concrete median barriers, and did not allocate the risk of such cancellations.

Judgment AFFIRMED.

CASE A.14

E.B. Harvey & Company, Inc. v. Protective Systems, Inc.,

1989 Tenn. App. Lexis 105 (1989)
Court of Appeals of Tennessee
Sanders, Presiding Judge

The plaintiff-appellant, E.B. Harvey Company, Inc. (Harvey), is engaged in the manufacture and wholesale of fine jewelry in Chattanooga. It has been engaged in this business for about 10 years. It maintains an inventory in excess of $1 million of gold, silver, precious stones, pearls, and other such materials related to the manufacture of jewelry. A considerable amount of its jewelry is on consignment and, by the very nature of its business, it requires a great deal of insurance. However, the insurance companies will not write the insurance unless it maintains an Underwriters Laboratories (U.L.)–approved AA burglary protection alarm system. The defendant-appellee, Protective Systems, Inc. (Protective), is one of two companies in Hamilton County which furnishes and maintains a U.L.–approved AA burglar protection system. In June 1981, Harvey entered into a three-year contract with Protective to install and maintain a burglar protection system. The contract provided:

It is agreed that Protective is not an insurer and that the payments hereinbefore named are based solely upon the value of the services herein described and it is not the intention of the parties that Protective assume responsibility for any losses occasioned by malfeasance or misfeasance in the performance of the services under this contract or for any loss or damage sustained through burglary, theft, robbery, fire or other cause or any liability on the part of Protective by virtue of this Agreement or because of the relation hereby established.

If there shall at any time be or arise any liability on the part of Protective, by virtue of this Agreement or because of the relation hereby established, whether due to the negligence of Protective or otherwise, such liability is and shall be limited to a sum total in amount to the rental service charge hereunder for a period of service not to exceed six months, which sum shall be paid and received as liquidated damages.

The burglary and hold-up system provided to Harvey operated by means of Grade AA telephone lines between the central monitoring station of Protective and Harvey's premises. Said telephone lines were at all times owned and maintained by the South Central Bell Telephone Company. On July 22, 1984, at 11:14 P.M., an outage condition was indicated on the E.B. Harvey & Company account. For a period of two weeks prior to this date, Protective's computer had been registering an inordinate number of outage signals which had all been traced back to problems in telephone company equipment. For this reason, on July 22, 1984, Protective's president, Pendell Meyers, notified the telephone company of this condition and reported a potential problem to the police department but did not contact a representative of Harvey to notify them of the outage condition.

The phone company was unable to locate the exact nature of the problem despite several telephone conversations with Meyers. The Chattanooga Police Department patrolled the premises surrounding Harvey's place of business twice that evening but did not note any unusual activity. The following morning, when an employee of Harvey reported to work, it was discovered that a burglary had in fact taken place. Some $200,000 worth of jewelry and inventory was stolen. Harvey sued Protective for damages resulting from the burglary. It alleged that Protective was guilty of negligence for its failure to notify Harvey or its employees of the outage which appeared on the burglary monitoring equipment.

Protective, for answer, denied the allegations of Harvey's complaint and, as an affirmative defense, alleged the contract between the parties with its exculpatory and limitation of liability provisions was enforceable and binding upon Harvey. After hearing testimony, the trial court held the extent of Harvey's recovery against Protective would be 650 percent as liquidated damages. A final judgment was entered and Harvey has appealed.

There is nothing in public policy to render inoperative or nugatory the contractual limitations contained in the agreement. Limitations against liability for negligence or breach of contract have generally been upheld in this state in the absence of fraud or overreaching. Limitations such as those contained in the present contract have generally been deemed reasonable and have been sustained in actions against the providers of burglary and fire alarm systems. Such clauses do not ordinarily protect against liability for fraud or intentional misrepresentation.

We concur with the trial court. The issues are found in favor of the appellees. The judgment of the trial court is AFFIRMED. The cost of this appeal is taxed to the appellant and the case is remanded to the trial court for collection of cost.

CASE A.15
Toys "R" Us, Inc. v. Abir,

1999 WL 61817 (1999)
United States District Court, S.D. New York
Koeltl, Judge

In 1997, plaintiff Toys "R" Us, Inc., filed an action alleging violations of federal law related to trademark dilution against the defendants, Eli Abir and Website Management, who had registered the name *Toysareus.com* as their Internet domain name. The plaintiffs alleged that this domain name diluted the plaintiff's mark TOYS "R" US. In November 1997, this court issued a temporary restraining order enjoining the defendants from "using or inducing others to use the names or marks or any colorable imitation of Plaintiff's TOYS "R" US, KIDS "R" US, BABIES "R" US and/or the family of "R" US marks" pending a decision on the plaintiff's motion for a preliminary injunction.

In December 1997, this court heard argument on the motion for a preliminary injunction. At that time the plaintiffs alleged that the defendants had also registered the domain name *Kidsareus.com*. This court then issued a preliminary injunction enjoining the defendants from, among other things, using or inducing others to use any colorable imitation of the family of "R" US marks pending final judgment. On August 27, 1998, this court granted the plaintiff's motion for summary judgment on the

trademark dilution claims. The following day, the court issued a separate Judgment and Order permanently enjoining the defendants from further infringement of the family of "R" US marks and ordering the transfer of the *Toysareus.com* and *Kidsareus.com* Internet domain names to the plaintiff.

In addition, this court held that because the defendants' conduct in this case was willful, intentional, deliberate, and in bad faith, the plaintiff is entitled to recover attorneys' fees and costs. In order to determine what constitutes "reasonable" attorneys' fees, the starting point is the "lodestar amount," which is the number of hours reasonably expended on the litigation multiplied by a reasonable hourly rate for attorneys and paralegals.

In determining a reasonable hourly rate, courts consider, inter alia, the size and experience of the firm. In this case, Darby & Darby is a well-known New York firm which specializes in intellectual property; the rates charged for its attorneys are comparable to other specialized intellectual property firms in the New York City legal market. The plaintiff's counsel swore in her declaration in support of this application that care was taken to enhance efficiency by assigning, at any one time, only one partner, one mid- to senior-level associate, one to two junior associates, and one to two legal assistants to the prosecution of this case. Having carefully reviewed the itemized request for disbursements, the court finds them neither unnecessary nor excessive for a case of this duration and complexity. The plaintiff is also entitled to costs, as well as those reasonable out-of-pocket expenses incurred by the attorneys and which are normally charged fee-paying clients.

Defendant Eli Abir, who is the owner of defendant Website Management, does not argue that the award requested by the plaintiffs is excessive. Instead, he argues that due to his business and personal circumstances he has limited financial resources and would be unable to pay more than a "symbolic" amount in attorneys' fees. However, nothing in the record in this case justifies a financially based reduction in the award of attorneys' fees and costs. For the reasons stated above, the plaintiff's motion for attorneys' fees and costs is granted in the amount of $55,162.76. SO ORDERED.

CASE A.16
Cafazzo v. Central Medical Health Services, Inc.,

668 A.2d 521 (1995)
Supreme Court of Pennsylvania
Montemuro, Justice

In 1986, appellant Albert Cafazzo underwent surgery for implantation of a mandibular prosthesis. In 1992, some time after it was discovered that this device was defective, a complaint was filed against Dr. Norman Stern, the physician who performed the surgery, and the hospital where the operation took place, claiming that "all defendants sell, provide or use certain prosthetic devices," and that they should be held strictly liable as having "provided, sold or otherwise placed in the stream of commerce products manufactured by Vitek, Inc., known as Proplast TMJ Implants." The complaint alleged that the prosthesis was defectively designed, unsafe for its intended use, and lacked any warning necessary in order to ensure safety.

Section 402A of the Restatement (Second) of Torts, provides in relevant part as follows:

(1) One who sells any product in a defective condition unreasonably dangerous to the user or consumer or to his property is

subject to liability for physical harm thereby caused to the ultimate user or consumer, or to his property, if:

(a) the seller is engaged in the business of selling such a product, and

(b) it is expected to and does reach the consumer without substantial change in the condition in which it is sold.

The thrust of the inquiry is not on whether a separate consideration is charged for the physical material used in the exercise of medical skill, but what service is performed to restore or maintain the patient's health. The determinative question becomes not what is being charged, but what is being done. The provision of medical services is regarded as qualitatively different from the sale of products.

This distinction is made clearer by the fact that case law also supports the application of 402A where what has been provided is not medical service or products connected with diagnosis and treatment, but rather materials related to mechanical or administrative functions. See *Thomas v. St. Joseph Hospital*, 618 S.W.2d 791 (Tex. Civ. App. 1981) (hospital held strictly liable where hospital gown ignited when lighted match fell on it).

It must be noted that the "seller" need not be engaged solely in the business of selling products such as the defective one to be held strictly liable. An example supporting this proposition appears in comment *f* of the Restatement (Second) of Torts, §402A and concerns the owner of a motion picture theater who offers edibles such as popcorn and candy for sale to movie patrons. The analogue to the instant case is valid in one respect only: both the candy and the TMJ implant are ancillary to the primary activity, viewing a film or undergoing surgery respectively. However, beyond that any comparison is specious. A movie audience is free to purchase or not any food items on offer, and regardless of which option is exercised the primary activity is unaffected. On the other hand, while the implant was incidental to the surgical procedure here, it was a necessary adjunct to the treatment administered, as were the scalpel used to make the incision, and any other material objects involved in performing the operation, all of which fulfill a particular role in provision of medical service, the primary activity.

When one enters the hospital as a patient, he goes there, not to buy medicines or pills, not to purchase bandages or iodine or serum or blood, but to obtain a course of treatment in the hope of being cured of what ails him. We find, consistent with the decisions cited above which distinguish medical services from merchandising, that appellees are not sellers, providers, suppliers or distributors of products such as to activate 402A.

CASE A.17
Burnett vs. Purtell,

1992 Ohio App. Lexis 3467 (1992)
Court of Appeals of Ohio
Ford, Presiding Judge

Appellees agreed to purchase a mobile home with shed from appellant. On Saturday, March 3, 1990, appellees paid appellant $6,500 and in return were given the certificate of title to the mobile home as well as a key to the mobile home, but no keys to the shed. At the same time the certificate of title was transferred, the following items remained in the mobile home: the washer and dryer, mattress and box springs, two chairs, items in the refrigerator, and the entire contents of the shed. These items were to be retained by appellant and removed by appellant. To facilitate removal, the estate retained one key to the mobile home and the only keys to the shed.

On Sunday, March 4, 1990, the mobile home was destroyed by fire through the fault of neither party. At the time of the fire, appellant still had a key to the mobile home, as well as the keys to the shed and she had not removed the contents of the mobile home nor the shed. The contents of the shed were not destroyed and have now been removed by appellant. The referee determined that the risk of loss remained with appellant because there was no tender of delivery. Appellant objected to the conclusion of law, but the trial court overruled the objection and entered judgment in favor of appellee. First, the appellant argues that because the certificate of title was transferred, appellees were given a key to the mobile home and the full purchase price was paid by appellees, that the risk of loss had shifted from appellant to appellees. The risk of loss passes to the buyer on his receipt of the goods if the seller is a merchant: otherwise the risk passes to the buyer on tender of delivery.

Analyzing the foregoing elements it is clear that, as the trial court stated, appellant did not tender delivery. The parties agreed that appellees would purchase the mobile home and shed from appellant. The contents of both the shed and the mobile home were to be retained by appellant and removed by appellant. At the time of the fire, appellant had not removed the items that she was required to remove from either the mobile home or the shed. Additionally, all keys to the mobile home were not surrendered and none of the keys to the shed were relinquished. Under this scenario, appellant did not tender conforming goods free of items belonging to her which remained in the trailer, nor did she put the mobile home at appellee's disposition without being fettered with the items previously enumerated. Accordingly, the trial court was correct in determining that appellant did not tender delivery within the meaning of the statute, and consequently the risk of loss remained with her. The trial court was correct in determining that appellant did not tender delivery in a manner sufficient to shift the risk of loss to appellees. Therefore, when it ordered appellant to return appellee's purchase money, it effectually mandated that the contract was "avoided."

Based on the foregoing, the judgment of the trial court is AFFIRMED.

CASE A.18
LNS Investment Company, Inc. v. Phillips 66 Co.,

731 F. Supp. 1484 (1990)
United States District Court
O'Connor, Chief Judge

Plaintiff is the successor to a company known as CompuBlend Corporation ("CBC"), which blended, labeled, and packaged quart plastic bottles of motor oil for, among others, defendant Phillips 66 Company. On July 29, 1986, W. Peter Buhlinger, defendant's manager of lubricants ("Buhlinger"), wrote a letter to Dan Tutcher, Plaintiff's vice-president of operations ("Tutcher"), which read as follows: This will confirm our verbal agreement wherein Phillips will purchase additional quantities of plastic bottles from CBC during 1986. CBC, in an effort to increase their packaging capacity has committed to purchase several additional molds to blow the Phillips plastic one-quart container. In order to amortize the cost of the additional equipment, Phillips has agreed to take delivery of a maximum of 4,000,000 bottles to be made available by December 31, 1986. This agreement includes the production available now and to be supplemented by the additional equipment. Should CBC not be able to produce the full 4,000,000 quarts by December 31, 1986, this agreement shall be considered satisfied. Phillips's desire is to receive as many bottles packaged with Phillips motor oil in 1986 from CBC as possible.

Plaintiff experienced numerous problems in maintaining even its precontract capacity. Moreover, the quality of goods plaintiff was able to deliver was frequently unacceptable to defendant. Laughlin reiterated defendant's dissatisfaction with plaintiff's products by letter dated October 15, 1986. Discussing bottles tendered by plaintiff, Laughlin stated that "we definitely do not want bottles on the shelf of the quality submitted." On December 16, 1986, Buhlinger wrote that defendant would not renew any commitments to purchase goods from plaintiff after March 31, 1987, due to plaintiff's poor performance under the July 29 agreement. Plaintiff filed this suit on March 12, 1987, alleging, inter alia, that defendant breached the July 29 agreement by failing to purchase plaintiff's full output of plastic bottles through December 31, 1986.

Plaintiff's failure to provide either the quantity or quality of goods contemplated by the July 29 agreement entitled defendant to suspend its performance. Section 84-2-609 of the Code states as follows: Right to adequate assurance of performance. (1) A contract for sale imposes an obligation on each party that the other's expectation of receiving due performance will not be impaired. When reasonable grounds for insecurity arise with respect to the performance of either party the other may in writing demand adequate assurance of due performance and until he receives such assurance may if commercially reasonable suspend any performance for which he has not already received the agreed return.

It was incumbent upon plaintiff to provide adequate assurance of its future performance to defendant. Plaintiff failed to provide defendant with adequate assurance of its future performance. Official UCC Comment 4 states that what constitutes "adequate" assurance of due performance is subject to the same test of factual conditions as what constitutes "reasonable grounds for insecurity." For example, where the buyer can make use of a defective delivery, a mere promise by a seller of good repute that he is giving the matter his attention and that the defect will not be repeated, is normally sufficient. Under the same circumstances, however, a similar statement by a known corner-cutter might well be considered insufficient without the posting of a guaranty or, if so demanded by the buyer, a speedy replacement of the delivery involved. By the same token where a delivery has defects, even though easily curable, which interfere with easy use by the buyer, no verbal assurance can be deemed adequate which is not accomplished by replacement, repair, money-allowance, or other commercially reasonable cure.

Plaintiff's continual excuses for failure to perform, unaccompanied by corresponding remedial action, cannot be deemed adequate assurance under the Code. Accordingly, defendant was entitled to suspend its own performance of the contract by refusing to place orders with plaintiff and/or canceling unfilled orders already placed, thirty days after either or both the September 18, 1986, and October 15, 1986, letters. In view of this conclusion, defendant did not breach the contract by suspending performance in December, 1986, and judgment will be entered in its favor.

Judgment for defendant.

CASE A.19
Johnson v. Chicago Pneumatic Tool Co.

607 So. 2d 615 (1992)
Court of Appeals of Louisiana
Crain, Judge

This is a products liability action in which William H. Johnson was injured in the course of his employment when a pipejack was accidentally propelled toward Johnson striking him in the back and pinning him between the edge of a large diameter pie which he was grinding and the pipejack. A pipejack is a large mechanical device which is inserted into large pipes which are in the process of being joined together. The pipejack applies pressure forcing the joints into an evenly rounded shape which can then be welded together. The movement of the pipejack was controlled by an air winch manufactured by Chicago Pneumatic Tool Company (Chicago Pneumatic) which had been utilized and incorporated by McDermott, Inc., Johnson's employer, into a system dedicated to the fitting or joining of large-diameter pipe. The accident occurred at the McDermott shipyard when a co-employee either tossed or laid a 50-gallon drum on the ground near the winch in the area where Johnson was working. The drum rolled and toppled over onto the winch throttle pushing the throttle downward which in turn activated the winch and caused the pipejack to move toward Johnson.

Johnson instituted this action against Chicago Pneumatic as manufacturer of the winch, alleging that the winch as designed and manufactured was unreasonably dangerous to normal use. McDermott intervened in this action. After trial on the merits, the jury rendered a special verdict in factor of defendant.

It is uncontroverted that at the time of the accident Johnson was working with his back to the pipejack and the winch; the winch was not being manually operated; and no one was standing at or adjacent to the winch controls. The clutch lever had previously been welded down by McDermott and as a result the clutch remained permanently engaged. Of the other winch controls, the throttle was set in the neutral position and neither the brake nor the safety lock was engaged.

In order to prevail in a products liability action a plaintiff must prove that his damage was a result of a condition of the product which made the product unreasonably dangerous to normal use. The "normal use" of a product encompasses all intended or foreseeable uses and misuses of the product. A manufacturer is obliged to adequately warn the user of any danger inherent in the normal use of the product which is not within the knowledge of or obvious to the normal user. The manufacture is also required to anticipate the environment in which the product will be used and to notify the user of the potential risks arising from foreseeable use or misuse in the foreseeable environment.

The finding of the jury that the winch was not employed in normal use at the time of the accident is a factual determination which should not be set aside unless clearly wrong. A review of the record reveals that McDermott modified the winch by permanently engaging the clutch; that this modification permanently removed one of the safety and control features designed for its safe and proper operation; the disengagement of the clutch without the engagement of the additional safety features would have prevented the accident; the basic safety mechanisms of the winch were not utilized; the winch was installed backwards, thereby requiring the operator to stand away from the controls; and the employees/operators were uninformed regarding familiarity with the controls and proper operation of the winch. After careful review of the record we conclude that the jury's determination in this matter is not manifestly erroneous.

AFFIRMED.

CASE A.20
Federal Deposit Insurance Corporation v. Woodside Construction, Inc.,

979 F.2d 172 (1992)
United States Court of Appeals for the Ninth Circuit
Hug, Circuit Judge

This case arose when Donald Galt signed a deed of trust note twice and signed a contract of guaranty twice. The FDIC claims that Galt is liable for $912,000, first because he signed the note as an indorser or, alternatively, because he signed the contract of guaranty as a guarantor. Galt claims that all of his signatures were in a representative capacity and that he did not sign individually as an indorser or as a guarantor. The FDIC maintains that one of the signatures on the note and one of the signatures on the contract of guaranty were signed in Galt's individual capacity, making him liable as an indorser on the note or, alternatively, as a guarantor on the contract of guaranty. The district court granted summary judgment for Galt on both the indorsement issue and the guaranty issue.

Galt obtained a loan from Alaska Mutual Bank for $912,000 on behalf of Woodside Construction of which he was an officer. The loan was evidenced by a promissory note, a deed of trust, a loan agreement, and a contract of guaranty. The signatures appeared on the note as follows:

> *(signature of Galt)*
> *Woodside Construction, Inc.*
> *signature(s)*
> *(signature of Galt)*
> *Donald A. Galt, President*

The contract of guaranty appears on the form as follows:

> *Woodside Construction, Inc.*
> *(signature of Galt)*
> *by Donald A. Galt*
> *Title Vice President*
> *by (signature of Galt)*
> *Title*
> *Guarantors:*
> *Guarantor*
> *Donald A. Galt*

As can be seen, the note bore Galt's signature below the name of the corporation, on the line designating his representative capacity as president. It also bore Galt's signature above the name of the corporation with no representative capacity designated.

The contract of guaranty bore Galt's signature below the name of the corporation, on the line designating his representative capacity, and then bore his signature on a line where no representative capacity was indicated. He did not sign on the line designated for his signature as guarantor.

Alaska National Bank merged with two other banks and became Alliance Bank, which retained this Woodside obligation. The loan was declared to be in default, and Alliance Bank instituted this action in state court. Alliance Bank was closed by the Alaska Department of Commerce and Economic Development, and the FDIC was appointed receiver. This Woodside obligation was sold by FDIC, as receiver, to FDIC in its corporate capacity. The FDIC then removed this case to federal court. The district court entered summary judgment for the FDIC against Woodside Construction on the note but entered summary judgment for Galt against the FDIC. The FDIC appeals the judgment rendered for Galt.

The manner in which Galt signed the promissory note bound him as an indorser in his individual capacity. He signed the note under the corporate name with the designation of his representative capacity. He also signed the note above the corporate name with no designation of any representative capacity. It is this latter signature that creates Galt's liability.

UCC Sec. 3-403(2) provides:

An authorized representative who signs his own name to an instrument:

(a) is personally obligated if the instrument neither names the person represented nor shows that the representative signed in a representative capacity:

(b) except as otherwise established between the immediate parties, is personally obligated if the Instrument names the person represented but does not show that the representative signed in a representative capacity, or if the instrument does not name the person represented but does show that the representative signed in a representative capacity.

Here, the first signature above the principal designation fails to indicate the representative capacity, and the second signature above the representative capacity fails to indicate the principal. Because the FDIC is the holder of the note here, parol evidence of intent is inadmissible, and Galt is personally liable.

The FDIC argues that Galt is liable for attorneys' fees. The note makes the indorser liable for the costs of collection, including attorneys' fees. Because we hold that Galt is the indorser, he is liable for attorneys' fees.

The judgment is REVERSED.

CASE A.21
Kedzie & 103rd Currency Exchange, Inc. v. Hodge,

601 N.E.2d 803 (Ill. App. I Dist. [1921])
Appellate Court of Illinois
Linn, Justice

Plaintiff, Kedzie & 103rd Street Currency Exchange, Inc., cashed a check for defendant Fred Fentress (who is not a party to this appeal). Defendant Beula M. Hodge, drawer of the check, notified her bank to stop payment on the check when Fentress, engaged to perform plumbing services, did not appear at her home to begin work. As a holder in due course, plaintiff sought damages from Hodge. The trial court, however, granted Hodge's motion to dismiss based on the defense of illegality.

Plaintiff states the issue as whether a holder in due course of a check takes the check free from the defense of illegality where the drawer of the check issued it as a partial advance payment for plumbing services to be rendered, but the payee was not licensed as a plumber.

Background

Plaintiff, an Illinois corporation doing business as a currency exchange, filed suit after the $500 check it had cashed for Fentress was returned marked "payment stopped." Hodge had made out the check to "Fred Fentress—A-OK Plumbing" as partial payment, in advance for plumbing services at her residence. When he failed to appear on the date work was to begin, Hodge directed her bank to stop payment on the check. Fentress, in the meantime, cashed the check at plaintiff currency exchange, indorsing the back as "Fred Fentress A-OK Plumbing Sole Owner." Plaintiff obtained a default judgment against Fentress.

Hodge filed a motion to dismiss the action as to her, asserting the defense of illegality. She had discovered that Fentress was not a licensed plumber listed with either the state or Chicago. Under An Act in Relation to the Licensing and Regulation of Plumbers (Plumber's Licensing Act), plumbers must obtain a license before practicing their trade. A violation of the act is a Class B misdemeanor for the first offense. According to Hodge, the plumbing contract was illegal and void; therefore, plaintiff took the check subject to the illegality defense. The trial court agreed and entered judgment in favor of Hodge.

Opinion

Under the Uniform Commercial Code (UCC), commercial instruments including checks are meant to be freely negotiable, and to that end a holder in due course will take the instrument free from "all defenses of any party to the instrument with whom the holder has not dealt except such incapacity, or duress, or illegality of the transaction, as renders the obligation of the party a nullity."

Comment 6 to UCC Sec. 3-305 explains that the question of illegality is a matter of state law and if under the law governing the contract the effect of the illegality is to make the obligation entirely null and void, the defense is good.

The dispositive issue before us, therefore, is whether under Illinois law the contract between Hodge and the plumber was null and void. If so, the defense of illegality was properly asserted and applied in this case. If the underlying obligation was merely voidable, however, the defense fails.

The Illinois legislature, by adopting Sec. 3-305 of the UCC, has expressly declared that illegality is an available defense against a holder in due course, as long as the effect of the illegality is to render the obligation sued upon null and void.

Illinois courts should not apply the illegality defense against holders in due course unless the illegal transaction is of the type that wholly nullifies the contract and thereby renders the instrument subject to the illegality defense.

In this state, the legislature has passed extensive legislation relating to the licensing of many trades and professions, recognizing that the regulation of these professions is essential to the public health, safety and welfare. In furtherance of the legislative goals of providing standards and protecting the public health, the Plumber's Licensing Act provides that one who attempts to practice plumbing without a license may suffer substantial penalties, including criminal prosecution and fines. By judicial construction, the unlicensed plumber also forfeits his right to compensation for illegal services rendered. The contract in question is not void unless the Plumber's Licensing Act or other legislation expressly declares it to be.

As a matter of policy, plaintiff argues that it is unfair to expect a currency exchange to police the negotiable instruments it receives to ferret out possible illegalities in the underlying contracts. While the argument is reasonable enough, the same could be made for all of the defenses which defeat the rights of holders in due course. The currency exchange does not have a way to ascertain if a check has been drafted under duress, if it represents a gambling debt, or if it is the check of one without legal capacity to be bound. The so-called "real" defenses are nonetheless valid and cut off the rights of the innocent holder of the instrument to obtain recourse against makers or endorsers of the instrument in question. Currency exchanges are in the business of cashing checks and undertake the attendant risks.

We conclude that the illegality defense asserted in this case is of the type to render the obligation a nullity under Sec. 3-305 of the Code. Therefore, we affirm the trial court's dismissal of the action against Hodge, as maker of the check.

AFFIRMED.

CASE A.22

First American Bank and Trust v. Rishoi,

553 So.2d 1387 (Fla. App. 5 Dist. 1990)
District Court of Appeals of Florida
Daniel, Chief Judge

First American Bank and Trust appeals a summary judgment in favor of William M. Rishoi as receiver for Clara Lamstein and the business she operated under the name of Interamerican Business Consultants and Associates, Inc.

In *Crosby v. Lewis*, the Crosbys had purchased $180,000 in cashier's checks, payable to Lamstein, from various banks and financial institutions. The checks were all delivered to Lamstein as investments. Lamstein's business was later closed down by the state on the ground that it was an illegal "ponzi" or pyramiding scheme. The assets of the business were placed in the control of Rishoi as receiver. Eighty thousand dollars of the cashier's checks from the Crosbys had been cashed and deposited by Lamstein prior to the receivership. However, $100,000 in cashier's checks remained uncashed in Lamstein's possession. The Crosby's requested that the banks not pay the cashier's checks. The banks issued stop payment orders on the outstanding cashier's checks and subsequently dishonored the checks when presented by the receiver for payment.

Although the issuing banks were not parties to that action, this court stated:

The banks which issued the cashier's checks are primarily liable to the receiver, and by refusing to honor the checks, they have prima facie violated the duties imposed on them.

Rishoi thereafter instituted suit against First American Bank and Trust claiming that the bank had improperly refused to honor the cashier's checks. The court below concluded that the bank had no right to stop payment on the cashier's checks and entered summary judgment in favor of Rishoi.

On appeal, the bank argues that Rishoi is not a holder in due course and therefore it was justified in refusing to honor the cashier's checks. The bank acknowledges that a cashier's check presented by a holder in due course may not be countermanded after issue. It also acknowledges that cashier's checks are treated as the next best thing to cash in the business community. On public policy grounds, however, the bank urges that it should be able to assist its customers by stopping payment on a cashier's check which has been obtained from a customer by a criminal act.

Warren Finance, Inc. v. Barnett Bank of Jacksonville, N.A., (552 So.2d 194 (Fla. 1989), the Florida Supreme Court recently held that, in accordance with common commercial practice and the use of a cashier's check as a cash substitute, any defenses which a bank may assert to avoid payment must be narrowly limited. The court concluded that, upon presentment for payment by a holder, a bank may only assert its real and personal defenses in order to refuse payment on a cashier's check issued by the bank. The bank may not, however, rely on a third party's defenses to refuse payment. The only inquiry a bank may make on presentment of a cashier's check is whether the payee or indorsee is in fact a legitimate holder, that is, whether the cashier's check is being presented by a thief or one who simply found a lost check, or whether the check has been materially altered. The court concluded that this approach maintains the validity and use of cashier's checks yet acknowledges the valid concerns of banks.

In the present case, the receiver was a legitimate holder and the bank had no real or personal defenses to assert against his claim for payment. Thus, the bank wrongfully dishonored its own obligation and is liable for payment. Accordingly, the trial court properly entered summary judgment in favor of the receiver.

AFFIRMED.

CASE A.23
Davenport v. Chrysler Credit Corporation,

818 S.W. 2d 23 (1991)
Court of Appeals of Tennessee
Koch, Judge

Larry and Debbie Davenport purchased a new 1987 Chrysler LeBaron from Gary Mathews Motors on October 28, 1987. They obtained financing through Chrysler Credit Corporation (Chrysler Credit) and signed a retail installment contract requiring them to make the first of 60 monthly payments on or before December 8, 1987.

The automobile developed mechanical problems before the Davenports could drive it off the dealer's lot. Even before their first payment was due, the Davenports had returned the automobile to the dealer seven times for repair. They were extremely dissatisfied and, after consulting a lawyer, decided to withhold their monthly payments until the matter was resolved.

Chrysler Credit sent the Davenports a standard delinquency notice when their first payment was 10 days late. The Davenports did not respond to the notice, and on December 23, 1987, Chrysler Credit telephoned the Davenports to request payment. Mrs. Davenport recounted the problems with the automobile and told Chrysler Credit that she would consult her lawyer and "would let them know about the payment." After consulting with the dealer, Chrysler Credit informed Mrs. Davenport that it would repossess the automobile if she did not make the payment.

Employees of American Lender Service arrived at the Davenports' home on the evening of January 14, 1988. They informed the Davenports that they were "two payments in default" and requested the automobile. The Davenports insisted they were not in default and, after a telephone call to their lawyer, refused to turn over the automobile until Chrysler Credit obtained the "proper paperwork." The American Lender Service employees left without the car.

Before leaving for work the next morning, Mr. Davenport parked the automobile in their enclosed garage and chained its rear end to a post using a logging chain and two padlocks. He also closed the canvas flaps covering the entrance to the garage and secured the flaps with cinder blocks. When the Davenports returned from work, they discovered that someone had entered the garage, cut one of the padlocks, and removed the automobile.

American Lender Service informed Chrysler Credit on January 18, 1988, that it had repossessed the automobile. On the same day, Chrysler Credit notified the Davenports that they could redeem the car before it was offered for sale. The Davenports never responded to the notice. Instead of selling the automobile immediately, Chrysler Credit held it for more than a year because of the Davenports' allegations that the automobile was defective. In July 1989, Chrysler Credit informed the Davenports that the automobile had been sold and requested payment of the $6,774.00 deficiency. The proof supports the trial court's conclusion that Chrysler Credit had a legal right to initiate repossession procedures.

The Davenport's dissatisfaction with their automobile did not provide them with a basis to unilaterally refuse to honor their payment obligations in the retail installment contract. At the time the repossession took place, the Davenports had not requested rescission of the contract, attempted to revoke their acceptance of the automobile, pursued their remedies under the "lemon law," or taken any other formal steps to resolve their dispute with the dealer concerning the automobile. The Davenports' conduct gave Chrysler Credit an adequate basis to consider the loan to be in default and to decide to protect its collateral by repossessing the automobile.

The Tennessee General Assembly preserved the secured parties' self-help remedies when it enacted the Uniform Commercial Code in 1963. It also preserved the requirement that repossession must be accomplished without a breach of the peace. The term "breach of the peace" is a generic term that includes all violations or potential violations of the public peace and order. We can find no support for limiting "breach of the peace" to criminal context.

Secured parties may repossess their collateral at a reasonable time and in a reasonable manner. Self-help procedures such as repossession are the product of a careful balancing of the interests of secured parties and debtors. Chrysler Credit and American Lender Service do not dispute that they obtained the automobile by entering a closed garage and by cutting a lock on a chain that would have prevented them from removing the automobile. The Davenports are only entitled to recover their damages stemming directly from the manner in which American Lender Service repossessed their automobile.

We REVERSE the trial court's judgment dismissing the Davenports' complaint.

CASE A.24
Dewsnup v. Timm,

116 L.Ed. 2d 903, 112 S. Ct. 773 (1992)
Supreme Court of the United States
Blackmun, Justice

We are confronted in this case with an issue concerning §506(d) of the Bankruptcy Code. May a debtor "strip down" a creditor's lien on real property to the value of the collateral, as judicially determined, when that value is less than the amount of the claim secured by the lien?

On June 1, 1978, respondents loaned $119,000 to petitioner Aletha Dewsnup and her husband, T. LaMar Dewsnup, since deceased. The loan was accompanied by a Deed of Trust granting a lien on two parcels of Utah farmland owned by the Dewsnups. Petitioner defaulted the following year. Under the terms of the Deed of Trust, respondents at that point could have proceeded against the real property collateral by accelerating the maturity of the loan, issuing a notice of default, and selling the land at a public foreclosure sale to satisfy the debt.

Respondents did issue a notice of default in 1981. Before the foreclosure sale took place, however, petitioner sought reorganization under Chapter 11 of the Bankruptcy Code. That bankruptcy petition was dismissed, as was a subsequent Chapter 11 petition. In June 1984, petitioner filed a petition seeking liquidation under Chapter 7 of the Code. Because of the pendency of these bankruptcy proceedings, respondents were not able to proceed to the foreclosure sale.

Petitioner-debtor takes the position that §506(a) and §506(d) are complementary and to be read together. Because, under §506(a), a claim is secured only to the extent of the judicially determined value of the real property on which the lien is fixed, a debtor can void a lien on the property pursuant to §506(d) to the extent the claim is no longer secured and thus is not "an allowed secured claim." In other words, §506(a) bifurcates classes of claims allowed under §502 into secured claims and unsecured claims; any portion of an allowed claim deemed to be unsecured under §506(a) is not an "allowed secured claim" within the lien-voiding scope of §506(d). Petition argues that there is no exception for unsecured property, abandoned by the trustee.

We conclude that respondents' alternative position, espoused also by the United States, although not without its difficulty, generally is the best of the several approaches. Therefore, we hold that §506(d) does not allow petitioner to "strip down" respondents' lien, because respondents' claim is secured by a lien and has been fully allowed pursuant to §502.

The practical effect of petitioner's argument is to freeze the creditor's secured interest at the judicially determined valuation. By this approach, the creditor would lose the benefit of any increase in the value of the property by the time of the foreclosure sale. The increase would accrue to the benefit of the debtor, a result some of the parties describe as a "windfall."

We think, however, that the creditor's lien stays with the real property until the foreclosure. That is what was bargained for by the mortgagor and the mortgagee. Any increase over the judicially determined valuation during bankruptcy rightly accrues to the benefit of the creditor, not to the benefit of the debtor and not to the benefit of other unsecured creditors whose claims have been allowed and who had nothing to do with the mortgagor–mortgagee bargain.

No provision of the pre-Code statute permitted involuntary reduction of the amount of a creditor's lien for any reason other than payment on the debt.

The judgment of the court of appeals is AFFIRMED.

CASE A.25
District of Columbia v. Howell,

607 A.2d 501 (D.C. Pap. 1992)
District of Columbia Court of Appeals
Farrell, Associate Judge

The Murch School Summer Discovery Program was designed to provide hands-on education for gifted and talented eight- and nine-year-old children. The program originated in 1985 when Mrs. Gill, the Murch School principal, attended a reception at Mount Vernon College arranged by Greg Butta, a Ph.D. candidate at The American University, to advertise the success of a summer program he had conducted at Mount Vernon. The program interested Mrs. Gill, and after several discussions, Butta sent her a formal proposal for conducting a similar program at the Murch School. Gill made changes to the proposal, then solicited and received approval for the program from the Assistant Superintendent for the District of Columbia Public Schools.

Butta hired the staff for the summer program, including some of the instructors who had taught in the Mount Vernon program. Mrs. Gill, however, reviewed all of the instructors' resumes, had veto authority over their hiring, and interviewed most of the staff, including A. Louis Jagoe, before the hiring was made final. Jagoe, who was hired to teach chemistry to the eight- and nine-year-olds in the program, held a master's degree in chemistry and was a Ph.D. candidate at The American University. Before the first general staff meeting, he told Butta that as part of the class he would do a luminescence experiment and a "cold-pack" experiment and wanted to make sparklers with the children. Jago and Butta discussed the safety of the sparker experiment only in regard to the location where the children would be allowed to light the sparklers.

On August 1, 1985, a staff meeting was held at which Gill, Butta, and all instructors and counselors were present. Each instructor gave a brief talk about what he or she intended to do in class. Several instructors testified that Jagoe told the group, including Mrs. Gill, that he planned to make sparklers as one of the chemistry experiments. Gill, who was in and out of the meeting, did not remember hearing Jagoe discuss the experiment, although notes she took at the meeting reflect that she heard him discuss the luminescence and cold pack experiments and asked him questions about these. Gill spoke and emphasized the "hands-on" nature of the program and her hopes for its success.

One child attending the program was nine-year-old Dedrick Howell, whose parents enrolled him after receiving the school brochure in the mail. The accident occurred on August 12, 1985. At the beginning of the chemistry class, Jagoe distributed his "recipe" for sparklers to the children and also wrote it on the blackboard. Along with other chemical ingredients, the recipe called for the use of potassium perchlorate as the oxidizing agent. Potassium perchlorate was described at trial as an extremely unstable and highly volatile chemical often used to make rocket fuel. Commercially made sparklers are not made with potassium perchlorate.

The children scooped the chemicals, including the potassium perchlorate, out of jars and, using pestles, ground up the mixture in mortars. While they were combining the chemicals, Jagoe ignited three different chemical mixtures at the front of the room with a butane lighter. Butta was present for one of the ignitions when he entered the room to drop off metal hangers for use in the experiment. Mrs. Gill also entered the room at one point, and saw the children working at tables wearing goggles or glasses. She also saw Jagoe at the front of the room lighting the chemicals with a fire extinguisher on the table next to him.

The children continued to grind the material while a counselor, Rebecca Seashore, distributed pieces of metal hangers to be dipped into the mixture at a later time. Dedrick Howell was specifically told not to dip the hanger into the material until instructed to do so. Moments later the chemicals exploded in front of Dedrick. The chemicals burned at 5000 degrees Fahrenheit, and Dedrick was burned over 25 percent of his body including his hands, arms, chest, and face.

An employer generally is not liable for injuries to third parties caused by an independent contractor over whom (or over whose work) the employer has reserved no control. There are exceptions to the rule, however, one of which is that one who employs an independent contractor to do work involving a special danger to others which the employer knows or has reason to know to be inherent in or normal to the work, or which he contemplates or has reason to contemplate when making the contract, is subject to liability for physical harm caused to such others by the contractor's failure to take reasonable precautions against such danger.

It is sufficient that work of any kind involves a risk, recognizable in advance, of physical harm to others which is inherent in the work itself, or normally to be expected in the ordinary course of the usual or prescribed way of doing it, or that the employer has special reason to contemplate such a risk *under the particular circumstances under which the work is to be done.*

The sparkler experiment combined flammable, combustible chemicals, open flames, and children; for that very reason, presumably, the children had been equipped with goggles. Though sparklers are explosives of a lesser order, conducting controlled explosions is a textbook example of an inherently dangerous activity. It was not unreasonable for the jury to conclude that the manufacture of sparklers by nine-year-old children was an inherently dangerous activity.

Therefore, the jury was well within its authority in finding that Jagoe was an independent contractor performing inherently dangerous work of which the district had actual or constructive knowledge.

The judgment is AFFIRMED as to liability and as to the award of $8 million in damages both for pain and suffering and for past medical expenses.

CASE A.26
Catalina Mortgage Co., Inc. v. Monier,

166 Ariz. 71, 800 P.2d 574 (1990)
Supreme Court of Arizona
Feldman, Vice Chief Judge

In 1984, Michael Monier and Talon Financial Corporation (Talon) formed the Coronado Partnership (Coronado). Monier and Talon were general partners; other individuals and entities were limited partners in the venture.

Shortly after its formation, Coronado purchased an office and warehouse complex in Tucson. In 1986, the partnership refinanced this property with a loan from Catalina Mortgage Company (Catalina). Talon's president, Roger Howard, executed a promissory note in the amount of $675,000 on behalf of Coronado. In mid-1987, Talon withdrew as a general partner, leaving Monier as the sole general partner in Coronado. The promissory note matured and $687,935 plus interest is now due and owing. Coronado filed for protection pursuant to Chapter 11 of the Bankruptcy Code.

In January 1989, Catalina filed a complaint against Monier in United States District Court, seeking judgment for the amount due on the promissory note plus interest, costs, and attorneys' fees. Catalina alleged that Monier was jointly and severally liable with the partnership entity for the debt. Monier answered, contending, among other things, that because the note was an obligation of the

partnership, the partnership assets had to be exhausted before the creditor sought recovery from an individual general partner.

Discussion

If a partnership's debt is contractual in nature, common law requires creditors to resort to and exhaust partnership assets before reaching the partners' individual assets. At common law, a partner is only jointly liable for the partnership's contractual debts, though partners are jointly and severally liable for tort obligations.

As adopted in most states, the Uniform Partnership Act (UPA) preserves this common law rule. The Arizona version of the UPA, however, provides that all partners are liable jointly and severally for everything chargeable to the partnership, and for all other debts and obligations of the partnership; but any partner may enter into a separate obligation to perform a partnership contract.

Catalina maintains that because the statute imposes joint and several liability on all partners, it may proceed against Monier without exhausting partnership assets. Catalina distinguishes cases from other jurisdictions that have considered the issue on the grounds that the applicable law imposed only joint liability as opposed to joint and several liability, that some states specifically provide by statute that partnership assets must be exhausted prior to imposing liability on individual partners for contractual obligations, and that the bankruptcy courts in some instances have misconstrued the state law involved.

Several liability is separate and distinct from liability of another to the extent that an independent action may be brought without joinder of others. The individual liability associated with partners that are jointly liable is not separate and distinct from the liability of all the partners jointly. Rather, that individual liability arises only after it has been shown that the partnership assets are inadequate. No direct cause of action may be maintained against the individual partners until the above condition is met. Several liability, on the other hand, imposes no such conditions precedent before one can be held individually liable.

Conclusion

We hold, therefore, that the scheme imposed by Arizona statutes is simply that a general partner is jointly and severally liable for partnership debts. The partner may be sued severally and his assets reached even though the partnership or other partners are not sued and their assets not applied to the debt. Under Arizona law a creditor may obtain a judgment against an individual general partner on a partnership debt and may reach the partner's assets prior to exhausting partnership assets.

CASE A.27
Johnson v. Dodgen,

451 N.W.2d. 168 (1990)
Supreme Court of Iowa
Lavorato, Justice

This breach of contract action is the aftermath of a bank failure caused by the embezzlement of $16.7 million by Des Moines stockbroker Gary Lewellyn. In 1967, Joe W. Dodgen agreed to buy controlling interest in the First National Bank of Humboldt under a stock purchase agreement (agreement) calling for monthly payments. Ben P. and Adeline G. St. John, the sellers, died shortly thereafter. Two trusts were then established to receive payments under the agreement.

Dodgen assigned the agreement to his company, Humboldt Realty Insurance Co., Inc. (Humboldt Realty), which was not in existence at the time the agreement was executed, and underwent several name changes until it became known as Iowa Growthland Financial Corporation. After the bank was closed in 1982, Iowa Growthland continued to make payments under the agreement until 1984.

The trusts then sued Dodgen and Iowa Growthland for the payments that were in arrears. Dodgen and Iowa Growthland filed an answer in which they raised failure of consideration as an affirmative defense. Simply put, they were claiming that the consideration for the agreement failed when the bank went out of existence. In addition, Dodgen asserted that he was not personally liable because he signed the agreement as an agent for Humboldt Realty. In its counterclaim, Iowa Growthland sought damages on the theory of unjust enrichment for payments it made after the bank was closed. The case was tried to a jury. By way of answers to special verdict forms, the jury found that the trustees were not entitled to recover for breach of contract, that Dodgen was indeed acting as an agent when he signed the agreement, and that Iowa Growthland was not entitled to damages for its claim of unjust enrichment.

The district court granted new trial on all the issues. Dodgen and Iowa Growthland appealed; the trustees cross-appealed.

We reverse and remand with directions to enter judgment in favor of the trustees pursuant to Iowa Rule of Appellate Procedure 26.

I. Failure of Consideration

Dodgen and Iowa Growthland contend that the continued existence of the bank was the essence or root of the agreement—the thing Dodgen really bargained for. They argue that when the bank was closed the consideration for Dodgen's promise to pay failed. This failure of consideration, they assert, excused any future performance on their part. There is a difference between lack of consideration and failure of consideration. A lack of consideration means no contract is ever formed. In contrast, a failure of consideration means the contract is valid when formed but becomes unenforceable because the performance bargained for has not been rendered. In our view the potential failure of any business that is being sold is always a risk in the contemplation of the parties. If the buyer wants protection against the risk, the simple solution is to hedge against it in the agreement. That was not done here. Consequently, Dodgen assumed that risk.

What Dodgen bargained for was control of the bank through the stock he purchased; he got it and had it for fifteen years. The fact that his investment later turned out worthless does not, in our view, constitute failure of consideration.

A. Essence of the Agreement

Under the agreement here, Dodgen agreed to purchase from St. John 506 shares of capital stock of the bank. The 506 shares represented 50.6 percent of the issued and outstanding stock of the bank. By this purchase, Dodgen was acquiring controlling interest in the bank.

B. The Executory Nature of the Agreement

This issue is inextricable intertwined with the essence of the agreement issue. Dodgen and Iowa Growthland contend that the agreement was still executory when the bank was closed because the trustees had physical possession of the stock. While the trustees are still able to turn over the stock, Dodgen and Iowa Growthland argue such a gesture would be meaningless because the asset that the stock represents is nonexistent. So, they argue, there was a failure of consideration when the bank was closed.

Here we think the parties intended title to the stock to pass to Dodgen once the stock was registered in his name. At this point several things had occurred. Dodgen had made the down payment called for in the agreement and began exercising control of the bank. Likewise, St. John had substantially performed his part of the agreement. Only two promises remained unperformed: Dodgen's full payment of the purchase price and St. John's delivery of physical possession of the stock.

In these circumstances, we think there was a constructive delivery of the stock to Dodgen. Although the collateral provision of the agreement denied Dodgen physical possession of the stock, it did give him the right to such possession upon full payment. The provision also gave him rights of ownership in all other respects. Risk of loss passed with this constructive delivery. The decline in the stock's value gave Dodgen no greater right to avoid his obligation to pay than an enhanced value would have given St. John an excuse for not delivering the stock.

C. Inability to Pledge the Stock as Security

It is true that under the agreement Dodgen could not borrow against the stock. Dodgen and Iowa Growthland assert this constraint as further evidence that consideration for the agreement failed. The short answer to this argument is that Dodgen should not be allowed to take advantage of a provision he agreed to.

II. Unjust Enrichment

We have already determined that there was not, as a matter of law, a failure of consideration. In view of our holding on the failure of consideration issue, we think the district court should have sustained the trustees' motion for directed verdict on the unjust enrichment counterclaim.

III. Agency

The trustees moved for a directed verdict against Dodgen personally because the record showed he signed the agreement. Dodgen resisted the motion, contending there was enough evidence in the record to generate a jury question on his agency defense. The only evidence on this point was Dodgen's testimony. Dodgen testified that when he signed the agreement St. John agreed that Humboldt Realty—Iowa Growthland's precedessor—would be the responsible party. The district court overruled the motion. The jury then determined that Dodgen was acting as an agent for Humboldt Realty when he signed the agreement. For reasons that follow, we think the district court should have sustained the motion for directed verdict.

At the time Dodgen and St. John signed the agreement, Humboldt Realty was not in existence. Ordinarily, in these circumstances Dodgen would be personally liable. The law is clear that an agent who purports to act on behalf of a nonexistent principal is liable as a party to the agreement. The rationale for the rule is simply that in such circumstances there is no agency. This situation frequently happens when a corporate promoter enters into contracts before the corporation is actually incorporated. There is, however, an exception to this rule. If the other contracting party knows that the principal does not exist and looks to the principal alone for responsibility, the promoter is relieved of personal liability.

Here the pivotal question is whether St. John agreed to look to Humboldt Realty alone for payment. We think reasonable minds would conclude from this record that he did not. We have substantial evidence that establishes Dodgen was acting in his personal capacity. First, as the district court ruled, the language of the agreement is unequivocal on this point. For example, the opening paragraph states that "This agreement made and entered into by and between B. P. St. John and Joe W. Dodgen said B. P. St. John being hereafter referred to as the seller and the said Joe W. Dodgen being hereafter referred to as the buyer." Moreover, Dodgen ostensibly signed the agreement in his individual capacity.

Second, St. John and Dodgen were, at the time of the agreement, very knowledgeable in financial and legal matters. It is inconceivable to us that St. John would turn over valuable assets and look solely to a nonexistent corporation for payment. It is also equally inconceivable to us that Dodgen would fail to insist on express language in the agreement that would relieve him of personal liability. Simply put, we think reasonable minds would conclude that the absence of such language meant that St. John was looking to Dodgen for payment, and Dodgen knew it.

Last, in 1982 Dodgen acknowledged his personal liability. In a letter to one of the trustees—a letter we previously mentioned—Dodgen said:

> You are also correct in that the contract between me and Ben and Adeline St. John is a personal obligation even though it was later assigned to First Investors Services, Inc.

This damaging admission coupled with the other evidence leads us to conclude that the district court should have sustained the motion for directed verdict on the agency issue.

IV. Disposition

We reverse the posttrial ruling of the district court. We remand the case to the district court with directions to enter judgment in favor of the trustees for $160,976—the delinquent amount at the time of the trial—together with interest and costs.

CASE A.28
United States v. WRW Corporation,

986 F.2d 138 (1993)
United States Court of Appeals for the Sixth Circuit
Peck, Judge

In 1985, civil penalties totaling $90,350 were assessed against WRW Corporation (WRW), a Kentucky corporation, for serious violations of safety standards under the Federal Mine Safety and Health Act (the Act) which resulted in the deaths of two miners. Following the imposition of civil penalties, WRW liquidated its assets and went out of business.

Three individual defendants, who were the sole shareholders, officers, and directors of WRW, were later indicted and convicted for willful violations of mandatory health and safety standards under the Act. Roger Richardson, Noah Woolum, and William Woolum each served prison sentences and paid criminal fines. After his release from prison, Roger Richardson filed for bankruptcy under Chapter 7 of the Bankruptcy Code.

The United States (the Government) brought this action in May of 1988 against WRW and Roger Richardson, Noah Woolum, and William Woolum to recover the civil penalties previously imposed against WRW. The district court denied the individual defendants' motion to dismiss and granted summary judgment to the Government piercing the corporate veil under state law and holding the individual defendants liable for the civil penalties assessed against WRW. For the reasons discussed herein, we affirm.

Piercing the Corporate Veil

Having determined that the imposition of a $90,350 sanction upon the defendants does not violate principles of double jeopardy, we turn to the defendants' argument that the district court erred in holding the individual defendants liable for the penalty by piercing the corporate veil of WRW under Kentucky law.

The district court held that it was appropriate to pierce WRW's corporate veil under either an equity theory or an alter ego theory, both of which are recognized under Kentucky law. Under either theory, the following factors must be considered when determining whether to pierce the corporate veil: (1) undercapitalization; (2) a failure to observe the formalities of corporate existence; (3) nonpayment or overpayment of dividends; (4) a siphoning off of funds by dominant shareholders; and (5) the majority shareholders having guaranteed corporate liabilities in their individual capacities.

The court first found that WRW was undercapitalized because it was incorporated with only $3,000 of capital, which the record indicates was insufficient to pay normal expenses associated with the operation of a coal mine. The district court next found that WRW failed to observe corporate formalities, noting that no bylaws were produced by the defendants, and all corporate actions taken by the individual defendants were without corporation authorization. Finally, although WRW never distributed any dividends to the individual defendants, and there was no evidence that the individual defendants siphoned off corporate funds, these factors alone do not mitigate against piercing the corporate veil in this case because WRW was never sufficiently capitalized and operated at a loss during its two years of active existence.

In addition to holding that the equities of this case support piercing the corporate veil, the district court held that the corporate veil should be pierced under the "alter ego" theory, because WRW and the defendants did not have separate personalities. In light of the lack of observance of corporate formalities or distinction between the individual defendants and the corporation, we agree with the district court's conclusion that "there was a complete merger of ownership and control of WRW with the individual Defendants."

The specific factual findings made by the district court amply support piercing the corporate veil of WRW and holding the individual defendants liable for the penalty assessed against the corporate entity. For all of the foregoing reasons, judgment of the district court is AFFIRMED.

CASE A.29
Neal v. Alabama By-Products Corporation,

No. 8282, 1990. Del. Ch. Lexis 127 (1990)
Court of Chancery of Delaware
Chandler, Vice Chancellor

Alabama By-Products Corporation (ABC) is a Delaware corporation engaged, during the 1970s and 1980s (and for many years before that), primarily in three lines of business. It mined coal on a cost plus basis for Alabama Power Company (a major utility in Alabama); it mined coal for its own account from surface and underground mines that it owned, and it manufactured and sold foundry coke from a plant in Birmingham called the Tarrant plant. To a certain extent ABC was also engaged in the development and sale of timber and forestry products on lands it owned.

ABC's two classes of stock traded in the over-the-counter market and were not listed on an exchange. Trading history in the stock was sporadic, but shows that the average bid price between 1977 and 1984 ranged from $47 to $75 per share. Class A stock had voting rights, while class B did not. At all times relevant to this lawsuit, there were about 757,300 class A shares and 1 million class B shares authorized, issued, and outstanding.

Drummond, an Alabama Corporation, is also engaged in the mining and sale of coal in the state of Alabama. In 1977 it became interested in acquiring ABC. Between September 1977 and February 1978 Drummond acquired, in privately negotiated transactions, about 75,800 class A shares of ABC stock and 188,167 class B shares. Drummond also obtained a controlling interest in Alabama Chemical Products Company (ACPC), a holding company which at the time held 476,420 class A shares of ABC stock (about 63% of those outstanding). Drummond paid the equivalent of $110 per share of ABC stock in these transactions. The book value of ABC's common stock on December 31, 1977, was $55.47 per share. Drummond eventually caused the liquidation of ACPC, with the resulting distribution of the ABC class A stock to Drummond and other ACPC stockholders.

Drummond reconstituted ABC's board of directors in December 1977, replacing five of the nine ABC directors with Drummond designees. At all relevant times for purposes of this litigation, a majority of ABC's directors were also directors or executive officers of Drummond. Around the time that it gained control of ABC's board, Drummond created an executive committee consisting of Gary Neal Drummond, E. A. Drummond and the then current president of ABC. The executive committee had authority to act on behalf of ABC's board of directors. From its controller position, Drummond caused ABC to lease some of its coal reserves to Drummond. Drummond also purchased ABC mined coal and resold it in certain markets.

In late December 1977, Drummond presented a merger proposal to ABC's board, proposing the acquisition of all outstanding shares not owned by Drummond. This proposal was later withdrawn. Three years later, in 1981, Drummond discussed with Goldman, Sachs and Company (Goldman Sachs), its investment banker, the possibility of acquiring the remaining equity in ABC. Goldman Sachs recommended at the time that Drummond propose a cash merger at a minimum price of $85 per share. Nevertheless, Drummond decided not to pursue the acquisition at that time.

On March 17, 1983, Drummond again proposed a merger to ABC's board of directors, a proposal by which each share of ABC not owned by Drummond would have been converted into the right to receive $65 in cash and ABC would have become a wholly owned subsidiary of Drummond. A special committee of ABC's board of directors (consisting of three ABC directors who were not directors or executive officers of Drummond) recommended the retention of the firm of Kidder, Peabody and Company, Inc. (Kidder Peabody), to evaluate the 1983 merger proposal and to determine whether it was fair to unaffiliated ABC shareholders from a financial point of view. Kidder Peabody's report, submitted in September 1983, concluded that Drummond's $65 cash merger offer was not fair to unaffiliated ABC shareholders from a financial point of view. Drummond's 1983 proposal was later withdrawn.

Drummond acquired additional shares of ABC class A and class B stock in 1984 for $54.40 and $55 per share, respectively. Although it was provided, in connection with the 1984 acquisitions, that additional payments would be made by Drummond if its board of directors formally approved a tender offer for shares or a merger with ABC within stipulated time limits, no tender offer or merger proposal was made during the time limits.

In December 1984, Drummond made a tender offer for any and all outstanding shares of class A and class B common stock of ABC at $75 per share. Neither Drummond nor ABC sought a fairness opinion from an independent investment banker or financial adviser with respect to the tender offer. Nor was a committee of outside ABC directors appointed to review or comment upon the fairness of the proposed transaction. ABC's board decided it would take no position with respect to the fairness of the tender offer price, leaving the ultimate determination to the judgment of the individual shareholder.

As a result of the tender offer, Drummond became the holder of more than 90 percent of ABC's outstanding and issued shares. Then, on August 13, 1985, Drummond effected a short-form merger under Delaware law, pursuant to which the minority shareholders were cashed out at $75.60 per share. This amount was determined by adopting the 1984 tender offer price ($75) and adding a 60-cent quarterly dividend that had been missed in 1985.

Following the August 13, 1985, merger, certain minority shareholders perfected their appraisal rights pursuant to §262 of Title 8 of the Delaware Code. These minority shareholders own approximately 50,000 class A shares and 75,000 class B shares. Neal characterizes this proceeding as a two-pronged action in which separate claims for appraisal and for unfair dealing have been joined. Drummond, as successor to ABC, is the only necessary and appropriate defendant, say petitioners, as to both the unfair dealing claim and the appraisals claim.

Neal argues they have avoided the risk of double recovery by limiting the relief requested for the unfair dealing claim to (1) costs of the proceeding, (2) reasonable attorneys fees and disbursements, and (3) expert witness fees incurred by petitioners as part of the appraisal claim.

Neal also accuses Drummond of postmerger unfair dealing, complaining that Drummond's defense of the $75.60 merger price is based on contrived liabilities and transparent efforts to ascribe negative values to certain ABC assets, all of which were not disclosed to shareholders at the time of the merger. These allegedly manipulative tactics, added to the unfair dealing associated with the notice of merger and merger price, form the basis for petitioners' unfair dealing claim and, they insist, warrant an award of litigation costs.

Neal challenges the fairness of the merger price, noting that it was fixed unilaterally by Drummond without the benefit of independent expert opinion as to its fairness. They also point out that no committee, special or otherwise, was appointed to review the fairness of the merger proposal, that the merger notice to stockholders failed to disclose certain allegedly material financial information, causing stockholders to make decisions with regard to accepting the merger price or seeking appraisal on the basis of very limited information about the assets and prospects of ABC.

Neal contends that ABC's fair value was $193.40 per share on August 13, 1985. That conclusion rests upon the testimony of their valuation expert, Mr. Kenneth McGraw, based on an analysis performed by Benchmark Valuation Consultants, a division of the accounting firm Peat Marwick Maine & Co. (Benchmark), which in turn was based in part on an analysis and valuation of ABC's coal reserves and coal mining operations by Dames & Moore, a firm with expertise in geologic, mining, and natural resource engineering.

McGraw testified that Benchmark valued ABC using three alternative methods: historical earnings, net asset value, and discounted cash flow. By the historical earnings approach, Benchmark arrived at a value of $166 per share of ABC stock. The net asset methodology resulted in a value of $205 per share. The discounted cash flow approach resulted in a valuation of $225 per share. Benchmark then applied a weighted average, assigning the greatest weight (40%) to the historical earnings and net asset value approaches and the lowest weight (20%) to the discounted cash flow methodology, to arrive at a valuation based on all three valuation methodologies of $193.40 per share.

Respondents assert that the merger price was fair. The merger price, in fact, was extremely generous, because respondents contend that ABC's statutory fair value is only $64 per share, more than $11 less than Drummond paid in the merger. Respondents' valuation is based upon the testimony of their expert trial witnesses, Arnold Spangler, a general partner at Lazard Freres & Co. (Lazard), and Robert Wilken of Paul Weir Company (Weir), who estimated the company's coal reserves.

Lazard's valuation appears to have been based on a hybrid discounted cash flow and net asset methodology. The analysis was designed to predict the value of future cash flows from ABC's continuing operations, including ABC-owned mines, power company mines, and the Tarrant coke plant, over a 13-year period from 1985 through 1997. This period corresponded to either the life of a variety of ABC's long-term contracts or to the exhaustion of its coal reserves, leaving only its Tarrant coke operation viable in 1997. Lazard arrived at a net after-tax cash flow that ABC's continuing operations were expected to generate from 1985 to 1997, to which Lazard applied a multiple of five against the 1997 projected net cash flow (the terminal value), arriving at a value for ABC's activities following the terminal year.

The contrasting opinions regarding ABC's value in August 1985 demonstrate how differently petitioners and respondents view the business prospect and asset valuations of ABC. These starkly contrasting views have been presented to the court through expert witnesses who have relied on complex business valuation methodologies. Although Benchmark relied on three different methodologies, there has been remarkably little disagreement over the illegitimacy of the valuation techniques used by the parties in this case. Dispute has been over the assumptions on which the methodologies have been based as well as the underlying information supplied to the experts. With expert opinions arrayed on each side of widely divergent arguments about the worth of certain assets, or the scope of certain liabilities, the court is forced to pick and choose among the competing contentions, in search of a reasonable, and fair, value. That is this court's mandate: determine the fair value of the stock of ABC on August 13, 1985.

Both sides have relied on a discounted future returns model and a net asset model, with petitioners' expert also using a historical earnings analysis. Other valuation approaches, with equivalent theoretical legitimacy, could have been used. But I am satisfied that respondents discounted future cash flow methodology is the appropriate valuation model in this case, especially since it was also used by petitioners' expert.

The more difficult task is to move beyond the analytical framework in order to test the underlying assumptions about ABC that the experts poured into the valuation models. This is the heart of the matter, for, as one commentator has noted, methods of valuation, including a discounted cash flow analysis, are only as good as the inputs to the model. A valuation methodology can produce a correct answer for any type of input. So, the relevant question is not how correct the resulting answer is, but how correct was the input or datum that produced the answer? Accordingly this court must view the assumptions and underlying factual premises for the valuation methodology actually used by both respondents and petitioners. Not every assumption need be scrutinized, however, for the parties have managed to agree, despite their best efforts, on certain assumptions and facts. Serious disputes exist in about eight different areas. The four principal areas of disagreement concern the value of ABC's coal reserves, the value of ABC's investment in the VP-5 mine in Virginia, the amount of ABC's excess working capital and, finally, the EME report on the purported environmental liability at ABC's Tarrant coke plant. The court is satisfied that respondents' discounted future cash flow methodology is the appropriate valuation model in this case, especially since it was also used by petitioners' expert.

The fair value of the petitioners' shares subject to the court's appraisal was $180.67 per share on August 13, 1985. Petitioners shall be entitled to simple interest upon that amount at a rate of 12-½ percent, payable from the date of the merger to the date of payment. The costs of this proceeding, other than expert witness costs and attorneys' fees, shall be assessed against the surviving corporation.

An Order consistent with this Memorandum Opinion has been entered.

CASE A.30
Water, Waste & Land, Inc., dba Westec v. Lanham,

955 P.2d 997 (1998)
Supreme Court of Colorado
Scott, Justice

Water, Waste, & Land, Inc., the petitioner, is a land development and engineering company doing business under the name "Westec." At the time of the events in this case, Donald Lanham and Larry Clark were managers and also members of Preferred Income Investors, LLC (Company or P.I.I.). The Company is a limited liability company organized under the Colorado Limited Liability Company Act.

In March 1995, Clark contacted Westec about the possibility of hiring Westec to perform engineering work in connection with a development project, which involved the construction of a fast-food restaurant known as Taco Cabana. In the course of preliminary discussions, Clark gave his business card to representatives of Westec. The business card included Lanham's address, which was also the address listed as the Company's principal office and place of business in its articles of organization filed with the secretary of state. While the Company's name was not on the business card, the letters "P.I.I." appeared above the address on the card. However, there was no indication as to what the acronym meant or that P.I.I. was a limited liability company.

After further negotiations, an oral agreement was reached concerning Westec's involvement with the Company's restaurant project.

Although Westec never received a signed contract, in mid-August it did receive verbal authorization from Clark to begin work. Westec completed the engineering work and sent a bill for $9,183 to Lanham. No payments were made on the bill. Westec filed a claim against Clark and Lanham individually as well as against the Company. At trial, the Company admitted liability for the amount claimed by Westec.

Under the common law of agency, an agent is liable on a contract entered on behalf of a principal if the principal is not fully disclosed. In other words, an agent who negotiates a contract with a third party can be sued for any breach of the contract unless the agent discloses both the fact that he or she is acting on behalf of a principal and the identity of the principal. Westec did not know Clark was acting as an agent for the Company or that the letters "P.I.I." stood for "Preferred Income Investors," a limited liability company registered under Colorado law. Clark and Lanham failed to disclose the existence as well as the identity of the limited liability company they represented.

Section 7-80-208 of the Colorado Limited Liability Company Act (1997) states:

> The fact that the articles of organization are on file in the office of the secretary of state is notice that the limited liability company is a limited liability company and is notice of all other facts set forth therein which are required to be set forth in the articles of organization.

In order to relieve Lanham of liability, this provision would have to be read to establish a conclusive presumption that a third party who deals with the agent of a limited liability company always has constructive notice of the existence of the agent's principal. We are not persuaded that the statute can bear such an interpretation.

Such a construction exaggerates the plain meaning of the language in the statute. This broad interpretation would be an invitation to fraud, because it would leave the agent of a limited liability company free to mislead third parties into the belief that the agent would bear personal financial responsibility under any contract, when in fact, recovery would be limited to the assets of a limited liability company not known to the third party at the time the contract was made. This construction would open the door to sharp practices and outright fraud. We may presume that in adopting section 7-80-208, the General Assembly did not intend to create a safe harbor for deceit.

In sum, then, section 7-80-208 places third parties on constructive notice that a fully identified company—that is, identified by a name such as "Preferred Income Investors, LLC," or the like—is a limited liability company provided that its articles of organization have been filed with the secretary of state. Section 7-80-208 is of little force, however, in determining whether a limited liability company's agent is personally liable on the theory that the agent has failed to disclose the identity of the company.

If Clark or Lanham had told Westec's representatives that they were acting on behalf of an entity known as "Preferred Income Investors, LLC," the failure to disclose the fact that the entity was a limited liability company would be irrelevant by virtue of the statute, which provides that the articles of organization operate as constructive notice of the company's limited liability form. Lanham and Clark did not identify Preferred Income Investors, LLC, as the principal in the transaction. The "missing link" between the limited disclosure made by Clark and the protection of the notice statute was the failure to state that "P.I.I.," the Company, stood for "Preferred Income Investors, LLC."

We see no legal basis to excuse the agents of the LLC from liability and therefore we REVERSE the judgment of the district court that found them not liable.

CASE A.31
Little v. Howard Johnson Co.,

183 Mich. App. 675
455 N.W. 2d 390 (1990)
Court of Appeals of Michigan
MacKenzie, Judge

Plaintiff Joy Little was injured on January 23, 1982, when she slipped on a walkway which allegedly had not been adequately cleared of ice and snow. The walkway was located on property on which a restaurant business was being operated as a franchise of defendant, Howard Johnson Company. Plaintiff filed suit alleging liability for her injuries. In district court Howard Johnson moved for summary disposition. The circuit court denied defendant's subsequent motion for summary disposition and the case proceeded to mediation. When it mediated at less than $10,000, the case was removed to district court for lack of circuit court jurisdiction. The district court found no factual dispute and ruled as a matter of law that defendant was neither directly nor vicariously liable for plaintiff's injuries and, accordingly, granted the motion. The circuit court reversed without elaboration.

Little posited three theories under which she claimed Howard Johnson as a franchisor may be held liable for the injuries she sustained at the franchisee's restaurant: (1) direct liability as a possessor of the land, (2) vicarious liability based on agency principles, and (3) liability based on an apparent agency theory.

1. Direct Liability

The general rule in Michigan is that invitors are liable for known dangerous conditions of property and for dangerous conditions which might be discovered with reasonable care. However, an invitor's direct liability requires the presence of both possession and control over the land.

Little contends that defendant should be deemed a "possessor" of the land as a result of the rights of control it retained in its franchise agreement with the restaurant's franchisee. We disagree. The franchise agreement merely provides that the franchisee "at all times will maintain the interior and exterior of the building's and surrounding premises in a clean, orderly, and sanitary condition satisfactory to Howard Johnson." In short, there is no issue of fact that defendant was a possessor of the premises who could be held directly liable for plaintiff's injuries.

2. Vicarious Liability

Generally, a principal is responsible for the negligence of its agent. In Michigan, the test for a principal–agent relationship is whether the principal has the right to control the agent. The threshold question here is what constitutes "control" sufficient to deem a franchisee to be an agent of a franchisor. Howard Johnson argues that a franchisor must have the right to control the day-to-day operations of a franchisee in order to establish an agency relationship. Little, on the other hand, maintains that an agency relationship is created where the franchisor retains the right to set standards regarding the products and services offered by the franchisee, the right to regulate such items as the furnishings and advertising used by the franchisee, and the right to inspect for conformance with the agreement. We agree with defendant.

This court has repeatedly held that in order to establish vicarious liability in such actions, the landowner must have retained some control and direction over the actual day-to-day work. It is not enough that the owner retained mere contractual control, the right to make safety inspections, or general oversight. The franchise agreement in this case primarily insured the uniformity and standardization of products and services offered by a Howard Johnson restaurant. These obligations do not affect the control of daily operations.

3. Apparent Agency

Howard Johnson argues that the district court properly concluded that no genuine issue of fact existed regarding its liability under an agency theory. We agree. Here, Little has failed to offer any documentary evidence that she was harmed as a result of relying on the perceived fact that the franchise was an agent of Howard Johnson. No evidence was presented which indicated that plaintiff justifiably expected that the walkway would be free of ice and snow because she believed that Howard Johnson operated the restaurant. REVERSED.

CASE A.32
Lampf, Pleva, Lipkind, Prupis & Petigrow v. Gilbertson,

111 S.CT. 2773, 115 L.Ed.2d 321 (1991)
United States Supreme Court
Blackmun, Justice

The controversy arises from the sale of seven Connecticut limited partnerships formed for the purpose of purchasing and leasing computer hardware and software. Petitioner Lampf, Pleva, Lipkind, Prupis & Petigrow is a West Orange, New Jersey, law firm that aided in organizing the partnerships and that provided additional legal services, including the preparation of opinion letters addressing the tax consequences of investing in the partnerships. The several plaintiff-respondents purchased units in one or more of the partnerships during the years 1979 through 1981 with the expectation of realizing federal income tax benefits therefrom.

The partnerships failed, due in part to the technological obsolescence of their wares. In late 1982 and early 1983, Gilbertson et al., received notice that the United States Internal Revenue Service was investigating the partnerships. The IRS subsequently disallowed the claimed tax benefits because of overvaluation of partnership assets and lack of profit motive. On November 3, 1986, and June 4, 1987, Gilbertson et al., filed their respective complaints in the United States District Court for the District of Oregon, naming as defendant's petitioner and others involved in the preparation of offering memoranda for the partnerships. The complaints alleged that plaintiff-respondents were induced to invest in the partnerships by misrepresentations in the offering memoranda, in violation of, among other things, §10(b) of the 1934 Securities Exchange Act and Rule 10b-5. The claimed misrepresentations were said to include assurances that the investments would entitle the purchasers to substantial tax benefits; that the leasing of the hardware and software packages would generate a profit; that the software was readily marketable; and that certain equipment appraisals were accurate and reasonable. Gilbertson et al., asserted that they became aware of the alleged misrepresentations only in 1985 following the disallowance by the IRS of the tax benefits claimed.

After consolidating the actions for discovery and pretrial proceedings, the district court granted summary judgment for the defendants on the ground that the complaints were not timely filed. The Court of Appeals for the Ninth Circuit reversed and remanded the cases. In view of the divergence of opinion among the circuits regarding the proper limitations period for Rule 10b-5 claims, we granted certiorari to address this important issue.

It is the usual rule that when Congress has failed to provide a statute of limitations for a federal cause of action, a court "borrows" or "absorbs" the local time limitation most analogous to the case at hand. This practice, derived from the Rules of Decision Act, has enjoyed sufficient longevity that we may assume that, in enacting remedial legislation, Congress ordinarily "intends by its silence that we borrow state law." The rule, however, is not without exception.

First, the court must determine whether a uniform statute of limitations is to be selected. Where a federal cause of action tends in practice to "encompass numerous and diverse topics and subtopics," such that a single state limitations period may not be consistently applied within a jurisdiction, we have concluded that the federal interests in predictability and judicial economy counsel the adoption of one source, or class of sources, for borrowing purposes.

Second, assuming a uniform limitations period is appropriate, the court must decide whether this period should be derived from a state or federal source. In making this judgment, the court should accord particular weight to the geographic character of the claim.

Finally, even where geographic considerations counsel federal borrowing, the aforementioned presumption of state borrowing that requires that a court determine that an analogous federal source truly affords a "closer fit" with the cause of action at issue than does any available state-law source. Although considerations pertinent to this determination will necessarily vary depending upon the federal cause of action and the available state and federal analogues, such factors as commonality of purpose and similarity of elements will be relevant.

We conclude that where, as here, the claim asserted is one implied under a statute that also contains an express cause of action with its own time limitation, a court should look first to the statute of origin to ascertain the proper limitations period. In the present litigation, there can be no doubt that the contemporaneously enacted express remedial provisions represent "a federal statute of limitations actually designed to accommodate a balance of interests very similar to that at stake here—a statute that is, in fact, an analogy to the present lawsuit more apt than any of the suggested state-law parallels." The 1934 Act contained a number of express causes of action, each with an explicit limitations period. With only one more restrictive exception, each of these includes some variation of a one-year period after discovery combined with a three-year period of repose. In adopting the 1934 Act, the 73rd Congress also amended the limitations provision of the 1933 Act, adopting the one- and three-year structure for each cause of action contained therein. We therefore conclude that we must reject the Commission's contention that the five-year period contained in §20A, added to the 1934 Act in 1988, is more appropriate for §10(b) actions than is the one- and three-year structure in the act's original remedial provisions.

Litigation instituted pursuant to §10(b) and Rule 10b-5 therefore must be commenced within one year after the discovery of the facts constituting the violation and within three years after such violation. As there is no dispute that the earliest of plaintiff-respondents' complaints was filed more than three years after petitioners' alleged misrepresentations, Gilbertson et al., claims were untimely.

The judgment of the court of appeals is REVERSED.

CASE A.33
Texaco, Inc. v. Hasbrouck dba Rick's Texaco,

496 U.S. 543
110 S.Ct. 2535, 110 L.Ed. 2d 492 (1990)
United States Supreme Court
Stevens, Justice

Petitioner (Texaco) sold gasoline directly to respondents and several other retailers in Spokane, Washington, at its retail tank wagon prices (RTW) while it granted substantial discounts to two distributors. During the period between 1972 and 1981, the stations supplied by the two distributors increased their sales volume dramatically, while respondents' sales suffered a corresponding decline. Respondents filed an action against Texaco under the Robinson-Patman Amendment to the Clayton Act (Act), alleging that the distributor discounts violated Section 2(a) of the Act. Respondents recovered treble damages, and the Court of Appeals for the Ninth Circuit affirmed the judgment. We granted certiorari, to consider Texaco's contention that legitimate functional discounts do not violate the act because a seller is not responsible for its customers' independent resale pricing decisions. While we agree with the basic thrust of Texaco's argument, we conclude that in this case it is foreclosed by the facts of record.

Respondents are 12 independent Texaco retailers. They displayed the Texaco trademark, accepted Texaco credit cards, and bought their gasoline products directly from Texaco. Texaco delivered the gasoline to respondents' stations. The retail gasoline market in Spokane was highly competitive throughout the damages period, which ran from 1972 to 1981. Stations marketing the nationally advertised Texaco gasoline competed with other major brands as well as with stations featuring independent brands. Moreover, although discounted prices at a nearby Texaco station would have the most obvious impact on a respondent's trade, the cross-city traffic patterns and relatively small size of Spokane produced a city-wide competitive market. Texaco's throughput sales in the Spokane market declined from a monthly volume of 569,269 gallons in 1970 to 389,557 gallons in 1975. Texaco's independent retailers' share of the market for Texaco gas declined from 76 percent to 49 percent. Seven of the respondents' stations were out of business by the end of 1978.

The respondents tried unsuccessfully to increase their ability to compete with lower priced stations. Some tried converting from full service to self-service stations. Two of the respondents sought to buy their own tank trucks and haul their gasoline from Texaco's supply point, but Texaco vetoed that proposal.

While the independent retailers struggled, two Spokane gasoline distributors supplied by Texaco prospered. Gull Oil Company (Gull) had its headquarters in Seattle and distributed petroleum products in four western states under its own name. In Spokane it purchased its gas from Texaco at prices that ranged from six to four cents below Texaco's RTW price. Gull resold that product under its own name; the fact that it was being supplied by Texaco was not known by either the public or the respondents. In Spokane, Gull supplied about 15 stations; some were "consignment stations" and some were "commission stations." In both situations Gull retained title to the gasoline until it was pumped into a motorist's tank. In the consignment stations, the station operator set the retail prices, but in the commission stations Gull set the prices and paid the operator a commission. Its policy was to price its gasoline at a penny less than the prevailing price for major brands. Gull employed two truck drivers in Spokane who picked up product at Texaco's bulk plant and delivered it to the Gull Stations. It also employed one supervisor in Spokane. Apart from its trucks and investment in retail facilities, Gull apparently owned no assets in that market. At least with respect to the commission stations, Gull is fairly characterized as a retailer of gasoline throughout the relevant period.

The Dompier Oil Company (Dompier) started business in 1954 selling Quaker State Motor Oil. In 1960 it became a full line distributor of Texaco products, and by the mid-1970s its sales of gasoline represented over three-quarters of its business. Dompier purchased Texaco gasoline at prices of 3.95 cents to 3.65 cents below the RTW price. Dompier thus paid a higher price than Gull, but Dompier, unlike Gull, resold its gas under the Texaco brand names. It supplied about eight to ten Spokane retail stations. In the period prior to October 1974, two of those stations were owned by the president of Dompier but the others were independently operated. In the early 1970s, Texaco representatives encouraged Dompier to enter the retail business directly, and in 1974 and 1975 it acquired four stations. Dompier's president estimated at trial that the share of its total gasoline sales made at retail during the middle 1970s was "probably 84 to 90 percent."

Like Gull, Dompier picked up Texaco's product at the Texaco bulk plant and delivered directly to retail outlets. Unlike Gull, Dompier owned a bulk storage facility, but it was seldom used because its capacity was less than that of many retail stations. Again, unlike Gull, Dompier received from Texaco the equivalent of the common carrier rate for delivering the gasoline product to the retail outlets. Thus, in addition to its discount from the RTW price, Dompier made a profit on its hauling function.

The stations supplied by Dompier regularly sold at retail at lower prices than respondents. Even before Dompier directly entered the retail business in 1974, its customers were selling to consumers at prices barely above the RTW price. Dompier's sales volume increased continuously and substantially throughout the relevant period. Between 1970 and 1975 its monthly sales volume increased from 155,152 gallons to 462,956 gallons; this represented an increase from 20.7 percent to almost 50 percent of Texaco's sales in Spokane.

There was ample evidence that Texaco executives were well aware of Dompier's dramatic growth and believed that it was attributable to "the magnitude of the distributor discount and the hauling allowance." In response to complaints from individual respondents about Dompier's aggressive pricing, however, Texaco representatives professed that they couldn't understand it.

Respondents filed suit against Texaco in July 1976. After a four-week trial, the jury awarded damages measured by the difference between the RTW price and the price paid by Dompier. As we subsequently decided in *J. Truett Payne Co. v. Chrysler Motors Corp.*, this measure of damages was improper. Accordingly, although it rejected

Texaco's defenses on the issue of liability, the Court of Appeals for the Ninth Circuit remanded the case for a new trial.

At the second trial, Texaco contended that the special prices to Gull and Dompier were justified by cost savings, were the product of a good faith attempt to meet competition, and were lawful "functional discounts." The district court withheld the cost justification defense from the jury because it was not supported by the evidence. It awarded respondents actual damages of $449,900. The jury apparently credited the testimony of respondents' expert witness who had estimated what the respondents' profits would have been if they had paid the same prices as the four stations owned by Dompier.

In Texaco's motion for judgment notwithstanding the verdict, it claimed as a matter of law that its functional discounts did not adversely affect competition within the meaning of the act because any injury to respondents was attributable to decisions made independently by Dompier. The district court denied the motion. In an opinion supplementing its oral ruling denying Texaco's motion for a directed verdict, the court assumed, arguendo, that Dompier was entitled to a functional discount, even on the gas that was sold at retail, but nevertheless concluded that the "presumed legality of functional discounts" had been rebutted by evidence that the amount of the discounts to Gull and Dompier was not reasonably related to the cost of any function that they performed.

The court of appeals affirmed. It reasoned: "As the Supreme Court long ago made clear, and recently affirmed, there may be a Robinson-Patman violation even if the favored and disfavored buyers do not compete, so long as the customers of the favored buyer compete with the disfavored buyer or its customers. Despite the fact that Dompier and Gull, at least in their capacities as wholesalers, did not compete directly with Hasbrouck, a Section 2(a) violation may occur if (1) the discount they received was not cost-based and (2) all or a portion of it was passed on by them to customers of theirs who competed with Hasbrouck. "Hasbrouck presented ample evidence to demonstrate that the services performed by Gull and Dompier were insubstantial and did not justify the functional discount."

The court of appeals concluded its analysis by observing: "To hold that price discrimination between a wholesaler and a retailer could never violate the Robinson-Patman Act would leave immune from antitrust scrutiny a discriminatory pricing procedure that can effectively serve to harm competition. We think such a result would be contrary to the objectives of the Robinson-Patman Act."

In order to establish a violation of the act, respondent had the burden of proving four facts: (1) that Texaco's sales to Gull and Dompier were made in interstate commerce; (2) that the gasoline sold to them was of the same grade and quality as that sold to respondents; (3) that Texaco discriminated in price as between Gull and Dompier on the one hand and respondents on the other; and (4) that the discrimination had a prohibited effect on competition. Moreover, for each respondent to recover damages, he had the burden of proving the extent of his actual injuries.

The first two elements of respondents' case are not disputed in this court, and we do not understand Texaco to be challenging the sufficiency of respondents' proof of damages. Texaco does argue, however, that although it charged different prices, it did not "discriminate in price" within the meaning of the act, and that, at least to the extent that Gull and Dompier acted as wholesalers, the price differentials did not injure competition. We consider the two arguments separately.

A supplier need not satisfy the rigorous requirements of the cost justification defense in order to prove that a particular functional discount is reasonable and accordingly did not cause any substantial lessening of competition between a wholesaler's customers and the suppliers' direct customers. The record in this case, however, adequately supports the finding that Texaco violated the act.

The proof established that Texaco's lower prices to Gull and Dompier were discriminatory throughout the entire nine-year period; that at least Gull, and apparently Dompier as well, was selling at retail during that entire period; that the discounts substantially affected competition throughout the entire market; and that they injured each of the respondents. There is no doubt that respondents proof of a continuing violation of the act throughout the nine year period was sufficient.

The judgment is AFFIRMED.

CASE A.34
FMC Corp. v. U.S. Department of Commerce,

786 F. Supp. 471 (E.D. Pa. 1992)
United States District Court
Newcomer, District Judge

This action is brought pursuant to the Comprehensive Environmental Response, Compensation and Liability Act of 1980, as amended (CERCLA), and the Declaratory Judgment Act. Plaintiff FMC Corporation (FMC) owned and operated, from 1963 to 1976, the Avtex site in Front Royal, Virginia, (the Facility), a site which has been listed on the National Priorities List since 1986. FMC seeks indemnification from the defendants for some portion of its present and future response costs of response in performing removal actions and other response actions at the Facility. FMC bases its claim on the United States Government (Government) activities during the period of January 1942 through 1945 relating to the operation of a rayon manufacturing facility at the Avtex site, and contends that these activities render the Government liable as an "owner," "operator," and/or "arranger" under section 107 of the CERCLA.

During World War II, after the bombing of Pearl Harbor and the Japanese conquest of Asia, the United States suffered a loss of 90 percent of its crude rubber supply. An urgent need arose for natural rubber substitute to be used in manufacturing airplane tires, jeep tires, and other war related items. The best rubber substitute available was high tenacity rayon tire cord. The Facility was one of the major producers of high tenacity rayon yarn, which was twisted and woven into high tenacity rayon tire cord. FMC presented evidence at trial showing that during the World War II period, the Government participated in managing and controlling the Facility, which was then owned by American Viscose Corporation (American Viscose), requiring the Facility to manufacture increasing quantities of high tenacity rayon yarn, which involved the treatment of hazardous materials, and necessitated the disposal of hazardous materials. FMC also presented evidence showing that the Government owned "facilities" and equipment at the plant used in the treatment and disposal of hazardous materials.

The evidence included the following:

(1) During World War II, the Government took over numerous plants which, for a multitude of reasons, failed to meet production requirements, including a plant producing high tenacity rayon yarn. Beginning no later than 1943, the rayon tire cord program received constant attention from the highest officials of the War Production Board (WPB), as well as top officials of the War Department and other Government departments and agencies.

(2) Once the WPB determined that there was a need for substantial expansion of the production capabilities at the Facility, Government personnel were assigned to facilitate and expedite construction. The rayon tire cord program, in general, and the implementation of the program at the Facility, in particular, required and received far more involvement, participation, and control by the Government than the vast majority of the production programs implemented during World War II.

(3) The disposal or treatment of hazardous substance is inherent in the production of high tenacity rayon yarn. The Government was familiar with the Facility's process for producing high tenacity rayon yarn. The Government knew or should have known that the disposal or treatment of hazardous substances was inherent in the manufacture of high tenacity rayon yarn and that its production requirements caused a significant increase in the amount of hazardous substances generated and disposed of at the Facility.

The district court concluded that the United States, through the actions and authority of WPB and other departments, agencies, and instrumentalities of the United States Government, "operated" the Facility, from approximately January 1942 to at least November 1945, as defined by section 101(2) of the CERCLA. During the period the Government operated the Facility, wastes containing "hazardous substances," as defined by section 101(14) of CERCLA, and as identified in 40 C.F.R. Part 302, Table 302.4 (1990), were "disposed of" at the Facility.

There has been a "release or threatened release" of hazardous substances from the facilities which were owned by the United States. Such release or threatened release of hazardous substances has caused and will continue to cause FMC to incur "necessary costs of response" within the meaning of Section 107 of CERCLA, including without limitation the costs which FMC has incurred and will incur in monitoring, assessing, and evaluating the release or threatened release of hazardous substances and performing removal and/or remedial activities and taking other actions required or requested by the EPA, as well as attorneys' fees and expenses associated with this lawsuit.

Liability of an owner or operator of a facility as defined by §107(a) for the cost of removal "is strict and joint and several." The United States Government as owner is responsible for costs resulting from responses to the release of hazardous substances.

And it is SO ORDERED.

CASE A.35
Wiljef Transportation, Inc. v. NLRB,

946 F.2d 1308 (1991)
United States Court of Appeals for the Seventh Circuit
Cudahy, Circuit Judge

This case presents an interesting question concerning the balance between an employer's right of expression and it's employees' right of association. Approximately two months before a vote on unionization, the employer, Wiljef Transportation, Inc. (Wiljef), read to its employees a corporate bylaw which states:

Section 2—Corporate Dissolution. Wiljef Transportation, Inc. hereby expresses as matter of corporate policy that operations will cease and the corporation will be dissolved in the event of unionization of its employees. As hereby authorized by the Board of Directors, this by-law may be announced to the employees of Wiljef Transportation, Inc. at any time deemed appropriate by the Board.

The by-law was adopted in 1979, and the announcement occurred in 1988. In the ensuing union representation election, the employees rejected unionization. The issue in this case is whether the announcement of the by-law constituted a "permitted prediction" of plant closure or a "proscribed threat." The NLRB held that the announcement was a threat in violation of Section 8(a)(1) of the National Labor Relations Act (NLRA), and Wiljef appealed to this court.

An employer's right to communicate its views to its employees is firmly established in the First Amendment and is recognized in Section 8(c) of the NLRA, which provides that "the expressing of any views, argument, or opinion shall not constitute or be evidence of an unfair labor practice if such expression contains no threat of reprisal or force or promise of benefit." On the other hand, the exceptions to the freedom of expression recognized in Section 8(c) reflect the right of employees to associate free of coercion by the employer. Section 8(a)(1) of the NLRA codifies that right by declaring that it is an unfair labor practice to interfere with, restrain or coerce employees exercising their right to organize in unions. The difficulty in cases attempting to relate to these two rights is in determining when speech becomes essentially coercive rather than factually informative or predictive so as to fall outside the protection of the First Amendment and violate the NLRA. The real issue, however, remains credibility and bona fides. A by-law purporting to be a management decision to close a business in the event of unionization is not protected expression unless objective factors demonstrate that it is really controlling on the question of closure. This holding preserves the balance between free expression and the right to organize.

Absent some persuasive evidence of other measures indicating that Wiljef intends to implement the corporate policy described in the by-law, the announcement of the by-law to the employees is coercive and in violation of the NLRA. Objective evidence to lend credibility to the by-law need not be based on economics and need not necessarily indicate circumstances beyond the employer's control.

Analytically the line is clear. To predict a consequence that will occur no matter how well disposed the company is toward unions is not to threaten retaliation; to predict a consequence that will occur because the company wants to punish workers for voting for the union—a consequence desired and freely chosen by a company rather than compelled by economic forces over which it has no control—is.

In light of our conclusion that Wiljef used the by-law in an attempt to coerce its employees and that no objective evidence indicated an intent to implement the by-law, the relief granted by the NLRB is proper. The petition for review is denied, and the order of the NLRB requiring Wiljef to expunge the by-law, cease further coercive activity, and post a notice to employees indicating that it had violated the law and will cease such violations is enforced.

CASE A.36
Robinson v. Jacksonville Shipyards, Inc.,

760 F. Supp. 1486 (1991)
United States District Court
Melton, District Judge

Plaintiff Lois Robinson (Robinson) is a female employee of Jacksonville Shipyards, Inc. (JSI). She has been a welder since September 1977. Robinson is one of a very small number of female skilled craftworkers employed by JSI. Between 1977 and the present, Robinson was promoted from third-class welder to second-class welder and from second-class welder to her present position as a first-class welder.

JSI is a Florida corporation that runs several shipyards engaged in the business of ship repair, including the Commercial Yard and the Mayport Yard. As a federal contractor, JSI has affirmative action and nondiscrimination obligations. Defendant Arnold McIlwain (McIlwain) held the office of President at JSI from the time Robinson was hired by the company through the time of the trial of this case.

In addition to a welding department, JSI's other craft departments including shipfitting, sheetmetal, electrical, transportation, shipping, and receiving (including toolroom), carpenter, boilermaker, inside machine, outside machine, rigging, quality assurance, and pipe. Employees in these craft departments may be assigned to work at either the Mayport Yard, situated at the Mayport Naval Station, or the Commercial Yard, situated at a riverfront site in downtown Jacksonville and sometimes referred to as the downtown yard. Robinson's job assignments at JSI have required her to work at both the Commercial Yard and the Mayport yard. Ship repair work is a dangerous profession; JSI acknowledges the need to "provide a working environment that is safe and healthful."

JSI is, in the words of its employees, "a boys club" and "more or less a man's world." Women craftworkers are an extreme rarity. The company's EEO-1 reports from 1980 to 1987 typically show that women form less than 5 percent of the skilled crafts.

Pictures of nude and partially nude women appear throughout the JSI work place in the form of magazines, plaques on the wall, photographs torn from magazines and affixed to the wall or attached to calendars supplied by advertising tool supply companies (vendors' advertising calendars). JSI has never distributed nor tolerated the distribution of a calendar or calendars with pictures of nude or partially nude men. Management employees from the very top down condoned these displays; often they had their own pictures.

Robinson credibly testified to the extensive, pervasive posting of pictures depicting nude women, partially nude women or sexual conduct and to the occurrence of other forms of harassing behavior perpetrated by her male co-workers and supervisors. Her testimony covered the full term of her employment, from 1977 to 1988.

Reported incidents included the following:

(1) pictures in the fab shop area, in January 1985, including one of a woman wearing black tights, the top pulled down to expose her breasts to view, and one of a nude woman in an outdoor setting apparently playing with a piece of cloth between her legs.

(2) a picture of a nude woman left on the tool box where Robinson returned her tools in the summer of 1986. The photograph depicted the woman's legs spread apart, knees bent up toward her chest, exposing her breasts and genitals. Several men were present and laughed at Robinson when she appeared upset by the picture.

(3) a drawing on a heater control box, approximately one foot square, of a nude woman with fluid coming from her genital area, in 1987, at the Commercial Yard.

(4) a dart board with a drawing of a woman's breast with her nipple as the bull's eye, in 1987 or 1988, at the Commercial Yard.

Robinson also testified about comments of a sexual nature she recalled hearing at JSI from co-workers. In some instances these comments were made while she also was in the presence of the pictures of nude or partially nude women. Among the remarks Robinson recalled are, "Hey pussycat, come here and give me a whiff," "The more you lick it, the harder it gets," "I'd like to get in bed with that," "I'd like to have some of that," "Black women taste like sardines," "It doesn't hurt women to have sex right after

childbirth," and so on. Defendants have admitted that pictures of nude or partially nude women have been posted in the shipfitters' trailer at the Mayport Yard during Robinson's employment at JSI.

Based on the foregoing, the court finds that sexually harassing behavior occurred through the JSI working environment with both frequency and intensity over the relevant time period. Robinson did not welcome such behavior.

In April 1987, during the pendency of this lawsuit, JSI adopted a new sexual harassment policy. It was instituted unilaterally, without consulting or bargaining with the union. The official policy statement, signed by Vice-President for Operations Larry Brown, endorses the following policy:

> *(1) It is illegal and a violation of Jacksonville Shipyards, Inc., Policy for any employee, male or female, to sexually harass another employee by:*
> *a. making unwelcomed sexual advances or request for sexual favors or other verbal or physical conduct of a sexual nature, a condition of an employee's continued employment, or*
> *b. making submission to or rejection of such conduct the basis for employment decisions affecting the employee, or*
> *c. creating an intimidating, hostile, or offensive working environment by such conduct.*
> *(2) Any employee who believes he or she has been the subject of sexual harassment, should report the alleged act immediately to John Stewart Ext. 3716 in our Industrial Relations Department. An investigation of all complaints will be undertaken immediately. Any supervisor, agent or other employee who has been found by the Company to have sexually harassed another employee will be subject to appropriate sanctions, depending on the circumstances, from a warning in his or her file up to and including termination.*

The 1987 policy had little or no impact on the sexually hostile work environment at JSI. Employees and supervisors lacked the knowledge and training in the scope of those acts that might constitute sexual harassment.

The court finds that the policies and procedures at JSI for responding to complaints of sexual harassment are inadequate. The company has done an inadequate job of communicating with employees and supervisors regarding the nature and scope of sexually harassing behavior. This failure is compounded by a pattern of unsympathetic response to complaints by employees who perceive that they are victims of harassment. This pattern includes an unwillingness to believe the accusations, an unwillingness to take prompt and stern remedial action against admitted harassers, and an express condonation of behavior that is and encourages sexually harassing conduct (such as the posting of pictures of nude and partially nude women). In some instances, the process of registering a complaint about sexual harassment became a second episode of harassment.

Ordered and Adjudged

That defendant Jacksonville Shipyards, Inc., is hereby enjoined to cease and desist from the maintenance of a work environment that is hostile to women because of their sex and to remedy the hostile work environment through the implementation, forthwith, of the Sexual Harassment Policy, which consists of the "Statement of Policy," "Statement of Prohibited Conduct," "Schedule of Penalties for Misconduct," "Procedures for Making, Investigating and Resolving Sexual Harassment and Retaliation Complaints," and "Procedures and Rules for Education and Training."

Jacksonville Shipyards, Inc., Sexual Harassment Policy
Statement of Policy

Title VII of the Civil Rights Act of 1964 prohibits employment discrimination on the basis of race, color, sex, age, or national origin. Sexual harassment is included among the prohibitions.

Sexual harassment, according to the federal Equal Employment Opportunity Commission (EEOC), consists of unwelcome sexual advances, requests for sexual favors or other verbal or physical acts of a sexual or sex-based nature where (1) submission to such conduct is made either explicitly or implicitly a term or condition of an individual's employment; (2) an employment decision is based on an individual's acceptance or rejection of such conduct; or (3) such conduct interferes with an individual's work performance or creates an intimidating, hostile or offensive working environment.

CASE A.37
Michigan Mutual Insurance Co. v. Marriott Corporation,

1992 WL 82498 N.D.Ill. (1992)
United States District Court, N.D. Illinois
Rovner, District Judge

During the period from October 15 through October 22, 1988, Jack Sonneveldt, president of Sonneveldt, Inc., was a paying guest at the O'Hare Marriott Hotel in Chicago, Illinois. He and his party arrived at the hotel in the company's 1984 Probe Prevost 40-foot, customized coach. Sonneveldt unsuccessfully attempted to park the Prevost coach in the hotel's valet parking area. At the request of hotel officials, he moved the Prevost coach to the hotel's general parking lot across the street, in front of the hotel.

Sometime during the evening of October 22, 1988, or the next morning, the Prevost coach was stolen from the Marriott parking lot. Sonneveldt, Inc.'s insurer, Michigan Mutual, paid the company $265,000 in full settlement of the resulting claim. As subrogee of Sonneveldt, Inc., Michigan Mutual brought the instant suit. Michigan Mutual asserts liability under a theory of bailment.

Illinois law requires a plaintiff to establish the following in order to make out a prima facie claim of bailment: (1) an agreement, express or implied, to take possession of the plaintiff's property; (2) delivery and acceptance of the property (in good condition) into the exclusive possession and control of the bailee; and (3) failure to return the property or re-delivery in a damaged state. The bailment claim fails because the complaint does not sufficiently allege that Marriott ever accepted delivery and possession, either actual or constructive, of the Prevost coach.

The Illinois Supreme Court considered delivery and acceptance in the parking lot context in *Wall v. Airport Parking Co. of Chicago*, 41 Ill.2d 506, 244 N.E.2d 190 (1969). The parking lot at issue in *Wall* was lighted, paved, and marked into parking spaces. Motorists entered through an unattended electronic gate where they received a ticket noting the time of their arrival. Motorists also retained the keys to their vehicles and locked them at their own discretion. An attendant was observed only while paying at check-out. Plaintiff's car was stolen while it was parked in this lot, and he sued under a theory of bailment.

Ruling that these facts showed neither delivery nor acceptance, the court affirmed the lower courts' holdings that no bailment had been established.

Michigan Mutual's pleadings do not inferentially suggest that Marriott exercised even the most remote control over the Prevost coach. The complaint indicates that the Sonneveldt driver drove the Prevost coach into the lot and parked the vehicle himself. Nowhere does it suggest that Marriott was left with a set of keys to the coach, or that the hotel otherwise accepted or obtained actual control over the vehicle. Without the keys, Marriott had neither partial nor complete control over the Prevost coach.

Failure to allege some degree of control over the Prevost coach by Marriott necessitates the conclusion that no delivery or acceptance took place. Insofar as Illinois law requires proof of delivery and acceptance in order to establish a prima facie claim of bailment, Michigan Mutual's complaint fails as a matter of law. Consequently, the defendant's motion for judgment on the pleadings is granted.

CASE A.38
Walker V. Quillen,

622 A.2d 1097 (1993)
Supreme Court of Delaware
Moore, Justice

Pursuant to Supreme Court Rule 25(a), appellees, Elizabeth Stay Ayres and Clara Louise Quillen, have moved to affirm a judgment of the Court of Chancery granting an implied easement in favor of appellees' servient estate, as against the dominant estate of appellant, Irvin C. Walker (Walker). The appellees content that sufficient evidence supports the findings of the Court of Chancery and that there was no abuse of discretion in granting the implied easement. We agree and affirm.

The appellees own in fee simple absolute a tract of land in Sussex County known as "Bluff Point." The tract is surrounded on three sides by Rehoboth Bay and is landlocked on the fourth side by Walker's land. At one time, the two tracts in question were held by a common owner. In 1878, Bluff Point was sold in fee simple absolute apart from the other holdings, thereby landlocking the parcel. A narrow dirt road, which traverses Walker's land, connects Bluff Point to a public road, and is its only means of access.

Under the doctrine of implied easement or easement by necessity the Court of Chancery found that the appellees were entitled to cross over a portion of Walker's land for access to Bluff Point. The court also found that water access, even if a reasonable substitute for land access, was not feasible because of the shallowness of the water surrounding Bluff Point. There is ample evidence in the record to support the finding that the two tracts originated from the unified holdings of one owner, and that an implied easement was created by the severance which landlocked Bluff Point. The record also sufficiently supports the finding that navigable access to Bluff Point was not feasible. NOW, THEREFORE, IT IS ORDERED that the judgment of the Court of Chancery be, and the same hereby is, AFFIRMED.

CASE A.39
In re Estate of Vallerius,

629 N.E.2d 1185 (1994)
Appellate Court of Illinois
Lewis, Presiding Judge

On December 22, 1987, Douglas White murdered his grandmother, Adella G. Vallerius. On the same day, at the same time, and in the same house, Douglas's brother, Craig White, murdered his grandmother's friend, Carroll Pieper. Douglas was convicted of Mrs. Vallerius's murder. Craig entered a negotiated plea of guilty to, and was convicted of, the murder of Carroll Pieper. Craig testified for the state in Douglas's murder trial as part of his negotiated guilty plea.

Mrs. Vallerius died testate, naming Douglas and Craig as her sole beneficiaries. Mrs. Vallerius's only heir was her daughter Renie White, Douglas and Craig's mother. On January 11, 1988, Mrs. Vallerius's will was admitted to probate. In compliance with the terms of the will, Douglas White and Dennis Johnson were appointed legal representatives of Mrs. Vallerius's estate. About 2-½ months after Mrs. Vallerius was murdered, on March 7, 1988, Renie White died, intestate, of natural causes. She left as her only heirs her two sons, Douglas and Craig.

On March 12, 1990, the appellees, Peter M. Vallerius, Glenna F. Giacoletto, Lawrence Joe Davis, Helen L. Vallerius, Gail Kadavi, Iione V. Henry, Janis Murray, Terrie L. Illies, and Duffy Joe Vallerius, filed a petition to intervene and to consolidate the estates of Mrs. Vallerius and Renie White and an "Objection to Distribution" in the estate of Mrs. Vallerius, wherein they alleged that "Douglas Keith White and Craig Steven White, having intentionally and unjustifiably caused the death of Adella G. Vallerius, cannot lawfully receive any property, benefit or other interest" by reason of her death, through the estate of Mrs. Vallerius or through the estate of Renie White.

After an evidentiary hearing on the appellees' objection to distribution, the court entered an order granting the appellees' request. The trial court found that the issue in the case was whether Douglas and Craig could receive any property or interest by reason of the death of Mrs. Vallerius, whether through her estate or through the estate of Renie White. The court determined that, under both statue and common law, the public policy of Illinois has long been to prevent wrongdoers from profiting from intentionally committed wrongful acts. The court further found that the petitioner-objectors (appellees herein) had sustained their burden of proof, by clear and convincing evidence, that Douglas and Craig intentionally caused the death of their grandmother, Mrs. Vallerius.

Appellants argue that the law does not preclude a murderer from inheriting property from a person other than the victim. The obvious intent of the law is that persons like Douglas and Craig White must not profit from their brutal murder of their grandmother. The fact that there is an intervening estate should not expurgate the wrong of the murderer.

The appellants argue that Craig cannot be held accountable for Douglas' murder of Mrs. Vallerius, since Craig did not actually swing the sledgehammer that killed Mrs. Vallerius but only killed Carroll Pieper after Douglas killed Mrs. Vallerius. Appellants argue that even though Craig "may have borne criminal responsibility for the actions of Douglas White under the criminal accountability statute," Craig cannot be denied his right of inheritance from his mother.

Craig White cannot be permitted to receive any benefit by reason of the death of Mrs. Vallerius, whether through her estate directly or indirectly through the estate of her daughter, Renie White. If we were to allow Craig White to receive any property, benefit, or interest from the estate of Renie White, our decision would directly contravene the state's unambiguous mandate that he not receive any property by reason of his grandmother's death in any capacity or by any circumstance.

CASE A.40
United States v. Natelli,

527 F.2d 311 (1975)
United States Court of Appeals, Second Circuit
Gurfein, Circuit Judge

Anthony M. Natelli and Joseph Scansaroli appeal from judgments of conviction entered in the United States District Court for the Southern District of New York on December 27, 1974, after a four-week trial before the Hon. Harold R. Tyler and a jury. Judge Tyler imposed a one-year sentence and a $10,000 fine upon Natelli, suspending all but 60 days imprisonment, and a one-year sentence and a $2,500 fine upon Scansaroli, suspending all but 10 days of the imprisonment.

Both appellants are certified public accountants. Natelli was the partner in charge of the Washington, D.C., office of Peat, Marwick, Mitchell & Co. (Peat), a large independent firm of auditors, and the engagement partner with respect to Peat's audit engagement for National Student Marketing Corporation (Marketing). Scansaroli was an employee of Peat, assigned as audit supervisor on that engagement.

Count Two of the indictment charged that, in violation of Section 32(a) of the Securities Exchange Act of 1934, four of Marketing's officers and the appellants, as independent auditors, "willfully and knowingly made and caused to be made false and misleading statements with respect to material facts" in a proxy statement for Marketing dated September 27, 1969, and filed with the Securities and Exchange Commission (SEC) in accordance with Section 14 of the 1934 Act.

The proxy statement was issued by Marketing in connection with a special meeting of its stockholders to consider *inter alia* a charter amendment increasing its authorized capital stock and the merger of six companies, including Interstate National Corporation (Interstate) into Marketing.

Marketing was formed in 1966 by Cortes W. Randell. It provided to major corporate accounts a diversified range of advertising, promotional and marketing services designed to reach the youth market.

In late September or early October 1968 (after the close of the fiscal year), Randell and Bernard Kurek, Marketing's Comptroller, met with both appellants and discussed the method of accounting that Marketing had been using with respect to fixed-fee programs. In the fixed-fee program, Marketing would develop overall marketing programs for the client to reach the youth market by utilizing a combination of the mailings, posters and other advertising services offered by Marketing.

The difficulty immediately encountered was that the client "commitments" had not been booked during the fiscal year, and were not in writing. The Marketing stock which had initially been sold at $6 per share was selling in the market by September 1968 for $80, an increase of $74 in five months. A refusal to book the oral "commitments" would have resulted in Marketing's showing a large loss for the fiscal year—according to Kurek's computations, a loss of $232,000.

Pursuant to Randell's urging, Scansaroli did not seek any written verifications. He accepted a schedule prepared by Kurek which showed about $1.7 million in purported "commitments."

On the basis of the above, Natelli decided not only to recognize income on a percentage-of-completion basis, but to permit adjustment to be made on the books after the close of the fiscal year in the amount of $1.7 million for such "unbilled accounts receivable." This adjustment turned the loss for the year into a handsome profit of $388,031, showing an apparent doubling of the profit of the prior year.

After the 1968 audit had been given a full certificate by the auditors on November 14, 1968, things began to happen with respect to the $1.7 million of "sales" that had been recorded as income after fiscal year end. Within five months of publication of the annual report, by May 1969, Marketing had written off over $1 million of the $1.7 million in "sales" which the auditors had permitted to be booked.

Appellants were asked to design the writeoff . . . Instead of reducing 1968 earnings commensurately, however, no such reduction was made. Appellants were informed by tax accountants in Peat's employ that a certain deferred tax item should be reversed, resulting in a tax credit that happened to be approximately the same amount as the profit to be written off. Scansaroli "netted" this extraordinary item (the tax credit) with an unrelated ordinary item (the write-off of sales and profits). By this procedure, he helped to conceal on the books the actual write-off of profits, further using the device of rounding off the tax item to make it conform exactly to the write-off. The effect of the netting procedure was to bury the retroactive adjustment which should have shown a material decrease in earnings for the fiscal year ended August 31, 1968.

The Proxy Statement

As part of the proxy statement, appellants set about to draft a footnote purporting to reconcile the Company's prior reported net sales and earnings from the 1968 report with restated amounts resulting from pooled companies reflected retroactively. The earnings summary in the proxy statement included companies acquired after fiscal 1968 and their pooled earnings. The footnote was the only place in the proxy statement which would have permitted an interested investor to see what Marketing's performance had been in its preceding fiscal year 1968, as retroactively adjusted, separate from the earnings and sales of the companies it had acquired in fiscal 1969.

At Natelli's direction, Scansaroli subtracted the written-off Marketing sales from the 1968 sales figures for the seven later acquired pooled companies without showing any retroactive adjustment for Marketing's own fiscal 1968 figures. There was no disclosure in the footnote that over $1 million of previously reported 1968 sales of Marketing had been written off. All narrative disclosure in the footnote was stricken by Natelli. This was a violation of Accounting Principles Board Opinion Number 9, which requires disclosure of prior adjustments which affect the net income of prior periods.

The proxy statement also required an unaudited statement of nine months' earnings through May 31, 1969. This was prepared by the Company, with the assistance of Peat on the same percentage of completion basis as in the 1968 audited statement. A commitment from Pontiac Division of General Motors amounting to $1.2 million was produced two months after the end of the fiscal period. It was dated April 28, 1969.

The proxy statement was to be printed at the Pandick Press in New York on August 15, 1969. At about 3 A.M. on that day, Natelli informed Randell that the "sale" to the Pontiac Division for more than $1 million could not be treated as a valid commitment because the letter from Pontiac was not a legally binding obligation. Randell responded at once that he had a "commitment from Eastern Airlines" in a somewhat comparable amount attributable to the nine months fiscal period (which had ended more than two

months earlier). Kelly, a salesman for Marketing, arrived at the printing plant several hours later with a commitment letter from Eastern Airlines, dated August 14, 1969, purporting to confirm an $820,000 commitment ostensibly entered into on May 14, just before the end of the nine-month fiscal period of September 1, 1968 through May 31, 1969. When the proxy statement was printed in final form the Pontiac "sale" had been deleted, but the Eastern "commitment" had been inserted in its place.

The proxy statement was filed with the SEC on September 30, 1969.

Natelli—Sufficiency of Evidence

It is hard to probe the intent of a defendant. Circumstantial evidence, particularly with proof of motive, where available, is often sufficient to convince a reasonable man of criminal intent beyond a reasonable doubt. When we deal with a defendant who is a professional accountant, it is even harder, at times, to distinguish between simple errors of judgment and errors made with sufficient criminal intent to support a conviction, especially when there is no financial gain to the accountant other than his legitimate fee.

The original action of Natelli in permitting the booking of unbilled sales after the close of the fiscal period in an amount sufficient to convert a loss into a profit was contrary to sound accounting practice, . . . When the uncollectability, and indeed, the nonexistence of these large receivables was established in 1969, the revelation stood to cause Natelli severe criticism and possible liability. He had a motive, therefore, intentionally to conceal the write-offs that had to be made.

Whether or not the deferred tax item was properly converted to a tax credit, the jury had a right to infer that "netting" the extraordinary item against ordinary earnings on the books in a special journal entry was, in the circumstances, motivated by a desire to conceal.

Honesty should have impelled appellants to disclose in the footnote which annotated their own audited statement for fiscal 1968 that substantial write-offs had been taken, after year end, to reflect a loss for the year. A simple desire to right the wrong that had been perpetrated on the stockholders and others by the false audited financial statement should have dictated that course. The failure to make open disclosure could hardly have been inadvertent, or a jury at least could so find, for appellants were themselves involved in determining the write-offs and their accounting treatment. The concealment of the retroactive adjustments to Marketing's 1968 year revenues and earnings could properly have been found to have been intentional for the very purpose of hiding earlier errors. There was evidence that Natelli himself changed the footnote to its final form.

The Eastern contract was a matter for deep suspicion because it was substituted so rapidly for the Pontiac contract to which Natelli had objected, and which had, itself, been produced after the end of the fiscal period, though dated earlier. It was still another unbilled commitment produced by Marketing long after the close of the fiscal period. Its spectacular appearance, as Natelli himself noted at the time, made its replacement of the Pontiac contract "weird." The Eastern "commitment" was not only in substitution for the challenged Pontiac "commitment" but strangely close enough in amount to leave the projected earnings figures for the proxy statement relatively intact. Nevertheless, it was booked as if more than $500,000 of it had already been earned. Natelli contends that he had no duty to verify the Eastern "commitment" because the earnings statement within which it was included was "unaudited."

This raises the issue of the duty of the CPA in relation to an unaudited financial statement contained within a proxy statement where the figures are reviewed and to some extent supplied by the auditors. It is common ground that the auditors were "associated" with the statement and were required to object to anything they actually "knew" to be materially false. We reject the argument of insufficiency of evidence as to Natelli, who could have pointed out the error of his previous certification and deliberately failed to do so. . . .

Scansaroli—Sufficiency of Evidence

There is some merit to Scansaroli's point that he was simply carrying out the judgments of his superior Natelli. The defense of obedience to higher authority has always been troublesome. There is no sure yardstick to measure criminal responsibility except by measurement of the degree of awareness on the part of a defendant that he is participating in a criminal act, in the absence of physical coercion such as a soldier might face. Here the motivation to conceal undermines Scansaroli's argument that he was merely implementing Natelli's instructions, at least with respect to concealment of matters that were within his own ken.

We think the jury could properly have found him guilty on the specification relating to the footnote.

With respect to the major item, the Eastern commitment, we think Scansaroli stands in a position different from that of Natelli. . . . Since in the hierarchy of the accounting firm it was not his responsibility to decide whether to book the Eastern contract, his mere adjustment of the figures to reflect it under orders was not a matter for his discretion. He cannot be held to have acted in reckless disregard of the facts.

We have considered the other arguments raised by appellants and find them without merit.

CASE A.41
OHG v. Kolodny

NY County, Supreme Court,
1st Jud. Dept., IA Part II (1992)
Baer, Justice

Plaintiff is an auction house dealing in works of art. Defendant is an art dealer. His gallery has purchased fine art from the plaintiff over the years, presumably with happier results than in this case. In 1988, defendant received, in New York, a catalogue sent by plaintiff that described works of art that would be put up for auction by plaintiff. Among these, defendant says, was "a bronze sculpture produced by Hiliare Germain Edgar Degas before 1900," to wit, the "Dancer Gazing." Plaintiff phoned defendant in New York during the auction and solicited a bid for the "Dancer." Without ever having set eyes on the right foot or any other part of the sculpture, plaintiff offered a bid of DM 220,000 and triumphed. Defendant was never told the identity of the consignor of the Degas. Defendant wired to plaintiff the purchase price and a commission.

The "Dancer" arrived shortly thereafter in New York, where she immediately did a pirouette and departed for London. Defendant wished to let no grass grow under either of his feet; he would put the Degas up for resale at Christie's and would, he was confident, earn a great deal of not bronze, but sterling. Eagle eyes at Christie's surveyed the work. Defendant was told, to his horror, that Christie's suspected that the statue was ersatz, in a word, a

fake. Defendant contacted Herr Hanstein and advised that his heart was heavy and his wallet, he was afraid, too light. Defendant sought a refund.

Defendant allegedly secured the agreement of plaintiff that the "Dancer" would be given the once or twice over by the world's foremost expert of Degas Bronzes, whose determination would be binding. The statue was brought to New York, where the expert, like many another world's foremost experts, resides. His conclusion unfortunately was that the work was not genuine.

A German court decided in favor of plaintiff, rejected defendant's contention that he was entitled to an offset for the purchase price of the pseudo-Degas. The court held that plaintiff had disclaimed any warranty as to the authenticity of the "Dancer"; that since the job of an auction house is to sell as commission agent many items owned by others, the authenticity of which the auctioneer cannot readily confirm, disclaimers do not violate the law; and that defendant in his letter on the Riopelle had disavowed any offset.

After plaintiff launched its "Blitzkrieg" here in New York, defendant responded with a lawsuit of his own. Defendant seeks to recover the purchase price of the ill-fated Degas. Defendant, relying inter alia upon Article 15 of the New York Arts and Cultural Affairs Law (the "Art Law"), contends that plaintiff is liable for having provided inaccurate information about the Degas and that the German judgment contravenes New York public policy, as a consequence of which its enforcement in favor of plaintiff is *verboten*. The argument, while creative and well presented, must fail.

CPLR Sec. 5304(b)(4) provides that a monetary judgment of a foreign country need not be recognized by New York if the cause of action on which the judgment is based is "repugnant to the public policy of this state." Normally, the judgment of a foreign nation will be given effect. Differences between the laws of New York and those of the many sovereign nations of the world are likely to arise often, but such differences alone cannot constitute a violation of public policy. As Judge Cardozo said, "We are not so provincial as to say that every solution of a problem is wrong because we deal with it otherwise at home." Were we New Yorkers to be overly provincial, we might well inspire foreign nations to reject enforcement of New York judgments, precisely the opposite of the purpose Article 53 was created to achieve and an outcome particularly undesirable as the economy of this country grows every day more intertwined with those of other nations.

The German court applied German law in this case. This is not unreasonable since the auction occurred in Germany and defendant placed his bid during a telephone call with the auction house in Germany. In addition, plaintiff's conditions of sale stated that legal relations between plaintiff and the bidder would be governed by German law. Defendant appeared in the German action, defended, and lost. There is, of course, no claim that German law and procedures are unfair and unworthy of respect here.

The Germans are less Bismarcian than defendant contends. German law, as exemplified by the decision of the Cologne court in this case, is not indifferent to the general sale of fakes by art merchants. The court relied upon the warranty exclusion that formed a condition of sale.

Enforcement of the German judgment would not undermine the public interest, public confidence in the law or security for individual rights, nor violate fundamental notions of what is decent and fair. The German judgment is enforceable.

Appendix B   The Constitution of the United States of America

We the People of the United States, in Order to form a more perfect Union, establish Justice, insure domestic Tranquility, provide for the common defense, promote the general Welfare, and secure the Blessings of Liberty to ourselves and our Posterity, do ordain and establish this Constitution for the United States of America.

ARTICLE I

Section 1. All legislative Powers herein granted shall be vested in a Congress of the United States, which shall consist of a Senate and House of Representatives.

Section 2. The House of Representatives shall be composed of Members chosen every second Year by the People of the several states, and the Electors in each State shall have the Qualifications requisite for Electors of the most numerous Branch of the State Legislature.

No Person shall be a Representative who shall not have attained to the Age of twenty five Years, and been seven Years a Citizen of the United States, and who shall not, when elected, be an Inhabitant of that State in which he shall be chosen.

Representatives and direct Taxes shall be apportioned among the several states which may be included within this Union, according to their respective Numbers, which shall be determined by adding to the whole Number of free Persons, including those bound to Service for a Term of Years, and excluding Indians not taxed, three fifths of all other Persons. The actual Enumeration shall be made within three Years after the first Meeting of the Congress of the United States, and within every subsequent Term of ten Years, in such Manner as they shall by Law direct. The number of Representatives shall not exceed one for every thirty Thousand, but each State shall have at Least one Representative; and until such enumeration shall be made, the State of New Hampshire shall be entitled to chuse three, Massachusetts eight, Rhode Island and Providence Plantations one, Connecticut five, New York six, New Jersey four, Pennsylvania eight, Delaware one, Maryland six, Virginia ten, North Carolina five, South Carolina five, and Georgia three.

When vacancies happen in the Representation from any State, the Executive Authority thereof shall issue Writs of Election to fill such vacancies.

The House of Representatives shall chuse their Speaker and other Officers; and shall have the sole Power of Impeachment.

Section 3. The Senate of the United States shall be composed of two Senators from each State, chosen by the Legislature thereof, for six Years; and each Senator shall have one Vote.

Immediately after they shall be assembled in Consequence of the first Election, they shall be divided as equally as may be into three Classes. The Seats of the Senators of the first Class shall be vacated at the Expiration of the second Year, of the second Class at the Expiration of the fourth Year, and the third Class at the Expiration of the sixth Year, so that one third may be chosen every second Year; and if Vacancies happen by Resignation, or otherwise, during the Recess of the Legislature of any State, the Executive thereof may make temporary Appointments until the next meeting of the Legislature, which shall then fill such Vacancies.

No person shall be a Senator who shall not have attained to the Age of thirty Years, and been nine Years a Citizen of the United States, and who shall not, when elected, be an Inhabitant of that State for which he shall be chosen.

The Vice President of the United States shall be President of the Senate, but shall have no Vote, unless they be equally divided.

The Senate shall chuse their other Officers, and also a President pro tempore, in the Absence of the Vice President, or when he shall exercise the Office of President of the United States.

The Senate shall have the sole power to try all Impeachments. When sitting for that Purpose, they shall be an Oath or Affirmation. When the President of the United States is tried, the Chief Justice shall preside: And no Person shall be convicted without the Concurrence of two thirds of the Members present.

Judgment in Cases of Impeachment shall not extend further than to removal from Office, and disqualification to hold and enjoy any Office of honor, Trust or Profit under the United States: but the Party convicted shall nevertheless be liable and subject to Indictment, Trial, Judgment and Punishment, according to Law.

Section 4. The Times, Places and Manner of holding Elections for Senators and Representatives, shall be prescribed in each State by the Legislature thereof: but the Congress may at any time by Law make or alter such Regulations, except as to the Places of choosing Senators.

The Congress shall assemble at least once in every Year, and such Meeting shall be on the first Monday in December, unless they shall by Law appoint a different day.

Section 5. Each House shall be the Judge of the Elections, Returns and Qualifications of its own Members, and a Majority of each shall constitute a Quorum to do Business; but a smaller Number may adjourn from day to day, and may be authorized to compel the Attendance of absent Members, in such Manner, and under such Penalties as each House may provide.

Each House may determine the Rules of its Proceedings, punish its Members for disorderly Behaviour, and, with the Concurrence of two thirds, expel a Member.

Each House shall keep a Journal of its Proceedings, and from time to time publish the same, excepting such

Parts as may in their Judgment require Secrecy; and the Yeas and Nays of the Members of either House on any question shall, at the Desire of one fifth of those Present, be entered on the Journal.

Neither House, during the Session of Congress, shall, without the Consent of the other, adjourn for more than three days, nor to any other Place than that in which the two Houses shall be sitting.

Section 6. The Senators and Representatives shall receive a Compensation for their Services, to be ascertained by Law, and paid out of the Treasury of the United States. They shall in all Cases, except Treason, Felony and Breach of the Peace, be privileged from Arrest during their Attendance at the Session of their respective Houses, and in going to and returning from the same; and for any Speech or Debate in either House, they shall not be questioned in any other Place.

No Senator or Representative shall, during the Time for which he was elected, be appointed to any civil Office under the Authority of the United States, which shall have been created, or the Emoluments whereof shall have been encreased during such time; and no Person holding any Office under the United States, shall be a Member of either House during his Continuance in Office.

Section 7. All Bills for raising Revenue shall originate in the House of Representatives; but the Senate may propose or concur with Amendments as on other Bills.

Every Bill which shall have passed the House of Representatives and the Senate, shall, before it become a Law, be presented to the President of the United States; If he approve he shall sign it, but if not he shall return it, with his Objections to that House in which it shall have originated, who shall enter the Objections at large on their Journal, and proceed to reconsider it. If after such Reconsideration two thirds of that House shall agree to pass the Bill, it shall be sent, together with the Objections, to the other House, by which it shall likewise be reconsidered, and if approved by two thirds of that House, it shall become a Law. But in all such Cases the Votes of both Houses shall be determined by Yeas and Nays, and the Names of the Persons voting for and against the Bill shall be entered on the Journal of each House respectively. If any Bill shall not be returned by the President within ten Days (Sundays excepted) after it shall have been presented to him, the Same shall be a Law, in like Manner as if he had signed it, unless the Congress by their Adjournment prevent its Return, in which Case it shall not be a Law.

Every Order, Resolution, or Vote to which the Concurrence of the Senate and House of Representatives may be necessary (except on a question of Adjournment) shall be presented to the President of the United States; and before the Same shall take Effect, shall be approved by him, or being disapproved by him, shall be repassed by two thirds of the Senate and House of Representatives, according to the Rules and Limitations prescribed in the Case of a Bill.

Section 8. The Congress shall have Power to lay and collect Taxes, Duties, Imposts and Excises, to pay the Debts and provide for the common Defence and general Welfare of the United States; but all Duties, Imposts and Excises shall be uniform throughout the United States;

To borrow Money on the credit of the United States;

To regulate Commerce with foreign Nations, and among the several States, and with the Indian Tribes;

To establish an uniform Rule of Naturalization, and uniform Laws on the subject of Bankruptcies throughout the United States;

To coin Money, regulate the Value thereof, and of foreign Coin, and fix the Standard of Weights and Measures;

To provide for the Punishment of counterfeiting the Securities and current Coin of the United States;

To establish Post Offices and post Roads;

To promote the Progress of Science and useful Arts, by securing for limited Times to Authors and Inventors the exclusive Right to their respective Writings and Discoveries;

To constitute Tribunals inferior to the supreme Court;

To define and punish Piracies and Felonies committed on the high Seas, and Offenses against the Law of Nations;

To declare War, grant Letters of Marque and Reprisal, and make Rules concerning Captures on Land and Water;

To raise and support Armies, but no Appropriation of Money to that Use shall be for a longer Term than two Years;

To provide and maintain a Navy;

To make Rules for the Government and Regulation of the land and naval Forces;

To provide for calling forth the Militia to execute the Laws of the Union, suppress Insurrections and repel Invasions;

To provide for organizing, arming, and disciplining, the Militia, and for governing such Part of them as may be employed in the Service of the United States, reserving to the States respectively, the Appointment of the Officers, and the Authority of training the Militia according to the discipline prescribed by Congress;

To exercise exclusive Legislation in all Cases whatsoever, over such District (not exceeding ten Miles square) as may, by Cession of particular States, and the Acceptance of Congress, become the Seat of the Government of the United States, and to exercise like Authority over all Places purchased by the Consent of the Legislature of the State in which the Same shall be, for the Erection of Forts, Magazines, Arsenals, dock-Yards, and other needful Buildings;—And

To make all Laws which shall be necessary and proper for carrying into Execution the foregoing Powers, and all other Powers vested by this Constitution in the Government of the United States, or in any Department or Officer thereof.

Section 9. The Migration or Importation of such Persons as any of the States now existing shall think proper to admit, shall not be prohibited by the Congress prior to the Year one thousand eight hundred and eight, but a Tax or

Duty may be imposed on such Importation, not exceeding ten dollars for each Person.

The Privilege of the Writ of Habeas Corpus shall not be suspended, unless when in Cases of Rebellion or Invasion the public Safety may require it.

No Bill of Attainder or ex post facto Law shall be passed.

No Capitation, or other direct, Tax shall be laid, unless in Proportion to the Census or Enumeration herein before directed to be taken.

No Tax or Duty shall be laid on Articles exported from any State.

No Preference shall be given by any Regulation of Commerce or Revenue to the Ports of one State over those of another; nor shall Vessels bound to, or from, one State, be obliged to enter, clear, or pay Duties in another.

No Money shall be drawn from the Treasury, but in Consequence of Appropriations made by Laws; and a regular Statement and Account of the Receipts and Expenditures of all public Money shall be published from time to time.

No Title of Nobility shall be granted by the United States: And no Person holding any Office of Profit or Trust under them, shall, without the Consent of the Congress, accept of any present, Emolument, Office, or Title, of any kind whatever, from any King, Prince, or foreign State.

Section 10. No State shall enter into any Treaty, Alliance, or Confederation; grant Letters of Marque and Reprisal; coin Money; emit Bills of Credit; make any Thing but gold and silver Coin a Tender in Payment of Debts; pass any Bill of Attainder, ex post facto Law, or Law impairing the Obligation of Contracts, or grant any Title of Nobility.

No State shall, without the Consent of the Congress, lay any Imposts or Duties on Imports or Exports, except what may be absolutely necessary for executing its inspection Laws: and the net Produce of all Duties and Imposts, laid by any State on Imports or Exports, shall be for the Use of the Treasury of the United States; and all such Laws shall be subject to the Revision and Control of the Congress.

No State shall, without the Consent of Congress, lay any Duty of Tonnage, keep Troops, or Ships of War in time of Peace, enter into any Agreement or Compact with another State, or with a foreign Power, or engage in War, unless actually invaded, or in such imminent Danger as will not admit of delay.

ARTICLE II

Section 1. The executive Power shall be vested in a President of the United States of America. He shall hold his Office during the Term of four Years, and, together with the Vice President, chosen for the same Term, be elected, as follows:

Each State shall appoint, in such Manner as the Legislature thereof may direct, a Number of Electors, equal to the whole Number of Senators and Representatives to which the State may be entitled in the Congress: but no Senator or Representative, or Person holding an Office of Trust or Profit under the United States, shall be appointed an Elector.

The Electors shall meet in their respective States, and vote by Ballot for two Persons, of whom one at least shall not be an Inhabitant of the same State with themselves. And they shall make a list of all the Persons voted for, and of the Number of Votes for each; which List they shall sign and certify, and transmit sealed to the Seat of the Government of the United States, directed to the President of the Senate. The President of the Senate shall, in the presence of the Senate and House of Representatives, open all the Certificates, and the Votes shall be counted. The Person having the greatest Number of Votes shall be the President, if such Number be a Majority of the whole Number of Electors appointed; and if there be more than one who have such Majority, and have an equal Number of Votes, then the House of Representatives shall immediately choose by Ballot one of them for President; and if no Person have a Majority, then from the five highest on the List the said House shall in like Manner choose the President. But in chusing the President, the Votes shall be taken by States, the Representation from each State having one Vote; A quorum for this Purpose shall consist of a Member or Members from two thirds of the States, and a Majority of all the States shall be necessary to a Choice. In every Case, after the Choice of the President, the Person having the greatest Number of Votes of the Electors shall be the Vice President. But if there should remain two or more who have equal Votes, the Senate shall chuse from them by Ballot the Vice President.

The Congress may determine the Time of Chusing the Electors, and the Day on which they shall give their Votes; which Day shall be the same throughout the United States.

No Person except a natural born Citizen, or a Citizen of the United States, at the time of the Adoption of this Constitution, shall be eligible to the Office of President; neither shall any Person be eligible to that Office who shall not have attained to the Age of thirty five Years, and been fourteen Years a Resident within the United States.

In Case of the Removal of the President from Office, or of his Death, Resignation, or Inability to discharge the Powers and Duties of the said Office, the Same shall devolve on the Vice President, and the Congress may by Law provide for the Case of Removal, Death, Resignation or Inability, both of the President and Vice President, declaring what Officer shall then act as President, and such Officer shall act accordingly, until the Disability be removed, or a President shall be elected.

The President shall, at stated Times, receive for his Services, a Compensation, which shall neither be increased nor diminished during the Period for which he shall have been elected, and he shall not receive within that Period any other Emolument from the United States, or any of them.

Before he enter on the Execution of his Office, he shall take the following Oath or Affirmation:—"I do solemnly swear (or affirm) that I will faithfully execute the Office of

President of the United States, and will to the best of my Ability, preserve, protect and defend the Constitution of the United States."

Section 2. The President shall be Commander in Chief of the Army and Navy of the United States, and of the Militia of the several States, when called into the actual Service of the United States; he may require the Opinion, in writing, of the principal Officer in each of the executive Departments, upon any Subject relating to the Duties of their respective Offices, and he shall have Power to grant Reprieves and Pardons for Offences against the United States, except in Cases of Impeachment.

He shall have Power, by and with the Advice and Consent of the Senate, to make Treaties, provided two thirds of the Senators present concur; and he shall nominate, and by and with the Advice and Consent of the Senate, shall appoint Ambassadors, other public Ministers and Consuls, Judges of the supreme Court, and all other Officers of the United States, whose Appointments are not herein otherwise provided for, and which shall be established by Law: but the Congress may by Law vest the Appointment of such inferior Officers, as they think proper, in the President alone, in the Courts of Law, or in the Heads of Departments.

The President shall have Power to fill up all Vacancies that may happen during the Recess of the Senate, by granting Commissions which shall expire at the End of their next Session.

Section 3. He shall from time to time give to the Congress Information of the State of the Union, and recommend to their Consideration such Measures as he shall judge necessary and expedient; he may, on extraordinary Occasions, convene both Houses, or either of them, and in Case of Disagreement between them, with Respect to the Time of Adjournment, he may adjourn them to such Time as he shall think proper; he shall receive Ambassadors and other public Ministers; he shall take Care that the Laws be faithfully executed, and shall Commission all the Officers of the United States.

Section 4. The President, Vice President and all civil Officers of the United States, shall be removed from Office on Impeachment for, and Conviction of, Treason, Bribery, or other high Crimes and Misdemeanors.

ARTICLE III

Section 1. The judicial Power of the United States, shall be vested in one supreme Court, and in such inferior Courts as the Congress may from time to time ordain and establish. The Judges, both of the supreme and inferior Courts, shall hold their Offices during good Behaviour, and shall, at Times, receive for their Services, a Compensation, which shall not be diminished during their Continuance in Office.

Section 2. The judicial Power shall extend to all Cases, in Law and Equity, arising under this Constitution, the Laws of the United States, and Treaties made, or which shall be made, under their Authority;—to all Cases affecting Ambassadors, other public Ministers and Consuls;—to all Cases of admiralty and maritime Jurisdiction;—to Controversies to which the United States shall be a Party;—to controversies between two or more States;—between a State and Citizens of another State;—between Citizens of different States;—between Citizens of the same State claiming Lands under Grants of different States, and between a State, or the Citizens thereof, and foreign States, Citizens or Subjects.

In all Cases affecting Ambassadors, other public Ministers and Consuls, and those in which a State shall be Party, the supreme Court shall have original Jurisdiction. In all the other Cases before mentioned, the supreme Court shall have appellate Jurisdiction, both as to Law and Fact, with such Exceptions, and under such Regulations as the Congress shall make.

The Trial of all Crimes, except in Cases of Impeachment, shall be by Jury; and such Trial shall be held in the State where the said Crimes shall have been committed; but when not committed within any State, the Trial shall be at such Place or Places as the Congress may by Law have directed.

Section 3. Treason against the United States, shall consist only in levying War against them, or in adhering to their Enemies, giving them Aid and Comfort. No Person shall be convicted of Treason unless on the Testimony of two Witnesses to the same overt Act, or on Confession in open Court.

The Congress shall have Power to declare the Punishment of Treason, but no Attainder of Treason shall work Corruption of Blood, or Forfeiture except during the Life of the Person attainted.

ARTICLE IV

Section 1. Full Faith and Credit shall be given in each State to the public Acts, Records, and judicial Proceedings of every other State. And the Congress may by general Laws prescribe the Manner in which such Arts, Records, and Proceedings shall be proved, and the Effect thereof.

Section 2. The Citizens of each State shall be entitled to all Privileges and Immunities of Citizens in the several States.

A person charged in any State with Treason, Felony, or other Crime, who shall flee from Justice, and be found in another State, shall on Demand of the executive Authority of the State from which he fled, be delivered up, to be removed to the State having Jurisdiction of the Crime.

No Person held to Service or Labour in one State, under the Laws thereof, escaping into another, shall, in Consequence of any Law or Regulation therein, be discharged from such Service or Labour, but shall be delivered up on Claim of the Party to whom such Service or Labour may be due.

Section 3. New States may be admitted by the Congress into this Union; but no new state shall be formed or erected within the Jurisdiction of any other State; nor any State be formed by the Junction of two or more States, or Parts of

States, without the Consent of the Legislatures of the States concerned as well as of the Congress.

The Congress shall have Power to dispose of and make all needful Rules and Regulations respecting the Territory or other Property belonging to the United States; and nothing in this Constitution shall be so construed as to Prejudice any Claims of the United States, or of any particular State.

Section 4. The United States shall guarantee to every State in this Union a Republican Form of Government, and shall protect each of them against Invasion; and on Application of the Legislature, or of the Executive (when the Legislature cannot be convened) against domestic Violence.

ARTICLE V

The Congress, whenever two thirds of both Houses shall deem it necessary, shall propose Amendments to this Constitution, or, on the Application of the Legislatures of two thirds of the several States, shall call a Convention for proposing Amendments, which, in either Case, shall be valid to all Intents and Purposes, as Part of this Constitution, when ratified by the Legislatures of three fourths of the several States, or by Conventions in three fourths thereof, as the one or the other Mode of Ratification may be proposed by the Congress; Provided that no Amendment which may be made prior to the Year One thousand eight hundred and eight shall in any Manner affect the first and fourth Clauses in the Ninth Section of the first Article; and that no State, without its Consent, shall be deprived of its equal Suffrage in the Senate.

ARTICLE VI

All Debts contracted and Engagements entered into, before the Adoption of this Constitution, shall be as valid against the United States under this Constitution, as under the Confederation.

This Constitution, and the Laws of the United States which shall be made in Pursuance thereof; and all Treaties made, or which shall be made, under the Authority of the United States, shall be the supreme Law of the Land; and the Judges in every State shall be bound thereby, any Thing in the Constitution or Laws of any State to the Contrary notwithstanding.

The Senators and Representatives before mentioned, and the Members of the several State Legislatures, and all executive and judicial Officers, both of the United States and of the Several States, shall be bound by Oath or Affirmation, to support this Constitution; but no religious Test shall ever be required as a Qualification to any Office or public Trust under the United States.

ARTICLE VII

The Ratification of the Conventions of nine States, shall be sufficient for the Establishment of this Constitution between the States so ratifying the Same.

AMENDMENT I [1791]

Congress shall make no law respecting an establishment of religion, or prohibiting the free exercise thereof; or abridging the freedom of speech, or the press; or the right of the people peaceably to assemble, and to petition the Government for a redress of grievances.

AMENDMENT II [1791]

A well regulated Militia, being necessary to the security for a free State, the right of the people to keep and bear Arms, shall not be infringed.

AMENDMENT III [1791]

No Soldier shall, in time of peace be quartered in any house, without the consent of the Owner, nor in time of war, but in a manner to be prescribed by law.

AMENDMENT IV [1791]

The right of the people to be secure in their persons, houses, papers, and effects, against unreasonable searches and seizures, shall not be violated, and no Warrants shall issue, but upon probable cause, supported by Oath or Affirmation, and particularly describing the place to be searched, and the persons or things to be seized.

AMENDMENT V [1791]

No person shall be held to answer for a capital, or otherwise infamous crime, unless on a presentment or indictment of a Grand Jury, except in cases arising in the land or naval forces, or in the Militia, when in actual service in time of War or public danger; nor shall any person be subject for the same offense to be twice put in jeopardy of life or limb; nor shall be compelled in any criminal case to be a witness against himself, nor be deprived of life, liberty, or property, without due process of law; nor shall private property be taken for public use, without just compensation.

AMENDMENT VI [1791]

In all criminal prosecutions, the accused shall enjoy the right to a speedy and public trial, by an impartial jury of the State and district wherein the crime shall have been committed, which district shall have been previously ascertained by law, and to be informed of the nature and cause of the accusation; to be confronted with the Witnesses against him; to have compulsory process for obtaining witnesses in his favor, and to have the Assistance of counsel for his defence.

AMENDMENT VII [1791]

In suits at common law, where the value in controversy shall exceed twenty dollars, the right of trial by jury shall be preserved, and no fact tried by a jury, shall be otherwise re-examined in any Court of the United States, than according to the rules of the common law.

AMENDMENT VIII [1791]

Excessive bail shall not be required, nor excessive fines imposed, nor cruel and unusual punishments inflicted.

AMENDMENT IX [1791]

The enumeration in the Constitution, of certain rights, shall not be construed to deny or disparage others retained by the people.

AMENDMENT X [1791]

The powers not delegated to the United States by the Constitution, nor prohibited by it to the States, are reserved to the States respectively, or to the people.

AMENDMENT XI [1798]

The judicial power of the United States shall not be construed to extend to any suit in law or equity, commenced or prosecuted against one of the United States by Citizens of another State, or by Citizens or Subjects of any Foreign State.

AMENDMENT XII [1804]

The Electors shall meet in their respective states and vote by ballot for President and Vice President, one of whom, at least, shall not be an inhabitant of the same state with themselves; they shall name in their ballots the person voted for as President, and in distinct ballots the person voted for as Vice President, and they shall make distinct lists of all persons voted for as President, and of all persons voted for as Vice President, and of the number of votes for each, which lists they shall sign and certify, and transmit sealed to the seat of the government of the United States, directed to the President of the Senate;—The President of the Senate shall, in the presence of the Senate and House of Representatives, open all the certificates and the votes shall then be counted;—The person having the greatest number of votes for President, shall be the President, if such number be a majority of the whole number of Electors appointed; and if no person have such majority, then from the persons having the highest numbers not exceeding three on the list of those voted for as President, the House of Representatives shall choose immediately, by ballot, the President. But in choosing the President, the votes shall be taken by states, the representation from each state having one vote; a quorum for this purpose shall consist of a member or members from two-thirds of the states, and a majority of all the states shall be necessary to a choice. And if the House of Representatives shall not choose a President whenever the right of choice shall devolve upon them, before the fourth day of March next following, then the Vice President shall act as President, as in the case of the death or other constitutional disability of the President. The person having the greatest number of votes as Vice President, shall be the Vice President, if such number be a majority of the whole number of Electors appointed, and if no person have a majority, then from the two highest numbers on the list, the Senate shall choose the Vice President; a quorum for the purpose shall consist of two-thirds of the whole number of Senators, and a majority of the whole number shall be necessary to a choice. But no person constitutionally ineligible to the office of President shall be eligible to that of the Vice President of the United States.

AMENDMENT XIII [1865]

Section 1. Neither slavery nor involuntary servitude, except as a punishment for crime whereof the party shall have been duly convicted, shall exist within the United States, or any place subject to their jurisdiction.

Section 2. Congress shall have power to enforce this article by appropriate legislation.

AMENDMENT XIV [1868]

Section 1. All persons born or naturalized in the United States, and subject to the jurisdiction thereof, are citizens of the United States and of the State wherein they reside. No State shall make or enforce any law which shall abridge the privileges or immunities of citizens of the United States; nor shall any State deprive any person of life, liberty, or property, without due process of law; nor deny to any person within its jurisdiction the equal protection of the laws.

Section 2. Representatives shall be appointed among the several States according to their respective numbers, counting the whole number of persons in each State, excluding Indians not taxed. But when the right to vote at any election for the choice of electors for President and Vice President of the United States, Representatives in Congress, the Executive and Judicial officers of a State, or the members of the Legislature thereof, is denied to any of the male inhabitants of such State, being twenty-one years of age, and citizens of the United States, or in any way abridged, except for participation in rebellion, or other crime, the basis of representation therein shall be reduced in the proportion which the number of such male citizens shall bear to the whole number of male citizens twenty-one years of age in such State.

Section 3. No person shall be a Senator or Representative in Congress, or elector of President and Vice President, or hold any office, civil or military, under the United States, or under any State, who, having previously taken an oath, as a member of Congress, or as an officer of the United States, or as a member of any State legislature, or as an executive or judicial officer of any State, to support the Constitution of the United States, shall have engaged in insurrection or rebellion against the same, or given aid or comfort to the enemies thereof. But Congress may by a vote of two-thirds of each House, remove such disability.

Section 4. The validity of the public debt of the United States, authorized by law, including debts incurred for payment of pensions and bounties for services in suppressing insurrection or rebellion, shall not be questioned.

But neither the United States nor any State shall assume or pay any debt or obligation incurred in aid of insurrection of rebellion against the United States, or any claim for the loss or emancipation of any slave; but all such debts, obligations and claims shall be held illegal and void.

Section 5. The Congress shall have power to enforce, by appropriate legislation, the provisions of this article.

AMENDMENT XV [1870]

Section 1. The right of citizens of the United States to vote shall not be denied or abridged by the United States or by any State on account of race, color, or previous condition of servitude.

Section 2. The Congress shall have power to enforce this article by appropriate legislation.

AMENDMENT XVI [1913]

The Congress shall have power to lay and collect taxes on incomes, from whatever source derived, without apportionment among the several States, and without regard to any census or enumeration.

AMENDMENT XVII [1913]

The Senate of the United States shall be composed of two Senators from each State, elected by the people thereof, for six years; and each Senator shall have one vote. The electors in each State shall have the qualifications requisite for electors of the most numerous branch of the State legislatures.

When vacancies happen in the representation of any State in the Senate, the executive authority of each State shall issue writs of election to fill such vacancies; *Provided,* That the legislature of any State may empower the executive thereof to make temporary appointments until the people fill the vacancies by election as the legislature may direct.

This amendment shall not be so construed as to affect the election or term of any Senator chosen before it becomes valid as part of the Constitution.

AMENDMENT XVIII [1919]

Section 1. After one year from the ratification of this article the manufacture, sale, or transportation of intoxicating liquors within, the importation thereof into, or the exportation thereof from the United States and all territory subject to the jurisdiction thereof for beverage purposes is hereby prohibited.

Section 2. The Congress and the several States shall have concurrent power to enforce this article by appropriate legislation.

Section 3. This article shall be inoperative unless it shall have been ratified as an amendment to the Constitution by the legislatures of the several States, as provided in the Constitution, within seven years from the date of the submission hereof to the States by the Congress.

AMENDMENT XIX [1920]

The right of citizens of the United States to vote shall not be denied or abridged by the United States or by any State on account of sex.

Congress shall have power to enforce this article by appropriate legislation.

AMENDMENT XX [1933]

Section 1. The terms of the President and Vice President shall end at noon on the 20th day of January, and the terms of Senators and Representatives at noon on the 3rd day of January, of the years in which such terms would have ended if this article had not been ratified; and the terms of their successors shall then begin.

Section 2. The Congress shall assemble at least once in every year, and such meeting shall begin at noon on the 3rd day of January, unless they shall by law appoint a different day.

Section 3. If, at the time fixed for the beginning of the term of the President, the President elect shall have died, the Vice President elect shall become President. If a President shall not have been chosen before the time fixed for the beginning of his term, or if the President elect shall have failed to qualify, then the Vice President elect shall act as President until a President shall have qualified; and the Congress may by law provide for the case wherein neither a President elect nor a Vice President elect shall have qualified, declaring who shall then act as President, or the manner in which one who is to act shall be selected, and such person shall act accordingly until a President or Vice President shall have qualified.

Section 4. The Congress may by law provide for the case of the death of any of the persons from whom the House of Representatives may choose a President whenever the right of choice shall have devolved upon them, and for the case of the death of any of the persons from whom the Senate may choose a Vice President whenever the right of choice shall have devolved upon them.

Section 5. Sections 1 and 2 shall take effect on the 15th day of October following the ratification of this article.

Section 6. This article shall be inoperative unless it shall have been ratified as an amendment to the Constitution by the legislatures of three-fourths of the several States within seven years from the date of its submission.

AMENDMENT XXI [1933]

Section 1. The eighteenth article of amendment to the Constitution of the United States is hereby repealed.

Section 2. The transportation or importation into any State, Territory, or possession of the United States for delivery or use therein of intoxicating liquors, in violation of the laws thereof, is hereby prohibited.

Section 3. This article shall be inoperative unless it shall have been ratified as an amendment to the Constitution by conventions in the several States, as provided in the

Constitution, within seven years from the date of the submission hereof to the States by the Congress.

AMENDMENT XXII [1951]

Section 1. No person shall be elected to the office of the President more than twice, and no person who has held the office of President, or acted as President, for more than two years of a term to which some other person was elected President shall be elected to the office of the President more than once. But this Article shall not apply to any person holding the office of President when this article was proposed by the Congress, and shall not prevent any person who may be holding the office of President, or acting as President, during the term within which this Article becomes operative from holding the office of President, or acting as President during the remainder of such term.

Section 2. This article shall be inoperative unless it shall have been ratified as an amendment to the Constitution by the legislatures of three-fourths of the several States within seven years from the date of its submission to the States by the Congress.

AMENDMENT XXIII [1961]

Section 1. The District constituting the seat of government of the United States shall appoint in such manner as the Congress may direct:

A number of electors of President and Vice President equal to the whole number of Senators and Representatives in Congress to which the District would be entitled if it were a State, but in no event more than the least populous State; they shall be in addition to those appointed by the States, but they shall be considered, for the purposes of the election of President and Vice President, to be electors appointed by a State; and they shall meet in the District and perform such duties as provided by the twelfth article of amendment.

Section 2. The Congress shall have power to enforce this article by appropriate legislation.

AMENDMENT XXIV [1964]

Section 1. The right of citizens of the United States to vote in any primary or other election for President or Vice President, for electors for President or Vice President, or for Senator or Representative in Congress, shall not be denied or abridged by the United States or any State by reason of failure to pay any poll tax or other tax.

Section 2. The Congress shall have power to enforce this article by appropriate legislation.

AMENDMENT XXV [1967]

Section 1. In case of the removal of the President from office or of his death or resignation, the Vice President shall become President.

Section 2. Whenever there is a vacancy in the office of the Vice President, the President shall nominate a Vice President who shall take office upon confirmation by a majority vote of both Houses of Congress.

Section 3. Whenever the President transmits to the President pro tempore of the Senate and the Speaker of the House of Representatives his written declaration that he is unable to discharge the powers and duties of his office, and until he transmits to them a written declaration to the contrary, such powers and duties shall be discharged by the Vice President as Acting President.

Section 4. Whenever the Vice President and a majority of either the principal officers of the executive departments or of such other body as Congress may by law provide, transmit to the President pro tempore of the Senate and the Speaker of the House of Representatives their written declaration that the President is unable to discharge the powers and duties of his office, the Vice President shall immediately assume the powers and duties of the office as Acting President.

Thereafter, when the President transmits to the President pro tempore of the Senate and the Speaker of the House of Representatives his written declaration that no inability exists, he shall resume the powers and duties of his office unless the Vice President and a majority of either the principal officers of the executive department or of such other body as Congress may by law provide, transmit within four days to the President pro tempore of the Senate and the Speaker of the House of Representatives their written declaration that the President is unable to discharge the powers and duties of his office. Thereupon Congress shall decide the issue, assembling within forty-eight hours for that purpose if not in session. If the Congress, within twenty-one days after receipt of the latter written declaration, or, if Congress is not in session, within twenty-one days after Congress is required to assemble, determines by two-thirds vote of both Houses that the President shall continue to discharge the same as Acting President; otherwise, the President shall resume the powers and duties of his office.

AMENDMENT XXVI [1971]

Section 1. The right of citizens of the United States, who are 18 years of age or older, to vote, shall not be denied or abridged by the United States or any State on account of age.

Section 2. The Congress shall have the power to enforce this article by appropriate legislation.

AMENDMENT XXVII [1992]

No law, varying the compensation for the services of the Senators and Representatives, shall take effect, until an election of Representatives shall have intervened.

Appendix C Uniform Commercial Code (2000 Official Text), Article 2

Table of Sections

Article 2 Sales

Article 2 Sales

Part 1. Short Title, General Construction and Subject Matter

§2–101. Short Title.

This Article shall be known and may be cited as Uniform Commercial Code—Sales.

§2–102. Scope; Certain Security and Other Transactions Excluded From This Article.

Unless the context otherwise requires, this Article applies to transactions in goods; it does not apply to any transaction which although in the form of an unconditional contract to sell or present sale is intended to operate only as a security transaction nor does this Article impair or repeal any statute regulating sales to consumers, farmers or other specified classes of buyers.

§2–103. Definitions and Index of Definitions.

(1) In this Article unless the context otherwise requires

(a) "Buyer" means a person who buys or contracts to buy goods.

(b) "Good faith" in the case of a merchant means honesty in fact and the observance of reasonable commercial standards of fair dealing in the trade.

(c) "Receipt" of goods means taking physical possession of them.

(d) "Seller" means a person who sells or contracts to sell goods.

(2) Other definitions applying to this Article or to specified Parts thereof, and the sections in which they appear are:

"Acceptance"	Section 2–606.
"Banker's credit"	Section 2–325.
"Between merchants"	Section 2–104.
"Cancellation"	Section 2–106(4).
"Commercial unit"	Section 2–105.
"Confirmed credit"	Section 2–325.
"Conforming to contract"	Section 2–106.
"Contract for sale"	Section 2–106.
"Cover"	Section 2–712.
"Entrusting"	Section 2–403.
"Financing agency"	Section 2–104.
"Future goods"	Section 2–105.
"Goods"	Section 2–105.
"Identification"	Section 2–501.
"Installment contract"	Section 2–612.
"Letter of Credit"	Section 2–325.
"Lot"	Section 2–105.
"Merchant"	Section 2–104.
"Overseas"	Section 2–323.
"Person in position of seller"	Section 2–707.
"Present sale"	Section 2–106.
"Sale"	Section 2–106.
"Sale on approval"	Section 2–326.
"Sale or return"	Section 2–326.
"Termination"	Section 2–106.

(3) The following definitions in other Articles apply to this Article:

"Check"	Section 3–104.
"Consignee"	Section 7–102.
"Consignor"	Section 7–102.
"Consumer goods"	Section 9–102.
"Dishonor"	Section 3–502.
"Draft"	Section 3–104.

(4) In addition Article 1 contains general definitions and principles of construction and interpretation applicable throughout this Article.

§2–104. Definitions: "Merchant"; "Between Merchants"; "Financing Agency".

(1) "Merchant" means a person who deals in goods of the kind or otherwise by his occupation holds himself out as having knowledge or skill peculiar to the practices or goods involved in the transaction or to whom such knowledge or skill may be

attributed by his employment of an agent or broker or other intermediary who by his occupation holds himself out as having such knowledge or skill.

(2) "Financing agency" means a bank, finance company or other person who in the ordinary course of business makes advances against goods or documents of title or who by arrangement with either the seller or the buyer intervenes in ordinary course to make or collect payment due or claimed under the contract for sale, as by purchasing or paying the seller's draft or making advances against it or by merely taking it for collection whether or not the documents of title accompany the draft. "Financing agency" includes also a bank or other person who similarly intervenes between persons who are in the position of seller and buyer in respect to the goods (Section 2–707).

(3) "Between merchants" means in any transaction with respect to which both parties are chargeable with the knowledge or skill of merchants.

§2–105. Definitions: Transferability; "Goods"; "Future" Goods; "Lot"; "Commercial Unit".

(1) "Goods" means all things (including specially manufactured goods) which are movable at the time of identification to the contract for sale other than the money in which the price is to be paid, investment securities (Article 8) and things in action. "Goods" also includes the unborn young of animals and growing crops and other identified things attached to realty as described in the section on goods to be severed from realty (Section 2–107).

(2) Goods must be both existing and identified before any interest in them can pass. Goods which are not both existing and identified are "future" goods. A purported present sale of future goods or of any interest therein operates as a contract to sell.

(3) There may be a sale of a part interest in existing identified goods.

(4) An undivided share in an identified bulk of fungible goods is sufficiently identified to be sold although the quantity of the bulk is not determined. Any agreed proportion of such a bulk or any quantity thereof agreed upon by number, weight or other measure may to the extent of the seller's interest in the bulk be sold to the buyer who then becomes an owner in common.

(5) "Lot" means a parcel or a single article which is the subject matter of a separate sale or delivery, whether or not it is sufficient to perform the contract.

(6) "Commercial unit" means such a unit of goods as by commercial usage is a single whole for purposes of sale and division of which materially impairs its character or value on the market or in use. A commercial unit may be a single article (as a machine) or a set of articles (as a suite of furniture or an assortment of sizes) or a quantity (as a bale, gross, or carload) or any other unit treated in use or in the relevant market as a single whole.

§2–106. Definitions: "Contract"; "Agreement"; "Contract for Sale"; "Sale"; "Present Sale"; "Conforming" to Contract; "Termination"; "Cancellation".

(1) In this Article unless the context otherwise requires "contract" and "agreement" are limited to those relating to the present or future sale of goods. "Contract for sale" includes both a present sale of goods and a contract to sell goods at a future time. A "sale" consists in the passing of title from the seller to the buyer for a price (Section 2–401). A "present sale" means a sale which is accomplished by the making of the contract.

(2) Goods or conduct including any part of a performance are "conforming" or conform to the contract when they are in accordance with the obligations under the contract.

(3) "Termination" occurs when either party pursuant to a power created by agreement or law puts an end to the contract otherwise than for its breach. On "termination" all obligations which are still executory on both sides are discharged but any right based on prior breach or performance survives.

(4) "Cancellation" occurs when either party puts an end to the contract for breach by the other and its effect is the same as that of "termination" except that the cancelling party also retains any remedy for breach of the whole contract or any unperformed balance.

§2–107. Goods to Be Severed from Realty: Recording.

(1) A contract for the sale of minerals or the like (including oil and gas) or a structure or its materials to be removed from realty is a contract for the sale of goods within this Article if they are to be severed by the seller but until severance a purported present sale thereof which is not effective as a transfer of an interest in land is effective only as a contract to sell.

(2) A contract for the sale apart from the land of growing crops or other things attached to realty and capable of severance without material harm thereto but not described in subsection (1) or of timber to be cut is a contract for the sale of goods within this Article whether the subject matter is to be severed by the buyer or by the seller even though it forms part of the realty at the time of contracting, and the parties can by identification effect a present sale before severance.

(3) The provisions of this section are subject to any third party rights provided by the law relating to realty records, and the contract for sale may be executed and recorded as a document transferring an interest in land and shall then constitute notice to third parties of the buyer's right under the contract for sale.

Part 2. Form, Formation and Readjustment of Contra

§2–201. Formal Requirements; Statute of Frauds.

(1) Except as otherwise provided in this section a contract for the sale of goods for the price of $500 or more is not enforceable by way of action or defense unless there is some writing sufficient to indicate that a contract for sale has been made between the parties and signed by the party against whom enforcement is sought or by his authorized agent or broker. A writing is not insufficient because it omits or incorrectly states a term agreed upon but the contract is not enforceable under this paragraph beyond the quantity of goods shown in such writing.

(2) Between merchants if within a reasonable time a writing in confirmation of the contract and sufficient against the sender is received and the party receiving it has reason to know its contents, it satisfies the requirements of subsection (1) against such party unless written notice of objection to its contents is given within 10 days after it is received.

(3) A contract which does not satisfy the requirements of subsection (1) but which is valid in other respects is enforceable

    (a) if the goods are to be specially manufactured for the buyer and are not suitable for sale to others in the ordinary course of the seller's business and the seller, before notice of repudiation is received and under circumstances which reasonably indicate that the goods are for the buyer, has made either a substantial beginning of their manufacture or commitments for their procurement; or

(b) if the party against whom enforcement is sought admits in his pleading, testimony or otherwise in court that a contract for sale was made, but the contract is not enforceable under this provision beyond the quantity of goods admitted; or

(c) with respect to goods for which payment has been made and accepted or which have been received and accepted (Section 2–606).

§2–202. Final Written Expression: Parol or Extrinsic Evidence.

Terms with respect to which the confirmatory memoranda of the parties agree or which are otherwise set forth in a writing intended by the parties as a final expression of their agreement with respect to such terms as are included therein may not be contradicted by evidence of any prior agreement or of a contemporaneous oral agreement but may be explained or supplemented

(a) by course and dealing or usage of trade (Section 1–205) or by course of performance (Section 2–208); and

(b) by evidence of consistent additional terms unless the court finds the writing to have been intended also as a complete and exclusive statement of the terms of the agreement.

§2–203. Seals Inoperative.

The affixing of a seal to a writing evidencing a contract for sale or an offer to buy or sell goods does not constitute the writing a sealed instrument and the law with respect to sealed instruments does not apply to such a contract or offer.

§2–204. Formation in General.

(1) A contract for sale of goods may be made in any manner sufficient to show agreement, including conduct by both parties which recognizes the existence of such a contract.

(2) An agreement sufficient to constitute a contract for sale may be found even though the moment of its making is undetermined.

(3) Even though one or more terms are left open a contract for sale does not fail for indefiniteness if the parties have intended to make a contract and there is a reasonably certain basis for giving an appropriate remedy.

§2–205. Firm Offers.

An offer by a merchant to buy or sell goods in a signed writing which by its terms gives assurance that it will be held open is not revocable, for lack of consideration, during the time stated or if no time is stated for a reasonable time, but in no event may such period of irrevocability exceed three months; but any such term of assurance on a form supplied by the offeree must be separately signed by the offeror.

§2–206. Offer and Acceptance in Formation of Contract.

(1) Unless otherwise unambiguously indicated by the language or circumstances

(a) an offer to make a contract shall be construed as inviting acceptance in any manner and by any medium reasonable in the circumstances;

(b) an order or other offer to buy goods for prompt or current shipment shall be construed as inviting acceptance either by a prompt promise to ship or by the prompt or current shipment of conforming or non-conforming goods, but such a shipment of non-conforming goods does not constitute an acceptance if the seller seasonably notifies the buyer that the shipment is offered only as an accommodation to the buyer.

(2) Where the beginning of a requested performance is a reasonable mode of acceptance an offeror who is not notified of acceptance within a reasonable time may treat the offer as having lapsed before acceptance.

§2–207. Additional Terms in Acceptance or Confirmation.

(1) A definite and seasonable expression of acceptance or a written confirmation which is sent within a reasonable time operates as an acceptance even though it states terms additional to or different from those offered or agreed upon, unless acceptance is expressly made conditional on assent to the additional or different terms.

(2) The additional terms are to be construed as proposals for addition to the contract. Between merchants such terms become part of the contract unless:

(a) the offer expressly limits acceptance to the terms of the offer;

(b) they materially alter it; or

(c) notification of objection to them has already been given or is given within a reasonable time after notice of them is received.

(3) Conduct by both parties which recognizes the existence of a contract is sufficient to establish a contract for sale although the writings of the parties do not otherwise establish a contract. In such case the terms of the particular contract consist of those terms on which the writings of the parties agree, together with any supplementary terms incorporated under any other provisions of this Act.

§2–208. Course of Performance or Practical Construction.

(1) Where the contract for sale involves repeated occasions for performance by either party with knowledge of the nature of the performance and opportunity for objection to it by the other, any course of performance accepted or acquiesced in without objection shall be relevant to determine the meaning of the agreement.

(2) The express terms of the agreement and any such course of performance, as well as any course of dealing and usage of trade, shall be construed whenever reasonable as consistent with each other; but when such construction is unreasonable, express terms shall control course of performance and course of performance shall control both course of dealing and usage of trade (Section 1–205).

(3) Subject to the provisions of the next section on modification and waiver, such course of performance shall be relevant to show a waiver or modification of any term inconsistent with such course of performance.

§2–209. Modification, Rescission and Waiver.

(1) An agreement modifying a contract within this Article needs no consideration to be binding.

(2) A signed agreement which excludes modification or rescission except by a signed writing cannot be otherwise modified or rescinded, but except as between merchants such a requirement on a form supplied by the merchant must be separately signed by the other party.

(3) The requirements of the statute of frauds section of this Article (Section 2–201) must be satisfied if the contract as modified is within its provisions.

(4) Although an attempt at modification or rescission does not satisfy the requirements of subsection (2) or (3) it can operate as a waiver.

(5) A party who has made a waiver affecting an executory portion of the contract may retract the waiver by reasonable notification received by the other party that strict performance will be required of any term waived, unless the retraction would be unjust in view of a material change of position in reliance on the waiver.

§2–210. Delegation of Performance; Assignment of Rights.

(1) A party may perform his duty through a delegate unless otherwise agreed or unless the other party has a substantial interest in having his original promisor perform or control the acts required by the contract. No delegation of performance relieves the party delegating of any duty to perform or any liability for breach.

(2) Except as otherwise provided in Section 9–406, unless otherwise agreed all rights of either seller or buyer can be assigned except where the assignment would materially change the duty of the other party, or increase materially the burden or risk imposed on him by his contract, or impair materially his chance of obtaining return performance. A right to damages for breach of the whole contract or a right arising out of the assignor's due performance of his entire obligation can be assigned despite agreement otherwise.

(3) The creation, attachment, perfection, or enforcement of a security interest in the seller's interest under a contract is not a transfer that materially changes the duty of or increases materially the burden or risk imposed on the buyer or impairs materially the buyer's chance of obtaining return performance within the purview of subsection (2) unless, and then only to the extent that, enforcement actually results in a delegation of material performance of the seller. Even in that event, the creation, attachment, perfection, and enforcement of the security interest remain effective, but (i) the seller is liable to the buyer for damages caused by the delegation to the extent that the damages could not reasonably be prevented by the buyer, and (ii) a court having jurisdiction may grant other appropriate relief, including cancellation of the contract for sale or an injunction against enforcement of the security interest or consummation of the enforcement.

(4) Unless the circumstances indicate the contrary a prohibition of assignment of "the contract" is to be construed as barring only the delegation to the assignee of the assignor's performance.

(5) An assignment of "the contract" or of "all my rights under the contract" or an assignment in similar general terms is an assignment of rights and unless the language or the circumstances (as in an assignment for security) indicate the contrary, it is a delegation of performance of the duties of the assignor and its acceptance by the assignee constitutes a promise by him to perform those duties. This promise is enforceable by either the assignor or the other party to the original contract.

(6) The other party may treat any assignment which delegates performance as creating reasonable grounds for insecurity and may without prejudice to his rights against the assignor demand assurances from the assignee (Section 2–609).

Part 3. General Obligation and Construction of Contract

§2–301. General Obligations of Parties.

The obligation of the seller is to transfer and deliver and that of the buyer is to accept and pay in accordance with the contract.

§2–302. Unconscionable Contract or Clause.

(1) If the court as a matter of law finds the contract or any clause of the contract to have been unconscionable at the time it was made the court may refuse to enforce the contract, or it may enforce the remainder of the contract without the unconscionable clause, or it may so limit the application of any unconscionable clause as to avoid any unconscionable result.

(2) When it is claimed or appears to the court that the contract or any clause thereof may be unconscionable the parties shall be afforded a reasonable opportunity to present evidence as to its commercial setting, purpose and effect to aid the court in making the determination.

§2–303. Allocation or Division of Risks.

Where this Article allocates a risk or a burden as between the parties "unless otherwise agreed", the agreement may not only shift the allocation but may also divide the risk or burden.

§2–304. Price Payable in Money, Goods, Realty, or Otherwise.

(1) The price can be made payable in money or otherwise. If it is payable in whole or in part in goods each party is a seller of the goods which he is to transfer.

(2) Even though all or part of the price is payable in an interest in realty the transfer of the goods and the seller's obligations with reference to them are subject to this Article, but not the transfer of the interest in realty or the transferor's obligations in connection therewith.

§2–305. Open Price Term.

(1) The parties if they so intend can conclude a contract for sale even though the price is not settled. In such a case the price is a reasonable price at the time for delivery if
  (a) nothing is said as to price; or
  (b) the price is left to be agreed by the parties and they fail to agree; or
  (c) the price is to be fixed in terms of some agreed market or other standard as set or recorded by a third person or agency and it is not so set or recorded.

(2) A price to be fixed by the seller or by the buyer means a price for him to fix in good faith.

(3) When a price left to be fixed otherwise than by agreement of the parties fails to be fixed through fault of one party the other may at his option treat the contract as cancelled or himself fix a reasonable price.

(4) Where, however, the parties intend not to be bound unless the price be fixed or agreed and it is not fixed or agreed there is no contract. In such a case the buyer must return any goods already received or if unable so to do must pay their reasonable value at the time of delivery and the seller must return any portion of the price paid on account.

§2–306. Output, Requirements and Exclusive Dealings.

(1) A term which measures the quantity by the output of the seller or the requirements of the buyer means such actual output or requirements as may occur in good faith, except that no quantity unreasonably disproportionate to any stated estimate or in the absence of a stated estimate to any normal or otherwise comparable prior output or requirements may be tendered or demanded.

(2) A lawful agreement by either the seller or the buyer for exclusive dealing in the kind of goods concerned imposes unless

otherwise agreed an obligation by the seller to use best efforts to supply the goods and by the buyer to use best efforts to promote their sale.

§2–307. Delivery in Single Lot or Several Lots.

Unless otherwise agreed all goods called for by a contract for sale must be tendered in a single delivery and payment is due only on such tender but where the circumstances give either party the right to make or demand delivery in lots the price if it can be apportioned may be demanded for each lot.

§2–308. Absence of Specified Place for Delivery.

Unless otherwise agreed
  (a) the place for delivery of goods is the seller's place of business or if he has none, his residence; but
  (b) in a contract for sale of identified goods which to the knowledge of the parties at the time of contracting are in some other place, that place is the place for their delivery; and
  (c) documents of title may be delivered through customary banking channels.

§2–309. Absence of Specific Time Provisions; Notice of Termination.

(1) The time for shipment or delivery or any other action under a contract if not provided in this Article or agreed upon shall be a reasonable time.

(2) Where the contract provides for successive performance but is indefinite in duration it is valid for a reasonable time but unless otherwise agreed may be terminated at any time by either party.

(3) Termination of a contract by one party except on the happening of an agreed event requires that reasonable notification be received by the other party and an agreement dispensing with notification is invalid if its operation would be unconscionable.

§2–310. Open Time for Payment or Running of Credit; Authority to Ship Under Reservation.

Unless otherwise agreed
  (a) payment is due at the time and place at which the buyer is to receive the goods even though the place of shipment is the place of delivery; and
  (b) if the seller is authorized to send the goods he may ship them under reservation, and may tender the documents of title, but the buyer may inspect the goods after their arrival before payment is due unless such inspection is inconsistent with the terms of the contract (Section 2–513); and
  (c) if delivery is authorized and made by way of documents of title otherwise than by subsection (b) then payment is due at the time and place at which the buyer is to receive the documents regardless of where the goods are to be received; and
  (d) where the seller is required or authorized to ship the goods on credit the credit period runs from the time of shipment but post-dating the invoice or delaying its dispatch will correspondingly delay the starting of the credit period.

§2–311. Options and Cooperation Respecting Performance.

(1) An agreement for sale which is otherwise sufficiently definite (subsection (3) of Section 2–204) to be a contract is not made invalid by the fact that it leaves particulars of performance to be specified by one of the parties. Any such specification must be made in good faith and within limits set by commercial reasonableness.

(2) Unless otherwise agreed specifications relating to assortment of the goods are at the buyer's option and except as otherwise provided in subsections (1) (c) and (3) of Section 2–319 specifications or arrangements relating to shipment are at the seller's option.

(3) Where such specification would materially affect the other party's performance but is not seasonably made or where one party's cooperation is necessary to the agreed performance of the other but is not seasonably forthcoming, the other party in addition to all other remedies
  (a) is excused for any resulting delay in his own performance; and
  (b) may also either proceed to perform in any reasonable manner or after the time for a material part of his own performance treat the failure to specify or to cooperate as a breach by failure to deliver or accept the goods.

§2–312. Warranty of Title and Against Infringement; Buyer's Obligation Against Infringement.

(1) Subject to subsection (2) there is in a contract for sale a warranty by the seller that
  (a) the title conveyed shall be good, and its transfer rightful; and
  (b) the goods shall be delivered free from any security interest or other lien or encumbrance of which the buyer at the time of contracting has no knowledge.

(2) A warranty under subsection (1) will be excluded or modified only by specific language or by circumstances which give the buyer reason to know that the person selling does not claim title in himself or that he is purporting to sell only such right or title as he or a third person may have.

(3) Unless otherwise agreed a seller who is a merchant regularly dealing in goods of the kind warrants that the goods shall be delivered free of the rightful claim of any third person by way of infringement or the like but a buyer who furnishes specifications to the seller must hold the seller harmless against any such claim which arises out of compliance with the specifications.

§2–313. Express Warranties by Affirmation, Promise, Description, Sample.

(1) Express warranties by the seller are created as follows:
  (a) Any affirmation of fact or promise made by the seller to the buyer which relates to the goods and becomes part of the basis of the bargain creates an express warranty that the goods shall conform to the affirmation or promise.
  (b) Any description of the goods which is made part of the basis of the bargain creates an express warranty that the goods shall conform to the description.
  (c) Any sample or model which is made part of the basis of the bargain creates an express warranty

that the whole of the goods shall conform to the sample or model.

(2)   It is not necessary to the creation of an express warranty that the seller use formal words such as "warrant" or "guarantee" or that he have a specific intention to make a warranty, but an affirmation merely of the value of the goods or a statement purporting to be merely the seller's opinion or commendation of the goods does not create a warranty.

§2–314. Implied Warranty: Merchantability; Usage of Trade.

(1)   Unless excluded or modified (Section 2–316), a warranty that the goods shall be merchantable is implied in a contract for their sale if the seller is a merchant with respect to goods of that kind. Under this section the serving for value of food or drink to be consumed either on the premises or elsewhere is a sale.

(2)   Goods to be merchantable must be at least such as

    (a)   pass without objection in the trade under the contract description; and

    (b)   in the case of fungible goods, are of fair average quality within the description; and

    (c)   are fit for the ordinary purposes for which such goods are used; and

    (d)   run, within the variations permitted by the agreement, of even kind, quality and quantity within each unit and among all units involved; and

    (e)   are adequately contained, packaged, and labeled as the agreement may require; and

    (f)   conform to the promises or affirmations of fact made on the container or label if any.

(3)   Unless excluded or modified (Section 2–316) other implied warranties may arise from course of dealing or usage of trade.

§2–315. Implied Warranty: Fitness for Particular Purpose.

Where the seller at the time of contracting has reason to know any particular purpose for which the goods are required and that the buyer is relying on the seller's skill or judgment to select or furnish suitable goods, there is unless excluded or modified under the next section an implied warranty that the goods shall be fit for such purpose.

§2–316. Exclusion or Modification of Warranties.

(1)   Words or conduct relevant to the creation of an express warranty and words or conduct tending to negate or limit warranty shall be construed wherever reasonable as consistent with each other, but subject to the provisions of this Article on parol or extrinsic evidence (Section 2–202) negation or limitation is inoperative to the extent that such construction is unreasonable.

(2)   Subject to subsection (3), to exclude or modify the implied warranty of merchantability or any part of it the language must mention merchantability and in case of a writing must be conspicuous, and to exclude or modify any implied warranty of fitness the exclusion must be by a writing and conspicuous. Language to exclude all implied warranties of fitness is sufficient if it states, for example, that "There are no warranties which extend beyond the description on the face hereof."

(3)   Notwithstanding subsection (2)

    (a)   unless the circumstances indicate otherwise, all implied warranties are excluded by expression like "as is", "with all faults" or other language which in common understanding calls the buyer's attention to the exclusion of warranties and makes plain that there is no implied warranty; and

    (b)   when the buyer before entering into the contract has examined the goods or the sample or model as fully as he desired or has refused to examine the goods there is no implied warranty with regard to defects which an examination ought in the circumstances to have revealed to him; and

    (c)   an implied warranty can also be excluded or modified by course of dealing or course of performance or usage of trade.

(4)   Remedies for breach of warranty can be limited in accordance with the provisions of this Article on liquidation or limitation of damages and on contractual modification of remedy (Sections 2–718 and 2–719).

§2–317. Cumulation and Conflict of Warranties Express or Implied.

Warranties whether express or implied shall be construed as consistent with each other and as cumulative, but if such construction is unreasonable the intention of the parties shall determine which warranty is dominant. In ascertaining that intention the following rules apply:

    (a)   Exact or technical specifications displace an inconsistent sample or model or general language of description.

    (b)   A sample from an existing bulk displaces inconsistent general language of description.

    (c)   Express warranties displace inconsistent implied warranties other than an implied warranty of fitness for a particular purpose.

§2–318. Third Party Beneficiaries of Warranties Express or Implied.

Note: If this Act is introduced in the Congress of the United States this section should be omitted. (States to select one alternative.)

Alternative A.   A seller's warranty whether express or implied extends to any natural person who is in the family or household of his buyer or who is a guest in his home if it is reasonable to expect that such person may use, consume or be affected by the goods and who is injured in person by breach of the warranty. A seller may not exclude or limit the operation of this section.

Alternative B.   A seller's warranty whether express or implied extends to any natural person who may reasonably be expected to use, consume or be affected by the goods and who is injured in person by breach of the warranty. A seller may not exclude or limit the operation of this section.

Alternative C.   A seller's warranty whether express or implied extends to any person who may reasonably be expected to use, consume or be affected by the goods and who is injured by breach of the warranty. A seller may not exclude or limit the operation of this section with respect to injury to the person of an individual to whom the warranty extends.

§2–319. F.O.B. and F.A.S. Terms.

(1)   Unless otherwise agreed the term F.O.B. (which means "free on board") at a named place, even though used only in connection with the stated price, is a delivery term under which

(a) when the term is F.O.B. the place of shipment, the seller must at that place ship the goods in the manner provided in this Article (Section 2–504) and bear the expense and risk of putting them into the possession of the carrier; or

(b) when the term is F.O.B. the place of destination, the seller must at his own expense and risk transport the goods to that place and there tender delivery of them in the manner provided in this Article (Section 2–503);

(c) when under either (a) or (b) the term is also F.O.B. vessel, car or other vehicle, the seller must in addition at his own expense and risk load the goods on board. If the term is F.O.B. vessel the buyer must name the vessel and in an appropriate case the seller must comply with the provisions of this Article on the form of bill of lading (Section 2–323).

(2) Unless otherwise agreed the term F.A.S. vessel (which means "free alongside") at a named port, even though used only in connection with the stated price, is a delivery term under which the seller must

(a) at his own expense and risk deliver the goods alongside the vessel in the manner usual in that port or on a dock designated and provided by the buyer; and

(b) obtain and tender a receipt for the goods in exchange for which the carrier is under a duty to issue a bill of lading.

(3) Unless otherwise agreed in any case falling within subsection (1)(a) or (c) or subsection (2) the buyer must seasonally give any needed instructions for making delivery, including when the term is F.A.S. or F.O.B. the loading berth of the vessel and in an appropriate case its name and sailing date. The seller may treat the failure of needed instructions as a failure of cooperation under this Article (Section 2-311). He may also at his option move the goods in any reasonable manner preparatory to delivery or shipment.

(4) Under the term F.O.B. vessel or F.A.S. unless otherwise agreed the buyer must make payment against tender of the required documents and the seller may not tender nor the buyer demand delivery of the goods in substitution for the documents.

§2–320. C.I.F. and C. & F. Terms.

(1) The term C.I.F. means that the price includes in a lump sum the cost of the goods and the insurance and freight to the named destination. The term C. & F. or C.F. means that the price so includes cost and freight to the named destination.

(2) Unless otherwise agreed and even though used only in connection with the stated price and destination, the term C.I.F. destination or its equivalent requires the seller at his own expense and risk to

(a) put the goods into the possession of a carrier at the port for shipment and obtain a negotiable bill or bills of lading covering the entire transportation to the named destination; and

(b) load the goods and obtain a receipt from the carrier (which may be contained in the bill of lading) showing that the freigt has been paid or provided for; and

(c) obtain a policy or certificate of insurance, including any war risk insurance, of a kind and on terms then current at the port of shipment in the usual amount, in the currency of the contract, shown to

cover the same goods covered by the bill of lading and providing for payment of loss to the order of the buyer or for the account of whom it may concern; but the seller may add to the price the amount of the premium for any such war risk insurance; and

(d) prepare an invoice of the goods and procure any other documents required to effect shipment or to comply with the contract; and

(e) forward and tender with commercial promptness all the documents in due form and with any indorsement necessary to perfect the buyer's rights.

(3) Unless otherwise agreed the term C. & F. or its equivalent has the same effect and imposes upon the seller the same obligations and risks as a C.I.F. term except the obligation as to insurance.

(4) Under the term C.I.F. or C. & F. unless otherwise agreed the buyer must make payment against tender of the required documents and the seller may not tender nor the buyer demand delivery of the goods in substitution for the documents.

§2–321. C.I.F. or C. & F.: "Net Landed Weights"; "Payment on Arrival"; Warranty of Condition on Arrival.

Under a contract containing a term C.I.F. or C. & F.

(1) Where the price is based on or is to be adjusted according to "net landed weights", "delivered weights", "out turn" quantity or quality or the like, unless otherwise agreed the seller must reasonably estimate the price. The payment due on tender of the documents called for by the contract is the amount so estimated, but after final adjustment of the price a settlement must be made with commercial promptness.

(2) An agreement described in subsection (1) or any warranty of quality or condition of the goods on arrival places upon the seller the risk of ordinary deterioration, shrinkage and the like in transportation but has no effect on the place or time of identification to the contract for sale or delivery or on the passing of the risk of loss.

(3) Unless otherwise agreed where the contract provides for payment on or after arrival of the goods the seller must before payment allow such preliminary inspection as is feasible; but if the goods are lost delivery of the documents and payment are due when the goods should have arrived.

§2–322. Delivery "Ex-Ship".

(1) Unless otherwise agreed a term for delivery of goods "ex-ship" (which means from the carrying vessel) or in equivalent language is not restricted to a particular ship and requires delivery from a ship which has reached a place at the named port of destination where goods of the kind are usually discharged.

(2) Under such a term unless otherwise agreed

(a) the seller must discharge all liens arising out of the carriage and furnish the buyer with a direction which puts the carrier under a duty to deliver the goods; and

(b) the risk of loss does not pass to the buyer until the goods leave the ship's tackle or are otherwise properly unloaded.

§2–323. Form of Bill of Lading Required in Overseas Shipment; "Overseas".

(1) Where the contract contemplates overseas shipment and contains a term C.I.F. or C. & F. or F.O.B. vessel, the seller unless

otherwise agreed must obtain a negotiable bill of lading stating that the goods have been loaded on board or, in the case of a term C.I.F. or C. & F., received for shipment.

(2)   Where in a case within subsection (1) a bill of lading has been issued in a set of parts, unless otherwise agreed if the documents are not to be sent from abroad the buyer may demand tender of the full set; otherwise only one part of the bill of lading need be tendered. Even if the agreement expressly requires a full set

    (a)   due tender of a single part is acceptable within the provisions of this Article on cure of improper delivery (subsection (1) of Section 2–508); and

    (b)   even though the full set is demanded, if the documents are sent from abroad the person tendering an incomplete set may nevertheless require payment upon furnishing an indemnity which the buyer in good faith deems adequate.

(3)   A shipment by water or by air or a contract contemplating such shipment is "overseas" insofar as by usage of trade or agreement it is subject to the commercial, financing or shipping practices characteristic of international deep water commerce.

§2-324. "No Arrival, No Sale" Term.

Under a term "no arrival, no sale" or terms of like meaning, unless otherwise agreed.

    (a)   the seller must properly ship conforming goods and if they arrive by any means he must tender them on arrival but he assumes no obligation that the goods will arrive unless he has caused the non-arrival; and

    (b)   where without fault of the seller the goods are in part lost or have so deteriorated as no longer to conform to the contract or arrive after the contract time, the buyer may proceed as if there had been casualty to identified goods (Section 2–613).

§2-325. "Letter of Credit" Term; "Confirmed Credit".

(1)   Failure of the buyer seasonably to furnish an agreed letter of credit is a breach of the contract for sale.

(2)   The delivery to seller of a proper letter of credit suspends the buyer's obligation to pay. If the letter of credit is dishonored, the seller may on seasonable notification to the buyer require payment directly from him.

(3)   Unless otherwise agreed the term "letter of credit" or "banker's credit" in a contract for sale means an irrevocable credit issued by a financing agency of good repute and, where the shipment is overseas, of good international repute. The term "confirmed credit" means that the credit must also carry the direct obligation of such an agency which does business in the seller's financial market.

§2-326. Sale on Approval and Sale or Return; Rights of Creditors.

(1)   Unless otherwise agreed, if delivered goods may be returned by the buyer even though they conform to the contract, the transaction is

    (a)   a "sale on approval" if the goods are delivered primarily for use, and

    (b)   a "sale or return" if the goods are delivered primarily for resale.

(2)   Goods held on approval are not subject to the claims of the buyer's creditors until acceptance; goods held on sale or return are subject to such claims while in the buyer's possession.

(3)   Any "or return" term of a contract for sale is to be treated as a separate contract for sale within the statute of frauds section of this Article (Section 2–201) and as contradicting the sale aspect of the contract within the provisions of this Article on parol or extrinsic evidence (Section 2–202).

§2-327. Special Incidents of Sale on Approval and Sale or Return.

(1)   Under a sale on approval unless otherwise agreed

    (a)   although the goods are identified to the contract the risk of loss and the title do not pass to the buyer until acceptance; and

    (b)   use of the goods consistent with the purpose of trial is not acceptance but failure seasonably to notify the seller of election to return the goods is acceptance, and if the goods conform to the contract acceptance of any part is acceptance of the whole; and

    (c)   after due notification of election to return, the return is at the seller's risk and expense but a merchant buyer must follow any reasonable instructions.

(2)   Under a sale or return unless otherwise agreed

    (a)   the option to return extends to the whole or any commercial unit of the goods while in substantially their original condition, but must be exercised seasonably; and

    (b)   the return is at the buyer's risk and expense.

§2-328. Sale by Auction.

(1)   In a sale by auction if goods are put up in lots each lot is the subject of a separate sale.

(2)   A sale by auction is complete when the auctioneer so announces by the fall of the hammer or in other customary manner. Where a bid is made while the hammer is falling in acceptance of a prior bid the auctioneer may in his discretion reopen the bidding or declare the goods sold under the bid on which the hammer was falling.

(3)   Such a sale is with reserve unless the goods are in explicit terms put up without reserve. In an auction with reserve the auctioneer may withdraw the goods at any time until he announces completion of the sale. In an auction without reserve, after the auctioneer calls for bids on an article or lot, that article or lot cannot be withdrawn unless no bid is made within a reasonable time. In either case a bidder may retract his bid until the auctioneer's announcement of completion of the sale, but a bidder's retraction does not revive any previous bid.

(4)   If the auctioneer knowingly receives a bid on the seller's behalf or the seller makes or procures such a bid, and notice has not been given that liberty for such bidding is reserved, the buyer may at his option avoid the sale or take the goods at the price of the last good faith bid prior to the completion of the sale. This subsection shall not apply to any bid at a forced sale.

Part 4. Title, Creditors and Good Faith Purchasers

§2-401. Passing of Title; Reservation for Security; Limited Application of This Section.

Each provision of this Article with regard to the rights, obligations and remedies of the seller, the buyer, purchasers or other third parties applies irrespective of title to the goods except where the provision refers to such title. Insofar as situations are not covered by the other provisions of this Article and matters concerning title become material the following rules apply:

(1) Title to goods cannot pass under a contract for sale prior to their identification to the contract (Section 2–501), and unless otherwise explicitly agreed the buyer acquires by their identification a special property as limited by this Act. Any retention or reservation by the seller of the title (property) in goods shipped or delivered to the buyer is limited in effect to a reservation of a security interest. Subject to these provisions and to the provisions of the Article on Secured Transactions (Article 9), title to goods passes from the seller to the buyer in any manner and on any conditions explicitly agreed on by the parties.

(2) Unless otherwise explicitly agreed title passes to the buyer at the time and place at which the seller completes his performance with reference to the physical delivery of the goods, despite any reservation of a security interest and even though a document of title is to be delivered at a different time or place; and in particular and despite any reservation of a security interest by the bill of lading

    (a) if the contract requires or authorizes the seller to send the goods to the buyer but does not require him to deliver them at destination, title passes to the buyer at the time and place of shipment; but

    (b) if the contract requires delivery at destination, title passes on tender there.

(3) Unless otherwise explicitly agreed where delivery is to be made without moving the goods.

    (a) if the seller is to deliver a document of title, title passes at the time when and the place where he delivers such documents; or

    (b) if the goods are at the time of contracting already identified and no documents are to be delivered, title passes at the time and place of contracting.

(4) A rejection or other refusal by the buyer to receive or retain the goods, whether or not justified, or a justified revocation of acceptance revests title to the goods in the seller. Such revesting occurs by operation of law and is not a "sale".

§2–402. Rights of Seller's Creditors Against Sold Goods.

(1) Except as provided in subsections (2) and (3), rights of unsecured creditors of the seller with respect to goods which have been identified to a contract for sale are subject to the buyer's rights to recover the goods under this Article (Sections 2–502 and 2–716).

(2) A creditor of the seller may treat a sale or an identification of goods to a contract for sale as void if as against him a retention of possession by the seller is fraudulent under any rule of law of the state where the goods are situated, except that retention of possession in good faith and current course of trade by a merchant-seller for a commercially reasonable time after a sale or identification is not fraudulent.

(3) Nothing in this Article shall be deemed to impair the rights of creditors of the seller

    (a) under the provisions of the Article on Secured Transactions (Article 9); or

    (b) where identification to the contract or delivery is made not in current course of trade but in satisfaction of or as security for a pre-existing claim for money, security or the like and is made under circumstances which under any rule of law of the state where the goods are situated would apart from this Article constitute the transaction a fraudulent transfer or voidable preference.

§2–403. Power to Transfer; Good Faith Purchase of Goods; "Entrusting".

(1) A purchaser of goods acquires all title which his transferor had or had power to transfer except that a purchaser of a limited interest acquires rights only to the extent of the interest purchased. A person with voidable title has power to transfer a good title to a good faith purchaser for value. When goods have been delivered under a transaction of purchase the purchaser has such power even though

    (a) the transferor was deceived as to the identity of the purchaser, or

    (b) the delivery was in exchange for a check which is later dishonored, or

    (c) it was agreed that the transaction was to be a "cash sale", or

    (d) the delivery was procured through fraud punishable as larcenous under the criminal law.

(2) Any entrusting of possession of goods to a merchant who deals in goods of that kind gives him power to transfer all rights of the entruster to a buyer in ordinary course of business.

(3) "Entrusting" includes any delivery and any acquiescence in retention of possession regardless of any condition expressed between the parties to the delivery or acquiescence and regardless of whether the procurement of the entrusting or the possessor's disposition of the goods have been such as to be larcenous under the criminal law.

(4) The rights of other purchasers of goods and of lien creditors are governed by the Articles on Secured Transactions (Article 9). [Bulk Transfers/Sales (Article 6)* and Documents of Title (Article 7)].

Part 5. Performance

§2–501. Insurable Interest in Goods; Manner of Identification of Goods.

(1) The buyer obtains a special property and an insurable interest in goods by identification of existing goods as goods to which the contract refers even though the goods so identified are non-conforming and he has an option to return or reject them. Such identification can be made at any time and in any manner explicitly agreed to by the parties. In the absence of explicit agreement identification occurs.

    (a) when the contract is made if it is for the sale of goods already existing and identified;

    (b) if the contract is for the sale of future goods other than those described in paragraph (c), when goods are shipped, marked or otherwise designated by the seller as goods to which the contract refers;

    (c) when the crops are planted or otherwise become growing crops or the young are conceived if the contract is for the sale of unborn young to be born within twelve months after contracting or for the sale of crops to be harvested within twelve months or the next normal harvest season after contracting, whichever is longer.

(2) The seller retains an insurable interest in goods so long as title to or any security interest in the goods remains in him and where the identification is by the seller alone he may until default or insolvency or notification to the buyer that the identification is final substitute other goods for those identified.

(3) Nothing in this section impairs any insurable interest recognized under any other statute or rule of law.

§2–502. Buyer's Right to Goods on Seller's Insolvency.

(1)   Subject to subsections (2) and (3) and even though the goods have not been shipped a buyer who has paid a part or all of the price of goods in which he has a special property under the provisions of the immediately preceding section may on making and keeping good a tender of any unpaid portion of their price recover them from the seller if:

    (a)   in the case of goods bought for personal, family, or household purposes, the seller repudiates or fails to deliver as required by the contract; or

    (b)   in all cases, the seller becomes insolvent within ten days after receipt of the first installment on their price.

(2)   The buyer's right to recover the goods under subsection (1)(a) vests upon acquisition of a special property, even if the seller had not then repudiated or failed to deliver.

(3)   If the identification creating his special property has been made by the buyer he acquires the right to recover the goods only if they conform to the contract for sale.

§2–503. Manner of Seller's Tender of Delivery.

(1)   Tender of delivery requires that the seller put and hold conforming goods at the buyer's disposition and give the buyer any notification reasonably necessary to enable him to take delivery. The manner, time and place for tender are determined by the agreement and this Article, and in particular

    (a)   tender must be at a reasonable hour, and if it is of goods they must be kept available for the period reasonably necessary to enable the buyer to take possession; but

    (b)   unless otherwise agreed the buyer must furnish facilities reasonably suited to the receipt of the goods.

(2)   Where the case is within the next section respecting shipment tender requires that the seller comply with its provisions.

(3)   Where the seller is required to deliver at a particular destination tender requires that he comply with subsection (1) and also in any appropriate case tender documents as described in subsections (4) and (5) of this section.

(4)   Where goods are in the possession of a bailee and are to be delivered without being moved

    (a)   tender requires that the seller either tender a negotiable document of title covering such goods or procure acknowledgment by the bailee of the buyer's right to possession of the goods; but

    (b)   tender to the buyer of a non-negotiable document of title or of a written direction to the bailee to deliver is sufficient tender unless the buyer seasonably objects, and receipt by the bailee of notification of the buyer's rights fixes those rights as against the bailee and all third persons; but risk of loss of the goods and of any failure by the bailee to honor the non-negotiable document of title or to obey the direction remains on the seller until the buyer has had a reasonable time to present the document or direction, and a refusal by the bailee to honor the document or to obey the direction defeats the tender.

(5)   Where the contract requires the seller to deliver documents

    (a)   he must tender all such documents in correct form, except as provided in this Article with respect to

bills of lading in a set (subsection (2) of Section 2–323); and

    (b)   tender through customary banking channels is sufficient and dishonor of a draft accompanying the documents constitutes non-acceptance or rejection.

§2–504. Shipment by Seller.

Where the seller is required or authorized to send the goods to the buyer and the contract does not require him to deliver them at a particular destination, then unless otherwise agreed he must

    (a)   put the goods in the possession of such a carrier and make such a contract for their transportation as may be reasonable having regard to the nature of the goods and other circumstances of the case; and

    (b)   obtain and promptly deliver or tender in due form any document necessary to enable the buyer to obtain possession of the goods or otherwise required by the agreement or by usage of trade; and

    (c)   promptly notify the buyer of the shipment.

Failure to notify the buyer under paragraph (c) or to make a proper contract under paragraph (a) is a ground for rejection only if material delay or loss ensues.

§2–505. Seller's Shipment Under Reservation.

(1)   Where the seller has identified goods to the contract by or before shipment:

    (a)   his procurement of a negotiable bill of lading to his own order or otherwise reserves in him a security interest in the goods. His procurement of the bill to the order of a financing agency or of the buyer indicates in addition only the seller's expectation of transferring that interest to the person named.

    (b)   a non-negotiable bill of lading to himself or his nominee reserves possession of the goods as security but except in a case of conditional delivery (subsection (2) of Section 2–507) a non-negotiable bill of lading naming the buyer as consignee reserves no security interest even though the seller retains possession of the bill of lading.

(2)   When shipment by the seller with reservation of a security interest is in violation of the contract for sale it constitutes an improper contract for transportation within the preceding section but impairs neither the rights given to the buyer by shipment and identification of the goods to the contract nor the seller's powers as a holder of a negotiable document.

§2–506. Rights of Financing Agency.

(1)   A financing agency by paying or purchasing for value a draft which relates to a shipment of goods acquires to the extent of the payment or purchase and in addition to its own rights under the draft and any document of title securing it any rights of the shipper in the goods including the right to stop delivery and the shipper's right to have the draft honored by the buyer.

(2)   The right to reimbursement of a financing agency which has in good faith honored or purchased the draft under commitment to or authority from the buyer is not impaired by subsequent discovery of defects with reference to any relevant document which was apparently regular on its face.

§2-507. Effect of Seller's Tender; Delivery on Condition.

(1) Tender of delivery is a condition to the buyer's duty to accept the goods and, unless otherwise agreed, to his duty to pay for them. Tender entitles the seller to acceptance of the goods and to payment according to the contract.

(2) Where payment is due and demanded on the delivery to the buyer of goods or documents of title, his right as against the seller to retain or dispose of them is conditional upon his making the payment due.

§2-508. Cure by Seller of Improper Tender or Delivery; Replacement.

(1) Where any tender or delivery by the seller is rejected because non-conforming and the time for performance has not yet expired, the seller may seasonably notify the buyer of his intention to cure and may then within the contract time make a conforming delivery.

(2) Where the buyer rejects a non-conforming tender which the seller had reasonable grounds to believe would be acceptable with or without money allowance the seller may if he seasonably notifies the buyer have a further reasonable time to substitute a conforming tender.

§2-509. Risk of Loss in the Absence of Breach.

(1) Where the contract requires or authorizes the seller to ship the goods by carrier

    (a) if it does not require him to deliver them at a particular destination, the risk of loss passes to the buyer when the goods are duly delivered to the carrier even though the shipment is under reservation (Section 2–505); but

    (b) if it does require him to deliver them at a particular destination and the goods are there duly tendered while in the possession of the carrier, the risk of loss passes to the buyer when the goods are there duly so tendered as to enable the buyer to take delivery.

(2) Where the goods are held by a bailee to be delivered without being moved, the risk of loss passes to the buyer

    (a) on his receipt of a negotiable document of title covering the goods; or

    (b) on acknowledgment by the bailee of the buyer's right to possession of the goods; or

    (c) after his receipt of a non-negotiable document of title or other written direction to deliver, as provided in subsection (4)(b) of Section 2–503.

(3) In any case not within subsection (1) or (2), the risk of loss passes to the buyer on his receipt of the goods if the seller is a merchant; otherwise the risk passes to the buyer on tender of delivery.

(4) The provisions of this section are subject to contrary agreement of the parties and to the provisions of this Article on sale on approval (Section 2–327) and on effect of breach on risk of loss (Section 2–510).

§2-510. Effect of Breach on Risk of Loss.

(1) Where a tender or delivery of goods so fails to conform to the contract as to give a right of rejection the risk of their loss remains on the seller until cure or acceptance.

(2) Where the buyer rightfully revokes acceptance he may to the extent of any deficiency in his effective insurance coverage treat the risk of loss as having rested on the seller from the beginning.

(3) Where the buyer as to conforming goods already identified to the contract for sale repudiates or is otherwise in breach before risk of their loss has passed to him, the seller may to the extent of any deficiency in his effective insurance coverage treat the risk of loss as resting on the buyer for a commercially reasonable time.

§2-511. Tender of Payment by Buyer; Payment by Check.

(1) Unless otherwise agreed tender of payment is a condition to the seller's duty to tender and complete any delivery.

(2) Tender of payment is sufficient when made by any means or in any manner current in the ordinary course of business unless the seller demands payment in legal tender and gives any extension of time reasonably necessary to procure it.

(3) Subject to the provisions of this Act on the effect of an instrument on an obligation (Section 3-310), payment by check is conditional and is defeated as between the parties by dishonor of the check on due presentment.

§2-512. Payment by Buyer Before Inspection.

(1) Where the contract requires payment before inspection nonconformity of the goods does not excuse the buyer from so making payment unless

    (a) the non-conformity appears without inspection; or

    (b) despite tender of the required documents the circumstances would justify injunction against honor under this Act (Section 5–109(b)).

(2) Payment pursuant to subsection (1) does not constitute an acceptance of goods or impair the buyer's right to inspect or any of his remedies.

§2-513. Buyer's Right to Inspection of Goods.

(1) Unless otherwise agreed and subject to subsection (3), where goods are tendered or delivered or identified to the contract for sale, the buyer has a right before payment or acceptance to inspect them at any reasonable place and time and in any reasonable manner. When the seller is required or authorized to send the goods to the buyer, the inspection may be after their arrival.

(2) Expenses of inspection must be borne by the buyer but may be recovered from the seller if the goods do not conform and are rejected.

(3) Unless otherwise agreed and subject to the provisions of this Article on C.I.F. contracts (subsection (3) of Section 2–321), the buyer is not entitled to inspect the goods before payment of the price when the contract provides

    (a) for delivery "C.O.D." or on other like terms; or

    (b) for payment against documents of title, except where such payment is due only after the goods are to become available for inspection.

(4) A place or method of inspection fixed by the parties is presumed to be exclusive but unless otherwise expressly agreed it does not postpone identification or shift the place for delivery or for passing the risk of loss. If compliance becomes impossible, inspection shall be as provided in this section unless the place or method fixed was clearly intended as an indispensable condition failure of which avoids the contract.

§2-514. When Documents Deliverable on Acceptance; When on Payment.

Unless otherwise agreed documents against which a draft is drawn are to be delivered to the drawee on acceptance of the draft if it is payable more than three days after presentment; otherwise, only on payment.

§2–515. Preserving Evidence of Goods in Dispute.

In furtherance of the adjustment of any claim or dispute

    (a) either party on reasonable notification to the other and for the purpose of ascertaining the facts and preserving evidence has the right to inspect, test and sample the goods including such of them as may be in the possession or control of the other; and

    (b) the parties may agree to a third party inspection or survey to determine the conformity or condition of the goods and may agree that the findings shall be binding upon them in any subsequent litigation or adjustment.

Part 6. Breach, Repudiation and Excuse

§2–601. Buyer's Rights on Improper Delivery.

Subject to the provisions of this Article on breach in installment contracts (Section 2–612) and unless otherwise agreed under the sections on contractual limitations of remedy (Sections 2–718 and 2–719), if the goods or the tender of delivery fail in any respect to conform to the contract, the buyer may

    (a) reject the whole; or

    (b) accept the whole; or

    (c) accept any commercial unit or units and reject the rest.

§2–602. Manner and Effect of Rightful Rejection.

(1) Rejection of goods must be within a reasonable time after their delivery or tender. It is ineffective unless the buyer seasonably notifies the seller.

(2) Subject to the provisions of the two following sections on rejected goods (Sections 2–603 and 2–604),

    (a) after rejection any exercise of ownership by the buyer with respect to any commercial unit is wrongful as against the seller; and

    (b) if the buyer has before rejection taken physical possession of goods in which he does not have a security interest under the provisions of this Article (subsection (3) of Section 2–711), he is under a duty after rejection to hold them with reasonable care at the seller's disposition for a time sufficient to permit the seller to remove them; but

    (c) the buyer has no further obligations with regard to goods rightfully rejected.

(3) The seller's rights with respect to goods wrongfully rejected are governed by the provisions of this Article on Seller's remedies in general (Section 2–703).

§2–603. Merchant Buyer's Duties as to Rightfully Rejected Goods.

(1) Subject to any security interest in the buyer (subsection (3) of Section 2–711), when the seller has no agent or place of business at the market of rejection a merchant buyer is under a duty after rejection of goods in his possession or control to follow any reasonable instructions received from the seller with respect to the goods and in the absence of such instructions to make reasonable efforts to sell them for the seller's account if they are perishable or threaten to decline in value speedily. Instructions are not reasonable if on demand indemnity for expenses is not forthcoming.

(2) When the buyer sells goods under subsection (1), he is entitled to reimbursement from the seller or out of the proceeds for reasonable expenses of caring for and selling them, and if the expenses include no selling commission then to such commission as is usual in the trade or if there is none to a reasonable sum not exceeding ten percent on the gross proceeds.

(3) In complying with this section the buyer is held only to good faith and good faith conduct hereunder is neither acceptance nor conversion nor the basis of an action for damages.

§2–604. Buyer's Options as to Salvage of Rightfully Rejected Goods.

Subject to the provisions of the immediately preceding section on perishables if the seller gives no instructions within a reasonable time after notification of rejection the buyer may store the rejected goods for the seller's account or reship them to him or resell them for the seller's account with reimbursement as provided in the preceding section. Such action is not acceptance or conversion.

§2–605. Waiver of Buyer's Objections by Failure to Particularize.

(1) The buyer's failure to state in connection with rejection a particular defect which is ascertainable by reasonable inspection precludes him from relying on the unstated defect to justify rejection or to establish breach

    (a) where the seller could have cured it if stated seasonably; or

    (b) between merchants when the seller has after rejection made a request in writing for a full and final written statement of all defects on which the buyer proposes to rely.

(2) Payment against documents made without reservation of rights precludes recovery of the payment for defects apparent on the face of the documents.

§2–606. What Constitutes Acceptance of Goods.

(1) Acceptance of goods occurs when the buyer

    (a) after a reasonable opportunity to inspect the goods signifies to the seller that the goods are conforming or that he will take or retain them in spite of their non-conformity; or

    (b) fails to make an effective rejection (subsection (1) of Section 2–602), but such acceptance does not occur until the buyer has had a reasonable opportunity to inspect them; or

    (c) does any act inconsistent with the seller's ownership; but if such act is wrongful as against the seller it is an acceptance only if ratified by him.

(2) Acceptance of a part of any commercial unit is acceptance of that entire unit.

§2–607. Effect of Acceptance; Notice of Breach; Burden of Establishing Breach After Acceptance; Notice of Claim or Litigation to Person Answerable Over.

(1) The buyer must pay at the contract rate for any goods accepted.

(2) Acceptance of goods by the buyer precludes rejection of the goods accepted and if made with knowledge of a non-conformity cannot be revoked because of it unless the acceptance was on the reasonable assumption that the non-conformity would be seasonably cured but acceptance does not of itself impair any other remedy provided by this Article for non-conformity.

(3) Where a tender has been accepted

    (a) the buyer must within a reasonable time after he discovers or should have discovered any breach notify the seller of breach or be barred from any remedy; and

    (b) if the claim is one for infringement or the like (subsection (3) of Section 2-312) and the buyer is sued as a result of such a breach he must so notify the seller within a reasonable time after he receives notice of the litigation or be barred from any remedy over for liability established by the litigation.

(4) The burden is on the buyer to establish any breach with respect to the goods accepted.

(5) Where the buyer is sued for breach of a warranty or other obligation for which his seller is answerable over

    (a) he may give his seller written notice of the litigation. If the notice states that the seller may come in and defend and that if the seller does not do so he will be bound in any action against him by his buyer by any determination of fact common to the two litigations, then unless the seller after seasonable receipt of the notice does come in and defend he is so bound.

    (b) if the claim is one for infringement or the like (subsection (3) of Section 2–312) the original seller may demand in writing that his buyer turn over to him control of the litigation including settlement or else be barred from any remedy over and if he also agrees to bear all expense and to satisfy any adverse judgment, then unless the buyer after seasonable receipt of the demand does turn over control the buyer is so barred.

(6) The provisions of subsection (3), (4) and (5) apply to any obligation of a buyer to hold the seller harmless against infringement or the like (subsection (3) of Section 2–312).

§2-608. Revocation of Acceptance in Whole or in Part.

(1) The buyer may revoke his acceptance of a lot or commercial unit whose non-conformity substantially impairs its value to him if he has accepted it

    (a) on the reasonable assumption that its non-conformity would be cured and it has not been seasonably cured; or

    (b) without discovery of such non-conformity if his acceptance was reasonably induced either by the difficulty of discovery before acceptance or by the seller's assurances.

(2) Revocation of acceptance must occur within a reasonable time after the buyer discovers or should have discovered the ground for it and before any substantial change in condition of the goods which is not caused by their own defects. It is not effective until the buyer notifies the seller of it.

(3) A buyer who so revokes has the same rights and duties with regard to the goods involved as if he had rejected them.

§2-609. Right to Adequate Assurance of Performance.

(1) A contract for sale imposes an obligation on each party that the other's expectation of receiving due performance will not be impaired. When reasonable grounds for insecurity arise with respect to the performance of either party the other may in writing demand adequate assurance of due performance and until he receives such assurance may if commercially reasonable suspend any performance for which he has not already received the agreed return.

(2) Between merchants the reasonableness of grounds for insecurity and the adequacy of any assurance offered shall be determined according to commercial standards.

(3) Acceptance of any improper delivery or payment does not prejudice the aggrieved party's right to demand adequate assurance of future performance.

(4) After receipt of a justified demand failure to provide within a reasonable time not exceeding thirty days such assurance of due performance as is adequate under the circumstances of the particular case is a repudiation of the contract.

§2-610. Anticipatory Repudiation.

When either party repudiates the contract with respect to a performance not yet due the loss of which will substantially impair the value of the contract to the other, the aggrieved party may

    (a) for a commercially reasonable time await performance by the repudiating party; or

    (b) resort to any remedy for breach (Section 2–703 or Section 2–711), even though he has notified the repudiating party that he would await the latter's performance and has urged retraction; and

    (c) in either case suspend his own performance or proceed in accordance with the provisions of this Article on the seller's right to identify goods to the contract notwithstanding breach or to salvage unfinished goods (Section 2–704).

§2-611. Retraction of Anticipatory Repudiation.

(1) Until the repudiating party's next performance is due he can retract his repudiation unless the aggrieved party has since the repudiation cancelled or materially changed his position or otherwise indicated that he considers the repudiation final.

(2) Retraction may be by any method which clearly indicates to the aggrieved party that the repudiating party intends to perform, but must include any assurance justifiably demanded under the provisions of this Article (Section 2–609).

(3) Retraction reinstates the repudiating party's rights under the contract with due excuse and allowance to the aggrieved party for any delay occasioned by the repudiation.

§2-612. "Installment Contract"; Breach.

(1) An "installment contract" is one which requires or authorizes the delivery of goods in separate lots to be separately accepted, even though the contract contains a clause "each delivery is a separate contract" or its equivalent.

(2) The buyer may reject any installment which is non-conforming if the non-conformity substantially impairs the value of that installment and cannot be cured or if the non-conformity is a defect in the required documents; but if the non-conformity does not fall within subsection (3) and the seller gives adequate assurance of its cure the buyer must accept that installment.

(3) Whenever non-conformity or default with respect to one or more installments substantially impairs the value of the whole contract there is a breach of the whole. But the aggrieved party reinstates the contract if he accepts a non-conforming installment without seasonably notifying of cancellation or if he brings an

action with respect only to past installments or demands performance as to future installments.

§2–613. Casualty to Identified Goods.

Where the contract requires for its performance goods identified when the contract is made, and the goods suffer casualty without fault of either party before the risk of loss passes to the buyer, or in a proper case under a "no arrival, no sale" term (Section 2-324) then

    (a) if the loss is total the contract is avoided; and

    (b) if the loss is partial or the goods have so deteriorated as no longer to conform to the contract the buyer may nevertheless demand inspection and at his option either treat the contract as avoided or accept the goods with due allowance from the contract price for the deterioration or the deficiency in quantity but without further right against the seller.

§2–614. Substituted Performance.

(1) Where without fault of either party the agreed berthing, loading, or unloading facilities fail or an agreed type of carrier becomes unavailable or the agreed manner of delivery otherwise becomes commercially impracticable but a commercially reasonable substitute is available, such substitute performance must be tendered and accepted.

(2) If the agreed means or manner of payment fails because of domestic or foreign governmental regulation, the seller may withhold or stop delivery unless the buyer provides a means or manner of payment which is commercially a substantial equivalent. If delivery has already been taken, payment by the means or in the manner provided by the regulation discharges the buyers obligation unless the regulation is discriminatory, oppressive or predatory.

§2–615. Excuse by Failure of Presupposed Conditions.

Except so far as a seller may have assumed a greater obligation and subject to the preceding section on substituted performance:

    (a) Delay in delivery or non-delivery in whole or in part by a seller who complies with paragraphs (b) and (c) is not a breach of his duty under a contract for sale if performance as agreed has been made impracticable by the occurrence of a contingency the non-occurrence of which was a basic assumption on which the contract was made or by compliance in good faith with any applicable foreign or domestic governmental regulation or order whether or not it later proves to be invalid.

    (b) Where the causes mentioned in paragraph (a) affect only a part of the seller's capacity to perform, he must allocate production and deliveries among his customers but may at his option include regular customers not then under contract as well as his own requirements for further manufacture. He may so allocate in any manner which is fair and reasonable.

    (c) The seller must notify the buyer seasonably that there will be delay or non-delivery and, when allocation is required under paragraph (b), of the estimated quota thus made available for the buyer.

§2–616. Procedure on Notice Claiming Excuse.

(1) Where the buyer receives notification of a material or indefinite delay or an allocation justified under the preceding

section he may by written notification to the seller as to any delivery concerned, and where the prospective deficiency substantially impairs the value of the whole contract under the provisions of this Article relating to breach of installment contracts (Section 2-612), then also as to the whole,

    (a) terminate and thereby discharge any unexecuted portion of the contract; or

    (b) modify the contract by agreeing to take his available quota in substitution.

(2) If after receipt of such notification from the seller the buyer fails so to modify the contract within a reasonable time not exceeding thirty days the contract lapses with respect to any deliveries affected.

(3) The provisions of this section may not be negated by agreement except in so far as the seller has assumed a greater obligation under the preceding section.

Part 7. Remedies

§2–701. Remedies for Breach of Collateral Contracts Not Impaired.

Remedies for breach of any obligation or promise collateral or ancillary to a contract for sale or not impaired by the provisions of this Article.

§2–702. Seller's Remedies on Discovery of Buyer's Insolvency.

(1) Where the seller discovers the buyer to be insolvent he may refuse delivery except for cash including payment for all goods therefore delivered under the contract, and stop delivery under this Article (Section 2-705).

(2) Where the seller discovers that the buyer has received goods on credit while insolvent he may reclaim the goods upon demand made within ten days after the receipt, but if misrepresentation of solvency has been made to the particular seller in writing within three months before delivery the ten day limitation does not apply. Except as provided in this subsection the seller may not base a right to reclaim goods on the buyer's fraudulent or innocent misrepresentation of solvency or of intent to pay.

(3) The seller's right to reclaim under subsection (2) is subject to the rights of a buyer in ordinary course or other good faith purchaser under this Article (Section 2-403). Successful reclamation of goods excludes all other remedies with respect to them.

§2–703. Seller's Remedies in General.

Where the buyer wrongfully rejects or revokes acceptance of goods or fails to make a payment due on or before delivery or repudiates with respect to a part or the whole, then with respect to any goods directly affected and, if the breach is of the whole contract (Section 2-612), then also with respect to the whole undelivered balance, the aggrieved seller may

    (a) withhold delivery of such goods;

    (b) stop delivery by any bailee as hereafter provided (Section 2-705);

    (c) proceed under the next section respecting goods still unidentified to the contract;

    (d) resell and recover damages as hereafter provided (Section 2-706);

    (e) recover damages for non-acceptance (Section 2-708) or in a proper case the price (Section 2-709);

    (f) cancel.

§2–704. Seller's Right to Identify Goods to the Contract Notwithstanding Breach or to Salvage Unfinished Goods.

(1) An aggrieved seller under the preceding section may

    (a) identify to the contract conforming goods not already identified if at the time he learned of the breach they are in his possession or control;

    (b) treat as the subject of resale goods which have demonstrably been intended for the particular contract even though those goods are unfinished.

(2) Where the goods are unfinished an aggrieved seller may in the exercise of reasonable commercial judgment for the purposes of avoiding loss and of effective realization either complete the manufacture and wholly identify the goods to the contract or cease manufacture and resell for scrap or salvage value or proceed in any other reasonable manner.

§2–705. Seller's Stoppage of Delivery in Transit or Otherwise.

(1) The seller may stop delivery of goods in the possession of a carrier or other bailee when he discovers the buyer to be insolvent (Section 2–702) and may stop delivery of carload, truckload, planeload or larger shipments of express or freight when the buyer repudiates or fails to make a payment due before delivery or if for any other reason the seller has a right to withhold or reclaim the goods.

(2) As against such buyer the seller may stop delivery until

    (a) receipt of the goods by the buyer; or

    (b) acknowledgment to the buyer by any bailee of the goods except a carrier that the bailee holds the goods for the buyer; or

    (c) such acknowledgment to the buyer by a carrier by reshipment or as warehouseman; or

    (d) negotiation to the buyer of any negotiable document of title covering the goods.

(3) (a) To stop delivery the seller must so notify as to enable the bailee by reasonable diligence to prevent delivery of the goods.

    (b) After such notification the bailee must hold and deliver the goods according to the directions of the seller but the seller is liable to the bailee for any ensuing charges or damages.

    (c) If a negotiable document of title has been issued for goods the bailee is not obliged to obey a notification to stop until surrender of the document.

    (d) A carrier who has issued a non-negotiable bill of lading is not obliged to obey a notification to stop received from a person other than the consignor.

§2–706. Seller's Resale Including Contract for Resale.

(1) Under the conditions stated in Section 2–703 on seller's remedies, the seller may resell the goods concerned or the undelivered balance thereof. Where the resale is made in good faith and in a commercially reasonable manner the seller may recover the difference between the resale price and the contract price together with any incidental damages allowed under the provisions of this Article (Section 2–710), but less expenses saved in consequence of the buyer's breach.

(2) Except as otherwise provided in subsection (3) or unless otherwise agreed resale may be at public or private sale including sale by way of one or more contracts to sell or of identification to an existing contract of the seller. Sale may be as a unit or in parcels and at any time and place and on any terms but every aspect of the sale including the method, manner, time, place and terms must be commercially reasonable. The resale must be reasonably identified as referring to the broken contract, but it is not necessary that the goods be in existence or that any or all of them have been identified to the contract before the breach.

(3) Where the resale is at private sale the seller must give the buyer reasonable notification of his intention to resell.

(4) Where the resale is at public sale

    (a) only identified goods can be sold except where there is a recognized market for a public sale of futures in goods of the kind; and

    (b) it must be made at a usual place or market for public sale if one is reasonably available and except in the case of goods which are perishable or threaten to decline in value speedily the seller must give the buyer reasonable notice of the time and place of the resale; and

    (c) if the goods are not to be within the view of those attending the sale the notification of sale must state the place where the goods are located and provide for their reasonable inspection by prospective bidders; and

    (d) the seller may buy.

(5) A purchaser who buys in good faith at a resale takes the goods free of any rights of the original buyer even though the seller fails to comply with one or more of the requirements of this section.

(6) The seller is not accountable to the buyer for any profit made on any resale. A person in the position of a seller (Section 2–707) or a buyer who has rightfully rejected or justifiably revoked acceptance must account for any excess over the amount of his security interest, as hereinafter defined (subsection (3) of Section 2-711).

§2–707. "Person in the Position of a Seller".

(1) A "person in the position of a seller" includes as against a principal an agent who has paid or become responsible for the price of goods on behalf of his principal or anyone who otherwise holds a security interest or other right in goods similar to that of a seller.

(2) A person in the position of a seller may as provided in this Article withhold or stop delivery (Section 2–705) and resell (Section 2–706) and recover incidental damages (Section 2–710).

§2–708. Seller's Damages for Non-Acceptance or Repudiation.

(1) Subject to subsection (2) and to the provisions of this Article with respect to proof of market price (Section 2–723), the measure of damages for non-acceptance or repudiation by the buyer is the difference between the market price at the time and place for tender and the unpaid contract price together with any incidental damages provided in this Article (Section 2–710), but less expenses saved in consequence of the buyer's breach.

(2) If the measure of damages provided in subsection (1) is inadequate to put the seller in as good a position as performance would have done then the measure of damages is the profit (including reasonable overhead) which the seller would have made from full performance by the buyer, together with any incidental damages provided in this Article (Section 2–710), due allowance for costs reasonably incurred and due credit for payments or proceeds of resale.

§2-709. Action for the Price.

(1) When the buyer fails to pay the price as it becomes due the seller may recover, together with any incidental damages under the next section, the price

    (a) of goods accepted or of conforming goods lost or damaged within a commercially reasonable time after risk of their loss has passed to the buyer; and

    (b) of goods identified to the contract if the seller is unable after reasonable effort to resell them at a reasonable price or the circumstances reasonably indicate that such effort will be unavailing.

(2) Where the seller sues for the price he must hold for the buyer any goods which have been identified to the contract and are still in his control except that if resale becomes possible he may resell them at any time prior to the collection of the judgment. The net proceeds of any such resale must be credited to the buyer and payment of the judgment entitles him to any goods not resold.

(3) After the buyer has wrongfully rejected or revoked acceptance of the goods or has failed to make a payment due or has repudiated (Section 2–610), a seller who is held not entitled to the price under this section shall nevertheless be awarded damages for non-acceptance under the preceding section.

§2-710. Seller's Incidental Damages.

Incidental damages to an aggrieved seller include any commercially reasonable charges, expenses or commissions incurred in stopping delivery, in the transportation, care and custody of goods after the buyer's breach, in connection with return or resale of the goods or otherwise resulting from the breach.

§2-71. Buyer's Remedies in General; Buyer's Security Interest in Rejected Goods.

(1) Where the seller fails to make delivery or repudiates or the buyer rightfully rejects or justifiably revokes acceptance then with respect to any goods involved, and with respect to the whole if the breach goes to the whole contract (Section 2–612), the buyer may cancel and whether or not he has done so may in addition to recovering so much of the price as has been paid

    (a) "cover" and have damages under the next section as to all the goods affected whether or not they have been identified to the contract; or

    (b) recover damages for non-delivery as provided in this Article (Section 2–713).

(2) Where the seller fails to deliver or repudiates the buyer may also

    (a) if the goods have been identified recover them as provided in this Article (Section 2–502); or

    (b) in a proper case obtain specific performance or replevy the goods as provided in this Article (Section 2–716).

(3) On rightful rejection of justifiable revocation of acceptance a buyer has a security interest in goods in his possession or control for any payments made on their price and any expenses reasonably incurred in their inspection, receipt, transportation, care and custody and may hold such goods and resell them in like manner as an aggrieved seller (Section 2–706).

§2-712. "Cover"; Buyer's Procurement of Substitute Goods.

(1) After a breach within the preceding section the buyer may "cover" by making in good faith and without unreasonable delay any reasonable purchase of or contract to purchase goods in substitution for those due from the seller.

(2) The buyer may recover from the seller as damages the difference between the cost of cover and the contract price together with any incidental or consequential damages as hereinafter defined (Section 2–715), but less expenses saved in consequence of the seller's breach.

(3) Failure of the buyer to effect cover within this section does not bar him from any other remedy.

§2-713. Buyer's Damages for Non-Delivery or Repudiation.

(1) Subject to the provisions of this Article with respect to proof of market price (Section 2–723), the measure of damages for nondelivery or repudiation by the seller is the difference between the market price at the time when the buyer learned of the breach and the contract price together with any incidental and consequential damages provided in this Article (Section 2–715), but less expenses saved in consequence of the seller's breach.

(2) Market price is to be determined as of the place for tender or, in cases of rejection after arrival or revocation of acceptance, as of the place of arrival.

§2-714. Buyer's Damages for Breach in Regard to Accepted Goods.

(1) Where the buyer has accepted goods and given notification (subsection (3) of Section 2–607) he may recover as damages for any non-conformity of tender the loss resulting in the ordinary course of events from the seller's breach as determined in any manner which is reasonable.

(2) The measure of damages for breach of warranty is the difference at the time and place of acceptance between the value of the goods accepted and the value they would have had if they had been as warranted, unless special circumstances show proximate damages of a different amount.

(3) In a proper case any incidental and consequential damages under the next section may also be recovered.

§2-715. Buyer's Incidental and Consequential Damages.

(1) Incidental damages resulting from the seller's breach include expenses reasonably incurred in inspection, receipt, transportation and care and custody of goods rightfully rejected, any commercially reasonable charges, expenses or commissions in connection with effecting cover and any other reasonable expense incident to the delay or other breach.

(2) Consequential damages resulting from the seller's breach include

    (a) any loss resulting from general or particular requirements and needs of which the seller at the time of contracting had reason to know and which could not reasonably be prevented by cover or otherwise; and

    (b) injury to person or property proximately resulting from any breach of warranty.

§2-716. Buyer's Right to Specific Performance or Replevin.

(1) Specific performance may be decreed where the goods are unique or in other proper circumstances.

(2) The decree for specific performance may include such terms and conditions as to payment of the price, damages, or other relief as the court may deem just.

(3) The buyer has a right of replevin for goods identified to the contract if after reasonable effort he is unable to effect cover

for such goods or the circumstances reasonably indicate that such effort will be unvailing or if the goods have been shipped under reservation and satisfaction of the security interest in them has been made or tendered. In the case of goods bought for personal, family, or household purposes, the buyer's right of replevin vests upon acquisition of a special property, even if the seller had not then repudiated or failed to deliver.

§2-717. Deduction of Damages From the Price.

The buyer on notifying the seller of his intention to do so may deduct all or any part of the damages resulting from any breach of the contract from any part of the price still due under the same contract.

§2-718. Liquidation or Limitation of Damages; Deposits.

(1) Damages for breach by either party may be liquidated in the agreement but only at an amount which is reasonable in the light of the anticipated or actual harm caused by the breach, the difficulties of proof of loss, and the inconvenience of nonfeasibility of otherwise obtaining an adequate remedy. A team fixing unreasonably large liquidated damages is void as a penalty.

(2) Where the seller justifiably withholds delivery of goods because of the buyer's breach, the buyer is entitled to restitution of any amount by which the sum of his payments exceeds

    (a) the amount to which the seller is entitled by virtue of terms liquidating the seller's damages in accordance with subsection (1), or

    (b) in the absence of such terms, twenty percent of the value of the total performance for which the buyer is obligated under the contract or $500, whichever is smaller.

(3) The buyer's right to restitution under subsection (2) is subject to offset to the extent that the seller establishes

    (a) a right to recover damages under the provisions of this Article other than subsection (1), and

    (b) the amount or value of any benefits received by the buyer directly or indirectly by reason of the contract.

(4) Where a seller has received payment in goods their reasonable value or the proceeds of their resale shall be treated as payments for the purposes of subsection (2); but if the seller has notice of the buyer's breach before reselling goods received in part performance, his resale is subject to the conditions laid down in this Article on resale by an aggrieved seller (Section 2–706).

§2-719. Contractual Modification or Limitation of Remedy.

(1) Subject to the provisions of subsections (2) and (3) of this section and of the preceding section on liquidation and limitation of damages,

    (a) the agreement may provide for remedies in addition to or in substitution for those provided in this Article and may limit or alter the measure of damages recoverable under this Article, as by limiting the buyer's remedies to return of the goods and repayment of the price or to repair and replacement of non-conforming goods or parts; and

    (b) resort to a remedy as provided is optional unless the remedy is expressly agreed to be exclusive, in which case it is the sole remedy.

(2) Where circumstances cause an exclusive or limited remedy to fail of its essential purpose, remedy may be had as provided in this Act.

(3) Consequential damages may be limited or excluded unless the limitation or exclusion is unconscionable. Limitation of consequential damages for injury to the person in the case of consumer goods is prima facie unconscionable but limitation of damages where the loss is commercial is not.

§2-720. Effect of "Cancellation" or "Rescission" on Claims for Antecedent Breach.

Unless the contrary intention clearly appears, expressions of "cancellation" or "rescission" of the contract or the like shall not be construed as a renunciation or discharge of any claim in damages for an antecedent breach.

§2-721. Remedies for Fraud.

Remedies for material misrepresentation or fraud include all remedies available under this Article for non-fraudulent breach. Neither rescission or a claim for rescission of the contract for sale nor rejection or return of the goods shall bar or be deemed inconsistent with a claim for damages or other remedy.

§2-722. Who Can Sue Third Parties for Injury to Goods.

Where a third party so deals with goods which have been identified to a contract for sale as to cause actionable injury to a party to that contract

    (a) a right of action against the third party is in either party to the contract for sale who has title to or a security interest or a special property or an insurable interest in the goods; and if the goods have been destroyed or converted a right of action is also in the party who either bore the risk of loss under the contract for sale or has since the injury assumed that risk as against the other,

    (b) if at the time of the injury the party plaintiff did not bear the risk of loss as against the other party to the contract for sale and there is no arrangement between them for disposition of the recovery, his suit or settlement is, subject to his own interest, as a fiduciary for the other party to the contract;

    (c) either party may with the consent of the other sue for the benefit of whom it may concern.

§2-723. Proof of Market Price: Time and Place.

(1) If an action based on anticipatory repudiation comes to trial before the time for performance with respect to some or all of the goods, any damages based on market price (Section 2–708 or Section 2–713) shall be determined according to the price of such goods prevailing at the time when the aggrieved party learned of the repudiation.

(2) If evidence of a price prevailing at the times or places described in this Article is not readily available the price prevailing within any reasonable time before or after the time described or at any other place which in commercial judgment or under usage of trade would serve as a reasonable substitute for the one described may be used, making any proper allowance for the cost of transporting the goods to or from such other place.

(3) Evidence of a relevant price prevailing at a time or place other than the one described in this Article offered by one party is not admissible unless and until he has given the other party such notice as the court finds sufficient to prevent unfair surprise.

§2-724. Admissibility of Market Quotations.

Whenever the prevailing price or value of any goods regularly bought and sold in any established commodity market is in issue, reports in official publications or trade journals or in newspapers or periodicals of general circulation published as the reports of such market shall be admissible in evidence. The circumstances of the preparation of such a report may be shown to affect its weight but not its admissibility.

§2-725. Statute of Limitations in Contracts for Sale.

(1) An action for breach of any contract for sale must be commenced within four years after the cause of action has accrued. By the original agreement the parties may reduce the period of limitation to not less than one year but may not extend it.

(2) A cause of action accrues when the breach occurs, regardless of the aggrieved party's lack of knowledge of the breach. A breach of warranty occurs when tender of delivery is made, except that where a warranty explicitly extends to future performance of the goods and discovery of the breach must await the time of such performance the cause of action accrues when the breach is or should have been discovered.

(3) Where an action commenced within the time limited by subsection (1) is so terminated as to leave available a remedy by another action for the same breach such other action may be commenced after the expiration of the time limited and within six months after the termination of the first action unless the termination resulted from voluntary discontinuance or from dismissal for failure or neglect to prosecute.

(4) This section does not alter the law on tolling of the statute of limitations nor does it apply to causes of action which have accrued before this Act becomes effective.

Appendix D Sarbanes-Oxley Act of 2002 (Excerpts)

Title I—Public Company Accounting Oversight Board

Sec. 101 Establishment; Administrative Provisions.

(a) Establishment of Board.—There is established the Public Company Accounting Oversight Board, to oversee the audit of public companies that are subject to the securities laws, and related matters, in order to protect the interests of investors and further the public interest in the preparation of informative, accurate, and independent audit reports for companies the securities of which are sold to, and held by and for, public investors. The Board shall be a body corporate, operate as a nonprofit corporation, and have succession until dissolved by an Act of Congress.

Sec. 102 Registration with the Board.

(a) Mandatory Registration.—It shall be unlawful for any person that is not a registered public accounting firm to prepare or issue, or to participate in the preparation or issuance of, any audit report with respect to any issuer.

(b) Application for Registration.—

(1) Form of application.—A public accounting firm shall use such form as the Board may prescribe, by rule, to apply for registration under this section.

Sec. 104 Inspections of Registered Public Accounting Firms.

(a) In General.—The Board shall conduct a continuing program of inspections to assess the degree of compliance of each registered public accounting firm and associated persons of that firm with this Act, the rules of the Board, the rules of the Commission, or professional standards, in connection with its performance of audits, issuance of audit reports, and related matters involving issuers.

(b) Inspection Frequency.—

(1) In general.—Subject to paragraph (2), inspections required by this section shall be conducted—

(A) annually with respect to each registered public accounting firm that regularly provides audit reports for more than 100 issuers; and

(B) not less frequently than once every 3 years with respect to each registered public accounting firm that regularly provides audit reports for 100 or fewer issuers.

Sec. 105 Investigations and Disciplinary Proceedings.

(a) In General.—The Board shall establish, by rule, subject to the requirements of this section, fair procedures for the investigation and disciplining of registered public accounting firms and associated persons of such firms.

(c) Disciplinary Procedures.—

(4) Sanctions.—If the Board finds, based on all of the facts and circumstances, that a registered public accounting firm or associated person thereof has engaged in any act or practice, or omitted to act, in violation of this Act, the rules of the Board, the provisions of the securities laws relating to the preparation and issuance of audit reports and the obligations and liabilities of accountants with respect thereto, including the rules of the Commission issued under this Act, or professional standards, the Board may impose such disciplinary or remedial sanctions as it determines appropriate, subject to applicable limitations under paragraph (5), including—

(A) temporary suspension or permanent revocation of registration under this title;

(B) temporary or permanent suspension or bar of a person from further association with any registered public accounting firm;

(C) temporary or permanent limitation on the activities, functions, or operations of such firm or person (other than in connection with required additional professional education or training);

(D) a civil money penalty for each such violation, in an amount equal to—

(i) not more than $100,000 for a natural person or $2,000,000 for any other person; and

(ii) in any case to which paragraph (5) applies, not more than $750,000 for a natural person or $15,000,000 for any other person;

(E) censure;

(F) required additional professional education or training; or

(G) any other appropriate sanction provided for in the rules of the Board.

(5) Intentional or other knowing conduct.—The sanctions and penalties described in subparagraphs (A) through (C) and (D)(ii) of paragraph (4) shall only apply to—

(A) intentional or knowing conduct, including reckless conduct, that results in violation of the applicable statutory, regulatory, or professional standard; or

(B) repeated instances of negligent conduct, each resulting in a violation of the applicable statutory, regulatory, or professional standard.

Title II—Auditor Independence

Sec. 201 Services Outside the Scope of Practice of Auditors.

(a) Prohibited Activities.—Section 10A of the Securities Exchange Act of 1934 (15 U.S.C. 78j–1) is amended by adding at the end of the following:

"(g) Prohibited Activities.—Except as provided in subsection (h), it shall be unlawful for a registered public accounting firm (and any associated person of that firm, to the extent determined appropriate by the Commission) that performs for any issuer any audit required by this title or the rules of the Commission under this title or, beginning 180 days after the date of commencement of the operations of the Public Company Accounting Oversight Board established under section 101 of the Sarbanes-Oxley Act of 2002 (in this section referred to as the 'Board'), the rules of the Board, to provide to that issuer, contemporaneously with the audit, any non-audit service, including—

"(1) bookkeeping or other services related to the accounting records or financial statements of the audit client;

"(2) financial information systems design and implementation;

"(3) appraisal or valuation services, fairness opinions, or contribution-in-kind reports;

"(4) actuarial services;

"(5) internal audit outsourcing services;

"(6) management functions or human resources;

"(7) broker or dealer, investment adviser, or investment banking services;

"(8) legal services and expert services unrelated to the audit; and

"(9) any other service that the Board determines, by regulation, is impermissible.

"(h) Preapproval Required for Non-Audit Services.—A registered public accounting firm may engage in any non-audit service, including tax services, that is not described in any of paragraphs (1) through (9) of subsection (g) for an audit client, only if the activity is approved in advance by the audit committee of the issuer, in accordance with subsection (i)."

Sec. 206 Conflicts of Interest.

Section 10A of the Securities Exchange Act of 1934 (15 U.S.C. 78j–1), as amended by this Act, is amended by adding at the end the following:

"(1) Conflicts of Interest.—It shall be unlawful for a registered public accounting firm to perform for an issuer any audit service required by this title, if a chief executive officer, controller, chief financial officer, chief accounting officer, or any person serving in an equivalent position for the issuer, was employed by that registered independent public accounting firm and participated in any capacity in the audit of that issuer during the 1-year period preceding the date of the initiation of the audit."

Title III—Corporate Responsibility

Sec. 301 Public Company Audit Committees.

Section 10A of the Securities Exchange Act of 1934 (15 U.S.C. 78f) is amended by adding at the end the following:

"(m) Standards Relating to Audit Committees.—

"(2) Responsibilities relating to registered public accounting firms.—The audit committee of each issuer, in its capacity as a committee of the board of directors, shall be directly responsible for the appointment, compensation, and oversight of the work of any registered public accounting firm employed by that issuer (including resolution of disagreements between management and the auditor regarding financial reporting) for the purpose of

preparing or issuing an audit report or related work, and each such registered public accounting firm shall report directly to the audit committee.

"(3) Independence.—

"(A) In general.—Each member of the audit committee of the issuer shall be a member of the board of directors of the issuer, and shall otherwise be independent.

"(B) Criteria.—In order to be considered to be independent for purposes of this paragraph, a member of an audit committee of an issuer may not, other than in his or her capacity as a member of the audit committee, the board of directors, or any other board committee—

"(i) accept any consulting, advisory, or other compensatory fee from the issuer; or

"(ii) be an affiliated person of the issuer or any subsidiary thereof.

Sec. 302 Corporate Responsibility for Financial Reports.

(a) Regulations Required.—The Commission shall, by rule, require, for each company filing periodic reports under section 13(a) or 15(d) of the Securities Exchange Act of 1934 (15 U.S.C. 78m, 78o(d)), that the principal executive officer or officers and the principal financial officer or officers, or persons performing similar functions, certify in each annual or quarterly report filed or submitted under either such section of such Act that—

(1) the signing officer has reviewed the report;

(2) based on the officer's knowledge, the report does not contain any untrue statement of a material fact or omit to state a material fact necessary in order to make the statements made, in light of the circumstances under which such statements were made, not misleading;

(3) based on such officer's knowledge, the financial statements, and other financial information included in the report fairly present in all material respects the financial condition and results of operations of the issuer as of, and for, the periods presented in the report;

(4) the signing officers—

(A) are responsible for establishing and maintaining internal controls;

(B) have designed such internal controls to ensure that material information relating to the issuer and its consolidated subsidiaries is made known to such officers by others within those entities, particularly during the period in which the periodic reports are being prepared;

(C) have evaluated the effectiveness of the issuer's internal controls as of a date within 90 days prior to the report; and

(D) have presented in the report their conclusions about the effectiveness of their internal controls based on their evaluation as of that date;

(5) the signing officers have disclosed to the issuer's auditors and the audit committee of the board

of directors (or persons fulfilling the equivalent function)—

    (A) all significant deficiencies in the design or operation of internal controls which could adversely affect the issuer's ability to record, process, summarize, and report financial data and have identified for the issuer's auditors any material weaknesses in internal controls; and

    (B) any fraud, whether or not material, that involves management or other employees who have a significant role in the issuer's internal controls; and

  (6) the signing officers have indicated in the report whether or not there were significant changes in internal controls or in other factors that could significantly affect internal controls subsequent to the date of their evaluation, including any corrective actions with regard to significant deficiencies and material weaknesses.

Sec. 303 Improper Influence on Conduct of Audits.

  (a) Rules to Prohibit.—It shall be unlawful, in contravention of such rules or regulations as the Commission shall prescribe as necessary and appropriate in the public interest or for the protection of investors, for any officer or director of an issuer, or any other person acting under the direction thereof, to take any action to fraudulently influence, coerce, manipulate, or mislead any independent public or certified accountant engaged in the performance of an audit of the financial statements of that issuer for the purpose of rendering such financial statements materially misleading.

Title IV—Enhanced Financial Disclosures

Sec. 401 Disclosures in Periodic Reports.

  (a) Disclosures Required.—Section 13 of the Securities Exchange Act of 1934 (15 U.S.C. 78m) is amended by adding at the end the following:

"(i) Accuracy of Financial Reports.—Each financial report that contains financial statements, and that is required to be prepared in accordance with (or reconciled to) generally accepted accounting principles under this title and filed with the Commission shall reflect all material correcting adjustments that have been identified by a registered public accounting firm in accordance with generally accepted accounting principles and the rules and regulations of the Commission.

"(j) Off–Balance Sheet Transactions.—Not later than 180 days after the date of enactment of the Sarbanes-Oxley Act of 2002, the Commission shall issue final rules providing that each annual and quarterly financial report required to be filed with the Commission shall disclose all material off-balance sheet transactions, arrangements, obligations (including contingent obligations), and other relationships of the issuer with unconsolidated entities or other persons, that may have a material current or future effect on financial condition, changes in financial condition, results of operations, liquidity, capital expenditures, capital resources, or significant components of revenues or expenses."

  (b) Commission Rules on Pro Forma Figures.—Not later than 180 days after the date of enactment of the Sarbanes-Oxley Act of 2002, the Commission shall issue final rules providing that pro forma financial information included in any periodic or other report filed with the Commission pursuant to the securities laws, or in any public disclosure or press or other release, shall be presented in a manner that—

    (1) does not contain an untrue statement of a material fact or omit to state a material fact necessary in order to make the pro forma financial information, in light of the circumstances under which it is presented, not misleading; and

    (2) reconciles it with the financial condition and results of operations of the issuer under generally accepted accounting principles.

Sec. 402 Enhanced Conflict of Interest Provisions.

  (a) Prohibition on Personal Loans to Executives.—Section 13 of the Securities Exchange Act of 1934 (15 U.S.C. 78m), as amended by this Act, is amended by adding at the end the following:

"(k) Prohibition on Personal Loans to Executives.—

    "(1) In general.— It shall be unlawful for any issuer (as defined in section 2 of the Sarbanes-Oxley Act of 2002), directly or indirectly, including through any subsidiary, to extend or maintain credit, to arrange for the extension of credit, or to renew an extension of credit, in the form of a personal loan to or for any director or executive officer (or equivalent thereof) of that issuer. An extension of credit maintained by the issuer on the date of enactment of this subsection shall not be subject to the provisions of this subsection, provided that there is no material modification to any term of any such extension of credit or any renewal of any such extension of credit on or after that date of enactment.

Sec. 406 Code of Ethics for Senior Financial Officers.

  (a) Code of Ethics Disclosure.—The Commission shall issue rules to require each issuer, together with periodic reports required pursuant to section 13(a) or 15(d) of the Securities Exchange Act of 1934, to disclose whether or not, and if not, the reason therefor, such issuer has adopted a code of ethics for senior financial officers, applicable to its principal financial officer and comptroller or principal accounting officer, or persons performing similar functions.

  (b) Changes in Codes of Ethics.—The Commission shall revise its regulations concerning matters requiring prompt disclosure on Form 8-K (or any successor thereto) to require the immediate disclosure by means of the filing of such form, dissemination by the Internet or by other electronic means, by any issuer of any change in or waiver of the code of ethics for senior financial officers.

  (c) Definition.—In this section, the term "code of ethics" means such standards as are reasonably necessary to promote—

    (1) honest and ethical conduct, including the ethical handling of actual or apparent conflicts of interest between personal and professional relationships;

(2) full, fair, accurate, timely, and understandable disclosure in the periodic reports required to be filed by the issuer; and

(3) compliance with applicable governmental rules and regulations.

Title V—Analyst Conflicts of Interest

Sec. 501 Treatment of Securities Analysts by Registered Securities Associations and National Securities Exchanges.

(a) Rules Regarding Securities Analysts.—The Securities Exchange Act of 1934 (15 U.S.C. 78a et seq.) is amended by inserting after section 15C the following new section:

"Sec. 15D. *Securities Analysts and Research Reports.*

"(a) Analyst Protections.—The Commission, or upon the authorization and direction of the Commission, a registered securities association or national securities exchange, shall have adopted, not later than 1 year after the date of enactment of this section, rules reasonably designed to address conflicts of interest that can arise when securities analysts recommend equity securities in research reports and public appearances, in order to improve the objectivity of research and provide investors with more useful and reliable information, including rules designed—

"(1) to foster greater public confidence in securities research, and to protect the objectivity and independence of securities analysts, by—

"(A) restricting the prepublication clearance or approval of research reports by persons employed by the broker or dealer who are engaged in investment banking activities, or persons not directly responsible for investment research, other than legal or compliance staff;

"(B) limiting the supervision and compensatory evaluation of securities analysts to officials employed by the broker or dealer who are not engaged in investment banking activities; and

"(C) requiring that a broker or dealer and persons employed by a broker or dealer who are involved with investment banking activities may not, directly or indirectly, retaliate against or threaten to retaliate against any securities analyst employed by that broker or dealer or its affiliates as a result of an adverse, negative, or otherwise unfavorable research report that may adversely affect the present or prospective investment banking relationship of the broker or dealer with the issuer that is the subject of the research report, except that such rules may not limit the authority of a broker or dealer to discipline a securities analyst for causes other than such research report in accordance with the policies and procedures of the firm;

"(2) to define periods during which brokers or dealers who have participated, or are to participate, in a public offering of securities as underwriters or dealers should not publish or otherwise distribute research reports relating to such securities or to the issuer of such securities;

"(3) to establish structural and institutional safeguards within registered brokers or dealers to assure that securities analysts are separated by appropriate informational partitions within the firm from the review, pressure, or oversight of those whose involvement in investment banking activities might potentially bias their judgment or supervision; and

"(4) to address such other issues as the Commission, or such association or exchange, determines appropriate.

"(b) Disclosure.—The Commission, or upon the authorization and direction of the Commission, a registered securities association or national securities exchange, shall have adopted, not later than 1 year after the date of enactment of this section, rules reasonably designed to require each securities analyst to disclose in public appearances, and each registered broker or dealer to disclose in each research report, as applicable, conflicts of interest that are known or should have been known by the securities analyst or the broker or dealer, to exist at the time of the appearance or the date of distribution of the report, including—

"(1) the extent to which the securities analyst has debt or equity investments in the issuer that is the subject of the appearance or research report;

"(2) whether any compensation has been received by the registered broker or dealer, or any affiliate thereof, including the securities analyst, from the issuer that is the subject of the appearance or research report, subject to such exemptions as the Commission may determine appropriate and necessary to prevent disclosure by virtue of this paragraph of material non-public information regarding specific potential future investment banking transactions of such issuer, as is appropriate in the public interest and consistent with the protection of investors;

"(3) whether an issuer, the securities of which are recommended in the appearance or research report, currently is, or during the 1-year period preceding the date of the appearance or date of distribution of the report has been, a client of the registered broker or dealer, and if so, stating the types of services provided to the issuer;

"(4) whether the securities analyst received compensation with respect to a research report, based upon (among any other factors) the investment banking revenues (either generally or specifically earned from the issuer being analyzed) of the registered broker or dealer; and

"(5) such other disclosures of conflicts of interest that are material to investors, research analysts, or the broker or dealer as the Commission, or such association or exchange, determines appropriate.

"(c) Definitions.—In this section—

"(1) the term 'securities analyst' means any associated person of a registered broker or dealer that is principally responsible for, and any associated person who reports directly or indirectly to a securities analyst in connection with, the preparation of the substance of a research report, whether or not any such person has the job title of 'securities analyst'; and

"(2) the term 'research report' means a written or electronic communication that includes an analysis of equity securities of individual companies or industries, and that provides information reasonably sufficient upon which to base an investment decision."

(b) Enforcement.—Section 21B(a) of the Securities Exchange Act of 1934 (15 U.S.C. 78u–2(a)) is amended by inserting "15D," before "15B".

(c) Commission Authority.—The Commission may promulgate and amend its regulations, or direct a registered securities association or national securities exchange to promulgate and amend its rules, to carry out section 15D of the Securities Exchange Act of 1934, as added by this section, as is necessary for the protection of investors and in the public interest.

Title VI—Commission Resources and Authority

Sec. 602 Appearance and Practice Before the Commission.

The Securities Exchange Act of 1934 (15 U.S.C. 78a et seq.) is amended by inserting after section 4B the following:

"Sec 4C. Appearance and Practice Before the Commission

"(a) Authority to Censure.—The Commission may censure any person, or deny, temporarily or permanently, to any person the privilege of appearing or practicing before the Commission in any way, if that person is found by the Commission, after notice and opportunity for hearing in the matter—

"(1) not to possess the requisite qualifications to represent others;

"(2) to be lacking in character or integrity, or to have engaged in unethical or improper professional conduct; or

"(3) to have willfully violated or willfully aided and abetted the violation of, any provision of the securities laws or the rules and regulations issued thereunder.

Title VII—Studies and Reports

Sec. 705 Study of Investment Banks.

(a) GAO Study.—The Comptroller General of the United States shall conduct a study on whether investment banks and financial advisers assisted public companies in manipulating their earnings and obfuscating their true financial condition. The study should address the rule of investment banks and financial advisers—

(1) in the collapse of the Enron Corporation, including with respect to the design and implementation of derivatives transactions, transactions involving special purpose vehicles, and other financial arrangements that may have had the effect of altering the company's reported financial statements in ways that obscured the true financial picture of the company;

(2) in the failure of Global Crossing, including with respect to transactions involving swaps of fiberoptic

cable capacity, in the designing transactions that may have had the effect of altering the company's reported financial statements in ways that obscured the true financial picture of the company; and

(3) generally, in creating and marketing transactions which may have been designed solely to enable companies to manipulate revenue streams, obtain loans, or move liabilities off balance sheets without altering the economic and business risks faced by the companies or any other mechanism to obscure a company's financial picture.

Title VIII—Corporate and Criminal Fraud Accountability

Sec. 801 Short Title.

This title may be cited as the "Corporate and Criminal Fraud Accountability Act of 2002".

Sec. 802 Criminal Penalties for Altering Documents.

(a) In General.—Chapter 73 of title 18, United States Code, is amended by adding at the end the following:

§1519. Destruction, alteration, or falsification of records in Federal investigations and bankruptcy

"Whoever knowingly alters, destroys, mutilates, conceals, covers up, falsifies, or makes a false entry in any record, document, or tangible object with the intent to impede, obstruct, or influence the investigation or proper administration of any matter within the jurisdiction of any department or agency of the United States or any case filed under Title 11, or in relation to or contemplation of any such matter or case, shall be fined under this title, imprisoned not more than 20 years, or both.

§1520. Destruction of corporate audit records

"(a) (1) Any accountant who conducts an audit of an issuer of securities to which section 10A(a) of the Securities Exchange Act of 1934 (15 U.S.C. 78j–l(a)) applies, shall maintain all audit or review workpapers for a period of 5 years from the end of the fiscal period in which the audit or review was concluded.

Sec. 807 Criminal Penalties for Defrauding Shareholders of Publicly Traded Companies.

(a) In General.—Chapter 63 of title 18, United States Code, is amended by adding at the end the following:

§1348. Securities fraud

"Whoever knowingly executes, or attempts to execute, a scheme or artifice—

"(1) to defraud any person in connection with any security of an issuer with a class of securities registered under section 12 of the Securities Exchange Act of 1934 (15 U.S.C. 78l) or that is required to file reports under section 15(d) of the Securities Exchange Act of 1934 (15 U.S.C. 78o(d)); or

"(2) to obtain, by means of false or fraudulent pretenses, representations, or promises, any money or property in connection with the purchase or sale of any security of an issuer with a class of securities registered under section 12 of the Securities Exchange Act of 1934 (15 U.S.C. 78l) or that is required to file reports under section 15(d) of the Securities Exchange Act of 1934 (15 U.S.C. 78o(d)); shall be fined under this title, or imprisoned not more than 25 years, or both."

Title IX—White-Collar Crime Penalty Enhancements

Sec. 901 Short Title.

This title may be cited as the "White-Collar Crime Penalty Enhancement Act of 2002".

Sec. 906 Corporate Responsibility for Financial Reports.

(a) In General.—Chapter 63 of title 18, United States Code, is amended by inserting after section 1349, as created by this Act, the following:

§1350. *Failure of corporate officers to certify financial reports*

(a) Certification of Periodic Financial Reports.—Each periodic report containing financial statements filed by an issuer with the Securities Exchange Commission pursuant to section 13(a) or 15(d) of the Securities Exchange Act of 1934 (15 U.S.C. 78m(a) or 78o(d)) shall be accompanied by a written statement by the chief executive officer and chief financial officer (or equivalent thereof) of the issuer.

"(b) Content.—The statement required under subsection (a) shall certify that the periodic report containing the financial statements fully complies with the requirements of section 13(a) or 15(d) of the Securities Exchange Act of 1934 (15 U.S.C. 78m or 78o(d)) and that information contained in the periodic report fairly presents, in all material respects, the financial condition and results of operations of the issuer.

"(c) Criminal Penalties.—Whoever—

"(1) certifies any statement as set forth in subsections (a) and (b) of this section knowing that the periodic report accompanying the statement does not comport with all the requirements set forth in this section shall be fined not more than $1,000,000 or imprisoned not more than 10 years, or both; or

"(2) willfully certifies any statement as set forth in subsections (a) and (b) of this section knowing that the periodic report accompanying the statement does not comport with all the requirements set forth in this section shall be fined not more than $5,000,000, or imprisoned not more than 20 years, or both."

(b) Clerical Amendment.—The table of sections at the beginning of chapter 63 of title 18, United States Code, is amended by adding at the end the following:

"1350". Failure of corporate officers to certify financial reports."

Title X—Corporate Tax Returns

Sec. 1001 Sense of the Senate Regarding the Signing of Corporate Tax Returns by Chief Executive Officers.

It is the sense of the Senate that the Federal income tax return of a corporation should be signed by the chief executive officer of such corporation.

Title XI—Corporate Fraud Accountability

Sec. 1101 Short Title.

This title may be cited as the "Corporate Fraud Accountability Act of 2002".

Sec. 1102 Tampering with a Record or Otherwise Impeding an Official Proceeding.

Section 1512 of title 18, United States Code, is amended—

(1) by redesignating subsections (c) through (i) as subsections (d) through (j), respectively; and

(2) by inserting after subsection (b) the following new subsection:

"(c) Whoever corruptly—

"(1) alters, destroys, mutilates, or conceals a record, document, or other object, or attempts to do so, with the intent to impair the object's integrity or availability for use in an official proceeding; or

"(2) otherwise obstructs, influences, or impedes any official proceeding, or attempts to do so,

shall be fined under this title or imprisoned not more than 20 years, or both."

Sec. 1105 Authority of the Commission to Prohibit Persons from Serving as Officers or Directors.

(a) Securities Exchange Act of 1934.—Section 21C of the Securities Exchange Act of 1934 (15 U.S.C. 78u–3) is amended by adding at the end the following:

"(f) Authority of the Commission to Prohibit Persons from Serving as Officers or Directors.—In any cease-and-desist proceeding under subsection (a), the Commission may issue an order to prohibit, conditionally or unconditionally, and permanently or for such period of time as it shall determine, any person who has violated section 10(b) or the rules or regulations thereunder, from acting as an officer or director of any issuer that has a class of securities registered pursuant to section 12, or that is required to file reports pursuant to section 15(d), if the conduct of that person demonstrates unfitness to serve as an officer or director of any such issuer."

(b) Securities Act of 1933.—Section 8A of the Securities Act of 1933 (15 U.S.C. 77h–l) is amended by adding at the end of the following:

"(f) Authority of the Commission to Prohibit Persons from Serving as Officers or Directors.—In any cease-and-desist proceeding under subsection (a), the Commission may issue an order to prohibit, conditionally or unconditionally, and permanently or for such period of time as it shall determine, any person who has violated section 17(a)(1) or the rules or regulations thereunder, from acting as an officer or director of any issuer that has a class of securities registered pursuant to section 12 of the Securities Exchange Act of 1934, or that is required to file reports pursuant to section 15(d) of that Act, if the conduct of that person demonstrates unfitness to serve as an officer or director of any such issuer."

Glossary

abandoned property Property that an owner has discarded with the intent to relinquish his or her rights in it and mislaid or lost property that the owner has given up any further attempts to locate.

abatement If the property the testator leaves is not sufficient to satisfy all the beneficiaries named in a will and there are both general and residuary bequests, the residuary bequest is abated first (i.e., paid last).

absolute priority rule A rule that says a reorganization plan is fair and equitable to an impaired class of unsecured creditors or equity holders if no class below it receives anything in the plan.

acceptance A manifestation of assent by the offeree to the terms of the offer in a manner invited or required by the offer as measured by the objective theory of contracts. (Section 50 of the Restatement (Second) of Contracts.) Occurs when a buyer or lessee takes any of the following actions after a reasonable opportunity to inspect the goods: (1) signifies to the seller or lessor in words or by conduct that the goods are conforming or that the buyer or lessee will take or retain the goods despite their nonconformity or (2) fails to effectively reject the goods within a reasonable time after their delivery or tender by the seller or lessor. Acceptance also occurs if a buyer acts inconsistently with the seller's ownership rights in the goods.

acceptance method The bankruptcy court must approve a plan of reorganization if (1) the plan is in the best interests of each class of claims and interests, (2) the plan is feasible, (3) at least one class of claims votes to accept the plan, and (4) each class of claims and interests is nonimpaired.

accession Occurs when the value of personal property increases because it is added to or improved by natural or manufactured means.

accommodation A shipment that is offered to the buyer as a replacement for the original shipment when the original shipment cannot be filled.

accommodation party A party who signs an instrument and lends his or her name (and credit) to another party to the instrument.

accord An agreement whereby the parties agree to accept something different in satisfaction of the original contract.

accord and satisfaction The settlement of a contract dispute.

accountant malpractice Occurs when the accountant breaches the duty of reasonable care, knowledge, skill, and judgment that he or she owes to a client when providing auditing and other accounting services to the client.

act of monopolizing A required act for there to be a violation of Section 2 of the Sherman Act. Possession of monopoly power without such act does not violate Section 2.

act of state doctrine States that judges of one country cannot question the validity of an act committed by another country within that other country's borders. It is based on the principle that a country has absolute authority over what transpires within its own territory.

action for an accounting A formal judicial proceeding in which the court is authorized to (1) review the partnership and the partners' transactions and (2) award each partner his or her share of the partnership assets.

actus reus "Guilty act"—the actual performance of the criminal act.

ademption A principle that says if a testator leaves a specific devise of property to a beneficiary, but the property is no longer in the estate when the testator dies, the beneficiary receives-nothing.

adequate assurance of performance A party to a sales or lease contract may demand an adequate assurance of performance from the other party if there is an indication that the contract will be breached by that party.

adjudged insane A person who has been adjudged insane by a proper court or administrative agency. A contract entered into by such a person is void.

administrative agencies Agencies that the legislative and executive branches of federal and state governments establish.

administrative dissolution Involuntary dissolution of a corporation that is ordered by the secretary of state if the corporation has failed to comply with certain procedures required by law.

administrative law judge (ALJ) A judge, presiding over administrative proceedings, who decides questions of law and fact concerning the case.

Administrative Procedure Act (APA) An act that establishes certain administrative procedures that federal administrative agencies must follow in conducting their affairs.

administrative subpoena An order that directs the subject of the subpoena to disclose the requested information.

adverse action A denial or revocation of credit or a change in the credit terms offered.

adverse possession When a person who wrongfully possesses someone else's real property obtains title to that property if certain statutory requirements are met.

advertisement A general advertisement is an invitation to make an offer. A specific advertisement is an offer.

affirmative action Policy that provides that certain job preferences will be given to minority or other protected class applicants when an employer makes an employment decision.

AFL-CIO The 1955 combination of the AFL and the CIO.

after-acquired property Property that the debtor acquires after the security agreement is executed.

agency The principal-agent relationship: the fiduciary relationship "which results from the manifestation of consent by one person to another that the other shall act in his behalf and subject to his control, and consent by the other so to act."

agency by ratification An agency that occurs when (1) a person misrepresents him- or herself as another's agent when in fact he or she is not and (2) the purported principal ratifies the unauthorized act.

agency law The large body of common law that governs agency; a mixture of contract law and tort law.

agency shop An establishment where an employee does not have to join the union, but must pay a fee equal to the union dues.

agent A person who has been authorized to sign a negotiable instrument on behalf of another person. The party who agrees to act on behalf of another.

agreement The manifestation by two or more persons of the substance of a contract.

agreement of conversion Document that states the terms for converting an existing business to an LLC.

aiding and abetting the commission of a crime Rendering support, assistance, or encouragement to the commission of a crime; harboring a criminal after he or she has committed a crime.

air pollution Pollution caused by factories, homes, vehicles, and the like that affects the air.

alien corporation A corporation that is incorporated in another country.

alien LLC An LLC that is organized in another country.

allonge A separate piece of paper attached to the instrument on which the indorsement is written.

altered check A check that has been altered without authorization that modifies the legal obligation of a party.

alternative dispute resolution (ADR) Methods of resolving disputes other than litigation.

Americans with Disabilities Act (ADA) of 1990 Imposes obligations on employers and providers of public transportation, telecommunications, and public accommodations to accommodate individuals with disabilities.

annual financial statement A statement provided to the shareholders that contains a balance sheet, an income statement, and a statement of changes in shareholder equity.

annual shareholders' meeting Meeting of the shareholders of a corporation that must be held annually by the corporation to elect directors and to vote on other matters.

answer The defendant's written response to the plaintiff's complaint that is filed with the court and served on the plaintiff.

anti-assignment clause A clause that prohibits the assignment of rights under the contract.

anticipatory breach A breach that occurs when one contracting party informs the other that he or she will not perform his or her contractual duties when due.

anticipatory repudiation The repudiation of a sales or lease contract by one of the parties prior to the date set for performance.

antideficiency statute A statute that prohibits deficiency judgments regarding certain types of mortgages, such as those on residential property.

anti-delegation clause A clause that prohibits the delegation of duties under the contract.

antidilution statutes State laws that allow persons and companies to register trademarks and service marks.

antitrust laws A series of laws enacted to limit anticompetitive behavior in almost all industries, businesses, and professions operating in the United States.

apparent agency Agency that arises when a principal creates the appearance of an agency that in actuality does not exist. Agency that arises when a franchisor creates the appearance that a franchisee is its agent when in fact an actual agency does not exist.

appeal The act of asking an appellate court to overturn a decision after the trial court's final judgment has been entered.

appellant The appealing party in an appeal. Also known as petitioner.

appellate body A panel of seven judges selected from WTO member nations that hears and decides appeals from decisions by the dispute settlement body.

apellee The responding party in an appeal. Also known as respondent.

appropriate bargaining unit The group that a union seeks to represent.

approval clause A clause that permits the assignment of the contract only upon receipt of an obligor's approval.

arbitration A form of ADR in which the parties choose an impartial third party to hear and decide the dispute. A nonjudicial method of dispute resolution whereby a neutral third party decides the case.

arbitration clause A clause in contracts that requires disputes arising out of the contract to be submitted to arbitration. A clause contained in many international contracts that stipulates that any dispute between the parties concerning the performance of the contract will be submitted to an arbitrator or arbitration panel for resolution.

arraignment A hearing during which the accused is brought before a court and is (1) informed of the charges against him or her and (2) asked to enter a plea.

arrest warrant A document for a person's detainment based upon a showing of probable cause that the person committed the crime.

arson Willfully or maliciously burning another's building.

Article 2A (Leases) Article of the UCC that governs lease of goods.

Article 4 of the UCC Establishes the rules and principles that regulate bank deposit and collection procedures.

Article 7 of the UCC An article of the Uniform Commercial Code that provides a detailed statutory scheme for the creation, perfection, and foreclosure on common carriers' and warehouse operators' liens. Article of the Uniform Commercial Code that governs documents of title.

Article 8 of the UCC The article of the UCC that governs transfer of securities.

Article 9 of the UCC An article of the Uniform Commercial Code that governs secured transactions in personal property.

articles of incorporation The basic governing documents of the corporation. These documents must be filed with the secretary of state of the state of incorporation.

articles of organization The formal documents that must be filed at the secretary of state's office of the state of organization of an LLC to form the LLC.

articles of termination Document that is filed with the secretary of state that terminates the LLC as of the date of filing or upon a later effective date specified in the document.

assault The threat of immediate harm or offensive contact or (2) any action that arouses reasonable apprehension of imminent harm. Actual physical contact is unnecessary.

assent Assent to enter into a contract may be manifested in any manner sufficient to show agreement, including express words or conduct of the parties.

assignee The party to whom the right has been transferred. The transferee in an assignment situation. The party to whom rights have been transferred.

assignment The transfer of contractual rights by the obligee to another party. The transfer of rights under a contract. A transfer by a tenant of his or her rights under a lease to another.

assignment and delegation Transfer of both rights and duties under the contract.

assignor The party who transfers the rights. The transferor in an assignment situation. The obligee who transfers the right.

assumption of duties When a delegation of duties contains the term assumption, I assume the duties, or other similar language; the delegatee is legally liable to the obligee for nonperformance.

assumption of the risk A defense a defendant can use against a plaintiff who knowingly and voluntarily enters into or participates in a risky activity that results in injury. A defense in which the defendant must prove that (1) the plaintiff knew and appreciated the risk and (2) the plaintiff voluntarily assumed the risk

Attachment The creditor has an enforceable security interest against the debtor and can satisfy the debt out of the designated collateral.

attempt to commit a crime When a crime is attempted but not completed.

attestation The action of a will being witnessed by two or three objective and competent people.

attorney-client privilege A rule that says a client can tell his or her lawyer anything about the case without fear that the attorney will be called as a witness against the client.

attribution procedure A procedure using codes, algorithms, identifying words or numbers, encryption, callback, or other acknowledgment to verify an authentication of a record.

at-will employees Employees who do not have employment contracts.

at-will LLC An LLC that has no specified term of duration.

auction with reserve Unless expressly stated otherwise, an auction is an auction with reserve; that is, the seller retains the right to refuse the highest bid and withdraw the goods from sale.

auction without reserve An auction in which the seller expressly gives up his or her right to withdraw the goods from sale and must accept the highest bid.

audit The verification of a company's books and records pursuant to federal securities laws, state laws, and stock exchange rules that must be performed by an independent CPA.

authenticate Signing the contract or executing an electronic symbol, sound, or message attached to, included in, or linked with the record.

authorized shares The number of shares provided for in the articles of incorporation.

automatic stay The result of the filing of a voluntary or involuntary petition; the suspension of certain actions by creditors against the debtor or the debtor's property.

backward vertical merger A vertical merger in which the customer acquires the supplier.

bailee A holder of goods who is not a seller or a buyer (e.g., a warehouse or common carrier). A holder of goods who is not a seller or a buyer (e.g., a warehouse).

bailee's rights Depending on the type of bailment, bailees may have the right to (1) exclusive possession of the bailed property, (2) use of the bailed property, and (3) compensation for work done or services provided.

bailment A transaction where an owner transfers his or her personal property to another to be held, stored, delivered, or for some other purpose. Title to the property does not transfer.

bailment at will A bailment without a fixed term; can be terminated at any time by either party.

bailment for a fixed term A bailment that terminates at the end of the term or sooner by mutual consent of the parties.

bailment for the sole benefit of the bailee A gratuitous bailment that benefits only the bailee. The bailee owes a duty of utmost care to protect the bailed property.

bailment for the sole benefit of the bailor A gratuitous bailment that benefits only the bailor. The bailee owes only a duty of slight care to protect the bailed property.

bailor The owner of property in a bailment.

bait and switch A type of deceptive advertising that occurs when a seller advertises the availability of a low-cost discounted item but then pressures the buyer into purchasing more expensive merchandise.

bank check A certified check, a cashier's check, or a traveler's check, the payment for which the bank is solely or primarily liable.

Bankruptcy Code The name given to the Bankruptcy Reform Act of 1978, as amended.

bankruptcy estate An estate created upon the commencement of a Chapter 7 proceeding that includes all the debtor's legal and equitable interests in real, personal, tangible, and intangible property, wherever located, that exist when the petition is filed, minus exempt property.

bargained-for exchange Exchange that parties engage in that leads to an enforceable contract.

battery Unauthorized and harmful or offensive physical contact with another person. Direct physical contact is not necessary.

bearer paper Bearer paper is negotiated by delivery; indorsement is not necessary.

beneficiary A person or organization designated in the will that receives all or a portion of the testator's property at the time of the testator's death. The person who is to receive the life insurance proceeds when the insured dies. Person for whose benefit a trust is created.

bequest A gift of personal property by will. Also known as a legacy.

bilateral contract A contract entered into by way of exchange of promises of the parties; "a promise for a promise."

bill of lading A document of title that is issued by a carrier when goods are received for transportation.

blank indorsement An indorsement that does not specify a particular indorsee. It creates bearer paper.

board of directors A panel of decision makers, the members of which are elected by the shareholders.

bona fide occupational qualification (BFOQ) Employment discrimination based on a protected class (other than race or color) is lawful if it is job related and a business necessity. This exception is narrowly interpreted by the courts.

bond A long-term debt security that is secured by some form of collateral.

breach Failure of a party to perform an obligation in a sales or lease contract.

breach of contract If a contracting party fails to perform an absolute duty owed under a contract.

breach of the duty of care A failure to exercise care or to act as a reasonable person would act.

bribery When one person gives another person money, property, favors, or anything else of value for a favor in return. Often referred to as a payoff or "kickback."

building A structure constructed on land.

building codes State and local statutes that impose specific standards on property owners to maintain and repair leased premises.

burglary Taking personal property from another's home, office, commercial or other type of building.

Business Brief Laws cannot be written in advance to anticipate every dispute that could arise in the future. Therefore, general principles are developed to be applied by courts and juries to individual disputes. This flexibility in the law leads to some uncertainty in predicting results of lawsuits.

business judgment rule A rule that protects the decisions of the board of directors, who act on an informed basis, in good faith, and in the honest belief that the action taken was in the best interests of the corporation and its shareholders. A rule that says directors and officers are not liable to the corporation or its shareholders for honest mistakes of judgement.

buyer in the ordinary course of business A person who in good faith and without knowledge of another's ownership or security interest in goods buys the goods in the ordinary course of business from a person in the business of selling goods of that kind [UCC 1-201(9)].

bylaws A detailed set of rules adopted by the board of directors after the corporation is incorporated that contains provisions for managing the business and the affairs of the corporation.

cancellation The termination of a contract by a contracting party upon the material breach of the contract by the other party. A buyer or lessee may cancel a sales or lease contract if the seller or lessor fails to deliver conforming goods or repudiates the contract or if the buyer or lessee rightfully rejects the goods or justifiably revokes acceptance of the goods.

case brief A summary of each of the following items of a case: 1. Case name and citation 2. Key facts 3. Issue presented 4. Holding of the court 5. Court's reasoning.

cashier's check A check issued by a bank where the customer has paid the bank the amount of the check and a fee. The bank guarantees the payment of the check.

causation A person who commits a negligent act is not liable unless his or her act was the cause of the plaintiff's injuries. The two types of causation that must be proven are (1) causation in fact (actual cause) and (2) proximate cause (legal cause).

causation in fact or actual cause The actual cause of negligence. A person who commits a negligent act is not liable unless causation in fact can be proven.

caveat emptor "Let the buyer beware," the traditional guideline of sales transactions.

certificate of amendment A document that keeps the certificate of limited partnership current.

certificate of authority Formal document that must be issued by the secretary of state of a state before a foreign LLC may conduct business in that state.

certificate of deposit (CD) A two-party negotiable instrument that is a special form of note created when a depositor deposits money at a financial institution in exchange for the institution's promise to pay back the amount of the deposit plus an agreed-upon rate of interest upon the expiration of a set time period agreed upon by the parties.

certificate of interest Document that evidences a member's ownership interest in an LLC.

certificate of limited partnership A document that two or more persons must execute and sign that makes the limited partnership legal and binding.

certificate of partnership A document that a partnership must file with the appropriate state government agency in some states to acknowledge that the partnership exists.

certificate of registration A document permitting a foreign limited partnership to transact business in a foreign state.

certified check A type of check where a bank agrees in advance (certifies) to accept the check when it is presented for payment.

certified public accountant (CPA) An accountant who has met certain educational requirements, has passed the CPA examination, and has had a certain number of years of audit experience.

chain of distribution All manufacturers, distributors, wholesalers, retailers, lessors, and subcomponent manufacturers involved in a transaction.

chain-style franchise The franchisor licenses the franchisee to make and sell its products or distribute services to the public from a retail outlet serving an exclusive territory.

changing conditions defense A price discrimination defense that claims prices were lowered in response to changing conditions in the market for or the marketability of the goods.

Chapter 7 liquidation bankruptcy The most familiar form of bankruptcy; the debtor's nonexempt property is sold for cash, the cash is distributed to the creditors, and any unpaid debts are discharged.

Chapter 11 A bankruptcy method that allows reorganization of the debtor's financial affairs under the supervision of the Bankruptcy Court.

Chapter 13 A rehabilitation form of bankruptcy that permits the courts to supervise the debtor's plan for the payment of unpaid debts by installments.

charging order A document that the court issues against the debtor-partner's partnership interest in order to satisfy a debt.

check An order by the drawer to the drawee bank to pay a specified sum of money from the drawer's checking account to the named payee (or holder). A distinct form of draft drawn on a financial institution and payable on demand.

choice of forum clause Clause in an international contract that designates which nation's court has jurisdiction to hear a case arising out of the contract. Also known as a forum-selection clause.

choice of law clause Clause in an international contract that designates which nation's laws will be applied in deciding a dispute.

closely held corporation A corporation owned by one or a few shareholders.

closing The finalization of a real estate sales transaction that passes title to the property from the seller to the buyer.

codicil A separate document that must be executed to amend a will. It must be executed with the same formalities as a will.

C.O.D. shipment A type of shipment contract where the buyer agrees to pay the shipper cash upon the delivery of the goods.

collateral Security against repayment of the note that lenders sometimes require; can be a car, a house, or other property. The property that is subject to the security interest.

collateral contract A promise where one person agrees to answer for the debts or duties of another person.

collecting bank The depository bank and other banks in the collection process (other than the payor bank).

collective bargaining The act of negotiating contract terms between an employer and the members of a union.

collective bargaining agreement The resulting contract from a collective bargaining procedure.

collision insurance Insurance that a car owner purchases to insure his or her car against risk of loss or damage.

coming and going rule A rule that says a principal is generally not liable for injuries caused by its agents and employees while they are on their way to or from work.

Commerce Clause A clause of the U.S. Constitution that grants Congress the power "to regulate commerce with foreign nations, and among the several states, and with Indian tribes."

commercial impracticability Nonperformance that is excused if an extreme or unexpected development or expense makes it impractical for the promisor to perform.

commercial speech Speech used by businesses, such as advertising. It is subject to time, place, and manner restrictions.

common carrier A firm that offers transportation services to the general public. The bailee. Owes a duty of strict liability to the bailor.

common law Developed by judges who issued their opinions when deciding a case. The principles announced in these cases became precedent for later judges deciding similar cases.

common law of contracts Contract law developed primarily by state courts.

common stock A type of equity security that represents the residual value of the corporation.

common stock certificate A document that represents the common shareholder's investment in the corporation.

common stockholder A person who owns common stock.

comparative negligence A doctrine under which damages are apportioned according to fault. A doctrine that applies to strict liability actions that says a plaintiff who is contributorily negligent for his or her injuries is responsible for a proportional share of the damages.

compensatory damages An award of money intended to compensate a nonbreaching party for the loss of the bargain; they place the nonbreaching party in the same position as if the contract had been fully performed by restoring the "benefit of the bargain." Damages that are generally equal to the difference between the value of the goods as warranted and the actual value of the goods accepted at the time and place of acceptance.

competent party's duty of restitution If a minor has transferred money, property, or other valuables to the competent party before disaffirming the contract, that party must place the minor back into status quo.

complaint The document the plaintiff files with the court and serves on the defendant to initiate a lawsuit.

complete performance Occurs when a party to a contract renders performance exactly as required by the contract; discharges that party's obligations under the contract.

comprehensive insurance A form of property insurance that insures an automobile from loss or damage from causes other than collision.

conciliation A form of mediation in which the parties choose an interested third party to act as the mediator.

concurrent condition A condition that exists when the parties to a contract must render performance simultaneously; each party's absolute duty to perform is conditioned on the other party's absolute duty to perform.

concurrent jurisdiction Jurisdiction shared by two or more courts.

condition A qualification of a promise that becomes a covenant if it is met. There are three types of conditions: conditions precedent, conditions subsequent, and concurrent conditions.

condition precedent based on satisfaction Clause in a contract that reserves the right to a party to pay for the items or services contracted for only if they meet his or her satisfaction.

condition subsequent A condition, if it occurs or doesn't occur, that automatically excuses the performance of an existing contractual duty to perform.

condominium A common form of ownership in a multiple-dwelling building where the purchaser has title to the individual unit and owns the common areas as a tenant in common with the other condominium owners.

confirmation The bankruptcy court's approval of a plan of reorganization.

confusion Occurs if two or more persons commingle fungible goods; title is then acquired by confusion.

conglomerate merger A merger that does not fit into any other category; a merger between firms in totally unrelated businesses.

consequential damages Foreseeable damages that arise from circumstances outside the contract. To be liable for these damages, the breaching party must know or have reason to know that the breach will cause special damages to the other party.

consideration Something of legal value given in exchange for a promise.

consignee The person to whom the bailed goods are to be delivered.

consignment An arrangement where a seller (the consignor) delivers goods to a buyer (the consignee) for sale.

consignor The person shipping the goods. The bailor.

Consolidated Omnibus Budget Reconciliation Act (COBRA) Federal law that permits employees and their beneficiaries to continue their group health insurance after an employee's employment has ended.

consolidation The act of a court to combine two or more separate lawsuits into one lawsuit. Occurs when two or more corporations combine to form an entirely new corporation.

conspicuous A requirement that warranty disclaimers be noticeable to the average person.

Constitution of the United States of America The supreme law of the United States.

constructive trust An equitable trust that is imposed by law to avoid fraud, unjust enrichment, and injustice.

consumer expectation test A test to determine merchantability based on what the average consumer would expect to find in food products.

Consumer Leasing Act (CLA) An amendment to the TILA that extends the TILA's coverage to lease terms in consumer leases.

Consumer Product Safety Act (CPSA) A federal statute that regulates potentially dangerous consumer products and created the Consumer Product Safety Commission.

Consumer Product Safety Commission (CPSC) An independent federal regulatory agency Aempowered to (1) adopt rules and regulations to interpret and enforce the Consumer Product Safety Act. (2) conduct research on safety, and (3) collect data regarding injuries.

consumer protection laws Federal and state statutes and regulations that promote product safety and prohibit abusive, unfair, and deceptive business practices.

contracts contrary to public policy Contracts that have a negative impact on society or that interfere with the public's safety and welfare.

contributory negligence A doctrine that says a plaintiff who is partially at fault for his or her own injury cannot recover against the negligent defendant. A defense that says a person who is injured by a defective product but has been negligent and has contributed to his or her own injuries cannot recover from the defendant.

controlling shareholder A shareholder that owns a sufficient number of shares to control the corporation effectively.

convenant of good faith and fair dealing Under this implied covenant, the parties to a contract not only are held to the express terms of the contract but are also required to act in "good faith" and deal fairly in all respects in obtaining the objective of the contact.

Convention Treaty that is sponsored by an international organization.

conversion of personal property A tort that deprives a true owner of the use and enjoyment of his or her personal property by taking over such property and exercising ownership rights over it.

cooling-off period Requires a union to give an employer at least 60 days' notice before a strike can commence.

cooperative A form of co-ownership of a multiple-dwelling building where a corporation owns the building and the residents own shares in the corporation.

co-ownership When two or more persons own a piece of real property. Also called concurrent ownership.

copyright infringement When a party copies a substantial and material part of the plaintiff's copyrighted work without permission. A copyright holder may recover damages and other remedies against the infringer.

Copyright Revision Act of 1976 Federal statute that (1) establishes the requirements for obtaining a copyright and (2) protects copyrighted works from infringement.

corporate citizenship A theory of responsibility that says a business has a responsibility to do good.

corporate seal A design containing the name of the corporation and the date of incorporation that is imprinted by the corporate secretary using a metal stamp on certain legal documents.

corporation A fictitious legal entity that is created according to statutory requirements.

corporations codes State statutes that regulate the formation, operation, and dissolution of corporations.

cost justification defense A defense in Section 2(a) action that provides that a seller's price discrimination is not unlawful if the price differential is due to "differences in the cost of manufacture, sale, or delivery" of the product.

counteroffer A response by an offeree that contains terms and conditions different from or in addition to those of the offer. A counteroffer terminates an offer.

Court of Appeals for the Federal Circuit A court of appeals in Washington, DC, that has special appellate jurisdiction to review the decisions of the Claims Court, the Patent and Trademark Office, and the Court of International Trade.

Court of Chancery Court that granted relief based on fairness. Also called equity court.

covenant An unconditional promise to perform.

covenant of good faith and fair dealing Under this implied covenant, the parties to a contract not only are held to the express terms of the contract but also are required to act in "good faith" and deal fairly in all respects in obtaining the objective of the contract.

covenant of quiet enjoyment A covenant that says a landlord may not interfere with the tenant's quiet and peaceful possession, use, and enjoyment of the leased premises.

cover Right of a buyer or lessee to purchase or lease substitute goods if a seller or lessor fails to make delivery of the goods or repudiates the contract or if the buyer or lessee rightfully rejects the goods or justifiably revokes their acceptance. The licensee's right to engage in a commercially reasonable substitute transaction after the licensor has breached the contract.

cram down method A method of confirmation of a plan of reorganization where the court forces an impaired class to participate in the plan of reorganization.

crashworthiness doctrine A doctrine that says automobile manufacturers are under a duty to design automobiles so they take into account the possibility of harm from a person's body striking something inside the automobile in the case of a car accident.

credit report Information about a person's credit history that can be secured from a credit bureau.

creditor The lender in a credit transaction.

creditor beneficiary Original creditor who becomes a beneficiary under the debtor's new contract with another party.

creditor beneficiary contract A contract that arises in the following situation: (1) a debtor borrows money, (2) the debtor signs an agreement to pay back the money plus interest, (3) the debtor sells the item to a third party before the loan is paid off, and (4) the third party promises the debtor that he or she will pay the remainder of the loan to the creditor.

creditor–debtor relationship Created when a customer deposits money into the bank; the customer is the creditor and the bank is the debtor.

creditors' committee The creditors holding the seven largest unsecured claims are usually appointed to the creditors' committee. Representatives of the committee appear at Bankruptcy Court hearings, participate in the negotiation of a plan of reorganization, assert objections to proposed plans and so on.

crime A crime is a violation of a statute for which the government imposes a punishment.

criminal conspiracy When two or more persons enter into an agreement to commit a crime and an overt act is taken to further the crime.

criminal fraud Obtaining title to property through deception or trickery. Also known as false pretenses or deceit.

critical legal thinking The process of specifying the issue presented by a case, identifying the key facts in the case and applicable law, and then applying the law to the facts to come to a conclusion that answers the issue presented.

cross-complaint Filed by the defendant against the plaintiff to seek damages or some other remedy.

crossover worker A person who does not honor a strike who either (1) chooses not to strike or (2) returns to work after joining the strikers for a time.

crown jewel A valuable asset of the target corporation's that the tender offeror particularly wants to acquire in the tender offer.

cruel and unusual punishment A clause of the Eighth Amendment that protects criminal defendants from torture or other abusive punishment.

cumulative voting A shareholder can accumulate all of his or her votes and vote them all for one candidate or split them among several candidates.

cure An opportunity to repair or replace defective or nonconforming goods.

custom The second source of international law, created through consistent, recurring practices between two or more nations over a period of time that have become recognized as binding.

damages A buyer or lessee may recover damages from a seller or lessor who fails to deliver the goods or repudiates the contract; damages are measured as the difference between the contract price (or original rent) and the market price (or rent) at the time the buyer or lessee learned of the breach.

damages for accepted nonconforming goods A buyer or lessee may accept nonconforming goods and recover the damages caused by the breach from the seller or lessor or deduct the damages from any part of the purchase price or rent still due under the contract.

danger invites rescue doctrine Doctrine that provides that a rescuer who is injured while going to someone's rescue can sue the person who caused the dangerous situation.

debenture A long-term unsecured debt instrument that is based on the corporation's general credit standing.

debt collector An agent who collects debts for other parties.

debt securities Securities that establish a debtor-creditor relationship in which the corporation borrows money from the investor to whom the debt security is issued.

debtor The borrower in a credit transaction.

debtor-in-possession A debtor who is left in place to operate the business during the reorganization proceeding.

declaration of duties If the delegatee has not assumed the duties under a contract, the delegatee is not legally liable to the obligee for nonperformance.

decree of judicial dissolution A decree of dissolution that is granted to a partner whenever it is not reasonably practical to carry on the business in conformity with the limited partnership agreement.

deed A writing that describes a person's ownership interest in a piece of real property.

deed of trust An instrument that gives the creditor a security interest in the debtor's property that is pledged as collateral.

defamation of character False statement(s) made by one person about another. In court, the plaintiff must prove that (1) the defendant made an untrue statement of fact about the plaintiff and (2) the statement was intentionally or accidentally published to a third party.

default Failure to make scheduled payments when due, bankruptcy of the debtor, breach of the warranty of ownership as to the collateral, and other events defined by the parties to constitute default.

defect Something wrong, inadequate, or improper in manufacture, design, packaging, warning, or safety measures of a product.

defect in design A defect that occurs when a product is improperly designed.

defect in manufacture A defect that occurs when the manufacturer fails to (1) properly assemble a product, (2) properly test a product, or (3) adequately check the quality of the product.

defect in packaging A defect that occurs when a product has been placed in packaging that is insufficiently tamperproof.

defective formation Occurs when (1) a certificate of limited partnership is not properly filed, (2) there are defects in a certificate that is filed, or (3) some other statutory requirement for the creation of a limited partnership is not met.

deferred posting rule A rule that allows banks to fix an afternoon hour of 2:00 P.M. or later as a cutoff hour for the purpose of processing items.

deficiency judgment Judgment of a court that permits a secured lender to recover other property or income from a defaulting debtor if the collateral is insufficient to repay the unpaid loan. A judgment that allows a secured creditor to successfully bring a separate legal action to recover a deficiency from the debtor entitles the secured creditor to recover the amount of the judgment from the debtor's other property.

delegatee The party to whom the duty has been transferred.

delegation doctrine A doctrine that says when an administrative agency is created, it is delegated certain powers; the agency can only use those legislative, judicial, and executive powers that are delegated to it.

delegation of duties A transfer of contractual duties by the obligor to another party for performance.

delegator The obligor who transferred his or her duty.

demand instrument An instrument payable on demand.

demand note A note payable on demand.

deponent Party who gives his or her deposition.

deposition Oral testimony given by a party or witness prior to trial. The testimony is given under oath and is transcribed.

depository bank The bank where the payee or holder has an account.

derivative lawsuit A lawsuit a shareholder brings against an offending party on behalf of the corporation when the corporation fails to bring the lawsuit.

destination contract A sales contract that requires the seller to deliver conforming goods to a specific destination. The seller bears the risk of loss during transportation. A contract that requires the seller to deliver the goods either to the buyer's place of business or to another destination specified in the sales contract.

devise A gift of real estate by will.

direct lawsuit A lawsuit that a shareholder can bring against the corporation to enforce his or her personal rights as a shareholder.

disability insurance Insurance that provides a monthly income to an insured who is disabled and cannot work.

disaffirmance The act of a minor to rescind a contract under the infancy doctrine. Disaffirmance may be done orally, in writing, or by the minor's conduct.

discharge Actions or events that relieve certain parties from liability on negotiable instruments. There are three methods of discharge: (1) payment of the instrument; (2) cancellation; and (3) impairment of the right of recourse. The termination of the legal duty of a debtor to pay debts that remain unpaid upon the completion of a bankruptcy proceeding. Creditors' claims that are not included in a Chapter 11 reorganization are discharged. A discharge is granted to a debtor in a Chapter 13 consumer debt adjustment bankruptcy only after all the payments under the plan are completed by the debtor.

discharge in bankruptcy A real defense against the enforcement of a negotiable instrument; bankruptcy law is intended to relieve debtors of burdensome debts, including negotiable instruments.

disclosure statement A statement that must contain adequate information about the proposed plan of reorganization that is supplied to the creditors and equity holders.

discovery A legal process during which both parties engage in various activities to discover facts of the case from the other party and witnesses prior to trial.

dishonored Occurs when an instrument has been presented for payment and payment has been refused.

disparate impact discrimination Occurs when an employer discriminates against an entire protected class. An example would be where a facially neutral employment practice or rule causes an adverse impact on a protected class.

disparate treatment discrimination Occurs when an employer discriminates against a specific individual because of his or her race, color, national origin, sex, or religion.

disposition of collateral If a secured creditor repossesses collateral upon a debtor's default, he or she may sell, lease, or otherwise dispose of it in a commercially reasonable manner.

disposition of goods A seller or lessor who is in possession of goods at the time the buyer or lessee breaches or repudiates the contract may in good faith resell, release, or otherwise dispose of the goods in a commercially reasonable manner and recover damages, including incidental damages, from the buyer or lessee.

dispute settlement body A board comprised of one representative from each WTO member nation that reviews panel reports.

dissension When an individual director opposes the action taken by the majority of the board of directors.

dissenting shareholder appraisal rights Shareholders who object to a proposed merger, share exchange, or sale or lease of all or substantially all of the property of a corporation have a right to have their shares valued by the court and receive cash payment of this value from the corporation.

dissolution "The change in the relation of the partners caused by any partner ceasing to be associated in the carrying on of the business" [UPA § 29].

distinctive A brand name that is unique and fabricated.

distribution of assets Upon the winding-up of a dissolved partnership, the assets of the partnership are distributed in the following order [UPA § 40(b)]: (1) Creditors (except partners who are creditors), (2) Creditor-partners, (3) Capital contributions, (4) Profits.

distribution of property Nonexempt property of the bankruptcy estate must be distributed to the debtor's secured and unsecured creditors pursuant to the statutory priority established by the Bankruptcy Code.

distributional interest A member's ownership interest in an LLC that entitles the member to receive distributions of money and property from the LLC. The ownership interest that a member has in an LLC.

distributorship franchise The franchisor manufactures a product and licenses a retail franchisee to distribute the product to the public.

diversity of citizenship A case between (1) citizens of different states, (2) a citizen of a state and a citizen or subject of a foreign country, and (3) a citizen of a state and a foreign country where a foreign country is the plaintiff.

dividend Distribution of profits of the corporation to shareholders.

division of markets When competitors agree that each will serve only a designated portion of the market.

doctrine of sovereign immunity States that countries are granted immunity from suits in courts of other countries.

doctrine of strict liability in tort A tort doctrine that makes manufacturers, distributors, wholesalers, retailers, and others in the chain of distribution of a defective product liable for the damages caused by the defect irrespective of fault.

document of title An actual piece of paper, such as warehouse receipt or bill of lading, that is required in some transactions of pick up and delivery. A negotiable instrument developed to represent the interests of the different parties in a transaction that uses storage or transportation between the parties.

domain name A unique name that identifies an individual's or company's Web site.

domestic corporation A corporation in the state in which it was formed.

domestic limited partnership A limited partnership in the state in which it was formed.

domestic LLC An LLC in the state in which it is organized.

donee A person who receives a gift.

donee beneficiary The third party on whom the benefit is to be conferred.

donee beneficiary contract A contract entered into with the intent to confer a benefit or gift on an intended third party.

donor A person who gives a gift.

double jeopardy clause A clause of the Fifth Amendment that protects persons from being tried twice for the same crime.

draft A three-party instrument that is an unconditional written order by one party that orders the second party to pay money to a third party.

Dram Shop Act Statute that makes taverns and bartenders liable for injuries caused to or by patrons who are served too much alcohol.

drawee of a check The bank where the drawer has his or her account.

drawee of a draft The party who must pay the money stated in the draft. Also called the acceptor of a draft.

drawer of a check The checking account holder and writer of the check.

drawer of a draft The party who writes the order for a draft.

dual-purpose mission An errand or other act that a principal requests of an agent while the agent is on his or her own personal business.

due diligence defense A defense to a Section 11 action that, if proven, makes the defendant not liable.

Due Process Clause A clause that provides that no person shall be deprived of "life, liberty, or property" without due process of the law.

duress Occurs where one party threatens to do a wrongful act unless the other party enters into a contract.

duty not to willfully or wantonly injure The duty an owner owes a trespasser to prevent intentional injury or harm to the trespasser when the trespasser is on his or her premises.

duty of accountability A duty that an agent owes to maintain an accurate accounting of all transactions undertaken on the principal's behalf.

duty of care The obligation we all owe each other not to cause any unreasonable harm or risk of harm. The obligation partners owe to use the same level of care and skill that a reasonable person in the same position would use in the same circumstances. A breach of the duty of care is negligence. A duty owed by a member of a member-managed LLC and a manager of a manager-managed LLC to not engage in (1) a known violation of law, (2) intentional conduct, (3) reckless conduct, or (4) grossly negligent conduct that injures the LLC. A duty that corporate directors and officers have to use care and diligence when acting on behalf of the corporation.

duty of loyalty A duty owed by a member of a member-managed LLC and a manager of a manager-managed LLC to be honest in his or her dealings with the LLC and to not act adversely to the interests of the LLC. A duty that a partner owes not to act adversely to the interests of the partnership. A duty that directors and officers have not to act adversely to the interests of the corporation and to subordinate their personal interests to those of the corporation and its shareholders.

duty of notification An agent's duty to notify the principal of information he or she learns from a third party or other source that is important to the principal.

duty of obedience A duty that partners must adhere to the provisions of the partnership agreement and the decisions of the partnership. A duty that directors and officers of a corporation have to act within the authority conferred upon them by the state corporation statute, the articles of incorporation, the corporate bylaws, and the resolutions adopted by the board of directors.

duty of ordinary care The duty an owner owes an invitee or a licensee to prevent injury or harm when the invitee or licensee steps on the owner's premises. Collecting banks are required to exercise ordinary care in presenting and sending checks for collection.

duty of performance An agent's duty to a principal that includes (1) performing the lawful duties expressed in the contract and (2) meeting the standards of reasonable care, skill, and diligence implicit in all contracts.

duty of reasonable care The duty that a reasonable bailee in like circumstances would owe to protect the bailed property.

duty of slight care A duty not to be grossly negligent in caring for something in one's responsibility.

duty of strict liability A duty that common carriers owe that says if the goods are lost, damaged, destroyed, or stolen, the common carrier is liable even if it was not at fault for the loss.

duty of utmost care A duty of care that goes beyond ordinary care that says common carriers and innkeepers have a responsibility to provide security to their passengers or guests.

duty to compensate A duty that a principal owes to pay an agreed-upon amount to the agent either upon the completion of the agency or at some other mutually agreeable time.

duty to cooperate A duty that a principal owes to cooperate with and assist the agent in the performance of the agent's duties and the accomplishment of the agency.

duty to indemnify A duty that a principal owes to protect the agent for losses the agent suffered during the agency because of the principal's misconduct.

duty to inform A duty a partner owes to inform his or her co-partners of all information he or she possesses that is relevant to the affairs of the partnership.

duty to reimburse A duty that a principal owes to repay money to the agent if the agent spent his or her own money during the agency on the principal's behalf.

easement A right to use someone else's land without owning or leasing it. A given or required right to make limited use of someone else's land without owning or leasing it.

easement appurtenant A situation created when the owner of one piece of land is given an easement over an adjacent piece of land.

easement in gross An easement that authorizes a person who does not own adjacent land to use another's land.

e-commerce The sale of goods and services by computer over the Internet.

economic duress Occurs when one party to a contract refuses to perform his or her contractual duties unless the other party pays an increased price, enters into a second contract with the threatening party, or undertakes a similar action.

electronic mail (e-mail) Electronic written communication between individuals using computers connected to the Internet.

elements of a bailment The following three elements are necessary to create a bailment: (1) personal property, (2) delivery of possession, and (3) a bailment agreement.

emancipation When a minor voluntarily leaves home and lives apart from his or her parents.

embezzlement The fraudulent conversion of property by a person to whom that property was entrusted.

eminent domain Power of the government to acquire private property for public purposes. The taking of private property by the government for public use, provided just compensation is paid to the private property holder.

Employee Retirement Income Security Act (ERISA) A federal act designed to prevent fraud and other abuses associated with private pension funds.

employer-employee relationship A relationship that results when an employer hires an employee to perform some form of physical service.

employer lockout Act of the employer to prevent employees from entering the work premises when the employer reasonably anticipates a strike.

employment relationships (1) Employer–employee. (2) principal–agent, and (3) principal–independent contractor.

endorsement An addition to an insurance policy that modifies it.

engagement A formal entrance into a contract between a client and an accountant.

entity theory A theory that holds that partnerships are separate legal entities that can hold title to personal and real property, transact business in the partnership name, sue in the partnership name, and the like.

entrepreneur A person who forms and operates a new business either by him- or herself or with others.

entrustment rule: buyer in the ordinary course of business A person who in good faith and without knowledge that the sale violates the ownership or security interests of a third party buys the goods in the ordinary course of business from a person in the business of selling goods of that kind. A buyer in the ordinary course of business takes the goods free of any third-party security interest in the goods.

enumerated powers Certain powers delegated to the federal government by the states.

Environmental Protection Agency (EPA) An administrative agency created by Congress in 1970 to coordinate the implementation and enforcement of the federal environmental protection laws.

Equal Access to Justice Act An act that was enacted to protect persons from harassment by federal administrative agencies.

Equal Credit Opportunity Act (ECOA) A federal statute that prohibits discrimination in the extension of credit based on sex, marital status, race, color, national origin, religion, age, or receipt of income from public assistance programs.

equal dignity rule A rule that says that agents' contracts to sell property covered by the Statute of Frauds must be in writing to be enforceable.

Equal Employment Opportunity Commission (EEOC) The federal administrative agency responsible for enforcing most federal antidiscrimination laws.

equal opportunity in employment The right of all employees and job applicants (1) to be treated without discrimination and (2) to be able to sue employers if they are discriminated against.

Equal Pay Act of 1963 Protects both sexes from pay discrimination based on sex; extends to jobs that require equal skill, equal effort, equal responsibility, and similar working conditions.

Equal Protection Clause A clause that provides that a state cannot "deny to any person within its jurisdiction the equal protection of the laws."

equity A doctrine that permits judges to make decisions based on fairness, equality, moral rights, and natural law.

equity securities Representation of ownership rights to the corporation. Also called stocks.

Establishment Clause A clause to the First Amendment that prohibits the government from either establishing a state religion or promoting one religion over another.

estate Ownership rights in real property; the bundle of legal rights that the owner has to possess, use, and enjoy the property.

estate pour autre vie A life estate measured in the life of a third party.

ethical fundamentalism When a person looks to an outside source for ethical rules or commands.

ethical relativism A moral theory that holds that individuals must decide what is ethical based on their own feelings as to what is right or wrong.

ethics A set of moral principles or values that governs the conduct of an individual or a group.

European Court of Justice The Judicial branch of the European Union, located in Luxembourg. It has jurisdiction to enforce European Union law.

European Union (Common Market) Comprises many countries of Western Europe; created to promote peace and security plus economic, social, and cultural development.

exclusionary rule A rule that says evidence obtained from an unreasonable search and seizure can generally be prohibited from introduction at a trial or administrative proceeding against the person searched.

exclusive agency contract A contract a principal and agent enter into that says the principal cannot employ any agent other than the exclusive agent.

exclusive jurisdiction Jurisdiction held by only one court.

exclusive license A license that grants the licensee exclusive rights to use informational rights for a specified duration.

exculpatory clause A contractual provision that relieves one (or both) of the parties to the contract from tort liability for ordinary negligence.

executed contract A contract that has been fully performed on both sides; a completed contract.

executive branch The part of the government that consists of the President and Vice President.

executive order An order issued by a member of the executive branch of the government.

executive powers Powers that administrative agencies are granted, such as the investigation and prosecution of possible violations of statutes, administrative rules, and administrative orders.

executory contract A contract that has not been fully performed. With court approval, executory contracts may be rejected by a debtor in bankruptcy.

exempt property Property that may be retained by the debtor pursuant to federal or state law; debtor's property that does not become part of the bankruptcy estate.

express agency An agency that occurs when a principal and an agent expressly agree to enter into an agency agreement with each other.

express authorization A stipulation in the offer that says the acceptance must be by a specified means of communication.

express contract An agreement that is expressed in written or oral words.

express partnership General partnership created by words, either verbal or written.

express powers Powers given to a corporation by (1) the U.S. Constitution, (2) state constitutions, (3) federal statutes, (4) state statutes, (5) articles of incorporation, (6) bylaws, and (7) resolutions of the board of directors.

express trust A trust created voluntarily by the settlor.

express warranty Any affirmation of fact or promise by the licensor about the quality of its software or information. A warranty that is created when a seller or lessor makes an affirmation that the goods he or she is selling or leasing meet certain standards of quality, description, performance, or condition.

extortion Threat to expose something about another person unless that other person gives money or property. Often referred to as "blackmail."

extradition Sending a person back to a country for criminal prosecution.

extreme duress Extreme duress, but not ordinary duress, is a real defense against enforcement of a negotiable instrument.

failure to provide adequate instructions A defect that occurs when a manufacturer does not provide detailed directions for safe assembly and use of a product.

failure to warn A defect that occurs when a manufacturer does not place a warning on the packaging of products that could cause injury if the danger is unknown.

Fair Credit and Charge Card Disclosure Act of 1988 An amendment to the TILA that requires disclosure of certain credit terms on credit- and charge-card solicitations and applications.

Fair Credit Reporting Act (FCRA) An amendment to the TILA that protects customers who are subjects of a credit report by setting out guidelines for credit bureaus.

Fair Debt Collection Practices Act (FDCPA) An act enacted in 1977 that protects consumer-debtors from abusive, deceptive, and unfair practices used by debt collectors.

Fair Labor Standards Act (FLSA) A federal act enacted in 1938 to protect workers; prohibits child labor and establishes minimum wage and overtime pay requirements.

Fair Packaging and Labeling Act A federal statute that requires the labels on consumer goods to identify the product; the manufacturer, processor, or packager of the product and its address; the net quantity of the contents of the package; and the quantity of each serving.

fair price rule A rule that says any increase in price paid for shares tendered must be offered to all shareholders, even those who have previously tendered their shares.

fair use doctrine A doctrine that permits certain limited use of a copyright by someone other than the copyright holder without the permission of the copyright holder.

false imprisonment The intentional confinement or restraint of another person without authority or justification and without that person's consent.

federal administrative agencies Administrative agencies that are part of the executive or legislative branch of government.

Federal Insurance Contributions Act (FICA) A federal act that says employees and employers must make contributions into the Social Security fund.

Federal Patent Statute of 1952 Federal statute that establishes the requirements for obtaining a patent and protects patented inventions from infringement.

federal question A case arising under the U.S. Constitution, treaties, or federal statutes and regulations.

Federal Reserve System A system of 12 regional Federal Reserve banks that assist banks in the collection of checks.

Federal Trade Commission (FTC) Federal government agency empowered to enforce federal franchising rules. Federal administrative agency empowered to enforce the Federal Trade Commission Act and other federal consumer protection statutes.

Federal Unemployment Tax Act (FUTA) A federal act that requires employers to pay unemployment taxes; unemployment compensation is paid to workers who are temporarily unemployed.

federalism The U.S. form of government; the federal government and the 50 state governments share powers.

fee simple absolute A type of ownership of real property that grants the owner the fullest bundle of legal rights that a person can hold in real property.

fee simple defeasible A type of ownership of real property that grants the owner all the incidents of a fee simple absolute except that it may be taken away if a specified condition occurs or does not occur.

felony The most serious type of crime; inherently evil crime. Most crimes against the person and some business-related crimes are felonies.

fictitious payee rule A rule that says that a drawer or maker is liable on a forged or unauthorized indorsement of a fictitious payee.

fiduciary duty Duty of loyalty, honesty, integrity, trust, and confidence owed by directors and officers to their corporate employers. The duty the directors of a corporation owe to act carefully and honestly when acting on behalf of the corporation.

final order rule A rule that says the decision of an administrative agency must be final before judicial review can be sought.

final prospectus A final version of the prospectus that must be delivered by the issuer to the investor prior to or at the time of confirming a sale or sending a security to a purchaser.

final settlement Occurs when the payor bank (1) pays the check in cash, (2) settles for the check without having a right to revoke the settlement, or (3) fails to dishonor the check within certain statutory time periods.

finance lease A three-party transaction consisting of the lessor, the lessee, and the supplier.

financing statement A document filed by a secured creditor with the appropriate government office that constructively notifies the world of his or her security interest in personal property.

fixed amount A requirement of a negotiable instrument that ensures that the value of the instrument can be determined with certainty.

fixed amount of money A negotiable instrument must contain a promise or order to pay a fixed amount of money.

fixtures Goods that are affixed to real estate so as to become part thereof.

fixtures Personal property that is permanently affixed to the real property, such as built-in cabinets in a house.

floating lien A security interest in property that was not in the possession of the debtor when the security agreement was executed; includes after-acquired property, future advances, and sale proceeds.

Food and Drug Administration (FDA) Federal administrative agency that administers and enforces the federal Food, Drug, and Cosmetic Act (FDCA) and other federal consumer protection laws.

Food, Drug, and Cosmetic Act (FDCA) A federal statute enacted in 1938 that provides the basis for the regulation of much of the testing, manufacture, distribution, and sale of foods, drugs, cosmetics, and medicinal products.

Foreclosure Legal procedure by which a secured creditor causes the judicial sale of the secured real estate to pay a defaulted loan.

Foreign Commerce Clause Clause of the U.S. Constitution that vests Congress with the power "to regulate commerce with foreign nations."

foreign corporation A corporation in any state or jurisdiction other than the one in which it was formed.

foreign limited partnership A limited partnership in all other states than the one in which it was formed.

foreign LLC An LLC in any state other than the one in which it is organized.

Foreign Sovereign Immunities Act Exclusively governs suits against foreign nations that are brought in federal or state courts in the United States; codifies the principle of qualified or restricted immunity.

foreign substance test A test to determine merchantability based on foreign objects that are found in food.

foreseeability standard A rule that an accountant is liable for negligence to third parties who are foreseeable users of the client's financial statements. Provides the broadest standard for holding accountants liable to third parties for negligence.

forged indorsement The forged signature of a payee or holder on a negotiable instrument.

forged instrument A check with a forged drawer's signature on it.

forgery Fraudulently making or altering a written document that affects the legal liability of another person. A real defense against the enforcement of a negotiable instrument; the unauthorized signature of a maker, drawer, or indorser.

formal contract A contract that requires a special form or method of creation.

forum-selection clause Contract provision that designates a certain court to hear any dispute concerning nonperformance of the contract.

forward vertical merger A vertical merger in which the supplier acquires the customer.

four legals Four notices or actions that prevent the payment of a check if they are received by the payor bank before it has finished its process of posting the check for payment.

Fourteenth Amendment Amendment that was added to the U.S. Constitution in 1868. It contains the Due Process, Equal Protection, and Privileges and Immunities clauses.

franchise Established when one party licenses another party to use the franchisor's trade name, trademarks, commercial symbols, patents, copyrights, and other property in the distribution and selling of goods and services.

franchise agreement An agreement that the franchisor and the franchisee enter into that sets forth the terms and conditions of the franchise.

fraud by concealment Occurs when one party takes specific action to conceal a material fact from another party.

fraud in the inception Occurs if a person is deceived as to the nature of his or her act and does not know what he or she is signing. A real defense against the enforcement of a negotiable instrument; a person has been deceived into signing a negotiable instrument thinking that it is something else.

fraud in the inducement Occurs when the party knows what he or she is signing, but has been fraudulently induced to enter into the contract. A personal defense against the enforcement of a negotiable instrument; a wrongdoer makes a false statement to another person to lead that person to enter into a contract with the wrongdoer.

fraudulent transfer Occurs when (1) a debtor transfers property to a third person within one year before the filing of a petition in bankruptcy and (2) the transfer was made by the debtor with an intent to hinder, delay, or defraud creditors.

Free Exercise Clause A clause to the First Amendment that prohibits the government from interfering with the free exercise of religion in the United States.

Freedom of Information Act An act that was enacted to give the public access to documents in the possession of federal administrative agencies. There are many exceptions to disclosure.

freedom of speech The right to engage in oral, written, and symbolic speech protected by the First Amendment.

freehold estate An estate where the owner has a present possessory interest in the real property.

fresh start The goal of federal bankruptcy law: To discharge the debtor from burdensome debts and allow him or her to begin again.

frolic and detour When an agent does something during the course of his employment to further his own interests rather than the principal's.

frustration of purpose A doctrine which excuses the performance of contractual obligations if (1) the object or benefit of a contract is made worthless to a promisor, (2) both parties knew what the purpose was, and (3) the act that frustrated the purpose was unforeseeable.

FTC franchise rule A rule set out by the FTC that requires franchisors to make full presale disclosures to prospective franchisees.

future advances Personal property of the debtor that is designated as collateral for future loans from a line of credit.

future goods Goods not yet in existence (ungrown crops, unborn stock animals).

future interest The interest that the grantor retains for him- or herself or a third party.

gambling statutes Statutes that make certain forms of gambling illegal.

gap-filling rule A rule that says an open term can be "read into" a contract.

general duty A duty that an employer has to provide a work environment "free from recognized hazards that are causing or are likely to cause death or serious physical harm to his employees."

general gift Gift that does not identify the specific property from which the gift is to be made.

general partners Partners in a limited partnership who invest capital, manage the business, and are personally liable for partnership debts.

general partnership An association of two or more persons to carry on as co-owners of a business for profit [UPA § 6(1)].

general principles of law The third source of international law, consisting of principles of law recognized by civilized nations. These are principles of law that are common to the national law of the parties to the dispute.

general-jurisdiction trial court A court that hears cases of a general nature that are not within the jurisdiction of limited-jurisdiction trial courts. Testimony and evidence at trial are recorded and stored for future reference.

generally accepted accounting principles (GAAPs) Standards for the preparation and presentation of financial statements.

generally accepted auditing standards (GAASs) Standards for the methods and procedures that must be used to conduct audits.

generally known dangers A defense that acknowledges that certain products are inherently dangerous and are known to the general population to be so.

general-purpose clause A clause often included in the articles of incorporation that authorizes the corporation to engage in any activity permitted corporations by law.

generic name A term for a mark that has become a common term for a product line or type of service and therefore has lost its trademark protection.

genuineness of assent The requirement that a party's assent to a contract be genuine.

gift A transfer of property from one person to another without exchange of money. A voluntary transfer of title to property without payment of consideration by the donee. To be a valid gift, three elements must be shown: (1) donative intent, (2) delivery, and (3) acceptance.

gift *causa mortis* A gift that is made in contemplation of death.

gift *inter vivos* A gift made during a person's lifetime that is an irrevocable present transfer of ownership.

gift promise An unenforceable promise because it lacks consideration.

good faith Honesty in fact in the conduct or transaction concerned. The good faith test is subjective.

good faith purchaser for value A person to whom good title can be transferred from a person with voidable title. The real owner cannot reclaim goods from a good faith purchaser for value.

good faith subsequent lessee A person to whom a lease interest can be transferred from a person with voidable title. The real owner cannot reclaim the goods from the subsequent lessee until the lease expires.

Good Samaritan law Statute that relieves medical professionals from liability for ordinary negligence when they stop and render aid to victims in emergency situations.

good title Title that is free from any encumbrances or other defects that are not disclosed but would affect the value of the property.

goods Tangible things that are movable at the time of their identification to the contract.

government contractor defense A defense that says a contractor who was provided specifications by the government is not liable for any defect in the product that occurs as a result of those specifications.

Government in the Sunshine Act An act that was enacted to open certain federal administrative agency meetings to the public.

grace period A period of time after the actual expiration date of a payment but during which the insured can still pay an overdue premium without penalty.

grantee The party to whom an interest in real property is transferred.

grantor The party who transfers an ownership interest in real property.

greenmail The purchase by a target corporation of its stock from an actual or perceived tender offeror at a premium.

group boycott When two or more competitors at one level of distribution agree not to deal with others at another level of distribution.

group insurance plan An insurance plan that is sold to all the members of a single group, often all the employees of one employer.

guaranteeing collection A form of accommodation where the accommodation party guarantees collection of a negotiable instrument; the accommodation party is secondarily liable on the instrument.

guaranteeing payment A form of accommodation where the accommodation party guarantees payment of a negotiable instrument; the accommodation party is primarily liable on the instrument.

guarantor The person who agrees to pay the debt if the primary debtor does not. The third person who agrees to be liable in a guaranty arrangement.

guaranty arrangement An arrangement where a third party promises to be secondarily liable for the payment of another's debt.

guaranty contract The contract between the guarantor and the original creditor.

guest statute Statute that provides that if a driver of a vehicle voluntarily and without compensation gives a ride to another person, the driver is not liable to the passenger for injuries caused by the driver's ordinary negligence.

hardship discharge A discharge granted if (1) the debtor fails to complete the payments due to unforeseeable circumstances, (2) the unsecured creditors have been paid as much as they would have been paid in a Chapter 7 liquidation proceeding, and (3) it is not practical to modify the plan.

Hart-Scott-Rodino Antitrust Improvement Act Requires certain firms to notify the FTC and the Justice Department in advance of a proposed merger. Unless the government challenges the proposed merger within 30 days, the merger may proceed.

hazardous waste Solid waste that may cause or significantly contribute to an increase in mortality or serious illness or pose a hazard to human health or the environment if improperly managed.

health insurance Purchased to help cover the costs of medical treatment, surgery, or hospital care.

holder What the transferee becomes if a negotiable instrument has been transferred by negotiation. A person who is in possession of a negotiable instrument that is drawn, issued, or indorsed to him or his order, or to bearer, or in blank.

holder in due course (HDC) A holder who takes a negotiable instrument for value, in good faith, and without notice that it is defective or is overdue.

holographic will Will that is entirely handwritten and signed by the testator.

homeowners policy A comprehensive insurance policy that includes coverage for the risks covered by a fire insurance policy as well as personal liability insurance.

honor Payment of a drawer's properly drawn check by the drawee bank.

horizontal merger A merger between two or more companies that compete in the same business and geographical market.

horizontal restraint of trade A restraint of trade that occurs when two or more competitors at the same level of distribution enter into a contract, combination, or conspiracy to restrain trade.

hung jury A jury that cannot come to a unanimous decision about the defendant's guilt. The government may choose to retry the case.

identification of goods Distinguishing the goods named in the contract from the seller's or lessor's other goods.

illegal consideration A promise to refrain from doing an illegal act. Such a promise will not support a contract.

illusory promise A contract into which both parties enter, but one or both of the parties can choose not to perform their contractual obligations. Thus the contract lacks consideration.

Immigration Reform and Control act of 1986 (IRCA) A federal statute that makes it unlawful for employers to hire illegal immigrants.

immoral contract A contract whose objective is the commission of an act that is considered immoral by society.

immunity from prosecution The government agrees not to use any evidence given by a person granted immunity against that person.

impairment of right of recourse Certain parties (holders, indorsers, accommodation parties) are discharged from liability on an instrument if the holder (1) releases an obligor from liability or (2) surrenders collateral without the consent of the parties who would benefit by it.

implied agency An agency that occurs when a principal and an agent do not expressly create an agency, but it is inferred from the conduct of the parties.

implied authorization Mode of acceptance that is implied from what is customary in similar transactions, usage of trade, or prior dealings between the parties.

implied exemptions Exemptions from antitrust laws that are implied by the Federal courts.

implied partnership General partnership implied from the conduct of the parties.

implied powers Powers beyond express powers that allow a corporation to accomplish its corporate purpose.

implied term A term in a contract that can reasonably be supplied by the courts.

implied trust A trust that is implied by law or from the conduct of the parties.

implied warranties The law implies certain warranties on transferors of negotiable instruments There are two types of implied warranties: transfer and presentment.

implied warranty of authority An agent who enters into a contract on behalf of another party impliedly warrants that he or she has the authority to do so.

implied warranty of fitness for a particular purpose An implied warranty that information is fit for the licensee's purpose that applies if the licensor (1) knows of any particular purpose for which the computer information is required and (2) knows that the licensee is relying on the licensor's skill or judgment to select or furnish suitable information.

implied warranty of fitness for human consumption A warranty that applies to food or drink consumed on or off the premises of restaurants, grocery stores, fast-food outlets, and vending machines.

implied warranty of habitability A warranty that provides that the leased premises must be fit, safe, and suitable for ordinary residential use.

implied warranty of informational content An implied warranty that there is no inaccuracy in the informational content caused by the merchant-licensor's failure to perform with reasonable care.

implied warranty of merchantability Unless properly disclosed, a warranty that is implied that sold or leased goods are fit for the ordinary purpose for which they are sold or leased, and other assurances.

implied warranty of merchantability of the computer program An implied warranty that the copies of the computer program are within the parameters permitted by the licensing agreement, that the computer program has been adequately packaged and labeled, and that the program conforms to any promises or affirmations of fact on the container or label.

implied-in-fact condition A condition that can be implied from the circumstances surrounding a contract and the parties' conduct.

implied-in-fact contract A contract where agreement between parties has been inferred because of their conduct.

impossibility of performance Nonperformance that is excused if the contract becomes impossible to perform; must be objective impossibility, not subjective.

imposter A person who impersonates a payee and induces a maker or drawer to issue an instrument in the payee's name and to give it to the imposter.

imposter rule A rule that says if an imposter forges the indorsement of the named payee, the drawer or maker is liable on the instrument and bears the loss.

imputed knowledge Information that is learned by the agent that is attributed to the principal.

in pari delicto When both parties are equally at fault in an illegal contract.

in personam jurisdiction Jurisdiction over the parties to a lawsuit.

in rem jurisdiction Jurisdiction to hear a case because of jurisdiction over the property of the lawsuit.

in transit A state in which goods are in the possession of a bailee or carrier and not in the hands of the buyer, seller, lessee, or lessor.

inaccessibility exception A rule that permits employees and union officials to engage in union solicitation on company property if the employees are beyond reach of reasonable union efforts to communicate with them.

incidental beneficiary A party who is unintentionally benefited by other people's contracts.

incidental damages When goods are resold or released, incidental damages are reasonable expenses incurred in stopping delivery, transportation charges, storage charges, sales commissions, and so on.

incontestability clause A clause that prevents insurers from contesting statements made by insureds in applications for insurance after the passage of a stipulated number of years.

incorporation by reference When integration is made by express reference in one document that refers to and incorporates another document within it.

incorporator The person or persons, partnerships, or corporations that are responsible for incorporation of a corporation.

indemnification Right of a partner to be reimbursed for expenditures incurred on behalf of the partnership.

indenture agreement A contract between the corporation and the holder that contains the terms of a debt security.

independent contractor A person who contracts with another to do something for him who is not controlled by the other nor subject to the other's right to control with respect to his physical conduct in the performance of the undertaking. [Restatement (Second) of Agency].

indictment The charge of having committed a crime (usually a felony), based on the judgment of a grand jury.

indirect price discrimination A form of price discrimination (e.g., favorable credit terms) that is less readily apparent than direct forms of price discrimination.

indorsee The party to whom a check is indorsed. The person to whom a negotiable instrument is indorsed.

indorsement The signature (and other directions) written by or on behalf of the holder somewhere on the instrument.

indorsement for deposit or collection An indorsement that makes the indorsee the indorser's collecting agent (e.g., "for deposit only").

indorsement of a check Occurs when a payee indorses a check to another party by signing the back of the check.

indorser The person who indorses a negotiable instrument. The payee who indorses a check to another party.

indorsers' liability Unqualified indorsers are secondarily liable on negotiable instruments they indorse; qualified indorsers disclaim liability and are not secondarily liable on instruments they indorse.

infancy doctrine A doctrine that allows minors to disaffirm (cancel) most contracts they have entered into with adults.

inferior performance Occurs when a party fails to perform express or implied contractual obligations that impair or destroy the essence of the contract.

informal contract A contract that is not formal. Valid informal contracts are fully enforceable and may be sued upon if breached.

information The charge of having committed a crime (usually a misdemeanor), based on the judgment of a judge (magistrate).

injunction A court order that prohibits a person from doing a certain act.

injury The plaintiff must suffer personal injury or damage to his or her property to recover monetary damages for the defendant's negligence.

innkeepers' statutes State statutes that limit an innkeeper's common law liability. An innkeeper can avoid liability for loss caused to a guest's property if (1) a safe is provided in which the guest's valuable property may be kept and (2) the guest is notified of this fact.

innocent misrepresentation Occurs when a person makes a statement of fact that he or she honestly and reasonably believes to be true, even though it is not. Occurs when an agent makes an untrue statement that he or she honestly and reasonably believes to be true.

INS Form 1-9 A form that must be filled out by all U.S. employers for each employee; states that the employer has inspected the employee's legal qualifications to work.

insane, but not adjudged insane A person who is insane but has not been adjudged insane by a court or administrative agency. A contract entered into by such person is generally voidable. Some states hold that such a contract is void.

Insecticide, Fungicide, and Rodenticide Act A federal statute that requires pesticides, herbicides, fungicides, and rodenticides to be registered with the EPA; the EPA may deny, suspend, or cancel registration.

inside director A member of the board of directors who is also an officer of the corporation.

insider trading When an insider makes a profit by personally purchasing shares of the corporation prior to public release of favorable information or by selling shares of the corporation prior to the public disclosure of unfavorable information.

Insider Trading Sanctions Act of 1984 A federal statute that permits the SEC to obtain a civil penalty of up to three times the illegal benefits received from insider trading.

installment contract A contract that requires or authorizes the goods to be delivered and accepted in separate lots.

instrument Term that means negotiable instrument.

insurable interest A person who purchases insurance must have a personal interest in the insured item or person.

insurance A means for persons and businesses to protect themselves against the risk of loss.

insured The party who pays a premium to a particular insurance company for insurance coverage.

insurer The insurance company that underwrites the insurance coverage.

intangible property Rights that cannot be reduced to physical form such as stock certificates, certificates of deposit, bonds, and copyrights.

integration The combination of several writings to form a single contract.

intellectual property rights Intellectual property rights, such as patents, copyrights, trademarks, trade secrets, trade names, and domain names are very valuable business assets. Federal and state laws protect intellectual property rights from misappropriation and infringement.

intended beneficiary A third party who is not in privity of contract but who has rights under the contract and can enforce the contract against the obligor.

intentional infliction of emotional distress A tort that says a person whose extreme and outrageous conduct intentionally or recklessly causes severe emotional distress to another person is liable for that emotional distress. Also known as the tort of outrage.

intentional interference with contractual relations A tort that arises when a third party induces a contracting party to breach the contract with another party.

intentional misrepresentation Intentionally defrauding another person out of money, property, or something else of value. When a seller or lessor fraudulently misrepresents the quality of a product and a buyer is injured thereby. Occurs when one person consciously decides to induce another person to rely and act on a misrepresentation. Also called fraud. Occurs when an agent makes an untrue statement that he or she knows is not true.

intentional tort A category of torts that requires that the defendant possessed the intent to do the act that caused the plaintiff's injuries. Occurs when a person has intentionally committed a wrong against (1) another person or his or her character, or (2) another person's property.

inter vivos trust A trust that is created while the settlor is alive.

intermediary bank A bank in the collection process that is not the depository or payor bank.

intermediate appellate court An intermediate court that hears appeals from trial courts.

intermediate scrutiny test Test that is applied to classifications based on protected classes other than race (e.g., sex or age).

International Court of Justice The judicial branch of the United Nations that is located in The Hague, the Netherlands. Also called the World Court.

International law Law that governs affairs between nations and that regulates transactions between individuals and businesses of different countries.

Internet A collection of millions of computers that provide a network of electronic connections between computers.

interpretive rules Rules issued by administrative agencies that interpret existing statutory language.

interrogatories Written questions submitted by one party to another party. The questions must be answered in writing within a stipulated time.

interstate commerce Commerce that moves between states or that affects commerce between states.

intervention The act of others to join as parties to an existing lawsuit.

intoxicated person A person who is under contractual incapacity because of ingestion of alcohol or drugs to the point of incompetence.

intrastate offering exemption An exemption from registration that permits local businesses to raise capital from local investors to be used in the local economy without the need to register with the SEC.

invasion of the right to privacy A tort that constitutes the violation of a person's right to live his or her life without being subjected to unwarranted and undesired publicity.

involuntary petition A petition filed by creditors of the debtor; alleges that the debtor is not paying his or her debts as they become due.

issued shares Shares that have been sold by the corporation.

joint and several liability Partners are jointly and severally liable for tort liability of the partnership. This means that the plaintiff can sue one or more of the partners separately. If successful, the plaintiff can recover the entire amount of the judgment from any or all of the defendant-partners.

joint liability Partners are jointly liable for contracts and debts of the partnership. This means that a plaintiff must name the partnership and all of the partners as defendants in a lawsuit.

joint tenancy A form of co-ownership that includes the right of survivorship.

joint will A will that is executed by two or more testators.

judgment on the underlying debt A right granted to a secured creditor to relinquish his or her security interest in the collateral and sue a defaulting debtor to recover the amount of the underlying debt.

judicial branch The part of the government that consists of the Supreme Court and other federal courts.

judicial decision A decision about an individual lawsuit issued by federal and state courts.

judicial decisions and teachings The fourth source of international law, consisting of judicial decisions and writings of the most qualified legal scholars of the various nations involved in the dispute.

judicial decree of dissolution Order of the court that dissolves a partnership. An application or petition must be filed by a partner or an assignee of a partnership interest with the appropriate state court; the court will issue a judicial decree of dissolution if warranted by the circumstances.

judicial dissolution Occurs when a corporation is dissolved by a court proceeding instituted by the state.

jurisdiction The authority of a court to hear a case.

jurisprudence The philosophy or science of law.

Just Compensation Clause Clause in the U.S. Constitution that mandates that the government must compensate owners and lessees for property taken under the power of eminent domain.

Kantian or duty ethics A moral theory that says that people owe moral duties that are based on universal rules, such as the categorical imperative "do unto others as you would have them do unto you."

land The most common form of real property; includes the land and buildings and other structures permanently attached to the land.

land pollution Pollution of the land that is generally caused by hazardous waste being disposed of in an improper manner.

land sales contract Arrangement where the owner of real property agrees to sell the property to a purchaser, who agrees to pay the purchase price to the owner-seller over an agreed-upon period of time.

land use control The collective term for the laws that regulate the possession, ownership, and use of real property.

landlord The owner who transfers the leasehold.

landlord–tenant relationship A relationship created when the owner of a freehold estate (landlord) transfers a right to exclusively and temporarily possess the owner's property to another (tenant).

Lanham Trademark Act (as amended) Federal statute that (1) establishes the requirements for obtaining a federal mark and (2) protects marks from infringement.

lapse of time An offer terminates when a stated time period expires. If no time is stated, an offer terminates after a reasonable time.

larceny Taking another's personal property other than from his or her person or building.

law That which must be obeyed and followed by citizens subject to sanctions or legal consequences; a body of rules of action or conduct prescribed by controlling authority, and having binding legal force.

law court A court that developed and administered a uniform set of laws decreed by the kings and queens after

William the Conqueror; legal procedure was emphasized over merits at this time.

lease The transfer of the right to use real property for a specified period of time. A transfer of the right to the possession and use of the named goods for a set term in return for certain consideration. A transfer of the right to the possession and use of the real property for a set term in return for certain consideration; the rental agreement between a landlord and a tenant.

leasehold A tenant's interest in the property.

legal entity An LLC is a separate legal entity—an artificial person—that can own property, sue and be sued, enter into and enforce contracts, and such.

legal insanity A state of contractual incapacity as determined by law.

legally enforceable contract If one party fails to perform as promised, the other party can use the court system to enforce the contract and recover damages or other remedy.

legislative branch The part of the government that consists of Congress (the Senate and the House of Representatives).

lessee The person who acquires the right to possession and use of goods under a lease.

lessor The person who transfers the right of possession and use of goods under the lease.

liability insurance Automobile insurance that covers damages that the insured causes to third parties.

libel A false statement that appears in a letter, newspaper, magazine, book, photograph, movie, video, and so on.

license A contract that transfers limited rights in intellectual property and informational rights. Grants a person the right to enter upon another's property for a specified and usually short period of time.

licensee The party who is granted limited rights in or access to intellectual property or informational rights owned by the licensor.

licensing agreement Detailed and comprehensive written agreement between the licensor and licensee that sets forth the express terms of their agreement.

licensing statute Statute that requires a person or business to obtain a license from the government prior to engaging in a specified occupation or activity.

licensor The owner of intellectual property or informational rights who transfers rights in the property or information to the licensee.

licensor's damages If a licensee breaches a contract, the licensor may sue and recover monetary damages from the licensee caused by the breach.

life estate An interest in the land for a person's lifetime; upon that person's death, the interest will be transferred to another party.

life insurance A form of insurance where the insurer is obligated to pay a specific sum of money upon the death of the insured.

limited liability Members are liable for the LLC's debts, obligations, and liabilities only to the extent of their capital contributions. Liability that shareholders have only to the extent of their capital contribution. Shareholders are generally not personally liable for debts and obligations of the corporation.

limited liability company (LLC) An unincorporated business entity that combines the most favorable attributes of general partnerships, limited partnerships, and corporations.

limited liability company codes State statutes that regulate the formation, operation, and dissolution of LLCs.

limited liability partnership (LLP) A type of partnership that has no general partner. All partners have limited liability. A special form of partnership where all partners are limited partners and there are no general partners.

limited partners Partners in a limited partnership who invest capital but do not participate in management and are not personally liable for partnership debts beyond their capital contributions.

limited partnership A special form of partnership that has both limited and general partners.

limited partnership agreement A document that sets forth the rights and duties of the general and limited partners; the terms and conditions regarding the operation, termination, and dissolution of the partnership; and so on.

limited-jurisdiction trial court A court that hears matters of a specialized or limited nature.

line of commerce Includes products or services that consumers use as substitutes. If an increase in the price of one product or service leads consumers to purchase another product or service, the two products are substitutes for each other.

lineal descendants Children, grandchildren, great-grandchildren, and so on of the testator.

liquidated damages Damages to which parties to a contract agree in advance if the contract is breached. Damages that are specified in the contract rather than determined by the court. Damages that will be paid upon a breach of contract and that are established in advance

litigation The process of bringing, maintaining, and defending a lawsuit.

long-arm statute A statute that extends a state's jurisdiction to nonresidents who were not served a summons within the state.

lost property When a property owner leaves property somewhere because of negligence, carelessness, or inadvertence.

mail fraud The use of mail to defraud another person.

mailbox rule A rule that states that an acceptance is effective when it is dispatched, even if it is lost in transmission.

main purpose or leading object exception If the main purpose of a transaction and an oral collateral contract is to provide pecuniary benefit to the guarantor, the collateral contract does not have to be in writing to be enforced.

maker of a CD The bank (borrower).

maker of a note The party who makes the promise to pay (borrower).

management Unless otherwise agreed, each partner has a right to participate in the management of the partnership and has an equal vote on partnership matters.

manager-managed LLC An LLC that has designated in its articles of organization that it is a manager-managed LLC.

marine insurance Insurance that owners of vessels purchase to insure against loss or damage to the vessel and its cargo caused by perils at sea.

Marine Protection, Research, and Sanctuaries Act A federal statute enacted in 1972 that extends environmental protection to the oceans.

mark The collective name for trademarks, service marks, certification marks, and collective marks that all can be trademarked.

market extension merger A merger between two companies in similar fields whose sales do not overlap.

material alteration A partial defense against enforcement of a negotiable instrument by an HDC. An HDC can enforce an altered instrument in the original amount for which the drawer wrote the check.

material breach A breach that occurs when a party renders inferior performance of his or her contractual duties.

maximizing profits A theory of social responsibility that says a corporation owes a duty to take actions that maximize profits for shareholders. [156]

mediation A form of ADR in which the parties choose a neutral third party to act as the mediator of the dispute.

Medicinal Device Amendment to the FDCA An amendment enacted in 1976 that gives the FDA authority to regulate medicinal devices and equipment.

meeting of the creditors A meeting of the creditors in a bankruptcy case that must occur not less than 10 days nor more than 30 days after the court grants an order for relief.

meeting the competition defense A defense provided in Section 2(b) that says a seller may lawfully engage in price discrimination to meet a competitor's price.

member An owner of an LLC.

member-managed LLC An LLC that has not designated that it is a manager-managed LLC in its articles of organization.

mens rea "Evil intent"—the possession of the requisite state of mind to commit a prohibited act.

merchant A person who (1) deals in the goods of the kind involved in the transaction or (2) by his or her occupation holds himself or herself out as having knowledge or skill peculiar to the goods involved in the transaction.

merger Occurs when one corporation is absorbed into another corporation and ceases to exist.

merger clause A clause in a contract that stipulates that it is a complete integration and the exclusive expression of the parties' agreement. Parol evidence may not be introduced to explain, alter, contradict, or add to the terms of the contract.

midnight deadline The midnight of the next banking day following the banking day on which the bank received the "on them" check for collection.

minor A person who has not reached the age of majority.

minor breach A breach that occurs when a party renders substantial performance of his or her contractual duties.

minor's duty of restoration As a general rule, a minor is obligated only to return the goods or property he or she has received from the adult in the condition it is in at the time of disaffirmance.

mirror image rule States that for an acceptance to exist, the offeree must accept the terms as stated in the offer.

misdemeanor A less serious crime; not inherently evil but prohibited by society. Many crimes against property are misdemeanors.

mislaid property When an owner voluntarily places property somewhere and then inadvertently forgets it.

misrepresentation An assertion that is made that is not in accord with the facts.

misuse A defense that relieves a seller of product liability if the user abnormally misused the product. Products must be designed to protect against foreseeable misuse.

mitigation A nonbreaching party is under a legal duty to avoid or reduce damages caused by a breach of contract.

mixed sale A sale that involves the provision of a service and a good in the same transaction.

mobile sources Sources of air pollution such as automobiles, trucks, buses, motorcycles, and airplanes.

Model Business Corporation Act (MBCA) A model act drafted in 1950 that was intended to provide a uniform law for regulation of corporations.

monetary damages An award of money.

money A "medium of exchange authorized or adopted by a domestic or foreign government." [UCC 1–201(24)]

monopoly power The power to control prices or exclude competition measured by the market share the defendant possesses in the relevant market.

moral minimum A theory of social responsibility that says a corporation's duty is to make a profit while avoiding harm to others.

mortgage A collateral arrangement where a property owner borrows money from a creditor who uses a deed as collateral for repayment of the loan.

mortgagee The creditor in a mortgage transaction.

mortgagor The owner-debtor in a mortgage transaction.

motion for judgment on the pleadings Motion that alleges that if all the facts presented in the pleadings are taken as true, the party making the motion would win the lawsuit when the proper law is applied to these asserted facts.

motion for summary judgment Motion that asserts that there are no factual disputes to be decided by the jury; if so, the judge can apply the proper law to the undisputed facts and decide the case without a jury. These motions are supported by affidavits, documents, and deposition testimony.

motivation test A test to determine the liability of the principal; if the agent's motivation in committing the intentional tort is to promote the principal's business, then the principal is liable for any injury caused by the tort.

mutual benefit bailment A bailment for the mutual benefit of the bailor and bailee. The bailee owes a duty of ordinary care to protect the bailed property.

mutual mistake of fact A mistake made by both parties concerning a material fact that is important to the subject matter of the contract.

mutual mistake of value A mistake that occurs if both parties know the object of the contract, but are mistaken as to its value.

mutual wills Occur where two or more testators execute separate wills that leave their property to each other on the condition that the survivor leave the remaining property on his or her death as agreed by the testators.

national courts The courts of individual nations.

National Labor Relations Board (NLRB) A federal administrative agency that oversees union elections, prevents employers and unions from engaging in illegal and unfair labor practices, and enforces and interprets certain federal labor laws.

necessaries of life A minor must pay the reasonable value of food, clothing, shelter, medical care, and other items considered necessary to the maintenance of life.

negligence A tort related to defective products where the defendant has breached a duty of due care and caused harm to the plaintiff. Failure of a corporate director or officer to exercise the duty of care while conducting the corporation's business.

negligence per se Tort where the violation of a statue or ordinance constitutes the breach of the duty of care.

negligent infliction of emotional distress A tort that permits a person to recover for emotional distress caused by the defendant's negligent conduct.

negotiable instrument Commercial paper that must meet these requirements: (1) be in writing, (2) be signed by the maker or drawer, (3) be an unconditional promise or order to pay, (4) state a fixed amount of money, (5) not require any undertaking in addition to the payment of money, (6) be payable on demand or at a definite time, and (7) be payable to order or to bearer. A special form of contract that satisfies the requirement established by Article 3 of the UCC. Also called commercial paper.

negotiation Transfer of a negotiable instrument by a person other than the issuer to a person who thereby becomes a holder.

New York standard fire insurance form A standard fire insurance policy that protects the homeowner from loss caused by fire, lightning, smoke, and water damage.

no evidence of forgery, alteration, or irregularity requirement A holder cannot become an HDC to an instrument that is apparently forged or altered or is so otherwise irregular or incomplete as to call into question its authenticity.

Noise Control Act A federal statute enacted in 1972 that authorizes the EPA to establish noise standards for products sold in the United States.

noise pollution Unwanted sound from planes, manufacturing plants, motor vehicles, construction equipment, stereos, and the like.

nominal damages Damages awarded when the non-breaching party sues the breaching party even though no financial loss has resulted from the breach; usually consists of $1 or some other small amount.

nonattainment areas Regions that do not meet air quality standards.

nonconforming uses Uses and buildings that already exist in the zoned area that are permitted to continue even though they do not fit within new zoning ordinances.

noncupative will Oral will that is made before a witness during the testator's last illness.

nonfreehold estate An estate in which the tenant has a right to possession of the property but not title to the property.

nonnegotiable contract Fails to meet the requirements of a negotiable instrument and, therefore, is not subject to the provisions of UCC Article 3.

nonpossessory interest When a person holds an interest in another person's property without actually owning any part of the property.

nonprice vertical restraints Restraints of trade that are unlawful under Section 1 of the Sherman Act if their anti-competitive effects outweigh their procompetitive effects.

nonprofit corporation A corporation that is formed to operate charitable institutions, colleges, universities, and other not-for-profit entities.

nonrestrictive indorsement An indorsement that has no instructions or conditions attached to the payment of the funds.

note An instrument that evidences the borrower's debt to the lender. A debt security with a maturity of five years or less.

notice of dishonor The formal act of letting the party with secondary liability to pay a negotiable instrument know that the instrument has been dishonored.

novation An agreement that substitutes a new party for one of the original contracting parties and relieves the exiting party of liability on the contract.

Nuclear Regulatory Commission (NRC) Federal agency that licenses the construction and opening of commercial nuclear power plants.

Nuclear Waste Policy Act of 1982 A federal statute that says the federal government must select and develop a permanent site for the disposal of nuclear waste.

objective theory of contracts A theory that says that the intent to contract is judged by the reasonable person standard and not by the subjective intent of the parties.

obligation An action a party to a sales or lease contract is required by law to carry out.

obscene speech Speech that (1) appeals to the prurient interest, (2) depicts sexual conduct in a patently offensive way, and (3) lacks serious literary, artistic, political, or scientific value.

Occupational Safety and Health Act A federal act enacted in 1970 that promotes safety in the workplace.

offensive speech Speech that is offensive to many members of society. It is subject to time, place, and manner restrictions.

offer The manifestation of willingness to enter into a bargain, so made as to justify another person in understanding that his assent to that bargain is invited and will conclude it. (Section 24 of Restatement (Second) of Contracts.)

offeree The party to whom an offer to enter into a contract is made. The party to whom an offer has been made.

offeror The party who makes an offer to enter into a contract. The party who makes an offer.

officers Employees of the corporation who are appointed by the board of directors to manage the day-to-day operations of the corporation.

on them item A check presented for payment by the payee or holder where the depository bank and the payor bank are not the same bank.

on us item A check that is presented for payment where the depository bank is also the payor bank. That is, the drawer and payee or holder have accounts at the same bank.

one year rule An executory contract that cannot be performed by its own terms within one year of its formation must be in writing.

one-year "on sale" doctrine A doctrine that says a patent may not be granted if the invention was used by the public for more than one year prior to the filing of the patent application.

operating agreement An agreement entered into among members that governs the affairs and business of the LLC and the relations among members, managers, and the LLC.

order Decision issued by an administrative law judge.

order for relief The filing of either a voluntary petition, an unchallenged involuntary petition, or a grant of an order after a trial of a challenged involuntary petition.

order paper Order paper is negotiated by (1) delivery and (2) indorsement.

order to pay A drawer's unconditional order to a drawee to pay a payee.

ordinances Laws enacted by local government bodies such as cities and municipalities, countries, school districts, and water districts.

ordinary bailments (1) Bailments for the sole benefit of the bailor, (2) bailments for the sole benefit of the bailee, and (3) bailments for the mutual benefit of the bailor and bailee.

organizational meeting A meeting that must be held by the initial directors of the corporation after the articles of incorporation are filed.

original tenor The original amount for which the drawer wrote the check.

outside director A member of the board of directors who is not an officer of the corporation.

outstanding shares Shares of stock that are in shareholder hands.

overdraft The amount of money a drawer owes a bank after it has paid a check despite insufficient funds in the drawer's account.

pac-man tender offer Occurs when a corporation that is the target of a tender offer makes a reverse tender offer for the stock of the tender offeror.

palming off Unfair competition that occurs when a company tries to pass one of its products as that of a rival.

panel A panel of three WTO judges that hears trade disputes between member nations and issues a "panel report."

parol evidence Any oral or written words outside the four corners of the written contract.

parol evidence rule A rule that says if a written contract is a complete and final statement of the parties' agreement, any prior or contemporaneous oral or written statements that alter, contradict, or are in addition to the terms of the written contract are inadmissible in court regarding a dispute over the contract. There are several exceptions to this rule.

part performance An equitable doctrine that allows the court to order an oral contract for the sale of land or transfer of another interest in real property to be specifically performed if it has been partially performed and performance is necessary to avoid injustice.

partner's interest A partner's share of profits and surplus of the partnership.

partnership agreement A written partnership agreement that the partners sign. Also called articles of partnership.

partnership at will A partnership with no fixed duration.

partnership capital Money and property contributed by partners for the permanent use of the partnership.

partnership for a term A partnership with a fixed duration.

partnership property Property that is originally brought into the partnership on account of the partnership and property that is subsequently acquired by purchase or otherwise on account of the partnership or with partnership funds.

past consideration A prior act or performance. Past consideration (e.g., prior acts) will not support a new contract. New consideration must be given.

patent infringement Unauthorized use of another's patent. A patent holder may recover damages and other remedies against a patent infringer.

payable on demand or at a definite time requirement A negotiable instrument must be payable either on demand or at a definite time.

payee of a CD The depositor (lender).

payee of a check The party to whom the check is written.

payee of a draft The party who receives the money from a draft.

payee of a note The party to whom the promise to pay is made (lender).

payor bank The bank where the drawer has a checking account and on which the check is drawn.

penal codes A collection of criminal statutes.

per capita A distribution of the estate that makes each grandchild and great-grandchild of the deceased inherit equally with the children of the deceased.

per se rule A rule that is applicable to those restraints of trade considered inherently anticompetitive. Once this determination is made, the court will not permit any defenses or justifications to save it.

per stirpes A distribution of the estate that makes grandchildren and great-grandchildren of the deceased inherit by representation of their parent.

perfect tender rule A rule that says if the goods or tender of a delivery fail in any respect to conform to the contract, the buyer may opt either (1) to reject the whole shipment, (2) to accept the whole shipment, or (3) to reject part and accept part of the shipment.

perfection by possession of the collateral If a secured creditor has physical possession of the collateral, no financing statement has to be filed; the creditor's possession is sufficient to put other potential creditors on notice of his or her secured interest in the property.

perfection of a security interest Establishes the right of a secured creditor against other creditors who claim an interest in the collateral.

periodic tenancy A tenancy created when a lease specifies intervals at which payments are due but does not specify how long the lease is for.

permanency requirement A requirement of negotiable instruments that says they must be in a permanent state, such as written on ordinary paper.

permanent trustee A legal representative of the bankruptcy debtor's estate, usually an accountant or lawyer; elected at the first meeting of the creditors.

personal articles floater An addition to the homeowners policy that covers specific valuable items.

personal defense A defense that can be raised against enforcement of a negotiable instrument by an ordinary holder but not against an HDC.

personal property Property that consists of tangible property such as automobiles, furniture, and jewelry; intangible property such as securities, patents, and copyrights; and instruments, chattel paper, documents of title, and accounts.

personal satisfaction test Subjective test that applies to contracts involving personal taste and comfort.

petition A document filed with the bankruptcy court that sets the bankruptcy proceedings into motion.

petition for certiorari A petition asking the Supreme Court to hear one's case.

petitioner The party appealing the decision of an administrative agency.

physical or mental examination A court may order another party to submit to a physical or mental examination prior to trial.

picketing The action of strikers walking in front of the employer's premises carrying signs announcing their strike.

piercing the corporate veil A doctrine that says if a shareholder dominates a corporation and uses it for improper purposes, a court of equity can disregard the corporate entity and hold the shareholder personally liable for the corporation's debts and obligations.

plaintiff The party who files the complaint.

plan of reorganization A plan that sets forth a proposed new capital structure for the debtor to have when it emerges from reorganization bankruptcy. The debtor has the exclusive right to file the first plan of reorganization; any party of interest may file a plan thereafter.

plant life and vegetation Real property that is growing in or on the surface of the land.

plea bargain When the accused admits to a lesser crime than charged. In return, the government agrees to impose a lesser sentence than might have been obtained had the case gone to trial.

pleadings The paperwork that is filed with the court to initiate and respond to a lawsuit.

point sources Sources of water pollution such as paper mills, manufacturing plants, electric utility plants, and sewage plants.

police power The power of states to regulate private and business activity within their borders.

policy The insurance contract.

portability requirement A requirement of negotiable instruments that says they must be able to be easily transported between areas.

possession A lease grants the tenant exclusive possession of the leased premises for the term of the lease or until the tenant defaults on the obligations under the lease.

possessory lien Lien obtained by a bailee on bailed property for the compensation owed by the bailor to the bailee.

Postal Reorganization Act An act that makes the mailing of unsolicited merchandise an unfair trade practice.

posteffective period The period of time that begins when the registration statement becomes effective and runs until the issuer either sells all of the offered securities or withdraws them from sale.

potential competition theory A theory that reasons that the real or implied threat of increased competition keeps businesses more competitive. A merger that would eliminate this perception can be enjoined under Section 7.

potential reciprocity theory A theory that says if Company A, which supplies materials to Company B, mergers with Company C (which in turn gets its supplies from Company B), the newly merged company can coerce Company B into dealing exclusively with it.

power of attorney An express agency agreement that is often used to give an agent the power to sign legal documents on behalf of the principal.

precedent A rule of law established in a court decision. Lower courts must follow the precedent established by higher courts.

preemption doctrine The concept that federal law takes precedence over state or local law.

preemptive rights Rights that give existing shareholders the option of subscribing to new shares being issued in proportion to their current ownership interest.

preexisting duty A promise lacks consideration if a person promises to perform an act or do something he or she is already under an obligation to do.

preferential lien Occurs when (1) a debtor gives an unsecured creditor a secured interest in property within 90 days before the filing of a petition in bankruptcy, (2) the transfer is made for a preexisting debt, and (3) the creditor would receive more because of this lien than it would as an unsecured creditor.

preferential transfer Occurs when (1) a debtor transfers property to a creditor within 90 days before the filing of a petition in bankruptcy, (2) the transfer is made for a preexisting debt, and (3) the creditor would receive more from the transfer than it would from Chapter 7 liquidation.

preferential transfer to an insider A transfer of property by an insolvent debtor to an "insider" within one year before the filing of a petition in bankruptcy.

preferred stock A type of equity security that is given certain preferences and rights over common stock.

preferred stock certificate A document that represents a shareholder's investment in preferred stock in the corporation.

preferred stockholder A person who owns preferred stock.

prefiling period A period of time that begins when the issuer first contemplates issuing the securities and ends when the registration statement is filed. The issuer may not condition the market during this period.

Pregnancy Discrimination Act Amendment to Title VII that forbids employment discrimination because of "pregnancy, childbirth, or related medical conditions."

premises liability The liability of landlords and tenants to persons injured on their premises.

premium The money paid to the insurance company.

presentment A demand for acceptance or payment of an instrument made upon the maker, acceptor, drawee, or other payor by or on behalf of the holder.

presentment across the counter When a depository physically presents the check for payment at the payor bank instead of depositing an "on them" check for collection.

presentment warranties Any person who presents a draft or check for payment or acceptance makes the following three warranties to a drawee or acceptor who pays or accepts the instrument in good faith: (1) The presenter has good title to the instrument or is authorized to obtain payment or acceptance of the person who has good title, (2) the instrument has not been materially altered, and (3) the presenter has no knowledge that the signature of the maker or drawer is unauthorized.

pretrial hearing A hearing before the trial in order to facilitate the settlement of a case. Also called a settlement conference.

pretrial motion A motion a party can make to try to dispose of all or part of a lawsuit prior to trial.

price-fixing Occurs where competitors in the same line of business agree to set the price of the goods or services they sell: raising, depressing, fixing, pegging, or stabilizing the price of a commodity or service.

primary liability Absolute liability to pay a negotiable instrument, subject to certain real defenses.

principal A person who authorizes an agent to sign a negotiable instrument on his or her behalf. The party who employs another person to act on his or her behalf.

principal–agent relationship An employer hires an employee and gives that employee authority to act and enter into contracts on his or her behalf.

priority The order in which conflicting claims of creditors in the same collateral are solved.

Privacy Act An act stipulating that federal administrative agencies can maintain only information about an individual that is relevant and necessary to accomplish a legitimate agency purpose.

private corporation A corporation formed to conduct privately owned business.

private nuisance A nuisance that affects or disturbs one or a few people.

private placement exemption An exemption from registration that permits issuers to raise capital from an unlimited number of accredited investors and no more than 35 nonaccredited investors without having to register the offering with the SEC.

Private Securities Litigation Reform Act of 1995 Provides a safe harbor from liability for companies that make forward-looking statements that are accompanied by meaningful cautionary statements of risk factors.

Privileges and Immunities Clause A clause that prohibits states from enacting laws that unduly discriminate in favor of their residents.

privity of contract The state of two specified parties being in a contract.

pro rata rule A rule that says shares must be purchased on a pro rata basis if too many shares are tendered.

probability of a substantial lessening of competition If there is a probability that a merger will substantially lessen competition or create a monopoly, the court may prevent the merger under Section 7 of the Clayton Act.

probate court A specialized state court that supervises the administration and settlement of an estate.

procedural due process Due process that requires the respondent to be given (1) proper and timely notice of the allegations or charges against him or her and (2) an opportunity to present evidence on the matter.

process of certification The accepting bank writes or stamps the word certified on the ordinary check of an account holder and sets aside funds from that account to pay the check.

processing plant franchise The franchisor provides a secret formula or process to the franchisee, and the franchisee manufactures the product and distributes it to retail dealers.

production of documents Request by one party to another party to produce all documents relevant to the case prior to the trial.

products liability The liability of manufacturers, sellers, and others for the injuries caused by defective products.

professional corporation A corporation formed by lawyers, doctors, or other professionals.

professional malpractice The liability of a professional who breaches his or her duty of ordinary care.

profit Grants a person the right to remove something from another's real property.

profit corporation A corporation created to conduct a business for profit that can distribute profits to shareholders in the form of dividends.

promise to pay A maker's (borrower's) unconditional and affirmative undertaking to repay a debt to a payee (lender).

promissory estoppel An equitable doctrine that prevents the withdrawal of a promise by a promisor if it will adversely affect a promisee who has adjusted his or her position in justifiable reliance on the promise. An equitable doctrine that permits enforcement of oral contracts that should have been in writing. It is applied to avoid injustice.

promissory note A two-party negotiable instrument that is an unconditional written promise by one party to pay money to another party.

promoter A person or persons who organize and start the corporation, negotiate and enter into contracts in advance of its formation, find the initial investors to finance the corporation, and so forth.

promoters' contracts A collective term for such things as leases, sales contracts, contracts to purchase property, and employment contracts entered into by promoters on behalf of the proposed corporation prior to its actual incorporation.

proof of claim A document required to be filed by unsecured creditors that states the amount of their claim against the debtor.

proper dispatch An acceptance must be properly addressed, packaged, and posted to fall within the mailbox rule.

prospectus A written disclosure document that must be submitted to the SEC along with the registration statement and given to prospective purchasers of the securities.

provisional credit Occurs when a collecting bank gives credit to a check in the collection process prior to its final settlement. Provisional credits may be reversed if the check does not "clear."

proximate cause or legal cause A point along a chain of events caused by a negligent party after which this party is no longer legally responsible for the consequences of his or her actions.

proxy The written document that a shareholder signs authorizing another person to vote his or her shares at the shareholders' meetings in the event of the shareholder's absence.

proxy card Written document signed by a shareholder that authorizes another person to vote the shareholder's shares.

proxy contest When opposing factions of shareholders and managers solicit proxies from other shareholders, the side that receives the greatest number of votes wins the proxy contest.

proxy statement A document that fully describes (1) the matter for which the proxy is being solicited, (2) who is soliciting the proxy, and (3) any other pertinent information.

public corporation A corporation formed to meet a specific governmental or political purpose.

public nuisance A nuisance that affects or disturbs the public in general.

public policy exception An exception to the employment at-will doctrine that states an employee cannot be discharged if such discharge violates the public policy of the jurisdiction.

publicly held corporation A corporation that has many shareholders and whose securities are often traded on national stock exchanges.

punitive damages Damages that are awarded to punish the defendant, to deter the defendant from similar conduct in the future, and to set an example for others.

purchase money security interest An interest a creditor automatically obtains when it extends credit to a consumer to purchase consumer goods.

purchasing property The most common method of acquiring title to personal property.

qualified individual with a disability A person who (1) has a physical or mental impairment that substantially limits one or more of his or her major life activities, (2) has a record of such impairment, or (3) is regarded as having such impairment.

quasi contract An equitable doctrine that permits the recovery of compensation even though no enforceable contract exists between the parties.

quasi in rem jurisdiction Jurisdiction allowed a plaintiff who obtains a judgment in one state to try to collect the judgment by attaching property of the defendant located in another state.

quasi- or implied-in-law contract An equitable doctrine whereby a court may award monetary damages to a plaintiff for providing work or services to a defendant even

though no actual contract existed. The doctrine is intended to prevent unjust enrichment and unjust detriment.

quiet title action An action brought by a party seeking an order of the court declaring who has title to disputed property. The court "quiets title" by its decision.

quorum The required number of shares that must be represented in person or by proxy to hold a shareholders' meeting. The RMBCA establishes a majority of outstanding shares as a quorum. The number of directors necessary to hold a board of directors' meeting or transact business of the board.

Racketeer Influenced and Corrupt Organizations Act (RICO) A federal statute that provides for both criminal and civil penalties.

radiation pollution Emissions from radioactive wastes that can cause injury and death to humans and other life and can cause severe damage to the environment.

ratification The act of a minor after the minor has reached the age of majority by which he or she accepts a contract entered into when he or she was a minor. When a principal accepts an agent's unauthorized contract. The acceptance by a corporation of an unauthorized act of a corporate officer or agent.

rational basis test Test that is applied to classifications not involving a suspect or protected class.

Rawls's social contract A moral theory that says each person is presumed to have entered into a social contract with all others in society to obey moral rules that are necessary for people to live in peace and harmony.

real defense A defense that can be raised against both holders and HDCs.

real property The land itself as well as buildings, trees, soil, minerals, timber, plants, crops, and other things permanently affixed to the land.

reasonable person test Objective test that applies to commercial contracts and contracts involving mechanical fitness.

receiving stolen property A person (1) knowingly receives stolen property and (2) intends to deprive the rightful owner of that property.

reclamation The right of a seller or lessor to demand the return of goods from the buyer or lessee under specified situations.

record date A date specified in the corporate bylaws that determines whether a shareholder may vote at a shareholders' meeting. A date that determines whether a shareholder receives payment of a declared dividend.

recording statute A state statute that requires the mortgage or deed of trust to be recorded in the county recorder's office of the county in which the real property is located.

recovery of damages A seller or lessor may recover damages measured as the difference between the contract price (or rent) and the market price (or rent) at the time and place the goods were to be delivered, plus incidental damages, from a buyer or lessee who repudiates the contract or wrongfully rejects tendered goods.

recovery of goods from an insolvent seller or lessor A buyer or lessee who has wholly or partially paid for goods before they are received may recover the goods from a seller or lessor who becomes insolvent within 10 days after receiving the first payment; the buyer or lessee must tender the remaining purchase price or rent due under the contract.

recovery of lost profits If the recovery of damages would be inadequate to put the seller or lessor in as good a position as if the contract had been fully performed by the buyer or lessee, the seller or lessor may recover lost profits, plus an allowance of overhead and incidental damages, from the buyer or lessee.

recovery of the purchase price or rent A seller or lessor may recover the contracted-for purchase price or rent from the buyer or lessee if the buyer or lessee (1) fails to pay for accepted goods, (2) breaches the contract and the seller or lessor cannot dispose of the goods, or if (3) the goods are damaged or lost after the risk of loss passes to the buyer or lessee.

red light doctrine A doctrine that says a holder cannot qualify as an HDC if he or she has notice of an unauthorized signature or an alteration of the instrument or any adverse claim against or defense to its payment.

redeemable preferred stock Stock that permits the corporation to buy back the preferred stock at some future date.

reformation An equitable doctrine that permits the court to rewrite a contract to express the parties' true intentions.

registered agent A person or corporation that is empowered to accept service of process on behalf of the corporation.

registration statement Document that an issuer of securities files with the SEC that contains required information about the issuer, the securities to be issued, and other relevant information.

regular meeting A meeting held by the board of directors at the time and place established in the bylaws.

regulatory statute A licensing statute enacted to protect the public.

rejection Express words or conduct by the offeree that rejects an offer. Rejection terminates the offer.

rejection of nonconforming goods If the goods or the seller's or lessor's tender of delivery fails to conform to the contract, the buyer or lessee may (1) reject the whole, (2) accept the whole, or (3) accept any commercial unit and reject the rest.

relevant geographical market A relevant market that is defined as the area in which the defendant and its competitors sell the product or service.

relevant product or service market A relevant market that includes substitute products or services that are reasonably interchangeable with the defendant's products or services.

relief from stay May be granted in situations involving depreciating assets where the secured property is not adequately protected during the bankruptcy proceedings; asked for by a secured creditor.

religious discrimination Discrimination against a person solely because of his or her religion or religious practices.

remainder If the right of possession returns to a third party upon the expiration of a limited or contingent estate.

replacement cost insurance Insurance that pays the cost to replace the damaged or destroyed property up to the policy limits.

replacement workers Workers who are hired to take the place of striking workers. They can be hired on either a temporary or permanent basis.

replevin An action by a buyer or lessor to recover scarce goods wrongfully withheld by a seller or lessor.

reply Filed by the original plaintiff to answer the defendant's cross-complaint.

Repossession A right granted to a secured creditor to take possession of the collateral upon default by the debtor.

res ipsa loquitur Tort where the presumption of negligence arises because (1) the defendant was in exclusive control of the situation and (2) the plaintiff would not have suffered injury but for someone's negligence. The burden switches to the defendant(s) to prove they were not negligent.

resale price maintenance A per se violation of Section 1 of the Sherman Act; occurs when a party at one level of distribution enters into an agreement with a party at another level to adhere to a price schedule that either sets or stabilizes prices.

rescission An action to undo the contract. An action to rescind (undo) the contract. Rescission is available if there has been a material breach of contract, fraud, duress, undue influence, or mistake.

residence contents broad form Insurance that renters purchase to cover loss or damage to their possessions.

residuary gift Gift of the estate left after the debts, taxes, and specific and general gifts have been paid.

Resource Conservation and Recovery Act (RCRA) A federal statute that authorizes the EPA to regulate facilities that generate, treat, store, transport, and dispose of hazardous wastes.

respondeat superior A rule that says an employer is liable for the tortious conduct of its employees or agents while they are acting within the scope of its authority.

Restatement of the Law of Contracts A compilation of model contract law principles drafted by legal scholars. The Restatement is not law.

restitution Returning of goods or property received from the other party to rescind a contract; if the actual goods or property is not available, a cash equivalent must be made.

restricted securities Securities that were issued for investment purposes pursuant to the intrastate, private placement, or small offering exemption.

restrictive covenant A private agreement between landowners that restricts the use of their land.

restrictive indorsement An indorsement that contains some sort of instruction from the indorser.

resulting trust A trust that is created by the conduct of the parties.

retained earnings Profits retained by the corporation and not paid out as dividends.

retention of collateral If a secured creditor repossesses collateral upon a debtor's default, he or she may propose to retain the collateral in satisfaction of the debtor's obligation.

revenue-raising statute A licensing statute with the primary purpose of raising revenue for the government.

reverse discrimination Discrimination against a group that is usually thought of as a majority.

reversion A right of possession that returns to the grantor after the expiration of a limited or contingent estate.

Revised Model Business Corporation Act (RMBCA) A revision of the MBCA in 1984 that arranged the provisions of the act more logically, revised the language to be more consistent, and made substantial changes in the provisions.

Revised Uniform Limited Partnership Act (RULPA) A 1976 revision of the ULPA that provides a more modern, comprehensive law for the formation, operation, and dissolution of limited partnerships.

revocation Withdrawal of an offer by the offeror terminates the offer. Reversal of acceptance. Termination of a will.

reward To collect a reward, the offeree must (1) have knowledge of the reward offer prior to completing the requested act and (2) perform the requested act.

right of inspection A right that shareholders have to inspect the books and records of the corporation.

right of redemption A right that says the mortgagor has the right to redeem real property after default and before foreclosure. Requires the mortgagor to pay the full amount of the debt incurred by the mortgagee because of the mortgagor's default. A right granted to a defaulting debtor or other secured creditor to recover the collateral from a secured creditor before he or she contracts to dispose of it or exercises his or her right to retain the collateral. Requires the redeeming party to pay the full amount of the debt and expenses caused by the debtor's default.

right to cure A licensor has the right to cure a contract under certain conditions.

River and Harbor Act A federal statute enacted in 1886 that established a permit system for the discharge of refuse, wastes, and sewage into U.S. navigable waterways.

robbery Taking personal property from another person by use of fear or force.

Rule 10b-5 A rule adopted by the SEC to clarify the reach of Section 10(b) against deceptive and fraudulent activities in the purchase and sale of securities.

rule of reason A rule that holds that only unreasonable restraints of trade violate Section 1 of the Sherman Act. The court must examine the pro- and anticompetitive effects of the challenged restraint.

rules and regulations Adopted by administrative agencies to interpret the statutes that they are authorized to enforce.

Sabbath law A law that prohibits or limits the carrying on of certain secular activities on Sundays.

Safe Drinking Water Act A federal statute enacted in 1974 and amended in 1986 that authorizes the EPA to establish national primary drinking water standards.

sale The passing of title from a seller to a buyer for a price. Also called a conveyance.

sale on approval A type of sale in which there is no actual sale unless and until the buyer accepts the goods.

sale or return contract A contract that says that the seller delivers goods to a buyer with the understanding that the buyer may return them if they are not used or resold within a stated or reasonable period of time.

sale proceeds The resulting assets from the sale, exchange, or disposal of collateral subject to a security agreement.

satisfaction The performance of an accord.

scienter Means international conduct. Scienter is required for there to be a violation of Section 10(b) and Rule 10b-5.

search warrant A warrant issued by a court that authorizes the police to search a designated place for specified contraband, articles, items, or documents. The search warrant must be based on probable cause.

secondary boycott picketing A type of picketing where unions try to bring pressure against an employer by picketing his or her suppliers or customers.

secondary liability Liability on a negotiable instrument that is imposed on a party only when the party primarily liable on the instrument defaults and fails to pay the instrument when due.

secondary meaning When an ordinary term has become a brand name.

Section 1 of the Sherman Act Prohibits contracts, combinations, and conspiracies in restraint of trade.

Section 10(b) A provision of the Securities Exchange Act of 1934 that prohibits the use of manipulative and deceptive devices in the purchase or sale of securities in contravention of the rules and regulations prescribed by the SEC.

Section 11 A provision of the Securities Act of 1933 that imposes civil liability on persons who intentionally defraud investors by making misrepresentations or omissions of material facts in the registration statement or who are negligent for not discovering the fraud.

Section 11(a) A section of the Securities Act of 1933 that imposes civil liability on accountants and others for (1) making misstatements or omissions of material facts in a registration statement or (2) failing to find such misstatements or omissions.

Section 12 A provision of the Securities Act of 1933 that imposes civil liability on any person who violates the provisions of Section 5 of the act.

Section 14(a) Provision of the Securities Exchange Act of 1934 that gives the SEC the authority to regulate the solicitation of proxies.

Section 14(e) A provision of the Williams Act that prohibits fraudulent, deceptive, and manipulative practices in connection with a tender offer.

Section 16(a) A section of the Securities Exchange Act of 1934 that defines any person who is an executive officer, a director, or a 10 percent shareholder of an equity security of a reporting company as a statutory insider for Section 16 purposes.

Section 2 of the Sherman Act Prohibits the act of monopolization and attempts or conspiracies to monopolize trade.

Section 2(a) of the Robinson-Patman Act Prohibits direct and indirect price discrimination by sellers of a commodity of a like grade and quality where the effect of such discrimination may be to substantially lessen competition or to tend to create a monopoly in any line of commerce.

Section 3 of the Clayton Act Prohibits tying arrangements involving sales and leases of goods.

Section 5 of the FTC Act Prohibits unfair and deceptive practices.

Section 7 of the NLRA A law that gives employees the right to join together and form a union.

Section 8(a) of the NLRA A law that makes it an unfair labor practice for an employer to interfere with, coerce, or restrain employees from exercising their statutory right to form and join unions.

Section 8(b) of the NLRA A law that prohibits unions from engaging in unfair labor practices that interfere with a union election.

Section 16(b) A section of the Securities Exchange Act of 1934 that requires that any profits made by a statutory insider on transactions involving short-swing profits belong to the corporation.

Section 18(a) A section of the Securities Exchange Act of 1934 that imposes civil liability on any person who makes false or misleading statements in any application, report, or document filed with the SEC.

Section 24 A section of the Securities Act of 1933 that makes it a criminal offense for any person to (1) willfully make any untrue statement of material fact in a registration statement filed with the SEC, (2) omit any material fact necessary to ensure that the statements made in the registration statement are not misleading, or (3) willfully violate any other provision of the Securities Act of 1933 or rule or regulation adopted thereunder.

Section 32 A provision of the Securities Exchange Act of 1934 that imposes criminal liability on any person who willfully violates the 1934 act or the rules or regulations adopted thereunder.

Section 32(a) A section of the Securities Exchange Act of 1934 that makes it a criminal offense for any person willfully and knowingly to make or cause to be made any false or misleading statement in any application, report, or other document required to be filed with the SEC pursuant to the Securities Exchange Act of 1934 or any rule or regulation adopted thereunder.

Section 552 of the Restatement (Second) of Torts A rule that an accountant is liable only for negligence to third parties who are members of a limited class of intended users of the client's financial statements. Provides a broader standard for holding accountants liable to third parties for negligence than the Ultramares doctrine.

section of the country A division of the country that is based on the relevant geographical market; the geographical area that will feel the direct and immediate effects of the merger.

secured credit Credit that requires security (collateral) that secures payment of the loan.

secured transaction A transaction that is created when a creditor makes a loan to a debtor in exchange for the debtor's pledge of personal property as security.

Securities Act of 1933 A federal statute that primarily regulates the issuance of securities by corporations, partnerships, associations, and individuals.

Securities and Exchange Commission (SEC) Federal administrative agency that is empowered to administer federal securities laws. The SEC can adopt rules and regulations to interpret and implement federal securities laws.

Securities Exchange Act of 1934 A federal statute that primarily regulates the trading in securities.

security An interest or instrument that is common stock, preferred stock, a bond, a debenture, or a warrant, (2) an interest or instrument that is expressly mentioned in securities acts, and (3) an investment contract. [744]

security agreement The agreement between the debtor and the secured party that creates or provides for a security interest.

self-dealing If the directors or officers engage in purchasing, selling, or leasing of property with the corporation, the contract must be fair to the corporation; otherwise, it is voidable by the corporation. The contract or transaction is enforceable if it has been fully disclosed and approved.

Self-Employment Contributions Act A federal act that says self-employed persons must pay Social Security taxes equal to the combined employer-employee amount.

self-incrimination The Fifth Amendment states that no person shall be compelled in any criminal case to be a witness against him- or herself.

service mark A mark that distinguishes the services of the holder from those of its competitors.

service of process A summons is served on the defendant to obtain personal jurisdiction over him or her.

settlement of the estate The process of a deceased's property being collected, debts and taxes being paid, and the remainder of the estate being distributed.

settlor or trustor Person who creates a trust.

sex discrimination Discrimination against a person solely because of his or her gender.

sexual harassment Lewd remarks, touching, intimidation, posting pinups, and other verbal or physical conduct of a sexual nature that occur on the job.

share exchange When one corporation acquires all the shares of another corporation and both corporations retain their separate legal existence.

shareholder voting agreements Agreement between two or more shareholders agreeing on how they will vote their shares.

shipment contract A contract that requires the seller to ship the goods to the buyer via a common carrier. The buyer bears the risk of loss during transportation. A sales contract that requires the seller to send the goods to the buyer, but not a specifically named destination.

short-form merger A merger between a parent corporation and a subsidiary corporation that does not require the vote of the shareholders of either corporation or the board of directors of the subsidiary corporation.

sight draft A draft payable on sight. Also called a demand draft.

signature Any name, word, or mark used in lieu of a written signature; any symbol that is (1) handwritten, typed, printed, stamped, or made in almost any other manner and (2) executed or adopted by a party to authenticate a writing.

signature liability A person cannot be held contractually liable on a negotiable instrument unless his or her signature appears on the instrument. Also called contract liability.

signature requirement A negotiable instrument must be signed by the drawer or maker. Any symbol executed or adopted by a party with a present intent to authenticate a writing qualifies as his or her signature.

signer A person signing an instrument who acts in the capacity of (1) a maker of notes and certificates of deposit, (2) a drawer of drafts and checks, (3) a drawee who certifies or accepts checks and drafts, (4) an indorser who indorses an instrument, (5) an agent who signs on behalf of others, or (6) an accommodation party.

slander Oral defamation of character.

small claims court A court that hears civil cases involving small dollar amounts.

small offering exemption For the sale of securities not exceeding $1 million during a 12-month period.

social host liability Rule that provides that social hosts are liable for injuries caused by guests who become intoxicated at a social function. States vary as to whether they have this rule in effect.

Social Security Federal system that provides limited retirement and death benefits to covered employees and their dependents.

sole proprietorship A form of business where the owner is actually the business; the business is not a separate legal entity.

sources of international law Those things that international tribunals rely on in settling international disputes.

special bailees Includes common carriers, warehouse companies, and innkeepers.

special federal courts Federal courts that hear matters of specialized or limited jurisdiction.

special indorsement An indorsement that contains the signature of the indorser and specifies the person (indorsee) to whom the indorser intends the instrument to be payable. Creates order paper.

special meeting A meeting convened by the board of directors to discuss new shares, merger proposals, hostile takeover attempts, and so forth.

special shareholders' meetings Meetings of shareholders that may be called to consider and vote on important or emergency issues, such as a proposed merger or amending the articles of incorporation.

specific duty An OSHA standard that addresses a safety problem of a specific duty nature (e.g., requirement for a safety guard on a particular type of equipment).

specific gift Gift of a specifically named piece of property.

specific performance A remedy that orders the breaching party to perform the acts promised in the contract; usually awarded in cases where the subject matter is unique, such as in contracts involving land, heirlooms, and paintings. Judgment of the court ordering a licensor to specifically perform the license by making the contracted-for unique information available to the licensee. A decree of the court that orders a seller or lessor to perform his or her obligations under the contract; usually occurs when the goods in question are unique, such as art or antiques.

stakeholder interest A theory of social responsibility that says a corporation must consider the effects its actions have on persons other than its stockholders.

stale check A check that has been outstanding for more than six months.

standing to sue The plaintiff must have some stake in the outcome of the lawsuit.

stare decisis Latin: "to stand by the decision." Adherence to precedent.

state action exemptions Business activities that are mandated by state law are exempt from federal antitrust laws.

state administrative agencies Administrative agencies that states create to enforce and interpret state law.

state antitakeover statutes Statutes enacted by state legislatures that protect corporations incorporated in or doing business in the state from hostile takeovers.

state supreme court The highest court in a state court system; it hears appeals from intermediate state courts and certain trial courts.

statement of disassociation A document filed with the secretary of state that gives constructive notice that a member has disassociated from an LLC.

statement of policy A statement issued by administrative agencies announcing a proposed course of action that an agency intends to follow in the future.

stationary sources Sources of air pollution such as industrial plants, oil refineries, and public utilities.

statute Written law enacted by the legislative branch of the federal and state governments that establishes certain courses of conduct that must be adhered to by covered parties.

Statute of Frauds State statute that requires certain types of contracts to be in writing.

statute of limitations Statute that establishes the time period during which a lawsuit must be brought; if the lawsuit is not brought within this period, the injured party loses the right to sue.

statute of repose A statute that limits the seller's liability to a certain number of years from the date when the product was first sold.

Statute of Wills A state statute that establishes the requirements for making a valid will.

statutory exemptions Exemptions from antitrust laws that are expressly provided in statutes enacted by Congress.

stock dividend Additional shares of stock paid as a dividend.

stop-payment order An order by a drawer of a check to the payor bank not to pay or certify a check.

stopping delivery of goods in transit A seller or lessor may stop delivery of goods in transit if he or she learns of the buyer's or lessee's insolvency or if the buyer or lessee repudiates the contract, fails to make payment when due, or gives the seller or lessor some other right to withhold the goods.

straight voting Each shareholder votes the number of shares he or she owns on candidates for each of the positions open.

strict liability Liability without fault.

strict liability standard Common law duty that says innkeepers are liable for lost, damaged, or stolen goods of guests even if they were not at fault for the loss.

strict or absolute liability Standard for imposing criminal liability without a finding of mens rea (intent).

strict scrutiny test Test that is applied to classifications based on race.

strike A cessation of work by union members in order to obtain economic benefits or correct an unfair labor practice.

subject matter jurisdiction Jurisdiction over the subject matter of a lawsuit.

sublease When a tenant transfers only some of his or her rights under the lease.

sublessee The new tenant in a sublease situation.

sublessor The original tenant in a sublease situation.

subrogation If an insurance company pays a claim to an insured for liability or property damage caused by a third party, the insurer succeeds to the right of the insured to recover from the third party.

substantial performance Performance by a contracting party that deviates only slightly from complete performance.

substantive due process Due process that requires that the statute or rule that the respondent is charged with violating be clearly stated.

substantive rules Government regulation that has the force of law and must be adhered to by covered persons and businesses.

subsurface rights Rights to the earth located beneath the surface of the land.

summons A court order directing the defendant to appear in court and answer the complaint.

superseding event A defendant is not liable for injuries caused by a superseding or intervening event for which he or she is not responsible.

supervening event An alteration or modification of a product by a party in the chain of distribution that absolves all prior sellers from strict liability.

supervening illegality The enactment of a statute, regulation, or court decision that makes the object of an offer illegal. This action terminates the offer.

supramajority voting requirement A requirement that a greater than majority of shares constitutes a quorum of the vote of the shareholders.

Supremacy Clause A clause of the U.S. Constitution that establishes that the federal Constitution, treaties, federal laws, and federal regulations are the supreme law of the land.

Surety The third person who agrees to be liable in a surety arrangement.

surety arrangement An arrangement where a third party promises to be primarily liable with the borrower for the payment of the borrower's debt.

taking for value requirement A holder must give value for the negotiable instrument to qualify as an HDC.

taking in good faith requirement A holder must take the instrument in good faith to qualify as an HDC.

taking possession A method of acquiring ownership of unowned personal property.

taking without notice of defect requirement A person cannot qualify as an HDC if he or she has notice that the instrument is defective in certain ways.

tangible property All real property and physically defined personal property such as buildings, goods, animals, and minerals.

target corporation The corporation that is proposed to be acquired in a tender offer situation.

Tax Reform Act (1976) An act that imposes criminal liability on accountants and others who prepare federal tax returns if they (1) willfully understate a client's tax liability, (2) negligently understate the tax liability, or (3) wrongfully indorse a client's tax refund check.

tax sale A method of transferring property ownership that involves a lien on property for unpaid property taxes. If the lien remains unpaid after a certain amount of time, a tax sale is held to satisfy the lien.

tenancy at sufferance A tenancy created when a tenant retains possession of property after the expiration of another tenancy or a life estate without the owner's consent.

tenancy at will A lease that may be terminated at any time by either party.

tenancy by the entirety A form of co-ownership of real property that can be used only by married couples.

tenancy for years A tenancy created when the landlord and the tenant agree on a specific duration for the lease.

tenancy in common A form of co-ownership where the interest of a surviving tenant in common passes to the deceased tenant's estate and not to the co-tenants.

tenant The party to whom the leasehold is transferred.

tender of delivery The obligation of the seller to transfer and deliver goods to the buyer in accordance with the sales contract.

tender of performance Tender is an unconditional and absolute offer by a contracting party to perform his or her obligations under the contract. Occurs when a party who has the ability and willingness to perform offers to complete the performance of his or her duties under the contract.

tender offer An offer that an acquirer makes directly to a target corporation's shareholders in an effort to acquire the target corporation.

tender offeror The party that makes a tender offer.

term LLC An LLC that has a specified term of duration.

termination The ending of a corporation that occurs only after the winding-up of the corporation's affairs, the liquidation of its assets, and the distribution of the proceeds to the claimants.

termination by acts of the parties An agency may be terminated by the following acts of the parties: (1) mutual agreement, (2) lapse of time, (3) purpose achieved, and (4) occurrence of a specified event.

termination by operation of law An agency is terminated by operation of law, including: (1) death of the principal or agent, (2) insanity of the principal or agent, (3) bankruptcy of the principal, (4) impossibility of performance, (5) changed circumstances, and (6) war between the principal's and agent's countries.

termination statement A document filed by the secured party that ends a secured interest because the debt has been paid.

testamentary trust A trust created by will: the trust comes into existence when the settlor dies.

testator The person who makes a will.

thermal pollution Heated water or material discharged into waterways that upsets the ecological balance and decreases the oxygen content.

through bill of lading A bill of lading that provides that connecting carriers may be used to transport the goods to their destination.

time draft A draft payable at a designated future date.

time instrument An instrument payable (1) at a fixed date, (2) on or before a stated date, (3) at a fixed period after sight, or (4) at a time readily ascertainable when the promise or order is issued. An instrument that specifies a definite date for payment of the instrument.

time note A note payable at a specific time.

tippee The person who receives material nonpublic information from a tipper.

tipper A person who discloses material nonpublic information to another person.

title Legal, tangible evidence of ownership of goods.

Title I of the Landrum-Griffin Act Referred to as labor's "bill of rights" that gives each union member equal rights and privileges to nominate candidates for union office, vote in elections, and participate in membership meetings.

title insurance Insurance that owners of real property purchase to insure that they have clear title to the property.

Title VII of the Civil Rights Act of 1964 (Fair Employment Practices Act) Intended to eliminate job discrimination based on five protected classes: race, color, religion, sex, or national origin.

tort A wrong. There are three categories: (1) intentional torts, (2) unintentional torts (negligence), and (3) strict liability.

tort of misappropriation of the right to publicity An attempt by another person to appropriate a living person's name or identity for commercial purposes.

toxic air pollutants Air pollutants that cause serious illness or death to humans.

toxic substances Chemicals used for agricultural, industrial, and mining uses that cause injury to humans, birds, animals, fish, and vegetation.

Toxic Substances Control Act A federal statute enacted in 1976 that requires manufacturers and processors to test new chemicals to determine their effect on human health and the environment before the EPA will allow them to be marketed.

trade acceptance A sight draft that arises when credit is extended (by a seller to a buyer) with the sale of goods. The seller is both the drawer and the payee, and the buyer is the drawee.

trade secret A product formula, pattern, design, compilation of data, customer list, or other business secret. Ideas that make a franchise successful but that do not qualify for trademark, patent, or copyright protection.

trademark A distinctive mark, symbol, name, word, motto, or device that identifies the goods of a particular business.

trademark infringement Unauthorized use of another's mark. The holder may recover damages and other remedies from the infringer.

transfer Any passage of an instrument other than its issuance and presentment for payment.

transfer warranties Any of the following five implied warranties: (1) The transferor has good title to the instrument or is authorized to obtain payment or acceptance on behalf of one who does have good title; (2) all signatures are genuine or authorized; (3) the instrument has not been materially altered; (4) no defenses of any party are good against the transferor; and (5) the transferor has no knowledge of any insolvency proceeding against the maker, or acceptor, or the drawer of an unaccepted instrument.

traveler's check A form of check sold by banks and other issuers. They are issued without a named payee. The purchaser fills in the payee's name when he or she uses the check to purchase goods or services.

Treaty Clause Clause of the U.S. Constitution that states the president "shall have the power . . . to make treaties, provided two-thirds of the senators present concur."

treasury shares Shares of stock repurchased by the company itself.

treaties The first source of international law, consisting of agreements or contracts between two or more nations that are formally signed by an authorized representative and ratified by the supreme power of each nation.

trespass to land A tort that interferes with an owner's right to exclusive possession of land.

trespass to personal property A tort that occurs whenever one person injures another person's personal property or interferes with that person's enjoyment of his or her personal property.

trial briefs Documents submitted by the parties' attorneys to the judge that contain legal support for their side of the case.

trier of fact The jury in a jury trial; the judge where there is not a jury trial.

trust A legal arrangement established when one person transfers title to property to another person to be held and used for the benefit of a third person.

trust corpus The property held in trust.

trustee Person who holds legal title to the trust corpus and manages the trust for the benefit of the beneficiary or beneficiaries.

tying arrangement A restraint of trade where a seller refuses to sell one product to a customer unless the customer agrees to purchase a second product from the seller.

ultra vires act An act by a corporation that is beyond its express or implied powers.

ultramares doctrine A rule that an accountant is liable only for negligence to third parties who are in privity of contract or a privity-like relationship with the accountant. Provides the narrowest standard for holding accountants liable to third parties for negligence.

unauthorized signature A signature made by a purported agent without authority from the purported principal.

unconditional Promises to pay and orders to pay must be unconditional in order for them to be negotiable.

unconditional promise or order to pay requirement A negotiable instrument must contain either an unconditional promise to pay (note or CD) or an unconditional order to pay (draft or check).

unconscionable disclaimer A disclaimer that is so oppressive or manifestly unfair that it will not be enforced by the court.

undue influence Occurs where one person takes advantage of another person's mental, emotional, or physical weakness and unduly persuades that person to enter into a contract; the persuasion by the wrongdoer must overcome the free will of the innocent party.

unenforceable contract A contract where the essential elements to create a valid contract are met, but there is some legal defense to the enforcement of the contract.

unfair advantage theory A theory that holds that a merger may not give the acquiring firm an unfair advantage over its competitors in finance, marketing, or expertise.

unfair competition Competition that violates the law.

Uniform Commercial Code Comprehensive statutory scheme that includes laws that cover aspects of commercial transactions.

UCC Statute of Frauds A rule that requires all contracts for the sale of goods costing $500 or more and lease contracts involving payments of $1,000 or more to be in writing.

UCC statute of limitations A rule that provides that an action for breach of any written or oral sales or lease contract must commence within four years after the cause of action accrues. The parties may agree to reduce the limitations period to one year.

Uniform Computer Information Transactions Act (UCITA) A model act that provides uniform and comprehensive rules for contracts involving computer information transactions and software and information licenses.

Uniform Franchise Offering Circular (UFOC) A uniform disclosure document that requires the franchisor to make specific presale disclosures to prospective franchisees.

Uniform Gift to Minors Act and Revised Uniform Gift to Minors Act Acts that establish procedures for adults to make gifts of money and securities to minors.

The Uniform Limited Liability Company Act (ULLCA) A model act that provides comprehensive and uniform laws for the formation, operation, and dissolution of LLCs.

Uniform Partnership Act (UPA) Model act that codifies partnership law. Most states have adopted the UPA in whole or in part.

Uniform Probate Code (UPC) A model law promulgated to establish uniform rules for the creation of wills, the administration of estates, and the resolution of conflicts in settling estates.

Uniform Securities Act An act that has been adopted by many states; it was drafted to coordinate state securities laws with federal securities laws.

Uniform Simultaneous Death Act An act that provides that if people who would inherit property from each other die simultaneously, each person's property is distributed as though he or she survived.

unilateral contract A contract in which the offeror's offer can be accepted only by the performance of an act by the offeree; a "promise for an act."

unilateral mistake When only one party is mistaken about a material fact regarding the subject matter of the contract.

unilateral refusal to deal A unilateral choice by one party not to deal with another party. This does not violate Section 1 of the Sherman Act because there is not concerted action.

uninsured motorist coverage Automobile insurance that provides coverage to the driver and passengers who are injured by an uninsured motorist or hit-and-run driver.

unintentional tort or negligence A doctrine that says a person is liable for harm that is the foreseeable consequence of his or her actions.

union shop An establishment where an employee must join the union within a certain number of days after being hired.

United Nations An international organization created by multilateral treaty in 1945 to promote social and economic cooperation among nations and to protect human rights.

U.S. Constitution The fundamental law of the United States of America. It was ratified by the states in 1788.

U.S. courts of appeals The federal court system's intermediate appellate courts.

U.S. district courts The federal court system's trial courts of general jurisdiction.

U.S. Supreme Court The Supreme Court was created by Article III of the U.S. Constitution. The Supreme Court is the highest court in the land. It is located in Washington, DC.

unprotected speech Speech that is not protected by the First Amendment and may be forbidden by the government.

unqualified indorsement An indorsement whereby the indorser promises to pay the holder or any subsequent indorser the amount of the instrument if the maker, drawer, or acceptor defaults on it.

unqualified indorser An indorser who signs an unqualified indorsement to an instrument.

unreasonable search and seizure Any search and seizure by the government that violates the Fourth Amendment.

unsecured credit Credit that does not require any security (collateral) to protect the payment of the debt.

usurping a corporate opportunity A director or officer steals a corporate opportunity for him- or herself.

usury law A law that sets an upper limit on the interest rate that can be charged on certain types of loans.

utilitarianism A moral theory that dictates that people must choose the action or follow the rule that provides the greatest good to society.

valid contract A contract that meets all of the essential elements to establish a contract; a contract that is enforceable by at least one of the parties.

variance An exception that permits a type of building or use in an area that would not otherwise be allowed by a zoning ordinance.

venue A concept that requires lawsuits to be heard by the court with jurisdiction that is nearest the location in which the incident occurred or where the parties reside.

vertical merger A merger that integrates the operations of a supplier and a customer.

vertical restraint of trade A restraint of trade that occurs when two or more parties on different levels of distribution enter into a contract, combination, or conspiracy to restrain trade.

violation A crime that is neither a felony nor a misdemeanor that is usually punishable by a fine.

voidable contract A contract where one or both parties have the option to avoid their contractual obligations. If a contract is avoided, both parties are released from their contractual obligations.

voidable title Title that a purchase has if the goods were obtained by (1) fraud, (2) a check that is later dishonored, or (3) impersonating another person.

voidable transfer An unusual payment or transfer of property by the debtor on the eve of bankruptcy that would unfairly benefit the debtor or some creditors at the expense of other creditors. Such transfer may be avoided by the bankruptcy court.

void contract A contract that has no legal effect; a nullity.

void title A thief acquires no title to the goods he or she steals.

voluntary dissolution A corporation that has begun business or issued shares can be dissolved upon recommendation of the board of directors and a majority vote of the shares entitled to vote.

voluntary petition A petition filed by the debtor; states that the debtor has debts.

voting trust The shareholders transfer their stock certificates to a trustee who is empowered to vote the shares.

waiting period A period of time that begins when the registration statement is filed with the SEC and continues until the registration statement is declared effective. Only certain activities are permissible during the waiting period.

warehouse company A bailee engaged in the business of storing property for compensation. Owes a duty of reasonable care to protect the bailed property.

warehouse receipt A written document issued by a person who is engaged in the business of storing goods for hire.

warranties of quality Seller's or lessor's assurance to buyer or lessee that the goods meet certain standards of quality. Warranties may be expressed or implied.

warranty A buyer's or lessee's assurance that the goods meet certain standards. A representation of the insured that is expressly incorporated in the insurance contract.

warranty against infringements A seller or lessor who is a merchant who regularly deals in goods of the kind sold or leased automatically warrants that the goods are delivered free of any third-party patent, trademark, or copyright claim.

warranty against interference The lessor warrants that no person holds a claim or interest in the goods that arose from an act or omission of the lessor that will interfere with the lessee's enjoyment of his or her leasehold interest.

warranty disclaimer Statements that negate express and implied warranties.

warranty of fitness for a particular purpose A warranty that arises where a seller or lessor warrants that the goods will meet the buyer's or lessee's expressed needs.

warranty of good title Sellers warrant that they have valid title to the goods they are selling and that the transfer of title is rightful.

warranty of no security interests Sellers of goods warrant that the goods they sell are delivered free from any third-party security interests, liens, or encumbrances that are unknown to the buyer.

waste Occurs when a tenant causes substantial and permanent damage to the leased premises that decreases the value of the property and the landlord's reversionary interest in it.

water pollution Pollution of lakes, rivers, oceans, and other bodies of water.

wetlands Areas that are inundated or saturated by surface water or ground water that support vegetation typically adapted for life in such conditions.

white-collar crimes Crimes usually involving cunning and deceit rather than physical force.

will A declaration of how a person wants his or her property distributed upon death.

will or inheritance A way to acquire title to property that is a result of another's death. If a person dies with a will, his or her property is distributed to the beneficiaries as designated in the will. If a person dies without a will, his or her property is distributed to the heirs as stipulated in the state's intestate statute.

Williams Act An amendment to the Securities Exchange Act of 1934 made in 1968 that specifically regulates all tender offers.

winding-up Process of liquidating the partnership's assets and distributing the proceeds to satisfy claims against the partnership. The process of preserving and selling the assets of the LLC and distributing the money and property to creditors and members.

winding-up and liquidation The process by which a dissolved corporation's assets are collected, liquidated, and distributed to creditors, shareholders, and other claimants.

wire fraud The use of telephone or telegraph to defraud another person.

withholding delivery The act of the seller or lessor purposefully refusing to deliver goods to the buyer or lessee upon breach of the sales or lease contract by the buyer or lessee or the insolvency of the buyer or lessee.

work product immunity A state statute that says an accountant's work papers cannot be used in a court action in that state; federal courts do not recognize this statute.

workers' compensation acts Acts that compensate workers and their families if workers are injured in connection with their jobs.

work-related test A test to determine the liability of a principal; if an agent commits an intentional tort within a work-related time or space, the principal is liable for any injury caused by the agent's intentional tort.

World Trade Organization (WTO) An international organization of more than 130 member nations created to promote and enforce trade agreements among member nations.

World Wide Web An electronic connection of millions of computers that support a standard set of rules for the exchange of information.

writ of certiorari An official notice that the Supreme Court will review one's case.

written order A stop-payment order that is good for six months after the date it is written.

wrongful disassociation Occurs when a member withdraws from (1) a term LLC prior to the expiration of the term or (2) an at-will LLC when the operating agreement eliminates a member's power to withdraw.

wrongful discharge The discharge of an employee in violation of a statute, an employment contract, or public policy, or tortiously. As a result, the employee can recover damages and other remedies.

wrongful dishonor Occurs when there are sufficient funds in a drawer's account to pay a properly payable check, but the bank does not do so.

wrongful dissolution When a partner withdraws from a partnership without having the right to do so at that time.

wrongful eviction A violation of the covenant of quiet enjoyment. Also called unlawful eviction.

wrongful termination The termination of an agency contract in violation of the terms of the agency contract. The nonbreaching party may recover damages from the breaching party. Termination of a franchise without just cause.

zoning commission A local administrative body that formulates zoning ordinances, conducts public hearings, and makes recommendations to the city council.

zoning ordinances Local laws that are adopted by municipalities and local governments to regulate land use within their boundaries. Zoning ordinances are adopted and enforced to protect the health, safety, morals, and general welfare of the community.

Case Index

Cases cited or discussed are in roman type. Principal cases are in **bold type**.

Subject Index

Q

Qualified individual with disability, defined, 1028
Qualified indorsements, 524–525
Qualified indorsers, 524, 542
Qualified opinions, auditor's, 1161
Quasi-contracts, 250–251, 296
Quenay, Francois, 1076
Quiet title action, 1084–1085
Qui tam lawsuits, 219
Quitclaim deeds, 1083
Quorums, 778

R

Race discrimination, 1014–1015
Racketeer Influenced and Corrupt Organizations Act (RICO), 163, 1170
Radiation pollution, 965–966
Railway Labor Act (1926), 992
Rand, Ayn, 1045
Ratification, 294
  agency by, 684
Rational basis test, 51
Rawls, John, 223–225
Rawls' social justice theory, 223–225
Reaffirmation agreement, 638
Real defenses. *See* Universal defenses
Real estate
  Americans with Disabilities Act and, 1102–1104
  Civil Rights Act and, 1102
  Fair Housing Act and, 1102
Real estate sales contracts, 1083
Realists, 8
Real property, 1077
  adverse possession of, 1086–1088
  concurrent ownership of, 1080–1081
  condominiums, 1081
  contracts involving, 326–327
  cooperatives, 1082
  eminent domain and, 1104–1106
  estates in land and, 1078–1079
  future interests rights and, 1083
  nonpossessory interests in, 1089–1091
  sale of, 1083–1086
  security interests in, 595–599
  tax sales of, 1086
  transfer of, by gift, 1086
  transfer of ownership of, 1083–1088
  types of, 1077–1078
Reasonable accommodations, 1028
Reasonable person standard, 244
Reasonable professional standard, 122
Rebuttal, 91–92
Receiving stolen property, 159
Reclaim goods, right to, 453–454
Recognizances, 251
Record date, 778
Recording statutes, 596–598, 1084, 1085
Redeemable preferred stock, 763
Redemption
  period of, 1086
  right of, 598, 614
  statutory period of, 598
Re-direct examination, 91
Red light doctrine, 541
Reference, incorporation by, 332
Reformation, 379
Registered agents, 758
Registration, certificate, 734
Registration, Evaluation and Authorization of Chemicals (REACH), 963–964
Registration statements, 882

Regulation A offerings, 887
Regulation Fair Disclosure (Reg FD), SEC, 898
Regulation Z, 617–618
Regulatory statutes, 149, 305
Rehabilitation alimony, 1127
Rehnquist, William, 16–17, 39, 49, 170
Reimbursement, principal's duty of, 685
Rejection, of offers, by offeree, 266, 267
Rejoinder, 91–92
Relevant market, defining, 925
Relief of stay, 637
Religious discrimination, 1021
Remainder, 1083
Remainder beneficiary, 1083, 1141, 1143
Remedies
  agreements affecting, 460
  for breach of licensing agreements, 399–440
  for breach of sales and lease contracts, 447–451
  buyers, 456–458
  for buyers, 453–456
  collection, 620
  enforcement of, 375
  equitable, 377–380
  for lessors, 453–456
  limitations of, 401–402
  seller's, 453–456
Remittur, 92
Rental arrangements, types of, 1094
Rent control ordinances, 1099
Renters' insurance, 1061
Renunciation of authority, 704
Reorganization, plan of, 659
Reorganization bankruptcy. *See* Chapter 11 reorganization bankruptcy
Replacement cost insurance, 1060
Replacement workers, 1000
Replevin actions, 457
Reply, 84
Repossession, 612
Repudiation, anticipatory, 459
Requirement contracts, 281
Resale price maintenance, 921–922
Rescission, 316, 375–377
  mutual, 354
Reserve
  auctions with, 264, 265
  auctions without, 264, 265
Residuary clause, 1136
Residuary gifts, 1136
Res ipsa loquitor, 130
Resolutions, shareholders, 810–812
Resource Conservation and Recovery Act (RCRA) (1976), 965
Respondeat superior, doctrine of of, 687
Respondent (appellee), 19, 93
Responding brief, 93
Restatement of the Law Contracts, 244
Restatement (Second) of Torts, 481
  Section 552 of, 1165–1166
Restatement (Third) of Torts, 481–492
Restitution
  defined, 375
  minor's duty of, 294
Restoration, competent party's duty of, 293
Restraints of trade, 915–925
  horizontal, 916–921
  vertical, 921–922
Restricted securities, 891–892
Restrictive indorsements, 525
Resulting trusts, 1141
Revenue-raising statutes, 305
Reverse discrimination, 1032
Reversion, 1083

Review, standards of, 51
Revised Article 2A (Leases), UCC, 413, 418, 424
  electronic contracts and, 459
Revised Article 3 (Negotiable Instruments), 566
Revised Article 2 (Sales), UCC, 413, 418, 424
  electronic contracts and, 431, 459
  electronic signatures and, 431
Revised Article 9 (Secured Transactions), 600, 612
Revised Model Business Corporation Act (RMBCA) (1984), 752
  Model Statutory Close Corporation Supplement, 765
  voting requirements and, 778
Revised Uniform Gift to Minors Act, 1044
Revised Uniform Limited Partnership Act (RULPA) (1976), 729
Revocation
  of acceptance, 452–453
  of authority, 704
  of offers, by offeror, 266, 267
Rewards, 262
Riders, 1056
Right(s)
  air, 1078
  appraisal, 814–815
  assignment of future, 345
  to cancel contracts, 457
  to cover, 457
  to cure, licensor's, 400–401
  to die, 1143
  to dispose of goods, 454
  of first refusal, 780
  future interest, 1083
  to inspect, 452
  mineral, 1077
  preemptive, 780–781
  to reclaim goods, 453–454
  to recover damages for accepted nonconforming goods, 458
  to recover damages for breach of contract, 455
  to recover damages for nondelivery, 458
  to recover lost profits, 455
  to recover purchase price or rent, 454–455
  of redemption, 598, 614
  to replevy goods, 457
  to stop delivery of goods in transit, 453
  subsurface, 1077
  successive assignments of same, 347
  to sue letter, 1012
  surface, 1077
  of survivorship, 728
  to-work laws, 998
  visitation, 1129
  to withhold delivery, 453
Risk of loss
  breach of sales contract, 436
  conditional sales, 434–436
  no breach sales contract, 433–434
Risk(s)
  assumption of, 494
  assumption of the, 135–137
Robbery, 159
Roberts, John G., 66
Robinson-Patman Act (1930), 913
  Section 2(a) of, 932–934
Romano-Germanic civil law system, 11
Rousseau, Jean-Jacques, 223, 1045
Royalty fees, 859
Rule 144, SEC, 892
Rule 147, SEC, 891
Rule 144A, SEC, 891